HEALTH CARE LAW AND ETHICS

HEALTH CARE LAW AND ETHICS

Ninth Edition

Mark A. Hall
Fred D. and Elizabeth L. Turnage Professor of Law and Public Health
Wake Forest University

David Orentlicher
Cobeaga Law Firm Professor of Law
UNLV William S. Boyd School of Law

Mary Anne Bobinski
Professor
Allard School of Law University of British Columbia

Nicholas Bagley
Professor of Law
University of Michigan

I. Glenn Cohen
Professor of Law
Harvard University

Wolters Kluwer

To contact Customer Service, e-mail customer.service@wolterskluwer.com, call 1-800-234-1660, fax 1-800-901-9075, or mail correspondence to:

Wolters Kluwer
Attn: Order Department
PO Box 990
Frederick, MD 21705

Printed in the United States of America.

2 3 4 5 6 7 8 9 0

ISBN 978-1-4548-8180-3

Library of Congress Cataloging-in-Publication Data

Names: Hall, Mark A., 1955- author. | Orentlicher, David, 1955- author. | Bobinski, Mary Anne, author. | Bagley, Nicholas, author. | Cohen, I. Glenn author.
Title: Health care law and ethics / Mark A. Hall, Fred D. and Elizabeth L. Turnage Professor of Law and Public Health, Wake Forest University; David Orentlicher, Cobeaga Law Firm Professor of Law, UNLV William S. Boyd School of Law; Mary Anne Bobinski, Professor, Allard School of Law, University of British Columbia; Nicholas Bagley, Professor of Law, University of Michigan; I. Glenn Cohen, Professor of Law, Harvard University.
Description: Ninth edition. | New York : Wolters Kluwer, [2018] | Includes bibliographical references and index.
Identifiers: LCCN 2017057070 | ISBN 9781454881803 (hardcover)
Subjects: LCSH: Medical laws and legislation—United States. | Medical care—Law and legislation—United States. | Medical ethics—United States.
Classification: LCC KF3821 .H35 2018 | DDC 344.7304/1—dc23
LC record available at https://lccn.loc.gov/2017057070

To Larry C. Hall, Ph.D., for showing me the joys of an academic life.
—*M.A.H.*

To the memory of Prof. Herman I. Orentlicher, for his commitment to "neutral skepticism," rigorous standards, and, above all, decency.
—*D.O.*

To my partner Holly and our daughter Anna, and to my parents, for their encouragement.
—*M.A.B.*

To Celia and Sebastian, who have brought so much joy and meaning to my life.
—*N.B.*

To Jesse. You and I and no one else.
—*I.G.C.*

To Bill Curran, for his guiding light.

Summary of Contents

Part III
Institutions, Providers, and the State   1019

Contents

Part I
■

The Provider and the Patient

2
■

The Treatment Relationship: Formation and Termination

4

■

Medical Malpractice

Part II

■

The Patient, the Provider, and the State   **495**

5

■

The Right and "Duty" to Die   *503*

6

■

*Organ Transplantation: The Control, Use, and Allocation
of Body Parts*   **629**

7

■

Reproductive Rights and Genetic Technologies   *699*

Part III

■

Institutions, Providers, and the State   1019

9

■

10

■

Regulation of Health Care Facilities and Transactions   *1247*

Preface

The Content and Organization of This Book

As this book passes its half-century anniversary, we pause to reflect on the remarkable metamorphosis of health care law from a subspecialty of tort law, to a mushrooming academic and practice field whose tentacles reach into myriad scholarly disciplines and areas of substantive law. This book's eight prior editions reflect important stages in this evolutionary growth. Health care law originated as a separate field of professional practice and academic inquiry during the 1960s, when this book was first published. Under the somewhat grandiose label of "medical jurisprudence," the primary focus at first was on medical proof in all kinds of criminal and civil litigation, on medical malpractice actions against physicians, and on public health regulation. The principal concern was how traditional bodies of legal doctrine and practice—such as criminal, tort, and evidence law—should apply in medical settings.

During the 1970s, bioethics became a major additional area of concern as a consequence of the right to die movement spawned by the *Quinlan* case, and the focus on individual autonomy contained in the informed consent doctrine and the landmark decision on reproductive decisionmaking in Roe v. Wade. Law courses during this and earlier periods were taught under the heading of "law and medicine."

In the 1980s, economic and regulatory topics formed the third component of health care law, as exemplified by the increasing application of antitrust laws to the health care industry and the growing body of legal disputes under

Medicare and Medicaid. This newer dimension accelerated its growth into the 1990s with the spread of HMOs and other managed care organizations, which propelled various corporate and contractual restructurings. These newer topics found their way into courses described as "health law."

New developments present continuing challenges to each of these areas of health care law and ethics. Biotechnology, consumer-driven health care, and bioterrorism are examples of emerging issues that receive increased attention in the previous edition. Currently, there is an explosion of interest in health care public policy, coinciding with Affordable Care Act, whose importance reverberates throughout the field yet whose survival remains uncertain.

This path of development has resulted in an academic discipline defined more by an accretion of topics drawn from historical events than by a systematic conceptual organization of issues. Each of the four major branches—malpractice, bioethics, public health, and financing/regulation—stands apart from the others and is thought to be dominated by a distinct theme. The principal concern of malpractice law is quality of care; bioethics is concerned with individual autonomy; public health poses the rights of patients against the state; and the primary focus of financing and regulatory law is access to care and the cost of care. As a consequence, health care law has yet to become a truly integrated and cohesive discipline.[1] It is too much the creature of history and not of systematic and conceptual organization.

Our major ambition in this book is to improve this state of disarray. This field has reached a stage of maturity that calls for stepping back and rethinking how all of its parts best fit together as a conceptual whole. In our view that conceptual whole is best organized according to the fundamental structural relationships that give rise to health care law. These relationships are:

1. The patient/physician relationship, which encompasses the duty to treat, confidentiality, informed consent, and malpractice
2. State oversight of doctors and patients, which encompasses the right to die, reproductive rights, physician licensure, and public health
3. The institutions that surround the treatment relationship, encompassing public and private insurance, hospitals and HMOs, and more complex transactions and organizational forms

We develop the traditional themes of quality, ethics, access, and cost throughout each of these three divisions. We also address cutting-edge and controversial topics such as health care reform, genetics, managed care, and rationing, but not as discrete topics; instead, we integrate these developments within a more permanent, overarching organizational structure, which is capable of absorbing unanticipated new developments as they occur.

---

1. This disarray is reflected by the ongoing confusion over competing names for the field. Although "law and medicine" and "health care law" appear to signify the same topic, the first term is understood to mean older style malpractice subject matter, and the second term is used to refer to newer economic and regulatory issues. Paradoxically, whereas "health care law" and "health law" might be thought to signify somewhat different fields—the latter is not restricted to medical treatment and therefore encompassing public health issues—in fact they are taken to mean the same thing.

In deciding which topics to present in each section and in what depth, our basic guide has been to focus on the essential attributes of the medical enterprise that make it uniquely important or difficult in the legal domain. Health care law is about the delivery of an extremely important, very expensive, and highly specialized professional service. If it were otherwise, this book would likely not exist. Some lawyers and scholars maintain that there is no unifying concept or set of ideas for health care law; instead, it is merely a disparate collection of legal doctrines and public policy responses, connected only by the happenstance that they involve doctors and hospitals in some way—much as if one had a course on the law of green things or the law of Tuesdays. It would be far more satisfying to find one or more organizing principles that explain not only what makes the disparate parts of health care law cohere, but also why that coherence distinguishes health care law from other bodies of integrated legal thought and professional practice.

We believe those organizing principles can, in part, be found in the phenomenology of what it is to be ill and to be a healer of illness. These two human realities are permanent and essential features that distinguish this field from all other commercial and social arenas. They permeate all parts of health care law, giving it its distinctive quality and altering how generic legal doctrine and conventional theories of government respond to its problems and issues. Health care law might still be worth studying even without these unique attributes of medical encounters, but it is much more engaging and coherent because of them. It is these attributes that give rise to an interrelated set of principles that justify classifying health care law as a coherent and integrated academic and professional discipline. Elaborating this perspective, see Mark A. Hall, The History and Future of Health Care Law: An Essentialist View, 41 Wake Forest L. Rev. 347 (2006).[2]

Accordingly, we stress the essential attributes of medical encounters throughout these materials by incorporating insights from other academic disciplines and theoretical perspectives. Behavioral disciplines such as psychology, sociology, and anthropology help to illuminate the nature of medical knowledge and the lived experience of illness, dependency, and trust as they occur in real-life medical encounters. Findings from health services research published in the health policy literature create a stronger empirical and theoretical base

---

2. For additional discussion of the overall content of health care law and approaches to teaching and understanding it, see Clark Havighurst, American Health Care and the Law: We Need to Talk!, 19(4) Health Aff. 84 (July 2000); William M. Sage, Relational Duties, Regulatory Duties, and the Widening Gap Between Individual Health Law and Collective Health Policy, 96 Geo. L. J. 497-522 (2008); Theodore W. Ruger, Health Law's Coherence Anxiety, 96 Geo. L. J. 625-648 (2008); Wendy Mariner, Toward an Architecture of Health Law, 35 Am. J. L. & Med. 67 (2009); M. Gregg Bloche, the Emergent Logic of Health Law, 82 S. Cal. L. Rev. 389-480 (2009); Andrew Fichter, The Law of Doctoring: A Study of the Codification of Medical Professionalism, 19 Health Matrix 317-385 (2009); Sandra Johnson, Regulating Physician Behavior: Taking Doctors' "Bad Law" Claims Seriously, 53 St. Louis U. L. J. 973 (2009); Maxwell Mehlman, Can Law Save Medicine?, 36 J. Leg. Med. 121 (2015); Teaching Health Law, J. L. Med. & Ethics (recurring column); Symposium, Teaching Health Law , 61 St. Louis U. L. J. 371 (2017); Symposium, Jurisprudence and the Body, 63 Syracuse L. Rev. 327 (2013) Symposium, 19 Ann. Health L. 1 (2010); Symposium, Patient-Centered Law and Ethics, 45 Wake Forest L. Rev. 1429 (2010); Symposium, Rethinking Health Law, 41 Wake Forest L. Rev. 341 (2006); Symposium, The Field of Health Law: Its Past and Future, 14 Health Matrix 1 (2004); William J. Curran, Titles in the Medicolegal Field: A Proposal for Reform, 1 Am. J. L. & Med. 1 (1975).

for exploring health care law, one that better exposes its broad social impact. Analytical disciplines, such as economics and moral and political theory, create the foundation for understanding developments in financing, regulation, and bioethics. And, the perspectives of feminist, communitarian, and critical race theory demonstrate the limitations of conventional analytical models and help us understand how health care law must evolve to accommodate viewpoints and concerns that have been excluded in the past.

Course Coverage

Clearly, it is not possible (or, if possible, not desirable) to cover the entirety of this book in a single course. The course coverage offered at different schools varies widely according to the curricular structure at each school and each teacher's interest and expertise. Accordingly, we have organized this book in a manner that lends itself to compartmentalization for use in a number of different courses, taught both in law schools and in schools of medicine, public health, and health care administration. The following are the most common sequences and groupings. Many courses contain a combination of several of these:

Malpractice	Chapters 2, 3, and 4
Bioethics	Chapters 3, 5, 6, and 7
Public Health	Chapter 8, and portions of Chapters 3 and 7
Health Care Finance and Regulation	Chapters 2, 9, and 10

In the first chapter, we have collected background and introductory readings that are relevant in a number of places throughout the book.

Authorship and Bibliography

The 1992 death of Bill Curran, the original author of this casebook, left us with a considerable burden to shoulder. Although Prof. Curran was involved in the conceptual reorganization of these materials, he was unable to contribute to their selection and editing. Still, his presence is felt in every part of these materials through the inspiration of his mentoring, his friendship, and his vast body of work. Primary responsibility for editing each chapter is divided as follows: Hall—Chapters 1, 4, and 10; Bobinski—Chapters 3, 7, and 8; Orentlicher—Chapters 2, 5, and 6; Bagley—Chapter 9; Cohen—portions of 2, 3, 6, and 8. However, we each contributed important portions to the others' materials and have worked collectively on the overall organization and thematic plan.

We intend that this book will continue to serve as both a teaching tool and an ongoing resource for conducting research in health care law. To that end, we provide substantial bibliographic notes in each section. Also, we have created a dedicated Web site to serve this book: www.health-law.org. It extends the book's content with interesting background materials, updates of important events since publication, additional relevant topics that were excluded due to space constraints, and links to other resources on the internet.

The following is a bibliography of resources and readings that relate to research in health care law generally. Additional bibliographic references that relate to particular parts of health care law, such as malpractice, bioethics, public health, or financing and regulation, can be found at pages 77, 280, 898, and 1190, and on the casebook Web site.

Treatises and Texts: Barry Furrow et al., Health Law (2d ed. 2001); Mark A. Hall, David Orentlicher, and Ira Mark Ellman, Health Care Law and Ethics in a Nutshell (3d ed. 2011); Eleanor Kinney, Administrative Law of Health care in a Nutshell (2016); Hooper, Lundy & Bookman, Treatise on Health Care Law; John H. Robinson, Roberta M. Berry & Kevin McDonnell, eds., A Health Law Reader: An Interdisciplinary Approach (1999); World Health Organization, International Digest of Health Legislation .

Health Care Law Journals: American Journal of Law and Medicine (Boston Univ.); Annals of Health Law (Loyola-Chicago); DePaul Journal of Health Care Law; Food, Drug and Cosmetic Law Journal; Health Law & Policy Abstracts and Public Health Law Abstracts (SSRN online journals); Health Matrix (Case Western Univ.); Houston Journal of Health Law & Policy; Indiana Health Law Review (Indiana Univ.-Indianapolis); Journal of Contemporary Health Law and Policy (Catholic Univ.); Journal of Health & Biomedical Law (Suffolk), Journal of Health and Life Sciences Law (St. Louis Univ., AHLA); Journal of Health Care Law & Policy (Univ. of Maryland); Journal of Law and Health (Cleveland-Marshall); Journal of Law, Medicine and Ethics (ASLME); Journal of Legal Medicine (So. Illinois Univ.); Medical Trial Technique Quarterly; Journal of Medicine and Law; St. Louis Univ. Law Journal (recurring symposia); Seton Hall Law Review (same); Quinnipiac Health Law Journal; Whittier Law Review; Yale Journal of Health Policy, Law and Ethics.

Leading Medical, Industry, and Health Policy Journals: American Journal of Public Health; American Medical News (AMA); Health Affairs (published by Project Hope); Health Care Financing and Delivery (SSRN online journal), Medicare & Medicaid Research Review (DHHS/CMS); Health Economics, Policy and Law (Cambridge Press); Health Services Research; Inquiry (published by Excellus, a Blue Cross plan in Rochester, NY); Hospitals and Health Networks (AHA); Journal of the American Medical Association; Journal of Health Politics, Policy and Law; Medical Care; Milbank Quarterly; Modern Healthcare; New England Journal of Medicine.

Health Law Societies, Digests, and Newsletters: ABA Section on Health Law (newsletter and journal); American College of Legal Medicine (journal); American Society of Law, Medicine, and Ethics (two journals); BNA Health Law Reporter (weekly); American Health Lawyers Association (monthly digest and newsletter, bimonthly journal).

Acknowledgments

This manuscript could not have been prepared without the diligent help of those students and staff who assisted us over the past few years (Hailey Cleek, Travis Edwards, Victoria Hall-Palerm, Dorothy Hector, Colin Herd, Amy Lai, John Minkley, Robert Petito, Lena Rieke, Michael Shapiro, and Jacob Steiner), and without the superhuman patience of our families (who, curiously, wish to remain anonymous). We also thank the authors and publishers who granted permission to use each of the excerpts of copyrighted material in these readings.

American Health Lawyers Association Public Interest Committee, "A Public Policy Discussion: Taking the Measure of the Stark Law" (2009). Copyright © 2009 by the American Health Lawyers Association. Reprinted by permission. All rights reserved.

Bagley, Nicholas, "Bedside Bureaucrats: Why Medicare Reform Hasn't Worked," Georgetown Law Journal 101, no. 3 (2013): 519-80. Copyright © 2013 by Georgetown Law Journal. Reprinted by permission. All rights reserved.

Baker, Tom, The Medical Malpractice Myth (2005). Copyright © 2005 by the University of Chicago Press. Reprinted by permission. All rights reserved.

Beauchamp, Tom L., and James F. Childress, "The Right to a Decent Minimum of Health Care" in Principles of Biomedical Ethics (4th ed., 1994). Copyright © 1994 by Oxford University Press. Reprinted by permission. All rights reserved.

Bennett, Amanda, "End-of-life Warning at $618,616 Makes Me Wonder Was It Worth It." Bloomberg News (March 4, 2010). Copyright © 2010 by Bloomberg BNA. Reprinted by permission. All rights reserved.

Berenson, Robert A., and Rachel A. Burton, "Accountable Care Organizations in Medicare and the Private Sector: A Status Update" (2011). Copyright © 2011 by the Urban Institute. Reprinted by permission. All rights reserved.

Blumenthal, David, "Making Medical Errors into 'Medical Treasures.'" JAMA 272, no. 23 (1994): 1867-68. Copyright © 1994 by the American Medical Association. Reprinted by permission. All rights reserved.

Bobinski, Mary Anne, "Autonomy and Privacy: Protecting Patients from Their Physicians." University of Pittsburgh Law Review 55 (1993): 291. Copyright © 1993 by the University of Pittsburgh Law Review. Reprinted by permission. All rights reserved.

Bodenheimer, Thomas, and Kevin Grumbach, "Reimbursing Physicians and Hospitals." JAMA 272, no. 12 (1994): 971-77. Copyright © 1994 by the American Medical Association. Reprinted by permission. All rights reserved.

Buckman, Robert, and Karl Sabbagh, Magic or Medicine? An Investigation of Healing and Healers (1995). Copyright © 1995 by Prometheus Books. Reprinted by permission. All rights reserved.

Butterfield, Bruce, and Gerard O'Neill, "Regulatory System in Shambles; Negligent Doctors Stay on Job." Boston Globe (October 2, 1994). Copyright © 1994 by the Boston Globe. Reprinted by permission. All rights reserved.

Cohodes, Donald R., "Where You Stand Depends on Where You Sit: Musings on the Regulation/Competition Dialogue." Journal of Health Politics, Policy and

White, Joseph, "Competing Solutions: American Health Care Proposals and International Experience" (1995). Copyright © 1995 by the Brookings Institution. Reprinted by permission. All rights reserved.

Mark Hall
David Orentlicher
Mary Anne Bobinski
Nick Bagley
Glenn Cohen

January 2018

1

■

Introduction

These readings introduce background information and overarching perspectives that are important for understanding the legal issues developed throughout this book. All of us have had some exposure to the world of medicine, but few law students have reason to understand the intricacies of this financing and delivery system and how it has developed. This understanding is essential in a course that focuses on the full range of legal and public policy issues pertaining to the delivery and payment for medical care. Those issues have naturally taken shape according to the structural components and historical growth of the health care sector and its various institutions.

As you read through what sometimes seems to be an alphabet soup of actors, institutions, and acronyms, rather than memorizing all the details, try to construct a coherent story line of how the health care sector took shape over time and how its various pieces interconnect at present. You don't need to master all the details now, as they will reemerge throughout the course, but it will be easier to remember them at the end if you have an initial framework to which you can attach them.

A. THE NATURE OF MEDICAL PRACTICE

We begin with a description of the human condition of illness and the professional practice of medicine, since these are what distinguish health care law from other fields of legal study. It is essential throughout this book to have some appreciation of the impact that illness has on how people function, the intricacies of medical decisionmaking, and how doctors and patients interact. To focus your thoughts on these issues, reflect on your own experiences with medical care, and consider the following list of popular "misconceptions" (developed by Alain Enthoven). What observations and evidence emerge from these readings to rebut or qualify each of these commonly held notions?

1. The doctor should be able to know what conditions the patient has, to answer the patient's questions precisely, and to prescribe the right treatment. If the doctor doesn't, that is incompetence or even malpractice.
2. For each medical condition, there is a "best" treatment. It is up to the doctor to know about that treatment and to use it. Anything else is unnecessary surgery, waste, fraud, or underservice.
3. Medicine is an exact science. Unlike 50 or 100 years ago, there is now a firm scientific base for what the doctor does. Standard treatments are supported by scientific proof of efficiency.
4. Medical care consists of standard products that can be described precisely and measured meaningfully in standard units such as "inpatient days," "outpatient visits," or "doctor office visits."
5. Much of medical care is a matter of life and death or serious pain or disability.
6. More medical care is better than less care.
7. People have no control over the timing of their need for medical care. Whatever care is needed is needed right away.

1. Patients, Doctors, and Hospitals

■ HEALTH CARE PAST AND PRESENT
Robert Rhodes
Health Care Politics, Policy, and Distributive Justice:
*The Ironic Triumph**

Death before the nineteenth century was an ever-looming presence in our ancestors' thoughts and a frequent visitor to their families. They feared it and had little control over it. Sudden death was as central to attitudes prior to the twentieth century as the cemetery was to every village and town. . . .

Resignation and fatalism toward natural occurrences characterize preindustrial societies, just as a sense of self-direction and control characterize modern society. . . . Modern societies have faith that they can control the future. A futurist orientation allows for savings, capital formation, long periods of education, and lifestyles that deny instant gratification for future health. Preindustrial conditions do not reward such faith. . . . Uncontrollable natural or supernatural forces took away life, and one needed to reconcile one's fate to the four horsemen of the apocalypse: disease, famine, pestilence, and drought.

The twentieth century represents perhaps the clearest triumph of science over fatalism. . . . The modern hospital, the professionalism of physicians and nurses, and

*Copyright © 1992, State University of New York Press. Reprinted by permission.

effective pharmaceuticals have dramatically altered mortality rates and improved the quality of life in postindustrial states.

For those entering a hospital prior to 1900, the probability of treatment helping, rather than harming, would be less than fifty-fifty, and the odds would be considerably poorer prior to 1870. Today, we identify hospitals as technologic citadels of sophisticated medical practice. But their preindustrial origins were as religious and charitable institutions for the hopelessly sick and poor. They were places to comfort the indigent dying.

For the first three quarters of the nineteenth century, medical personnel were not in charge of hospitals. . . . In the main, hospitals at that time were places for the homeless poor and insane to die. The affluent classes were treated at home. For a variety of reasons, however, hospitals became central to medical practice and education between 1870 and 1910.[1] . . .

[T]he development of the medical profession parallels particular developments of the hospital. This is especially true of surgery, which enjoyed a dramatic increase of prestige and precision during this time. Technological advances played a major role in changing surgery. Before painkilling drugs, surgical methods in the first half of the nineteenth century depended upon powerful and swift physicians whose craft and tools were closer to the corner butcher. Mortality rates of about 40 percent followed amputation.

Three developments altered the brutality and mortality rates and allowed abdominal surgery, which was rarely performed prior to 1890. Dentist William Morton's demonstration of ether at Massachusetts General Hospital in 1846 ushered in a means of eliminating pain and allowed more careful and delicate surgery. Joseph Lister's discovery of antisepsis in 1867 gradually led to new procedures during surgery to prevent infection. However, antisepsis was poorly understood. Lister's technique was based on the use of carbolic acid spray, but his methods were adopted only over a long period of time. Fatal infections continued even after using the spray because antiseptic procedures were not followed carefully until after 1880. Soon, sterile procedures were properly followed and surgery rapidly expanded. Finally, the development of the X-ray in 1895, along with other diagnostic tools, opened the way for abdominal surgery for appendicitis, gallbladder, and stomach ulcers. Thoracic surgery and surgery of the nervous and cardiovascular systems developed in the early 1900s.

TRIUMPH AND TRAGEDY

By 1950, the cliché a "medical miracle" had rich meaning. Infant mortality rates in the United States were fewer than 15 per 100,000 births, down from 300 or so per 100,000 at the turn of the century. Pneumonia, once whispered by medical staff who witnessed the suffering of the dying to be the "old man's relief," now was easily controlled with penicillin. Infectious diseases in particular dramatically declined in the first half of the twentieth century. Improvement in health was a triumph of modernity, and part of that triumph was a consequence of modern medicine. There is, however, much debate about the weight of medicine's contribution, compared to other modern factors. . . .

1. Paul Starr, The Social Transformation of American Medicine 151 (1982).

Our dramatic advances in health are also related to improved nutrition, lifestyle, and education, as well as to medical advancements. The literature of health care points, in particular, to . . . proper diet, minimal tension, absence of smoking or heavy drinking, daily exercise, and a life-style that provides low-risk factors for accidents. Advances in health and longevity are more closely tied to higher income, better diets, and especially greater education than to advances in medicine. . . .

Yet, American perception of well-being is closely identified with medicine. Paradoxically, much of the public's present disenchantment with medicine is the consequence of this identification. Modern medicine has advanced to the frontiers of preserving life, but only by increasingly more expensive therapies and diagnoses to preserve life "on its margins." That is, additional expenditures and efforts to treat disease produce diminishing results in proportion to the effort. We are just beginning to learn that our scientific capacity to triumph over illness, physical anomalies, and death, on many occasions with medical miracles, brings with it a special brand of tragedy.

We have become totally modern. No more can we explain death and suffering as a consequence of fate. It is our medicine, or lack of it, that denies death and suffering. We know we must choose who receives scarce resources and who does not. No longer can we attribute to fate or to God the responsibility for making life-and-death decisions. Yet, these life-and-death decisions involve very expensive procedures and technologies and often contribute only marginally to extending life. Examples are well known and regularly make front-page newspaper drama: organ transplants, aggressive treatment of terminal patients, neonates under 750 grams, or long-term comatose patients.

These new choices challenge our basic values and frequently produce conflict. . . . Conflict is father to politics and law, and politics determines who gets what, when, and how. Conflict also forces moral reassessment of traditional attitudes and postures, including the justice question: "Who *should* get what, when and how."

How do we distribute health care? How should we? How does political power within the present economic system determine the distribution of health care? These questions obviously spill over the boundaries of economics, politics, sociology, law, medicine, history, and philosophy. In particular, looming over the politics of health care is a sense of the tragic, as well as the majestic. Tragedy points to human endeavors that are virtuous and honorable, yet carry the seeds of their own downfall. Our efforts to lessen the suffering and lengthen the lives of Americans through accessible, affordable, quality health care represent the best of our traditions and have been, on balance, an American success story. Sometimes we fall short in that effort because some group is unreasonably left behind in the political shuffle. The [45] million Americans who [have] no health coverage represent[] such a group. At other times, our very success leads to exasperating dilemmas of bioethics and distributive justice that would cross the eyes of a Solomon. Our dilemma over public financing for costly organ transplants at the expense of other badly needed programs or continued aggressive treatment of comatose or terminally ill loved ones are poignant, modern examples. It is here where triumph merges with tragedy.

■END-OF-LIFE WARNING AT $618,616 MAKES ME WONDER WAS IT WORTH IT
Amanda Bennett
Bloomberg News, Mar. 4, 2010*

It was some time after midnight on Dec. 8, 2007, when [the doctor] told me my husband might not live till morning. The kidney cancer that had metastasized almost six years earlier was growing in his lungs. He was in intensive care at the Hospital of the University of Pennsylvania in Philadelphia, and had begun to spit blood.

Terence Bryan Foley, 67 years old, my husband of 20 years, father of our two teenagers, a Chinese historian who earned his Ph.D. in his 60s, a man who played more than 15 musical instruments and spoke six languages, a San Francisco cable car conductor and sports photographer, an expert on dairy cattle and swine nutrition, film noir and Dixieland jazz, was confused. He knew his name, but not the year. He wanted a Coke.

Should Terence begin to hemorrhage, the doctor asked, what should he do? This was our third end-of-life warning in seven years. We fought off the others. Perhaps we could dodge this one too. [Terence's oncologist] and I both believed that a new medicine he had just begun to take would buy him more time. Keep him alive if you can, I said. Let's see what the drug, Pfizer Inc.'s Sutent, can do.

Terence died six days later, on Friday, Dec. 14, 2007. What I couldn't know then was that the thinking behind my request—along with hundreds of decisions we made over seven years—was a window on the impossible calculus at the core of the U.S. health-care debate.

EXPENSIVE LAST CHANCES

Terence and I didn't have to think about money, allocation of medical resources, the struggles of [millions of] uninsured Americans, or the impact on corporate bottom lines. Backed by medical insurance provided by my employers, we were able to fight his cancer with a series of expensive last chances like the one I asked for that night.

How expensive? The bills totaled $618,616, almost two-thirds of it for the final 24 months, much of it for treatments that no one can say for sure helped extend his life. In just the last four days of trying to keep him alive—two in intensive care, two in a cancer ward—our insurance was charged $43,711 for doctors, medicines, monitors, X-rays and scans. Two years later, the only thing I know for certain that money bought was confirmation that he was dying.

Some of the drugs probably did Terence no good at all. At least one helped fewer than 10 percent of all those who took it. Pharmaceutical companies and insurers will have to sort out the economics of treatments that end up working for only a small subset. Should everyone have the right to try them? Terence and I answered yes. Each drug potentially added life. Yet that too led me to a question I can't answer. When is it time to quit?   *JESUS*

---

*Excerpted with permission. For a fuller account, see Amanda Bennett, The Cost of Hope (2012).

SCIENCE, EMOTION, COSTS

Congress didn't touch the issue in [the Patient Protection and Affordable Care Act of 2010]. The mere hint of somehow limiting the ability to choose care as aggressively as Terence and I did, created a whirlwind of accusations that the ill, aged and infirm would be forced before government "death panels."

As the debate heated up, I remembered the fat sheaf of insurance statements that arrived after Terence's death . . . [from] six hospitals, four insurers, Medicare, three oncologists, and a surgeon. Those papers tell the story of a system filled with people doing their best. And they raise complex questions about a health-care system that consumes 17 percent of the economy. As I leafed through the stack of documents, it was easy to see why 31 percent of the money spent on health care goes to paperwork and administration. . . .

The documents revealed an economic system in which the sellers don't set and the buyers don't know the prices. The University of Pennsylvania hospital charged more than 12 times what Medicare at the time reimbursed for a chest scan. One insurer paid a hospital for 80 percent of the $3,232 price of a scan, while another covered 24 percent. Insurance companies negotiated their own rates, and neither my employers nor I paid the difference between the sticker and discounted prices.

'IT'S COMPLETELY INSANE'

In this economic system, prices of goods and services bear little relation to the demand for them or their cost to make — or, as it turns out, the good or harm they do. "No other nation would allow a health system to be run the way we do it. It's completely insane," said Uwe E. Reinhardt, a political economy professor at Princeton University. . . . Taking it all into account, the data showed we had made a bargain that hardly any economist looking solely at the numbers would say made sense. Why did we do it?

I was one big reason. Not me alone, of course. The medical system has a strong bias toward action. My husband, too, was unusual . . . in his passionate willingness to endure discomfort for a chance to see his daughter grow from a child to a young woman, and his son graduate from high school.

After Terence died, [his doctor] drew me a picture of a bell curve, showing the range of survival times for kidney cancer sufferers. Terence was way off in the tail on the right-hand side, an indication he had indeed beaten the odds. An explosion of research had made it possible to extend lives for years — enough to keep our quest from having been total madness.

Terence used to tell a story, almost certainly apocryphal, about his Uncle Bob. Climbing aboard a landing craft before the invasion of Normandy, so the story went, Bob's sergeant told the men that by the end of the day, nine out of 10 would be dead. Said Bob, on hearing that news: "Each one of us looked around and felt so sorry for those other nine poor sonsabitches."

For me, it was about pushing the bell curve. Knowing that if there was something to be done, we couldn't not do it. Believing beyond logic that we were going to escape the fate of those other poor sonsabitches. It is very hard to put a price on that kind of hope.

PRICING HOPE

We found the cancer by accident [a decade ago]. . . . Within a month, Terence was in surgery, and [another doctor] had taken out the diseased kidney. . . . "We got it all," he said. Terence was visibly moved. "Thank you for saving my life," he said. . . . The statistics looked good. By the traditional method of staging—a 7-centimeter tumor with no sign of having spread—Terence had an 85 percent chance of surviving five years.

The bills from Regence Blue Cross & Blue Shield of Oregon show the operation was relatively inexpensive, too, just over $25,000, or only about 4 percent of the total [eventually] charged to keep Terence alive. Insurance paid a discounted $14,084. Terence and I paid $209.87. The lab soon cast a chill on our optimism.

Terence had "collecting duct" cancer, the rarest and most aggressive form. . . . If that was correct, Terence had almost no chance of making it to the end of the year. . . . "Watchful waiting" was the recommended path. Waiting for him to die was what we feared. He didn't die. He got better. We didn't know why. We tried not to think about it. . . .

Then, on May 6, 2002, I was at work when [our son] Terry called, panic in his voice. "Mom, come home. Dad is very sick." . . . His father was in bed, his face flaming with fever, shaking with chills under a pile of blankets. He could barely speak. "The cancer is in my lungs," he said. "I've got six to nine months left."

A scan had spotted the cancer's spread. Not wanting to worry us, Terence had secretly begun taking Interleukin-2. If he recovered, he figured, we would never know how close he came; if he died, he would have spared us months of anguish. . . . What he didn't reckon on was that the drug would make him violently ill. But it was the only possible therapy at that time. Injections of the protein—at $735 a dose—were intended to stimulate the immune response to help fight off the cancer's invasion. The overall response rate was about 10 percent. For most, it did nothing.

That evening, for the one and only time, I felt pure terror. I spent the night awake in our dark living room. . . . Knowing the long odds, [the oncologist later] told me he had prescribed Interleukin-2 simply because it was all there was. Terence stopped taking it after just a few weeks, unable to stand the side effects.

I shook off my fear and plunged into the Internet. If there was something out there that could save him, I was going to find it. One colleague had been snatched from dying of AIDS by a chance introduction to a doctor who prescribed an experimental antiviral cocktail. Another had beaten leukemia with a cutting-edge bone marrow transplant. We could defeat this, too. . . .

The entire medical bill for seven years . . . was steeply discounted. The $618,616 became $254,176 when the insurers paid their share and imposed their discounts. Of that, Terence and I were responsible for $9,468—less than 4 percent. . . .

[A]s summer in Philadelphia turned to autumn. Terence resumed [another treatment which he had ceased earlier due to side effects]. Because he wasn't in a clinical trial, our insurance company was billed: $27,360 a dose, for four treatments. [But that also failed to stop the cancer's spread.] . . .

READING THEIR GOODBYES

[A few months later] I signed the papers transferring Terence to hospice. The next day, Tuesday, the hospital staff took away the machines and the monitors. The oncologists and radiologists and lab technicians disappeared. Another group of people—hospice nurses, social workers, chaplains and counselors for me and the children—began to arrive one by one, as the focus shifted from treating Terence to easing our transition.

For the next three days, with Terence in the same hospital bed, we spent $14,022 on [pain and anxiety medications], and on monitoring for him and counseling for a different kind of pain management for the children and me. The cost was less than a third of the previous four days' $43,711.

Terence drifted into a coma on Tuesday. I e-mailed his friends and read their goodbyes aloud, hoping he could hear and understand. I slept in a chair. At about 2:30 A.M. Friday, a noise in the hall startled me. I awoke just in time to hold his hand as he died. They gave me back his wedding ring the next day.

Looking back, memories of my zeal to treat are tinged with sadness. Since I didn't believe my husband was going to die, I never let us have the chance to say goodbye. . . .

Would I do it all again? Absolutely. I couldn't not do it again. But I think had he known the costs, Terence would have fought the insurers spending enough, at roughly $200,000, to vaccinate almost a quarter-million children in developing countries. That's how he would have thought about it. . . .

Did we help Terence? Or harm him? . . . [His doctor] and I looked at the numbers. The average patient in his [clinical] trial got 14 months of extra life. Without any treatment, [his doctor] estimates that for someone at Terence's stage of the disease it was three months. Terence got 17 months—still within the realm of chance, but way, way up on the bell curve.

There's another bell curve that starts about where Terence's left off. It charts the survival times for patients treated not just with [the dugs Terence received] but also Novartis's Afinitor and GlaxoSmithKline's Votrient, made available within the past three years. Doctors and patients now are doing what we dreamed of, staggering one drug after another and buying years more of life. . . .

[Terence's] 17 months included an afternoon looking down at the Mediterranean with Georgia from a sunny balcony in Southern Spain. Moving Terry into his college dorm. Celebrating our 20th anniversary with a carriage ride through Philadelphia's cobbled streets. A final Thanksgiving game of charades with cousins Margo and Glenn.

And one last chance for Terence to pave the way for all those other poor sonsabitches.

■ DOCTORS, PATIENTS, AND HEALTH INSURANCE: THE ORGANIZATION AND FINANCING OF MEDICAL CARE
Herman Miles Somers & Anne Ramsay Somers
1961

. . . The popular conception of the doctor-patient relationship is a mixture of fact and fancy. Until World War II the general practitioner family doctor was still in the majority. The one-to-one relationship of a personally chosen physician—where economic and other factors permitted any choice—with his patient was the most common form of medical practice. In big cities, the doctor had an office, usually mahogany and leather, sparsely equipped with simple diagnostic aids, a few surgical tools, and some antiseptic drugs. But, especially in rural areas and suburbs, he was more often found in the homes of his patients doing his rounds, working at the bedside of the sick and injured. His black bag held almost all his equipment. His records were kept partly in a small notebook, mostly in his mind and heart. He appeared indefatigable, compassionate, and available wherever and whenever needed. . . .

This doctor of the past has been idealized in story, picture, and legend. . . . Despite its apparent anachronisms, the picture still appeals to people's sentiments—even to those fully aware of its use as a public relations device. It has the warmth and intimate concern that no hypodermic needle—no complex of steel and tubing—can replace, however effective they may be. Although medical miracles are now performed successfully between strangers, doctors and patients both believe that the absence of continuity, personal concern, and individual attention are detrimental to the best medical care. This is not without foundation.

The origin of the "traditional" doctor-patient relationship reaches deep into the past. From the beginning of medical history, the practicing physician has been part priest, part technician, part personal or family counselor. In early days, when medicine had very little in the way of scientific knowledge to rely on, it was inevitable that the subjective priestly element should be dominant. . . .

In modern times medicine has become more scientific. But the traditional reliance on mystical forces and a highly authoritarian doctor-patient relationship persists to a degree unknown in other contemporary human relations. . . . The relationship of citizen and state, of employer and employee, of teacher and pupil, parent and child, even of husband and wife, have undergone profound and acknowledged changes as a result of the technological and socio-economic trends of the past few centuries. But there is no general acknowledgment or acceptance of the significant change that has, in fact, been taking place in the doctor-patient relationship. Of the manifold and complex reasons, only a few of the more important can be noted here.

First and basic is the persistence—in spite of scientific progress—of large elements of uncertainty and fear regarding illness and medical care which are conducive to continued reliance on hope, faith, confidence and other subjective factors on the part of both doctor and patient. "Honor thy physician because of the need thou hast of him," so said apocryphal Ecclesiastes to the Hebrews thousands of years ago. And still, today, patients yearn to have confidence in their doctors, to idealize them, to endow them with superhuman powers. Talcott Parsons, the Harvard sociologist, reconciles the use of such subjective factors—the use of "modern magic"—with the scientific basis of modern medicine by calling it a "functional bias."

> The basic function of magic is to bolster the self-confidence of actors in situations where energy and skill *do* make a difference but where, because of uncertainty factors, outcomes cannot be guaranteed. This fits the situation of the doctor, but in addition on the side of the patient it may be argued the *belief* in the possibility of recovery is an important factor in it. If from purely a technical point of view both the individual doctor and the general tradition are optimistically biased it ought to help. . . . Of course, this argument must not be pressed too far.

As the boundaries of medical ignorance and uncertainty are pushed back, one would expect this resort to supra-scientific factors to decline, and, indeed, it has in the case of bacterial and other diseases where the cause and cure are clearly established. But the reduced role of subjective factors in the treatment of specific cases has been more than offset by an increasing interest in the role of the emotions in illness. A widespread increase in psychotherapy and psychosomatic medicine has renewed the emphasis on a personal doctor and a personal doctor-patient relationship of a type that permits knowledge of the "whole [person]." . . .

Moreover, it is now widely believed that illness, *per se*, tends to create—even in the most intellectual of patients—an attitude of dependence, of "regression" to helplessness, and perhaps to childlike behavior. . . . In this state, confidence in the authority and benevolence of the doctor, as well as in his scientific knowledge and technical skill—the now-familiar "father-image"—is generally desired and often desirable.

Finally, there is the impenetrable mystery of death. The physician's relation to this event—however helpless he in fact may be—has endowed him, in the eyes of centuries of patients, with an aura of the mystery. To the extent that the physician identifies himself with this priestly role and takes on himself the burden associated therewith, or at least appears to do so through the gravity of his personal demeanor and behavior, his supra-scientific role continues to be respected and perpetuated, reinforcing in the eyes of individual patients and society at large his status as a dispenser of increasingly scientific medicine.

■ COMPETING SOLUTIONS: AMERICAN HEALTH CARE PROPOSALS AND INTERNATIONAL EXPERIENCE
Joseph White
1995

America's systems for delivering and paying for medical care are notably more complex than those of most other countries. Many doctors work in more than one hospital, making governance of medical staffs difficult; specialists are harder to coordinate because there are more of them; and the proliferation of forms of managed care means rapid change in patterns of gatekeeping and referral.

PHYSICIANS

American doctors go through extensive training to work long hours for high pay. The typical medical school program requires, after four years of college, four more years of "undergraduate" medical education. During the final two years, students receive some clinical training. Virtually all graduates then must complete some graduate medical education in order to be licensed to practice medicine. This education is obtained in residency programs, mainly in hospitals affiliated with medical schools. Normally only one year of residency (as an intern) is needed for licensure, but up to eight years (for neurosurgeons) may be required for certification as a specialist.

. . . Given the length of their training and the size of their debts, it is understandable that most physicians feel entitled to incomes that are much higher than those of most other Americans. . . . [The median physician salary is about $200,000, roughly five times that of the average American worker. The range across specialties is broad. Pediatricians and general practitioners typically earn around $175,000, common medical specialists (cardiology, dermatology, anesthesiology) are in the $250,000-$350,000 range, while heart surgeons and brain surgeons can earn well over $500,000. Some doctors earn substantially more from entrepreneurial activities such as medical patents and investments in various health care organizations.]

An unusually high proportion of American doctors are trained to specialize. Fewer than 10 percent of American doctors [call] themselves general practitioners (GPs), the standard term for primary care physicians. But because a specialist such as a family practitioner, internist, pediatrician, or obstetrician-gynecologist may be a person's regular physician, between 33 and 40 percent of physicians (depending on who is counting) are mainly primary care providers. [Specialists who receive several years of extra training and pass additional exams are designated as "Board Certified," meaning that they comply with voluntary, private standards set by the American Specialty Boards, which operate under the auspices of the AMA. At one time, board certification was relatively rare, but now the vast majority of new doctors obtain certification. About two dozen boards now exist, covering not only standard specialties but also areas of general practice such as family medicine and internal medicine.] . . .

Two-thirds of physicians practice in offices, the vast majority with admitting privileges to a hospital. Many practice in more [than one hospital] (for example, a nice suburban hospital for simple cases, and a high-tech academic medical center for difficult ones). Hospitals therefore must compete for admissions by making those physicians happy, such as by having the fanciest equipment. . . .

INSTITUTIONAL CARE

Long-term or chronic care, especially for the aged, is a complicated system on its own, and the potential expenses of long-term care are so great that it is highly unlikely that any reform will do much about it. [Therefore, the focus here is] on the costs of the current American health care system, of which one major component is hospital services for acute care.

The American supply of hospitals is dominated by private nonprofit hospitals—many owned by religious organizations. [About two-thirds] of hospital beds [are] provided by the nonprofits, 10 percent by the for-profit sector. The rest, just over a quarter of the beds, [are] in federal, state, or local facilities. It is hard to identify much difference between the behavior and efficiency of the for-profit and private nonprofits. If private institutions are more efficient, the savings go largely or entirely to investors.

Americans spend a great deal of money on hospitals: [about 40 percent] of all spending on patient care. But . . . the hospital is not as dominant a provider as it once was or still is in other countries. Hospitals and doctors tried to avoid regulation by moving care to ostensibly freestanding ambulatory care facilities. Examples include kidney dialysis units, and radiology group practices with close relations with hospitals. Some payers encouraged the shift, believing those facilities would be cheaper. . . .

Back in the traditional hospitals, the nature of care depends greatly on hospitals' relationships with doctors and medical schools, and on hospitals' catchment areas — the areas from which they get most of their patients. . . .

A suburban hospital can generally provide sophisticated care, such as cardiac bypass surgery, but it is not as likely to have clinical professors who are able to provide extremely specialized care for "interesting" cases. All hospitals want the most advanced equipment, but the academic medical centers must have it for research and training. These centers rely heavily on residents and interns for delivery of care and, most important, are likely to have a much lower-class population of patients.

Many of the [academic medical centers] are in inner cities. They are likely to have large outpatient departments to train the students (residents) and serve the local population, which feeds into the inpatient wards; the emergency room not only gets emergencies but also serves as an outpatient clinic for some of the population. All of this is the good news: If a major teaching hospital is in the inner city, then either a large and endowed institution or a state government pays for some care for the inner-city poor.

When local hospitals receive little funding for education, poor populations must frequently rely on a hospital financed by a strapped city or county budget. Such hospitals — for example, Cook County in Chicago, Boston City, and Charity in New Orleans — have interns and residents to do the work because of their relationship with a training program, but nowhere near the resources of a freestanding university hospital. All hospitals in the inner city try to convince Medicare that they deserve an extra subsidy for treating a poorer, less-insured, and often sicker population. The federal government calls these disproportionate share payments. One of the huge issues for American health care reform is what will happen to the academic medical centers and the remaining urban public hospitals if payment systems allow competing insurers to favor hospitals that are less expensive because they have lesser teaching and subsidy burdens.

Another major issue is how a bias toward specialized, high-technology medicine, created in part by how medical education is financed and how physicians are paid, is reinforced by arrangements for capital investment in American medicine. There are hardly any measures in place to prevent a "medical arms race" among hospitals that seek the most advanced technology in order to attract physicians and generate revenue. . . .

Because for years insurers would pay whatever physicians and hospitals billed, and hospitals relied on physicians to provide patients, hospitals competed for patients by having the best equipment, and insurers ended up paying for excess treatments and higher charges per treatment. Also, at one time, physicians could refer patients to any specialist they wished, and patients could go directly to a specialist without referral.

The rise of managed care and of more aggressive bargaining by insurers has change[d] this basic pattern. Insurers have become more likely to refuse to approve a given service or to insist on a lower price. Hospitals still need to attract physicians by offering the best equipment, however, so they are caught between the demands of doctors and payers. Meanwhile insurers are limiting choice of and access to specialists by building closed panels, in which a person covered by a plan either cannot use or must pay a surcharge to use any provider who is not on special contract to the plan. A patient might find that her doctor of 20 years' standing is no longer part of her insurance plan; a physician might find that many of his patients can afford referral only to three nephrologists whom he does not know. One of the key issues in reform is whether these . . . restrictions on choice of physician are necessary.

◼ DOCTORS, PATIENTS, AND HEALTH INSURANCE: THE ORGANIZATION AND FINANCING OF MEDICAL CARE
Herman Miles Somers & Anne Ramsay Somers
1961

[T]he conflict between [hospital] medical staff and [hospital] management has become both sharper and more open in recent years. The roots of this conflict—the basic dichotomy in hospital organization—go back to eighteenth century Britain and the establishment of the Anglo-American tradition of voluntary hospitals. There was no such dichotomy in medieval days when hospitals were operated, with little medical assistance, by monastic orders for the sick poor. There is generally no such duality in the major Continental hospitals which are usually run, with unquestioned authority, by full-time chiefs of medical services. The distinguishing feature of the Anglo-American voluntary hospital, however, has been its use by private physicians for private patients with little or no accompanying administrative or financial responsibility. . . .

Recent developments—the hospital's changing role, its increase in size, complexity, utilization, cost, and its greatly altered financial base—have intensified the inherent instability of this administrative structure. . . . Lay influences on hospital administration and policy are clearly increasing. Ultimate policy responsibility has always rested with lay trustees. Traditionally, they limited their oversight to balancing the books. With the tremendous increase in hospital costs, however, this single concern has led to increasing surveillance over the hospital's total functioning, including the organization of the medical staff. The hospital administrator, traditionally an untrained individual content to play a fairly subservient role and socially outranked by doctor and trustee alike, is being transformed into a professional with increasing self-confidence and authority. . . .

At the same time the hospital has become an indispensable workshop for the modern physician, who finds it virtually impossible to practice good medicine without hospital affiliation. The hospital is the center of his professional world, and he is acknowledged to be its key figure. Fully 40 percent of private physician income is now earned in the hospital. Naturally he wants "his" institution equipped with the latest scientific and technological facilities. But the doctor's relationship to the hospital is peculiarly ambiguous. As a rule he assumes neither administrative nor financial responsibility. Yet, in practice, his is the most powerful voice in the organization. He alone admits and discharges patients; he alone can diagnose, prescribe, and treat patients—still the chief purpose for which the hospital exists. With his high professional status, he may, in most hospitals, countermand administrative orders and defy lay authority with relative impunity. The result is the confusing duality that prevails today throughout the hospital system, public and private. . . .

It is sometimes proposed that hiring the medical staff on a salary or contract basis would increase the doctors' sense of responsibility for hospital administration and help clarify lines of accountability. It could integrate the administrative structure without restricting professional integrity. This is the general pattern in a few of the nation's best hospitals, such as the Henry Ford in Detroit and the Cleveland Clinic Hospital. Most of the profession is, however, vigorously opposed to such practice, alleging "hospital domination," "lay control," or the "corporate practice of medicine." Some hospitals have taken a middle road — employing full-time medical directors (this is frequently the practice in government hospitals) and in a few instances, full-time chiefs of medical services. This too is generally frowned on by physicians in private practice. . . .

Many hospital spokesmen, however, content themselves with pleading for physician cooperation in assuring some responsibility for hospital operations and costs. . . . But such recommendations are usually set in a purely hortatory context. It is not clear how such preachments are to influence the individual doctor. The "medical staff" of which he is a member is in most instances simply a term for the collectivity of physicians authorized to practice in a particular hospital. The staff can be as disciplinary an instrument as it chooses to be, but in most places it has chosen minimal responsibility. . . . By and large the staff still prefers not to interfere with the practices of the individual physician.

■ CLINICAL DECISION MAKING: FROM THEORY TO PRACTICE
David M. Eddy
1996

Medical practice is in the middle of a profound transition. Most physicians can remember the day when, armed with a degree, a mission, and confidence, they could set forth to heal the sick. Like Solomon, physicians could receive patients, hear their complaints, and determine the best course of action. While not every patient could be cured, everyone could be confident that whatever was done was the best possible. Most important, each physician was free, trusted, and left alone to determine what was in the best interest of each patient.

All of that is changing. . . . Now physicians must deal with second opinions, precertification, skeptical medical directors, variable coverage, outright denials, utilization review, threats of cookbook medicine, and letters out of the blue chiding that Mrs. Smith is on two incompatible drugs. Solomon did not have to call anyone to get permission for his decisions. What is going on?

What is going on is that one of the basic assumptions underlying the practice of medicine is being challenged. This assumption is not just a theory about cholesterol, antiarrhythmia, or estrogens. This assumption concerns the intellectual foundation of medical care. Simply put, the assumption is that whatever a physician decides is, by definition, correct. The challenge says that while many decisions no doubt *are* correct, many are not, and elaborate mechanisms are needed to determine which are which. Physicians are slowly being stripped of their decisionmaking power.

Notes: Doctors and Hospitals

1. *The Two-Headed Monster.* The unique structure of American hospitals, in which doctors are independent but essential to their financial well-being, has been described as "attractive as a two-headed monster" and as "stable as a three-legged stool." See

H. L. Smith, Two Lines of Authority Are One Too Many, 84 Modern Hosp. 59 (Mar. 1955). This division of authority is mirrored throughout the organizational structure of the health care system. For instance, hospitals, unlike any other business organization, are required by state licensure laws and private accreditation standards to have *two* sets of corporate bylaws; one for the hospital administration and a second for the medical staff. Similarly, health insurance traditionally pays hospitals separately from doctors, as reflected in the distinctions between Blue Cross (hospital insurance) vs. Blue Shield (physician insurance) and between Medicare Part A vs. Part B.

2. *Power Relationships in Medicine.* Medical sociologists and organizational theorists have produced a rich literature discussing the role of physicians within medical institutions. Leading examples are Eliot Freidson, Doctoring Together (1975); Eliot Freidson, Profession of Medicine (1970); Paul Starr, The Social Transformation of American Medicine (1982); Jeffrey Harris, The Internal Organization of Hospitals: Some Economic Implications, 8 Bell J. Econ. 467 (1977). For an exploration of how these insights illuminate a variety of legal doctrines and public policy debates, see Mark A. Hall, Institutional Control of Physician Behavior: Legal Barriers to Health Care Cost Containment, 137 U. Pa. L. Rev. 431 (1988) ("Because the law absorbs and reflects the values and relationships of traditional medicine, it has codified the ethic of professional dominance, effectively shielding physicians from the institutional influence contemplated by revolutionary changes in health care policy."); Sara Rosenbaum, The Impact of United States Law on Medicine as a Profession, 289 JAMA 1546 (2003); Symposium, 29 J. Health Pol. Pol'y & L. 557 (2004); Symposium, 4 Ind. Health L. Rev. 205-286 (2007).

3. *History and Description.* For **general histories and descriptions** of the health care delivery system, see David Smith & Arnold Kaluzny, The White Labyrinth: A Guide to the Health Care System (2d ed. 2000); Kristina M. Young & Philip J. Kroth, Health Care USA: Understanding Its Organization and Delivery (9th ed. 2018); David Johnson & Nancy Kane, The U.S. Health Care System: A Product of American History and Values, *in* E. Elhauge ed., The Fragmentation of U.S. Health Care (2010); Hamilton Moses et al., The Anatomy of US Health Care, 310 JAMA 1947 (2013). For more extensive historical accounts of the transformation of hospitals and their role in modern medicine, see Guenter B. Risse, Mending Bodies, Saving Souls: A History of Hospitals (1999); Charles Rosenberg, The Care of Strangers (1987); David Rosner, A Once Charitable Enterprise (1982); Rosemary Stevens, In Sickness and in Wealth: American Hospitals in the Twentieth Century (1989).

2. Medicine, Illness, and Healing

■ MAGIC OR MEDICINE? AN INVESTIGATION OF HEALING AND HEALERS*
Robert Buckman & Karl Sabbagh
1995

[S]ome may find surprising . . . that the exact definition of what constitutes a disease or an illness is determined not by biology but by society. Certainly, there is a class of health problems that are seen in a similar way in all societies. For instance, if a previously fit man suddenly clutches his chest, looks white and sweaty and is acutely short of breath even at rest, then in Western society we would say that this man has probably had a heart attack, and we would prove it with ECGs and blood tests. It might be that in another society that episode is regarded as a visitation from a malevolent spirit . . . .

Some [diseases] are far more difficult to define and pigeon-hole and are classified differently in different societies. In Germany, for example, doctors prescribe six times the amount of heart drugs per person than in England or France. This is not because of a greater incidence of coronary artery disease in Germany . . . . One of the major reasons is that the German language doesn't have a way of distinguishing heart problems from any other kind of chest pain. . . . Thus, *Herzinsuffizienz* is an illness-label that is almost exclusive to Germany . . . .

In the same way, in France, a large number of nonspecific symptoms are attributed to a *crise de foie*—a "crisis of the liver." In fact, approximately 80 percent of problems attributed to a crisis of the liver are actually migraine. . . . Similarly, in the American medical view, minor illnesses are much more likely to be ascribed to (unspecified) viral illnesses. This is in line with the prevailing mood of the times in America in which disease is seen as an external invasive threat and there is a predilection for diagnosing infections since they can often be dealt with actively and quickly. . . .

Now consider a common event—bereavement. We expect to be sad after the death of someone we love—if the bereaved person cries continuously for a week, is that an illness? If he or she cries for six months, is that an illness? And what about adolescence? In Montana, a change in financing of private hospitals led to many general hospitals quickly changing themselves into psychiatric hospitals. Unfortunately, there were not enough patients to fill them, so there was a sudden epidemic of new diagnoses. Teenagers who had falling grades at school were now diagnosed as psychiatrically disturbed (with a major advertising campaign to get the point across to the parents) and were admitted to a hospital—at four times the rate that occurred in neighboring Utah. . . .

These [examples] again emphasize the partly arbitrary—and rather parochial—definitions of disease and illness. Each society decides for itself at the time what are legitimately regarded as diseases or illnesses. Those definitions vary from culture to culture. Furthermore, those conditions that we regard as normal today may be diagnosed as illnesses tomorrow.

■ THE TYRANNY OF HEALTH*
Faith T. Fitzgerald
331 New Eng. J. Med. 196 (1994)

There has recently been much in both lay and medical literature on the promotion of healthy lifestyles. Once upon a time people did not have lifestyles;

they had lives. Those lives were filled with work and play, battle and respite, excitement and boredom, but principally with the day-to-day struggle for existence, centered largely around the family, birth, death, disease, and health. What is the difference between a lifestyle and a life? Central to it, I believe, is the concept that lifestyle is something one chooses, and life is something that happens to one. This distinction will affect the future of medicine, and certainly health care reform, in this country. The emphasis on healthy lifestyles, although salutary in many ways, has a very dark side to it and has led to the increasing peril of a tyranny of health in the United States. To explain the potential dangers of the emphasis on healthy lifestyles, I here review the concept of health and its role in the fabric of our society.

A healthy lifestyle is said to be essential to the promotion of wellness. What is wellness? In 1946, the World Health Organization, largely in revulsion against the activities of Nazi physicians and the creatures who worked with them, redefined health as "a state of complete physical, mental, and social well being, and not merely the absence of disease or infirmity." This has become known as "wellness," a highly desirable state. A well or healthy person is one who is not only physically whole and vigorous, but also happy and socially content. What a good idea! . . .

Concurrently, and perhaps naively, both the lay public and the medical profession began to confuse the ideal of health with the norm for health. That is, we went from "Wouldn't it be great to have this be the definition of health" to "This *is* the definition of health." Having accepted the view that health should be a perfect state of wellness, we went on to declare that it was. But if one accepts the idea that physical vigor and emotional and social contentment are not only desirable, but also expected, there is a problem. If health is normal, then sickness and accidents are faults. Who or what is at fault varies: environmental pollution, for example, or government plots, doctors themselves, diet, radon, or political bias. We now act as if we really believe that disease, aging, and death are unnatural acts and all things are remediable. All we have to do, we think, is know enough (or spend enough), and disease and death can be prevented or fixed. . . .

In his paper "Medical Nemesis," [Lancet 1974;1:918-921,] Illich wrote in 1974 that classifying all the troubles of humanity as medical problems is actually antithetical to true health, in that it limits the ability of people to learn to cope with pain, sickness, and death as integral parts of life. Health, he maintained, is not freedom from the inevitability of death, disease, unhappiness and stress, but rather the ability to cope with them in a competent way. If this is true, then the more medicine and society direct individual behavior, the less autonomous, and therefore the less healthy, the individual may become.

We must beware of developing a zealotry about health, in which we take ourselves too seriously and believe that we know enough to dictate human behavior, penalize people for disagreeing with us, and even deny people charity, empathy, and understanding because they act in a way of which we disapprove. Perhaps the health care crisis could be resolved, in part, if we [health care professionals realized that] . . . we cannot fix everything (though we do some things marvelously well), nor can our patients—no matter how intelligent or attentive—prevent all disease and death. We may be trying to do too much and thus diluting an awareness and application of what we can do well.

■ THE MACHINE AT THE BEDSIDE*
Stanley Joel Reiser & Michael Anbar
1984

Technology has altered significantly the form and meaning of the medical relationship. It allows us to direct our vision and attention to variables singled out by it as significant. Thus, stethoscopes increase the significance of chest sounds, X-rays of anatomic shadows, electrocardiograms of waves on a graph, computers of printouts, dialysis machines of chemical balances, and so forth. Such evidence is important for diagnosis and therapy, and the more precisely it can be stated, the more valuable it becomes. In comparison, evidence given by patients, and altered by its passage through the prism of their experience and personality, has seemed to the technological age of the past two centuries less substantive, accurate, and meaningful as a basis for clinical decisionmaking and actions. Increasingly, practitioners encounter patients for relatively brief and intermittent periods—such as the consultant visiting a hospitalized patient whom he or she has never before met. In such visits the technical aspects often dominate, for there is no time or prior relationship to determine much about who the patient is, or what the patient thinks about the illness or the needs it engenders. And even in medical relationships that are not so discontinuous, technological measurements and measures tend to crowd out other dimensions of evaluation and therapeutics. To speak so of the attention focused on the technological features of practice does not diminish their great significance and benefit. Rather, it points out that they do not encompass all critical aspects of diagnosis or treatment. . . .

From the beginning of their introduction in the mid-nineteenth century, automated machines that generated results in objective formats such as graphs and numbers were thought capable of purging from health care the distortions of subjective human opinion. They were supposed to produce facts free of personal bias, and thus to reduce the uncertainty associated with human choice. This view, held by both practitioners and patients, stimulated the intense use of these devices, sometimes to excess. This excess has been characterized by overreliance on technologically depicted features of illness, inadequate understanding of the capabilities and limits of machines and the information they generate, and relative inattention to those aspects of medicine learned by inquiry into the patient's experiences and views. Machines can seem so accurate, so right. They can make us forget who made them, and who designed into them—with all the possibilities of human frailty and error—the programs that dictate their function. They can make us forget the hands and minds behind their creation; they can make us forget ourselves.

Notes: The Social Construction of Disease

1. *Is Anyone Healthy?* Students, especially younger ones, often fail to appreciate the extent to which health issues pervade society. According to one survey, in a typical *month*, 80 percent of adults report some type of medical symptom, 20 percent visit

a doctor, 6 percent visit an alternative (nontraditional) health care provider, and 4 percent go to a hospital. Larry Green et al., The Ecology of Medical Care Revisited, 344 New Eng. J. Med. 2021 (2001). See also H. Gilbert Welch et al., Overdiagnosed: Making People Sick in the Pursuit of Health (2011); Nortin M. Hadler, Worried Sick (2008); Otis Brawley & Paul Goldberg, How We Do Harm: A Doctor Breaks Ranks About Being Sick in America (2012); Nortin M. Hadler, The Last Well Person (2004); Clifton Meador, The Last Well Person, 330 New Eng. J. Med. 440 (1994).

2. For additional views on the meaning of health and illness and the impact of medical technology, see Peter Conrad, The Medicalization of Society (2007); Nancy King et al. eds., The Social Medicine Reader (2d ed. 2005); R. A. Deyo & D. L. Patrick, Hope or Hype: The Obsession with Medical Advances and the High Cost of False Promises (2005); Robert A. Aronowitz, Making Sense of Illness: Science, Society, and Disease (1998); Daniel Callahan, False Hopes: Why America's Quest for Perfect Health Is a Recipe for Failure (1998); Rene Dubos, Man, Medicine, and Environment (1968); Michel Foucault, The Birth of the Clinic (1963); David Mechanic, Symptoms, Illness Behavior, and Help Seeking (1982); Roy Porter, The Greatest Benefit to Mankind (1998); David Rothman, Beginnings Count: The Technological Imperative in American Health Care (1997); Wm. B. Schwartz, Life Without Disease: The Pursuit of Medical Utopia (1998); Susan Sontag, Illness as Metaphor (1988); Richard A. Miller, Extending Life: Scientific Prospects and Political Obstacles, 80(2) Milbank Q. (2002); Lars Noah, Pigeonholing Illness: Medical Diagnosis as a Legal Construct, 50 Hastings L. Rev. 241 (1999); Talcott Parsons, The Sick Role and the Role of the Physician Reconsidered, 53 Health & Soc'y 257 (1975); Symposium, The Price of Medical Technology, 27(6) Health Aff. (Nov. 2008); Symposium, 21(2) Health Aff. (Mar. 2002); Symposium, 20(5) Health Aff. (Sept. 2001); Symposium, 25 J. Med. & Phil. 519 (2000); Developments, Medical Technology and the Law, 103 Harv. L. Rev. 1519 (1990).

■MAKING MEDICAL SPENDING DECISIONS*
Mark A. Hall
1997

THE ONTOLOGICAL ASSAULT OF ILLNESS

Illness is frequently described as an "ontological assault." It undermines one's personal identity by attacking the fundamental unity of mind and body. In a state of health, our body is part of an integrated sense of self that responds instinctively to our will and serves our inner purposes almost effortlessly. When illness strikes, our body becomes an enemy of self. It does not respond as we wish and its frailties dominate our conscious thoughts. Illness strikes at one of our most fundamental assumptions in everyday life—that we will continue to exist and function much as we have in the past. Serious illness shatters our "primordial sense of invulnerability" (Silberman 1991).

The profound incapacitating effect of this assault on our very being is much more debilitating than any of life's other major disruptions, whether they be divorce, incarceration or impoverishment. Physician and philosopher Edmund Pellegrino observes correctly that:

> In no other deprivation is the dissolution of the person so intimate that it impairs the capacity to deal with all other deprivations. The poor man can still hope for a change of fortune, the prisoner for a reprieve, the lonely for a friend. But the ill person remains impaired even when freed of these other constraints on the free exercise of his humanity. (Pellegrino 1982, at 159)

Consider also this account by a philosopher and patient who herself suffers from a severe chronic illness, multiple sclerosis:

> The most deeply held assumption of daily life is the assumption that I, personally, will continue to be alive and it is in light of this assumption that one engages in daily activities. The onset of illness, however, brings one concretely face-to-face with personal vulnerability. . . . Thus, the person who is ill . . . is unable readily to fit illness into the typified schema used to organize and interpret experience. . . . One finds oneself preoccupied with the demands of the here and now, confined to the present moment, unable effectively to project into the future. (Toombs 1992, at 21, 69)

In addition to these profound internal effects, . . . when ill we are often immobilized and confined to bed in a prone position and subjected to mind-altering medications. This compromises our physical ability to act and deliberate and places us in a psychological state of dependency. Treatment also compromises physical integrity and exposes us to singular vulnerability by giving physicians unprecedented access to our bodies and personal histories. Treatment requires us to expose every part of ourselves, down to our very blood and guts, while we remain prostrate or unconscious.

Typically, when ill, we do not resist what would otherwise be viewed as utterly repugnant invasions and vulnerabilities. Sickness returns us to an infantile state where our strongest desire is usually to be cared for and to be relieved of the responsibility and anxiety of deciding and acting. "Such sick people . . . may plausibly prefer not to take on any kind of work, much less the fierce, foreign, and forbidding labor of medical decisions" (Schneider 1997). This is true even for the most knowledgeable of patients—physicians themselves. Franz Ingelfinger, M.D., long time editor of the eminently prestigious New England Journal of Medicine and an expert in diseases of the esophagus, found himself in a dilemma of how best to treat his own difficult case of cancer of the esophagus. His doctors, respecting their patient's world renowned expertise, were leaving this vexing decision to him:

> As a result, not only I but my wife, my son and daughter-in-law (both doctors), and other family members became increasingly confused and emotionally distraught. Finally, when the pangs of indecision had become nearly intolerable, one wise physician friend said, "What you need is a doctor." . . . When that excellent advice was followed, my family and I sensed immediate and immense relief. . . .

[M]y description of the real experience of illness applies to simple and serious conditions alike. Sickness does not have to be life threatening for it to profoundly affect thinking and functioning. A bad flu bug, a relentless shooting pain, a case of food poisoning, an inconsolable child, or even an unexplained lump or a persistent bad cough can have these menacing and incapacitating effects at least to some degree. Even if this state of mind is the exception in medical treatment encounters, it nevertheless is the dominant explanation of why the medical system exists. . . . Medical ethics and health care policy should have its primary focus on the quintessential features of the treatment relationship even if those features account for only a fraction of [medical] decisions.

THE MYSTICAL POWER OF HEALING

[The condition of illness is only half of the story in a medical encounter. We must also understand something about the experience of healing. Modern medicine thinks of healing as occurring mainly through biochemical processes activated by medical interventions chosen based on diagnostic analysis and professional experience.] . . . Much of medicine is of this rational quality, but [this account ignores] an essential nonrational component of medicine. . . . This essential component is the mystical power of healing. By this, I mean the hidden elements of the treatment encounter that result in healing through what might be termed charismatic or self-healing means. The power of healing I refer to is the dimension of doctoring that enables physicians to confer relief through spiritual or emotional means akin to those used by parents or priests.[2]

Before alienating the skeptical reader entirely, let me illustrate with an everyday example from my own experience. Last year when my six-year-old daughter was suffering from a common ear ache, her distress brought her to inconsolable tears while waiting more than an hour to be seen by the doctor. I convinced a nurse to take her temperature, give her an aspirin, and say a few kind words of reassurance. Instantaneously, my daughter felt much better, far quicker than any possible pharmacological effect could have taken hold. I was puzzled by this abrupt improvement until I had my own excruciating ear ache a few weeks later and experienced exactly the same sort of instantaneous relief as soon as the doctor examined me and wrote a prescription. Knowing that I was in the good hands of a trained professional who offered the prospect of relief produced in me a sense of exhilaration and a release of anxiety accompanied by a pronounced improvement of my symptoms. This instantaneous recovery might be attributed simply to excessive nerves or to a more complex type of placebo effect but, however labeled or explained, it was effective. The pain was not just more bearable; it went away.

Researchers and physicians have documented countless similar examples of mundane and miraculous relief caused by a largely nonscientific or "nonspecific" process of healing. This placebo effect is not limited to purely psychological states, bizarre conditions, especially susceptible patients, or to manipulative physicians. This effect has been documented in the treatment of diabetes, cancer, and heart disease, for instance, and without the physicians even intending to cause the effect. In one scientific study, two sets of patients were subjected to different surgical operations to treat angina (chest pain), one that performed the standard chest operation,

---

2. On the prevalence of the image of physician as parent or priest, see May 1983.

and the other that only pretended to do so by cutting the skin under anesthesia. Both the sham and the real procedure produced equal relief of physical symptoms (Beecher 1961). A review of other surgical and medical procedures once firmly believed to be effective but later discarded as entirely unfounded led one author to speculate that placebo healing effects may be present to a significant extent in 70 percent of clinical encounters (Roberts 1993).

Those who have studied this nonspecific healing effect conclude that it pervades medicine, both in modern times and in prescientific and primitive cultures. This is because the effect is connected more to the intervention of the healer than it is to the particular therapeutic agent used. Put another way, the doctor himself is a therapeutic agent, regardless of the actual effectiveness of the particular drug or procedure (Suchman & Matthews 1988; Houston 1938). In each culture and each era, there has been a prevailing theory of medical treatment, many of which are pure fantasy if not dangerous, yet remarkably few have been proven to be wholly without benefit. Doctors and healers have been universally respected throughout the ages and across primitive and advanced societies; we can only assume that most of them have offered some form of relief despite the now apparent quackery they once practiced. Indeed, it has often been commented that the history of medicine until this century has been the history of the placebo effect. Now that medicine has a firm scientific foundation, this mystical or charismatic element has been surpassed by technological skill, but it will never be entirely displaced. One of the prominent trends in modern medicine is the revival of both popular and scientific interest in these poorly understood domains of caring for patients through alternative or holistic schools of medicine (Frohoch 1992; Cousins 1979).

The best scientific explanation for this charismatic healing effect is that the process of treatment, and not its specific content, has universal benefit for many or most illnesses, regardless of the specific physiological effects of the treatment. The treatment process has this universal healing power by virtue of the archetypal characteristics that activate the patient's own healing mechanisms—mechanisms that are still largely undiscovered and unexplained. This is best demonstrated by the fact that the basic structure of the treatment encounter is remarkably the same across all systems of medicine, including Western, Eastern, religious, herbal, and primitive. In each of these belief systems, society recognizes the healing powers of a professional elite (physicians or shamans), who administer personally to the patient with physical touching and healing agents (drugs or herbs), often in a dramatic and cathartic ritualistic setting (surgery or exorcism) specially designed for the purpose (hospital or bonfire). In the process, patients feel cared for (nurses or mystics), they are given an explanation for their condition (diagnosis or demonization) that is consistent with their prevailing belief system (scientific medicine or spirit worship), and they are assigned tasks of self care in which they take responsibility in part for their own improvement (dietary regimen or prayer).[3]

These many symbolic structural elements are thought to activate patients' internal healing powers through a variety of psychological channels. A patient who

---

3. The leading work developing this explanation is Frank 1973. See also Brody 1992; Novack 1987.

knows someone is devoted to caring for him is able to release the dread and anxiety that may be heightening discomfort and weakening the body's resistance. Believing in the power of the healer may enable the patient to regress to an earlier, more infantile state of mind that enhances this release and the resulting comfort. This confidence in the healer is elevated by the healer's status in society, his invocation of methods consistent with that society's belief system, and his offering an explanation of the otherwise troubling and disorienting disease that makes sense to the patient. And, this belief is further cemented by the ritualistic and dramatic elements of laying on of hands, taking of medication, climactic performance, and hallowed setting. . . .

Critical to this healing power is the patient's confidence and trust in the healer. "The image of omnipotence is an essential component of the healer" (see Cassell 1991). The healer appears able to activate the patient's own healing mechanisms because the patient turns himself over both in mind and body to the healer. "A patient's hope and trust lead to a 'letting go' that counteracts stress and is often the key to getting well" (Siegel 1986). Psychiatrists, starting with Freud, have described this phenomenon as "transference," in which patients foist on their healers qualities they formerly attributed to their parents in infancy when parents were viewed as all powerful and all knowing. "Deep in patients' unconscious, physicians are viewed as miracle workers, patterned after the fantasied all-caring parents of infancy. Medicine, after all, was born in magic and religion, and the doctor-priest-magician-parent unity that persists in patients' unconscious cannot be broken" (Katz 1984, at 142-47, 192). . . .

I hasten to concede that none of these assertions are known with any degree of empirical confidence. We are forced into this highly speculative reading of anecdotal accounts from physicians, anthropologists, and ethnographic researchers since empirical testing of this nonspecific healing power is very difficult and has not been widely attempted.[4] Nevertheless, many informed observers and patients view the charismatic dimension of healing as fundamental to the treatment relationship (e.g., Brody 1992; Schenck & Churchill 2011).

[PARTIAL BIBLIOGRAPHY, UPDATED]

Beecher, H. (1961). "Surgery as Placebo," 176 JAMA 1102.

Brody, H. (1992). The Healer's Power (New Haven, CT: Yale Univ. Press).

Cassell, E.J. (1991). The Nature of Suffering and the Goals of Medicine (Oxford Univ. Press).

Cousins, N. (1979). Anatomy of an Illness as Perceived by the Patient: Reflections on Healing and Regeneration (New York: W.W. Norton).

Frank, J.D. (1973). Persuasion and Healing: A Comparative Study of Psychotherapy (Baltimore: Johns Hopkins Univ. Press).

Frohoch, F.M. (1992). Healing Powers: Alternative Medicine, Spiritual Communities, and the State (Univ. Chicago Press).

Houston, R. (1938). "The Doctor Himself as a Therapeutic Agent," 11 Annals Int. Med. 1415.

Katz, J. (1984). The Silent World of Doctor and Patient (New York: The Free Press).

4. There are some scattered scientific studies demonstrating the placebo effect and the effect of certain of these healing rituals, but no scientific studies exploring what ingredients make this process work . . . [or are counterproductive].

Kleinman, A. (1988). The Illness Narratives: Suffering, Healing, and the Human Condition (Basic Books).

Miller, F. et al. (eds.). The Placebo (2013).

Novack, D.H. (1987). "Therapeutic Aspects of the Clinical Encounter," 2 J. Gen. Intern. Med. 346.

Pellegrino, E.D. (1979). "Toward a Reconstruction of Medical Morality: The Primacy of the Act of Profession and the Fact of Illness," 4 J. Med. & Philo. 32.

Pellegrino, E.D. and Thomasma, D.C. (1981). A Philosophical Basis of Medical Practice (Oxford Univ. Press).

Roberts, A.H. et al. (1993). "The Power of Nonspecific Effects in Healing," 12 Clin. Psychol. Rev. 375.

Schenck, D. & Churchill, L. (2011). Healers: Extraordinary Clinicians at Work.

Schneider, C.E. (1997). The Practice of Autonomy: Patients, Doctors, and Medical Decisions (Oxford Univ. Press).

Spiro, H.M. (1986). Doctors, Patients, and Placebos (New Haven, CT: Yale Univ. Press).

Suchman, A.L., and Matthews, D.A. (1988). "What Makes the Doctor-Patient Relationship Therapeutic? Exploring the Connexional Dimension of Medical Care," 108 Ann. Intern. Med. 125.

Toombs, S.K. (1992). The Meaning of Illness, A Phenomenological Account of the Different Perspectives of Physician and Patient (Boston: Kluwer Academic Publishers).

Notes: The Phenomenology of Sickness and Healing

1. *Illness.* Does your own experience with illness confirm or rebut the incapacitating and dehumanizing effects described by Mark Hall? Consider the additional accounts, both analytical and narrative, on the Web site for this book, www.health -law.org.

2. *Doctors, Patients, and Placebos.* These readings explain that the placebo effect is not isolated to a few psychologically susceptible individuals or conditions. It permeates medical encounters and typifies the doctor-patient relationship in ways that scientific medicine tends to ignore or deny. The mere encounter with a doctor appears to activate internal, self-healing mechanisms across a wide range of medical conditions, regardless of the actual treatments rendered. In short, doctors do not just administer placebos; they *are* placebos. Considering this, should the FDA deny approval for a drug because it acts "only" as a placebo? How does a doctor obtain informed consent from a patient when he knows the treatment is partially or totally intended to invoke a placebo effect?

In 2006, the AMA issued an ethics opinion that it is unprofessional to use placebos deceptively. Taking issue with this position, see Adam J. Kolber, A Limited Defense of Clinical Placebo Deception, 26 Yale L. & Pol'y Rev. 75-134 (2007); Rachel Sherman & John Hickner, Academic Physicians Use Placebos in Clinical Practice and Believe in the Mind-Body Connection, 23 J. Gen. Intern. Med. 7 (2007).

3. *Alternative and Conventional Healers.* There is now widespread social interest in alternative healing, both as a separate area of professional practice and as a component of conventional scientific practice. For further exploration, see the casebook Web site, www.health-law.org and the sources in note 5.

4. *Therapeutic Jurisprudence.* Consider the various implications these provocative readings have for law and public policy. Do they alter conventional legal notions about who should control decisionmaking in the treatment encounter? Do they

suggest that health insurance should more freely cover untested or unorthodox therapies? When disputes arise over treatment decisions or insurance coverage, are patients capable of aggressively pursuing their legal rights? Are patients capable of acting as informed consumers in a medical marketplace in which they evaluate the costs and benefits of different treatment options? Questions like these are addressed by a branch of legal thought known as "therapeutic jurisprudence," which views law as a therapeutic agent. This perspective asks whether normal social and behavioral assumptions realistically fit the medical arena, and whether legal rules do a good job of fostering the therapeutic goals of medicine.

5. *Bibliography.* For additional descriptions and analyses of the **phenomenology of illness (note 1)**, see Howard Brody, Stories of Sickness (1987); Kathy Charmaz, Good Days, Bad Days: The Self in Chronic Illness and Time (1991); Norman Cousins, The Healing Heart (1983); Michael C. Dohan, Reflections on a Bone Marrow Transplant, 132 Annals Intern. Med. 587 (2000). Discussing how issues of trust and vulnerability affect a number of issues in health care law, see Mark A. Hall, Law, Medicine, and Trust, 55 Stan. L. Rev. 463 (2002); Robert Gatter, Faith, Confidence, and Health Care: Fostering Trust in Medicine Through Law, 39 Wake Forest L. Rev. 395 (2004).

For additional discussion of the **placebo effect (note 2)**, see Anup Malani, Regulation with Placebo Effects, 58 Duke L.J. 411 (2008); Kathleen M. Boozang, The Therapeutic Placebo: The Case for Patient Deception, 54 Fla. L. Rev. 687 (2002); Anne Harrington, The Placebo Effect: An Interdisciplinary Exploration (1997); The Science of the Placebo (Harry A. Guess et al. eds., 2002). See generally Amitai Aviram, The Placebo Effect of Law: Law's Role in Manipulating Perceptions, 75 Geo. Wash. L. Rev. 54 (2006) (discussing how, "like the placebo effect of medicine, a law may impact social welfare beyond its objective effects by manipulating the public's subjective perception of the law's effectiveness").

On **alternative medicine (note 3),** see Anne Harrington, The Cure Within: A History of Mind-Body Medicine (2007); Michael H. Cohen, Complementary and Alternative Medicine: Legal Boundaries and Regulatory Perspectives (1998); Michael Ruggio & Lauren DeSantis-Then, Complementary and Alternative Medicine: Longstanding Legal Obstacles to Cutting Edge Treatment, 2 J. Health & Life Sci. L. 137 (2009); Barbara L. Atwell, Mainstreaming Complementary and Alternative Medicine in the Face of Uncertainty, 72 UMKC L. Rev. 593 (2004); Symposium, 31 J.L. Med. Ethics 183 (2003); Michael H. Cohen & Mary C. Ruggie, Integrating Complementary and Alternative Medical Therapies in Conventional Medical Settings, 72 U. Cin. L. Rev. 671-729 (2003); Joseph A. Barrette, The Alternative Medical Practice Act, 77 St. John's L. Rev. 75 (2003); James A. Bulen, Complementary and Alternative Medicine: Ethical and Legal Aspects of Informed Consent to Treatment, 24 J. Leg. Med. 331 (2003); Kathleen M. Boozang, Is the Alternative Medicine? Managed Care Apparently Thinks So, 32 Conn. L. Rev. 567 (2000); notes on pages 1266-1268.

For leading examples of **therapeutic jurisprudence (note 4),** focused mainly on mental health and criminal law, see Law in a Therapeutic Key (David B. Wexler & Bruce J. Winnick eds., 1996); Marshall B. Kapp, The Law and Older Persons: Is Geriatric Jurisprudence Therapeutic? (2003). For an attempt to further develop this perspective in health care law, see Hall, supra, 55 Stan. L. Rev. 463 (2002).

END

3. The Nature of Medical Judgment

■ CLINICAL DECISION MAKING: FROM THEORY TO PRACTICE
David M. Eddy*
1996

. . . Why do physicians vary so much in the way they practice medicine? At first view, there should be no problem. There are diseases—neatly named and categorized by textbooks, journal articles, and medical specialty societies. There are various procedures physicians can use to diagnose and treat these diseases. It should be possible to determine the value of any particular procedure by applying it to patients who have a disease and observing the outcome. And the rest should be easy—if the outcome is good, the procedure should be used for patients with that disease; if the outcome is bad, it should not. Some variation in practice patterns can be expected due to differences in the incidence of various diseases, patients' preferences, and the available resources, but these variations should be small and explainable.

The problem of course is that nothing is this simple. Uncertainty, biases, errors, and differences of opinions, motives, and values weaken every link in the chain that connects a patient's actual condition to the selection of a diagnostic test or treatment. . . . Uncertainty creeps into medical practice through every pore. Whether a physician is defining a disease, making a diagnosis, selecting a procedure, observing outcomes, assessing probabilities, assigning preference, or putting it all together, he is walking on very slippery terrain. It is difficult for nonphysicians, and for many physicians, to appreciate how complex these tasks are, how poorly we understand them, and how easy it is for honest people to come to different conclusions.

DEFINING A DISEASE

If one looks at patients who are obviously ill, it is fairly easy to identify the physical and chemical disorders that characterize that illness. On the other hand, a large part of medicine is practiced on people who do not have obvious illnesses, but rather have signs, symptoms, or findings that may or may not represent an illness that should be treated. Three closely related problems make it difficult to determine whether or not a patient actually has a disease that needs to be diagnosed or treated.

One problem is that the dividing line between "normal" and "abnormal" is not nearly as sharp as a cursory reading of a textbook would suggest. . . . A second problem is that many "diseases," at least at the time they are diagnosed, do not by themselves cause pain, suffering, disability, or threat to life. They are considered diseases only because they increase the probability that something else that is truly bad will happen in the future. . . .

The difficulty of defining a disease is compounded by the fact that many of the signs, symptoms, findings, and conditions that might suggest a disease are extremely

*Reprinted with permission. Dr. Eddy is a physician researcher, formerly on the faculty of Duke University, and now a consultant in Jackson Hole, Wyoming.

common. If a breast biopsy were performed on a random sample of senior citizens, fully 90 percent of them could have fibrocystic disease. If obesity is a disease, the average American is diseased. . . . Morbid obesity is defined as 100 percent above the ideal weight. But what is "ideal," and why 100 percent? The lesson is that for many conditions a clinician faces, there is no clear definition of disease that provides an unequivocal guide to action, and there is wide room for differences of opinion and variations in practice. . . .

[E]ven when sharp criteria are created, physicians vary widely in their application of these criteria—in their ability to ask about symptoms, observe signs, interpret test results, and record the answers. The literature on "observer variation" has been growing for a long time. . . . Thirteen pathologists were asked to read 1,001 specimens obtained from biopsies of the cervix, and then to repeat the readings at a later time. On average, each pathologist agreed with himself only 89 percent of the time (intraobserver agreement), and with a panel of "senior" pathologists only 87 percent of the time (interobserver agreement). Looking only at the patients who actually had cervical pathology, the intraobserver agreement was only 68 percent and the interobserver agreement was only 51 percent. The pathologists were best at reading more advanced disease and normal tissue, but were labeled "unsatisfactory" in their ability to read the precancerous and preinvasive stages.

Similar studies have been reported for . . . many other signs, symptoms, and procedures. Even if there were no uncertainty about what constitutes a disease and how to define it, there would still be considerable uncertainty about whether or not a patient has the signs, symptoms, and findings needed to fit the definition.

SELECTING A PROCEDURE

The task of selecting a procedure is no less difficult. There are two main issues. First, for any patient condition there are dozens of procedures that can be ordered, in any combination, at any time. The list of procedures that might be included in a workup of chest pain or hypertension would take more than a page, spanning the spectrum from simply asking questions, to blood studies, to X-rays. Even for highly specific diagnostic problems, there can be a large choice of procedures. For example, if a woman presents with a breast mass and her physician wants to know its approximate size and architecture, the physician might contemplate an imaging procedure. The choice could include mammography, ultra-sonography, thermography, diaphanography, computed tomography, lymphography, Mammoscan, and magnetic resonance imaging. . . . And why should a diagnostic workup be limited to one test? Why not follow a negative mammogram with a computed tomogram (or vice versa)? For the detection of colorectal cancer, a physician can choose any combination of fecal occult blood tests (and there are more than a dozen brands), digital examination, rigid sigmoidoscopy, flexible 30 cm sigmoidoscopy, flexible 60 cm sigmoidoscopy, barium enema (either plain or air contrast), and colonoscopy. These choices are not trivial. Most procedures have different mechanisms of action and a long list of pros and cons. . . . These procedures are for relatively well-defined diseases; imagine the problems of selecting procedures to evaluate symptoms like fatigue, headache, or fever that can have about a dozen causes. . . .

In theory, much of the uncertainty just described could be managed if it were possible to conduct enough experiments under enough conditions, and observe the outcomes. Unfortunately, measuring the outcomes of medical procedures is one of the most difficult problems we face. The goal is to predict how the use of a procedure in a particular case will affect that patient's health and welfare. Standing in the way are at least a half dozen major obstacles. The central problem is that there is a natural variation in the way people respond to a medical procedure. Take two people who, to the best of our ability to define such things, are identical in all important respects, submit them to the same operative procedure, and one will die on the operating table while the other will not. Because of this natural variation, we can only talk about the probabilities of various outcomes — the probability that a diagnostic test will be positive if the disease is present (sensitivity), the probability that a test will be negative if the disease is absent (specificity), the probability that a treatment will yield a certain result, and so forth.

One consequence of this natural variation is that to study the outcomes of any procedure it is necessary to conduct the procedure on many different people, who are thought to represent the particular patients we want to know about, and then average the results. . . . Some diseases are so rare that, in order to conduct the ideal clinical trials, it would be necessary to collect tens of thousands, if not hundreds of thousands, of participants. A good example concerns the frequency of the Pap smear. One might wonder why the merits of a three-year versus one-year frequency cannot be settled by a randomized controlled trial. Because of the low frequency of cervical cancer, and the small difference in outcomes expected for the two frequencies, almost one million women would be required for such a study. . . .

Finally, even when the best trials are conducted, we still might not get an answer. Consider the value of mammography in women under fifty, and consider just one outcome — the effect on breast cancer mortality. Ignore for the time being the radiation hazard, false-positive test results, inconvenience, financial costs, and other issues. This is one of the best-studied problems in cancer prevention, benefiting from the largest (60,000 women) and longest (more than 15 years) completed randomized controlled trial, and an even larger uncontrolled study involving 270,000 women screened for five years in 29 centers around the country. Yet we still do not know the value of mammography in women under 50. . . .

Unable to turn to a definitive body of clinical and epidemiological research, a clinician or research scientist who wants to know the value of a procedure is left with a mixture of randomized controlled trials, nonrandomized trials, uncontrolled trials, and clinical observations. The evidence from different sources can easily go in different directions, and it is virtually impossible for anyone to sort things out in his or her head. Unfortunately, the individual physician may be most impressed by observations made in his or her individual practice. This source of evidence is notoriously vulnerable to bias and error. What a physician sees and remembers is biased by the types of patients who come in; by the decisions of the patients to accept a treatment and return for follow-up; by a natural desire to see good things; and by a whole series of emotions that charge one's memory. On top of these biases, the observations are vulnerable to large statistical errors because of the small number of patients a physician sees in a personal practice. . . .

Now assume that a physician can know the outcomes of recommending a particular procedure for a particular patient. Is it possible to declare whether those outcomes are good or bad? Unfortunately, no. The basic problem is that any procedure has multiple outcomes, some good and some bad. The expected reduction in chest pain that some people will get from coronary artery bypass surgery is accompanied by a splitting of the chest, a chance of an operative mortality, days in the hospital, pain, anxiety, and financial expense. Because the outcomes are multiple and move in different directions, tradeoffs have to be made. And making tradeoffs involves values. . . . Imagine the variation in how different people value pain, disability, operative mortality, life expectancy, a day in a hospital, and who is going to feed the dogs. . . .

PUTTING IT ALL TOGETHER

The final decision about how to manage a patient requires synthesizing all the information about a disease, the patient, signs and symptoms, the effectiveness of dozens of tests and treatments, outcomes and values. All of this must be done without knowing precisely what the patient has, with uncertainty about signs and symptoms, with imperfect knowledge of the sensitivity and specificity of tests, with no training in manipulating probabilities, with incomplete and biased information about outcomes, and with no language for communicating or assessing values. If each piece of this puzzle is difficult, it is even more difficult for anyone to synthesize all the information and be certain of the answer. It would be an extremely hard task for a research team; there is no hope that it could occur with any precision in the head of a busy clinician. Hence the wide variability in the estimates physicians place on the values of procedures.

[A] final example document[s] how difficult it is to combine information from many sources to estimate the value of a particular procedure. . . . A survey of 1,000 11-year-old schoolchildren in New York City found that 65 percent had undergone tonsillectomy. The remaining children were sent for examinations to a group of physicians and 45 percent were selected for tonsillectomy. Those rejected were examined by another group of physicians and 46 percent were selected for surgery. When the remaining children were examined again by another group of physicians, a similar percent were recommended for tonsillectomy, leaving only 65 students. At that point, the study was halted for lack of physicians.

CONSEQUENCES

The view of anyone who wants a close look at the consequences of different medical procedures is, at best, smoky. Some procedures may present a clear picture, and their value, or lack of it, may be obvious; putting a finger on a bleeding carotid artery is an extreme example. But for many, if not most medical procedures, we can only see shadows and gross movements. . . . We certainly do not know how a particular individual will respond. Words like "rare," "common," and "a lot" must be used instead of "one out of 1,000," or "seven on a scale of one to ten." . . .

In the end, given all the uncertainties, incentives, and heuristics, a physician will have to do what is comfortable. If it is admitted that the uncertainty surrounding the use of a procedure is great, and that there is no way to identify for certain what is best, or to prove that any particular action is right or wrong, the safest and most comfortable position is to do what others are doing. The applicable maxim is "safety in numbers." A physician who follows the practices of his or her colleagues is safe from criticism, free from having to explain his or her actions, and defended by the concurrence of colleagues.

▉ COMPLICATIONS: A SURGEON'S NOTES ON AN IMPERFECT SCIENCE
Atul Gawande*
2002

THE CASE OF THE RED LEG

Seeing patients with one of the surgery professors in his clinic one afternoon, I was struck by how often he had to answer his patients' questions, "I do not know." These are four little words a doctor tends to be reluctant to utter. We're supposed to have the answers. We want to have the answers. But there was not a single person he did not have to say those four little words to that day. . . . The core predicament of medicine — the thing that makes being a patient so wrenching, being a doctor so difficult, and being a part of a society that pays the bills they run up so vexing — is uncertainty. With all that we know nowadays about people and diseases and how to diagnose and treat them, it can be hard to see this, hard to grasp how deeply the uncertainty runs. As a doctor, you come to find, however, that the struggle in caring for people is more often with what you do not know than what you do. Medicine's ground state is uncertainty. And wisdom — for both patients and doctors — is defined by how one copes with it.

This is the story of one decision under uncertainty.

It was two o'clock on a Tuesday afternoon in June. . . . I had just finished admitting someone with a gallbladder infection and was attempting to sneak out for a bite to eat when one of the emergency room physicians stopped me with yet another patient to see: a twenty-three-year-old, Eleanor Bratton, with a red and swollen leg. . . . "It's probably only a cellulitis" [he said] — a simple skin infection. . . . But he wanted me to make sure there wasn't anything "surgical" going on — an abscess that needed draining or some such. "Would you mind taking a quick look?" Groan. No. Of course not. . . .

She looked fit, athletic, and almost teenage, with blond hair tight in a ponytail, nails painted gold, and her eyes fixed on a television. There did not seem anything seriously ill about her. . . . That weekend she had gone back home to Hartford, Connecticut, to attend a wedding . . . and she had kicked off her shoes and danced the whole night. The morning after, however, she woke up with her left foot feeling sore. She had a week-old blister on the top of her foot from some cruddy sandals she had worn, and now the skin surrounding the blister was red and puffy. . . . The redness spread, and during the night she got chills and sweats and a fever of one hundred and three degrees. . . . I asked Eleanor if she had had any pus or drainage from her leg.

No. Any ulcers open up in her skin? No. A foul smell or blackening of her skin? No. Any more fevers? Not in the last two days. I let the data roll around in my head. . . . Objectively, the rash had the exact appearance of a cellulitis, something antibiotics would take care of. But another possibility lodged in my mind now, one that scared the hell out of me. . . .

---

*Excerpted with permission, Henry Holt and Company. The author is a physician on the faculty of Harvard's Schools of Medicine and of Public Health. This true story uses fictionalized names.

Decisions in medicine are supposed to rest on concrete observations and hard evidence. But just a few weeks before, I had taken care of a patient I could not erase from my mind. . . . He was found to have a small and very ordinary skin rash on his chest and was sent home with antibiotic pills for cellulitis. That night the rash spread eight inches. The following morning he spiked a fever of one hundred and two degrees. By the time he returned to the emergency room, the skin involved had become numb and widely blistered. Shortly after, he went into shock. He was transferred to my hospital and we quickly took him to the OR.

He didn't have a cellulitis but instead an extremely rare and horrendously lethal type of infection known as necrotizing fasciitis (fah-shee-EYE-tiss). The tabloids have called it a disease of "flesh-eating bacteria" and the term is not an exaggeration. Opening the skin, we found a massive infection, far worse than what appeared from the outside. All the muscles of the left side of his chest, going around to his back, up to his shoulder, and down to his abdomen, had turned gray and soft and foul with invading bacteria and had to be removed. . . . The next day we had to remove his arm. For a while, we actually thought we had saved him. . . . One by one, however, his kidneys, lungs, liver, and heart went into failure, and then he died. It was among the most awful cases I have ever been involved in.

What we know about necrotizing fasciitis is this: it is highly aggressive and rapidly invasive. It kills up to 70 percent of the people who get it. No known antibiotic will stop it. . . . It is an organism that usually causes little more than a strep throat, but in certain strains it has evolved the ability to do far worse. No one knows where these strains come from. As with a cellulitis, they are understood to enter through breaks in the skin. The break can be as large as a surgical incision or as slight as an abrasion. . . . Survival is possible only with early and radical excisional surgery, often requiring amputation. To succeed, however, it must be done early. By the time signs of deep invasion are obvious—such as shock, loss of sensation, widespread blistering of the skin—the person is usually unsalvageable.

Standing at Eleanor's bedside, bent over examining her leg, I felt a little foolish considering the diagnosis. . . . True, in the early stages, a necrotizing fasciitis can look just like a cellulitis, presenting with the same redness, swelling, fever, and high white blood cell count. But . . . [o]nly about a thousand cases of necrotizing fasciitis occur in the entire United States each year, mainly in the elderly and chronically ill—and well over *three million* cases of cellulitis.

What's more, Eleanor's fever had gone away; she didn't look unusually ill; and I knew I was letting myself be swayed by a single, recent, anecdotal case. If there were a simple test to tell the two diagnoses apart, that would have been one thing. But there is none. The only way is to go to the operating room, open the skin, and look—not something you want to propose arbitrarily. . . .

Eleanor and her father looked on with new dread when [the general surgeon, Dr.] Studdert arrived in his scrubs and operating hat to see her. He had her tell her story again and then uncovered her leg to examine it. He didn't seem too impressed. Talking by ourselves, he told me that the rash looked to him only "like a bad cellulitis." But could he say for sure that it was not necrotizing fasciitis? He could not. It is a reality of medicine that choosing to *not* do something—to not order a test, to not give an antibiotic, to not take a patient to the operating room—is far harder than choosing to do it. . . .

Studdert sat down on the edge of her bed . . . and, in a quiet and gentle voice, he went on to explain the unquiet and ungentle effects of necrotizing fasciitis. . . . "I think it is unlikely you have it," he told Eleanor. "I'd put the chances"—he was guessing here—"at well under five percent." But, he went on, "without a biopsy, we cannot rule it out." He paused for a moment to let her and her father absorb this. Then he started to explain what the procedure involved. . . .

Eleanor went rigid. "This is crazy," she said. "This doesn't make any sense." She looked frantic, like someone drowning. "Why don't we just wait and see how the antibiotics go?" Studdert explained that this was a disease that you cannot sit on, that you had to catch it early to have any chance of treating it. Eleanor just shook her head and looked down at her covers.

Studdert and I both turned to her father to see what he might have to say. He . . . asked what would happen if the biopsy were positive for the disease. Studdert . . . hesitated before going on. "This can mean an amputation," he said. Eleanor began to cry. "I don't want to do this, Dad." Mr. Bratton swallowed hard, his gaze fixed somewhere miles beyond us.

In recent years, we in medicine have discovered how discouragingly often . . . medicine still lacks the basic organization and commitment to make sure we do what we know to do. But spend almost any amount of time with doctors and patients, and you will find that the larger, starker, and more painful difficulty is the still abundant uncertainty that exists over what should be done in many situations. The gray zones in medicine are considerable, and every day we confront situations like Eleanor's—ones in which clear scientific evidence of what to do is missing and yet choices must be made.

Exactly which patients with pneumonia, for example, should be hospitalized and which ones sent home? Which back pains treated by surgery and which by conservative measures alone? Which patients with a rash taken to surgery and which just observed on antibiotics? For many cases, the answers can be obvious. But for many others, we simply do not know. . . . In the absence of algorithms and evidence about what to do, you learn in medicine to make decisions by feel. You count on experience and judgment. And it is hard not to be troubled by this. . . . But in the face of uncertainty, what other than judgment does a physician have—or a patient have, for that matter? . . .

Eleanor and her dad now agreed to go ahead. "Let's get it over with," she said. But then I brought her the surgical consent form to sign. On it, I had written not only that the procedure was a "biopsy of the left lower extremity" but also that the risks included a "possible need for amputation." She cried out when she saw the words. It took her several minutes alone with her father before she could sign. . . .

There is, in fact, another approach to decision making, one advocated by a small and struggling coterie in medicine. The strategy, long used in business and the military, is called decision analysis, and the principles are straightforward. On a piece of paper (or a computer), you lay out all your options, and all the possible outcomes of those options, in a decision tree. You make a numeric estimate of the probability of each outcome, using hard data when you have it and a rough prediction when you don't. You weigh each outcome according to its relative desirability (or "utility") to the patient. Then you multiply out the numbers for each option and choose the one with the highest calculated "expected utility." The goal is to use explicit, logical, statistical thinking instead of just your gut. The decision to recommend annual mammograms for all women over age fifty was made this way and so was the U.S. decision to bail out Mexico when its economy tanked. Why not, the advocates ask, individual patient decisions?

Recently, I tried "treeing out" (as the decision buffs put it) the choice Eleanor faced. The options were simple: to biopsy or not biopsy. The outcomes quickly got complicated, however. There was: not being biopsied and doing fine; not being biopsied, getting diagnosed late, going through surgery, and surviving anyway; not being biopsied and dying; being biopsied and getting only a scar; being biopsied and getting a scar plus bleeding from it; being biopsied, having the disease and an amputation, but dying anyway; and so on. When all the possibilities and consequences were penciled out, my decision tree looked more like a bush. Assigning the probabilities for each potential twist of fate seemed iffy. I found what data I could from the medical literature and then had to extrapolate a good deal. And determining the relative desirability of the outcomes seemed impossible after talking to Eleanor about them. Is dying a hundred times worse than doing fine, a thousand times worse, a million? Where does a scar with bleeding fit in? Nonetheless, these are the crucial considerations, the decision experts argue, and when we decide by instinct, they say, we are only papering this reality over.

Producing a formal analysis in any practical time frame proved to be out of the question, though. It took a couple of days—not the minutes that we had actually had—and a lot of back and forths with two decision experts. But it did provide an answer. According to the final decision tree, we should *not* have gone to the OR for a biopsy. The likelihood of my initial hunch being right was too low, and the likelihood that catching the disease early would make no difference anyway was too high. Biopsy could not be justified, the logic said. I don't know what we would have made of this information at the time. We didn't have the decision tree, however. And we went to the OR. . . .

At first glance beneath her skin, there was nothing apparent to alarm us. . . . When we probed with the tip of a clamp inside the calf incision, however, it slid unnaturally easily along the muscle, as if bacteria had paved a path. This is not a definitive finding, but enough of one that Studdert let out a sudden, disbelieving, "Oh shit." . . . The features he saw were "consistent with necrotizing fasciitis[.]" . . . "She's got it," he finally announced grimly. . . .

Decisions compound themselves, in medicine like in anything else. No sooner have you taken one fork in the road than another and another come upon you. The critical question now was what to do. . . . "I thought about a BKA," a below-knee amputation, Studdert says, "even an AKA," an above-knee amputation. No one would have faulted him for doing either. But he found himself balking. "She was such a young girl," he explains. "It may seem harsh to say, but if it was a sixty-year-old man I would've taken the leg without question." This was partly, I think, a purely emotional unwillingness to cut off the limb of a pretty twenty-three-year-old—the kind of sentimentalism that can get you in trouble. But it was also partly instinct again, an instinct that her youth and fundamentally good health might allow him to get by with just removing the most infested tissue (a "debridement") and washing out her foot and leg. Was this a good risk to take, with one of the deadliest bacteria known to man loose in her leg? Who knows? But take it he did. . . . We ended up operating on her leg four times in four days. . . . Only then was Studdert confident that not only had Eleanor survived, but her foot and leg had, too. . . .

For close to thirty years, Dartmouth physician Jack Wennberg has studied decision making in medicine, . . . [a]nd what he has found is a stubborn, overwhelming, and embarrassing degree of inconsistency in what we do. His research has shown, for example, that the likelihood of a doctor sending you for a gallbladder-removal operation varies 270 percent depending on what city you live in; for a hip replacement, 450 percent; for care in an intensive care unit during the last six months of your life, 880 percent. A patient in Santa Barbara, California, is five times more likely to be recommended back surgery for a back pain than one in Bronx, New York. This is, in the main, uncertainty at work, with the varying experience, habits, and intuitions of individual doctors leading to massively different care for people.

How can this be justified? The people who pay for the care certainly do not see how. (That is why insurers bug doctors so constantly to explain our decisions.) Nor might the people who receive it. Eleanor Bratton, without question, would have been treated completely differently depending on where she went, who she saw, or even just when she saw me (before or after that previous necrotizing fasciitis case I'd seen; at 2 A.M. or 2 P.M.; on a quiet or a busy shift). She'd have gotten merely antibiotics at one place, an amputation at another, a debridement at a third. This result seems unconscionable.

People have proposed two strategies for change. One is to shrink the amount of uncertainty in medicine—with research, not on new drugs or operations (which already attracts massive amounts of funding) but on the small but critical everyday decisions that patients and doctors make (which gets shockingly little funding). Everyone understands, though, that a great deal of uncertainty about what to do for people will always remain. (Human disease and lives are too complicated for reality to be otherwise.) So it has also been argued, not unreasonably, that doctors must agree in advance on what should be done in the uncertain situations that arise—spell out our actions ahead of time to take the guesswork out and get some advantage of group decision. This last goes almost nowhere, though. For it runs counter to everything we doctors believe about ourselves as individuals, about our personal ability to reason out with patients what the best course of action for them is. . . .

The possibilities and probabilities are all we have to work with in medicine, though. What we are drawn to in this imperfect science, what we in fact covet in our way, is the alterable moment—the fragile but crystalline opportunity for one's know-how, ability, or just gut instinct to change the course of another's life for the better. In the actual situations that present themselves, however—a despondent woman arrives to see you about a newly diagnosed cancer, a victim bleeding from a terrible injury is brought pale and short of breath from the scene, a fellow physician asks for your opinion about a twenty-three-year-old with a red leg—we can never be sure whether we have such a moment or not. Even less clear is whether the actions we choose will prove either wise or helpful. That our efforts succeed at all is still sometimes a shock to me. But they do. . . .

Notes: Medical Decisionmaking

1. *The Nature of Medical Judgment.* Medical decisionmaking is best appreciated by examining a range of particular medical cases. One example of a full-length case

discussion, which illustrates many of the dimensions of uncertainty of judgment described by Doctors Gawande and Eddy is linked on the Web site for this book, www.health-law.org. For additional readings on the nature of medical judgment, see Kathryn Montgomery, How Doctors Think (2006); Jerome Groopman, How Doctors Think (2007); Kathryn Hunter, Doctors' Stories: The Narrative Structure of Medical Knowledge (1991).

Dr. Gawande mentions the work of Dartmouth researchers documenting dramatic variations in physicians' practice styles in different communities. Dr. Gawande brought this research to widespread attention in The Cost Conundrum: What a Texas Town Can Teach Us About Health Care, The New Yorker, June 1, 2009. Efforts to standardize medical practice and reduce variations in practice are discussed in Chapters 4.A and 9.D. For additional discussion of treatment variation, see Institute of Medicine, Variation in Health Care Spending (2013). For discussion of differential treatment based on race, see Chapter 2.A.2.

2. *Medical Terminology.* Early editions of this book contained information about medical terminology, medical science, and anatomy. Lawyers who practice in this field must eventually acquire a fair amount of medical knowledge, and many law students enjoy learning something about a different profession's specialized vocabulary. Others see medical terminology as an obstacle to understanding what's really happening in these cases. We have chosen to cater to the latter group; our feeling is that if you end up working in this field, you will have plenty of opportunity to learn the terminology later. Here, when cases contain uncommon medical terms, we will define them for you. If we fail to do so, most terms used in this book are contained in better-quality general dictionaries. For those who want more specialized information, here is a sampling of various medical texts and treatises, some written especially for lawyers and others for medical professionals or for the lay public. **Medical Dictionaries:** Dorland's Illustrated Medical Dictionary; Stedman's Medical Dictionary; Taber's Cyclopedic Medical Dictionary. Links to the online versions of these can be found on this casebook's Web site, www.health-law.org. A comprehensive guide to medical research for legal purposes is Caroline Young, Medico-Legal Research Using Evidence-Based Medicine, 102 L. Libr. J. 449 (2010).

B. THE "CRISIS" IN ACCESS, COST, AND QUALITY

■ HEALTH AND MEDICAL CARE REFORM IN THE UNITED STATES: ETHICAL QUESTIONS AND CONCERNS
Thomas W. Merrill, David G. Miller, Joseph A. Raho & Ginger Gruters
President's Council on Bioethics, Staff Background Paper
2008

The reform of health and medical care in the United States has been a topic on our national agenda for decades now. . . . [A]t present, we seem to be witnessing a remarkable coalescence — of the public, health professionals and organizations, and policymakers — around the conclusion that the American "system" of health and medical care is ailing. Three problems — of access and coverage, of quality, and of cost—are usually cited as the signs and symptoms of this increasingly worrisome state. . . . [W]e offer a purely descriptive account of the problems of access, quality, and cost, in order to illustrate their complexity and to draw out their implications for ethical questioning. . . .

I. THE PROBLEM OF ACCESS TO HEALTH AND MEDICAL CARE

In [2010], according to the Current Population Survey of the U.S. Census Bureau, [50] million Americans were uninsured. This statistic is often cited in ways that suggest that it—and it alone—constitutes the whole of the problem of access to health and medical care in the United States. . . . There are other dimensions to the problem of access. The underinsured, who have some coverage but are inadequately protected against high out-of-pocket costs, are the subjects of a growing literature. Difficulties with the supply and geographical distribution of health care professionals, along with some types of health care facilities (for example, emergency rooms), are also constituents of the problem of access. Our focus here, however, is on the uninsured. . . .

According to one estimate, some 18,000 premature deaths per year in the United States (as well as a number of other serious health conditions) could have been prevented by better access to health care.[3] To be sure, the uninsured do have access to emergency room care . . . , but care through this source tends to be less than optimal. Conditions are often treated only when they have become very serious. Moreover, the use of emergency care by the uninsured exacerbates the burdens placed on often strained emergency rooms and centers. . . . Those hospitals and professionals incur costs that eventually lead to higher charges for the insured or to increasing outlays of federal and state funds for uncompensated care. . . .

The preceding review of statistical data underscore[s] one conclusion: the situation of the uninsured in the United States is a complicated one, far more so than the oft-cited figure of [50] million reveals. As this review has shown, that number does not capture how long the uninsured lack this essential component of access to care, nor does it provide important information on who the uninsured are. The number of individuals who lack insurance for a year or more is lower than [50] million—probably somewhere between 30 and 40 million. Nor is it the case that the uninsured are all poor and thus unable to purchase insurance. More than one-third have household incomes above the median national income. Moreover, about a fifth are not citizens. . . . It is also noteworthy that the rates of uninsurance are higher among the poor and among African-American and Hispanic communities. . . .

II. THE PROBLEM OF HEALTH CARE COSTS AND FINANCING

Just as few, if any, would dispute the fact that there are many millions of uninsured Americans, so too would few take issue with the claims that health care costs

---

3. See the Institute of Medicine report *Hidden Costs, Value Lost: Uninsurance in America* (2003). Other scholars point out, however, that it is difficult to establish clear evidence of causation (as opposed to correlation) between insurance status and health status. . . .

in the United States are high compared to other industrialized nations and that these costs are increasing in seemingly unconstrained ways. These facts are cause for concern on a number of fronts. Such broad measures of population health as infant mortality and life expectancy, for example, indicate that the U.S. does no better, and in some cases does far worse, than similar countries that spend less on health care: we may not be getting good value for our money. . . . [T]he current situation is made more worrying still by the historical trends in the growth of health care spending. . . . According to some estimates made by the Congressional Budget Office, if current trends continue, health care spending could rise to almost 50 percent of total Gross Domestic Product (GDP) by 2082. . . .

There is much controversy, of course, over the causes of those increases and the ways we might address those causes. Here, we simply lay out some well-known facts about health care spending in the United States: as a portion of GDP and per capita; as it affects employees and employers; and as it affects federal and state budgets.

Today [as of 2016], the United States spends about [$3.3] trillion per year on health care, which amounts to [18] percent of GDP and about [$10,000] per person. Of course, compared with the poorer nations of the world, all of the wealthier nations spend a greater proportion of their income on health care. The United States, however, spends more on health care—both on a per capita basis and as a percentage of its GDP—than *any* other nation in the world. . . . National spending on health care as a share of GDP increased from about 5 percent in 1960 to our current level of [18] percent today and is projected to continue to grow. . . . The cumulative effect of those growth rates is this: The United States has experienced a *twenty-fold increase* in health care expenditures—a four-fold increase over the consumer price index over the same period. . . .

Of course, the rising share of health care as a portion of GDP may not necessarily be cause for concern. As mentioned above, as countries become wealthier, their citizens tend to spend more money on health care, and there is no way to determine *a priori* what the "appropriate" level of spending on health care may be. Moreover, the percentage of GDP representing health care also depends on the size and character of what happens in other sectors of the economy. Above all, the costs by themselves do not tell us anything about the quality or value of the care being provided. . . . Nevertheless, as the cost of health care rises so quickly relative to growth in GDP, it cannot fail to strain private and public budgets and to make it ever more difficult to solve or ameliorate other problems. . . .

For individuals, rising health care costs lead to increased premiums and to insurance plans that attempt to restrain *their* costs by using higher deductibles, co-pays, and the like. Because individuals and families in the United States tend to get their insurance through their employers, who choose and purchase coverage from an insurer, those employers are often in the middle between the insurance companies and their employees who actually use the insurance. For this reason, employers are often the parties that complain most loudly about rising costs. They also tend to look to devices for holding down costs through cost sharing and the like. In [2017] the average cost of [group] insurance (including both the part of the premium paid by the employer and the employee) was [over $6,000] per year for an individual and [over $18,000] per year for a family. . . .

Most economists argue that, despite appearances, employers are not really paying the insurance premiums of their employees. Rather, the insurance premium is simply part of the total compensation package for the employee. Because of the tax exemption for health insurance, it makes sense for an employee to take part of their compensation as (untaxed) health benefits. For most Americans, our employer picks the insurance company, chooses the plan, and sends in the check, but the employer does not bear the final cost of the insurance premiums. That comes out of whatever the total amount of compensation the employer is willing to pay to the employee. In times of rising health care costs, that means that more of the total compensation has to go to insurance and less can go to increased wages. . . . Rather than coming out of corporate profits, the increasing cost of health care has resulted in relatively flat real wages for 30 years. That is the real health care cost-wage trade-off. . . .

Increased health care costs also put a burden on federal and state governments, primarily through Medicare and Medicaid. . . . [P]ublic funds, including Medicare, Medicaid, Veterans health care, and other programs account for about 45 percent of total health spending in any given year. For the governments that pay for these programs, rising health care costs mean some hard choices: reducing benefits, restricting eligibility, cutting other public programs, raising taxes.

For the states, health care costs are already the single largest part of state budgets. . . . Not surprisingly, states have tended to respond by cutting other programs, most commonly funding for public higher education. . . . For the federal government, rising health care costs . . . could threaten to swamp the budget. . . .

III. The Problem of Health Care Quality

In light of the fact that the United States spends much more on health care than other countries, it is reasonable to ask: Are we getting good value for the money? But with respect to the question of the quality of our health care, we find significant division between, on the one hand, those who cite the technological marvels produced in America and the outcomes in the treatment of complex diseases and, on the other hand, those who look to various aggregate measures of population health and find significant defects. . . . Of course, these seemingly opposed arguments are not mutually incompatible: America could produce the world's best technologies while also failing to provide the right care in many routine instances, not to mention the problems of the uninsured. And so we ask: What do we know about the quality of American health care?

On the one hand, it is true that by many measures of population health, the United States does quite poorly: infant mortality rates are higher in the United States than in many other comparable nations, and life expectancy rates are also low compared to other industrialized nations. A study by the World Health Organization (WHO) found that the United States ranked 37th . . . behind many other industrialized nations, all of which, as we have seen, spend far less per capita on health care than the U.S. does. . . .

Yet there is controversy over these facts. Some scholars argue, for example, that the cross-national comparisons fail to take into account differences in the underlying populations in different countries. They suggest that if we control for factors like homicide rates and car accidents—both of which are higher in the United States than in other countries—the measures of population health begin to look more similar to other nations. They also point out that rates of survival after the diagnosis of various serious ailments like cancer tend to be higher in the U.S. than elsewhere. Moreover, defenders of health care in United States point to the medical technologies and innovations developed here: The United States has produced more winners of the Nobel Prize in medicine than any other country. . . . Additionally, the U.S. spends far more of its public and private monies on biomedical research and development than does the European Union. Thus, defenders of U.S. health care argue that we cannot evaluate the level of quality of health care in the United States without keeping in mind the increased quality of the technologies used in health care.

As is often noted, Americans tend to be strongly attached to medical innovation and new medical technologies, more so than citizens of other countries. And there is a respectable body of literature which argues that the benefits of new technologies far outweigh their costs (as heavy as the latter may be). The [Harvard] economist David Cutler . . . and colleagues find that the cost of treating a heart attack has increased by some $10,000 in the 1990s, but that life expectancy after heart attack also rose by about one year. The treatment for low-birth weight infants presents a similarly positive picture. Cutler and colleagues conclude that "technological changes have proved to be worth far more than their costs."[35] . . .

Of course, . . . even the best technology cannot help very much if a particular patient does not have access to it—or does not have *timely* access. [Moreover], with respect to three different indicators—patient safety, receipt of recommended care, and variations in the intensity and outcomes of treatment—evidence suggests troublesome inadequacies in the quality of health care in America.

Patient Safety: Marked and seemingly widespread deficiencies in patient safety were the focus of the Institute of Medicine's *To Err Is Human*, a report published in 2000. According to the IOM, as many as 98,000 deaths are the result of medical error each year in the United States. That is more deaths from medical error than from motor vehicle accidents (around 45,000 deaths annually), from breast cancer (also around 45,000 deaths annually), or from AIDS (around 16,000 deaths annually). . . .

Receipt of Recommended Care: In the last few decades, professional societies along with such government agencies as the Agency for Healthcare Research and Quality have sought to develop and promulgate clinical practice guidelines and clinical pathways that stipulate the evidence-based recommendations for the most effective diagnosis and treatment of a wide range of diseases and disorders, from childhood asthma to adult hypertension. Nonetheless, [the] first national,

35. David Cutler, *Your Money or Your Life: Strong Medicine for America's Healthcare System* (New York: Oxford University Press, 2004).

41. McGlynn, Asch, Adams, et al., "The Quality of Health Care Delivered to Adults in the United States," *New England Journal of Medicine,* vol. 328: 2635-2645, June 26, 2003.

comprehensive study on quality of care for adults in the U.S. . . . found that patients received the recommended care only 54.9 percent of the time.[41]. . . As [the author] testified before the U.S. Senate, "We spend nearly $2 trillion annually on health care and we get it right about half the time. That may be the best in the world, but I think you would agree that we can and should do better."

Variations in Intensity and Outcomes of Treatment: A substantial body of evidence also supports the finding of wide variations of the amount of money spent and of treatments performed between different areas of the country, but without any corresponding variations in health outcomes. In fact, the evidence seems to suggest that geographical areas that spend more actually have lower levels of quality of care. Researchers at Dartmouth led by Jack Wennberg and Elliott Fisher have shown, for example, that the amount of money spent per capita on Medicare recipients varies widely between different areas of the country, by almost as much as a threefold difference, even after controlling for differences in age, race, and sex. But, . . . the correlation with quality is low.

Many researchers have concluded that increased spending does not translate into better outcomes—in fact it may translate into worse outcomes. Wennberg and Fisher contend that much of the health care spending in Medicare, perhaps as much as 20 percent to 30 percent, does not bring added health benefits and that there may well be a similar proportion of private spending on health care that does not bring better outcomes. Economists suggest that in many cases Americans may be at the "flat of the curve," that is, at that place in a cost-benefit analysis when further resources may not only bring added benefit but may, in fact, bring less benefit. . . . Peter Orszag, director of the Congressional Budget Office, has recently written: "With health care spending currently representing 16 percent of gross domestic product (GDP), [Wennberg and Fisher's results] would suggest that nearly 5 percent of GDP—or roughly $700 billion each year—goes to health care spending that can't be shown to improve health outcomes." Of course, as Orszag observes, trying to figure out how to reduce inappropriate or unnecessary care is no easy task. . . .

Leaving aside the difficult problems of designing the right policies to make American health care more efficient, however, there is a more fundamental question about what we—as patients and as citizens—expect from modern medical technology. Do we have extravagant expectations from medical science? Are we so accustomed to having someone else pay the bill that we no longer question whether a particular intervention is worth its cost? While evaluating the cost-effectiveness of various interventions or organizing the health care system to be more cost effective will not solve all of our health care problems, it may be a necessary condition of a more sustainable system that we come to see that more is not always better.

A variety of problems—access, cost, and quality—make health care in the United States an unavoidably complicated affair, and this is not the place to elaborate specific policy proposals. But we should remember that the health care system is one in which each of us will find ourselves in various capacities at various points in our lives, and the decisions we make about the various aspects of health care reflect our identity as a nation and the type of social union we wish to create and advance. . . .

International Comparsion of Spending on Health, 1980–2010

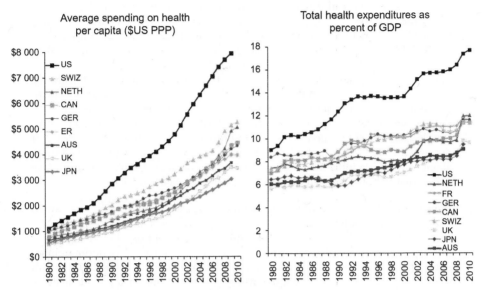

Notes: PPP = purchasing power parity; GDP = gross domestic product.
Source: Commonweath Fund, based on OECD Health Data 2012.

Notes: The Crisis in American Medicine

1. *The Perpetual Crisis.* American medicine has been declared to be in a "crisis" since at least the early 1960s. See Marion Sanders, The Crisis in American Medicine (1961). Can things really be all that bad if they've been like this so long? Note the competing viewpoint of Harvard economist David Cutler, cited above, that major increases in medical spending can be traced to substantial gains in health that, at least in certain areas, are clearly worth their costs.

Even if there is not a "crisis," there is still clearly a serious problem in American medicine. In case you're still not convinced, consider the following additional facts, opinions, and anecdotes.

> Medicine, like many other American institutions, suffered a stunning loss of confidence in the 1970s. Previously, two premises had guided government health policy: first, that Americans needed more medical care—more than the market alone would provide; and second, that medical professionals and private voluntary institutions were best equipped to decide how to organize those services. . . . In the 1970s this mandate ran out. The economic and moral problems of medicine displaced scientific progress at the center of public attention. Enormous increases in cost seemed ever more certain; corresponding improvements in health ever more doubtful. The prevailing assumptions about the need to expand medical care were reversed: The need now was to curb its apparently insatiable appetite for resources. In a short time, American medicine seemed to pass from stubborn shortages to irrepressible excess, without ever having passed through happy sufficiency. [Paul Starr, The Social Transformation of American Medicine 379 (1982).]

> How much does an overnight stay at a Virginia hospital cost? . . . A year ago, Mr. Shipman, a 43-year-old former furniture salesman from Herndon, Va., experienced

severe chest pains during the night. . . . Suspecting a heart attack, doctors first performed a cardiac catheterization to examine and unblock the coronary arteries. Then, they inserted a stent, a small metal device that props open a blocked artery so the blood flows better to the heart. Lacking health insurance, Mr. Shipman . . . checked himself out of the hospital against medical advice. Since then, Mr. Shipman and his wife, Alina, have received hospital bills totaling $29,500. . . . In addition, there were other bills: some $1,000 for the ambulance trip, $6,800 from the cardiologist who performed the stent procedure, and several thousand dollars for the local emergency-room visit. In all, the two-day health crisis left the Shipmans saddled with medical bills totaling nearly $40,000. Once solidly middle class, the couple says the debt triggered a gradual unraveling of their lives. "Middle class or not, when you have a bill of $37,000 hanging over your head, that's all you think about," says Ms. Shipman. . . . "You eat, sleep and breathe that bill." [Lucette Lagnado, Anatomy of a Hospital Bill, Wall St. J., Sept. 21, 2004, at B1.]

In its technical brilliance, American health care is unsurpassed. Its best care would have seemed miraculous just a few years ago. But the bad side of American health care is very bad, and there is reason to think that it will get worse before it gets better. For one thing, the coming years will see a further increase in both the number of the elderly in the population and their percentage of the population. The growth will be particularly great among those over 85, the people most likely to make heavy use of the medical system. New technology, for which one can almost always read "expensive" new technology, continues to invade medicine. [Henry T. Greely, The Future of the American Health Care System, 3 Stan. L. & Pol'y Rev. 16 (1991).]

There are few other areas of the U.S. economy where waste is so apparent and the possibility of savings is so tangible. . . . Perhaps the most troubling . . . [fact] is the amount spent on administration. For every office-based physician in the United States, there are 2.2 administrative workers. That exceeds the number of nurses, clinical assistants, and technical staff put together. One large physician group in the United States estimates that it spends 12 percent of revenue just collecting revenue. . . . The situation is no better in hospitals. . . . Duke University Hospital, for example, has 900 hospital beds and 1,300 billing clerks. On top of this are the administrative workers in health insurance. [David Cutler & Dan P. Ly, The (Paper) Work of Medicine, 25 J. Econ. Perspect. 3 (2011).]

There is no U.S. health care system. What we call our health care system is, in daily practice, a hodgepodge of historic legacies, philosophical conflicts, and competing economic schemes. Health care in America combines the tortured, politicized complexity of the U.S. tax code with a cacophony of intractable political, cultural, and religious debates about personal rights and responsibilities. Every time policymakers, corporate health benefits purchasers, or entrepreneurs try to fix something in our health care system, they run smack into its central reality: the primary producers and consumers of medical care are uniquely, stubbornly self-serving as they chew through vast sums of other people's money. Doctors and hospitals stumble their way through irresolvable conflicts between personal gain and ethical responsibilities; patients struggle with the acrimony and anguish that accompany life-and-death medical decisions; consumers, paying for the most part with everybody's money but their own, demand that the system serve them with the immediacy and flexibility of other industries; and health insurers are trapped in the middle, trying to keep everybody happy. A group of highly imaginative, energetic people armed with the world's largest Mark-n-Wipe board could not purposefully design a more complex, dysfunctional system if they tried. It is a $1.3 trillion per year fiasco narrated with moral shrillness and played out one competing anecdote after another. [J. D. Kleinke, Oxymorons: The Myth of a U.S. Health Care System 1 (2001).]

2. *International Comparisons and Medical Tourism.* According to one analysis, the poor U.S. performance on aggregate health statistics noted above (life expectancy, infant death rate) is not due to major differences in health habits or lifestyles, since the United States is similar in many ways to the comparison European countries. Instead, this author argues that the lower U.S. rankings are due in large part to the relatively inadequate system of primary care physicians and the overuse of high-risk procedures. Barbara Starfield, Is U.S. Health Really the Best in the World?, 284 JAMA 483 (2000). Another prominent study found that the British are much healthier than Americans in all major disease areas, such as diabetes, heart disease, stroke, lung disease, and cancer, even after controlling for all relevant sociodemographic factors. J. Banks, M. Marmot et al., Disease and Disadvantage in the United States and England, 295 JAMA 2037 (2006). Consider also, the following, from a health policy expert at Harvard:

> Finally, if you take a big step back and look at the data, Americans do better than average in timely access [to care], especially to specialty services and "elective" surgery (which is often not that elective). They tend to be among the [world] leaders in acute care quality, when healthcare means the difference between life and death, although the quality of primary care could surely be better. And America is the innovation engine of the world, pumping out new drugs and treatments that benefit the whole world. . . . [O]verall, while the U.S. healthcare system has a lot of work ahead, we should not overlook its strengths – and they are sizeable.

Ashish Jha, Judging Health Systems: Focusing on What Matters (Sept. 2017). See Chapter 9.F for additional international discussion.

One sign of better medical value elsewhere is the extent to which Americans who are footing the bill are willing to receive care in other countries, even lesser-developed ones such as India, Mexico, or the Caribbean. See note 3 for readings on this growing phenomenon of "medical tourism" and its host of legal issues.

3. *More Facts, Figures, and Opinions.* There is seemingly an endless appetite for **facts and figures** about the U.S. health care delivery system. Those who wish for more, or more recent numbers, can find them in the annual reports of the Medicare Payment Advisory Commission (MedPac), in periodic issues of Health Affairs, and on the Web pages for the U.S. Census Bureau and the Centers for Medicare and Medicaid Services (CMS), which are linked to the Web page for this book, www.health-law.org.

For more discussion of **what's right or wrong with the U.S. health care system (note 1)**, see Elisabeth Rosenthal, An American Sickness (2017); Jonathan Cohn, Sick: The Untold Story of America's Health Care Crisis (2007); Shannon Brownlee, Overtreated: Why Too Much Medicine Is Making Us Sicker and Poorer (2007); David Goldhill, How American Health Care Killed My Father, The Atlantic, Sept. 2009; Tom Daschle, Critical: What We Can Do About the Health-Care Crisis (2008); Einer Elhauge ed., The Fragmentation of U.S. Health Care (2010); Julius B. Richmond & Rashi Fein, The Health Care Mess: How We Got into It and What It Will Take to Get Out (2005); Paul Krugman & Robin Wells, The Health Care Crisis and What to Do About It, 53 N.Y. Review of Books No. 5 (Mar. 23, 2006); Jonathan Gruber & Helen Levy, The Evolution of Medical Spending Risk, 23 J. Econ. Perspec. 25 (2009); Robert E. Hall & Charles I. Jones, The Value of Life and the Rise in Health Spending, 122 Q. J. Econ. 39 (2007); Kevin Murphy & Robert Topel eds., Measuring the Gains from Medical Research (2003); Elliott S. Fisher, Medical Care: Is More Always Better?, 349 New Eng. J. Med. 1665 (2003); Nortin M. Hadler, The Last Well Person (2004); Henry Aaron & Paul Ginsburg, Is Health Spending Excessive? If So, What Can We Do About It?, 28(5) Health Aff. 1260 (Oct. 2009); Symposium, 39 J.L. Med. & Ethics 111 (2011); President's Council of Economic Advisors, The Economic Case for Health Care Reform (2009); Thomas Bodenheimer, High and Rising Health Care Costs, 142 Annals Intern. Med. 847, 932 (2005); Symposium, 28 Health Aff. 1250 (Oct. 2009); Symposium, 362 New Eng. J. Med. 1 (2010); Symposium, 22(1) Health Aff. 1 (Jan. 2003).

On **international comparisons (note 2)**, see Cathy Schoen et al., U.S. Health System Performance: A National Scorecard, 25 Health Aff. w457 (Sept. 2006); David Squires, Explaining High Health Care Spending in the United States: An International Comparison (Commonwealth Fund 2012); S. H. Woolf, U.S. Health in International Perspective: Shorter Lives, Poorer Health (Institute of Medicine, 2013).

On **medical tourism (note 2)**, see Glenn Cohen & Holly Lynch, Patients with Passports: Medical Tourism, Law and Ethics (2013); Glenn Cohen, Protecting Patients with Passports: Medical Tourism and the Patient Protective Argument, 95 Iowa L. Rev. 1467 (2010); Nathan Cortez, Cross-Border Health Care and the Hydraulics of Health Reform (2012); Nathan Cortez, Recalibrating the Legal Risks of Cross-Border Health Care, 10 Yale J. Health Pol'y L. & Ethics 1 (Winter 2010); Nicolas P. Terry, Under-Regulated Health Care Phenomena in a Flat World: Medical Tourism and Outsourcing, 29 W. New Eng. L. Rev. 421 (2007); Kerrie S. Howze, Medical Tourism: Symptom or Cure?, 41 Ga. L. Rev. 1013 (2007); Thomas R. McLean, The Offshoring of American Medicine, 14 Annals Health L. 205 (2005); Note, 18 Kennedy Inst. Ethics J. 193 (2008) (bibliography); Symposium, 26 Wis. Int'l L.J. 591-964 (2008).

C. COMPETING PARADIGMS IN HEALTH LAW

This section briefly introduces various analytical perspectives that give greater depth to our understanding of health care law, ethics, and public policy. Most of these analytical frameworks spring from some branch of moral and political theory that addresses fundamental questions of individual and social justice, such as how best to distribute scarce medical resources, and whose decision over medical treatment should govern when there is conflict. Necessarily, this must be a grab bag of somewhat disconnected lines of thought drawn from many different intellectual disciplines—primarily philosophy, economics, and political science. This is due to what Einer Elhauge below calls the "paradigm pathology" of health care law: See also the sources cited in note 2 of the Preface.

Although health law may have a core set of concerns, it lacks a dominant analytical mode. In classic fields of law such as contracts or torts, most people seem at least to be asking the same sorts of questions, even if they don't arrive at the same answers. Health care law has so many interdisciplinary, intellectual currents that courts and scholars sound at times like the mythical builders of the Tower of Babel. Some order can be brought to this mélange of ideologies by categorizing and critiquing different "paradigms" of thought. As the second and third readings in this section explain, the dominant paradigms in past decades have been professionalism and patient autonomy, and the contending analytical paradigms respond to these. Rather than attempt any neat packaging of the contenders, for they are still very untidy, try to identify throughout the course which currents of thought are consistent with or opposed to the professionalism or patient autonomy paradigms and in what ways.

■ALLOCATING HEALTH CARE MORALLY*
Einer Elhauge
82 Cal. L. Rev. 1449 (1994)

Health law policy suffers from an identifiable pathology. . . . [I]t employs four different paradigms for how decisions to allocate resources should be made: the market paradigm, the professional paradigm, the moral paradigm, and the political paradigm. . . . [R]ather than coordinate these decisionmaking paradigms, health law policy employs them inconsistently, such that the combination operates at cross-purposes.

This inconsistency results in part because, intellectually, health care law borrows haphazardly from other fields of law, each of which has its own internally coherent conceptual logic, but which in combination results in an incoherent legal framework and perverse incentive structures. In other words, health care law has not—at least not yet—established itself to be a field of law with its own coherent conceptual logic, as opposed to a collection of issues and cases from other legal fields connected only by the happenstance that they all involve patients and health care providers.

In other part, the pathology results because the various scholarly disciplines focus excessively on their favorite paradigms. Scholars operating in the disciplines of economics, medicine, political science, and philosophy each tend to assume that their discipline offers a privileged perspective. This leads them either to press their favored paradigm too far or to conceptualize policy issues solely in terms of what their paradigm can and cannot solve.

Instead, health law policy issues should be conceived in terms of comparative paradigm analysis. Such analysis focuses on the strengths and weaknesses of the various decisionmaking paradigms, determining which is *relatively* better suited to resolving various decisions, and then assigning each paradigm to the roles for which it is best suited. . . .

Luckily, this is a mode of analysis in which legal scholars, as cross-disciplinary generalists, have some plausible claim to comparative scholarly advantage. Unluckily, it is hard and arduous. Nevertheless, it offers the promise that health law scholars will provide insights into health policy that so far have been missed. In a field as intellectually new as modern health law, it should hardly be surprising that this task has only begun.

■ THE PROFESSIONAL PARADIGM OF MEDICAL CARE: OBSTACLE TO DECENTRALIZATION*
Clark C. Havighurst
30 Jurimetrics J. 415 (1990)

The thesis of this article is that, despite all the organizational and financial changes that occurred in the health care sector in the 1980s, we still cannot fight the battle for efficiency effectively because we are saddled as a society with a particular paradigmatic conception of the medical care enterprise. The source of this paradigm is a deep-seated belief, long fostered by the medical profession, that medical care is not a commodity, that its characteristics are scientifically determined, and that decisions concerning it must be entrusted exclusively to professionals. That this paradigm is ideologically attractive and contains some significant kernels of truth simply complicates the problem of adapting it to accord with current economic realities.

The professional paradigm of the medical enterprise is a venerable one, stemming from the days early in this century when the medical profession rose to what sociologist Paul Starr has called a position of "cultural authority, economic power, and political influence."[5] Although its tenets are nowhere officially set down, some of them can be deduced from the profession's performance during the era when it exercised rather complete hegemony over health care and its financing. Judging from that experience, the profession's ideology has included the following themes:

- medical care should be evaluated only on the basis of safety and efficacy;
- cost considerations should not enter into medical decisionmaking because counting costs implies both a willingness to trade off a patient's welfare against other societal needs and a tolerance for differences based on ability to pay;
- decisions on the appropriate utilization of medical services should be based exclusively on scientific evidence and expert opinion;
- although patient preferences should be honored under the principle of informed consent, there is no similar urgency about giving people opportunities to express their preferences qua consumers, with cost differences in view; and
- professional norms alone should set the limits of a physician's judgment.

Under these general principles, the role of payers was long limited to ensuring that professional norms were followed, so that only care that was virtually useless or positively harmful was excluded. . . .

The professional paradigm derives much of its force from the egalitarian ideal in medicine—the belief that every citizen is entitled to medical care of the same quality and that "two-tier" medicine is unthinkable. Even though society has not seen fit to adopt an egalitarian policy by accepting either the heavy tax burden or the stringent rationing necessary to achieve it, the egalitarian ideal colors much

---

5. P. Starr, The Social Transformation of American Medicine 5 (1982).

thinking about medical care. Indeed, even in the absence of any actual legal or contractual entitlement, a powerful entitlement mentality must be confronted by anyone seeking to economize in the provision of health services. The professional paradigm generally supports this view of things, while the profession as a whole resists most of the measures that would be necessary to create an affordable, truly egalitarian system. There is here a marriage of convenience—between physicians' desires to resist infringements on their clinical freedom and a particularly extreme view of the requirements of social justice.

The scientific character of medicine has also provided vital support for the professional paradigm. Indeed, the success of the medical profession in establishing its scientific character in the early part of the century—in the Flexner Report,[6] for example—laid the groundwork for its claim of exemption from market forces and for its autonomy as a profession. Once medical care was viewed as the application of science to human problems rather than as a commercial service to be bought and sold in market transactions, the profession was able to resist most of the pressures that naturally arose and to head off, by effective lobbying or collective action, market developments that might have threatened its hegemony. . . .

Residues of the professional paradigm can be found in many places but are particularly significant in the legal system. Not only does the law tend to defer to the medical profession's presumed scientific authority on many points, but it is often administered with an egalitarian mentality that tends to define issues in terms of abstract rights. Indeed, the law frequently goes to great lengths to avoid appearing to concede that some persons might ever have a legal or even a contractual right to better medical care than someone else. This refusal to recognize the reality that some consumers might choose, or wish to choose, to purchase more or better health care than others—or have a lesser entitlement because of inability or unwillingness to pay—greatly complicates efforts to economize in the private sector. It also raises, perhaps inappropriately, the cost to government of providing for those who cannot support themselves. As long as the legal system does not acknowledge inequality or recognize efforts to escape the costly standards implicit in the professional/scientific/egalitarian paradigm, neither self-supporting consumers nor taxpayers are in a good position to economize on health care by refusing to buy too much of a good thing.

■ THE PRACTICE OF AUTONOMY: PATIENTS, DOCTORS, AND MEDICAL DECISIONS
Carl E. Schneider
1998

Bioethicists, like lawyers, live in danger of what I once called "hyper-rationalism." Hyper-rationalism has both a methodological and a substantive aspect. As a method, [h]yper-rationalism is essentially the substitution of reason for information and analysis. It has two components: First, the belief that reason can reliably be used to infer facts where evidence is unavailable or incomplete, and second, the practice of interpreting facts through a narrow set of artificial analytic categories.

6. A. Flexner, *Medical Education in the United States and Canada* (Carnegie Foundation for the Advancement of Technology, Bull. No. 4, 1910).

Hyper-rationalism, in other words, tempts us to believe that we can understand how people think and act merely by reasoning, and not by investigating. . . .

For one thing, the assumptions of hyper-rationalism can lead us into a tendency to see human nature and conduct as verging on the uniform. . . . As empiricists in fields ranging from sociology to psychology to anthropology have been at pains to show, this view exaggerates human rationality and understates the role of social and cultural factors in patient's lives. . . .

Hyper-rationalists' . . . picture of human nature is too simple, too disembodied, to be convincing. They present a bloodless, flat, distant, abstract, depersonalized, impoverished view of the way people think, feel, and act, of the social circumstances in which people live, of the ethical lives they lead. And hyper-rationalism's simplifications are particularly injurious in [health law and ethics], a field that treats people in their least rational moments, in their most emotional travails, in their most contextual complexity.

Hyper-rationalism, of course, has its uses. It promotes the kind of generalization that frees courts and commentators to reason logically about the normative problems that are, after all, one of their central concerns. And some simplification of life's complexity is necessary if human problems are to be dealt with practically and promptly, if comprehensible rules are to be devised, if useful precedent is to be developed, if institutions are to function smoothly. But we should want to insinuate as much of that complexity as possible into normative discourse. A failure to do so perilously distances norms from the people and circumstances they seek to govern.

This is a peril with which law is all too familiar. [7] . . . One of the great truths about law is that, with unnerving frequency, it fails to achieve the effects intended for it, and sometimes quite fails to have any effect at all. Some of the most fascinating modern legal scholarship reminds lawyers how removed their talk is from the world's ken. That literature reveals that, to the lawyer's chagrin, businesses resist using contracts, ranchers do not know what rules of liability govern damage done by wandering cattle, suburbanites do not summon the law to resolve neighborhood disputes, engaged couples do not know the law governing how they will own property when they marry, citizens repeatedly reject the due process protections proffered them, and, what is worse, all these people simply don't care what the law says. . . .

What is going on here? Well, of course, lots of things. But central among them is society's enormous complexity and the narrow relevance of the law to it. People are enticed by many pressures beyond those the law creates. They have their own agendas and, more important, their own normative systems. The law writes rules, but the governed—when they know the rules—often have the incentives, time, and energy to avoid them.

Consider advance directives [for end-of-life care]. They offer an apparently irresistible way of speaking in one of life's greatest crises. Yet people spurn them. They do so because they have their own lives to lead. Momentous as the crisis may be, it will generally not seem urgent until it arrives. People resist contemplating their own mortality. They heartily dislike and don't easily understand legal forms; they find them obscure and darkly imagine how they might be misused. For that matter,

---

7. The remainder of this excerpt interpolates parts of another publication by the same author, Bioethics in the Language of the Law, 24(4) Hastings Center Rep. (July 1994).

people may doubt that they will be used at all. Further, many people have trouble envisioning their circumstances years into the future or how they would respond to those hypothetical circumstances. And I suspect that people expect that decisions about their welfare would in any case fall to people they trust—to their families. In short, advance directives were formulated and promoted by people—bioethicists, lawyers, and doctors, for instance—who know what they want to do through them and keenly want to do it. But many of us are not clear about what we want and about whether getting it is worth the costs.

In short, while the language of the law may have penetrated into the bosom of society, it must still, in quotidian life, compete with the many other languages that people speak more comfortably, more fluently, and with much more conviction. These are languages of religion and morality, of love and friendship, of pragmatism and social accommodation, of custom and compromise. The danger for [health law and ethics], then, is believing too deeply that law can pierce the Babel, can speak with precision, can be heard. . . .

But what is the antidote to hyper-rationalism? There are several. For instance, [Howard] Brody writes that philosophy of medicine "can indeed advance by . . . abstract discussions; but it can advance only so far. At some point we will require a richer context for the discussion to proceed fruitfully. This context can be provided by stories of sickness." . . .

We need, then, to inhabit all the mansions available in the house of bioethics. And among the least inhabited of those mansions is that of empirical research. Such research offers a breadth, rigor, and precision of understanding that is available in no other way. It provides a disciplined way of reviewing our assumptions and a systematic means of identifying neglected issues. In sum, empirical research provides a fruitful means of obtaining a more detailed, complex, and acute understanding of what patients want, think, and do which can deepen—and darken—our understanding of bioethical problems.

Notes: Professionalism, Empiricism, and Other Paradigms

1. *Defending Professionalism.* Contrasting with Prof. Havighurst's views, a number of scholars have defended the important role that professionalism plays in medicine and analyzed how law should promote or accommodate desirable features of professionalism. See, e.g., Andrew Fitcher, The Law of Doctoring: A Study of the Codification of Medical Professionalism, 19 Health Matrix 317 (2009); Gail Agrawal, Resuscitating Professionalism: Self-Regulation in the Medical Marketplace, 66 Mo. L. Rev. 341 (2001). On professionalism generally, see Eliot Freidson, Professionalism: The Third Logic (2001).

2. *Outsider Jurisprudence.* Feminist critique, critical race theory, and critical legal studies are flourishing in health care law, as they are elsewhere in legal analysis. See, e.g., Symposium, Deconstructing Traditional Paradigms in Bioethics: Race, Gender, Class, and Culture, 15 St. Louis U. Pub. L. Rev. 183 (1996). Leading critical legal scholars are David Frankford and Gregg Bloche. Examples of their work include Privatizing Health Care: Economic Magic to Cure Legal Medicine, 66 S. Cal. L. Rev. 1 (1992) (Frankford); The Invention of Health Law, 91 Cal. L. Rev. 247 (2003) (Bloche). Professors Dorothy Roberts and Lisa Ikemoto have been especially prominent scholars on critical race theory. Examples of their work include Killing

the Black Body: Race, Reproduction, and the Meaning of Liberty (1997) (Roberts); The Genetic Tie, 62 U. Chi. L. Rev. 209 (1995) (Roberts); In the Shadow of Race: Women of Color in Health Disparities Policy, 39 U.C. Davis L. Rev. 1023 (2006) (Ikemoto). See also Michele Goodwin, Black Markets: The Supply and Demand of Body Parts (2006); David B. Smith, Health Care Divided: Race and Healing a Nation (1999); Vernellia R. Randall, Slavery, Segregation and Racism: An African American Perspective on Bioethics, 15 St. Louis U. Pub. L. Rev. 191 (1996). Feminist critique is multidisciplinary, but is especially rich with respect to reproductive issues. For a broad introduction, see articles published in Symposium, Feminist Bioethics, 26 J. Med. & Phil. 339 (2001) and the materials in Chapter 7 of this casebook. See also Susan M. Wolf, Feminism & Bioethics: Beyond Reproduction (1996); Symposium, 44 U. Balt. L. Rev. 163 (2015); Symposium, 9 Duke J. Gender L. & Pol'y 1 (2002).

3. *Empiricism and Narratives.* Whichever philosophical or analytical camp one hails from, all agree that legal and public policy analysis is greatly enhanced with good empirical information. That is why we try to provide a good amount of empirical data throughout the notes in this book. For other general overviews of empirical work relevant to health care law and ethics, see Michelle M. Mello & Kathryn Zeiler, Empirical Health Law Scholarship: The State of the Field, 96 Geo. L.J. 649-702 (2008); Jeremy Sugarman et al., A Quarter Century of Empirical Research in Biomedical Ethics, *in* Methods in Medical Ethics (2d ed. 2010); Scott Burris, From Health Care Law to the Social Determinants of Health: A Public Health Law Research Perspective, 159 U. Pa. L. Rev. 1649 (2011).

Empiricism can also take a more anecdotal form, by deepening understanding of legal and public policy problems through the rhetorical device of narrative. Telling personal stories can be a powerful way to demonstrate how law actually affects people in real lives. Several compelling examples are contained in these materials, see pages 5, 30, 255, and others are cited in the bibliography at page 24 and are discussed in Carl Schneider's book. For additional narratives, see Elizabeth A. Pendo, Images of Health Insurance in Popular Film: The Dissolving Critique, 37 J. Health L. 267 (2004); Stacey A. Tovino, Incorporating Literature into a Health Law Curriculum, 9 J. Med. & L. 213 (2005); Dena Davis, Tell Me a Story: Using Short Fiction in Teaching Law, 47 J. Leg. Educ. 240 (1997); and a recurring column in Health Affairs. Narrative approaches have also been criticized as excessively anecdotal and tending to be misrepresentative. See David A. Hyman, Patient Dumping: Lies, Damned Lies, and Narrative, 73 Ind. L.J. 797 (1998).

PART I

THE PROVIDER AND
THE PATIENT

This first part of the book explores the legal issues that lie at the core of the provider-patient relationship. By provider, we mean doctors, hospitals, and other people and institutions that deliver health care services. Chapter 2 examines the basic structure of the treatment relationship, including topics such as the duty to treat and the formation and termination of the treatment relationship. Chapter 3 considers the fiduciary nature of the treatment relationship, with coverage including confidentiality, informed consent, and conflicts of interest. Chapter 4 is devoted to medical malpractice liability. These patient care issues all spring directly from how providers and patients interact at the point of treatment. Although these interactions are certainly influenced by institutional, financial, and regulatory forces, this external environment is not explored in depth until the later parts of the book.

The provider-patient relationship is governed primarily by contract, tort, and fiduciary law—all aspects of private law. Within the sphere of public law, constitutional law is of very limited relevance in this part. It affects primarily the end-of-life and reproductive issues discussed in Part II, Chapters 5 and 7. Public law does influence the provider-patient relationship through important regulatory constraints, but for the most part these are extensions of or reactions to the basic private law framework. So that is where we begin.

The treatment relationship starts and ends in contract law. Contract principles determine whether there is a duty to accept a patient and whether treatment can be terminated. But, between these defining points, the *content* of the treatment relationship is determined primarily by tort and fiduciary law, not by contract. That is because the treatment encounter creates what is known as a "relational contract," one that governs a complex relationship by incorporating external social norms rather than by specifying detailed performance requirements and standards. Cf. Mark A. Hall, Toward Relationship-Centered Health Law, 50 Wake Forest L. Rev. 233 (2015). Tort and fiduciary law are richer sources for social and professional norms relating to medicine than the law generated by commercial sales, although the legal framework for imposing those norms remains that of contract law.

To better understand this interconnected web of legal doctrine, we begin this part of the book with a chapter on the basic structure of the treatment relationship: how it is formed, how it is terminated, and the extent to which it can be altered and defined by private agreement. In the following two chapters, we look more at the content of treatment relationships, starting first with the fiduciary duties of confidentiality, candor, and loyalty, and then in the next chapter considering the full extent of malpractice liability.

While the focus of these first three chapters is, respectively, contract, fiduciary, and tort law, the divisions among these bodies of law are not so neatly confined. Each set of private law concepts, as well as various public law influences, can be felt throughout this first part of the book. Thus, there is a broad inquiry that connects all of these chapters: To what extent should the structure and content of medical relationships be defined by the parties themselves, by legal norms based in conventional common law doctrine, or by explicit legislative oversight tailored specifically to the medical context?

2

![black square]

The Treatment Relationship:
Formation and Termination

Ordinarily, the patient-provider relationship is a consensual one to which both parties must agree. Therefore, an individual physician may, generally speaking, refuse to accept patients for any reason or for no reason. The same is true to a lesser extent for hospitals and other institutions. But this general freedom of contract is limited in several important ways. Hospitals may not turn patients away in emergencies until they have at least stabilized the patient's condition. Neither may doctors or hospitals refuse patients for certain discriminatory reasons, such the patient's race, sex, or HIV status. Once treatment has begun, it may not be ceased without proper arrangements being made. And providers may not impose unreasonable conditions on their agreement to treat. While historically a physician's freedom to turn away patients found its limitations primarily in the law, the growth of formal arrangements between managed care health plans and physicians means that a provider's obligation to treat is being increasingly defined by the private agreements among the patient, insurance plan, and provider. The following materials explore the origins of, and limits on, this freedom of contract between providers and patients.

A. THE DUTY TO TREAT

1. The Duty to Accept Patients

■ **HURLEY v. EDDINGFIELD**
59 N.E. 1058 (Ind. 1901)

BAKER, Justice.

The appellant sued appellee for $10,000 damages for wrongfully causing the death of his intestate. The court sustained appellee's demurrer to the complaint, and this ruling is assigned as error.

The material facts may be summarized thus: At and for years before decedent's death appellee was a practicing physician at Mace, in Montgomery county, duly licensed under the laws of the state. He held himself out to the public as a general practitioner of medicine. He had been decedent's family physician. Decedent became dangerously ill, and sent for appellee. The messenger informed appellee of decedent's violent sickness, tendered him his fee for his services, and stated to him that no other physician was procurable in time, and that decedent relied on him for attention. No other physician was procurable in time to be of any use, and decedent did rely on appellee for medical assistance. Without any reasons whatever, appellee refused to render aid to decedent. No other patients were requiring appellee's immediate service, and he could have gone to the relief of decedent if he had been willing to do so. Death ensued, without decedent's fault, and wholly from appellee's wrongful act. The alleged wrongful act was appellee's refusal to enter into a contract of employment. Counsel do not contend that, before the enactment of the law regulating the practice of medicine, physicians were bound to render professional service to everyone who applied. The act regulating the practice of medicine provides for a board of examiners, standards of qualification, examinations, licenses to those found qualified, and penalties for practicing without license. The act is a preventive, not a compulsive, measure. In obtaining the state's license (permission) to practice medicine, the state does not require, and the licensee does not engage, that he will practice at all or on other terms than he may choose to accept. Counsel's analogies, drawn from the obligations to the public on the part of innkeepers, common carriers, and the like, are beside the mark. Judgment affirmed.

■ **WILMINGTON GENERAL HOSPITAL v. MANLOVE**
174 A.2d 135 (Del. 1961)

SOUTHERLAND, Chief Justice.

This case concerns the liability of a private hospital for the death of an infant who was refused treatment at the emergency ward of the hospital. The facts are these:

On January 4, 1959, Darien E. Manlove, the deceased infant, then four months old, developed diarrhea. The next morning his parents consulted Dr. Hershon. They asked whether the medicine they had for him was all right and the doctor said that it was. In the evening of the same day Mrs. Manlove took the baby's temperature.

It was higher than normal. They called Dr. Hershon, and he prescribed additional medication (streptomycin), which he ordered delivered by a pharmacy.

Mrs. Manlove stayed up with the child that night. He did not sleep. On the morning of January 6th, the parents took the infant to Dr. Hershon's office. Dr. Thomas examined the child and treated him for sore throat and diarrhea. He prescribed a liquid diet and some medicine. . . .

On the morning of January 7th (a Wednesday) [the infant's] temperature was still above normal — 102. Mr. and Mrs. Manlove determined to seek additional medical assistance. They knew that Dr. Hershon and Dr. Thomas were not in their offices on Wednesdays, and they took their infant to the emergency ward of the Wilmington General Hospital.

There is no real conflict of fact as to what occurred at the hospital. The parents took the infant into the reception room of the Emergency Ward. A nurse was on duty. They explained to the nurse what was wrong with the child, that is, that he had not slept for two nights, had a continuously high temperature, and that he had diarrhea. Mr. Manlove told the nurse that the child was under the care of Dr. Hershon and Dr. Thomas, and showed the nurse the medicines prescribed. The nurse explained to the parents that the hospital could not give treatment because the child was under the care of a physician and there would be danger that the medication of the hospital might conflict with that of the attending physician. The nurse did not examine the child, take his temperature, feel his forehead, or look down his throat. The child was not in convulsions, and was not coughing or crying. There was no particular area of body tenderness.

The nurse tried to get in touch with Dr. Hershon or Dr. Thomas in the hospital and at their offices, but was unable to do so. She suggested that the parents bring the baby Thursday morning to the pediatric clinic.

Mr. and Mrs. Manlove returned home. Mrs. Manlove made an appointment by telephone to see Dr. Hershon or Dr. Thomas that night at eight o'clock. At eight minutes past three o'clock in the afternoon the baby died of bronchial pneumonia. . . .

It was assumed by both parties below that the hospital was a private hospital and not a public one — that is, an institution founded and controlled by private persons and not by public authority. The trial court disagreed, finding a quasi-public status in the receipt of grants of public money and tax exemptions. . . . Hence, the court concluded, liability may be imposed on the defendant in an emergency case.

We are compelled to disagree with the view that the defendant has become a public (or quasi-public) hospital. It is admitted (although the record does not show it) that it is privately owned and operated. We find no dissent from the rule that such a hospital is a private hospital, and may, at least in the absence of control by the legislature, conduct its business largely as it sees fit. . . .

Moreover, the holding that the receipt of grants of public money requires the hospital to care for emergency cases, as distinguished from others, is not logical. Why emergency cases? If the holding is sound it must apply to all the hospital services, and that conclusion, as we shall see, is clearly unsound. . . .

We are of opinion that the defendant is a private and not a public hospital, in so far as concerns the right of a member of the public to demand admission or treatment. What, then, is the liability of a private hospital in this respect?

Since such an institution as the defendant is privately owned and operated, it would follow logically that its trustees or governing board alone have the right to determine who shall be admitted to it as patients. No other rule would be sensible or workable. Such authority as we have found supports this rule. "A private hospital owes the public no duty to accept any patient not desired by it, and it is not necessary to assign any reason for its refusal to accept a patient for hospital service." 41 C. J. S. Hospitals §8, p.345. . . .

. . . Does that rule apply to the fullest extent to patients applying for treatment at an emergency ward? . . .

It may be conceded that a private hospital is under no legal obligation to the public to maintain an emergency ward, or, for that matter, a public clinic. But the maintenance of such a ward to render first-aid to injured persons has become a well-established adjunct to the main business of a hospital. If a person, seriously hurt, applies for such aid at an emergency ward, relying on the established custom to render it, is it still the right of the hospital to turn him away without any reason? In such a case, it seems to us, such a refusal might well result in worsening the condition of the injured person, because of the time lost in a useless attempt to obtain medical aid. Such a set of circumstances is analogous to the case of the negligent termination of gratuitous services, which creates a tort liability. Restatement, Law of Torts, "Negligence," §323. . . .

As above indicated, we are of opinion that liability on the part of a hospital may be predicated on the refusal of service to a patient in case of an unmistakable emergency, if the patient has relied upon a well-established custom of the hospital to render aid in such a case. . . .

Applying this rule here, we inquire, was there an unmistakable emergency? Certainly, the record does not support the view that the infant's condition was so desperate that a layman could reasonably say that he was in immediate danger. The learned judge indicated that the fact that death followed in a few hours showed an emergency; but with this we cannot agree. It is hindsight. And it is to be noted that the attending physician, after prescribing for the child one morning before, did not think another examination that night or the next morning was required. If this case had gone to the jury on the record here made, we would have been required to hold that it was insufficient to establish liability. We cannot agree that the mere recitation of the infant's symptoms was, in itself, evidence of an emergency sufficient to present a question for the jury. Before such an issue could arise there would have to be evidence that an experienced nurse should have known that such symptoms constituted unmistakable evidence of an emergency. . . .

The possibility that the case might turn on additional evidence respecting the matters we have touched upon was not considered either by the court or counsel. In these circumstances, we think the case should go back for further proceedings. We should add, however, that if plaintiff cannot adduce evidence showing some incompetency of the nurse, or some breach of duty or some negligence, his case must fail. Like the learned judge below, we sympathize with the parents in their loss of a child; but this natural feeling does not permit us to find liability in the absence of satisfactory evidence.

For the reasons above set forth the order denying summary judgment is affirmed, without approving the reasons therefor set forth in the court's opinion.

■WIDEMAN v. SHALLOWFORD COMMUNITY HOSPITAL
826 F.2d 1030 (11th Cir. 1987)

HILL, Circuit Judge.

This case presents the novel question of whether a county government's alleged practice of using its emergency medical vehicles only to transport patients to certain county hospitals which guarantee the payment of the county's medical bills violates a right protected by the federal constitution. We hold that such a practice, even if proved, would not violate any established constitutional right. . . .

I. BACKGROUND

The facts underlying this case are undeniably tragic. On April 12, 1984, Toni Wideman, who at the time was four months pregnant, began experiencing abdominal pain. She called her obstetrician, Dr. John Ramsey, who instructed her to come immediately to Piedmont Hospital. Ms. Wideman called the 911 emergency telephone number in DeKalb County and requested an ambulance to take her to Piedmont. Three employees of the DeKalb County Emergency Medical Service (EMS) responded to this call. Ms. Wideman claims that she again informed the EMS employees to take her to Piedmont where her doctor was waiting, but they refused and, instead, took her against her wishes to Shallowford Community Hospital. After a substantial delay, during which the attending physician at Shallowford spoke by phone with Dr. Ramsey, Ms. Wideman was transferred to Piedmont. At that point, however, Dr. Ramsey was unable to stop her labor, and Ms. Wideman gave birth to a premature baby, named Ebony Laslun Wideman, who survived for only four hours. . . .

. . . It seems that both parties, as well as the district court, have assumed that the alleged policy violates a cognizable constitutional right, which the plaintiffs characterize as their right to the provision of essential medical treatment and services by the county.[1] However, . . . the proper resolution of this case requires us first to determine whether the Constitution grants a right to medical care and treatment in these circumstances. . . .

III. A. EXISTENCE OF A CONSTITUTIONAL RIGHT TO ESSENTIAL MEDICAL CARE

Beginning from the broadest prospective, we can discern no general right, based upon either the Constitution or federal statutes, to the provision of medical treatment and services by a state or municipality. If such a right exists at all, it must derive from the Fourteenth Amendment's due process clause, which forbids a state to deprive anyone of life, liberty or property without due process of law. The due process clause, however, has traditionally been interpreted as protecting certain

---

1. The constitutional right alleged by the plaintiffs arguably may be characterized as the much more specific right to the medical care and services of their choice. Ms. Wideman was provided with medical care in this case; indeed, she was rushed to a hospital in an ambulance provided by the county. Her claim appears to be that she should have been able to direct the ambulance wherever she wanted to go. For purposes of our analysis, however, we shall consider the plaintiffs' alleged constitutional right as they have characterized it.

"negative liberties," i.e., an individual's right to be free from arbitrary or discriminatory action taken by a state or municipality. This circuit has recognized the "well established notion that the Constitution limits the actions the states can take rather than mandating specific obligations." Bradberry v. Pinellas County, 789 F.2d 1513, 1517 (11th Cir. 1986). . . .

Two Supreme Court decisions dealing with access to abortions also support our conclusion that there is no general right to medical care or treatment provided by the state. In Maher v. Roe, 432 U.S. 464 (1977), two indigent women brought suit challenging a Connecticut regulation prohibiting the funding of abortions that were not medically necessary. The plaintiffs argued under the Fourteenth Amendment that the state regulation impinged on their constitutional right to an abortion, as recognized in Roe v. Wade, 410 U.S. 113 (1973). The Court upheld the state regulation, concluding that *Roe* did not declare an unqualified constitutional right to an abortion; rather, that case declared a woman's right to be protected from unduly burdensome interference with her freedom to decide whether to terminate her pregnancy. Significantly, in reaching this result, the Court noted that "the Constitution imposes no obligation on the states to pay the pregnancy-related medical expenses of indigent women, or indeed to pay any of the medical expenses of indigents." *Maher*, 432 U.S. at 469 (footnote omitted).

The Court's subsequent decision in Harris v. McRae, 448 U.S. 297 (1980), reinforced the constitutional distinction between requiring the state to provide medical services and prohibiting the state from impeding access to such services. The plaintiffs in *Harris* challenged the constitutionality of the Hyde amendment, which denied public funding for certain medically necessary abortions, as violating their due process liberty interest in deciding whether to terminate a pregnancy. The Supreme Court held that although the liberty protected by the due process clause prohibits unwarranted government interference with freedom of choice in the context of certain personal decisions, "it does not confer an entitlement to such funds as may be necessary to realize all the advantages of that freedom." . . . More recently, the Court has interpreted *Maher* and *Harris* as standing for the proposition that, "as a general matter, the state is under no constitutional duty to provide substantive services for those within its border." Youngberg v. Romeo, 457 U.S. 307, 317 (1982).

Several courts of appeals decisions have addressed the issue of whether a state or municipality has a duty under the Fourteenth Amendment to provide various protective services to its citizens. Almost without exception, these courts have concluded that governments are under no constitutional duty to provide police, fire, or other public safety services. . . .

B

That there exists no such general right to the provision of medical care and services by the state, however, does not end our inquiry. Both the Supreme Court and various circuit courts have indicated that the existence of a "special custodial or other relationship" between an individual and the state may trigger a constitutional duty on the part of the state to provide certain medical or other services. In these special circumstances, the state's failure to provide such services might implicate constitutionally protected rights.

EXAMPLES

For example, the Supreme Court has held that the Eighth Amendment prohibition against cruel and unusual punishments, applicable to the states via the Fourteenth Amendment, requires states to provide medical care for those whom it is punishing by incarceration. . . . Similarly, the Court has held that an involuntarily committed mental patient retains . . . a clear Fourteenth Amendment right "to adequate food, shelter, clothing, and medical care." *Youngberg*, 457 U.S. at 315. . . .

Following this rationale, a constitutional duty can arise only when a state or municipality, by exercising a significant degree of custody or control over an individual, places that person in a worse situation than he would have been had the government not acted at all. Such a situation could arise by virtue of the state affirmatively placing an individual in a position of danger, effectively stripping a person of her ability to defend herself, or cutting off potential sources of private aid. The key concept is the exercise of coercion, dominion, or restraint by the state. . . .

In the present case, we conclude that DeKalb County did not exercise a degree of coercion, dominion, or restraint over Ms. Wideman sufficient to create a "special relationship." . . . The county did not force or otherwise coerce her into its ambulance; it merely made the ambulance available to her, and she entered it voluntarily. Ms. Wideman's physical condition at the time might have required her to seek immediate medical help, and that need might have induced her to make use of the service provided by the county, hoping that she could convince the EMS employees to take her where she wanted to go. Her physical condition, however, cannot be attributed to the county. . . . Therefore, the county was under no affirmative constitutional duty to provide any particular type of emergency medical service for her. . . .

. . . Because the Constitution does not require municipalities to provide any emergency medical services at all, it would be anomalous indeed to hold them liable for providing limited services which happen to be less extensive than a particular citizen may desire. . . .

Notes: The Differing Obligations of Physicians and Hospitals; Hospitals as Quasi-Public Facilities

1. *The "No Duty" Rule.* The complaint and brief in Hurley v. Eddingfield reveal that the deceased patient was in distress during childbirth, yet, as the *Hurley* court suggests, physicians are not obligated to provide care to a particular patient unless they have agreed to do so. A standard characterization of this principle appears in Oliver v. Brock, 342 So. 2d 1, 3 (Ala. 1976):

> A physician is under no obligation to engage in practice or to accept professional employment, but when the professional services of a physician are accepted by another person for the purposes of medical or surgical treatment, the relation of physician and patient is created. The relation is a consensual one wherein the patient knowingly seeks the assistance of a physician and the physician knowingly accepts him as patient. The relationship between a physician and patient may result from an express or implied contract, either general or special, and the rights and liabilities of the parties thereto are governed by the general law of contract. . . . 61 Am. Jur. 2d, Physicians, Surgeons, and Other Healers, §96.

This "no duty" rule is consistent with tort law's normal "Good Samaritan" doctrine, which does not require individuals, even professionals, to come to the aid of strangers in distress. A physician's *ethical*, as opposed to legal, duty is somewhat more demanding, however. The American Medical Association's Principles of Medical Ethics state that a "physician shall, in the provision of appropriate patient care, except in emergencies, be free to choose whom to serve. . . ." (Principle VI). Why couldn't this ethical pledge to provide emergency care be converted into an implied promise that physicians make to the public at large? See William E. May, Medical Ethics: Code and Covenant or Philanthropy and Contract? 5(6) Hastings Ctr. Rep. 29 (1975). Doesn't the public rely on physicians as much as they do on hospital emergency departments? Consider especially Dr. Eddingfield's status as the plaintiff's family physician. Despite these qualms, *Hurley* is still thought to state the prevailing law for physicians.

2. *Triggering a Treatment Relationship.* A physician's complete freedom to refuse treatment exists only if a treatment relationship has not been initiated. We discuss below what actions constitute the initiation of treatment; but here, the fact that Dr. Eddingfield may have treated the *Hurley* patient in the past did not suffice, because the law considers treatment relationships to coincide with "spells of illness." Thus, once a patient recovers from an illness or stops seeking treatment, a new treatment relationship must be formed in order to invoke a duty of continuing treatment. See, e.g., Grubbs v. Rawls, 369 S.E.2d 683, 685-686 (Va. 1988).

Consider how this issue might come out differently when the patient receives medical care from a health maintenance organization (HMO). In this regard, see Hand v. Tavera, 864 S.W.2d 678 (Tex. Ct. App. 1993) (holding that "when the healthcare plan's insured shows up at a participating hospital emergency department, and the plan's doctor on call is consulted about treatment or admission, there is a physician-patient relationship between the doctor and the insured").

3. *The Hospital's Duty.* Despite the reluctance of the *Manlove* court to find a duty to treat, it is considered a groundbreaking case in that it paved the way for other courts to make more definitive findings of hospital liability for the refusal of emergency care. See, e.g., Stanturf v. Sipes, 447 S.W.2d 558 (Mo. 1969) (hospital may be liable for refusing to treat frostbite victim who could not post $25 deposit); Mercy Medical Center v. Winnebago County, 206 N.W.2d 198 (Wis. 1973) ("It would shock the public conscience if a person in need of medical emergency aid would be turned down at the door of a hospital."); but see Campbell v. Mincey, 413 F. Supp. 16 (N.D. Miss. 1975) (no obligation of hospital emergency department to care for pregnant woman in labor). Many states impose a requirement of open emergency departments by statute or regulation. See generally Karen Rothenberg, Who Cares? The Evolution of the Legal Duty to Provide Emergency Care, 26 Hous. L. Rev. 21 (1989).

How do you explain the fact that hospitals have a duty to provide emergency care to all who seek it while physicians are under no such obligation? Arguably, it does not make sense to expect physicians to be available at all times, while hospitals can reasonably be expected to always have someone staffing their emergency departments. But what about just expecting physicians to be available during their regular office hours for emergencies? Can't doctors factor into their scheduling the possibility of emergencies? Don't they in fact already do that? Is part of the issue that physicians may not necessarily have the expertise for any emergency patient that comes through the door? Suppose the physician is a dermatologist and is confronted with a cardiac emergency. Is there anything the doctor reasonably could do besides call 911? How might it actually not serve patients' interests in less populated areas if physicians have a duty to provide care to those in need?

Hospitals, too, may be able to limit their obligation according to their capacity or expertise. Suppose a hospital has no emergency department because it specializes in elective surgeries. Or suppose the emergency department is full. When this happens, hospital emergency departments often place themselves on "drive-by" status, which means they alert ambulances not to stop there. One court held this was permissible in the case of a child who consequently suffered brain damage, even though the hospital had treated the child many times in the past and had encouraged his parents to pass up other closer hospitals and come there if he had serious problems. Davis v. Johns Hopkins Hospital, 622 A.2d 128 (Md. 1993). Regulations under the Emergency Medical Treatment and Active Labor Act (EMTALA) come to the same conclusion. 42 C.F.R. §489.24(b)(4).

4. *The Meaning of Reliance.* Why is the *Manlove* reliance theory limited to just emergency care? Observe the court's reasoning that "such a refusal [of treatment] might well result in worsening the condition of the injured person, because of the time lost in a useless attempt to obtain medical aid." Presumably, this is true only in a very serious or "unmistakable" emergency. It might be possible, however, to argue for other types of reliance. Suppose, for instance, that a prospective patient chose to live in the community because of the presence of a hospital, and it would thereby frustrate his or her reliance if the hospital could deny care in nonemergencies as well as emergencies. On the other hand, while such patients may have a psychological reliance, they would not suffer a *detrimental* reliance in the sense of a material change in one's position for the worse.

Where reliance is detrimental, should the patient have to demonstrate actual reliance in the particular case, rather than reliance being assumed? The *Manlove* court appeared to treat only the detriment part as requiring proof, not the psychological expectation. Should we presume that patients always legitimately expect emergency departments to be open to them? Consider, for instance, Guerrero v. Copper Queen Hospital, 537 P.2d 1329 (Ariz. 1975), which found that a hospital in a border town owned by a local mining company had a duty to render emergency aid to two severely burned Mexican children who were injured in their home across the border.

5. *Physicians "On Call."* *Hurley* and *Manlove* appear consistent because one is about doctors and the other is about hospitals. But does it make sense for hospitals to have a duty to accept emergency patients if the doctors who work there are free to refuse treatment? Courts generally have resolved this problem by holding that a doctor who is "on call" for a hospital emergency department voluntarily undertakes the hospital's greater duty of care. The leading decision is Hiser v. Randolph, 617 P.2d 774 (Ariz. 1980). At 11:45 P.M. one night, Bonita Hiser came to the emergency department at Mojave County General Hospital in a semi-comatose condition arising out of an exacerbation of her juvenile onset diabetes. Along with the seven other doctors in the area, Dr. Randolph took turns as the on-call physician for the emergency department, a duty for which he was paid $100 per 12-hour shift, and he was on call when Mrs. Hiser came to the hospital. When the emergency department nurse called Dr. Randolph, he refused to come in. He claimed this was because he

lacked the expertise to treat diabetes, but there was also evidence that his refusal was based on personal animosity toward Mrs. Hiser or the fact that Mrs. Hiser's husband was a lawyer. Mrs. Hiser died because of the delay in treatment. The court found that Dr. Randolph breached his duty of care arising from his status as an on-call physician. According to the court,

> the obviously intended effect of the [hospital's] bylaws and rules and regulations was to obligate the emergency room doctor "on call" to provide emergency treatment to the best of the doctor's ability to any emergency patient of the hospital. Under these circumstances, the lack of a consensual physician-patient relationship before a duty to treat can arise has been waived by the signatory doctors.

But see Childs v. Weis, 440 S.W.2d 104 (Tex. Ct. App. 1969) (physicians on emergency call were under no specific duty to see all patients who presented themselves to the emergency department).

    A similar analysis is possible for HMO physicians. See St. Charles v. Kender, 646 N.E.2d 411 (Mass. Ct. App. 1995) (HMO subscriber is a third-party beneficiary of an HMO's contracts with its physicians; contract was breached when physician failed to return patient's calls for an appointment). In Hand v. Tavera, 864 S.W.2d 678 (Tex. Ct. App. 1993), Lewis Hand went to the Humana Hospital (Village Oaks) emergency department because of a three-day headache. He also had high blood pressure, and his medical history revealed that his father had died of an aneurysm. The emergency department physician was able to control Mr. Hand's blood pressure and headache temporarily with medication but ultimately concluded that Mr. Hand should be admitted to the hospital. Hospital admissions required the approval of another physician under the Humana Health Care Plan, so the emergency department physician called Dr. Robert Tavera, the physician responsible that evening for authorizing admissions of Humana patients. Dr. Tavera decided that Mr. Hand should be treated as an outpatient. A few hours after returning home, Mr. Hand suffered a stroke. The trial court granted Dr. Tavera summary judgment on the ground that no patient-physician relationship had been formed, but the appellate court held that a patient-physician relationship existed by virtue of Mr. Hand's membership in the Humana Health Care Plan and Dr. Tavera's designation "as the doctor acting for the Humana plan that night." As the court observed, "Hand paid premiums to Humana to purchase medical care in advance of need . . . and Tavera's medical group agreed to treat Humana enrollees in exchange for the fees received from Humana. In effect, Hand had paid in advance for the services of the Humana plan doctor on duty that night, who happened to be Tavera, and the physician-patient relationship existed." Which actions constitute the formation of a doctor-patient relationship is discussed further at pages 93-107. As discussed there, when physicians serve as on-call *consultants* to the emergency department, courts generally require some involvement in the patient's care before finding a duty to treat. See pages 102-103.

    6. *The Quasi-Public Status of Hospitals.* Another basis for imposing a duty to treat, distinct from the reliance theory, is the assertion that physicians or hospitals owe duties to the public at large simply by virtue of their having chosen to become licensed health care providers. It is a version of this argument that the *Hurley* court rejects with the cryptic comment that "analogies, drawn from the obligations to the

public on the part of innkeepers, common carriers, and the like, are beside the mark."

In ancient common law, certain occupations and businesses were considered to be "common callings," meaning that they could not turn away customers without a good reason. Innkeepers and public transport ("common carriers") were the classic examples. The reasons for these heightened public service duties were the importance of the service, the monopoly status of the business, and the support it received from the government. See Charles Burdick, The Origin of the Peculiar Duties of Public Service Companies, 11 Colum. L. Rev. 514, 616, 742 (1911); O. W. Holmes, Jr., Common Carriers and the Common Law, 13 Am. L. Rev. 40 (1879).

In modern times, these "businesses affected with a public interest" are the public utilities (electric, phone, trains, etc.), and common-law duties of public service have been supplanted by overt government regulation. This body of common law has therefore become somewhat archaic, but it is still sometimes invoked against trade associations or labor unions that refuse membership. See generally Comment, 49 U. Chi. L. Rev. 840 (1982); Note, 102 Harv. L. Rev. 1993 (1989).

In Chapter 10, we will see that this body of law has been used to characterize hospitals as "quasi-public" facilities for purposes of giving *physicians* rights of access to their medical staffs. Considering that patients are the ultimate customers for whom public benefit is intended, shouldn't this analogy have even more application to them? It would be ironic indeed to insist on physician access but deny patient access. Nevertheless, the *Manlove* court rejected this view. In other states, later decisions have been more receptive to the quasi-public characterization. For instance, in Thompson v. Sun City Community Hospital, 688 P.2d 605 (Ariz. 1984), the court found that a cause of action exists against a hospital that stabilized a patient with a severed artery and then transferred him for financial reasons. The court based the duty to treat on the general public policy embodied in hospital licensing regulations and private accreditation standards. Also, in Payton v. Weaver, considered at page 114, the court suggested in dictum that this public service theory could be used to impose a community-wide obligation on kidney dialysis centers to share the burden of treating an unwanted disruptive patient. Cf. A. J. G. Priest, Possible Adaptation of Public Utility Concepts in the Health Care Field, 35 Law & Contemp. Probs. 839 (1970).

7. *The Private Status of Physicians.* Reconsider the situation of physicians. Why shouldn't medical practice by physicians be considered a "common calling" or a quasi-public service? Indeed, it turns out that, in fifteenth-century English law, physicians were included on the list of common callings along with blacksmiths and other important professions. Perhaps today, the missing ingredient is that a physician rarely has a local monopoly; usually there are several in town. But not always. One court found a common-law duty to treat where the sole physician practice group in town refused to accept a patient who had filed a complaint against one of the doctors in the group. Leach v. Drummond Medical Group, 192 Cal. Rptr. 650 (Cal. Ct. App. 1983).

There is an alternative explanation for the law no longer treating physicians as being engaged in a common calling. Consider this perspective:

> Although the law was ambiguous, there is a substantial argument that the duty to serve the public extended to all businesses that held themselves out as open to the public. Only around the time of the Civil War did this rule begin formally to

narrow, and only after the Civil War, when civil rights were extended to African-Americans for the first time, did the courts clearly state for the first time that most businesses had no common-law duties to serve the public. The rule achieved its present form only when the issue became enmeshed in the problem of race relations. This change in the law had the effect – and without doubt the purpose – of enabling businesses to continue to serve white customers while choosing to exclude black customers. [Joseph W. Singer, No Right to Exclude: Public Accommodations and Private Property, 90 Nw. U. L. Rev. 1283, 1294-1295 (1996).]

In a few state statutes, regulatory law imposes some limited duties on physicians to provide care for patients. In Massachusetts, for instance, physicians, as a condition of being licensed, must agree to charge Medicare patients no more than Medicare's "reasonable charge." This has been held not to violate the constitutional rights of physicians. Dukakis v. Massachusetts Medical Society, 815 F.2d 790 (1st Cir. 1987).

8. *Paying vs. Indigent Patients.* Perhaps this body of law is not more developed because doctors and hospitals rarely turn away patients who can pay. For patients who cannot pay, the public service theory is usually no help, since the common law never required common callings to serve people for free. Only the reliance theory reaches this result, but it is restricted to serious emergencies, those in which the patient is worse off for having made a futile attempt to secure service. Only in Arizona have courts used a public service theory to impose a duty to treat patients who cannot pay, and there too the duty is limited to emergency care. (Should it be?) For the view that physicians, hospitals, and other providers should be regulated as a public utility, both to promote access and contain costs, see Nicholas Bagley, Medicine as a Public Calling, 114 Mich. L. Rev. 57 (2015).

9. *Enforcement of Public Rights.* For patients who cannot pay, regulatory law may place hospitals under somewhat greater duties than the common law to treat both emergency and nonemergency patients, but these public law duties have been limited and are not enforceable by individual patients.

Consider, for example, tax law. Nonprofit hospitals are considered to be "charities" that are exempt from property and income tax. Part of this charitable status includes an obligation to treat some patients for free. As discussed in Chapter 10.B.2, federal law restricts this free-care obligation to emergency patients, as do most states, but a few states are beginning to require hospitals to devote a certain percentage of their overall services to patients who cannot pay. Once again, however, this is a community service obligation owed to the public at large, not to individual patients, and so it cannot be enforced very easily by private action. Finally, the Joint Commission on Accreditation of Healthcare Organizations (JCAHO) private accreditation standards require hospitals to accept patients without regard to "source of payment," but this is interpreted to mean accepting all patients with some source of payment (e.g., not turning away Medicaid patients) rather than a duty to accept patients who cannot pay.

This leaves us with the following patchwork of laws: for physicians, no common-law duty to treat, even in emergencies. For hospitals: (1) a common-law duty to treat emergency patients regardless of payment, but only in serious emergencies; (2) common law and regulatory duties to treat all patients who can pay; but (3) no enforceable duty to treat nonemergency or mild emergency patients who cannot pay. This set the stage for enactment of a new federal statute, the Emergency Medical Treatment and Active Labor Act (EMTALA), discussed in the *Burditt* case at page 67.

Notes: Moral and Constitutional Rights to Health Care

1. *Moral Rights to Treatment.* The discussion of legal rights to treatment surely must be informed by how our society views moral rights to health care. What message does society send when the law limits the right to treatment so narrowly as to encompass only serious emergencies? Does the emergency care limitation suggest that we are trying to limit care to the most compelling needs and to avoid people demanding too much care (emergencies being thought of as unpredictable)? This might be seen as a partial embodiment of the "rescue principle" discussed in Chapter 9.D.1, which declares that the strongest ethical demand in medicine is to help those in greatest need. In this regard, the moral dimension of medicine is stronger than in any other commercial arena, because there is no equivalent requirement that grocers, restaurants, or hotels provide their services for free to people in dire straits. What justifies this distinction? Is it that if food and housing were available on demand, it would be too easy to abuse the privilege? But what kinds of incentives for patients does a right only to emergency care generate? Is the reluctance of the courts to find even broader rights to health care a reflection of the difficulty in deciding who to hold responsible for vindicating these rights? Or perhaps it reflects the difficulty in defining what a right to health care would include. Consider in this regard the difference between defining a right to food or housing and a right to health care.

The moral issue can also be debated from a broader, social perspective. So far, we have thought only about whether patients have a right to demand treatment from particular doctors and hospitals. Even where they do not have these private rights, perhaps they have a claim to a more public right, one that society as a whole owes to provide minimally decent health care to all. Arguments to this effect are explored in Chapter 9. For some time, we have recognized this claim to basic social support for education and to a more limited extent for food and housing. But for health care, there was no national safety net until the enactment of the Patient Protection and Affordable Care Act in 2010. Importantly, the Act expands Medicaid coverage to all persons whose family income is no more than 138 percent of the federal poverty level. Still, even with the Act's implementation, more than 25 million Americans (many of them undocumented immigrants) lack health insurance of any kind. Perhaps it was politically and morally sustainable to deny coverage to so many people before enactment of the Affordable Care Act—and to continue denying coverage to millions of Americans—only because private hospital emergency departments exist as a last resort for those without insurance. Could it be, then, that the heightened private law duties of hospitals weakened our nation's public law commitment to health care access? See Mark A. Hall, The Unlikely Case in Favor of Patient Dumping, 28 Jurimetrics 389 (1988). For an argument that private law duties tend to undermine voluntary charity, see Richard Epstein, Mortal Peril: Our Inalienable Right to Health Care? (1997). For responses to Epstein, see Symposium: Is America's Health Care System in Mortal Peril?, 1998 U. Ill. L. Rev. 683.

2. *Positive vs. Negative Liberty.* If there is a moral right to health care generally, it is clearly not vindicated as a substantive due process right by the U.S. Constitution. *Wideman* is a classic statement of the principle that the Bill of Rights embodies primarily negative, not positive, liberties, that is, it is concerned mainly with freedoms from government imposition, not rights to government assistance. Thus, the Constitution becomes relevant to health care when the government bans treatment choices or forces treatment, but not when it simply declines to assist in obtaining treatment. In this regard, the U.S. Constitution differs markedly from constitutional models in Europe. B. Jessie Hill, What Is the Meaning of Health? Constitutional Implications of Defining "Medical Necessity" and "Essential Health Benefits" Under the Affordable Care Act, 38 Am. J.L. & Med. 445 (2012); John A. Robertson, Controversial Medical Treatment and the Right to Health Care, 36(6) Hastings Center Rep. 15 (2006).

Wideman was followed by an important Supreme Court opinion confirming its general analysis in this regard. In DeShaney v. Winnebago County Department of Social Services, 489 U.S. 189 (1989), the Court held that no constitutional violation occurred in a case where a child was left with permanent brain damage when a state social services agency failed to intervene aggressively enough to prevent child abuse. The state had received several reports of severe beatings by the father. The Court reaffirmed "that the due process clauses generally confer no affirmative right to governmental aid," and it reasoned that the state agency had not assumed a "special relationship" with the child by virtue of having made some ineffectual efforts to protect him since the agency did nothing to make him more vulnerable to the danger. See also Archie v. Racine, 847 F.2d 1211 (7th Cir. 1988) (en banc) (§1983 action not maintainable for city rescue service's negligent failure to dispatch ambulance; no constitutional right to treatment exists).

As *Wideman* indicates, government will assume duties to provide health care when it confines individuals in psychiatric hospitals, prisons, or other facilities. Before the enactment of the Affordable Care Act, occasional press reports described cases of uninsured people committing crimes so they would have access to health care while incarcerated. Katie Moisse & James Verone, The Medical Motive for His $1 Bank Robbery, ABC News, June 23, 2011.

3. *Equal Protection.* In Maher v. Roe, 432 U.S. 464, 469-470 (1977), discussed in *Wideman*, the Court identified another possible source of a constitutional duty to treat: "The Constitution imposes no obligation on the states to pay . . . any of the medical expenses of indigents. But when a state decides to alleviate some of the hardships of poverty by providing medical care, the manner in which it dispenses benefits is subject to constitutional limitations." For example, in Memorial Hospital v. Maricopa County, 415 U.S. 250 (1974), the Court struck down Arizona's requirement of a year's residence in a county as a condition of receiving nonemergency medical care at county expense as infringing on the right to travel. Might a state be subject to an equal protection attack for funding some procedures but not others? See Doe v. Colautti, 592 F.2d 704 (3d Cir. 1978) (finding no violation of the equal protection clause when Pennsylvania's medical assistance program provided less generous benefits for psychiatric care than for general medical care). See Chapter 9.D.1 for discussion of statutory protections against discrimination in access to health care.

4. *Legislative Mandates.* In Harris v. McRae, 448 U.S. 297 (1980), another abortion funding case discussed in *Wideman*, the Court addressed a nonconstitutional

theory for compelling government funding of health care. States that participate in Medicaid are, generally speaking, required to fund most medically necessary forms of treatment. Beal v. Doe, 432 U.S. 438, 444 (1977). Although *McRae* found this statutory requirement to be inapplicable to abortions, in other cases the medical necessity mandate has proved to be an effective tool for obtaining Medicaid coverage. Pittman v. Secretary, Florida Dept. Health & Rehab. Services; 998 F.2d 887 (11th Cir. 1993) (requiring coverage of a liver-intestine transplant for a child); Rush v. Parham, 625 F.2d 1150 (5th Cir. 1980) (requiring funding for sex change operations in certain circumstances). However, there is no statutory requirement that Medicaid be funded at a level sufficient to cover all people who need it. See Chapter 9.D for additional discussion.

■ BURDITT v. U.S. DEPARTMENT OF HEALTH AND HUMAN SERVICES
934 F.2d 1362 (5th Cir. 1991)

REAVLEY, Circuit Judge.

Hospitals that execute Medicare provider agreements with the federal government pursuant to 42 U.S.C. §1395cc must treat all human beings who enter their emergency departments in accordance with the Emergency Medical Treatment and Active Labor Act (EMTALA), 42 U.S.C. §1395dd. Hospitals and responsible physicians found to have violated EMTALA's requirements are subject to civil money penalties. [This case is an appeal by Dr. Burditt of a $20,000 fine assessed against him by the Department of Health and Human Services. EMTALA also provides for a private cause of action, with prevailing plaintiffs entitled to monetary damages from the offending hospital and appropriate equitable relief. Damages may not be recovered from physicians in a private cause of action, however.]

I.A. FACTS

Mrs. Rosa Rivera arrived in the emergency room of DeTar Hospital in Victoria, Texas at approximately 4:00 P.M. on December 5, 1986. At or near term with her sixth child, she was experiencing one-minute, moderate contractions every three minutes and her membranes had ruptured. Two obstetrical nurses, Tammy Kotsur and Donna Keining, examined her and found indicia of labor and dangerously high blood pressure. Because Rivera had received no prenatal care, and had neither a regular doctor nor means of payment, Kotsur telephoned Burditt, who was next on DeTar's rotating call-list of physicians responsible for such "unaligned" obstetrics patients. Upon hearing Rivera's history and condition, Burditt told Kotsur that he "didn't want to take care of this lady" and asked her to prepare Rivera for transfer to John Sealy Hospital in Galveston, Texas, 170 miles away. Burditt agreed to call back in five to ten minutes.

Kotsur and Keining told the nursing supervisor, Jean Herman, and DeTar's administrator, Charles Sexton, of their belief that it would be unsafe to transfer Rivera. When Burditt called back, Keining told him that, according to Sexton's understanding of hospital regulations and federal law, Burditt would have to examine Rivera and personally arrange for John Sealy to receive her before he could legally transfer her. Keining asked Burditt for permission to start an intravenous push of magnesium sulfate as a precaution against convulsive seizures. Burditt told Keining to begin administering this medication only if Rivera could be transported by ambulance. . . .

Burditt arrived at approximately 4:50 to examine Rivera. He confirmed her blood pressure to be the highest he had ever seen, 210/130, and he assumed that she had been hypertensive throughout her pregnancy. As the experienced head of DeTar's obstetrics and gynecology department, Burditt knew that there was a strong possibility that Rivera's hypertension would precipitate complications which might kill both Rivera and her baby. He also knew that the infants of hypertensive mothers are at higher-than-normal risk of intrauterine growth retardation. He estimated that Rivera's baby was six pounds—less than normal weight—and arranged her transfer to John Sealy, a perinatal facility better equipped than DeTar to care for underweight infants. . . .

KNEW

At approximately 5:00, Herman showed Burditt DeTar's guidelines regarding EMTALA, but he refused to read them. Burditt told Herman that Rivera represented more risk than he was willing to accept from a malpractice standpoint. Herman explained that Rivera could not be transferred unless Burditt signed a DeTar form entitled "Physician's Certificate Authorizing Transfer." Burditt asked for "that dang piece of paper" and signed his name under the following:

> I have examined the patient, _____, and have determined that, based upon the information available to me at this time, the medical benefits reasonably expected from the provision of appropriate medical treatment at another medical facility outweigh the increased risks to the patient's medical condition from effecting [the] transfer. The basis for my conclusion is as follows: _____

Burditt listed no basis for his conclusion and remarked to Herman that "until DeTar Hospital pays my malpractice insurance, I will pick and choose those patients that I want to treat."

Burditt then went to care for another unaligned patient, Sylvia Ramirez, while the nurses arranged Rivera's transfer. They found another obstetrical nurse, Anita Nichols, to accompany Rivera to John Sealy. Burditt returned to the nurses' station and stayed there from 5:30 to 6:18. He never again examined Rivera or asked about her medical condition, though he inquired several times about the status of her transfer. Burditt delivered the Ramirez baby at 6:22. Afterward, Nichols told him the results of her examination of Rivera and informed him that the ambulance had arrived. Based exclusively on Nichols' statements, Burditt concluded that Rivera's condition had not changed since his examination two hours before. Burditt did not reexamine Rivera though he saw her being wheeled to the ambulance. He did not order any medication or life support equipment for Rivera during her transfer.

Nichols delivered Rivera's healthy baby in the ambulance approximately 40 miles into the 170-mile trip to John Sealy. She directed the driver to nearby Ganado Hospital to get a drug called pitocin to staunch Rivera's bleeding. While there, Nichols telephoned Burditt, who ordered her to continue to John Sealy despite the birth. Instead, per Rivera's wishes, Nichols returned Rivera to DeTar, where Burditt refused to see her because she failed to proceed to John Sealy in accordance with his instructions. Burditt directed that Rivera be discharged if she was stable and not bleeding excessively. A DeTar official pressed Burditt to allow Dr. Shirley Pigott to examine Rivera. Rivera stayed at DeTar under Pigott's care for three days and left in good health. . . .

II.A.1. SCREENING

Because Rivera presented herself to DeTar's emergency department and a request was made on her behalf for care, EMTALA required DeTar to

provide for an *appropriate* medical screening examination *within the capability of the hospital's emergency department* to determine whether or not an emergency medical condition . . . exists or to determine if the individual is in active labor . . . .

42 U.S.C. §1395dd(a) (emphasis added). The parties agree that DeTar appropriately screened Rivera and discovered that she had an "emergency medical condition"—severe hypertension—within the meaning of 42 U.S.C. §1395dd(e)(1).[2]

II.A.2. EMERGENCY MEDICAL CONDITION AND ACTIVE LABOR

Patients diagnosed with an "emergency medical condition" or "active labor" must either be treated or be transferred in accordance with EMTALA. Burditt claims that Rivera received all of the care that she was due under EMTALA because he stabilized her hypertension sufficiently for transfer and she was not in active labor when she left DeTar for John Sealy.

II.A.2.a. Unstable Emergency Medical Condition

Rivera's blood pressure was 210/130 at 4:00 and 5:00. This was the last reading known to Burditt before he facilitated her transfer. Nurses also measured her blood pressure as 173/105 at 5:30, 178/103 at 5:45, 186/107 at 6:00, and 190/110 at 6:50. Experts testified that Rivera's hypertension put her at high risk of suffering serious complications, including seizures, heart failure, kidney dysfunction, tubular necrosis, stroke, intracranial bleeding, placental abruption, and fetal hypoxia. This is substantial, if not conclusive evidence that Rivera entered and exited DeTar with an emergency medical condition.

Burditt argues that he fulfilled EMTALA's requirements with respect to Rivera's hypertension by "stabilizing" it, or

provid[ing] such medical treatment of the condition as may be necessary to assure, within reasonable medical probability, that no material deterioration of the condition is likely to result from [a] transfer. . . .

DRS ARGUMENT

42 U.S.C. §1395dd(e)(4)(A). He claims that the magnesium sulfate that he ordered for Rivera has an antihypertensive effect that complements its primary anticonvulsive purpose.

2. EMTALA defines "emergency medical condition" as
a medical condition manifesting itself by acute symptoms of sufficient severity (including severe pain) such that the absence of immediate medical attention could reasonably be expected to result in—
    (A) placing the patient's health in serious jeopardy,
    (B) serious impairment to bodily functions, or
    (C) serious dysfunction of any bodily organ or part.
42 U.S.C. §1395dd(e)(1) (Supp. IV 1987).

DEFINITION OF "EMERGENCY MEDICAL CONDITION"

Development of any of the possible complications could have killed or seriously injured Rivera, her baby, or both, and thus would constitute a "material deterioration" under 42 U.S.C. §1395dd(e)(4)(A). Any deterioration would "result" from transfer in that Rivera would have received better care for any complication at DeTar than in the ambulance. Thus, Burditt could not have stabilized Rivera unless he provided treatment that medical experts agree would prevent the threatening and severe consequences of Rivera's hypertension while she was in transit. [The HHS appeals board] could properly disregard Burditt's testimony and accept that of all other testifying experts in holding that Burditt provided no such treatment, and thus did not stabilize Rivera's emergency medical condition. . . .

II.A.2.b. Active Labor

EMTALA defines "active labor" as labor at a time when

> (B) there is inadequate time to effect safe transfer to another hospital prior to delivery, or
> (C) a transfer may pose a threat [to] the health and safety of the patient or the unborn child.

42 U.S.C. §1395dd(e)(2)(B)-(C). This statutory definition renders irrelevant any medical definition of active labor. . . .

Burditt challenges the ALJ's finding that, at approximately 5:00, there was inadequate time to safely transfer Rivera to John Sealy before she delivered her baby. Dr. Warren Crosby testified that, based on Burditt's own examination results, Rivera would, more likely than not, deliver within three hours after Burditt [made the decision to transfer her to] John Sealy. . . . Burditt does not challenge [the] conclusion that the ambulance trip from DeTar to John Sealy takes approximately three hours. We therefore hold that [the HHS appeals board] properly concluded that Rivera was in active labor under 42 U.S.C. §1395dd(e)(2)(B).

The ALJ also found that Rivera was in active labor under clause C at the time Burditt examined her. There is always some risk of a vehicular accident in transit, so transfer always "may" pose a threat to the health and safety of the patient or fetus. . . . We believe that Congress intended clause C to extend EMTALA's . . . protection to women in labor who have any complication with their pregnancies regardless of delivery imminency. Because better medical care is available in a hospital than in an ambulance, whether a transfer "may pose a threat" under 42 U.S.C. §1395dd(e)(2)(C) depends on whether the woman in labor has any medical condition that could interfere with the normal, natural delivery of her healthy child. Under the statutory language, a woman in labor is entitled to EMTALA's . . . protections upon a showing of possible threat; it does not require proof of a reasonable medical probability that any threat will come to fruition. . . .

The record overwhelmingly confirms that Rivera's hypertension could have interfered with a normal delivery, and she was thus in active labor under 42 U.S.C. §1395dd(e)(2)(C). . . .

II.A.3. TREAT OR TRANSFER

Upon discovery of active labor or an emergency medical condition, EMTALA usually requires hospitals to treat the discovered condition. Under certain circumstances, however, EMTALA allows hospitals to transfer patients instead of treating them. 42 U.S.C. §1395dd(b)(1)(B). . . . [The court went on to find that Burditt had not satisfied the requirements under EMTALA for a transfer before stabilization. Under EMTALA, transfer is permitted if the patient requests transfer *or* the physician has certified in writing that the medical benefits of transfer outweigh the increased risks to the patient. In addition, the receiving hospital must be capable of providing the needed treatment and must have agreed to accept the transfer. Finally, the transfer must occur with appropriate personnel and transportation, including appropriate life support measures. While Burditt had obtained consent from John Sealy before the transfer, he had not reasonably concluded that the benefits of transfer outweighed the risks nor had he arranged for the transfer with appropriate personnel and transportation.]

II.C. EMTALA's Constitutionality

As his final attempt to escape [liability], Burditt claims that EMTALA effects a public taking of his services without just compensation in contravention of the Constitution's Fifth Amendment.

Assuming *arguendo* that professional services constitute property protected by the takings clause, Burditt has not shown that EMTALA effects a taking. EMTALA imposes no responsibilities directly on physicians; it unambiguously requires hospitals to examine and stabilize, treat, or appropriately transfer all who arrive requesting treatment. Its provision for sanctions against physicians who knowingly violate its requirements is merely an enforcement mechanism that does not alter its explicit assignment of duties.

Governmental regulation that affects a group's property interests "does not constitute a taking of property where the regulated group is not required to participate in the regulated industry." Whitney v. Heckler, 780 F.2d 963, 972 (11th Cir.), *cert. denied*, 479 U.S. 813 (1986).

Two levels of voluntariness undermine Burditt's taking assertion. Only hospitals that voluntarily participate in the federal government's Medicare program must comply with EMTALA. Hospitals must consider the cost of complying with EMTALA's requirements in deciding whether to continue to participate in the Medicare program.

Second, Burditt is free to negotiate with DeTar or another hospital regarding his responsibility to facilitate a hospital's compliance with EMTALA. Thus, physicians only voluntarily accept responsibilities under EMTALA if they consider it in their best interest to do so. Accordingly, Burditt's claim under the takings clause is without merit. . . .

Notes: The Federal Patient Dumping Statute

1. *Historical Background.* Congress passed the Emergency Medical Treatment and Active Labor Act (EMTALA) as part of the Consolidated Omnibus Reconciliation Act of 1986 (COBRA), in response to the perception that state law was too weak to prevent widespread patient dumping. While EMTALA, or COBRA, has worked better than previous legal efforts, in part because of the private right of action, there are still concerns that patient dumping persists at unacceptable levels. One scholar argues, however, that

EMTALA is a virtual catalogue of how to get a statute wrong. First, generalize from unrepresentative anecdotal evidence in identifying the problem. Draft the statute sloppily, and leave the most important words undefined or defined too broadly. Finance the resulting open-ended entitlement with an unfunded mandate imposed on private parties.... [Design the enforcement system] to reward the wrong people. Finally, apply the statute even after the world on which it depended has vanished. Any one of these problems would be bad enough in isolation, but their combined effect is devastating to the interests EMTALA was intended to protect.

David A. Hyman, Dumping EMTALA: When Bad Laws Happen to Good People (1998) (unpublished). As you read the following notes, see if you can determine why someone might reach such a conclusion. Nevertheless, Prof. Hyman acknowledges that

the statute is wildly popular across the entirety of the political spectrum and among such disparate interest groups as physicians, advocates for the poor, [academics,] and consumer groups. Unlike many reforms, EMTALA does not create a new administrative bureaucracy; it does not favor the interests of the well-connected against the less fortunate; its on-budget costs are modest; and it seems to be no more intrusive than is absolutely necessary to accomplish its objectives.

David A. Hyman, Patient Dumping and EMTALA: Past Imperfect/Future Shock, 8 Health Matrix 29, 29 (1998).

As the *Burditt* court indicated, courts have not thought EMTALA poses constitutional problems. But not everyone agrees. E. Haavi Morreim, EMTALA: Medicare's Unconstitutional Condition on Hospitals, 43 Hastings Const. L.Q. 61 (2015).

Dr. Michael Burditt was the first physician fined for an EMTALA violation, and his actions were vigorously defended by the Texas Medical Association. For a critical view of the Fifth Circuit's decision in the *Burditt* case, see David Hyman, Lies, Damned Lies, and Narrative, 73 Ind. L.J. 797, 824-832 (1998). As a general matter, the government rarely penalizes individual physicians under EMTALA, levying most of its fines on hospitals. Sophie Terp et al., Individual Physician Penalties Resulting from Violation of Emergency Medical Treatment and Labor Act, 24 Academic Emergency Med. 442 (2017).

2. *Screening and Stabilizing.* EMTALA creates two distinct duties. First, the duty to screen patients is triggered by their arrival at the hospital, and it ceases if it is determined they are not in what the statute defines as an "emergency" condition. Second, if patients are in an emergency condition, then the hospital must stabilize them. (The statutory requirements are similar for patients in active labor.) Most litigation has arisen at the first stage, in cases where patients claim the hospital failed entirely to evaluate or recognize their emergency condition.

But that is not our main concern in this note. Our concern is, if there clearly is an emergency, how far does the duty to treat extend? Do hospitals have to perform bypass surgery after they halt a heart attack? Although *Burditt* found that "stabilizing" care was not rendered in that case, what about other typical situations? Consider whether the outcome would be any different under EMTALA than it was under this state law decision: Joyner v. Alton Ochsner Medical Foundation, 230 So. 2d 913 (La. Ct. App. 1970) (auto accident victim did not "require immediate admission" after stabilizing care was rendered, despite "multiple deep facial lacerations, a possible head injury, traumatic damage to the teeth and multiple bruises and contusions of the body, resulting in considerable loss of blood"). Consider whether the duty to treat under EMTALA is as strong as it is under this state law decision: Thompson v. Sun City Community Hospital, 688 P.2d 605 (Ariz. 1984) (a cause of action exists against a hospital that stabilized a patient with a severed artery and then transferred him for financial reasons). Is the federal statute any more demanding than the *Manlove* reliance theory?

Moreover, courts have applied the stabilization requirement of EMTALA only when a hospital discharges a patient or transfers the patient to another hospital, and not when the hospital provides care. Harry v. Marchant, 291 F.3d 767, 770-772 (11th Cir. 2002) (en banc) (observing that the stabilization requirement of EMTALA is defined in terms of transfer or discharge). See also Alvarez-Torres v. Ryder Memorial Hospital, Inc., 582 F.3d 47, 51-52 (1st Cir. 2009); Bryan v. Rectors and Visitors of the University of Virginia, 95 F.3d 349, 352 (4th Cir. 1996).

For a view that EMTALA has blocked blatantly discriminatory practices without actually improving the quality of health care received by disadvantaged populations, see Karin V. Rhodes & Kristofer L. Smith, Short-term Care with Long-term Costs, 69 Annals Emergency Med. 163 (2017). For proposals to make EMTALA work more effectively, see Katharine Van Tassel, Modernizing the Emergency Medical Treatment & Labor Act to Harmonize with the Affordable Care Act to Improve Equality, Quality and Cost of Emergency Care, 15 Hous. J. Health L. & Pol'y 131 (2015).

There are other consequences of an obligation only to stabilize. For example, hospitals may send undocumented immigrants back to their home countries, and many of these patients die because of their inability to access follow-up care upon their return.

Although EMTALA only requires stabilization, other federal rules may extend the duty to provide care. Medicare's conditions for participation require safe discharge planning for hospitalized patients, and it may not be safe to discharge a patient who has only been stabilized. Jennifer L. Herbst, Permanent Patients, 47(1) Hastings Center Rep. 6 (2017).

In its requirement to stabilize emergency patients, EMTALA does not require the impossible. If a hospital does not have the facilities or personnel necessary to fully stabilize a patient, and the patient must be transferred to a more sophisticated hospital to receive needed care, the first hospital can transfer the patient to the more sophisticated hospital without violating EMTALA. The transferring hospital must do all it can to stabilize the patient's condition, but it need not do what it cannot do. Cherukuri v. Shalala, 175 F.3d 446 (6th Cir. 1999) (absolving physician at small rural hospital after the physician transferred two patients who needed surgery to stop internal bleeding from an automobile accident).

And to ensure that potential receiving hospitals do not undermine patient protections, EMTALA imposes on those hospitals a duty to accept appropriate transfers (no "reverse dumping"). St. Anthony Hospital v. U.S. Dept. HHS, 309 F.3d 680 (10th Cir. 2002).

3. *The Patient's Indigency.* While the passage of EMTALA was motivated by concerns about private hospitals "dumping" indigent or uninsured patients on public hospitals, the statutory language imposes no requirement that patients show that they were denied emergency services because of indigency or lack of insurance. See

42 U.S.C. §1395dd(a) ("if any individual . . . comes to the emergency department . . . , the hospital must provide for an appropriate medical screening examination within the capability of the hospital's emergency department").

Accordingly, courts have generally held that it is irrelevant why a person did not receive an appropriate screening exam or, if an emergency was identified, why a person did not receive stabilizing care before discharge or transfer. As one court observed, "[EMTALA] applies to any and all patients, not just to patients with insufficient resources." Brooker v. Desert Hospital Corp., 947 F.2d 412, 415 (9th Cir. 1991). Accord Summers v. Baptist Medical Center, 91 F.3d 1132 (8th Cir. 1996); Gatewood v. Washington Healthcare Corp., 933 F.2d 1037, 1040 (D.C. Cir. 1991).

The Supreme Court addressed the motive question in the context of EMTALA's stabilization requirement and rejected any need to show an improper motive. Roberts v. Galen of Virginia, Inc., 525 U.S. 249 (1999). The Court "express[ed] no opinion" on the need to show an improper motive for a claim of inappropriate medical screening.

Perhaps the most controversial extension of EMTALA beyond economic discrimination occurred in the Baby K case, which involved a baby with anencephaly—a baby missing the major part of the brain that is necessary for conscious thought. In In re Baby K, 16 F.3d 590 (4th Cir. 1994), parents of an anencephalic child sought ventilatory treatment of their child during periodic bouts of respiratory distress. After the second of three such episodes, the hospital sought judicial permission to withhold the ventilator when the child next came to the emergency department. In the view of the hospital, it was medically and ethically inappropriate to ventilate the child given her limited life expectancy, her total absence of consciousness, and the futility of treatment at improving her condition. According to the hospital, the only appropriate treatment for the child was the treatment "it would provide other anencephalic infants—supportive care in the form of warmth, nutrition, and hydration." The court rejected the hospital's argument. It observed that EMTALA requires stabilizing treatment in the event of a medical emergency, and the child's respiratory distress met EMTALA's definition of a medical emergency. If there was to be an exception for "futile" care under EMTALA, Congress would have to write that exception into the statute. The court's opinion in Baby K is presented in Chapter 5 with additional discussion.

The Baby K decision raises serious questions about the ability of society to contain health care costs. If the hospital in the case could not deny a ventilator to an anencephalic child, how could any emergency medical care be withheld on the ground that its high costs were not justified by its minimal benefit? Is there a distinction between the economic or other discrimination prohibited by EMTALA and the denial of care that results when a hospital is concerned about the limits of society's resources?

Perhaps in recognition of these concerns, the Fourth Circuit limited the impact of Baby K two years later. In Bryan v. Rectors and Visitors of the University of Virginia, 95 F.3d 349 (4th Cir. 1996), an EMTALA claim was brought on behalf of a patient who died of a heart attack after her physicians decided that "no further efforts to prevent her death should be made." Twenty days before the heart attack, the patient had been admitted to the hospital in respiratory distress. Eight days before the heart attack, apparently because of the hopelessness of the patient's condition, her physicians decided to withhold further life-sustaining treatment, including cardiopulmonary resuscitation, in the event of a cardiac arrest. When she suffered her heart attack, no efforts were made to prevent her death. According to the court, there was no EMTALA violation because EMTALA "was intended to regulate the hospital's care of the patient only in the immediate aftermath of the act of admitting her for emergency treatment and while it considered whether it would undertake longer-term full treatment or instead transfer the patient to a hospital that could and would undertake that treatment." Id. at 352.

4. *Preventive Dumping.* There has been concern that hospitals would try to evade their EMTALA obligations by dumping patients before they reach the emergency department. For example, when called by a paramedic or emergency medical technician who is transporting a patient by ambulance, the emergency department staff might direct the ambulance to another hospital. Early cases suggested that hospitals would have considerable freedom to prevent patients from reaching the emergency department. See Miller v. Medical Center of Southwest Louisiana, 22 F.3d 626 (5th Cir. 1994) (hospital not liable under EMTALA for refusing to accept the transfer of a patient who needed specialized emergency care beyond the capabilities of the transferring hospital); Johnson v. University of Chicago Hospitals, 982 F.2d 230 (7th Cir. 1992) (hospital not liable for diverting an ambulance to another hospital).

Subsequent amendment of the EMTALA regulations and case law interpreting the amendment have limited the ability of hospitals to engage in preventive dumping. Under one regulation, patients have come to the hospital's emergency department for purposes of EMTALA once they have reached any part of the hospital's property, including a hospital-owned ambulance service. 42 C.F.R. §489.24(b) (2011) (applied in Hernandez v. Starr County Hospital District, 30 F. Supp. 2d 970 (S.D. Tex. 1999); Preston v. Meriter Hospital, Inc., 700 N.W.2d 158 (Wis. 2005)). The same regulation permits hospitals to divert non-hospital-owned ambulance services if the emergency department "does not have the staff or facilities to accept any additional emergency patients." 42 C.F.R. §489.24(b)(4). The Ninth Circuit has interpreted this provision to mean that a hospital violates EMTALA when it diverts a non-hospital-owned ambulance in the absence of an inability to provide treatment for the patient. Arrington v. Wong, 237 F.3d 1066 (9th Cir. 2001); see also Morales v. Sociedad Espanola de Auxilo Mutuo y Beneficencia, 524 F.3d 54 (1st Cir. 2008). See Caroline J. Stalker, Comment, How Far Is Too Far?: EMTALA Moves from the Emergency Room to Off-Campus Entities, 36 Wake Forest L. Rev. 823 (2001).

Note that there is some ambiguity to §489.24(b). Although the regulation seems to limit the ability of hospitals to divert non-hospital-owned ambulances, it also states that "[a]n individual in a non-hospital-owned ambulance off hospital property is not considered to have come to the hospital's emergency department even if a member of the ambulance staff contacts the hospital by telephone or telemetry communications and informs the hospital that they want to transport the individual to the hospital for examination and treatment."

As indicated, under 42 C.F.R. §489.24(b), EMTALA is triggered when an individual comes to areas of the hospital other than the emergency department. Thus, a First Circuit decision emphasizes the point that a hospital's duty to stabilize before transfer applies to any patient in the hospital, "regardless of how that person enters the institution or where within the walls he may be when the hospital identifies the problem." Lopez-Soto v. Hawayek, 175 F.3d 170, 173 (1st Cir. 1999) (observing that the stabilization requirement of EMTALA applies to an individual who "comes to a hospital" and holding that EMTALA applies when a pregnant woman is admitted to the maternity ward and taken to the operating room for a cesarean section, and her infant is born with respiratory distress and needs emergency care).

5. *Dumping After Admission to the Hospital.* Courts disagree as to whether EMTALA's stabilization requirement continues to apply once the patient has been admitted to the hospital. Cases have arisen in which patients were admitted to the hospital for treatment and, after a few or more days of treatment, been transferred to another hospital or discharged before their illness was fully treated. Or as in *Lopez-Soto, supra* note 4, the emergency condition may develop after the individual has become an inpatient or outpatient at the hospital.

Some courts have concluded that the obligation to stabilize exists throughout the patient's visit to the hospital. In addition to *Lopez-Soto*, see Thornton v. Southwest Detroit Hospital, 895 F.2d 1131 (6th Cir. 1990).

Other courts have concluded that the stabilization requirement ceases upon the patient's admission to the regular hospital. Bryan v. Rectors and Visitors of the University of Virginia, 95 F.3d 349, 352 (4th Cir. 1996); James v. Sunrise Hospital, 86 F.3d 885 (9th Cir. 1996); Bryant v. Adventist Health Systems/West, 289 F.3d 1162 (9th Cir. 2002). Note that in *Bryan* and *Bryant*, the courts were deciding about the stabilization requirement for care rendered during the patient's hospital stay and not in the context of a transfer or discharge. Hence, it is not surprising that the courts were especially concerned about converting state malpractice claims into federal EMTALA claims. See note 6, infra, pages 76-77. In *Bryant*, the Court observed that the stabilization requirement would not cease upon the patient's admission to the hospital "if a patient demonstrates in a particular case that inpatient admission was a ruse to avoid EMTALA's requirements." 289 F.3d at 1169. A federal district court invoked that point in a case in which a patient was sent home after admission but before his injuries had been stabilized. Morgan v. North Mississippi Medical Center, Inc., 403 F. Supp. 2d 1115, 1130 (S.D. Ala. 2005). Although the court denied the hospital's motion to dismiss the EMTALA claim, it ultimately concluded on summary judgment that the hospital had not engaged in a ruse to avoid EMTALA's requirements when it admitted the patient. Morgan v. North Mississippi Medical Center, Inc., 458 F. Supp. 2d 1341 (S.D. Ala. 2006).

In a final rule that took effect in 2003, the Centers for Medicare & Medicaid Services took the position that EMTALA does not apply to individuals who are inpatients or outpatients at a hospital. 42 C.F.R. §489.24(b), (d)(2). The Sixth Circuit, which concluded in the *Thornton* case, supra, that the obligation to stabilize persists through the patient's hospitalization, has rejected the regulation. Moses v. Providence Hospital & Medical Centers, Inc., 561 F.3d 573, 583 (6th Cir. 2009). The Third Circuit, on the other hand, has upheld the regulation. Torretti v. Main Line Hospitals, Inc., 580 F.3d 168, 174-176 (3d Cir. 2009) (interpreting 42 C.F.R. §489.24(b) when an EMTALA claim was brought by an outpatient). So too have many district courts. Thornhill v. Jackson Parish Hospital, 184 F. Supp. 3d 392, 399-400 (W.D. La. 2016) (citing cases).

6. *Appropriate Medical Screening.* In interpreting EMTALA's requirement of an "appropriate medical screening examination," courts have recognized an important tension between ensuring access to emergency care for all persons and creating a federal cause of action for charges of malpractice in the emergency department. If a

person is sent home from the emergency department after a physician wrongly concludes that there is no serious health problem, the mistaken diagnosis may reflect either the negligent provision of care or the purposeful denial of care. A hospital trying to evade its EMTALA obligations might do so by giving undesired patients short shrift when screening them. At the same time, patients who have been injured by malpractice may try to bring their claim under both state tort law and federal EMTALA law, thereby increasing their potential recovery, gaining access to a federal forum and its quicker judgments, and increasing their bargaining power with the hospitals by virtue of the latter's possible loss of its participation in Medicare. EMTALA claims are often appended to state tort claims when people sue for injuries allegedly caused by inadequate emergency care. Singer, supra note 1, 33 Hous. L. Rev. at 118 & n.22.

Courts have consistently stated that EMTALA cannot be used to bring claims for medical malpractice, and they have tried to distinguish between a denial of care and the negligent provision of care by looking at whether the hospital screened the patient in the same way it screens similarly situated patients. As the D.C. Circuit explained, the issue is whether the hospital "conform[ed] its treatment of a particular patient to its standard screening procedures. . . . [A]ny departure from standard screening procedures constitutes inappropriate screening." Gatewood v. Washington Healthcare Corp., 933 F.2d 1037, 1041 (D.C. Cir. 1991). Similarly, the Fourth Circuit has stated that EMTALA's screening requirement is designed to prevent "disparate treatment." Vickers v. Nash General Hospital, Inc., 78 F.3d 139, 143 (4th Cir. 1996). Hospitals are obligated only to "apply uniform screening procedures to all individuals coming to the emergency room." In re Baby K, 16 F.3d 590, 595 (4th Cir. 1994). Accord Correa v. Hospital San Francisco, 69 F.3d 1184 (1st Cir. 1995); Summers v. Baptist Medical Center, 91 F.3d 1132, 1138 (8th Cir. 1996); Repp v. Anadarko Municipal Hospital, 43 F.3d 519, 522 (10th Cir. 1994); Holcomb v. Monahan, 30 F.3d 116, 117 (11th Cir. 1994).

The Sixth Circuit has adopted a similar standard, although it has indicated that the departure from the hospital's standard screening procedures must have resulted from some invidious motive like bias against the patient on the basis of "race, sex, politics, occupation, education, personal prejudice, drunkenness, spite . . . distaste for the patient's condition (e.g., AIDS patients). . . ." Cleland v. Bronson Health Care Group, Inc., 917 F.2d 266, 271-272 (6th Cir. 1990); Roberts v. Galen of Virginia, 111 F.3d 405, 408-409 (6th Cir. 1997), rev'd in part, 525 U.S. 249 (1999). Even if the Sixth Circuit requires some invidious motive, would it ever be difficult to find a bias lurking that would be unacceptable under the *Cleland* standard? Perhaps not often, but see Garrett v. Detroit Medical Center, 2007 U.S. Dist. LEXIS 17584 (E.D. Mich. Mar. 14, 2007) (dismissing patient's EMTALA claim on grounds that the defendant hospital transferred the patient to a hospital so he could be treated at a hospital that was "in-network" for his insurance).

Since EMTALA requires hospitals to apply their standard screening procedures, cases can turn on whether the defendant hospital had established standard screening guidelines and whether the defendant physician had followed those guidelines. See, e.g., Delibertis v. Pottstown General Hospital, 152 F. Supp. 3d 394, 399-400 (E.D. Pa. 2016) (rejecting summary judgment since hospital presented evidence that treating physician followed his own standard practices rather than the hospital's standard practices).

For an argument that trial courts are too quick to grant summary judgment for hospitals on the question of whether patients received an appropriate screening, see Note, 87 N.Y.U. L. Rev. 591 (2012).

Despite the courts' admonition that EMTALA does not create a federal malpractice cause of action, there inevitably will be some overlap between EMTALA claims and malpractice claims. Do you see how a requirement that hospitals provide all patients with their standard screening procedures amounts to requiring that the hospitals provide nonnegligent care? See Demetrios G. Metropoulos, Note, Son of COBRA: The Evolution of a Federal Malpractice Law, 45 Stan. L. Rev. 263 (1992).

As the preceding discussion indicates, courts have interpreted the requirement of an appropriate screening examination as an equal treatment right rather than an entitlement right. But isn't EMTALA a statute that grants an entitlement rather than a right of equal treatment? Is there a way to define appropriate screening examination as an entitlement without turning it even more clearly into the equivalent of nonnegligent care?

7. *Further Reading.* On EMTALA and its **role in the health care system** (note 1), see Russell Korobkin, Determining Health Care Rights from Behind a Veil of Ignorance, 1998 U. Ill. L. Rev. 801; Paul T. Menzel, Justice and Fairness, 40 J.L. Med. & Ethics 582 (2012); Sara Rosenbaum, The Enduring Role of the Emergency Medical Treatment and Active Labor Act, 32 Health Aff. 2075 (2013); Sara Rosenbaum et al., EMTALA and Hospital "Community Engagement," 53 Buff. L. Rev. 499 (2005); Karen Rothenberg, Who Cares? The Evolution of the Legal Duty to Provide Emergency Care, 26 Hous. L. Rev. 21 (1989); Dana E. Schaffner, Note, EMTALA: All Bark and No Bite, 2005 U. Ill. L. Rev. 1021; Lawrence E. Singer, Look What They've Done to My Law, Ma: COBRA's Implosion, 33 Hous. L. Rev. 113 (1996); Annot., 104 A.L.R. Fed. 166.

On the **duty to stabilize** (note 2), see Mark A. Hall, The Unlikely Case in Favor of Patient Dumping, 28 Jurimetrics J. 389 (1990) ("In the great majority of cases, the federal standard will do nothing to prevent patient dumping. . . . Even for those patients who do require stabilization prior to transfer, the federal law will result only in a delay in the transfer."); Kenneth R. Wing & John R. Campbell, The Emergency Room Admission: How Far Does the "Open Door" Go?, 63 U. Det. L. Rev. 119 (1985); Will Jay Pirkey, Shameful Practice, 39 L.A. Law. 20 (July/Aug. 2016).

On the ethical and financial concerns with **undocumented immigrants** (note 2), see Maya Babu & Joseph Wolpin, Undocumented Immigrants, Healthcare Access and Medical Repatriation Following Serious Medical Illness, 3 J. Health & Life Sci. L. 83 (2009); Janet L. Dolgin & Katherine R. Dieterich, When Others Get Too Close, 19 Cornell J.L. & Pub. Pol'y 283 (2010); Svetlana Lebedinski, EMTALA: Treatment of Undocumented Aliens and the Financial Burden It Places on Hospitals, 7 J.L. Soc'y 146 (2005-2006); Jennifer M. Smith, Screen, Stabilize, and Ship: EMTALA, U.S. Hospitals, and Undocumented Immigrants, 10 Hous. J. Health L. & Pol'y 309 (2010); Michael J. Young & Lisa Soleymani Lehmann, Undocumented Injustice, 370 New Eng. J. Med. 669 (2014).

2. *Wrongful Reasons to Reject Patients*

While physicians or hospitals may, for most patients, refuse to treat for "good" reasons (such as inability to pay), or even for no particular reason, they may not deny care for the wrong reasons. For example, Title VI of the Civil Rights Acts of 1964 makes it unlawful for hospitals that receive federal money (such as Medicare and Medicaid) to discriminate on the basis of a patient's race, color, or national origin. On the other hand, without a statute that specifically prohibits the particular reason for discrimination, morally problematic denials of care are generally permissible, as the first case demonstrates.

■ WALKER v. PIERCE
560 F.2d 609 (4th Cir. 1977)

BRYAN, Senior Circuit Judge.

Violation of their civil rights was laid in this action for damages and declaratory and injunctive relief by Virgil Walker and Shirley Brown, black females, to Clovis H. Pierce, the attending obstetrician at the Aiken County Hospital in South Carolina for sterilizing them, or threatening to do so, solely on account of their race and number of their children, while they were receiving medical assistance under the [state's] Medicaid program. . . .

Centering the controversy is the policy previously announced and constantly pursued in practice by the doctor, testified to by him as follows:

> My policy was with people who were unable to financially support themselves, whether they be on Medicaid or just unable to pay their own bills, if they were having a third child, to request they voluntarily submit to sterilization following the delivery of the third child. If they did not wish this as a condition for my care, then I requested that they seek another physician other than myself.

There is no question of his professional qualifications or experience.

As drawn by the plaintiffs, he is the arch-offender. The accusation is incursion upon their constitutional rights of privacy, due process of law, and equal protection of the law as well as of their statutory privileges against discrimination on account of their race and color, all by subjecting or threatening the plaintiffs as citizens of the United States with involuntary sterilization. . . .

Virgil Walker had completed the seventh grade, was separated from her husband, and was receiving Aid to Families with Dependent Children and Medicaid benefits. Expecting her fourth child, she first went to Pierce on January 7, 1972. During this consultation, he discussed family planning and his sterilization policy. Walker refused to consent. The issue again came up at the second visit and she again declined. Walker testified that Pierce threatened to have her state assistance terminated unless she cooperated. She called another doctor, but he was not taking new patients.

On February 4, 1972, Spears, a Department of Social Services caseworker assigned to Walker, received a note from Pierce's office asking that he talk with Walker about sterilization. Thereupon, Spears, according to his testimony, spoke with her on February 17th, offering to get her a second doctor. On the other hand, Walker stated that Spears had said there was nothing he could do. Then she returned to Pierce and subsequently signed a consent form for sterilization.

Her fourth child was delivered at the Aiken County Hospital April 16, 1972 by Dr. Billy Burke, an obstetrician who substituted for Pierce on occasion. Burke discussed tubal ligation with Walker. Her response was that she did not want additional children and understood that it would be a permanent sterilization. Two more consent forms were then signed. Pierce performed the operation April 17, 1972. She protested no further because, she said, it would have been futile.

Walker's hospital bills and doctor's fees were paid by Medicaid. Under the South Carolina plan operated by the Department of Social Services, the patient-physician relationship is one of free choice for both parties. The physician, under no contract with the state, simply submits his bill when treatment is concluded to the Medicaid insurance carrier instead of the patient. . . .

We perceive no reason why Dr. Pierce could not establish and pursue the policy he has publicly and freely announced. Nor are we cited to judicial precedent or statute inhibiting this personal economic philosophy. Particularly is this so when all persons coming to him as patients are seasonably made fully aware of his professional attitude toward the increase in offspring and his determination to see it prevail. At no time is he shown to have forced his view upon any mother. Indeed, quite the opposite appears. In the single occasion in this case of a sterilization by this doctor, not just one but three formal written consents were obtained — the first before delivery of the fourth child and two afterwards. . . .

[The court also held that Dr. Pierce was not a state actor and therefore could not be found to have violated his patients' constitutional rights. Also, as an aside (not addressed by the court), recognize that, although hospitals were subject to Title VI of the federal Civil Rights Act, at the time physicians were not, due to political obstacles and administrative complexities that prompted a strained reading of Title VI's application to payments to physicians. David Barton Smith, Health Care Divided: Race and Healing a Nation 161-164, 227-278 (1999).

Notes: Discriminatory Denials of Care

1. *Racial Discrimination in Health Care.* As with other parts of society, the health care system has suffered from a long history of discrimination on the basis of race. At one time, it was commonplace, especially in the South, for hospitals to refuse admission to blacks. These and other forms of overt discrimination have now largely disappeared as the result of various prohibitions contained in federal and state regulatory law, as well as in the hospital industry's own private accreditation code. See generally Sara Rosenbaum et al., U.S. Civil Rights Policy and Access to Health Care by Minority Americans, 57 Med. Care Res. & Rev. 226 (2000); Symposium, 42(5) J. Health Pol. Pol'y L. 739 (Oct. 2017).

Serious concerns remain, however, over more subtle forms of racial bias in the delivery of health care services. One form occurs in the location of health care facilities, which in inner cities are sometimes older, less accessible, or not as well equipped. See Sara J. Rosenbaum & Sara Schmucker, Viewing Health Equity Through a Legal Lens, 42 J. Health Pol. Pol'y L. 771 (2017).

Discrimination can also arise in individual treatment decisions. Numerous studies have documented that physicians treat blacks, and sometimes women, differently for the same medical conditions. For instance, blacks are less likely than whites to receive a kidney transplant, coronary artery bypass surgery, or other major surgical procedures. See Dayna Bowen Matthew, Just Medicine: A Cure for Racial Inequality in American Health Care (2015); R. Yearby, Breaking the Cycle of Unequal Treatment with Health Care Reform, 44 U. Conn. L. Rev. 1281 (2010); Symposium, 42 (5) J. Health Pol. Pol'y L. (2017); Symposium, 25 Health Matrix 1 (2015); Symposium, 55 How. L.J. 679 (2012).

2. *Race-Based Medicine.* Some analysts respond that the studies just cited are not as conclusive as they may appear because of real or possible differences among racial groups in income, medical considerations, biological factors, and patient preferences. Jonathan Klick & Sally Satel, The Health Disparities Myth (2006); Kimani Paul-Emile, Patient Racial Preferences and the Medical Culture of Accommodation, 60 UCLA L. Rev. 462 (2012). See also Nancy Kressin & Peter Groeneveld, Race/ Ethnicity and Overuse of Care, 93 Milbank Q. 112 (2015) (reporting that whites are more *over*treated than others).

Is it *ever* legitimate for doctors to take race into account as relevant in deciding how best to treat patients? Critics argue that skin color is an imperfect proxy for genetic or environmental factors that are relevant to choosing the best treatment for each patient. Defenders of "race-based medicine" say that ethnic heritage is a reasonably accurate indicator of a variety of medical risk factors that physicians should and do take into account.

For policy and legal analysis race-based medicine, see Michael J. Malinowski, Dealing with the Realities of Race and Ethnicity, 45 Hous. L. Rev. 1415 (2009); D. Wasserman, The Justifiability of Racial Classification and Generalizations in Contemporary Clinical and Research Practice, 9 Law, Probability & Risk 215 (2010); Erik Lillquist & Charles A. Sullivan, The Law and Genetics of Racial Profiling in Medicine, 39 Harv. C.R.-C.L. L. Rev. 393 (2004); Sharona Hoffman, "Racially-Tailored" Medicine Unraveled, 55 Am. U. L. Rev. 395-456 (2005) ("'race-based' medicine might violate numerous anti-discrimination provisions contained in federal law, state law, and federal research regulations and guidelines"); Symposium, 34 J.L. Med. & Ethics 483 (2006); Symposium, 36 J.L. Med. & Ethics 443 (2008); and articles by Jonathan Kahn in 4 Yale J. Health Pol'y L. & Ethics 1 (2004); and 92 Iowa L. Rev. 353 (2007).

3. *Filling the legal void.* No cases have yet arisen that attack differential treatment patterns by physicians as forms of racial discrimination. In part, that is because, prior to now, Title VI of the Civil Rights Act, which applies to federally funded services, has been interpreted as not applying to physicians, supra page 80. And no federal statute prohibited discrimination on the basis of sex in health care services. The Affordable Care Act closes these gaps by broadening the definition of federally funded activities and the kinds of discrimination that are prohibited. Sandra H. Johnson, The ACA's Provision on Nondiscrimination Takes Shape, 46(5) Hastings Center Rep. 5 (2016); Symposium, 42(5) J. Health Pol. Pol'y L. (2017).

4. *Conscience Defense to Discrimination.* When a patient is protected from discrimination by a civil rights statute, may a physician nevertheless refuse to treat on grounds of religious belief? The California Supreme Court answered that question for a patient denied fertility services, allegedly on the basis of her sexual orientation.

The Court held that a physician may not refuse treatment if it is on a basis protected from discrimination by statute. However, the Court left open the possibility for denying treatment based on an unprotected status (e.g., unmarried status of parents). North Coast Women's Care Medical Group, Inc. v. Superior Court, 189 P.3d 959 (Cal. 2008). For further discussion, see Symposium: The Future of Rights of Conscience in Health Care: Legal and Ethical Perspectives, 9(1) Ave Maria Law Rev. (2010).

5. *Discrimination on the Basis of Disability.* While Congress waited until 2010 to close the gaps in Title VI's protection against treatment that discriminates on the basis of race or sex, Congress enacted protections against discrimination on the basis of disability in two important statutes much earlier, the Rehabilitation Act of 1973 and the Americans with Disabilities Act of 1990.

The analysis of discrimination under disability statutes is inherently complicated. Often a person's disability is relevant in deciding whether the person is a candidate for treatment. For example, it would not make much sense to transplant a kidney or liver into a patient dying of cancer. Accordingly, while physicians or hospitals rarely would acknowledge that they discriminate on the basis of race or sex, they often will be comfortable citing a patient's disability as a reason for denying care. As we will see, unlawful denials of care can occur both from a refusal to treat at all or a refusal to provide certain kinds of care after the patient-physician relationship is formed.

■ UNITED STATES v. UNIVERSITY HOSPITAL
729 F.2d 144 (2d Cir. 1984)

PRATT, Circuit Judge.

. . . Baby Jane Doe was born on October 11, 1983 at St. Charles Hospital in Port Jefferson, New York. She was suffering from multiple birth defects, the most serious of which were myelomeningocele, commonly known as spina bifida, a condition in which the spinal cord and membranes that envelop it are exposed; microcephaly, an abnormally small head; and hydrocephalus, a condition characterized by an accumulation of fluid in the cranial vault. In addition, she exhibited a "weak face," which prevents the infant from closing her eyes or making a full suck with her tongue; a malformed brain stem; upper extremity spasticity; and a thumb entirely within her fist.

As a result of the spina bifida, the baby's rectal, bladder, leg, and sensory functions were impaired. Due to the combination of microcephaly and hydrocephalus, there was an extremely high risk that the child would be so severely retarded that she could never interact with her environment or with other people.

At the direction of the first pediatric neurosurgeon to examine her, the baby was immediately transferred to University Hospital for dual surgery to correct her spina bifida and hydrocephalus. Essentially, this would entail excising a sac of fluid and nerve endings on the spine and closing the opening, and implanting a shunt to relieve pressure caused by fluid build-up in the cranial cavity. The record indicates that these dual, corrective surgical procedures were likely to prolong the infant's life, but would not improve many of her handicapping conditions, including her anticipated mental retardation.

After consulting with several physicians, nurses, religious advisors, a social worker, and members of their family, the parents of the baby decided to forego the corrective surgery. Instead, they opted for a "conservative" medical treatment consisting of good nutrition, the administration of antibiotics, and the dressing of the baby's exposed spinal sac.

Litigation surrounding Baby Jane Doe began on October 16, when A. Lawrence Washburn, Jr., a Vermont attorney unrelated to the child and her family, commenced a proceeding in New York State Supreme Court seeking appointment of a guardian ad litem for the child and an order directing University Hospital to perform the corrective surgery, [contending that failure to do so would violate Section 504 of the Rehabilitation Act of 1973, 29 U.S.C. §794] . . .

. . . The Appellate Division found that the "concededly concerned and loving parents have made an informed, intelligent, and reasonable determination based upon and supported by responsible medical authority." As the court elaborated:

> The record confirms that the failure to perform the surgery will not place the infant in imminent danger of death, although surgery might significantly reduce the risk of infection. On the other hand, successful results could also be achieved with antibiotic therapy. Further, while the mortality rate is higher where conservative medical treatment is used, in this particular case the surgical procedures also involved a great risk of depriving the infant of what little function remains in her legs, and would also result in recurring urinary tract and possibly kidney infections, skin infections and edemas of the limbs.

Thus, the Appellate Division determined that the parents' decision was in the best interest of the infant and that there was, therefore, no basis for judicial intervention. . . . [The Appellate Division's decision was affirmed by the New York Court of Appeals, but on the ground that the trial court had abused its discretion in permitting the case to go forward. The Court of Appeals observed that (a) Mr. Washburn (the petitioner) had no direct interest in the case, (b) Mr. Washburn had not contacted the State Department of Social Services, which had primary responsibility under state law for initiating child abuse proceedings, and (c) the trial court had failed to seek the Department of Social Service's assistance.]

[Meanwhile, as the state court proceedings were unfolding, HHS received a complaint that Baby Jane Doe was being denied medical treatment because of her handicap. In response to the complaint, HHS obtained the record of the state court proceedings and, after personal review by the Surgeon General, requested the infant's medical records from the hospital. When the hospital refused to provide the records, HHS brought its case in federal court, alleging that the hospital was violating Section 504 of the Rehabilitation Act. The federal district court granted summary judgment for the hospital on two grounds: first, the hospital refused to operate on Baby Jane Doe, not because of her handicap, but because her parents did not consent to the procedures; and second, the parents' refusal of treatment was reasonable given the medical options. The federal government appealed, resulting in this opinion.]

To focus more sharply on this central issue, it is first necessary to examine the theory upon which the government predicates its [claim]. The theory rests on two premises. First, the government draws a distinction between decisionmaking based on a "bona fide medical judgment," which without definition it concedes to be beyond the reach of §504, and decisionmaking based solely on an individual's handicap, which it argues is covered by §504. Second, the government identifies Baby

Jane Doe's microcephaly, which the record indicates will result in severe mental retardation, as the handicapping condition. From these premises, the government reasons that if a newborn infant suffering from spina bifida and hydrocephalus, but not microcephaly, would receive treatment or services that differ from those provided to an infant suffering from all three defects, or alternatively, if the hospital would seek a state court order compelling surgery in the former case, but not in the latter, then a violation of §504 would have been established. . . .

With this unsettled regulatory background in mind, we turn to the statutory language, which is fundamental to any issue of statutory construction. Section 504 provides in pertinent part as follows:

> No otherwise qualified handicapped individual in the United States, as defined in section 706(7) of this title, shall, solely by reason of his handicap, be excluded from the participation in, be denied the benefits of, or be subjected to discrimination under any program or activity receiving federal financial assistance.

Under 29 U.S.C. §706(7)(B), "the term 'handicapped individual' means . . . any person who (i) has a physical or mental impairment which substantially limits one or more of such person's major life activities, (ii) has a record of such an impairment, or (iii) is regarded as having such an impairment." . . .

[We] next consider whether [Baby Jane Doe] possibly can be considered an "otherwise qualified" handicapped individual or to have been "subjected to discrimination" under §504. These two issues are intertwined.

The leading cases construing the "otherwise qualified" criterion of §504 have involved allegedly discriminatory denials of admission to certain educational programs. Southeastern Community College v. Davis, 442 U.S. 397 (1979); Doe v. New York University, 666 F.2d 761 (2d Cir. 1981). In that context, this court in Doe v. New York University recognized that

> it is now clear that [the phrase "otherwise qualified handicapped individual"] refers to a person who is qualified *in spite of* her handicap and that an institution is not required to disregard the disabilities of a handicapped applicant, provided the handicap is relevant to reasonable qualifications for acceptance, or to make substantial modifications in its reasonable standards or program to accommodate handicapped individuals but may take an applicant's handicap into consideration, along with all other relevant factors, in determining whether she is qualified for admission. [Id. at 775 (emphasis in original).]

Doe establishes that §504 prohibits discrimination against a handicapped individual only where the individual's handicap is unrelated to, and thus improper to consideration of, the services in question. As defendants here point out, however, where medical treatment is at issue, it is typically the handicap itself that gives rise to, or at least contributes to, the need for services. Defendants thus argue, and with some force, that the "otherwise qualified" criterion of §504 cannot be meaningfully applied to a medical treatment decision. Similarly, defendants argue that it would be pointless to inquire whether a patient who was affected by a medical treatment decision was, "solely by reason of his handicap, . . . subjected to discrimination."

The government's answer to both these arguments is that Baby Jane Doe can be viewed as suffering from not one, but multiple handicaps. Indeed, the crux of the government's case is that her microcephaly is the operative handicap, and that the requested records are necessary to determine whether she has been discriminated against solely for that reason.

Despite its superficial logic, the government's theory is flawed in at least two respects. First, the government's view of "otherwise qualified" is divorced from the statutory language. As the mainstream of cases under §504 exemplifies, the phrase "otherwise qualified" is geared toward relatively static programs or activities such as education, employment, and transportation systems. As a result, the phrase cannot be applied in the comparatively fluid context of medical treatment decisions without distorting its plain meaning. In common parlance, one would not ordinarily think of a newborn infant suffering from multiple birth defects as being "otherwise qualified" to have corrective surgery performed or to have a hospital initiate litigation seeking to override a decision against surgery by the infant's parents. If Congress intended §504 to apply in this manner, it chose strange language indeed.

Second, in arguing that Baby Jane may have been "subjected to discrimination" the government has taken an oversimplified view of the medical decisionmaking process. Where the handicapping condition is related to the (conditions) to be treated, it will rarely, if ever, be possible to say with certainty that a particular decision was "discriminatory." It is at this point that the analogy to race, relied on so heavily by the dissent, breaks down. Beyond the fact that no two cases are likely to be the same, it would invariably require lengthy litigation primarily involving conflicting expert testimony to determine whether a decision to treat, or not to treat, or to litigate or not to litigate, was based on a "bona fide medical judgment," however that phrase might be defined. Before ruling that congress intended to spawn this type of litigation under §504, we would want more proof than is apparent from the face of the statute.

The legislative history, moreover, indicates that congress never contemplated that §504 would apply to treatment decisions of this nature. . . . [According to t]he Senate Report accompanying the 1974 amendments:

> . . . Section 504 was enacted to prevent discrimination against all handicapped individuals . . . in relation to federal assistance in employment, housing, transportation, education, health services, or any other federally-aided programs. Examples of handicapped individuals who may suffer discrimination in receipt of federally-assisted services . . . are as follows: physically or mentally handicapped children who may be denied admission to federally-supported school systems on the basis of their handicap; handicapped persons who may be denied admission to federally-assisted nursing homes on the basis of their handicap; those persons whose handicap is so severe that employment is not feasible but who may be denied the benefits of a wide range of federal programs. . . .

S. Rep. No. 1297, supra at 6388-6389.

This passage provides the best clue to congressional intent regarding §504's coverage of "health services." As Judge Gesell noted in American Academy of Pediatrics v. Heckler, 561 F. Supp. at 401:

> The legislative history . . . [on this subject] focuses on discrimination against adults and older children and denial of access to federal programs. As far as can be determined, no congressional committee or member of the House or Senate ever even suggested that section 504 would be used to monitor medical treatment of defective

newborn infants or establish standards for preserving a particular quality of life. No medical group appeared alert to the intrusion into medical practice which some doctors apprehend from such an undertaking, nor were representatives of parents or spokesmen for religious beliefs that would be affected heard. . . .

We are aware, of course, that "where the words and purpose of a statute plainly apply to a particular situation, . . . the fact that the specific application of the statute never occurred to Congress does not bar us from holding that the situation falls within the statute's coverage." United States v. Jones, 607 F.2d 269, 273 (9th Cir. 1979), *cert. denied*, 444 U.S. 1085 (1980). Here, however, the government's theory not only strains the statutory language but also goes well beyond Congress's overriding concern with guaranteeing handicapped individuals access to programs or activities receiving federal financial assistance. Further, the situation in question is dramatically different in kind, not just in degree, from the applications of §504 discussed in the legislative history. . . .

This void in the legislative history is conspicuous for another reason. Prior to the enactment of the Rehabilitation Act, congress had passed a number of measures limiting federal involvement in medical treatment decisions. For example, the very first section of the Medicare law, . . . codified at 42 U.S.C. §1395, . . . provides that "nothing in this subchapter shall be construed to authorize any federal officer or employee to exercise any supervision or control over the practice of medicine or the manner in which medical services are provided." . . .

In view of this consistent congressional policy against the involvement of federal personnel in medical treatment decisions, we cannot presume that Congress intended to repeal its earlier announcements in the absence of clear evidence of congressional intent to do so. . . .

In the present case, Baby Jane Doe has been treated in an evenhanded manner at least to the extent that the hospital has always been and remains willing to perform the dual, corrective surgeries if her parents would consent. Requiring the hospital either to undertake surgery notwithstanding the parents' decision or alternatively, to petition the state court to override the parents' decision, would impose a particularly onerous affirmative action burden upon the hospital. . . .

WINTER, Circuit Judge, dissenting.

Since I believe that §504 applies to the provision of medical services to handicapped infants, I respectfully dissent. . . . Section 504 . . . states with as much clarity as is reasonably possible that in some circumstances recipients of federal financial assistance may not differentiate between individuals on grounds that one or more is handicapped. . . . Although modern courts frequently rely upon legislative history to reach results at odds with the seemingly plain language of a statute, only the most compelling reasons should induce a court to override statutory language because the legislative history is silent on a particular point. Such compelling circumstances might exist in the present case if Congress had no reason to address the questions at hand when it enacted §504. It hardly needs stating that the underlying issues brim with political and moral controversy and portend to extend the hand of the federal government into matters traditionally governed by an interaction of parental judgment and state authority. Were I able to conclude that Congress had no reason to address these issues in its consideration of §504, I would concur with the majority on the grounds that specific consideration by the Congress of this political and moral minefield would be appropriate before applying the statute as written.

However, such a conclusion is untenable since §504 is no first step into a hitherto uncharted legal wilderness. As the Senate Report stated:

> Section 504 was patterned after, and is almost identical to, the antidiscrimination language of section 601 of the Civil Rights Act of 1964, 42 U.S.C. 2000d-1 (relating to race, color, or national origin), and section 901 of the Education Amendments of 1972, 42 U.S.C. 1683 (relating to sex). The section therefore constitutes the establishment of a broad government policy that programs receiving federal financial assistance shall be operated without discrimination on the basis of handicap.

S. Rep. No. 1297, 93d Cong., 2d Sess., *reprinted* in 1974 U.S. Code Cong. & Ad. News 6373, 6390. Section 504 was thus enacted against a background of well understood law which was explicitly designated as a guide to interpretation. Congress was persuaded that a handicapped condition is analogous to race and that, so far as the administration of federal financial assistance is concerned, discrimination on the basis of a handicap should be on statutory par with discrimination on the basis of race.

Once §504's legislative heritage is acknowledged, the "void" in the legislative history is eliminated and the many issues raised by defendants with regard to medical decisions, parental judgments and state authority simply evaporate. The government has never taken the position that it is entitled to override a medical judgment. Its position rather is that it is entitled under §504 to inquire whether a judgment in question is a bona fide medical judgment. While the majority professes uncertainty as to what that means, application of the analogy to race eliminates all doubt. A judgment not to perform certain surgery because a person is black is not a bona fide medical judgment. So too, a decision not to correct a life threatening digestive problem because an infant has Down's Syndrome is not a bona fide medical judgment. The issue of parental authority is also quickly disposed of. A denial of medical treatment to an infant because the infant is black is not legitimated by parental consent. Finally, once the legislative analogy to race is acknowledged, the intrusion on state authority becomes insignificant. . . .

———————

Bragdon v. Abbott, 524 U.S. 624 (1998). Invoking the Americans with Disabilities Act's (ADA's) protection from discrimination based on disability, a woman with HIV infection challenged her dentist's refusal to fill her cavity unless he performed the procedure in a hospital. (The woman, Sidney Abbott, would have been responsible for the cost of using the hospital's facilities.) Important issues in the case were whether HIV infection constitutes a disability for purposes of the ADA and whether the dentist could nevertheless justify denying treatment in his office to protect himself from becoming infected with HIV during the procedure. (The ADA generally tracks the framework of the Rehabilitation Act's protection against discrimination based on disability but expands to more people the protection of the Rehabilitation Act.)

The Court concluded that Ms. Abbott's HIV infection constituted a disability under the ADA on the ground that HIV infection is a "physical . . . impairment that substantially limits one or more . . . major life activities." 42 U.S.C. §12102(2)(A). According to the Court, HIV infection is a physical impairment from the moment of infection because the virus immediately begins to damage an infected person's white blood cells and because of the severity of the disease. As to whether HIV infection substantially limits a major life activity, the Court observed that it might have identified many major life activities substantially limited by HIV infection. Since Ms. Abbott claimed that HIV infection substantially limited her ability to have children, the Court restricted its inquiry to that life activity. As an activity "central to the life process itself," reproduction constitutes a major life activity, wrote the Court. Moreover, HIV infection substantially limits reproduction in two ways: "First, a woman infected with HIV who tries to conceive a child imposes on the man a significant risk of becoming infected. . . . Second, an infected woman risks infecting her child during gestation and childbirth. . . ." The Court also noted that, even though the risk of transmission of HIV from mother to infant could be reduced by treatment to 8 percent, such a risk of transmitting a fatal disease rose to the level of a substantial limitation.

As to whether the dentist could defend his insistence on treatment at a hospital, he would have to show that Ms. Abbott "pose[d] a direct threat to [his] health or safety. . . ." 42 U.S.C. §12182(b)(3), with direct threat defined as "a significant risk to the health or safety of others that cannot be eliminated by a modification of policies, practices, or procedures or by the provision of auxiliary aids or services." Id. In assessing whether the dentist's fear of HIV transmission was objectively reasonable, "the views of public health authorities, such as the U.S. Public Health Service, CDC, and the National Institutes of Health, are of special weight and authority. The views of these organizations are not conclusive, however. A health care professional who disagrees with the prevailing medical consensus may refute it by citing a credible scientific basis for deviating from the accepted norm." The Court remanded the case for consideration of the dentist's defense of a direct threat to his health if he were to fill Ms. Abbott's cavity in his office instead of a hospital.

On remand, the First Circuit found in favor of Ms. Abbott. The court concluded that, because of the availability of universal precautions to prevent transmission of HIV infection from patient to dentist, the dentist could not justify his denial of treatment in terms of the need to protect himself from becoming infected with HIV. Abbott v. Bragdon, 163 F.3d 87 (1st Cir. 1998), cert. denied, 526 U.S. 1131 (1999). (Universal precautions are measures that health care providers are supposed to take with every patient to prevent the spread of infectious diseases like HIV and hepatitis. Examples of universal precautions are the wearing of gloves and other protective attire by health care providers, the use of special wastebaskets to dispose of used needles, and sterilization of medical instruments after each use.) The First Circuit decided that once physicians take universal precautions, no significant risk of HIV transmission remains.

■ GLANZ v. VERNICK
756 F. Supp. 632 (D. Mass. 1991)

MAZZONE, Judge.
In April, 1989, plaintiff's decedent, Raymond Vadnais, brought this suit alleging discrimination in violation of §504 of the Rehabilitation Act of 1973 (the "Act"), 29 U.S.C. §794. . . . The case is now before [this court] on the [defendants' motions for] summary judgment.

The allegations in the complaint can be briefly summarized as follows. In December, 1986, defendant Dr. Vernick saw Mr. Vadnais at the Ear, Nose, and Throat Clinic (the "ENT Clinic") at Beth Israel Hospital and treated him for severe pain in the right ear, at first by prescribing antibiotics and ear drops. In January, 1987, Dr. Vernick diagnosed a perforation in Mr. Vadnais's right ear and, at Mr. Vadnais's third visit, recommended surgery to repair the perforation. After Mr. Vadnais agreed to undergo surgery, Dr. Vernick learned that Mr. Vadnais was infected with HIV and in March, 1987, informed Mr. Vadnais that he would not perform the operation. The ear condition persisted, causing severe pain and discomfort, while Mr. Vadnais continued the ineffective use of antibiotics and ear drops.

In August, 1988, Dr. Yale Berry, unaware of Mr. Vadnais's HIV status, performed the surgery, curing Mr. Vadnais's ear problem. Subsequently, Mr. Vadnais brought this lawsuit seeking . . . compensatory damages for the pain and suffering and emotional distress caused by the delay in receiving corrective surgery, along with punitive damages and attorney's fees. . . .

Count I of the complaint charges that Dr. Vernick, . . . by refusing to perform surgery, unlawfully discriminated against Mr. Vadnais because of his handicap, HIV seropositivity, in violation of §504 of the Rehabilitation Act. . . .

Section 504 states in pertinent part that "no otherwise qualified handicapped individual in the United States . . . shall, solely by reason of his handicap, be excluded from the participation in, be denied the benefits of, or be subjected to discrimination under any program or activity receiving federal financial assistance. . . ." 29 U.S.C. §794.

The defendants argue that summary judgment is appropriate for several . . . reasons . . . [including] the ground that Mr. Vadnais was not "otherwise qualified" for elective ear surgery. They argue that it is proper for a doctor to consider a patient's handicap in determining whether a patient is qualified for surgery. On the basis of this argument, they conclude that Mr. Vadnais was not "otherwise qualified" for surgery because his HIV disease increased his risk of infection, and, furthermore, that the court should defer to the doctor's determination that it was in his patient's best interest to postpone surgery. . . .

As the Court made clear in *Arline*, the "otherwise qualified" determination requires an individualized inquiry and appropriate findings of fact. With respect to the defendants' assertions about the risks of surgery, the facts are in dispute. The defendants contend that surgery was postponed because Dr. Vernick thought that Mr. Vadnais was "AIDS positive," because the proposed ear surgery was elective, and because it would pose significant risks to the patient. In addition, they offer Dr. Berry's statement in his deposition that he would not have performed the surgery had he known that Mr. Vadnais had AIDS. The plaintiff offers the contradicting evidence that Mr. Vadnais was HIV-positive and had not yet been diagnosed as having AIDS when surgery was refused. Moreover, Dr. Vernick in answers to interrogatories and Dr. Berry in his deposition stated that they do not consider HIV seropositivity alone as a disqualifying factor for surgery. Based on the evidence that the plaintiff has produced, facts are certainly available to warrant the conclusion that Mr. Vadnais was "otherwise qualified" for surgery. Moreover, the defendants have not produced any evidence that reasonable accommodations could not have been made.

There is some merit to the argument that the court should defer to a doctor's medical judgment. Cf. *Arline*, 480 U.S. at 288 ("courts normally should defer to the reasonable medical judgments of public health officials" when conducting "otherwise qualified" inquiry). Accepting this argument at face value, however, would completely eviscerate §504's function of preventing discrimination against the disabled in the healthcare context. A strict rule of deference would enable doctors to offer merely pretextual medical opinions to cover up discriminatory decisions. The evidentiary approach to §504 cases discussed in Pushkin v. Regents of the Univ. of Colo., 658 F.2d 1372 (10th Cir. 1981), properly balances deference to sound medical opinions with the need to detect discriminatory motives. The plaintiff must first make out a prima facie case that he was otherwise qualified for surgery, and only then does the burden shift to the defendant to show that the plaintiff's handicap made him unqualified. The plaintiff, however, must still be given an opportunity "to prove either that the reason given by defendants is a pretext or that the reason . . . 'encompasses *unjustified* consideration of the handicap itself.'" *Leckelt*, 714 F. Supp. at 1385 (citing *Pushkin*, 658 F.2d at 1387) (emphasis added).

In sum, because . . . there are genuine issues of material fact surrounding the "otherwise qualified" inquiry, summary judgment on the §504 claim is inappropriate.

Notes: Denials of Care Because of Disability

1. *Subsequent Developments.* In the end, the parents in *University Hospital* agreed to have a shunt implanted to drain the fluid in their daughter's brain, although the surgery was delayed because of an infection that was likely related to the opening in her spine. The child, Keri-Lynn, has done much better than predicted. Although she is confined to a wheelchair and developmentally disabled, she can talk, and by age 30 in 2013, she was living in a group home Monday through Friday, taking academic classes, and receiving physical therapy. It is not clear whether surgery to close Keri-Lynn's spine would have improved her outcome.

2. *The Americans with Disabilities Act. University Hospital* and *Glanz* were decided under the Rehabilitation Act, which applies only to federally funded programs or services and federal executive agencies. Since those cases, the Americans with Disabilities Act (ADA) has gone into effect, and its provisions apply to all nonfederal providers of health care services, public or private. The statutory language of the ADA was designed to track the Rehabilitation Act and court decisions interpreting that Act.

For further discussion of the ADA and denials of health care, see Chapters 8.B.2 and 9.D.1; Carl H. Coleman, Conceiving Harm: Disability Discrimination in Assisted Reproductive Technologies, 50 UCLA L. Rev. 17 (2002); Mary A. Crossley, Of Diagnoses and Discrimination: Discriminatory Nontreatment of Infants with HIV Infection, 93 Colum. L. Rev. 1581 (1993); Wendy F. Hensel & Leslie E. Wolf, Playing God: The Legality of Plans Denying Scarce Resources to People with Disabilities in Public Health Emergencies, 63 Fla. L. Rev. 719 (2011); Kimberly M. Mutcherson, Disabling Dreams of Parenthood, 27 Law & Ineq. 311 (2009); David Orentlicher, Destructuring Disability: Rationing of Health Care and Unfair Discrimination Against the Sick, 31 Harv. C.R.-C.L. L. Rev. 49 (1996); Philip G. Peters, Jr., When Physicians Balk at Futile Care, 91 Nw. U. L. Rev. 798 (1997); and Philip G. Peters, Jr., Health Care Rationing and Disability Rights, 70 Ind. L.J. 491 (1995), which is excerpted in Chapter 9.

3. *Definition of Disability.* As indicated by the Supreme Court in *Bragdon*, one has to determine whether a person is in fact disabled under the ADA or Rehabilitation

Act before deciding whether there has been unlawful discrimination on account of disability. Until 1999, it did not seem to be very difficult for plaintiffs to prove that they were disabled under the ADA. Disability can be shown not only by the presence of a disabling condition but also by a history of a disabling condition or by showing that one is regarded by others as having a disabling condition. 42 U.S.C. §12102(2). Moreover, the legislative history indicated that the judgment whether a patient is disabled should be made assuming that no treatment is provided. Thus, even if a patient's disabling symptoms could be alleviated with medication, the patient would still be considered disabled under the ADA.

In 1999, the Supreme Court raised the bar on the definition of disability by holding that a person is not actually disabled if medications or medical devices can alleviate the disabling symptoms. Moreover, the Court established a relatively high threshold for showing that one is disabled because of being "regarded as having" a disabling condition. Sutton v. United Air Lines, 527 U.S. 471 (1999). The ADA Amendments Act of 2008 overrode *Sutton* and other narrowing decisions by the Supreme Court. As a result, the definition of disability is consistent again with the legislative history of the ADA. For a discussion of the 2008 Act, see Jeannette Cox, Crossroads and Signposts: The ADA Amendments Act of 2008, 85 Ind. L.J. 187 (2010). For a very helpful discussion about defining disability, see Mary Crossley, The Disability Kaleidoscope, 74 Notre Dame L. Rev. 621 (1999).

4. *When Denial of Treatment Is Discriminatory.* What standard does the *Glanz* court suggest for deciding whether a denial of care constitutes unlawful discrimination on the basis of disability? What theories does the *University Hospital* court use to find no unlawful discrimination when medical care is withheld from a severely disabled newborn? Which of the different approaches do you think makes the most sense?

Note that, while the court's decision in *University Hospital* rested in part on the fact that Baby Jane Doe's parents agreed to the withholding of care, there is much more to the opinion. In addition, another court reached the same result as *University Hospital* in a case in which the parents charged that the physicians' treatment recommendations were biased by the presence of the child's severe disability and that the physicians failed to disclose their bias when obtaining the parents' consent to withhold care. Johnson v. Thompson, 971 F.2d 1487, 1493-1494 (10th Cir. 1992) (citing *University Hospital* for the proposition that, "[w]here the handicapping condition is related to the condition(s) to be treated, it will rarely, if ever, be possible to say . . . that a particular decision was 'discriminatory'"). There are other reasons to discount parental agreement. As Judge Winter observed in his *University Hospital* dissent, parental agreement does not necessarily vitiate a discrimination claim. The parents may not be adequately representing the child's interests.

Both *Glanz* and *University Hospital* take the view that a person's disability can be a relevant consideration in the person's access to health care. If a disability affects the benefit that the patient can receive from health care, then the disability can be a factor in deciding how to treat the patient. But that leaves most disabled persons subject to denials of health care. The immune system compromise of an HIV-infected person, for example, will have wide-ranging effects on that person's response to medical or surgical therapy. Crossley, supra note 2, at 1650. Indeed, the argument in *Glanz* that Mr. Glanz's HIV infection would predispose him to infection would apply to any HIV-infected patient undergoing surgery. How do we consider the effects of a person's disability without discriminating unfairly against that person? What if it is true that a disabled person would not gain as much benefit from treatment as a nondisabled person? Is an appropriate analogy the educational services that states are required to provide in the primary public schools for children with disabilities? See New Mexico Association for Retarded Citizens v. New Mexico, 678 F.2d 847, 854-855 (10th Cir. 1982) (requiring special education to ensure that children with disabilities receive an education appropriate to their needs).

To what extent are the costs of care relevant to the analysis? If Baby Jane Doe's care cost thousands instead of hundreds of thousands of dollars, should that make a difference in deciding whether disability discrimination occurred? If you think social costs are relevant, then why does the denial of care by Dr. Pierce seem more troubling than the withholding of care from Baby Jane Doe? Wasn't he also concerned primarily about social costs? Is his decision worse because it was directed toward only the poor, or because welfare status is correlated with race? Or is it that sterilization is reminiscent of discredited eugenic social policies of the past?

Rather than avoiding the care of certain patients by claiming that the patient is not a candidate for care (as in *University Hospital* or *Glanz*), physicians might claim that the patient needs to be referred for more specialized care. In Lesley v. Chie, 250 F.3d 47 (1st Cir. 2001), the U.S. Court of Appeals for the First Circuit addressed a disability discrimination claim in the context of a physician's referral of the patient to a more specialized colleague. In *Leslie*, the court considered "the extent to which a court should defer to a physician's claim that he lacks the experience, knowledge, or other prerequisites necessary to address the medical conditions that allegedly prompted his referral of a patient to another physician." The case arose after an obstetrician referred an HIV-infected, pregnant woman to another hospital for drug therapy designed to prevent transmission of HIV to the woman's child. The other hospital had a special Women and Infants HIV Program. The court found no Rehabilitation Act violation, writing,

> Under the Rehabilitation Act, a patient may challenge her doctor's decision to refer her elsewhere by showing the decision to be devoid of any reasonable medical support. This is not to say, however, that the Rehabilitation Act prohibits unreasonable medical decisions as such. Rather, the point of considering a medical decision's reasonableness in this context is to determine whether the decision was unreasonable in a way that reveals it to be discriminatory. In other words, a plaintiff's showing of medical unreasonableness must be framed within some larger theory of disability discrimination. For example, a plaintiff may argue that her physician's decision was so unreasonable — in the sense of being arbitrary and capricious — as to imply that it was pretext for some discriminatory motive, such as animus, fear, or "apathetic attitudes." See, e.g., Howe v. Hull, 874 F. Supp. 779, 788-89 (N.D. Ohio 1994) (under ADA, jury could find doctor's diagnosis that plaintiff had extremely rare disorder requiring transfer was pretextual, where patient only had an allergic drug reaction, and doctor did not mention the rare disorder in requesting the transfer but only mentioned plaintiff's HIV-status). Or, instead of arguing pretext, a plaintiff may argue that her physician's decision was discriminatory on its face, because it rested on stereotypes of the disabled rather than an individualized inquiry into the patient's condition — and hence was "unreasonable" in that sense. [Id. at 55.]

5. *Infectious Patients.* As *Bragdon* indicates, an outright denial of care on account of the person's HIV status is unlawful disability discrimination. However, *Bragdon*

also indicates that in deciding whether to provide care, physicians may take into account the risk to the physician of becoming infected from the patient. How should the risk be taken into account? What if an orthopedic surgeon refuses to operate on an HIV-infected (or hepatitis-infected) patient on the grounds that orthopedic surgery is "bloody" and involves exposure to sharp edges of bone as well as to sharp surgical instruments? What if the surgeon already provides care to a significant number of HIV-infected patients and the surgeon is trying to have a child? Should it matter whether the denial of care is for elective rather than essential surgical procedures? Consider a dermatologist who refuses to perform a hair transplant on an HIV-infected person on the ground that the procedure invariably causes significant bleeding from the patient's scalp. It is important to note that the circuit courts disagree on exactly when a risk is serious enough to be "significant." For a discussion of the different standards, see Onishea v. Hopper, 171 F.3d 1289, 1296-1299 (11th Cir. 1999) (interpreting "significant risk" in the context of a Rehabilitation Act case).

Concerns about discrimination against HIV-infected physicians are discussed at pages 205-207.

B. THE STRUCTURE OF THE TREATMENT RELATIONSHIP

1. Forming a Patient-Physician Relationship

In general, it is clear when a patient-physician relationship has been created. A patient seeks care, and the physician provides the care. In many situations, however, it is not so clear whether a relationship was formed. There may have been some interaction between the patient and the physician, for example, a telephone call or conversation, but not enough interaction to create a professional relationship. Or the patient's physician may have consulted another physician, and the question is whether the second physician's participation creates a professional relationship between that physician and the patient. In some cases, as we saw in *Hiser*, pages 61-62, when physicians refuse to see patients, the patients will claim that the physicians had previously bound themselves to provide care. There will also be cases when the physician actually examines the patient, but the examination is arranged on behalf of an employer or insurer. Then the issue arises whether the physician's primary obligation is to the patient or to the company that retains him. Finally, when a physician clearly has obligations to a patient, issues arise over whether those obligations extend to third parties who might also be harmed by the physician's professional decisions. The following materials explore each of these issues in varying depth.

■ ADAMS v. VIA CHRISTI REGIONAL MEDICAL CENTER
19 P.3d 132 (Kan. 2001)

ALLEGRUCCI, Justice.
This is a personal injury and wrongful death action filed by Albert and Forestean Adams, the parents of Nichelle Adams, who died as a result of a ruptured ectopic pregnancy. [After settling with Via Christi, the plaintiffs proceeded to trial

against their daughter's physician, Dr. Louis Ohaebosim.] The jury returned a verdict in favor of the parents. . . .

In July 1992, Nichelle Adams was 22 years old and was living with her parents and her younger sister. On July 22, Mrs. Adams got home from work at approximately 8:40 P.M. to find that Nichelle had been complaining about her stomach and had gone to bed. Mrs. Adams was concerned because Nichelle generally was a very active person.

Dr. Ohaebosim, an osteopath, who had been a family practitioner for 22 years, had been the family physician for Mr. and Mrs. Adams and their three children for several years. He had a patient file on Nichelle, but he had not seen her in his office since 1988. On July 6, Nichelle completed a form for Planned Parenthood in which she answered "no" to the question "Do you have a family physician?" Dr. Ohaebosim continued to provide medical care to other members of the family. Mrs. Adams had gotten medical advice from Dr. Ohaebosim over the telephone on a number of occasions.

Until 1990, Dr. Ohaebosim included as part of his family practice the treatment of women through pregnancy, labor, and delivery. He delivered over a thousand babies. After 1990, he continued to treat pregnant women for nonpregnancy-related conditions and to make the determination for women that they were pregnant, but he referred women to other practitioners for prenatal care, labor, and delivery. Dr. Ohaebosim testified about sending a letter to his patients to advise them that he would no longer be providing obstetrical care. He also testified that he advised all the hospitals, "I don't deliver babies anymore." He further stated, "This is my notice written. I'm writing to inform you that I would cease delivering babies on January, 1990, on the 1st of January, 1990." Mrs. Adams testified that she did not receive a letter from the doctor advising that he no longer offered obstetrical care. She was unaware that Dr. Ohaebosim had eliminated obstetrical care from his practice.

At approximately 9 P.M. on July 22, Mrs. Adams called Dr. Ohaebosim. She got his answering service, and then the doctor called Mrs. Adams right back. She told Dr. Ohaebosim that Nichelle was 5 to 8 weeks pregnant and was experiencing abdominal pain. Mrs. Adams later told a doctor at the hospital that she mentioned shortness of breath to Dr. Ohaebosim in the telephone conversation, but Dr. Ohaebosim later denied it, and at the time of trial Mrs. Adams could not remember telling him anything other than Nichelle was pregnant and had abdominal pain.

Dr. Ohaebosim testified that 8 weeks is the typical time when an ectopic pregnancy becomes symptomatic because the fetus becomes too large for the fallopian tube. When Mrs. Adams told Dr. Ohaebosim of Nichelle's condition, he did not suspect that Nichelle might have an ectopic pregnancy. . . .

Dr. Ohaebosim testified that he told Mrs. Adams that abdominal pain is not abnormal during pregnancy but to take Nichelle to the emergency room if she got any worse. He also told her to have Nichelle see a doctor the next day. Mrs. Adams testified that Dr. Ohaebosim did not mention taking Nichelle to the emergency room, but that he did say to bring her into his office the next day. Dr. Ohaebosim and Mrs. Adams agreed that he did not ask her any questions about Nichelle's condition.

At approximately midnight, Mrs. Adams drove Nichelle to the hospital, where she was admitted into the emergency room at 12:25 A.M. on July 23. By the time Nichelle was taken into an examining room, she was agitated and thrashing around.

While Mrs. Adams was alone with Nichelle in the examination room, Nichelle vomited. Mrs. Adams called for help, and, when hospital personnel took over Nichelle's care, Mrs. Adams was taken to a nursing station to call her husband. . . . Before her husband arrived at the hospital, Mrs. Adams was told that Nichelle had gone into cardiac arrest. Later she was told that Nichelle was being taken to surgery.

Dr. Ohaebosim was not contacted with regard to Nichelle until approximately 4 P.M. on July 23. He immediately went to the hospital. Nichelle was on life support systems and nonreactive to the light Dr. Ohaebosim shined in her eyes. He discussed Nichelle's condition with her family, and at approximately 6:30 P.M. she died after being removed from the support systems pursuant to her family's decision. There was evidence that Nichelle might have lived if she had received medical care at 9 or 9:30 P.M. on July 22, instead of after midnight.

Mr. and Mrs. Adams, individually and as administrators of the estate of Nichelle Adams, sued St. Francis Regional Medical Center and Dr. Ohaebosim. . . .

Dr. Ohaebosim contends that there was no physician-patient relationship between him and Nichelle Adams on July 22, 1992, and that in the absence of a physician-patient relationship, no duty arose. . . .

The factors Dr. Ohaebosim advances in support of his position that no physician-patient relationship existed on July 22, 1992, between him and Nichelle Adams are the following:

1. A physician-patient relationship did exist on that date between him and Mrs. Adams.
2. He had not seen, talked to, or treated Nichelle for approximately four years prior to July 22.
3. He did not speak to Nichelle on July 22.
4. His only knowledge of Nichelle's obstetric history was the information provided by Mrs. Adams during the telephone conversation.
5. He no longer provided obstetrical care.
6. He "took no action other than discussing, in very general terms," Nichelle's condition with Mrs. Adams.
7. He did not consider Nichelle to be his patient, and Nichelle did not consider him to be her doctor.

Of these factors, the key to resolving this issue is Dr. Ohaebosim's own statement that he discussed Nichelle's condition with Mrs. Adams. In doing so, he consented to give medical advice about Nichelle's condition and he gave it. It is immaterial that he had not seen Nichelle for several years. It is immaterial that he did not speak directly to Nichelle on July 22. It is not significant in the circumstances that he states that he did not consider Nichelle to be his patient and that Nichelle did not consider him to be her doctor. He did consider Mrs. Adams to be his patient. He was a family physician, and in years past he had treated her daughter, Nichelle. When Mrs. Adams spoke to him by telephone on July 22 and told him that Nichelle was 5-8 weeks pregnant and experiencing abdominal pain, Dr. Ohaebosim did not say that he did not consider Nichelle to be his patient. He did not say that he no longer provided obstetrical care. Rather than suggesting to Mrs. Adams that she contact another doctor at that time, he listened to what Mrs. Adams told him about Nichelle and gave her his medical opinion in response. Dr. Ohaebosim's undertaking to render medical advice as to Nichelle's condition gave rise to a physician-patient relationship. Thus, even if the earlier physician-patient relationship between Dr. Ohaebosim and Nichelle had lapsed or been extinguished, it was renewed.

The essential difference between the facts of this case and those cited by Dr. Ohaebosim is his taking some action to give medical assistance. Typical of the cases he cites is *Ortiz v. Shah, 905 S.W.2d 609 (Tex. App. 1995)*. Ortiz was taken to the emergency room with a gunshot wound. The emergency room nurse paged Dr. Shah, who was the "on call" surgeon. Before Dr. Shah reached the hospital, Ortiz had been treated in the emergency room and taken to surgery, where he died. Dr. Shah had no prior relationship with Ortiz. Dr. Shah never saw the patient Ortiz. He never talked to him, and he never gave any advice to anyone about Ortiz's care. He simply told the nurse who contacted him that he was on his way to the hospital. Dr. Shah had taken no action that affected the medical treatment received by Ortiz. Dr. Ohaebosim, in contrast, gave his medical opinion about Nichelle Adams' condition. His opinion was that she was experiencing nothing unusual, which served to reassure Mrs. Adams about her daughter's condition and dissuade her from promptly seeking medical attention for Nichelle.

Dr. Ohaebosim contends that he declined to treat Nichelle. He did not decline to express his medical opinion about her condition. Thus, he cannot be said to have declined to treat her. A physician-patient relationship existed between Dr. Ohaebosim and Nichelle, and a duty of care was owed by Dr. Ohaebosim to Nichelle. . . .

■ ESTATE OF KUNDERT v. ILLINOIS VALLEY COMMUNITY HOSPITAL
964 N.E.2d 670 (Ill. App. 2012)

SCHMIDT, Justice

Plaintiffs, Dustin Kundert and Krista Grady, brought this medical malpractice suit on behalf of their deceased child, Kameryn Kundert, and his estate against defendant, Illinois Valley Community Hospital (Illinois Valley). The circuit court . . . dismissed the action. . . . Plaintiffs appeal, claiming the court erred when holding, as a matter of law, no relationship existed between the decedent, or his parents, and defendant sufficient to create a legal duty of care. We affirm.

FACTS

Given the procedural history of this case, the facts we recite are derived from plaintiffs' second amended complaint. On April 18, 2007, Krista Grady gave birth to Kameryn Kundert. . . . On May 31, 2007, Kameryn exhibited signs and symptoms of a serious illness. Unable to reach [Kameryn's pediatrician] Dr. Fess . . . Krista called Illinois Valley at 7:29 P.M. that night. She informed the operator that she needed to speak to a medical professional for advice about Kameryn's symptoms.

The operator transferred the call to an individual in the emergency room. Krista told this unknown individual that Dr. Fess . . . could not be reached. Krista then described Kameryn as a six-week-old newborn with a high temperature who was very fussy, unable to sleep and refusing to eat. The individual informed Krista that she was overreacting, which was typical for new mothers, to administer Tylenol and give Kameryn tepid baths. The individual was unsure of the proper dosage of Tylenol and, as such, instructed Krista to contact a pharmacy. The individual noted that the symptoms described did not require immediate medical attention and to follow up with Dr. Fess in the morning. Finally, "the individual on the telephone advised [Krista] that Illinois Valley did not have the equipment or medical personnel to provide medical services to infants." Krista called a pharmacy to determine the proper amount of Tylenol to give Kameryn.

Relying on the information received during the phone call, Krista postponed seeking medical treatment for Kameryn until Dr. Fess's office opened at 8 A.M. on June 1, 2007. Following an examination in Dr. Fess's office, Dr. Fess arranged for Kameryn to be transported via ambulance to Illinois Valley's emergency room. Dr. Fess advised the emergency room personnel that a septic six-week-old would be arriving. Once there, medical personnel performed a lumbar puncture, took a chest X-ray and administered intravenous fluids and oxygen. Within an hour of arriving, Kameryn was transferred to St. Francis Medical Center to receive a "higher level of specialized medical treatment not available at Illinois Valley." At St. Francis, Kameryn was treated for bacterial meningitis. He died on June 15, 2007. . . .

ANALYSIS

. . . Plaintiffs argue that their complaint unequivocally establishes: (1) "a direct connection" between Krista and defendant; (2) the fact that Krista knowingly sought medical advice from defendant; (3) that defendant's agent "consented to render medical advice," which equated to "accept[ing] Kameryn as a patient"; and (4) Krista "relied on that advice."

. . . [T]he "relationship of physician and patient is a consensual relationship in which the patient knowingly seeks the physician's assistance and the physician knowingly accepts the person as a patient." . . . Plaintiffs' second amended complaint specifically states that "the individual on the telephone advised [Krista] that Illinois Valley did not have the equipment or medical personnel to provide medical services to infants." We fail to see how the actions of the person on phone, even while viewing all the allegations of the complaint in the light most favorable to the plaintiffs, evince a "knowing acceptance" of Kameryn as a patient. Plaintiffs acknowledge that the person who took the phone call informed Krista that Illinois Valley did not have the equipment or personnel to treat Kameryn that evening.

Plaintiff argues that the act of recommending Tylenol and tepid baths is constructive acceptance of the patient. . . . Plaintiffs would have us hold that a physician-patient relationship is created anytime a physician dispenses advice. That is, the singular act of dispensing any quantum of advice equates to knowing or at least constructive acceptance of a patient. Case law does not support such a holding. [The court described previous cases in which the dispensation of medical advice] was insufficient to create a physician-patient relationship.

The unidentified person with whom Krista spoke was not asked to perform any tests, interpret any results or examine Kameryn. The circumstances surrounding the inquiry and response indicate that the person merely gave an informal opinion based upon rather common symptoms: those being a temperature, fussiness and refusal to eat or sleep.

. . . [The] "consequence" of finding that [a patient's inquiry coupled with an] informal opinion . . . creates a [treatment] relationship "would have a chilling effect upon the practice of medicine. It would stifle communication . . . to the detriment of the patient." . . . It is, we think, not unreasonable to expect medical providers would attempt to limit their tort exposure. We would expect that the result of finding that this phone call created a physician-patient relationship would be that anytime a parent called and reported a child with a fever, the response would be the same: "Hang up and call 911 or drive your child to an emergency room." We believe that this would benefit neither the providers nor consumers of medical care. We find public policy supports the trial court's decision.

. . . We can think of no other way to categorize the statement made to Krista that Illinois Valley "did not have the equipment or medical personnel to provide medical services to infants" than a refusal to provide services. . . . At a minimum, that allegation made by plaintiffs defeats any notion that Illinois Valley "knowingly accepted" Kameryn as a patient on the night in question. As such, we hold plaintiffs' second amended complaint fails to properly allege the existence of a hospital-patient relationship and as such no duty existed as a matter of law. Therefore, the trial court did not err in granting defendant's motion to dismiss.

Finally, citing to [two earlier Illinois cases] and *Adams v. Via Christi Regional Medical Center*, plaintiffs assert that the "common thread amongst cases imposing a duty of care is whether the patient sought and received medical advice during the telephone call." We disagree. The common thread running through these cases is whether a patient knowingly sought a physician's service and the physician knowingly accepted the patient. As detailed above, . . . the singular act of dispensing advice does not equate to knowing acceptance of a patient. A review and analysis of *Adams* does not change our opinion that no hospital-patient relationship was created in this case. . . .

While noting the question of whether a duty exists is a question of law, the *Adams* court found it proper to submit a question to the jury for it to determine whether the phone call from the mother to the doctor created a physician-patient relationship. The jury found it did. The *Adams* court found that the doctor "did not decline to express his medical opinion about her condition. Thus, he cannot be said to have declined to treat her." As such, the *Adams* court found a physician-patient relationship existed sufficient to create a duty of care.

. . . Even if we were bound by *Adams*, we see two major distinctions. First, as this matter comes to us following the granting of a motion to dismiss, there can be no question of fact; we must consider all well-pled facts as true. Secondly, and maybe most importantly for our analysis, that forces us to accept as true plaintiffs' contention that the person at the hospital "advised [Krista] that Illinois Valley did not have the equipment or medical personnel to provide medical services to infants." We see no way to interpret this language other than as declining to treat Kameryn.

■ REYNOLDS v. DECATUR MEMORIAL HOSPITAL
660 N.E.2d 235 (Ill. App. 1996)

McCULLOUGH, Judge.

. . . The only issue is whether, as a matter of law, a telephone conference between treating pediatrician Dr. Sharon Bonds and [Dr. Thomas] Fulbright concerning Kevin [Reynolds]'s condition created a physician-patient relationship between Kevin and Fulbright. . . . The trial court found there was no physician-patient relationship and, therefore, no duty was owed by Fulbright to plaintiffs. We affirm. . . .

At about 10:45 P.M. on November 29, 1990, Kevin was seen in the emergency room of Decatur Memorial Hospital by Dr. Terry Balagna. The history given indicated he was injured at 8:30 or 9 P.M. by falling while jumping on the couch in the family living room. Upon examination, an abnormal breathing pattern was observed. Tests were conducted to discover the possibility of an infection or an electrolyte or metabolic problem. Cervical spine X-rays were taken at about 1:05 A.M. which appeared normal. Nevertheless, Kevin was admitted to the hospital. Balagna called Bonds, a pediatrician, to examine him.

Bonds arrived at the hospital at about 1:45 A.M. on November 30, 1990. At that time, Kevin's temperature was 102 degrees Fahrenheit. Bonds made a quick assessment of plaintiff and took a history from Barbara [Reynolds, Kevin's mother], which indicated Kevin had jumped off the couch, landed on his arm, walked to his mother, and gradually become limp after that. Bond noticed the child's breathing difficulties and that he was flaccid. She reviewed the emergency room records and X-ray reports, conducted reflex tests, and noticed he was moving his head. His neck was not tender. Among the possible reasons for his condition which Bonds considered were neurologic, traumatic, metabolic, infectious, or post-infectious problem. Because of the fever, she was leaning toward the infectious process diagnosis, and she did not consider a spinal cord injury. A history of a two-foot fall with a normal 2 ½-year-old child did not indicate to her the existence of a cervical cord injury from trauma.

At 2:05 A.M., Bonds telephoned Fulbright[, a neurologist,] at his home. She advised Fulbright that Kevin walked following the fall, he had an elevated temperature and was flaccid and responsive, and the cervical spine X-rays were negative. She probably told him the child was flaccid from the neck down, including all four extremities. Fulbright inquired if the child had a stiff neck. Bonds said she did not know, went to check Kevin's neck, and returned to inform Fulbright that his neck was stiff. At the end of the conversation, Fulbright suggested a spinal tap to determine whether meningitis, encephalitis, or something similar was involved. Bonds did not ask Fulbright to treat Kevin, nor did Fulbright commit himself to further involvement with Kevin. Bonds was under the impression that Fulbright would see Kevin if she contacted him and requested that he treat Kevin.

Fulbright's recollection of his telephone conversation was as follows:

> Dr. Bonds called me regarding Kevin Reynolds. She related to me that the patient had presented with a history of a fall, I believe from a couch. The height estimated to be less than two feet. She related that the child was listless, and that the child was febrile with a fever of—on the order of 102 degrees Fahrenheit. I questioned Dr. Bonds regarding the history. My first concern was the veracity of the history. My major concern here was the question of child abuse. There was some report on her part that the history had been somewhat inconsistent. That in itself is a hallmark of abuse. I questioned her specifically as to whether or not she felt abuse was operative in this case. She stated relatively emphatically that she did not think that it was. She did not think that the fall was overly significant because of its apparently benign nature, that is, a fall from a low height of a young child as happens to every young child. The question of the cause of the fever and the possible neurological causes of the fever was raised. The question of meningitis was discussed. The question of an ascending neuritis was discussed. The performance of a lumbar puncture was discussed. The conclusion was that Dr. Bonds would perform the lumbar puncture

and let me know if she wanted me to see the child thereafter. I offered to make myself physically available if she wished. We elected to proceed with the plan of her performing the lumbar puncture and letting me know if she needed me there.

Fulbright often received informal inquiries from other doctors asking questions and seeking suggestions. These inquiries do not include a request to see a patient, review a patient, or render an opinion, but only to discuss the case. He considered this a courtesy service for which he did not bill. He offered to make himself available because the other physician may be inhibited about asking him to see the patient due to the late hour or the marginal neurosurgical nature of the case.

. . . Fulbright stated he did not receive another call from Bonds or anyone else at the hospital with regard to Kevin's condition or treatment. Kevin's family never asked Fulbright to treat Kevin, and he never saw, examined, or came to a diagnosis as to Kevin's condition. Fulbright did not bill for any services to Kevin. . . .

[Bonds concluded that Kevin had an infectious cause for his symptoms. In fact, he had suffered a spinal cord injury that left him with quadriplegia.]

In a negligence action for medical malpractice, there must be a duty owed by defendant to the plaintiff, a breach of duty, an injury proximately caused by the breach, and resultant damages. The determination of whether the parties stood in such a relationship to one another that the law would impose on defendant a duty of reasonable conduct for the benefit of the plaintiff is a question of law. That policy determination is based on consideration of the likelihood of injury, the magnitude of the burden of guarding against it, and the consequences of placing that burden on the defendant. . . .

The relationship of physician and patient is . . . a consensual relationship in which the patient knowingly seeks the physician's assistance and the physician knowingly accepts the person as a patient. A consensual relationship can exist where other persons contact the physician on behalf of the patient, but this is not a case in which Fulbright was asked to provide a service for Kevin, conduct laboratory tests, or review test results. Fulbright did nothing more than answer an inquiry from a colleague. He was not contacted again and he charged no fee. A doctor who gives an informal opinion at the request of a treating physician does not owe a duty of care to the patient whose case was discussed. . . .

Plaintiffs suggest that what needs to be done is to find a physician-patient relationship to result from every such conversation. The consequence of such a rule would be significant. It would have a chilling effect upon [the] practice of medicine. It would stifle communication, education and professional association, all to the detriment of the patient. The likely effect in adopting plaintiffs' argument also would be that such informal conferences would no longer occur. . . .

■ **LYONS v. GRETHER**
239 S.E.2d 103 (Va. 1977)

POFF, Justice.

. . . Plaintiff, a blind person, accompanied by her four-year-old son and her guide dog, arrived at defendant's "medical office" on the morning of October 18, 1975, a Saturday, to keep an appointment "for treatment of a vaginal infection."

She was told that defendant would not treat her unless the dog was removed from the waiting room. She insisted that the dog remain because she "was not informed of any steps which would be taken to assure the safety of the guide dog, its care, or availability to her after treatment." Defendant "evicted" plaintiff, her son, and her dog, refused to treat her condition, and failed to assist her in finding other medical attention. By reason of defendant's "wrongful conduct," plaintiff was "humiliated" in the presence of other patients and her young son, and "for another two days while she sought medical assistance from other sources," her infection became "aggravated" and she endured "great pain and suffering." . . . [P]laintiff demanded damages resulting from "breach of his duty to treat." [The trial court dismissed the case.] . . .

Although there is some conflict of authority, the courts are in substantial accord upon the rules concerning the creation of a physician-patient relationship and the rights and obligations arising therefrom. In the absence of a statute, a physician has no legal obligation to accept as a patient everyone who seeks his services. A physician's duty arises only upon the creation of a physician-patient relationship; that relationship springs from a consensual transaction, a contract, express or implied, general or special, and a patient is entitled to damages resulting from a breach of a physician's duty. Whether a physician-patient relationship is created is a question of fact, turning upon a determination whether the patient entrusted his treatment to the physician and the physician accepted the case.

We consider first whether the facts stated in the motion for judgment, and the reasonable inferences deducible therefrom, were sufficient to allege the creation of a physician-patient relationship and a duty to treat. Standing alone, plaintiff's allegation that she "had an appointment with defendant" would be insufficient, for it connotes nothing more than that defendant had agreed to see her. But plaintiff alleged further that the appointment she had been given was "for treatment of a vaginal infection." The unmistakable implication is that plaintiff had sought and defendant had granted an appointment at a designated time and place for the performance of a specific medical service, one within defendant's professional competence, viz., *treatment* of a particular ailment. It is immaterial that this factual allegation might have been contradicted by evidence at trial. Upon demurrer, the test of the sufficiency of a motion for judgment is whether it states the essential elements of a cause of action, not whether evidence might be adduced to defeat it. . . . [The court went on to observe that, on remand, there was also a factual question as to whether Dr. Grether's refusal to treat Ms. Lyons amounted to a lawful termination of their professional relationship.]

Notes: Creating the Patient-Physician Relationship

1. *Telephone Calls by a Prospective Patient.* Are *Adams* and *Kundert* consistent with each other? In what way was the argument for the existence of a patient-physician relationship stronger in *Kundert* than in *Adams*? Is there another way to interpret the *Kundert* court's statement that the hospital "did not have the equipment or medical personnel to provide medical services to infants," other than as a refusal to provide care? Is it appropriate to read *Lyons* as holding that scheduling a specific appointment creates a professional relationship, or was this case driven by the physician's reason for cancelling the appointment? Compare Weaver v. University of Michigan

Board of Regents, 506 N.W.2d 264, 266 (Mich. App. 1993) (merely scheduling an appointment does not by itself establish a patient-physician relationship).

The ease with which a treatment relationship can be formed perhaps explains why hospital emergency department staff have been accused of engaging in what is known as a "wallet biopsy"—asking the patient or family more detailed questions about insurance and financial responsibility when they first come in than they do about the patient's condition, in order to be sure they can refuse treatment if the patient cannot pay and is not in a serious condition. For additional examples and discussion from the case law, see Annot., What Constitutes Physician-Patient Relationship for Malpractice Purposes, 17 A.L.R. 4th 132 (1982).

2. *Consultations by a Patient's Physician.* As the *Reynolds* court concluded, when a colleague of a patient's physician is informally consulted for advice rather than being asked to see the patient, conduct laboratory tests, or render a formal opinion, the "curbside" consultation does not create a patient-physician relationship between the patient and the colleague. In one case, which is probably at the extreme, the court so held even though the treating physician consulted a colleague in response to concerns expressed by the patient's mother about the appropriateness of care being provided her daughter. In that case, the treating physician reassured the mother on the basis of the consultation and also mentioned the consultation on his discharge summary. Oliver v. Brock, 342 So. 2d 1 (Ala. 1976). See also Irvin v. Smith, 31 P.3d 934 (Kan. 2001); Jennings v. Badgett, 230 P.3d 861 (Okla. 2010).

However, if a physician assumes some responsibility for diagnostic or treatment decisions, then a patient-physician relationship may be created. See Crisp Regional Hospital v. Oliver, 621 S.E.2d 554, 560-561 (Ga. App. 2005) (jury could conclude that a patient-physician relationship was formed when the physician wrote an order for an MRI scan before patient's first appointment with the physician). Or if a physician sees a patient as part of a formal consultation, supplies a diagnostic impression, and recommends a treatment plan, a limited doctor-patient relationship may be created, which carries with it some duties of care, even though the physician has no further involvement in the patient's care. White v. Harris, 36 A.3d 203 (Vt. 2011) (psychiatrist met with patient via a 90-minute video conference and in so doing "assumed a duty to act in a manner consistent with the applicable standard of care so as not to harm decedent through the consultation services provided"). But a simple, formal consultation without any further involvement by the physician need not trigger a patient-physician relationship. Gilbert v. Miodovnik, 990 A.2d 983 (D.C. 2010) (no relationship for an obstetrician who conducted a routine "chart review" of a case and wrote notes with his advice on a form inserted into the patient's medical record). A recent case from Georgia sets some useful parameters: while recognizing that a doctor "does not have to physically examine a patient in order for the doctor-patient relationship to arise," and "[m]erely listening to another physician's description of a patient's problem and offering a professional opinion regarding the course of treatment is not enough," a relationship is formed when the doctor "essentially directs the course of that patient's treatment." Smith v. Rodillo, 765 S.E.2d 432 (Ga. App. 2015).

For a sense of the distinction between informal, curbside consultations and more formal consultations, see Farrin A. Manian & David A. Janssen, Curbside Consultations: A Closer Look at a Common Practice, 275 JAMA 145 (1996).

Do you agree with the policy reasons given by the *Reynolds* court for its holding? Given the principle that a patient-physician relationship is not created by a consultation, does this effectively mean that patients receive the benefit of free consultations but they "pay" for the consultations by "waiving" their right to sue the consulted physician? If that is what is going on here, does it follow that patients should be able to waive their right to sue their treating physician in exchange for a lower fee for their care? See discussion of Tunkl v. Regents of the University of California and related cases at pages 107-110.

Phone consultations with a medical specialist are much more likely to lead to the formation of a patient-physician relationship when the physician is serving as an "on-call" physician to the hospital's emergency department, as illustrated by two Missouri cases. In Corbet v. McKinney, 980 S.W.2d 166 (Mo. App. 1998), a patient sued an emergency department physician for misdiagnosis of an ear problem and also sued an ear, nose, and throat specialist who had been telephoned by the emergency department physician. Since the specialist had not seen or billed the patient and was not under any contractual obligation to participate in the patient's care, the court held that no patient-physician relationship had been created. In contrast, in Millard v. Corrado, 14 S.W.3d 42 (Mo. App. 1999), the court found a patient-physician relationship between a patient and an on-call physician who never saw the patient and who allegedly failed to respond quickly enough to his pages, on the ground that the hospital bylaws required on-call physicians to respond to calls within a reasonable amount of time.

While the Missouri court in *Millard* found a duty to treat for the on-call consultant based solely on the physician's preexisting contractual obligation, courts in Georgia and Michigan have followed an Ohio decision, McKinney v. Schlatter, 692 N.E.2d 1045 (Ohio App. 1997), in requiring some involvement by the physician in the patient's care. See Anderson v. Houser, 523 S.E.2d 342 (Ga. App. 1999); Oja v. Kin, 581 N.W.2d 739 (Mich. App. 1998). (Note that the Ohio Supreme Court rejected the *McKinney* test in a later case, *Lownsbury*, mentioned below.)

Kundert is not the only example of how Illinois courts have extended the principle in *Reynolds* from a conversation between two doctors to apply as well to a conversation between a patient and a doctor. In Siwa v. Koch, the court of appeals also held that the mere dispensation of advice does not create a treatment relationship even when a physician gives advice directly to the patient in person. According to the *Siwa* court, plaintiffs must show additional evidence demonstrating that the health care provider chose to enter into a patient-provider relationship. 902 N.E.2d 1173 (Ill. App. 2009) (no relationship when a hospital employee volunteered to undergo a CT scan so the hospital and radiologist could test out new computer software for the scanner).

Some courts avoid the entire debate over whether a full-scale doctor-patient relationship has been triggered and hold simply that the physician owes a duty of care to the extent of his or her involvement, whatever that is. Diggs v. Arizona Cardiologists, 8 P.3d 386 (Ariz. App. 2000). For instance, in Mozingo v. Pitt County Memorial Hospital, 415 S.E.2d 341 (N.C. 1992), the court allowed suit against a physician who merely supervised the obstetrical residents who made an error. The supervising physician was at home "on call" when the difficulty arose and responded immediately when asked to come to the hospital. By the time he arrived, the delivery had been completed. The court accepted the plaintiff's allegations that supervising physicians have a duty to check in periodically when they know that a difficult case is in the hospital. Thus, duty was imposed by virtue of the physician's supervising status even though he never saw the patient until it was too late. Accord Lownsbury v. Van Buren, 762 N.E.2d 354 (Ohio 2001). But see Prosise v. Foster 544 S.E.2d 331 (Va. 2001) (no patient-physician relationship solely on account of on-call physician's obligation to supervise medical residents in the emergency department).

3. *Employment or Insurance Physicals.* Patients are often examined by physicians in situations in which the physician is retained by a third party. For example, a company may require a preemployment examination, or an insurer may require an examination before issuing a policy or paying benefits. In general, no patient-physician relationship is created when the physician examines a patient at the request and for the benefit of a third party, and the patient therefore has no cause of action if the physician fails to diagnose a disease or disclose abnormal findings. Smith v. Radecki, 238 P.3d 111, 115 (Alaska 2010) (rejecting malpractice claim when independent medical exam after a workplace accident failed to detect abnormalities); Payne v. Sherrer, 458 S.E.2d 916 (Ga. App. 1995) (no cause of action for breach of confidentiality against a physician who examined employee on behalf of employer); Murphy v. Blum, 554 N.Y.S.2d 640 (App. Div. 1990) (no cause of action for basketball referee who was not told of abnormal EKG findings by physician who performed yearly physical examinations for the NBA).

However, there are important exceptions to this general principle. For example, the physician may have a duty "to take reasonable steps to make information available timely to the examinee of any findings that pose an imminent danger to the examinee's physical or mental well-being." Green v. Walker, 910 F.2d 291, 296 (5th Cir. 1991) (interpreting Louisiana law in case in which a physician allegedly failed to diagnose lung cancer during an annual employment examination). Accord Stanley v. McCarver, 92 P.3d 849 (Ariz. 2004); Reed v. Bojarski, 764 A.2d 433 (N.J. 2001) (both imposing a duty of care on physicians who find evidence of serious illness); Daly v. United States, 946 F.2d 1467 (9th Cir. 1991) (interpreting Washington state law in a case in which a job applicant had undergone a preemployment examination, and the radiologist failed to inform the applicant of an abnormal X-ray). A patient-physician relationship may also be found if the physician "affirmatively" advises the patient on "how to be treated." Hickey v. Travelers Insurance Co., 558 N.Y.S.2d 554 (App. Div. 1990) (workers' compensation physician mistakenly advised employee that surgery was not necessary to treat work-related injuries). See also Webb v. T.D., 951 P.2d 1008 (Mont. 1997) (liability when physician negligently diagnoses a patient's condition and communicates the misdiagnosis directly to the patient). Such advice need not be extensive. See Dugan v. Mobile Medical Testing Services, 830 A.2d 752 (Conn. 2003) (denying the defendant summary judgment when an employee, during his employment physical, asked "about the results of his EKG" and the defendant's employee said, "Everything looks fine. We only found one irregular heartbeat.").

While the physician may not have an affirmative duty to the patient, the physician does have a duty not to harm the patient. Greenberg v. Perkins, 845 P.2d 530 (Colo. 1993) (physician referred patient for an evaluation that aggravated an old back injury); Dyer v. Trachtman, 679 N.W.2d 311 (Mich. 2004) (physician allegedly tore shoulder cartilage that had been recently repaired surgically by another physician).

A few states permit malpractice claims to be brought in the absence of a patient-physician relationship. Ritchie v. Krasner, 211 P.2d 1272 (Ariz. 2009) (permitting negligence claim against physician who performed an independent medical examination after a workplace injury on ground that the physician did not adequately "investigate the symptoms of a cervical spine injury"); Berry v. National Medical Services, Inc., 205 P.3d 745 (Kan. Ct. App. 2009) (allowing claim of employee who lost job after enrolling in alcohol treatment program and failing test administered by third party for its negligence in test administration). Finally, even where the examining physician has no duty to the patient, the third party that requires the exam and chooses the physician may have a duty of care. Dornak v. Lafayette General Hospital, 399 So. 2d 168 (La. 1981) (employer liable for failing to disclose tuberculosis diagnosed during preemployment examination).

For further discussion, see Patrick D. Blake, Note, Redefining Physicians' Duties: An Argument for Eliminating the Physician-Patient Relationship Requirement in Actions for Medical Malpractice, 40 Ga. L. Rev. 573 (2006).

4. *Telemedicine.* In telemedicine, the patient and physician are in separate places (indeed in some instances in separate states or countries) and care is provided over the telephone or the Web. The level of interaction and technology can vary greatly from the relatively low-tech (such as telepsychiatry) to the high-tech (telerobotics for surgery) to something in between (teleradiology). Because telemedicine necessarily deviates from the traditional context of a physician-patient relationship, even seemingly straightforward telemedicine interactions can add ambiguity to the formation of a legal relationship. According to the Federation of State Medical Boards' Model Policy for the Appropriate Use of Telemedicine Technologies in the Practice of Medicine, the physician-patient relationship "tends to begin when an individual with a health-related matter seeks assistance from a physician who may provide assistance. However, the relationship is clearly established when the physician agrees to undertake diagnosis and treatment of the patient, and the patient agrees to be treated, whether or not there has been an encounter in person between the physician (or other appropriately supervised health care practitioner) and patient." Federation of State Medical Boards, Model Policy for the Appropriate Use of Telemedicine Technologies in the Practice of Medicine, Apr. 2014. For further discussion see John D. Blum, Internet Medicine and the Evolving Legal Status of the Physician-Patient Relationship, 24 J. Legal Med. 413 (2003); Paul Spradley, Comment, Telemedicine: The Law Is the Limit, 14 Tul. J. Tech. & Intell. Prop. 307 (2011).

5. *Retail Clinics.* Increasingly, Americans receive health care through retail health clinics in drug stores, grocery stores, or big-box retailers like Wal-Mart. These clinics typically offer on-demand primary care from nurse practitioners (NPs) or physician assistants (PAs) at a lower cost than a typical physician visit. Visits to retail clinics have eclipsed 10 million annually and make up about 2 percent of all primary care visits in the United States. Bachrach et al., Building a Culture of Health: The Value Proposition of Retail Clinics, RWJF, Apr. 2015. The inherent nature of these clinics, however, featuring the use of non-physicians in administering care, raises questions as to the type of treatment relationship created and the required standard of care. If no physician is involved, no physician-patient relationship is created. Is the correct standard of care in a malpractice action that of a reasonable PA? See Annie Hsu, Legal Issues Concerning Retail Clinics, 20 Health Law 13 (2008). Most retail

clinic practitioners communicate frequently with a consulting physician. Indeed, many states require physicians to supervise and/or collaborate with NPs and PAs. Traditionally, when physicians are supervising the work of NPs and PAs, physicians can be liable for inadequate supervision, or under *respondeat superior,* negligent acts performed by the NP or PA. Should a collaborative relationship between a physician and NP in the retail clinic setting establish the requisite control for vicarious liability? See Lauren E. Battaglia, Supervision and Collaboration Requirements: The Vulnerability of Nurse Practitioners and Its Implications for Retail Health, 87 Wash. U. L. Rev. 1127 (2010); Kristen E. Schleiter, Retail Medical Clinics: Increasing Access to Low Cost Medical Care Amongst a Developing Legal Environment, 19 Annals of Health Law 527 (2010).

6. *Duties to Third Parties.* Similar issues arise when physicians have a clear treatment relationship with a patient but their treatment decisions affect third parties. The question then is whether physicians owe a duty of care to someone who is not their patient and who may be a complete stranger. For example, if a physician negligently stops prescribing a drug to control a patient's seizures, and the patient injures a third party because of a seizure while driving an automobile, does the third party have a malpractice cause of action against the physician?

The issue here is similar to the question of a physician's duty to warn third parties who might be injured by the physician's patient (because the patient may act on a psychotic delusion, for example), or who share a health risk with the patient (either because the patient carries an infectious disease, or because the patient and third party share a genetic risk of disease). That issue is taken up in Chapter 3. In both kinds of cases, there is a common issue as to whether the physician owes a duty of care to the third party. The two kinds of cases differ in that here the issue is whether a physician owes a duty of nonnegligence to third parties, while in the other cases the issue is whether the physician has a duty to warn third parties of their risk.

While courts generally recognize some duty of nonnegligence to third parties, they differ on the extent of that duty. In Welke v. Kuzilla, 375 N.W.2d 403 (Mich. App. 1985), the court found liability simply because the injury to the third party was reasonably foreseeable. In that case, a woman driving her car was killed in an automobile collision that was allegedly precipitated by medication given by the physician to the driver of the other car. See also Hardee v. Biomedical Applications of South Carolina, 636 S.E.2d 629 (S.C. 2006). Other states find a duty only when there is a "special relationship" between the third party and either the patient or the physician. Thus, in Renslow v. Mennonite Hospital, 367 N.E.2d 1250 (Ill. 1977), the court held a hospital and physician liable for prenatal injuries to a child from blood transfusions that nine years earlier had caused Rh-sensitization in the child's mother. However, the same court rejected liability when a passenger was injured in an automobile accident allegedly caused because the car's driver was impaired by medications that the physician negligently prescribed, observing that the relationship between driver and passenger does not have the intimacy of mother and fetus. Kirk v. Michael Reese Hospital, 513 N.E.2d 387, 399 (Ill. 1987).

A New York court has required the additional showing that the physician had "sufficient ability and authority to control the conduct" of the patient before finding a duty of care to third parties. The court found no duty of care to the children of a driver who crashed into a bridge abutment after losing consciousness, allegedly because of negligently prescribed medication, on the ground that the driver "was free to accept or reject defendant's diagnosis and advice and she was at liberty to seek a second opinion. . . . [S]he had the right to decide what treatment and advice she would accept or reject." Conboy v. Mogeloff, 567 N.Y.S.2d 960, 961-962 (App. Div. 1991). Is this a fair characterization of the way patients respond when physicians prescribe medication for them?

In an interesting twist on the third-party question, courts have considered whether a kidney donor can sue a physician on the ground that the physician's negligence caused the recipient's need for the kidney transplant. The courts generally have rejected such claims on the ground that no patient-physician relationship existed between the donor and the recipient's physician. See, e.g., Dabdoub v. Ochsner Clinic, 802 So. 2d 651 (La. App. 2000); Moore v. Shah, 458 N.Y.S.2d 33 (N.Y. App. Div. 1982). However, a Massachusetts court allowed a donor to claim that a physician wrongly concluded that a transplant was needed by the recipient when the donor had established his own patient-physician relationship with the physician. Montalto v. Stoff, 2007 Mass. Super LEXIS 404 (Super. Ct. 2007). In an Ohio case, the donor was able to sue the hospital when the recipient of a kidney donation died from negligence shortly after the transplant was performed. Siebe v. Univ. of Cincinnati, 766 N.E.2d 1070 (Ohio Ct. Cl. 2001).

Third-party questions also arise in the context of reproductive medicine, as discussed in Chapter 7.

2. Limiting the Scope of the Treatment Relationship

In contrast with finding that a provider has no obligation to a third party or ostensible patient, it might be conceded that a treatment relationship exists but that the provider's obligation is limited in some important respects. The section considers both limitations on the standard of care that determines liability and limitations on other obligations such as the scope of practice.

■ TUNKL v. REGENTS OF THE UNIVERSITY OF CALIFORNIA
383 P.2d 441 (Cal. 1963)

TOBRINER, Justice.

. . . Hugo Tunkl brought this action to recover damages for personal injuries alleged to have resulted from the negligence of two physicians in the employ of the University of California Los Angeles Medical Center, a hospital operated and maintained by the Regents of the University of California as a nonprofit charitable institution . . . for the primary purpose of aiding and developing a program of research and education in the field of medicine. . . . Upon his entry to the hospital, Tunkl signed a document setting forth certain "Conditions of Admission." The crucial condition number six reads as follows:

> RELEASE: The hospital is a nonprofit, charitable institution. In consideration of the hospital and allied services to be rendered and the rates charged therefor, the patient or his legal representative agrees to and hereby releases The Regents of the

University of California, and the hospital from any and all liability for the negligent or wrongful acts or omissions of its employees, if the hospital has used due care in selecting its employees. . . .

Plaintiff at the time of signing the release was in great pain, under sedation, and probably unable to read. At trial plaintiff contended that the release was invalid, asserting that a release does not bind the releasor if at the time of its execution he suffered from so weak a mental condition that he was unable to comprehend the effect of his act. The jury, however, found against plaintiff on this issue. Since the verdict of the jury established that plaintiff either knew or should have known the significance of the release, this appeal raises the sole question of whether the release can stand as a matter of law. . . .

We begin with the dictate of the relevant Civil Code §1668. The section states: "All contracts which have for their object, directly or indirectly, to exempt anyone from responsibility for his own fraud, or willful injury to the person or property of another, or violation of law, whether willful or negligent, are against the policy of the law."

The course of §1668, however, has been a troubled one. . . . Some of the cases have applied the statute strictly, invalidating any contract for exemption from liability for negligence. . . . Other cases hold that the statute prohibits the exculpation of gross negligence only; still another case states that the section forbids exemption from active as contrasted with passive negligence. In one respect, as we have said, the decisions are uniform. The cases have consistently held that the exculpatory provision may stand only if it does not involve "the public interest."[3] . . . [C]ourts [have] struck down exculpatory clauses as contrary to public policy in the case of a contract to transmit a telegraph message and in the instance of a contract of bailment. . . .

If, then, the exculpatory clause which affects the public interest cannot stand, we must ascertain those factors or characteristics which constitute the public interest. The social forces that have led to such characterization are volatile and dynamic. No definition of the concept of public interest can be contained within the four corners of a formula. The concept, always the subject of great debate, has ranged over the whole course of the common law. . . .

In placing particular contracts within or without the category of those affected with a public interest, the courts have revealed a rough outline of that type of transaction in which exculpatory provisions will be held invalid. Thus, the attempted but invalid exemption involves a transaction which exhibits some or all of the following characteristics. It concerns a business of a type generally thought suitable for public regulation. The party seeking exculpation is engaged in performing a service of great importance to the public, which is often a matter of practical necessity for some members of the public. The party holds himself out as willing to perform this service for any member of the public who seeks it, or at least for any member coming within certain established standards.[4] As a result of the essential nature of

---

3. The view that the exculpatory contract is valid only if the public interest is not involved represents the majority holding in the United States. . . .

4. . . . There is a close historical relationship between the duty of common carriers, public warehousemen, innkeepers, etc. to give reasonable service to all persons who apply, and the refusal of courts to permit such businesses to obtain exemption from liability for negligence. . . .

the service, in the economic setting of the transaction, the party invoking exculpation possesses a decisive advantage of bargaining strength against any member of the public who seeks his services. In exercising a superior bargaining power the party confronts the public with a standardized adhesion contract of exculpation, and makes no provision whereby a purchaser may pay additional reasonable fees and obtain protection against negligence. Finally, as a result of the transaction, the person or property of the purchaser is placed under the control of the seller, subject to the risk of carelessness by the seller or his agents. . . .

In the light of the decisions, we think that the hospital-patient contract clearly falls within the category of agreements affecting the public interest. To meet that test, the agreement need only fulfill some of the characteristics above outlined; here, the relationship fulfills all of them. . . . The would-be patient is in no position to reject the proffered agreement, to bargain with the hospital, or in lieu of agreement to find another hospital. The admission room of a hospital contains no bargaining table where, as in a private business transaction, the parties can debate the terms of their contract. As a result, we cannot but conclude that the instant agreement manifested the characteristics of the so-called adhesion contract. . . .

Defendant [next] contends that while the public interest may possibly invalidate the exculpatory provision as to the paying patient, it certainly cannot do so as to the charitable one. . . . [W]e see no distinction in the hospital's duty of due care between the paying and nonpaying patient. The duty, emanating not merely from contract but also tort, imports no discrimination based upon economic status. . . . To immunize the hospital from negligence as to the charitable patient because he does not pay would be as abhorrent to medical ethics as it is to legal principle. . . .

In substance defendant here asks us to modify our decision in Malloy v. Fong, 37 Cal. 2d 356, 232 P.2d 241 (1951), which removed the charitable immunity; defendant urges that otherwise the funds of the research hospital may be deflected from the real objective of the extension of medical knowledge to the payment of claims for alleged negligence. Since a research hospital necessarily entails surgery and treatment in which fixed standards of care may not yet be evolved, defendant says the hospital should in this situation be excused from such care. But the answer lies in the fact that possible plaintiffs must prove negligence; the standards of care will themselves reflect the research nature of the treatment; the hospital will not become an insurer or guarantor of the patient's recovery. To exempt the hospital completely from any standard of due care is to grant it immunity by the side-door method of a contractual clause exacted of the patient. We cannot reconcile that technique with the teaching of *Malloy*. . . .

The judgment is reversed.

Notes: Limiting the Standard of Care and Scope of Practice

1. *Limiting Liability.* Other courts that have disallowed contractual provisions that would relieve doctors of malpractice liability include Emory University v. Porubiansky, 282 S.E.2d 903 (Ga. 1981) (university dental clinic's liability release was void as against public policy even though the clinic was used for training purposes as part of the dental school); Meiman v. Rehabilitation Center, Inc., 444 S.W.2d 78 (Ky. 1969) (rehabilitation facility's liability release was invalid as being against public policy); Olson v. Molzen, 558 S.W.2d 429 (Tenn. 1977) (physician's liability release for an abortion patient was invalid as contrary to public policy).

Nevertheless, partial waivers may be allowed in some situations. The leading example is Madden v. Kaiser Foundation Hospitals, 552 P.2d 1178 (Cal. 1976), excerpted and discussed at page 401, which upheld a provision in an HMO contract that required malpractice claims to be decided by arbitration. Unlike in *Tunkl*, arbitration does not alter the standard of care, only the process of dispute resolution; the limitation was imposed on healthy employees as part of their health insurance, not on a sick patient coming to the hospital; and the limitation was part of a contract negotiated by a very large employer on behalf of its workers in a situation where the employees had a choice of other health insurance that did not contain this limitation.

Waivers or limitations of liability are also commonly enforced when, for good reason, physicians depart from standard medical practice. This might occur, for instance, if a patient insists on leaving the hospital "against medical advice" (a so-called discharge A.M.A.). Such patients are asked to sign a waiver or release from liability for harm resulting from refusing recommended treatment. Consider also a patient, who for religious or other reasons, insists on a type of treatment that is not medically recommended, or one who agrees to participate in a medical experiment. See, e.g., Colton v. New York Hospital, 414 N.Y.S.2d 866 (Sup. Ct. 1979) (permitting release from liability for injury resulting from nonnegligent care when the treatment—a kidney transplant—was experimental); Shorter v. Drury, 695 P.2d 116 (Wash. 1985) (permitting a hospital to require a Jehovah's Witness patient who refused blood transfusions to release the hospital, its personnel, and the patient's physician from liability for any injury resulting from the refusal); see generally 6 A.L.R.3d 704.

Separate from contractual waiver, there are also cases of de facto waiver. One example comes from so-called "medical tourism," where a patient might travel from Milwaukee to Bangkok to receive a cardiac bypass. Given civil procedural difficulties in suing in U.S. courts (personal jurisdiction, forum non conveniens, choice of law, enforcement of judgments) and the difficulty in bringing suit abroad, many patients will not recover. How should our public policy differentiate between these de facto waivers and contractual ones? For a discussion see I. Glenn Cohen, Protecting Patients with Passports: Medical Tourism and the Patient Protective-Argument, 95 Iowa L. Rev. 1467 (2010).

2. *Scope of Practice; Futility.* The remainder of these notes explore other types of limitations on a physician's or hospital's treatment obligation. One such limitation concerns the scope of practice. Physicians are entitled to limit their practice to a particular specialty and geographic area. See, e.g., McNamara v. Emmons, 97 P.2d 503 (Cal. 1939) (physician absolved of responsibility for follow-up care when patient had gone to stay 20 miles out-of-town, and the physician arranged for care with another physician where the patient was staying); Thaddeus Mason-Pope, Medical Futility Statutes: No Safe Harbor to Unilaterally Refuse Treatment, 75 Tenn. L. Rev. 1 (2007).

Also, physicians are not obligated to provide care that offers no medical benefit. As discussed in Chapter 5, however, there is considerable disagreement as to when medical treatment becomes futile.

3. *Conscientious Objection.* In some situations, physicians or other medical workers may have a conscientious objection to providing care. For example, obstetrician-gynecologists often are unwilling to perform abortions. Congress and many state

legislatures have enacted so-called conscience clause statutes that protect medical personnel from retaliatory measures for refusing to participate in abortions. See 42 U.S.C. §300a-7 (2011) (known as the "Church Amendment"); Lara Cartwright-Smith, HHS Provider Conscience Regulation, Health Reform GPS (Apr. 12, 2011); Chapter 7. Because only a minority of obstetrician-gynecologists perform abortions, abortions are not available in many parts of the country. Should a state respond to the poor access of its residents to abortion by requiring that, as a condition of licensure, obstetrician-gynecologists must be willing to perform abortions?

A physician who is morally opposed to abortion may be not only unwilling to perform abortions but also unwilling to facilitate abortions by referring patients to an abortion provider or informing them of the option to have an abortion. Would a refusal to discuss abortion violate the patient's right to informed consent? See Rust v. Sullivan, 500 U.S. 173, 195 (1991) (permitting the federal government to refuse family planning funds to organizations that counsel or refer for abortions where there is no medical need); see Chapter 7.

In recent years, many states have enacted or considered legislation dealing with pharmacists' objections to filling prescriptions for birth control pills, emergency contraception, or other drugs. The majority of the laws permit pharmacists to exercise their conscience and not fill a prescription, but some states require pharmacists or emergency departments to fill the prescriptions. National Conference of State Legislatures, Pharmacist Conscience Clauses: Laws and Information (updated May 2012).

Professor Sepper explains how conscience clause legislation modifies the common law and the current lay of the land:

[T]he legislation shifts the burden of any harm caused by refusal onto specific patients and the general public by immunizing refusing institutions and individuals from civil and criminal liability or professional discipline. Patients harmed by refusal have no recourse to courts or state medical boards. Under all but a few conscience clauses, patients may be refused care even in emergencies. For example . . . delaying an abortion procedure for a woman who is miscarrying—as Catholic hospitals often require—may contravene the standard of care; yet, under conscience legislation, the patient's injuries—from, for example, going septic—go unremedied. In recent years, legislatures across the United States have expanded the reach of conscience laws substantially. More procedures have been specified as appropriate subjects of conscientious objection. Several states have moved from abortion to sterilization to contraception. The broadest legislation—in Mississippi, Illinois, and Washington—permits conscientious objections to any medical treatment at all. In these states, Jehovah's Witnesses could refuse to transfuse patients. A vegan could withhold vaccines that contain egg proteins on the ground that the use of animal products is morally wrong. Under some statutes, healthcare providers may withhold information, refuse to refer for treatment, and deny patients care distant from the contested procedure. With the country's broadest conscience legislation, Mississippi permits refusal to participate in "patient referral, counseling, therapy, testing, diagnosis or prognosis" for any medical procedure. . . A clinic could withhold information about HIV testing. A doctor could fail to tell a patient about the terminal nature of his cancer in order to ensure aggressive treatment, instead of hospice care. Under such broad conscience laws, these actions could generate no tort liability, professional discipline, or adverse employment action. Finally, a growing number of individuals and entities can claim rights to accommodation. In addition to direct providers like doctors and nurses, the new generation of conscience legislation covers pharmacists, medical secretaries, orderlies, billing clerks, and the like. The category of entities covered has also widened from hospitals to other healthcare facilities and even to insurance companies.

Elizabeth Sepper, Conscientious Refusals of Care, in The Oxford Handbook of U.S. Healthcare Law (I. Glenn Cohen, Allison K. Hoffman, William M. Sage eds. 2015).

For further discussion of these issues, see Alta Charo, The Celestial Fire of Conscience—Refusing to Deliver Medical Care, 352 New Eng. J. Med. 2471 (2005); Farr A. Curlin et al., Religion, Conscience, and Controversial Clinical Practices, 356 New Eng. J. Med. 593 (2007); Kent Greenawalt, Refusals of Conscience, What Are They and When Should They Be Accommodated, 9 Ave Maria L. Rev. 47 (2010); David Orentlicher, Law, Religion, and Health Care, 8 UC Irvine L. Rev. (2018). Joanna K. Sax, Access to Prescription Drugs: A Normative Economic Approach to Pharmacist Conscience Clause Legislation, 63 Me. L. Rev. 89 (2010); Martha S. Swartz, "Conscience Clauses" or "Unconscionable Clauses," 6 Yale J. Health Pol'y L. & Ethics 269 (2006); Lynn D. Wardle, Protection of Health-Care Providers' Rights of Conscience in American Law, 9 Ave Maria L. Rev. 1 (2010); Pamela H. Del Negro and Stephen W. Aronson, Religious Accommodations for Employees in the Health Care Workplace, 8 J. Health & Life Sci. L. 72 (2015).

As discussed in Chapter 5 of this text, issues about conscientious objection also arise when patients request that life-sustaining treatment be withdrawn, and may arise in other circumstances as well. For a thorough analysis of different contexts and legal implications, see Anne Dellinger & Anne Vickery, When Staff Object to Participating in Care, 28 J. Health & Hosp. L. 269 (1995). The impact of religious freedom claims on access to contraceptives is also discussed in Chapter 7.

3. Terminating the Treatment Relationship

■ RICKS v. BUDGE
64 P.2d 208 (Utah 1937)

HANSON, Justice.

This is an action for malpractice against the defendants who are physicians and surgeons at Logan, Utah, and are copartners doing business under the name and style of the "Budge Clinic." . . . [P]laintiff alleges that he was suffering from an infected right hand and was in immediate need of medical and surgical care and treatment, and there was danger of his dying unless he received such treatment; that defendants for the purpose of treating plaintiff sent him to the Budge Memorial Hospital at Logan, Utah; that while at the hospital and while he was in need of medical and surgical treatment, defendants refused to treat or care for plaintiff and abandoned his case. . . .

The evidence shows that on or about March 8, 1935, plaintiff caught the middle finger of his right hand on a barbed wire. Soon thereafter the finger and hand began to swell and became reddened. In the early morning of March 11th, plaintiff went to the Budge Memorial Hospital to seek treatment from the defendants. Dr. S. M. Budge . . . made two lateral incisions in the finger, waited a few hours to see the result, and then later the same morning deepened the incisions in order to reach the pus, which he believed had developed. . . .

The plaintiff remained in the hospital from March 11th until March 15th, during which time he was under the care of Dr. S. M. Budge. . . . On the morning of March 15th, plaintiff told the nurse and Dr. Budge that he intended leaving the hospital that morning. Dr. Budge advised plaintiff against leaving, but notwithstanding the protests of Dr. Budge, plaintiff left the hospital after paying the amount that was due at that time. . . .

[T]he evidence shows that when plaintiff left the hospital on March 15th, Dr. Budge advised him to continue the same treatment that had been given him at the hospital, and that if the finger showed any signs of getting worse at any time, plaintiff was to return at once to Dr. Budge for further treatment; that on the morning of March 17th, plaintiff telephoned Dr. Budge, and explained the condition of his hand; that he was told by the doctor to come to his office. . . . Dr. Budge again examined the hand[,] told plaintiff the hand was worse and . . . said to plaintiff: "You have got to go back to the hospital." . . . Plaintiff left immediately for the hospital. . . . Within a short time after the arrival of plaintiff, Dr. [Budge] arrived at the hospital. Plaintiff testified: "He [meaning Dr. S. M. Budge] came into my room and said, 'You are owing us. I am not going to touch you until that account is taken care of.'" (The account referred to was, according to plaintiff, of some years' standing and did not relate to any charge for services being then rendered.) Plaintiff testified that he did not know what to say to the doctor, but that he finally asked the doctor if he was going to take care of him, and the doctor replied: "No, I am not going to take care of you. I would not take you to the operating table and operate on you and keep you here 30 days, and then there is another $30.00 at the office, until your account is taken care of." Plaintiff replied: "If that is the idea, if you will furnish me a little help, I will try to move."

Plaintiff testified that this help was furnished, and that after being dressed, he left the Budge Memorial Hospital to seek other treatment. . . . He walked to the Cache Valley Hospital, a few blocks away, and there met Dr. Randall, who examined the hand. Dr. Randall testified that when the plaintiff arrived at the Cache Valley Hospital, the hand was swollen with considerable fluid oozing from it; that the lower two-thirds of the forearm was red and swollen from the infection which extended up in the arm, . . . and that plaintiff required immediate surgical attention. . . . Plaintiff remained under the care of Dr. Randall for approximately a month. About two weeks after the plaintiff entered the Cache Valley Hospital, it became necessary to amputate the middle finger and remove about an inch of the metacarpal bone.

Dr. S. M. Budge testified that at the time he sent the plaintiff to the Budge Memorial Hospital on March 17th, plaintiff was in a dangerous condition and needed immediate surgical and medical attention; that the reason for sending him to that hospital was in order to give him the necessary immediate surgical and medical attention. . . . There can be no question from the evidence that it was the intention of Dr. S. M. Budge to operate at once on plaintiff's hand.

Defendants contend: (1) That there was no contract of employment between plaintiff and defendants and that defendants in the absence of a valid contract were not obligated to proceed with any treatment. . . . We cannot agree. . . . The evidence shows that plaintiff had been under the care and treatment of the defendants at the Budge Memorial Hospital from March 11th to March 15th; that when he left that hospital on March 15th, Dr. S. M. Budge said to him: "If you are going home, you had better follow out the treatment at home just as near as you can the same as you were doing here. Here is another thing I want to tell you, if you see any signs of that finger getting worse at any time, you come in and see me immediately." On March 17th, plaintiff, realizing that his condition was getting worse, telephoned Dr. S. M. Budge and was told by that doctor to come to the doctor's office, which plaintiff did; that there both Dr. S. M. Budge and Dr. D. C. Budge examined the hand; that Dr. D. C. Budge indicated on it where it should be opened; and that under the instructions of these doctors, plaintiff was returned to the hospital for no other purpose than having his hand operated upon at once.

Under this evidence, it cannot be said that the relation of physician and patient did not exist on March 17th. It had not been terminated after its commencement on March 11th. When the plaintiff left the hospital on March 15th, he understood that he was to report to Dr. S. M. Budge if the occasion required and was so requested by the doctor. Plaintiff's return to the doctor's office was on the advice of the doctor. While at the doctor's office, both Dr. S. M. Budge and Dr. D. C. Budge examined plaintiff's hand and they ordered that he go at once to the hospital for further medical attention. That plaintiff was told by the doctor to come to the doctor's office and was there examined by him and directed to go to the hospital for further treatment would create the relationship of physician and patient. That the relationship existed at the time the plaintiff was sent to the hospital on March 17th cannot be seriously questioned.

We believe the law is well settled that a physician or surgeon, upon undertaking an operation or other case, is under the duty, in the absence of an agreement limiting the service, of continuing his attention, after the first operation or first treatment, so long as the case requires attention. The obligation of continuing attention can be terminated only by the cessation of the necessity which gave rise to the relationship, or by the discharge of the physician by the patient, or by the withdrawal from the case by the physician after giving the patient reasonable notice so as to enable the patient to secure other medical attention. A physician has the right to withdraw from a case, but if the case is such as to still require further medical or surgical attention, he must, before withdrawing from the case, give the patient sufficient notice so the patient can procure other medical attention if he desires. . . .

[The court remanded the case for consideration of whether Mr. Ricks suffered any physical and mental suffering by virtue of having to go to Cache Valley Hospital for care. The outcome on remand was not reported.]

■ PAYTON v. WEAVER
182 Cal. Rptr. 225 (Cal. Ct. App. 1982)

GRODIN, Judge.

Occasionally a case will challenge the ability of the law, and society, to cope effectively and sensitively with fundamental problems of human existence. This is such a case. Appellant, Brenda Payton, is a 35-year-old black woman who suffers from a permanent and irreversible loss of kidney function, a condition known as chronic end stage renal disease. To stay alive, she must subject herself two or three times a week to hemodialysis (dialysis), a process in which the patient's circulatory system is connected to a machine through which the blood is passed . . . [and] artificial kidneys . . . drain the blood of excess liquids and accumulated impurities. Without such treatment, . . . liquid will begin to fill the lungs, making breathing difficult and possibly leading to heart failure. The resulting toxic waste buildup and chemical imbalances can also threaten the function of the heart and other organs.

Brenda has other difficulties. Unable to care for her children, she lives alone in a low-income housing project in West Oakland, subsisting on a $356 per month Social Security check. She has no family support; one brother is in prison and another is a mental patient. She confesses that she is a drug addict, having been addicted to heroin and barbiturates for over 15 years. She has alcohol problems, weight problems and, not surprisingly, emotional problems as well.

Despite these difficulties, Brenda appears from the record to be a marvelously sympathetic and articulate individual who in her lucid moments possesses a great sense of dignity and is intent upon preserving her independence and her integrity as a human being. At times, however, her behavior is such as to make extremely difficult the provision of medical care which she so desperately requires.

The other principal figure in this case is respondent John C. Weaver, Jr., a physician specializing in kidney problems. He conducts his practice through respondent Biomedical Application of Oakland, Inc. (BMA), which operates an outpatient dialysis treatment unit on the premises of respondent Providence Hospital.

Dr. Weaver began treating Brenda in 1975 when, after the birth of Brenda's twin daughters, her system rejected a transplanted kidney. . . . On December 12, 1978, Dr. Weaver sent Brenda a letter stating he would no longer permit her to be treated at BMA because of her "persistent uncooperative and antisocial behavior over . . . more than . . . three years . . . her persistent refusal to adhere to reasonable constraints of hemodialysis, the dietary schedules and medical prescriptions . . . the use of barbiturates and other illicit drugs and because all this resulted in disruption of our program at BMA."

In the latter part of 1978, Brenda applied for admission to the regular dialysis treatment programs operated by respondents Alta Bates and Herrick Hospitals, and was refused.

For several months, Dr. Weaver continued to provide Brenda with necessary dialysis on an emergency basis, through Providence. On April 23, 1979, he again notified her by letter that he would no longer treat her on an outpatient basis. This letter led to Brenda's filing of a petition for mandate to compel Dr. Weaver, BMA, and Providence to continue to provide her with outpatient dialysis services. That litigation was settled by a stipulated order which called for continued treatment provided Brenda met certain conditions: that she keep all appointments at their scheduled time; that she refrain from use of alcohol and drugs; that she maintain prescribed dietary habits; and that she "in all respects cooperate with those providing her care and abide by her physician's prescribed medical regimen." Later, a sixth stipulation was added: that Brenda would "enter into and participate in good faith in a program of regular psychotherapy and/or counselling."

Dr. Weaver and BMA continued treatment of Brenda as an outpatient pursuant to the stipulation, but on March 3, 1980, Dr. Weaver, contending that Brenda had failed to fulfill any part of the bargain, again notified her that treatment would be terminated. He provided her with a list of dialysis providers in San Francisco and the East Bay, and volunteered to work with her counsel to find alternative care.

Brenda then instituted a second proceeding, . . , this time naming Herrick and Alta Bates Hospitals as respondents, along with Dr. Weaver, BMA and Providence. . . .

The trial court, after a lengthy evidentiary hearing, found that Brenda had violated each and every condition which she had accepted as part of the stipulated order providing for continued treatment, and that finding is basically undisputed. There was evidence that Brenda continued [to abuse alcohol and drugs, not adhere to dietary restrictions or her counseling program, miss numerous dialysis appointments thereby triggering 30 emergencies requiring hospitalization in the 11 months preceding trial, and in general display] "gross non-cooperation with her treating physician, BMA of Oakland and Providence Hospital." The trial court found that her behavior in these respects was "knowing and intentional."

Brenda's behavior was found to affect not only Dr. Weaver but the other patients and the treating staff as well. Dialysis treatment is typically provided to several patients at a time, all of them connected to a single dialysis machine. There was evidence that Brenda would frequently appear for treatment late or at unscheduled times in a drugged or alcoholic condition, that she used profane and vulgar language, and that she had on occasion engaged in disruptive behavior, such as bothering other patients, cursing staff members with obscenities, screaming and demanding that the dialysis be turned off and that she be disconnected before her treatment was finished, pulling the dialysis needle from the connecting shunt in her leg causing blood to spew, and exposing her genitals in a lewd manner. . . .

DISCUSSION

We begin our analysis by considering the trial court's conclusion that Dr. Weaver and the clinic with which he is associated have no present legal obligation to continue providing Brenda with dialysis treatment. . . . Brenda relies upon the general proposition that a physician who abandons a patient may do so "only . . . after due notice, and an ample opportunity afforded to secure the presence of other medical attendance." Lathrope v. Flood, 63 P. 1007, 1008 (1901). The trial court found, however, that Dr. Weaver gave sufficient notice to Brenda, and discharged all his obligations in that regard, and that finding, also, is amply supported. Dr. Weaver supplied Brenda with a list of the names and telephone numbers of all dialysis providers in San Francisco and the East Bay, and it is apparent from the record that nothing would have pleased him more than to find an alternative facility for her, but there is no evidence that there is anything further he could have done to achieve that goal under the circumstances.

During the proceedings, the trial court observed that Dr. Weaver "is one of the most sensitive and honest physicians that I have been exposed to either in a courtroom or out of a courtroom," that he was "in fact sensitive to [Brenda's] needs, that he has attempted to assist her to the best of his medical abilities, that he continues to have concern for her as a person and has continued to serve her medical needs," and that "[the] man has the patience of Job." It appears that Dr. Weaver has behaved according to the highest standards of the medical profession, and that there exists no basis in law or in equity to saddle him with a continuing sole obligation for Brenda's welfare. The same is true of the clinic, the BMA.

We turn now to Brenda's contention that Herrick and Alta Bates Hospitals violated their obligations under Health and Safety Code §1317 [to provide emergency care] by denying her admission to their regular outpatient dialysis programs in late 1978. The trial court found that at the time Brenda applied for admission to these programs she was not in an "emergency condition," by which the court obviously meant that she was in no imminent physical danger on the day she applied. Brenda contends, however, that her illness is itself "a chronic/acute emergency which requires that she receive medical treatment every third day to avoid death," and that such a condition qualifies for mandated service under §1317. . . .

. . . While end stage renal disease is an extremely serious and dangerous disease, which can create imminent danger of loss of life if not properly treated, the need for continuous treatment as such cannot reasonably be said to fall within the scope of §1317. There are any number of diseases or conditions which could be fatal to the patient if not treated on a continuing basis. If a patient suffering from such a disease or condition were to appear in the emergency room of a hospital in need of immediate life-saving treatment, §1317 would presumably require that such treatment be provided. But it is unlikely that the legislature intended to impose upon whatever health care facility such a patient chooses the unqualified obligation to provide continuing preventive care for the patient's lifetime.

It does not necessarily follow that a hospital, or other health care facility, is without obligation to patients in need of continuing medical services for their survival. While it has been said that "[a] private hospital owes the public no duty to accept any patient not desired by it, and it is not necessary to assign any reason for its refusal to accept a patient for hospital service" (41 C.J.S. Hospitals, §8, p.345), it is questionable whether a hospital which receives public funding under the Hill-Burton Act (42 U.S.C. §291), and perhaps from other sources, can reasonably be said to be "private" in that sense. Rather, where such a hospital contains a unique, or scarce, medical resource needed to preserve life, it is arguably in the nature of a "public service enterprise," and should not be permitted to withhold its services arbitrarily, or without reasonable cause. And, while disruptive conduct on the part of a patient may constitute good cause for an individual hospital to refuse continued treatment, since it would be unfair to impose serious inconvenience upon a hospital simply because such a patient selected it, it may be that there exists a *collective* responsibility on the part of the providers of scarce health resources in a community, enforceable through equity, to *share* the burden of difficult patients over time, through an appropriately devised contingency plan.

This argument was not presented to the trial court, however, and the record is not adequate to support relief on that ground as a matter of law. . . . Whatever collective responsibility may exist, it is clearly not absolute, or independent of the patient's own responsibility.

Notes: Abandonment Liability

1. *The* Payton *Case.* After the court decided the *Payton* case, dialysis providers in the area did arrange to share the responsibility for treating Ms. Payton. The court's suggestion of a public service obligation is mentioned at the end of its opinion. For additional discussion, see Stella Smetanka, Who Will Protect the "Disruptive" Dialysis Patient?, 32 Am. J.L. & Med. 53 (2006).

How might Ms. Payton have challenged Dr. Weaver's decision to discontinue care under the Americans with Disabilities Act? See David Orentlicher, Denying

Treatment to the Noncompliant Patient, 265 JAMA 1579 (1991). Is it so clear that noncompliance is a legitimate basis for a physician to stop treating a patient? Why might a patient not follow the physician's recommendations? If noncompliance is an accepted justification for terminating the patient-physician relationship, what implications does that have for the patient's right to refuse medical treatment?

What do you think about the fact that the court decided to mention the plaintiff's race? Is her race relevant to a full assessment of the case? For a critical view of the court's discussion of Ms. Payton and Dr. Weaver, see Lois Shepherd & Margaret Mohrmann, Welcome, Healing, and Ethics, 50 Wake Forest L. Rev. 259 (2015).

For a discussion of termination of care on grounds of conscience, see John K. Davis, Conscientious Refusal and a Doctor's Right to Quit, 29 J. Med. Philos. 75 (2004) (arguing that a physician can terminate care only if "the doctor's refusal does not make the patient worse off than she would have been had she gone to another doctor in the first place").

2. *Ricks v. Budge.* What are the critical factors that resulted in the courts coming to different conclusions in *Ricks* and *Payton* as to the physician's liability? Was it fair to hold the Drs. Budge responsible for Mr. Ricks's difficulties when he originally left the hospital against their advice? Why not conclude that the patient-physician relationship ended when Mr. Ricks left the hospital and that the Drs. Budge refused to renew the relationship when they found that Mr. Ricks had an unpaid bill?

3. *Abandonment Liability.* Once a patient-physician relationship is formed, it is implicit that the relationship continues as long as the patient needs treatment for the condition that brought the patient to the physician. Once the need is satisfied, the relationship ends. The professional relationship can also be ended explicitly if the patient unilaterally chooses to dispense with the physician's services or if both parties agree to the termination of the relationship. Finally, as the *Payton* case demonstrates, physicians can terminate the patient-physician relationship as long as they give notice to the patient such that the patient has sufficient opportunity to secure care from another physician. Failure to adhere to the required notice can result in abandonment liability if the patient is injured as a result.

Strictly speaking, abandonment liability results from purposefully ceasing treatment for primarily nonmedical reasons, not from mistakenly ceasing treatment due to medical error. In other words, it is more akin to breach of contract than to medical malpractice. Nevertheless, courts and lawyers often confuse the two theories when patients are injured by failure to treat. See generally Comment, The Action of Abandonment in Medical Malpractice Litigation, 36 Tulane L. Rev. 834 (1962); Annot., Liability of Physician Who Abandons Care, 57 A.L.R.2d 432 (1958).

4. *Lack of Payment.* As the *Ricks* case indicates, failure of a patient to pay does not permit the physician to discontinue care before satisfying the usual requirements for terminating the patient-physician relationship. This principle contrasts with the physician's freedom to take a patient's ability to pay into account when deciding whether to commence a professional relationship. As one court observed in a case in which a physician treated a patient for a miscarriage but suspended his care before the end of her need for treatment,

> Whether the patient be a pauper or a millionaire, whether he be treated gratuitously or for reward, the physician owes him precisely the same measure of duty, and the same degree of skill and care. He may decline to respond to the call of a patient

> unable to compensate him; but if he undertakes the treatment of such a patient, he cannot defeat a suit for malpractice, nor mitigate a recovery against him, upon the principle that the skill and care required of a physician are proportioned to his expectation of pecuniary recompense.

Becker v. Janinski, 15 N.Y.S. 675, 677 (Civ. Ct. 1891). For further discussion of the effects of cost containment on the standard of care, see pages 310-317.

While a physician may not simply discontinue care because of nonpayment, nonpayment is an acceptable basis for a physician to terminate the patient-physician relationship so long as the termination is accomplished properly. See, e.g., Surgical Consultants, P.C. v. Ball, 447 N.W.2d 676, 682 (Iowa App. 1989) (terminating care for nonpayment is permissible because there is no "evidence that the physician has terminated the relationship at a critical stage of the patient's treatment [or] that the termination was done without reason or sufficient notice to enable the patient to procure another physician"). The critical issue is whether proper termination entails only notice or also requires that the patient actually secure another physician. The usual practice is for physicians to find a substitute and arrange the transfer themselves if, for instance, they are retiring from practice or going on vacation. This avoids any question of liability. There is little legal guidance where another willing physician cannot be located but a patient who cannot pay still receives ample notice. What does *Payton* suggest as the answer? See Mark A. Hall, A Theory of Economic Informed Consent, 31 Ga. L. Rev. 511, 527-533 (1997); Mark A. Hall & Carl E. Schneider, When Patients Say No (to Save Money): An Essay on the Tectonics of Health Law, 41 Conn. L. Rev. 743 (2009).

3

The Treatment Relationship: Confidentiality, Consent, and Conflicts of Interest

A. THE FIDUCIARY NATURE OF THE TREATMENT RELATIONSHIP

The interactions between healers and those hoping to be healed are complex. Science, sociology, and psychology all provide important perspectives on the rich character of these important relationships. As noted in Chapter 1.A.2 and the Somers & Somers excerpt at page 8, the experience of illness may include anxiety and physical distress that, combined with the patient's relative lack of knowledge, create a substantial power imbalance between the patient and her caregiver. Moreover, many aspects of the treatment relationship involve sensitive personal matters, ranging from one's weight to one's sexual history and mental health needs. This chapter initially explores the implications of these special vulnerabilities for the laws governing confidentiality of medical information, informed consent, and conflicts of interest. The final section of the chapter explores the implications of this power imbalance for the rules governing research on human subjects, where risks to participants may eventually result in advances in treatment.

Traditional contract and tort norms have been radically altered in many of these areas through the interventions of courts, legislatures, and administrative agencies. Courts have found protections for patients in the implied or expressed belief that the treatment relationship is a fiduciary one, in which physicians in particular, but perhaps some other providers as well, owe heightened duties to protect the vulnerable patient's interests. This chapter explores the extent to which physicians have fiduciary obligations to their patients as well as the implications of those obligations. The chapter also examines when and how special protections for patients have been extended—often by legislation or regulation—beyond the physician-patient relationship to other health care providers and institutional actors.

Fiduciary law is not usually a topic of thorough study in the law school curriculum and it is worth considering its key elements before turning to legislative, regulatory, and judicial approaches to protecting patients' interests. As a common law doctrine, fiduciary law can be thought of as a separate source of distinct legal duties or as a legal status that heightens or alters ordinary contract and tort law duties. Fiduciary principles impose a special measure of loyalty and devotion on several classes of professionals (lawyers, trustees, and general agents) by virtue of their control over an important subject matter, the vulnerability of their clients and the resulting potential for abuse. The materials in Chapter 1.A.2 explain why some courts have found that "the relationship of patients and physicians is a fiduciary one of the highest degree. It involves every element of trust, confidence and good faith."[1] Doctors have a complex body of knowledge and skills that are critical to preserving the life and restoring the health of their patients. Doctors control their patients' welfare in the most vital aspects imaginable. Sick patients, by virtue of their debilitated and vulnerable state, are dependent on their physicians' judgments and actions. Accurate diagnosis requires patients to reveal the most personal details of their lives, and effective treatment often entails invasion of the most essential aspects of bodily intimacy, invading the very blood and guts of our integrated sense of self. Thus many legal decisions and commentators have recognized doctors' fiduciary status.[2] For a sampling of the literature, see Robert Gatter, Faith, Confidence, and Health Care: Fostering Trust in Medicine Through Law, 39 Wake Forest L. Rev. 395, 396 (2004); Thomas L. Hafemeister & Sarah P. Bryan, Beware Those Bearing Gifts: Physicians' Fiduciary Duty to Avoid Pharmaceutical Marketing, 57 U. Kan. L. Rev. 491 (2009); Mark A. Hall, Law, Medicine, and Trust, 55 Stan. L. Rev. 463 (2002); Dayna Bowen Matthew, Implementing American Health Care Reform: The Fiduciary Imperative, 59 Buff. L. Rev. 715 (2011); Maxwell J. Mehlman, Why Physicians Are Fiduciaries for Their Patients, 12 Ind. Health L.J. 1 (2015); and Marc A. Rodwin, Medicine, Money & Morals: Physicians' Conflicts of Interest (1993).

Classifying physicians as fiduciaries might appear to be a simple matter; it is much more difficult, however, to say precisely what obligations result. Fiduciary law is far from a seamless web. There is no integrated body of principles or precise doctrine that applies uniformly to all forms of fiduciary relationships.[3] Nonetheless,

---

1. Lockett v. Goodill, 430 P.2d 589, 591 (Wash. 1967).

2. Some authorities, however, distinguish confidential relations from fiduciary relations and declare that physicians are subject only to the former. See, e.g., Restatement (Third) of Trusts §2 *cmt b(1)* (2003); 1 Austin W. Scott & William F. Fratcher, The Law of Trusts §2.5, at 43 (4th ed. 1987). The primary thrust of the distinction, however, is one of burden of proof, not scope of obligation. The law does not assume that a position of trust exists in a confidential relation as quickly as it does in a fiduciary one, but where such trust exists, the duties are essentially the same.

3. See L. S. Sealy, Fiduciary Relationships, 1962 Cambridge L.J. 69, 73 (observing that labelling a relationship fiduciary "does not warrant the inference that any particular fiduciary principle or remedy can be applied"). For other works that address fiduciary principles at this more general level, see Paul D. Finn, Fiduciary Obligations 15-76 (1977); Tamar Frankel,

there are basic principles of fiduciary obligation that share a broad, familial resemblance across many categories of relationships. One of the common themes is a modification of the ordinary rules of contract. In a classic contractual relationship, neither party has a duty to maintain the secrecy of information provided by the other party, nor a duty to disclose information to the other about the qualities of the product or service sold or the particular needs of the purchaser. *Caveat emptor*, let the buyer beware, is the most common rule associated with classic contract law. Parties to the contract can impose additional obligations on each other only by bargaining for specific contract terms.

As noted in Chapter 2, courts have modified the ordinary contract regime by limiting the ability to alter or waive the basic standard of care or by limiting the ability to terminate the relationship. This chapter explains that courts have modified these pure contract principles to provide additional special protections for patients. Courts have used ordinary tort law as well as fiduciary law to achieve these protections, holding, for example, that physicians can be sued for damages if they fail to maintain patient confidences or to disclose important information about any proposed treatment. State and federal regulators also have responded to the special characteristics of the treatment relationship and the concomitant special duties of health care providers by enacting a wide range of statutes and regulations designed to protect patient confidentiality and to control conflicts of interest.

As you read the following materials, consider how well courts and legislatures have responded to the unique attributes and requirements of the doctor-patient relationship. Are the protections sufficient? Are they excessive or dysfunctional? Should federal or state law be used to address these concerns? When and how should similar obligations be imposed on other types of health care providers? Should similar rules be applied to facilities and institutions such as hospitals and HMOs?

B. CONFIDENTIALITY OF MEDICAL INFORMATION

Both patients and health care providers have long believed that the health care relationship creates a special duty on the part of the provider to protect the patient's interests. One example is the duty to protect the confidentiality of patient information, which was thought necessary to encourage patients to seek treatment and to disclose personal information fully and truthfully. The common belief that there was such a duty obscured a significant number of important legal questions. What is the source of the obligation? On whom is the duty imposed? What are the limits of the duty? What remedies are available for breaches of confidentiality? Does the system of legal protections effectively balance patient rights, provider duties, and social interests? Historically state courts and legislatures attempted to protect patients' interests in medical privacy by imposing duties to maintain confidentiality on individual health care providers, primarily physicians. There has been a sea change in the last 15 years, as the federal government has flooded the health care

Fiduciary Law, 71 Cal. L. Rev. 795, 808-816 (1983); Tamar Frankel, Fiduciary Duties as Default Rules, 74 Or. L. Rev. 1209 (1995); Philosophical Foundations of Fiduciary Law (Andrew S. Gold and Paul B. Miller eds. 2014); Marc Rodwin, Medicine, Money & Morals 179-211 (1993); Symposium, The Role of Fiduciary Law and Trust in the Twenty-First Century: A Conference Inspired by the Work of Tamar Frankel, 91 Boston U. L. Rev. 833-1299 (2011).

system with detailed regulations designed to protect patients' interests in controlling disclosure and use of their medical information. Yet federal regulations—even of the intense sort that will begin this chapter—have not totally displaced the importance of state laws, which in many cases still provide the best avenue for aggrieved patients to challenge breaches of confidentiality.

1. The Federal Duty to Maintain Medical Privacy: Federal Privacy Regulations (HIPAA)

The confidentiality of health information was protected in varying ways by a patchwork of state common law and regulatory approaches for many decades. Critics and patients' rights advocates contended that the framework was seriously deficient because protections varied from place to place and because the narrow focus on physician obligations left vast swaths of the health care system without effective constraints on the disclosure of medical information. At the same time as the complexity and range of participants in the health care system were expanding, technological advances were moving health care records from often illegible paper notes and files found in a single physician's office to comprehensive electronic health records (EHRs) stored in databases that could be accessed by many individuals and institutional participants in health care.

The Health Insurance Portability and Accountability Act of 1996 (HIPAA) was concerned mainly with improving how health insurance is designed and sold, see Chapter 9.A—but it also included a set of provisions facilitating the electronic processing of insurance claims and other types of medical information. In order to ensure that greater use of electronic health information would not compromise privacy, the HIPAA statute also required the Secretary of Health and Human Services to issue rules improving privacy protections. The key privacy regulations, which were first issued in 2006 and substantially revised in 2013, are found at 45 C.F.R. §160 et seq.

In general, the federal privacy regulations (the "Privacy Rule") require certain "covered entities" to maintain the confidentiality of defined types of "protected health information" (PHI). Covered entities include health insurers, claims-processing clearinghouses, and health care providers. 45 C.F.R. §160.102(a). These entities must (1) adopt internal procedures to protect the privacy of protected health information; (2) train employees regarding privacy procedures; (3) designate a privacy officer; (4) secure patient records that contain protected information; and (5) establish and enforce agreements with certain third parties (called "business associates") that ensure that they maintain privacy protection for information they have access to. The HITECH Act of 2009 expanded the reach of the Act by imposing many of the Privacy Rule's requirements to business associates. 45 C.F.R. §160.102(b). A "business associate" is "a person [defined to include various organizations and businesses] who" is not an employee of a covered entity but "creates, receives, maintains, or transmits protected health information for a function or activity . . . including claims processing or administration . . . or . . . provides" services such as legal, accounting, or management services. 45 C.F.R. §160.103. The current version of the rule makes clear that a "subcontractor that creates, receives, maintains, or transmits protected health information on behalf of the business associate" also qualifies as a business associate. Id.

The definition of "health information" is comprehensive. The term means:

> any information, including genetic information, whether oral or recorded in any form or medium, that
>> (1) Is created or received by a health care provider . . . [or a broad range of other entities]; and
>> (2) Relates to the past, present, or future physical or mental health or condition of an individual; the provision of health care to an individual; or the past, present, or future payment for the provision of health care to an individual.

45 C.F.R. §160.103. The Privacy Rule focuses on the protection of a particular subset of health information, called "protected health information," defined as "individually identifiable health information" held or transmitted in electronic media or "transmitted or maintained in any other form or medium." Id. (noting specific exceptions).

The central requirements for using or disclosing PHI are found in a single section, 45 C.F.R. §164.502, but this provision links to and incorporates definitions, standards, and exceptions found in more than 25 other sections or subsections in the Privacy Rule. The Rule thus has gained a reputation for complexity; handbooks, seminars, and training sessions have sprung up to help those working with health care information to master the technical details. A broad summary of the disclosure aspects of the Rule is nonetheless possible.

The standard for the use and disclosure of PHI by covered entities establishes a strict baseline rule of confidentiality, essentially prohibiting *any* use or disclosure of patient medical information, unless a specific regulatory exception applies. The standard provides seven general avenues for disclosure:

1. PHI can be disclosed to the individual or the individual's personal representative (with special rules if there are concerns about abuse or neglect).
2. The information can be used for "treatment, payment, or health care operations" with the patient's general consent (called "TPO" in the increasingly common HIPAA lingo of health lawyers and consultants).
3. The information can be disclosed where the entity receives a more specific "valid authorization," typically via a written and signed document, the nature of which may vary depending on whether the general authorization rule or special rules governing psychotherapy notes, marketing, or sale of PHI apply.
4. A specified subset of PHI can be disclosed without written authorization in certain defined situations after giving the patient an opportunity to object. For example, basic information about an individual's identity and condition can be added to the hospital directory and made available to callers based on an oral agreement after the individual has been given an opportunity to object and can even be provided in emergency circumstances when the individual is unable to communicate approval or disapproval if this would be consistent with any known patient preferences and in the best interests of the patient.
5. An individual's PHI can be disclosed without his or her authorization or agreement in roughly a dozen categories of special circumstances, e.g., where the disclosure is required by law.

6. A "limited data set" that excludes most identifying information can be disclosed for use in public health, research, and operations. Limited types of PHI may also be disclosed in carefully circumscribed circumstances for institutional fundraising and by health plans involved in underwriting decisions.

7. Covered entities are also permitted to disclose PHI "incident to use[s] or disclosures otherwise permitted or required" so long as the covered entity has followed the standards governing the minimum necessary disclosure of information and has put in place proper administrative, physical, and technical safeguards.

45 C.F.R. §164.502. The complex regulatory framework addresses a host of other issues, ranging from the rules governing the creation of de-identified health information that can be used without consent, to the use of health information in research, to the responsibility of the covered entities to ensure that business associates comply with privacy requirements.

Any use or transfer of medical information that does not comply with these detailed rules violates the law, even if completely inadvertent and resulting in no actual harm to the patient, but many such technical violations went unpunished. Thus, enforcement of the Privacy Rule initially appeared lax to some critics, until passage of the HITECH Act in 2009 required the imposition of penalties for all violations. The new regulations issued under the HITECH Act provide that DHHS "will impose a civil money penalty upon a covered entity or business associate" for violations. 45 C.F.R. §160.402(a). The civil penalties begin at a minimum of $100 for inadvertent breaches but rise to a minimum of $50,000 for offenses committed with a higher level of culpability. 45 C.F.R. §160.404. The Rule establishes factors for the Secretary to consider in setting the penalty between the established minimums and maximums. These civil penalty provisions create significant financial exposure for covered entities, even at the lowest dollar level. For example, continuing violations generate a separate violation each day, 45 C.F.R. 160.406. The risk is lessened somewhat by a cap of $1,500,000 placed on the total penalty for identical violations in a calendar year.

Knowing violations of the privacy rules that involve using unique health identifiers or obtaining or disclosing identifiable health information can result in fines and imprisonment. 42 U.S.C. §1320d-6. Notably, the most severe penalties (fines up to $250,000 and ten years imprisonment) are reserved for persons who commit the offense with the "intent to sell, transfer or use individually identifiable health information for commercial advantage, personal gain, or malicious harm . . . ." Id.

The Privacy Rule does not explicitly create a private cause of action or remedy and courts have been unwilling to find an implied right of action for individuals harmed by disclosures. Acara v. Banks, 470 F.3d 569 (5th Cir. 2006); Bonney v. Stephens Memorial Hospital, 17 A.3d 123 (Me. 2011); Espinoza v. Gold Cross Services, 234 P.3d 156 (Utah 2010).

The Privacy Rule includes important preemption rules that ultimately reinforce the role of states in establishing and enforcing strict privacy protections. First, HIPAA preemption applies only to state laws that provide weaker protections of privacy; states remain free to adopt and to enforce more protective regimes. 45 C.F.R. §160.201-.205. Second, the Privacy Rule provides that in cases involving civil penalties, the federal penalty "is in addition to any other penalty prescribed by law," 45 C.F.R. §160.418. Plaintiffs are therefore free to pursue whatever damage claims might otherwise be available under state law. This is particularly important given that the federal Privacy Rule does not provide a direct cause of action for individuals injured by improper disclosures. Courts have begun to wrestle with the potential impact of the Privacy Rule on a wide range of state provisions and practices.

■ IN THE MATTER OF MIGUEL M. v. BARRON
950 N.E.2d 107 (N.Y. 2011)

SMITH, J.

We hold that the Privacy Rule adopted by the federal government pursuant to the Health Insurance Portability and Accountability Act (HIPAA) prohibits the disclosure of a patient's medical records to a state agency that requests them for use in a proceeding to compel the patient to accept mental health treatment, where the patient has neither authorized the disclosure nor received notice of the agency's request for the records. . . .

Dr. Charles Barron, as designee of the New York City Department of Health and Mental Hygiene, applied for an order under Mental Hygiene Law §9.60 requiring "assisted outpatient treatment" (AOT) for Miguel M. The petition alleged that Miguel was suffering from a mental illness; that he was unlikely to survive safely in the community without supervision; that he had a history of failing to comply with treatment; that he was unlikely to participate in necessary treatment voluntarily; and that he needed, and would benefit from, AOT to prevent a relapse or deterioration of his mental status, which would be likely to result in serious harm to Miguel or to others.

At the hearing on the petition, Barron offered in evidence records from two hospitals relating to three occasions on which Miguel was hospitalized. A witness called by Barron testified that the hospitals had furnished the records in response to a request—a request made, it is clear from the record, without notice to Miguel. The witness acknowledged that Miguel had not authorized the release of the records, and that no court order for their disclosure had been sought or obtained.

The records were received in evidence over Miguel's objection and Barron's witness described their contents. After the hearing, [the] Supreme Court directed that Miguel "receive and accept assisted outpatient treatment" for a period of six months. The Appellate Division affirmed. We granted leave to appeal, and now reverse. . . .

Mental Hygiene Law §9.60, known as "Kendra's Law," was enacted in 1999. It is named for Kendra Webdale, who was killed by a mentally ill man who pushed her off a subway platform. It says that, on a proper showing, a mentally ill person whose lack of compliance with treatment has, twice within the last 36 months, caused him or her to be hospitalized may be the subject of AOT pursuant to a plan stated in a court order. Public officials identified as "directors of community services" are given the duty of enforcing Kendra's Law, and a petition to require AOT may be filed by a director of community services or his or her designee. [The] Mental Hygiene Law permits disclosure of medical records to a director of community services who requests it in the exercise of his or her duties. Thus, the disclosure of a patient's medical records for purposes of an AOT proceeding is permitted by state law, unless the applicable state law is preempted. Miguel argues that it is.

Miguel says that preemption is found in HIPAA and the Privacy Rule. The Privacy Rule prohibits disclosure of an identifiable patient's health information without the patient's authorization, subject to certain exceptions (45 CFR 164.508[a] [1]). HIPAA . . . and the Privacy Rule say that contrary state laws are preempted unless they offer privacy protections that are "more stringent" than those of the federal law; New York does not offer any more stringent protection that is relevant here. The preemption issue thus comes down to whether the disclosure of Miguel's medical records was permitted by one of the exceptions to the Privacy Rule.

Barron relies on two exceptions, those permitting disclosure for purposes of "public health" and "treatment." It is possible to read the language of both exceptions as covering the disclosure now at issue, but in both cases the reading is strained. Considering the apparent purposes of these two exceptions, we conclude that neither fits these facts.

The public health exception permits disclosure of protected information to:

> [a] public health authority that is authorized by law to collect or receive such information for the purpose of preventing or controlling disease, injury, or disability, including, but not limited to, the reporting of disease, injury, vital events such as birth or death, and the conduct of public health surveillance, public health investigations, and public health interventions.

Barron reasons that disclosure of a mentally ill person's hospital records for purposes of requiring that person to accept AOT protects the public health, because mentally ill people might kill or injure other people — like Kendra Webdale — who, of course, are members of the public. Thus Barron, a person designated to enforce Kendra's Law, would be a "public health authority," collecting information for the "purpose of preventing . . . injury," and his action to require AOT in Miguel's case could be called a public health intervention. We are not convinced, however, that the authors of the Privacy Rule meant "public health" in this literal, but counterintuitive, sense.

The apparent purpose of the public health exception is to facilitate government activities that protect large numbers of people from epidemics, environmental hazards, and the like, or that advance public health by accumulating valuable statistical information. To disclose private information about particular people, for the purpose of preventing those people from harming themselves or others, effects a very substantial invasion of privacy without the sort of generalized public benefit that would come from, for example, tracing the course of an infectious disease. The disclosure to Barron of Miguel's hospital records was not within the scope of the public health exception.

The treatment exception permits disclosure of protected health information "for treatment activities of a health care provider." "Treatment" is defined as:

> the provision, coordination, or management of health care and related services by one or more health care providers, including the coordination or management of health care by a health care provider with a third party; consultation between health care providers relating to a patient; or the referral of a patient for health care from one health care provider to another.

Again, Barron's argument is literalistic: AOT — assisted outpatient treatment — is literally "treatment" — "the provision . . . of health care . . . by one or more health care providers." But the thrust of the treatment exception is to facilitate the sharing of information among health care providers working together. We see no indication that the authors of the regulation meant to facilitate "treatment" administered by a volunteer "provider" over the patient's objection. Disclosure for that purpose is a more serious invasion of privacy than, for example, the transmission of medical records from a patient's primary care physician to a specialist—the sort of activity for which the treatment exception seems primarily designed. The treatment exception is inapplicable here.

We find support for our conclusion that the two exceptions Barron relies on are inapposite in the existence of other exceptions that Barron might have invoked but did not. The Privacy Rule authorizes disclosure of health information, subject to certain conditions, "in the course of any judicial or administrative proceeding," in response to either "an order of a court or administrative tribunal" or "a subpoena, discovery request, or other lawful process" (45 CFR 164.512[e]). Thus, Barron could have pursued Miguel's records either by seeking a court order or by serving a subpoena. To do so in compliance with the Privacy Rule, however, Barron would have had to give notice to Miguel of his request for the records. He could not, absent extraordinary circumstances, have obtained a court order requiring disclosure without giving such notice. And the Privacy Rule's exception for subpoenas and the like is conditioned on "satisfactory assurance" from the person seeking the information to the entity providing it either "that reasonable efforts have been made . . . to ensure that the individual who is the subject of the protected health information . . . has been given notice of the request," or that an order protecting the confidentiality of the information has been sought. In a case, like this one, to which the patient is a party, a request for a protective order would require notice to the patient.

We can see no reason, and Barron has suggested none, why notice should not have been given here. It may well be, in this case as in many others, that no valid ground for withholding the records exists; courts ruling on disclosure issues will surely be conscious, as we are, of the strong public interest in seeing that mentally ill people who might otherwise be dangerous receive necessary treatment. But it seems only fair, and no great burden on the public agencies charged with enforcing Kendra's Law, to give patients a chance to object before the records are delivered.

We emphasize that it is far from our purpose to make the enforcement of Kendra's Law difficult. It may often be possible to avoid all disclosure problems by getting the patient to authorize the disclosure in advance; surely many mentally ill people will, while they are under proper care, recognize that disclosure is very much in their own interest. When there is no advance authorization, patients who are given notice that their records are being sought often may not object; when they do object, their objections may often be overruled. We hold only that unauthorized disclosure without notice is, under circumstances like those present here, inconsistent with the Privacy Rule. . . .

Barron argues in the alternative that, even if the disclosure of the records to him was unlawful—as we have held it was—the Supreme Court did not err by admitting the records into evidence at the AOT hearing. HIPAA, as Barron points out, contains its own remedies for violations: civil penalties and, for the knowing and wrongful disclosure of individually identifiable health information, fines and imprisonment. Neither exclusion of the records from evidence nor suppression of evidence obtained by use of the records is among the remedies listed. Barron cites decisions from other states holding that evidence obtained as a result of a HIPAA violation need not be suppressed in a criminal case. . . .

We assume it is correct that, in a criminal case, a HIPAA or Privacy Rule violation does not always require the suppression of evidence. . . . But this case is different. It is one thing to allow the use of evidence resulting from an improper disclosure of information in medical records to prove that a patient has committed a crime; it is another to use the records themselves, or their contents, in a proceeding to subject to unwanted medical treatment a patient who is not accused of any wrongdoing. Using the records in that way directly impairs, without adequate justification, the interest protected by HIPAA and the Privacy Rule: the interest in keeping one's own medical condition private. We therefore hold that medical records obtained in violation of HIPAA or the Privacy Rule, and the information contained in those records, are not admissible in a proceeding to compel AOT.

Accordingly, the order of the Appellate Division should be reversed, with costs, and the case remitted to Supreme Court for further proceedings in accordance with this opinion.

Notes: HIPAA Privacy Protections

1. *Preempting Patient Access?* Should the preemption analysis of *Miguel M.* turn on who is seeking the records? In Marabello ex rel Marabello v. State of New York, 964 N.Y.S.2d 863 (N.Y. Ct. Cl. 2013), a New York claims court case read *Miguel M.* narrowly as applying to patients seeking to shield disclosure of health records to *third parties* without notice. The *Marabello* court denied plaintiff's request to access incident reports and other records related to his stay in a group home operated by New York State. Plaintiff argued that a state education law, which allowed institutions not to disclose health information collected solely for internal quality assurance purposes, was preempted by the HIPAA Privacy Rule. Id, at 239. The court disagreed, holding that although under *Miguel M.,* HIPAA preempted state law as to disclosure of health information to third parties, it did not similarly preempt state law as to patient access, particularly when the information was not relevant to making medical decisions concerning the patient.

2. *Challenges to HIPAA.* Efforts to challenge HIPAA on constitutional or statutory grounds have failed. In South Carolina Med. Assn. v. Thompson, 327 F.3d 346 (4th Cir. 2003), the court rejected the plaintiffs' claims that the HIPAA regulations constituted an unconstitutionally vague and improper, standardless delegation of legislative authority. See also Citizens for Health v. Leavitt, Secretary U.S. Department Health and Human Services, 428 F.3d 167 (3d Cir. 2005). For a summary of litigation under HIPAA, see Annot., 194 A.L.R. Fed. 133 (2004).

3. *The Special Nature of Medical Information and EHRs.* The HIPAA privacy standard and related provisions regulating the security of electronic health records (EHRs) represent a very significant investment of public and private resources into the privacy of health care information. The Privacy Rule protects a broad range of information created and held by individual health care providers, practice groups, hospitals, HMOs, and other entities. HIPAA compliance efforts undoubtedly impose hundreds of millions of dollars in costs across the health care system. In theory, our willingness to bear these costs is based on the special character of medical information as distinct from other types of personal information and the nature of the health care provider-patient relationship. See, e.g., Mark A. Rothstein, The

Hippocratic Bargain and Health Information Technology, 38 J.L. Med. & Ethics 7 (2010). Do the costs of the HIPAA privacy regime seem commensurate with the benefits privacy generates for individuals? Are broader social goals served by the Privacy Rule? Are the notice and authorization provisions of HIPAA effective mechanisms for protecting privacy and autonomy or do they merely result in a meaningless flurry of additional paperwork? For a critique, see Fred H. Cate, Protecting Privacy in Health Research: The Limits of Individual Choice, 98 Cal. L. Rev. 1766 (2010).

The Privacy Rule is focused on "covered entities" and "business associates." Some non-health care providers have attempted to establish Web-based medical records databases, arguing that HIPAA rules do not apply to the arrangements. Perhaps to address consumer concerns about privacy, Microsoft named its product "Microsoft Vault." Should these databases be covered by the Privacy Rule? Eric S. Pasternack, HIPAA in the Age of Electronic Health Records, 41 Rutgers L.J. 817 (2010) (suggesting amendment of HIPAA to address electronic medical records companies).

4. *Big Data and Patient Privacy*. To what extent can individuals' personal medical data be used to improve medical care for all patients in keeping with ethical privacy standards? To what extent *should* it be used? HIPAA and the HITECH Act were designed to increase the use of EHRs as a method of reducing costs and improving efficiency and quality of health care, explicitly providing incentive payments to hospitals that effectively utilized EHRs to streamline their care delivery processes. See David Blumenthal & Marilyn Tavenner, The "Meaningful Use" Regulation for Electronic Health Records, 363 New Eng. J. Med. 501 (2010). The power of the data collected through EHRs exceeds the ability to provide more effective care for each specific patient. With the use of predictive analytics, hospitals with access to thousands of patients' medical records will be able to ascertain the probable risk, at any given moment, of harm for any potential patient. This capability would allow hospitals to allocate their resources more equitably and precisely when making rapid, life-or-death decisions.

The privacy concerns that could accompany this broader use of individuals' data, however, are large, and the current HIPAA Privacy Rule may not be well equipped to protect against them. HIPAA's regulations are geared toward protecting data from use and theft by entities outside of the health sphere and include specific provisions designed to protect the security of electronic health records from such threats. 45 C.F.R. §§164.302-.318. Fears of improper use are legitimate given the frequency of breaches, whether intentional, see Doe v. Walgreens, 2010 WL 4823212 (Tenn. Ct. App.) (Walgreens employee wrongfully accessed Walgreens database and shared co-worker's HIV status with others), or merely negligent, see Milt Freudenheim, Breaches Lead to Push to Protect Medical Data, N.Y. Times, May 30, 2011.

In contrast, reliance on big data and predictive analytics will increase the likelihood that patients' data will be purposefully disseminated within the medical community, against which HIPAA would not guard. There are measures hospitals can take to "launder" the data, that is strip it of most identifying information, but laundering the data too carefully may come at the price of reducing its usefulness. How comfortable are we risking the privacy of individuals' personal medical information in exchange for better care across the board? For a discussion of HIPAA's shortcomings with respect to intra-hospital data privacy, see Nicolas P. Terry, Big Data Proxies and Health Privacy Exceptionalism, 24 Health Matrix 65 (2014). See also I. Glenn

Cohen, et. al., The Legal and Ethical Concerns that Arise from Using Complex Predictive Analytics in Health Care, 33 Health Affairs 1139 (2014) (suggesting additional safeguards, such as establishing a third party to verify when data is sufficiently unlikely to risk re-identification and notifying patients prior to treatment that their data may be used but not necessarily requiring explicit consent).

5. *Genetic Information.* Advances in genetics may create additional privacy concerns. Scientists are increasingly able to link human genes with the risk of developing various human maladies. Individuals have a definite interest in maintaining the confidentiality of their genetic predisposition for a variety of ills. At the same time, other affected family members, insurers, and others have an interest in gaining access to this information. Lawrence O. Gostin & James G. Hodge, Jr., Genetic Privacy and the Law: An End to Genetics Exceptionalism, 40 Jurimetrics J. 21 (1999); Mark A. Hall, Legal Rules and Industry Norms: The Impact of Laws Restricting Health Insurers' Use of Genetic Information, 40 Jurimetrics J. 93 (1999). Indeed, researchers have shown that it is possible to re-identify some anonymized genetic samples through using publicly available databases. Melissa Gymrek et al., Identifying Personal Genomes by Surname Inference, 339 Science 321, 321 (2013). The federal Genetic Information Nondiscrimination Act of 2008 (GINA), Pub. L. 110-233, 122 Stat. 881, established special rules protecting the confidentiality of genetic information and restricting the use of this information by insurers and employers. See Jessica L. Roberts, Preempting Discrimination: Lessons from the Genetic Information Nondiscrimination Act, 63 Vand. L. Rev. 439 (2010). In the first case of its kind, two employees were awarded $2.2 million when their employer asked them to undergo a cheek swab and DNA test, in violation of GINA, to determine if they were the employees who had habitually defecated in the warehouse (earning the memorable moniker of "the case of the devious defecator"). Lowe v. Atlas Logistics Grp. Retail Servs. (Atlanta), LLC, 102 F. Supp. 3d 1360 (N.D. Ga. 2015); Daniel Weissner, Georgia Workers Win $2.2 million in "Devious Defecator" Case, Reuters, June 23, 2015. The HIPAA Privacy Rule includes certain types of genetic information, including information about family members, in the definition of health information subject to the Rule's protections. 45 C.F.R. §160.103.

6. *The (Limited) Right of Individuals to Control Medical Records.* HIPAA establishes a large reservoir of PHI presumptively under the control of an individual but also establishes significant escape valves through which the flow of PHI is controlled by others. The Rule permitting use of PHI for treatment purposes is a major example: Under this provision no separate patient consent is required. The presumption of confidentiality is reduced in some circumstances where common practices and likely preferences of patients would create a default rule of disclosure. 45 C.F.R. §§164.502(a)(1)(v); 164.510. As noted above, this provision eases disclosure of PHI in hospital directories; it also facilitates disclosure to family members and friends involved in the patient's care and to disaster relief organizations. The Rule also establishes that disclosures can be made without any authorization or opportunity to agree or object in any one of a dozen important categories of circumstances. As noted above, this provision establishes that PHI can be disclosed where required by law. Other permitted disclosures include: disclosures for public health activities (a broad category including specific examples such as disease surveillance, notification of exposure to contagious diseases, or FDA-related reports of adverse events); disclosures about victims of abuse, neglect, or domestic violence; disclosures for judicial and administrative proceedings; and disclosures for research or law enforcement

purposes, among others. See 45 C.F.R. §164.512. See also U.S. v. Wilk, 572 F.3d 1229 (11th Cir. 2009) (law enforcement and judicial proceedings exception).

Given HIPAA's protective purposes, the court in *Miguel* took a narrow approach to interpreting the scope of HIPAA's exceptions. Does the court's analysis seem persuasive? What will be the impact of the court's ruling on New York's ability to carry out the purposes of Kendra's Law? The court suggests that patients could be asked to pre-authorize release of their medical records. Would this approach cure the harm to an individual's right to control disclosure, given that the records were going to be used to mandate treatment over the patient's current objections? The Privacy Rule allows covered entities to rely on an authorization unless it is known to have been revoked; revocations must be written. 45 C.F.R. §164.508.

7. *Patients' Rights and Medical Records.* Medical records have traditionally been deemed the property of the health care provider who creates them, though patients and others may have access to the information within them. EHRs and the collection and transmission of electronic databases of information have created new challenges and opportunities, including questions about who owns the information contained in a record, as distinct from the physical medium in which the information is stored. See, e.g., Mark A. Hall, Property, Privacy, and the Pursuit of Interconnected Electronic Medical Records, 95 Iowa L. Rev. 631 (2010) (arguing that patients should be given right to monetize access and control rights over medical records); Marc A. Rodwin, Patient Data: Property, Privacy & the Public Interest, 36 Am. J.L. & Med. 586 (2010); Frank Pasquale, Grand Bargains for Big Data: The Emerging Law of Health Information, 72 Md. L. Rev. 682 (2013). Cf. Sorrell v. IMS Health, 564 U.S. 552 (2011) (discussing economic value of data on physicians' prescription practices; striking down on First Amendment grounds a state ban on sale of information). The HITECH Act gives patients the right to restrict sale of their PHI. 42 U.S.C. §17935(d); 45 C.F.R. §164.508(a)(4) (authorization required).

The Privacy Rule establishes that patients must be given access to most types of their own PHI, with some exceptions, including psychotherapy notes. 45 C.F.R. §164.524. The Rule establishes timelines and procedures for access, including whether or not the denial of access will be considered to be reviewable and the procedures for review. For example, a correctional facility's denial of access on safety grounds would be unreviewable. Also unreviewable would be a denial of an individual's access to "protected health information created or obtained . . . in the course of research that includes treatment" during the research, "provided that the individual . . . agreed to the denial of access" during the consent process for the research. Id. Among other things, this rule protects the integrity of double-blind clinical trials, see section D. Reviewable grounds for denial of access include concerns that "access . . . is reasonably likely to endanger the life or physical safety of the individual or another person." Id. Reviews generally are conducted by licensed health professionals who were not part of the original access decision.

The Privacy Rule also gives individuals a right to amend PHI held within a particular record set. 45 C.F.R. §164.526. Covered entities can deny a request to amend where, for example, the entity believes the PHI "[i]s accurate and complete." The individual retains the right to submit a written statement disagreeing with the denial; the individual's statement must thereafter be transmitted with the disputed PHI along with any rebuttal from the entity. Where the entity accepts the amendment, the Rule creates a process for communicating the correction to persons or entities identified by the individual.

The Privacy Rule gives patients information about different types of disclosures of their PHI. The concept of disclosing disclosures is called "accounting." 45 C.F.R. §164.528. There are numerous exclusions from the accounting duty. One major exclusion involves disclosures made for treatment, payment, and health care operations. Id. Section 13405(c) of the HITECH Act expanded accounting to include treatment-related disclosures through an EHR. Covered entities argued that the expanded accounting provisions might be unduly onerous, but the more stringent revisions to the Privacy Rule were successfully finalized in January 2013. See 78 Fed. Reg. 5599–5600 (Jan. 25, 2013). The HITECH Act strengthened protections for patients by requiring notification of data breaches. 42 U.S.C. §17932. "Breach" means the "acquisition, access, use or disclosure of" PHI not otherwise permitted under the Privacy Rule "which compromises the security or privacy of" the PHI. 45 C.F.R. §164.402. Certain inadvertent disclosures within the health care environment are excluded. Id. Outside of these exclusions, covered entities or business associates must disclose breaches unless they can "demonstrate [] that there is a low probability that the protected health information has been compromised based on a risk assessment." Id. The risk assessment must consider: "[t]he nature and extent of the . . . [PHI] involved including the types of identifiers and the likelihood of re-identification"; "[t]he unauthorized person who used the . . . [PHI] or to whom the disclosure was made"; "[w]hether the . . . [PHI] was actually acquired or viewed"; and "[t]he extent to which the risk to the . . . [PHI] has been mitigated." Id. Covered entities must notify the individuals and the Secretary of HHS about breaches; "prominent media outlets" must be notified about breaches "involving more than 500 residents." 45 C.F.R. §§164.404-.408; see also §164.410 (notification by business associates).

Notwithstanding the legal protections for patient access to their own records, many patients find securing such access difficult. Elizabeth Rosenthal recounted such an episode in the New York Times: "Many readers were shocked by my recent article about Peter Drier, who received a surprise bill of $117,000 from an out-of-network assistant surgeon who helped out during his back operation. But almost as surprising was how difficult it was during my reporting for Mr. Drier to extract his own records from the hospital." Elizabeth Rosenthal, Medical Records: Top Secret, N.Y. Times Nov. 8, 2014, SR5. As Rosenthal wrote, "Hospitals are computerized, and patients have a right to their own records, so I assumed getting the chart would be easy. I was wrong. The six-week ordeal included requests that needed to be made via regular mail, numerous phone calls, consent forms and an estimate for copying fees that totaled $100. This was topped off by an actual visit to the hospital by Mr. Drier, who sat in an office until he had paper documents in hand."

8. *The Standards for Business Associates.* Covered entities are permitted to disclose PHI to "business associates" after "obtain[ing] satisfactory assurance that the business associate will appropriately safeguard the information." 45 C.F.R. §164.502(e)(1). Business associates perform a range of functions from claims management to quality assurance. 45 C.F.R. §160.103 ("business associate"). Critics argued that permitting disclosure of PHI to business associates created a significant risk, as those entities were not directly subject to regulation under HIPAA. The HITECH Act tightened the rules governing business associates by, among other things, directly imposing both security and privacy standards and civil and criminal penalties for violations. 42 U.S.C. §17934; 45 C.F.R. §164.502(a)(3), (4). Disclosures by business

associates remain a significant issue. See Kevin Sack, Medical Data of Thousands Posted Online, N.Y. Times, Sept. 9, 2011.

9. *The Intersection of HIPAA with Other Laws Governing Disclosure.* HIPAA interacts with a wide range of federal and state legislation, such as rules governing financial records, public records laws, and state discovery rules. See, e.g., Holman v. Rasak, 785 N.W.2d 98 (Mich. 2010) (HIPAA does not preempt state discovery rules permitting ex parte discovery from plaintiff's treating physician where "reasonable efforts have been made . . . to secure a protective order that meets" HIPAA requirements); State ex rel. Proctor v. Messina, 320 S.W.3d 145 (Mo. 2010) (en banc) (trial court lacked authority to issue order authorizing ex parte communications under HIPAA); Abbott v. Texas Department of Mental Health and Mental Retardation, 212 S.W.3d 648 (Tex. App. 2006) (HIPAA does not preempt state Public Information Act); State ex rel. Cincinnati Enquirer v. Daniels, 844 N.E.2d 1181 (Ohio 2006) (lead-risk-assessment reports did not count as PHI, and even if they did, the public records law requiring disclosure of lead-risk-assessment reports was permissible under the "required by law" exception to the HIPAA privacy rule); see also Thomas v. 1156729 Inc., 979 F.Supp. 2d 780, 783 (2013) (while HIPAA preempted the state's law regarding ex parte discovery from plaintiff's physician, HIPAA itself "neither prohibits nor permits" ex parte interviews, and therefore granting ex parte discovery subject to a qualified protective order was not inconsistent with HIPAA). That said, even within a jurisdiction, the preemption determination often turns on particularities of the case. Cuyahoga County Board of Health v. Lipson O'Shea Legal Group, 50 N.E.3d 499 (Ohio 2016) distinguishing *Daniels* and holding that the requested "documentation or information of all homes . . . in Cuyahoga County where a minor child was found to have elevated blood levels in excess of 10 [mg/dl]" could qualify as PHI, unlike the information requested in *Daniels*, because the address information could be used to identify specific individuals based on their physical status or condition); see also Brown v. Mortensen, 253 P.3d 522 (Cal. 2011) (analyzing interaction between HIPAA, the federal Fair Credit Act, and state law in claim involving alleged unlawful disclosure of medical records by debt collector). At least one author has proposed that the HIPAA Privacy Rule prohibits "pharmacies from selling de-identified prescription information to data miners for use by drug manufacturers to market their brand-name drugs." Beverly Cohen, Regulating Data Mining Post-Sorrell: Using HIPAA to Restrict Marketing Uses of Patients' Private Medical Information, 47 Wake Forest L. Rev. 1141 (2012).

10. *The Enforcement Record.* The Privacy Rule is enforced by DHHS's Office of Civil Rights (OCR). The incentives created by the HITECH Act appear to have spurred enforcement, with thousands of complaints investigated and resolved each year. In its first use of the civil monetary damages provisions of the HITECH Act, the OCR imposed a $4.3 million civil penalty against Cignet Health in Maryland based on Cignet's refusal to provide 41 patients with access to their medical records and Cignet's failure to cooperate with the OCR investigation. The OCR secured a $1 million settlement from the Massachusetts General Hospital, one of the nation's most prestigious institutions, based on the breach of privacy arising from an employee leaving records of 192 infectious-disease clinic patients on a subway train. And more recently, the OCR made clear that it would also be bringing enforcement actions against both covered business associates and their parent companies. In 2016, HHS imposed fines of $400,000 and $650,000, respectively, against Care New

England (for actions taken by its business associate) and the Catholic Health Care Services (CHCS) of the Archdiocese of Pennsylvania (itself a business associate of Catholic Clinical Consultants). The settlement with CHCS marked the OCR's first direct settlement with a business associate. In both cases, OCR implemented a corrective action plan in addition to the fine, involving HHS monitoring of the covered associate for an indefinite period. For more on these enforcement actions, see www. hhs.gov/hipaa/newsroom/.

Notes: Beyond HIPAA—Constitutional, Common Law, and Statutory Duties to Maintain Confidentiality

1. *Overview.* Long before HIPAA, state courts and legislatures grappled with whether and how information arising from the treatment relationship would be protected from disclosure. The Privacy Rule does not displace other laws that are more protective of privacy. Moreover, the absence of a private cause of action in HIPAA means that patients injured by disclosures must look primarily to other sources of law to secure compensation. It is therefore important to (1) understand the scope and implications of the federal Privacy Rule; (2) determine whether other federal and state privacy protections are available; and (3) carefully consider the scope of the privacy protections, the persons or entities subject to duties, the limits of the duties, and the available remedies. There are three major sources of duties to maintain the confidentiality of medical information outside the Privacy Rule: federal and state constitutions, statutes, and the common law.

2. *A Constitutional Right of Confidentiality.* The issue of patient confidentiality is of special importance to state and federal health care providers or agencies. Several courts have found that individuals have a constitutionally protected interest in maintaining the privacy of their medical information. See, e.g., Alfred v. Corrections Corp. of America, 437 Fed. Appx. 281 (5th Cir. 2011) (overturning dismissal of prisoner's claim of potential constitutional violation arising from disclosure of his HIV status to another prisoner); Doe v. City of New York, 15 F.3d 264 (2d Cir. 1994) (individuals have a constitutional right of privacy in their medical information; court employs a balancing test to determine whether the government entity's interest in disclosure is "substantial" enough to outweigh the individual's privacy interest). This "informational privacy" interest has its roots in the Supreme Court's decision in Whalen v. Roe, 429 U.S. 589 (1977). In that case, the Court upheld a state program that created a centralized data bank with the names of all persons in the state who had been prescribed certain controlled substances. In dicta, however, the Court noted that the state might have some constitutional obligation to maintain the confidentiality of the information it collected. Constitutional aspects of the obligation to maintain confidentiality will be addressed in more detail in Chapter 8, at pages 950-955.

3. *The Doctrinal Basis for a Common-Law Duty to Maintain Confidentiality.* Most states provide a private cause of action against licensed health care providers who impermissibly disclose confidential information obtained in the course of the treatment relationship to third parties. See Annot., 48 A.L.R.4th 668 (1986). Generally, a physician-patient relationship must be formed before the duty to maintain confidences arises. See Howes v. United States, 887 F.2d 729 (6th Cir. 1989) (psychologist and psychiatrist not liable for disclosing information about husband's drug and

alcohol use that had been provided by nonpatient wife). Depending on the jurisdiction, the claim may be phrased as a breach of contract, as an act of malpractice, as a breach of fiduciary duty, as an act of fraud/misrepresentation, or as a breach of a specific civil statute permitting the award of damages. See Biddle v. Warren General Hospital, 715 N.E.2d 518 (Ohio 1999) (finding breach of confidentiality to be an independent tort); Givens v. Mullikin ex rel. Estate of McElwaney, 75 S.W.3d 383 (Tenn. 2002) (implied covenant of confidentiality found in contract for treatment.) The duty to maintain confidentiality generally includes the obligation to have in place policies and procedures designed to reduce the risk of accidental or intentional disclosures. Compare Behringer v. The Medical Center at Princeton, 592 A.2d 1251 (N.J. Super. Ct. Law Div. 1991) (hospital liable for failing to have in place policies to protect the confidentiality of the HIV status of a patient-surgeon), with Rosen v. Montgomery Surgical Center, 825 So. 2d 735 (Ala. 2001) (court rejects invasion of privacy claim based on actions of non-physician employee of hospital) and Doe v. Guthrie Clinic Ltd., 5 N.E.3d 578 (N.Y. 2014) (clinic liability for disclosure limited to reasonably foreseeable acts within scope of employment).

In addition, licensed health care providers who breach the confidentiality of their patients run the risk of professional disciplinary action. See, e.g., Salerian v. Maryland State Board of Physicians, 932 A.2d 1225 (Md. App. 2007) (finding unprofessional conduct where forensic psychiatrist engaged by defense in espionage case disclosed information to subject's wife and media). State privacy rules may also be applied outside the treatment relationship. See Washburn v. Rite Aid Corp., 695 A.2d 495 (R.I. 1997).

The doctrinal basis of the common-law claim can be important to prospective plaintiffs. If the claim arises in contract, plaintiffs will have the benefit of the (generally longer) contract statute of limitations. Plaintiffs alleging breaches of contract will also avoid some of the procedural barriers to malpractice suits established as part of tort reform efforts in many states. See, e.g., Pierce v. Caday, 422 S.E.2d 371 (Va. 1992) (breach of confidentiality claim is subject to notice requirements imposed by malpractice reform statutes). See also Chapter 4.H. A few courts have considered whether breach of confidentiality claims should be subject to the ordinary negligence statute of limitations or the special statute of limitations imposed for malpractice claims. See, e.g., Tighe v. Ginsberg, 540 N.Y.S.2d 99 (App. Div. 1989) (disclosure of medical records is a breach of fiduciary duty subject to the longer negligence statute of limitations). Finally, plaintiffs in contract suits need prove only that the physician failed to honor the degree of confidentiality that was promised. They need not find and present expert medical testimony on the question of whether the health care provider defendant violated the applicable standard of care. Cf. Berger v. Sonneland, 26 P.3d 257 (Wash. 2001) (expert medical testimony required in malpractice claim). Plaintiffs have begun to use the HIPAA Privacy Rule as the source of the standard of care in common-law claims for damages. Compare Byrne v. Avery Center for Obstetrics & Gynecology, PC, 314 Conn. 433 (2014) (HIPAA standards may inform the standard of care) with Sheldon v. Kettering Health Network, 40 N.E.3d 661 (Ohio Ct. App. 2015) (violation of HIPAA standards does not constitute negligence per se). See also Sharona Hoffman & Andy Podgurski, E-Health Hazards: Provider Liability and Electronic Health Record Systems, 24 Berkeley Tech. L.J. 1523, 1558-1560 (2009).

4. *Statutory Protection.* HIPAA is not the only federal statute protecting the confidentiality of information. The federal Privacy Act of 1974 governs the use of

information by federal agencies. See, e.g., FAA v. Cooper, 132 S. Ct. 1441 (2012) (interagency exchange of information relating to an individual's HIV status may have violated Act but sovereign immunity applied to bar claims for emotional or mental distress damages). Many states have passed statutes governing the confidentiality of information provided in the health care provider-patient relationship. Some of these state statutes were enacted to build upon the federal Privacy Rule. See Symposium, 2 Yale J. Health Pol'y L. & Ethics 325 (2002). Other state provisions protect certain types of health information. See, e.g., Annot., 12 A.L.R.5th 149 (1993). Do state rules providing additional protection for certain types of health care information, such as information regarding HIV status, represent good public policy?

5. *Confidentiality as a Rule of Evidence.* The confidentiality of patient-physician communications is often also protected under rules of evidence. This evidentiary "privilege" prohibits the discovery of protected information. State rules of evidence almost always provide for a physician-patient privilege. The rule may be invoked by the physician on behalf of the patient or by the patient, but only the patient generally has the power to waive the privilege. See 81 Am. Jur. 2d Witnesses §§444, 452. The privilege may be limited to communications with physicians. In Buchanan v. Mayfield, 925 S.W.2d 135 (Tex. App. 1996), for example, the court held that the statutory privilege accorded to "confidential communications between a physician and a patient" did not apply to the communications between a dentist and a patient.

The Federal Rules of Evidence do not include a physician-patient privilege, see Charles Alan Wright & Kenneth W. Graham, Jr., 25 Fed. Prac. & Proc. Evid. §5521 (RR 504) (discussing the rejection of a physician-patient privilege under the Federal Rules of Evidence); Ralph Ruebner & Leslie Ann Reis, Hippocrates to HIPAA: A Foundation for a Federal Physician-Patient Privilege, 77 Temp. L. Rev. 505 (2004). The Supreme Court recognized a "psychotherapist-patient" privilege under Rule 501 of the Federal Rules of Evidence in Jaffee v. Redmond, 116 S. Ct. 1923 (1996). Justice Stevens, writing for the majority, found that the privilege was "rooted in the imperative need for confidence and trust" and that it served important public and private interests. The majority applied the privilege to shield communications between a police officer and her social worker therapist, who provided counseling after the police officer shot an allegedly innocent person. Justice Scalia's dissent focused on the injustice created by the application of the privilege, including the loss of evidence of possible wrongdoing. There is no dangerous-patient exception to the federal psychotherapist-patient testimonial privilege even though the psychotherapist may have the statutory discretion to disclose confidential information about the patient to prevent harm to a third party or to the patient. U.S. v. Chase, 340 F.3d 978 (9th Cir. 2003).

Is the privilege necessary? Will people seek care from physicians or therapists without its protection? Empirical evidence suggests that perhaps they will. See Daniel W. Shuman, The Origins of the Physician-Patient Privilege and Professional Secret, 39 Sw. L.J. 661, 664-665 (1985) (noting the empirical evidence does not fully support utilitarian proponents of a privilege).

6. *Waiver and Other Exceptions.* The duty to maintain confidentiality is not ordinarily absolute under either common law or statute. Where the duty is derived from medical ethics and practice, for example, it will be limited by policies that permit disclosure for the protection of third parties. Statutes protecting the confidentiality

of patient information often contain a general rule of confidentiality and then list situations under which that confidentiality can be breached. The "exceptions" to the duty to maintain confidentiality can be quite broad. Generally, patient information *may* be revealed when the patient consents, or when disclosure is necessary to protect the health and safety of either the patient or third parties. In some circumstances, health care providers may even have a *duty* to breach confidentiality imposed by common law or statute. This issue is discussed in more detail at pages 134-152.

Whether or not a patient has waived his or her right to confidentiality is a significant issue in litigation. See Annot., 21 A.L.R.3d 912 (1968); compare Reda v. Advocate Health Care, 765 N.E.2d 1002 (Ill. 2002) (plaintiff in neurological injury action had not placed mental condition at issue and had not waived privilege with respect to his mental health records) with Deprizio v. Memorial Hospital Association, 12 N.E.3d 782, 790 (Ill. App. Ct. 2014) (plaintiff waived his privilege to confidentiality when he brought an action for pain and suffering and presented evidence referring to his mental health status, including direct references to documents and mental health services). Should asserting one's fitness to be a parent in a child custody dispute constitute a waiver of the psychiatrist-patient privilege? See Laznovsky v. Laznovsky, 745 A.2d 1054 (Md. 2000) (no); Culbertson v. Culbertson, 455 S.W.3d 107, 131-135 (Ct. App. Tenn. 2014) (surveying jurisdictions). See also Annot., 50 A.L.R.4th 714 (1986).

Should a patient be able to gain access to the identity of other patients? Rogers v. New York University Hospitals Cntr., 795 N.Y.S.2d 438 (N.Y. Sup. 2005) (identity of fellow patient can be released without violating HIPAA privacy); Baptist Memorial Hospital-Union County v. Johnson, 754 So. 2d 1165 (Miss. 2000) (hospital must disclose identity of patient who mistakenly breast-fed another patient's baby); Falco v. Institute of Living, 757 A.2d 571 (Conn. 2000) (psychiatrist-patient privilege prevented disclosure of identity of patient who attacked plaintiff in psychiatric hospital). See also Annot., 66 A.L.R.5th 591 (1999).

7. *Adherence to Confidentiality.* Despite the legal rules, studies regularly demonstrate that patient confidentiality is often breached. See, e.g., Elizabeth A. Kitsis, Shining a Light on Shadowing, 305 JAMA 1029 (2011) (shadowing of physicians by university students and patient privacy); Rebecca Shore et al., Report of the AMA Council on Ethical and Judicial Affairs: Professionalism in the Use of Social Media, 22 J. Clin. Ethics 165 (2011) (noting breaches of patient confidentiality); John C. Moskop, From Hippocrates to HIPAA: Privacy and Confidentiality in Emergency Medicine, 45 Ann. Emerg. Med. 60 (2005); P. A. Ubel et al., Elevator Talk: Observational Study of Inappropriate Comments in a Public Space, 99 Am. J. Med. 190 (1995). What explains the gulf between legal standards and medical practice in this area?

2. The Duty to Breach Confidentiality

The duty to maintain confidentiality exists in an uneasy equilibrium with a potentially conflicting duty to breach confidentiality in some circumstances. Recall that the federal Privacy Rule permits some disclosures without patient authorization or opportunity to agree or object. Covered entities:

1. "[M]ay use or disclose protected health information to the extent that such use of disclosure is required by law";
2. "[M]ay disclose . . . [PHI] for . . . public health activities and purposes . . . to" public health authorities for, e.g., disease surveillance activities, prevention of child abuse or neglect, or drug safety monitoring;
3. May disclose PHI to "[a] person who may have been exposed to a communicable disease or may otherwise be at risk of contracting or spreading a disease or condition, if the covered entity or public health authority is authorized by law to notify such person as necessary in the conduct of a public health intervention or investigation"; and
4. [M]ay, consistent with applicable law and standards of ethical conduct, use or disclose protected health information, if the covered entity, in good faith, believes that the use or disclosure: [] [i]s necessary to prevent or lessen a serious and imminent threat to the health or safety of a person or the public; and [] [is] to a person or persons reasonably able to prevent or lessen the threat, including the target of the threat. . . .

45 C.F.R. §164.512 (a), (b), (c), (j).

Health care providers sometimes have not only a common-law or statutory *authority* to breach confidentiality; they also have the *duty* to do so. Failure to meet this obligation can lead to criminal or civil liability. As you read the following materials, consider the perspective of health care providers. Are the rules governing confidentiality and disclosure in hopeless conflict, subjecting health care providers to "Catch-22" liability? Consider also the perspective of patients. Are the limits of confidentiality clear for patients? Is the protection afforded patient-provider communication sufficient to encourage necessary medical treatment? Finally, consider the costs to society created by duties to maintain confidentiality and duties to disclose. When should the interests of third parties be sufficient to outweigh the interests of patients in the confidentiality of medical information?

Florida provides a typical example of laws regarding the mandatory reporting of abuse, neglect, or exploitation of vulnerable adults:

(1) Mandatory reporting.—
(a) Any person, including, but not limited to, any:
1. Physician, osteopathic physician, medical examiner, chiropractic physician, nurse, paramedic, emergency medical technician, or hospital personnel engaged in the admission, examination, care, or treatment of vulnerable adults;
2. Health professional or mental health professional other than one listed in subparagraph 1;
3. Practitioner who relies solely on spiritual means for healing;
4. Nursing home staff; assisted living facility staff; adult day care center staff; adult family-care home staff; social worker; or other professional adult care, residential, or institutional staff; . . . who knows, or has reasonable cause to suspect, that a vulnerable adult has been or is being abused, neglected, or exploited shall immediately report such knowledge or suspicion to the central abuse hotline.

Fla. Stat. Ann. §415.1034. Section 415.1034(b) describes specific types of information about the alleged victim, perpetrator, and types of injuries. Persons who knowingly and willfully fail to make reports or who prevent others from doing so are subject to misdemeanor criminal liability. Id. §415.111. Persons who report matters in good faith are immune from statutory liability.

Notes: Statutory Disclosure Obligations

1. *Structure of Statutory Obligations.* Each state imposes disclosure obligations on health care professionals by statute. The statute typically will establish (1) who has the duty to disclose information; (2) the events or information that must be disclosed; (3) to whom the information must be disclosed; and (4) the immunities or liabilities associated with the disclosure obligation. State disclosure obligations generally apply to a wide range of licensed health professions, such as physicians, nurses, nursing home staff members, social workers, and others. The HIPAA Privacy Rules permit providers to make these disclosures. 45 C.F.R. §164.512.

2. *Types of Disclosure Duties.* Most disclosure obligations are associated with the risk of harm to others through criminal activity or the transmission of disease. The Florida statute focuses on the danger of elder abuse, a matter of particular concern in retirement communities. The disclosure duty stems from concerns that members of this group may not be able to communicate their abuse to others. Like other states, Florida imposes a similar disclosure obligation for instances of suspected child abuse. Fla. Stat. Ann. §39.201.

States also require physicians and others to report gunshot or knife wounds to police authorities. See, e.g., N.Y. Penal Law §265.25. See generally Mark A. Hall, Hospital and Physician Disclosure of Information Concerning a Patient's Crime, 63 U. Det. L. Rev. 145 (1985). The disclosure will alert appropriate authorities to the probability that a crime has occurred, but it is not especially helpful in preventing imminent harm. Citizens do not have a general obligation to disclose possible criminal activity; what justifies the existence of a disclosure obligation here? Arguably, the health care provider who gives medical treatment to a gunshot victim is more than a passive bystander, insofar as he or she may help perpetrators to elude law enforcement officers. In addition, the ordinary rules favoring confidentiality may not apply; individuals who have been shot or knifed may be highly motivated to seek health care whether or not their treatment will be confidential.

What about wounds not serious enough to fall within the scope of a reporting statute but which might nonetheless reveal evidence of criminal activity? Suppose that a district attorney serves grand jury subpoenas duces tecum on nearly two dozen hospitals, seeking "[a]ny and all records pertaining to any male Caucasian patient between the ages of 30 to 45 years, . . . [treated during a two-day period] for a laceration, puncture wound or slash, or other injury caused by or possibly caused by a cutting instrument and/or sharp object, said injury being plainly observable to a lay person without expert or professional knowledge. . . ." The subpoenas expressly exclude from discovery information obtained by licensed health care professionals while attending the patient and necessary to provide care for the patient. Should the hospitals comply? See In re Grand Jury Investigation in New York County, 779 N.E.2d 173 (N.Y. 2002) (upholding appellate decision quashing the subpoenas); In re Grand Jury Subpoena for Medical Records of Payne, 839 A.2d 837 (N.H. 2004) (statute requiring physicians to report bodily injuries arising from criminal acts insufficient to provide unilateral authority for government subpoena of medical records). Finally, states also require health care providers to report information about individuals who have been diagnosed with certain contagious or transmissible diseases. See pages 958-964.

3. *Disclose to Whom?* States require disclosures to different types of state authorities. Some disclosures are made directly to law enforcement personnel. See, e.g., N.Y. Penal Law §265.25 (gunshot wounds disclosed to police). States have also established special "hotlines" for certain types of disclosures, such as those regarding child or elder abuse. See, e.g., Fla. Stat. Ann. §39.201. Contagious or transmissible disease reports are most often directed to state public health authorities. See, e.g., Fla. Stat. Ann. §384.25 (sexually transmissible diseases reported to health department). The statutes generally provide that the confidentiality of some types of reported information will be protected from further disclosure. See, e.g., id. These confidentiality protections may be constitutionally required. See pages 950-955.

4. *Immunities and Liabilities.* Providers who file mandatory reports about diseases or abuse are usually immune from damages for any mistake and resulting harm. See Zamstein v. Marvasti, 692 A.2d 781 (Conn. 1997). But see Runyon v. Smith, 749 A.2d 852 (N.J. 2000). Less clear is the legal exposure for a professional who is in a position to file a report, but who fails to do so. Under some statutes, a failure to comply with statutory reporting requirements can lead to criminal or civil liability. New York's child abuse reporting statute provides one example of a typical statutory scheme:

> 1. Any person, official or institution required by this title to report a case of suspected child abuse or maltreatment who willfully fails to do so shall be guilty of a class A misdemeanor.
> 2. Any person, official or institution required by this title to report a case of suspected child abuse or maltreatment who knowingly and willfully fails to do so shall be civilly liable for the damages proximately caused by such failure.

N.Y. Social Services Law §420.

Should children injured by a provider's failure to report child abuse be permitted to bring suit in jurisdictions where the reporting statute does not include a specific civil remedy? Courts are divided. See Annot., 73 A.L.R.4th 782 (1989). Should a subsequent child abuse victim be permitted to sue the provider on the theory that if the provider had reported the first victim the second victim would not have been at risk? Marcelletti v. Bathani, 500 N.W.2d 124 (Mich. Ct. App. 1993) (no); Yates v. Mansfield Board of Education, 102 Ohio St.3d 205 (2005) (yes). A provider's failure to follow reporting rules can also spark professional disciplinary action. In the Matter of Schroeder, 415 N.W.2d 436 (Minn. Ct. App. 1988). Should a health care provider have a duty to disclose the limits of confidentiality before providing services to her patients? See Marks v. Tenbrunsel, 910 So. 2d 1255 (Alabama 2005) (patient not permitted to pursue claim against psychologist who reported alleged child abuse even though patient claims he was assured of confidentiality); Hayes v. State, 667 N.E.2d 222 (Ind. Ct. App. 1996) (holding that therapist had no duty to warn client that disclosures of child sexual abuse would be reported to state authorities).

5. *Common-Law Disclosure Requirements.* As the next case reveals, disclosure obligations also arise under common law.

■BRADSHAW v. DANIEL
854 S.W.2d 865 (Tenn. 1993)

ANDERSON, Justice.

We granted this appeal to determine whether a physician has a legal duty to warn a nonpatient of the risk of exposure to the source of his patient's noncontagious disease—Rocky Mountain Spotted Fever. . . .

On July 19, 1986, Elmer Johns went to the emergency room at Methodist Hospital South in Memphis, Tennessee, complaining of headaches, muscle aches, fever, and chills. He was admitted to the hospital under the care and treatment of the defendant, Dr. Chalmers B. Daniel, Jr. Dr. Daniel first saw Johns on July 22, 1986, at which time he ordered the drug Chloramphenicol, which is the drug of choice for a person in the latter stages of Rocky Mountain Spotted Fever. Johns' condition rapidly deteriorated, and he died the next day, July 23, 1986. An autopsy was performed, and the Centers for Disease Control in Atlanta conclusively confirmed, in late September 1986, that the cause of death was Rocky Mountain Spotted Fever. Although Dr. Daniel communicated with Elmer Johns' wife, Genevieve, during Johns' treatment, he never advised her of the risks of exposure to Rocky Mountain Spotted Fever, or that the disease could have been the cause of Johns' death.

A week after her husband's death, on August 1, 1986, Genevieve Johns came to the emergency room of Baptist Memorial Hospital in Memphis, Tennessee, with similar symptoms of chills, fever, mental disorientation, nausea, lung congestion, myalgia, and swelling of the hands. She was admitted to the hospital and treated for Rocky Mountain Spotted Fever, but she died three days later, on August 4, 1986, of that disease. It is undisputed that no patient-physician relationship existed between Genevieve Johns and Dr. Daniel.

The plaintiff, William Jerome Bradshaw, is Genevieve Johns' son. He filed this suit alleging that the defendant's negligence in failing to advise Genevieve Johns that her husband died of Rocky Mountain Spotted Fever, and in failing to warn her of the risk of exposure, proximately caused her death. . . . Dr. Gelfand [an expert witness for the defense] testified that the medical standard of care did not require a physician treating a patient infected with, or suspected of being infected with, Rocky Mountain Spotted Fever to treat the family of the patient in contact with him, or to warn them of the risk of exposure to the disease or the risk of exposure to ticks or tick bites. The plaintiff responded with the affidavit of Dr. Burt Prater. Dr. Prater testified that because of the clustering effect of the disease, the medical standard of care required that a physician treating a patient with symptoms of Rocky Mountain Spotted Fever advise the family of the patient as to the incubation period, the symptoms of the disease, and the need for immediate medical attention upon manifestation of the symptoms. Dr. Prater further testified that the defendant, Dr. Daniel, negligently failed to diagnose Elmer Johns' fatal disease of Rocky Mountain Spotted Fever and failed to warn his wife, Genevieve Johns, of the incubation period of the disease, the symptoms, and the need to seek medical treatment upon manifestation of the symptoms. He also testified that the disease, if untreated, has a 40 percent mortality rate, but if treated promptly, has a 4 percent mortality rate. Based on the affidavits, the defendant's motion for summary judgment was denied. The case was . . . tried before a jury, which returned a verdict of $50,000 against the defendant. . . .

LEGAL DUTY

The defendant physician argues that he owed his patient's wife no legal duty because first, there was no physician-patient relationship, and second, Rocky Mountain Spotted Fever is not a contagious disease and, therefore, there is no duty to warn of the risk of exposure.

We begin our analysis by examining how we determine when a legal duty may be imposed upon one for the benefit of another. While duty was not part of the early English common law jurisprudence of tort liability, it has since become an essential element in negligence cases. . . . [T]he imposition of a legal duty reflects society's contemporary policies and social requirements concerning the right of individuals and the general public to be protected from another's act or conduct. Indeed, it has been stated that " 'duty' is not sacrosanct in itself, but is only an expression of the sum total of those considerations of policy which lead the law to say that the plaintiff is entitled to protection." W. Keeton, Prosser and Keeton on the Law of Torts §53 at 358. . . .

The defendant contends that the absence of a physician-patient relationship negates the existence of a duty in this case. While it is true that a physician-patient relationship is necessary to the maintenance of a medical malpractice action, it is not necessary for the maintenance of an action based on negligence, and this Court has specifically recognized that a physician may owe a duty to a nonpatient third party for injuries caused by the physician's negligence, if the injuries suffered and the manner in which they occurred were reasonably foreseeable. Wharton Transport Corp. v. Bridges, 606 S.W.2d 521, 526 (Tenn. 1980) (physician owed duty to third party injured by disabled truck driver's negligence, where the physician was negligent both in his physical examination and certification of the truck driver for the employer).

Here, we are asked to determine whether a physician has an affirmative duty to warn a patient's family member about the symptoms and risks of exposure to Rocky Mountain Spotted Fever, a noncontagious disease. Insofar as we are able to determine, there is no reported decision from this or any other jurisdiction involving circumstances exactly similar to those presented in this case.

We begin by observing that all persons have a duty to use reasonable care to refrain from conduct that will foreseeably cause injury to others. In determining the existence of a duty, courts have distinguished between action and inaction. Professor Prosser has commented that "the reason for the distinction may be said to lie in the fact that by 'misfeasance' the defendant has created a new risk of harm to the plaintiff, while by 'nonfeasance' he has at least made his situation no worse, and has merely failed to benefit him by interfering in his affairs." Prosser, §56 at 373.

Because of this reluctance to countenance nonfeasance as a basis of liability, as a general rule, under the common law, one person owed no affirmative duty to warn those endangered by the conduct of another. Prosser, §56 at 374; Tarasoff v. Regents of University of California, 17 Cal. 3d 425 (1976). To mitigate the harshness of this rule, courts have carved out exceptions for cases in which the defendant stands in some special relationship to either the person who is the source of the danger, or to the person who is foreseeably at risk from the danger. Accordingly,

> while an actor is always bound to prevent his acts from creating an unreasonable risk to others, he is under the affirmative duty to act to prevent another from sustaining

harm only when certain socially recognized relations exist which constitute the basis for such legal duty.

Harper & Kime, The Duty to Control the Conduct of Another, 43 Yale L. J. 886, 887 (1934).

One of the most widely known cases applying that principle is *Tarasoff*, supra, in which the California Supreme Court held that when a psychotherapist determines or, pursuant to the standards of his profession, should determine that his patient presents a serious danger of violence to another, the therapist has an affirmative duty to use reasonable care to protect the intended victim against such danger, and the duty may require the physician to warn the intended victim of the danger. The special relationship of the patient to his psychotherapist supported imposition of the affirmative duty to act for the benefit of third persons. . . .

Decisions of other jurisdictions have employed the same analysis and held that the relationship of a physician to his patient is sufficient to support the duty to exercise reasonable care to protect third persons against foreseeable risks emanating from a patient's physical illness. Specifically, other courts have recognized that physicians may be liable to persons infected by a patient, if the physician negligently fails to diagnose a contagious disease, or having diagnosed the illness, fails to warn family members or others who are foreseeably at risk of exposure to the disease. . . . [S]ee generally Annot., 3 A.L.R.5th 370 (1992). . . .

Returning to the facts of this case, first, it is undisputed that there was a physician-patient relationship between Dr. Daniel and Elmer Johns. Second, here, as in the contagious disease context, it is also undisputed that Elmer Johns' wife, who was residing with him, was at risk of contracting the disease. This is so even though the disease is not contagious in the narrow sense that it can be transmitted from one person to another. Both Dr. Daniel and Dr. Prater, the plaintiff's expert, testified that family members of patients suffering from Rocky Mountain Spotted Fever are at risk of contracting the disease due to a phenomenon called clustering, which is related to the activity of infected ticks who transmit the disease to humans. Dr. Prater also testified that Dr. Daniel negligently failed to diagnose the disease and negligently failed to warn his patient's wife, Genevieve Johns, of her risk of exposure to the source of disease. Dr. Daniel's expert disputed these conclusions, but Dr. Daniel conceded there is a medical duty to inform the family when there is a diagnosis of the disease. Thus, this case is analogous to the *Tarasoff* line of cases adopting a duty to warn of danger and the contagious disease cases adopting a comparable duty to warn. Here, as in those cases, there was a foreseeable risk of harm to an identifiable third party, and the reasons supporting the recognition of the duty to warn are equally compelling here.

We, therefore, conclude that the existence of the physician-patient relationship is sufficient to impose upon a physician an affirmative duty to warn identifiable third persons in the patient's immediate family against foreseeable risks emanating from a patient's illness. Accordingly, we hold that under the factual circumstances of this case, viewing the evidence in a light most favorable to the plaintiff, the defendant physician had a duty to warn his patient's wife of the risk to her of contracting Rocky Mountain Spotted Fever, when he knew, or in the exercise of reasonable care, should have known, that his patient was suffering from the disease. Our holding here is necessarily limited to the conclusion that the defendant physician owed

Genevieve Johns a legal duty. We express no opinion on the other elements which would be required to establish a cause of action for common-law negligence in this case.

Accordingly . . . this cause is remanded to the trial court for proceedings consistent with this opinion. . . .

Notes: Common-Law Duty to Warn

1. *Overview.* Was Dr. Daniel negligent in his treatment of his patient, Elmer Johns? Daniel appropriately identified the cause of Johns' illness and provided treatment. On what basis can he be held liable for injuries to someone who was not his patient? The court notes that the existence of a physician-patient relationship generally is a prerequisite to the maintenance of a malpractice action. It finds, however, that the absence of a relationship is no barrier to an ordinary negligence action. See Chapter 2.B.1, discussing a physician's duty to third parties. However, the court still must confront whether there is a "special relationship," due to the oft-described distinction between "misfeasance" and "nonfeasance" (creating a risk of harm vs. failing to protect others from a risk of harm created by another). As a general rule, nonfeasance does not constitute actionable negligence. The "special relationship" rule is an exception to this principle. See, e.g., Restatement (Second) Torts §§314, 314A; W. Jonathan Cardi, A Pluralistic Analysis of the Therapist/Physician Duty to Warn Third Parties, 44 Wake Forest L. Rev. 877 (2009); Aaron D. Twerski, The Cleaver, the Violin, and the Scalpel: Duty and the Restatement (Third) of Torts, 60 Hastings L.J. 1 (2008). The key in many third-party liability cases therefore is whether there is a "special relationship" that justifies the imposition of liability for nonfeasance. Note that some jurisdictions are hostile toward the expansion of physicians' duties to third parties. See, e.g., Thapar v. Zezulka, 994 S.W.2d 635 (Tex. 1999).

Once the existence of a duty is established, the court must determine its scope. The scope of the duty is determined in large part by the nature of the risk and the physician's ability to reduce the risk reasonably. Note that in duty to warn situations, some risks can be reduced simply by warning the patient. As an example, suppose that a physician treats a patient for epilepsy and fails to tell the patient to refrain from driving. The patient has a seizure and runs into an oncoming car. Although the physician may have a duty to the driver of the other car, the accident and injury could easily have been avoided by warning the patient not to drive. If the patient had been warned, and had refrained from driving, no breach of confidentiality would have been required and there would have been no conflict between the duty to maintain confidentiality and the duty to protect others from harm. The discussion in this section focuses on the more difficult cases where physicians might have to breach patient confidentiality in order to protect third parties. Note that the federal Privacy Rules permit covered entities to disclose personally identifiable health information in some circumstances to prevent or reduce the risk of a "serious and imminent threat to health and safety" 45 C.F.R. §164.512(j), supra page 140.

Just how far does the duty described in *Bradshaw* extend? The Supreme Court of Connecticut addressed the issue in Jarmie v. Troncale, 306 Conn. 578 (Conn. 2012). In that case, a pedestrian was struck by a car, which the defendant's patient was driving. The victim brought a negligence claim against the doctor for failing to warn his patient that a medication the doctor had prescribed might cause drowsiness. The court concluded that the doctor had no duty to the third party and dismissed the case. Should the outcome have been different if the patient had sued, rather than the third-party victim?

2. *Categorizing Cases: A General Theory of Liability or a Laundry List?* The first problem in these common-law liability cases lies in determining the existence of a "special relationship." The *Bradshaw* court notes that the physician-patient relationship has been used to support the imposition of liability in cases involving dangerous psychiatric patients and patients with contagious illnesses. Courts have also noted the importance of the physician-patient relationship in some automobile and child abuse cases. Does this indicate that physicians will always be held liable for injuries caused by or to their patients? Or are courts developing a list of situations in which physicians may be held liable? If so, what principles or factors determine whether the physician owes a duty to the third party? Are disclosure obligations limited to physicians, or do other types of health care professionals face the same threat of liability?

a. *Contagious Diseases.* One well-developed line of cases holds physicians liable for injuries to nonpatients caused by communicable diseases. Physicians have been held liable for failing to diagnose the contagious condition. See, e.g., Jones v. Stanko, 160 N.E. 456 (Ohio 1928) (physician fails to diagnose smallpox and puts neighbors at risk for infection). But see Ellis v. Peter, 627 N.Y.S.2d 707 (App. Div. 1995) (failure to diagnose TB; no duty to warn). Liability has also been imposed for failure to warn others about the risk of transmission. See, e.g., Skillings v. Allen, 173 N.W. 663 (Minn. 1919) (negligent failure to disclose risk of transmission of scarlet fever); Gammill v. United States, 727 F.2d 950, 954 (10th Cir. 1984) (physician may be found liable for failing to warn persons at risk for exposure of the danger). By contrast, see McNulty v. City of New York, 792 N.E.2d 162 (N.Y. 2003) (defendant physicians did not owe friend of person infected with meningitis a duty to warn her of the risk of infection); Santa Rosa Health Care Corp. v. Garcia, 964 S.W.2d 940 (Tex. 1998) (no duty to warn wife of hemophiliac of risk of HIV). See generally Annot., 3 A.L.R.5th 370 (1992). Note that *Bradshaw* is an extension of this principle — Rocky Mountain Spotted Fever is not contagious but it is likely that others in the patient's household may have come into contact with infected ticks.

The duty to protect third parties from harm in contagious disease cases has become highly controversial because of the risk of HIV transmission. Do physicians have an obligation to warn third parties when their patients continue to engage in activities that present the risk of HIV transmission? The answer is complicated somewhat by the existence of special statutes protecting the confidentiality of HIV-related information, which may restrict the ability to disclose information even when others may be at risk, and by variations in the risk of transmission related to use of condoms and anti-retroviral therapies. See generally Guion L. Johnstone, A Social Worker's Dilemma When a Client Has a Sexually Transmitted Disease, 49 U. Louisville L. Rev. 111 (2010) (reviewing physician obligations); Bernard Friedland, HIV Confidentiality and the Right to Warn — The Health Care Provider's Dilemma, 80 Mass. L. Rev. 3 (1995).

b. *Mental Illness.* Another set of cases concern a mental health professional's duty to protect third parties from his or her patient. The leading case is Tarasoff v. Regents of University of California, 551 P.2d 334 (Cal. 1976), discussed briefly in *Bradshaw*. In *Tarasoff*, a therapist knew that a patient had made threats of violence toward a young woman. The therapist unsuccessfully attempted to commit the patient for treatment. The patient murdered the young woman, whose parents then sued the patient's mental health care providers. The California Supreme Court, relying in part on Restatement (Second) of Torts §315, supra, held that psychotherapists could be held liable for failing to exercise reasonable care to protect a third party where the therapists know or should know that their patient presents a serious danger of violence to another. The court held that therapists might have an obligation to warn those at risk and specifically rejected the defendants' contention that such a warning would impermissibly breach client confidentiality. *Tarasoff* was much discussed by commentators through the late 1970s and 1980s.

Tarasoff is an important opinion, almost always cited by courts and legislative bodies whether it is followed or rejected. See, e.g., Munstermann v. Alegent Health-Immanuel Medical Center, 716 N.W.2d 73 (Neb. 2006) (establishing scope of psychiatrist's liability to third parties); Powell v. Catholic Medical Center, 749 A.2d 301 (N.H. 2000) (discussing implications of state codification of *Tarasoff*-type rule); Estates of Morgan v. Fairfield Family Counseling Center, 673 N.E.2d 1311 (Ohio 1997) (psychiatrist-outpatient relationship is a "special relationship" justifying imposition of duty to protect third parties).

Many jurisdictions have adopted only a narrow reading of *Tarasoff* or have rejected it completely. See, e.g., Dawe v. Dr. Reuven Bar-Levav & Associates, 780 N.W.2d 272 (Mich. 2010) (statute codifying narrow mental health professional's duties to warn did not completely abrogate common-law duty of care to other patients). Indeed, California itself has partially limited it by statute. Ann. Cal. Civ. Code §43.92. In Nasser v. Parker, 455 S.E.2d 502 (Va. 1995), for example, the court considered whether the defendant physician and hospital had a duty to warn a victim about the impending release of a former boyfriend who had threatened to kill her. The court noted the special relationship rule found in §315, but held that no special relationship existed without an additional showing of an ability to control the patient's conduct:

> Accordingly, we disagree with the holding of *Tarasoff* that a doctor-patient relationship or a hospital-patient relationship alone is sufficient, as a matter of law, to establish a "special relation" under Restatement §315(a). Within the context of the Restatement, there is nothing special about the ordinary doctor-patient relationship or hospital-patient relationship. We think there must be added to those ordinary relationships the factor, required by [Restatement] §319, of taking charge of the patient, meaning that the doctor or hospital must be vested with a higher degree of control over the patient than exists in the ordinary doctor-patient or hospital-patient relationship before a duty arises concerning the patient's conduct.

Id. at 506. See also Boulanger v. Pol, 900 P.2d 823 (Kan. 1995) (no special relationship between psychiatrist and voluntary mental patient); Thapar v. Zezulka, 994 S.W.2d 635 (Tex. 1999) (no duty to warn). But see Volk v. DeMeerleer, 187 Wash. 2d 241 (2016) (arguably expanding *Tarasoff*-type liability by holding that psychiatrist may be liable to outpatient's foreseeable victims).

c. *Driving Impairments.* Most driving impairment cases involve the physician's obligation to warn the patient about the risks of driving. See, e.g., Weigold v. Patel, 840 A.2d 19 (Conn. App. 2004) (no liability where patient aware of tendency to fall asleep while driving). See generally Annot., 43 A.L.R.4th 153 (1986). Where a state statute requires physicians to report certain driving impairments, physicians can be held liable for injuries to third parties. See, e.g., Harden by Harden v. Allstate Insurance Co., 883 F. Supp. 963 (D. Del. 1995). But see Praesel v. Johnson, 967 S.W.2d 391 (Tex. 1998) (no negligence per se or common-law duty).

d. *Genetic Risks?* How should the duty to warn apply to genetic disorders? Does a physician who diagnoses a hereditary disorder in a person have obligations to disclose that disorder to the patient's children or siblings (often called the "proband")? Compare Pate v. Threlkel, 661 So.2d 278 (Fla. 1995) (physician owed a duty to children of patient diagnosed with a hereditary disease, but that duty was satisfied by warning the patient and did not require warning children directly) with Safer v. Estate of Pack, 677 A.2d 1188 (N.J. Super. 1996) (declining to follow *Pate* because the court could not say that "in all circumstances, the duty to warn will be satisfied by informing the patient. It may be necessary, at some stage, to resolve a conflict between the physician's broader duty to warn and his fidelity to an expressed preference of the patient that nothing be said to family members about the details of the disease.") See also Molloy v. Meier, 679 N.W.2d 711 (Minn. 2004) ("physician's duty regarding genetic testing and diagnosis extends beyond the patient to biological parents who foreseeably may be harmed by a breach of that duty"). Should the law turn on what most patients would want in terms of information? See K. Wolff et al., Confidentiality Versus Duty to Inform—An Empirical Study on Attitudes Toward the Handling of Genetic Information, 143 Am. J. Med. Genet. A. 142 (2007) (most respondents wished to be informed about a hereditary disease in their family; study included consideration of conditions under which breach of confidentiality would be deemed acceptable). Suppose that a sperm bank or egg brokerage later determines that one of its donors has a hereditary disease. Should it have an obligation to track down all the donor-conceived children of that donor? What if doing so would require informing the child that their maternity or paternity is different from what he or she believes?

e. *Incidental Findings in Research.* These materials focus on duties to disclose within a clinical relationship. There is also a well-established literature on somewhat analogous duties in the research context, what are often called "incidental findings." For a good discussion, see Symposium, The Law of Incidental Findings in Human Subjects Research: Establishing Researchers' Duties, 36 J.L. Med. & Ethics 361 (2008). See also, section D. Human Experimentation and Research, below.

3. *A Risk of Harm.* The risk of harm is clear in some cases, particularly those involving serious contagious diseases. The issue is more problematic in the case of psychiatric patients. See, e.g., Douglas Mossman, The Imperfection of Protection Through Detection and Intervention, 30 J. Leg. Med. 109 (2009). Can mental health professionals accurately predict which patients will present a risk of harm to others? The *Tarasoff* court used a professional standard of care to measure the scope of the physicians' obligation to third parties: If the defendant knew or should have known of the risk, using professional judgment, then liability may follow. Tarasoff v. Regents of University of California, 551 P.2d 334 (Cal. 1976). See also Estates of Morgan v. Fairfield Family Counseling Center, 673 N.E.2d 1311, 1325 (Ohio 1997) (psychotherapists need not have perfect predictive power), superseded by statute, Ohio Rev. Code Ann. §2305.51 (West 2014) (expressly limiting mental health professionals' liability for failure to warn to circumstances where the patient has made explicit threats of harm to a clearly identifiable victim and the physician did not take one of four enumerated steps).

4. *Foreseeable and Identifiable Third Parties.* Many contagious disease and psychiatric dangerousness cases suggest that a health care provider's duty to disclose

is established by a specific risk to foreseeable and identifiable third parties. See, e.g., *Bradshaw* and *Tarasoff*, supra. This requirement serves at least two purposes: It bolsters the sense that the risk of harm is imminent, and it suggests that a disclosure requirement is reasonable. Where a health care provider knows the identity of the person at risk of harm, it seems reasonable to require that that person be warned about the risk. A few courts have also been willing to impose a duty to breach confidentiality even where the risk is more generalized, however. In Schuster v. Altenberg, 424 N.W.2d 159 (Wis. 1988), the court held that a duty to breach confidentiality existed even in cases where there was no "readily identifiable target" of the patient's violent tendencies. Id. at 172-174. In such cases, the therapist has the duty to inform police so that emergency commitment proceedings can be initiated.

In cases where the claim is based on the physician's failure to disclose information to the *patient* rather than to the injured third parties, courts have not limited liability to situations in which the third party is known or identifiable. See, e.g., Reisner v. Regents of the University of California, 37 Cal. Rptr. 2d 518 (Cal. Ct. App. 1995) (physicians owed a duty to HIV-infected boyfriend to disclose to patient or her parents her HIV status; failure to disclose occurred long before sexual relationship between young people began).

5. *Disclose to Whom?* As noted above, in most cases a physician's duty to third parties is discharged by disclosing the risk to his or her patient. See, e.g., Emerich v. Philadelphia Center for Human Development, Inc., 720 A.2d 1032 (Pa. 1999) (duty satisfied by statement to victim that she should not go to patient's apartment); Pate v. Threlkel, 661 So. 2d 278 (Fla. 1995) ("in any circumstances in which the physician has a duty to warn . . . that duty will be satisfied by warning the patient."). Where the patient presents a risk of harm to an identifiable third party, many jurisdictions also will impose a duty to disclose the risk to that person. See, e.g., *Tarasoff*, supra. Sometimes the provider's disclosure obligation can be met through an institutional disclosure mechanism. In Casarez v. NME Hospital, 883 S.W.2d 360 (Tex. App. 1994), for example, a nurse who allegedly contracted HIV from a patient sued the patient's physician for failing to warn him of the patient's condition. The court held that the physician complied with his obligations by notifying the hospital's infection control and quality assurance committees of his patient's condition.

In the absence of a statute, should a court require a physician, who knows that a patient presents a risk of harm through driving, to disclose this information to state authorities? What if the patient is informed of the risk and states that she will continue to drive despite the danger?

6. *Zone of Reasonable Judgment.* Given the conflicting nature of the duties to disclose and to protect confidentiality, and the ambiguities associated with each duty, do physicians have enough guidance to allow them to avoid liability? Even if the duties were precisely defined, it would be tricky at best to walk the narrow line between them. But where the extent of each duty is uncertain, it may be impossible to avoid liability. Disclosing may give rise to damages or ethical sanctions for breach of confidentiality, whereas keeping quiet may result in damages for injuries caused to others. What's a doctor to do? Should the law provide for a neutral zone between these two duties, in which disclosure is discretionary, but not mandatory? In other words, doctors would have a qualified privilege to disclose if they do so in the good faith belief that disclosure is necessary to prevent harm, but could not be sued for failing to disclose unless _____. The issue then becomes: How would you fill

in the blank? See Mark A. Hall, Hospital and Physician Disclosure of Information Concerning a Patient's Crime, 63 U. Det. L. Rev. 145 (1985) (advocating a qualified privilege with respect to the duty to report serious crimes committed by patients).

7. *Further Reading.* On the *Tarasoff* case and its progeny, see Mark Rothstein, Tarasoff Duties after Newton, 42 J. L., Med. & Ethics 104 (2014); Symposium, *Tarasoff* at Thirty, 75 U. Cin. L. Rev. 497-661 (2006); W. Jonathon Cardi, A Pluralistic Analysis of the Therapist/Physician Duty to Warn Third Parties, 44 Wake Forest L. Rev. 877 (2009); Annot., 83 A.L.R.3d 1201 (1978). On disclosure obligations as to genetic risks, see Mary L. Kovalesky, To Disclose or Not to Disclose: Determining the Scope and Exercise of a Physician's Duty to Warn Third Parties of Genetically Transmissible Conditions, 76 U. Cin. L. Rev. 1019 (2007-2008); Gillian Nycum et al., Intra-Familial Obligations to Communicate Genetic Risk Information: What Foundations? What Forms?, 3 McGill J.L. & Health 21 (2009) (providing international comparisons); Kenneth Offit et al., The "Duty to Warn" a Patient's Family Members About Hereditary Disease Risks, 292 JAMA 1469 (2004).

Discussion Problems

Consider how you would analyze the following problems. What law(s) or regulations would apply in your state? Will the health care provider have a duty to maintain confidentiality, the authority to breach confidentiality, or a duty to disclose the information?

- A 30-year-old woman meets with a physician who had also treated her mother. The woman asks the physician for specific information about her mother's medical history. The woman argues that she needs the information to determine whether she is at a significantly higher risk for (a) cancer, (b) high blood pressure, or (c) glaucoma. Should it matter whether the woman's mother is deceased? On this last point, see 45 C.F.R. §164.502(f) ("A covered entity must comply with the [privacy] requirements . . . with respect to the [PHI] of a deceased individual for a period of 50 years following the death of the individual."); and Jessica Berg, Grave Secrets: Legal and Ethical Analysis of Post-mortem Confidentiality, 34 Conn. L. Rev. 81 (2001).
- A drug treatment center's admission form includes the following notice:

  > We understand that persons who have problems with drugs and alcohol may fear that treatment information will be disclosed to others, including family members or employers. Rest assured that your medical treatment information will be protected from disclosure as provided by law.

  A patient undergoes voluntary HIV testing and receives a positive test result. May or must the treatment center disclose the patient's HIV status to other patients? What if it appears that the HIV-infected patient has begun a sexual relationship with another patient? What if the patient is taking anti-retroviral therapies, which reduce the risk of transmission, and claims that she or he is using safer sexual practices?
- Law enforcement officials are concerned about another possible anthrax bioterrorism event. Local authorities approach pharmacies in a particular town, seeking information about recent prescriptions for antibiotics. May the phar-

macies release the information to law enforcement officials? Suppose that a physician in the town recently received a call from a patient, inquiring about a prescription for an antibiotic thought to be effective against anthrax. May or must the physician disclose this information to anyone?

C. INFORMED CONSENT

1. Goals, Aspirations, Policies

In Chapter 1.A.2 and in the introduction to this chapter we observed that the physician-patient relationship is characterized by a huge imbalance of power, owing to the vulnerability of illness and treatment and physicians' vastly superior knowledge and skills. This power imbalance may be further accentuated by economic and cultural factors. See Chapter 1.C. What should the medical and legal response be to these inequalities in the physician-patient relationship? Historically, or perhaps apocryphally, a patient's reverence for her physician was a source of comfort and an important underpinning to the psychology of a cure. A wide range of factors—perhaps among them the anti-establishment views of the 1960s, the consumer movement of the 1970s, the patient advocacy movements of the 1980s and 1990s, the ready availability of health-related information on the Internet beginning in the 2000s, the startling advances and lingering failures of medical progress, and the expansion of specialties such as "bioethics" and "health law"—have combined to challenge the authority and supremacy of the physician. The most prominent legal tool used by those seeking to reform the physician-patient relationship is the doctrine of informed consent. It is believed that requiring physicians to provide more information to their patients will help to redress the power imbalance problems created by the inequality of knowledge. As you read the materials on informed consent, consider how effective the law has been, or conceivably could be, in accomplishing this reformist mission. Consider also what model the reformists envision for the ideal patient-physician interaction, and whether all (or many) patients actually subscribe to that model.

■ PATIENT-CENTERED MEDICINE:
A PROFESSIONAL EVOLUTION
Christine Laine & Frank Davidoff*
275 JAMA 152, 152-153 (1996)

In the past, physicians commonly withheld diagnostic information from patients with patients' tacit consent. Hippocrates advocated "concealing most things from the patient while you are attending to him . . . revealing nothing of the patient's future or present condition." . . . The attitude[] of Hippocrates . . . would

---

* Dr. Laine is Editor in Chief, and Dr. Davidoff is an Editor Emeritus, at the Annals of Internal Medicine, published by the American College of Physicians. Dr. Laine is also affiliated with the Division of Internal Medicine at Jefferson Medical College, Thomas Jefferson University.

undoubtedly get [him] into trouble today. Patients increasingly expect to know not only their diagnoses, but also details of pathophysiology, treatment options, and prognosis. . . . Patients expect and often demand information that used to be only within physicians' reach, and physicians increasingly expect to share such information with patients.

The transformation in attitudes surrounding disclosure of diagnoses is particularly striking when one considers cancer. . . . A 1961 study . . . revealed that . . . 90 percent of physicians surveyed preferred not to tell cancer patients their diagnoses. . . . [B]y 1979 . . . 97 percent of physicians surveyed preferred to disclose a diagnosis of cancer. . . .

Beyond "honesty is the best policy," the argument for informing patients is that information enables patients to participate in medical decisions. In more physician-centered days, physicians would decide what was best for their patients, and patient participation was limited to compliance with physicians' orders. As medicine becomes more patient centered, participation begins with the patient helping to decide what the physician will order, and the emphasis shifts from compliance to participation.

■ RETHINKING INFORMED CONSENT
Peter H. Schuck*
103 Yale L.J. 899, 900-905 (1994)

The doctrine requiring physicians to obtain a patient's informed consent before undertaking treatment is relatively young, having first appeared in a recognizable, relatively robust form only in 1957.[1] Yet the values that underlie the doctrine have an ancient pedigree. The consent norm had occupied a prominent and honored place in our legal thought for many centuries before the courts began to develop a jurisprudence of informed consent in health care.[2] Also well established was the cognate notion that consent must be informed or knowledgeable in some meaningful sense if we are to accord it legal or moral significance. . . .

The doctrine of informed consent in health care shared in the more general expansion of American tort liability that proceeded well into the 1980s and that now appears to have stabilized. Everyone, it seems, favors the principle of informed consent; it is "only" the specific details and applications of the doctrine that arouse serious debate. In order to map and enlarge this debate, it is useful to distinguish three different versions of informed consent doctrine. The first is the letter and spirit of the doctrine as developed primarily by courts—the law "in books." The second is the doctrine as imagined, feared, and often caricatured by some physicians—the

* Reprinted by permission of The Yale Law Journal Company and Fred B. Rothman & Company. The author is the Simeon E. Baldwin Professor Emeritus of Law at Yale Law School.

1. See Jay Katz, The Silent World of Doctor and Patient 48-84 (1984); see also Ruth R. Faden & Tom L. Beauchamp, A History and Theory of Informed Consent 235-273 (1986).

2. See, e.g., Ford v. Ford, 10 N.E. 474, 475 (Mass. 1887) [assault defined in part by absence of consent].

law "in the mind." The third version, a consequence both of the gap between the first two and of other situational constraints, is the doctrine as actually practiced by clinicians—the law "in action." (Of course, there are almost as many laws-in-action as there are distinct physician-patient relationships.)

Most commentators on informed consent deploy one or more of these versions of the law. Generally (and crudely) speaking, these commentators fall into two camps: idealists and realists. Informed consent idealists—primarily some judges and medical ethicists—advocate a relatively expansive conception of the physician's obligation to disclose and elicit information about risks and alternatives.[18] More specifically, the idealists tend to define informed consent law's pivotal concepts—materiality of risk, disclosure, alternatives, and causation—broadly and subjectively from the perspective of the individual patient rather than that of the professional, while defining the law's exceptions to the duty narrowly. Perhaps most important, idealists emphasize the qualitative dimension of physician-patient interactions concerning treatment decisions. They insist that these interactions be dialogic rather than authoritative, tailored to the individual patient's emotional needs and cognitive capacities rather than formulaic, aimed at maximizing patient autonomy and comprehension rather than mere information flow, and sensitive to the distortions that can be created by power differentials between physician and patient.

The idealists employ a distinctive rhetorical strategy. Capitalizing on the universal support for the principles and goals of informed consent, they point to the often striking difference between the law in books and the law in action—a difference that I call the "informed consent gap." The existence of this gap, they argue, shows that the law in action falls far short of the law in books. Since the law that they think should be in the books is often even more demanding, the true gap is wider still. The problem, then, is not so much the law in books, which tends to demand too little of physicians; rather, it is the laws in action and in the mind. For the idealist, therefore, the goal of reform must be to close the informed consent gap by conforming the law in action, at the very least, to the law now in books.

The realists—primarily practicing physicians—harbor a different vision of informed consent.[20] Although they emphatically do not contest the principle and goals of informed consent, they do question whether most patients really desire the kind of dialogue that the idealists propose. They also question whether, whatever patients desire, the gains in patient autonomy and improved outcomes produced by the dialogue are worth the additional time, money, and needless patient anxiety

---

18. See, e.g., Canterbury v. Spence, 464 F.2d 772, 787 (D.C. Cir. 1972) (principle of informed consent requires that physician disclose information that reasonable patient would wish to know in making treatment decisions); Truman v. Thomas, 611 P.2d 902, 906-907 (Cal. 1980) (patient must be apprised of risks of not undergoing treatment, even if she has refused treatment); see also Katz, supra note 1, at 48-84.

20. Perhaps the most articulate of the realists is Dr. Thomas P. Duffy. See Thomas P. Duffy, Agamemnon's Fate and the Medical Profession, 9 W. New Eng. L. Rev. 21 (1987) (reviewing and criticizing Jay Katz's approach). Dr. Sherwin Nuland advances a more moderate realist position in his . . . book. See Sherwin B. Nuland, How We Die: Reflections on Life's Final Chapter 258-261, 265-267 (1994) (distinguishing inter alia, between family physicians, who can and should engage in meaningful informed consent dialogue with patients, and specialists, who cannot realistically be expected to do so).

and confusion that informed consent may entail. Like the idealists, many realists employ a characteristic rhetoric. Rather than master the doctrinal details of the informed consent law in books, they point instead to the law in their minds, which they can easily caricature in order to demonstrate the law's folly. Although some realists do not concede that the law in action actually deviates from the law in their minds, many others readily admit that a gap does in fact exist. To them, however, this gap simply demonstrates how impractical the idealists' vision is and why it cannot be implemented in the demanding world of contemporary clinical practice.

In a real sense, then, informed consent idealists and realists argue past one another, producing a debate that is oblique and inconclusive rather than pointed and fruitful. For several related reasons, it is time to revisit this debate. These reasons include the intense public concern about rising health care costs, the bureaucratization of the physician-patient relationship, and the organization of health care delivery into units with some degree of market power over providers. Is the informed consent gap to be deplored or tolerated? Should physicians' legal obligations to disclose be further expanded, retained in their present form, or reduced? . . .

Notes: The Theory and Practice of Informed Consent

1. *Using Legal Rules to Foster Autonomy.* Peter Schuck suggests that informed consent idealists seek to promote individual autonomy while informed consent realists argue that the goals of complete individual autonomy cannot be met, at least not without great cost. As you read the following materials, identify the interests protected by the informed consent doctrine. A number of commentators have concluded that the doctrine fails to protect individual interests or to promote individual autonomy. See, e.g., Jay Katz, Informed Consent — Must It Remain a Fairy Tale?, 10 J. Contemp. Health L. & Pol'y 69 (1993).

Should we blame the law for this shortcoming, or is it inherently incapable of regulating the subtle and minute interactions between doctors and patients? Dr. Jay Katz, one of the law's most visionary and respected advocates of heightened informed consent, believed that "the radically different climate of physician-patient decisionmaking . . . cannot be implemented by judicial, legislative, or administrative orders." Jay Katz, The Silent World of Doctor and Patient 228 (1984). Similarly, a prestigious blue-ribbon ethics commission recognized that

> further evolution of legal standards toward a firmer protection of individual self-determination in medical decisions must be tempered by a recognition of the law's limits as an instrument of social control. . . . [T]he Commission is concerned that efforts to draw the law further into regulating the subtler aspects of relations between patients and health care professionals may prove ineffective, burdensome and ultimately counterproductive.

President's Commission for the Study of Ethical Problems in Medicine and Biomedical and Behavioral Research, Making Health Care Decisions: A Report on the Ethical and Legal Implications of Informed Consent in the Patient-Practitioner Relationship 30, 204, 252 (1982).

2. *Informed Consent in Practice.* Also consider the problems raised by the implementation of the doctrine. The process of health care decisionmaking described

in narratives by physicians often suggests the irrelevance of the legal framework. See, e.g., Atul Gawande, Complications: A Surgeon's Notes on an Imperfect Science (2002), which is excerpted at pages 30-34. Has the process of providing informed consent through signed consent forms become as ritualized and meaningless as the exchange of a peppercorn in land transactions? Empirical studies often cast doubt on the efficacy of the practice of informed consent. In one pathbreaking article, Alan Meisel and Loren H. Roth reviewed the empirical data on informed consent. Alan Meisel & Loren H. Roth, Toward an Informed Discussion of Informed Consent: A Review of the Empirical Studies, 25 Ariz. L. Rev. 265 (1983). They found that few patients understood or remembered what they had been told about their medical condition and treatment options. Other research confirms these findings. In one typical study, patients facing either anterior cervical fusion or lumbar laminectomy were given a training session on the procedures by a neurosurgeon and a clinical nurse specialist with a master's degree in neurosurgery. D. A. Herz et al., Informed Consent: Is It a Myth?, 30 Neurosurgery 453 (1992). Patients were given a "simple" written test immediately after the training session; the mean patient score was only 43.5 percent. Six weeks later, the mean test score dropped to 38.4 percent. The authors concluded that health care providers "cannot necessarily expect accurate patient or family recall or comprehension. Fulfillment of the doctrine of informed consent by neurosurgeons may very well be mythical."

There are a number of explanations for the gap between disclosure and comprehension/retention. Patients are often sick or emotionally vulnerable at the time of the disclosure; information may be presented in a highly technical and incomprehensible fashion; patients may not have the intelligence or educational background necessary to understand medical information; and patients may not feel able to ask important follow-up questions. See, e.g., Yael Schenker et al., Interventions to Improve Patient Comprehension in Informed Consent for Medical and Surgical Procedures: A Systematic Review, 31 Med. Decis. Making 151 (2011). Despite these problems, patients often report that they are satisfied with the informed consent process. See, e.g., F. W. Verheggen et al., Patients' Perceptions on Informed Consent and the Quality of Information Disclosure in Clinical Trials, 29 Patient Educ. Couns. 137 (1996).

Finally, the capacity of patients to understand and to make decisions may be greater than their capacity to participate in carrying out those decisions. A. D. Naik and colleagues note that the "clinical application of the concept of patient autonomy has centered on the ability to deliberate and make treatment decisions (decisional autonomy) to the virtual exclusion of the capacity to execute the treatment plan (executive autonomy)." A. D. Naik et al., Patient Autonomy for the Management of Chronic Conditions: A Two-Component Re-Conceptualization, 9(2) Am. J. Bioethics 23-30 (2009). For responses, see Symposium, 9(2) Am. J. Bioethics 31-35 (2009).

3. *Information That Is Harmful.* Information is not always welcome. Some types of information may increase anxiety and decrease enjoyment of life without appreciably adding to decisionmaking ability. See generally, Symposium, The Right Not to Know, 42 J. L., Med. & Ethics 6-63 (2014). Imagine a genetic condition associated with the early onset of severe dementia and death for which there is no effective preventive treatment. How many people would want to know how and when they are going to die? The empirical evidence is mixed:

What studies have been done are not at all clear on the psychological effects of predictive genetic testing. Some commentators have suggested that genetic testing can cause depression and suicide. Studies have demonstrated at least some negative impact on family functioning from predictive testing for Huntington's Disease—a test that can confirm with near-certainty whether one will develop this disabling disease. The data are inconclusive, but likely suffer from substantial selection bias. It may well be that living with the knowledge that one will develop an incurable disease turns out to be better than living with uncertainty. At least it may only be different, rather than "worse." When asked what it was like finally to know that she had Huntington's, one young woman replied that " '[i]t's hard to think the other way anymore of not knowing,' . . . 'It's become a part of my life.'"

Christian Turner, The Burden of Knowledge, 43 Ga. L. Rev. 297, 315 (2009).

Assuming that individuals will have different values and preferences in this area, how do you ask whether someone wants to know without tipping them off to the truth? One solution to this dilemma is to have a more elaborate informed consent process before giving the test, in which patients are told that the information obtained might be upsetting or might affect their personal relationships, etc. Then patients could choose not to be tested at all. See Mark E. Robson et al., American Society of Clinical Oncology Policy Statement Update: Genetic and Genomic Testing for Cancer Susceptibility, 28 J. Clin. Oncol. 893 (2010); Consensus Statement, Genetic Testing for Susceptibility to Adult-Onset Cancer: The Process and Content of Informed Consent, 277 JAMA 1467 (1997). This expansive approach to pretest counseling obviously would put a crimp in the approach that many clinicians take toward routine testing, in which screening tests are done with hardly any notice at all, much less with elaborate informed consent.

Advances in genetics raise an additional dilemma. If one patient wants the information and consents to testing, does this invade the privacy of family members who may not want to know the information or even to have the information created? These family members might suffer psychological effects or, absent special legal protections, adverse financial effects from insurance or employment. Professor Roger Dworkin has argued that genetic medicine requires us to adapt our individual autonomy model of informed consent so that it becomes more family centered. Roger B. Dworkin, Medical Law and Ethics in the Post-Autonomy Age, 68 Ind. L. J. 727 (1993). How would one obtain consent from an extended family? Is agreement by every competent adult required, or only a critical mass, or only a single-family matriarch or patriarch?

4. *Do Patients Want Decisional Autonomy?* Several commentators have argued that patients want to be informed but do not actually want to make their own health care decisions. Carl Schneider, a law professor at the University of Michigan, after reviewing empirical studies of patient interest in medical decisionmaking, concluded:

Taken as a whole, these studies surveyed a considerable variety of populations—from the perfectly well to the dangerously sick. They asked patients about their own conditions and about hypothetical illnesses. They framed their respondent's choices in a variety of ways. And their virtually universal conclusion was that, while patients commonly wish to be informed about their medical circumstances, at least a quite substantial number of them did not want to make their own medical decisions, or perhaps even to participate in those decisions in any very significant way. . . .

One might suppose that if patients were ever to assert their decisional authority it would be after hearing the alarming recitation of risks that characterizes the process of informed consent. Yet a number of studies of that process "strongly suggest that refusals attributable to disclosures are rarely, if ever, seen." Similarly, a study of why patients refuse treatment found an average of 4.6 refusals per 100 patient days. The reasons for refusal were complex, and generally there was more than one "cause" per patient. But two kinds of reasons stood out: first, a failure to tell the patient about the purpose of what was proposed; second, psychological factors, prominently including "characterological factors" (for example, using a refusal to accept treatment as a way of expressing a wish to be cared for) and "other psychoses." While the first of these causes reconfirms the wish for information we have so frequently encountered, neither of them is inconsistent with a reluctance to take control of medical decisions. And the dog that did not bark in the night is the absence of any significant number of patients who heard a doctor's recommendation and reached a different conclusion on the merits.

Carl E. Schneider, Bioethics with a Human Face, 69 Ind. L.J. 1075, 1097, 1099 (1994). Professor Schneider also noted significant evidence that "the more severe a patient's illness, the less likely the patient is to want to make medical decisions." Id. at 1101. See also, Marc D. Ginsberg, Beyond *Canterbury*: Can Medicine and Law Agree about Informed Consent? And Does It Matter? 45 J. L., Med & Ethics 106 (2017). Some have argued that informed consent represents an obsession with Western values and norms that seem less relevant to those from other cultures. See sources cited in note 7 below.

5. *Informed Consent vs. Traditional Malpractice.* Despite academic interest, informed consent theories play a role in a relatively small percentage of claims against physicians, at least as measured by opinions published in computerized databases such as Westlaw. As you read these materials, consider the role that informed consent theories appear to play in traditional malpractice litigation. Of what relevance is it that informed consent claims are rarely brought alone but are most often seen in cases where plaintiffs also are asserting traditional negligence claims?

6. *The Spectrum of Informed Consent Standards.* Both courts and legislatures have participated in the redefinition of the roles in the physician-patient relationship. They have responded to the inequality of knowledge between providers and patients in at least four distinct ways. Some jurisdictions, about half in fact, use some version of a "material risk" or "reasonable patient" standard, which requires disclosure of risks that a reasonable patient would consider to be material in making a medical treatment decision. An almost equal number use the "professional malpractice" standard, under which physicians are required to disclose to patients that information which would have been disclosed by the reasonable, minimally competent physician. (See Chapter 4 for a detailed discussion of the theory of malpractice claims.) A small number of jurisdictions take an even more protective approach, requiring disclosure of information that a particular patient (as contrasted with a "rational" patient) would have wanted to make his or her decision. Finally, courts seeking tools to regulate the nature of the physician-patient relationship have recently turned to fiduciary law as a source of additional disclosure obligations for physicians.

7. *Additional Commentaries.* The literature on informed consent is voluminous. Some particularly useful commentaries (in addition to those cited in Schuck's

article) include Janet L. Dolgin, The Legal Development of Informed Consent Doctrine: Past and Present, 19 Cambridge Q. Healthcare Ethics 97 (2010); Christine Grady, Enduring and Emerging Challenges of Informed Consent, 372 New Eng. J. Med. 855 (2015); Marjorie Maguire Schultz, From Informed Consent to Patient Choice: A New Protected Interest, 95 Yale L. J. 219 (1985). The major treatise is Fay A. Rozovsky, Consent to Treatment: A Practical Guide (2015). There are several important books on the subject, including Carl E. Schneider, The Practice of Autonomy: Patients, Doctors, and Medical Decisions (1998); Ruth R. Faden & Tom L. Beauchamp, A History and Theory of Informed Consent (1986); Jessica W. Berg et al., Informed Consent: Legal Theory and Practice (2001). For general discussions of informed consent, see Annot., 88 A.L.R.3d 1008 (1978).

For a classic **attack on the fundamental theory of informed consent liability**, see Richard Epstein, Medical Malpractice: The Case for Contract, 1976 Am. B. Found. Res. J. 87 (1976). For a critique of informed consent law's application to **racial, religious, and ethnic minority patients**, see Dayna Bowen Matthew, Race, Religion, and Informed Consent—Lessons from Social Science, 36 J.L. Med. & Ethics 150 (2008). For **critiques of prevailing views of patient autonomy** and the physician-patient fiduciary relationship see: Omri Ben-Shahar & Carl E. Schneider, The Failure of Mandated Disclosure, 159 U. Pa. L. Rev. 647 (2011); Roger B. Dworkin, Getting What We Should from Doctors: Rethinking Patient Autonomy and the Doctor-Patient Relationship, 13 Health Matrix 235 (2003); Joan H. Krause, Can Health Law Truly Become Patient-Centered?, 45 Wake Forest L. Rev. 1489 (2010); Symposium, Under Attack: Reconceptualizing Informed Consent, 45 J. L., Med. & Ethics 6-111 (2017); Symposium, Contemporary Challenges in Informed Consent, 44 J. L., Med. Ethics 371-461 (2016).

For more on **informed consent in practice** (note 2), see Lisa I. Iezzoni, Survey Shows That at Least Some Physicians Are Not Always Open or Honest with Patients, 31 Health Aff. 383 (2012) (more than 10 percent of surveyed physicians reported telling "patients something untrue in the previous year"); C.J. Manta, J. Ortiz, B.W. Moulton, and S.S. Sonnad, From the Patient Perspective, Consent Forms Fall Short of Providing Information to Guide Decision Making, _ J Patient Safety _ (Aug. 3, 2016); A. Sherlock & S. Brownie, Patients' Recollection and Understanding of Informed Consent: A Literature Review, 84 ANZ J Surg 207 (2014); J. Bester, C. Cole & E. Kodish, The Limits of Informed Consent for an Overwhelmed Patient: Clinicians' Role in Protecting Patients and Preventing Overwhelm, 18 AMA J. Ethics 869 (2016); Barbara A. Noah, The (Ir)Rationality of (Un)Informed Consent, 34 Quinn. L Rev. 691 (2016); and Ada C. Stefanescu Schmidt, Ami Bhatt & Cass Sunstein, Boundedly Rational Patients? Health and Patient Mistakes in a Behavioral Framework, 1 J. Beh. Econ. for Pol'y 13-17, 19-25 (2017) (Pts 1 & 2).

Exploring various issues **relating to genetics and medical testing** (note 3), see Bartha Maria Knoppers, From the Right to Know to the Right Not to Know, 42 J. L., Med. & Ethics 6 (2014); Gina Kolata, How Do You Live Knowing You Might Have an Alzheimer's Gene?, N.Y. Times, June 7, 2012; Stewart Justman, Uninformed Consent: Mass Screening for Prostate Cancer, 26 Bioethics 143 (2012) (noting that widespread PSA screening creates risk of overdiagnosis and overtreatment for sons of men tested, without demonstrable improvements in health care outcomes).

For **cultural and comparative perspectives** (note 4), see Leslie J. Blackhall et al., Ethnicity and Attitudes Toward Patient Autonomy, 274 JAMA 820 (1995);

Joseph A. Carrese & Lorna A. Rhodes, Western Bioethics on the Navajo Reservation: Benefit or Harm?, 274 JAMA 826 (1995); Lawrence O. Gostin, Informed Consent, Cultural Sensitivity, and Respect for Persons, 274 JAMA 844 (1995); George J. Annas & Frances H. Miller, The Empire of Death: How Culture and Economics Affect Informed Consent in the U.S., U.K. and Japan, 20 Am. J. L. & Med. 357 (1994); Kristina Orfali & Elisa J. Gordon, Autonomy Gone Awry: A Cross-Cultural Study of Parents' Experiences in Neonatal Intensive Care Units, 25 Theoretical Med. & Bioethics 329 (2004).

Commentators have been particularly concerned with the role of informed consent in **medical research**. See, e.g., George J. Annas, Questing for Grails: Duplicity, Betrayal and Self-Deception in Postmodern Medical Research, 12 J. Contemp. Health L. & Pol'y 297 (1996); Ruth R. Faden & Tom L. Beauchamp, A History and Theory of Informed Consent 151-232 (1986). The issue is explored in greater depth in section D of this text.

Note: Informed Consent and the First Amendment

The First Amendment to the U.S. Constitution protects "freedom of speech." Yet states directly or indirectly regulate physician speech through the informed consent doctrine as well as through legislative requirements covering disclosures relating to a broad range of conditions or potential therapies. See, e.g., N.J.S. 26:5C-16 (requiring that primary care physicians provide pregnant women with specified information including the recommendation that they undergo testing for HIV). Like state regulation of the medical profession more generally, these disclosure requirements typically are deemed to further the state's compelling interest in the protection of public health. For particularly thoughtful, recent analyses of the relationship between the First Amendment and informed consent, see David Orentlicher, Abortion and Compelled Physician Speech, 43 J. L., Med. & Ethics 9 (2015); and Nadia N. Sawicki, Toward a Healthy First Amendment, 50 Wash. U. J.L. & Pol'y 11 (2016).

When do governmental efforts to regulate the content of physician-patient communication violate the First Amendment? The "Docs v. Glocks" litigation provides a good example of the complexity of this issue. In 2011, after learning about six anecdotal examples of patients concerned about actions or comments from health care providers related to firearm ownership, Florida enacted the Firearm Owners' Privacy Act (FOPA). F.S. §790.338. The Act prohibited physicians from (a) routinely inquiring about or keeping records of patient firearm ownership; (b) discriminating against patients exercising their "constitutional right to own or possess firearms or ammunition"; or (c) "unnecessarily harassing [] patient[s] about firearm ownership during an examination." Id. Violations of the Act were to be addressed through professional disciplinary action. Wollschlaeger v. Governor, Florida, 848 F.3d 1293, 1303 (11th Cir. 2017) (en banc). Firearm ownership is associated with substantial health risks and various medical organizations recommend that physicians inquire about gun ownership and counsel patients regarding gun safety measures. Id. at 1316. A group of physicians and medical organizations challenged the legislation under the First and Fourteenth Amendments.

The complex procedural history of the case, which includes a divided Court of Appeals panel issuing three different opinions employing three different standards of review, demonstrates significant uncertainty about the intersection of state power over professional regulation with First Amendment protections for physician speech. The Court of Appeals sitting en banc rejected the state's argument that "the First Amendment is not implicated because any effect on speech is merely incidental to the regulation of professional conduct," holding that "we do not think it is appropriate to subject content-based restrictions on speech by those engaged in a certain profession to mere rational basis review." 848 F.3d at 1308, 1311. However, the court determined that it did not need to resolve whether state regulation of professional speech should be tested using heightened scrutiny or strict scrutiny as FOPA's record-keeping, inquiry, and anti-harassment provisions failed the more generous heightened scrutiny review. Id. at 1311. Under the heightened scrutiny standard, states must show that specific speaker- and content-based restrictions directly advance a substantial government interest and that the measures are drawn to achieve that interest and that there is a "fit" between the means and ends chosen by the legislation. Id. at 1311-1312 (citing Sorrell v. IMS Health, Inc, 564 U.S. 552 (2011) (quotations omitted)).

The court found that the record-keeping, inquiry, and anti-harassment provisions did not directly advance the state's asserted substantial interests in protecting citizens' Second Amendment rights, individual privacy or access to health care or its substantial interests in regulating the medical profession. (Of these, the state's interest in regulating the medical profession to protect public health would likely be relevant to the typical informed consent requirement). The court also found that the FOPA measures were not narrowly drawn to achieve these interests. After limiting the FOPA's anti-discrimination provision to apply to "non-expressive conduct," the court upheld the anti-discrimination provision. Id. at 1317. In a second majority opinion, the court also found that the anti-harassment provisions were unconstitutionally vague. Id. at 1319. For more on the case and its implications, see Claudia E. Haupt, Professional Speech and the Content-Neutrality Trap, 127 Yale L. J. Forum 150 (2017); and Wendy E. Parmet, Jason A. Smith & Matthew Miller, Physicians, Firearms, and Free Speech—Overturning Florida's Firearm-Safety Gag Rule, 376 New Eng. J. Med. 1901 (2017).

For additional examples of the debate about the appropriate scope of state control see King v. Governor of N.J., 767 F.3d 216 (3rd Cir. 2014) (upholding NJ prohibition of use of "sexual orientation change efforts" ("SOCE") therapy to children in an analysis that offers less constitutional protection for professional speech than for public speech or the expression of opinions to patients); Pickup v. Brown, 740 F.3d 1208, 1225-29 (9th Cir. 2013) (upholding California law prohibiting use SOCE therapy to children); and Conant v. Walters, 309 F.3d 629 (9th Cir. 2002) (striking down policy threatening physicians who recommended medicinal use of marijuana with the loss of DEA prescriptive authority).

The power of states to direct physician speech has been particularly tested in the area of abortion. The Supreme Court has upheld the constitutional validity of state laws that impose specific informed consent obligations on physicians performing abortions. Planned Parenthood of Southeastern Pennsylvania v. Casey, 505 U.S. 833, 884 (1992). There have been successive waves of state informed consent regulations involving matters ranging from fetal development and pain to asserted mental health consequences for women who choose to undergo abortion. See Wendy K. Mariner & George J. Annas, Informed Consent and the First Amendment, 372

New Eng. J. Med. 1285 (2015). Courts have typically upheld special abortion-related informed consent requirements against First Amendment challenges so long as the required disclosures are found to be relevant, truthful, and non-misleading. The issue is explored further in Chapter 7 at pages 753-755.

2. *The Competing Disclosure Standards*

■ CANTERBURY v. SPENCE
464 F.2d 772 (D.C. Cir.), cert. denied, 409 U.S. 1064 (1972)

[Appellant Canterbury, a 19-year-old clerk-typist who had experienced persistent back pain, sought care from Dr. Spence. Dr. Spence conducted a number of tests to determine the cause of the back pain and eventually recommended that Canterbury undergo a laminectomy. According to the court, Canterbury "did not raise any objection to the proposed operation nor did he probe into its exact nature." Dr. Spence spoke with Canterbury's mother by telephone. She asked "if the recommended operation was serious and Dr. Spence replied 'not any more than any other operation.'" It is unclear whether Mrs. Canterbury consented to the operation before it took place; she did sign a consent form afterward. The laminectomy was performed without any apparent difficulties. During the recovery period, however, hospital personnel failed to assist Canterbury during the process of voiding, and Canterbury fell out of his bed while attempting to void. Canterbury developed signs of partial paralysis a few hours after the fall, which were only partially improved by another operation.]

At the time of the trial . . . [he] required crutches to walk, still suffered from urinal incontinence and paralysis of the bowels, and wore a penile clamp. . . . [H]e [had] held a number of jobs, but had constant trouble finding work because he needed to remain seated and close to a bathroom. The damages appellant claims include extensive pain and suffering, medical expenses, and loss of earnings.

Appellant filed suit in the district court on March 7, 1963, four years after the laminectomy and approximately two years after he attained his majority. The complaint stated several causes of action against each defendant. Against Dr. Spence it alleged, among other things, negligence in the performance of the laminectomy and failure to inform him beforehand of the risk involved. Against the hospital the complaint charged negligent postoperative care in permitting appellant to remain unattended after the laminectomy, in failing to provide a nurse or orderly to assist him at the time of his fall, and in failing to maintain a side rail on his bed. . . .

At the close of appellant's case in chief, each defendant moved for a directed verdict and the trial judge granted both motions. . . . The judge did not allude specifically to the alleged breach of duty by Dr. Spence to divulge the possible consequences of the laminectomy.

We reverse. The testimony of appellant and his mother that Dr. Spence did not reveal the risk of paralysis from the laminectomy made out a prima facie case of violation of the physician's duty to disclose which Dr. Spence's explanation did not negate as a matter of law. . . .

Suits charging failure by a physician[6] adequately to disclose the risks and alternatives of proposed treatment are not innovations in American law. They date back a good half-century, and in the last decade they have multiplied rapidly. There is, nonetheless, disagreement among the courts and the commentators on many major questions, and there is no precedent of our own directly in point. For the tools enabling resolution of the issues on this appeal, we are forced to begin at first principles.

The root premise is the concept, fundamental in American jurisprudence, that "[e]very human being of adult years and sound mind has a right to determine what shall be done with his own body. . . ."[12] True consent to what happens to one's self is the informed exercise of a choice, and that entails an opportunity to evaluate knowledgeably the options available and the risks attendant upon each. The average patient has little or no understanding of the medical arts, and ordinarily has only his physician to whom he can look for enlightenment with which to reach an intelligent decision. From these almost axiomatic considerations springs the need, and in turn the requirement, of a reasonable divulgence by physician to patient to make such a decision possible.[15]

A physician is under a duty to treat his patient skillfully but proficiency in diagnosis and therapy is not the full measure of his responsibility. The cases demonstrate that the physician is under an obligation to communicate specific information to the patient when the exigencies of reasonable care call for it. . . .

A reasonable revelation in these respects is not only a necessity but, as we see it, is as much a matter of the physician's duty. It is a duty to warn of the dangers lurking in the proposed treatment, and that is surely a facet of due care. It is, too, a duty to impart information which the patient has every right to expect. The patient's reliance upon the physician is a trust of the kind which traditionally has exacted obligations beyond those associated with arms length transactions. His dependence upon the physician for information affecting his well-being, in terms of contemplated treatment, is well-nigh abject. As earlier noted, long before the instant litigation arose, courts had recognized that the physician had the responsibility of satisfying the vital informational needs of the patient. More recently, we ourselves have found "in the fiducial qualities of [the physician-patient] relationship the physician's duty to reveal to the patient that which in his best interests it is important that he should

---

6. Since there was neither allegation nor proof that the appellee hospital failed in any duty to disclose, we have no occasion to inquire as to whether or under what circumstances such a duty might arise.

12. Schloendorff v. Society of New York Hospital, 211 N.Y. 125, 105 N.E. 92, 93 (1914). . . .

15. In duty-to-disclose cases, the focus of attention is more properly upon the nature and content of the physician's divulgence than the patient's understanding or consent. Adequate disclosure and informed consent are, of course, two sides of the same coin — the former a sine qua non of the latter. But the vital inquiry on duty to disclose relates to the physician's performance of an obligation, while one of the difficulties with analysis in terms of "informed consent" is its tendency to imply that what is decisive is the degree of the patient's comprehension. As we later emphasize, physician discharges the duty when he makes a reasonable effort to convey sufficient information although the patient, without fault of the physician, may not fully grasp it. . . .

know." We now find, as a part of the physician's overall obligation to the patient, a similar duty of reasonable disclosure of the choices with respect to proposed therapy and the dangers inherently and potentially involved.

This disclosure requirement, on analysis, reflects much more of a change in doctrinal emphasis than a substantive addition to malpractice law. It is well established that the physician must seek and secure his patient's consent before commencing an operation or other course of treatment. It is also clear that the consent, to be efficacious, must be free from imposition upon the patient. It is the settled rule that therapy not authorized by the patient may amount to a tort—a common law battery—by the physician. And it is evident that it is normally impossible to obtain a consent worthy of the name unless the physician first elucidates the options and the perils for the patient's edification. Thus the physician has long borne a duty, on pain of liability for unauthorized treatment, to make adequate disclosure to the patient.[36] . . .

Duty to disclose has gained recognition in a large number of American jurisdictions, but more largely on a different rationale. The majority of courts dealing with the problem have made the duty depend on whether it was the custom of physicians practicing in the community to make the particular disclosure to the patient. . . . We agree that the physician's noncompliance with a professional custom to reveal, like any other departure from prevailing medical practice, may give rise to liability to the patient. We do not agree that the patient's cause of action is dependent upon the existence and nonperformance of a relevant professional tradition.

There are, in our view, formidable obstacles to acceptance of the notion that the physician's obligation to disclose is either germinated or limited by medical practice. To begin with, the reality of any discernible custom reflecting a professional consensus on communication of option and risk information to patients is open to serious doubt. We sense the danger that what in fact is no custom at all may be taken as an affirmative custom to maintain silence, and that physician-witnesses to the so-called custom may state merely their personal opinions as to what they or others would do under given conditions. . . . Respect for the patient's right of self-determination on particular therapy demands a standard set by law for physicians rather than one which physicians may or may not impose upon themselves.

More fundamentally, the majority rule overlooks the graduation of reasonable-care demands in Anglo-American jurisprudence and the position of professional custom in the hierarchy. . . .

There is . . . no basis for operation of the special medical standard where the physician's activity does not bring his medical knowledge and skills peculiarly into play. . . .

---

36. We discard the thought that the patient should ask for information before the physician is required to disclose. Caveat emptor is not the norm for the consumer of medical services. Duty to disclose is more than a call to speak merely on the patient's request, or merely to answer the patient's questions; it is a duty to volunteer, if necessary, the information the patient needs for intelligent decision. The patient may be ignorant, confused, over-awed by the physician or frightened by the hospital, or even ashamed to inquire. See generally Note, Restructuring Informed Consent: Legal Therapy for the Doctor-Patient Relationship, 79 Yale L.J. 1533, 1545-1551 (1970). . . .

[T]he physician's duty to disclose is governed by the same legal principles applicable to others in comparable situations, with modifications only to the extent that medical judgment enters the picture. We hold that the standard measuring performance of that duty by physicians, as by others, is conduct which is reasonable under the circumstances.

Once the circumstances give rise to a duty on the physician's part to inform his patient, the next inquiry is the scope of the disclosure the physician is legally obliged to make. The courts have frequently confronted this problem but no uniform standard defining the adequacy of the divulgence emerges from the decisions. . . .

The larger number of courts, as might be expected, have applied tests framed with reference to prevailing fashion within the medical profession. . . .

In our view, the patient's right of self-decision shapes the boundaries of the duty to reveal. That right can be effectively exercised only if the patient possesses enough information to enable an intelligent choice. The scope of the physician's communications to the patient, then, must be measured by the patient's need, and that need is the information material to the decision. Thus the test for determining whether a particular peril must be divulged is its materiality to the patient's decision: All risks potentially affecting the decision must be unmasked. And to safeguard the patient's interest in achieving his own determination on treatment, the law must itself set the standard for adequate disclosure.

Optimally for the patient, exposure of a risk would be mandatory whenever the patient would deem it significant to his decision, either singly or in combination with other risks. Such a requirement, however, would summon the physician to second-guess the patient, whose ideas on materiality could hardly be known to the physician. That would make an undue demand upon medical practitioners, whose conduct, like that of others, is to be measured in terms of reasonableness. Consonantly with orthodox negligence doctrine, the physician's liability for nondisclosure is to be determined on the basis of foresight, not hindsight; no less than any other aspect of negligence, the issue on nondisclosure must be approached from the viewpoint of the reasonableness of the physician's divulgence in terms of what he knows or should know to be the patient's informational needs. . . .

From these considerations we derive the breadth of the disclosure of risks legally to be required. The scope of the standard is not subjective as to either the physician or the patient; it remains objective with due regard for the patient's informational needs and with suitable leeway for the physician's situation. In broad outline, we agree that "[a] risk is thus material when a reasonable person, in what the physician knows or should know to be the patient's position, would be likely to attach significance to the risk or cluster of risks in deciding whether or not to forego the proposed therapy."

The topics importantly demanding a communication of information are the inherent and potential hazards of the proposed treatment, the alternatives to that treatment, if any, and the results likely if the patient remains untreated. The factors contributing significance to the dangerousness of a medical technique are, of course, the incidence of injury and the degree of the harm threatened. A very small chance of death or serious disablement may well be significant; a potential disability which dramatically outweighs the potential benefit of the therapy or the detriments of the existing malady may summon discussion with the patient.

There is no bright line separating the significant from the insignificant; the answer in any case must abide a rule of reason. Some dangers—infection, for example—are inherent in any operation; there is no obligation to communicate those of which persons of average sophistication are aware. Even more clearly, the physician bears no responsibility for discussion of hazards the patient has already discovered, or those having no apparent materiality to patients' decision on therapy. . . .

No more than breach of any other legal duty does nonfulfillment of the physician's obligation to disclose alone establish liability to the patient. An unrevealed risk that should have been made known must materialize, for otherwise the omission, however unpardonable, is legally without consequence. Occurrence of the risk must be harmful to the patient, for negligence unrelated to injury is nonactionable. And, as in malpractice actions generally, there must be a causal relationship between the physician's failure to adequately divulge and damage to the patient.

A causal connection exists when, but only when, disclosure of significant risks incidental to treatment would have resulted in a decision against it. The patient obviously has no complaint if he would have submitted to the therapy notwithstanding awareness that the risk was one of its perils. On the other hand, the very purpose of the disclosure rule is to protect the patient against consequences which, if known, he would have avoided by foregoing the treatment. The more difficult question is whether the factual issue on causality calls for an objective or a subjective determination. . . .

It has been assumed that the issue is to be resolved according to whether the factfinder believes the patient's testimony that he would not have agreed to the treatment if he had known of the danger which later ripened into injury. . . .

In our view, this method of dealing with the issue on causation comes in second-best. It places the physician in jeopardy of the patient's hindsight and bitterness. It places the factfinder in the position of deciding whether a speculative answer to a hypothetical question is to be credited. It calls for a subjective determination solely on testimony of a patient-witness shadowed by the occurrence of the undisclosed risk.

Better it is, we believe, to resolve the causality issue on an objective basis: in terms of what a prudent person in the patient's position would have decided if suitably informed of all perils bearing significance. If adequate disclosure could reasonably be expected to have caused that person to decline the treatment because of the revelation of the kind of risk or danger that resulted in harm, causation is shown, but otherwise not. The patient's testimony is relevant on that score of course but it would not threaten to dominate the findings. . . .

In the context of trial of a suit claiming inadequate disclosure of risk information by a physician, the patient has the burden of going forward with evidence tending to establish prima facie the essential elements of the cause of action, and ultimately the burden of proof—the risk of nonpersuasion—on those elements. . . . The burden of going forward with evidence pertaining to a privilege not to disclose, however, rests properly upon the physician. . . .

We now delineate our view on the need for expert testimony in nondisclosure cases. . . .

The guiding consideration our decisions distill, however, is that medical facts are for medical experts and other facts are for any witnesses—expert or not—having sufficient knowledge and capacity to testify to them. It is evident that many of the issues typically involved in nondisclosure cases do not reside peculiarly within the medical domain. Lay witness testimony can competently establish a physician's failure to disclose particular risk information, the patient's lack of knowledge of the risk, and the adverse consequences following the treatment. Experts are unnecessary to a showing of the materiality of a risk to a patient's decision on treatment, or to the reasonably, expectable effect of risk disclosure on the decision. These conspicuous examples of permissible uses of nonexpert testimony illustrate the relative freedom of broad areas of the legal problem of risk nondisclosure from the demands for expert testimony that shackle plaintiffs' other types of medical malpractice litigation. . . .

This brings us to the remaining question . . . whether appellant's evidence was of such caliber as to require a submission to the jury. [T]he evidence was clearly sufficient to raise an issue as to whether Dr. Spence's obligation to disclose information on risks was reasonably met or was excused by the surrounding circumstances. Appellant testified that Dr. Spence revealed to him nothing suggesting a hazard associated with the laminectomy. His mother testified that, in response to her specific inquiry, Dr. Spence informed her that the laminectomy was no more serious than any other operation. When, at trial, it developed from Dr. Spence's testimony that paralysis can be expected in 1 percent of laminectomies, it became the jury's responsibility to decide whether that peril was of sufficient magnitude to bring the disclosure duty into play. There was no emergency to frustrate an opportunity to disclose, and Dr. Spence's expressed opinion that disclosure would have been unwise did not foreclose a contrary conclusion by the jury. There was no evidence that appellant's emotional makeup was such that concealment of the risk of paralysis was medically sound. Even if disclosure to appellant himself might have bred ill consequences, no reason appears for the omission to communicate the information to his mother, particularly in view of his minority. The jury, not Dr. Spence, was the final arbiter of whether nondisclosure was reasonable under the circumstances. . . .

Reversed and remanded for new trial.

■ CULBERTSON v. MERNITZ
602 N.E.2d 98 (Ind. 1992)

KRAHULIK, Justice.

Roland B. Mernitz, M.D., (Appellee-Defendant) seeks transfer from the Court of Appeals' reversal of a summary judgment entered in his favor. Culbertson v. Mernitz (1992), Ind. App., 591 N.E.2d 1040. The issue squarely presented in this petition is whether expert medical testimony is required to establish the standard of care of health care providers on the issue of informed consent. . . .

The facts of the case are as follows. Dr. Mernitz first saw Patty Jo Culbertson on March 28, 1988. Her chief complaint was that of uncontrollable leakage of urine and discharge from the vagina. After performing a physical examination, Dr. Mernitz . . . recommend[ed] . . . that she . . . undergo a surgical procedure known as a[n] MMK [Marshall Marchetti Krantz] procedure in order to suspend the bladder and either a hysterectomy or cryosurgery to freeze the infected tip of the cervix. Dr. Mernitz contends that he advised her of the general risks of any surgery, viz. infection, bleeding, and death, and that, with respect to the bladder suspension, he explained to her the risk that the procedure could fail and the possibility that she would be unable to void. . . . Both parties . . . agree that Dr. Mernitz did not advise her of a risk that the cervix could become adhered to the wall of the vagina.

Following this office visit, Mrs. Culbertson decided to proceed with the bladder suspension and cryosurgery. She was admitted to the hospital and underwent these procedures. Post-surgically, Mrs. Culbertson's cervix adhered to the wall of her vagina. Dr. Mernitz prescribed medication for this condition, but Mrs. Culbertson became dissatisfied with his care and saw another surgeon who eventually performed a total abdominal hysterectomy, bilateral salpingo-oophorectomy which involves the removal of both ovaries, and another bladder suspension.

Following this surgery, Mr. and Mrs. Culbertson filed a proposed complaint against Dr. Mernitz with the Indiana Department of Insurance in four counts. . . . Count II alleged that Dr. Mernitz failed to inform Mrs. Culbertson of the alternatives to surgery and the inherent risks and complications of surgery. . . .

A medical review panel was convened and, after submission of evidence to it, issued its written opinion. . . . With respect to the informed consent issue alleged in Count II, the panel ruled:

> The Panel determines that [Dr. Mernitz] did not advise [Mrs. Culbertson] of the complication of cervical adhesion to the vagina; the Panel further determines that such non-disclosure does not constitute a failure to comply with the appropriate standard of care, as such complication is not considered a risk of such surgery requiring disclosure to the patient.

The Culbertsons filed their civil action in a complaint that mirrored the allegations of the proposed complaint. After answering this complaint, Dr. Mernitz moved for summary judgment relying on the expert opinion issued by the medical review panel. The Culbertsons did not file an affidavit or other evidence in opposition to the motion for summary judgment, but argued to the trial court that the "prudent patient" standard should be utilized in evaluating informed consent claims. The trial court entered summary judgment [for the defendants]. . . . [W]e must determine the role, if any, played by expert medical opinion in resolving claims of medical malpractice premised upon a failure to obtain an informed consent.

The courts, historically, have established the standard of care required of physicians when treating patients. The law requires that a physician treating a patient possess and exercise that degree of skill and care ordinarily possessed and exercised by a physician treating such maladies.

. . . In order for a lay jury to know whether a physician complied with the legally prescribed standard of care, expert testimony has generally been held to be required. This requirement was premised on the logical belief that a non-physician could not know what a reasonably prudent physician would or would not have done under the circumstances of any given case. Therefore, an expert familiar with the practice of medicine needed to establish what a reasonably prudent physician would or would not have done in treating a patient in order to set before the jury a depiction of the reasonably prudent physician against which to judge the actions of the defendant physician. An exception was created in cases of res ipsa loquitur on the premise that in such cases a lay jury did not need guidance from a physician familiar with medical practice as to what was required of a reasonably prudent physician because the deficiency of practice "spoke for itself." Kranda v. Houser-Norborg

Med. Corp., 419 N.E.2d 1024, 1042 (Ind. App. 1981). This was the settled law of most American jurisdictions, including Indiana, prior to the early 1970s when two cases on the opposite coasts carved out an additional exception to the requirement of expert medical testimony in the area of "informed consent." [The court summarized Cobbs v. Grant, 8 Cal. 3d 229 (1972), and Canterbury v. Spence, 464 F.2d 772 (D.C. Cir.), cert. denied, 409 U.S. 1064 (1972).]

INFORMED CONSENT IN INDIANA JURISPRUDENCE

[The court reviewed Indiana case law and concluded that Indiana followed the medical malpractice standard in informed consent cases. Under this standard, physicians are required to disclose that which the reasonably careful, skillful, and prudent physician would disclose under the same or similar circumstances. In general, medical expert testimony will be required to determine whether a physician has violated her duty, "unless the situation is clearly within the realm of laymen's comprehension."]

Resolution of the issue of the necessity of expert medical testimony in informed consent cases depends on whether the issue is viewed through the eyes of the physician or the patient. When viewed through the eyes of the physician, it is easy to see that a physician should not be required to guess or speculate as to what a hypothetical "reasonably prudent patient" would "need to know" in order to make a determination. A physician should only be required to do that which he is trained to do, namely, conduct himself as a reasonably prudent physician in taking a history, performing a physical examination, ordering appropriate tests, reaching a diagnosis, prescribing a course of treatment, and in discussing with the patient the medical facts of the proposed procedure, including the risks inherent in either accepting or rejecting the proposed course of treatment. From a physician's viewpoint, he should not be called upon to be a "mind reader" with the ability to peer into the brain of a prudent patient to determine what such patient "needs to know," but should simply be called upon to discuss medical facts and recommendations with the patient as a reasonably prudent physician would.

On the other hand, from the patient's viewpoint, the physician should be required to give the patient sufficient information to enable the patient to reasonably exercise the patient's right of self-decision in a knowledgeable manner. Viewed from this vantage point, the patient does not want the medical profession to determine in a paternalistic manner what the patient should or should not be told concerning the course of treatment. Thus, such a patient would view the reasonably prudent physician standard as destroying the patient's right of self-decision and, impliedly, placing such decision under the exclusive domain of the medical profession. While this viewpoint may or may not have been justified in 1972 when *Canterbury* and *Cobbs* were decided, a review of medical ethics standards of care in 1992 should assuage this fear.

The 1992 Code of Medical Ethics, as prepared by the Council on Ethical and Judicial Affairs of the American Medical Association, sets forth the medical profession's standard on informed consent. It reads as follows:

> The patient's right of self-decision can be effectively exercised only if the patient possesses enough information to enable an intelligent choice. The patient should

make his own determination on treatment. The physician's obligation is to present the medical facts accurately to the patient or to the individual responsible for his care and to make recommendations for management in accordance with good medical practice. The physician has an ethical obligation to help the patient make choices from among the therapeutic alternatives consistent with good medical practice. Informed consent is a basic social policy for which exceptions are permitted (1) where the patient is unconscious or otherwise incapable of consenting and harm from failure to treat is imminent; or (2) when risk-disclosure poses such a serious psychological threat of detriment to the patient as to be medically contraindicated. Social policy does not accept the paternalistic view that the physician may remain silent because divulgence might prompt the patient to forego needed therapy. Rational, informed patients should not be expected to act uniformly, even under similar circumstances, in agreeing to or refusing treatment.

We recognize this statement as a reasonable statement on the issue of informed consent. There is no need to change Indiana law on this issue. We therefore hold that, except in those cases where deviation from the standard of care is a matter commonly known by lay persons, expert medical testimony is necessary to establish whether a physician has or has not complied with the standard of a reasonably prudent physician.

In the present case we cannot say that the risk of the adherence of the cervix to the vaginal wall is a matter commonly known to lay persons. Therefore, the Culbertsons needed to provide expert medical testimony to refute the unanimous opinion issued by the medical review panel in order to present a material issue of fact as to what a reasonably prudent physician would have discussed concerning this proposed surgery. Without the presentation of such expert medical opinion, the trial court could only conclude that there was no genuine issue of material fact and that summary judgment should be entered for Dr. Mernitz.

[Justice Dickson's dissenting opinion is omitted.]

Notes: Competing Disclosure Standards

1. *The Objective Patient-Centered Standard vs. the Professional Standard.* Why did the *Canterbury* court reject the professional standard of disclosure? One criticism of the malpractice standard is that it measures the scope of required disclosures by customary practice rather than by the patient's need to know. The *Culbertson* court considered and rejected this argument, noting that the 1992 Code of Medical Ethics promulgated by the American Medical Association recognized a physician's duty to provide information to patients. See also, AMA Code of Medical Ethics 1.1.3 Patient Rights & 2.1 Informed Consent & Shared Decision Making (2016). Does *Canterbury*'s material risk standard provide any significant additional protections given current norms of medical practice? An empirical study suggests that informed consent claims are more likely to succeed in jurisdictions that have adopted the "patient-centered" standard of disclosure. David M. Studdert et al., Geographic Variation in Informed Consent Law: Two Standards for Disclosure of Treatment Risks, 4 J. Empirical Legal Stud. 103 (2007).

2. *The Implications of* Canterbury's *Patient-Centered or Material Risk Standard.* How are providers to know whether a risk should be deemed material? Is there any way for a physician to make this determination before providing care for the patient

or before litigating the issue? See American College of Surgeons, Surgical Risk Calculator, at https://riskcalculator.facs.org/RiskCalculator/. What factors does the court suggest are relevant to the determination of materiality? How would you advise a physician who is considering whether to inform patients about the following risks associated with a particular type of cosmetic surgery: (1) a .01 percent risk of death from anesthesia; (2) a 1 percent risk of severe bleeding that would require a blood transfusion (which carries additional risks, ranging from fever to heart failure to transmission of bloodborne pathogens); (3) a 3 percent risk of postoperative infection (which would require treatment by antibiotics, which carry a small risk of adverse reactions); (4) a 5 percent risk of nerve damage that could lead to localized paralysis and/or loss of sensation; and (5) a 10 percent risk that the cosmetic flaw will not be significantly improved.

Some legislatures have provided "safe harbors" for physicians. In Texas, for example, a Medical Disclosure Panel determines what disclosures should be made for certain types of procedures. Physicians disclosing risks pursuant to the Panel's guidelines enjoy a rebuttable presumption that their informed consent obligations have been met. Failure to follow the guidelines creates a rebuttable presumption of negligence. Tex. Civ. Prac. & Rem. Code §74.106. See also Louisiana Medical Disclosure Panel, LSA-R.S. 40:1157.2.

3. *Assessing the Disclosure Landscape.* The patient-centered, material risk standard has been adopted in roughly half of the states and the District of Columbia. The professional disclosure standard has been adopted in the bulk of the remaining states. Two states use a "hybrid" approach. Robin Fretwell Wilson, The Promise of Informed Consent, in the Oxford Handbook of U.S. Health Law 218 (I. Glenn Cohen, Allison K. Hoffman & William M. Sage eds. 2017). In some states, the disclosure standard has been adopted by the courts; in others, it has been imposed by the legislature. In jurisdictions following the professional or reasonable physician disclosure standard, medical practice determines whether a particular type of information will be disclosed to patients. The standard protects physicians from liability so long as they disclose that which would be disclosed by the reasonably prudent physician under like or similar circumstances. In *Culbertson*, the court suggests that the professional malpractice standard will protect individual autonomy because it incorporates the view that individuals must be given enough information to make intelligent decisions. Was Mrs. Culbertson given enough information in this case?

4. *The Subjective Patient-Centered Disclosure Standard.* Note that the material risk standard requires the disclosure of information that a reasonable person would consider material in making a determination about treatment. In most circumstances, physicians are not required to provide information about risks that might be considered significant by an individual patient. The *Canterbury* court recognizes this potential defect but finds that the imposition of a subjective disclosure standard would pose an "undue burden" on a physician—unless the physician knows of the patient's idiosyncratic views. See, e.g., Stowell v. Huddleston, 643 F.3d 631 (8th Cir. 2011) (applying state informed consent standard requiring disclosure of risks of particular significance to patient); Lugenbuhl v. Dowling, 676 So. 2d 602 (La. Ct. App. 1996) (subjective considerations potentially relevant even in objective standard jurisdiction). The overwhelming majority of those jurisdictions that use the "material risk" standard have followed the *Canterbury* approach by measuring the scope of disclosure by the objective patient. But cf. Macy v. Blatchford, 8 P.3d 204

(Or. 2000) (evidence of sexual relationship between physician and patient relevant to determine whether physician had met his statutory duty to "explain" proposed treatment because of the possible impact of the relationship on the patient's ability to understand).

5. *Expert Testimony Under the Material Risk and Professional Disclosure Standards.* In jurisdictions following the professional disclosure standard, testimony by medical experts obviously will be required to determine whether the defendant met the standard of care. University of Maryland Medical System Corp. v. Waldt, 983 A.2d 112 (Md. 2009) (proposed expert not qualified to testify regarding informed consent claim); Foster v. Oral Surgery Ass'n, 940 A.2d 1102 (Maine 2008) (medical ethicist not qualified as expert). Will a plaintiff in a "material risk" jurisdiction be able to avoid this requirement? Testimony by medical experts will still be required to provide the fact finder with information about the nature and degree of risk associated with particular treatments. See Dunn v. Yager, 58 So. 3d 1171 (Miss. 2011); but see Shortell v. Cavanagh, 15 A.3d 1042 (Conn. 2011) (expert testimony not always required). Experts may also be needed to help the fact finder determine whether the harm suffered by the plaintiff was caused by the procedure or by the plaintiff's underlying injury. See, e.g., Suhadolnik v. Pressman, 254 P.3d 11 (Idaho 2011) (expert testimony and local standard of care); Griffin v. Moseley, 234 P.3d 869 (Mont. 2010) (physician qualified to testify about neurosurgeon's duty to disclose alternative treatments). In some cases, the plaintiff's evidentiary burden can be met through the "expert testimony" provided by the defendant physician. Garcia v. Robinson, 375 P.3d 167 (Hawai'i 2016). See generally Annot., 52 A.L.R.3d 1084 (1973).

6. *Whose Duty? Disclosure as a "Professional" Rather Than "Institutional" Obligation.* Courts typically focus on the physician-patient relationship in establishing and defining disclosure obligations. See, e.g., Shinal v. Toms, 162 A.3d 429 (Pa. 2017) ("physician may not delegate to others his or her obligation to provide sufficient information in order to obtain a patient's informed consent"). Another important consequence of the doctrinal origins of the informed consent claim is that its application has been restricted to a limited range of health care professionals. See, e.g., Blotner v. Doreika, 678 S.E.2d 80 (Ga. 2009) (no common-law informed consent duty applicable to chiropractors); Foster v. Traul, 120 P.3d 278 (Idaho 2005) (physician has duty to obtain informed consent; hospital merely assists in documentation). Should health care institutions have a duty to disclose some types of risks? Should there be an institutional duty to ensure that patients have given their informed consent to care? If so, what should be the doctrinal source of this obligation? The role of hospitals is further discussed infra at page 179 note 4.

7. *Informed Consent and Battery.* Why couldn't claims of this type be resolved using principles from battery cases? Plaintiffs pleading informed consent violations as battery actions have two key advantages: They do not have to prove a deviation from the standard of care and they have greater access to punitive damages awards. There are drawbacks, of course; a battery theory is difficult to apply where the medical treatment is noninvasive, and a defendant's insurance policy may exclude coverage for intentional torts.

In the typical informed consent claim, the patient has given technical consent to being "touched" by the defendant but argues that consent would not have been given if appropriate disclosures had been made. Courts generally reject battery claims because the patient has "consented" to the touching. In most jurisdictions, battery claims are reserved for those situations in which (1) the patient has not consented to any treatment at all, (2) the health care provider performs a completely different procedure than that for which consent was given, (3) the health care provider performs a procedure on the wrong area of the body, or (4) a different, unconsented-to provider performs the procedure. See, e.g., Coulter v. Thomas, 33 S.W.3d 522 (Ky. 2000) (physician's failure to remove blood pressure cuff as requested by patient addressed in battery claim, not under state informed consent statute); Humboldt Gen. Hosp. v. Sixth Jud. Dist. Ct., 376 P.3d 167 (Nev. 2016) (physician inserted non-FDA approved IUD; battery applicable where consent absent, informed consent governs this dispute over scope); but see Linog v. Yampolosky, 656 S.E.2d 355 (S.C. 2008) (no cause of action for medical battery); and Allison v. Brown, 801 S.E.2d 761 (Va. 2017) (surgeon allegedly improperly operated on both breasts rather than one; plaintiff failed to plead claim for battery and failed to establish proximate cause for informed consent; case remanded for retrial on whether it was negligent to operate without consent); Mayr v. Osborne, 795 S.E.2d 731 (Va. 2017) (claim that physician operated on the "wrong area" by fusing incorrect level of patient's spine properly addressed through informed consent and negligence rather than battery). See generally Annot., 39 A.L.R.4th 1034 (1985). For a discussion from a medical perspective, see David C. Ring et al., Case 34-2010: A 65-Year-Old Woman with an Incorrect Operation on the Left Hand, 363 New Eng. J. Med. 1950 (2010).

8. *Fraud, Misrepresentation and Violation of Consumer Protection Legislation.* Health care providers who misrepresent the risks associated with treatments could be held liable for fraud, misrepresentation, or violation of consumer protection statutes. See, e.g., Annot., 42 A.L.R.4th 543 (1985); Jones v. Clinch, 73 A.3d 80 (D.C. Ct. App. 2013) (noting differential treatment of patient claims under consumer protection legislation in Maryland and D.C.). However, courts are reluctant to permit use of these theories, particularly where they may be asserted in an effort to avoid procedural or substantive requirements applicable to medical negligence claims. See Chapter 4.H. See Sanchez v. Martin, 378 S.W.3d 581 (Tex.-App.-Dallas 2017).

Notes: The Other Elements of a Nondisclosure Claim

1. *Elements of a Cause of Action.* Plaintiffs in informed consent claims generally will be required to prove (1) that the medical procedure carried a specific risk that was not disclosed, (2) that the physician violated the applicable standard of disclosure, (3) that the undisclosed risk materialized, and (4) that the failure to disclose the information caused the patient's injury.

2. *The Materialization of the Undisclosed Risk.* The plaintiff must show that the undisclosed risk actually materialized into harm. As a result, many failures to disclose information are never litigated. Does this make sense? Can you draw a parallel to the concept of proximate cause in traditional negligence actions? If the purpose of the informed consent doctrine is to protect individual autonomy and to encourage the transfer of information, doesn't a violation of the disclosure obligation cause a cognizable injury even without a physical harm? See Parris v. Limes, 277 P.3d 1259 (Okla. 2012) (patient who underwent post-surgical treatments alleges physician erred in failing to disclose that surgically removed prostate was cancer

free; court finds that the emergence of an undisclosed risk is not required where
the patient would not have undergone treatment if he or she had been properly
"informed of all the material facts").

Several commentators have argued that individual autonomy would be better
protected through the adoption of a "dignitary tort" doctrine, in which the failure
to disclose information would be actionable even in the absence of any physical
injury. See, e.g., Alan Meisel, A "Dignitary Tort" as a Bridge Between the Idea of
Informed Consent and the Law of Informed Consent, 16 L. Med. & Health Care
210, 211-214 (1988); Aaron D. Twerski & Neil B. Cohen, Informed Decision-Making
and the Law of Torts: The Myth of Justiciable Causation, 1988 U. Ill. L. Rev. 607, 655;
Alan J. Weisbard, Informed Consent: The Law's Uneasy Compromise with Ethical
Theory, 65 Neb. L. Rev. 749, 763-764 (1986).

How should damages be measured? "The damages analysis . . . involves a comparison between the condition a plaintiff would have been in had he or she been
properly informed and not consented to the risk, with the plaintiff's impaired condition as a result of the risk's occurrence." Howard v. University of Medicine &
Dentistry of N.J., 800 A.2d 73 (N.J. 2002). The damages calculations can be more
difficult when the patient's initial condition is serious and there are no other alternative treatments.

3. *Objective Causation.* The causation issues associated with informed consent
actions are somewhat complex. Most jurisdictions—including those applying the
material risk standard—will require proof of objective causation. That is, a plaintiff
will be required to show that a reasonable patient would not have undergone the
treatment had the material risks been disclosed. Cf. White v. Beeks, 469 S.W.3d 517
(Tenn. 2015) (expert testimony about risks relevant whether or not the risks materialized). Does the informed consent doctrine coupled with an objective causation
requirement adequately protect the patient's right to the information necessary
to participate in medical decisionmaking? Consider the range of circumstances in
which the defendant will be found liable for failing to disclose information. The
defendant will be held liable only where he or she suggests that a patient undergo
a procedure that, had the true risks been disclosed, a reasonable patient would
have refused to undergo. Why wouldn't this simply constitute ordinary malpractice? Should plaintiffs be required to show that they would not have undergone
the procedure or is it enough to show that a reasonable patient might have sought
another opinion or considered a different provider? Compare Spencer v. Goodill,
17 A.3d 552 (Del. 2011) (jury entitled to consider all options that reasonable person
might have considered, including seeking second opinion, a different doctor, or a
better equipped hospital, even though same operation might ultimately have been
pursued) with Orphan v. Pilnik, 940 N.E.2d 555 (N.Y. 2010) (evidence insufficient
where "plaintiff . . . alleged only that, if fully informed, she would have sought second opinion").

How much of the "plaintiff's position" is the jury to consider within the limits
of objective causation? See Bernard v. Char, 903 P.2d 667, 675-676 (Haw. 1995) (jury
permitted to consider whether a reasonable person who was in great pain and who
had no health insurance would have opted for tooth extraction or a more expensive root canal procedure); Ashe v. Radiation Oncology Associates, 9 S.W.3d 119,
123-124 (Tenn. 1999) (fact finder applying objective causation rules may take into
account characteristics of plaintiff, including "idiosyncrasies, fears, age, medical

condition, and religious beliefs"). At what point does the objective causation standard dissolve into a subjective standard?

4. *The Critique of Objective Causation.* Critics of the objective causation standard argue that it undercuts the goal of protecting individual autonomy. The standard is only a rough approximation or a surrogate device for the protection of individual autonomy because it works only so long as the individual is "reasonable." The Oklahoma Supreme Court has agreed:

> The *Canterbury* view certainly severely limits the protection granted an injured patient. To the extent the plaintiff, given an adequate disclosure, would have declined the proposed treatment, and a reasonable person in similar circumstances would have consented, a patient's right of self-determination is irrevocably lost. This basic right to know and decide is the reason for the full-disclosure rule. Accordingly, we decline to jeopardize this right by the imposition of the "reasonable man" standard. . . .
>
> If a plaintiff testifies he would have continued with the proposed treatment had he been adequately informed, the trial is over under either the subjective or objective approach. If he testifies he would not, then the causation problem must be resolved by examining the credibility of plaintiff's testimony. The jury must be instructed that it must find the plaintiff would have refused the treatment if he is to prevail.
>
> Although it might be said this approach places a physician at the mercy of a patient's hindsight, a careful practitioner can always protect himself by insuring that he has adequately informed each patient he treats. If he does not breach this duty, a causation problem will not arise.

Scott v. Bradford, 606 P.2d 554, 559 (Okla. 1979); see also Parris v. Lime, 277 P.3d 1259 (Okla. 2012). Oklahoma's "subjective causation" approach has not gained many adherents. But see Zalazar v. Vercimak, 633 N.E.2d 1223, 1227 (Ill. App. Ct. 1993) (severely limiting the use of objective causation and expert opinion in informed consent cases arising from cosmetic surgery); and Allison v. Brown, 293 Va. 617 (2017) (noting issue remains open in state). For academic commentaries on the causation problem, see Aaron D. Twerski & Neil B. Cohen, Informed Decision-Making and the Law of Torts: The Myth of Justiciable Causation, 1988 U. Ill. L. Rev. 607; Evelyn M. Tenenbaum, Revitalizing Informed Consent and Protecting Patient Autonomy: An Appeal to Abandon Objective Causation, 64 Okla. L. Rev. 697 (2012).

3. Limiting Liability for Failure to Disclose

■ RIZZO v. SCHILLER
445 S.E.2d 153 (Va. 1994)

HASSELL, Justice.

In this appeal, we consider whether the plaintiffs presented sufficient evidence to establish a prima facie case of medical malpractice against a physician who allegedly failed to obtain the mother's informed consent to use obstetrical forceps to deliver her baby.

Michael Sean Rizzo, Jr., by Pamela Rizzo, his mother and next friend, Pamela Rizzo, individually, and Michael Sean Rizzo, Sr., filed this action against Maurice Schiller, M.D. The plaintiffs alleged that Dr. Schiller, an obstetrician and gynecologist, breached the standard of care owed to them when he assisted Ms. Rizzo with the delivery of Michael. Specifically, the plaintiffs alleged that Dr. Schiller was negligent in the use of obstetrical forceps during the delivery and that he failed to obtain Ms. Rizzo's informed consent to use the forceps.

The case was tried before a jury. The trial court granted Dr. Schiller's motion to strike the plaintiffs' informed consent claim. The case proceeded to the jury on the theory that Dr. Schiller was negligent in the use of the obstetrical forceps. The jury returned a verdict in favor of Dr. Schiller, and we awarded the plaintiffs an appeal on issues related to their informed consent claim.

Pamela Rizzo was admitted to Fairfax Hospital on November 7, 1989, about 9:00 A.M. She was in active labor, and Dr. Schiller was notified of her admission. Upon admission to the hospital, Ms. Rizzo signed the following form:

Authorization for Medical and Surgical Procedures

Patient History No. /P/9456

I hereby authorize Dr. Schiller, and/or other members of the Medical Staff of The Fairfax Hospital of his choice, to perform diagnostic or therapeutic medical and surgical procedures on and to administer anesthetics to Pamela Rizzo. I further authorize The Fairfax Hospital to dispose of any removed tissue or amputated parts.

11/07/89   [Signed] *Pamela S. Rizzo*

_____   _____
(Date)   (Signature)

[Signed] *Vera Thomas*

_____   _____
(Witness)   (Relationship)

About 12 hours later, Ms. Rizzo's fetal membranes were artificially ruptured at 8:50 P.M., and about 10:00 P.M., she was "pushing with contractions." At 10:15 P.M., Dr. Schiller ordered that Ms. Rizzo be taken to the delivery room. While in the delivery room, Ms. Rizzo made a few, but unsuccessful, attempts to "push" the baby through the birth canal with her abdominal muscles. When Ms. Rizzo's attempts to "push" were unsuccessful, Dr. Schiller told her that he was going to use forceps to deliver the baby. Ms. Rizzo testified that "before I could even get my composure together, ask what they were for, why, [the forceps] were inside me. And my son's head was out, just the head."

[Michael Rizzo developed a subdural hematoma after his birth. Experts testified that the forceps injured his head, causing the hematoma and Michael's subsequently diagnosed cerebral palsy.]

Dr. Arner qualified as an expert witness on the subjects of obstetrics and gynecology and gave the following testimony. Even though Ms. Rizzo had been given certain medication, she was capable of making medical decisions. Ms. Rizzo would have been able to deliver Michael spontaneously, without the use of forceps, had Dr. Schiller simply waited. If forceps are used in "non-emergent situations," the patient should be informed about the use of the forceps and should be given the opportunity to participate in the decision regarding whether the forceps will be used. Dr. Arner opined that Dr. Schiller breached the standard of care owed to Ms. Rizzo because he failed to allow her to participate in the decision to use forceps.

The plaintiffs contend that the trial court erred by striking their evidence because they established a prima facie case that Dr. Schiller failed to obtain Ms. Rizzo's informed consent for the use of obstetrical forceps during Michael's delivery. Dr. Schiller, however, argues that the plaintiffs' evidence fails to establish a prima facie case and that the plaintiffs failed to present evidence of proximate causation. Furthermore, Dr. Schiller asserts that Ms. Rizzo was allowed to participate in the decision to use forceps because she signed the authorization form. We disagree with Dr. Schiller.

In Hunter v. Burroughs, 96 S.E. 360, 366-367 (1918), we held that "it is the duty of a physician in the exercise of ordinary care to warn a patient of the danger of possible bad consequences of using a remedy," but that the physician's failure to warn "is not per se an act of negligence." Rather, the physician owes a duty to make a reasonable disclosure to the patient of all significant facts under the circumstances. This duty is limited to those disclosures that a reasonable medical practitioner would provide under the same or similar circumstances. Bly v. Rhoads, 222 S.E.2d 783, 785-787 (1976). In most cases, expert testimony is necessary to establish those instances where the duty to disclose arises and what disclosures a reasonable medical practitioner would have made under the same or similar circumstances. Id.

We are of opinion that the plaintiffs presented sufficient evidence to establish a prima facie case that Dr. Schiller failed to obtain Ms. Rizzo's informed consent to use the obstetrical forceps. As we have already mentioned, Dr. Arner testified that the appropriate standard of care required that Dr. Schiller inform Ms. Rizzo about the use of the forceps and that she be given an opportunity to participate in the decision whether to use forceps. Ms. Rizzo testified that Dr. Schiller did not disclose any information to her about the use of the forceps and that he used the forceps without her consent.

It is true that Ms. Rizzo signed a document that purportedly is a consent form. However, this form did not inform her of any specific procedures that Dr. Schiller intended to perform; nor did it inform her of foreseeable risks associated with any procedures or risks in failing to perform any procedures. As Dr. Arner observed, the form is so general in nature that "you could also justify amputating her foot." We hold that the duty imposed upon a physician to obtain a patient's informed consent requires more than simply securing the patient's signature on a generalized consent form, similar to the form present here. The law requires informed consent, not mere consent, and the failure to obtain informed consent is tantamount to no consent.

We are also of opinion that the plaintiffs presented sufficient evidence of proximate causation as an element of their prima facie case. Here, the plaintiffs presented evidence from which the jury might have inferred that had Ms. Rizzo been informed of the possible consequences associated with the use of obstetrical forceps, she would have continued to assist in the birth process by "pushing" and that Michael would have been born spontaneously. The plaintiffs also presented evidence from which the jury could have found that but for the use of the forceps, Michael would not have suffered the brain injury.

Accordingly, we will remand this case for a trial of the plaintiffs' claims of lack of informed consent.

Notes: Limiting Liability for Failure to Disclose

1. *Informed Consent and Competence.* The patient's capacity is an important factor in informed consent cases. Physicians must secure consent from someone who has the legal capacity to give it. See Chapter 5.A.1.

Where the patient is incapable of giving consent him- or herself, alternative decisionmaking methods have been adopted by courts and legislatures. These are discussed in Chapter 5.A.3. Did Pamela Rizzo have the capacity to make intelligent health care decisions? Her medical expert testified affirmatively.

2. *The Limits of the Duty to Inform.* Courts and commentators have discussed five general limitations to the duty to disclose:

- *Common Knowledge.* There is no duty to disclose risks "of which persons of average sophistication are aware."
- *Patient Knowledge.* The patient cannot recover for the physician's failure to disclose a risk already known by the patient.
- *Emergencies.* There is no duty to disclose information in an emergency situation where the patient is not competent, immediate treatment is required to prevent more serious harm, and no substitute decisionmaker is available. See Stewart-Graves v. Vaughn, 170 P.3d 1151 (Wash. 2007) (physician's continued resuscitation of newborn child fell within emergency exception to informed consent). The issue of decisionmaking for incompetent persons is considered in more detail at pages 536-582.
- *Therapeutic Privilege.* There is no duty to disclose information where the disclosure process would "foreclose rational decision" or "pose psychological damage" to the patient. The *Canterbury* court was particularly concerned about the need to circumscribe this exception lest it swallow the general rule. The AMA Code of Ethics (2016) limits withholding information from patients. See §2.1.3 ("Except in emergency situation in which a patient is incapable of making an informed decision, withholding information without the patient's knowledge of consent is ethically unacceptable. When information has been withheld in such circumstances, physicians[] should convey that information once the emergency situation has been resolved" in accordance with certain guidelines). For academic commentary on the therapeutic exception, see, e.g., Kathleen M. Boozang, The Therapeutic Placebo: The Case for Patient Deception, 54 Fla. L. Rev. 687 (2002). There are few reported applications of the rule. See, e.g., Barrai v. Betwee, 50 P.3d 946 (Haw. 2002) (psychiatrist fails to establish therapeutic privilege exception); and Marsingill v. O'Malley, 58 P.3d 495 (Alaska 2002) (plaintiffs essentially claim that physician should have applied the therapeutic privilege by withholding information about the likelihood that emergency room treatment would be painful or uncomfortable; patient allegedly suffered injuries from her decision to delay seeking emergency medical assistance after hearing about the nature of the likely treatment).
- *Waiver.* Although there are few court decisions on the issue, the disclosure doctrine's grounding in autonomy suggests that patients should be able to

refuse information offered by the physician. See Spar v. Cha, 907 N.E.2d 974, 983 (Ind. 2009); and Mark A. Hall, A Theory of Economic Informed Consent, 31 Ga. L. Rev. 511 (1997).

These limitations on the duty to disclose may be announced by courts or, in professional disclosure standard jurisdictions, may be established by the testimony of medical experts. The defendant generally has the burden of proving that an exception to the duty to inform is present. For a general discussion of exceptions to the duty to disclose, see Alan Meisel, The "Exceptions" to the Informed Consent Doctrine: Striking a Balance Between Competing Values in Medical Decisionmaking, 1979 Wis. L. Rev. 413.

3. *The "Consent" Process, or the Use of Forms.* Critics of the informed consent process argue that the ideal of a meaningful exchange of information between patient and physician has been replaced with the ritual of the informed consent form. How does the *Rizzo* court analyze the validity of the informed consent document signed by the plaintiff? Why shouldn't a physician be entitled to rely upon informed consent forms as a shield to liability? How was the document defective? Who should draft informed consent documents—health care providers or attorneys? Would a physician relying on the validity of an informed consent form have a malpractice claim against the drafter? Should a physician's failure to obtain a signed consent form give rise to liability? Holley v. Huang, 284 P.3d 81 (Colo. App. 2011) ("because documentation is not required, a failure to document does not constitute a failure to meet the standard of care").

Physician defendants hope that a signed consent form will foreclose any informed consent claim. It is true that a properly completed form can establish at least a presumption that a patient has consented to treatment. Sometimes the presumption is established by statute. See, e.g., Ohio Rev. Code Ann. §2317.54. A form indicating only that a patient has received information and consents is probably not sufficient to benefit from the presumption. See, e.g., Havens v. Hoffman, 902 P.2d 219, 223 (Wyo. 1995) (overturning physician's summary judgment; hospital form is an acknowledgment of the receipt of information but does not indicate the nature of the information disclosed).

4. *Informed Consent Forms in Hospitals.* Hospital employees, such as nurses, often procure patients' signatures on informed consent forms prior to surgery. Does this mean that hospitals have a duty to obtain the informed consent of patients? Courts routinely find that the answer is "no." The duty to obtain informed consent is the physician's; the hospital's involvement in the process normally is considered to be merely facilitative. Annot., 88 A.L.R.3d 1008 (1978). For a cogent critique, see Robert Gatter, The Mysterious Survival of the Policy Against Informed Consent Liability for Hospitals, 81 Notre Dame L. Rev. 1203 (2006). The physician's duty may not be delegable, even to his or her employees. See, e.g., Shinal v. Toms, 162 A.2d 429 (Pa. 2017) ("[A] physician may not delegate to others his or her obligation to provide sufficient information in order to obtain a patient's informed consent. Informed consent requires direct communication between physician and patient, and contemplates a back-and-forth, face-to-face exchange, which might include questions that the patient feels the physician must answer personally before the patient feels informed and becomes willing to consent. The duty to obtain the patient's informed consent belongs solely to the physician.")

5. *Comparative Negligence and Assumption of Risk.* Should patients have an obligation to truthfully disclose information to their physicians? Should the obligation arise only in response to a physician's inquiries, or should patients have a duty to affirmatively disclose matters that a reasonable patient would think might be relevant to his or her medical treatment? In Brown v. Dibbell, 595 N.W.2d 358 (Wis. 1999), the court held that

> for patients to exercise ordinary care, they must tell the truth and give complete and accurate information about personal, family, and medical histories to a doctor to the extent possible in response to the doctor's requests for information when the requested information is material to a doctor's duty as prescribed by . . . [the informed consent statute] and that a patient's breach of that duty might, under certain circumstances, constitute contributory negligence.

Id. at 368-369. The court did not consider whether patients had a duty to disclose information sua sponte. See also, Piatek v. Beale, 999 N.E.2d 68, 70 (Ind. App. 2013) ("a patient may be contributorily negligent if she gives her doctor false or incomplete information when she is capable of providing an accurate history").

Should a defendant physician be able to argue for contributory or comparative negligence where the plaintiff signs a blank consent form, or signs a consent form without reading it? What if a patient fails to ask for clarifications where the consent documents contain inconsistencies or gaps? See Oghia v. Hollan, 363 S.W.3d 30 (Ky. Ct. App. 2012) (comparative negligence applies to informed consent only in extraordinary circumstances not present in case).

An informed consent form is essentially a written documentation of the patient's assumption of the disclosed risks, assumed in order to achieve a procedure's potential benefits. See Karp v. Cooley, 493 F.2d 408 (5th Cir. 1974) (directed verdict for the defendant affirmed; patient undergoing first attempted implantation of a mechanical heart had been given extensive information and counseling about the experimental nature of the treatment and its risks). Patients ordinarily are not permitted, however, to assume the risk that a procedure will be negligently recommended or performed; they assume only the risks that are non-negligently produced. In the typical case, then, a signed informed consent form signifies that the patient was informed of the required risks and agreed to accept those risks; a form is powerful evidence of a physician's compliance with the duty to disclose but is irrelevant to an ordinary malpractice action brought against a physician for delivering substandard care. See Spar v. Cha, 907 N.E.2d 974 (Ind. 2009) ("a waiver of informed consent does not assume risks associated with negligent performance of the underlying procedure or treatment").

As is often true in legal matters, things are not quite this simple, however. As noted at pages 408-410, informed consent and ordinary malpractice overlap and interact in several important respects. Where there are alternative standards of care or courses of treatment, obtaining informed consent may be important to the physician's malpractice defense that the physician complied with a "respectable minority" point of view. For instance, informed consent can justify departing from customary practice in order to participate in medical research or to try out an untested procedure. Similarly, informed consent might be used to bolster an affirmative defense that the patient assumed the risk or was contributorily negligent.

See, e.g., Smith v. Hull, 659 N.E.2d 185 (Ind. Ct. App. 1995) (in a case involving injuries from treatment for baldness, a contributory negligence finding "was supported by evidence that patient sought out physician and hair injection procedure, received extensive literature and discussed risks with physician, and signed consent forms prior to undergoing procedures, . . . leav[ing] us with little doubt that Smith's desire to sport a full head of hair motivated him to pursue remedies that he knowingly undertook at his own peril"); Schneider v. Revici, which is excerpted and discussed at page 394. In traditional malpractice cases not involving informed consent claims, should courts exclude evidence of the consent process to avoid confusion about whether the patient had accepted the risks of his or her injuries? See Brady v. Urbas, 111 A.3d 1155 (Pa. 2015) (yes).

6. *Injury and Causation.* Note that Ms. Rizzo's claim would have failed if the undisclosed risk had not materialized, that is, if the use of forceps had not resulted in her son's injuries. How did Dr. Schiller's failure to disclose the risks associated with using forceps cause Michael Rizzo's injuries? The court holds that the plaintiffs presented sufficient evidence of proximate causation for a jury to decide in their favor. A jury could have decided that Ms. Rizzo, had she been appropriately informed, might have rejected the use of forceps and continued to "push" and that Michael's brain injuries would not have occurred. Assume that you represent the defendant. What types of counter-evidence might you want to present on this issue?

7. *Alternative Treatments.* Under the professional malpractice standard, a physician must disclose treatment alternatives if the reasonable, competent physician would have done so. The existence of alternative treatments would also be considered "material" under the patient-centered standard of disclosure. See, e.g., Allen v. Harrison, 374 P.3d 812 (Okla. 2016) (physician has duty to provide information about all medically reasonable alternatives, including those not being recommended to the patient); Annot., 38 A.L.R.4th 900 (1985). But see Cline v. Kresa-Reahl, 728 S.E.2d 87 (W. Va. 2012) (traditional medical malpractice rather than informed consent applies where physician does not disclose information about non-recommended treatment). What should be the physician's disclosure obligation where a treatment alternative is not readily available, perhaps because of cost considerations or geographic location? See, e.g., Mark Hall, A Theory of Economic Informed Consent, 31 Ga. L. Rev. 511 (1997). Should physicians have an obligation to inform patients about promising but as yet untested potential therapies? See J. Lowenthal, S. C. Hull & S. D. Pearson, The Ethics of Early Evidence—Preparing for a Possible Breakthrough in Alzheimer's Disease, 367 New Eng. J. Med. 488 (2012). Should the physician be required to disclose the option of "doing nothing"? See, e.g., Wecker v. Amend, 918 P.2d 658 (Kan. Ct. App. 1996) (yes).

8. *Precision Medicine.* Recent advances in what is sometimes called "personalized" or "precision" medicine may create additional challenges. Much of the discussion in this section has been premised on the concept of average benefits and risks, such as the likelihood that a particular form of treatment will be successful or that a patient will have an adverse outcome in surgery. An individual patient may not be—and in fact probably is not—"average." A patient's personal risk and benefit profile may differ from the average profile in significant ways. Precision medicine involves first developing and then offering "treatments targeted to the needs of individual patients on the basis of genetic, biomarker, phenotypic, or psychosocial characteristics that distinguish a given patient from other patients

with similar clinical presentations." J. Larry Jameson & Dan L. Longo, Precision Medicine—Personalized, Problematic, and Promising, 372 New Eng. J. Med. 2229 (2015). See also, Francis S. Collins & Harold Varmus, A New Initiative on Precision Medicine, 372 New Eng. J. Med. 793 (2015) (describing plans for significant investment of federal funds). The "development" part of the initiative involves investments in research on the implications of personal factors or characteristics. The "offering" component will require individual physicians to understand when and how to apply a more personalized approach to assessing risks and benefits for patients. As Jameson and Longo note, "[t]he extent to which . . . [advances in precision medicine] are constructive or disruptive depends on our ability to harness vast amounts of new knowledge and treatment options within the framework of everyday clinical practice." Id. at 2233. See also, id. at 2232 (noting the difficulties faced by physicians who must "adapt to this daunting explosion of information and the associated clinical guidelines," suggesting use of informatics and referral pathways for patients from primary care providers to those with expertise in the data and guidelines relevant to the patient's condition); and A. D. Sniderman, R. B. D'Agostino & M. J. Pencina, The Role of Physicians in the Era of Predictive Analytics, 314 JAMA 25 (2015) (discussing importance of understanding individualized risk and implications for clinical practice). What role should the informed consent doctrine play in this process? Will the risk of liability help to "push" physicians to move toward more individualized approaches to the assessment of benefits and risks? How will courts apply the professional standard and material risk standard when patients contend that their physician should have provided a more personalized assessment of treatment alternatives, risks, and benefits? See Gary E. Marchant, Kathryn Scheckel & Doug Campos-Outcalt, Contrasting Medical and Legal Standards of Evidence: A Precision Medicine Case Study, 44 J. L. Med. & Ethics 194 (2016).

9. *Informed Consent and the Therapeutic Placebo.* Physicians and medical researchers have long believed in the "placebo effect," under which some patients appear to improve after the administration of spurious "treatment." Recent research explores the forms and limits of placebo effects. See Damien G. Finniss et al., Placebo Effects: Biological, Clinical, and Ethical Advances, 375 Lancet 686 (2010); Ted J. Kaptchuk & Franklin G. Miller, Placebo Effects in Medicine, 373 New Eng. J. Med. 8 (2015). As noted above, the *Canterbury* court established but sought to limit the therapeutic privilege. Does the informed consent doctrine implicitly prohibit the use of placebos? Can you design a method of using placebos that would allow physicians (and patients) to gain the benefits of the placebo effect without violating the disclosure doctrine?

10. *Misdiagnoses and Diagnostic Tests vs. Treatments.* How should courts view informed consent claims brought in cases involving a health care practitioner's failure to diagnose a patient's condition, which then leads to a failure to provide information about appropriate treatments, alternatives, risks, and benefits? Compare Gomez v. Sauerwein, 331 P.3d 19 (Wash. 2014) (where "provider rules out a particular diagnosis . . . there is no duty to inform the patient on treatment options pertaining to the ruled out diagnosis") with Marsingill v. O'Malley, 58 P.3d 495 (Alaska 2002) (plaintiff may claim both that physician failed to appreciate the seriousness of her condition and that he failed to properly inform her of the risks associated with her condition); and Downs v. Trias, 49 A.3d 180 (Conn. 2012) ("A physician who fails to apprise a patient of a certain fact may . . . be held liable for failing to know

the fact in the first place (medical negligence) and for failing to convey the fact to the patient . . . (lack of informed consent)" (emphasis omitted).

Should the duty to disclose alternatives depend on whether a treatment or a diagnostic test is at issue? See Jandre v. Wisconsin Injured Patients and Families Compensation Fund, 813 N.W.2d 627 (2012). The patient in *Jandre* was brought to the emergency room after he had trouble swallowing his coffee and began drooling; he also experienced slurred speech, facial drooping on the left side, dizziness, and leg weakness. The emergency room physician considered many possible causes, including Bell's Palsy and some form of stroke. She performed a number of diagnostic tests, including using a stethoscope on Jandre's carotid arteries to listen for a blocked artery, but did not order the more reliable carotid ultrasound diagnostic test. She also did not inform Jandre about the availability of the test. The physician incorrectly, but non-negligently, found that Jandre had Bell's palsy. About 11 days after leaving the ER, Jandre suffered a full-blown stroke that caused physical and cognitive injuries. In a fractured decision, the Wisconsin Supreme Court found that the ER physician had a duty to disclose the availability of the carotid ultrasound under the reasonable patient standard. Id. A concurring justice agreed with the result but expressed strong concerns about the policy implications of the decision. Id. at 666. A vigorous dissent warned that the decision would result in strict liability for physicians.

Should physicians be shielded from liability for failure to discuss diagnostic tests for alternative conditions that they have non-negligently eliminated from consideration? Physicians frequently engage in a differential diagnosis analysis, moving from a range of possible conditions of greater or lesser probability to a final diagnosis by analyzing the patient's symptoms, family history, and the results of various diagnostic tests. What are the implications of this decision for physicians engaged in this process? Is the type of fully informed consent the majority imagines a practical possibility in already-overburdened hospital emergency rooms? Will health care costs increase as patients are informed about and demand more diagnostic tests?

11. *Law in Books, Law in Action, and the "New" Model of Shared Decisionmaking.* Does the informed consent duty established under malpractice principles provide adequate protection for patient autonomy? Does it protect physicians from unwarranted intrusions into professional autonomy?

There have been flurries of reformist proposals over the past 15 years exploiting the many weaknesses of the current legal approach to informed consent and advocating some form of "shared medical decisionmaking." New models of "shared decisionmaking" in health care promote a dialogue with physicians providing information about risks and probabilities while patients contribute information about values and preferences with the goal of jointly developing a treatment plan. Although the model has many variations, this description is typical:

> Shared medical decision-making is a process in which the physician shares with the patient all relevant risk and benefit information on all treatment alternatives and the patient shares with the physician all relevant personal information that might make one treatment or side effect more or less tolerable than others. Then, both parties use this information to come to a mutual medical decision.

Jamie Staples King & Benjamin W. Moulton, Rethinking Informed Consent: The Case for Shared Medical Decision-Making, 32 Am. J.L. & Med. 429, 431 (2006) (citations omitted). For a critique, see Carl E. Schneider, Void for Vagueness, Hastings Center Rep. 10 (Jan.-Feb. 2007). Is shared decisionmaking simply a variation on the reasonable patient standard? See Erica S. Spatz, Harlan M. Krumholtz & Benjamin W. Moulton, The New Era of Informed Consent: Getting to a Reasonable-Patient Standard Through Shared Decision Making, 315 JAMA 2063 (2016). Could implementation of shared decisionmaking expand physician liability for failure to disclose low risks that could become relevant in light of a patient's shared values and preferences?

The shared decisionmaking process is often assisted by the use of computer-based or audiovisual "decision aids." This approach may be particularly appropriate for elective procedures or areas in which there are multiple treatment options with varying risks and benefits. Courts typically find, however, that physicians are not required to use any particular means of communicating risk information. Holley v. Huang, 284 P.3d 81 (Colo. App. 2011) ("A doctor may employ any means of communication—such as conversation, writings, video and audio recordings, or some combination of these—that will yield a properly informed consent."). See also Jessica Berg, The E-Health Revolution and the Necessary Evolution of Informed Consent, 11 Ind. Health L. Rev. 589 (2014); Nadia N. Sawicki, Informed Consent Beyond the Physician-Patient Encounter: Tort Implications of Extra-Clinical Decision Support Tools, 21 Ann. Health L. 1 (2012).

Shared decisionmaking has advanced somewhat in recent years through several state and federal initiatives. See Erica S. Spatz, Harlan M. Krumholz & Benjamin W. Moulton, Prime Time for Shared Decision Making, 317 JAMA 1309 (2017). Is shared decisionmaking a recalibration of the role of physicians and patients that addresses the critique of traditional informed consent's focus on information transfer and patient autonomy? For a clinician's contrary view, see Lisa Rosenbaum, The Paternalism Preference—Choosing Unshared Decision Making, 373 New Eng. J. Med. 589 (2015).

12. *Further Reading.* On patients' **competency to consent** (note 1), see S. Boettger et al., Assessment of Decisional Capacity: Prevalence of Medical Illness and Psychiatric Comorbidities, 13 Palliat Support Care 1275 (2015); Laura B. Dunn et al., Assessing Decisional Capacity for Clinical Research or Treatment: A Review of Instruments, 163 Am. J. Psychiatry 1323 (2006); Marsha Garrison, The Empire of Illness: Competence and Coercion in Health-Care Decision Making, 49 Wm. & Mary L. Rev. 781 (2007); Bruce J. Winick, Competency to Consent to Treatment: The Distinction Between Assent and Objection, 28 Hous. L. Rev. 15 (1991); Annot., 25 A.L.R.3d 1439 (1969). Consent issues are particularly acute in the treatment of minors. See generally Note, Mature Minors, Medical Choice, and the Constitutional Right to Martyrdom, 102 Va. L. Rev. 1355 (2016); Jennifer L. Rosato, Let's Get Real: Quilting a Principled Approach to Adolescent Empowerment in Health Care Decision-Making, 51 DePaul L. Rev. 769 (2002).

Regarding **physicians' use of placebos** (note 9), see Kathleen M. Boozang, The Therapeutic Placebo: The Case for Patient Deception, 54 U. Fla. L. Rev. 687 (2002); S. C. Hull et al., Patients' Attitudes about the Use of Placebo Treatments: Telephone Survey, 347 BMJ f3757 (2013) (50–84% of respondents found placebo use acceptable in a range of fact situations; 21.9% found placebo use by physicians unacceptable in all circumstances); Adam J. Kolber, A Limited Defense of Clinical Placebo Deception, 26 Yale L & Pol'y Rev. 75 (2007); Anup Malani, Regulation with Placebo Effects, 58 Duke L.J. 411 (2008); Franklin Miller & Luana Colloca, The Legitimacy of Placebo Treatments in Clinical Practice: Evidence and Ethics, 9 Am. J. Bioethics 39 (2009).

On **shared decisionmaking** (note 11), see Dominick L. Frosch et al., Authoritarian Physicians and Patients' Fear of Being Labeled "Difficult" Among Key Obstacles to Shared Decision Making, 31 Health Aff. 1030 (2012); Jaime S. King et al., The Potential of Shared Decision Making to Reduce Health Disparities, 39 J.L. Med. & Ethics 30 (2011); Dayna Bowen Matthew, Implementing American Health Care Reform: The Fiduciary Imperative, 59 Buff. L. Rev. 715, 798-800 (2011); Symposium, 70 Med. Care Res. & Rev. 35 (2013).

Discussion Problem: Informed Refusals?

Dr. Claude R. Thomas was Mrs. Rena Truman's personal physician from 1963 to 1969. In 1969, another physician discovered that Mrs. Truman had advanced cervical cancer. Mrs. Truman died in 1970, at the age of 30. Rena Truman's children sued Dr. Thomas for failing to perform a Pap test on Mrs. Truman between 1964 and 1969. Trial testimony indicated that (1) if the Pap smear had been performed during this time period, Mrs. Truman's condition would have been discovered at an earlier stage and she probably would have lived; (2) medical practice required physicians to inform women of the purpose of a Pap test; and (3) Dr. Thomas repeatedly advised Mrs. Truman to undergo the test but did not specifically explain the possible consequences of her refusal. Consider this case under the professional and material risk standards of disclosure. What arguments can you make on behalf of Mrs. Truman's children? What arguments or defenses might you raise on behalf of Dr. Thomas? See Truman v. Thomas, 611 P.2d 902 (Cal. 1980). See also Providence Health Center v. Dowell, 262 S.W.3d 324, 334-335 (Tex. 2008) (O'Neill, dissenting).

4. Fiduciary Obligations, Conflicts of Interest, and Novel Disclosure Obligations

Depending on the jurisdiction, the informed consent doctrine has grown out of the rich soil of cases involving battery, malpractice, and fiduciary law. The doctrine has the potential for continued expansive growth, particularly in those jurisdictions emphasizing a physician's fiduciary obligations over the professional standard of care. In these states, the scope of informed consent is not limited by the current standard of professional conduct. As you read the following cases, consider whether the courts have gone too far or not far enough in regulating the scope of physician disclosure. Does the imposition of liability in these cases seem "just"? Do the courts' decisions seem consistent with the informed consent doctrine they purport to apply? What is the likely impact of these decisions on the nature of physician-patient communications? Are patients more likely to receive important information? What will physicians do to minimize liability?

■ AUTONOMY AND PRIVACY: PROTECTING PATIENTS FROM THEIR PHYSICIANS
Mary Anne Bobinski
55 U. Pitt. L. Rev. 291, 347-356 (1994)

. . . Jurisdictions with more generous disclosure requirements typically rely, at least in part, on fiduciary principles as a basis for the disclosure obligation. Fiduciary law thus presents a possible avenue for future growth of a more vibrant disclosure duty. Tort law and the law governing fiduciary relationships are similar in that they impose extra-contractual duties on individuals. The two regulatory schemes, however, differ in conception of those duties. Tort law most often imposes general duties irrespective of the status of the parties. The law of fiduciaries, in contrast, is based on the special character of the relationship between two parties. Courts struggling to define the scope of tort-based disclosure duties have often noted the fiducial characteristics of the doctor-patient relationship as a justification for disclosure. This linkage between ordinary tort and fiduciary principles creates the opportunity for both growth and confusion. Ordinary tort duties may be expanded or amplified because of the perceived relevance of fiduciary principles. To date, few courts have explicitly considered the implications of wholesale acceptance of the doctor-patient relationship as one subject to fiduciary law. There has been little judicial analysis of the appropriateness of applying fiduciary-based disclosure obligations to the physician-patient relationship, and virtually no judicial analysis of the special problems presented by provider-associated risk.

The first question is whether the relationship between physicians and patients is a fiduciary one. Fiduciary relationships are generally described as those in which some aspect of the relationship between the parties [such as an imbalance of power or knowledge] justifies the imposition of special obligations on one of them. Several treatises on fiduciary law name the physician-patient relationship as a fiduciary one and the courts have tended to concur. [See pages 122-123.]

Next, the fiduciary duties that physicians owe to patients must be determined. Generally, a fiduciary must act for the benefit of another, but the specific duties imposed on a fiduciary will vary with the scope of the relationship between the parties. The fiduciary owes a duty of loyalty, "good faith, trust, special confidence and candor" to the other party. Obviously, it is not a breach of the fiduciary relationship for the fiduciary to receive compensation for her services. However, the fiduciary can breach her duty by engaging in self-dealing, by receiving bribes or kickbacks, or by misappropriating that knowledge or property which belongs to the entrustor. The role of disclosure in fiduciary law is somewhat complicated. The fiduciary's failure to disclose information to the entrustor can constitute an independent breach of fiduciary duty when the information was gathered in the course of the fiduciary's duties. Disclosure may also help determine whether an apparent breach of fiduciary duties has been "cured" by the consent of the entrustor. The validity of the entrustor's consent will be the important question because the fiduciary's influence over. the entrustor may make any consent presumptively invalid. Disclosure in these cases is of evidentiary significance; it may bolster the fiduciary's claim that the entrustor's consent to the transaction was valid. As a substantive matter, disclosure may not be sufficient where the fiduciary's influence over the entrustor makes any—even informed—consent illusory. . . .

This analysis of fiduciary principles assumes that a breach will provide some effective remedy for patients. A fiduciary is liable to the entrustor for a breach of fiduciary duties. A breach of a fiduciary obligation can be remedied by voiding a transaction, by payment by the fiduciary to the trusting party of any impermissible benefits or profits, or by payment by the fiduciary to compensate the other party for actual damages, which may include compensation for personal injury. Courts are divided on whether the entrustor is required to show some specific injury flowed from the fiduciary's breach of her duties.

The significant number of courts that have applied fiduciary principles to the physician-patient relationship can be deceiving. Most courts have failed to consider the broader policy implications of classifying the physician-patient relationship as a fiduciary one; most have also failed to analyze the range of physicians' required fiduciary duties. Some courts have responded to these problems by hedging, noting that the relationship has fiducial "qualities" or "characteristics" or finding that it is a "confidential" relationship. . . .

The . . . [most important] judicial consideration of common law economic disclosure obligations occurred in Moore v. Regents of the University of California. . . .

■ MOORE v. THE REGENTS OF THE UNIVERSITY OF CALIFORNIA
793 P.2d 479 (Cal. 1990), cert. denied, 499 U.S. 936 (1991)

PANELLI, Justice.

We granted review in this case to determine whether plaintiff has stated a cause of action against his physician and other defendants for using his cells in potentially lucrative medical research without his permission. Plaintiff alleges that his physician failed to disclose preexisting research and economic interests in the cells before obtaining consent to the medical procedures by which they were extracted. . . . We hold that the complaint states a cause of action for breach of the physician's disclosure obligations, but not for conversion.

FACTS

. . . The plaintiff is John Moore (Moore), who underwent treatment for hairy-cell leukemia at the Medical Center of the University of California at Los Angeles (UCLA Medical Center). The five defendants are: (1) Dr. David W. Golde (Golde), a physician who attended Moore at UCLA Medical Center; (2) the Regents of the University of California (Regents), who own and operate the university; (3) Shirley G. Quan, a researcher employed by the Regents; (4) Genetics Institute, Inc. (Genetics Institute); and (5) Sandoz Pharmaceuticals Corporation and related entities (collectively Sandoz).

Moore first visited UCLA Medical Center on October 5, 1976, shortly after he learned that he had hairy-cell leukemia. After hospitalizing Moore and "withdrawing extensive amounts of blood, bone marrow aspirate, and other bodily substances," Golde confirmed that diagnosis. At this time all defendants, including Golde, were aware that "certain blood products and blood components were of great value in a number of commercial and scientific efforts" and that access to a patient whose blood contained these substances would provide "competitive, commercial, and scientific advantages."

On October 8, 1976, Golde recommended that Moore's spleen be removed. Golde informed Moore "that he had reason to fear for his life, and that the proposed splenectomy operation . . . was necessary to slow down the progress of his disease." Based upon Golde's representations, Moore signed a written consent form authorizing the splenectomy.

Before the operation, Golde and Quan "formed the intent and made arrangements to obtain portions of [Moore's] spleen following its removal" and to take them to a separate research unit. Golde gave written instructions to this effect on October 18 and 19, 1976. These research activities "were not intended to have . . . any relation to [Moore's] medical . . . care." However, neither Golde nor Quan informed Moore of their plans to conduct this research or requested his permission. Surgeons at UCLA Medical Center, whom the complaint does not name as defendants, removed Moore's spleen on October 20, 1976.

Moore returned to the UCLA Medical Center several times between November 1976 and September 1983. He did so at Golde's direction and based upon representations "that such visits were necessary and required for his health and well-being, and based upon the trust inherent in and by virtue of the physician-patient relationship. . . ." On each of these visits Golde withdrew additional samples of "blood, blood serum, skin, bone marrow aspirate, and sperm." On each occasion Moore travelled to the UCLA Medical Center from his home in Seattle because he had been told that the procedures were to be performed only there and only under Golde's direction.

"In fact, [however,] throughout the period of time that [Moore] was under [Golde's] care and treatment, . . . the defendants were actively involved in a number of activities which they concealed from [Moore]. . . ." Specifically, defendants were conducting research on Moore's cells and planned to "benefit financially and competitively . . . [by exploiting the cells] and [their] exclusive access to [the cells] by virtue of [Golde's] on-going physician-patient relationship. . . ."

Sometime before August 1979, Golde established a cell line from Moore's T-lymphocytes.[2] On January 30, 1981, the Regents applied for a patent on the cell line, listing Golde and Quan as inventors. "[B]y virtue of an established policy . . . , [the] Regents, Golde, and Quan would share in any royalties or profits . . . arising out of [the] patent." The patent issued on March 20, 1984, naming Golde and Quan as the inventors of the cell line and the Regents as the assignee of the patent. The Regent's patent also covers various methods for using the cell line to produce lymphokines. Moore admits in his complaint that "the true clinical potential of each of the lymphokines . . . [is] difficult to predict, [but] . . . competing commercial firms

----

2. A T-lymphocyte is a type of white blood cell. T-lymphocytes produce lymphokines, or proteins that regulate the immune system. Some lymphokines have potential therapeutic value. If the genetic material responsible for producing a particular lymphokine can be identified, it can sometimes be used to manufacture large quantities of the lymphokine through the techniques of recombinant DNA. . . . Moore's T-lymphocytes were interesting to the defendants because they overproduced certain lymphokines, thus making the corresponding genetic material easier to identify. . . .

in these relevant fields have published reports in biotechnology industry periodicals predicting a potential market of approximately $3.01 billion by the year 1990 for a whole range of [such lymphokines]. . . ." [Golde and his associates received several hundred thousand dollars over the next three years plus shares of stock, under agreements with Genetics Institute to develop the cell line products.]

Based upon these allegations, Moore attempted to state 13 causes of action.[4] . . . [T]he superior court sustained a general demurrer to the entire complaint. . . .

DISCUSSION

A. BREACH OF FIDUCIARY DUTY AND LACK OF INFORMED CONSENT

Moore repeatedly alleges that Golde failed to disclose the extent of his research and economic interests in Moore's cells[6] before obtaining consent to the medical procedures by which the cells were extracted. These allegations, in our view, state a cause of action against Golde for invading a legally protected interest of his patient. This cause of action can properly be characterized either as the breach of a fiduciary duty to disclose facts material to the patient's consent or, alternatively, as the performance of medical procedures without first having obtained the patient's informed consent.

Our analysis begins with three well-established principles. First, "a person of adult years and in sound mind has the right, in the exercise of control over his own body, to determine whether or not to submit to lawful medical treatment." Cobbs v. Grant, 8 Cal. 3d 229, 242 (1972). Second, "the patient's consent to treatment, to be effective, must be an informed consent." *Cobbs*, 8 Cal. 3d at 242. Third, in soliciting the patient's consent, a physician has a fiduciary duty to disclose all information material to the patient's decision.

These principles lead to the following conclusions: (1) A physician must disclose personal interests unrelated to the patient's health, whether research or economic, that may affect the physician's professional judgment; and (2) a physician's failure to disclose such interests may give rise to a cause of action for performing medical procedures without informed consent or breach of fiduciary duty. . . .

Indeed, the law already recognizes that a reasonable patient would want to know whether a physician has an economic interest that might affect the physician's professional judgment. As the Court of Appeal has said, "[c]ertainly a sick patient deserves to be free of any reasonable suspicion that his doctor's judgment is influenced by a profit motive." Magan Medical Clinic v. Cal. State Bd. of Medical Examiners, 249 Cal. App. 2d 124, 132 (1967). The desire to protect patients from possible conflicts of interest has also motivated legislative enactments. Among these

---

4. (1) "Conversion"; (2) "lack of informed consent"; (3) "breach of fiduciary duty"; (4) "fraud and deceit"; (5) "unjust enrichment"; (6) "quasi-contract"; (7) "bad faith breach of the implied covenant of good faith and fair dealing"; (8) "intentional infliction of emotional distress"; (9) "negligent misrepresentation"; (10) "intentional interference with prospective advantageous economic relationships"; (11) "slander of title"; (12) "accounting"; and (13) "declaratory relief."

6. In this opinion we use the inclusive term cells to describe all of the cells taken from Moore's body, including blood cells, bone marrow, spleen, etc.

is Business and Professions Code §654.2. Under that section, a physician may not charge a patient on behalf of, or refer a patient to, any organization in which the physician has a "significant beneficial interest, unless [the physician] first discloses in writing to the patient, that there is such an interest and advises the patient that the patient may choose any organization for the purposes of obtaining the services ordered or requested by [the physician]." Similarly, under Health and Safety Code §24173, a physician who plans to conduct a medical experiment on a patient must, among other things, inform the patient of "[t]he name of the sponsor or funding source, if any, . . . and the organization, if any, under whose general aegis the experiment is being conducted."

It is important to note that no law prohibits a physician from conducting research in the same area in which he practices. Progress in medicine often depends upon physicians, such as those practicing at the university hospital where Moore received treatment, who conduct research while caring for their patients.

Yet a physician who treats a patient in whom he also has a research interest has potentially conflicting loyalties. This is because medical treatment decisions are made on the basis of proportionality—weighing the benefits to the patient against the risks to the patient. As another court has said, "the determination as to whether the burdens of treatment are worth enduring for any individual patient depends upon the facts unique in each case," and "the patient's interests and desires are the key ingredients of the decision-making process." A physician who adds his own research interests to this balance may be tempted to order a scientifically useful procedure or test that offers marginal, or no, benefits to the patient.[8] The possibility that an interest extraneous to the patient's health has affected the physician's judgment is something that a reasonable patient would want to know in deciding whether to consent to a proposed course of treatment. It is material to the patient's decision and, thus, a prerequisite to informed consent. . . .

We acknowledge that there is a competing consideration. To require disclosure of research and economic interests may corrupt the patient's own judgment by distracting him from the requirements of his health.[9] But California law does not grant physicians unlimited discretion to decide what to disclose. . . .

Accordingly, we hold that a physician who is seeking a patient's consent for a medical procedure must, in order to satisfy his fiduciary duty[10] and to obtain the

8. This is, in fact, precisely what Moore has alleged with respect to the postoperative withdrawals of blood and other substances.

9. . . . [A] physician who orders a procedure partly to further a research interest unrelated to the patient's health should not be able to avoid disclosure with the argument that the patient might object to participation in research. In some cases, however, a physician's research interest might play such an insignificant role in the decision to recommend a medically indicated procedure that disclosure should not be required because the interest is not material. By analogy, we have not required disclosure of "remote" risks that "are not central to the decision to administer or reject [a] procedure." Truman v. Thomas, 27 Cal. 3d 285, 293 (1980).

10. In some respects the term fiduciary is too broad. In this context the term fiduciary signifies only that a physician must disclose all facts material to the patient's decision. A physician is not the patient's financial adviser. As we have already discussed, the reason why a physician must disclose possible conflicts is not because he has a duty to protect his patient's financial interests, but because certain personal interests may affect professional judgment.

patient's informed consent, disclose personal interests unrelated to the patient's health, whether research or economic, that may affect his medical judgment.

1. Dr. Golde

We turn now to the allegations of Moore's third amended complaint to determine whether he has stated such a cause of action. . . . Moore alleges that Golde actively concealed his economic interest in Moore's cells during this time period.

> [D]uring each of these visits . . . , and even when [Moore] inquired as to whether there was any possible or potential commercial or financial value or significance of his Blood and Bodily Substances, or whether the defendants had discovered any-thing . . . which was or might be . . . related to any scientific activity resulting in commercial or financial benefits . . . , the defendants repeatedly and affirmatively repre-sented to [Moore] that there was no commercial or financial value to his Blood and Bodily Substances . . . and in fact actively discouraged such inquiries.

. . . In these allegations, Moore plainly asserts that Golde concealed an economic interest in the postoperative procedures. Therefore, applying the principles already discussed, the allegations state a cause of action for breach of fiduciary duty or lack of informed consent.

We thus disagree with the superior court's ruling that Moore had not stated a cause of action . . . [because he] failed to allege that the operation lacked a therapeutic purpose or that the procedure was totally unrelated to therapeutic purposes. In our view, neither allegation is essential. Even if the splenectomy had a therapeutic purpose, it does not follow that Golde had no duty to disclose his additional research and economic interests. As we have already discussed, the existence of a motivation for a medical procedure unrelated to the patient's health is a potential conflict of interest and a fact material to the patient's decision.

2. The Remaining Defendants

The Regents, Quan, Genetics Institute, and Sandoz are not physicians. In contrast to Golde, none of these defendants stood in a fiduciary relationship with Moore or had the duty to obtain Moore's informed consent to medical procedures. If any of these defendants is to be liable for breach of fiduciary duty or performing medical procedures without informed consent, it can only be on account of Golde's acts and on the basis of a recognized theory of secondary liability, such as respondeat superior. The procedural posture of this case, however, makes it unnecessary for us to address the sufficiency of Moore's secondary-liability allegations. . . .

B. CONVERSION

[The portion of the opinion rejecting Moore's attempt to characterize the invasion of his rights as a conversion is excerpted at page 667. The court reasoned that such an unprecedented extension of property law concepts is not warranted because strict liability would be too threatening to legitimate and socially useful scientific research.] For these reasons, we hold that the allegations of Moore's third amended complaint state a cause of action for breach of fiduciary duty or lack of informed consent, but not conversion.

MOSK, Justice, dissenting.

. . . I disagree with the majority's . . . conclusion that in the present context a nondisclosure cause of action is an adequate—in fact, a superior—substitute for a conversion cause of action. In my view the nondisclosure cause of action falls short on at least three grounds. First, . . . the majority's theory apparently is that the threat of [a damages action based on nondisclosure] . . . will have a prophylactic effect: It will give physician-researchers incentive to disclose any conflicts of interest before treatment, and will thereby protect their patients' right to make an informed decision about what may be done with their body parts.

The remedy is largely illusory. . . . There are two barriers to recovery. First, the patient must show that if he or she had been informed of all pertinent information, he or she would have declined to consent to the procedure in question. . . . The second barrier to recovery is still higher, and is erected on the first: It is not even enough for the plaintiff to prove that he personally would have refused consent to the proposed treatment if he had been fully informed; he must also prove that in the same circumstances no reasonably prudent person would have given such consent. . . . Few if any judges or juries are likely to believe that disclosure of . . . a possibility of research or development would dissuade a reasonably prudent person from consenting to the treatment. For example, in the case at bar no trier of fact is likely to believe that if defendants had disclosed their plans for using Moore's cells, no reasonably prudent person in Moore's position—i.e., a leukemia patient suffering from a grossly enlarged spleen—would have consented to the routine operation that saved or at least prolonged his life. Here . . . a motion for nonsuit for failure to prove proximate cause will end the matter. In this context, accordingly, the threat of suit on a nondisclosure cause of action is largely a paper tiger.

The second reason why the nondisclosure cause of action is inadequate for the task that the majority assign to it is that it fails to solve half the problem before us: It gives the patient only the right to refuse consent, i.e., the right to prohibit the commercialization of his tissue; it does not give him the right to grant consent to that commercialization on the condition that he share in its proceeds. . . . Third, the nondisclosure cause of action fails to reach a major class of potential defendants: all those who are outside the strict physician-patient relationship with the plaintiff. . . .

In sum, the nondisclosure cause of action (1) is unlikely to be successful in most cases, (2) fails to protect patients' rights to share in the proceeds of the commercial exploitation of their tissue, and (3) may allow the true exploiters to escape liability. It is thus not an adequate substitute, in my view, for the conversion cause of action. . . .

BROUSSARD, Justice, concurring and dissenting.

. . . I disagree with the suggestion in [Justice Mosk's] dissenting opinion that defendants will be able to avoid all liability under the breach-of-fiduciary-duty theory simply by showing that plaintiff would have proceeded with the surgical removal of his diseased spleen even if defendants had disclosed their research and commercial interest in his cells. . . . [I]n this context [of a breach of fiduciary duty]—unlike in the traditional "informed consent" context of *Cobbs*—a plaintiff should not be required to establish that he would not have proceeded with the medical treatment in question if his physician had made full disclosure, but only that the doctor's wrongful failure to disclose information proximately caused the plaintiff some type of compensable damage. . . . [I]n appropriate circumstances, punitive as well as compensatory damages would clearly be recoverable in such an action. Accordingly, [Justice Mosk] underestimates the potential efficacy of the breach-of-fiduciary-duty cause of action in dismissing the action as a "paper tiger."

■ HOWARD v. UNIVERSITY OF MEDICINE & DENTISTRY OF NEW JERSEY
800 A.2d 73 (N.J. 2002)

LaVecchia, J.

In this appeal we consider what causes of action will lie when a plaintiff contends that a physician misrepresented his credentials and experience at the time he obtained the plaintiff's consent to surgery. . . .

[The plaintiff suffered serious and progressive back injuries in an automobile accident but decided to forgo recommended surgery. The plaintiff was referred to Dr. Heary, a professor at the defendant University, after the plaintiff sustained additional back injuries in a second car accident.] Dr. Heary had two pre-operative consultations with plaintiff. In the first consultation, Dr. Heary determined that plaintiff needed surgery to correct a cervical myelopathy secondary to cervical stenosis and a significantly large C3 C4 disc herniation. Because of the serious nature of the surgery, Dr. Heary recommended that plaintiff's wife attend a second consultation. The doctor wanted to explain again the risks, benefits, and alternatives to surgery, and to answer any questions concerning the procedure.

Plaintiff returned with his wife for a second consultation, but what transpired is disputed. An "Office Note" written by Dr. Heary detailing the contents of the consultation states that "[a]ll alternatives have been discussed and patient elects at this time to undergo the surgical procedure, which has been scheduled for March 5, 1997." Dr. Heary asserts that he informed plaintiff and his wife that the surgery entailed significant risks, including the possibility of paralysis. Plaintiffs dispute that they were informed of such risks. Further, they contend that during the consultation plaintiff's wife asked Dr. Heary whether he was Board Certified and that he said he was. Plaintiffs also claim that Dr. Heary told them that he had performed approximately sixty corpectomies in each of the eleven years he had been performing such surgical procedures. According to Mrs. Howard, she was opposed to the surgery and it was only after Dr. Heary's specific claims of skill and experience that she and her husband decided to go ahead with the procedure.

Dr. Heary denies that he represented that he was Board Certified in Neurosurgery.[1] He also denies that he ever claimed to have performed sixty corpectomies per year for the eleven years he had practiced neurosurgery.

Dr. Heary performed the surgical procedure on March 5, 1997, but it was unsuccessful. A malpractice action was filed alleging that Mr. Howard was rendered quadriplegic as a result of Dr. Heary's negligence. [The plaintiffs sought leave to add a fraud claim to their complaint. The trial court rejected the motion, the appellate division reversed, and the matter was appealed to the state supreme court.]

---

1. Although he was Board Eligible at the time of Mr. Howard's surgery, Dr. Heary did not become Board Certified in Neurosurgery until November 1999. . . .

Presently, a patient has several avenues of relief against a doctor: (1) deviation from the standard of care (medical malpractice); (2) lack of informed consent; and (3) battery. . . . Plaintiffs' motion to amend the complaint to add a fraud claim raises the question whether a patient's consent to surgery obtained through alleged misrepresentations about the physician's professional experience and credentials is properly addressed in a claim of lack of informed consent, or battery, or whether it should constitute a separate and distinct claim based on fraud.

We focus first on the distinction between lack of informed consent and battery as they are recognized in New Jersey. The doctrine of informed consent was tied initially to the tort of battery, but its evolution has firmly established it as a negligence concept. . . . By the mid-twentieth century, as courts began to use a negligence theory to analyze consent causes of action, the case law evolved from the notion of consent to *informed* consent, balancing the patient's need for sufficient information with the doctor's perception of the appropriate amount of information to impart for an informed decision. . . . The doctrine of informed consent continued to be refined. See Natanson v. Kline, 350 P.2d 1093, 1106, modified on other grounds, 354 P.2d 670 (1960) (holding that doctor's required disclosure was "limited to those disclosures which a reasonable medical practitioner would make under the same or similar circumstances," known as the "professional standard"). Eventually, the "prudent patient," or "materiality of risk" standard was introduced. Canterbury v. Spence, 464 F.2d 772, 786-88 (D.C. Cir. 1972), cert. denied, 409 U.S. 1064 (1972). That patient-centered view of informed consent stresses the patient's right to self-determination, and the fiduciary relationship between a doctor and his or her patients. . . . [New Jersey originally followed the professional standard of disclosure but later adopted the patient-centered material risk standard discussed in *Canterbury*.]

Our common law also authorizes a medical battery cause of action where a doctor performs a surgery without consent, rendering the surgery an unauthorized touching. . . . In circumstances where the surgery that was performed was authorized with arguably inadequate information, however, an action for negligence is more appropriate. . . . Thus, although a claim for battery will lie where there has been "ghost surgery"* or where no consent has been given for the procedure undertaken, if consent has been given for the procedure only a claim based on lack of informed consent will lie. A claim based on lack of informed consent properly will focus then on the adequacy of the disclosure, its impact on the reasonable patient's assessment of the risks, alternatives, and consequences of the surgery, and the damages caused by the occurrence of the undisclosed risk. . . .

Few jurisdictions have confronted the question of what cause of action should lie when a doctor allegedly misrepresents his credentials or experience. Research has revealed only one jurisdiction that has allowed a claim based on lack of informed consent under similar circumstances. See Johnson v. Kokemoor, 545 N.W.2d 495 (Wis. 1996) (analyzing doctor's affirmative misrepresentation as claim for lack of informed consent and finding that reasonable person would have considered information regarding doctor's relative lack of experience in performing surgery to have

---

* ["Ghost surgery" occurs if the patient consents to a surgical procedure to be performed by Physician A but the surgery actually is performed by Physician B.—EDS.]

been material in making intelligent and informed decision). Although some suggest that a claim based in fraud may be appropriate if a doctor actively misrepresents his or her background or credentials, we are aware of no court that has so held. . . .

The thoughtful decision of the Appellate Division notwithstanding, we are not convinced that our common law should be extended to allow a novel fraud or deceit-based cause of action in this doctor-patient context that regularly would admit of the possibility of punitive damages, and that would circumvent the requirements for proof of both causation and damages imposed in a traditional informed consent setting. We are especially reluctant to do so when plaintiff's damages from this alleged "fraud" arise exclusively from the doctor-patient relationship involving plaintiff's corpectomy procedure. . . . Accordingly, we hold that a fraud or deceit-based claim is unavailable to address the wrong alleged by plaintiff. We next consider whether a claim based on lack of informed consent is the more appropriate analytical basis for the amendment to the complaint permitted by the Appellate Division. . . .

Our case law never has held that a doctor has a duty to detail his background and experience as part of the required informed consent disclosure; nor are we called on to decide that question here. . . . Courts generally have held that claims of lack of informed consent based on a failure to disclose professional-background information are without merit. . . . Although personal credentials and experience may not be a required part of an informed consent disclosure under the current standard of care required of doctors, the question raised in this appeal is whether significant misrepresentations concerning a physician's qualifications can affect the validity of consent obtained. The answer obviously is that they can.

In certain circumstances, a serious misrepresentation concerning the quality or extent of a physician's professional experience, viewed from the perspective of the reasonably prudent patient assessing the risks attendant to a medical procedure, can be material to the grant of intelligent and informed consent to the procedure. See 1 Dan B. Dobbs, *The Law of Torts*, §251 at 660-61 (2001) (citing *Kokemoor, supra,* and discussing that some authority has begun to suggest that patient is entitled to information concerning doctor's experience in performing specific surgery). In *Kokemoor, supra,* the Supreme Court of Wisconsin reviewed a case in which the plaintiff alleged that her surgeon did not obtain her informed consent to perform a surgical procedure because he had misrepresented his experience in response to a direct question during a pre-operative consultation. 545 N.W.2d at 505. At trial, evidence was introduced suggesting that the type of surgery performed — basilar bifurcation aneurysm — was "among the most difficult in all of neurosurgery." Ibid. The court found that evidence of the defendant's lack of experience was relevant to an informed consent claim because "[a] reasonable person in the plaintiff's position would have considered such information material in making an intelligent and informed decision about the surgery." Ibid.

The allegation here is that defendant's misrepresentations concerning his credentials and experience were instrumental in overcoming plaintiff's reluctance to proceed with the surgery. The theory of the claim is not that the misrepresentation induced plaintiff to proceed with unnecessary surgery. . . . Rather, plaintiff essentially contends that he was misled about material information that he required in order to grant an intelligent and informed consent to the performance of the procedure because he did not receive accurate responses to questions concerning defendant's experience in performing corpectomies and whether he was "Board Certified." Plaintiff allegedly was warned of the risk of paralysis from the corpectomy procedure; however, he asserts that if he had known the truth about defendant's qualifications and experience, it would have affected his assessment of the risks of the procedure. Stated differently, defendant's misrepresentations induced plaintiff to consent to a surgical procedure, and its risk of paralysis, that he would not have undergone had he known the truth about defendant's qualifications. Stripped to its essentials, plaintiff's claim is founded on lack of informed consent.

As noted earlier, a patient-specific standard of what is material to a full disclosure does not apply in a claim based on lack of informed consent. Thus, plaintiff's subjective preference for a Board Certified physician, or one who had performed more corpectomies than defendant had performed, is not the actionable standard. Nonetheless, assuming the misrepresentations are proved, if an objectively reasonable person could find that physician experience was material in determining the medical risk of the corpectomy procedure to which plaintiff consented, and if a reasonably prudent person in plaintiff's position informed of the defendant's misrepresentations about his experience would not have consented, then a claim based on lack of informed consent may be maintained.

Modern advances in medicine coupled with the increased sophistication of medical consumers require an evolving notion of the reasonably prudent patient when assessing a claim based on lack of informed consent. . . . That said, most informed consent issues are unlikely to implicate a setting in which a physician's experience or credentials have been demonstrated to be a material element affecting the risk of undertaking a specific procedure. The standard requires proof on which an objectively reasonable person would base a finding that physician experience could have a causal connection to a substantial risk of the procedure. . . .

The alleged misrepresentations in this case about "physician experience" (credentials and surgical experience) provide a useful context for demonstrating the difficulty inherent in meeting the materiality standard required in order for physician experience to have a role in an informed consent case. We recognize that a misrepresentation about a physician's experience is not a perfect fit with the familiar construct of a claim based on lack of informed consent. The difficulty arises because physician experience is not information that directly relates to the procedure itself or one of the other areas of required medical disclosure concerning the procedure, its substantial risks, and alternatives that must be disclosed to avoid a claim based on lack of informed consent. But the possibility of materiality is present. If defendant's true level of experience had the capacity to enhance substantially the risk of paralysis from undergoing a corpectomy, a jury could find that a reasonably prudent patient would not have consented to that procedure had the misrepresentation been revealed. That presumes that plaintiff can prove that the actual level of experience possessed by defendant had a direct and demonstrable relationship to the harm of paralysis, a substantial risk of the procedure that was disclosed to plaintiff. Put differently, plaintiff must prove that the additional undisclosed risk posed by defendant's true level of qualifications and experience increased plaintiff's risk of paralysis from the corpectomy procedure.

The standard for causation that we envision in such an action will impose a significant gatekeeper function on the trial court to prevent insubstantial claims concerning alleged misrepresentations about a physician's experience from proceeding to a jury. We contemplate that misrepresented or exaggerated physician experience would have to significantly increase a risk of a procedure in order for it to affect the judgment of a reasonably prudent patient in an informed consent case. As this case demonstrates, the proximate cause analysis will involve a two-step inquiry.

The first inquiry should be, assuming a misrepresentation about experience, whether the more limited experience or credentials possessed by defendant could have substantially increased plaintiff's risk of paralysis from undergoing the corpectomy procedure. We envision that expert testimony would be required for such a showing. The second inquiry would be whether that substantially increased risk would cause a reasonably prudent person not to consent to undergo the procedure. If the true extent of defendant's experience could not affect materially the risk of paralysis from a corpectomy procedure, then the alleged misrepresentation could not cause a reasonably prudent patient in plaintiff's position to decline consent to the procedure. The court's gatekeeper function in respect of the first question will require a determination that a genuine issue of material fact exists requiring resolution by the factfinder in order to proceed to the second question involving an assessment by the reasonably prudent patient. Further, the trial court must conclude that there is a genuine issue of material fact concerning both questions in order to allow the claim to proceed to trial.

Finally, to satisfy the damages element in a claim based on lack of informed consent, a plaintiff typically has to show a causal connection between the inadequately disclosed risk of the procedure and the injury sustained. . . . If that risk materialized and harmed plaintiff, damages for those injuries are awarded. . . . Here, if successful in his claim based on lack of informed consent, plaintiff may receive damages for injuries caused by an inadequately disclosed risk of the corpectomy procedure. However, as noted, to be successful plaintiff must prove that defendant's allegedly misrepresented qualifications and experience can satisfy the stringent test for proximate causation that is required for physician experience to be material to the substantial risk of the procedure that occurred (paralysis) and injured plaintiff. If he can, then plaintiff may be compensated for that injury caused by the corpectomy irrespective of whether defendant deviated from the standard of care in performing the surgical procedure.

In conclusion, plaintiff's medical malpractice action will address any negligence in defendant's performance of the corpectomy procedure. We hold that in addition plaintiff may attempt to prove that defendant's alleged misrepresentation about his credentials and experience presents a claim based on lack of informed consent to the surgical procedure, consistent with the requirements and limitations that we have imposed on such a claim. . . .

Notes: Fiduciary Principles and the Disclosure of Provider-Associated Risks

1. *Do Fiduciary Principles Add Anything?* Why couldn't the *Moore* court analyze the facts solely using traditional informed consent analysis? Read the opinion to determine (1) the theory underlying the imposition of fiduciary obligations; (2) the scope of the fiduciary duty; (3) the actions that might constitute a breach of the duty; (4) the injury requirements, if any; and (5) the remedies for a breach of fiduciary duty. Do fiduciary duties expand or merely parallel the duties already created

under the material risk standard in informed consent cases? What should Golde have done to avoid liability? Why doesn't the court impose disclosure duties on the other defendants? Would a conversion claim have been an easier basis of recovering damages from all of the defendants? Moore's conversion claim is discussed in more detail in Chapter 6, at pages 667-672. Fiduciary claims might be limited or eliminated where specific legislation governs informed consent actions. Daniels v. Gamma West Brachytherapy, 221 P.3d 256 (Utah 2009).

2. *Causation Problems in* Moore. Who has the better of the causation and damages arguments between Justice Mosk and Justice Broussard? On remand, Moore's claim was settled before going to trial, so the court never had to resolve these issues. The *Howard* court directly confronts the knotty causation questions created by provider-associated risk disclosure claims. Will Mr. Howard be able to recover on his informed consent claim without expert proof that the surgeon violated the standard of care in the conduct of the surgery? Why or why not? See Starozytnyk v. Reich, 871 A.2d 733 (N.J. Super. 2005) (affirming dismissal of plaintiff's informed consent and fiduciary duty claims due to absence of proximate cause). Would the fiduciary character of the physician-patient relationship be better protected through the adoption of a new statutory claim that would focus on dignitary harm rather than the types of damages ordinarily recognized in malpractice or fiduciary claims? For a proposal see Caroline Forell & Anna Sortun, The Tort of Betrayal of Trust, 42 U. Mich. J.L. Reform 557 (2008–2009).

3. *Disclosure vs. Prohibition.* Provider-associated risks are distinguishable from risks associated with medical treatment because informed patients may be able to avoid a specific risk entirely through, e.g., seeking a second opinion, in the case of conflicts created by financial interests, or by seeking care elsewhere, in the case of other risks. Moreover, physicians might be the most knowledgeable source of information about some types of provider-associated risks and patients might have difficulty accessing this information unless physicians have an affirmative duty to disclose. However, individual patient decisions to avoid some types of risks might have a cumulative negative impact. As one example, physicians will not be able to train and to acquire experience with procedures if patients demand care only from experienced providers. Requiring disclosure of provider-associated risks and benefits can also infringe on the privacy interests of health providers.

The fiduciary conception of the physician-patient relationship suggests that physicians must set aside self-interest to serve their patients' interests. In other fiduciary contexts, some types of conflicts of interest can be addressed through disclosure and knowing acceptance by the vulnerable party. Other types of conflicts are simply prohibited. See infra, at page 186. Should provider-associated risks presumptively be dealt with through one mechanism or the other? What information would you want to have to answer this question? One of many possible areas of research might be to understand better the impact of disclosures on patients. Compare, Roy Spece et al., An Empirical Method for Materiality: Would Conflict of Interest Disclosures Change Patient Decisions?, 40 Amer. J. L. & Medicine 253 (2014) (experiment finds that disclosure of physician financial interests "significantly and substantially increased the probability that the mock patient would reject the conflicted physician's recommendations") with C. P. DiPaola et al., Surgeon-Industry Conflict of Interest: Survey of North Americans' Opinions Regarding Consulting with Industry, 14 Spine J. 584 (2014) (80% of survey respondents "felt it was ethical and either beneficial or of no influence to the quality of health care if surgeons were consultants for surgical device companies"); and Christine Grady et al., The Limits of Disclosure: What Research Subjects Want to Know About Investigator Financial Interests, 34 J. L. Med. & Ethics 592 (2006) (majority of respondents wanted to know about investigators' interest but "only a minority thought such financial information would influence their decisions about research participation in any way"). For recent commentaries on the role of fiduciary principles in medicine, see Maxwell J. Mehlman, Why Physicians are Fiduciaries for Their Patients, 12 Ind. Health L. Rev. 1 (2015). For a thoughtful examination of the problem of provider-associated risk, see Nadia N. Sawicki, Modernizing Informed Consent: Expanding the Boundaries of Materiality, 2016 U. Ill. L. Rev. 821.

Notes: Financial Conflicts of Interest

1. *Financial Conflicts of Interest.* Different types of financial and nonfinancial conflicts of interest permeate medical relationships, as they do most human affairs. (For example, the authors of this book receive modest royalties when their own students purchase it.) How assiduous should physicians be in avoiding or disclosing them? The AMA Code of Ethics provides that "The primary objective of the medical profession is to render service to humanity; reward of financial gain is a subordinate consideration. Under no circumstances may physicians place their own financial interests above the welfare of their patients." AMA Code of Ethics 11.2.2 (2016). This general standard is supplemented by specific statements relating to different types of potential conflicts. The Code provides, for example, that "physicians should . . . [d]isclose any financial and other factors that could affect the patient's care." Id. at 11.2.4. What types of financial arrangements can create a real or perceived conflict of interest? Financial conflicts have been addressed through a number of research studies, working groups, and symposia.

2. *Conflicts Arising from Financial Arrangements Favoring Additional Care.* The issue of conflicts of interest in medical research identified in *Moore* has continued to attract scrutiny and is discussed further infra at page 241. But aside from research studies, what does *Moore* mean for ordinary medical treatment settings? Does it establish a common-law duty for physicians to disclose to patients financial conflicts of interest that could reasonably affect routine treatment recommendations? No one supposes that doctors must disclose the distorting effects of fee-for-service reimbursement, which might result in harms from unnecessary treatment. Cf. Ambach v. French, 216 P.3d 405 (Wash. 2009) (rejecting Consumer Protection Act claim by patient against physician based in part on extra expense of shoulder surgery compared with alternative treatment). Should courts be more receptive to claims based on financial incentives created by additional commercial arrangements? Compare Wright v. Jeckle, 144 P.3d 301 (Wash. 2006) (rejecting claim that physician's direct sale of anti-obesity drug constituted a violation of fiduciary duty under state anti-kickback legislation merely because physician profited from sales) with Bigler-Engler v. Breg, Inc, 7 Cal. App. 5th 276 (2017) (breach of fiduciary duty claim arising from physician recommendation of device to be rented or purchased from his medical group; physician did not disclose his financial interest in the transaction, note that the device was available from other sources, or disclose known risks to the patient).

As *Moore* briefly indicates, statutory law sometimes requires disclosure of certain kinds of financial conflicts of interest. A prime example is when physicians receive payments from third parties related to treatment decisions or have investment or ownership interests in the facilities to which they refer their patients. State and federal laws prohibit or regulate these investment interests in many circumstances. Which approach strikes you as more appropriate: disclosure or prohibition/regulation? See Chapters 9.E.3 and 10.E for further discussion.

Consider as well the many tactics that drug and medical device companies have used to encourage physicians to prescribe their products. Kickbacks and direct financial incentives are illegal; other types of arrangements have elicited increasing attention. The Affordable Care Act includes "sunshine" provisions that require drug, device, and medical supply companies to report their payments to physicians. 42 U.S.C.A. §1320a-7h. See the CMS Open Payments Web site, www.cms.gove/openpayments. The federal provisions preempt most state statutes or regulations requiring manufacturers to disclose payments but do not preempt disclosure obligations placed on physicians. Can pharmaceutical companies spur sales by redirecting funds toward marketing their wares directly to consumers, who will then pressure their physicians to prescribe the latest cures? See Thomas L. Hafemeister & Richard M. Gulbrandsen, The Fiduciary Obligation of Physicians to "Just Say No" if an "Informed" Patient Demands Services That Are Not Medically Indicated, 39 Seton Hall L. Rev. 335 (2009).

3. *Discussing the Costs of Care.* Curiously, there is virtually no legal or ethical guidance on whether physicians should tell patients how much treatment options cost. In the distant past, this may have been because physicians followed an ethic of treat first and bill later, letting patients pay what they were able. In the more recent past, this may be because insurance usually pays for the majority of costs. In the future, however, these cost-insulating features may soon recede, under the influence of "consumer-driven" health insurance plans that expose patients to much greater cost-sharing obligations. See pages 1104-1107. This will likely generate disputes by patients who feel they were not adequately informed about the costs of the treatments to which they agreed. Under the informed consent and fiduciary principles you have learned, should physicians have to volunteer information about costs, or only wait for patients to ask first? Does the answer differ for the costs of the physicians' own services vs. costs charged by other providers, goods, or services the physician may recommend (such as lab tests, drugs, or specialist referrals)?

4. *Conflicts Arising from Incentives to Deny Care.* Should there be a duty to disclose incentives related to managed care? Could you argue that incentives to reduce health care expenses in managed care are "common knowledge"? If there is a financial disclosure obligation on the part of physicians participating in managed care arrangements, how great should the financial incentive be before it is considered "material"? Should the plaintiff be required to prove that the incentive was sufficient to affect physician decisionmaking in individual cases? Or can we presume that managed care companies would not use financial incentives unless they worked, by affecting physician decisions at least to some extent? Managed care physicians might argue that incentives are designed only to reduce unnecessary medical care and are not large enough to induce physicians to refrain from making necessary medical referrals. Even if incentives potentially affect necessary care, isn't the threat of a malpractice claim enough to ensure that physicians will still make

appropriate referrals, or a sufficient remedy when they fail to do so? Should any duty to disclose managed care incentives be satisfied by a global disclosure when the patient first enrolls (and perhaps once a year thereafter), or must the incentives be repeated each time the patient seeks treatment? For an argument that disclosure at enrollment satisfies the fiduciary obligation, or perhaps acts as a waiver of subsequent disclosures, see Mark A. Hall, A Theory of Economic Informed Consent, 31 Ga. L. Rev. 511 (1997). Other aspects of managed care incentives are discussed at Chapter 9.E.3.

5. *Fiduciary Duties and Managed Care in the Courts.* *Moore* appeared to open the door to using informed consent and/or fiduciary theories to protect patients from the risks created by a provider's financial arrangements with third parties, such as managed care organizations. Subsequent courts have tried to push the door shut, at least on some types of claims. In Neade v. Portes, 739 N.E.2d 496 (Ill. 2000), for example, the Illinois Supreme Court rejected the use of fiduciary theories in a case involving managed care incentives. Mr. Neade was only 37 but had a number of significant risk factors for heart disease. Mr. Neade began to experience radiating chest pain and shortness of breath. Mr. Neade's primary physician, Dr. Portes, authorized Mr. Neade's hospitalization. While hospitalized, Mr. Neade underwent a battery of tests that appeared to rule out heart disease. Thereafter, Dr. Portes failed to refer Mr. Neade for more specific tests for heart disease, despite recurring symptoms. Mr. Neade had a heart attack and died. Mr. Neade's estate brought claims for breach of fiduciary duty and medical negligence against Dr. Portes and others. Dr. Portes participated in a risk-sharing agreement with the patient's HMO that arguably gave the physician an incentive to deny referrals to his patients.

Relying in part on some of the language found in the United States Supreme Court's opinion in Pegram v. Herdrich, 530 U.S. 211 (2000) (exploring fiduciary duty under federal ERISA statute), discussed infra at page 1189, the Illinois Supreme Court rejected the breach of fiduciary duty claim. The Illinois Supreme Court held that a cause of action for breach of fiduciary duty based on a physician's failure to reveal a financial interest in a medical incentive fund essentially duplicated the underlying medical negligence claim:

> [I]t is operative facts together with the injury that we look to in order to determine whether a cause of action is duplicative. In the case at bar, the operative fact in both [the malpractice and fiduciary duty] counts is Dr. Portes' failure to order an angiogram for Mr. Neade. Plaintiff alleges in both counts that Mr. Neade's failure to receive an angiogram is the ultimate reason for his subsequent death. Plaintiff also alleges the same injury in both her medical negligence claim and her breach of fiduciary duty claim, namely, Mr. Neade's death and its effect on plaintiff and her family. We determine that plaintiff's breach of fiduciary duty claim is a re-presentment of her medical negligence claim.
>
> An examination of the elements of a medical negligence claim and breach of fiduciary duty claim illustrates the way in which a breach of fiduciary duty claim would "boil down to a malpractice claim." *Herdrich*, 530 U.S. at —, 120 S. Ct. at 2157. To sustain an action for medical negligence, plaintiff must show: (1) the standard of care in the medical community by which the physician's treatment was measured; (2) that the physician deviated from the standard of care; and (3) that a resulting injury was proximately caused by the deviation from the standard of care. . . . Thus, the standard of care is the relevant inquiry by which we judge a physician's actions in a medical negligence case. . . .

In contrast to an action for medical negligence, in order to state a claim for breach of fiduciary duty, it must be alleged that a fiduciary duty exists, that the fiduciary duty was breached, and that such breach proximately caused the injury of which the plaintiff complains. . . .

In order to sustain a breach of fiduciary duty claim against Dr. Portes, plaintiff would have to allege, inter alia, that: (1) had she known of the Medical Incentive Fund she would have sought an opinion from another physician; (2) that the other physician would have ordered an angiogram for Mr. Neade; (3) that the angiogram would have detected Mr. Neade's heart condition; and (4) that treatment could have prevented his eventual myocardial infarction and subsequent death. In order to prove the second element, plaintiff would have been required to present expert testimony that the expert, after examining Mr. Neade and considering his history, would have ordered an angiogram. This requirement relates to the standard of care consideration—the first prong in a traditional medical negligence claim—under which a physician is held to "the reasonable skill which a physician in good standing in the community would use." That is precisely what plaintiff must prove to support her breach of fiduciary duty claim. As the Supreme Court stated in *Herdrich*, the breach of fiduciary duty claim "would boil down to a malpractice claim, and the fiduciary standard would be nothing but the malpractice standard traditionally applied in actions against physicians." *Herdrich*, 530 U.S. at —, 120 S. Ct. at 2157. Thus, we need not recognize a new cause of action for breach of fiduciary duty when a traditional medical negligence claim sufficiently addresses the same alleged misconduct. The breach of fiduciary duty claim in the case at bar would be duplicative of the medical negligence claim.

Our decision to refrain from permitting the creation of this new cause of action finds additional support in statutory law. The Illinois legislature has placed the burden of disclosing HMO incentive schemes on HMOs themselves. . . .

Moreover, the outcome that would result if we were to allow the creation of a new cause of action for breach of fiduciary duty against a physician in these circumstances may be impractical. For example, physicians often provide services for numerous patients, many of whom may be covered by different HMOs. In order to effectively disclose HMO incentives, physicians would have to remain cognizant at all times of every patient's particular HMO and that HMO's policies and procedures. See, e.g., Mark Hall, A Theory of Economic Informed Consent, 31 Ga. L. Rev. 511, 525-26 (1997). . . . If we were to recognize a breach of fiduciary duty claim in the context of the case at bar, we fear the effects of such a holding may be unworkable.

Neade v. Portes, 739 N.E.2d. at 502-506. The court also held that evidence of the physician's financial incentives could be relevant on issues relating to interest and bias, in the event that physician testified in the medical negligence trial. Id. at 506.

Chief Justice Harrison dissented:

A complaint against a lawyer for professional malpractice may be couched in either contract or tort. . . . The same rule should apply here. Although this case involves medical rather than legal malpractice, that distinction is insignificant. . . . The right to assert claims for breach of fiduciary duty and negligence in the same professional malpractice action is not unfettered. When the same operative facts support a negligence count and a count for breach of fiduciary duty based on the same injury to the client, the counts are identical and the fiduciary duty count should be dismissed as duplicative. . . . In this case, however, the negligence and breach of fiduciary duty counts asserted by plaintiff are not identical. . . . As the appellate court correctly recognized,

> [i]t is conceivable that a trier of fact could find both that Dr. Portes was within the standard of care and therefore not negligent in relying on the thallium stress test and the EKG in deciding that an angiogram was not necessary and also that Dr. Portes did breach his fiduciary duty in not disclosing his financial incentive arrangement and, as a proximate result thereof, Neade did not obtain a second opinion, suffered a massive coronary infarction, and died.

710 N.E.2d 418. . . .

Id. at 506.

6. *Institutional Disclosure Obligations Under Fiduciary Law.* Under common-law principles, as *Moore* holds, institutions are generally free from the disclosure duties imposed on physicians. A federal statute, the Employee Retirement Income Security Act of 1974 (ERISA), regulates health plans provided as a benefit of employment. This statute has a number of important implications for the organization and delivery of health care in the United States that are considered in more detail in Chapters 4.G.2 and 9.C. For present purposes, it is enough to note that the Supreme Court's decision in *Pegram* left the door open to efforts to use ERISA's fiduciary principles as a tool for imposing disclosure obligations on managed care employee benefit plans. See infra, at page 1189.

7. *Further Reading.* On **financial conflicts of interest generally**, see Maxwell J. Mehlman, Can Law Save Medicine?, 36 J. Legal Med. 121 (2015); Lisa Rosenbaum, Three Part Conflict of Interest Series, 372 New Eng. J. Med. 1860-1864, 1959-1963, 2064-2068 (2015); Special Issue, Conflicts of Interest, 317 JAMA 1705-1797 (2017); Symposium, Conflicts of Interest in the Practice of Medicine, 40 J. L. Med. & Ethics 436-522 (2012). For a popular account by a former long-time reporter for the New York Times, see Elisabeth Rosenthal, An American Sickness: How Healthcare Became Big Business and How You Can Take It Back (2017).

For more about **drug company marketing to physicians** (note 2), see Christopher Robertson, Susannah Rose & Aaron S. Kesselheim, Effect of Financial Relationships on the Behaviors of Health Care Professionals: A Review of the Evidence, 40 J. L. Med. & Ethics 452 (2012); Thomas L. Hafemeister & Sarah P. Bryan, Beware Those Bearing Gifts: Physicians' Fiduciary Duty to Avoid Pharmaceutical Marketing, 57 U. Kan. L. Rev. 491 (2009).

On the ACA's **"sunshine" provisions** (note 2), see Shantanu Agrawal & Douglas Brown, The Physician Payments Sunshine Act—Two Years of the Open Payments Program, 374 New Eng. J. Med. 906 (2016); Charles Ornstein, Public Disclosure of Payments to Physicians from Industry, 317 JAMA 1749 (2017).

Considering whether physicians should discuss **the costs of treatment** (note 3), see Barak D. Richman, Mark A. Hall & Kevin A. Schulman, Overbilling and Informed Financial Consent—A Contractual Solution, 367 New Eng. J. Med. 396 (2012)(noting possible relevance of fiduciary principles); and Nadia N. Sawicki, Modernizing Informed Consent: Expanding the Boundaries of Materiality, 2016 U. Ill. L. Rev. 821, 849-850; Mark A. Hall & Carl E. Schneider, Professional Obligations When Patients Pay Out of Pocket, 58 J. Fam. Prac. E1 (2009).

Regarding **incentives to withhold care** (note 4), see Isaac D. Buck, Furthering the Fiduciary Metaphor: The Duty of Providers to the Payers of Medicare, 104 Cal. L. Rev. 1043 (2016) (arguing that the fiduciary concept should be expanded to include a physician duty of loyalty to Medicare as a payer); Jessica Mantel, A Defense of Physicians' Gatekeeping Role: Balancing Patients' Needs with Society's Interests, 42 Pepp. L. Rev. 633 (2015) (arguing that physicians as gatekeepers have dual duties to patients and society); and Maxwell J. Mehlman, Why Physicians are Fiduciaries for Their Patients, 12 Ind. Health L. Rev. 1 (2015) (critiquing *Neade* and contending that physicians' fiduciary duties should be recognized and strengthened).

Notes: Nonfinancial Provider-Associated Risks

1. *Nonfinancial Provider-Associated Risks.* Should physicians have a duty to disclose risks to patients that arise from the identity and characteristics of the provider rather than the type of procedure? In some ways, this topic is the natural corollary of advances in precision medicine, supra at page 181. The development of "big data" means that it is now possible to track experience levels, success rates, and other aspects of physician performance. See, e.g., Nikhil R. Sahni et al., Surgeon Specialization and Operative Mortality in the United States: Retrospective Analysis, 354 BMJ i3571 (2016) ("for six of the eight procedures examined . . . ., we found surgeon specialization to be an important predictor of mortality"). *Howard* is part of a small new line of cases considering whether physicians have any duty to disclose provider risks, as distinguished from procedural risks.

2. *Experience and Success Rates.* Consumers of health care services can now access a wide range of data about the quality of care and health care outcomes produced by health care institutions. As discussed at pages 1203–1204, health care organizations and purchasers are developing and collecting information about health care outcomes for individual practitioners. Should health care providers have a duty to disclose their own "scorecards" to patients? How does the *Howard* court distinguish between informed consent and misrepresentation claims in this area? Courts generally have considered cases involving misrepresentation of experience under informed consent rather than misrepresentation law. See, e.g., Roderer v. Dash, 233 P.3d 1101 (Alaska 2010); Ray v. Kapiolani Medical Specialists, 259 P.3d 569 (Haw. 2011); Kelly v. Vinzant, 197 P.3d 803 (Kan. 2008); Willis v. Bender, 596 F.3d 1244 (10th Cir. 2010). At least one court has rejected an intentional misrepresentation claim in which the plaintiff did not present expert testimony establishing that his injuries were caused by inexperience. Wooding v. U.S., 2010 WL 781303 (3d Cir. 2010).

For other cases involving physician experience, see Duffy v. Flagg, 905 A.2d 15 (Conn. 2006) (informed consent does not require physician to give detailed account of her past experience with a procedure when answers would not have been relevant to key informed consent issues); DeGennaro v. Tandon, 873 A.2d 191 (Conn. App. 2005) (reasonable patient would consider lack of experience in using equipment, and lack of assistance, to be material information about provider-specific risk); Goldberg v. Boone, 912 A.2d 698 (Md. 2006) (jury should determine whether physician experience is material); Wlosinski v. Cohn, 713 N.W.2d 16 (Mich. App. 2005) ("raw success rates" need not be disclosed; interesting concurring and dissenting opinions); Duttry v. Patterson, 771 A.2d 1255 (Pa. 2001) (physician's personal characteristics and experience irrelevant in informed consent claim; misrepresentation claim possible); Johnson v. Kokemoor, 545 N.W.2d 495 (Wis. 1996) (applying informed consent principles to a case involving a physician's relative lack of experience).

3. *Ghost Surgery and Concurrent Surgery.* The *Howard* court, at page 194, notes that a cause of action for battery may be appropriate to address the issue of "ghost surgery," where a patient consents to surgery with one surgeon but another actually performs the procedure. The battery claim can often be defeated by demonstrating that the patient signed consent forms that establish that a procedure may be performed by the surgeon or by others. Assuming that a patient has agreed to the possibility that others might be involved in the surgery, would the informed consent doctrine nonetheless require that the original surgeon provide additional information about the likelihood that others will be involved in the surgery, their experience level, and the degree of supervision that will be provided by the original surgeon? See Hurley v. Kirk, 398 P.3d 7 (2017) (physician has "duty to inform the patient 'who' will be performing significant portions of the procedure or surgical tasks"). These questions were brought into focus by the Boston Globe's "Spotlight" team, which released an investigative report on the use of concurrent surgeries at the well-regarded Massachusetts General Hospital. Jenn Abelson et al., Clash in the Name of Care, Boston Globe (2015) (describing controversies arising from scheduling concurrent surgeries, during which a surgeon may move back and forth between two surgical procedures, without disclosure to patients).

4. *Conscience Rights and Disclosure Duties.* Physicians may have personal beliefs and values that affect their views about the delivery of some forms of health care. The "conscience rights" of health care providers are often protected through legislation that allows physicians and others to refrain from participating in care and, in some circumstances, from providing information about types of care, that conflicts with their beliefs. See Chapter 7.B. But see Ronit Y. Stahl & Ezekiel J. Emanuel, Physicians, Not Conscripts — Conscientious Objection in Health Care, 376 New Eng. J. Med. 1380 (2017) (arguing that recognition of conscience rights should be limited). Do physicians have an obligation to disclose their beliefs and the possible impact of those beliefs on their treatment recommendations? Would such a requirement be too great an intrusion into the privacy interests of physicians? Could a physician's discussion of moral or religious principles create a different form of harm for patients concerned about the disapproval of their physicians?

5. *Abuse of Drugs or Alcohol.* Would the reasonable patient consider a physician's cocaine addiction to be a material fact in deciding whether or not to undergo surgery? Would the professional standard of care require such a disclosure? Compare Rice v. Brakel, 310 P.3d 16 (Ariz. Ct. App. 2013) (surgeon's failure to disclose prescription drug dependency not actionable under informed consent; plaintiff failed to prove that he would have declined treatment or that defendant's acts caused his injury); and Albany Urology Clinic, P.C. v. Cleveland, 528 S.E.2d 777 (Ga. 2000) (no duty to disclose drug use under common law or state informed consent statute), with Hidding v. Williams, 578 So. 2d 1192 (La. Ct. App. 1991) (physician has duty to reveal his alcoholism; concurring opinion raises interesting causation problem).

6. *Infection with HIV.* In the early years of the HIV epidemic, there was a vigorous debate about whether a physician had or should have a duty to disclose his or her HIV status. See, e.g., Mary Anne Bobinski, Autonomy and Privacy: Protecting Patients from Their Physicians, 55 U. Pitt. L. Rev. 291 (1994). The application of the informed consent doctrine to the problem of HIV disclosure in health care was complicated by the fact that many patients were more fearful about the very low risk of HIV transmission from health care worker to patient than they were about other,

larger risks. In addition, persons with HIV infection are protected from discrimination under a variety of statutes, including the Americans with Disabilities Act, unless they pose a "significant risk" to the health or safety of others. 42 U.S.C. §§12111-12113; see infra at page 935. From the perspective of the infected physician, disclosure ought not be required unless there is a significant risk of transmission. From the perspective of the patient, even a "less than significant" risk could be avoided by selecting an (apparently) uninfected health care provider. One court resolved the conflict in favor of the patient's right to know:

> [Dr. Behringer, a surgeon] argues: (1) the risk of transmission of HIV from surgeon to patient is too remote to require informed consent, and (2) the law of informed consent does not require disclosure of the condition of the surgeon. . . : [Dr. Behringer] argues that the use of the informed consent form is tantamount to a de facto termination of surgical privileges. [Dr. Behringer] further urges that patient reaction is likely to be based more on public hysteria than on a studied assessment of the actual risk involved.
>
> The answer to these arguments is two-fold. First, it is the duty of the surgeon utilizing the informed consent procedure to explain to the patient the real risk involved. If the patient's fear is without basis, it is likewise the duty of the surgeon to allay that fear. . . . .
>
> [Dr. Behringer] further argues that there is no requirement under the doctrine of informed consent that a surgeon's physical condition be revealed as a risk of the surgery itself. The informed consent cases are not so narrow as to support that argument. In [a prior New Jersey Supreme Court case] . . . the court spoke of not only an evaluation of the nature of the treatment, but of "any attendant substantial risks." . . .
>
> [Dr. Behringer] urges that these issues should be dealt with on a case-by-case basis, wherein the hospital or medical staff monitors an HIV-positive surgeon and makes a determination as to the surgeon's ability to perform a particular invasive procedure. . . . The position [Dr. Behringer] seeks to implement is replete with the "anachronistic paternalism" rejected in both Canterbury v. Spence, supra, and by the [New Jersey] Supreme Court. . . .
>
> The obligation of a surgeon performing invasive procedures, such as [Dr. Behringer], to reveal his AIDS condition, is one which requires a weighing of [Dr. Behringer's] rights against the patient's rights. New Jersey's strong policy supporting patient rights, weighed against [Dr. Behringer's] individual right to perform an invasive procedure as a part of the practice of his profession, requires the conclusion that the patient's rights must prevail. At a minimum, the physician must withdraw from performing any invasive procedure which would pose a risk to the patient. Where the ultimate harm is death, even the presence of a low risk of transmission justifies the adoption of a policy which precludes invasive procedures when there is "any" risk of transmission. In the present case, the debate raged as to whether there was "any" risk of transmission, and the informed-consent procedure was left in place. If there is to be an ultimate arbiter of whether the patient is to be treated invasively by an AIDS-positive surgeon, the arbiter will be the fully-informed patient. The ultimate risk to the patient is so absolute—so devastating—that it is untenable to argue against informed consent combined with a restriction on procedures which present "any risk" to the patient.

Estate of Behringer v. Medical Center at Princeton, 592 A.2d 1251, 1279-1283 (N.J. Super. Ct. Div. 1991). The federal Centers for Disease Control issued recommendations in 1991 that advised HIV-infected health care workers seeking to engage in "exposure-prone" procedures to (a) secure advice from an expert review panel; and (b) inform patients of their HIV status. Lawrence O. Gostin, Rights and Duties of HIV-Infected Health Care Professionals, 10 Health Care Anal. 67 (2002) (recommending revision of national policy). The CDC has since "retired" its guidance on HIV HCWs, and current anti-retroviral therapies can reduce a patient's viral load and ability to transmit HIV to others. How would courts resolve a case involving the disclosure duties of an HIV-infected surgeon today?

7. *Further Reading.* For commentaries on **disclosing experience and success rates** (note 2), see Aaron D. Twerski, The Second Revolution in Informed Consent: Comparing Physicians to Each Other, 94 Nw. U. L. Rev. 1 (1999); Aaron D. Twerski & Neil B. Cohen, Comparing Medical Providers: A First Look at the New Era of Medical Statistics, 58 Brook. L. Rev. 5 (1992); Nadia N. Sawicki, Modernizing Informed Consent: Expanding the Boundaries of Materiality, 2016 U. Ill. L. Rev. 821; Robert Weinstein et al., Infection-Control Report Cards—Ensuring Patient Safety, 353 New Eng. J. Med. 225 (2005); J. Wilks et al., Surgeon with Worst Performance Figures Might Be the Best Option, 323 Brit. Med. J. 1071 (2001).

On **ghost and concurrent surgery** (note 3), see American College of Surgeons, Statements on Principles, https://www.facs.org/about-acs/statements (2016) (discussing intraoperative responsibility of primary surgeon); and Michelle M. Mello & Edward H. Livingston, Managing the Risks of Concurrent Surgeries, 315 JAMA 1563 (2016).

For a detailed consideration of the issues relating to **disclosing physicians' personal beliefs** (note 4), see Nadia Sawicki, Mandating Disclosure of Conscience-Based Limitations on Medical Practice, 42 Amer. J. L. & Med. 85 (2016).

Problem: *Moore* Liability?

What types of disclosures would be required in the following situations, under either a physician-centered or patient-centered approach? Would the result differ under fiduciary theories?

1. A physician recommending a surgical procedure necessary to save the patient's life will earn about $15,000 from the surgery and follow-up care. What if the surgery is for cosmetic purposes?
2. A physician recommends that a patient see a specialist for her condition. The physician is married to the specialist.
3. A physician providing care for an HMO patient with back pain suggests that the patient take a conservative approach to treatment, delaying expensive diagnostic tests and surgery for as long as possible. The physician's financial arrangements with the HMO include provisions that decrease the physician's income if the physician spends more than an allocated amount on diagnostic tests or hospitalization.
4. A physician describes herself as a social drinker. She only drinks during the evenings and on weekends. On average, she consumes about 21 mixed drinks per week.
5. A surgeon fails to maintain medical malpractice liability coverage despite the fact that coverage is mandatory in the jurisdiction. See Jarrell v. Kaul, 123 A.3d 1022 (N.J. 2015).

6. A physician fails to inform a patient suffering from pancreatic cancer of the patient's low statistical life expectancy. The patient does not make the proper financial arrangements, causing substantial real estate and tax losses. See Arato v. Avedon, 858 P.2d 598 (Cal. 1993).

7. A physician discovers a medical error in a patient's care. Should it matter whether the physician caused the error or whether it occurred under someone else's care? See Chapter 4.A.

D. HUMAN EXPERIMENTATION AND RESEARCH

The *Moore* litigation arose because of the alleged conflicts of interest created by the research interests of the defendants. Media sources and pharmaceutical company advertisements regularly highlight the results of medical research, touting the next great cures for long-feared diseases (as well as informing us about cures for diseases that we never knew existed). Medical research is conducted in a range of public and private settings, funded by public and private sources, and regulated either by different federal regulatory entities or by much more diffuse common-law rules. Funding for medical research totaled $116.5 billion in the United States in 2012. Medical device, biotechnology, and pharmaceutical firms contributed $67.9 billion, or about 58% of the total. The National Institutes of Health contributed $30.9 billion, or 27%. Foundations and charities, state and local government, and non-NIH federal funders contributed $17.6 billion, or 15%. Hamilton Moses et al., The Anatomy of Medical Research: US and International Comparisons, 313 JAMA 174 (2015). The United States is the global leader in spending on medical research, but its share of the world's public and private spending total decreased from 57% in 2004 to 44% in 2012. Id. See also, Justin Chakma et al., Asia's Ascent — Global Trends in Biomedical R & D Expenditures, 370 New Eng. J. Med. 3 (2014).

Medical research involving human experimentation typically takes place in clinical trials, defined as "research stud[ies] in which human volunteers are assigned to interventions (for example, a medical product, behavior, or procedure) based on a protocol (or plan) and then evaluated for effects on biomedical or health outcomes." NIH, ClinicalTrials.gov Background. Data on clinical research has become much more available due to changes in legal requirements, conditions imposed by funders, and new ethical standards that either require or encourage the registration of clinical research trials and in some cases also require the posting of results. The ClinicalTrials.gov database listed 254,668 studies being carried out in 201 countries as of September 2017, with 105,033 studies located in the United States. Millions of people in the United States take part in medical research every year. See "Tom Abate, Experiments on Humans: Business of Clinical Trials Soars, but Risk Unknown, S.F. Chron., Aug. 4, 2002, at A1 (citing "an estimated 20 million Americans tak[ing] part in more than 41,000 clinical trials and uncounted more federally funded experiments").

There are two central concerns in the research context. The first is that experimental treatment is often not done for the patient's immediate benefit. Some patients may approach medical research thinking they will receive better care because it is "state of the art," but this is usually a false impression. Instead, the treatment that is being studied may be riskier; almost certainly its risks are less well known than standard treatment. Also, in randomized controlled trials (RCTs), patients are often "randomized" "blindly" between an "experimental arm" and a "control arm." This means that, by luck of the draw, a significant percentage will receive ordinary treatment or even, in some cases, a placebo; participants generally will not know which type of care they will receive. See generally, Laura E. Bothwell et al., Assessing the Gold Standard—Lessons from the History of RCTs, 374 New Eng. J. Med. 2175 (2016). Moreover, the innovation in treatment may have nothing at all to offer their condition, but may be intended solely to provide an improvement for other patients. The relevant distinction is between "therapeutic" and "nontherapeutic research." Only in the former is there something that a patient might benefit from immediately, but even then, patients are often asked to undergo risks that are greater than the potential rewards in order to further the aims of science.

Fully informed patients may be more than willing to accept these arrangements out of a sense of altruism and a desire to be a part of progress. But there is a second difficulty: How well informed are they, and how freely do they make their decision? Some patients may feel pressured in subtle ways without the knowledge of their physicians. Imagine a physician who eagerly pitches her pet research project, and a patient who fears (irrationally or not?) that disappointing his doctor will jeopardize his treatment. For other patients, coercion could be more overt. The reluctance of well-informed patients to participate in risky experiments might lead researchers either to conceal the experiment or to use patients from vulnerable or socially disadvantaged groups. Cf. Lee Black et al., Physician Recruitment of Patients to Non-Therapeutic Oncology Trials: Ethics Revisited, 4 Frontiers in Pharmacol. 1 (2013).

These concerns are not merely speculative. The history of medical research reveals both astounding advances and disquieting practices. Scientists have sought to expand our knowledge of human biology, illness, and treatment, often at the expense of the least fortunate in society: slaves, the poor, criminals, and other institutionalized persons. Several twentieth-century examples have left a legacy of fear and mistrust. Nazi scientists conducted a vigorous program of medical research on prisoners and internees during World War II. Their appalling lack of respect for human life and humane principles resulted in the Nuremberg Code. The Code's central tenet is a requirement that human research subjects give consent to participation in any research project. See Jonathan D. Moreno, Ulf Schmidt & Steve Joffe, The Nuremberg Code 70 Years Later, 318 JAMA 795 (2017).

Violations of human rights by researchers are not limited, however, to some distant time and far-off place. Two examples of research abuses in the United States have had a profound impact. In the Tuskegee Study, which ran from the 1950s until the early 1970s, researchers studied the effects of untreated syphilis in a group of African-American men. The researchers purported to treat the men for their ailments but never disclosed to their subjects that they continued to suffer from a highly treatable, yet debilitating illness. The researchers' apparently cavalier disregard for their subjects has resulted in a legacy of distrust among minority and poor communities.

In the mid-1990s, the federal government revealed that hundreds of persons had been involuntarily, and in some cases unknowingly, subjected to research in which they were exposed to radiation and harmful substances. President Clinton was forced to announce the adoption of newly strengthened protections for human subjects participating in classified research projects. Strengthened Protections for Human Subjects of Classified Research, 62 Fed. Reg. 26,367 (1997). See generally U.S. Advisory Comm. on Human Radiation Experiments, Final Report of the Advisory Committee on Human Radiation Experiments (Ruth Faden ed., 1996).

More recently, public attention has been drawn to the case of Henrietta Lacks, an African-American woman who died of cancer in 1951. Cell samples extracted from Ms. Lacks for research without her knowledge or consent were used to create the HeLa cell line, which became widely used in biomedical research, including commercial activities. Ms. Lack's family finally became aware of the cell line in the 1970s. Rebecca Skloot, The Immortal Life of Henrietta Lacks (2011). Additional controversy arose in 2013, when researchers published information about the genome of HeLa cells, which raised privacy concerns for Ms. Lacks' living relatives. Kathy L. Hudson & Francis S. Collins, Family Matters, 500 Nature 141 (2013).

A special set of rules governs the disclosure and consent process in medical research. For more than a quarter of a century, medical research has been governed by federal regulations that required an elaborate consent process in order for research to receive federal funding. U.S. Dep't Health & Human Servs. (DHHS), Protection of Human Subjects, 45 C.F.R. Part 46, subparts A through E. Subpart A, originally adopted in 1991, is known as the "Common Rule" because more than a dozen federal agencies and departments agreed to incorporate its provisions into their own regulations or otherwise had agreed to be bound by the same rules. 45 C.F.R. §46.101-.124. Parts B through D of the DHHS regulations provide special protections for specific groups: pregnant women, neonates, and fetuses (subpart B, 45 C.F.R. §46.201-.207), prisoners (subpart C, §46.301-.306), and children (subpart D, §46.401-.409); not all agencies and departments have adopted these provisions. Part E governs the registration of the institutional review boards (IRBs) that are responsible for certain aspects of protecting human research subjects, including particularly the adequacy of the informed consent process. Importantly, the FDA has maintained separate provisions governing the informed consent process. U.S. Food & Drug Admin., 21 C.F.R. §§50.1-.56 (protection of human subjects); 54.1-.6 (financial disclosure by clinical investigators); and 56.101-.124 (IRBs).

Under this long-standing framework, entities that accept federally funded research projects have assured that they would protect human subjects in research projects. 45 C.F.R. §46.103(b). In part due to additional requirements imposed by some federal agencies, entities typically have applied these protections to non-federally-funded research involving human subjects as well. Private foundations usually have similar requirements for funded research projects. The end result has been that the federal regulations effectively have governed most planned medical research in the United States. These federal rules, while influential, do not preempt state laws providing greater protection of human subjects. The federal government announced a process for revising the Common Rule in 2011, and the final regulations were released in early 2017, with most provisions effective as of January of 2018.

■ WHY INFORMED CONSENT? HUMAN EXPERIMENTATION AND THE ETHICS OF AUTONOMY
Richard W. Garnett*
36 Cath. Law. 455 (1996)

. . . Why does consent have such moral power? Accept for now that our deference to consent is—perhaps mistakenly—rooted in a commitment to human dignity, expressed through respect for autonomy. Is consent's justifying role necessarily required by this commitment to human dignity? Why have we come to think that it is? Does our dignity as persons follow from, or does it instead create and condition, our autonomy? Do we respect consent because one feature of our dignity is that we always know what is best for us? Clearly we do not. . . .

III. REGULATING HUMAN EXPERIMENTATION THROUGH CONSENT

A. THE NUREMBERG CODE AND "INFORMED CONSENT"

The Nuremberg Code and the memory of the Nazi doctors' trial animate and permeate modern thinking about regulation of human experimentation. The Code was our most morally rigorous attempt to limit human experimentation. Its most memorable command was that, in medical research, "[t]he voluntary consent of the human subject is absolutely essential."[70] But while the Code has come to stand for "informed consent," it required more. It focused as much on the experiment itself, on the welfare of the subject, and on the conduct of the researcher as it did on the need for the subject's consent. Sadly, this broad focus has received relatively short shrift, and the consent principle has eclipsed the others.

The Code stands tall in memory but its influence has never lived up to its aims. Seen by many as a product of and reaction to Nazi terror, the Code is often dismissed as a context-bound relic, no longer useful for today's researchers. Pragmatists argue that the Code is simply too demanding, that its standards are too high for necessary research to meet, and that its absolutism cannot compete with the utilitarian and impersonal ethics of modern medicine. . . .

B. REGULATING EXPERIMENTATION AFTER NUREMBERG: THE STANDARD MODEL OF INFORMED CONSENT

. . . Today, human experimentation is regulated by a crazy-quilt of hortatory codes and maxims, scattered federal laws and regulations, and most importantly, by Institutional Review Boards,[85] which provide peer review of proposed experiments. "Informed consent" is still the touchstone, but modern regulations and procedures

---

* Law professor at Notre Dame Law School.

70. The Nazi Doctors and the Nuremberg Code: Human Rights in Human Experimentation 2 (George J. Annas & Michael A. Grodin eds., 1992).

85. For a complete review of the structure and function of Institutional Review Boards, see, e.g., 45 C.F.R. §§46.107-111 (1994); 21 C.F.R. §§56.101-114 (1994). "IRB approval means the determination of the IRB that the research has been reviewed and may be conducted at an institution within the constraints set forth by the IRB and by other institutional and federal requirements." 45 C.F.R. §46.102(h).

tolerate and expect deviations from this ideal. Thus, when addressing human experimentation—and they rarely do—courts occasionally mention the [Nuremberg] Code, but generally apply and enforce the more flexible informed consent requirements of later regulations.

The legal doctrine of informed consent as it has developed is quite different from the dignity-based commitment to self-determination animating the Nuremberg Code. The most important feature of today's regulatory regime is that it focuses on the subject's state of mind more than on the experiment itself. What is referred to here as the "Standard Model" of informed consent is this subjectively oriented informed consent in the context of peer review. In practice, research peers have proven insufficiently critical when evaluating proposed experiments. In addition, the informed consent "requirement" is viewed as a chore and a ritual, an impersonal incantation, a hurried signing of papers. We know this is true, yet we cherish the myth of informed consent, skating over its lack of real content or impact. But because the Standard Model is a subterfuge aimed more at easing our consciences than at protecting research subjects, it fails both as a necessary condition for proposed experiments and as a justification for them.

IV. THE STANDARD MODEL IN ACTION: INFORMED CONSENT IN HARD CASES

. . . The Standard Model regulates experiments by requiring the subjects' informed consent. Comparatively little attention is given to the nature of the experiment itself—apart from its riskiness—or to the researcher's goals and intentions. Under the Standard Model, concern may be triggered by some characteristic of the subject (age, health, mental capabilities) or by the experiment's location (prison, hospital, university). These characteristics and locations, however, relate less to whether the researcher's plan is itself ethical, than whether the subject's consent was really given, or was truly informed. When experiments are prohibited, it is due to the quality, or lack thereof, of the consent given, not the propriety of the experiment itself. In these situations, whatever it is that gives the subject's consent its justificatory power—the mysterious indicia of autonomy worth respecting—is deemed lacking. To illustrate this dynamic at work, I review below the operation of the Standard Model in three paradigmatically hard cases.

A. PRISONERS

Prisoners have long been conveniently immobile, docile, and hence ideal subjects for research and experimentation. . . . Accordingly, experimentation on prisoners is carefully scrutinized under the Standard Model. The Department of Health and Human Services warns that "prisoners may be under constraints because of their incarceration which could affect their ability to make a truly voluntary and uncoerced decision whether or not to participate as subjects in research." . . .

B. THE TERMINALLY ILL

. . . As with prisoners, experimentation with terminally or grieviously ill patients distorts the Standard Model. Like children or the mentally handicapped, dying persons are often thought of as incapable of making informed decisions; and like prisoners, they are viewed as not "really" free, but instead, captive to the course of their disease and therefore under duress. Even when these patients are lucid, we fear their assessment of an experiment's benefits and risks may be skewed; we worry they might submit to quackery in a hopeless and desperate attempt to beat the inevitable. We also worry that the dying may, having abandoned all hope, submit to immoral experiments out of misplaced or entirely genuine altruism. Finally, we fear that we may be tempted to exploit these subjects' despair, incapacity, or altruism, and to railroad through experiments which might not otherwise pass ethical muster. . . .

C. CHILDREN

The use of children poses even thornier problems for research. We need to experiment on children; their problems and illnesses are often sui generis and can only be solved through experiments on them. However, the Standard Model assumes children cannot give adequate consent, and so it gives in to necessity, though the Nuremberg Code insisted that the subject's consent was essential. Because children cannot, by definition, give consent, we settle for less. In addition, because children are a necessary and unique research class, we are forced to face the steely utilitarian calculus that hides beneath the Standard Model's veneer of respect for persons.

The Standard Model requires someone's consent, and parents are the most obvious candidates. However, even parents might not be able to isolate and protect an individual child's safety and dignity, especially when another child is thrown into the equation. The same considerations that call into question whether a prisoner's consent was voluntary or informed might undermine a desperate parent's consent as well. . . .

■ GRIMES v. KENNEDY KRIEGER INSTITUTE, INC.
782 A.2d 807 (Md. 2001)

Opinion by CATHELL, J.

PROLOGUE

We initially note that these are cases of first impression for this Court. For that matter, precious few courts in the United States have addressed the issues presented in the cases at bar. . . .

In these present cases, a prestigious research institute, associated with Johns Hopkins University, based on this record, created a nontherapeutic research program whereby it required certain classes of homes to have only partial lead paint abatement modifications performed, and in at least some instances, including at least one of the cases at bar, arranged for the landlords to receive public funding by way of grants or loans to aid in the modifications. The research institute then encouraged, and in at least one of the cases at bar, required, the landlords to rent the premises to families with young children. In the event young children already resided in one of the study houses, it was contemplated that a child would remain in the premises, and the child was encouraged to remain, in order for his or her blood to be periodically analyzed. In other words, the continuing presence of the children that were the subjects of the study was required in order for the study to be complete. Apparently, the children and their parents involved in the[se] cases . . . were from a lower economic strata and were, at least in one case, minorities.

The purpose of the research was to determine how effective varying degrees of lead paint abatement procedures were. Success was to be determined by periodically, over a two-year period of time, measuring the extent to which lead dust remained in, or returned to, the premises after the varying levels of abatement modifications, and, as most important to our decision, by measuring the extent to which the theretofore healthy children's blood became contaminated with lead, and comparing that contamination with levels of lead dust in the houses over the same periods of time. [Some evidence suggests that families with young children were given priority in renting abated apartments.] . . .

The same researchers had completed a prior study on abatement and partial abatement methods that indicated that lead dust remained and/or returned to abated houses over a period of time. . . . [The researchers also acknowledged that exposure to lead was "particularly hazardous for children."] . . . After publishing this report, the researchers began the present research project in which children were encouraged to reside in households where the possibility of lead dust was known to the researcher to be likely, so that the lead dust content of their blood could be compared with the level of lead dust in the houses at periodic intervals over a two-year period.

Apparently, it was anticipated that the children, who were the human subjects in the program, would, or at least might, accumulate lead in their blood from the dust, thus helping the researchers to determine the extent to which the various partial abatement methods worked. There was no complete and clear explanation in the consent agreements signed by the parents of the children that the research to be conducted was designed, at least in significant part, to measure the success of the abatement procedures by measuring the extent to which the children's blood was being contaminated. It can be argued that the researchers intended that the children be the canaries in the mines but never clearly told the parents. . . .

The researchers and their Institutional Review Board apparently saw nothing wrong with the research protocols that anticipated the possible accumulation of lead in the blood of otherwise healthy children as a result of the experiment, or they believed that the consents of the parents of the children made the research appropriate. Institutional Review Boards (IRB) are oversight entities [that are within the organizational structure of the institution conducting the research]. In research experiments, an IRB can be required in some instances by either federal or state regulation, or sometimes by the conditions attached to governmental grants that are used to fund research projects. Generally, their primary functions are to assess the protocols of the project to determine whether the project itself is appropriate, whether the consent procedures are adequate, whether the methods to be employed meet proper standards, whether reporting requirements are sufficient, and the assessment of various other aspects of a research project. One of the most important objectives of such review is the review of the potential safety and the health hazard impact of a research project on the human subjects of the experiment, especially on vulnerable subjects such as children. Their function is not to help researchers seek funding for research projects.

In the instant case, as is suggested by some commentators as being endemic to the research community as a whole, infra, the IRB involved here, the Johns Hopkins

University Joint Committee on Clinical Investigation, in part, abdicated that responsibility, instead suggesting to the researchers a way to miscast the characteristics of the study in order to avoid the responsibility inherent in nontherapeutic research involving children. . . .

While the suggestion of the IRB would not make this experiment any less nontherapeutic or, thus, less regulated, . . . [its action] shows two things: (1) that the IRB had a partial misperception of the difference between therapeutic and nontherapeutic research and the IRB's role in the process and (2) that the IRB was willing to aid researchers in getting around federal regulations designed to protect children used as subjects in nontherapeutic research. An IRB's primary role is to assure the safety of human research subjects — not help researchers avoid safety or health-related requirements. The IRB, in this case, misconceived, at least partially, its own role.

The provisions or conditions imposed by the federal funding entities, pursuant to federal regulations, are conditions attached to funding. As far as we are aware, or have been informed, there are no federal or state (Maryland) statutes that mandate that all research be subject to certain conditions. Certain international "codes" or "declarations" exist (one of which is supposedly binding but has never been so held) that, at least in theory, establish standards. We shall describe them, infra. Accordingly, we write on a clean slate in this case. We are guided, as we determine what is appropriate, by those international "codes" or "declarations," as well as by studies conducted by various governmental entities, by the treatises and other writings on the ethics of using children as research subjects, and by the duties, if any, arising out of the use of children as subjects of research.

Otherwise healthy children, in our view, should not be enticed into living in, or remaining in, potentially lead-tainted housing and intentionally subjected to a research program, which contemplates the probability, or even the possibility, of lead poisoning or even the accumulation of lower levels of lead in blood, in order for the extent of the contamination of the children's blood to be used by scientific researchers to assess the success of lead paint or lead dust abatement measures. Moreover, in our view, parents, whether improperly enticed by trinkets, food stamps, money or other items, have no more right to intentionally and unnecessarily place children in potentially hazardous nontherapeutic research surroundings, than do researchers. In such cases, parental consent, no matter how informed, is insufficient.

While the validity of the consent agreement and its nature as a contract, the existence or nonexistence of a special relationship, and whether the researchers performed their functions under that agreement pursuant to any special relationships are important issues in these cases that we will address, the very inappropriateness of the research itself cannot be overlooked. It is apparent that the protocols of research are even more important than the method of obtaining parental consent and the extent to which the parents were, or were not, informed. If the research methods, the protocols, are inappropriate then, especially when the IRB is willing to help researchers avoid compliance with applicable safety requirements for using children in nontherapeutic research, the consent of the parents, or of any consent surrogates, in our view, cannot make the research appropriate or the actions of the researchers and the Institutional Review Board proper.

The research relationship proffered to the parents of the children the researchers wanted to use as measuring tools, should never have been presented in a nontherapeutic context in the first instance. Nothing about the research was designed for treatment of the subject children. They were presumed to be healthy at the commencement of the project. As to them, the research was clearly nontherapeutic in nature. The experiment was simply a "for the greater good" project.[6] The specific children's health was put at risk, in order to develop low-cost abatement measures that would help all children, the landlords, and the general public as well. . . .

The research project at issue here, and its apparent protocols, differs in large degree from, but presents similar problems as those in the Tuskegee Syphilis Study conducted from 1932 until 1972 . . . the intentional exposure of soldiers to radiation in the 1940s and 50s . . . the tests involving the exposure of Navajo miners to radiation . . . and the secret administration of LSD to soldiers by the CIA and the Army in the 1950s and 60s. . . . [In] the Tuskegee Syphilis Study . . . patients infected with syphilis were not subsequently informed of the availability of penicillin for treatment of the illness, in order for the scientists and researchers to be able to continue research on the effects of the illness. . . . [P]erhaps [the] most notorious . . . [nontherapeutic research project was] the deliberate use of infection . . . in order to study the degree of infection and the rapidity of the course of the disease in the . . . typhus experiments at Buchenwald concentration camp during World War II. These programs were somewhat alike in the vulnerability of the subjects; uneducated African American men, debilitated patients in a charity hospital, prisoners of war, inmates of concentration camps and others falling within the custody and control of the agencies conducting or approving the experiments. In the present case, children, especially young children, living in lower economic circumstances, albeit not as vulnerable as the other examples, are nonetheless, vulnerable as well.

It is clear to this Court that the scientific and medical communities cannot be permitted to assume sole authority to determine ultimately what is right and appropriate in respect to research projects involving young children free of the limitations and consequences of the application of Maryland law. The Institutional Review Boards, IRBs, are, primarily, in-house organs. In our view, they are not designed, generally, to be sufficiently objective in the sense that they are as sufficiently concerned

---

6. The ultimate goal was to find the cost of the minimal level of effective lead paint or lead dust abatement costs so as to help landlords assess, hopefully positively, the commercial feasibility of attempting to abate lead dust in marginally profitable, lower-rent urban housing, in order to help preserve such housing in the Baltimore housing market. . . . The tenants involved, presumably, would be from a lower-rent urban class. . . . The children of middle class or rich parents apparently were not involved.

> Indeed, the literature on the law and ethics of human experimentation is replete with warnings that all subjects, but especially vulnerable subjects, are at risk of abuse by inclusion [as research subjects]. Those vulnerable subjects included prisoners, who are subject to coercion, . . . children and the elderly . . . and racial minorities, ethnic minorities, and women . . . whom history shows to be the most frequent victims of abuses in human experimentations.

R. Alta Charo, Protecting Us to Death: Women, Pregnancy and Clinical Research Trials, 38 St. Louis U. L.J. 135, 135 (Fall, 1993). . . .

with the ethicality of the experiments they review as they are with the success of the experiments. . . . Here, the IRB, whose primary function was to insure safety and compliance with applicable regulations, encouraged the researchers to misrepresent the purpose of the research in order to bring the study under the label of "therapeutic" and thus under a lower safety standard of regulation. The IRB's purpose was ethically wrong, and its understanding of the experiment's benefit incorrect.

The conflicts are inherent. This would be especially so when science and private industry collaborate in search of material gains. Moreover, the special relationship between research entities and human subjects used in the research will almost always impose duties.

In respect to examining that special relationship, we are obliged to further examine its nature and its ethical constraints. In that regard, when contested cases arise, the assessment of the legal effect of research on human subjects must always be subject to judicial evaluation. One method of making such evaluations is the initiation of appropriate actions bringing such matters to the attention of the courts, as has been done in the cases at bar. It may well be that in the end, the trial courts will determine that no damages have been incurred in the instant cases and thus the actions will fail for that reason. In that regard, we note that there are substantial factual differences in the . . . [separate cases under review]. But the actions, themselves, are not defective on the ground that no legal duty can, according to the trial courts, possibly exist. For the reasons discussed at length in the main body of the opinion, a legal duty normally exists between researcher and subject and in all probability exists in the cases at bar. Moreover, as we shall discuss, the consents of the parents in these cases under Maryland law constituted contracts creating duties. Additionally, under Maryland law, to the extent parental consent can ever be effective in research projects of this nature, the parents may not have been sufficiently informed and, therefore, the consents ineffective and, based on the information contained in the sparse records before this court, the research project . . . may have invaded the legal rights of the children subjected to it. . . .

II. FACTS & PROCEDURAL BACKGROUND . . .

The research study [giving rise to these cases] was sponsored jointly by the EPA and the Maryland Department of Housing and Community Development (DHCD). It was thus a joint federal and state project. The Baltimore City Health Department and Maryland Department of the Environment also collaborated in the study. It appears that, because the study was funded and sponsored in part by a federal entity, certain federal conditions were attached to the funding grants and approvals. There are certain uniform standards required in respect to federally funded or approved projects. We, however, are unaware of, and have not been directed to, any federal or state statute or regulation that imposes limits on this Court's powers to conduct its review of the issues presented. None of the parties have questioned this Court's jurisdiction in these cases. Moreover, 45 Code Federal Regulations (C.F.R.) 46.116(e) specifically provides: "The informed consent requirements in this policy are not intended to preempt any applicable federal, state, or local laws which require additional information to be disclosed in order for informed consent to be legally effective." Those various federal or state conditions, recommendations, etc., may well be relevant at a trial on the merits as to whether any breach of a contractual or other duty occurred, or whether negligence did, in fact, occur; but have no limiting effect on the issue of whether, at law, legal duties, via contract or "special relationships" are created in Maryland in experimental nontherapeutic research involving Maryland children. . . .

In summary, KKI conducted a study of five test groups of twenty-five houses each. The first three groups consisted of houses known to have lead present. The amount of repair and maintenance conducted increased from Group 1 to Group 2 to Group 3. The fourth group consisted of houses, which had at one time lead present but had since allegedly received a complete abatement of lead dust. The fifth group consisted of modern houses, which had never had the presence of lead dust. The twenty-five homes in each of the first three testing levels were then to be compared to the two control groups: the twenty-five homes in Group 4 that had previously been abated and the 25 modern homes in Group 5. The research study was specifically designed to do less than full lead dust abatement in some of the categories of houses in order to study the potential effectiveness, if any, of lesser levels of repair and maintenance.

If the children were to leave the houses upon the first manifestation of lead dust, it would be difficult, if not impossible, to test, over time, the rate of the level of lead accumulation in the blood of the children attributable to the manifestation. In other words, if the children were removed from the houses before the lead dust levels in their blood became elevated, the tests would probably fail, or at least the data that would establish the success of the test—or of the abatement results, would be of questionable use. Thus, it would benefit the accuracy of the test, and thus KKI, the compensated researcher, if children remained in the houses over the period of the study even after the presence of lead dust in the houses became evident. . . .

[The consent form for the study provided:]

PURPOSE OF STUDY

As you may know, lead poisoning in children is a problem in Baltimore City and other communities across the country. Lead in paint, house dust and outside soil are major sources of lead exposure for children. Children can also be exposed to lead in drinking water and other sources. We understand that your house is going to have special repairs done in order to reduce exposure to lead in paint and dust. On a random basis, homes will receive one of two levels of repair. We are interested in finding out how well the two levels of repair work. The repairs are not intended, or expected, to completely remove exposure to lead.

We are now doing a study to learn about how well different practices work for reducing exposure to lead in paint and dust. We are asking you and over one hundred other families to allow us to test for lead in and around your homes up to 8 to 9 times over the next two years provided that your house qualifies for the full two years of study. Final eligibility will be determined after the initial testing of your home. We are also doing free blood lead testing of children aged 6 months to 7 years, up to 8 to 9 times over the next two years. We would also like you to respond to a short questionnaire every 6 months. This study is intended to monitor the effects of the repairs and is not intended to replace the regular medical care your family obtains. . . .

BENEFITS

To compensate you for your time answering questions and allowing us to sketch your home we will mail you a check in the amount of $5.00. In the future we would mail you a check in the amount of $15 each time the full questionnaire is completed. The dust, soil, water, and blood samples would be tested for lead at the Kennedy Krieger Institute at no charge to you. We would provide you with specific blood-lead results. We would contact you to discuss a summary of house test results and steps that you could take to reduce any risks of exposure. . . .

On appeal, appellant[s] seek[] review of the Circuit Court's decision granting KKI summary judgment. . . . [They] contend[] that KKI owed a duty of care . . . based on the nature of its relationship with [the children and parents participating in the study] . . . arising out of: (1) a contract between the parties; (2) a voluntary assumption by KKI; (3) a "special relationship" between the parties; and (4) a Federal regulation. . . . [The appellants argued that KKI was negligent in, for example, failing to notify a parent about elevated lead levels in a rental property for nine months, by which time her child had elevated blood levels of lead.]

III. DISCUSSION

A. STANDARD OF REVIEW

We resolve these disputes in the context of the trial court's granting of the appellee's motions for summary judgment in the two distinct cases. The threshold issues before this Court are whether, in the two cases presented, appellee, KKI, was entitled to summary judgment as a matter of law on the basis that no contract existed and that there is inherently no duty owed to a research subject by a researcher. Perhaps even more important is the ancillary issue of whether a parent in Maryland, under the law of this State, can legally consent to placing a child in a nontherapeutic research study that carries with it any risk of harm to the health of the child. We shall resolve all of these primary issues. . . .

B. GENERAL DISCUSSION

Initially, we note that we know of no law, nor have we been directed to any applicable in Maryland courts, that provides that the parties to a scientific study, because it is a scientific, health-related study, cannot be held to have entered into special relationships with the subjects of the study that can create duties, including duties, the breach of which may give rise to negligence claims. We also are not aware of any general legal precept that immunizes nongovernmental "institutional volunteers" or scientific researchers from the responsibility for the breaches of duties arising in "special relationships." Moreover, we, at the very least, hold that, under the particular circumstances testified to by the parties, there are genuine disputes of material fact concerning whether a special relationship existed between KKI and . . . [the appellants]. Concerning this issue, the granting of the summary judgment motions was clearly inappropriate. When a "special relationship" can exist as a matter of law, the issue of whether, given certain facts, a special relationship does exist, when there is a dispute of material fact in that respect, is a decision for the finder of fact, not the trial judge. We shall hold initially that the very nature of nontherapeutic scientific research on human subjects can, and normally will, create special relationships out of which duties arise. Since World War II the specialness or nature of such relationships has been frequently of concern in and outside of the research community.

As a result of the atrocities performed in the name of science during the Holocaust, and other happenings in the World War II era, what is now known as the Nuremberg Code evolved. Of special interest to this Court, the Nuremberg Code, at least in significant part, was the result of legal thought and legal principles, as opposed to medical or scientific principles, and thus should be the preferred standard for assessing the legality of scientific research on human subjects. Under it, duties to research subjects arise. . . . [The court cited a work by distinguished Boston University Professor George Annas detailing the history of the Nuremberg Code and explaining the lack of U.S. case law regarding the regulation of research under the Nuremberg Code or any other source of regulation.] . . .

In arguing that a fuller disclosure should be made when consent is sought for nontherapeutic research, as opposed to therapeutic research, [ethicist Karine] Morin notes:

> Furthermore, as long as courts continue to interpret the doctrine of informed consent in experimentation as it applies in the context of treatment, the uniqueness of the protection needed for human research subjects will be overlooked. Failing to recognize that subjects who volunteer for the sake of the advancement of science are differently situated from patients who stand to benefit from treatment results in an analysis that misconceives the purpose of disclosure. Beyond informing the patient as to means available to treat him or her, a subject must become a voluntary and willing participant in an endeavor that may yield no direct benefit to him or her, or worse, that may cause harm.

Karine Morin, The Standard of Disclosure in Human Subject Experimentation, 19 J. Legal Med. 157, 220 (1998). . . .

[T]here is no[t] [a] complete record of the specific compensation of the researchers involved. Although the project was funded by the EPA, at the request of KKI the EPA has declined to furnish such information to the attorney for one of the parties, who requested it under the federal Freedom of Information Act. Whether the research's character as a co-sponsored state project opens the records under the Maryland Public Information Act has apparently not been considered. Neither is there in the record any development of what pressures, if any, were exerted in respect to the researchers obtaining the consents of the parents and conducting the experiment. Nor, for the same reason, is there a sufficient indication as to the extent to which the Institute has joined with commercial interests, if it has, for the purposes of profit, that might potentially impact upon the researcher's motivations and potential conflicts of interest—motivations that generally are assumed, in the cases of prestigious entities such as Johns Hopkins University, to be for the public good rather . . . [than] a search for profit.

We do note that the institution involved, the respondent here . . . is a highly respected entity, considered to be a leader in the development of treatments, and treatment itself, for children infected with lead poisoning. With reasonable assurance, we can note that its reputation alone might normally suggest that there was no realization or understanding on the Institute's part that the protocols of the experiment were questionable, except for the letter from the IRB requesting that the researchers mischaracterize the study.

We shall further address both the factual and legal bases for the findings of the trial courts, holding, ultimately, that the respective courts erred in both respects.

C. NEGLIGENCE

It is important for us to remember that appellants allege that KKI was negligent. Specifically, they allege that KKI, as a medical researcher, owed a duty of care to them, as subjects in the research study, based on the nature of the agreements between them and also based on the nature of the relationship between the parties. They contend specifically that KKI was negligent because KKI breached its duty to: (1) design a study that did not involve placing children at unnecessary risk; (2) inform participants in the study of results in a timely manner; and (3) to completely and accurately inform participants in the research study of all the hazards and risks involved in the study. . . .

Because this is a review of the granting of the two summary judgments based solely on the grounds that there was no legal duty to protect the children, we are primarily concerned with . . . whether KKI was under a duty to protect appellants from injury.[33] . . .

The relationship that existed between KKI and both sets of appellants in the case at bar was that of medical researcher and research study subject. Though not expressly recognized in the Maryland Code or in our prior cases as a type of relationship which creates a duty of care, evidence in the record suggests that such a relationship involving a duty or duties would ordinarily exist, and certainly could exist, based on the facts and circumstances of each of these individual cases. . . .

IV. THE SPECIAL RELATIONSHIPS

A. THE CONSENT AGREEMENT CONTRACT

Both sets of appellants signed a similar Consent Form prepared by KKI in which KKI expressly promised to: (1) financially compensate (however minimally) appellants for their participation in the study; . . . (2) collect lead dust samples from appellants' homes, analyze the samples, discuss the results with appellants, and discuss steps that could be taken, which could reduce exposure to lead; and (3) collect blood samples from children in the household and provide appellants with the results of the blood tests. In return, appellants agreed to participate in the study, by: (1) allowing KKI into appellants' homes to collect dust samples; (2) periodically filling out questionnaires; and (3) allowing the children's blood to be drawn, tested, and utilized in the study. If consent agreements contain such provisions, and the trial court did not find otherwise, and we hold from our own examination of the record that such provisions were so contained, mutual assent, offer, acceptance, and consideration existed, all of which created contractual relationships imposing

---

33. We note that there was little suggestion of actual permanent injury to the children involved with these two cases. Our opinion is not directed to the matter of whether damages can be proven in the present cases.

duties by reason of the consent agreement . . . (as well, as we discuss elsewhere, by the very nature of such relationships).

By having appellants sign this Consent Form, both KKI and appellants expressly made representations, which, in our view, created a bilateral contract between the parties. At the very least, it suggests that appellants were agreeing with KKI to participate in the research study with the expectation that they would be compensated, albeit, more or less, minimally, be informed of all the information necessary for the subject to freely choose whether to participate, and continue to participate, and receive promptly any information that might bear on their willingness to continue to participate in the study. This includes full, detailed, prompt, and continuing warnings as to all the potential risks and hazards inherent in the research or that arise during the research. KKI, in return, was getting the children to move into the houses and/or to remain there over time, and was given the right to test the children's blood for lead. As consideration to KKI, it got access to the houses and to the blood of the children that had been encouraged to live in a "risk" environment. In other words, KKI received a measuring tool — the children's blood. Considerations existed, mainly money, food coupons, trinkets, bilateral promises, blood to be tested in order to measure success. "Informed consent" of the type used here, which imposes obligation and confers consideration on both researcher and subject (in these cases, the parents of the subjects) may differ from the more one-sided "informed consent" normally used in actual medical practice. Researcher/subject consent in nontherapeutic research can, and in this case did, create a contract.[35]

B. THE SUFFICIENCY OF THE CONSENT FORM

The consent form did not directly inform the parents of the fact that it was contemplated that some of the children might ingest lead dust particles, and that one of the reasons the blood of the children was to be tested was to evaluate how effective the various abatement measures were.

A reasonable parent would expect to be clearly informed that it was at least contemplated that her child would ingest lead dust particles, and that the degree to which lead dust contaminated the child's blood would be used as one of the ways in which the success of the experiment would be measured. The fact that if such information was furnished, it might be difficult to obtain human subjects for the research, does not affect the need to supply the information, or alter the ethics of failing to provide such information. A human subject is entitled to all material information. The respective parent should also have been clearly informed that in order for the measurements to be most helpful, the child needed to stay in the house until the conclusion of the study. Whether assessed by a subjective or an objective standard, the children, or their surrogates, should have been additionally informed that the researchers anticipated that, as a result of the experiment, it was possible that there might be some accumulation of lead in the blood of the children. The "informed" consent was not valid because full material information was not furnished to the subjects or their parents.

---

35. We make no determination as to whether informed consent in a therapeutic medical context can generate contractual obligations.

C. SPECIAL RELATIONSHIP

In Case Number 128, Ms. Hughes signed a Consent Form in which KKI agreed to provide her with "specific blood-lead results" and discuss with her "a summary of house test results and steps that [she] could take to reduce any risks of exposure." She contends that this agreement between the parties gave rise to a duty owed by KKI to provide her with that information in a timely manner. She signed the Consent Form on March 10, 1993. The project began almost simultaneously. KKI collected dust samples in the Monroe Street property on March 9, 1993, August 23, 1993, March 9, 1994, September 19, 1994, April 18, 1995, and November 13, 1995. The March 9, 1993 dust testing revealed what the researchers referred to as "hot spots," where the level of lead was "higher than might be found in a completely renovated house." . . . [T]his information was not furnished to Ms. Hughes until December 16, 1993, more than nine months after the samples had been collected and not until after Ericka Grimes's blood was found to contain elevated levels of lead. She contends that not only did KKI have a duty to report such information in a timely manner but that it breached this duty by delaying to such a time that her daughter was allowed to contract lead poisoning. Looking at the relevant facts of Case Number 128, they are susceptible to inferences supporting the position of appellant, Ericka Grimes, and, moreover, that, if true, would create a "special relationship" out of which duties would be created. Therefore, for this reason alone, the grant of summary judgment was improper. . . .

[T]he trial courts appear to have held that special relationships out of which duties arise cannot be created by the relationship between researchers and the subjects of the research. While in some rare cases that may be correct, it is not correct when researchers recruit people, especially children whose consent is furnished indirectly, to participate in nontherapeutic procedures that are potentially hazardous, dangerous, or deleterious to their health. As opposed to compilation of already extant statistics for purposes of studying human health matters, the creation of study conditions or protocols or participation in the recruitment of otherwise healthy subjects to interact with already existing, or potentially existing, hazardous conditions, or both, for the purpose of creating statistics from which scientific hypotheses can be supported, would normally warrant or create such special relationships as a matter of law.

It is of little moment that an entity is an institutional volunteer in a community. If otherwise, the legitimacy of the claim to noble purpose would always depend upon the particular institution and the particular community it is serving in a given case. As we have indicated, history is replete with claims of noble purpose for institutions and institutional volunteers in a wide variety of communities.

Institutional volunteers may intend to do good or, as history has proven, even to do evil and may do evil or good depending on the institution and the community they serve. Whether an institutional volunteer[36] in a particular community should

---

36. Moreover, it is not clear that KKI was a mere volunteer in any event. It received funding for developing and conducting the research. Whether it recognized a profit is unknown from the record. The "for profit" nature of some research may well increase the duties of researchers to insure the safety of research subjects, and may well increase researchers' or an institution's susceptibility for damages in respect to any injuries incurred by research subjects.

be granted exceptions from the application of law is a matter that should be scrutinized closely by an appropriate public policy maker. Generally, but not always, the legislative branch is appropriately the best first forum to consider exceptions to the tort laws of this State—even then it should consider all ramifications of the policy—especially considering the general vulnerability of subjects of such studies—in this case, small children. In the absence of the exercise of legislative policymaking, we hold that special relationships, out of which duties arise, the breach of which can constitute negligence, can result from the relationships between researcher and research subjects.

D. THE FEDERAL REGULATIONS

A duty may be prescribed by a statute, or a special relationship creating duties may arise from the requirement for compliance with statutory provisions. Although there is no duty of which we are aware prescribed by the Maryland Code in respect to scientific research . . . , federal regulations have been enacted that impose standards of care that attach to federally funded or sponsored research projects that use human subjects. See 45 C.F.R. Part 46 (2000). 45 C.F.R. Part 46, Subpart A, is entitled "Basic HHS Policy for Protection of Human Research Subjects" and Subpart D of the regulation is entitled "Additional Protections for Children Involved as Subjects in Research." . . . [T]his study was funded, and co-sponsored, by the EPA and presumably was therefore subject to these federal conditions. These conditions, if appropriate administrative action has been taken, require fully informed consent in any research using human subjects conducted, supported, or otherwise subject to any level of control or funding by any federal department or agency. . . .

These federal regulations, especially the requirement for adherence to sound ethical principles, strike right at the heart of KKI's defense of the granting of the Motions for Summary Judgment. Fully informed consent is lacking in these cases. The research did not comply with the regulations. There clearly was more than a minimal risk involved. Under the regulations, children should not have been used for the purpose of measuring how much lead they would accumulate in their blood while living in partially abated houses to which they were recruited initially or encouraged to remain, because of the study. . . .

Clearly, KKI, as a research institution, is required to obtain a human participant's fully informed consent, using sound ethical principles. It is clear from the wording of the applicable federal regulations that this requirement of informed consent continues during the duration of the research study and applies to new or changing risks. In this case, a special relationship out of which duties might arise might be created by reason of the federally imposed regulations. The question becomes whether this duty of informed consent created by federal regulation, as a matter of state law, translates into a duty of care arising out of the unique relationship that is researcher-subject, as opposed to doctor-patient. We answer that question in the affirmative. In this State, it may, depending on the facts, create such a duty.

Additionally, the Nuremberg Code, intended to be applied internationally, and never expressly rejected in this country, inherently and implicitly, speaks strongly to the existence of special relationships imposing ethical duties on researchers who conduct nontherapeutic experiments on human subjects. The Nuremberg Code specifically requires researchers to make known to human subjects of research "all inconveniences and hazards reasonably to be expected; and the effects upon his health or person which may possibly come from his participation in the experiment." The breach of obligations imposed on researchers by the Nuremberg Code, might well support actions sounding in negligence in cases such as those at issue here. We reiterate as well that, given the facts and circumstances of both of these cases, there were, at the very least, genuine disputes of material facts concerning the relationship and duties of the parties, and compliance with the regulations.

V. The Ethical Appropriateness of the Research

The World Medical Association in its Declaration of Helsinki . . . included a code of ethics for investigative researchers and was an attempt by the medical community to establish its own set of rules for conducting research on human subjects. . . .[39]

The determination of whether a duty exists under Maryland law is the ultimate function of various policy considerations as adopted by either the Legislature, or, if it has not spoken, as it has not in respect to this situation, by Maryland courts. In our view, otherwise healthy children should not be the subjects of nontherapeutic experimentation or research that has the potential to be harmful to the child. It is, first and foremost, the responsibility of the researcher and the research entity to see to the harmlessness of such nontherapeutic research. Consent of parents can never relieve the researcher of this duty. We do not feel that it serves proper public policy concerns to permit children to be placed in situations of potential harm, during nontherapeutic procedures, even if parents, or other surrogates, consent. Under these types of circumstances, even where consent is given, albeit inappropriately, policy considerations suggest that there remains a special relationship between researchers and participants to the research study, which imposes a duty of care. This is entirely consistent with the principles found in the Nuremberg Code.

Researchers cannot ever be permitted to completely immunize themselves by reliance on consents, especially when the information furnished to the subject, or the party consenting, is incomplete in a material respect. A researcher's duty is not created by, or extinguished by, the consent of a research subject or by IRB approval. The duty to a vulnerable research subject is independent of consent, although the obtaining of consent is one of the duties a researcher must perform. All of this is especially so when the subjects of research are children. Such legal duties, and legal protections, might additionally be warranted because of the likely conflict of interest between the goal of the research experimenter and the health of the human subject, especially, but not exclusively, when such research is commercialized. There is always a potential substantial conflict of interest on the part of researchers as between them and the human subjects used in their research. If participants in the study withdraw from the research study prior to its completion, then the results of

---

39. . . . Declaration of Helsinki, World Medical Assembly (WMA) 18th Assembly (June 1964), amended by 29th WMA Tokyo, Japan (October 1975), 35th WMA Venice, Italy (October 1983) and the 41st WMA Hong Kong (September 1989). [Eds. Note: For the current WMA Declaration of Helsinki, see 310 JAMA 2191 (2013).]

the study could be rendered meaningless. There is thus an inherent reason for not conveying information to subjects as it arises, that might cause the subjects to leave the research project. That conflict dictates a stronger reason for full and continuous disclosure. . . .

A special relationship giving rise to duties, the breach of which might constitute negligence, might also arise because, generally, the investigators are in a better position to anticipate, discover, and understand the potential risks to the health of their subjects. . . .

This duty requires the protection of the research subjects from unreasonable harm and requires the researcher to completely and promptly inform the subjects of potential hazards existing from time to time because of the profound trust that participants place in investigators, institutions, and the research enterprise as a whole to protect them from harm. . . .

While we acknowledge that foreseeability does not necessarily create a duty, we recognize that potential harm to the children participants of this study was both foreseeable and potentially extreme. A "special relationship" also exists in circumstances where such experiments are conducted.

VI. Parental Consent for Children to Be Subjects of Potentially Hazardous Nontherapeutic Research

The issue of whether a parent can consent to the participation of her or his child in a nontherapeutic health-related study that is known to be potentially hazardous to the health of the child raises serious questions with profound moral and ethical implications. What right does a parent have to knowingly expose a child not in need of therapy to health risks or otherwise knowingly place a child in danger, even if it can be argued it is for the greater good? The issue in these specific contested cases does not relate primarily to the authority of the parent, but to the procedures of KKI and similar entities that may be involved in such health-related studies. The issue of the parents' right to consent on behalf of the children has not been fully presented in either of these cases, but should be of concern not only to lawyers and judges, but to moralists, ethicists, and others. The consenting parents in the contested cases at bar were not the subjects of the experiment; the children were. Additionally, this practice presents the potential problems of children initiating actions in their own names upon reaching majority, if indeed, they have been damaged as a result of being used as guinea pigs in nontherapeutic scientific research. Children, it should be noted, are not in our society the equivalent of rats, hamsters, monkeys, and the like. Because of the overriding importance of this matter and this Court's interest in the welfare of children—we shall address the issue.

Most of the relatively few cases in the area of the ethics of protocols of various research projects involving children have merely assumed that a parent can give informed consent for the participation of their children in nontherapeutic research. . . .

It is not in the best interest of a specific child, in a nontherapeutic research project, to be placed in a research environment, which might possibly be, or which proves to be, hazardous to the health of the child . . . in order to test methods that may ultimately benefit all children. . . .

One simply does not expose otherwise healthy children, incapable of personal assent (consent), to a nontherapeutic research environment that is known at the inception of the research, might cause the children to ingest lead dust. It is especially troublesome, when a measurement of the success of the research experiment is, in significant respect, to be determined by the extent to which the blood of the children absorbs, and is contaminated by, a substance that the researcher knows can, in sufficient amounts, whether solely from the research environment or cumulative from all sources, cause serious and long term adverse health effects. Such a practice is not legally acceptable. . . .

In the[se] case[s], no impartial judicial review or oversight was sought by the researchers or by the parents. . . . Science cannot be permitted to be the sole judge of the appropriateness of such research methods on human subjects, especially in respect to children. We hold that in these contested cases, the research study protocols [presented to the court] . . . were not appropriate. . . .

VII. Conclusion

We hold that in Maryland a parent, appropriate relative, or other applicable surrogate, cannot consent to the participation of a child or other person under legal disability in nontherapeutic research or studies in which there is any risk of injury or damage to the health of the subject.

We hold that informed consent agreements in nontherapeutic research projects, under certain circumstances can constitute contracts; and that, under certain circumstances, such research agreements can, as a matter of law, constitute "special relationships" giving rise to duties, out of the breach of which negligence actions may arise. We also hold that, normally, such special relationships are created between researchers and the human subjects used by the researchers. Additionally, we hold that governmental regulations can create duties on the part of researchers towards human subjects out of which "special relationships" can arise. Likewise, such duties and relationships are consistent with the provisions of the Nuremberg Code.

The determination as to whether a "special relationship" actually exists is to be done on a case by case basis. . . . The determination as to whether a special relationship exists, if properly pled, lies with the trier of fact. We hold that there was ample evidence in the cases at bar to support a fact finder's determination of the existence of duties arising out of contract, or out of a special relationship, or out of regulations and codes, or out of all of them, in each of the cases.

We hold that on the present record, the Circuit Courts erred in their assessment of the law and of the facts as pled in granting KKI's motions for summary judgment in both cases before this Court. Accordingly, we vacate the rulings of the Circuit Court for Baltimore City and remand these cases to that court for further proceedings consistent with this opinion. . . .

RAKER, J., concurring in result only:

These appeals present the narrow question of whether the Circuit Courts erred in granting summary judgments to appellee, the Kennedy Krieger Institute, a research entity, on the ground that, as a matter of law, it owed no duty to warn appellants, Ericka Grimes and Myron Higgins, et al., human subjects participating in its research study. I concur in the judgment of the Court only and join in the Court's judgment that the Circuit Courts erred in granting summary judgments to appellee. These cases should be remanded for further proceedings.

I concur in the Court's judgment because I find that appellants have alleged sufficient facts to establish that there existed a special relationship between the parties in these cases, which created a duty of care that, if breached, gives rise to an action in negligence. . . . I would hold that a special relationship giving rise to a duty of care, the breach of which would be the basis for an action in negligence, existed in these cases and would remand the cases at bar to the Circuit Courts for further proceedings. I agree with the majority that this duty includes the protection of research subjects from unreasonable harm and requires the researcher to inform research subjects completely and promptly of potential hazards resulting from participation in the study. . . . As a result of the existence of this tort duty, I find it unnecessary to reach the thorny question, not even raised by any of the parties, of whether the informed consent agreements in these cases constitute legally binding contracts. . . .

As I have indicated, this case presents a narrow question of whether a duty in tort exists between the plaintiffs and the defendants. . . . Nonetheless, the majority appears to have decided the issue of whether such duty of care was, in fact, breached as a matter of law, without a hearing or a trial on the merits.

I cannot join in the majority's sweeping factual determinations. . . .

ON MOTION FOR RECONSIDERATION

PER CURIAM.

The Court has considered the motion for reconsideration and the submissions by the various amici curiae. The motion is denied, with this explanation.

Some of the issues raised in this case, in the briefs and at oral argument, were important ones of first impression in this State, and the Court therefore attempted to address those issues in a full and exhaustive manner. The case reached us in the context of summary judgments entered by the Circuit Court, which entailed rulings that the evidence presented by the plaintiffs, for purposes of the motions, even when taken in a light most favorable to them, was insufficient as a matter of law to establish the prospect of liability. We disagreed with that determination. Although we discussed the various issues and arguments in considerable detail, the only conclusion that we reached as a matter of law was that, on the record currently before us, summary judgment was improperly granted—that sufficient evidence was presented in both cases which, if taken in a light most favorable to the plaintiffs and believed by a jury, would suffice to justify verdicts in favor of the plaintiffs. Thus, the cases were remanded for further proceedings in the Circuit Court. Every issue bearing on liability or damages remains open for further factual development, and any relevant evidence not otherwise precluded under our rules of evidence is admissible.

Much of the argument in support of and in opposition to the motion for reconsideration centered on the question of what limitations should govern a parent's authority to provide informed consent for the participation of his or her minor child in a medical study. In the Opinion, we said at one point that a parent "cannot consent to the participation of a child . . . in nontherapeutic research or studies in which there is any risk of injury or damage to the health of the subject." As we think is clear from Section VI of the Opinion, by "any risk," we meant any articulable risk beyond the minimal kind of risk that is inherent in any endeavor. The context of the statement was a non-therapeutic study that promises no medical benefit to the child whatever, so that any balance between risk and benefit is necessarily negative. As we indicated, the determination of whether the study in question offered some benefit, and therefore could be regarded as therapeutic in nature, or involved more than that minimal risk is open for further factual development on remand.

RAKER, Judge, dissenting.

I respectfully dissent from the order denying the motions for reconsideration. I adhere to the views previously expressed in my concurring opinion filed herein. . . . The majority's discussion of the ability of a parent or guardian to consent to the participation of a minor child in a nontherapeutic research study and the discussion regarding the ethics of the research conducted in these cases involve serious public policy considerations. The statements are a declaration of public policy that, in the posture of this case, are best left to the General Assembly. . . .

■ FEDERAL POLICY FOR THE PROTECTION OF HUMAN SUBJECTS
82 Fed. Reg. 7149 (Jan. 19, 2017)

PURPOSE OF THE REGULATORY ACTION

Individuals who are the subjects of research may be asked to contribute their time and assume risk to advance the research enterprise, which benefits society at large. U.S. federal regulations governing the protection of human subjects in research have been in existence for more than three decades. The Department of Health, Education, and Welfare first published regulations for the protection of human subjects in 1974, and the Department of Health and Human Services (HHS) revised them in the early 1980s. During the 1980s, HHS began a process that eventually led to the adoption of a revised version of the regulations by 15 U.S. federal departments and agencies in 1991. The purpose of this effort was to promote uniformity, understanding, and compliance with human subject protections as well as to create a uniform body of regulations across federal departments and agencies (subpart A of 45 Code of Federal Regulations [CFR] part 46), often referred to as the "Common Rule" or "Protection of Human Subjects Regulations." Those regulations were last amended in 2005, and have remained unchanged until the issuance of this final rule.

Since the Common Rule was promulgated, the volume and landscape of research involving human subjects have changed considerably. Research with human subjects has grown in scale and become more diverse. Examples of developments include: an expansion in the number and types of clinical trials, as well as observational studies and cohort studies; a diversification of the types of social and behavioral research being used in human subjects research; increased use of sophisticated analytic techniques to study human biospecimens; and the growing use of electronic health data and other digital records to enable very large datasets to be rapidly analyzed and combined in novel ways. Yet these developments have not been accompanied by major change in the human subjects research oversight system, which has remained largely unaltered over the past two decades.

On July 26, 2011, the Office of the Secretary of HHS, in coordination with the Executive Office of the President's Office of Science and Technology Policy (OSTP), published an advance notice of proposed rulemaking (ANPRM) to request comment on how current regulations for protecting those who participate in research might be modernized and revised to be more effective.

On September 8, 2015, HHS and 15 other federal departments and agencies published a Notice of Proposed Rulemaking (NPRM) proposing revisions to the regulations for protection of human subjects in research.[2] Like the ANPRM, the NPRM sought comment on how to better protect research subjects while facilitating valuable research and reducing burden, delay, and ambiguity for investigators. Public comments on both the ANPRM and the NPRM have informed the final rule that is now being promulgated.

The final rule is designed to more thoroughly address the broader types of research conducted or otherwise supported by all of the Common Rule departments and agencies such as behavioral and social science research. It also benefits from continuing efforts to harmonize human subjects policies across federal departments and agencies.

SUMMARY OF THE MAJOR CHANGES IN THE FINAL RULE

The final rule differs in important ways from the NPRM [proposed rule]. Most significantly, several proposals are not being adopted:

- The final rule does not adopt the proposal to require that research involving nonidentified biospecimens be subject to the Common Rule, and that consent would need to be obtained in order to conduct such research. . . .
- The final rule does not expand the policy to cover clinical trials that are not federally funded. . . .
- The final rule does not include the proposed standardized privacy safeguards for identifiable private information and identifiable biospecimens. Aspects of proposals that relied on those safeguards have been modified or are not being adopted.
- The final rule does not adopt the most restrictive proposed criteria for obtaining a waiver of the consent requirements relating to research with identifiable biospecimens.

The final rule makes the following significant changes to the Common Rule:

- Establishes new requirements regarding the information that must be given to prospective research subjects as part of the informed consent process.
- Allows the use of broad consent (i.e., seeking prospective consent to unspecified future research) from a subject for storage, maintenance, and secondary research use of identifiable private information and identifiable biospecimens.

2. HHS. Federal Policy for the Protection of Human Subjects. 80 FR 53931 (Sept. 8, 2015). Retrieved from https://www.federalregister.gov/documents/2015/09/08/2015 -21756/federal-policy-for-the-protection-of-human-subjects.

Broad consent will be an optional alternative that an investigator may choose instead of, for example, conducting the research on nonidentified information and nonidentified biospecimens, having an institutional review board (IRB) waive the requirement for informed consent, or obtaining consent for a specific study.

- Establishes new exempt categories of research based on their risk profile. Under some of the new categories, exempt research would be required to undergo limited IRB review to ensure that there are adequate privacy safeguards for identifiable private information and identifiable biospecimens.
- Creates a requirement for U.S.-based institutions engaged in cooperative research to use a single IRB for that portion of the research that takes place within the United States, with certain exceptions. This requirement becomes effective 3 years after publication of the final rule.
- Removes the requirement to conduct continuing review of ongoing research for studies that undergo expedited review and for studies that have completed study interventions and are merely analyzing study data or involve only observational follow up in conjunction with standard clinical care.

Other minor changes have been to improve the rule and for purposes of clarity and accuracy. . . .

THE RATIONALE FOR MODERNIZING THE COMMON RULE . . .

THE CHANGING NATURE OF RESEARCH

This final rule recognizes that in the past two decades a paradigm shift has occurred in how research is conducted. Evolving technologies—including imaging, mobile technologies, and the growth in computing power—have changed the scale and nature of information collected in many disciplines. Computer scientists, engineers, and social scientists are developing techniques to integrate different types of data so they can be combined, mined, analyzed, and shared. The advent of sophisticated computer software programs, the Internet, and mobile technology has created new areas of research activity, particularly within the social and behavioral sciences. In biomedical science, the Human Genome Project laid the foundation for precision medicine and promoted an environment of data sharing and innovation in analytics and technology, and drew attention to the need for policies that support a changing research landscape. New technologies, including genomic sequencing, have quickly led to exponential growth in the data to which investigators have access. The sheer volume of data that can be generated in research, the ease with which it can be shared, and the ways in which it can be used to identify individuals were simply not possible, or even imaginable, when the Common Rule was first adopted.

Research settings are also shifting. Although much biomedical research continues to be conducted in academic medical centers, more research is being conducted in clinical care settings, thus combining research and medical data. Biospecimen repositories and large databases have made it easier to do research on existing (stored) biospecimens and data. Clinical research networks connected through electronic health records have developed methods for extracting clinical data for research purposes and are working toward integration of research data into electronic health records in a meaningful way. The scientific community recognizes the value of data sharing and open-source resources and understands that pooling intellectual resources and capitalizing on efficient uses of data and technology represent the best ways to advance knowledge.

At the same time, the level of public engagement in the research enterprise has changed. More people want to play an active role in research, particularly related to health.

As technology evolves, so does the nature of the risks and benefits of participating in certain types of research. Many studies do not involve interaction with research subjects, but instead involve secondary analysis of data or biospecimens. Risks related to these types of research studies are largely informational, not physical; that is, harms could result primarily from the inappropriate disclosure of information and not from the research interventions themselves. Nonetheless, those harms can be significant.

Because of these shifts in science, technology, and public engagement and expectations, a wide range of stakeholders have raised concerns about the limitations of the existing regulatory framework, arguing for a re-evaluation of how the fundamental principles of the 1979 Belmont Report that underlie the Common Rule—respect for persons, beneficence, and justice—are applied in practice to the myriad new contexts in which U.S. research is conducted in the 21st century. The changes that are being implemented in the final rule continue to be shaped by those principles. . . .

Finally, it is important to note that, to the extent appropriate, the intent is to eventually amend the other subparts of the HHS human subjects protection regulations in 45 CFR part 46 (subparts B, C, D, and E), and consider the need for updates to FDA regulations and other relevant federal departmental or agency regulations with overlapping scope.

Notes: Human Subjects Research

1. *Federal Regulation.* As described above, most of the field of clinical investigation is now very closely regulated by the DHHS's Office for Human Research Protections, 45 C.F.R. §§46.101 et seq, and the federal Food and Drug Administration (FDA), 21 C.F.R. §§50.1-.56; 54.1-.6; and 56.101-.124. The federal regulatory structure differs from informed consent law in that the penalty for violation is disqualification from federal funding rather than a claim for damages. The regulatory focus, however, mirrors the informed consent themes already introduced in our discussion of fiduciary liability. The federal regulations are designed to safeguard individual autonomy from overreaching by researchers. The mechanism used to provide protection is a combination of mandatory disclosure and individual assent. The researcher is charged with a special obligation to care for his or her research subject and to protect the subject from harm. The federal regulations require prior approval of the informed consent process that typically includes written disclosures and consents. These documents are reviewed by interdisciplinary ethical review committees (called "institutional review boards" or "IRBs") located in hospitals, in other medical research centers, and in universities where research is conducted using human subjects. The Common Rule explicitly preserves from preemption foreign, state, tribal, or local laws providing additional protections. 45 C.F.R. §46.101(f), (g).

The relevant federal agency may also permit federal agencies to apply equivalent or more protective internationally recognized protections for human research subjects in research conducted in foreign countries. Id. at §46.101(h).

The Common Rule has played an extremely important role in establishing norms for human subjects research and specific standards for consent. The revision process began with a detailed advance notice of proposed rulemaking in 2011, which was followed by a notice of the proposed rulemaking that offered specific proposed revisions in 2015. These announcements generated significant attention. The proposed rule generated more than 2,100 public comments along with two major reports. See National Research Council of the National Academies, Proposed Revisions to the Common Rule for the Protection of Human Subjects in the Behavioral and Social Sciences (2014); National Academies of Sciences, Engineering, and Medicine, Optimizing the Nation's Investment in Academic Research: A New Regulatory Framework for the 21st Century (2016). The Final Rule differs from the original proposed rule in a number of ways, and further changes are anticipated in related DHHS rules and in the FDA rules governing human subjects research. See, 21st Century Cures Act, P.L. No. 114-255 (2016) (sec. 3023, DHHS and FDA harmonization). The notes in this section will focus on the Common Rule, using the provisions effective as of January 2018, unless otherwise noted.

2. *Basic Definitions: What Is Research?* The federal regulations establish a broad definition of *research* as "a systematic investigation, including research development, testing, and evaluation, designed to develop or contribute to generalizable knowledge." 45 C.F.R. §46.102(l). A "[h]uman subject" is "a living individual about whom an investigator (whether professional or student) conducting research: (i) Obtains information or biospecimens through intervention or interaction with the individual, and uses, studies, or analyzes the information or biospecimens; or (ii) Obtains, uses, studies, analyzes, or generates identifiable private information or identifiable biospecimens." Id. §46.102(e). Is the line between medical treatment and medical research always clear? See Lars Noah, Informed Consent and the Elusive Dichotomy Between Standard and Experimental Therapy, 28 Am. J. L. & Med. 361 (2002).

Although the revised Common Rule maintains the previous broad definition of *research*, the Rule now includes additional provisions carving out activities "deemed not to be research," such as: (1) certain scholarly and journalistic activities (including legal research); (2) specifically defined public health surveillance activities; (3) collection and analysis of information, biospecimens, or records by criminal justice authorities for specific purposes; and (4) authorized operational activities supporting certain "intelligence, homeland security, defense or other national security missions." 45 C.F.R. §46.102(l). The new Common Rule also broadens the category of "exempt research," which generally involves research considered to present low risks to participants, that will ordinarily be exempt from most Part A (Common Rule) requirements. 45 C.F.R. §46.104. One particularly important category of exemptions involves a new process for securing broad consent for secondary use of personally identifiable information or biospecimens, which will be considered further below.

3. *General Requirements for Funded Research.* The federal regulations establish several criteria for approval of most forms of research:

> (a) In order to approve research covered by this policy the IRB shall determine that all of the following requirements are satisfied:

(1) Risks to subjects are minimized: (i) By using procedures that are consistent with sound research design and that do not unnecessarily expose subjects to risk, and (ii) Whenever appropriate, by using procedures already being performed on the subjects for diagnostic or treatment purposes.

(2) Risks to subjects are reasonable in relation to anticipated benefits, if any, to subjects, and the importance of the knowledge that may reasonably be expected to result. In evaluating risks and benefits, the IRB should consider only those risks and benefits that may result from the research (as distinguished from risks and benefits of therapies subjects would receive even if not participating in the research). The IRB should not consider possible long-range effects of applying knowledge gained in the research (e.g., the possible effects of the research on public policy) as among those research risks that fall within the purview of its responsibility.

(3) Selection of subjects is equitable. In making this assessment the IRB should take into account the purposes of the research and the setting in which the research will be conducted. The IRB should be particularly cognizant of the special problems of research that involves a category of subjects who are vulnerable to coercion or undue influence, such as children, prisoners, individuals with impaired decision-making capacity, or economically or educationally disadvantaged persons.

(4) Informed consent will be sought from each prospective subject or the subject's legally authorized representative, in accordance with, and to the extent required by, §46.116.

(5) Informed consent will be appropriately documented or appropriately waived in accordance with §46.117.

(6) When appropriate, the research plan makes adequate provision for monitoring the data collected to ensure the safety of subjects.

(7) When appropriate, there are adequate provisions to protect the privacy of subjects and to maintain the confidentiality of data. (i) The Secretary of HHS will, after consultation with the Office of Management and Budget's privacy office and other Federal departments and agencies that have adopted this policy, issue guidance to assist IRBs in assessing what provisions are adequate to protect the privacy of subjects and to maintain the confidentiality of data. . . .

(b) When some or all of the subjects are likely to be vulnerable to coercion or undue influence, such as children, prisoners, individuals with impaired decision-making capacity, or economically or educationally disadvantaged persons, additional safeguards have been included in the study to protect the rights and welfare of these subjects.

45 C.F.R. §46.111 (specific provisions governing research involving "storage or maintenance of identifiable private information or identifiable biospecimens for potential secondary research use" omitted).

Therapeutic research provides the possibility of benefit to the research subject; some risk to the subject might therefore be tolerated so long as it is outweighed by the anticipated benefit and other criteria are met. Nontherapeutic research does not offer a benefit to the subject; the research therefore cannot proceed unless the risks are minimal. The *Grimes* court characterized the lead abatement research as involving more than minimal risk and suggested that parents might not be permitted to consent to nontherapeutic research involving children that poses more than a minimal risk. What is a minimal risk? Federal regulations in place since 1991 provide that "minimal risk means that the probability and magnitude of harm or discomfort anticipated in the research are not greater in and of themselves than those ordinarily encountered in daily life or during the performance of routine physical or psychological examinations or tests." 45 C.F.R. §46.102(j). Is this the definition used by the *Grimes* court? Why didn't the *Grimes* court consider the risk to be minimal, given that children who live in older housing frequently are exposed to the risk of lead paint?

The Rule authorizes "expedited" review (by the IRB chair or one more designated members) for "certain kinds of research involving no more than minimal risk, and for minor changes in approved research." 45 C.F.R. §46.110 (noting that the Secretary of DHHS has published a "list of categories of research that may be reviewed by the IRB through an expedited review procedure" and that "the Secretary will evaluate the list at least every 8 years").

4. *Institutional Review Boards (IRBs).* Under federal law, the membership of an IRB is supposed to be diverse and professionally knowledgeable about research proposals and research ethics. 45 C.F.R. §46.107. IRBs that regularly consider research proposals involving vulnerable subjects should consider including "one or more individuals who are knowledgeable about and experienced in working with these subjects." Id. The IRB must include at least one member who is unaffiliated with the institution. IRB members may not participate in the review of a research project in which they have a conflict of interest. Id.

The *Grimes* court was skeptical about the independence of IRBs. Commentators have raised many questions about the ability of potentially overworked and conflicted IRBs to safeguard research subjects. The federal government implemented expanded oversight of IRBs in 2009. 45 C.F.R. §46.501-.505. Some of the provisions found in the new Common Rule were designed to allow IRBs to focus attention on higher risk studies. Other mechanisms designed to protect the safety of research subjects include reporting requirements for adverse events and the use of data and safety monitoring committees.

5. *Informed Consent in Research.* The federal regulations focus on the informed consent process as the major tool for protecting human subjects. The informed consent rules are much more detailed in some areas than common-law rules but do not preempt those laws. 45 C.F.R. §46.116. Note that federal law prohibits research sponsors from requiring waivers of liability for negligence. Id. Examine the informed consent form excerpted in the *Grimes* decision: In what way(s) was it deficient?

The Common Rule includes "general," "basic," and "additional" consent requirements. "General" informed consent provisions require (with various exceptions) that (1) human subjects or their legal representatives must provide consent; (2) investigators should ensure that subjects have "sufficient opportunity to discuss and consider" participation and should "minimize the possibility of coercion or undue influence"; (3) information should be provided in "understandable language"; and (4) the information should include what "a reasonable person would want to have in order to make an informed decision . . . and an opportunity to discuss that information." 45 C.F.R. §46.116(a). New provisions also require that, for most forms of consent, the process "begin with a concise and focused presentation of the key information that is most likely to assist a prospective subject . . . in understanding the reasons why one might or might not want to participate in the research. This part of the informed consent must be presented in a way that facilitates comprehension." Id. at §46.116(a)(5). The consent as a whole must provide sufficient detail within an organizational structure that "facilitates the prospective subject's . . . understanding." Id.

The Common Rule establishes "basic elements" of informed consent that should be provided for research not covered by an exception. The basic elements include the purposes of the research, a description of reasonably foreseeable risks and benefits, a disclosure of appropriate alternative procedures or treatments, notice of confidentiality protections, an explanation regarding the availability of compensation for any injuries, contact information for the project, and notice that participation is voluntary. Id. at §46.116(b). In addition, for research involving private information or biospecimens, the consent must include one of two options: "(i) A statement that identifiers might be removed from the identifiable private information or identifiable biospecimens and that, after such removal, the information or biospecimens could be used for future research studies or distributed to another investigator for future research studies without additional informed consent from the subject or the legally authorized representative, if this might be a possibility; or (ii) A statement that the subject's information or biospecimens collected as part of the research, even if identifiers are removed, will not be used or distributed for future research studies." Id. at at §46.116(b)(9).

The Common Rule also includes "additional elements of consent" that are to be provided for research not carried out under one of the Rule's exceptions. Id. at §46.116(c). For example, where appropriate, the consent should include language indicating that the research may involve unforeseeable risks. The new Rule makes some significant additions to this list of potentially required disclosures in areas that had previously created controversy and concern. For example, the consent must provide "[a] statement that the subject's biospecimens (even if identifiers are removed) may be used for commercial profit and whether the subject will or will not share in this commercial profit." Id. at §46.116(c)(7). Where relevant, the new Rule also requires statements about the circumstances, if any, in which "clinically relevant research results, including individual research results, will be disclosed to subjects." Id. at §46.116(c)(8). Potential subjects must also be told whether research involving biospecimens "will or might include whole genome sequencing." Id. at §46.116(c)(9).

Finally, the Common Rule now requires "one IRB-approved informed consent form used to enroll subjects" be posted on a publicly accessible Web site for clinical trials that are "conducted or supported by a Federal department or agency." 45 C.F.R. §46.116(h). This provision will dramatically improve transparency regarding the informed consent process and could result in the development and recognition of model provisions that could reduce the costs of compliance for researchers.

6. *Exceptions to the Regular Informed Consent Principles.* There are a number of important exceptions to the Common Rule's general, basic, and additional informed consent provisions, three of which will be briefly summarized here:

a. *The "Broad Consent" Option.* The new Common Rule offers researchers the option of seeking broad consent for the storage, maintenance, and secondary research use of identifiable private information or identifiable biospecimens (collected for either research studies other than the proposed research or nonresearch purposes). Research carried out using the broad consent provisions that meets certain other requirements, including adequate protection to protect the privacy of subjects and the confidentiality of the data, see §46.111(a)(7), may be found to be exempt under 45 C.F.R. 46.104(d)(8). The broad consent process includes a small subset of the general, basic, and additional consent rules described in Note 5 (e.g., notices regarding the possibility of commercialization or the use of whole genome sequencing) along with seven separate requirements targeting key issues in the use of biospecimens. 45 C.F.R. §46.116(d).

b. *The General Waiver or Alteration of Consent Rule.* The Common Rule permits IRBs to waive or alter consent requirements in certain circumstances. 45 C.F.R. §46.116(f). Before waiving or altering the requirements, the IRB must determine and document that: "(i) The research involves no more than minimal risk to the subjects; (ii) The research could not practicably be carried out without the requested waiver or alteration; (iii) If the research involves using identifiable private information or identifiable biospecimens, the research could not practicably be carried out without using such information or biospecimens in an identifiable format; (iv) The waiver or alteration will not adversely affect the rights and welfare of the subjects; and (v) Whenever appropriate, the subjects or legally authorized representatives will be provided with additional pertinent information after participation." Id. at §46.116(f)(3). An IRB cannot waive consent for storage, maintenance, or secondary research with identifiable private information or biospecimens where individuals have already declined to provide broad consent. Id. §46.116(f)(1). An IRB approving alteration of some of the consent requirements must still adhere to the general consent requirements (45 C.F.R. §46.116(a)), and, where broad consent is at issue (45 C.F.R. §46.116(d)), may not alter any of the specific broad consent requirements established in the Rule.

c. *The Screening or Recruiting Rule.* The Common Rule also authorizes IRBs to permit researchers to "obtain information or biospecimens for the purpose of screening, recruiting, or determining the eligibility of prospective subjects without informed consent" if (1) the researchers "obtain information through oral or written communication with the prospective subject or . . . representative"; or (2) the researchers will obtain the information "by accessing records or stored biospecimens." 45 C.F.R. §46.116(g). Consent must be carried out and documented in accordance with 45 C.F.R. §46.117.

7. *Research Involving Biospecimens.* Assume that you are a researcher hoping to use biospecimens in research. Would you be likely to use the Common Rule's much discussed, new broad consent provisions? Or, would you prefer to secure waiver of the consent requirements or de-identification of the biospecimens? See Holly Fernandez Lynch & Michelle Meyer, Hastings Center Rep. 3 (May-June 2017) (arguing that use of broad consent provisions will be limited in light of other mechanisms available within the Rule).

The new Common Rule provisions regarding biospecimens defer for the time being a major area of debate involving the "identifiability" of biospecimens, that is, whether most biospecimens are inherently identifiable as they contain genetic material that is uniquely associated with a particular individual. The early drafts of the revised rules would have treated non-identified biospecimens the same as identified biospecimens, considering both to be research involving human subjects. That proposal proved very controversial, as the following explains:

> [T]he use of existing (left over from clinical care or earlier research) human biospecimens (and associated data) traditionally has been deemed not to be human

subjects research under the Common Rule if the identity of the subject may not readily be ascertained by the investigator, and to be exempt from most forms of regulatory oversight if the specimens or data are themselves identifiable but information is recorded by the investigator in a non-identifiable manner. This is because the framers of the Common Rule felt confident that these mechanisms of segregating specimens and data from identifiers were adequate to protect any interests of the individuals from which they were derived. Any risk, such as the remote risk of re-identification, was small in comparison to the promise of scientific and medical advances that depended upon the specimens.

Today, this is a matter of considerable controversy. On one hand, technological advances, such as whole-genome sequencing and increasing access to big data, have made it possible for a scientist with access to both sophisticated equipment and a reference key to take an otherwise unidentified human biospecimen and re-identify it using the unique data gleaned from a person's DNA. Although such equipment is expensive and not widely available, and there is no universal reference key of everyone's DNA, the potential for unauthorized re-identification has caused some to argue that there is a pervasive and unavoidable risk of "informational harm" to specimen sources that requires a tightening of the rules. Those who want more restrictions are concerned about protecting individual liberties and most importantly privacy, and want to maximize the principle of autonomy.

On the other hand are those who advocate for fewer restrictions on and greater sharing of biospecimens and data to maximize their utility in solving important problems. This camp is a mix of scientists, ethicists, and disease-oriented patient advocates, each of whom views the risks of unauthorized re-identification as relatively small and better addressed through penalties for violations rather than tighter restrictions that could impede important scientific progress. People who want fewer restrictions on use of biospecimens typically believe that a more communitarian approach to research will increase beneficence and justice.

Despite the lack of consensus around these issues, millions of human biospecimens are collected and stored each year. Most are obtained during routine clinical encounters with patients for diagnostic and treatment purposes, while a minority are collected with explicit research intent following informed consent by a donor. Regardless of the circumstances, it is not possible to know with certainty at the time of collection all the possible future uses for which a specimen could be of value. Thus, the only way to guarantee full informed consent would be to re-approach donors each time a new use is imagined (which notably is not even possible once a specimen has been de-identified). Science is evolving more quickly than our regulatory procedures can accommodate. A permissive stance would be to allow unforeseen future uses without obtaining new, specific consent unless there is an obvious risk of harm, on the premise that such uses might contribute to important medical discoveries. A conservative approach would be to discard biospecimens immediately following the original use for which they were collected to avoid even the appearance of violating donor's expectations. The current regulatory approach—maintained following revisions finalized in 2017. . .—requires consent from the specimen source only for the active collection of specimens and data for research use, and for the secondary use of only identified specimens and data. In light of technological advancement and changing patient attitudes, however, the challenge is how best to balance the importance of protecting individual interests against the value of promoting the good of the larger human community.

The federal agencies that oversee human subjects research made an attempt to address this challenge by proposing a major revision to the research rules in 2015 via a Notice of Proposed Rule Making (NPRM) to amend the Common Rule . . . .

The NPRM proposed an approach on one side of the spectrum of possibilities and generated substantial dialogue regarding the best path forward . . . .

In particular, the NPRM proposed to expand the definition of the term "human subject" to include a living individual about whom the investigator "obtains, uses, studies, or analyzes biospecimens" even when those biospecimens have been stripped of all the traditional pieces of identifying information. The presumption underlying this proposal was that all genetic material can potentially serve as a unique personal identifier—if not now, then in the relatively near future. The proposal also was based on the notion that individuals have greater autonomy interests in controlling their biospecimens than previously had been acknowledged. The consequence of this regulatory redefinition would be that secondary research with de-identified biospecimens would no longer be permissible without some form of consent, a dramatic change from the status quo. Under the NPRM's proposal, that consent could be "broad," applying to future unspecified use, rather than specific for each study, but the conditions for waiver of consent for biospecimen research would have been dramatically tightened, such that waiver would become "rare."

Suzanne M. Rivera, Barbara E. Bierer, Holly Fernandez Lynch & I. Glenn Cohen, Introduction, in Specimen Science 5-8 (Holly Fernandez Lynch et al. eds. 2017). Based on numerous comments, the final revised Common Rule reverted to regarding non-identified biospecimens as not constituting "human subjects," meaning that no consent or even IRB review is required, but the issue of what constitutes identifiability remains unresolved. The final Rule requires regulatory agencies, alongside relevant experts, to reexamine the Rule's definition of "identifiable private information" and "identifiable biospecimen" within one year and thereafter at least every four years. Research involving "whole genome sequencing" is likely to be caught up in this review process.

8. *The Role of Randomized Clinical Trials (RCTs) and Placebos.* The randomized clinical trial is a core feature of biomedical research. In an RCT, research subjects are randomly assigned to receive the treatment under study or to receive another form of treatment or, in some cases, no treatment or a placebo. The Common Rule recognizes the use of placebos. 45 C.F.R. §46.102(b) (definition of "clinical trial" includes possible placebo use). From an ethical standpoint, an RCT is justified when there is "clinical equipoise," that is, when the differential benefits of the various forms of treatment or non-treatment are not known or are roughly the same. The legitimacy of equipoise has been challenged, in part because of concerns that it is difficult to know when equipoise truly exists. See, e.g., Franklin G. Miller & Stephen Joffe, Equipoise and the Dilemma of Randomized Clinical Trials, 364 New Eng. J. Med. 476 (2011).

Concerns about RCTs are particularly acute in medical research involving placebos, where some level of patient deception about treatment is inherent in the research design. Does the problem of deception run both ways? Should researchers be able to bring claims against research participants who deceive researchers in order to become eligible to participate in trials? Cf. Rebecca Dresser, Subversive Subjects: Rule Breaking and Deception in Clinical Trials, 41 J. L. Med. & Ethics 829 (2013); David B. Resnik & David J. McCann, Deception by Research Participants, 373 New Eng. J. Med. 1192 (2015).

9. *The Aftermath of* Grimes. The *Grimes* decision was understandably controversial. Imagine how medical researchers might feel about a decision that appears

to compare a research study sponsored by the federal government and conducted by a leading research institution with Nazi war crimes. The *Grimes* decision sparked a number of commentaries, including Lainie Friedman Ross, In Defense of the Hopkins Lead Abatement Studies, 30 J. L. Med. & Ethics 50 (2002). See also L. Song Richardson, When Human Experimentation Is Criminal, 99 J. Crim. L. & Criminology 89 (2009) (arguing that medical researchers who "conduct experiments on individuals without their knowledge" or who "deliberately fail to disclose to individuals the known and obvious risks of participation in an experiment" should face criminal punishment).

What did the court actually hold in *Grimes*? The lengthy opinion (more than 70 pages, heavily edited here) explores the broad terrain of human subjects research and appears to hold that (1) parents/surrogates cannot consent to the participation of their children/incompetents in nontherapeutic research where there is any risk of injury or damage to the health of the subject; (2) informed consent agreements in nontherapeutic research trials may create "special relationships," and violation of the agreements may be addressed in breach of contract and negligence; and (3) other sources of the "special relationship" include the researcher-subject relationship itself and governmental research regulations. How much does the court majority take back in the per curiam opinion rejecting reconsideration? The court suggests that the parties are free to present evidence on any of these issues. What evidence would you present for either side? The Maryland courts have subsequently considered a number of claims arising from lead-related research carried out in Baltimore in the 1990s. See, e.g., Smith v. Kennedy Krieger Institute, 2017 WL 1076481 (Md. Ct. App. 2017) (affirming a jury verdict in favor of Kennedy Krieger Institute on claims); and Ward v. White v. Kennedy Krieger Institute, Inc 110 A.3d 724 (Md. Ct. App. 2015) (fraudulent and negligent misrepresentation claims must fail as a matter of law as "lead safe" houses were not presented as "lead free"; institution accurately described lead in homes and did not engage in unfair or deceptive trade practices).

10. *Litigating Claims of Research-Related Harms.* There have been a relatively small number of lawsuits involving experimental medicine using either negligence or informed consent theories, despite the huge volume of activity involving research subjects. A few courts have considered whether clinical trial sponsors owe a fiduciary duty to participants. See, e.g., Suthers v. Amgen Inc., 441 F. Supp. 2d 478 (S.D.N.Y. 2006) (plaintiffs' complaint dismissed in case challenging drug company's decision to terminate clinical trial and deny access to experimental drug; no fiduciary duty owed); and Abney v. Amgen Inc., 443 F.3d 540 (6th Cir. 2006) (no fiduciary duty as the clinical trial sponsors were not acting primarily for the benefit of the participants).

11. *Incidental Findings.* Should researchers have any obligation to inform patients about "incidental findings," such as health issues discovered unexpectedly during the course of research, e.g., tumors discovered during scans for other purposes, or genetic anomalies discovered during testing for something else? Among the "additional elements" for informed consent established in the new Common Rule is a requirement that researchers provide information about whether, and under what conditions, clinically relevant research results will be disclosed to the subjects. 45 C.F.R. §§46.116(c)(8). How should this process be handled in research that might involve biobanks and other forms of archived data sets that may have

been collected long ago? Should there be a duty to inform patients that is enforceable under state law? Should different rules apply to international research? Should there be an obligation to inform research subjects if later research reveals that a particular genetic finding is associated with heightened risks to health? Cf. Reed E. Pyeritz, The Coming Explosion in Genetic Testing—Is There a Duty to Recontact?, 365 New Eng. J. Med. 1367 (2011).

12. *Conflicts of Interest.* The *Grimes* court repeatedly expressed concerns about the conflicts of interest between human subjects and researchers. Researchers may have a financial interest in the subject matter of their research that puts their research subjects at risk or affects the reliability of research results. See *Moore,* supra and note 3 at pages 199-204. News stories regularly reveal shocking conflicts of interest that can jeopardize patient safety and the integrity of research results. A number of influential organizations and scholars have focused on methods of identifying and limiting conflicts of interest between researchers and research subjects. See, e.g., Bernard Lo & Marilyn J. Field eds., Conflict of Interest in Medical Research, Education, and Practice (Institute of Medicine, 2009).

Federal regulations require covered institutions to put in place a conflicts of interest policy that includes a requirement that researchers report, and make publicly accessible, significant financial interests (generally $5,000 or more) "that could directly and significantly affect the design, conduct, or reporting of PHS [Public Health Service]-funded research." 42 C.F.R. §50.601-50.607. The Affordable Care Act includes provisions requiring manufacturers of drugs, biologics, and medical devices to report payments to physicians. 42 U.S.C.A. §1320a-7h; 42 C.F.R. §403.904. The economic aspects of medical research may also be regulated under the federal fraud and abuse laws, discussed infra, at Chapter 10.E.

13. *The Economic Interests of Clinical Research Subjects.* As noted above, the Common Rule's consent provisions require that subjects be notified about the possibility that identified or de-identified biospecimens will be used for commercial profit and whether the subject will share in that profit. 45 C.F.R. §46.116(c)(7). Should clinical research subjects share in the economic value of discoveries? The ownership issue, famously raised in Moore v. Regents of the University of California, 793 P.2d 479 (Cal. 1990), supra, at page 187, resurfaced in Washington University v. Catalona, 490 F.3d 667 (8th Cir. 2007). The case arose when a researcher at Washington University accepted a position elsewhere and sought donor consent to take biological specimens that had been donated for research with him to his new position. Universities were keenly interested in the case due to fears that research biobanks would be severely restricted if donor-patients could control the use of their donated tissues. The district court found for the university and the court of appeals agreed, holding that "individuals who make an informed decision to contribute their biological materials voluntarily to a particular research institution for the purpose of medical research" do not "retain an ownership interest allowing the individuals to direct or authorize the transfer of such materials to a third party." 490 F.3d at 673. See also Chapter 6.B.

The economic interests of research subjects have also been debated in the domain of intellectual property law. See, e.g., Greenberg v. Miami Children's Hospital Research Institute, Inc., 264 F. Supp. 2d 1064 (S.D. Fla. 2003), excerpted at page 672 (dismissing all but unjust enrichment claims brought by families whose samples had been used to develop a genetic test for Canavan's Disease). See also Eliot Marshall, Genetic Testing: Families Sue Hospital, Scientist for Control of

Canavan Gene, 290 Science 1062 (2000); Charlotte H. Harrison, Neither *Moore* nor the Market: Alternative Models for Compensating Contributors of Human Tissue, 28 Am. J. L. & Med. 77 (2002).

14. *Research on Vulnerable Populations.* As Professor Richard Garnett notes, much of the controversy in human research has surrounded projects involving groups viewed as particularly vulnerable to coercion or abuse. Historically, the Common Rule addressed the need to ensure equity in the selection of research subjects while being mindful of the risks of research involving "children, prisoners, pregnant women, mentally disabled persons, or economically or educationally disadvantaged persons." 45 C.F.R. §46.111(3) (pre-revision). The revised Rule continues this basic approach while shifting the focus of attention to "subjects who are vulnerable to coercion or undue influence, such as children, prisoners, individuals with impaired decision-making capacity, or economically or educationally disadvantaged persons." Id. (as of January 2018). Where research involves members of vulnerable groups, the study should include additional safeguards to protect the rights and welfare of these subjects. Id. In Parts B–D of the DHHS human subjects have not yet been amended to reflect this new focus, though revisions are anticipated. See 45 C.F.R. §46.201-.207(subpart B pregnant women, neonates, and fetuses), prisoners (subpart C, §46.301-.306), and children (subpart D, §46.401-.409).

Somewhat counterintuitively, the focus on vulnerability is also reflected in concerns about exclusion. Commentators have criticized the failure of medical researchers to include children, women, and members of minority groups in research protocols. Exclusion can be harmful when, for example, conditions particularly affecting disadvantaged or vulnerable groups simply aren't studied or where the exclusion of certain categories of research subjects results in failures to identify possible differences in treatment effectiveness across the population. There are a number of federal initiatives to encourage the inclusion of children, women, minorities, and others in research trials.

a. *Children and Pregnant Women.* The use of children in research presents special problems because the only "consent" available is parental consent, and because the risks of research many may not be fully known or understood. Federal regulations provide special protections for children serving as research subjects. See 45 C.F.R. §§46.401-.409 (DHHS regulations); 21 C.F.R. §§50.50-.56 (FDA regulations). Although pregnant women are no longer automatically considered to be "vulnerable" subjects under the Common Rule, Part B currently still retains specific protections for pregnant women, fetuses, and neonates. 45 C.F.R. §§46.201-.207.

There are conflicting objectives of scientific research involving children: (1) ensuring that children benefit from the progress in medical care made possible by such research and (2) minimizing the risks to children from their participation in scientific research. Many drugs have been tested only in adults, leaving physicians to choose between denying children access to potentially useful medications and guessing about the correct dosage for pediatric use. Congress has become very involved in the issue. The FDA Web site includes a collection of material on pediatric issues, www.fda.gov/cder/pediatric/. Most of the commentaries on research involving children assume the existence of an underlying disease or condition that the research seeks to address. Should research on human enhancement, such as through the use of drugs to improve memory or intelligence, be governed by similar rules? See Maxwell J. Mehlman & Jessica W. Berg, Human Subjects Protections in Biomedical Enhancement Research: Assessing Risk and Benefit and Obtaining Informed Consent, 36 J. L. Med. & Ethics 546 (2008).

b. *Patients with Life-Threatening Illnesses.* Research is an important issue for persons with terminal conditions. Where the current, tested treatments are ineffective, people are often tempted to view "research" as providing the best treatment. They may be particularly vulnerable to coercion and the implicit promises and hopes offered by researchers. On the other hand, of course, research in these areas is extremely important for current and future patients. See, e.g., Michael Malinowski, Throwing Dirt on Doctor Frankenstein's Grave: Access to Experimental Treatments at the End of Life, 65 Hastings L. J. 615 (2014); Jerry Menikoff, The Vulnerability of the Very Sick, 37 J. L. Med. & Ethics 51 (2009). The issue is addressed again in Chapter 8's discussion of the power of the state to protect terminally ill persons from potentially harmful drugs, at pages 988-998.

c. *Individuals with Impaired Decisionmaking Capacity.* Similar concerns exist about whether surrogates can give consent for research on patients with impaired decisionmaking capacity, with the additional concern about who is an appropriate surrogate.

d. *Prisoners.* Should prisoners be permitted to participate in research, even when they "consent"? DHHS regulations provide special protections for prisoners. See 45 C.F.R. §§46.301-.306; and https://humansubjects.nih.gov/prisoners. The special rules require, for example, that a majority of the IRB members have no other association with the prison and that one member be a prisoner or prisoner representative. Another provision requires assurance that parole boards will not take the prisoner's participation into account; prisoners must also be informed of this policy.

15. *Emergency Research.* FDA regulations permit research experimentation on patients who have not consented, personally or through surrogates, in certain circumstances. Under the Rule, an independent physician and an IRB must agree that the clinical trial concerns a life-threatening condition and that there is no proven, available treatment; that obtaining consent is not feasible; that the research cannot be carried out in another manner; and that the risks and benefits of the experimental procedure are reasonable under the circumstances. 21 C.F.R. §50.24. The emergency research regulations are somewhat controversial because they explicitly abandon the Nuremberg Code's requirement of informed consent. See Nuremberg Code, available at http://ohsr.od.nih.gov/guidelines/nuremberg.html. Some commentators also maintain that these regulations allow research that has no therapeutic benefit for the immediate patient since they include patients who are near death with no hope of recovery.

16. *Research in Other Countries.* As noted above, many trials are conducted in whole or part in countries outside the United States. Cf. ClinicalTrials.gov (listing nearly 150,000 studies located in 200 countries outside of the United States as of September 2017). Proponents of this research argue that it is increasingly difficult to manage drug trials and to recruit a statistically meaningful number of study subjects in the United States and other high income countries. Yet, as noted in the beginning of this section, the history of medical research suggests a need to guard against the risks of exploitation and abuse. Foreign jurisdictions thus have a strong interest in local regulation. For efforts to address alleged abuses through U.S. courts, see Abdullahi v. Pfizer, 562 F.3d 163 (2d Cir. 2009) (permitting claims under Alien Tort

Statute, which alleged violation of customary international law norms regarding consent to medical experimentation); and Estate of Alvarez v. Johns Hopkins Univ., 205 F. Supp.3d 681 (D. Md. 2016) (affirming dismissal of claims arising from non-consensual medical experimentation in Guatemala).

What rules should apply to human subjects research conducted outside the United States by companies affiliated with U.S. companies, or where the study results will be used to seek approval to market a drug in the United States? These concerns gained additional public attention in 2011 with the release of a report by the Presidential Commission for the Study of Bioethical Issues, Research Across Borders, which considered the protections offered to participants in research supported by the federal government and carried out in countries around the world.

The Common Rule applies to federally funded research wherever it is carried out; any applicable foreign laws or regulations "that provide additional protections to human subjects of research" are not preempted. 45 C.F.R. §46.101(f). See also, 21 C.F.R. §50.1(the FDA's protection of human subjects extends to "all clinical investigations regulated by the [FDA under provisions of the Federal Food, Drug, and Cosmetic Act], as well as clinical investigations that support applications for research or marketing permits for products regulated by the [FDA]"). International standards are also important. The CIOMS and Declaration of Helsinki standards offer somewhat different approaches to key issues such as openness to the inclusion of vulnerable subjects in research and the types of community benefits that should be integrated into research projects carried out in moderate- or low-resources countries. Johannes J.M. van Delden & Rieke van de Graaf, Revised CIOMS International Ethical Guidelines for Health-Related Research Involving Humans, 317 JAMA 135 (2017); Joseph Millum, David Wendler & Ezekiel J. Emanuel, The 50th Anniversary of the Declaration of Helsinki: Progress but Many Remaining Challenges, 310 JAMA 2143 (2013).

17. *Resources and Commentaries.* The DHHS's Office for Human Research Protections maintains a Web site with links **to key federal regulations and documents**; www.hhs.gov/ohrp/. Important books on human subjects research in addition to those noted above include Baruch A. Brody, The Ethics of Biomedical Research: An International Perspective (1998); Claire Foster, The Ethics of Medical Research on Humans (2001); Jerry Menikoff & Edward P. Richards, What the Doctor Didn't Say: The Hidden Truth About Medical Research (2006).

For influential **criticisms of human subjects research**, see the articles cited in *Grimes* and George J. Annas, Questing for Grails: Duplicity, Betrayal and Self-Deception in Research, 12 J. Contemp. Health L. & Pol'y 297 (1996); Carl Elliot, Whatever Happened to Human Experimentation?, Hastings Center Rep. 8 (Jan.-Feb. 2016); Christine Grady et al., Informed Consent, 376 New Eng. J. Med. 856-867 (2017) (reviewing challenges and opportunities for novel, e-technology-based informed consent); Jay Katz, Human Experimentation and Human Rights, 38 St. Louis U. L.J. 7 (1993).

For resources or commentaries on **the revised Common Rule**, see (in addition to the sources cited above) James G. Hodge & Lawrence O. Gostin, Revamping the US Federal Common Rule: Modernizing Human Participant Research Regulations, 317 JAMA 1521 (2017); I. Glenn Cohen & Holly Fernandez Lynch, Human Subjects Research Regulation: Perspectives on the Future (MIT Press 2014); Barbara E. Bierer Mark Barnes & Holly Fernandez Lynch, Revised "Common Rule" Shapes

Protections for Research Participants, 36 Health Affairs 784 (2017); and Jerry Menikoff, Julie Kaneshiro & Ivor Pritchard, The Common Rule, Updated, 367 New Eng. J. Med. 613 (2017).

On **safety monitoring** (note 4), see Rachel Berhman Sherman et al., New FDA Regulation to Improve Safety Reporting in Clinical Trials, 365 New Eng. J. Med. 3 (2011); and Charles J. Kowalski & Jan L. Hewett, Data and Safety Monitoring Boards: Some Enduring Questions, 37 J. L. Med. & Ethics 496 (2009).

On the **use of placebos in research** (note 8), compare Clifford J. Rosen & Sundeep Khosia, Placebo-Controlled Trials in Osteoporosis—Proceeding with Caution, 363 New Eng. J. Med. 1365 (2010), with C. Michael Stein & Wayne A. Ray, The Ethics of Placebo in Studies with Fracture End Points in Osteoporosis, 363 New Eng. J. Med. 1367 (2010). See also S.L. Niemansburg et al., Reconsidering the Ethics of Sham Interventions in an Era of Emerging Technologies, 157 Surgery 801 (2015); Elana A. Bertam, How Current Informed Consent Protocols Flunk the Sham Surgery Test: A New Frontier in Medicine and Ethics, 14 Quinnipiac Health L. J. 131 (2010).

On **claims for research-related harms** (note 10), see Valerie Gutmann Koch, A Private Right of Action for Informed Consent in Research, 45 Seton Hall L. Rev. 173 (2015); Paul B. Miller & Charles Weijer, Fiduciary Obligation in Clinical Research, 34 J. L. Med. & Ethics 424 (2006); E. Haavi Morreim, The Clinical Investigator as Fiduciary: Discarding a Misguided Idea, 33 J. L. Med. & Ethics 586 (2005); E. Haavi Morreim, Litigation in Clinical Research: Malpractice Doctrines Versus Research Realities, 32 J. L. Med. & Ethics 474 (2004).

Regarding how to handle **incidental findings** (note 11), see President's Commission for the Study of Bioethical Issues, Anticipate and Communicate: Ethical Management of Incidental and Secondary Findings in the Clinical, Research, and Direct-to-Consumer Contexts (2013); Lisa Eckstein, Jeremy R. Garrett & Benjamin E. Berkman, A Framework for Analyzing the Ethics of Disclosing Genetic Research Findings, 42 J. L. Med & Ethics 190 (2014); Elizabeth Pike, Karen Rothenberg & Benjamin E. Berkman, Finding Fault? Exploring Legal Duties to Return Incidental Findings in Genomic Research, 102 Geo. L. J. 795 (2014).

On researchers' **conflicts of interest** (note 12), see Barry Meier & Duff Wilson, Spine Experts Repudiate Medtronic Studies, N.Y. Times, June 29, 2011; Special Issue, The Evolving Safety Profile of rhBMP-2 Use in the Spine, 11 Spine J. A1-A14, 463-539 (2011); Robin Fretwell Wilson, The Death of Jesse Gelsinger: New Evidence of the Influence of Money and Prestige in Human Research, 36 Am. J. L. & Med. 295-325 (2010); Symposium, Dangerous Liaisons? Industry Relations with Health Professionals, 37 J. L. Med. & Ethics 398-460 (2009); Stacey A. Tovino, Conflicts of Interest in Medicine, Research, and Law: A Comparison, 117 Penn. St. L. Rev. 1291 (2013); Bernard Lo & Marilyn J. Field eds., Conflict of Interest in Medical Research, Education, and Practice (Institute of Medicine, 2009); Robert Steinbrook, Controlling Conflict of Interest—Proposals from the Institute of Medicine, 360 New Eng. J. Med. 2160 (2009); Kevin P. Weinfurt, Disclosure of Financial Relationships to Participants in Clinical Research, 361 New Eng. J. Med. 916 (2009).

Regarding **research on vulnerable populations** (note 14), see Joseph Millum, David Wendler & Ezekiel J. Emanuel, The 50th Anniversary of the Declaration of Helsinki: Progress but Many Remaining Challenges, 310 JAMA 2143 (2013) (noting revised Declaration's greater openness to research involving vulnerable populations but critiquing limitations); Michelle Goodwin, Vulnerable Subjects: Why Does Informed Consent Matter?, 44 J. L. Med. & Ethics 371 (2016); and Symposium, Vulnerability in Biomedical Research, 37 J. L. Med. & Ethics 6-82 (2009). With regard to **children**, see Kristien Hens et al., Children and Biobanks: A Review of the Ethical and Legal Discussion, 130 Hum. Genet. 403 (2011); Valarie Blake et al., Harmonization of Ethics Policies in Pediatric Research, 39 J. L. Med. & Ethics 70 (2011); Ruqaiijah Yearby, Missing the "Target": Preventing the Unjust Inclusion of Vulnerable Children for Medical Research Studies, 42 Amer. J. L. & Med. 797 (2016). Regarding **people with impairments,** see Benedict Carey, An N.Y.U. Study Gone Wrong, and a Top Researcher Dismissed, New York Times, June 27, 2016 (discussing study at psychiatric research center); Carl H. Coleman, Research with Decisionally Incapacitated Human Subjects: An Argument for a Systemic Approach to Risk-Benefit Assessment, 83 Ind. L. J. 743 (2008); P. C. Candia & A. C. Barba, Mental Capacity and Consent to Treatment in Psychiatric Patients: The State of the Research, 24 Curr Opin Psychiatry 442 (2011).

On **making research more inclusive** (note 14), see NIH Human Subjects Policies and Guidance; P. Kanakamedala & S. Haga, Characterization of Clinical Study Populations by Race and Ethnicity in Biomedical Literature, 22 Ethn. Dis. 96 (2012) (though increasingly common, "reporting of race/ethnicity of study populations is relatively low, ambiguous, and inconsistent"); Marianne J. Legato, Paula A. Johnson & JoAnne E. Manson, Consideration of Sex Differences in Medicine to Improve Health Care and Patient Outcomes, 316 JAMA 1865 (2016); and Special Issue, Research Ethics and Minority Populations 103 Am. J. Pub. Health 2118-2199, 2207-2251 (2013). With regard to **women**, see Sara F. Goldkind et al., Enrolling Pregnant Women in Research—Lessons from the H1N1 Influenza Epidemic, 362 New Eng. J. Med. 2241 (2010); Anna C. Mastroianni at al., Research with Pregnant Women, Hastings Center Rep 38 (May-June 2017); and Chapter 7, at pages 758-762, 861-865.

On **research in emergency settings** (note 15), see Gail H. Javitt, Old Legacies and New Paradigms: Confusing "Research" and "Treatment" and Its Consequences in Responding to Emergent Health Threats, 8 J. Health Care L. & Pol'y 38 (2005); Richard S. Saver, Critical Care Research and Informed Consent, 75 N.C. L. Rev. 205 (1996); Symposium, In Case of Emergency: No Need for Consent, 27(1) Hastings Center Rep. 7-12 (1997). See also Ian Roberts et al., Effect of Consent Rituals on Mortality in Emergency Care Research, 377 Lancet 1071 (2011) (arguing that UK rules can be unethical if "consent rituals delay the start of a trial treatment such that the treatment effect could be reduced or obscured").

Discussing research **internationally, including in developing countries** (note 16), see M.K. Mallath & T. Chawla, Investigators' Viewpoint of Clinical Trials in India: Past, Present and Future, 8 Perspect. Clin. Res. 31 (2017); Gerard Porter, Regulating Clinical Trials in India: The Economics of Ethics, __ Dev. World Bioeth. __ (2017); Dennis M. Coyne, International Pharmaceutical Mistrials: Existing Law for the Protection of Human Subjects and a Proposal for Reform, 29 B. U. Int'l L. J. 427 (2011); Darby Hull, Reining in the Commercialized Foreign Clinical Trial, 36 J. Leg. Med. 367 (2015); World Medical Association Declaration of Helsinki: Ethical Principles for Medical Research Involving Human Subjects, 310 JAMA 2191 (2013); and Paul Ndebele, The Declaration of Helsinki, 50 Years Later, 310 JAMA 2145 (2013).

Problem: The SUPPORT Trial

New concerns have arisen about the appropriateness of informed consent procedures for research at least arguably falling with the standard of care. Consider the following facts:

The University of Alabama at Birmingham was the lead study site for a national clinical research trial known as the Surfactant, Positive Pressure, and Oxygenation Randomized Trial ("SUPPORT"). Designed by Dr. Carlo and approved by the IBR Defendants, the SUPPORT study was created to analyze the effects of differing oxygen saturation levels on premature infants. At the time of the study, it was nationally accepted (and neither party contests) that the recognized standard of care was to keep the oxygen saturation levels of low-birth-weight infants at between 85% and 95%. This standard notwithstanding, it was also known that a prolonged period of high oxygen saturation can result in oxygen toxicity which leads to an increased risk of "retinopathy of prematurity".[1] On the other hand, a prolonged period of low oxygen saturation can result in neuro-developmental impairment and death. Given the difficulties of calibrating the optimal oxygen range, the SUPPORT study sought to determine whether, within the accepted standard of care, there was a more precise range of oxygen saturation that would better reduce the risk of exposing an infant to either too much or too little oxygen.

The SUPPORT study randomly divided eligible and enrolled premature infants into two groups. One group was to be kept at an oxygen saturation level between 85-89%, which is the low end of the standard-of-care range, while the other would be kept at an oxygen saturation level between 90-95%, which is the high end of that range. Further, to ensure double-blind data collection, the study would employ specialized oximeters . . . that would "mask" to an onlooker the true oxygen saturation levels of the infants. The oximeters would, however, signal an alarm whenever an infant's oxygen level strayed below 85% or above 95%.

Publishing the results of the study in the New England Journal of Medicine, the study authors concluded that infants in the high-oxygen group were more likely to be diagnosed with retinopathy while infants in the low-oxygen group were more likely to die. There was no statistically significant difference in the incidence of neuro-developmental impairments between the high and low groups.

To enroll in the study, Plaintiffs' guardians had to execute informed consent documents that were drafted and approved by Defendants. After the study's completion, however, the Department of Health and Human Services authored a letter questioning whether these informed consent documents had properly disclosed all of the risks associated with enrollment in the SUPPORT study.

Plaintiffs filed the operative Fifth Amended Complaint in the United States District Court for the Northern District of Alabama asserting claims against Defendants for negligence, negligence per se, breach of fiduciary duty, products liability, and lack of informed consent. Plaintiffs allege that they suffered serious injuries as a result of their participation in the study. Specifically, Plaintiffs Lewis and Malone were assigned to the low-oxygen group, with prolonged periods of low oxygen saturation being associated with neuro-developmental impairment and death.

---

1. Retinopathy of prematurity is a disease that occurs in premature babies. It causes abnormal blood vessels to grow in the retina, and can lead to the retina detaching from the back of the eye, resulting in blindness.

Fortunately, neither infant died, but they did develop neurological issues. Plaintiff Collins was assigned to the high-oxygen group, with prolonged high-oxygen saturation being associated with retinopathy, which can lead to blindness. Plaintiff Collins did develop retinopathy, but fortunately he did not suffer permanent vision loss. Following discovery, Defendants moved for summary judgment asserting that, based on the undisputed material facts, Plaintiffs had failed to demonstrate that participation in the SUPPORT study had caused the injuries alleged in the Complaint. The district court agreed that Plaintiffs had failed to prove that their injuries were caused by participation in the SUPPORT study, as opposed to being a consequence of their premature births.

Looney v. Moore, 861 F.3d 1303, 1306-07 (11th Cir. 2017). The Court of Appeals certified a question to the Alabama Supreme Court regarding whether state law required proof of injury in an informed consent case.

Are you troubled by any aspects of the research trial? The consent forms for the research did not alert parents to the known risks of higher or lower levels of oxygen and instead identified "possible skin breakdown at the oximeter site as the only increased risk of participation in the study." Looney v. Moore, 2015 WL 4773747, *3 (N.D. Ala.). Should parents have been informed about the association of higher or lower levels of oxygen with particular types of risks? Should parents have been informed that their children would not receive individualized treatment in the same way that they would have outside the trial and that the caregivers would not know the infants' oxygen saturation level so long as it was within the broad band of the study? See John D. Lantos, Vindication for SUPPORT, 373 New Eng. J. Med. 1393 (2015); Chana A. Sacks & Celestine E. Warren, Foreseeable Risks? Informed Consent for Studies within the Standard of Care, 372 New Eng. J. Med. 306 (2015); Sabrina Tavernise, Premature Babies Study Raises Debate Over Risks and Ethical Consent, New York Times, Sept. 7, 2015; Robin Fretwell Wilson & Robert John Morse, Realizing Informed Consent in Times of Controversy 44 J. L. Med. Ethics 402 (2016).

Problem: Compensation for Research-Related Injuries

Who should bear the risks of research-related injuries: research subjects, researchers, or society more broadly? Would it make sense to require that clinical trials provide some form of insurance coverage or compensation given the risks borne by participants and the benefits accrued by society? What are the barriers or risks of addressing the compensation issue? The Common Rule prohibits waivers of negligence. 45 C.F.R. §46.116(a)(6). Where risks are more than minimal, participants should ordinarily be provided with "an explanation as to whether any compensation and an explanation as to whether any medical treatments are available if injury occurs and, if so, what they consist of, or where further information may be obtained." 45 C.F.R. §46.116(b)(6). The Helsinki Declaration goes further, providing that "[a]ppropriate compensation and treatment for subjects who are harmed as a result of participating in research must be ensured." Helsinki Declaration, 310 JAMA 2191 (2013) (§15). See also, Elizabeth R. Pike, Recovering from Research: A No-Fault Proposal to Compensate Injured Research Participants, 38 Am. J. L. & Med. 7 (2012).

Problem: Medical Research, Biobanks, and the Privacy Rule

This chapter began with an exploration of the special character of medical information and the complex web of privacy regulations designed to give individuals the right to control use of their protected health information. Privacy concerns pervade medical research. How will medical researchers be able to identify potentially appropriate medical research subjects without having access to medical records? How confidential are the records of medical research projects? These issues are growing increasingly complex, in part due to large-scale research involving medical records, biological samples, and genetic testing. The availability of large sets of patient data and biological samples creates the opportunity to carry out new research strategies that hold great promise for identifying causes and cures for human conditions.

Does the Privacy Rule, discussed supra at pages 124-127, create inordinate barriers to research, particularly research involving large collections of patient data or biobanking? A study by the Institute of Medicine found that the answer was "yes"; the resulting report made a series of recommendations to address the problem. Institute of Medicine, Beyond the HIPAA Privacy Rule: Enhancing Privacy, Improving Health Through Research (2009). The report recommended that HIPAA's Privacy Rule not be applied to research; that PHI related to direct, interventional research with human subjects be regulated under the Common Rule for research; and that "information-based" research (including biobanks) be regulated under a new scheme that would emphasize administrative safeguards rather than requiring patient consent. As one commentator on the report has noted:

> Autonomy and informed consent are vital ethical and legal principles undergirding . . . experimentation on human subjects. But these principles are implicated less strongly, if at all, by data-based health research—research that is becoming more common and more important as more patient data is captured and stored electronically. . . . [T]here is no ethical principle that requires choice as the basis for research involving patient data, especially if identifying information is masked and the use of the data is subject to strong, substantive security and privacy requirements. Regulatory insistence on choice is quite literally allowing people to die and suffer unnecessarily without even providing the benefit of aiding privacy.

Fred Cate, Protecting Privacy in Health Research: The Limits of Individual Choice, 98 Cal. L. Rev. 1765, 1802 (2010). For a pointed critique of the IOM Report, see Mark A. Rothstein, Improve Privacy in Research by Eliminating Informed Consent? IOM Report Misses the Mark, 37 J. L. Med. & Ethics 507 (2009) (The IOM Report "underestimates the risk to individuals, . . . fail[s] to justify abandonment of informed consent . . . overvalues researchers' interests . . . [and] overlook[s] the betrayal of [patient] trust"). Would you support the IOM Report's approach? Do you think that the Privacy Rule's authorization process is realistic and viable for large-scale medical records research projects? Do you think that medical records research conducted without specific patient authorization would injure patient autonomy and the trust necessary to the treatment relationship? What types of evidence would you need to answer these questions? Professors Cate and Rothstein cite to a range of evidence to support their positions, from the meaninglessness of many patient consumer choices, as evidenced by the ubiquitous clicking of "I agree" to software licensing notices (noted by Professor Cates) to surveys demonstrating that most people want to decide whether their PHI is used for research (noted by Professor Rothstein).

The DHHS has modified the Privacy Rule provisions relating to research, though not to the extent advocated by the IOM Report. As of 2013, the Privacy Rule provides three avenues for the use of PHI for research:

1. *De-identification.* The PHI can be "de-identified" by removing more than 18 types of information, ranging from name to any biometric identifiers. De-identified information is not considered to be PHI subject to the protections of the Rule. 45 C.F.R. §164.502(d).

2. *Authorization.* Individuals can provide specific authorization for the use of their PHI in research. 45 C.F.R. §164.508. The authorization for research now is slightly less demanding than the usual authorization provisions under the Privacy Rule. For example, the authorization can be combined with the informed consent form for the research study. The provider may require completion of the authorization before providing research-related treatment. The authorization need not have a specific expiration date, but instead can state " 'end of the research study,' 'none,' or similar language . . . if the authorization is for . . . research, including the creation and maintenance of a research database or research repository." Id. at §164.508(c)(1)(v). The 2013 revisions to the federal Privacy Rule moved closer to the Common Rule by, for example, 45 C.F.R. §164.508(b)(3) (permitting use of compound authorization for the use of protected health information for research studies with a consent to participate in the research or authorization to create a research database). See also Mark A. Rothstein, HIPAA Privacy Rule 2.0, 41 J. L. Med. & Ethics 525 (2013).

3. *Substituted Consent by IRB or Privacy Board.* The Privacy Rule permits use of PHI for research where either an IRB or Privacy Board (as defined in the regulations) approves a waiver of the authorization requirement; where the review is necessary to prepare a research protocol and no PHI will leave the entity; or where the research involves decedent's PHI. 45 C.F.R. §164.512(i). An IRB or Privacy Board may waive authorization where (1) "the use or disclosure . . . involves no more than minimal risk to the privacy of individuals"; (2) "The research could not practicably be conducted without the waiver or alteration"; (3) "The research could not practicably be conducted without access to and use of the protected health information; and (4) certain other procedural requirements have been met." Id.

The Common Rule revision process originally contemplated a number of privacy-related changes. As noted above, at page 230, the "final rule does not include the proposed standardized privacy safeguards for identifiable private information and identifiable biospecimens." Instead, the Rule simply provides that the IRB should ensure [w]hen appropriate, [that] there are adequate provisions to protect the privacy of subjects and to maintain the confidentiality of data." 45 C.F.R. 46.111(a)(7). After consultation, the Secretary of DHHS will issue "guidance to assist IRBs in assessing what provisions are adequate to protect the privacy of subjects and to maintain the confidentiality of data."

Do the current Rules achieve the correct balance between individual control of PHI and the promotion of research, which may improve health care for all? What changes, if any, would you suggest? What types of guidance would be of assistance to IRBs? For international aspects of these issues, see Symposium, Parts I & II: Harmonizing Privacy Law to Enable International Biobank Research, 43 J. L. Med. & Ethics 673-826 (2015) & 44 J. L. of Med. & Ethics 7-172 (2016).

Problem: DNA Research and Indigenous Communities

The Havasupai people, who live in the Grand Canyon, have been embroiled in a conflict with Arizona State University over the use of the tribe's DNA samples. University researchers took DNA samples from the Havasupai with the hope of finding genetic clues to the tribe's high rate of diabetes. The Havasupai believed that the blood samples were collected solely for diabetes research. However, tribe members discovered that their blood samples were used to study many other issues, including mental illnesses and the tribe's historical migration pattern, which threatened to create conflicts with the tribe's traditional beliefs about its origin.

What types of legal claims might be available to the Havasupai? Who would have standing to bring the claims? How would damages be measured? See Amy Harmon, Indian Tribe Wins Fight to Limit Research of Its DNA, N.Y. Times, April 21, 2010; Michelle M. Mello & Leslie Wolf, The Havasupai Indian Tribe Case—Lessons for Research Involving Stored Biologic Samples, 363 New Eng. J. Med. 204 (2010). See also Debra Harry, Indigenous Peoples and Gene Disputes, 84 Chi.-Kent L. Rev. 147 (2009); Bette Jacobs et al., Bridging the Divide Between Genomic Science and Indigenous Peoples, 38 J. L. Med. & Ethics 684 (2010).

4

Medical Malpractice

This chapter addresses those theories of physician and institutional liability that relate directly to the quality of care rendered, in short, classic medical malpractice actions. Other related types of liability arising from somewhat different theories of tort or contract are covered in Chapters 2 and 3; for instance, liability for refusing to accept patients, for releasing confidential medical information, or for failing to obtain informed consent. Chapter 9 addresses the liability of health insurers for failing to pay for or approve covered services, and Chapter 10 addresses liabilities arising from purely business transactions, such as those under antitrust law.

This medical malpractice chapter begins with a general overview of what we mean by medical mistakes or bad quality, and what other mechanisms besides tort liability exist for preventing or correcting bad quality. This is intended to prompt you to think about the proper aims of malpractice liability and how the tort system should function in the medical arena. We return to these themes at the end of the chapter with an examination of medical malpractice reform.

The core of the chapter develops the various components of the malpractice cause of action against physicians. It begins with the basic standard of care and how it is proved and then develops alternative theories of liability. Next, causation and affirmative defenses are surveyed, followed by a discussion of damages and settlement. The chapter then explores how these theories of liability apply to hospitals, and finally how hospital liability theories apply to managed care entities such as HMOs. Throughout, we try to achieve a useful mix of (1) explaining the basic elements of legal doctrine and its complexities, (2) outlining the pragmatics of litigating these types of cases, and (3) considering the implications for public policy.

Bibliography

There are several useful texts and treatises on medical malpractice, both from a practicing lawyer perspective and from a public policy perspective. The leading multi-volume treatise is D. Louisell & H. Williams, Medical Malpractice. A good source on trial techniques and medical issues is the multi-volume treatise, Lee S. Goldsmith, Medical Malpractice: Guide to Medical Issues. Another useful resource is D. Danner et al., Medical Malpractice: Checklists and Discovery. For a briefer text addressed to law students, see M. Boumil & Hattis, Medical Liability in a Nutshell Series (3d ed. 2011). A good practical overview is Thomas M. O'Toole et al., The Anatomy of a Medical Malpractice Verdict, 70 Mont. L. Rev. 57 (2009). For a broad theoretical overview, see Alex Stein, Toward a Theory of Medical Malpractice, 97 Iowa L. Rev. 1201 (2012).

For **historical and social accounts** of the development and impact of medical malpractice law, see Kenneth Allen DeVille, Medical Malpractice in Nineteenth-Century America (1990); Iain Hay, Money, Medicine, and Malpractice in American Society (1992); James C. Mohr, American Medical Malpractice Litigation in Historical Perspective, 283 JAMA 1731 (2000); Theodore Silver, One Hundred Years of Harmful Error: The Historical Jurisprudence of Medical Malpractice, 1992 Wis. L. Rev. 1193; Catherine T. Struve, Doctors, the Adversary System, and Procedural Reform in Medical Liability Litigation, 72 Fordham L. Rev. 944 (2004); Robert Field, The Malpractice Crisis Turns 175: What Lessons Does History Hold for Reform, 4 Drexel L. Rev. 7 (2011); Maxwell Mehlman, Professional Power and the Standard of Care in Medicine, 44 Ariz. St. L. J. 1165 (2012); G. Annas, Doctors, Patients and Lawyers: Two Centuries of Health Law, 367 New Eng. J. Med. 445 (2012).

Descriptions and analyses of malpractice **liability systems abroad** can be found in B. A. Koch ed., Medical Liability in Europe (2011); Symposium, 4 Drexel L. Rev. 1-296 (2011); Symposium, 86 Chi.-Kent. L. Rev. 1021-1301 (2011); 87 Chi.-Kent. L. Rev. 1-198 (2012).

A. MEDICAL MISTAKES AND QUALITY

1. The Nature and Extent of Medical Error

We begin with this inquiry: Why do medical mistakes occur, and what kinds of legal responses are appropriate? You should first read or review Chapter 1.A.3, which discusses the nature of medical decisionmaking in general. Then, consider the following accounts of why medical errors and injuries are so widespread.

■ HEALTH AND MEDICAL CARE REFORM IN THE UNITED STATES: ETHICAL QUESTIONS AND CONCERNS
Thomas W. Merrill, David G. Miller, Joseph A. Raho & Ginger Gruters
President's Council on Bioethics, Staff Background Paper, 2008

[Read Part III of this excerpt, on pages 38-41.]

■ MAKING MEDICAL ERRORS INTO "MEDICAL TREASURES"
David Blumenthal*
272 JAMA 1867 (1994)

Throughout most of this century, the public has granted physicians extraordinary autonomy and power in return for an implied promise that, among other things, physicians would guarantee the quality of care patients receive. Implicit in this social contract was the belief on both sides that physicians have the capability to practice error-free or nearly error-free medicine themselves and to ensure that the rest of the system functions just as well. This belief has served the interests of both parties to this contract. Physicians have enjoyed the resulting status, freedom, and material rewards. Patients have enjoyed the reassuring fantasy that when they are ill, they can expect their physicians to make the health care system perform flawlessly.

Comfortable as this arrangement has been, it is proving dysfunctional. Physicians are encouraged to hold themselves to unattainable standards, to deny evidence of error, and thus to overlook opportunities for improving themselves and the health care system as a whole. When inevitable errors occur, patients feel betrayed and enraged. These feelings fuel the malpractice crisis that is itself a major deterrent to the openness required for quality improvement.

The paradox of modern quality improvement is that only by admitting and forgiving error can its rate be minimized. For error reduction to occur, physicians must become more comfortable with their fallibility, and patients must become more accepting of their own vulnerability.

■ COMPLICATIONS: A SURGEON'S NOTES ON AN IMPERFECT SCIENCE
Atul Gawande**
2002

WHEN DOCTORS MAKE MISTAKES

To much of the public—and certainly to lawyers and the media—medical error is fundamentally a problem of bad doctors. The way that things go wrong in medicine is normally unseen and, consequently, often misunderstood. Mistakes do happen. We tend to think of them as aberrant. They are, however, anything but.

At 2 A.M. on a crisp Friday in winter a few years ago, I was in sterile gloves and gown, pulling a teenage knifing victim's abdomen open, when . . . the emergency medical technicians wheeled in a woman who appeared to be in her thirties and to weigh more than two hundred pounds. She lay motionless on a hard orange plastic spinal board—eyes closed, skin pale, blood running out of her nose. . . .

---

* M.D., formally at Massachusetts General Hospital and Harvard Medical School.

** Excerpted with permission, Henry Holt and Company. The author is a physician on the faculty of Harvard's Schools of Medicine and of Public Health. This true story uses fictionalized names.

"What's the story?" I asked.

An EMT rattled off the details: "Unidentified white female unrestrained driver in high-speed rollover. Ejected from the car. Found unresponsive to pain. Pulse a hundred, BP a hundred over sixty, breathing at thirty on her own . . ." This woman's breaths were shallow and rapid. An oximeter, by means of a sensor placed on her finger, measured the oxygen saturation of her blood. The "02 sat" is normally more than 95 percent [but hers was low]. . . .

"She's not oxygenating well," I announced in the flattened-out, wake-me-up-when-something-interesting-happens tone. . . . I got hold of a bag mask, pressed its clear facepiece over her nose and mouth, and squeezed the bellows, a kind of balloon with a one-way valve, shooting a liter of air into her with each compression. After a minute or so, her oxygen came up to a comfortable 98 percent. She obviously needed our help with breathing. "Let's tube her," I said. That meant putting a tube down through her vocal cords and into her trachea, which would insure a clear airway and allow for mechanical ventilation.

Johns, the [supervising physician], wanted to do the intubation. . . . He sucked out about a cup of blood and clot. Then he picked up the endotracheal tube—a clear rubber pipe about the diameter of an index finger and three times as long—and tried to guide it between her [vocal] cords. After a minute, her sat started to fall.

"You're down to seventy percent," a nurse announced.

Johns kept struggling with the tube, trying to push it in, but it banged vainly against the cords. The patient's lips began to turn blue. . . . When you're having trouble getting the tube in, the next step is to get specialized expertise. "Let's call anesthesia," I said. . . . Somewhere in my mind, I must have been aware of the possibility that her airway was shutting down because of vocal cord swelling or blood. If it was, and we were unable to get a tube in, then the only chance she'd have to survive would be an emergency tracheotomy: cutting a hole in her neck and inserting a breathing tube into her trachea. Another attempt to intubate her might even trigger a spasm of the cords and a sudden closure of the airway—which is exactly what did happen.

If I had actually thought this far along, I would have recognized how ill-prepared I was to do an emergency "trache." As the one surgeon in the room, it's true, I had the most experience doing tracheotomies, but that wasn't saying much. . . . I should have immediately called [a more experienced surgeon] for backup. . . . [Then we could have] done a tracheotomy while things were still relatively stable and I had time to proceed slowly. But for whatever reasons—hubris, inattention, wishful thinking, hesitation, or the uncertainty of the moment—I let the opportunity pass.

Johns hunched over the patient, trying intently to insert the tube through her vocal cords. When her sat once again dropped into the 60s, he stopped and put the mask back on. We stared at the monitor. The numbers weren't coming up. Her lips were still blue. Johns squeezed the bellows harder to blow more oxygen in.

"I'm getting resistance," he said.

The realization crept over me: this was a disaster. "Damn it, we've lost her airway," I said. "Trache kit! Light! . . ." I pulled on a gown and a new pair of gloves while trying to think through the steps. . . . [But] I was beset by uncertainty—where should I cut? Should I make a horizontal or vertical incision? . . .

There was no time to wait. Four minutes without oxygen would lead to permanent brain damage, if not death. Finally, I took the scalpel and cut. I hit a vein . . . [Because of the blood], I couldn't see anything . . . I called for suction but the suction wasn't working . . . [W]orking blindly, because of the blood and the poor light—I cut down through the overlying fat and tissue until I felt the blade scrape against the almost bony cartilage . . . I searched with the tip of the knife, walking it along until I felt it reach a gap. I hoped it was the [right spot], and pressed down firmly. I felt the tissue suddenly give, and I cut an inch-long opening. . . [But] was this deep enough? Was I even in the right place?

"I think I'm in," I said, to reassure myself as much as anyone else. "I hope so," [the anesthesiologist] said. "She doesn't have much longer."

I took the tracheostomy tube and tried to fit it in, but something seemed to be blocking it. I twisted it and turned it, and finally jammed it in. Just then [Dr. Ball, the supervising surgeon] arrived. He rushed up to the bed and leaned over for a look. "Did you get it?" he asked. I said that I thought so. The bag mask was plugged onto the open end of the trache tube. But when the bellows were compressed the air just gurgled out of the wound. Ball quickly put on gloves and a gown. . . . "I'm not going to get her an airway in time," he said. . . . Essentially, he was admitting my failure. Trying an oral intubation again was pointless—just something to do instead of watching her die. I was stricken, and concentrated on doing chest compressions, not looking at anyone. It was over, I thought.

And then, amazingly, . . . "I'm in." He had managed to slip a pediatric-size endotracheal tube through the vocal cords. In thirty seconds, with oxygen being manually ventilated through the tube, her heart was back, racing at a hundred and twenty beats a minute. Her [oxygen level] registered at 60 and then climbed. Another thirty seconds and it was at 97 percent. All the people in the room exhaled, as if they, too, had been denied their breath. . . .

We eventually identified the woman, whom I'll call Louise Williams; she was thirty-four years old and lived alone in a nearby suburb. Her alcohol level on arrival had been three times the legal limit, and had probably contributed to her unconsciousness. . . . When Ball came out and talked to family members, he told them of the dire condition she was in when she arrived, the difficulties "we" had had getting access to her airway, the disturbingly long period of time that she had gone without oxygen and thus his uncertainty about how much brain function she still possessed. They listened without protest; there was nothing for them to do but wait. . . .

I felt a sense of shame like a burning ulcer. This was not guilt: guilt is what you feel when you have done something wrong. What I felt was shame: I was what was wrong. And yet I also knew that a surgeon can take such feelings too far. It is one thing to be aware of one's limitations. It is another to be plagued by self-doubt. . . . Even worse than losing self-confidence, though, is reacting defensively. There are surgeons who will see faults everywhere except in themselves. They have no questions and no fears about their abilities. As a result, they learn nothing from their mistakes and know nothing of their limitations. . . .

Consider some other surgical mishaps. In one, a general surgeon left a large metal instrument in a patient's abdomen, where it tore through the bowel and the wall of the bladder. In another, a cancer surgeon biopsied the wrong part of a woman's breast and thereby delayed her diagnosis of cancer for months. A cardiac surgeon skipped a small but key step during a heart valve operation, thereby killing the patient. A general surgeon saw a man racked with abdominal pain in the emergency room and, without taking a CT scan, assumed that the man had a kidney stone; eighteen hours later, a scan showed a rupturing abdominal aortic aneurysm, and the patient died not long afterward.

How could anyone who makes a mistake of that magnitude be allowed to practice medicine? We call such doctors "incompetent," "unethical," and "negligent." We want to see them punished. And so we've wound up with the public system we have for dealing with error: malpractice lawsuits, media scandal, suspensions, firings.

There is, however, a central truth in medicine that complicates this tidy vision of misdeeds and misdoers: all doctors make terrible mistakes. Consider the cases I've just described. I gathered them simply by asking respected surgeons I know—surgeons at top medical schools—to tell me about mistakes they had made just in the past year. Every one of them had a story to tell.

In 1991, the *New England Journal of Medicine* published a series of landmark papers from a project known as the Harvard Medical Practice Study—a review of more than thirty thousand hospital admissions in New York State. The study found that nearly 4 percent of hospital patients suffered complications from treatment which either prolonged their hospital stay or resulted in disability or death, and that two-thirds of such complications were due to errors in care. One in four, or 1 percent of admissions, involved actual negligence. . . . [S]ubsequent investigations around the country have confirmed the ubiquity of error. In one . . . study, mistakes in administering drugs—giving the wrong drug or the wrong dose, say—occur, on average, about once every hospital admission, mostly without ill effects, but 1 percent of the time with serious consequences.

If error were due to a subset of dangerous doctors, you might expect malpractice cases to be concentrated among a small group, but in fact they follow a uniform, bell-shaped distribution. Most surgeons are sued at least once in the course of their careers. Studies of specific types of error, too, have found that repeat offenders are not the problem. The fact is that virtually everyone who cares for hospital patients will make serious mistakes, and even commit acts of negligence, every year. For this reason, doctors are seldom outraged when the press reports yet another medical horror story. They usually have a different reaction: That could be me. The important question isn't how to keep bad physicians from harming patients; it's how to keep good physicians from harming patients.

Medical malpractice suits are a remarkably ineffective remedy. Troyen Brennan, [formerly] a Harvard professor of law and public health, points out that research has consistently failed to find evidence that litigation reduces medical error rates. In part, this may be because the weapon is so imprecise. Brennan led several studies following up on the patients in the Harvard Medical Practice Study. He found that fewer than 2 percent of the patients who had received substandard care ever filed suit. Conversely, only a small minority among the patients who did sue had in fact been the victims of negligent care. And a patient's likelihood of winning a suit depended primarily on how poor his or her outcome was, regardless of whether that outcome was caused by disease or unavoidable risks of care.

The deeper problem with medical malpractice suits is that by demonizing errors they prevent doctors from acknowledging and discussing them publicly. The tort system makes adversaries of patient and physician, and pushes each to offer a heavily slanted version of events. When things go wrong, it's almost impossible for a physician to talk to a patient honestly about mistakes. Hospital lawyers warn doctors that, although they must, of course, tell patients about injuries that occur, they are never to intimate that they were at fault, lest the "confession" wind up in court as damning evidence in a black-and-white morality tale. At most, a doctor might say, "I'm sorry that things didn't go as well as we had hoped."

There is one place, however, where doctors can talk candidly about their mistakes, if not with patients, then at least with one another. It is called the Morbidity and Mortality Conference—or, more simply, M & M—and it takes place, usually once a week, at nearly every academic hospital in the country. This institution survives because laws protecting its proceedings from legal discovery have stayed on the books in most states, despite frequent challenges. . . .

In its way, the M & M is an impressively sophisticated and human institution. Unlike the courts or the media, it recognizes that human error is generally not something that can be deterred by punishment. The M & M sees avoiding error as largely a matter of will—of staying sufficiently informed and alert to anticipate the myriad ways that things can go wrong and then trying to head off each potential problem before it happens. It isn't damnable that an error occurs, but there is some shame to it. In fact, the M & M's ethos can seem paradoxical. On the one hand, it reinforces the very American idea that error is intolerable. On the other hand, the very existence of the M & M, its place on the weekly schedule, amounts to an acknowledgment that mistakes are an inevitable part of medicine.

But why do they happen so often? Lucian Leape, medicine's leading expert on error, points out that many other industries—whether the task is manufacturing semiconductors or serving customers at the Ritz-Carlton—simply wouldn't countenance error rates like those in hospitals. The aviation industry has reduced the frequency of operational errors to one in a hundred thousand flights, and most of those errors have no harmful consequences. The buzz-word at General Electric these days is "Six Sigma," meaning that its goal is to make product defects so rare that in statistical terms they are more than six standard deviations away from being a matter of chance—almost a one-in-a-million occurrence.

Of course, patients are far more complicated and idiosyncratic than airplanes, and medicine isn't a matter of delivering a fixed product or even a catalogue of products; it may well be more complex than just about any other field of human endeavor. Yet everything we've learned in the past two decades—from cognitive psychology, from "human factors" engineering, from studies of disasters like Three Mile Island and Bhopal—has yielded the same insights: not only do all human beings err, but they err frequently and in predictable, patterned ways. And systems that do not adjust for these realities can end up exacerbating rather than eliminating error. . . .

Medicine teems with examples. Take writing out a prescription, a rote procedure that relies on memory and attention, which we know are unreliable. Inevitably, a physician will sometimes specify the wrong dose or the wrong drug. Even when the prescription is written correctly, there's a risk that it will be misread. (Computerized ordering systems can almost eliminate errors of this kind, but only a small minority of hospitals have adopted them.) . . . You can also make the case that onerous workloads, chaotic environments, and inadequate team communication all represent [flaws] in the system. . . . When things go wrong, it is usually because a series of failures conspires to produce disaster. . . . The doctor is often only the final actor in a chain of events that set him or her up to fail. Error experts, therefore, believe that it's the process, not the individuals in it, that requires closer examination and correction. In a sense, they want to industrialize medicine. . . .

But the story doesn't have to end here, as the cognitive psychologists and industrial error experts have demonstrated. . . . It would be deadly for us, the individual actors, to give up our belief in human perfectibility. The statistics may say that someday I will sever someone's main bile duct [while removing a gallbladder], but each time I [do the] operation I believe that with enough will and effort I can beat the odds. This isn't just professional vanity. It's a necessary part of good medicine, even in superbly "optimized" systems. . . .

This may explain why many doctors take exception to talk of "systems problems," "continuous quality improvement," and "process re-engineering." It is the dry language of structures, not people. I'm no exception: something in me, too, demands an acknowledgment of my autonomy, which is also to say my ultimate culpability. Go back to that Friday night in the ER, to the moment when I stood, knife in hand, over Louise Williams, her lips blue, her throat a swollen, bloody, and suddenly closed passage. A systems engineer might have proposed some useful changes. Perhaps a backup suction device should always be at hand, and better light more easily available. Perhaps the institution could have trained me better for such crises, could have required me to have operated on a few more goats. . . .

Yet although the odds were against me, it wasn't as if I had no chance of succeeding. Good doctoring is all about making the most of the hand you're dealt, and I failed to do so. The indisputable fact was that I hadn't called for help when I could have, and when I plunged the knife into her neck and made my horizontal slash my best was not good enough. It was just luck, hers and mine, that [another doctor] somehow got a breathing tube into her in time.

There are all sorts of reasons that it would be wrong to take my license away or to take me to court. These reasons do not absolve me. Whatever the limits of the M & M, its fierce ethic of personal responsibility for errors is a formidable virtue. No matter what measures are taken, doctors will sometimes falter, and it isn't reasonable to ask that we achieve perfection. What is reasonable is to ask that we never cease to aim for it.

Notes: Medical Mistakes

1. *The Extent of Medical Error.* Are you surprised or shocked by the nearly 100,000 annual deaths caused by medical mistakes that is estimated by the Institute of Medicine? This estimate is based primarily on the influential Harvard study, mentioned by Dr. Gawande. Realize, though, that most people who die as the result of medical treatment do not die in the prime of life; many are old or feeble patients whose prospects for long-term survival are dim at best. For full details and analysis, see Paul Weiler et al., A Measure of Malpractice (1993). Similar studies were conducted in California in 1974, and in Utah and Colorado in the late 1990s, producing remarkably similar findings. The Institute of Medicine's report, To Err Is Human: Building a Safer Health System (2000), called widespread attention to these findings, and its recommendations spurred renewed efforts to improve medical care systems to prevent many common mistakes.

Professor Mark Grady reasons that medical mistakes are common because medical science has progressed so rapidly and is capable of much more than it once was. "New technology can enlarge people's opportunities to forget to use precaution and thereby be negligent." Why Are People Negligent? Technology, Nondurable Precautions, and the Medical Malpractice Explosion, 82 Nw. U. L. Rev. 293, 295 (1988). Renowned philosophers Samuel Gorovitz and Alasdair MacIntyre also argue that a high error rate is inevitable in medicine because of the human condition and the limits of technology. Toward a Theory of Medical Fallibility, 5(6) Hastings Center Rep. 13 (Dec. 1975). Lucien Leape (whom Gawande mentions) illustrates from one study of an intensive care unit, which documented "an average of 178 activities per day [for each patient]. The 1.7 errors per day thus indicate that hospital personnel were functioning at a 99 percent level of proficiency. However, a 1 percent failure rate is substantially higher than is tolerated in industry, particularly in hazardous fields such as aviation and nuclear power. As W. E. Deming points out, even 99.9 percent may not be good enough: 'If we had to live with 99.9 percent, we would have: 2 unsafe plane landings per day at O'Hare, 16,000 pieces of lost mail every hour, 32,000 bank checks deducted from the wrong bank account every hour.'" Error in Medicine, 272 JAMA 1851 (1994).

Are these views consistent with commonly held attitudes and expectations about modern medicine as conveyed by mass media? Could there be some therapeutic or social benefit to the blind faith that people sometimes place in their doctors? See Chapter 1.A.2. Viewed in this light, is it good to counter mass delusion by debunking the myth of infallibility?

2. *Conceptual Distinctions.* Roughly a third of malpractice claims are for diagnostic errors (especially failure to diagnose cancer), a third are for surgical errors (improper technique, slip of knife, foreign objects left inside); and a third are for improper medical treatment (e.g., drug reaction, anesthesia error, birth injury). Regardless of the type of medical treatment involved, consider, as you read the cases in the remainder of this chapter, how you would classify the various mistakes that led to injury. One useful analysis distinguishes between skill-based errors ("slips") and those based on decisionmaking (mental "mistakes"). Lucian L. Leape, Error in Medicine, 272 JAMA 1851 (1994). Realize that judgment mistakes might be due to misperception of the problem, choice of the wrong rule of action, or misapplication of the rule. Which kinds of error does Dr. Gawande's account illustrate? As you read the cases in this chapter, consider also whether the errors are the responsibility of any one actor, or do they result from flaws in the overall *system* for coordinating and delivering care? For more on the latter distinction, see Institute of Medicine, supra; Michelle Mello & David Studdert, Deconstructing Negligence: The Role of Individual and System Factors in Causing Medical Injuries, 96 Georgetown L. J. 599 (2008); and a series of articles exploring the nature of medical error, running in the Annals of Internal Medicine (2002–2003).

Renowned medical sociologist Elliot Friedson introduces another distinction in Doctoring Together (1975):

"Normal," excusable mistakes are those that every physician could conceive of making because of lack of information, the uncertainty of medical knowledge, the limitation of available techniques, and the uniqueness of the case. Many physicians would not even call these "mistakes"; in the interviews, some called them "so-called mistakes." Such normal mistakes are less mistakes than they are unavoidable events; they are not so much committed by the doctor as they are suffered or risked. They do not reflect on the physician's competence so much as on his luck. Thus, one should not judge or criticize a colleague's apparent mistakes because "there but for the grace of God go I."

In contrast to normal mistakes are deviant mistakes. Essentially, deviant mistakes seemed to be those that are thought to be due to a practitioner's negligence, ignorance, or ineptitude, reflecting upon his lack of basic or reasonable competence, ethicality, conscientiousness, and judgment. They consist in failures to follow the widely agreed-on rules of good practice. These are the mistakes that are frequently called "blatant" or "gross," "serious" being an adjective more often used to delineate the consequence of a mistake rather than its analytic character.

Timothy Stolzfus Jost, in the article on page 279, introduces two additional relevant distinctions:

A patient may receive a medical procedure that is technically appropriate but . . . [still] suffer a variety of affronts to dignity from health care professionals [such as failure to explain what is happening]. . . . A doctor may be unnecessarily rude or abrupt with a patient, or show contempt for the value of a patient's time. . . . These violations of social values and norms . . . seldom result in litigation or regulatory action, but frequently result in patient dissatisfaction. . . .

Finally, medical errors must be distinguished from medical failures. Some medical failures are not errors in the sense that anyone is culpable for their occurrence. They are simply due to unforeseeable reactions of a particular patient to treatment, unavoidable failure of equipment, the current limits of medical knowledge, or the ultimately intractable complexity of the human body. Even though such failures should in most instances not result in either tort or regulatory sanctions, an effective quality assurance system can discover them, and identify their causes, and perhaps assure they do not happen again.

3. *The Patient's Perspective.* Popular opinion sometimes thinks that malpractice plaintiffs are just trying to capitalize on their misfortune in order to hit the jackpot by suing a rich or well-insured doctor, or that plaintiffs are seduced into this attitude by personal injury lawyers looking for a big contingency fee. Certainly, there is some element of truth in this account, but to a large extent many patients also feel genuinely angry and wronged by how they were treated. In one law office (the one that represented the plaintiff in the first case below), 56 percent of inquiries about malpractice over a ten-year period were prompted by the doctor's referring unpaid bills to a collection agency, and 60 percent of potential clients were told by a nurse that malpractice had occurred. J. Reagan McLaurin et al., Pitfalls for the Practitioner: A Claimant's View of Medical Malpractice, Carolina Health Serv. Res. 97 (Summer 1994). A review of deposition transcripts found that, in 70 percent of the cases, the patients complained of one or more of the following behaviors by the doctor: devaluing patients' views, deserting the patient, and delivering information poorly. See Wendy Levinson, Physician-Patient Communication: A Key to Malpractice Prevention, 272 JAMA 1619 (1994). See also Debra Roter, The Patient-Physician Relationship and Its Implications for Malpractice Litigation, 9 J. Health Care L. & Pol'y 304 (2006).

4. *Physicians' Attitudes Toward Making Mistakes.* A classic study of how medical professionals respond to error is Charles Bosk, Forgive and Remember: Managing Medical Failure (2d ed. 2003). Reflecting on Dr. Gawande's narrative, how would you, or most people, feel if you learned that a perfectly human slip or mental error caused a patient to die or endure great suffering? Would you (or others) be defensive, self-loathing, in denial of your responsibility, deeply regretful and apologetic, "philosophical"? Which of these (or other) attitudes is most constructive? Which help doctors to carry on in the face of inevitability? Which attitudes are likely to lead to constructive change?

5. *Telling Patients and Apologizing.* Dr. Gawande comments that, due to the threat of liability, "it's almost impossible for a physician to talk to a patient honestly about mistakes." See also Sagit Mor & Orna Rabinovich-Einy, Relational Malpractice, 42 Seton Hall L. Rev. 601 (2012). But, should physicians be required, as an aspect of their fiduciary duty to patients, to inform patients when a bad outcome is due to a medical mistake? This question is receiving considerable ethical and public policy attention. The private accreditation body in charge of hospitals (the JCAHO, Joint Commission on the Accreditation of Healthcare Organizations) has instituted a "sentinel events" reporting policy that requires hospitals to make physicians inform patients or their families when unexpected death or serious injury is caused by medical care rather than by the natural course of disease. See Symposium, 35 J. Health L. 179 (2002). A few states require the same. William Sage et al., Bridging the Relational-Regulatory Gap: A Pragmatic Information Policy for Patient Safety and Medical Malpractice, 59 Vand. L. Rev. 1263 (2006).

When doctors reveal medical errors to patients, should they also apologize, either from a genuine feeling of remorse, or as a strategic way to head off medical malpractice litigation?

> Doctors' apologies for medical mistakes may not be a cure-all for litigation, but explaining unforeseen outcomes and making early settlement offers have proven effective, say lawyers who have participated in the process in the last decade. The concept is called "full disclosure/early offer," and it's spreading. The U.S. Department of Veterans Affairs' Veterans Health Administration—as well as a number of hospital systems and insurers across the nation—are among the entities that have adopted variations of the policy. . . . Plaintiffs' and defense attorneys agree that the program—often referred to as Sorry Works! from The Sorry Works! Coalition, . . . —is a sound strategy miscast in the public perception as a touchy-feely ritual. . . . [H]ealth care providers willing to admit when they have made an error and quickly get on top of it cut down on the anger that leads to litigation. . . .
>
> Michael A. Stidham, whose Jackson, Ky., practice includes representing Department of Veterans Affairs (V.A.) patients, has settled three cases with the Veterans Affairs Medical Center in Lexington, Ky.—two on the same morning—and lost a bench trial in a medical malpractice case that involved a suicide. Stidham said that he likes the system and thinks that its wider application could help to reduce docket backlogs. In contrast, a case against a local hospital can take three to four years to get to trial. "The only thing I really find lacking in it at this point is that I don't believe they tell the prospective plaintiffs that they have the right to discuss their offers with an attorney. A lot of men and women don't understand why they're receiving these offers," he said. Stidham noted that "I didn't always get everything I wanted, but I didn't leave with a bad taste in my mouth, and left with a satisfied client, which is the most important thing."

Ginny M. Hamm, the special assistant U.S. attorney assigned to the V.A. medical center in Lexington who worked with the former hospital chief of staff, Dr. Steve S. Kraman, to introduce a centerwide disclosure program in 1987, said that a full and lengthy explanation always precedes an offer. Since Hamm did her first disclosure case in 1989, the "golden rule" has been to tell veterans or their families that they should seek counsel when the hospital meets with them to disclose what went wrong, she said. Kraman, as chief of staff, would speak to the veteran and his family on behalf of the entire medical center, offering an apology and explaining the error, then "hand off to me for the settlement," she said. Hamm added that if the V.A. determined that no mistake was made, it would hold a "closure" meeting explaining its finding to the veteran. Kraman, who now serves on the board of The Sorry Works! Coalition, said that he was aware of only two cases in which angry patients sued for damages. "The vast majority of people respond in kind. If treated honestly, they don't even want money. They want to see that some good comes out of a bad situation," Kraman said.

Peter Geier, Emerging Med-Mal Strategy: "I'm Sorry," National L. J., July 24, 2006.

6. *Physicians' Attitudes Toward Being Sued.* In contrast with their private regret over poor medical outcomes, most doctors view a malpractice suit as an unjustified affront to their professional integrity and reputation, as revealed in the article that follows. Another doctor graphically depicts his feeling of violation after a string of suits in quick succession: "From being a virgin for 20 years, all of a sudden I was gang raped." N. Hupert et al., Processing the Tort Deterrent Signal: A Qualitative Study, 43 Soc. Sci. & Med. 1 (1996). See also Peter Kowey, A Piece of My Mind, 306 JAMA 18 (2011). Does this type of response cause you concern about whether malpractice law is having its intended social effect? How constructive are physicians' responses to this deterrent signal likely to be? Consider how constructive are the suggestions made by the physician in the following article. Also, see page 330 for a discussion of the meaning and extent of the "defensive medicine" caused by the threat of liability.

7. *Bibliography.* For critique of the Institute of Medicine's findings (note 1), see Rodney A. Hayward & Timothy P. Hofer, Estimating Hospital Deaths Due to Medical Errors: Preventability Is in the Eye of the Reviewer, 286 JAMA 415 (2001); Clement J. McDonald et al., Deaths Due to Medical Errors Are Exaggerated in Institute of Medicine Report, 284 JAMA 93 (2000). Additional discussions of the **extent and cause of medical error**, and of **measuring and improving quality**, can be found at Tom Baker, The Medical Malpractice Myth (2005); Michelle M. Mello & Troyen A. Brennan, Deterrence of Medical Errors: Theory and Evidence for Malpractice Reform, 80 Tex. L. Rev. 1595 (2002); Michael Saks, Medical Malpractice: Facing Real Problems and Finding Real Solutions, 35 Wm. & Mary L. Rev. 693 (1994); Peter Jacobson, Medical Liability and the Culture of Technology, *in* Medical Malpractice and the U.S. Health Care System (W. Sage & R. Kersh eds., 2006); Christopher Landrigan et al., Temporal Trends in Rates of Patient Harm Resulting from Medical Care, 363 New Eng. J. Med. 2124 (2011); Rosemary Gibson & Janardan Prasad Singh, Wall of Silence: The Untold Story of Medical Mistakes That Kill and Injure Millions of Americans (2003); Robert M. Wachter & Kaveh G. Shojania, Internal Bleeding: The Truth Behind America's Terrifying Epidemic of Medical Mistakes (2004); Marianne Paget, A Complex Sorrow: Reflections on Cancer and an Abbreviated Life (1993); Symposium, 29(9) Health Aff. (Sept. 2010); Symposium, 22(2) Health Aff. (March

2003); Symposium, 46 Perspect. Biol. Med. 1 (Winter 2003); Symposium, Patient Injury, Medical Errors, Liability and Reform, 29 J. L. Med. & Ethics 248 (2001). For additional discussion, pro and con, of **disclosing and apologizing for medical error**, and whether doing so increases litigation risk (note 5), see K. M. Mazor et al., Communicating with Patients About Medical Errors: A Review of the Literature, 164 Arch. Intern. Med. 1690 (2003); Aaron Lazare, The Healing Forces of Apology in Medical Practice and Beyond, 57 DePaul L. Rev. 251 (2008); Thomas Gallagher et al., Disclosing Harmful Medical Errors to Patients, 356 New Engl. J. Med. 2713 (2007); Symposium, 166 Arch. Intern. Med. 1585 (2006); Symposium, 33(1) Health Aff. 11-52 (Jan. 2014); see Jonathan Todres, Toward Healing and Restoration for All: Reframing Medical Malpractice Reform, 39 Conn. L. Rev. 667 (2006); Richard Bourne, Medical Malpractice: Should Courts Force Doctors to Confess Their Own Negligence to Their Patients?, 61 Ark. L. Rev. 621 (2009); Steven Raper, No Role for Apology: Remedial Work and the Problem of Medical Injury, 11 Yale J. Health Pol'y L. & Ethics 267 (2011); Erin Ann O'Hara, Apology and Thick Trust: What Spouse Abusers and Negligent Doctors Might Have in Common, 79 Chi.-Kent L. Rev. 1055 (2004); Lee Taft, Apology and Medical Mistake: Opportunity or Foil?, 14 Ann. Health L. 55 (2005).

2. Critiquing and Measuring the Malpractice System

■ SUITS FOR ALLEGED MALPRACTICE
George W. Gay, M.D.
165 Bos. Med. & Surg. J. 353 (1911)*

Suits at law against reputable physicians for alleged malpractice have attracted unusual attention in late years by reason of their increasing frequency and by the absence of a reasonable foundation of truth and justice in the charges usually brought against the defendant. Litigation, like legislation, was never so rampant as it is today. The multitude of lawyers, the bewildering mass of statutes, and the ever-increasing volume of both only tend to aggravate a condition which would seem already to be too complicated for the public welfare . . . What a large and growing number of litigants want is not a resort to justice, but a resort to chance; not the establishment of truth and the enforcement of whatever rights based on the truth have been infringed upon, but a verdict or a decision obtained from ignorance, prejudice, or favor . . .

[Courts have become so congested] in many states that the President of the United States, the American Bar Association, and many of the acute legal minds of the country are trying to devise some method of correcting this unfortunate state of affairs. . . Thus far, there seems to be no relief from this deplorable state of affairs, nor are the prospects for such relief encouraging . . .

---

* The author was a prominent surgeon in Boston. Thanks to Rob Field for pointing out this gem of an article, a full copy of which can be found on the Web site for this casebook, www.health-law.org. It is fascinating reading.

However faithful and efficient may be the physician . . . [he] is in no way protected from a suit by the fact that the mode of treatment pursued in any case was the one accepted and approved by the leading authorities, or that, from the nature of the disease or injuries, no known method of treatment could have improved the results obtained. These facts do not protect a physician from an unjust, vexatious, and expensive suit . . . Having rendered faithful, skillful service through a long and perhaps critical illness, and having obtained the best result possible under the circumstances, nothing can be more disheartening, more aggravating, and more demoralizing to one's faith in human nature than a suit for malpractice. . . .

To assert that physicians never make mistakes under any circumstances is to claim a degree of perfection which no profession nor vocation possesses. From the nature of our calling and of the conditions with which we have to deal, an occasional error is inevitable. The wonder is that the mistakes are so few. . . . Nature's processes are often obscure, and the danger signals may not be in evidence until too late to avert disaster . . . As the Supreme Court of a neighboring state has well said, "the medical practitioner is necessarily surrounded by doubt and uncertainties and unavoidably exposed to errors and mistakes, which may well furnish a satisfactory explanation of unfavorable results." . . . .

The members of the medical profession stand ready to make reasonable amends for errors and to adjust proper claims. They strongly object, however, to being mulcted and fleeced by sharpers and unreasonable people, as is attempted in a vast majority of the malpractice suits of the present day . . .

Malpractice suits are brought from various motives, as for example, to extort money from the defendant, to escape the payment of his bill, to avenge the disappointment at the termination of the case, to deliberately injure the reputation of the defendant out of spite, and to attract the notice and sympathy of friends and neighbors. The sanctimonious excuse of desiring to protect others from the incompetency of the defendant is occasionally offered as a reason for bringing suit. It is doubtful if a patient of his own motion often brings an action for damages in these cases . . .

A very important factor in many of these cases is the perniciously active attorney, who is constantly on the watch for opportunities to instigate and foment claims of all sorts with little regard to right and justice . . . It would be difficult to devise a scheme, or a mode of procedure, more conducive to the instigation and presentation of bogus claims, than is the so-called contingent suit of the present day. It is a game of chance, a gamble, having stakes that are especially alluring, when the defendants are timid, or rich, or both . . .

Not infrequently, a malpractice suit is brought against the consultant either separately or in conjunction with the attending physician. This is especially noticeable when the former has attachable property, or the reputation of wealth." . . . Holding the consultant equally responsible with the regular attendant for the treatment, especially if the patient be seen but once by the former . . . may be good law, but in many instances, it is neither justice nor common sense . . . It may subject physicians of the highest skill, who have rendered faithful and intelligent service, to the necessity of defending themselves in blackmailing suits against charges having no foundation in fact, or for conditions over which they never had any control and for which they are in no way responsible. It encourages false claims and fake suits . . .

Of course, there is another side to this matter, and no one will deny the fact that malpractice suits are justified under certain conditions [example omitted] . . . This paper makes no plea in defense of such work, but confines itself to those cases in which there is little or no just cause for complaint as to the treatment . . .

The writer much regrets that he is unable to suggest any escape from this unjust and aggravating state of affairs. So long as there are ungrateful patients and pernicious lawyers and doctors, physicians, however accomplished and renowned, must run the risk of being hauled into court upon the most unjust charges and put to the trouble and expense of defending themselves, their reputation, their character, and their bank account, if they be so fortunate as to have one, against the blackmailers and "ambulance chasers" that infest every community . . .

Care, forethought, and discretion would seem to be our only safeguards . . . In the first place, it is essential that the physician . . . should undertake only such cases as he can properly manage with or without available assistance. A reasonably-correct diagnosis is the basis of satisfactory clinical work and no pains should be spared to obtain it. Prompt and repeated consultations should be requested in difficult and obscure cases for the double purpose of avoiding error and dividing responsibility. In these days of highly-developed specialism, it is incumbent upon the family practitioner to avail himself of the services of experts upon all proper occasions, not only for the benefit of the patient, but for his own as well . . .

Let the public understand that reputable physicians . . . will stand by each other in their defense of the right as against the wrong, regardless of time, trouble, and expense; that we mean to do our best for the welfare of our patients, and having done that, we naturally resent being called upon to defend such action at law. Let the people fully comprehend the above facts and conditions, and these unjust and uncalled for suits for alleged malpractice should disappear from the calendars of our courts.

■ THE MEDICAL MALPRACTICE MYTH
Tom Baker*

Medical malpractice premiums are skyrocketing. "Closed" signs are sprouting on health clinic doors. Doctors are leaving the field of medicine, and those who remain are practicing in fear and silence. Pregnant women cannot find obstetricians. Billions of dollars are wasted on defensive medicine. And angry doctors are marching on state capitols across the country. All this is because medical malpractice litigation is exploding. Egged on by greedy lawyers, plaintiffs sue at the drop of a hat. Juries award eye-popping sums to undeserving claimants, leaving doctors, hospitals, and their insurance companies no choice but to pay huge ransoms. . . .

This is the medical malpractice myth. . . . None of this bears even a passing resemblance to reality. In fact, the research is so clearly to the contrary that the most interesting question is why the research has not changed people's minds. . . .

Built on a foundation of urban legend mixed with the occasional true story, supported by selective references to academic studies, and repeated so often that even the mythmakers forget the exaggeration, half truth, and outright misinformation employed in the service of their greater good, the medical malpractice myth has filled doctors, patients, legislators, and voters with the kind of fear that short circuits critical thinking.

This fear has inspired legislative action on a nationwide scale three times in my lifetime: [the mid-1970s, the mid-1980s, and the early 2000s]. . . . This time around we have a lot more information. First, we know from [various] studies that the real problem is too much medical malpractice, not too much litigation. . . . The real costs of medical malpractice are the lost lives, extra medical expenses, time out of work, and pain and suffering of tens of thousands of people every year, the vast majority of whom do not sue. . . . "[U]ndeserving" people sometimes bring medical malpractice claims because they do not know that the claims lack merit and because they cannot find out what happened to them (or their loved ones) without making a claim. Most undeserving claims disappear before a trial; most trials end in a verdict for the doctor; doctors almost never pay claims out of their own pockets; and hospitals and insurance companies refuse to pay claims unless there is a good evidence of malpractice. If a hospital or insurance company does settle a questionable claim to avoid a huge risk, there is a very large discount. This means that big payments to undeserving claimants are the very rare exception, not the rule. . . .

This is a book with a mission. My goal is reframing the public discussion about medical malpractice lawsuits . . . [so that] the people who know a lot about medicine and the people who know a lot about law can start to talk *to* each other, rather than *at* each other, about the role that law can play in improving the quality of health care.

Notes: Facts and Figures

1. *The History and "Epidemiology" of Malpractice Suits.* Are you surprised by the fact that Dr. Gay wrote his article a century ago? His perspective is still shared by a large portion of the medical profession today. To appreciate the concern that doctors have about being sued in the modern legal climate, consider that, prior to 1960, only one in seven doctors had ever been sued in their entire career. Today, claims are filed against about one in seven doctors *each year*. This explains why malpractice law is often the focal point for discussion of tort reform in state and federal legislatures, and why tort reform is one of the AMA's highest legislative priorities, sometimes appearing to rank above other social concerns such as universal access to health care.

Although most doctors complain about the threat of malpractice suits, they are not all equally affected. Malpractice claims are not spread uniformly. Some specialties (surgery, anesthesiology, obstetrics, and emergency medicine) produce claims much more frequently than others and some doctors within the same specialty are sued more often than others.

2. *Plaintiffs' Lawyers.* As Prof. Baker summarizes, and as his book thoroughly documents, a flurry of empirical research over the past decade or more allows us to address the contentious debate over malpractice litigation with something more than anecdotal opinion. For instance, the claim Dr. Gay made a century ago that

too many frivolous suits are filed is belied today by the fact that most experienced malpractice lawyers are very selective in the cases they agree to take, due to the costs of litigation and the uncertainty of prevailing. In one study of six firms, 502 potential plaintiffs called over a ten-day period. Of these, 85 (17 percent) were selected for expert review of the medical records. Sixty-two percent of these were rejected, usually for insufficient damages, and only one-quarter for lack of negligence. For callers who were rejected without medical review, the overwhelming reason (73 percent) was insufficient damages. L. Huycke & M. Huycke, Characteristics of Potential Plaintiffs in Malpractice Litigation, 120 Ann. Intern. Med. 792 (1994). Naturally, less established malpractice attorneys may decide not to be this selective.

3. *Jury Bias.* It appears that physicians' concerns about juries being biased in favor of injured patients are exaggerated. For the most part, research findings are much more supportive of juries than is popular opinion. When malpractice complaints go to trial, plaintiffs win only 20 to 30 percent of the time. This compares with an overall success rate of about 50 percent for plaintiffs in general civil litigation. Interviews with jurors in malpractice cases also confirm that, generally speaking, they enter the case sympathetic to doctors and suspicious of plaintiffs' motives to "make a fast buck." Neil Vidmar, Medical Malpractice and the American Jury (1995).

Although doctors win most of the time, how accurate these verdicts are is another question. Accuracy, of course, is in the eye of the beholder, since there is no agreement on what the proper "gold standard" should be for evaluating jury verdicts. The best that researchers can do is to ask expert neutral physicians whether the medical records reveal any substandard care causing injury. When they do so, researchers find a statistically significant, but far from perfect, correlation between the expert reviewer's opinion and the jury's verdict in the same case. For instance, one study compared how cases were resolved by juries with how the physician-run insurer had evaluated the case before trial for purposes of settlement negotiations. It found that plaintiffs won 42 percent of the cases that the insurer's consultants considered "indefensible," but plaintiffs won only 21 percent of those considered "defensible." This study also found that wins and losses were not influenced by the severity of injury, indicating that juries were not swayed purely by sympathy for the plaintiff. The amount of damages did vary with the strength of the liability case, even after controlling for the severity of the injury. Therefore, the expected value of a malpractice claim (i.e., the expected award times the chances of winning) was 25 times larger for claims that reviewers judged to be meritorious than for ones they judged to be without merit. This gives contingent fee lawyers a strong incentive to weed out weaker or "frivolous" claims. Mark I. Taragin et al., The Influence of Standard of Care and Severity of Injury on the Resolution of Medical Malpractice Claims, 117 Ann. Intern. Med. 780 (1992). Other studies show that, when plaintiffs win, damages are appropriately correlated with the patients' age and severity of injury.

Finding a statistical association between jury results and expert opinion means only that jury verdicts as a whole are not entirely random or unpredictable. Results in individual cases are still highly erratic. Also, as the numbers from the study by Taragin and colleagues reflect, depending on how one conceives of the correct "gold standard," juries produce a large number of both false positives (incorrect findings of negligence) and false negatives (incorrect findings of no liability), perhaps more of the latter than the former. The materials in section D outline alternatives for liability determination other than the jury trial that rely more on expert opinion. Even if these alternatives were to produce greater accuracy, what other values would they sacrifice?

Another measure of the accuracy and rationality of the malpractice system is lawyers' behavior in settling cases. As discussed in section F, many more cases settle than go to trial. Lawyers take their clues for when and how much to settle by observing how juries behave. If juries don't reach accurate results or if their behavior is unpredictable, then settlement decisions are not likely to be accurate. As summarized in Philip G. Peters, Jr., What We Know About Malpractice Settlements, 92 Iowa L. Rev. 1783 (2007), "weak claims are much less likely to result in a settlement payment than strong claims. Only 10% to 20% of the weak cases result in a payment, and it is typically only a token amount, such as forgiveness of any unpaid doctor bills. Strong cases settle at a much higher rate (85% to 90%) and for a much larger average payment. Borderline cases fall in the middle." See also David M. Studdert et al., Claims, Errors, and Compensation Payments in Medical Malpractice Litigation, 354 New Eng. J. Med. 2024 (2006) (malpractice claims involving verifiable errors are much more likely to result in a payment to the patient, and such payments are substantially higher than in claims without medical errors that are settled).

4. *Further Reading.* On medical **malpractice attorneys and their case selection** (note 2), see Kenneth DeVille, Act First and Look Up the Law Afterward? Medical Malpractice and the Ethics of Defensive Medicine, 19 Theoretical Med. & Bioethics 569 (1998) (an excellent overview, both for doctors and lawyers, of the factors that influence patients' decisions to consult a lawyer, lawyers' decisions to bring a case, the chances of success, and the likely recovery); L. Laska, Medical Malpractice Cases Not to File, 20 Mem. St. U. L. Rev. 27 (1989); Catherine T. Harris et al., Who Are Those Guys? An Empirical Examination of Medical Malpractice Plaintiffs' Attorneys, 58 SMU L. Rev. 225 (2005); Stephen Daniels & Joanne Martin, Plaintiff's Lawyers, Specialization, and Medical Malpractice, 59 Vand. L. Rev. 1051 (2006).

For additional views and research on **jury bias and accuracy** (note 3), see Philip G. Peters, The Role of the Jury in Modern Malpractice Law, 87 Iowa L. Rev. 911 (2002) (thorough review of the evidence, concluding that juries, on balance, reach defensible results and are not biased against physicians; if anything, juries are biased in doctors' favor); Philip G. Peters, Doctors and Juries, 105 Mich. L. Rev. 1453 (2007) (multiple studies are "startlingly consistent," that "the probability of a plaintiff's verdict grows as the evidence of negligence improves"); Thomas M. O'Toole et al., The Anatomy of a Medical Malpractice Verdict, 70 Mont. L. Rev. 57 (2009); William M. Sage & Rogan Kersh, Medical Malpractice and the U.S. Health Care System (2006); Frank Sloan & Lindsey M. Chepke, Ill-Suited? Medical Malpractice at a Crossroads (2008); David A. Hyman & Charles Silver, Medical Malpractice Litigation and Tort Reform: It's the Incentives, Stupid, 59 Vand. L. Rev. 1085 (2006); Symposium, 4 J. Empirical Legal Stud. 1 (2007). Compare Jeffrey O'Connell & Christopher Pohl, How Reliable Is Medical Malpractice Law? A Review of "Medical Malpractice and the American Jury," 12 J. L. & Health 359 (1998) (insightful review of both Neil Vidmar's research of jury verdicts and the Harvard study findings, concluding that malpractice law is not well designed to produce accurate and fair results, and

Relationship Between Injuries & Claims

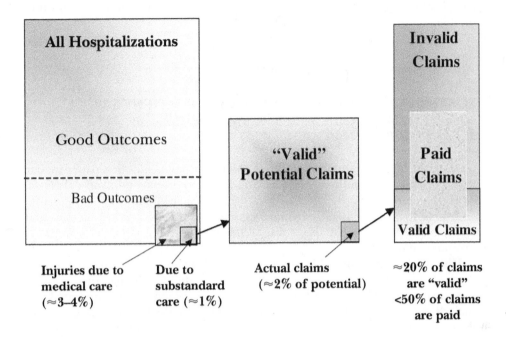

Note: Diagram scale is only approximate.

advocating instead a no-fault compensation system), with David A. Hyman, Medical Malpractice and the Tort System: What Do We Know and What (If Anything) Should We Do About It?, 80 Tex. L. Rev. 1639 (2002) (criticizing malpractice system but also expressing skepticism about no-fault compensation).

5. *Piecing It All Together.* Based on the data and concepts discussed in these notes, Randall Bovbjerg has created the accompanying diagram above, adapted from an earlier version by Don Harper Mills (who ran the California study). The diagram is conceptual, not to scale, but it provides some rough scope for the issues addressed throughout this chapter.

In any medical encounter, there is a considerable chance of a disappointing outcome. However, most of these poor results are the unavoidable consequence of the disease itself and the inherent limits of medical science. Of all hospital admissions, only about 4 percent involve an injury caused by medical treatment. Of these, only about one-fourth (1 percent of the total) are the result of substandard care. Only about 2 percent of negligent injuries result in claims being filed with insurers. In part, this is because the great majority of these injuries are temporary or minor. Importantly, however, most claims are for injuries not caused by negligence. Fewer than half of all claims result in payment, usually through settlement.

6. *Looking Ahead.* The next reading considers the full range of possible legal responses that are available for medical mistakes and other deficiencies in the

quality of health care delivery. As you read it, consider which responses are appropriate for which types of mistakes, and how malpractice suits compare with other types of legal oversight.

3. Approaches to Improving Quality of Care

■ FOSTERING RATIONAL REGULATION OF PATIENT SAFETY
Michelle M. Mello, Carly N. Kelly & Troyen A. Brennan
30 J. Health Pol. Pol'y & L. 375 (2005)

After decades of inattention to the problem of medical injuries, patient safety is now occupying a prominent place on the health policy agenda and garnering renewed regulatory interest. . . . This article reviews the evolution of the regulatory environment for patient safety, examines some of the tensions and challenges that currently dene patient safety oversight, and suggests strategies for more rational and responsive regulation. . . .

Historically, the relationship between government and the health care industry has been characterized by an unparalleled faith in the ability of medical professionals to regulate themselves. Recently, however, three developments have invigorated policy makers' interest in health care quality oversight. First, the Institute of Medicine's (IOM's) reports on patient safety (Kohn, Corrigan, and Donaldson 2000) and quality of care (Institute of Medicine 2001) have focused public attention on the current deficiencies in health care and, by implication, the deciencies of existing regulatory efforts. These wake-up calls have created signicant political momentum for new forms of regulation. Second, the steady erosion of professionalism in medicine has suggested to legislators and the public that physicians are no longer equipped to self-regulate. Third, the escalating intrusion of the market into health care has raised public suspicion about corner cutting by prot-driven entities. . . .

In this article, we seek to assess the new regulation of patient safety. We dene regulation broadly to include any organized and deliberate leveraging of power or authority to effect changes in the behavior of health care providers. . . . *Patient safety* specically refers to prevention of iatrogenic injury — that is, injuries caused by medical management as opposed to the patient's underlying disease process. Quality assurance aims more broadly at improving health outcomes by improving care processes, with an emphasis on basing medical decisions on the best available evidence and ensuring that patients receive needed services. . . . Safety focuses on inadvertent harm to patients, whereas effectiveness focuses on the production of afrmative benet. Yet the two are frequently conflated. . . .

[S]everal major studies conducted over the past thirty years have gradually built an empirical case that iatrogenic injuries are a serious public health problem warranting intervention. The 2000 IOM report on medical errors catapulted this research into the public eye and energized public and private regulators to undertake such interventions. . . . [I]n the mid-1980s, a group of [Harvard] investigators . . . undertook a review of thirty thousand medical records and sixty-seven thousand malpractice claims (Weiler et al. 1993). The results, which were . . . replicated in

Utah and Colorado in the late 1990s by some of the same investigators, . . . were strikingly similar: 3 percent of hospitalizations resulted in an adverse event and about 1 percent involved an adverse event attributable to negligence (Thomas et al. 2000). . . . The IOM's report on medical errors, which extrapolated injury prevalence gures from the Harvard studies, generated publicity at a level virtually unparalleled in health services research. In particular, the IOM's estimate that forty-four thousand to ninety-eight thousand deaths per year were attributable to medical errors shocked the public. . . .

The science of error prevention in other industries turns out to produce few ready-made solutions to medical injuries. . . . [U]nlike nuclear plant failures or air crashes, medical injuries are diffuse and often difcult to disentangle from bad outcomes unrelated to medical management. . . . Thus, we must begin by acknowledging that there is presently very little evidence of measures that can give rise to patient safety regulation. This nearly ensures that the regulation will be a complicated story, as the enthusiasm of regulators exceeds the range of tools available to them. With this background in mind, we now turn to that story as it has unfolded to date.

THE PLURALISTIC REGULATORY ENVIRONMENT

The current regulatory environment for patient safety is highly pluralistic in nature. Traditional, top-down forms of regulation such as statutes and agency oversight are supplemented with private and quasi-private, bottom-up approaches including tort law and the market. Individually, each of these regulatory mechanisms has well-recognized strengths and weaknesses, but often overlooked are the interactive effects. . . .

Government regulation of health care quality has traditionally been limited, dominated by a philosophy that medical professionals can and should regulate themselves. Historically, quality assurance in hospitals was largely left to the medical staff, whose primary mechanism for ensuring quality was the careful selection and oversight of the clinicians who were given staff privileges. . . . Hospitals' medical leadership reviews the credentials of physician applicants, admits only those who are believed to meet high standards, and periodically reviews the care provided by individual doctors to determine whether to continue their staff privileges.

Hospitals have also self-regulated through accreditation by the Joint Commission on Accreditation of Healthcare Organizations (JCAHO). . . . Although the JCAHO has influential lay commissioners, it remains dominated by hospital and physician representatives. . . . States formally retain responsibility for hospital licensure decisions, but most states have incorporated JCAHO accreditation standards into their licensure standards, and the large majority accepts JCAHO accreditation as the basis for a license. Similarly, the federal government has made JCAHO accreditation a sufficient condition for certification for Medicare participation. . . .

The JCAHO inspects hospitals every two to three years to ensure that they are in compliance with a series of structural and process-oriented quality measures. . . . It is not clear that the[se] standards address the problems that are most important for patient safety. . . . The standards may have been favored because most of them are relatively easy to articulate and measure. . . . Some have expressed doubts that its accreditation inspections have meaningful effects on hospital quality. . . .

To some extent, research and policy organizations are beginning to step in to address the information deficiency and assist policy makers in crafting substantive patient safety legislation. For example, the National Quality Forum (NQF), a public-private partnership in Washington, DC, has begun to develop a list of adverse events that should not occur and should be reported to governmental—as well as a list of safety-enhancing interventions. However, many of the proposed interventions are from the effectiveness domain, and quite a few of those from the safety domain are admittedly best shots rather than evidence based. . . .

BOTTOM-UP REGULATION

Tort Law. Tort law, or personal injury law, is intended to serve two regulatory functions. First, it provides a social insurance function; that is, it is a mechanism to compensate injured persons for the costs of injuries caused by the inadequate precaution taking of others. Second, it serves a deterrent function: in requiring that a defendant pay money to persons injured by the defendant's conduct, tort liability creates an economic incentive for safer behavior.

Tort law is a bottom-up regulatory approach because it relies upon individual patients to initiate malpractice claims. Although it bears little resemblance to statutory and administrative regulation in terms of its source or scope of application, in our view it can reasonably be considered a form of regulation. . . . Beginning in the 1940s, leading judges began to modify existing tort doctrine by eliminating principles that made it difficult for patients to sue doctors (Weiler 1991). Making lawsuits more attractive to potential plaintiffs was part of a general strategy to strengthen the deterrent signal tort law sent to health care providers. By 1960, these changes in malpractice law had led to a significant increase in claims frequency. These changes have had the intended effect of making providers more conscious of the threat of malpractice litigation, but whether this awareness has translated into improved patient safety is hotly disputed.

Tort law has certain advantages over other forms of health care regulation. Unlike agency oversight, litigation is not vulnerable (except at the margins) to capture by the regulated parties, fluctuations in political and bureaucratic agendas, or underfunded regulatory mandates. Unlike industry self-regulation, it is not constrained by the inherent conflict of interest involved in policing one's own profession.

However, several factors have made the relationship between tort law and patient safety a troubled and increasingly uncomfortable one. First, courts face significant structural constraints in serving as regulators. Judges lack specic expertise about health care quality and must rely on litigants to supply the facts of disputes and suggest remedies. In contrast, agency regulators typically have extensive experience in health care. Courts cannot engage in problem detection and initiate cases on their own; they must wait for an aggrieved litigant to present himself or herself—after the harm has already been done. Furthermore, they are limited in the remedies at their disposal: whereas agencies can promulgate new rules that will apply to all providers under their jurisdiction, and conduct inspections and impose sanctions for violating the rules, court decisions in tort cases bind only the particular defendant at bar (though landmark rulings may influence the behavior of other providers). All of these design features of the judiciary make tort law a relatively inefcacious mechanism in general. Several additional problems make it especially problematic for regulating patient safety.

One concern is that there is scant evidence that physicians process the deterrent signal sent by malpractice litigation in a constructive way (Danzon 1985; Mello and Brennan 2002). Physicians have long maintained that most malpractice suits are unwarranted, that patterns of suing are haphazard, and that as a result malpractice litigation does not create a rational and systematic deterrent signal. Contributing to the perception of haphazardness are findings from the California, New York, and Utah/Colorado studies showing that most patients who are injured due to negligence never bring claims, whereas a large proportion of malpractice claims do not actually involve a negligent injury. . . .

As a result, rather than viewing lawsuits as an indication that their clinical practices require modification, physicians tend to view suits as unrelated to the quality of care rendered. This is largely a modern view. Prior to the dissemination of the [Harvard study's] New York results, physician groups were more inclined to consider patient safety improvement a good risk-management strategy. Certainly there is no better example of this than . . . anesthesiologists responding to the mid-1980s tort crisis with a massive effort to understand and reduce anesthesia injuries. In contrast, providers in today's malpractice crisis seek merely to limit their liability. . . .

Finally, the deterrent signal is weakened by the fact that nearly all health care providers carry professional liability insurance and are therefore insulated from at least the economic consequences of malpractice (Danzon 1985). Experience rating—adjusting premiums to reflect an insured's claims experience—can get around this problem, but is not considered feasible for individual physicians (Mello and Brennan 2002). Owing to these and other problems, tort law as a form of regulation has not had much of an impact on patient safety. Although few systematic studies of the deterrent value of the tort law have been conducted, the existing analyses provide only very limited evidence that providers who experience malpractice claims have fewer adverse events and instances of negligence in the future. . . .

[T]he critical twist on the tort crisis today is that it has begun to create a siege mentality among physicians. This in turn has led to increased defensiveness regarding any initiative designed to bring more awareness to medical injuries, in particular patient safety initiatives that aim to encourage physician self-reporting of adverse events (Liang 2000). There is a dynamic tension between the general belief that greater transparency about adverse events is a good thing and the need to keep information about reported adverse events confidential in order to encourage reporting.

. . . We expect the conflict between patient safety regulation and malpractice to persist, because both are impelled by the increasingly widely accepted notion that patients are endangered by errors in medical care. The tort system presumes that punishment through economic sanctions is the best approach to deterrence, especially because the tort system is essentially uncapturable by the regulated industry. Members of the patient safety movement within the health care industry, however, rely on motivated professional commitment and a sanction-free environment to cultivate greater safety. As the public's awareness of errors deepens, plaintiffs' attorneys will grow more empowered and aggressive, which will in turn increase the pressure of the tort crisis and the defensiveness of the medical profession.

Market and Business Approaches. Regulation is usually contrasted with the market as an approach to social change, so it is perhaps odd to describe market approaches in an article on regulation. But if regulation is conceived of broadly as a rational structure of incentives set in place to accomplish a particular purpose, then regulation can proceed through market forces. . . . It has become de rigueur to refer to this regulatory strategy as building a "business case for quality."

The theory of value-based purchasing is that purchasers—employers, the government, health care organizations, and, to a lesser extent, individual patients—can gather, analyze, and use quality, safety, and cost information on health care providers for the purpose of selectively contracting with providers based on their performance. Individual patients in a consumer-driven health care marketplace can vote with their feet by choosing health plans or hospitals based on quality and safety report cards. Employers and the government can mandate or encourage providers to pursue specific objectives through the use of contractual provisions, direct financial incentives, and ongoing quality monitoring.

How well does this theory translate into practice? With regard to shopping behavior by individual patients, the findings are rather discouraging. Considerable energy has been spent generating quality report cards on health care organizations and making this information available to consumers, . . . [but] few consumers actually use quality information in selecting providers. For the most part, patients continue to pick their providers based on personal recommendations or convenience. . . .

[V]alue-based purchasing is presently being pursued vigorously by only a handful of large employers and employer coalitions. Other employers have been reluctant to venture down this path due to a number of obstacles including inadequate manpower and expertise, the difficulty of collecting quality and outcomes data, questions about the credibility of existing quality measures, and financial constraints that drive employers to shop for providers and health plans primarily based on cost rather than quality. Additionally, employers in small markets or markets dominated by small businesses generally do not have sufficient leverage with hospitals to successfully push for improved patient safety.

Some employers have attempted to increase their collective bargaining power by forming coalitions to pursue patient safety initiatives. One coalition that has garnered considerable attention is the Leapfrog Group, a consortium of more than one hundred large employers . . . representing more than 31 million employees. [The] Leapfrog Group has announced the intention of steering these employees toward health care institutions that have instituted specic safety measures. Rather than rating [or picking] individual hospitals, the group has chosen to give consumers information about comparative institutional performance on three processes or practices believed to be associated with high-safety care: [computerized entry of physicians' orders, referral of patients for high-risk procedures to hospitals that perform a high volume of these procedures, and round-the-clock coverage of intensive care units by ICU physician specialists]. . . .

It appears that Leapfrog chose clear standards, for which compliance can be readily monitored to be able to rely largely on self-reporting. But the evidence that the standards themselves are the most effective approaches to improving safety has been questioned. . . . [Also, the] investments required to implement Leapfrog's recommendations are substantial, and the business case requires strong evidence that Leapfrog certification will raise market demand for a hospital's services enough to recoup these expenditures. . . . To create strong financial incentives for hospitals, initiatives such as Leapfrog need to significantly expand their purchaser and patient base and select safety standards that are possible for most or all hospitals to meet with a reasonable investment.

. . . Business-case advocates discouraged by this situation might articulate a business case along a second angle: rather than emphasizing the potential for increased market share as a result of safety improvement, as Leapfrog does, they might emphasize the costs of medical injuries and the potential for hospitals to avoid those costs by reducing injuries. . . . However, an often-missed nuance is that medical injury costs generally do not redound in a significant way to hospitals. Most of these costs—which include additional acute care costs, the cost of long-term care and maintenance of the disabled, lost income, and lost household production—fall on patients and their families, their health insurers, their employers, and state disability and income-support programs. Although the costs of poor safety are largely externalized to other parties, the costs of implementing safety improvement fall squarely on hospitals. For this reason . . . hospitals have little to gain financially from putting improvements in place. . . .

Presently, the tort system focuses liability heavily on individuals; the circumstances in which health care organizations are held liable are relatively limited. This approach makes sense if we believe that individual negligence is responsible for most preventable medical injuries. But if research reveals that errors often tend to be attributable not to individual carelessness or incompetence but to breakdowns in larger systems of care (which hospitals are in a much better position than individuals to x), then the wisdom of regulating patient safety through our current tort system may be cast into doubt. Such a finding would suggest, at a minimum, the need to refashion tort doctrine to incorporate greater enterprise liability. . . .

The Implications of Regulatory Pluralism

We have described a regulatory landscape in patient safety consisting of two streams of regulation—one from the top down and one from the bottom up—each of which is populated by multiple regulators. State and federal legislatures, state and federal administrative agencies, industry accrediting, professional and peer review organizations, courts and litigants, and purchaser organizations are all active regulators of patient safety today. Pluralistic regulation is a choice, not an inevitability. In other industries in which safety is a concern, we have limited the number of regulators. Dedicated national-level agencies have exclusive jurisdiction over nuclear power and aviation, for example; and the tort liability system has been largely eliminated as a regulator of workplace safety, replaced by the workers' compensation system and agency oversight. Who should regulate patient safety?

There is reason to hope that greater coordination and consensus on effective safety measures will emerge naturally over time, because many of the same experts advise the various regulators and because so much of this regulatory activity is quite new. There are already signs of moves in this direction: the JCAHO, [National Quality Forum, Agency for Healthcare Research and Quality] and Leapfrog are now collaborating on various measures and standards. However, all are adding new requirements, and there is still the sense on the part of the entities that they have a responsibility to serve the public by issuing mandates, even if that means that they cannot always wait for evidence to develop. . . .

All of the regulators on the scene today have a valuable contribution to make to safety improvement. However, as we have articulated, their collective impact has been somewhat enervated by lack of coordination and evidence-based standard setting. An optimal model of regulatory pluralism would address these concerns by better leveraging the distinctive institutional strengths of the various regulators. This capacity-leveraging model, as it might be called, recognizes that evidence-based patient safety regulation proceeds through a number of distinct steps, each of which calls for particular kinds of expertise and institutional capabilities. . . .

It is worth noting that despite its historical preeminence as a patient safety regulator, the tort liability system['s] . . . ability to set new standards for patient safety is circumscribed by the continued reliance of most states' courts on medical custom to set the standard of care. . . . The courts' ability to enforce compliance with standards is [also] limited by the fact that they can only address cases of noncompliance that come before them, and only a tiny fraction of patients injured by negligence le lawsuits. Thus, it is a mistake to rely on the tort system as a frontline regulator of patient safety. At best, it is a regulator of last resort, seeking to make whole those who have suffered injuries that other forms of regulation have tried and failed to prevent. . . .

REFERENCES

Danzon, P. 1985. *Medical Malpractice: Theory, Evidence, and Public Policy.* Cambridge, MA: Harvard University Press.

Institute of Medicine. 2001. *Crossing the Quality Chasm: A New Health System for the Twenty-First Century.* Washington, DC: National Academies Press. 2002. *Fostering Rapid Advances in Health Care: Learning from System Demonstrations.* Washington, DC: Institute of Medicine.

Kohn, L. T., J. M. Corrigan, and M. S. Donaldson, eds. 2000. *To Err Is Human: Building a Safer Health System.* Washington, DC: National Academies Press.

Liang, B. A. 2000. Risks of Reporting Sentinel Events. *Health Affairs* 19(5): 112-120.

Mello, M. M., and T. A. Brennan. 2002. Deterrence of Medical Errors: Theory and Evidence for Malpractice Reform. *University of Texas Law Review* 80: 1595-1637.

Studdert, D. M., M. M. Mello, and T. A. Brennan. 2004. Medical Malpractice. *New England Journal of Medicine* 350: 283-292.

Thomas, E. J., D. M. Studdert, H. R. Burstin, E. J. Orav, T. Zeena, E. J. Williams, K. M. Howard, P. C. Weiler, and T. A. Brennan. 2000. Incidence and Types of Adverse Events and Negligent Care in Utah and Colorado. *Medical Care* 38: 261-271.

Weiler, P. C. 1991. *Medical Malpractice on Trial.* Cambridge, MA: Harvard University Press.

Weiler, P. C., H. H. Hiatt, J. P. Newhouse, W. G. Johnson, T. A. Brennan, and L. L. Leape. 1993. *A Measure of Malpractice: Medical Injury, Malpractice Litigation, and Patient Compensation.* Cambridge, MA: Harvard University Press.

■ THE NECESSARY AND PROPER ROLE OF REGULATION TO ASSURE THE QUALITY OF HEALTH CARE*
Timothy Stolzfus Jost
25 Hous. L. Rev. 525 (1988)

A consideration of strategies for quality assurance should begin with an examination of the meaning of quality and error. Donabedian, the leading theorist of health care quality, . . . categorizes [quality] evaluation mechanisms in his famous

---

* This excerpt is a combination of three articles, the second one entitled Regulatory Approaches to Problems in the Quality of Medical Care: Diagnosis and Prescription (Copyright © 1989 by the Regents of the University of California), and the third one entitled Oversight of the Quality of Medical Care: Regulation, Management, or the Market? They are reprinted with permission. Headings, footnote numbering, and to some extent the structure of the argument have been altered from the original.

typology as concerned with structure, process, or outcome.[2] A structural evaluation (e.g., a licensure examination) focuses on underlying capacity to deliver quality care: How much does the doctor know; how well is the hospital equipped? . . . [S]tructural aspects of care are the easiest to define and to evaluate; thus, many strategies rely, at least in part, on structural evaluation.

Process evaluation studies the process through which care is delivered. It considers, for example, whether a drug was properly prescribed in the appropriate dosage given the patient's symptoms. Process is more difficult to evaluate than structure. Process evaluation is usually based on professional consensus as to appropriate procedures for a given problem. It forms the basis for many peer review programs. It has been criticized as overemphasizing the technical nature of care and contributing to health care cost inflation through this emphasis. Moreover, process norms are model treatments for model cases. It is difficult to adapt them to address the wide variations found in patients and their conditions.

Finally, outcome analysis considers the results of care: Did the patient get better; did the condition improve? Comparing hospital mortality and morbidity statistics for treatment of a particular condition is a form of outcome analysis. Outcome analysis is the most difficult form of quality evaluation because the duration, timing, or extent of outcomes of optimal care are often hard to specify. Data on the outcomes of care delivered by professionals or institutions cannot be compared usefully unless adjustments are made for variations in case mix and severity of conditions. It is often difficult to relate a specific outcome to a particular medical intervention, and outcomes are often clear only when it is too late to affect practice. Yet outcome analysis looks at the ends of medical care rather than the means, and is thus ultimately most telling. The medical malpractice system has always begun its inquiry with a bad outcome, though it ultimately relies on process analysis. . . .

Notes: Quality Measurement and Control

1. *Overview.* The purpose of this section is to put in broader context the role that malpractice law plays in the deterrence and punishment of medical error and in the improvement of medical quality. To sharpen your focus, review the types of bad medical outcomes identified earlier, the dimensions of quality surveyed by Jost, and the various social and legal responses available, noting which responses are addressed to which types and dimensions of poor quality. Based on the resulting patterns and gaps, how would you articulate the strongest case for the role of tort law? What types of medical mistakes should it be most concerned with? Which types should it ignore?

2. *Medical Licensure.* Professor Mello and colleagues fail to mention another source of medical quality regulation — physician licensure. As discussed in Chapter 10.A, each state has a disciplinary process to consider complaints against physicians

---

2. Donabedian, Criteria and Standards for Quality Assessment and Monitoring, 12 Quality Rev. Bull. 99 (1986); Donabedian, Commentary on Some Studies on the Quality of Care, Health Care Fin. Ref., 1987 Supp., at 75, 76-77; 1 A. Donabedian, Explorations in Quality Assessment and Monitoring: The Definition of Quality and Approaches to Its Assessment 4-6 (1980).

from either patients or other physicians. Much like state bars for attorney discipline, these boards of medical examiners are composed of other physicians and therefore are subject to the limits of self-regulation noted above. As summarized by Prof. Sawicki in the article excerpted at page 1259, "medical boards rarely take disciplinary action on the basis of incompetent medical practice or poor quality of care." Instead, many of their actions are based on financial misdeeds, substance abuse, or inappropriate relationships with patients. Character, Competence, and the Principles of Medical Discipline, 13 J. Health Care L. & Pol'y 285 (2010).

3. *Donabedian's Categories.* To sharpen your understanding of the structure/process/outcome categories developed by Donabedian, consider which category best describes the way that each of the following measures ensures the quality of motor vehicle driving: (1) requiring drivers to pass a written exam; (2) requiring an on-road test; (3) vehicle inspection laws that check brake lights, windshield wipers, etc.; (4) enforcing speed limits; (5) increasing insurance premiums when drivers are involved in accidents.

4. *The Information Explosion.* Other influential standards-setting organizations, in addition to those that Professor Mello and colleagues mention, include the National Committee for Quality Assurance (NCQA), which focuses on performance measures for HMOs and other health plans using what is known as the Health Plan and Employer Data and Information Set (HEDIS). HEDIS entails measures such as consumer satisfaction, rates of childhood immunization and cancer screening, and management of asthma and diabetes. Medicare does something similar using its Consumer Assessment of Health Plans and Systems (CAHPS) survey.

The federal government has also taken strides to rank hospitals according to how well their patients do. The Center for Medicare and Medicaid Services (CMS), which oversees Medicare and Medicaid, rewards hospitals that report a variety of quality measures focused on process steps in caring for heart attacks, pneumonia, and surgery patients. CMS also reports hospital mortality statistics, adjusted for various risk factors (so that hospitals are not rated poorly simply for treating sicker patients). In addition to simply reporting this information, CMS is implementing payment policies that reward better-performing hospitals or penalize worse ones. See Chapter 9.E.2 and the casebook Web site for further details, www.health-law.org.

So far, these "report card" efforts have not extended (much) to physicians. Medicare is beginning to move in this direction, but a variety of concerns will likely slow progress. Physician organizations have objected to (1) the burden of providing all the relevant information, and (2) how valid the information is. On validity, consider the situation of a physician who complains that his poor surgical outcomes scorecard is due to the fact that his colleagues refer him the most difficult cases, in recognition of his being the very best in the community at what he does. A related concern is that, if outcome measures (like death) are not appropriately adjusted for patient risk factors, then physicians will avoid patients who are likely to hurt their scorecards. See Timothy Hofer et al., The Unreliability of Individual Physician "Report Cards" for Assessing the Costs and Quality of Care of a Chronic Disease, 281 JAMA 2098 (1999) (finding that report cards "were unable to detect reliably true practice differences" and that their use "may foster an environment in which physicians can most easily avoid being penalized by avoiding . . . [more difficult patients who have not responded well to treatment]").

5. *Total Quality Management.* Central to any comprehensive discussion of health care quality is the concept of "continuous quality improvement" (CQI), also known as "total quality management" (TQM). This is a managerial concept imported from manufacturing industries that owes its popularity to management gurus whose ideas were first implemented by Japanese companies and are considered an important reason why they so quickly surpassed American quality standards in consumer electronics and automobile manufacturing. In health care, CQI signals a paradigm shift away from identifying isolated mistakes and deterring malefactors, to improving the quality of all outcomes through systems improvements. CQI assumes that professionals generally are diligent and well motivated and so only need better information and support in order to do a better job. Its philosophy is captured in the title of the first reading in this chapter, Making Medical Errors into "Medical Treasures," since it views mistakes as opportunities to learn, not occasions for blame and punishment. CQI attempts to target the entire range of medical outcomes, not simply to eliminate the "bad apples," and it sees errors as resulting more from system flaws than from individual misfeasance. Institute of Medicine, Crossing the Quality Chasm: A New Health System for the Twenty-first Century (2001).

Troyen Brennan, co-author with Professor Mello, supra, teamed up with Donald Berwick, a proponent of quality improvement who now heads CMS, to write New Rules: Regulation, Markets, and the Quality of American Health Care (1996). They argue that the entire legal regime is antithetical to the philosophy of quality improvement. Can you imagine how that might be the case? For a contrary argument, see David A. Hyman & Charles Silver, The Poor State of Health Care Quality in the U.S.: Is Malpractice Liability Part of the Problem or Part of the Solution?, 90 Corn. L. Rev. 893 (2005).

6. *Bibliography.* On **modernizing quality regulation in the information age** (note 4), see Kristin Madison, Regulating Health Care Quality in an Information Age, 40 U.C. Davis L. Rev. (2007); Kristin Madison, Donabedian's Legacy: The Future of Health Care Quality Law and Policy, 10 Ind. Health L. Rev. 325 (2013); William M. Sage, Regulating Through Information: Disclosure Laws and American Health Care, 99 Colum. L. Rev. 1701 (1999); Symposium, 31 J. Leg. Med. 9 (2010); Symposium, 24(1) Health Aff. (Jan. 2005); Symposium, 23 Health Aff. (Oct. 2004) (special supp.).

For studies that examine the **impact of comparative outcomes measures on actual consumer and provider behavior**, see Mark Chassin, Achieving and Sustaining Improved Quality, 21(4) Health Aff. 40 (July 2002) (finding some impact); Ashish K. Jha & Arnold M. Epstein, The Predictive Accuracy of the New York State Coronary Artery Bypass Surgery Report-Card System, 25(3) Health Aff. 844 (June 2006) (finding no impact); David Dranove et al., Is More Information Better? The Effects of "Report Cards" on Health Care Providers, 111 J. Pol. Econ. 555 (2003) (finding negative impact by prompting physicians and hospitals to avoid sicker or more severe cases); Symposium, 35 Health Aff. 563 (2016).

On **quality measurement and improvement generally**, see Stephen R. Latham, System Responsibility: Three Readings of the IOM Report on Medical Error, 27 Am. J. L. & Med. 145 (2001); 335 New Eng. J. Med., issues 12-15 (1996); Symposium, 16(3) Health Aff. (May 1997); Symposium, 12 Widener L. Rev. 1 (2005); Katharine Tassell, Harmonizing the Affordable Care Act with the Three Main National Systems for Healthcare Quality Improvement, 78 Brook L. Rev. 883 (2013).

B. PHYSICIAN LIABILITY

1. The Custom-Based Standard of Care

■ McCOURT v. ABERNATHY
457 S.E.2d 603 (S.C. 1995)

SHAW, Acting Associate Justice.

[The following facts are quoted from Wendy McCourt's medical record: "This patient is a 23-year-old white female who was admitted to the hospital with shortness of breath and chest wall pain. The patient states about five days prior to admission, she was working with some horses doing castrations. While trying to hold a horse, the horse suddenly bolted and hyperextended her left shoulder. . . . The patient also relates that about two days prior to the horse incident, she pricked her finger with a pin. She continued working around manure and other agents in the barns with the horses. She had developed a slight redness around the pin prick over the fat pad of the left second finger."]

[Doctors Abernathy and Clyde are board certified family practitioners who practice together in Anderson, South Carolina.] . . . There is evidence Wendy was seen by Dr. Abernathy in his office at the time [of the horse incident] and was treated for a pulled muscle. [Three or four days later,] on Sunday, March 13, her condition worsened and Wendy went to the Anderson Memorial Hospital emergency room. She was experiencing greater pain and had difficulty breathing. Dr. Clyde examined Wendy at that time and treated her for a pulled chest muscle. There is evidence Dr. Clyde treated the puncture wound to Wendy's finger at that time.[2] She was given prescriptions for Motrin and Co-Tylenol. She returned to her home.

The following day, March 14, Wendy's condition became significantly worse and she again sought treatment at the emergency room. She was examined by an emergency room physician who ran some blood tests. This physician indicated an immediate need to admit Wendy to the hospital. He telephoned Dr. Abernathy and was given permission to admit Wendy. At 6:30 that evening, Dr. Abernathy examined Wendy and observed the injured finger, for which he prescribed Keflex, an oral antibiotic.

At 9:00 the following morning, both Dr. Abernathy and Dr. Clyde saw Wendy while making rounds at the hospital. By that time, Wendy's condition had worsened yet more and the doctors consulted Dr. Kovaz, an internist. Although appellants requested a consult from Dr. Kovaz, they did not express any urgency in his seeing her. After examining Wendy, Dr. Kovaz immediately moved her to the intensive care unit with a diagnosis of sepsis, a bacterial infection. Although treatment with intravenous antibiotics was begun at that time, her condition continued to deteriorate. Over the next four days, her skin began to slough off, her eyes filled with blood,

---

2. Steven McCourt testified Dr. Clyde pointed out the puncture wound on Wendy's finger which Dr. Clyde proceeded to clean and dress. He stated the finger was red and swollen to almost twice the normal size, and was having some sort of discharge. He further testified the wound was very noticeable and Wendy indicated it was a result of a pin prick that occurred a couple of days earlier.

her feet turned black, she bled from her nose, mouth and pores, and she became bloated beyond recognition. On March 19, 1988, Wendy McCourt died from beta strep septicemia with multiple organ system failure secondary to the sepsis.*

Respondent presented expert testimony from Dr. Neal Craine and Dr. Kenneth DeHart. Dr. Craine stated Wendy's illness was caused by "an unfortunate circumstance where transient bacteria in the bloodstream landed in an area already traumatized by the injury with the horse." He testified, assuming, as the "Death Summary" indicates, Dr. Abernathy saw Wendy on the ninth, she had a puncture wound to the finger and it was known she was working around horses, he should have put her on preventive antibiotics on that day. He stated it would also have been below the standard of care for Dr. Clyde to have observed an infected finger on the thirteenth and not treat her with antibiotics nor order laboratory tests. He stated he felt Wendy had a 100 percent chance of survival on the thirteenth had she been started on antibiotics at that time. Based on the test results received on the afternoon of the fourteenth, he stated that a doctor should know the patient was seriously ill and should have suspected sepsis. He concluded Wendy's life could have been saved if antibiotics had been started on the ninth, which would have prevented or treated an early infection of the finger. He also stated, more likely than not, Wendy could have been saved on the thirteenth by treatment with antibiotics as well as on the fourteenth with aggressive antibiotic therapy. He stated it was also below the standard of care to wait until the fifteenth to call in a specialist.

Dr. DeHart likewise testified [that] . . . failure to treat [the infected finger] prophylactically fell below the standard of care. . . . As to Dr. Abernathy's treatment on the fourteenth, he testified it was "profoundly below the standard of care," not because he missed the diagnosis, but because he failed to order aggressive observation and failed to request consultation intervention.

This matter was tried by a jury and on January 7, 1993 the jury returned the following verdicts for appellant: [$700,000 in actual damages and $1,000,000 in punitive damages against Dr. Abernathy, and $350,000 in actual damages and $500,000 in punitive damages against Dr. Clyde.] TOTAL VERDICTS: $2,550,000. . . .

Appellants first contend the trial judge erred in failing to charge several jury instructions relating to mistake in diagnosis or error in judgment in a medical malpractice cause of action.[4] . . . [T]he appellants assert all of the charges stand for

---

* [In the popular press, beta strep is known as the "flesh-eating" bacteria, as described by Dr. Gawande at page 255. Septicemia is an extremely serious condition in which an infection invades the bloodstream and spreads throughout the body, much like a localized cancer can metastasize. — Eds.]

4. Oral request #1: When a physician exercises ordinary care and skill in keeping within recognized and proven methods, he is not liable for the result of a bona fide mistake of judgment. There is no responsibility unless it is negligent, as I have defined that to you, so as to be inconsistent with that degree of skill which is the duty of every physician practicing in his specialty to possess and use. . . . Request #13: Ladies and Gentlemen, when a physician exercises ordinary care and skill in keeping within recognized and proven methods, he is not liable for the result of a mere mistake of judgment or for a bad result which does not occur because of any negligence on his part. There is no responsibility for error of judgment or for a bad result unless it is so negligent as to be inconsistent with that degree of skill which it is the duty of every practitioner practicing in his specialty to possess.

the proposition that a physician is not liable for a mistake in diagnosis or error in judgment if he acts within the appropriate standard of care. . . . We disagree. . . . [T]he requested charges may have a tendency to confuse the jury. Some of the charges imply to the jury that an error in judgment is actionable only if made in bad faith. Such an instruction would impose an unrealistic burden on the plaintiff to prove the doctor's judgment was rendered with less than good faith.

. . . [T]he trial judge gave the following relevant charges:

> . . . The mere fact that the plaintiff's expert may use a different approach is not considered a deviation from the recognized standard of medical care. Nor is the standard violated because the expert disagrees with a defendant as to what is the best or better approach in treating a patient. Medicine is an inexact science, and generally qualified physicians may differ as to what constitutes a preferable course of treatment. Such differences due to preference . . . do not amount to malpractice.
>
> I further charge you that the degree of skill and care that a physician must use in diagnosing a condition is that which would be exercised by competent practitioners in the defendant doctor's field of medicine. In South Carolina the question of whether a physician, in making a diagnosis deviated from the applicable standard of care either by not employing a particular procedure or by not ordering a particular test is to be determined by what an ordinary careful and prudent physician would have done under the same or similar circumstances. . . .
>
> Negligence may not be inferred from a bad result. Our law says that a physician is not an insurer of health, and a physician is not required to guarantee results. He undertakes only to meet the standard of skill possessed generally by others practicing in his field under similar circumstances.

Even if we were to assume the appellants' requested charges were the current and correct law of the state, we find the instructions [given] as a whole clearly intimate that a mere mistake in diagnosis or error in judgment alone is insufficient to support a finding of malpractice. Accordingly, we find no error.

Appellants next contend the trial judge erred in denying their motions for new trial . . . on the basis of the excessiveness of the punitive damages awards. They contend the damages are excessive and, because there was no evidence of conduct rising to the level of recklessness, the verdict was the result of passion and prejudice. We disagree.

In order for a plaintiff to recover punitive damages, there must be evidence the defendant's conduct was willful, wanton, or in reckless disregard of the plaintiff's rights. A conscious failure to exercise due care constitutes willfulness. . . .

We find the record before us contains evidence that both Dr. Abernathy and Dr. Clyde consciously failed to exercise due care in treating Wendy. This evidence includes, but is not limited to: (1) failure to properly diagnose and treat Wendy within the standard of care on three separate occasions; (2) failure to order timely diagnostic tests in light of continual complaints and no improvement of Wendy's condition; (3) failure to appreciate the seriousness of Wendy's deteriorating condition in the face of highly abnormal blood work; (4) failure to aggressively monitor Wendy's deteriorating condition; and (5) failure to promptly seek the immediate aid of a specialist once the seriousness of Wendy's condition became apparent. While the evidence indicates a more severe degree of culpability on the part of Dr. Abernathy than Dr. Clyde, the record contains sufficient evidence of conduct on the part of both doctors to support the awards of punitive damages. The jury's determination of damages is entitled to substantial deference. We find no abuse of the trial judge's discretion in this respect. . . . Affirmed.

■ LOCKE v. PACHTMAN
521 N.W.2d 786 (Mich. 1994)

MALLETT, Justice.

In this medical malpractice action, the trial judge granted defendants' motion for a directed verdict at the close of the plaintiff's proofs. The court of appeals affirmed, finding that plaintiff had failed to make a prima facie showing of the standard of care related to defendants' allegedly negligent conduct. We affirm.

I

On August 5, 1981, plaintiff Shirley Locke underwent a vaginal hysterectomy with entocele and rectocele repair at the University of Michigan Hospital.* The procedure was performed by defendant, Dr. Judith Pachtman, then a fourth-year resident in gynecology. Codefendant, Dr. James Roberts, was the attending physician and was present for most of the surgery.**

Dr. Pachtman testified that she performed the first two procedures, the hysterectomy and entocele repair, without complication, although the entocele repair took longer than expected. Following the entocele repair, Dr. Roberts left the room to attend another operation that had been previously scheduled.

Dr. Pachtman then began the rectocele repair. Upon Dr. Pachtman's initial insertion into the levator ani muscle, the needle she was using broke. One-half to two-thirds of the needle, a length of about 1.5 cm, broke off and lodged somewhere within that muscle. Dr. Pachtman searched unsuccessfully for the broken portion of the needle for 15 to 20 minutes. At that time, Dr. Roberts returned and joined Dr. Pachtman in searching for the needle fragment.

Drs. Pachtman and Roberts utilized a silver probe to X-ray the affected area, in an attempt to locate the broken portion of the needle. After ascertaining the approximate location of the fragment, they decided to close the old incision and to continue their search through a new incision. After unsuccessfully searching for the needle for another 45 minutes to one hour, they abandoned the search and closed the second incision. Both doctors indicated that they felt it was in the plaintiff's best interest to terminate the surgery at that point, even though they had failed to locate the needle fragment.

---

* As explained at trial, an entocele is an out-pouching or hernia of the peritoneal cavity where the bowel protrudes into the area between the vagina and the rectum. A rectocele is a hernial protrusion of the rectum through the posterior vaginal wall.

** At trial, Dr. Roberts explained that he was the senior medical officer involved in the procedure. However, he also stated that, as attending physician, his role was to act as assistant and consultant to Dr. Pachtman, who actually performed the surgery. Dr. Pachtman essentially agreed with Dr. Roberts' characterization of his role in the procedure, but asserted nevertheless that, as attending physician, Dr. Roberts had "ultimate responsibility" for the surgery.

Plaintiff testified that after the surgery Dr. Pachtman informed her of the needle breakage and stated that the needle was entrenched in the muscle and therefore could remain there without causing her any problems. However, after experiencing considerable pain and discomfort, plaintiff consulted with another physician, Dr. Frances Couch. Dr. Couch advised removing the needle fragment, and, subsequently, she performed the surgical procedure, successfully locating and removing the broken portion of the needle.

Plaintiff filed suit against Drs. Pachtman and Roberts, alleging negligence on various grounds, including the use of a needle that they knew or should have known was too small and failing to locate and remove the needle fragment. Plaintiff claimed that she suffers from severe pain, disfigurement, and limitation of body movement and functions, as well as experiencing mental and emotional distress. Plaintiff's husband, Danny Locke, filed a derivative claim.

In testimony presented at trial, plaintiff's expert witness, Dr. Couch, was unable to identify any negligent conduct on the part of either Dr. Pachtman or Dr. Roberts. Dr. Couch also stated that she could not give an opinion regarding the adequacy of the needle size, because she had never viewed the needle intact. She explained that she could not identify the size of the needle without viewing the needle in its entirety.

When questioned generally regarding the cause of needle breakage and its relation to the standard of care, Dr. Couch made two separate statements. At one point Dr. Couch stated that the standard of care did not relate to needle breakage at all, but rather to how one dealt with it, suggesting that needle breakage was simply one of the risks of surgery. Later, without relating this point to a standard of care, she noted that a surgeon's "incorrect technique" often causes a needle to break. When asked to describe what she meant by incorrect technique, Dr. Couch described instances in which a surgeon fails to manipulate the needle correctly, such as by inserting it at the wrong angle or applying too much force. Dr. Couch also testified that she had previously had a needle break while performing surgery.

In addition to Dr. Couch's expert testimony, plaintiff introduced evidence regarding a number of statements allegedly made by Dr. Pachtman following the surgery. Plaintiff's brother, Reverend Gary Heniser, testified that, while he was at the hospital visiting his sister, Dr. Pachtman told him, " 'I knew the needle was too small when I used it.' " Coplaintiff Danny Locke testified that Dr. Pachtman had also spoken to him about the surgery: "[S]he told me that it was her fault, that she used the wrong needle, and she was sorry." Finally, Shirley Locke testified that Dr. Pachtman had told her: "I knew that needle was too small when the new scrub nurse handed it to me. It wasn't her fault because she was new, but I chose to use it anyway and it's my fault and I am really sorry. . . ."

Both Dr. Pachtman and Dr. Roberts testified at trial. Neither acknowledged any negligent behavior in the choice of needle, the needle breakage, or their subsequent search for the needle fragment.

At the close of plaintiff's proofs, the trial court granted defendants' motion for directed verdict on the ground that plaintiff had failed to make a prima facie showing regarding the standard of care. Plaintiff's motion for a new trial was denied, and, in a divided opinion, the court of appeals affirmed. . . .

II

Proof of a medical malpractice claim requires the demonstration of the following four factors: (1) the applicable standard of care, (2) breach of that standard of care by the defendant, (3) injury, and (4) proximate causation between the alleged breach and the injury.[6] To survive a motion for directed verdict, the plaintiff must make a prima facie showing regarding each of the above elements.

Plaintiff argues that the lower courts erred in finding that she had failed to demonstrate the standard of care applicable to defendants' conduct. Plaintiff contends that expert testimony was sufficient to establish this point, and, further, that the standard of care and breach of that standard were inferable under the doctrine of res ipsa loquitur and because the alleged negligence was within the common understanding of the jury.

We agree with the lower courts' determination that no prima facie showing was made, and therefore we affirm the directed verdict entered for the defendants.

A

. . . Plaintiff argues first that the standard of care attributable to Dr. Pachtman was established by way of expert testimony. This court has long recognized the importance of expert testimony in establishing a medical malpractice claim, and the need to educate the jury and the court regarding matters not within their common purview. As we have previously explained:

> In a case involving professional service the ordinary layman is not equipped by common knowledge and experience to judge of the skill and competence of that service and determine whether it squares with the standard of such professional practice in the community. For that, the aid of expert testimony from those learned in the profession involved is required.

While we have recognized exceptions to this requirement, the benefit of expert testimony, particularly in demonstrating the applicable standard of care, cannot be overstated.

In this case, plaintiff contends that the standard of care applicable to Dr. Pachtman was established by Dr. Couch's expert testimony. For this point, plaintiff relies on Dr. Couch's statement that needle breakage often occurs because of the surgeon's "incorrect technique." Plaintiff asserts that this testimony, coupled with Dr. Pachtman's admissions regarding use of a needle she knew to be too small, were sufficient to establish the standard of care and breach of that standard.

---

6. [Michigan statutes state:]

In an action alleging malpractice the plaintiff shall have the burden of proving that in light of the state of the art existing at the time of the alleged malpractice: (a) The defendant, if a general practitioner, failed to provide the plaintiff the recognized standard of acceptable professional practice in the community in which the defendant practices or in a similar community, and that as a proximate result of the defendant failing to provide that standard, the plaintiff suffered an injury. (b) The defendant, if a specialist, failed to provide the recognized standard of care within that specialty as reasonably applied in light of the facilities available in the community or other facilities reasonably available under the circumstances, and as a proximate result of the defendant failing to provide that standard, the plaintiff suffered an injury.

Dr. Couch's testimony with regard to the standard of care associated with needle breakage was rather confused. At one point she suggested that needle breakage was merely one of the risks of surgery, and that needle breakage did not ordinarily signal a violation of the standard of care. . . . Dr. Couch later testified that needle breakage may be attributable to a surgeon's "incorrect technique":

Q. From your experience and your training can the manner in which a surgeon utilizes a needle cause it to break?
A. I would say most of the time that's the case. It's a matter of incorrect technique.
Q. Could you discuss that?
A. Well, a needle is curved. If you forget the needle is curved and you push against the curve instead of with the curve the needle will break. If you try to put a needle through an instrument it doesn't go through steel. If it's not positioned correctly in a tissue and you're trying to draw it through against a clamp it will break. . . . Generally, that's most of the reason why they break. You are putting force against where it wasn't made to be put against.

As the lower courts found, it is indeed questionable whether Dr. Couch's latter testimony on this point was sufficient to establish a standard of care with regard to "incorrect technique." Dr. Couch, while presenting one way in which needles break, never went so far as to relate that discussion to a standard of care. In effect, she never explained what a reasonably prudent surgeon would do, in keeping with the standards of professional practice, that might not have been done by Dr. Pachtman. Accordingly, the jury would have had no standard against which to measure Dr. Pachtman's conduct. This factor, coupled with the conflicting nature of Dr. Couch's testimony, leads us to believe that the standard of care was not sufficiently established. . . .

B

Plaintiff next argues that the statements allegedly made by Dr. Pachtman were themselves sufficient to establish the standard of care and breach of that standard. Plaintiff contends that her case is governed by this court's decision in Orozco v. Henry Ford Hosp., 408 Mich. 248, 290 N.W.2d 363 (1980). . . . Plaintiff's reliance upon *Orozco* is misplaced. In *Orozco*, the plaintiff testified that during his hernial surgery he heard one of the surgeons say, "Oops, I cut in the wrong place." Following the surgery, one of his testicles atrophied. At trial, an expert witness testified that this injury was likely due to an impairment of the blood supply to the testicles during the surgery.

At the close of Orozco's proofs, the trial court granted the defendants' motion for a directed verdict, and the court of appeals affirmed, finding that the plaintiff had failed to make a prima facie showing of the applicable standard of care.[9] This court reversed the court of appeals by per curiam opinion. The court found that

---

9. In reaching this conclusion, the court of appeals relied on Lince v. Monson. In Lince, this court held that expert testimony was required in order for the jury to determine whether the defendants violated the standard of care when they mistakenly sutured the plaintiff's ureter in responding to excessive bleeding. 363 Mich. at 142, 108 N.W.2d 845.

expert testimony was not necessary because jury members would be able to determine, from their own common knowledge, whether the defendants' actions violated the applicable standard of care. As the court explained:

> Here Orozco offered the fact of the injury, a medical explanation of how that injury likely occurred, and an admission by the surgeon that he cut in the wrong place. Paraphrasing *Lince*, "[t]he question is whether the action of defendants conformed to standards of good practice in the community. Common knowledge and the experience of ordinary laymen do . . . equip them to give the answer in a case such as this" when an expert testifies that the likely cause of injury was an impairment of the blood supply to the testicles in the course of the operation and the plaintiff testifies that the surgeon said, "Oops, I cut in the wrong place."

. . . This decision was in line with previous case law holding that expert testimony is not normally required where the defendant mistakenly treated or did injury to a portion of the body that was free of disease and not designated for treatment. Sullivan v. Russell, 417 Mich. 398, 408, 338 N.W.2d 181 (1983) (no expert testimony was necessary where a dentist mistakenly ground three of the plaintiff's teeth not intended for treatment); Higdon v. Carlebach, 348 Mich. 363, 374, 83 N.W.2d 296 (1957) (expert testimony was not required where a dentist, using a rotating disk to separate two of the plaintiff's teeth, mistakenly cut into her tongue).

Turning to the present case, we hold that the lower courts correctly concluded that Dr. Pachtman's statements were insufficient to make a prima facie showing. While the statements may have indicated Dr. Pachtman's belief that she made a mistake or acted in error, a jury could not reasonably infer from those statements alone that Dr. Pachtman's actions did not conform to the standard of professional practice for the community as a whole.

Unlike the situation presented in *Orozco*, the standard of care associated with needle choice and needle breakage is not accessible to the jury absent expert guidance. Plaintiff has provided no guidance with regard to what options were available to Dr. Pachtman and which of them she should have chosen. In short, there was no testimony regarding what a reasonably prudent surgeon would have done in Dr. Pachtman's situation. We agree with the court of appeals determination that the jury should not be left to speculate in this regard. It is precisely to avoid such speculation that expert testimony is ordinarily required. . . .

E

Plaintiff asserts liability against Dr. Roberts on grounds . . . [of] negligent supervision. However, . . . plaintiff's negligent supervision claim is also not supported by the record. There was uncontroverted testimony, including testimony from plaintiff's own expert, to the fact that it was not unusual for an attending physician at University of Michigan Hospital to leave a resident alone during portions of a procedure. There was no testimony suggesting that such action was violative of a standard of care, nor do we find that point inferable by the jury. Therefore this claim is also without merit. . . .

CAVANAGH, C.J., and RILEY, BRICKLEY, BOYLE, and ROBERT P. GRIFFIN, JJ., concur.

LEVIN, Justice (dissenting). . . .

The question presented is whether Pachtman's statements—in effect admitting error but not in lawyer jargon such as "standard medical practice in this community"—are prima facie evidence of the standard of care and breach. . . .

The majority concludes that Pachtman's statements may have expressed her belief that she violated her personal standard of care, and her personal standard of care may have been higher than the prevailing standard of care among physicians in the community. . . . It is no more probable, however, that the statements concerned her personal standard of care than that they concerned the generally applicable standard of care. The statements refer neither to a personal nor a general standard of care. The statements can reasonably be read either way, and a jury should decide the meaning of Pachtman's statements.[10] . . . This is not a case in which a physician merely expressed general dissatisfaction with her overall performance or merely expressed regret.

Cases from other jurisdictions indicate that statements like Pachtman's—that confess error with reasonable specificity—are prima facie evidence of the standard of care and breach.

In Greenwood v. Harris, 362 P.2d 85, 87-88 (Okla. 1961), the plaintiff alleged that the physician erroneously diagnosed her pregnancy as a tumor, and then performed unnecessary surgery that left the plaintiff with an unsightly and painful scar. The plaintiff's only evidence concerning the standard of care was the physician's statements to the plaintiff and her husband that he "should have made more tests," and that he "wasn't satisfied with the lab report [and] should have had the tests run again, . . . should have made some other tests." The Oklahoma Supreme Court held that those statements alone were prima facie evidence of the standard of care and breach. The court said: We can interpret these statements in no other way than as an admission that a faulty diagnosis had been made due to the failure of the defendant to use and apply the customary and usual degree of skill exercised by physicians in the community. . . .

In Sheffield v. Runner, 163 Cal. App. 2d 48, 328 P.2d 828 (1958), a physician's statement that he should have put the patient in a hospital was held to be prima facie evidence of the standard of care and breach. In Wickoff v. James, 159 Cal. App. 2d 664, 324 P.2d 661 (1958), a physician's statement that he "sure messed up" was held to be prima facie evidence of the standard of care and breach. In Robertson v. LaCroix, 534 P.2d 17, 19 (Okla. App., 1975), a physician's statement that he "just made a mistake and got over too far" during surgery was held to be prima facie evidence of the standard of care and breach. . . .

Other state supreme courts have found that the standard of care was not established by statements that fail to explain with relative precision what the physician should have done. . . . In Maxwell v. Women's Clinic, 102 Idaho 53, 54, 625 P.2d 407 (1981), the plaintiff claimed that the defendant physician negligently performed a

10. In Wooten v. Curry, 50 Tenn. App. 549, 552, 554, 362 S.W.2d 820 (1961), as distinguished from the instant case, the physician, under the law of Tennessee, was subject to liability for malpractice if his conduct fell below his personal standard of care. . . . [See also Burton v. Brooklyn Doctor's Hospital, 452 N.Y.S.2d 875 (1982) (modifying treatment to conduct a medical experiment violates duty to exercise physicians' best judgment, even though treatment rendered was within existing standard of care).]

tubal ligation. The plaintiff's only evidence regarding the standard of care was the physician's statement that he "obviously messed up." The Idaho Supreme Court held that summary judgment against the plaintiff was properly granted because the plaintiff did not present sufficient evidence of breach of the standard of care. In Cobbs v. Grant, 104 Cal. Rptr. 505, the physician's statement that he "blamed himself for [the plaintiff] being back in there [the hospital]" was held not to be prima facie evidence of the standard of care and breach. In both *Maxwell* and [*Cobbs*], the physicians' statements did not explain relatively precisely—as did Pachtman's—how they had erred.

I conclude, consistent with precedent from other jurisdictions, that Pachtman's statement satisfied Locke's burden of presenting prima facie evidence of the standard of care and breach.

◼ THE ROLE OF THE JURY IN MODERN MALPRACTICE LAW
Philip G. Peters, Jr.
87 Iowa L. Rev. 909 (2002)

A. TRADITIONAL DEFERENCE TO MEDICAL CUSTOMS

For more than a century, courts have given physicians the power to set their own standard of care. This delegation of standard-setting authority to private parties dramatically distinguished malpractice actions from other negligence litigation. . . . In most negligence actions, the defendant's compliance with industry customs is simply one factor for the jury to consider. . . . Since the late nineteenth century, courts have treated physicians quite differently. Medical customs are not merely admissible; they define the physician's legal standard of care.[2] In the words of Dean Prosser, the custom-based standard of care "gives the medical profession . . . the privilege, which is usually emphatically denied to other groups, of setting their own legal standards of conduct, merely by adopting their own practices."

By deferring conclusively to medical customs, the courts materially changed the function that the jury would perform in malpractice actions. In an ordinary negligence action, the jury must consider all of the evidence adduced and then determine whether the defendant has behaved reasonably under the circumstances. To do so, the jury must make important judgments about the value of life and personal safety and about the proper level of safety precautions. In a malpractice action, by contrast, the jury does not make these value judgments. Instead, they have been

2. See, e.g., James A. Henderson, Jr. & John A. Siliciano, Universal Health Care and the Continued Reliance on Custom in Determining Medical Malpractice, 79 Cornell L. Rev. 1382, 1384 (1994) (stating custom is rule in medical malpractice); Alan H. McCoid, The Care Required of Medical Practitioners, 12 Vand. L. Rev. 549, 560, 605-606 (1959) (same); Clarence Morris, Custom and Negligence, 42 Colum. L. Rev. 1147, 1158 (1942) (stating custom normally should define standard of care); Theodore Silver, One Hundred Years of Harmful Error: The Historical Jurisprudence of Medical Malpractice, 1992 Wis. L. Rev. 1193, 1212 (stating custom determines standard of care).

delegated to the medical profession. The jury's job is merely to determine whether the defendant has complied with the norms set by the industry.

B. THE RECENT RETREAT FROM A CUSTOM-BASED STANDARD

Gradually, quietly and relentlessly, state courts are abandoning the custom-based standard of care.* Thus far, a dozen states have expressly refused to equate reasonable care with customary practices. . . . These states now use a "reasonable physician" test. Another nine states, although not explicitly addressing the role of custom, have also endorsed the "reasonable physician" test. In these states, . . . the jury decides whether the physician behaved reasonably, not whether she complied with custom. Although experts still battle in the courtroom, they argue about what physicians *should* do, not what physicians *ordinarily* do.

In addition to the states that have moved to a reasonability standard, several other states have case law that is too ambiguous or inconsistent to classify confidently. As a consequence, the fraction of states that unambiguously endorse the custom-based standard of care has fallen from a clear majority to a shrinking plurality.

Finally, courts in states that purportedly endorse the custom-based standard often allow plaintiffs more latitude than the law on the books would imply. Plaintiffs in these states commonly reach a jury even when their experts have stated only that the defendant's conduct is not "acceptable" or "appropriate" or fails to meet the "standard of care." The experts in these cases have not been required to testify that the defendant deviated from customary practice. . . .

Whatever the explanation, it is clear today that courts defer less to physicians than they once did and are less willing to erect special rules for health care providers. For example, physicians are no longer exempt from the antitrust laws. In many states, physicians no longer enjoy the protection from corporate competition once provided by the corporate practice prohibitions. In tort law, physicians have lost the protection of the strict locality rule and are also required to obtain informed consent. In addition, courts appear to be retreating from some of the special "no duty" rules that once typified medical malpractice law, such as the rule that pharmacists have no duty to warn patients about incompatible prescriptions and the rule that "on call" doctors have no duty to emergency patients until they establish a physician-patient relationship. Abandonment of the custom-based standard of care is consistent with this trend away from special rules for health care providers. The weakening of support for the custom-based standard of care is also consistent with the gradual movement of twentieth century tort law away from special duties tailored for specific social contexts and toward a general obligation of reasonable care. . . .

D. IMPLICATIONS

Whether de jure or de facto, the shift away from the customary standard and to a reasonable physician standard takes the task of standard-setting away from the

---

* This migration away from the custom-based standard of care is described at much greater length in Philip G. Peters, Jr., The Quiet Demise of Deference to Custom: Malpractice Law at the Millennium, 57 Wash. & Lee L. Rev. 163, 166-168 (2000).

profession and assigns it to the jury. The centrality of this doctrinal shift cannot be overstated. The delegation of standard-setting authority to the professions is unique in tort law. It is the foundation upon which the field of medical malpractice law has been built. Under the custom-based standard of care, . . . the jury determines what the customary practice *is*. It does not decide what the custom *ought* to be. The law assigns the normative judgment to the medical profession. . . . Under the jury-applied reasonable physician standard, by contrast, the *jury* determines what a reasonable physician would have done under similar circumstances, not the profession. Medical customs, to the extent that they exist, are admissible, but they are not binding on the jury. . . . The crucial unanswered question is whether jurors can handle that task responsibly. . . .

E. CONFIDENCE IN MEDICAL CUSTOMS

Scholars and courts have articulated two quite distinct rationales for trusting clinical practices. The first is faith in the professionalism of physicians. The second is faith in the power of the market to make medical practices efficient. In the real world, however, medical practices live up to neither ideal. Historically, both courts and scholars have trusted physicians to put the welfare of patients above all other interests. . . .

Regrettably, much of this confidence in physician norms is misplaced. Recent research demonstrates that physicians, like the rest of us, are driven not only by science and fidelity to patient interests, but also by habit, self-interest and other competing considerations. . . . As a result, medical customs have a veneer of scientific validity that is too often undeserved. . . . Medicine has also undergone a recent structural transformation. . . . Insurers are using a variety of strategies to make physicians more cost-conscious. . . .

Under these circumstances, it seems reasonable to revisit the assumption that medical customs are uniquely reliable. The unwavering faith that the law once placed in physicians was probably naive from the outset and predictably has weakened in a more realistic and cynical age. . . .

[Moreover, the] argument in favor of a custom-based standard of care turns on [a] fundamental assumption . . . that medical customs will be readily ascertainable. . . . In reality, however, medical practices rarely provide [a] stable, ascertainable benchmark. . . . In the past few decades, medical researchers have learned that clinical practices vary dramatically and inexplicably. A number of studies, starting with the classic work of John Wennberg,* have demonstrated that physician practices vary widely, even within narrow geographic limits. . . . [A] Medicare study found that procedure rates varied by more than three hundred percent for more than one-half of the procedures studied.

In addition to the geographic variation that permeates clinical medicine, the highly-differentiated nature of medical problems is also a barrier to the formation of medical customs. Patients vary in ways that resist standardization. This variation in patients is matched by a similar variety in possible therapeutic responses, each with its own mix of benefits, risks and costs. At the same time, physicians vary in their

* See, e.g., John Wennberg, Dealing with Medical Malpractice Variations: A Proposal for Action, Health Aff. 6, 7 (1984).

preferences and in their knowledge of the medical literature. Finally, the movement of many employers away from fee-for-service health plans and toward managed care plans has produced significant differences among health plans in their resources and their cost-containment philosophies. Under these circumstances, there will rarely be a "custom" that provides a clear rule of decision. . . .

There is an additional erroneous assumption underlying the idea that a custom-based standard will provide a more ascertainable and predictable standard. In truth, few trial experts can be expected to have an accurate sense of what most physicians are doing. As David Eddy notes, "[I]t is a major research task to figure out what practitioners in a community are doing."* As a consequence, experts who are asked questions about the standard of care are unlikely to have a reliable understanding of customary norms across the nation or even in similar communities. Instead, their testimony is more likely to be a barometer of their own practices. . . .

H. SUMMARY OF POTENTIAL ADVANTAGES OF JURY STANDARD-SETTING

Abandonment of the custom-based standard of care in favor of a reasonable physician standard offers several potential advantages. Most importantly, the reasonable physician standard assigns the task of legal standard-setting to representatives of the community, rather than to the regulated industry. Jury decision-making is more likely to incorporate community values. Moreover, the flexibility of the reasonable physician standard provides more protection for innovators and less shelter for those adhering to antiquated customs. Furthermore, the reasonable physician standard is a more honest way to accomplish these goals than bending the custom-based standard to cure its shortcomings. The reasonable physician standard of care also gives the health care industry an incentive to engage the community in a dialogue about health care resources. At the same time, it allows the courts to supervise the influence of the managed care industry on clinical practices.

Notes: The Custom-Based Standard of Care

1. *Overview.* These readings introduce a number of complexities and nuances in the basic malpractice standard of care: the error-in-judgment rule, the standard of care for residents and specialists, the availability of punitive damages, the liability of consulting and attending physicians, admissions of error, and sensitivity to resource constraints. These detailed issues are taken up later in this chapter. The main focus of these notes is this more general inquiry: How does malpractice law define which bad results are compensated and which are not? On this point, in what respects are *McCourt* and *Locke* in agreement? In what respects do they disagree? If each of their respective facts and procedural histories were presented to the other court, would you expect a similar result?

2. *Verbal Formulations.* Courts constantly tinker with the precise verbal formulation of the basic standard of care that should be instructed to the jury and uttered by the expert witnesses. This creates havoc for the imprecise lawyer or judge. Illustrative is McCarty v. Mladineo, 636 So. 2d 377 (Miss. 1994), where the court reversed a verdict in favor of the defendant physician, holding that it was error to

---

* David M. Eddy, The Use of Evidence and Cost Effectiveness by the Courts: How Can It Help Improve Health Care?, 26 J. Health Pol. Pol'y & L. 387, 396 (2001).

instruct that the standard is that of a "minimally competent physician." Instead, the court ruled that the jury should be instructed in terms of the "reasonably prudent, minimally competent" physician.

An error in the opposite direction occurred in the trial in Smith v. Menet, 530 N.E.2d 277 (Ill. App. Ct. 1988). There, the plaintiff's lawyer had his favorable verdict reversed because, in questioning his expert witness, he asked whether the defendant's conduct "fell within the standard of *good* medical care." Because the only negative testimony was in response to this defective question, the court ruled there was insufficient evidence to sustain the verdict, explaining, "when good is interpreted to mean better than average, it contradicts the applicable standard," even though in prior cases the same court had used phrases such as "the reasonable skill which a physician in good standing would use."

Deposition testimony Dr. Abernathy gave in the *McCourt* case indicates that he was on academic probation for a time while a student at the University of South Carolina Medical School. Are "below average" doctors automatically liable for their mistakes, or are we to suppose that, as in Garrison Keillor's Lake Wobegon, most doctors are at or above average? The focus on "average" skill and judgment should not mislead one into thinking that any sort of numerical dividing line or litmus test exists. See Hood v. Phillips, 554 S.W.2d 160, 165 (Tex. 1977) (rejecting an instruction to the jury that creates the impression that "the standard for malpractice is to be determined by a poll of the medical profession").

Similarly, it has been observed that the custom-based standard is not strictly determined by actual practice. Instead, it is one that inquires whether existing practices are "accepted" within the profession. Professor Joseph King explains that the distinction between accepted and actual practice is the focus of much of this linguistic debate. Joseph King, In Search of a Standard of Care for the Medical Profession: The "Accepted Practice" Formula, 28 Vand. L. Rev. 1213 (1975). By way of analogy, consider whether, if the automobile driving standard of care were determined by custom, should someone who speeds up through a yellow light be found negligent? Many, or even a majority, of drivers in some communities may actually do this, but we all know they are not supposed to.

3. *Supervising Physicians.* As *Locke* indicates, supervising physicians are liable under a standard of care for reasonable supervision. Other cases explore the extent of liability when a physician is consulted on an informal basis. Consider, for instance, a doctor discussing a difficult case with her colleagues in the physician's lounge, or in a passing conversation in the hallway. These cases frequently turn on whether any doctor-patient relationship was ever established, for, as explained in Chapter 2.B.1, no professional duty of care attaches unless such a relationship was formed.

4. *Saying You're Sorry.* Dr. Pachtman is lucky that her expression of regret at making a mistake was not used against her in court. Other jurisdictions are more willing to do so. David M. Studdert et al., Disclosure of Medical Injury to Patients: An Improbable Risk Management Strategy, 26(1) Health Aff. 215 (Jan. 2007). Accordingly, there is a movement to enact "apology shield" statutes that protect physicians who disclose errors to patients and/or express regret for bad outcomes. However, most of these statutes cover only statements of sympathy but not admissions of responsibility. Anna Mastroianni et al., The Flaws in State "Apology" and "Disclosure" Laws Dilute Their Intended Impact, 29(9) Health Aff. 1611 (2010). Ronan v. Sanford Health, 809 N.W.2d 834 (S.D. 2012) applied one such statute to exclude a hospital employee's statements to a bereaved wife that "I'm sorry we failed

you, we let you down. [The doctor] got the whole thing off on the wrong track and it snowballed. . . . [That's what happens] when people don't do their jobs." Without this evidence, the jury issued a defense verdict.

5. *Is Medical Consensus Real or Imagined?* What do you think about Prof. Peters's argument that the law often imagines a professional consensus that in fact does not exist? Here are the similar views of a practicing physician:

> To be quite candid, I have no idea what the standard of care really is, and my point is that neither does anyone else. . . . The implementation of the term in the judicial setting . . . disregards in large part the intangible and interpersonal patient variables that so often affect the medical outcome. . . . In fact, there is no standard of care. The medical body of knowledge contains both fact and opinion. Each case must be assessed on its individual merits, including intangible factors and only from a prospective viewpoint.

Robert P. Nirschl, Delving into the Myth of "Standard of Care," Am. Med. News, Dec. 16, 1988, at 24. If law really is this disconnected from reality, what difficulties and dangers does this create? Consider the issue from both the plaintiff's and the defendant's perspectives.

Suppose the "snowflake" attitude in the previous quote (every patient is unique) is correct. Does this mean that the custom-based standard is entirely a figment of the judicial imagination? Even if custom is not nearly so unitary and precise as we might sometimes imagine, does this negate the fact that, for any set of clinical facts, however unique, there are decisions or actions that virtually no doctor would find acceptable? In other words, do these sentiments do anything more than establish that, in many cases, the actual standard of care is very broad and allows for major differences of opinion?

Assuming the latter is correct, how do we make sure that expert witnesses are honestly testifying to a breach of (or compliance with) the standard of care and not merely expressing a strong personal preference or opinion? See Travers v. District of Columbia, 672 A.2d 566 (D.C. 1996) (holding that the expert testimony established only personal preference or opinion, not prevailing custom). More than this, even experts' personal opinions may overstate what they themselves do in actual practice. Several studies have shown that most doctors are actually less thorough, prompt, or accurate than experts have claimed they are in particular lawsuits. William Meadow & Cass Sunstein, Statistics, Not Experts, 51 Duke L. J. 629 (2001). These authors conclude, therefore, that proof of custom should be even more rigorous, using statistical or survey evidence rather than expert opinion. See also Tim Cramm et al., Ascertaining Customary Care in Malpractice Cases: Asking Those Who Know, 37 Wake Forest L. Rev. 699 (2002). However, others agree with Prof. Peters that the persistent failure of actual practice to measure up to accepted medical standards reinforces the case for a reasonable physician standard for liability. Richard Lempert, Following the Man on the Clapham Omnibus: Social Science Evidence in Malpractice Litigation, 37 Wake Forest L. Rev. 903 (2002).

Keep these problems in mind as we consider the locality rule, respectable minority rule, and evidentiary rules introduced in later readings.

6. *Punitive Damages.* Do you think Drs. Abernathy and Clyde in the *McCourt* case deserved to be hit with punitive damages? In many states, public policy forbids liability insurance from covering punitives because this would dilute the intended

impact on the defendant, so punitives have to be paid from the doctors' own personal assets. Would this change your opinion?

Regardless of your opinion about the *McCourt* case, it contains (according to allegations in the plaintiffs' brief) several inflammatory elements that are frequently seen in cases that receive punitives: failure to treat aggressively a seriously ill patient; failure to admit promptly and candidly to the seriousness of the mistake; and suggestions that the medical records might have been altered after the fact. Compare this with the account from Dr. Gawande at page 255, whose patient appears to have had a very similar kind of infection.

Punitive damages are still rare in medical malpractice cases, owing to the complexity of medical judgment, the good motives of virtually all doctors, and the high regard in which most juries hold doctors in general. However, there is a noted trend toward more punitive damage awards against doctors—in large cities, they are now awarded in over 10 percent of malpractice cases that reach a verdict. In recent years, a number of states have enacted limits on the amount of punitives relative to compensatory damages (for instance, no more than three times compensatory damages).

In a rare decision, one court reduced from $5 million to $2 million a punitive award against a nursing home for the death of a patient, finding that there was no evidence of recklessness, and that the amount was ten times the compensatory damage and several times the defendant's net worth. Stogsdill v. Healthmark Partners, 377 F.3d 827 (8th Cir. 2004).

7. *Further Reading.* On the **standard of care** generally, see Page Keeton, Medical Negligence: The Standard of Care, 10 Tex. Tech. L. Rev. 351 (1979); 18 A.L.R.4th 603 (1982); Leonard J. Nelson, Helling v. Carey Revisited: Physician Liability in Age of Managed Care, 25 Seattle U. L. Rev. 775 (2002); Ben A. Rich, Medical Custom and Medical Ethics: Rethinking the Standard of Care, 14 Cambridge Q. Healthcare Ethics 27 (2005); and the sources cited in n.2 of the Peters article.

On the **empirical basis for the standard of care** (note 5), see Symposium, 37 Wake Forest L. Rev. 663 (2002) (thorough discussion of the problem, with multiple critiques and proposals for reform); Bryan A. Liang, Medical Malpractice: Do Physicians Have Knowledge of Legal Standards and Assess Cases as Juries Do?, 3 U. Chi. L. Sch. Roundtable 59, 90 (1996); Caroline Young, Medico-Legal Research Using Evidence-Based Medicine, 102 Law Libr. J. 449 (2010); Lars Noah, Medicine's Epistemology: Mapping the Haphazard Diffusion of Knowledge in the Biomedical Community, 44 Ariz. L. Rev. 373 (2002).

On **punitive damages** in medical malpractice cases (note 6) see Frank M. McClellan, Medical Malpractice: Law, Tactics, and Ethics ch. 8 (1994); M. Rustad & T. Koenig, Reconceptualizing Punitive Damages in Medical Malpractice: Targeting Amoral Corporations, Not "Moral Monsters," 47 Rutgers L. Rev. 975 (1995); Robert Shaw, Punitive Damages in Medical Malpractice: An Economic Evaluation, 81 N.C. L. Rev. 2371 (2003).

2. Variations in the Standard of Care

The black-letter law is simple to utter, but more difficult to implement. Physicians are judged by the standard of care that is established by prevailing practice and professional consensus. But seldom can one find a monolithic, clearly defined "right way" of doing things that almost all doctors agree to. Medical practice is highly variable and judgmental. This leads us to consider which variations in practice or opinion can legitimately be used to adjust the standard of care in a given case, and which cannot. The following materials explore variations that are structured around (1) schools of thought and training, (2) practice location and specialization, and (3) source of payment.

■ JONES v. CHIDESTER
610 A.2d 964 (Pa. 1992)

PAPADAKOS, Justice.

We granted review in this case in order to reexamine our test for the defense of the so-called two schools doctrine in a medical malpractice case arising in the context of a jury instruction. The necessity of our reexamination arises from the vacillation of the Superior Court and our court in applying the appropriate standard.

A medical practitioner has an absolute defense to a claim of negligence when it is determined that the prescribed treatment or procedure has been approved by one group of medical experts even though an alternate school of thought recommends another approach, or it is agreed among experts that alternative treatments and practices are acceptable. The doctrine is applicable only where there is more than one method of accepted treatment or procedure. In specific terms, however, we are called upon in this case to decide once again whether a school of thought qualifies as such when it is advocated by a "considerable number" of medical experts or when it commands acceptance by "respect[ed], reputable and reasonable" practitioners. The former test calls for a quantitative analysis, while the latter is premised on qualitative grounds.

The facts indicate that in November, 1979, Appellant, Billy Jones, underwent orthopedic surgery on his leg performed by Dr. John H. Chidester. In order to create a bloodless field for the surgery, the surgeon employed a tourniquet which was elevated and released at various intervals. Because of subsequent problems with the leg, the patient was referred to a neurosurgeon who determined that Jones had suffered nerve injury to the leg. Additional examinations by other doctors confirmed that the nerve injury had resulted in a condition known as "drop foot."

At trial in June, 1988, Jones complained, inter alia, that his nerve injury was the result of Dr. Chidester's use of the tourniquet. Both sides presented testimony by medical experts supporting their positions. Unsurprisingly, Dr. Chidester's experts told the court and jury that his technique was acceptable medically in this particular case, and the plaintiffs' experts insisted that it constituted unacceptable practice. At the close of the evidence, the court gave the following instruction to the jury:

> . . . Ladies and gentlemen, I instruct you upon this additional principle of law known as the two schools of thought doctrine. This principle provides that it is improper for a jury to be required to decide which of two schools of thought as to proper procedure should have been followed in this case, when both schools have their respective and respected advocates and followers in the medical profession. . . . Thus, under the two schools of thought doctrine, a physician in the position of Dr. Chidester will not be held liable to a plaintiff merely for exercising his judgment in applying the course of treatment supported by a reputable and respected body

of medical experts, even if another body of medical experts' opinion would favor a different course of treatment. . . .

The jury returned a verdict in favor of Dr. Chidester. . . . On appeal, Jones argues that under Pennsylvania law, the test for the doctrine is "considerable number" rather than "reputable and respected" as the court had charged the jury.

We note at the outset of our analysis that there appears to be confusion and contradiction in the use of these standards—a confusion apparent even between the trial court's charge to the jury ("reputable and respected") and its subsequent opinion denying the post-trial motion ("considerable number"). . . . The initial modern case in this jurisdiction on the subject of the two schools of thought doctrine was Remley v. Plummer, 79 Pa. Superior Ct. 117 (1922). Relevant portions of that opinion are as follows:

> The question actually passed upon by the jury was not whether the defendants, in their handling of the case, had been guilty of negligence in not following a well-recognized and established mode of treatment, but rather, which of two methods, both having their respective advocates and followers of respectable authority, was the safer and better from a surgical standpoint. . . . Where competent medical authority is divided, a physician will not be held responsible if in the exercise of his judgment he followed the course of treatment advocated by a considerable number of his professional brethren in good standing in his community. . . .
>
> Thus practitioners of a reputable school of medicine are not to be harassed by litigation and mulcted in damages because the course of treatment prescribed by that school differs from that adopted by another school: (citations omitted) . . . As we said in Patten v. Wiggin, "The jury are not to judge by determining which school, in their judgment, is the best." "If the treatment is in accordance with a recognized system of surgery, it is not for the court or jury to undertake to determine whether that system is best, nor to decide questions of surgical science on which surgeons differ among themselves:" . . . The testimony clearly showed a difference of medical opinion expressed by physicians and surgeons of unquestioned standing and reputation, and the defendants were not negligent for having adopted the view held by the majority of their brethren who testified.

. . . Other jurisdictions also appear to waffle between the two standards. . . . In Borja v. Phoenix General Hospital, Inc., 727 P.2d 355 (Az. 1986), the court [held] that the doctrine requires only support by a "respectable minority." California has defined its standard as one where "a physician chooses one of alternative accepted methods of treatment, with which other physicians agree." Meier v. Ross General Hospital, 445 P.2d 519 (Cal. 1968). Florida has adopted the "respectable minority" test in Schwab v. Tolley, 345 So. 2d 747 (Fla. App. 1977), while Arkansas accepts the doctrine when any alternative "recognized method" is employed by the physician. Rickett v. Hayes, 511 S.W.2d 187 (Ark. 1974). . . .

It is incumbent upon us to settle this confusion. The "two schools of thought doctrine" provides a complete defense to malpractice. It is therefore insufficient to show that there exists a "small minority" of physicians who agree with the defendant's questioned practice. Thus, the Superior Court's "reputable and respected by reasonable medical experts" test is improper. Rather, there must be a considerable number of physicians, recognized and respected in their field, sufficient to create another "school of thought." . . . A school of thought should be adopted not only by "reputable and respected physicians" in order to insure quality but also by a "considerable number" of medical practitioners for the purpose of meeting general acceptance even if it does not rise to the level of a majority. . . .

In recognizing this doctrine, we do not attempt to place a numerical certainty on what constitutes a "considerable number." The burden of proving that there are two schools of thought falls to the defendant. The burden, however, should not prove burdensome. The proper use of expert witnesses should supply the answers. Once the expert states the factual reasons to support his claim that there is a considerable number of professionals who agree with the treatment employed by the defendant, there is sufficient evidence to warrant an instruction to the jury on the two "schools of thought." It then becomes a question for the jury to determine whether they believe that there are two legitimate schools of thought such that the defendant should be insulated from liability.

Reversed and remanded for a new trial consistent with this opinion.

McDermott, Justice, concurring.

. . . [W]hether it [is] best to chill or heat, use medicines, intervene with scalpel or await nature, or approach from back, front, top or bottom to reach the site of ill, are questions over which doctors disagree. One group of doctors of skill and competence may withhold the scalpel, another group of equal competence may believe in quick response. When each group has its advocates, and each has its arguable reasons, a doctor of either cannot be faulted if he properly administers the one to his knowledge and experience seems the better, so long as that group is comprised of a sufficient number of reputable and respected members.

Thus, an isolated expert cannot argue it was his own belief that a procedure was inappropriate, because then this belief would be elevated, against experience and knowledge, to a separate level, though a considerable portion of the world of medicine be against it.

I join in the opinion of the majority.

Zappala, Justice, concurring.

While I join in the opinion, I vehemently disagree with the majority that the existence of two schools of medical thought may ever be a question of fact to be submitted to a jury. . . . It is the responsibility of the trial judge to determine in the first instance whether there are two schools of medical thought so that competent medical authority as to a course of treatment is divided. It is a question of law for the trial judge. It is not a question of fact. In all other respects, I agree with the majority's analysis of the two schools of medical thought doctrine.

■ CHAPEL v. ALLISON
785 P.2d 204 (Mont. 1990)

Sheehy, Justice.

. . . Lawrence A. Chapel was injured when he was kicked by a horse on February 18, 1983. He was taken to the emergency room at Livingston Memorial Hospital where he was treated by Dr. James G. Allison [for a severe leg fracture]. . . . He applied a long leg cast extending from Chapel's mid-thigh down to and including his foot. . . . The cast was removed May 2, 1983. Chapel's leg exhibited a varus deformity (bow-leggedness) which required surgery, a procedure called an "osteotomy," to straighten the bowed leg. . . .

Chapel had been a patient of Dr. Allison's for nearly 20 years, the doctor treating ailments from common illnesses up to and including sprains, fractures, and an initial treatment for a ruptured disc. Chapel's injury was of the kind which would fall within the area of practice of an orthopedic surgeon. It would also fall within the area of practice of a properly qualified general practitioner. . . . Dr. Allison claimed during the litigation that he possessed the requisite degree of knowledge for treating Chapel because of his 24 years of practice in which he had treated 1,000 fractures, 50 of which involved the tibia and 15 of which involved the tibial plateau, and one instance of the same injury, but without the wound overlying the fracture site.

The expert testimony produced by the plaintiff Chapel came from an orthopedic surgeon from Denman, Massachusetts, Dr. Stephen Sand, board-certified in the specialty of orthopedic surgery. His testimony was as follows:

Q. Based upon what you have learned by reviewing all of the documents that we mentioned, have you been able to form a reasonable judgment on what the standards of care are in the Livingston-Bozeman area in Montana for the care and treatment of an injury such as was sustained by Mr. Chapel by a general practitioner? . . .

A. My opinion, based on the review of the information that you have stated, and my contact with a general practitioner in the area, is that a general practitioner would not, under ordinary circumstances, handle this type of case or injury.

. . . At the close of Chapel's case in chief, . . . the court granted Dr. Allison's motion for a directed verdict. . . . The district court said that proof of the competency of Dr. Sand to testify in the matter was "very shaky"; that the plaintiff did not call Dr. Kurtz, a Bozeman doctor, upon whom Dr. Sand had relied for information as to the area of practice for a general practitioner; that Dr. Allison had testified that in his opinion Chapel was bow-legged before the accident and despite the leg injury and disc surgery the same year, that Chapel was able to go elk hunting in the mountains for a two-week period; that the other doctors whose testimony appeared in the case have all in effect said that there was no fault. . . .

During pretrial procedures before the district court, the plaintiff made a motion in limine that the "same locality rule" (infra) was not applicable in this case. The court denied the motion, saying:

> The court specifically determines that the rule applicable in this case is that Dr. Allison will be held to the standard of care in February 1983 of a licensed general practitioner, who is not board certified, in the same or similar communities within Montana. Provided, however, experts from elsewhere and in other specialties will be considered competent to testify if they are medically qualified and if they are in fact familiar with the standards for a general practitioner in Livingston or similar communities in Montana at the time in question. . . .

Formerly, the standard of care required of a physician or surgeon in treating a patient was to exercise as reasonable care and skill which "is usually exercised by physicians or surgeons of good standing of the same system or school of practice in the community in which he resides, having due regard to the condition of medical or surgical science at that time." The "same locality rule" restricted the geographical area from which the degree of care exercised by a physician or surgeon could be determined to the community in which the doctor resided.

In Tallbull v. Whitney, 564 P.2d 162 (Mont. 1977), this court examined the "same locality rule" and determined that the foundation for it no longer existed. The reasons given were that the accessibility of medical literature, the frequency and availability of national, regional and state medical meetings, advances of communication of medical knowledge, transportation advances, and the opportunity for rural community doctors to gain medical knowledge in the same manner as doctors in more populous regions in the state, all made the "same locality rule" outdated. In *Tallbull*, this court expanded the rule saying:

> For the foregoing reasons, we hold that Montana's "locality rule" imposes on a physician undertaking the care of a patient the legal duty of possessing and exercising that reasonable and ordinary degree of learning, skill and care possessed and exercised by physicians of good standing of the same school of practice in the same or similar locality in Montana. A similar locality in Montana within the meaning of this rule is a locality of similar geographical location, size and character in a medical context.

The *Tallbull* rule was modified insofar as it applied to an orthopedic surgeon in Aasheim v. Humberger, 695 P.2d 824 (Mont. 1985). There, this court recognized that the defendant was a nationally board-certified orthopedic surgeon and had received comparable training and passed the same national board certification tests as all other board-certified orthopedic specialists in the nation. On that basis, this Court held that when a defendant in a medical negligence action was a board-certified specialist, his skill and learning would be measured by "the skill and learning possessed by other doctors in good standing, practicing in the same specialty and who hold the same national board certification." Thenceforth, board certified specialists in Montana would be subject to a national standard of care.

In Glover v. Ballhagen, 756 P.2d 1166 (Mont. 1988), . . . the doctor was a board-certified family practitioner. In *Glover*, we concluded that: ". . . the standard of care to which a board certified family practitioner will be held is that skill and learning possessed by other doctors in good standing, practicing with the same national board certification." . . .

Not answered in the foregoing cases, and raised as an issue in this case, is whether a non-board-certified general practitioner, practicing in a Montana community, who treats a patient for an injury of a kind which would fall within an area of practice of an orthopedic surgeon should be held to the degree of care, knowledge and skill of the specialist. . . . Because of the broad implications to the medical community and to injured patients lurking in whatever decision we made on this issue, we ordered rebriefing and oral argument on the issue and invited briefs from amici curiae. Here are the arguments marshalled by each side:

Counsel for Chapel maintains that in an age of increasing specialization, a doctor in general practice is under a legal duty, in diagnosing or treating a patient, to seek consultation with or refer a patient to a specialist when the doctor knows or should know in the exercise of reasonable care that the services of a specialist are indicated. Chapel further argues that if there is another mode of treatment that is likely to be more successful for which the physician does not have the facilities or the training to administer, but which is available from specialists, it is the doctor's duty to so advise the patient, and failure to apprise the patient of these facts would constitute a breach of that duty. . . .

Dr. Allison contends that restricting the degree of care to the same or similar communities in Montana is proper because he confronts illnesses and injuries in serving his community whereas practitioners in a larger city devote much of their practice to initial diagnoses with referral to a specialist for anything beyond routine care. Dr. Allison also contends that it would be impracticable to require a general practitioner to be held to the standard of care of whatever area of expertise in which his treatment might fall, including an orthopedic surgeon, a dermatologist, a neurologist, an obstetrician, an internist, and so on.

An amicus brief filed by the Montana Trial Lawyers Association . . . contend[s] that there is a trend away from the locality rule in most states which apply a national standard of care, typically defined as "a physician is under a duty to use that degree of care and skill which is expected of a reasonable competent practitioner in the same class to which it belongs, acting in the same or similar circumstances." Trial Lawyers contend that the phrase "the same or similar circumstances" allows the trier of fact to take into account and to weigh local conditions when the standard is applied, so as to reflect the same "general facilities, services, and options" which were available to the treating doctor. . . .

An amicus brief was received from the Montana Hospital Association. Essentially, this brief points out the rather dire prospects faced by rural hospitals in Montana. It states that all of Montana's 64 hospitals were only marginally profitable for the past five years but that rural hospitals experienced increasing financial losses. The losses are occurring primarily because of reduced utilization of rural hospitals. Some of the reductions are due to public policies and issues undertaken at both the federal and state levels with cutbacks in federal and state Medicare and Medicaid programs. The importance of a rural doctor to a rural hospital is emphasized in the brief and the hospitals contend that the similar locality rule is needed in rural areas to keep physicians there providing essential health services and utilizing local rural hospital services. . . .

The brief of the Montana Medical Association recognizes the implications of the problem and seems to be seeking a middle ground for its resolution. Thus, with regard to general practitioners, its brief recommends that we continue to adopt the "same or similar locality" standard, without geographical limitations for general practitioners but allow the "national" specialist standard to be applied to any physician who holds himself or herself out as a specialist. . . . The brief suggests that the elimination of the Montana boundary restriction on the locality rule is warranted. . . . It points out that if the "same or similar locality" rule for general practitioners is any locality similar in the United States, sound policy reasons support such a change, including . . . the increased availability of expert witnesses, the lack of which would be some justification for alterations in the law. The brief contends for a balance to be struck between the right of a negligently injured patient to receive compensation through the availability of expert testimony and the right of a doctor to due process and a fair hearing, by insuring that those experts who do testify possess solid practical experience in the type of practice at issue.

On balance, the position asserted by the Montana Medical Association as to the standard of care applicable in cases of this type, with slight modification, appears suitable for adoption by us. . . . [W]e abandon the "locality" rule which is limited to Montana communities. . . . The geographical restriction of the state boundary is too narrow in view of the necessity of expert testimony; yet, as the Association contends, the national standard should not exclude local considerations which face rural general practitioners. Accordingly, we hold that a non-board-certified general practitioner is held to the standard of care of a "reasonably competent general practitioner acting in the same or similar community in the United States in the same or similar circumstances." See Shilkret v. Annapolis Emergency Hospital Association, 349 A.2d 245 (Md. 1975). "Similar circumstances" permits consideration by the trier of fact of legitimate local factors affecting the ordinary standard of care including the knowledge and experience of the general practitioner, commensurate with the skill of other competent physicians of similar training and experience, with respect to the type of illness or injury he confronts and the resources, facilities and options available to him at the time. . . . This opinion applies only to general practitioners, and does not affect board-certified specialists or board-certified general or family practitioners. . . .

Reversed and remanded for further proceedings in accordance with this opinion.

Notes: Variations in the Standard of Care — Location, Schools of Thought, Experiments, and Specialization

1. *The Respectable Minority Rule.* Reaching a different result from that in *Jones* on the quantitative vs. qualitative standard is Hood v. Phillips, 554 S.W.2d 160 (Tex. 1977). Even more demanding than Jones, see Yates v. Univ. of W. Virginia Bd. of Trustees, 549 S.E.2d 681 (W. Va. 2001) (doctrine does not apply unless the alternative method "enjoys such substantial support within the medical community that it is, in fact, widely and generally recognized").

Intertwined with the "respectable minority" or "two schools of thought" doctrine is the "error in judgment" concept discussed in the *McCourt* case (page 282), since it conveys the same notion of absence of negligence when doctors make an educated choice among two or more reasonable paths. Many courts shy away from the "error in judgment" language, however, because it seems to convey to the jury that doctors are liable only if they act in bad faith, but other courts find the instruction permissible. Reviewing jurisdictions, in a divided opinion, see Passarello v. Grumbine, 87 A.3d 285 (Pa. 2014). Some scholars have argued that doctors should be given discretion similar to business managers to make mistakes as long as they act in good faith. E.g., Jeffrey O'Connell & Andrew S. Boutros, Treating Medical Malpractice Claims Under a Variant of the Business Judgment Rule, 77 Notre Dame L. Rev. 373 (2002); Charles Caldwell & Evan Seamone, Excusable Neglect in Malpractice Suits Against Radiologists, 16 Ann. Health L. 43 (2007).

2. *Medical Experiments.* Does the "considerable number" formulation allow sufficient room for medical experimentation? Requiring that a sizeable number of doctors follow a practice means that the first few to innovate do so at their own risk. Is strict liability an appropriate standard for medical experimentation? Early decisions generally held "yes," but most modern courts say "no," holding that doctors

are bound by a standard of reasonable experimentation. Brook v. St. John's Hickey Memorial Hospital, 380 N.E.2d 72 (Ind. 1978) (no liability for hitting a nerve while injecting needle in the leg instead of the arm; "therapeutic innovation has long been recognized as permissible; . . . even where there is an established mode of treatment, the physician may be permitted to innovate somewhat if he can establish that, in his best judgment, this was for the benefit of his patient"); Hood v. Phillips, 554 S.W.2d 160 (Tex. 1977) ("physicians should be allowed to experiment in order that medical science can provide greater benefits for humankind"; jury should have been allowed to decide based on expert testimony that controversial surgery was unreasonable and discredited). In order for this justification to hold, however, the innovation must be done for therapeutic reasons, not purely for research curiosity. This usually means the deviation from standard therapy is fairly minor or existing treatment is wholly inadequate. As a German authority explains:

> [T]hree different types of procedure must be distinguished: (i) *Therapeutic treatment*, whereby the patient is treated with [one of the] normal and approved (or orthodox) procedures; (ii) *Therapeutic experiments*, whereby the patient is treated with new methods and techniques for primarily (though not exclusively) therapeutic purposes. This is also known as therapeutic research or "innovative therapy"; (iii) *Research experiments*, whereby persons, either patients or test subjects, are treated with new methods and drugs for purely scientific purposes.

Dieter Giesen, Civil Liability of Physicians for New Methods of Treatment and Experimentation: A Comparative Examination, 3 Med. L. Rev. 22 (1995). See also Nancy King, Experimental Treatment: Oxymoron or Aspiration?, 25(4) Hastings Center Rep. 6 (July 1995).

Liability for experimental deviations from customary practice is more often avoided by resorting to informed consent law. Because modern experiments are usually accompanied by careful disclosure of the risks and procedures, in most instances the patient has been informed of the therapy's experimental status and has consented to the increased risks. In order for this consent to be effective, is it sufficient to disclose simply (1) the risks of the experimental therapy (which, by definition, are not well known), (2) the fact that this is an experiment, or also (3) the comparative risks and benefits of the alternative, standard procedure? In practice, only (1) and (2) are usually done. Nevertheless, the consent is usually sufficient to avoid liability, unless of course the procedure itself was improperly performed. See Slater v. Optical Radiation Corp., 961 F.2d 1330 (7th Cir. 1992) (experiment okay if patient is informed of risks); Karp v. Cooley, 493 F.2d 408 (5th Cir. 1974) (first patient to receive an artificial heart expressly consented to all aspects of operation); Fiorentino v. Wenger, 280 N.Y.S.2d 373 (N.Y. 1967) (doctor liable where he failed to disclose he was the only one in the country who performed a discredited operation).

Even if doctors and hospitals are not legally obligated to compensate fully informed patients who are injured in medical experiments, should they do so voluntarily, as a matter of public policy, considering the sacrifice the patient has made for the benefit of science? Many hospitals and drug companies agree to pick up at least the costs of treatment for injuries in experiments they conduct or fund.

3. *Excessive Innovation.* A contrasting concern is that the custom standard unduly speeds up adoption of expensive and unproven innovations. Prof. Gibson

argues that the custom standard creates a "feedback effect" in which some doctors first start to use unproven precautions, such as electronic fetal heart monitoring, in order to, rightly or wrongly, reduce the likelihood of suit, then others start to do the same, which creates the basis for an emerging new custom, which then forces all doctors to follow suit. "Instead of discouraging wasteful practices, then, the law feeds them back into doctrine, . . . ratcheting up the standard of care. Overcautious physicians consequently have to do even more to steer clear of liability, and the cycle begins anew." James Gibson, Doctrinal Feedback and (Un)reasonable Care, 94 Va. L. Rev. 1641 (2008). See also Michelle Lewis et al., The Locality Rule and the Physician's Dilemma: Local Medical Practices vs. the National Standard of Care, 297 JAMA 2633 (2007) (claiming that a locality standard might be more demanding than a national standard, when local physicians' practices are excessive). Does that seem plausible? If so, is there any way to modulate or restate the custom standard to avoid that effect?

4. *Unorthodox Medicine.* Less frequently litigated is whether the "schools of thought" doctrine protects doctors who practice completely unorthodox or unscientific medicine, such as homeopathy, naturopathy, or even faith healing. If the practitioner is not a licensed M.D., then presumably only the standards of that group apply. If a physician incorporates alternative theories, or uses them exclusively, then a tougher issue is presented. In the leading, and virtually the only, case—one involving a cancer patient who died after her doctor treated her with nutritional therapy—the court held that "we see no reason why a patient should not be allowed to make an informed decision to go outside currently approved medical methods in search of an unconventional treatment." Schneider v. Revici, 817 F.2d 987 (2d Cir. 1987). In that case, the doctor had carefully documented a consent form that advised the patient to seek conventional treatment as well, and the jury rejected the claim that the doctor had fraudulently misrepresented the prospects of success for the treatment. In a licensing case not involving malpractice, however, the court held that a doctor who uses homeopathic medicines prepared from "moss, the night shade plant, and various other . . . substances" can be disciplined for engaging in unprofessional conduct, even though his patients were fully informed and there was no evidence that he posed a risk of harm to anyone. In re Guess, 393 S.E.2d 833 (N.C. 1990). See also Brown v. Shyne, 151 N.E. 197 (N.Y. 1926) (chiropractor who practices medicine will be held to the standard of a physician). See generally Michael H. Cohen, Complementary and Alternative Medicine: Legal Boundaries and Regulatory Perspectives (1998); J. Brad Kallmyer, A Chimera in Every Sense: Standard of Care for Physicians Practicing Complementary and Alternative Medicine, 2 Ind. Health L. Rev. 225 (2005).

5. *Legal Effect of Schools-of-Thought Rules.* In conventional cases, more important than how exactly the "two schools" or "error in judgment" rules are phrased is their legal effect. Do you agree with the majority or with Justice Zappala's concurrence in *Jones*? Also, do you agree that the defendant should bear the burden of proof; in other words, is this doctrine an affirmative defense, or must the plaintiff negate the existence of alternative schools as part of his prima facie case? If the defendant bears the burden and the doctrine merely results in instructing the jury, how does one avoid the concern expressed in Justice McDermott's concurrence in *Jones* that an "isolated expert" should not be allowed to elevate his mere personal belief to a binding standard of care?

A minority of courts give the doctrine greater force by using it to direct a verdict where the conflicting expert testimony merely shows a "difference of opinion" and not that the defendant was beyond the bounds of any respectable practice. See, e.g., Chumbler v. McClure, 505 F.2d 489 (6th Cir. 1974) (directed verdict for defendant is proper despite conflict in testimony and the fact that Dr. McClure was the only doctor in town who followed the disputed practice; "the test for . . . community standards is not to be determined solely by a plebiscite").

Even if this harder stance is taken, however, it is still relatively simple for the plaintiff's expert to create a jury issue on the question of "respectability." Consider which of the following is sufficient to get the case in front of the jury:

1. "I would never do it that way."
2. "No one I know of does it that way."
3. "In my opinion, no respectable doctor should do it that way; some may do so, but that's not considered good medical practice."

How difficult do you suppose it is for an expert who starts at the first position to move to the third?

6. *Locality Rules.* A classic statement of the reasons for the old "strict" locality rule can be found in Small v. Howard, 128 Mass. 131, 136 (1880) ("It is a matter of common knowledge that a physician in a small country village . . . [is] but seldom called upon as a surgeon to perform difficult operations. He would have but few opportunities of observation and practice in that line such as public hospitals or large cities would afford."). Have these conditions really changed that much? Another reason the strict locality rule has been overturned is that the "conspiracy of silence" among medical professionals made it extremely difficult for a plaintiff to find a qualified expert witness, even in cases of egregious negligence. The seminal decision on liberalizing the locality rule is Pederson v. Dumouchel, 431 P.2d 973 (Wash. 1967) ("The fact that several careless practitioners might settle in the same place cannot affect the standard of [care]. . . . Negligence cannot be excused on the ground that others in the same locality practice the same kind of negligence. No degree of antiquity can give sanction to usage bad in itself.").

Chapel indicates that the differences among the modern locality rules may be more in appearance than in substance. A national standard tends to be "lowered" (or, more properly, varied) by its inclusion of a "similar circumstances" qualifier, while a local standard tends to be "raised" (or universalized) when applied to board-certified specialists. The meaning and significance of board certification is explained further below. Of the following three factors, which do you think is *most* relevant in defining "similarity" of location or circumstances: (1) population density; (2) medical facilities (consider similar towns with and without a teaching hospital); or (3) socioeconomics, such as portion of population without insurance or on Medicaid? See generally Annots., 18 A.L.R.4th 603 (1982); 99 A.L.R.3d 1133 (1980).

It may be possible to raise even the strict locality standard to a national level with testimony in the particular case that local doctors follow the national practice. Idaho is one of the few states to retain the strict locality standard, where it is codified by statute. Plaintiff's efforts to circumvent it by attempting to qualify national experts have resulted in about a dozen state supreme court decisions clarifying when national standards apply. Symposium, 44 Idaho L. Rev. 291 (2008). At first, it appeared the court had adopted the Montana rule that board certification automatically invokes a national standard, but it later retreated to holding that this depends on the testimony in each case. See Grimes v. Green, 746 P.2d 978 (Idaho 1987). See also Henning v. Thomas, 366 S.E.2d 109 (Va. 1988) (expert from another part of the country allowed to testify to a statewide standard of care for orthopedic surgeons by asserting that uniform national standards apply in all states).

As these cases indicate, the primary significance of the locality dimension of the standard of care is not the influence these words have when instructed to the jury, but instead is on who is qualified to testify on both sides of the case. Issues of witness qualification are discussed below. It suffices for now to observe that, in most jurisdictions today, experts need not actually practice in the specialty or locational category that defines the standard of care, they need only demonstrate some acquaintance with the relevant standard of care. This liberalization in expert qualification may be just as or more important in practical effect than how the standard of care is defined in theory.

7. *The Specialization Dimension of the Standard of Care.* In addition to geography and schools of practice, the custom-based standard is adjusted according to the physician's specialization. Thus, a surgeon or obstetrician is held to a higher standard than is a general practitioner who performs the same procedure. Specialty practice is usually designated by "board certification," meaning that the physician has passed special training and testing requirements set by one of the two dozen American Boards of Medical Specialties. Observe how the *Chapel* court deals with the question of board certified family practitioners. Do you agree, considering that family practice is one of the classic forms of general practice?

What about subspecialties? Rather than just general surgery, suppose a physician is regarded as a specialist in cardiac surgery, or pediatric cardiac surgery, or in a particular heart valve replacement for children. How does one square the notion that the standard is elevated for specialists with the rule that the standard should not be elevated simply because the defendant is more highly skilled or experienced than average? In resolving this dilemma, it may help to observe that one basis for elevating the standard of care to begin with — to that of a reasonably prudent physician as opposed to a reasonably prudent person — is that doctors hold themselves out as specially trained professionals. If this is key to the initial elevation, then how doctors hold themselves out as specialists and subspecialists may determine how many further gradations are possible. See, e.g., Aves v. Shah, 997 F.2d 762 (10th Cir. 1993) (general practitioner held to an obstetrics standard because she considered herself a specialist, and so did her patient).

Plaintiffs sometimes attempt to elevate a generalist standard by arguing that a doctor should be held to a specialist standard if she extends her practice to procedures or conditions that are not within the competence of an ordinary generalist, thereby becoming a de facto specialist. Although this does not usually succeed in just these terms, plaintiffs sometimes are able to conflate the generalist and specialist standards to some extent by arguing, as in *Chapel,* that, although a generalist might have rendered treatment as well as could be expected, he failed to recognize his own limitations and call in a specialist when one was needed.

Locke v. Pachtman, in the prior set of cases, raises the additional complication of what standard applies to a doctor-in-training. Licensure of M.D.s occurs only after they complete four years of medical school and pass a series of standardized exams.

They then go through a period of apprenticeship, partially or wholly in a hospital setting, in which they are known as "residents" (the older term is "interns"). Those who seek board certification go through much longer residencies. Even though residents have just received their M.D.s and practice only under supervision, most courts, as in *Locke*, hold them to at least a normal standard of care for general practitioners, reasoning that, if they aren't ready to practice as full-fledged doctors, they should not be represented as such to patients. Many courts go further and hold them to an elevated standard, somewhere between generalists and specialists, since they are usually in specialty training at highly sophisticated teaching and research hospitals. See Justin Ward, Medical Residents: Should They Be Held to a Different Standard of Care?, 22 J. Leg. Med. 283 (2001). See, e.g., Jistarri v. Nappi, 549 A.2d 210 (Pa. Super. Ct. 1988) (orthopedic resident held to an intermediate standard of care). Prof. King argues that, following informed consent principles, residents who disclose their status as trainees should be held to a trainee standard, whereas those who don't should be held to a fully practicing specialist standard. Joseph H. King, The Standard of Care for Residents and Other Medical School Graduates in Training, 55 Am. U. L. Rev. 683-751 (2006). See also Phelps v. Physicians Insurance Co. of Wisconsin, Inc., 698 N.W.2d 643 (Wis. 2005) (holding first-year obstetrics resident to standard of care of other such residents).

8. *Further Reading*. For additional discussion of **medical experimentation** (note 2), see Chapter 3.C.4; President's Commission, Compensating for Research Injuries (1982); Comment, 78 Wash. L. Rev. 229 (2003); Anna Mastroianni, Liability, Regulation and Policy in Surgical Innovation, 16 Health Matrix 351 (2006); Michael D. Greenberg, Medical Malpractice and New Devices: Defining an Elusive Standard of Care, 19 Health Matrix 423 (2009); Anna Laakmann, When Should Physicians Be Liable for Innovation?, 36 Cardozo L. Rev. 913 (2015). For historical discussion of the **locality rule** (note 6), see T. Silver, One Hundred Years of Harmful Error: The Historical Jurisprudence of Medical Malpractice, 1992 Wis. L. Rev. 1193 (arguing that locality originally was just a relevant factor but mistakenly was converted into an absolute rule); Marc Ginsberg, The Locality Rule Lives!, 61 Drake L. Rev. 321 (2013).

Problem: What Is the Standard of Care?

Imagine a law school grading regime in which your final grade could be docked from one to five points each time you failed to answer correctly a question posed to you in class, but only if you had failed to meet the prevailing "standard of care" in preparation for the class. (In other words, you are penalized only if you are at "fault" for not knowing, with fault defined as not preparing.) Write a statement of what you view as the prevailing standard of care in your school for class preparation. What is the highest standard to which you might be held? Are there "accepted" alternative or "minority" standards? Does the standard vary according to 1L vs. 2L vs. 3L, or for first vs. second semester 1Ls, or according to full-time vs. night students? Should the prevailing standard differ in top-ten national schools as opposed to non-ABA-accredited schools?

In an evidentiary hearing, who should be allowed to testify about such a standard: only current students at the same school; students at another school; anyone who has graduated from law school within ten years; faculty; administrators?

Would such a regime cause you to prepare excessively, that is, more than you needed to in order to do well on the exam?

■ MURRAY v. UNMC PHYSICIANS
806 N.W.2d 118 (Neb. 2011)

GERRARD, J.

This case involves a failure to provide medical treatment. The treatment at issue is a very expensive drug that must be administered indefinitely. But it also may cause serious and even deadly symptoms if its administration is interrupted. In this case, the patient's treating physicians, wary of those health risks, decided not to administer the drug until the patient's insurer approved it or another source of payment could be found. But, regrettably, the patient died before either happened. The question presented in this appeal is whether under such circumstances, an expert medical witness is permitted to opine that under the customary standard of care, a physician should consider the health risks to a patient who may be unable to pay for continued treatment. We conclude that such testimony is admissible and, therefore, reverse the district court's order granting a new trial. . . .

Pulmonary arterial hypertension is a chronic medical condition in which the blood vessels in the lungs constrict, and the resulting pressure on the heart leads to heart failure. Flolan is a vasodilator that relaxes blood vessels and prevents blood clotting. It is administered by a pump, connected to a port and catheter usually inserted above the collarbone. Flolan is very expensive and short-acting, so patients on Flolan treatment need a constant supply of the drug, because if its administration stops, pulmonary blood pressure rebounds and can be life threatening. And because Flolan is a chronic treatment, patients who begin Flolan need to remain on it, essentially, for the rest of their lives—it must be administered 24 hours a day and costs approximately $100,000 a year. The parties do not seem to disagree that generally, Flolan therapy is the appropriate course of treatment for chronic pulmonary arterial hypertension. . . .

The course of treatment relevant to this case began in late June 2006, as [Mary Murray's] treating physician, Austin Thompson, M.D., was preparing to treat Mary's pulmonary arterial hypertension with Flolan. . . . [After evaluating Mary's condition, Dr. Thompson approved her for Flolan.] She was discharged [to wait for insurance approval] and was supposed to begin Flolan after port placement the following week. But on July 10, she reported to the emergency room with a rapid heartbeat and shortness of breath. She began to seize, then her heartbeat stopped, and medical efforts failed to resuscitate her.

At trial, the parties disputed both the cause of Mary's death and whether [the University of Nebraska Medical Center (UNMC)] had breached the standard of care. Robert [Murray, Mary's husband,] presented expert medical testimony that . . . UNMC's treatment of Mary fell below the relevant standard of care after June 29, because the medical center should have paid for and provided Flolan by July 4 or 5—in other words, that the standard of care for a patient as sick as Mary was to start Flolan and obtain insurance approval afterward. UNMC's witnesses, on the other hand, testified that . . . their practice was to wait for insurance approval before beginning Flolan, because most patients are not able to pay for the drug without insurance and it can be more dangerous if treatment is started and then stopped. . . . [Dr.] Thompson testified to "horror stories" about patients who had been forced to discontinue treatment, and he said it would be "irresponsible" not to have lifelong financial support for the drug, because it could be "devastating" if discontinued. . . .

The jury returned a general verdict for UNMC. But Robert filed a motion for new trial that the district court granted. The court explained:

> . . . that, as a matter of law, a medical standard of care cannot be tied to or controlled by an insurance company or the need for payment. The "bean counters" in an insurance office are not physicians. Medicine cannot reach the point where an insurance company determines the medical standard of care for the treatment of a patient. Nor, can we live in a society where the medical care required is not controlled by the physicians treating the patient. The position advanced by [UNMC's] expert tells us that the standard of care is different for those with money than for those without. This is neither moral nor just. It is wrong. . . .

ANALYSIS

It is important, from the outset, to carefully note what issues this appeal does *not* present. This appeal arises against a backdrop of increasing concern about the costs of health care, among health care providers, insurers, government officials, and consumers. That concern has prompted a great deal of discussion, among commentators and in the public arena, about what should be done to control health care costs or to allocate potentially limited resources. As we will explain below, the question presented in this appeal is narrow and does not require us to address the more sweeping issues that are the subject of greater public policy debate. But some discussion of the broader picture will help us clarify what this case is about—or, more precisely, what it is not about.

In Nebraska, [the legislature has adopted the standard similar to the locality rule]. That standard is consistent with the general common-law rule and is a so-called unitary, or wealth-blind, standard of care. In other words, the standard of care is found in the customary practices prevailing among reasonable and prudent physicians and must not be compromised simply because the patient cannot afford to pay.[8] That standard of care, however, developed in a world of fee-for-service medicine and persisted while health insurance still primarily provided first-dollar unlimited coverage.[9] . . .

But "[b]ecause tort law expects physicians to provide the same standard of care regardless of patients' ability to pay, and because this standard sometimes encompasses costly technologies no longer readily available for the poorest citizens," physicians are "caught in a bind between legal expectations and economic realities."[11] Courts have been accused of being "oblivious to the costs of care, essentially

8. See E. Haavi Morreim, Cost Containment and the Standard of Medical Care, 75 Cal. L. Rev. 1719 (1987); John A. Siliciano, Wealth, Equity, and the Unitary Medical Malpractice Standard, 77 Va. L. Rev. 439 (1991).

9. See E. Haavi Morreim, Stratified Scarcity: Redefining the Standard of Care, 17 L. Med. & Health Care 356 (1989).

11. E. Haavi Morreim, Medicine Meets Resource Limits: Restructuring the Legal Standard of Care, 59 U. Pitt. L. Rev. 1, 4-5 (1997).

requiring physicians to commandeer resources that may belong to other parties, regardless of whether those other parties owe the patient these resources." *Id.*

It has been suggested that at a fundamental level, a unitary, wealth-blind standard of care cannot be reconciled with the growth of technology and the stratification of available health care. Custom is increasingly difficult to identify in today's medical marketplace, as resource distinctions produce fragmentation and disintegration.[13] It has also been suggested that maintaining a unitary standard of care disadvantages those who may not be able to pay for health care. Physicians remain free, for the most part, to decline to treat those who cannot pay, and "an outright refusal to treat an indigent patient, in contrast to a decision to treat in a manner inconsistent with the unitary malpractice standard, rarely creates the threat of liability." Siliciano, supra note 8, at 457. So, it has been argued that rather than assume the burden of paying for a patient's treatment, or the potential liability of providing some but not all possible care, the unitary standard makes it more likely that "providers will now sidestep the entire problem simply by refusing to accept some, or all, of such patients for treatment." *Id.*

On the other hand, it has been argued that permitting physicians to make medical decisions based on resource scarcity would compromise the fiduciary relationship between patient and physician, creating a conflict of interest because the patient's well-being would no longer be the physician's focus.[16] The question is how the value judgments inherent in the development of the standard of care might evolve in response to a societal interest in controlling health care costs. It has been explained that . . .

> [p]hysicians do not do everything conceivably possible in caring for a patient—they draw what they consider to be reasonable boundary lines. For example, physicians do not order every diagnostic test available for a patient that requests a physical examination, even though doing so might reveal interesting information. Instead, they order tests which are indicated given the age and physical characteristics of the patient. Hirshfeld, *supra* note 16, at 1835.

A physician's initial value judgment, in other words, is constrained by reason but does not include a societal interest in conserving costs or resources, and certainly does not include weighing the physician's own economic interests.

In short, the traditional ethical norms of the medical profession and the legal demands of the customary standard of care impose significant restrictions on a physician's ability to consider the costs of treatment, despite significant and increasing pressure to contain those costs. Whether the legal standard of care should change to alleviate that conflict, and how it might change, has been the subject of considerable discussion. It has been suggested that the customary standard of care could evolve

13. See James A. Henderson, Jr. & John A. Siliciano, Universal Health Care and the Continued Reliance on Custom in Determining Medical Malpractice, 79 Cornell L. Rev. 1382 (1994).

16. See Maxwell J. Mehlman, The Patient-Physician Relationship in an Era of Scarce Resources: Is There a Duty to Treat?, 25 Conn. L. Rev. 349 (1993); Edward B. Hirshfeld, Should Ethical and Legal Standards for Physicians Be Changed to Accommodate New Models for Rationing Health Care?, 140 U. Pa. L. Rev. 1809 (1992).

to permit the denial of marginally beneficial treatment—in other words, when high costs would not be justified by minor expected benefits.[20] Others have suggested that the standard of care should evolve to consider two separate components: (1) a skill component, addressing the skill with which diagnoses are made and treatment is rendered, that would not vary by a patient's financial circumstances and (2) a resource component, addressing deliberate decisions about how much treatment to give a patient, that would vary so as to not demand more of physicians than is reasonable.[21] . . . And many have suggested that custom should no longer be the benchmark for the standard of care; instead, practice standards or guidelines could be promulgated that would settle issues of resource allocation.[24]

All of the concerns discussed above are serious, and they present difficult questions that courts will be required to confront in the future. But we do not confront them here, because under the unique facts of this case, they are not presented. Contrary to the district court's belief, this is not a case in which insurance company "bean counters" overrode the medical judgment of a patient's physicians or in which those physicians allowed their medical judgment to be subordinated to a patient's ability to pay for treatment.[26] Nor is this a case in which the parties disputed the cost-effectiveness of the treatment at issue. Rather, UNMC's evidence was that its decision to wait to begin Flolan treatment was not economic—it was a medical decision, based on the health consequences to the patient if the treatment is interrupted. . . .

UNMC's witnesses testified that UNMC's treatment of Mary was consistent with the statutory standard of care—in other words, that health care providers in the same community or in similar communities and engaged in the same or similar lines of work would ordinarily defer Flolan treatment until payment for a continuous supply had been secured. We cannot depart from the customary standard of care on policy grounds, even if it is subject to criticism, because the standard of care is defined by statute and public policy is declared by the Legislature. . . .

Finally, and more fundamentally, the district court's concerns about health care policy, while understandable, are misplaced in a situation in which the patient's ability to continue to pay for treatment is still a *medical* consideration. . . . This case does not involve a conflict of interest between the physician and patient—there was no evidence, for instance, of a financial incentive for UNMC's physicians to control costs. As explained by UNMC's witnesses, the decision to defer Flolan treatment was not based on its financial effect on UNMC, or subordinating Mary's well-being to the interests of other patients, or even considering Mary's own financial interest. Instead, when making its initial value judgment regarding Mary's treatment,

20. See Mark A. Hall, Rationing Health Care at the Bedside, 69 N.Y.U. L. Rev. 693 (1994).

21. See Mark A. Hall, Paying for What You Get and Getting What You Pay For: Legal Responses to Consumer-Driven Health Care, 69 Law & Contemp. Probs. 159 (Autumn 2006).

24. See Daniel W. Shuman, The Standard of Care in Medical Malpractice Claims, Clinical Practice Guidelines, and Managed Care: Towards a Therapeutic Harmony?, 34 Cal. W. L. Rev. 99 (1997); Peter H. Schuck, Malpractice Liability and the Rationing of Care, 59 Tex. L. Rev. 1421 (1981).

26. Compare Wickline v. State, 192 Cal. App. 3d 1630 (1986) [which is excerpted at page 454 infra].

UNMC's physicians were not weighing the risk to Mary's health against the risk to her pocketbook, or UNMC's budget, or even a general social interest in controlling health care costs. UNMC's physicians were weighing the *risk to Mary's health* of delaying treatment against the *risk to Mary's health* of potentially interrupted treatment. . . .

As explained by [Mary's doctors], the reason for waiting to begin Flolan until after insurance approval had been obtained was out of concern for the health of the patient. That was not meaningfully different from any number of other circumstances in which a health care provider might have to base a treatment decision upon the individual circumstances of a patient. For instance, a physician with concerns about a particular patient's ability to follow instructions, or report for appropriate followup care, might treat the patient's condition differently in the first instance. And a health care provider who is told that a patient cannot afford a particular treatment may recommend a less expensive but still effective treatment, reasoning that a treatment that is actually used is better than one that is not. These are difficult decisions, and there may be room to disagree, but it is hard to say they are unreasonable as a matter of law, or that an expert cannot testify that such considerations are consistent with the customary standard of care. . . .

UNMC's evidence and opinion testimony reflect difficult medical decisions — but still *medical* decisions. Therefore, the scope of our holding is limited. We need not and do not decide whether the standard of care can or should incorporate considerations such as cost control or allocation of limited resources. Although the decision (or lack thereof) of a third-party payor contributed to the circumstances of this case, UNMC's decisions were still (according to its evidence) premised entirely upon the medical well-being of its patient. In a perfect world, difficult medical decisions like the one at issue in this case would be unnecessary. But we do not live in a perfect world, and we cannot say as a matter of law that UNMC's decisions in this case violated the standard of care.

Notes: The Impact of Economic Constraints

1. *Damned If You Do.* It may seem surprising that more courts have not previously considered more squarely a question as fundamental as whether the costs of treatment can affect the legal standard of care. The one case that comes closest to being on point is Wickline v. State, 239 Cal. Rptr. 810 (Cal. Ct. App. 1986), cited in *Murray* and reprinted at page 454. It found that no malpractice occurred when a Medicaid patient lost her leg as the result of being released from the hospital in four days rather than the eight days her doctors requested. The treating physicians blamed the state Medicaid program because it refused to pay for any more than four days. The court's rejection of liability says very little about the legal standard of care, however, since the patient chose not to sue her doctors, only Medicaid. She relied on her doctors as her expert witnesses against the state, and they naturally were not willing to testify that they gave her substandard medicine. Therefore, the key issue was not litigated. This case does illustrate, however, that there is often a wide range in acceptable standards of practice from the minimum to the optimal — here, from four to eight days — so that there may be plenty of room to accommodate economically constrained practice patterns within existing standards of care, especially under the "respectable minority rule."

The absence of case law on point is also due to the fact that defense counsel are highly reluctant to raise resource constraints as an excuse for omitting potentially beneficial treatment, for fear that plaintiffs might turn this defense against them by inflaming the jury to impose punitive damages, as discussed at page 464. Indeed, in a series of lawsuits, plaintiffs' lawyers have argued that an HMO physician's decision to withhold treatment, such as a Pap smear or biopsy to detect cancer, was inappropriately influenced by how the doctor was paid. The common law is still undeveloped because most of these cases have been settled or dismissed for procedural reasons prior to trial. In the few reported decisions, one court ruled that it was proper to exclude evidence that profit motivation might have caused an HMO physician to fail to hospitalize a patient with labor complications, observing that such evidence "was only marginally relevant [to malpractice] and potentially very prejudicial." Madsen v. Park Nicollet Medical Center, 419 N.W.2d 511, 515 (Minn. Ct. App. 1988), rev'd on other grounds, 431 N.W.2d 855 (Minn. 1988). However, Neade v. Portes, 739 N.E.2d 496 (Ill. 2000), ruled that evidence of economic motivation is admissible in a medical malpractice case. Is it possible to reconcile these conflicting decisions by observing that, where negligent treatment exists, a financial inducement can be found to be a contributing factor, but, standing alone, it does not constitute an independent tort? Would the second point hold true, however, if the financial inducement is not known to the patient? The discussion at page 200 addresses whether an informed consent cause of action exists for failure to disclose payment methods that create a conflict of interest.

2. *Ducking the Hard Questions.* Are you convinced by the *Murray* court's assertion that the doctor's decision was purely medical? Why would treatment necessarily need to stop just because insurance might not pay? If the patient refuses treatment because of the costs, then of course doctors must comply. Mark Hall & Carl Schneider, When Patients Say No (To Save Money): An Essay on the Tectonics of Health Law, 41 Conn. L. Rev. 743 (2009). But what if the Murrays would have wanted to continue the treatment and try to find ways to raise the funds? What would the law of "patient abandonment," discussed in Chapter 2.B.3, say about stopping treatment against the patient's wishes simply because they cannot pay?

In any event, the *Murray* court suggests that the custom rule provides leeway to consider costs, when doctors in fact think that it is medically relevant to consider costs. Does the similar locality version of the custom rule provide more leeway for this defense — by allowing lawyers to argue that physicians who practice under unconstrained, fee-for-service insurance are not from sufficiently similar situations to give relevant testimony in more cost-constrained settings? How would you evaluate such an argument based on the cases above? In Moss v. Miller, 625 N.E.2d 1044 (Ill. App. Ct. 1993), the court reversed a defense verdict against a prisoner who alleged negligent failure to refer him to a specialist. The fatal flaw in the trial was simply the inclusion of an ordinary similar locality standard in the jury instructions. The court was concerned that the jury would be misled, in light of counsel's arguments that prisons are a distinct locality. The court held:

> [T]hose practicing the medical arts in the penitentiary are held to the same standard of care as [other doctors]. To hold otherwise would be to abandon reason and common sense. . . . [W]e recognize constraints necessarily exist in correctional institutions which may well have a negative effect on the ability to delivery medical

services. . . . However, those types of constraints, while interfering with proper medical care, do not lessen the standards required of the medical arts practitioner.

Are these questions easier if patients are thought to have a choice over the matter? Consider, for instance, whether subscribers to an HMO plan should be allowed to contractually specify a lower but acceptable standard of care than that which prevails elsewhere in their community, so that their health insurance will be more affordable. That topic is discussed further at page 407.

3. *Bibliography.* In 1975, Randall Bovbjerg first analyzed these issues in relation to HMOs: The Medical Malpractice Standard of Care: HMOs and Customary Practice, 1975 Duke L. J. 1375. In 1981, the Texas Law Review published a lengthy debate among James Blumstein, Rand Rosenblatt, and Peter Schuck about precisely this set of issues. Symposium, 59 Tex. L. Rev. 1345 (1981). Haavi Morreim collects and expands her several articles (cited in *Murray*) into the book, Holding Health Care Accountable (2001). Considering how the issues take shape in the era of increased patient cost-sharing, see Isaac Buck, The Cost of High Prices: Embedding an Ethic of Expense into the Standard of Care, 58 B.C. L. Rev. 101 (2017) (developing the concept of "financial toxicity" as justification for physicians to consider costs to patients).

Problem: Economic Malpractice

You are legal counsel to Metropolis Inner City Hospital (MICH), a public facility that is bound by statute to treat all patients regardless of their ability to pay. Naturally, the hospital is chronically strapped for funds. Controversy is fast developing within the medical staff over the use of high osmolar contrast media (HOCM) vs. low osmolar contrast media (LOCM) in diagnostic imaging procedures, such as angiography. This is an invasive procedure to visualize the blockage in blood vessels by injecting a substance that shows up under X-ray (the "contrast media"). The substance's "osmolarity" affects its safety, with lower being better. Toxic effects are usually temporary (pain, nausea, altered kidney or nervous functions), but some are permanent, and some deaths have been documented. Although HOCMs are approved as safe and effective by the FDA, they have osmolarities of up to seven times that of blood plasma and consequently produce undesirable effects in some patients. Concerns over the toxicity of HOCMs led to the development of LOCMs, the first of which became commercially available ten years ago. Although all adverse reactions can be reduced by using LOCMs instead of HOCMs, HOCMs are usually well tolerated and affected patients respond quickly to treatment. Fortunately, fatal adverse reactions appear to be very infrequent. However, on a purely medical basis, with no cost considerations taken into account, there is no scientific reason to use anything other than LOCMs owing to the significant reduction in the prevalence of all degrees of adverse reactions.

The higher incidence of adverse reactions to HOCMs can be reduced by identifying patients at highest risk, such as those with asthma, allergies, renal or cardiac impairment, diabetes, etc. The American College of Radiology issued a set of guidelines for use of HOCMs vs. LOCMs based on various risk factors. However, risk stratification schemes cannot identify all persons who will react adversely to HOCMs. There is still a statistical benefit that can be realized by giving LOCM to patients who are placed in a low-risk category.

Both HOCMs and LOCMs produce images of similar quality. LOCMs, however, are about 10 to 20 times higher cost per dose than HOCMs ($20 vs. $200–$400). Although the higher cost may not be viewed as outrageous per procedure, if all procedures at MICH were to use LOCMs, costs would total over $500,000 a year.

Five years ago, about 9 percent nationally of radiological exams requiring contrast media were done with LOCMs. By this year, this number had climbed to 70 percent. Previously, MICH has used LOCMs only for high-risk patients. Physicians at MICH have expressed liability concerns about the continued use of HOCMs for any patients. Despite adherence to risk stratification procedures, the very availability of LOCMs concerns them. LOCM manufacturers have helped to fuel these concerns by telling the radiologists that the use of any contrast agent other than LOCMs could constitute malpractice.

How would you advise the hospital on the physicians' demands to eliminate all use of HOCMs? See Jacobson & Rosenquist, The Introduction of Low-Osmolar Contrast Agents in Radiology, 260 JAMA 1586 (1988).

3. Res Ipsa and Negligence Per Se

◼ LOCKE v. PACHTMAN
521 N.W.2d 786 (Mich. 1994)

[The facts are stated in the main excerpt at page 285. Briefly, a long, flexible needle broke off while Dr. Pachtman was performing surgery. After searching, she could not find it, and so a second operation was required to remove it. The court held there was insufficient expert testimony from the plaintiff for the case to go to the jury.]

Plaintiff next argues that even if expert testimony was insufficient, her case against Dr. Pachtman should have proceeded to the jury on the theory of res ipsa loquitur. Specifically, plaintiff contends, under this doctrine, a prima facie case was made, with regard to both the needle breakage and the fact that defendant terminated the surgery without having recovered the needle. The lower courts rejected these arguments, as do we. . . .

The following four factors a[re] necessary to a res ipsa loquitur claim:

(1) the event must be of a kind which ordinarily does not occur in the absence of someone's negligence;

(2) it must be caused by an agency or instrumentality within the exclusive control of the defendant;

(3) it must not have been due to any voluntary action or contribution on the part of the plaintiff . . .

(4) [e]vidence of the true explanation of the event must be more readily accessible to the defendant than to the plaintiff.

In the medical malpractice context, the crucial element, and that most difficult to establish, will often be the first factor, i.e., that the event is of a kind that does not ordinarily occur in the absence of negligence. A bad result will not itself be sufficient to satisfy that condition. . . . This does not mean that a bad result cannot be presented by plaintiffs as part of their evidence of negligence, but, rather, that, standing alone, it is not adequate to create an issue for the jury. Something more is required, be it the common knowledge that the injury does not ordinarily occur without negligence or expert testimony to that effect. . . . Neither standard was met here. . . . Even plaintiff's own expert acknowledged at one point that needle breakage is one of the risks of surgery, suggesting that faulty equipment might be a cause of breakage. . . .

Plaintiff relies on this court's holding in LeFaive v. Asselin, 262 Mich. 443, 247 N.W. 911 (1933). In *LeFaive*, the court held that a jury could determine, without the aid of expert testimony, that the defendant's action in inadvertently leaving a needle within the plaintiff's incision violated the applicable standard of care. Plaintiff's analogy to *LeFaive* is inapposite. In *LeFaive*, the act of leaving the needle within the incision was one of carelessness, from which negligence may easily be discerned. However, a far different situation is presented where a needle breaks off, and the surgeon, despite attempts to locate the fragment is unable to. One could not reasonably conclude, on the basis of common knowledge, that such an event does not ordinarily occur in the absence of negligence. . . .

Notes: Res Ipsa Loquitur and Negligence Per Se

1. *Other Examples. Locke* is an example of one of several typical, recurring situations in which courts will sometimes allow the case to go to the jury without expert testimony on deviation from customary practice. Other typical scenarios involve: leaving other foreign objects behind after surgery, such as clamps and sponges; injury to a part of the body that was not involved in the operation; and removal of the wrong organ or appendage. These cases are argued and decided under several doctrinal categories that overlap with res ipsa loquitur: "negligence per se"; the "common knowledge rule"; and "obvious negligence." As noted in Flowers v. Torrance Memorial Hospital Medical Center, 35 Cal. Rptr. 2d 685 (Cal. 1994), the gist of all these doctrines is captured in Bob Dylan's *Subterranean Homesick Blues* (Columbia Records 1965): "[Y]ou don't need a weatherman to know which way the wind blows." In the words of a Tennessee court, however, the medical negligence must be "as plain as a fly floating in a bowl of buttermilk." German v. Nichopoulos, 577 S.W.2d 197 (Tenn. Ct. App. 1978).

These various doctrinal categories are not all identical, however, and they are often applied somewhat differently in medical malpractice cases than they are in conventional tort cases. The "common knowledge" rule allows the jury to make simple factual findings from its own experience and knowledge base. It allows some facts to be found even though there are gaps in the supporting evidence, but it usually does not allow a finding of negligence without any expert testimony at all. Res ipsa loquitur is a stronger rule because it does allow this result, in proper circumstances. Negligence per se is stronger still; it can result in the judge directing a verdict of negligence as a matter of law. Note that this use of negligence per se differs from the standard application, which finds negligence as a matter of law only when a statute is violated; here, no statutory violation is required. Negligence per se in malpractice cases tends to be restricted, however, to certain extreme factual situations, such as incorrect sponge counts or amputating the wrong leg, in which negligence is so obvious as to be beyond dispute. Compare Guilbeau v. St. Paul Fire and Marine Insurance Co., 325 So. 2d 395 (La. Ct. App. 1976) ("the general rule

. . . is that a surgeon's failure to remove a sponge or pad before closing an incision may be regarded as negligence per se" justifying a directed verdict for plaintiff), with Nazar v. Branham, 291 S.W.3d 599 (Ky. 2009) (res ipsa, and not negligence per se, applies to foreign object cases due to the complexity who precisely is responsible within surgical teams for counting and retrieving surgical objects). For a case-by-case comparison among these rules, see Annot., 49 A.L.R.4th 63 (1986); Joseph H. King, The Common Knowledge Exception to the Expert Testimony Requirement for Establishing the Standard of Care in Medical Malpractice, 59 Ala. L. Rev. 51 (2007).

Notice how these three doctrines, without meaning to do so, tend to shift the focus from what physicians ordinarily do in similar cases, to what the jury thinks was reasonable in the particular case. Therefore, these doctrines do not simply overcome a gap in the evidence; they tend to alter the substantive standard of liability.

2. *Doctrinal Variations.* Res ipsa loquitur potentially applies to any type of medical mistake, as long as the elements of the rule are met. Because some of these elements are matters that are not usually in the common knowledge of jurors, however, plaintiffs frequently need expert testimony to establish them, as illustrated in *Locke.* Res ipsa loquitur in such cases allows the jury to fill in by inference the gaps that remain in expert testimony rather than displacing expert testimony entirely.

For a contrasting view that takes a more expansive approach than *Locke* to the availability of res ipsa loquitur and the "common knowledge rule," see Jones v. Harrisburg Polyclinic Hospital, 437 A.2d 1134 (Pa. 1981) (res ipsa applies whenever there is a "fund of common knowledge" from which to draw lay inferences), and an excellent student note on the case, 21 Duq. L. Rev. 547 (1983). Compare generally De Leon Lopez v. Corporacion Insular de Seguros, 931 F.2d 116 (1st Cir. 1991) (expert not needed where hospital switched babies born at same time), and Seavers v. Methodist Medical Center, 9 S.W.3d 86 (Tenn. 1999) (where patient suffered nerve damage in arm while being restrained in a hospital bed, res ipsa applies even when the issue is not within "the fund of common knowledge" but requires expert testimony to establish its elements), and Toppino v. Herhahn, 673 P.2d 1297 (N.M. 1983) (it is common knowledge that reconstructive breast surgery should result in breast of same size and shape as the other one), with Miller v. Jacoby, 33 P.3d 68 (Wash. 2001) (res ipsa applies to failure to fully remove a surgical drain but not to negligence in inserting the drain), and Sisson v. Elkins, 801 P.2d 722 (Okla. 1990) (res ipsa does not apply to surgeon who cut the wrong blood vessel, despite testimony he was negligent), and Bearfield v. Hauch, 595 A.2d 1320 (Pa. Super. Ct. 1991) (severing nerve during gallbladder surgery does not raise inference of negligence absent expert testimony to that effect, because usual results from this surgery are not within "fund of common knowledge").

Is the first element of res ipsa satisfied by the mere fact that, statistically speaking, a harmful effect rarely occurs if the procedure is performed properly? See Clark v. Gibbons, 426 P.2d 525 (Cal. 1967) (the rarity of the problem alone is not enough, but coupled with actual evidence of possible negligent acts this does suffice to support a jury verdict; operation had to be terminated prematurely because anesthesia wore off too early).

The factor requiring exclusive control is often not applied literally in medical malpractice actions, under the reasoning that it is unduly demanding considering that the team approach to treatment often means that no single defendant is exclusively responsible and the plaintiff is often not in a position to observe who performs which tasks. The classic case is Ybarra v. Spangard, 208 P.2d 445 (Cal. Ct. App. 1949), which allowed res ipsa to be instructed where a patient suffered a shoulder injury while under anesthesia for an appendectomy. The court observed that it should be the defendants' burden to come forward with evidence about who among those present in the operating room was and was not responsible for the injury. For a review of the application of these rules in cases of multiple medical defendants, see Annot., 67 A.L.R.4th 544 (1989).

3. *Legal Effect.* Locke v. Pachtman focuses on the conditions required for applying the res ipsa doctrine. Also at issue in these cases are the legal effects of the doctrine when it does apply. In *Locke,* the doctrine would have resulted in presenting the case to the jury. Other courts go further and use the doctrine to instruct the jury to find liability against at least one of the defendants, although this is much more controversial. See, e.g., Anderson v. Somberg, 338 A.2d 1 (N.J. 1975) (adopting this approach in a case similar to *Locke,* over a heated dissent accusing the majority of forcing the jury to act without "any semblance of rationality, . . . as the whimsy of the moment dictates, . . . no more a rational process than were trial by ordeal or trial by combat"). But see Salgo v. Leland Stanford Jr. University Board of Trustees, 317 P.2d 170 (Cal. Ct. App. 1957) (improper to direct verdict for plaintiff where factual dispute existed over whether needle injection hit the spinal cord and where experts disagreed over whether such a mistake would constitute negligence). An intermediate approach, followed by a substantial minority of states, is to create some type of rebuttable presumption or shift in the burden of proof when the elements of res ipsa are met.

4. *"Never Events."* Medicare now has a policy of not paying for certain "never events" — those that should never happen, such as administering the wrong drug or dosage or operating on the wrong body part. Should this federal payment rule determine state courts' applications of negligence per se or res ipsa loquitur? Somewhat surprisingly, the federal list also includes patients injured by falling, certain infections resulting from treatment, and pulmonary embolisms (blood clots to the lung) caused by certain surgeries.

5. *Legal Trend.* In earlier years, many legal commentators urged that res ipsa loquitur and similar liberalizing rules were necessary to aid plaintiffs with legitimate claims who were confronted with "the conspiracy of silence" on the part of physicians refusing to appear as expert witnesses. See, e.g., *Salgo,* supra. In more recent times, now that it is much easier to find qualified experts, the attitudes of commentators in both legal and medical journals have all but completely reversed. These rules are now often described as unfair to defendant physicians. Many of the statutory reforms adopted in the mid-1970s and mid-1980s include modifications of the res ipsa loquitur doctrine in medical malpractice litigation. See references and discussion in section H. A particularly outspoken expression of the modern view is found in Priest v. Lindig, 583 P.2d 173, 175 n.7 (Alaska 1976), where the court asserted that the legislative history of the Alaska statute abolishing res ipsa loquitur in medical malpractice cases was intended to counteract "the *intolerable* rule of law resulting in astronomically high malpractice insurance rates" (emphasis added). For commentary on these rules, see K. Albin, Res Ipsa Loquitur and Expert Opinion Evidence in Medical Malpractice Cases, 82 Va. L. Rev. 325 (1996).

4. Ordinary Negligence

It is one thing to argue that medical custom is common knowledge or its violation can be presumed from the outrageousness of the doctor's behavior. It is another thing altogether to argue that liability should be imposed *regardless* of medical custom or *contrary* to known medical custom. That is the result in the following decision, which is the most infamous of all medical malpractice cases.

◼ HELLING v. CAREY
519 P.2d 981 (Wash. 1974)

HUNTER, Associate Justice.

This case arises from a malpractice action instituted by the plaintiff (petitioner), Barbara Helling.

The plaintiff suffers from primary open angle glaucoma. Primary open angle glaucoma is essentially a condition of the eye in which there is an interference in the ease with which the nourishing fluids can flow out of the eye. Such a condition results in pressure gradually rising above the normal level to such an extent that damage is produced to the optic nerve and its fibers with resultant loss in vision. The first loss usually occurs in the periphery of the field of vision. The disease usually has few symptoms and, in the absence of a pressure test, is often undetected until the damage has become extensive and irreversible.

The defendants (respondents), Dr. Thomas F. Carey and Dr. Robert C. Laughlin, are partners who practice the medical specialty of ophthalmology. Ophthalmology involves the diagnosis and treatment of defects and diseases of the eye.

The plaintiff first consulted the defendants for myopia, nearsightedness, in 1959. At that time she was fitted with contact lenses. She next consulted the defendants in September, 1963, concerning irritation caused by the contact lenses. Additional consultations occurred in October, 1963; February, 1967; September, 1967; October, 1967; May, 1968; July, 1968; August, 1968; September, 1968; and October, 1968. Until the October 1968 consultation, the defendants considered the plaintiff's visual problems to be related solely to complications associated with her contact lenses. On that occasion, the defendant, Dr. Carey, tested the plaintiff's eye pressure and field of vision for the first time. This test indicated that the plaintiff had glaucoma. The plaintiff, who was then 32 years of age, had essentially lost her peripheral vision and her central vision was reduced to approximately 5 degrees vertical by 10 degrees horizontal.

Thereafter, in August of 1969, after consulting other physicians, the plaintiff filed a complaint against the defendants alleging, among other things, that she sustained severe and permanent damage to her eyes as a proximate result of the defendants' negligence. During trial, the testimony of the medical experts for both the plaintiff and the defendants established that the standards of the profession for that specialty in the same or similar circumstances do not require routine pressure tests for glaucoma upon patients under 40 years of age. The reason the pressure test for glaucoma is not given as a regular practice to patients under the age of 40 is that the disease rarely occurs in this age group. Testimony indicated, however, that the standards of the profession do require pressure tests if the patient's complaints and symptoms reveal to the physician that glaucoma should be suspected.

The trial court entered judgment for the defendants following a defense verdict. . . .

We find this to be a unique case. The testimony of the medical experts is undisputed concerning the standards of the profession for the specialty of ophthalmology. It is not a question in this case of the defendants having any greater special ability, knowledge and information than other ophthalmologists which would require the defendants to comply with a higher duty of care than that "degree of care and skill which is expected of the average practitioner in the class to which he belongs, acting in the same or similar circumstances." Pederson v. Dumouchel, 72 Wash. 2d 73, 79, 431 P.2d 973 (1967). The issue is whether the defendants' compliance with the standard of the profession of ophthalmology, which does not require the giving of a routine pressure test to persons under 40 years of age, should insulate them from liability under the facts in this case where the plaintiff has lost a substantial amount of her vision due to the failure of the defendants to timely give the pressure test to the plaintiff.

The defendants argue that the standard of the profession, which does not require the giving of a routine pressure test to persons under the age of 40, is adequate to insulate the defendants from liability for negligence because the risk of glaucoma is so rare in this age group. The testimony of the defendant, Dr. Carey, however, is revealing as follows:

Q.   Now, when was it, actually, the first time any complaint was made to you by her of any field or visual field problem?

A.   Really, the first time that she really complained of a visual field problem was the August 30th date. [1968.]

Q.   And how soon before the diagnosis was that?

A.   That was 30 days. We made it on October 1st.

Q.   And in your opinion, how long, as you nor have I the whole history and analysis and the diagnosis, how long had she had this glaucoma?

A.   I would think she probably had it ten years or longer.

Q.   Now, Doctor, there's been some reference to the matter of taking pressure checks of persons over 40. What is the incidence of glaucoma, the statistics, with persons under 40?

A.   In the instance of glaucoma under the age of 40, is less than 100 to one percent. The younger you get, the less the incidence. It is thought to be in the neighborhood of one in 25,000 people or less.

Q.   How about the incidence of glaucoma in people over 40?

A.   Incidence of glaucoma over 40 gets into the 2 to 3 percent category, and hence, that's where there is this great big difference and that's why the standards around the world has been to check pressures from 40 on.

The incidence of glaucoma in one out of 25,000 persons under the age of 40 may appear quite minimal. However, that one person, the plaintiff in this instance, is entitled to the same protection, as afforded persons over 40, essential for timely detection of the evidence of glaucoma where it can be arrested to avoid the grave and devastating result of this disease. The test is a simple pressure test, relatively inexpensive. There is no judgment factor involved, and there is no doubt that by giving the test the evidence of glaucoma can be detected. The giving of the test is harmless if the physical condition of the eye permits. The testimony indicates that although the condition of the plaintiff's eyes might have at times prevented the defendants from administering the pressure test, there is an absence of evidence in the record that the test could not have been timely given.

Justice Holmes stated in Texas & Pac. Ry. v. Behymer, 189 U.S. 468, 470, 23 S. Ct. 622, 623, 47 L. Ed. 905 (1903): "What usually is done may be evidence of what ought to be done, but what ought to be done is fixed by a standard of reasonable prudence, whether it usually is complied with or not." In The T. J. Hooper, 60 F.2d 737, on page 740 (2d Cir. 1932), Justice Hand stated: "(I)n most cases reasonable prudence is in fact common prudence; but strictly it is never its measure; a whole calling may have unduly lagged in the adoption of new and available devices. It never may set its own tests, however persuasive be its usages. *Courts must in the end say what is required; there are precautions so imperative that even their universal disregard will not excuse their omission.*" (Italics ours.)

Under the facts of this case reasonable prudence required the timely giving of the pressure test to this plaintiff. The precaution of giving this test to detect the incidence of glaucoma to patients under 40 years of age is so imperative that irrespective of its disregard by the standards of the opthalmology profession, it is the duty of the courts to say what is required to protect patients under 40 from the damaging results of glaucoma.

We therefore hold, as a matter of law, that the reasonable standard that should have been followed under the undisputed facts of this case was the timely giving of this simple, harmless pressure test to this plaintiff and that, in failing to do so, the defendants were negligent, which proximately resulted in the blindness sustained by the plaintiff for which the defendants are liable.

There are no disputed facts to submit to the jury on the issue of the defendants' liability. Hence, a discussion of the plaintiff's proposed instructions would be inconsequential in view of our disposition of the case.

The judgment of the trial court and the decision of the court of appeals is reversed, and the case is remanded for a new trial on the issue of damages only.

■ MEDICAL UNCERTAINTY, DIAGNOSTIC TESTING, AND LEGAL LIABILITY*
Eric E. Fortess & Marshall B. Kapp
13 L. Med. & Health Care 213 (1985)

Health care cost considerations exert increasing influence today over clinical decisionmaking. One way to help contain costs while maintaining the quality of

* Reprinted with the permission of the American Society of Law, Medicine & Ethics.

health care may be to increase among both physicians and patients an acknowledgment of, and tolerance for, a reasonable degree of medical uncertainty. By medical uncertainty we mean here those clinical situations in which, based on available data, absolute scientific proof regarding some aspect of a patient's health status cannot be obtained. . . .

For a variety of reasons, physicians are generally reluctant to acknowledge openly the existence and role of uncertainty in medical care. Traditional medical training does not go deeply into the theory, mathematics, and management of uncertainty. Moreover, physicians tend to insist on maintaining professional control and dominance, to believe in the potential therapeutic efficacy of both the patients' and the professionals' unquestioning confidence in a treatment, and to perceive that many patients will not accept a physician who claims not to be omniscient. . . . The main impetus for physicians' overuse of diagnostic and therapeutic modalities is their intellectual desire to know as much as possible about the facts of each case, whether or not any of the additional data generated will materially affect the course of treatment or the ultimate outcome. Other factors are the Western philosophy that action is superior to inaction and the "technological imperative" perspective that whatever technology can do should be done. See V. Fuchs, Who Shall Live? Health, Economics and Social Change (1974). . . .

A physician comfortable with his or her own uncertainty can usually convince the patient to accept incomplete or indefinite answers and explanations. This acceptance implies a change in emphasis from a Mechanistic Paradigm to a . . . Probabilistic Paradigm. This conceptual framework recognizes that absolute certainty is neither obtainable, identifiable, nor always desirable. . . . Put simply, past a certain point, the chance of achieving a small gain in certainty is not worth the costs—in any respect—of the effort. . . .

Most physicians appreciate the logic of diagnostic and therapeutic restraint in the face of inescapable medical uncertainty. Yet many argue that such restraint could result in patient-initiated medical malpractice suits predicated on provision of less than maximal care. To protect themselves, they resort to "defensive medicine," one cause of rising health care costs. "Defensive medicine" is an ambiguous, often carelessly used term for which Hershey has supplied the most useful working definition: "Poor practice (a deviation from what the physician believes is sound practice and which is generally so regarded) induced by a threat of liability." N. Hershey, The Defensive Practice of Medicine: Myth or Reality, Milbank Memorial Fund Quarterly 50(1):69, 72 (January 1972). A 1983 American Medical Association study claims that 40 percent of the AMA's members prescribe additional tests and 27 percent provide additional treatment at least in part because of the perceived threat of litigation. . . .

Most importantly, our public policymakers assume that uncontrolled health care costs are indeed due partially to a medical malpractice system that engenders defensive medicine. This perception has led to the introduction in Congress of bills that would substantially alter the medical malpractice system in an attempt to control one aspect of federal health care costs.

In spite of the furor over defensive medicine, cost-effective medical practice and the prudent management of legal risks can co-exist. An examination of malpractice jurisprudence supports this thesis and refutes many widespread but incorrect perceptions. . . . By expressly recognizing that the same clinical problem can be approached in a range of different but equally acceptable ways (based either on the physician's philosophical convictions or on recognition of the limited state of medical knowledge), the legal system in essence respects and condones medical uncertainty and embraces the Probabilistic Paradigm. . . .

Contrary to popular medical belief, the mere existence of a particular diagnostic or treatment technology does *not* automatically create a legal imperative to use that technology indiscriminately. . . . The case most often cited to prove that rampant judicial intervention has wreaked havoc with medical standard-setting and necessitated the defensive practice of medicine is Helling v. Carey. . . . The medical profession reacted to the *Helling* decision with somber predictions that the quality of medical practice would fall and the cost of health care would rise, due to the overuse and misuse of diagnostic testing. It was argued that money, time, and other resources would be diverted from real needs and that patients would be unnecessarily exposed to iatrogenic risks. These predictions have in large measure gone unfulfilled. Whatever surge in defensive medicine and costs can be traced directly to *Helling* is attributable to a misperception, rather than to an accurate appraisal of the current status of the law and its requirements.

Basically, the *Helling* case, for all its attendant publicity, simply represents a legal anomaly. With the exception of *Gates v. Jensen*, 595 P.2d 919 (Wash. 1979), in which the same Washington Supreme Court ignored a legislative attempt to return to the professional standard and instead ratified the *Helling* approach, the *Helling* precedent has not been applied in any reported malpractice lawsuit in any jurisdiction. . . .

[Nevertheless], *Helling*, as almost the sole example of direct legal intervention in setting the stringency of a medical standard, bears closer scrutiny. . . . We propose the following method of analysis, based on the mathematics of diagnostic testing, as a model . . . that may be applied to other tests to demonstrate that cost-effective medicine is also legally defensible. . . .

[Glaucoma] is diagnosed with one or more of three tests: tonometry, to measure intraocular pressure; perimetry, to evaluate the patient's field of vision; and funduscopy of the optic disc to detect "cupping" of the head of the optic nerve. In screening for glaucoma, ophthalmologists customarily use a tonometric test first. Tonometry usually involves light contact of the pressure-measuring instrument, the tonometer, on the anesthetized eye. If a pressure greater than 22 millimeters of mercury is found, the other tests may then be used to confirm or reject a diagnosis of glaucoma. Diagnosis is complicated by the fact that some people can have glaucoma without high intraocular pressure, while others can have high pressure (ocular hypertension) without developing glaucoma. . . . If glaucoma is diagnosed, treatment may include drugs to lower intraocular pressure, laser therapy, or surgery.

The diagnostic tests for glaucoma are thus not perfect, and actual disease states do not correspond totally with test results. Two major types of diagnostic error can occur: false negative test results with diseased patients and false positive test results with disease-free individuals. The ability of a test to correctly identify people with a disease is called its *sensitivity*, and its ability to correctly identify people without disease is its *specificity*. A test with few false negative results is highly sensitive, while one with few false positives is very specific. [Screening tests, like the tonometry pressure test used to detect possible glaucoma, are usually designed to err on the side of false positives, considering that false negatives — missing an actual case — are worse than falsely suspecting a number of healthy cases. In addition, even a low false positive *rate*, that is, very good test specificity, will produce a high *number* of false positives if the underlying incidence of the disease is very low, because lots of people have to be tested in order to ferret out the few true positives.] . . .

How do the probabilities of diagnostic testing relate to the *Helling* case? . . . Let us consider a hypothetical population of 25,000 individuals under age forty, of whom one has glaucoma. . . . Applying the estimates representing the best test performance, sensitivity of 70 percent and specificity of [95] percent, to our hypothetical population produces 1,250 false positive results. . . . If one is a true positive and 1,250 are false positives, then we can calculate that [the probability of truly having glaucoma when there is a positive test result is about 0.0008.] . . . Repeating the test, or performing the other two tests—perimetry and funduscopy, each with its own imperfect sensitivity and specificity—will shrink the pool of [false positives] but may never separate the one diseased person from the others. [Therefore, all may need to be treated. In addition, we must consider, even the one true positive may not be detected because of the rate of false negatives. Finally, when detected, treatment for the one true positive may not be safe and effective.] . . .

We have seen that in our hypothetical population, tonometry will probably produce [1,251] positive test results, of which only one truly identifies a person with glaucoma. Several disturbing issues arise. . . . What does the physician do with these patients, over 99.99 percent of whom don't have glaucoma? Does the physician have a duty to inform every patient of the possibility of glaucoma, causing great anxiety in many? Must the physician carefully monitor the thousands of patients identified as being at "increased risk" for glaucoma? What are the costs to society of mislabeling many people as "at risk" and then following and retesting them, perhaps for years? . . .

In retrospect, the *Helling* plaintiff should have been tested on the basis of her complaints and symptoms, despite her youth. But what would constitute good practice in one specific and unusual medical situation should not in itself be sufficient reason to institute a broad policy to test [all] young people for glaucoma.

■ ONE HUNDRED YEARS OF HARMFUL ERROR: THE HISTORICAL JURISPRUDENCE OF MEDICAL MALPRACTICE*
Theodore Silver
1992 Wis. L. Rev. 1193

A medical malpractice action is identical in all vital respects to any and every suit sounding in negligence. That simple truth, however, has been lost in a maze of judicial mistakes one century in the making. . . . Courts do not frequently offer a rationale for the professional custom rule. A few have suggested that medicine is too complex and the human body too temperamental to allow that a doctor be held to the simple standard of reasonableness. . . . Such explanations might at first seem sensible, but sensible they surely are not. First, medicine is no more complex than scores of other professional undertakings. . . . Organ transplantation is

* Reprinted by permission of the Wisconsin Law Review.

glamorous, but surely it is no more complicated or unpredictable in outcome than taming wild animals, designing a nation-wide marketing plan, or evaluating a new corporate security. All these pursuits are prey to the unknown and unknowable, and all demand expertise of a high order. With regard to medicine, complexity and uncertainty provides no greater reason for fashioning a standard of care after custom than they would in any other professional endeavor. . . .

Negligence is nothing more nor less than a failure to do what a reasonable person would under the prevailing circumstance. From a more refined perspective it is a failure to assess reasonably the costs and benefits associated with a given course of conduct, and thus to decide on its advisability. Justice Learned Hand . . . reduced the matter to quasi-mathematical terms, creating the famed Hand calculus: "Possibly it serves to bring this notion into relief to state in algebraic terms: if the probability be called P; the injury, L; and the burden, B; liability depends upon whether B is less than L multiplied by P: i.e., whether $B < PL$." Conway v. O'Brien, 111 F.2d 611 (2nd Cir. 1940).

The complexity of any technical field, medicine included, may well disable a lay juror who seeks independently to assess the relative risks and benefits attending a given course of conduct. That, however, only means that the juror needs advice from experts (genuine experts) who can identify the risks and benefits at issue. Thus informed, there is no reason that a juror cannot and should not pass on the appropriateness of anyone's conduct, including a physician's.

Without expert assistance, a lay juror cannot determine whether it is negligent to discharge a particular cardiac patient from the hospital without prescribing anticoagulants. Yet, to make the determination, the juror requires only that an expert explain how the omission affects the matter of risks and benefits. An expert might explain that, according to standard medical wisdom, anticoagulants present a variety of risks and adverse effects, and, to the extent competent information allows, he might provide estimates of such risks in quantitative terms. . . . Armed with this knowledge, the jury would be competent to determine, as it does in any other negligence suit, whether the defendant physician had acted with reasonable care. . . .

Notes: Ordinary Negligence and the "Hand Formula"; Defensive Medicine

1. *Helling* met with an immediate storm of criticism in the legal and medical literature and upset the insurance industry even more, causing many insurers to feel that the deluge of expanded legal liability had reached revolutionary levels of social and political policy. This decision, along with the concurrence printed below, was credited with contributing to the withdrawal in the mid-1970s of many insurers from the medical malpractice market and the resulting "crisis" in medical malpractice, discussed in section H.

Is *Helling* really all that revolutionary? Can it be justified, for instance, using the res ipsa loquitur and negligence per se rules articulated in the previous notes, or is it simply an example, noted above at page 292, of courts rejecting a medical custom standard of liability in favor of a reasonable physician standard? See, e.g., United Blood Services v. Quintana, 827 P.2d 509 (Colo. 1992) (plaintiff is entitled to show that blood bank's methods for screening for AIDS virus, which were standard at the time, were not sufficiently protective because blood banks had failed to quickly adopt new safer methods). There is an obvious difference, however, between allowing a plaintiff to reach the jury without an expert on a contested question of fact and conceding that all medical opinion is opposed to the plaintiff's position. There is also an obvious difference between allowing the case to go to the jury and finding negligence as a matter of law. Did the defendant have a fair chance to present the data described in the Fortess and Kapp article? Do you think this information would have mattered to the *Helling* court? Prof. Peters explains that

> in one respect, the *Helling* decision was and remains genuinely aberrant. No other court has endorsed the Washington Supreme Court's decision to take the issue of medical negligence away from the jury and to rule, without the benefit of expert testimony, that a customary practice is negligent as a matter of law. This aspect of *Helling* was deeply flawed and has justly contributed to its reputation as a rogue case. However, *Helling*'s rejection of customary norms was not aberrant. Not only has *Helling*'s rejection of customary standards survived in Washington with the eventual blessing of the legislature, but many other courts have reached the same conclusion. Although few of these courts have expressly relied on *Helling*, perhaps because of its notoriety, many have agreed with its rejection of customary standards.

Philip G. Peters, The Quiet Demise of Deference to Custom: Malpractice Law at the Millennium, 57 Wash. & Lee L. Rev. 163, 171 (2000).

Immediately following *Helling*, the Washington legislature attempted to explicitly overrule it by a statute, but the state supreme court interpreted the statute as being consistent with its decision in *Helling*, since the statute refers to the skill and care "possessed" by physicians rather than "practiced" by them. Gates v. Jensen, 595 P.2d 919 (Wash. 1979). A subsequent decision clarifies, however, that "absent exceptional circumstances such as were present in *Helling*, expert testimony will be necessary to show whether or not a particular practice is reasonably prudent" and to clarify what skill and knowledge Washington physicians actually possess. Harris v. Groth, 663 P.2d 113 (Wash. 1983). The net effect, then, is to adopt the same "reasonable physician" standard that exists in many other states.

2. *The Technological Imperative.* It is often said that medicine in general, and doctors in particular, operate under a "technological imperative," which compels the use of all available technology, regardless of the economic, and sometimes even the medical, costs. This imperative is reinforced by the threat of liability, because doctors who want to obtain and use a new piece of equipment or new surgical technique that others are using can always point to the liability concerns of being the last one on the block to innovate. For instance, in Washington v. Washington Hospital Center, 579 A.2d 177 (D.C. 1990), a brain-damaged patient won $4.5 million because the hospital failed to acquire a newer, better machine for monitoring oxygen levels during surgery. The monitor was in use in some, perhaps many, other hospitals, but not in all, and the plaintiff's expert equivocated on whether the new monitor was required by the standard of care at the time of the injury. However, there was evidence that the hospital's chief anesthesiologist, prior to the accident, had asked the hospital to purchase the new monitor, citing as support the potential legal threat of not complying with the emerging national standard of care.

When the technology in question is diagnostic, it produces information relevant to additional courses of treatment. This information often leads to a "clinical cascade," in which further testing is required to confirm or reject the initial test, and then to various paths of treatment. Along the way, other potential or actual problems are often uncovered or created, which precipitate additional testing or treatment. Thus, early intervention and additional information in medicine often spawns greater, not lesser, costs. For instance, one study found that women undergoing annual mammograms have a 50 percent chance of receiving a false positive result over the course of ten years, and a 19 percent chance of undergoing an unnecessary biopsy. One HMO spent $33 to evaluate false positive results for every $100 spent on breast cancer screening. J. G. Elmore et al., Ten-Year Risk of False Positive Screening Mammograms and Clinical Breast Examinations, 338 New Eng. J. Med. 1089 (1998). An accompanying editorial argues that these results do not justify refusing to do routine mammograms for women under age 50, but they do support informing younger women of these odds and giving them the opportunity to decline. Are there any practical difficulties in resolving these issues simply by presenting the choice to patients? See H. Gilbert Welch, Informed Choice in Cancer Screening, 285 JAMA 2776 (2001) (criticizing this approach). Reviewing the evidence, the U.S. Preventive Services Task Force initially recommended routine mammograms starting at age 40. Then, in late 2009, in the midst of national debate over federal health care reform, the Task Force recommended against routine mammograms below age 50. A storm of controversy erupted, amid shouts that government was already starting to ration health care, so the government quickly clarified that the recommendation still leaves doctors and patients free to opt for mammogram screening at younger ages and that most insurance would still continue to pay for this, but the controversy still has not been quelled. See Jessica Mantel, Setting National Coverage Standards for Health Plans Under Healthcare Reform, 58 UCLA L. Rev. 221 (2010).

Given the financial and professional impetus for doing all that is possible in medicine, why do you suppose eye doctors in 1974 had restrained themselves from routinely testing all patients for glaucoma? How likely is this collective restraint to be exercised after *Helling*? Is this kind of collective restraint — selective use of new technology — good or bad for society? Who should make these decisions: doctors, patients, courts, or regulators?

A questionnaire administered several years after *Helling* revealed that it had not affected ophthalmology practice as much as had been expected. Doctors reported that they often performed the glaucoma test on patients under 40, but this was true both within and outside Washington State, and both before and after the court's decision. It appears that the testimony given in the case, that routine testing for younger patients was never done, was simply wrong. Jerry Wiley, The Impact of Judicial Decision on Professional Conduct: An Empirical Study, 55 S. Cal. L. Rev. 345 (1982). In 2005, the U.S. Preventive Services Task Force reviewed all available evidence and concluded that there was "insufficient evidence to recommend for or against screening adults for glaucoma." Due to "uncertainty of the magnitude of benefit from early treatment and given the known harms of screening and early treatment," the task force "could not determine the balance between the benefits and harms of screening for glaucoma." What does this suggest about the accuracy and utility of using tort law to evaluate and regulate medical practice?

3. *The Hand Formula.* Consider how the Hand formula might actually come out in the *Helling* case, using the numbers in Fortess and Kapp and additional reasonable assumptions. Start with the value for L, which represents the injury loss.

What do you think reasonable compensation would be for the partial loss of vision Helling suffered (tunnel vision, but still functional eyesight) — $100,000, $250,000, $500,000, or more? What are the possible values for the other factors? Starting with B, the burden of injury prevention, assume 25,000 people are screened at a cost of $10 each. How much should be added to B for the unnecessary treatment and anxiety caused by false positives — $100 per person? $200? $500? Next, what value should be used for P, the probability of loss prevention? Realize that screening all 25,000 does not guarantee detecting the one bad case, and if it is detected, it is not always possible to treat it effectively. Suppose detection and treatment are only 70 percent effective. Suppose they are only 50 percent effective. What would the value of the loss have to be in order to balance out these costs and probabilities? See Schwartz & Komesar, Doctors, Damages and Deterrence, infra.

4. *Defensive Medicine.* Despite all the controversy, some type of pressure testing has in fact become routine in all eye exams. Perhaps the costs are lower than supposed or the sensitivity and specificity have been improved. Or perhaps this is an example of the phenomenon described as "defensive medicine." This phrase is often used by doctors in a highly pejorative way to accuse the legal system of fostering unnecessary or harmful medical practice adopted solely to avoid liability and not for patient welfare. On the other hand, defensive medicine might be characterized as a perfectly appropriate result of the deterrent effect of liability, which encourages safer practices and more vigilance against error. In the middle ground, defensive medicine might be defined as medical practices adopted for liability reasons that are marginally or potentially beneficial but that, on balance, are wasteful. One must try to be clear in this debate about which understanding of the term is meant.

One place to start is to ask why the worst form of defensive medicine would ever occur. Since nonbeneficial medical procedures impose medical risks from side effects and cost more money, why don't these counterpressures force doctors to resist the legal pressures? One answer is that, under fee-for-service reimbursement, the economic costs of extra procedures are borne by insurance and contribute to doctors' revenues. Observe that liability concerns conceivably could also manifest themselves through lengthier counseling with patients (to acquire greater insight into their lifestyle habits and past medical history) or through more library research (to learn more about difficult, borderline cases) — much like we see in law firms that are paid by the hour — but this is not the sort of behavior complained of. Instead, it is said that physicians manifest defensive concerns by increasing the number of tests and procedures — no surprise since they are paid on a fee-for-service basis. Given this, is defensive medicine likely to abate, or at least assume a different form, as payment shifts to a different form? See Daniel Kessler & Mark McClellan, Malpractice Law and Health Care Reform: Optimal Liability Policy in an Era of Managed Care, 84 J. Public Econ. 175 (2002) (finding that managed care restrictions and liability reforms have similar and reinforcing effects in reducing defensive practices, which suggests that both payment incentives and liability pressures contribute to excess medical costs); Michael Frakes, The Surprising Relevance of Medical Malpractice Law, 82 U. Chicago L. Rev. 317 (2015) (arguing that medical costs would be more responsive to legal rules if underlying payment methods were not so inflationary).

Another reason doctors may minimize or ignore the medical risks created by nonbeneficial defensive medicine is that these risks may be less likely to result in large damage verdicts. A single omitted diagnosis concentrates the harms of omission in a single case. A mild side effect spreads the harms of commission over a large number of cases, none of which is likely to result in suit. Also, side effects from unnecessary procedures may be more difficult to prove. Consider, for instance, that while too many X-rays may cause an increased risk of cancer, it is almost impossible to detect the specific origin of any particular case of cancer. Occasionally, however, one does see a successful suit for the harmful effects of unnecessary treatment, especially surgery. E.g., Riser v. American Med. Int'l, 620 So. 2d 372 (La. Ct. App. 1993) (liability for unnecessary arteriogram that caused patient to die from a stroke).

5. *The Extent of Defensive Medicine.* How precisely to define defensive medicine and the extent to which it contributes to the total costs of health care are still matters very much in debate. Based on estimates of tens of billions of dollars, the AMA and other interest groups continue to press for sweeping federal relief from state malpractice laws as one means to lower health care costs, but others sharply criticize the methodology behind the estimates. Also, they note that even tens of billions of dollars is considerably less than 10 percent of the nation's $2.5 trillion health care bill.

6. *Negative Defensive Medicine.* Perhaps the most serious harm of defensive medicine, however, is when it operates in the opposite direction, to discourage doctors from doing certain procedures. This is known as "negative" defensive medicine. Because the malpractice liability threat is especially high for labor and delivery, many general practitioners have stopped delivering babies, some obstetricians refuse to take certain high-risk cases or restrict their practice to gynecology, and others refuse to accept Medicaid patients for whom the reimbursement is too low to compensate for the liability risk. This aggravates the serious shortage of physicians in rural areas and creates barriers to care for other disadvantaged population groups who are more prone to premature births or to being on Medicaid.

A large and prominent medical group in San Diego adopted a policy of transferring patients and all their family members if they filed a malpractice claim. In one case, the court ruled that this could constitute illegal abandonment, interference with the doctor-patient relationship, and breach of fiduciary duties if the transfer hampered access to care or lacked sufficient notice and opportunity to find a new physician. Scripps Clinic v. Superior Court, 108 Cal. App. 4th 917, 134 Cal. Rptr. 2d 101 (Cal. App. 2003). In Williams v. St. Joseph Hospital, 629 F.2d 448 (7th Cir. 1980), the court found that this could constitute an antitrust violation.

7. *Further Reading.* For discussion of **technological imperative** issues (note 2) relating to electronic fetal monitoring during childbirth, see Note, 51 Stan. L. Rev. 807 (1999); James Gibson, Doctrinal Feedback and (Un)reasonable Care, 94 Va. L. Rev. 1641 (2008). See generally, H. Gilbert Welch et al., Overdiagnosed: Making People Sick in the Pursuit of Health (2011); Richard A. Deyo, Cascade Effects of Medical Technology, 23 Ann. Rev. Pub. Health 23 (2002).

For additional discussion of the **empirical issues in *Helling***, see J. F. Bovin et al., Cost-Effectiveness of Screening for Primary Open Angle Glaucoma, 3 J. Med. Screening 154 (1996); Comment, Rational Health Policy and the Legal Standard of Care: A Call for Judicial Deference to Medical Practice Guidelines, 77 Cal. L. Rev. 1483 (1989); William Schwartz & Neil Komesar, Damages and Deterrence: An Economic View of Medical Malpractice, 298 New Eng. J. Med. 1282 (1978).

For additional discussion of **defensive medicine** and physicians' perceptions of the legal system (note 5), see page 264; Tom Baker, The Medical Malpractice

Myth (2005); Michelle Mello et al., National Costs of the Medical Liability System, 29(9) Health Aff. 1569 (Sept. 2010) (estimating defensive costs of (only) $45 billion); James Reschovsky & Cynthia Saiontz-Martinez, Malpractice Claim Fears and the Costs of Treating Medicare Patients, Health Serv. Res. (2017) (estimating that physicians' liability concerns add $1,000–$2,000 per year to the cost of Medicare patients); William Thomas et al., Low Costs of Defensive Medicine, Small Savings from Tort Reform, 29(9) Health Aff. 1578 (Sept. 2010); Troyen A. Brennan et al., Liability, Patient Safety, and Defensive Medicine, *in* Medical Malpractice and the U.S. Health Care System 93, 109-110 (W. Sage & R. Kersh eds., 2006); David Studdert et al., Defensive Medicine Among High-Risk Specialist Physicians, 293 JAMA 2609 (2005); D. Kessler & M. McClellan, Do Doctors Practice Defensive Medicine?, 8 Q. J. Econ. 353 (1996).

Problem: To Test or Not to Test

Older women are at higher risk of giving birth to children with certain congenital defects such as Down syndrome. Amniocentesis, the test for these defects, itself poses risks of causing a miscarriage. The universal, accepted practice for pregnant women without a family history of defects is to use amniocentesis routinely only for women age 35 or over. The logic is that, under 35, the statistical risk of miscarriage is greater than the chance of detecting serious birth defects. Also, amniocentesis can have false positives, which can result in erroneously aborting a healthy fetus.

How would you evaluate the age-35 rule of thumb under *Helling*? Under the Hand formula? Under informed consent law? Consider this both from the situation of a younger woman who is not tested who delivers a baby with Down syndrome, and an older woman who is tested, resulting in the miscarriage of a healthy fetus.

C. QUALIFICATION AND EXAMINATION OF MEDICAL EXPERTS

Earlier editions of this casebook devoted hundreds of pages to issues of medical proof in civil and criminal litigation generally. Medical and similar scientific expertise is critical in areas as diverse as criminal law, paternity disputes, and competency hearings. Lawyers in these cases draw from countless scientific disciplines and specific techniques such as autopsies, genetics and DNA fingerprinting, polygraphs, and hypnosis-induced memory. See generally D. H. Kaye, Science in Evidence (1997); David Faigman et al., Modern Scientific Evidence (1997); Federal Judicial Center, Reference Manual on Scientific Evidence (1994); Jason Payne-James et al. eds., Encyclopedia of Forensic and Legal Medicine (2006). Earlier in this century, issues like these dominated the field of law and medicine, which was then known as "medical jurisprudence." See James C. Mohr, Doctors and the Law: Medical Jurisprudence in Nineteenth-Century America (1993). Today, it is no longer possible to adequately summarize each of these branches of forensic medicine. Instead, they are addressed in the law school curriculum as specialized aspects of advanced evidence law, or of law and science more generally. For those who are interested, a sampling of these issues can be found on the Web site for this book, www.health-law. org, where we have provided an edited version of the Supreme Court's landmark decision on scientific evidence, Daubert v. Merrell Dow Pharmaceuticals, Inc., 509 U.S. 579 (1993), with notes relevant to medical issues.

Even though medical proof in general is no longer a major part of this course, it is still important to understand the fundamentals of medical proof as one aspect of litigating medical malpractice cases. For this reason, we survey in this section a variety of common evidentiary and discovery issues encountered in malpractice litigation, primarily, how litigants in medical malpractice cases prove or dispute the standard of care.

■ TREES V. ORDONEZ
311 P3d 848 (Or. 2013)

BALMER, C. J.

In this medical malpractice case, . . . Plaintiff presented expert testimony from a biomechanical engineer familiar with use of the medical device installed on plaintiff's cervical spine by defendant, a neurosurgeon. For the reasons set out below, we conclude that plaintiff introduced sufficient evidence from an expert witness who is not a medical doctor to present a jury question on at least one aspect of her negligence claim.

Dr. Ordonez, a neurosurgeon, performed surgery on plaintiff that involved installing a plate made by Synthes on plaintiff's cervical spine . . . Plaintiff brought this negligence action against Dr. Ordonez . . . alleging, among other things, that Dr. Ordonez had failed to properly place and secure the Synthes plate and its screws, resulting in damage to plaintiff's esophagus that led to other injuries. At trial, plaintiff presented expert testimony from Dr. Tencer, a biomechanical engineer who is not a medical doctor, about the design, use, and installation of the Synthes plate; however, no medical doctor testified that defendant had breached the standard of care. At the close of plaintiff's evidence, the court granted defendant's motion for a directed verdict on the standard of care and breach because, although Dr. Tencer's testimony established the "ideal" placement of the Synthes plate, the court determined that defendant's conduct had to be compared to that of other neurosurgeons . . . We conclude that Dr. Tencer's testimony was sufficient for plaintiff to survive a motion for a directed verdict, and we reverse . . .

The Synthes plate that defendant used is a titanium plate designed to provide stability to allow for cervical fusion . . . To install the plate, the surgeon inserts a set of two screws into each of the six holes in the plate . . . For plaintiff's surgery, defendant used the smallest available plate, ...

At trial, plaintiff presented expert testimony from Dr. Tencer, a biomechanical engineer who works as a professor in the Department of Orthopedic Surgery at the medical school at the University of Washington. Dr. Tencer has a Ph.D. in mechanical engineering and is not a medical doctor. He testified, however, that there is overlap between the two disciplines because biomechanical engineering involves "engineering devices for the human body," and "surgeon[s] put[ ] in mechanical devices to hold bones together."

In his current position as a professor, Dr. Tencer lectures medical residents who are learning to become orthopedists on various topics, including "what types of things to watch out for" when using implants, and he guides some of those residents through research projects. He acts as a scientific reviewer for a variety of academic journals, including the journal Spine, and he has lectured to the National Association of Orthopedic Surgeons. In addition, he conducts his own research and has developed an implant system for spinal surgeries. Dr. Tencer testified that in the course of conducting research comparing the Synthes plate to other similar devices, he had watched and participated in the placement of a Synthes plate on a cadaver, but had not participated in such a surgery involving a living person . . . Outside the research and patient care context, Dr. Tencer testified that he also had experience with Synthes devices because he had done biomechanical testing of some of those devices as part of the FDA approval process, and he had helped Synthes come up with ways to improve their products.

Dr. Tencer testified about . . . defendant's placement of the plate on plaintiff's cervical spine, and he identified two related concerns. His first concern was that, unlike a correctly installed plate, the plate had not been bent to follow the curvature of plaintiff's spine. As a result, the plate was not close enough to the cervical spine to allow the screws to be fully seated in the plate. His second concern was that some of the screw heads protruded above the plate.

Dr. Tencer focused on the second concern, testifying that the plate that defendant had selected was the incorrect size. The plate was too short, and, as a result, the screws used to secure the plate were "over angled," and five of the six screws did not sit flush with the plate. Dr. Tencer went on to state that "it's very well defined as a step that the screw head must sit underneath down below the plates so it doesn't present any sharp edges" because "obviously [sharp edges] can lead to damage to the tissue." Specifically, he noted that a protruding screw head could come into contact with the esophagus. Given that risk, Dr. Tencer testified that, because there were screws protruding above the plate used on plaintiff, "it's pretty clear it's a go/no-go situation. In other words, any protrusion above the plate is essentially no-go, because it's clear that it can cause damage of some type, and it's very well described in all the literature that there should be no protrusion.". . .

[T]he issue is whether the testimony of an expert who is not a medical doctor can establish "that degree of care, skill and diligence that is used by ordinarily careful physicians . . . in the same or similar circumstances" and a breach of that standard. . . . [Oregon Rule of Evidence 702] provides that "a witness qualified as an expert by knowledge, skill, experience, training or education" may testify "[i] f scientific, technical or other specialized knowledge will assist the trier of fact to understand the evidence or to determine a fact in issue." . . .

Other jurisdictions have split on the issue: some jurisdictions have required expert testimony from a medical doctor to establish the standard of care, and others have held that experts who are not medical doctors may, in certain cases, provide testimony sufficient to establish the standard of care for a medical doctor. Compare Bell v. Hart, 516 So.2d 562, 570 (Ala.1987) (finding pharmacist and psychologist could not testify to standard of care in negligent prescription case against physician because "the standard of care must be established by medical testimony," meaning "testimony by physicians or properly introduced medical treatises"), with Thompson v. Carter, 518 So.2d 609, 614–15 (Miss.1987) (toxicologist and pharmacologist should have been allowed to testify regarding the standard of care for physician prescribing a drug because an expert on the standard of care must possess medical knowledge, but need not possess a medical degree) . . .

This court's medical malpractice cases . . . focus on whether the expert has the necessary knowledge to support his or her testimony, rather than whether the expert has a particular degree or specialty. See, e.g., Sheppard v. Firth, 334 P.2d 190 (Or. 1959) (finding that trial court erred in allowing orthopedic surgeon, who had no training in treatment using chiropractic adjustments, to testify that chiropractor's treatment was improper). For example, unlike decisions from some other jurisdictions, our cases have allowed experts from schools of medicine different from the defendant's to testify to the standard of care, if they have the necessary knowledge . . .

In Creasey v. Hogan, 637 P.2d 114 (Or. 1981), for example, this court held that two orthopedic surgeons could testify regarding the standard of care for a podiatrist in performing a bunionectomy. The court based its decision on evidence that orthopedic surgeons as well as podiatrists perform bunionectomies, use similar methods of treatment, rely on some of the same texts, and attend the same medical conferences. The court also noted that at least one of the methods that the podiatrist had used in that case was commonly used by both disciplines. Thus, in determining the qualifications of experts in medical malpractice cases, our cases have looked to substance, rather than form, and have focused on the knowledge of the expert, see id., rather than on an expert's particular medical degree or area of specialty . . .

Based on our cases, testimony from a qualified expert, who has knowledge about the standard of care that is helpful to the trier of fact, is admissible, and we see no principled reason why such testimony is necessarily insufficient to establish the standard of care in a medical malpractice case merely because that testimony comes from an expert who is not a medical doctor. . . . [M]any of defendant's concerns about allowing a nonphysician to establish the standard of care can be addressed through cross-examination of the nonphysician experts and through a defendant doctor's own testimony or that of his or her experts. That is, a defendant can challenge the weight that the trier of fact should afford to testimony from an expert who is not a medical doctor, and then the jury—not this court—ultimately must determine what weight to afford that testimony . . .

Based on Dr. Tencer's testimony, a reasonable jury could infer that an "ordinarily careful" surgeon would not leave screws protruding above the plate because that would present a "no-go" situation, particularly when those screws specifically are designed to sit below the surface of the plate due to the risk of damage to the soft tissue . . . [Thus], the evidence that the screw heads in this case were protruding above the plate could allow a jury to find that defendant breached the standard of care . . . .

■ CRUZ-VAZQUEZ v. MENNONITE GENERAL HOSPITAL
613 F.3d 54 (1st Cir. 2010)

Lipez, Circuit Judge.

In this action filed pursuant to Puerto Rico's medical malpractice law, . . . the district court excluded the testimony of the plaintiffs' lone expert witness at trial. [We reverse.] . . .

The plaintiffs brought this [malpractice] action against Mennonite General Hospital, two physicians, and several others, alleging that the defendants' negligence caused the premature birth of their daughter and her death two days later. . . .

[T]he plaintiffs proposed to introduce testimony from one expert witness, Dr. Carlos E. Ramírez. . . . In response to an oral motion by the defendants, however, the court . . . ruled that Dr. Ramírez was not a qualified expert and would not be permitted to testify. The court then determined that the plaintiffs lacked evidence to support their claims and granted the defendants' motion for judgment as a matter of law on that basis. . . .

[T]he judge's task in determining whether to admit or exclude expert testimony is "to ensure that the expert's testimony 'both rests on a reliable foundation and is relevant to the task at hand.'" Although a district court has substantial discretion to make admissibility determinations on expert testimony, that discretion is not without bounds. An expert "with appropriate credentials and an appropriate foundation for the opinion at issue must be permitted to present testimony as long as the testimony has a 'tendency to make the existence of any fact that is of consequence to the determination of the action more probable or less probable than it would be without the evidence.'" (quoting Fed. R. Evid. 401). Generally, if an expert has "scientific, technical, [and] other specialized knowledge" that "will assist the trier better to understand a fact in issue," and that knowledge "rests on a reliable foundation," that testimony must be admitted.

Dr. Ramírez received his medical degree in 1981 from the University of Puerto Rico, . . . [and] became board certified in obstetrics and gynecology in 1987 and was re-certified in 1997. . . . Dr. Ramírez served as a [part-time] faculty member in gynecology and obstetrics for twenty-six years [at the University of Puerto Rico, and did both general gynecology and obstetrics]. In 2000, after being diagnosed with cancer, Dr. Ramírez left his private practice. . . . Since that time, he has . . . served as an expert witness in approximately 150 medical malpractice cases in the past ten years . . . primarily for plaintiffs because . . . defendants are reluctant to hire experts who have testified for plaintiffs in medical malpractice actions.

The district court excluded Dr. Ramírez's testimony on the ground that Dr. Ramírez was biased in favor of plaintiffs in medical malpractice cases. . . . The court also highlighted the fact that "Dr. Ramírez has begun collaborating with the distinguished attorney for Plaintiffs in this case . . . to give lectures regarding medical-malpractice and EMTALA." The Court noted that those lectures were "for profit, thereby focusing [Dr. Ramírez's] work further on assisting plaintiffs who seek to sue doctors and hospitals for various alleged violations of the law." This too "indicate[d] to the Court that Dr. Ramírez is not an impartial witness" because "he has a significant stake in the successful outcome of cases brought by alleged victims of medical malpractice."

In a similar vein, the Court described . . . a "trend" in which "supposed experts" do not "utiliz[e] scientific methods to render an opinion" but instead "twist[] scientific methods to produce a result that will support the case of those footing the bill." [T]he district court explained that it evaluated such experts "with a highly critical eye in order to preserve the sanctity of the common law legal system." . . .

The district court cited as the basis for excluding Dr. Ramírez's testimony aspects of his work that are typically established through cross-examination of an expert witness at trial in an effort to discredit his or her testimony. The court's reasoning had nothing to do with the scientific validity of the opinion that Dr. Ramírez proposed to offer or the principles that underlie it. . . . By excluding Dr. Ramírez's testimony due to its own determination that Dr. Ramírez would be a biased witness on the grounds cited, the district court abused its discretion. Assessing the potential bias of an expert witness, as distinguished from his or her specialized training or knowledge or the validity of the scientific underpinning for the expert's opinion, is a task that is "properly left to the jury." . . . Thus, considerations such as an expert witness's pecuniary interest in the outcome of a case, or his status as an expert witness only for one side of an issue, or the extent to which a doctor currently sees patients, go to the probative weight of testimony, not its admissibility. Furthermore, specific credentials, such as an up-to-date board certification, are not required for an expert to be qualified to testify. . . . The judgment is therefore vacated.

Notes: Qualification and Impeachment of Experts

1. *The Practice Dimension.* Observe that the requirements for qualifying an expert to testify on the standard of care are distinct from those for testifying about causation or extent of injuries. The former is our primary focus here. On the latter, see sections E.1 and F.

As the *Trees* court explains, the American courts are split on the issue of the competency of nonphysicians to testify on the standards of patient care required of medical practitioners. For other examples of the more restrictive viewpoint see Boehm v. Mayo Clinic Rochester, 690 N.W.2d 721 (Minn. 2005) (nurse practitioner lacked sufficient training or practical experience to testify about the standard of care for restraining the head movement of a patient after surgery by a thoracic surgeon); Wexler v. Hecht, 928 A.2d 973 (Pa. 2007) (under state statute, podiatrist may not testify about bunion surgery done by orthopedist).

Similar objections can be lodged against physicians as well. See, e.g., Williams v. Wadsworth, 503 N.W.2d 120 (Minn. 1993) (cardiologist who had not performed lymphangiogram in ten years could not testify against endocrinologist); Chase v. Mary Hitchcock Memorial Hospital, 668 A.2d 50 (N.H. 1995) (general practitioner who did not usually handle premature deliveries could not testify against obstetrician). However, most courts do not require physician experts to practice in precisely the same specialty as the defendant.

It is also curious to observe how courts react when physicians are called to testify against nonphysicians. Again, decisions are split. Creekmore v. Maryview Hospital, 662 F.3d 686 (4th Cir. 2011) (physician may testify about nursing standard for monitoring high-risk maternity patient); Sullivan v. Edward Hospital, 806 N.E.2d 645 (Ill. 2004) (physician may not testify about the standard of care for nurses in restraining a patient from falling out of bed); Wilkins v. Conn. Childbirth & Women's Ctr., 104 A.3d 671 (Ct. 2014) (physician may testify against a nurse midwife); Hankla v. Postell, 749 S.E.2d 726 (Ga. 2013) (physician who does not supervise or train nurse midwives may not testify against them).

2. *The Geographic Dimension.* Another dimension of an expert's qualification in addition to specialty and licensure is geographic location of practice. Where the jurisdiction follows a local or statewide standard of care, is it necessary for the expert to actually live and practice in that location? Generally, no; courts allow experts to assert knowledge of local practices through professional contacts in addition to actual practice. In Idaho, this has been elevated to a high art form in about a half dozen state supreme court cases that clarify precisely what extent of local inquiry will suffice for properly educating an out-of-area expert. See Symposium, 44 Idaho

L. Rev. 291 (2008); Suhadolnik v. Pressman, 254 P.3d 11 (Idaho 2011) (expert's bare statement that he is familiar with local practice does not suffice; must show he talked with a local specialist; not sufficient merely to review medical records and depositions in the case); Gubler v. Boe, 815 P.2d 1034 (Idaho 1991) (plaintiff must show that the local doctors his expert consulted were practicing in the same town the year the treatment was rendered). See also Shipley v. Williams, 350 S.W.3d 527 (Tenn. 2011) (lengthy opinion explaining all the ways in which an out-of-state expert can show actual knowledge of local practice). Another technique for qualifying out-of-state experts is for them to assert that national standards apply equally in every location. See, e.g., Henning v. Thomas, 366 S.E.2d 109 (Va. 1988). But see Falcon v. Cheung, 848 P.2d 1050 (Mont. 1993) (university physician may not testify to rural standard of care if he has never practiced in that setting).

3. *Impeaching Hired Guns.* Cruz-Vazquez v. Mennonite General Hospital adopts the prevailing approach of allowing "professional experts" to testify, subject to impeachment. Some courts go further, however, by restricting insinuations of an "opinion for sale." For instance, one court ordered a new trial where plaintiff's counsel unfairly characterized the hospital's expert as a " 'hired gun' who peddles his expertise randomly" and where plaintiff's counsel introduced extensive evidence about all of the defense expert's various sources of income, including fees from patient care and from consulting unrelated to malpractice litigation. The court reasoned that "there must be, and is, a point beyond which inquiry is/will be held to be prejudicial, too intrusive and only serving to divert the case into collateral matters." Mohn v. Hahnemann Medical College, 515 A.2d 920-923 (Pa. Super. Ct. 1986).

For a survey of legal and regulatory actions that can be taken to reprimand or control medical experts, see Gary N. McAbee, Improper Expert Medical Testimony: Existing and Proposed Mechanisms of Oversight, 19 J. Leg. Med. 257 (1998); Fred L. Cohen, The Expert Medical Witness in Legal Perspective, 25 J. Leg. Med. 185 (2004). See also Austin v. American Ass'n of Neurological Surgeons, 253 F.3d 967 (7th Cir. 2001) (expert witness had no right to challenge his suspension from a professional medical association for giving "irresponsible" testimony). For a general analysis and critique, with proposals for reform, see Jody Menon, Adversarial Medical and Scientific Testimony and Lay Jurors, 21 Am. J. L. & Med. 282 (1995).

4. *Statutory Reforms.* A number of states have cracked down on the perceived abuses of hired-gun, out-of-state, and inexperienced experts by enacting statutes that set more demanding qualifications. Common examples include requiring the expert (1) to reside in or near the state; (2) to have been in active practice in recent years (which excludes full-time teachers and researchers as well as "consultants"); (3) to practice in the same or overlapping specialty, or to have performed the same type of procedure, in recent years; and/or (4) to be licensed in the same professional category. Following these criteria, courts are becoming more stringent about expert qualifications. One court, for instance, refused to allow an osteopathic family physician to testify against another osteopathic family physician because their board certifications were from different professional organizations. Dale v. Kolb, 61 So. 3d 251 (Ala. 2010). See also Stowell v. Huddleston, 643 F.3d 631 (Minn. 2011) (refusing to allow an ophthalmologist to testify against a surgeon regarding failure to warn a patient about the risk of blindness from a procedure).

These statutes often contain "escape valves" that give trial courts limited discretionary authority to waive these requirements for just cause. See, e.g., Jackson v. Qureshi, 671 S.E.2d 163 (Va. 2009) (out-of-state pediatrician may testify against a pediatric emergency physician); Sutphin v. Platt, 720 S.W.2d 455 (Tenn. 1986) (upholding constitutionality of residency rule because escape clause avoided hardship). But, where there is no judicial escape valve, one court has declared statutory restrictions on expert qualifications to be unconstitutional because they invaded the judiciary's "sole . . . province" to determine procedural matters. Broussard v. St. Edward Mercy Health System, Inc., 386 S.W.3d (Ark. 2012).

■ TRIAL TACTICS AND METHODS*
Robert E. Keeton**
1973

Plaintiff Peter Park alleges that Defendant David Dell, an anesthesiologist, negligently injected liquid anaesthesia into tissues of plaintiff's arm rather than into the vein, causing damage to nerves and producing disability. At trial, a professor of neurology, who did not treat plaintiff and does not have personal knowledge of the relevant medical history, is called as an expert witness for the plaintiff. [The following demonstrates how] hypothetical questions [might] be framed as to the cause of plaintiff's disability and as to whether the defendant's conduct failed to measure up to professional standards:

Doctor, as the basis for my next question, please assume the following as facts:

(1) Peter Park, on January 6, 19X3, went to the Dental Clinic of Ames Memorial Hospital for an operation to be conducted by Dr. John Rogers, an oral surgeon, the operation having been scheduled to treat a serious infection of Peter Parks' gums, which had been diagnosed by Dr. Rogers as advanced gingivitis;

(2) Defendant, Dr. David Dell, was the attending anesthesiologist at that operation;

(3) Defendant, Dr. Dell, began to anesthetize Peter Park for the operation by an injection of a liquid anesthesia, called Brevitol, into Peter Park's left arm;

(4) The first injection produced no effect of drowsiness; also, immediately after that injection, Peter Park complained of severe pain in the arm and requested that the proposed operation not be done and that he be released;

(5) Defendant, Dr. David Dell, with the assistance of others, restrained Peter Park forcefully, and, without checking again to be sure the needle was properly seated, so as to cause the injection to go into the vein where it was supposed to go Dr. Dell injected additional liquid anesthesia, called Brevitol, into plaintiff's left arm;

(6) After the second injection of Brevitol failed to produce the intended effect, Dr. Dell and others again restrained Peter Park forcibly, and Dr. Dell administered gas as an anesthetic;

(7) Dr. Rogers, the oral surgeon, then proceeded with the operation;

(8) Peter Park remained at the Dental Clinic after the operation for about four hours, and during that time continued to complain of pain in his left arm and

---

* Adapted from materials developed by the Instructors in Trial Practice at Harvard Law School. Reprinted with permission.

** Formerly Professor at Harvard Law School and subsequently a trial court judge.

of what he described to attendants as a crawling sensation in the fingers of his left hand and in his left arm; . . .

(9) The pain gradually went away during the next few days, but Peter Park was, and is, still not able to straighten into the full open position the third and fourth fingers of his left hand;

(10) In February, 19X3, Peter Park came to you, on the recommendation of a friend, and his condition was as you found it to be and as you have described it in your testimony today in this court, including sensory and motor deprivation in the left arm, centering in the region of the third and fourth fingers, and damage to the ulnar and median nerves.

Doctor, given these assumptions and findings, have you an opinion, with reasonable certainty, as to the cause of the condition of Peter Park's arm?

Yes, I do.

What is that opinion?

Brevitol injected into his arm missed the vein and entered the tissues, causing nerve damage.

Doctor, given the same set of assumptions and findings, have you an opinion, with reasonable certainty, as to whether the attending anesthesiologist, Dr. Dell, acted in accordance with the professional standards of medical practice among anesthesiologists in this and similar communities while attending Peter Park on January 6, 19X3?

I do.

What is that opinion?

He did not.

Please explain in what way Dr. Dell did not act in accordance with these professional standards.

He missed the vein with the needle, shot a batch of Brevitol into the tissues of the arm, and failed to check the placement of the needle before injecting a second batch, after the first failed to have its expected effect.

■McCOURT v. ABERNATHY
457 S.E.2d 603 (S.C. 1995)

[The following is part of the examination of one of the plaintiff's experts in the case excerpted at page 282, taken from the trial court record. The expert is a physician practicing emergency medicine in South Carolina.]

Q. Did you have an opportunity to go over the medical records thoroughly?
A. I have.
Q. Did you have an opportunity to read the deposition of Steve McCourt?
A. I have.
Q. Did you have an opportunity to read the deposition of Dr. David Potts?
A. Yes.
Q. Would you tell the jury, please, what your opinions are in regards to the treatment that Mrs. McCourt received on March the 9th, if you have any opinions in that regard?

A.   The opinion I form is based on the information that has been given to me; in part the death summary, and in part the comments that have been made today. But I feel that indeed if an infectious finger was presented on the 9th, if indeed the individual was evaluated on the 9th, I feel that it falls below the standard of care not to have treated that prophylactically.

Q.   All right. Tell us what the standard of care, meaning the proper practice, for March the 9th would have been if done correctly.

A.   . . . I would view this as a dirty wound . . . or contaminated. There are a number of guidelines promulgated in part by the American College of Surgeons and others that would suggest that individuals who are showing signs of infection, which could be localized tenderness or pain, with a contaminated wound, would benefit from prophylactic antibiotics.

■ STANG-STARR v. BYINGTON

532 N.W.2d 26 (Neb. 1995)

CAPORALE, Justice. . . .

Pursuant to verdict, the district court dismissed this action wherein [] Teri Stang-Starr claims she was damaged by the negligent failure of [] Dr. Robert T. Byington to properly diagnose and treat abnormalities in her cervix. [Over a period of eight months, Byington obtained three Pap smears. The first showed moderate cellular abnormalities. The second report incorrectly stated no malignant cells were present. The lab made a mistake and should have said the sample was unsatisfactory and therefore the evaluation was inconclusive. The third Pap smear, followed by a biopsy, found stage IV cervical cancer. The defense disputed whether a correct diagnosis would have made a difference, arguing that it was not possible for moderate abnormalities to progress to full scale cancer so quickly. The jury found in favor of the defendant doctor.] Stang-Starr . . . here asserts that the district court erred by refusing to permit her to question her medical experts regarding medical texts and treatises upon which they relied in their testimony. . . .

During the trial, Stang-Starr called two physicians to testify on her behalf as expert witnesses: Dr. Manford Oliphant and Dr. William Woodard. . . . Based on his knowledge and information obtained from textbooks, medical literature, and personal experience, Oliphant formed an opinion, to a reasonable medical probability, as to the standard of care required of a board-certified obstetrician in May 1986 in Lincoln or similar communities. He then testified that he had read a particular technical bulletin issued by the [American College of Obstetrics] as a predicate to formulating some of the opinions on dysplasia to which he had testified. When Stang-Starr offered that bulletin into evidence, Byington successfully interposed a hearsay objection.

Stang-Starr then made an offer of proof of the bulletin and of material found in more than 12 textbooks concerning gynecology and colposcopy. She proposed that Oliphant would identify the text as authority in the field, identify the text as a basis of opinion, and identify and read specific passages of the material upon which Oliphant relied in testifying. The district court sustained Byington's hearsay objections to the offers.

Woodard then took the stand and testified that in forming his opinion, he had reviewed five or six textbooks, other specifically named textbooks, 15 to 18 journal articles, and the college bulletin identified earlier. In making an offer of proof, Stang-Starr represented that were Woodard allowed to respond to questions about those medical authorities, he would describe the textbooks by title, author, and date of publication, but would not attempt to quote from the actual text. Byington's hearsay objection to the offer was sustained. . . .

On cross-examination, Woodard testified generally as to what the medical literature suggested. When asked on cross-examination whether he had experienced a patient's cancer to progress from normal to invasive within nine months, he replied that the "literature suggests that the original Pap smear was improper or was one of those false negatives, from 15 to 40 percent, and that the cancer doesn't go that rapidly." . . .

On redirect examination, Woodard was asked whether in his opinion there existed in May 1986 diagnostic chaos as to how a gynecologist should have responded to moderate dysplasia in Pap smears. Woodard responded that there was no confusion as to what to do about dysplasia from a gynecologist's standpoint. When asked what the basis for his statement was, Woodard began to reply about the technical bulletin referred to earlier. Byington objected on the basis of hearsay and lack of foundation. Stang-Starr then withdrew the question, and the redirect examination continued with the following questions and answers: . . .

Q.   Okay. Let me hand you, Dr. Woodard, a copy—first of all, will you verify what's been marked as . . . the . . . technical bulletin . . . and refer you to page 3 under "Evaluation of Abnormalities." . . .
Q.   Do those two paragraphs address the approach to an abnormal Pap smear when the report comes back?
A.   Yes, they do.
Q.   Would you please give us your interpretation of those two paragraphs from that . . . bulletin? . . .

The objection was sustained. . . .

When offered to prove the truth of matters asserted in them, learned writings, such as treatises, books, and articles regarding specialized areas of knowledge, are clearly hearsay. 2 McCormick on Evidence §321 (John W. Strong 4th ed. 1992). There was no exception for learned treatises at common law, and medical textbooks and professional articles are not admissible to prove the substantive facts stated therein. . . . We have permitted the use of standard medical texts and other authorities for the purpose of impeaching, contradicting, or discrediting a witness through cross-examination. . . . We have not, however, permitted the use of such materials as independent evidence of the opinions and theories advanced by the parties. As explained in Van Skike v. Potter, 73 N.W. 295, 299 (Neb. 1887):

> [E]ven if they are regarded as authoritative, [medical texts] cannot be read to the jury as independent evidence of the opinions and theories therein expressed or advocated. One objection to such testimony is that it is not delivered under oath; a second objection is that the opposite party is thereby deprived of the benefit of a cross-examination; and a third and perhaps a more important reason for rejecting

such testimony is that the science of medicine is not an exact science. There are different schools of medicine, the members of which entertain widely different views, and it frequently happens that medical practitioners belonging to the same school will disagree as to the cause of a particular disease, or as to the nature of an ailment with which a patient is afflicted, even if they do not differ as to the mode of treatment. Besides, medical theories, unlike the truths of exact science, are subject to frequent modification and change, even if they are not altogether abandoned. For these reasons it is very generally held that when, in a judicial proceeding, it becomes necessary to invoke the aid of medical experts it is safer to rely on the testimony of competent witnesses who are produced, sworn, and subjected to a cross-examination, than to permit medical books or pamphlets to be read to the jury.

. . . While it is likely that the practice of medicine is more of a science today than it was almost a century ago when we decided *Van Skike*, the fact remains that the *Van Skike* reasoning continues to be sound. We are thus not persuaded that we should abandon our longstanding rule in this regard.

Nor does the fact that the out-of-court statements contained in the authorities were offered in the guise of forming the bases for the testifying experts' opinions alchemically transmute them from inadmissible hearsay into admissible nonhearsay. When Stang-Starr attempted to elicit testimony from her witness concerning what a particular authority has reported about an issue, she was attempting to use her witness to recite the opinion of each authority cited instead of eliciting her witness' expert opinion derived from the witness' own knowledge and experience. The witness was merely seeking to act as a conduit for inadmissible hearsay. The recitation of a passage by a nontestifying authority, even if such is in conformity with the opinion of the testifying expert, is hearsay.

As observed in United States v. Williams, 431 F.2d 1168, 1172 (5th Cir. 1970):

> If the witness has gone to only one hearsay source and seeks merely to summarize the content of that source, then he is acting as a summary witness, not an expert. . . . When, however, the witness has gone to many sources—although some or all be hearsay in nature—and rather than introducing mere summaries of each source he uses them all, along with his own professional experience, to arrive at his opinion, that opinion is regarded as evidence in its own right and not as an attempt to introduce hearsay in disguise.

. . . Accordingly, the district court did not err in sustaining Byington's objections to the proffered evidence or the offers of proof made in regard to the evidence. . . .

Notes: Examination of Experts; Introduction of Treatises and Guidelines

1. *Hypothetical Questions.* The rigors of evidence rules governing the questioning of expert witnesses have been considerably loosened over the past two generations. The excerpt from Robert Keeton's 1973 book displays the older form in which (1) each factual underpinning for the expert's opinion was explicitly stated hypothetically prior to eliciting the expert's opinion, and (2) each hypothetical foundation point had to be independently proved in evidence. This hypothetical question approach produced a horribly complex chain of thought for the jury to absorb and, for lawyers, meant agonizing decisions about strategy and heightened chances for

error. The lawyer's task was to decide whether to state as part of the hypothetical basis for an expert's opinion facts in dispute or facts based on evidence that might not be admitted. If the jury were to find that one of the subsidiary assumptions was false, or the court were to exclude the source of evidence for that point, then it could easily be argued that the expert's entire testimony was worthless.

The modern approach, embodied in Federal Rules of Evidence 701, 702, 703, and 705, and followed now in most states, is demonstrated in the testimony taken from the *McCourt* case. Both aspects of the older approach stated above are now rejected. Instead, experts' opinions may be based on information that is not in evidence if it is the type of information experts in that field normally rely on in forming opinions. These foundation points do not have to be disclosed before giving an opinion. All of these matters are left to cross-examination by the opposing lawyer. Still, do you think some of the older technique might be valuable in direct examination? Selective restatement of the foundational points, either prior to or following the expert's statement of opinion, could help to reinforce strengths in the case and how well reasoned the opinion is. For additional discussion, see David M. Malone & Paul J. Zwier, Effective Expert Testimony (3d ed. 2014).

2. *Learned Treatises.* Modern practice has also loosened somewhat with respect to the use of learned treatises. The emerging approach, adopted in Federal Rules of Evidence 803(18), is to allow testimony, either in direct or cross-examination, from learned treatises, guidelines, or other similar authoritative sources that the expert acknowledges are reliable. The court may also take judicial notice of their reliability. However, these statements may not be received as exhibits but only read into evidence. Naturally, the states vary in the extent to which they have adopted this liberalization. They also vary considerably in the extent to which, under the older practice, these authorities could be used in cross-examination. Some states require the expert to admit he relied on the authority; others require only that he acknowledge the general authoritativeness of the treatise or other written source. See Annot., 38 A.L.R.2d 77 (1958 & Supp.).

3. *Practice Guidelines.* One type of documentary evidence that has unique status in medical malpractice actions is the "package inserts" for prescription drugs (compiled in the Physicians' Desk Reference (PDR)), which contain FDA-required warnings and instructions for use. As noted at page 372, these written guidelines are directly admissible as independent evidence on the standard of care under the hearsay exception for tabulations, lists, and directories generally relied on by persons in particular occupations. Fed. R. Evid. 803(17). Some courts treat package inserts as especially authoritative by declaring that they are prima facie proof of the standard of care, subject to rebuttal that physicians commonly depart from the instructions in particular situations.

Observe in *Stang-Starr* that it is much more difficult to introduce other officially promulgated statements of medical standards adopted by professional societies such as the AMA and the various certification boards for medical specialties. These "practice guidelines" are also being issued in greater numbers by government research agencies such as the National Institutes of Health (NIH), which convene experts in the field to deliberate on an area of medical practice and issue a consensus statement advising physicians of the best approach to particular clinical situations. Should explicit statements of consensus standards of care from these authoritative national sources be subjected to the same hearsay hurdles as medical treatises and scholarly articles written by only one or a few individuals? Even under the modern treatment of medical authorities illustrated in the McCourt v. Abernathy testimony, courts often rule that practice guidelines can only be referred to and recited by testifying experts, not introduced directly as independent proof. Many commentators, however, argue that if the source is sufficiently authoritative, and the guidelines sufficiently relevant, they should not only be admitted as independent evidence of the standard of care, they should be taken as conclusive, or at least presumptive, proof of the standard of care.

Practice guidelines are usually used offensively by plaintiffs against doctors who deviate from them, but they can also be used defensively by doctors to justify their treatment decisions. Thousands of these detailed practice guidelines currently exist, and their numbers are rapidly proliferating as a consequence of the perceived need to bring greater rationality and standardization to medical practice. Guidelines issued by government agencies and professional societies are used not only to advise physicians of proper practice, but increasingly are being adapted by public and private insurers as a basis for conducting utilization review activities that determine what treatments are paid for by health insurance. These newer guidelines are geared toward determining when treatment is unnecessary, and therefore are more relevant to defending than to prosecuting a malpractice claim. Some states have viewed these guidelines as a possible way to blunt the impact of defensive medicine — the tendency of physicians to perform unnecessary procedures out of a fear of liability. Maine was the first state to declare by statute (which is no longer in effect) that certain officially promulgated guidelines were directly admissible and create an "affirmative defense," but Maine did not allow plaintiffs to use these designated guidelines unless they were put in issue by the defense. Is this differential weight justifiable? Consider the argument in Mark A. Hall, The Defensive Effect of Medical Practice Policies in Malpractice Litigation, 54 Law & Contemp. Probs. 119 (Spring 1991):

> This difference in the [offensive vs. defensive] posture of the [case] is critical because of the possibility that two schools of practice might prevail. With this possibility in mind, it makes eminent sense to hold that it is not conclusive for a plaintiff to establish that the defendant violated *one* established standard. However, the opposite holds for a defendant who complies with at least one established professional guideline: Because it is not necessary for a doctor to show that unanimous professional consensus supports his conduct, a defense is sufficiently established if the doctor shows only that she complied with *at least* one respectable body of opinion.

Observe also that most guidelines purport to state optimal, not minimally acceptable, practice. Does this mean, though, that guidelines should be inadmissible by plaintiffs or only receive lesser weight?

If authoritative medical practice guidelines were to be given special weight in more states, then one must consider which organizations have authoritative stature. Are guidelines issued by a national association or government agency relevant under a similar locality standard in a rural setting? May guidelines adopted by insurers (including HMOs) be considered? In many hospitals and HMOs, efforts are being made to develop treatment protocols that are based on specific scientific evidence from actual patients at the facility rather than being based on broad professional opinion. This movement toward evidence-based, institution-specific guidelines is seen as desirable for three reasons: (1) decentralized efforts will generate many more guidelines, (2) these guidelines are likely to be more useful because they are more clinically specific, and (3) physicians who participate in their development are more likely to comply with them. What objections do you imagine, however, from the plaintiff's lawyer when a physician attempts to defend himself with the institution's own guideline? See Adams v. Laboratory Corporation of America, 760 F.3d 1322 (11th Cir. 2014) (refusing to follow "litigation guideline" from pathology association that required "blinded" review of challenged slides (to determine whether original misreading was negligent), because this "industry group has promulgated a set of guideless that attempts to define and limit the evidence courts should accept when the group's members are sued.").

4. *Physician Report Cards.* Another emerging source of evidence are the "report cards" discussed in section A.3 that are beginning to emerge on individual doctors. These reports contain statistics on the number of good and bad outcomes for particular types of high-profile treatment such as cardiac bypass surgery. These statistics are not unlike the kind of information hospital peer review committees traditionally compile on infection rates, blood loss, tissue analysis, and other technical aspects of surgery, but those sources of information are cloaked in the peer review privilege discussed at page 328, which keeps them confidential. The newer report cards are discoverable, but are they admissible? One commentator predicts not, based on irrelevance. Courts are cautious about admitting evidence of previous similar wrongdoing because of the potential for undue prejudice and the reluctance to greatly expand the scope of litigation. This type of evidence is generally limited to instances involving the very same mistake. See Paul D. Rheingold, The Admissibility of Evidence in Malpractice Cases: The Performance Records of Practitioners, 58 Brook. L. Rev. 75 (1992).

5. *Empirical Evidence of Medical Custom.* With so many available and emerging sources of empirical evidence regarding medical custom, one must wonder why courts have not been more demanding regarding the foundation for experts who testify about medical custom. Courts traditionally have allowed experts to testify based on their general experience and opinion rather than requiring them to show they have actually studied or researched in a scientific or methodical fashion how physicians usually behave in similar circumstances. Perhaps this is a holdover from a century ago when, under a local standard of care, nothing more could be expected. However, as noted above, at page 307, this often results in testimony that is demonstrably inaccurate. Accordingly, several scholars have advocated either allowing or encouraging experts to conduct surveys of physicians, or to analyze databases reflecting actual physician practices, in order to support their expert opinions. Could this help to overcome difficulties that plaintiffs face in finding qualified experts? Might this be *required* as a basic element of the scientific validity of experts' assertions about professional practice, under Daubert v. Merrell Dow Pharmaceuticals, Inc., 509 U.S. 579 (1993)? See Adams v. Laboratory Corporation of America, 760 F.3d 1322 (11th Cir. 2014) (suggesting not, because *Daubert* allows qualified experts to rely on their "experience and general knowledge in the field"). For a thorough analysis of these proposals and their many problems, see Symposium, Empirical Approaches to Proving the Standard of Care in Medical Malpractice Cases, 37 Wake Forest L. Rev. 663 (2002).

6. *Further Reading.* For various analyses and critiques of existing law regarding **practice guidelines** (note 3), and proposals for change, see generally Michelle Mello & Allen Kachalia, Medical Malpractice: Evidence on Reform Alternatives and Claims Involving Elderly Patients (MedPac, 2016); Maxwell Mehlman, Professional Power and the Standard of Care in Medicine, 44 Ariz. St. L. J. 1165 (2012); K. Van Tassel, Harmonizing the Accountable Care Act with the Three Main National Systems for Healthcare Quality Improvement, 78 Brook. L. Rev. 883 (2013); Ronen Avraham, Clinical Practice Guidelines: The Warped Incentive in the U.S. Healthcare System, 37 Am. J. L. & Med. 7 (2011); Ronen Avraham, Private Regulation, 34 Harv. J. L. & Pub. Pol'y 543 (2011); S. Mangalmurti et al., Medical Malpractice in the Age of Electronic Health Records, 363 New Eng. J. Med. 2060 (2010); Jodi Finder, The Future of Practice Guidelines: Should They Constitute Conclusive Evidence of the Standard of Care?, 10 Health Matrix 67 (2000); R. E. Leahy, Rational Health Policy and the Legal Standard of Care: A Call for Judicial Deference to Medical Practice Guidelines, 77 Cal. L. Rev. 1483 (1989); Michelle Mello, Of Swords and Shields: The Use of Clinical Practice Guidelines in Medical Malpractice Litigation, 149 U. Pa. L. Rev. 645 (2000); Note, 61 Wash. & Lee L. Rev. 479 (2004); Arnold J. Rosoff, The Role of Clinical Practice Guidelines in Health Care Reform, 5 Health Matrix 369 (1995).

On the use of **physician report cards** in litigation (note 4), see Symposium, 58 Brook. L. Rev. 85 (1992); Aaron S. Kesselheim et al., Will Physician-Level Measures of Clinical Performance Be Used in Medical Malpractice Litigation?, 295 JAMA 1831 (2007).

Notes: Discovery and Confidentiality

1. *Medical Records.* Investigation of a potential malpractice claim by a plaintiff's lawyer starts with obtaining and reviewing his client's own medical records. The initial review may be conducted inside the law firm by someone such as a nurse paralegal who has some medical training, but thorough investigation usually entails sending the record out for expert review prior to initiating suit. Hospital medical records are too large, complex, and various to adequately summarize in the context of this book. An illustration of the types of documents and sorts of information one might find in a typical hospital chart can be found on the Web site for this book, www.health-law.org, which contains excerpts from the trial record in McCourt v. Abernathy, page 282. Take a look at these samples. On first inspection, they may be hard to digest, but see if you can read them in a way that tells a story. The usual components of a medical story are: (1) history and symptoms; (2) exam, testing, and diagnosis; (3) treatment; and (4) outcome. Following that structure, see if you can identify in these records how Wendy first presented her symptoms, what additional symptoms her physicians observed, what tests they performed and why, where the diagnosis went wrong, and what the resulting effect was on her treatment.

2. *Spoliation of Evidence.* Medical malpractice cases frequently contain allegations that medical records have been altered to cover up mistakes. If true, this obviously creates problems for the defense, which is then subject to various damaging presumptions or waivers of defenses, if not penalties for outright fraud and deceit. See generally Comment, Spoliation of Evidence and Medical Malpractice, 14 Pace L. Rev. 235 (1994).

3. *Confidentiality and Ex Parte Contacts.* Not only must medical malpractice lawyers master certain specialized evidence rules, they must also be familiar with several rules of confidentiality and discovery that are of unique importance in this type of litigation. Most obvious is the privilege against disclosing confidential medical information, discussed in Chapter 2.B. Clearly, patients who sue their doctors are held to have waived this privilege with respect to their own medical records, but the privilege bars them from inquiring into the treatment of other, similar patients. Less obvious is the rule that, despite this waiver, defense counsel cannot informally inquire into the plaintiff's medical records. Several courts have ruled that the privilege remains intact until defense counsel conducts formal discovery, since this allows the plaintiff a chance to pose an objection if the inquiry is excessive, for instance, looking into aspects of the plaintiff's past treatment that are not relevant to the case. Defense counsel who violate this ban on "ex parte" communications with a plaintiff's physicians can find, to their surprise, that evidence otherwise perfectly accessible to them is barred from the proceedings. Additional discussion and a sample case on this topic can be found in the softbound edition of this portion of the casebook, Medical Liability and Treatment Relationships (3d ed. 2012).

4. *Peer Review Confidentiality.* Other sources of confidentiality and evidentiary privilege protect the defendant in a malpractice action. The primary sources are: (1) peer review confidentiality statutes; (2) the attorney-client communication privilege; and (3) the lawyer's work product privilege. We will discuss only the first of these, and only briefly. See the Web site for this book, www.health-law.org, for additional information.

Peer review confidentiality attaches by statute in most states to various standing hospital committees that investigate the competence of individual practitioners and the quality of care rendered within the institution. In order to ensure candor and vigorous participation in these activities, state statutes protect from discovery any records generated by these committees. A few decisions have recognized a common-law privilege protecting self-evaluation or self-improvement efforts even in the absence of such statutes. The peer review confidentiality statutes produce a steady stream of litigation over precisely which committees and records they cover. See generally Annots., 60 A.L.R.4th 1273 (1988); 81 A.L.R.3d 944 (1977).

One major area of dispute concerns "incident reports" and investigations conducted by hospital risk management departments. Compare Krusac v. Covenant Medical Center, 865 N.W.2d 908 (Mich. 2015) (incident reports are privileged), with Valley Health System v. Eighth Judicial District Court, 252 P.3d 676 (Nev. 2011) (some incident reports are discoverable). The hospital might also seek to protect these reports as attorney work product, or to protect the communications they report under the attorney-client privilege. These claims are not always successful, for reasons summarized on the Web site. See, e.g., Collins v. Braden, 384 S.W.3d 154 (Ky. 2012) (hospital lawyers who interviewed nurse witnesses were not acting as lawyers for the nurses, only for the hospital).

Out of concern that state law too narrowly protects the ability of health care institutions to investigate, correct, and report medical safety issues, Congress adopted a discovery privilege and liability protection in 2005. The Patient Safety and Quality Improvement Act protects from discovery any reports of medical errors made by health care providers to certified "patient safety organizations," such as the JCAHO. However, any such records must be maintained only for patient safety evaluation purposes, and not for patient care or billing purposes. The goal is to encourage efforts to improve medical quality in arenas outside the traditional peer review process, for instance, by sharing information among different facilities or with private accreditation organizations.

5. *The Costs of Litigation.* The complexity of medical malpractice cases, and the costs of medical expertise, mean that these are expensive cases to litigate, often costing at least $50,000 in out-of-pocket expenses. Overall, less than half of medical malpractice premiums collected end up in the pockets of injured patients.

6. *Further Reading.* For commentary and analysis of **ex parte contacts** (note 3), see Beverly Cohen, Reconciling the HIPAA Privacy Rule with State Laws Regulating Ex Parte Interviews of Plaintiffs' Treating Physicians, 43 Hous. L. Rev. 1091 (2006); Comment, 34 Cap. U. L. Rev. 775 (2006); Annot., 50 A.L.R.4th 714 (1986).

On **peer review confidentiality and immunity** (note 4), see Gregory Nowakowski et al., Health Care Quality Improvement Act: Peer Review, Procedure, Process, and Privacy, 33 Cooley L. Rev. 1 (2016); Lisa M. Nijm, Pitfalls of Peer Review, 24 J. Leg. Med. 541 (December 2003); Gail Friend et al., Identifying and Protecting the Peer Review and Medical Committee Privilege, 49 Baylor L. Rev. 607 (1997); Comment, 11 Mich. St. U. J. Med. & L. 177 (2007); Note, 17 Health Matrix 319 (2007); Note, 4 Ind. Health L. Rev. 151 (2007).

Attacking the view that **liability exposure deters error reporting or quality improvement** (note 4), see David A. Hyman & Charles M. Silver, The Poor State of Health Care Quality in the U.S.: Is Malpractice Liability Part of the Problem or Part of the Solution?, 90 Cornell L. Rev. 893 (2005); Stephan Landsman, Reflections on Juryphobia and Medical Malpractice Reform, 57 DePaul L. Rev. 221 (2008).

D. ALTERNATIVE THEORIES OF LIABILITY

Observing the difficulties that plaintiffs often have in qualifying expert witnesses and proving a breach of the standard of care, it is understandable that their lawyers are eager to find theories of liability that do not rely on the custom-based standard of care. The following readings survey several such theories.

1. Breach of Contract

■ SULLIVAN v. O'CONNOR
296 N.E.2d 183 (Mass. 1973)

KAPLAN, Justice.

The plaintiff patient secured a jury verdict of $13,500 against the defendant surgeon for breach of contract in respect to an operation upon the plaintiff's nose. . . . The declaration was in two counts. In the first count, the plaintiff alleged that she, as patient, entered into a contract with the defendant, a surgeon, wherein the defendant promised to perform plastic surgery on her nose and thereby to enhance her beauty and improve her appearance; that he performed the surgery but failed to achieve the promised result; rather the result of the surgery was to disfigure and deform her nose, to cause her pain in body and mind, and to subject her to other damage and expense. The second count, based on the same transaction, was in the conventional form for malpractice, charging that the defendant had been guilty of negligence in performing the surgery. . . . The jury returned a verdict for the plaintiff on the contract count, and for the defendant on the negligence count. The judge then instructed the jury on the issue of damages.

As background to the instructions and the parties' exceptions, we mention certain facts as the jury could find them. The plaintiff was a professional entertainer, and this was known to the defendant. The agreement was as alleged in the declaration. More particularly, judging from exhibits, the plaintiff's nose had been straight, but long and prominent; the defendant undertook by two operations to reduce its prominence and somewhat to shorten it, thus making it more pleasing in relation to the plaintiff's other features. Actually, the plaintiff was obliged to undergo three operations, and her appearance was worsened. Her nose now had a concave line to about the midpoint, at which it became bulbous; viewed frontally, the nose from bridge to midpoint was flattened and broadened, and the two sides of the tip had lost symmetry. This configuration evidently could not be improved by further surgery. The plaintiff did not demonstrate, however, that her change of appearance had resulted in loss of employment. Payments by the plaintiff covering the defendant's fee and hospital expenses were stipulated at $622.65. . . .

By his exceptions, the defendant contends that the judge erred in allowing the jury to take into account anything but the plaintiff's out-of-pocket expenses (presumably at the stipulated amount). The defendant excepted to the judge's refusal of his request for a general charge to that effect, and, more specifically, to the judge's refusal of a charge that the plaintiff could not recover for pain and suffering connected with the third operation or for impairment of the plaintiff's appearance and associated mental distress. . . . We conclude that the defendant's exceptions should be overruled.

It has been suggested on occasion that agreements between patients and physicians by which the physician undertakes to effect a cure or to bring about a given result should be declared unenforceable on grounds of public policy. But there are many decisions recognizing and enforcing such contracts, see annotation, 43 A.L.R.3d 1221, and the law of Massachusetts has treated them as valid, although we have had no decision meeting head on the contention that they should be denied legal sanction. These causes of action are, however, considered a little suspect, and thus we find courts straining sometimes to read the pleadings as sounding only in tort for negligence, and not in contract for breach of promise, despite sedulous efforts by the pleaders to pursue the latter theory.

It is not hard to see why the courts should be unenthusiastic or skeptical about the contract theory. Considering the uncertainties of medical science and the variations in the physical and psychological conditions of individual patients, doctors can seldom in good faith promise specific results. Therefore, it is unlikely that physicians of even average integrity will in fact make such promises. Statements of opinion by the physician with some optimistic coloring are a different thing, and may indeed have therapeutic value. But patients may transform such statements into firm promises in their own minds, especially when they have been disappointed in the event, and testify in that sense to sympathetic juries.[2] If actions for breach of promise can be readily maintained, doctors, so it is said, will be frightened into practising "defensive medicine." On the other hand, if these actions were outlawed, leaving only the possibility of suits for malpractice, there is fear that the public might be exposed to the enticements of charlatans, and confidence in the profession might ultimately be shaken. See Miller, The Contractual Liability of Physicians and Surgeons, 1953 Wash. L.Q. 413, 416-423. The law has taken the middle of the road position of allowing actions based on alleged contract, but insisting on clear proof. Instructions to the jury may well stress this requirement and point to tests of truth, such as the complexity or difficulty of an operation as bearing on the probability that a given result was promised. See annotation, 43 A.L.R.3d 1225, 1225-1227.

If an action on the basis of contract is allowed, we have next the question of the measure of damages to be applied where liability is found. Some cases have taken the simple view that the promise by the physician is to be treated like an ordinary commercial promise. . . . Thus in Hawkins v. McGee, 84 N.H. 114, 146 A. 641, the defendant doctor was taken to have promised the plaintiff to convert his damaged hand by means of an operation into a good or perfect hand, but the doctor so operated as to damage the hand still further. The court, following the usual expectancy formula, would have asked the jury to estimate and award to the plaintiff the difference between the value of a good or perfect hand, as promised, and the value of the hand after the operation. . . . Other cases, including a number in New York, without distinctly repudiating the *Hawkins* type of analysis, have indicated that a different and generally more lenient measure of damages is to be applied. . . .

The factors, already mentioned, which have made the cause of action somewhat suspect, also suggest moderation as to the breadth of the recovery that should be permitted. Where, as in the case at bar and in a number of the reported cases, the doctor has been absolved of negligence by the trier, an expectancy measure may be thought harsh. We should recall here that the fee paid by the patient to the doctor for the alleged promise would usually be quite disproportionate to the putative expectancy recovery. To attempt, moreover, to put a value on the condition that would or might have resulted, had the treatment succeeded as promised, may sometimes put an exceptional strain on the imagination of the factfinder. . . .

The question of recovery on a reliance basis for pain and suffering or mental distress requires further attention. We find expressions in the decisions that pain and suffering (or the like) are simply not compensable in actions for breach of contract. The defendant seemingly espouses this proposition in the present case. True, if the buyer under a contract for the purchase of a lot of merchandise, in suing for the seller's breach, should claim damages for mental anguish caused by his disappointment in the transaction, he would not succeed; he would be told, perhaps, that the asserted psychological injury was not fairly foreseeable by the defendant as a probable consequence of the breach of such a business contract. See Restatement: Contracts, §341, and comment *a*. But there is no general rule barring such items of damage in actions for breach of contract. It is all a question of the subject matter

---

2. Judicial skepticism about whether a promise was in fact made derives also from the possibility that the truth has been tortured to give the plaintiff the advantage of the longer period of limitations sometimes available for actions on contract as distinguished from those in tort or for malpractice.

and background of the contract, and when the contract calls for an operation on the person of the plaintiff, psychological as well as physical injury may be expected to figure somewhere in the recovery, depending on the particular circumstances. . . .

In the light of the foregoing discussion, all the defendant's exceptions fail: The plaintiff was not confined to the recovery of her out-of-pocket expenditures; she was entitled to recover also for the worsening of her condition, and for the pain and suffering and mental distress involved in the third operation. . . .

Notes: Liability Based on Contract or Fraud

1. *Strategic Choice of Theories.* The application of a contractual theory of liability in medical malpractice is rare, and, as illustrated in *Sullivan,* the courts usually impose a very high standard for proving a contractual breach. Nevertheless, plaintiffs persist for four reasons: raising the standard of care and avoiding the need to produce expert medical testimony; seeking a longer statute of limitations; avoiding restrictions imposed by medical malpractice reform statutes; and avoiding doctrines of sovereign or charitable immunity. Even where a contract action exists, the second and third strategies do not always work. Courts tend to impose the tort-law requirements when an action sounds in medical malpractice, regardless of the precise legal theory, and many statutory reforms define "medical malpractice actions" to include both tort and contract theories.

2. *Promises, Imagined and Real.* The *Sullivan* case involves an allegation of contractual guarantee of a particular result in plastic surgery. Another common situation involves a woman who conceives a child following a sterilization procedure. See generally Annot., 43 A.L.R.3d 1221 (1972 & Supp.). Courts express hostility to these and other contract theories in a variety of ways. In addition to raising the standard of proof to clear and convincing evidence and lowering damages to a reliance rather than an expectation measure, some courts also require the plaintiff to show separate consideration for the promise of a cure, apart from the doctor's normal fee for performing the procedure, or they require the guarantee to be in writing. See, e.g., Herrera v. Roessing, 533 P.2d 60 (Colo. 1975). Other states have achieved the same policy by statute. But see Burns v. Wannemaker, 343 S.E.2d 27 (S.C. 1986) (no separate consideration required for dentist's breach of express warranty with respect to fitting dentures).

What type of communication is sufficient to meet a clear and convincing proof standard? Compare Ferlito v. Cecola, 419 So. 2d 102 (La. Ct. App. 1982) (dentist's promise to "make your teeth real pretty" does not create a promise of complete satisfaction with respect to repairing crooked and discolored teeth), and Anglin v. Kleeman, 665 A.2d 747 (N.H. 1995) (alleged statements that surgery would make knee stronger and enable patient to resume football were opinions and not promises), with Doerr v. Villate, 220 N.E.2d 767 (1966) (assurance that sterilization will prevent pregnancy sufficient to support contract cause of action). As a practical matter, most surgeons avoid these disputes by including in the signed informed consent form a statement that specifically denies any guarantee of results and asserts only that the surgeon will use his professional skills in the accepted manner. After signing such a document, can the patient claim not to have understood its plain language? Is such a document similar to a release or covenant not to sue, which generally are not enforced? See section E.3 and Chapter 2.B.2.

3. *Advertising.* HMOs and other forms of managed care insurance create an arena in which contractual theories may have much greater prominence. Garden variety contract claims naturally arise when HMO subscribers complain that deliberate decisions to refuse treatment breached the promise of covered services contained in their insurance contract. Where the complaint sounds more in classic malpractice due to poorly performed treatment, mistaken diagnoses, or the like, contract theory might be based on advertising or promotional statements. Explicit image-building efforts with the public at large were once a rarity in medicine, but now there is a glut of ads in newspapers, on billboards, and over the airwaves touting the quality of various medical institutions such as hospitals or HMOs. Even if these and similar assertions cannot be taken as warranting specific results from particular procedures, they can be argued to heighten the ordinary standard of care. Consider, for instance, an HMO that advertises "total health care" or that it has "over 1000 of the best doctors" in the region. See Allan S. Brett, The Case Against Persuasive Advertising by HMOs, 326 New Eng. J. Med. 1353 (1992). As George Anders explains,

> HMOs don't present themselves as the medical equivalent of a tawdry motel chain or a discount clothing store in a rundown part of town, blithely selling an inferior product in the name of having the cheapest possible price, Managed-care companies promise to uphold standards through their cost cutting, simply by targeting wasteful practices.

Health Against Wealth: HMOs and the Breakdown of Medical Trust 59 (1996).

Should the same concerns expressed in *Sullivan* about allowing doctors to give "therapeutic assurances" cause courts to take a protective view of quality assurances issued by medical institutions? Giordano v. Ramirez, 503 So. 2d 947 (Fla. Dist. Ct. App. 1987), held that a health care plan that promised a "high standard of competence, care, and concern for the welfare and needs of subscribers" did not undertake a higher than normal standard of care. However, in Dunn v. Praiss, 656 A.2d 413 (N.J. 1995), the court accepted for purposes of argument that a contractual theory might be maintained based on language in an HMO's description of benefits that "Plan members receive health care from a large number of well-qualified, highly trained physicians." Nevertheless, the court dismissed the claim on technical grounds for failure to raise it in time. See also McClellan v. Health Maintenance Organization of Pennsylvania, 604 A.2d 1053 (Pa. Super. Ct. 1992) (allowing patient to plead HMO breached contract by misrepresenting that physicians were qualified and would make appropriate referrals).

4. *Abandonment and Switching Doctors.* Contractual theories also arise frequently in the form of allegations that physicians "abandoned" a patient by totally neglecting the patient or by failing to give the required attention. Abandonment claims may sound like negligence, but they also can be said to be grounded in the contractual obligation to attend the patient properly and continuously until care for the particular illness is no longer needed. In this respect, the physician has failed to provide the personal professional services demanded under the contract of medical care. See Chapter 2.B.3. Employing a somewhat different theory, Maryland's high court ruled that a breach of contract action can be stated, based on informed consent principles, against a doctor who allows a training physician to perform part of an operation, where the patient alleges that the more experienced doctor expressly stated he would do the operation. Dingle v. Belin, 749 A.2d 157 (Md. 2000).

5. *Fraud.* Closely related to the contract and guarantee situations represented by *Sullivan* are situations where a physician is accused of fraudulent statements or intentional misrepresentation of the results that can be expected from treatment. Most of these cases involve unethical practices and criminal activities by charlatans who are not licensed physicians or are persons who have had medical licenses revoked in the past for improper practices. There are many alleged "doctors" who offer unorthodox treatment for weight loss, baldness, cancer, or other conditions where afflicted patients are especially susceptible to false hopes for cure. The most well-known action in this field was the prosecution of a chiropractor "faith healer" for murder in the case of a young child with cancer in her eye. The prosecutor obtained a conviction for first-degree murder under a felony-murder theory that characterized the chiropractor's false promises as "grand theft." The California Supreme Court reversed, asserting that grand theft is not the type of felony that usually creates personal danger to human life and so could not support the felony-murder rule. People v. Phillips, 414 P.2d 353 (Cal. 1966). The case did not end at this point, however. The prosecutor persisted and in a second jury trial the chiropractor was convicted of second-degree murder. On appeal, the intermediate appellate court upheld the conviction on grounds that the defendant maliciously caused the child's death by fraudulently discouraging the parents from seeking proper treatment. People v. Phillips, 270 Cal. App. 2d 381, 75 Cal. Rptr. 720 (Cal. Ct. App. 1969). For a review of the background of the case see W. Curran, Law-Medicine Notes—Program in Medicolegal Relations 161-164 (1989).

Some cases do not involve frankly criminal conduct but rather overzealous assurances to patients before or after treatment, or both. In order to sustain liability for fraud, however, the plaintiff would be required to prove that statements of fact, not opinion, were knowingly false. Practitioners can often claim they have an honest belief based on a few documented "miraculous" cures. See, e.g., Schneider v. Revici, excerpted at page 395.

6. *Implied Warranties.* Contractual theories based on express statements should be distinguished from those based on implied warranties. Implied warranties that arise automatically from the sale of consumer products do not generally attach to professional services. Where products are involved in medical care, they are usually considered by the courts as incidental to medical services and therefore as not giving rise to implied warranties or other forms of products liability on the part of doctors or hospitals. Products liability theories may, however, be stated against manufacturers of medical drugs and devices. For additional discussion, see section D.3.

2. Vicarious Liability

■ FRANKLIN v. GUPTA
567 A.2d 524 (Md. App. 1990)

WILNER, Judge.

. . . Appellant, an unfortunate soul with a host of physical and emotional problems, also developed carpal tunnel syndrome—a condition that causes pain in the wrist and muscle weakness in the hand. He consulted Dr. Shanker L. Gupta, a general surgeon, who recommended surgical treatment for that condition.

... Dr. Herbert S. T. Lee, an anesthesiologist, and Gary J. Sergott, a certified registered nurse anesthetist, were assigned by the hospital to administer and monitor the anesthesia. Unfortunately, Dr. Lee was also scheduled to administer and monitor anesthesia to another patient in another operating room at the hospital at the same time. Dr. Lee chose to tend to the other patient, and so the actual administration and monitoring of the anesthesia to appellant fell to Nurse Sergott. As we shall see, things did not go as planned. The anesthesia administered by Nurse Sergott was not only not effective, but appellant suffered certain physical and emotional trauma from it, and the surgery was eventually cancelled.

As a result of this experience, appellant filed a claim with the Health Claims Arbitration Office against Dr. Gupta, Dr. Lee, Nurse Sergott, and the hospital. After an evidentiary hearing, the arbitration panel found no liability on the part of any of the defendants and entered an award in their favor. Appellant rejected the award and filed suit in the Circuit Court for Baltimore City.

After a de novo trial, the jury agreed with the arbitration panel that there was no liability on the part of Dr. Gupta, but it concluded that the other defendants were culpable. It returned a verdict in favor of Dr. Gupta but against Dr. Lee, Nurse Sergott, and the hospital in the amount of $375,000. . . . [The trial court granted the three losing defendants' motions for a new trial or, in the alternative, remittitur of all but $50,000, citing the failure of appellant to show convincing evidence that the treatment rendered caused most of his injuries. Plaintiff appealed.]

I. Underlying Facts

We mean no disrespect when we say that appellant was not a picture of health when he presented himself at the hospital on July 16, 1981—the day before his scheduled surgery. He had a history of syncope (temporary blackouts), asthma, emphysema, bronchitis, hyperthyroidism, chronic depression, and a nervous condition. He was also excessively—"morbidly"—obese; five feet, five inches tall, he weighed 295 pounds. He was permanently and totally disabled from employment and subsisted from Social Security disability benefits.

Dr. Lee, as we indicated, was designated by the hospital as the anesthesiologist for appellant's surgery, along with Nurse Sergott. Dr. Lee visited appellant on the afternoon of the 16th for an "anesthesia evaluation." Because of the patient's asthma, obesity, and hyperthyroidism, Dr. Lee recognized that appellant was a "high risk patient for anesthesia"; he therefore decided against a general anesthesia and opted instead for an axillary or brachial block.[1] He did not, however, . . . discuss the case in any way with Nurse Sergott. . . . Nurse Sergott independently decided to use a brachial block; he decided, by himself, which drug to use for that purpose; and he also decided, by himself, what analgesic to use and how it was to be administered. . . .

At some point, shortly after administering the third dose of [local anesthesia], Nurse Sergott noticed that the block was "patchy"—i.e., "[t]he media flesh was not completely blocked on his hand." He wanted to give appellant another block, but

---

1. An axillary or brachial block is designed to anesthetize the entire arm, but nothing more.

Dr. Gupta insisted that he put appellant to sleep. Believing that general anesthesia was inappropriate and that, "being a surgeon, [Dr. Gupta] is not aware of anesthesia," Nurse Sergott decided to consult Dr. Lee who, . . . then busy with another patient under anesthesia and unable to leave, agreed that appellant should be given another brachial block and not put to sleep.

. . . While Nurse Sergott was conferring with Dr. Lee, appellant's breathing became shallow. Indeed, according to the medical record, he became cyanotic—i.e., his skin turned blue because of lack of oxygen in the body. He then became bradycardic (slow heartbeat) and had a period of asystole (his heart stopped beating entirely). . . . Appellant was promptly intubated and given Atropine and cardiopulmonary resuscitation, and his heartbeat returned to normal. At that point, Dr. Lee appeared and instructed Dr. Gupta to cancel the surgery.

Appellant remained in the hospital until his discharge on July 21, 1981. He never did have the surgery on his wrist. [He alleged that the delay caused by the nurse anesthesist's indecision and inability to properly anesthetize him aggravated his underlying medical conditions and caused permanent injury. . . .]

IV. JURY INSTRUCTIONS

. . . At the close of the evidence, appellant submitted . . . Proposed Instruction No. 11, captioned "Responsibility and Liability of Surgeon—the Captain of the Ship Doctrine." The relevant part of it is as follows:

> While Mr. Franklin was being prepared to undergo surgery, Dr. Gupta, the surgeon, is ordinarily regarded in law as having the exclusive responsibility and control over the case. . . . [H]e can thus be held responsible for any acts of negligence committed during the operation by any nurse anesthetist or assisting physician who is under his direction, no matter whether or not such assistant is an employee of [the] Hospital. For the purposes of the surgery, nurse Sergott and the other members of the operating room staff are referred to as "borrowed servants" for whose acts the surgeon and the employer ([the] Hospital) must be responsible. . . .

The court declined to give . . . instructions . . . about any vicarious liability on the part of Dr. Gupta for the acts or omissions of Dr. Lee or Nurse Sergott. Instead, it told the jury, in relevant part that . . . "Dr. Gupta is to be judged in his capacity as a surgeon. Dr. Lee is to be judged in his capacity as an anesthesiologist; and Mr. Sergott is to be judged in his capacity as a certified, registered nurse anesthetist. . . ."

[No] expert witness asserted any direct negligence on the part of Dr. Gupta. Nor did . . . any expert witness assert, as a matter of standard medical or hospital practice, that Dr. Gupta, as the surgeon employed to operate on appellant's wrist, had the expertise, the duty, or the right to supervise or control the method of anesthesia, the agents used to achieve the anesthesia, the dosages of those agents, the preoperative examination and evaluation of appellant by Lee and/or Sergott, the extent of communication and collaboration between them, or the precise manner in which Sergott conducted himself in the holding area and in the operating room.[5] There was no evidence that Dr. Gupta actually exercised, or attempted to exercise, any such supervision or control. Proposed Instruction No. 11, then, was not based on any factual predicate but on an assumed principle of law.

The principle underpinning the instruction has become popularly—and sometimes erroneously or misleadingly—called the "captain of the ship" doctrine. As explained in Thomas v. Raleigh General Hosp., 358 S.E.2d 222, 224 (W. Va. 1987): "Under this doctrine, a surgeon is likened to the captain of a ship, in that it is his duty to control everything going on in the operating room. Thus, liability is imposed by virtue of the surgeon's status and without any showing of actual control by the surgeon." As pointed out by Price, The Sinking of the "Captain of the Ship," 10 J. Legal Med. 323 (1989), this "Captain of the Ship" doctrine is but one of several theories of vicarious liability on the part of hospitals and surgeons for acts of negligence committed in the operating room. It is helpful, in examining the doctrine, to consider its context, its purpose, its scope, and how the courts have dealt with it.

A hospital, like any "master" or employer, is liable under agency principles for the negligence of its servants or employees. That would include nurses, physicians, and other medical and nonmedical personnel employed by it. Until fairly recently, however, in Maryland and in many states, this vicarious liability under agency law was of little assistance to plaintiffs injured by malpractice because of the eleemosynary (or governmental) immunity enjoyed by most hospitals. See Annotation, 25 A.L.R.2d 29 (1952).

Whether for that reason or whether because hospitals in earlier days were regarded less as comprehensive health care providers in their own right than as "innkeeper[s], providing a facility for patients to be treated by their privately retained physicians" (Price, supra, 10 J. Legal Med. at 340), courts began to impose liability on the surgeon for what went on in the operating room. The first theory employed was the traditional "borrowed servant" doctrine now expressed in Restatement (Second) of Agency §227.[6] The notion was that the surgeon acted as a special employer who borrowed nurses and other attendants from their general employer—the hospital—and thus became liable for their negligence. See, in general, Annotation, 12 A.L.R.3d 1017 (1967). Liability under that doctrine, of course, requires a showing that the surgeon actually controlled or had a right to control the details of the servant's conduct.

In McConnell v. Williams, 361 Pa. 355, 65 A.2d 243 (1949), the Pennsylvania Court essentially applied that doctrine, but in doing so it likened the surgeon to the captain of a ship. Unfortunately, that simile came to receive more attention than the actual holding in the case. The defendant was an obstetrician employed to attend the plaintiff during her pregnancy. The delivery, by cesarian section, was a difficult one. When the baby was removed from the womb, the defendant handed her to an intern to tie the cord and administer silver nitrate to the eyes. The intern

---

5. Dr. Gupta . . . conceded only that it was part of his duty to see that the patient is properly anesthetized before beginning to operate.

6. A servant directed or permitted by his master to perform services for another may become the servant of such other in performing the services. He may become the other's servant as to some acts and not as to others.

performed the latter task negligently; he put too much solution in the eyes and failed to irrigate, thereby causing severe damage to the child's eyes. The intern was a hospital employee but had been designated by the obstetrician to assist. The action against the obstetrician was based solely on a theory of vicarious liability for the intern's negligence. At the time the case reached the Pennsylvania Supreme Court, the hospital enjoyed charitable immunity and therefore could not be made to answer for the intern's negligence.

Unlike most cases, the obstetrician acknowledged in his testimony that his liability "was to continue until the baby was turned over to the family doctor" and that "he had complete control of the operating room and of every person within it while the operation was in progress." It was in that light that the court, after reciting the general law relating to borrowed servants, including the requirement of control, made the statement that

> it can readily be understood that in the course of an operation in the operating room of a hospital, and until the surgeon leaves that room at the conclusion of the operation . . . he is in the same complete charge of those who are present and assisting him as is the captain of a ship over all on board, and that such supreme control is indeed essential in view of the high degree of protection to which an anaesthetized, unconscious patient is entitled. . . . [I]f operating surgeons were not to be held liable for the negligent performance of the duties of those then working under them, the law would fail in large measure to afford a means of redress for preventable injuries sustained during the course of such operations.

McConnell is sometimes credited with having spawned a new "separate and independent concept of agency" in hospital settings. Price, supra, 10 J. Legal Med. at 331. That may be giving *McConnell* too much credit. . . . [T]he *McConnell* court made clear that the issue of control by the surgeon was one of fact, not of law. In its concluding paragraph, it said that "[i]t is for the jury to determine whether the relationship between defendant and the intern, at the time the child's eyes were injured, was that of master and servant." 65 A.2d at 48.

Some courts that seemingly have made surgeons strictly liable for the negligence of others in the operating room, or that have used the expression "captain of the ship," have in reality done nothing more than apply res ipsa loquitur or a doctrine of negligence per se to the physician. Most of these cases involved the leaving of sponges or other foreign substances in the body, and the court adopted the view that, in such circumstances, negligence on the part of the surgeon can be inferred from the mere happening of the event. The surgeon's negligence, in other words, was direct, not vicarious. References in these cases to the "captain of the ship" are usually in the context of rejecting as a defense to such inferred negligence that the surgeon relied on an erroneous sponge count by the nurse.

In summary, a careful analysis of the cases cited as "captain of the ship" cases generally reveals that the court has applied traditional agency concepts and that, where the surgeon has been held liable, the liability has either been direct (even if inferred) or based on evidence that the negligent actors were, in fact, under his direct supervision and control. As in *McConnell,* the rhetoric often tends to obscure the factual underpinning of the holding.[7]

To the extent that the doctrine is regarded as an expansion of the traditional borrowed servant rule, most courts have either expressly rejected it or have declared it inapplicable when the negligent actor is an anesthesiologist or nurse anesthetist. Two theories have been advanced for the rejection or limitation. The first was well expressed in Thomas v. Raleigh General Hosp., supra, 358 S.E.2d 222, 225:

> We reject the captain of the ship doctrine. The trend toward specialization in medicine has created situations where surgeons do not always have the right to control all personnel within the operating room. . . . An assignment of liability based on a theory of actual control more realistically reflects the actual relationship which exists in a modern operating room.[8]

. . . Compare Baird v. Sickler, 69 Ohio St. 2d 652, 433 N.E.2d 593 (1982) (surgeon could be liable for the negligent conduct of a nurse anesthetist where the evidence showed that the surgeon "exercised and possessed" the right to control the nurse's actions and actually "participated in the administering of the anesthetic.")

The second theory, applied by some courts, is that, with the curtailment or abolition of the hospital's charitable or governmental immunity, by statute or judicial decision, an expanded liability on the part of the surgeon is no longer necessary. . . .

Maryland ventured into these waters only once — 76 years ago. In Hunner v. Stevenson, supra, 122 Md. 40, 89 A. 418, . . . [the plaintiff] sued the doctor, not for anything he did or didn't do directly, but on the theory that, as the surgeon, he was responsible for the negligence of other hospital personnel in the post-operative treatment and dressing of the wound. The court said as to that issue: . . . "It would

7. The Texas Court in Sparger v. Worley Hospital, Inc., 547 S.W.2d 582, 584 (Tex. 1977), put its judicial finger on the problem:

> way of being canonized and of growing until they can stand and walk independently of the usual general rules. Mr. Justice Frankfurter once wrote concerning such phrasemaking in judicial opinions: "The phrase . . . is an excellent illustration of the extent to which uncritical use of words bedevils the law. A phrase begins life as a literary expression; its felicity leads to its lazy repetition; and repetition soon establishes it as a legal formula, undiscriminatingly used to express different and sometimes contradictory ideas." Tiller v. Atlantic Coast Line R. Co., 318 U.S. 54, 68, 63 S. Ct. 444, 452, 87 L. Ed. 610 (1943). The result in the use of captain of the ship is that a surgeon or physician may be held liable, not as others upon the basis of the general rule of borrowed servant, but as captain of the ship.

8. May v. Broun, 261 Or. 28, 492 P.2d 776, 781 (1972), also espoused the first theory, pointing out at 781:

> Changes have also been occurring in the confines of operating rooms. Surgeons are operating more and more in a highly-mechanized environment wholly created by hospitals. Much highly technical equipment, now considered necessary, is furnished by the hospital and operated by personnel which the hospital hires and trains. As a result, in most instances, a surgeon cannot actually have direct supervision or control over such equipment and the persons who operate it even when he is present, if he is going to give the concentration and attention to the surgery which his patient has the right to expect.

be unreasonable to expect such a one as the record shows the appellant to be — performing operations in five different hospitals in Baltimore, and in one at Frederick, in addition to his other practice — to continue to dress the wounds and have personal charge of the after-treatment in all cases until the patient is discharged from the hospital."

... From our analysis of how other courts have dealt with the issue at hand, we reject any "captain of the ship" theory of liability. ... The correct doctrine to apply is the traditional "borrowed servant" rule. Where the evidence suffices to support a finding that the surgeon in fact had or exercised the right to control the details of another person's work or conduct in the operating room and the other elements of the rule are satisfied, the trier of fact may find that the surgeon was the "special employer" and is therefore liable for the negligence of the borrowed servant.

That was not the case here, however. As we indicated, there was no evidence that Dr. Gupta in any way supervised or controlled, attempted to supervise or control, or had the right or power to supervise or control, the conduct and decisions of Dr. Lee or Nurse Sergott. Proposed Instruction No. 11 was therefore properly rejected. ...

Notes: Physicians' Vicarious Liability; "Captain of the Ship"

1. *The* Franklin *Case.* Cutting against the grain of *Franklin* and other modern cases, a California court reasoned that the "captain of the ship" doctrine still survives, even without evidence of actual control, in a case involving a sponge left behind due to negligence of the nurse who conducted the sponge count. The court reasoned that, even though it is not the surgeon's responsibility to conduct or check the sponge count, a "helpless patient on the operating table who cannot understand or control what is happening reasonably expects a surgeon to oversee her care and to look out for her interests. We find this special relationship sufficient justification for . . . [a] nondelegable duty to remove all sponges from the patient's body." The court contrasted this situation with anesthesia, which it acknowledged is conducted by "an independent specialist. . . . By contrast, an assisting nurse is obligated to follow the commands of a surgeon. . . ." Baumgardner v. Yusuf, 144 Cal. App. 4th 1381 (2006).

Similarly, under *Franklin*'s borrowed servant rule, acknowledging that Dr. Gupta did not actually determine which anesthesia to use and how to administer it, are you convinced beyond any reasonable dispute that he lacked the *right* and *power* to do so? It was agreed that he could at least halt the operation if he was not satisfied. What about Dr. Lee, the anesthesiologist? Was he any more responsible, in actuality or in theory, for what the nurse did wrong? As it turns out, he and the nurse were found liable, along with the hospital (albeit, for only $50,000). How strong is the "captain of the ship" case against Dr. Lee? See generally Nancy King, The Physician as Captain of the Ship: A Critical Appraisal (1988); Annot., 12 A.L.R.3d 1017 (1967).

2. *The Effect on Hospital Liability.* "Captain of the ship" and borrowed servant are not only theories of liability against doctors, they are also theories of defense asserted by hospitals. Where a surgeon controls a negligent nurse, hospitals assert that they are not vicariously liable even though they are the nurse's employer because they lent their "servant" to the physician. See Krane v. St. Anthony Hospital System, 738

P.2d 75 (Colo. Ct. App. 1987). However, most courts hold the hospital jointly liable unless the doctor instructs the nurse to do an act that is not within the general scope of duty. Restatement (Second) of Agency §227; Annot., 29 A.L.R.3d 1065 (1970).

The erosion of hospitals' charitable immunity and the rise of complex, technologically dependent team treatment are discussed further in section H.1. Are there any other theories of liability that you think should be affected by these developments? Some in the academic and public policy community contend that hospitals should be *exclusively* liable for all negligent medical care rendered on their premises, without regard to the physician's specialty or relationship with the hospital, thus absolving individual physicians from any liability, even for their own mistakes. See page 514.

3. *Professional Corporations.* Physicians' vicarious liability is not restricted to the borrowed servant rule. It can also arise by virtue of being an employer of or partner with the medical professional who makes a negligent mistake. In the partnership setting, doctors are not individually liable for negligence committed by their colleagues unless they are involved in the treatment. The partnership as an entity however, is, liable, and doctors who are general partners have unlimited individual liability for making good the partnership's debts, so the liability exposure effectively exists in general partnerships. See Annot., 85 A.L.R.2d 889 (1962 & Supp.). This is one reason doctors seek to organize as professional corporations, which combine the tax advantages of a partnership with the liability protections of a corporate form. However, many state professional corporations' statutes protect physicians only from contractual or business obligations, not tort obligations, or have been interpreted in this fashion by restrictive court decisions. Thus, physicians continue to be jointly and severally liable for the professional torts of member physicians. See, e.g., Pediatric Neurosurgery v. Russell, 44 P.3d 1063 (Colo. 2002).

More recently, states have enacted "limited liability corporation" statutes that make it even easier to combine the tax benefits of partnerships with the liability protections of the corporate form. As discussed in Chapter 10.B.3, these have proven to be wildly popular. Although they retain the same constraints on the ability to avoid professional liability, some of these statutes adopt the innovation that physicians are vicariously liable only if they supervise the physician at fault.

Moreover, these liability rules affect only the obligation to patients. They can always be altered internally by indemnification agreements among partnering physicians or with their corporate entities.

3. Strict Liability, Products Liability, and Preemption

This chapter focuses on the professional liability of those who deliver health care services: doctors, hospitals, and HMOs. Also important in the medical arena is the institutional liability of those who manufacture and sell medical drugs and equipment. Length constraints do not allow an in-depth treatment of these additional sources of liability, so we provide only a cursory survey of products liability. For more, see also Lars Noah, This Is Your Products Liability Restatement on Drugs, 74 Brook. L. Rev. 839 (2009).

Also, because products liability is a form of strict liability, we consider here whether conventional negligence liability could be replaced or supplemented by some form of "no-fault" liability. Finally, this intersection of issues also raises the question of federal preemption of state tort law.

Rather than attempt to master all the twists and turns of these various complex doctrines, read this case and the following notes with these more general questions in mind: Why is strict liability justified for medical products but not for medical services? Where products liability exists, how is it shared among the responsible parties (manufacturer, hospital, and physician)? Should doctors and hospitals also be subject to a form of no-fault liability? Should regulatory oversight of medical safety displace the traditional role that juries play in balancing the competing concerns over cost, quality, fairness, and innovation?

■ BRUESEWITZ v. WYETH
562 U.S. 223 (2011)

SCALIA, J.

For the last 66 years, vaccines have been subject to the same federal premarket approval process as prescription drugs, and compensation for vaccine-related injuries has been left largely to the States. Under that regime, . . . vaccines became, one might say, victims of their own success. They had been so effective in preventing infectious diseases that the public became much less alarmed at the threat of those diseases, and much more concerned with the risk of injury from the vaccines themselves.

Much of the concern centered around vaccines against diphtheria, tetanus, and pertussis (DTP), which were blamed for children's disabilities and developmental delays. This led to a massive increase in vaccine-related tort litigation. Whereas between 1978 and 1981 only nine product-liability suits were filed against DTP manufacturers, by the mid-1980's the suits numbered more than 200 each year. This destabilized the DTP vaccine market, causing two of the three domestic manufacturers to withdraw; and the remaining manufacturer, Lederle Laboratories, estimated that its potential tort liability exceeded its annual sales by a factor of 200. . . .

To stabilize the vaccine market and facilitate compensation, Congress enacted the [National Childhood Vaccine Injury Act of 1986 (NCVIA)]. The Act establishes a no-fault compensation program designed to work faster and with greater ease than the civil tort system. A person injured by a vaccine, or his legal guardian, may file a petition for compensation. . . . A special master then makes an informal adjudication of the petition. . . . [After appeal to an administrative court], a claimant has two options: to accept the court's judgment and forgo a traditional tort suit for damages, or to reject the judgment and seek tort relief from the vaccine manufacturer. Fast, informal adjudication is made possible by the Act's Vaccine Injury Table, which lists the vaccines covered under the Act; describes each vaccine's compensable, adverse side effects; and indicates how soon after vaccination those side effects should first manifest themselves. Claimants who show that a listed injury first manifested itself at the appropriate time are prima facie entitled to compensation. No showing of causation is necessary; the [government] bears the burden of disproving causation. A claimant may also recover for unlisted side effects, and for listed side effects that occur at times other than those specified in the Table, but for those the claimant must prove causation. Unlike in tort suits, claimants under the Act are not required to show that the administered vaccine was defectively manufactured, labeled, or designed.

Successful claimants receive compensation for medical, rehabilitation, counseling, special education, and vocational training expenses; diminished earning capacity; pain and suffering; and $250,000 for vaccine-related deaths. Attorney's fees are provided, not only for successful cases, but even for unsuccessful claims that are not frivolous. These awards are paid out of a fund created by an excise tax on each vaccine dose.

The *quid pro quo* for this, designed to stabilize the vaccine market, was the provision of significant tort-liability protections for vaccine manufacturers. The Act requires claimants to seek relief through the compensation program before filing suit for more than $1,000. Manufacturers are generally immunized from liability for failure to warn if they have complied with all regulatory requirements (including but not limited to warning requirements) and have given the warning either to the claimant or the claimant's physician. . . . And most relevant to the present case, the Act expressly eliminates liability for a vaccine's unavoidable, adverse side effects:

> No vaccine manufacturer shall be liable in a civil action for damages arising from a vaccine-related injury or death associated with the administration of a vaccine after October 1, 1988, if the injury or death resulted from side effects that were unavoidable even though the vaccine was properly prepared and was accompanied by proper directions and warnings.

The vaccine at issue here is a DTP vaccine. . . . Hannah Bruesewitz was born on October 20, 1991. Her pediatrician administered doses of the DTP vaccine according to the Center for Disease Control's recommended childhood immunization schedule. Within 24 hours of her April 1992 vaccination, Hannah started to experience seizures. She suffered over 100 seizures during the next month, and her doctors eventually diagnosed her with "residual seizure disorder" and "developmental delay." Hannah, now a teenager, is still diagnosed with both conditions. . . .

A Special Master denied [the parents'] claims on various grounds, . . . [and the Bruesewitzes elected to file suit in state court]. Their complaint alleged (as relevant here) that defective design of [Wyeth's] DTP vaccine caused Hannah's disabilities, and that [Wyeth] was subject to strict liability, and liability for negligent design, under Pennsylvania common law. [The complaint also made claims based upon failure to warn and defective manufacture, but those were no longer at issue. After removal to federal court, the case was dismissed], holding that the Pennsylvania law providing those causes of action was preempted by [the NCVIA]. . . .

[Under the statute], [p]rovided that there was proper manufacture and warning, any remaining side effects, including those resulting from design defects, are deemed to have been unavoidable. State-law design-defect claims are therefore preempted. . . . The language of the provision thus suggests that the *design* of the vaccine is a given, not subject to question in the tort action. What the statute establishes as a complete defense must be unavoidability (given safe manufacture and warning) *with respect to the particular design.* Which plainly implies that the design itself is not open to question.[1]

A further textual indication leads to the same conclusion. Products-liability law establishes a classic and well known triumvirate of grounds for liability: defective manufacture, inadequate directions or warnings, and defective design. If all three were intended to be preserved, it would be strange to mention specifically only two, and leave the third to implication. . . . *Expressio unius, exclusio alterius.* . . .

Petitioners' and the dissent's textual argument also rests upon the proposition that the word "unavoidable" in [the statute] is a term of art that incorporates comment *k* to Restatement (Second) of Torts §402A (1963-1964). The Restatement generally holds a manufacturer strictly liable for harm to person or property caused by "any product in a defective condition unreasonably dangerous to the user." Comment *k* exempts from this strict-liability rule "unavoidably unsafe products." An unavoidably unsafe product is defined by a hodge-podge of criteria and a few examples, such as the Pasteur rabies vaccine and experimental pharmaceuticals. Despite this lack of clarity, petitioners seize upon one phrase in the comment *k* analysis, and assert that by 1986 a majority of courts had made this a *sine qua non* requirement for an "unavoidably unsafe product": a case-specific showing that the product was "quite incapable of being made safer for [its] intended . . . use."[2]

We have no need to consider the finer points of comment *k*. Whatever consistent judicial gloss that comment may have been given in 1986, there is no reason to believe that [the NCVIA] was invoking it. . . . The structure of the NCVIA and of vaccine regulation in general reinforces what the [statutory] text suggests. A vaccine's license spells out [in great detail] the manufacturing method that must be followed and the directions and warnings that must accompany the product. Manufacturers ordinarily must obtain the Food and Drug Administration's (FDA) approval before modifying either. . . . Design defects, in contrast, do not merit a single mention in the NCVIA or the FDA's regulations. Indeed, the FDA has never even spelled out in regulations the criteria it uses to decide whether a vaccine is safe and effective for its intended use. And the decision is surely not an easy one. Drug manufacturers often could trade a little less efficacy for a little more safety, but the safest design is not always the best one. Striking the right balance between safety and efficacy is especially difficult with respect to vaccines, which affect public as well as individual health. Yet the Act, which in every other respect micromanages manufacturers, is silent on how to evaluate competing designs, . . . leaving the universe of alternative designs to be limited only by an expert's imagination.

1. The dissent advocates for another possibility: "[A] side effect is 'unavoidable' . . . where there is no feasible alternative design that would eliminate the side effect of the vaccine without compromising its cost and utility." . . . We have no idea how much more expensive an alternative design can be before it "compromis[es]" a vaccine's cost or how much efficacy an alternative design can sacrifice to improve safety. Neither does the dissent. And neither will the judges who must rule on motions to dismiss.

2. Restatement §402A, Comment *k*, p. 353. Petitioners cite, *inter alia, Kearl* v. *Lederle Labs.*, 218 Cal. Rptr. 453, 463-464 (1985); *Belle Bonfils Memorial Blood Bank* v. *Hansen*, 665 P. 2d 118, 122 (Colo. 1983). Though it is not pertinent to our analysis, we point out that a large number of courts disagreed with that reading of comment *k*, and took it to say that manufacturers did not face strict liability for side effects of properly manufactured prescription drugs that were accompanied by adequate warnings. See, *e.g., Brown* v. *Superior Court*, 751 P. 2d 470 (Cal. 1988); . . .

Jurors, of course, often decide similar questions with little guidance, and we do not suggest that the absence of guidance alone suggests preemption. But the lack of guidance for design defects combined with the extensive guidance for the two grounds of liability specifically mentioned in the Act strongly suggests that design defects were not mentioned because they are not a basis for liability. . . . And, of course, whenever the FDA concludes that a vaccine is unsafe, it may revoke the license.

These provisions for federal agency improvement of vaccine design, and for federally prescribed compensation, once again suggest that [the statute's] silence regarding design-defect liability was not inadvertent. It instead reflects a sensible choice to leave complex epidemiological judgments about vaccine design to the FDA and the National Vaccine Program rather than juries. . . .

The dissent's legislative history relies on the following syllogism: A 1986 House Committee Report states that [the statute] "sets forth the principle contained in Comment *k* of Section 402A of the Restatement of Torts (Second);" in 1986 comment *k* was "commonly understood" to require a case-specific showing that "no feasible alternative design" existed; Congress therefore must have intended [the statute] to require that showing. The syllogism ignores . . . [that] Comment *k* did not have a "commonly understood meaning" in the mid-1980's. Some courts thought it required a case-specific showing that a product was "unavoidably unsafe"; many others thought it categorically exempted certain types of products from strict liability. . . .

For the foregoing reasons, we hold that the National Childhood Vaccine Injury Act preempts all design-defect claims against vaccine manufacturers brought by plaintiffs who seek compensation for injury or death caused by vaccine side effects.

Justice SOTOMAYOR, Justice GINSBURG joins, dissenting.

Vaccine manufacturers have long been subject to a legal duty, rooted in basic principles of products liability law, to improve the designs of their vaccines in light of advances in science and technology. Until today, that duty was enforceable through a traditional state-law tort action for defective design. . . . [The Court's] decision leaves a regulatory vacuum in which no one ensures that vaccine manufacturers adequately take account of scientific and technological advancements when designing or distributing their products. . . .

Blackletter products liability law generally recognizes three different types of product defects: design defects, manufacturing defects, and labeling defects (e.g., failure to warn). The reference in the "even though" clause to a "properly prepared" vaccine "accompanied by proper directions and warnings" is an obvious reference to two such defects — manufacturing and labeling defects. . . . [I]t follows that the "even though" clause requires a vaccine manufacturer in each civil action to demonstrate that its vaccine is free from manufacturing and labeling defects to fall within the liability exemption of [the NCVIA]. Given that the "even though" clause requires the absence of manufacturing and labeling defects, the "if" clause's reference to "side effects that were unavoidable" must refer to side effects caused by something other than manufacturing and labeling defects. The only remaining kind of product defect recognized under traditional products liability law is a design defect. Thus, "side effects that were unavoidable" must refer to side effects caused by a vaccine's *design* that were "unavoidable." . . . Accordingly, . . . Congress must also have intended a vaccine manufacturer to demonstrate in each civil action that the particular side effects of a vaccine's design were "unavoidable." . . .

The legislative history . . . expressly adopts comment *k* of §402A of the Restatement of Torts (Second) (1963-1964) (hereinafter Restatement), which provides that "unavoidably unsafe" products—i.e., those that "in the present state of human knowledge, are quite incapable of being made safe for their intended and ordinary use"—are not defective.[3] As "[a]n outstanding example" of an "[u]navoidably unsafe" product, comment *k* cites "the vaccine for the Pasteur treatment of rabies, which not uncommonly leads to very serious and damaging consequences when it is injected"; "[s]ince the disease itself invariably leads to a dreadful death, both the marketing and the use of the vaccine are fully justified, notwithstanding the unavoidable high degree of risk which they involve." Comment *k* thus provides that "seller[s]" of "[u]navoidably unsafe" products are "not to be held to strict liability" provided that such products "are properly prepared and marketed, and proper warning is given." As the [legislative history of the NCVIA] explains, Congress intended that the "principle in Comment K regarding 'unavoidably unsafe' products" apply to the vaccines covered in the bill. . . . By the time of the Vaccine Act's enactment in 1986, numerous state and federal courts had interpreted comment *k* to mean that a product is "unavoidably unsafe" when, given proper manufacture and labeling, no feasible alternative design would reduce the safety risks without compromising the product's cost and utility.[4] . . . By explaining what Congress meant by the term "unavoidable," moreover, the [Congressional] Report also confirms that whether a side effect is "unavoidable" . . . involves a specific

3. Comment *k* provides as follows: "*Unavoidably unsafe products.* There are some products which, in the present state of human knowledge, are quite incapable of being made safe for their intended and ordinary use. These are especially common in the field of drugs. An outstanding example is the vaccine for the Pasteur treatment of rabies, which not uncommonly leads to very serious and damaging consequences when it is injected. Since the disease itself invariably leads to a dreadful death, both the marketing and the use of the vaccine are fully justified, notwithstanding the unavoidable high degree of risk which they involve. Such a product, properly prepared, and accompanied by proper directions and warning, is not defective, nor is it *unreasonably* dangerous. The same is true of many other drugs, vaccines, and the like, many of which for this very reason cannot legally be sold except to physicians, or under the prescription of a physician. It is also true in particular of many new or experimental drugs as to which, because of lack of time and opportunity for sufficient medical experience, there can be no assurance of safety, or perhaps even of purity of ingredients, but such experience as there is justifies the marketing and use of the drug notwithstanding a medically recognizable risk. The seller of such products, again with the qualification that they are properly prepared and marketed, and proper warning is given, where the situation calls for it, is not to be held to strict liability for unfortunate consequences attending their use, merely because he has undertaken to supply the public with an apparently useful and desirable product, attended with a known but apparently reasonable risk."

4. . . . See 1 L. Frumer & M. Friedman, Products Liability §§8.07[1]-[2], pp. 8-277 to 8-278 (2010) (comment *k* applies "only to defects in design," and there "must be no feasible alternative design which on balance accomplishes the subject product's purpose with a lesser risk" (internal quotation marks omitted)). To be sure, a number of courts at the time of the Vaccine Act's enactment had interpreted comment *k* to preclude design defect claims categorically for certain kinds of products, see *Hill v. Searle Labs.*, 884 F. 2d 1064, 1068 (CA8 1989) (collecting cases), but as indicated by the sources cited above, the courts that had construed comment *k* to apply on a case-specific basis generally agreed on the basic elements of what constituted an "unavoidably unsafe" product. . . .

inquiry in each case as to whether the vaccine "in the present state of human skill and knowledge cannot be made safe,"—i.e., whether a feasible alternative design existed that would have eliminated the adverse side effects of the vaccine without compromising its cost and utility. . . . Accordingly, I believe [the statute] exempts vaccine manufacturers from tort liability only upon a showing by the manufacturer in each case that the vaccine was properly manufactured and labeled, and that the side effects stemming from the vaccine's design could not have been prevented by a feasible alternative design that would have eliminated the adverse side effects without compromising the vaccine's cost and utility.

[T]he majority's position elides a significant difference between state tort law and the federal regulatory scheme. . . . [N]either the Act nor any other provision of federal law places a legal duty on vaccine manufacturers to improve the design of their vaccines to account for scientific and technological advances. Indeed, the FDA does not condition approval of a vaccine on it being the most optimally designed among reasonably available alternatives, nor does it (or any other federal entity) ensure that licensed vaccines keep pace with technological and scientific advances.[5] Rather, the function of ensuring that vaccines are optimally designed in light of existing science and technology has traditionally been left to the States through the imposition of damages for design defects. Cf. *Wyeth* v. *Levine*, 555 U.S. 555 (2009) (noting that the FDA has "traditionally regarded state law as a complementary form of drug regulation" as "[s]tate tort suits uncover unknown drug hazards and provide incentives for drug manufacturers to disclose safety risks promptly"). . . .

I respectfully dissent.

Notes: Designing a No-Fault Liability System

1. *Overview.* The type of no-fault compensation programs used for childhood vaccines has also received considerable discussion as a possible basis for an administrative compensation system that could apply to all medical injuries, including those caused by physicians or hospital staff. These no-fault liability proposals resemble the workers' compensation schemes that replaced negligence suits against employers in the first half of the twentieth century. The basic structure is to define a range of compensable events, establish a schedule of economic and noneconomic damages, and create an administrative system for filing claims and resolving factual disputes and questions of interpretation. See generally Paul C. Weiler, Medical Malpractice on Trial (1991). Each of these components offers potential advantages over current tort law, but also presents sources of controversy and difficulties in design and implementation, as explored in the following notes.

2. *Defining Compensable Events.* Defining compensable events in terms of negative medical outcomes, without regard to fault or the standard of care, has the

5. See, *e.g.*, *Hurley* v. *Lederle Labs.*, 863 F. 2d 1173, 1177 (CA5 1988) ("[T]he FDA is a passive agency: it considers whether to approve vaccine designs only if and when manufacturers come forward with a proposal"); . . . Conk, Is There a Design Defect in the Restatement (Third) of Torts: Products Liability? 109 Yale L.J. 1087, 1128-1129 (1999-2000) ("The FDA does not claim to review products for optimal design. . . . FDA review thus asks less of drug . . . manufacturers than the common law of products liability asks of other kinds of manufacturers").

advantages of greater simplicity, the reduction of pejorative accusations against well-meaning professionals, and the increased social justice of covering seriously injured patients regardless of the behavior that caused the injury. Proponents of no-fault argue that traditional malpractice liability does a poor job of deterrence because doctors perceive lawsuits as largely random and uncontrollable events, medical malpractice insurance is widespread and not experience-rated, and deterrent signals create unnecessary and costly "defensive medicine." See generally Michelle M. Mello & Troyen A. Brennan, Deterrence of Medical Errors: Theory and Evidence for Malpractice Reform, 80 Tex. L. Rev. 1595 (2002). The hope is that a well-crafted no-fault system could correct some or all of these deficiencies. Sagit Mor & Orna Rabinvich-Einy, Relational Malpractice, 42 Seton Hall L. Rev. 610 (2012).

The difficulty with designing a no-fault compensation system, however, is defining exactly which events trigger compensation. As vaccine injuries illustrate, medical causation is complex and not all failures to achieve perfect results are avoidable. Subjecting these questions to litigation would prove costly, but they are essential to defining the scope of strict liability. Therefore, causation and injury questions continue to complicate no-fault systems even though they are designed to be simple and expedient. Claims to the vaccine compensation program, for instance, have become increasingly litigious and protracted. Betsy Grey, The Plague of Causation in the National Childhood Vaccine Injury Act, 48 Harv. J. on Legis. 343 (2011); Peter H. Meyers, Fixing the Flaws in the Federal Vaccine Injury Compensation Program, 63 Admin. L. Rev. 785 (2011).

Moreover, in the context of physician care, it is difficult to define which bad results are avoidable or unexpected without allowing concepts of fault to creep back in, since a less than perfect outcome is compensable only if "correct" medical procedures would have avoided it. Consider, for instance, how you would determine which of various versions of the following events is subject to no-fault compensation: misdiagnosis; adverse drug reactions; and post-surgical infections. Can you make such a determination without suggesting the doctors did something wrong? Can you do so without alluding to what most other doctors do in the same situation?

One way to circumvent these difficulties is simply to list for each major category of treatment or illness which outcomes are considered abnormal enough to warrant compensation as a medical injury. This is what the vaccine compensation fund does, but doing this for all of medicine would be a huge, complex undertaking. Still, methods have been proposed, as documented in note 6.

3. *Costs and Administrative Efficiency.* The other two components of proposals for no-fault compensation attempt to make damages more predictable and dispute resolution speedier and less costly. These advantages are articulated further in sections E.4 and H. Of particular note is the fact that, under the conventional tort system, less than 50 percent of malpractice insurance premiums end up in the pockets of injured patients. Aaron Carroll et al., The Impact of Defense Expenses in Medical Malpractice Claims, 40 J. L. Med. & Ethics 135 (2012). The hope is that savings in administrative and legal costs and the somewhat lower awards from a no-fault system will largely offset the increase in the number of claims that are filed, so that the total costs of the system remain the same but it covers more people and operates more fairly. These virtues alone are substantial enough that in the 1980s the AMA proposed a *fault-based* administrative compensation system. There is the potential, however, that as the system becomes less costly and more accessible, the number of

claims will skyrocket, since research has shown that the number of patients who now sue is a tiny fraction (1 to 2 percent) of the total number who are injured by medical care. Accordingly, the AMA has stopped promoting its administrative reform proposal. However, the idea has been taken up by others, in the form of resolving malpractice disputes through administrative hearings or specialized "health courts." See note 6.

The other drawback to no-fault schemes is their costs and how they are distributed. Even with administrative efficiencies, full compensation for all medical injuries would be much more expensive in total than the present system because so many injuries now are entirely uncompensated. To keep a no-fault system affordable, proponents usually set tight caps on total recoverable damages. As discussed in section F, this resolution of the funding dilemma in essence shifts compensation from the most severely to the least severely injured victims of medical error.

4. *Childbirth Injuries.* All-encompassing administrative no-fault systems for the full range of medical injuries have been adopted in Sweden, Finland, and New Zealand (the latter as part of a compensation system for all accidental injuries). See K. Oliphant & R. Wright eds., Medical Malpractice and Compensation in Global Perspective (2013); J. Dute et al. eds. No-Fault Compensation in the Health Care Sector (2004).

In the United States, the closest real-world application of these ideas has occurred in Florida and Virginia, with their limited no-fault schemes that cover only designated injuries from child birth—the arena that produces the greatest liability exposure. Both programs cover only severe, permanent brain damage. Other injuries in obstetrics such as death, birth defects, and non-neurological physical injury are left to the regular tort system. Because of this limited scope, few claims have been filed or paid. See note 6. Compensation for these cases is focused primarily on the unreimbursed costs of medical care; compensation for lost earnings and for pain and suffering are severely limited.

5. *Neo-No Fault.* A final variation is no fault by voluntary agreement, also known as "neo-no fault." Jeffrey O'Connell is the architect of this idea, in Neo-No Fault Remedies for Medical Injuries: Coordinated Statutory and Contractual Alternatives, 49 Law & Contemp. Probs. 125 (Spring 1986). The gist is that if doctors or hospitals promptly volunteer to cover the uncompensated economic consequences of a medical injury, then patients would be precluded from suing in tort for noneconomic damages (or, in other versions, they would be taxed various costs if they then sued and failed to recover more than the offer). If you had as a client the doctors in the *Locke* case (page 285), would you advise making this type of voluntary offer of payment?

6. *Bibliography.* On the pros and cons of **no-fault** (note 3), see Catherine Struve, Doctors, the Adversary System, and Procedural Reform in Medical Liability Litigation, 72 Fordham L. Rev. 943 (2004); Eleanor D. Kinney, Administrative Law Approaches to Medical Malpractice Reform, 49 St. Louis U. L. J. 45 (2004); Michelle Mello et al., "Health Courts" and Accountability for Patient Safety, 84 Milbank Q. 459 (2006); Maxwell Mehlman & Dale Nance, Medical Injustice: The Case Against Health Courts (2007); Philip G. Peters, Jr., Health Courts? 88 B.U. L. Rev. 227 (2008); Note, 7 Yale J. Health Pol'y L. & Ethics 387 (2007); Symposium, 33 J. Health Pol. Pol'y & L. 725 (2008); Symposium, J. Health Care L. & Policy 217 (2006).

On **childbirth injury compensation** programs (note 4), see Randall R. Bovbjerg & Frank A. Sloan, No Fault for Medical Injury: Theory and Evidence, 67 Univ. Cin.

L. Rev. 53 (1998); David M. Studdert et al., The Jury Is Still In: Florida's Birth-Related Neurological Injury Compensation Plan After a Decade, 25 J. Health Pol. Pol'y & L. 499 (June 2000); Gil Siegal et al., Adjudicating Severe Birth Injury Claims in Florida and Virginia, 34 Am. J. L. & Med. 493 (2008). For additional discussion of the federal vaccine compensation program, see Peter H. Meyers, Fixing the Flaws in the Federal Vaccine Injury Compensation Program, 63 Admin. L. Rev. 785 (2011).

On "neo-no fault" (note 5), see Jeffrey O'Connell & Evan Stephenson, Binding Statutory Early Offers by Defendants, Not Plaintiffs, *in* Personal Injury Suits, 54 DePaul L. Rev. 233 (2005); J. Hersch et al., An Empirical Assessment of Early Offer Reform for Medical Malpractice, 36 J. Leg. Stud. 119 (2007).

Notes: Products Liability for Defective Drugs and Medical Devices

1. *Mass Torts.* Defective drugs and devices have given rise to several massive rounds of litigation when it was discovered that a widely used drug or medical device has a previously unknown potential harm. Notable examples include DES (prenatal miscarriage prevention), Vioxx (arthritis treatment), silicone breast implants, Bendectin (a pregnancy antinausea drug), Dalkon Shield (an intrauterine contraceptive device), and the birth control pill. Some manufacturers, such as Dow-Corning in the breast implant cases, have declared bankruptcy when faced with billions of dollars in liability claims. See generally Michael D. Green, Bendectin and Birth Defects: The Challenges of Mass Toxic Substances Litigation (1996); Jonathan Van O'Steen, The FDA Defense: Vioxx and the Argument Against Federal Preemption of State Claims for Injuries Resulting from Defective Drugs, 48 Ariz. L. Rev. 67 (2006); Frank M. McClellan, The Vioxx Litigation: A Critical Look at Trial Tactics, the Tort System, and the Roles of Lawyers in Mass Tort Litigation, 57 DePaul L. Rev. 509 (2008).

2. *Medical Devices.* The only example comment *k* cites of unavoidably unsafe products is medical drugs, but its rationale might also apply to medical devices such as pacemakers and various artificial implants. Is there any basis on which to distinguish these two categories of medical products? Most courts conclude "no," and so refuse to apply strict liability to medical devices as well. See Tansy v. Dacomed Corp., 890 P.2d 881 (Okla. 1994) (penile implant that failed due to overuse); Annot., 70 A.L.R.4th 16 (1989). Should the same be true for medical devices available to consumers in stores, such as thermometers, heating pads, and crutches? Are tampons "medical devices"? What about condoms? Where do each of these lie on the line drawn by one court between products "used to make work easier or to provide pleasure" vs. those "necessary to alleviate pain and suffering" or prevent illness? Brown v. Superior Court, 751 P.2d 470 (Cal. 1988). See O'Gilvie v. International Playtex Inc., 821 F.2d 1438 (10th Cir. 1987) (applying ordinary strict liability to toxic shock syndrome allegedly caused by tampons); Artiglio v. Superior Court, 27 Cal. Rptr. 2d 589 (Ct. App. 1994) (comment *k* covers breast implants despite their use for cosmetic purposes); Hufft v. Horowitz, 5 Cal. Rptr. 2d 377 (Ct. App. 1992) (distinguishing implanted medical devices that, like drugs, are available only from physicians and go inside the body, from ordinary commercial medical products such as wheelchairs).

3. *Litigating Unavoidability.* *Bruesewitz* resolves what "unavoidably unsafe" means under the childhood vaccine statute, but controversy still rages in state courts,

where common-law products liability still prevails. Notice the reference in *Bruesewitz* to two distinct positions: (1) *per se:* all drugs and devices covered by comment *k* are free from design defect claims; (2) *case-by-case:* each case inquires whether the particular drug or device could have been designed more safely without sacrificing any substantial benefit or cost advantage. For a while, the case-by-case rule appeared to be the majority position, but the newer Restatement (Third) of the Law of Torts: Products Liability (1998) leans more heavily in favor of the per se rule. Still, it is not decisive, so debate continues.

4. *Blood Shield Statutes.* The one instance where manufacturers and distributors of medical supplies have avoided strict liability even for *manufacturing* defects is contaminated blood transfusions. Despite careful screening, a certain portion of donated or purchased blood is contaminated with impurities such as hepatitis or AIDS viruses. For a while, courts wrestled with whether blood banks or hospitals that sell defective blood are selling a product or instead only performing a service. See Brody v. Overlook Hospital, 332 A.2d 596 (N.J. 1975) (blood banks not subject to strict liability; reversing contrary decision by lower court). To resolve the legal uncertainty produced by these inconsistent holdings, virtually all states have enacted "blood shield" statutes declaring that blood products are not subject to strict products liability. These statutes often apply as well to human organs and tissues used for transplants. Annot., 75 A.L.R.5th 229 (2000); Annot., 24 A.L.R.4th 508 (1982); Comment, 2 Ind. Health L. Rev. 295 (2005).

Several courts have ruled that these statutes do not cover companies that manufacture drugs from blood products, such as the "clotting factor" that pharmaceutical companies produce to keep hemophiliacs from bleeding. See In re Rhone-Poulenc Rorer, Inc., 51 F.3d 1293 (7th Cir. 1995). Because this manufacturing process requires combining blood from many different donors in order to distill a single batch of clotting factor, virtually all severe hemophiliacs—some 10,000 in all—were infected with the AIDS virus during the early 1980s before adequate screening tests were available. The manufacturers agreed to settle a class action suit for roughly $100,000 for each person infected. See Conk, infra, 109 Yale L. J. 1087 (2000).

5. *Hospital and Physician Liability.* The comment *k* defense applies only to design and warning defects. When drugs and medical devices suffer from manufacturing defects, strict products liability clearly applies, but only to manufacturers and distributors, not to hospitals or doctors, so long as the product is not altered by the provider. Consider, for instance, the needle that broke during surgery in the Locke v. Pachtman case (page 285). If the needle had broken due to a manufacturing flaw, as opposed to misuse, the hospital and doctor would not have been responsible, even though they were in the chain of distribution. The reason is that, in this context, the needle is seen as merely a supply that is incidental to the sale of a service, and therefore the doctor, not the patient, is the end user. Magrine v. Krasnico, 97 N.J. 228 (1967) (dentist not responsible for broken needle); Note, The Physician as Consumer, 79 Nw. U. L. Rev. 460 (1984); Annot., 100 A.L.R.3d 1205 (1980). The same reasoning does not apply as strongly when considering other medical supplies such as pacemakers and neck braces that are more clearly sold by hospitals as individual products. Most courts, however, find that hospitals generally are not covered by products liability law for defects in their supplies or equipment that are used directly for patient care. See, e.g., Cafazzo v. Central Medical Health Service,

Inc., 668 A.2d 521 (Pa. 1995) (neither doctor nor hospital strictly liable for defective prosthesis implanted in patient's jaw). Naturally, hospitals can be held liable for failing to reasonably inspect and maintain equipment and medical devices.

6. *Learned Intermediaries and Direct-to-Consumer Advertising.* Warnings for prescription drugs generally need to be given only to doctors, not to patients. Under tort law's "learned intermediary" rule, it is up to physicians to determine how these warnings should be incorporated into their treatment decisions and which warnings should be passed along to patients. Reyes v. Wyeth Labs, 498 F.2d 1264 (5th Cir. 1974). The learned intermediary rule does not apply to "over-the-counter" drugs purchased directly by consumers, however, and several courts have held it does not apply to mass immunization vaccines or to prescription drugs that are commonly available just for the asking, without any particular medical problem. The classic instance of the latter is the birth control pill. In these situations, manufacturers can be sued for failures to warn consumers directly. See Davis v. Wyeth Labs, 399 F.2d 121 (9th Cir. 1968) (polio); MacDonald v. Ortho Pharmaceutical Corp., 475 N.E.2d 65 (Mass. 1985) (birth control pills).

Increasingly, drug companies are advertising directly to the public a wide range of pharmaceuticals for common maladies, encouraging people to ask their doctor to prescribe drugs for seasonal allergies, baldness, and heartburn, for instance. This is partly in response to restrictions imposed by managed care insurers. Symposium, 346 New Eng. J. Med. 523 (2002). One influential court has held, with respect to birth control implants, that advertising directly to consumers precludes application of the learned intermediary rule. Perez v. Wyeth Laboratories, 734 A.2d 1245 (N.J. 1999). In a potentially groundbreaking decision, the West Virginia Supreme Court went much further, holding that the learned intermediary doctrine no longer applies generally, due to the pharmaceutical industry's widespread use of direct-to-consumer advertising. State v. Karl, 647 S.E.2d 899 (W. Va. 2007). Criticizing this decision, see Note, 48 Jurimetrics J. 285 (2008).

7. *Package Inserts and "Off-Label" Use.* Where the learned intermediary rule applies, patients can still sue drug manufacturers for inadequate warnings to their physicians, and naturally patients can also sue their physicians who ignore drug risks or fail to warn them personally. These suits against physicians are brought as standard negligent practice or breach of informed consent actions, however. In such actions, the FDA's required warning to physicians, known as the "package insert," becomes one possible source of evidence against the physician. The instructions on package inserts do not strictly bind physicians; FDA law allows them to use approved drugs in any fashion they want, even if the particular use is not approved (so-called off-label use). This is particularly common, for instance, in cancer treatment and, to a lesser extent, AIDS treatment. Nevertheless, as discussed above at page 344, most courts have held that plaintiffs may introduce package inserts directly into evidence on the standard of care as an exception to the hearsay rule, and a few have held that package inserts create a rebuttable, prima facie case for liability when the defendant doctor deviates from the instructions, shifting the burden of proof to the doctor to show that the departure was accepted practice. See Hyman & Armstrong, P.S.C. v. Gunderson, 279 S.W.3d 93 (Ky. 2008) (package insert admissible but not conclusive of standard of care); Cuc Thi Ngo v. Queen's Med. Ctr., 358 P.3d 26 (Hawaii 2015) (same); Garvey v. O'Donoghue, 530 A.2d 1141 (D.C. App. 1987) (package insert is prima facie evidence of standard of care); Note, 51 Stan. L. Rev.

1343 (1999). If physicians intentionally and nonnegligently use a drug for purposes other than those approved by the FDA, or in a manner that contradicts the manufacturer's warnings, does this absolve the manufacturer from products liability? See K. Stoffelmayr, Products Liability and "Off-Label" Uses of Prescription Drugs, 63 U. Chi. L. Rev. 275 (1996) (finding that the cases split into five different lines, from no liability, to liability if off-label use is widespread, to full liability).

8. *"Detail Men."* The FDA requires pharmaceutical manufacturers to continue monitoring adverse reactions to their products even after approval, and to change or intensify warnings if different or greater risks materialize. As described in Sterling Drug, Inc. v. Yarrow, 408 F.2d 978 (8th Cir. 1969), this information is collected and these after-market warnings are distributed through pharmaceutical "detail men" who permeate hospitals and doctors' offices trying to encourage doctors to use their products. The court upheld a jury verdict finding a manufacturer liable for failing to use this means of communication where, one year prior to the plaintiff's starting treatment with the drug, medical publications began to report an association between the drug and certain serious side effects:

> Appellant usually communicates its product information to physicians prescribing its products: (1) by "detail men," who are specially trained field representatives engaged in selling and promoting the use of its products by personal calls in which oral presentations are made and literature and samples delivered, (2) by listings of drugs in an annually published advertising medium known as Physicians' Desk Reference, (3) by "product cards" which are mailed and distributed by detail men to physicians and are available at medical conventions and hospital exhibits, and (4) by special letters mailed to physicians. . . . Nevertheless, the detail men who made regular personal calls on prescribing physicians and customers were never, in the relevant period, instructed to invite attention of the physicians and customers to the reported dangers. . . . The warnings of side effects . . . were limited to the product cards, the Physicians' Desk Reference and to the "Dear Doctor" letter dated February 1963 . . . [that were sent] to all [248,000] physicians and hospital personnel in the United States. . . .
>
> The direct and circumstantial evidence amply supports a finding that . . . Dr. Olson (and other general practitioners) receive so much literature on drugs that it is impossible to read all of it; that Dr. Olson relied on detail men, medical conventions, medical journals and conversations with other doctors for information on drugs he was prescribing; that Dr. Olson was inundated with literature and product cards of various manufacturers; that a change in literature and an additional letter were insufficient to present new information to Dr. Olson; that detail men visit physicians at frequent intervals and could give an effective warning which would affirmatively notify the doctor of the dangerous side effects of chloroquine phosphate on the retina. These findings of fact were not clearly erroneous. . . .
>
> This does not mean that every physician in the United States must have been given an immediate warning by a personal messenger. But it does mean that the trial court was justified in finding that it was unreasonable to fail to instruct the detail men, at least, to warn the physicians on whom they regularly called of the dangers of which appellant had learned, or in the exercise of reasonable care should have known. . . . [Moreover], the "Dear Doctor" letter could have been reasonably found to be lacking in emphasis, timeliness and attention inviting qualities. A reasoning mind could find that appellant's warning actions were unduly delayed, reluctant and lacking in a sense of urgency.

Drug company "detail men" can also be a source of liability when they minimize the significance of official warnings in their eagerness to sell their product. See, e.g., Incollingo v. Ewing, 282 A.2d 206 (Pa. 1971) (official warning ineffective where detail men emphasized antibiotic's effectiveness and wide acceptance while downplaying known side effects). For additional discussion, see the incredible saga of the 15-year litigation (two trials and three state supreme court decisions) in Feldman v. Lederle Labs, 625 A.2d 1066 (N.J. 1993), concerning the failure to warn that a common antibiotic can cause teeth to turn gray.

9. *Computerized Medicine.* The computerization of medicine creates novel opportunities for design defect and related theories of products liability. Physicians and nurses increasingly are using software programs that prescribe or recommend diagnostic and treatment decisions, for instance, by analyzing lists of symptoms and assigning probabilities to alternative diagnoses. If these computer algorithms are found to contain an error, perhaps the designer, seller, or hospital purchaser can be found liable. Related issues arise from medical information or advice given on Web sites that are proliferating rapidly. For discussion and analysis, see B. H. Lamkin, Medical Expert Systems and Publisher Liability: A Cross-Contextual Analysis, 43 Emory L.J. 731 (1994); Nicolas P. Terry, Cyber-Malpractice: Legal Exposure for Cybermedicine, 25 Am. J. L. Med. 327 (1999); S. Mangalmurti et al., Medical Malpractice in the Age of Electronic Health Records, 363 New Eng. J. Med. 2060 (2010); Nadia Sawicki, Patient Protection and Decision-Aid Quality: Regulatory and Tort Law Approaches, 54 Ariz. L. Rev. 621 (2012).

10. *Federal Preemption.* Displacement of state tort law might also result from FDA regulation. The FDA imposes extensive testing requirements for safety and effectiveness before prescription drugs and potentially dangerous medical devices can be marketed. After approval, the FDA also extensively regulates the labeling instructions and warnings that manufacturers must give doctors. Is there any basis in public policy for holding manufacturers liable for design defects or warning deficiencies that the FDA finds acceptable? Consider the discussion in Chapter 8.D.1 of the FDA approval process, which notes that the FDA relies primarily on information supplied by and tests commissioned by the pharmaceutical manufacturers themselves, rather than the FDA conducting its own investigations.

FDA regulation might absolve manufacturers of liability in one of two ways. First, regulatory compliance might act as a substantive defense to liability under state tort law by demonstrating actual reasonableness or nondefectiveness. Second, federal law might be found to preempt state tort liability. There are different responses to these two arguments. For the substantive defense, state courts usually allow regulatory compliance only as evidence, but not as conclusive proof, of reasonable care. A few states by statute declare that regulatory compliance creates a rebuttable presumption of nonliability or protects manufacturers from punitive damages. See Garcia v. Wyeth-Ayerst Labs., 385 F.3d 961 (6th Cir. 2004); Note, 84 N.C. L. Rev. 737 (2006).

As for federal preemption, courts' positions are complex, differing between drugs and devices and between different types of claimed defects. For drugs, most cases find no federal preemption because the federal statute overrides state law only where "there is a direct and positive conflict." Such a conflict might be found with respect to warnings of risk if the FDA labeling requirements were exclusive, that is, if the FDA were to preclude any additional warnings than those it imposes. See Pliva, Inc. v. Mensing, 131 S. Ct. 1672 (2011) (state law preempted for labeling of *generic* drugs because generic manufacturers must use the same labels as those approved for brand name equivalents). But, for non-generic drugs, the FDA has been unclear about whether its labeling requirements can be varied by manufacturers or whether its labeling rules preempt state tort law. Given this uncertainty, the Court held in Wyeth v. Levine, 555 U.S. 555 (2009), that FDA oversight does not preempt a suit claiming inadequate warning for a drug administered by injection. Nevertheless, manufacturers remain reluctant to depart from the FDA script. Could that be because doing so might itself expose them to suit? How so?

For medical devices, the preemptive effect of federal regulation is equally complex. The Food, Drug and Cosmetics Act appears to expressly preempt state law in §360k(a), which declares that states may not impose any "requirement which is different from or in addition to" those imposed by the FDA. Based on this, a number of circuit courts found products liability actions preempted, but others did not. The Supreme Court ruled 5-4 that no preemption occurs for medical devices that receive only cursory FDA review. Medtronic Inc. v. Lohr, 518 U.S. 470 (1996). The precise reasoning is obscure due to fractured voting, but preemption still does hold for devices that receive more thorough pre-market review by the FDA. E.g., Riegel v. Medtronic, 552 U.S. 312 (2008) (suit preempted regarding balloon catheter that burst during surgery). Also, claims that device manufacturers were not honest with the FDA in obtaining approval are preempted. Buckman Co. v. Plaintiffs' Legal Committee, 531 U.S. 341 (2001).

11. *Further Reading.* On **design defects** (note 3), see George W. Conk, Is There a Design Defect in the Restatement (Third) of Torts: Products Liability?, 109 Yale L. J. 1087 (2000); James A. Henderson & Aaron D. Twerski, Drug Designs Are Different, 111 Yale L. J. 151 (2001); Symposium, 30 Seton Hall L. Rev. 202 (1999).

On **direct-to-consumer advertising** (note 6), see Richard C. Ausness, Will More Aggressive Marketing Practices Lead to Greater Tort Liability for Prescription Drug Manufacturers?, 37 Wake Forest L. Rev. 97 (2002); Jack Karns, Direct Advertising of Prescription Drugs: The Duty to Warn and the Learned Intermediary Rule, 3 DePaul J. Health Care L. 273 (2000); Note, 51 Stan. L. Rev. 1343 (1999).

On **federal preemption** (note 10), see Symposium, 32 Hamline L. Rev. 657 (2009); Richard Epstein, What Tort Theory Tells Us About Federal Preemption: The Tragic Saga of Wyeth v. Levine, 65 N.Y.U. Ann. Surv. Am. L. 485 (2010); Catherine M. Sharkey, What *Riegel* Portends for FDA Preemption of State Law Products Liability Claims, 103 Nw. U. L. Rev. 437 (2009); Mary J. Davis, The Battle over Implied Preemption: Products Liability and the FDA, 48 B.C. L. Rev. 1089 (2007); William Dreier, Liability for Drug Advertising, Warnings, and Frauds, 58 Rutgers L. Rev. 615 (2006); Richard Ausness, Should the Courts Defer to the FDA's New Interpretation of the Medical Device Amendments?, 80 Tul. L. Rev. 727 (2006); Note, Cardozo L. Rev. 38 (2005); Annot., 98 A.L.R. Fed. 124 (1990).

Review Questions: Products Liability

Under the majority rule, what is the potential liability of the manufacturer (Mfg.) and the physician (Dr.) or hospital in each of the following situations? What attitudes of public policy support liability or nonliability in each situation?

1. Dr. implants a pacemaker. Before doing so, he fails to ascertain that it is operational. It turns out to be a dud.
2. With FDA approval, Mfg. markets a new, powerful chemotherapy drug for kidney cancer. The package insert warns that it is not intended for use in any other cancer. Dr. decides to use the drug for pancreatic cancer, which, using standard treatment, currently has an extremely dim prognosis (10 percent chance of survival). The drug's toxic effects kill the cancer patient. Dr. obtains only generic, routine informed consent ("We'll be treating you with various chemical agents that have a significant risk of toxic side effects, including death"), but does not say anything about using a new drug intended for a different purpose.
3. Korkafine is a widely used and recommended over-the-counter drug for hay-fever-type allergies. Mfg. widely advertises it both to the public under the brand name Snuffle, and also directly to physicians, since many people consult physicians about their allergies. After five years on the market, it was discovered that, when korkafine is taken in conjunction with okra (a southern vegetable), a bizarre chemical reaction occasionally happens that causes mild hair loss. After some deliberation, the FDA allows the drug to remain on the market as long as Mfg. adds the okra warning to others on the package and in any written promotional materials. Three years later, suit is brought against Mfg. by a rapidly balding Southerner who, with his Dr.'s knowledge, decided to use Snuffle every spring and fall during pollen season.

E. CAUSATION AND AFFIRMATIVE DEFENSES

Having surveyed numerous theories that can be used to establish a physician's breach of duty, we now turn to other elements of the basic medical malpractice cause of action: causation, affirmative defenses, and damages.

1. Causation

■ HERSKOVITS v. GROUP HEALTH COOPERATIVE OF PUGET SOUND
664 P.2d 474 (Wash. 1983)

DORE, Justice.
. . . The personal representative of Leslie Herskovits' estate initiated this survivorship action against Group Health Cooperative of Puget Sound (Group Health),

alleging failure to make an early diagnosis of her husband's lung cancer. Group Health moved for summary judgment for dismissal on the basis that Herskovits probably would have died from lung cancer even if the diagnosis had been made earlier, which the trial court granted.

The complaint alleged that Herskovits came to Group Health Hospital in 1974 with complaints of pain and coughing. . . . Plaintiff contends that Herskovits was treated thereafter only with cough medicine. . . . In the early spring of 1975, Mr. and Mrs. Herskovits went south in the hope that the warm weather would help. Upon his return to the Seattle area with no improvement in his health, Herskovits visited Dr. Jonathan Ostrow on a private basis for another medical opinion. Within three weeks, Dr. Ostrow's evaluation and direction to Group Health led to the diagnosis of cancer. In July of 1975, Herskovits' lung was removed, but no radiation or chemotherapy treatments were instituted. Herskovits died 20 months later, on March 22, 1977, at the age of 60.

At hearing on the motion for summary judgment, plaintiff was unable to produce expert testimony that the delay in diagnosis "probably" or "more likely than not" caused her husband's death. . . . Dr. Ostrow testified that if the tumor was a "stage 1" tumor in December 1974, Herskovits' chance of a five-year survival would have been 39 percent. In June 1975, his chances of survival were 25 percent assuming the tumor had progressed to "stage 2" . Thus, the delay in diagnosis may have reduced the chance of a five-year survival by 14 percent. . . . It is Group Health's contention that plaintiff must prove that Herskovits "probably" would have survived had the defendant not been allegedly negligent; that is, the plaintiff must prove there was at least a 51 percent chance of survival. . . .

This court has held that a person who negligently renders aid and consequently increases the risk of harm to those he is trying to assist is liable for any physical damages he causes. Restatement (Second) of Torts §323. . . . This court heretofore has not faced the issue of whether, under §323(a), proof that the defendant's conduct increased the risk of death by decreasing the chances of survival is sufficient to take the issue of proximate cause to the jury. Some courts in other jurisdictions have allowed the proximate cause issue to go to the jury on this type of proof. These courts emphasized the fact that defendants' conduct deprived the decedents of a "significant" chance to survive or recover, rather than requiring proof that with absolute certainty the defendants' conduct caused the physical injury. The underlying reason is that it is not for the wrongdoer, who put the possibility of recovery beyond realization, to say afterward that the result was inevitable.

Other jurisdictions have rejected this approach, generally holding that unless the plaintiff is able to show that it was more likely than not that the harm was caused by the defendant's negligence, proof of a decreased chance of survival is not enough to take the proximate cause question to the jury. These courts have concluded that the defendant should not be liable where the decedent more than likely would have died anyway. . . .

III

We are persuaded by the reasoning of the Pennsylvania Supreme Court in Hamil v. Bashline, 392 A.2d 1280 (Pa. 1978). While *Hamil* involved an original survival chance of greater than 50 percent, we find the rationale used by the *Hamil* court to apply equally to cases such as the present one, where the original survival chance is less than 50 percent. The plaintiff's decedent was suffering from severe chest pains. His wife transported him to the hospital where he was negligently treated in the emergency unit. The wife, because of the lack of help, took her husband to a private physician's office, where he died. In an action brought under the wrongful death and survivorship statutes, the main medical witness testified that if the hospital had employed proper treatment, the decedent would have had a substantial chance of surviving the attack. The medical expert expressed his opinion in terms of a 75 percent chance of survival. . . .

The *Hamil* court distinguished the facts of that case from the general tort case in which a plaintiff alleges that a defendant's act or omission set in motion a force which resulted in harm. In the typical tort case, the "but for" test, requiring proof that damages or death probably would not have occurred "but for" the negligent conduct of the defendant, is appropriate. In *Hamil* and the instant case, however, the defendant's act or omission failed in a duty to protect against harm from another source. Thus, as the *Hamil* court noted, the factfinder is put in the position of having to consider not only what did occur, but also what might have occurred. "Such cases by their very nature elude the degree of certainty one would prefer and upon which the law normally insists before a person may be held liable." . . . The *Hamil* court held that once a plaintiff has demonstrated that the defendant's acts or omissions have increased the risk of harm to another, such evidence furnishes a basis for the jury to make a determination as to whether such increased risk was in turn a substantial factor in bringing about the resultant harm.

. . . The following quotation from Hicks v. United States, 368 F.2d 626, 632 (4th Cir. 1966), is frequently cited in cases adopting loss of a chance because it succinctly defines the doctrine:

> Rarely is it possible to demonstrate to an absolute certainty what would have happened in circumstances that the wrongdoer did not allow to come to pass. The law does not in the existing circumstances require the plaintiff to show to a certainty that the patient would have lived had she been hospitalized and operated on promptly. . . .

The recent case of James v. United States, 483 F. Supp. 581 (N.D. Cal. 1980), concerned the failure to diagnose and promptly treat a lung tumor. The court concluded that the plaintiff sustained its burden of proof even without statistical evidence, stating:

> As a proximate result of defendant's negligence, James was deprived of the opportunity to receive early treatment and the chance of realizing any resulting gain in his life expectancy and physical and mental comfort. *No matter how small that chance may have been*—and its magnitude cannot be ascertained—no one can say that the chance of prolonging one's life or decreasing suffering is valueless.
>
> . . . We hold that medical testimony of a reduction of chance of survival from 39 percent to 25 percent is sufficient evidence to allow the proximate cause issue to go to the jury. . . . To decide otherwise would be a blanket release from liability for doctors and hospitals any time there was less than a 50 percent chance of survival,

regardless of how flagrant the negligence. . . . We reverse the trial court and reinstate the cause of action.

PEARSON, Justice (concurring).

. . . In medical malpractice cases such as the one before us, cause in fact must usually be established by expert medical testimony, and must be established beyond the balance of probabilities. In a case such as this, medical testimony must be relied upon to establish the causal relationship between the liability-producing situation and the claimed physical disability resulting therefrom. The evidence will be deemed insufficient to support the jury's verdict, if it can be said that considering the whole of the medical testimony the jury must resort to speculation or conjecture in determining such causal relationship. In many recent decisions of this court we have held that such determination is deemed based on speculation and conjecture if the medical testimony does not go beyond the expression of an opinion that the physical disability "might have" or "possibly did" result from the hypothesized cause. To remove the issue from the realm of speculation, the medical testimony must at least be sufficiently definite to establish that the act complained of "probably" or "more likely than not" caused the subsequent disability.

The issue before the court, quite simply, is whether Dr. Ostrow's testimony satisfies th[is] standard. . . . In order to make this determination, we must first define the "subsequent disability" suffered by Mr. Herskovits. Therein lies the crux of this case. . . .

If the injury is determined to be the death of Mr. Herskovits, then under the established principles of proximate cause plaintiff has failed to make a prima facie case. Dr. Ostrow was unable to state that probably, or more likely than not, Mr. Herskovits' death was caused by defendant's negligence. On the contrary, it is clear from Dr. Ostrow's testimony that Mr. Herskovits would have probably died from cancer even with the exercise of reasonable care by defendant. . . .

If, on the other hand, we view the injury to be the reduction of Mr. Herskovits' chance of survival, our analysis might well be different. Dr. Ostrow testified that the failure to diagnose cancer in December 1974 probably caused a substantial reduction in Mr. Herskovits' chance of survival. The . . . standard of proof is therefore met.

I note here that two other problems are created by the latter analysis. First, we have never before considered whether the loss or reduction of a chance of survival is a compensable injury. And second, this analysis raises the issue of whether an action for reduction of the chance of survival can be brought under the wrongful death statute. Confronted with these problems, . . . I turn to consider how other jurisdictions have dealt with similar cases. . . .

Having concluded this somewhat detailed survey of the cases cited by plaintiff, what conclusions can we draw? First, the critical element in each of the cases is that the defendant's negligence either deprived a decedent of a chance of surviving a potentially fatal condition or reduced that chance. To summarize, in Hicks v. United States the decedent was deprived of a probability of survival; in Jeanes v. Milner the decedent's chance of survival was reduced from 35 percent to 24 percent; in O'Brien v. Stover, the decedent's 30 percent chance of survival was reduced by an indeterminate amount; in McBride v. United States the decedent was deprived of the probability of survival; in Kallenberg v. Beth Israel Hospital the decedent was deprived of a 20 percent to 40 percent chance of survival; in Hamil v. Bashline the decedent was deprived of a 75 percent chance of survival; and in James v. United States the decedent was deprived of an indeterminate chance of survival, no matter how small.

The three cases where the chance of survival was greater than 50 percent (*Hicks*, *McBride*, and *Hamil*) are unexceptional in that they focus on the death of the decedent as the injury, and they require proximate cause to be shown beyond the balance of probabilities. Such a result is consistent with existing principles in this state, and with cases from other jurisdictions cited by defendant. The remaining four cases allowed recovery despite the plaintiffs' failure to prove a probability of survival. . . . I am convinced that these cases reflect a trend to the most rational, least arbitrary, rule by which to regulate cases of this kind. I am persuaded to this conclusion not so much by the reasoning of these cases themselves, but by the thoughtful discussion of a recent commentator. King, Causation, Valuation, and Chance in Personal Injury Torts Involving Preexisting Conditions and Future Consequences, 90 Yale L.J. 1353 (1981).

King's basic thesis is explained in the following passage, which is particularly pertinent to the case before us:

> . . . A plaintiff ordinarily should be required to prove by the applicable standard of proof that the defendant caused the loss in question. What caused a loss, however, should be a separate question from what the nature and extent of the loss are. This distinction seems to have eluded the courts, with the result that lost chances in many respects are compensated either as certainties or not at all. . . . A more rational approach, however, would allow recovery for the loss of the chance of cure even though the chance was not better than even. The probability of long-term survival would be reflected in the amount of damages awarded for the loss of the chance. . . .

Under the all or nothing approach, typified by Cooper v. Sisters of Charity of Cincinnati, Inc., 27 Ohio St. 2d 242, 272 N.E.2d 97 (1971), a plaintiff who establishes that but for the defendant's negligence the decedent had a 51 percent chance of survival may maintain an action for that death. The defendant will be liable for all damages arising from the death, even though there was a 49 percent chance it would have occurred despite his negligence. On the other hand, a plaintiff who establishes that but for the defendant's negligence the decedent had a 49 percent chance of survival recovers nothing. . . .

These reasons persuade me that the best resolution of the issue before us is to recognize the loss of a less than even chance as an actionable injury. Therefore, I would hold that plaintiff has established a prima facie issue of proximate cause by producing testimony that defendant probably caused a substantial reduction in Mr. Herskovits' chance of survival.

The decedent's personal action for loss of this chance will survive to his personal representatives. The family of the decedent should also be allowed to maintain an action for the lost chance of recovery by the decedent. I would interpret the wrongful death statute to apply to cases of this type. Under this interpretation, a person will "cause" the death of another person whenever he causes a substantial reduction in that person's chance of survival.

Finally, it is necessary to consider the amount of damages recoverable in the event that a loss of a chance of recovery is established. Once again, King's discussion provides a useful illustration of the principles which should be applied:

> To illustrate, consider a patient who suffers a heart attack and dies as a result. Assume that the defendant-physician negligently misdiagnosed the patient's condition, but that the patient would have had only a 40 percent chance of survival even with a timely diagnosis and proper care. Regardless of whether it could be said that the defendant caused the decedent's death, he caused the loss of a chance, and that chance-interest should be completely redressed in its own right. Under the proposed rule, the plaintiff's compensation for the loss of the victim's chance of surviving the heart attack would be 40 percent of the compensable value of the victim's life had he survived (including what his earning capacity would otherwise have been in the years following death). The value placed on the patient's life would reflect such factors as his age, health, and earning potential, including the fact that he had suffered the heart attack and the assumption that he had survived it. The 40 percent computation would be applied to that base figure. . . .

BRACHTENBACH, Justice (dissenting).

. . . Malpractice suits represent a class of controversies where extreme caution should be exercised in relaxing causation requirements. The physician serves a vital function in our society, a function which requires the assumption of a duty to the patient. Yet, his profession affords him only an inexact and often experimental science by which to discharge his duty. Moreover, the tendency to place blame on a physician who fails to find a cure is great. Thus, policy considerations do not, on balance, weigh in favor of abandoning the well-established requirements of proximate cause.[13]

. . . Usually the substantial factor test has been applied only in situations where there are two causes, either of which could have caused the event alone, and it cannot be determined which was the actual cause. For example, A and B both start separate fires which combine to burn C's house. Either fire alone would have caused the same result, but C cannot prove that "but-for" the negligence of either A or B the house would not have burned. Therefore, to prevent both A and B being relieved of liability, the "but-for" test is abandoned, and the question becomes whether the conduct of A or B was a substantial factor in causing the fire that injured C. Under this test, either A or B could be held liable for the damage. Except in situations where there are coequal causes, however, defendant's act cannot be a substantial factor when the event would have occurred without it. . . .

Thus, I would not resolve the instant case simply by focusing on the 14 percent differentiation in the chance to survive five years for the different stages of cancer.

---

13. There is also a difference between the standard of proof for proximate cause to show liability and the standard of proof to show the amount of damages after liability is established. Courts are willing to relax proof requirements on the issue of damages, once liability is shown. Therefore, statistical data may be of greater value at the damage stage, especially with regard to future damages that are necessarily subject to some uncertainties and contingencies.

Instead, I would accept this as an admissible fact, but not as proof of proximate cause. To meet the proximate cause burden, the record would need to reveal other facts about the patient that tended to show that he would have been a member of the 14 percent group whose chance of five years' survival could be increased by early diagnosis. . . .

Other statistics admitted into evidence also tend to show the inconclusiveness of the statistics relied on by the majority. One study showed the two-year survival rate for this type of cancer to be 46.6 percent for stage one and 39.8 percent for stage two. Mr. Herskovits lived for 20 months after surgery, which was 26 months after defendant allegedly should have discovered the cancer. Therefore, regardless of the stage of the cancer at the time Mr. Herskovits was examined by defendant, it cannot be concluded that he survived significantly less than the average survival time. Hence, it is pure speculation to suppose that the doctor's negligence "caused" Mr. Herskovits to die sooner than he would have otherwise. . . .

Cases alleging misdiagnosis of cancer are increasing in number, perhaps because of the increased awareness of the importance of early detection. These cases, however, illustrate no more than an inconsistency among courts in their treatment of the problems of proof. See Annot., Malpractice in Connection with Diagnosis of Cancer, 79 A.L.R.3d 915 (1977). Perhaps as medical science becomes more knowledgeable about this disease and more sophisticated in its detection and treatment of it, the balance may tip in favor of imposing liability on doctors who negligently fail to promptly diagnose the disease. But, until a formula is found that will protect doctors against liability imposed through speculation as well as afford truly aggrieved plaintiffs their just compensation, I cannot favor the wholesale abandonment of the principle of proximate cause. For these reasons, I dissent.

Notes: Causation and Loss of Chance

1. *Life Is Complicated.* Unlike conventional personal injury litigation where the victim first encounters the defendant in a generally healthy condition, malpractice plaintiffs usually start out sick. Moreover, the injury is more often failure to improve rather than a more garden-variety bodily injury. These factors, coupled with the complexities of human biology, result in causation issues demanding as much or more of a lawyer's time and attention as do issues regarding standard of care.

2. *The Traditional Test.* Under the traditional "more likely than not test," plaintiffs sometimes lose on summary judgment or have their verdicts overturned because the expert testimony is expressed in terms of "reasonable possibility" rather than "probability." A few courts have gone further, however, and required expert testimony of a "reasonable medical certainty." See, e.g., Steineke v. Share Health Plan of Nebraska, 518 N.W.2d 904 (Neb. 1994). One court insisted:

> The issue is not merely one of semantics. There is a logical reason for the rule [requiring "reasonable medical certainty"]. For a factfinder to award damages for a particular condition to a plaintiff, he must find as a fact that the condition was legally caused by the defendant's conduct. Here, the only evidence offered was that it was "probably caused," and that is not enough. Perhaps in the world of medicine nothing is absolutely certain. Nevertheless, doctors must make decisions in their own profession every day based on their own expert opinions. Physicians must un-

derstand that it is the intent of our law that if the plaintiff's medical expert cannot form an opinion with sufficient certainty so as to make a medical judgment, there is nothing on the record with which a jury can make a decision with sufficient certainty so as to make a legal judgment.

McMahon v. Young, 276 A.2d 534 (Pa. 1971). Going in the other direction, one court allowed a physician to testify that a radiologic dye caused an injury despite the long statistical odds against this happening, based on the expert's "differential diagnosis" that concluded that other possible causes were not present, so the dye was the most likely cause. Marcum v. Adventist System/West, 193 P.3d 1 (2008). See generally Jeff Lewin, The Genesis and Evolution of Legal Uncertainty About "Reasonable Medical Certainty," 57 Md. L. Rev. 380 (1998).

3. *The Concurrence.* Oddly, Justice Pearson's concurring opinion is actually the plurality opinion since it garnered four votes, in contrast with the two votes for Justice Dore. The dissent had three. Subsequently, the Washington Supreme Court endorsed the plurality's opinion, and extended the rule to cover cases where a patient is disabled but does not die. Mohr v. Grantham, 262 P.3d 490 (Wash. 2011). What is the difference between Justice Pearson's and Justice Dore's conception of the loss-of-chance theory? Does this conceptual debate make any practical difference in the fact patterns that are actionable, the case's procedural posture, or the measure of damages? The concurrence specifies the measure of damages rather clearly (or does it)? How should damages be measured under the main opinion?

Most courts agree that full damages should not be awarded under a loss-of-chance theory, but rather should be discounted by the portion of chance that was lost. What is the correct portion in *Herskovits*, however: 39 percent, 25 percent, or 14 percent? Some courts might reason that he lost all, not just a portion, of his preexisting 39 percent since he in fact died. Even if this is not correct in theory, in practice it may be difficult to know the precise chance of survival that results *after* the mistake (i.e., in this case, the 25 percent). Absent this evidence, do damages become too speculative to award? Note the comment in note 13 of the dissent. For thoughtful analysis generally, see Lars Noah, An Inventory of Mathematical Blunders in Applying the Loss-of-a-Chance Doctrine, 70 Mo. L. Rev. (2005); Robert Rhee, Loss of Chance, Probabilistic Cause, and Damage Calculations, 1 Suffolk U. L. Rev. 39 (2013).

Why should damages be discounted only if the chance of survival was less than 50 percent? Aren't full damages at 51 percent but half damages at 49 percent just as arbitrary as the causation/no-causation line the plurality complains of? Despite this concern, there has been no movement to reduce full damages under ordinary but-for causation.

4. *Wrongful Death Actions.* Another complication, noted by the concurrence, is whether the loss-of-chance theory applies under wrongful death statutes, in contrast with the patient's own survival action. Consider, again, whether it matters which theory of loss of chance one adopts, the majority or concurrence. These statutes vary in their precise wording and the precise theory of damages, so predictably courts reach different results. For a contrasting view, see Kramer v. Lewisville Memorial Hospital, 858 S.W.2d 397 (Tex. 1993).

5. *Causation vs. Breach of Duty.* Observe that loss of chance is not, strictly speaking, a theory of liability. It is a theory of causation or injury. Breach of duty must still be positively demonstrated under the normal "more likely than not" standard.

Thus, testimony that if a procedure or test had been done the patient's chances would have improved does not suffice to establish that the treatment is required by the standard of care.

6. *Fear of Death or Disease.* Following the argument in the *Herskovits* concurrence, can a loss-of-chance theory be applied even if the loss has not yet occurred? Most courts have not yet taken loss of chance this far. In Fabio v. Bellomo, 504 N.W.2d 758 (Minn. 1993), the court held that a delayed diagnosis of cancer was not actionable where chemotherapy successfully brought the cancer into remission, even though the patient might prove that the delay shortened her life expectancy by increasing the odds that cancer would recur. The obstacle in such actions is that the loss complained of—shortened life—has not yet happened, but query whether there has not been some loss of the "chance interest" described in the *Herskovits* concurrence. Following that logic, the same court that decided *Fabio* subsequently allowed a loss-of-chance theory (over a vigorous dissent) in a case where delay in cancer diagnosis reduced the patient's chance of survival from 60 to 40 percent, but the patient remained in remission at the time of suit. Dickhoff v. Green, 836 N.W.2d 321 (Minn. 2013). But such cases remain rare.

Contrast this mistake-without-injury scenario with cases where there is some actual, present medical injury. Then, plaintiffs may recover for the possibility that the harms may get worse in the future. For instance, Fein v. Permanente Medical Group, excerpted at page 410, allowed recovery for the economic costs from a shortened life expectancy and increased risk of disease caused by the misdiagnosis of a heart attack that left the patient in a weakened condition. These elements of damage do not require any unique theory of liability since actual injury is already established and the only issue is its full extent. Also, where there is present injury, it may be possible to recover as an element of damages the emotional distress over worrying about future death or disease.

It may be possible to avoid showing present injury if the only damages being sought are economic, for the costs of monitoring future health problems caused by increased risk of disease. See, e.g., Sutton v. St. Jude Medical S.C., Inc., 419 F.3d 568 (6th Cir. 2005) (recognizing a right to recover for increased risk of future harm when a possibly defective implanted medical device required medical monitoring). These "medical monitoring" theories have been tested in a number of lawsuits, usually involving toxic exposures rather than medical errors. Victor E. Schwartz et al., Medical Monitoring: Should Tort Law Say Yes?, 34 Wake Forest L. Rev. 1057 (1999); Symposium, 88 Va. L. Rev. 1921 (2002); Comment, 32 Wm. Mitchell L. Rev. 1095 (2006).

Recovery is not as readily available, however, where the *only* injury is *emotional.* In such cases, another body of precedent addresses whether tort actions can be maintained for negligent infliction of a purely emotional injury. Traditionally this was not actionable except in specialized cases such as the mishandling of a corpse. In recent decades, however, courts have liberalized this theory of action, but in a highly complex and contradictory fashion that is impossible to summarize here. See Andrew R. Klein, Fear of Disease and the Puzzle of Futures Cases in Tort, 35 U.C. Davis L. Rev. 965 (2002). In general, courts require that the distress be especially severe and that some special relationship or characteristic exist that limits the range of potential claimants. In the medical context, the doctor-patient relationship and the act of medical treatment can easily satisfy the special relationship requirement.

The severe distress element has been found to be satisfied in two notable medical situations: fear of cancer and fear of AIDS. A few cases have ruled that doctors or institutions can be sued when their negligence reasonably causes patients to fear they have a dread disease, even if the evidence fails to establish that negligence worsened their prospects. Hedgepeth v. Whitman Walker Clinic, 22 A.2d 789 (D.C. Cir. 2011) (en banc); Roes v. FHP, Inc., 985 P.2d 661 (Haw. 1999); 50 A.L.R.4th 12 (1986). See S. Lochlann Jain, Fear of Cancer, 44 Loy. L.A. L. Rev. 233 (2010).

Fear of AIDS exposure has produced considerable litigation. The typical scenario involves a patient who discovers after surgery that her doctor carried the AIDS virus (HIV) and the patient then suffers a period of great distress until receiving a series of conclusive negative HIV tests. Courts are divided on whether these claims are actionable (usually stated as informed consent actions), with disputes centering on whether the fear is reasonable in light of the extent of actual exposure during treatment. Another version of AIDS phobia involves a false positive HIV test result such that, for a period of time, the patient falsely thinks he has AIDS. With certain limitations, courts have allowed these versions of negligent infliction of distress actions as well. See Chizmar v. Mackie, 896 P.2d 196 (Alaska 1995) (actionable despite no physical injury); R.J. v. Humana of Florida, 652 So. 2d 360 (Fla. 1995) (actionable if some physical harm can be shown from unnecessary treatment).

7. *Other States.* Most jurisdictions to consider the issue have accepted some form of the loss-of-chance doctrine. For a particularly thorough review of decisions and theories, see Delaney v. Cade, 873 P.2d 175 (Kan. 1994). One loss-of-chance case allowed this theory to go to the jury even though the deceased patient had only a 10 percent chance of survival, at best. Wendland v. Sparks, 574 N.W.2d 327 (Iowa 1998). For an example of a contrary decision, see Williams v. Spring Hill Memorial Hospital, 646 So. 2d 1373 (Ala. 1994). A compromise position is to allow recovery for an increased risk of harm, but only if there is "reasonable medical certainty" that the defendant's negligence caused the increased risk. Holton v. Memorial Hospital, 679 N.E.2d 1202 (Ill. 1997). A full collection of decisions is contained in Annot., 54 A.L.R.4th 10 (1987). For recent commentary, see Todd Aagaard, Note, Identifying and Valuing the Injury in Lost Chance Cases, 96 Mich. L. Rev. 1335 (1998); David A. Fischer, Tort Recovery for Loss of a Chance, 36 Wake Forest L. Rev. 60 (2001); Margaret Berger & Aaron D. Twerski, Uncertainty and Informed Choice, 104 Mich. L. Rev. 258 (2005).

Problem: Loss of a Chance

Group Health, the *Herskovits* defendant, is an HMO. HMOs attempt to reduce costs of medical care by eliminating marginal tests, where the potential "yield" of the tests in accurate findings of disease is low compared to the unit cost of the diagnostic testing. If these cost containment policy decisions render some "missed diagnoses" statistically inevitable, should the health care provider be liable under the "lost chance" doctrine? Consider, for instance, Pap smears, which detect cervical cancer. Suppose the HMO were to calculate that testing every second year rather than every year would save $5 million for its population of 50,000 women patients and, statistically, would increase the number of untreatable cases from ten to eleven per year and decrease the treatable cases from ten to nine per year. That is, assume that, in this population, the HMO can expect 20 cases of cervical cancer a year. With testing every year, ten could be detected in time and successfully treated, but with testing every two years, only nine could be. Can any woman covered by the HMO who then has untreatable cervical cancer sue under a loss-of-chance theory? Assume that, once incurable cervical cancer is found, there is no way after the fact to be sure whether it is one of the cases that could have been successfully detected and treated.

2. Statutes of Limitations

■ RATHJE v. MERCY HOSPITAL
745 N.W.2d 443 (Iowa 2008)

CADY, J.

On March 19, 1999, Kelly and Richard Rathje admitted their sixteen-year-old daughter, Georgia, to an outpatient alcohol abuse treatment center at Mercy Hospital in Cedar Rapids. Part of the treatment plan developed for Georgia called for the [ongoing] administration of a drug called Antabuse [twice a week]. This drug causes the body to produce an alcohol sensitivity that results in a highly unpleasant reaction to the ingestion of beverages containing alcohol. . . . Around a week later [back at home], Georgia began to feel sick and nauseated [even though she was not consuming any alcohol]. She also began to experience cramps and was constipated. . . . [T]he family's physician, Dr. Jerome Janda . . . prescribed medication for Georgia's stomach pain.

[Still], Georgia would not eat or drink. She was suffering from abdominal pain and was vomiting a green substance. She was also fatigued. . . . On April 26, Georgia returned to Dr. Janda's office. She had been bedridden for most of the time since the previous office visit on April 23. She was nauseated, vomiting, and constipated. At this visit, Dr. Janda noticed Georgia's skin color was "mildly yellow or jaundiced and the whites of her eyes were yellowish or icteric." . . . Georgia was admitted to St. Luke's Hospital [the next day, where] Dr. Janda consulted with a surgeon about his concern that Georgia could have gallbladder stones. . . . The gastroenterologist determined the jaundice and elevated liver enzymes experienced by Georgia were secondary to hepatitis. He believed Georgia's condition might be a "drug-induced hepatitis secondary to Antabuse." He recommended Georgia stop taking all prior medications. Georgia['s] . . . condition continued to deteriorate over the passing days. On May 5, she was transferred to the University of Iowa Hospitals and Clinics Pediatric Intensive Care Unit. She later received a liver transplant as a result of end-stage liver disease secondary to Antabuse.

On April 26, 2001, Georgia and her parents filed a petition against numerous health care providers, including Mercy and Dr. Dwight Schroeder, the medical director at the Alcohol Treatment Center at Mercy. The lawsuit claimed Dr. Schroeder and the hospital were negligent in prescribing Antabuse and in their treatment of Georgia for alcohol abuse, and this negligence was the cause of her irreversible liver damage and transplant. . . . The district court granted summary judgment for Mercy Hospital and Dr. Schroeder. It found the facts were undisputed that Georgia's injury had physically manifested itself well prior to April 26, 1999, more than two years before the Rathjes filed suit. Consequently, it concluded the lawsuit filed by the Rathjes was barred by the statute of limitations. . . .

III. Statute of Limitations for Medical Malpractice Actions.

This case requires us once again to visit the medical malpractice statute of limitations and apply it to the facts of a particular case. We have done this on a number of occasions since the special statute was enacted in 1975, . . . [y]et, this law has raised some questions about the fairness of the outcome of a number of these cases. This perception has not gone unnoticed by us, for we have freely acknowledged the statute can "severely restrict[] the rights of unsuspecting patients." Nevertheless, we have declined to change course, recognizing it is the role of the legislature to "address this problem."

It is, of course, the role of the legislature to write [and amend] statutes, . . . [y]et, these general principles of separation of powers and fundamental duties do not totally absolve us from our continued responsibility to interpret applicable statutes in each case and, more importantly, to revisit our past interpretations if we are convinced they have not clearly captured the intent of our legislature. . . .

We begin . . . by returning to the original statute of limitations for personal injury actions enacted by our legislature in the Nineteenth Century, . . . [which] used the "accrual" of the claim as a starting point for the limitation period. In doing so, the legislature determined a two-year period was sufficient for a reasonably diligent person to file a [tort] claim with the judicial system. . . . While the legislature prescribes the period of limitation, courts have generally been called upon to determine when a claim accrues to start the running of the statute of limitations. This task has been formidable, largely due to the manifold sequences in which the elements of a tort action can unfold and become discernible to a plaintiff as a signal to pursue a legal remedy for a wrong.

The first rule to emerge from our early statute-of-limitations cases was that a claim accrued when the injured party had a "right to institute and maintain a suit." This approach meant the statute was triggered when the commission of a tortious act caused a legally recognized injury. It reflected the general rule of law around the country. We also observed early on that the tortious act committed by a defendant was not always immediately followed by the resulting injury. Thus, in response to a number of statute-of-limitations cases in which the injury did not occur until long after the wrongful act, our general rule for the accrual of a claim was more specifically described to commence the running of the statute of limitations for personal injury actions at the time the injury occurred. This approach was logical because the injury would not always occur at the same time as the wrongful act, but no cause of action could accrue until the injury occurred. . . . Of course, there was no change in the rule that the statute of limitations began to run even if the plaintiff had not discovered the injury or its cause. The early case of [Ogg v. Robb, 181 Iowa at 147 (1917)] illustrates this approach.

In *Ogg*, the plaintiff suffered burns on his arms as a result of x-rays taken by the doctor after he broke his wrist. This event occurred in 1901. In 1912, the plaintiff developed cancer in his arm, resulting in amputation. In 1915, he brought a negligence action against the doctor, alleging the x-rays caused the cancer. After finding no evidence of fraudulent concealment of the tort by the physician, the court concluded the cause of action accrued at the time of the burn in 1901, and the action was therefore barred by the statute of limitations. This approach reaffirmed the bright-line rule, but frequently left victims who were unable to discover their injuries within the statute-of-limitations period, through no fault of their own, without any remedy.

[This "injury" rule] was followed well into the Twentieth Century. The individual hardship visited on those plaintiffs who failed to discover the injury before the end of the statute-of-limitations period was largely considered to be the price paid to achieve the greater societal goals of the statute of limitations. *See* W. Page Keeton et. al, *Prosser and Keeton on the Law of Torts* §30, at 165 (5th ed. 1984). . . . Other jurisdictions, however, began to apply [a] "discovery rule" . . . in response to the harshness of the prevailing rule to unsuspecting plaintiffs who were blamelessly ignorant of their legal rights. In the same year we rejected the discovery rule in *Ogg*, Maryland became the first . . . state in the nation to apply the discovery rule to a medical malpractice case. In *Hahn v. Claybrook*, 130 Md. 179 (1917), a plaintiff brought a malpractice action against her doctor, claiming the doctor negligently prescribed argentum oxide for a six-year period between 1904 and 1910. The plaintiff claimed the excessive quantities of the drug caused silver poisoning, a chronic discoloration of the skin. . . . Consequently, the court held the statute of limitations began to run at the time the plaintiff first noticed her skin discoloration in 1908, not when the doctor began prescribing the drug. . . .

[Eventually], Iowa joined the parade of states to apply the discovery rule to the general statute of limitations. . . . We also observed with approval that the discovery rule as defined in other jurisdictions meant the statute of limitations did not begin to run until the date "the wrongful act" was discovered or should have been discovered. Yet, we ultimately held that actions for negligence do not accrue until the plaintiff discovers or should have discovered "the injury to his interest." The distinction between "the wrongful act" and "the injury" as the triggering event went unnoticed.

. . . In *Baines v. Blenderman*, 223 N.W.2d 199 (Iowa 1974), the plaintiff, Baines, awoke from surgery on a herniated disk and was unable to see out of his right eye. The surgery took place on March 30, 1970. A treating physician told Baines the condition was temporary. Baines, however, was eventually examined by another doctor on July 15, 1970. This doctor informed Baines his vision loss could have been caused by the deprivation of blood to his eye during the surgery and his condition was permanent. Baines filed an action against the surgeon more than two years after the surgery but less than two years after he was informed of the probable cause of his condition and that his condition was permanent. . . . Baines claimed he was unaware of his cause of action . . . until he was informed on July 15, 1970, that his injury was permanent and he learned how it likely occurred. The doctor claimed the statute of limitations began to run when Baines awoke from surgery because this was the date he knew of his injury (blindness) and knew it resulted from surgery.

. . . [W]e held a plaintiff must not only discover the injury and its cause, but must also discover the physician was negligent. Yet, we reached this conclusion without acknowledging the rule followed in [some] other jurisdictions that discovery [simply] of the injury and its factual cause triggers the statute of limitations. . . . Conceptually, the national movement responsible for introducing the discovery rule into the statute of limitations merely transformed the commencement of the limitation period from the date the elements of the cause of action *occurred* to the date the elements were [or reasonably should have been] *discovered.* The difficult subissue, however, was how the discovery rule should be applied to the elements of the claim, i.e. whether or not it should be applied to *all* of the elements. Most state courts, as we did in *Baines*, triggered the discovery rule upon knowledge of the cause of action, including at least some knowledge that the conduct of the physician was negligent or wrongful. Other courts interpreted the discovery rule more narrowly to require only knowledge of the injury and its factual cause, without requiring discovery of any negligence or possible wrongdoing. In fact, many courts made the choice between the two theories without recognizing there was even a choice to be made, and others vacillated back and forth with little recognition they were doing so, . . . [or] failed to precisely describe the full meaning of their rule governing the breadth of knowledge required to trigger the statute of limitations, which has made it difficult at times to discern which rule was actually followed. . . . This phenomenon was aptly described by the New Hampshire Supreme Court:

> One might read several discovery cases and conclude that the courts are applying two substantively distinct rules. In most cases the courts frame the rule in terms of the plaintiff's discovery of the causal relationship between his injury and the defendant's conduct. In some cases, . . . a court will state simply that, under the discovery rule, a cause of action accrues when the plaintiff discovers or should have discovered his injury. Still other courts use both statements of the rule within the same case. The reason for these apparent differences is that in most cases in which the court states the rule in terms of the discovery of the injury, the injury is the kind that puts the plaintiff on notice that his rights have been violated. Thus, there is no reason for the court to express the rule in terms of the discovery of the causal connection between the harm and the defendant's conduct. . . .

Raymond v. Eli Lilly & Co., 117 N.H. 164 (1977).

The national trend of using the term "injury" to describe the triggering event under the discovery rule . . . gave rise to the suggestion from time to time that the discovery rule only looked to the injury to commence the running of the period of limitation, without any requirement of knowledge of its cause or the physician's wrongdoing. . . . [But no] court at the time [actually] expressed a principled notion that the cause of action accrued under the discovery rule based on mere knowledge of the injury.

The second circumstance of importance at the time *Baines* was decided was the concomitant drumbeat of tort reform sweeping the country, predicated on claims of a mounting medical malpractice crisis. One common reform centered on the need to tighten the statute of limitations to reduce a physician's exposure to future liability for malpractice lawsuits. In particular, as the popularity of the discovery rule . . . picked up steam in the 1960s, the medical malpractice insurance industry began to increase premiums to protect against the resulting "long tail" of potential liability. In response to this problem, various state and national commissions recommended placing an outside limit on the discovery rule in medical malpractice cases. As a result, statutes of repose, which bar medical malpractice claims after a specific period of time regardless of the date of discovery, were proposed to reduce malpractice premiums by eliminating the insurance companies' inability to predict future claims and losses. . . .

In 1975, one year following *Baines*, the Iowa legislature enacted Iowa Code section 614.1(9)(*a*) as a specific exception to the general statute of limitations for malpractice actions against a specific group of medical personnel and medical facilities.

The statute maintained the two-year limitation period, adopted the discovery rule, and placed a six-year period of repose on the applicability of the discovery rule as proposed by the reform movement. The statute of repose provided an outside limitation for all lawsuits, even though the injury had not been discovered.

Since the enactment of the statute, the dispute in Iowa has not involved the adoption of the discovery rule or the six-year period of repose. Instead, the dispute has mostly centered on the extent to which the legislature intended to restrict the triggering event for the two-year limitation. While the Iowa legislature adopted the discovery rule concept, it defined the rule to begin the two-year statute of limitations when the patient "knew, or through the use of reasonable diligence should have known . . . *the injury or death* for which damages are sought in the action" [emphasis added]. In contrast, the definition of the discovery rule in *Baines* provided for the cause of action to accrue not only upon the discovery of the injury and its cause, but also the discovery of the negligent conduct.

In our first cases to address section 614.1(9) following its enactment, we . . . focused on the triggering event used by the legislature under the statute—injury or death—and found neither the plain language of the statute nor the history of the statute permitted us to inject any modifying language that the injury or death be wrongful. . . . We also formally read inquiry notice into the application of the statute and indicated the duty to investigate begins "once a person is aware that a problem exists." The "injury" claimed to have been suffered in [one case] was posttraumatic stress disorder allegedly caused, in part, by the rude bedside statements of a treating psychiatrist. The plaintiff's "problem" surfaced so as to give rise to a duty to investigate at the time the conduct of the psychiatrist hurt her feelings, even though she did not understand the medical reasons why the conduct adversely affected her. . . . [In another case, we] concluded that the constant pain experienced by [the patient] following [an] operation was sufficient to put her on notice of the injury for which she claimed damages.

We next faced the statute in *Schlote v. Dawson*, 676 N.W.2d 187 (Iowa 2004). In that case, the patient brought a malpractice action against a physician based on a claim that the physician negligently treated a throat condition by unnecessarily removing his voice box. However, the patient did not discover the surgery may have been unnecessary until more than two years later and, consequently, filed the lawsuit more than two years after the voice box was removed. . . . [We] determined the legislature intended the word "injury," to refer to its common dictionary meaning of physical harm, as opposed to its legal meaning involving the violation of a right or protected interest. . . . Consequently, we found the statute of limitations began to run when the plaintiff knew the fact of his injury, even though the plaintiff did not know of the physician's wrongful conduct. . . .

In applying this case law to the undisputed facts of the summary judgment proceedings in this case, it is clear the Rathjes were placed on inquiry notice when Georgia was suffering from physical harm prior to April 26, 1999, more than two years prior to filing the petition. She was experiencing increasing signs of physical harm to her body, which an investigation revealed within two years from the time of the onset of the symptoms was caused by the administration of Antabuse. Under the rule applied in *Schlote*, the Rathjes failed to timely file their petition, even though they had no idea of the cause of the harm prior to the commencement of the statute of limitations. . . .

Understanding the consequences of this state of the law, the Rathjes attempt to sidestep this result by arguing the relevant injury for the purpose of the statute of limitations is not the symptoms Georgia experienced prior to April 26, 1999, but the later damage to her liver. They claim the liver damage is the injury that is the basis for the lawsuit, and this injury was not discovered, or could not have been reasonably discovered, until after April 26, 1999. The approach advocated by the Rathjes gives rise to concerns about allowing plaintiffs to separate injuries [or "split causes of action"] and only leads to additional problems in an already troubled area of the law. . . .

Clearly, the [Iowa] legislature intended to reject discovery of the physician's negligence as a triggering event for the discovery rule, but there was . . . no indication our legislature sought to narrow the triggering event to something other than the two prevailing schools of thought. . . . This dispute over the triggering event was aptly illustrated in *U.S. v. Kubrick*, 444 U.S. 111 (1979). In *Kubrick*, a patient brought a medical malpractice action under the Federal Tort Claims Act to recover for a loss of hearing that allegedly resulted from prior treatment he received for an infection to his leg. The patient knew of his hearing loss more than two years before filing his petition and knew it was most likely caused by the drug used to irrigate the leg infection. However, the patient did not discover the treating physician should have known that using the drug to treat the infection would cause hearing loss until less than two years before filing the petition. . . . [The Court] explained the rationale for only using discovery of the injury and its factual cause to trigger the discovery rule for purposes of the statute of limitations instead of also requiring knowledge of negligent treatment, as follows:

> That [the plaintiff] has been injured in fact may be unknown or unknowable until the injury manifests itself; and the facts about causation may be in the control of the putative defendant, unavailable to the plaintiff or at least very difficult to obtain. The prospect is not so bleak for a plaintiff in possession of the critical facts that he has been hurt and who has inflicted the injury. He is no longer at the mercy of the latter. There are others who can tell him if he has been wronged, and he need only ask. If he does ask and if the defendant has failed to live up to minimum standards of medical proficiency, the odds are that a competent doctor will so inform the plaintiff. . . .

In some instances, the cause of medical malpractice injuries may be evident from facts of the injury alone, but in other cases it may not. Yet, in all cases, a plaintiff must at least know the cause of the injury resulted or may have resulted from medical care in order to be protected from the consequences of the statute of limitations by seeking expert advice from the medical and legal communities. . . . Thus, the discovery of relevant facts about the injury to commence the statute of limitations must include its cause in order to justify the commencement of the limitation period. . . .

We think it is clear our legislature intended the medical malpractice statute of limitations to commence upon actual or imputed knowledge of both the injury and its cause in fact. Moreover, it is equally clear this twin-faceted triggering event must at least be identified by sufficient facts to put a reasonably diligent plaintiff on notice to investigate. This approach rejects the claim made by the Rathjes that "the injury" that will trigger the statute can be separated into different degrees of harm or different categories of harm that separately give rise to different triggering dates. The statute does not work in that manner. We adhere to the rule that a plaintiff does not need to know the full extent of the injury before the statute of limitations begins to run. The statute begins to run only when the injured party's actual or imputed knowledge of the injury and its cause reasonably suggest an investigation is warranted. *See* Annot., 101 A.L.R. Fed. 27 (1991). The symptoms experienced by a patient can be sufficient to alert a reasonable person to the existence of the injury, but those symptoms may not always alert the plaintiff to the cause of the injury. These elements must be considered together to allow the statute of limitations to operate in its intended manner to protect unsuspecting plaintiffs.

The general approach we adopt today is consistent with the framework followed in other jurisdictions. . . . While these jurisdictions reach different conclusions on the question whether discovery of causation involves the relationship between the injury and the factual cause or the relationship between the injury and negligence (or some evidence of wrongdoing), they all recognize causation to be an essential component of the analysis. Although some courts appear to state a rule, from time to time, that the statute of limitations begins to run upon discovery of the injury alone, as we have done in the past, the validity of those holdings are suspect. . . .

In applying the medical malpractice statute of limitations, as we now interpret it, to the undisputed facts in this case, it is clear the Rathjes knew Georgia was suffering from physical harm. However, a reasonable jury could find they did not know the cause of the harm until, at the earliest, April 27, 1999, the date the gastroenterologist made a diagnosis of "drug-induced hepatitis secondary to Antabuse." . . .

Notes: Statutes of Limitations

1. *Discovery Rule.* Why exactly did Georgia's earlier visits to Dr. Janda (the family doctor) not indicate actual notice of a possible injury related to taking Antabuse? There was no suggestion that Georgia was consuming alcohol at home, so perhaps it was because Dr. Janda believed the cause might be an unrelated gallstone problem. But, don't doctors usually consider a variety of possible causes? Perhaps a more definitive diagnosis is required because only then might it be reasonable to consult a lawyer. Is that really what a reform-minded legislature probably intended, in contrast with a rule that a patient simply must have reason to think that something isn't right? Compare Wilson v. El-Daief, 964 A.2d 354 (Pa. 2009) (excruciating pain after surgery is sufficient notice where patient admitted that she thought "something was wrong"). And, do you agree with the Iowa court's resolution that these questions should be resolved by a jury's factual determinations rather than by the court as a matter of law? The debate surely will continue, even in Iowa.

Notice how the Iowa court's resolution differs from the formulation advanced by the Rathjes. Rather than argue that they failed to discover the cause of an earlier injury, they argued that the actual injury in question did not occur until later, as the effects of the drug became serious enough to destroy Georgia's liver. Therefore, no discovery rule is needed to extend the limitations period. Other courts have been more receptive to creative attempts to "split the cause of action." See, e.g., Cleaveland v. Gannon, 655 S.E.2d 662 (2007) (when undiagnosed cancer started to metastasize, this restarted the clock because spreading cancer constitutes a new "injury"). Also consider situations (like those reviewed by the Iowa court) where the slowly growing nature of an injury means that it accrues over a period of time. See generally Annots., 70 A.L.R.3d 7 (1976); 50 A.L.R.4th 250 (1986); Neal F. Eggeson, Snatching Confusion from the Jaws of Clarity: The Puzzling Evolution of the Discovery Rule, 8 Ind. Health L. Rev. 95 (2011).

2. *Statute of Repose; Fraudulent Concealment.* Notice that the six-year outer limit would bar suit regardless of any failure to discover injury. It runs from the "date on which occurred the act or omission . . . [alleged] to have been the cause of the injury." Although Iowa creates an exception for foreign objects left in the body (which remain subject to an indefinite discovery rule), other states apply their statutes of repose even to those situations. See, e.g., Walters v. Cleveland Regional Medical Center, 307 S.W.3d 292 (Tex. 2010) (ten-year statute of repose is absolute, even in foreign object case). Statutes of repose usually do not apply, however, in situations of "fraudulent concealment." When might that arise in medical malpractice cases? What if, during follow-up treatment, a doctor simply fails to tell the patient the full extent of injury or its true cause?

3. *Constitutional Challenges.* Several state supreme courts have struck down shortened statutes of limitations as unconstitutional, usually on grounds of equal protection, because they target only one type of tort action — medical malpractice. Some of these decisions find an absence of rational basis for this selective restriction, while others justify fundamental-interest heightened scrutiny based on an "open courts" constitutional provision that guarantees the right to sue for personal injury. See, e.g., Kenyon v. Hammer, 688 P.2d 961 (Ariz. 1984) (shorter limitations period for medical malpractice than for other tort cases violates equal protection); Martin v. Richey, 711 N.E.2d 1273 (Ind. 1999) (a two-year period does not give a reasonable opportunity to sue for a patient who claimed that her physician negligently failed to diagnose breast cancer that she did not discover until three years later). Contra Deen v. Egleston, 597 F.3d 1223 (11th Cir. 2010) (applying a two-year limitation to a mentally incompetent patient is constitutional under the rational basis test); Jennings v. Burgess, 917 S.W.2d 790 (Tex. 1996) (statute valid if it does not produce unreasonable result in the particular case). For discussion of the Indiana case, see Symposium, Indiana's Medical Malpractice Reform, 31 Ind. L. Rev. 1043 (1998). See generally section H of this chapter.

4. *Continuing Treatment.* Another tolling doctrine adopted by some state courts is the "continuing course of treatment" rule, which suspends the clock as long as a patient continues to receive treatment from the defendant doctor (or institution). Courts differ on whether this rule survives the malpractice reform statutes. Compare Forshey v. Jackson, 671 S.E.2d 748 (W. Va. 2008) (continuing treatment rule is still in effect) with Dickey v. Vermette, 960 A.2d 1178 (Me. 2008) (rule implicitly abolished by statute). See Note, 62 Ala. L. Rev. 439 (2011).

Where the rule applies, there are two versions: The conventional one applies even to a single act of negligence. It holds that the statute does not start to run until treatment for the same condition has been completed. The rationale is well stated in Watkins v. Fromm, 488 N.Y.S.2d 768 (App. Div. 1985):

> It would be absurd to require a wronged patient to interrupt corrective efforts by serving a summons on the physician or hospital superintendent. . . . [T]he trust and confidence that marks the physician-patient relationship puts the patient at

a disadvantage to question the doctor's techniques and gives the patient the right to rely upon the doctor's professional skill without the necessity of interrupting a continuing course of treatment by instituting suit. The exception not only provides the patient with the opportunity to seek corrective treatment from the doctor, but also gives the physician a reasonable chance to identify and correct errors made at an earlier stage of treatment.

The second version applies only where there is continuing negligence, such as a doctor who repeatedly prescribes the wrong medication. Here, the rationale for the doctrine is more formal: it is to operationalize the statutory definition of the injury event that triggers the statute running. Strictly speaking, then, this second version is not a tolling doctrine; it is a rule about when injury actually occurs. Where the mistake is failure to diagnose, does the negligence continue until the doctor makes the correct diagnosis? Fabio v. Bellomo, 504 N.W.2d 758 (Minn. 1993) (no, for failure to diagnose lump as breast cancer, even though patient saw her doctor 60 times over four years and misdiagnosis was repeated several times); Sander v. Geib, Elseton, Frost P.A., 506 N.W.2d 107 (S.D. 1993) (yes, where incorrect reading of a Pap smear was repeated and subsequent visits were for general gynecological exams); Chambers v. Conaway, 883 S.W.2d 156 (Tex. 1993) (yes, under similar facts, even past the point where misdiagnosis was repeated).

Under the first version of the doctrine, what kind of treatment will toll the statute? Treatment for any condition, or only for the condition in question? Consider the various rationales for the doctrine, and what they would suggest. See Konstantikis v. Kassipidis, 602 N.Y.S.2d 67 (App. Div. 1993) (no continuing treatment occurred for surgery that accidentally caused infertility where subsequent treatment of infertility addressed other problems).

What if the subsequent negligence is not by the same exact doctor, but by someone the doctor practices with? In Watkins v. Fromm, supra, the court held that continued treatment by a medical group tolled the statute against two doctors even though the two doctors left the group more than three years before it concluded its treatment of the patient.

3. Affirmative Defenses

All of the standard affirmative defenses available in other tort actions can be used in medical malpractice cases. The following decision reviews a number of these, as well as other strands of doctrine from earlier in the chapter. Focus your attention on the aspects of the case that concern release from liability, contributory negligence or comparative fault, and assumption of risk.

■ SCHNEIDER v. REVICI
817 F.2d 987 (2d Cir. 1987)

MINER, Circuit Judge.

Emanuel Revici, M.D. and the Institute of Applied Biology, Inc. (the "Institute") appeal from a judgment . . . arising from Dr. Revici's treatment of plaintiff Edith

Schneider's breast cancer with unconventional, noninvasive cancer therapy, after she had been advised by numerous doctors to undergo a biopsy and had refused to do so. Edith Schneider and her husband asserted . . . : (1) fraud, premised on Dr. Revici's alleged promise to cure Mrs. Schneider of breast cancer; and (2) medical malpractice. . . . After the district judge refused to charge the jury on the affirmative defense of express assumption of risk, the jury . . . awarded Edith Schneider and her husband $1,000,000.00 and $50,000.00 respectively. Because the jury found that Mrs. Schneider was equally responsible, through her own culpable conduct, for the damages she suffered, the awards were halved to $500,000.00 and $25,000.00, pursuant to New York's comparative negligence statute.

On appeal, Dr. Revici and the Institute challenge the district court's refusal to charge with respect to an alleged covenant not to sue and express assumption of risk as affirmative defenses, either of which would serve as a total bar to recovery. Appellants also contend that numerous evidentiary rulings were erroneous. . . .

I. BACKGROUND

In October 1981, Dr. Cocoziello discovered a lump in appellee Edith Schneider's right breast during her annual gynecological checkup. . . . Mrs. Schneider was examined by Dr. Abessi and Dr. Volke, who both separately advised her to undergo a biopsy and possibly a partial mastectomy, depending upon the analysis of the biopsied tissue. She refused.

In November 1981, Mrs. Schneider consulted with Dr. Emanuel Revici, . . . a physician and researcher who treats cancer patients with "non-toxic," noninvasive methods that have not been adopted by the medical community. Mrs. Schneider had learned of Dr. Revici and his novel cancer therapy from a radio program. After Mrs. Schneider signed a detailed consent form,[1] Dr. Revici diagnosed cancer of the right breast and began treatment with selenium [a nonmetallic element used in electronic devices] and dietary restrictions. . . . After 14 months of treatment, the tumor had increased in size, and cancer had spread to her lymph system and left breast. Mrs. Schneider finally underwent a bilateral mastectomy at Memorial Sloan-Kettering Hospital in January 1983, followed by 16 months of conventional chemotherapy. . . .

---

1. Mrs. Schneider signed a consent form that reads as follows: Dr. Revici testified that Mrs. Schneider had told him that she had not seen other doctors and had not yet had a mammogram. He testified that because of this, he explained the consent form to her in great detail. . . .

> . . . I fully understand that some of the treatment procedures and medications are still investigatory awaiting further research and submission for F.D.A. approval. . . . I am aware that the practice of medicine is not an exact science and I acknowledge that no guaranties have been made to me as to the results of the treatment procedures and medications. . . . I therefore release Dr. Emanuel Revici from all liabilities to me, including all claims and complaints by me or by other members of my family. I am here because I wish to try the Revici methods and preparations for disease control. . . .

A. EVIDENTIARY RULINGS

. . . The trial court excluded records of patients successfully treated by Dr. Revici on the grounds that the issue in medical malpractice is not whether a particular treatment is effective but whether that treatment is a deviation from accepted medical practice in the community. The trial court's statement of the law of medical malpractice is correct. However, evidence as to the effectiveness of Dr. Revici's treatment method was relevant to show that he did not make a false representation with intent to defraud. Any error in excluding the patient records was clearly harmless, however, in light of the jury's finding that Dr. Revici was not liable on the claim of common law fraud. Dr. Revici's sole liability was founded on medical malpractice, which is amply supported by the record, and the evidence of the effectiveness of his treatment was not relevant to that issue. . . .

Defendants' expert witness, Gerhard Schrauzer, had testified about the nutritional value of selenium — testimony directed at negating the fraud claim against Dr. Revici. To rebut that testimony, plaintiffs called Victor Herbert, M.D., who authored two books concerning health and nutrition fads. . . . Appellants object to the trial court's failure to strike his testimony in the following exchange:

Q. Could you tell us whether Dr. Emanuel Revici is recognized by the National Council Against Health Fraud and in what manner? [Objection]
A. We recognize him as a quack, we recognize his treatment as snake oil. We consider him, in quotes, one of the cruelest killers in the United States.

. . . The labels applied to Dr. Revici by Dr. Herbert should not have been countenanced by the district judge. Dr. Herbert was entitled to furnish his opinion on the efficacy of Dr. Revici's treatment and on the consequences likely to befall patients who accepted it in lieu of traditional treatment. These views could have been forcefully expressed without the incendiary labels "quack" and "one of the cruelest killers." However, viewing the testimony in the context of the emphatic opinions that were properly expressed, we do not believe the failure to strike the use of inflammatory characterizations warrants reversal. The labels, though improper, added but slight impact to the force of Dr. Herbert's testimony.

We have considered the other evidentiary arguments of appellants and find them to be without merit.

B. COVENANT NOT TO SUE

New York law recognizes the efficacy of a covenant not to sue in the context of medical treatment:

> Specifically, where a patient voluntarily agrees to undergo an experimental and inherently dangerous surgical procedure, the parties may covenant to exempt the physician from liability for those injuries which are found to be the consequences of the non-negligent, proper performance of the procedure. . . . That is to say, that an experimental procedure which, because of its inherent dangers, may ordinarily be in and of itself a departure from customary and accepted practice (and thus possibly actionable as malpractice) even if performed in a non-negligent manner, may be rendered unactionable by a covenant not to sue.

Colton v. New York Hospital, 414 N.Y.S.2d 866, 876 (Sup. Ct. 1979), and cases there cited. However, New York requires that "a covenant not to sue . . . must be strictly construed against the party asserting it. Moreover, its wording must be 'clear and unequivocal.'" The form signed by Mrs. Schneider lacks the precision required by New York law.

In the first place, the form was not labeled a covenant or agreement not to sue but was instead captioned "CONSENT FOR MEDICAL CARE." . . . Second, the one paragraph of the consent form that bears on legal liability is not "clear and unequivocal." . . . To "release . . . from all liabilities" can plausibly be understood only to relinquish claims currently existing, rather than to promise not to sue in the future on claims that may subsequently arise. . . .

The district judge did not err in declining to submit the covenant not to sue issue to the jury.

C. ASSUMPTION OF RISK

. . . In 1975, New York adopted a comparative negligence statute eliminating contributory negligence as a total bar to recovery. Prior to adoption of the statute a plaintiff was required to be free of any negligence contributing in the slightest degree to his injury, in order to recover. The plaintiff's own negligence was viewed as an intervening cause, between the defendant's negligent act and the plaintiff's injury, which prevented any recovery. Dowd v. New York, Ontario & W. Ry. Co., 63 N.E. 541 (N.Y. 1902). See generally Arbegast v. Board of Educ., 480 N.E.2d 365, 368 (N.Y. 1985).

The doctrine of assumption of risk was a defense to an action for the recovery of damages for personal injuries, prior to the adoption of the comparative negligence statute. . . . While assumption of risk, like contributory negligence, barred recovery, it was predicated on a theory of contract rather than on a theory of culpable conduct: the plaintiff's agreement, either express or implied, to absolve the defendant from responsibility. "Express" assumption of risk resulted from an advance agreement that the defendant need not use reasonable care for the plaintiff's benefit. "Implied" assumption of risk, on the other hand, was founded on plaintiff's unreasonable and voluntary consent to the risk of harm from defendant's conduct with full understanding of the possible harm. Restatement (Second) of Torts §§496B, 496E.

In 1975, New York's Civil Practice Law and Rules were amended by the addition of a pure comparative negligence statute. . . . In accord with the plain language of the statute . . . commentators assumed that under the new comparative negligence statute assumption of risk was no longer a total bar to recovery, but simply diminished the amount of damages recoverable. . . . [However,] [i]n 1985, the Court of Appeals of New York . . . held that express assumption of risk would provide a complete defense, while implied assumption of risk was subsumed by [the comparative negligence statute]: "[The statute] requires diminishment of damages in the case of an implied assumption of risk but, except as public policy proscribes an agreement limiting liability, does not foreclose a complete defense that by express consent of the injured party no duty exists and, therefore, no recovery may be had." Arbegast, 480 N.E.2d at 371. . . .

In the case before us, appellees contend that it is against public policy for one expressly to assume the risk of medical malpractice and thereby dissolve the physician's duty to treat a patient according to medical community standards. . . . [W]e see no reason why a patient should not be allowed to make an informed decision to go outside currently approved medical methods in search of an unconventional treatment. While a patient should be encouraged to exercise care for his own safety, we believe that an informed decision to avoid surgery and conventional chemotherapy is within the patient's right "to determine what shall be done with his own body," Schloendorff v. Society of the New York Hospital, 105 N.E. 92 (N.Y. 1914) (Cardozo, J.). . . .

While we do not determine, in the case before us, whether Mrs. Schneider expressly assumed the risk of Dr. Revici's treatment, we hold that there existed sufficient evidence—in the language of the Consent for Medical Care form that she signed, and in testimony relating to specific consent informed by her awareness of the risk of refusing conventional treatment to undergo the Revici method—to allow the jury to consider express assumption of risk as an affirmative defense that would totally bar recovery. It was therefore error for the district court to deny the defendants' request for a jury charge on the issue, and we reverse and remand for that reason.

Notes: Affirmative Defenses

1. Schneider v. Revici introduces a complex thicket of doctrines that overlap to a large extent but that are also conceptually distinct: (1) the standard of care for experimental care or "alternative" practitioners; (2) informed consent (the discussion of which is omitted in this excerpt); (3) release from liability, or waiver of the right to sue; (4) contributory negligence or comparative fault; and (5) assumption of risk. (1) and (2) are explored elsewhere because they go to basic elements in the cause of action. See section B.2 and Chapter 3.C. In addition, the fraud action mentioned in the decision is explored at page 377, and the evidentiary point is addressed in section C.

The focus here is on the affirmative defenses stated in (3), (4), and (5). Observe the extent of both overlap and independence among these. Even though the release was not effective, the court still found the consent form could establish assumption of risk. And even though there was no instruction on assumption of risk, the jury found 50 percent comparative fault. For a contrasting decision from over a century ago, see Nelson v. Harrington, 40 N.W. 228 (Wis. 1888) (patient not contributorily negligent in seeking care from "clairvoyant physician" even though he knew in advance what the treatment was; "the proposition that one holding himself out as a medical practitioner, . . . because he resorts to some peculiar method . . . [is] exonerated from all liability for unskillfulness on his part, no matter how serious the consequences may be, cannot be entertained" and is contrary to public policy).

2. *Waiver of Liability.* Generally speaking, releases of liability or waivers of the right to sue for medical negligence, signed at the time of treatment, are unenforceable as contrary to public policy, even if they are correctly worded. The seminal decision is Tunkl v. Regents, discussed in the next case and excerpted at page 107. See Annot., 6 A.L.R.3d 704 (1966 & Supp.). *Revici* is consistent with this law because it holds only that a release of liability prior to a claim arising is potentially valid only to the extent that it specifies *nonnegligent* performance of nonstandard care. Releases

are also commonly obtained and enforced when patients leave the hospital against medical advice ("AMA").

Releases from liability or covenants not to sue for negligent care are also valid if signed *after* the harm occurs and the claim arises. This is how parties settle a dispute. A critical aspect of legal practice is to correctly distinguish between the two forms—release vs. covenant—because of the effect on the liability of joint tortfeasors. Many malpractice actions are brought against more than one defendant—several doctors or a hospital as well as the doctors. Plaintiffs often agree to settle with one or more of the less culpable or less well insured parties while keeping the others on the hook. At common law, a release from liability of one joint tortfeasor had the automatic effect of releasing all the others, even if the release stated to the contrary, because it was seen as extinguishing a single, indivisible cause of action; covenants not to sue do not have this effect, however. This rule has been reversed in most states, but releases are still dangerous in some states. See, e.g., Gilbert v. Sycamore Municipal Hospital, 622 N.E.2d 788 (Ill. 1993) (settlement with doctor extinguishes vicarious liability of hospital even though settling parties expressly reserved the right to sue hospital); Fiakpoey v. Middlesworth, 118 A.D.3d 743 (NY App. Div. 2014) (release of hospital also releases independent physician who is agent of hospital).

3. *Contributory Fault and Mitigation of Damages.* *Revici* addresses comparative fault and contributory negligence only in passing, but this was obviously a large part of the case since it resulted in halving the jury verdict. Presumably, this finding was based on Ms. Schneider's foolishness in believing Dr. Revici's claims and ignoring advice to seek conventional treatment at the same time.[1] What other actions might constitute contributory fault, either during, before, or following treatment? Notice in note 1 that Ms. Schneider misled Dr. Revici about her medical history. See also Fall v. White, 449 N.E.2d 628 (Ind. Ct. App. 1983) (patient contributed to his own death by heart attack when he failed to reveal to the doctor that he was experiencing chest pains); Annot., 33 A.L.R.4th 790 (1984). Consider also that, where a doctor is given an inaccurate or incomplete medical history, this may also negate any primary finding of negligence on the doctor's part.

In other cases, courts have found contributory fault where the patient blatantly ignored doctors' orders or failed to return for follow-up visits, as instructed. See Dennis v. Jones, 928 A.2d 672 (D.C. 2007) (patient may have contributed to her post-surgical complications by continuing to smoke contrary to doctor's instructions); Shinholster v. Annapolis Hospital, 685 N.W.2d 275 (Mich. 2004) (patient is 20 percent at fault for failure to diagnose mini-strokes leading to massive stroke because she failed to take her prescribed blood pressure medication); Harlow v. Chin, 545 N.E.2d 602 (Mass. 1989) (13 percent fault found where patient failed to contact doctor when pain got much worse. But see Tobia v. Cooper Hospital

---

1. Subsequent studies have shown, however, that selenium in fact inhibits several types of cancer. In one study, it cut cancer deaths in half. The benefit was so dramatic, the researchers felt compelled to halt the placebo wing of the study. Graham Colditz, Selenium and Cancer Prevention: Promising Results Indicate Further Trials Required, 276 JAMA 1984 (1996). On the other hand, Dr. Revici also treated cancer patients with vinegar, baking soda, soft boiled eggs, and coffee. See Revici v. Comm'r of Educ., 546 N.Y.S.2d 240 (1989) (upholding revocation of Dr. Revici's medical license).

University Medical Center, 643 A.2d 1 (N.J. 1994) (doctors' duty of care includes protecting patients from harming themselves, in a case where an 85-year-old fell off a stretcher trying to go to the bathroom unattended); Durphy v. Kaiser Foundation Health Plan, 698 A.2d 459 (D.C. 1997) (patient's failure to follow instructions, resulting in foot amputation, does not bar recovery for prior act of negligence by doctor). See generally Michele Goodwin & L. Richardson, Patient Negligence, 72 Law & Contemp. Probs. 223 (Fall 2009); Annot., 84 A.L.R.5th 619 (2000). Patient negligence that occurs *after* the doctor's can also go to mitigation of damages rather than mitigation of fault. See George Washington University v. Waas, 648 A.2d 178 (D.C. 1994) (patient's failure to follow instructions and cooperate with follow-up treatment mitigates damages from failure to diagnose cancer but does not bar recovery).

Can patients be found at fault for their behavior *leading up to* their medical condition? In general, no. Doctors take their patients as they find them. See Mercer v. Vanderbilt University, Inc., 134 S.W.3d 121 (Tenn. 2004) (no contributory fault by patient who suffered brain damage from a negligent medical mistake during treatment for a car accident caused by the patient's own alcohol consumption); Jensen v. Archbishop Bergan Mercy Hospital, 459 N.W.2d 178 (Neb. 1990) (no contributory negligence even though patient's failure to lose weight may have caused the pulmonary embolism that was negligently treated). But see Cobo v. Raba, 495 S.E.2d 362 (N.C. 1998) (a patient who was also a doctor could be found contributorily negligent for engaging in repeated unprotected homosexual intercourse with prostitutes and for delays in seeking treatment once he became HIV-infected). Similarly, in the context of mitigation of damages, patients do not have to submit to risky surgery or medication to correct a negligent injury, even if medically advised. See, e.g., Robins v. Katz, 391 N.W.2d 495 (Mich. Ct. App. 1986) (patient could refuse second foot surgery to correct mistakes made the first time). But see Corlett v. Caserta, 562 N.E.2d 257 (Ill. App. Ct. 1990) (Jehovah's Witness who refused blood transfusion to correct gastric bleeding following colon surgery must "bear a proportionate share of tort liability").

4. *Good Samaritans.* Another affirmative defense of unique importance to medical malpractice is the "Good Samaritan" immunity statutes enacted in all states. These laws are intended to encourage doctors to come to the aid of injured strangers ("Is there a doctor in the house?") by reducing the standard of care to gross negligence or recklessness when they respond to an emergency or render first aid. Usually, one thinks of these accident scenes occurring on the highway or in public places, but because the wording of these statutes varies, it is sometimes possible to argue they apply in hospital settings or in doctors' offices. See Annot., 68 A.L.R.4th 294 (1989); Paul A. Hattis, Overcoming Barriers to Physician Volunteerism, 2004 U. Ill. L. Rev. 167. The case for this interpretation is stronger if the physician who claims immunity is a true volunteer, that is, not the patient's usual doctor and not assigned to emergency care. In a few states, these statutes cover all types of treatment, not just emergencies, but they apply to ordinary medical care only when physicians treat indigent patients for free. See, e.g., Rodas v. Seidlin, 56 F.3d 610 (7th Cir. 2011) (salaried physicians at low-income clinic not entitled to immunity).

These statutes first arose during the 1960s after a flurry of press reports discussing the legal vulnerability of doctors who aid accident or heart attack victims on the scene. In fact, there were no recorded malpractice suits against doctors in such situations. William J. Curran, The Not-So-Good Samaritan Laws, 270 New Eng. J. Med. 1003 (1964). What about physicians who respond to a public health emergency, such as bioterrorism or a flu pandemic? Some scholars are concerned that existing laws and precedents do not protect sufficiently against liability claims in those potential doomsday scenarios. Sharona Hoffman, Responders' Responsibility: Liability and Immunity in Public Health Emergencies, 96 Geo. L. J. 1913 (2008); Eleanor Kinney et al., Altered Standards of Care for Health Care Providers in the Pandemic Influenza, 6 Ind. Health L. Rev. 1 (2009); Victoria Sutton, Is There a Doctor (and a Lawyer) in the House? Why Our Good Samaritans Laws Are Doing More Harm Than Good for a National Public Health Security Strategy: A Fifty-State Survey, 6 J. Health & Biomed. L. 261 (2010); Comment, 14 J. Health Care L. & Pol'y 209 (2011).

5. *Hospital Immunity*. Other sources of potential immunity have more relevance for hospitals than for physicians and so are discussed later in this chapter. These include charitable immunity for nonprofit facilities, and governmental immunity for state and municipal facilities. In most states, these immunities have disappeared or have been greatly scaled back.

4. Arbitration and Waiver of Liability

The next case concerns arbitration. It is important in its own right, since various forms of alternative dispute resolution are increasingly being used for medical care. But it has broader importance as well. It explains the legal framework in which contractual agreements might be used to alter the core standard of care or to waive malpractice liability entirely. The key question is how far this precedent might extend in those directions.

■ MADDEN v. KAISER FOUNDATION HOSPITAL
552 P.2d 1178 (Cal. 1976)

TOBRINER, Justice.
Defendants appeal from an order denying enforcement of an arbitration provision in a medical services contract entered into between the Board of Administration of the State Employees Retirement System (hereafter board) and defendant Kaiser Foundation Health Plan. Plaintiff, a state employee who enrolled under the Kaiser plan, contends that she is not bound by the provision for arbitration. The instant appeal presents the issue whether an agent or representative, contracting for medical services on behalf of a group of employees, has implied authority to agree to arbitration of malpractice claims of enrolled employees arising under the contract. . . .

When plaintiff first enrolled under the Kaiser plan in 1965, it did not contain an arbitration provision. On April 1, 1971, however, the Kaiser Foundation Health Plan, anticipating the inclusion of an arbitration provision, mailed to all subscribers a brochure which, in describing the terms and benefits of the plan, stated that claims involving professional liability and personal injury must be submitted to arbitration. Shortly thereafter, on May 28, 1971, the Kaiser Foundation Health Plan and the board amended their contract in several respects and included a provision for binding arbitration of "any claim arising from the violation of a legal duty incident to this Agreement."[2]

On August 1, 1971, plaintiff underwent a hysterectomy at the Kaiser Hospital in Los Angeles. During the surgery, her bladder was perforated; blood transfusions were required; plaintiff thereafter contracted serum hepatitis.

Plaintiff filed a malpractice complaint against Kaiser and the blood banks. Kaiser moved to stay the action and compel arbitration. Opposing this motion, plaintiff filed a declaration stating that because of absence from work by reason of illness she had not received the April 1971 brochure, that she was not aware of the execution of the arbitration agreement in May of 1971, and thus had no knowledge that the Kaiser plan, at the time of her operation, required arbitration of malpractice claims. By order of April 22, 1974, the trial court denied the motion to stay the action and compel arbitration. Kaiser appeals from that order.

2. *The board, as agent for the employees, had implied authority to provide for arbitration of malpractice claims.*

Government Code §§22774, 22790 and 22793 authorize the board to negotiate contracts for group medical plans for state employees. In negotiating such agreements and amendments the board acts as the agent or representative of the employees. . . .

We shall explain that although the courts in the past regarded arbitration as an unusual and suspect procedure, they now recognize it as an accepted method of settlement of disputes. Since Civil Code §2319 grants an agent the authority to do whatever is "proper and usual" to carry out his agency, the board enjoyed an implied authority to agree to arbitration of malpractice claims of enrolled employees. . . .

In Crofoot v. Blair Holding Corp., 260 P.2d 156, 170 (Cal. App. 1953), Justice Peters summarized the evolution of legal attitudes toward arbitration.

> Arbitration has had a long and troubled history. The early common law courts did not favor arbitration, and greatly limited the powers of arbitrators. But in recent times a great change in attitude and policy has taken place. Arbitrations are now usually covered by statutory law, as they are in California. Such statutes evidence a strong public policy in favor of arbitrations, which policy has frequently been approved and enforced by the courts.

Subsequent decisions confirm the self-evident fact that arbitration has become an accepted and favored method of resolving disputes, praised by the courts as an expeditious and economical method of relieving overburdened civil calendars.

The transformation of legislative and judicial attitudes toward arbitration has encouraged a dramatic development in the use of this procedure. A 1952 study estimated that "aside from personal injury cases and cases in which the government is a party, more than 70 percent of the total civil litigation is decided

---

2. The arbitration agreement stated that it was retroactive to April 1, 1971, the date of the Kaiser brochure advising subscribers of the arbitration clause. Since plaintiff's claim arose after May 28, 1971, we need not consider whether the agreement can be retroactively effective to require arbitration of claims arising before it was finally approved.

through arbitration rather than by the courts" (Mentschikoff, The Significance of Arbitration—A Preliminary Inquiry (1952) 17 Law & Contemp. Prob. 698). In the following decades arbitration further expanded its role to encompass in certain circumstances disputes requiring evaluation of personal injury claims: California and many other states now require arbitration of uninsured motorist claims, and proposals for no-fault automobile insurance frequently provide for arbitration. . . .

The matter becomes even clearer if we narrow our focus to arbitration of disputes arising under group contracts. In collective bargaining agreements, which, like the present contract, are negotiated by elected representatives on behalf of a group of employees, arbitration has become a customary means of resolving disputes. . . .

Finally, we observe the growing interest in and use of arbitration to cope with the increasing volume of medical malpractice claims. Henderson, Contractual Problems in the Enforcement of Agreements to Arbitrate Medical Malpractice, 58 Va. L. Rev. 947, 956 (1972). . . .

We therefore conclude that an agent or other fiduciary who contracts for medical treatment on behalf of his beneficiary retains the authority to enter into an agreement providing for arbitration of claims for medical malpractice.[11]

3. *The principles that govern contracts of adhesion do not bar enforcement of the arbitration amendment.*

. . . Contending that the Kaiser contract is one of adhesion, plaintiff argues that the courts should refuse to enforce its arbitration clause on the ground that the clause is inconspicuous, unexpected, and disrupts the members' reasonable expectation that a malpractice claim will be adjudicated by trial by jury. We explain our reason for concluding that the principles governing adhesion contracts do not cover the present case. . . .

In the characteristic adhesion contract case, the stronger party drafts the contract, and the weaker has no opportunity, either personally or through an agent, to negotiate concerning its terms. The Kaiser plan, on the other hand, represents the product of negotiation between two parties, Kaiser and the board, possessing parity of bargaining strength. Although plaintiff did not engage in the personal negotiation of the contract's terms, she and other public employees benefitted from representation by a board, composed in part of persons elected by the affected

---

11. Amicus suggests that we should fashion a new rule to the effect that no arbitration provision in a group insurance policy will bind the beneficiary absent proof of the beneficiary's actual knowledge of that provision. In the present case, Kaiser provided plaintiff with a brochure describing the Kaiser plan, including the arbitration provision. Apart from plaintiff's own testimony, neither the board nor Kaiser have any way of proving whether or not plaintiff read all or part of that brochure. The orderly administration of the plan would be impossible if it were to depend on such proof. Amicus acknowledges as much; it does not maintain that no provision of the Kaiser plan can be enforced against a beneficiary who enrolls without actual knowledge of that provision; it would, instead provide only that arbitration provisions cannot be enforced without actual knowledge. But Amicus' proposal for a special rule which discriminates against enforcement of arbitration clauses would be viable only if arbitration were an extraordinary procedure, and one especially disadvantageous for the beneficiary—propositions which we have rejected in . . . cases cited in this opinion.

employees, which exerted its bargaining strength to secure medical protection for employees on more favorable terms than any employee could individually obtain.

In many cases of adhesion contracts, the weaker party lacks not only the opportunity to bargain but also any realistic opportunity to look elsewhere for a more favorable contract; he must either adhere to the standardized agreement or forego the needed service. Plaintiff, on the other hand, enjoyed the opportunity to select from among several medical plans negotiated and offered by the board, some of which did not include arbitration provisions, or to contract individually for medical care. . . .

To support her contract of adhesion argument, plaintiff points to Tunkl v. Regents of University of California, 383 P.2d 441 (Cal. 1963); that decision, however, serves instead to illuminate by contrast the nonoppressive character of the contract in the present case. In *Tunkl*, defendant hospital presented to all incoming patients a document entitled "Conditions of Admission," which provided that the patient release the hospital from liability for negligent or wrongful acts. We observed that the "would-be patient is in no position to reject the proffered agreement, to bargain with the hospital, or in lieu of agreement to find another hospital." Thus, the patient had no realistic choice but to assent to a standardized agreement under which he waived his right to recover for negligently inflicted injuries.

As we have explained, plaintiff, in contrast to *Tunkl*, benefitted from the board's assertion of equal power on her behalf, enjoyed the opportunity to choose from among alternative medical plans, and waived no substantive right. We conclude that *Tunkl* is not controlling in the instant setting; the principles of adhesion contracts, as elucidated and applied in *Tunkl* and the other cases we have cited, do not bar enforcement of terms of a negotiated contract which neither limit the liability of the stronger party nor bear oppressively upon the weaker. Accordingly, such principles do not bar enforcement of the arbitration amendment against plaintiff Madden.

4. Enforcement of the arbitration provision does not violate constitutional or statutory protections of the right to trial by jury. . . .

Plaintiff further contends that the arbitration provision in the Kaiser contract fails because it does not expressly waive the parties' constitutional right to jury trail. But to predicate the legality of a consensual arbitration agreement upon the parties' express waiver of jury trial would be as artificial as it would be disastrous.

When parties agree to submit their disputes to arbitration they select a forum that is alternative to, and independent of, the judicial—a forum in which, as they well know, disputes are not resolved by juries. Hence there are literally thousands of commercial and labor contracts that provide for arbitration but do not contain express waivers of jury trial. Courts have regularly enforced such agreements; in [one case], for example, we unanimously affirmed an order compelling an employer to submit a contract dispute to arbitration, although the arbitration provision did not expressly waive the employer's right to trial by jury. Relying on this consistent pattern of judicial decision, contracting parties, such as Kaiser and the board in the case at bar, continue to draft arbitration provisions without express mention of any right to jury trial. Before today no one has so much as imagined that such agreements are consequently invalid; to destroy their viability upon an extreme hypothesis that they fail expressly to negative jury trials would be to frustrate the parties' interests and destroy the sanctity of their mutual promises. . . .

We conclude that the trial court erred in denying Kaiser's motion to compel arbitration and in refusing to stay the action against Kaiser. . . .

MOSK, Justice (dissenting).

I dissent. . . .

It must be emphasized that the plaintiff enrolled in the Kaiser plan in 1965, at a time when the master contract between Kaiser and the Board of Administrators of the State Employees Retirement System contained no arbitration clause and apparently none was contemplated. . . . Six years after plaintiff's original enrollment in the plan, without her knowledge or consent, the board purporting to act on her behalf agreed with Kaiser to amend the master contract to provide that plaintiff's claims must be submitted to arbitration. . . . Had the original master contract executed by the board and Kaiser provided for arbitration, plaintiff might have been bound thereby when she signed a written enrollment in the program. But six years after enrollment by plaintiff an amendment providing for abdication of fundamental rights can be effective only if plaintiff consents thereto in writing. This is manifest when the two rights purportedly abandoned by the board on behalf of plaintiff are as fundamental as recourse to the courts of the state and trial by jury. . . .

Notes: Alternative Dispute Resolution; Contractually Set Standards of Care

1. *Pros and Cons of Arbitration.* Professor Thomas Metzloff explains:

> Arbitration in and of itself does not radically change how a dispute is litigated apart from the identity of the decisionmaker. Discovery may be somewhat limited and the hearing itself is hopefully shorter. But beyond such tinkering, the use of an arbitration format does not usually alter many of the procedural elements that malpractice defenders find objectionable. . . . Significantly, arbitration does not change the basic tort theory of liability.

Thomas B. Metzloff, The Unrealized Potential of Malpractice Arbitration, 31 Wake Forest L. Rev. 203, 215 (1996). Where arbitration differs is in the formality of the proceedings and the length of the hearing. Based on the experience at Kaiser, when cases are arbitrated they are resolved in about half the time and the hearings often last only one or two days. However, arbitration can also be more expensive because the parties have to split the costs of the arbitrators, in contrast with the judicial system, which is essentially free. Arbitration also tends to produce different results than litigation. Plaintiffs win about 50 percent more often than in jury trials; however, very large recoveries are rare. Conventional wisdom is that arbitration more often produces "compromise verdicts," although Metzloff's experience is to the contrary.

Professor Metzloff explains that, "in the simplistic nature of the tort reform debates, patient advocates are against [arbitration] because doctors are for it; arbitration has become a prisoner of war." Accordingly, arbitration of medical malpractice disputes is rare, except in the HMO context. Even then, it is still the exception. To understand why, consider whether, on balance, arbitration really is pro-plaintiff or pro-defendant? Does it depend on the facts of the case? Consider small claims vs. very large ones; cases where liability is hotly disputed; the parties' feelings about justice and vindication; and the interests of the lawyers on each side. If litigation truly were made speedier, less costly, and more predictable, would you expect an increase or decrease in the number of claims submitted? See generally Marc Ginsberg, The Execution of an Arbitration Provision as a Condition Precedent to Medical Treatment: Legally Enforceable? Medically Ethical?, 42 Mitchell Hamline L. Rev. 273 (2016); Kenneth DeVille, The Jury Is Out: Pre-Dispute Binding Arbitration Agreements for Medical Malpractice Claims, 28 J. Leg. Med. 333 (2007); Kathy L. Cerminara, Contextualizing ADR in Managed Care: A Proposal Aimed at Easing Tensions and Resolving Conflict, 33 Loy. U. Chi. L. J. 547 (2002); Symposium, 74 Law & Contemp. Probs. 1 (Summer 2011); Symposium: Medical Malpractice Dispute Resolution, 28 Cap. U. L. Rev. 249 (2000); Annot., 24 A.L.R.5th 1 (1994).

2. *Mediation.* In contrast with the *Madden* setting, agreements to arbitrate made after a claim arises are not controversial; this is a standard form of alternative dispute resolution. Also of growing significance are voluntary agreements to mediate malpractice disputes. In mediation, the parties go through a structured process designed to sharpen their understanding of the other side's perspective and to search for common ground. The process is entirely nonbinding, but some jurisdictions mandate that parties pursue mediation before litigating. Lydia Nussbaum, Trial and Error: Legislating ADR for Medical Malpractice Reform, 76 Md. L. Rev. 247 (2017). In contrast with voluntary binding arbitration and voluntary nonbinding mediation are mandatory nonbinding screening panels. As discussed in section H, many states require malpractice parties to submit their disputes to panels composed of doctors and lawyers that render advisory opinions on the merits, with the hope of encouraging settlement or early dismissal. This has proven to be a failure. Can you see why?

3. *Varying the* Madden *Facts.* Is it crucial to the holding in *Madden* that the plaintiff had several insurance options available, not all of which required arbitration? What about an employee who is offered only a single HMO insurance policy at work? If an employer chooses a single plan for workers that requires arbitration, is the employer doing this as the workers' agent? See Siopes v. Kaiser Foundation Health Plan, 312 P.3d 869 (Haw. 2013) (no, unless workers are specifically informed of the provision). Many state statutes encouraging malpractice arbitration allow these agreements to be revoked retroactively within one to three months of signing. Does this provide the element of choice required to avoid adhesion contract characterization? What if revocation is allowed only prospectively, that is, for disputes that have not yet arisen or treatment not yet rendered?

More controversial than the *Madden* setting are agreements to arbitrate signed at the point of treatment, that is, upon admission to the hospital or when arriving at the doctor's office. Typically, the patient is given no obvious choice (although in fact the provider may provide treatment anyway if the patient refuses to sign). In different versions of this context, courts have been more inclined to follow *Tunkl* and find unconscionability. See, e.g., Sosa v. Paulos, 924 P.2d 357 (Utah 1996) (unconscionable where given to patient when she was already in surgical gown, even though she had right to revoke within 14 days). The Supreme Court, however, has ruled that states go too far in declaring point-of-treatment arbitration illegal as a matter of law, since doing so contravenes the Federal Arbitration Act, which declares that arbitration agreements connected with commerce are enforceable. Marmet Health Care Center, Inc. v. Brown, 132 S. Ct. 1201 (2012). Similarly, the

Trump administration has proposed that nursing homes participating in Medicare be allowed to require binding arbitration, reserving a ban on arbitration that the government had imposed during the last months of the Obama administration.

These federal rules, however, do not preclude a state court finding that a particular agreement's terms are unconscionable. For instance, King v. Bryant, 795 S.E.2d 340 (N.C. 2017) refused to enforce an arbitration agreement with a surgeon because it was too obscure for the patient to notice or understand, and Gessa v. Manor Care of Florida, Inc., 86 So. 3d 484 (Fla. 2011) invalidated an arbitration agreement by a nursing home patient because it precluded any award of punitive damages. But see Hayes v. Oakridge Home, 908 N.E.2d 408 (Ohio 2009) (over a vigorous dissent, enforcing an arbitration agreement and waiver of punitive damages signed by a 95-year-old nursing home resident).

In one decision, the court struck down an arbitration agreement as applied, ruling that Kaiser fraudulently ran its arbitration process to strategically gain an unfair advantage on the panel and to create needless delay so that the plaintiff would die before the decision, resulting in lower damages. Engalla v. The Permanente Medical Group, 938 P.2d 903 (Cal. 1997). See also Sosa v. Paulos, supra (agreement unconscionable where losing claimant is required to pay all the arbitration costs, but requiring all the arbitrators to be physicians is not per se unconscionable).

4. *Altering Tort Law by Contract.* The *Tunkl* decision discussed in *Madden* is excerpted at page 107. It states the general law that providers cannot enforce waivers of malpractice liability. In contrast with total waivers, however, are agreements to alter the prevailing legal standards. If parties can agree to arbitrate, can they also agree to change the substantive rules that determine liability during arbitration, assuming that other elements of unconscionability are avoided (adequate notice and some element of choice)? Clark Havighurst is the leading advocate of contractually determined standards of care. He proposes the following language to be included in HMO-type health insurance contracts:

> Because the costs of unlimited legal rights (and their enforcement) must ultimately be borne by you and other plan subscribers, you agree that, in any legal action brought by you against a Plan Provider for injury suffered in the course of your treatment, you will be entitled to recover damages only if such injury was caused by gross negligence on the part of the Provider. Gross negligence is distinguishable from ordinary negligence and is characterized by willful neglect of your personal well-being or reckless disregard for the consequences of some act or omission.

Health Care Choices: Private Contracts as Instruments of Health Reform 296 (1995).

Would the assumption of risk doctrine applied in Schneider v. Revici, page 395, validate these types of agreement? What else might be determined by contract? Consider: the statute of limitations; the allowable elements of recoverable damages; who is entitled to testify as an expert; and anything else from the long list of legal reforms discussed in section H. Even if these are not contrary to public policy, is it plausible to assume that ordinary consumers will focus their attention on this many discrete elements of their insurance policies or hospital admission forms? Even if these are noticed by consumers, can it be said they have meaningful choice if they lack the opportunity to bargain over each component of the package? In theory, the private market could offer a differentially priced checklist of legal options, but in practice this is never done. Why not? See generally Mark A. Hall, Making Medical Spending Decisions ch. 7 (1997).

5. *Consumer-Directed Health Care.* As discussed at page 1104, health insurers and employers are turning more to types of coverage that place more responsibility on patients to pay for treatment themselves out of pocket. If a patient refuses treatment his physician recommends due to expense, what defenses might protect the physician if he or she continues to treat the patient with less effective care (assuming that the less expensive treatment does not work or causes harm)? For in-depth discussion, see Mark Hall & Carl Schneider, When Patients Say No (To Save Money): An Essay on the Tectonics of Health Law, 41 Conn. L. Rev. 743 (2009); Haavi Morreim, High-Deductible Health Plans: New Twists on Old Challenges from Tort and Contract, 59 Vand. L. Rev. 1207 (2006); Mark A. Hall, Paying for What You Get and Getting What You Pay For, 69 Law & Contemp. Prob. 159 (Autumn 2006).

6. *Further Reading.* On **different forms of ADR for medical malpractice** generally (notes 1 and 2), see Nussbaum supra; Kathy L. Cerminara, Contextualizing ADR in Managed Care: A Proposal Aimed at Easing Tensions and Resolving Conflict, 33 Loy. U. Chi. L. J. 547 (2002); Symposium, 74 Law & Contemp. Probs. 1 (Summer 2011); Symposium: Medical Malpractice Dispute Resolution, 28 Cap. U. L. Rev. 249 (2000).

On the **enforceability of arbitration** (note 3), Marc Ginsberg, The Execution of an Arbitration Provision as a Condition Precedent to Medical Treatment: Legally Enforceable? Medically Ethical?, 42 Mitchell Hamline L. Rev. 273 (2016); Kenneth DeVille, The Jury Is Out: Pre-Dispute Binding Arbitration Agreements for Medical Malpractice Claims, 28 J. Leg. Med. 333 (2007); Annot., 24 A.L.R.5th 1 (1994).

On **contractual specification** of the standard of care (note 4), see Richard A. Epstein, Medical Malpractice: The Case for Contract, 1976 Am. B. Found. Res. J. 87 (1976). Professor Maxwell Mehlman is a leading opponent of these agreements, arguing that principles of fiduciary contracting prohibit them. M. Mehlman, Fiduciary Contracting: Limitations on Bargaining Between Patients and Health Care Providers, 51 U. Pitt. L. Rev. 365 (1990). See also Chapter 2.B.2; Jennifer Arlen, Contracting over Liability: Medical Malpractice and the Cost of Choice, 158 U. Pa. L. Rev. 957 (2010); Tom Baker & Timothy Lytton, Allowing Patients to Waive the Right to Sue for Malpractice: A Response to Thaler and Sunstein, 104 Nw. U. L. Rev. 233 (2010); Note, 83 N.Y.U. L. Rev. 850 (2009).

5. *Informed Consent Law*

Informed consent law is covered in Chapter 3. This body of law is usually not thought of as a defense to malpractice liability; rather, it is an alternative theory of liability. Nevertheless, we mention informed consent law here because its principles have important similarities to various defenses, and because the complex relationship between informed consent liability and ordinary malpractice liability cannot be fully understood until this point. See generally Jerry Menikoff, Demanded Medical Care, 30 Ariz. St. L. J. 1091 (1998).

Earlier, we saw that a number of alternative theories of physician liability potentially avoid the need for expert testimony about the standard of care. Informed consent liability is another such alternative theory, and it is the one that is most frequently tried. Typically, plaintiffs' lawyers allege breach of informed consent along with breach of the standard of care. Liability rarely is found to rest exclusively on this allegation, however, separate from ordinary malpractice. This is because informed consent liability is distinct from negligence liability only within a limited range of circumstances. This can be illustrated by distributing physicians' competency in responding to any given condition across a range of treatment options, as follows:

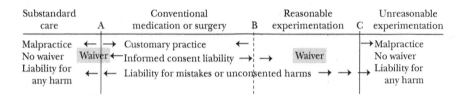

Ordinary malpractice liability exists for harms that result from doing less than or more than what most reasonable physicians would do (to the left of A and the right of C), or for making a mistake while giving conventional treatment (between A and C). Ordinary malpractice liability does not exist for unavoidable side effects that result from conventional treatment done competently. Informed consent liability, in contrast, might apply across this full range of treatment options. Where it overlaps with ordinary malpractice, however, it is mostly redundant. Deviations from customary practice are negligent, regardless of the presence or absence of consent. We have just seen that the prevailing standard of care generally speaking cannot be waived.

For the most part, then, informed consent law has unique effect only where treatment decisions comply with customary practice. The main exceptions to this generalization are for treatments at the two borders between customary and nonstandard care. At the right-hand border, B, which leads into experimental treatment, physicians who are purposefully more aggressive than is customary can avoid malpractice liability if they obtain informed consent for experiments that are considered reasonable innovations. At point C, however, experiments become too radical to permit consent.

Informed consent law also operates at the left-hand border with customary care, to help resolve ambiguous cases in what in fact is a large gray zone rather than a bright line. For instance, where there are competing schools of thought or alternative courses of acceptable treatment, informed consent can play a strong defensive role for a physician who follows an unorthodox approach or one subscribed to by only a minority of physicians. An example is found above in Schneider v. Revici. Finally, informed consent can be used defensively by physicians to disclaim any promise of a guaranteed result, thereby foreclosing possible contract liability as discussed in section D.1.

We return now to the middle zone, where informed consent operates separately from ordinary malpractice. Informed consent liability attaches to unavoidable side effects from competent treatment if the harms were not sufficiently disclosed to the patient. The key question is what standard of disclosure applies? This is discussed at length in Chapter 3, as part of the law that defines the structure of the physician-patient relationship. There, we learn that informed consent law has four different doctrinal foundations: battery law; custom-based negligence; patient-centered negligence; and fiduciary law. Only one of these four—custom-based negligence—determines disclosure obligations according to what other doctors commonly disclose to their patients, thereby requiring expert testimony just like regular medical malpractice. The other theories can be established through patient testimony and common knowledge. But the custom-based version of informed consent liability prevails in many, perhaps most, states. Moreover, in all states informed consent liability is difficult to demonstrate because, in order for causation to be established, it must be shown that the patient would have opted to decline treatment that is generally acceptable. Also, the jury must conclude that the alternative treatment would not have caused a worse outcome due to its own risks of failure or side effects.

F. DAMAGES AND SETTLEMENT

■ FEIN v. PERMANENTE MEDICAL GROUP
695 P.2d 665 (Cal. 1985)

KAUS, Justice.

In this medical malpractice action, both parties appeal from a judgment awarding plaintiff about $1 million in damages. Defendant claims that the trial court committed reversible error . . . in failing to order that the bulk of plaintiff's award be paid periodically rather than in a lump sum. Plaintiff . . . maintains that the trial court, in fixing damages, should not have applied two provisions of the Medical Injury Compensation Reform Act of 1975 (MICRA): Civil Code §3333.2, which limits noneconomic damages in medical malpractice cases to $250,000, and Civil Code §3333.1, which modifies the traditional "collateral source" rule in such litigation. Plaintiff's claims are based on a constitutional challenge similar to the challenges to other provisions of MICRA that we recently addressed and rejected in Roa v. Lodi Medical Group, Inc., 695 P.2d 164 (Cal. 1985) [upholding the following limits on lawyers' contingency fees in medical malpractice cases: 40 percent of the first $50,000, 33 percent of the next $50,000, 25 percent of the next $100,000, and 10 percent of any amounts above $200,000]. We conclude that the judgment should be affirmed in all respects.

I

On Saturday, February 21, 1976, plaintiff Lawrence Fein, a 34-year-old attorney, . . . felt a brief pain in his chest as he was riding his bicycle to work. [The pain returned several times and worsened over the next few days. He saw two doctors and a nurse practitioner with the defendant, which is affiliated with Kaiser-Permanente, but each time the pain was treated as a muscle spasm. It turned out to be a heart attack.] . . .

Following a period of hospitalization and medical treatment without surgery, plaintiff returned to his job on a part-time basis in October 1976, and resumed full-time work in September 1977. By the time of trial, he had been permitted to return to virtually all of his prior recreational activities—e.g., jogging, swimming, bicycling and skiing.

In February 1977, plaintiff filed the present action, alleging that his heart condition should have been diagnosed earlier and that treatment should have been given either to prevent the heart attack or, at least, to lessen its residual effects. The case went to judgment only against Permanente. . . .

At trial, Dr. Harold Swan, . . . testified to the damage caused by the attack. He stated that as a result of the attack a large portion of plaintiff's heart muscle had died, reducing plaintiff's future life expectancy by about one-half, to about 16 or 17 years. Although Dr. Swan acknowledged that some of plaintiff's other coronary arteries also suffer from disease, he felt that if plaintiff had been properly treated his future life expectancy would be decreased by only 10 to 15 percent, rather than half. . . .

The jury awarded $24,733 for wages lost by plaintiff to the time of trial, $63,000 for future medical expenses, and $700,000 for wages lost in the future as a result of the reduction in plaintiff's life expectancy.[1] Finally, the jury awarded $500,000 for "noneconomic damages," to compensate for pain, suffering, inconvenience, physical impairment and other intangible damages sustained by plaintiff from the time of the injury until his death. . . .

The trial court . . . reduced the noneconomic damages to $250,000, reduced the award for past lost wages to $5,430—deducting $19,303 that plaintiff had already received in disability payments as compensation for such lost wages—and ordered defendant to pay the first $63,000 of any future medical expenses not covered by medical insurance provided by plaintiff's employer, as such expenses were incurred. At the same time, the court declined to order that the award for future lost wages or noneconomic damages be paid periodically pursuant to Code of Civil Procedure §667.7, determining that the statute was not "mandatory" and that "under the unique facts and circumstances of this case" a periodic payment award of such damages would "defeat[ ] rather than promote[ ]" the purpose of §667.7. [The following excerpt focuses on how these various components of damages were calculated. Other portions of the opinion address whether the statutory limits are constitutional.] . . .

V

Defendant . . . argues that the trial court erred in permitting the jury to award damages for the loss of earnings attributable to plaintiff's so-called lost years, i.e., the period of time by which his life expectancy was diminished as a result of defendant's negligence. We believe that this was clearly a proper element of plaintiff's damages. . . . [R]ecovery of such damages is consistent with the general rule permitting an award based on the loss of future earnings a plaintiff is likely to suffer

---

1. Plaintiff did not claim that the heart attack would reduce his earning capacity during his lifetime.

because of inability to work for as long a period of time in the future as he could have done had he not sustained the accident.[10] . . .

Defendant alternatively argues that the jury should have been instructed to deduct from plaintiff's prospective gross earnings of the lost years, the "saved" cost of necessities that plaintiff would not incur during that period. Although there is some authority to support the notion that damages for the lost years should be assessed on the basis of plaintiff's "net" loss, we need not decide that issue in this case because defendant neither requested such an instruction at trial nor presented any evidence of anticipated cost savings that would have supported such an instruction. . . .

After the jury returned its verdict, defendant requested the trial court to enter a judgment—pursuant to §667.7 of the Code of Civil Procedure—providing for the periodic payment of future damages, rather than a lump-sum award. . . . The statute provides that "[i]n any [medical malpractice action], a superior court shall, at the request of either party, enter a judgment ordering that money damages or its equivalent for future damages of the judgment creditor be paid in whole or in part by periodic payments rather than by a lump-sum payment if the award equals or exceeds fifty thousand dollars ($50,000) in future damages."[11] . . .

---

10. The comments in the Restatement 2d Torts §924 state:

d. Loss or impairment of earning capacity for the future. The extent of future harm to the earning capacity of the injured person is measured by the difference, viewed as of the time of trial, between the value of the plaintiff's services as they will be in view of the harm and as they would have been had there been no harm. This difference is the resultant derived from reducing to present value the anticipated losses of earnings during the expected working period that the plaintiff would have had during the remainder of his prospective life, but for the defendant's act. Accordingly, the trier of fact must ascertain, as nearly as can be done in advance, the difference between the earnings that the plaintiff would or could have received during his life expectancy but for the harm and the earnings that he will probably be able to receive during the period of his life expectancy as now determined. . . .

11. Section 667.7 provides in relevant part:

As a condition to authorizing periodic payments of future damages, the court shall require the judgment debtor who is not adequately insured to post security adequate to assure full payment of such damages awarded by the judgment. . . . Such payments shall only be subject to modification in the event of the death of the judgment creditor. . . . However, money damages awarded for loss of future earnings shall not be reduced or payments terminated by reason of the death of the judgment creditor, but shall be paid to persons to whom the judgment creditor owed a duty of support, as provided by law, immediately prior to his death. . . . By authorizing periodic payment judgments, it is the further intent of the legislature that the courts will utilize such judgments to provide compensation sufficient to meet the needs of an injured plaintiff and those persons who are dependent on the plaintiff for whatever period is necessary while eliminating the potential windfall from a lump-sum recovery which was intended to provide for the care of an injured plaintiff over an extended period who then dies shortly after the judgment is paid, leaving the balance of the judgment award to persons and purposes for which it was not intended. It is also the intent of the legislature that all elements of the periodic payment program be specified with certainty in the judgment ordering such payments and that the judgment not be subject to modification at some future time which might alter the specifications of the original judgment.

Nonetheless, for several reasons relating to the specific facts of this case, we conclude that the trial court judgment should not be reversed on this ground. To begin with, although the court formally rejected defendant's motion for a periodic payment order, its judgment did provide for the periodic payment of the damages which the jury awarded for plaintiff's future medical expenses, directing the defendant to pay such expenses "as [they] are incurred up to the amount of $63,000."

Second, with respect to the award of noneconomic damages, . . . the jury was not instructed to designate the portion of the noneconomic damage award that was attributable to future damages, and it did not do so. Instead, it returned an undifferentiated special verdict awarding noneconomic damages of $500,000. Because of defendant's failure to raise the periodic payment issue earlier, plaintiff was deprived of the opportunity to seek a special verdict designating the amount of "future noneconomic damage." . . .

Third and finally, there is the question of the $700,000 award for lost future earnings. Although in general lost future earnings are a type of future damage particularly suitable to a periodic payment judgment, this case presents a somewhat unusual situation because the damages awarded are solely attributable to the earnings of plaintiff's lost years. If the trial court had ordered such damages paid periodically over the time period when the loss was expected to be incurred, the damages would have been paid in their entirety after plaintiff's expected death, and thus—if the life expectancy predictions were accurate—plaintiff would not have received any of this element of damages. . . .

Thus, in sum, we conclude that none of the defendant's contentions call for a reversal of the judgment.

VII

We now turn to plaintiff's contentions.

As noted, although the jury by special verdict set plaintiff's noneconomic damages at $500,000, the trial court reduced that amount to $250,000 pursuant to Civil Code §3333.2. Plaintiff challenges this ruling, contending that §3333.2 is unconstitutional on a number of grounds. In many respects, plaintiff's argument tracks the constitutional objections to other provisions of MICRA that we have recently rejected in *Roa*. . . .

For similar reasons, plaintiff's constitutional challenge to Civil Code §3333.1—which modifies this state's common law "collateral source" rule—is also without merit. Under the traditional collateral source rule, a jury, in calculating a plaintiff's damages in a tort action, does not take into consideration benefits—such as medical insurance or disability payments—which the plaintiff has received from sources other than the defendant—i.e., "collateral sources"—to cover losses resulting from the injury. Under §3333.1, subdivision (a), a medical malpractice defendant is permitted to introduce evidence of such collateral source benefits received by or payable to the plaintiff; when a defendant chooses to introduce such evidence, the plaintiff may introduce evidence of the amounts he has paid—in insurance premiums, for example—to secure the benefits. Although §3333.1, subdivision (a)—as ultimately adopted—does not specify how the jury should use such evidence, the legislature apparently assumed that in most cases the jury would set plaintiff's damages at a lower level because of its awareness of plaintiff's "net" collateral source benefits. . . .

In addition, §3333.1, subdivision (b) provides that whenever such collateral source evidence is introduced, the source of those benefits is precluded from obtaining subrogation either from the plaintiff or from the medical malpractice defendant. As far as the malpractice plaintiff is concerned, subdivision (b) assures that he will suffer no "double deduction" from his tort recovery as a result of his receipt of collateral source benefits; because the jury that has learned of his benefits may reduce his tort award by virtue of such benefits, the legislature eliminated any right the collateral source may have had to obtain repayment of those benefits from the plaintiff. . . .

[T]he legislature clearly did not act irrationally in choosing to modify the collateral source rule as one means of lowering the costs of malpractice litigation. In analyzing the collateral source rule more than a decade ago, we acknowledged that most legal commentators had severely criticized the rule for affording a plaintiff a "double recovery" for "losses" he had not in reality sustained, and we noted that many jurisdictions had either restricted or repealed it. . . .

The judgment is affirmed.

■ ROBERTS v. STEVENS CLINIC HOSPITAL
345 S.E.2d 791 (W. Va. 1986)

NEELY, Justice.

In this appeal we decide whether we should sustain a McDowell County Circuit Court $10,000,000 jury award [for compensatory damages] in favor of the parents and two siblings of Michael Joseph Roberts, a 2 1/2-year-old child who died as the result of medical malpractice. [A surgeon punctured his bowel trying to correct a problem that was causing severe diarrhea. He died from the resulting infection.] . . .

Kenneth and Joyce Roberts are a young couple who . . . gave birth to Michael Joseph Roberts. . . . Michael was the darling of the whole family. He was both an intelligent and happy little boy who was particularly close to his mother. The jury had before it substantial evidence that since Michael's death Joyce has been overwhelmed by grief and that the Roberts' family is no longer a happy household. . . . Joyce spent many nights crying and writing poems to Michael, and there was evidence that she continues to suffer from chronic diarrhea and vomiting. . . .

At trial the plaintiff introduced into evidence a professionally prepared, twenty minute, videotape that combined "home movie" video recordings of Michael taken by a neighbor with a series of still, colored, photographs of Michael and the family. The audio background for this video presentation consisted of tape recordings of the child's voice as well as Joyce's voice singing and talking to the child. It is the defendant's contention that this film was a "theatrical" presentation that artistically highlighted certain aspects of Michael's life and Joyce's relationship to Michael in an inaccurate way.

We have reviewed the tape in its entirety and we find nothing inflammatory or prejudicial about it. . . . The purpose of the videotape was to demonstrate that Michael was a healthy, intelligent, enthusiastic, and well-loved child. So, as a preliminary matter, the videotape was relevant. In our review of the tape, we find no artistic highlighting that emphasizes some scenes or photographs more than others, and we find no merit in the defendant's assertion that because the mother's voice went on several seconds after the screen turned black, an unduly sentimental atmosphere was evoked that would have prejudiced the jury.

This court has not previously addressed the admissibility of videotape "Day-in-the-Life" films. . . . We are not unmindful of the potential dangers inherent in such presentations. As one court has explained: Almost always an edited tape necessarily raises issues as to every sequence portrayed of whether the event shown is fairly representative of fact, after the editing process, and whether it is unduly prejudicial because of the manner of presentation. Bolstridge v. Central Maine Power Co., 621 F. Supp. 1202 (D.C. Me. 1985) (plaintiff's "Day-in-the-Life" videotape excluded when open court testimony could demonstrate similar evidence, and admission of videotape would create risk of distracting jury and unfairly prejudicing defendant). . . . But, we shall not reverse a trial court's decision in these matters unless the record shows a clear abuse of discretion. . . .

We now come to the most serious problem in this case, namely the closing argument of plaintiff's counsel. In a nutshell, the reason that we are compelled to reduce the jury's award from $10,000,000 to $3,000,000 is that plaintiff's counsel implied, in his closing argument, that the duty of the jury was to place a value on Michael's life. No objection along those lines, however, was made during the closing argument, and for that reason we are undisposed to reverse the entire trial because, technically, the error was waived.[5] . . .

[Plaintiff's counsel] argued that if a $10,000,000 race horse had been killed through the negligence of a veterinary hospital, the measure of damages would be exactly $10,000,000. At another point in the argument counsel asked what would have happened if someone had approached Michael's parents with an envelope containing ten, $1,000,000 winning lottery tickets and asked the parents if they would trade Michael's life for the tickets. Finally, counsel made reference to the American space program where billions of dollars are spent to avoid the loss of a single life. Representative excerpts from counsel's closing argument are as follows:

> . . . Now if Michael were a race horse and the Stevens Clinic Hospital operated a veterinarian hospital and a race horse named Michael died as a result of the negligence of a veterinary doctor, you wouldn't have any trouble in returning a verdict for millions of dollars because you know that that's what race horses are worth. You tell me, you tell the family, are horses entitled to better care than children? And are children less valuable than horses? . . .

Our wrongful death statute specifically sets forth the losses for which damages can be recovered.[8] Obviously, if the measure of damages were the value of a human

---

5. . . . In the roughly seven seconds available to counsel to make the strategic decision whether to object, it probably dawned on counsel that an objection and "curative" instruction would serve only to reinforce plaintiff's counsel's point.

8. W. Va. Code §55-7-6 [1982] provides:

> The verdict of the jury shall include, but may not be limited to, damages for the following: (A) Sorrow, mental anguish, and solace which may include society, companionship, comfort, guidance, kindly offices and advice of the decedent; (B) compensation for reasonably expected loss of (i) income of the decedent, and (ii) services, protection, care and assistance provided by the decedent; (C) expenses for the care, treatment and hospitalization of the decedent incident to the injury resulting in death; and (D) reasonable funeral expenses. . . .

life then, arguably, no jury verdict could be excessive. The death of a family member, particularly a child, involves inconsolable grief for which no amount of money can compensate. . . . We believe that our conclusion in this regard is grounded in sound public policy, which we now proceed to discuss.[9] . . .

[B]ecause less than 6 percent of all serious lawsuits are tried, the most important thing that courts do is to cast a shadow of legal rules within which litigants can craft their own custom-made settlements. . . . Without the occasional jury award that is at least ten times greater than what the parties would have settled for immediately after the tragedy, there would be no incentive on the part of clients to temper the . . . anti-settlement proclivities of their lawyers by urging quick payment of just claims. . . .

Ideally, in a case such as the one before us where the negligence of the defendants is palpable, some just compensation for Michael's death would have been forthcoming within 30 days. Yet Michael died in July, 1982 and it is now April, 1986 without the Roberts' having received any compensation whatsoever for Michael's loss.

When the defendants moved for leave to file an appeal in this court, the court asked the parties to describe the settlement negotiations that preceded the trial. Such information is generally inadmissible and incompetent to show liability or set the measure of damages. But we believe that settlement discussions have some bearing on the necessarily subjective criteria that appellate courts use to determine a proper remittitur, because such a determination affects future settlement negotiations. . . .

About two months before trial plaintiff's counsel made a written offer to both defendants to settle for $5,000,000, which was approximately half of the total available insurance coverage of $10,250,000. No response was received from the defendants until the Friday afternoon before the Monday morning trial date! At that time defendant Magnus offered $100,000 and the offer was rejected. The next day the offer was increased to $125,000, and after one week of trial, when most of the plaintiff's evidence was in, and both defendants had reason to expect a substantial verdict, defendant Magnus increased the offer to $220,000.

In light of the statistically demonstrable fact that settlement rather than litigation is the true cynosure of the whole judicial process, in this case, then, we not only ask ourselves how much money the Roberts family should receive to compensate them for the losses enumerated under the Wrongful Death Statute; we also ask ourselves what jury award in a case of this type will establish the proper climate for out-of-court settlements. . . . Accordingly, . . . the case is remanded to the circuit court with directions to enter a remittitur of $7,000,000 and enter judgment on the verdict for $3,000,000 or, in the alternative, at the option of the plaintiff, to award a new trial.

Reversed and remanded with directions.

9. While the plaintiffs furnished us with a number of cases where jury verdicts of this magnitude have been approved, the plaintiffs in those cases had suffered severe personal injuries that necessitated enormous future medical care costs and also loss of earning capacity. These elements are absent in this case.

Notes: Damages; Wrongful Life Cases

1. *Hedonic Damages.* Damages for loss of enjoyment of life are sometimes referred to as "hedonic damages." One must distinguish carefully among versions of hedonic damages in order to make an accurate statement of the law. The situation in which they are the most readily recoverable is as an element of pain and suffering, where an injury has left the plaintiff alive and aware but disabled. The situation in which they are least recoverable is where the plaintiff is killed or left comatose. The inability to experience the loss of life's pleasures usually means that they cannot be claimed as a form of pain and suffering. But a few courts disagree. For a thorough review of the law with majority and dissenting views, see generally McDougald v. Garber, 536 N.E.2d 372 (N.Y. 1989). See also Annot., 34 A.L.R.4th 293 (1984). *Fein* presents a third situation, where a plaintiff is fully abled in the present, but is likely to die early. Here, it is possible to receive some form of compensation for lost enjoyment of life by characterizing the damages as distress and anguish in the present over realizing that one's life is shortened. The traditional view, however, is that no recovery is allowed for the value of life itself, under the view that it is impossible or unseemly to place a value on life.

Measurable *economic* damages, however, do pertain to a shortened life. Review *Fein* to clarify the difference between economic damages during life and as a result of a shortened life. Which set of economic damages raises the possibility of a "necessities-of-living" offset? Which set relies on diminished earning capacity?

Other exceptions to the general rule that loss of life is not compensated arise by virtue of wrongful death statutes. Review the version of this statute in the *Roberts* case and the components of damages that were recognized and rejected there. You will observe that these statutes do not directly overturn the general rule. How, then, do they justify noneconomic damages in cases of instantaneous death?

2. *Wrongful Life and Wrongful Birth.* "Wrongful life" and "wrongful birth" cases are where these concepts are put to their greatest test in medical malpractice litigation. In contrast to wrongful death actions that ask what is the value of a *lost* life, wrongful life and birth actions ask what are the damages for a life *brought into being* that *should not* have been. There are two typical scenarios. First, if a doctor fails to identify or avoid a birth defect, a claim can result for the expenses and anguish of living life with a severe handicap. Second, if a sterilization procedure fails, an action can result for the expenses of raising a normal, healthy child, as well as for any harms attendant to pregnancy and childbirth.[1] The first scenario presents the greatest conceptual difficulties.

The first difficulty is causation. Usually, the only way to avoid a birth defect once it is detected is by aborting. Of course, there is always the question whether the parents would have made this decision, but there is the more fundamental realization that the only way *this* child could have avoided the severe defect is to not be born at all. Therefore, one must measure damages by comparing the two states of severe disability with nonexistence.

---

1. A third scenario, which entails wrongfully maintaining an existing life by refusing to disconnect life support, is presented in Anderson v. St. Francis-St. George Hospital, 671 N.E.2d 225 (Ohio 1996), which is discussed at page 570.

At first, these causation and damages difficulties were insurmountable for the courts. Shortly after abortions became commonplace, however, courts began to allow limited forms of these actions. See William J. Curran, Genetic Counseling and Wrongful Life, 68 Am. J. Public Health 501 (1978). They distinguished between "wrongful life" actions, which are the child's own claims for the suffering and expenses of being alive, and "wrongful birth" actions, which are the parents' claims for having to raise a handicapped child. Most courts allow only the latter — the parents' claim — and even then limit the damages to mostly economic ones, such as the "extraordinary" costs of intensive care and treatment. (Query why not the "ordinary" costs as well?) Emotional distress damages are not recoverable in a number of states because it is thought that the emotional benefits of having a child at all outweigh the emotional harms of the severe handicap. Again, it is usually not factually possible to make a claim for failure to have a healthy child. Nevertheless, a number of other states allow juries to weigh the competing benefits and burdens of having the child at all and award damages for a net emotional loss.

A very few states also allow the handicapped child to maintain his own action, but the damages are similarly constrained to the economic costs of managing life as a disabled adult. The leading case is Turpin v. Sortini, 643 P.2d 954 (Cal. 1982). This is no different, however, than allowing the parents to recover the costs of care for the child's *entire* lifetime rather than for only the years of dependency. A very few courts have rejected both causes of action entirely. See, e.g., Atlanta Obstetrics & Gynecology Group v. Abelson, 398 S.E.2d 557 (Ga. 1990). Also, several state legislatures, motivated by antiabortion sentiments, have restricted or abolished these causes of action. Note, Wrongful Birth Actions: The Case Against Legislative Curtailment, 100 Harv. L. Rev. 2017 (1987) (arguing these statutes are unconstitutional).

In "wrongful conception" cases (i.e., those involving failed sterilizations), courts usually allow only the medical expenses of birth but not the economic costs of raising a normal, healthy child. Although child-rearing costs clearly result from the failed sterilization, as a matter of social policy most courts are not willing to allow a jury to find that children, on balance, are a burden. Other courts, however, allow recovery of both the economic and the emotional costs of having an unexpected child, subject to the jury's views on the value of offsetting benefits. One court went so far as to allow recovery of child-rearing costs with no offset, under the view that emotional benefits are usually offset only against emotional, not economic, burdens. Marchiniak v. Lundborg, 450 N.W.2d 243 (Wis. 1990).

There are a host of cases, and almost as many law review articles, on this topic. For a sampling of the latter, see note 8. For cases, see Annot., 74 A.L.R.4th 798 (1989).

The potential for wrongful life litigation is greatly increasing with the explosion in genetic tests, not only for congenital defects but also for "normal" diseases later in life such as cancer. Far-reaching genetic mapping projects currently under way are likely to increase exponentially our current ability to detect predisposition to genetic conditions. For additional discussion, see Chapter 7.D.

3. *The Size of Awards.* Most years, medical malpractice cases regularly produce some of the highest verdicts in the country, in the range of $20 million to $50 million or more. Usually, these involve severely damaged newborns. But, focusing on these extreme cases gives a false impression of what typical damages awards are in medical malpractice cases. Even a more systematic reading of reported decisions

can give a false impression since only the rare claim reaches appellate review and review is more likely when the actual or potential damages award is high. Substantial empirical research sheds considerable light on the experience in more typical malpractice claims.

When claims are filed, only about a third result in payment, most by settlement. Fewer than 10 percent of malpractice claims are tried, and only about 20 to 30 percent of these produce plaintiff verdicts. Most jury verdicts are well below $1 million. A study of verdicts from large cities in 2001 found that the median award was $77,000 for temporary injuries, $412,000 for permanent injuries, and $837,000 for death; no plaintiff with a temporary injury received a jury verdict exceeding $1 million. David A. Hyman & Charles Silver, Medical Malpractice Litigation and Tort Reform: It's the Incentives, Stupid, 59 Vand. L. Rev. 1085, 1105 (2006). Considering all of this, injured patients have difficulty finding a lawyer willing to take their case when their potential damages are less than $50,000. Id.

Combining both jury verdicts and claims settled outside of litigation, the average payment in 2015 was about $400,000 nationally, but this does not represent the typical case because the average is skewed by a relatively few number of very high awards. More representative is the median payout, which (in 2015) was $225,000. Settlement amounts have held fairly steady over the past decade, but the number of paid claims has dropped by about 40 percent since 2005. See note 8.

4. *Settlements.* Additional research indicates that, when cases go to trial, the variation in jury awards *in the aggregate* is broadly consistent with the severity of injury, although for a given category of injury, *individual* jury awards are highly erratic, varying by a factor of ten or more. See Symposium, 54 Law & Contemp. Probs. 1 (Winter 1991). This unpredictability makes it difficult to settle cases, even where liability is relatively clear. Also, doctors are often reluctant to settle because of the negative publicity and their desire for personal vindication. Accordingly, medical malpractice cases are twice as likely to go to trial as are other personal injury suits. Michael Saks, Do We Really Know Anything About the Behavior of the Tort Litigation System—And Why Not?, 140 U. Pa. L. Rev. 1147, 1128 (1992).

Nevertheless, most malpractice awards are obtained through settlement. Settlement amounts are influenced by the reputation and experience of the particular lawyers and expert witnesses representing plaintiffs, with lawyers receiving significantly more if their track record in front of juries shows they are able to land sizeable verdicts. Also, studies show that settlement amounts tend to correlate with the strength of a case, although the degree of injury has more influence than the degree of fault. For sources, see note 8.

On the other hand, settlement tends to suppress the average amount of the award. Settlements rarely are for amounts greater than the limits of physicians' liability insurance, so physicians almost never have to use personal assets to pay claims. In a study from Florida, only about a fifth of paid claimants recovered more than their economic loss, and most recovered less, on account of the discounting that occurs in settlement negotiations. The average pretrial settlement paid about half of economic losses. Even those who won at trial recovered on average only 22 percent more than economic losses. Frank Sloan et al., Suing for Medical Malpractice (1993). Again, this is due in part to settlement. Plaintiffs often settle even after receiving favorable jury verdicts, since a post-trial settlement avoids the cost and delay of an appeal. The vast majority of $1 million-plus verdicts are settled for somewhat less. An insurer is likely to insist on appealing only if it is confident in the merits or if it sees the case as a good opportunity to set a favorable precedent for future cases. Review the facts in McCourt v. Abernathy at page 282. As defense counsel, what would you have settled the case for after trial?

5. *Dropping a Claim.* As just noted, over half of malpractice claims filed are closed (resolved) without payment, some by court dismissal, but many because the insurer refuses to pay and the plaintiff simply drops the claim. See Dwight Golann, Dropped Medical Malpractice Claims, 30(7) Health Aff. 1343 (2011). How can a lawyer ethically drop a case, though, once she learns it is not possible to settle? Generally, there are two options: (1) have an agreement (preferably written) with the client that the case is being taken on for purposes of settlement only; (2) seek the judge's permission to withdraw. The latter is necessary only if suit has been filed. Many judges will be reluctant to grant this permission if diligent investigation before suit would have disclosed the case's weaknesses.

6. *Scheduled Damages.* One notable proposal to make jury awards more predictable is to create a schedule of pain and suffering damages according to a matrix of the following factors: whether the injury is temporary or permanent; life expectancy; and whether the injury is minor, significant, major, or grave. These scheduled damages could then either be mandated, given to the jury as advisory guidelines, or used by the judge to police excessively large or small verdicts. Moreover, the scheduled amounts could be based on a collection of actual prior jury verdicts rather than on legislative or administrative assessments. See note 8.

7. *The Collateral Source Rule.* It may seem difficult on the surface to justify the traditional collateral source rule that allows plaintiffs double recovery of their medical bills or lost income, but in theory this is sensible because most third-party health and disability insurers have a contractual right of subrogation that allows them to be reimbursed for their payments from the tort award. In practice, however, such subrogation claims are fairly rare, owing to the difficulty in allocating lump sum tort awards or settlements among various damages components. Moreover, many states have statutes that limit or preclude the ability of insurers to enforce these contractual provisions. A more practical justification for not offsetting collateral source recoveries is the need to provide plaintiffs a source for paying their attorneys' fees. This is also a practical justification for unlimited pain and suffering awards. This perhaps best explains why physicians push so strongly for malpractice reform statutes that limit these elements of damage, since they go a long way toward removing lawyers' economic motivation for taking the case in the first place. Note that the *Roa* case decided the same day as *Fein* upheld California's statutory limits on the size of contingency fees.

Recall from section A.1 the research that indicates many injured patients sue because they are worried primarily about the costs of medical treatment or in response to hospitals' or doctors' attempts to collect on their overdue bills. How does this information bear on this debate? Would you advise hospitals and doctors to voluntarily pick up the costs of extended treatment for injured patients without admitting liability?

8. *Bibliography.* For discussion of **wrongful life/birth** cases and related theories (note 2), see Alexander M. Capron, Tort Liability in Genetic Counseling, 79 Colum. L. Rev. 618 (1979); Wendy F. Hensel, The Disabling Impact of Wrongful Life and Wrongful Birth Actions, 40 Harv. C.R.-C.L. L. Rev. 141 (2005); Daniel Whitney &

Kenneth Rosenbaum, Recovery of Damages for Wrongful Birth, 32 J. Leg. Med. 167 (2011); Dov Fox, Reproductive Negligence, 117 Colum. L. Rev. 149 (2017).

On the **size of awards** (note 3) and **settlements** (4), see Michelle Mello & Allen Kachalia, Medical Malpractice: Evidence on Reform Alternatives and Claims Involving Elderly Patients (MedPac, 2016); David A. Hyman et al., Settlement at Policy Limits and the Duty to Settle, 8 J. Empirical Legal Stud. 48 (2011); Catherine Harris et al., Placing "Standard of Care" in Context: The Impact of Witness Potential and Attorney Reputation in Medical Malpractice Litigation, 3 J. Empirical Legal Stud. 467 (2006); Catherine Harris et al., Does Being a Repeat Player Make a Difference?, 8 Yale J. Health Pol'y L. & Ethics 253 (2008); Philip Peters, What We Know About Malpractice Settlements, 92 Iowa L. Rev. 1783 (2007); Kathryn Zeiler et al., Physicians' Insurance Limits and Malpractice Payments, 36 J. Leg. Stud. 9 (2007); Neil Vidmar et al., Million Dollar Medical Malpractice Cases in Florida: Post-Verdict and Pre-Suit Settlements, 59 Vand. L. Rev. 1343 (2006); David Hyman et al., Do Defendants Pay What Juries Award?, J. Empirical Legal Stud. 3 (2007).

Regarding **hedonic damages** (note 1), see generally R. Pallin & B. Danninger, Hedonic Damages: Proving Damages for Lost Enjoyment of Living (1990); Eric A. Posner & Cass R. Sunstein, Dollars and Death, 72 U. Chi. L. Rev. 537 (2005). On **scheduled damages** (note 6), see Randall R. Bovbjerg et al., Valuing Life and Limb in Tort: Scheduling "Pain and Suffering," 83 Nw. U. L. Rev. 908 (1989); David M. Studdert et al., Rationalizing Noneconomic Damages, 74 Law & Contemp. Probs. 57 (Summer 2011). On the **collateral source rule** (note 7), see Adam Todd, An Enduring Oddity: The Collateral Source Rule in the Face of Tort Reform, the Affordable Care Act, and Increased Subrogation, 43 McGeorge L. Rev. 965 (2012); Comment, 60 UCLA L. Rev. 736 (2013).

Exercise: "A Day in the Life"

Interview someone you know who suffers from a physical or mental infirmity, or someone who lives with such a person. Write a script for a demonstrative exhibit (video, charts, still photographs, etc.) that details a day or week in the life of this individual. Explain your strategic decisions regarding what to highlight or dramatize and what to leave out or avoid, in order to maximize the exhibit's emotional impact without having it excluded altogether.

Exercise: Damages Settlement

Conduct a settlement negotiation with one of your classmates in the following hypothetical:*

> Joe Jenks is paralyzed from the waist down as a result of negligently performed surgery on his back. At the time of the surgery he was 30 years of age and employed as a forklift operator for Wheeling Manufacturing Co. He graduated from high school at age 18, spent two years in the army (receiving an honorable discharge), and

* This is adapted from Frank M. McClellan, Medical Malpractice: Law, Tactics, and Ethics (1994). Another excellent source for practical trial techniques is Thomas M. O'Toole et al., The Anatomy of a Medical Malpractice Verdict, 70 Mont. L. Rev. 57 (2009).

immediately after discharge went to work for Wheeling. Before the surgery he was in good health, except for chronic back pain that plagued him for six months after he fell while playing basketball. He earned $40,000 as a forklift operator in the year before the accident. In addition, that same year he earned $30,000 moonlighting as a security guard on evenings and weekends. He has never been married and lives alone. He was a below-average student in high school, graduating at the bottom of his class. He was, however, a well-liked and ambitious young man who had a strong aptitude for mechanics. His paralysis is permanent.

Take the lawyer's position on one side or the other in a suit against the orthopedic surgeon. Make up and stick to the client facts you need that aren't given. Assume that investigating and trying the case will cost the plaintiff's lawyer $50,000 in out-of-pocket expenses and will cost the doctor's insurer $150,000 in legal fees and expenses. Assume further that your jurisdiction has no damages cap, but does have statutes that allow period payments and offset of collateral source payments. Engage in negotiations attempting to reach a definite settlement. If successful, then reveal to the other side the actual "bottom line" or "top dollar" you would have been willing to agree to. If you haven't reached a settlement after half an hour, then determine how far apart you are by stating your final best offers.

■ BLEDAY v. OUM GROUP
645 A.2d 1358 (Pa. Super. Ct. 1994)

HUDOCK, Judge.

. . . Appellants secured malpractice insurance through Insurers for the period of February, 1988, through February, 1989. The policy obtained by Appellants contained the following [provision]:

> The company shall have the right and duty to defend any suit against the insured seeking damages because of such injury even if any of the allegations of the suit are groundless, false or fraudulent. The company may make such investigation and settlement of any claim or suit as it deems expedient.

Within the time period covered by said policy, Tracey Worchesky (Worchesky) instituted an action against Appellants. The nature of her claim was that she had to seek corrective surgery from another podiatrist because she never properly recovered from surgery performed by Dr. Bleday. . . . [O]ver the objection of Appellants, Insurers settled Worchesky's claim for $10,000.[1] Insurers stated that the settlement was a result of a business decision which was made to "avoid the cost of litigation and the uncertainties of a jury trial."

. . . Appellants filed a complaint against Insurers and Adjusters . . . alleg[ing] that Insurers breached their duty of good faith to Appellants by settling Worchesky's claim without their consent. . . . With respect to damages, Appellants assert that they

---

1. As one of the grounds for objecting to the settlement, Appellants assert that Worchesky, at no time, submitted an expert report to support her claim of injury. The only expert report was secured by [Insurers], and it stated that Dr. Bleday was not negligent.

will be subjected to increased insurance premiums, loss of earnings, and harm to reputation since Dr. Bleday's name will be placed on the National Physician Data Bank, a list of doctors who have been involved in malpractice actions. . . . The trial court granted the [defendants' motion to dismiss]. . . . Appellants assert that Insurers, despite the policy language "deems expedient," have the duty to act in good faith in the handling of its claims. . . .

After a thorough review of case law from other jurisdictions, we conclude that, although judicial deference must be given to the decision of an insurance company to settle a claim within the policy limits, a claim for bad faith may, in limited circumstances, be asserted against the insurance company notwithstanding a "deems expedient" provision. A "deems expedient" provision in an insurance contract cannot be interpreted to convey to an insurance company an absolute right to settle a claim within the policy limits if such settlement was contrary to the intent and expectation of the parties. However, after a thorough review of the complaint filed by Appellants, we find that Appellants did not sufficiently plead a cause of action in bad faith against Insurers, and, thus, the trial court properly granted Insurers' preliminary objections.

Several jurisdictions hold that a "deems expedient" provision in an insurance contract conveys to an insurer an absolute right to settle the claims of the insured within the insurance policy limits. . . . In Feliberty v. Damon, 527 N.E.2d 261 (N.Y. 1988), a medical malpractice panel found that the appellant committed malpractice and was liable in the amount of $743,000. Before judgment was entered and without his consent, the appellant's insurer settled the claim for $700,000, an amount within the policy limits. The appellant sought compensatory and punitive damages from the insurer, asserting that his reputation was damaged as a result of the settlement. The New York court, in granting the insurer's motion to dismiss the complaint, held that the insurance company had an absolute right to settle under the language of the policy. . . .

In Shuster v. South Broward Hospital, 591 So.2d 174 (Fla. 1992), . . . the court opined:

> The language of the ["deems expedient"] provision is clear and the insured was put on notice that the agreement granted the insurer the exclusive authority to control settlement and to be guided by its own self-interest when settling the claim for amounts within the policy limits. The obvious intent behind placing the provision in the agreement was to grant the insurer the authority to decide whether to settle or defend the claim based on its own self-interest, and this authority includes settling for the nuisance value of the claim. Therefore, we interpret the provision as granting the insurer the discretion to settle cases for amounts within the policy limits, regardless of whether the claim is frivolous or not. . . .

However, the court further stressed that every contract that is entered into requires the good faith performance of its provisions, and, thus, the "deems expedient" provision is not absolute. . . .

Based on the facts in the case herein, we find that Appellants have not sufficiently pled a cause of action in bad faith. . . . We believe, as the Supreme Court of Florida did in Shuster, that something more is required to maintain a cause of action for bad faith when a claim is settled within the policy limits. However, we leave for another day to define what circumstances constitute bad faith; it is enough to say that they are not present in the instant case. . . .

■ REGULATORY SYSTEM IN SHAMBLES; NEGLIGENT DOCTORS STAY ON JOB
Bruce Butterfield & Gerard O'Neill
Boston Globe, Oct. 2, 1994*

A nine-month investigation of malpractice by the Boston Globe Spotlight Team examined more than 1,000 court cases of scores of doctors across the state who have been sued repeatedly over the last ten years—some more than ten times. Yet nearly all continue to practice virtually unregulated and unpenalized. . . . Records of the most-sued doctors reveal a malpractice trail of anguish and suffering across the state: children maimed for life; babies dead from botched deliveries; women dying needlessly of breast and cervical cancers; patients left paraplegic, incontinent or crippled. . . . In case after case, the story is the same. Doctors at the center of the malpractice problem are frequently sued, but never admit wrongdoing regardless of the severity of the case.

And there is nobody willing to force them: not fellow doctors, not medical insurers, and not even the courts where settlements are almost always subject to secrecy agreements. . . . Deficient doctors in Massachusetts rarely lose their licenses. They never lose malpractice insurance. When they get in trouble in one hospital, they are often passed to another. The result is a medical monitoring system turned on its head. . . .

Take the case of Dr. Grahshyam P. Massand—currently practicing at Somerville Hospital. Massand has been sued 10 times since 1985, been subject to hospital restrictions on his work, lost privileges at one hospital, and moved to another. . . . If patients should have been able to find out about any problem doctor, it should have been about Massand. His record was well known by medical, regulatory and insurance officials alike. But in many cases, the slow-footed Board of Registration in Medicine doesn't even know who the repeatedly sued doctors are. Insurers know, but shroud nearly everything they do—and everything they fail to do—in confidentiality. The agency that insures two-thirds of all doctors is the quasi-public Massachusetts Professional Insurance Association, established in the mid-1970s and dominated by doctors and hospital executives who sit on its board of directors. Despite its public mission, it is protective and secretive to its core. . . . Its executives say they process the paper and pay the bills, but don't get involved with discipline. "I mean, it's not our job," says Tracy Gehan Leu, spokeswoman for the agency.

The real job of disciplining bad doctors is left to the Board of Registration in Medicine. But the board's efforts on the malpractice front have all but collapsed. Massand is one of only a handful of repeatedly sued doctors who have been formally

---

* This is the first of a five-part series of articles. The last two paragraphs of this excerpt are from another article in the same series, Brian C. Mooney, Doctors with Dubious Records Start Fresh in Other States, *Boston Globe*, Oct. 5, 1994.

charged by the board. Still, after a decade marked by disastrous cases, he continues to hang onto his license.

Far more common are doctors like Sherman Stein—untouched by the board despite frequent and severe malpractice complaints. . . . Stein was sued for negligence, and his insurers settled in a secret agreement in 1992. By then, Stein had left a trail of lawsuits and patients claiming they were injured or maimed by him. But he was no longer around—he had moved on to become head of neurosurgery at Cooper Hospital in Camden, N.J., with an ostensibly spotless record. In all, Stein has had 11 malpractice suits filed against him since 1985, and a twelfth filed only months before that—one of the worst records of any doctor in the state. At least six of those suits resulted in secret settlements to avoid trial. . . .

Judges as well as lawyers routinely sidestep a 1986 state law banning confidential settlements, which occur in about one third of all medical malpractice suits. . . . [I]n the overwhelming majority of cases in which plaintiffs are paid, the settlement is masked by a bland order "stipulating dismissal" of the complaint and a patient's promise not to talk about it under a threat of forfeiture. . . . In many cases, the record is a sham: Judgment is recorded for the doctor even though the insurer paid a substantial sum to the plaintiff. . . .

These clamps on the flow of information to the public outrage activists in the small but growing health consumer movement. "This is ultimately a question of the right to know," said U.S. Rep. Ron Wyden (D.-Or.), principal sponsor of the bill that created the national data bank and cosponsor of a pending bill that would open up some of its information to the public. . . . Wyden's bill, opposed by the AMA, would disclose information about physicians and others who have had medical privileges restricted or had two or more payouts in malpractice suits.

Notes: Settlement; National Practitioner Data Bank; Insurance

1. *Bleday* reflects the prevailing law that insurers with "deems expedient" language control the decision to settle. Other courts have ruled, however, that as soon as the defendant's lawyer determines that the insurer and the doctor are at odds on settlement, the lawyer has a conflict of interest and therefore a duty to notify the doctor and give him a chance to obtain other counsel. Even if the doctor cannot block the insurer's decision, he might want to release the insurer from further involvement and bear the costs of defending himself. Breach of this duty to disclose could result in an action for legal malpractice. Rogers v. Robson, Masters, Ryan, Brumund & Belon, 407 N.E.2d 47 (Ill. 1980). The physician-owned malpractice insurers that exist in many states are more sympathetic to allowing physicians to control the decision to go to trial than are independent, "commercial" insurers. In many states, insurance is available with language that requires the doctor's consent to settle, but in other states, insurers prohibit such clauses because they deter settlement. Interestingly, where such clauses exist, they increase the cost of insurance by 1 to 3 percent, which physicians are often willing to pay so they can have more control over whether they will be reported to the National Practitioner Data Bank (NPDB). For an exploration of the psychology of settlement in this context, see Ralph Peeples et al., Settlement Has Many Faces: Physicians, Attorneys and Medical Malpractice, 41 J. Health & Soc. Behav. 333 (2000). See generally Scott Thomas,

An Insurer's Right to Settle Versus Its Duty to Defend Nonmeritorious Medical Malpractice Claims, 16 J. Leg. Med. 545 (1995).

When doctors want to settle, they have more legal leverage because insurers can be held liable for exposing doctors to uninsured damages beyond their policy limits. See generally Kent D. Syverud, The Duty to Settle, 76 Va. L. Rev. 1113 (1990); Annot., 18 A.L.R.5th 474 (1995).

2. *Secrecy.* As the *Boston Globe* article reflects, some doctors very much want to settle malpractice suits to avoid attracting attention. Even though the NPDB was implemented in 1989 to require disclosure of all payments in claims against doctors, defense lawyers are often able to avoid these laws by (1) stipulating that payment will come from an institutional defendant such as a hospital or medical clinic rather than the doctor; (2) stipulating that the doctor is not at fault; and (3) presenting an uncontested motion to seal the court records for cause. See Haavi Morreim, Malpractice, Mediation, and Moral Hazard: The Virtues of Dodging the Data Bank, 27 Ohio St. J. on Disp. Resol. 1 (2012). Query whether it is ethically permissible for a plaintiff's lawyer to participate in such a stipulation or motion that neither she nor her client actually believes.

Public outrage following the *Boston Globe*'s investigative reporting led to a 1996 law in Massachusetts requiring the medical licensing board to collect and provide on request information about each complaint against a doctor in which any payment is made to the plaintiff. Well over a dozen other statutes have followed suit, and most require that this information be made available to the public through the Internet. See this casebook's Web site for links, www.health-law.org, and see generally E. Helland, Bargaining in the Shadow of the Website: Disclosure's Impact on Medical Malpractice Litigation, 12 Am. L. & Econ. Rev. 423 (2010); Matthew E. Brown, Redefining the Physician Selection Process and Rewriting Medical Malpractice Settlement Disclosure Webpages, 31 Am. J. L. & Med. 479 (2005). Many commentators view these mandatory reporting requirements as an obstacle to settlement. E.g., William Sage et al., Bridging the Relational-Regulatory Gap: A Pragmatic Information Policy for Patient Safety and Medical Malpractice, 59 Vand. L. Rev. 1263 (2006). But see Helland, supra. At present, the NPDB requires settlements of *any* size to be reported, even those of "nuisance value." Unlike the Massachusetts system, however, the NPDB does not allow public access to this information. Instead, the information is collected only for use by state licensing boards or by medical institutions when they review physicians' competence for licensing or credentialing purposes. Litigants have access only in cases that allege a hospital was negligent in allowing a doctor to use its facilities.

3. *Malpractice Insurance.* One might think that physicians who are repeatedly sued would be put out of business because they could no longer afford their malpractice insurance, much like high-risk automobile drivers. Malpractice insurance, however, is not generally "experience-rated," that is, premiums usually are not set according to each doctor's track record. Instead, premiums are usually adjusted only for the doctor's location and practice specialty. Premiums can vary by as much as fivefold based on location and tenfold based on specialty. See Frank Sloan et al., Insuring Medical Malpractice (1991); William M. Sage, Medical Malpractice Insurance and the Emperor's Clothes, 54 DePaul L. Rev. 463 (2005). For the most part, the lack of a rating system for physicians individually is in keeping with empirical evidence that malpractice claims, on average, are largely unpredictable events. In one study, doctors who were sued in a six-year baseline period had only

a 3 percent chance of being sued in a subsequent three-year period. Randall R. Bovbjerg & Kenneth R. Petronis, The Relationship Between Physicians' Malpractice Claims History and Later Claims, 272 JAMA 1421 (1994). Of course, this does not excuse the failure of physician-owned insurers to do something about the few doctors who are sued and lose repeatedly. Additional discussion about the structure of the medical malpractice insurance market is in section H.

G. INSTITUTIONAL LIABILITY

While most doctors are well insured, some are not; and even those who are do not always make the most attractive targets for suit. Moreover, many medical errors do not result from physicians' mistakes. Therefore, plaintiffs are sometimes eager to hold the institutions in which physicians practice responsible for bad medical outcomes. There are two prominent institutions: hospitals and insurers, especially HMOs. These institutional targets of suit entail both unique theories of liability and unique defenses against liability, which the following sections explore.

You will learn shortly that two distinct theories of liability have emerged: vicarious and direct. In the former, the institution is held strictly liable for acts of negligence by member physicians, based on the physician's relationship with the institution. Observe how this branch of liability takes shape according to differences in how types of physicians are connected with hospitals. Direct liability, the second branch, depends on showing some wrongdoing by the institution's management with respect to physician competence and patient care. Here, the issue is what responsibility is it realistic to assign to lay managers with respect to clinical matters? Overarching this development of legal doctrine is an evolution in judicial and public attitudes about the role that institutions play in the delivery of health care. This change has occurred both with respect to hospital liability and in the migration of liability from hospitals to HMOs. To set these materials in their historical context, then, we begin with a now outmoded but still seminal decision.

1. Hospital Liability

■ SCHLOENDORFF v. SOCIETY OF NEW YORK HOSPITAL
105 N.E. 92 (N.Y. 1914)

CARDOZO, J.

In the year 1771, by royal charter of George III, the Society of the New York Hospital was organized for the care and healing of the sick. During the century and more which has since passed, it has devoted itself to that high task. It has no capital stock; it does not distribute profits; and its physicians and surgeons, both the visiting and the resident staff, serve it without pay. Those who seek it in search of health are charged nothing if they are needy, either for board or for treatment. The well-to-do are required by its by-laws to pay $7 a week for board, an amount insufficient to cover the per capita cost of maintenance. Whatever income is thus received is added to the income derived from the hospital's foundation, and helps to make it possible for the work to go on. The purpose is not profit, but charity. . . .

To this hospital, the plaintiff came in January, 1908. She was suffering from some disorder of the stomach. She asked the superintendent or one of his assistants what the charge would be, and was told that it would be $7 a week. She became an inmate of the hospital, and after some weeks of treatment, the house physician, Dr. Bartlett, discovered a lump, which proved to be a fibroid tumor. He consulted the visiting physician, Dr. Stimson, who advised an operation. The plaintiff's testimony is that the character of the lump could not, so the physicians informed her, be determined without an ether examination. She consented to such an examination, but notified Dr. Bartlett, as she says, that there must be no [surgical removal]. She was taken at night from the medical to the surgical ward and prepared for an operation by a nurse. On the following day ether was administered, and, while she was unconscious, a tumor was removed. Her testimony is that this was done without her consent or knowledge. She is contradicted both by Dr. Stimson and by Dr. Bartlett, as well as by many of the attendant nurses. For the purpose of this appeal, however, since a verdict was directed in favor of the defendant, her narrative, even if improbable, must be taken as true. Following the operation, and, according to the testimony of her witnesses, because of it, gangrene developed in her left arm, some of her fingers had to be amputated, and her sufferings were intense. She now seeks to charge the hospital with liability for the wrong.

Certain principles of law governing the rights and duties of hospitals, when maintained as charitable institutions have, after much discussion, become no longer doubtful. It is the settled rule that such a hospital is not liable for the negligence of its physicians and nurses in the treatment of patients. Hillyer v. St. Bartholomew's Hospital, [1909] 2 K.B. 820. This exemption has been placed upon two grounds. The first is that of implied waiver. It is said that one who accepts the benefit of a charity enters into a relation which exempts one's benefactor from liability for the negligence of his servants in administering the charity. The hospital remains exempt, though the patient makes some payment to help defray the cost of board. Such a payment is regarded as a contribution to the income of the hospital, to be devoted, like its other funds to the maintenance of the charity. The second ground of the exemption is the relation subsisting between a hospital and the physicians who serve it. It is said that this relation is not one of master and servant, but that the physician occupies the position, so to speak, of an independent contractor, following a separate calling, liable, of course, for his own wrongs to the patient whom he undertakes to serve, but involving the hospital in no liability, if due care has been taken in his selection. On one or the other, and often on both of these grounds, a hospital has been held immune from liability to patients for the malpractice of its physicians. The reasons that have led to the adoption of this rule are, of course, inapplicable where the wrong is committed by a servant of the hospital and the sufferer is not a patient. It is therefore also a settled rule that a hospital is liable to strangers—i. e., to persons other than patients—for the torts of its employees committed within the line of their employment.

In the case at hand, the wrong complained of is not merely negligence. It is trespass. Every human being of adult years and sound mind has a right to determine what shall be done with his own body; and a surgeon who performs an operation without his patient's consent commits an assault, for which he is liable in damages. This is true, except in cases of emergency where the patient is unconscious, and where it is necessary to operate before consent can be obtained. The fact that the wrong complained of here is trespass, rather than negligence, distinguishes this case from most of the cases that have preceded it. . . . [The plaintiff] had never waived the right to recover damages for any wrong resulting from this operation, for she had forbidden the operation. In this situation, the true ground for the defendant's exemption from liability is that the relation between a hospital and its physicians is not that of master and servant. The hospital does not undertake to act through them, but merely to procure them to act upon their own responsibility. . . .

The wrong was not that of the hospital; it was that of physicians, who were not the defendant's servants, but were pursuing an independent calling, a profession sanctioned by a solemn oath, and safeguarded by stringent penalties. If, in serving their patient, they violated her commands, the responsibility is not the defendant's; it is theirs. There is no distinction in that respect between the visiting and the resident physicians. Whether the hospital undertakes to procure a physician from afar, or to have one on the spot, its liability remains the same. . . .

It is true, I think, of nurses, as of physicians, that, in treating a patient, they are not acting as the servants of the hospital. The superintendent is a servant of the hospital; the assistant superintendents, the orderlies, and the other members of the administrative staff are servants of the hospital. But nurses are employed to carry out the orders of the physicians, to whose authority they are subject. The hospital undertakes to procure for the patient the services of a nurse. It does not undertake, through the agency of nurses, to render those services itself. The reported cases make no distinction in that respect between the position of a nurse and that of a physician and none is justified in principle. If there are duties performed by nurses foreign to their duties in carrying out the physician's orders, and having relation to the administrative conduct of the hospital, the fact is not established by this record, nor was it in the discharge of such duties that the defendant's nurses were then serving. The acts of preparation immediately preceding the operation are necessary to its successful performance, and are really part of the operation itself. They are not different in that respect from the administration of the ether. Whatever the nurse does in those preliminary stages is done, not as the servant of the hospital, but in the course of the treatment of the patient, as the delegate of the surgeon to whose orders she is subject. The hospital is not chargeable with her knowledge that the operation is improper any more than with the surgeon's.

If, however, it could be assumed that a nurse is a servant of the hospital, . . . [w]as she to infer from the plaintiff's words that a distinguished surgeon intended to mutilate the plaintiff's body in defiance of the plaintiff's orders? Was it her duty, as a result of this talk, to report to the superintendent of the hospital that the ward was about to be utilized for the commission of an assault? I think that no such interpretation of the facts would have suggested itself to any reasonable mind. The preparation for an ether examination is to some extent the same as for an operation. The hour was midnight, and the plaintiff was nervous and excited. . . . There may be cases where a patient ought not to be advised of a contemplated operation until shortly before the appointed hour. To discuss such a subject at midnight might cause needless and even harmful agitation. About such matters a nurse is not qualified to judge. She is drilled to habits of strict obedience. She is accustomed to rely unquestioningly upon the judgment of her superiors. No woman occupying such a position would reasonably infer from the plaintiff's words that it was the purpose of the surgeons to operate whether the plaintiff forbade it or not. I conclude, therefore, that the plaintiff's statements to the nurse on the night before the operation are insufficient to charge the hospital with notice of a contemplated wrong. . . .

The conclusion, therefore, follows that the trial judge did not err in his direction of a verdict. A ruling would, indeed, be an unfortunate one that might constrain charitable institutions, as a measure of self-protection, to limit their activities. A hospital opens its doors without discrimination to all who seek its aid. It gathers in its wards a company of skilled physicians and trained nurses, and places their services at the call of the afflicted, without scrutiny of the character or the worth of those who appeal to it, looking at nothing and caring for nothing beyond the fact of their affliction. In this beneficent work, it does not subject itself to liability for damages, though the ministers of healing whom it has selected have proved unfaithful to their trust.

Notes: Hospital Liability; Charitable and Governmental Immunity

1. Schloendorff. For a fascinating account of the history of this famous case, see Paul Lombardo, Phantom Tumors and Hysterical Women: Revising Our View of the Schloendorff Case, 33 J. L. Med. Ethics 791 (2005). He reveals that the unconsented operation was a hysterectomy.

Is Justice Cardozo's rejection of hospital liability as absolute as it first appears? What about the qualification, "if due care has been taken in [the doctor's] selection"? What if the court were more demanding about the nurse's duty to speak up? Compare these potential theories of liability with those introduced in the modern landmark case of Darling v. Charleston Community Hospital, excerpted at page 439.

2. *Charitable Immunity.* The rule of charitable immunity was subjected to an increasing number of exceptions—distinguishing between paying and nonpaying patients, patients and strangers, and administrative vs. professional acts—until it eventually crumbled in most states. The leading decision is President of Georgetown College v. Hughes, 130 F.2d 810 (D.C. Cir. 1942), which observed that charitable hospitals could simply purchase insurance to protect themselves from economic catastrophe. The gist of this changed attitude is best captured in a colorful dissent by the renowned Pennsylvania Justice Musmanno in Michael v. Hahnemann Medical College and Hospital of Philadelphia, 172 A.2d 769 (Pa. 1961):

> Hospitals then were little better than hovels in which the indigent were gathered for the primitive cures available. The wealthy and the well-to-do were cared for in their homes. The hospital or infirmary was more often than not part of the village parish. Charity in the biblical sense prevailed. And if it happened that some poor mortal was scalded by a sister of mercy, who exhausted from long hours of vigil and toil, accidentally spilled a ladle of hot soup on a hand extended for nourishment, there was no thought of lawsuits against the philanthropists who made the meager refuge possible. But if, following such a mishap, litigation should have been initiated in the courts, it is not difficult to understand why judges would be reluctant to honor such a complaint, convinced on the basis of humanity, that an enterprise utterly devoid of worldly gain should be exempt from liability. A successful lawsuit against such a feeble structure might well have demolished it and have thus paralyzed the only helping hand in the world of unconcern for the rag-clothed sick and the crutchless disabled.

The situation today is quite different. Charitable enterprises are not housed in ramshackle wooden structures. They are not mere storm shelters to succor the traveler and temporarily refuge those stricken in a common disaster. Hospitals today, to a large extent, are mighty edifices, in stone, glass and marble. They maintain large staffs, they use the best equipment that science can devise, they utilize the most modern methods of helping themselves to the noblest purpose of man, that of helping one's stricken brother. But they do all this on a business basis, and properly so. . . . And if the hospital is a business for the purpose of collecting money, it must be a business for the purpose of meeting its obligations. . . .

So be it for hospitals, but what about physician groups? In an unusual but important decision, the Virginia Supreme Court considered whether faculty at the state's premier medical school qualified for charitable immunity. The Court held no, despite the organization's charitable tax exemption, because it operated much more as a normal for-profit business than as a charity. University of Virginia Health Services Foundation v. Morris, Va., 657 S.E.2d 512 (Va. 2008). Despite this shift in attitude, a number of states retain a version of charitable immunity in statutes that limit the amount of damages that can be recovered against nonprofit hospitals or charities generally. See Conners v. Northeast Hospital Corp., 439 Mass. 469 (2003) ($20,000 cap on damages against any charitable corporation protects a hospital in a suit by someone who slipped in its icy parking lot); Annot., 25 A.L.R.4th 517 (1983).

3. *Governmental Immunity.* Public hospitals might also claim governmental immunity under the common-law concept that "the king can do no wrong." See, e.g., Withers v. University of Kentucky, 939 S.W.2d 340 (Ky. 1997) (university hospital is a "state agency" immune from suit). Most states, however, have abrogated governmental immunity to some degree by statute, as has the federal government. This abrogation is often limited, though, to "ministerial" or "proprietary" functions, thus preserving many of the same arcane distinctions that arose under charitable immunity and the *Schloendorff* rule. See, e.g., Moser v. Heistand, 681 A.2d 1322 (Pa. 1996) (immunity exists only for suits based simply on physician error, not for suits based on failures in administration that result in physician error). See generally John Akula, Sovereign Immunity and Health Care: Can Government Be Trusted?, 19(6) Health Aff. 152 (Dec. 2000). Substantial immunity is still common in many states for psychiatric hospitals, and full immunity is still preserved for injuries suffered during the course of active military duty. See Feres v. United States, 340 U.S. 135 (1950). In sharp contrast, Veterans Administration (VA) hospitals are subject by statute to a form of strict liability, without regard to negligence. See Brown v. Gardner, 513 U.S. 113 (1994).

4. *Subsequent Developments in Vicarious Liability.* The refusal to apply ordinary principles of respondeat superior even to employed nurses gave way in later decades to a rule that held the hospital responsible for "administrative" errors, in contrast with errors in medical judgment. What resulted was a string of arcane distinctions and inconsistent decisions concerning such routine medical acts as administering medication, giving injections, and applying casts. For instance, giving a blood transfusion to the wrong patient was considered "administrative," whereas giving the wrong blood to the right patient was labeled an error of medical judgment. See generally Bing v. Thunig, 143 N.E.2d 3 (N.Y. 1957). As will be seen in the next case, these cracks in hospitals' liability armor eventually led to the outright reversal of

Schloendorff by *Bing.* The modern issue, then, becomes how does standard respondeat superior apply to physicians who are not, strictly speaking, employees.

On the modern status of hospital liability generally, see James Smith, Hospital Liability; Mary Bertolet & Lee Goldsmith, Hospital Liability: Law and Practice; Aspen Hospital Law Manual. Documenting a sharp rise in suits against nursing homes, see David G. Stevenson & David M. Studdert, The Rise of Nursing Home Litigation: Findings from a National Survey of Attorneys, 22(2) Health Aff. 219 (Mar. 2003).

■ DIGGS v. NOVANT HEALTH, INC.
628 S.E.2d 851 (N.C. App. 2006)

GEER, Judge.

In September 1999, plaintiff, who was in her early eighties, was diagnosed [with gall stone disease]. . . . Plaintiff chose to have [a surgeon] perform the gall bladder surgery [who] had hospital privileges at Forsyth Medical Center ("FMC") . . . [which] in turn is owned by Novant Health Inc. Plaintiff's gall bladder surgery required general anesthesia. Piedmont Anesthesia & Pain Consultants, P.A. ("Piedmont") had a contract . . . that granted Piedmont the exclusive right to provide anesthesia services at FMC. Piedmont employees Dr. Joseph McConville and nurse Sheila Crumb were responsible for administering anesthesia to plaintiff through an induction and intubation process. Ms. Crumb performed the intubation, which involved inserting a tube into plaintiff's trachea, under the supervision of Dr. McConville. Ms. Crumb made three attempts before successfully completing the intubation. At some point during the attempts, Ms. Crumb perforated plaintiff's esophagus, a fact that was not discovered until many hours after the gall bladder surgery was over. Plaintiff contends that as a result of that perforation, she has suffered severe and permanent injuries.

On 11 October 2002, plaintiff filed suit against not only the hospital defendants, but also Ms. Crumb, Dr. McConville, and Piedmont, . . . [alleging] that the hospital defendants were vicariously liable for the anesthesiology defendants' negligence, as well as the negligence of the hospital floor nurses who, following plaintiff's surgery, failed to immediately notice the perforation. . . . [The trial court granted summary judgment for the hospital defendants.]

A. LIABILITY BASED ON ACTUAL AGENCY

As this Court has held, "[u]nder the doctrine of *respondeat superior,* a hospital is liable for the negligence of a physician or surgeon acting as its agent. There will generally be no vicarious liability on an employer for the negligent acts of an independent contractor." This Court has established that "[t]he vital test in determining whether an agency relationship exists is to be found in the fact that the employer has or has not retained the right of control or superintendence over the contractor or employee as to details." Specifically, the principal must have the right to control *both the means and the details of the process* by which the agent is to accomplish his task in order for an agency relationship to exist.

In arguing that an agency relationship existed, plaintiff relies exclusively on two contracts entered into between Piedmont and FMC: the Anesthesia Agreement and the Anesthesia Services Agreement. The Anesthesia Services Agreement specifically provided, however, that FMC "shall neither have nor exercise any control or direction over the methods by which [Piedmont] or any Physician shall perform it or his work and functions." . . . Further, under the agreements, (1) the physicians associated with Piedmont are not prohibited from practicing outside of the Hospital; (2) Piedmont and the hospital bill patients separately for their respective services; (3) Piedmont is responsible for meeting its own hiring needs; and (4) Piedmont is responsible for managing its own scheduling. . . .

We hold that the provisions in the agreements between Piedmont and FMC are materially indistinguishable from those in . . . *Hoffman v. Moore Reg'l Hosp., Inc.*, 114 N.C. App. 248, 251, 441 S.E.2d 567, 569 (1994) (upholding grant of summary judgment when the physician was a member of a private group, the physician's schedule was determined by the group rather than the hospital, and the patient was billed for the physician's services by the group and not the hospital). . . . Plaintiff has, therefore, failed to present sufficient evidence to establish a *prima facie* case of actual agency.

B. LIABILITY BASED ON APPARENT AGENCY

It is well-established that even in the absence of an agency relationship, "'[w]here a person, by words or conduct, represents or permits it to be represented that another is his agent, he will be estopped to deny the agency as against third persons, who have dealt, on the faith of such representation, with the person so held out as agent, even if no agency exists in fact.'" This doctrine of apparent agency was first considered by our Supreme Court as a basis for hospital liability for malpractice in *Smith v. Duke Univ.*, 14 S.E.2d 643 (NC 1941): . . . [Citing *Schloendorff*, the court rejected both actual and apparent agency on the part of Duke University, even though it employed the doctor in question as a member of its medical school faculty, because he was employed to teach and treat indigent patients, and this patient was seen as part of his private practice, for which the patient paid the doctor separately.] . . .

Our Supreme Court has since recognized that, in the years following *Smith*, the nature of hospitals has substantially changed. After observing that the *Smith* assumptions regarding hospitals were "no longer appropriate in this era," the Court explained: "First of all, hospitals are now in the business of treatment. As stated in [Bing v. Thunig, 143 N.E.2d 3 (NY 1957), which overturned *Schloendorff*]:

> The conception that the hospital does not undertake to treat the patient, does not undertake to act through its doctors and nurses, but undertakes instead simply to procure them to act upon their own responsibility, no longer reflects the fact. Present day hospitals, as their manner of operation plainly demonstrates, do far more than furnish facilities for treatment. They regularly employ on a salary basis a large staff of physicians, nurses and internes [sic], as well as administrative and manual workers, and they charge patients for medical care and treatment, collecting for such services, if necessary, by legal action. Certainly, the person who avails himself of hospital facilities' expects that the hospital will attempt to cure him, not that its nurses or other employees will act on their own responsibility.

In applying the doctrine of apparent agency, courts throughout the country have struggled with this change in the nature of hospitals from institutions providing only facilities to institutions actually providing medical services, such as emergency room care or, as in this case, anesthesia. In *Sword v. NKC Hosps., Inc.*, 714 N.E.2d 142 (Ind. 1999), the Indiana Supreme Court . . . noted that courts have employed apparent agency to hold hospitals liable for the negligence of independent contractors in both emergency room and anesthesia contexts. The court . . . pointed out that some jurisdictions ask whether the plaintiff reasonably believed that the hospital was providing the pertinent medical care, while other jurisdictions presume reliance. Overall, the court concluded that "[c]entral to both of these factors — that is, the hospital's manifestations and the patient's reliance — is the question of whether the hospital provided notice to the patient that the treating physician was an independent contractor and not an employee of the hospital." . . . According to *Sword*, . . . "a hospital generally will be able to avoid liability by providing meaningful written notice to the patient, acknowledged at the time of admission." The court noted, however, that written notice might not suffice if the patient did not have an adequate opportunity to make an informed choice, such as in the case of a medical emergency.

After conducting a similar survey of the development of the law nationwide, the South Carolina Supreme Court also chose to adopt [an apparent agency] approach. *Simmons v. Tuomey Reg'l Med. Ctr.*, 533 S.E.2d 312, 322 (SC 2000). . . . The court limited application of this test "to those situations in which a patient seeks services at the hospital as an institution, and is treated by a physician who reasonably appears to be a hospital employee." It stressed that its holding did "not extend to situations in which the patient is treated in an emergency room by the patient's own physician after arranging to meet the physician there. Nor does our holding encompass situations in which a patient is admitted to a hospital by a private, independent physician whose only connection to a particular hospital is that he or she has staff privileges to admit patients to the hospital. Such patients could not reasonably believe his or her physician is a hospital employee." Comparable tests have been adopted in numerous other jurisdictions, particularly with respect to the rendering of anesthesia or emergency services. . . .

Defendants point to [our prior decision in] *Hoffman* as establishing a different test. . . . Although the plaintiff in *Hoffman*, who was admitted to a hospital at the request of her private physician for a particular procedure, did not choose the doctor who would perform that procedure, the consent form specifically listed five possible doctors and the patient was looking to one of those doctors to provide her care. The case fell squarely within the traditional *Smith* analysis regarding treating physicians. There was no indication in the opinion that the hospital was holding itself out as providing the services involved as opposed to simply providing facilities for the performance of the procedure by private practitioners. Under those circumstances, this Court required evidence "that Mrs. Hoffman would have sought treatment elsewhere or done anything differently had she known for a fact that [the doctor] was not an employee of the hospital."

When, however, a hospital does hold itself out as providing services, we . . . are . . . persuaded by the weight of authority from other jurisdictions. Under this approach, a plaintiff must prove that (1) the hospital has held itself out as providing medical services, (2) the plaintiff looked to the hospital rather than the individual medical provider to perform those services, and (3) the patient accepted those services in the reasonable belief that the services were being rendered by the hospital or by its employees. A hospital may avoid liability by providing meaningful notice to a patient that care is being provided by an independent contractor. *See, e.g., Cantrell v. Northeast Ga. Med. Ctr.*, 235 Ga. App. 365, 368, 508 S.E.2d 716, 719-20 (1998) (concluding that trial court did not err in granting a directed verdict to hospital when "conspicuous signage was posted and forms signed by the patient or representative revealed the independent contractor status of the doctor").

Plaintiff has submitted sufficient evidence to meet this test. The hospital had a Department of Anesthesiology with a Chief of Anesthesiology and a Medical Director, a fact that a jury could reasonably find indicated to the public that FMC was providing anesthesia services to its patients. Further, defendants chose to provide those services by contracting with Piedmont to provide anesthesia services to the hospital on an exclusive basis. Piedmont doctors served as the hospital's Chief of Anesthesiology and anesthesia Medical Director. As Dr. McConville put it, his group "provide[d] the anesthesia services for the operating room at Forsyth." . . . Plaintiff and other surgical patients had no choice as to who would provide anesthesia services for their operations.

Plaintiff's affidavit states that she was unaware that Dr. McConville and Ms. Crumb were not employees of the hospital. . . . In addition, plaintiff pointed to the form on FMC letterhead that she signed entitled "Consent to Operation and/or Other Procedures." The form specified: "I therefore authorize *my physician*, his or her associates or assistants to perform such surgical procedures as they, in the exercise of their professional judgment, deem necessary and advisable." (Emphasis added.) By contrast, with respect to anesthesia services, the form stated: "I authorize the administration of such anesthetics as may be necessary or advisable *by the anesthetist/anesthesiologist responsible for this service and I request the administration of such anesthetics.*" . . . A jury could decide based on this form that plaintiff was, through this form, requesting anesthesia services from FMC and that—given the distinction made between plaintiff's personal physician and the unnamed anesthesiologist—plaintiff was accepting those services in the reasonable belief that the services would be provided by the hospital and its employees. . . .

Given the current record, we hold that the trial court erred in granting summary judgment with respect to plaintiff's claims based on apparent agency. . . . Plaintiff has also argued (1) that the hospital defendants owed plaintiff a non-delegable duty and (2) that the hospital defendants are liable, even apart from agency principles, for the failure to obtain informed consent from plaintiff regarding anesthesia services. . . . [B]ecause of our resolution of this appeal, we need not address these alternative arguments. . . .

Notes: Hospital Vicarious Liability

1. *Employed Physicians.* Under modern law, there is universal agreement that hospitals are vicariously liable for their employed physicians and nurses. Principles of actual agency determine when doctors are hospital agents even when they are not official employees. Notice how the hospital in *Diggs* had carefully arranged its anesthesiology contract to avoid actual agency, following factors specified in an earlier N.C. appellate court decision. But, what about different contracts at other hospitals? In Adamski v. Tacoma General Hospital, 579 P.2d 970 (Wash. App. 1978), the court allowed a jury trial on actual agency for emergency room physicians when the hospital billed patients for their services, among other factors.

2. *Hospital Control.* Is it consistent with the corporate practice of medicine doctrine, discussed in Chapter 10.B.3, to hold a hospital responsible for the professional mistakes of its agent-physicians? The corporate practice of medicine doctrine holds that it is illegal for corporations to subject physicians to the control of lay management because this would constitute the unlicensed practice of medicine. If respondeat superior liability is premised on the principal's control of an agent's actions, how can it coexist with this prohibition of corporate control of physicians? One court, agreeing with this logic, surprisingly held that a health center cannot, as a matter of law, be held responsible for a physician's negligence. Daly v. Aspen Center for Women's Health, 134 P.3d 450 (Colo. App. 2005). Another decision, issued with respect to an HMO, found it necessary to declare the corporate practice of medicine doctrine "totally abolished" in order to hold the HMO vicariously liable for an employed physician's mistake. Sloan v. Metropolitan Health Council of Indianapolis, 516 N.E.2d 1104 (Ind. Ct. App. 1987). The court also reasoned, consistent with other decisions, that respondeat superior does not require actual control but merely a finding that the negligent acts occurred within the course and scope of employment. Otherwise, hospitals could not be held responsible for employed nurses, or airlines for employed pilots. Perhaps based on this thinking, other courts have not found it necessary to abolish the corporate practice of medicine doctrine in order to hold hospitals liable for physicians' errors. See, e.g., McDonald v. Hampton Training School for Nurses, 486 S.E.2d 299 (Va. 1997) (vicarious liability attaches even though hospital does not control actual medical judgment); Dias v. Brigham Medical Associates, Inc., 438 Mass. 317 (2002) (same, for a medical group).

3. *"Captain of the Ship."* One hospital defense against vicarious liability that still remains is the "captain of the ship" or borrowed servant doctrine discussed at page 360. The effect of this doctrine is not only to hold physicians (usually surgeons) responsible for subordinate doctors and nurses, but sometimes also to relieve the hospital from vicarious responsibility. This occurs when a hospital employee's negligent acts are directed or supervised by a physician who is not an agent of the hospital; then, the independent physician can be found to have temporarily "borrowed" the hospital's employee. Courts usually find that the hospital and the physician in charge share the employee and therefore share liability. See, e.g., Tonsic v. Wagner, 329 A.2d 497 (Pa. 1974). However, courts sometimes hold the doctor solely liable if he instructs the nurse to perform an act that contravenes hospital policy. See, e.g., Hoffman v. Wells, 397 S.E.2d 696 (Ga. 1990). See also Restatement (Second) of Agency §227.

4. *Indemnification Agreements.* The principles of vicarious liability introduced here apply to other medical institutions than just hospitals. Materials below explore for instance how vicarious liability applies to HMOs. Earlier, it was observed that physician practice groups or clinics can be held liable as an entity for the negligence of one of their members. It is possible in all of these circumstances, however, to reallocate liability among the parties through the use of indemnification agreements. These agreements do not alter the rights of the injured patient, but they do affect which of several joint tortfeasors can seek contribution or indemnification from the others. Negotiating these indemnification agreements is a major aspect of contract drafting, especially in managed care settings.

5. *Ostensible Agency.* Even though the *Diggs* court claims that facts and circumstances matter, how different would the next case be if the surgical consent form

refers to "*my* anesthesiologist" rather than "*the* anesthesiologists"? Or, what if the hospital were to have patients sign a separate disclaimer form acknowledging that all doctors are independent contractors and not hospital agents? In the emergency room context, most modern courts hold that hospitals are subject to a jury finding of ostensible agency for emergency room physicians regardless of the specifics of the arrangement. The courts' reasoning is reflected in the following cases: Gilbert v. Sycamore Municipal Hospital, 622 N.E.2d 788 (Ill. 1993) (hospital advertising itself as offering quality care contributes to the impression that doctors work for the hospital); Simmons v. Tuomey Regional Medical Center, 533 S.E.2d 312 (S.C. 2000) (patient did not specifically choose any of the emergency room physicians that treated her); Whitlow v. Rideout Memorial Hospital, 237 Cal. App. 4th 631 (2015) (disclaimer of agency in admission form and on wall signs may not have been adequate notice for patient in excruciating pain). To the contrary, see Frezados v. Ingalls Memorial Hosp., 991 N.E.2d 817 IIll. App. 2013) ("Nearly everyone who seeks emergency treatment is in some physical or emotional distress, and were we to hold that such distress could operate to nullify provisions in an otherwise duly signed treatment consent form, hospitals would always be required to proceed to trial on claims of vicarious liability.").

In non-emergency contexts like that in *Diggs*, where ostensible agency is applied to hospital-based specialists such as radiologists and anesthesiologists, some courts are more open to argument both ways, depending on the facts and circumstances. See, e.g., Milliron v. Francke, 793 P.2d 824 (Mont. 1990) (providing radiologist with office, equipment, personnel, and billing is not sufficient to establish agency relationship; in a rural setting, it is understood this is necessary to maintain adequate staffing). However, most courts find their way to allowing the case to go to trial. E.g., Burless v. West Virginia University Hospitals, Inc., 601 S.E.2d 85 (W. Va. 2004) (disclaimer in a consent form was not sufficient to inform patient giving birth that university physicians were not hospital employees); Sword v. NKC Hospitals, 714 N.E.2d 142 (Ind. 1999) (anesthesiologist could be found to be an apparent agent of a hospital that "aggressively marketed its services to the public . . . [as] 'the most technically sophisticated birthplace in the region' and touted the 'full availability of a special anesthesiology team, experienced and dedicated exclusively to OB patients'"); York v. Rush-Presbyterian-St. Luke's Medical Center, 854 N.E.2d 635 (Ill. 2006) (similar, based on 28-page analysis of detailed testimony, even for a patient who himself was a surgeon and who picked most of his own doctors).

6. *Office-Based Physicians.* Do you think the ostensible agency doctrine could apply to specialists who are not entirely hospital based, such as surgeons or consultants referred by a patient's primary care physician? After all, hospitals also have departments of cardiology and surgery, and patients often do not pick their own surgeons or cardiologists (for instance, if their heart or surgical problem develops while they're in the hospital for a different problem, or if they enter the hospital through the emergency room before being transferred to a regular hospital room). So far, only Puerto Rico courts have not gone this far, holding hospitals vicariously liable whenever a patient "goes directly to the hospital seeking medical aid and the hospital 'provides' the physicians who treat him [or her], . . . because [then] the patient has entrusted his or her health to the hospital." Casillas-Sanchez v. Ryder Memorial Hosp., 960 F.Supp.2d 362 (D.P.R. 2013). In contrast, this court held that the hospital cannot be held vicariously liable "when the patient has first

gone directly to the physician's private office and then is treated at the hospital on the physician's recommendation merely because said institution is one of several which the physician has the privilege of using." At present, this is a distinctly minority position, but a few other courts appear willing to expand vicarious liability to any situation where "a patient seeks treatment from a hospital and not from a particular physician of the patient's choosing." Syracuse v. Diao, 707 N.Y.S.2d 570 (App. Div. 2000) (allowing case to go to trial where a patient simply called a specialized surgery center to request an appointment but did not ask for a particular physician).

7. *Enterprise Liability.* Notice the *Diggs* court's brief mention at the end of an argument based on "non-delegable duty," also known as "enterprise liability." This concept would hold hospitals automatically liable for all acts of negligence, either within particular departments or for all physicians within their walls, regardless of the specifics of actual or apparent agency—even if the doctor is conceded to be an obvious independent contractor. The rationale for a nondelegable duty is that the public policy supporting hospital responsibility is so strong that, as a matter of law, the hospital may not avoid responsibility by delegating the function to an independent contractor. The classic example is an airline that attempts to shield itself from liability by retaining pilots as independent contractors.

So far, this nondelegable duty concept has been applied in only a few cases and only to emergency room care. The leading case is Jackson v. Power, 743 P.2d 1376 (Alaska 1987). Based on hospital licensing statutes and Joint Commission accreditation standards, the court observed that the hospital had assumed a duty to ensure adequate emergency room services. The court then concluded that a hospital "may not shield itself from liability by claiming that it is not responsible for the results of negligently performed health care when the law imposes a duty on the hospital to provide that health care. . . . We simply cannot fathom why liability should depend upon the technical employment status of the emergency room physician who treats the patient." Is this reasoning necessarily limited to emergency room care? So far, this is as far as courts have taken it. See Fletcher v. South Peninsula Hospital, 71 P.3d 833 (Alaska 2003) (refusing to extend the doctrine to surgeons).

8. *The Next Stage.* Falling between vicarious liability for some physicians and enterprise liability for all physicians is a position known as "direct institutional liability," in which hospitals are held liable even for acts of independent physicians, but only if the hospital management breached a duty of care owed directly to patients with respect to selecting or supervising the physician. That theory of liability is thought to have been introduced by the next case. See if you can discern in this case a major shift in liability, or instead whether its holding rests on a more conventional application of vicarious liability. To the extent it presages a new duty of hospitals, precisely what is the content of that duty?

■ DARLING v. CHARLESTON COMMUNITY MEMORIAL HOSPITAL
211 N.E.2d 253 (Ill. 1965), cert. denied, 383 U.S. 946 (1966)

SCHAEFER, Justice.

. . . On November 5, 1960, the plaintiff, who was 18 years old, broke his leg while playing in a college football game. He was taken to the emergency room at the defendant hospital where Dr. Alexander, who was on emergency call that day, treated him. Dr. Alexander, with the assistance of hospital personnel, applied traction and placed the leg in a plaster cast. A heat cradle was applied to dry the cast. Not long after the application of the cast plaintiff was in great pain and his toes, which protruded from the cast, became swollen and dark in color. They eventually became cold and insensitive. On the evening of November 6, Dr. Alexander "notched" the cast around the toes, and on the afternoon of the next day he cut the cast approximately three inches up from the foot. On November 8, he split the sides of the cast with a Stryker saw; in the course of cutting the cast the plaintiff's leg was cut on both sides. Blood and other seepage were observed by the nurses and others, and there was a stench in the room, which one witness said was the worst he had smelled since World War II. The plaintiff remained in Charleston Hospital until November 19, when he was transferred to Barnes Hospital in St. Louis and placed under the care of Dr. Fred Reynolds, head of orthopedic surgery at Washington University School of Medicine and Barnes Hospital. Dr. Reynolds found that the fractured leg contained a considerable amount of dead tissue which in his opinion resulted from interference with the circulation of blood in the limb caused by swelling or hemorrhaging of the leg against the construction of the cast. Dr. Reynolds performed several operations in a futile attempt to save the leg but ultimately it had to be amputated eight inches below the knee.

The evidence before the jury is set forth at length in the opinion of the Appellate Court and need not be stated in detail here. The plaintiff contends that it established that the defendant was negligent in permitting Dr. Alexander to do orthopedic work of the kind required in this case, and not requiring him to review his operative procedures to bring them up to date; in failing, through its medical staff, to exercise adequate supervision over the case, especially since Dr. Alexander had been placed on emergency duty by the hospital, and in not requiring consultation, particularly after complications had developed. Plaintiff contends also that in a case which developed as this one did, it was the duty of the nurses to watch the protruding toes constantly for changes of color, temperature and movement, and to check circulation every ten to twenty minutes, whereas the proof showed that these things were done only a few times a day. Plaintiff argues that it was the duty of the hospital staff to see that these procedures were followed, and that either the nurses were derelict in failing to report developments in the case to the hospital administrator, he was derelict in bringing them to the attention of the medical staff, or the staff was negligent in failing to take action. Defendant is a licensed and accredited hospital, and the plaintiff contends that the licensing regulations, accreditation standards, and its own bylaws define the hospital's duty, and that an infraction of them imposes liability for the resulting injury.

The defendant's position is stated in the following excerpts from its brief:

> It is a fundamental rule of law that only an individual properly educated and licensed, and not a corporation, may practice medicine. . . . Accordingly, a hospital is powerless under the law to forbid or command any act by a physician or surgeon in the practice of his profession. . . . A hospital is not an insurer of the patient's recovery, but only owes the patient the duty to exercise such reasonable care as his known condition requires and that degree of care, skill and diligence used by hospitals generally in that community. . . . Where the evidence shows that the hospital care was in accordance with standard practice obtaining in similar hospitals, and

Plaintiff produces no evidence to the contrary, the jury cannot conclude that the opposite is true even if they disbelieve the hospital witnesses. . . . A hospital is not liable for the torts of its nurse committed while the nurse was but executing the orders of the patient's physician, unless such order is so obviously negligent as to lead any reasonable person to anticipate that substantial injury would result to the patient from the execution of such order. . . . The extent of the duty of a hospital with respect to actual medical care of a professional nature such as is furnished by a physician is to use reasonable care in selecting medical doctors. When such care in the selection of the staff is accomplished, and nothing indicates that a physician so selected is incompetent or that such incompetence should have been discovered, more cannot be expected from the hospital administration.

The basic dispute, as posed by the parties, centers upon the duty that rested upon the defendant hospital. That dispute involves the effect to be given to . . . hospital regulations adopted by the State Department of Public Health under the Hospital Licensing Act, to the Standards for Hospital Accreditation of the American Hospital Association, and to the bylaws of the defendant. . . .

The conception that the hospital does not undertake to treat the patient, does not undertake to act through its doctors and nurses, but undertakes instead simply to procure them to act upon their own responsibility, no longer reflects the fact. Present-day hospitals, as their manner of operation plainly demonstrates, do far more than furnish facilities for treatment. They regularly employ on a salary basis a large staff of physicians, nurses and internes, as well as administrative and manual workers, and they charge patients for medical care and treatment, collecting for such services, if necessary, by legal action. Certainly, the person who avails himself of "hospital facilities" expects that the hospital will attempt to cure him, not that its nurses or other employees will act on their own responsibility. (Fuld, J., in Bing v. Thunig (1957), 2 N.Y.2d 656, 163 N.Y.S.2d 3, 11, 143 N.E.2d 3, 8.)

The Standards for Hospital Accreditation, the state licensing regulations and the defendant's bylaws demonstrate that the medical profession and other responsible authorities regard it as both desirable and feasible that a hospital assume certain responsibilities for the care of the patient.

We now turn to an application of these considerations to this case. . . . [W]e need not analyze all of the issues submitted to the jury. Two of them were that the defendant had negligently:

5. Failed to have a sufficient number of trained nurses for bedside care of all patients at all times capable of recognizing the progressive gangrenous condition of the plaintiff's right leg, and of bringing the same to the attention of the hospital administration and to the medical staff so that adequate consultation could have been secured and such conditions rectified; . . .

7. Failed to require consultation with or examination by members of the hospital surgical staff skilled in such treatment; or to review the treatment rendered to the plaintiff and to require consultants to be called in as needed.

We believe that the jury verdict [against the hospital] is supportable on either of these grounds. On the basis of the evidence before it the jury could reasonably have concluded that the nurses did not test for circulation in the leg as frequently as necessary, that skilled nurses would have promptly recognized the conditions that signalled a dangerous impairment of circulation in the plaintiff's leg, and would have known that the condition would become irreversible in a matter of hours. At that point, it became the nurses' duty to inform the attending physician, and if he failed to act, to advise the hospital authorities so that appropriate action might be taken. As to consultation, there is no dispute that the hospital failed to review Dr. Alexander's work or require a consultation; the only issue is whether its failure to do so was negligence. On the evidence before it the jury could reasonably have found that it was. . . .

Judgment affirmed.

■ JOHNSON v. MISERICORDIA COMMUNITY HOSPITAL
301 N.W.2d 156 (Wis. 1981)

COFFEY, Justice.

. . . This action arose out of a surgical procedure performed at Misericordia by Dr. Salinsky on July 11, 1975, in which he unsuccessfully attempted to remove a pin fragment from Johnson's right hip. During the course of this surgery, the plaintiff's common femoral nerve and artery were damaged causing a permanent paralytic condition of his right thigh muscles with resultant atrophy and weakness and loss of function. . . .

[T]he jury found that Salinsky was negligent with respect to the medical care and treatment he afforded the plaintiff and attributed 20 percent of the causal negligence to him and 80 percent to the hospital. . . . [T]he only facts material to this review are those connected with Misericordia Hospital in appointing Dr. Salinsky to the medical staff with orthopedic privileges.

The record establishes that Misericordia was formerly . . . a nursing home known as Downtown Nursing Home, Inc. Subsequently, . . . all of the nursing home services were discontinued and the name "Misericordia Community Hospital" was adopted. The hospital known as Misericordia Community Hospital was not and has not been accredited by the Joint Commission on Accreditation of Hospitals. . . .

Dr. Salinsky applied for orthopedic privileges on the medical staff. In his application, Salinsky stated that . . . his privileges at other hospitals had never "been suspended, diminished, revoked, or not renewed." In another part of the application form, he failed to answer any of the questions pertaining to his malpractice insurance. . . .

Mrs. Jane Bekos, Misericordia's medical staff coordinator (appointed April of 1973), testifying from the hospital records, noted that Salinsky's appointment to the medical staff was recommended by the then hospital administrator, David A. Scott, Sr., on June 22, 1973. Salinsky's appointment and requested orthopedic privileges, according to the hospital records, were not marked approved until August 8, 1973. This approval of his appointment was endorsed by Salinsky himself. Such approval would, according to accepted medical administrative procedure, not be signed by the applicant but by the chief of the respective medical section. Additionally, the record establishes that Salinsky was elevated to the position of Chief of Staff shortly after he joined the medical staff. However, the court record and the hospital records are devoid of any information concerning the procedure utilized by the

Misericordia authorities in approving either Salinsky's appointment to the staff with orthopedic privileges, or his elevation to the position of Chief of Staff.

Mrs. Bekos, testified that . . . she failed to contact any of the references in Salinsky's case. . . . Further, Mrs. Bekos stated that an examination of the Misericordia records reflected that at no time was an investigation made by anyone of any of the statements recited in his application. . . .

Dr. A. Howell, the hospital's medical director, stated that the hospital did not have a functioning credentials committee at this time, and therefore the executive committee . . . assume[d] the responsibility of evaluating and approving applications for medical staff privileges. . . . [T]he minutes of [the June 21st] meeting list Salinsky as an attending member of the defendant's medical staff at the meeting despite the fact that Salinsky's application for staff privileges had neither been recommended for approval, nor approved by the committee as of this date. . . .

At trial, the representatives of two Milwaukee hospitals, . . . gave testimony concerning the accepted procedure for evaluating applicants for medical staff privileges. Briefly, they stated that the hospital's governing body, i.e., the board of directors or board of trustees, has the ultimate responsibility in granting or denying staff privileges. However, the governing board delegates the responsibility of evaluating the professional qualifications of an applicant for clinical privileges to the medical staff. The credentials committee (or committee of the whole) conducts an investigation of the applying physician's or surgeon's education, training, health, ethics and experience through contacts with his peers in the specialty in which he is seeking privileges, as well as the references listed in his application to determine the veracity of his statements and to solicit comments dealing with the applicant's credentials. Once the credentials committee (or committee of the whole) has conducted their investigation and reviewed all of the information bearing on the applicant's qualifications, it relays its judgment to the governing body, which, as noted, has the final appointing authority.

The record demonstrates that had the executive committee of Misericordia, in the absence of a current credentials committee, adhered to the standard and accepted practice of investigating a medical staff applicant's qualifications and thus examined Salinsky's degree, postgraduate training, and contacted the hospitals referred to in his application, it would have found, contrary to his representations, that he had in fact experienced denial and restriction of his privileges, as well as never having been granted privileges at the very same hospitals he listed in his application. This information was readily available to Misericordia, and a review of Salinsky's associations with various Milwaukee orthopedic surgeons and hospital personnel would have revealed that they considered Salinsky's competence as an orthopedic surgeon suspect, and viewed it with a great deal of concern. . . .

[W]e hold that a hospital has a duty to exercise due care in the selection of its medical staff. . . . [O]ur holding is supported by the decisions of a number of courts from other jurisdictions. See . . . Annot., 51 A.L.R.3d 981 (1973). These cases hold that a hospital has a direct and independent responsibility to its patients, over and above that of the physicians and surgeons practicing therein, to take reasonable steps to (1) insure that its medical staff is qualified for the privileges granted and/or (2) to evaluate the care provided. . . .

The resolution of the issue of whether the hospital was negligent in granting Salinsky orthopedic surgical privileges and appointing him to its medical staff depends on whether Misericordia exercised that degree of care and skill as the average hospital exercises in selecting its medical staff. Applying this standard to the facts of this case, Johnson was only required to show that the defendant did not exercise reasonable care (that degree of care ordinarily exercised by the average hospital) to determine whether Salinsky was competent. . . . Therefore, the trial court's instruction that the hospital was required to exercise reasonable care in the granting of medical staff privileges and that reasonable care "meant that degree of care, skill and judgment usually exercised under like or similar circumstances by the average hospital," was proper.

Turning to the plaintiff's proof requirements, since the procedures ordinarily employed by hospitals in evaluating applications for staff privileges are not within the realm of the ordinary experience of mankind, we agree with the ruling of the appellate court that expert testimony was required to prove the same. . . .

There was credible evidence to the effect that a hospital, exercising ordinary care, would not have appointed Salinsky to its medical staff. Mr. Harden, administrator for Family Hospital, testified a hospital governing board with knowledge that an applicant for medical staff privileges had his orthopedic surgical privileges revoked at one hospital, on the recommendation of a panel of three orthopedic surgeons, and that his orthopedic privileges at another hospital were confined to simple operative procedures, would not, on the basis of this information, have granted him surgical privileges in that specialty. Dr. Sam Neeseman stated that a hospital's credentials committee, with knowledge of such events would not, in the exercise of ordinary care, have approved the applicant's request for orthopedic privileges. . . . Thus, the jury's finding of negligence on the part of Misericordia must be upheld as the testimony of Mr. Harden and Dr. Neeseman constituted credible evidence which reasonably supports this finding. . . .

[A]lthough [a hospital] must rely on the medical staff and in particular the credentials committee (or committee of the whole) to investigate and evaluate an applicant's qualifications for the requested privileges, . . . this delegation of the responsibility to investigate and evaluate the professional competence of applicants for clinical privileges does not relieve the governing body of its duty to appoint only qualified physicians and surgeons to its medical staff and periodically monitor and review their competency. . . . The facts of this case demonstrate that a hospital should, at a minimum, require completion of the application and verify the accuracy of the applicant's statements, especially in regard to his medical education, training and experience. Additionally, it should: (1) solicit information from the applicant's peers, including those not referenced in his application, who are knowledgeable about his education, training, experience, health, competence and ethical character; (2) determine if the applicant is currently licensed to practice in this state and if his licensure or registration has been or is currently being challenged; and (3) inquire whether the applicant has been involved in any adverse malpractice action and whether he has experienced a loss of medical organization membership or medical privileges or membership at any other hospital. The investigating committee must also evaluate the information gained through its inquiries and make a reasonable judgment as to the approval or denial of each application for staff privileges. The hospital will be charged with gaining and evaluating the knowledge that would have been acquired had it exercised ordinary care in investigating its medical staff applicants. . . . This is not to say that hospitals are insurers of the competence of their medical staff, for a hospital will not be negligent if it exercises the noted standard of care in selecting its staff.

Notes: Hospitals' Direct Liability; Risk Management Programs

1. *Direct vs. Vicarious Liability. Darling* is undoubtedly the most significant hospital liability case in the past 50 years. It is frequently referred to as a landmark decision in the field of hospital liability because it placed at least some degree of direct responsibility on the hospital for the maintenance of an acceptable standard of care of patients. Direct or "corporate" liability contrasts with vicarious liability in that it imposes on hospitals a duty of care owed directly to patients with respect to medical judgment. Conventional forms of direct liability entail primarily administrative, not medical, functions such as maintaining safe premises, sterile equipment, and adequate rules and regulations. *Darling* is recognized as extending direct corporate liability to substandard medical care rendered by independent doctors. Hospitals thus can be found liable for some act of negligence on their part with respect to patient care decisions made by independent doctors; vicarious liability, on the other hand, attaches regardless of the degree of hospital care but only when doctors are actual or apparent agents.

2. *Darling's Progeny.* Consider whether the *Darling* court actually intended to announce a new theory of liability. How else could the case have been reasoned, using principles from the previous case and notes? Commentators have observed that *Darling* achieved its status largely by virtue of the importance that academic commentators and subsequent decisions attached to it, and the vocal reaction of hospitals and physicians. The leading commentator was health law professor Arthur Southwick, in The Hospital's New Responsibility, 17 Clev.-Marshall L. Rev. 146 (1968); and The Hospital as an Institution — Expanding Responsibilities Change Its Relationship with the Staff Physician, 9 Cal. W. L. Rev. 429 (1973). See generally Annot., 62 A.L.R. 4th 692 (1988).

3. *Enterprise Liability and the Balance of Power.* What reaction to *Darling* would you expect from the medical profession and the hospital industry? Surprisingly, *Darling* was openly embraced by hospitals but vehemently attacked by physicians. It greatly influenced the standards of the Joint Commission and virtually became the official philosophy of the American Hospital Association. The AMA's reaction to the *Darling* decision was immediate and negative. In considering why this would be so, consider what *Darling* signals about the power relationship between hospitals and physicians. Would it be fair to impose hospital responsibility for patient care without allowing hospital authority? In its comment on the case in 12 Citation 82 (1965), the AMA said, "The effect of this decision is unfortunate since it appears to place a hospital in a position where it must exercise control over the practice of medicine by physicians on its attending staff in order to avoid liability. This is apt to encourage control of the practice of medicine by persons who are not licensed physicians."

A similar reaction occurred in 1993 when President Clinton's health care reform task force aired an idea for medical malpractice reform known as exclusive enterprise liability. As discussed at pages 465 and 491, exclusive enterprise liability would change existing law in two ways: (1) it would hold hospitals and HMOs vicariously liable for all negligent injuries caused by any member physician, regardless of status or contractual relationship with the institution; and (2) the institution would be solely liable, letting doctors entirely off the hook. Surprisingly, the hospital industry was interested in this idea but the AMA vehemently opposed it, causing the Clinton administration to quickly back away. Even though the AMA was clamoring for relief from medical malpractice, it viewed this proposal for abolishing physician liability as a Trojan Horse because of its implications for the relative power balance between doctors and medical institutions. See Frances Miller, Malpractice Liability and Physician Autonomy, 342 Lancet 973 (1993); Robert A. Berenson, Do Physicians Recognize Their Own Best Interests?, 13(2) Health Aff. 185 (1994).

Despite this hostility, some HMOs, most teaching hospitals, and virtually all government hospitals implement a de facto form of exclusive enterprise liability in which the institution pays for the physicians' malpractice insurance (usually as part of its own self-insured retention fund), defends all suits, and pays all judgments for claims arising from treatment at the institution. Reinforcing the policy argument in favor of a more general form of hospital enterprise liability, recall the readings at pages 276 and 281 explaining that many medical errors in hospitals are due to flaws in the system of care rather than purely individual physician mistakes, but that hospitals lack a sufficient "business case" to improve patient safety because they internalize only a small percentage of the costs of medical error. See also Michelle M. Mello et al., Who Pays for Medical Errors? An Analysis of Adverse Event Costs, the Medical Liability System, and Incentives for Patient Safety Improvement, 4 J. Empirical Legal Stud. 835 (2007).

For these reasons, most legal scholars strongly favor broader hospital enterprise liability. See, e.g., Kenneth Abraham & Paul Weiler, Enterprise Liability and the Evolution of the American Health Care System, 108 Harv. L. Rev. 381 (1994); Barry Furrow, Patient Safety and the Fiduciary Hospital, 1 Drexel L. Rev. 439 (2009); Philip G. Peters, Resuscitating Hospital Enterprise Liability, 73 Mo. L. Rev. 369-397 (2008).

4. *Duty to Supervise and Nursing Negligence. Darling* and its progeny identify two forms of hospital negligence with respect to physicians: negligent selection and retention, and negligent supervision. The first of these, which is developed in Johnson v. Misericordia Community Hospital, is much less controversial. Observe that it was recognized in passing even in *Schloendorff,* supra. It entails reviewing physicians' competency and performance history before admission to the medical staff and periodically (typically every two years) thereafter. Surprisingly, however, one modern court has refused to recognize a tort for negligent credentialing, reasoning that regulatory oversight of hospitals suffices. Paulino v. QHG of Springdale, Inc., 386 S.W.3d 462 (Ark. 2012).

The duty to supervise, in contrast, assumes *contemporaneous* supervision of daily treatment decisions *as they are made.* Several subsequent decisions have alluded to this duty of contemporaneous supervision, but few have squarely imposed it, distinct from the duty of care in selection and retention. Indeed, subsequent decisions in Illinois have expressly disavowed any such duty arising from *Darling.* See Essig v. Advocate BroMenn Medical Center, 33 N.E.3d 288 (Ill. App. Ct. 2015) ("the only logical inference from [plaintiffs'] argument is that [the hospital] should have appointed . . . a fully trained and licensed urologist to oversee [the surgeon] . . . and to veto the allegedly negligent course of treatment . . . . Of course, the law does not impose such a duty on hospitals").

Other courts, however, have rather explicitly imposed such a duty of active supervision, at least in dictum. See, e.g., Thompson v. Nason Hospital, 591 A.2d 703 (Pa. 1991). Usually, these are cases of gross negligence in which the departure from medical standards is so blatant that it is possible to attribute to hospital administrators' constructive knowledge of the error in progress. One route for attributing this knowledge is through nurses, under the logic that, at some point, nurses should object to or call to a supervisor's attention treatment that is going extremely badly. Because nurses are hospital employees, this theory essentially holds hospitals vicariously liable for nurses' failure to speak up or intervene. See Strubhart v. Perry Memorial Hospital, 903 P.2d 263 (Okla. 1995); T. Hardy, 61 Tul. L. Rev. 86 (1986) (the test under *Darling* should be "whether in a given situation a reasonable, prudent nurse would have spoken up about a physician's negligence"). Is this explanation consistent with the facts in *Darling*? Is it consistent with the practical realities of the doctor-nurse relationship? Recall Justice Cardozo's treatment of this very same theory of liability in *Schloendorff*, supra. See also Essig v. Advocate, supra ("it would be entirely inconsistent with both the scope of nursing practice and the applicable standard of care for an attending nurse to attempt to interfere with a surgeon, *in the midst of an ongoing surgery*").

5. *Risk Management.*

The newly created role in hospitals of "risk manager" marks the official recognition of a role that has become central to the way hospitals are run. Their role is clearly defined . . . "to avoid or minimize potential legal, and hence, financial loss for the health care provider." Although they may fulfill several different administrative functions, . . . I contend that current risk management practices in hospitals have risen to a pitch of near hysteria. They embody actions that are unprecedented in their intrusiveness into the doctor-patient relationship and are unethical in violating the rights of patients. . . . The typical responses of risk managers are wildly overactive. If people in ordinary life were to act in accordance with the minuscule probabilities on which risk management bases its decisions, we would all be in a constant state of paralysis. . . . Hospital administrators have refused to permit competent adult patients to reject burdensome treatment even when physicians concur with the patient's wish. It is not uncommon for administrators to request that a court order be obtained whenever there is a shred of doubt (which almost always exists) about what the law says. Where it was once physicians who overtreated patients because they believed it was their moral obligation to continue therapy, it is now hospital administrators and risk managers who more often insist on overtreatment out of fear of medical-legal liability. It is not a great exaggeration to view risk managers as enemies of patients. . . .

Who are these risk managers, and what is the origin of their role in the hospital? Some risk managers have law degrees, but most do not. Some are nurses who rose to the rank of supervisor and then moved into hospital administration, often after obtaining a master's degree. Others come from the ranks of hospital administrators, some with a degree in hospital or business administration. More rare are individuals with an advanced degree in a field such as sociology, and still others made their career in health planning or administration and were around long before the occupation of risk manager was invented. Large medical centers typically have an office of risk management in addition to in-house counsel. The staff of lawyers works together with risk management both in devising hospital policies that affect patients and in dealing with individual cases in which anyone suspects that there may be a risk of some sort.

The overall movement can be traced back to the late 1960s and early 1970s, when efforts were begun in industrial and other workplaces to reduce the costs of liability payments by underwriters and insurance companies. The trend widened, and in the 1980s risk management offices began to be established in hospitals . . . to deal with concerns about possible liability arising out of incident reports in the hospital: a patient falling out of bed, a visitor slipping in a puddle of water in the corridor, an inadvertent injury to a patient in the course of treatment. . . . The original worries about legal liability have now expanded to encompass everything that might place the hospital in a bad light. Risk managers are now charged with the task of minimizing risks other than those of liability. They look out for the projected risks of bad publicity, the actions of a disgruntled employee, or the possible political ramifications of a medical decision or hospital policy. . . . Even when the patient has no family, and there is no one around who would sue the hospital, risk management is brought into the case. One of the peculiar features of this situation is the nearly automatic response by many physicians to call risk management whenever the slightest uncertainty is voiced about an ethical matter or vaguely perceived to have legal implications. . . .

Ruth Macklin, Enemies of Patients (1993). Does this account confirm the fears of the AMA about the consequences for physicians of exposing hospitals to liability?

Hospitals are now required to have risk management programs by Joint Commission accreditation standards, and, in a few states, by hospital licensing laws. Risk management programs are now common also in nursing homes and HMOs. On their structure and content generally, see American Society for Healthcare Risk Management, Risk Management Handbook for Health Care Facilities (1990); B. Youngberg, Essentials of Hospital Risk Management (1990).

6. *Informed Consent Liability.* One form of physician supervision for which courts have been especially reluctant to impose hospital liability is the duty to obtain informed consent. One might suppose that it easily falls within the hospital's administrative functions to ensure that patients have signed the proper paperwork before major operations are conducted, especially since nurses usually have a central role in obtaining informed consent. Most courts, however, hold that informed consent is solely the responsibility of the physician because the delicate considerations of what exactly to tell the patient and when are matters "particularly calling for the exercise of medical judgment." Valles v. Albert Einstein Medical Center, 805 A.2d 1232 (Pa. 2002) (no liability even for employed physician because "a medical facility cannot maintain control over this aspect of the physician-patient relationship"). For a critique, see Robert Gatter, The Mysterious Survival of the Policy Against Informed Consent Liability for Hospitals, 81 Notre Dame L. Rev. 1203 (2006); Note, 1 Ind. Health L. Rev. 253 (2004).

7. *Self-Imposed Standards.* The hospital licensing regulations, accreditation standards, and hospital bylaws referred to in the *Darling* opinion contained statements such as the following:

[REGULATIONS]

The [hospital] board [of directors] shall be responsible for the maintenance of proper standards of professional work in the hospital and shall require that the medical staff function in conformity with reasonable standards of competency. . . .

[ACCREDITATION STANDARDS]

Maintaining high standards of medical care will depend upon the character of the [medical] staff and the effectiveness of its organization to carry out the following duties: 1. Selection of those recommended for staff appointments and hospital privileges. 2. Constant analysis and review of the clinical work done in the hospital. . . . It is the duty of the hospital [medical] staff through its chiefs of service and Executive Committee to see that members of the staff do not fail in the matter of calling consultants as needed.

[MEDICAL STAFF BYLAWS]

The purpose of this organization shall be to insure that all patients admitted to the hospital or treated in the outpatient department receive the best possible care.

Another important aspect of the court's holding is that standards such as these, to which the hospital subscribed or was bound, can be introduced as evidence, but not conclusive proof, of the customary standard of administrative care that prevails in the hospital industry. See also the discussion at page 345 of practice guidelines and other written standards used to establish the medical standard of care against physicians. Is the effect of these standards to make a hospital strictly liable for any mistakes that doctors make? How would you revise these standards in order to perform their intended function in these various legal documents while at the same time moderating their liability effect?

8. *Hospital Custom.* Most courts hold hospitals to a national standard of care in selecting medical staff members. Would a similar locality standard be more appropriate? Consider the history and accreditation status of Misericordia Community Hospital, which was a very small hospital with relatively few medical staff. Under the national standard, are these factors relevant to the "like or similar circumstances" qualifier? See Note, 1983 Wis. L. Rev. 453 (arguing that the *Misericordia* standards are too demanding for some hospitals). Observe, though, that the duty to fully investigate physicians' credentials is greatly eased now that hospitals can obtain records of past malpractice lawsuits and disciplinary actions by other hospitals from the National Practitioner Data Bank, described at page 425.

Hospital negligence cases are not as dependent on expert witnesses as are physician negligence cases, despite the *Johnson* court's holding on this point. Once the issue of physician negligence is established, issues of administrative care and proper oversight are subject to the "reasonable person" standard. Other courts sometimes hold that these issues are subject to commonsense understanding. If you were on a jury, would you consider a hospital negligent if it approved a physician who had been sued for malpractice three times in the past five years? If he had lost or settled two of the three suits for substantial amounts?

9. *Medical Staff Committees.* Observe the brief discussion at the end of *Johnson* concerning the legal effect of the hospital's delegating the task of medical staff credentialing to members and committees of the medical staff. Recall that medical staff members are, generally speaking, not agents of the hospital. Therefore, could a hospital not claim in a typical case, where it merely follows the medical staff's recommendation, that it is not responsible for their sloppiness or poor judgment? Assume the hospital board has no way to know that the medical staff did a poor job or made a bad decision. This defense does not work for two reasons: (1) Although medical

staff members are independent contractors in their medical status as practicing doctors, they are agents of the hospital in their administrative status while sitting on medical staff committees. Therefore, ordinary respondeat superior applies to their committee mistakes. (2) The duty to screen medical staff members is considered nondelegable.

Distributing liability in the opposite direction, would it be possible to hold medical staff members individually liable for doing a poor job in evaluating an applicant? Alternatively, could the medical staff be held liable as an entity? In practice, physicians are not individually exposed since hospitals usually assume responsibility for liability arising from medical staff review activities. See generally J. Horty & D. Mulholland, The Legal Status of the Hospital Medical Staff, 22 St. Louis U. L. J. 485 (1978).

10. *Puzzles to Ponder.* In *Johnson,* the jury found Dr. Salinsky negligent. Is this necessary to hold the hospital liable for its own negligence? If a hospital negligently admits a bad doctor to the medical staff, shouldn't it be liable for any injury the doctor causes, under the notion that the hospital's negligence is distinct from the doctor's? This question seems to never have been addressed directly by the courts. Uniformly, they find hospital negligence only where the doctor is also negligent. The best explanation for this limitation is one of proximate cause. A hospital's negligent screening of a physician is not sufficiently proximate to a patient's injury, even if it literally causes the injury, unless the injury results from the physician's own negligence as well.

Another doctrinal puzzle is whether hospitals who negligently credential a physician are liable to patients who are injured off premises in the doctor's private office. Although standard foreseeability and but-for causation tests would appear to be met, most courts hold that hospitals are liable only for injuries to hospital patients, even where the plaintiff can prove she relied on the hospital credentials in selecting the doctor. Again, the notion appears to be one of proximate cause, influenced by older notions of privity of contract. See Insinga v. LaBella, 543 So. 2d 209 (Fla. 1989) (no hospital liability for giving admitting privileges to a person masquerading as a physician, where injury occurred outside hospital). But see Copithorne v. Framingham Union Hospital, 520 N.E.2d 139 (Mass. 1988) (hospital duty extends to medical staff member who drugged and raped patient in her home). Should it make any difference if the doctor practices in a hospital-owned and -leased medical office building right next door? What if the hospital owns an HMO that the doctor and patient belong to?

11. Other important sources of hospital liability are surveyed at Chapters 2.A and 3.B. Of particular importance is the federal Emergency Medical Treatment and Labor Act (EMTALA), which creates a form of strict liability for hospitals that refuse to treat patients who are in labor or in a serious emergency condition. Much of the litigation under EMTALA has addressed whether it essentially federalizes malpractice actions arising out of the emergency room (or potentially anywhere in the hospital). For the most part, courts have said "no," holding that the statute was intended to apply only to purposefully refusing standard care, not to errors in judgment or skill in carrying out treatment. See page 77.

2. Managed Care Liability

We turn now to a new form of institution, one that combines medical delivery with medical financing. When confronted with HMOs' institutional liability, courts quickly applied the same structure of analysis that had developed for hospitals. Because HMOs differ in important respects from hospitals, however, the result of this analysis may not be the same. In the following materials, consider how different types of managed care entities and arrangements should be treated under the various theories and branches of no liability, vicarious liability, and direct liability.

■ BOYD v. ALBERT EINSTEIN MEDICAL CENTER
547 A.2d 1229 (Pa. Super. Ct. 1988)

OLSZEWSKI, Judge:

This is an appeal from the trial court's order granting summary judgment in favor of defendant/appellee, Health Maintenance Organization of Pennsylvania (hereinafter HMO). Appellant asserts that the trial court erred in granting the motion for summary judgment when there existed a question of material fact as to whether participating physicians are the ostensible agents of HMO. For the reasons stated below, we reverse the grant of summary judgment.

The facts, as averred by the parties in their pleadings and elicited through deposition testimony, reveal that at the time of her death, decedent and her husband were participants in the HMO. HMO is a medical insurance provider that offers an alternative to the traditional Blue Cross/Blue Shield insurance plan.[1] Decedent's husband became eligible for participation in a group plan provided by HMO through his employer. Upon electing to participate in this plan, decedent and her husband were provided with a directory and benefits brochure which listed the participating physicians. Restricted to selecting a physician from this list, decedent chose Doctor David Rosenthal and Doctor Perry Dornstein as her primary care physicians.

In June of 1982, decedent contacted Doctor David Rosenthal regarding a lump in her breast. Doctor Rosenthal ordered a mammogram to be performed which revealed a suspicious area in the breast. Doctor Rosenthal recommended that decedent undergo a biopsy and referred decedent to Doctor Erwin Cohen for that purpose. Doctor Cohen, a surgeon, is also a participating HMO physician. The referral to a specialist in this case was made in accordance with the terms and conditions of HMO's subscription agreement.[2]

On July 6, 1982, Doctor Cohen performed a biopsy of decedent's breast tissue at Albert Einstein Medical Center. During the procedure, Doctor Cohen perforated decedent's chest wall with the biopsy needle, causing decedent to sustain a left hemothorax. Decedent was hospitalized for treatment of the hemothorax at Albert Einstein Hospital for two days.

---

1. A Health Maintenance Organization is an organized system of health care which provides or arranges for a comprehensive array of basic and supplemental health care services. These services are provided on a prepaid basis to voluntarily enrolled members living within a prescribed geographic area. Responsibility for the delivery, quality and payment of health care falls to the managing organization — the HMO.

2. Doctor Rosenthal admitted in his deposition that HMO limited specifically the doctors to whom decedent could have been referred.

In the weeks following this incident decedent complained to her primary care physicians, Doctor David Rosenthal and Doctor Perry Dornstein, of pain in her chest wall, belching, hiccoughs, and fatigue. On August 19, 1982, decedent awoke with pain in the middle of her chest. Decedent's husband contacted her primary care physicians, Doctors Rosenthal and Dornstein, and was advised to take decedent to Albert Einstein Hospital where she would be examined by Doctor Rosenthal. Upon arrival at Albert Einstein emergency room, decedent related symptoms of chest wall pain, vomiting, stomach and back discomfort to Doctor Rosenthal. Doctor Rosenthal commenced an examination of decedent, diagnosed Tietz's syndrome,[3] and arranged for tests to be performed at his office where decedent underwent X-rays, EKG, and cardiac isoenzyme tests.[4] Decedent was then sent home and told to rest.[5]

During the course of that afternoon, decedent continued to experience chest pain, vomiting and belching. Decedent related the persistence and worsening of these symptoms by telephone to Doctors Rosenthal and Dornstein, who prescribed, without further examination, Talwin, a pain medication. At 5:30 that afternoon decedent was discovered dead in her bathroom by her husband, having expired as a result of a myocardial infarction.

Appellant's complaint and new matter aver that HMO advertised that its physicians and medical care providers were competent, and that they had been evaluated for periods of up to six months prior to being selected to participate in the HMO program as a medical provider. The complaint further avers that decedent and appellant relied on these representations in choosing their primary care physicians. The complaint then avers that HMO was negligent in failing to

> qualify or oversee its physicians and hospital who acted as its agents, servants, or employees in providing medical care to the decedent nor did HMO of Pa. require its physicians, surgeons and hospitals to provide adequate evidence of skill, training and competence in medicine and it thereby failed to furnish the decedent with competent, qualified medical care as warranted.

Finally, appellant's new matter avers that HMO furnished to its subscribers documents which identify HMO as the care provider and state that HMO guarantees the quality of care.

---

3. Tietze's Syndrome is an inflammatory condition affecting the costochondral cartilage. It occurs more commonly in females, generally in the 30 to 50 age range.

4. HMO avers that decedent was returned to the doctor's office for testing because it was more comfortable and convenient for her. Appellant, however, asserts that the tests were performed in the doctor's office, rather than the hospital, in accordance with the requirements of HMO whose primary interest was in keeping the medical fees within the corporation.

5. Appellant contends that Doctor Rosenthal acted negligently in ordering the tests to be performed in his office when decedent exhibited symptoms of cardiac distress. The safer practice, avers appellant, would have been to perform the tests at the hospital where the results would have been more quickly available. Appellant further contends that, despite Doctor Rosenthal's diagnosis of Tietze's Syndrome, the nature of the tests he ordered indicates that he was concerned about the possibility of a heart attack.

Appellant's theory of recovery before the trial court was primarily one of vicarious liability under the ostensible agency theory. In granting defendant HMO's motion for summary judgment, the trial court found that plaintiff/appellant had failed to establish either of the two factors on which the theory of ostensible agency, as applied to hospitals in *Capan*, is based. On appeal, appellant contends that the evidence indicates that there exists a question of fact regarding whether HMO may be held liable under this theory. . . .

The group master contract provides that HMO "operates a comprehensive prepaid program of health care which provides health care services and benefits to Members in order to protect and promote their health, and preserve and enhance patient dignity." HMO was incorporated in 1975 under the laws of Pennsylvania and converted from a nonprofit to a for-profit corporation in 1981. HMO is based on the individual practice association model (hereinafter IPA), which means that HMO is comprised of participating primary physicians who are engaged in part in private practice in the HMO service area. Under the plan, IPA contracts with HMO to provide medical services to HMO members. IPA selects its primary and specialist physicians and enters into an agreement with them obligating the physician to perform health services for the subscribers of HMO.

The primary physician's role is defined as the "gatekeeper into the health care delivery system." "An HMO member must consult with his primary physician before going to a specialist and/or the hospital." If the primary physician deems it necessary, he arranges a consultation with an HMO participating specialist, which constitutes a second opinion. "Basically, with the primary physicians 'screening' the members' illnesses, excessive hospitalization and improper use of specialists can be reduced."

Member-patients use a physician directory and choose a conveniently located office of a participating primary physician. HMO members will only receive reimbursement from nonparticipating providers when the condition requiring treatment was of an immediate nature. Determinations of immediacy are made by the HMO quality assurance committee. In any event, persons desiring emergency non-provider benefits must notify HMO or their primary physician of the emergency within 48 hours and must give written proof of the occurrence within ninety days after service is rendered. . . .

Primary physicians are paid through a mechanism termed "capitation." Capitation is an actuarially determined amount prepaid by HMO to the primary physician for each patient who has chosen his office. The dollar amount is based upon a predetermined rate per age group. The primary physicians are paid 80 percent of the capitation amount and the remaining 20 percent is pooled by IPA and goes back into a pooled risk-sharing fund as a reserve against specialty referral costs and hospital stays. Each primary care office has its own specialist fund and hospital fund established by allocating a predetermined amount each month for each member who has chosen that primary care office. The surplus from the specialist fund is returned to the primary care office. The hospital fund, however, is governed by a hospital risk/incentive-sharing scheme which anticipates a number of inpatient days per members per year. If the actual hospital utilization is less than anticipated, the HMO and IPA each receive 50 percent of the savings. IPA must place the savings in the Special IPA risk-sharing account and must use the funds to offset losses resulting from unanticipated physician costs. If utilization is greater than anticipated, IPA is responsible for 50 percent of the loss up to the amount of uncommitted funds in the Special IPA risk sharing account. . . .

HMO asserts that because the theory of ostensible agency has been applied in Pennsylvania only to the relationship between hospitals and independent contractor physicians, the theory is not appropriate in the instant situation. We emphasize, however, that when this court introduced the concept of ostensible agency to this Commonwealth in *Capan*, supra, we based that decision in large part upon "the changing role of the hospital in society [which] creates a likelihood that patients will look to the institution" for care. Because the role of health care providers has changed in recent years, the *Capan* rationale for applying the theory of ostensible agency to hospitals is certainly applicable in the instant situation. . . .

We find that the facts indicate an issue of material fact as to whether the participating physicians were the ostensible agents of HMO. HMO covenanted that it would "[provide] health care services and benefits to Members in order to protect and promote their health. . . . " "HMOPA operates on a direct service rather than an indemnity basis." Appellant paid his doctor's fee to HMO, not to the physician of his choice. Then, appellant selected his primary care physicians from the list provided by HMO. Regardless of who recommended appellant's decedent to choose her primary care physician, the fact remains that HMO provides a limited list from which a member must choose a primary physician. Moreover, those primary physicians are screened by HMO and must comply with a list of regulations in order to honor their contract with HMO.

Further, as mandated by HMO, appellant's decedent could not see a specialist without the primary physician's referral. As HMO declares, the primary physician is the "gatekeeper into the health care delivery system." "An HMO member must consult with his primary physician before going to a specialist and/or the hospital." Moreover, appellant's decedent had no choice as to which specialist to see. In our opinion, because appellant's decedent was required to follow the mandates of HMO and did not directly seek the attention of the specialist, there is an inference that appellant looked to the institution for care and not solely to the physicians; conversely, that appellant's decedent submitted herself to the care of the participating physicians in response to an invitation from HMO. See comment (a), Restatement (Second) Agency §267. . . .

We conclude, therefore, that the trial court erred when it granted HMO's motion for summary judgment on the ground that the participating physicians were not the ostensible agents of HMO. . . .

McEwen, Judge, concurring.

I concur in the result reached by the majority since the author, after a very careful analysis of the issues presented in this appeal, reaches the quite basic principle that issues of material fact may not be resolved by summary judgment.

I write only because it appears to me that the learned trial court improperly resolved by summary judgment the basic factual issue of whether the literature, in which HMO "guaranteed" and "assured" the quality of care provided to its subscribers, had been distributed to appellant or to other subscribers of HMO.

It might also be mentioned that while the court was understandably uncertain as to the theories upon which plaintiff was proceeding,[1] it appears that the amended complaint of plaintiff does contain factual averments supporting a breach of warranty claim.

■ WICKLINE v. STATE
239 Cal. Rptr. 810 (Cal. Ct. App. 1986)

Rowen, Associate Justice.

[Lois Wickline, who was treated under California's Medicaid program (known as "Medi-Cal"), sued the State, but not her physician, for negligently causing her premature discharge from the hospital, resulting in complications that eventually necessitated amputation of her right leg. Wickline alleged that her premature discharge was the fault of Medi-Cal's erroneous withholding of its authorization for her continued hospitalization.] This is an appeal from a judgment for plaintiff entered after a trial by jury. For the reasons discussed below, we reverse the judgment.

Principally, this matter concerns itself with the legal responsibility that a third party payor, in this case, the State of California, has for harm caused to a patient when a cost containment program is applied in a manner which is alleged to have affected the implementation of the treating physician's medical judgment. . . .

I

Responding to concerns about the escalating cost of health care, public and private payors have in recent years experimented with a variety of cost containment mechanisms. We deal here with one of those programs: The prospective utilization review process.

At the outset, this court recognizes that this case appears to be the first attempt to tie a health care payor into the medical malpractice causation chain and that it, therefore, deals with issues of profound importance to the health care community and to the general public. For those reasons we have permitted the filing of amicus curiae briefs in support of each of the respective parties in the matter to assure that due consideration is given to the broader issues raised before this court by this case. . . .

Early cost containment programs utilized the retrospective utilization review process. In that system the third party payor reviewed the patient's chart after the fact to determine whether the treatment provided was medically necessary. If, in the judgment of the utilization reviewer, it was not, the health care provider's claim for payment was denied.

---

1. The trial court noted in its opinion that

the gravamen of plaintiff's complaint is that HMO of PA guaranteed or warranted the quality of care provided. . . . Plaintiff's theory of recovery . . . is not entirely clear. A reading of the complaint suggests Plaintiff is proceeding upon grounds of corporate liability. However, in his answer to the motion of HMO of PA for summary judgment, plaintiff contends HMO of PA is vicariously liable through ostensible agency.

In the cost containment program in issue in this case, prospective utilization review, authority for the rendering of health care services must be obtained before medical care is rendered. Its purpose is to promote the well-recognized public interest in controlling health care costs by reducing unnecessary services while still intending to assure that appropriate medical and hospital services are provided to the patient in need. However, such a cost containment strategy creates new and added pressures on the quality assurance portion of the utilization review mechanism. The stakes, the risks at issue, are much higher when a prospective cost containment review process is utilized than when a retrospective review process is used.

A mistaken conclusion about medical necessity following retrospective review will result in the wrongful withholding of payment. An erroneous decision in a prospective review process, on the other hand, in practical consequences, results in the withholding of necessary care, potentially leading to a patient's permanent disability or death.

II

Though somewhat in dispute, the facts in this case are not particularly complicated. In 1976, Wickline a married woman in her mid-40's, with a limited education, was being treated by Dr. Stanley Z. Daniels (Dr. Daniels), a physician engaged in a general family practice, for problems associated with her back and legs. Failing to respond to the physical therapy type of treatment he prescribed, Dr. Daniels had Wickline admitted to Van Nuys Community Hospital (Van Nuys or Hospital) in October 1976 and brought in another physician, Dr. Gerald E. Polonsky (Dr. Polonsky), a specialist in peripheral vascular surgery, to do a consultation examination. Peripheral vascular surgery concerns itself with surgery on any vessel of the body, exclusive of the heart.

Dr. Polonsky examined plaintiff and diagnosed her condition as arteriosclerosis obliterans with occlusion of the abdominal aorta, more generally referred to as Leriche's Syndrome. . . .

According to Dr. Polonsky, the only treatment for Leriche's Syndrome is surgical. In Wickline's case her disease was so far advanced that Dr. Polonsky concluded that it was necessary to remove a part of the plaintiff's artery and insert a synthetic (Teflon) graft in its place.

After agreeing to the operation, Wickline was discharged home to await approval of her doctor's diagnosis and authorization from Medi-Cal for the recommended surgical procedure and attendant acute care hospitalization. It is conceded that at all times in issue in this case, the plaintiff was eligible for medical benefits under California's medical assistance program, the "Medi-Cal Act," which is more commonly referred to as Medi-Cal. (Welf. & Inst. Code, §§14000 et seq., 14000.4.)

As required, Dr. Daniels submitted a treatment authorization request to Medi-Cal, sometimes referred to as form "161," "MC-161" or "TAR." In response to Dr. Daniels' request, Medi-Cal authorized the surgical procedure and 10 days of hospitalization for that treatment.

On January 6, 1977, plaintiff was admitted to Van Nuys by Dr. Daniels. On January 7, 1977, Dr. Polonsky performed a surgical procedure in which a part of plaintiff's artery was removed and a synthetic artery was inserted to replace it. Dr. Polonsky characterized that procedure as "a very major surgery."

Later that same day Dr. Polonsky was notified that Wickline was experiencing circulatory problems in her right leg. He concluded that a clot had formed in the graft. As a result, Wickline was taken back into surgery, the incision in her right groin was reopened, the clot removed and the graft was resewn. Wickline's recovery subsequent to the two January 7th operations [was] characterized as "stormy." She had a lot of pain, some spasm in the vessels in the lower leg and she experienced hallucinating episodes. On January 12, 1977, Wickline was returned to the operating room where Dr. Polonsky performed a lumbar sympathectomy.

A lumbar sympathectomy is a major operation in which a section of the chain of nerves that lie on each side of the spinal column is removed. The procedure causes the blood vessels in the patient's lower extremity to become paralyzed in a wide open position and was done in an attempt to relieve the spasms which Wickline was experiencing in those vessels. Spasms stop the outflow of blood from the vessels causing the blood to back up into the graft. Failure to relieve such spasms can cause clotting.

Dr. Polonsky was assisted in all three surgeries by Dr. Leonard Kovner (Dr. Kovner), a board-certified specialist in the field of general surgery and the chief of surgery at Van Nuys. Dr. Daniels was present for the initial graft surgery on January 7, 1977, and for the right lumbar sympathectomy operation on January 12, 1977.

Wickline was scheduled to be discharged on January 16, 1977, which would mean that she would actually leave the hospital sometime before 1 P.M. on January 17, 1977. On or about January 16, 1977, Dr. Polonsky concluded that "it was medically necessary" that plaintiff remain in the hospital for an additional eight days beyond her then scheduled discharge date. Drs. Kovner and Daniels concurred in Dr. Polonsky's opinion.

Dr. Polonsky cited many reasons for his feeling that it was medically necessary for plaintiff to remain in an acute care hospital for an additional eight days, such as the danger of infection and/or clotting. His principal reason, however, was that he felt that he was going to be able to save both of Wickline's legs and wanted her to remain in the hospital where he could observe her and be immediately available, along with the hospital staff, to treat her if an emergency should occur.

In order to secure an extension of Wickline's hospital stay, it was necessary to complete and present to Medi-Cal a form called "Request for Extension of Stay in Hospital," commonly referred to as an "MC-180" or "180." . . .

At Van Nuys, Patricia N. Spears (Spears), an employee of the hospital and a registered nurse, had the responsibility for completing 180 forms. In this case, as requested by Dr. Polonsky, Spears filled out Wickline's 180 form and then presented it to Dr. Daniels, as plaintiff's attending physician, to sign, which he did, in compliance with Dr. Polonsky's recommendation. All of the physicians who testified agreed that the 180 form prepared by Spears was complete, accurate and adequate for all purposes in issue in this matter.

Doris A. Futerman (Futerman), a registered nurse, was, at that time, employed by Medi-Cal as a Health Care Service Nurse, commonly referred to as an "on-site nurse." . . .

Futerman, after reviewing Wickline's 180 form, felt that she could not approve the requested eight-day extension of acute care hospitalization. While conceding that the information provided might justify some additional time beyond the scheduled discharge date, nothing in Wickline's case, in Futerman's opinion, would have warranted the entire eight additional days requested and, for those reasons, she telephoned the Medi-Cal Consultant. She reached Dr. William S. Glassman (Dr. Glassman), one of the Medi-Cal Consultants on duty at the time in Medi-Cal's Los Angeles office. The Medi-Cal Consultant selection occurred randomly. As was the practice, whichever Medi-Cal Consultant was available at the moment took the next call that came into the office. . . .

After speaking with Futerman on the telephone, Dr. Glassman rejected Wickline's treating physician's request for an eight-day hospital extension and, instead, authorized an additional four days of hospital stay beyond the originally scheduled discharge date. . . .

After review of Wickline's 180 form, Dr. Glassman testified that the factors that led him to authorize four days, rather than the requested eight days, was that there was no information about the patient's temperature which he, thereupon, assumed was normal; nothing was mentioned about the patient's diet, which he then presumed was not a problem; nor was there any information about Wickline's bowel function, which Dr. Glassman then presumed was functioning satisfactorily. Further, the fact that the 180 form noted that Wickline was able to ambulate with help and that whirlpool treatments were to begin that day caused Dr. Glassman to presume that the patient was progressing satisfactorily and was not seriously or critically ill. . . .

In essence, respondent argues, Dr. Glassman based his decision on signs and symptoms such as temperature, diet and bowel movements, which were basically irrelevant to the plaintiff's circulatory condition for which she was being treated and did not concern himself with those symptoms and signs which an ordinary prudent physician would consider to be pertinent with regard to the type of medical condition presented by Wickline.

Complying with the limited extension of time authorized by Medi-Cal, Wickline was discharged from Van Nuys on January 21, 1977. Drs. Polonsky and Daniels each wrote discharge orders. At the time of her discharge, each of plaintiff's three treating physicians were aware that the Medi-Cal Consultant had approved only four of the requested eight-day hospital stay extension. While all three doctors were aware that they could attempt to obtain a further extension of Wickline's hospital stay by telephoning the Medi-Cal Consultant to request such an extension, none of them did so. . . .

At trial, Dr. Polonsky testified that in the time that had passed since the first extension request had been communicated to Medi-Cal, on January 16th or 17th, and the time of her scheduled discharge on January 21, 1977, Wickline's condition had neither deteriorated nor become critical. In Dr. Polonsky's opinion no new symptom had presented itself and no additional factors had occurred since the original request was made to have formed the basis for a change in the Medi-Cal Consultant's attitude regarding Wickline's situation. In addition, he stated that at the time of Wickline's discharge it did not appear that her leg was in any danger.

Dr. Polonsky testified that at the time in issue he felt that Medi-Cal Consultants had the state's interest more in mind than the patient's welfare and that that belief influenced his decision not to request a second extension of Wickline's hospital stay. In addition, he felt that Medi-Cal had the power to tell him, as a treating doctor, when a patient must be discharged from the hospital. Therefore, while still of the subjective, noncommunicated, opinion that Wickline was seriously ill and that the danger to her was not over, Dr. Polonsky discharged her from the hospital on January 21, 1977. He testified that had Wickline's condition, in his medical judgment, been critical or in a deteriorating condition on January 21, he would have made some effort to keep her in the hospital beyond that day even if denied authority by Medi-Cal and even if he had to pay her hospital bill himself. . . .

All of the medical witnesses who testified at trial agreed that Dr. Polonsky was acting within the standards of practice of the medical community in discharging Wickline on January 21, 1977. . . .

Wickline testified that in the first few days after she arrived home she started feeling pain in her right leg and the leg started to lose color. In the next few days the pain got worse and the right leg took on a whitish, statue-like marble appearance. Wickline assumed she was experiencing normal recovery symptoms and did not communicate with any of her physicians. Finally, when "the pain got so great and the color started changing from looking like a statue to getting a grayish color," her husband called Dr. Kovner. It was Wickline's memory that this occurred about the third day after her discharge from the hospital and that Dr. Kovner advised Mr. Wickline to give extra pain medicine to the plaintiff.

Thereafter, gradually over the next few days, the plaintiff's leg "kept getting grayer and then it got bluish." The extra medication allegedly prescribed by Dr. Kovner over the telephone did not relieve the pain Wickline was experiencing. She testified that "by then the pain was just excruciating, where no pain medicine helped whatsoever." Finally, Wickline instructed her husband to call Dr. Kovner again and this time Dr. Kovner ordered plaintiff back into the hospital. Wickline returned to Van Nuys that same evening, January 30, 1977, nine days after her last discharge therefrom. . . .

Attempts to save Wickline's leg through the utilization of anticoagulants, antibiotics, strict bed rest, pain medication and warm water whirlpool baths to the lower extremity proved unsuccessful. On February 8, 1977, Dr. Polonsky amputated Wickline's leg below the knee because had he not done so "she would have died." The condition did not, however, heal after the first operation and on February 17, 1977, the doctors went back and amputated Wickline's leg above the knee. . . .

In Dr. Polonsky's opinion, to a reasonable medical certainty, had Wickline remained in the hospital for the eight additional days, as originally requested by him and her other treating doctors, she would not have suffered the loss of her leg. . . .

Dr. Polonsky testified that in his medical opinion, the Medi-Cal Consultant's rejection of the requested eight-day extension of acute care hospitalization and his authorization of a four-day extension in its place did not conform to the usual medical standards as they existed in 1977. He stated that, in accordance with those standards, a physician would not be permitted to make decisions regarding the care of a patient without either first seeing the patient, reviewing the patient's chart or discussing the patient's condition with her treating physician or physicians.

III

From the facts thus presented, appellant takes the position that it was not negligent as a matter of law. Appellant contends that the decision to discharge was made by each of the plaintiff's three doctors, was based upon the prevailing standards of practice, and was justified by her condition at the time of her discharge. It argues that Medi-Cal had no part in the plaintiff's hospital discharge and therefore was not liable even if the decision to do so was erroneously made by her doctors. . . .

As to the principal issue before this court, i.e., who bears responsibility for allowing a patient to be discharged from the hospital, her treating physicians or the health care payor, each side's medical expert witnesses agreed that, in accordance with the standards of medical practice as it existed in January 1977, it was for the patient's treating physician to decide the course of treatment that was medically necessary to treat the ailment. It was also that physician's responsibility to determine whether or not acute care hospitalization was required and for how long. Finally, it was agreed that the patient's physician is in a better position than the Medi-Cal Consultant to determine the number of days medically necessary for any required hospital care. The decision to discharge is, therefore, the responsibility of the patient's own treating doctor.

Dr. Kaufman testified that if, on January 21, the date of the plaintiff's discharge from Van Nuys, any one of her three treating doctors had decided that in his medical judgment it was necessary to keep Wickline in the hospital for a longer period of time, they, or any of them, should have filed another request for extension of stay in the hospital, that Medi-Cal would expect those physicians to make such a request if they felt it was indicated, and upon receipt of such a request further consideration of an additional extension of hospital time would have been given.

Title 22 of the California Administrative Code §51110, provided, in pertinent part, at the relevant time in issue here, that: "The determination of need for acute care shall be made in accordance with the usual standards of medical practice in the community."

The patient who requires treatment and who is harmed when care which should have been provided is not provided should recover for the injuries suffered from all those responsible for the deprivation of such care, including, when appropriate, health care payors. Third party payors of health care services can be held legally accountable when medically inappropriate decisions result from defects in the design or implementation of cost containment mechanisms as, for example, when appeals made on a patient's behalf for medical or hospital care are arbitrarily ignored or unreasonably disregarded or overridden. However, the physician who complies without protest with the limitations imposed by a third-party payor, when his medical judgment dictates otherwise, cannot avoid his ultimate responsibility for his patient's care. He cannot point to the health care payor as the liability scapegoat when the consequences of his own determinative medical decisions go sour.

There is little doubt that Dr. Polonsky was intimidated by the Medi-Cal program but he was not paralyzed by Dr. Glassman's response nor rendered powerless to act appropriately if other action was required under the circumstances. If, in his medical judgment, it was in his patient's best interest that she remain in the acute care hospital setting for an additional four days beyond the extended time period originally authorized by Medi-Cal, Dr. Polonsky should have made some effort to keep Wickline there. He himself acknowledged that responsibility to his patient. It was his medical judgment, however, that Wickline could be discharged when she was. All the plaintiff's treating physicians concurred and all the doctors who testified at trial, for either plaintiff or defendant, agreed that Dr. Polonsky's medical decision to discharge Wickline met the standard of care applicable at the time. Medi-Cal was not a party to that medical decision and therefore cannot be held to share in the harm resulting if such decision was negligently made.

In addition, thereto, while Medi-Cal played a part in the scenario before us in that it was the resource for the funds to pay for the treatment sought, and its input regarding the nature and length of hospital care to be provided was of paramount importance, Medi-Cal did not override the medical judgment of Wickline's treating physicians at the time of her discharge. It was given no opportunity to do so. Therefore, there can be no viable cause of action against it for the consequences of that discharge decision. . . .

V

This court appreciates that what is at issue here is the effect of cost containment programs upon the professional judgment of physicians to prescribe hospital treatment for patients requiring the same. While we recognize, realistically, that cost consciousness has become a permanent feature of the health care system, it is essential that cost limitation programs not be permitted to corrupt medical judgment. We have concluded, from the facts in issue here, that in this case it did not.

For the reasons expressed herein, this court finds that appellant is not liable for respondent's injuries as a matter of law. That makes unnecessary any discussion of the other contentions of the parties.

Notes: Managed Care Liability

1. *The Components of Managed Care.* Managed care is a term that applies broadly to a wide variety of arrangements that restrict the generosity of traditional health insurance. Managed care (1) restricts choice of physicians through networks and gatekeepers, (2) alters discrete treatment decisions through utilization review and prior authorization requirements, and (3) creates cost-constrained financial incentives through capitation payments and risk-sharing pools. Each of these components has distinct liability implications and can exist separately from the others. For instance, "managed indemnity" insurance does (2) but not (1) or (3), simply by adding utilization review to traditional insurance. Preferred provider organizations (PPOs) do (1) but not (3), and may do (2) but not necessarily. HMOs are the fullest embodiment of managed care because they incorporate all three components. In analyzing these cases and others that are likely to arise in the future, however, be sure to think individually about each of these components and observe how they might arise in a variety of different institutional forms.

2. *HMO Immunity.* In a few jurisdictions, HMOs are immune from suit for negligent treatment, in some states by statute and in one state formerly by court decision. Williams v. Good Health Plus, Inc., 743 S.W.2d 373 (Tex. Ct. App. 1987), resonates with hospital decisions early in the century by holding that an HMO logically cannot be held liable because the corporate practice of medicine doctrine prevents it from controlling physicians' treatment decisions. That decision has since been overturned by statute, however. Comment, 30 Tex. Tech. L. Rev. 1227 (1999). But California, by statute, declares that health insurers may not be held vicariously liable for medical decisions by independent physicians. Martin v. PacifiCare of California, 198 Cal. App. 4th 1390 (2011). Economist Patricia Danzon is one who

argues for HMO immunity under the theory that holding physicians individually liable is sufficient, unless the HMO agrees by contract to assume liability. Patricia M. Danzon, Tort Liability: A Minefield for Managed Care, 24 J. Leg. Stud. 491 (1997). Do you agree?

3. *Vicarious Liability.* There are two basic types of HMOs, with several permutations. The HMO type in *Boyd* was an Independent Practice Association (IPA), which is composed of a large contractual network of physicians who maintain practices in their own offices and see patients with many different types of insurance. For a decision similar to *Boyd*, see Villazon v. Prudential Health Care Plan, 843 So. 2d 842 (Fla. 2003). An agency relationship is much easier to establish with the other type of HMO, a staff or group model, in which a smaller number of physicians work exclusively for a single HMO in a centralized clinic. What about a PPO (preferred provider organization) or POS (point of service) plan with an open network in which patients are encouraged to stay with the designated physicians but are free to go outside the network and select any doctor they want by paying a higher deductible or copayment? What about a closed network that is very large but has no gatekeeping restrictions, that is, patients can see anyone they want when they want, but only within the network? See generally Comment, Managed Health Care: HMO Corporate Liability, Independent Contractors, and the Ostensible Agency Doctrine, 15 J. Corp. L. 535 (1990).

How might an IPA HMO alter its structure or operations to avoid the attribution of agency and vicarious liability? See Chase v. Independent Practice Ass'n, 583 N.E.2d 251 (Mass. App. Ct. 1991) (vicarious liability rejected where HMO contract stated the IPA only "arranged for" services but did not provide services directly); Jones v. U.S. Healthcare, 723 N.Y.S.2d 478 (App. Div. 2001) (an HMO "cannot be held vicariously liable for defendant doctors' and hospital's alleged malpractice in discharging plaintiff and her baby prematurely, where the . . . Group Master Contract, membership card and Member Handbook clearly state that doctors and hospitals participating in defendant's health care program are independent contractors"). But see Petrovich v. Share Health Plan, 719 N.E.2d 756 (Ill. 1999) (exculpatory language in insurance documents does not control if the patient didn't actually read or understand the documents). Because IPAs are now the dominant form of HMOs, and because HMO lawyers have widely adopted these techniques, the working assumption among both plaintiff's and defense lawyers is that HMOs generally cannot be held vicariously liable simply by virtue of forming a network and requiring gatekeeping. This is also confirmed in several of the state managed care liability statutes discussed in the next note. See Agrawal & Hall, infra.

4. *HMO Direct Liability.* The focus of *Boyd* is vicarious liability, but HMOs have also been held to the same type of direct corporate liability ushered in by Darling v. Charleston Community Memorial Hospital, page 439. Recall that for hospitals, direct corporate liability takes two basic forms: a duty of care in the selection of physicians, and a duty of care in the contemporaneous supervision of physicians. The former is readily applicable to HMOs as well. Several courts have held that they have the same obligation hospitals do to review the credentials and competency of physicians that they select for their network. See, e.g., McClellan v. Health Maintenance Organization, 604 A.2d 1053 (Pa. Super. Ct. 1992); Pagarigan v. Aetna, 2005 WL 2742807 (Cal. Ct. App. 2005). HMOs are required under their own accreditation standards to engage in a hospital-like credentialing

process, and increasingly they are required to do so by state regulation as well. Nevertheless, many managed care networks accept virtually "any willing provider," that is, anyone with a license who agrees to the network's payment terms. A "Dear Doctor" letter sent by one PPO to California physicians stated, "Welcome to the PPO network. You are now part of a carefully selected panel of more than 300 hospitals and 21,000 physicians." Robert A. Berenson, Beyond Competition, 16(2) Health Aff. 171, 175 (1997). Some states require by statute that HMOs accept any qualified provider. Does either voluntary or mandatory nonselectivity undermine the basis for a duty of care in selection?

Recall that the second branch of *Darling*—the duty of contemporaneous supervision—is highly controversial with respect to hospitals and is accepted in only a very limited fashion in most jurisdictions because it doesn't make sense to require hospital administrators to actively intervene in medical treatment decisions. Is the case for an HMO's duty to supervise any stronger? Even if there is no such mandatory duty, however, consider whether HMOs have voluntarily assumed such a duty through their utilization review function. Is this not the essential point of *Wickline*, that when insurance companies choose to intervene in treatment decisions, they assume a duty of care in doing so? Accord Shannon v. McNulty, 718 A.2d 828 (Pa. Super. Ct. 1998) ("When . . . an insurer interjects itself into the rendering of medical decisions affecting a subscriber's care it must do so in a medically reasonable manner.").

To remove any doubt about this issue, about a dozen states have adopted statutes that hold insurers liable for personal injuries caused by negligent or inappropriate administration of health insurance benefits. See Agrawal & Hall, infra; Note, 74 Temp. L. Rev. 507 (2001). It is unlikely, however, that these statutes can be applied to employer-provided health insurance, due to the federal preemption doctrine discussed in the following case.

5. *Medical Tourism.* Complex medical care can be quite good in some less developed countries such as India and Malaysia, but considerably less expensive, even factoring in travel costs—with net savings of tens of thousands of dollars per procedure for many common surgeries. See page 43. Thus, it may be just a matter of time before insurers, or self-insured employers, begin offering strong incentives (in the form of discounts or rebates) to people who opt to use "preferred providers" overseas. Would doing only that give rise to insurer liability for any medical injuries? If so, under what theory(ies) of institutional liability? And, what standard of care (domestic or foreign) should determine the provider's underlying negligence? For discussion, but no resolution, of these fascinating questions, see Glenn Cohen, Protecting Patients with Passports, 95 Iowa L. Rev. 1467 (2010).

6. Wickline's *Holding.* The precise holding or nonholding of *Wickline* has been a source of considerable confusion, both in the courts and among lawyers and commentators. This confusion is due in part to the unusual tactical decision by the plaintiff's lawyer not to sue the treating physicians. As a result, the plaintiff was able to use the treating physicians as experts for her side, but the physicians were unwilling to indict themselves by testifying that the four-day stay fell below a minimally acceptable standard of care. Without such testimony, the court was forced to find no liability. Without any basis in the clinical evidence for finding anyone liable, much of what the court said about the competing responsibilities of physicians and insurers was rendered dictum.

Nevertheless, *Wickline* is still the seminal case on the issues it addresses. In trying to make sense of what the opinion means for future disputes, distinguish these two issues: (1) whether insurers are potentially on the liability hook for making bad coverage decisions, and (2) whether physicians are off the liability hook when insurers are at fault. Realize it is possible to answer "yes" to (1) and "no" to (2); in other words, both can be held liable at the same time. Others sometimes interpret *Wickline* to mean, however, that the doctor's ultimate responsibility absolves the insurance company from blame. The most prominent instance of this reading of *Wickline* is a subsequent California decision, Wilson v. Blue Cross of Southern California, 271 Cal. Rptr. 876 (Cal. Ct. App. 1990). There, a psychiatric patient committed suicide after being released from the hospital when his private insurer stopped paying for his hospitalization benefits due to lack of medical necessity. The court found it necessary to distinguish and disapprove *Wickline* in order to allow the case to be tried against the insurer under a negligence theory. Is anything in *Wickline* opposed to such a holding? For a sampling of the extensive commentary on these two cases, see John Blum, An Analysis of Legal Liability in Health Care Utilization Review and Case Management, 26 Hous. L. Rev. 191 (1989); Comment, 52 Ohio St. L. J. 1289 (1991).

Under *Wickline*, could insurer liability be imposed not only based on the substance of the utilization review decision, but also based on the process? What flaws were present in Medi-Cal's UR process? How feasible would it be to improve on that process?

If insurers can be found liable for negligent failures to approve necessary care, can they also be held accountable for negligent approvals of harmful care?

7. *Bringing Liability and Payment into Sync.* Does the potential liability under *Wickline* make sense from the physician's perspective? Physicians complain that it is unfair to hold them responsible for failing to provide treatment that insurance will not pay for. See Note, 59 Duke L. Rev. 955 (2010). What realistic options did Mrs. Wickline's physicians have? How might the tort standard of medical appropriateness be brought more into sync with the insurance standard? One possibility is by referring to the law of abandonment, which is discussed in Chapter 2.B.3. There, we learn that physicians are able to terminate care in certain circumstances if they give proper notice and an opportunity to locate another physician. Whether lack of payment is a permissible reason to give this notice has not yet clearly been decided.

See also section B.2 for consideration of whether physicians practicing under managed care constraints should be held to a lower standard of care than under fee-for-service insurance.

8. *Few Cases but Big Verdicts.* One reason for the lack of clarity about the respective responsibilities of physicians and insurers is that there have been surprisingly few cases like *Wickline* and *Wilson* with decisions on the merits. This suggests that perhaps in practice insurers rarely deny coverage for care that is required by the minimal standard of medical practice. The paucity of suits may also be due to the preemption of state law by the federal ERISA statute, discussed in the next case. Others attribute the favorable malpractice record of staff model HMOs like Kaiser to their detailed programs of malpractice prevention and physician monitoring and to the availability of a grievance process for dissatisfied patients. These characteristics typically do not exist, however, in the broad network model HMOs that currently prevail in the market. Further explanation for the small number of suits

comes from the fact that plaintiffs' lawyers are reluctant to name health insurers in medical malpractice suits since this greatly complicates the litigation and is usually unnecessary given the fact that the treating physician is "on the hook" in any event (for reasons explained in *Wickline*). Also, plaintiffs' lawyers report seeing few or no cases where harm results from health insurers' refusing to pay for treatment that physicians request. Agrawal & Hall, infra.

Although there have been few successful cases against health insurers, when plaintiffs have succeeded, they sometimes win very large punitive damages awards, in the range of $50 million to $100 million or more. For instance, in Fox v. Health Net (1993), a California jury awarded $77 million in punitive damages (plus $12 million compensatory) against an HMO that had refused to pay for an innovative cancer treatment, which the surviving family claimed resulted in the patient's death. This was eclipsed by the $120 million verdict in Goodrich v. Aetna U.S. Healthcare (1999), $116 million of which were punitive damages. Like *Fox*, the *Goodrich* verdict was based on an HMO's reluctance to authorize expensive, state-of-the-art treatment for terminal cancer that it considered to be experimental. Then, in 2013, a Nevada jury returned a whopping $524 million verdict against an HMO for contracting with a physician whose sloppy procedures resulted in infecting the patient with Hepatitis C, Meyer v. Health Plan of Nevada.

Does this track record of very few successful verdicts, but some that are extremely large, create appropriate incentives for plaintiffs to sue? Is it likely to send appropriate deterrence signals to health insurers? Does the small number of suits suggest a need to remove barriers to suing health plans? Would a "floodgate" of litigation threaten the viability of the managed care industry or of its core cost-containment practices? For discussion from various perspectives, see the literature cited in note 14.

9. *Financial Incentives.* Another potential basis for direct liability against HMOs and managed care arrangements is the use of financial incentives to encourage physicians to economize. An insurer might avoid the entire issue of liability for second-guessing medical judgment by paying doctors in a way that encourages them to economize in their own clinical decisionmaking. Using *Wickline*'s notion of "defects in the design or implementation of cost containment mechanisms," is it possible nevertheless to argue that some financial incentives are too strong per se, or that in practice they caused a physician to err? Answering "yes," see Pagarigan v. Aetna, 2005 WL 2742807 (Cal. Ct. App. 2005). Consider by analogy the suits in the 1990s against Domino's Pizza for pressuring its deliverers to drive too fast. As discussed in section B.1, financial incentives might also lead to claims for punitive damages in medical malpractice cases against physicians. Section B.2 discusses whether incentives give rise to a claim for breach of fiduciary duty.

10. *Breach of Contract.* The *Boyd* concurrence suggests that HMO liability might also be based on a contractual or quasi-promissory theory, such as warranty or fraud. This possibility is explored in the notes following Sullivan v. O'Connor, at page 350. Is there a difference between the nature of the promises an HMO makes and those made by typical hospitals or doctors? Professor Brewbaker argues that, because HMOs, unlike hospitals, sell medical services, they undertake an implied warranty of quality which, as with doctors, promises nonnegligent care. Therefore, he argues that HMOs should be automatically liable for any negligent care delivered under their auspices, regardless of whether they fall under the theories of liability

devised for hospitals. William Brewbaker, Medical Malpractice and Managed Care Organizations: The Implied Warranty of Quality, 60 Contemp. Probs. 117 (Spring 1997).

11. *Employer Liability.* If insurers can be held liable for lack of care in selecting physicians and supervising treatment decisions, how about employers who construct their own managed care plans? Many large employers eliminate the "middle man" by contracting directly with hospitals and physicians on a self-insured basis. In doing so, an employer may either "rent a network," that is, contract with an existing network of providers, or it might form its own network. In either event, is it plausible to impose the same type of managed care liability on employers as on the insurers they have ousted? If such liability existed under state law, it would likely be preempted for reasons addressed in the following case. For discussion, see Dana M. Muir, Fiduciary Status as an Employer's Shield: The Perversity of ERISA Fiduciary Law, 2 U. Pa. J. Lab. & Emp. L. 391 (2000).

12. *Exclusive Enterprise Liability.* The furthest extension of the concepts of enterprise liability developed for hospitals, HMOs, and other forms of managed care would be to hold a network of hospitals, doctors, and insurers exclusively liable at the highest institutional level for any medical mistake that occurs within any component part. If the health care delivery system were to move toward the "integrated delivery system" structure described in Chapter 10, commentators have speculated whether these networks should or will be the final point of liability focus. So far, most networks are only loosely formed contractual affiliations in which the parties (hospitals, doctors, and insurers) agree on a nonexclusive basis to market their services collectively to employers or other insurers. Does this entail sufficient integration, coordination, selection, and supervision to justify imposition of enterprise liability? Consider whether it is feasible for integrated delivery systems to influence the quality of care if these affiliations are nonexclusive, that is, if doctors and hospitals belong to several such networks. As Mello & Kachalia, infra page 479, explain:

> [T]he plan's liability could be limited to injuries caused by physicians who receive the greatest share of their reimbursement from that payer, or could extend to any injury incurred by the plan's insured patients. The former would better peg liability to the plan's ability to influence the physician's practice, since the plan's threat not to contract with physicians in the future if they did not improve would have greater financial consequence for the physician. However, it could allow plans that did not have a large market share to evade liability altogether.

13. *Consumer-Driven Health Care.* As insurers recede from aggressive managed care, will these liability threats likewise recede, or will they be replaced with new theories of liability? According to one professor, consumer-driven health care opens up an entirely new arena of potential health plan liability in the form of failure to provide full or accurate information about health care options. Kristin Madison, ERISA and Liability for Provision of Medical Information, 84 N.C. L. Rev. 471-546 (2006). See also E. Haavi Morreim, High-Deductible Health Plans: Litigation Hazards for Health Insurers, 18 Health Matrix 1 (2008).

14. *Further Reading.* For commentary and analysis on **managed care liability** generally, see Haavi Morreim, Holding Health Care Accountable (2001); Jennifer Arlen & William MacLeod, Malpractice Liability for Physicians and Managed Care

Organizations, 78 N.Y.U. L. Rev. 1929 (2003); Gail Agrawal & Mark Hall, What If You *Could* Sue Your HMO? Managed Care Liability Beyond the ERISA Shield, 47 St. Louis U. L. J. 235 (2003); Clark Havighurst, Vicarious Liability: Relocating Responsibility for the Quality of Medical Care, 26 Am. J. L. Med. 7 (2000); Peter Jacobson & Neena Patil, Managed Care Litigation: Legal Doctrine at the Boundary of Tort and Contract, 57 Med. Care Res. & Rev. 440 (2000); David Studdert et al., Expanded Managed Care Liability: What Impact on Employer Coverage?, 18(6) Health Aff. 7 (Dec. 1999); Richard A. Epstein & Alan O. Sykes, The Assault on Managed Care: Vicarious Liability, Class Actions, and the Patient's Bill of Rights, 30 J. Leg. Stud. 625 (2002).

On **enterprise liability** (note 12), see K. Abraham & P. Weiler, Enterprise Medical Liability and the Choice of the Responsible Enterprise, 20 Am. J. L. & Med. 29 (1994); Clark C. Havighurst, Making Health Plans Accountable for the Quality of Care, 31 Ga. L. Rev. 587 (1997); William Sage, Enterprise Liability and the Emerging Managed Care Health Care System, 60 Law & Contemp. Probs. 159 (Spring 1997); Randall R. Bovbjerg & Robert Berenson, Enterprise Liability in the Twenty-First Century, *in* Medical Malpractice and the U.S. Health Care System (W. Sage & R. Kersh eds., 2006); Note, 121 Harv. L. Rev. 1192 (2008).

Problem: Enterprise Liability

Mike Mulligan is administrator of Florence Nightingale Hospital, a large facility in a metropolitan area. Mary Anne is the local lawyer. Mike has a plan to protect the hospital from the erosion of business that has resulted from managed care contracts taking more and more patients into the larger facilities nearby. Mulligan's plan is for the hospital to form its own managed care network. Mulligan would like to include as many of the local physicians as possible in the network. (Assume this is legal under antitrust law.) The network will then sell HMO-type insurance to local residents. The premium revenues will be split 50/50 between the hospital and the doctors, with the physician half going mostly to the primary care physicians. These primary care physicians will act as gatekeepers for hospitalization decisions, referrals to specialists in town, and referrals to larger hospitals for more complex care.

Mulligan consults Mary Anne about advice on the liability implications of this plan. The hospital has been named in a number of suits recently, and he is concerned at the formation stage about what new liability exposure the network will create and what steps are possible to manage or reduce that exposure. Taking the position of Mike Mulligan, how desirable would each of the following alternative ideas be from a business or practical perspective? Taking the position of Mary Anne, how desirable would each be from a legal perspective?

1. Automatically accept into the network any doctor with medical staff privileges at the hospital.
2. In contracting with doctors, insist on an indemnification clause that requires them to compensate the hospital system for any paid claims that arise from the doctor's own fault.
3. Agree to purchase malpractice insurance for network physicians, defend any claims brought by patients, and pay for any resulting liability. Consider this option both for hospital-based care only and for all medical care.

4. Increase the size and authority of the risk management department, school them in the techniques of quality assurance and "total quality management," and impose a passel of practice guidelines that cover liability-sensitive areas of medicine.

5. Write insurance contracts so as to notify subscribers that network physicians are independent contractors. Post similar statements in doctors' waiting rooms, at hospital entrances, on hospital admission forms, and on informed consent forms. Review stationery, billing forms, and uniform dress to avoid creating the unintended impression of an agency relationship between the hospital system and network physicians.

6. Have the risk management department and Mary Anne review all advertising and marketing materials to eliminate any statements that might create an expectation or image of receiving quality care.

7. Write insurance contracts so as to specifically promise an "adequate level of care, consistent with the coverage provided by this insurance and within the standards of care that prevail in other, similar locations in this state."

◼ AETNA HEALTH INC. v. DAVILA
542 U.S. 200 (2004)

Justice THOMAS delivered the opinion of the Court.

In these consolidated cases, two individuals sued their respective HMOs for alleged failures to exercise ordinary care in the handling of coverage decisions, in violation of a duty imposed by the Texas Health Care Liability Act (Texas Act). We granted certiorari to decide whether the individuals' causes of action are completely preempted by the . . . Employee Retirement Income Security Act of 1974 (ERISA) . . .

[Davila was covered by Aetna through his employer, and Calad was covered by CIGNA through her husband's employer.] Respondents both suffered injuries allegedly arising from Aetna's and CIGNA's decisions not to provide coverage for certain treatment and services recommended by respondents' treating physicians. Davila's treating physician prescribed Vioxx to remedy Davila's arthritis pain, but Aetna refused to pay for it. Davila did not appeal or contest this decision, nor did he purchase Vioxx with his own resources and seek reimbursement. Instead, Davila began taking Naprosyn, from which he allegedly suffered a severe reaction that required extensive treatment and hospitalization. [Editors' note: The Court fails to mention that Davila nearly died from bleeding ulcers and that, although Vioxx is much more expensive than Naprosyn, it has fewer side effects relating to bleeding ulcers.]

Calad underwent surgery, and although her treating physician recommended an extended hospital stay, a CIGNA discharge nurse determined that Calad did not meet the plan's criteria for a continued hospital stay. CIGNA consequently denied coverage for the extended hospital stay. Calad experienced postsurgery complications forcing her to return to the hospital. She alleges that these complications would not have occurred had CIGNA approved coverage for a longer hospital stay.

[In separate state-court suits,] respondents . . . argued that petitioners' refusal to cover the requested services violated their "duty to exercise ordinary care when making health care treatment decisions," and that these refusals "proximately caused" their injuries. Petitioners removed the cases to Federal District Courts, arguing that respondents' causes of action fit within the scope of, and were therefore completely preempted by, ERISA . . . The United States Court of Appeals for the Fifth Circuit consolidated their cases with several others raising similar issues . . . After examining the causes of action available under [ERISA], the Court of Appeals determined that respondents' claims could possibly fall under . . . §502(a)(1)(B), which provides a cause of action for the recovery of wrongfully denied benefits. . . . [However, the court ruled that this case does not fall under ERISA because] respondents "are not seeking reimbursement for benefits denied them," but rather request "tort damages" arising from "an external, statutorily imposed duty of 'ordinary care.'" . . .

II

Congress enacted ERISA to "protect . . . the interests of participants in employee benefit plans and their beneficiaries" by setting out substantive regulatory requirements for employee benefit plans and to "provid[e] for appropriate remedies, sanctions, and ready access to the Federal courts." 29 U.S.C. §1001(b). The purpose of ERISA is to provide a uniform regulatory regime over employee benefit plans. To this end, ERISA includes expansive preemption provisions, see ERISA §514, which are intended to ensure that employee benefit plan regulation would be "exclusively a federal concern." ERISA's "comprehensive legislative scheme" includes "an integrated system of procedures for enforcement." . . . As the Court said in *Pilot Life Ins. Co. v. Dedeaux*, 481 U.S. 41 (1987):

> [T]he detailed provisions of §502(a) set forth a comprehensive civil enforcement scheme that represents a careful balancing of the need for prompt and fair claims settlement procedures against the public interest in encouraging the formation of employee benefit plans. The policy choices reflected in the inclusion of certain remedies and the exclusion of others under the federal scheme would be completely undermined if ERISA-plan participants and beneficiaries were free to obtain remedies under state law that Congress rejected in ERISA. The six carefully integrated civil enforcement provisions found in §502(a) of the statute as finally enacted . . . provide strong evidence that Congress did *not* intend to authorize other remedies that it simply forgot to incorporate expressly.

Therefore, any state-law cause of action that duplicates, supplements, or supplants the ERISA civil enforcement remedy conflicts with the clear congressional intent to make the ERISA remedy exclusive and is therefore pre-empted. . . . It follows that if an individual brings suit complaining of a denial of coverage for medical care, where the individual is entitled to such coverage only because of the terms of an ERISA-regulated employee benefit plan, and . . . if an individual, at some point in time, could have brought his claim under ERISA §502(a) . . . then the individual's cause of action is completely preempted by ERISA. . . .

III

The only action [Davila] complained of was Aetna's refusal to approve payment for Davila's Vioxx prescription. Further, the only relationship Aetna had with

Davila was its partial administration of Davila's employer's benefit plan. Similarly . . . Calad contests only CIGNA's decision to refuse coverage for her hospital stay . . . It is clear, then, that respondents complain only about denials of coverage promised under the terms of ERISA-regulated employee benefit plans. Upon the denial of benefits, respondents could have paid for the treatment themselves and then sought reimbursement through a §502(a)(1)(B) action, or sought a preliminary injunction. . . .[1]

Respondents contend, however, that the complained-of actions violate legal duties that arise independently of ERISA or the terms of the employee benefit plans at issue in these cases. Both respondents brought suit specifically under the Texas Act, alleging that petitioners "controlled, influenced, participated in and made decisions which affected the quality of the diagnosis, care, and treatment provided" in a manner that violated "the duty of ordinary care." . . . The Texas Act does impose a duty on managed care entities to "exercise ordinary care when making health care treatment decisions," and makes them liable for damages proximately caused by failures to abide by that duty. However, if a managed care entity correctly concluded that, under the terms of the relevant plan, a particular treatment was not covered, the managed care entity's denial of coverage would not be a proximate cause of any injuries arising from the denial. Rather, the failure of the plan itself to cover the requested treatment would be the proximate cause.[2] More significantly, the Texas Act clearly states that "[it] . . . create[s] no obligation on the part of the health insurance . . . entity to provide to an insured or enrollee treatment which is not covered by the health care plan of the entity." Hence, . . . interpretation of the terms of respondents' benefit plans forms an essential part of their [state law] claim, and [state law] liability would exist here only because of petitioners' administration of ERISA-regulated benefit plans. Petitioners' potential liability under the Texas Act in these cases, then, derives entirely from the particular rights and obligations established by the benefit plans. . . . [R]espondents bring suit only to rectify a wrongful denial of benefits promised under ERISA-regulated plans, and do not attempt to remedy any violation of a legal duty independent of ERISA. . . .

[T]he Court of Appeals found significant that respondents "assert a tort claim for tort damages" rather than "a contract claim for contract damages," and that respondents "are not seeking reimbursement for benefits denied them." But, distinguishing between preempted and non-preempted claims based on the particular label affixed to them would "elevate form over substance and allow parties to evade" the preemptive scope of ERISA simply "by relabeling their contract claims as claims for tortious breach of contract." . . . In [previous Supreme Court cases

---

1. Respondents also argue that the benefit due under their ERISA-regulated employee benefit plans is simply the membership in the respective HMOs, not coverage for the particular medical treatments that are delineated in the plan documents. Respondents did not identify this possible argument in their brief in opposition to the petitions for certiorari, and we deem it waived.

2. To take a clear example, if the terms of the health care plan specifically exclude from coverage the cost of an appendectomy, then any injuries caused by the refusal to cover the appendectomy are properly attributed to the terms of the plan itself, not the managed care entity that applied those terms.

finding preemption], the plaintiffs all brought state claims that were labeled either tort or tort-like. . . .

Respondents also argue—for the first time in their brief to this Court—that the Texas Act is a law that regulates insurance, and hence that ERISA §514(b)(2)(A) saves their causes of action from preemption.[3] This argument is unavailing. . . . ERISA §514(b)(2)(A) must be interpreted in light of the congressional intent to create an exclusive federal remedy in ERISA §502(a). Under ordinary principles of conflict preemption, then, even a state law that can arguably be characterized as "regulating insurance" will be preempted if it provides a separate vehicle to assert a claim for benefits outside of, or in addition to, ERISA's remedial scheme.

IV

Respondents, their *amici*, and some Courts of Appeals have relied heavily upon Pegram v. Herdrich, 530 U.S. 211 (2000), in arguing that ERISA does not preempt or completely preempt state suits such as respondents'. . . . *Pegram* cannot be read so broadly. In *Pegram*, the plaintiff sued her physician-owned-and-operated HMO (which provided medical coverage through plaintiff's employer pursuant to an ERISA-regulated benefit plan) and her treating physician, both for medical malpractice and for a breach of an ERISA fiduciary duty. The plaintiff's treating physician was also the person charged with administering plaintiff's benefits; it was she who decided whether certain treatments were covered. We reasoned that the physician's "eligibility decision and the treatment decision were inextricably mixed." We concluded that "Congress did not intend [the defendant HMO] or any other HMO to be treated as a fiduciary to the extent that it makes mixed eligibility decisions acting through its physicians." . . .

[I]it was essential to *Pegram*'s conclusion that the decisions challenged there were truly "mixed eligibility and treatment decisions," *i.e.*, medical necessity decisions made by the plaintiff's treating physician *qua* treating physician and *qua* benefits administrator. Put another way, the reasoning of *Pegram* "only make[s] sense where the underlying negligence also plausibly constitutes medical maltreatment by a party who can be deemed to be a treating physician or such a physician's employer." Cicio v. Does, 321 F.3d 83, 109 (C.A.2 2003) (Calabresi, J., dissenting in part). Here, however, petitioners are neither respondents' treating physicians nor the employers of respondents' treating physicians. Petitioners' coverage decisions, then, are pure eligibility decisions, and *Pegram* is not implicated. . . .

Justice GINSBURG, with whom Justice BREYER joins, concurring.

. . . [This] decision is consistent with our governing case law on ERISA's preemptive scope. I therefore join the Court's opinion. But, with greater enthusiasm . . . I also join "the rising judicial chorus urging that Congress and [this] Court revisit what is an unjust and increasingly tangled ERISA regime." DiFelice v. AETNA U.S. Healthcare, 346 F.3d 442, 453 (C.A.3 2003) (Becker, J., concurring). Because the Court has coupled an encompassing interpretation of ERISA's preemptive force

---

3. ERISA §514(b)(2)(A) reads, as relevant: "[N]othing in this subchapter shall be construed to exempt or relieve any person from any law of any State which regulates insurance, banking, or securities."

with a cramped construction of the "equitable relief" allowable under §502(a)(3), a "regulatory vacuum" exists: "[V]irtually all state law remedies are preempted but very few federal substitutes are provided."

A series of the Court's decisions has yielded a host of situations in which persons adversely affected by ERISA-proscribed wrongdoing cannot gain make-whole relief [because] "there is a stark absence in [ERISA] itself and in its legislative history of any reference to an intention to authorize the recovery of extracontractual damages" for consequential injuries. . . . [F]resh consideration of the availability of consequential damages under §502(a)(3) is plainly in order. See 321 F.3d, at 106, 107 (Calabresi, J., dissenting in part) ("gaping wound" caused by the breadth of preemption and limited remedies under ERISA, as interpreted by this Court, will not be healed until the Court "start[s] over" or Congress "wipe[s] the slate clean"); DiFelice, 346 F.3d, at 467 ("The vital thing . . . is that either Congress or the Court act quickly, because the current situation is plainly untenable."); Langbein, What ERISA Means by "Equitable": The Supreme Court's Trail of Error in *Russell, Mertens,* and *Great-West,* 103 Colum. L. Rev. 1317, 1365 (2003). . . . The Government notes a potential amelioration. . . . [It] suggests that the Act, as currently written and interpreted, may "allo[w] at least some forms of 'make-whole' relief." . . . As the Court points out, respondents here declined the opportunity to amend their complaints to state claims for relief under §502(a). . . . But the Government's suggestion may indicate an effective remedy others similarly circumstanced might fruitfully pursue.

"Congress . . . intended ERISA to replicate the core principles of trust remedy law, including the make-whole standard of relief." *Langbein* 1319. I anticipate that Congress, or this Court, will one day so confirm.

Notes: ERISA Preemption

1. *Damages Under ERISA.* Under ERISA, patients who are wrongly denied health insurance benefits can recover compensation only for the costs of treatment, but not for consequential damages, pain and suffering, wrongful death, or punitive damages. Corcoran v. United Healthcare, Inc., 965 F.2d 1321 (5th Cir. 1992), dramatically illustrates the hardship caused by this restriction in available remedies. There, a woman miscarried late in her pregnancy due, she alleged, to the HMO's refusal to authorize hospitalization for pregnancy complications. The court limited her potential remedies under ERISA to an order for treatment or compensation for treatment costs. But, because the fetus had died, these remedies were meaningless. This restriction of damages is much more severe even than that imposed by ordinary contract law. See Sullivan v. O'Connor, page 350. Therefore, it is important to note the concurring Justices' argument in *Davila* that this limitation can and should be revisited. See Sarah Spisich, The Aftermath of *Davila:* Are Healthcare Enrollees Now in a Sinking Ship Without a Paddle?, 17(4) The Health Lawyer 22 (Aug. 2005); Comment, 2006 B.Y.U. L. Rev. 1589 (2007).

The majority in *Davila* appears to think the outcome makes perfect sense according to congressional intent. Legislative history, however, reveals that Congress wrote ERISA primarily with pension benefits in mind, and long before managed care health insurance existed. Do you see why limiting damages to the costs of treatment might have made a lot more sense under traditional insurance? Assuming, as the concurrence argues, that ERISA's remedies no longer make sense for managed care insurance, whose responsibility is it to fix the problem: Congress's or the courts'? See Andrews-Clarke v. Travelers Insurance Co., 948 F. Supp. 49 (D. Mass. 1997) ("Although the [failure of the utilization reviewer to approve hospitalization for a deeply troubled alcoholic who later committed suicide] is extraordinarily troubling, even more disturbing to this Court is the failure of Congress to amend a statute that, due to the changing realities of the modern health care system, has gone conspicuously awry from its original intent. Does anyone care? Do you?").

2. *ERISA Terminology Is Obscure and Confusing.* Essentially, an ERISA "plan" exists any time an employer pays for health insurance. If the employer simply purchases health insurance, then technically there may be a distinction between the "plan," which is the decision to purchase, and the insurance, which is the contracted-for benefit. Would it be possible, using this distinction, to argue that ERISA preempts only suits against employers for failing to provide insurance, but not suits against insurers for failing to provide the benefits covered by the insurance? Observe how *Davila* avoids this issue in footnote 2 of the opinion, but a few lower courts have adopted this position. See, e.g., Washington Physicians Service Ass'n v. Gregoire, 147 F.3d 1039 (9th Cir. 1998) ("The mere fact that many [employers] choose to buy health insurance for their [employees] does not cause a regulation of health insurance automatically to 'relate to' any employee benefit plan—just as a decision to buy an apple a day for every employee, or to offer employees a gym membership, does not cause all state regulation of apples and gyms to 'relate to' employee benefit plans."). But see Hotz v. Blue Cross & Blue Shield of Massachusetts, 292 F.3d 57, 59-60 (1st Cir. 2002) ("Although the [employer plan/insurance plan] distinction is linguistically possible, it would mean that numerous past ERISA suits brought to secure payment for medical services from third-party providers under ERISA plans lacked a legal basis."). See generally Russell Korobkin, The Failed Jurisprudence of Managed Care, and How to Fix It: Reinterpreting ERISA Preemption, 51 UCLA L. Rev. 457 (2003).

Regardless, ERISA preemption would still apply to situations where the employer self-insures, that is, pays for health care directly out of its own funds. In that case, ERISA clearly preempts state law liability against the employer. So far, courts have applied ERISA preemption equally to both purchased and self-funded health insurance, where tort and contract claims are concerned. This distinction is relevant, however, for purposes of preemption of state insurance regulation, as discussed in Chapter 9.C.

3. *Which Claims Are Preempted?* The end of the *Davila* opinion briefly alludes to ERISA's effect on more conventional medical malpractice claims that arise under managed care insurance. Lower court decisions clarify the following: ERISA clearly does not apply to a malpractice claim against only the treating physician for a medical mistake that is unaffected by health insurance. . . . Likewise, courts usually find no preemption if a plaintiff attempts to hold a health insurer vicariously liable for a treating physician's mistake. Pacificare of Oklahoma v. Burrage, 59 F.3d 151 (10th Cir. 1995); Rice v. Panchal, 65 F.3d 637 (7th Cir. 1995). This helps to explain *Davila*'s reference to the fact that the plaintiffs' physicians in that case were not employees of the health plans.

The law is unsettled, however, when there is a medical treatment mistake and the plaintiff attempts to hold the insurer *directly* responsible because it selected bad physicians or influenced their treatment decisions. This is similar to the situation in Pegram v. Herdrich, 530 U.S. 211 (2000), which is discussed in *Davila*. There, the patient claimed that her doctor was influenced by profit distributions from the HMO and that this financial tie violates ERISA fiduciary standards. In the course of rejecting that claim under ERISA, the Court noted that the patient was free to pursue her claim in state court in the form of a medical malpractice suit. This strongly suggests that direct liability actions against HMOs for care provided by treating physicians are not preempted by ERISA, even after *Davila*.

In short, courts must distinguish between tort claims based on insurance coverage decisions, which are preempted, and medical malpractice liability, which is not preempted. In drawing this line, many lower courts have followed a rule of thumb that distinguishes between claims based on the *quantity* of care and those based on its *quality*. See, e.g., Dukes v. U.S. Healthcare, 57 F.3d 350 (3d Cir. 1995); Bauman v. U.S. Healthcare, Inc., 193 F.3d 151 (3d Cir. 1999). The *Davila* case makes no reference to this concept, however. Instead, it focuses on whether the insurer or the treating physician made the critical decision. Is that distinction likely to be sufficiently clear in most cases? What about situations where the treating physician is employed full time by an HMO, and the HMO instructs the physician that a particular treatment option is not approved, for instance, that women should not remain in the hospital longer than 48 hours following normal childbirth? That might be regarded as a quantity decision based on the insurance policy's medical appropriateness criteria, or it might be regarded as a form of direct HMO liability for interfering with physicians' ability to make good treatment decisions. Does *Davila* resolve which is the correct characterization?

One further complication: If it is possible to find an agency relationship between the HMO and the treating physician, should it matter that the HMO is not the physician's employer? Isn't the critical factor whether or not the physician agreed with, or acquiesced in, the HMO's decision? In *Davila*, the HMO refused to pay for treatments the physicians ordered, but, in many other cases, physicians may not order treatment they know the HMO won't pay for or that will cost the physician money under the HMO's payment incentives. Shouldn't patients be able to blame the HMO, at least in part, when this happens? In such cases, should *Davila* apply?

There is a large amount of academic literature discussing these issues, but most of it predates *Davila*. For subsequent analysis, see Aaron S. Kesselheim & Troyen A. Brennan, The Swinging Pendulum: The Supreme Court Reverses Course on ERISA and Managed Care, 5 Yale J. Health Pol'y L. & Ethics 451 (2005); Leonard A. Nelson, Aetna v. Davila: A Missed Opportunity, 31 Wm. Mitchell L. Rev. 843-896 (2005); Comment, 88 U. Colo. L. Rev. 1169 (2017); Note, 84 Tex. L. Rev. 1347-1383 (2006).

4. *Medicare Preemption.* Preemption issues might also arise under Medicare, which has a restrictive set of remedies for beneficiaries (discussed in Chapter 9.D.2). One court has held that Medicare's administrative review process does not preempt a state tort action against a private HMO that contracted to deliver Medicare services. McCall v. Pacificare of California, Inc., 21 P.3d 1189 (Cal. 2001). But, a later court has disagreed, finding that Medicare's 2006 amendments preempt liability suits against private Medicare insurers. Morrison v. Health Plan of Nevada, 328 P.3d 1165 (Nev. 2014).

H. MEDICAL MALPRACTICE REFORM

■ *McCall v. United States*
  134 So.3d 894 (Fla. 2014)

Lewis, J.

This case is before the Court to answer four questions of Florida law certified by the United States Court of Appeals for the Eleventh Circuit: [does the state's $1,000,000 cap on noneconomic damages in medical malpractice wrongful death cases violate any of four provisions of Florida's constitution: (1) the right to equal protection; (2) the right of access to the courts; (3) the right to trial by jury; and (4) the separation of powers? The court answered the first question in the affirmative, finding an equal protection violation, and so the court decided that it is unnecessary to answer the remaining constitutional questions.] . . .

Facts And Procedural History

[As described by the trial court, Michelle McCall was a "bright, beautiful, and healthy, 20-year-old woman" who, while living at home, became pregnant with her high school sweetheart. Because one or both parents were in the Air Force, she received care from military medical personnel. Tragically, during delivery, she bled to death because, as the trial court found, her nurses failed to recognize, or convey to the physicians in time, the seriousness of her blood loss over the span of two hours. Under Florida's wrongful death statute, the trial court awarded damages for economic loss of almost $1 million, plus noneconomic damages totaling $2 million — with $750,000 of the latter going to each of her parents and $500,000 going to her newborn son. Florida's malpractice reform statute, however, limits noneconomic damages to $1 million in wrongful death cases, regardless of the number of recovering family members. The federal court of appeals (11th Cir.) ruled that this limit does not violate the U.S. Constitution, but it certified to the Florida Supreme Court whether a different result obtains under the state's constitution.]

Equal Protection

. . . The Florida Constitution provides, in pertinent part: "All natural persons, female and male alike, are equal before the law." . . . Unless a suspect class or fundamental right protected by the Florida Constitution is implicated by the challenged provision, the rational basis test will apply to evaluate an equal protection challenge. To satisfy the rational basis test, a statute must bear a rational and reasonable relationship to a legitimate state objective, and it cannot be arbitrary or capriciously imposed. . . The statutory cap on wrongful death noneconomic damages fails because it imposes unfair and illogical burdens on injured parties when an act of medical negligence gives rise to multiple claimants. . . Further, the statutory cap on wrongful death noneconomic damages does not bear a rational relationship to the stated purpose that the cap is purported to address, the alleged medical malpractice insurance crisis in Florida.

Arbitrary Distinctions

. . . The plain language of this statutory plan irrationally impacts circumstances which have multiple claimants/survivors differently and far less favorably than circumstances in which there is a single claimant/survivor. . . Applying the cap, the federal court then reduced the amounts of damages so each claimant would receive only half of his or her respective damages. . . [T]he greater the number of survivors and the more devastating their losses are, the less likely they are to be fully compensated for those losses.

Other state supreme courts have struck down caps on noneconomic damages based upon a similar rationale. . . The Supreme Court of New Hampshire condemned on equal protection grounds a $250,000 cap on noneconomic damages in medical malpractice cases, concluding that it is "simply unfair and unreasonable to impose the burden of supporting the medical care industry solely upon those persons who are most severely injured and therefore most in need of compensation." Carson v. Maurer, 120 N.H. 925, 424 A.2d 825, 837 (1980). [The Florida cap likewise] has the effect of saving a modest amount for many by imposing devastating costs on a few—those who are most grievously injured, those who sustain the greatest damage and loss, and multiple claimants for whom judicially determined noneconomic damages are subject to division and reduction simply based upon the existence of the cap. . .

Our holding today is not inconsistent with the decisions in . . . University of Miami v. Echarte, 618 So.2d 189 (Fla.1993) . . . . [I]n Echarte this Court considered whether a $250,000 cap on noneconomic damages for medical malpractice claims where a party requested arbitration violated the access to courts provision of the Florida Constitution. . . In upholding the constitutionality of the cap in medical malpractice arbitration proceedings, this Court in Echarte noted that arbitration provided commensurate benefits in exchange for the cap, such as saving the expense of attorney fees and expert witnesses. Conversely, under [the wrongful death cap], survivors receive absolutely no benefit whatsoever from the cap on noneconomic damages, but only arbitrary reductions based upon the number of survivors. . . .

THE ALLEGED MEDICAL MALPRACTICE CRISIS

In addition to arbitrary and invidious discrimination between medical malpractice claimants, the cap on noneconomic damages also violates the Equal Protection Clause of the Florida Constitution because it bears no rational relationship to a legitimate state objective. . . The Florida Legislature attempted to justify the cap on noneconomic damages by claiming that "Florida is in the midst of a medical malpractice insurance crisis of unprecedented magnitude." The Legislature asserted that the increase in medical malpractice liability insurance premiums has resulted in physicians leaving Florida, retiring early from the practice of medicine, or refusing to perform high-risk procedures, thereby limiting the availability of health care. . .

Although assertions of a malpractice insurance crisis are often accompanied by images of runaway juries entering verdicts in exorbitant amounts of noneconomic damages, one study revealed that in Florida cases which resulted in payments of $1 million or more over a fourteen-year period, only 7.5 percent involved a jury trial verdict [citing Vidmar et al., page 421 supra]. . . . Not only do jury trials constitute only a small portion of $1 million payments, [but] the settlements following verdicts tend to be substantially less than the jury awards." According to the authors, with one exception, cases with verdicts in excess of $4 million settled for, on average, 37 percent less than the verdict. Thus, available data indicates the Task Force's finding that noneconomic damage awards by juries are a primary cause of the purported medical malpractice crisis in Florida is most questionable.

Even the Task Force whose report was relied upon by the Florida Legislature . . . recognized that there are other explanations for the dramatic rise in medical malpractice insurance premiums. For example, the Task Force Report notes that, [according to one witness]:

[T]his so-called "crisis" is nothing more than the underwriting cycle of the insurance industry, and driven by the same factors that caused the "crises" in the 1970s and 1980s. According to . . . [this witness], with each crisis, there has been a severe drop in the investment income for insurers, which has been compounded by sever [sic] under-pricing of insurance premiums in the prior years. . . . [D]uring years of high interest rates or excellent insurer profits that are invested for maximum return, the insurance companies engage in fierce competition for premium dollars by selling under-priced premiums and insuring very poor risks. Then . . . when investment income drops, either due to increases in interest rates or the stock market, or due to low income resulting from unbearably low premiums, the insurance industry responds by sharply increasing premiums and reducing coverage. . . The tort reform changes in the 1980s had nothing to do with the flattening of rates. The flattening was caused instead by modulations in the insurance cycle throughout the country. . .

See also Tom Baker, THE MEDICAL MALPRACTICE MYTH 53–54 (2005) ("[T]he two most recent medical liability insurance crises did not result from sudden or dramatic increases in medical malpractice settlements or jury verdicts. . . . [T]he crises resulted from dramatic increases in the amount of money that the insurance industry put in reserve for claims. Those reserve increases were so big because the insurance industry systematically underreserved in the years leading up to the crisis."). . . Based upon these statements and reports, although medical malpractice premiums in Florida were undoubtedly high in 2003, we conclude the Legislature's determination that . . . Florida was in the midst of a bona fide medical malpractice crisis, threatening the access of Floridians to health care, is dubious and questionable at the very best.

THE IMPACT OF DAMAGE CAPS ON THE ALLEGED CRISIS

Even if these conclusions by the Legislature are assumed to be true, . . . [r]eports have failed to establish a direct correlation between damages caps and reduced malpractice premiums. [Various insurance officials testified during legislative deliberations that, if a cap were enacted, they would not necessarily reduce malpractice premiums immediately, or would do so only slightly, in part because they would need to see if the cap survives in court.] . . . While the cap on noneconomic damages limits the amount of money that insurance companies must pay injured victims of medical malpractice, [it] does not require insurance companies to use the acquired savings to lower malpractice insurance premiums for physicians. . . . [Although Florida's insurance regulator required insurers to take the cap into account in formulating their rates], [t]here was no mandated rate reduction [and Florida's malpractice premiums remain high compared to other states, with Florida insurers earning substantial profits.]. . . . With such impressive [profits], the insurance industry should pass savings onto Florida physicians in the form of reduced malpractice insurance premiums.[10] . . .

THE CURRENT STATUS OF MEDICAL MALPRACTICE IN FLORIDA

Lastly, even if a "crisis" existed when [the cap] was enacted, a crisis is not a permanent condition. Conditions can change, which remove or negate the justification for a law, transforming what may have once been reasonable into arbitrary and irrational legislation. . . Having evaluated current data, we conclude that no rational basis exists to justify continued application of the noneconomic damages cap . . . . [M]edical malpractice filings in Florida have decreased significantly, [more than 60 percent since 2003-2004. Moreover, the number and amount of malpractice claims paid by insurers has dropped about 30 percent.] . . .

Based on the foregoing, we . . . hold that the cap on wrongful death noneconomic damages violates the Equal Protection Clause of the Florida Constitution. We defer answering the remaining certified questions.

[One other Justice joined this opinion. Three other justices concurred only in the result, making this merely a plurality opinion, because: "Although this Court is not bound to blindly defer to all legislative findings, I disagree with the plurality's independent evaluation and reweighing of reports and data . . . ."].

POLSTON, C.J., with CANADAY, J., dissenting.

. . . On appeal, the Eleventh Circuit . . . reasoned as follows [under the U.S. Constitution]:

> Plaintiffs ask us to second guess the legislature's judgment in enacting a "per incident" rather than "per claimant" statutory cap. However, equal protection is not a license for courts to judge the wisdom, fairness, or logic of legislative choices. The legislature identified a legitimate governmental purpose in passing the statutory cap, namely to reduce the cost of medical malpractice premiums and health care. The means that Florida chose, a per incident cap on noneconomic damages, bears a rational relationship to that end. The Florida legislature could reasonably have concluded that such a cap would reduce damage awards and in turn make medical malpractice insurance more affordable and healthcare more available. . .

[Similarly], multiple state courts have rejected equal protection challenges to statutory caps on noneconomic damages. . . In fact, it is hard to conceive a more rational means of assuaging the fear of huge damage awards and reining in insurance costs in the case of a victim's death than by limiting noneconomic wrongful death damages. More specifically, the Florida Legislature could have rationally believed that the cap on noneconomic damages would reduce malpractice damage awards,

---

10. Despite such increases in net income, in 2012 one medical malpractice insurance company nonetheless charged obstetricians in Miami–Dade County more than $190,000 for $1 million of coverage. The company charged obstetricians in other Florida counties approximately $98,000 for the same coverage. During 2012, the same company charged orthopedists in Miami–Dade County more than $115,000 for $1 million of coverage, whereas orthopedists in other Florida counties were charged approximately $59,000.

which would thereby increase predictability in the medical malpractice insurance market and lead to reduced insurance premiums. . . In fact, the Governor's Task Force, upon which the Legislature expressly relied, concluded as much:

> [I]mposing caps on non-economic damages in medical malpractice cases will significantly reduce the exposure of Florida healthcare providers to risk of loss from jury awards of inherently subjective damages. Such a reduction of risk will make malpractice losses much more predictable, and thereby lead to stability in malpractice insurance premium rates. A reduction in potential liability and resulting stability will encourage more malpractice insurers to participate in the Florida market. This, along with the reduced exposure to risk, will permit insurers to charge lower premiums, on a sound financial basis . . .

The Task Force received specific testimony indicating that "[i]n Georgia, physicians pay from $5,000 to $6,000 for $1,000,000 of coverage. Thirty miles south, in Jacksonville, that costs $27,000." And the Task Force . . . found that "[i]n Miami, evidence reflects that 80 percent of the OB/GYNs carry no insurance and those who do are paying over $207,000 per year for $1 million dollars worth of coverage." . . . The Task Force also described testimony indicating that, as a result of these issues, over half the doctors in Florida that carry insurance can only afford to carry a $250,000 policy . . . .

The Task Force also stated its belief that "caps on non-economic damages are particularly effective, because they limit the escalation of awards for pain and suffering, which fuels large increases for all awards and settlements." In fact, the Task Force thought that a cap on noneconomic damages was so important to alleviating the crisis and lowering premiums that it recommended a $250,000 per incident cap on noneconomic damages, rather than the $1 million per incident cap at issue in this case. . .

Justice Lewis notes that medical malpractice filings have decreased significantly since fiscal year 2003–04 and that Florida, according to a 2011 report, is now retaining a fairly high percentage of Florida-trained medical students. While he uses this information to support the plurality's argument that the statutory caps are no longer justified because a medical malpractice crisis does not currently exist, this information just as easily (and perhaps more likely) supports the argument that the cap has had its intended effect and that, if the cap is eliminated, the medical malpractice crisis would return in full force. . .

While the plurality clearly would have come to a different policy choice than the Legislature based upon the hardly unambiguous data that the plurality could cull from the record and the Internet, that is not the point. Instead, our precedent dictates that we employ the rational basis test, which is a relatively easy test for a statute to pass. . .

[For various reasons, the dissent also reasoned that the cap does not infringe the right of access to the courts; the right to trial by jury; or the separation of powers.]

■EVALUATION OF OPTIONS FOR MEDICAL MALPRACTICE SYSTEM REFORM

Michelle M. Mello & Allen Kachalia*

Report to the Medicare Payment Advisory Commission, 2010

The objective of this report is to evaluate the prospects for several leading medical malpractice reform proposals to positively affect the performance of the medical liability system and the system's impact on health care. . . . This report describes the essential features of each proposed reform [in Table 1] and synthesizes the best available evidence about the likely effects of each of 6 outcome variables:

1. **Claims:** malpractice claim outcomes, including the number of claims filed, including the ease and equity with which patients receive compensation, and claims costs
2. **Overhead costs:** malpractice system administrative costs, including litigation costs and insurers' overhead expenses
3. **Liability costs:** malpractice liability costs for health care providers (i.e., malpractice insurance premiums)
4. **Defensive medicine:** defensive medical practices and overall health care spending and utilization
5. **Supply:** health care provider supply and patient access to care, including health insurance coverage and cost
6. **Quality of care:** potential to foster evidence-based care and improve patient safety

TRADITIONAL STATE REFORMS

CAPS ON NONECONOMIC DAMAGES

. . . The rationale for this reform is to reduce the number of multi-million dollar awards, which are difficult for liability insurers to plan for and pay and which may pose special difficulties for health care facilities that are self-insured. It is also motivated by a desire to reduce the high degree of variation and perceived arbitrariness in jury awards for "pain and suffering." Twenty-six states currently impose a cap on noneconomic damages and 6 cap total damages. Medical professional societies strongly desire to see noneconomic damages caps adopted in the remaining states, through state legislation or imposition of a federal cap. . . .

---

* This excerpt contains a few passages from the authors' updated version of this report, Medical Malpractice: Evidence on Reform Alternatives and Claims Involving Elderly Patients (MedPac, 2016).

Table 1.
Reform Options Evaluated

Reform	Basic Description
Traditional State Reforms	*Reforms that have been widely implemented at the state level*
Caps on noneconomic damages	Limit the amount of money that a plaintiff can take as an award for noneconomic losses, or "pain and suffering," in a malpractice suit. The cap may apply to the plaintiff, limiting the amount she may receive, or to each defendant, limiting the total amount for which each may be liable.
Pretrial screening panels	Panel reviews a malpractice case at an early stage and provides an opinion about whether a claim has sufficient merit to proceed to trial. Typically, a negative opinion does not bar a case from going forward, but can be introduced by the defendant as evidence at the trial.
Certificate of merit	Requires a plaintiff to present, at the time of filing the claim or soon thereafter, an affidavit certifying that a qualified medical expert believes that there is a reasonable and meritorious cause for the suit.
Attorney fee limits	Limits the amount of a malpractice award that a plaintiff's attorney may take in a contingent-fee arrangement. The limitation is typically expressed as a percentage of the award; it may also incorporate a maximum dollar value.
Joint-and-several liability reform	In cases involving more than one defendant, such as a physician and a hospital, this reform limits the financial liability of each defendant to the percentage fault that the jury allocates to that defendant. Without this reform, the plaintiff may collect the entire amount of the judgment from one defendant if the other(s) default on their obligation to pay, even if the paying defendant bore only a small share of the responsibility for what happened to the plaintiff.
Collateral-source rule reform	Eliminates a traditional rule that if an injured plaintiff receives compensation for her injury from other sources, such as health insurance, that payment should not be deducted from the amount that a defendant who is found liable for that injury must pay.
Periodic payment	Allows or requires insurers to pay out malpractice awards over a long period of time, rather than in a lump sum. This enables insurers to purchase annuities (sometimes called "structured settlements") from other insurance companies which cost less than paying the whole award up front. Insurers are also able to retain any amounts that the plaintiff does not actually collect during her lifespan.
Statutes of limitations/repose	

Reform	Basic Description
Innovative Reforms	*Reforms that have had limited or no implementation in the U.S.*
Schedule of noneconomic damages	A hierarchy or tiering system is created for purposes of categorizing medical injuries and creating a relative ranking of severity. A dollar value range for noneconomic damages is then assigned to each severity tier. The schedule is used by juries and judges either as an advisory document or as a binding guideline.
Administrative compensation systems or "health courts"	Routes medical injury claims into an alternative adjudication process involving specialized judges, decision and damages guidelines, neutral experts, and (under most proposals) a compensation standard that is broader than the negligence standard.
Disclosure-and-offer programs	Institutional programs that support clinicians in disclosing unanticipated care outcomes to patients and that make rapid offers of modest compensation in appropriate cases.
Enterprise medical liability	Broadens the prospects for holding health care organizations, such as hospitals and managed care organizations, directly liable for medical injuries, in addition to or instead of holding individual clinicians liable.

Although the oldest and most widely publicized example of a noneconomic damages cap, California's, is $250,000, most states have found it politically difficult to implement such a stringent cap in more recent rounds of reform. It is more common for states to set the cap at $500,000 or more, and to opt for a tiered cap in which different amounts apply to different kinds of injuries. The appeal of a flat cap is its simplicity and, when set at a low amount, greater potential for cost control. The appeal of a tiered cap is its greater vertical equity—that is, more severe injuries are eligible for a higher award. . . .

The evidence increasingly suggests that noneconomic damages caps are associated with a statistically significant decrease in the frequency of claims, whether the measure used is paid claims or all claim filings. Six studies have returned such findings, 22, 26-31, while two have found no association. Mechanistically, the . . . link is that caps discourage plaintiff's attorneys from filing claims by lowering the expected value of the case, which in a contingent-fee system affects the attorney's expected return on investment. Overall, the evidence is too equivocal at this time to support a conclusion about the effect of caps on claim frequency.

Most studies of the effects of caps on claims payouts have found a significant effect, typically on the order of a 20 to 30 percent reduction in average award size. . . . The effect of damages caps on malpractice insurance premiums has been the subject of intense controversy. The issue has been exhaustively studied, with mixed findings among well-designed studies. [Five] studies have identified significant effects of caps, while four older studies found no effect. A reasonable conclusion based on strong, recent studies is that caps moderately constrain the growth of premiums over time, with an effect on the order of 6 to 13 percent. . . .

[Regarding defensive medicine, there] is good, but not uniform, evidence that damages caps are associated with lower rates of utilization of services that are considered to be indicators of defensive medicine [such as cesarean sections and evaluation for heart problems]. . . . [A] fairly large evidence base suggests that non-economic damages caps effect statistically significant increases in the supply of physicians in a state — though some evidence suggests the effect may be concentrated among high-risk specialist physicians, rural areas, and/or caps at the most stringent level (around $250,000). . . Examining the studies with positive findings, the effect sizes have varied dramatically, but have clustered around 2-5%. . . .

Overall, the . . . weight of the evidence suggests that caps reduce claims frequency, achieve substantial savings in average claims payments, modestly constrain the growth of malpractice insurance premiums, moderately improve physician supply, and reduce at least some defensive medical practices. Evidence concerning their effects on health insurance and quality of care is too limited or equivocal to support firm conclusions. . . .

PRETRIAL SCREENING PANELS

The function of pretrial screening panels is to review a malpractice case at an early stage and provide an opinion about whether or not the claim has sufficient merit to proceed to trial. Typically, a negative opinion does not bar a case from going forward, but can be introduced by the defendant as evidence at the trial. The rationale for this reform is to reduce the number of nonmeritorious malpractice claims, and the litigation expenses incurred in defending them, by bringing expert judgment to bear before a large amount of legal expenses are incurred. Additionally, panel decisions can provide juries with a neutral source of expertise in cases that go to trial. About 20 states currently have pretrial screening panels of some kind. Screening panels have been repealed in at least 7 states and overturned by courts on constitutional grounds in at least another 5. . . .

A handful of well-designed studies have examined the effects of pretrial screening panels, and the weight of the evidence suggests that they are not effective in reducing claims costs, claim frequency, or malpractice insurance premiums. They may help reduce defensive medicine. The evidence concerning their effects on defense costs, physician supply, health insurance premiums, and quality of care is too limited or equivocal to support conclusions about those relationships. Panels involve their own administrative costs.

CERTIFICATE OF MERIT

Certificate of merit (COM) reforms require the plaintiff in a malpractice suit to present, at the time of filing the claim or soon thereafter, an affidavit certifying that a qualified medical expert believes that there is a reasonable and meritorious cause for the suit. Like pretrial screening panels, the rationale for COM requirements is to reduce the number of nonmeritorious malpractice claims and associated expenses by bringing expert judgment to bear early in the litigation. At least 11 states have adopted COM requirements, but Washington State's COM law was recently struck down on constitutional grounds. . . .

Only one methodologically-strong study has examined the effects of COM requirements and did not find an effect on the number of paid claims or payment amounts on large claims. On their face, COM requirements add a modest amount to the cost of litigation. Theoretically, the prospects for affecting the key outcome variables appear quite weak.

ATTORNEY FEE LIMITS

Attorney fee limits cap the amount of a malpractice award that a plaintiff's attorney may take as a contingency fee. Nearly all medical malpractice cases are handled by plaintiff's attorneys on a contingent-fee basis. . . . The rationale for attorney fee limits is to discourage plaintiff's attorneys from accepting cases of marginal or no merit by altering the attorney's expected return on investment in the case. Sixteen states currently have limits on attorney fees in medical malpractice cases. . . . [The evidence shows weak or no effects for this and the remainder of the "traditional" reforms. See Table 3 below.]

INNOVATIVE REFORMS . . .

ADMINISTRATIVE COMPENSATION SYSTEMS OR "HEALTH COURTS"

The use of administrative compensation systems or "health courts" for medical injury has frequently been proposed over the last 40 years. Proposals for administrative systems or health courts can contain several differing features, but most fit into one of two general models. In one model, often described as a *medical court*, a jury is replaced with a . . . medically trained judge to adjudicate the negligence determination. Most of the other features of the present tort process are kept without much change. In the second model, an administrative agency investigates and adjudicates claims for medical injury. . . . The medical court model is a smaller departure from the present tort system than an administrative model . . . [in that] most medical court proposals [change only the adjudicator but] keep the remainder of the tort process intact. This model is rooted in the notion that better equipped judges and fact-finders would make quicker and more accurate decisions. The objective is not necessarily to improve patient access to compensation, but rather to handle the claims filed more accurately and efficiently.

In the administrative model, . . . the agency would act as a neutral fact-finder and adjudicator so that the process would not be slowed down by an adversarial fact-finding process. Decisions could theoretically be rendered more cost-effectively because neither attorneys nor experts to represent each point of view would be required. Because filing a claim should be easier, administrative models can have the additional benefit of increasing the number of patients with access to the compensation system. To further boost access to compensation, most administrative models call for the use of a compensation standard broader than negligence, such as "avoidability." . . . A no-fault standard would not compensate all injuries caused by medical care, but just those that are not "necessary and ordinary to" medical care (e.g., the loss of hair due to chemotherapy would not be compensable but a post-surgical infection would be). A no-fault standard would, however, be more expensive because a greater proportion of claims would be paid. It also would not align as well with patient safety principles that focus on preventability of harm. . . .

The design of an administrative compensation system will need to include whether or not limits on damages (economic, noneconomic, or punitive) will be applied. One option is to . . . create a schedule of noneconomic damages and award full or close to full economic damages. . . .

[Another key design question is] whether the system will be patients' only legal remedy for malpractice, or whether claimants can opt to pursue their claims in the administrative system or in the courts. . . . A detailed constitutional analysis [of a mandatory design] is beyond the scope of this report, but . . . [o]ther exclusive administrative systems, such as workers' compensation systems, have been successfully designed and implemented while withstanding constitutional challenges. A voluntary design avoids these constitutional difficulties for the most part, but has other disadvantages. Due-process rights would still require that a mechanism for informing patients about their choice and eliciting informed consent to participation be developed. Laws in some states may prohibit such pre-injury agreements. . . . [Also, providing a choice] perpetuates the current inefficiencies of the tort system and essentially creates two tracks for compensation, leading to greater complexity. . . . Additionally, legal wrangling may arise over whether a particular claim meets the defined categories for jurisdiction. . . .

Very little actual experience on administrative systems for medical injury in the United States exists, but . . . modeling has predicted that total costs in an administrative compensation system may remain unchanged or slightly decline as compared to the negligence based tort system. Total costs, nevertheless, will vary based on the compensation standard and award limits (if any). Effects on defensive medicine and quality of care are likely to be positive, while effects on insurance premiums and physician supply are difficult to predict.

DISCLOSURE-AND-OFFER PROGRAMS

Disclosure and offer (D&O) [or apology] programs support clinicians in disclosing unanticipated care outcomes to patients and make rapid offers of compensation in appropriate cases. [These are also known as "communication and resolution" programs.] Presently, they are operated by a [limited number] of hospitals and liability insurers (predominantly self-insured hospital systems). . . . D&O programs vary in their structures and processes, but contain some common elements: When an unanticipated outcome occurs, clinicians are asked to promptly report it to . . . patients and/or their families. A disclosure occurs when a provider reveals and explains an adverse event and apologizes. . . . A rapid investigation into the cause of the error is conducted, and further disclosures are made regarding the findings of the investigation. . . . The institution makes an expedited decision about whether compensation in some form is appropriate, based on the compensation standard it has adopted. If the standard is met, an offer is made to the patient. Incidents not resolved through settlement after this process can go on to become malpractice claims in the tort system. . . .

D&O programs . . . appeal to many clinicians because they are consonant with principles of medical ethics (fiduciary duty, patient autonomy, and justice). . . . On the other hand, [l]iability risk is widely regarded to be among the chief barriers, and the number of institutions with formal D&O programs remains limited. Other barriers to disclosure include the emotional difficulty of the conversation, shame and guilt, the stress of a possible lawsuit, potential consequences in credentialing processes, and reputational harm. . . .

[T]he evidence base for evaluating the effects of such programs on the key outcome variables is [small]. However, . . . the available reports suggest that [these programs] are a highly promising approach, which can return substantial benefits in terms of reductions in claim frequency, payouts, and overhead costs and at the same time improve patient access to compensation and patient safety. . . , there is some risk associated with experimentation with this approach. . . . [P]oorly executed disclosures or inadequate offers of compensation may inflame patients and families, prompting additional claims. . . .

ENTERPRISE MEDICAL LIABILITY

Enterprise medical liability is a legal doctrine assigning liability to a health care organization for tortious injuries that occur within its facilities or are caused by its clinical staff affiliates, including but not limited to its employees. Under this system, the liability of individual physicians and other clinicians is reduced or eliminated. . . . Although some judicial loosening in this area has been visible over time, it remains difficult to hold health care facilities directly liable for medical malpractice outside of a few narrow circumstances. . . .

The two most important rationales for imposing enterprise medical liability are economic efficiency and fairness. In the malpractice context, enterprise medical liability addresses the perceived unfairness of holding individual health care providers liable for "systems failures" within an organization that lead to preventable injuries and that the individuals have little or no ability to control. The efficiency rationale is that placing liability on the organization provides economic incentives for the organization—which does have control over the "systems failures" and is in a position to prevent injuries at a lower cost than the clinician—to invest in cost-justified changes to improve patient safety. Future injuries will therefore be prevented at a socially efficient level. Without enterprise medical liability, the tort system sends an economic signal to actors who arguably are not in a good position to effect the kind of changes that are needed to prevent injuries. . . .

A fourth rationale is that enterprise medical liability permits more effective use of experience rating in insurance. Experience rating is the practice of pricing insurance premiums to reflect the insured's past claims experience. This is actuarially difficult to do for individual physicians because they are sued so infrequently, but it is considerably easier at the level of the health care organization. The advantages of experience rating are that it more fairly apportions insurance costs to those who create losses and that it more accurately targets the "deterrent signal" of the tort system to those who most need to modify their behavior in order to prevent injuries. . . .

A proposal for demonstration projects of health-plan-based enterprise medical liability was part of the Clinton health reform package. However, the proposal did not advance due to adverse reactions, ranging from disinterest to strong opposition, on the part of key stakeholder groups, including physician organizations, liability insurers, plaintiff's attorneys, and managed care organizations. . . .

Some proposals for enterprise medical liability have focused on health plans as the locus of liability, while others have suggested that hospitals and other health care provider organizations serve as the responsible enterprise. Today, the latter formulation receives more attention in policy debates, largely due to the ascendency of network-model managed care organizations in the market, which have less control over their affiliated physicians than closed-panel HMOs. The "accountable care organization" (ACO) is another, more modern concept with potential applicability for this reform. Economic theory suggests that liability should be placed on an organization that can realistically be expected to have the power to institute systemic patient safety improvements within health care systems and influence individual physician behavior. . . . Health insurers' leverage may vary considerably depending on their market share and the nature of their affiliation with physicians, and many community hospitals (as opposed to academic medical centers) may not have close relationships with the physicians they credential. On the other hand, placing liability on health plans is argued to serve as a counterweight to health plans' extant incentives to provide less care than might be medically optimal. . . .

Most proposals for enterprise medical liability specify that there would no longer be any liability for individual clinicians. An alternative would be to greatly expand the potential for holding health care organizations liable while retaining the possibility of holding individuals liable as well. Different rules could be imposed depending on whether the care was rendered within the walls of a hospital or other health facility as opposed to a non-hospital-affiliated physician office. . . . [An] argument against retaining individual liability is that pure enterprise medical liability [is] a simpler regime that avoids fights among defendants in a malpractice case about who was responsible for the injury. . . .

Enterprise medical liability is generally discussed in the literature as a mandatory scheme imposed by statute. An alternative is that health plans or health care facilities could voluntarily elect to assume liability for some or all of their affiliated physicians, with the physicians agreeing by contract to the necessary financial adjustments to finance the new arrangement. . . . One drawback would be . . . the fragmentation of incentives that would occur if not all physicians affiliated with the sponsoring hospital or health plan agreed to participate in the new arrangement. . . .

[In summary, enterprise medical liability] is promising on theoretical grounds, but existing examples of this arrangement in the U.S. are limited and have not been evaluated in a way that supports inferences about its effect on any of the key outcome variables.

Conclusions

The findings of this analysis concerning the effects of traditional and innovative tort reforms are summarized in Tables 3 and 4 [which have been edited somewhat]. . . . [T]he evidence base for evaluating most *traditional* state tort reforms is large and mature. However, studies have generated limited or no evidence that most reforms have significant effects on the key outcome variables examined in this report. The exception is caps on noneconomic damages, which have well-documented effects on several of the outcomes. . . .

The Congressional Budget Office (CBO) recently estimated the cost of a package of 5 reforms implemented together in all states: a $250,000 noneconomic damages cap, a punitive damages cap of $500,000 or twice the economic damages award, collateral-source offsets, a 1-year statute of limitations for adults and 3-year limit for

Table 3.

Summary of Evidence Concerning the Effects of Traditional Tort Reforms

	Claims frequency and costs	Overhead costs	Liability costs	Defensive medicine	Supply	Quality of care
Caps on noneconomic damages	↓ for frequency ↓↓ for costs	↑	↓ for premiums	↓	↑ for physician supply 0 for health insurance premiums	0
Pretrial screening panels	0	↑	0	↓	0	0
Certificate of merit	0	↑	0	0	0	0
Attorney fee limits	0	↑	0	0	0	0
Joint-and-several liability reform	0	0	0	0	0 for physician supply 0 for health insurance premiums	0
Collateral-source rule reform	0	0	0	0	0 for physician supply 0 for health insurance premiums	0
Periodic payment	0	0	0	0	0	0
Shorter statute of limitations/ repose	0	0	↓	0	0	0

Notes: Effects are classified as large increase (↑↑), modest increase (↑), no change (0), modest decrease (↓), or large decrease (↓↓). [This table is updated with information from the authors' 2016 report.]

Table 4.

Summary of Probable Effects of Innovative Tort Reforms

	Claims frequency and costs	Overhead costs	Liability costs	Defensive medicine	Supply	Quality of care
Schedule of noneconomic damages	0 (highly dependent on award levels)	↓	↓	↓	0	0
Administrative compensation systems or "health courts"	Medical court model: 0 Administrative model: ↑↑ for frequency, 0 for costs	Medical court model: ↓ Administrative model: ↓	0	Medical court model: 0 Administrative model: ↓	0	Medical court model: 0 Administrative model: ↑
Disclosure-and-offer programs	↓	↓↓	↓	0	0	↑
Safe harbors for adherence to evidence-based practice guidelines	0	↓	0	↓↓		↑↑
Enterprise liability	0	↓	↓	↓	0	↑

Notes: Effects are classified as large increase (↑↑), modest increase (↑), no change (0), modest decrease (↓), or large decrease (↓↓).

children, and joint-and-several liability reform. . . . Its current cost model estimates that nationwide implementation of [this package of 5 reforms] would result in a 0.5 percent decrease in total national health care expenditures. . . .

The evidence base for evaluating the *innovative* tort reforms is extremely small. . . . However, based on theoretical predictions and the limited evidence available, most of these reforms show sufficient promise for impacting some of the key outcome variables to merit controlled experimentation, such as through demonstration projects. . . .

In closing, tort reform in the states to date has been characterized by a pattern of imitation of reforms implemented in other jurisdictions—even in the absence of evidence that they are effective in achieving their goals. Reform initiatives have often been driven by health care providers' and insurers' urgent demands that policy makers do something to ameliorate the effects of highly volatile liability environments. Today, most states are experiencing at least a moderate easing of the "crisis" conditions of the last decade. This environment presents more favorable conditions for experimentation with more novel reforms.

Notes: Medical Malpractice Reform Statutes

1. *Deja Vu All Over Again.* With each previous edition of this casebook, it seems we were in the midst of, or just exiting from, yet another crisis in medical liability. But, for whatever reason, this issue has not flared up much over the past decade. Malpractice reform was not included as part of President Obama's Affordable Care Act. Prior to that, President George W. Bush proposed a national set of reforms similar to those in California, but Congress failed to act. In 2003, Prof. Bill Sage aptly commented that "it is striking . . . that Congress is actively debating whether to adopt [a package of reforms] enacted in California in 1975, . . . [yet] the health care system has undergone revolutionary change since [then]. It is as if Rip van Winkle awoke from his twenty-year nap and went about his business equipped with antique weapons and dressed in yesteryear's fashions without the current townspeople thinking anything was amiss." William M. Sage, Unfinished Business: How Litigation Relates to Health Care Regulation, 28 J. Health Pol. Pol'y & L. 387, 392 (2003).

2. *Statutory Scope.* An important legal issue created by all malpractice reform statutes is precisely which actions they apply to and whether plaintiffs can state their claims in a manner that avoids these restrictions. These statutes typically are written to apply to professional negligence actions against practitioners of the healing arts. One route for avoiding them that appeared open for a while was the federal anti-dumping legislation discussed in Chapter 2.A. Some state limitations do not apply to actions under the federal statute. See Draper v. Chiapuzio, 9 F.3d 1391 (9th Cir. 1993). But courts have restricted the federal anti-dumping statute so that, for the most part, it does not apply to garden-variety malpractice complaints. Other avoidance techniques include framing the action with an alternative common-law theory, such as breach of contract, fraud, or battery, or as institutional rather than professional negligence. See, e.g., Atkinson v. Lammico Insurance Co., 63 So. 3d 1176 (3d Cir. 2011) (malpractice reform statute does not apply to physician's failure to advise testing the patient's son for genetic disease since the victim was not the doctor's patient); David v. Our Lady of the Lake Hospital, Inc., 849 So. 2d 38 (La.

2003). Courts also sometimes find that these statutes do not apply to nonphysicians. See, e.g., Lane v. Health Options, Inc., 796 So. 2d 1234 (Fla. App. 2001) (negligence action against an HMO is not a medical malpractice action). Another court found that a damages cap does not apply to a physician's professional corporation because the corporation is not a licensed professional, even though the doctor was a sole practitioner and the liability of his wholly owned corporation was purely vicarious. Schwartz v. Brownlee, 482 S.E.2d 827 (Va. 1997). However, courts are sharply split on most of these issues, and courts sometimes apply reform statutes even to suits that do not relate to patient care. E.g., Texas West Oaks Hospital v. Williams, 371 S.W.3d 171 (Tex. 2012) (malpractice statute applies to suit by employee over unsafe work conditions). See generally Annots., 12 A.L.R. 5th 1 (1993); 89 A.L.R. 4th 887 (1992).

3. *Constitutional Challenges.* Damages caps have received the most constitutional scrutiny, with well over half the states having a supreme court decision on point. The cases are split approximately evenly, and some states have reversed themselves, e.g., Watts v. Lester E. Cox Medical Centers, 376 S.W.3d 633 (Mo. 2012) (overruling earlier case that upheld noneconomic damage cap of $350,000). See the casebook Web site, www.health-law.org, for the latest. See also Annot., 26 A.L.R. 5th 245 (1995), and note 8.

Other reform elements generally fare better in the courts, but nevertheless encounter substantial opposition. The usual objections are either of the equal protection stripe, or are based on separation of powers (protecting inherently judicial functions) or on a constitutional right to court access and to a jury trial, which were mentioned in *McCall.* See, e.g., Zeier v. Zimmer, 152 P.3d 861 (Okla. 2006) (declaring unconstitutional the requirement to obtain a certificate of merit prior to filing suit); Putman v. Wenatchee Valley Medical Center, 166 Wn. 2d 974, 216 P.3d 374 (Wash. 2009) (same).

One maneuver to avoid constitutional objections is for the legislature to authorize parties to elect an alternative dispute resolution mechanism by contract. This is already common in the form of arbitration statutes. This could also be done for damages caps, limitations periods, and all the rest. See, e.g., Ralph Peeples & Catherine T. Harris, Learning to Crawl: The Use of Voluntary Caps on Damages in Medical Malpractice Litigation, 54 Cath. U. L. Rev. 703 (2005). Is there any constitutional barrier to the legislature authorizing the enforcement of contracts that courts would ordinarily find to be unconscionable adhesion contracts? Note the *McCall* court's discussion of an earlier decision in that state which upheld a damage cap that applies to voluntary arbitration.

4. *Public Policy Rhetoric vs. Evidence.* Consider again the complaints that doctors typically make against the legal system. How accurate are they, in light of the notes and materials in sections A and F, as well as the facts and figures mentioned in *McCall?* And, as the *McCall* court asks, how likely are any of these reforms to abate these criticisms? One reputable national survey reports that variation across states in doctors' concerns about malpractice risk have no obvious relationship to objective indicators of actual risk, or to the extent of statutory reforms. Emily Carrier et al., Physicians' Fears of Malpractice Lawsuits Are Not Assuaged by Tort Reforms, 29(9) Health Aff. 1585 (Sept. 2010).

If a convincing case for reform cannot be made based on these arguments, how about one based simply on the need to contain overall health care spending?

As the *McCall* decision documents, malpractice insurance premiums vary considerably by location and by physicians' practice specialties. Overall, malpractice premiums total roughly $10 billion (hospitals and doctors combined, in 2008), but this is substantially less than 1 percent of all health care spending. Of potentially greater significance are the "shadow" costs of malpractice litigation that occur in the form of defensive medical practices. Doctors argue they cannot hold down the costs of treatment as long as they are exposed to the potential liability for omitting expensive but marginally beneficial care. Review the notes at page 330 to consider whether this is a compelling argument, and see Michelle Mello et al., National Costs of the Medical Liability System, 29(9) Health Aff. 1569 (Sept. 2010).

5. *Screening Panels.* Why do you think advisory screening panels have been so ineffective? As Mello and Kachalia mention, their purpose is to give litigants a more accurate view of the merits of their case in order to promote settlement. Consider that these panels usually are composed of lawyers and doctors. How helpful are their views on the merits likely to be in predicting jury verdicts? In some states, plaintiffs' lawyers simply refuse to show up during the screening panel process, believing the information is not worth the time and effort and that any negative finding will not be that damaging even if it comes to the attention of the jury. Two states have declared screening panels unconstitutional based on evidence of their poor performance in practice. See note 8.

6. *Exclusive Enterprise Liability.* As Mello and Kachalia note, even if exclusive enterprise liability is not officially enacted, it already exists in "virtual" form through private agreement. Some HMOs and many government and teaching hospitals purchase insurance for all their doctors and defend all lawsuits arising from treatment under their auspices. The HMO or hospital assuming full responsibility for all negligent medical care within the institution has the same effect as shifting liability entirely from the doctor. See Kenneth S. Abraham & Paul C. Weiler, Enterprise Liability and the Evolution of the American Health Care System, 108 Harv. L. Rev. 381 (1994).When Harvard's teaching hospitals implemented this scheme, the liability insurer began to monitor patterns of litigation and noticed recurring problems in anesthesia. The insurer asked the Harvard anesthesiologists to analyze the causes. Rather than blaming others or acting defensively, the group devised new techniques and equipment to lower the risk of mishap. As a result, anesthesia mortality dropped tenfold, and the Harvard anesthesia protocols have become standard across the country. Based on experiences such as this, some scholars advocate that newly emerging "Accountable Care Organizations" should also take on enterprise liability, in order to encourage better teamwork among care providers. Laura Hermer, Aligning Incentives in Accountable Care Organizations: The Role of Medical Malpractice Reform, 17 J. Health care L. & Pol'y 271 (2014) ("It remains to be seen, however, whether physicians would be prepared to accept the impact these changes may have on professional autonomy . . .").

7. *What You See Depends on Where You Stand.* What perspectives do you think each of the following groups has on what are the fundamental social purposes of malpractice litigation and how well they are being achieved: (1) injured patients and their lawyers; (2) doctors; (3) patients who have not been injured (but some day may be), that is, the general public? Try answering this question in terms of these three purposes: (1) compensating injured patients; (2) making wrongdoers pay for their harms; and (3) improving the quality of medicine.

8. *Bibliography.* On **the purposes of malpractice liability** generally (note 7), see Michael J. Saks et al., A Multiattribute Utility Analysis of Legal System Response to Medical Injuries, 54 DePaul L. Rev. 277 (2005); Roger B. Dworkin, The Process Paradigm: Rethinking Medical Malpractice, 41 Wake Forest L. Rev. 509 (2006); Alex Stein, Toward a Theory of Medical Malpractice, 97 Iowa L. Rev. 1201 (2012).

On the **malpractice crisis generally,** see Michelle Mello et al., The New Medical Malpractice Crisis, 348 New Eng. J. Med. 2281 (2003); Marc A. Rodwin et al., Why the Medical Malpractice Crisis Persists Even When Malpractice Insurance Premiums Fall, 25 Health Matrix 163 (2015). Advocating for a stronger federal role in reform, see Abigail R. Moncrieff, Federalization Snowballs: The Need for National Action in Medical Malpractice Reform, 109 Colum. L. Rev. 844 (2009). On malpractice **insurance premiums**, see Bernard Black, et al., Medical Liability Insurance Premia: 1990-2016 Dataset, with Literature Review and Summary Information, 14 J. Empirical Leg. Stud. 238 (2017).

For additional reviews of or proposals for both **traditional and innovative reforms** and their effects, see Daniel Kessler, Evaluating the Medical Malpractice System and Options for Reform, 25 J. Econ. Perspect. 93 (2011); Myungho Paik et al., Will Tort Reform Bend the Cost Curve?, 9 J. Empirical Legal Stud. 173 (2012); Leonard Nelson et al., Medical Liability and Health Care Reform, 21 Health Matrix 443 (2011); Jan Ambrose & Anne Carroll, Medical Malpractice Reform and Insurer Claims Defense, 32 J. Health Pol. Pol'y L. 843 (2007); Michelle Mello & Troyen Brennan, Medical Malpractice, 350 New Eng. J. Med. 283 (2004); Ronen Avraham & Max Schanzenbach, The Impact of Tort Reform on Private Health Insurance Coverage, 12 Am. L. & Econ. Rev. 319 (2010); Mary Coombs, How Not to Do Medical Malpractice Reform: A Florida Case Study, 18 Health Matrix 373 (2008); Frank Sloan & Lindsey M. Chepke, Ill-Suited? Medical Malpractice at a Crossroads (2008); W. Sage & Rogan Kersh eds., Medical Malpractice and the U.S. Health Care System (2006); Symposium, 37 U. Mem. L. Rev. 455 (2007); Symposium, 59 Vand. L. Rev. 1017 (2006); Symposium, 27 J. Leg. Med. 1 (2006); Symposium, 33 J. L. Med. & Ethics 414 (2005); Symposium, 5 Yale J. Health Pol'y L. & Ethics 341 (2005); Symposium, 23(4) Health Aff. (Aug. 2004); Symposium, 54 DePaul L. Rev. 203 (2005); Symposium, 26 N. Ill. U. L. Rev. 439 (2006); David Studdert, Note, 56 Duke L. J. 611 (2006).

On **constitutional challenges** (note 3), see Carly Kelly & Michelle Mello, Are Medical Malpractice Damages Caps Unconstitutional?, 33 J. L. Med. & Ethics 515 (2005); Elizabeth Stewart Poisson, Addressing the Impropriety of Statutory Caps on Pain and Suffering Awards in the Medical Liability System, 82 N.C. L. Rev. 759 (2004); Michelle M. Mello et al., Policy Experimentation with Administrative Compensation for Medical Injury: Issues Under State Constitutional Law, 45 Harv. J. on Legis. 59 (2008).

On **screening panels** (note 5), see Jona Goldschmidt, Where Have All the Panels Gone? A History of the Arizona Medical Liability Review Panel, 23 Ariz. St. L. J. 1013 (1992); Catherine Struve, Doctors, the Adversary System, and Procedural Reform in Medical Liability Litigation, 72 Fordham L. Rev. 943 (2004).

Problem: Malpractice Reform Legislation

Look up the various components of the medical malpractice reform statute in your (or another) state in an annotated statute book. Categorize these components according to the chart on page 487. Which interest groups appear to have prevailed with the legislature—doctors, personal injury lawyers, or insurers? What has been the judicial reaction? When was the statute first enacted, and have there been subsequent amendments?

PART II

THE PATIENT, THE PROVIDER, AND THE STATE

The next four chapters continue to focus on the core patient-provider treatment relationship, but with an important new dimension added: that of the state and other third parties. It should be clear by now that medical decisions do not occur in a vacuum. They affect the interests of society and other individuals in many tangible and direct ways. Therefore, society often constrains allowable treatment options, either foreclosing some or mandating others. The social element in medical treatment becomes increasingly obvious as we progress through these chapters. In Chapter 5, we look at treatment decisions that bring about or forestall death. Chapter 6 examines how scarce life-saving organs are procured and allocated for transplantation. Chapter 7 examines reproductive medical decisionmaking. Chapter 8 explores a variety of issues in the arena of public health, mostly centered on avoiding the spread of contagious diseases. In each chapter, one of the core questions is how much ethical and legal protection should be given to individual value choices when they conflict with broader social objectives. But each chapter also continues to examine two other kinds of conflict: conflicts between patients' values and providers' values and conflicts between societal rules and individual provider autonomy.

■ MEDICAL LAW AND ETHICS IN THE POST-AUTONOMY AGE
Roger B. Dworkin *68 Ind. L.J. 727 (1993)*

Patient autonomy has long been the dominant rhetorical value in American medical law and medical ethics. It has been far less dominant in fact. Now, developments in genetics raise serious questions about the scientific validity of the assumptions on which autonomy-based law and ethics rest, and new attention to the values of civic republicanism, community, and inclusiveness raises questions about the extent to which the dominance of autonomy is desirable. Yet a move away from autonomy is frightening, especially when no one can be sure what will take its place. In this essay, I shall examine, in a preliminary way, the extent to which autonomy really dominates our medical law and ethics, the extent to which reformulation seems desirable in light of scientific developments and changing values, and the direction medical law and ethics might safely move in a post-autonomy age.

RHETORIC AND REALITY

Autonomy can mean a number of different things. To the liberal individualist (that is, the typical American), it means the ability and the opportunity to choose one's course of action and to act to effectuate one's choice. It means freedom from constraint, as long as one's behavior does not injure others. It tends not to recognize the extent to which most actions, even the most apparently private ones, have an impact on others,[8] and the more apparently private an activity is, the more liberal individual autonomy insists that it not be regulated.

Concern for patient autonomy in the liberal individualist sense dominates the rhetoric of American medical law and medical ethics. Cardozo's dictum that "[e]very human being of adult years and sound mind has a right to determine what shall be done with his own body"[9] is ubiquitous. The entire law of informed consent is premised on the dominance of patient autonomy over competing values, including the value of good medical care. Abortion law, right-to-die law, and even some wrongful birth and life opinions are explained textually as reflecting respect for patient autonomy. . . .

Yet, in reality, autonomy does not seem to be as dominant a value as rhetoric would suggest. . . . Of course, the law allows autonomy to be sacrificed when important public needs are at stake. Thus, compulsory vaccination laws are plainly valid. However, their existence does not really challenge autonomy's dominant position. It simply demonstrates that even a dominant value must sometimes be sacrificed for the public good.

Often, however, autonomy yields in the face of less, clearly public concerns. The most obvious rejections of autonomy are professional licensure statutes and the regulation of drugs and medical devices by Congress and the Food and Drug Administration. Licensure and the control of allegedly beneficial medicines and devices are designed to protect persons from themselves; that is, to paternalistically prevent individuals from autonomously making bad choices. . . .

---

8. *See generally* MARY ANN GLENDON, RIGHTS TALK (1991).
9. Schloendorff v. Society of N.Y. Hosp., 105 N.E. 92, 93 (N.Y. 1914).

The law does not honor the freely entered into agreements of doctors and patients. The law of tort, not contract, determines the quality of medical care to which a person is entitled, and a patient may not contract away the right to receive reasonable care. A patient's informed consent to receive medical care does not exempt a health care provider from liability if a consented to risk occurs through negligence. . . .

At first blush, autonomy may seem to be the primary value underlying the Supreme Court's abortion jurisprudence. However, . . . under *Roe*, abortion may be regulated after the end of the first trimester to the extent necessary to protect maternal health. Further, the Court allowed states to prohibit anybody other than doctors from performing abortions even during the first trimester, a restriction that can only be understood as reflecting a paternalistic concern for maternal well-being. . . .

To some extent, right-to-die law reflects a real concern for individual autonomy, yet here too the law remains unwilling to go where the autonomy principle would push it. . . . A patient may effectively ask not to be resuscitated and perhaps not to be fed, but a request for a lethal injection will not be honored. Refusal to honor such a request is inconsistent with a law based on patient autonomy. Patient autonomy has even less to do with right-to-die cases about patients who have never been competent and once-competent patients who did not express their treatment desires before becoming incompetent. . . .

New drug regulation, injury compensation law, informed consent cases, abortion decisions, right-to-die law, and organ transplantation decisions all demonstrate that American medical law, even as it has developed in the heyday of liberal individualism, is not nearly as autonomy-centered as it claims to be. If that is true, what can we expect as liberalism loses its lustre and science challenges its foundations? . . .

Unlike liberal individualism, a second possible meaning of autonomy is rooted not so much in choice, as in being let alone. It is a physical concept rather than an intellectual one. If you touch me or eavesdrop on me, you have injured my autonomy by invading my space. If you actually do something to change my body, you have injured my autonomy by changing the very constitution of what I am. This view might be called physical essentialist autonomy. . . .

[Dworkin explains that a virtue of this approach is its more general application. The right to choose may work well for the competent patient, but makes little sense for the many patients who lack decisionmaking capacity. Dworkin refers to former California Chief Justice Rose Bird, who reasoned that we should focus on rights] rooted in *bodily* autonomy, a right which Chief Justice Bird said was constitutional in the deepest sense. That is, it is part of what constitutes the human being . . . .

Juxtaposing the . . . liberal individualist autonomy with Chief Justice Bird's physical essentialist autonomy highlights the need for an alternative approach. The [liberal individualist] makes the mistake of treating a person as if she is nothing more than a choice maker and actor. As noted previously, . . . [cases] involving incompetent persons make plain the insufficiency of that approach. However, the approach is also inadequate for competent persons. Choice making is a characteristic of healthy persons, but it is not their only characteristic. We must be cautious not to factually overrate even healthy persons' abilities to choose and not to ethically overvalue that capacity. Overvaluation risks dehumanizing incompetent persons and creating an ethical vacuum if and when we learn that healthy persons' abilities to choose are more constrained than we like to think.

Yet Chief Justice Bird's approach is also unsatisfying. Her physical essentialist view [ignores other values at stake. Protecting bodily autonomy is important, but patient interests also can be served by invasions of their body. What good does it do to protect a patient's right to bodily integrity if she thereby loses her opportunity to develop to her maximum potential?]

Liberal individualist autonomy and physical essentialist autonomy thus seem to impale us on the horns of a dilemma. A third approach to autonomy would treat the individual as dominant, but attempt to avoid the failings of both liberal individualism and physical essentialism. This approach would be rooted in respect for the individual as a complete being. It would deviate from common linguistic meanings of the word *autonomy* by focusing neither on the freedom to choose and act, nor on the freedom from physical intrusion. It would simply be an approach that put the interests of the person most affected by an action or proposed action first. It would be a highly realistic approach because it would examine what really happens to a person. Thus, it could avoid resort to rhetorical fictions (like liberal individualism) and sacrifice of a person's well-being to someone else's principles (like physical essentialism). Such an approach might be called respectful paternalism. It would be paternalistic because it would involve someone making decisions for somebody else, presumably in that person's best interest. It would be respectful because it would consider the real impact of an action on the person affected, thus avoiding the imposition of one's principles on another to her detriment, and because it would consider the preferences and choices of the affected person, to the extent they can be ascertained, as part of the decisionmaking process. . . .

This weak version of autonomy seems an improvement over either of the other two approaches. Yet it is not without its shortcomings. By focusing solely on the individual, respectful paternalism, like all forms of autonomy, ignores both reality and important personal and social interests. All autonomy-centered approaches ignore the fact that nobody is autonomous. Everybody lives in groups — families, workplaces, clubs, labor unions, towns, states, countries — and almost everything that affects one person affects others as well.

Insights offered by feminist,[10] republican,[11] and communitarian[12] scholars have demonstrated the impoverishment of an exclusively individual-rights based approach to social issues, and developments in genetics cast doubt on the factual underpinnings of such an approach. . . .

The same point can be made in every area of bioethics: Pregnant women have fetuses, mates, and parents. . . . Persons with healthy organs may have siblings with unhealthy ones. Potential surrogate mothers may have husbands, preexisting children, the new child, men with whom they have contracted and those men's wives, all of whom are affected by the surrogate mother's behavior. Dying persons have families with both emotional and financial needs.

Autonomy-based systems undervalue those other persons' needs. They assume that it is possible to ascertain who is most affected by an action or condition and then

---

10. *E.g.*, Leslie Bender, *A Lawyer's Primer on Feminist Theory and Tort*, 38 J. LEGAL ED. 3 (1988).

11. *E.g.*, MICHAEL J. SANDEL, LIBERALISM AND THE LIMITS OF JUSTICE (1982).

12. *E.g.*, MARY ANN GLENDON, RIGHTS TALK (1991).

allow that person's interests to trump all others. The factual assumption is true sometimes, but only sometimes. Who is most affected by a decision about whether to use a kidney from an incompetent "donor" to save a dying competent sibling with end stage renal disease? Who is most affected by a decision whether to perform a Caesarian section delivery that may shorten the life of a terminally ill, episodically competent pregnant woman by a few days in order to run an *x* percent chance of saving her fetus? . . .

[M]odern genetics compounds the difficulties by simultaneously reemphasizing the poverty of autonomy-based approaches and highlighting the risks in surrendering the focus on individuals. . . . Genetic medical practice challenges the conventional notion of the individually-based, doctor-patient relationship. Genetic medicine only makes sense if it is understood as a family-centered, rather than an individually-focused form of medical practice. Typically, physicians and other genetic counselors are consulted by couples who want to learn their risk of having a child with a genetic disease, by couples and their already-affected children, or by persons who seek information about their own health based on the condition of their relatives. Each of these situations requires learning about one person to help another. Each may present the diagnostician with information about persons whom he has never seen and may raise serious questions about his obligations. To what individual does the doctor owe a duty when tests of husband, wife, and child reveal that the husband is not the child's father? What are the doctor's duties when diagnosis of a person present in the doctor's office necessarily informs him that relatives of that person are at risk for developing avoidable colon cancer or having a child with hemophilia? In a profession whose raison d'être is doing family studies to reveal family information, these questions cannot be answered by thoughtless recitation of tired slogans about the doctor owing an exclusive obligation to his patient. Indeed, often it is not even clear who the patient is.

Modern genetic research compounds the inadequacy of the individual autonomy model by rekindling the debates between free will and determinism and between nature and nurture. As scientists map the human genome, they increasingly discover not only the genes for well-known genetic diseases, but also uncover the genetic roots of a wide variety of diseases and behaviors that are often not thought of as genetic. What does it mean to talk of an autonomous individual if the individual's genotype predisposes him to alcoholism, schizophrenia, crime, cancer, or heart disease? To the extent that most American law and ethics are based on assumptions about personal moral accountability, modern genetics throws those legal and ethical positions into question.

However, . . . [r]ecognizing that there are limits to what individuals can do or control is not a concession to total determinism. The danger of modern genetics, like the danger of the old eugenics, is that society will mistakenly believe it proves more than it does and use it as an excuse to injure further those who are already disadvantaged. Thus, again the challenge is to incorporate new understandings in a way that moves away from the excesses of individual autonomy and its frequent inability to help solve problems, without legitimating imposition on underdogs. How is that to be done?

RESPECT FOR ALL INDIVIDUALS

I suggest that a useful way to begin would be (1) to refocus our rhetoric and our rules away from concern for individual choice and toward respect for individuals, while (2) recognizing that individuals live in groups whose individual members deserve respect too. In other words, we should combine what I have called respectful paternalism with respect for all affected members of society. Respect for individuals requires valuing their apparently freely-made choices, even if we do not always follow them. Respect for individual affected members of society recognizes the reality of the social condition but reduces risks of imposition by insisting on finding real impacts on real persons before those interests may be weighed against others. Respect for all individuals rejects as unacceptably dangerous a focus on the alleged interests of society as a whole. . . .

In determining an individual's interests, his ability to choose and the negative impact of taking that away from him are relevant. . . . To put it differently, the choices of competent persons are worth points in the legal and ethical calculus. However, choices do not end the inquiry. They may be illusory; the person may no longer be aware of them; and other people count too. Therefore, the way to make a decision is to consider what is best for everyone concerned, while specifically assigning a value to choices in order to avoid running roughshod over affected persons. . . .

Perhaps the approach suggested here can be made clearer by applying it to a few examples. . . . Respect for all affected individuals would require that before consenting to treatment, patients be given the amount of information that a person who cared about their well-being (including their psychological and dignitary well-being) would give them—not the amount a hypothetical reasonable doctor would provide or a reasonable patient would want. Conversation with close family members of the patient and some attention to their desires would be relevant as well. Failure to provide adequate information under such a vague standard should be viewed as an ethical lapse. Whether it makes sense also to treat it as a tort is beyond the scope of this essay.

Terminally ill patients who are incompetent and have expressed no choices about withholding or withdrawing medical care deserve respect. They retain an interest in dignity and in avoiding unnecessary suffering. However, their loved ones' interests are also strong and should be accorded great weight. Suffering from watching a close relative die a prolonged death is real. On the other hand, the anguish of believing one was premature in letting the loved one die is real as well. Respect for relatives requires that they be accorded significant discretion in deciding whether to allow the patient to die. The doctor's sense that he is wasting his time in a futile exercise is probably worth something, especially if the patient is past suffering and the family is split. An identified salvable patient's need for the dying person's hospital bed is also relevant. A generalized concern about not wasting resources is not. Society cannot be allowed to solve its health care cost crisis by running roughshod over its sickest members.

Medical law and ethics based on individual autonomy are rooted in fiction and ignore important values. The salutary role of the autonomy focus is that it avoids state imposition and abuse of the weak. As the illustrations here suggest, an approach rooted in respect for all individuals would avoid fiction and increase the chance of sound results by considering all relevant persons and values in each case while keeping the door to state imposition and abuse of the powerless tightly closed.

Notes: Bioethics, Law, and the Relevant Values

1. *The Role of Autonomy.* As the *Dworkin* excerpt indicates, many scholars have questioned the weight that patient autonomy should be given, partly because other important values may conflict with patient self-determination and also because individual rights-based analyses provide a limited understanding of the relationship between the individual and other people, especially family and friends, but also society more generally. Our connections with members of different communities play a critical role in the way we live our lives.

2. *The Attack on "Principlism."* Concerns about the standard analysis are rooted not only in the weight that autonomy should be given, but also in terms of how the analysis should be structured. For example, commenters often frame issues of medical ethics in terms of the conflict between core principles, as when patient self-determination (autonomy) runs up against the duty of care providers to promote the patient's interests (beneficence), and then ask which of the conflicting principles is more pertinent and to what degree. This approach grew primarily out of the foundational work of Tom Beauchamp and James Childress at Georgetown University's Kennedy Institute of Ethics and at the University of Virginia, and it is presented in their now classic Principles of Biomedical Ethics. This framework has become so dominant that it is sometimes referred to as the "Georgetown mantra." But this approach's ordering of discussion according to core principles has come under attack in recent years from several directions.

Some argue that principles are too abstract, and so the focus should be on a more intuitive or pragmatic analysis of individual cases. This is known as "casuistry." Others argue that when most analyses resort primarily to the two principles of autonomy and beneficence, they are being too arbitrary or ad hoc and not sufficiently founded in rigorous philosophical analysis. Still others advance a "virtue ethics," which holds that we must look not only at the rightness or goodness of an action, but also the character of the actor in order to identify and cultivate good moral traits such as honesty and compassion. Beauchamp and Childress respond that their principles framework is more malleable than their critics recognize and so is capable of adapting to all of these competing positions.

3. *Further Reading.* On patient **autonomy** (note 1), see Jurrit Bergsma & David Thomasma, Autonomy and Clinical Medicine (2010); Benjamin Levi, Respecting Patient Autonomy (1999); Carl Schneider, The Practice of Autonomy (1998); Rebecca Kukla, Conscientious Autonomy, 35(2) Hastings Center Rep. 34 (2005); Carl Schneider, The Practice of Autonomy (1998); Alfred I. Tauber, Patient Autonomy and the Ethics of Responsibility (2005).

On **principlism** and its alternatives (note 2), see Nancy S. Jecker et al., Bioethics: An Introduction to the History, Methods, and Practice (3d ed. 2011); Edmund D. Pellegrino & David C. Thomasma, The Virtues in Medical Practice (1993); Symposium: Emerging Paradigms in Bioethics, 69 Ind. L. J. 945 (1994); Edmund Pellegrino, The Metamorphosis of Medical Ethics, 269 JAMA 1158 (1993).

On the **role of law** in deciding bioethics questions, see George Annas, Standard of Care: The Law of American Bioethics (1993); Roger Dworkin, Limits: The Role of Law in Bioethical Decision Making (1996); David Rothman, Strangers at the Bedside: A History of How Law and Bioethics Transformed Medical Decisionmaking

(1992); Charity Scott, Why Law Pervades Medicine, 14 Notre Dame J. L. Ethics & Pub. Pol'y, 245 (2000); Michael H. Shapiro, Is Bioethics Broke? On the Idea of Ethics and Law "Catching Up" with Technology, 33 Ind. L. Rev. 17 (1999).

On the field of **bioethics** more generally, there is a wide range of useful sources: Journals: Bioethics Reporter; Bioethics; Cambridge Quarterly of Health Care Ethics; Kennedy Institute of Ethics Journal; Hastings Center Report; Issues in Law and Medicine; Journal of Clinical Ethics; Journal of Medical Ethics; Journal of Medical Humanities and Bioethics; Journal of Medicine and Philosophy; and the general medical and legal journals listed in the Preface. Treatises and Monographs: T. Beauchamp & J. Childress, Principles of Biomedical Ethics (7th ed. 2012); Baruch A. Brody et al., Medical Ethics: Analysis of the Issues Raised by the Codes, Opinions & Statements (2001); J. Childress & R. Gaare, BioLaw: A Legal and Ethical Reporter on Medicine, Health Care, and Bioengineering; H. Tristram Englehardt, The Foundations of Biomedical Ethics (2d ed. 1996); Bernard Gert et al., Bioethics: A Return to Fundamentals (1997); A. Jonsen et al., Clinical Ethics: A Practical Approach to Ethical Decisions in Clinical Medicine (8th ed. 2015); David Orentlicher, Matters of Life and Death: Making Moral Theory Work in Medical Ethics and the Law (2002); W. Reich, Encyclopedia of Bioethics; Robert Veatch, A Theory of Medical Ethics (1981).

5

■

The Right and "Duty" to Die

A. REFUSAL OF LIFE-SUSTAINING TREATMENT

In Chapter 3 we saw that patients enjoy a right of informed consent: Physicians may not deliver care to a patient without first informing the patient about the care and its alternatives and obtaining the patient's voluntary and competent consent to the treatment. If the patient must consent to treatment, it follows that the patient also enjoys a right to *withhold* consent and refuse the treatment.

Ordinarily, this corollary right to refuse treatment is not controversial. Patients with lower back pain from a slipped disk are free to choose between surgery to remove the disk and alternatives like anti-inflammatory drugs, exercise, and chiropractic manipulation. Patients with coronary artery disease may choose among invasive procedures, such as coronary artery bypass surgery and coronary angioplasty, and medical therapies, such as antianginal drugs.

In many cases, however, a refusal of treatment will result in the patient's death. In such cases, the state (or the health care provider) may want to invoke its interest in preserving life to ensure that the patient receives the treatment necessary to sustain life. The issue, then, is how we balance the individual's right to refuse treatment with the state's or other persons' interest in preserving the patient's life.

It is useful to begin the analysis with the right to accept or refuse life-sustaining treatment when only the patient's interests are directly at stake. For example, an adult patient dying of cancer might reject additional rounds of chemotherapy on the grounds that the treatment is unlikely to provide much benefit but will likely cause significant discomfort. In such a case, the health of another person is not jeopardized by the refusal of treatment.

In later sections and chapters, we will consider whether the patient's right to make treatment decisions becomes circumscribed as we move beyond the core right. Does it matter that a pregnant woman's refusal of a blood transfusion will jeopardize the health of her fetus? Does it matter that a patient's refusal of treatment for tuberculosis would place other persons at risk? What if the patient is not refusing offered treatment but is requesting treatment that has not been offered? Does it matter, for example, that the patient is trying to take a lethal drug to end life? Similarly, does it matter that the patient is requesting treatment to sustain life that the patient's physician is unwilling to provide on the ground that the treatment provides little benefit?

Social recognition of the right to refuse life-sustaining treatment reflected the confluence of several factors. In recent decades, advances in medical technology have permitted physicians to save many lives that once were lost to disease or accident. In some cases, however, the person survives with a very poor quality of life and no hope of recovery. While medical care can maintain the person's life for weeks, months, or even years, the greatly diminished quality of life and the burdensomeness of the treatment mean to some individuals that the treatment is not desired. In addition, these life-saving advances in technology have become very costly. If the life that can be saved has a very poor quality and society's limited resources could be used for other patients who would have a better quality of life and who want treatment, then it is not clear that the state has an interest in always preserving the patient's life. Finally, the law not only had recognized a right of informed consent, it also had recognized a right of pregnant women to choose an abortion. In 1973, the U.S. Supreme Court handed down its decision in Roe v. Wade. If the state's interest in preserving the life of a fetus does not overcome the woman's interest in personal autonomy, then it becomes more difficult to justify a state interest in preserving the life of a dying person against the person's will.

There is an extensive literature on the refusal of life-sustaining treatment, including Allen E. Buchanan & Dan W. Brock, Deciding for Others (1989); Robert Burt, Taking Care of Strangers (1979); Norman Cantor, Legal Frontiers of Death & Dying (1987); Nancy Berlinger et al., The Hastings Center Guidelines for Decisions on Life-Sustaining Treatment and Care Near the End of Life (2d ed. 2013); Alan Meisel, Kathy L. Cerminara & Thaddeus M. Pope, The Right to Die (3d ed. 2004); President's Commission for the Study of Ethical Problems in Medicine, Deciding to Forego Life-Sustaining Treatment (1983); Paul Ramsey, Ethics at the Edges of Life (1978).

1. The Competent Patient

The right to refuse life-sustaining treatment is most straightforward when the patient possesses decisionmaking capacity and therefore is able to make informed and voluntary decisions about medical care. If the patient is incompetent, we confront an additional issue of how to decide whether the patient's right to refuse treatment is being exercised properly. While we directly consider that issue in the next section, we nevertheless begin our analysis here with cases involving incompetent patients, since it was in those cases that the courts developed the law governing treatment refusals by competent patients.

◼ IN THE MATTER OF KAREN QUINLAN
355 A.2d 647 (N.J. 1976)

HUGHES, Chief Justice.

On the night of April 15, 1975, for reasons still unclear, Karen Quinlan ceased breathing for at least two 15 minute periods. She received some ineffectual mouth-to-mouth resuscitation from friends. She was taken by ambulance to Newton Memorial Hospital. There she had a temperature of 100 degrees, her pupils were unreactive and she was unresponsive even to deep pain. The history at the time of her admission to that hospital was essentially incomplete and uninformative. . . . Dr. Morse and other expert physicians who examined her characterized Karen as being in a "chronic persistent vegetative state." Dr. Fred Plum, one of such expert witnesses, defined this as a "subject who remains with the capacity to maintain the vegetative parts of neurological function but who . . . no longer has any cognitive function." . . . In this respect it was indicated by Dr. Plum that the brain works in essentially two ways, the vegetative and the sapient. He testified:

> We have an internal vegetative regulation which controls body temperature, which controls breathing, which controls to a considerable degree blood pressure, which controls to some degree heart rate, which controls chewing, swallowing and which controls sleeping and waking. We have a more highly developed brain which is uniquely human which controls our relation to the outside world, our capacity to talk, to see, to feel, to sing, to think. Brain death necessarily must mean the death of both of these functions of the brain, vegetative and the sapient. Therefore, the presence of any function which is regulated or governed or controlled by the deeper parts of the brain which in laymen's terms might be considered purely vegetative would mean that the brain is not biologically dead.

. . . The experts believe that Karen [who is 22 years old] cannot now survive without the assistance of the respirator; that exactly how long she would live without it is unknown; that the strong likelihood is that death would follow soon after its removal, and that removal would also risk further brain damage and would curtail the assistance the respirator presently provides in warding off infection. . . .

The further medical consensus was that Karen in addition to being comatose is in a chronic and persistent "vegetative" state, having no awareness of anything or anyone around her and existing at a primitive reflex level. Although she does have some brain stem function (ineffective for respiration) and has other reactions one normally associates with being alive, such as moving, reacting to light, sound and noxious stimuli, blinking her eyes, and the like, the quality of her feeling impulses is unknown. She grimaces, makes stereotyped cries and sounds and has chewing motions. Her blood pressure is normal. . . .

Karen is described as emaciated, having suffered a weight loss of at least 40 pounds, and undergoing a continuing deteriorative process. Her posture is described as fetal-like and grotesque; there is extreme flexion-rigidity of the arms, legs and related muscles and her joints are severely rigid and deformed.

. . . No form of treatment which can cure or improve that condition is known or available. As nearly as may be determined, considering the guarded area of remote uncertainties characteristic of most medical science predictions, she can *never* be restored to cognitive or sapient life. . . .

She is debilitated and moribund and although fairly stable at the time of argument before us (no new information having been filed in the meanwhile in expansion of the record), no physician risked the opinion that she could live more than a year and indeed she may die much earlier. Excellent medical and nursing care so far has been able to ward off the constant threat of infection, to which she is peculiarly susceptible because of the respirator, the tracheal tube and other incidents of care in her vulnerable condition. Her life accordingly is sustained by the respirator and tubal feeding, and removal from the respirator would cause her death soon, although the time cannot be stated with more precision. . . .

[Ms. Quinlan's father asked the superior court to appoint him the guardian of his daughter and to be given the express power to "authorize the discontinuance of all extraordinary medical procedures" sustaining his daughter's life. Ms. Quinlan's father also asked that the treating physicians and hospitals and the local prosecutor be enjoined from interfering with the discontinuation and that the local prosecutor also be enjoined from bringing a criminal prosecution after a discontinuation of treatment. The father's requests were opposed by the doctors, the hospital, the county prosecutor, the State of New Jersey, and Ms. Quinlan's guardian ad litem. The superior court denied the father's request for power to stop treatment.]

III. THE RIGHT OF PRIVACY

It is the issue of the constitutional right of privacy that has given us most concern, in the exceptional circumstances of this case. Here a loving parent, . . . seeks authorization to abandon specialized technological procedures which can only maintain for a time a body having no potential for resumption or continuance of other than a "vegetative" existence.

We have no doubt, in these unhappy circumstances, that if Karen were herself miraculously lucid for an interval (not altering the existing prognosis of the condition to which she would soon return) and perceptive of her irreversible condition, she could effectively decide upon discontinuance of the life-support apparatus, even if it meant the prospect of natural death. To this extent we may distinguish [John F. Kennedy Memorial Hospital v. Heston, 279 A.2d 670 (N.J. 1971)], which concerned a severely injured young woman (Delores Heston), whose life depended on surgery and blood transfusion; and who was in such extreme shock that she was unable to express an informed choice (although the court apparently considered the case as if the patient's own religious decision to resist transfusion were at stake), but most importantly a patient apparently salvable to long life and vibrant health;—a situation not at all like the present case.

We have no hesitancy in deciding, in the instant diametrically opposite case, that no external compelling interest of the state could compel Karen to endure the unendurable, only to vegetate a few measurable months with no realistic possibility of returning to any semblance of cognitive or sapient life. We perceive no thread of logic distinguishing between such a choice on Karen's part and a similar choice which, under the evidence in this case, could be made by a competent patient terminally ill, riddled by cancer and suffering great pain; such a patient would not be resuscitated or put on a respirator . . . , and a fortiori would not be kept *against his will* on a respirator.

Although the Constitution does not explicitly mention a right of privacy, Supreme Court decisions have recognized that a right of personal privacy exists and that certain areas of privacy are guaranteed under the Constitution. . . .

Presumably this right is broad enough to encompass a patient's decision to decline medical treatment under certain circumstances, in much the same way as it is broad enough to encompass a woman's decision to terminate pregnancy under certain conditions.

Nor is such right of privacy forgotten in the New Jersey Constitution. N.J. Const. (1947), Art. I, par. 1.

The claimed interests of the state in this case are essentially the preservation and sanctity of human life and defense of the right of the physician to administer medical treatment according to his best judgment. In this case, the doctors say that removing Karen from the respirator will conflict with their professional judgment. The plaintiff answers that Karen's present treatment serves only a maintenance function; that the respirator cannot cure or improve her condition but at best can only prolong her inevitable slow deterioration and death; and that the interests of the patient, as seen by her surrogate, the guardian, must be evaluated by the court as predominant, even in the face of an opinion *contra* by the present attending physicians. Plaintiff's distinction is significant. The nature of Karen's care and the realistic chances of her recovery are quite unlike those of the patients discussed in many of the cases where treatments were ordered. In many of those cases the medical procedure required (usually a transfusion) constituted a minimal bodily invasion and the chances of recovery and return to functioning life were very good. We think that the state's interest *contra* weakens and the individual's right to privacy grows as the degree of bodily invasion increases and the prognosis dims. Ultimately there comes a point at which the individual's rights overcome the state interest. It is for that reason that we believe Karen's choice, if she were competent to make it, would be vindicated by the law. Her prognosis is extremely poor,—she will never resume cognitive life. And the bodily invasion is very great,—she requires 24 hour intensive nursing care, antibiotics, the assistance of a respirator, a catheter and feeding tube. . . .

IV. THE MEDICAL FACTOR

Having declared the substantive legal basis upon which plaintiff's rights as representative of Karen must be deemed predicated, we face and respond to the assertion on behalf of defendants that our premise unwarrantably offends prevailing medical standards. . . .

We glean from the record here that physicians distinguish between curing the ill and comforting and easing the dying; that they refuse to treat the curable as if they were dying or ought to die, and that they have sometimes refused to treat the hopeless and dying as if they were curable. . . . [M]any [physicians] have refused to inflict an undesired prolongation of the process of dying on a patient in irreversible condition when it is clear that such "therapy" offers neither human nor humane benefit. We think these attitudes represent a balanced implementation of a profoundly realistic perspective on the meaning of life and death and that they respect the whole Judeo-Christian tradition of regard for human life. No less would they seem consistent with the moral matrix of medicine, "to heal." . . .

Yet this balance, we feel, is particularly difficult to perceive and apply in the context of the development by advanced technology of sophisticated and artificial life-sustaining devices. For those possibly curable, such devices are of great value, and, as ordinary medical procedures, are essential. Consequently, as pointed out by Dr. Diamond, they are necessary because of the ethic of medical practice. But in light of the situation in the present case (while the record here is somewhat hazy in distinguishing between "ordinary" and "extraordinary" measures), one would have to think that the use of the same respirator or like support could be considered "ordinary" in the context of the possibly curable patient but "extraordinary" in the context of the forced sustaining by cardio-respiratory processes of an irreversibly doomed patient. . . .

The evidence in this case convinces us that the focal point of decision should be the prognosis as to the reasonable possibility of return to cognitive and sapi-ent life, as distinguished from the forced continuance of that biological vegetative existence to which Karen seems to be doomed. [The court granted Mr. Quinlan's request, authorizing him to discontinue his daughter's life support. Surprisingly, Karen ended up living for another ten years without ventilator support.]

■ IN RE CONROY
486 A.2d 1209 (N.J. 1985)

SCHREIBER, Justice.

In 1979 Claire Conroy, who was suffering from an organic brain syndrome that manifested itself in her exhibiting periodic confusion, was adjudicated an incompe-tent, and plaintiff, her nephew, was appointed her guardian. . . .

During [a July 21–November 17, 1982] hospitalization, Dr. Kazemi observed that Ms. Conroy was not eating adequately, and therefore, on July 23, he inserted a nasogastric tube that extended from her nose through her esophagus to her stom-ach. Medicines and food were then given to her through this tube. On October 18, the tube was removed, and Ms. Conroy was fed by hand through her mouth for two weeks. However, she was unable to eat a sufficient amount in this manner, and the tube was reinserted on November 3. . . .

At the time of trial, Ms. Conroy [age 84] was no longer ambulatory and was confined to bed, unable to move from a semi-fetal position. She suffered from arte-riosclerotic heart disease, hypertension, and diabetes mellitus; her left leg was gan-grenous to her knee; she had several necrotic decubitus ulcers (bed sores) on her left foot, leg, and hip; an eye problem required irrigation; she had a urinary cathe-ter in place and could not control her bowels; she could not speak; and her ability to swallow was very limited. On the other hand, she interacted with her environment in some limited ways: she could move her head, neck, hands, and arms to a minor extent; she was able to scratch herself, and had pulled at her bandages, tube, and catheter; she moaned occasionally when moved or fed through the tube, or when her bandages were changed; her eyes sometimes followed individuals in the room; her facial expressions were different when she was awake from when she was asleep;

and she smiled on occasion when her hair was combed, or when she received a comforting rub. . . .

[This case arose when Ms. Conroy's guardian, who was also her nephew, petitioned the trial court for permission to discontinue Ms. Conroy's feeding tube. The guardian ad litem opposed the petition, and the trial court granted permission. The guardian ad litem appealed, and the intermediate court of appeals reversed. At issue in the case was whether Ms. Conroy's feeding tube could be withdrawn. While this case was before the intermediate court of appeals, Ms. Conroy died with her feeding tube in place. The N.J. Supreme Court nevertheless heard the case, as one involving a matter "of substantial importance and . . . capable of repetition but evad[ing] review."]

III

The starting point in analyzing whether life-sustaining treatment may be withheld or withdrawn from an incompetent patient is to determine what rights a competent patient has to accept or reject medical care. It is therefore necessary at the outset of this discussion to identify the nature and extent of a patient's rights that are implicated by such decisions.

The right of a person to control his own body is a basic societal concept, long recognized in the common law. . . .

The doctrine of informed consent is a primary means developed in the law to protect this personal interest in the integrity of one's body. "Under this doctrine, no medical procedure may be performed without a patient's consent, obtained after explanation of the nature of the treatment, substantial risks, and alternative therapies." Cantor, A Patient's Decision to Decline Life-Saving Medical Treatment: Bodily Integrity Versus the Preservation of Life, 26 Rutgers L. Rev. 228, 237 (1973). . . .

The patient's ability to control his bodily integrity through informed consent is significant only when one recognizes that this right also encompasses a right to informed refusal. Thus, a competent adult person generally has the right to decline to have any medical treatment initiated or continued.

The right to make certain decisions concerning one's body is also protected by the federal constitutional right of privacy. . . . While this right of privacy might apply in a case such as this, we need not decide that issue since the right to decline medical treatment is, in any event, embraced within the common-law right to self-determination.

Whether based on common-law doctrines or on constitutional theory, the right to decline life-sustaining medical treatment is not absolute. In some cases, it may yield to countervailing societal interests in sustaining the person's life. Courts and commentators have commonly identified four state interests that may limit a person's right to refuse medical treatment: preserving life, preventing suicide, safeguarding the integrity of the medical profession, and protecting innocent third parties.

The state's interest in preserving life is commonly considered the most significant of the four state interests. It may be seen as embracing two separate but related concerns: an interest in preserving the life of the particular patient, and an interest in preserving the sanctity of all life.

While both of these state interests in life are certainly strong, in themselves they will usually not foreclose a competent person from declining life-sustaining medical treatment for himself. This is because the life that the state is seeking to protect in such a situation is the life of the same person who has competently decided to forego the medical intervention; it is not some other actual or potential life that cannot adequately protect itself.

In cases that do not involve the protection of the actual or potential life of someone other than the decisionmaker, the state's indirect and abstract interest in preserving the life of the competent patient generally gives way to the patient's much stronger personal interest in directing the course of his own life. . . .

[As to the state interest in preventing suicide], declining life-sustaining medical treatment may not properly be viewed as an attempt to commit suicide. Refusing medical intervention merely allows the disease to take its natural course; if death were eventually to occur, it would be the result, primarily, of the underlying disease, and not the result of a self-inflicted injury. In addition, people who refuse life-sustaining medical treatment may not harbor a specific intent to die; rather, they may fervently wish to live, but to do so free of unwanted medical technology, surgery, or drugs, and without protracted suffering. . . . The difference is between self-infliction or self-destruction and self-determination. . . .

The third state interest that is frequently asserted as a limitation on a competent patient's right to refuse medical treatment is the interest in safeguarding the integrity of the medical profession. . . . Medical ethics do not require medical intervention in disease at all costs. . . . Indeed, recent surveys have suggested that a majority of practicing doctors now approve of passive euthanasia and believe that it is being practiced by members of the profession.

Moreover, even if doctors were exhorted to attempt to cure or sustain their patients under all circumstances, that moral and professional imperative, at least in cases of patients who were clearly competent, presumably would not require doctors to go beyond advising the patient of the risks of foregoing treatment and urging the patient to accept the medical intervention. If the patient rejected the doctor's advice, the onus of that decision would rest on the patient, not the doctor. . . .

The fourth asserted state interest in overriding a patient's decision about his medical treatment is the interest in protecting innocent third parties who may be harmed by the patient's treatment decision. [The court cites cases involving minor children who would be abandoned by a parent's death or involving threats to public health or prison security.] . . .

On balance, the right to self-determination ordinarily outweighs any countervailing state interests, and competent persons generally are permitted to refuse medical treatment, even at the risk of death. Most of the cases that have held otherwise, unless they involved the interest in protecting innocent third parties, have concerned the patient's competency to make a rational and considered choice of treatment. . . .

In view of the case law, we have no doubt that Ms. Conroy, if competent to make the decision and if resolute in her determination, could have chosen to have her nasogastric tube withdrawn. Her interest in freedom from nonconsensual invasion of her bodily integrity would outweigh any state interest in preserving life or in safeguarding the integrity of the medical profession. In addition, rejecting her artificial means of feeding would not constitute attempted suicide, as the decision would probably be based on a wish to be free of medical intervention rather than a specific intent to die, and her death would result, if at all, from her underlying medical condition, which included her inability to swallow. Finally, removal of her feeding tube would not create a public health or safety hazard, nor would her death leave any minor dependents without care or support.

It should be noted that if she were competent, Ms. Conroy's right to self-determination would not be affected by her medical condition or prognosis. . . . Of course, a patient's decision to accept or reject medical treatment may be influenced by his medical condition, treatment, and prognosis; nevertheless, a competent person's common-law and constitutional rights do not depend on the quality or value of his life.

[In the section on the incompetent patient, at page 537, we consider the second half of the court's opinion, which discusses how decisions about life-sustaining treatment should be made for patients like Ms. Conroy.]

■ CRUZAN v. DIRECTOR, MISSOURI DEPARTMENT OF HEALTH
497 U.S. 261 (1990)

REHNQUIST, Chief Justice.

. . . On the night of January 11, 1983, Nancy Cruzan lost control of her car as she traveled down Elm Road in Jasper County, Missouri. The vehicle overturned, and Cruzan was discovered lying face down in a ditch without detectable respiratory or cardiac function. Paramedics were able to restore her breathing and heartbeat at the accident site, and she was transported to a hospital in an unconscious state. An attending neurosurgeon diagnosed her as having sustained probable cerebral contusions compounded by significant anoxia (lack of oxygen). The Missouri trial court in this case found that permanent brain damage generally results after six minutes in an anoxic state; it was estimated that Cruzan was deprived of oxygen from 12 to 14 minutes. She remained in a coma for approximately three weeks and then progressed to an unconscious state in which she was able to orally ingest some nutrition. In order to ease feeding and further the recovery, surgeons implanted a gastrostomy feeding and hydration tube in Cruzan with the consent of her then husband. Subsequent rehabilitative efforts proved unavailing. [Now age 31, she] lies in a Missouri state hospital in what is commonly referred to as a persistent vegetative state: generally, a condition in which a person exhibits motor reflexes but evinces no indications of significant cognitive function. The state of Missouri is bearing the cost of her care.

After it had become apparent that Nancy Cruzan had virtually no chance of regaining her mental faculties, her parents asked hospital employees to terminate the artificial nutrition and hydration procedures. . . . The employees refused to honor the request without court approval. [Ms. Cruzan's parents then sought judicial authorization from a state trial court. The trial court granted approval, but the Missouri Supreme Court reversed that decision.] . . .

We granted certiorari to consider the question whether Cruzan has a right under the United States Constitution which would require the hospital to withdraw life-sustaining treatment from her under these circumstances.

At common law, even the touching of one person by another without consent and without legal justification was a battery. Before the turn of the century, this Court observed that "[n]o right is held more sacred, or is more carefully guarded, by the common law, than the right of every individual to the possession and control of his own person, free from all restraint or interference of others, unless by clear and unquestionable authority of law." Union Pacific R. Co. v. Botsford, 141 U.S. 250, 251 (1891). This notion of bodily integrity has been embodied in the requirement that informed consent is generally required for medical treatment. Justice Cardozo, while on the Court of Appeals of New York, aptly described this doctrine: "Every human being of adult years and sound mind has a right to determine what shall be done with his own body; and a surgeon who performs an operation without his patient's consent commits an assault, for which he is liable in damages." Schloendorff v. Society of New York Hospital, 105 N.E. 92, 93 (N.Y. 1914). The informed consent doctrine has become firmly entrenched in American tort law.

The logical corollary of the doctrine of informed consent is that the patient generally possesses the right not to consent, that is, to refuse treatment. Until about 15 years ago and the seminal decision in In re Quinlan, the number of right-to-refuse-treatment decisions was relatively few. Most of the earlier cases involved patients who refused medical treatment forbidden by their religious beliefs, thus implicating First Amendment rights as well as common law rights of self-determination. More recently, however, with the advance of medical technology capable of sustaining life well past the point where natural forces would have brought certain death in earlier times, cases involving the right to refuse life-sustaining treatment have burgeoned. . . .

As these cases demonstrate, the common law doctrine of informed consent is viewed as generally encompassing the right of a competent individual to refuse medical treatment. Beyond that, these cases demonstrate both similarity and diversity in their approaches to decision of what all agree is a perplexing question with unusually strong moral and ethical overtones. . . . This is the first case in which we have been squarely presented with the issue whether the United States Constitution grants what is in common parlance referred to as a "right to die." . . .

The Fourteenth Amendment provides that no state shall "deprive any person of life, liberty, or property, without due process of law." The principle that a competent person has a constitutionally protected liberty interest in refusing unwanted medical treatment may be inferred from our prior decisions. In Jacobson v. Massachusetts, 197 U.S. 11, 24-30 (1905), for instance, the Court balanced an individual's liberty interest in declining an unwanted smallpox vaccine against the state's interest in preventing disease. Decisions prior to the incorporation of the Fourth Amendment into the Fourteenth Amendment analyzed searches and seizures involving the body under the due process clause and were thought to implicate substantial liberty interests.

Just this Term, in the course of holding that a state's procedures for administering antipsychotic medication to prisoners were sufficient to satisfy due process concerns, we recognized that prisoners possess "a significant liberty interest in avoiding the unwanted administration of antipsychotic drugs under the due process clause of the Fourteenth Amendment." Washington v. Harper, 494 U.S. 210, 221-222 (1990). Still other cases support the recognition of a general liberty interest in refusing medical treatment. Vitek v. Jones, 445 U.S. 480, 494 (1980) (transfer to mental hospital coupled with mandatory behavior modification treatment implicated liberty interests); Parham v. J.R., 442 U.S. 584, 600 (1979) ("[A] child, in common with adults, has a substantial liberty interest in not being confined unnecessarily for medical treatment").

But determining that a person has a "liberty interest" under the due process clause does not end the inquiry; "whether respondent's constitutional rights have been violated must be determined by balancing his liberty interests against the relevant state interests." Youngberg v. Romeo, 457 U.S. 307, 321 (1982).

Petitioners insist that under the general holdings of our cases, the forced administration of life-sustaining medical treatment, and even of artificially delivered food and water essential to life, would implicate a competent person's liberty interest. Although we think the logic of the cases discussed above would embrace such a liberty interest, the dramatic consequences involved in refusal of such treatment would inform the inquiry as to whether the deprivation of that interest is constitutionally permissible. But for purposes of this case, we assume that the United States Constitution would grant a competent person a constitutionally protected right to refuse lifesaving hydration and nutrition. . . .

[While the Court assumed for purposes of the case that Nancy Cruzan had a right to refuse her treatment, it also upheld Missouri's imposition of treatment on the ground that the Missouri Supreme Court had adopted a reasonable procedural standard for deciding when an incompetent person's right to refuse treatment should be invoked. That part of the decision is considered at page 547, in the section on the incompetent patient.]

O'CONNOR, Justice, concurring.

I agree that a protected liberty interest in refusing unwanted medical treatment may be inferred from our prior decisions, and that the refusal of artificially-delivered food and water is encompassed within that liberty interest. . . .

Artificial feeding cannot readily be distinguished from other forms of medical treatment. See, e.g., Council on Ethical and Judicial Affairs, American Medical Association, AMA Ethical Opinion 2.20, Withholding or Withdrawing Life-Prolonging Medical Treatment, Current Opinions 13 (1989); The Hastings Center, Guidelines on the Termination of Life-Sustaining Treatment and the Care of the Dying 59 (1987). Whether or not the techniques used to pass food and water into the patient's alimentary tract are termed "medical treatment," it is clear they all involve some degree of intrusion and restraint. Feeding a patient by means of a nasogastric tube requires a physician to pass a long flexible tube through the patient's nose, throat, and esophagus and into the stomach. . . . A gastrostomy tube (as was used to provide food and water to Nancy Cruzan) or jejunostomy tube must be surgically implanted into the stomach or small intestine. Requiring a competent adult to endure such procedures against his or her will burdens the patient's liberty, dignity, and freedom to determine the course of their own treatment. Accordingly, the liberty guaranteed by the Due Process Clause must protect, if it protects anything, an individual's deeply personal decision to reject medical treatment, including the artificial delivery of food and water. . . .

SCALIA, Justice, concurring.

. . . While I agree with the Court's analysis today, and therefore join in its opinion, I would have preferred that we announce, clearly and promptly, that the federal courts have no business in this field; that American law has always accorded the state the power to prevent, by force if necessary, suicide — including suicide by refusing to take appropriate measures necessary to preserve one's life; that the point at which life becomes "worthless," and the point at which the means necessary to preserve it become "extraordinary" or "inappropriate," are neither set forth in the Constitution nor known to the nine Justices of this Court any better than they are known to nine people picked at random from the Kansas City telephone directory; and hence that . . . [when] a patient no longer wishes certain measures to be taken to preserve his or her life, it is up to the citizens of Missouri to decide, through their elected representatives, whether that wish will be honored. It is quite impossible (because the Constitution says nothing about the matter) that those citizens will decide upon a line less lawful than the one we would choose; and it is unlikely (because we know no more about "life and death" than they do) that they will decide upon a line less reasonable. . . .

Petitioners rely on three distinctions to separate Nancy Cruzan's case from ordinary suicide: (1) that she is permanently incapacitated and in pain; (2) that she would bring on her death not by any affirmative act but by merely declining treatment that provides nourishment; and (3) that preventing her from effectuating her presumed wish to die requires violation of her bodily integrity. None of these suffices. Suicide was not excused even when committed "to avoid those ills which [persons] had not the fortitude to endure." 4 Blackstone, supra, at 189. "The life of those to whom life has become a burden — of those who are hopelessly diseased or fatally wounded — nay, even the lives of criminals condemned to death, are under the protection of the law, equally as the lives of those who are in the full tide of life's enjoyment, and anxious to continue to live." Blackburn v. State, 23 Ohio St. 146, 163 (1873). . . . [Assisted suicide] is declared by the law to be murder, irrespective of the wishes or the condition of the party to whom the poison is administered. . . ." Blackburn, supra, at 163.

The second asserted distinction — suggested by the recent cases canvassed by the Court concerning the right to refuse treatment — relies on the dichotomy between action and inaction. Suicide, it is said, consists of an affirmative act to end one's life; refusing treatment is not an affirmative act "causing" death, but merely a passive acceptance of the natural process of dying. I readily acknowledge that the distinction between action and inaction has some bearing upon the legislative judgment of what ought to be prevented as suicide — though even there it would seem to me unreasonable to draw the line precisely between action and inaction, rather than between various forms of inaction. It would not make much sense to say that one may not kill oneself by walking into the sea, but may sit on the beach until submerged by the incoming tide; or that one may not intentionally lock oneself into a cold storage locker, but may refrain from coming indoors when the temperature drops below freezing. Even as a legislative matter, in other words, the intelligent line does not fall between action and inaction but between those forms of inaction that consist of abstaining from "ordinary" care and those that consist of abstaining from "excessive" or "heroic" measures. Unlike action versus inaction, that is not a line to be discerned by logic or legal analysis, and we should not pretend that it is.

. . . Of course, the common law rejected the action-inaction distinction in other contexts involving the taking of human life as well. In the prosecution of a parent for the starvation death of her infant, it was no defense that the infant's death was "caused" by no action of the parent but by the natural process of starvation, or by the infant's natural inability to provide for itself. A physician, moreover, could be criminally liable for failure to provide care that could have extended the patient's life, even if death was immediately caused by the underlying disease that the physician failed to treat.

It is not surprising, therefore, that the early cases considering the claimed right to refuse medical treatment dismissed as specious the nice distinction between "passively submitting to death and actively seeking it. The distinction may be merely verbal, as it would be if an adult sought death by starvation instead of a drug. If the state may interrupt one mode of self-destruction, it may with equal authority interfere with the other." John F. Kennedy Memorial Hosp. v. Heston, 279 A.2d 670, 672-673 (N.J. 1971).

The third asserted basis of distinction — that frustrating Nancy Cruzan's wish to die in the present case requires interference with her bodily integrity — is likewise inadequate, because such interference is impermissible only if one begs the question whether her refusal to undergo the treatment on her own is suicide. It has always been lawful not only for the state, but even for private citizens, to interfere with bodily integrity to prevent a felony. That general rule has of course been applied to suicide. . . . The state-run hospital, I am certain, is not liable under 42 U.S.C. §1983 for violation of constitutional rights, nor the private hospital liable under general tort law, if, in a state where suicide is unlawful, it pumps out the stomach of a person who has intentionally taken an overdose of barbiturates, despite that person's wishes to the contrary. . . .

What I have said above is not meant to suggest that I would think it desirable, if we were sure that Nancy Cruzan wanted to die, to keep her alive by the means at issue here. I assert only that the Constitution has nothing to say about the subject. To raise up a constitutional right here we would have to create out of nothing (for it exists neither in text nor tradition) some constitutional principle whereby, although the state may insist that an individual come in out of the cold and eat food, it may not insist that he take medicine; and although it may pump his stomach empty of poison he has ingested, it may not fill his stomach with food he has failed to ingest. Are there, then, no reasonable and humane limits that ought not to be exceeded in requiring an individual to preserve his own life? There obviously are, but they are not set forth in the due process clause. What assures us that those limits will not be exceeded is the same constitutional guarantee that is the source of most of our protection — what protects us, for example, from being assessed a tax of 100% of our income above the subsistence level, from being forbidden to drive cars, or from being required to send our children to school for 10 hours a day, none of which horribles is categorically prohibited by the Constitution. Our salvation is the equal protection clause, which requires the democratic majority to accept for themselves and their loved ones what they impose on you and me. This Court need not, and has no authority to, inject itself into every field of human activity where irrationality and oppression may theoretically occur, and if it tries to do so it will destroy itself.

Notes: The Individual Interest in Refusing Treatment

1. *Karen Quinlan*. Even though Karen Quinlan's family won the right to have her ventilator discontinued, her physician and the hospital administration refused to comply with the decision of the New Jersey Supreme Court. Rather than turning off the ventilator immediately, Ms. Quinlan's physician, Dr. Morse, spent the next

five months "weaning" her from the ventilator so she could breathe on her own. Ms. Quinlan eventually lived for another ten years. Gregory E. Pence, Medical Ethics: Accounts of Ground-Breaking Cases 62-63 (7th ed. 2015). See also Annette E. Clark, The Right to Die: The Broken Road from *Quinlan* to *Schiavo*, 37 Loy. U. Chi. L. J. 383 (2006).

As the *Quinlan* case illustrates, physicians may incorrectly believe that a patient will be permanently dependent on a ventilator or other medical treatment. Similarly, physicians may incorrectly believe that a patient is terminally ill. People may therefore decline life-sustaining treatment on the basis of mistaken assumptions about their prognoses. How would you respond to the argument that this kind of uncertainty should preclude a patient from refusing life-sustaining treatment?

2. *Persistent Vegetative State, Coma, and Brain Death.* The persistent vegetative state of Karen Quinlan and Nancy Cruzan is often confused with coma and brain death. There is some similarity among the three conditions. With all three, the person suffers a total and sustained loss of consciousness. That is, the cerebral hemispheres, which are responsible for conscious behavior, do not function. Accordingly, the person has no thoughts, feelings, sensations, desires, or emotions. There is no purposeful action, social interaction, memory, pain, or suffering. The person has lost all awareness of self and environment.

Brain death, coma, and the persistent vegetative state differ in the extent to which there is function of the brain stem, the part of the brain that controls unconscious activity. In brain death, there is a nearly complete and an irreversible loss of brain stem function (as well as a complete and irreversible loss of cerebral hemisphere function). As a result, the brain is no longer able to regulate what are known as the body's "vegetative" functions, which include the functions of the heart, lungs, kidneys, intestinal tract, and certain reflex actions. Brain-dead persons appear to be in a deep coma in which they generally do not engage in any spontaneous movement. Moreover, they do not respond to stimuli such as pain, touch, sound, or light. Mechanical measures and other artificial support can maintain a brain-dead person's heartbeat, breathing, and other vegetative functions temporarily, but usually only for a few days or weeks after brain death occurs. As discussed at the end of this chapter, a patient who is brain dead is legally, not just figuratively, dead. As a consequence, patients and families have no choice over "life support"; treatment *must* be withdrawn, not as a matter of the patient's rights, but simply as a matter of medical routine and out of proper respect for the deceased. The one important qualification is when the patient and family have authorized organ donation, in which case "life support" may be continued even though the patient is dead in order to keep the organs from deteriorating before "harvesting." See pages 621 and 646 for further discussion of brain death and its role in organ transplantation.

In contrast to brain-dead persons, patients in a persistent vegetative state are still alive. Because they maintain relatively normal brain stem function, they can usually breathe air, digest food, and produce urine without any assistance. They experience cycles of sleeping, in which their eyes are closed, and waking, in which their eyes are open. They may smile, utter unintelligible sounds, or move their eyes, arms, and legs sporadically. Vegetative state patients also manifest a range of reflex reactions to different stimuli; they will grimace, cough, gag, and move their arms and legs. While all of this activity gives the appearance of consciousness, there is none.

Coma may be viewed as a condition intermediate between brain death and the vegetative state. The brain stem retains some function, but not the range of activity seen in the vegetative state. For example, coma is a sleep-like state in which the eyes remain closed. The patient's breathing is impaired, and many reflexes are absent. Coma and the vegetative state also differ in their duration. Comas rarely last more than two to four weeks, by which time the patient either dies, enters a vegetative state, or regains some degree of consciousness. The duration of the vegetative state, on the other hand, frequently lasts for more than a few weeks. Once it has existed for several months, it is characterized as a persistent vegetative state. Patients can survive for years, even decades, in a persistent vegetative state. In rare cases, patients have regained consciousness from a persistent vegetative state, but these patients usually remain severely disabled neurologically. The Multi-Society Task Force on PVS, Medical Aspects of the Persistent Vegetative State (Second of Two Parts), 330 New Eng. J. Med. 1572 (1994). See also Bryan Jennett, The Vegetative State: Medical Facts, Ethical and Legal Dilemmas (2002).

3. *Sources of a Right to Refuse Life-Sustaining Treatment.* In the early cases that recognized a right to refuse treatment, courts rested the right on two individual interests: the common-law right to be free of nonconsensual bodily invasion (i.e., the right to informed consent) and the substantive due process right to make decisions of critical importance to one's destiny (i.e., the right to privacy). As the U.S. Supreme Court began to narrow the reach of the right to privacy, state courts relied more heavily on common-law principles of informed consent to find a right to refuse life-sustaining treatment. This trend is reflected in the excerpts printed above from the *Quinlan* and *Conroy* decisions of the New Jersey Supreme Court. After the *Cruzan* decision, however, courts are again relying on the substantive due process right, although now framed as a liberty interest rather than a privacy right. It is true that the *Cruzan* majority only assumed for purposes of the case that individuals enjoy a constitutional right to refuse life-sustaining treatment. Nevertheless, the decision has been read by courts and commentators as establishing such a right. See, e.g., State v. Pelham, 824 A.2d 1082, 1087 (N.J. 2003) (observing that "[s]ince the 1976 decision in *Quinlan,* numerous other courts, including the United States Supreme Court, have recognized the so-called 'right to die.'"); Browning v. Herbert, 568 So. 2d 4, 10 (Fla. 1990) ("A competent individual has the constitutional right to refuse medical treatment regardless of his or her medical condition," citing *Cruzan*); John A. Robertson, *Cruzan* and the Constitutional Status of Nontreatment Decisions for Incompetent Patients, 25 Ga. L. Rev. 1139 (1991); Donald H. J. Hermann, Artificial Nutrition and Hydration and the Patient in Persistent Vegetative State, 40 U. Dayton L. Rev. 407, 410 (2016).

Although we can easily view the informed consent right and the substantive due process right as independent rights—the first, a right to be free of unwanted bodily invasion; the second, a right to make important personal decisions—the *Cruzan* Court collapsed the two. There, as we saw, the Court turned to common-law principles of informed consent as the basis for finding a constitutional liberty interest in refusing life-sustaining treatment. Yet, in terms of underlying principles, it arguably makes more sense to collapse the rights in the other direction. Do you see how the right to informed consent ultimately comes down to a notion of privacy or liberty in making important personal decisions? See, e.g., Schloendorff v. Society of New York Hospital, 105 N.E. 92, 93 (N.Y. 1914) (Cardozo, J.) (holding that surgery without consent is an unlawful assault because "[e]very human being of adult years and sound mind has a right to determine what shall be done with his own body"). In terms of future implications, why do you think the *Cruzan* Court preferred to rest its constitutional right on principles of informed consent rather than on the kind of privacy analysis employed in its abortion cases, Roe v. Wade or Planned Parenthood of Southeastern Pennsylvania v. Casey?

4. *State Action.* In *Cruzan*, the patient was being treated in a state rehabilitation facility, so the Supreme Court did not need to worry whether the state action requirement of the Fourteenth Amendment was satisfied (i.e., the Fourteenth Amendment protects against government, not private, action). Yet, in many cases, it is a private physician or hospital refusing to discontinue life-sustaining treatment. In those cases, it is not clear how the patients could invoke their federal constitutional right to refuse treatment. See Blum v. Yaretsky, 457 U.S. 991, 1004 (1982) (no state action implicated by a private nursing home's decision to transfer a patient despite a reduction in the patient's Medicaid benefits by the state in response to the transfer; "a state normally can be held responsible for a private decision only when it has exercised [such] coercive power . . . that the choice must in law be deemed to be that of the state"). Most likely, state action has not been viewed as an issue in treatment withdrawal cases both because state common-law grounds are available to justify withdrawal and because the courts recognize that the state is doing more than refusing to intervene but is also using the threat of criminal liability to effectively force the physician or hospital to treat. See, e.g., In re Colyer, 660 P.2d 738, 742 (Wash. 1983) (finding state action in part because of the state's "capability of imposing criminal sanctions on the hospital and its staff"). In some cases, a court's finding of state action is difficult to reconcile with the U.S. Supreme Court's state action decisions. See, e.g., Rasmussen v. Fleming, 741 P.2d 674, 682 n.9 (Ariz. 1987) (finding state action on the basis of the state's regulation and licensing of hospitals and physicians and the state's supervisory authority over the guardianship of incapacitated persons).

5. *Withdrawing vs. Withholding.* The *Quinlan* opinion suggests that if the issue had been whether to put Karen Quinlan on a ventilator, she clearly would have enjoyed a right to have the ventilator withheld. At one time, some commentators argued that it was permissible to withhold life-sustaining treatment but not to withdraw such treatment, just as there is no obligation to come to someone's rescue, but there is an obligation not to abandon a rescue. Over time, however, in both ethics and the law, the distinction between withdrawing and withholding was rejected. Indeed, as many commentators have observed, it is arguably worse to withhold than to withdraw. If treatment is withheld, then an opportunity is lost to see if the treatment would provide unexpected benefit. Withdrawal presumably occurs only after it becomes clear that the treatment provides insufficient benefit. Moreover, as suggested by Justice Brennan in his dissent in *Cruzan*, 497 U.S. at 314, if we did not recognize a right to have treatment withdrawn, many people might not seek care in the first place because they would be afraid of not being able to stop treatment once it was started. If the treatment ended up not working and causing greater suffering, the person would be stuck. Do you agree with this latter argument? Is it likely that people would hesitate to seek potentially life-saving care because they might not be able to stop the care at some later time?

Despite years of ethicists and courts rejecting the distinction between withholding and withdrawing, health care providers feel very differently about the two acts.

Many physicians believe it is ethically and legally less acceptable to withdraw care than to withhold it. See, e.g., Neil J. Farber et al., Physicians' Decisions to Withhold and Withdraw Life-Sustaining Treatment, 166 Arch. Intern. Med. 560 (2006); Dominic Wilkinson & Julian Savulescu, A Costly Separation Between Withdrawing and Withholding Treatment in Intensive Care, 28 Bioethics 127 (2014).

These feelings are not surprising. It is hard not to feel responsible for a patient's death when you turn off a ventilator and the patient dies within minutes. Two ethics consultants wrote about their experience in discontinuing a ventilator from a competent, 67-year-old patient, Mr. Larson, who was irreversibly dependent on the ventilator because of "post-polio syndrome."

> Although we received grateful hugs from the family and thanks from the health care team, we were struck by the gravity of what we had done. Doubts kept creeping into our minds. We each experienced a wave of disquieting emotion, feelings that we had killed this patient who would have otherwise continued to live connected to the ventilator. We knew intellectually that he had the legal and ethical right to refuse this medical treatment, but the gravity of the decision and our participation haunted us. We returned to our immediate commitments of caring for other patients, one of us responding next to the need of a patient who wanted medical help for a pulmonary problem to prolong his life. Both of us remained preoccupied throughout the afternoon thinking about Mr. Larson and what we had done. Our respective medical careers have generally been devoted to responding to patient wishes to postpone death and to prolong life. We've seen our patients die of their various diseases, but now our acquiescence in allowing his death caused us much anguish. This anguish continued in both of us for several days. One of us sought counsel from a psychiatrist who reinforced our belief that we did the right thing, counteracting those deep feelings that somehow we had killed this patient. Gradually we came to terms with what had happened. . . . Our consciences were clear, but we were left feeling very impressed with how difficult it had been to honor this man's request.

Miles J. Edwards & Susan W. Tolle, Disconnecting a Ventilator at the Request of a Patient Who Knows He Will Then Die: The Doctor's Anguish, 117 Ann. Intern. Med. 254, 256 (1992).

How should the law take account of these feelings?

6. *Type of Treatment at Stake.* As the *Quinlan* and *Cruzan* cases suggest, it was once unclear legally whether artificial ventilation or artificial nutrition and hydration could be discontinued, and there were many commentators opposed to withdrawal of feeding tubes. See, e.g., Daniel Callahan, On Feeding the Dying, 13(5) Hastings Center Rep. 22 (1983); Mark Siegler & Alan J. Weisbard, Against the Emerging Stream: Should Fluids and Nutritional Support Be Discontinued?, 145 Arch. Intern. Med. 129 (1985). The *Cruzan* case essentially resolved the debate in terms of the law, and now it is widely accepted that patients can refuse any medical treatment. Nevertheless, many health care providers are still slow to withdraw feeding tubes because of their personal moral concerns.

Not all treatment decisions have been so controversial. In particular, do-not-resuscitate (DNR) orders have been accepted medical practice for decades. Such orders, often called DNAR (do-not-attempt-resuscitation) orders, were developed because dying patients do not always want physicians to try to restart their heartbeat when their illness results in the terminal event of cardiac arrest. A DNR order means that cardiopulmonary resuscitation (CPR) will be withheld from the patient. The acceptance of DNR orders is reflected in the hospital accreditation standards of the Joint Commission for the Accreditation of Healthcare Organizations, which *require* hospitals to maintain a specific policy for DNR orders. What is controversial about DNR orders is whether physicians may write them over the objection of the patient or the patient's family, on the ground that CPR serves no useful purpose. This issue will be discussed in greater depth in the section on futility, pages 610-627.

7. *Costs of Care.* While the right to refuse treatment coincides with a trend toward greater recognition of patients' rights, it also coincides, as mentioned in the introduction to this section, with concerns about the high cost of medical care. When the *Cruzan* case was working its way through the courts, it was common to hear people justify withdrawal of care on the ground that it was costing more than $100,000 a year to keep her alive and that money could be better spent on other kinds of medical care. Does the right to refuse treatment simply reflect the economic cost to society of enforcing a duty to receive life-sustaining treatment?

Much has been made about the high percentage of health care costs that are consumed at the end of life. One often hears that close to a third of Medicare spending occurs during the last six months of patients' lives. Overall, however, end-of-life spending is not so high. According to estimates, only 7 to 13 percent of total medical expenditures occur during the last year of patients' lives. In addition, physicians tend to treat people aggressively during the last six or twelve months of life when it appears that the patient has a reasonable chance of a good recovery. For patients with poor prognoses, most of the costs of care go to cover nursing home and home health care; in other words, basic supportive care.

8. *Further Reading.* On withdrawing **feeding tubes** (note 6), see Elise Piot et al., Caregivers Confronted with the Withdrawal of Artificial Nutrition at the End of Life, 32 Am. J. Hospice & Palliative Med. 732 (2015). See also Susan E. Hickman et al., The Consistency Between Treatments Provided to Nursing Facility Residents and Orders on the Physician Orders for Life-Sustaining Treatment Form, 59 J. Amer. Geriatrics Soc. 2091 (2011) (finding that treatment decisions were consistent with POLST orders 94 percent of the time overall but only 64 percent of the time for feeding tubes).

On **end-of-life costs** (note 7), see Melissa D. Aldridge & Amy S. Kelley, The Myth Regarding the High Cost of End-of-Life Care, 105 Am. J. Public Health 2411 (2015); Mariacristina De Nardi et al., Medical Spending of the US Elderly, 37 Fiscal Studies 717 (2016); Anne A. Scitovsky, Medical Care in the Last Twelve Months of Life: The Relation Between Age, Functional Status, and Medical Care Expenditures, 66 Milbank Q. 640 (1988); Samuel S. Richardson et al., Use of Aggressive Medical Treatments Near the End of Life: Differences Between Patients With and Without Dementia, 42 Health Serv. Res. 183 (2007) (concluding that "during the final 30 days of life, acute care patients with dementia are treated substantially less aggressively than patients without dementia").

Notes: The State's Interest in Preserving Life

1. *The State's Interest.* In *Conroy,* the New Jersey Supreme Court essentially argued that the state's interest in preserving patients' lives is sufficient to justify the

imposition of medical treatment only when patients want their lives preserved. The state's primary interest is to protect patients from having their lives taken involuntarily. Similarly, in his dissent in *Cruzan*, Justice Brennan wrote:

> The only state interest asserted here is a general interest in the preservation of life. But the state has no legitimate general interest in someone's life, completely abstracted from the interest of the person living that life, that could outweigh the person's choice to avoid medical treatment. . . . [T]he state's general interest in life must accede to Nancy Cruzan's particularized and intense interest in self-determination in her choice of medical treatment. There is simply nothing legitimately within the state's purview to be gained by superseding her decision.

Cruzan, 497 U.S. at 313-314 (Brennan, J., with Marshall, J., and Blackmun, J., dissenting).

David Blake argues that such a view conflates the value of life with the ability to exercise individual autonomy. Self-determination surely is a critical value, he observes, but there is intrinsic value to a person's life above and beyond the value recognized by that person. David Blake, State Interests in Terminating Medical Treatment, 19(3) Hastings Center Rep. 5 (1989). Why might the state have interests in preserving life even when a competent adult rejects continued life? Consider concerns about preserving the moral worth of society (if patients are allowed to die when they consent, people may have less respect for life and be less troubled when death comes about involuntarily); about preserving freedom of choice in areas of profound consequence to happiness (we do not permit people to become slaves or renounce their right to a divorce); and about avoiding the domination of one group by another (here, preventing the victimization of severely disabled persons). David Orentlicher, Physician-Assisted Dying: The Conflict with Fundamental Principles of American Law, *in* Medicine Unbound: The Human Body and the Limits of Medical Intervention 256 (Blank & Bonnicksen eds., 1994).

2. *Balancing the Individual and State Interests.* If the state's interest in preserving a patient's life exists only insofar as the patient wishes to continue living, then there is no need to balance the state's interest against the individual interest. If the state's interest has some content that is independent of the individual's interest, then that raises the question of how we should balance the state's interest in preserving life with the individual's interest in being able to refuse treatment. Should the right to refuse life-sustaining treatment be unlimited or should it be restricted according to the type of treatment at issue (e.g., antibiotics vs. a ventilator) or the patient's medical condition (e.g., pneumonia in an otherwise healthy person vs. widely metastatic cancer). Do you agree with the *Quinlan* court's view that the right to refuse life-sustaining treatment should grow as the degree of bodily invasion increases and the prognosis dims? Should it matter whether the patient is terminally ill or might be able to live for many years?

As the case law has developed, courts have seemingly abandoned any effort to balance the individual's right to refuse treatment with the state's interest in preserving life, almost without exception permitting competent patients to refuse life-sustaining treatment. In the early cases, including *Quinlan*, the courts had suggested that the right to refuse life-sustaining treatment was a right that existed when life could be prolonged for only a short time, with a poor quality of life and at considerable cost to the patient (with cost being measured in terms of pain, other suffering, and economic burden). However, later cases have not so limited the right.

As we saw, the New Jersey Supreme Court in *Conroy* concluded that:

> the right to self-determination ordinarily outweighs any countervailing state interests, and competent persons generally are permitted to refuse medical treatment, even at the risk of death. . . . Ms. Conroy's right to self-determination would not be affected by her medical condition or prognosis. . . . [A] competent person's common-law and constitutional rights do not depend on the quality or value of his life.

486 A.2d at 1225-1226. Two years later, in In re Peter, 529 A.2d 419 (N.J. 1987), involving the removal of a feeding tube from a patient in a persistent vegetative state, the same court wrote:

> Medical choices . . . are not to be decided by societal standards of reasonableness or normalcy. Rather, it is the patient's preferences—formed by his or her unique personal experiences—that should control.
>
> The privacy that we accord medical decisions does not vary with the patient's condition or prognosis. The patient's medical condition is generally relevant only to determine whether the patient is or is not competent. . . . [529 A.2d at 423.]

Other courts have taken the same view of the state's interest in preserving life. In the case of Elizabeth Bouvia, an intermediate appeals court permitted a 28-year-old college graduate who retained her full intellectual capacity to refuse a feeding tube. Because of severe cerebral palsy, Ms. Bouvia was quadriplegic, confined to bed, and dependent on others for all of her needs. She also was in continual pain from severe arthritis. She had suffered a series of emotional setbacks when her husband left her and her physical deterioration forced her to drop out of school and become dependent on others. Despondent, she admitted herself to a public hospital as a psychiatric patient, with the apparent intent of starving herself to death using the assistance of pain relief and other comfort care provided by the hospital. After a trial court denied her judicial assistance, she abandoned that effort and lived at several different facilities before seeking permission from a trial court to have her feeding tube withdrawn. In addressing the fact that Ms. Bouvia was not terminally ill, the appellate court wrote,

> If her right to choose may not be exercised because there remains to her, in the opinion of the court, a physician or some committee, a certain arbitrary number of years, months, or days, her right will have lost its value and meaning. Who shall say what the minimum amount of available life must be? Does it matter if it be 15 to 20 years, 15 to 20 months, or 15 to 20 days, if such life has been physically destroyed and its quality, dignity and purpose be gone? As in all matters lines must be drawn at some point, somewhere, but that decision must ultimately belong to the one whose life is in issue. Here Elizabeth Bouvia's decision to forego medical treatment or life-support through a mechanical means belongs to her. It is not a medical decision for her physicians to make. Neither is it a legal question whose soundness is to be resolved by lawyers or judges. It is not a conditional right subject to approval by ethics committees or courts of law. It is a moral and philosophical decision that, being a competent adult, is hers alone.

Bouvia v. Superior Court, 225 Cal. Rptr. 297, 304-305 (Ct. App. 1986)..

According to the *Bouvia* court, a competent adult "has the right to refuse *any* medical treatment, even that which may save or prolong her life." 225 Cal. Rptr. at 300 (emphasis in original). Despite winning her case, Ms. Bouvia did not exercise her right to refuse life-sustaining treatment.

The Nevada Supreme Court also has given little weight to the state's interest in preserving life. In McKay v. Bergstedt, 801 P.2d 617 (Nev. 1990), a 31-year-old man, Kenneth Bergstedt, sought permission to discontinue a ventilator. Mr. Bergstedt had been quadriplegic, and therefore ventilator-dependent, since a swimming accident at age ten. He was able to read, watch television, write poetry by orally operating a computer, and move around in a wheelchair. His quadriplegia was irreversible, but he was not terminally ill. When the death of his father appeared imminent, Mr. Bergstedt wanted to end his life because "he despaired over the prospect of life without the attentive care, companionship and love of his devoted father." Id. at 620. His mother had died several years earlier. The court observed that Mr. Bergstedt's desire to end his life was driven primarily by "[f]ear of the unknown," that he was preoccupied with concern "over the quality of his life after the death of his father." Id. at 624. In concluding that Mr. Bergstedt's right to refuse treatment overrode the state's interest in preserving life, the court "attach[ed] great significance to the quality of Kenneth's life as he perceived it under the particular circumstances that were afflicting him." Id. at 625.[1] Like many of the decisions in this area, the Nevada Supreme Court's opinion came down after Mr. Bergstedt died. About a month before the decision, and a week before his father died, Mr. Bergstedt's father disconnected his son's ventilator. Father Succumbs to Cancer After Fulfilling Son's Death Wish, San Diego Union-Tribune, October 12, 1990, at A15.

Although there are some early cases to the contrary,[2] courts have approved refusals of treatments necessary to sustain life even when the treatment is simple and minimally invasive, and the person could readily be restored to good health. In Fosmire v. Nicoleau, 551 N.E.2d 77 (N.Y. 1990), the court recognized the right of a 36-year-old adult to refuse blood transfusions that could restore her to good health following blood loss during a cesarean section. The patient refused the transfusions both because she was a Jehovah's Witness and because she feared that a transfusion would transmit HIV or other infectious organisms. In Stamford Hospital v.

---

1. The *Bergstedt* court also recognized a fifth state interest beyond the four generally relied on by courts. According to the court, there is an interest "in encouraging the charitable and humane care of afflicted persons." 801 P.2d at 628. Patients contemplating refusal of life-sustaining treatment therefore must be fully informed of the care alternatives that would be available to them if they remained alive. Id.

2. See, e.g., Application of President & Directors of Georgetown College, Inc., 331 F.2d 1000 (D.C. Cir.), *cert. denied*, 377 U.S. 968 (1964) (25-year-old required to accept a blood transfusion to treat severe blood loss from a perforated ulcer); John F. Kennedy Memorial Hospital v. Heston, 279 A.2d 670 (N.J. 1971) (22-year-old required to accept a blood transfusion during surgery that was performed because her spleen was ruptured in an automobile accident).

Vega, 674 A.2d 821, 824-825 (Conn. 1996), the court also recognized a patient's right to refuse blood transfusions after she had lost a good deal of blood during the vaginal delivery of her child. The patient refused the transfusions because she was a Jehovah's Witness.[3] It is important to recognize that, while a blood transfusion does not have the intrusiveness of a ventilator, Jehovah's Witnesses are expressing a central tenet of their religion when they refuse transfusions. See Dena S. Davis, Does "No" Mean "Yes"? The Continuing Problem of Jehovah's Witnesses and Refusal of Blood Products, 19(3) Second Opinion 34 (1994); Richard Singelenberg, The Blood Transfusion Taboo of Jehovah's Witnesses: Origin, Development and Function of a Controversial Doctrine, 31 Soc. Sci. Med. 515 (1990).

Prisoner cases are an area in which courts will require continuation of treatment.[4] In In re Caulk, 480 A.2d 93 (N.H. 1984), a 36-year-old prisoner in good health stopped eating with the intent to end his life because he was serving a 15- to 30-year sentence and was facing additional charges that could ultimately add up to a sentence of life without parole. The court permitted the state to forcibly feed Mr. Caulk, citing concerns about institutional order and the fact that Mr. Caulk was not suffering from any illness. The court also observed that Mr. Caulk's attempt at starvation was frustrating the criminal justice system. Because of his condition, two states that had pending indictments against Mr. Caulk were forced to postpone his trials. As a result, the two states could not meet their duty "to bring to finality pending investigations in such a way that the public knows that the criminal justice system has successfully responded to accusations of criminal behavior." 480 A.2d at 96. See also Polk County Sheriff v. Iowa District Court, 594 N.W.2d 421 (Iowa 1999) (rejecting a pretrial detainee's request to discontinue chronic dialysis); Laurie v. Senecal, 666 A.2d 806 (R.I. 1995) (rejecting healthy prisoner's request to die by refusing food and water); McNabb v. Department of Corrections, 180 P.3d 1257 (Wash. 2008) (rejecting a healthy prisoner's refusal of nutrition and hydration).

Note that courts have upheld the right of prisoners to refuse life-sustaining treatment when they are doing so for reasons similar to nonincarcerated persons. Thor v. Superior Court, 855 P.2d 375 (Cal. 1993) (permitting prisoner who was quadriplegic from a neck fracture to refuse a feeding tube); Stouffer v. Reid, 993 A.2d 104 (Md. 2010) (permitting inmate with end-stage renal disease to refuse kidney dialysis); Commonwealth Department of Corrections v. Lindsey, 984 A.2d 573 (Pa. Commw. Ct. 2009) (permitting inmate with "severe kidney ailment" and "gastrointestinal bleeding problem" to refuse blood transfusions).

3. *Burdensome Treatment vs. Burdensome Life.* The nearly unlimited recognition of a right to refuse life-sustaining treatment means that courts have not distinguished between patients who refuse treatment because the treatment itself is not desired and patients who refuse treatment because their life with treatment has become undesirable. The former category includes Jehovah's Witnesses who reject a blood transfusion or a patient with end-stage cancer who rejects an experimental drug

3. In both *Fasmire* and *Stamford Hospital*, the patient had received transfusions by virtue of a lower court's order before winning on appeal.

4. As discussed in Chapters 7 and 8, courts have also been much more willing to impose treatment when a third party's interest is at stake, for example, when a woman is pregnant or there is a threat to public health.

with severe side effects. The latter category includes patients like Elizabeth Bouvia and Kenneth Bergstedt. Does it make sense to distinguish between patients who reject treatment and patients who reject life? When a person with kidney failure who is dependent on dialysis becomes tired of the dependency and decides to stop receiving dialysis treatments, is the person rejecting the treatment or life? Even if we could distinguish between rejecting treatment and rejecting life, why does that distinction matter if the right to refuse treatment is based on principles of self-determination and concerns about avoiding suffering?

4. *Practice vs. the Law.* Despite the fairly clear message from appellate courts that competent patients have the right to refuse life-sustaining treatment, irrespective of the prognosis or the type of treatment, actual practices by physicians and lower court judges retain some of the *Quinlan* kind of balancing. For example, as discussed in more detail in the note on innocent third parties, pages 529-530, some trial court judges will order blood transfusions for Jehovah's Witnesses despite the religiously based refusal of the patient, only to have the decision reversed on appeal after it is impossible to undo the transfusion. See, e.g., In re Duran, 769 A.2d 497 (Pa. Super. Ct. 2001) (patient received blood transfusion following liver transplant surgery despite written statement before surgery refusing any transfusions). Similarly, in a leading medical ethics guide for practicing physicians, the authors present the following case and analysis:

> Mr. Cure, a 24-year-old graduate student, has been brought to the emergency room by a friend. Previously in good health, he is complaining of a severe headache and a stiff neck. . . . [Based on physical examination and laboratory tests, a] diagnosis of bacterial meningitis is made. . . .
>
> [Mr. Cure] is informed that he needs immediate hospitalization and administration of antibiotics. Although drowsy, he appears to understand the physician's explanation. He refuses treatment and says he wants to go home. The physician explains the extreme dangers of going untreated and the minimal risks of treatment. [Without treatment, there is a likelihood of death of 60 to 80 percent, with survivors generally having major and permanent neurologic damage. With treatment, there is a greater than 90 percent chance of full recovery.] The young man persists in his refusal. . . .
>
> This patient should be treated despite his refusal. His refusal is enigmatic, insofar as he offers no reason for refusing. Certainly, the clinician should suspect an altered mental status due to high fever and brain infection, [but] this patient . . . communicates articulately, and appears to understand the consequences of his refusal. There is no time for a thorough psychiatric examination. Given the enigmatic nature of his refusal and the urgent, serious need for treatment, the patient should be treated with antibiotics, even against his will. Should there be time, legal authorization should be sought. . . .
>
> . . . It is difficult to believe that this young man wishes to die or become permanently damaged neurologically.

Albert R. Jonsen et al., Clinical Ethics: A Practical Approach to Ethical Decisions in Clinical Medicine §§1.0.8, 2.2.4 (8th ed. 2015).

How should we view the willingness of physicians and courts to override treatment refusals by persons who easily could be restored to good health? Is this a reasonable safeguard against taking too far the important ethical and legal principle of patient autonomy? Or should we worry about physicians and courts going too far the other way in frustrating patient autonomy? In explaining their willingness to override Mr. Cure's refusal of treatment, Jonsen and colleagues gave a reason that is perfectly consistent with respect for patient autonomy. How did they justify their action in terms of individual self-determination? For a similar argument, see Richard A. Epstein, Moral Peril: Our Inalienable Right to Health Care? 300-305 (1997).

Notes: The State's Interest in Preventing Suicide

While we will save most of our analysis of the relationship between withdrawal of life-sustaining treatment and suicide for the section on physician aid in dying, at pages 582-610, it is worth thinking about the distinction now:

1. *The State's Interest in Preventing Suicide.* In discussing the state's interest in preventing suicide, the courts almost summarily dismiss this objection to the withdrawal of life-sustaining treatment. In the *Saikewicz* case, the Massachusetts Supreme Court relegated the concern about suicide to a footnote, began its analysis by stating that "[t]he interest in protecting against suicide seems to require little if any discussion," and completed its analysis by stating that "[t]here is no connection between the conduct here in issue and any state concern to prevent suicide." Superintendent of Belchertown State School v. Saikewicz, 370 N.E.2d 417, 426 n.11 (Mass. 1977). Yet, under a dictionary definition of suicide, would it not be suicide if a patient on a ventilator flipped a switch that turned off the ventilator? (According to Merriam-Webster's Collegiate Dictionary 1249 (11th ed. 2012), suicide is "the act or an instance of taking one's own life voluntarily and intentionally esp. by a person of years of discretion and of sound mind.")

The *Saikewicz* court and the *Conroy* court emphasized that, with withdrawal, the cause of death is natural and the patient has no intent to die. In addition, the *Saikewicz* court observed that "the underlying state interest in this area lies in the prevention of irrational self-destruction." Note that this "irrational self-destruction" argument is a different kind of argument than the "natural cause" and "intent" arguments. Which of these three arguments do you find persuasive? Do you see how the three arguments might play out differently on the question of permitting physician aid in dying? (As discussed in the section on physician aid in dying, this text prefers that term to physician-assisted suicide.)

2. *Distinguishing Treatment Withdrawal from Aid in Dying.* In contrast to the usual judicial analysis, Justice Scalia in his dissent in *Cruzan* saw no distinction between the refusal of life-sustaining treatment and suicide. Indeed, in his view, refusing life-sustaining treatment is a form of suicide. As his analysis suggests, the categories of treatment refusal and suicide are not self-defining but are labels we apply once we have decided whether a particular life-ending act should be permitted. If we do not approve of a life-ending act, we characterize it as suicide or euthanasia; if we approve of a life-ending act, we find some other term to describe it, for example, the withdrawal of life-sustaining treatment. Indeed, at one time, when its propriety was still in question, the withdrawal of life-sustaining treatment was commonly characterized as "passive euthanasia." Conroy, supra, at page 510; John A. Robertson, Involuntary Euthanasia of Defective Newborns, 27 Stan. L. Rev. 213, 214-215 & n.16 (1975). Can we find any content to the concept of suicide, or is it simply a way to express a moral conclusion that we have reached on other grounds? One way to answer this question would be to consider two other questions: Do you think that

Kenneth Bergstedt was suicidal when he sought discontinuation of his ventilator? Why wouldn't a physician who discontinued Mr. Bergstedt's ventilator be guilty of active euthanasia?

Notes: The Ethical Integrity of the Medical Profession

1. *Professional Objection to Withdrawal.* The state's interest in preserving the ethical integrity of the medical profession has rarely been invoked to prevent the withdrawal of life-sustaining treatment. Courts either conclude that withdrawing treatment is consistent with the ethics of the medical profession (as in *Quinlan* and *Conroy*) and/or indicate that the weight of the interest in professional integrity is not sufficient to override the individual interest in refusing life-sustaining treatment (as in *Conroy*).

Still, there may be cases in which the physician has a personal, moral objection to discontinuing life-sustaining treatment. If the patient's right to refuse treatment rests on a principle of individual autonomy, how do we resolve the conflict when the physician invokes the same principle of individual autonomy to resist participation in the patient's death? We might say that the physician's rights are not violated since the physician need only refrain from acting, but is that an answer to the physician who is morally opposed to helping cause a patient's death? There also may be situations in which the hospital or nursing home has an institutional policy against withdrawing life-sustaining treatment. How should these cases be handled?

Courts have responded to this problem in different ways. In Brophy v. New England Sinai Hospital, 497 N.E.2d 626, 639 (Mass. 1986), the court wrote:

> There is nothing in *Saikewicz* and its progeny which would justify compelling medical professionals, in a case such as this, to take active measures which are contrary to their view of their ethical duty toward their patients. There is substantial disagreement in the medical community over the appropriate medical action. It would be particularly inappropriate to force the hospital, which is willing to assist in a transfer of the patient, to take affirmative steps to end the provision of nutrition and hydration to him. A patient's right to refuse medical treatment does not warrant such an unnecessary intrusion upon the hospital's ethical integrity in this case.

Similarly, in Gray v. Romeo, 697 F. Supp. 580 (D.R.I. 1988), the court allowed the hospital to arrange for a transfer of the patient but held that the hospital must accede to the patient's refusal of artificial nutrition and hydration if the patient could not be "promptly transferred to a health care facility that will respect her wishes." Id. at 591.

Two New Jersey courts have refused to permit a transfer of the patient even though a transfer might have been feasible. In both cases, there was no warning of the hospital's policy when the patient was admitted for care; the policy was not formalized until the request was made to stop treatment and the patient had been hospitalized for some time. According to the court in In re Jobes, 529 A.2d 434, 450 (N.J. 1987):

> Mrs. Jobes' family had no reason to believe they were surrendering the right to choose among medical alternatives when they placed her in the nursing home [in 1980]. The nursing home apparently did not inform Mrs. Jobes' family about its

policy toward artificial feeding until May of 1985 when they requested that [her feeding tube] be withdrawn. In fact, there is no indication that this policy has ever been formalized. Under these circumstances, Mrs. Jobes and her family were entitled to rely on the nursing home's willingness to defer to their choice among courses of medical treatment.

We do not decide the case in which a nursing home gave notice of its policy not to participate in the withdrawal or withholding of artificial feeding at the time of a patient's admission. Thus, we do not hold that such a policy is never enforceable. But we are confident in this case that it would be wrong to allow the nursing home to discharge Mrs. Jobes. . . . [Id. at 450.]

Accord In re Requena, 517 A.2d 886 (N.J. Super. Ct. Ch. Div.), aff'd, 517 A.2d 869 (N.J. Super. Ct. App. Div. 1986) (patient had been in the hospital for 17 months and was admitted before the hospital merged with a Catholic hospital).

This issue is also addressed in advance directive statutes. Typically, the statutes direct the physician to arrange for transfer of the patient's care to another physician, without speaking to situations in which a transfer cannot be arranged. Those statutes that do address that situation generally require the physician to comply with the patient's request or bring the case before a court. But see Ind. Code Ann. §16-36-4-13(f) ("If the attending physician, after reasonable investigation, finds no other physician willing to honor the patient's declaration, the attending physician may refuse to withhold or withdraw life prolonging procedures.").

2. *Legal Liability.* In addition to moral considerations, provider objection to treatment withdrawal may reflect legal concerns. Although the right to refuse life-sustaining treatment is now well established, in 1983, prosecutors brought criminal charges against two physicians for withdrawing life-sustaining treatment at the behest of the patient's family. Barber v. Superior Court, 195 Cal. Rptr. 478 (Ct. App. 1983). The patient, Clarence Herbert, had suffered a cardiac arrest after intestinal surgery, causing "severe brain damage" and leaving him "in a vegetative state, which was likely to be permanent." Three days later, the family requested that all life-sustaining "machines" be discontinued. The physicians immediately withdrew Mr. Herbert's ventilator, and, two days later, after further consultation with the family, they withdrew Mr. Herbert's feeding tube. After Mr. Herbert died, prosecutors brought murder charges against Mr. Herbert's surgeon and internist. The court recognized the authority of Mr. Herbert's family to refuse life-sustaining treatment on his behalf and therefore concluded that "the [physicians'] omission to continue treatment under the circumstances, though intentional and with knowledge that the patient would die, was not an unlawful failure to perform a legal duty." Id. at 493.

Although no physician has suffered civil or criminal liability for withdrawing life-sustaining treatment at the request of a patient or the patient's family, physicians may express concerns about the risks of legal liability when faced with a request to withdraw treatment. Mildred Z. Solomon et al., Decisions Near the End of Life: Professional Views on Life-Sustaining Treatments, 83 Am. J. Public Health 14, 19 (1993). Part of this concern may reflect the fact that, in *Barber*, Mr. Herbert's physicians were in fact prosecuted, but consider whether physicians may rebuff a request to discontinue treatment by pointing to legal concerns as a camouflage, conscious or not, of their moral disagreement with the request. In other words, physicians who think it is morally wrong to discontinue treatment may find it easier—and more persuasive — to say that they cannot stop treatment rather than to acknowledge that they can, but do not want to do so.

3. *Further Reading.* On **physician objection to withholding care** (note 1), see George Annas, When Suicide Prevention Becomes Brutality: The Case of Elizabeth Bouvia, 14(2) Hastings Center Rep. 20 (1984); John K. Davis, Conscientious Refusal and a Doctor's Right to Quit, 29 J. Med. Philos. 75 (2004); Anne M. Dellinger & Ann Morgan Vickery, When Staff Object to Participating in Care, 28 J. Health Hosp. Law 269 (1995); Brian C. Kalt, Death, Ethics, and the State, 23 Harv. J. L. & Pub. Pol'y 487 (2000); Note, Life-Sustaining Treatment Law, 47 B.C. L. Rev. 815 (2006); David Orentlicher, Law, Religion, and Health Care, 8 UC Irvine L. Rev. (2018); Nadia Sawicki, Mandating Disclosure of Conscience-based Limitations on Medical Practice, 42 Am. J. L. & Med. 85 (2016); Nadia Sawicki, The Hollow Promise of Freedom of Conscience, 33 Cardozo L. Rev. 1389 (2012); Elizabeth Sepper, Taking Conscience Seriously, 98 Va. L. Rev. 1501 (2012); page 110-112 .

Notes: The Protection of Innocent Third Parties

1. *Protecting the Interests of Third Parties.* Courts regularly cite the state's interest in protecting the interests of innocent third parties when a patient wants to refuse life-sustaining medical treatment, particularly when the patient has minor children who would arguably suffer from the loss of a parent. At one time, courts would invoke the interest in innocent third parties to impose treatment. For example, in Application of the President and Directors of Georgetown College, 331 F.2d 1000 (D.C. Cir. 1964), the court ordered blood transfusions for Mrs. Jesse E. Jones, a 25-year-old married woman who was the mother of a seven-month-old child. Mrs. Jones had "lost two thirds of her body's blood supply from a ruptured ulcer" and was refusing transfusion because of her religious beliefs as a Jehovah's Witness. Id. at 1006. The court cited the state's interest in preventing the abandonment of Mrs. Jones' child, as well as other grounds, including the fact that "Mrs. Jones was *in extremis* and hardly *compos mentis* at the time in question," Mrs. Jones did not want to die even if she did not want a blood transfusion, and "a life hung in the balance." Id. at 1008-1009.

In more recent cases, courts have generally recognized a parent's right to refuse life-sustaining treatment even though the parent has young children. In In re Debreuil, 629 So. 2d 819 (Fla. 1993), Patricia Debreuil, an otherwise healthy woman, suffered life-threatening bleeding after delivering her fourth child by cesarean section. The trial court ordered transfusions, which were administered, but, on appeal, the Florida Supreme Court held that the trial court erred. According to the court, concerns about the children, who were newborn, 4, 6, and 12 years of age, did not justify the transfusions since the children could be cared for by their father. However, the court "decline[d] at this time to rule out the possibility that some case not yet before us may present a compelling interest to prevent abandonment." Id. at 827. In a similar case, Fosmire v. Nicoleau, 551 N.E.2d 77 (N.Y. 1990), the New York court of appeals also held that the parent had the right to refuse life-sustaining treatment. In that case, Denise Nicoleau had lost a substantial amount of blood after delivering a baby boy via cesarean section. Ms. Nicoleau was married and otherwise in good health. She refused transfusions because of both her religious beliefs as a Jehovah's Witness and her fear of contracting AIDS or other communicable diseases. After the hospital obtained a court order, Ms. Nicoleau received two blood transfusions. The court of appeals held that the trial court erred in ordering the transfusions. Moreover, the court suggested in its dicta that its holding would have been the same even if she had been the only parent available to care for her child: "The state does not prohibit parents from engaging in dangerous activities because there is a risk that their children will be left orphans." Id. at 84. See also Stamford Hospital v. Vega, 674 A.2d 821 (Conn. 1996) (Jehovah's Witness had the right to refuse a blood transfusion needed after she delivered a child although, again, she won on appeal after receiving blood transfusions ordered by the trial court). Still, courts have not yet faced the issue whether a parent would have to receive life-sustaining treatment if the parent's death would leave a minor child as an orphan.

How should courts respond to a single parent's refusal of life-sustaining treatment when the parent has young children? Would it depend on whether the treatment would restore the parent to good health or would only maintain the parent in a severely disabled condition? What if the parent has arranged for a grandparent, aunt, and/or uncle to take care of the children? Is the refusal of life-sustaining treatment by a single parent any different from single parents who engage in risky vocations or avocations? Should we prohibit single parents from being soldiers, police, firefighters, or coal miners? Should exercising your right to procreate require you to forfeit your right to refuse life-sustaining treatment?

2. *Law on the Books vs. Law in Practice.* While appellate courts in recent years have consistently upheld the right of healthy people to refuse blood transfusions, the courts typically do so only after the person has received the transfusion because of an order by a lower court. See Fosmire v. Nicoleau, 551 N.E.2d at 79; Stamford Hospital v. Vega, 674 A.2d at 826; In re Dubreuil, 629 So. 2d at 821. The *Dubreuil* case is particularly striking because the Florida Supreme Court had previously held that a young woman could refuse blood transfusions even though she had minor children. Wons v. Public Health Trust, 541 So. 2d 96 (Fla. 1989). The only apparent difference between the *Dubreuil* and *Wons* cases was that Ms. Dubreuil was estranged from her husband while Ms. Wons was apparently living amicably with her husband. *Dubreuil,* 629 So. 2d at 826. On the other hand, the Florida Supreme Court stated in *Wons* that "these cases demand individual attention. No blanket rule is feasible which could sufficiently cover all occasions in which this situation will arise." 541 So. 2d at 98.

What should we make of the fact that the appellate courts consistently recognize a right of healthy persons to refuse blood transfusions while some trial courts order the blood transfusions? If you were a hospital lawyer, and a physician in your hospital wanted to obtain a court order to transfuse a parent of young children against the parent's wishes, what action would you pursue?

2. The Patient Whose Competence Is Uncertain

In the vast majority of cases, it is clear whether the patient is competent. Most patients either clearly possess decisionmaking capacity or they clearly do not. In some cases, however, whether the patient can competently consent to or refuse treatment is not so easily decided. While patient competence has been a long-standing issue, physicians, lawyers, and other professionals have not yet developed a readily applied standard for assessing competence, perhaps because of its elusive nature. Important considerations include whether the patient's decision is based on "rational" reasons and whether the patient has the ability to understand or has demonstrated actual understanding. For example, the New Jersey Supreme Court has written that "[a] competent patient has a clear understanding of the nature of his or her illness and prognosis, and of the risks and benefits of the proposed treatment, and has the capacity to reason and make judgments about that information." In re Farrell, 529 A.2d 404, 413 n.7 (N.J. 1987). But it is not a simple matter to assess a person's capacity for reasoning and understanding nor is it clear what level of understanding a person must be able to exercise to be considered competent.

■ LANE v. CANDURA
376 N.E.2d 1232 (Mass. App. Ct. 1978)

PER CURIAM.

[Ms. Rosaria Candura was a 77-year-old woman with gangrene in her right foot and lower leg. Her physicians recommended amputation without delay, but Ms. Candura refused after originally agreeing to the surgery. She already had undergone two amputative operations on her right foot, losing a toe in one and part of her foot in the other. In explaining her reasons for refusing a third amputative surgery, she said] that she has been unhappy since the death of her husband [two years earlier]; that she does not wish to be a burden to her children; that she does not believe that the operation will cure her; that she does not wish to live as an invalid or in a nursing home; and that she does not fear death but welcomes it. . . .

[The court further found that Ms. Candura] is discouraged by the failure of the earlier operations to arrest the advance of the gangrene. She tends to be stubborn and somewhat irrascible [sic]. . . . [S]he expressed a desire to get well but indicated that she was resigned to death and was adamantly against the operation. . . . [S]he is lucid on some matters and confused on others. Her train of thought sometimes wanders. Her conception of time is distorted. She is hostile to certain doctors. She is on occasion defensive and sometimes combative in her responses to questioning. But she has exhibited a high degree of awareness and acuity. . . . [One psychiatrist testified that Ms. Candura lacked decisionmaking capacity, in part because she would not discuss her reasons for refusal with him and because he thought her gangrene might be compromising her thinking. Another psychiatrist, who was able to elicit Ms. Candura's reasons for refusing treatment, testified that she possessed decisionmaking capacity.]

[The court held that Ms. Candura was competent to refuse treatment, noting that her competence had not been questioned until she withdrew her original consent to the surgery; that she had a right to make her own decisions about medical treatment, even if the decisions seemed unwise; that, while she might have symptoms of senility, there was no evidence that her confusion or forgetfulness was interfering with her ability to decide about the surgery; and that her case did not involve] the uninformed decision of a person incapable of appreciating the nature and consequences of her act. . . .

■ DEPARTMENT OF HUMAN SERVICES v. NORTHERN
563 S.W.2d 197 (Tenn. Ct. App. 1978)

TODD, Judge.

[Ms. Mary Northern was a 72-year-old woman with gangrene of both feet who refused her physicians' recommendation of amputative surgery of the feet to prevent her death. A physician reported that] he found the patient to be generally lucid and sane, . . . [but that] she is functioning on a psychotic level with respect to her gangrenous feet. She tends to believe that her feet are black because of soot or dirt. . . . There is an adamant belief that her feet will heal without surgery. . . . There is no desire to die, yet her judgment concerning recovery is markedly impaired. If she appreciated the seriousness of her condition, heard her physicians' opinions, and concluded against an operation, then I would believe she understood and could decide for herself. But my impression is that she does not appreciate the dangers to her life. . . .

[The court found Ms. Northern incompetent to decide about the surgery, basing its decision on her failure to appreciate the nature of her medical condition and her refusal to make a choice between living and keeping her feet. In the view of the court, Ms. Northern was resorting to the "device of denying" her medical condition to avoid having to choose between losing her life and losing her feet.] If, as repeatedly stated, this patient could and would give evidence of a comprehension of the facts of her condition and could and would express her unequivocal desire in the face of such comprehended facts, then her decision, however unreasonable to others, would be accepted and honored by the courts and her doctors. The difficulty is that she cannot or will not comprehend the facts. . . .

[Because of "complications rendering surgery more dangerous," the amputations were not performed. Approximately three months after the court's decision, Ms. Northern died from her gangrene.]

Notes: Assessing Competence

1. *Applying the Tests for Competence.* It makes good sense to consider a patient's degree of understanding and rationality of reasoning, but how should we respond to patients who do not want to explain their decision? What if the patient says, "I don't want the surgery, and it's none of your business why"? The court in *Northern* makes much of Ms. Northern's misunderstanding of what was going on with her feet, but what if she appreciated that her feet were gangrenous but misunderstood other issues? What if she had said that she understood that her feet were gangrenous but that they became that way because she had sinned and that the good Lord would heal them for her now that she was repenting? Would that constitute an incompetent refusal of surgery? For an interesting discussion of religious beliefs and decisionmaking capacity, see Adrienne M. Martin, Tales Publicly Allowed: Competence, Capacity, and Religious Beliefs, 37(1) Hastings Center Rep. 33 (2007) (arguing that religious beliefs that interfere with understanding may make the patient incapacitated but that respect for the patient's religious values may lead us to accept the patient's decision).

In a case similar to *Northern*, a woman refused further dialysis, and cited the burden of the treatment, as well as her belief that Jesus would heal her. Two psychiatrists testified that the woman was depressed and not making a competent decision; a third psychiatrist believed that the woman was making a competent and voluntary refusal of dialysis. The court ordered dialysis, observing that the woman "demonstrated a lack of understanding of the high risk of death without dialysis. She refused to acknowledge the risk inherent in her refusal of treatment and through her other medical choices had demonstrated an unequivocal desire to live." In re J.M., 3 A.3d 651 (N.J. Super. Ct. Ch. Div. 2010).

How accurate are physicians at detecting a patient's incapacity? In a review-of-the-literature study, researchers found that physicians "missed the diagnosis in 58% of patients who were judged incapable" in a formal, independent assessment. In other words, the physicians incorrectly concluded that the patients possessed decisionmaking capacity in more than half of the patients who lacked such capacity. On the other hand, physicians generally were correct when they made a diagnosis of incapacity. The researchers also found that the best formal assessment tool for measuring capacity to decide is the Aid to Capacity Evaluation. Laura L. Sessums, Does This Patient Have Medical Decision-Making Capacity?, 306 JAMA 420 (2011).

2. *Adolescents.* Issues of competence also arise for adolescents. There are two separate questions that must be answered: (1) Do minors have capacity to decide for themselves? (2) If not, is the decision one that parents can make for them? In general, the answer to (1) is "no" and to (2) is "yes": Minors usually are held to lack decisionmaking capacity, and parents usually have authority to make decisions on their behalf. Both rules have important exceptions, however. The exceptions to the second rule are discussed below at pages 574-578, where we learn that courts often deny parents authority to refuse life-sustaining treatment for their children. These notes discuss exceptions to the first rule, that is, situations where minors may make important medical decisions for themselves.

While minors generally lack decisionmaking capacity, "mature minors" may be accorded decisionmaking authority if they can show decisionmaking capacity despite their age. For example, in a medical malpractice case, Caldwell v. Bechtol, 724 S.W.2d 739 (Tenn. 1987), the Tennessee Supreme Court considered whether a woman five months shy of her eighteenth birthday could give consent to treatment by an osteopathic physician for her lower back pain. The court stated:

> Several relevant principles from these cases may be stated for this case. Whether a minor has the capacity to consent to medical treatment depends upon the age, ability, experience, education, training, and degree of maturity or judgment obtained by the minor, as well as upon the conduct and demeanor of the minor at the time of the incident involved. Moreover, the totality of the circumstances, the nature of the treatment and its risks or probable consequences, and the minor's ability to appreciate the risks and consequences are to be considered. Guided by the presumptions in the Rule of Sevens, these are questions of fact for the jury to decide. [Id. at 748.]

The Rule of Sevens holds that "under the age of seven, no capacity; between seven and fourteen, a rebuttable presumption of no capacity; between fourteen and twenty-one, a rebuttable presumption of capacity." Id. at 745.

The Supreme Court of Appeals of West Virginia adopted a test very similar to that of the *Caldwell* court in the context of a life-sustaining treatment decision. In Belcher v. Charleston Area Medical Center, 422 S.E.2d 827 (W. Va. 1992), Larry Belcher, a minor of 17 years and 8 months, suffered from muscular dystrophy, and it appeared that he would become ventilator dependent imminently. His physician and parents decided that Mr. Belcher would not be ventilated or resuscitated in the event of a respiratory arrest, and Mr. Belcher died the following day from a respiratory arrest. An issue before the court was whether his physician should have consulted Mr. Belcher before a decision was made about ventilation and resuscitation. The court wrote:

> Whether the child has the capacity to consent depends upon the age, ability, experience, education, training, and degree of maturity or judgment obtained by the child, as well as upon the conduct and demeanor of the child at the time of the procedure or treatment. The factual determination would also involve whether the minor has the capacity to appreciate the nature, risks, and consequences of the medical procedure to be performed, or the treatment to be administered or withheld. Where there is a conflict between the intentions of one or both parents and the minor, the physician's good faith assessment of the minor's maturity level would immunize him or her from liability for the failure to obtain parental consent. [Id. At 838.]

In In re Swan, 569 A.2d 1202 (Me. 1990), the Maine Supreme Court relied on the statements of a minor, Chad Swan, to permit the withholding of a feeding tube. Mr. Swan was 18 years old at the time of the decision but had become permanently unconscious from an automobile accident at age 17. In permitting the withholding, the court relied on statements that Mr. Swan had made about his wishes regarding life-sustaining treatment. At age 16 he had spoken to his mother about a highly publicized local case in which the patient had also become permanently unconscious from a motor vehicle accident and said, "If I can't be myself . . . no way . . . let me go to sleep." In addition, eight days before his accident, after visiting a comatose friend in the hospital, Mr. Swan told his brother, "I don't ever want to get like that. . . . I would want somebody to let me leave—to go in peace." Id. at 1205. According to the court,

> The fact that Chad made these declarations as to medical treatment before he reached the age of eighteen is at most a factor to be considered by the fact finder in assessing the seriousness and deliberativeness with which his declarations were made. . . . Capacity exists when the minor has the ability of the average person to understand and weigh the risks and benefits. [Id.]

Another leading case discussing the mature minor doctrine in the context of life-sustaining treatment is In re E.G., 549 N.E.2d 322 (Ill. 1989). In that case, a 17-year-old woman with an acute leukemia consented to treatment for her leukemia except for blood transfusions. Her refusal was based on her religious beliefs as a Jehovah's Witness. Her physician testified that, without blood transfusions, E.G. would likely die within a month. With blood transfusions, her chemotherapy had an 80 percent chance of achieving a remission of her leukemia but only a 20 to 25 percent chance of giving E.G. a long-term survival. After the trial court appointed one of the hospital's counsel as E.G.'s temporary guardian, blood transfusions were administered. On appeal, the Illinois Supreme Court held that mature minors enjoy a right to refuse life-sustaining medical treatment. In deciding when that right can be exercised, the court first concluded that, "[w]hen a minor's health and life are at stake," proof of a minor's maturity must be made "by clear and convincing evidence." Id. at 327. In addition, the state's interest in protecting the minor's health "will vary depending upon the nature of the medical treatment involved. Where the health care issues are potentially life threatening, the state's *parens patriae* interest is greater than if the health care matter is less consequential." Id. Minors should be considered mature enough to make their own life-sustaining treatment decisions "[i]f the evidence is clear and convincing that the minor is mature enough to appreciate the consequences of her actions, and . . . the minor is mature enough to exercise the judgment of an adult." Invoking the state's interest in protecting the interests of third parties, the court also wrote that "[i]f a parent or guardian opposes an unemancipated mature minor's refusal to consent to treatment for a life-threatening health problem, this opposition would weigh heavily against the minor's right to refuse." Id. at 328. Since E.G.'s mother agreed with her decision, the court did not indicate how the balance between the minor's right to decide and the state's interest in third parties would play out. In addition, since E.G. had become an adult by the time the decision was issued, the court did not remand the case for determination of her maturity.

Do you agree with the *E.G.* court that the minor's right should depend on whether the "health care issues are potentially life-threatening"? Note that this standard would result in mature minors being governed by something akin to the *Quinlan* substantive standard ("the state's interest *contra* weakens and the individual's right to privacy grows as the degree of bodily invasion increases and the prognosis dims," *Quinlan*, 355 A.2d at 664) and adults by the *Conroy* substantive standard (a competent patient's right to refuse life-sustaining treatment "would not be affected by her medical condition or prognosis," *Conroy*, 486 A.2d at 1226).

Which court do you think has the better approach on the issue of parental disagreement with the child, *E.G.* or *Belcher*?

Not all states recognize a mature minor doctrine. For example, a federal district court in Georgia concluded that Georgia state law grants decisionmaking capacity only in certain statutorily specified situations (e.g., minors who are married, pregnant, or have children) but does not include a mature minor doctrine. Novak v. Cobb County-Kennestone Hospital Authority, 849 F. Supp. 1559, 1575-1576 (N.D. Ga. 1994). Other states have not decided one way or another whether maturity serves as the basis for decisionmaking capacity for a minor. In re Cassandra C., 112 A.3d 158 (Conn. 2015); In re Conner, 140 P.3d 1167 (Or. Ct. App. 2006).

3. *Reliability of Patient Decisions.* While a patient may be competent to decide, there still is the question whether the patient has in fact reached a firm and settled decision. We might expect patients to express a good deal of ambivalence when making life-sustaining treatment decisions. When faced with a patient who has come to a decision with some difficulty and gone back and forth on the matter, should we require some kind of waiting period to ensure that the decision really is a reliable one? As discussed in the section on physician aid in dying at page 594, when Oregon adopted its physician aid in dying law, it included a requirement that patients wait at least 15 days from the time they request physician assistance until they can obtain a prescription for a lethal dose of a drug. Should there be a similar waiting period for refusals of life-sustaining treatment? Recall that Kenneth Bergstedt sought and received permission to disconnect his ventilator because he feared what his life would be like after his father died. In that case, Mr. Bergstedt died one week before

his father died and one month before the court issued its ruling, apparently because his father disconnected the ventilator. If Mr. Bergstedt had been alive when the court decided the case, should the court have required that Mr. Bergstedt see what his life was like after his father died before deciding whether to refuse the ventilator? How long a trial of living without his father would be sufficient?

There are studies that have considered whether patients' treatment preferences are stable over time. In a review of these studies, researchers found that in most studies, more than two-thirds of patients had stable preferences, that preferences to forgo treatment were generally more stable than preferences to receive treatment, and that advance care planning was associated with greater stability. Among patients with declines in health status, studies found both increases and decreases in the desired aggressiveness of care. Catherine L. Auriemma et al., Stability of End-of-Life Preferences, 174 JAMA Internal Med. 1085 (2014). There also is stability over time in terms of how much patients want their treatment preferences to control once they become unable to decide for themselves and how much they want their medical decisions to be based on what their loved ones or physicians think is in their best interests. Daniel P. Sulmasy et al., How Would Terminally Ill Patients Have Others Make Decisions for Them in the Event of Decisional Incapacity? A Longitudinal Study, 55 J. Am. Geriatrics Soc'y 1981 (2007).

4. *Further Reading.* On **determining capacity** (note 1), see Jalayne J. Arias, A Time to Step In: Legal Mechanisms for Protecting Those with Declining Capacity, 39 Am. J. L. & Med. 134 (2013); Jessica Wilen Berg et al., Constructing Competence, 48 Rutgers L. Rev. 345 (1996); Marsha Garrison, The Empire of Illness: Competence and Coercion in Health-Care Decision Making, 49 Wm. & Mary L. Rev. 781 (2007).

On **adolescents** (note 2), see Rhonda Gay Hartman, Adolescent Decisional Autonomy for Medical Care, 8 U. Chi. L. Sch. Roundtable 87 (2001); Kimberly M. Mutcherson, Whose Body Is It Anyway?, 14 Cornell J. L. & Pub. Pol'y 251 (2005); Michelle Oberman, Minor Rights and Wrongs, 24 J. L. Med. & Ethics 127 (1996); Jennifer L. Rosato, Let's Get Real: Quilting a Principled Approach to Adolescent Empowerment in Health Care Decision-Making, 51 DePaul L. Rev. 769 (2002); Elizabeth S. Scott, Judgment and Reasoning in Adolescent Decisionmaking, 37 Vill. L. Rev. 1607 (1992); Symposium, 38 J. Med. & Philo. 249-340 (2013); Symposium, Roundtable on Adolescent Decision Making, 15 J. Health Care L. & Pol'y 1-172 (2012).

3. The Incompetent Patient

When a patient is incompetent, as is common when decisions about life-sustaining treatment are made, a few questions arise: Does the right to refuse life-sustaining treatment survive incompetence? If it does, is the right the same? How is the right invoked on behalf of the patient? You should pay particular attention to the procedural safeguards that the courts have adopted to govern life-sustaining treatment decisions for incompetent patients.

We will begin with two cases from the New Jersey Supreme Court. By way of background, the New Jersey Supreme Court has also adopted procedural safeguards for withdrawal decisions involving competent patients. It is useful to consider how these safeguards change when we move from the competent to the incompetent patient. New Jersey's safeguards for competent patients were developed in In re Farrell, 529 A.2d 404 (N.J. 1987). That case involved a woman, Kathleen Farrell, who became ventilator dependent from amyotrophic lateral sclerosis (ALS, or Lou Gehrig's disease). ALS is a disorder of the nervous system that results in degeneration of the nerves controlling voluntary muscle movements. The disease, whose cause is unknown, gradually leaves people unable to move their muscles. Ultimately, this means that they cannot move their arms or legs, swallow, speak intelligibly, or breathe. At the time of Ms. Farrell's diagnosis, a victim's life expectancy even with life-sustaining treatment was usually one to three years. For "competent patients who are living at home" and "who request the discontinuance of life-sustaining medical treatment," the *Farrell* court adopted the following procedural safeguards:

> First, it must be determined that the patient is competent and properly informed about his or her prognosis, the alternative treatments available, and the risk involved in the withdrawal of the life-sustaining treatment. Then it must be determined that the patient made his or her choice voluntarily and without coercion. . . . These issues are more easily resolved when the patient is in a hospital, nursing home, or other institution, because in those settings the patient is observed by more people. To protect the patient who is at home, we require that two non-attending physicians examine the patient to confirm that he or she is competent and is fully informed about his or her prognosis, the medical alternatives available, the risks involved, and the likely outcome if medical treatment is disconnected.[8] . . . The two independent confirmations of competency that we require should satisfy any questions that might later arise about the propriety of the withholding or withdrawal of treatment. Additionally, this procedural requirement should serve to forestall hasty medical decisions made while a patient is in an emotionally disturbed state because of a sudden illness or major catastrophe. [529 A.2d at 413-415.]

The *Farrell* court also held that there is no need to seek court approval before treatment is withdrawn.

■ IN RE CONROY
486 A.2d 1209 (N.J. 1985)

SCHREIBER, Justice.

Plaintiff, Thomas C. Whittemore, nephew and guardian of Claire Conroy, an incompetent, sought permission to remove a nasogastric feeding tube, the primary conduit for nutrients, from his ward, an eighty-four-year-old bedridden woman with serious and irreversible physical and mental impairments who resided in a nursing home. [Additional medical facts for this case are presented in the case excerpt at pages 508-509 in the section on the competent patient. As mentioned there, Ms. Conroy died while her case was before the intermediate court of appeals, but the New Jersey Supreme Court still heard the case as one involving a matter "of substantial importance and . . . capable of repetition but evad[ing] review."]

---

8. The procedure we hereby establish for determining the competency of a patient at home who has decided to forgo life-sustaining treatment is likewise applicable to patients in hospitals and nursing homes.

. . . Ms. Conroy had lived a rather cloistered life. She had been employed by a cosmetics company from her teens until her retirement at age 62 or 63. She had lived in the same home from her childhood until she was placed in the nursing home, had never married, and had very few friends. She had been very close to her three sisters, all of whom had died. . . .

Mr. Whittemore testified that Ms. Conroy feared and avoided doctors and that, to the best of his knowledge, she had never visited a doctor until she became incompetent in 1979. He said that on the couple of occasions that Ms. Conroy had pneumonia, "[y]ou couldn't bring a doctor in," and his wife, a registered nurse, would "try to get her through whatever she had." He added that once, when his wife took Ms. Conroy to the hospital emergency room, "as foggy as she was she snapped out of it, she would not sign herself in and she would have signed herself out immediately." According to the nephew, "[a]ll [Ms. Conroy and her sisters] wanted was to . . . have their bills paid and die in their own house." He also stated that he had refused to consent to the amputation of her gangrenous leg in 1982 and that he now sought removal of the nasogastric tube because, in his opinion, she would have refused the amputation and "would not have allowed [the nasogastric tube] to be inserted in the first place."

Ms. Conroy was a Roman Catholic. The Rev. Joseph Kukura, a Roman Catholic priest and an associate professor of Christian Ethics at the Immaculate Conception Seminary in Mahwah, New Jersey, testified that acceptable church teaching could be found in a document entitled "Declaration of Euthanasia" published by the Vatican Congregation for the Doctrine of the Faith, dated June 26, 1980. The test that this document espoused required a weighing of the burdens and the benefits to the patient of remaining alive with the aid of extraordinary life-sustaining medical treatment. Father Kukura said that life-sustaining procedures could be withdrawn if they were extraordinary, which he defined to embrace "all procedures, operations or other interventions which are excessively expensive, burdensome or inconvenient or which offer no hope of benefit to a patient." Here, he said, the hope of recovery and of returning to cognitive life, even with the nasogastric feeding, was not a reasonable possibility. The means of care were not adding to the value of her life, which was outweighed by the burdens of that life. He therefore considered the use of the nasogastric tube extraordinary. It was his judgment that removal of the tube would be ethical and moral, even though the ensuing period until her death would be painful. . . .

II

This case requires us to determine the circumstances under which life-sustaining treatment may be withheld or withdrawn from an elderly nursing-home resident who is suffering from serious and permanent mental and physical impairments, who will probably die within approximately one year even with the treatment, and who, though formerly competent, is now incompetent to make decisions about her life-sustaining treatment and is unlikely to regain such competence. Subsumed within this question are two corollary issues: what substantive guidelines are appropriate for making these treatment decisions for incompetent patients, and what procedures should be followed in making them. . . .

The *Quinlan* decision dealt with a special category of patients: those in a chronic, persistent vegetative or comatose state. In a footnote, the opinion left open the question whether the principles it enunciated might be applicable to incompetent patients in "other types of terminal medical situations . . . , not necessarily involving the hopeless loss of cognitive or sapient life." 355 A.2d at 671 n.10. We now are faced with one such situation: that of elderly, formerly competent nursing-home residents who, unlike Karen Quinlan, are awake and conscious and can interact with their environment to a limited extent, but whose mental and physical functioning is severely and permanently impaired and whose life expectancy, even with the treatment, is relatively short. The capacities of such people, while significantly diminished, are not as limited as those of irreversibly comatose persons, and their deaths, while no longer distant, may not be imminent. Large numbers of aged, chronically ill, institutionalized persons fall within this general category.

Such people . . . are unable to speak for themselves on life-and-death issues concerning their medical care. This does not mean, however, that they lack a right to self-determination. The right of an adult who, like Claire Conroy, was once competent, to determine the course of her medical treatment remains intact even when she is no longer able to assert that right or to appreciate its effectuation. As one commentator has noted:

> Even if the patient becomes too insensate to appreciate the honoring of his or her choice, self-determination is important. After all, law respects testamentary dispositions even if the testator never views his gift being bestowed. [Cantor, supra, 30 Rutgers L. Rev. at 259.]
> Any other view would permit obliteration of an incompetent's panoply of rights merely because the patient could no longer sense the violation of those rights. [Id. at 252.]

Since the condition of an incompetent patient makes it impossible to ascertain definitively his present desires, a third party acting on the patient's behalf often cannot say with confidence that his treatment decision for the patient will further rather than frustrate the patient's right to control his own body. Nevertheless, the goal of decisionmaking for incompetent patients should be to determine and effectuate, insofar as possible, the decision that the patient would have made if competent. Ideally, both aspects of the patient's right to bodily integrity — the right to consent to medical intervention and the right to refuse it — should be respected.

In light of these rights and concerns, we hold that life-sustaining treatment may be withheld or withdrawn from an incompetent patient when it is clear that the particular patient would have refused the treatment under the circumstances involved. The standard we are enunciating is a subjective one, consistent with the notion that the right that we are seeking to effectuate is a very personal right to control one's own life. The question is not what a reasonable or average person would have chosen to do under the circumstances but what the particular patient would have done if able to choose for himself.

The patient may have expressed, in one or more ways, an intent not to have life-sustaining medical intervention. Such an intent might be embodied in a written document, or "living will," stating the person's desire not to have certain types of life-sustaining treatment administered under certain circumstances. It might also be evidenced in an oral directive that the patient gave to a family member, friend, or health care provider. It might consist of a durable power of attorney or appointment of a proxy authorizing a particular person to make the decisions on the patient's behalf if he is no longer capable of making them for himself. It might take the form of reactions that the patient voiced regarding medical treatment administered to others. It might also be deduced from a person's religious beliefs and the tenets of that religion, or from the patient's consistent pattern of conduct with respect to prior decisions about his own medical care. Of course, dealing with the matter in advance in some sort of thoughtful and explicit way is best for all concerned.

Any of the above types of evidence, and any other information bearing on the person's intent, may be appropriate aids in determining what course of treatment the patient would have wished to pursue. . . .

Although all evidence tending to demonstrate a person's intent with respect to medical treatment should properly be considered by surrogate decisionmakers, . . . the probative value of such evidence may vary depending on the remoteness, consistency, and thoughtfulness of the prior statements or actions and the maturity of the person at the time of the statements or acts. Thus, for example, an offhand remark about not wanting to live under certain circumstances made by a person when young and in the peak of health would not in itself constitute clear proof 20 years later that he would want life-sustaining treatment withheld under those circumstances. In contrast, a carefully considered position, especially if written, that a person had maintained over a number of years or that he had acted upon in comparable circumstances might be clear evidence of his intent.

Another factor that would affect the probative value of a person's prior statements of intent would be their specificity. Of course, no one can predict with accuracy the precise circumstances with which he ultimately might be faced. Nevertheless, any details about the level of impaired functioning and the forms of medical treatment that one would find tolerable should be incorporated into advance directives to enhance their later usefulness as evidence.

Medical evidence bearing on the patient's condition, treatment, and prognosis, like evidence of the patient's wishes, is an essential prerequisite to decisionmaking under the subjective test. . . . [S]ince the goal is to effectuate the patient's right of informed consent, the surrogate decisionmaker must have at least as much medical information upon which to base his decision about what the patient would have chosen as one would expect a competent patient to have before consenting to or rejecting treatment. . . . Particular care should be taken not to base a decision on a premature diagnosis or prognosis.

We recognize that for some incompetent patients it might be impossible to be clearly satisfied as to the patient's intent either to accept or reject the life-sustaining treatment. Many people may have spoken of their desires in general or casual terms, or, indeed, never considered or resolved the issue at all. In such cases, a surrogate decisionmaker cannot presume that treatment decisions made by a third party on the patient's behalf will further the patient's right to self-determination, since effectuating another person's right to self-determination presupposes that the substitute decisionmaker knows what the person would have wanted. Thus, in the absence of adequate proof of the patient's wishes, it is naive to pretend that the right to self-determination serves as the basis for substituted decisionmaking.

We hesitate, however, to foreclose the possibility of humane actions, which may involve termination of life-sustaining treatment, for persons who never clearly expressed their desires about life-sustaining treatment but who are now suffering a prolonged and painful death. An incompetent, like a minor child, is a ward of the state, and the state's *parens patriae* power supports the authority of its courts to allow decisions to be made for an incompetent that serve the incompetent's best interests, even if the person's wishes cannot be clearly established. . . . We therefore hold that life-sustaining treatment may also be withheld or withdrawn from a patient in Claire Conroy's situation if either of two "best interests" tests—a limited-objective or a pure-objective test—is satisfied.

Under the limited-objective test, life-sustaining treatment may be withheld or withdrawn from a patient in Claire Conroy's situation when there is some trustworthy evidence that the patient would have refused the treatment, and the decision-maker is satisfied that it is clear that the burdens of the patient's continued life with the treatment outweigh the benefits of that life for him. By this we mean that the patient is suffering, and will continue to suffer throughout the expected duration of his life, unavoidable pain, and that the net burdens of his prolonged life (the pain and suffering of his life with the treatment less the amount and duration of pain that the patient would likely experience if the treatment were withdrawn) markedly outweigh any physical pleasure, emotional enjoyment, or intellectual satisfaction that the patient may still be able to derive from life. . . .

In the absence of trustworthy evidence, or indeed any evidence at all, that the patient would have declined the treatment, life-sustaining treatment may still be withheld or withdrawn from a formerly competent person like Claire Conroy if a third, pure-objective test is satisfied. Under that test, as under the limited-objective test, the net burdens of the patient's life with the treatment should clearly and markedly outweigh the benefits that the patient derives from life. Further, the recurring, unavoidable and severe pain of the patient's life with the treatment should be such that the effect of administering life-sustaining treatment would be inhumane. Subjective evidence that the patient would not have wanted the treatment is not necessary under this pure-objective standard. Nevertheless, even in the context of severe pain, life-sustaining treatment should not be withdrawn from an incompetent patient who had previously expressed a wish to be kept alive in spite of any pain that he might experience. . . .

We are aware that it will frequently be difficult to conclude that the evidence is sufficient to justify termination of treatment under either of the "best interests" tests that we have described. Often, it is unclear whether and to what extent a patient such as Claire Conroy is capable of, or is in fact, experiencing pain. Similarly, medical experts are often unable to determine with any degree of certainty the extent of a nonverbal person's intellectual functioning or the depth of his emotional life. When the evidence is insufficient to satisfy either the limited-objective or pure-objective standard, however, we cannot justify the termination of life-sustaining treatment as clearly furthering the best interests of a patient like Ms. Conroy. . . .

The decisionmaking procedure for comatose, vegetative patients suggested in *Quinlan*, namely, the concurrence of the guardian, family, attending physician, and hospital prognosis committee, is not entirely appropriate for patients such as Claire Conroy, who are confined to nursing homes. There are significant differences in the patients, the health-care providers, and the institutional structures of nursing homes and hospitals. . . .

[The court went on to discuss special concerns with treatment withdrawal in nursing homes, including the vulnerability of nursing home residents, the fact that residents are often without any surviving family, the limited role that physicians play in nursing home care, and the occurrence of neglectful and abusive care in nursing homes. Because of these concerns, the court required the involvement of New Jersey's Office of the Ombudsman before the discontinuation of life-sustaining treatment from a patient like Claire Conroy. In addition, two physicians, unaffiliated with the nursing home or with the attending physician, would have to have confirmed the patient's medical condition and prognosis.]

Provided that the two physicians supply the necessary medical foundation, the guardian, with the concurrence of the attending physician, may withhold or withdraw life-sustaining treatment if he believes in good faith, based on the medical evidence and any evidence of the patient's wishes, that it is clear that the subjective, limited-objective or pure-objective test is satisfied. In addition, the ombudsman must concur in that decision. . . . Finally, if the limited-objective or pure-objective test is being used, the family—that is, the patient's spouse, parents, and children, or in their absence, the patient's next of kin, if any—must also concur in the decision to withhold or withdraw life-sustaining treatment. . . .

[The court then concluded that the evidence about Ms. Conroy's condition was insufficient to find that any of these three tests was met in this case. The court did not believe that it was sufficiently clear what decision she personally would have made, nor was it satisfied by the available information about the extent of pleasure or pain she was experiencing before she died. Therefore, were she still alive, the court would have instructed her guardian to find out more about her prior preferences and the benefits and burdens of her life before deciding whether any of the three standards for withdrawing treatment were satisfied.]

■ IN RE JOBES
529 A.2d 434 (N.J. 1987)

GARIBALDI, Justice.

. . . This appeal requires us to develop the guidelines and procedures under which life-sustaining medical treatment may be withdrawn from a non-elderly nursing home patient in a persistent vegetative state who, prior to her incompetency, failed to express adequately her attitude toward such treatment. . . .

[The case arose when the husband and parents of Nancy Jobes asked the nursing home to withdraw Ms. Jobes's feeding tube. The nursing home refused on moral grounds, and the husband sought judicial authorization of the withdrawal. After a seven-day trial, the court approved the removal of the feeding tube but held that the nursing home could refuse to participate in the removal and could require transfer of Ms. Jobes to another facility for discontinuation of the feeding. When the court entered its judgment, it stayed relief pending final determination on appeal, which went directly to this court.]

II

Nancy Ellen Jobes is thirty-one years old. . . . Prior to March of 1980, Mrs. Jobes had no significant mental or physical handicap. She was employed as a certified laboratory technologist, and was four and one-half months pregnant with her first child.

On March 11, 1980, Mrs. Jobes was admitted to Riverside Hospital for treatment of injuries sustained in an automobile accident. Doctors soon determined that her fetus had been killed. During the course of an operation to remove the dead fetus, she sustained a severe loss of oxygen and blood flow to her brain. She suffered massive and irreversible damage to the part of her brain that controls thought and movement. She has never regained consciousness. . . .

She cannot swallow. Originally, she was fed and hydrated intravenously, then through a nasogastric tube, then a gastrotomy tube. In June 1985, complications with the gastrotomy tube necessitated an even more direct approach. Since then, Mrs. Jobes has been fed through a j-tube inserted—through a hole cut into her abdominal cavity—into the jejunum of her small intestine. Water and a synthetic, pre-digested formula of various amino acids are pumped through the j-tube continuously. . . .

IV

Mrs. Jobes' closest friends, her cousin, her clergyman, and her husband offered testimony that was intended to prove that if she were competent, Mrs. Jobes would refuse to be sustained by the j-tube. Deborah Holdsworth, a registered nurse and life-long friend of Mrs. Jobes, recalled a conversation in 1971 in which Mrs. Jobes stated that if she were ever crippled like the children with multiple sclerosis and muscular dystrophy that Ms. Holdsworth cared for, she would not want to live. Ms. Holdsworth also recalled telling Mrs. Jobes on numerous occasions that she, Holdsworth, would not want to live like Karen Quinlan did after the removal of her respirator. She recalled that Mrs. Jobes had not disagreed with her, but could not recall Mrs. Jobes' position any more clearly than that. Finally, Holdsworth recalled that in late 1979 Mrs. Jobes specifically stated that she would not want to be kept alive on a respirator like a patient suffering from amyotrophic lateral sclerosis whom Ms. Holdsworth had described to her.

Another friend of Mrs. Jobes' since childhood, Donna DeChristofaro, testified that in Autumn 1979 Mrs. Jobes had told her that "it was a shame that [Karen Quinlan] hadn't died when they removed the respirator; that that wasn't living, it was existing; that she had wished that God had taken her then. . . ."

Mrs. Jobes' first cousin, Dr. Cleve Laird, recalled a discussion he had with her in the summer of 1975 about a victim of an automobile accident who was being kept alive by a cardiac stimulator:

> She said that she wouldn't want those measures taken in her case and that she certainly wouldn't want to live that way. I said, well, they wouldn't do that to me because I carried and still carry a form of identification that says that I do not wish to have any heroic measures taken in case of massive injury.
>
> Subsequent to that she became interested in where I had gotten that and I told her that it was pretty common both at Baylor where I had taught prior to going up to Massachusetts and also at Harvard. I said that I would send her a card. My wife was there and I turned around to her and told her why didn't she send one. Then we moved on into discussion of other technical things.

Dr. Laird testified that his wife had sent the card to Mrs. Jobes, and that Mrs. Jobes thanked them for it in a note she sent them at Christmas. The card has not been found.

John Jobes testified that if his wife were competent, she would "definitely" choose to terminate the artificial feeding that sustains her in her present condition. He generally recalled her having stated that she would not want to be kept alive under Karen Quinlan's circumstances. She did this frequently when the *Quinlan* case was in the news, mostly during 1976-1977.

The Reverend George A. Vorsheim, minister of the Morris Plains Presbyterian Church, testified that he had married the Jobes, and that he was familiar with them and with Mrs. Jobes' parents. They are all members of the Presbyterian Church (U.S.A.). The Reverend Mr. Vorsheim testified that Mrs. Jobes was raised in the Presbyterian Faith, and that in the Presbyterian Faith there is no religious requirement to perpetuate life by artificial means nor is there any doctrine prohibiting life-sustaining medical treatment. The Presbyterian Church leaves decisions like the one at issue here to the individual conscience. . . .

V

In *Conroy* and *Peter*, we have described the type of evidence that can establish a person's medical preferences under the "subjective test." We have explained that the probative value of prior statements offered to prove a patient's inclination for or against medical treatment depends on their specificity, their "remoteness, consistency and thoughtfulness . . . [,] and the maturity of the person at the time of the statements. . . ." *Conroy*, 486 A.2d at 1230. All of the statements about life-support that were attributed to Mrs. Jobes were remote, general, spontaneous, and made in casual circumstances. Indeed, they closely track the examples of evidence that we have explicitly characterized as unreliable.

Other than her prior statements, the only evidence of Mrs. Jobes' intent that the trial court relied on was her membership in the Presbyterian Church. There is no specific evidence of her personal belief in the tenets of that Church; nevertheless, we have consistently recognized that "a person's religious affiliation and the tenets of that religion may furnish evidence of his or her intent with regard to medical decisions." *Conroy*, supra, 98 N.J. at 362. In this case, however, Mrs. Jobes' minister testified that her religion neither requires nor forbids medical treatment like that at issue here. Therefore, Mrs. Jobes' religious affiliation does not offer much guidance in determining what her preference would be in this situation.

Thus, we conclude that although there is some "trustworthy" evidence that Mrs. Jobes, if competent, would want the j-tube withdrawn, it is not sufficiently "clear and convincing" to satisfy the subjective test. Therefore, we must determine the guidelines and procedures under which life-sustaining medical treatment may be withdrawn from a patient like Mrs. Jobes when there is no clear and convincing proof of her attitude toward such treatment.

VI

Because of the unique problems involved in decisionmaking for any patient in the persistent vegetative state, we necessarily distinguish their cases from cases involving other patients. Accordingly, in *Peter* we held that neither the life-expectancy test nor the balancing tests set forth in *Conroy* are appropriate in the case of a persistently vegetative patient. Those holdings are equally relevant in this case. In any case involving a patient in the persistent vegetative state, "we look instead primarily to *Quinlan* for guidance." *Peter*, 529 A.2d at 425 [observing that "[w]hile a benefits-burdens analysis is difficult with marginally cognitive patients like Claire Conroy, it is essentially impossible with patients in a persistent vegetative state. By definition such patients, like Ms. Peter, do not experience any of the benefits or burdens that the *Conroy* balancing tests are intended or able to appraise"]. . . .

In light of Karen Quinlan's inability to assert her right to decline continued artificial respiration, we determined that "[t]he only practical way to prevent destruction of the right [was] to permit the guardian and family of Karen to render their best judgment, subject to the qualifications [t]hereinafter stated, as to whether she would exercise it in [her] circumstances." 355 A.2d at 664. The term *substituted judgment* is commonly used to describe our approach in *Quinlan*. This approach is intended to ensure that the surrogate decisionmaker effectuates as much as possible the decision that the incompetent patient would make if he or she were competent. Under the substituted judgment doctrine, where an incompetent's wishes are not clearly expressed, a surrogate decisionmaker considers the patient's personal value system for guidance. The surrogate considers the patient's prior statements about and reactions to medical issues, and all the facets of the patient's personality that the surrogate is familiar with—with, of course, particular reference to his or her relevant philosophical, theological, and ethical values—in order to extrapolate what course of medical treatment the patient would choose.

In *Quinlan*, we held that the patient's family members were the proper parties to make a substituted medical judgment on her behalf. We make the same determination today. Almost invariably the patient's family has an intimate understanding of the patient's medical attitudes and general world view and therefore is in the best position to know the motives and considerations that would control the patient's medical decisions. . . .

Family members are best qualified to make substituted judgments for incompetent patients not only because of their peculiar grasp of the patient's approach to life, but also because of their special bonds with him or her. Our common human experience informs us that family members are generally most concerned with the welfare of a patient. It is they who provide for the patient's comfort, care, and best interests, and they who treat the patient as a person, rather than a symbol of a cause. Where strong and emotional opinions and proponents exist on an issue involving the treatment of an incompetent, extreme care must be exercised in determining who will act as his or her surrogate decisionmaker. We believe that a family member is generally the best choice. . . .

As we stated in *Farrell*: . . .

Competent patients usually actively solicit the advice and counsel of family members in decisionmaking. Family members routinely ask questions of the medical staff about the patient's condition and prognosis; one study found they frequently asked more questions than patients themselves did. Family members, in fact, commonly act as advocates for patients in the hospital. . . . [Newman, Treatment Refusals for the Critically Ill: Proposed Rules for Family, the Physician and the State, III N.Y. L. Sch. Human Rights Annual 35 (1985).]

The law has traditionally respected the private realm of family life which the state cannot enter. . . . We believe that this tradition of respect for and confidence in the family should ground our approach to the treatment of the sick. [*Farrell*, 529 A.2d at 414. . . .]

Normally those family members close enough to make a substituted judgment would be a spouse, parents, adult children, or siblings. Generally, in the absence of such a close degree of kinship, we would not countenance health care professionals deferring to the relatives of a patient, and a guardian would have to be appointed. However, if the attending health care professionals determine that another relative, e.g., a cousin, aunt, uncle, niece, or nephew, functions in the role of the patient's nuclear family, then that relative can and should be treated as a close and caring family member.

There will, of course, be some unfortunate situations in which family members will not act to protect a patient. We anticipate that such cases will be exceptional. Whenever a health-care professional becomes uncertain about whether family members are properly protecting a patient's interests, termination of life-sustaining treatment should not occur without the appointment of a guardian. . . .

Mrs. Jobes is blessed with warm, close, and loving family members. It is entirely proper to assume that they are best qualified to determine the medical decisions she would make. Moreover, there is some trustworthy evidence that supports their judgment of Mrs. Jobes' personal inclinations. Therefore, we will not presume to disturb their decision.

Thus, we hold that the right of a patient in an irreversibly vegetative state to determine whether to refuse life-sustaining medical treatment may be exercised by the patient's family or close friend. If there are close and caring family members who are willing to make this decision there is no need to have a guardian appointed. We require merely that the responsible relatives comply with the medical confirmation procedures that we henceforth establish. . . .

VII

. . . For non-elderly non-hospitalized patients in a persistent vegetative state who, like Mrs. Jobes, have a caring family or close friend, or a court-appointed guardian in attendance, we hold that the surrogate decisionmaker who declines life-sustaining medical treatment must secure statements from at least two independent physicians knowledgeable in neurology that the patient is in a persistent vegetative state and that there is no reasonable possibility that the patient will ever recover to a cognitive, sapient state. If the patient has an attending physician, then that physician likewise must submit such a statement. These independent neurological confirmations will substitute for the concurrence of the prognosis committee for patients who are not in a hospital setting and thereby prevent inappropriate withdrawal of treatment. In a proper case, however, they should not be difficult to obtain, and this requirement should not subject the patient to undesired treatment.

As long as the guidelines we hereby establish are followed in good faith, no criminal or civil liability will attach to anyone involved in the implementation of a surrogate decision to decline medical treatment. Accordingly, judicial review of such decisions is not necessary or appropriate. . . .

IX

... If a disagreement arises among the patient, family, guardian, or doctors, or if there is evidence of improper motives or malpractice, judicial intervention will be required. We expect, however, that disagreements will be rare and that intervention seldom will be necessary. We emphasize that even in those few cases in which the courts may have to intervene, they will not be making the ultimate decision whether to terminate medical treatment. Rather, they will be acting to insure that all the guidelines and procedures that we have set forth are properly followed. . . .

◼ CRUZAN v. DIRECTOR, MISSOURI DEPARTMENT OF HEALTH
497 U.S. 261 (1990)

REHNQUIST, Chief Justice.

[The facts of this case and the Court's discussion of the existence of a right to refuse treatment are excerpted at pages 511-515 in the section on the competent patient. Ms. Cruzan suffered severe brain damage from an automobile accident that left her in a persistent vegetative state. A few years later, when her parents sought to have Ms. Cruzan's feeding tube discontinued, the Missouri Supreme Court found there to be insufficient evidence that Ms. Cruzan would want the treatment withdrawn. The primary evidence of her wishes were thoughts expressed about a year before the accident "in somewhat serious conversation with a housemate friend that if sick or injured she would not wish to continue her life unless she could live at least halfway normally."]

... Petitioners go on to assert that an incompetent person should possess the same right in this respect as is possessed by a competent person. . . .

The difficulty with petitioners' claim is that in a sense it begs the question: An incompetent person is not able to make an informed and voluntary choice to exercise a hypothetical right to refuse treatment or any other right. Such a "right" must be exercised for her, if at all, by some sort of surrogate. Here, Missouri has in effect recognized that under certain circumstances a surrogate may act for the patient in electing to have hydration and nutrition withdrawn in such a way as to cause death, but it has established a procedural safeguard to assure that the action of the surrogate conforms as best it may to the wishes expressed by the patient while competent. Missouri requires that evidence of the incompetent's wishes as to the withdrawal of treatment be proved by clear and convincing evidence. The question, then, is whether the United States Constitution forbids the establishment of this procedural requirement by the state. We hold that it does not.

Whether or not Missouri's clear and convincing evidence requirement comports with the United States Constitution depends in part on what interests the state may properly seek to protect in this situation. Missouri relies on its interest in the protection and preservation of human life, and there can be no gainsaying this interest. As a general matter, the states—indeed, all civilized nations—demonstrate their commitment to life by treating homicide as a serious crime. Moreover, the majority of states in this country have laws imposing criminal penalties on one who assists another to commit suicide. We do not think a state is required to remain neutral in the face of an informed and voluntary decision by a physically able adult to starve to death.

But in the context presented here, a state has more particular interests at stake. The choice between life and death is a deeply personal decision of obvious and overwhelming finality. We believe Missouri may legitimately seek to safeguard the personal element of this choice through the imposition of heightened evidentiary requirements. It cannot be disputed that the due process clause protects an interest in life as well as an interest in refusing life-sustaining medical treatment. Not all incompetent patients will have loved ones available to serve as surrogate decisionmakers. And even where family members are present, "[t]here will, of course, be some unfortunate situations in which family members will not act to protect a patient." In re Jobes, 529 A.2d 434, 447 (N.J. 1987). A state is entitled to guard against potential abuses in such situations. . . . Finally, we think a state may properly decline to make judgments about the "quality" of life that a particular individual may enjoy, and simply assert an unqualified interest in the preservation of human life to be weighed against the constitutionally protected interests of the individual.

In our view, Missouri has permissibly sought to advance these interests through the adoption of a "clear and convincing" standard of proof to govern such proceedings. . . . "This Court has mandated an intermediate standard of proof—'clear and convincing evidence'—when the individual interests at stake in a state proceeding are both 'particularly important' and 'more substantial than mere loss of money.' " Santosky v. Kramer, 455 U.S. 745, 756 (1982) (quoting Addington, supra, [441 U.S.] at 424). Thus, such a standard has been required in deportation proceedings, in denaturalization proceedings, in civil commitment proceedings, and in proceedings for the termination of parental rights. . . .

We think it self-evident that the interests at stake in the instant proceedings are more substantial, both on an individual and societal level, than those involved in a run-of-the-mine civil dispute. But not only does the standard of proof reflect the importance of a particular adjudication, it also serves as "a societal judgment about how the risk of error should be distributed between the litigants." Santosky, 455 U.S., at 755. The more stringent the burden of proof a party must bear, the more that party bears the risk of an erroneous decision. We believe that Missouri may permissibly place an increased risk of an erroneous decision on those seeking to terminate an incompetent individual's life-sustaining treatment. An erroneous decision not to terminate results in a maintenance of the status quo; the possibility of subsequent developments such as advancements in medical science, the discovery of new evidence regarding the patient's intent, changes in the law, or simply the unexpected death of the patient despite the administration of life-sustaining treatment at least create the potential that a wrong decision will eventually be corrected or its impact mitigated. An erroneous decision to withdraw life-sustaining treatment, however, is not susceptible of correction.

It is also worth noting that most, if not all, states simply forbid oral testimony entirely in determining the wishes of parties in transactions which, while important, simply do not have the consequences that a decision to terminate a person's life does. . . . There is no doubt that statutes requiring wills to be in writing, and statutes of frauds which require that a contract to make a will be in writing, on occasion frustrate the effectuation of the intent of a particular decedent, just as Missouri's requirement of proof in this case may have frustrated the effectuation of the not fully-expressed desires of Nancy Cruzan. But the Constitution does not require general rules to work faultlessly; no general rule can.

In sum, we conclude that a state may apply a clear and convincing evidence standard in proceedings where a guardian seeks to discontinue nutrition and hydration of a person diagnosed to be in a persistent vegetative state.

Petitioners alternatively contend that Missouri must accept the "substituted judgment" of close family members even in the absence of substantial proof that their views reflect the views of the patient. . . .

No doubt is engendered by anything in this record but that Nancy Cruzan's mother and father are loving and caring parents. If the state were required by the United States Constitution to repose a right of "substituted judgment" with anyone, the Cruzans would surely qualify. But we do not think the due process clause requires the state to repose judgment on these matters with anyone but the patient herself. Close family members may have a strong feeling—a feeling not at all ignoble or unworthy, but not entirely disinterested, either—that they do not wish to witness the continuation of the life of a loved one which they regard as hopeless, meaningless, and even degrading. But there is no automatic assurance that the view of close family members will necessarily be the same as the patient's would have been had she been confronted with the prospect of her situation while competent. All of the reasons previously discussed for allowing Missouri to require clear and convincing evidence of the patient's wishes lead us to conclude that the State may choose to defer only to those wishes, rather than confide the decision to close family members.

O'CONNOR, Justice, concurring.
[In her concurrence, Justice O'Connor suggested that the Constitution gives individuals the right to have their life-sustaining treatment decisions made by a formally appointed surrogate decisionmaker (e.g., through a durable power of attorney).]

BRENNAN, Justice, with whom MARSHALL, Justice, and BLACKMUN, Justice, join, dissenting.
. . . As the majority recognizes, Missouri has a *parens patriae* interest in providing Nancy Cruzan, now incompetent, with as accurate as possible a determination of how she would exercise her rights under these circumstances. Second, if and when it is determined that Nancy Cruzan would want to continue treatment, the state may legitimately assert an interest in providing that treatment. But until Nancy's wishes have been determined, the only state interest that may be asserted is an interest in safeguarding the accuracy of that determination.

Accuracy, therefore, must be our touchstone. Missouri may constitutionally impose only those procedural requirements that serve to enhance the accuracy of a determination of Nancy Cruzan's wishes or are at least consistent with an accurate determination. The Missouri "safeguard" that the Court upholds today does not meet that standard. The determination needed in this context is whether the incompetent person would choose to live in a persistent vegetative state on life support or to avoid this medical treatment. Missouri's rule of decision imposes a markedly asymmetrical evidentiary burden. Only evidence of specific statements of treatment choice made by the patient when competent is admissible to support a finding that the patient, now in a persistent vegetative state, would wish to avoid further medical treatment. Moreover, this evidence must be clear and convincing.

No proof is required to support a finding that the incompetent person would wish to continue treatment.

A

The majority offers several justifications for Missouri's heightened evidentiary standard. First, the majority explains that the state may constitutionally adopt this rule to govern determinations of an incompetent's wishes in order to advance the state's substantive interests, including its unqualified interest in the preservation of human life. Missouri's evidentiary standard, however, cannot rest on the state's own interest in a particular substantive result. To be sure, courts have long erected clear and convincing evidence standards to place the greater risk of erroneous decisions on those bringing disfavored claims. In such cases, however, the choice to discourage certain claims was a legitimate, constitutional policy choice. In contrast, Missouri has no such power to disfavor a choice by Nancy Cruzan to avoid medical treatment, because Missouri has no legitimate interest in providing Nancy with treatment until it is established that this represents her choice. Just as a state may not override Nancy's choice directly, it may not do so indirectly through the imposition of a procedural rule. . . .

The majority claims that the allocation of the risk of error is justified because it is more important not to terminate life support for someone who would wish it continued than to honor the wishes of someone who would not. An erroneous decision to terminate life support is irrevocable, says the majority, while an erroneous decision not to terminate "results in a maintenance of the status quo." But, from the point of view of the patient, an erroneous decision in either direction is irrevocable. An erroneous decision to terminate artificial nutrition and hydration, to be sure, will lead to failure of that last remnant of physiological life, the brain stem, and result in complete brain death. An erroneous decision not to terminate life support, however, robs a patient of the very qualities protected by the right to avoid unwanted medical treatment. His own degraded existence is perpetuated; his family's suffering is protracted; the memory he leaves behind becomes more and more distorted.

Even a later decision to grant him his wish cannot undo the intervening harm. But a later decision is unlikely in any event. "[T]he discovery of new evidence," to which the majority refers, is more hypothetical than plausible. The majority also misconceives the relevance of the possibility of "advancements in medical science," by treating it as a reason to force someone to continue medical treatment against his will. The possibility of a medical miracle is indeed part of the calculus, but it is a part of the patient's calculus. If current research suggests that some hope for cure or even moderate improvement is possible within the lifespan projected, this is a factor that should be and would be accorded significant weight in assessing what the patient himself would choose.[18]

18. For Nancy Cruzan, no such cure or improvement is in view. So much of her brain has deteriorated and been replaced by fluid, see App. to Pet. for Cert. A94, that apparently the only medical advance that could restore consciousness to her body would be a brain transplant.

B

Even more than its heightened evidentiary standard, the Missouri court's categorical exclusion of relevant evidence dispenses with any semblance of accurate fact finding. The court adverted to no evidence supporting its decision, but held that no clear and convincing, inherently reliable evidence had been presented to show that Nancy would want to avoid further treatment. In doing so, the court failed to consider statements Nancy had made to family members and a close friend. The court also failed to consider testimony from Nancy's mother and sister that they were certain that Nancy would want to discontinue artificial nutrition and hydration, even after the court found that Nancy's family was loving and without malignant motive. The court also failed to consider the conclusions of the guardian ad litem, appointed by the trial court, that there was clear and convincing evidence that Nancy would want to discontinue medical treatment and that this was in her best interests. The court did not specifically define what kind of evidence it would consider clear and convincing, but its general discussion suggests that only a living will or equivalently formal directive from the patient when competent would meet this standard.

Too few people execute living wills or equivalently formal directives for such an evidentiary rule to ensure adequately that the wishes of incompetent persons will be honored. While it might be a wise social policy to encourage people to furnish such instructions, no general conclusion about a patient's choice can be drawn from the absence of formalities. The probability of becoming irreversibly vegetative is so low that many people may not feel an urgency to marshal formal evidence of their preferences. Some may not wish to dwell on their own physical deterioration and mortality. Even someone with a resolute determination to avoid life support under circumstances such as Nancy's would still need to know that such things as living wills exist and how to execute one. Often legal help would be necessary, especially given the majority's apparent willingness to permit states to insist that a person's wishes are not truly known unless the particular medical treatment is specified.

. . . When Missouri enacted a living will statute, it specifically provided that the absence of a living will does not warrant a presumption that a patient wishes continued medical treatment. Thus, apparently not even Missouri's own legislature believes that a person who does not execute a living will fails to do so because he wishes continuous medical treatment under all circumstances.

The testimony of close friends and family members, on the other hand, may often be the best evidence available of what the patient's choice would be. It is they with whom the patient most likely will have discussed such questions and they who know the patient best. . . .

. . . The rules by which an incompetent person's wishes are determined must represent every effort to determine those wishes. The rule that the Missouri court adopted and that this Court upholds, however, skews the result away from a determination that as accurately as possible reflects the individual's own preferences and beliefs. It is a rule that transforms human beings into passive subjects of medical technology. . . .

D

Finally, I cannot agree with the majority that where it is not possible to determine what choice an incompetent patient would make, a state's role as *parens patriae* permits the state automatically to make that choice itself. Under fair rules of evidence, it is improbable that a court could not determine what the patient's choice would be. Under the rule of decision adopted by Missouri and upheld today by this Court, such occasions might be numerous. But in neither case does it follow that it is constitutionally acceptable for the state invariably to assume the role of deciding for the patient. A state's legitimate interest in safeguarding a patient's choice cannot be furthered by simply appropriating it.

The majority justifies its position by arguing that, while close family members may have a strong feeling about the question, "there is no automatic assurance that the view of close family members will necessarily be the same as the patient's would have been had she been confronted with the prospect of her situation while competent." I cannot quarrel with this observation. But it leads only to another question: Is there any reason to suppose that a state is more likely to make the choice that the patient would have made than someone who knew the patient intimately? To ask this is to answer it. . . .

. . . A state may ensure that the person who makes the decision on the patient's behalf is the one whom the patient himself would have selected to make that choice for him. And a state may exclude from consideration anyone having improper motives. But a state generally must either repose the choice with the person whom the patient himself would most likely have chosen as proxy or leave the decision to the patient's family.

Notes: Deciding for the Incompetent Patient

1. *Nancy Cruzan.* After the U.S. Supreme Court upheld the Missouri Supreme Court's holding that there was not sufficient evidence to show that Nancy Cruzan would want her feeding tube withdrawn, Ms. Cruzan's family returned to a state trial court with new evidence of her wishes. Because of wide publicity about her case, friends who had discussed end-of-life decisionmaking with Ms. Cruzan came forward with additional testimony about her wishes. These friends had not come forward sooner because they knew Ms. Cruzan under her married name, Nancy Davis, and she had taken her maiden name back when she divorced her husband shortly before her accident. The state did not oppose withdrawal of the feeding tube, and the court ruled in favor of the family. The feeding tube was withdrawn, and Ms. Cruzan died shortly thereafter, five months after the U.S. Supreme Court's decision. Gregory E. Pence, Medical Ethics: Accounts of Ground-Breaking Cases 66 (7th ed. 2015).

2. *The Right of Incompetent Patients.* In *Conroy,* the court held that a competent adult's right to refuse life-sustaining medical treatment remains intact when the person loses competence. Similarly, the *Saikewicz* court wrote that "[t]he recognition of that right must extend to the case of an incompetent, as well as a competent, patient because the value of human dignity extends to both." Superintendent of Belchertown State School v. Saikewicz, 370 N.E.2d 417, 427 (Mass. 1977). Is it so clear that the right to refuse life-sustaining treatment should survive incompetence? If the right is justified by principles of self-determination, why should the right exist for individuals who can no longer express their preferences?

Consider the following explanations for a right to refuse life-sustaining treatment for incompetent persons:

a. We can justify the extension of the right to refuse treatment by analogy to a person's right to dispose of property at death through a will. By letting people pass their wealth on to their family or other chosen beneficiaries, we do not discourage people from engaging in socially desirable activities while they are alive (e.g., wealth-generating activities.) In addition, we want people to be able to ensure the financial security of their loved ones. Both justifications arguably apply to treatment withdrawals. Do you see how this is so?

b. To properly understand the right to refuse treatment, we need to consider not only who gets to make the treatment decision but also who does not get to make the decision. When individuals enjoy a right to refuse treatment, they gain personal control over an important aspect of their lives, and they also are freed from government control over that important aspect. This anti-totalitarian justification for the right to refuse treatment is still very much present for incompetent persons. Giles Scofield, The Calculus of Consent, 20(1) Hastings Center Rep. 44 (1990); Jed Rubenfeld, The Right of Privacy, 102 Harv. L. Rev. 737 (1989).

c. Incompetent persons may not have any interests in self-determination, but they do have interests in being spared from suffering and in being treated with dignity. A right to refuse treatment is essential to ensure that incompetent persons do not undergo unjustified suffering from the imposition of medical treatment. It is also essential to ensure that incompetent persons are not robbed of their dignity.

Which of these statements do you think explain(s) or should explain the right to refuse treatment for incompetent persons? Would the nature of the right vary depending on which of the explanations actually is at work? That is, do any of the explanations justify a broader right than the other explanations? Would explanation c. justify withdrawal of Nancy Jobes's or Nancy Cruzan's feeding tube?

In thinking about why we permit the right to refuse treatment to survive incompetence, does your explanation account for why we do not permit the right to vote to survive incompetence? Suppose a person had voted consistently as a Democrat and explained such voting on the basis that Democrats were more likely to provide adequate funding for nursing homes and other long-term care. Should that person's ballot be cast for Democratic candidates even after the person becomes incompetent?

3. *Variation in Procedural Rules.* The recognition of a right to refuse treatment for incompetent persons still leaves the question as to how the right should be implemented. In *Cruzan*, the U.S. Supreme Court gave states broad leeway to adopt procedural rules for deciding when life-sustaining treatment can be withdrawn from incompetent persons.

In general, states will permit withdrawal of treatment if there is clear and convincing evidence of the patient's treatment preferences from written or oral statements made by the patient before losing competence. Evidence of the patient's wishes is clear and convincing when it is "sufficient to persuade the trier of fact that the patient had a firm and settled commitment" to decline treatment. In re Westchester County (O'Connor), 531 N.E.2d 607, 613 (N.Y. 1988). If clear and convincing evidence does not exist, there is considerable variation from state to state as to whether treatment may be discontinued.

As we have seen, New Jersey has adopted different standards for patients in different conditions. For patients who are permanently unconscious and who did not leave clear and convincing evidence of their wishes, family members may decide on the patient's behalf under a "substituted judgment" standard in which the family members draw on their knowledge of the patient to reach "as much as possible the decision that the incompetent patient would make if he or she were competent." *Jobes*, 529 A.2d at 444. For patients who have some degree of consciousness and have a short life expectancy (but are not expected to die imminently), treatment withdrawals must be justified either by clear and convincing evidence that this is what the patient would have wanted (*Conroy*'s "subjective" standard) or by a demonstration that the pain and suffering of continued treatment markedly outweigh the benefits of continued treatment (*Conroy*'s two "objective" or "best interests" standards).

Other states have not varied their standard in terms of the patient's condition. Some courts, for example, have adopted a simple best interests standard for cases in which the patient's preferences cannot be established. See, e.g., Rasmussen v. Fleming, 741 P.2d 674, 689 (Ariz. 1987) (observing that "[w]here no reliable evidence of a patient's intent exists, as here, the substituted judgment standard provides little, if any, guidance to the surrogate decisionmaker and should be abandoned in favor of the 'best interests' standard"); In re Torres, 357 N.W.2d 332, 338-339 (Minn. 1984).

A good illustration of the best interests standard is the court's discussion in *Saikewicz*. Although the court stated that it was employing a substituted judgment approach, it actually was employing a best interests approach. Indeed, inasmuch as Mr. Saikewicz had never been competent, it made no sense to employ a substituted judgment. The analysis of the *Saikewicz* court follows:

> . . . In short, the decision in cases such as this should be that which would be made by the incompetent person, if that person were competent, but taking into account the present and future incompetency of the individual as one of the factors which would necessarily enter into the decisionmaking process of the competent person. . . .
>
> The two factors considered by the probate judge to weigh in favor of administering chemotherapy were: (1) the fact that most people elect chemotherapy and (2) the chance of a longer life. . . . With regard to the second factor, the chance of a longer life carries the same weight for Saikewicz as for any other person, the value of life under the law having no relation to intelligence or social position. Intertwined with this consideration is the hope that a cure, temporary or permanent, will be discovered during the period of extra weeks or months potentially made available by chemotherapy. The guardian ad litem investigated this possibility and found no reason to hope for a dramatic breakthrough in the time frame relevant to the decision.
>
> The probate judge identified six factors weighing against administration of chemotherapy. Four of these—Saikewicz's age,[17] the probable side effects of treatment, the low chance of producing remission, and the certainty that treatment will cause immediate suffering—were clearly established by the medical testimony to be considerations that any individual would weigh carefully. A fifth factor—Saikewicz's inability to cooperate with the treatment—introduces those considerations that are unique to this individual and which therefore are essential to the proper exercise

---

17. This factor is relevant because of the medical evidence in the record that people of Saikewicz's age do not tolerate the chemotherapy as well as younger people and that the chance of remission is decreased. Age is irrelevant, of course, to the question of the value or quality of life.

of substituted judgment. The judge heard testimony that Saikewicz would have no comprehension of the reasons for the severe disruption of his formerly secure and stable environment occasioned by the chemotherapy. He therefore would experience fear without the understanding from which other patients draw strength. The inability to anticipate and prepare for the severe side effects of the drugs leaves room only for confusion and disorientation. The possibility that such a naturally uncooperative patient would have to be physically restrained to allow the slow intravenous administration of drugs could only compound his pain and fear, as well as possibly jeopardize the ability of his body to withstand the toxic effects of the drugs.

The sixth factor identified by the judge as weighing against chemotherapy was "the quality of life possible for him even if the treatment does bring about remission." To the extent that this formulation equates the value of life with any measure of the quality of life, we firmly reject it. A reading of the entire record clearly reveals, however, the judge's concern that special care be taken to respect the dignity and worth of Saikewicz's life precisely because of his vulnerable position. The judge, as well as all the parties, was keenly aware that the supposed inability of Saikewicz, by virtue of his mental retardation, to appreciate or experience life had no place in the decision before them. Rather than reading the judge's formulation in a manner that demeans the value of the life of one who is mentally retarded, the vague, and perhaps ill-chosen, term "quality of life" should be understood as a reference to the continuing state of pain and disorientation precipitated by the chemotherapy treatment. Viewing the term in this manner, together with the other factors properly considered by the judge, we are satisfied that the decision to withhold treatment from Saikewicz was based on a regard for his actual interests and preferences and that the facts supported this decision. Superintendent of Belchertown State School v. Saikewicz, 370 N.E.2d 417, 431-432 (Mass. 1977).

Other states permit family members or guardians to employ a *Jobes*-like substituted judgment standard for all incompetent patients. Brophy v. New England Sinai Hospital, Inc., 497 N.E.2d 626, 634-635 (Mass. 1986); In re Tavel, 661 A.2d 1061, 1068-1069 (Del. 1995). As the Indiana Supreme Court wrote:

> Respect for patient autonomy does not end when the patient becomes incompetent. In our society, health care decisionmaking for patients typically transfers upon incompetence to the patient's family. . . . Even when they have not left formal advance directives or expressed particular opinions about life-sustaining medical treatment, most Americans want the decisions about their care, upon their incapacity, to be made for them by family and physician, rather than by strangers or by government.
> [In re Lawrence, 579 N.E.2d 32, 39 (Ind. 1991).]

Illinois also relies on family decisionmaking, although not for all patients. The Illinois Supreme Court struggled with the question of treatment withdrawal in In re Estate of Longeway, 549 N.E.2d 292 (Ill. 1989), and In re Greenspan, 558 N.E.2d 1194 (Ill. 1990), and Rudy Linares highlighted the need for better legal guidance when he discontinued a ventilator from his 15-month-old child while holding medical staff at bay with a gun. John D. Lantos et al., The Linares Affair, 17 L. Med. & Health Care 308 (1989). In response, the Illinois legislature passed its Health Care Surrogate Act. 755 Ill. Comp. Stat. 40. The Act applies to incompetent patients who have not executed a living will or durable power of attorney for health care and who either are terminally ill, are permanently unconscious, or have some other incurable or irreversible condition "that imposes severe pain or otherwise imposes an inhumane burden on the patient," and for which life-sustaining medical treatment "provides only minimal medical benefit." 755 Ill. Comp. Stat. 40/10. For persons covered by the Act, life-sustaining treatment decisions are to be made by family members or close friends. The Act instructs surrogate decisionmakers to decide first on the basis of how they believe the patient would have decided. Essentially, then, surrogates are governed first by New Jersey's "subjective" and "substituted judgment" standards. If surrogates are unable to figure out what the patient would have wanted, decisions for the patient "shall be made on the basis of the patient's best interests *as determined by the surrogate decision maker.*" 755 Ill. Comp. Stat. 40/20(b) (1) (emphasis added). The best interests judgment is to be made by weighing the benefits to and burdens on the patient from treatment against the burdens and benefits of the treatment itself.

At one time New York employed essentially the same standard for all patients that Missouri adopted for cases like the *Cruzan* case—a strict version of *Conroy's* subjective standard. The New York Court of Appeals not only required clear and convincing evidence of the patient's wishes, as in *Conroy*, but also adopted a strict view of clear and convincing evidence, requiring

> proof sufficient to persuade the trier of fact that the patient held a firm and settled commitment to the termination of life supports *under the circumstances like those presented.* As a threshold matter, the trier of fact must be convinced, as far as is humanly possible, that the strength of the individual's beliefs and the durability of the individual's commitment to those beliefs makes a recent change of heart unlikely. The persistence of the individual's statements, the seriousness with which those statements were made and the inferences, if any, that may be drawn from the surrounding circumstances are among the factors which should be considered.

O'Connor, 531 N.E.2d at 613 (emphasis added).

In 2010, the New York legislature replaced the *O'Connor* standard with an approach much like that of New Jersey. Under the Family Health Care Decisions Act, family members or close friends may refuse life-sustaining treatment for patients who are terminally ill or permanently unconscious. In addition, for patients who have an incurable condition, family members or close friends may refuse life-sustaining treatment that is inhumane or extraordinarily burdensome. N.Y. Pub. Health Law §2994-d. The legislative language comes largely from the recommendations of the New York State Task Force on Life and the Law's report, When Others Must Choose: Deciding for Patients Without Capacity (1992 and 1993 Supplement).

Most states now have statutes authorizing surrogate decisionmaking in the event that the patient did not execute an advance directive. Like Illinois and New York, they tend to restrict the surrogate's authority in terms of the patient's condition. For example, in Maryland, the patient must be terminally ill or permanently unconscious, or must have an "end-stage condition," defined as an "advanced, progressive, irreversible condition . . . [t]hat has caused severe and permanent deterioration indicated by incompetency and complete physical dependency." Md. Code Ann., Health Gen. §5-601(i). Still, the Uniform Health Care Decisions Act and surrogate statutes in some states recognize the authority of surrogates to make life-sustaining treatment decisions without qualification in terms of the patient's condition. See, e.g., Uniform Health Care Decisions Act §5(a) (1993); D.C. Code Ann. §21-2210; Va. Code Ann. §54.1-2986. Which of the different approaches for deciding about end-of-life care for incompetent persons make the most sense to you? Or, is it better, in a pluralistic society, to have different approaches in different states?

4. *General Trends in Procedural Rules.* Despite the state-to-state variation, some patterns do emerge. In particular, states tend to adopt stricter procedural rules when the incompetent patient is neither terminally ill nor permanently unconscious. In such cases, the patient has some degree of consciousness and may live for a year or more. The *Conroy* case falls into this category, and the New Jersey Supreme Court adopted a stricter standard than it did in the *Jobes* case for patients who are permanently unconscious. The California Supreme Court also has adopted strict standards for patients who are neither terminally ill nor permanently unconscious. In *Wendland,* the court required clear and convincing evidence that patients would have refused treatment under the circumstances in which they now find themselves, or clear and convincing evidence that withdrawal of treatment would be in the patient's best interests. Conservatorship of Wendland, 28 P.3d 151 (Cal. 2001). (The court did not "attempt to define the extreme factual predicates that, if proved by clear and convincing evidence, might support a [surrogate's] decisions that withdrawing life support would be in the best interest of a conscious [patient]." Id. at 174. The court did observe that a surrogate's "own subjective judgment that the [patient] d[oes] not enjoy a satisfactory quality of life" is insufficient. Id.)

Other courts have adopted the strict subjective standard of *Conroy* and *Wendland* but have not included an alternative objective standard. For example, in the *Martin* case, the Michigan Supreme Court adopted a purely subjective standard for patients who are neither terminally ill nor permanently unconscious, a standard similar to New York's old *O'Connor* standard. For such patients in Michigan, in the absence of a written directive expressing the patient's preferences, prior oral statements will be sufficient to justify withdrawal of treatment "[o]nly when the patient's prior statements clearly illustrate a serious, well thought out, consistent decision to refuse treatment under these exact circumstances or circumstances highly similar to the current situation." In re Martin, 538 N.W.2d 399, 411 (Mich. 1995).

In Michael Martin's case, this test was not satisfied despite considerable testimony suggesting he would not want treatment provided. Mr. Martin had suffered serious injuries, including a head injury, from an automobile accident that left him "unable to walk or talk, and rendered him dependent on a colostomy for defecation and a gastrostomy tube for nutrition." He was able to understand "only very short and very simple questions." He could not "accurately comprehend questions that are lengthy, verbose, or that require the retention of multiple thoughts." In particular, he could not understand "his physical capabilities and medical condition." Id. at 402-404. Mr. Martin's wife testified to eight years of discussions regarding his wishes in the event of a serious accident or disabling illness, the most recent discussion occurring one month before his accident. These discussions took place after the Martins watched movies about people who could no longer take care of themselves because of an accident or illness.

> Mike stated to me on several occasions: "That's bullshit. I would never want to live like that." He also said to me, "Please don't ever let me exist that way because those people don't even have their dignity." . . . [Regarding a movie about a football player with a terminal illness,] Mike said to me after we saw it together: "If I ever get

sick don't put me on any machines to keep me going if there is no hope of getting better." He also said that if I ever put him on machines to keep him alive: "I'll always haunt you, Mary." Then he would say, "Do you understand?" I always said "Yes." We watched this movie at least two or three times and had virtually the same discussion each time. . . . Mike was an avid hunter and frequently expressed concerned [sic] about a hunting accident. Mike frequently told me that if he ever had an accident from which he would "not recover" and "could not be the same person," he did "not want to live that way." He would say, "Mary, promise me you wouldn't let me live like that if I can't be the person I am right now, because if you do, believe me I'll haunt you every day of your life." [Id. at 412.]

The Michigan court found that this testimony did not represent clear and convincing evidence of Mr. Martin's wishes. Two of his co-workers stated that, while Mr. Martin had indicated his desire not to be kept alive if in a vegetative state, Mr. Martin's present condition was not "the type referred to in conversations with them before his injury." In addition, several witnesses testified that, after his accident, Mr. Martin would shake his head no "when asked if he ever felt that he did not want to continue living." Id. at 412-413. For discussion of the *Martin* case, see the articles by Andrew J. Broder and Ronald E. Cranford, and by Thomas J. Marzen and Daniel Avila in Symposium Issue: Assisted Suicide, Health Care and Medical Treatment Choices, 72 U. Det. Mercy L. Rev. 719 (1995). For another case requiring clear evidence of the patient's wishes before removing a life-sustaining treatment from a patient who is neither terminally ill nor permanently unconscious, see Spahn v. Eisenberg, 563 N.W.2d 485 (Wis. 1997). Cf. In re D.L.H., 2 A.3d 505 (Pa. 2010) (interpreting Pennsylvania's health care representative statute to require the provision of life-preserving treatment for incompetent patients who are neither terminally ill nor permanently unconscious and who have not appointed a health care agent).

Does it make sense to vary the procedural rules depending on the patient's medical condition? If we have a different procedural standard for patients like Mr. Martin or Ms. Conroy than we do for patients like Ms. Jobes, have we maintained the principle that the substantive right to refuse life-sustaining treatment is not altered by incompetence? Should we be concerned about the fact that stricter procedural standards are likely to affect people differently depending on their socioeconomic status?

Although it is controversial whether clear and convincing evidence of the patient's wishes should be required before discontinuing life-sustaining treatment, it is less controversial when courts impose strict standards for establishing the patient's prognosis. If life-sustaining treatment is withdrawn because the patient is terminally ill or permanently unconscious, for example, we would want to be reasonably sure that the patient really is terminally ill or permanently unconscious. The Alabama Supreme Court came to that conclusion when it adopted a clear and convincing evidence standard for deciding that a patient is permanently unconscious for purposes of carrying out the patient's advance directive in the event of permanent unconsciousness. Knight v. Beverly Health Care Bay Manor Health Care Center, 820 So. 2d 92, 102 (Ala. 2001).

5. *The Patient's Best Interests.* While most courts and commentators believe that decisions for incompetent patients should reflect a judgment of what the patient would have wanted based on the patient's statements and values while competent, others disagree. Rebecca Dresser and John Robertson contend that medical

decisions for incompetent persons should be based on an assessment of the patient's current best interests, that the incompetent person is very different from the person's previously competent self:

> It is wrong to assume that the incompetent patient's prior competent preferences are the best indicator of the patient's current interests. If we could determine the choice that these patients would make if suddenly able to speak—if they could tell us what their interests in their compromised states are—such choices would reflect their current and future interests as incompetent individuals, not their past preferences. . . . When people become incompetent and seriously ill, . . . their interests may radically change. With their reduced mental and physical capacities, what was once of extreme importance to them no longer matters, while things that were previously of little moment assume much greater significance. An existence that seems demeaning and unacceptable to the competent person may still be of value to the incompetent patient, whose abilities, desires and interests have greatly narrowed.

Rebecca S. Dresser & John A. Robertson, Quality of Life and Non-Treatment Decisions for Incompetent Patients: A Critique of the Orthodox Approach, 17 L. Med. & Health Care 234 (1989).

Some support for this view comes from the empirical literature. Studies indicate that healthy persons underestimate the quality of life of disabled persons. That is, when healthy persons are asked to estimate the quality of life of disabled persons, they give a lower quality of life than that given by the disabled persons about their own quality of life. In addition, people who become disabled find that they have a higher quality of life than they thought they would.

Which approach do you prefer, a "subjective" and/or "substituted judgment" approach based on the patient's statements and values while competent, or an "objective" approach based on the patient's current best interests?

In a study of patients on dialysis because of kidney failure, the patients were asked to consider whether they would want dialysis continued if they developed advanced Alzheimer's disease. They were then asked how much leeway they would want their family and physician to have in terms of overriding their wishes if overriding would be in their best interests. The researchers found that 39 percent of the patients would want their family and physicians to have "no leeway" in overriding their wishes, 31 percent of the patients would want their family and physicians to have "complete leeway" in overriding their wishes, and the remaining 30 percent of patients would want their family and physician to have some leeway (19 percent a "little leeway" and 11 percent a "lot of leeway"). Ashwini Sehgal et al., How Strictly Do Dialysis Patients Want Their Advance Directives Followed?, 267 JAMA 59 (1992). In another study of patients who were either seriously ill or at least 80 years old, researchers asked the patients about their wishes for CPR in the event of cardiac arrest. They then asked the patients whether their wishes about CPR should be followed if they lost decisionmaking capacity, or whether the CPR decision should be made by their family and physician. More than 70 percent of the patients preferred that their family and physician decide about CPR. Christina M. Puchalski, Patients Who Want Their Family and Physician to Make Resuscitation Decisions for Them, 48(5) J. Am. Geriatrics Soc'y S84 (2000).

How do these studies affect your feelings about a subjective vs. objective standard?

6. *Family Decisionmaking.* For an argument in favor of family decisionmaking in all cases of incompetent persons, see Nancy K. Rhoden, Litigating Life and Death, 102 Harv. L. Rev. 375, 437-439 (1988) (emphasis in original):

> Families have historically exercised and continue to exercise a great deal of autonomy over decisions about procreation, education, and the upbringing of children. Family members have likewise attended to other members during their illnesses and have helped make their treatment choices for them. Not surprisingly, polls repeatedly show that patients, and members of society in general, believe that family members should function as surrogate decisionmakers. In short, there is a deep-rooted and almost instinctual sense that a close family member should make decisions. Most readers will understand this if they consider whom they would want to make treatment decisions for themselves—their families or physicians and hospital administrators.
>
> Moreover, because of the nature of the family as an association, its members are in the best position to reproduce preferences of an incompetent patient. . . . Not only are family members most likely to be privy to any relevant statements that patients have made on the topics of treatment or its termination, but they also have longstanding knowledge of the patient's character traits. Although evidence of character traits may seem inconclusive to third parties, closely related persons may, quite legitimately, "just know" what the patient would want in a way that transcends purely logical evidence. . . . Family members also *care* most: . . . humans naturally care most for those closest to them.
>
> Moreover, no patient is an island. The family is the context within which a person first develops her powers of autonomous choice, and the values she brings to these choices spring from, and are intertwined with, the family's values. A parent may understand a child's values because she helped to form them, a child may grasp a parent's values because the parent imparted them to her, and a couple may have developed and refined their views in tandem.

Rhoden recommends a presumption in favor of the family's choice, except that when "the patient recognizes caretakers and can interact with her environment in some way—even if she is completely nonverbal—then the patient has an interest in living, and foregoing treatment, unless it is excessively burdensome, is not a reasonable choice." Id. at 442.

Is Rhoden correct in her belief that family members will do a good job reflecting a patient's preferences? According to a review of studies on this question, surrogates are accurate about two-thirds of the time. David I. Shalowitz et al., The Accuracy of Surrogate Decision Makers, 166 Arch. Intern. Med. 493 (2006).

Interestingly, Rhoden's approach and the best interests approach of Dresser and Robertson may not be that different in the end in terms of the kinds of decisions that would be made for incompetent persons. Dresser and Robertson generally would respect families' judgments as to whether treatment is in the patient's best interests except that it would not be acceptable for a family to decline treatment when the patient is a conscious, incompetent person "who can experience enjoyment and pleasure, and whose conditions and necessary treatment interventions impose on them small or moderate burdens." Dresser & Robertson, 17 L. Med. & Health Care at 242. In other words, Dresser and Robertson defer to the family as a general matter, as does Rhoden, and they limit the family's authority in essentially the same situations.

How do you respond to the concern of the *Cruzan* majority that family members are not disinterested parties to the decision? How might a patient's children react to the prospects of several more months or years of hospital or nursing home costs for the patient?

Note that family decisionmaking and substituted judgment approaches overlap substantially. In *Jobes*, for example, the court approved substituted judgments by families, and other courts or statutes also authorize family members to make substituted judgments for incompetent patients.

7. *Other People's Interests.* Courts and scholars typically justify family decisionmaking on the ground that family members are best suited to represent the patient's interests. But maybe their own interests ought to count. Recall this argument from Roger B. Dworkin, Medical Law and Ethics in the Post-Autonomy Age, 68 Ind. L. J. 727 (1993), supra, at pages 498-500:

> All autonomy-centered approaches ignore the fact that nobody is autonomous. Everybody lives in groups—families, workplaces, clubs, labor unions, towns, states, countries—and almost everything that affects one person affects others as well. . . .
>
> Autonomy-based systems undervalue those other persons' needs. They assume that it is possible to ascertain who is most affected by an action or condition and then allow that person's interests to trump all others. . . .
>
> RESPECT FOR ALL INDIVIDUALS
>
> I suggest that a useful way to begin would be (1) to refocus our rhetoric and our rules away from concern for individual choice and toward respect for individuals, while (2) recognizing that individuals live in groups whose individual members deserve respect too. . . . .
>
> Terminally ill patients who are incompetent and have expressed no choices about withholding or withdrawing medical care deserve respect. They retain an interest in dignity and in avoiding unnecessary suffering. However, their loved ones' interests are also strong and should be accorded great weight. Suffering from watching a close relative die a prolonged death is real. [So is] the anguish of believing that one was premature in letting the loved one die. . . . Respect for relatives requires that they be accorded significant discretion in deciding whether to allow the patient to die. . . .
>
> Medical law and ethics based on individual autonomy . . . ignore important values. The salutary role of the autonomy focus is that it avoids state imposition and abuse of the weak. As the illustrations here suggest, an approach rooted in respect for all individuals would . . . increase the chance of sound results by considering all relevant persons and values in each case, while keeping the door to state imposition and abuse of the powerless tightly closed.

8. *Disagreements Among Family Members.* An important concern with family decisionmaking is how to resolve disagreements among family members. To some extent, this issue is addressed by state statutes governing surrogate decisionmaking. Typically, these statutes establish a hierarchy of family members according to their authority to make decisions on behalf of the patient. See, e.g., Md. Code Ann., Health-Gen. §5-605(a)(2) (establishing a hierarchy of legal guardian (if one has been appointed), spouse, adult child, parent, adult brother or sister, other close relative, or friend). However, not all states have such statutes, and even when they

exist, physicians may be reluctant to implement a request by some family members to discontinue treatment over the objections of other family members.

Courts also are reluctant to permit withdrawal of treatment in the presence of a disagreement among family members. Indeed, the reluctance to order withdrawal of treatment in the midst of a family dispute may explain many of the court decisions that seem most at odds with the ethical and legal principles underlying the law in this area. For example, in the *Martin* case, supra pages 557-558, in which Mr. Martin's wife seemed to be acting on repeatedly expressed wishes of her husband when she asked that treatment be discontinued, the court's decision to require treatment may have reflected the opposition of Mr. Martin's parents to withdrawal as much as it reflected a desire for stricter standards for patients who are neither terminally ill nor permanently unconscious. Similarly, in *Spahn*, supra page 558, there was a disagreement between the patient's sister and niece. Even more problematic is the court's decision in Couture v. Couture, 549 N.E.2d 571, 576 (Ohio Ct. App. 1989). In that case, a patient's divorced parents disagreed as to whether his artificial nutrition and hydration should be discontinued. The patient was in a persistent vegetative state, and the appellate court upheld the lower court's finding of clear and convincing evidence that Mr. Couture would want the treatment discontinued. Nevertheless, the court ordered that the treatment be continued.

Perhaps the most extreme family dispute occurred in the case of Terri Schiavo in Florida. A dispute between Ms. Schiavo's husband and parents resulted in nearly seven years of litigation with more than a dozen state and federal court decisions, statutes by the Florida Legislature and Congress, and intervention by Governor Jeb Bush and President George W. Bush. Ms. Schiavo's husband requested the withdrawal of her feeding tube after she had been in a persistent vegetative state for several years. After reviewing the testimony, the trial court judge concluded that there was clear and convincing evidence that Terri would not want a feeding tube, based on her prior oral statements to family members. In re Schiavo, 780 So. 2d 176, 179-180 (Fla. Ct. App. 2001). Ms. Schiavo's parents petitioned successfully for reinsertion of the feeding tube, and after a second removal and reinsertion in 2003, Ms. Schiavo's feeding tube was finally removed in March 2005. Her death ensued 13 days later.

In many cases of disagreement among family members (or with providers of care), mediation or other alternative dispute resolution processes may be useful.

9. *Ethics Committees and Consultants.* Many commentators and courts have encouraged resort to ethics committees and/or ethics consultants to help resolve disagreements among patients, family members, and health care providers. Indeed, the *Quinlan* court suggested that physicians might routinely turn to a hospital ethics committee for guidance when faced with requests by a patient or family to discontinue life-sustaining treatment. *Quinlan*, 355 A.2d at 668-669 (citing Karen Teel, The Physician's Dilemma, 27 Baylor L. Rev. 6 (1975)). There are two basic types of committees, with many variations. "Prognosis committees" are composed primarily of medical personnel and their principal role is to help clinicians resolve questions about the patient's medical condition and likely outcomes of treatment. Full-fledged "ethics committees" include physicians, nurses, social workers, ethicists, lawyers, clergy, and others, including community representatives, and they serve as an interface between clinicians and families. Whereas ethics committees tend to be ongoing, standing committees, prognosis committees may be ad hoc committees

constituted as particular cases arise. In re Colyer, 660 P.2d 738, 749 & n.7 (Wash. 1983). Note too that courts in some cases require or recommend confirmation of prognosis by independent consulting physicians rather than a committee. In re Conroy, 486 A.2d 1209, 1242 (N.J. 1985).

Prodded partly by accreditation requirements, hospitals are increasingly likely to have the full-fledged ethics committees that are available to consider ethical questions that arise in the hospital, and to serve in an advisory role to the patients and physicians involved. In their advisory role, they make no formal decisions and issue nothing of binding force. Ethics committees may, however, develop binding hospital policies and protocols for dealing with specific recurring ethical issues. They also provide ethics education to clinicians. Committee on Bioethics, Institutional Ethics Committees, 107 Pediatrics 205 (2001) (reaffirmed October 2008, 123 Pediatrics 1421 (2009)). It is also becoming more common for hospitals to have ethics consultants, who are physician or nonphysician ethicists whom treating physicians can call on for advice, much as they call on medical specialists for consultation.

An important question is what the goals of the ethics committee or consultant should be. Is it to reach the ethically "correct" result, or is it to guide the involved parties to a result that all can accept? While these two goals may be compatible, they may also be in conflict, and there is often a tendency to view compromise as a desirable goal. The issue whether to aim for the right result or an amicable outcome raises the further question as to whether ethics can lead us to a correct answer or only provide analytic tools to better understand the issues at stake. There are also important legal issues, including whether committee proceedings are confidential and whether committee members are subject to tort liability for their decisions.

For an interesting historical perspective on hospital ethics committees, including discussion of their use to approve abortions, allocate limited kidney dialysis slots, and review decisions to withdraw life-sustaining treatment from seriously disabled newborns, see George J. Annas, Ethics Committees: From Ethical Comfort to Ethical Cover, 21(3) Hastings Center Rep. 18 (1991).

10. *Resort to the Courts.* Courts routinely discourage judicial intervention into end-of-life cases, on the basis either that these are matters for legislatures to work out or that these are matters that are best resolved by patients, families, and physicians. Two typical statements follow:

> . . . Because the issue with all its ramifications is fraught with complexity and encompasses the interests of the law, both civil and criminal, medical ethics and social morality, it is not one which is well-suited for resolution in an adversary judicial proceeding. It is the type [of] issue which is more suitably addressed in the legislative forum, where fact finding can be less confined and the viewpoints of all interested institutions and disciplines can be presented and synthesized. In this manner only can the subject be dealt with comprehensively and the interests of all institutions and individuals be properly accommodated. [Satz v. Perlmutter, 379 So. 2d 359, 260 (Fla. 1980).]

> . . . [J]udicial review of a competent patient's refusal of life-sustaining medical treatment is generally not appropriate. Only unusual circumstances, such as a conflict among the physicians, or among the family members, or between the physicians and the family or other health care professionals, would necessitate judicial intervention. . . .

No matter how expedited, judicial intervention in this complex and sensitive area may take too long. Thus, it could infringe the very rights that we want to protect. The mere prospect of a cumbersome, intrusive, and expensive court proceeding during such an emotional and upsetting period in the lives of a patient and his or her loved ones would undoubtedly deter many persons from deciding to discontinue treatment. And even if the patient or the family were willing to submit to such a proceeding, it is likely that the patient's rights would nevertheless be frustrated by judicial deliberation. Too many patients have died before their right to reject treatment was vindicated in court. Even in this case—where the judicial system acted in an extremely prompt and efficient manner (only 14 days elapsed between the filing of the complaint and the grant of the petition for certification)—we were unable to act in time. Mrs. Farrell died shackled to the respirator. [In re Farrell, 529 A.2d 404, 415 (N.J. 1987).]

Other concerns with judicial involvement include the consequences of forcing the family and physicians into an adversarial posture and the requirement that the court issue its decision based on the state of affairs that existed at the time the record was made despite the possibility of rapidly changing facts. See In re L.H.R., 321 S.E.2d 716, 720-721 (Ga. 1984); William J. Curran, The *Saikewicz* Decision, 298 New Eng. J. Med. 499 (1978).

Nevertheless, some courts have required judicial review of treatment withdrawal cases, requirements that have proven to be short-lived. The Massachusetts Supreme Court, in the *Saikewicz* case, required probate court approval before life-sustaining treatment could be withdrawn from incompetent persons. *Saikewicz*, 370 N.E.2d at 433-434. Not surprisingly, medical reaction to the *Saikewicz* court's requirement of judicial involvement was immediate and overwhelmingly disapproving. Hospital attorneys were also generally opposed to the decision. Civil rights groups and many academic lawyers, on the other hand, supported the court's holding. Impassioned debate took up many pages of volumes 4 and 5 of the American Journal of Law & Medicine (1978-1979). Ultimately, the issue was dissipated two years later by a subsequent Massachusetts Supreme Court decision in which the court wrote that "our opinions should not be taken to establish any requirement of prior judicial approval that would not otherwise exist." In re Spring, 405 N.E.2d 115, 120 (Mass. 1980).

In 1989, the Illinois Supreme Court also imposed a requirement of a court order for cases in which family members or other surrogate decisionmakers seek to discontinue artificial nutrition and hydration from an incompetent person. In re Longeway, 549 N.E.2d 292, 300-301 (Ill. 1989). Despite the court's holding, there was no surge in petitions for court orders to withdraw feeding tubes. Some hospitals and nursing homes continued to stop artificial nutrition and hydration without seeking judicial approval; others may have simply continued to provide artificial nutrition and hydration. In 1991, the Illinois legislature eliminated the need for judicial approval when it passed the state's Health Care Surrogate Act, 755 Ill. Comp. Stat. 40.

11. *Further Reading.* On the **Cruzan** case, see Yale Kamisar, When Is There a Constitutional "Right to Die"? When Is There No Constitutional "Right to Live"?, 25 Ga. L. Rev. 1203 (1991); Thomas W. Mayo, Constitutionalizing the "Right to Die," 49 Md. L. Rev. 103 (1990).

On **surrogate decisionmaker statutes** (note 3), see Diane E. Hoffmann, The Maryland Health Care Decisions Act, 53 Md. L. Rev. 1064 (1994); Nina A. Kohn

& Jeremy A. Blumenthal, Designating Health Care Decisionmakers for Patients without Advance Directives, 42 Ga. L. Rev. 979 (2008); Jerry A. Menikoff et al., Beyond Advance Directives—Health Care Surrogate Laws, 327 New Eng. J. Med. 1165 (1992); Charles P. Sabatino, The New Uniform Health Care Decisions Act, 53 Md. L. Rev. 1238 (1994); Marah Stith, The Semblance of Autonomy: Treatment of Persons with Disabilities Under the Uniform Health-Care Decisions Act, 22 Issues L. & Med. 39 (2006).

On **best interests** (note 5), see Norman F. Boyd et al., Whose Utilities for Decision Analysis?, 10 Med. Decis. Making 58 (1990); Norman L. Cantor, Discarding Substituted Judgment and Best Interests, 48 Rutgers L. Rev. 1193 (1996); Rebecca Dresser, Missing Persons, 46 Rutgers L. Rev. 609 (1994); Terri R. Fried et al., Prospective Study of Health Status Preferences and Changes in Preferences over Time in Older Adults, 166 Arch. Intern. Med. 890 (2006) (finding that patients become more accepting of diminished health status as their own health declines); David Orentlicher, Destructuring Disability: Rationing of Health Care and Unfair Discrimination Against the Sick, 31 Harv. C.R.-C.L. L. Rev. 49, 69 (1996); Daniel P. Sulmasy et al., How Would Terminally Ill Patients Have Others Make Decisions for Them in the Event of Decisional Incapacity?, 55 J. Am. Geriatrics Soc'y 1981 (2007) (finding that most patients wanted their decisions to be based on a mix of their expressed preferences and what their loved ones and physicians thought was in their best interests); Peter A. Ubel et al., Mismanaging the Unimaginable: The Disability Paradox and Health Care Decision Making, 24(4) Health Psychol. S57 (2005).

On **family decisionmaking** (note 6), see Kathleen M. Boozang, An Intimate Passing: Restoring the Role of Family and Religion in Dying, 58 U. Pitt. L. Rev. 549 (1997); Allen E. Buchanan, The Limits of Proxy Decisionmaking for Incompetents, 29 UCLA L. Rev. 386 (1981); Jacqueline J. Glover, Should Families Make Health Care Decisions?, 53 Md. L. Rev. 1158 (1994); John Hardwig, What About the Family?, 20(2) Hastings Center Rep. 5 (1990); Katherine A. Hinderer et al., Withdrawal of Life-Sustaining Treatment: Patient and Proxy Agreement, 34 Dimensions Crit. Care Nurs. 91 (2015); Nancy S. Jecker, The Role of Intimate Others in Medical Decision Making, 30 Gerontologist 65 (1990); Sara M. Moorman & Deborah Carr, Spouses' Effectiveness as End-of-Life Health Care Surrogates, 48 Gerontologist 811 (2008); James L. Nelson, Taking Families Seriously, 22(4) Hastings Center Rep. 6 (1992).

On the **Schiavo** case (note 8), see symposia at 22 Const. Commentary 383 (2005) and 35 Stetson L. Rev. 1 (2005); Barbara A. Noah, Politicizing the End of Life, 59 U. Miami L. Rev. 107 (2004); Lois Shepherd, Shattering the Neutral Surrogate Myth in End-of-Life Decisionmaking, 35 Cumb. L. Rev. 575 (2004/2005). For a timeline of the case and links to key documents and other resources, see the University of Miami Bioethics Program's Web site.

On **mediation and other alternative dispute resolution** (note 8), see I. Glenn Cohen, Negotiating Death, 9 Harv. Negotiation L. Rev. 253 (2004); Nancy Neveloff Dubler & Carol B. Liebman, Bioethics Mediation (2004); Robert Gatter, Unnecessary Adversaries at the End of Life, 79 B.U. L. Rev. 1091 (1999); Diane E. Hoffmann, Mediating Life and Death Decisions, 36 Ariz. L. Rev. 821 (1994); Symposium, 15(2) Cardozo J. Conflict Resol. (2014).

On **ethics committees and consultants** (note 9), see Alan Meisel & Kathy L. Cerminara, The Right to Die §3.25 (3d ed. 2004 & Supps.); David C. Blake, The

Hospital Ethics Committee: Health Care's Moral Conscience or White Elephant?, 22(1) Hastings Center Rep. 5 (1992); John C. Fletcher & Mark Siegler, What Are the Goals of Ethics Consultation?, 7 J. Clin. Ethics 122 (1996); Diane Hoffmann & Anita Terzian, The Role and Legal Status of Health Care Ethics Committees in the U.S., *in* Legal Perspectives in Bioethics (Ana Ilitis et al. eds., 2008); Thaddeus Pope, Multi-Institutional Healthcare Ethics Committees, 31 Campbell L. Rev. 257 (2009); Bethany Spielman, Has Faith in Health Care Ethics Consultants Gone Too Far?, 85 Marq. L. Rev. 161 (2001); Robin Wilson, Hospital Ethics Committees as the Forum of Last Resort: An Idea Whose Time Has Not Come, 76 N.C. L. Rev. 353 (1998); Symposium: Hospital Ethics Committees and the Law, 50 Md. L. Rev. 742 (1991).

Notes: Advance Planning

As the court opinions regularly observe, people can avoid many of the problems with end-of-life decisionmaking by executing a living will, durable power of attorney for health care, or other advance directive while competent. All states have either a living will or power of attorney statute and almost all states have both. Alan Meisel, Kathy L. Cerminara & Thaddeus M. Pope, The Right to Die §§7.01, 7.13 (3d ed. 2004 & Supps.). The statutes typically state that the rights granted therein are cumulative with other rights individuals might have with respect to end-of-life medical decisions.

1. *Living Wills.* The first living will statute was enacted in California in 1976; the document is called a "living" will because it takes effect while the testator is still alive. With a living will, also called a treatment directive, a person describes the circumstances under which treatment would not be desired. A person also might use a living will to indicate a desire that treatment *not* be withheld as long as life can be prolonged. Indeed, Indiana's living will statute includes two forms, one a typical "living will declaration" to express a desire that treatment be withheld, the other a "life prolonging procedures declaration" to express a desire that treatment be provided. Ind. Stat. Ann. §§16-36-4-10, 16-36-4-11. The Indiana statute also states that a life prolonging procedures declaration has conclusive weight while a living will declaration has "great weight." Ind. Stat. Ann. §16-36-4-8 (f)-(g). In many other states, statutory forms offer patients a choice between forgoing or requesting care.

Living wills have several drawbacks. If a person gives specific instructions, the document will not provide guidance in unanticipated situations. If a person instead tries to give general guidance that can be applied to any particular situation, then there will likely be a good deal of ambiguity in the living will, ambiguity that may lead different people to different interpretations of the person's wishes. Some statutes apply only to patients with terminal illnesses and persistent vegetative states, and some statutes restrict the circumstances under which artificial nutrition and hydration may be withdrawn. People can avoid such limitations by attaching addenda or using one of the model forms available from national organizations, although most people are likely to use the statutory form out of either convenience or unawareness of the alternatives. For a case illustrating the problems that patients can experience with having their living wills followed, see Wright v. Johns Hopkins Health Systems Corp., 728 A.2d 166 (Md. 1999) (discussed, infra, page 570). For an argument that living wills should be treated as medical documents rather than legal documents, see Joshua A. Rolnick et al., Delegalizing Advance Directives—Facilitating Advance

Care Planning, 376 New Eng. J. Med. 2105 (2017). For a gripping account by a law professor who underwent a heart transplant of why advance directives should not be conclusive, see Louis J. Sirico, Jr., Life and Death: Stories of a Heart Transplant Patient, Real Prop. Prob. & Trust J. 554 (2002).

2. *Proxy Appointments.* Rather than giving treatment instructions, a person might choose to appoint a proxy or surrogate decisionmaker by executing a durable power of attorney for health care. By doing so, the individual can transfer authority to make medical decisions to someone else. Durable powers of attorney were created because under the common law, all agency power ceases when the principal becomes incompetent. With a "durable" power of attorney, the proxy's agency authority survives the incompetence of the patient. Technically, durable powers of attorney for health care are actually "springing" powers of attorney. In other words, strictly speaking, a durable power of attorney takes effect while the principal is still competent and continues to have effect if the principal becomes incompetent. A springing power of attorney, on the other hand, does not take effect until the principal becomes incompetent. Despite the inaccuracy of the term, powers of attorney for health care are universally characterized as durable powers of attorney.

With a power of attorney, a person can avoid many of the problems with living wills. Power of attorney statutes generally apply to patients in any condition and with regard to any treatment. It is unusual for them to qualify the surrogate's authority to situations in which the patient is terminally ill or to restrict the surrogate's authority to decline artificial nutrition and hydration. Accordingly, people can provide for the exercise of their right to refuse treatment in all circumstances. Since proxies have broad authority, they are able to make decisions even when patients have not expressed their wishes or expressed them in too vague a way to be sure what the patient intended. Of course, some people may not have anyone whom they trust enough to appoint as a proxy. For a decision recognizing broad surrogate authority, see Stein v. County of Nassau, 642 F. Supp. 2d 135 (E.D.N.Y. 2009), in which the court held that under New York's health care proxy statute, surrogates have authority to make medical decisions in any setting, including the patient's home, not just in hospitals. The court of appeals vacated the trial court's holding on the ground that the New York statute required the attending physician to certify in writing that the patient lacked decisionmaking capacity, and no such certification had been made. Stein v. Barthelson, 419 Fed. Appx. 617 (2d Cir. 2011).

Some people choose to combine a treatment directive with a power of attorney, giving some instructions and leaving authority to the surrogate for situations not covered by their instructions. What do you see as the problem with this approach?

Recall that when patients do not leave a living will to express their wishes about the use of a ventilator, feeding tube, or other treatment, courts will consider oral statements by patients to see whether there is clear and convincing evidence of the patients' treatment preferences. If courts will follow patient wishes for a treatment decision when patients have expressed their preferences through clear oral statements rather than through a formal written document, shouldn't courts also consider oral statements by patients regarding their choice of surrogate? For example, wasn't it clear that Michael Martin expected his wife to make medical decisions for him? Why require written authorization (or a state surrogate statute) before recognizing a surrogate decisionmaker in such cases?

3. *Statutory Forms.* Advance directive laws typically include a statutory form but generally state that individuals need not use the statutory form. However, in a few states, the statutes require compliance with the statutory form. See, e.g., Texas Medical Power of Attorney, Tex. Health & Safety Code §§166.163, 166.164. What would be the legal significance of a handwritten living will that does not follow the statutory format?

4. *Limitations of Advance Directives.* For many years, advance directives were disappointing in practice. Most people did not fill them out, even when encouraged to do so by physicians. Moreover, as indicated, when living wills were executed, they often were too vague to give sufficient guidance. And even when living wills gave sufficient guidance, they often were overridden by physicians.

Thus, for example, while courts clearly recognized that end-of-life decisions should be based on patient preferences and values, empirical studies indicated that the physician's preferences and values seemed to drive decisions regarding the withdrawal of life-sustaining medical treatment. David Orentlicher, The Limitations of Legislation, 53 Md. L. Rev. 1255, 1280-1288 (1994). In one study, after nursing home residents completed living wills, researchers followed the residents to determine whether subsequent medical decisions were consistent with them. The researchers found that physicians overrode the living wills 25 percent of the time. Marion Danis et al., A Prospective Study of Advance Directives for Life-Sustaining Care, 324 New Eng. J. Med. 882 (1991). While a 75 percent agreement may seem good, the study suggests that physicians overrode the patient's preferences the majority of the time when there was a disagreement between the patient's choice and the physician's preferences:

> [I]n most end-of-life situations, physicians and patients probably agree on whether treatment should be provided, and much of the 75 percent consistency between the living wills and the physicians' decisions can be explained by a sharing of values between patients and physicians. When there is disagreement between physicians and patients, however, it follows that the physicians' preferences generally prevail. Assuming that there is a 60 percent agreement rate and a 40 percent disagreement rate between patients and physicians, then a 25 percent override rate means that physicians prevail in 62.5 percent of the disagreements (25 percent/40 percent).

Orentlicher, The Limitations of Legislation, at 1282. This predominance of physicians' values also could be found in situations involving competent patients or in which family members have decisionmaking authority.

In recent years, there has been improvement. Dying patients are much more likely to have completed an advance directive, and studies have found closer agreement between patient preferences and the care they received. But the data are mixed on agreement between patient preferences and care received, and failures to respect patient preferences seem to be more likely when patients request aggressive care.

Moreover, physicians' personal values often diverge from the principles that have become widely recognized in ethics and the law. Even though patients are as free to have treatment withdrawn as to have it withheld, many physicians believe it is ethically and legally less acceptable to withdraw care than to withhold it, as discussed at pages 518-519 in the section on the competent patient. Similarly, even though the patient's right to refuse treatment applies to all medical treatments, whether the decision to withhold or withdraw involves a ventilator, CPR, or a feeding tube, physicians often express a greater reluctance to withdraw some treatments than others, particularly artificial nutrition and hydration. Jesse W. Delaney & James Downar, How Is Life Support Withdrawn in Intensive Care Units? 35 J. Crit. Care 12 (2016).

It is not only physicians who view feeding tubes differently than dialysis, ventilators, or other treatments. Statutory treatment of end-of-life decisions indicates that this view is shared more widely. In one study, researchers found that 20 states set more stringent standards for withdrawal of artificial nutrition and hydration than for withdrawal of other treatments. Carol E. Sieger et al., Refusing Artificial Nutrition and Hydration, 50 J. Am. Geriatrics Soc'y 544 (2002). Not all of those standards have been constitutionally valid. According to an opinion by the Oklahoma Attorney General, Oklahoma's advance directive statute was unconstitutional when it limited the withholding of artificial nutrition and hydration from patients who were terminally ill or persistently unconscious. Okla. Att'y Gen. Op., No. 06-7 (Apr. 6, 2006). In response, the Oklahoma legislature amended its statute to create a presumption that patients wish to have artificial nutrition and hydration provided unless they give contrary directions in an advance directive or leave other clear and convincing evidence of their wishes, their physician knows that the patient would not want these treatments, or it would be futile or inhumane to provide artificial nutrition and hydration. 63 Okla. Stat. tit. 63, §§3080.3-3080.4.

Knowing that physicians may not follow instructions in an advance directive and that they may also impose their views on surrogate decisionmakers, what advice might you give to clients who want to ensure that their wishes are carried out?

For an interesting study of efforts to ensure that patients have advance directives or surrogates, see Daniel P. Kessler & Mark B. McClellan, Advance Directives and Medical Treatment at the End of Life, 23 J. Health Econ. 111 (2004) (finding that state laws with incentives for physicians or hospitals to comply with advance directives reduce the probability of patients dying in an acute care hospital, that laws requiring the appointment of a surrogate in the absence of an advance directive increase the probability of receiving acute care in the last month of life, but decrease the probability of receiving nonacute care, and that neither type of law leads to any savings in medical expenditures).

5. *Patient Self-Determination Act.* The federal government has tried to facilitate advance planning with the enactment of the Patient Self-Determination Act. The Act applies to health care institutions that receive Medicare or Medicaid funds. Under the Act, people must be informed of their rights regarding medical decisionmaking, including the right to refuse life-sustaining treatment, when they are admitted to a hospital or nursing home, come under the care of a home health agency or hospice, or enroll in a health maintenance organization (HMO). These institutions must also inquire as to whether patients have an advance directive and document any directive in the patient's medical record. The institutions must ensure that they are in compliance with state law regarding advance directives and must not condition their provision of care on whether a patient has an advance directive.

Studies during the first 15 years after passage of the Patient Self-Determination Act generally suggested a limited impact of the Act and problems with compliance by health care facilities. More recent data show very good compliance by facilities. General Accounting Office, Advance Directives: Information on Federal Oversight, Provider Implementation and Prevalence, GAO-15-416 (Apr. 2015). In addition, it is possible that the Act has contributed to the significant increase in completion of advance directives in recent years by dying patients.

6. *Physician Orders for Life-Sustaining Treatment.* If treatment can be withdrawn based on clear and convincing evidence of the patient's wishes, does it matter whether the wishes are documented by the patient or by someone else?

Physicians can create advance directives for their patients by documenting patient preferences in their medical records. While this option followed from principles of end-of-life law, states also have passed statutes recognizing "physician orders for life-sustaining treatment" or POLST. POLST translate the general guidance that patients might provide in a living will into specific physician orders regarding treatment. Because POLST take the form of physician orders, they have the potential for being more effective than patient-written advance directives in carrying out the patient's wishes. In particular, POLST address the problem of physicians overriding patient advance directives (discussed, supra, note 4).

7. *Enforcement of the Legal Standards.* As discussed at pages 528 and 568-569, end-of-life decisions may be driven more by the physician's views or the hospital's legal defensiveness than by the patient's preferences. One way to address the failure to follow patients' wishes is to hold physicians and institutions liable in tort suits when they ignore the patient's preferences. Individuals or their families have sued providers for administering unwanted life-sustaining treatment, but courts have generally refused to impose liability.

In an Ohio case, for example, the patient, a Mr. Winter, had stated his desire not to be resuscitated in the event of cardiac arrest. He wanted to avoid the fate of his wife, whose health seriously deteriorated after she received cardiopulmonary resuscitation (CPR). Mr. Winter's physician wrote a do-not-resuscitate (DNR) order in the medical chart, but Mr. Winter was resuscitated nevertheless. Two days later, Mr. Winter suffered a stroke, and he required nursing home care until his death two years later. The court permitted nominal damages only for the battery of receiving unwanted CPR, holding that the stroke was not a direct result of the CPR. Anderson v. St. Francis-St. George Hospital, 671 N.E.2d 225 (Ohio 1996).

Maryland's supreme court also rejected a claim based on wrongful administration of life-sustaining care. In Wright v. Johns Hopkins Health Systems Corp., 728 A.2d 166 (Md. 1999), a man with HIV disease, Robert Lee Wright, Jr., had executed a living will declining life-sustaining care, and he had also requested a DNR order on the hospital's HIV Case Management Plan of Care. More than a year later, when he was terminally ill with AIDS, Mr. Wright received a blood transfusion on what was supposed to be the final day of a three-day hospitalization for treatment of his AIDS. Immediately following the transfusion, Wright suffered a cardiac arrest and was resuscitated despite his advance planning. The cardiac arrest left him with severe brain damage, and he died ten days later, still in the hospital. The court upheld summary judgment in favor of the hospital on two grounds. First, by its language, the living will took effect when Wright had been "certified [to have] a terminal condition by two (2) physicians," and that certification had not occurred. Id. at 175. Second, although Wright had requested a DNR order, hospital policy set forth the physician's responsibility to discuss the withholding of CPR when patients had an irreversible disease and death was imminent or there was a high probability of cardiac arrest during the current hospitalization. Although Wright's life expectancy was less than six months, his death was not imminent. Id. at 177.

Other cases rejecting damages include Duarte v. Chino Community Hospital, 85 Cal. Rptr. 2d 521 (Ct. App. 1999); Taylor v. Muncie Medical Investors, 727 N.E.2d

466, 471 (Ind. Ct. App. 2000). For a case rejecting a lawsuit by parents for the undesired resuscitation of a premature infant, see Miller v. HCA, Inc., 118 S.W.3d 758 (Tex. 2003).

Courts have not only been reluctant to authorize damages for the imposition of unwanted life-sustaining treatment, they have sometimes required families to pay hospital bills that accrued during the time between the family's request that treatment be stopped and the issuance of a court order upholding the family's request. Grace Plaza of Great Neck, Inc. v. Elbaum, 623 N.E.2d 513 (N.Y. 1993); First Healthcare Corp. v. Rettinger, 467 S.E.2d 243 (N.C. 1996).

But the cases go in both directions. While some courts have rejected damages, others have permitted them. See, e.g., Gragg v. Calandra, 696 N.E.2d 1282 (Ill. Ct. App. 1998); Scheible v. Joseph L. Morse Geriatric Center, Inc., 988 So. 2d 1130 (Fla. Ct. App. 2008).

Since some of the courts' reluctance to award damages reflected a sense that the law regarding withdrawal of treatment was not well established when the cases arose, courts may become more willing to allow damages for the unwanted imposition of treatment. In Doctors Hospital of Augusta v. Alicea, 788 S.E.2d 392 (Ga. 2016), for example, the Georgia Supreme Court rejected a claim of statutory immunity by the defendants when they failed to comply with a surrogate decisionmaker's instructions. Even when damages are permitted, tort law principles often will yield low recoveries, but there are exceptions. Andrew J. Broder, "She Don't Want No Life Support," 75 U. Det. Mercy L. Rev. 595 (1998) (reporting a jury award in excess of $16 million, reduced to $1.43 million by the trial court, and ultimately settled while the appeal was pending).

Why do you suppose that some courts have been reluctant to impose damages in these cases?

Courts' reluctance to award damages for unwanted life-sustaining treatment may explain in part why some hospitals will not honor a patient's request to discontinue treatment in the absence of a court order. Court cases arise even when the patient's wishes and the law clearly support withdrawal. See, e.g., Bartling v. Superior Court, 209 Cal. Rptr. 220 (Ct. App. 1984) (hospital refused to remove ventilator upon request of competent adult patient). To some extent, the hospitals are likely acting on the basis of religious or other moral scruples. It may also be the case that the hospital's attorneys view the legal risks, however minimal, as existing primarily on the side of withdrawing treatment. As discussed at page 528, regarding the ethical integrity of the medical profession, even though no physician or hospital has been held civilly or criminally liable for withdrawing life-sustaining treatment at the behest of the patient or family, criminal charges were lodged against two physicians in Barber v. Superior Court, 195 Cal. Rptr. 478 (Ct. App. 1983). Moreover, most lawyers would probably prefer to explain to a jury why they kept someone alive too long than why they let someone die prematurely.

For a related issue, consider "wrongful life" and "wrongful birth" causes of action when a child is born with a disability that could have been detected with prenatal screening. This issue is discussed at pages 417-418.

8. *Further Reading.* On **advance directives** (notes 1 and 2), see Norman L. Cantor, Advance Directives and the Pursuit of Death with Dignity (1993); Lesley S. Castillo et al., Lost in Translation: The Unintended Consequences of Advance Directive Law on Clinical Care, 154 Ann. Intern. Med. 121 (2011); Rebecca Dresser, Precommitment:

A Misguided Strategy for Securing Death with Dignity, 81 Tex. L. Rev. 1823 (2003); Angela Fagerlin & Carl E. Schneider, Enough: The Failure of the Living Will, 34(2) Hastings Center Rep. 30 (2004); Leslie Francis, The Evanescence of Living Wills, 14 J. Contemp. L. 27 (1988); Bernard Lo & Robert Steinbrook, Resuscitating Advance Directives, 164 Arch. Intern. Med. 1501 (2004); David Orentlicher, Advance Medical Directives, 263 JAMA 2365 (1990); Symposium, Advance Directive Instruments for End-of-Life and Health Care Decision Making, 4 Psychol. Pub. Pol'y & L. 579 (1998); Katherine Taylor, Compelling Pregnancy at Death's Door, 7 Colum. J. Gender & L. 85 (1997); Joan M. Teno et al., Association Between Advance Directives and Quality of End-of-Life Care, 55 J. Am. Geriatrics Soc'y 189 (2007).

On **respect for patient choices** (note 4), see Susan Adler Channick, The Myth of Autonomy at the End-of-Life, 44 Vill. L. Rev. 577 (1999); Kenneth E. Covinsky et al., Communication and Decision-Making in Seriously Ill Patients, 48(5) J. Am. Geriatrics Soc'y S187 (2000) (reporting that physicians wrote DNR orders for only 52 percent of patients who said they did not want CPR and that physicians frequently misjudged patient willingness to live in a nursing home); Karen Detering et al., The Impact of Advance Care Planning on End of Life Care in Elderly Patients, 340 BMJ c1345 (2010); Erika R. Manu et al., Advance Directives and Care Received by Older Nursing Home Residents, 34 Amer. J. Hospice & Palliative Med. 105 (2017); David Orentlicher, The Illusion of Patient Choice in End-of-Life Decisions, 267 JAMA 2101, 2101-2102 (1992); Maria J. Silveira, Advance Directives and Outcomes of Surrogate Decision Making Before Death, 362 New Eng. J. Med. 1211 (2010); Maria J. Silveira et al., Advance Directive Completion by Elderly Americans, 62 J. Amer. Geriatrics Soc. 706 (2014).

On the **Patient-Self Determination Act** (note 5), see John La Puma, David Orentlicher & Robert J. Moss, Advance Directives on Admission, 266 JAMA 402 (1991); Practicing the PSDA: A Hastings Center Report Special Supplement, 21(5) Hastings Center Rep. S1-S16 (1991); Susan M. Wolf et al., Sources of Concern About the Patient Self-Determination Act, 325 New Eng. J. Med. 1666 (1991).

On **POLST** (note 6), see Susan E. Hickman et al., Use of the Physician Orders for Life-Sustaining Treatment Program in the Clinical Setting, 63 J. Am. Geriatrics Soc. 341 (2015); Diane Meier & Larry Beresford, POLST Offers Next State in Honoring Patient Preferences, 12 J. Palliative Med. 291 (2009). (While POLST is the original name, states have chosen a variety of names, including Medical Order for Life-Sustaining Treatment (MOLST) and Physician Order Regarding Treatment (PORT). Alan Meisel, Kathy L. Cerminara & Thaddeus M. Pope, The Right to Die §1A.07[D] (3d ed. 2009 Supp.). For a cautionary view, see Kendra A. Moore et al., The Problems with Physician Orders for Life-Sustaining Treatment, 315 JAMA 259 (2016).

On **liability for failing to honor an advance directive** (note 7), see Holly Fernandez Lynch et al., Compliance with Advance Directives, 29 J. Leg. Med. 133 (2008); Rose Gasner, Financial Penalties for Failing to Honor Patient Wishes to Refuse Treatment, 11 St. Louis U. Pub. L. Rev. 499 (1992); Alan Meisel, Kathy L. Cerminara & Thaddeus M. Pope, The Right to Die §11.01[A] (3d ed. 2017 Supp.); Adam A. Milani, Better Off Dead Than Disabled?, 54 Wash. & Lee L. Rev. 149 (1997); Philip G. Peters, Jr., The Illusion of Autonomy at the End of Life, 45 UCLA L. Rev. 673 (1998); Thaddeus Mason Pope, Legal Briefing: New Penalties for Disregarding Advance Directives and Do-Not-Resuscitate Orders, 28 J. Clin. Ethics 74 (2017).

Problems: Interpreting and Drafting Advance Directives

1. Karen Thomas was a 65-year-old woman with a severe narrowing of her left carotid artery (one of the two main arteries that carries blood to the brain). Because of the high risk of a disabling stroke, her physician recommended surgery to correct the narrowing. When he explained that there was a small risk that the surgery itself would precipitate a stroke or heart attack, Ms. Thomas told her physician about her living will. Four years earlier, after her husband had died of a prolonged illness, Ms. Thomas had executed the will, and she told her surgeon that she wished her will to be carried out in the event that she became incapacitated as a result of the surgery. She also told the surgeon that she considered life to be worth living only if she could live independently. Her living will included the following passage:

> If a situation should arise in which there is no reasonable expectation of my recovery from physical or mental disability, I request that I be allowed to die and not be kept alive by artificial means or heroic measures. I do not fear death itself as much as the indignities of deterioration, dependence, and hopeless pain. I therefore ask that medications be mercifully administered to me to alleviate suffering, even though this may hasten the moment of death. This request is made after careful consideration. I hope that you who care for me will feel morally bound to follow its mandate.

Ms. Thomas's surgery went well, and she awoke with full neurological function. However, shortly thereafter, she began to experience progressively worsening weakness on her right side and other abnormalities consistent with a serious stroke on the left side of her brain. She was taken back to the operating room, and her surgeons removed a large clot in a main artery that delivers blood to the left side of the brain. Nevertheless, Ms. Thomas continued to manifest signs of a severe stroke, with paralysis of her right side and loss of consciousness with responsiveness only to painful stimuli. Over the next week, Ms. Thomas showed no improvement in her condition, and, because of a pneumonia, needed a ventilator to ensure adequate oxygenation. Ms. Thomas's brother reminded the hospital of her living will and requested that the ventilator be discontinued. Her physician asked for a neurology consult, and the neurologists indicated that it could take several months before her ultimate prognosis became clear. They felt there was a 10 percent chance that she could recover most of her mental and physical capacity, although she might always need a wheelchair, a 30 percent chance that she would die without recovering consciousness, and a 60 percent chance that she would be seriously and permanently disabled. If you were the hospital's attorney, and Ms. Thomas's physician asked for your guidance, what would you say and/or do? (This case is a modified version of a case presented in Stuart J. Eisendrath & Albert R. Jonsen, The Living Will: Help or Hindrance?, 249 JAMA 2054 (1983).)

2. As an exercise to promote understanding of advance directives, you will serve as the "attorney" of a layperson you know and assist your "client" in filling out an advance directive. The exercise also requires you to write a one-page, single-spaced report about the reasoning behind the choices made and your impressions of the process. Your responsibility is to help your client understand the advance directive process and reach some resolution of the necessary decisions (e.g., whom to appoint as an agent, in what circumstances treatment may be withdrawn). If

the person you approach is willing to discuss these decisions with you but unwilling to commit to any definitive answers, that is all right. Just leave the form blank and explain the client's reasoning in your report. It is your responsibility to select an advance directive form to be used. You may want to use the statutory form for your state, which you can find in your state's statutory code, or you may want to use a generic form. The Web site for this book (www.health-law.org) also has a list of discussion questions you may want to use with your client. After your completed advance directive and one-page report are due, you will be given a patient scenario. You should then write down what would be the effect of your client's advance directive and ask your client whether that effect is consistent with what the client would want done if the client were ever in the condition described in the scenario. If it is unclear what outcome would result from the advance directive, or if the result would depend on information not available, then you should indicate that such is the case.

Notes: Young Children and Adolescents (Not Competent)

1. *Presumption of Parental Authority.* As mentioned at page 533, parents generally have authority to make medical decisions, including decisions about life-sustaining medical treatment on behalf of their children. The usual standard for parental decisionmaking is a best interests standard. Alan Meisel, Kathy L. Cerminara & Thaddeus M. Pope, The Right to Die §9.05[A] (3d ed. 2016 Supp.). The child's lack of decisionmaking capacity precludes the adoption of a standard based solely on the child's wishes. Still, one can consider the child's desires even if they are not determinative. Over time, courts have refined the best interests standard for children, as illustrated by the following standard from California:

> We conclude that a court making the decision of whether to withhold or withdraw life-sustaining medical treatment from a dependent child should consider the following factors: (1) the child's present levels of physical, sensory, emotional and cognitive functioning; (2) the quality of life, life expectancy and prognosis for recovery with and without treatment, including the futility of continued treatment; (3) the various treatment options, and the risks, side effects, and benefits of each; (4) the nature and degree of physical pain or suffering resulting from the medical condition; (5) whether the medical treatment being provided is causing or may cause pain, suffering, or serious complications; (6) the pain or suffering to the child if the medical treatment is withdrawn; (7) whether any particular treatment would be proportionate or disproportionate in terms of the benefits to be gained by the child versus the burdens caused to the child; (8) the likelihood that pain or suffering resulting from withholding or withdrawal of treatment could be avoided or minimized; (9) the degree of humiliation, dependence and loss of dignity resulting from the condition and treatment; (10) the opinions of the family, the reasons behind those opinions, and the reasons why the family either has no opinion or cannot agree on a course of treatment; (11) the motivations of the family in advocating a particular course of treatment; and (12) the child's preference, if it can be ascertained, for treatment. [In re Christopher I, 106 Cal. App. 4th 533, 551 (Ct. App. 2003) (followed by J. N. v. Superior Court, 156 Cal. App. 4th 523, 534 (Ct. App. 2007).]

As the best interests standard suggests, parents will be denied authority to refuse life-sustaining treatment in some situations. The classic cases are those involving families of Jehovah's Witnesses where the children need blood transfusions and their parents decline the transfusions on religious grounds. In those cases, the courts have held that the children must be given the transfusions. See, e.g., In re McCauley, 565 N.E.2d 411 (Mass. 1991) (eight-year-old child needed blood transfusion as part of treatment for an acute leukemia); In re Cabrera, 552 A.2d 1114 (Pa. Super. Ct. 1989) (six-year-old child with sickle cell anemia who had already suffered two strokes needed weekly blood transfusions over at least a year's time to reduce the risk of a recurrence of her strokes from 70 percent to 10 percent). In ordering treatment, the courts typically cite Prince v. Massachusetts, 321 U.S. 158, 170 (1944), where the Court wrote:

> Parents may be free to become martyrs themselves. But it does not follow they are free, in identical circumstances, to make martyrs of their children before they have reached the age of full and legal discretion when they can make that choice for themselves.

As the *Prince* excerpt indicates, the theory of these cases is that the children must be given an opportunity to reach adulthood to decide for themselves which religious tenets they will follow. What is the problem with this theory?

2. *Applying the Best Interests Standard to Children.* The hard question in this area is where the limits of parental authority end, and when a refusal of treatment becomes child neglect or abuse. At either end of the spectrum, the law is fairly clear.

Courts have had no trouble holding that, when a child can readily be restored to good health or when treatment poses little risk, parents may *not* refuse a life-sustaining treatment, such as a blood transfusion (*McCauley* and *Cabrera*, supra, In re L.S., 87 P.3d 521 (Nev. 2004)), antibiotics (Walker v. Superior Court, 763 P.2d 852 (Cal. 1988) (upholding conviction of Christian Science parents of involuntary manslaughter for withholding treatment for meningitis from nine-month-old child)), or abdominal surgery (Commonwealth v. Twitchell, 617 N.E.2d 609 (Mass. 1993) (finding that Christian Science parents were not entitled to withhold intestinal surgery from their two-year-old child, but overturning their conviction for involuntary manslaughter on grounds that they were prevented from presenting the affirmative defense that they were misled as to their risk of prosecution by an opinion of the state's Attorney General)). For another case in which statutory ambiguity resulted in a dropping of charges, see Hermanson v. State, 604 So. 2d 775 (Fla. 1992).

Similarly, courts have had no trouble holding that parents *may* refuse life-sustaining ventilators or feeding tubes when the child is irreversibly unconscious. See, e.g., In re L.H.R., 321 S.E.2d 716 (Ga. 1984) (permitting the removal of a ventilator from a several-month-old child in an irreversible coma); In re P.V.W., 424 So. 2d 1015 (La. 1982) (permitting the removal of artificial life supports from an infant who had been irreversibly comatose since birth); In re Guardianship of Crum, 580 N.E.2d 876 (Ohio Prob. Ct. 1991) (permitting the removal of a feeding tube from a 17-year-old who was irreversibly unconscious); In re Guardianship of Myers, 610 N.E.2d 663 (Ohio Prob. Ct. 1993) (permitting the removal of a feeding tube from a minor, apparently an adolescent, who was irreversibly unconscious).

Other decisions, however, are not so clear. Some treatments will have a low likelihood of success and may carry substantial risks. As the following cases indicate, the courts have not come to a consensus on the extent of parental discretion:

Newmark v. Williams, 588 A.2d 1108 (Del. 1991). A three-year-old boy was diagnosed as having an aggressive malignancy of the immune system, Burkitt's lymphoma. By the time a diagnosis was made during surgery for an intestinal obstruction, the cancer had spread elsewhere in the boy's body. His physician recommended that he be treated with a heavy regimen of chemotherapy. According to the medical testimony, there was a 40 percent chance of a "cure." Without treatment, he would likely die within six to eight months. Medical testimony also indicated that the treatment itself was quite toxic and might prove fatal. The boy's parents declined the chemotherapy in favor of care from a Christian Science practitioner. Given the substantial risks of treatment and the less than 50 percent chance of success, the court upheld the parental refusal of treatment.

In re Hamilton, 657 S.W.2d 425 (Tenn. Ct. App. 1983). A 12-year-old girl was diagnosed with Ewing's sarcoma, a bone cancer for which the girl had a 25 to 50 percent chance of long-term remission with treatment. Without treatment, she would likely die within six to nine months. Her father, a lay minister of the Church of God of the Union Assembly, refused treatment on religious grounds. Given the apparent certainty of death without treatment, and the reasonable possibility of long-term success with treatment, the court overrode the parental refusal of treatment. The court seemed to consider the fact that the family's religious sect did not refuse all kinds of medical treatment.

In re Hofbauer, 393 N.E.2d 1009 (N.Y. 1979). A seven-year-old boy developed Hodgkin's lymphoma, and his parents rejected conventional radiation and chemotherapy in favor of metabolic therapy, which included injections of laetrile. The parents explained that they were concerned about the side effects of conventional treatment and that they would agree to conventional therapy if the boy's physician, who was a proponent of metabolic therapy, so advised. The physician testified that the boy was responding well to the metabolic therapy and indicated that he would use conventional treatment if there was a significant deterioration in the boy's condition. The court found that, given these considerations, the family was acting reasonably.

Custody of a Minor, 393 N.E.2d 836 (Mass. 1979). A three-year-old boy was being treated with conventional medical therapy for an acute leukemia, and the leukemia was in remission with a chance of cure as high as 80 percent. However, the boy's parents decided to discontinue his chemotherapy and substitute metabolic therapy, involving the daily taking of enzymes, laetrile, and megadoses of vitamins. The child's leukemia reappeared, and the trial court ordered resumption of conventional chemotherapy, whereupon the leukemia went back into remission, albeit with the chance of cure now at 50 percent. The parents agreed to continue with conventional chemotherapy but also wanted to continue with the metabolic therapy. The trial court ordered the parents to stop the metabolic therapy. The state supreme court affirmed the trial court's order, observing that the metabolic therapy was not only ineffective in treating the leukemia but also posed significant risks of toxicity from the megadoses of vitamins and from the laetrile. In particular, noted the court, laetrile can be broken down in the body to cyanide, leading to chronic cyanide poisoning and eventually to blindness, deafness, and an inability to walk.

In re Phillip B., 156 Cal. Rptr. 48 (Ct. App. 1979). A 12-year-old boy with Down syndrome suffered from a congenital heart defect that, without surgical correction, would result in gradually worsening incapacity and, ultimately, an early death. The parents opposed surgery. Because of the child's Down syndrome and the fact that his heart defect had caused changes in his lung's blood vessels over time, his risk of death from the surgery—5 to 10 percent—was higher than usual, and he had a higher than usual risk of postoperative complications. Because of the child's elevated risks from surgery, the court upheld the parents' decision to refuse surgery. (Subsequently, volunteers at a facility where Phillip B. resided successfully petitioned to become his guardians and for authorization for medical testing, Guardianship of Phillip B., 188 Cal. Rptr. 781 (Ct. App. 1983).)

Which of these court decisions do you think are correctly decided?

For other interesting cases, see In re Nicholas E., 720 A.2d 562 (Me. 1998) (permitting mother to refuse aggressive antiviral drug therapy to treat HIV infection in her four-year-old son); In re Gianelli, 834 N.Y.S.2d 623 (N.Y. Sup. Ct. 2007) (denying parents' request to withdraw ventilator from a 14-year-old child who had a lethal genetic disease and a life expectancy of no more than two years but who was still "aware and enjoy[ed] TV and videos"); In re Martin F. v. D. L., 820 N.Y.S.2d 759 (N.Y. Sup. Ct. 2006) (deferring to parent's refusal of antipsychotic drug for three-year-old child). For two cases imposing treatment for cancers that can be quite responsive to treatment, see In re Cassandra C., 112 A.3d 158 (Conn. 2015) (Hodgkin's lymphoma); P. J. ex rel Jensen v. Wagner, 603 F.3d 1182 (10th Cir. 2010) (Ewing's sarcoma).

Many states provide exemptions in their child abuse and neglect laws for parents who refuse medical treatment on religious grounds. In some of these states, the exemptions excuse parents from liability when their children suffer from the denial of care, though generally not when the child's life is endangered. But courts often read the exemptions narrowly, relying on a couple of theories. First, many of the exemptions state that parents cannot be held accountable "solely" for relying on prayer, or for relying on prayer "alone," rather than on medical care, so liability can be upheld on the ground that the charges are brought because of the harm rather than because of the use of prayer. In addition, the exemptions typically apply to child and abuse laws but not so often to other laws under which parents may be held accountable, such as involuntary manslaughter statutes. State v. Neumann, 832 N.W. 2d 560 (Wis. 2013). And of course, the exemptions speak to the ability of the state to punish parents. Even if a court cannot sanction the parents, it still may order that treatment be provided to the child. Indeed, the federal regulation that led to the adoption of the religious exemptions explicitly drew a line between holding parents liable and ensuring access to care for children. The regulation, which no longer is in effect, tied federal funding for child abuse programs to the enactment of religious exemptions. But the regulation also stated that the exemptions "shall not preclude a court from ordering that medical services be provided to the child, where his health requires it." And state law exemptions typically track this requirement. In practice, though, the judicial power to order treatment may not provide adequate protection for children.

3. Further Reading. Good discussions of this topic include Annamaria Del Buono, Living on a Prayer, 17 Rutgers J. L. & Religion 449 (2016); Erwin Chemerinsky & Michele Goodwin, Religion Is Not a Basis for Harming Others, 104 Geo. L. J.

1111 (2016); Joseph Goldstein, Medical Care for the Child at Risk, 86 Yale L. J. 645 (1977); Martin T. Harvey, Adolescent Competency and the Refusal of Medical Treatment, 13 Health Matrix 297 (2003); David Orentlicher, Law, Religion, and Health Care, 8 UC Irvine L. Rev. (2018); Jennifer L. Rosato, Using Bioethics Discourse to Determine When Parents Should Make Health Care Decisions for Their Children, 73 Temp. L. Rev. 1 (2000); Lainie Ross, Children, Families, and Health Care Decision Making (1998); Walter Wadlington, Medical Decision Making for and by Children, 1994 U. Ill. L. Rev. 311.

Notes: Severely Disabled Newborns

1. *Historical Background and Congressional Action.* Treatment of severely disabled newborns generated considerable debate in the 1980s in conjunction with several celebrated cases in which parents sought to withhold life-sustaining treatment from children born with Down syndrome or other, more serious conditions. One case involved the death in 1982 of a Bloomington, Indiana, infant with Down syndrome. The child suffered from several congenital abnormalities associated with Down syndrome, including an esophageal obstruction that prevented oral feeding but that could have been corrected by surgery. The parents declined surgery, and the child died after a trial court and the local Child Protection Committee upheld the parents' decision. In response to the case, the U.S. Department of Health and Human Services adopted rules under the Rehabilitation Act of 1973 to regulate treatment decisions for severely disabled newborns, but the Supreme Court invalidated the rules as not justified by any evidence that such persons were being discriminated against in the provision of health care. Bowen v. American Hospital Association, 476 U.S. 610 (1986).

Also in response to the controversy generated by the Bloomington case, Congress enacted provisions of the Child Abuse Amendments of 1984 to address concerns about the "withholding of medically indicated treatment from disabled infants with life-threatening conditions." 42 U.S.C.A. §5106a(b)(10) (West 1995) (now §5106a(b)(2)(B)). Regulations adopted under this legislation are in effect; the regulations condition federal grants for child abuse prevention on whether states establish programs or procedures to respond to cases of alleged "medical neglect." (45 C.F.R. §1340.15). As to the definition of medical neglect,

> The term "medical neglect" includes, but is not limited to, the withholding of medically indicated treatment from a disabled infant with a life-threatening condition.
>
> The term "withholding of medically indicated treatment" means the failure to respond to the infant's life-threatening conditions by providing treatment . . . which, in the treating physician's . . . reasonable medical judgment, will be most likely to be effective in ameliorating or correcting all such conditions, except that the term does not include the failure to provide treatment (other than appropriate nutrition, hydration, or medication) to an infant when, in the treating physician's . . . reasonable medical judgment any of the following circumstances apply:
>
> (i) The infant is chronically and irreversibly comatose;
>
> (ii) The provision of such treatment would merely prolong dying, not be effective in ameliorating or correcting all of the infant's life-threatening conditions, or otherwise be futile in terms of the survival of the infant; or

(iii) The provision of such treatment would be virtually futile in terms of the survival of the infant and the treatment itself under such circumstances would be inhumane. [45 C.F.R. §1340.15(b).]

In the interpretive guidelines to these regulations, the Department of Health and Human Services observed that the "third key feature" of the definition of "withholding of medically indicated treatment" is "that even when one of [the] three circumstances is present, and thus failure to provide treatment is not a 'withholding of medically indicated treatment,' the infant must nonetheless be provided with appropriate nutrition, hydration, and medication." 45 C.F.R. pt. 1340, app.

While the interpretive guidelines suggest that nutrition and hydration may never be withheld from a newborn, some commentators have argued that there is ambiguity in the qualifying use of "appropriate" before "nutrition, hydration, and medication." One could interpret the term as meaning that nutrition and hydration must be provided and that the way in which it is provided must be appropriate for the child (e.g., the composition of the feedings must meet the dietary needs of the child or the method of feeding, by oral feeding or a feeding tube, must be tailored to the child's condition). Alternatively, one could interpret "appropriate" as meaning that nutrition and hydration must be provided only when it is appropriate given the child's overall medical condition and that, for some newborns, parents may reasonably conclude that artificial nutrition and hydration should be withdrawn. Lawrence J. Nelson et al., Forgoing Medically Provided Nutrition and Hydration in Pediatric Patients, 23 J. L. Med. & Ethics 33, 40-41 (1995).

The reach of the federal regulations is limited because it is a condition for grants, not a substantive standard directly applicable to parents, physicians, or hospitals. Indeed, as indicated in the previous notes section, courts do permit parents to decline artificial nutrition and hydration for their irreversibly unconscious children. Moreover, while there have been cases in which the regulations were at issue, the courts generally have concluded that the parents could proceed with their decision to decline treatment. In re AMB, 640 N.W.2d 262 (Mich. Ct. App. 2001) (finding the Child Abuse Amendments inapplicable for a newborn with heart defects incompatible with long-term survival); Mary A. Crossley, Of Diagnoses and Discrimination, 93 Colum. L. Rev. 1581, 1613-1614 n.134 (1993) (describing a case in which parents could decline CPR for a child who was irreversibly unconscious and a case in which parents could decline ventilation for a terminally ill child with severe mental and physical disabilities); Carol R. Leicher & Francis J. DiMario, Termination of Nutrition and Hydration in a Child with Vegetative State, 148 Arch. Pediatr. Adolesc. Med. 87 (1994) (describing a case in which parents could decline artificial nutrition and hydration for a permanently unconscious child).

However, a decision by a Wisconsin court of appeals took a strict view of the Child Abuse Amendments. In a case involving a child born after 23 weeks of gestation who was given maximal life-prolonging treatment, the parents sued, claiming that they were not sufficiently informed of their child's prognosis when they agreed to some of the life-saving measures. The court rejected the parents' claim, concluding that under both the Amendments and Wisconsin end-of-life law, the parents did not have the right to refuse life-sustaining treatment for their infant. Montalvo v. Borkovec, 647 N.W.2d 413 (Wis. Ct. App. 2002).

Even if courts defer to parental decisions, parental wishes may be frustrated by the unwillingness of physicians to withdraw or withhold care, either out of personal conviction or because of a belief that the federal regulations mandate care. Early data suggested that the regulations were having a significant impact on physician practices. In a survey of pediatric neurologists, researchers found that 75 percent of the responders stated that "they 'never' recommend the withholding of fluids and nutrition." Stephen Ashwal et al., The Persistent Vegetative State in Children: Report of the Child Neurology Society Ethics Committee, 32 Ann. Neurol. 570, 573 (1992). In a survey in which neonatologists were asked to consider cases of infants with a short life expectancy and severe neurologic disabilities, many responders reported that the federal regulations required the provision of treatment that was not in the best interests of the child. Many also reported that the regulations had led them to change their practices. Loretta M. Kopelman et al., Neonatologists Judge the "Baby Doe" Regulations, 318 New Eng. J. Med. 677 (1988). More recent reports suggest that there may not have been a substantial impact overall from the Child Abuse Amendments on clinical practice. Charity Scott, Baby Doe at Twenty-Five, 25 Ga. St. U. L. Rev. 801, 807-811 (2009).

For a discussion of the potential use of EMTALA (the federal law providing a right to emergency medical care, see Chapter 2.A.1) to override parental decision-making, see Sadath A. Sayeed, The Marginally Viable Newborn: Legal Challenges, Conceptual Inadequacies, and Reasonableness, 34 J. L. Med. & Ethics 600 (2006) (discussing the interaction of EMTALA with the Born Alive Infant Protection Act of 2002).

2. *Rehabilitation Act and Americans with Disabilities Act.* While there has not been much litigation over the regulations implementing the Child Abuse Amendments of 1984, there has been some important litigation of treatment decisions for severely disabled newborns under §504 of the Rehabilitation Act of 1973. Section 504 prohibits recipients of federal funds from discriminating against "otherwise qualified" disabled persons solely on the basis of their disability. 29 U.S.C. §794. The Americans with Disabilities Act of 1990 extends the protections of §504 to virtually all health care settings. In the §504 cases, the claim is that denying treatment to the newborn is an unlawful act of discrimination. In these cases, the courts have permitted the withholding of treatment. For example, in United States v. University Hospital, 729 F.2d 144 (2d Cir. 1984), the issue was whether surgery could be withheld from an infant with spina bifida, a condition of variable severity in which there is incomplete closure of the tissues surrounding the spinal cord. In this case, the infant had serious physical problems like impaired bowel and bladder function and was thought to have such compromised mental function that she would "never interact with her environment or other people." Id. at 146. The surgery, which would have closed the opening in her spine and implanted a shunt to drain excessive fluid buildup in her brain, was likely to prolong the infant's life but not do anything to treat her disabilities. A state appellate court had refused to intervene, noting that, while the surgery would enhance the infant's chances of living, it also might aggravate her disabilities. In also refusing to intervene, the Second Circuit wrote:

> *Doe* [v. New York University, 666 F.2d 761 (2d Cir. 1981),] establishes that §504 prohibits discrimination against a handicapped individual only where the individual's handicap is unrelated to, and thus improper to consideration of, the services

in question. As defendants here point out, however, where medical treatment is at issue, it is typically the handicap itself that give rise to, or at least contributes to, the need for services. Defendants thus argue, and with some force, that the "otherwise qualified" criterion of §504 cannot be meaningfully applied to a medical treatment decision. Similarly, defendants argue that it would be pointless to inquire whether a patient who was affected by a medical treatment decision, was "solely by reason of his handicap . . . subjected to discrimination."

. . . Where the handicapping condition is related to the condition(s) to be treated, it will rarely, if ever, be possible to say with certainty that a particular decision was "discriminatory."

729 F.2d at 156-157. See also Johnson v. Thompson, 971 F.2d 1487 (10th Cir. 1992) (finding no violation of §504 when surgery was withheld from children with spina bifida).

In the end, the parents in *University Hospital* agreed to have a shunt implanted to drain the fluid in their daughter's brain, although the surgery was delayed because of an infection that was likely related to the opening in her spine. The child, Keri-Lynn, has done much better than predicted. Although she is confined to a wheelchair and developmentally disabled, she can talk, and by age 30 in 2013, she was living in a group home Monday through Friday taking academic classes and receiving physical therapy. It is not clear whether surgery to close Keri-Lynn's spine would have improved her outcome. The *University Hospital* decision is excerpted on pages 82-87 and discussed on pages 90-92. The ADA is discussed further in Chapter 9.D.1.

3. *The Role of Physicians.* There have been important changes with respect to parental discretion over the past two decades because of changes in physicians' views as to what constitutes appropriate care for seriously disabled newborns. Partly because advances in medical care are resulting in better outcomes and partly because of changing social attitudes about disabled infants, physicians are becoming more aggressive in recommending treatment. For example, while many physicians once believed it reasonable to withhold surgery to correct an intestinal obstruction in a child with Down syndrome and allow the child to die, it would probably be very difficult today to find a physician taking that position. Sarah Glazer, Born Too Soon, Too Small, Too Sick; Whatever Happened to Baby Doe?, Washington Post, Apr. 2, 1991, at Z8; Betty Wolder Levin et al., Treatment Choice for Infants in the Neonatal Intensive Care Unit at Risk for AIDS, 265 JAMA 2976, 2978 Table 3 (1991). Since courts are likely to defer to physicians as to whether treatment is necessary, the range of parental discretion has been narrowing. Indeed, it is not clear that the *Phillip B.* case discussed at page 577 would come out the same way if it were decided today.

4. *Further Readings.* See "Baby Doe at Twenty-Five" symposium in 25(4) Georgia State Law Review (2008); Target article and commentaries in 11(2) Am. J. Bioethics (2011); Loretta Kopelman, The Best Interests Standard for Incompetent or Incapacitated Patients of All Ages, 35 J. L. Med. & Ethics 187 (2007); Dianne Koller Fine, Government as God, 34 New Eng. L. Rev. 343 (2000); Legislative Workshop, Baby Doe: Problems and Legislative Proposals, 1984 Ariz. St. L. J. 601; Benjamin H. Levi, Withdrawing Nutrition and Hydration from Children, 42 Clin. Pediatr. 139 (2003); Martha Minow, Beyond State Intervention in the Family: For Baby Jane Doe, 18 U. Mich. J. L. Reform 933 (1985); Nancy K. Rhoden, Treatment Dilemmas

for Imperiled Newborns, 58 S. Cal. L. Rev. 1283 (1985); Carl E. Schneider, Rights Discourse and Neonatal Euthanasia, 76 Cal. L. Rev. 151 (1988); George P. Smith, II, Murder, She Wrote or Was It Merely Selective Nontreatment?, 8 J. Contemp. Health L. & Pol'y 49 (1992); Robert F. Weir, Selective Nontreatment of Handicapped Newborns (1984).

B. PHYSICIAN AID IN DYING

We have seen that the competent patient has an almost unlimited right to refuse medical treatment even though death might result. An important question is whether this strong right should be extended to permit a patient to hasten death by taking a lethal dose of a drug.

As a preliminary matter, it is worth considering the different descriptive terms used for this topic. Although courts commonly talk about "physician-assisted suicide," others prefer "physician aid in dying," "death with dignity," or similar terms. Choice of terms depends a good deal on whether one views decisions by dying persons to manage their deaths with self-administered medications as "suicides" or more like decisions to refuse life-sustaining medical treatment. Following the recommendation of the American Public Health Association, this text will use the term "physician aid in dying."

■ WASHINGTON v. GLUCKSBERG
521 U.S. 702 (1997)

REHNQUIST, Chief Justice.

The question presented in this case is whether Washington's prohibition against "causing" or "aiding" a suicide offends the Fourteenth Amendment to the United States Constitution. We hold that it does not.

It has always been a crime to assist a suicide in the state of Washington. In 1854, Washington's first Territorial Legislature outlawed "assisting another in the commission of self-murder." Today, Washington law provides: "A person is guilty of promoting a suicide attempt when he knowingly causes or aids another person to attempt suicide." Wash. Rev. Code §9A.36.060(1) (1994). "Promoting a suicide attempt" is a felony, punishable by up to five years' imprisonment and up to a $10,000 fine. . . .

Petitioners in this case are the state of Washington and its Attorney General. Respondents Harold Glucksberg, M.D., Abigail Halperin, M.D., Thomas A. Preston, M.D., and Peter Shalit, M.D., are physicians who practice in Washington. These doctors occasionally treat terminally ill, suffering patients, and declare that they would assist these patients in ending their lives if not for Washington's assisted-suicide ban. In January 1994, respondents, along with three gravely ill, pseudonymous plaintiffs who have since died and Compassion in Dying, a nonprofit organization that counsels people considering physician-assisted suicide, sued in the United States district court, seeking a declaration that Wash. Rev. Code §9A.36.060(1) (1994) is, on its face, unconstitutional.

The plaintiffs asserted "the existence of a liberty interest protected by the Fourteenth Amendment which extends to a personal choice by a mentally competent, terminally ill adult to commit physician-assisted suicide." . . . [T]he district court agreed and concluded that Washington's assisted-suicide ban is unconstitutional because it "places an undue burden on the exercise of [that] constitutionally protected liberty interest." . . .

A panel of the court of appeals for the Ninth Circuit reversed. . . . Compassion in Dying v. Washington, 49 F.3d 586, 591 (1995). The Ninth Circuit reheard the case en banc, reversed the panel's decision, and affirmed the district court. Compassion in Dying v. Washington, 79 F.3d 790, 798 (1996). . . . The court . . . concluded that "the Constitution encompasses a due process liberty interest in controlling the time and manner of one's death . . ." [and] that the state's assisted-suicide ban was unconstitutional "as applied to terminally ill competent adults who wish to hasten their deaths with medication prescribed by their physicians." . . . We granted certiorari and now reverse.

I

We begin, as we do in all due-process cases, by examining our nation's history, legal traditions, and practices. In almost every state—indeed, in almost every Western democracy—it is a crime to assist a suicide. The states' assisted-suicide bans are not innovations. Rather, they are longstanding expressions of the states' commitment to the protection and preservation of all human life. . . .

More specifically, for over 700 years, the Anglo-American common-law tradition has punished or otherwise disapproved of both suicide and assisting suicide. [The court continues by noting that English law initially treated suicide as a form of murder, with the person's real and personal property being forfeited to the king. Only the personal property was forfeited, however, if the suicide was motivated by serious illness. Beginning in 1701, the colonies, and later the states, rescinded their laws criminalizing suicide because of the unfairness to the decedent's family, rather than out of any acceptance of suicide.]

That suicide remained a grievous, though nonfelonious, wrong is confirmed by the fact that colonial and early state legislatures and courts did not retreat from prohibiting assisting suicide. . . . And the prohibitions against assisting suicide never contained exceptions for those who were near death. . . . By the time the Fourteenth Amendment was ratified, it was a crime in most states to assist a suicide. . . . In this century, the Model Penal Code also prohibited "aiding" suicide, prompting many states to enact or revise their assisted-suicide bans. . . .

The Washington statute at issue in this case, Wash. Rev. Code §9A.36.060 (1994), was enacted in 1975 as part of a revision of that state's criminal code. . . . In 1991, Washington voters rejected a ballot initiative which, had it passed, would have permitted a form of physician-assisted suicide. . . .

California voters rejected an assisted-suicide initiative similar to Washington's in 1993. On the other hand, in 1994, voters in Oregon enacted, also through ballot initiative, that state's "Death with Dignity Act," which legalized physician-assisted suicide for competent, terminally ill adults. Since the Oregon vote, many proposals to legalize assisted-suicide have been and continue to be introduced in the states' legislatures, but none has been enacted. And just last year, Iowa and Rhode Island joined the overwhelming majority of states explicitly prohibiting assisted suicide. . . .

Attitudes toward suicide itself have changed since [the thirteenth century], but our laws have consistently condemned, and continue to prohibit, assisting suicide. . . . Against this backdrop of history, tradition, and practice, we now turn to respondents' constitutional claim.

II

The due process clause guarantees more than fair process, and the "liberty" it protects includes more than the absence of physical restraint. The clause also provides heightened protection against government interference with certain fundamental rights and liberty interests. In a long line of cases, we have held that, in addition to the specific freedoms protected by the Bill of Rights, the "liberty" specially protected by the due process clause includes the rights to marry, to have children, to direct the education and upbringing of one's children, to marital privacy, to use contraception, to bodily integrity, and to abortion. We have also assumed, and strongly suggested, that the due process clause protects the traditional right to refuse unwanted lifesaving medical treatment. *Cruzan*, 497 U.S., at 278-279.

But we "have always been reluctant to expand the concept of substantive due process because guideposts for responsible decisionmaking in this unchartered area are scarce and open-ended." *Collins*, 503 U.S., at 125. By extending constitutional protection to an asserted right or liberty interest, we, to a great extent, place the matter outside the arena of public debate and legislative action. We must therefore "exercise the utmost care whenever we are asked to break new ground in this field," ibid., lest the liberty protected by the due process clause be subtly transformed into the policy preferences of the members of this Court.

Our established method of substantive-due-process analysis has two primary features: First, we have regularly observed that the due process clause specially protects those fundamental rights and liberties which are, objectively, "deeply rooted in this nation's history and tradition," *Moore*, 431 U.S. at 503 (plurality opinion), and "implicit in the concept of ordered liberty," such that "neither liberty nor justice would exist if they were sacrificed," Palko v. Connecticut, 302 U.S. 319, 325, 326 (1937). Second, we have required in substantive-due-process cases a "careful description" of the asserted fundamental liberty interest. *Flores*, 507 U.S. at 302. . . .

Turning to the claim at issue here, the court of appeals stated that "properly analyzed, the first issue to be resolved is whether there is a liberty interest in determining the time and manner of one's death," or, in other words, "is there a right to die?" Similarly, respondents assert a "liberty to choose how to die" and a right to "control of one's final days," and describe the asserted liberty as "the right to choose a humane, dignified death," and "the liberty to shape death." . . .

Respondents contend that in *Cruzan* we "acknowledged that competent, dying persons have the right to direct the removal of life-sustaining medical treatment and thus hasten death" and that "the constitutional principle behind recognizing the patient's liberty to direct the withdrawal of artificial life support applies at least as strongly to the choice to hasten impending death by consuming lethal medication." . . .

The right assumed in *Cruzan*, however, was not simply deduced from abstract concepts of personal autonomy. Given the common-law rule that forced medication was a battery, and the long legal tradition protecting the decision to refuse unwanted medical treatment, our assumption was entirely consistent with this nation's history and constitutional traditions. The decision to commit suicide with the assistance of another may be just as personal and profound as the decision to refuse unwanted medical treatment, but it has never enjoyed similar legal protection. Indeed, the two acts are widely and reasonably regarded as quite distinct. In *Cruzan* itself, we recognized that most states outlawed assisted suicide—and even more do today—and we certainly gave no intimation that the right to refuse unwanted medical treatment could be somehow transmuted into a right to assistance in committing suicide.

Respondents also rely on *Casey*. There, the Court's opinion concluded that "the essential holding of Roe v. Wade should be retained and once again reaffirmed." *Casey*, 505 U.S., at 846. . . . In reaching this conclusion, the opinion discussed in some detail this Court's substantive-due-process tradition of interpreting the due process clause to protect certain fundamental rights and "personal decisions relating to marriage, procreation, contraception, family relationships, child rearing, and education," and noted that many of those rights and liberties "involve the most intimate and personal choices a person may make in a lifetime."

The court of appeals, like the district court, found *Casey* "highly instructive" and "almost prescriptive" for determining "what liberty interest may inhere in a terminally ill person's choice to commit suicide":

> Like the decision of whether or not to have an abortion, the decision how and when to die is one of "the most intimate and personal choices a person may make in a lifetime," a choice "central to personal dignity and autonomy." [79 F.3d, at 813-814.]

Similarly, respondents emphasize the statement in *Casey* that:

> At the heart of liberty is the right to define one's own concept of existence, of meaning, of the universe, and of the mystery of human life. Beliefs about these matters could not define the attributes of personhood were they formed under compulsion of the State. [*Casey*, 505 U.S., at 851.]

By choosing this language, the Court's opinion in *Casey* described, in a general way and in light of our prior cases, those personal activities and decisions that this Court has identified as so deeply rooted in our history and traditions, or so fundamental to our concept of constitutionally ordered liberty, that they are protected by the Fourteenth Amendment. The opinion moved from the recognition that liberty necessarily includes freedom of conscience and belief about ultimate considerations to the observation that "though the abortion decision may originate within the zone of conscience and belief, it is more than a philosophic exercise." *Casey*, 505 U.S., at 852. That many of the rights and liberties protected by the due process clause sound in personal autonomy does not warrant the sweeping conclusion that any and all important, intimate, and personal decisions are so protected, and *Casey* did not suggest otherwise.

The history of the law's treatment of assisted suicide in this country has been and continues to be one of the rejection of nearly all efforts to permit it. That being the case, our decisions lead us to conclude that the asserted "right" to assistance in committing suicide is not a fundamental liberty interest protected by the due process clause. The Constitution also requires, however, that Washington's assisted-suicide ban be rationally related to legitimate government interests. This requirement is unquestionably met here. As the court below recognized, Washington's assisted-suicide ban implicates a number of state interests.

First, Washington has an "unqualified interest in the preservation of human life." The state's prohibition on assisted suicide, like all homicide laws, both reflects and advances its commitment to this interest. . . .

. . . The court of appeals also recognized Washington's interest in protecting life, but held that the "weight" of this interest depends on the "medical condition and the wishes of the person whose life is at stake." Washington, however, has rejected this sliding-scale approach and, through its assisted-suicide ban, insists that all persons' lives, from beginning to end, regardless of physical or mental condition, are under the full protection of the law. As we have previously affirmed, the states "may properly decline to make judgments about the 'quality' of life that a particular individual may enjoy," *Cruzan*, 497 U.S., at 282. This remains true, as *Cruzan* makes clear, even for those who are near death.

Relatedly, all admit that suicide is a serious public-health problem, especially among persons in otherwise vulnerable groups. . . . The state has an interest in preventing suicide, and in studying, identifying, and treating its causes.

Those who attempt suicide—terminally ill or not—often suffer from depression or other mental disorders. Research indicates, however, that many people who request physician-assisted suicide withdraw that request if their depression and pain are treated. The New York Task Force, however, expressed its concern that, because depression is difficult to diagnose, physicians and medical professionals often fail to respond adequately to seriously ill patients' needs. Thus, legal physician-assisted suicide could make it more difficult for the state to protect depressed or mentally ill persons, or those who are suffering from untreated pain, from suicidal impulses.

The state also has an interest in protecting the integrity and ethics of the medical profession. In contrast to the court of appeals' conclusion that "the integrity of the medical profession would [not] be threatened in any way by [physician-assisted suicide]," the American Medical Association, like many other medical and physicians' groups, has concluded that "physician-assisted suicide is fundamentally incompatible with the physician's role as healer." American Medical Association, Code of Ethics §2.211 (1994). And physician-assisted suicide could, it is argued, undermine the trust that is essential to the doctor-patient relationship by blurring the time-honored line between healing and harming.

Next, the state has an interest in protecting vulnerable groups—including the poor, the elderly, and disabled persons—from abuse, neglect, and mistakes. . . . We have recognized [in *Cruzan*] . . . the real risk of subtle coercion and undue influence in end-of-life situations. . . . If physician-assisted suicide were permitted, many might resort to it to spare their families the substantial financial burden of end-of-life health-care costs.

The state's interest here goes beyond protecting the vulnerable from coercion; it extends to protecting disabled and terminally ill people from prejudice, negative and inaccurate stereotypes, and "societal indifference." The state's assisted-suicide ban reflects and reinforces its policy that the lives of terminally ill, disabled, and elderly people must be no less valued than the lives of the young and healthy, and that a seriously disabled person's suicidal impulses should be interpreted and treated the same way as anyone else's.

Finally, the state may fear that permitting assisted suicide will start it down the path to voluntary and perhaps even involuntary euthanasia. The court of appeals struck down Washington's assisted-suicide ban only "as applied to competent, terminally ill adults who wish to hasten their deaths by obtaining medication prescribed by their doctors." Washington insists, however, that the impact of the court's decision will not and cannot be so limited. . . . The court of appeals' decision, and its expansive reasoning, provide ample support for the state's concerns. The court noted, for example, that the "decision of a duly appointed surrogate decision maker is for all legal purposes the decision of the patient himself," that "in some instances, the patient may be unable to self-administer the drugs and . . . administration by the physician . . . may be the only way the patient may be able to receive them,' " and that not only physicians, but also family members and loved ones, will inevitably participate in assisting suicide. Thus, it turns out that what is couched as a limited right to "physician-assisted suicide" is likely, in effect, a much broader license, which could prove extremely difficult to police and contain.

This concern is further supported by evidence about the practice of euthanasia in the Netherlands. The Dutch government's own study revealed that in 1990, there were 2,300 cases of voluntary euthanasia (defined as "the deliberate termination of another's life at his request"), 400 cases of assisted suicide, and more than 1,000 cases of euthanasia without an explicit request. In addition to these latter 1,000 cases, the study found an additional 4,941 cases where physicians administered lethal morphine overdoses without the patients' explicit consent. This study suggests that, despite the existence of various reporting procedures, euthanasia in the Netherlands has not been limited to competent, terminally ill adults who are enduring physical suffering, and that regulation of the practice may not have prevented abuses in cases involving vulnerable persons, including severely disabled neonates and elderly persons suffering from dementia. . . . Washington, like most other states, reasonably ensures against this risk by banning, rather than regulating, assisting suicide.

We need not weigh exactingly the relative strengths of these various interests. They are unquestionably important and legitimate, and Washington's ban on assisted suicide is at least reasonably related to their promotion and protection. We therefore hold that Wash. Rev. Code §9A.36.060(1) (1994) does not violate the Fourteenth Amendment, either on its face or "as applied to competent, terminally ill adults who wish to hasten their deaths by obtaining medication prescribed by their doctors." 79 F.3d, at 838.[24]

. . . Throughout the nation, Americans are engaged in an earnest and profound debate about the morality, legality, and practicality of physician-assisted suicide. Our holding permits this debate to continue, as it should in a democratic society. The decision of the en banc court of appeals is reversed, and the case is remanded for further proceedings consistent with this opinion. . . .

---

24. . . . We emphasize that we today reject the court of appeals' specific holding that the statute is unconstitutional "as applied" to a particular class. Justice Stevens agrees with this holding, but would not "foreclose the possibility that an individual plaintiff seeking to hasten her death, or a doctor whose assistance was sought, could prevail in a more particularized challenge." Our opinion does not absolutely foreclose such a claim. However, given our holding that the due process clause of the Fourteenth Amendment does not provide heightened protection to the asserted liberty interest in ending one's life with a physician's assistance, such a claim would have to be quite different from the ones advanced by respondents here.

■ VACCO v. QUILL
521 U.S. 793 (1997)

REHNQUIST, Chief Justice.

In New York, as in most states, it is a crime to aid another to commit or attempt suicide, but patients may refuse even lifesaving medical treatment. The question presented by this case is whether New York's prohibition on assisting suicide therefore violates the equal protection clause of the Fourteenth Amendment. We hold that it does not.

Petitioners are various New York public officials. Respondents Timothy E. Quill, Samuel C. Klagsbrun, and Howard A. Grossman are physicians who practice in New York. They assert that although it would be "consistent with the standards of [their] medical practices" to prescribe lethal medication for "mentally competent, terminally ill patients" who are suffering great pain and desire a doctor's help in taking their own lives, they are deterred from doing so by New York's ban on assisting suicide. Respondents, and three gravely ill patients who have since died, sued the state's Attorney General in the United States district court. They urged that because New York permits a competent person to refuse life-sustaining medical treatment, and because the refusal of such treatment is "essentially the same thing" as physician-assisted suicide, New York's assisted-suicide ban violates the equal protection clause.

The district court disagreed: "It is hardly unreasonable or irrational for the state to recognize a difference between allowing nature to take its course, even in the most severe situations, and intentionally using an artificial death-producing device." . . .

The court of appeals for the Second Circuit reversed. The court determined that, despite the assisted-suicide ban's apparent general applicability, "New York law does not treat equally all competent persons who are in the final stages of fatal illness and wish to hasten their deaths," because "those in the final stages of terminal illness who are on life-support systems are allowed to hasten their deaths by directing the removal of such systems; but those who are similarly situated, except for the previous attachment of life-sustaining equipment, are not allowed to hasten death by self-administering prescribed drugs." . . . We granted certiorari and now reverse.

The equal protection clause commands that no state shall "deny to any person within its jurisdiction the equal protection of the laws." This provision creates no substantive rights. Instead, it embodies a general rule that states must treat like cases alike but may treat unlike cases accordingly. If a legislative classification or distinction "neither burdens a fundamental right nor targets a suspect class, we will uphold [it] so long as it bears a rational relation to some legitimate end." Romer v. Evans, 517 U.S. (slip op., at 10) (1996).

New York's statutes outlawing assisting suicide affect and address matters of profound significance to all New Yorkers alike. They neither infringe fundamental rights nor involve suspect classifications. These laws are therefore entitled to a "strong presumption of validity." Heller v. Doe, 509 U.S. 312, 319 (1993).

On their faces, neither New York's ban on assisting suicide nor its statutes permitting patients to refuse medical treatment treat anyone differently than anyone else or draw any distinctions between persons. Everyone, regardless of physical condition, is entitled, if competent, to refuse unwanted lifesaving medical treatment;

no one is permitted to assist a suicide. Generally speaking, laws that apply evenhandedly to all "unquestionably comply" with the equal protection clause. New York City Transit Authority v. Beazer, 440 U.S. 568, 587 (1979).

The court of appeals, however, concluded that some terminally ill people—those who are on life-support systems—are treated differently than those who are not, in that the former may "hasten death" by ending treatment, but the latter may not "hasten death" through physician-assisted suicide. This conclusion depends on the submission that ending or refusing lifesaving medical treatment "is nothing more nor less than assisted suicide." Unlike the court of appeals, we think the distinction between assisting suicide and withdrawing life-sustaining treatment, a distinction widely recognized and endorsed in the medical profession and in our legal traditions, is both important and logical; it is certainly rational.

The distinction comports with fundamental legal principles of causation and intent. First, when a patient refuses life-sustaining medical treatment, he dies from an underlying fatal disease or pathology; but if a patient ingests lethal medication prescribed by a physician, he is killed by that medication.

Furthermore, a physician who withdraws, or honors a patient's refusal to begin, life-sustaining medical treatment purposefully intends, or may so intend, only to respect his patient's wishes and "to cease doing useless and futile or degrading things to the patient when [the patient] no longer stands to benefit from them." Assisted Suicide in the United States, Hearing before the Subcommittee on the Constitution of the House Committee on the Judiciary, 104th Cong., 2d Sess., 368 (1996) (testimony of Dr. Leon R. Kass). The same is true when a doctor provides aggressive palliative care; in some cases, painkilling drugs may hasten a patient's death, but the physician's purpose and intent is, or may be, only to ease his patient's pain. A doctor who assists a suicide, however, "must, necessarily and indubitably, intend primarily that the patient be made dead." Id. at 367. Similarly, a patient who commits suicide with a doctor's aid necessarily has the specific intent to end his or her own life, while a patient who refuses or discontinues treatment might not.

The law has long used actors' intent or purpose to distinguish between two acts that may have the same result. Put differently, the law distinguishes actions taken "because of" a given end from actions taken "in spite of" their unintended but foreseen consequences. . . .

Given these general principles, it is not surprising that many courts, including New York courts, have carefully distinguished refusing life-sustaining treatment from suicide. . . . Similarly, the overwhelming majority of state legislatures have drawn a clear line between assisting suicide and withdrawing or permitting the refusal of unwanted lifesaving medical treatment by prohibiting the former and permitting the latter. . . .

For all these reasons, we disagree with respondents' claim that the distinction between refusing lifesaving medical treatment and assisted suicide is "arbitrary" and "irrational." Granted, in some cases, the line between the two may not be clear, but certainty is not required, even were it possible. Logic and contemporary practice support New York's judgment that the two acts are different, and New York may therefore, consistent with the Constitution, treat them differently. By permitting everyone to refuse unwanted medical treatment while prohibiting anyone from assisting a suicide, New York law follows a longstanding and rational distinction.

New York's reasons for recognizing and acting on this distinction—including prohibiting intentional killing and preserving life; preventing suicide; maintaining physicians' role as their patients' healers; protecting vulnerable people from indifference, prejudice, and psychological and financial pressure to end their lives; and avoiding a possible slide towards euthanasia—are discussed in greater detail in our opinion in *Glucksberg*. These valid and important public interests easily satisfy the constitutional requirement that a legislative classification bear a rational relation to some legitimate end.

The judgment of the court of appeals is reversed. . . .

O'CONNOR, Justice, concurring [joined by Justices GINSBURG and BREYER in substantial part.]

Death will be different for each of us. For many, the last days will be spent in physical pain and perhaps the despair that accompanies physical deterioration and a loss of control of basic bodily and mental functions. Some will seek medication to alleviate that pain and other symptoms.

The Court frames the issue in this case as whether the due process clause of the Constitution protects a "right to commit suicide which itself includes a right to assistance in doing so," and concludes that our nation's history, legal traditions, and practices do not support the existence of such a right. I join the Court's opinions because I agree that there is no generalized right to "commit suicide." But respondents urge us to address the narrower question whether a mentally competent person who is experiencing great suffering has a constitutionally cognizable interest in controlling the circumstances of his or her imminent death. I see no need to reach that question in the context of the facial challenges to the New York and Washington laws at issue here. The parties and amici agree that in these states a patient who is suffering from a terminal illness and who is experiencing great pain has no legal barriers to obtaining medication, from qualified physicians, to alleviate that suffering, even to the point of causing unconsciousness and hastening death. In this light, even assuming that we would recognize such an interest, I agree that the state's interests in protecting those who are not truly competent or facing imminent death, or those whose decisions to hasten death would not truly be voluntary, are sufficiently weighty to justify a prohibition against physician-assisted suicide.

Every one of us at some point may be affected by our own or a family member's terminal illness. There is no reason to think the democratic process will not strike the proper balance between the interests of terminally ill, mentally competent individuals who would seek to end their suffering and the state's interests in protecting those who might seek to end life mistakenly or under pressure. As the Court recognizes, states are presently undertaking extensive and serious evaluation of physician-assisted suicide and other related issues. In such circumstances, "the . . . challenging task of crafting appropriate procedures for safeguarding . . . liberty interests is entrusted to the 'laboratory' of the states . . . in the first instance." Cruzan v. Director, Missouri Department of Health, 497 U.S. 261, 292 (1990) (O'Connor, J., concurring) (citing New State Ice Co. v. Liebmann, 285 U.S. 262, 311 (1932)). . . .

STEVENS, Justice, concurring in the judgments.

The Court ends its opinion with the important observation that our holding today is fully consistent with a continuation of the vigorous debate about the "morality, legality, and practicality of physician-assisted suicide" in a democratic society. I write separately to make it clear that there is also room for further debate about the limits that the Constitution places on the power of the states to punish the practice.

I

The morality, legality, and practicality of capital punishment have been the subject of debate for many years. In 1976, this Court upheld the constitutionality of the practice in cases coming to us from Georgia, Florida, and Texas. In those cases we concluded that a state does have the power to place a lesser value on some lives than on others; there is no absolute requirement that a state treat all human life as having an equal right to preservation. Because the state legislatures had sufficiently narrowed the category of lives that the state could terminate, and had enacted special procedures to ensure that the defendant belonged in that limited category, we concluded that the statutes were not unconstitutional on their face. In later cases coming to us from each of those states, however, we found that some applications of the statutes were unconstitutional.

Today, the Court decides that Washington's statute prohibiting assisted suicide is not invalid "on its face," that is to say, in all or most cases in which it might be applied. That holding, however, does not foreclose the possibility that some applications of the statute might well be invalid. . . .

History and tradition provide ample support for refusing to recognize an open-ended constitutional right to commit suicide. Much more than the state's paternalistic interest in protecting the individual from the irrevocable consequences of an ill-advised decision motivated by temporary concerns is at stake. There is truth in John Donne's observation that "No man is an island." The state has an interest in preserving and fostering the benefits that every human being may provide to the community—a community that thrives on the exchange of ideas, expressions of affection, shared memories and humorous incidents as well as on the material contributions that its members create and support. . . .

But just as our conclusion that capital punishment is not always unconstitutional did not preclude later decisions holding that it is sometimes impermissibly cruel, so is it equally clear that a decision upholding a general statutory prohibition of assisted suicide does not mean that every possible application of the statute would be valid. . . .

III

. . . Although as a general matter the state's interest in the contributions each person may make to society outweighs the person's interest in ending her life, this interest does not have the same force for a terminally ill patient faced not with the choice of whether to live, only of how to die. Allowing the individual, rather than the state, to make judgments "about the 'quality' of life that a particular individual may enjoy," does not mean that the lives of terminally-ill, disabled people have less value than the lives of those who are healthy. Rather, it gives proper recognition to the individual's interest in choosing a final chapter that accords with her life story, rather than one that demeans her values and poisons memories of her.

Similarly, the state's legitimate interests in preventing suicide, protecting the vulnerable from coercion and abuse, and preventing euthanasia are less significant in this context. I agree that the state has a compelling interest in preventing persons from committing suicide because of depression, or coercion by third parties. But the state's legitimate interest in preventing abuse does not apply to an individual who is not victimized by abuse, who is not suffering from depression, and who makes a rational and voluntary decision to seek assistance in dying. . . .

Relatedly, the state and amici express the concern that patients whose physical pain is inadequately treated will be more likely to request assisted suicide. Encouraging the development and ensuring the availability of adequate pain treatment is of utmost importance; palliative care, however, cannot alleviate all pain and suffering. See Orentlicher, Legalization of Physician Assisted Suicide: A Very Modest Revolution, 38 Boston College L. Rev. 443, 454 (1997) ("Greater use of palliative care would reduce the demand for assisted suicide, but it will not eliminate [it]"). An individual adequately informed of the care alternatives thus might make a rational choice for assisted suicide. For such an individual, the state's interest in preventing potential abuse and mistake is only minimally implicated.

The final major interest asserted by the state is its interest in preserving the traditional integrity of the medical profession. The fear is that a rule permitting physicians to assist in suicide is inconsistent with the perception that they serve their patients solely as healers. But for some patients, it would be a physician's refusal to dispense medication to ease their suffering and make their death tolerable and dignified that would be inconsistent with the healing role. For doctors who have long-standing relationships with their patients, who have given their patients advice on alternative treatments, who are attentive to their patient's individualized needs, and who are knowledgeable about pain symptom management and palliative care options, heeding a patient's desire to assist in her suicide would not serve to harm the physician-patient relationship. Furthermore, because physicians are already involved in making decisions that hasten the death of terminally ill patients—through termination of life support, withholding of medical treatment, and terminal sedation—there is in fact significant tension between the traditional view of the physician's role and the actual practice in a growing number of cases.

As the New York State Task Force on Life and the Law recognized, a state's prohibition of assisted suicide is justified by the fact that the "ideal" case in which "patients would be screened for depression and offered treatment, effective pain medication would be available, and all patients would have a supportive committed family and doctor" is not the usual case. New York State Task Force on Life and the Law, When Death Is Sought: Assisted Suicide and Euthanasia in the Medical Context 120 (May 1994). Although, as the Court concludes today, these potential harms are sufficient to support the state's general public policy against assisted suicide, they will not always outweigh the individual liberty interest of a particular patient. Unlike the court of appeals, I would not say as a categorical matter that these state interests are invalid as to the entire class of terminally ill, mentally competent patients. I do not, however, foreclose the possibility that an individual plaintiff seeking to hasten her death, or a doctor whose assistance was sought, could prevail in a more particularized challenge. Future cases will determine whether such a challenge may succeed. . . .

Notes: Physician Aid in Dying

1. *Factual Background.* The debate over physician aid in dying was sparked anew in March 1989, when a distinguished group of physicians argued in favor of physician aid in dying as a last resort for relieving patient suffering. Sidney H. Wanzer et al., The Physician's Responsibility Toward Hopelessly Ill Patients, 320 New Eng. J. Med. 844 (1989), and in June 1990 when Dr. Jack Kevorkian, a retired pathologist living in Michigan, assisted the dying of Janet Adkins. Ms. Adkins was a 54-year-old woman in the early stages of Alzheimer's disease who decided to end her life before she became even more affected.

While Kevorkian's license to practice medicine was revoked, he continued to aid patient dying. By December 1997, he had disclosed his assistance in more than 50 deaths, and his attorney indicated that he had assisted in the range of 100 deaths.

Kevorkian lost his constitutional challenge to Michigan's prohibition of physician aid in dying, People v. Kevorkian, 527 N.W.2d 714 (Mich. 1994), and was prosecuted four different times, but juries acquitted him in three trials and a mistrial was declared in the fourth prosecution. When he crossed the line from aid in dying to euthanasia, however, Kevorkian was convicted. On March 26, 1999, a jury found him guilty of second-degree murder for administering a fatal injection to Thomas Youk, a 52-year-old man suffering from amyotrophic lateral sclerosis (ALS or Lou Gehrig's disease). This was the case in which Kevorkian taped the patient's death, and the tape was televised by *60 Minutes* in November 1998. The trial court judge sentenced Kevorkian to 10 to 25 years in prison, and 8 years later, Kevorkian was released from prison on parole. On June 3, 2011, Kevorkian died of natural causes at the age of 83.

The fact that Kevorkian was convicted despite his earlier escapes from punishment can be attributed to a few factors: (1) this was a case of euthanasia rather than aid in dying; (2) during his interview on *60 Minutes*, Kevorkian indicated that he chose euthanasia rather than aid in dying to advance his agenda rather than to serve the patient's needs (and Youk could have chosen aid in dying); (3) Kevorkian was aggressively flouting the law with the televising of Youk's death; and (4) Kevorkian defended himself rather than relying on a lawyer to make his case.

Dr. Timothy Quill also focused discussion on physician aid in dying by disclosing in 1991 that he prescribed a lethal dose of barbiturates for a cancer patient who was terminally ill. Timothy E. Quill, Death and Dignity, 324 New Eng. J. Med. 691 (1991). In Quill's case, prosecutors were unable to persuade a grand jury to bring an indictment.

The absence of a conviction for either Kevorkian or Quill for aid in dying did not reflect a gap in the law. In both Michigan and New York, the law prohibited aid in dying. However, juries are generally unwilling to convict physicians who help dying patients self-administer a lethal dose of drugs. Prosecutions of a physician for either aid in dying or euthanasia are rare. Convictions are almost unheard of, with only one case reported in the literature before Kevorkian's, a case in which a physician injected his mother-in-law with a fatal dose of Demerol. The mother-in-law suffered from advanced Alzheimer's disease, and the physician pled guilty to a charge of manslaughter and was sentenced to two years' probation after a plea-bargain. Maria T. CeloCruz, Aid-in-Dying, 18 Am. J. L. & Med. 369, 377-383 (1992); Leonard Glantz, Withholding and Withdrawing Treatment, 15 L. Med. & Health Care 231, 232 (1987). For a case in which a physician was acquitted of charges of performing euthanasia, on grounds that his treatment fell within the standard of care for palliative care, see State v. Naramore, 965 P.2d 211 (Kan. 1998).

The legal system is also sympathetic to cases of aid in dying and euthanasia involving family members or close friends of the patient, but to a lesser extent than with physicians. Family members have been convicted of criminal charges, but they are likely to be sentenced leniently.

2. *Legalized Aid in Dying in Oregon.* In November 1994, Oregon voters approved by referendum the Oregon Death with Dignity Act, a law that permits mentally competent, terminally ill persons to obtain a prescription from their physicians for a lethal dose of a drug. The statute requires patients to make their request for aid in dying orally and in writing and to reiterate their request orally at least 15 days after the initial request. The physician is required to inform the patient of the medical diagnosis, prognosis, and alternatives to aid in dying, and must refer the patient to a consulting physician to confirm both the diagnosis and that the patient is competent and making a voluntary and informed decision. If either physician believes that the patient suffers from a psychiatric disorder or from a depression that impairs judgment, the patient must be referred for counseling. Or. Rev. Stat. §§127.800-.897.

A constitutional challenge to the statute was brought, and the district court judge enjoined the law. According to the court, terminally ill persons were denied equal protection by the statute because the state did not employ the same safeguards to protect terminally ill persons from impaired judgment or abuse as used to protect nonterminally ill persons. Lee v. Oregon, 891 F. Supp. 1429 (D. Or. 1995). On appeal, the Ninth Circuit held that the plaintiffs did not have standing to challenge the Oregon statute and so vacated the district court judgment and remanded with instructions to dismiss for lack of jurisdiction. Lee v. Oregon, 107 F.3d 1382, 1392 (9th Cir. 1997). After the Ninth Circuit's decision, the Oregon legislature voted to send the Death with Dignity Act back to the electorate for a second vote by referendum in November 1997. Oregon's voters reaffirmed their earlier approval, this time by a larger margin, 60 to 40 percent versus 51 to 49 percent in 1994.

The first public report of a death under Oregon's aid in dying law came on March 25, 1998. After the report, it was disclosed that the law had been invoked earlier by another patient. On August 18, 1998, the state released data on the first ten patients who exercised their rights under the Death with Dignity Act, and since then Oregon has issued annual reports describing its experience with aid in dying. The full reports are available at the Web site of the Oregon Health Authority's Public Health Division; summaries have been published for the earlier years in the New England Journal of Medicine.

Through December 31, 2016, physicians had written 1,749 prescriptions under the Death with Dignity Act, and 1,127 patients had taken the lethal medication (64 percent), a small number were still alive, and the rest died of their illnesses). Less than two-fifths of 1 percent of deaths in Oregon are by aid in dying. The most common diagnosis has been cancer (77 percent), and the patients have been similar to other dying patients with regard to sex, race, urban or rural residence, health insurance coverage, and hospice enrollment. The level of education has been higher for patients who choose aid in dying. The most common concerns of patients choosing aid in dying have been loss of autonomy, decreased ability to participate in enjoyable activities, and loss of dignity.

Researchers studying patients' reasons for aid in dying have found similar results to those of the state. According to one study, loss of independence, a desire to control the circumstances of death, and concerns about future pain and quality of life are leading reasons for patients to invoke the Death with Dignity Act. Linda Ganzini et al., Oregonians' Reasons for Requesting Physician Aid in Dying, 169 Arch. Intern. Med. 489 (2009). Similarly, another study found that reasons for pursuing aid in dying included loss of function and other physical consequences of illness, loss of sense of self and a desire for control, and fears about the future. Depression was not a significant factor. Robert A. Pearlman et al., Motivations for Physician-Assisted Suicide, 20 J. Gen. Intern. Med. 234 (2005).

Researchers also have looked at physicians' responses to requests under the Oregon Act. A study found that physicians in Oregon grant roughly one in six requests for a lethal prescription and that one in ten requests actually result in aid in dying. Physicians did not provide a prescription in 82 percent of cases because the physician was not willing to aid in dying ever (29 percent), the physician was not willing to assist in the particular case (24 percent), the patient died before meeting Oregon's legal requirements or before receiving a prescription (22 percent), the patient had a change of mind before meeting Oregon's legal requirements or before receiving a prescription (17 percent), or the patient did not meet Oregon's legal requirements (15 percent). While 20 percent of requests came from patients with depression, none of their requests were granted. Linda Ganzini et al., Physicians' Experiences with the Oregon Death with Dignity Act, 342 New Eng. J. Med. 557 (2000). Data from the Netherlands suggest that physicians there are more likely to grant a patient's request for physician aid in dying or euthanasia. Jansen-van der Weide et al., Granted, Undecided, Withdrawn, and Refused Requests for Euthanasia and Physician-Assisted Suicide, 165 Arch. Intern. Med. 1698 (2005) (finding in a physician survey that 44 percent of explicit requests for physician aid in dying or euthanasia were granted).

The Task Force to Improve the Care of Terminally Ill Oregonians has published a 91-page guidebook on the Oregon law, Oregon's Death with Dignity Act: A Guidebook for Health Care Providers. The Task Force represents 25 health care professional organizations, state agencies, and health care systems. You can find the Guidebook at the Web site of the Center for Ethics at Oregon Health Sciences University. For an article observing that efforts to address patients' concerns can diminish the desire for physician aid in dying, see Paul B. Bascom & Susan W. Tolle, Responding to Requests for Physician-Assisted Suicide, 288 JAMA 91 (2002).

3. *Aid in Dying in Other States.* Even before Oregon legalized aid in dying, studies suggested that physician aid in dying and physician-caused euthanasia occur on a regular, albeit infrequent, basis in the United States. Anthony L. Back et al., Physician-Assisted Suicide and Euthanasia in Washington State, 275 JAMA 919 (1996); Ezekiel J. Emanuel et al., The Practice of Euthanasia and Physician-Assisted Suicide in the United States, 280 JAMA 506 (1998); Diane E. Meier et al., A National Survey of Physician-Assisted Suicide and Euthanasia in the United States, 338 New Eng. J. Med. 1193 (1998).

In a national survey regarding requests for physician aid in dying or euthanasia, physicians reported that patients receiving aid in dying had a "substantial burden of physical pain and distress," and were "expected to die of their illness within a short time." For euthanasia, physicians reported that the patients were "imminently dying, bedridden, and severely uncomfortable." About 20 to 30 patients who died by aid in dying or euthanasia were reported to be depressed, but patients with depression were significantly less likely to have their requests granted. Diane E. Meier et al., Characteristics of Patients Requesting and Receiving Physician-Assisted Death, 163 Arch. Intern. Med. 1537 (2003).

Once the Supreme Court rejected a federal constitutional right, the aid in dying debate shifted back to state courts and legislatures. For more than a decade, legalization did not extend beyond Oregon's borders. In 1998, voters in Michigan rejected aid in dying by referendum on a 71 percent to 29 percent vote, and Maine rejected aid in dying by referendum in 2000 on a 51.5 percent to 48.5 percent vote.

In November 2008, Washington became the second state to permit physician aid in dying. A voter initiative—the Washington Death with Dignity Act—that was patterned on the Oregon Death with Dignity Act passed with 58 percent support. Rev. Code Wash. §70.245. Through December 31, 2016, 1,186 patients had received a prescription for life-ending medication, and patients in Washington are more likely than in Oregon to take the medication. Among the patients who died, whether by taking the prescribed medication or not, more than 75 percent had cancer, and the main concerns of the patients were loss of autonomy, diminished ability to engage in activities that made life enjoyable, and a loss of dignity. Reports are available at the Web site of the Washington State Department of Health.

Aid in dying laws also have been enacted in Vermont (2013), California (2015), Colorado (2016), and Washington, D.C. (2016), either by referendum or legislative passage, and bills to legalize aid in dying have been introduced in other state legislatures. On the other hand, several states have enacted or reaffirmed their prohibitions of aid in dying. For updates on legislative activity, see the Death with Dignity National Center Web site.

Seriously ill persons also have gone to state court for relief, arguing for a right to aid in dying under state constitutional law. In December 2009, the Montana Supreme Court held that physician aid in dying is permissible under state law. Baxter v. State, 224 P.3d 1211 (Mont. 2009). The trial court had recognized a right to physician aid in dying under the Montana constitution, but the Supreme Court vacated the constitutional ruling and rested its holding on Montana statutory law. According to the Supreme Court, "a terminally ill patient's consent to physician aid in dying constitutes a statutory defense to a charge of homicide against the aiding physician."

Litigation in other states has been unsuccessful so far. See Sampson v. Alaska, 31 P.3d 88 (Alaska 2001); Donorovich-O'Donnell v. Harris, 194 Cal. Rptr. 3d 579 (Ct. App. 2015); Krischer v. McIver, 697 So. 2d 97 (Fla. 1997); State v. Melchert-Dinkel, 844 N.W.2d 13 (Minn. 2014); Morris v. Brandenburg, 376 P.3d 836 (N.M. 2016); Myers v. Schneiderman, __ N.E.3d __ (N.Y. 2017).

Whether recognized through a court decision, legislature enactment, or public referendum, the right to aid in dying in the United States has been limited to terminally ill adults possessing the mental capacity to make an informed choice. For a comparison with legalization in Belgium, the Netherlands, and Canada, see David Orentlicher, International Perspectives on Physician Assistance in Dying, 46(6) Hastings Center Report 6 (2016).

4. *States' Rights and the Right to Die.* As controversial end-of-life decisions have worked their way through state courts and legislatures, federal government officials

have sometimes tried to intervene. Earlier, on page 562, the *Schiavo* discussion referenced congressional and presidential involvement. Federal intervention also occurred with respect to Oregon's Death with Dignity Act.

In November 2001, Attorney General John Ashcroft tried to reverse the federal government's policy on physician aid in dying in Oregon. Under a June 1998 declaration by Ashcroft's predecessor, Janet Reno, the Drug Enforcement Administration (DEA) did not intervene when physicians used federally controlled prescription drugs to assist a patient's death under Oregon law. Ashcroft's directive to the DEA specifically allowed for the revocation of drug prescription licenses of doctors who participated in aid in dying using federally controlled substances. His directive did not speak to criminal prosecution of the doctors, but they could have been subjected to severe prison sentences under the Controlled Substances Act.

The U.S. Court of Appeals for the Ninth Circuit rejected Attorney General Ashcroft's effort to override Oregon's law, holding that he lacked authority under the Controlled Substances Act to intervene. Oregon v. Ashcroft, 368 F.3d 1118 (9th Cir. 2004). In January 2006, the Supreme Court affirmed the Ninth Circuit, concluding that the Controlled Substances Act does not give the Attorney General authority to declare "illegitimate a medical standard for care and treatment of patients that is specifically authorized under state law." Gonzales v. Oregon, 546 U.S. 243 (2006).

Previously, members of Congress were unsuccessful in their efforts to override Oregon's law. Companion bills were introduced in the U.S. House and Senate that would have permitted the DEA to revoke a physician's registration to prescribe federally controlled substances if the physician prescribed a lethal dose of drugs under Oregon's law. Neither bill was passed, and Congress considered a new bill, the Pain Relief Promotion Act, during 1999 and 2000, that would have overridden Oregon's law by stating that no drugs regulated as controlled substances by the federal government could be used to aid in dying. For a discussion of the Act, see David Orentlicher & Arthur Caplan, The Pain Relief Promotion Act of 1999: A Serious Threat to Palliative Care, 283 JAMA 255 (2000).

Many commentators have criticized federal involvement in end-of-life decisions as being politically motivated; others see value in the federal oversight. Similar issues arise with federal intrusion into state decisions to allow marijuana use for medical purposes. See Chapter 8.

5. *Substantive Due Process.* As discussed in *Glucksberg*, a right to aid in dying can be analogized to the right to refuse unwanted medical treatment and the right to abortion.

The right to refuse treatment: The Supreme Court had no trouble upholding the traditional distinction between the withdrawal of life-sustaining treatment and physician aid in dying. The Ninth and Second Circuits in *Glucksberg* and *Quill*, however, found the distinction to be unconstitutional, at least for persons who are terminally ill. Consider the following arguments for the distinction. Do they really explain why treatment withdrawal and aid in dying should be treated differently?

> a. "[D]eclining life-sustaining medical treatment may not properly be viewed as an attempt to commit suicide. Refusing medical intervention merely allows the disease to take its natural course; if death were eventually to occur, it would be the result, primarily, of the underlying disease, and not the result of a self-inflicted injury." In re Conroy, 486 A.2d 1209, 1224 (N.J. 1985).

b. "A physician who withdraws . . . life-sustaining medical treatment purposefully intends . . . only to respect his patient's wishes and 'to cease doing useless and futile or degrading things to the patient.'. . . A doctor who assists a suicide, however, 'must, necessarily and indubitably, intend primarily that the patient be made dead.'" Vacco v. Quill, supra.

c. The right to die is only a right to refuse unwanted bodily invasion. As the Massachusetts Supreme Court wrote in the *Saikewicz* case, "[A] person has a strong interest in being free from nonconsensual invasion of his bodily integrity." Superintendent of Belchertown v. Saikewicz, 370 N.E.2d 417, 424 (Mass. 1977). Similarly, the right to abortion is essentially the right to avoid an unwanted invasion of the body by a fetus. Aid in dying in contrast is a right to demand a bodily invasion, and there is no tradition in the law of such a right.

d. If physicians began to dispense death-causing agents, patients would develop a profound distrust of the medical profession. "[I]f physicians become killers or are even merely licensed to kill, the profession—and, therewith, each physician—will never again be worthy of trust and respect as healer and comforter and protector of life in all its frailty." Willard Gaylin et al., Doctors Must Not Kill, 259 JAMA 2140, 2141 (1988).

e. "How easily will [physicians] be able to care wholeheartedly for patients when it is always possible to think of killing them as a 'therapeutic option'? Shall it be penicillin and a respirator one more time, or perhaps just an overdose of morphine this time? Physicians get tired of treating patients who are hard to cure, who resist their best efforts, who are on their way down—'gorks,' 'gomers,' and 'vegetables' are only some of the less than affectionate names they receive from the house officers. Won't it be tempting to think that death is the best treatment for the little old lady 'dumped' again on the emergency room by the nearby nursing home?" Leon Kass, Neither for Love nor Money: Why Doctors Must Not Kill, 94 Pub. Int. 25, 35 (Winter 1989).

f. Many physicians lack training in the relief of pain and other symptoms of suffering, and many terminally ill patients receive inadequate palliative care to relieve their suffering. Craig D. Blinderman & J. Andrew Billings, Comfort Care for Patients Dying in the Hospital, 373 New Eng. J. Med. 2549 (2015). It is dangerous to legalize aid in dying before we ensure that physicians are providing appropriate palliative care to their patients.

g. "Two strong movements have each begun to enlist many enthusiastic adherents throughout the nation: a movement toward managed care as a means of cost control and a movement toward managed death through euthanasia and assisted suicide. . . . In managed care, . . . [physicians] are usually given financial incentives to control costs while maintaining quality. . . . As providers of managed care, many physicians will be motivated by concern for quality, but concerns about cost will also be significant. Their concern for quality will probably be made explicit, but their concern for cost will generally be left unspoken. As providers of managed death, many physicians will be sincerely motivated by respect for patient autonomy, but the cost factor will always lurk silently in the background. This will be especially true if they are providing managed death in a setting of managed care." Daniel P. Sulmasy, Managed Care and Managed Death, 155 Arch. Intern. Med. 133, 133, 134 (1995).

h. "Is this the kind of choice, assuming that it can be made in a fixed and rational manner, that we want to offer a gravely ill person? Will we not sweep up, in the process, some who are not really tired of life, but think others are tired of them; some who do not really want to die, but who feel they should not live on, . . . Will not some feel an obligation to have themselves 'eliminated' in order that funds allocated for their terminal care might be better used by their families or, financial worries aside, in order to relieve their families of the emotional strain involved?" Yale Kamisar, Some Non-Religious Views Against Proposed "Mercy-Killing" Legislation, 42 Minn. L. Rev. 669, 690 (1958).

i. Among terminally ill patients, those with depression are much more likely to have a strong desire for death to come soon. Keith G. Wilson et al., Mental Disorders and the Desire for Death in Patients Receiving Palliative Care for Cancer, 6 BMJ Supportive & Palliative Care 170 (2016). Yet many physicians fail to recognize treatable depression in their patients, particularly the elderly. Some patients will receive aid in dying when they really need mental health care.

j. "Slavery was long ago outlawed on the ground that one person should not have the right to own another, even with the other's permission. Why? Because it is a fundamental moral wrong for one person to give over his life and fate to another, whatever the good consequences, and no less a wrong for another person to have that kind of total, final power. Like slavery, dueling was long ago banned on similar grounds: even free, competent individuals should not have the power to kill each other, whatever their motives, whatever the circumstances. Consenting adult killing, like consenting adult slavery or degradation, is a strange route to human dignity." Daniel Callahan, When Self-Determination Runs Amok, 22(2) Hastings Center Rep. 52, 52 (1992).

k. "It is not medicine's place to determine when lives are not worth living or when the burden of life is too great to be borne. Doctors have no conceivable way of evaluating such claims on the part of patients, and they should have no right to act in response to them. Medicine should try to relieve human suffering, but only that suffering which is brought on by illness and dying as biological phenomena, not that suffering which comes from anguish or despair at the human condition." Callahan, supra, at 52, 55.

The right to abortion: In some ways, a right to aid in dying seems more defensible than a right to abortion. The life being ended is the life of the person making the decision rather than the life of a third party. Moreover, what is being taken away is a short period of great suffering rather than a potential for a full span of a healthy and productive life. In other ways, the right to aid in dying is the harder case. In particular, the life of a person rather than a pre-viable fetus is being taken.

How well the analogy works depends on which theory you accept for the right to abortion. Consider the following arguments for a right to abortion. How well do they support a right to aid in dying?

a. "Our law affords constitutional protection to personal decisions relating to marriage, procreation, contraception, family relationships, child rearing and education. [These] matters, involving the most intimate and personal choices a person may make in a lifetime, choices central to personal dignity and autonomy, are central to the liberty protected by the Fourteenth Amendment. At the heart of liberty is the right to define one's own concept of existence, of meaning, of the universe, and of the mystery of human life. Beliefs about these matters could not define the attributes of personhood were they formed under compulsion of the state." Planned Parenthood of Southeastern Pennsylvania v. Casey, 505 U.S. 833, 851 (1992).

b. "It is a deeply rooted principle of American law that an individual is ordinarily not required to volunteer aid to another individual who is in danger or in need of assistance. In brief, our law does not require people to be Good Samaritans. . . . [I]f we require a pregnant woman to carry the fetus to term and deliver it—if we forbid abortion, in other words—we are compelling her to be a Good

Samaritan. . . . [I]f we consider the generally very limited scope of obligations of samaritanism under our law, and if we consider the special nature of the burdens imposed on pregnant women by laws forbidding abortion, we must eventually conclude that the equal protection clause forbids imposition of these burdens on pregnant women." Donald H. Regan, Rewriting Roe v. Wade, 77 Mich. L. Rev. 1569, 1569 (1979).

c. "The distinctive and singular characteristic of the laws against which the right to privacy has been applied lies in their *productive or affirmative* consequences. There are perhaps no legal proscriptions with more profound, more extensive, or more persistent affirmative effects on individual lives than the laws struck down as violations of the right to privacy. Anti-abortion laws . . . involve the forcing of lives into well-defined and highly confined institutional layers. . . . They affirmatively and very substantially shape a person's life; they direct a life's development along a particular avenue. These laws do not simply proscribe one act or remove one liberty; they inform the totality of a person's life. . . . Anti-abortion laws produce motherhood: They take diverse women with every variety of career, life-plan, and so on, and make mothers of them all. . . . For a period of months and quite possibly years, forced motherhood shapes women's occupations and preoccupations in the minutest detail; it creates a perceived identity for women and confines them to it. . . ." Jed Rubenfeld, The Right of Privacy, 102 Harv. L. Rev. 737, 784, 788 (1989).

6. *The Patient's Condition.* An important question in determining due process rights in end-of-life care is whether the critical issue is the physician's action or the patient's condition. We have seen that the courts permit withdrawal of treatment regardless of the patient's condition but are generally unwilling to recognize a right to aid in dying (or euthanasia), also regardless of the patient's condition. In contrast, when the Ninth and Second Circuits in *Glucksberg* and *Quill* recognized a right to aid in dying, the courts suggested that the critical question is not the nature of the physician's action but the condition of the patient. That is, the critical issue is whether the patient has an irreversible and fatal medical problem, not whether there is a withdrawal of treatment or aid in dying. Consider the following perspectives:

Suppose the doctor agrees to withhold treatment [from a dying patient], as the conventional doctrine says he may. The justification for his doing so is that the patient is in terrible agony, and since he is going to die anyway, it would be wrong to prolong his suffering needlessly. But now notice this. If one simply withholds treatment, it may take the patient longer to die, and so he may suffer more than he would if more direct action were taken and a lethal injection given. This fact provides strong reason for thinking that, once the initial decision not to prolong his agony has been made, active euthanasia is actually preferable to passive euthanasia, rather than the reverse. To say otherwise is to endorse the option that leads to more suffering rather than less, and is contrary to the humanitarian impulse that prompts the decision not to prolong his life in the first place. [James Rachels, Active and Passive Euthanasia, 292 New Eng. J. Med. 78, 78 (1975).]

There are two individuals, one of whom is twenty-eight years old, is despondent from a recent romantic breakup and, because of an acute asthma attack, is temporarily ventilator dependent. Other than the asthma, this person is in good health. The other individual is eighty-two years old, is wracked with pain from widely metastatic cancer and has no more than a few weeks to live. Assume that both of these individuals wish to end their lives, the twenty-eight-year-old by refusing the ventilator and the eighty-two-year-old by suicide. Under current law, the twenty-eight-year-old may have the ventilator discontinued while the eighty-two-year-old generally lacks a right to suicide assistance.

Yet, in terms of the reasons why we recognize a right to refuse life-sustaining treatment, it would be more justifiable for a physician to assist the eighty-two-year-old's suicide than to accede to the twenty-eight-year-old's refusal of the ventilator. . . . [T]he right to refuse life-sustaining treatment arose out of a sense that hopelessly ill patients should be able to refuse treatment that provides little, if any, benefit and merely prolongs the dying process. Society's interest in preserving a patient's life becomes attenuated when there is little life left to save, and treatment becomes burdensome rather than beneficial. In the same way, society's interest in preserving the life of the eighty-two-year-old becomes attenuated — the patient's remaining life is very short and overcome by severe suffering. Conversely, imposing a ventilator on the twenty-eight-year-old would not result in the brief prolongation of a dying process but the long extension of a life that likely would become very much valued by the patient. If we were to decide these cases strictly on their own merits, we would probably permit physicians to assist the suicide of the eighty-two-year-old but not permit them to withdraw the ventilator from the twenty-eight-year-old. [David Orentlicher, The Legalization of Physician-Assisted Suicide: A Very Modest Revolution, 38 B.C. L. Rev. 443, 462-463 (1997).]

If the patient's condition is more critical than the nature of the physician's act, does this imply that the appropriate standard for both the right to refuse life-sustaining treatment and a right to aid in dying is the standard of the *Quinlan* court, that the individual's right should "grow [] as the degree of bodily invasion increases and the prognosis dims. Ultimately there comes a point at which the individual's rights overcome the state interest. . . ." *Quinlan*, 355 A.2d at 664.

7. *Equal Protection.* The *Quill* court addressed the question whether a right to refuse life-sustaining treatment implies a right to physician aid in dying under the equal protection clause. In the lawsuit over Oregon's statute legalizing physician aid in dying, on the other hand, the federal district court in *Lee* used the equal protection clause to limit the ability of states to permit aid in dying. See supra, at page 594.

If the Second Circuit in *Quill* used the equal protection clause to strike down a prohibition on aid in dying, and the district court in *Lee* used the equal protection clause to strike down a statute permitting aid in dying, do the two opinions simply demonstrate that the equal protection clause is hopelessly indeterminate, or is there a way to reconcile the two rulings?

If we accept the logic of the *Lee* court, must we require the same safeguards for withdrawal of life-sustaining treatment that we require for aid in dying? Aren't patients on life-sustaining treatment given less protection from abuse or impaired judgment than persons who are not being sustained by medical treatment but who want to die? Isn't it easier for a patient like Kenneth Bergstedt, at page 523, to end his life involuntarily than a person who isn't dependent on a ventilator?

8. *Limiting a Right to Aid in Dying.* In *Glucksberg* and *Quill,* the Supreme Court echoed concerns from many commentators that a right to aid in dying cannot be easily cabined. As one scholar has observed,

[i]f personal autonomy and the termination of suffering are supposed to be the touchstones for physician-assisted suicide, why exclude those with nonterminal illnesses or disabilities who might have to endure greater pain and suffering *for much*

longer periods of time than those who are expected to die in the next few weeks or months? If the terminally ill do have a right to assisted suicide, doesn't someone who must continue to live what *she considers* an intolerable or unacceptable existence *for many years* have an equal—or even greater—right to assisted suicide? . . . [I]f, as proponents of assisted suicide maintain, there is no significant difference between the right to assisted suicide and the right to reject unwanted life-saving treatment, it is fairly clear that, once established, the right to assisted suicide would not be limited to the terminally ill. For the right of a person to reject life-sustaining medical treatment *has not been so limited.*

Yale Kamisar, Against Assisted Suicide—Even a Very Limited Form, 72 U. Det. Mercy L. Rev. 735, 740-741 (1995) (emphasis in original).

Is the Court's observation in *Glucksberg* correct that, if we permit physician aid in dying for terminally ill persons, we must also permit euthanasia for terminally ill persons who lack the physical ability to self-administer a lethal dose of medication? Is the Court also correct that we must honor the living will of a patient who requested euthanasia in the event of terminal illness? Must we permit aid in dying for patients who are not terminally ill but who have an incurable and irreversible illness and are suffering greatly?

For an argument that a right to aid in dying is not readily susceptible to expansion, see David Orentlicher & Christopher M. Callahan, Feeding Tubes, Slippery Slopes, and Physician-Assisted Suicide, 25 J. Leg. Med. 389 (2004).

9. *Palliative Sedation.* In her concurring opinion, Justice O'Connor suggested that dying patients have a constitutional right to alleviate their suffering, but that such a right would not imply a right to aid in dying since patients are able to obtain medications to relieve their suffering "even to the point of causing unconsciousness and hastening death."

It is well accepted in ethics and law that physicians can administer medications to relieve pain or other suffering even if doing so poses some increased risk of death for the patient. Under this principle of "double effect," the risk of death is acceptable as long as the medication is used in a reasonable effort to treat the patient's suffering. By way of analogy, we permit physicians to perform open heart surgery, despite the risk of patient death, because the primary purpose of the surgery is to treat the patient's heart disease, and the benefits of the surgery are reasonable when compared with the risks.

In some cases, as Justice O'Connor noted, the patient must be sedated into unconsciousness to relieve the suffering. In these cases, the patient is sedated into a coma from which the patient usually dies in a few days, either because the patient is at the end stage of the underlying illness or because food and water are withheld.

Is there a good reason to permit palliative sedation (once, and at the time of *Glucksberg* and *Quill*, called "terminal sedation") but not to permit aid in dying? From the patient's perspective, which is the more desirable approach? Do you see how palliative sedation could be viewed as a form of euthanasia? See David Orentlicher, The Supreme Court and Physician-Assisted Suicide: Rejecting Assisted Suicide but Embracing Euthanasia, 337 New Eng. J. Med. 1236 (1997) (and a fuller version of the argument in 24 Hastings Const. L.Q. 947 (1997)).

In the Netherlands, where palliative sedation and aid in dying both are permitted, one study found that palliative sedation is "typically used to address severe physical and psychological suffering in dying patients, whereas perceived loss of dignity during the last phase of life is a major problem for patients requesting euthanasia." Judith A. C. Rietjens et al., Terminal Sedation and Euthanasia, 166 Arch. Intern. Med. 749 (2006). But see Jean-Jacques Georges et al., Differences Between Terminally Ill Cancer Patients Who Died After Euthanasia Had Been Performed and Terminally Ill Cancer Patients Who Did Not Request Euthanasia, 19 Palliative Med. 578 (2005) (finding that patients choosing euthanasia had much higher levels of severe pain, vomiting, and nausea than patients who did not choose euthanasia).

States have begun to recognize a right to palliative care in their legislatures and courts. Florida, California, New York, and other states have passed statutes requiring physicians to advise terminally ill patients of their options for end-of-life care, including hospice care, and treatment to relieve pain and other symptoms. Alan Meisel, Kathy L. Cerminara & Thaddeus M. Pope, The Right to Die §6.03[I] (3d ed. 2015 Supp.); Fla. Stat. §765.1103; Cal. Health & Safety Code §442.5; N.Y. Pub. Health Law §2997-c. In addition to these statutory rights, patients may be able to recover damages from doctors and other health care providers for the failure to provide adequate pain relief. Tolliver v. Visiting Nurse Ass'n of Midlands, 771 N.W. 2d 908 (Neb. 2009); Ben Rich, Physicians' Legal Duty to Relieve Suffering, 175 West. J. Med. 151 (2001).

If there is a right to receive medications to alleviate the symptoms of disease, is there also a right to receive medications to treat the disease itself? In a surprising decision in favor of patients' rights based on *Cruzan* and *Glucksberg*, a panel of the D.C. Circuit initially found a limited constitutional right of terminally ill persons to receive experimental cancer chemotherapy or other potentially therapeutic drugs without Food and Drug Administration (FDA) approval when there are no other therapeutic options left. Abigail Alliance v. Eschenbach, 445 F.3d 470 (D.C. Cir. 2006). This decision was reversed by the en banc court, however, 495 F.3d 695 (D.C. Cir. 2007), which reasoned that such a right is not deeply rooted in the nation's history and tradition, considering the long history of the regulation of pharmacists and pharmaceuticals. During the litigation, the FDA proposed a new rule to give terminally ill patients greater access to experimental drugs. 71 Fed. Reg. 75147 (2006).

10. *Predicting Patient Outcome.* An important concern about a right of terminally ill persons to aid in dying is the reliability of a physician's prediction that a patient will die soon (e.g., within six months). For many patients, it is difficult to predict when they will die. Certainty varies not only from patient to patient but also from disease to disease—while predictions are fairly reliable for patients with cancers, they are not as reliable for patients with dementia, emphysema, or heart failure. Ellen Fox et al., Evaluation of Prognostic Criteria for Determining Hospice Eligibility in Patients with Advanced Lung, Heart, or Liver Disease, 282 JAMA 1638 (1999); Susan L. Mitchell et al., The Advanced Dementia Prognostic Tool: A Risk Score to Estimate Survival in Nursing Home Residents with Advanced Dementia, 40 J. Pain Symptom Mgmt. 639 (2010).

Still, among all patients certified as likely to die within six months for purposes of hospice benefits under Medicare, only 20 percent receive the benefits for more than six months. Medicare Payment Advisory Commission, Healthcare Spending and the Medicare Program: A Data Book 188 (June 2016). (And physicians might be quicker to diagnose a patient as terminally ill to establish eligibility for Medicare benefits than to establish eligibility for physician aid in dying.)

If we reject a right to aid in dying for the terminally ill because of uncertainties as to when a patient is terminally ill, does it follow that we should reject a right to refuse life-sustaining treatment because patients might refuse treatment on the mistaken assumption either that they are terminally ill or that, while not terminally ill, they will be permanently dependent on a ventilator or other treatment?

11. *Refusing Food and Water.* Some commentators have argued that patients who are not dependent upon life-sustaining treatment but who desire aid in dying can always end their lives by refraining from eating and drinking. James L. Bernat et al., Patient Refusal of Hydration and Nutrition, 153 Arch. Intern. Med. 2723 (1993).

While some courts and commentators have suggested that death by starvation is painful, Brophy v. New England Sinai Hospital, 497 N.E.2d 626, 641 n.2 (Mass. 1986) (Lynch, J., dissenting), there actually seems to be little discomfort from dying by withdrawal of nutrition and hydration, and the discomfort can easily be relieved with appropriate care. Robert J. Sullivan, Accepting Death Without Artificial Nutrition or Hydration, 8 J. Gen. Intern. Med. 220, 221 (1993). In most cases, death will occur within a few days.

If people can end their lives by starvation, or, for that matter, by a number of ways described in Derek Humphrey, Final Exit (1991), why do patients request aid in dying? Note that, even with cessation of eating and drinking, it still may take several weeks in rare cases for the patient to die. Sullivan, supra, at 221-222.

Note also that in their advance directive and surrogate decisionmaking statutes, several states prohibit the withholding of food and water that can be ingested normally from patients who lack decisionmaking capacity. Thaddeus Mason Pope & Lindsey E. Anderson, Voluntarily Stopping Eating and Drinking, 17 Widener L. Rev. 363 (2011). Do these prohibitions pass constitutional muster?

12. *Conscientious Objection.* Living will statutes routinely recognize a conscientious objection on the part of physicians who are unwilling to participate in a withdrawal of life-sustaining treatment. Cal. Prob. Code §4734; Ohio Rev. Code Ann. §2133.10(A); Pa. Cons. Stat. tit. 20, §5424(a). If the physician believes that it is morally wrong to discontinue life-sustaining treatment, then the physician may withdraw from the case and arrange for another physician to carry out the patient's request. To the physician with a conscientious objection of this sort, withdrawal of treatment is understood to cause the patient's death; it does not matter that the physician is doing so by omission or "inaction." To the conscientious objector, withdrawing treatment is just as much an action as aiding in dying. If the physician who opposes withdrawal of treatment may equate it to aid in dying, does it follow that the physician who supports aid in dying may equate it to withdrawal of treatment?

13. *Euthanasia.* While most of the legal activity surrounding this issue in the United States has focused on aid in dying, some statutory proposals and cases seek a right to euthanasia. As mentioned, the California and Washington legislative initiatives that were defeated would have granted a right to both aid in dying and euthanasia. Also, a California man sought a declaratory judgment permitting him to have his body preserved cryogenically before he died in the hope that physicians could reanimate his body once a cure was found for his brain cancer. Since the "freezing" process would result in the man's death, his claim rested on the existence of a constitutional right to euthanasia, but the court held that no such right exists.

Donaldson v. Van de Kamp, 4 Cal. Rptr. 2d 59 (Ct. App. 1992). (Normally, cryo-preservation takes place after the person dies.)

14. *Other Countries.* Australia's Northern Territory became the first jurisdiction to legalize euthanasia when it enacted the Rights of the Terminally Ill Act in May 1996. The legislation took effect on July 1, 1996, and the first reported death under the Act occurred on September 22, 1996. The law permitted euthanasia and aid in dying for terminally ill persons after evaluation by two physicians, including a psychiatrist, and after a nine-day waiting period. Robert L. Schwartz, Rights of the Terminally Ill Act of the Australian Northern Territory, 5 Cambridge Q. Healthcare Ethics 157 (1996). In March 1997, after four persons had invoked the law, the Australian Parliament repealed the legislation.

In the Netherlands, euthanasia and aid in dying were treated as criminal acts, but they were not prosecuted if performed under guidelines that were developed between 1973 and 1984 by the legal system and the medical profession. In 2001, legislation formally legalized aid in dying and euthanasia in accordance with existing practices, with some extension of those practices. The legislation took effect in April 2002.

In the Netherlands, the patient must be competent and have made a consistent, persistent, and voluntary request for euthanasia or aid in dying. The patient need not be terminally ill but must be incurably ill and experiencing unbearable suffering that cannot be relieved. The patient's physician must consult with an experienced colleague before acceding to the patient's request. Maurice A. M. Wachter, Active Euthanasia in the Netherlands, 262 JAMA 3316 (1989).

As discussed in *Glucksberg*, there is evidence that the guidelines for euthanasia and aid in dying were not rigorously followed in a substantial number of cases before 2002. Empirical data indicate that in about one-fourth of cases of euthanasia or aid in dying, physicians did not observe the strict criteria for those procedures. In these cases, the patient "had in a previous phase of his or her illness expressed a wish for euthanasia should suffering become unbearable," the patient was "near to death and clearly suffering grievously, yet verbal contact had become impossible," or the decision had been discussed with the patient but the patient's wishes had not been expressed explicitly and persistently. Paul J. van der Maas et al., Euthanasia and Other Medical Decisions Concerning the End of Life, 338 Lancet 669, 672 (1991); Paul J. van der Maas et al., Euthanasia, Physician-Assisted Suicide, and Other Medical Practices Involving the End of Life in the Netherlands, 1990-1995, 335 New Eng. J. Med. 1699, 1701 (1996).

In response to this evidence, the Royal Dutch Medical Association issued new guidelines in August 1995 that emphasized that existing rules needed to be followed and that stated that euthanasia should not be performed unless aid in dying is not an option (e.g., because the patient is too sick to swallow the lethal drug) and that the consulting physician may not have a professional or family relationship with the patient or physician. A subsequent study found that rates of aid in dying and euthanasia had stabilized between 1995 and 2001, with physicians becoming somewhat more reluctant to engage in the two practices. Bregje D. Onwuteaka-Philipsen, Euthanasia and Other End-of-Life Decisions in the Netherlands in 1990, 1995, and 2001, 362 Lancet 395 (2003).

After the 2002 legalization of euthanasia and aid in dying, there was an initial decline in euthanasia cases, perhaps as physicians were adjusting to the new law, but by 2010, rates had returned to their pre-legislation levels. For example, the euthanasia rate in 2010 was 2.8 percent of all deaths, slightly up from 2.6 percent in 2001, while aid in dying changed little, from 0.2 percent in 2001 to 0.1 percent in 2010. On the other hand, the rate of life-ending acts without a current explicit request from the patient dropped from 0.7 percent in 2001 to 0.2 percent in 2010. Bregje D. Onwuteaka-Philipsen, Trends in End-of-life Practices before and after the Enactment of the Euthanasia Law in the Netherlands from 1990 to 2010, 380 Lancet 908 (2012).

Dutch patients who request aid in dying or euthanasia are more likely to be depressed than comparable patients who do not make such a request. However, doctors refuse the requests most of the time for depressed patients, and the prevalence of depression among those who receive aid in dying or euthanasia is no higher than among similar patients who do not request aid in dying or euthanasia. Ilana Levene & Michael Parker, Prevalence of Depression in Granted and Refused Requests for Euthanasia and Assisted Suicide, 37 J. Med. Ethics 205 (2011).

In addition to legalizing existing rules for non-prosecuted euthanasia and aid in dying for competent persons, the 2002 law also permits euthanasia by advance directive. But that option appears to have limited impact. In a survey of physicians who care for nursing home patients, researchers found no examples of euthanasia performed on a patient with dementia who had requested euthanasia in an advance directive. Marike E. de Boer et al., Advance Directives for Euthanasia in Dementia, 59 J. Am. Geriatrics Soc'y 989 (2011).

In Belgium, final approval was given in 2002 to legislation permitting euthanasia under rules like those in the Netherlands. Data from a survey of physicians in Flanders (the Dutch part of Belgium) indicate a higher rate of euthanasia than in the Netherlands — 4.6 percent of deaths in 2013. Kenneth Chambaere et al., Recent Trends in Euthanasia and Other End-of-Life Practices in Belgium, 372 New Eng. J. Med. 1179 (2015).

By not requiring a terminal illness for euthanasia or aid in dying, the Netherlands and Belgium make it possible for patients whose primary illness is psychiatric to choose euthanasia or aid in dying, and that has raised concerns about practices in the two countries. Scott Y. H. Kim et al., Euthanasia and Assisted Suicide of Patients With Psychiatric Disorders in the Netherlands 2011 to 2014, 73 JAMA Psychiatry 362 (2016); Barron H. Lerner & Arthur L. Caplan, Euthanasia in Belgium and the Netherlands: On a Slippery Slope?, 175 JAMA Intern. Med. 1640 (2015).

Canada is the most recent country to legalize euthanasia and aid in dying, though with greater restrictions than in the Netherlands and Belgium. David Orentlicher, International Perspectives on Physician Assistance in Dying, 46(6) Hastings Center Report 6 (2016).

In Germany, euthanasia is prohibited by law, but aid in dying is not. However, physicians are legally obligated to try to resuscitate persons who have attempted suicide. Consequently, while aid in dying is practiced in Germany, the assistance is usually provided by family members or friends rather than physicians. The German Society for Humane Dying is a large, private, nonmedical organization that provides advice to members about aid in dying after they have been members for at least a year. Margaret P. Battin, Assisted Suicide: Can We Learn from Germany?, 22(2) Hastings Center Rep. 44 (1992).

Switzerland permits aid in dying with or without the involvement of a physician; there, too, lay assistance is common. Stephen J. Ziegler, Collaborated Death: An Exploration of the Swiss Model, 37 J. L. Med. & Ethics 318 (2009). Concerns have been raised by the practice of "suicide tourism," in which individuals from other countries where physician aid in dying is illegal travel to Switzerland to end their lives. For further discussion, see Alan Meisel, Kathy L. Cerminara & Thaddeus M. Pope, The Right to Die §12.07[D] (3d ed. 2017 Supp.).

15. *Additional Arguments.* Consider the following additional arguments regarding aid in dying (or euthanasia):

> The common concern that assisted suicide will shorten life may be mistaken. Seriously ill patients often face an option of treatment that has a small but still significant chance of prolonging life. At the same time, there may be a substantial risk that the treatment will fail and only cause painful and debilitating side effects. The prospect of the treatment failure and the side effects will discourage many patients from accepting the treatment. A small chance of success may not be enough to overcome a high risk of great suffering. If a right to assisted suicide existed, however, those same patients would be more likely to accept the treatment. The patients would know that, if the treatment did not work, they would always have the option of ending their suffering through physician assisted suicide. The patients would not have to fear the consequences of treatment failure. They also would know that, with their physician's guidance, their suicide attempt would be more dignified, less painful and less likely to fail and leave the patient in a condition of even greater suffering. [David Orentlicher, The Legalization of Physician-Assisted Suicide: A Very Modest Revolution, 38 B.C. L. Rev. 443, 452-453 (1997).]

> There is an important distinction between withdrawal of treatment and aid in dying, but not for the reasons usually given. The bare distinction between pulling the plug and writing a prescription for lethal drugs is not morally meaningful, but the distinction has served as a useful "proxy" for the distinction between morally justified patient deaths and morally unjustified deaths. The right to refuse treatment reflects a societal sentiment that people should be able to take life-shortening action when they are suffering greatly from serious and irreversible illness. Recall, for example, that the *Quinlan* court recognized the right only when the patient had a "dim" prognosis. But it isn't feasible to judge on a case-by-case basis whether someone is seriously enough ill to choose death. If courts must decide when a patient is so sick that the patient can refuse life-sustaining treatment, then the government ends up deciding who must live and who may die based on judgments about a person's quality of life. When case-by-case judgments are too problematic, we implement our moral and legal principles through generally valid rules, recognizing that the rules will not fit every case perfectly but also recognizing the infeasibility of case-by-case determinations. The distinction between suicide assistance and treatment withdrawal was an example of rule-based lawmaking that, in the view of the public and the courts, was an effective way to ensure that patients could end their lives only when they were morally justified in doing so. The typical patient who refuses life-sustaining treatment is suffering from a serious and irreversible illness while the typical person who attempts suicide has a treatable mental health condition.

> But while generally valid, the withdrawal-suicide distinction left an important gap. There are many patients desiring aid in dying who are suffering greatly from serious and irreversible illness and whose wishes to end their lives therefore are morally justified in society's view. By allowing aid in dying only for terminally ill patients,

the law can do a better job sorting morally valid from morally invalid requests by patients to end their lives and still avoid case-by-case determinations. Id. at 445, 465-70; David Orentlicher, Matters of Life and Death: Making Moral Theory Work in Medical Ethics and the Law 16-23 (2001); David Orentlicher et al., The Changing Legal Climate for Physician Aid in Dying, 311 JAMA 1961 (2014).

16. *Further Readings*. On **physician aid in dying** (note 2), see Margaret P. Battin, Physician-Assisted Dying and the Slippery Slope, 45 Willamette L. Rev. 91 (2008); Daniel Callahan & Margot White, The Legalization of Physician-Assisted Suicide, 30 U. Rich. L. Rev. 1 (1996); Ronald Dworkin, Life's Dominion (1993); Leonard M. Fleck, Just Caring, 72 U. Det. Mercy L. Rev. 873 (1995); Sylvia A. Law, Physician-Assisted Death, 55 Md. L. Rev. 292 (1996); Thomas Marzen, "Out, Out Brief Candle," 21 Hastings Const. L.Q. 799 (1994); Physician-Assisted Suicide (Margaret P. Battin et al. eds., 1998); Robert A. Sedler, Constitutional Challenges to Bans on "Assisted Suicide," 21 Hastings Const. L.Q. 777 (1994); Symposium, 106 Mich. L. Rev. 1453 (2008); Symposium: Physician-Assisted Suicide, 82 Minn. L. Rev. 885 (1998); Symposium: Visions of Death and Dying, 24 Hastings Const. L.Q. 833 (1997); Symposium, Physician-Assisted Suicide, 35 Duq. L. Rev. 1 (1996).

On the **U.S. experience** with aid in dying (notes 2 and 3), see Herbert Hendin & Kathleen Foley, Physician-Assisted Suicide in Oregon, 106 Mich. L. Rev. 1613 (2008); Barbara Coombs Lee, Oregon's Experience with Aid in Dying, 1330 Annals N.Y. Acad. Sciences 94 (2014); Susan Okie, Physician-Assisted Suicide—Oregon and Beyond, 352 New Eng. J. Med. 1627 (2005); Jackson Pickett, Can Legalization Improve End-of-Life Care? An Empirical Analysis, 16 Elder L. J. 333 (2009); Kathryn Tucker, In the Laboratory of the States, 106 Mich. L. Rev. 1593 (2008).

On **states' rights** (note 4), see Brian Bix, Physician-Assisted Suicide and Federalism, 17 Notre Dame J. L. Ethics & Pub Pol'y 53 (2003); Steven G. Calabresi, The Terri Schiavo Case: In Defense of the Special Law Enacted by Congress and President Bush, 100 Nw. U. L. Rev. 151 (2006); Lars Noah, Ambivalent Commitments to Federalism in Controlling the Practice of Medicine, 53 U. Kan. L. Rev. 149 (2004); Adam M. Samaha, Undue Process: Congressional Referral and Judicial Resistance in the Schiavo Controversy, 22 Const. Commentary 505 (2005); Marc Spindelman, A Dissent from the Many Dissents from Attorney General Ashcroft's Interpretation of the Controlled Substances Act, 19 Issues L. & Med. 3 (2003).

On **palliative sedation** (note 9), see Nathan I. Cherny & Russell K. Portenoy, Sedation in the Management of Refractory Symptoms, 10(2) J. Palliative Care 31 (1994); National Ethics Committee, Veterans Health Administration, The Ethics of Palliative Sedation as a Therapy of Last Resort, 23 Am. J. Hosp. Palliat. Care 483 (2007); Henk ten Have & Jos V. M. Welie, Palliative Sedation Versus Euthanasia, 47 J. Pain & Symptom Mgmt. 123 (2014); Bernard Lo & Gordon Rubenfeld, Palliative Sedation in Dying Patients, 294 JAMA 1810 (2005); Timothy E. Quill et al., Last-Resort Options for Palliative Sedation, 154 Ann. Intern. Med. 421 (2009); Robert D. Truog et al., Barbiturates in the Care of the Terminally Ill, 327 New Eng. J. Med. 1678 (1992). See also George P. Smith, II, Refractory Pain, Existential Suffering, and Palliative Care, 20 Cornell J. L. & Pub. Pol'y 469 (2011).

On *Abigail Alliance* (note 9), see Chapter 8.D.1; Rebecca Dresser, Investigational Drugs and the Constitution, 36(6) Hastings Center Rep. 9 (2006); Peter Jacobson

& Wendy Parmet, A New Era of Unapproved Drugs, 297 JAMA 205 (2007); John Robertson, Controversial Medical Treatment and the Right to Health Care, 36(6) Hastings Center Rep. 15 (2006).

Problem: Is It Aid in Dying or Is It Withdrawal of Treatment?*

Laura is a chronically depressed woman in her late 60s who has very symptomatic arthritis and is seriously overweight. The arthritis causes her chronic pain, which in turn has led her to become addicted to pain medications. Her arthritis and obesity have also caused her to be nonambulatory. Four days ago, Robert, Laura's husband, came into the room at home where Laura appeared injured. Robert called the paramedics, and Laura was brought to the hospital. Robert says that, at the time he called the paramedics, he had not realized that Laura had shot herself with a pistol to the head (actually under her chin with an exit wound in the forehead). He says if he had known, he would not have called them. What happened next was that Laura was taken to surgery and found to have sustained considerable damage to her head but not much damage to the brain except some to the frontal lobes. The surgeons indicate that although the patient is intubated and ventilator-dependent, it is because of the mechanical damage and edema in her neck, and they feel they will be able to take her off the ventilator shortly. Because her brain damage is minimal and involving only the frontal lobes, without the development of meningitis, she is not expected to have any loss of movement or sensation. [Injuries to the frontal lobes can cause a number of personality changes. People with such injuries may become indifferent to the problems of others, give little thought to the effects of their conduct on others, exhibit socially inappropriate behavior like telling silly or tasteless jokes, and become distractible and given to euphoria and emotional outbursts. There also is often a reduction in worry, anxiety, depression, and sensitivity to stressful stimuli, and patients who suffer from chronic pain often complain less of the pain after a frontal lobe injury. There may be compromise of memory or intellectual skills, including problem solving ability, or there may be very little effect on memory and intellect.]

Shortly after Laura's arrival to the hospital, Robert brought a copy of the state's standard Durable Power of Attorney for Health Care (DPAHC) form, which was signed by Laura, duly witnessed, and dated three months before the date of her gunshot wound. Laura had designated Robert as her DPAHC agent. Robert told the hospital doctors and staff that he and his family were aware of the emotional and physical pain and suffering that Laura had experienced over the years and understood that she was depressed (indeed, she had attempted suicide in the 1970s with pills), but she really did not want to live and suffer from her infirmities any longer and she wanted to end the suffering, and, as her agent, he wanted them to stop the emergency treatment and let her die.

Emergency treatment was continued despite the protestations of Robert and the family, who wanted to let Laura die. Currently, Laura is under morphine pain

---

* This problem was adapted from a case originally presented by Maurice Bernstein, M.D., University of Southern California School of Medicine, and Scott Rae, Ph.D., Talbot School of Theology, Biola University (California).

management in the intensive care unit, still ventilator-dependent and unable to communicate, is not deteriorating and indeed her doctors are optimistic about a possible recovery. "A recovery . . . , but to what?" Robert and family say. "A return to the misery of her life before she shot herself and possibly with some additional impairments?" What Robert and the family want the medical staff to do is take Laura off the ventilator and let her die.

You work in the office of the hospital's legal counsel who receives a call from the physicians taking care of Laura asking for legal advice. They want to know whether the law permits, requires, or forbids them to comply with the family's request to discontinue the ventilator. The legal counsel asks you for a memo analyzing the legal issues raised by this case. What would you write in the memo? In considering whether discontinuation of the ventilator would constitute withdrawal of life-sustaining treatment or aid in dying, do you see how the answer depends on your theory as to why aid in dying is different from withdrawal of treatment?

C. FUTILITY

While cases about life-sustaining medical treatment have generally involved situations in which the patient or patient's proxy wanted to stop treatment over the objection of physicians or the hospital, cases are also arising in which the positions are reversed: the patient or proxy wants to continue with treatment, but the physicians or hospital want to stop providing care. In such cases, the patient or family asserts the patient's right to make medical decisions; the physicians or hospital argue that the treatment is medically "futile," that it does not provide sufficient—or any—medical benefit and therefore ought not to be offered to the patient.

■ IN RE BABY K
16 F.3d 590 (4th Cir. 1994)

WILKINS, Circuit Judge.

The Hospital instituted this action against Ms. H, Mr. K, and Baby K, seeking a declaratory judgment that it is not required under the Emergency Medical Treatment and Active Labor Act (EMTALA), 42 U.S.C.A. §1395dd (West 1992),[2] to

---

2. The Hospital also sought declaratory relief under §504 of the Rehabilitation Act of 1973 (Rehabilitation Act), 29 U.S.C.A. §794 (West Supp. 1993); the Americans with Disabilities Act of 1990 (ADA), 42 U.S.C.A. §§12101 et seq. (West 1993); the Child Abuse Prevention and Treatment Act (Child Abuse Act), 42 U.S.C.A. §§5101-5106h (West Supp. 1993); and the statutes and common law of Virginia. In addressing these provisions, the district court concluded that a failure to provide respiratory support to Baby K because of her condition of anencephaly would constitute discrimination in violation of the ADA and the Rehabilitation Act but declined to rule on the application of the Child Abuse Act or Virginia law. Because we conclude that the Hospital has a duty to render stabilizing treatment under EMTALA, we need not address its obligations under the remaining federal statutes or the laws of Virginia.

provide treatment other than warmth, nutrition, and hydration to Baby K, an anencephalic infant. Because we agree with the district court that EMTALA gives rise to a duty on the part of the Hospital to provide respiratory support to Baby K when she is presented at the Hospital in respiratory distress and treatment is requested for her, we affirm.

I

Baby K was born at the Hospital in October of 1992 with anencephaly, a congenital malformation in which a major portion of the brain, skull, and scalp are missing. While the presence of a brain stem does support her autonomic functions and reflex actions, because Baby K lacks a cerebrum, she is permanently unconscious. Thus, she has no cognitive abilities or awareness. She cannot see, hear, or otherwise interact with her environment.

When Baby K had difficulty breathing on her own at birth, Hospital physicians placed her on a mechanical ventilator. This respiratory support allowed the doctors to confirm the diagnosis and gave Ms. H, the mother, an opportunity to fully understand the diagnosis and prognosis of Baby K's condition. The physicians explained to Ms. H that most anencephalic infants die within a few days of birth due to breathing difficulties and other complications. Because aggressive treatment would serve no therapeutic or palliative purpose, they recommended that Baby K only be provided with supportive care in the form of nutrition, hydration, and warmth. Physicians at the Hospital also discussed with Ms. H the possibility of a "Do Not Resuscitate Order" that would provide for the withholding of lifesaving measures in the future.

The treating physicians and Ms. H failed to reach an agreement as to the appropriate care. Ms. H insisted that Baby K be provided with mechanical breathing assistance whenever the infant developed difficulty breathing on her own, while the physicians maintained that such care was inappropriate. As a result of this impasse, the Hospital sought to transfer Baby K to another hospital. This attempt failed when all of the hospitals in the area with pediatric intensive care units declined to accept the infant. In November of 1992, when Baby K no longer needed the services of an acute-care hospital, she was transferred to a nearby nursing home.

Since being transferred to the nursing home, Baby K has been readmitted to the Hospital three times due to breathing difficulties. Each time she has been provided with breathing assistance and, after stabilization, has been discharged to the nursing home. Following Baby K's second admission, the Hospital filed this action to resolve the issue of whether it is obligated to provide emergency medical treatment to Baby K that it deems medically and ethically inappropriate. Baby K's guardian ad litem and her father, Mr. K, joined in the Hospital's request for a declaration that the Hospital is not required to provide respiratory support or other aggressive treatments. . . .

II

Congress enacted EMTALA in response to its "concern that hospitals were 'dumping' patients [who were] unable to pay, by either refusing to provide emergency medical treatment or transferring patients before their emergency conditions were stabilized." Brooks v. Maryland General Hospital Inc., 996 F.2d 708, 710 (4th Cir. 1993). Through EMTALA, Congress sought "to provide an 'adequate first response to a medical crisis' for all patients," Baber v. Hospital Corp. of America, 977 F.2d 872, 880 (4th Cir. 1992), by imposing two duties on hospitals that have entered into Medicare provider agreements.

First, those hospitals with an emergency medical department must provide an appropriate medical screening to determine whether an emergency medical condition exists for any individual who comes to the emergency medical department requesting treatment. A hospital fulfills this duty if it utilizes identical screening procedures for all patients complaining of the same condition or exhibiting the same symptoms.

An additional duty arises if an emergency medical condition is discovered during the screening process. EMTALA defines an "emergency medical condition" as including:

> a medical condition manifesting itself by acute symptoms of sufficient severity (including severe pain) such that the absence of immediate medical attention could reasonably be expected to result in —
>
> (i)   placing the health of the individual . . . in serious jeopardy,
> (ii) serious impairment to bodily functions, or
> (iii) serious dysfunction of any bodily organ or part. [42 U.S.C.A. §1395dd(e)(1)(A).]

When an individual is diagnosed as presenting an emergency medical condition:

> the hospital must provide either—
>   (A) within the staff and facilities available at the hospital, for such further medical examination and such treatment as may be required to stabilize the medical condition, or
>   (B) for the transfer of the individual to another medical facility in accordance with subsection (c) of this section. [42 U.S.C.A. §1395dd(b)(1).]

The treatment required "to stabilize" an individual is that treatment "necessary to assure, within reasonable medical probability, that no material deterioration of the condition is likely to result from or occur during the transfer of the individual from a facility." 42 U.S.C.A. §1395dd(e)(3)(A). Therefore, once an individual has been diagnosed as presenting an emergency medical condition, the hospital must provide that treatment necessary to prevent the material deterioration of the individual's condition or provide for an appropriate transfer to another facility.

In the application of these provisions to Baby K, the Hospital concedes that when Baby K is presented in respiratory distress a failure to provide "immediate medical attention" would reasonably be expected to cause serious impairment of her bodily functions. Thus, her breathing difficulty qualifies as an emergency medical condition, and the diagnosis of this emergency medical condition triggers the duty of the hospital to provide Baby K with stabilizing treatment or to transfer her in accordance with the provisions of EMTALA. Since transfer is not an option available to the Hospital at this juncture,[5] the Hospital must stabilize Baby K's condition. . . .

III

. . . As the Hospital acknowledged during oral argument, Baby K resides at the nursing home for months at a time without requiring emergency medical attention. Only when she has experienced episodes of bradypnea or apnea[9] has Baby K required respiratory support to prevent serious impairment of her bodily functions. It is bradypnea or apnea, not anencephaly, that is the emergency medical condition that brings Baby K to the Hospital for treatment. . . . The Hospital does not allege that it would refuse to provide respiratory support to infants experiencing bradypnea or apnea who do not have anencephaly. Indeed, a refusal to provide such treatment would likely be considered as providing no emergency medical treatment. . . .

[The Hospital argues] that, in redressing the problem of disparate emergency medical treatment, Congress did not intend to require physicians to provide medical treatment outside the prevailing standard of medical care. The Hospital asserts that, because of their extremely limited life expectancy and because any treatment of their condition is futile, the prevailing standard of medical care for infants with anencephaly is to provide only warmth, nutrition, and hydration. Thus, it maintains that a requirement to provide respiratory assistance would exceed the prevailing standard of medical care. However, the plain language of EMTALA requires stabilizing treatment for any individual who comes to a participating hospital, is diagnosed as having an emergency medical condition, and cannot be transferred. . . . The Hospital has been unable to identify, nor has our research revealed, any statutory language or legislative history evincing a congressional intent to create an exception to the duty to provide stabilizing treatment when the required treatment would exceed the prevailing standard of medical care. We recognize the dilemma facing physicians who are requested to provide treatment they consider morally and ethically inappropriate, but we cannot ignore the plain language of the statute because

---

5. In order for a hospital to transfer a patient prior to stabilization, EMTALA requires: (1) the patient or a person acting on the patient's behalf to request a transfer in writing after being informed of the risks involved and the obligations of the hospital under EMTALA; or (2) a proper certification that the medical benefits expected from the transfer outweigh the risks involved. 42 U.S.C.A. §1395dd(c)(1). In addition, the transfer must meet the criteria for an appropriate transfer which include the requirement that a qualified receiving facility agree to accept that the patient and to provide appropriate medical treatment. 42 U.S.C.A. §1395dd(c)(1)(B), (c)(2). Since Ms. H objects to the transfer of Baby K, since the Hospital has not obtained a certificate that the benefits of a transfer would outweigh the medical risks involved, and since no qualified medical facility has agreed to accept Baby K, the requirements for transfer prior to stabilization have not been met. If Ms. H requests a transfer or the Hospital obtains a certification that the benefits of a transfer would outweigh the risks involved, and all of the requirements for an appropriate transfer are met, then the Hospital could, of course, transfer Baby K to another qualified medical facility prior to stabilization.

9. Bradypnea is an "abnormal slowness of breathing." Dorland's Illustrated Medical Dictionary 230 (27th ed. 1988). In an infant who has established and sustained spontaneous breathing, apnea describes the cessation of respiration for more than sixty seconds. Id. at 112.

"to do so would 'transcend our judicial function.' " *Baber*, 977 F.2d at 884. The appropriate branch to redress the policy concerns of the Hospital is Congress. . . .

IV

It is beyond the limits of our judicial function to address the moral or ethical propriety of providing emergency stabilizing medical treatment to anencephalic infants. We are bound to interpret federal statutes in accordance with their plain language and any expressed congressional intent. Congress rejected a case-by-case approach to determining what emergency medical treatment hospitals and physicians must provide and to whom they must provide it; instead, it required hospitals and physicians to provide stabilizing care to any individual presenting an emergency medical condition. EMTALA does not carve out an exception for anencephalic infants in respiratory distress any more than it carves out an exception for comatose patients, those with lung cancer, or those with muscular dystrophy—all of whom may repeatedly seek emergency stabilizing treatment for respiratory distress and also possess an underlying medical condition that severely affects their quality of life and ultimately may result in their death. Because EMTALA does not provide for such an exception, the judgment of the district court is affirmed.

■ CAUSEY v. ST. FRANCIS MEDICAL CENTER
719 So. 2d 1072 (La. Ct. App. 1998)

Brown, J.

The facts of this end of life drama are not materially disputed. Believing it medically and ethically inappropriate, a physician and hospital withdrew life- sustaining care to a 31-year-old, quadriplegic, end-stage renal failure, comatose patient over the strongly expressed objections of the patient's family. . . .

Facts

Having suffered cardiorespiratory arrest, Sonya Causey was transferred to St. Francis Medical Center (SFMC) from a nursing home. She was comatose, quadriplegic and in end-stage renal failure. Her treating physician, Dr. Herschel R. Harter, believed that continuing dialysis would have no benefit. Although Dr. Harter agreed that with dialysis and a ventilator Mrs. Causey could live for another two years, he believed that she would have only a slight (1% to 5%) chance of regaining consciousness. Because Mrs. Causey's family demanded aggressive life-sustaining care, Dr. Harter sought unsuccessfully to transfer her to another medical facility willing to provide this care.

Dr. Harter enlisted support from SFMC's Morals and Ethics Board. The Board agreed with Dr. Harter's opinion to discontinue dialysis, life-support procedures, and to enter a "no-code" status (do not resuscitate). Mrs. Causey was taken off a feeding tube and other similar devices. The day the ventilator was removed, Mrs. Causey died of respiratory and cardiac failure.

Plaintiffs, the husband, father and mother of Sonya Causey, brought this petition for damages against SFMC and Dr. Harter. Defendants filed an exception of prematurity asserting that this action was covered under Louisiana's Medical

Malpractice Act, which requires that malpractice claims be first submitted to a medical review panel before any action can be filed. . . .

DISCUSSION

Patient participation in medical decision-making is now well-established. Recognizing individual autonomy and the right to self-determination, our state legislature enacted a statute granting a competent, terminally ill person the right to *refuse* medical treatment.

In the *Karen Quinlan* case the court rejected a physician's adamant stand that he had a moral duty to treat to the last gasp. In that case, the father, not the physician, was given the power to decide whether his comatose daughter's life-prolonging care was beneficial. . . .

Now the roles are reversed. Patients or, if incompetent, their surrogate decision-makers, are demanding life-sustaining treatment regardless of its perceived futility, while physicians are objecting to being compelled to prolong life with procedures they consider futile. . . .

The problem is not with care that the physician believes is harmful or literally has no effect. For example, radiation treatment for Mrs. Causey's condition would not have been appropriate. This is arguably based on medical science. Rather, the problem is with care that has an effect on the dying process, but which the physician believes has no benefit. Such life-prolonging care is grounded in beliefs and values about which people disagree. Strictly speaking, if a physician can keep the patient alive, such care is not medically or physiologically "futile;" however, it may be "futile" on philosophical, religious or practical grounds.

Placement of statistical cut-off points for futile treatment involves subjective value judgments. The difference in opinion as to whether a 2% or 9% probability of success is the critical point for determining futility can be explained in terms of personal values, not in terms of medical science. When the medical professional and the patient, through a surrogate, disagree on the worth of pursuing life, this is a conflict over values, i.e., whether extra days obtained through medical intervention are worth the burden and costs.

SFMC had in place a Futile Care Policy which allowed for the discontinuance of medical care over and above that necessary for comfort and support if the probability of improving the patient's condition was slight and would serve only to prolong life in that condition. The inclusion of non-medical persons on the Morals and Ethics Board signals that this is not strictly a physiological or medical futility policy, but a policy asserting values and beliefs on the worth of sustaining life, even in a vegetative condition.

Futility is a subjective and nebulous concept which, except in the strictest physiological sense, incorporates value judgments. Obviously, in this case, subjective personal values of the benefit of prolonging life with only a slight possibility of improvement dictated SFMC's and Dr. Harter's decision.

To focus on a definition of "futility" is confusing and generates polemical discussions. We turn instead to an approach emphasizing the standard of medical care.

Physicians are professionals and occupy a special place in our community. They are licensed by society to perform this special role. No one else is permitted to use life-prolonging technology, which is considered by many as "fundamental" health care. The physician has an obligation to present all medically acceptable treatment options for the patient or her surrogate to consider and either choose or reject; however, this does not compel a physician to provide interventions that in his view would be harmful, without effect or "medically inappropriate." In recognizing a terminal patient's right to refuse care, La. R.S. 40:1299.58.1(a)(4) states that the statute is not to be construed "to require the application of *medically inappropriate* treatment or life-sustaining procedures to any patient or to interfere with *medical judgment* with respect to the application of medical treatment or life-sustaining procedures." (Emphasis added). Unfortunately, "medically inappropriate" and "medical judgment" are not defined. . . .

Standards of medical malpractice require a physician to act with the degree of skill and care ordinarily possessed by those in that same medical specialty acting under the same or similar circumstances. Departure from this prevailing standard of care, coupled with harm, may result in professional malpractice liability. A finding that treatment is "medically inappropriate" by a consensus of physicians practicing in that specialty translates into a standard of care. Thus, in this case, whether Dr. Harter and SFMC met the standard of care concerning the withdrawal of dialysis, life-support procedures and the entering of a "no code" status must be determined. . . . [T]he Medical Malpractice Act is applicable and the matter should first be submitted to a medical review panel.

[Although multiple experts supported the withdrawal of care in their testimony to the medical review panel, the *Causey* case was settled before trial on remand.]

Notes: Medical Futility

1. *What Really Happened in* Baby K? Baby K, whose name was Stephanie Keene, ultimately lived for two-and-a-half years in a pediatric nursing facility. She died in the emergency room of Fairfax Hospital in Fairfax, Virginia—the same hospital that brought the *Baby K* case—after being taken there by ambulance for the sixth time. Her anencephaly had been diagnosed by ultrasound during the sixteenth week of her gestation, and her mother, Contrenia Harrell, decided to carry her to term, believing (according to press accounts) that " 'all life is precious' " and that God would guide Stephanie's life. Other local hospitals reportedly refused to accept a transfer of Baby K shortly after her birth.

Baby K's medical bills ultimately reached almost $1 million. They were covered in part by her mother's insurance with an HMO and in part by Medicaid. These financing systems are described in Chapter 9. They often do not pay the full costs of treatment. Nevertheless, hospital officials stated that the costs of Baby K's care were not a factor in the hospital's lawsuit. Even so, the hospital may have been thinking about the implications of the case for future patients, and the cost of caring for patients like Baby K are likely to be an issue for other hospitals as health insurers increasingly employ capitation rates for reimbursement, and as Medicare and Medicaid continue to limit their reimbursement rates.

An important question is who should make the treatment decision for a patient like Baby K? Do you think the insurers should have a stake in the decision? Would it be reasonable to tell Baby K's mother she can insist on treatment but not on payment, thereby remaining liable for the bills? If she still insisted on treatment, but the hospital knew she could never pay, should it still have to treat?

For a report on family objections to futility determinations at a major teaching hospital, see Ellen M. Robinson et al., After the DNR: Surrogates Who Persist in Requesting Cardiopulmonary Resuscitation, 47(1) Hastings Ctr. Rep. 10 (2017).

2. *A Medical Miracle?* Some might scoff at Ms. Harrell's reported belief in a medical miracle, but one may in fact have occurred here. As the court noted, anencephalic children generally do not live very long; fewer than 10 percent of such children survive more than a week. Baby K may be the longest-lived child with anencephaly. Rather than a miracle, however, her length of life may indicate that the general lack of aggressive treatment for anencephalic children results in their actual lifespans being considerably shorter than their potential lifespans.

3. *Disability Discrimination.* An important issue raised by the *Baby K* case is whether a denial of treatment would violate the Americans with Disabilities Act (and the Rehabilitation Act). Although the Fourth Circuit declined to decide this issue, supra page 610 n.2, the court did allude to the issue in its opinion, supra page 613. There, the Court observes that the hospital would provide ventilator support to infants in respiratory distress who were not anencephalic. This argument is analogous to the argument raised in the *University Hospital* case, reprinted at pages 82-87 and discussed at pages 90-92 and 580-581. In *University Hospital,* there were charges of discrimination when potentially life-prolonging treatments were withheld from a seriously disabled infant. The crux of the argument is as follows: Anti-discrimination law requires similarly situated persons to be treated alike. Is *Baby K* similarly situated to other infants needing ventilator treatment because she is also in respiratory distress, or is she not similarly situated because her respiratory distress is related to her anencephaly rather than to a condition that is more responsive to medical treatment? A major concern in these cases is whether scarce resources can be allocated. For a relevant discussion of this concern in the context of allocating organs for transplantation, see pages 691-696 For further discussion of the Americans with Disabilities Act, see Chapter 9.D.1.

The implications of *Baby K* for hospitals trying to limit health care costs is serious. Perhaps in recognition of that fact, the Fourth Circuit cabined the holding of *Baby K* two years later in Bryan v. Rectors and Visitors of the University of Virginia, 95 F.3d 349 (4th Cir. 1996) (discussed at pages 74-75). In *Bryan,* the court rejected the family's claim when physicians withheld resuscitative treatment from a hopelessly ill patient who died of a heart attack 20 days after her hospital admission.

4. *Defining Futility.* Futility is generally analyzed under two rubrics: qualitative and quantitative futility. Under qualitative futility, the claim is that medical treatment cannot provide a sufficient benefit to justify its use. Some commentators argue that there is qualitative futility when the patient would not recover enough to go home from the hospital, some find qualitative futility when the patient is permanently unconsciousness, and others believe there is futility only when treatment cannot provide a physiological benefit. In this third view, treatment is not futile as long as it can prolong life or affect the quality of life in any way.

Under quantitative futility, the claim is that there is too low a likelihood that medical treatment will have its desired effect. Here, too, there is disagreement as to when futility exists. Some would find futility when a particular treatment has been consistently unsuccessful for at least 100 tries. Lawrence J. Schneiderman et al., Medical Futility: Its Meaning and Ethical Implications, 112 Ann. Intern. Med. 949 (1990). Others would place it at different likelihoods of success. In one study, researchers discussed with internal medicine residents the reasons why the residents wrote do-not-resuscitate (DNR) orders for their patients. In two-thirds of the cases in which quantitative futility was a contributing factor to the DNR order, the likelihood that the patient would be resuscitated and be able to go home from the hospital was 1 percent or less. In 9 percent of cases, on the other hand, the likelihood of success was 20 percent or more. J. Randall Curtis et al., Use of the Medical Futility Rationale in Do-Not-Attempt-Resuscitation Orders, 273 JAMA 124, 126-127 (1995). Of course, one's view about quantitative futility depends on the qualitative benefit to be gained. The greater the potential qualitative benefit, the lower the likelihood of benefit before a treatment would be considered futile.

5. *Comparison with* Quinlan. In 1991, doctors at Hennepin County Medical Center unsuccessfully invoked futility to discontinue a ventilator from a patient in a persistent vegetative state. In re Wanglie, No. PX-91-283 (Hennepin County Prob. Ct. Minn., July 1, 1991), discussed in Steven H. Miles, Informed Demand for "Nonbeneficial" Medical Treatment, 325 New Eng. J. Med. 512 (1991).

The *Wanglie* case is exactly the reverse of the *Quinlan* case. Both cases involved a patient who was permanently unconscious and thought to be ventilator dependent. In *Quinlan*, the family was in court trying to have the ventilator stopped. In *Wanglie*, the family was in court trying to have the ventilator continued. If ventilator treatment for Mrs. Wanglie was futile, how could it not have been futile for Ms. Quinlan? Why do you suppose the hospital in *Wanglie* asked the court to appoint a conservator for Mrs. Wanglie rather than simply to authorize discontinuation of her ventilator?

6. *Other Futility Cases.* In futility cases, courts so far have split between siding with the patient or the patient's family and siding with the physicians and hospital.

For cases rejecting futility, in addition to *Baby K* and *Wanglie*, there is In re Jane Doe, 418 S.E.2d 3 (Ga. 1992). In that case, an adolescent suffered from a severe and degenerative neurological disease that left her comatose or nearly comatose. Jane Doe's physicians and hospital wanted to de-escalate life support and enter a DNR order, and her parents split on the issue. Although the case was brought at least in part as a futility case, the positions of the parties changed during the judicial proceedings such that the Georgia Supreme Court ended up deciding the case on the issue of resolving parental disagreements over CPR. The court held that a DNR order could not be written without the consent of both parents.

In another unreported case, In re Ryan N. Nguyen, #94206074-5 (Wash. Super. Ct., Spokane County, Nov. 22, 1994), the futility argument also was rejected. Ryan Nguyen was born six weeks early and was diagnosed with severe brain damage, an intestinal blockage, and malfunctioning kidneys. The hospital where he was being treated could not provide the necessary dialysis, and two academic medical centers refused to accept a referral, in at least one case on the ground that the child had such a dismal prognosis. The family obtained a court order for treatment, and the publicity resulted in a hospital offering to provide care. Ultimately, Ryan's intestinal blockage was cleared, his kidney problems resolved, and it turned out that he had not suffered any irreversible brain injury. Alexander Morgan Capron, Baby Ryan and Virtual Futility, 25(2) Hastings Center Rep. 20 (1995).

For a case accepting futility in addition to *Bryan* and *Causey*, consider the *Gilgunn* case. Gilgunn v. Massachusetts General Hospital, No. 92-4820 (Mass. Super. Ct. Suffolk Cty., April 22, 1995). In that case, Catherine Gilgunn became comatose and terminally ill at age 71, and her physicians decided to write a do-not-resuscitate order and discontinue her ventilator over the objections of one of her children. Alexander Morgan Capron, Abandoning a Waning Life, 25(4) Hastings Center Rep. 24 (1995). After Mrs. Gilgunn died, her daughter sued the hospital and physician, and the jury decided in favor of the defendants. This case, however, may not tell us very much about the law on futility since the verdict was not appealed, and the jury may have sided with the hospital and physicians on any of several theories. Capron, supra, at 25-26.

Nearly a decade after the *Gilgunn* case, Massachusetts General Hospital sought judicial permission to discontinue aggressive treatment of a patient severely disabled by ALS (Lou Gehrig's disease), over the objections of the patient's daughter. For the most part in this case, the hospital did not succeed with its futility argument. The trial court upheld the patient's appointment of her daughter as health care proxy and also ordered the writing of a do-not-resuscitate order (which by the time of the decision had been agreed to by the daughter) on the grounds that CPR would be both "inappropriate and harmful." The court also instructed the daughter to make future medical decisions based on the daughter's assessment of the patient's best interests. The court felt that the patient's condition had deteriorated in ways unanticipated by the patient and that the patient's wishes were no longer ascertainable. (In the appointment, the patient directed her daughter to decide on the basis of her wishes unless her wishes were unknown, in which case her daughter was supposed to decide on the basis of an assessment of best interests.) In re Barbara Howe, No. 03 P 1255 (Mass. Prob. & Fam. Ct., Suffolk Div., March 22, 2004). A year later, the daughter and hospital were back in court and settled the dispute with an agreement that the hospital would maintain ventilator support for three more months and then be free to discontinue treatment. Ms. Howe died 26 days before the expiration of the three-month period. John J. Paris et al., *Howe v. MGH* and *Hudson v. Texas Children's Hospital*: Two Approaches to Resolving Family-Physician Disputes in End-of-Life Care, 26 J. Perinatology 726 (2006).

Betancourt v. Trinitas Hospital involved a patient in a persistent vegetative state for whom physicians wanted to write a DNR order and discontinue dialysis. Family members sought an injunction against these steps, and the New Jersey trial court rejected the hospital's futility argument. While the appeal was pending, the patient died, and the court of appeals dismissed the case as moot. The court also called on the legislature, executive branch, and appropriate commissions to develop policy for cases involving claims of futility. 1 A.3d 823 (N.J. Ct. App. 2010). Note that the New Jersey Supreme Court did not dismiss the *Conroy* case as moot even though Ms. Conroy died while the appeal was pending in her case.

7. *Futility Statutes.* As in Louisiana, some states have addressed futility by statute. See, e.g., Ark. Code § 20-6-109; Tenn. Code § 68-11-1808; Tex. Health & Safety Code Ann. §166.046; Va. Code Ann. §54.1-2990.

The Texas statute is notable for the procedures it sets out to invoke futility. In Texas, a physician's refusal to honor a request for treatment requires review by an ethics or medical committee, and the patient or surrogate decisionmaker is entitled to attend the committee's meeting and receive a written explanation for the committee's decision. If the patient or family disagrees with a committee's decision affirming the refusal, the physician must make a reasonable effort to transfer the patient to a physician who will provide the desired treatment. Although treatment must be provided pending transfer, there is no obligation to provide treatment beyond the tenth day after a committee decision in favor of refusing treatment.

While some view the Texas approach as a model, Paris et al., *Howe v. MGH*, supra, it has provoked considerable controversy in some cases when doctors and hospitals have invoked it, and family members have been able to delay the withdrawal of treatment through court challenges.

While Texas clearly recognizes futility as a basis for withholding treatment, other statutes tend to authorize withholding treatment only under a very narrow or uncertain definition of futility or require the provision of treatment pending transfer to a facility that is willing to provide care. Cal. Prob. Code §§4735-4736 (modifying §7(f) of the Uniform Health Care Decisions Act (1993)); Idaho Code §39-4514; Md. Code Ann., Health—General §5-611; N.Y. Pub. Health L. §§2994-f(3).

Virginia's statute, Va. Code Ann. §54.1-2990, seems to clearly authorize physicians to withhold care they deem futile, and some hospitals have implemented futility policies without incident. Other hospitals in the state, however, see uncertainty in the statutory authorization, and there have been efforts to clarify the law. Similarly, in other states, such as Arkansas and Tennessee, whose statutes seem to authorize physicians to withhold care they deem futile, some hospitals are comfortable implementing the statutory authorization while other hospitals are not.

8. *Futility in Practice.* What do you make of the fact that the physicians in *Baby K* were willing to provide the child with nutrition and hydration but not a ventilator to ensure adequate oxygenation? If a ventilator is futile because the child is anencephalic, then why isn't a feeding tube futile? Conversely, if we say that Mrs. Wanglie is entitled to a ventilator because it could maintain her life, would we also say she is entitled to a heart valve replacement if one were needed to maintain her life?

Is there some difference between *Bryan, Causey,* and *Gilgunn,* on one hand, and many of the other cases presented (e.g., *Baby K, Howe, Jane Doe, Wanglie,* and *Ryan Nguyen*) that might explain why the two groups of cases came out differently?

9. *Additional Views.* Consider the following perspectives on futility:

> a. "In the event that the patient or surrogate requests a treatment that the responsible health care professional regards as clearly futile in achieving its physiological objective and so offering no physiological benefit to the patient, the professional has no obligation to provide it. However, the health care professional's value judgment that although a treatment will produce physiological benefit, the benefit is not sufficient to warrant the treatment, should not be used as a basis for determining a treatment to be futile." Guidelines on the Termination of Life-Sustaining Treatment and the Care of the Dying: A Report of the Hastings Center 32 (1987).
>
> b. "The argument that physician judgments about the futility of CPR are improper simply because they incorporate value judgments relies on a principle that has implausible implications for the rest of medical practice. . . . If the physician cannot refuse because, as a matter of principle, he or she is forbidden to employ 'value judgments,' then no justification can remain for refusal to provide a computed tomographic scan for the anxious patient with a headache, who also may have attached symbolic importance to the procedure, and no justification is available for resisting a family's demand that even 'physiologically futile' resuscitation efforts must continue indefinitely. . . . The real question can no longer be *whether* value judgments can be made concerning the provision of CPR or other medical

techniques; rather, the question is *which* value judgments physicians may use in deciding whether to meet patients' demands." Tom Tomlinson & Howard Brody, Futility and the Ethics of Resuscitation, 264 JAMA 1276, 1277-1278 (1990)

c. Claims that a particular treatment is "futile" are really claims that the treatment is too expensive at a time when health care resources are severely strained. Physicians prefer to characterize a treatment as futile rather than as too costly for the same reason that judges prefer to justify a decision on the ground that it is compelled by precedent rather than to acknowledge the indeterminacy in the law and concede that they are deciding on the basis of personal philosophy. By characterizing a treatment as medically futile and therefore of no purpose, physicians can hide the fact that they are rationing care, and thereby avoid patient challenges to their rationing decisions. It is much easier for a patient to challenge a rationing decision than a "medical" decision. Calling a treatment futile serves another purpose. It permits physicians to regain some of the authority they have lost since the mid-1960s when medical ethics and the law began to give greater recognition to patient autonomy. If a treatment decision is viewed as a medical decision rather than a value judgment, then physicians can colorably claim that the decision is exclusively for them to make.

10. *Further Reading.* While there are a relatively small number of court cases involving "futility," there is an extensive literature on the topic of **medical futility**. Useful readings on the issue include an official policy statement of several professional societies at 191 Am. J. Resp. & Crit. Care Med. 1318 (2015); Mary Ann Baily, Cost and End-of-Life-Care, 39 J. L. Med. & Ethics 172 (2011); Leslie Blackhall, Must We Always Use CPR?, 317 New Eng. J. Med. 1281 (1987); Paul R. Helft et al., The Rise and Fall of the Futility Movement, 343 New Eng. J. Med. 293 (2000); Jerry Menikoff, Demanded Medical Care, 30 Ariz. St. L. J. 1091 (1998); David Orentlicher, Matters of Life and Death, 123-166 (2002); Thaddeus Mason Pope, Dispute Resolution Mechanisms for Intractable Medical Futility Disputes, 58 N.Y.L. Sch. L. Rev. 347 (2013/2014).Tom Tomlinson & Howard Brody, Futility and the Ethics of Resuscitation, 264 JAMA 1276 (1990); Robert Truog, Medical Futility, 25 Ga. St. U. L. Rev. 985 (2009); and a symposium in the June 2011 issue of the Journal of Bioethical Inquiry.

Other useful articles include contributions to a Symposium on Medical Futility, 25 Seton Hall L. Rev. 873-1026 (1995); Mary A. Crossley, Medical Futility and Disability Discrimination, 81 Iowa L. Rev. 179 (1995); Philip G. Peters, Jr., When Physicians Balk at Futile Care, 91 Nw. U. L. Rev. 798 (1997); and Lance K. Stell, Stopping Treatment on Grounds of Futility, 11 St. Louis U. Pub. L. Rev. 481 (1992).

Notes: Brain Death

Although futility has been debated seriously as an issue only since the late 1980s, the development of the concept of brain death in the late 1960s and early 1970s can be seen as an early manifestation of the futility concern.

1. *Medical Background.* Traditionally, death was pronounced based on the cessation of the beating of the heart and the breathing of the lungs. In other words, death was determined on the basis of "cardiopulmonary" criteria. Typically at death, a person's heart stops functioning because of injury or illness. The person's lungs and brain also stop functioning because they are deprived of their blood flow. Since

it is a much simpler matter to detect loss of heart and lung function than to detect loss of brain function, cardiopulmonary criteria for death were adopted. In some cases, injury or illness causes loss of brain function first, and without the regulation of the brain, the lungs also stop functioning (i.e., the breathing of the lungs is controlled by the brain stem—the beating of the heart is also regulated by the brain stem, but the heart can pump an adequate amount of blood in the absence of brain stem function). When the lungs stop, the heart is deprived of oxygen, and it then ceases beating. Historically, loss of lung and heart function followed within minutes of the loss of brain function, and patients who had lost brain function satisfied cardiopulmonary criteria for death.

With advances in medical technology, however, it became possible to support a person's heart and lungs with mechanical ventilation even after cessation of brain function. According to cardiopulmonary criteria, these persons were not dead, but to many observers, they seemed to have lost their vitality. Patients who have lost all brain function appear to be in a very deep coma. (Interestingly, spontaneous movements are more common in brain-dead patients than once thought. In a study, researchers found that 39 percent of their brain-dead patients exhibited spontaneous movements of their fingers, toes, and arms. These movements are believed to reflect spinal cord reflexes, and, in fact, no brain activity was seen on EEGs during the movements. Gustavo Saposnik et al., Spontaneous and Reflex Movements in Brain Death, 54 Neurology 221 (2000).) Mechanical measures and other artificial support can maintain brain-dead patients' heartbeat and breathing temporarily, but usually only for a few weeks or months, after cessation of brain function. But see D. Alan Shewmon, Chronic "Brain Death": Meta-Analysis and Conceptual Consequences, 51 Neurology 1538 (1998) (describing the maintenance of a heartbeat in brain-dead patients for more than a year, including one patient for more than 14 years). Because of the profound loss of functioning, the permanence of the condition, and the inability to prolong the state for very long, many observers questioned whether it made sense to provide treatment to these patients.

Ordinarily, such questioning might lead to a right to have medical treatment withdrawn when a person's brain stops functioning, just as Karen Quinlan's persistent vegetative state led the New Jersey Supreme Court to recognize her right to have her ventilator withdrawn. Instead, "brain" criteria for death were developed. In a report that was highly influential in leading to the acceptance of "brain death," the authors wrote:

> Our primary purpose is to define irreversible coma as a new criterion for death. There are two reasons why there is need for a definition: (1) Improvements in resuscitative and supportive measures have led to increased efforts to save those who are desperately injured. Sometimes these efforts have only partial success so that the result is an individual whose heart continues to beat but whose brain is irreversibly damaged. The burden is great on patients who suffer permanent loss of intellect, on their families, on the hospitals, and on those in need of hospital beds already occupied by these comatose patients. (2) Obsolete criteria for the definition of death can lead to controversy in obtaining organs for transplantation.

Report of the Ad Hoc Committee of the Harvard Medical School to Examine the Definition of Brain Death, A Definition of Irreversible Coma, 205 JAMA 85, 85 (1968).

As this excerpt suggests, the adoption of brain criteria for death may have been motivated primarily by futility-type concerns—the high burdens and low benefits of treatment—as well as by concerns about the shortage of organs for transplantation. Philosophical considerations about the meaning of life seemingly played little role in the change.

In the next chapter, we take up the issues of organ transplantation related to brain death. Here, we consider the implications for patient autonomy of brain criteria for death. By defining patients as dead when they lose brain function, it would seem to follow that one could not choose for oneself or one's family member to have mechanical ventilation continued after cessation of brain function. That implication has been confirmed by the law.

2. *Adoption of Brain Criteria for Death.* Kansas was the first state to adopt a brain death statute, and its constitutionality was upheld in State v. Schaffer, 574 P.2d 205 (1977). It did so in the context of a murder prosecution, where the defendant had argued that the doctors who removed life support, and not himself, caused the death of the victim. A later case adopting the brain death definition as a matter of common law provides a particularly thorough explanation of the relationship between the definition of death and homicide statutes. People v. Eulo, 472 N.E.2d 286 (N.Y. 1984). Death by brain criteria is accepted in every state as well as the District of Columbia. Alan Meisel, Kathy L. Cerminara & Thaddeus M. Pope, The Right to Die §6.04[A] (3d ed. 2017 Supp.). The Uniform Determination of Death Act has been enacted by statute in a majority of states. Several states, like Washington, have adopted brain death by court decision, and the remainder of the states have enacted brain death legislation without relying on the uniform law.

In re Bowman, 617 P.2d 731 (Wash. 1980) (en banc), provides a good discussion of the principles undergirding brain death. According to the court,

> [d]eath is both a legal and medical question. Traditionally, the law has regarded the question of at what moment a person died as a question of fact to be determined by expert medical testimony. However, recognizing that the law has independent interests in defining death which may be lost when deference to medicine is complete, courts have established standards which, although based on medical knowledge, define death as a matter of law. Thus, the law has adopted standards of death but has turned to physicians for the criteria by which a particular standard is met. [Id. at 734.]

3. *The Meaning of Adopting Brain Criteria for Death.* It is not clear what the significance has been of changing the definition of death to include cessation of brain function. We could characterize the change as substituting brain death for cardiopulmonary death. Under this view, the essence of personhood is found in the functioning of the mind rather than the body, so that death occurs when the brain stops functioning. We can identify brain death either directly, by showing the absence of brain function, or indirectly, by showing the absence of cardiac function (i.e., once the heart stops pumping blood to the brain, the brain cells die). According to another view, life requires the presence of both brain and cardiopulmonary function. Once one of the two functions is lost, the person is dead.

A third view, and the one given by most commentators to explain the development of neurological criteria for death, is that death has always meant loss of the body's integrative capacity. Under this view, death occurs when the body loses its ability to function as an integrated whole rather than as a collection of independently functioning cells or tissues. After all, a person's cells can be maintained indefinitely in the laboratory, but we would not therefore say that the person is still alive. The body retains some ability to integrate bodily functions as long as there is some brain function, but once the brain ceases all function, the body has lost its integrative capacity. Again, we can measure loss of integrative function either directly, by establishing loss of brain function, or indirectly, by establishing loss of cardiopulmonary function. According to this view, we always thought of death as the loss of integrative capacity, but, until recently, we were able to determine its existence only when the heart stopped beating. Once we were able to support cardiopulmonary function artificially even after loss of brain function, we were able to have different ways to measure death. Under the integrative capacity view, the definition of death did not change; rather, we have only changed the criteria for ascertaining death. President's Commission for the Study of Ethical Problems in Medicine and Biomedical and Behavioral Research, Defining Death 32-38 (1981); Alexander M. Capron & Leon Kass, A Statutory Definition of the Standards for Determining Human Death, 121 U. Pa. L. Rev. 87, 102 (1972).

4. *Loss of Integrative Capacity.* While the President's Commission and others accept integrative capacity as the basis for life, there are serious problems with this theory. First, it turns out that people who are dead according to neurological criteria still maintain some integrative capacity. For example, their brains still regulate water retention by the kidneys to ensure the appropriate balance among water, blood cells, and other components of blood in the body's bloodstream. In addition, many patients who are dead by brain criteria have some electrical activity on their electroencephalograms (EEGs), and they "frequently respond to surgical incision at the time of organ procurement with a significant rise in both heart rate and blood pressure." Robert D. Truog, Is It Time to Abandon Brain Death?, 27(1) Hastings Center Rep. 29, 29-30 (1997). Proponents of the integrative capacity theory respond that death occurs when there is loss of all critical or essential bodily functions. James L. Bernat, Brain Death, 49 Arch. Neurol. 569, 569 (1992), but that begs the question of what bodily functions are critical.

A second problem with the integrative capacity theory is that it does not seem to explain how people think about death. The fact that we still use the term "brain death" and speak of keeping "brain dead" patients on "life support" suggests that people think of death by neurological criteria differently than death by cardiopulmonary criteria. Indeed, in one study, physicians and nurses likely to be involved in organ procurement for transplantation were asked to explain why they thought a person was dead when the brain stopped functioning. While 25 percent of the physicians and nurses gave loss of integrative capacity as their reason, 36 percent spoke in terms of loss of consciousness and 32 percent indicated that they really did not believe the patient was dead, explaining that the patient would die soon no matter what was done or that the patient's quality of life was unacceptable. Stuart J. Youngner, Defining Death: A Superficial and Fragile Consensus, 49 Arch. Neurol. 570, 571 (1992). See also Richard Willing, Brain-Dead Woman Dies After Baby Born, USA Today, Aug. 4, 2005, at 3A (marking woman's death when ventilator was discontinued nearly three months after declaration of death by brain criteria).

5. *Choosing a Definition of Death.* How should we define death? How do we choose among cardiopulmonary death, brain death, and upper brain death (i.e., loss of consciousness)? What is the moral, philosophical, or legal principle that helps us decide what it means to be dead? If the issue is whether the person has the essential characteristics of a human being, why not require only permanent loss of consciousness before declaring someone dead? Is it because unconscious persons do things that make them appear to be conscious (e.g., random or reflexive movements of the eyes, arms, or legs)? Or is it that we cannot be sure they are really unconscious and therefore those things that look like conscious activity may really reflect conscious activity?

For useful readings on these issues, see Alexander Morgan Capron, Brain Death, 344 New Eng. J. Med. 1244 (2001); Michael B. Green & Daniel Wikler, Brain Death and Personal Identity, 9 Phil. & Pub. Aff. 105 (1980); Jeff McMahan, An Alternative to Brain Death, 34 J. L. Med. & Ethics 44 (2006); President's Commission for the Study of Ethical Problems in Medicine and Biomedical and Behavioral Research, Defining Death (1981); President's Council on Bioethics, Controversies in the Determination of Death (2008); Tom Stacy, Death, Privacy, and the Free Exercise of Religion, 77 Cornell L. Rev. 490 (1992); Robert M. Veatch, The Whole-Brain-Oriented Concept of Death, 3 J. Thanatology 13 (1975); Stuart J. Youngner et al., eds., The Definition of Death (1999).

6. *Lack of Patient or Family Choice.* When a person has been declared dead, that person's legal representative (in this case the guardian ad litem) cannot insist that the patient be maintained on a ventilator. Indeed, in In re *Bowman*, the court automatically assumed that the declaration of death by brain criteria foreclosed a choice of continued treatment. 617 P.2d at 420-421.

Nevertheless, cases continue to arise in which families challenge the determination of death by brain criteria, arguing that the determination of death was not properly made, though their primary concern may be with the use of neurologic criteria to determine death. The case of Jahi McMath received considerable public attention in 2014 when a teenager suffered a cardiac arrest after surgery and was declared dead by brain criteria. Her parents sued to maintain her medical care, and an agreement was reached in which the parents were able to transfer her to a facility that would provide continued care. For further reading, see Seema K. Shah, Piercing the Veil: The Limits of Brain Death as a Legal Fiction, 48 U. Mich. J. L. Reform 301 (2015).

Does it necessarily follow from the fact that a person is dead that we do not respect the person's or the family's wishes for ventilation to be continued until the heart stops beating? We can point to public health concerns to explain why a person must be buried or cremated after cardiopulmonary death, but what is the justification for insisting that a ventilator be discontinued after brain death? Would it matter if the person could pay for the costs of the continued treatment, through either an insurance policy or personal wealth?

7. *Single or Multiple Definitions.* Must we have a standard definition of death to which everyone subscribes? In New Jersey, under the determination of death statute, people are dead when either their heart and lungs or their brain stops functioning. However,

[t]he death of an individual shall not be declared upon the basis of neurological criteria . . . when the licensed physician authorized to declare death, has reason to believe, on the basis of information in the individual's available medical records, or information provided by a member of the individual's family or any other person knowledgeable about the individual's personal religious beliefs that such a declaration would violate the personal religious beliefs of the individual. In these cases, death shall be declared, and the time of death fixed, solely upon the basis of cardio-respiratory criteria. . . . [N.J. Stat. Ann. 26:6A-5.]

In New York, a New York State Department of Health Regulation provides that hospitals shall establish "a procedure for the reasonable accommodation of the individual's religious or moral objection to the determination" of death by neurological criteria. N.Y. Comp. Codes R. & Regs. tit. 10, §400.16(e)(3). New York physicians and hospitals vary in the extent to which they will continue treatment of a brain-dead person under that provision, but the regulation's requirement of reasonable accommodation does not mandate the continuation of treatment beyond the time necessary for the family to obtain an independent medical opinion and try to arrange for transfer of the patient to another facility. In re Long Island Jewish Medical Center, 641 N.Y.S.2d 989, 992 (Sup. Ct. 1996). California also has an accommodation provision much like the New York provision. Under California law, families that have "any special religious or cultural practices or concerns" about brain death are entitled to a "reasonably brief period of accommodation." Cal. Health & Safety Code §1254.4.

Could we permit all persons to decide when they are dead, as long as their definition of death falls within a reasonable range, say as long as the definition is permanent unconsciousness, brain death, or cardiac death? Would this be any different from the current status of abortion law, which essentially allows women to decide when their fetus becomes a person, as long as the woman chooses some point between conception and viability? For an argument that the free exercise clause of the First Amendment gives patients and their families a right to determine when death occurs, see Stacy, supra page 625.

We might also want to have different definitions of death depending on the reasons for wanting to know whether the patient is still alive. In this regard, see Roger Dworkin, Death in Context, 48 Ind. L.J. 623 (1975). Dworkin argues that "the effort devoted to defining death is wasted at best, counterproductive at worst," because of the variety of contexts in which the issue is relevant, namely: (1) procedural issues such as when the statutes of limitations begin to run for wrongful death actions and murder prosecutions; (2) numerous property and wealth devolution issues such as who died first for purposes of probating the wills of two people with interests in each other's estates; and (3) status relationships such as when remarriage is valid. Consider, for instance, that one accepted departure from the uniform definition of death is the presumption in many states that a person is dead who is missing for more than seven years.

8. *Criteria for Brain Death.* Guidelines for determining brain death have been published by medical specialty societies. Guidelines and discussion of brain death in adults and children can be found at Eelco F.M. Wijdicks et al., Evidence-Based Guideline Update: Determining Brain Death in Adults, 74 Neurology 1911 (2010);

Thomas A. Nakagawa et al., Clinical Report—Guidelines for the Determination of Brain Death in Infants and Children, 128 Pediatrics e720 (2011). Even with guidelines, the diagnosis of death by brain criteria is not a simple one, and there is considerable variation among neurologists in making the diagnosis. Shivani Ghoshal & David M. Greer, Why Is Diagnosing Brain Death So Confusing?, 21 Current Opinion Crit. Care 107 (2015).

6

Organ Transplantation: The Control, Use, and Allocation of Body Parts

This chapter explores another dimension of personal control over medical decisions: the supply and distribution of lifesaving organs for transplantation. Because of the serious shortage of transplantable organs, this is a topic that sparks much debate: Can financial payments to organ donors be used to increase the supply of organs? Can organs or other tissues be taken without permission after a person dies? When organs are in short supply and lives of those who need them are at stake, who gets them first and who decides? These questions range broadly among issues and themes that are addressed elsewhere in this book, but they are more compelling here because the stakes are so clearly life-and-death, and because the use of body parts is so infused with moral and emotional value.

We start by focusing on who controls the decision for organ donation. We have seen that patients may refuse unwanted offers of medical treatment even if doing so results in death. Courts have concluded that the state has a weaker interest than the patient in deciding how to balance concerns about bodily integrity with concerns about the preservation of the patient's own life. What if, on the other hand, there are other lives at stake? Does the state have a greater interest than the patient in making medical decisions when the issue is balancing the individual's concerns with the needs of other persons? That question extends beyond this chapter since an individual's medical decisions can implicate the interests of other persons in a number of ways. In Chapter 5, we considered situations in which a person's death would leave minor children without one of their parents. In Chapters 7 and 8, we consider situations in which a fetus's health is at stake or in which a person's illness poses a public health threat to other persons.

In this chapter, the question is how the balance of affected interests is struck with respect to organs and tissues. The state may perceive an interest in overriding a person's desire to maintain bodily integrity after death by taking the deceased's organs or tissues for people who need a transplant. Or the state may perceive an interest in protecting individuals from unwise decisions to give up their organs while they are still alive. In some cases, then, the question is whether the state can require a transfer (e.g., remove corneas from cadavers for transplantation); in other cases, the question is whether the state can make it harder for people to give up their organs (e.g., prohibit sales of kidneys). Should the balance be struck by individuals since it is their body, or by the state since it has a longer- and broader-range view of both individual and collective interests, or should there be a division of responsibility? As we will see, much of the law in this area has developed in response to the shortage of organs for transplantation, so before we begin, it is helpful to understand more about the need for organ donation and the existing sources of supply.

Good background readings include Michelle Goodwin, Black Markets: The Supply and Demand of Body Parts (2006); Organ Transplantation in Times of Shortage (Ralf Jox et al., eds., 2016); Organ Substitution Technology (Deborah Matheiu ed., 1988); The Ethics of Organ Transplantation (Wayne Shelton & John Balint eds., 2001); Organ and Tissue Donation (Bethany Spielman ed., 1996); Robert M. Veatch & Lainie F. Ross, Transplantation Ethics (2d ed. 2015); Organ Transplantation (Stuart J. Youngner et al., eds., 1996).

Note: The Shortage of Organs for Transplantation

The shortage of organs for transplantation is substantial. In October 2017, there were more than 127,000 registrations, and nearly 117,000 people on waiting lists for transplantation of a kidney, liver, heart, lung, intestine, or pancreas. (The number of registrations exceeds the number of people waiting since individuals may register on the waiting lists of more than one transplant center. On the other hand, many candidates are temporarily classified as "inactive" by their transplant programs because "they are medically unsuitable for transplantation or need to complete other eligibility requirements.")

About 7,000 people die each year waiting for an organ to become available, and more than 6,000 people are removed from the waiting list because they become too sick to receive a transplant. Even these statistics understate the problem. Given the serious shortage of organs for transplantation, many individuals never make it onto a waiting list since it is clear that they will not have sufficient priority to receive a transplant. (Current and historical data on organ transplantation can be found on the Web site of the Organ Procurement and Transplantation Network (OPTN). Other useful information can be found at the Web site of the United Network for Organ Sharing (UNOS).)

The gap between need and supply reflects a number of considerations. First, in a substantial percentage of cases in which a person dies and the person's organs could be transplanted, there is no transplantation. Physicians may neglect to ask for permission, or family members may refuse to donate the decedent's organs. Physicians are often uncomfortable raising the issue of transplantation, fearing that it will only exacerbate the family's grief. Families may deny permission for transplantation because they have religious or other objections to the removal of a body's organs after death. Efforts have been made to encourage people to register as organ donors, and now a majority of Americans have done so, but many people do not sign up, sometimes because of fears that their physicians will hasten their death, sometimes because of unwillingness to consider their mortality, sometimes because of religious conviction or a desire for an intact body. James R. Rodrigue et al., Organ Donation Decision, 6 Am. J. Transplantation 190 (2006); Wendy Walker et al., Factors Influencing Bereaved Families' Decisions About Organ Donation, 35 West. J. Nursing Res. 1339 (2013).

But even when people do register as donors and physicians know that they have done so, their decision may not ensure organ retrieval unless family consent can be obtained. Many physicians will not remove a deceased person's organs without family consent despite the fact that ethics and the law give priority to the decedent's previously expressed wishes. Indeed, according to the Revised Uniform Anatomical Gift Act, if a person does not revoke a decision to donate before dying, other persons are generally barred from amending or revoking the decedent's consent to donate. Rev. Unif. Anatomical Gift Act §8(a) (2006). This provision is designed to strengthen a similar provision in the previous Uniform Act, according to which a decedent's decision to donate is "irrevocable and does not require the consent or concurrence of any person after the donor's death." Unif. Anatomical Gift Act §2(h) (1987). Even before the 2006 revision a number of states enacted legislation to firmly indicate that the decedent's wishes control. See, e.g., Ind. Code §29-2-16-2.5. But see Ana S. Iltis, Organ Donation, Brain Death and the Family, 43 J. L. Med. & Ethics 369 (2015) (arguing that the usual authorization through donor registration should not count as valid consent).

The gap between need and supply of organs also reflects the fact that, while the number of transplants each year has been increasing, the number of waiting list registrations has been growing twice as fast. The number of waiting list registrations rose from 16,000 to nearly 128,000 between 1988 and 2017, but the number of transplants rose from about 13,000 to less than 35,000. This continually growing gap between candidates for transplant and available organs reflects several factors. The number of persons who die in a way that leaves their organs suitable for transplantation has been reduced by the enactment of laws requiring seat belts or motorcycle helmets, the use of air bags in automobiles, gun control legislation, and the stricter enforcement of laws that prohibit driving under the influence of alcohol. At the same time, progress in medicine is increasing the number of persons who could benefit from a transplant.

A. ORGAN DONATION

1. Competent Organ Donors

Traditionally, organ donation has been governed by state law. The National Organ Transplant Act of 1984 added a good deal of federal regulation. The Act created the Organ Procurement and Transportation Network as a private, nonprofit entity to determine standards for organ allocation and to establish a system for matching organ donors with recipients. 42 U.S.C. §274(b). The Act also imposed a ban on the sale of organs or other tissues used in transplantation. 42 U.S.C. §274e. However, the ban does not apply to blood, sperm, or ova.

When patients are alive, they are free to donate renewable tissues (e.g., blood and semen) and tissues that are not necessary to maintain health (e.g., ova). They may also sell these tissues (though there is controversy about the selling of ova). On the other hand, people may not donate or sell life-necessary organs (e.g., hearts). In between these two extremes are donations — but not sales — of organs or parts of organs where there may be a significant health risk to the donor.

For example, a person might want to donate a kidney to a family member. Since people typically have two kidneys, the donor ordinarily would function reasonably well without the second kidney. As with any major surgery, however, there are some risks from the donation — the chance of dying from the operation is about 0.03 percent. In addition, if something happened to the remaining kidney, there would be no backup. Over the long term, kidney donors experience a several-fold increase in risk of kidney failure compared to non-donors, though the absolute risk appears to be less than one percent for most donors. For female donors who later become pregnant, kidney donation raises the risk of hypertensive disorders of pregnancy. Kidney donors also may find that donation affects their access to health or life insurance. On the other hand, state law may protect living donors from being fired for having to take time off from their jobs, even in at-will employment states. Delaney v. Signature Health Care Foundation, 376 S.W.3d 55 (Mo. App. 2012).

Because of the risks to the donor — even if small — and concerns about donor motivation, donation of kidneys by living persons still provokes some controversy. When the donation occurs within the family, there are concerns about coercion; when the donation is extrafamilial, there are concerns about hidden payments or psychological stability of the donor. Nevertheless, transplant centers generally welcome donation of kidneys within families. Extrafamilial donations also are becoming more common, and studies suggest that transplant centers can screen potential donors to ensure that their desire to donate does not reflect psychopathology.

Similar issues are raised with regard to donations of a partial liver, which can be done since the liver can grow new tissue after it has been divided. But the concerns are accentuated since the risks to the donor from the surgery are greater than with kidney donation. Consequently, there is greater reluctance among transplant centers to accept donors who do not have a close relationship with the recipient. Data on long-term effects of partial liver donation are starting to emerge and are reassuring so far. But it's still too early to draw firm conclusions.

Partial lung transplants are not commonly performed in the United States, but are more important in countries that do not rely as much on deceased donors. Ethical concerns are heightened because two donors are needed for each recipient. Roger D. Yusen et al., Morbidity and Mortality of Live Lung Donation, 14 Am. J. Transplantation 1846 (2014).

People also may agree while competent to have their organs (and other tissues) taken for transplantation after they die. These donations are governed by the relevant state's version of the 2006 Revised Uniform Anatomical Gift Act or the 1968 or 1987 Uniform Anatomical Gift Act. Some version of the 1968 Act was adopted by every state and the District of Columbia within four years of the Act's issuance. By the time the 1987 Act was issued, some states had already adopted at least one of the new provisions, and by 1992, 46 states and the District of Columbia had done so. Fred H. Cate, Human Organ Transplantation: The Role of Law, 20 Iowa J. Corp. L.

69, 71-74 (1994). The 2006 Revised Act quickly elicited interest. By 2012, 45 states had adopted the Act, with an additional state since then.

Under all versions of the Act, competent adults may make a gift of their organs, with the gift to take effect upon their deaths. The gift may be for education, research, transplantation, or other therapy. For individuals who have not made a gift and who have not expressed opposition to the use of their organs, family members may authorize the taking of their organs. The 1987 Act added a few new provisions: hospitals must ask adult patients whether they want to be organ donors after death (routine inquiry); hospitals must discuss with family members their authority to authorize the taking of organs from deceased patients (routine request); medical examiners may authorize the taking of organs after autopsy if they do not find any objection after reasonable efforts to ascertain the person's or family's wishes; and, as with federal law, sales are prohibited. There is also duplication of federal law with respect to routine requests. That step is required of hospitals as a condition of receiving Medicare and Medicaid reimbursement. 42 U.S.C. §1320b-8. The 2006 Revised Act eliminated the ability of medical examiners to authorize organ retrieval in the absence of consent, in light of case law questioning that authority (discussed in section B.1, infra). Rev. Unif. Anatomical Gift Act §23 (2006). It also expanded the list of persons who may consent to organ donation after a person's death to include adult grandchildren, adults who "exhibited special care and concern for the decedent," and health care agents. Id. at §9(a).

Traditionally, organ donation focused on life-extending transplants. More recently, patients have received life-enhancing transplants, including transplants of hands, faces, and uteri. A uterus can be transplanted from a living or deceased donor, while other life-enhancing transplants involve deceased donors. Critics have questioned whether life enhancement without life extension can justify the risks of transplantation to the recipient, particularly from the immunosuppressive drugs that must be taken to prevent "rejection" of the transplant and that increase the risk of cancer. Nevertheless, life-enhancing transplants are becoming more common, and there have been births to recipients of a uterus transplant.

An even more controversial kind of transplant may be in the offing—whole body transplant to the recipient's head. In that case, the transplant can be both life-enhancing and life-extending, but it is not clear that the chances of success are high enough to justify a procedure that would kill the recipient if unsuccessful. Ana Iltis, The First Human Body Transplant, Bill of Health blog (May 30, 2017).

Further Reading. On **discomfort with living organ donation** among transplant professionals, see Adnan Sharif, Unspecified Kidney Donation, 95 Transplantation 1425 (2013); Allison Tong et al., Living Kidney Donor Assessment, 13 Am. J. Transplantation 2912 (2013).

On **living kidney donation,** see Brian J. Boyarsky et al., Experiences Obtaining Insurance after Live Kidney Donation, 14 Am. J. Transplantation 2168 (2014); Amit X. Garg et al., Gestational Hypertension and Preeclampsia in Living Kidney Donors, 372 New Eng. J. Med. 124 (2015); Morgan E. Grams et al., Kidney-Failure Risk Projection for the Living Kidney-Donor Candidate, 374 New Eng. J. Med. 411 (2016); Martin D. Jendrisak et al., Altruistic Living Donors, 6 Am. J. Transplantation 115 (2006); Ngan M. Lam, Long-term Medical Risks to the Living Kidney Donor, 11 Nature Rev. Nephrology 411, 414 (2015); Paul E. Morrissey et al., Good Samaritan Kidney Donation, 27 Transplantation 1369 (2005); Dorry L. Segev et al.,

Perioperative Mortality and Long-Term Survival Following Live Kidney Donation, 303 JAMA 959 (2010).

On **partial-liver donation**, see Vanessa R. Humphreville et al., Longterm Health-Related Quality of Life after Living Liver Donation, 22 Liver Transplantation 53 (2016); Abimereki D. Muzaale, Estimates of Early Death, Acute Liver Failure, and Long-term Mortality among Live Liver Donors, 142 Gastroenterology 273 (2012); Lainie Friedman Ross et al., Ethics in Living Donor Transplantation, in Transplantation of the Liver 65 (Ronald W. Busuttil & Göran B.G. Klintmalm eds., 3d ed. 2015).

On **obstacles to donation** facing willing donors, see Andrea DiMartini, Social and Financial Outcomes of Living Liver Donation, 17 Am. J. Transplantation 1081 (2017); James R. Rodrigue, Predonation Direct and Indirect Costs Incurred by Adults Who Donated a Kidney, 15 Am. J. Transplantation 2387 (2015); Lara Tushla et al., Living-Donor Kidney Transplantation: Reducing Financial Barriers to Live Kidney Donation—Recommendations from a Consensus Conference, 10 Clinical J. Am. Soc. Nephrology 1696 (2015).

On **life-enhancing** transplants, see a target article and comments on face transplants, 4(3) Am. J. Bioethics (2004); Kavita Arora & Valarie Blake, Uterus Transplantation, 125 Obstetrics & Gynecology 971 (2015); David Orentlicher, Toward Acceptance of Uterus Transplants, 42(6) Hastings Center Rep. 12 (2012); Brendan Parent, Informing Donors About Hand and Face Transplants, 10 J. Health & Biomedical L. 309 (2015); Maria Siemionow et al., Successes and Lessons Learned after More Than a Decade of Upper Extremity and Face Transplantation, 18 Curr. Opin. Organ Transplantation 633 (2013).

2. Incompetent Organ "Donors"

An important issue is whether the right of a competent person to donate organs survives incompetence. Is the issue analogous to whether the right to refuse life-sustaining treatment survives incompetence? We worry about abuse with organ transplantation—society might be too willing to take organs from incompetent persons to give the organs to competent persons—but we also worry about life-sustaining treatment being withdrawn too quickly from incompetent persons. Are there any important differences between the two concerns about abuse?

■ STRUNK v. STRUNK
445 S.W.2d 145 (Ky. Ct. App. 1969)

OSBORNE, Judge.

The specific question involved upon this appeal is: Does a court of equity have the power to permit a kidney to be removed from an incompetent ward of the state upon petition of his . . . mother, for the purpose of being transplanted into the body of his brother, who is dying of a fatal kidney disease? We are of the opinion it does.

The facts of the case are as follows: Arthur L. Strunk, 54 years of age, and Ava Strunk, 52 years of age, of Williamstown, Kentucky, are the parents of two sons. Tommy Strunk is 28 years of age, married, an employee of the Penn State Railroad and a part-time student at the University of Cincinnati. Tommy is now suffering from chronic glomerulus nephritis, a fatal kidney disease. He is now being kept alive by frequent treatment on an artificial kidney, a procedure which cannot be continued much longer.

Jerry Strunk is 27 years of age, incompetent, and through proper legal proceedings has been committed to the Frankfort State Hospital and School, which is a state institution maintained for the feebleminded. He has an I.Q. of approximately 35, which corresponds with the mental age of approximately six years. He is further handicapped by a speech defect, which makes it difficult for him to communicate with persons who are not well acquainted with him. When it was determined that Tommy, in order to survive, would have to have a kidney the doctors considered the possibility of using a kidney from a cadaver if and when one became available or one from a live donor if this could be made available. The entire family, his mother, father and a number of collateral relatives were tested. Because of incompatibility of blood type or tissue none were medically acceptable as live donors. As a last resort, Jerry was tested and found to be highly acceptable. . . . The mother . . . petitioned the county court for authority to proceed with the operation. The court found that the operation was necessary, that under the peculiar circumstances of this case it would not only be beneficial to Tommy but also beneficial to Jerry because Jerry was greatly dependent upon Tommy, emotionally and psychologically, and that his well-being would be jeopardized more severely by the loss of his brother than by the removal of a kidney. . . .

A psychiatrist, in attendance to Jerry, who testified in the case, stated in his opinion the death of Tommy under these circumstances would have "an extremely traumatic effect upon him" (Jerry).

The Department of Mental Health of this Commonwealth has entered the case as amicus curiae and on the basis of its evaluation of the seriousness of the operation as opposed to the traumatic effect upon Jerry as a result of the loss of Tommy, recommended to the court that Jerry be permitted to undergo the surgery. Its recommendations are as follows:

> . . . Jerry Strunk, a mental defective, has emotions and reactions on a scale comparable to that of normal person. He identifies with his brother Tom; Tom is his model, his tie with his family. Tom's life is vital to the continuity of Jerry's improvement at Frankfort State Hospital and School. The testimony of the hospital representative reflected the importance to Jerry of his visits with his family and the constant inquiries Jerry made about Tom's coming to see him. Jerry is aware he plays a role in the relief of this tension. We the Department of Mental Health must take all possible steps to prevent the occurrence of any guilt feelings Jerry would have if Tom were to die.
>
> The necessity of Tom's life to Jerry's treatment and eventual rehabilitation is clearer in view of the fact that Tom is his only living sibling and at the death of their parents, now in their fifties, Jerry will have no concerned, intimate communication so necessary to his stability and optimal functioning.
>
> The evidence shows that at the present level of medical knowledge, it is quite remote that Tom would be able to survive several cadaver transplants. Tom has a much better chance of survival if the kidney transplant from Jerry takes place.

Upon this appeal we are faced with the fact that all members of the immediate family have recommended the transplant. The Department of Mental Health has likewise made its recommendation. The county court has given its approval. The circuit court has found that it would be to the best interest of the ward of the state that the procedure be carried out. Throughout the legal proceedings, Jerry has been represented by a guardian ad litem, who has continually questioned the power of the state to authorize the removal of an organ from the body of any incompetent who is a ward of the state. . . .

The renal transplant is becoming the most common of the organ transplants. This is because the normal body has two functioning kidneys, one of which it can reasonably do without, thereby making it possible for one person to donate a kidney to another. Testimony in this record shows that there have been over 2,500 kidney transplants performed in the United States up to this date. The process can be effected under present techniques with minimal danger to both the donor and the donee. Doctors Hamburger and Crosneir describe the risk to the donor as follows:

> This discussion is limited to renal transplantation, since it is inconceivable that any vital organ other than the kidney might ever be removed from a healthy living donor for transplantation purposes. The immediate operative risk of unilateral nephrectomy in a healthy subject has been calculated as approximately 0.05 percent. The long-term risk is more difficult to estimate, since the various types of renal disease do not appear to be more frequent or more severe in individuals with solitary kidneys than in normal subjects. On the other hand, the development of surgical problems, trauma, or neoplasms, with the possible necessity of nephrectomy, do increase the long-term risks in living donors; the long-term risk, on this basis, has been estimated at 0.07 percent. These data must, however, be considered in the light of statistical life expectancy which, in a healthy 35-year-old adult, goes from 99.3 percent to 99.1 percent during the next five succeeding years; this is an increase in risk equal to that incurred by driving a car for 16 miles every working day. The risks incurred by the donor are therefore very limited, but they are a reality, even if, until now, there have been no reports of complications endangering the life of a donor anywhere in the world. Unfortunately, there is no doubt that, as the number of renal transplants increases, such an incident will inevitably be recorded. Hamburger and Crosneir, Moral and Ethical Problems in Transplantation, *in* Human Transplantation 37 (Rapaport and Dausset ed. 1968). . . .

We are of the opinion that a chancery court does have sufficient inherent power to authorize the operation. The circuit court having found that the operative procedures in this instance are to the best interest of Jerry Strunk and this finding having been based upon substantial evidence, we are of the opinion the judgment should be affirmed. . . .

STEINFELD, Judge, dissenting.

Apparently because of my indelible recollection of a government which, to the everlasting shame of its citizens, embarked on a program of genocide and experimentation with human bodies I have been more troubled in reaching a decision in this case than in any other. My sympathies and emotions are torn between a compassion to aid an ailing young man and a duty to fully protect unfortunate members of society. . . .

The majority opinion is predicated upon the finding of the circuit court that there will be psychological benefits to the ward but points out that the incompetent has the mentality of a six-year-old child. It is common knowledge beyond dispute that the loss of a close relative or a friend to a six-year-old child is not of major impact. Opinions concerning psychological trauma are at best most nebulous. Furthermore, there are no guarantees that the transplant will become a surgical success, it being well known that body rejection of transplanted organs is frequent. The life of the incompetent is not in danger, but the surgical procedure advocated creates some peril. . . .

Unquestionably the attitudes and attempts of the . . . members of the family of the two young men whose critical problems now confront us are commendable, natural and beyond reproach. However, they refer us to nothing indicating that they are privileged to authorize the removal of one of the kidneys of the incompetent for the purpose of donation, and they cite no statutory or other authority vesting such right in the courts. The proof shows that less compatible donors are available and that the kidney of a cadaver could be used, although the odds of operational success are not as great in such case as they would be with the fully compatible donor brother.

I am unwilling to hold that the gates should be open to permit the removal of an organ from an incompetent for transplant, at least until such time as it is conclusively demonstrated that it will be of significant benefit to the incompetent. The evidence here does not rise to that pinnacle. To hold that . . . guardians or courts have such awesome power even in the persuasive case before us, could establish legal precedent, the dire result of which we cannot fathom. Regretfully I must say no.

■ IN RE PESCINSKI
226 N.W.2d 180 (Wis. 1975)

WILKIE, Chief Justice.

Does a county court have the power to order an operation to be performed to remove a kidney of an incompetent ward, under guardianship of the person, and transfer it to a sister where the dire need of the transfer is established but where no consent has been given by the incompetent or his guardian ad litem, nor has any benefit to the ward been shown?

That is the issue presented on appeal here. The trial court held that it did not have that power and we agree. The appellant, Janice Pescinski Lausier, on her own petition, was appointed guardian of the person of her brother, the respondent, Richard Pescinski. In 1958, Richard was declared incompetent and was committed to Winnebago State Hospital. He has been a committed mental patient since that date, classified as a schizophrenic, chronic, catatonic type.

On January 31, 1974, Janice Pescinski Lausier petitioned for permission to Dr. H. M. Kauffman to conduct tests to determine whether Richard Pescinski was a suitable donor for a kidney transplant for the benefit of his sister, Elaine Jeske. Elaine had both kidneys surgically removed in 1970, because she was suffering from kidney failure diagnosed as chronic glomerulonephritis. In order to sustain her life, she was put on a dialysis machine, which functions as an artificial kidney. Because of the deterioration of Elaine, the petition contended that a kidney transplant was needed. Subsequent tests were completed establishing that Richard was a suitable donor, and a hearing was then held on the subject of whether permission should be granted to perform the transplant. The guardian ad litem would not give consent to the transplant and the county court held that it did not have the power to give consent for the operation.

At the time of the hearing Elaine was 38 and her brother Richard was 39. Evidence was produced at the hearing that the other members of the Pescinski family had been ruled out as possible donors on the basis of either age or health. The father, aged 70, and the mother, aged 67, were eliminated as possible donors by Dr. Kauffman because, as a matter of principle, he would not perform the operation on a donor over 60. A similar rationale was applied by Dr. Kauffman as to all of the six minor children of Elaine, the doctor concluding that he "would not personally use their kidneys" as a matter of his "own moral conviction." Mrs. Jeske's sister, Mrs. Lausier, was excluded as a donor because she has diabetes. Another brother, Ralph Pescinski, testified that he was 43 years old, had been married 20 years and had 10 children, 9 of whom remained at home. He is a dairy farmer and did not care to be a donor because there would be nobody to take over his farm and he felt he had a duty to his family to refuse. He further testified that he had a stomach disorder which required a special diet and had a rupture on his left side. He had been to see Dr. Capati at the Neillsville Clinic, who told him he should not get involved and that his family should come first.

The testimony showed that Richard was suffering from schizophrenia — catatonic type, and that while he was in contact with his environment there was marked indifference in his behavior. Dr. Hoffman, the medical director at the Good Samaritan Home, West Bend, Wisconsin, testified that in layman's terms Richard's mental disease was a flight from reality. He estimated Richard's mental capacity to be age 12. No evidence in the record indicates that Richard consented to the transplant. Absent that consent, there is no question that the trial court's conclusion that it had no power to approve the operation must be sustained.

"A guardian of the person has the care of the ward's person and must look to the latter's health, education, and support." 39 Am. Jur. 2d, Guardian and Ward, p.60, §68. The guardian must act, if at all, "loyally in the best interests of his ward." Guardianship of Nelson, 123 N.W.2d 505, 509 (Wis. 1963). There is absolutely no evidence here that any interests of the ward will be served by the transplant.

. . . We decline to adopt the concept of "substituted judgment" which was specifically approved by the Kentucky Court of Appeals in Strunk v. Strunk. . . .

As the dissenting opinion in Strunk v. Strunk points out, "substituted judgment" is nothing more than an application of the maxim that equity will speak for one who cannot speak for himself. Historically, the substituted judgment doctrine was used to allow gifts of the property of an incompetent. If applied literally, it would allow a trial court, or this court, to change the designation on a life insurance policy or make an election for an incompetent widow, without the requirement of a statute authorizing these acts and contrary to prior decisions of this court.

We conclude that the doctrine should not be adopted in this state.

We, therefore, must affirm the lower court's decision that it was without power to approve the operation, and we further decide that there is no such power in this court. An incompetent particularly should have his own interests protected. Certainly no advantage should be taken of him. In the absence of real consent on his part, and in a situation where no benefit to him has been established, we fail to find any authority for the county court, or this court, to approve this operation. . . .

DAY, Justice, dissenting. . . .

. . . The guardian ad litem for the incompetent in this case has interposed strong objection to the transplant from Richard Pescinski to his sister, who . . . has now deteriorated to the point of confinement in a wheelchair. We were advised that without a kidney transplant death for her is quite imminent. The brother, on the other hand, the incompetent, is in good health. The medical testimony is that the removal of one of his kidneys would be of minimal risk to him and that he would function normally on one kidney for the rest of his natural life, as do thousands of others in similar circumstances. . . . To avoid the concerns expressed by the guardian ad litem, there are certain definite standards which could and should be imposed. First of all, a strong showing should be made that without the kidney transplant the proposed donee or recipient stands to suffer death. This is certainly the evidence here. Secondly, that reasonable steps have been taken to try and acquire a kidney from other sources and the record is clear that such attempt was made here. Because of the fact that the donee has had six children, she has built up certain chemical resistance to the receipt of foreign tissue into her body which can be overcome only by a transplant from one close to her by blood such as a brother or sister. The testimony showed the impracticality of acquiring a kidney from either her other brother or her sister. No suitable kidney from a cadaver has been found since her kidneys were removed in 1970. The next showing that should be made is that the incompetent proposed donor is closely related by blood to the proposed donee, such as a brother or sister, which of course is the case here. Showing should be made that the donor, if competent, would most probably consent because of the normal ties of family. Here, the trial court specifically found ". . . the conclusion would appear to be inescapable that the ward [the incompetent proposed donor] would so consent and that such authorization should be granted." Another showing should be that the proposed incompetent donor is in good health and that was shown here. And lastly, that the operation is one of minimal risk to the donor and that the donor could function normally on one kidney following such operation. The medical testimony is all to the effect that the donor would undergo minimal risk and would be able to function normally on one kidney. In fact, the testimony is that a person can function on as little as one tenth of one normal kidney.

With these guidelines, the fear expressed that institutions for the mentally ill will merely become storehouses for spare parts for people on the outside is completely unjustified. I agree with the trial court that if the brother here were competent in all probability he would be willing to consent to the transplant to save his sister's life. For him it would be a short period of discomfort which would not affect his ability either to enjoy life or his longevity. . . .

Notes: The Incompetent Organ Donor

1. *The Appropriate Legal Standard.* Which decision do you prefer, *Strunk* or *Pescinski?* There are a small number of reported cases, and the majority permit the organ transplant. 4 A.L.R. 5th 1000; Doriane Lambelet Coleman, Testing the Boundaries of Family Privacy, 35 Cardozo L. Rev. 1289 (2014). Consider the following perspective:

> Despite widespread acceptance in the United States, few other nations allow routine use of minors or mentally incompetent persons as organ donors. Judicial decisions

of United States courts seem to be without parallel in any other country. . . . The Council of Europe has recommended that organ donation from wards be forbidden except when the donor, having capacity of understanding, has given consent. . . .

Rodney K. Adams, Live Organ Donors and Informed Consent: A Difficult Minuet, 8 J. Leg. Med. 555, 572 (1987). (The Council of Europe does condone removal of regenerative tissue like bone marrow from persons lacking capacity to consent in limited circumstances (e.g., the recipient must be a sibling of the donor). Council of Europe, Additional Protocol to the Convention on Human Rights and Biomedicine, on Transplantation of Organs and Tissues of Human Origin (January 24, 2002).)

Thus, while there have been dozens of transplants in the United States from minor donors, they are much less common in other countries, and they are forbidden by law in a number of countries. Kristof Thys et al., Could Minors Be Living Kidney Donors?, 26 Transplant Int'l 949 (2013); Nicholas J. A. Webb & Peter-Marc Fortune, Should Children Ever Be Living Kidney Donors?, 10 Pediatric Transplantation 851 (2006).

Are the decisions in *Strunk* and *Pescinski* actually consistent with each other? Is the dissent in *Strunk* correct that we should not base the decision on supposed psychological benefit to Jerry Strunk inasmuch as such benefit is highly speculative? What about having Strunk's brother not visit him for a couple of weeks to see if he is adversely affected by his brother's absence? Were the outcomes different in *Strunk* and *Pescinski* because Strunk could relate to his sibling while Pescinski could not? Or because the recipient in *Strunk* would have been a man, and the recipient in *Pescinski* a woman? What incentives do you think the court in *Pescinski* might have been trying to avoid? After the Wisconsin Supreme Court denied her request for organ transplantation, Elaine Jeske died of kidney failure.

Which of the following factors should a court consider in deciding whether to order a transplantation from an incompetent person, and how should they be weighed: benefit to the recipient of the organ; risk to the donor; the relationship between the donor and recipient; the availability of alternative donors; and the feelings of the donor about the procedure? Do you agree with Justice Day's dissent in *Pescinski* on this question? Why do you suppose he believed that Richard Pescinski, if competent, would agree to be a donor when the other brother, Ralph Pescinski, did not agree to be a donor?

2. *Further Reading*. For additional discussion of these issues, see Charles Baron et al., Live Organ and Tissue Transplants from Minor Donors in Massachusetts, 55 B.U. L. Rev. 159 (1975); Cara Cheyette, Note, Organ Harvests from the Legally Incompetent, 41 B.C. L. Rev. 465 (2000); Michelle Goodwin, My Sister's Keeper, 29 W. New Eng. L. Rev. 357 (2007); Michael T. Marley, Note, Proxy Consent to Organ Donation by Incompetents, 111 Yale L. J. 1215 (2002); Sara Lind Nygren, Note, Organ Donation by Incompetent Patients, 2006 U. Chi. Legal F. 471; John Robertson, Organ Donations by Incompetents and the Substituted Judgment Doctrine, 76 Colum. L. Rev. 48 (1976).

Problem: Conceiving a Child to Make Tissue Available for Transplantation

A couple, John and Joanne, have a 10-year-old daughter with leukemia who will almost certainly die within five years without a stem cell transplant. (Historically, stem cells for transplantation were taken from the donor's bone marrow, but now stem cells can often be retrieved as well from a donor's circulating blood or a new-born's umbilical cord blood.) With a transplant, there is a 70 percent chance of a long-term survival. Family members and friends have been tested to see if their stem cells are compatible, but none are candidates for transplantation. Despite a nationwide search to find a compatible donor, none has been found. John and Joanne decide to conceive another child in the hope that this child's stem cells will be suitable for transplantation in their daughter. There is a 25 percent chance that a new child will have compatible cells, but the odds can be improved to 100 percent with preimplantation genetic screening. With this approach, a couple can create embryos through in vitro fertilization. The embryos can then be tested to see if the new child's stem cells will be compatible with the existing child. Yury Verlinsky et al., Preimplantation HLA Testing, 291 JAMA 2079 (2004). If John and Joanne bear a child, and the child's cells are compatible, then physicians would perform a transplant with stem cells from umbilical cord blood after birth or other stem cells when the new child is older. There is no risk to the child from using its umbilical cord blood; the risk that the child would die from a surgery to remove stem cells is unknown, but probably not more than 1/10,000. The risk of serious complications from using stem cells from circulating blood is also very low. Should John and Joanne be able to conceive the child and consent to the transplantation? [This problem is based on the *Ayala* case, in which a couple conceived a child to serve as a bone marrow donor for their daughter. Diane M. Gianelli, Bearing a Donor?, American Medical News, Mar. 2, 1990, at 3.]

For further discussion, see Katrien Devolder, Preimplantation HLA Typing: Having Children to Save Our Loved Ones, 31 J. Med. Ethics 582 (2005); Marley McClean, Children's Autonomy v. Children's Autonomy," 43 Pepp. L. Rev. 837 (2016); Susan M. Wolf et al., Using Preimplantation Genetic Diagnosis to Create a Stem Cell Donor, 31 J. L. Med. & Ethics 327 (2003).

3. Redefining Death

According to the law of every state, organs necessary for life (e.g., the heart or an entire liver) cannot be removed from a person for transplantation unless the person is dead (the "dead donor" rule). Moreover, even with kidneys, which can be donated while the person is alive, more than half of organs for transplantation come from decedents. This is both because two kidneys can be taken from dead persons and only one kidney from a living person, and also because persons are more reluctant to donate a kidney while alive than once dead. Most kidney transplants from a live donor go to a family member or friend.

In the United States, most organs taken from dead persons come from patients whose death is diagnosed by cessation of brain function ("brain death") rather than from patients whose death is diagnosed by cessation of cardiopulmonary function (loss of heart and lung function). This is because the blood flow of brain-dead patients can be maintained with the provision of artificial life supports until the organs are removed for transplantation. Without continued blood supply, organs in the body deteriorate and quickly become unavailable for transplantation.

As discussed in Chapter 5, when a person is brain dead, the heart and lungs will ordinarily also stop working unless the person is maintained on a ventilator. Artificial ventilation and other medical support can maintain a brain-dead person's heartbeat and breathing for days to months but not indefinitely. Pregnant women have been maintained in brain death until their fetuses mature enough to be delivered by cesarean section. David R. Field et al., Maternal Brain Death During Pregnancy, 260 JAMA 816 (1988) (describing a case in which a brain-dead, pregnant woman was maintained on a ventilator for nine weeks). There is some question whether cessation of heartbeat and respiration are really inevitable after brain death. While it appears that most brain-dead patients cannot be maintained more than two or three months, some have been maintained for more than a year, including one patient for more than 14 years. D. Alan Shewmon, Chronic "Brain Death," 51 Neurology 1538 (1998).

Some commentators have proposed that death be redefined so that more persons would be candidates for organ transplantation. In particular, it has been argued that brain death should be defined by whether there is brain function sufficient to achieve consciousness, not by whether there is brain function at all. If brain death were defined by the absence of consciousness, then anencephalic children and permanently unconscious persons would be dead, and their organs could be removed for transplantation. Other commentators have suggested that we no longer use death as the sole criterion for removing life-necessary organs but permit removal of life-necessary organs from living persons in limited situations. See, e.g., Zoe Fritz, Can 'Best Interests' Derail the Trolley?, J. Med. Ethics Online First (August 31, 2016) (organ retrieval on basis of patient's best interests); Robert D. Truog, Defining Death, 93 Tex. L. Rev. 1885, 1905-1908 (2015) (suggesting a focus on the ethical concerns of consent and harm to allow organ retrieval from patients who are permanently unconscious or whose death is imminent).

The question, then, for this section is whether the need for more organs is sufficient reason for the state to either change the definition of death or permit individuals to donate their own organs or the organs of family members before death occurs. Does the individual's right to control bodily integrity and to make decisions about important personal matters include a right to decide when life-necessary organs may be given to others?

■ IN RE T.A.C.P.

609 So. 2d 588 (Fla. 1992)

KOGAN, Justice.

We have for review an order of the trial court certified by the Fourth District Court of Appeal as touching on a matter of great public importance requiring immediate resolution by this court. We frame the issue as follows: Is an anencephalic newborn considered "dead" for purposes of organ donation solely by reason of its congenital deformity? We have jurisdiction.

I. FACTS

At or about the eighth month of pregnancy, the parents of the child T.A.C.P. were informed that she would be born with anencephaly. This is a birth defect invariably fatal, in which the child typically is born with only a "brain stem" but otherwise lacks a human brain. In T.A.C.P.'s case, the back of the skull was entirely missing and the brain stem was exposed to the air, except for medical bandaging. The risk of infection to the brain stem was considered very high. Anencephalic infants sometimes can survive several days after birth because the brain stem has a limited capacity to maintain autonomic bodily functions such as breathing and heartbeat. This ability soon ceases, however, in the absence of regulation from the missing brain.

In this case, T.A.C.P. actually survived only a few days after birth. . . .

On the advice of physicians, the parents continued the pregnancy to term and agreed that the mother would undergo cesarean section during birth. The parents agreed to the cesarean procedure with the express hope that the infant's organs would be less damaged and could be used for transplant in other sick children. Although T.A.C.P. had no hope of life herself, the parents both testified in court that they wanted to use this opportunity to give life to others. However, when the parents requested that T.A.C.P. be declared legally dead for this purpose, her health care providers refused out of concern that they thereby might incur civil or criminal liability.

The parents then filed a petition in the circuit court asking for a judicial determination. After hearing testimony and argument, the trial court denied the request on grounds that §382.009(1), Florida Statutes (1991), would not permit a determination of legal death so long as the child's brain stem continued to function. On appeal, the Fourth District summarily affirmed but then certified the trial court's order to this court for immediate resolution of the issue. We have accepted jurisdiction to resolve this case of first impression.

II. The Medical Nature of Anencephaly

Although appellate courts appear never to have confronted the issues there already is an impressive body of published medical scholarship on anencephaly. From our review of this material, we find that anencephaly is a variable but fairly well defined medical condition. Experts in the field have written that anencephaly is the most common severe birth defect of the central nervous system seen in the United States, although it apparently has existed throughout human history.

A statement by the Medical Task Force on Anencephaly ("Task Force") printed in the New England Journal of Medicine generally described "anencephaly" as "a congenital absence of major portions of the brain, skull, and scalp, with its genesis in the first month of gestation" David A. Stumpf et al., The Infant with Anencephaly, 322 New Eng. J. Med. 669, 669 (1990). The large opening in the skull accompanied by the absence or severe congenital disruption of the cerebral hemispheres is the characteristic feature of the condition.

> The Task Force defined anencephaly as diagnosable only when all of the following four criteria are present:
> (1) A large portion of the skull is absent. (2) The scalp, which extends to the margin of the bone, is absent over the skull defect. (3) Hemorrhagic, fibrotic tissue is exposed because of defects in the skull and scalp. (4) Recognizable cerebral hemispheres are absent. [Id. at 670.]

Anencephaly is often, though not always, accompanied by defects in various other body organs and systems, some of which may render the child unsuitable for organ transplantation. . . .

The Task Force stated that most reported anencephalic children die within the first few days after birth, with survival any longer being rare. After reviewing all available medical literature, the Task Force found no study in which survival beyond a week exceeded 9 percent of children meeting the four criteria. Two months was the longest confirmed survival of an anencephalic, although there are unconfirmed reports of one surviving three months and another surviving fourteen months. [This decision preceded the *Baby K* case, page 610, involving an anencephalic child who lived for two years.] The Task Force reported, however, that these survival rates are confounded somewhat by the variable degrees of medical care afforded to anencephalics. Some such infants may be given considerable life support while others may be given much less care.

The Task Force reported that the medical consequences of anencephaly can be established with some certainty. All anencephalics by definition are permanently unconscious because they lack the cerebral cortex necessary for conscious thought. Their condition thus is quite similar to that of persons in a persistent vegetative state. Where the brain stem is functioning, as it was here, spontaneous breathing and heartbeat can occur. In addition, such infants may show spontaneous movements of the extremities, "startle" reflexes, and pupils that respond to light. Some may show feeding reflexes, may cough, hiccup, or exhibit eye movements, and may produce facial expressions.

The question of whether such infants actually suffer from pain is somewhat more complex. It involves a distinction between "pain" and "suffering." The Task Force indicated that anencephaly in some ways is analogous to persons with cerebral brain lesions. Such lesions may not actually eliminate the reflexive response to a painful condition, but they can eliminate any capacity to "suffer" as a result of the condition. Likewise, anencephalic infants may reflexively avoid painful stimuli where the brain stem is functioning and thus is able to command an innate, unconscious withdrawal response; but the infants presumably lack the capacity to suffer. It is clear, however, that this incapacity to suffer has not been established beyond all doubt. . . .

There appears to be general agreement that anencephalics usually have ceased to be suitable organ donors by the time they meet all the criteria for "whole brain death," i.e., the complete absence of brain-stem function. There also is no doubt that a need exists for infant organs for transplantation. Nationally, between 30 and 50 percent of children under two years of age who need transplants die while waiting for organs to become available.

III. LEGAL DEFINITIONS OF "DEATH" & "LIFE"

[The court discussed the history of the cardiopulmonary definition of death and the development of a definition of death based on cessation of brain function. The court then discusses Florida's approach to defining death.]

Indeed, Florida appears to have struck out on its own. The statute cited as controlling by the trial court does not actually address itself to the problem of anencephalic infants, nor indeed to any situation other than patients actually being sustained by artificial life support. The statute provides:

> For legal and medical purposes, *where respiratory and circulatory functions are maintained by artificial means of support* so as to preclude a determination that these

functions have ceased, the occurrence of death *may* be determined where there is the irreversible cessation of the functioning of the entire brain, including the brain stem, determined in accordance with this section.

§382.009(1), Fla. Stat. (1991) (emphasis added). A later subsection goes on to declare:

Except for a diagnosis of brain death, the standard set forth in this section is not the exclusive standard for determining death or for the withdrawal of life-support systems.

§382.009(4), Fla. Stat. (1991). This language is highly significant for two reasons.

First, the statute does not purport to codify the common law standard applied in some other jurisdictions, as does the uniform act. The use of the permissive word *may* in the statute in tandem with the savings clause of §382.009(4) buttresses the conclusion that the legislature envisioned other ways of defining "death." Second, the statutory framers clearly did not intend to apply the statute's language to the anencephalic infant not being kept alive by life support. To the contrary, the framers expressly limited the statute to that situation in which "respiratory and circulatory functions are maintained by artificial means of support." . . .

The parties have cited to no authorities directly dealing with the question of whether anencephalics are "alive" or "dead." Our own research has disclosed no other federal or Florida law or precedent arguably on point or applicable by analogy. We thus are led to the conclusion that no legal authority binding upon this court has decided whether an anencephalic child is alive for purposes of organ donation. In the absence of applicable legal authority, this court must weigh and consider the public policy considerations at stake here.

IV. COMMON LAW & POLICY

Initially, we must start by recognizing that §382.009, Florida Statutes (1991), provides a method for determining death in those cases in which a person's respiratory and circulatory functions are maintained artificially. §382.009(4), Fla. Stat. (1991). Likewise, we agree that a cardiopulmonary definition of death must be accepted in Florida as a matter of our common law, applicable whenever §382.009 does not govern. Thus, if cardiopulmonary function is not being maintained artificially as stated in §382.009, a person is dead who has sustained irreversible cessation of circulatory and respiratory functions as determined in accordance with accepted medical standards. We have found no credible authority arguing that this definition is inconsistent with the existence of death, and we therefore need not labor the point further.

The question remaining is whether there is good reason in public policy for this court to create an additional common law standard applicable to anencephalics. Alterations of the common law, while rarely entertained or allowed, are within this court's prerogative. However, the rule we follow is that the common law will not be altered or expanded unless demanded by public necessity, or where required to vindicate fundamental rights. We believe, for example, that our adoption of the cardiopulmonary definition of death today is required by public necessity and, in any event, merely formalizes what has been the common practice in this state for well over a century.

Such is not the case with petitioners' request. Our review of the medical, ethical, and legal literature on anencephaly discloses absolutely no consensus that public necessity or fundamental rights will be better served by granting this request. . . .

There is an unquestioned need for transplantable infant organs. Yet some medical commentators suggest that the organs of anencephalics are seldom usable, for a variety of reasons, and that so few organ transplants will be possible from anencephalics as to render the enterprise questionable in light of the ethical problems at stake — even if legal restrictions were lifted.

Others note that prenatal screening now is substantially reducing the number of anencephalics born each year in the United States and that, consequently, anencephalics are unlikely to be a significant source of organs as time passes. And still others have frankly acknowledged that there is no consensus and that redefinition of death in this context should await the emergence of a consensus.

A presidential commission in 1981 urged strict adherence to the Uniform Determination of Death Act's definition, which would preclude equating anencephaly with death. President's Commission for the Study of Ethical Problems, Biomedical, and Behavioral Research, Defining Death: Medical, Legal and Ethical Issues in the Determination of Death 2 (1981). Several sections of the American Bar Association have reached much the same conclusion. National Conference on Birth, Death, and Law, Report on Conference, 29 Jurimetrics J. 403, 421 (Lori B. Andrews et al. eds., 1989).

Some legal commentators have urged that treating anencephalics as dead equates them with "nonpersons," presenting a "slippery slope" problem with regard to all other persons who lack cognition for whatever reason. Others have quoted physicians involved in infant-organ transplants as stating, "The slippery slope is real," because some physicians have proposed transplants from infants with defects less severe than anencephaly.

We express no opinion today about who is right and who is wrong on these issues — if any "right" or "wrong" can be found here. The salient point is that no consensus exists as to: (a) the utility of organ transplants of the type at issue here; (b) the ethical issues involved; or (c) the legal and constitutional problems implicated.

V. Conclusions

Accordingly, we find no basis to expand the common law to equate anencephaly with death. We acknowledge the possibility that some infants' lives might be saved by using organs from anencephalics who do not meet the traditional definition of "death" we reaffirm today. But weighed against this is the utter lack of consensus, and the questions about the overall utility of such organ donations. The scales clearly tip in favor of not extending the common law in this instance. . . .

Notes: Redefining Death

1. *The* T.A.C.P. *Decision.* At the end of Section III of the opinion, the court observed that there was no binding legal authority on the issue of whether an anen-

cephalic child is alive for purposes of organ donation. Accordingly, said the court, it was an issue for the court to decide after weighing the public policy considerations at stake. What standard did the court employ for deciding whether to expand the common law in this case? Is it so clear that organ retrieval from anencephalic infants did not satisfy the court's standard? Why isn't the desire to avoid needless deaths a sufficiently strong basis for changing the common law? Were the justifications behind the court's adoption of the cardiopulmonary definition of death any more compelling? The court points to the lack of consensus on the issue, but doesn't the lack of consensus cut both ways (i.e., how should the court decide when there is no consensus for either position)? Should the court feel bound by its perception of academic opinion?

2. *The Role of Utilitarian Justifications.* Although it may seem too utilitarian to change the definition of death in order to facilitate organ transplantation, we saw in Chapter 5 that utilitarian concerns essentially were responsible when the definition of death was changed to include the cessation of brain function. In justifying a change in the definition of death, the influential Harvard Medical School report cited the burdens of treating brain-dead persons, including the diversion of resources from other patients, and the difficulty in obtaining organs for transplantation. Report of the Ad Hoc Committee of the Harvard Medical School to Examine the Definition of Brain Death, A Definition of Irreversible Coma, 205 JAMA 85, 85 (1968), excerpted at page 622. In other words, there are two important questions here. First, is there a principled difference between permitting organ retrieval from anencephalic infants now and permitting organ retrieval from brain-dead persons 35 years ago? Or is the real difference the fact that many more organs can be retrieved from brain-dead persons than from anencephalic infants? Second, even if there is no principled difference, might we still want to say that it would be wrong to retrieve organs from anencephalic infants?

3. *Modifying the "Dead Donor" Rule.* As mentioned earlier, some commentators have proposed that, rather than change the definition of death to facilitate organ donation, we should modify the dead donor rule. Instead of insisting that people be dead before taking their heart, liver, lungs, and kidneys for transplantation, we would permit organ donation before death, in limited circumstances. For example, people could direct in a living will that, in the event of a condition of permanent unconsciousness, they want their organs taken for transplantation. Or, parents of anencephalic children could be given the opportunity to choose among continuing treatment, stopping treatment, or donating their child's organs before the child dies.

Would this approach be more acceptable than changing the definition of death? Do you think that the reasons for having the dead donor rule apply when a person is permanently unconscious? Can we distinguish the removal of organs from permanently unconscious persons from other actions that we already permit? For example, can we really distinguish taking a ventilator away from a permanently unconscious person, because the ventilator could be better used by someone else, from taking the lungs from a permanently unconscious person, because the lungs could be better used by someone else? Indeed, if we had consent to take the lungs from the person's advance directive, would it be less troublesome than taking away a ventilator when doing so would be over the objections of the family and in disregard of the patient's advance directive?

4. *Donation after "Cardiopulmonary Death."* Given the substantial shortage of organs for transplantation, greater efforts are being made to increase the number of organs taken from persons who die from cessation of cardiopulmonary function. One approach is to infuse cold fluids into the dead body to rapidly cool the organs and prevent their deterioration. Another approach, for patients whose ventilators are being withdrawn, is to perform the withdrawal in an operating room. That way, once the ventilator is withdrawn and the patient dies, action can be taken quickly to maintain the vitality of the organs before they are removed for transplantation.

The ratio of "cardiopulmonary death" donors to "brain death" donors is about 1:5 in the United States, 2:3 in the United Kingdom, and 3:2 in the Netherlands. Data so far indicate that kidney transplants fare as well after cardiopulmonary death as after brain death but that liver transplants are not as successful after cardiopulmonary death. Janet M. Bellingham et al., Donation After Cardiac Death: A 29-Year Experience, 150 Surgery 692 (2011); Laura A. Siminoff et al., A Comparison of Request Process and Outcomes in Donation after Cardiac Death and Donation after Brain Death, 17 Am. J. Transplantation 1278 (2017).

While donation after cardiopulmonary death is becoming more common, critics argue the patients may not be truly dead when they are declared dead. When organ donation is planned for someone after cardiopulmonary death, physicians typically declare death after cardiopulmonary function has ceased for five minutes. (Data indicate that hearts do not spontaneously resume circulatory function after two minutes of cessation.) But does it matter that cardiopulmonary resuscitation can restore circulatory function? In addition, it usually takes more than five minutes without blood flow for the brain to die. Jerry Menikoff, The Importance of Being Dead, 18 Issues L. & Med. 3 (2002).

5. *Further Reading.* On **anencephalic donors** (note 2), see Jay A. Friedman, Taking the Camel by the Nose: The Anencephalic as a Source for Pediatric Organ Transplants, 90 Colum. L. Rev. 917 (1990); Fazal Khan & Brian Lea, Paging King Solomon: Towards Allowing Organ Donation from Anencephalic Infants, 6 Ind. Health L. Rev. 17 (2009); Margaret Lock, Twice Dead (2002); D. Alan Shewmon et al., The Use of Anencephalic Infants as Organ Sources, 261 JAMA 1773 (1989).

On modifying the **dead donor rule** (note 3), see Robert M. Arnold & Stuart J. Youngner, The Dead Donor Rule: Should We Stretch It, Bend It, or Abandon It?, 2 Kennedy Inst. Ethics J. 263 (1993); Council on Ethical and Judicial Affairs, American Medical Association, The Use of Anencephalic Neonates as Organ Donors, 273 JAMA 1614 (1995) (position reversed in Charles W. Plows, Reconsideration of AMA Opinion on Anencephalic Neonates as Organ Donors, 275 JAMA 443 (1996)); Sheldon F. Kurtz & Michael J. Saks, Living Organ Donor Act, 18 Iowa J. Corp. L. 523, 561 (1993).

On donation after **cardiopulmonary death** (note 4), see James L. Bernat, Controversies in Defining and Determining Death in Critical Care, 9 Nature Rev. Neurology 164 (2013); Institute of Medicine, Organ Donation: Opportunities for Action 127-160 (2006); Procuring Organs for Transplant (Robert M. Arnold et al. eds., 1995); David J. Reich et al., ASTS Recommended Practice Guidelines for Controlled Donation after Cardiac Death Organ Procurement and Transplantation, 9 Am. J. Transplantation 2004 (2009); President's Council on Bioethics, Controversies in the Determination of Death (2008); Markus Weber et al., Kidney Transplantation from Donors Without a Heartbeat, 347 New Eng. J. Med. 248 (2002).

B. OWNERSHIP AND CONTROL OF THE BODY

1. Mandates or Incentives for Organ Donation

At one time, states commonly permitted the removal of corneas and other tissues or organs from persons who died and were undergoing an autopsy by a coroner or medical examiner. In such cases, the legislatures probably reasoned, the body was being cut open and some tissue permanently removed anyway as part of the autopsy. The 1987 Uniform Anatomical Gift Act encouraged the passage of such statutes in its §4. But the 2006 Revised Uniform Anatomical Gift Act eliminated §4, and most states have followed the 2006 Act. Still, some states have retained the coroner/medical examiner authority, particularly for corneas.

If an organ or tissue can be used to improve the health of a living person, particularly if the tissue is the cornea, whose absence would not be detectable by looking at the corpse, then should we not give preference to the living person over the dead person? Is there any reason to limit mandatory "donation" to cadavers undergoing an autopsy? Why not take organs and tissues from every cadaver? Why not require living persons to give up renewable tissues, like bone marrow, for transplantation? To the extent that takings of organs or tissues raise concerns about people being deprived of their body parts without their consent and without compensation, can we answer those concerns by offering financial incentives for organ donation?

■ STATE v. POWELL
497 So. 2d 1188 (Fla. 1986)

OVERTON, Justice.

This is a petition to review a circuit court order finding unconstitutional §732.9185, Florida Statutes (1983), which authorizes medical examiners to remove corneal tissue from decedents during statutorily required autopsies when such tissue is needed for transplantation. The statute prohibits the removal of the corneal tissue if the next of kin objects, but does not require that the decedent's next of kin be notified of the procedure. The Fifth District Court of Appeal certified that this case presents a question of great public importance requiring immediate resolution by this court. We accept jurisdiction . . . , and, for the reasons expressed below, find that the statute is constitutional.

The challenged statute provides:

> Corneal removal by medical examiners.—
>
> (1) In any case in which a patient is in need of corneal tissue for a transplant, a district medical examiner or an appropriately qualified designee with training in ophthalmologic techniques may, upon request of any eye bank authorized under s. 732.918, provide the cornea of a decedent whenever all of the following conditions are met:
>> (a) A decedent who may provide a suitable cornea for the transplant is under the jurisdiction of the medical examiner and an autopsy is required in accordance with s. 406.11.
>> (b) No objection by the next of kin of the decedent is known by the medical examiner.

(c) The removal of the cornea will not interfere with the subsequent course of an investigation or autopsy.

(2) Neither the district medical examiner nor his appropriately qualified designee nor any eye bank authorized under s. 732.918 may be held liable in any civil or criminal action for failure to obtain consent of the next of kin.

The trial court decided this case by summary judgment. The facts are not in dispute. On June 15, 1983, James White drowned while swimming at the city beach in Dunellon, Florida. Associate Medical Examiner Dr. Thomas Techman, who is an appellant in this cause, performed an autopsy on James' body at Leesburg Community Hospital. On July 11, 1983, Anthony Powell died in a motor vehicle accident in Marion County. Medical Examiner Dr. William H. Shutze, who is also an appellant in this cause, performed an autopsy on Anthony's body. In each instance, under the authority of §732.9185, the medical examiner removed corneal tissue from the decedent without giving notice to or obtaining consent from the parents of the decedent.

James' and Anthony's parents, who are the appellees in this case, each brought an action claiming damages for the alleged wrongful removal of their sons' corneas and seeking a judgment declaring §732.9185 unconstitutional. . . .

In addressing the issue of the statute's constitutionality, we begin with the premise that a person's constitutional rights terminate at death. If any rights exist, they belong to the decedent's next of kin.

Next, we recognize that a legislative act carries with it the presumption of validity and the party challenging a statute's constitutionality must carry the burden of establishing that the statute bears no reasonable relation to a permissible legislative objective. In determining whether a permissible legislative objective exists, we must review the evidence arising from the record in this case.

The unrebutted evidence in this record establishes that the state of Florida spends approximately $138 million each year to provide its blind with the basic necessities of life. At present, approximately 10 percent of Florida's blind citizens are candidates for cornea transplantation, which has become a highly effective procedure for restoring sight to the functionally blind. As advances are made in the field, the number of surgical candidates will increase, thereby raising the demand for suitable corneal tissue. The increasing number of elderly persons in our population has also created a great demand for corneas because corneal blindness often is age-related. Further, an affidavit in the record states:

> Corneal transplants are particularly important in newborns. The brain does not learn to see if the cornea is not clear. There is a critical period in the first few months of life when the brain "learns to see." If the cornea is not clear, the brain not only does not "learn to see," but the brain loses its ability to "learn to see." Hence, corneal transplant in children must be made as soon as practicable after the problem is discovered. Without the medical examiner legislation, there would be virtually no corneal tissue available for infants and these children would remain forever blind.

The record reflects that the key to successful corneal transplantation is the availability of high-quality corneal tissue and that corneal tissue removed more than ten hours after death is generally unsuitable for transplantation. The implementation of §732.9185 in 1977 has, indisputably, increased both the supply and quality of tissue available for transplantation. Statistics show that, in 1976, only 500 corneas were obtained in Florida for transplantation while, in 1985, more than 3,000 persons in Florida had their sight restored through corneal transplantation surgery.

The record also demonstrates that a qualitative difference exists between corneal tissue obtained through outright donation and tissue obtained pursuant to §732.9185. In contrast to the tissue donated by individuals, which is largely unusable because of the advanced age of the donor at death, approximately 80 to 85 percent of tissue obtained through medical examiners is suitable for transplantation. The evidence establishes that this increase in the quantity and quality of available corneal tissue was brought about by passage of the statute and is, in large part, attributable to the fact that §732.9185 does not place a duty upon medical examiners to seek out the next of kin to obtain consent for cornea removal. An affidavit in the record reveals that, before legislation authorized medical examiners in California to remove corneas without the consent of the next of kin, the majority of the families asked by the Los Angeles medical examiner's office responded positively; however, approximately 80 percent of the families could not be located in sufficient time for medical examiners to remove usable corneal tissue from the decedents.

An autopsy is a surgical dissection of the body; it necessarily results in a massive intrusion into the decedent. This record reflects that cornea removal, by comparison, requires an infinitesimally small intrusion which does not affect the decedent's appearance. With or without cornea removal, the decedent's eyes must be capped to maintain a normal appearance.

Our review of §732.9185 reveals certain safeguards which are apparently designed to limit cornea removal to instances in which the public's interest is greatest and the impact on the next of kin the least: corneas may be removed only if the decedent is under the jurisdiction of the medical examiner; an autopsy is mandated by Florida law; and the removal will not interfere with the autopsy or an investigation of the death. Further, medical examiners may not automatically remove tissue from all decedents subject to autopsy; rather, a request must be made by an eye bank based on a present need for the tissue.

We conclude that this record clearly establishes that this statute reasonably achieves the permissible legislative objective of providing sight to many of Florida's blind citizens.

We next address the trial court's finding that §732.9185 deprives appellees of a fundamental property right. All authorities generally agree that the next of kin have no property right in the remains of a decedent. Although, in Dunahoo v. Bess, 200 So. 541, 542 (1941), this court held that a surviving husband had a "property right" in his wife's body which would sustain a claim for negligent embalming, . . . [m]ore recently, we affirmed the district court's determination that the next of kin's right in a decedent's remains is based upon "the personal right of the decedent's next of kin to bury the body rather than any property right in the body itself." Jackson v. Rupp, 228 So. 2d 916, 918 (Fla. 4th DCA 1969), *affirmed*, 238 So. 2d 86 (Fla. 1970). The view that the next of kin has no property right but merely a limited right to possess the body for burial purposes is universally accepted by courts and commentators. Prosser states:

> A number of decisions have involved the mishandling of dead bodies. . . . In these cases the courts have talked of a somewhat dubious "property right" to the body, usually in the next of kin, which did not exist while the decedent was living, cannot be conveyed, can be used only for the one purpose of burial, and not only has no

pecuniary value but is a source of liability for funeral expenses. It seems reasonably obvious that such "property" is something evolved out of thin air to meet the occasion, and that it is in reality the personal feelings of the survivors which are being protected, under a fiction likely to deceive no one but a lawyer.

W. Prosser, The Law of Torts, 43-44 (2d ed. 1955). . . .

Under the facts and circumstances of these cases, we find no taking of private property by state action for a non-public purpose in violation of article X, §6, of the Florida Constitution. We note that the right to bring an action in tort does not necessarily invoke constitutional protections. Decisions of the United States Supreme Court have clearly established that the loss of a common law right by legislative act does not automatically operate as a deprivation of substantive due process. Tort actions may be restricted when necessary to obtain a permissible legislative objective.

Appellees also assert that their right to control the disposition of their decedents' remains is a fundamental right of personal liberty protected against unreasonable governmental intrusion by the due process clause. Appellees argue that, because the statute permits the removal of a decedent's corneas without reference to his family's preferences, it infringes upon a right, characterized as one of religion, family, or privacy, which is fundamental and must be subjected to strict scrutiny. . . .

We reject appellees' argument. The cases cited recognize only freedom of choice concerning personal matters involved in existing, ongoing relationships among living persons as fundamental or essential to the pursuit of happiness by free persons. We find that the right of the next of kin to a tort claim for interference with burial, established by this court in *Dunahoo*, does not rise to the constitutional dimension of a fundamental right traditionally protected under either the United States or Florida Constitution. Neither federal nor state privacy provisions protect an individual from every governmental intrusion into one's private life, especially when a statute addresses public health interests.

The record contains no evidence that the appellees' objections to the removal of corneal tissues for human transplants are based on any "fundamental tenets of their religious beliefs." Wisconsin v. Yoder, 406 U.S. at 218. . . .

In conclusion, we hold that §732.9185 is constitutional because it rationally promotes the permissible state objective of restoring sight to the blind. In so holding, we note that laws regarding the removal of human tissues for transplantation implicate moral, ethical, theological, philosophical, and economic concerns which do not readily lend themselves to analysis within a traditional legal framework. Applying constitutional standards of review to §732.9185 obscures the fact that at the heart of the issue lies a policy question which calls for a delicate balancing of societal needs and individual concerns more appropriately accomplished by the legislature. . . .

■BROTHERTON v. CLEVELAND
923 F.2d 477 (6th Cir. 1991)

Martin, Circuit Judge.

Deborah S. Brotherton, the wife of decedent Steven Brotherton, appeals the dismissal of her §1983 claim for wrongful removal of her deceased husband's corneas. Because we find that Deborah Brotherton has a protected property interest in her husband's corneas and that the removal of those corneas was caused by established state procedures, we reverse.

On February 15, 1988, Steven Brotherton was found "pulseless" in an automobile and was taken to Bethesda North Hospital in Cincinnati, Ohio. He was pronounced dead on arrival. The hospital asked Deborah Brotherton to consider making an anatomical gift; she declined, based on her husband's aversion to such a gift, and her refusal was documented in the hospital's "Report of Death."

Because Steven Brotherton's death was considered a possible suicide, his body was taken to the Hamilton County coroner's office. An autopsy of Steven Brotherton's body was performed on February 16, 1988; after the autopsy, the coroner permitted Steven Brotherton's corneas to be removed and used as anatomical gifts. The coroner's office had called the Cincinnati Eye Bank, which sent the technician who removed the corneas. Deborah Brotherton did not learn that her husband's corneas had been removed until she read the autopsy report.

Bethesda North Hospital made no attempt to inform the coroner's office of Deborah Brotherton's objection to making an anatomical gift, and the coroner's office did not inquire into whether there was an objection. Ohio Rev. Code §2108.60 permits a coroner to remove the corneas of autopsy subjects without consent, provided that the coroner has no knowledge of an objection by the decedent, the decedent's spouse, or, if there is no spouse, the next of kin, the guardian, or the person authorized to dispose of the body. The custom and policy of the Hamilton County coroner's office is not to obtain a next of kin's consent or to inspect the medical records or hospital documents before removing corneas. [Indeed, when personnel at the eye bank started asking about the existence of objections to removals, the coroner instructed his staff to withhold information about next of kin. Brotherton v. Cleveland, 173 F.3d 552, 556 (6th Cir. 1999).]

Deborah Brotherton, on her own behalf and on behalf of her children, as well as a purported class of similarly situated plaintiffs, filed this case under 42 U.S.C. §1983, alleging that her husband's corneas were removed without due process of law and in violation of the equal protection clause. She also asserted pendent state law claims for emotional distress. . . .

A majority of the courts confronted with the issue of whether a property interest can exist in a dead body have found that a property right of some kind does exist and often refer to it as a "quasi-property right." . . . However, two Ohio appellate courts which have been confronted with determining the nature of the right have avoided characterizing it in this manner.

In *Carney*, an appellate court ruled on who has standing to bring a claim for mishandling a dead body. The court stated that calling the right to control the dead body of a relative a "quasi-property right" would create a legal fiction and concluded:

> This court rejects the theory that a surviving custodian has quasi-property rights in the body of the deceased, and acknowledges the cause of action for mishandling of a dead body as a subspecies of the tort of infliction of emotional distress. *Carney*, 33 Ohio App. 3d at 37. . . .

In *Everman*, an appellate court rejected the argument that a husband's right to possession of his deceased wife's body for purposes of preparation, mourning, and burial is protected against unreasonable search or seizure. In so ruling, the court stated:

> There is no issue in this case of the possessory right of a spouse or other appropriate member of the family of a deceased for the purposes of preparation, mourning and burial. This right is recognized by law and by the decisions. This is not the [sic] say that a person has a property right in the body of another, living or dead, or that a corpse may not be temporarily held for investigation as to the true cause of death. *Everman*, 54 Ohio App. 3d at 122.

Evading the question of whether to call the spouse's interest "property," the *Everman* court recognized that Ohio does grant that right which resides at the very core of a property interest: the right to possess.

The concept of "property" in the law is extremely broad and abstract. The legal definition of "property" most often refers not to a particular physical object, but rather to the legal bundle of rights recognized in that object. Thus, "property" is often conceptualized as a "bundle of rights." The "bundle of rights" which have been associated with property include the rights to possess, to use, to exclude, to profit, and to dispose. . . .

Though some early American cases adopted the English common-law rule that there was no property right in a dead body, other cases held that the rule was unsound in light of the rights of next of kin with regard to burial. The tendency to classify the bundle of rights granted by states as a property interest of some type was a direct function of the increased significance of those underlying rights. The prevailing view of both English and American courts eventually became that next of kin have a "quasi-property" right in the decedent's body for purposes of burial or other lawful disposition. . . .

Thankfully, we do not need to determine whether the Supreme Court of Ohio would categorize the interest in the dead body granted to the spouse as property, quasi-property or not property. Although the existence of an interest may be a matter of state law, whether that interest rises to the level of a "legitimate claim of entitlement" protected by the due process clause is determined by federal law. This determination does not rest on the label attached to a right granted by the state but rather on the substance of that right.

Ohio Rev. Code §2108.02(B), as part of the Uniform Anatomical Gift Act governing gifts of organs and tissues for research or transplants, expressly grants a right to Deborah Brotherton to control the disposal of Steven Brotherton's body. *Everman* expresses the recognition that Deborah Brotherton has a possessory right to his body. *Carney* allows a claim for disturbance of his body. Although extremely regulated, in sum, these rights form a substantial interest in the dead body, regardless of Ohio's classification of that interest. We hold the aggregate of rights granted by the state of Ohio to Deborah Brotherton rises to the level of a "legitimate claim of entitlement" in Steven Brotherton's body, including his corneas, protected by the due process clause of the Fourteenth Amendment.

We also hold the removal of Steven Brotherton's corneas were caused by established state procedures and that Ohio failed to provide the necessary predeprivation process. The Supreme Court has often reiterated that a property interest may not be destroyed without a hearing. See, e.g., Logan v. Zimmerman Brush Co.,

455 U.S. 422, 434 (1982). In *Logan*, the Supreme Court ruled that the timing of a hearing depends upon the accommodation of competing interests involved, which include: the importance of the private interests, the length and finality of deprivation, and the magnitude of governmental interest. The Court added that deprivation of property resulting from an established state procedure can only satisfy due process if there is a predeprivation hearing. . . .

It is the policy and custom of the Hamilton County coroner's office not to review medical records or paperwork pertaining to a corpse prior to the removal of corneas. This intentional ignorance is induced by Ohio Rev. Code §2108.60 which allows the office to take corneas from the bodies of deceased without considering the interest of any other parties, as long as they have no knowledge of any objection to such a removal. After the cornea is removed, it is not returned and the corpse is permanently diminished. The only governmental interest enhanced by the removal of the corneas is the interest in implementing the organ/tissue donation program; this interest is not substantial enough to allow the state to consciously disregard those property rights which it has granted. Moreover, predeprivation process undertaken by the state would be a minimal burden to this interest. This court does not at this time need to establish the type or extent of predeprivation process required by the due process clause; we merely hold that the policy and custom of the Hamilton County coroner's office is an established state procedure necessitating predeprivation process. . . .

[The litigation in *Brotherton* was finally settled ten years after this decision with a change in policy at the coroner's office and the payment of $5.25 million into a settlement fund to compensate the class of people harmed by the coroner's practices. Brotherton v. Cleveland, 141 F. Supp. 2d 894 (S.D. Ohio 2001).]

McFALL v. SHIMP
10 Pa. D. & C. 3d 90 (Allegheny County 1978)

FLAHERTY, Judge.
Plaintiff, Robert McFall, suffers from a rare bone marrow disease and the prognosis for his survival is very dim, unless he receives a bone marrow transplant from a compatible donor. Finding a compatible donor is a very difficult task and limited to a selection among close relatives. After a search and certain tests, it has been determined that only defendant [David Shimp] is suitable as a donor. Defendant refuses to submit to the necessary transplant, and before the court is a request for a preliminary injunction which seeks to compel defendant to submit to further tests, and, eventually, the bone marrow transplant. [McFall had aplastic anemia, and Shimp was his first cousin.]

Although a diligent search has produced no authority, plaintiff cites the ancient statute of King Edward I, 811 Westminster 2, 13 Ed. I, c.24, pointing out, as is the case, that this court is a successor to the English courts of Chancery and derives power from this statute, almost 700 years old. The question posed by plaintiff is that, in order to save the life of one of its members by the only means available, may society infringe upon one's absolute right to his "bodily security"?

The common law has consistently held to a rule which provides that one human being is under no legal compulsion to give aid or to take action to save another human being or to rescue. A great deal has been written regarding this rule which, on the surface, appears to be revolting in a moral sense. Introspection, however, will demonstrate that the rule is founded upon the very essence of our free society. It is noteworthy that counsel for plaintiff has cited authority which has developed in other societies in support of plaintiff's request in this instance. Our society, contrary to many others, has as its first principle, the respect for the individual, and that society and government exist to protect the individual from being invaded and hurt by another. Many societies adopt a contrary view which has the individual existing to serve the society as a whole. In preserving such a society as we have, it is bound to happen that great moral conflicts will arise and will appear harsh in a given instance. In this case, the chancellor is being asked to force one member of society to undergo a medical procedure which would provide that part of that individual's body would be removed from him and given to another so that the other could live. Morally, this decision rests with defendant, and, in the view of the court, the refusal of defendant is morally indefensible. For our law to *compel* defendant to submit to an intrusion of his body would change every concept and principle upon which our society is founded. To do so would defeat the sanctity of the individual, and would impose a rule which would know no limits, and one could not imagine where the line would be drawn.

This request is not to be compared with an action at law for damages, but rather is an action in equity before a chancellor, which, in the ultimate, if granted, would require the forceable submission to the medical procedure. For a society which respects the rights of *one* individual, to sink its teeth into the jugular vein or neck of one of its members and suck from it sustenance for *another* member, is revolting to our hard-wrought concepts of jurisprudence. Forceable extraction of living body tissue causes revulsion to the judicial mind. Such would raise the spectre of the swastika and the Inquisition, reminiscent of the horrors this portends.

This court makes no comment on the law regarding plaintiff's rights in an action at law for damages, but has no alternative but to deny the requested equitable relief. An order will be entered denying the request for a preliminary injunction. . . .

[Mr. McFall died two weeks after the court's opinion was issued. For details about the case, see Fordham E. Huffman, Comment, Coerced Donation of Body Tissues: Can We Live with *McFall v. Shimp?*, 40 Ohio St. L. J. 409 (1979); Alan Meisel & Loren H. Roth, Must a Man Be His Cousin's Keeper?, 8(5) Hastings Center Rep. 5 (1978) (observing that newspaper accounts reported strong pressures from Shimp's wife and mother for him not to donate and that Shimp explained his refusal in terms of the risks of anesthesia, concerns that the procedure would aggravate existing aches and pains, and the possibility that his job-related exposure to chemicals might interfere with the regeneration of his bone marrow).]

Notes: Obligations to Give Up Organs and Tissues; Autopsies

1. *The Family's Property Rights.* Which of the two courts, *Powell* or *Brotherton*, has the better analysis on the issue of whether the family has a property right? If the family can choose whether or not to donate the organs of a person who has just died, doesn't that make it clear that the family possesses a property right in the decedent's organs?

The *Powell* court cited the various safeguards in the Florida statute "which are apparently designed to limit cornea removal to instances in which the public's interest is greatest and the impact on the next of kin the least." The opinion suggests that these safeguards played an important role in the court's decision, but are they required under the court's standard that a statute is valid unless it "bears no reasonable relation to a permissible legislative objective"?

2. *Authority for Autopsies.* As the first two cases illustrate, state law gives broad authority for coroners or medical examiners to perform autopsies in cases of unnatural death or for public health reasons, despite any objection by the family. In a full autopsy, internal organs are removed, examined, and placed back in the body, but not necessarily reattached with any care or precision. These statutes are widely regarded as constitutional and are rarely challenged. See, e.g., Rielly v. City of New York, 1992 WL 368082 (E.D.N.Y. 1992) (autopsy statute that permits performance of procedure without consent of relatives when part of a criminal homicide investigation is "plainly" constitutional). The reasoning is both that important public health and law enforcement objectives outweigh any private interests, and also that opening and examining a corpse does not clearly infringe any constitutionally protected interest. An autopsy may not constitute a deprivation of "property" at all since, after the body is examined, it is returned to the family more or less intact. The constitutionality of autopsy statutes is buttressed by the fact that they frequently allow the family to object for religious reasons.

While there is no constitutional obstacle to performing autopsies in the proper manner, if this authority is abused, courts do recognize that families have protected interests in the nature of a quasi-property right to respectful treatment and to exercise some control over the disposition of the decedent's body. In one case, a court allowed a constitutional tort action against a part-time coroner who also ran an eye bank and was allegedly caught stealing eyeballs from corpses before sewing the eyelids shut. Whaley v. County of Tuscola, 58 F.3d 1111 (6th Cir. 1995). See also Whitehair v. Highland Memory Gardens, 327 S.E.2d 438 (W. Va. 1985) (tort suit allowed for mishandling of corpse during interment process). But see Hinkle v. City of Clarksburg, 81 F.3d 416 (4th Cir. 1996) (medical examiners entitled to qualified immunity on claim that they improperly disposed of decedent's internal organs); Arnaud v. Odom, 870 F.2d 304, 309 (5th Cir. 1989) (no §1983 due process claim against physician for performing unauthorized experiments on decedent during autopsy because state law provided adequate postdeprivation remedy of action for tampering with a corpse); Albrecht v. Treon, 617 F.3d 890 (6th Cir. 2010) (no §1983 due process claim when coroner discarded decedent's brain after an autopsy because no property rights of the family were infringed).

3. *The Process Due the Family.* Powell, Brotherton, and other cases have clearly established the state's right to take corneas for transplantation from bodies that are undergoing an autopsy by the state (in the absence of an objection). *Brotherton,* however, requires some kind of process before the corneas can be taken. What kind of process do you think *Brotherton* requires? Would it have been sufficient if the coroner had reviewed Mr. Brotherton's medical records to see if an objection to tissue removal had been registered? Should the coroner have to contact the family to ascertain their wishes before taking any corneas? What if, after reasonable efforts to contact family members, they cannot be reached before the autopsy? (Perhaps

family members are out of town or overseas and are not responding to messages left on their telephone.)

For a case with a result similar to that in *Brotherton*, see Newman v. Sathyavaglswaran, 287 F.3d 786 (9th Cir. 2002) (expressing great concern with the absence of pre-removal process before retrieval of corneas, but leaving for future proceedings exactly what process is due). Before the *Newman* litigation commenced, and in response to an article in the *Los Angeles Times* about alleged trafficking in corneas by the Los Angeles County Coroner's Office, California amended its cornea removal statute to require consent by the decedent or a surrogate decisionmaker. 1998 Cal. Adv. Legis. Serv. 887. The current statute can be found at Cal. Gov't Code §27491.47. (Mr. Newman had been under the custody of the Los Angeles County Coroner's Office when his corneas were taken.)

In response to *Brotherton* and *Newman*, the Revised Uniform Anatomical Gift Act §23 (2006) removed the authority of coroners to release corneas (or other tissues or organs) in the absence of consent. For more background, see the discussion of Sections 22 and 23 of the Revised Act in the "Summary of the Changes in the Revised Act." The Revised Act has substantially curtailed the use of cornea removal statutes in the United States. Almost all states have enacted the 2006 Revision, though not all of them repealed their cornea provisions. Thus, *Powell* and *Brotherton* now serve as constitutional baselines in the event that attitudes change, and states reconsider the use of coroner statutes.

4. *Retrieving Visceral Organs in Coroners' Cases.* A number of states had gone even further than Florida and Ohio and enacted statutory provisions allowing coroners or medical examiners to remove hearts, lungs, kidneys, livers, and other visceral organs for transplantation if (a) there had been no objection by the decedent while alive or by family members either before or after the decedent's death, and (b) efforts to contact the family had not been successful. The widespread adoption of the 2006 Act has eliminated most of these provisions. But even when in effect, they did not necessarily result in the retrieval of organs. Coroners and medical examiners were reluctant to remove visceral organs for transplantation without the family's permission. In Texas, in the first year after medical examiners were given authority to remove visceral organs without consent, that authority was used only twice. Coroners and medical examiners are not the only persons reluctant to remove organs without family consent. Even in cases in which a person has registered as an organ donor, transplant surgeons often will not remove the person's organs without the family's permission.

While the 2006 Act has led states to revoke the authority of coroners or medical examiners to remove hearts, livers, kidneys, and other organs in the absence of consent, some states retained their cornea removal provisions when they adopted the 2006 Act. See, e.g., Ind. Code §29-2-16.1-3 (requiring consent for organs); Ind. Code §36-2-14-19 (allowing cornea removal). Interestingly, in Montana, the legislature followed the provisions of the Revised Uniform Anatomical Gift Act on coroners and medical examiners, but also retained its statutory provision granting authority to retrieve organs and tissues in the absence of consent. Compare Mont. Code Ann. §72-17-215 with §72-17-217.

5. *Presumed Consent More Broadly.* A number of commentators have argued that retrieval of organs should not have been limited to coroners' cases but should become a routine practice for all deceased persons. Under this "presumed consent" approach, the law would shift the presumption that people do not want to donate

their organs in the absence of explicit consent to a presumption that people do want to donate their organs in the absence of an explicit refusal. Instead of having to "opt in" to organ donation, people would be treated as willing donors unless they "opted out" of donation.

If we allow states to conduct autopsies without permission in criminal cases, does it follow that we should allow removal of organs from all dead persons without permission for transplantation? If the relevant issues are the violation of the person's bodily integrity and the benefit to society, how does an autopsy to solve a crime compare with a removal of organs to save a life or to improve someone's health? How does being subject to organ removal after death compare to being subject to a military draft while alive? Would a presumed consent law be constitutional assuming an adequate option to register objection?

Even if policy and constitutional objections to presumed consent laws could be overcome, it is not clear how great an impact they would have. Consider this take on presumed consent:

> While it is true that organ retrieval rates are higher in countries with presumed consent laws, the reasons for the higher retrieval rates may lie elsewhere than in the presumption of consent. Some studies find a meaningful effect from presumed consent legislation — organ donation rates may increase by a quarter to a third from presumed consent. Other studies, however, do not find that presumed consent legislation increases donation rates. Other factors, such as the infrastructure for organ transplantation or the likelihood that a person's organs will be suitable for transplantation, may explain the differences in retrieval rates between presumed consent and actual consent countries. Indeed, it is clear that countries can achieve high retrieval rates without presuming consent.
>
> The Spanish experience is illustrative. Spain has had the highest rates for organ retrieval, and its high rates often are attributed to presumed consent legislation that was enacted in 1979. However, . . . families always are asked for consent, and the family's wishes prevail. Spain's retrieval rate did not actually rise until 1989—ten years after adoption of presumed consent—when other changes were implemented. In particular, Spain has a highly organized national transplant system, with active and well-trained transplant coordinators at every hospital where organs are retrieved. It may be that these other policy changes rather than presumed consent are responsible for Spain's high retrieval rates.
>
> The U.S. experience is consistent with this view. Organ procurement rates vary from state to state and can be increased by greater efforts to ensure that organ procurement organizations are aware of potential donors and that health care providers involve organ procurement professionals in discussions with family members. . . . [David Orentlicher, Presumed Consent to Organ Donation, in Nudging Health: Health Law and Behavioral Economics (Glenn Cohen, Holly Lynch & Christopher Robertson eds., Johns Hopkins University Press, 2016).]

In addition, it seems difficult for professionals or the public to implement presumed consent fully even when it has been adopted. Presumed consent has been enacted in many countries, but as in Spain, next-of-kin are informed of the intention to remove organs. And in almost all of the countries, family objections will prevent removal. Amanda M. Rosenblum et al., The Authority of Next-of-kin in Explicit and Presumed Consent Systems for Deceased Organ Donation, 27 Nephrology Dialysis Transplantation 2533 (2012).

Similarly, as mentioned in the previous note, the state laws permitting coroners to remove organs and tissues did not seem to have been employed very much for visceral organs despite their widespread use for removal of corneas.

For an argument that the enactment of the coroner provisions represented a limited experiment with presumed consent in the United States and that the repeal of those provisions after the 2006 Act reflects a societal judgment against presumed consent, see David Orentlicher, Presumed Consent to Organ Donation: Its Rise and Fall in the United States, 61 Rutgers L. Rev. 295 (2009).

6. *Required Request.* States have tried to increase organ donation through the adoption of "required request" laws. These laws, which almost all states have, require hospitals to ensure that families are asked for permission to retrieve organs from patients who die. Required request is also a condition for hospitals to receive Medicare and Medicaid reimbursement. 42 U.S.C. §1320b-8. Required request was designed to overcome the reluctance of physicians to raise the issue of organ donation with families, but the laws did not have much impact on their own. In a study to ascertain why required request was not working, researchers found that families were generally asked about organ donation, but family members frequently refused consent. Laura A. Siminoff et al., Public Policy Governing Organ and Tissue Procurement in the United States, 123 Ann. Intern. Med. 10 (1995). See also Ellen Sheehy et al., Estimating the Number of Potential Organ Donors in the United States, 349 New Eng. J. Med. 667 (2003) (finding that "[l]ack of consent to a request for donation was the primary cause of the gap between the number of potential donors and the number of actual donors").

Organ procurement organizations have been able to raise the consent rate for family members by improving the way they discuss the possibility of donation. Heather M. Traino et al., Regional Differences in Communication Process and Outcomes of Requests for Solid Organ Donation, 17 Am J. Transplantation 1620 (2017).

7. *Mandated Choice.* "Mandated choice" laws, under which all competent adults have to explicitly state whether or not they wish to be organ donors after they die, also are common. Almost all states ask applicants whether they want to be an organ donor when they obtain a driver's license. Supporters of mandated choice observe that it places the decision in the hands of the individual rather than in the hands of family members.

Critics worry that mandated choice usually is implemented without the prospective donor receiving much information, preventing genuine informed consent and causing many people to refuse consent. While there has been an increase in the percentage of people who have registered as organ donors, mandated choice does not appear to have increased the number of organ transplants. Paula Chatterjee et al., The Effect of State Policies on Organ Donation and Transplantation in the United States, 175 JAMA Internal Med. 1323 (2015).

8. *Taking Tissue from Living Persons.* The *McFall* case may have come from a local Pennsylvania court, but it nevertheless represents the state of the law. There is no case that has required one person to give up tissue for the benefit of another person over the first person's objection. A subsequent case went even further and denied access to the name of a potential donor, whom the dying person wanted to contact and try to persuade to serve as a donor. In Head v. Colloton, 331 N.W.2d 870 (Iowa 1983), William Head, who was living in Texas, needed a bone marrow transplant to treat his leukemia. He had heard that the University of Iowa maintained a registry

of potential bone marrow donors, and through conversations with a staff member, discovered that a woman in the registry might have compatible tissue for donation. The woman had been entered into the registry without her knowledge—she had been tested at one time to see if she could be a blood platelet donor to a family member—and the registry's practice was to ask potential donors whether they were willing as a general matter to participate in bone marrow transplants. When this woman was contacted, she indicated that she would consider donation but only for a family member. Mr. Head then filed suit, seeking disclosure of the woman's name to the court or his attorney so the woman could be informed about Mr. Head's situation and asked if she would consider donation in this particular case. The court held that, while the bone marrow registry was a public record under Iowa law, it was a confidential record to which public access must be denied.

If we consider just the case itself, the result in *Head* may seem problematic. However, from a broader perspective, why do you think the court felt it had to preserve the confidentiality of the woman's name? Does your answer explain why the court was not even willing to require the bone marrow registry to send the woman a letter about Mr. Head without disclosing the woman's name to Mr. Head?

9. *The Other Side of the Argument.* Is it so obvious that *McFall* and *Head* are correctly decided? Most persons share the *McFall* court's abhorrence at the idea of an involuntary taking of a person's tissue for use by another person. Yet, our society already condones behavior that is arguably more coercive. If given the choice between paying taxes and donating blood every three months, which would you choose? Of course, there are health risks with bone marrow donation. Common side effects include bone pain and fatigue. Life-threatening problems occur between 0.1 and 0.3 percent of the time, and the risk of death is probably somewhere between 0.01 and 0.03 percent. Annelies Billen et al., A Review of the Haematopoietic Stem Cell Donation Experience, 49 Bone Marrow Transplantation 729 (2014); Dennis L. Confer et al., Bone Marrow and Peripheral Blood Cell Donors and Donor Registries, *in* Thomas' Hematopoietic Cell Transplantation 423, 427-428 (Stephen J. Forman et al. eds., 5th ed. 2016). Consider also the following argument:

> [I]f you are talking about fairness, I really do not understand why the fact that I have inherited good kidneys, or good bone marrow, . . . or indeed inherited a good environment, gives me more rights than the person who has inherited bad ones. I am not sure that a person deserves inherited desirable body parts any more than he or she deserves inherited wealth. . . . Consider this situation from a Rawlsian point of view. If one did not know whether or not one would have good marrow or kidneys, then what would one say if asked whether one preferred the right to obtain somebody else's bone marrow or kidneys or the right to retain one's own? In the real world, where there are more people who have good kidneys than there are people who need them, it is all too easy to vote against a law which mandates donation. But what about voting behind a Rawlsian veil, where we would not know whether we were the needy or the well-endowed?

Guido Calabresi, Do We Own Our Bodies?, 1 Health Matrix 5, 16 (1991). Calabresi observes that laws requiring organ or tissue donation might only be passed by the majority if the potential donors were relatively weak politically and the potential recipients were relatively powerful politically, and that such laws would therefore "have to be constitutionally suspect." Id. at 11-12. But what if discrimination were not an issue?

> Now consider a communitarian-based law under which . . . *everyone* would have to be donors because we wanted to show that we are *all* willing to take on the burden. . . . Of course, it is unlikely that a legislature would actually do this, which again says something about whether or not we as a society are sufficiently concerned about "life" to be *nondiscriminating* communitarians. If we were, then I would argue the law might well be constitutional. [Id. at 13.]

Advances in medicine have resulted in a procedure that replaces bone marrow transplants in most cases. Rather than harvesting adult blood stem cells from bone marrow for transplantation in cases like *McFall*, doctors can retrieve stem cells from the donor's circulating blood after giving the donor a drug to stimulate stem cell production. Like bone marrow donation, this peripheral blood stem cell donation is generally safe, although rare serious complications can occur, including death. It is not clear whether the risk of death differs between bone marrow and peripheral cell donation. Confer et al., supra, at 429. Because it is less invasive to retrieve stem cells from peripheral blood, recovery time is generally shorter. While researchers have worried about a theoretical risk of leukemia or other cancers of the blood system from the drugs used to stimulate peripheral stem cell production, studies have not found any elevation in risk among donors. Bronwen E. Shaw et al., A Review of the Genetic and Long-term Effects of G-CSF Injections in Healthy Donors, 50 Bone Marrow Transplantation 334 (2015).

Once peripheral stem cell donation became possible, so did payment for donors. The federal law that prohibits payments for organs includes bone marrow but not blood in the definition of organ. 42 U.S.C. §274e(c)(1). While the government opposed payments for peripheral stem cell donors, a federal court of appeals concluded that because peripheral stem cells are components of circulating blood rather than of bone marrow, payments are permissible. Flynn v. Holder, 684 F.3d 852 (9th Cir. 2012).

10. *The "Trolley Problem."* Moral theorists have posed the following dilemma: If a trolley conductor is steering a runaway car through a crowded city and must choose between two tracks, it is morally permissible, and perhaps mandatory, to choose the track that will result in harm to fewer people, even if in doing so the conductor will purposefully kill someone? That being the case, why can't a physician take five life-necessary organs from one person in order to save the lives of five other persons, or even take tissue from a person for whom it is not life-necessary to give it to another person for whom it would be life-sustaining? The possible answers turn out to be more complicated than you would first think, and lead to fascinating extrapolations.

For discussion, see Michael J. Costa, The Trolley Problem Revisited, 24 S. J. Phil. 437 (1986); Frances M. Kamm, Harming Some to Save Others, 57 Phil. Stud. 227 (1989); Adam Kolber, A Matter of Priority: Transplanting Organs Preferentially to Registered Donors, 55 Rutgers L. Rev. 671 (2003); James A. Montmarquet, On Doing Good, 79 J. Phil. 439 (1982); Eric Rakowski, Taking and Saving Lives, 93 Colum. L. Rev. 1063 (1993); Judith Jarvis Thomson, The Trolley Problem, 94 Yale L. J. 1395 (1985); Judith Jarvis Thomson, The Realm of Rights 176-202 (1990).

11. *Further Reading.* On **presumed consent** (note 5), see Maxwell J. Mehlman, Presumed Consent to Organ Donation, 1 Health Matrix 31 (1991); Paul T. Menzel, Strong Medicine (1990); Jesse Dukeminier & David Sanders, Organ Transplantation: A Proposal for Routine Salvaging of Cadaver Organs, 279 New Eng. J. Med. 413 (1968); Arthur J. Matas et al., A Proposal for Cadaver Organ Procurement, 10 J. Health Pol. Pol'y & L. 231 (1985); Theodore Silver, The Case for a Post-Mortem Organ Draft and a Proposed Model Organ Draft Act, 68 B.U. L. Rev. 681 (1988); Robert M. Veatch & J. B. Pitt, The Myth of Presumed Consent, 27 Transplant. Proc. 1888 (1995).

On **mandated choice** (note 7), Council on Ethical and Judicial Affairs, American Medical Association, Strategies for Cadaveric Organ Procurement: Mandated Choice and Presumed Consent, 272 JAMA 809 (1994); Ana S. Ilitis, Organ Donation, Brain Death and the Family: Valid Informed Consent, 43 J. L. Med. & Ethics 369 (2015); Sheldon F. Kurtz & Michael J. Saks, Cadaveric Organ Donor Act, 18 Iowa J. Corp. L. 523, 527 (1993); Aaron Spital, Mandated Choice for Organ Donation, 125 Ann. Intern. Med. 66 (1996).

On **payments for stem cells** (note 9), see I. Glenn Cohen, Selling Bone Marrow—*Flynn v. Holder*, 366 New Eng. J. Med. 296 (2012); Seema Mohapatra, Cutting the Cord to Private Cord Blood Banking, 84 U. Colo. L. Rev. 933 (2013).

Problem: Obligatory Stem Cell Donation

Suppose a legislature, concerned about the shortage of stem cell donors for transplants, passed a law requiring that all persons be included in a national stem cell registry. People would automatically be registered at birth by having a small amount of additional blood taken at the time that blood was taken for routine newborn medical testing. Other persons would have to bring a certificate showing that they had registered before they could obtain or renew a driver's license or begin a new academic year in school. When someone needed a stem cell transplant (either from bone marrow or peripheral blood), the person's physician could check with the registry for a match. If a match was found, the person who matched would have to donate stem cells for a transplant. People could be excused from having to donate if they had religious objections or had a medical reason that disqualified them as a donor (just as the military excuses conscientious objectors and those with health problems from the draft). Should this law be constitutional? If constitutional, is it good policy? Would it matter whether the state paid some compensation to the donors as it does with military or jury duty? Would any constitutional concerns be eliminated if the law simply required automatic registration, leaving with the individual the decision whether to donate stem cells if a match occurred?

Consider the following variation on the facts: A Chernobyl-like disaster occurs in the United States, and, because of the nuclear fallout, tens or hundreds of thousands of persons need stem cell transplants. In response to the disaster, Congress passes a law requiring all healthy adults to register as potential stem cell donors. Do your answers to the previous questions come out any differently?

Notes: Financial Incentives for Organ Donation

1. *Proposals for Financial Incentives.* Another obvious way to increase the supply of transplantable organs is with financial inducement. A number of commentators have criticized the federal law that prohibits payment for organs. 42 U.S.C. §274e. They propose that people should be able either to sell their tissues and body parts that are not essential for life, as they now do with blood products, semen, or ova, or to receive payment for a promise to give up their organs when they die.

In 2000, Pennsylvania enacted a statute authorizing payments of $3,000 to families for medical or funeral expenses of the decedent. 20 Pa. Cons. Stat. Ann. §8622. The federal prohibition against sales of organs has prevented the statute from taking effect. In June 2002, the American Medical Association called for pilot studies of financial incentives for organ donation. Deborah Josefson, AMA Considers Whether to Pay for Donation of Organs, 324 Brit. Med. J. 1541 (2002).

In January 2004, Wisconsin enacted a state tax deduction for live organ donors that passes muster under federal law. Organ donors can deduct up to $10,000 from adjusted gross income for travel expenses, lodging expenses, or lost wages that are not reimbursed (a donor can claim the deduction only once). Wis. Stat. §71.05(10)(i). Under federal law, "valuable consideration" may not be paid for a human organ, but valuable consideration does not include "the expenses of travel, housing, and lost wages incurred by the donor of a human organ in connection with the donation of the organ." 42 U.S.C. §274e(c)(2). Since Wisconsin's enactment, several states have passed similar statutes. With regard to the concern that payments will have a coercive effect on poor people, why is Wisconsin's approach particularly good?

Such incentives would increase the organ supply, it is argued. But empirical evidence indicates that payments would have to be higher than currently allowed. Paula Chatterjee et al., The Effect of State Policies on Organ Donation and Transplantation in the United States, 175 JAMA Internal Med. 1323 (2015); Nicola Lacetera et al., Removing Financial Barriers to Organ and Bone Marrow Donation, 33 J. Health Econ. 43 (2014).

Considerations of justice also can support payments to donors. Noting that transplant surgeons, organ recipients, and others involved in transplantation benefit, commentators argue that donors also ought to benefit. A third argument in favor of some kind of payment is that we may have fewer problems with donors or their families wanting to be involved with recipients or feeling that the recipient owes them something. Thomas Murray has observed that gift-giving, unlike business dealings, can result in open-ended human relationships:

> In short, gifts create moral relationships that are much more open-ended, less specifiable, and less contained than contracts. Contracts are well suited to the marketplace where a strictly limited relationship for a narrow purpose — trading goods or services — is desired. Gifts are better for initiating and sustaining more rounded human relationships, where future expectations are unknown, and where the exchange of goods is secondary in importance to the relationship itself.

Thomas H. Murray, Gifts of the Body and the Needs of Strangers, 17(2) Hastings Center Rep. 30, 31 (1987) (but preferring a system of donation for organs because of the important social values that it promotes).

After studying the relations between organ recipients and the donor or the donor's family, Renée Fox and Judith Swazey concluded that

> [w]hat recipients believe they owe to donors and the sense of obligation they feel about repaying "their" donor for what has been given, weigh heavily on them. This psychological and moral burden is especially onerous because the gift the recipient has received from the donor is so extraordinary that it is inherently unreciprocal. It has no physical or symbolic equivalent. As a consequence, the giver, the receiver, and their families may find themselves locked in a creditor-debtor vise that binds them one to another in a mutually fettering way. We have called these aspects of the gift-exchange dimensions of transplantation, "the tyranny of the gift." . . . In the case of a live kidney donation, for example, the donor may exhibit a great deal of "proprietary interest" in the health, work, and private life of the close relative who has received his or her organ. . . .
>
> Recipients of cadaveric organ transplants also suffer from the magnitude of the gift they have received and from its unrequitable nature. . . . [T]he import of what has been given may not only drive close relatives of a cadaver donor to seek out the recipient but also, especially with heart transplants, to relate to this person as if he or she embodied the living spirit of the donor. However painful it may be for the recipients and their families to be united with their organ donors' kin, they are likely to feel obligated to yield to them because of their ineffable sense of indebtedness. . . .

Renée C. Fox & Judith P. Swazey, Spare Parts 40-41 (1992).

Do we want open-ended relationships between organ donors and recipients?

2. *Concerns with Financial Incentives.* Opponents of organ sales claim that it will undermine altruistic sentiments in society. Proponents counter that we do not lose altruism by using tax deductions to encourage charitable contributions and that, in any event, altruism in society is not based on what kind of organ donation system we have. Opponents also worry that organ sales "commodify" the body (i.e., turn the body into a commodity). Proponents respond that society already permits a great deal of commodification when it permits people to work for a wage. Should we be more worried about commodifying people by buying their organs than commodifying people when we pay them for the fruits of their minds? There is also a concern about desperate persons taking unacceptable risks for pay. In response to this concern, there have been proposals to pay people for their organs, but only if the organs are taken after death, with payment to the person's heirs:

> My proposed solution is a futures market in which healthy individuals would be given the opportunity to contract for the sale of their body tissue for delivery after their death. If the vendor's organs are harvested and transplanted, a payment in the range of $5,000 for each major organ and lesser amounts for minor tissue would be made to his estate or designee. The hospital in which the vendor dies, as any bailee entrusted with valuable property, would have the legal duty to preserve his cadaver in a manner suitable for organ harvesting and to notify the purchasing agency of the decedent's condition so that it may harvest his organs. The proposal speaks only to increasing the supply of organs, not to allocating them. . . . The futures market I propose avoids three potential ethical and political pitfalls. First, because there will be no acquisition of organs from live donors, it does not raise the spectre of exploiting the poor. Second, because the market need not be used to allocate the

harvested organs, the rich need have no greater access than the poor. Finally, because people will be selling their own organs, their next of kin will not be required to traffic in the decedents' remains.

Lloyd R. Cohen, Increasing the Supply of Transplant Organs, 58 Geo. Wash. L. Rev. 1, 2 (1989).

Are there in fact good reasons for denying a person the freedom to sell a kidney? We might be concerned about a system in which the wealthy are able to obtain kidneys more easily than the poor, but suppose we permit sales of organs only if the organ is sold to the United Network for Organ Sharing (UNOS), which in turn would allocate the organ according to its customary criteria? Organ selling seems ghoulish, but is there more than an aesthetic preference that underlies the opposition to sales? Are the reasons for opposing sales sufficient to deny poor persons the means to purchase basic necessities for their families? Might the prohibition on sales exist so that we can, as a society, avoid having to deal with the reality of people being so desperately poor as to want to sell a kidney?

3. *Costs of Financial Incentives.* In considering the option of financial incentives, you may be concerned about the added cost to organ transplantation from the need to pay donors. But why is that a problem if a life is saved? Is it clear that the cost of transplantation will go up? Finally, consider the fact that educational campaigns to increase organ donation also are costly. For a study finding that education campaigns are cost-effective, see Manik Razdan et al., Promoting Organ Donor Registries Through Public Education, 100 Transplantation 1332 (2016).

4. *Further Reading.* There is a rich literature on **incentives to provide organs** for transplantation, including the symposium, Organs and Inducements, 77(3) Law & Contemp. Probs. (2014), and Robert Arnold et al., Financial Incentives for Cadaver Organ Donation, 73 Transplantation 1361 (2002) (representing the ethics committee of the American Society of Transplant Surgeons).

For the **proponent side**, see T. Randolph Beard & David L. Kaserman, On the Ethics of Paying Organ Donors, 55 DePaul L. Rev. 827 (2006); Richard A. Epstein, Mortal Peril: Our Inalienable Right to Health Care? 249-261 (1997); Sigrid Fry-Revere, The Kidney Sellers: A Journey of Discovery in Iran (2014); Henry Hansmann, The Economics and Ethics of Markets for Human Organs, 14 J. Health Pol. Pol'y & L. 57 (1989); Jamila Jefferson-Jones, The Exchange of Inmate Organs for Liberty, 16 J. Gender Race & Just. 105 (2013); Mark S. Nadel & Carolina A. Nadel, Using Reciprocity to Motivate Organ Donors, 5 Yale J. Health Pol'y L. & Ethics 293 (2005); Richard Schwindt & Aidan R. Vining, Proposal for a Future Delivery Market for Transplant Organs, 11 J. Health Pol. Pol'y & L. 483 (1986); James S. Taylor, Stakes and Kidneys (2005); Evelyn M. Tenenbaum, Bartering for a Compatible Kidney Using Your Incompatible, Live Kidney Donor, 42 Am. J. L. & Med. 129 (2016); Note, The Sale of Human Body Parts, 72 Mich. L. Rev. 1182 (1974).

For the **critical side**, see Arthur L. Caplan, Trafficking and Markets in Kidneys, in the Future of Bioethics: International Dialogues (2014); Gabriel M. Danovitch, The High Cost of Organ Transplant Commercialism, 85 Kidney Int'l 248 (2014); F. Daniel Davis & Samuel J. Crowe, Organ Markets and the Ends of Medicine, 34 J. Med. Philos. 586 (2009); Francis L. Delmonico et al., Living and Deceased Organ Donation Should Be Financially Neutral Acts, 15 Am. J. Transplantation 1187 (2015); Julian Koplin, Assessing the Likely Harms to Kidney Vendors in Regulated

Organ Markets, 14(10) Am. J. Bioethics 7 (2014); Margaret Jane Radin, Market-Inalienability, 100 Harv. L. Rev. 1849 (1987); Simon Rippon, Imposing Options on People in Poverty, 40 J. Med. Ethics 145 (2014); Debra Satz, Why Some Things Should Not Be for Sale (2010).

For empirical evidence on **organ selling in other countries,** legally in Iran for live donors and in Saudi Arabia for cadaveric donors, and illegally in other countries, see Jennifer M. Babik & Peter Chin-Hong, Transplant Tourism, 17 Curr. Infectious Dis. Rep. 18 (2015); I. Glenn Cohen, Transplant Tourism, J. L. Med. & Ethics 269 (2013); Debra A. Budiani-Saberi, Human Trafficking for Organ Removal in India, 97 Transplantation 380 (2014); Nasrollah Ghahramani, Paid Living Donation and Growth of Deceased Donor Programs, 100 Transplantation 1165 (2016); Benita S. Padilla, Regulation Compensation for Kidney Donors in the Philippines, 14 Curr. Opin. Organ Transplant. 120 (2009); Adibul Hasan S. Rizvi et al., Regulated Compensated Donation in Pakistan and Iran, 14 Curr. Opin. Organ Transplant. 124 (2009); Mohammed Al Sebayel et al., Donor Organ Shortage Crisis: A Case Study Review of a Financial Incentive-Based System, 46 Transplantation Proceedings 2030 (2014).

2. Ownership and Control of Human Tissue

Whether organs and other tissues can be taken involuntarily or can be willingly sold depends in part on whether we think people have a property interest in their body. That issue is explored in the following case, but in a somewhat different context: using human tissue for research purposes rather than for transplantation. As you read this case, consider whether the court's answers to the ownership and control questions can be generalized to other contexts, or whether the court creates a special rule just for medical research.

■ MOORE v. THE REGENTS OF THE UNIVERSITY OF CALIFORNIA
793 P.2d 479 (Cal. 1990)

PANELLI, Justice.

[The facts of this case are presented at page 187. After holding that people have a right of informed consent when a researcher profits from studying and using their cells, the court considered whether use of a person's cells without permission violates the person's property rights.]

. . . Moore also attempts to characterize the invasion of his rights as a conversion—a tort that protects against interference with possessory and ownership interests in personal property. He theorizes that he continued to own his cells following their removal from his body, at least for the purpose of directing their use, and that he never consented to their use in potentially lucrative medical research. . . .

No court, however, has ever in a reported decision imposed conversion liability for the use of human cells in medical research. While that fact does not end our inquiry, it raises a flag of caution. In effect, what Moore is asking us to do is to impose a tort duty on scientists . . . [that] would affect medical research of importance to all of society, implicat[ing] policy concerns far removed from the traditional, two-party ownership disputes in which the law of conversion arose. . . .

"To establish a conversion, plaintiff must establish an actual interference with his *ownership or right of possession*. . . . Where plaintiff neither has title to the property alleged to have been converted, nor possession thereof, he cannot maintain an action for conversion." (Del E. Webb Corp. v. Structural Materials Co., 123 Cal. App. 3d 593, 610-611 (1981)) (emphasis added).

Moore . . . argues that "[i]f the courts have found a sufficient proprietary interest in one's persona, how could one not have a right in one's own genetic material, something far more profoundly the essence of one's human uniqueness than a name or a face?" However, . . . the goal and result of defendants' efforts has been to manufacture lymphokines. Lymphokines, unlike a name or a face, have the same molecular structure in every human being and the same important functions in every human being's immune system. Moreover, the particular genetic material which is responsible for the natural production of lymphokines, and which defendants use to manufacture lymphokines in the laboratory, is also the same in every person; it is no more unique to Moore than the number of vertebrae in the spine or the chemical formula of hemoglobin.

. . . [T]he Court of Appeal in this case concluded that "[a] patient must have the ultimate power to control what becomes of his or her tissues. To hold otherwise would open the door to a massive invasion of human privacy and dignity in the name of medical progress." Yet one may earnestly wish to protect privacy and dignity without accepting the extremely problematic conclusion that interference with those interests amounts to a conversion of personal property. Nor is it necessary to force the round pegs of "privacy" and "dignity" into the square hole of "property" in order to protect the patient, since the fiduciary-duty and informed-consent theories protect these interests directly by requiring full disclosure. . . .

Finally, the subject matter of the Regents' patent—the patented cell line and the products derived from it—cannot be Moore's property. This is because the patented cell line is both factually and legally distinct from the cells taken from Moore's body. Federal law permits the patenting of organisms that represent the product of "human ingenuity," but not naturally occurring organisms. Human cell lines are patentable because "[l]ong-term adaptation and growth of human tissues and cells in culture is difficult—often considered an art . . . ," and the probability of success is low. U.S. Congress, Office of Technology Assessment, New Developments in Biotechnology: Ownership of Human Tissues and Cells 33 (1987). It is this *inventive effort* that patent law rewards, not the discovery of naturally occurring raw materials. . . .

Of the relevant policy considerations, two are of overriding importance. The first is protection of a competent patient's right to make autonomous medical decisions. . . . This policy weighs in favor of providing a remedy to patients when physicians act with undisclosed motives that may affect their professional judgment. The second important policy consideration is that we not threaten with disabling civil liability innocent parties who are engaged in socially useful activities, such as researchers who have no reason to believe that their use of a particular cell sample is, or may be, against a donor's wishes. . . .

We need not, however, make an arbitrary choice between liability and nonliability. Instead, an examination of the relevant policy considerations suggests an appropriate balance: Liability based upon existing disclosure obligations, rather than an unprecedented extension of the conversion theory, protects patients' rights of privacy and autonomy without unnecessarily hindering research. . . .

Research on human cells plays a critical role in medical research. This is so because researchers are increasingly able to isolate naturally occurring, medically useful biological substances and to produce useful quantities of such substances through genetic engineering. These efforts are beginning to bear fruit. Products developed through biotechnology that have already been approved for marketing in this country include treatments and tests for leukemia, cancer, diabetes, dwarfism, hepatitis-B, kidney transplant rejection, emphysema, osteoporosis, ulcers, anemia, infertility, and gynecological tumors, to name but a few.

The extension of conversion law into this area will hinder research by restricting access to the necessary raw materials. Thousands of human cell lines already exist in tissue repositories. . . . These repositories respond to tens of thousands of requests for samples annually. Since the patent office requires the holders of patents on cell lines to make samples available to anyone, many patent holders place their cell lines in repositories to avoid the administrative burden of responding to requests. At present, human cell lines are routinely copied and distributed to other researchers for experimental purposes, usually free of charge. This exchange of scientific materials, which still is relatively free and efficient, will surely be compromised if each cell sample becomes the potential subject matter of a lawsuit. . . .

[T]he theory of liability that Moore urges us to endorse threatens to destroy the economic incentive to conduct important medical research. If the use of cells in research is a conversion, then with every cell sample a researcher purchases a ticket in a litigation lottery. Because liability for conversion is predicated on a continuing ownership interest, "companies are unlikely to invest heavily in developing, manufacturing, or marketing a product when uncertainty about clear title exists." (OTA Rep., supra, at p. 27.) . . .

BROUSSARD, Justice, concurring and dissenting.

. . . If this were a typical case in which a patient consented to the use of his removed organ for general research purposes and the patient's doctor had no prior knowledge of the scientific or commercial value of the patient's organ or cells, I would agree that the patient could not maintain a conversion action. In that common scenario, the patient has abandoned any interest in the removed organ and is not entitled to demand compensation if it should later be discovered that the organ or cells have some unanticipated value. I cannot agree, however, with the majority that a patient may never maintain a conversion action for the unauthorized use of his excised organ or cells, even against a party who knew of the value of the organ or cells before they were removed and breached a duty to disclose that value to the patient. . . .

Although the majority opinion, at several points, appears to suggest that a removed body part, by its nature, may never constitute "property" for purposes of a conversion action, there is no reason to think that the majority opinion actually intends to embrace such a broad or dubious proposition. If, for example, another medical center or drug company had stolen all of the cells in question from the UCLA Medical Center laboratory and had used them for its own benefit, there would be no question but that a cause of action for conversion would properly lie against the thief, and the majority opinion does not suggest otherwise. Thus, the majority's analysis cannot rest on the broad proposition that a removed body part is not property, but rather rests on the proposition that a *patient* retains no ownership interest in a body part once the body part has been removed from his or her body. . . .

MOSK, Justice, dissenting.

. . . The majority's third and last reason for their conclusion that Moore has no cause of action for conversion under existing law is that "the subject matter of the Regents' patent—the patented cell line and the products derived from it—cannot be Moore's property." The majority then offer a dual explanation: "This is because the patented cell line is both *factually* and *legally* distinct from the cells taken from Moore's body" (emphasis added). Neither branch of the explanation withstands analysis.

. . . For present purposes no distinction can be drawn between Moore's cells and the Mo cell line. It appears that the principal reason for establishing a cell line is not to "improve" the quality of the parent cells but simply to extend their life indefinitely, in order to permit long-term study and/or exploitation of the qualities already present in such cells. The complaint alleges that Moore's cells naturally produced certain valuable proteins in larger than normal quantities; indeed, that was why defendants were eager to culture them in the first place. Defendants do not claim that the cells of the Mo cell line are in any degree more productive of such proteins than were Moore's own cells. . . .

I do not question that the cell line is primarily the product of defendants' inventive effort. Yet likewise no one can question Moore's crucial contribution to the invention—an invention named, ironically, after him: But for the cells of Moore's body taken by defendants, there would have been no Mo cell line. Thus the complaint alleges that Moore's "Blood and Bodily Substances were absolutely essential to defendants' research and commercial activities . . . and that defendants could not have applied for and had issued to them the Mo cell-line patent and other patents described herein without obtaining and culturing specimens of plaintiff's Blood and Bodily Substances." . . . Defendants admit this allegation by their demurrers, as well they should: For all their expertise, defendants do not claim they could have extracted the Mo cell line out of thin air.

Nevertheless the majority conclude that the patent somehow cut off all Moore's rights—past, present, and future—to share in the proceeds of defendants' commercial exploitation of the cell line derived from his own body tissue. The majority cite no authority for this unfair result, and I cannot believe it is compelled by the general law of patents: A patent is not a license to defraud. Perhaps the answer lies in an analogy to the concept of "joint inventor." . . .

> Although a patient who donates cells does not fit squarely within the definition of a "joint inventor," the policy reasons that inform joint inventor patents should also apply to cell donors. Neither John Moore nor any other patient whose cells become the basis for a patentable cell line qualifies as a "joint inventor" because he or she did not further the development of the product in any intellectual or conceptual sense. Nor does the status of patients as sole owners of a component part make them deserving of joint inventorship status. What the patients did do, knowingly or unknowingly, is collaborate with the researchers by donating their body tissue. . . . By providing the researchers with unique raw materials, without which the resulting product could not exist, the donors become necessary contributors to the product. Concededly, the patent is not granted for the cell as it is found in nature, but for

the modified biogenetic product. However, the uniqueness of the product that gives rise to its patentability stems from the uniqueness of the original cell. *A patient's claim to share in the profits flowing from a patent would be analogous to that of an inventor whose collaboration was essential to the success of a resulting product. The patient was not a coequal, but was a necessary contributor to the cell line.* (Danforth, Cells, Sales, and Royalties: The Patient's Right to a Portion of the Profits, 6 Yale L. & Pol'y Rev. 179, 197 (1988) (emphasis added).) . . .

The majority begin their analysis by stressing the obvious facts that research on human cells plays an increasingly important role in the progress of medicine, and that the manipulation of those cells by the methods of biotechnology has resulted in numerous beneficial products and treatments. Yet it does not necessarily follow that, as the majority claim, application of the law of conversion to this area "will hinder research by restricting access to the necessary raw materials," i.e., to cells, cell cultures, and cell lines. . . .

To begin with, if the relevant exchange of scientific materials was ever "free and efficient," it is much less so today. Since biological products of genetic engineering became patentable in 1980, human cell lines have been amenable to patent protection and, as the court of appeal observed in its opinion below, "The rush to patent for exclusive use has been rampant." Among those who have taken advantage of this development, of course, are the defendants herein. . . . With such patentability has come a drastic reduction in the formerly free access of researchers to new cell lines and their products: The "novelty" requirement for patentability prohibits public disclosure of the invention at all times up to one year before the filing of the patent application. Thus defendants herein recited in their patent specification, "At no time has the Mo cell line been available to other than the investigators involved with its initial discovery." . . .

Secondly, to the extent that cell cultures and cell lines may still be "freely exchanged," e.g., for purely research purposes, it does not follow that the researcher who obtains such material must necessarily remain ignorant of any limitations on its use: By means of appropriate recordkeeping, the researcher can be assured that the source of the material has consented to his proposed use of it, and hence that such use is not a conversion. . . . "Record keeping would not be overly burdensome because researchers generally keep accurate records of tissue sources for other reasons: to trace anomalies to the medical history of the patient, to maintain title for other researchers and for themselves, and to insure reproducibility of the experiment." Toward the Right of Commerciality, 34 UCLA L. Rev. at 241. As the Court of Appeal correctly observed, any claim to the contrary "is dubious in light of the meticulous care and planning necessary in serious modern medical research." . . .

A second policy consideration adds notions of equity to those of ethics. Our society values fundamental fairness in dealings between its members, and condemns the unjust enrichment of any member at the expense of another. This is particularly true when, as here, the parties are not in equal bargaining positions. We are repeatedly told that the commercial products of the biotechnological revolution "hold the promise of tremendous profit." Toward the Right of Commerciality, 34 UCLA L. Rev. at 211. In the case at bar, for example, the complaint alleges that the market for the kinds of proteins produced by the Mo cell line was predicted to exceed $3 billion by 1990. . . .

There is, however, a third party to the biotechnology enterprise — the patient who is the source of the blood or tissue from which all these profits are derived. While he may be a silent partner, his contribution to the venture is absolutely crucial. . . . Yet defendants deny that Moore is entitled to any share whatever in the proceeds of this cell line. This is both inequitable and immoral. . . .

The majority's final reason for refusing to recognize a conversion cause of action on these facts is that "there is no pressing need" to do so because the complaint also states another cause of action that is assertedly adequate to the task [—the nondisclosure cause of action]. . . .

I disagree . . . with the majority's . . . conclusion that in the present context a nondisclosure cause of action is an adequate—in fact, a superior—substitute for a conversion cause of action. [Justice Mosk then goes on to point out how difficult it is for patients to win damages in informed consent cases. He also points out that an informed consent claim would be good only against the patient's physician, in this case Dr. Golde, but not against other persons or institutions outside the patient-physician relationship who benefited from the patient's cells.]

■ GREENBERG v. MIAMI CHILDREN'S HOSPITAL RESEARCH INSTITUTE, INC.
264 F. Supp. 2d 1064 (S.D. Fla. 2003)

MORENO, Judge . . .

I. BACKGROUND . . .

The Complaint alleges a tale of a successful research collaboration gone sour. In 1987, Canavan disease still remained a mystery—there was no way to identify who was a carrier of the disease, nor was there a way to identify a fetus with Canavan disease. Plaintiff Greenberg approached Dr. Matalon, a research physician . . . for assistance. Greenberg requested Matalon's involvement in discovering the genes that were ostensibly responsible for this fatal disease, so that tests could be administered to determine carriers and allow for prenatal testing for the disease. [Canavan disease is a genetic disorder of the neurologic system that usually causes death by age 4 and is more common among Jews from Eastern Europe and among Saudi Arabians. If both parents carry the gene for Canavan disease, their children face a 25 percent chance of developing the disease.]

At the outset of the collaboration, Greenberg and the Chicago Chapter of the National Tay-Sachs and Allied Disease Association, Inc. ("NTSAD") located other Canavan families and convinced them to provide tissue (such as blood, urine, and autopsy samples), financial support, and aid in identifying the location of Canavan families internationally. The other individual Plaintiffs began supplying Matalon with the same types of information and samples beginning in the late 1980s. . . .

The individual Plaintiffs allege that they provided Matalon with these samples and confidential information "with the understanding and expectations that such samples and information would be used for the specific purpose of researching Canavan disease and identifying mutations in the Canavan disease which could lead to carrier detection within their families and benefit the population at large." Plaintiffs further allege that it was their "understanding that any carrier and prenatal testing developed in connection with the research for which they were providing essential support would be provided on an affordable and accessible basis, and that Matalon's research would remain in the public domain to promote the discovery of more effective prevention techniques and treatments and, eventually, to effectuate a cure for Canavan disease." This understanding stemmed from their "experience in community testing for Tay-Sachs disease, another deadly genetic disease that occurs most frequently in families of Ashkenazi Jewish descent."

There was a breakthrough in the research in 1993. Using Plaintiffs' blood and tissue samples, familial pedigree information, contacts, and financial support, Matalon and his research team successfully isolated the gene responsible for Canavan disease. After this key advancement, Plaintiffs allege that they continued to provide Matalon with more tissue and blood in order to learn more about the disease and its precursor gene.

In September 1994, unbeknownst to Plaintiffs, a patent application was submitted for the genetic sequence that Defendants had identified. This application was granted in October 1997, and Dr. Matalon was listed as an inventor on the gene patent and related applications for the Canavan disease, Patent No. 5,679,635 (the "Patent"). Through patenting, Defendants acquired the ability to restrict any activity related to the Canavan disease gene, including without limitation: carrier and prenatal testing, gene therapy and other treatments for Canavan disease and research involving the gene and its mutations.

Although the Patent was issued in October 1997, Plaintiffs allege that they did not learn of it until November 1998, when MCH (Miami Children's Hospital) revealed their intention to limit Canavan disease testing through a campaign of restrictive licensing of the Patent. . . . Defendant MCH also began restricting public accessibility through negotiating exclusive licensing agreements and charging royalty fees. . . .

. . . Plaintiffs generally seek a permanent injunction restraining Defendants from enforcing their patent rights, damages in the form of all royalties Defendants have received on the Patent as well as all financial contributions Plaintiffs made to benefit Defendants' research. Plaintiffs allege that Defendants have earned significant royalties from Canavan disease testing in excess of $75,000 through enforcement of their gene patent, and that Dr. Matalon has personally profited by receiving a recent substantial federal grant to undertake further research on the gene patent. . . .

III. ANALYSIS . . .

A. LACK OF INFORMED CONSENT

[The court rejected a duty for researchers to disclose their economic interests, distinguishing Moore v. Regents of the University of California on the ground that the researcher in that case also provided care to Mr. Moore, while Dr. Matalon did not provide care to any of the plaintiffs.] . . .

C. UNJUST ENRICHMENT

In Count III of the Complaint, Plaintiffs allege that MCH is being unjustly enriched by collecting license fees under the Patent. Under Florida law, the elements of a claim for unjust enrichment are (1) the plaintiff conferred a benefit on the defendant, who had knowledge of the benefit; (2) the defendant voluntarily accepted and retained the benefit; and (3) under the circumstances it would be inequitable for the defendant to retain the benefit without paying for it. The Court finds that Plaintiffs have sufficiently alleged the elements of a claim for unjust enrichment to survive Defendants' motion to dismiss.

While the parties do not contest that Plaintiffs have conferred a benefit to Defendants, including, among other things, blood and tissue samples and soliciting financial contributions, Defendants contend that Plaintiffs have not suffered any detriment, and note that no Plaintiff has been denied access to Canavan testing. Furthermore, the Plaintiffs received what they sought—the successful isolation of the Canavan gene and the development of a screening test. Plaintiffs argue, however, that when Defendants applied the benefits for unauthorized purposes, they suffered a detriment. Had Plaintiffs known that Defendants intended to commercialize their genetic material through patenting and restrictive licensing, Plaintiffs would not have provided these benefits to Defendants under those terms.

Naturally, Plaintiffs allege that the retention of benefits violates the fundamental principles of justice, equity, and good conscience. While Defendants claim that they have invested significant amounts of time and money in research, with no guarantee of success and are thus entitled to seek reimbursement, the same can be said of Plaintiffs. Moreover, Defendants' attempt to seek refuge in the endorsement of the U.S. Patent system, which gives an inventor rights to prosecute patents and negotiate licenses for their intellectual property fails, as obtaining a patent does not preclude the Defendants from being unjustly enriched. The Complaint has alleged more than just a donor-donee relationship for the purposes of an unjust enrichment claim. Rather, the facts paint a picture of a continuing research collaboration that involved Plaintiffs also investing time and significant resources in the race to isolate the Canavan gene. Therefore, given the facts as alleged, the Court finds that Plaintiffs have sufficiently pled the requisite elements of an unjust enrichment claim and the motion to dismiss for failure to state a claim is DENIED as to this count. . . .

E. CONVERSION

The Plaintiffs allege in Count V of their Complaint that they had a property interest in their body tissue and genetic information. . . . The Court disagrees and declines to find a property interest for the body tissue and genetic information voluntarily given to Defendants. These were donations to research without any contemporaneous expectations of return of the body tissue and genetic samples, and thus conversion does not lie as a cause of action.

In Florida, the tort of "conversion is an unauthorized act which deprives another of his property permanently or for an indefinite time." Using property given for one purpose for another purpose constitutes conversion.

First, Plaintiffs have no cognizable property interest in body tissue and genetic matter donated for research under a theory of conversion. This case is similar to *Moore v. Regents of the University of California*, where the Court declined to extend liability under a theory of conversion to misuse of a person's excised biological materials. The plaintiff in *Moore* alleged that he had retained a property right in excised bodily material used in research, and therefore retained some control over the results of that research. The California Supreme Court, however, disagreed and held that the use of the results of medical research inconsistent with the wishes of the donor was not conversion, because the donor had no property interest at stake after the donation was made. . . .

Second, limits to the property rights that attach to body tissue have been recognized in Florida state courts. For example, *in State v. Powell, 497 So. 2d 1188, 1192 (Fla. 1986)*, the Florida Supreme Court refused to recognize a property right in the body of another after death. Similarly, the property right in blood and tissue samples also evaporates once the sample is voluntarily given to a third party.

. . . Plaintiffs cite a litany of cases in other jurisdictions that have recognized that body tissue can be property in some circumstances. *See, e.g., Brotherton v. Cleveland, 923 F.2d 477, 482 (6th Cir. 1991)* (aggregate of rights existing in body tissue is similar to property rights); *York v. Jones, 717 F. Supp. 421, 425 (E.D. Va. 1989)* (couple granted property rights in their frozen embryos). These cases, however, do not involve voluntary donations to medical research. . . .

The Court finds that Florida . . . law do[es] not provide a remedy for Plaintiffs' donations of body tissue and blood samples under a theory of conversion liability. Indeed, the Complaint does not allege that the Defendants used the genetic material for any purpose but medical research. Plaintiffs claim that the *fruits* of the research, namely the patented material, was commercialized. This is an important distinction and another step in the chain of attenuation that renders conversion liability inapplicable to the facts as alleged. If adopted, the expansive theory championed by Plaintiffs would cripple medical research as it would bestow a continuing right for donors to possess the results of any research conducted by the hospital. At the core, these were donations to research without any contemporaneous expectations of return. Consequently, the Plaintiffs have failed to state a claim upon which relief may be granted on this issue. Accordingly, this claim is DISMISSED. . . .

Notes: Human Tissue in Research

1. *Subsequent Developments.* When the *Moore* case went back to the trial court on remand, the parties settled for an undisclosed amount of money. Ultimately, researchers figured out how to produce large amounts of lymphokines without using Mr. Moore's cell line. The *Greenberg* case also was settled, with Miami Children's Hospital permitted to license and collect royalty fees for the laboratory test for the Canavan gene, but obligated to allow license-free use of the Canavan gene in research to cure Canavan disease. Note, 93 Geo. L. J. 365, 376 (2004).

2. Washington University v. Catalona. In his partial dissent in *Moore*, Judge Broussard poses a hypothetical theft of cells from the UCLA laboratory to argue that "the majority's analysis cannot rest on the broad proposition that a removed body part is not property, but rather rests on the proposition that a *patient* retains no ownership interest in a body part once the body part has been removed from his or her body." On the other hand, even Judge Mosk's dissent concedes that when "the source of the material has consented to [the researcher's] proposed use of it, such use is not a conversion." To what extent is human tissue treated more or less like property once it has been left or "removed from the body"?

In *Washington University v. Catalona*, a highly respected researcher of prostate cancer, Dr. William Catalona, moved from Washington University, St. Louis, to Northwestern University, he wanted to take a repository of prostate tissue, blood, and DNA samples that he had collected from patients and that he used in his research. On summary judgment, a federal trial court concluded that the patients had donated their tissue samples to Washington University, which enjoyed ownership rights over those samples. The court therefore held that neither the patients nor Dr. Catalona could insist that Washington University transfer the samples to Northwestern University. Wash. Univ. v. Catalona, 437 F. Supp. 2d 985 (E.D. Mo. 2006). For further discussion of this case, see Lori Andrews, Who Owns Your Body? A Patient's Perspective on *Washington University v. Catalona*, 34 J. L. Med. Ethics 398 (2006). What factors might lead a court to accept property rights in tissue or genetic material stored in a biobank or a research lab? How do the public policy arguments over property rights change once the donor is no longer involved?

Should individuals retain rights in biological material or information that looks even less like property than human tissue? Some states have passed legislation endowing individuals with a property interest in their genetic data, while the majority of those addressing the issue have granted a privacy interest. See Anya E. R. Prince, Comprehensive Protection of Genetic Information: One Size Privacy or Property Models May Not Fit All, 79 Brooklyn L. Rev. 175, 195-201 (2013). What protections, constitutional or otherwise, exist for DNA that has been "abandoned"? Elizabeth Joh has characterized the government's use in criminal investigations of "abandoned" DNA as "covert involuntary DNA sampling"; see Reclaiming "Abandoned" DNA: The Fourth Amendment and Genetic Privacy, 100 Nw. U. L. Rev. 857, 880-882, (2006), and calls for the recognition of nonconsensual DNA theft as a crime, Elizabeth E. Joh, DNA Theft: Recognizing the Crime of Nonconsensual Genetic Collection and Testing, 91 B.U. L. REV. 665, 670 (2011). Extending the discussion of individual protections to other biomaterials including reproductive material further tests our intuitive understanding of the "property" at stake. For a systematic application of moral and political theory to rights in genetic material see Cohen, I. Glenn, The Right Not to Be a Genetic Parent?, 81 S. Cal. L. Rev. 1115, 1148-1151 (2008).

3. *Reconciling* Moore *and* Greenberg *with* McFall. Are the results in *Moore* and *Greenberg* consistent with the result in McFall v. Shimp, supra page 655? If the state cannot force Mr. Shimp to give up his bone marrow for the greater good of society, why can it force Mr. Moore and others to relinquish control over their cells for the same reason? Does Shimp win and the others lose only because the cells were already outside their bodies, and they therefore suffered no invasion of their bodily integrity? But didn't Moore consent to subsequent invasions of his bodily integrity after the surgery only because of Dr. Golde's deception? Does the *Moore* case simply prove Judge Calabresi's point at page 661 that we see ourselves as the Shimps and users of lymphokines of society, but not as the McFalls or Moores of society?

4. *The Immortal Life of Henrietta Lacks and Theories of Property.* Consider the story of Henriett Lacks, as detailed in Rebecca Skloot's prize-winning book The Immortal Life of Henrietta Lacks (2010)

> [I]n 1951, Henrietta Lacks, a poor black woman from Baltimore, sought treatment
> at Johns Hopkins for cervical cancer. Before administering radium for the first time,

the attending doctor cut two dime-size samples of tissue, one cancerous and one healthy, from Lacks' cervix. As was the custom of the day, no one specifically asked Lacks' permission for collection of the tissue or informed her that her specimens might be studied. The treating physician gave the tissue to Dr. George Gey, a scientist who had been trying to establish a continuously reproducing, or immortal, human cell line for use in cancer research. According to protocol, a lab assistant scribbled an abbreviation of Lacks' name, HeLa, on the sample tubes. HeLa cells succeeded where all other human samples had failed, and Gey gave away laboratory-grown cells to interested colleagues. Scientists grew HeLa cells in mass quantities to test the new polio vaccine among other uses, and soon a commercial enterprise was growing batches for large-scale use. More than half a century later, Lacks' tissue has yielded an estimated 50 million metric tons of HeLa cells, and more than 60,000 scientific and medical studies, and are in continued use today. If the specimens had been truly anonymized, Lacks' identity would not be known.

Suzanne M. Rivera, Barbara E. Bierer, Holly Fernandez Lynch, & I. Glenn Cohen, Introduction, in Specimen Science 3 (H. Lynch et al. eds. 2017).

Until the publication of Skloot's book, Lacks' family received no recognition and certainly no remuneration for their mother's cells, which had fueled a significant amount of scientific advancement in the 20th Century. Was that morally problematic? Do the theories of property, addressed in the next note, help answer the question?

5. *Applying Theories of Property to Human Tissue.* Once it is removed from the body, do individuals deserve property interests in their tissue? Does the answer depend on one's theory of property? How might one justify a property claim here?

One view is that I "deserve" the entitlement to profit from my genetic material. But why do I deserve that? The idea of deserving is often thought to be a function of effort: I deserve my paycheck and you do not because I have worked for it. But when it comes to my genetic material I have invested no effort giving me a claim. It just is. The same problem is evident when the theory is framed in economic rather than moral terms, as is familiar in intellectual property discourse, using entitlement as an economic incentive for productive labor. Unlike with copyright, for example, there is no productive labor to incentivize here; one's genetic material is not something to invest in or develop.

Perhaps we do not need incentives here. One might instead argue for the allocation of the entitlement from a starting point of self-ownership—that my body is my property. This is where John Locke starts, with a thesis that "every man has a property in his own person," John Locke, The Second Treatise of Government, ¶27 (1690), and from this derives his theory that an individual also can claim property in whatever he mixes his labor. But even if we grant the Lockean postulate of self-ownership, does it clearly resolve the cases that interest us? Imagine the tissue is that which has been separated and discarded, like hair after a haircut or a tumor removed from the body. Why should we not instead think of discarded genetic material as relegated to the commons, at least until another individual mixes his or her labor with the material to make something of it? Or is this more like a farmer who owns land under which a geologist discovers oil or gas?

A different set of theories are what we might call the personhood theories of property. Margaret Jane Radin is one of the best-known expositors of this view of property close to personhood, suggesting the law does not and should not treat all forms of property the same. Radin suggests one's family home, one's wedding ring, and one's blood are examples of property "closely bound up with personhood because they are part of the way we constitute ourselves as continuing personal entities." Margaret Jane Radin, Property and Personhood, 34 Stan. L. Rev. 957, 966-967 (1982). On this theory, one's entitlement to one's genetic information flows directly from it being part of one's person. But as a descriptive and a normative matter how convincing is this argument? Descriptively do we really think individuals are the genetic information, that Henrietta Lacks is the HeLA cells such that whatever we do to one we do to the other? Normatively do we want people to so heavily identify with their genes? Especially with tissue that is removed, transformed, etc? Would it be better instead to stop emphasizing the idea that our genes are in a deep or fundamental way ourselves? More generally are existing theories of real and intellectual property a good fit for genes?

Returning to the *Moore* case, why should everyone but Moore be able to benefit financially from the use of his cells? We might argue that the difference between paying researchers and paying patients is the fact that we worry about patients assuming undue health risks for pay, but we do not have to worry about researchers putting themselves at risk of personal harm if they benefit financially from their work. What is the counter to this argument?

Does the *Greenberg*'s theory of unjust enrichment provide adequate protection for patients?

Just as researchers can earn substantial sums by manipulating a person's cells in research, so can companies realize large profits by processing a cadaver's tissues for transplantation. Although federal law prohibits payments to the decedent's family for skin, tendons, bone, heart valves, and other tissues, 42 U.S.C. §274e, tissue banks can receive reasonable payments for their retrieval and storage costs, and tissue processors can charge what the market will bear for tissues used in transplants. In contrast to the substantial regulation of the organ transplant system, the law provides considerably less oversight of the tissue processing and transplant industry.

6. *The Scope of Consent.* When individuals consent to donating tissue or genetic material for a specific use but researchers go beyond that consent what do researchers owe to donors? In Havasupai Tribe of Havasupai Reservation v. Arizona Bd. of Regents, 220 Ariz. 214, 204 P.3d 1063 (Ct. App. 2008), the Havasupai Tribe asked researchers at Arizona State University to look into possible genetic and dietary impacts on diabetes rates in the Tribe. Informed-consent documents were signed and blood samples were taken from more than 200 Havasupai. After the project ended, the samples were subsequently used for several research projects and article publications. After contentious discussions, the Tribe brought suit against ASU for the alleged misuse of their blood samples. The court initially dismissed the complaint on procedural grounds but was overruled by the court of appeals. In 2010, the University settled agreeing to "pay $700,000 to 41 of the tribe's members, return the blood samples and provide other forms of assistance to the impoverished Havasupai." Should the law view researchers using samples without consent for the purpose of publication differently than their use for profit?

7. *Research on Minority Groups.* As noted in *Moore*, the court is concerned over how extending property rights might hinder research efforts. How does this policy argument minimize the rights of the individual? Of a group (such as Ashkenazi Jews or the Havasupai Tribe)? Kristen Carpenter notes how majority interests in

policy making are often automatically classified in hierarchy above tribal interests. See Kristen Carpenter, Real Property and Personhood, 27 Stan. Envtl. L. J. 313, 380 (2008). Should courts allow conversion claims for minority groups who donate their biological material in good faith?

8. *Changing Regulation.* When the "Common Rule," the main human subjects research ethics regulation in the United States, was first promulgated in 1991, it was generally considered a fair assumption that a human biospecimen, free of any identifying information like a name or patient identification number, could not reasonably be re-identified by a scientist in a laboratory (or anyone else). Research involving "de-identified" biospecimens was therefore not considered to be human subjects research under the Common Rule. Advances in genetics and big data have challenged this assumption. The result has been a protracted battle over whether the Common Rule's protective requirements should be applied to the use of both identified and de-identified biospecimens. See Suzanne M. Rivera, Barbara E. Bierer, Holly Fernandez Lynch, & I. Glenn Cohen, Introduction, in Specimen Science 5-8 (H. Lynch et al. eds., 2017). For the time being, research involving de-identified biospecimens may be carried out without the typical consent and IRB review requirements imposed on human subjects research under the Common Rule. See Chapter 3.D, note 7.

9. *From Ownership and Control to Patent. Moore, Greenberg,* and our discussion thus far focuses on ownership and control of the actual tissue. What about intellectual property in its underlying genetic information? In Ass'n for Molecular Pathology v. Myriad Genetics, Inc. 133 S. Ct. 2107 (2013), several nonprofit organizations and university researchers sued Myriad claiming that its patents on isolated and synthesized DNA molecules impeded their research. Myriad had obtained several patents in connection with the BRCA1 and BRCA2 genes, mutations of which can dramatically increase breast and ovarian cancer. Myriad's discovery enabled it to develop medical tests to detect mutations and assess whether a patient has an increased risk of cancer. The question was whether isolated molecules as well as synthetically created ones were patentable subject matter within the meaning of the Patent Act. The Supreme Court held that DNA molecules that were isolated were not patentable subject matter under the Patent Act, while synthetically created exons-only strands of nucleotides known as complementary DNA (cDNA) were patentable subject matter. Ass'n for Molecular Pathology v. Myriad Genetics, Inc.. 133 S. Ct. 2107 (2013). However, the Court "devoted minimal space to policy analysis" in its opinion. See Patent Act of 1952 — Patentable Subject Matter — Ass'n for Molecular Pathology v. Myriad Genetics, Inc., 127 Harv. L. Rev. 388, 393 (2013). Whether courts should extend patent protections to genetic material, or instead try to keep more of this knowledge unpatentable and thus in the public domain, depends on your "vision of scientific progress" and the role incentives play to encourage innovation, as well as the economic realities of developing different kinds of products in this space.

10. *Further Reading.* On **interests of the tissue donor** (note 2), see George J. Annas, Outrageous Fortune: Selling Other People's Cells, 20(6) Hastings Center Rep. 36 (1990); R. Alta Charo, Body of Research — Ownership and Use of Human Tissue, 355 New Eng. J. Med. 1517 (2006); Donna M. Gitter, Ownership of Human Tissue: A Proposal for Federal Recognition of Human Research Participants' Property Rights in Their Biological Material, 61 Wash. & Lee L. Rev. 257 (2004); Michele

Goodwin, Formalism and the Legal Status of Body Parts, 2006 U. Chi. Legal F. 317; Natalie Ram, Assigning Rights and Protecting Interests: Constructing Ethical and Efficient Legal Rights in Human Tissue, 23 Harv. J. L. & Tech. 119 (2009).

On the **regulation of the tissue industry** (note 5), see Robert A. Katz, The Re-Gift of Life: Can Charity Law Prevent For-Profit Firms from Exploiting Donated Tissue and Nonprofit Tissue Banks?, 55 DePaul L. Rev. 943 (2006); Michelle Oberman, When the Truth Is Not Enough: Tissue Donation, Altruism, and the Market, 55 DePaul L. Rev. 903 (2006).

On **group rights** and informed consent in genetics research (notes 6 and 7), see Jenny Reardon & Kim TallBear, "Your DNA Is Our History" Genomics, Anthropology, and the Construction of Whiteness as Property, 53 S5 Current Anthropology S233, 238 (2012); Radhika Rao, Genes and Spleens: Property, Contract, or Privacy Rights in the Human Body?, 35 J. L. Med. & Ethics 371, 378 (2007); Debra Harry & Le'a Malia Kanehe, Assessing Tribal Sovereignty over Cultural Property: Moving Towards Protection of Genetic Material and Indigenous Knowledge, 5 Seattle J. Soc. Just. 27 (2006).

To learn more about **patent law and genetic materials** (note 9), see Samantak Ghosh, The Taking of Human Biological Products, 102 Cal. L. Rev. 511 (2014) and Daryl Pullman & George P. Nicholas, Intellectual property and the ethical/legal status of human DNA: The (ir)relevance of context, 35 Études/Inuit/Studies 143 (2011).

C. ALLOCATION OF ORGANS

So far, we have been discussing issues about organ procurement and proposals to increase the supply of organs. Another critical issue is organ allocation: Among those in need of an organ transplant, to whom will an available organ be given? Three key questions impact whether individuals receive a transplant: whether they get on a waitlist, how they are prioritized on a waitlist, and whether they can afford the transplant and post-transplant care (including the availability of public and private insurance). The important law for this issue is the National Transplant Act of 1984. As mentioned above, the Act created the OPTN as a private, nonprofit entity to oversee the recovery and allocation of organs for transplantation. Since 1986, the Secretary of Health and Human Services has awarded successive contracts to the United Network for Organ Sharing (UNOS) to operate the OPTN. UNOS is a membership organization that includes the 58 organ procurement organizations throughout the country, as well as more than 300 transplant surgery centers, medical laboratories that perform tests for organ matching, volunteer and advocacy groups, and members of the general public. The organ procurement organizations are responsible for recovering organs in their geographic area and allocating the organs to patients in need. OPTN/UNOS issues allocation guidelines for the procurement organizations to follow, and while the guidelines differ for hearts, livers, kidneys, and other organs, they generally rely on criteria such as the likelihood of a successful transplant, time spent on the waiting list, and medical urgency (i.e., is the person likely to die or suffer irreparable injury if a transplant is not performed soon). A person's place of residence may also play a critical role. Preference for a transplant is given to people on the local waiting list, and people tend to appear only on the waiting list for their area. Often the different criteria come into conflict. Patients can gain high priority because of an urgent need for a liver transplant, but then have the priority offset by a shorter life expectancy even with a transplant (as, for example, when patients with chronic liver failure are not eligible for the highest priority status and thereby receive lower priority than patients with acute liver failure).

While OPTN/UNOS guidelines govern the allocation of organs for persons who are on a waiting list for a transplant, there are no standard rules for deciding when a person is added to a waiting list. Accordingly, while transplant centers exhibit considerable agreement in their policies, they also vary in their approaches. In deciding whom to place on the waitlist, transplant centers tend to consider several factors: the likelihood that the transplant surgery will go well, the length of time that the recipient will benefit from the transplant before either the transplant is "rejected" by the patient or the patient dies, and the quality of life that the recipient will experience with the transplant. For indirect measures of these factors, transplant centers look at the severity and cause of organ failure, the presence in the recipient of other illnesses that affect either life expectancy or the ability to tolerate major surgery, the patient's age, and psychosocial criteria (e.g., alcohol or other drug abuse, psychiatric illness, mental retardation, and lack of compliance with treatment regimens in the past).

With liver transplantation, for example, a number of unofficial policies have developed. Patients with liver cancer generally do not do well with a transplant because of recurrence of the cancer, and transplant centers typically limit transplants to liver cancer patients whose cancers are found early and have not yet spread. Maria Reig et al., Hepatocellular Carcinoma, in Medical Care of the Liver Transplant Patient 121, 124 (Pierre-Alain Clavien et al. eds., 4th ed. 2012). Other patients who are denied liver transplants are those who currently engage in drug abuse, have severe infections, or have a non-liver, non-skin cancer. Audrey Coilly & Didier Samuel, Selection and Evaluation of the Recipient (Including Retransplantation), in Medical Care of the Liver Transplant Patient, supra, at 3, 6-10. Transplantation for patients with liver failure from alcohol abuse is common, but there is variation among centers in deciding which persons with alcoholic liver disease should be considered for transplantation. Factors that are used to select candidates include documented abstinence from alcohol (typically at least six months), evidence of social stability (e.g., employment, permanent residence, and marriage), presence of a good family or social support system, absence of illicit substance use, absence of psychiatric illness, and compliance with recommendations by the patient's treating physicians. See Elisa A. Moreno, et al., Psychiatric Assessment of Liver Transplant Candidates, in Transplantation of the Liver 381, 401 (Ronald W. Busuttil & Goran B.G. Klintmalm eds., 3d ed. 2015); see also Seonaid McCallum & George Masterton, Liver Transplantation for Alcoholic Liver Disease: A Systematic Review of Psychosocial Selection Criteria, 41 Alcohol & Alcoholism 358 (2006) (finding that social stability, past compliance with medical care, and other variables, but not duration of pre-transplant abstinence from alcohol use, are good predictors of post-transplant success). Some transplant centers are now performing transplants for some patients with HIV infection. Vandana Khungar et al., Current Indications, Contraindications, Delisting Criteria, and Timing for Transplantion, in Transplantion of the Liver, supra, at 94.

Ability to pay is also an obstacle for many potential organ transplant recipients. As discussed in Chapter 9, Medicare pays for kidney transplants, but not for all of the associated costs (e.g., coverage is temporary for drugs to prevent rejection of the transplanted organ by the recipient's immune system that have to be taken as long as the organ is still functioning). Medicare also pays for heart, lung, and liver transplants, but restricts the pool of potential recipients by requiring them to meet certain medical criteria and to qualify for Social Security disability benefits. In addition, with these organs, Medicare also does not pay all of the associated medical costs. Some recipients can rely on private insurance or Medicaid, but those patients too may receive only partial reimbursement for the costs of the transplant and its follow-up care. Accordingly, for some people, the costs of a transplant may preclude its availability. Even for people who receive a transplant, financial considerations may compromise the long-term success of the procedure. Data suggest that an important reason for failure of organs a few years after transplantation is the unaffordability of the drugs to suppress the recipient's immune system. Lisa M. Willoughby et al., Health Insurance Considerations for Adolescent Transplant Recipients as They Transition to Adulthood, 11 Pediatric Transplantation 127 (2007).

■ OPTN/UNOS POLICY FOR ORGAN DISTRIBUTION AND ALLOCATION

OPTN/UNOS prescribes policies for allocation of each type of organ. Below you will find an excerpt from the liver allocation policy. The excerpt reflects the OPTN/UNOS policy for ranking adults waiting for liver transplants. There are additional provisions for children waiting for transplants that can be found at the OPTN Web site.

The overarching principle of liver allocation is to prioritize the sickest first, with the sickest intended to be those at the greatest risk of dying without a transplant. The method of prioritizing patients on the liver transplant waiting list is based on the MELD score, which is a calculated score based on four common lab values. The lowest score is a 6, and the maximum is capped at 40. Importantly, though, there are exceptions to a patient's priority being based on the calculated score: a) status 1A—the highest priority awarded to patients expected not to live beyond 7 days without a transplant; and b) patients awarded MELD exception points—these extra priority points are awarded to patients for whom the MELD score calculation underestimates their medical urgency.

Geography also matters. Unlike deceased-donor kidneys, which can safely remain on ice for 24 hours, or even more and still be usable, the ideal cold time for a liver is less than 8 hours, with 12 hours thought to be the extreme upper-limit for livers from young, otherwise healthy donors. Accordingly, it makes sense to favor potential recipients who live closer to the donor.

As you work through the policy, consider the following questions. If a liver becomes available after a death in Chicago, and there is a person waiting for a liver in Gary, IN, Indianapolis, IN, Fargo, ND, and Los Angeles, CA, each with a MELD score of 20, how will OPTN/UNOS rank the four people who are waiting? What if the person from Indianapolis is Status 1A, and the person from Fargo has a MELD score of 6? For a map of the organ procurement regions, see the OPTN

Web site. You can also find a list of organ procurement organizations (OPOs) (the local geographic units in the policy) there. Note that some OPOs cross state boundaries (e.g., the New England Organ Bank), some follow a state's boundaries (e.g., Alabama Organ Center), and some serve part of a single state (e.g., OneLegacy in the Los Angeles area).

The OPTN/UNOS policy ranks potential recipients in the following allocation order from highest to lowest priority:

Combined local and regional status 1A

Local/regional MELD scores 35-40 (offers made locally then regionally for each MELD score)

Local MELD score 29-34

Local MELD score 15-28

Regional MELD score 15-34

National status 1A

National MELD score > 15

Local MELD score < 15

Regional MELD score <15

National MELD score <15

Sale Elwir & John Lake, Current Status of Live Allocation in the United States, 12 Gastroenterology & Hepatology 166, 167 tbl 2 (2016)

OPTN/UNOS Policy 9: Allocation of Livers and Liver-Intestines — November 1, 2017

9.1 Status and Score Assignments Each liver transplant candidate is assigned a score that reflects the probability of death within a 3-month period as determined by the Model for End-Stage Liver Disease (MELD) scoring system . . . Liver candidates can also be assigned a priority status if the candidate meets the requirements for that status.

Liver candidates at least 18 years old at the time of registration may be assigned any of the following:

- Adult status 1A
- Calculated MELD score
- Exception MELD score
- Inactive status

. . . .

9.1.A Adult Status 1A Requirements

. . .

The candidate's transplant program may assign the candidate adult status 1A if *all* the following conditions are met:

1. The candidate is at least 18 years old at the time of registration
2. The candidate has a life expectancy without a liver transplant of less than 7 days and has at least *one* of the following conditions:
   a. Fulminant liver failure, without pre-existing liver disease and currently in the intensive care unit (ICU) . . .
   c. Primary non-function [primary non-function is to be distinguished from secondary non-function, or loss of function from problems external to the liver, like heart disease] of a transplanted whole liver within 7 days of transplant . . .
   d. Primary non-function within 7-days of transplant of a transplanted liver segment from a deceased or living donor . . .
   e. Hepatic artery thrombosis (HAT) within 7-days of transplant . . .
   f. Acute decompensated Wilson's disease [a rare, inherited disease that results in damage to the liver and the brain].

[The Policy then describes the MELD scoring system, which is based on three laboratory values, with a maximum score of 40. The three laboratory values are serum bilirubin (a measure of liver function), INR (a measure of blood-clotting ability that reflects liver function), and serum creatinine (a measure of kidney function).]

. . . .

9.5 Liver Allocation Points

Points are used for sorting liver candidates according to *Policy 9.6.D: Sorting Within Each Classification.*

9.5.A Points for Waiting Time

Points are assigned so that the status 1A . . . candidate with the longest waiting time receives the most points as follows:

- 10 points for the candidate with the greatest total status 1A . . . waiting time within each classification
- A fraction of 10 points divided up among the remaining status 1A . . . candidates within each classification, based on the potential recipient's total waiting time

9.5.B Points Assigned by Blood Type

For status 1A . . . transplant candidates, those with the same blood type as the deceased liver donor will receive 10 points. Candidates with compatible but not identical blood types will receive 5 points, and candidates with incompatible types will receive 0 points. . . .

Within each MELD... score, donor livers will be offered to transplant candidates with blood types identical to the deceased donor first, then to candidates who are blood type compatible, followed by candidates who are blood type incompatible with the deceased donor.

9.6 LIVER ALLOCATION, CLASSIFICATIONS, AND RANKINGS

. . . .

9.6.D SORTING WITHIN EACH CLASSIFICATION

Within each status 1A allocation classification, candidates are sorted in the following order:

1. Total points, highest to lowest (waiting time points, plus blood type compatibility points)
2. Total waiting time at status 1A (highest to lowest) . . .

[Most] other candidates are sorted in the following order:

1. MELD [] score (highest to lowest)
2. Identical blood types, compatible blood types, then incompatible blood types
3. Waiting time at the current or higher MELD... score (highest to lowest)
4. Total waiting time (highest to lowest).

Notes: Criteria for Rationing Organs

1. *Local vs. National Standards for Listing.* As we have seen, UNOS guidelines kick in only after patients have been selected for the waiting list. Getting on the waiting list can be a much more important step, and transplant centers are free to develop their own policies. Is that appropriate, or should UNOS issue national guidelines for determining when a patient will be added to the waiting list?

In the past, UNOS has suggested it would develop standard criteria for deciding when a person should be placed on the waiting list for either a kidney or liver. Such criteria would help address the problem of some transplant centers being too quick to place a patient on a waiting list (sometimes doing so on the theory that, by the time the patient reaches the top of the list, the patient will be ready for a transplant).

Note that to some extent, the allocation guidelines also give guidance for adding people to the waiting list. For example, if a patient's liver disease is severe enough for the patient to qualify for Status 1A once listed or the patient has a high MELD score, the disease is also severe enough that the patient should be listed.

For an example of professional guidelines for listing candidates for organ transplantation, see Michael R. Lucey et al., Minimal Criteria for Placement of Adults on the Liver Transplant Waiting List: A Report of the National Conference Organized by the American Society of Transplant Physicians and the American Association for the Study of Liver Diseases, 3 Liver Transplantation 628 (1997); Mandeep R. Mehra et al., Listing Criteria for Heart Transplantation: International Society for Heart and Lung Transplantation Guidelines for the Care of Cardiac Transplant Candidates—2006, 25 J. Heart & Lung Transplantation 1024 (2006).

For a discussion of the inequities in listing, see Michele Goodwin, Altruism's Limits: Law, Capacity, and Organ Commodification, 56 Rutgers L. Rev. 305, 330-339 (2004).

If recipients can be listed on multiple waitlists nationally and organs can be transported across state lines, should the United States participate in an international organ transplant network? Relatedly, should non-resident non-citizens be eligible for U.S. organs? While the United States does not currently participate in a multinational organ-allocation system, non-resident aliens are eligible to receive transplants and are considered based on the same factors as U.S. citizens. For a further discussion proposing a normative prescription for this asymmetry, see I. Glenn Cohen, Organs Without Borders? Allocating Transplant Organs, Foreigners, and the Importance of the Nation-State (?), 77 Law & Contemp. Probs. 175 (2014).

2. *Relative Weights of Different Criteria.* Under the UNOS policy for liver transplantation, the greatest weights are given to medical urgency and the length of time that the recipient will benefit from the transplant. Medical urgency comes into play through the criteria for Status 1A and the MELD score ranking. Patients do not qualify for Status 1A unless their life expectancy without a transplant is less than seven days, and sicker patients have higher MELD scores.

The length of time that the recipient will benefit from the transplant is reflected in two ways. First, and more importantly, there is consideration of the patient's life expectancy with a transplant. Adult patients qualify for Status 1A only if they suffer from "fulminant" liver failure. These patients, whose liver failure has usually come on suddenly, typically live longer with a liver transplant than patients with "chronic" or long-standing liver failure. If the liver failure has existed for only a short time, then almost all of its harm to the body can be reversed with a liver transplant. When the liver failure has been long-standing, then much of its damage to the body is permanent and cannot be reversed. As a result, the patient might die even though the new liver is functioning well. (Note that some patients qualify for Status 1A if they've experienced unsuccessful liver transplant surgery. These patients might have developed their initial need for a transplant after chronic liver failure.)

Length of benefit from the transplant is also reflected in consideration of the likelihood that the liver will be rejected by the recipient's immune system. Under Policy 3.6.2, points are given for blood type similarity (maximum of ten points) since rejection of the transplant is less likely when blood types are compatible.

Some consideration in the UNOS liver policy is given to concerns of equity in access; this is done in the awarding of points for time on the waiting list and for blood type similarity. The relationship between equity and points for blood type similarity is somewhat complicated. First, Policy 9.5.B has special rules for blood type O patients. Second, under Policy 9.5.B, if the donor and recipient have *identical* blood types, ten points are given. Five points are given for *compatible* blood types. These rules in Policy 9.5.B exist because patients with blood type O would be disadvantaged if livers were allocated only on the basis of blood type compatibility. Livers from type O donors are good transplants for recipients of any blood type (i.e., type O people are "universal" donors), but type O recipients must rely almost exclusively on livers from type O donors. If only compatibility mattered, livers from type O donors would be scattered among recipients of all blood types, thereby decreasing the pool of "good" livers for blood type O patients and increasing the pool of "good" livers for patients of other blood types.

For suggestions to improve the use of MELD scores, see Kiran M. Bambha & Scott W. Biggins, Inequities of the Model for End-Stage Liver Disease, 13 Curr. Opin. Organ Transplant. 227 (2008).

For allocation of kidneys, UNOS assigns different relative weights. The most important difference is the diminished role of medical urgency. Urgency plays a much smaller role in kidney allocation decisions because of the availability of dialysis. Length of benefit and equity both are important aspects of kidney allocation. For example, a key factor is matching kidneys and recipients based on their expected longevity. Donor kidneys that are expected to function the longest are given to patients who are expected to have the longest survival after transplant. The goal is to avoid the problem of less healthy recipients dying with transplants that still function well and healthier recipients needing a second transplant. This matching applies to 20 percent of kidneys. For the other 80 percent, waiting time is the most important consideration, and equity is further promoted in the way waiting time is calculated—a patient's time on dialysis before being added to the wait list is included in the patient's waiting time to protect patients who are slower to be added to the list. There also is some consideration of tissue compatibility between kidney and recipient, which is associated with a greater length of time in which the kidney functions in the recipient. Significant consideration is given as well to the fact that some potential recipients are highly "sensitized" to foreign tissues (i.e., tissues from other persons) and are therefore much less likely to find a kidney that they would not reject immediately. Common causes of tissue sensitization are blood transfusions, pregnancy, and receipt of an organ transplant previously (i.e., situations in which the patient has been exposed to tissue from another person). Bhayna Chopra & Kalathil K. Sureshkumar, Changing Organ Allocation Policy, 5(2) World J. Transplant. 38 (2015).

3. *The Controversial Nature of Allocation Criteria.* Since the allocation of organs may have life and death consequences, there often is considerable controversy over the selection criteria, as occurred in November 1996 when UNOS proposed an amendment of the criteria for allocation of livers. The proposed policy gave greater weight to the patient's life expectancy with a transplant and less weight to the patient's medical urgency. Under the pre-proposal policy, urgency was the dominant consideration. Patients were classified as Status 1 if they were expected to die within seven days without a transplant, regardless of whether they suffered from fulminant or chronic liver failure. To give greater weight to expected benefit, the proposed policy limited Status 1 only to patients whose need for a transplant was urgent *and* who were suffering from fulminant liver failure. Patients with chronic liver failure could not qualify for Status 1 even if their need for a liver was urgent. When the 1996 proposal was announced, there were charges of discrimination against alcoholics since alcohol abuse is one of the most common causes of chronic liver failure.

Because of the public outcry, the liver allocation rules underwent multiple modifications between 1996 and 2002. The U.S. Department of Health and Human Services provided guidance through amendment of its regulations governing organ transplantation at 42 C.F.R. 6 §§121.1 et seq. (2002). For discussion of the controversy, see Dulcinea A. Grantham, Transforming Transplantation: The Effect of the Health and Human Services Final Rules on the Organ Allocation System, 35 U.S.F. L. Rev. 751 (2001).

4. *Legal Rights to a Transplant.* Does a potential recipient of an organ ever enjoy a legal right to the organ?

The rights of a potential recipient were explored to some extent in Colavito v. New York Organ Donor Network, Inc., 860 N.E.2d 713 (N.Y. 2006) and 486 F.3d 78 (2d Cir. 2007). That case arose after a widow tried to donate a kidney from her deceased husband to the husband's longtime friend. One of the kidneys was sent to the friend's hospital, but anatomical abnormalities (renal artery aneurysms) made the kidney unsuitable for transplantation. When the friend's surgeon asked for the second kidney, he was told that it had already been transplanted into another person. The widow argued that she intended for any donation to be limited to the longtime friend, and there were questions whether the second kidney had in fact been transplanted when the call came from the friend's doctor. As it turned out, immunological testing demonstrated that the kidneys were not compatible with the friend and could not have been transplanted into him. For that reason, the New York Court of Appeals did not decide whether a disappointed transplant recipient might have a cause of action under New York public health law for failure to receive the transplant. The court did conclude that a disappointed transplant recipient is not able to bring a cause of action for conversion.

Whether or not potential recipients enjoy legal rights to a transplant, they may have a valid claim if they lose an opportunity for an organ because of a transplant program's malfeasance. Litigation against the liver transplant program at University of California-Irvine precipitated a shutting down of the program by the federal government. A patient sued the program, claiming that it wrongfully denied her an organ on many occasions over a four-year period. In supporting her claim, the patient cited a UNOS document indicating that the transplant program had declined organs offered by UNOS for the woman approximately 40 times. Irvine v. Regents of the University of California, 57 Cal. Rptr. 3d 500 (Ct. App. 2007) (reinstating claim and remanding for consideration by the trial court). During its investigation of the program, Medicare found that the program lacked adequate staffing, resulting in a very high level of deaths among patients on the waiting list. Charles Ornstein & Alan Zarembo, Hospital Halts Liver Transplant Program, L.A. Times, Nov. 11, 2005, at A1.

5. *Local vs. National Waiting Lists.* Another controversial issue has been the use of local, regional, and national waiting lists rather than a single national list. As the liver allocation policy indicates, people on the local waiting list generally have priority over people on the regional waiting list, who in turn have priority over people on the national waiting list. Some people are listed on multiple local waiting lists, and some health care plans require their members to be listed on the local waiting list for transplant "centers of excellence," but most people are listed only on the local waiting list where they reside. In recent years, the emphasis on geography has been reduced. In December 2010, for example, Status 1A patients on the regional waiting list were given parity with Status 1A patients on the local waiting list.

As a result of the emphasis on local lists, patients in some parts of the country may wait only a few days for a new organ while patients in other parts of the country may wait a few months or longer, or die while waiting. This disparity explained in part why former baseball star Mickey Mantle received a liver two days after going on the waiting list. In the region for his organ procurement agency, there was a waiting list at the time of only 3.3 days for someone with Mantle's severity of illness, while the national average was 78 days. For all liver transplants, regardless of severity of illness, the average wait varied across the country from 18 to 443 days.

   The use of local waiting lists also means that persons with a relatively low priority for an organ transplant will receive organs before persons with a higher priority who live in other parts of the country. At one time, local waiting lists primarily reflected the inability to transport an organ from one part of the country to another before the organ deteriorated, but currently, kidneys and livers generally can be retrieved from a deceased person in one region and flown to a recipient in another region. (Hearts and lungs can be preserved outside the body for 4-6 hours, livers for 12-24 hours, and kidneys for 48-72 hours.) Why do you suppose, then, that priority is given first to people in the local area or region?

   6. *Social Worth.* When kidney dialysis first became available, there were not enough dialysis machines for all those who needed treatment. Hospitals therefore established committees to decide who would receive dialysis. One member of such a committee was quoted as follows:

> The choices were hard. . . . I remember voting against a young woman who was a known prostitute. I found I couldn't vote for her, rather than another candidate, a young wife and mother. I also voted against a young man who, until he learned he had renal failure, had been a ne'er do-well, a real playboy. He promised he would reform his character, go back to school, and so on, if only he were selected for treatment. But I felt I'd lived enough to know that a person like that won't really do what he was promising at the time.

Renée C. Fox & Judith P. Swazey, The Courage to Fail 232 (1974). Discomfort with the selection process led Congress in 1972 to provide Medicare coverage for any person with kidney failure who needed dialysis. Roger W. Evans et al., Implications for Health Care Policy: A Social and Demographic Profile of Hemodialysis Patients in the United States, 245 JAMA 487 (1981).

   Most commentators reject social worth as a criterion for organ allocation. Some of the reasons are presented in the following passage:

> A patient's contribution to society—or social worth—should not be a factor in allocation decisions. Such judgments are usually defended as attempts to maximize the return on society's investment in medical resources. One common use is to justify the denial of care to the elderly, who some argue no longer make a positive contribution to the social good. . . .
>
>   A social worth criterion can also be used to justify discrimination against the young and virtually any other group not actively involved in the economic productivity of society, on the grounds that those who have put the most into society are entitled to get the most back out of it. Distinctions can be made among economic contributions as well; for instance, white collar workers with higher salaries may be favored over blue collar workers or the working poor. Social worth can also be measured by noneconomic criteria. Artists, writers, musicians, and other cultural elite may be favored over average citizens, and people with dependents may be preferred over those without families.
>
>   Because of the pluralistic values of society, any single definition of social contribution or social worth is inherently suspect. Social worth judgments often reflect the preferences and values of individual decision makers rather than any objective criteria. In addition, by assuming that members of a certain group make greater social contributions than others, a social worth criterion ignores diversity and the value of each individual.

Council on Ethical and Judicial Affairs, American Medical Association, Ethical Considerations in the Allocation of Organs and Other Scarce Medical Resources Among Patients, 155 Arch. Intern. Med. 29 (1995).

While social worth criteria may generally be inappropriate, might there be some circumstances when they are relevant? Consider the following perspective:

> Yet Dr. [Mark] Siegler said he would exempt Mickey Mantle from his rule [that people with liver failure from alcoholism should go to the bottom of the transplant waiting list] because the baseball legend is "a real American hero." He said Mr. Mantle, "who captured the imagination of a generation through his skill and ability and personality," should not be lumped in with the rest of the population. . . . "I think we have to give deference to the rare heroes in American life," he added. "We don't have enough of these people in America, and when one comes along, we have got to take them with all their warts and failures and treat them differently."

Gina Kolata, Transplants, Morality and Mickey, N.Y. Times, June 11, 1995, §4, at 5.

Is Dr. Siegler's proposal any different than our country's practice of spending millions of dollars more to protect the President from assassination than to protect the lives of citizens living in high crime areas? Or what if you were a hospital attorney and you received a call from the transplant service because a liver was available for transplantation but the person at the top of the waiting list was someone who had been convicted multiple times for child sex abuse? Would it matter if the person was still in prison? Would it matter if the person was serving a life sentence without parole?

Is it consistent to consider costs when rationing care but not to consider social value? For example, assume we would deny someone care because the costs of the care are very high (e.g., $500,000), and the benefits of care seem very low (e.g., an extra few months of life in a permanently unconscious state). If the costs to society of the person's medical treatment matter, then why doesn't it matter whether the person will recover with treatment, return to work, and benefit society?

As mentioned, commentators generally reject social worth as a legitimate criterion. Nevertheless, it is still an unwritten consideration employed by physicians who refer patients for transplants or by transplant surgeons who accept patients on referral.

7. *Individual Responsibility.* Should we take into account the extent to which people are "responsible" for their need for an organ transplant? For example, should people who need a liver because of alcoholic liver disease be given lower priority than people who need a transplant because of a congenital defect in their liver? Consider the following affirmative response to this question:

> We suggest that patients who develop ESLD [end-stage liver disease] through no fault of their own (e.g., those with congenital biliary atresia or primary biliary cirrhosis) should have a higher priority in receiving a liver transplant than those whose liver disease results from failure to obtain treatment for alcoholism. . . . Although alcoholics cannot be held responsible for their disease, once their condition has been diagnosed they can be held responsible for seeking treatment and preventing the complication of ARESLD [alcohol-related end-stage liver disease]. . . . We are not suggesting that some lives and behaviors have greater value than others. . . . But we are holding people responsible for their personal effort. . . .

Much of the initial success in securing public and political approval for liver transplantation was achieved by focusing media and political attention not on adults but on children dying of ESLD. The public may not support transplantation for patients with ARESLD in the same way that they have endorsed this procedure for babies born with biliary atresia. . . . Just because a majority of the public holds these views does not mean they are right, but the moral intuition of the public . . . reflects community values that must be seriously considered.

Alvin H. Moss & Mark Siegler, Should Alcoholics Compete Equally for Liver Transplantation?, 265 JAMA 1296-1297 (1991).

In response to the argument that persons with alcohol-related liver failure are being singled out when other persons become sick as a result of voluntary behavior, including smokers with chronic lung disease, athletes who sustain injuries, and people who develop coronary artery disease from poor diet and insufficient exercise, Moss and Siegler respond,

[t]he critical distinguishing factor for treatment of ARESLD is the scarcity of the resource needed to treat it. The resources needed to treat most of these other conditions are only moderately or relatively scarce, and patients with these diseases or injuries can receive a share of the resources . . . roughly equivalent to their need. [Id. at 1296.]

In a companion article a different perspective was presented:

We could rightly preclude alcoholics from transplantation only if we assume that qualification for a new organ requires some level of moral virtue or is canceled by some level of moral vice. But there is absolutely no agreement—and there is likely to be none—about what constitutes moral virtue and vice and what rewards and penalties they deserve. The assumption that undergirds the moral argument for precluding alcoholics is thus unacceptable. Moreover, even if we could agree . . . upon the kind of misconduct we would be looking for, the fair weighting of such a consideration would entail highly intrusive investigations into patients' moral habits—investigations universally thought repugnant. . . . We do not seek to determine whether a particular transplant candidate is an abusive parent or a dutiful daughter, whether candidates cheat on their income taxes or their spouses, or whether potential recipients pay their parking tickets or routinely lie when they think it is in their best interests. We refrain from considering such judgments for several good reasons: (1) We have genuine and well-grounded doubts about comparative degrees of voluntariness and, therefore, *cannot pass judgment fairly*. (2) Even if we could assess degrees of voluntariness reliably, we *cannot know what penalties different degrees of misconduct deserve*. (3) *Judgments of this kind could not be made consistently in our medical system*—and a fundamental requirement of a fair system in allocating scarce resources is that it treat all in need of certain goods on the same standard, without unfair discrimination by group.

Carl Cohen et al., Alcoholics and Liver Transplantation, 265 JAMA 1299, 1299-1300 (1991) (emphasis in original).

8. *Quality of Life.* The UNOS guidelines do not include a criterion for quality of life, perhaps because persons with a permanently low quality of life never make it onto a waiting list. In a survey of pediatric transplant centers, researchers found that

more than 40 percent of programs would automatically deny an organ transplant to a child suffering from severe (IQ < 35) or profound (IQ < 20) neurodevelopmental delay. Christopher T. Richards et al., Use of Neurodevelopmental Delay in Solid Organ Transplant Decisions, 13 Pediatric Transplantation 843, 847-848 (2009).

Should quality of life matter?

> . . . If for example some people were given life-saving treatment in preference to others because they had a better quality of life than those others, or more dependents and friends, or because they were considered more useful, this would amount to regarding such people as more valuable than others on that account. Indeed, it would be tantamount, literally, to sacrificing the lives of others so that they might continue to live.
>
> Because my own life would be better and even of more value to me if I were healthier, fitter, had more money, more friends, more lovers, more children, more life expectancy, more everything I want, it does not follow that others are entitled to decide that because I lack some or all of these things I am less entitled to health care resources, or less worthy to receive those resources, than others, or that those resources would somehow be wasted on me.

John Harris, QALYfying the Value of Life, 13 J. Med. Ethics 117, 121 (1987).

> The appeal of considering [duration and quality of life] can be brought out by a contrast with an alternative position, namely that what is valuable are lives, not life-years or their quality. From this point of view society should aim purely and simply to keep the number of deaths to a minimum. It would follow that one should strive to save a baby who can only live another hour of acute suffering just as much as one who will have a happy and fruitful existence for three score years and ten. The two individuals are both human and subjects of consciousness; and surely at least some of the significance that is attributed to these characteristics is adventitious. An evaluation of life and lives without regard to actual or potential [length and quality of life] seems very incomplete. . . . Surely health is a *sine qua non* for the whole gamut of activities, experiences, aspirations and attainment of goals which make our lives valuable to us.

John Cubbon, The Principle of QALY Maximisation as the Basis for Allocating Health Care Resources, 17 J. Med. Ethics 181, 182 (1991).

9. *The Tension Between Social Utility and Equality.* As the previous notes suggest, in choosing criteria for allocating organs, a critical concern is the tension between maximizing social utility and treating all persons equitably. The local guidelines used by transplant programs to decide whether a patient should be placed on the waiting list tend to emphasize utilitarian criteria, including likelihood that the transplant surgery will go well and expected duration of benefit for the recipient. The UNOS guidelines for ranking persons on the waiting list give more weight to equitable considerations like time spent waiting for an organ. How do you think the balance should be drawn? In that regard, consider the following perspectives.

> Allocation of very scarce medical interventions such as organs and vaccines is a persistent ethical challenge. We evaluate eight simple allocation principles that

can be classified into four categories: treating people equally, favouring the worst-off, maximising total benefits, and promoting and rewarding social usefulness. No single principle is sufficient to incorporate all morally relevant considerations and therefore individual principles must be combined into multiprinciple allocation systems. . . .

Some people wrongly suggest that allocation can be based purely on scientific or clinical facts, often using the term "medical need". There are no value-free medical criteria for allocation. Although biomedical facts determine a person's post-transplant prognosis or the dose of vaccine that would confer immunity, responding to these facts requires ethical, value-based judgments. . . This paper identifies and evaluates eight simple principles that have been suggested[:]

[1] Treating people equally

    1) *Lottery*[:] . . . Equal moral status supports an equal claim to scarce resources.

    2) *First-come, first-served*[:] Within health care, many people endorse a first-come, first-served distribution of beds in intensive care units or organs for transplant.

[2] Favouring the worst-off: prioritarianism

    3) *Sickest first*[:] Treating the sickest people first prioritises those with the worst future prospects if left untreated.

    4) *Youngest first*[:] Although not always recognised as such, youngest-first allocation directs resources to those who have had less of something supremely valuable — life-years.

[3] Maximizing total benefits: utilitarianism

    5) *Save the most lives*[:] One maximising strategy involves saving the most individual lives. . . Other things being equal, we should always save five lives rather than one. . .

    6) *Prognosis or life-years*[:] Rather than saving the most lives, prognosis allocation aims to save the most life-years. . .

[4] Promoting and rewarding social usefulness

    7) *Instrumental value*[:] Instrumental value allocation prioritises specific individuals to enable or encourage future usefulness. . .

    8) *Reciprocity*[:] Reciprocity allocation is backward-looking, rewarding past usefulness or sacrifice. . . For important health-related values, reciprocity might involve preferential allocation to past organ donors. . . [while] [p]riority to military veterans embodies reciprocity for promoting non-health values. . .

Govind Persad, Alan Wertheimer & Ezekiel J. Emanuel, Principles for Allocation of Scarce Medical Interventions, 373 The Lancet 423, 423-426 (2009).

What allocation principles or combination should be applied to organ waiting lists? Do you agree with their critique of the UNOS points system?

The UNOS points systems. . . combine three principles: sickest-first (current medical condition); first-come, first-served (waiting time); and prognosis (antigen, antibody, and blood type matching between recipient and donor). UNOS weights principles differently depending on the organ distributed. Kidney and pancreas allocation is mainly by waiting time, with some weight given to sickest-first and prognosis. Conversely, heart allocation weights sickest-first principles heavily and waiting time less so. Lung and liver allocation takes into account waiting time, sickest-first, and prognosis. . .

Current UNOS systems incorporate two flawed simple principles: first-come, first-served and sickest first. They are also vulnerable to additional exploitation. Taking advantage of the first-come, first-served principle, well-off patients place themselves on multiple waiting lists. Exploiting the sickest-first element, some transplant centres have temporarily altered or misrepresented their patients' health state to get them scarce organs, making sickest-first both practically and inherently flawed.

Furthermore, UNOS points systems do not appropriately consider the benefit-maximising principles, prognosis, and saving the most lives, nor do they include youngest-first allocation. Most dramatically, multiple- organ transplants to one individual are permitted, even when a heart-lung-liver combination could save three lives if transplanted separately. Similarly, policy revisions during the 1990s de-emphasised organ-recipient matching even though poorer matching leads to fewer lives saved.

Attempts to remedy these deficiencies have been covert and haphazard. In an effort to implement prognosis allocation tacitly, ill or old people have been excluded from supposedly first-come, first-served waiting lists. Physicians can misdiagnose comorbidities as contra- indications, wrongly implying that transplants will harm recipients, rather than explicitly practising prognosis- based allocation. Some have proposed so-called old-for-old policies that match donor organ age to recipient age—misrepresenting both youngest-first and prognosis-based allocation as biological fact. Others have advocated local rather than national waiting lists to circumvent sickest-first allocation. Explicit and public acknowledgment of allocation strategies would be preferable to this surreptitious and piecemeal approach.

Id. at 426-427.

As the previous article acknowledges, there are no "value-free medical criteria for allocation." In that regard, consider the following argument:

. . . [T]he environment is shaped not simply by natural, inevitable forces but also has been shaped to serve the interests of some segments of society at the expense of others. The socio-political environment cannot always be justified by the operation of neutral or objective principles or by principles that are otherwise morally valid.

. . . Social norms develop not because they are pre-ordained, but because they serve the needs of social groups that are dominant either in numbers or power. . . .

Social forces cause disability by commission when environmental pollution leads to lung diseases or cancers, when lead-based paint damages the neurological systems of children, or when unchecked violence results in traumatic injury.

Social organization causes disability by omission when priorities are established for medical research and treatment. Some illnesses, such as heart disease and cancer, are the subject of vast research expenditures, while other illnesses receive disproportionately little federal research funding. Patients with intensively studied diseases are much more likely to be saved from disabling symptoms than patients with neglected diseases. . . . Moreover, when treatments are developed for a particular disease, they are often based on the norm of a patient without any coexisting illnesses. As a result, patients with multiple illnesses are less able to benefit from treatment. For example, persons with chronic lung disease are less likely to be viewed as appropriate candidates for coronary artery surgery. . . .

David Orentlicher, Destructuring Disability: Rationing of Health Care and Unfair Discrimination Against the Sick, 31 Harv. C.R.-C.L. L. Rev. 49, 66-71 (1996).

While it is useful to frame the debate in terms of the trade-off between social utility and social equality, it is also important to understand how unhelpful this framing can be. It is not clear what content exists in the idea that people need to be treated as equals. Peter Westen, The Empty Idea of Equality, 95 Harv. L. Rev. 537 (1982). We can all agree that equal treatment is a moral imperative, but we can also agree that we do not want to treat everyone in the same way. People are different, and those differences need to be recognized. For example, we require all children to attend school (or be schooled at home), but we do not impose the same requirement on adults. Accordingly, we need to decide when people are the same for purposes of organ transplantation and when they are different. In this regard, it is not clear whether differences in expected length of life or expected quality of life mean that people should be treated differently for purposes of kidney transplantation or whether length and quality of life are irrelevant to organ allocation decisions.

10. *Racial Inequity.* One important area of concern in terms of equity is the evidence that African Americans are disadvantaged when it comes to receiving kidney transplants. Despite the fact that African Americans are more likely than whites to need a kidney transplant, they are less likely to receive a transplant. The disparity in access to kidney transplants remains even after researchers control for confounding variables like cause of the kidney failure, age, and family income. Much of the difference may reflect the fact that white persons waiting for a kidney are more likely to have a good tissue match with an available organ since most organs come from whites. Important questions are whether the effects of poorer tissue matching can be overcome by immunosuppressive drugs and whether achieving more successful transplants is sufficient reason to disadvantage a racial group that is already disadvantaged in the health care system. See Ian Ayres et al., Unequal Racial Access to Kidney Transplantation, 46 Vand. L. Rev. 805 (1993); Council on Ethical and Judicial Affairs, Black-White Disparities in Health Care, 263 JAMA 2344 (1990); Arnold M. Epstein et al., Racial Disparities in Access to Renal Transplantation, 343 New Eng. J. Med. 1537 (2000); Sayeed K. Malek et al., Racial and Ethnic Disparities in Kidney Transplantation, 24 Transplant International 419 (2011).

The inequities in allocation may reflect and/or contribute to a lower trust in the organ retrieval and allocation systems and a lower willingness to donate organs among African Americans. Laura A. Siminoff et al., Racial Disparities in Preferences and Perceptions Regarding Organ Donation, 21 J. Gen. Intern. Med. 995 (2006). These issues are compounded by organ procurement organization staff being less likely to discuss organ donation or to discuss the details of organ donation with African American family members. Laura A. Siminoff et al., Comparison of Black and White Families' Experiences and Perceptions Regarding Organ Donation Requests, 31 Crit. Care Med. 146 (2003).

In response to the concerns about racial disparities in kidney transplantation, OPTN/UNOS amended its allocation policy in November 2002 to increase minority access to kidney transplants. Recent studies had indicated that OPTN/UNOS could reduce its emphasis on tissue matching while still maintaining a high rate of long-term success. Accordingly under the new policy, tissue matching is relevant only in a few areas (i.e., when the donor and recipient match perfectly or when there is matching at the "DR locus"). The change in policy has reduced the magnitude of the disparities. Malek et al., supra, at 421.

Racial disparities also existed in liver transplantation, but adoption of the MELD scores has resulted in elimination of an association between race and the receipt of a liver transplant once patients are added to the waitlist. However, disparities based on the sex of the patient remain, with women less likely than men to receive a transplant. Cynthia A. Moylan et al., Disparities in Liver Transplantation Before and After Introduction of the MELD Score, 300 JAMA 2371 (2008). In addition, disparities on the basis of race still exist with respect to being referred to a transplant center for evaluation. A. K. Mathur et al., Race and Ethnicity in Access to and Outcomes of Liver Transplantation, 9 Am. J. Transplantation 2662 (2009).

11. *The Americans with Disabilities Act.* The Americans with Disabilities Act (ADA), 42 U.S.C. §§12101-12213, prohibits discrimination against persons with disabilities in employment, education, housing, health care, and other services on account of their disabilities, unless the disabilities are relevant to the decision being made. Thus, for example, a construction company could refuse to hire someone confined to a wheelchair as a roofer but could not refuse to hire that person as a desk clerk. Similarly, an organ transplant program could not deny a kidney transplant to a blind person simply because the person is blind. Discrimination is also prohibited when it results from more "neutral" criteria that have a disproportionate effect (disparate impact) on persons with disabilities. For example, it might violate the ADA to deny an organ transplant to persons without a driver's license since a requirement to have a driver's license disadvantages blind persons. Which of the criteria for organ allocation discussed above potentially implicate the ADA? So far, no cases have been decided on this question.

Even if the person's disability is relevant to the decision being made, the person may not be denied the benefit if "reasonable accommodations" would overcome the effects of the disability. In some cases, a person's psychiatric condition might interfere with the success of an organ transplant. If psychiatric counseling would keep the condition under control, the organ transplant program might have to provide the counseling as part of its treatment program.

Another important question is whether the ADA limits the ability of transplant programs to take into account unrelated medical considerations that affect a person's likelihood of benefiting from a new organ. For example, would it violate the ADA if a transplant candidate is denied a kidney because the candidate has lung disease in addition to kidney failure, and the lung disease will shorten the person's life expectancy? Most likely, the lung disease would be considered a "relevant" difference under the ADA, but other criteria used by transplant programs (e.g., lack of mental retardation) are suspect under the ADA.

12. *Absolute vs. Relative Scarcity.* Organ allocation presents a compelling case to consider criteria for rationing limited medical resources because the short supply of organs creates a situation of absolute scarcity: We know that giving an organ to

one person rather than others means some people will die. Financial resources are also scarce, and affect organ transplantation as well as other life-saving medical procedures, but they are not scarce in the same absolute sense. Instead, we must decide in more relative terms which medical conditions or procedures deserve more funding than others, and whether medical needs are more demanding than other social needs. Resource allocation issues at this broader level are debated in many of the same moral terms as have been introduced here, but the legal context is framed in terms of the right to payment under public and private insurance, and in terms of disability discrimination. See Chapter 9.D.

13. *Further Reading.* On **ethical issues** in organ allocation, (notes 6-9), see Douglas J. Besharov & Jessica Dunsay Silver, Rationing Access to Advanced Medical Techniques, 8 J. Leg. Med. 507 (1987); F. Daniel Davis, The Ethics of Organ Allocation (2007) (paper prepared for the President's Council on Bioethics); Richard A. Epstein, Mortal Peril: Our Inalienable Right to Health Care? 263-282 (1997); John F. Kilner, Who Lives? Who Dies? Ethical Criteria in Patient Selection (1990); David L. Weimer, Medical Governance (2010); Robert M. Veatch & Lainie F. Ross, Transplantation Ethics (2d ed. 2015).

On the relationship between **organ allocation and the ADA** (note 11), see David Orentlicher, Psychosocial Assessment of Organ Transplant Candidates and the Americans with Disabilities Act, 18 Gen. Hosp. Psychiatry 5S (1996); David Orentlicher, Destructuring Disability: Rationing of Health Care and Unfair Discrimination Against the Sick, 31 Harv. C.R.-C.L. L. Rev. 49 (1996). The role of the ADA in governing other kinds of rationing decisions is also taken up in Chapter 9.D.1.

7

Reproductive Rights and Genetic
Technologies

This chapter examines both the state's right to regulate individual reproductive capacity and the use of genetic technologies. We treat reproduction as a discrete subject area, separate from the state's ability to control other sorts of human behavior, because human reproduction raises especially controversial moral, ethical, and legal issues. Reproduction is not just another bodily function; the creation of human life implicates profound moral and religious issues not encountered in other medical arenas. Therefore, many special constitutional, statutory, and common-law rules have been developed to resolve disputes arising from human reproductive capacity. As you study this chapter, consider whether the rules adopted differ significantly from the rules used in other, similar disputes and whether these differences are warranted from a public policy or legal standpoint. Reproduction is at least partly a question of genetics, but advances in genetics have profound implications beyond reproduction. The final section of this chapter will focus on the legal implications of advances in genetics outside of reproduction.

This chapter will focus initially on four broad aspects of reproductive health law. The first two sections of the chapter explore the conflict between state and individual interests in controlling reproductive capacity. Do people have a constitutionally protected interest in either procreating or in refraining from procreation? Do states have the power to control or to influence personal reproductive decisions? The third section explores the legal recognition of fetal interests as distinguishable from and sometimes conflicting with those of parents. Should pregnant women be subjected to criminal or civil sanctions where their behavior presents risks of fetal injury? The fourth section focuses on the moral, ethical, and legal implications of new reproductive technologies. Who should be considered to be the legal parents of a child who is conceived from donor sperm and egg and gestated by a willing surrogate? The fifth and final section of the chapter explores the legal implications of advances in genetics and the regulation of genetic technologies. Should cloning and related procedures be allowed for reproductive, research, or therapeutic purposes? Should scientists be permitted to patent life forms and genes?

Note: Many Streams or One River: Reproductive Rights and Substantive Due Process

We all have an interest in controlling our own reproductive capacity. Through reproduction, we transmit our individual genetic heritage to a new generation, and in the process are likely to experience the rewards and pains of parenting. Biological reproduction is also associated with cultural reproduction: the ability to pass along values, religious beliefs, and one's cultural heritage. The burdens of reproduction are well known. For women, pregnancy and delivery present certain health risks. For both women and men, unwanted parenthood can be emotionally and financially burdensome. Techniques for avoiding reproduction, such as abstinence, condoms, and oral contraceptives, each have their drawbacks.

Government entities can also have an interest in controlling the reproductive capacity of certain individuals or groups. In societies struggling with overpopulation, the government may have an interest in discouraging reproduction. What is more, historically many governments have expressed an interest in preventing reproduction by some individuals, such as persons with disabilities or members of disfavored ethnic or racial minorities. Other societies, on the other hand, may wish to encourage stable or increasing rates of reproduction. This can be accomplished by restricting access to technologies designed to prevent reproduction. Additionally, many societies have sought to protect the new life created through procreation, sometimes at the very earliest stages of its existence within a woman's body. Finally, legislation in these areas often reflects moral and religious perspectives on sexuality, procreation, and fetal interests.

It is therefore not surprising that courts and legislatures have been occupied with the task of balancing these often conflicting individual and social interests. What is the nature of a person's interest in controlling reproduction? Do we have a constitutional right to control procreative capacity that is distinguishable from the right to control medical treatment? Is the right to procreate the mirror image of the right not to procreate? When may the state intrude on personal procreative choice, by either attempting to prevent or to encourage procreation?

Judicial review of state policies under the Constitution's Fourteenth Amendment due process clause raises some troubling constitutional history. You will recall from basic constitutional law that, in the early part of the last century, the Supreme Court took an "activist" approach to reviewing the constitutional validity of state economic regulation under the due process clause. In Lochner v. New York, 198 U.S. 45 (1905), the Court struck down a state's regulation of maximum work hours as a violation of the fundamental right to contract. However, the onslaught of programs in the late 1930s designed to ameliorate the Depression caused the Court to retreat by substituting a more deferential, rationally basis, standard of review of state economic regulation. Thereafter, the *Lochner* era of "substantive due process" was thoroughly repudiated as a valid form of judicial review for economic regulation. See Ferguson v. Skrupa, 372 U.S. 726 (1963). But what about "substantive due process" as applied to non-economic interests? Today, the language of "substantive due process" is largely shunned, but in some circumstances its animating ideas have survived. For example, much of the Supreme Court's recent case law on gay rights—such as viewing anti-sodomy laws as unconstitutional and interpreting the Constitution to require gay marriage—owe an undeniable intellectual lineage to doctrines of "substantive due process." But make no mistake, this remains a hotly contested issue in constitutional law and indeed in some instances has served as a litmus test for judicial confirmation.

Courts attempting to define the nature of individual interests in procreation and to mark the permissible scope of state regulation have struggled in the shadow of the *Lochner* era. Judges have been forced to confront three important issues. What is the constitutional source of the right to procreate? What are the permissible limits of state regulation? Will the judiciary be able to avoid another *Lochner* debacle in which there is widespread criticism of its fundamental authority to engage in searching substantive due process review?

Academics have also wondered whether the framing of a "right to procreate," is all that helpful in understanding these disputes. In particular, in reproductive technology cases, the courts are frequently confronted with multiple rights to and not to procreate. I. Glenn Cohen, The Constitution and the Rights Not to Procreate, 60 Stan. L. Rev. 1135 (2008). We return to this issue at pages 802 -804 when we discuss reproductive technologies in greater detail.

A. RIGHT TO PROCREATE?

■ BUCK v. BELL
274 U.S. 200 (1927)

HOLMES, Justice.

This is a writ of error to review a judgment of the Supreme Court of Appeals of the State of Virginia, affirming a judgment of the Circuit Court of Amherst County, by which the defendant in error, the superintendent of the State Colony for Epileptics and Feeble Minded, was ordered to perform the operation of salpingectomy upon Carrie Buck, the plaintiff in error, for the purpose of making her sterile. 130 S.E. 516. The case comes here upon the contention that the statute authorizing the judgment is void under the Fourteenth Amendment as denying to the plaintiff in error due process of law and the equal protection of the laws.

Carrie Buck is a feeble-minded white woman who was committed to the State Colony above mentioned in due form. She is the daughter of a feeble-minded mother in the same institution, and the mother of an illegitimate feeble-minded child. She was 18 years old at the time of the trial of her case in the Circuit Court in the latter part of 1924. An Act of Virginia approved March 20, 1924 recites that the health of the patient and the welfare of society may be promoted in certain cases by the sterilization of mental defectives, under careful safeguard, etc.; that the sterilization may be effected in males by vasectomy and in females by salpingectomy, without serious pain or substantial danger to life; that the Commonwealth is supporting in various institutions many defective persons who if now discharged would become a menace but if incapable of procreating might be discharged with safety and become self-supporting with benefit to themselves and to society; and that experience has shown that heredity plays an important part in the transmission of insanity, imbecility, etc. The statute then enacts that whenever the superintendent of certain institutions including the above named State Colony shall be of opinion that it is for the best interest of the patients and of society that an inmate under his care should be sexually sterilized, he may have the operation performed upon any patient afflicted with hereditary forms of insanity, imbecility, etc., on complying with the very careful provisions by which the act protects the patients from possible abuse.

The superintendent first presents a petition to the special board of directors of his hospital or colony, stating the facts and the grounds for his opinion, verified by affidavit. Notice of the petition and of the time and place of the hearing in the institution is to be served upon the inmate, and also upon his guardian, and if there is no guardian the superintendent is to apply to the Circuit Court of the County to appoint one. If the inmate is a minor notice also is to be given to his parents, if any, with a copy of the petition. The board is to see to it that the inmate may attend the hearings if desired by him or his guardian. The evidence is all to be reduced to writing, and after the board has made its order for or against the operation, the superintendent, or the inmate, or his guardian, may appeal to the Circuit Court of the County. The Circuit Court may consider the record of the board and the evidence before it and such other admissible evidence as may be offered, and may affirm, revise, or reverse the order of the board and enter such order as it deems just. Finally any party may apply to the Supreme Court of Appeals, which, if it grants the appeal, is to hear the case upon the record of the trial in the Circuit Court and may enter such order as it thinks the Circuit Court should have entered. There can be no doubt that so far as procedure is concerned the rights of the patient are most carefully considered, and as every step in this case was taken in scrupulous compliance with the statute and after months of observation, there is no doubt that in that respect the plaintiff in error has had due process at law.

The attack is not upon the procedure but upon the substantive law. It seems to be contended that in no circumstances could such an order be justified. It certainly is contended that the order cannot be justified upon the existing grounds. The judgment finds the facts that have been recited and that Carrie Buck "is the probable potential parent of socially inadequate offspring, likewise afflicted, that she may be sexually sterilized without detriment to her general health and that her welfare and that of society will be promoted by her sterilization," and thereupon makes the order. In view of the general declarations of the Legislature and the specific findings of the Court obviously we cannot say as matter of law that the grounds do not exist, and if they exist they justify the result. We have seen more than once that the public welfare may call upon the best citizens for their lives. It would be strange if it could not call upon those who already sap the strength of the state for these lesser sacrifices, often not felt to be such by those concerned, in order to prevent our being swamped with incompetence. It is better for all the world, if instead of waiting to execute degenerate offspring for crime, or to let them starve for their imbecility, society can prevent those who are manifestly unfit from continuing their kind. The principle that sustains compulsory vaccination is broad enough to cover cutting the Fallopian tubes. Jacobson v. Massachusetts, 197 U.S. 11. Three generations of imbeciles are enough.

But, it is said, however it might be if this reasoning were applied generally, it fails when it is confined to the small number who are in the institutions named and is not applied to the multitudes outside. It is the usual last resort of constitutional arguments to point out shortcomings of this sort. But the answer is that the law does all that is needed when it does all that it can, indicates a policy, applies it to all within the lines, and seeks to bring within the lines all similarly situated so far and so fast as its means allow. Of course so far as the operations enable those who otherwise must be kept confined to be returned to the world, and thus open the asylum to others, the equality aimed at will be more nearly reached.

Judgment affirmed.

SKINNER v. OKLAHOMA
316 U.S. 535 (1942)

DOUGLAS, Justice.

This case touches a sensitive and important area of human rights. Oklahoma deprives certain individuals of a right which is basic to the perpetuation of a race—the right to have offspring. Oklahoma has decreed the enforcement of its law against petitioner, overruling his claim that it violated the Fourteenth Amendment. Because that decision raised grave and substantial constitutional questions, we granted the petition for certiorari.

The statute involved is Oklahoma's Habitual Criminal Sterilization Act. Okla. Stat. Ann. tit. 57, §171, et seq. That Act defines an "habitual criminal" as a person who, having been convicted two or more times for crimes "amounting to felonies involving moral turpitude" either in an Oklahoma court or in a court of any other state, is thereafter convicted of such a felony in Oklahoma and is sentenced to a term of imprisonment in an Oklahoma penal institution. Machinery is provided for the institution by the Attorney General of a proceeding against such a person in the Oklahoma courts for a judgment that such person shall be rendered sexually sterile. Notice, an opportunity to be heard, and the right to a jury trial are provided. The issues triable in such a proceeding are narrow and confined. If the court or jury finds that the defendant is an "habitual criminal" and that he "may be rendered sexually sterile without detriment to his or her general health," then the court "shall render judgment to the effect that said defendant be rendered sexually sterile," by the operation of vasectomy in case of a male and of salpingectomy in case of a female. Only one other provision of the Act is material here and that is [the section] which provides that "offenses arising out of the violation of the prohibitory laws, revenue acts, embezzlement, or political offenses, shall not come or be considered within the terms of this Act."

Petitioner was convicted in 1926 of the crime of stealing chickens and was sentenced to the Oklahoma State Reformatory. In 1929 he was convicted of the crime of robbery with fire arms and was sentenced to the reformatory. In 1934 he was convicted again of robbery with firearms and was sentenced to the penitentiary. He was confined there in 1935 when the Act was passed. In 1936 the Attorney General instituted proceedings against him. Petitioner in his answer challenged the Act as unconstitutional by reason of the Fourteenth Amendment. A jury trial was had. The court instructed the jury that the crimes of which petitioner had been convicted were felonies involving moral turpitude and that the only question for the jury was whether the operation of vasectomy could be performed on petitioner without detriment to his general health. The jury found that it could be. A judgment directing that the operation of vasectomy be performed on petitioner was affirmed by the Supreme Court of Oklahoma by a 5-4 decision. 115 P.2d 123.

Several objections to the constitutionality of the Act have been pressed upon us. It is urged that the Act cannot be sustained as an exercise of the police power in view of the state of scientific authorities respecting inheritability of criminal traits. It is argued that due process is lacking because under this Act, unlike the act upheld in Buck v. Bell, 274 U.S. 200, the defendant is given no opportunity to be heard on the issue as to whether he is the probable potential parent of socially undesirable offspring. It is also suggested that the Act is penal in character and that the sterilization provided for is cruel and unusual punishment and vocative of the Fourteenth Amendment. We pass those points without intimating an opinion on them, for there is a feature of the Act which clearly condemns it. That is its failure to meet the requirements of the equal protection clause of the Fourteenth Amendment.

We do not stop to point out all of the inequalities in this Act. A few examples will suffice. In Oklahoma grand larceny is a felony. Larceny is grand larceny when the property taken exceeds $20 in value. Embezzlement is punishable "in the manner prescribed for feloniously stealing property of the value of that embezzled." Hence he who embezzles property worth more than $20 is guilty of a felony. A clerk who appropriates over $20 from his employer's till and a stranger who steals the same amount are thus both guilty of felonies. If the latter repeats his act and is convicted three times, he may be sterilized. But the clerk is not subject to the pains and penalties of the Act no matter how large his embezzlements nor how frequent his convictions. A person who enters a chicken coop and steals chickens commits a felony; and he may be sterilized if he is thrice convicted. If, however, he is a bailee of the property and fraudulently appropriates it, he is an embezzler. Hence no matter how habitual his proclivities for embezzlement are and no matter how often his conviction, he may not be sterilized. Thus the nature of the two crimes is intrinsically the same and they are punishable in the same manner. Furthermore, the line between them follows close distinctions. . . . Whether a particular act is larceny by fraud or embezzlement turns not on the intrinsic quality of the act but on when the felonious intent arose. . . .

It was stated in Buck v. Bell, supra, that the claim that state legislation violates the equal protection clause of the Fourteenth Amendment is "the usual last resort of constitutional arguments." Under our constitutional system the states in determining the reach and scope of particular legislation need not provide "abstract symmetry." They may mark and set apart the classes and types of problems according to the needs and as dictated or suggested by experience. . . . Thus, if we had here only a question as to a state's classification of crimes, such as embezzlement or larceny, no substantial federal question would be raised. For a state is not constrained in the exercise of its police power to ignore experience which marks a class of offenders or a family of offenses for special treatment. Nor is it prevented by the equal protection clause from confining "its restrictions to those classes of cases where the need is deemed to be clearest." . . .

But the instant legislation runs afoul of the equal protection clause, though we give Oklahoma that large deference which the rule of the foregoing cases requires. We are dealing here with legislation which involves one of the basic civil rights of man. Marriage and procreation are fundamental to the very existence and survival of the race. The power to sterilize, if exercised, may have subtle, far reaching and devastating effects. In evil or reckless hands it can cause races or types which are inimical to the dominant group to wither and disappear. There is no redemption for the individual whom the law touches. Any experiment which the state conducts is to his irreparable injury. He is forever deprived of a basic liberty. We mention these matters not to reexamine the scope of the police power of the states. We advert to them merely in emphasis of our view that strict scrutiny of the classification which a state makes in a sterilization law is essential, lest unwittingly or otherwise invidious discriminations are made against groups or types of individuals in violation of the constitutional guaranty of just and equal laws. The guaranty of "equal protection of the laws is a pledge of the protection of equal laws." Yick Wo v. Hopkins, 118 U.S. 356, 369. When the law lays an unequal hand on those who have committed intrinsically the same quality of offense and sterilizes one and not the other, it has made as an invidious a discrimination as if it had selected a particular race or nationality for oppressive treatment. Sterilization of those who have thrice committed grand larceny with immunity for those who are embezzlers is a clear, pointed, unmistakable discrimination. Oklahoma makes no attempt to say that he who commits larceny by trespass or trick or fraud has biologically inheritable traits which he who commits embezzlement lacks. Oklahoma's line between larceny by fraud and embezzlement is determined, as we have noted, "with reference to the time when the fraudulent intent to convert the property to the taker's own use" arises. We have not the slightest basis for inferring that that line has any significance in eugenics nor that the inheritability of criminal traits follows the neat legal distinctions which the law has marked between those two offenses. In terms of fines and imprisonment the crimes of larceny and embezzlement rate the same under the Oklahoma code. Only when it comes to sterilization are the pains and penalties of the law different. The equal protection clause would indeed be a formula of empty words if such conspicuously artificial lines could be drawn. In Buck v. Bell, supra, the Virginia statute was upheld though it applied only to feebleminded persons in institutions of the state. But it was pointed out that "so far as the operations enable those who otherwise must be kept confined to be returned to the world, and thus open the asylum to others, the equality aimed at will be more nearly reached." Here there is no such saving feature. Embezzlers are forever free. Those who steal or take in other ways are not. If such a classification were permitted, distinctions which are "very largely dependent upon history for explanation" could readily become a rule of human genetics.

Reversed.

STONE, Chief Justice, concurring.

I concur in the result, but I am not persuaded that we are aided in reaching it by recourse to the equal protection clause.

If Oklahoma may resort generally to the sterilization of criminals on the assumption that their propensities are transmissible to future generations by inheritance, I seriously doubt that the equal protection clause requires it to apply the measure to all criminals in the first instance, or to none.

Moreover, if we must presume that the legislature knows—what science has been unable to ascertain—that the criminal tendencies of any class of habitual offenders are transmissible regardless of the varying mental characteristics of its individuals, I should suppose that we must likewise presume that the legislature, in its wisdom, knows that the criminal tendencies of some classes of offenders are more likely to be transmitted than those of others. And so I think the real question we have to consider is not one of equal protection, but whether the wholesale condemnation of a class to such an invasion of personal liberty, without opportunity to any individual to show that his is not the type of case which would justify resort to it, satisfies the demands of due process. . . .

Science has found and the law has recognized that there are certain types of mental deficiency associated with delinquency which are inheritable. But the state does not contend—nor can there be any pretense—that either common knowledge or experience, or scientific investigation, has given assurance that the criminal tendencies of any class of habitual offenders are universally or even generally inheritable. In such circumstances, inquiry whether such is the fact in the case of any particular individual cannot rightly be dispensed with. Whether the procedure by which a statute carries its mandate into execution satisfies due process is a matter of judicial cognizance. A law which condemns, without hearing, all the individuals of a class to so harsh a measure as the present because some or even many merit condemnation, is lacking in the first principles of due process. . . .

[Justice Jackson's concurring opinion is omitted.]

Notes: The Right to Procreate

1. *The Right to Procreate.* Did Justice Holmes suggest that there was a "fundamental" right to procreate? What standard of review did the *Buck* court apply to its review of the Virginia sterilization statute? The Court cites Jacobson v. Massachusetts, 197 U.S. 11 (1904), for the proposition that the state's interest in protecting public health was sufficient to support a program of compulsory vaccination. Are there any significant differences between the intrusions to individual liberty created by vaccination as opposed to sterilization? Note that the historical record suggests that Carrie Buck and her family did not actually suffer from "feeble-mindedness." See University of Virginia, Eugenics Historical Materials, available at www.hsl. virginia.edu/historical/eugenics/. See also Paul A. Lombardo, Three Generations, No Imbeciles: Eugenics, the Supreme Court, and *Buck v. Bell* (2008); Edward J. Larson, Putting Buck v. Bell in Scientific and Historical Context, 39 Pepp. L. Rev. 119 (2011); Victoria Nourse, Buck v. Bell: A Constitutional Tragedy from a Lost World, 39 Pepp. L. Rev. 101 (2011). See also Thomas v. Hickman, 2009 WL 1273190 (E.D. Cal. 2009) (prisoner claims Fourteenth Amendment violation of right to procreate, alleging medical procedure resulted in sterilization without consent).

The *Skinner* decision is often thought to have overruled Buck v. Bell. Is this so? Does Justice Douglas identify the right to procreate as "fundamental"? Of what significance is the fact that *Skinner* was decided as an equal protection case rather than a substantive due process case? What was the flaw in the Oklahoma statute? Does the Court's analysis suggest that mandatory sterilization statutes could be upheld if they were supported by sufficiently rigorous scientific evidence about the heritability of a socially costly trait? There was no evidence of a hereditable condition in Jack Skinner's case. He had lost a foot in an accident and had difficulty finding work to support himself and his wife. See Lombardo, supra. For recent explorations of the right to procreate, see Carter J. Dillard, Rethinking the Procreative Right, 10 Yale Hum. Rts. & Dev. L. J. 1, 3 (2007) (suggesting narrow definition of right); John A. Robertson, Assisting Reproduction, Choosing Genes, and the Scope of Reproductive Freedom, 76 Geo. Wash. L. Rev. 1490 (2009) (right to procreate, assisted reproductive technologies, and gene selection).

2. *Eugenics. Buck* and *Skinner* arose from what might be called the first wave of the genetic revolution. Public interest in genetics and Darwinism was high during the early 1900s. Leading commentators suggested that individuals and society should consider whether patterns of reproductive behavior were likely to "improve" or lead to the "deterioration" of the human stock. These eugenic theories were combined with fears about the "quality" of immigrants and other disfavored members of society, whose reproductive tendencies were viewed as a potential assault upon society. The sterilization statutes at issue in *Buck* and *Skinner* were the legislative outgrowth of these popular concerns.

During and after World War II, eugenic theories became closely associated with Nazi atrocities, which included forced sterilizations and the extermination of those deemed to sap the strength of the "Aryan race." The scientific and moral flaws of early eugenic theories were exposed and publicized. Public reaction against state-organized eugenic policies became quite strong. Despite this change in public attitudes, some social programs designed to "encourage" sterilization among poor persons or those with mental disabilities continued well into the 1960s. See, e.g., The Oxford Handbook of the History of Eugenics (Alison Bashford & Philippa Levine eds., 2010); Genes and Human Self-Knowledge: Historical and Philosophical Reflections on Modern Genetics (Robert F. Weir et al. eds., 1994); Note, 72 Geo. Wash. L. Rev. 862 (2004).

We are now in the second wave of the genetic revolution. At the turn of the century, scientists in the United States and elsewhere joined together to identify and map the human "genome," the sequence of genes found in human beings. The Genetic Information Nondiscrimination Act of 2008, P.L. 110-233, 122 Stat. 881 (2008), prohibits some forms of genetic discrimination in employment and insurance and is discussed in greater depth in Chapter 3. Many ethicists argue that people will benefit as advances in genetics produce better information to use in making decisions about whether and how to reproduce. Does it matter, from an ethical or legal standpoint, whether efforts to avoid the reproduction of certain "traits" arise from public or private action? Should it matter whether advances in genetics are used to avoid traits considered to be harmful or to acquire traits considered to be desirable? See, e.g., Bernard G. Prusak, Rethinking "Liberal Eugenics": Reflections and Questions on Habermas on Bioethics, 35(6) Hastings Center Rep. 31 (Nov.–Dec. 2005). We will return to these questions as we consider the connections between genetic information and the use of abortion or assisted reproduction.

3. *Sterilization of Incompetent Persons. Buck* explored the state's ability to impose sterilization upon the mentally incompetent. The issue still arises. See Vaughn v. Ruoff, 253 F.3d 1124 (8th Cir. 2001) (government social worker not entitled to qualified immunity on claim that she violated clearly established constitutional rights of mildly retarded woman by threatening loss of children if woman refused to consent

to sterilization). The modern debate has centered on the ability of courts to authorize sterilizations when sought by the family or guardian of an incompetent person. In these cases, the "state" is involved only in the sense that the guardians seek judicial authorization of the sterilization procedure. Courts have been confronted with two separate issues: (1) Does this court have jurisdiction over the subject matter of the dispute? (2) What substantive and procedural rules should be applied to resolve the dispute? The resolution of the second issue is particularly difficult because of the potential conflict between the incompetent's rights to procreate and to refrain from procreation. See, e.g., In re Hayes, 608 P.2d 635 (Wash. 1980).

In *Hayes*, the mother of a girl with severe mental retardation sought a court order specifically authorizing her daughter's sterilization. The trial court held that it did not have the authority to authorize the sterilization. On appeal, the Washington Supreme Court held that the lower court did have jurisdiction over the question and that a petition for sterilization could be granted "in the rare and unusual case that sterilization is in the best interest of the retarded person." 608 P.2d at 637. The court established a framework of procedural and substantive protections designed to ensure that sterilization was necessary to serve the best interests of the individual rather than for the convenience of her caretakers. See also Guardianship of Mary Moe, 960 N.E.2d 350 (Mass. App. 2012) (overturning abortion order under substituted judgment standard and sterilization order where "judge appears to have simply produced the requirement out of thin air"); In re Valerie N., 707 P.2d 760 (Cal. 1985) (en banc) (ban on sterilization of incompetent persons violates their constitutionally protected liberty interests); In re Wirsing, 573 N.W.2d 51 (Mich. 1998) (probate court had jurisdiction to authorize guardian's consent to sterilization; clear and convincing evidence not required). Note that the vast majority of these sterilizations are performed on women. Does this present any ethical or legal concerns? Do statutes prohibiting disability-based discrimination affect the legality of these sterilizations? See Kerry Lynn Macintosh, Brave New Eugenics: Regulating Assisted Reproductive Technologies in the Name of Better Babies, 2010 U. Ill. J. L. Tech. & Pol'y 257 (2010) (drawing connection between constraints on use of assisted reproduction and eugenic sterilizations); Vanessa Volz, A Matter of Choice: Women with Disabilities, Sterilization, and Reproductive Autonomy in the Twenty-First Century, 27 Women's Rts. L. Rep. 203 (2006), and pages 935-937.

Title II of the Americans with Disabilities Act (ADA) prohibits disability-based discrimination in the provision of public services. 42 U.S.C.A. §§12131-12165. Some rulings by the Supreme Court have raised doubts about whether Title II could be applied to secure monetary damages from states without running afoul of the sovereign immunity provisions of the Eleventh Amendment to the U.S. Constitution. See Tennessee v. Lane, 124 S. Ct. 1978 (2004).

4. *"Temporary Mandatory Sterilization" or Mandatory Birth Control.* Is the state also precluded from mandating birth control? Most cases have arisen when judges have ordered defendants to refrain from reproducing or have ordered defendants to use long-acting contraceptives as a condition of probation. See, e.g., State v. Talty, 814 N.E.2d 1201 (Ohio 2004) (invalidating condition where there was no provision to lift anti-procreation order even when plaintiff became up to date on his child support payments); and State v. Oakley, 629 N.W. 2d 200 (Wis. 2001) (upholding probation condition that defendant avoid having another child absent showing his willingness to provide financial support for children). See also A. Felecia Epps,

Unacceptable Collateral Damage: The Danger of Probation Conditions Restricting the Right to Have Children, 38 Creighton L. Rev. 611 (2005); Symposium, Long Term Contraception, Hastings Center Rep. S1-S33 (Jan.–Feb. 1995). Women are much more likely to be the targets of reproductive restrictions than men. See Rachel Roth, "No New Babies?" Gender Inequality and Reproductive Control in the Criminal Justice and Prison Systems, 12 Am. U. J. Gender & Soc. Pol'y & L. 391 (2004). But see Smith v. Superior Court, 725 P.2d 1101 (Ariz. 1986).

5. *Governmental Encouragement.* More subtle problems are raised when governmental action is not overtly coercive, but merely seeks to encourage reproductive restraint by structuring government benefit or taxation programs to discriminate against large families. In Dandridge v. Williams, 397 U.S. 471 (1970), the Supreme Court upheld a Maryland regulation limiting payments under the state's Aid for Dependent Children program (AFDC) to no more than $240 or $250 per family. As a result of the regulation, AFDC payments equaling a calculated subsistence standard went only to families with fewer than five or six children, there was no additional payment for children beyond that point. 397 U.S. at 509-510 n.2 (Marshall, J., dissenting). This case is a good example of how, as discussed in this chapter's introduction, the shadow of *Lochner* majority looms large: the Court stated that it was fearful of invalidating state economic or social regulations because it was "far too reminiscent of an era when the Court thought the Fourteenth Amendment gave it power to strike down state laws because they may be unwise, improvident, or out of harmony with a particular school of thought." Dandridge, 397 U.S. at 484 (internal quotation marks omitted). The Court did not answer plaintiffs' contentions that the regulation infringed parents' rights "to freedom of choice concerning procreation and reproduction and to marital privacy." Brief for Appellees at 31. See Yvette Barksdale, And the Poor Have Children: A Harm-Based Analysis of Family Caps and the Hollow Procreative Rights of Welfare Beneficiaries, 14 Law & Ineq. 1 (1995); Rebekah J. Smith, Family Caps in Welfare Reform: Their Coercive Effects and Damaging Consequences, 29 Harv. J. L. & Gender 151 (2006).

6. *"Private" Coercion.* In Walker v. Pierce, 560 F.2d 609 (4th Cir. 1977), cert. denied, 434 U.S. 1075 (1978), two African-American women claimed that the defendant, obstetrician Pierce, had sterilized or threatened to sterilize them because of their race, number of children, and status as recipients of publicly funded Medicaid benefits. Dr. Pierce's policy was to refuse to provide obstetrical services to poor women with more than two children unless the women agreed to undergo sterilization after delivery of their third child. The plaintiffs argued that Dr. Pierce had acted "under the color of state law" and that this policy violated their constitutional rights to privacy, due process, and equal protection. The court rejected the claims, in part because it found that Dr. Pierce's connection to the state Medicaid program and a hospital that had received federal funds was not sufficient to make him a state actor subject to liability for the violation of constitutional rights under 42 U.S.C. §1983. The court noted:

> We perceive no reason why Dr. Pierce could not establish and pursue the policy he has publicly and freely announced. Nor are we cited to judicial precedent or statute inhibiting this personal economic philosophy. Particularly is this so when all persons coming to him as patients are seasonably made fully aware of his professional attitude toward the increase in offspring and his determination to see it prevail. At

no time is he shown to have forced his view upon any mother. Indeed, quite the opposite appears. In the single occasion in this case of a sterilization by this doctor, not just one but three formal written consents were obtained, the first before delivery of the fourth child and two afterwards.

560 F.2d at 613. Federal regulations now require specific informed consent and other procedures to reduce the risk of coerced sterilizations in programs supported by federal funds. 42 C.F.R. §§50.201-210.

7. Skinner *and Reproductive Technologies.* Should the right to procreate recognized in *Skinner* be applied to cutting-edge reproductive technologies that do not involve sexual (i.e., coital) reproduction? The infertile have the same desire for reproduction as fertile persons, but should the fact that they have to rely on technology to reproduce make a difference? See, e.g., Judith Daar, Reproductive Technologies and the Law, 141 (2006); I. Glenn Cohen and Daniel L. Chen, Trading-Off Reproductive Technology and Adoption: Does Subsidizing IVF Decrease Adoption Rates and Should It Matter? 95 Minn. L. Rev. 485 (2010). Would the Supreme Court view the constitutional claims to be the same? Does it depend on one's theory of constitutional interpretation? This topic is dealt with in greater depth below in Part D.

Problem: Sterilization and Advances in Genetics

Scientists completed the map of the human genome sequence—part of the billion-dollar Human Genome Project—in 2000. The functional significance of the gene sequences and their implications for our understanding disease and non-diseased traits remain vague at the moment, despite frequent news stories touting the discovery of the "gene for" fill-in-the-blank. But there are certainly major success stories, like the discovery of the association between BRCA1 and BRCA 2 gene mutations and dramatically increased risk of breast cancer. AMP v. Myriad, 569 U.S. 576 (2013).

Consider the development and use of genetic tests for the following conditions:

1. Gene A is a "dominant" trait. Because we ordinarily carry two copies of each gene, only one of which is passed to our offspring, a child of someone who carries one of these genes has a 50 percent chance of receiving this gene and of experiencing its bad effects. Gene A is a late-onset genetic disorder. Persons with the defective gene will develop Alzheimer's disease in their 50s. See Gina Kolata, How Do You Live Knowing You Might Have an Alzheimer's Gene?, N.Y. Times, June 7, 2012.

2. Gene B is a recessive trait and will be expressed only if a child receives the "defective" gene from each parent. Statistically speaking, for two parents who each carry one of these genes, there is a 25 percent chance of their passing two defective genes to their offspring. Children with two B genes develop a painful disorder that leads to death, usually by the age of five. See Emily Rapp, Notes from a Dragon Mom, N.Y. Times, Oct. 15, 2011.

3. Genetic trait C is caused by a large number of different genetic mutations. Scientists have developed a test that will identify 75 percent of these

mutations, but trait C is not always expressed in persons who have these mutations and it is also found in persons who do not have these mutations. Persons with C have shortened life spans; with proper medical care they may live into their 20s or beyond.

4. Hypothetical genetic trait D is associated with higher rates of criminal conduct. Persons who inherit one copy of the gene are 10 percent more likely to be convicted of a violent crime than the general population. Persons with two copies of the gene are 30 percent more likely to be convicted of a violent crime. Although geneticists cannot completely explain the correlation between this gene and criminal conduct, they do believe that the gene is associated with greater risk taking and lower social empathy. Cf. A. Reif et al., Nature and Nurture Predispose to Violent Behavior: Serotonergic Genes and Adverse Childhood Environment, 32 Neuropsychopharmacology 2375 (2007); K. Blum et al., Sex, Drugs, and Rock 'N' Roll: Hypothesizing Common Mesolimbic Activation as a Function of Reward Gene Polymorphisms, 44 J. Psychoactive Drugs 38 (2012).

Is there any basis for restricting the reproduction of any of these persons? Could the risks of reproduction be used to justify premarital screening for one or more of these conditions? See Chapter 8 at page 943. Could a state require individuals who carry one or more of these genes to be counseled about the possible reproductive consequences? The ethical norms governing genetic counselors typically prohibit coercion or directive counseling while encouraging focus on the patient's values and preferences. See Robert Wachbroit & David Wasserman, Patient Autonomy and Value—Neutrality in Nondirective Genetic Counseling, 6 Stan. L. & Pol'y Rev. 103 (1995).

Could a state prohibit reproduction for persons who carry two copies of the hypothetical gene associated with trait D? With one copy? Does *Skinner* stand for the proposition that the state can never prohibit reproduction? Or must the state merely have an adequate scientific basis and apply its standard uniformly? Could the state argue that it has a compelling interest in protecting the child from being born? See Dena Davis, Genetic Dilemmas: Reproductive Technology, Parental Choices, and Children's Futures (2009); Perfecting Pregnancy: Law, Disability and the Future of Reproduction (Isabel Karpin & Kristin Savell eds., 2012); Mary Anne Bobinski, Genetics and Reproductive Decision Making, *in* The Human Genome Project and the Future of Health Care 79-107 (1996); Lois Shepherd, Protecting Parents' Freedom to Have Children with Genetic Differences, 1995 U. Ill. L. Rev. 761. Genetic progress may not provide benefits to all groups in society. See Mary Briody Mahowald, Genes, Women, Equality (1999); Sonia Suter, A Brave New World of Designer Babies, 22 Berkeley Tech. L. J. 897 (2007); Symposium, Communities of Color and Genetic Testing: Purpose, Voice & Values, 27 Seton Hall L. Rev. 887 (1997).

Problem: The Ashley Treatment

Ashley is a profoundly disabled six-year-old with the mental capacity of a three-month-old whose parents have asked a Seattle-area hospital for surgery to remove her uterus and to prevent breast growth, along with hormone treatments to restrain her growth. Should the treatment be provided? With what procedural and substantive protections? See Peter Singer, A Convenient Truth, N.Y. Times, Jan. 26, 2007 (discussing the Ashley case and the hospital's agreement with the parents' requests).

Ashley's parents argued that the procedures were in her best interests, as she would avoid the discomfort of menstruation and the expected development of large breasts; moreover, her smaller stature would permit the parents to include her more readily in family outings and activities. A state investigation later concluded that the procedures should not have been done without a court order. Christine Ryan, Revisiting the Legal Standards That Govern Requests to Sterilize Profoundly Incompetent Children: In Light of the "Ashley Treatment," Is a New Standard Appropriate?, 77 Fordham L. Rev. 287 (2008) (noting investigation report available at www.disability-rightswa.org). See also Alicia Ouellette, Shaping Parental Authority over Children's Bodies, 85 Ind. L. J. 955 (2010); Ed Pilkington & Karen McVeigh, "Ashley Treatment" on Rise amid Concerns from Disability Groups, The Guardian, Mar. 15, 2012.

Problem: Incompetent Persons and Long-Term Contraception

Grace and Tony Jones have a daughter, Alice, who is 17 years old. Alice has a low IQ. She attends school along with other children in the neighborhood, but she takes part in special classes designed to meet her intellectual and emotional needs. Alice is a friendly person who takes a great interest in others and in animals. She has an ordinary interest in sexual activity and often talks about looking forward to having her own child. On the other hand, she is not fond of going to her physician and has a low tolerance for pain. She is easily distractible and must be reminded by others to bathe and eat. Alice's parents are concerned about her future, particularly because they are entering their 50s and can foresee a period of declining health. They want to ensure that Alice is not "burdened by the trauma and responsibility of childrearing or the loss of a child by adoption." They have heard that forced sterilization of minors and incompetents is very controversial. (See discussion at page 707.) As an alternative, they have approached Alice's physician to have Alice undergo insertion of an IUD contraceptive, which could prevent against pregnancy for several years. If this is not possible, they want Alice to be given a birth control pill prescription. How would you advise Alice's physician? Are there any potential sources of liability? In what ways is this situation similar to the sterilization cases? In what ways is it different? Are the differences legally significant? What sources of law would you examine to determine the physician's obligations? Could the ADA be relevant? Would you seek a court order, and if so, of what type?

Problem: Chemical or Surgical Castration of Male Sex Offenders

Should the government's purpose matter in sterilization cases? In most of the cases discussed above, the state intended to restrict a person's ability to procreate, either because of eugenic ideology or because of a judgment that the individual would not provide properly for a child. Consider the movement in the 1990s to require male sex offenders to undergo "chemical castration" as a condition of probation. See, e.g., Daniel L. Icenogle, Sentencing Male Sex Offenders to the Use of

Biological Treatments, 15 J. Leg. Med. 279 (1994). Courts and legislatures hoped to reduce recidivism rates by reducing the offender's sexual drive; the effect on reproduction, therefore, was merely incidental. Appellate courts struck down early efforts to impose chemical castration in the criminal context. See, e.g., People v. Gauntlett, 352 N.W.2d 310 (Mich. Ct. App.), modified on other grounds, 353 N.W.2d 463 (Mich. 1984) (unlawful condition of probation). Legislatures responded by explicitly authorizing the use of chemical castration as a condition of probation for certain sex offenders. See, e.g., Cal. Penal Code §645 (authorizing chemical castration). Should prisoners be entitled to voluntarily consent to castration? See Tex. Gov't Code Ann. §§501.061-.062 (repeat sex offenders authorized to voluntarily undergo orchiectomy, also known as surgical castration). Could a physician ethically perform an orchiectomy on a physically healthy male? If so, under what circumstances? Compare your views with the provisions of the Texas law. For a discussion on the efficacy of treatments for sexual offenders, see Abby Goodnough & Monica Davey, For Sex Offenders, Dispute on Therapy's Benefits, N.Y. Times, Mar. 6, 2007.

Assume that your client, Greg Aya, has been convicted of child molestation on three different occasions. His female victims were all less than 13 years old. Under the applicable California statute, chemical castration must be imposed as a condition of probation. The procedure will require Greg to receive regular shots of a drug that will reduce his sex drive and which will likely impair his sexual functioning. The treatment is to continue until the state's experts certify that it is "no longer necessary." Can you devise a challenge to the California statute and its application to Greg? Will cases such as *Skinner* be useful? Should it matter whether Greg will have an opportunity to "bank" frozen sperm for possible future procreation? Are there any other sources of relevant law? Will you be successful? See Houston v. State, 852 So. 2d 425 (Fla. App. 2003) (trial court failed to follow requirements of chemical castration statute); Bruno v. State, 837 So. 2d 521 (Fla. App. 2003) (surgical castration not authorized for violation of statute at issue in case; illegal sentence resulting from negotiated plea agreement must be set aside). For more on the legal and ethical issues surrounding chemical castration of male sex offenders, see Lystra Batchoo, Voluntary Surgical Castration of Sex Offenders: Waiving the Eighth Amendment Protection from Cruel and Unusual Punishment, 72 Brook. L. Rev. 689 (2007); Karen Harrison, Legal and Ethical Issues When Using Antiandrogenic Pharmacotherapy with Sex Offenders, 3 Sexual Offender Treatment (2008); Marnie E. Rice & Grant T. Harris, Is Androgen Deprivation Therapy Effective in the Treatment of Sex Offenders?, 17 Psychol. Pub. Pol'y & L. 315 (2011); Catherine Rylyk, Note: Lest We Regress to the Dark Ages: Holding Voluntary Surgical Castration Cruel and Unusual, Even for Child Molesters, 16 Wm. & Mary Bill Rts. J. 1305 (2008).

B. RIGHT TO AVOID PROCREATION?

Court decisions identifying a constitutionally protected interest in being able to procreate without impermissible state interference are relatively uncontroversial since state efforts to limit procreation are quite intrusive. The procedure at issue in *Skinner* involved surgery and the permanent alteration of reproductive capacity. In contrast, state restrictions on access to contraception implicate individual interests in a fashion that is arguably less intrusive. Do individuals have a right to *avoid* reproduction that includes the right to use contraceptive technology? Does the right extend to postconception techniques of avoiding reproduction, such as abortion? The next set of cases considers the constitutional validity of state efforts to restrict access to contraception and abortion. As you read these cases, try to identify the source and scope of an individual's right to avoid procreation. What types of state regulation are permissible? Does the validity of state regulation depend on its purpose or effect?

1. Contraception

■ GRISWOLD v. CONNECTICUT
381 U.S. 479 (1965)

DOUGLAS, Justice.

. . . The statutes whose constitutionality is involved in this appeal are §§53-32 and 54-196 of the General Statutes of Connecticut (1958 rev.). The former provides: "Any person who uses any drug, medicinal article or instrument for the purpose of preventing conception shall be fined not less than fifty dollars or imprisoned not less than sixty days nor more than one year or be both fined and imprisoned." Section 54-196 provides: "Any person who assists, abets, counsels, causes, hires or commands another to commit any offense may be prosecuted and punished as if he were the principal offender."

The appellants[, physicians who prescribed contraceptives to married persons,] were found guilty as accessories and fined $100 each, against the claim that the accessory statute as so applied violated the Fourteenth Amendment. . . .

[W]e are met with a wide range of questions that implicate the due process clause of the Fourteenth Amendment. Overtones of some arguments suggest that Lochner v. State of New York, 198 U.S. 45, should be our guide. But we decline that invitation. . . . We do not sit as a super-legislature to determine the wisdom, need, and propriety of laws that touch economic problems, business affairs, or social conditions. This law, however, operates directly on an intimate relation of husband and wife and their physician's role in one aspect of that relation.

The association of people is not mentioned in the Constitution nor in the Bill of Rights. The right to educate a child in a school of the parents' choice—whether public or private or parochial—is also not mentioned. Nor is the right to study any particular subject or any foreign language. Yet the First Amendment has been construed to include certain of those rights.

By Pierce v. Society of Sisters, 268 U.S. 510, the right to educate one's children as one chooses is made applicable to the states by the force of the First and Fourteenth Amendments. By Meyer v. State of Nebraska, 262 U.S. 390, the same dignity is given the right to study the German language in a private school. In other words, the state may not, consistently with the spirit of the First Amendment, contract the spectrum of available knowledge. The right of freedom of speech and press includes not only the right to utter or to print, but the right to distribute, the right to receive, the right to read. . . . Without those peripheral rights the specific rights would be less secure. . . .

The foregoing cases suggest that specific guarantees in the Bill of Rights have penumbras, formed by emanations from those guarantees that help give them life and substance. Various guarantees create zones of privacy. The right of association contained in the penumbra of the First Amendment is one, as we have seen. The Third Amendment in its prohibition against the quartering of soldiers "in any house" in time of peace without the consent of the owner is another facet of that privacy. The Fourth Amendment explicitly affirms the "right of the people to be secure in their persons, houses, papers, and effects, against unreasonable searches and seizures." The Fifth Amendment in its self-incrimination clause enables the citizen to create a zone of privacy which government may not force him to surrender to his detriment. The Ninth Amendment provides: "The enumeration in the Constitution, of certain rights, shall not be construed to deny or disparage others retained by the people." The Fourth and Fifth Amendments were described in Boyd v. United States, 116 U.S. 616, 630, as protection against all governmental invasions "of the sanctity of a man's home and the privacies of life." We have had many controversies over these penumbral rights of "privacy and repose." These cases bear witness that the right of privacy which presses for recognition here is a legitimate one.

The present case, then, concerns a relationship lying within the zone of privacy created by several fundamental constitutional guarantees. And it concerns a law which, in forbidding the use of contraceptives rather than regulating their manufacture or sale, seeks to achieve its goals by means having a maximum destructive impact upon that relationship. Such a law cannot stand in light of the familiar principle, so often applied by this Court, that a "governmental purpose to control or prevent activities constitutionally subject to state regulation may not be achieved by means which sweep unnecessarily broadly and thereby invade the area of protected freedoms." NAACP v. Alabama, 377 U.S. 288, 307. Would we allow the police to search the sacred precincts of marital bedrooms for telltale signs of the use of contraceptives? The very idea is repulsive to the notions of privacy surrounding the marriage relationship.

We deal with a right of privacy older than the Bill of Rights—older than our political parties, older than our school system. Marriage is a coming together for better or for worse, hopefully enduring, and intimate to the degree of being sacred. It is an association that promotes a way of life, not causes; a harmony in living, not political faiths; a bilateral loyalty, not commercial or social projects. Yet it is an association for as noble a purpose as any involved in our prior decisions.

Reversed.

GOLDBERG, Justice, whom the CHIEF JUSTICE and BRENNAN, Justice, join, concurring.

I agree with the Court that Connecticut's birth-control law unconstitutionally intrudes upon the right of marital privacy, and I join in its opinion and judgment. . . . I do agree that the concept of liberty protects those personal rights that are fundamental, and is not confined to the specific terms of the Bill of Rights. My conclusion that the concept of liberty is not so restricted and that it embraces the right of marital privacy though that right is not mentioned explicitly in the Constitution is supported both by numerous decisions of this Court, referred to in the Court's opinion, and by the language and history of the Ninth Amendment. . . .

[I]t should be said of the Court's holding today that it in no way interferes with a state's proper regulation of sexual promiscuity or misconduct [such as "adultery, homosexuality, and the like"]. . . .

HARLAN, Justice, concurring.

. . . In my view, the proper constitutional inquiry in this case is whether this Connecticut statute infringes the due process clause of the Fourteenth Amendment because the enactment violates basic values "implicit in the concept of ordered liberty," Palko v. State of Connecticut, 302 U.S. 319, 325. . . . I believe that it does. While the relevant inquiry may be aided by resort to one or more of the provisions of the Bill of Rights, it is not dependent on them or any of their radiations. The due process clause of the Fourteenth Amendment stands, in my opinion, on its own bottom.

WHITE, Justice, concurring.

In my view this Connecticut law as applied to married couples deprives them of "liberty" without due process of law, as that concept is used in the Fourteenth Amendment. I therefore concur in the judgment of the Court reversing these convictions under Connecticut's aiding and abetting statute. . . .

In these circumstances one is rather hard pressed to explain how the ban on use by married persons in any way prevents use of such devices by persons engaging in illicit sexual relations and thereby contributes to the state's policy against such relationships. . . . I find nothing in this record justifying the sweeping scope of this statute, with its telling effect on the freedoms of married persons, and therefore conclude that it deprives such persons of liberty without due process of law.

STEWART, Justice, whom BLACK, Justice, joins, dissenting.

Since 1879 Connecticut has had on its books a law which forbids the use of contraceptives by anyone. I think this is an uncommonly silly law. As a practical matter, the law is obviously unenforceable, except in the oblique context of the present case. As a philosophical matter, I believe the use of contraceptives in the relationship of marriage should be left to personal and private choice, based upon each individual's moral, ethical, and religious beliefs. As a matter of social policy, I think professional counsel about methods of birth control should be available to all, so that each individual's choice can be meaningfully made. But we are not asked in this case to say whether we think this law is unwise, or even asinine. We are asked to hold that it violates the United States Constitution. And that I cannot do.

In the course of its opinion the Court refers to no less than six Amendments to the Constitution: the First, the Third, the Fourth, the Fifth, the Ninth, and the Fourteenth. But the Court does not say which of these Amendments, if any, it thinks is infringed by this Connecticut law.

We are told that the due process clause of the Fourteenth Amendment is not, as such, the "guide" in this case. With that much I agree. There is no claim that this law, duly enacted by the Connecticut legislature, is unconstitutionally vague. There is no claim that the appellants were denied any of the elements of procedural due process at their trial, so as to make their convictions constitutionally invalid. And, as the Court says, the day has long passed since the due process clause was regarded as a proper instrument for determining "the wisdom, need, and propriety" of state laws. *Compare* Lochner v. State of New York, 198 U.S. 45, *with* Ferguson v. Skrupa, 372 U.S. 726. . . .

As to the First, Third, Fourth, and Fifth Amendments, I can find nothing in any of them to invalidate this Connecticut law. . . . [Moreover] the Ninth Amendment . . . was . . . adopted by the states simply to make clear that the adoption of the Bill of Rights did not alter the plan that the Federal Government was to be a government of express and limited powers, and that all rights and powers not delegated to it were retained by the people and the individual states. . . .

What provision of the Constitution, then, does make this state law invalid? The Court says it is the right of privacy "created by several fundamental constitutional guarantees." With all deference, I can find no such general right of privacy in the Bill of Rights, in any other part of the Constitution, or in any case ever before decided by this Court.

At the oral argument in this case we were told that the Connecticut law does not "conform to current community standards." But it is not the function of this Court to decide cases on the basis of community standards. We are here to decide cases "agreeably to the Constitution and laws of the United States." It is the essence of judicial duty to subordinate our own personal views, our own ideas of what legislation is wise and what is not. If, as I should surely hope, the law before us does not reflect the standards of the people of Connecticut, the people of Connecticut can freely exercise their true Ninth and Tenth Amendment rights to persuade their elected representatives to repeal it. That is the constitutional way to take this law off the books.

Notes: A Right to Avoid Procreation

1. *Another Constitutional Right?* Does the Court settle on the source of a constitutional right to avoid procreation in *Griswold?* Justice Douglas reviews a number of different parts of the Bill of Rights before concluding that their "penumbra" was sufficiently broad to encompass the right of married couples to use contraceptives. Is Douglas's attempt to find textual support for this right persuasive? Note that Justices Goldberg and White were dissatisfied with Douglas's analysis, preferring to rest the decision on the Ninth Amendment and the "liberty" clause of the Fourteenth Amendment, respectively. Justice Stewart raises the specter of *Lochner* in his dissent, arguing that the majority is substituting its own judgment for the will of the people of Connecticut, as delivered by their elected representatives. See generally I. Glenn Cohen, The Constitution and the Rights Not to Procreate, 60 Stan. L. Rev. 1135 (2008) (exploring unbundling of right not to procreate).

2. *Individuals or Married Couples.* Left unresolved in *Griswold* was the question whether the right to use contraceptives belonged to the individual or was instead some protected aspect of the marital relationship. In Eisenstadt v. Baird, 405 U.S. 438 (1972), Baird was convicted for "exhibiting contraceptive[s] . . . in the course of delivering a lecture on contraception to . . . students at Boston University" and "for giving a young woman a package of [contraceptive] foam at the end of his address." The Massachusetts statute at issue imposed a maximum five-year prison term for distribution of contraceptives unless certain statutory requirements were met. The statute permitted a physician to prescribe contraceptives to married persons to prevent pregnancy. Single persons were denied access to contraceptives to prevent pregnancy; however, any adult could obtain contraceptives to prevent the spread of disease. The Court struck down the statutory scheme under a rationally basis, equal protection standard. The Court's holding suggested, without explicitly deciding, that individuals might have a fundamental liberty interest in decisions to avoid procreation:

[W]hatever the rights of the individual to access to contraceptives may be, the rights must be the same for the unmarried and the married alike.

If under Griswold [v. Connecticut, 381 U.S. 479 (1965),] the distribution of contraceptives to married persons cannot be prohibited, a ban on distribution to unmarried persons would be equally impermissible. It is true that in *Griswold* the right of privacy in question inhered in the marital relationship. Yet the marital couple is not an independent entity with a mind and heart of its own, but an association of two individuals each with a separate intellectual and emotional makeup. If the right of privacy means anything, it is the right of the individual, married or single, to be free from unwarranted governmental intrusion into matters so fundamentally affecting a person as the decision whether to bear or beget a child.

On the other hand, if *Griswold* is no bar to a prohibition on the distribution of contraceptives, the state could not, consistently with the equal protection clause, outlaw distribution to unmarried but not to married persons. In each case the evil, as perceived by the state, would be identical, and the underinclusion would be invidious. . . . We hold that by providing dissimilar treatment for married and unmarried persons who are similarly situated, Massachusetts General Laws Ann., c. 272, §§21 and 21A, violate the equal protection clause.

Id. at 453-455.

3. *Judicial Review of Social Legislation.* According to some, the Supreme Court is essentially an antidemocratic institution in which life-tenured political appointees wield the potential power to reverse the will of the democratically elected representatives of the majority. Are you troubled by the Court's lack of deference to the will of the people as embodied in their statutes? What limits, if any, does the Court place upon itself? Are those limits meaningful? Does the very process of judicial review of social legislation betray our society's ultimate discomfort with democracy?

4. *Paying for Contraceptives.* Contraceptives remain controversial, largely due to religious and moral views regarding the procreative purpose of sexual activity. See, e.g., R. Alta Charo, Warning: Contraceptive Drugs May Cause Political Headaches, 366 New Eng. J. Med. 1361 (2012). Should public and private insurers provide coverage for contraceptives? Is this a policy argument or could a failure to provide contraceptive coverage be considered impermissible sex discrimination? See Sylvia A. Law, Sex Discrimination and Insurance for Contraception, 73 Wash. L. Rev. 363 (1998). Courts have also been asked to determine whether the failure to pay for prescription contraceptives under various health plans violates federal or state law. See, e.g., Catholic Charities of Sacramento, Inc. v. Superior Court, 85 P.3d 67 (Cal.), cert. denied, 125 S. Ct. 53 (2004) (upholding state Women's Contraceptive Equity Act in constitutional challenge brought by employer which opposed contraceptives on religious grounds); and Standridge v. Union Pac. R.R. Co. (In re Union Pac. R.R. Employment Practices Litigation), 479 F. 3d 936 (8th Cir. Neb. Mar. 15, 2007) (finding employer did not violate Title VII by failing to cover prescription contraception for women). State and federal legislative initiatives in this area are summarized in the National Conference of State Legislatures, Health Insurance Coverage for Contraceptives (available at NCSL Web site, www.ncsl.org). Following the recommendations of an Institute of Medicine panel, the Obama administration announced in 2012 that contraception coverage without co-pays or deductibles should be provided in the basic package of health care benefits required in the Affordable Care Act. The initial proposal, which exempted churches but not other

institutions with religious affiliations, such as universities and hospitals, was modified to insulate certain religiously affiliated organizations from paying for or providing information about the coverage, 45 C.F.R. §147.130(a)(1)(iv). Challenges to the eventual policy resulted in two important Supreme Court cases, Burwell v. Hobby Lobby Stores, Inc., 134 S. Ct. 2751 (2014) and Zubik v. Burwell, 136 S. Ct. 1557 (2016) (per curiam):

> Several for-profit corporations with religious owners subsequently filed suit under [the Religious Freedom Restoration Act of 1993 (RFRA)], requesting exemption from the mandate, and eventually reached the Supreme Court in consolidated cases brought by chain store Hobby Lobby and cabinet manufacturer Conestoga Wood. The Court's analysis of their claims proceeded in four steps, resulting in a 5-4 decision. First came the threshold question of whether for-profit corporations count as "persons" capable of exercising religion under RFRA. Relying on the near universal acceptance that RFRA's use of the word "persons" includes non-profit corporations, the Court determined that "persons" should equally encompass for-profit corporations. It concluded that—like religious non-profits—closely held, secular for-profit corporations can equally "further[] individual religious freedom" of individuals united in the enterprise.
>
> As RFRA requires, the Court then evaluated whether: (1) the mandate imposed a substantial burden on the objecting corporations' free exercise rights; (2) the government had a compelling interest in the mandate; and (3) the government had less restrictive alternatives. The majority determined that the objecting corporations were indeed substantially burdened by the mandate, because they faced a choice between paying potentially large tax penalties for noncompliance and violating their religious beliefs. It was irrelevant that they were not required themselves to buy or use contraceptives, as they sincerely objected to being complicit in helping pay, arrange, or contract for those services. The dissent, in contrast, concluded that the "connection between the [owners'] religious objections and the contraceptive coverage requirement is too attenuated to rank as substantial."
>
> The Court assumed, without deciding, that the governmental interest in guaranteeing cost-free access to contraceptives was compelling. It then assessed whether the mandate was the least restrictive means of furthering that interest, concluding that the mandate could not satisfy the "exceptionally demanding" least-restrictive-means standard of RFRA. Because the government had accommodated non-profit religious organizations, the Court determined that it could equally accommodate for-profit corporations. But the Court refused to confirm that the accommodation—which at that time required notification to the employer's insurer—"complie[d] with RFRA for purposes of all religious claims"—leaving the door open to ongoing litigation by nonprofits against the accommodation itself.
>
> In July 2015, in response to the Supreme Court's *Hobby Lobby* decision, HHS issued a new version of the rule that allowed certain closely-held for-profit entities the same accommodation available to eligible religious non-profits. The new rule also provided an alternative accommodation mechanism, permitting employers to notify HHS in writing of their religious objection, rather than deliver a specific form to their insurance issuer or third-party administrator.
>
> Despite this expansion, several employers continued to object, claiming that the required process under the accommodation was still a substantial burden in two ways. First, they argued, submitting notice directly to the insurance issuer, third-party administrator, or even the government simply triggers another party to engage in the objectionable activity without removing the employer entirely from the chain of

complicity. Second, they claimed that their religious convictions forbid them from contracting with companies that will provide free coverage for the contraceptive services, so it is problematic for them to retain relationships with these insurance companies and third party administrators at all. Thus, the objecting employers sought an outright exemption, rather than an accommodation, arguing that the government has ample alternative means to provide access to cost-free contraceptives to their employees without burdening employers' religious exercise.

In response to these claims, eight out of nine courts of appeals to hear the cases concluded that no substantial burden on religious exercise existed under the accommodation. The accommodation, they decided, excused objecting employers from any involvement—that private insurers complied with their own legal obligations to offer contraceptive coverage could not substantially burden the plaintiffs.

In its October 2015 term, the Supreme Court took up a number of these non-profit cases, consolidated under the name Zubik v. Burwell. After oral argument, however, having taken the unusual step of proposing a possible alternative process for accommodation from the mandate and requesting supplemental briefing on that alternative, the Court issued a unanimous per curiam opinion remanding the cases to the appellate courts with the instruction to afford the parties "an opportunity to arrive at an approach going forward that accommodates petitioners' religious exercise while at the same time ensuring that women covered by petitioners' health plans 'receive full and equal health coverage, including contraceptive coverage.'" The Court took great pains to provide a list of matters it was explicitly not deciding, such as "whether petitioners' religious exercise has been substantially burdened, whether the Government has a compelling interest, or whether the current regulations are the least restrictive means of serving that interest." While many attributed the decision not to rule on the merits to the fact that the Court is currently faced with an even number of justices following the death of Justice Scalia, there is significant dispute as to what the Court did or did not signal through its opinion.

The cases—and the issues of substantial burden, compelling interest, and potential alternatives—will likely return to the Court shortly in the same, or similar, posture.

Introduction, Law, Religion, and Health in the United States (Holly Fernandez Lynch, I. Glenn Cohen, Elizabeth Sepper eds, 2017)(internal citations omitted).

5. *Minors and Contraception.* Particularly thorny disputes have arisen regarding the ability of the state to regulate access to contraceptives for minors. In Carey v. Population Services, 431 U.S. 678 (1977), the Court struck down a New York statute that criminalized distribution of condoms to persons under 16 years of age and provided that condoms could be distributed only by licensed pharmacists to persons over 16. Justice Brennan, writing for the plurality, found that minors had a limited constitutional right of access to contraceptives and that the state had failed to show that its regulation served a "significant state interest." Justices White and Powell would have invalidated the statute as irrational without finding that minors had a protected constitutional interest. Justice Rehnquist authored a spirited dissent. The Court's doctrinal difficulties in this case mirror its fractured decisionmaking in abortion cases involving minors, see page 749.

Do parents have a constitutional right to be consulted (or informed) when professional clinics offer contraceptive advice or services to minor children living with their parents? In Doe v. Irwin, 615 F.2d 1162 (6th Cir. 1980), the court held that there was no such parental right and reversed the district court's finding that a state-

funded family planning center's practice of distributing contraceptives to unemancipated minors without parental notice or consultation violated the parents' constitutional right to oversee the care, custody, and nurturing of their children. Do
parents have a constitutional right to prevent schools from distributing condoms to
their children? See Parents United for Better Schools, Inc. v. Board of Education,
148 F.3d 260 (3d Cir. 1998) (voluntary high school condom distribution program
does not violate parents' fundamental rights where parents could refuse to let children participate); Curtis v. School Committee of Falmouth, 652 N.E.2d 580 (Mass.
1995) (upholding program that did not allow parental opt out), cert. denied, 116
S. Ct. 753 (1996). Should schools learning that a minor is pregnant be required to
notify the minor's parents? Melissa Prober, Please Don't Tell My Parents: The Validity of School Policies Mandating Parental Notification of a Student's Pregnancy, 71
Brook. L. Rev. 557 (2005).

Family planning counseling for minors may raise special problems of medical ethics for physicians and other health care personnel. Elise D. Berlan & Ter-
rill Bravender, Confidentiality, Consent, and Caring for the Adolescent Patient, 21
Curr. Opin. Pediatr. 450 (2009); David A. Klein & Jeffrey W. Hutchinson, Providing
Confidential Care for Adolescents, 85 Am. Fam. Physician 556 (2012); Ryan E. Lawrence et al., Adolescents, Contraception and Confidentiality: A National Survey of
Obstetrician-Gynecologists, 84 Contraception 259 (2011). Should a physician who
discovers that a minor is engaged in sexual activity have a duty to report the situation as a case of potential child abuse? See Jodi Rudoren, Judge Blocks Law to
Report Sex Under 16, N.Y. Times, Apr. 19, 2006, at A16.

The Supreme Court's jurisprudence governing access to abortion for minors
has also influenced some legislatures to consider restrictions on minors' access to
contraception. Some research suggests that these proposals might cause minors to
turn to other, potentially less effective methods of avoiding pregnancy. Rachel K.
Jones et al., Adolescents' Reports of Parental Knowledge of Adolescents' Use of
Sexual Health Services and Their Reactions to Mandated Parental Notification for
Prescription Contraception, 293 JAMA 340 (2005). Currently, "21 states and the
District of Columbia explicitly allow all minors to consent to contraceptive services"
and "25 states explicitly permit minors to consent to contraceptive services in one
or more circumstances," leaving four states with "no explicit policy." Guttmacher
Institute, Minors' Access to Contraceptive Services, Feb. 1, 2013 (most recent brief-
ing available at www.guttmacher.org/sections/contraception.php).

6. *Emergency Contraception.* Emergency contraception, also known as the "morning-after pill," should be taken as soon as possible after unprotected intercourse to
prevent conception or the implantation of a fertilized egg in a woman's uterus. It
appears to work in most cases by "delaying or preventing ovulation, but prevention
of implantation cannot be ruled out." Alastair J. J. Wood et al., The Politics of Emergency Contraception, 366 New Eng. J. Med. 101 (2012). Those who believe that
human life begins at the fertilization of an ovum view the drug as an abortifacient
because it in some cases may work by preventing the implantation of a fertilized egg.
But see Pam Belluck, Abortion Qualms on Morning-After Pill May Be Unfounded,
N.Y. Times, June 5, 2012.

State regulations initially focused on the role of pharmacists in dispensing the
prescriptions, including providing "right of conscience" protections for pharmacists
who refused to dispense the drug based on their personal moral or religious beliefs.

See the National Conference of State Legislatures, Emergency Contraception Laws (available at the NCSL Web site); Noesen v. State Department of Regulation and Licensing, Pharmacy Examining Bd., 751 N.W.2d 385 (Wis. App. 2008) (state board permitted to discipline pharmacists who refused to refill a prescription for birth control pills and refused to transfer the prescription to another pharmacy). After some controversy, the FDA approved over-the-counter (OTC) sales of Plan B emergency contraception for women over age 17. Frank Davidoff & James Trussell, Plan B and the Politics of Doubt, 296 JAMA 1775 (2006); Cynthia Harper et al., Over-the-Counter Access to Emergency Contraception for Teens, 77 Contraception 230 (2008) (noting arguments supporting OTC for teens). See also Anspach v. City of Philadelphia, Department of Public Health, 503 F.3d 256 (3d Cir. 2007) (rejecting First and Fourteenth Amendment claims brought by parents and unemancipated minor against clinic that provided emergency contraception to minor at her request). The debate about whether the drug should be available OTC for minors flared up in 2012 when the Secretary of Health and Human Services initially ordered the FDA commissioner not to approve OTC sales for minors 16 and under. See Wood, supra.

2. Abortion

■ ROE v. WADE
410 U.S. 113 (1973)

BLACKMUN, Justice.

[Roe challenged the constitutional validity of a Texas statute that made it a crime to procure an abortion, except where necessary to save the life of the pregnant woman. The Court held that the statute violated the Fourteenth Amendment's due process clause. Justice Blackmun recognized that states had two separate interests in regulating abortion: (1) an interest in protecting the health and safety of women; and (2) an interest in protecting fetal life. These interests had to be weighed against the rights of the woman and her fetus. The Court first held that women had a protected "privacy" interest in the abortion decision:]

This right of privacy, whether it be founded in the Fourteenth Amendment's concept of personal liberty and restrictions upon state action, as we feel it is, . . . is broad enough to encompass a woman's decision whether or not to terminate her pregnancy. The detriment that the state would impose upon the pregnant woman by denying this choice altogether is apparent. Specific and direct harm medically diagnosable even in early pregnancy may be involved. Maternity, or additional offspring, may force upon the woman a distressful life and future. Psychological harm may be imminent. Mental and physical health may be taxed by child care. There is also the distress, for all concerned, associated with the unwanted child, and there is the problem of bringing a child into a family already unable, psychologically and otherwise, to care for it. In other cases, as in this one, the additional difficulties and continuing stigma of unwed motherhood may be involved. All these are factors the woman and her responsible physician necessarily will consider in consultation. . . .

[A] state may properly assert important interests in safeguarding health, in maintaining medical standards, and in protecting potential life. At some point in pregnancy, these respective interests become sufficiently compelling to sustain regulation of the factors that govern the abortion decision. The privacy right involved, therefore, cannot be said to be absolute. In fact, it is not clear to us that the claim asserted by some amici that one has an unlimited right to do with one's body as one pleases bears a close relationship to the right of privacy previously articulated in the Court's decisions. The Court has refused to recognize an unlimited right of this kind in the past. Jacobson v. Massachusetts, 197 U.S. 11 (1905) (vaccination); Buck v. Bell, 274 U.S. 200 (1927) (sterilization). [See also the assisted suicide cases in Chapter 5.B.]

We, therefore, conclude that the right of personal privacy includes the abortion decision, but that this right is not unqualified and must be considered against important state interests in regulation. . . .

Where certain "fundamental rights" are involved, the Court has held that regulation limiting these rights may be justified only by a "compelling state interest," and that legislative enactments must be narrowly drawn to express only the legitimate state interests at stake. . . .

The appellee and certain amici argue that the fetus is a "person" within the language and meaning of the Fourteenth Amendment. . . . If this suggestion of personhood is established, the appellant's case, of course, collapses, for the fetus' right to life would then be guaranteed specifically by the Amendment. . . . [The Court rejects this claim, noting that "person" in the Constitution is never used in a way that suggests it could have any prenatal application.] . . .

The pregnant woman cannot be isolated in her privacy. She carries an embryo and, later, a fetus, if one accepts the medical definitions of the developing young in the human uterus. The situation therefore is inherently different from [prior cases]. . . .

[W]e do not agree that, by adopting one theory of life, Texas may override the rights of the pregnant woman that are at stake. We repeat, however, that the state does have an important and legitimate interest in preserving and protecting the health of the pregnant woman . . . and that it has still another important and legitimate interest in protecting the potentiality of human life. These interests are separate and distinct. Each grows in substantiality as the woman approaches term and, at a point during pregnancy, each becomes "compelling."

With respect to the state's important and legitimate interest in the health of the mother, the "compelling" point, in the light of present medical knowledge, is at approximately the end of the first trimester. This is so because of the now-established medical fact that until the end of the first trimester mortality in abortion may be less than mortality in normal childbirth. It follows that, from and after this point, a state may regulate the abortion procedure to the extent that the regulation reasonably relates to the preservation and protection of maternal health. . . .

This means, on the other hand, that, for the period of pregnancy prior to this "compelling" point, the attending physician, in consultation with his patient, is free to determine, without regulation by the state, that, in his medical judgment, the patient's pregnancy should be terminated. If that decision is reached, the judgment may be effectuated by an abortion free of interference by the state.

With respect to the state's important and legitimate interest in potential life, the "compelling" point is at viability. This is so because the fetus then presumably has the capability of meaningful life outside the mother's womb. State regulation protective of fetal life after viability thus has both logical and biological justifications. If the state is interested in protecting fetal life after viability, it may go so far as to proscribe abortion during that period, except when it is necessary to preserve the life or health of the mother. . . .

[The Court then applied these standards to invalidate the Texas abortion statute.]

Affirmed in part and reversed in part.

REHNQUIST, Justice, dissenting.

The Court's opinion brings to the decision of this troubling question both extensive historical fact and a wealth of legal scholarship. While the opinion thus commands my respect, I find myself nonetheless in fundamental disagreement with those parts of it that invalidate the Texas statute in question, and therefore dissent. . . .

I would reach a conclusion opposite to that reached by the Court. I have difficulty in concluding, as the Court does, that the right of "privacy" is involved in this case. . . . If the Court means by the term *privacy* no more than that the claim of a person to be free from unwanted state regulation of consensual transactions may be a form of "liberty" protected by the Fourteenth Amendment, there is no doubt that similar claims have been upheld in our earlier decisions on the basis of that liberty. . . . The test traditionally applied in the area of social and economic legislation is whether or not a law such as that challenged has a rational relation to a valid state objective. Williamson v. Lee Optical Co., 348 U.S. 483, 491 (1955). The due process clause of the Fourteenth Amendment undoubtedly does place a limit, albeit a broad one, on legislative power to enact laws such as this. If the Texas statute were to prohibit an abortion even where the mother's life is in jeopardy, I have little doubt that such a statute would lack a rational relation to a valid state objective under the test stated in *Williamson*, supra. But the Court's sweeping invalidation of any restrictions on abortion during the first trimester is impossible to justify under that standard, and the conscious weighing of competing factors that the Court's opinion apparently substitutes for the established test is far more appropriate to a legislative judgment than to a judicial one. . . .

While the Court's opinion quotes from the dissent of Mr. Justice Holmes in Lochner v. New York, 198 U.S. 45, 74 (1905), the result it reaches is more closely attuned to the majority opinion of Mr. Justice Peckham in that case. As in *Lochner* and similar cases applying substantive due process standards to economic and social welfare legislation, the adoption of the compelling state interest standard will inevitably require this Court to examine the legislative policies and pass on the wisdom of these policies in the very process of deciding whether a particular state interest put forward may or may not be "compelling." The decision here to break pregnancy into three distinct terms and to outline the permissible restrictions the state may impose in each one, for example, partakes more of judicial legislation than it does of a determination of the intent of the drafters of the Fourteenth Amendment. . . .

To reach its result, the Court necessarily has had to find within the scope of the Fourteenth Amendment a right that was apparently completely unknown to the drafters of the Amendment. . . .

There apparently was no question concerning the validity of this provision or of any of the other state statutes when the Fourteenth Amendment was adopted. The only conclusion possible from this history is that the drafters did not intend to have the Fourteenth Amendment withdraw from the states the power to legislate with respect to this matter.

For all of the foregoing reasons, I respectfully dissent.

Notes: Roe v. Wade

1. *Abortion Statistics.* Abortion is a relatively common medical procedure in the United States. According to federal government statistics, "825,564 abortions were reported to CDC for 2008" from 47 states, the District of Columbia, and New York City, with about one-fifth of all pregnancies ending in abortion. Karen Pazol et al., Abortion Surveillance—United States, 2008, 60 MMWR 1, 11 (Nov. 25, 2011) (No. SS-15). For an overall review of the topic from a public health perspective, see Cynthia C. Harper et al., Abortion in the United States, 26 Annu. Rev. Public Health 501 (2005).

2. *Fetal Personhood.* The "personhood" of the fetus is an area of significant religious and philosophical debate. It is clear that many major religions treat an unborn child as a person from the moment of conception. Philosophers and bioethicists have also argued for the special, human nature of the fetus. Is it possible to argue that fetuses are "persons" for constitutional purposes? If a fetus is a constitutional person then it would be protected under the due process and equal protection clauses. How does the Court deal with this issue? Did the Texas criminal abortion statute indicate that Texas believed that fetuses were persons? See also Christopher Robert Kaczor, The Ethics of Abortion: Women's Rights, Human Life, and the Question of Justice (2011); Bonnie Steinbeck, Life Before Birth: The Moral and Legal Status of Embryos and Fetuses (2d ed. 2011); Note, What We Talk About When We Talk About Persons: The Language of a Legal Fiction, 114 Harv. L. Rev. 1745 (2001). Would a fetus's status as a person automatically mean that abortion would be prohibited by the constitution? In DeShaney v. Winnebago County Department of Social Services, 489 U.S. 189 (1989), the Supreme Court held that the state did not owe any affirmative duty to protect a child from private violence inflicted by his father. What are the implications of this in the abortion context? Would *DeShaney* be relevant if a plaintiff argued that the state's failure to criminalize abortion while criminalizing other types of homicide violated the Equal Protection Clause? See Lee v. Oregon, 107 F.3d 1382 (9th Cir. 1997) (raising equal protection challenge to Oregon's assisted suicide statute, but ultimately resolving the case on plaintiff's lack of standing), cert. denied sub nom. Lee v. Harcleroad, 522 U.S. 927 (1997).

3. *Sources of Authority in Constitutional Interpretation.* In the full opinion, Justice Blackmun engages in a painstaking analysis of historical, legal, medical, and religious attitudes toward abortion. By what theory is this discussion constitutionally relevant? Is this an argument that the framers of the Fourteenth Amendment considered procreative liberty to be fundamental? Even if this doubtful proposition were accurate, should it be determinative? In other contexts, some have argued that the Constitution should evolve over time; could not the controversy over abortion indicate heightened sensitivity to the rights of others that should be incorporated into the Constitution? If the Constitution can grow to recognize a woman's right to choose, can it also grow to recognize fetal rights? In the unedited opinion, Justice Blackmun also details the opinions of various medical organizations. Should the

medical profession have special influence on the establishment of constitutional norms where they concern biological processes?

4. *The "Right to Privacy."* What is the nature of the right to privacy? Does Justice Blackmun succeed in adequately describing its source, scope, and limits? Note that the Court adopts the theory that the source of the right is the liberty clause of the Fourteenth Amendment. How would Justice Rehnquist determine whether the right to choose abortion is "fundamental"? Does his charge of "Lochnerism" seem valid?

5. *The State's Interest.* Justice Blackmun contends that the interests of the pregnant woman and the state can be weighed and evaluated through the use of the trimester framework. Does he adequately explain what the state's interest is in the first trimester? What types of state regulation would be supported by this interest? Is Justice Blackmun's discussion of the importance of viability convincing? Or does it constitute *ipse dixit*?

6. *Additional Ethical or Moral Aspects of Abortion.* Abortion implicates our definition of personhood, the value of potential human life, and the obligations of health professionals to "do no harm" and to serve patients' medical needs. The law on abortion does not differentiate among the various possible nontherapeutic reasons underlying a woman's decision to end a pregnancy, but ethicists, philosophers, and religious groups often make these distinctions. Consider the following rationales for abortion:

a. Should abortion be used explicitly as a means of after-the-fact birth control? See Judith Jarvis Thomson, A Defense of Abortion, 1 Phil. & Pub. Aff. 47 (1971) (mounting a defense of abortion, but suggesting that abortion merely as birth control exceeds ethical bounds). The issue is of increasing importance to those who fear that the increasing availability of pharmaceutical abortions might increase use of abortion as a method of family planning. See, e.g., Karen Pazol et al., Abortion Surveillance—United States, 2008, 60 MMWR 1, 11 (Nov. 25, 2011) (No. SS-15) ("The use of medical abortion increased 17% from 2007 to 2008."). Many statutes that are aimed at restricting abortion differentiate abortions where pregnancy is the result of rape and incest from all other kinds of abortions. Is such a distinction tenable? See I. Glenn Cohen, Are All Abortions Equal? Should There Be Exceptions to the Criminalization of Abortion for Rape and Incest?, 43 J. L. Med. & Ethics 87 (2015) (rejecting the distinction).

b. Should abortion be used to eliminate multiple births? Pregnancies with multiple fetuses carry health risks for the fetuses and for the expectant mother. Obstetricians have the ability to selectively reduce the number of fetuses in multifetal pregnancies. Is there an ethical basis justifying selection reduction from triplets to twins that would not apply to the reduction of twins to a singleton fetus? For a discussion of the clinical and ethical issues, see Judith F. Daar, Selective Reduction of Multiple Pregnancy: Lifeboat Ethics in the Womb, 25 U.C. Davis L. Rev. 773 (1992); Mark Evans et al., Update on Selective Reduction, 25 Prenatal Diag. 807 (2005).

c. Should abortion be used to avoid the birth of a child with birth defects? If so, which defects? Why shouldn't this be considered an impermissible form of disability-based discrimination or eugenics? Genetic screening is already used to identify the sex of the fetus, sometimes to avoid a sex-linked genetic disorder but other times to ensure parental control over gender. Should parents be able to use genetic screening to identify the sex of a child so that they can abort a child of the "wrong" gender? See Ariz. Rev. Stat. §13-3603.02 (prohibiting performing or soliciting abortions based on sex or race of fetus). See also Susannah Baruch et al., Genetic Testing of Embryos: Practices and Perspectives of U.S. IVF Clinics, 89 Fertility & Sterility 1053 (2008); John F. Muller, Disability, Ambivalence, and the Law, 37 Am. J. L. & Med. 469 (2011); Erik Parens & Adrienne Asch, the Disability Rights Critique of Prenatal Genetic Testing, 29 Hastings Center Rep. 40 (Sept.–Oct. 1999) (special supp.); Stanford Symposium on Preimplantation Genetic Diagnosis, 85 Fertility & Sterility 1631-1660 (2006); Jennifer Steinhauer, House Rejects Bill to Ban Sex-Selective Abortions, N.Y. Times, May 31, 2012.

d. What about using abortion to "deselect" other characteristics, such as size, hair color, or personality, assuming that genetic science progressed to make this possible? At some point, prospective parents may be able to create even more detailed shopping lists. Is there anything ethically or legally wrong with permitting parents to abort pregnancies until they conceive a fetus with a projected IQ greater than 125? See Greer Conley et al., Prenatal Whole Genome Sequencing: Just Because We Can, Should We?, 42(4) Hastings Center Rep. 28 (July–Aug. 2012); Owen D. Jones, Reproductive Autonomy and Evolutionary Biology: A Regulatory Framework for Trait-Selection Technologies, 19 Am. J. L. & Med. 187 (1993); Maxwell J. Mehlman, The Law of Above Averages: Leveling the New Genetic Enhancement Playing Field, 85 Iowa L. Rev. 517 (2000); John A. Robertson, Genetic Selection of Offspring Characteristics, 76 B. U. L. Rev. 421 (1996); Stanford Symposium on Preimplantation Genetic Diagnosis, supra.

7. *Abortion Politics.* Those who hoped that a Supreme Court decision in this area would resolve the issue have been greatly disappointed. The *Roe* decision helped to fuel another 40 years of debate about abortion, the Constitution, and state regulation. "Pro-life" or "anti-choice" advocates were not vanquished, but in fact seemed invigorated by the Court's rejection of most types of state abortion regulation. Abortion continued to be a political issue; federal, state, and local political candidates announced their positions even in races where the controversy was largely irrelevant given the nature of the office being elected. "Pro-life" or "anti-choice" activists worked for a constitutional amendment. State legislatures continued to regulate abortion, sending test case after test case to the courts. "Pro-choice" or "pro-abortion" advocates fought in the courts and the legislatures to preserve constitutional protections for women seeking abortions. While it would be naive to imagine that the judicial selection process before *Roe* was apolitical, it is clear that the abortion debate produced a new "litmus test" for potential state and federal judicial nominees. Cf. Linda Greenhouse, Democracy and the Courts: The Case of Abortion, 61 Hastings L. J. 1333 (2010). The cases and notes in the remainder of this section will summarize the judicial response to changes in the political battle lines.

8. *Supreme Court Abortion Jurisprudence Between* Roe *and* Casey. For a summary of some of the important cases between *Roe* and *Casey,* see Rachael K. Pirner & Laurie B. Williams, *Roe* to *Casey:* A Survey of Abortion Law, 32 Washburn L. J. 166 (1993).

■ PLANNED PARENTHOOD OF SOUTHEASTERN PENNSYLVANIA v. CASEY
505 U.S. 833 (1992)

O'CONNOR, KENNEDY, and SOUTER, Justices.

I

Liberty finds no refuge in a jurisprudence of doubt. Yet 19 years after our holding that the Constitution protects a woman's right to terminate her pregnancy in its early stages, Roe v. Wade, 410 U.S. 113 (1973), that definition of liberty is still questioned. Joining the respondents as amicus curiae, the United States, as it has done in five other cases in the last decade, again asks us to overrule *Roe.*

At issue in these cases are five provisions of the Pennsylvania Abortion Control Act of 1982 as amended in 1988 and 1989. 18 Pa. Cons. Stat. §§3203-3220 (1990). The Act requires that a woman seeking an abortion give her informed consent prior to the abortion procedure, and specifies that she be provided with certain information at least 24 hours before the abortion is performed. For a minor to obtain an abortion, the Act requires the informed consent of one of her parents, but provides for a judicial bypass option if the minor does not wish to or cannot obtain a parent's consent. Another provision of the Act requires that, unless certain exceptions apply, a married woman seeking an abortion must sign a statement indicating that she has notified her husband of her intended abortion. The Act exempts compliance with these three requirements in the event of a "medical emergency." In addition to the above provisions regulating the performance of abortions, the Act imposes certain reporting requirements on facilities that provide abortion services. . . .

After considering the fundamental constitutional questions resolved by *Roe,* principles of institutional integrity, and the rule of stare decisis, we are led to conclude this: The essential holding of Roe v. Wade should be retained and once again reaffirmed. . . .

II

Constitutional protection of the woman's decision to terminate her pregnancy derives from the due process clause of the Fourteenth Amendment. . . .

Our law affords constitutional protection to [certain] personal decisions relating to marriage, procreation, contraception, family relationships, child rearing, and education. . . . These matters, involving the most intimate and personal choices a person may make in a lifetime, choices central to personal dignity and autonomy, are central to the liberty protected by the Fourteenth Amendment. At the heart of liberty is the right to define one's own concept of existence, of meaning, of the universe, and of the mystery of human life. Beliefs about these matters could not define the attributes of personhood were they formed under compulsion of the state.

These considerations begin our analysis of the woman's interest in terminating her pregnancy but cannot end it, for this reason: Though the abortion decision may originate within the zone of conscience and belief, it is more than a philosophic exercise. Abortion is a unique act. It is an act fraught with consequences for others: for the woman who must live with the implications of her decision; for the persons who perform and assist in the procedure; for the spouse, family, and society which must confront the knowledge that these procedures exist, procedures some deem nothing short of an act of violence against innocent human life; and, depending on one's beliefs, for the life or potential life that is aborted. Though abortion is conduct, it does not follow that the state is entitled to proscribe it in all instances. That is because the liberty of the woman is at stake in a sense unique to the human condition and so unique to the law. The mother who carries a child to full term is subject to anxieties, to physical constraints, to pain that only she must bear. That these sacrifices have from the beginning of the human race been endured by woman with a pride that ennobles her in the eyes of others and gives to the infant a bond of love cannot alone be grounds for the state to insist she make the sacrifice. Her suffering is too intimate and personal for the state to insist, without more, upon its own vision of the woman's role, however dominant that vision has been in the course of our history and our culture. The destiny of the woman must be shaped to a large extent on her own conception of her spiritual imperatives and her place in society.

It should be recognized, moreover, that in some critical respects the abortion decision is of the same character as the decision to use contraception, to which Griswold v. Connecticut, Eisenstadt v. Baird, and Carey v. Population Services International, afford constitutional protection. We have no doubt as to the correctness of those decisions. . . .

While we appreciate the weight of the arguments made on behalf of the state in the case before us, arguments which in their ultimate formulation conclude that *Roe* should be overruled, the reservations any of us may have in reaffirming the central holding of *Roe* are outweighed by the explication of individual liberty we have given combined with the force of stare decisis. We turn now to that doctrine.

[In Part III, the Justices reviewed the importance of *stare decisis* in constitutional cases, and concluded that *Roe* should not be overruled.]

IV

From what we have said so far it follows that it is a constitutional liberty of the woman to have some freedom to terminate her pregnancy. We conclude that the basic decision in *Roe* was based on a constitutional analysis which we cannot now repudiate. The woman's liberty is not so unlimited, however, that from the outset the state cannot show its concern for the life of the unborn, and at a later point in fetal development the state's interest in life has sufficient force so that the right of the woman to terminate the pregnancy can be restricted. . . .

We conclude the line should be drawn at *viability*, so that before that time the woman has a right to choose to terminate her pregnancy. We adhere to this principle for two reasons. First, as we have said, is the doctrine of *stare decisis*. Any judicial act of line-drawing may seem somewhat arbitrary, but *Roe* was a reasoned statement, elaborated with great care. We have twice reaffirmed it in the face of great opposition. . . .

The second reason is that the concept of viability, as we noted in *Roe*, is the time at which there is a realistic possibility of maintaining and nourishing a life outside the womb, so that the independent existence of the second life can in reason and all fairness be the object of state protection that now overrides the rights of the woman. See Roe v. Wade, 410 U.S., at 163. . . . [T]here may be some medical developments that affect the precise point of viability, but this is an imprecision within tolerable limits. . . . The viability line also has, as a practical matter, an element of fairness. In some broad sense it might be said that a woman who fails to act before viability has consented to the state's intervention on behalf of the developing child.

The woman's right to terminate her pregnancy before viability is the most central principle of Roe v. Wade. It is a rule of law and a component of liberty we cannot renounce. . . . On the other side of the equation is the interest of the state in the protection of potential life. The *Roe* Court recognized the state's "important and legitimate interest in protecting the potentiality of human life." The weight to be given this state interest, not the strength of the woman's interest, was the difficult question faced in *Roe*. . . . [W]e have concluded that the essential holding of *Roe* should be reaffirmed.

Yet it must be remembered that Roe v. Wade speaks with clarity in establishing not only the woman's liberty but also the state's "important and legitimate interest in potential life." That portion of the decision in *Roe* has been given too little acknowledgment and implementation by the Court in its subsequent cases. Those cases decided that any regulation touching upon the abortion decision must survive strict scrutiny, to be sustained only if drawn in narrow terms to further a compelling state interest. Not all of the cases decided under that formulation can be reconciled with the holding in *Roe* itself that the state has legitimate interests in the health of the woman and in protecting the potential life within her. In resolving this tension, we choose to rely upon *Roe*, as against the later cases. . . . Most of our cases since *Roe* have involved the application of rules derived from the trimester framework. . . .

We reject the trimester framework, which we do not consider to be part of the essential holding of *Roe*. Measures aimed at ensuring that a woman's choice contemplates the consequences for the fetus do not necessarily interfere with the right recognized in *Roe*, although those measures have been found to be inconsistent with the rigid trimester framework announced in that case. A logical reading of the central holding in *Roe* itself, and a necessary reconciliation of the liberty of the woman and the interest of the state in promoting prenatal life, require, in our view, that we abandon the trimester framework as a rigid prohibition on all provability regulation aimed at the protection of fetal life. The trimester framework suffers from these basic flaws: In its formulation it misconceives the nature of the pregnant woman's interest; and in practice it undervalues the state's interest in potential life, as recognized in *Roe*. . . .

The very notion that the state has a substantial interest in potential life leads to the conclusion that not all regulations must be deemed unwarranted. Not all burdens on the right to decide whether to terminate a pregnancy will be undue. In our view, the undue burden standard is the appropriate means of reconciling the state's interest with the woman's constitutionally protected liberty. . . . Because we set forth a standard of general application to which we intend to adhere, it is important to clarify what is meant by an undue burden.

A finding of an undue burden is a shorthand for the conclusion that a state regulation has the purpose or effect of placing a substantial obstacle in the path of a woman seeking an abortion of a nonviable fetus. A statute with this purpose is invalid because the means chosen by the state to further the interest in potential life must be calculated to inform the woman's free choice, not hinder it. And a statute which, while furthering the interest in potential life or some other valid state interest, has the effect of placing a substantial obstacle in the path of a woman's choice cannot be considered a permissible means of serving its legitimate ends. . . . Understood another way, we answer the question, left open in previous opinions discussing the undue burden formulation, whether a law designed to further the state's interest in fetal life which imposes an undue burden on the woman's decision before fetal viability could be constitutional. The answer is no.

Some guiding principles should emerge. What is at stake is the woman's right to make the ultimate decision, not a right to be insulated from all others in doing so. Regulations which do no more than create a structural mechanism by which the state, or the parent or guardian of a minor, may express profound respect for the life of the unborn are permitted, if they are not a substantial obstacle to the woman's exercise of the right to choose. Unless it has that effect on her right of choice, a state measure designed to persuade her to choose childbirth over abortion will be upheld if reasonably related to that goal. Regulations designed to foster the health of a woman seeking an abortion are valid if they do not constitute an undue burden. . . .

We give this summary:

(a) To protect the central right recognized by Roe v. Wade while at the same time accommodating the state's profound interest in potential life, we will employ the undue burden analysis as explained in this opinion. An undue burden exists, and therefore a provision of law is invalid, if its purpose or effect is to place a substantial obstacle in the path of a woman seeking an abortion before the fetus attains viability.

(b) We reject the rigid trimester framework of Roe v. Wade. To promote the state's profound interest in potential life, throughout pregnancy the state may take measures to ensure that the woman's choice is informed, and measures designed to advance this interest will not be invalidated as long as their purpose is to persuade the woman to choose childbirth over abortion. These measures must not be an undue burden on the right.

(c) As with any medical procedure, the state may enact regulations to further the health or safety of a woman seeking an abortion. Unnecessary health regulations that have the purpose or effect of presenting a substantial obstacle to a woman seeking an abortion impose an undue burden on the right.

(d) Our adoption of the undue burden analysis does not disturb the central holding of Roe v. Wade, and we reaffirm that holding. Regardless of whether exceptions are made for particular circumstances, a state may not prohibit any woman from making the ultimate decision to terminate her pregnancy before viability.

(e) We also reaffirm *Roe*'s holding that "subsequent to viability, the state in promoting its interest in the potentiality of human life may, if it chooses, regulate, and even proscribe, abortion except where it is necessary, in appropriate medical judgment, for the preservation of the life or health of the mother." Roe v. Wade, 410 U.S., at 164-165.

These principles control our assessment of the Pennsylvania statute, and we now turn to the issue of the validity of its challenged provisions.

V

A

Because it is central to the operation of various other requirements, we begin with the statute's definition of medical emergency. . . . [T]he court of appeals construed the phrase "serious risk" to include those circumstances. It stated: "we read the medical emergency exception as intended by the Pennsylvania legislature to assure that compliance with its abortion regulations would not in any way pose a significant threat to the life or health of a woman." . . . We adhere to that course today, and conclude that, as construed by the court of appeals, the medical emergency definition imposes no undue burden on a woman's abortion right.

B

We next consider the informed consent requirement. Except in a medical emergency, the statute requires that at least 24 hours before performing an abortion a physician inform the woman of the nature of the procedure, the health risks of the abortion and of childbirth, and the "probable gestational age of the unborn child." The physician or a qualified nonphysician must inform the woman of the availability of printed materials published by the state describing the fetus and providing information about medical assistance for childbirth, information about child support from the father, and a list of agencies which provide adoption and other services as alternatives to abortion. An abortion may not be performed unless the woman certifies in writing that she has been informed of the availability of these printed materials and has been provided them if she chooses to view them.

Our prior decisions establish that as with any medical procedure, the state may require a woman to give her written informed consent to an abortion. In this respect, the statute is unexceptional. Petitioners challenge the statute's definition of informed consent because it includes the provision of specific information by the doctor and the mandatory 24-hour waiting period. The conclusions reached by a majority of the Justices in the separate opinions filed today and the undue burden standard adopted in this opinion require us to overrule in part some of the Court's past decisions, decisions driven by the trimester framework's prohibition of all previability regulations designed to further the state's interest in fetal life. . . .

To the extent [that our prior decisions] find a constitutional violation when the government requires, as it does here, the giving of truthful, nonmisleading information about the nature of the procedure, the attendant health risks and those of childbirth, and the "probable gestational age" of the fetus, those cases go too far, are inconsistent with *Roe*'s acknowledgment of an important interest in potential life, and are overruled. . . .

Whether the mandatory 24-hour waiting period is . . . invalid because in practice it is a substantial obstacle to a woman's choice to terminate her pregnancy is a close question. The findings of fact by the district court indicate that because of the distances many women must travel to reach an abortion provider, the practical effect will often be a delay of much more than a day because the waiting period requires that a woman seeking an abortion make at least two visits to the doctor. The district court also found that in many instances this will increase the exposure of women seeking abortions to "the harassment and hostility of anti-abortion protestors demonstrating outside a clinic." As a result, the district court found that for those women who have the fewest financial resources, those who must travel long distances, and those who have difficulty explaining their whereabouts to husbands, employers, or others, the 24-hour waiting period will be "particularly burdensome."

These findings are troubling in some respects, but they do not demonstrate that the waiting period constitutes an undue burden. We do not doubt that, as the district court held, the waiting period has the effect of "increasing the cost and risk of delay of abortions," but the district court did not conclude that the increased costs and potential delays amount to substantial obstacles. . . .

We also disagree with the district court's conclusion that the "particularly burdensome" effects of the waiting period on some women require its invalidation. A particular burden is not of necessity a substantial obstacle. Whether a burden falls on a particular group is a distinct inquiry from whether it is a substantial obstacle even as to the women in that group. And the district court did not conclude that the waiting period is such an obstacle even for the women who are most burdened by it. Hence, on the record before us, and in the context of this facial challenge, we are not convinced that the 24-hour waiting period constitutes an undue burden. . . .

C

Pennsylvania's abortion law provides, except in cases of medical emergency, that no physician shall perform an abortion on a married woman without receiving a signed statement from the woman that she has notified her spouse that she is about to undergo an abortion. The woman has the option of providing an alternative signed statement certifying that her husband is not the man who impregnated her; that her husband could not be located; that the pregnancy is the result of spousal sexual assault which she has reported; or that the woman believes that notifying her husband will cause him or someone else to inflict bodily injury upon her. A physician who performs an abortion on a married woman without receiving the appropriate signed statement will have his or her license revoked, and is liable to the husband for damages. . . .

The spousal notification requirement is thus likely to prevent a significant number of women from obtaining an abortion. It does not merely make abortions a little more difficult or expensive to obtain; for many women, it will impose a substantial obstacle. We must not blind ourselves to the fact that the significant number of women who fear for their safety and the safety of their children are likely to be deterred from procuring an abortion as surely as if the Commonwealth had outlawed abortion in all cases. . . .

The husband's interest in the life of the child his wife is carrying does not permit the state to empower him with this troubling degree of authority over his wife. The contrary view leads to consequences reminiscent of the common law. A husband has no enforceable right to require a wife to advise him before she exercises her personal choices. If a husband's interest in the potential life of the child outweighs a wife's liberty, the state could require a married woman to notify her husband before she uses a postfertilization contraceptive. Perhaps next in line would be a statute requiring pregnant married women to notify their husbands before engaging in conduct causing risks to the fetus. After all, if the husband's interest in the fetus' safety is a sufficient predicate for state regulation, the state could reasonably conclude that pregnant wives should notify their husbands before drinking alcohol or smoking. Perhaps married women should notify their husbands before using contraceptives or before undergoing any type of surgery that may have complications affecting the husband's interest in his wife's reproductive organs. And if a husband's interest justifies notice in any of these cases, one might reasonably argue that it justifies exactly what the *Danforth* Court held it did not justify—a requirement of the husband's consent as well. A state may not give to a man the kind of dominion over his wife that parents exercise over their children.

[The statute] embodies a view of marriage consonant with the common-law status of married women but repugnant to our present understanding of marriage and of the nature of the rights secured by the Constitution. Women do not lose their constitutionally protected liberty when they marry. The Constitution protects all individuals, male or female, married or unmarried, from the abuse of governmental power, even where that power is employed for the supposed benefit of a member of the individual's family. These considerations confirm our conclusion that [the spousal notification provision] is invalid.

D

We next consider the parental consent provision. Except in a medical emergency, an unemancipated young woman under 18 may not obtain an abortion unless she and one of her parents (or guardian) provides informed consent as defined above. If neither a parent nor a guardian provides consent, a court may authorize the performance of an abortion upon a determination that the young woman is mature and capable of giving informed consent and has in fact given her informed consent, or that an abortion would be in her best interests.

We have been over most of this ground before. Our cases establish, and we reaffirm today, that a state may require a minor seeking an abortion to obtain the consent of a parent or guardian, provided that there is an adequate judicial bypass procedure. Under these precedents, in our view, the one-parent consent requirement and judicial bypass procedure are constitutional. . . .

VI

Our Constitution is a covenant running from the first generation of Americans to us and then to future generations. It is a coherent succession. Each generation must learn anew that the Constitution's written terms embody ideas and aspirations that must survive more ages than one. We accept our responsibility not to retreat from interpreting the full meaning of the covenant in light of all of our precedents. We invoke it once again to define the freedom guaranteed by the Constitution's own promise, the promise of liberty. . . .

BLACKMUN, Justice, concurring in part, concurring in the judgment in part, and dissenting in part.

Three years ago, in Webster v. Reproductive Health Serv., 492 U.S. 490 (1989), four Members of this Court appeared poised to "cas[t] into darkness the hopes and visions of every woman in this country" who had come to believe that the Constitution guaranteed her the right to reproductive choice. All that remained between the promise of *Roe* and the darkness of the plurality was a single, flickering flame. Decisions since *Webster* gave little reason to hope that this flame would cast much light. . . . But now, just when so many expected the darkness to fall, the flame has grown bright.

I do not underestimate the significance of today's joint opinion. Yet I remain steadfast in my belief that the right to reproductive choice is entitled to the full protection afforded by this Court before *Webster*. And I fear for the darkness as four Justices anxiously await the single vote necessary to extinguish the light. . . .

Make no mistake, the joint opinion of Justices O'Connor, Kennedy, and Souter is an act of personal courage and constitutional principle. . . .

Today, no less than yesterday, the Constitution and decisions of this Court require that a state's abortion restrictions be subjected to the strictest of judicial scrutiny. Our precedents and the joint opinion's principles require us to subject all non-de minimis abortion regulations to strict scrutiny. Under this standard, the Pennsylvania statute's provisions requiring content-based counseling, a 24-hour delay, informed parental consent, and reporting of abortion-related information must be invalidated. . . .

In one sense, the Court's approach is worlds apart from that of The Chief Justice and Justice Scalia. And yet, in another sense, the distance between the two approaches is short—the distance is but a single vote.

I am 83 years old. I cannot remain on this Court forever, and when I do step down, the confirmation process for my successor well may focus on the issue before us today. That, I regret, may be exactly where the choice between the two worlds will be made.

REHNQUIST, Chief Justice, with whom WHITE, SCALIA, and THOMAS, Justices, join, concurring in the judgment in part and dissenting in part.

The joint opinion, following its newly-minted variation on *stare decisis*, retains the outer shell of Roe v. Wade, but beats a wholesale retreat from the substance of that case. We believe that *Roe* was wrongly decided, and that it can and should be overruled consistently with our traditional approach to *stare decisis* in constitutional cases. We would adopt the approach of the plurality in Webster v. Reproductive Health Services, 492 U.S. 490 (1989), and uphold the challenged provisions of the Pennsylvania statute in their entirety. . . .

In construing the phrase *liberty* incorporated in the due process clause of the Fourteenth Amendment, we have recognized that its meaning extends beyond freedom from physical restraint. In Pierce v. Society of Sisters, 268 U.S. 510 (1925), we held that it included a parent's right to send a child to private school; in Meyer v. Nebraska, 262 U.S. 390 (1923), we held that it included a right to teach a foreign language in a parochial school. Building on these cases, we have held that the term *liberty* includes a right to marry, Loving v. Virginia, 388 U.S. 1 (1967); a right to procreate, Skinner v. Oklahoma ex rel. Williamson, 316 U.S. 535 (1942); and a right to use contraceptives. Griswold v. Connecticut, 381 U.S. 479 (1965); Eisenstadt v. Baird, 405 U.S. 438 (1972). But a reading of these opinions makes clear that they do not endorse any all-encompassing "right of privacy." . . .

Nor do the historical traditions of the American people support the view that the right to terminate one's pregnancy is "fundamental." . . .

We think, therefore, both in view of this history and of our decided cases dealing with substantive liberty under the due process clause, that the Court was mistaken in *Roe* when it classified a woman's decision to terminate her pregnancy as a "fundamental right" that could be abridged only in a manner which withstood "strict scrutiny." . . .

The joint opinion of Justices O'Connor, Kennedy, and Souter cannot bring itself to say that *Roe* was correct as an original matter, but the authors are of the view that "the immediate question is not the soundness of *Roe*'s resolution of the issue, but the precedential force that must be accorded to its holding." Instead of claiming that *Roe* was correct as a matter of original constitutional interpretation, the opinion therefore contains an elaborate discussion of *stare decisis*. This discussion of the principle of *stare decisis* appears to be almost entirely dicta, because the joint opinion does not apply that principle in dealing with *Roe*. *Roe* decided that a woman had a fundamental right to an abortion. The joint opinion rejects that view. *Roe* decided that abortion regulations were to be subjected to "strict scrutiny" and could be justified only in the light of "compelling state interests." The joint opinion rejects that view. *Roe* analyzed abortion regulation under a rigid trimester framework, a framework which has guided this Court's decisionmaking for 19 years. The joint opinion rejects that framework.

The sum of the joint opinion's labors in the name of *stare decisis* and "legitimacy" is this: Roe v. Wade stands as a sort of judicial Potemkin Village, which may be pointed out to passers by as a monument to the importance of adhering to precedent. But behind the facade, an entirely new method of analysis, without any roots in constitutional law, is imported to decide the constitutionality of state laws regulating abortion. Neither *stare decisis* nor "legitimacy" are truly served by such an effort.

We have stated above our belief that the Constitution does not subject state abortion regulations to heightened scrutiny. Accordingly, we think that the correct analysis is that set forth by the plurality opinion in *Webster*. A woman's interest in having an abortion is a form of liberty protected by the due process clause, but states may regulate abortion procedures in ways rationally related to a legitimate state interest. . . .

We therefore would hold that each of the challenged provisions of the Pennsylvania statute is consistent with the Constitution. It bears emphasis that our conclusion in this regard does not carry with it any necessary approval of these regulations. Our task is, as always, to decide only whether the challenged provisions of a law comport with the United States Constitution. If, as we believe, these do, their wisdom as a matter of public policy is for the people of Pennsylvania to decide.

■ GONZALES v. CARHART
550 U.S. 124 (2007)

KENNEDY, J.

These cases require us to consider the validity of the Partial-Birth Abortion Ban Act of 2003 (Act), 18 U.S.C. §1531, a federal statute regulating abortion procedures. In recitations preceding its operative provisions the Act refers to the Court's opinion in Stenberg v. Carhart, 530 U.S. 914 (2000), which [struck down Nebraska's restriction on] abortion procedures used in the later stages of pregnancy. Compared to the state statute at issue in *Stenberg*, the Act is more specific concerning the instances to which it applies and in this respect more precise in its coverage. We conclude the Act should be sustained against the objections lodged by the broad, facial attack brought against it. . . .

I

A

The Act proscribes a particular manner of ending fetal life, so it is necessary here, as it was in *Stenberg*, to discuss abortion procedures in some detail. . . .* Abortion methods vary depending to some extent on the preferences of the physician and, of course, on the term of the pregnancy and the resulting stage of the unborn child's development. Between 85 and 90 percent of the approximately 1.3 million abortions performed each year in the United States take place in the first three months of pregnancy, which is to say in the first trimester. . . . The Act does not regulate these procedures.

Of the remaining abortions that take place each year, most occur in the second trimester. The surgical procedure referred to as "dilation and evacuation" or "D & E" is the usual abortion method in this trimester. . . . Although individual techniques for performing D & E differ, the general steps are the same. . . . A doctor must first dilate the cervix at least to the extent needed to insert surgical instruments into the uterus and to maneuver them to evacuate the fetus. . . .

The abortion procedure that was the impetus for the numerous bans on "partial-birth abortion," including the Act, is a variation of this standard. . . . The medical community has not reached unanimity on the appropriate name for this D & E variation. It has been referred to as "intact D & E," "dilation and extraction" (D & X), and "intact D & X." . . . For discussion purposes this D & E variation will be referred to as intact D & E. The main difference between the two procedures is that in intact D & E a doctor extracts the fetus intact or largely intact with only a few passes [through the cervix, instead of extracting it in pieces]. . . . Intact D & E gained public notoriety when, in 1992, Dr. Martin Haskell gave a presentation describing his method of performing the operation. . . .

D & E and intact D & E are not the only second-trimester abortion methods. Doctors also may abort a fetus through medical induction. The doctor medicates the woman to induce labor, and contractions occur to deliver the fetus. Induction, which unlike D & E should occur in a hospital, can last as little as 6 hours but can take longer than 48. It accounts for about five percent of second-trimester abortions before 20 weeks of gestation and 15 percent of those after 20 weeks. Doctors turn to two other methods of second-trimester abortion, hysterotomy [removal of the fetus via an incision in the abdomen and uterine wall] and hysterectomy [removal of the uterus], only in emergency situations because they carry increased risk of complications. . . .

B

After Dr. Haskell's procedure received public attention, with ensuing and increasing public concern, bans on "partial birth abortion" proliferated. By the time

---

* [Justice Kennedy's opinion includes graphic descriptions of various second-term abortion procedures that have been shortented and summerized in the edited version of the opinion—EDS.]

of the *Stenberg* decision, about 30 States had enacted bans designed to prohibit the procedure. . . . In 1996, Congress also acted to ban partial-birth abortion. President Clinton vetoed the congressional legislation, and the Senate failed to override the veto. Congress approved another bill banning the procedure in 1997, but President Clinton again vetoed it. In 2003, after this Court's [5-4] decision in *Stenberg* [striking down Nebraska's ban], Congress passed [and President Bush signed] the Act at issue here. . . .

The Act responded to *Stenberg* in two ways. First, Congress made factual findings. Congress determined that this Court in *Stenberg* "was required to accept the very questionable findings issued by the district court judge," . . . but that Congress was "not bound to accept the same factual findings." Congress found, among other things, that "[a] moral, medical, and ethical consensus exists that the practice of performing a partial-birth abortion . . . is a gruesome and inhumane procedure that is never medically necessary and should be prohibited." . . . Second, and more relevant here, the Act's language differs from that of the Nebraska statute struck down in *Stenberg*. . . . [The court then summarized the provisions of the Act.]

II

The principles set forth in the joint opinion in *Planned Parenthood of Southeastern Pa. v. Casey*, [supra at page 728] did not find support from all those who join the instant opinion. . . . Whatever one's views concerning the *Casey* joint opinion, it is evident a premise central to its conclusion — that the government has a legitimate and substantial interest in preserving and promoting fetal life — would be repudiated were the Court now to affirm the judgments of the Courts of Appeals.

[Applying the principles of *Casey*] . . . we must determine whether the Act furthers the legitimate interest of the Government in protecting the life of the fetus that may become a child. . . . We assume the following principles for the purposes of this opinion. Before viability, a State "may not prohibit any woman from making the ultimate decision to terminate her pregnancy" [*Casey*, 505 U.S. at 879 (plurality opinion)]. It also may not impose upon this right an undue burden, which exists if a regulation's "purpose or effect is to place a substantial obstacle in the path of a woman seeking an abortion before the fetus attains viability." . . . On the other hand, "[r]egulations which do no more than create a structural mechanism by which the State, or the parent or guardian of a minor, may express profound respect for the life of the unborn are permitted, if they are not a substantial obstacle to the woman's exercise of the right to choose." . . . *Casey*, in short, struck a balance. The balance was central to its holding. We now apply its standard to the cases at bar. . . .

[The Act] regulates and proscribes, with exceptions or qualifications to be discussed, performing the intact D & E procedure. Respondents agree the Act encompasses intact D & E, but they contend its additional reach is both unclear and excessive. Respondents assert that, at the least, the Act is void for vagueness because its scope is indefinite. In the alternative, respondents argue the Act's text proscribes all D & Es. Because D & E is the most common second-trimester abortion method, respondents suggest the Act imposes an undue burden. In this litigation the Attorney General does not dispute that the Act would impose an undue burden if it covered standard D & E.

We conclude that the Act is not void for vagueness, does not impose an undue burden from any overbreadth, and is not invalid on its face.

The Act punishes "knowingly perform[ing]" a "partial-birth abortion." §1531(a). It defines the unlawful abortion in explicit terms. . . . "As generally stated, the void-for-vagueness doctrine requires that a penal statute define the criminal offense with sufficient definiteness that ordinary people can understand what conduct is prohibited and in a manner that does not encourage arbitrary and discriminatory enforcement." . . . The Act satisfies both requirements. . . .

Unlike the statutory language in *Stenberg* that prohibited the delivery of a " 'substantial portion' " of the fetus—where a doctor might question how much of the fetus is a substantial portion—the Act defines the line between potentially criminal conduct on the one hand and lawful abortion on the other. . . . Doctors performing D & E will know that if they do not deliver a living fetus to an anatomical landmark [referring to the delivery of the fetus to a certain point as specified in the statute] they will not face criminal liability. This conclusion is buttressed by the intent that must be proved to impose liability. The Court has made clear that scienter requirements alleviate vagueness concerns. . . .

We next determine whether the Act imposes an undue burden, as a facial matter, because its restrictions on second-trimester abortions are too broad. A review of the statutory text discloses the limits of its reach. The Act prohibits intact D & E; and, notwithstanding respondents' arguments, it does not prohibit the D & E procedure in which the fetus is removed in parts. . . .

IV

. . . The abortions affected by the Act's regulations take place both previability and postviability. . . . Under the principles accepted as controlling here, . . . the question is whether the Act, measured by its text in this facial attack, imposes a substantial obstacle to late-term, but previability, abortions. The Act does not on its face impose a substantial obstacle, and we reject this further facial challenge to its validity.

A

The Act's purposes are set forth in recitals preceding its operative provisions. A description of the prohibited abortion procedure demonstrates the rationale for the congressional enactment. The Act proscribes a method of abortion in which a fetus is killed just inches before completion of the birth process. Congress stated as follows: "Implicitly approving such a brutal and inhumane procedure by choosing not to prohibit it will further coarsen society to the humanity of not only newborns, but all vulnerable and innocent human life, making it increasingly difficult to protect such life." The Act expresses respect for the dignity of human life.

Congress was concerned, furthermore, with the effects on the medical community and on its reputation caused by the practice of partial-birth abortion. The findings in the Act explain: "Partial-birth abortion . . . confuses the medical, legal, and ethical duties of physicians to preserve and promote life, as the physician acts directly against the physical life of a child, whom he or she had just delivered, all but the head, out of the womb, in order to end that life." There can be no doubt the government "has an interest in protecting the integrity and ethics of the medical profession." Washington v. Glucksberg, 521 U.S. 702 (1997). . . .

Casey reaffirmed these governmental objectives. The government may use its voice and its regulatory authority to show its profound respect for the life within the woman. A central premise of the opinion was that the Court's precedents after *Roe* had "undervalue[d] the State's interest in potential life." 505 U.S. at 873 (plurality opinion). . . . The plurality opinion indicated "[t]he fact that a law which serves a valid purpose, one not designed to strike at the right itself, has the incidental effect of making it more difficult or more expensive to procure an abortion cannot be enough to invalidate it." Id. at 874. This was not an idle assertion. The three premises of *Casey* must coexist. . . . The third premise, that the State, from the inception of the pregnancy, maintains its own regulatory interest in protecting the life of the fetus that may become a child, cannot be set at naught by interpreting *Casey*'s requirement of a health exception so it becomes tantamount to allowing a doctor to choose the abortion method he or she might prefer. Where it has a rational basis to act, and it does not impose an undue burden, the State may use its regulatory power to bar certain procedures and substitute others, all in furtherance of its legitimate interests in regulating the medical profession in order to promote respect for life, including life of the unborn.

The Act's ban on abortions that involve partial delivery of a living fetus furthers the Government's objectives. No one would dispute that, for many, D & E is a procedure itself laden with the power to devalue human life. Congress could nonetheless conclude that the type of abortion proscribed by the Act requires specific regulation because it implicates additional ethical and moral concerns that justify a special prohibition. Congress determined that the abortion methods it proscribed had a "disturbing similarity to the killing of a newborn infant," and thus it was concerned with "draw[ing] a bright line that clearly distinguishes abortion and infanticide." . . . The Court has in the past confirmed the validity of drawing boundaries to prevent certain practices that extinguish life and are close to actions that are condemned. *Glucksberg* found reasonable the State's "fear that permitting assisted suicide will start it down the path to voluntary and perhaps even involuntary euthanasia." 521 U.S. at 732-35. . . .

Respect for human life finds an ultimate expression in the bond of love the mother has for her child. The Act recognizes this reality as well. Whether to have an abortion requires a difficult and painful moral decision. . . . While we find no reliable data to measure the phenomenon, it seems unexceptionable to conclude some women come to regret their choice to abort the infant life they once created and sustained. Severe depression and loss of esteem can follow. . . .

In a decision so fraught with emotional consequence some doctors may prefer not to disclose precise details of the means that will be used, confining themselves to the required statement of risks the procedure entails. From one standpoint this ought not to be surprising. Any number of patients facing imminent surgical procedures would prefer not to hear all details, lest the usual anxiety preceding invasive medical procedures become the more intense. This is likely the case with the abortion procedures here in issue. . . .

It is, however, precisely this lack of information concerning the way in which the fetus will be killed that is of legitimate concern to the State. *Casey*, 505 U.S. at 873 (plurality opinion) ("States are free to enact laws to provide a reasonable framework for a woman to make a decision that has such profound and lasting meaning"). The State has an interest in ensuring so grave a choice is well informed. It is self-evident that a mother who comes to regret her choice to abort must struggle with grief more anguished and sorrow more profound when she learns, only after the event, what she once did not know . . . [about how the procedure is performed].

It is a reasonable inference that a necessary effect of the regulation and the knowledge it conveys will be to encourage some women to carry the infant to full term, thus reducing the absolute number of late-term abortions. The medical profession, furthermore, may find different and less shocking methods to abort the fetus in the second trimester, thereby accommodating legislative demand. The State's interest in respect for life is advanced by the dialogue that better informs the political and legal systems, the medical profession, expectant mothers, and society as a whole of the consequences that follow from a decision to elect a late-term abortion. . . . In sum, we reject the contention that the congressional purpose of the Act was "to place a substantial obstacle in the path of a woman seeking an abortion." 505 U.S. at 878 (plurality opinion).

B

The Act's furtherance of legitimate government interests bears upon, but does not resolve, the next question: whether the Act has the effect of imposing an unconstitutional burden on the abortion right because it does not allow use of the barred procedure where " 'necessary, in appropriate medical judgment, for [the] preservation of the . . . health of the mother.' " [citing Ayotte v. Planned Parenthood of Northern New Eng., 546 U.S. 320] . . . The prohibition in the Act would be unconstitutional, under precedents we here assume to be controlling, if it "subject[ed] [women] to significant health risks." [Id. at 328.] . . . In *Ayotte* the parties agreed a health exception to the challenged parental-involvement statute was necessary "to avert serious and often irreversible damage to [a pregnant minor's] health." . . . Here, by contrast, whether the Act creates significant health risks for women has been a contested factual question. The evidence presented in the trial courts and before Congress demonstrates both sides have medical support for their position. . . .

The question becomes whether the Act can stand when this medical uncertainty persists. The Court's precedents instruct that the Act can survive this facial attack. The Court has given state and federal legislatures wide discretion to pass legislation in areas where there is medical and scientific uncertainty. [The Court cites, among other cases, Jacobson v. Commonwealth of Massachusetts, 197 U.S. 11 (1905), discussed in Chapter 8 at page 924.] . . . Physicians are not entitled to ignore regulations that direct them to use reasonable alternative procedures. The law need not give abortion doctors unfettered choice in the course of their medical practice, nor should it elevate their status above other physicians in the medical community. . . . Medical uncertainty does not foreclose the exercise of legislative power in the abortion context any more than it does in other contexts. . . . The medical uncertainty over whether the Act's prohibition creates significant health risks provides a sufficient basis to conclude in this facial attack that the Act does not impose an undue burden. . . .

In reaching the conclusion the Act does not require a health exception we reject certain arguments made by the parties on both sides of these cases. On the one hand, the Attorney General urges us to uphold the Act on the basis of the congressional findings alone. Although we review congressional factfinding under a deferential standard, we do not in the circumstances here place dispositive weight on Congress' findings. The Court retains an independent constitutional duty to review factual findings where constitutional rights are at stake. . . . As respondents have noted, and the District Courts recognized, some recitations in the Act are factually incorrect. . . .

On the other hand, relying on the Court's opinion in *Stenberg*, respondents contend that an abortion regulation must contain a health exception "if 'substantial medical authority supports the proposition that banning a particular procedure could endanger women's health.'" . . . As illustrated by respondents' arguments and the decisions of the Courts of Appeals, *Stenberg* has been interpreted to leave no margin of error for legislatures to act in the face of medical uncertainty. . . . A zero tolerance policy would strike down legitimate abortion regulations, like the present one, if some part of the medical community were disinclined to follow the proscription. This is too exacting a standard to impose on the legislative power, exercised in this instance under the Commerce Clause, to regulate the medical profession. Considerations of marginal safety, including the balance of risks, are within the legislative competence when the regulation is rational and in pursuit of legitimate ends. When standard medical options are available, mere convenience does not suffice to displace them; and if some procedures have different risks than others, it does not follow that the State is altogether barred from imposing reasonable regulations. The Act is not invalid on its face where there is uncertainty over whether the barred procedure is ever necessary to preserve a woman's health, given the availability of other abortion procedures that are considered to be safe alternatives. . . .

In these circumstances the proper means to consider exceptions is by as-applied challenge. . . . This is the proper manner to protect the health of the woman if it can be shown that in discrete and well-defined instances a particular condition has or is likely to occur in which the procedure prohibited by the Act must be used. In an as-applied challenge the nature of the medical risk can be better quantified and balanced than in a facial attack. . . .

Respondents have not demonstrated that the Act, as a facial matter, is void for vagueness, or that it imposes an undue burden on a woman's right to abortion based on its overbreadth or lack of a health exception. For these reasons the judgments of the Courts of Appeals for the Eighth and Ninth Circuits are reversed. . . .

[Justices Roberts, Scalia, Thomas, and Alito joined the majority opinion. Justice Thomas wrote a concurring opinion, joined by Justice Scalia, "reiterat[ing] my view that the Court's abortion jurisprudence . . . has no basis in the Constitution."]

GINSBURG, J., dissenting. . . .

Seven years ago, in *Stenberg*, . . . the Court invalidated a Nebraska statute criminalizing the performance of a medical procedure that, in the political arena, has been dubbed "partial-birth abortion." . . . [T]he Court held the Nebraska statute unconstitutional in part because it lacked the requisite protection for the preservation of a woman's health. . . .

Today's decision is alarming. It refuses to take *Casey* and *Stenberg* seriously. It tolerates, indeed applauds, federal intervention to ban nationwide a procedure found necessary and proper in certain cases by the American College of Obstetricians and Gynecologists (ACOG). It blurs the line, firmly drawn in *Casey* between previability and postviability abortions. And, for the first time since *Roe*, the Court blesses a prohibition with no exception safeguarding a woman's health.

I dissent from the Court's disposition. Retreating from prior rulings that abortion restrictions cannot be imposed absent an exception safeguarding a woman's health, the Court upholds an Act that surely would not survive under the close scrutiny that previously attended state-decreed limitations on a woman's reproductive choices.

I

As *Casey* comprehended, at stake in cases challenging abortion restrictions is a woman's "control over her [own] destiny." . . . Women, it is now acknowledged, have the talent, capacity, and right "to participate equally in the economic and social life of the Nation." . . . Their ability to realize their full potential, the Court recognized, is intimately connected to "their ability to control their reproductive lives." . . . Thus, legal challenges to undue restrictions on abortion procedures do not seek to vindicate some generalized notion of privacy; rather, they center on a woman's autonomy to determine her life's course, and thus to enjoy equal citizenship stature. See, e.g., Siegel, Reasoning from the Body: A Historical Perspective on Abortion Regulation and Questions of Equal Protection, 44 Stan. L. Rev. 261 (1992); Law, Rethinking Sex and the Constitution, 132 U. Pa. L. Rev. 955 (1984).

In keeping with this comprehension of the right to reproductive choice, the Court has consistently required that laws regulating abortion, at any stage of pregnancy and in all cases, safeguard a woman's health. . . . We have thus ruled that a State must avoid subjecting women to health risks not only where the pregnancy itself creates danger, but also where state regulation forces women to resort to less safe methods of abortion. . . .

[The courts below] made findings after full trials at which all parties had the opportunity to present their best evidence. . . . According to the expert testimony plaintiffs introduced, the safety advantages of intact D & E are marked for women with certain medical conditions, for example, uterine scarring, bleeding disorders, heart disease, or compromised immune systems. . . . Further, plaintiffs' experts testified that intact D & E is significantly safer for women with certain pregnancy-related conditions, such as placenta previa and accreta and for women carrying fetuses with certain abnormalities, such as severe hydrocephalus. . . . Based on thoroughgoing review of the trial evidence and the congressional record, each of the District Courts to consider the issue rejected Congress' findings as unreasonable and not supported by the evidence. . . . The District Courts' findings merit this Court's respect. . . .

II

The Court offers flimsy and transparent justifications for upholding a nationwide ban on intact D & E. . . . The law saves not a single fetus from destruction, for it targets only a *method* of performing abortion. . . . And surely the statute was not designed to protect the lives or health of pregnant women. . . . In short, the Court upholds a law that, while doing nothing to "preserv[e] . . . fetal life," . . . bars a woman from choosing intact D & E although her doctor "reasonably believes [that procedure] will best protect [her]." . . .

Ultimately, the Court admits that "moral concerns" are at work, concerns that could yield prohibitions on any abortion. . . . Notably, the concerns expressed are untethered to any ground genuinely serving the Government's interest in preserving life. By allowing such concerns to carry the day and case, overriding fundamental rights, the Court dishonors our precedent. . . .

Revealing in this regard, the Court invokes an antiabortion shibboleth for which it concededly has no reliable evidence: Women who have abortions come to regret their choices, and consequently suffer from "[s]evere depression and loss of esteem." . . .[7] Because of women's fragile emotional state and because of the "bond of love the mother has for her child," the Court worries, doctors may with-hold information about the nature of the intact D & E procedure. . . . The solution the Court approves, then, is *not* to require doctors to inform women, accurately and adequately, of the different procedures and their attendant risks. . . . Instead, the Court deprives women of the right to make an autonomous choice, even at the expense of their safety. . . . This way of thinking reflects ancient notions about women's place in the family and under the Constitution-ideas that have long since been discredited. . . .

One wonders how long a line that saves no fetus from destruction will hold in face of the Court's "moral concerns." . . . The Court's hostility to the right *Roe* and *Casey* secured is not concealed. Throughout, the opinion refers to obstetrician-gynecologists and surgeons who perform abortions not by the titles of their medical specialties, but by the pejorative label "abortion doctor." . . . A fetus is described as an "unborn child," and as a "baby," . . . second-trimester, previability abortions are referred to as "late-term," . . . ; and the reasoned medical judgments of highly trained doctors are dismissed as "preferences" motivated by "mere convenience." . . . Instead of the heightened scrutiny we have previously applied, the Court deter-mines that a "rational" ground is enough to uphold the Act. . . . And, most trou-bling, *Casey*'s principles, confirming the continuing vitality of "the essential holding of *Roe*" are merely "assume[d]" for the moment, . . . rather than "retained" or "reaf-firmed" . . . .

Though today's opinion does not go so far as to discard *Roe* or *Casey*, the Court, differently composed than it was when we last considered a restrictive abor-tion regulation, is hardly faithful to our earlier invocations of "the rule of law" and the "principles of *stare decisis.*" . . . In candor, the Act, and the Court's defense of it, cannot be understood as anything other than an effort to chip away at a right declared again and again by this Court. . . .

[This dissent was joined by Justices Stevens, Souter, and Breyer.]

Notes: The Post-*Casey* and Post-*Gonzales* Landscape, including *Whole Women's Health v. Hellerstedt*

1. *Stare Decisis.* Did *Casey* overturn *Roe*? Does the Court's discussion of *stare deci-sis* in the abortion cases seem persuasive? What does it mean to reaffirm Roe v. Wade while overturning the trimester framework, as the Court did in *Casey*? What types of cases are now likely to have different results?

7. The Court is surely correct that, for most women, abortion is a painfully difficult decision. . . . But "neither the weight of the scientific evidence to date nor the observable reality of 33 years of legal abortion in the United States comports with the idea that having an abortion is any more dangerous to a woman's long-term mental health than delivering and parenting a child that she did not intend to have. . . ." Cohen, Abortion and Mental Health: Myths and Realities, 9 Guttmacher Policy Rev. 8 (2006). . . .

The *Gonzales* Court clearly was forced to wrestle with the significance of *stare decisis* given the Court's invalidation of a similar statute in *Stenberg*. In *Stenberg*, the majority seemed to constrain the state's ability to prohibit abortion procedures:

> In sum, Nebraska has not convinced us that a health exception is "never necessary to preserve the health of women."... Rather, a statute that altogether forbids D & X [referred to as an "intact D & E" in *Gonzales*] creates a significant health risk. The statute consequently must contain a health exception. This is not to say ... that a State is prohibited from proscribing an abortion procedure whenever a particular physician deems the procedure preferable.... But where substantial medical authority supports the proposition that banning a particular abortion procedure could endanger women's health, *Casey* requires the statute to include a health exception when the procedure is " 'necessary, in appropriate medical judgment, for the preservation of the life or health of the mother.'"

530 U.S. 914 at 937-938. Does the *Gonzales* majority overturn *Stenberg*?

The *Gonzales* decision suggested that governments would be given more latitude to regulate abortion to protect "moral values" and women's interests (as defined by the *Gonzales* majority rather than by Justice Ginsburg). Justice Ginsburg explicitly discusses the impact of the changes in the Court's membership since *Casey* and *Stenberg* in her dissent and expresses concern about the future of the abortion right. See R. Alta Charo, The Partial Death of Abortion Rights, 356 New Eng. J. Med. 2125 (2007). Justices Souter and Stevens have since been replaced by Justices Kagan and Sotomayor, who support the continuation of constitutional protections; Justice Scalia has been replaced by Justice Gorsuch, who is expected to take a similar negative position.

2. *Abortion and Equal Protection.* Some commentators have argued that restrictions on abortion ought to be challenged under equal protection grounds. Restrictions on abortion impose a burden that is suffered exclusively by pregnant women. Several scholars have argued that the right recognized in *Roe* would have been better defended on equal protection grounds. They argue first that, forcing women to sacrifice their lives and health to bear children prevents them from full and equal enjoyment of the rights of citizenship. Abortion restrictions inhibit the economic independence of women, and embody a paternalistic perspective that confines women to the domestic sphere. Additionally, women of limited resources are acutely impacted by restrictions, and equal protection is unfulfilled in a system that "condemns the poor to a Hobson's choice of compulsory motherhood or illegal and unsafe abortion." Jack M. Balkin, (judgment of the Court), in What *Roe v. Wade* Should Have Said: The Nation's Top Legal Experts Rewrite America's Most Controversial Decision 31-62 (Jack M. Balkin ed., 2005). This Equal Protection approach finds some support in Justice Ginsburg's dissent in *Gonzales*, which begins with a description of the abortion right as necessary to ensure women's liberty and equality. Is there any other support for this view in the Court's recent decisions? See Jennifer S. Hendricks, Body and Soul: Equality, Pregnancy, and the Unitary Right to Abortion, 45 Harv. C.R.-C.L. L. Rev. 329 (2010); Priscilla J. Smith, Give Justice Ginsburg What She Wants: Using Sex Equality Arguments to Demand Examination of the Legitimacy of State Interests in Abortion Regulation, 34 Harv. J. L. & Gender 377 (2011). But see Charles I. Lugosi, Conforming to the Rule of Law: When Person and Human Being Finally Mean the Same Thing in Fourteenth Amendment Jurisprudence, 22 Issues L. & Med. 119 (2006) (arguing that the Supreme Court should reconsider its failure to

find fetuses protected under the Equal Protection Clause). For interesting alternative arguments, see Andrew Koppelman, Originalism, Abortion, and the Thirteenth Amendment, 112 Columbia L. Rev. 1917 (2012) (arguing that banning abortion and compelling women to bear children would violate the Thirteenth Amendment).

3. *The Personhood Movement.* The Personhood movement seeks to categorize fetuses as persons and adopts a definition of "person" that includes all homo sapiens, "without regard to sentience or stage of development." Jonathan F. Will, Beyond Abortion: Why the Personhood Movement Implicates Reproductive Choice, 39 Am. J. L. & Med. 573 (2013). Personhood USA, the main organizing force of the movement, identifies itself as a Christian ministry and operates at a national and state level seeking personhood rights for fetuses. The movement has not had much success with failed ballot initiatives in Colorado, North Dakota, and Mississippi, as well as a failed constitutional amendment in Mississippi. Opponents to the Personhood movement have highlighted the effects of the movement on reproductive technology, which has the support of some abortion opponents. The movement's definition of "personhood" is ambiguous, and it can have serious effects on other areas of health care. The Mississippi proposed constitutional amendment defined person as "every human being from the moment of fertilization, cloning, or the functional equivalent thereof." I. Glenn Cohen, Religion and Reproductive Technology, in Law, Religion, and Health in the United States (Holly Fernandez Lynch, I. Glenn Cohen, Elizabeth Sepper eds, 2017). This could mean a "penetration of the egg by a sperm, assembly of the new embryonic genome, successful activation of that genome, and implantation of the embryo in the uterus." Id. The definition of "person" would impact other areas of health care such as assistive reproductive technology, prenatal care, and ectopic pregnancies. This has thus far prevented the movement from enacting its legislative agenda. See Judith Daar, The Outdated Pregnancy, 35 J. Legal Med. 505, 527 (2014); Maya Manian, Lessons from Personhood's Defeat: Abortion Restrictions and Side Effects on Women's Health, 74 Ohio St. L. J. 75 (2013); Jonathan F. Will, Conscience Legislation, the Personhood Movement, and Access to Emergency Contraception, 4 Faulkner L. Rev. 411 (2013).

4. *The Undue Burden Standard.* The Supreme Court held in *Roe*, at least by implication, that states could require that first-trimester abortions be performed by physicians. 410 U.S. 113, 163 (1973). The state's interest in the health of a pregnant woman would become compelling at the point where the risks of the abortion outweighed the risks of carrying the pregnancy to term, or at the end of the first trimester. After this point, "a state may regulate the abortion procedure to the extent that the regulation reasonably relates to the preservation and protection of maternal health." States may establish requirements for providers and facilities. At the point of fetal viability, sometime around the end of the second trimester, a state may assert its compelling interest in protecting fetal life by prohibiting abortion, except where the procedure was necessary to preserve the life or health of the pregnant woman. Id. Is *Gonzales* consistent with this framework? What interests support regulation of the type of abortion procedure used prior to viability? The Supreme Court confirmed that states may require that physicians perform abortions in Mazurek v. Armstrong, 520 U.S. 968 (1997) (rejecting contention that requirement placed an undue burden on access to abortion). See also Guttmacher Institute, An Overview of Abortion Laws (Mar. 1, 2016) (38 states require use of licensed physicians). As might be expected, *Casey* has been cited in more than 1,400 judicial decisions since its publication. It has been used to uphold some state abortion regulations, see, e.g., Barnes v. Moore,

970 F.2d 12 (5th Cir. 1992), and to strike down others, see, e.g., Stenberg v. Carhart, supra. Litigants have sought to use *Casey* in other socially controversial areas. See, e.g., Washington v. Glucksberg, 521 U.S. 702 (1997) (Court rejects view that *Casey* supports a constitutional right to assisted suicide). Will the Court's decision in *Gonzales* have a ripple effect in other areas? See Abigail Alliance for Better Access to Developmental Drugs v. von Eschenbach, 495 F.3d 695, 714 (D.C. Cir. 2007) (en banc) (citing *Gonzales* in a case involving limiting patient access to experimental therapies for the power of legislatures to act even where scientific uncertainty exists).

5. Whole Women's Health v. Hellerstedt. In an important new chapter in its abortion jurisprudence, the Supreme Court decided Whole Women's Health v. Hellerstedt, 136 S. Ct. 2292 (2016). The case involved a challenge to two main provisions of Texas' H.B.2: the admitting privileges requirement and surgical-center requirement. "The 'admitting-privileges requirement' provide[d] that a 'physician performing or inducing an abortion . . . must, on the date [of service], have active admitting privileges at a hospital . . . located not further than 30 miles from the' abortion facility, "while" the 'surgical-center requirement' require[d] an 'abortion facility' to meet the 'minimum standards . . . for ambulatory surgical centers' under Texas law." Id. at 2296. The Supreme Court, in a 5-3 decision authored by Justice Breyer and joined by Justices Kennedy, Ginsburg, Sotomayor, and Kagan rejected Texas' attempt to defend the law as neutral regulation of physicians and facilities aimed at protecting health care quality. Instead, the Court held "[w]e agree with the District Court that the surgical-center requirement, like the admitting-privileges requirement, provides few, if any, health benefits for women, poses a substantial obstacle to women seeking abortions, and constitutes an 'undue burden' on their constitutional right to do so." Id. at 2318. Beyond the outcome, the case suggests two important doctrinal changes—though it is hard to tell whether they will take root. First, the opinion takes a very different attitude toward legislative deference than did *Gonzales*:

> The statement that legislatures, and not courts, must resolve questions of medical uncertainty is also inconsistent with this Court's case law. Instead, the Court, when determining the constitutionality of laws regulating abortion procedures, has placed considerable weight upon evidence and argument presented in judicial proceedings . . . Although [in *Gonzales*] we upheld a statute regulating abortion, we did not do so solely on the basis of legislative findings. Unlike in *Gonzales*, the relevant statute here does not set forth any legislative findings. Rather, one is left to infer that the legislature sought to further a constitutionally acceptable objective (namely, protecting women's health). For a district court to give significant weight to evidence in the judicial record in these circumstances is consistent with this Court's case law.

Id. at 2310. Second, the Court corrected the lower court's statement of the operative constitutional test, which "may be read to imply that a district court should not consider the existence or nonexistence of medical benefits when considering whether a regulation of abortion constitutes an undue burden. The rule announced in *Casey*, however, requires that courts consider the burdens a law imposes on abortion access together with the benefits those laws confer." Id. at 2309. Justice Thomas wrote a dissent for himself and joined Justice Alito's (as did Justice Roberts') separate dissent. Do you agree with the Court's majority that its approach is consistent with *Gonzales*?

6. *Later Abortions.* Second-trimester abortions are relatively rare. Karen Pazol et al., Abortion Surveillance—United States, 2012, 64 MMWR 1, 8 (Nov. 27, 2015) (No. SS-10) (7.2% of reported abortions occurred at 14 to 20 weeks of gestation;

only 1.3% occurred at 21 weeks or greater). See also Lisa Haddad et al., Changes in Abortion Provider Practices in Response to the Partial-Birth Abortion Ban Act of 2003, 79 Contraception 379 (2009).

What explains the significant legislative activity in this area, given the relative rarity of these procedures? The *Stenberg* decision discussed in *Gonzales* arguably presented a blueprint for states interested in enacting limits on late-term abortions, yet most legislatures did not review or revise their partial-birth abortion bans to conform with *Stenberg*'s criteria. Why did Congress finally enact the "partial-birth" abortion ban after the Court's decision in *Stenberg*?

Most states have enacted legislation limiting or prohibiting later abortions or banning "partial-birth" abortion. Guttmacher Institute, State Policies on Later Abortions (Nov. 1, 2012) (listing states and status of court challenges); Guttmacher Institute, Bans on "Partial-Birth" Abortion (Mar. 1, 2016) (32 states have enacted bans on partial-birth abortions), both available at www.guttmacher.org/. Late-term abortions remain extremely controversial. Joe Stumpe, Jurors Acquit Kansas Doctor in a Late-Term Abortion Case, N.Y. Times, Mar. 28, 2009, at A11; Monica Davey, Abortion Foe Found Guilty in Doctor's Killing, N.Y. Times, Jan. 30, 2010, at A12.

7. *New State Attempts at Restrictions.* Changes in the political climate and the composition of the Supreme Court have resulted in sharp increases in state legislation relating to abortion, including efforts to ban abortion preemptively should Roe v. Wade be overturned. According to a 2016 report by the Guttmacher Institute, "[i]n the 43 years since the U.S. Supreme Court handed down *Roe v. Wade*, states have enacted 1,074 abortion restrictions. Of these, 288 (27%) have been enacted just since 2010." See Elizabeth Nash et al., Laws Affecting Reproductive Health and Rights: 2015 State Policy Review; Guttmacher Institute, Last Five Years Account for More Than One-quarter of All Abortion Restrictions Enacted Since Roe (Jan. 13, 2016).

These restrictions have taken many forms but there are a few prominent types that have been challenged:

a. *Fetal Pain Laws.* A relatively new type of state legislation focuses on the concept of fetal pain as a basis for banning later abortions, typically after 20 weeks. See Neb. Rev. St. §38-2021 (unprofessional conduct includes performance of abortion in violation of Pain-Capable Unborn Child Protection Act). See I. Glenn Cohen & Sadath Sayeed, Fetal Pain, Abortion, Viability and the Constitution, 39 J. L. Med. & Ethics 235 (2011) (finding legislation unconstitutional but noting close question and discussing the lack of scientific evidence for its claims). The Supreme Court has stated that preservation of fetal life becomes compelling only at viability and has not addressed fetal pain. Fetal pain laws attempt to capitalize on this gap. In Isaacson v. Horne, 716 F.3d 1213 (9th Cir. 2013), cert. denied, 134 S. Ct. 905 (2014), the Court of Appeals identified viability as the critical factor for determining constitutionality and held that the state "may not deprive a woman of the choice to terminate her pregnancy at any point prior to viability." 716 F.3d 1231 (9th Cir. 2013).

b. *Targeted Restrictions on Abortion Providers ("TRAP") Laws.* States have increased reporting, facilities, and inspection requirements for abortion providers. These regulations generally reduce the number of abortion providers and increase the costs of providing the procedure. Twenty-four states have enacted TRAP laws. Requirements include room size, corridor width, and relationships with hospitals, and are outside the scope of what is necessary to ensure patient safety. Guttmacher Institute, Targeted Regulation of Abortion Providers (Mar. 4, 2016). Although many regulations will be upheld given the Supreme Court's explicit authorization of certain forms of state provider regulation, providers and activists have successfully challenged some provisions under the undue burden standard. In 2012, a lower court issued a preliminary injunction against enforcement of a new Mississippi statute requiring hospital admitting privileges and board certification in obstetrics and gynecology for abortion providers; the legislation had threatened to close the state's only abortion clinic. Jackson Women's Health Organization v. Currier, 2012 WL 2886715 (S.D. Miss.); and Dawn Johnson, "TRAP"ing *Roe* in Indiana and a Common-Ground Alternative, 118 Yale L. J. 1356 (2009) (noting impact of increasing regulation of providers). The Supreme Court recently addressed the constitutionality of TRAP laws in Whole Womans Health v. Hellerstedt, 136 S. Ct. 2292 (2016), discussed above.

8. *Medically Induced Abortions.* Women who face difficulties accessing surgical abortions may turn to mifepristone. In 2000, mifepristone was approved by the FDA for use in terminating pregnancies in accordance with particular dosing requirements developed in the 1980s. Subsequent research resulted in changes in the clinical practice for the use of the drug, including a reduction in the required dosage and a slight expansion of the gestational period during which the drug could be used. The change in dosing results in fewer side effects and requires fewer visits to a provider. In 2016, the FDA approved a revised regimen for the drug with smaller dosage. The revision increased in the number of days a woman would be able to take the medication, and decreased in the number of clinician visits required. Women may still face barriers to medication-induced abortions. Thirty-seven states require a licensed physician to provide the medication, and eighteen require clinicians to be physically present with the patient when prescribing abortion-inducing drugs. Guttmacher Institute, State Policies in Brief: Medication Abortion (Mar. 1, 2016). Can a state criminally prosecute a woman for terminating her pregnancy using a drug purchased over the Internet? McCormack v. Hiedeman, 694 F.3d 1004 (9th Cir. 2012) (finding undue burden where a state felony statute was used to prosecute a woman where the pregnancy was not terminated by a physician under a regulatory regime).

9. *Minors and Abortion.* Does the right established in Roe v. Wade apply to minors as well? Even if one accepts the proposition that women have a right to choose abortion, it does not necessarily follow that minors should be given the right to secure an abortion without parental notification or even consent. The Supreme Court has supported a minor's right of access to contraceptives, but the risks associated with an abortion clearly outweigh those created by the use of condoms. Parents ordinarily must give consent for their children to undergo medical procedures, absent an emergency, and abortion is a morally and religiously sensitive medical procedure. Notifying a parent of a child's pregnancy can, additionally, give parents important information about a child's participation in sexual activities. On

the other hand, children have constitutional rights in many circumstances. A significant percentage of teenagers may have the maturity to make their own abortion determinations. Further, a minor's right to make these decisions free from parental interference may be an important issue in abusive or incestuous homes.

The post-*Roe* Supreme Court struggled to determine whether and when a minor had a right to choose abortion. See, e.g., Ohio v. Akron Center for Reproductive Health, 497 U.S. 502 (1990); Hodgson v. Minnesota, 497 U.S. 417 (1990). These decisions were marked by deep divisions within the Court, with a majority of Justices upholding state parental notification or consent rules so long as they were accompanied by a judicial bypass procedure that permitted a mature minor to obtain judicial approval of her decision. The *Casey* court affirmed the continuing validity of *Hodgson* and *Akron* by upholding Pennsylvania's parental consent or judicial bypass procedure. More recently, the Supreme Court found that New Hampshire's parental notification law, which prohibited physicians from performing abortions on minors without prior written notice to a parent or guardian, could be unconstitutional in a medical emergency. The matter was remanded to the Court of Appeals for a determination of whether the remedy could be narrowed to prevent invalidation of the entire legislation. Ayotte v. Planned Parenthood, 546 U.S. 320 (2006). See Note, 119 Harv. L. Rev. 2552 (2006). See also State v. Planned Parenthood of Alaska, 171 P.3d 577 (Alaska 2007) (statute requiring parental consent struck down under state constitution; consent requirement more intrusive than notification and not the least restrictive way of achieving the state interests).

May states require minors to prove that they are mature enough to make a decision about abortion by clear and convincing evidence? See In re B. S., 74 P.3d 285 (Ariz. App. 2003) (applying this standard); In re Doe, 139 So. 3d 428 (Fla. 2d DCA 2014) (applying this standard). Can a trial court judge rely on a minor's failure to consult with her mother about proposed abortion as evidence for finding that she lacks the maturity required to make the decision? In re Doe, 33 A.3d 615 (Pa. 2011) (probably not, but see dissent); cf. In re Doe, 153 So. 3d 925 (Fla. 2d DCA 2014) (maturity required need not be the same as an adult). See also Zbaraz v. Madigan, 572 F.3d 370 (7th Cir. 2009) (rejecting facial challenge to judicial bypass standards for immature minors); and In re Petition of Anonymous 3, 782 N.W.2d 591 (Neb. 2010) (de novo review of record; no parental notification required as minor was emancipated). If a minor cannot prove she is mature enough to bypass the parental consent statute, the court must conduct an inquiry into whether the abortion without parental consent would nevertheless be in her best interest. 1 Am. Jur. 2d Abortion and Birth Control §38. For a summary of the law involving minors and abortion, see Guttmacher Institute, Parental Involvement in Minors' Abortions (as of March 1, 2016), available at: www.guttmacher.org; Carol Sanger, Decisional Dignity: Teenage Abortion, Bypass Hearings, and the Misuse of Law, 18 Colum. J. Gender & L. 409 (2009); and National Conference of State Legislatures, Parental Consent or Notification for Abortion (available at the NCSL Web site). See also Theodore Joyce et al., Changes in Abortions and Births and the Texas Parental Notification Law, 354 New Eng. J. Med. 1031 (2006) (analysis of data to determine impact of law on abortion rates).

10. *Disability and Sex Selective Abortions.* A number of states have enacted legislation prohibiting abortions for reasons of sex, disability, or genetic abnormality. See Guttmacher Institute, Abortion Bans in Cases of Sex or Race Selection or

Genetic Anomaly (2016). North Dakota was the first state to prohibit abortions in cases of fetal anomaly, making physicians criminally liable for violating the North Dakota statute, which applies even if the fetus has a condition that means it will die soon after birth. N.D. Cent. Code Ann. § 14-02.1-04.1. Indiana is the second state to ban abortions based on fetal anomalies; the law also prevents abortion based on race or national origin. The constitutionality of the Indiana statute is currently being litigated. Planned Parenthood of Indiana & Kentucky, Inc. v. Comm'r, No. 116CV00763TWPDML, 2016 WL 3556914 (S.D. Ind. June 30, 2016). Women are not required to state a reason for abortion, and some laws, like those in Kansas, are narrowly tailored to prohibit abortions by physicians with knowledge that the abortion is being sought on the basis of sex. See Thomas J. Molony, Roe, Casey, and Sex-Selection Abortion Bans, 71 Wash. & Lee L. Rev. 1089 (2014) (suggesting that narrowly tailored bans may be permissible under *Casey*). Aside from criminal penalties, could an equal protection claim be brought against sex or disability selective abortions? Who would have standing to bring such a claim? Could you argue that medical providers who permit the use of testing to identify and abort fetuses likely to be born with disabilities have violated the ADA? Would public health institutions engaging in the policy violate the equal protection clause? Would a challenger have to show that a fetus was a "person"? For further discussion on sex and disability selective abortions see Brian Citro et al. Replacing Myths with Facts: Sex-Selective Abortion Laws in the United States (2014); Alicia Ouellette, Selection against Disability: Abortion, ART, and Access, Symposium, Intersections in Reproduction: Perspectives on Abortion and Assisted Reproductive Technologies, 43 J. L. Med. & Ethics 211 (2015). Martha A. Field, Killing the "Handicapped"—Before and After Birth, 16 Harv. Women's L. J. 79 (1993); Dov Fox & Christopher Griffin, Jr., Disability-Selective Abortion and the Americans with Disabilities Act, 2009 Utah L. Rev. 845; Janet Malek, Deciding Against Disability: Does the Use of Reproductive Genetic Technologies Express Disvalue for People with Disabilities?, 36 J. Med. Ethics 217 (2010).

Notes: Funding, Speech, Religion, and Abortion

1. *Government Funding for Abortion.* Restrictions on government funding for abortions were the first real political and legal successes for abortion opponents. In Maher v. Roe, 432 U.S. 464 (1977), the Supreme Court upheld the constitutional validity of a Connecticut welfare rule that provided Medicaid recipients with coverage for pregnancy services but not for nontherapeutic abortion services. In Harris v. McRae, 448 U.S. 297 (1980), the Court upheld the "Hyde Amendment," which prohibited the use of federal Medicaid dollars to reimburse the cost of most abortions even when they were medically necessary. The Court found that funding restrictions did not violate the due process or equal protection clause because, while women had a constitutional right to choose abortion, they did not have a constitutional right to make the government pay for it. The government, the Court held, was free to establish programs that provided pregnancy benefits while denying coverage for abortion:

> But, regardless of whether the freedom of a woman to choose to terminate her pregnancy for health reasons lies at the core or the periphery of the due process liberty

recognized in [Roe v. Wade], it simply does not follow that a woman's freedom of choice carries with it a constitutional entitlement to the financial resources to avail herself of the full range of protected choices. . . . [A]lthough government may not place obstacles in the path of a woman's exercise of her freedom of choice, it need not remove those not of its own creation. Indigence falls in the latter category. The financial constraints that restrict an indigent woman's ability to enjoy the full range of constitutionally protected freedom of choice are the product not of governmental restrictions on access to abortions, but rather of her indigence. Although Congress has opted to subsidize medically necessary services generally, but not certain medically necessary abortions, the fact remains that the Hyde Amendment leaves an indigent woman with at least the same range of choice in deciding whether to obtain a medically necessary abortion as she would have had if Congress had chosen to subsidize no health care costs at all. We are thus not persuaded that the Hyde Amendment impinges on the constitutionally protected freedom of choice recognized in [Roe].

448 U.S. 297 at 316-317. Federal funding for abortion is the subject of regular congressional debate, and the abortion coverage exclusion occasionally expands and narrows as the result of political campaigns waged by pro-choice and anti-abortion forces.

State courts have sometimes found a state constitutional right to Medicaid funding for abortions, requiring that states fund these services even in the absence of federal assistance. See, e.g., State Department of Health & Human Services v. Planned Parenthood of Alaska, Inc., 28 P.3d 904 (Alaska 2001). Other states have statutory or constitutional provisions that *prohibit* expenditure of state funds on abortions. These jurisdictions have been confronted with somewhat of a dilemma because federal law requires that states provide funding for abortion in some limited circumstances, and federal law of course is supreme even when weighed against a state constitutional provision. See Dalton v. Little Rock Family Planning Services, 516 U.S. 474 (1996). See generally Guttmacher Institute, State Funding of Abortion Under Medicaid (Nov. 1, 2012).

Government funding returned as a controversial issue in the late 1980s with the adoption of new regulations implementing federal funding of family planning clinics under Title X of the Public Health Service Act. 42 U.S.C. §§300 to 300a-6. The Act specified that federal funds could not be "used in programs where abortion is a method of family planning." Id. §300a-6. The regulations placed three different conditions on recipients of Title X federal funds. The first, and most controversial, set of provisions came to be known as the "gag clause." Title X providers were prohibited from counseling about abortion or providing a referral even when specifically requested by a patient. Project personnel were permitted to state: "The project does not consider abortion an appropriate method of family planning and therefore does not counsel or refer for abortion." 42 C.F.R. §59.8(b)(5) (1989). The regulations also restricted Title X projects from encouraging, promoting, or advocating abortion as a method of family planning through lobbying, educational programs, or other activities. 42 C.F.R. §59.10(a) (1989). Finally, Title X projects had to be organized so that they were "physically and financially separate" from abortion activities. 42 C.F.R. §59.9 (1989). The Supreme Court rejected claims that the regulations violated the First Amendment in Rust v. Sullivan, 500 U.S. 173 (1991). The Court relied on the Harris v. McRae line of federal funding cases to hold that the regulations merely implemented a permissible governmental objective: ensuring that federal funds were used only for family planning purposes, not the promotion of abortion. Id. at 192-200. The gag rule was rescinded in the Clinton Administration. See Standards of Compliance for Abortion-Related Services in Family Services Projects, 65 Fed. Reg. 41,270 (2000).

There was intense debate over the coverage of abortion services in the federal Patient Protection and Affordable Care Act. The final legislation and regulations impose strict accounting requirements designed to ensure that federal funds are not used for abortion services. States may prohibit coverage of abortion services, but if they do not, the new insurance exchanges are permitted to sell insurance that covers abortion. However, no federal funds may be used to subsidize that portion of the coverage. See Susan A. Cohen, Insurance Coverage of Abortion, 13 Guttmacher Pol'y Rev. 2 (2010); Guttmacher Institute, Restricting Insurance Coverage of Abortion (2013). See also Lisa C. Ikemoto, Abortion, Contraception and the ACA, 55 How. L. J. 731 (2012); Roy G. Spece, Jr., The Purpose Prong of *Casey*'s Undue Burden Test and Its Impact on the Constitutionality of Abortion Insurance Restrictions in the Affordable Care Act or Its Progeny, 33 Whittier L. Rev. 77 (2011).

The latest round of the funding battle involves state efforts to cut off funding for Planned Parenthood's family planning and other health services because of the organization's involvement in providing abortion services. Compare Planned Parenthood Ass'n of Hidalgo County Texas, Inc. v. Suehs, 692 F.3d 343 (5th Cir. 2012) (regulation barring organization from receiving funds under state health program if it promotes elective abortion or is affiliated with organizations promoting elective abortion does not violate First Amendment) with Planned Parenthood of Indiana, Inc. v. Commissioner of Indiana State Department of Health, 699 F.3d 962 (7th Cir. 2012) (upholding preliminary injunction against state law excluding health care providers who performed abortion from participation in Medicaid because federal law gives patients freedom of choice among qualified providers; state permitted to ban abortion-related providers from receiving funds under separate federal block grant program).

2. *Informed Consent.* A number of state legislatures have sought to regulate the informed consent process for abortions by requiring abortion providers to disclose specific types of information about, for example, fetal age and development, or the availability of paternity support actions under state law. State legislatures have been particularly active in expanding informed consent provisions related to (1) the human status of the fetus under state law; (2) fetal development as assessed by sonogram results or heart auscultation; and (3) abortion and mental health. Opponents have argued that statements about the status of the fetus violate the First Amendment rights of physicians to avoid compelled speech; that the provisions requiring women to view sonograms or to listen to heart auscultation are not medically necessary; and that the required disclosures about fetal pain and mental health are inaccurate and misleading.

    a.   *Fetal Personhood.* The courts have not been sympathetic to claims that the disclosure requirements violate physicians' First Amendment rights. Citing Rust v. Sullivan, supra, Planned Parenthood v. Casey, supra, and Gonzales v. Carhart, supra, courts have held that physician speech can be subject to reasonable regulation via informed consent so long as the required information is relevant, truthful, and non-misleading. In Planned Parenthood of Minnesota, North Dakota, South Dakota v. Rounds, 653 F.3d 662 (8th Cir. 2011), the court upheld a South Dakota law requiring physicians to provide oral advisories about the human status of the fetus, the protected nature of the relationship between the woman and the fetus, and the fact that the abortion will terminate that relationship. This case has a complicated procedural history: The judgment was vacated, 662 F.3d 1072 (8th Cir. 2011), but a subsequent en banc decision noted that the panel holding on this issue was still in force, 686 F.3d 889, 893 n.1 (8th Cir. 2012) (en banc).

b. *Disclosure of Fetal Development.* The U.S. Court of Appeals for the Fifth Circuit reviewed and rejected claims that Texas' sonogram and heartbeat requirements violated physicians' First Amendment rights or constituted an undue burden on the woman's abortion right. Texas Medical Providers Performing Abortion Services v. Lakey, 667 F.3d 570, 580 (5th Cir. 2012) (rejecting physicians' First Amendment claims). The court noted that standard medical practice supported the use of sonograms and measures to hear the fetal heartbeat. The state law simply required that this relevant, truthful, and non-misleading information be shared with pregnant women unless they certified that they fell into one of three excluded groups (involving women whose pregnancy came from certain types of rapes, minors in a judicial bypass procedure, or fetuses with an "irreversible medical condition or abnormality"). Id. at 578-579. Similarly, the Eighth Circuit affirmed the Arkansas heartbeat disclosure requirement furthered a legitimate state interest. Edwards v. Beck, 8 F. Supp. 3d 1091 (E.D. Ark. 2014) aff'd, 786 F.3d 1113 (8th Cir. 2015). The statute required that a physician performing an abortion conduct an ultrasound to determine if a heartbeat was detectible. If a fetal heartbeat was detectible the physician was required to inform the pregnant woman in writing that the fetus possessed a heartbeat and the statistical probability of bringing the fetus to term based on is gestational age. Id. at 1097. Contrast these cases with Stuart v. Camnitz. 774 F.3d 238 (4th Cir. 2014). The Fourth Circuit held that North Carolina's sonogram requirement violated the physicians' First Amendment rights. The court found that requiring a physician to display and review a sonogram to a woman who is covering her ears and eyes constitutes compelled speech and lacks counterbalancing state interests. Id. at 252. See also John A. Robertson, Abortion and Technology: Sonograms, Fetal Pain, Viability, and Early Prenatal Diagnosis, 14 U. Pa. J. Const. L. 327, 349-357 (2011); Jeannie Suk, The Trajectory of Trauma: Bodies and Minds of Abortion Discourse, 110 Colum. L. Rev. 1193 (2010); Erin B. Bernstein, Disclosure Two Ways, Symposium, Intersections in Reproduction: Perspectives on Abortion and Assisted Reproductive Technologies, 43 J. L. Med. & Ethics 245 (2015).

c. *Abortion and Mental Health.* The *Gonzales* majority noted the possibility that women would suffer psychologically from participating in the abortion procedure. But see Trine Munk-Olsen et al., Induced First-Trimester Abortion and Risk of Mental Disorder, 364 New Eng. J. Med. 332 (2011) ("relative risk of psychiatric contact did not differ significantly after abortion as compared with before abortion . . . but did increase after childbirth"). State legislatures have begun to incorporate the idea of mental or emotional sequelae from abortion into their informed consent provisions. The Eighth Circuit reviewed and upheld a requirement that a physician disclose the "[i]ncreased risk of suicide ideation and suicide" to women considering abortion. Planned Parenthood Minnesota, supra, 686 F.3d at 894. The plaintiffs argued that most research demonstrated that there was no causal link between abortion and suicide and that any increased prevalence of suicide in women who had undergone abortion was related to other life factors rather than the abortion itself. The court found that the required disclosure was truthful and non-misleading, noting that physicians were free to explain the absence of scientific evidence that the abortion procedure itself leads to an increased risk of suicide. 686 F.3d 889, at 893-906.

Do physicians have a duty to warn patients about the "abortion trauma syndrome" under the common law? Does it matter whether a jurisdiction follows the "material risk" or "professional" standard of disclosure? See Emily Bazelon, Is There a Post-Abortion Syndrome?, N.Y. Times Magazine, Jan. 21, 2006, at 41. Nada L. Stotland, The Myth of the Abortion Trauma Syndrome, 268 JAMA 2078 (1992).

Physicians have always had a duty to disclose information to women undergoing the abortion procedure. The ordinary rules governing disclosure (see Chapter 3.C) apply unless a state has enacted a specific informed consent procedure for abortion. As you recall, the two major disclosure standards are the "malpractice" standard and the "material risk" standard. There are few reported decisions in which patients have brought informed consent claims against their physicians. See, e.g., Humes v. Clinton, 792 P.2d 1032 (Kan. 1990) (no recovery for emotional distress caused by physician's failure to disclose risks where no physical injury occurs); Acuna v. Turkish, 930 A.2d 416 (N.J. 2007) (physician has no duty to disclose human status of fetus); Rodriguez v. Epstein, 664 N.Y.S.2d 20 (App. Div. 1997) (physicians not required to refer patients in counseling on alternatives to elective abortion); Spencer v. Seikel, 742 P.2d 1126 (Okla. 1987) (physician has no duty to inform plaintiff that late-term abortion might be available in other states). See also Bendar v. Rosen, 588 A.2d 1264 (N.J. Super. Ct. App. Div. 1991) (facts are as complex as those found in the typical Torts final; court upholds jury award for psychological trauma following an abortion).

3. *Waiting Periods.* State legislatures have also enacted "waiting periods," in an effort to regulate the informed consent process. Under waiting periods, women are required to wait some statutorily established period of time (one to three days) between being given information about the abortion procedure and undergoing the procedure itself. Guttmacher Institute, Counseling and Waiting Periods for Abortion (as of March 1, 2016). Waiting periods can be particularly problematic for women who must travel significant distances to secure access to abortion services.

Before *Casey*, courts generally invalidated attempts to dictate the specifics of what doctors must disclose to their patients—particularly scripts that were blatant attempts to discourage the procedure. See Akron v. Akron Center for Reproductive Health, 462 U.S. 416 (1983) (striking requirement that woman be informed, inter alia, that "the unborn child is a human life from the moment of conception"). The *Casey* decision reopened this avenue for state regulation by upholding a Pennsylvania informed consent provision and 24-hour waiting rule because they did not impose an "undue burden" on women seeking an abortion. See, e.g., Cincinnati Women's Services, Inc. v. Taft, 468 F.3d 361 (6th Cir. 2006) (upholding Ohio's requirement of an informed consent process with physician 24 hours before procedure). See also Annot., 119 A.L.R.5th 315 (2004). How will the *Whole Women's Health* decision, discussed above, change these kinds of cases?

4. *Conscience Provisions.* Generally, private facilities and actors are not required to participate in abortions. See Lisa C. Ikemoto, When a Hospital Becomes Catholic, 47 Mercer L. Rev. 1087 (1996). Under federal law, private hospitals, which are not state actors, are free to decide for themselves not to perform abortions. See 20 U.S.C. §1688 ("Nothing in this chapter shall be construed to require or prohibit any person, or public or private entity, to provide or pay for any benefit or service, including the use of facilities, related to abortion."). But see Doe v. Bridgeton Hospital Ass'n, Inc., 389 A.2d 526 (N.J. Super. Ct. Law Div. 1978) (private hospitals required to provide access to abortions under state constitution). Corporations are not required to provide coverage for contraception if they are closely held and if it would violate their religious beliefs. In Burwell v. Hobby Lobby, 134 S. Ct. 2751 (2014), discussed above, the Court held that the mandated coverage of contraception violates the Religious Freedom Restoration Act as it does not satisfy the Act's least restrictive means requirement. See Elizabeth Sepper, Conscientious Refusals of Care, in The Oxford Handbook of U.S. Healthcare Law (2015) (arguing the decision has broad consequences for access to other medical services).

Consider also the rights of individual health care practitioners (as opposed to facilities) to refuse to participate in abortions. Following *Roe*, Congress and many state legislatures moved quickly to enact so-called conscience clause statutes that protect physicians, nurses, and other medical personnel from retaliatory measures for refusing to participate in abortions. See 42 U.S.C. §300a-7 (known as the "Church Amendment"); Shelton v. University of Medicine & Dentistry of New Jersey, 223 F.3d 220 (3d Cir. 2000) (hospital provided reasonable accommodations to nurse's religious beliefs regarding abortions); Judith F. Daar, A Clash at the Bedside: Patient Autonomy v. A Physician's Professional Conscience, 44 Hastings L. J. 1241, 1274 (1993) (comparing protection for physician conscience in death and dying and abortion cases); Mark L. Rienzi, The Constitutional Right Not to Participate in Abortions: *Roe, Casey,* and the Fourteenth Amendment Rights of Healthcare Providers, 87 Notre Dame L. Rev. 1 (2011) (arguing provider's right to refuse merits constitutional recognition). The FDA's approval of mifepristone and emergency contraception (which some argued served as an abortifacient) generated claims that pharmacists should have a similar right of conscience. See Kansas St. Ann. §65-443 (2012) (conscience provision amended to include coverage of prescriptions); and Robin Fretwell Wilson, The Limits of Conscience: Moral Clashes over Deeply Divisive Healthcare Procedures, 34 Am. J. L. & Med. 41 (2008). Justice Kennedy's opinion in *Gonzales,* supra, notes that states have the power to regulate abortion "to protect[] the integrity and ethics of the medical profession." Some commentators have argued that health care workers should also be deemed to have a right of conscience supporting their interest in providing abortion services. See, e.g., Lisa H. Harris, Recognizing Conscience in Abortion Provision, 367 New Eng. J. Med.

981 (2012); Elizabeth Sepper, Taking Conscience Seriously, 98 Va. L. Rev. 1501 (2012) (noting need to balance institutional and provider claims of conscience); Steph Sterling & Jessica L. Waters, Beyond Religious Refusals: The Case for Protecting Health Care Workers' Provision of Abortion Care, 34 Harv. J. L. & Gender 463 (2011).

5. *Abortion Protesters.* Courts and legislatures have also struggled to resolve the controversies created by abortion protesters. Anti-abortion protesters have sought to block clinic doors and to engage in "sidewalk counseling" of women attempting to gain access to abortion clinics. Theoretically, protesters might be charged with violation of state trespass laws. Compare Joan Teshima, Annot., Trespass: State Prosecution for Unauthorized Entry or Occupation, for Public Demonstration Purposes, of Business, Industrial, or Utility Premises, 41 A.L.R.4th 773 (1985), with James O. Pearson, Jr., Annot., "Choice of Evils," Necessity, Duress, or Similar Defense to State or Local Criminal Charges Based on Acts of Public Protest, 3 A.L.R.5th 521 (1992). Abortion clinics and their supporters have also sought to use the federal Racketeer Influenced and Corrupt Organizations Act (RICO). In Scheidler v. National Organization of Women, 547 U.S. 9 (2006), the Supreme Court rejected efforts to use RICO and the Hobbs Act's extortion provisions in a class action brought by NOW against individuals and organizations involved in anti-abortion protests.

State and local officials sometimes have been overwhelmed by the numbers and commitment of protesters. See Operation Save America v. City of Jackson, 275 P.3d 438 (Wyo. 2012) (TRO entered to restrict abortion protest in and around town square during Boy Scout festival found unconstitutional). Judges have issued injunctions designed to create a "buffer zone" around clinics, attempting to balance the need to protect free speech against the harms protesters inflict on the clinics and their patients. The Supreme Court opinions in this area are complex. See, e.g., Schenck v. Pro-Choice Network of Western New York, 519 U.S. 357 (1997) (upholding "fixed" 15-foot buffer zones but striking down "floating" buffer zone established around people and vehicles; floating buffer zones unnecessarily burdened speech); Madsen v. Women's Health Center, 512 U.S. 753 (1994) ("In evaluating a content-neutral injunction, the governing standard is whether the injunction's challenged provisions burden no more speech than necessary to serve a significant government interest."); McCullen v. Coakley, 134 S. Ct. 2158 (2014) (reversing lower court, finding buffer zone was not content-based, but statute lacked narrow tailoring and did not serve a significant government interest and was thus a violation of the First Amendment). See also Bray v. Alexandria Women's Health Clinic, 506 U.S. 263 (1993) (42 U.S.C. §1985 does not protect women seeking abortion from the concerted activities of abortion protesters).

Clinic defenders turned to other forums for additional relief. Congress enacted statutory protections in the Freedom of Access to Clinic Entrances Act of 1994. 18 U.S.C. §248. See also Planned Parenthood of Columbia/Williamette, Inc. v. American Coalition of Life Activists, 422 F.3d 949 (9th Cir. 2005), cert. denied, 126 S. Ct. 1912 (2006) (publication of names and addresses of abortion providers through "guilty" posters and Internet Web site are "threat[s] of force" giving rise to liability for punitive damages under FACE; amount reduced). See generally Guttmacher Institute, Protecting Access to Clinics (2016).

C. STATE OR FEDERAL RECOGNITION OF FETAL INTERESTS

1. Introduction

This section considers what steps government can take to protect potential life, apart from restricting abortions. There are a variety of alternative legal mechanisms for protecting fetal interests. Tort law could be used to recover damages for fetal injuries and to deter conduct that puts fetuses at risk of injury. Criminal law could be used to punish those who injure fetuses. Governments also may establish the importance of fetal interests via proclamations and even by the allocation of public funds. See generally Sara Dubow, Ourselves Unborn: A History of the Fetus in Modern America (2011). As noted in the last section, the Personhood movement is working to establish fetuses as persons at both the federal and state levels.

The Supreme Court's procreation jurisprudence presents no barrier to the preferential allocation of public funds toward childbearing rather than abortion or to the development of a particularized abortion informed consent statute. See supra at pages 751-753. Yet *Skinner, Roe, Casey,* and *Gonzales* do not resolve the validity of other governmental efforts to value and protect fetal interests. *Skinner* suggested that individuals have a fundamental liberty interest in deciding to procreate. *Roe* held that a fetus was not a "person" entitled to protection under the Fourteenth Amendment and prohibited the state from adopting a definition of fetal personhood that would infringe on a woman's right to choose abortion. However, *Casey* suggests that the Supreme Court will be much more deferential toward a state's asserted desire to protect fetuses, at least so long as the measures taken to protect the fetus do not "unduly" infringe a woman's abortion option. Furthermore, *Casey* reiterates *Roe*'s holding that a state's interest in fetal life becomes compelling at the point of viability. At viability, the state may prohibit abortion completely unless the procedure is necessary for the health or life of the pregnant woman. The Supreme Court's decision in *Gonzales* affirmed the government's ability to promote fetal interests and to define the scope of what might be medically appropriate, even before viability. See Randy Beck, *Gonzales, Casey,* and the Viability Rule, 103 Nw. U. L. Rev. 249 (2009) (criticizing Supreme Court's approach to viability). The abortion cases suggest that the Court would not permit states to value the fetus's potential life more than the life of the pregnant woman.

This brief summary demonstrates that the abortion cases are not very helpful in establishing the scope of governmental power to protect fetal life outside of the abortion context, when the risk to the fetus comes from something other than the pregnant woman's right to choose abortion. Courts have struggled to determine the appropriate constitutional balance between a state's interest in protecting fetal life and a woman's right to engage in activities that might put her fetus at risk. The first part of this section briefly summarizes state and federal recognition of fetal interests. The second part of the section focuses on two of the most difficult areas for courts and commentators: forced medical treatment for pregnant women and criminal prosecution of pregnant women for conduct presenting a risk to their fetus.

a. State Law and Fetal Personhood

State law protections for fetal interests have grown in recent years in areas ranging from tort law, to criminal law, to medical research. State courts generally resolve the question of a fetus's personhood by interpreting and applying the words of statutes or precedents rather than searching for a unitary definition of personhood that could be applied to fetuses in all areas of the law. Does this strike you as the correct approach? What prevents states from adopting a unitary concept of personhood that could be applied across different areas of law? Wouldn't such an approach comport more closely with the centrality of personhood to most ethical, moral, and jurisprudential theories? See, e.g., Saru M. Matambanadzo, Embodying Vulnerability: A Feminist Theory of the Person, 20 Duke J. Gender L. & Pol'y 45 (2012); Note, What We Talk About When We Talk About Persons: The Language of a Legal Fiction, 114 Harv. L. Rev. 1745 (2001). See also In the Matter of the Unborn Child of Starks, 18 P.3d 342 (Okla. 2001). States have taken up the issue through legislation, enacting provisions that define the fetus as a human being under state law. See 720 Ill. Comp. Stat. Ann. §510/1.

States have been particularly quick to recognize fetal interests in tort law. The old black-letter rule was that fetuses could only recover for injuries sustained in utero if they were born alive. Roland F. Chase, Annot., Liability for Prenatal Injuries, 40 A.L.R.3d 1222 (1971). Parents could not recover for the wrongful death of their unborn children. These tort rules have undergone significant revision. A majority of states now permit suits on behalf of injured fetuses, even when stillborn, if the injury was sustained after the point of viability. Annot., Right to Maintain Action or to Recover Damages for Death of Unborn Child, 84 A.L.R.3d 411 (1978). A few states even permit tort claims where the injury was sustained prior to viability. See, e.g., Nealis v. Baird, 996 P.2d 438 (Okla. 1999) (wrongful death statute covers nonviable fetus born alive); Wiersma v. Maple Leaf Farms, 543 N.W.2d 787 (S.D. 1996) (wrongful death statute provides cause of action for loss of nonviable unborn child).

Tort claims involving fetal injury often must address substantial causation issues: The plaintiff must prove that the tortfeasor actually caused legally cognizable harm. This burden of proof may be difficult to meet where the pregnancy is in the earliest stages at the time of the fetal injury because of the significant rate of spontaneous abortion or miscarriage during this period. See also Agota Peterfy, Commentary, Fetal Viability as a Threshold to Personhood: A Legal Analysis, 16 J. Leg. Med. 607 (1995).

Does a fetus have similar rights to be free of injuries caused by its mother? There are several problems with these claims: The parental immunity doctrine will protect the pregnant woman in some jurisdictions; there are difficulties establishing the appropriate standard of care; and there are also public policy concerns with imposing liability for maternal conduct. See Thomas M. Fleming, Annot., Right of Child to Action Against Mother for Infliction of Prenatal Injuries, 78 A.L.R.4th 1082 (1991). Only a handful of courts have even considered the issue; litigation of this sort typically arises only when mothers arrange to have their children sue them in order to draw resources from their homeowners' or automobile insurance policies. Most courts have rejected the claims. See Stallman v. Youngquist, 531 N.E.2d 355 (Ill. 1988) (car accident); Remy v. MacDonald, 801 N.E.2d 260 (Mass. 2004) (car accident; summarizing case law); Chenault v. Huie, 989 S.W.2d 474 (Tex. App. 1999) (grossly negligent use of illicit drugs). The *Stallman* court's criticism of the liability claim was pointed:

It is clear that the recognition of a legal right to begin life with a sound mind and body on the part of a fetus which is assertable after birth against its mother would have serious ramifications for all women and their families, and for the way in which society views women and women's reproductive abilities. The recognition of such a right by a fetus would necessitate the recognition of a legal duty on the part of the woman who is the mother; a legal duty, as opposed to a moral duty, to effectuate the best prenatal environment possible. . . . Any action which negatively impacted on fetal development would be a breach of the pregnant woman's duty to her developing fetus. Mother and child would be legal adversaries from the moment of conception until birth. . . .

The relationship between a pregnant woman and her fetus is unlike the relationship between any other plaintiff and defendant. No other plaintiff depends exclusively on any other defendant for everything necessary for life itself. No other defendant must go through biological changes of the most profound type, possibly at the risk of her own life, in order to bring forth an adversary into the world. It is, after all, the whole life of the pregnant woman which impacts on the development of the fetus. As opposed to the third-party defendant, it is the mother's every waking and sleeping moment which, for better or worse, shapes the prenatal environment which forms the world for the developing fetus.

531 N.E.2d at 359-360. But see Grodin v. Grodin, 301 N.W.2d 869 (Mich. Ct. App. 1980) (child's mother potentially liable to child for prenatal injuries); Tesar v. Anderson, 789 N.W.2d 351 (Wis. App. 2010) (public policy does not preclude action by father against mother's insurer where mother's negligent driving resulted in stillborn birth). A few courts have considered whether maternal negligence should be imputed to her child in the child's action against third parties for prenatal conduct. See, e.g., Hogle v. Hall, 916 P.2d 814 (Nev. 1996) (no).

States may also use the criminal law to protect fetal interests. Criminal prosecutions against "strangers" have generally fallen into two categories: (1) traditional crimes and (2) special criminal statutes protecting fetuses. Attempts to prosecute third parties for traditional crimes such as murder or manslaughter typically fail. Homicide convictions, for example, require the death of a "person," usually defined as a person born alive. A defendant who violently assaults a pregnant woman might be prosecuted for a homicide if the fetus is born alive but then dies as a result of the criminal conduct. Cf. Mamta K. Shah, Note, Inconsistencies in the Legal Status of an Unborn Child: Recognition of a Fetus as Potential Life, 29 Hofstra L. Rev. 931, 933-949 (2001). See also State v. Courchesne, 998 A.2d 1 (Conn. 2010) (infant born alive who subsequently dies due to injuries sustained in utero is "person" under murder statute); State v. Horne, 319 S.E.2d 703 (S.C. 1984) (death of unborn viable fetus supports manslaughter conviction).

A majority of states have enacted special statutes designed to criminalize conduct related to fetuses. Feticide statutes are a common example. Prosecutions under these provisions are less controversial, in part because legislative intent is clear. The statutes generally include specific exceptions for a woman exercising her right to choose abortion and for abortion providers. Lawrence J. Nelson, A Crisis for Women's Rights? Surveying Feticide Statutes for Content, Coverage, and Constitutionality, 6 U. Denv. Crim. L. Rev. 63 (2016); Mamta K. Shah, supra; Alan S. Wasserstrom, Annot., Homicide Based on Killing of Unborn Child, 64 A.L.R.5th 671 (1998). See also People v. Davis, 872 P.2d 591 (Cal. 1994). Many states reviewed and revised criminal laws governing fetuses in the aftermath of some highly publicized cases involving the murder of pregnant women. See also National Conference of State Legislatures, Fetal Homicide Laws (available at the NCSL Web site) (citing 38 states with legislation as of March 2015). Do feticide statutes demonstrate irreconcilable conflicts in the law given that third parties can be subjected to criminal penalties for conduct permissible when undertaken by the pregnant woman? See Luke M. Milligan, A Theory of Stability: John Rawls, Fetal Homicide, and Substantive Due Process, 87 B.U. L. Rev. 1177 (2007); Carolyn B. Ramsey, Restructuring the Debate over Fetal Homicide Laws, 67 Ohio St. L. J. 721 (2006) (arguing that abortion rights are not inconsistent with feticide prosecutions). Criminal prosecution of women for risky prenatal activity is a controversial area that will be considered in more detail below.

States can also show respect for fetuses, and indirectly disfavor abortion, by restricting the use of fetal tissue produced in spontaneous or planned abortions. A number of state legislatures have prohibited the use of fetal remains in medical research or have otherwise attempted to restrict fetal experimentation. Violators may be criminally prosecuted. See, e.g., Mo. Ann. Stat. §188.036 (purports to ban abortions performed to obtain fetal material for experimentation); N.D. Cent. Code §14-02.2-02 (fetal experimentation restrictions); 18 Pa. Cons. Stat. Ann. §3216 (fetal experimentation restrictions). These statutes may be implicated in stem cell research, discussed below at page 861.

b. Federal Recognition of Fetal Interests

The federal government has had fewer opportunities to show its interest in fetal well-being, but federal activity is prominent in three areas: (1) the allocation of funds designed to protect fetal health; (2) the adoption of legislation designed to criminally or civilly penalize risky conduct; and (3) the dramatic debates about the permissibility of embryonic stem cell research.

The federal government wields enormous power through its capacity to tie the expenditure of federal dollars to particular policy objectives. For many years, the eligibility rules for the federal-state Medicaid program were the most important federal expression of interest in fetal well-being through the provision of Medicaid coverage for pregnant women. Coverage for pregnant women near or below the federal poverty level has expanded over the past two decades. See 42 U.S.C. §§1396a(a)(10)(A)(III), 1396d(n). Health insurance coverage for pregnant women is an indirect indication of the value of fetal life. See also 42 C.F.R. §457.10 (unborn children eligible for health coverage under State Children's Health Insurance Program). The Affordable Care Act also enhanced coverage of maternity care in public and private health plans. Elizabeth Kukura, Giving Birth Under the ACA: Analyzing the Use of Law as a Tool to Improve Health Care, 94 Neb. L. Rev. 799 (2016). Federal funding for stem cell research, which raises the specter of the use and destruction of embryos, will be discussed in the final section of this chapter, at page 864.

Congress has also sought to recognize and to protect fetal interests more directly. The federal Partial-Birth Abortion Ban Act of 2003 discussed supra, at page 736, recognizes a private cause of action to protect fetal interests. The Act gives certain relatives of a fetus subjected to the prohibited procedure a right to recover civil damages. 18 U.S.C.A. §1531.

Congress also expanded federal criminal law to recognize the distinct offense of injuring or killing a fetus. The federal Unborn Victims of Violence Act of 2004, codified at 18 U.S.C.A. §1841, was enacted in the aftermath of a highly publicized murder of a pregnant woman. The Act provides:

> **(a)(1)** Whoever engages in conduct that violates any of [certain enumerated] . . . provisions of law . . . and thereby causes the death of, or bodily injury . . . [to] a child, who is in utero at the time the conduct takes place, is guilty of a separate offense under this section.
>
> **(2)(A)** Except as otherwise provided in this paragraph, the punishment for that separate offense is the same as the punishment provided under Federal law for that conduct had that injury or death occurred to the unborn child's mother.
>
> **(B)** An offense under this section does not require proof that
>
> **(i)** the person engaging in the conduct had knowledge or should have had knowledge that the victim of the underlying offense was pregnant; or
>
> **(ii)** the defendant intended to cause the death of, or bodily injury to, the unborn child.
>
> **(C)** If the person engaging in the conduct thereby intentionally kills or attempts to kill the unborn child, that person shall instead of being punished under subparagraph (A), be punished as provided under [sections of the federal criminal law relating to murder, manslaughter, and attempt to committee murder or manslaughter] . . . for intentionally killing or attempting to kill a human being.
>
> **(D)** Notwithstanding any other provision of law, the death penalty shall not be imposed for an offense under this section. . . .

Constitutionally protected abortion procedures are exempted. Id. See generally Carolyn B. Ramsey, Restructuring the Debate over Fetal Homicide Laws, 67 Ohio St. L.J. 721 (2006).

2. Pregnant Women and Forced Medical Treatment

A pregnant woman presents a unique dilemma for health care providers. The woman's autonomy interests must be fully recognized as a matter of law and medical ethics. Yet the woman's decisions about medical treatment can have an immediate impact on the fetus, whose interests also demand respect. The health care professional's legal and ethical obligations to the fetus, as a being separate and distinct from her mother, are a matter of greater controversy. Should a physician's duties to the fetus ever override the obligations to a pregnant patient? When and how should courts or legislatures intervene in this potential conflict? Are the rules developed in this area truly sui generis, or should they be applied to situations in which third parties make demands for biological support from other persons? Compare the following material, for instance, with the discussion in Chapter 6 of whether people can be forced to donate life-saving organs or tissue at little risk to themselves. For critiques of the focus on maternal risk to children, see Linda C. Fentiman, Are Mothers Hazardous to Their Children's Health?: Law, Culture and the Framing of Risk, 21 Va. J. Soc. Pol'y & L. 295 (2014); and Dara E. Purvis, The Rules of Maternity, 84 Tenn. L. Rev. 367 (2017).

▇THE COLONIZATION OF THE WOMB
Nancy Ehrenreich*
43 Duke L.J. 492 (1993)

Science has been called the religion of modern times, and probably only a fool would attempt to convince a reader, in the course of a law review article no less, that medicine, the form of science most widely used by the consuming public, is not "scientific." Yet that is what I must do here, for central to my argument is the notion that medicine is a hegemonic discourse—that it is laden with value choices and beliefs that masquerade as truth, nature, and biological "fact." My argument will be limited, however, to that part of medicine that deals with women and their reproductive processes, and I will not attempt to prove my point—a rather misguided effort anyway in an argument premised on profound skepticism about the notion of empirical proof itself—so much as to present a substantial amount of material suggestive of it. . . .

The scientific world view is accepted by scientists and laypeople alike. It is a belief system that denies its own reality as a world view, believing instead that it is a series of truths about knowing and controlling the unpredictable world we live in. . . . Through the use of the scientific method, it is thought, science can continually test and perfect the knowledge it acquires, moving ever closer to a "true" understanding of the world and the individuals who occupy it. . . . In the area of medicine, this theme of controlling nature is particularly evident. Technological advances have totally transformed what we mean by life and death, allowing tiny babies to survive and prosper after premature births and the elderly or those with permanent brain damage to exist (if not exactly "live") far beyond anything previously thought possible. Technology is extolled for enabling physicians to overcome "imperfections" in a woman's reproductive organs by removing eggs from ovaries, fertilizing them in petri dishes, and then returning them to the uterus. Physicians correct bad eyesight, replace torn ligaments, set broken bones, refashion hearts. Central to our notion of medicine is its role in controlling and transforming our bodies.

Upon examination, it can be seen that this view strongly associates science with many of the same terms that are traditionally associated with men; whereas, the opposite of science (anything that is unscientific) is associated with opposed and feminized terms. Science is thought to be an objective, neutral, rational, fact-based method of controlling nature, whereas non-"scientific" forms of knowledge are usually stigmatized as superstition and ignorance and thought to be based on subjective, biased, and emotional assessments of reality. Non-science is also clearly associated with women: the phrase "old wives' tale," for example, makes quite explicit the cultural equation between bad health care and women, simultaneously defining women's knowledge as nonscientific and dismissing it as erroneous. Moreover, women are seen not only as the source of dangerous medical advice but also as the sites of dangerous disease and decay. In short, . . . women are often treated as the prototypical embodiment of the natural world that science exists to control.

I can imagine many readers arriving at this point only to say, "So what? Medicine and science are, generally, objective and rational. Of course they are imperfect

* Nancy Ehrenreich is a Professor at the Sturm College of Law at the University of Denver.

and will continually improve, but they are nevertheless as close as we can get to a neutral and accurate understanding of the world." Many recent writings, however, have fundamentally challenged that confidence in medical knowledge. . . .

[T]hings are actually much more complicated. I will start from the fundamental assumption, long accepted in the social sciences, that biological science is a product of culture, rather than an entity existing separate and apart from the world it attempts to know. In other words, the very categories through which medical scientists comprehend the world are themselves the product of the culture in which they live. Medicine is a social construct, rather than a set of "truths" about the world. To accept this premise is not to say that medicine is "wrong" or that it never works but that its understanding is partial, its truths contingent.

Applying this insight to the reproductive context, I will contend, therefore, that the field of obstetrics is not a domain in which experts use generally unchallengeable "facts" about human reproduction to facilitate the birthing process, but rather that it is an arena of struggle over the role(s) of women in society and indeed over the meaning of the word *woman.* Before turning to that broader point, however, I must first add one last piece of the picture of how Western dualisms operate in the realm of medicine by discussing how the reproductive process itself is perceived. . . .

As many writers have pointed out, medicine (as practiced in the United States) conceives of female reproductive processes, from menstruation to childbirth to menopause, as pathological, disease-like conditions that need to be controlled to prevent them from harming the women in whose bodies they occur (or, in the case of childbirth, the fetuses those women are carrying). . . . Childbirth itself is also seen as a dangerous, pathological, and unpredictable medical event. The role of the physician during labor is conceptualized, therefore, as imposing control and predictability on this process (and, hence, on the women through whom it is played out). Physicians "manage" the labor, performing various interventions to ensure that it proceeds along the lines of "normal" births, lines that are derived by averaging the wide range of patterns that labor actually follows among different women into a standardized set of "stages" with their own prescribed durations and symptomatology. In addition, successful childbirth has increasingly become equated with only the production of a "perfect" product, a child free of infection or disabilities. . . .

Protecting a fetus often entails imposing certain risks on the woman carrying it; a cesarean section, for example, is at least twice as likely as a vaginal birth to result in the death of the mother. Yet this risk becomes irrelevant if the cultural norm already prescribes that she be willing to sacrifice anything and everything for her children (born or unborn). Given that norm, it is easy for the doctor to either (1) assume that she is a good mother and therefore not consider her preferences very much during labor, on the assumption that she would want to sacrifice for her child, or (2) assume that she is a bad mother and therefore not consider her preferences very much during labor, on the assumption that she has no right to have them respected. . . .

In recent years, however, the medical model of reproduction has come under sustained attack by a burgeoning (at the beginning, primarily white) women's health movement. . . . [T]here are essentially three ways in which such sets of opposing terms are usually criticized. First, one can argue that the dualisms unfairly stereotype members of the low status group. That is, they are inaccurate: most white women are not passive, most African-Americans are not lazy, and so on. Those presenting a parallel challenge to the medical model claim that it unfairly stigmatizes alternative birthing approaches as less scientific or successful than traditional medicine. Second, one can argue that the dualisms elevate traits that are actually unenviable and socially destructive and disparage traits that are good and valuable. Thus, for example, relational feminists have contended that pure logic is not necessarily superior to intuitive understanding and that striving for self-sufficiency may be less laudable than recognizing human interdependence, and race theorists have suggested that contextual facts and narrative are as powerful conceptual tools as abstract analytics. In the reproductive context, this criticism takes the form of an effort to elevate alternative birthing strategies, arguing that they are actually better—both in terms of quality of care and in terms of human fulfillment—than the traditional approach.

The third critique of Western dualisms, and the one that is most important to my argument, alleges that the distinctions the dualisms draw are themselves incoherent. That is, in any particular instance, it will not be readily apparent whether an individual's reaction to her circumstances is rational or emotional, active or passive. What seems absolutely illogical to one person, for example, might indeed seem perfectly rational to another. Because of this indeterminacy of meaning, the act of labeling conduct as one or the other is facilitated by unstated (and perhaps unconscious) assumptions that reflect and reinforce power disparities in society. In other words, the dualisms do not represent or identify "real" differences in the world but rather serve as vehicles for the deployment of social power.

I mean two things by this assertion. First, the power to decide what is rational (or whatever) and what is not devolves upon those with power in the society at large. Because their visions of the world are those most often conveyed through societal institutions such as law, the media, and schools, it is their interpretations of a particular incident that will seem most "true." Second, that power to name, to interpret the world, legitimates the position of the dominant group to which it belongs as well as that group's oppression of others. The consistent application of the dominant terms of the dualisms to those in power and the devalued terms to a variety of "others" reinforces negative images of those others that then seem to justify their subordination. Relying on these insights, much of the critical feminist and critical race theory scholarship in the last several years has been directed at revealing the ways in which the dominant belief system's interpretation of the world prevents judges from seeing the behavior and concerns of women (of all colors) or people of color (of both sexes) as rational, responsible, and legitimate. . . .

II. LAW AND MEDICINE AS MUTUALLY LEGITIMATING DISCOURSES AND PRACTICES

. . . Legal authorities in general pay great deference to medical expertise. The most obvious example of this deference, of course, is the retention of a custom standard to define medical malpractice. . . . In the area of reproduction, this judicial deference to medical authority is particularly marked. . . . This judicial tendency to subsume women's interest in controlling their reproductive capacities within physicians' right to practice medicine reflects a similar attitude in the society at large. . . .

When considered in light of the sets of associations previously described, law's great deference to medicine is perhaps not surprising. . . . [L]aw is associated with many of the same traits as medicine. Both are thought to be neutral and objective pursuits, devoid of personal bias or subjective self-interest. Both are seen as coldly rational — as based on facts and rules, rather than opinions and values. Moreover, both are seen as controlling people: Whereas medicine controls their physical bodies, law controls the body politic, providing a peaceful means for resolving disputes that otherwise might dissolve into warfare. Put another way, medicine controls physical nature, whereas law avoids a social "state of nature." Finally, both fields are populated by elite white men who enjoy very comfortable incomes and high status. Given these affinities, judicial trust in the medical profession to make dispassionate and value-free decisions in individual cases is not surprising. . . .

■ IN RE A.C.
573 A.2d 1235 (D.C. App. 1990) (en banc)

TERRY, Associate Judge.

I

. . . This case came before the trial court when George Washington University Hospital petitioned the emergency judge in chambers for declaratory relief as to how it should treat its patient, A.C., who was close to death from cancer and was twenty-six and one-half weeks pregnant with a viable fetus. After a hearing lasting approximately three hours, which was held at the hospital (though not in A.C.'s room), the court ordered that a cesarean section be performed on A.C. to deliver the fetus. Counsel for A.C. immediately sought a stay in this court, which was unanimously denied by a hastily assembled division of three judges. In re A.C., 533 A.2d 611 (D.C. 1987). The cesarean was performed, and a baby girl, L.M.C., was delivered. Tragically, the child died within two and one-half hours, and the mother died two days later.

Counsel for A.C. now maintain that A.C. was competent and that she made an informed choice not to have the cesarean performed. Given this view of the facts, they argue that it was error for the trial court to weigh the state's interest in preserving the potential life of a viable fetus against A.C.'s interest in having her decision respected. They argue further that, even if the substituted judgment procedure had been followed, the evidence would necessarily show that A.C. would not have wanted the cesarean section. Under either analysis, according to these arguments, the trial court erred in subordinating A.C.'s right to bodily integrity in favor of the state's interest in potential life. . . .

II

[A.C. had suffered from cancer for 14 years. During a period of remission, she married and conceived a child. At 25 weeks in her pregnancy, her doctors found a terminal, inoperable tumor in her lung. She decided to continue her pregnancy and to receive palliative treatment, apparently with the desire to extend her life at least to the twenty-eighth week of pregnancy, when the prognosis for the fetus would be much better if intervention were necessary. However, as her condition worsened during her twenty-sixth week, her stated desire to have the baby became more equivocal. Her mother opposed the operation, but her husband "was too distraught to testify and uttered only a few words at the hearing."]

After hearing this testimony and the arguments of counsel, the trial court made oral findings of fact. It found, first, that A.C. would probably die, according to uncontroverted medical testimony, "within the next twenty-four to forty-eight hours"; second, that A.C. was "pregnant with a twenty-six and a half week viable fetus who, based upon uncontroverted medical testimony, has approximately a 50 to 60 percent chance to survive if a cesarean section is performed as soon as possible"; third, that because the fetus was viable, "the state has [an] important and legitimate interest in protecting the potentiality of human life"; and fourth, that there had been some testimony that the operation "may very well hasten the death of [A.C.]," but that there had also been testimony that delay would greatly increase the risk to the fetus and that "the prognosis is not great for the fetus to be delivered post-mortem. . . ." Most significantly, the court found:

> The court is of the view that it does not clearly know what [A.C.'s] present views are with respect to the issue of whether or not the child should live or die. She's presently unconscious. As late as Friday of last week, she wanted the baby to live. As late as yesterday, she did not know for sure.

Having made these findings of fact and conclusions of law, and expressly relying on In re Madyun, 114 Daily Wash. L. Rptr. 2233 (D.C. Super. Ct. July 26, 1986), the court ordered that a cesarean section be performed to deliver A.C.'s child. . . .

[After the judge's order was communicated to A.C. by her doctors, she at first agreed to the operation, but shortly later she refused. Although she appeared lucid, her doctors differed in their opinions as to whether she had reached a truly competent and informed decision one way or the other.] After hearing this new evidence, the court found that it was "still not clear what her intent is" and again ordered that a cesarean section be performed. . . . The operation took place, but the baby lived for only a few hours, and A.C. succumbed to cancer two days later.

IV

A. INFORMED CONSENT AND BODILY INTEGRITY

A number of learned articles have been written about the propriety or impropriety of court-ordered cesarean sections. E.g., Johnsen, The Creation of Fetal Rights: Conflicts with Women's Constitutional Rights to Liberty, Privacy, and Equal Protection, 95 Yale L.J. 599 (1986); Kolder, Gallagher & Parsons, Court-Ordered Obstetrical Interventions, 316 New Eng. J. Med. 1192 (1987) (hereafter Obstetrical Interventions); Rhoden, The Judge in the Delivery Room: The Emergence of Court-Ordered Caesareans, 74 Cal. L. Rev. 1951 (1986); Robertson, Procreative Liberty and the Control of Conception, Pregnancy, and Childbirth, 69 Va. L. Rev. 405 (1983). Commentators have also considered how medical decisions for incompetent persons which may involve some detriment or harm to them should be made. . . . These and other articles demonstrate the complexity of medical intervention cases, which become more complex with the steady advance of medical technology. From a recent national survey, it appears that over the five years preceding the survey there were 36 attempts to override maternal refusals of proposed medical treatment, and that in 15 instances where court orders were sought to authorize cesarean interventions, 13 such orders were granted. Obstetrical Interventions, supra, 316 New Eng. J. Med. at 1192-1193. . . . Nevertheless, there is only one published decision from an appellate court that deals with the question of when, or even whether, a court may order a cesarean section: Jefferson v. Griffin Spalding County Hospital Authority, 247 Ga. 86, 274 S.E.2d 457 (1981).

Jefferson is of limited relevance, if any at all, to the present case. In *Jefferson* there was a competent refusal by the mother to undergo the proposed surgery, but the evidence showed that performance of the cesarean was in the medical interests of both the mother and the fetus.[7] . . .

[O]ur analysis of this case begins with the tenet common to all medical treatment cases: that any person has the right to make an informed choice, if competent to do so, to accept or forego medical treatment. . . .

[C]ourts do not compel one person to permit a significant intrusion upon his or her bodily integrity for the benefit of another person's health. See, e.g., . . . McFall v. Shimp, 10 Pa. D. & C.3d 90 (Allegheny County Ct. 1978). In *McFall* the court refused to order Shimp to donate bone marrow which was necessary to save the life of his cousin, McFall:

> The common law has consistently held to a rule which provides that one human being is under no legal compulsion to give aid or to take action to save another human being or to rescue. . . . For our law to compel defendant to submit to an intrusion of his body would change every concept and principle upon which our society is founded. To do so would defeat the sanctity of the individual, and would impose a rule which would know no limits, and one could not imagine where the line would be drawn.

Id. at 91. [This case is excerpted and discussed at page 655.] Even though Shimp's refusal would mean death for McFall, the court would not order Shimp to allow his body to be invaded. It has been suggested that fetal cases are different because a woman who "has chosen to lend her body to bring [a] child into the world" has an enhanced duty to assure the welfare of the fetus, sufficient even to require her to undergo cesarean surgery. Robertson, Procreative Liberty, supra, 69 Va. L. Rev. at 456. Surely, however, a fetus cannot have rights in this respect superior to those of a person who has already been born.[8] . . .

7. Because the patient in *Jefferson* had a placenta previa which blocked the birth canal, doctors estimated that without cesarean intervention there was a 99 percent chance that her full-term fetus would perish and a 50 percent chance that the mother would die as well. The mother was unquestionably competent to make her own treatment decisions, but refused a cesarean because of her religious beliefs. A trial court gave custody of the fetus to state human resources officials and ordered a cesarean section; the Georgia Supreme Court denied the parents' motion for a stay. [Nevertheless, the mother went into hiding, and both she and the child survived without the operation.]

8. There are also practical consequences to consider. What if A.C. had refused to comply with a court order that she submit to a cesarean? Under the circumstances she obviously could not have been held in civil contempt and imprisoned or required to pay a daily fine until compliance. . . . Enforcement could be accomplished only through physical force or its equivalent. A.C. would have to be fastened with restraints to the operating table, or perhaps involuntarily rendered unconscious by forcibly injecting her with an anesthetic, and then subjected to unwanted major surgery. Such actions would surely give one pause in a civilized society, especially when A.C. had done no wrong. Cf. Rochin v. California, 342 U.S. 165, 169, 72 S. Ct. 205, 208, 96 L. Ed. 183 (1952).

In those rare cases in which a patient's right to decide her own course of treatment has been judicially overridden, courts have usually acted to vindicate the state's interest in protecting third parties, even if in fetal state. . . .

We hold, however, that without a competent refusal from A.C. to go forward with the surgery, and without a finding through substituted judgment that A.C. would not have consented to the surgery, it was error for the trial court to proceed to a balancing analysis, weighing the rights of A.C. against the interests of the state.

There are two additional arguments against overriding A.C.'s objections to caesarean surgery. First . . . [court orders diminish the patient's trust in her physician and may deter women from seeking care]. . . . Second, and even more compellingly, any judicial proceeding in a case such as this will ordinarily take place—like the one before us here—under time constraints so pressing that it is difficult or impossible for the mother to communicate adequately with counsel, or for counsel to organize an effective factual and legal presentation in defense of her liberty and privacy interests and bodily integrity. . . .

In this case A.C.'s court-appointed attorney was unable even to meet with his client before the hearing. By the time the case was heard, A.C.'s condition did not allow her to be present, nor was it reasonably possible for the judge to hear from her directly. The factual record, moreover, was significantly flawed because A.C.'s medical records were not before the court and because Dr. Jeffrey Moscow, the physician who had been treating A.C. for many years, was not even contacted and hence did not testify.[17] . . .

C. THE TRIAL COURT'S RULING . . .

What a trial court must do in a case such as this is to determine, if possible, whether the patient is capable of making an informed decision about the course of her medical treatment. If she is, and if she makes such a decision, her wishes will control in virtually all cases. If the court finds that the patient is incapable of making an informed consent (and thus is incompetent), then the court must make a substituted judgment. This means that the court must ascertain as best it can what the patient would do if faced with the particular treatment question. Again, in virtually all cases the decision of the patient, albeit discerned through the mechanism of substituted judgment, will control. We do not quite foreclose the possibility that a conflicting state interest may be so compelling that the patient's wishes must yield, but we anticipate that such cases will be extremely rare and truly exceptional. This is not such a case.

Having said that, we go no further. We need not decide whether, or in what circumstances, the state's interests can ever prevail over the interests of a pregnant patient. We emphasize, nevertheless, that it would be an extraordinary case indeed

---

17. In an affidavit filed after the hearing, Dr. Moscow said that if he had been notified of the proceedings, he would have come to the hospital immediately and would have testified that a cesarean section was medically inadvisable *both for A.C. and for the fetus.* Dr. Moscow also viewed the hospital's handling of A.C.'s case as deficient in several other significant respects. In these circumstances we think it unfortunate that Dr. Moscow was not called by representatives of the hospital and made available to the court when the hospital decided to seek judicial guidance.

in which a court might ever be justified in overriding the patient's wishes and authorizing a major surgical procedure such as a cesarean section.[23]

. . . If the substituted judgment procedure were to be followed, there is evidence going both ways as to what decision A.C. would have made, and we see no point in requiring the court now to make that determination when it can have no practical effect on either A.C. or L.M.C.

Accordingly, we vacate the order of the trial court and remand the case for such further proceedings as may be appropriate.

BELSON, Associate Judge, concurring in part and dissenting in part.

I agree with much of the majority opinion, but I disagree with its ultimate ruling that the trial court's order must be set aside, and with the narrow view it takes of the state's interest in preserving life and the unborn child's interest in life. . . . I would hold that in those instances, fortunately rare, in which the viable unborn child's interest in living and the state's parallel interest in protecting human life come into conflict with the mother's decision to forgo a procedure such as a cesarean section, a balancing should be struck in which the unborn child's and the state's interests are entitled to substantial weight.

It was acknowledged in Roe v. Wade, 410 U.S. 113 (1973), that the state's interest in potential human life becomes compelling at the point of viability. . . . When the unborn child reaches the state of viability, the child becomes a party whose interests must be considered. . . .

The balancing test should be applied in instances in which women become pregnant and carry an unborn child to the point of viability. This is not an unreasonable classification because, I submit, a woman who carries a child to viability is in fact a member of a unique category of persons. Her circumstances differ fundamentally from those of other potential patients for medical procedures that will aid another person, for example, a potential donor of bone marrow for transplant. This is so because she has undertaken to bear another human being, and has carried an unborn child to viability. Another unique feature of the situation we address arises from the singular nature of the dependency of the unborn child upon the mother. A woman carrying a viable unborn child is not in the same category as a relative, friend, or stranger called upon to donate bone marrow or an organ for transplant. Rather, the expectant mother has placed herself in a special class of persons who

---

23. In particular, we stress that nothing in this opinion should be read as either approving or disapproving the holding in In re Madyun, supra. There are substantial factual differences between Madyun and the present case. In this case, for instance, the medical interests of the mother and the fetus were in sharp conflict; what was good for one would have been harmful to the other. In *Madyun*, however, there was no real conflict between the interests of mother and fetus; on the contrary, there was strong evidence that the proposed cesarean would be beneficial to both. Moreover, in *Madyun* the pregnancy was at full term, and Mrs. Madyun had been in labor for two and a half days; in this case, however, A.C. was barely two-thirds of the way through her pregnancy, and there were no signs of labor. If another *Madyun*-type case ever comes before this court, its result may well depend on facts that we cannot now foresee. For that reason (among others), we defer until another day any discussion of whether *Madyun* was rightly or wrongly decided. [Elsewhere the court also limited its reasoning to those cases involving "a major bodily invasion," reserving judgment on when "lesser invasions" would be permitted and on "where the line should be drawn between 'major' and 'minor' surgery."]

are bringing another person into existence, and upon whom that other person's life is totally dependent. Also, uniquely, the viable unborn child is literally captive within the mother's body. No other potential beneficiary of a surgical procedure on another is in that position.

For all of these reasons, . . . I cannot agree that in cases where a viable unborn child is in the picture, it would be extremely rare, within that universe, to require that the mother accede to the vital needs of the viable unborn child.[8]

For the reasons stated above, I would affirm.

Notes: Forced Medical Treatment

1. *Abortion and Cesareans.* How should the state's interest in protecting viable fetuses, recognized in *Roe, Casey,* and subsequent case law affect a woman's right to control her own medical treatment? Should these decisions be limited to the abortion context in which they arose? Does the underlying reasoning—that the state's compelling interest can override a woman's constitutionally protected right to choose abortion—seem transferable where the constitutional interests at stake are a woman's right to choose her own medical care and to be free from extreme invasions to her bodily integrity? Recall that Cruzan v. Director, Missouri Department of Health, 497 U.S. 261 (1990), suggests that the right to control end-of-life treatment decisions has a constitutional dimension. If a state interest is compelling in one circumstance, wouldn't it be compelling in the other? In which cases would the In re A.C. court permit forced medical interventions to preserve the fetus? For a thoughtful analysis of the state's interest in potential life, see Dov Fox, Interest Creep, 82 Geo Wash. L. Rev. 273 (2014) (arguing that the "state's interest in 'potential life'" should be understood to reflect four different types of interests: "prenatal welfare, postnatal welfare, social values and social effects").

2. *Moral or Legal Obligations to Protect Fetuses?* Generations of law students have considered the hypothetical of the champion swimmer who observes a person drowning offshore. The bystander is said to have a moral, but not a legal, obligation to attempt to save the drowning swimmer. Is the pregnant woman in the same position as the expert swimmer? Which of the following factors should be considered ethically or legally relevant to the resolution of these cases: Whether the woman became pregnant by choice? Whether she intends to carry the fetus to term? The gestational age of the fetus? The probability of harm to the fetus? The degree of harm to the fetus? The probability and degree of harm confronted by the pregnant woman? Whether the proposed medical treatment would benefit the woman as well as the fetus? The nature of the intrusion into the woman's autonomy? The rationale for the woman's refusal of treatment? What other factors might you consider? Do pregnant women have an

---

8. To the contrary, it appears that a majority of courts faced with this issue have found that the state's compelling interest in protection of the unborn child should prevail. See Noble-Allgire, Court-Ordered Cesarean Sections, 10 J. Legal Med. 211, 236 (1989). I add that in mapping this uncharted area of the law, we can draw lines, and a line I would draw would be to preclude the use of physical force to perform an operation. The force of the court order itself as well as the use of the contempt power would, I think, be adequate in most cases. See id. at 243.

ethical duty to protect their fetuses from harm? Should pregnant women have a legal obligation to protect their fetuses from harm, just as parents have a legal obligation to safeguard their children? For a detailed analysis of the ethical and legal aspects of these cases, see David Orentlicher, Matters of Life and Death: Making Moral Theory Work in Medical Ethics and the Law 91-120 (2001) (arguing that pregnant women may have both a moral and a legal obligation to protect their fetuses, at least under some circumstances, but noting that the creation of a legal obligation could create a perverse incentive for pregnant women to avoid prenatal care).

3. *Court-Ordered Medical Interventions.* The *A.C.* court implies, in dicta, that the state's interest in fetal life might override a woman's interest in avoiding some minimally intrusive medical interventions. Should the state's interest in preserving the life of a viable fetus outweigh a woman's right to refuse routine prenatal care? Antibiotics? A physician's recommendation of complete bed rest for three months? The use of forceps? A cesarean section delivery?

Most of the reported cases involve cesareans. The Kolder study described by the *A.C.* court also found:

> Among 21 cases in which court orders were sought, the orders were obtained in 86 percent; in 88 percent of those cases, the orders were received within six hours. Eighty-one percent of the women involved were black, Asian, or Hispanic, 44 percent were unmarried, and 24 percent did not speak English as their primary language. All the women were treated in a teaching-hospital clinic or were receiving public assistance. . . .

Veronica E. Kolder et al., Court-Ordered Obstetrical Interventions, 316 New Eng. J. Med. 1192, 1192 (1987).

The In re A.C. decision is regarded by most law review commentators as the dominant judicial approach, at least at the appellate level. See also In re Baby Boy Doe, a Fetus, 632 N.E.2d 326, 330 (Ill. App. Ct. 1994) (Illinois courts should not balance the rights of the viable fetus against the woman's right to control her treatment; "a woman's competent choice in refusing medical treatment as invasive as a cesarean section . . . must be honored, even in circumstances where the choice may be harmful to her fetus."). But see Pemberton v. Tallahassee Memorial Regional Center, 66 F. Supp. 2d 1247 (N.D. Fla. 1999).

In *Pemberton,* a woman subjected to a state-court-ordered cesarean section brought §1983 and §1985 claims in federal court against the regional hospital, claiming that its actions had violated her constitutional rights to "bodily integrity . . . to refuse unwanted medical treatment . . . to make important personal and family decisions without undue governmental interference . . . [and] her right to religious freedom." Id. at 1251. The court rejected the claims, noting:

> Ms. Pemberton was at full term and actively in labor. It was clear that one way or the other, a baby would be born (or stillborn) very soon, certainly within hours. Whatever the scope of Ms. Pemberton's personal constitutional rights . . . they clearly did not outweigh the interests of the State of Florida in preserving the life of the unborn child. . . . Bearing an unwanted child is surely a greater intrusion on the mother's constitutional interests than undergoing a caesarean section to deliver a child that the mother affirmatively desires to deliver. [Id. at 1251-1252.]

Could a woman's refusal of a cesarean section recommended by her physicians be used as evidence of neglect? New Jersey Division of Youth and Family Services v. V.M.

and B.G., 974 A.2d 448 (N.J. Super. 2009) (no); and Jessica L. Waters, In Whose Best Interest?, 34 Harv. J. L. & Gender 81 (2011).

Cases involving less intrusive measures are less common. See, e.g., Burton v. State, 49 So. 3d 263 (Fla. App. 2010) (overturning lower court order requiring pregnant woman "to submit to any medical treatment deemed necessary by the attending obstetrician, including detention in the hospital for enforcement of bed-rest . . ."); Barbara F. v. Bristol Division of the Juvenile Court Department, 735 N.E.2d 357 (Mass. 2000) (discussing case involving protective custody of pregnant woman who had religious objections to prenatal care); Taft v. Taft, 446 N.E.2d 395 (Mass. 1983) (rejecting husband's effort to obtain a court order requiring pregnant wife to undergo "purse string" operation on cervix). A maternal-fetal conflict may also arise when a woman needs medication that can negatively impact her fetus. See, e.g., Guardianship of J.D.S., 864 So. 2d 534 (Fla. App. 2004) (state law does not permit appointment of guardian for a fetus in case involving incompetent pregnant women whose medications posed risk to fetus). Will clashes between optimal fetal development and basic lifestyle choices, such as whether to smoke, what to eat, and how to conduct childbirth, arise with greater frequency in the future due to rapid advances in: (1) understanding the fetal developmental process; (2) refining diagnostic techniques that detect fetal problems; and (3) developing modes of surgical and medical intervention that allow in utero therapy? See, e.g., Bernard M. Dickens & Rebecca J. Cook, Legal and Ethical Issues in Fetal Surgery, 115 Int'l J. Gynecol. Obstet. 80 (2011).

4. *Medical Predictions and Medical Ethics.* In a surprising number of the reported cases, such as the principal case and *Jefferson,* described in n.7 of the opinion, the doctors' predictions of the need for fetal intervention proved completely wrong. Sometimes the strength of the medical evidence appears to be exaggerated by the court. See *Pemberton,* 66 F. Supp. at 1250 n.2 (noting that the underlying court order exaggerated the degree of certainty of the underlying medical testimony). The excerpt from Professor Ehrenreich's work offers a feminist analysis of science and medicine, noting as well the power given to medical pronouncements by the courts. Does this critical perspective offer either explanatory or normative insights about these cases?

The absence of predictive certainty has played at least some role in the development of the ethical guidelines of medical societies. See, e.g., Committee on Ethics Opinion, American College of Obstetricians and Gynecologists, Refusal of Medically Recommended Treatment During Pregnancy (No. 664, June 2016) ("The use of coercion is not only ethically impermissible but also medically inadvisable because of the realities of prognostic uncertainty and the limitations of medical knowledge. . . . . [I]t is never acceptable for obstetrician-gynecologists to attempt to influence patients toward a clinical decision using coercion. Obstetrician-gynecologists are discouraged in the strongest possible terms from the use of duress, manipulation, coercion, physical force, or threats, including threats to involve the courts or child protective services, to motivate women toward a specific clinical decision"), available at www.acog.org/Resources-And-Publications/Committee-Opinions. The American Medical Association House of Delegates–approved policy provides:

> Court Ordered Medical Treatments and Legal Penalties for Potentially Harmful Behavior by Pregnant Women: (1) Judicial intervention is inappropriate when a woman has made an informed refusal of a medical treatment designed to benefit her fetus. If an exceptional circumstance could be found in which a medical treatment poses an insignificant or no health risk to the woman, entails a minimal invasion of her bodily integrity, and would clearly prevent substantial and irreversible

harm to her fetus, it might be appropriate for a physician to seek judicial intervention. However, the fundamental principle against compelled medical procedures should control in all cases which do not present such exceptional circumstances.

AMA, H-420.969, Legal Interventions During Pregnancy (reaffirmed 2016), available through: https://policysearch.ama-assn.org/policyfinder.

5. *State or Private Interests.* Should it matter whether the action to force a cesarean is brought by private parties or by the state? In re A.C. was initiated by a hospital, which sought a declaratory judgment permitting the surgery. In re Baby Boy Doe, supra note 3, was pursued by the Illinois state attorney's office. Should the hospital be able to assert the state's interest in protecting fetuses? In the employment context, the Supreme Court has held that policies purportedly designed to protect fetuses that discriminate against fertile women constitute impermissible sex discrimination under Title VII of the Civil Rights Act. Int'l Union, United Automobile, Aerospace and Agricultural Implement Workers of America, UAW v. Johnson Controls, 499 U.S. 187 (1991). Johnson Controls argued that its policy of discriminating against fertile woman was justified as a "bona fide occupational qualification [BFOQ] necessary to the normal operation" of its business. The Court rejected the claim, holding that "Johnson Controls' professed moral and ethical concerns about the welfare of the next generation do not suffice to establish a BFOQ of female sterility." The Civil Rights Act provisions apply only to employment, not to a hospital's treatment of its patients, but the Court's reasoning suggests that private third parties might be restricted from discriminating against women in order to protect fetuses. For more information on the *Johnson Controls* decision, see Mary Becker, Reproductive Hazards After *Johnson Controls*, 31 Hous. L. Rev. 43 (1994); Elaine Draper, Reproductive Hazards and Fetal Exclusion Policies After *Johnson Controls*, 12 Stan. L. & Pol'y Rev. 117 (2001).

6. *Testing and Medical Treatment for HIV Transmission.* Many women with HIV infection are pregnant or hope to become pregnant. Pregnant women who take anti-retroviral drugs and deliver through cesarean section can reduce the risk of HIV transmission from 25-30 percent to a little over 2 percent. Is the risk of HIV transmission from woman to child sufficient to support a program of mandatory HIV testing for pregnant women? Does your answer depend on the use to be made of the test information? What if it is used to "encourage" HIV-infected pregnant women to abort? To get treatment for themselves or their children? Many states have enacted statutes designed to encourage the use of "routine" HIV testing for pregnant women. See Leslie E. Wolf et al., Legal Barriers to Implementing Recommendations for Universal Routine Prenatal HIV Testing, 32 J. L. Med. & Ethics 137 (2004). In 2006, the federal Centers for Disease Control and Prevention issued new guidelines encouraging HIV screening for pregnant women. Bernard M. Branson et al., Revised Recommendations for HIV Testing of Adults, Adolescents, and Pregnant Women in Health Care Settings, 55 MMWR Recomm. Rep. 1 (2006) (RR-14) (recommending directive counseling); and Lawrence O. Gostin, HIV Screening in Health Care Settings: Public Health and Civil Liberties in Conflict?, 296 JAMA 2023 (2006). See discussion at page 946.

Should women with HIV infection be forced to take anti-retroviral therapy? Is this the type of "lesser" invasion of liberty that a court might accept? See In re the Termination of Parental Rights to Aaliyah W. v. Abigail W., 2011 WL 446866 (Wis. App. 2011) (noting detention of pregnant woman in hospital to ensure HIV treatment necessary to protect unborn child). See also Michael A. Grizzi, Compelled Antiviral Treatment of HIV Positive Women, 5 UCLA Women's L. J. 473 (1995); Margot Kaplan, "A Special

Class of Persons": Pregnant Women's Right to Refuse Medical Treatment After *Gonzales v. Carhart*, 13 J. Const. L. 145 (2010). You should reconsider these problems after reading Chapter 8's discussion of public health laws under which people can be screened for diseases and forced to undergo treatment to protect the health of third parties. See pages 958-962. Are the rules governing forced medical treatment for pregnant women consistent with other public health policies? Are any differences explained by the lesser weight given to the state's interest in protecting fetuses, even viable ones?

7. *Further Reading.* For additional consideration of the **ethical and legal aspects of forced medical treatment** (note 2) see April L. Cherry, The Free Exercise Rights of Pregnant Women Who Refuse Medical Treatment, 69 Tenn. L. Rev. 563 (2002); Michelle Goodwin, Fetal Protection Laws: Moral Panic and the New Constitutional Battlefront, 102 Cal. L. Rev. 781 (2014); Michelle Oberman, Mothers and Doctors' Orders: Unmasking the Doctor's Fiduciary Role in Maternal-Fetal Conflicts, 94 Nw. U. L. Rev. 451 (2000). **Court ordered medical interventions** (note 3) are analyzed in April L. Cherry, *Roe*'s Legacy: The Nonconsensual Medical Treatment of Pregnant Women and Implications for Female Citizenship, 6 U. Pa. J. Const. L. 723 (2004); Linda C. Fentiman, The New "Fetal Protection": The Wrong Answer to the Crisis of Inadequate Health Care for Women and Children, 84 Denv. U. L. Rev. 537 (2006); Lynn M. Paltrow & Jeanne Flavin, Arrests of and Forced Interventions on Pregnant Women in the United States, 1973-2005, 38 J. Health Politics, Pol'y and L.299 (2013) (summarizing available data on 413 cases of "forced interventions," some of which involved forced medical treatment). Articles considering **less physically intrusive forms of forced medical care** (note 3) include Julie D. Cantor, Court-Ordered Care—A Complication of Pregnancy to Avoid, 366 New Eng. J. Med. 2237 (2012) (discussing *Burton*, supra, and reviewing cases); April L. Cherry, The Detention, Confinement, and Incarceration of Pregnant Women for the Benefit of Fetal Health, 16 Colum. J. Gender & L. 147 (2007).

Problem: Pregnancy, Advanced Directives, and Brain Death

Janet Kuan was 24 weeks pregnant when an aneurysm burst in her brain. She was rushed to the hospital and into surgery, but she experienced extensive brain damage. Although her brain stem is still functioning—and she can breathe without a respirator—all of her higher brain functions have irreversibly ceased. Janet's physicians agree that she is in a permanent vegetative state.

Two years ago, Janet filled out a living will form provided to her by her physician. The form indicated that she wished to refuse "life-sustaining treatments" if she were reliably diagnosed as suffering from a "terminal condition," which was defined to include a "permanent vegetative state." The form also included the following language: "Pursuant to state law, this document becomes null and void and will be given no effect if I am pregnant at the time I am diagnosed with the terminal condition." Janet had crossed out this language in the form and written: "I do not wish to be treated if I am terminally ill and pregnant."

Janet's husband, Nick, wants Janet to be kept alive using a feeding tube and whatever other means are necessary. He hopes that the child can be delivered alive. Janet's parents are repelled by the thought of their child being used as an incubator. What should Janet's physicians do? If the courts become involved, how should they rule and for what reasons?

Many states have enacted living will or advanced directives statutes that purport to restrict the ability of pregnant women to refuse life-sustaining treatment. Assess the validity of these statutes under *Cruzan*, supra at pages 547 and 511, and the majority and dissenting opinions in *A.C.* Should it matter whether the fetus is viable? Would the In re A.C. majority approve the application of the statute to void a pregnant woman's decision not to pursue life-sustaining treatment under the theory that the treatment would extend rather than diminish her life expectancy? Should it matter whether the life-sustaining treatment is more or less invasive than a cesarean section? For a discussion of these issues, see Timothy J. Burch, Incubator or Individual?: The Legal and Policy Deficiencies of Pregnancy Clauses in Living Will and Advanced Health Care Directive Statutes, 54 Md. L. Rev. 528 (1995); Katherine A. Taylor, Compelling Pregnancy at Death's Door, 7 Colum. J. Gender & L. 85 (1997). Could continued treatment against the wishes of the pregnant woman give rise to a successful tort claim? Nadia N. Sawicki, A New Life for Wrongful Living, 58 N.Y.L. Sch. L. Rev. 279 (2013/14) (suggesting new approaches).

What if Janet Kuan's brain injuries are so severe that she meets the requirements for brain death? Are there any legal or ethical problems associated with maintaining a brain-dead woman on life support to permit her fetus to mature with the hope that it can be delivered alive? See Manny Fernandez, Texas Woman Taken Off Life Support After Order, N.Y. Times, January 26, 2014 (court finds state law barring withdrawal of life sustaining treatment from pregnant women does not apply when woman is brain dead); David R. Field et al., Maternal Brain Death During Pregnancy, 260 JAMA 816 (1988) (patient maintained in a brain-dead state for nine weeks at a cost of $217,784 before delivery of an infant weighing about 3 pounds); Lawrence O. Gostin, Legal and Ethical Responsibilities Following Brain Death: The McMath and Muñoz Cases, 311 JAMA 903 (2014); Seema K. Shah, Piercing the Veil: The Limits of Brain Death as a Legal Fiction, 48 U. Mich. J. L. Ref. 301 (2015) (arguing that legal fiction of brain death should not be used in cases involving pregnant, brain-dead women).

Problem: Post-Cesarean Deliveries

Conflicts over cesarean births are also connected to debates about whether women who have had a cesarean delivery may subsequently deliver vaginally without undue risk to themselves or to their children. See, e.g., Jun Zhang et al., Contemporary Cesarean Delivery Practice in the United States, 203 Am. J. Obstet. Gynecol. 326.e1 (2010) (noting decline in rate of vaginal birth after cesarean delivery (VBAC) despite evidence supporting attempt at vaginal delivery). Concerns about the risks have led physicians and hospitals to refuse to offer vaginal delivery as an option to women who have had a cesarean section delivery in the past. See Anemona Hartocollis, Mother Accuses Doctors of Forcing C-Section and Files Suit, N.Y. Times, May 16, 2014; and E. L. Tilden et al., Vaginal Birth After Cesarean, 216 Am J. Obstet. Gynecol 403.e1 (2017) (noting lack of access to in-hospital VBAC options). Should a woman who has previously had a cesarean delivery have a right to give birth vaginally despite any increased risk? Is this a matter that can and should be dealt with using the informed consent process? If the informed consent process is legally adequate, would there be any heightened malpractice risk for the health care providers? See AMA, H-420.969, Legal Interventions During Pregnancy, supra ("To minimize the risk of legal action by a pregnant patient or an injured fetus, the physician should document medical recommendations made including the consequences of failure to comply with the physician's recommendation"). Can the woman waive her child's right to bring a claim for damages? Is the woman's right to choose vaginal birth related in any way to her right to refuse life-sustaining treatment?

Problem: Access to Drugs Associated with Birth Defects

How should the FDA regulate medications that could have a negative impact on fetuses if taken by pregnant women? Accutane® (used to treat acne), thalidomide (used to treat leprosy), and other products are associated with a significant risk of severe birth defects. Should the products be banned for all, prescribed only for those women who are willing to demonstrate that they are not pregnant and will not become pregnant, or prescribed for anyone with suitable warnings? See Ami E. Doshi, The Cost of Clear Skin: Balancing the Social and Safety Costs of IPledge with the Efficacy of Accutane (Isotretinoin), 37 Seton Hall L. Rev. 625 (2007); Richard A. Epstein, Regulatory Paternalism in the Market for Drugs: Lessons from Vioxx and Celebrex, 5 Yale J. Health Pol'y L. & Ethics 741 (2005); Lars Noah, Too High a Price for Some Drugs? The FDA Burdens Reproductive Choice, 44 San Diego L. Rev. 231 (2007); Toby L. Schonfeld et al., iPledge Allegiance to the Pill: Evaluation of Year 1 of a Birth Defect Prevention and Monitoring System, 37 J. L. Med. & Ethics 104 (2009). See also, Cerveny v. Aventis, Inc., 855 F.3d 1091 (2017) (analyzing whether state failure to warn claims are subject to preemption; case involves failure to warn that Clomid fertility drug could cause birth defects).

3. Pregnant Women and Drug Use

■ WHITNER v. SOUTH CAROLINA
492 S.E.2d 777 (S.C. 1997), cert. denied, 523 U.S. 1145 (1998)

TOAL, Justice.

This case concerns the scope of the child abuse and endangerment statute in the South Carolina Children's Code (the Code), S.C. Code Ann. §20-7-50 (1985) [the "statute"]. We hold the word child as used in that statute includes viable fetuses.

On April 20, 1992, Cornelia Whitner (Whitner) pled guilty to criminal child neglect for causing her baby to be born with cocaine metabolites in its system by reason of Whitner's ingestion of crack cocaine during the third trimester of her pregnancy. The circuit court judge sentenced Whitner to eight years in prison. Whitner did not appeal her conviction.

Thereafter, Whitner filed a petition for Post Conviction Relief (PCR), pleading the circuit court's lack of subject matter jurisdiction to accept her guilty plea. . . .

Under South Carolina law, a circuit court lacks subject matter jurisdiction to accept a guilty plea to a nonexistent offense. For the sentencing court to have had subject matter jurisdiction to accept Whitner's plea, criminal child neglect would have to include an expectant mother's use of crack cocaine after the fetus is viable. . . .

[The statute] provides:

Any person having the legal custody of any child or helpless person, who shall, without lawful excuse, refuse or neglect to provide . . . the proper care and attention for such child or helpless person, so that the life, health or comfort of such child or helpless person is endangered or is likely to be endangered, shall be guilty of a misdemeanor and shall be punished within the discretion of the circuit court.

The state contends this section encompasses maternal acts endangering or likely to endanger the life, comfort, or health of a viable fetus.

Under the Children's Code, "child" means a "person under the age of 18." The question for this Court, therefore, is whether a viable fetus is a "person" for purposes of the Children's Code.

In interpreting a statute, this court's primary function is to ascertain the intent of the legislature. Of course, where a statute is complete, plain, and unambiguous, legislative intent must be determined from the language of the statute itself. We should consider, however, not merely the language of the particular clause being construed, but the word and its meaning in conjunction with the purpose of the whole statute and the policy of the law. Finally, there is a basic presumption that the legislature has knowledge of previous legislation as well as of judicial decisions construing that legislation when later statutes are enacted concerning related subjects.

South Carolina law has long recognized that viable fetuses are persons holding certain legal rights and privileges. . . . [The court summarized the treatment of fetuses under state tort law, noting that the state wrongful death statute had been interpreted to permit actions brought on behalf of viable fetuses even where they were not born alive.]

More recently, we held the word *person* as used in a criminal statute includes viable fetuses. State v. Horne, 319 S.E.2d 703 (S.C. 1984), concerned South Carolina's murder statute, S.C. Code Ann. §16-3-10 (1976). The defendant in that case stabbed his wife, who was nine months' pregnant, in the neck, arms, and abdomen. Although doctors performed an emergency cesarean section to deliver the child, the child died while still in the womb. The defendant was convicted of voluntary manslaughter and appealed his conviction on the ground South Carolina did not recognize the crime of feticide.

This court disagreed. In a unanimous decision, we held it would be "grossly inconsistent . . . to construe a viable fetus as a 'person' for the purposes of imposing civil liability while refusing to give it a similar classification in the criminal context." 319 S.E.2d at 704. Accordingly, the court recognized the crime of feticide with respect to viable fetuses.

Similarly, we do not see any rational basis for finding a viable fetus is not a "person" in the present context. Indeed, it would be absurd to recognize the viable fetus as a person for purposes of homicide laws and wrongful death statutes but not for purposes of statutes proscribing child abuse. Our holding . . . that a viable fetus is a person rested primarily on the plain meaning of the word *person* in light of existing medical knowledge concerning fetal development. We do not believe that the plain and ordinary meaning of the word *person* has changed in any way that would now deny viable fetuses status as persons.

The policies enunciated in the Children's Code also support our plain meaning reading of "person." . . . The abuse or neglect of a child at any time during childhood can exact a profound toll on the child herself as well as on society as a whole. However, the consequences of abuse or neglect which takes place after birth often pale in comparison to those resulting from abuse suffered by the viable fetus before birth. This policy of prevention supports a reading of the word *person* to include viable fetuses. Furthermore, the scope of the Children's Code is quite broad. It applies "to all children who have need of services." When coupled with the comprehensive remedial purposes of the Code, this language supports the inference that the legislature intended to include viable fetuses within the scope of the Code's protection.

Whitner advances several arguments against an interpretation of "person" as used in the Children's Code to include viable fetuses. We shall address each of Whitner's major arguments in turn.

Whitner's first argument concerns the number of bills introduced in the South Carolina General Assembly in the past five years addressing substance abuse by pregnant women. . . . We disagree with Whitner's conclusion about the significance of the proposed legislation. Generally, the legislature's subsequent acts "cast no light on the intent of the legislature which enacted the statute being construed." . . .

Whitner also argues an interpretation of the statute that includes viable fetuses would lead to absurd results obviously not intended by the legislature. Specifically, she claims if we interpret "child" to include viable fetuses, every action by a pregnant woman that endangers or is likely to endanger a fetus, whether otherwise legal or illegal, would constitute unlawful neglect under the statute. For example, a woman might be prosecuted . . . for smoking or drinking during pregnancy. Whitner asserts these "absurd" results could not have been intended by the legislature and, therefore, the statute should not be construed to include viable fetuses.

We disagree for a number of reasons. First, the same arguments against the statute can be made whether or not the child has been born. After the birth of a child, a parent can be prosecuted . . . for an action that is likely to endanger the child without regard to whether the action is illegal in itself. For example, a parent who drinks excessively could, under certain circumstances, be guilty of child neglect or endangerment even though the underlying act—consuming alcoholic beverages—is itself legal. Obviously, the legislature did not think it "absurd" to allow prosecution of parents for such otherwise legal acts when the acts actually or potentially endanger the "life, health or comfort" of the parents' born children. We see no reason such a result should be rendered absurd by the mere fact the child at issue is a viable fetus.

Moreover, we need not address this potential parade of horribles advanced by Whitner. In this case, which is the only case we are called upon to decide here, certain facts are clear. Whitner admits to having ingested crack cocaine during the third trimester of her pregnancy, which caused her child to be born with cocaine in its system. Although the precise effects of maternal crack use during pregnancy are somewhat unclear, it is well documented and within the realm of public knowledge that such use can cause serious harm to the viable unborn child. . . . There can be no question here Whitner endangered the life, health, and comfort of her child. We need not decide any cases other than the one before us.

We are well aware of the many decisions from other states' courts throughout the country holding maternal conduct before the birth of the child does not give rise to criminal prosecution under state child abuse/endangerment or drug distribution statutes. . . . Many of these cases were prosecuted under statutes forbidding delivery or distribution of illicit substances and depended on statutory construction of the terms "delivery" and "distribution." . . . Obviously, such cases are inapplicable to the present situation. The cases concerning child endangerment statutes or construing the terms *child* and *person* are also distinguishable, because the states in which these cases were decided have entirely different bodies of case law from South Carolina. . . .

[Previous tort and criminal law cases] were decided primarily on the basis of the meaning of "person" as understood in the light of existing medical knowledge, rather than based on any policy of protecting the relationship between mother and child. As a homicide case, *Horne* also rested on the state's — not the mother's — interest in vindicating the life of the viable fetus. Moreover, the United States Supreme Court has repeatedly held that the states have a compelling interest in the life of a viable fetus [citing *Roe* and *Casey*]. . . . If, as Whitner suggests we should, we read *Horne* only as a vindication of the mother's interest in the life of her unborn child, there would be no basis for prosecuting a mother who kills her viable fetus by stabbing it, by shooting it, or by other such means, yet a third party could be prosecuted for the very same acts. We decline to read *Horne* in a way that insulates the mother from all culpability for harm to her viable child. . . .

[T]he dissent implies that we have ignored the rule of lenity requiring us to resolve any ambiguities in a criminal statute in favor of the defendant. The dissent argues that "[a]t most, the majority only suggests that the term *child* . . . is ambiguous," and that the ambiguity "is created not by reference to our decisions under the Children's Code or by reference to the statutory language and applicable rules of statutory construction, but by reliance on decisions in two different fields of the law, civil wrongful death and common law feticide."

Plainly, the dissent misunderstands our opinion. First, we do not believe the statute is ambiguous and, therefore, the rule of lenity does not apply. Furthermore, our interpretation of the statute is based primarily on the plain meaning of the word *person* as contained in the statute. We need not go beyond that language. However, because our prior decisions . . . support our reading of the statute, we have discussed the rationale underlying those holdings. We conclude that both statutory language and case law compel the conclusion we reach. We see no ambiguity. . . .

C. CONSTITUTIONAL ISSUES

[The court quickly disposed of any constitutional impediments to child endangerment prosecutions of drug-using pregnant women. It rejected Whitner's "notice" claim because the statute clearly and unambiguously covered viable fetuses and Whitner therefore had notice of the potential for prosecution. The court also rejected Whitner's claim that prosecution improperly violated her 14th Amendment "privacy" interests. The court found that the statute merely created an additional penalty for conduct that was already illegal — use of crack cocaine — and did not improperly penalize Whitner for choosing to carry her pregnancy to term.]

WALLER and BURNETT, JJ., concur.

FINNEY, Chief Justice:

I respectfully dissent, and would affirm the grant of post-conviction relief to respondent Whitner.

The issue before the court is whether a fetus is a "child" within the meaning of . . . a statute which makes it a misdemeanor for a "person having legal custody of any child or helpless person" to unlawfully neglect that child or helpless person. Since this is a penal statute, it is strictly construed against the state and in favor of respondent.

The term *child* . . . is defined as a "person under the age of 18" unless a different meaning is required by the circumstances. . . . More importantly, it is apparent from a reading of the entire statute that the word *child* . . . means a child in being and not a fetus. A plain reading of the entire child neglect statute demonstrates the intent to criminalize only acts directed at children, and not those which may harm fetuses. First, [the statute] . . . does not impose criminal liability on every person who neglects a child, but only on a person having legal custody of that child. The statutory requirement of legal custody is evidence of intent to extend the statute's reach only to children, because the concept of legal custody is simply inapplicable to a fetus. Second, [the statute refers to other statutory sections] . . . for the definition of neglect. [These sections] . . . define[] a neglected child as one harmed or threatened with harm, and further defines harm. The vast majority of acts which constitute statutory harm under [these provisions] are acts which can only be directed against a child, and not towards a fetus.[2] . . .

At most, the majority only suggests that the term *child* as used in [the child neglect statute at issue] is ambiguous. This suggestion of ambiguity is created not by reference to our decisions under the Children's Code or by reference to the statutory language and applicable rules of statutory construction, but by reliance on decisions in two different fields of the law, civil wrongful death and common law feticide. Even if these wrongful death, common law, and Children's Code decisions are sufficient to render the term *child* in [the statute] . . . ambiguous, it is axiomatic that the ambiguity must be resolved in respondent's favor.

I would affirm.

MOORE, Justice:

I concur with the dissent in this case but write separately to express my concerns with today's decision. In my view, the repeated failure of the legislature to pass proposed bills addressing the problem of drug use during pregnancy is evidence the child abuse and neglect statute is not intended to apply in this instance. This court should not invade what is clearly the sole province of the legislative branch. At the very least, the legislature's failed attempts to enact a statute regulating a pregnant woman's conduct indicate the complexity of this issue. While the majority opinion is perhaps an argument for what the law should be, it is for the General Assembly, and not this court, to make that determination by means of a clearly drawn statute. With today's decision, the majority not only ignores legislative intent but embarks on a course rejected by every other court to address the issue. . . .

■ FERGUSON v. CITY OF CHARLESTON
532 U.S. 67 (2001)

STEVENS, J.

In this case, we must decide whether a state hospital's performance of a diagnostic test to obtain evidence of a patient's criminal conduct for law enforcement purposes is an unreasonable search if the patient has not consented to the procedure. More narrowly, the question is whether the interest in using the threat of criminal sanctions to deter pregnant women from using cocaine can justify a departure from the general rule that an official nonconsensual search is unconstitutional if not authorized by a valid warrant.

2. Examples include condoning delinquency, using excessive corporal punishment, committing sexual offenses against the child, and depriving her of adequate food, clothing, shelter or education.

I

In the fall of 1988, staff members at the public hospital operated in the city of Charleston by the Medical University of South Carolina (MUSC) became concerned about an apparent increase in the use of cocaine by patients who were receiving prenatal treatment. In response to this perceived increase, as of April 1989, MUSC began to order drug screens to be performed on urine samples from maternity patients who were suspected of using cocaine. If a patient tested positive, she was then referred by MUSC staff to the county substance abuse commission for counseling and treatment. However, despite the referrals, the incidence of cocaine use among the patients at MUSC did not appear to change.

Some four months later, Nurse Shirley Brown, the case manager for the MUSC obstetrics department, heard a news broadcast reporting that the police in Greenville, South Carolina, were arresting pregnant users of cocaine on the theory that such use harmed the fetus and was therefore child abuse.[1] Nurse Brown discussed the story with MUSC's general counsel, Joseph C. Good, Jr., who then contacted Charleston Solicitor Charles Condon in order to offer MUSC's cooperation in prosecuting mothers whose children tested positive for drugs at birth.

After receiving Good's letter, Solicitor Condon took the first steps in developing the policy at issue in this case. . . . [The policy is called] "POLICY M-7," dealing with the subject of "Management of Drug Abuse During Pregnancy." . . .

The first three pages of Policy M-7 set forth the procedure to be followed by the hospital staff to "identify/assist pregnant patients suspected of drug abuse." . . . The first section, entitled the "Identification of Drug Abusers," provided that a patient should be tested for cocaine through a urine drug screen if she met one or more of nine criteria . . . [including no or late prenatal care]. It also stated that a chain of custody should be followed when obtaining and testing urine samples, presumably to make sure that the results could be used in subsequent criminal proceedings. The policy also provided for education and referral to a substance abuse clinic for patients who tested positive. Most important, it added the threat of law enforcement intervention that "provided the necessary 'leverage' to make the [p]olicy effective." . . . That threat was, as respondents candidly acknowledge, essential to the program's success in getting women into treatment and keeping them there.

The threat of law enforcement involvement was set forth in two protocols, the first dealing with the identification of drug use during pregnancy, and the second with identification of drug use after labor. Under the latter protocol, the police were to be notified without delay and the patient promptly arrested. Under the former, after the initial positive drug test, the police were to be notified (and the patient arrested) only if the patient tested positive for cocaine a second time or if she missed an appointment with a substance abuse counselor. . . . [although at least one patient was arrested after an initial positive drug screen]. In 1990, however, the policy was modified at the behest of the solicitor's office to give the patient who tested positive during labor, like the patient who tested positive during a prenatal care visit, an opportunity to avoid arrest by consenting to substance abuse treatment.

---

1. Under South Carolina law, a viable fetus has historically been regarded as a person; in 1995, the South Carolina Supreme Court held that the ingestion of cocaine during the third trimester of pregnancy constitutes criminal child neglect. Whitner v. South Carolina, 492 S.E.2d 777 (S.C. 1995), cert. denied, 523 U.S. 1145 (1998).

The last six pages of the policy contained forms for the patients to sign, as well as procedures for the police to follow when a patient was arrested. The policy also prescribed in detail the precise offenses with which a woman could be charged, depending on the stage of her pregnancy [, with the charges as well as their nature and severity changing with each stage]. . . . Other than the provisions describing the substance abuse treatment to be offered to women who tested positive, the policy made no mention of any change in the prenatal care of such patients, nor did it prescribe any special treatment for the newborns.

II

Petitioners are 10 women who received obstetrical care at MUSC and who were arrested after testing positive for cocaine. Four of them were arrested during the initial implementation of the policy; they were not offered the opportunity to receive drug treatment as an alternative to arrest. The others were arrested after the policy was modified in 1990; they either failed to comply with the terms of the drug treatment program or tested positive for a second time. Respondents include the city of Charleston, law enforcement officials who helped develop and enforce the policy, and representatives of MUSC.

Petitioners' complaint challenged the validity of the policy under various theories, including the claim that warrantless and nonconsensual drug tests conducted for criminal investigatory purposes were unconstitutional searches. Respondents advanced two principal defenses to the constitutional claim: (1) that, as a matter of fact, petitioners had consented to the searches; and (2) that, as a matter of law, the searches were reasonable, even absent consent, because they were justified by special non-law-enforcement purposes. . . . The District Court rejected the second defense because the searches in question "were not done by the medical university for independent purposes. [Instead,] the police came in and there was an agreement reached that the positive screens would be shared with the police." . . . Accordingly, the District Court submitted the factual defense to the jury with instructions that required a verdict in favor of petitioners unless the jury found consent. . . . The jury found for respondents.

Petitioners appealed, arguing that the evidence was not sufficient to support the jury's consent finding. The Court of Appeals for the Fourth Circuit affirmed, but without reaching the question of consent. . . .

We granted certiorari, 528 U.S. 1187 (2000), to review the appellate court's holding on the "special needs" issue. Because we do not reach the question of the sufficiency of the evidence with respect to consent, we necessarily assume for purposes of our decision—as did the Court of Appeals—that the searches were conducted without the informed consent of the patients. We conclude that the judgment should be reversed and the case remanded for a decision on the consent issue.

III

Because MUSC is a state hospital, the members of its staff are government actors, subject to the strictures of the Fourth Amendment. . . . Moreover, the urine tests conducted by those staff members were indisputably searches within the meaning of the Fourth Amendment. Skinner v. Railway Labor Executives' Assn., 489 U.S. 602, 617 (1989). . . . Neither the District Court nor the Court of Appeals concluded that any of the nine criteria used to identify the women to be searched provided either probable cause to believe that they were using cocaine, or even the basis for a reasonable suspicion of such use. Rather, the District Court and the Court of Appeals viewed the case as one involving MUSC's right to conduct searches without warrants or probable cause. . . . Furthermore, given the posture in which the case comes to us, we must assume for purposes of our decision that the tests were performed without the informed consent of the patients. . . .

Because the hospital seeks to justify its authority to conduct drug tests and to turn the results over to law enforcement agents without the knowledge or consent of the patients, this case differs from the four previous cases in which we have considered whether comparable drug tests "fit within the closely guarded category of constitutionally permissible suspicionless searches." Chandler v. Miller, 520 U.S. 305, 309 (1997). . . .

In each of . . . [the prior] cases, we employed a balancing test that weighed the intrusion on the individual's interest in privacy against the "special needs" that supported the program. As an initial matter, we note that the invasion of privacy in this case is far more substantial than in those cases. In the previous four cases, there was no misunderstanding about the purpose of the test or the potential use of the test results, and there were protections against the dissemination of the results to third parties. . . . The reasonable expectation of privacy enjoyed by the typical patient undergoing diagnostic tests in a hospital is that the results of those tests will not be shared with nonmedical personnel without her consent. . . .[2] In none of our prior cases was there any intrusion upon that kind of expectation.[3]

The critical difference between those four drug-testing cases and this one, however, lies in the nature of the "special need" asserted as justification for the warrantless searches. In each of those earlier cases, the "special need" that was advanced as a justification for the absence of a warrant or individualized suspicion was one divorced from the State's general interest in law enforcement. . . . In this case, however, the central and indispensable feature of the policy from its inception was the use of law enforcement to coerce the patients into substance abuse treatment. This fact distinguishes this case from circumstances in which physicians or psychologists, in the course of ordinary medical procedures aimed at helping the patient herself, come across information that under rules of law or ethics is subject to reporting requirements, which no one has challenged here. See, e.g., Council on Ethical and Judicial Affairs, American Medical Association, PolicyFinder, Current Opinions E-5.05 (2000) (requiring reporting where "a patient threatens to inflict serious bodily harm to another person or to him or herself and there is a reasonable probability that the patient may carry out the threat"). . . .

2. There are some circumstances in which state hospital employees, like other citizens, may have a duty to provide law enforcement officials with evidence of criminal conduct acquired in the course of routine treatment, see, e.g., S. C. Code Ann. §20-7-510 (2000) (physicians and nurses required to report to child welfare agency or law enforcement authority "when in the person's professional capacity the person" receives information that a child has been abused or neglected). While the existence of such laws might lead a patient to expect that members of the hospital staff might turn over evidence acquired in the course of treatment to which the patient had consented, they surely would not lead a patient to anticipate that hospital staff would intentionally set out to obtain incriminating evidence from their patients for law enforcement purposes.

3. In fact, we have previously recognized that an intrusion on that expectation may have adverse consequences because it may deter patients from receiving needed medical care. . . .

Respondents argue in essence that their ultimate purpose—namely, protecting the health of both mother and child—is a beneficent one. . . . In looking to the programmatic purpose, we consider all the available evidence in order to determine the relevant primary purpose. . . . Tellingly, the document codifying the policy incorporates the police's operational guidelines. It devotes its attention to the chain of custody, the range of possible criminal charges, and the logistics of police notification and arrests. Nowhere, however, does the document discuss different courses of medical treatment for either mother or infant, aside from treatment for the mother's addiction.

Moreover, throughout the development and application of the policy, the Charleston prosecutors and police were extensively involved in the day-to-day administration of the policy. . . .

While the ultimate goal of the program may well have been to get the women in question into substance abuse treatment and off of drugs, the immediate objective of the searches was to generate evidence for law enforcement purposes . . . in order to reach that goal. . . . The threat of law enforcement may ultimately have been intended as a means to an end, but the direct and primary purpose of MUSC's policy was to ensure the use of those means. In our opinion, this distinction is critical. Because law enforcement involvement always serves some broader social purpose or objective, under respondents' view, virtually any nonconsensual suspicionless search could be immunized under the special needs doctrine by defining the search solely in terms of its ultimate, rather than immediate, purpose. . . . Such an approach is inconsistent with the Fourth Amendment. Given the primary purpose of the Charleston program, which was to use the threat of arrest and prosecution in order to force women into treatment, and given the extensive involvement of law enforcement officials at every stage of the policy, this case simply does not fit within the closely guarded category of "special needs."[4]

The fact that positive test results were turned over to the police does not merely provide a basis for distinguishing our prior cases applying the "special needs" balancing approach to the determination of drug use. It also provides an affirmative reason for enforcing the strictures of the Fourth Amendment. While state hospital employees, like other citizens, may have a duty to provide the police with evidence of criminal conduct that they inadvertently acquire in the course of routine treatment, when they undertake to obtain such evidence from their patients for the specific purpose of incriminating those patients, they have a special obligation to make sure that the patients are fully informed about their constitutional rights, as standards of knowing waiver require. . . .

As respondents have repeatedly insisted, their motive was benign rather than punitive. Such a motive, however, cannot justify a departure from Fourth Amendment protections, given the pervasive involvement of law enforcement with the development and application of the MUSC policy. The stark and unique fact that characterizes this case is that Policy M-7 was designed to obtain evidence of criminal conduct by the tested patients that would be turned over to the police and that could be admissible in subsequent criminal prosecutions. While respondents are correct that drug abuse both was and is a serious problem, "the gravity of the threat

---

4. It is especially difficult to argue that the program here was designed simply to save lives. Amici claim a near consensus in the medical community that programs of the sort at issue, by discouraging women who use drugs from seeking prenatal care, harm, rather than advance, the cause of prenatal health. . . .

alone cannot be dispositive of questions concerning what means law enforcement officers may employ to pursue a given purpose." . . . The Fourth Amendment's general prohibition against nonconsensual, warrantless, and suspicionless searches necessarily applies to such a policy. . . .

Accordingly, the judgment of the Court of Appeals is reversed, and the case is remanded for further proceedings consistent with this opinion.

It is so ordered.

KENNEDY, J., concurring:

I agree that the search procedure in issue cannot be sustained under the Fourth Amendment. My reasons for this conclusion differ somewhat from those set forth by the Court, however, leading to this separate opinion. . . .

In my view, it is necessary and prudent to be explicit in explaining the limitations of today's decision. The beginning point ought to be to acknowledge the legitimacy of the State's interest in fetal life and of the grave risk to the life and health of the fetus, and later the child, caused by cocaine ingestion. Infants whose mothers abuse cocaine during pregnancy are born with a wide variety of physical and neurological abnormalities. . . . There should be no doubt that South Carolina can impose punishment upon an expectant mother who has so little regard for her own unborn that she risks causing him or her lifelong damage and suffering. The State, by taking special measures to give rehabilitation and training to expectant mothers with this tragic addiction or weakness, acts well within its powers and its civic obligations.

The holding of the Court, furthermore, does not call into question the validity of mandatory reporting laws such as child abuse laws which require teachers to report evidence of child abuse to the proper authorities, even if arrest and prosecution is the likely result. . . . [W]e must accept the premise that the medical profession can adopt acceptable criteria for testing expectant mothers for cocaine use in order to provide prompt and effective counseling to the mother and to take proper medical steps to protect the child. If prosecuting authorities then adopt legitimate procedures to discover this information and prosecution follows, that ought not to invalidate the testing. . . .

SCALIA, J., dissenting:

There is always an unappealing aspect to the use of doctors and nurses, ministers of mercy, to obtain incriminating evidence against the supposed objects of their ministration—although here, it is correctly pointed out, the doctors and nurses were ministering not just to the mothers but also to the children whom their cooperation with the police was meant to protect. But whatever may be the correct social judgment concerning the desirability of what occurred here, that is not the issue in the present case. . . . The question before us is a narrower one: whether, whatever the desirability of this police conduct, it violates the Fourth Amendment's prohibition of unreasonable searches and seizures. In my view, it plainly does not. . . .

It is rudimentary Fourth Amendment law that a search which has been consented to is not unreasonable. There is no contention in the present case that the urine samples were extracted forcibly. The only conceivable bases for saying that they were obtained without consent are the contentions (1) that the consent was coerced by the patients' need for medical treatment, (2) that the consent was uninformed because the patients were not told that the tests would include testing for drugs, and (3) that the consent was uninformed because the patients were not told that the results of the tests would be provided to the police. . . .

Until today, we have never held—or even suggested—that material which a person voluntarily entrusts to someone else cannot be given by that person to the police, and used for whatever evidence it may contain. . . . Today's holding would be remarkable enough if the confidential relationship violated by the police conduct were at least one protected by state law. . . . But today's holding goes even beyond that, since there does not exist any physician-patient privilege in South Carolina. . . .

There remains to be considered the first possible basis for invalidating this search, which is that the patients were coerced to produce their urine samples by their necessitous circumstances, to-wit, their need for medical treatment of their pregnancy. If that was coercion, it was not coercion applied by the government—and if such non-governmental coercion sufficed, the police would never be permitted to use the ballistic evidence obtained from treatment of a patient with a bullet wound. And the Fourth Amendment would invalidate those many state laws that require physicians to report gunshot wounds, . . . evidence of spousal abuse, . . . and (like the South Carolina law relevant here, see S. C. Code Ann. §20-7-510 (2000)) evidence of child abuse. . . .

I think it clear, therefore, that there is no basis for saying that obtaining of the urine sample was unconstitutional. The special-needs doctrine is thus quite irrelevant, since it operates only to validate searches and seizures that are otherwise unlawful. In the ensuing discussion, however, I shall assume (contrary to legal precedent) that the taking of the urine sample was (either because of the patients' necessitous circumstances, or because of failure to disclose that the urine would be tested for drugs, or because of failure to disclose that the results of the test would be given to the police) coerced. Indeed, I shall even assume (contrary to common sense) that the testing of the urine constituted an unconsented search of the patients' effects. On those assumptions, the special-needs doctrine would become relevant; and, properly applied, would validate what was done here. . . .

The cocaine tests started in April 1989, neither at police suggestion nor with police involvement. Expectant mothers who tested positive were referred by hospital staff for substance-abuse treatment . . .—an obvious health benefit to both mother and child. . . . Thus, in their origin—before the police were in any way involved—the tests had an immediate, not merely an "ultimate," . . . purpose of improving maternal and infant health. Several months after the testing had been initiated . . . [the hospital invited police involvement] . . . Why would there be any reason to believe that, once this policy of using the drug tests for their "ultimate" health benefits had been adopted, use of them for their original, immediate, benefits somehow disappeared, and testing somehow became in its entirety nothing more than a "pretext" for obtaining grounds for arrest?

In sum, there can be no basis for the Court's purported ability to "distinguish this case from circumstances in which physicians or psychologists, in the course of ordinary medical procedures aimed at helping the patient herself, come across information that . . . is subject to reporting requirements," . . . .

But as far as the Fourth Amendment is concerned: There was no unconsented search in this case. And if there was, it would have been validated by the special-needs doctrine. For these reasons, I respectfully dissent.

Notes: Maternal Substance Abuse

1. *Prevalence and Effect of Maternal Substance Abuse.* Thousands of children are born each year to women who have used tobacco, alcohol, or illegal drugs during

pregnancy. In 2016, 6.3 percent of pregnant women aged 15-44 reported using illicit drugs in the last month, compared to 13.2 percent of non-pregnant women in this age group. Tobacco use was higher, with 10.6 percent of pregnant women and 21.8 percent of non-pregnant women aged 15-44 reporting use of tobacco products within the past month. More than 8 percent of pregnant women and more than 53 percent of non-pregnant women reported drinking alcohol. In total, 20 percent of pregnant women in this age group reported using illicit drugs, tobacco products, or alcohol in the past month compared to 62 percent of non-pregnant women. Substance Abuse and Mental Health Services Administration, U.S. Department of Health and Human Services, 2016 National Survey on Drug Use and Health. The type of substance used varies by race and socioeconomic status, although there is some evidence that the overall use of potentially injurious substances is consistent across all groups. See S. L. Hans, Demographic and Psychosocial Characteristics of Substance-Abusing Pregnant Women, 26 Clin. Perinatology 55 (1999). The data can be interpreted in various ways. It suggests that pregnant women use potentially harmful substances at lower rates, potentially signaling that women act to reduce fetal risk. On the other hand, it is possible that at least a portion of the apparent difference reflects stigma rather than behavior change as pregnant women may be less likely to report potentially risky behavior. See J. C. Chang, et al., Perinatal Illicit Drug and Marijuana Use, 31 Am. J. Health Promot. 35 (2017) (study in five urban outpatient clinics demonstrated that pregnant women significantly underreported their use of drugs to their obstetricians). Regardless, the data demonstrates that a significant percentage of women who know they are pregnant report using illicit drugs, tobacco, or alcohol, and that rates of usage are higher in "nonpregnant" women who may unknowingly be in an early stage of pregnancy.

Illicit drugs, alcohol, tobacco, and other substances can injure developing fetuses. Research findings include higher rates of prematurity, lower birth weights, and cognitive/behavioral abnormalities. It is important to recognize, however, that other related factors may contribute to some of these problems, including inadequate diet, poor prenatal care, and a less than optimal developmental environment. See Cortney E. Lollar, 92 Ind. L. J. 947 (2017) (challenging link between use of illegal substances and harm to offspring); and Sonia Minnes et al., Prenatal Tobacco, Marijuana, Stimulant, and Opiate Exposure: Outcomes and Practical Implications, 6 Addict. Sci. Clin. Pract. 57 (2011). Should policies developed to deal with the use of illicit drugs by pregnant women be applied to the use of harmful, but legal, substances? The U.S. Centers for Disease Control (CDC) recommends that a significant proportion of women refrain from drinking alcohol to avoid the risk of fetal alcohol spectrum disorders. Daniel Victor, No Alcohol for Sexually Active Women Without Birth Control, C.D.C. Recommends, N.Y. Times, February 3, 2016 (noting potential risks to fetuses from alcohol exposure before a woman is aware of her pregnancy). Marijuana use is now legal in an increasing number of jurisdictions, yet health providers recommend that pregnant women or women considering pregnancy refrain from using the drug. Committee Opinion Summary No. 722: Marijuana Use During Pregnancy and Lactation, 130 Obstet. Gynecol. 931 (2017). The *Whitner* court suggests that prosecutions for risky, but legal behavior are possible but potentially problematic from a constitutional standpoint. Some jurisdictions nonetheless consider legal conduct presenting risks to fetuses as a sufficient basis for legal intervention. See Wis. Stat. 48.133, discussed further below.

2. *Two Views on Legislative Intent.* Determining whether traditional child endangerment, drug delivery, or other statutes apply to the problem of risky prenatal

conduct is initially a problem of statutory interpretation. Does the statute apply to fetuses explicitly or will a court find that the legislature intended for the provision to apply to fetuses? The vast majority of states that have considered the statutory interpretation questions in the criminal context have found that the legislature did not intend to include fetuses. For an excellent review of the relevant cases, see Linda C. Fentiman, In the Name of Fetal Protection: Why American Prosecutors Pursue Drug Users (and Other Countries Don't), 18 Colum. J. Gender & L. 647 (2009); and James G. Hodge, Jr., Annotation, Prosecution of Mother for Prenatal Substance Abuse Based on Endangerment of or Delivery of Controlled Substances to Child, 70 A.L.R.5th 461 (1999). See also, State v. Ikerd, 850 A.2d 516 (N.J. Super. 2004) (holding that "a pregnant, drug-addicted woman who has violated the conditions of her probation cannot be sentenced to prison for the avowed purpose of safeguarding the health of her fetus."). *Whitner*, therefore, represents the minority view. The decision could still be "right" for purposes of South Carolina law. Do you agree that the state legislature intended that the child endangerment statute be applied to a pregnant woman's behavior toward her fetus? Why would the legislature attempt to enact legislation on the subject if the child endangerment statute already provided a remedy? How persuasive is the majority's statutory interpretation? Is the legislature likely to "correct" the court if it is wrong?

South Carolina continues to follow the *Whitner* approach. In State v. McKnight, 576 S.E.2d 168 (S.C. 2003), the South Carolina Supreme Court cited *Whitner* in affirming a defendant's conviction of homicide by child abuse through prenatal use of cocaine. The defendant gave birth to a stillborn child estimated to be at 34-37 weeks of gestation; metabolites of cocaine were found during an autopsy of the fetus. The defendant was sentenced to a 20-year term of imprisonment. The court later determined that McKnight had received ineffective assistance of counsel and reversed her conviction. State v. McKnight, 661 S.E.2d 354 (S.C. 2008). Would a criminal prosecution for child abuse and neglect based on a pregnant women's use of drugs require proof that the woman knew she was pregnant? Dept. of Social Services v. Jennifer M., 744 S.E.2d 591 (S.C.App. 2013) (yes).

The defendant in *Whitner* argued that South Carolina's recognition of tort and criminal law actions arising from fetal injuries was an attempt to protect a woman's relationship with her fetus rather than an effort to protect a fetal right to be free from harm. The court rejected the argument, finding that state case law was based on the definition of "person" and noting the state's compelling interest in protecting fetal life. Other courts have accepted the defendant's view and have restricted actions brought against the woman, as opposed to some third party, on the theory that state criminal and tort rules are intended to protect the woman's relationship with the fetus.

State ex rel. Angela M.W. v. Kruzicki, 561 N.W.2d 729 (Wis. 1997), is typical of the majority approach. Angela M.W.'s obstetrician reported her to county authorities because of her persistent drug use during pregnancy. The county filed a motion to take Angela's unborn child (and, by necessity, Angela herself) into custody; the order was granted by the juvenile court. The county then filed a petition asserting that the unborn child was a "child in need of protection or services" under state law because Angela was endangering her fetus's health. The relevant statute defined "child" as a "person who is less than 18 years of age." Angela brought and lost an action in the court of appeals, seeking her release or a stay of the juvenile court proceedings. In the course of these proceedings, Angela gave birth to a baby boy.

The Wisconsin Supreme Court reversed the court of appeals, with three justices dissenting. 561 N.W.2d 729 (Wis. 1997) (The court issued its decision despite the child's birth and Angela's release from confinement under an exception to the mootness doctrine often used in litigation involving pregnancy. See Roe v. Wade, supra.). The court agreed that the definition of "child" was ambiguous under the statutory scheme but held that the legislature had not intended to include unborn fetuses in the definition. The court noted, for example, that the statute used "child" in a number of ways that were inconsistent with the inclusion of viable fetuses. The majority did not reach the constitutional issues because it was able to overturn the custodial order on statutory interpretation grounds alone. See also Ian Vandewalker, Taking the Baby Before It's Born: Termination of the Parental Rights of Women Who Use Illegal Drugs While Pregnant, 32 NYU Rev. L. & Soc. Change 423 (2008).

Note that some states have attempted to prosecute pregnant drug users under statutes that make it a criminal offense to "deliver" drugs to another "person." The prosecutions proceeded on the theory that a pregnant woman who had ingested illegal drugs within a few days of giving birth was capable of transmitting drug metabolites to her newborn during the brief time period between birth and the cutting of the umbilical cord—when the child was a "person." Courts have rejected these prosecutions, holding that the legislatures did not intend this application of the drug delivery statutes. See, e.g., Annotation, 70 A.L.R.5th 461 (1999); Johnson v. State, 602 So. 2d 1288 (Fla. 1992). Could a woman be charged with abuse and neglect after a child's birth based on prenatal drug use? See N.J. Dept of Child. and Families v. A.L., 59 A.3d 576 (N.J. 2013) (abuse and neglect applies to child not to fetus; insufficient evidence of actual harm or substantial risk of harm to the child presented to support finding of abuse and neglect).

3. *The Constitution and the Prosecution of Pregnant Women.* Most attempted prosecutions have failed on the basis of statutory interpretation and legislative intent. Courts, therefore, have rarely reached the constitutional objections to the prosecution of pregnant women. Of course a state legislature could easily surmount the statutory interpretation obstacles to criminal prosecution by enacting legislation that clearly imposes criminal punishments on pregnant women who injure their fetuses. Tennessee briefly enacted such a law, permitting the criminal prosecution of pregnant women whose infants were born addicted to or harmed by illegal drugs. The legislation established an affirmative defense for pregnant women who enrolled in a drug treatment program before childbirth, maintained enrollment after delivery, and successfully completed treatment. Note, A Velvet Hammer: The Criminalization of Motherhood and the New Maternalism, 104 Cal. L. Rev. 1299 (2016) (discussing Tenn. Code Ann. §39-13-107, in effect from 2014-2016). Courts reviewing this type of legislation would be forced to confront potential due process and equal protection challenges. How would you frame the constitutional questions?

The *Whitner* court's constitutional analysis was cursory. The majority defended child endangerment prosecutions from constitutional attack by noting that the underlying drug use was already criminal. Would it be unconstitutional to prosecute pregnant women for conduct that, while potentially injurious, was otherwise legal? How would you analyze the prosecution of a woman for smoking tobacco after fetal viability? The dissenting justices in State ex rel. Angela M.W. seemed to argue that such prosecutions would also be permissible under the due process and equal protection clauses:

Angela next contends that the custodial effect of the protective order violated her due process liberty interest under the United States Constitution. . . . In regard to the state interest implicated here, the United States Supreme Court has determined [that] . . . the state's interest in protecting the life and health of an unborn child becomes compelling and dominant once the fetus reaches viability. . . . In the present case, there is no dispute that Angela's child was a viable fetus when the petition was filed, that Angela was actively using cocaine, and that the use of cocaine put the child at substantial risk of great bodily harm or possibly death. As such, the state has a compelling state interest to protect Angela's fetus under *Roe* [and] *Casey*. . . . [If *Roe* stands for the proposition that the state's interest in a viable fetus can override a woman's wish to terminate the pregnancy, why shouldn't the state be able to] protect the viable fetus from maternal conduct which functionally presents the same risk and portends the same result, the death of the viable fetus? . . .

The next issue therefore is whether the infringement on Angela's liberty is narrowly tailored to further the compelling state interest. I conclude that it is. The Children's Code specifies the procedures necessary to further the state's compelling interest in the protection of children. These procedures must be complied with before the state can exercise its right to detain and ultimately protect a child. [The procedures include a post-detention hearing to determine whether there is probable cause to exercise jurisdiction over the child and whether the child will be "subject to injury if . . . not taken into protective custody."] . . . In light of all the statutorily imposed procedures necessary to detain a child, it is clear that the means by which the state's compelling interest is served are narrowly tailored to [meet the state's interest in protecting children]. . . .

Finally, Angela argues that if the state is allowed to intervene when the mother ingests cocaine, this will "open the door" for the state to intervene whenever a mother acts in any manner that is potentially harmful to her viable fetus. Angela cites as examples the possibility of state intervention if a mother smokes or refuses to take her prenatal vitamins. This argument is not a realistic one because [the statute] . . . contains the necessary protections against unreasonable or unjustified intervention by the state. . . . Clearly, the Children's Code enables the state to intervene only when a child faces substantial risk. Thus, [the statute] . . . contains the necessary stopping point to protect against Angela's slippery slope argument. In fact, if this were not true, then the same argument would have validity under the Children's Code even if the child has been born [citing Whitner v. State, supra].

State ex rel. Angela M.W. v. Kruzicki, 561 N.W.2d 729, 747-749 (Wis. 1997) (Crooks, J., dissenting).

Do you agree with the dissent's disposition of the constitutional questions? Do the abortion cases stand for the proposition that the state's compelling interest in fetal life can outweigh more than a woman's right to terminate her pregnancy? For a thoughtful analysis of the state's interests in these cases, see Dov Fox, Interest Creep, 82 Geo. Wash. L. Rev. 273 (2014) (noting that careful analysis reveals "four species of government concern," not all of which are compelling). How would you characterize the nature of the pregnant woman's interests? Is the use of forced confinement and drug treatment a measure narrowly tailored to achieve the state's objectives? Compare the dissent's analysis with the majority and dissenting opinions in In re A.C. See also Nancy Ehrenreich, The Colonization of the Womb, 43 Duke L. J. 492 (1993).

Following the *Angela M.W.* decision, the Wisconsin legislature specifically authorized the juvenile courts to intervene to protect fetuses:

> The [juvenile] court has exclusive original jurisdiction over an unborn child alleged to be in need of protection or services which can be ordered by the court whose expectant mother habitually lacks self-control in the use of alcohol beverages, controlled substances or controlled substance analogs, exhibited to a severe degree, to the extent that there is a substantial risk that the physical health of the unborn child, and of the child when born, will be seriously affected or endangered unless the expectant mother receives prompt and adequate treatment for that habitual lack of self-control. The court also has exclusive original jurisdiction over the expectant mother of an unborn child described in this section.

Wisc. Stat. §48.133. Pregnant women may be taken into custody and may be required to participate in an inpatient alcohol or drug treatment program. Wisc. Stat. Ch. 48. Does the legislation raise any constitutional concerns beyond those noted in *Whitner* and *Angela M. W.*? Loertscher v. Anderson, __ F. Supp.3d __ (2017), 2017 WL 1613654 (finding Act void for vagueness, holding that "habitual lack of self-control" and "substantial risk to the physical health of the unborn child" are "not subject to reasonably precise interpretation" and therefore do not provide fair warning or standard for enforcement). The district court order striking down the legislation is stayed pending disposition of the appeal by the Seventh Circuit. Anderson v. Loertscher, 137 S.Ct. 2328 (2017).

4. *Medical Care for Pregnant Women and the Fourth Amendment.* The *Ferguson* case might be viewed as the natural outgrowth of the criminalization of drug use by pregnant women. Note that the Court does not find fault with the state law criminalizing prenatal drug abuse. What were the constitutional defects of the hospital policy in *Ferguson*? State law often requires health care providers to report matters such as child abuse and gunshot wounds. See Chapter 3, at page 141. Do reports under these statutes present the same Fourth Amendment problems as the hospital policy in *Ferguson*? For a summary of state testing and reporting rules, see Guttmacher Institute, Substance Use During Pregnancy (Sept. 2017). See also The American College of Obstetricians and Gynecologists, Committee Opinion, Substance Abuse Reporting and Pregnancy: The Role of the Obstetrician-Gynecologist, 117 Obstet. Gynecol. 200 (2011, reaffirmed 2014) ("The use of the legal system to address perinatal alcohol and substance abuse is inappropriate . . . . In states that mandate reporting, policy makers, legislators, and physicians should work together to retract punitive legislation and identify and implement evidence-based strategies outside the legal system. . .").

On remand in *Ferguson*, the United States Court of Appeals for the Fourth Circuit issued a lengthy opinion holding that: (1) a mother's Fourth Amendment interests are not implicated by newborn urine testing; (2) the MUSC's policy of testing patients' urine for evidence of cocaine was not designed to further medical care; (3) the hospital's consent forms did not adequately inform patients about the use of urine tests for law enforcement purposes; and (4) patients who presented themselves to the hospital for treatment could not be said to have impliedly consented to the urine search policy. Ferguson v. City of Charleston, South Carolina, 308 F.3d 380 (4th Cir. 2002). The court also held that two patients had sufficient knowledge of the law enforcement purposes of the testing to imply consent. Id. Could a state require welfare recipients to undergo warrantless, suspicionless drug testing as a condition of receiving benefits? Marchwinski v. Howard, 113 F. Supp. 2d 1134 (E.D. Mich. 2000) (no), upheld on rehearing en banc, 60 Fed. Appx. 601 (6th Cir. 2003) (judgment of the district court reinstated by equally divided vote of the appeals court en banc).

5. *The Criminal Model vs. the Treatment Model.* Punitive prenatal substance abuse policies clearly might deter drug-addicted women from seeking prenatal care. Not surprisingly, the AMA's policy favors treatment over criminal liability: "Criminal sanctions or civil liability for harmful behavior by the pregnant woman toward her fetus are inappropriate. . . . Pregnant substance abusers should be provided with rehabilitative treatment appropriate to their specific physiological and psychological needs." AMA, H-420.969 Legal Interventions During Pregnancy. Critics of the criminal model also note that pregnant women had faced difficulties accessing treatment programs. See, e.g., Elaine W. v. Joint Diseases North General Hospital, 613 N.E.2d 523 (N.Y. 1993) (exclusion of pregnant women from treatment program). Despite improvements in policies and funding, gaps in treatment remain. Mishka Terpian, Nyaradzo Linginaker & Lindsay Appel, Women-Centered Drug Treatment Services and Need in the United States, 2002-2009, 105 Amer. J. Pub. Health. e50 (2015).

Whitner and *Ferguson* were followed by a new wave of legislation focused on the therapeutic solution to risky maternal conduct. See Guttmacher Institute, Substance Use During Pregnancy (Sept. 2017); Elizabeth E. Coleman & Monica K. Miller, Assessing Legal Responses to Prenatal Drug Use: Can Therapeutic Responses Produce More Positive Outcomes Than Punitive Responses?, 20 J. L. & Health 35 (2007). What would be the benefits and risks of a public policy employing a therapeutic approach in public hospitals? Jeremiah A. Ho & Alexander O. Rovzar, Preventing Neonatal Abstinence Syndrome within the Opioid Epidemic: A Uniform Facilitative Policy, 54 Harv. J. on Legis. 423 (2017) (focusing on early identification of opioid misuse and implementation of standardized treatment protocol in public hospitals).

One possible noncriminal approach to prenatal substance abuse is civil commitment. See Chapter 8, at pages 971-975. Does this approach avoid any of the drawbacks of criminal prosecution? See Linda C. Fentiman, The New "Fetal Protection": The Wrong Answer to the Crisis of Inadequate Health Care for Women and Children, 84 Denv. U. L. Rev. 537, 566 (2006) ("Thirty-four states and the District of Columbia currently permit pregnant women to be civilly committed for alcohol and other drug abuse").

6. *Further Reading.* For information about the **impact of substance use** by pregnant women (note 1), see National Institute on Drug Abuse, NIH, What Are the Effects of Maternal Cocaine Use? (2016 Update), at https://www.drugabuse.gov/publications/research-reports/cocaine/what-are-effects-maternal-cocaine-use; and Nora D. Volkow, Wilson M. Compton & Eric M. Wargo, The Risks of Marijuana Use During Pregnancy, 317 JAMA 129 (2017) (data suggests increased use, noting risks and need for further study). Additional analyses of cases involving state **criminal prosecutions of women for conduct during pregnancy** (note 2) can be found in Michele Goodwin, Precarious Moorings: Tying Fetal Drug Law Policy to Social Profiling, 42 Rutgers L. J. 659 (2011); Michelle Goodwin, Prosecuting the Womb, 76 Geo. Wash. L. Rev. 1657 (2008); Lynn M. Paltrow & Jeanne Flavin, Arrests of and Forced Interventions on Pregnant Women in the United States, 1973-2005, 38 J. Health Politics, Pol'y and L. 299 (2013) (analyzing 413 cases); Dara E. Purvis, The Rules of Maternity, 84 Tenn. L. Rev. 367 (2017). **Constitutional aspects** (note 3) of the issues are discussed further at Myrisha S. Lewis, Criminalizing Substance Abuse and Undermining Roe v. Wade: The Tension between Abortion Doctrine and the Criminalization of Prenatal Substance Abuse, 23 Wm. & Mary J. Women & L. 185 (2017). For an article further exploring the balance between **criminal and treatment models** (note 5), see April Cherry, Shifting Our Focus from Retribution to Compassion, 28 J. L. & Health

6 (2015); Andrew J. Weisberg & Frank E. Vandervort, *A Liberal Dilemma: Respecting Autonomy While Also Protecting Inchoate Children from Prenatal Substance Abuse*, 24 Wm. & Mary Bill Rts. J. 659 (2016) (arguing for "sufficient enforcement mechanisms to ensure inchoate children are ultimately protected").

D. USING REPRODUCTIVE TECHNOLOGIES TO CREATE NEW FAMILIES

Technological advances in reproduction have cast into question some long-established legal doctrines. Who is the father of a child conceived through artificial insemination (AI)? Who is the mother of a child born through the use of in vitro fertilization (IVF) techniques and surrogacy? Is it possible to have two fathers or two mothers? Is it possible to have more than two parents? These questions are intrinsically important because of the joys, legal rights, and obligations that go along with parenthood. Yet the answers to these questions also can have important consequences for our ideas of what "parenthood," "fatherhood," or "motherhood" means.

Some of the issues considered in this section build upon those discussed in section A of this chapter. Litigants often assert their constitutional right to control procreation, for example, in arguing for particular legal treatment of a reproductive technology. Moreover, the struggle for control between individuals and the state is a consistent theme of the cases in section A and in this section. Nonetheless, there are important differences in the cases in these sections.

In the earlier section, the state's attempt to control most often took the form of regulations or of outright prohibition of the use of the technology itself, such as state attempts to restrict access to abortion. In this section, we are concerned primarily with state attempts to control outcome rather than use. Most state regulation focuses on the manner in which the technology is used and seeks to establish the legal status of participants in the process. These efforts have been resisted by individuals who have sought to use contractual agreements or existing statutory mechanisms to establish legal status and relationships. The primary issue therefore has been whether individuals or the state controls the legal status of participants in reproductive ventures.

1. Parenting Possibilities

■ASSISTED REPRODUCTIVE TECHNOLOGY AND THE FAMILY*
John A. Robertson**
47 Hastings L.J. 911 (1996)

More than one in eight married couples in the United States suffer from infertility (defined as a lack of pregnancy after a year of unprotected intercourse). Although some couples adopt or choose to remain childless, many turn to physicians for help in forming families. The list of assisted reproductive techniques (ARTs)

---

* Copyright © 1996 by the University of California, Hastings College of Law. Reprinted by permission.

** John Robertson, one of the leading scholars in the development of health law in the United States, was Vinson & Elkins Chair, University of Texas Law School, until his death in 2017.

available for treating infertility now includes intrauterine insemination (IUI), ovulation induction, in vitro fertilization (IVF), intracytoplasmic sperm injection, sperm donation, egg donation, embryo donation, and gestational surrogacy. . . .

The use of assisted reproductive techniques by infertile couples is a family-centered act, reflecting couples' desire to form families with biologically related offspring. Although adoption and foster parenting can provide parenting experiences, only ARTs enable one or both partners to have some biologic tie, either genetic or gestational, to their children. While some critics of ARTs disapprove of the emphasis these technologies place on genetic ties, our culture, our law, and our social and psychological understandings of reproduction and parenting define parental and offspring roles largely though not exclusively in genetic or biologic terms. In this context, the development of safe and effective ARTs appears to be positive: It reduces the suffering of childless couples by making it possible for them to realize their procreative goals.

Yet many people have doubts about ARTs and the industry that has grown up around them. Some of these doubts concern the morality and consequences of interfering with nature or manipulating the earliest stages of life. Others focus on the consequences for offspring, for participants (including the couples directly involved and the collaborating donors and surrogates), and for women and families generally. Some have criticized the industry's emphasis on profits and its lack of regulation—which has recently received considerable attention because of allegations of the theft of eggs and embryos by leading doctors at a California fertility center. . . .

My basic premise is that ARTs support the traditional notion of the family, even though they depart from the conventional method of producing children through coital conception. Despite the differences in the method of conception, the goal of an ART is a child biologically related to one or both rearing parents—a goal similar to that sought through coital conception. The family project in each case should be treated equally. The use of gamete donors and surrogates, however, requires special attention because of the potential problems that the resulting desegregation of the genetic, gestational, and social aspects of procreation pose for participants and offspring. . . .

ARTs, FREEDOM, AND THE FAMILY

Before addressing current policy issues, it is useful to consider briefly the connection between the use of ARTs and personal and procreative liberty. Critics of ARTs have often called for prohibition or regulation without realizing the impact such restrictions would have on procreative freedom, a freedom that is highly valued in other contexts. Yet the right of infertile couples to use these techniques is as important as their right to conceive coitally or to avoid reproduction once pregnancy has occurred. The argument in support of the rights of infertile couples to use ARTs to form families can be briefly stated.

Although it is not mentioned explicitly in the Constitution, courts would no doubt recognize as fundamental the right of a married couple to reproduce coitally, because of the traditional association of reproduction and childbearing with marriage, and the independent importance of reproduction in people's lives. Since an infertile couple or individual has the same interest in bearing and rearing offspring as a fertile couples does, their right to use noncoital techniques to treat infertility should have equivalent respect. This is clearest when the couple's own gametes will be involved, such as IUI and IVF, but it should also be recognized when one partner does not contribute genetically or gestationally to reproduction. Thus laws that restrict or prohibit access to ARTs should be judged under the same exacting standard that would apply to direct restrictions on coital reproduction—the need to show a compelling state interest not achievable by less restrictive means. Under this standard, most objections to ARTs are insufficient to justify banning or unduly burdening their use, though there is considerable room for reasonable regulation designed to assure that consumers fully understand and freely choose the particular ART at issue. . . .

■ ASSISTED REPRODUCTIVE TECHNOLOGY SURVEILLANCE — UNITED STATES, 2014

Saswati Sunderam, et al.,

66(SS-6) *Morbidity & Mortality Weekly Rep. Surveill Summ* 1 (2017)

Since the birth of the first U.S. infant conceived with assisted reproductive technology (ART) in 1981, use of advanced technologies to overcome infertility has increased, as has the number of fertility clinics providing ART services and procedures in the United States. In 1992, Congress passed the Fertility Clinic Success Rate and Certification Act . . . which requires that all U.S. fertility clinics performing ART procedures report data to CDC annually on every ART procedure performed. . . . Several measures of success for ART are presented in the annual report, including the percentage of ART procedures and transfers that result in pregnancies, live-birth deliveries, singleton live-birth deliveries, and multiple live-birth deliveries.

Although ART helps millions of infertile couples to achieve pregnancy, it is associated with potential health risks to both mother and infant. Because multiple embryos are transferred in the majority of ART procedures, ART often results in multiple-gestation pregnancies and multiple births. Risks to the mother from multiple births include higher rates of caesarean deliveries, maternal hemorrhage, pregnancy-related hypertension, and gestational diabetes. Risks to the infant include prematurity, low birthweight, infant death, and elevated risk for birth defects and developmental disability. Further, even singleton infants conceived with ART have a higher risk for low birthweight and prematurity than singletons not conceived with ART.

This report was compiled on the basis of ART surveillance data reported to CDC's Division of Reproductive Health for procedures performed in 2014. . . .

ART includes fertility treatments in which eggs or embryos are handled in a laboratory (e.g., in vitro fertilization [IVF], gamete intrafallopian transfer, and zygote intrafallopian transfer). Approximately 99.0% of ART procedures performed are IVF. Because an ART procedure consists of several steps over an interval of approximately 2 weeks, a procedure often is referred to as a cycle of treatment. An ART cycle usually begins with drug-induced ovarian stimulation. If eggs are produced, the cycle progresses to the egg-retrieval stage, which involves surgical removal of the eggs from the ovaries. After the eggs are retrieved, they are combined with sperm in the laboratory during the IVF procedure. If successful, the most viable embryos (i.e., those that appear morphologically most likely to develop and implant) are selected for transfer back into the uterus by clinicians. If an embryo implants in the uterus, a clinical pregnancy is diagnosed by the presence of a gestational sac detectable by ultrasound. The majority of pregnancy losses occur within the first 12 weeks. Beyond 12 weeks of gestation, the pregnancy usually progresses to a live-birth delivery, defined as the delivery of one or more live-born infants. Survival of pregnancy ranges from 95.0% at 16 weeks to 98.0% at 20 weeks. ART does not include treatments in which only sperm are handled (i.e., intrauterine insemination) or procedures in which a woman takes drugs to stimulate egg production without the intention of having eggs retrieved.

ART procedures are classified into four types on the basis of the source of the egg (patient or donor) and the status of the embryos (fresh or thawed). Both fresh and thawed embryos can be derived from either the patient's eggs or the donor's eggs. Both patient and donor embryos can be created using sperm from a partner or from a donor. ART procedures involving fresh embryos include an egg-retrieval stage. ART procedures that use thawed embryos do not include egg retrieval because the eggs were fertilized during a previous procedure and the resultant embryos were frozen until the current procedure. An ART cycle can be discontinued at any step for medical reasons or by patient choice. . . .

Of 498 fertility clinics in the United States that performed ART procedures in 2014, a total of 458 (92.2%) provided data to CDC, with the majority located in or near major cities in the United States. . . .*

The use of ART has increased substantially in the United States since the beginning of ART surveillance. In 1996 (the first full year for which ART data were reported to CDC), a total of 20,597 infants were born from 64,036 ART procedures. Since then, the number of procedures reported to CDC and the number of infants born from ART procedures have approximately tripled. . . .

The contribution of ART on rates of multiple births and poor birth outcomes remained substantial in 2014, as approximately 39.0% of ART-conceived infants were born in multiple births (compared with only 3.5% of infants among the total birth population). The contribution of ART-conceived infants to all triplets and higher-order infants increased slightly from 25.2% in 2013 to 26.4% in 2014. ART-conceived twins accounted for approximately 95.3% (24,514 of 25,714) of all ART-conceived infants born in multiple-birth deliveries. On average, approximately two embryos were transferred among women aged <35 years, even though single embryo transfers have been associated with better perinatal outcomes among the majority of women in this age group. Although the rate of eSET** procedures was still relatively low among women aged <35 years, from 2013 to 2014, the eSET rate increased from 21.4% to 28.5%. This is the largest annual percentage increase (33.6%) in eSET rate in the U.S ever detected through NASS. The percentage of low birthweight and preterm birth was substantially higher among ART-conceived infants (27.8% and 33.2%, respectively) than among all infants (8.0% and 11.3%, respectively). Among ART-conceived infants, twins and triplets and higher-order infants were more likely than singletons to be born preterm (more than 4.5 times and seven times, respectively). Although infants conceived with ART accounted for approximately 1.6% of total

---

* There were 169,568 ART procedures reported in 2014, with 138,029 embryo transfers and 68,988 ART pregnancies resulting in 68,782 ART live birth infants. There were 2,646.5 ART procedures per 1 million women aged 15-44 years. 66(6) MMWR 1, 15 (2017) (Table 1)—ED].

** "Elective single-embryo transfer (eSET) is a procedure in which one embryo, selected from a larger number of available embryos, is placed in the uterus, with extra embryos cryopreserved. Fresh transfer procedures in which only one embryo was transferred but no embryos were cryopreserved are considered single-embryo transfer (SET) but not considered eSET." Id. at 4—ED.].

births in the United States in 2014, the proportions of twins and triplets and higher-order infants attributable to ART were 18.0% and 26.4%, respectively.

Comparable data on ART use and embryo transfer practices from 17 European countries indicate that in 2011, ART use as defined by the number of procedures performed per 1 million women of reproductive age was 6,556; this was approximately 2.7 times higher than the rate in the United States in 2011. Percentages of single-embryo transfers (eSET rates are not reported) varied widely in Europe, and a few countries reported a single-embryo transfer rate of over 50.0%. Overall, in these 17 reporting countries, approximately 81.0% of all IVF deliveries were singleton deliveries, compared with 72.0% in the United States. . . .

ART use (as measured by the number of ART procedures performed per 1 million women of reproductive age) varied widely by reporting area . . . . Importantly, residents of California, Illinois, Massachusetts, New Jersey, New York, and Texas accounted for nearly half (47.0%) of all ART-conceived infants. The large number of ART procedures performed in these states is a result of the large size of the general population (California, Texas), higher ART use (Massachusetts, New Jersey), or both (New York, Illinois). The contribution of ART to all infants born was 4.7% in Massachusetts and 1.7% in California.

Such differences might be explained in part by variations in state health insurance coverage. A total of 15 states . . . have passed legislation mandating insurance coverage for fertility treatments, although not all mandates require coverage for ART; mandates from four of these states . . . include comprehensive coverage for at least four cycles of IVF.[†] Three of the four states with comprehensive mandates (Illinois, Massachusetts, and New Jersey) had rates of ART use that were at least 50.0% higher than the national level. This type of mandated insurance has been associated with greater use of ART. Linkage of NASS data with birth certificate data in three states indicated that Massachusetts had a higher overall rate of ART use compared with Florida and Michigan, which do not have a comprehensive coverage mandate for ART. . . .

According to the American Society of Reproductive Medicine (ASRM) and SART [Society for Assisted Reproduction Technology], eSET is recommended for favorable prognosis patients . . . . The guidelines issued by ASRM/SART on the number of embryos transferred have been revised several times. However, ASRM/SART guidelines on the number of embryos transferred allow for up to two embryos to be transferred even among favorable prognosis patients with patient counseling regarding risks for multifetal pregnancies. A high number of double-embryo transfers occur among patients who might otherwise appear to be good candidates for transferring one embryo. Reducing the number of embryos transferred from two to one among those patients who have a good chance of pregnancy and live birth with single-embryo transfers will lower ART-conceived twin rates. . . .

The national percentage of eSET increased from 7.4% in 2009 to 28.5% in 2014 among women aged <35 years. From 2013 to 2014, the national percentage of eSET among women aged <35 years increased by approximately 33.0%. The percentage of eSET is still lower in the United States than in countries that impose restrictions on the number of embryos transferred and provide extensive public funding

† . . . Information [about insurance coverage] is available at http://www.resolve.org/family-building-options/insurance_coverage/state-coverage.html.

for ART services. The eSET rates are influenced by many factors (e.g., patient's age, diagnostic factors, and treatment costs); ART treatment costs are high and typically paid out-of-pocket by the patient. In the United States, even where mandated, coverage for infertility treatment can vary in scope. . . . Because ART procedures are expensive (out-of-pocket costs to achieve a live birth estimated at $27,000 for patients with no insurance), broad insurance mandates for IVF might increase the use of eSET and decrease multiple-embryo transfer procedures. Wider acceptance and use of eSET procedures still face considerable barriers in the United States and might require strengthening the guidelines on embryo transfer practices along with expansion of insurance coverage for ART services. . . .

Singleton live-birth deliveries have lower risks than multiple-birth deliveries for adverse birth outcomes such as prematurity, low birthweight, disability, and death. To optimize healthy birth outcomes, the transfer of fewer embryos should be encouraged, where appropriate, taking into consideration the patient's age and prognosis. The percentage of ART-conceived multiple-birth infants in the United States decreased from 53.1% in 2000 to 39.4% in 2014. A substantial decrease was noted in the percentage of ART-conceived triplets and higher-order infants (from 8.9% in 2000 to 1.8% in 2014), and a smaller decrease was noted in the percentage of ART-conceived twins (from 44.2% in 2000 to 37.5% in 2014). . . .

Despite th[e] increase in eSET use, ART-conceived twin infants still accounted for approximately 40.0% of all ART-conceived infants in 2014, and on average, 1.7 embryos were transferred among favorable prognosis patients aged <35 years. In addition to embryo transfer practices, high ART-conceived twin rates also might be partially explained by a desire for more than one child among couples experiencing infertility who might believe that the benefits of a multiple-gestation pregnancy outweigh the risks. . . . Studies indicate that patient education focusing on maternal and perinatal morbidity and mortality, as well as the economic costs of twin gestation, has been effective in reducing the preference for twins among patients.

The economic costs of multiple births also underscore the importance of efforts to reduce ART-related multiple births. In 2013, the mean health care cost to patients and insurers was estimated to be $26,922 for ART-conceived singleton deliveries, $115,238 for ART-conceived twins, and $434,668 for ART-conceived triplets and higher-order infants. . . . Evidence from other countries suggests that greater insurance coverage for ART when combined with restrictions on the number of embryos transferred per cycle can reduce multiple births. . . .

The percentage of low birthweight and very low birthweight infants was higher among ART-conceived infants than among infants in the total birth population. . . . In the United States, the contribution of ART to preterm births, the majority of which are also low birthweight, is a key concern. Fertility treatments, both ART and controlled ovarian stimulations, contribute substantially to preterm births. Preterm births are a leading cause of infant mortality and morbidity; preterm infants are at increased risk for death and have more health and developmental problems than full-term infants. The health risks associated with preterm birth have contributed to increased health care costs. The societal economic costs associated with all preterm births in the United States was last reported in 2005 and was estimated at $26 billion annually ($51,600 per infant born preterm). In 2012, the societal economic costs associated with ART-conceived preterm infants in the United States was estimated at approximately $1.3 billion.

In addition to the known multiple-birth risks associated with ART, even single-ton infants conceived from ART procedures are at increased risk for low birthweight and preterm delivery. In 2014, of all ART-conceived singleton infants, 9.0% were low birthweight, compared with 6.3% of infants in the total birth population. The per-centage of ART-conceived singletons born preterm was 13.2%, compared with 9.7% of infants in the total U.S. birth population. Therefore, adverse infant health out-comes (e.g., low birthweight and preterm delivery) among singletons also should be considered when assessing the effects of ART. . . .

CONCLUSION

Since 1996, the number of ART procedures performed in the United States and the number of infants born as a result of these procedures nearly tripled. With this increasing use, ART-conceived infants represented 1.6% of infants born in the United States in 2014 and noticeably contributed to the prevalence of low birthweight and preterm deliveries, as approximately two fifths of ART-conceived infants were multiple-birth deliveries. Furthermore, among ART-conceived infants, although the percentage of triplets or higher-order infants has decreased since 2000, the percent-age of twin infants has remained persistently high. Therefore, the impact of ART on poor birth outcomes remains substantial. This report documents the rates and contribution of ART to multiple-birth deliveries, low birthweight, and preterm birth by patient's reporting area of residence. It also highlights the differences in rates of low birthweight and prematurity between ART-conceived infants and all infants in the total birth population. These findings allow state health departments to moni-tor the extent of ART-related adverse perinatal outcomes among singletons, twins, and triplets and higher-order infants in their reporting areas.

Comprehensive insurance coverage of ART can help increase access to fertility treatments. Increased use of ART in reporting areas with insurance mandates also can result in higher numbers of ART-conceived multiple-birth deliveries. The findings in this report indicate that ART use was higher than the national rate in all four states with mandated comprehensive insurance coverage. . . . Further research is needed to ascertain the influence of state health insurance mandates on ART use, embryo transfer practices, infant outcomes, and economic and out-of-pocket patient costs of multiple births. Addressing the risk for multiple-birth deliveries also requires under-standing the perspectives of couples undergoing infertility treatments who might view a multiple birth, especially twins, as an acceptable or desired outcome or might lack awareness of the increased risks associated with multiple births to mothers and infants. Although the majority of clinicians acknowledge that the birth of a healthy singleton is the best outcome of ART, they might be sensitive to patient perspectives. Clinicians need to be aware of ongoing efforts to limit the number of embryos trans-ferred to reduce the rate of multiple births, particularly twins, and encourage wider implementation of eSET, when clinically appropriate, as mechanisms of promoting singleton infant births among ART-conceived pregnancies.

CDC has outlined a public health oriented strategy for detection, preven-tion, and management of infertility . . . Of public health importance is the role of infertility treatment on adverse birth outcomes, primarily because of higher rates of multiple births. ART only partially explains the overall prevalence of these adverse outcomes in the United States. Other factors influencing multiple births include maternal age at conception and non-ART fertility treatments. . . . (i.e., controlled ovarian stimulation such as superovulation-intrauterine insemination and conventional ovulation induction) . . . . In 2011, approximately 19.0% of twin births in the United States were attributable to non-IVF fertility treatments. . . .

Notes: Reproductive Technologies, Parenting Possibilities, and Advances in Genetics

1. *Overview and Reproductive Alternatives.* The Notes in this section provide an overview of some of the major issues and themes that will be considered in subsequent sections focusing on specific types of alternative reproductive techniques. One preliminary inquiry is the exploration of families and family creation. How important is it to have a child? How important is it to have a child who is genetically related to you or to your partner? See S. Hendriks, The Importance of Genetic Parenthood for Infertile Men and Women, 39 Human Reprod. 2076 (2017) (providing analysis of rationales for 98 percent of respondents at fertility clinic who preferred genetic parenthood for themselves and their partner); and Debora Spar & Anna Harrington, Building a Better Baby Business, 10 Minn. J. L. Sci. & Tech. 41 (2009) (discussing supply, demand, and the market for reproductive technologies). Professor Robertson reviews the prevalence of infertility in our society; estimates vary. Cf. Maria E. Thoma et al., Prevalence of Infertility in the United States as Estimated by the Current Duration Approach and A Traditional Constructed Approach, 99 Fertility & Sterility 1324 (2013) (noting range of different approaches to defining and estimating infertility prevalence and providing estimates of 15.5 percent and 7.0 percent using different methods). The data on infertility typically understate potential demand as single people and gay or lesbian couples have also sought to make use of alternative approaches to reproduction.

Current forms of alternative reproduction involve separating the contribution of gametes (eggs and sperm) from gestation. Reproductive projects therefore can involve:

- intended parent(s) (one or more),
- donors or providers of the sperm and oocytes (who may or may not be intended parents), and
- a provider of the womb (who may be a gestational surrogate or an intended parent).

New forms of ART, such as mitochondrial replacement technology, may expand the number of potential participants in the reproductive enterprise. See page 827. Other future developments, such as the potential for creating viable sperm and eggs from skin cells, may reduce the need for third-party gamete donors. See page 826.

The individuals making use of new approaches to reproduction may use the same technique in an effort to achieve different results. For example, a physician might use donor eggs and sperm along with IVF to create an embryo that is implanted into a woman. The parties participating in this process might intend in one case that the woman bearing the child be recognized as the legal mother of the child, while a different set of parties using the same techniques might hope that the woman bearing the child will be recognized only as a gestational surrogate who has no legal relationship or claim on the child to whom she gives birth. The CDC report excerpted above does not focus on this aspect of the use of ART but simply reports the total number of procedures and births.

The participants in alternative reproduction can be connected with each other through:

- formal legal ties (e.g., married or participants in domestic partnerships),
- informal agreements between family members or friends (such as when a sister or friend agrees to serve as an oocyte donor or gestational surrogate),
- more formalized agreements or contracts that seek to establish the rights and obligations of relatives, friends, and "strangers."

See, e.g., The Ethics Committee of ASRM, Using Family Members as Gamete Donors of Surrogates, 107 Fertility & Sterility 1136 (2017) (analyzing ethical aspects of specific intrafamilial arrangements). The reproductive endeavor can be facilitated or directed by third parties or health care providers who "package" arrangements for intended parents.

2. *ARTs and the Constitution: One Right or Many?* In the article excerpted above, Professor Robertson suggests that constitutional protection of the right to procreate extends to the use of new reproductive technologies, even where the resulting child will not be biologically related to the intended parents. See also John A. Robertson, Assisting Reproduction, Choosing Genes, and the Scope of Reproductive Freedom, 76 Geo. Wash. L. Rev. 1490 (2008). Others, like Radhika Rao, would limit *Skinner* to protecting the privacy of persons from state intrusions upon bodily integrity. Radhika Rao, Constitutional Misconceptions, 93 Mich. L. Rev. 1473, 1484 (1995). How would you characterize the source and dimensions of this constitutional right?

While the language in *Skinner* (page 703) is broad and general, the Supreme Court has been disinclined in recent years to find constitutional protection for activities not deeply rooted in history and tradition. See Troxel v. Granville, 530 U.S. 57 (2000) (parents have fundamental right to make child-rearing decisions; Constitution limits state's ability to presume interaction with grandparents is in the best interests of a child); Michael H. v. Gerald D., 491 U.S. 110 (1989) (rejecting claim of married woman's male lover that he had constitutional right to establish a parenting relationship with his genetic child, born of his lover during her marriage to another man).

In the context of coital reproduction, the courts often discuss a "right to procreate" and a "right not to procreate" as the cases discussed earlier in this chapter demonstrate. Is that concept of the right adequate when it comes to reproductive technologies, or do we need a more sophisticated mapping? For example, as one of us has written:

[W]hen we are discussing the right not to procreate, we need to recognize three possible rights not to be a parent—a right not to be a gestational parent, a right not to be a genetic parent, and a right not to be a legal parent. The tendency to view these rights as a monolithic bundle is an outgrowth of the fact that, in natural reproduction, the three rights tend to be clustered together: when a woman seeks an abortion, she is simultaneously exercising a right not to be a gestational, legal, and genetic parent, and we seldom have reason to try and disaggregate the three. But the world of reproductive technology allows us to see that the bundling of these three rights is not inherent. Conceptually, we can add the three rights not to be a parent and three possible opposing rights to be a parent, for a relationship of six possible rights:

A right not to be a gestational parent	A right to be a gestational parent
A right not to be a genetic parent	A right to be a genetic parent
A right not to be a legal parent	A right to be a legal parent . . .

. . .

More generally, even as to the rights not to procreate, one could imagine a legal regime that recognized one or two of these rights but not the remaining one or ones. Further, some disputes about assisted reproduction depend on one of the sticks in the bundle but not others, and in resolving them a court need only determine the existence and applicability of one of the sticks in the bundle.

[To see this, contrast two cases. Case 1:] A gestational surrogate is carrying the genetic offspring of the husband and wife. As part of her surrogacy agreement she has agreed that she will not do anything to endanger the fetus, including getting an abortion, without the permission of the husband and the wife. The agreement also provides that the husband and the wife will be the legal parents of the child, assuming all attendant financial obligations. Assume that the jurisdiction allows such assignments of parentage. Notwithstanding the agreement, in the third month of her pregnancy, the surrogate announces her intention to get an abortion, a course of action the husband and the wife attempt to prevent. If she argues that enforcing the agreement violates her rights by preventing her from getting an abortion, then her claim is really that the enforcement infringes her right not to be a gestational parent against her will. Thus, it is necessary and sufficient for her claim that she has a right not to be a gestational parent, it is neither necessary nor sufficient that she have a right not to be a legal parent or a genetic parent.

[Case 2:] A gestational surrogate is carrying the child of the husband and the wife. Prenatal testing indicates that the child has a significant genetic abnormality. The husband and the wife want the surrogate to have an abortion. She refuses to do so. If the husband and the wife argue that allowing her to continue with the pregnancy would violate their rights, their claim is really that it violates their right not to be genetic parents against their will (as well as their right not to be legal parents in any jurisdiction that would attach legal parentage to the genetic parents in this case). It is neither necessary nor sufficient that they have a right to be or not to be gestational parents.

I. Glenn Cohen, The Constitution and the Rights Not to Procreate, 60 Stan. L. Rev. 1135, 1140-1143 (2008). As you read the materials in the rest of this chapter, consider whether it is helpful to "unbundle" the rights to and not to procreate and what that unbundling reveals about the constitutional status of various rights claims.

Other commentators have noted the possibility of additional sources of constitutional protection in considering ARTs. The Court has been sensitive to the harmful impact of policies grounded in gender stereotyping and has also recognized same-sex marriage, in Obergefell v. Hodges, 135 S.Ct. 2584 (2015). Would the equal protection clause provide another possible line of argument to contest state regulations that, for example, "privilege biological over social connections" and thereby exclude some men and women and many same-sex couples seeking to create families through ARTs? See Douglas NeJaime, The Nature of Parenthood, 126 Yale L. J. 2260, 2347-62 (2017); and Courtney Megan Cahill, Reproduction Reconceived, 101 Minn. L. Rev. 617 (2016). See also, Pavan v. Smith, 137 S.Ct. 2075 (2017), discussed at page 814.

Once the appropriate standard of constitutional review has been identified, the next analytic steps require examining the nature of the state's interest in regulating ART and the "fit" between the state interest and the regulation. Professor Cohen has challenged the theoretical and philosophical bases for the regulation of many forms of ART. Professor Cohen is particularly skeptical of state regulations justified as furthering the "best interests of the child," pointing out that many forms of regulation would prevent the birth of a child and noting the difficulty with state claims that it would be better not to be born alive than to be born using a particular form of ART. I. Glenn Cohen, Regulating Reproduction: The Problem with Best Interests, 96 Minn. L. Rev. 423 (2011); and I. Glenn Cohen, Beyond Best Interests, 96 Minn. L. Rev. 1187 (2012).

How should the courts approach the application of constitutional principles to state laws and regulations involving ARTs? Will courts find that procreative liberty is limited to "natural" procreation via sexual reproduction? What will be the limits of constitutional protection for procreative liberty? Does our right to procreative liberty extend beyond genetic parenting to include the use of donated gametes? If genetic parenting is constitutionally significant, will cloning be given any constitutional protection? Are there special considerations where legal rules seem grounded in traditional gender-based or heteronormative views? We will return to questions about the uses and limits of constitutional protections as we consider these and other procreational approaches in the remaining sections of this chapter.

3. *Regulation.* Should states or the federal government regulate the use of reproductive technology? Do the risks associated with multiple embryo transfers support direct regulation or indirect regulation through the tort system? How should our legal system determine the legal rights and responsibilities of participants in reproductive activities? Consider some of the possible reproductive alternatives. Who do you think should be considered to be the "legal" parent(s) of the child produced by these arrangements? What factors motivate your judgments? Should states enact legislation regulating the use of alternative reproduction and defining the legal status of the participants? What should be the guiding principles of the legislation? What standards should courts use in the absence of legislation? Should the intent of the parties always govern the use of these techniques and the status of the parties? What should happen where the parties no longer agree on these matters? When, if ever, should states or courts override the intent of the parties? Is there any constitutional limit on state regulation or legislation that overrides the intent of the parties? The situation is made even more complex by the potential for human cloning, discussed below in section E.

ART regulation involves the intersection of matters typically within the jurisdiction of state governments (family law, medical practice) with issues controlled at the federal level (interstate commerce, human subjects research, the donation and use of human cells). Not surprisingly, regulation in the United States has been piecemeal, with significant regulatory gaps. Courts therefore have been forced to step in to resolve the implications of new reproductive technologies. See generally

Susan Frelich Appleton, Illegitimacy and Sex, Old and New, 20 Am. U. J. Gender Soc. Pol'y & L. 347 (2012) (noting similarities between old legal treatment of illegitimacy and regulation of ARTs); and David Adamson, Regulation of Assisted Reproductive Technologies in the United States, 39 Fam. L. Q. 727 (2005).

4. *Standards, Guidelines, and Studies.* Commissions and other advisory groups have issued numerous recommendations. The National Conference of the Commissioners on Uniform State Laws (hereinafter, "Uniform Law Commission") has issued three versions of the Uniform Parentage Act [UPA] (2017, 2002, 1973) over the past four decades, with each iteration grappling with some of the family law ramifications of advances in assisted reproductive technology. The UPA will be further discussed below. See also, Uniform Law Commission, Uniform Probate Code (2008); American Bar Association (ABA), Model Act Governing Assisted Reproductive Technology Agencies (2016); ABA, Model Act Governing Assisted Reproductive Technology (2008); President's Council on Bioethics, Reproduction and Responsibility: The Regulation of New Biotechnologies (2004). Professional societies and organizations have also issued guidelines. See, e.g., the various guidelines from the Society for Assisted Reproduction Technology (SART) and the American Society for Reproductive Medicine (ASRM) that are cited throughout this section.

5. *International Developments.* The development and use of ARTs has created controversy in countries around the world. For data on the use of ART worldwide, see International Committee for Monitoring Assisted Reproductive Technologies World Report: Assisted Reproductive Technology 2008, 2009, 2010, 31 Human Reprod. 1588 (2016) (providing data and estimating more than 404,364 children born with various types of ART worldwide in 2010). Several countries have enacted comprehensive legislation designed to cover the use of ARTs and new genetic technologies such as cloning. Canada enacted the Assisted Human Reproduction Act in 2004, see http://laws-lois.justice.gc.ca/eng/acts/A-13.4/. One major purpose of the Act is to prevent the commercialization of reproductive technologies. Thus, the Act prohibits payment for sperm or egg donors. Critics argue that the decommercialization will reduce the supplies of sperm and eggs available for use. See Barbara von Tigerstrom, Federal Health Legislation and the Assisted Human Reproduction Act Reference, 74 Sask. L. Rev. 33 (2011) (analyzing impact of Supreme Court of Canada decision striking down portions of Act but upholding restrictions on commercialization and posthumous reproduction).

6. *Reproductive Tourism.* As ART has developed and improved, couples have demonstrated willingness to travel, resulting in "reproductive tourism." Ethics Committee of the ASRM, Cross-Border Reproductive Care: An Ethics Committee Opinion, 106 Fertil. & Steril. 1627 (2016). The activities involved in the reproductive project can span the boundaries of states and countries, such as when intended parents from the United States, Canada, or the United Kingdom travel to other countries to access gestational surrogates and lower-cost services. I. Glenn Cohen, Patients with Passports: Medical Tourism, Law, and Ethics (2015); I. Glenn Cohen, Circumvention Tourism, 97 Cornell L. Rev. 1309 (2012). How should home countries that prohibit activities like commercial surrogacy treat their citizens who travel abroad to circumvent these laws? Should citizenship be recognized for the resulting children? See Cohen, supra, Patients with Passports; and page 860. The meaning of "reproductive tourism" can change quickly. Many of the most popular countries for reproductive tourism began restricting access to ARTs, particularly surrogacy,

in 2015. The United States has become a leading destination for patients who can afford the costs of care and who seek access to surrogacy and other ARTs. Tamar Lewin, Coming to the U.S. for Baby, and Womb to Carry It, N.Y. Times, July 5, 2014.

7. *Genetic Testing.* Reproductive and genetic technologies can be combined, thereby creating new policy dilemmas. Genetic testing can be employed at various stages in reproduction, with ethical and religious concerns generally increasing at each stage. Individuals can be tested before donating their gametes, the preembryo can be tested after conception but before implantation, or the embryo and fetus can be tested after implantation. Genetic testing after implantation clearly raises the possibility of abortion, with all the attendant controversy. Initially, genetic tests during pregnancy involved blood and ultrasound tests followed by a physically invasive amniocentesis test during the second trimester that carried some risk for the fetus. Z. Alfirevic, K. Navaratnam & F. Mujezinovic, Amniocentesis and Chorionic Villus Sampling for Prenatal Diagnosis, Cochrane Database Syst. Rev. (Sept. 2017) (comparing risks of various forms of prenatal diagnosis). The latest genetic tests use fetal DNA found in blood samples from the pregnant woman and can be performed at an earlier stage of pregnancy. Noninvasive prenatal genetic testing (NIPT) permits women to gain access to a wider range of fetal characteristics during a period of pregnancy when abortion is still relatively accessible. See Rachel Rebouché, Non-Invasive Testing, Non-Invasive Counseling, 43 J. L. Med. & Ethics 228 (2015). The ability to conduct genetic testing has advanced more quickly than the ability to translate the results into useable knowledge for clinicians or parents. Commentators note the potential challenges to providing adequate counseling and informed consent for pregnant women who may soon be offered fetal genetic sequencing. Josephine Johnston, Ruth M. Farrell & Erik Parens, Supporting Women's Autonomy and Prenatal Testing, 377 N. Eng. J. Med. 505 (2017) (noting that genetic sequencing may "reveal information about hundreds or thousands of genes" and that there is considerable uncertainty about the significance of genetic variations).

8. *"Negative" vs. "Positive" Eugenics.* Should it matter whether parents are engaging in "negative" versus "positive" eugenics? In the first, parents seek to avoid some abnormal and seriously disabling genetic condition. In the second, they hope to acquire a child with some particularly socially desirable traits. Persons who take advantage of prenatal screening may use information about their child's genetic characteristics in deciding whether to continue the pregnancy to term. NIPT now provides information about genetic conditions such as Down syndrome much earlier in pregnancy. H. Hume & S. T. Chasen, Trends in Timing of Prenatal Diagnosis and Abortion for Fetal Chromosomal Abnormalities, 213 Am. J. Obstet. Gynecol. 545 (2015) (discussing rate and earlier timing for abortions related to certain chromosomal variations, including Down syndrome); Darrin P. Dixon, Informed Consent or Institutionalized Eugenics?, 24 Issues L. & Med. 3 (2008) (arguing pressures result in high abortion rates for fetuses diagnosed with Down syndrome). Could a state restrict access to genetic screening tests in order to further its interest in protecting fetal life? The state would not restrict abortion, per se, but merely limit parental access to information.

Should similar reasoning be applied in the context of ARTs, where preimplantation genetic screening can be combined with IVF to ensure that only embryos without certain genetic variations are implanted in a woman's uterus? See Rebouché, supra, and related articles in Symposium, Intersections in Reproduction:

Perspectives on Abortion and Assisted Reproductive Technologies, 43 J. L. Med. & Ethics 174-362 (2015). Assuming that genetic testing is available, should parents have a duty to use preimplantation genetic diagnosis (PGD) to prevent the birth of a child with a seriously disabling condition? See Janet Malek & Judy Daar, The Case for a Parental Duty to Use Preimplantation Genetic Diagnosis for Medical Benefit, 12 Am. J. Bioethics 3 (2012) (ethical duty and potential parental duty under tort law). Would a "negative" eugenics program discriminate against non-implanted embryos on the basis of their disability? Alicia Ouelette, Selection Against Disability: Abortion, ART, and Access, 43 J. L. Med. & Ethics 211 (2015); and Note, Regulating Preimplantation Genetic Diagnosis: The Pathologization Problem, 118 Harv. L. Rev. 2770 (2005). What if the parents sought to use these technologies to choose the gender of their child, perhaps by implanting only the embryos of the "correct" gender? Compare the discussion of sex selection and abortion, supra, pages 750-751, and Judith F. Daar, ART and the Search for Perfectionism: On Selecting Gender, Genes, and Gametes, 9 J. Gender Race & Just. 241 (2005). Professional organizations are divided on the topic. Compare, AMA Code of Ethics, 4.2.3(3) (physicians should "[p]rovide sex selection of sperm only for purposes of avoiding a sex-linked inheritable disorder. Physicians should not participate in sex selection of sperm for reasons of gender preference") with Ethics Committee of the ASRM, Use of Reproductive Technology for Sex Selection for Nonmedical Reasons, 103 Fertil. & Steril. 1418 (2015) (no consensus within Committee; clinics encouraged to develop and make available their policies and to accommodate employee decisions about participation).

9. *Gene Therapy, Genetic Engineering, and Genetic Enhancement.* At some future point, effective genetic engineering and genetic therapy technologies may be developed. As will be discussed, at page 899, we are seeing the first breakthroughs in these areas with the CRISPR-Cas9 technology gene editing technologies. While the terms are not always used consistently, "gene therapy" most often refers to treating a genetic disorder, either through traditional medical or genetic means. Genetic engineering typically refers to altering an individual's genes. Somatic genetic engineering or therapy involves changing the genetic content of a person's non-reproductive cells. Germ-line genetic engineering or therapy involves changing the genetic content of a person's reproductive cells or gametes. Germ-line genetic engineering could be very appealing to those who have serious genetic conditions that limit their ability or desire to reproduce. Yet the scientific risks and ethical concerns related to genetic engineering are greatest when the "treatment," perhaps more realistically called an "experiment," also involves future generations.

Advances in genetics may also empower humans to "enhance" their offspring. Enhancement may occur by taking genes associated with desirable traits from third parties for incorporation into one's gametes or embryos. "Enhancement" might also be achieved through the use of non-human genetic materials or engineered materials. Although all such research would be controversial, incorporation of novel genes into the germ-line once again would be the most risky, controversial, and morally problematic. See, e.g., I. Glenn Cohen, What (If Anything) Is Wrong with Human Enhancement? What (If Anything) Is Right with It?, 49 Tulsa L. Rev. 645 (2014).

Should the federal government or state governments restrict access to these technologies? Should regulation distinguish between somatic cell therapy and germ-line therapy, assuming that researchers are able to confidently predict whether germ-line cells will be affected by a treatment? How should regulation proceed, perhaps with a permanent, total ban on germ-line research? See, David Baltimore et al., A Prudent Path Forward for Genomic Engineering and Germline Gene Modification, 348 Science 36 (2015); Edward Lampier et al., Don't Edit the Human Germline, 519 Nature 410 (2015).

Assuming that research goes forward, are you concerned about equality of access to genetic screening tests and/or genetic therapies? What if access to genetic technologies could reify class differences — permitting the wealthy to ensure the future success of their offspring through positive genetic engineering? Is this any different from current practices that permit the wealthy to send their children to expensive private schools? See generally Dov Fox, Silver Spoons and Golden Genes: Genetic Engineering and the Egalitarian Ethos, 33 Am. J. L. & Med. 567 (2007).

10. *Commentaries.* This is yet another area rich with commentaries. Early, influential articles relating to **reproductive alternatives** (note 1) include: R. Alta Charo, And Baby Makes Three — or Four, or Five, or Six: Redefining the Family After the Reprotech Revolution, 15 Wis. Women's L. J. 231 (2000); Janet L. Dolgin, Choice, Tradition, and the New Genetics: The Fragmentation of the Ideology of Family, 32 Conn. L. Rev. 523 (2000); Thomas H. Murray, What Are Families For? Getting to an Ethics of Reproductive Technology, 32(3) Hastings Center Rep. 41 (May–June 2002) (suggesting that emphasis on procreative liberty risks disregard for the interests of children); Dorothy E. Roberts, Race and the New Reproduction, 47 Hastings L. J. 935 (1996); John A. Robertson, Children of Choice: Freedom and the New Reproductive Technologies (1994); John A. Robertson, Procreative Liberty and the Control of Conception, Pregnancy, and Childbirth, 69 Va. L. Rev. 405 (1983). John A. Robertson, Procreative Liberty and Harm to Offspring in Assisted Reproduction, 30 Am. J. L. & Med. 7 (2004); John A. Robertson, Procreative Liberty in the Era of Genomics, 29 Am. J. L. & Med. 439 (2003).

For more on the **constitutionality** of regulating ART and possible regulatory schemes (note 2), in addition to the articles cited above, see Naomi R. Cahn, The New Kinship, 100 Geo. L. J. 367 (2012); Radhika Rao, Equal Liberty: Assisted Reproductive Technology and Reproductive Equality, 76 Geo. Wash. L. Rev. 1457 (2008); Marsha Garrison, Regulating Reproduction, 76 Geo. Wash. L. Rev. 1623 (2008); June Carbone, If I Say "Yes" to Regulations Today, Will You Still Respect Me in the Morning?, 76 Geo. Wash. L. Rev. 1747 (2008); Catherine A. Clements, What About the Children? A Call for Regulation of Assisted Reproductive Technology, 84 Ind. L. J. 331 (2008).

For more on **international regulation of ART and reproductive tourism** (notes 5 & 6), see the United Kingdom's Human Fertilisation & Embryology Authority, at www.hfea.gov.uk; Lisa C. Ikemoto, Reproductive Tourism: Equality Concerns in the Global Market for Fertility Services, 27 Law & Ineq. J. 277 (2009); Alicia Ouelette et al., Lessons Across the Pond: Assisted Reproductive Technology in the United Kingdom and the United States, 31 Am. J. L. & Med. 419 (2005); Richard F. Storrow, Religious, Feminism and Abortion: The Regulation of Assisted Reproduction in Two Catholic Countries, 42 Rutgers L. Rev. 725 (2011); and Richard F. Storrow, Travel into the Future of Reproductive Technology, 79 UKMC L. Rev. 295 (2010).

Readings relating to the implications of **genetic testing** (note 7) include: Barbara Katz Rothman, The Tentative Pregnancy: Prenatal Diagnosis and the Future of Motherhood (1986); President's Council on Bioethics, Reproduction and

Responsibility: The Regulation of New Biotechnologies (2004); Sonia M. Suter, The Routinization of Prenatal Testing, 28 Am. J. L. & Med. 233 (2002).

For additional commentaries on **negative or positive eugenics**, including **genetic enhancement** (notes 8 & 9), see Harry Adams, A Human Germline Modification Scale, 32 J. L. Med. & Ethics 164 (2004); Ronald M. Green, Babies by Design: The Ethics of Genetic Choice (2007); Robert Klitzman, Struggles in Defining and Addressing Requests for "Family Balancing": Ethical Issues Faced by Providers and Patients, 44 J. L. Med. & Ethics 616 (2016); Jessica Knouse, Reconciling Liberty and Equality in the Debate over Preimplantation Genetic Diagnosis, 2013 Utah L. Rev. 107 (2013); Maxwell J. Mehlman, Any DNA to Declare? Regulating Offshore Access to Genetic Enhancement, 28 Am. J. L. & Med. 179 (2002); Michael Sandel, The Case Against Perfection: Ethics in an Age of Genetic Engineering (2007); Daniel L. Tobey, What's Really Wrong with Genetic Enhancement: A Second Look at Our Posthuman Future, 6 Yale J. L. & Tech. 54 (2003-2004); and LeRoy Walters & Julie Palmer, The Ethics of Human Gene Therapy (1996).

2. Gamete Donation

The donation of gametes—sperm and ova—encompasses old and new uses of reproductive technology. Artificial insemination (AI), also known as intrauterine insemination (IUI), is the oldest assisted reproductive technique; in its simplest form, it requires no medical expertise or specialized equipment. The two major types of AI used today involve (1) using the sperm of the husband or male partner (AIH); or (2) using the sperm of a third-party donor (AID). AIH can compensate for certain types of male infertility. AID provides a substitute source of male gametes in the case of profound male infertility or compensates for the absence of a male partner for single heterosexual women or lesbians. See Leena Nahata, Nathanael Stanley & Gwendolyn Quinn, Gamete Donation: Current Practices, Public Opinion, and Unanswered Questions, 107 Fertility & Sterility 1298 (2017); Tamar Lewin, 10 Things to Know about Being a Sperm Donor, N.Y. Times, November 3, 2016 (noting that two largest sperm banks in the United States accept about 1/100 applicants). Most of the legal and policy debates have focused on AID. In the Internet age, it should not be surprising that sperm banks offer information about potential donors online. Couples or single women searching for a suitable donor may select various donor characteristics, may hear an audiotape of the donor's voice, and may even be able to see a donor's baby picture. See Anetta Pietrzak, The Price of Sperm, 14 J. L. & Fam. Stud. 121 (2012).

Donation of an egg (also called an oocyte) is much more medically complex and invasive. Prospective donors must undergo medical treatment to stimulate their ovaries to produce multiple eggs. The donor is monitored through ultrasound exams and blood tests to determine whether there are a sufficient number of eggs to warrant harvesting. The eggs must be retrieved from inside the woman's body using an ultrasound-guided needle or through a laparoscopic procedure. See Practice Committee of the ASRM, Prevention and Treatment of Moderate and Severe Ovarian Hyperstimulation Syndrome: A Guideline, 106 Fertility & Sterility 1634 (2016) (OHSS occurs in 1-5 percent of cycles); and Jane E. Brody, Do Egg Donors Face Longer-Term Risks, N.Y. Times, July 10, 2017 (noting calls to study long-term impact of hormone injections). In the early years of ART, the technical challenges associated with freezing oocytes meant that "fresh" donated eggs would need to be fertilized using sperm in the laboratory (using IVF), creating a preembryo that could either be frozen or implanted in a woman's uterus. (The legal and ethical aspects of embryo donation and use will be discussed in great detail below, at pages 828-838.) "Egg banks" are now available on the Internet, with Web sites offering to match infertile women with prospective egg donors having certain characteristics.

Recent advances in cryopreservation mean that eggs may now be frozen for possible future use in ART. Women may now use oocyte cryopreservation to preserve their reproductive potential, for medical reasons (such as before medical treatments that might affect fertility) or for non-medical reasons. See Society for Assisted Reproductive Technology (SART) and the Practice Committee of the American Society for Reproductive Medicine (ASRM), Mature Oocyte Cryopreservation: A Guideline, 99 Fertility & Sterility 37 (2013) (concluding cryopreservation of oocytes no longer experimental but, citing limited data, recommending that cryopreservation use be limited to women with the medical need to preserve capacity and not for women seeking to delay reproduction). Would egg banking by women present any special concerns? Compare John A. Robertson, Egg Freezing and Egg Banking: Empowerment and Alienation in Assisted Reproduction, 1 J. of Law & the Biosciences 113 (2014) (noting some concerns) with Imogen Goold, Trust Women to Choose, J. of L. & the Biosciences (2017) (a thoughtful response) available at: https://doi.org/10.1093/jlb/lsxOLO. Egg freezing remains an underutilized option. Lauren W. Milman et al., Assessing Reproductive Choices of Women and the Likelihood of Oocyte Preservation in the Era of Elective Oocyte Freezing, 107 Fertility & Sterility 1214 (2017) (exploring demand and willingness to pay for elective egg freezing); and Brody, supra (noting claims that a well-known tech company had offered a $20,000 egg freezing employee benefit).

Gamete donation is governed by federal regulations and the voluntary guidelines of professional organizations. 21 C.F.R. §§1271.45-1271.90 (donor eligibility and screening rules); Ethics Committee of the ASRM, Interests, Obligations, and Rights in Gamete Donation, 102 Fertility & Sterility 675 (2014); Practice Committees of ASRM and SART, Recommendations for Gamete and Embryo Donation: A Committee Opinion, 99 Fertility & Sterility 47 (2013). The federal regulations require entities that provide ART to register with the government; organizations that participate in gamete donation are subject to inspection and other oversight. The regulations and guidelines generally require quarantine of the donation and evaluation and testing of the gamete donor for certain communicable and genetic conditions. Interestingly, the quarantine requirement applies to sperm but not to oocytes. Recommendations for Gamete and Embryo Donation, supra, at 52-53 (cryopreservation of oocytes necessary for quarantine process "cannot be performed reliably," contrary to Mature Oocyte Cryopreservation: A Guideline, supra).

The Practice Committees' guidelines also require screening and evaluation of potential gamete recipients. Are health care providers who refuse to provide reproductive technology services to persons with hereditary conditions or disabilities engaged in impermissible disability-based discrimination under the ADA? See Ethics Committee of the ASRM, Human Immunodeficiency Virus (HIV) and Infertility Treatment: A Committee Opinion, 104 Fertility & Sterility e1 (2015) (no ethical reason to withhold fertility services from clinics with relevant resources where individuals and couples are willing to use risk reduction techniques); Carl

H. Coleman, Conceiving Harm: Disability Discrimination in Assisted Reproductive Technologies, 50 UCLA L. Rev. 17 (2002); and 21 C.F.R. §1271.90 (exceptions from donor screening requirements). Gamete providers have established systems that support parental efforts to use race as a factor in selecting donors. Should this be permissible? See Dov Fox, Note, Racial Classification in Assisted Reproduction, 118 Yale L. J. 1844 (2009) (practices legal but "pernicious").

Who is the father of a child produced through AI? Should a child produced within a marriage be presumed to be the child of the husband? Should genetic parentage govern over social norms or the parties' expectations? The AI provisions of the 1973 version of the Uniform Parentage Act (UPA), adopted in some form or another in most states, were designed to eliminate ambiguity and to relieve prospective donors of the risk of unwanted paternity. Uniform Law Commission, UPA §5 (1973). The 1973 Act provided a legal mechanism for recognizing the infertile husband as the father of a child born through insemination of his wife using donor sperm. The husband was required to give written consent, the procedure had to be performed under the supervision of a physician, and the records were subject to inspection by a court upon a showing of good cause. Under the 1973 UPA, the sperm donor was not considered the father so long as the sperm was provided to a licensed physician for insemination of a "married woman." This restrictive language placed the donor at risk if the sperm was used in the insemination of a woman who was not legally married—and consequently made AI for single or lesbian women difficult to obtain in some states. Other states adopted a version of the rule that simply omitted the word "married," eliminating the legal barrier to the use of AI for unmarried women. Many providers nonetheless continued to deny access to these services to unmarried women.

The 1973 UPA did not consider the legal consequences of egg donation, IVF, or gestational surrogacy; the woman who gave birth to a child was presumed to be the child's mother. Advances in reproductive technology led to the development of new legislative proposals in the late 1980s and states began to enact gamete and embryo donation provisions in the early 1990s. The 2002 UPA reflected these developments:

§701. Scope of Article. This [article] does not apply to the birth of a child conceived by means of sexual intercourse[, or as the result of a [lawful] gestational agreement . . .].

§702. Parental Status of Donor. A donor is not a parent of a child conceived by means of assisted reproduction.

§703. Paternity of Child of Assisted Reproduction. A man who provides sperm for, or consents to, assisted reproduction by a woman as provided in Section 704 with the intent to be the parent of her child, is a parent of the resulting child.

§704. Consent to Assisted Reproduction. (a) Consent by a woman, and a man who intends to be a parent of a child born to the woman by assisted reproduction must be in a record signed by the woman and the man. This requirement does not apply to a donor.

(b) Failure [sic] a man to sign a consent required by subsection (a), before or after birth of the child, does not preclude a finding of paternity if the woman and the man, during the first two years of the child's life resided together in the same household with the child and openly held out the child as their own.

The Act also limits the period of time in which the husband can challenge his paternity following the use of assisted conception, with some exceptions. UPA §705 (2002) (available at: http://uniformlaws.org/). How would the female partner of a woman who conceives via AI be treated under the 2002 UPA? As will be discussed below, the framework adopted in the 2002 UPA failed to address directly the ramifications of same-sex couples seeking to use donor gametes to create families. The 2017 UPA contains provisions intended to fill this gap.

Notes: Gamete Donation

1. *Gamete "Donation" and Compensation.* The trend in the law is to treat the donation of sperm and eggs as legally similar. Do you agree? Should the greater degree of medical and physical intrusion involved in egg donation have any legal significance? See generally Anne Reichman Schiff, Solomonic Decisions in Egg Donation: Unscrambling the Conundrum of Legal Maternity, 80 Iowa L. Rev. 265 (1995). Should it be permissible to compensate gamete donors? The 2002 UPA provides that a "donor" is "an individual who produces eggs or sperm used for assisted reproduction, whether or not for consideration." UPA §102(8) (2002). See also UPA §102(9) (2017) (donor is "an individual who provides gametes intended for use in assisted reproduction, whether or not for consideration").

Sperm donors typically are compensated less than $200 per deposit. Before mid-2016, the Ethics Committee of the ASRM suggested a cap on the level of compensation to egg donors. See Ethics Committee of the ASRM, Financial Compensation of Oocyte Donors, 88 Fertility & Sterility 305 (2007) (suggesting that payments over $5,000 required justification and that payments over $10,000 were inappropriate). What justified placing a cap on compensation for egg donors but not sperm donors? What types of concerns are raised by the cap? In 2011, four former oocyte donors brought a class action suit against the ASRM, SART, and various clinics and agencies claiming that the recommended cap constituted price-fixing under the Sherman Antitrust Act. Malinda S. Lee et al., Limitations on the Compensation of Gamete Donors: A Public Opinion Survey, 107 Fertility & Sterility 1355, 1356 (2017). The ASRM settled the claim in 2016 and withdrew its payment recommendations. The most recent ASRM guideline no longer includes a suggested cap on compensation but continues to express concerns about market-based compensation. Ethics Committee of the ASRM, Financial Compensation of Oocyte Donors: An Ethics Opinion, 106 Fertility & Sterility e15 (2016) (compensation level should be tied to time, inconvenience, and discomfort for donor; "[c]ompensation should not vary according to . . . [among other things] the donor's ethnic or other personal characteristics"). In contrast to the free-market ethos in the United States, compensation for gamete donors is completely banned or severely limited in other countries. See, e.g., the sources cited above; and Trudo Lemmens, The Commodification of Gametes: Why Prohibiting Untrammeled Commercialization Matters, in Trudo Lemmens et al., eds, Regulating Creation: The Law, Ethics, and Policy of Assisted Human Reproduction (2017).

The 1973, 2002, and 2017 versions of the UPA refuse to apply the "donation" rules when the child is conceived through sexual intercourse. See UPA §701 (2002, 2017). Why doesn't the UPA permit the parties to execute a document indicating that the sexual activity is for the purpose of donating gametes? In Ferguson v. McKiernan, the court noted the parental responsibilities created in sexual reproduction under state law and the differential treatment of non-coital reproduction:

> In the case of traditional sexual reproduction, there simply is no question that the parties to any resultant conception and birth may not contract between themselves to deny the child the support he or she requires. . . . In the institutional sperm donation case, however, there appears to be a growing consensus that clinical, institutional sperm donation neither imposes obligations nor confers privileges upon the sperm donor. Between these poles lies a spectrum of arrangements that exhibit characteristics of each extreme to varying degrees—informal agreements between friends to conceive a child via sexual intercourse; non-clinical non-sexual insemination; and so on.

940 A.2d 1236, 1246 (Pa. 2007) (upholding informal agreement and protecting sperm donor from parental support because facts most closely mirrored the institutional sperm donation arrangement). Should courts and legislatures extend gamete donation rules to embryo donations?

2. *Difficulties in the Application of the 1973 UPA Approach.* The 1973 UPA was adopted by 19 states. It imposed a variety of requirements for AI, such as physician supervision and written consent by the husband. Where the criteria were not satisfied, the donor might be given—or forced to accept—parental rights and obligations. Cf. Jhordan C. v. Mary K., 224 Cal. Rptr. 530 (Ct. App. 1986); Weaver v. Guinn, 31 P.3d 1119 (Or. Ct. App. 2001). In some cases involving technical violations of a state's AI statute, in a manner agreed to by the participants, courts sometimes have reached the statutory results through equitable doctrines such as estoppel or ratification. See, e.g., E.E. v. O.M.G.R., 20 A.3d 1171 (N.J. Super. 2011) (self-administered AI; best interests of child met through sole custody to biological mother without support order from biological father). Adherence to the criteria, on the other hand, did not necessarily shield the participants from the claims of presumed "donors" seeking parental rights. See Janssen v. Alicea, 30 So. 3d 680 (Fla. Dist. Ct. App. 2010) (reversing summary judgment were genuine issues of fact with respect to whether man was sperm donor or part of "commissioning couple"); McIntyre v. Crouch, 780 P.2d 239 (Or. Ct. App. 1989) (termination of donor's parental rights might be unconstitutional where "donor" argues that sperm was provided with understanding that he would be considered father). See generally Annot., 83 A.L.R.4th 295 (1991).

There was a resurgence of litigation surrounding some of the implications of AI for nontraditional families in the early 2000s. The use of AI by lesbian couples created a new wave of litigation testing the legal recognition of the nonbiological lesbian parent of the resulting child. See, e.g., Kristine H. v. Lisa R., 117 P.3d 690 (Cal. 2005) (birth mother estopped from contesting maternity of her former partner with whom she had previously obtained a stipulated judgment declaring that both were the parents of a child born through AI); K.M. v. E.G., 117 P.3d 673 (Cal. 2005) (woman who provided ova to her female partner for IVF is a legal parent of the children born through this arrangement along with the birth mother; law terminating parental rights of sperm donor not applied to the partner who donated ova); Elisa B. v. The Superior Court of El Dorado County, 117 P.3d 660 (Cal. 2005) (woman is legally a parent despite lack of biological connection based on conduct holding the children born to her female partner through AI as her own). See Ann K. Wooster, Adoption of Child by Same-Sex Partners, 61 A.L.R.6th 1 (2011).

3. *Continuing Challenges Under the 2002 UPA.* The 1973 UPA was adopted in whole or part by 19 states; the 2002 UPA or its amendments had been adopted by 11 states as of mid-2017. The 2002 UPA resolved some, but not all, of the gaps in the 1973 model act. The 2002 UPA made clear that a donor was not the legal parent, whether or not the assisted reproduction participants were married. The 2002 Act also eliminated the requirement that the donor provide his sperm to a physician. UPA §102(8) (2002). The 2002 UPA continued the presumption that a woman who gave birth to a child was the mother of the child, unless the child was conceived as part of a gestational surrogacy contract authorized and approved under state law. UPA §201 (2002). This presumption provided additional protection for egg donors, by creating a default rule establishing the woman who gave birth as the mother rather than the donor.

The 2002 UPA did not resolve all donor conflicts. The 2002 UPA provided that donors had no parental rights and no right to seek such rights, UPA §702 cmt., yet the language left open the possibility of claims for parental rights from sperm-contributors who claimed that they had been promised the opportunity to maintain a relationship with their biological offspring. See note 2, supra.

In addition, the 2002 UPA failed to provide same-sex couples using AI with the protections afforded to heterosexual couples. The issue reached the United States Supreme Court in Pavan v. Smith, 137 S.Ct. 2075 (2017). Two married same-sex couples who had conceived children through AI sought to obtain Arkansas birth certificates listing both spouses as the parents of the children. The state instead issued birth certificates recognizing the birth mothers as the legal parents, relying in part on state laws providing that the mother is the woman who gives birth to a child. In addition, the state cited statutory provisions establishing the "husband"—not a same-sex partner—as the father of a child born during marriage in most other circumstances, including where procreation was accomplished through AI, so long as the husband had consented in writing. 137 S.C.t at 2077. The Court reversed the judgment of the Arkansas Supreme Court, finding:

> The Arkansas Supreme Court's decision, we conclude, denied married same-sex couples access to the "constellation of benefits that the Stat[e] ha[s] linked to marriage." *Obergefell*, 135 S.Ct., at 2601. . . . W]hen a married woman in Arkansas conceives a child by means of artificial insemination, the State will—indeed, must—list the name of her male spouse on the child's birth certificate. See § 20–18–401(f)(1) . . . . And yet state law, as interpreted by the court below, allows Arkansas officials in those very same circumstances to omit a married woman's female spouse from her child's birth certificate. . . . As a result, same-sex parents in Arkansas lack the same right as opposite-sex parents to be listed on a child's birth certificate, a document often used for important transactions like making medical decisions for a child or enrolling a child in school. . . .
>
> *Obergefell* proscribes such disparate treatment. As we explained there, a State may not "exclude same-sex couples from civil marriage on the same terms and conditions as opposite-sex couples." 135 S.Ct., at 2605. Indeed, in listing those terms and conditions—the "rights, benefits, and responsibilities" to which same-sex couples, no less than opposite-sex couples, must have access—we expressly identified

"birth and death certificates." 135 S.Ct., at 2601. That was no accident: Several of the plaintiffs in *Obergefell* challenged a State's refusal to recognize their same-sex spouses on their children's birth certificates. . . . In considering those challenges, we held the relevant state laws unconstitutional to the extent they treated same-sex couples differently from opposite-sex couples. See 135 S.Ct., at 2605. That holding applies with equal force [here].

Echoing the court below, the State defends its birth-certificate law on the ground that being named on a child's birth certificate is not a benefit that attends marriage. Instead, the State insists, a birth certificate is simply a device for recording biological parentage—regardless of whether the child's parents are married. But Arkansas law makes birth certificates about more than just genetics. As already discussed, when an opposite-sex couple conceives a child by way of anonymous sperm donation—just as the petitioners did here—state law requires the placement of the birth mother's husband on the child's birth certificate. . . . And that is so even though (as the State concedes) the husband "is definitively not the biological father" in those circumstances. . . . Arkansas has thus chosen to make its birth certificates more than a mere marker of biological relationships: The State uses those certificates to give married parents a form of legal recognition that is not available to unmarried parents. Having made that choice, Arkansas may not, consistent with *Obergefell,* deny married same-sex couples that recognition

137 S.Ct. at 2078-79 (per curiam). Justices Gorsuch, Thomas, and Alito dissented (citing, in part, procedural concerns). See also, D.M.T. v. T.M.H., 129 So.3d 320 (Fla. 2013). In *D.M.T,* a woman who had donated an egg to her partner sought to establish her parental rights despite a state law providing that gamete donors had no parental rights outside narrow circumstances not considered to be applicable. Id. at 333 (the statutory scheme exempted "the commissioning couple," defined as "the intended mother and father of a child," "or a father who has executed a pre-planned adoption agreement"). The Florida Supreme Court rejected claims that the statutory scheme could be avoided based on the "intent" of the parties, which in this case likely would have confirmed that both parties intended the biological mother to retain her status as a parent. Instead, the court held that the application of the statutory scheme to the biological mother violated state and federal due process and equal protections, and further held that the biological mother had not waived her constitutional rights by signing a standard fertility clinic informed consent form. Id. at 347.

4. *The 2017 UPA.* The 2017 UPA has not yet been considered or adopted by any jurisdiction. It may nonetheless be influential for states interested in bringing their family law provisions into alignment with the Supreme Court's decisions in *Obergefell* and Pavan v. Smith, supra. The 2017 UPA donor provisions attempt to eliminate the differential treatment of same-sex and opposite-sex couples:

SECTION 702. PARENTAL STATUS OF DONOR. A donor is not a parent of a child conceived by assisted reproduction.

SECTION 703. PARENTAGE OF CHILD OF ASSISTED REPRODUCTION. An individual who consents under Section 704 to assisted reproduction by a woman with the intent to be a parent of a child conceived by the assisted reproduction is a parent of the child.

SECTION 704. CONSENT TO ASSISTED REPRODUCTION.

(a) Except as otherwise provided in subsection (b), the consent described in Section 703 must be in a record signed by a woman giving birth to a child conceived by assisted reproduction and an individual who intends to be a parent of the child.

(b) Failure to consent in a record as required by subsection (a), before, on, or after birth of the child, does not preclude the court from finding consent to parentage if:

(1) the woman or the individual proves by clear-and-convincing evidence the existence of an express agreement entered into before conception that the individual and the woman intended they both would be parents of the child; or

(2) the woman and the individual for the first two years of the child's life. . . resided together in the same household with the child and both openly held out the child as the individual's child, unless the individual dies or becomes incapacitated before the child attains two years of age or the child dies before the child attains two years of age, in which case the court may find consent under this subsection to parentage if a party proves by clear-and-convincing evidence that the woman and the individual intended to reside together in the same household with the child and both intended the individual would openly hold out the child as the individual's child, but the individual was prevented from carrying out that intent by death or incapacity.

The 2017 UPA also establishes limitations on a spouse's dispute of parentage, (§705), and allows withdrawal of consent "any time before a transfer that results in pregnancy" (§707). Do the revised provisions reflect the full range of possible donor arrangements? Will the revisions reduce the risk of litigation involving known "donors" claiming parental rights?

5. *Tort and Criminal Liability.* The regulations and professional standards governing gamete donation could at least theoretically be supplemented by tort or criminal law. Tort claims could arise from "product defects" or failure to observe the standard of care required in screening, storing, or using gametes. More egregious behavior, ranging from fraud to assault and misappropriation, might give rise to criminal prosecution. What theories of recovery and claims for damage might be permissible? Tamar Lewin, Sperm Banks Accused of Losing Samples and Lying about Donors, N.Y. Times, July 21, 2016 (discussing range of recent claims). Leaving aside the agreements between parties involved in gamete donations, which may purport to waive liability or require use of alternative dispute mechanisms, what are some of the barriers to successful tort claims? See George L. Blum, Liability of Cryobanks or Fertility Clinics for Negligence and Other Actions Related to Frozen Sperm or Embryos, 16 A.L.R. 7th Art. 8 (2016). Tort claims can be difficult to assert if donors can remain anonymous. But see Ethics Committee of the ASRM, Disclosure of Medical Errors Involving Gametes and Embryos, 106 Fertility & Sterility 59 (2016); and Johnson v. Superior Court, 95 Cal. Rptr. 2d 864 (2000) (tort action claiming failure to disclose sperm donor had family history of autosomal dominant polycystic kidney disease; court compels donor's deposition and record production).

Should sperm banks be held liable for the negligent destruction of donated sperm? Practice Committee of the ASRM, Recommendations for Development of an Emergency Plan for In Vitro Fertilization Programs: A Committee Opinion, 105 Fertility & Sterility e11 (2016) (all IVF programs and clinics should have a plan to protect fresh and cryopreserved human tissue in the event of an emergency or natural disaster). How would you measure the damages? See Kurchner v. State Farm Fire & Casualty Co, 858 So.2d 1220 (Fla. App. 2003) (destruction of sperm not "bodily injury" and loss not covered under insurance policy). Professor Dov Fox has suggested creation of a framework for "reproductive wrongs" recognizing "misconduct that (1) imposes unwanted pregnancy or parenthood, (2) deprives wanted pregnancy or parenthood, and (3) confounds efforts to have or avoid a child born with particular traits." Dov Fox, Reproductive Negligence, 117 Columbia L. Rev. 149 (2017) (noting as well that positive role that a right to recover could play given the lack of robust regulation and the current barriers to tort claims).

There have been isolated allegations of conduct that could at least theoretically give rise to criminal prosecution. For three bizarre cases, see James v. Jacobson, 6 F.3d 233 (4th Cir. 1993) (noting criminal prosecution of physician who used his own sperm in providing AI services to more than 70 women); Judy Siegel-Itkovich, Doctor's Licence Suspended After He Admitted Removing Ova Without Consent, 334 BMJ 557 (2007) (physician removed hundreds of ova without patient consent for use in ART); Stone v. Regents, University of California, 92 Cal. Rptr.2d 94 (Ct. App. 1999) (physician allegedly engaged in "egg stealing").

6. *Posthumous Reproduction.* The ability to donate and store gametes (and embryos) means that it is possible to parent a child after one's death. What ethical and legal issues are raised by this possibility? One key question involves control—who has the right to decide whether to use stored gametes for reproductive purposes? See Hecht v. Superior Court, 59 Cal. Rptr.2d 222 (Ct. App. 1996), review denied (Cal. 1997) (after a six-year battle, a deceased man's frozen sperm were awarded to his girlfriend as designated in his will, over the objections of the decedent's adult children). Should parents have the authority to direct collection of gametes from their children before or immediately after death? See Michelle Goodwin & Naomi Duke, Capacity and Autonomy: A Thought Experiment on Minors' Access to Assisted Reproductive Technology, 34 Harv. J. L. & Gender 503 (2011). See generally Sara E. Barton, Population-Based Study of Attitudes Toward Posthumous Reproduction, 98 Fertility & Sterility 735 (2012) ("[a]lmost 50% of the general population support posthumous reproduction in men and women" with a "majority favor[ing] prior consent from the deceased"); and Sharona Hoffman & Andrew P. Morriss, Birth After Death: Perpetuities and the New Reproductive Technologies, 38 Ga. L. Rev. 575 (2004).

The posthumous birth raises another set of issues: Should the child be considered the legal child of the decedent? What is the impact on the child's ability to inherit or to take part in family/survivors benefits programs? The traditional rule is that a man cannot be the father of a child born more than nine to ten months after his death. The 2002 UPA provided that an individual who had consented to be a parent by assisted reproduction would not be considered the parent of the child born of the process if she or he died before the "placement of eggs, sperm or embryos" unless the "deceased spouse" had also consented in a record to be the parent of a child born of assisted reproduction occurring after death. UPA §707 (2002). See also Uniform Law Commission, Uniform Probate Code §§2-120, 2-121 (2008 Amendments) (consent required; time limits established for posthumous reproduction); ABA Model Act Governing Assisted Reproductive Technology (2008) (decedent must have consented in record to become parent by posthumous reproduction); Kristine S. Knaplund, Children of Assisted Reproduction, 45 U.

Mich. J. L. Reform 899 (2012) (analyzing posthumous reproduction provisions of the UPC). The 2017 UPA includes similar provisions:

SECTION 708. PARENTAL STATUS OF DECEASED INDIVIDUAL.

(a) If an individual who intends to be a parent of a child conceived by assisted reproduction dies during the period between the transfer of a gamete or embryo and the birth of the child, the individual's death does not preclude the establishment of the individual's parentage of the child if the individual otherwise would be a parent of the child under this [act].

(b) If an individual who consented in a record to assisted reproduction by a woman who agreed to give birth to a child dies before a transfer of gametes or embryos, the deceased individual is a parent of a child conceived by the assisted reproduction only if:

    (1) either:

        (A) the individual consented in a record that if assisted reproduction were to occur after the death of the individual, the individual would be a parent of the child; or

        (B) the individual's intent to be a parent of a child conceived by assisted reproduction after the individual's death is established by clear-and-convincing evidence; and

    (2) either:

        (A) the embryo is in utero not later than [36] months after the individual's death; or

        (B) the child is born not later than [45] months after the individual's death.

UPA §708 (2017). Subdivision (a) is new but is described as "implicit" in the 2002 approach; (b) includes language adopted from parallel provisions in the Uniform Probate Code (2008). Id. (Comment).

Posthumous reproduction can also have an impact on benefits provided under private and public plans. The Supreme Court upheld the Social Security Administration's determination that state intestacy law determines whether posthumously conceived children qualify for federal benefits. Astrue v. Capato, 566 U.S. 541 (2012). See also Khabbaz v. Commissioner, Social Security Administration, 930 A.2d 1180 (N.H. 2007) (posthumously conceived child not considered surviving issue under state intestacy law); Woodward v. Commissioner of Social Security, 760 N.E.2d 257 (Mass. 2002) (children can inherit if wife establishes genetic relationship and decedent's consent to posthumous reproduction and support).

7. *Anonymity.* Artificial insemination has a long history, and the early presumption was that anonymity was a necessary part of the arrangement. Anonymity helped to ensure that the sperm donor would not be held liable for child support in an era of ambiguous obligations. Anonymity also allowed the receiving couple both to claim parentage over the child born as a result of AI and to conceal the male partner's infertility in a less sympathetic era. Walter Wadlington, Artificial Insemination: The Dangers of a Poorly Kept Secret, 64 Nw. U. L. Rev. 777 (1970). Yet the legal and social climate has changed considerably in the past few decades. Beginning in the 1970s, adopted children and those who have given children up for adoption pushed for the creation of mechanisms allowing adopted children to learn the identity of their birth parents.

In recent years, a parallel movement has advocated for children born from assisted reproduction to have access to information about their donor-conceived status as well as about the identity of their genetic parents. The major professional organizations recommend that parents disclose to their children that they were conceived with the use of donor gametes. The Ethics Committee of the ASRM, Interests, Obligations, and Rights of the Donor in Gamete Donation, 102 Fertility & Sterility 675 (2014). Some fertility programs now offer mutually voluntary contact arrangements. Joanna E. Scheib, Alice Ruby & Jean Benward, Who Requests Their Sperm Donor's Identity? The First Ten Years of Information Releases to Adults with Open-Identity Donors, 107 Fertility & Sterility 483 (2017) (approximately 35 percent of eligible offspring requested their donor's identity, most of those who learned the identity hoped to make contact). Should a donor who provides gametes in an open disclosure environment be permitted to withdraw his or her consent to disclosure?

Should the legal regimes developed for open adoption and adoption registry concepts be mirrored in the world of gamete donation? Do children born of AI have a right to information about their genetic parents? Is openness necessary to prevent accidental incest? See Jacqueline Mroz, From One Sperm Donor, 150 Children, N.Y. Times, Sept. 6, 2011. Will greater openness reduce the supply of gametes and, if so, should that influence the development of the law in this area? Cohen et al., supra; Naomi R. Cahn, The New Kinship, 100 Geo. L. J. 367 (2012) (advocating openness and registry process); I. Glenn Cohen, Response: Rethinking Sperm-Donor Anonymity: Of Changed Selves, Nonidentity, and One-Night Stands, 100 Geo. L. J. 431 (2012) (offering response to Prof. Cahn). The ASRM does not take a position on the issue. The Ethics Committee of the ASRM, Interests, Obligations, and Rights of the Donor in Gamete Donation, 102 Fertility & Sterility 675 (2014) (donors should be informed of information-sharing practices and cautioned "that promises of anonymity or future contact cannot be assured").

Some countries now require that gamete donor information be made available to offspring. See Glenn Cohen et al., Sperm Donor Anonymity and Compensation: An Experiment with American Sperm Donors, 3 J. of L. & the Biosciences 468, 469-472 (2016) (reviewing policy debate and approaches in other countries). Victoria, Australia removed anonymity retroactively, allowing offspring to access donor information even in cases where the donors had participated in ART with the understanding that they would remain anonymous. Melissa Davey, Victorian Egg and Sperm Donors to Lose Anonymity Under New Legislation, The Guardian, Feb. 24, 2016. Contact between donors and offspring requires additional consent process. Should similar legislation be adopted in your state and, if so, would it be vulnerable to a constitutional challenge?

The 2017 UPA includes a new Article on donor information, modeled on legislation from Washington State.

SECTION 901. DEFINITIONS. In this [article]:
(1) "Identifying information" means: (A) the full name of a donor; (B) the date of birth of the donor; and (C) the permanent and, if different, current address of the donor at the time of the donation.
(2) "Medical history" means information regarding any: (A) present illness of a donor; (B) past illness of the donor; and (C) social, genetic, and family history pertaining to the health of the donor.

SECTION 902. APPLICABILITY. This [article] applies only to gametes collected on or after [the effective date of this [act]].

SECTION 903. COLLECTION OF INFORMATION. A gamete bank or fertility clinic licensed in this state shall collect from a donor the donor's identifying information and medical history at the time of the donation. . . .

SECTION 904. DECLARATION REGARDING IDENTITY DISCLOSURE.
(a) A gamete bank or fertility clinic licensed in this state which collects gametes from a donor shall: (1) provide the donor with information in a record about the donor's choice regarding identity disclosure; and (2) obtain a declaration from the donor regarding identity disclosure.
(b) A gamete bank or fertility clinic . . . shall give a donor the choice to sign a declaration . . . that either: (1) states that the donor agrees to disclose the donor's identity to a child conceived by assisted reproduction with the donor's gametes on request once the child attains 18 years of age; or (2) states that the donor does not agree presently to disclose the donor's identity to the child.
(c) A gamete bank or fertility clinic licensed in this state shall permit a donor who has signed a declaration under subsection (b)(2) to withdraw the declaration at any time by signing a declaration under subsection (b)(1).

SECTION 905. DISCLOSURE OF IDENTIFYING INFORMATION AND MEDICAL HISTORY.
(a) On request of a child . . . who attains 18 years of age, a [covered bank or clinic] . . . shall make a good-faith effort to provide the child with identifying information of the donor who provided the gametes, unless the donor signed and did not withdraw a declaration under Section 904(b)(2). If the donor signed and did not withdraw the declaration, the gamete bank or fertility clinic shall make a good-faith effort to notify the donor, who may elect under Section 904(c) to withdraw the donor's declaration.
(b) Regardless whether a donor signed a declaration under Section 904(b)(2), on request by a child . . . who attains 18 years of age, or, if the child is a minor, by a parent or guardian of the child, a gamete bank or fertility clinic licensed in this state shall make a good-faith effort to provide the child or . . . the parent or guardian of the child, access to nonidentifying medical history of the donor.

UPA §901-905 (2017) (modeled on Wash. Rev. Code §26.26.750). Does the UPA permit a donor who consented to disclosure to withdraw his or her consent? Would you recommend adoption of UPA's voluntary, prospective approach?

Problem: Ovary Transplantation

Researchers have demonstrated some success in autologous transplantation of ovarian tissue. Alberto Revelli et al., Live Birth After Orthotopic Grafting of Autologous Cryopreserved Ovarian Tissue and Spontaneous Conception in Italy, 99 Fertility & Sterility 227 (2013); Michael Grynberg et al., Ovarian Tissue and Follicle Transplantation as an Option for Fertility Preservation, 97 Fertility & Sterility 1260

(2012). Heterologous transplantation is more complex because of the risk of tissue rejection and the need for the transplant recipient to take immunosuppressing drugs. Would transplantation of an ovary from a donor present any particular legal or ethical challenges? Should live donors be permitted to gift an ovary (women ordinarily have two)? Should an ovary donor be treated like an egg donor or should the person to whom the ovary is donated now be deemed to be the "owner" of the ova generated by the ovary despite the lack of genetic connection? See Roger G. Gosden, Ovary and Uterus Transplantation, 136 Reproduction 671 (2008) (reviewing advances supporting potential for transplantation); Mohamed A. Bedaiwy et al., Reproductive Organ Transplantation: Advances and Controversies, 90 Fertility & Sterility 2031 (2008). Should parents have the authority to initiate cryopreservation of a child's ovarian tissue to preserve potential future fertility where the child's fertility might be at risk due to illness or medical treatment? See Practice Committee of the ASRM, Ovarian Tissue Cryopreservation: A Committee Opinion, 101 Fertility & Sterility 1237 (2014) (noting procedure experimental but only option available for fertility preservation in young girls).

3. In Vitro Fertilization

In vitro fertilization (IVF) involves the fertilization of eggs by sperm in a laboratory setting. The first known "test tube" baby was born in the late 1970s. The birth was controversial. A congressional committee held hearings on the topic of federal funding for related research projects. See, e.g., Walter Wadlington, Artificial Conception: The Challenge for Family Law, 69 Va. L. Rev. 465 (1983). Critics argued that IVF was unnatural, that it supplanted God in the creation of new life, that it could lead to embryo farms, and that children born from IVF might have genetic or other health problems. Forty years later, IVF has become an accepted infertility procedure. Success rates approach those of natural reproduction for younger patients but are lower for older women using their own oocytes. Barbara Luke et al., Cumulative Birth Rates with Linked Assisted Reproductive Technology Cycles, 366 New Eng. J. Med. 2483 (2012). Does the broad acceptance of IVF illustrate what philosopher Bertrand Russell once observed (in An Outline of Intellectual Rubbish: A Hilarious Catalogue of Organized and Individual Stupidity 20 (1943)), that "[e]very advance in civilization has been denounced as unnatural while it was recent"?

IVF is physically and emotionally taxing for participants. The woman providing the eggs (who may either be a donor or the intended parent) must undergo the hormone therapy and egg-extraction procedures described supra at page 809. These hormone treatments cause ovarian hyperstimulation syndrome in less than 5 percent of IVF cycles; the syndrome ordinarily resolves within a few weeks but in very rare cases can lead to death. Bradley J. Van Voorhis, In Vitro Fertilization, 356 New Eng. J. Med. 379, 382 (2007) (video of oocyte extraction available online). The man providing the sperm (either the donor or the intended parent) must undergo screening and sample collection. The intended carrier of the embryo—either the gestational surrogate or the intended mother—must undergo treatment to ensure that her uterus is prepared to receive the embryo at the time of implantation (which may occur soon after fertilization or after unfreezing stored embryos).

"Multiple births are the most frequent complication of IVF, contributing to a virtual epidemic of multiple gestations in the United States." Bradley J. Van Voorhis, supra, at 382; see also Saswati Sunderam et al., Assisted Reproductive Technology Surveillance—United States, 2014, supra page 796. IVF is associated with multiple births because physicians seeking to achieve a pregnancy often transfer multiple embryos in one cycle in hopes that at least one will be retained and the pregnancy brought to term. Multiple gestations are more risky for both the pregnant woman and the resulting children, who may be born with low birth weight and other special medical needs. Yet even singleton pregnancies induced through IVF are associated with higher rates of complications, and some studies have suggested that assisted reproductive technology is associated with an increased risk of birth defects. Barbara Luke, Pregnancy and Birth Outcomes in Couples with Infertility with and without Assisted Reproductive Technology, 217 Amer. J. of Obstet. & Gynecol. 270 (2017). See also Louise M. Stewart, In Vitro Fertilization and Breast Cancer: Is There Cause for Concern?, 98 Fertility & Sterility 334 (2012) (increased rate of breast cancer for women beginning IVF at younger ages).

These procedures are fairly expensive. A single cycle of IVF can cost $19,000 or more. Ethics Committee of the ASRM, Disparities in Access to Effective Treatment for Infertility in the United States: An Ethics Committee Opinion, 104 Fertility & Sterility 1104 (2015). The overall success rate for the first cycle is 29.5 pecent; it is common to have 3–4 cycles of treatment and expenses of $40,000 to $50,000 per live birth. Andrew Smith et al., Live-Birth Rate Associated with Repeat In Vitro Fertilization Treatment Cycles, 314 JAMA 2654 (2015). Success rates are lower for older women; additional treatment cycles increase total costs and, in the end, may not be successful. Many people would not be able to afford IVF if required to pay out of pocket; health insurance coverage for IVF is therefore an important issue.

Historically, insurance companies argued that IVF procedures were excluded as "experimental" or that they were not covered "treatments" because they did not address the underlying medical condition of infertility and required "treatment" of third parties (such as the sperm donor). The more common current technique is to include a specific exclusion for infertility treatment within the health insurance plan or contract. Edward L. Raymond, Jr., Annot., Coverage of Artificial Insemination Procedures or Other Infertility Treatments by Health, Sickness, or Hospitalization Insurance, 80 A.L.R.4th 1059 (1990). A few states require that insurance contracts sold within the state provide coverage for IVF, although this requirement cannot be applied to self-insured employee benefit plans. The Affordable Care Act does not mandate coverage of infertility care. Kate Devine, Robert Stillman & Alan H. DeCherney, The Affordable Care Act: Early Implications for Fertility Medicine, 101 Fertility & Sterility 1224 (2014). Do health plans limiting or denying coverage for infertility treatment violate the ADA or the Pregnancy Discrimination Act? See infra at Chapter 9.D.1; and Saks v. Franklin Covey Co., 316 F.3d 337 (2d Cir. 2003) (holding that exclusions of coverage for male and female infertility treatments did not violate the Pregnancy Discrimination Act or Title VII's ban on sex discrimination). Should state IVF insurance mandates include coverage for women without male partners? See N.J.S.A. §17B:27-46.1x (2017) (coverage provided for women under 35 years of age without male partners who have been unable to conceive after 12 failed AI attempts under the supervision of a physician).

Consumers of infertility services may be vulnerable to unscrupulous practitioners. Congressional concern with this problem led to passage of the Fertility Clinic Success Rate and Certification Act of 1992, Pub. L. No. 102-493, codified at 42 U.S.C.A. §§263a-1 to -7 (2006). Clinic success rates are available online. CDC, Assisted Reproductive Technology (ART), at www.cdc.gov/art/ARTReports.htm. Some providers enter into shared risk agreements with patients under which, for example, patients pay a reduced fee after a set number of cycles of IVF or receive a refund of some fees if pregnancy is not achieved. See, e.g., Ethics Committee of the ASRM, Financial "Risk-Sharing" or Refund Programs in Assisted Reproduction: An Ethics Committee Opinion, 106 Fertility & Sterility e8 (2016) (recommending various practices to reduce the risks associated with conflicts of interest created by shared risk agreements).

Problems: Ethical Aspects of IVF

- *The Risk of Failure vs. the Risk of Sextuplets.* How many embryos should be transferred to a woman's uterus at one time? Should the number be set by individual physicians, ethical guidelines, or a standard of care enforceable in a malpractice action? As noted in Saswati Sunderam, et al., Assisted Reproductive Technology Surveillance — United States, 2014, supra page 796, the problem arises in part because of the relatively high expense and low success rate of IVF. Physicians might transfer two to three embryos in hopes of achieving a single live birth, depending on the age of the woman and other factors. But multiple embryo transfers increase the risk of a multiple pregnancy, which brings greater health risks for the woman and fetuses. The "remedy" is selective abortion, discussed supra at page 726. Should the birth of sextuplets become prima facie evidence of unethical or negligent conduct by an infertility center? See Practice Committee of the ASRM and Practice Committee of the SART, Guidance on the Limits to the Number of Embryos to Transfer: A Committee Opinion, 107 Fertility & Sterility 901 (2017) (providing guidelines for upper limits of embryo transfer; single-embryo transfer established as appropriate for many types of patients; additional embryos considered appropriate for some types of patients); and K. S. Acharya, Do Donor Oocyte Cycles Comply with ASRM/SART Embryo Transfer Guidelines?, 106 Fertility & Sterility 603 (2016) (88 percent of transfers met compliance criteria; multiple pregnancy rate significantly higher in non-compliant cycles). Should states limit the number of transfers by legislation? See Guidance on the Limits to the Number of Embryos to Transfer, supra, at 902 (expressing concern about legislative limits); S. Ory, The American Octuplet Experience: A Transformative Event, 93 Fertility & Sterility 337 (2010) (noting potential for state legislation after well-publicized birth of octuplets).
- *Postmenopausal Reproduction and Gatekeeping vs. Discrimination.* When may infertility treatment providers deny services to prospective patients based on concerns about risks or other factors? As one example, should access to IVF be restricted based on the age of the intended mother? Clinics can use donor eggs and hormone therapy to sustain a pregnancy even after menopause. The Ethics Committee of the ASRM recommends that physicians "discourage[]

or den[y]" embryo transfer for women over 45 "with underlying conditions that increase or exacerbate obstetrical risks." Morever, "[b]ecause of concerns related to the high risk nature of pregnancy, as well as longevity, treatment of women over the age of 55 should generally be discouraged." Oocyte or Embryo Donation to Women of Advanced Reproductive Age: An Ethics Opinion, 106 Fertility & Sterility e3 (2016). Should "longevity," along with some risks to the offspring of older men, be sufficient cause to discourage procreation? See Andrea Mechanick Braverman, Old, Older and Too Old: Age Limits for Medically Assisted Fatherhood?, 107 Fertility & Sterility 329 (2017). Should it be permissible for providers to refuse treatment to women who are at higher risk for pregnancy-related complications? See Ethics Committee of the ASRM, Provision of Fertility Services for Women at Increased Risk of Complications During Fertility Treatment or Pregnancy: An Ethics Committee Opinion, 106 Fertility & Sterility 1319 (2016) (providers may ethically treat women at elevated risk with certain conditions, e.g., regarding informed consent, but providers "may also conclude that the risks are too high for them to treat particular patients ethically").

Health care providers often act as gatekeepers for care, determining whether care is "medically necessary," for example. Gatekeeping can be controversial and contested. Fertility-related treatments may implicate providers' values, ethics, and religious beliefs. Patients have expressed concerns about the ability to seek care consistent with their own values and preferences, as well as about economic, social, racial, and other barriers to access. See, e.g., Tazina Vega, Infertility, Endured Through a Prism of Race, N.Y. Times, April 25, 2014. Discriminatory conduct by providers might violate ethical guidelines. See, e.g., Ethics Committee of the ASRM, Access to Fertility Services by Transgender Persons, 104 Fertility & Sterility 111(2015); and Access to Fertility Treatment by Gays, Lesbians, and Unmarried Persons, 100 Fertility & Sterility 1524 (2013).

There are a few cases involving claims of impermissible discrimination under state laws prohibiting, for example, discrimination by places of public accommodation or businesses. North Coast Women's Care Medical Group, Inc. v. San Diego Superior Court, 189 P.3d 959 (Cal. 2008) (upholding discrimination claim against fertility providers based on sexual orientation or marital status against claimed violation of free exercise of religious rights of defendants); Moon v. Michigan Reproductive & IVF Center, P.C., 810 N.W.2d 919 (2011) (physician may not reject unmarried patient based on discriminatory animus toward a protected characteristic). For an analysis of the potential tension between religious freedom and non-discrimination requirements, see I. Glenn Cohen, Religion and Reproductive Technology, in Law, Religion and Health in the United States (Holly Fernandez Lynch, I. Glenn Cohen & Elizabeth Sepper, eds. 2017).

- *Preimplantation Genetic Diagnosis (PGD).* Genetic tests can be used to select which preembryos will be implanted. PGD and preimplantation genetic screening (PGS) raise important issues related to informed consent and malpractice. See, e.g., Tochi Amagwula, Preimplantation Genetic Diagnosis: A Systematic Review of Litigation in the Face of New Technology, 98 Fertility & Sterility 1277 (2012); The Practice Committees of the SART & ASRM, Preimplantation

Genetic Testing, 90 Fertility & Sterility S136 (2008). Much of the commentary by ethicists has focused on the use of tests to avoid the implantation of embryos with disabling genetic conditions or to select offspring of a certain sex. See page 806. Are there any limits on parental ability to select for traits that might be considered to be disabilities? Should it be permissible for deaf parents to use PGD to ensure that they have deaf offspring? See Ethics Committee of the ASRM, Transferring Embryos with Genetic Anomalies Detected in Preimplantation Testing: An Ethics Committee Opinion, 107 Fertility & Sterility 1130 (2017) ("in most clinical cases it is ethically permissible to assist or decline to assist in transferring such embryos" however transfer of embryos "is ethically problematic and highly discouraged" where the "child is highly likely to be born with a life-threatening condition that causes severe and early debility with no possibility of reasonable function").

Consider the "rights-based" analysis of reproduction, which focuses on the right of the parent to reproduce and to use technology to achieve a healthy child. Under a rights-based approach, when may the state interfere with parental reproductive choices? Could a parent be held liable for intentionally selecting an injurious genetic characteristic for his or her child? Now consider an ethics-based approach to the problems of reproduction. What ethical norms would you apply to a parent's use of reproductive technologies? How would you capture the interests of the child and society? See Kirsten Rabe Smolensky, Creating Children with Disabilities, 60 Hastings L. J. 299 (2008) (exploring parental tort liability); I. Glenn Cohen, Intentional Diminishment, the Non-Identity Problem, and Legal Liability, 60 Hastings L. J. 347 (2008) (response to Smolensky); Alicia R. Ouellette, Insult to Injury, 60 Hastings L. J. 397 (2008) (response to Smolensky).

- *Savior Siblings.* A "savior sibling" is the name bioethicists give to a child created to serve as a stem cell or organ donor to the diseased sibling. See Susan M. Wolf, Jeffrey P. Kahn & John E. Wagner, Using Preimplantation Genetic Diagnosis to Create a Stem Cell Donor: Issues, Guidelines & Limits, 31 J. of L. Med. & Ethics 327, 327 (2003). The most critical ethical questions concern: (1) whether parents should be allowed to use Preimplantaiton Genetic Diagnosis (PGD) to choose an embryo to implant and gestate that is a tissue or bone marrow donor to the sibling; (2) the psychological harm or benefit to the child created as a savior sibling of this origin story (including feelings of guilt should transplant prove unsuccessful); and (3) under what circumstances parents should be allowed to authorize bone marrow or solid organ donation by the savior sibling to the ill sibling in circumstances where the child is not of the age or maturity to give true informed consent. In the United Kingdom, the use of PGD to create a savior sibling is permitted when that technology is needed to ensure that the child itself does not develop the ailment affecting his or her sibling, but not when its purpose is only for tissue typing. In the United States, no law regulates this reproductive practice, though ethicists have argued for certain internal guidelines, including that the sibling's condition should be life threatening or seriously disabling and likely to be ameliorated by creation of savior sibling, that there be psychological screening of the parents to ensure that they will have the right attitude toward the children and be able to raise them in a loving environment, that the kinds of donations a savior sibling may make be limited before the age of consent (e.g., no solid organ transplant), etc. Id. Even with these restrictions in place, do you agree that the practice should be permitted in the United State.? If you were asked to design a policy, what elements would you include?

• *Children of the Unborn.* Tissue from the ovaries of aborted female fetuses theoretically could be used to create a new life. Other than the obvious opportunities for impossible brain teasers, is there any moral or policy problem with being the child of someone who was never born? Would *Roe* and *Casey* bar state attempts to restrict the use of fetal reproductive tissue? See Jonathan Hersey, Comment, Enigma of the Unborn Mother: Legal and Ethical Considerations of Aborted Fetal Ovarian Tissue and Ova Transplantations, 43 UCLA L. Rev. 159 (1995); John A. Robertson, Ethical Issues in Ovarian Transplantation and Donation, 73 Fertility & Sterility 443, 445 (2000); see also Dori C. Woods & Jonathan L. Tilly, The Next (Re)Generation of Ovarian Biology and Fertility in Women: Is Current Science Tomorrow's Practice?, 98 Fertility & Sterility 3 (2012) (noting challenges to efforts to obtain oocytes from embryonic or induced pluripotent human stem cells).

• *In Vitro Gametogenesis (IVG)* or *Gametes from Skin Cells.* Researchers have made advances in generating sperm and oocytes from embryonic stem cells and induced pluripotent stem cells, special types of cells that will be discussed in more detail in section E of this chapter. For present purposes, these advances are important because they signal the possibility that—perhaps within the next 20 years—it might be possible to use adult human skin cells to create either eggs or sperm. Tamar Lewin, Babies From Skin Cells? Prospect Is Unsettling to Some Experts, N.Y. Times, May 16, 2017. As Professor Sonia Suter has observed:

> These scientific advances raise important questions about what IVG might mean for human procreation. In some ways, this technology is just another method to allow infertile individuals to have genetically related children. In other words, it is one of many forms of assisted reproductive technology (ART). On the other hand, it potentially allows for methods of procreation that have never been possible before. With IVG, same-sex couples may be able to have children who are biologically related to both of them. In addition, IVG could facilitate 'multiplex' parenting, where groups of more than two individuals (whether all male, all female, or a combination) procreate together, producing children who are the genetic progeny of them all. And finally, single individuals may be able to procreate without the genetic contribution of another individual, what I refer to as 'solo IVG'. IVG also presents the possibility of 'perfecting reproduction', by greatly improving the ability to screen for undesirable diseases or even traits.

Sonia Suter, *In Vitro* Gametogenesis: Just Another Way to Have a Baby?, 3 J. of L. & the Biosciences 87, 88 (2015). See also, June Carbone, Peer Commentary, 3 J. of L. & the Biosciences 673 (2015). What are the potential risks and benefits of these developments? Are there ethical concerns? How would the options that Professor Suter discusses be "digested" by our current system of laws and what changes in laws would you recommend? See also, articles collected in Stem Cell Derived Gametes, 40 J. of Medical Ethics 723-765 (2014).

Problem: Mitochondrial Replacement Technology

The most recent advance in ART resulted in news headlines around the world proclaiming the birth of a child with "three parents." See, Gina Kolata, Birth of Baby with Three Parents' DNA Marks Success for Banned Technique, N.Y. Times, Sept. 27, 2016. Unpacking the headline requires a brief detour into genetics and the IVF process.

Discussions about genetics usually focus on the 23 pairs of chromosomes found in a human cell's nucleus, or perhaps the 23 unpaired chromosomes found in human gametes. Less discussed, but still important, is the DNA found outside the cell nucleus in mitochondria, which are structures involved in energy production within cells. Mitochondrial DNA is passed on to children and future generations through a mother's oocytes and in zygotes (the cells formed by the union of two gametes). Errors in mitochondrial genes can cause serious and potentially fatal health conditions that may be passed on to children. Absent some intervention, women carriers of mitochondrial genetic disorders may feel constrained from genetic reproduction. Mitochondrial replacement provides a path to genetic parenthood for these women.

The two approaches to mitochondrial replacement both involve third-party donors. In the first approach, an oocyte is taken from a carrier of mitochondrial disease and the "spindle" (nuclear DNA) is removed and placed in an unfertilized oocyte from a donor with normal mitochondrial DNA. The egg is then fertilized with sperm from the intended father and IVF is used to implant the embryo into the woman who will carry the pregnancy. In the second approach, a donor's egg is fertilized and the pronucleous is removed and discarded. An egg from the carrier of mitochondrial disease is fertilized with sperm from the intended father and the pronucleous is removed and inserted into the donor's fertilized oocyte. IVF is then used to implant the embryo into the intended carrier. See Marni J. Falk, Alan Decherney & Jeffrey P. Kahn, Mitochondrial Replacement Techniques—Implications for the Clinical Community, 374 N. Eng. J. Med. 1103 (2016) (explaining mitochondrial replacement techniques and providing a helpful illustration); Eli Y. Adashi & I. Glenn Cohen, Going Germline: Mitochondrial Replacement as a Guide to Genome Editing, 164 Cell 832 (2016); US National Library of Medicine, Mitochondrial DNA, at https://ghr.nlm.nih.gov/mitochondrial-dna (providing useful background on mitochondrial DNA).

Mitochondrial replacement is controversial in several respects. First, this technique modifies the human germ-line by "pairing" mitochondrial DNA from one woman with the nuclear DNA of a different woman; this new pairing will be inherited by future generations. In this sense, the technique appears to violate a moratorium on human genome modification. See, Nicholas Wade, Scientists Seek Moratorium on Edits to Human Genome That Could be Inherited, N.Y. Times, Dec. 3, 2015. We will return to this topic in Chapter 9E's discussion of advances in genetics. Leaving this issue aside, what are the implications of mitochondrial donation for ART? The first issue involves access. The U.K. Parliament has approved the use of MRT but the United States has, as yet, not done so. See Y. Adashi & I. Glenn Cohen, supra. Could an individual in the United States sue claiming denial of access to the technology would violate her (or his) constitutional rights? How might the existing precedents answer the question? The second issue allows us to return to the news headlines mentioned at the beginning of this problem. Who would be the parents of a child born as a result of this technique? Would the woman who contributes mitochondrial DNA to the child have any legal relationship with the child under the UPA or other regulatory schemes? Should she? In the alternative, should the donor of mitochondrial DNA be considered to be similar to an organ donor? Will courts and legislatures that have used terms such as "genetic parent" need to clarify their language moving forward? For more discussion of the implications of this emerging technique, see, e.g., National Academies of Sciences, Engineering, and Medicine, Mitochondrial Replacement Techniques: Ethical, Social, and Policy Considerations (2016); and Special Issue: The Ethics of Mitochondrial Replacement, 31 Bioethics 1-69 (2017).

4. *Frozen Embryos*

■ J.B. v. M.B. & C.C.
783 A.2d 707 (N.J. 2001)

Poritz, C.J.

In this case, a divorced couple disagree about the disposition of seven preembryos . . . that remain in storage after the couple, during their marriage, undertook in vitro fertilization procedures. We must first decide whether the husband and wife have entered into an enforceable contract that is now determinative on the disposition issue. If not, we must consider how such conflicts should be resolved by our courts.

Although the reproductive technology to accomplish in vitro fertilization has existed since the 1970s, there is little case law to guide us in our inquiry. . . .

J.B. and M.B. were married in February 1992. After J.B. suffered a miscarriage early in the marriage, the couple encountered difficulty conceiving a child and sought medical advice from the Jefferson Center for Women's Specialties. Although M.B. did not have infertility problems, J.B. learned that she had a condition that prevented her from becoming pregnant. On that diagnosis, the couple decided to attempt in vitro fertilization at the Cooper Center for In Vitro Fertilization, P.C. (the Cooper Center). . . .

The Cooper Center's consent form describes the procedure. . . . The consent form also contains language discussing the control and disposition of the preembryos. . . .

The in vitro fertilization procedure was carried out in May 1995 and resulted in eleven preembryos. Four were transferred to J.B. and seven were cryopreserved. J.B. became pregnant . . . and gave birth to the couple's daughter on March 19, 1996. In September 1996, however, the couple separated, and J.B. informed M.B. that she wished to have the remaining preembryos discarded. M.B. did not agree.

J.B. filed a complaint for divorce on November 25, 1996, in which she sought an order from the court "with regard to the . . . frozen embryos." In a counterclaim filed on November 24, 1997, M.B. demanded judgment compelling his wife "to allow the . . . frozen embryos currently in storage to be implanted or donated to other infertile couples." J.B. filed a motion for summary judgment on the preembryo issue in April 1998 alleging, in a certification filed with the motion, that she had intended to use the preembryos solely within her marriage to M.B. She stated . . . "I endured the in vitro process and agreed to preserve the preembryos for our use in the context of an intact family." . . . M.B., in a cross-motion filed in July 1998, described his understanding very differently. . . . His certification stated: . . . "For me, as a Catholic, the I.V.F. procedure itself posed a dilemma. We discussed this issue extensively and had agreed that no matter what happened the eggs would be either utilized by us or by other infertile couples." . . .

The couple's final judgment of divorce, entered in September 1998, resolved all issues except disposition of the preembryos. Shortly thereafter, the trial court granted J.B.'s motion for summary judgment on that issue. . . . Because the husband was "fully able to father a child," and because he sought control of the preembryos "merely to donate them to another couple," the court concluded that the wife had "the greater interest and should prevail."

The Appellate Division affirmed. . . . We . . . now modify and affirm the judgment of the Appellate Division. . . .

M.B. contends that the judgment of the court below violated his constitutional rights to procreation and the care and companionship of his children. He also contends that his constitutional rights outweigh J.B.'s right not to procreate because her right to bodily integrity is not implicated, as it would be in a case involving abortion. He asserts that religious convictions regarding preservation of the preembryos, and the State's interest in protecting potential life, take precedence over his former wife's more limited interests. Finally, M.B. argues that the Appellate Division should have enforced the clear agreement between the parties to give the preembryos a chance at life. He believes that his procedural due process rights have been violated because he was not given an opportunity to introduce evidence demonstrating the existence of that agreement, and because summary judgment is inappropriate in a case involving novel issues of fact and law.

J.B. argues that the Appellate Division properly held that any alleged agreement between the parties to use or donate the preembryos would be unenforceable as a matter of public policy. She contends that New Jersey has "long recognized that individuals should not be bound by agreements requiring them to enter into family relationships or [that] seek to regulate personal intimate decisions relating to parenthood and family life." J.B. also argues that in the absence of an express agreement establishing the disposition of the preembryos, a court should not imply that an agreement exists. It is J.B.'s position that requiring use or donation of the preembryos would violate her constitutional right not to procreate. Discarding the preembryos, on the other hand, would not significantly affect M.B.'s right to procreate because he is fertile and capable of fathering another child. . . .

M.B. contends that he and J.B. entered into an agreement to use or donate the preembryos, and J.B. disputes the existence of any such agreement. As an initial matter, then, we must decide whether this case involves a contract for the disposition of the cryopreserved preembryos resulting from in vitro fertilization. We begin, therefore, with the consent form provided to J.B. and M.B. by the Cooper Center. . . . That form states, among other things:

> The control and disposition of the embryos belongs to the Patient and her Partner. You will be asked to execute the attached legal statement regarding control and disposition of cryopreserved embryos.

The attachment, executed by J.B. and M.B., provides further detail in respect of the parties' "control and disposition":

> I, J.B. (patient), and M.B. (partner) agree that all control, direction, and ownership of our tissues will be relinquished to the IVF Program under the following circumstances:
>
> 1. A dissolution of our marriage by court order, unless the court specifies who takes control and direction of the tissues, or
> 2. In the event of death of both of the above named individuals, or unless provisions are made in a Will, or
> 3. When the patient is no longer capable of sustaining a normal pregnancy, however, the couple has the right to keep embryos maintained for up to two years before making a decision [regarding a] "host womb" or
> 4. At any time by our/my election which shall be in writing, or
> 5. When a patient fails to pay periodic embryo maintenance payment.

The consent form, and more important, the attachment, do not manifest a clear intent by J.B. and M.B. regarding disposition of the preembryos in the event of "[a] dissolution of [their] marriage." Although the attachment indicates that the preembryos "will be relinquished" to the clinic if the parties divorce, it carves out an exception that permits the parties to obtain a court order directing disposition of the preembryos. . . . Clearly, the thrust of the document signed by J.B. and M.B. is that the Cooper Center obtains control over the preembryos unless the parties choose otherwise in writing, or unless a court specifically directs otherwise in an order of divorce.

The conditional language employed in the attachment stands in sharp contrast to the language in the informed consents provided by the hospital in Kass v. Kass, 696 N.E.2d 174 (N.Y. 1998). . . . In *Kass*, the New York Court of Appeals enforced a couple's memorialized decision to donate their preembryos for scientific research when they could not agree on disposition. . . . The court found that the parties had signed an unambiguous contract to relinquish control of their preembryos to the hospital for research purposes in the event of a dispute. . . . In that case, the parties executed several forms before undergoing in vitro fertilization. . . . Informed Consent No. 2 stated: "In the event of divorce, we understand that legal ownership of any stored . . . [preembryos] must be determined in a property settlement and will be released as directed by order of a court of competent jurisdiction." Addendum No. 2-1 further elaborated:

> In the event that we . . . are unable to make a decision regarding the disposition . . . we now indicate our desire for the disposition of . . . [preembryos] and direct the IVF Program to (choose one):
>
> Our frozen pre-zygotes may be examined by the IVF Program for biological studies and be disposed of by the IVF Program for approved research investigation as determined by the IVF Program.

Moreover, before the parties divorced, they drafted and signed an " 'uncontested divorce' agreement" indicating that their preembryos "should be disposed of [in] the manner outlined in our consent form and [neither party] will lay claim to custody of these . . . [preembryos]." . . .

The *Kass* court found that the parties had agreed to donate their preembryos for IVF research if they could not together decide on another disposition. . . . That holding is based on language entirely different from the language in the form in this case. Here, the parties have agreed that on the dissolution of their marriage the Cooper Center obtains control of the preembryos unless the court specifically makes another determination. Under that provision, the parties have sought another determination from the court.

M.B. asserts, however, that he and J.B. jointly intended another disposition. Because there are no other writings that express the parties' intentions, M.B. asks the Court either to remand for an evidentiary hearing on that issue or to consider his certified statement. . . .

We find no need for a remand to determine the parties' intentions at the time of the in vitro fertilization process. Assuming that it would be possible to enter into a valid agreement at that time irrevocably deciding the disposition of preembryos in circumstances such as we have here, a formal, unambiguous memorialization of the parties' intentions would be required to confirm their joint determination. The parties do not contest the lack of such a writing. We hold, therefore, that J.B. and M.B. never entered into a separate binding contract providing for the disposition of the cryopreserved preembryos now in the possession of the Cooper Center.

In essence, J.B. and M.B. have agreed only that on their divorce the decision in respect of control, and therefore disposition, of their cryopreserved preembryos will be directed by the court. In this area, however, there are few guideposts for decision-making. Advances in medical technology have far outstripped the development of legal principles to resolve the inevitable disputes arising out of the new reproductive opportunities now available. For infertile couples, those opportunities may present the only way to have a biological family. Yet, at the point when a husband and wife decide to begin the in vitro fertilization process, they are unlikely to anticipate divorce or to be concerned about the disposition of preembryos on divorce. As they are both contributors of the genetic material comprising the preembryos, the decision should be theirs to make. See generally Davis v. Davis, 842 S.W.2d 588, 597 (Tenn. 1992) (stating that donors should retain decision-making authority with respect to their preembryos). . . .

But what if, as here, the parties disagree. Without guidance from the Legislature, we must consider a means by which courts can engage in a principled review of the issues presented in such cases in order to achieve a just result. Because the claims before us derive, in part, from concepts found in the Federal Constitution and the Constitution of this State, we begin with those concepts.

Both parties . . . invoke the right to privacy in support of their respective positions. More specifically, they claim procreational autonomy as a fundamental attribute of the privacy rights guaranteed by both the Federal and New Jersey Constitutions. Their arguments are based on various opinions of the United States Supreme Court that discuss the right to be free from governmental interference with procreational decisions. . . . In Skinner v. Oklahoma [supra at page 703], the Court spoke of that most "basic liberty[]" when rejecting, on equal protection grounds, an Oklahoma statute that required sterilization of certain repeat criminal offenders. 316 U.S. at 541. . . .

This Court also has recognized the fundamental nature of procreational rights [when we] observed . . . that "the rights of personal intimacy, of marriage, of sex, of family, of procreation . . . are fundamental rights protected by both the federal and state Constitutions." . . .

Those decisions provide a framework within which disputes over the disposition of preembryos can be resolved. In *Davis, supra,* for example, a divorced couple could not agree on the disposition of their unused, cryopreserved preembryos . . . [842 S.W.2d 588, 589 (Tenn. 1992)]. The Tennessee Supreme Court balanced the right to procreate of the party seeking to donate the preembryos (the wife), against the right not to procreate of the party seeking destruction of the preembryos (the husband). . . .

We agree with the Tennessee Supreme Court that "ordinarily, the party wishing to avoid procreation should prevail." . . . M.B.'s right to procreate is not lost if he is denied an opportunity to use or donate the preembryos. M.B. is already a father and is able to become a father to additional children, whether through natural procreation or further in vitro fertilization. In contrast, J.B.'s right not to procreate may be lost through attempted use or through donation of the preembryos. Implantation, if successful, would result in the birth of her biological child and could have life-long emotional and psychological repercussions.[7] . . . Her fundamental right not to procreate is irrevocably extinguished if a surrogate mother bears J.B.'s child. We will not force J.B. to become a biological parent against her will.

The court below "concluded that a contract to procreate is contrary to New Jersey public policy and is unenforceable." . . . That determination follows the reasoning of the Massachusetts Supreme Judicial Court in A.Z. v. B.Z., wherein an agreement to compel biological parenthood was deemed unenforceable as a matter of public policy. 725 N.E.2d 1051, 1057-58 (2000). The Massachusetts court likened enforcement of a contract permitting implantation of preembryos to other contracts to enter into familial relationships that were unenforceable under the laws of Massachusetts, i.e., contracts to marry or to give up a child for adoption prior to the fourth day after birth. . . .

[T]he laws of New Jersey also evince a policy against enforcing private contracts to enter into or terminate familial relationships. . . .[8]

---

7. The legal consequences for J.B. also are unclear. See N.J.A.C. 8:2-1.4(a) (stating "the woman giving birth shall be recorded as a parent"). We note without comment that a recent case before the Chancery Division in Bergen County concluded that seventy-two hours must pass before a non-biological surrogate mother may surrender her parental rights and the biological mother's name may be placed on the birth certificate. A.H.W. v. G.H.B., 772 A.2d 948 (2000). In Arizona, an appellate court determined that a statute allowing a biological father but not a biological mother to prove paternity violated the Equal Protection Clause. Soos v. Superior Court, 897 P.2d 1356, 1361 (1995). In California, the legal mother is the person who "intended to bring about the birth of a child that she intended to raise as her own." Johnson v. Calvert, 851 P.2d 776, 782 (Cal. 1993), cert. denied, 510 U.S. 874, and cert. dismissed, Baby Boy J. v. Johnson, 510 U.S. 938 (1993).

8. Currently, a minority of states have passed legislation addressing in vitro fertilization. See, e.g., Cal. Penal Code §367g (West 1999) (permitting use of preembryos only pursuant to written consent form); Fla. Stat. ch. 742.17 (1997) (establishing joint decision-making authority regarding disposition of preembryos); La. Rev. Stat. Ann. §§ 9:121 to 9:133 (West 1991) (establishing fertilized human ovum as a biological human being that cannot be intentionally destroyed); Okla. Stat. Ann. tit. 10, §556 (West 2001) (requiring written consent for embryo transfer); Tex. Family code Ann. §151.103 (West 1996) (establishing parental rights over child resulting from preembryo).

Enforcement of a contract that would allow the implantation of preembryos at some future date in a case where one party has reconsidered his or her earlier acquiescence raises similar issues. If implantation is successful, that party will have been forced to become a biological parent against his or her will.

We note disagreement on the issue both among legal commentators and in the limited case law on the subject. *Kass*, supra, held that "agreements between progenitors, or gamete donors, regarding disposition of their . . . [preembryos] should generally be presumed valid and binding, and enforced in a dispute between them. . . ." 696 N.E.2d at 180. The New York court emphasized that such agreements would "avoid costly litigation," "minimize misunderstandings and maximize procreative liberty by reserving to the progenitors the authority to make what is in the first instance a quintessentially personal private decision."[9] . . . Yet, as discussed above, the Massachusetts Supreme Judicial Court as well as our Appellate Division have declared that when agreements compel procreation over the subsequent objection of one of the parties, those agreements are violative of public policy. *A.Z.*, *supra*, 725 N.E.2d at 1057-58; *J.B.*, *supra*, 331 N.J. Super. at 234. . . .

We recognize that persuasive reasons exist for enforcing preembryo disposition agreements. Both the *Kass* and *Davis* decisions pointed out the benefits of enforcing agreements between the parties. . . . We also recognize that in vitro fertilization is in widespread use, and that there is a need for agreements between the participants and the clinics that perform the procedure. We believe that the better rule, and the one we adopt, is to enforce agreements entered into at the time in vitro fertilization is begun, subject to the right of either party to change his or her mind about disposition up to the point of use or destruction of any stored preembryos.

The public policy concerns that underlie limitations on contracts involving family relationships are protected by permitting either party to object at a later date to provisions specifying a disposition of preembryos that that party no longer accepts. Moreover, despite the conditional nature of the disposition provisions, in the large majority of cases the agreements will control, permitting fertility clinics and other like facilities to rely on their terms. Only when a party affirmatively notifies a clinic in writing of a change in intention should the disposition issue be reopened. Principles of fairness dictate that agreements provided by a clinic should be written in plain language, and that a qualified clinic representative should review the terms with the parties prior to execution. Agreements should not be signed in blank, as in *A.Z.*, *supra*, 725 N.E.2d at 1057, or in a manner suggesting that the parties have not given due consideration to the disposition question. Those and other reasonable safeguards should serve to limit later disputes.

Finally, if there is disagreement as to disposition because one party has reconsidered his or her earlier decision, the interests of both parties must be evaluated. . . . Because ordinarily the party choosing not to become a biological parent will prevail, we do not anticipate increased litigation as a result of our decision. In this case, after having considered that M.B. is a father and is capable of fathering additional children,

---

9. The Supreme Court of Tennessee, in dicta, also stated "that an agreement regarding disposition of any untransferred preembryos in the event of contingencies (such as the death of one or more of the parties, divorce, financial reversals, or abandonment of the program) should be presumed valid and should be enforced as between the progenitors." *Davis*, *supra*, 842 S.W.2d at 597.

we have affirmed J.B.'s right to prevent implantation of the preembryos. We express no opinion in respect of a case in which a party who has become infertile seeks use of stored preembryos against the wishes of his or her partner, noting only that the possibility of adoption also may be a consideration, among others, in the court's assessment.

Under the judgment of the Appellate Division, the seven remaining preembryos are to be destroyed. It was represented to us at oral argument, however, that J.B. does not object to their continued storage if M.B. wishes to pay any fees associated with that storage. M.B. must inform the trial court forthwith whether he will do so; otherwise, the preembryos are to be destroyed.

The judgment of the Appellate Division is affirmed as modified.

VERNIERO, J., concurring.

I join in the disposition of this case and in all but one aspect of the Court's opinion. I do not agree with the Court's suggestion, in dicta, that the right to procreate may depend on adoption as a consideration. . . . I also write to express my view that the same principles that compel the outcome in this case would permit an infertile party to assert his or her right to use a preembryo against the objections of the other party, if such use were the only means of procreation. In that instance, the balance arguably would weigh in favor of the infertile party absent countervailing factors of greater weight. I do not decide that profound question today, and the Court should not decide it or suggest a result, because it is absent from this case.

[Justice Zazzali's concurring opinion is omitted.]

Notes: Frozen Embryo Disputes

1. *Family, Property, or Contract Law?* Should preembryos be treated as the property or as the children of one or both parents? The *Davis* litigation, cited in *J.B.*, has influenced all subsequent decisions. Davis v. Davis, 842 S.W.2d 588 (Tenn. 1992), on rehearing in part, 1992 WL 341632 (Tenn. 1992), cert. denied sub nom. Stowe v. Davis, 507 U.S. 911 (1993). As in most frozen embryo disputes, the litigants were divorcing and could not agree on the disposition of their frozen embryos, which had been produced in more hopeful times. The *Davis* trial court resolved the frozen embryo dispute as though the embryos were children of the marriage. 842 S.W.2d at 589. The wife was awarded "custody" so that she could arrange to have the embryos implanted. The trial court's holding was exceedingly controversial—in part because it implicitly challenged the characterization of embryos and fetuses as nonpersons in abortion law—and the decision was promptly appealed. The Tennessee Supreme Court rejected the notion that the preembryos were "persons," finding instead that the preembryos had a special status:

> To our way of thinking, the most helpful discussion on this point is found . . . in the ethical standards set by The American Fertility Society. . . .
>
> [T]he preembryo deserves respect greater than that accorded to human tissue but not the respect accorded to actual persons. The preembryo is due greater respect than other human tissue because of its potential to become a person and because of its symbolic meaning for many people. Yet, it should not be treated as a person, because it has not yet developed the features of personhood, is not yet established as developmentally individual, and may never realize its biologic potential. . . .

> We conclude that preembryos are not, strictly speaking, either "persons" or "property," but occupy an interim category that entitles them to special respect because of their potential for human life. It follows that any interest that [the genetic parents] . . . have in the preembryos in this case is not a true property interest. However, they do have an interest in the nature of ownership, to the extent that they have decisionmaking authority concerning disposition of the preembryos, within the scope of policy set by law. . . .

Davis, 842 S.W.2d at 596. What does it mean to give the embryos "special respect" because of their potential for human life? What are the practical implications of this "respect"? What does it mean to say that the progenitors have decisional authority, particularly since most disputes arise because the genetic parents disagree about the decision to make? Post-*Davis*, the Iowa Supreme Court has "identified three primary approaches to resolving disputes over the disposition of frozen embryos . . . (1) the contractual approach; (2) the contemporaneous mutual consent model; and (3) the [interests] balancing test [used in *J.B.* and in *Davis* where the parties had not executed an agreement]." In re Witten, 672 N.W.2d 768 (Iowa 2003).

2. *Disposing of Frozen Embryos by Contract or Mutual Agreement?* As noted in the *J.B.* decision, supra, there is substantial disagreement about whether the parties can contractually bind themselves to a particular form of embryo disposition even after one or both parties changes his or her preference. Does the *J.B.* court enforce the agreement signed by the parties? The informed consent form/disposition agreement appears to give the Cooper Center control over the embryos upon the divorce of the parties, absent a court order or a written agreement of the parties. Perhaps the court's decision actually fulfills the contract's terms. What about the alleged additional agreement between the parties, the one that M.B. claimed that he should have a right to prove? Why doesn't M.B. have a right to present evidence about his agreement with his wife regarding the disposition of the embryos? The court appears to impose a judicially constructed "statute of frauds," requiring that such agreements be written.

The New Jersey court also holds that "[w]e believe that the better rule, and the one we adopt, is to enforce agreements entered into at the time in vitro fertilization is begun, subject to the right of either party to change his or her mind about disposition up to the point of use or destruction of any stored preembryos." *J.B.*, supra. Does this mean that the court favors the use of binding predisposition contracts? Probably not, given that the court will only enforce agreements so long as the parties don't change their minds. This certainly is not the traditional legal approach to the enforcement of contracts.

It appears that other courts might enforce disposition agreements in some circumstances. The *Davis* court noted in dicta, for example:

> We believe, as a starting point, that an agreement regarding disposition of any untransferred preembryos in the event of contingencies (such as the death of one or more of the parties, divorce, financial reversals, or abandonment of the program) should be presumed valid and should be enforced as between the progenitors. This conclusion is in keeping with the proposition that the progenitors, having provided the gametic material giving rise to the preembryos, retain decisionmaking authority as to their disposition.
>
> At the same time, we recognize that life is not static, and that human emotions run particularly high when a married couple is attempting to overcome infertility

problems. It follows that the parties' initial "informed consent" to IVF procedures will often not be truly informed because of the near impossibility of anticipating, emotionally and psychologically, all the turns that events may take as the IVF process unfolds. Providing that the initial agreements may later be modified by agreement will, we think, protect the parties against some of the risks they face in this regard. But, in the absence of such agreed modification, we conclude that their prior agreements should be considered binding.

Davis, 842 S.W.2d at 597. See also Kass v. Kass, 696 N.E.2d 174 (N.Y. 1998) (enforcing dispositional terms of signed consents, which assigned preembryos for research purposes); In re Dahl and Angle, 194 P.3d 834 (Or. App. 2008) ("courts should give effect to a valid agreement evincing the parties' intent"); Roman v. Roman, 193 S.W.3d 40 (Tex. App. 2006) (embryo agreement terms should be enforced).

The contractual approach has been described as "[t]he currently prevailing view." In re Witten, 672 N.W.2d 768, 776 (Iowa 2003). The *Witten* court nonetheless rejected the contractual approach because it provides " 'insufficient[] protect[ion for] the individual and societal interests at stake.' " Id. at 777. The court agreed with critics of the contractual approach who argued that preferences regarding embryo disposition cannot be known in advance. Id. The court noted:

> We have considered and rejected the arguments of some commentators that embryo disposition agreements are analogous to antenuptial agreements and divorce stipulations, which courts generally enforce. . . . Whether embryos are viewed as having life or simply as having the potential for life, this characteristic or potential renders embryos fundamentally distinct from the chattels, real estate, and money that are the subjects of antenuptial agreements. Divorce stipulations are also distinguishable. While such agreements may address custody issues, they are contemporaneous with the implementation of the stipulation, an attribute noticeably lacking in disposition agreements.

In re Witten, 672 N.W.2d at 781-782. The court rejected the balancing of interests approach because it would require the court to make sensitive value judgments about procreation particularly within the dominion of individuals. The court thus adopted the contemporaneous agreement standard: "A better principle to apply . . . is the requirement of contemporaneous mutual consent. Under that model, no transfer, release, disposition, or use of the embryos can occur without the signed authorization of both donors. If a stalemate results, the status quo would be maintained. . . . Thus, any expense [for embryo storage] should logically be borne by the person opposing destruction." Id. at 783. See also A.Z. v. B.Z., 725 N.E.2d 1051 (Mass. 2000) (court expresses doubt about whether informed consent forms offered by clinic and signed by parties reflected their intent); Deborah L. Forman, Embryo Disposition and Divorce: Why Clinic Consent Forms Are Not the Answer, 24 J. Am. Acad. Matrim. L. 57 (2011) (offering critique of reliance on forms).

3. *Frozen Embryos and the Constitution.* Frozen embryos occupy a peculiar position under the law. Who should have power to exercise control over the embryos? Are these questions answered by an analysis of the "right to procreate" or the "right not to procreate"? Women invest more "sweat equity" in in vitro reproduction than men. Women must undergo arduous hormone therapy and ova retrieval procedures. Men must produce a sperm sample, typically under less harrowing

conditions. Should this difference in investments affect the outcome? See Ruth Colker, Pregnant Men Revisited or Sperm Is Cheap, Eggs Are Not, 47 Hastings L. J. 1063 (1996). If procreation had occurred in the ordinary fashion, a man's ability to decline the opportunity of fatherhood would have ended with the procreative act itself. A man cannot require that a woman undergo an abortion, for example; see pages 733-734. Should courts use a similar analogy when considering frozen embryo disputes, denying genetic parents the opportunity to reject parenthood once they have committed their gametes to the enterprise? See Kass v. Kass, 1995 WL 110368 (N.Y. Sup. Ct.) (unpublished opinion), rev'd, 663 N.Y.S.2d 581 (App. Div. 1997).

Most courts following the balancing of interests approach have favored the right not to procreate. In *J.B.*, supra, for example, the court anticipates that the party who does not wish to procreate will "ordinarily . . . prevail." The *Davis* court reached a similar result for cases not governed by a preexisting contractual agreement:

> If no prior agreement exists, then the relative interests of the parties in using or not using the preembryos must be weighed. Ordinarily, the party wishing to avoid procreation should prevail, assuming that the other party has a reasonable possibility of achieving parenthood by means other than use of the preembryos in question. If no other reasonable alternatives exist, then the argument in favor of using the preembryos to achieve pregnancy should be considered. However, if the party seeking control of the preembryos intends merely to donate them to another couple, the objecting party obviously has the greater interest and should prevail. But the rule does not contemplate the creation of an automatic veto, and in affirming the judgment of the court of appeals, we would not wish to be interpreted as so holding. . . .

842 S.W.2d at 604. See also A.Z. v. B.Z., 725 N.E.2d 1051 (Mass. 2000) (husband's interest in avoiding procreation outweighed defendant's interest in having additional children; husband should not be forced to become a parent). See also I. Glenn Cohen, The Right Not to Be a Genetic Parent, 81 S. Cal. Rev. 1115 (2008). When, if ever, would these courts authorize the use of embryos over the objection of one of the parties? What is the significance of the dispute between the majority and concurring opinions in *J.B.* regarding the ability to adopt? A Pennsylvania appellate court using a balancing of interests approach in a case where the parties had no disposition agreement awarded frozen embryos to a woman who had undergone cancer treatment and would not otherwise be able to bear a genetically related child. Reber v. Reiss, 42 A.3d 1131 (Pa. Super. 2012). The court considered but rejected the argument that the woman could achieve parenthood through adoption. Id. at 1138-1139 (adoption is "laudable" but not the same as genetic parenting and adoption option not practically available to woman due to her age and health history). See also, Szafranski v. Dunston, 34 N.E.3d 1132 (Ill App. 2016) (holding that trial court did not err in finding woman whose fertility had been affected by cancer treatment had a greater interest in using the preembryos than her ex-boyfriend's interest in preventing their use).

4. *Genetic Parenthood and Frozen Embryo Disputes.* In In re Litowitz, the Washington Supreme Court confronted a frozen embryo dispute in which one of the parties was not genetically related to the embryos. 48 P.3d 261 (Wash. 2002), opinion amended, 53 P.3d 516 (2002), cert. denied sub nom. Litowitz v. Litowitz, 537 U.S. 1191 (2003). Becky M. Litowitz was unable to produce oocytes or to bear a child. She and her then-husband David J. Litowitz entered into an agreement with an egg donor to obtain eggs that could be fertilized with David's sperm and then implanted in a gestational surrogate. The Litowitz marriage crumbled before the birth of their first child pro-

duced according to this arrangement. The parties could not agree to the disposition of the remaining frozen embryos. The trial court gave the embryos to the husband for implantation in another surrogate "based on the best interest of the child." Id. at 264.

The Washington Supreme Court took a different approach. The court held that Becky Litowitz's rights would be determined by contract because she had no biological connection to the preembryos. Id. at 267. Becky argued that she and David had equal rights to the embryos because the egg donor contract provided that the "intended parents" were the owners of the donated eggs. Id. at 267-268. The court rejected this claim, holding that the egg donor contract did not apply once the eggs had been fertilized. Id. at 268. The court then turned to the cryopreservation contract the parties entered into with the fertility clinic. That contract provided that the preembryos should be "thawed out and not allowed to undergo further development" after five years. Id. at 271. Given that the five years had expired, the court suggested that the embryos might already have been destroyed or could be destroyed in accordance with the parties' expressed wishes.

5. *Legislation.* Several states have enacted legislation establishing special consent and dispute resolution rules for the allocation of frozen embryos. See, e.g., N.J. Stat. Ann. §26:2Z-2 (persons providing infertility treatment must provide certain options for the disposal of embryos including for use in research). Some jurisdictions focus on regulating the informed consent process. See, e.g., Cal. H & S Code §125315 (patients must be given options for disposition in the event of separation or divorce); and Findley v. Lee, 2016 WL 270083 (Cal. Super.) (court holds that agreement signed pursuant to statute given conclusive effect regarding disposition of embryos). Other jurisdictions give the partner wishing to avoid procreation the right to withdraw consent any time before the use of the embryos. See, e.g., Colo. Rev. Stat. §19-4-106. Several states have enacted rules governing embryo adoption. See National Conference of State Legislatures, supra. Legislation may be helpful in some circumstances but is not likely to resolve the need for judicial determinations completely. How should courts resolve embryo disputes when the parties have failed to execute an agreement about the disposition of embryos as required by state law?

6. *Lost Embryos; Donated Embryos.* Should couples be permitted to sue infertility centers that lose or erroneously destroy frozen embryos? See Jeter v. Mayo Clinic Arizona, 121 P.3d 1256 (Ariz. 2005) (rejecting wrongful death claim but permitting certain other claims to go forward); Miller v. American Infertility Group of Illinois, S.C., 897 N.E.2d 837 (Ill. App. 2008) (no wrongful death claim before embryo is implanted). Couples may agree to have unused preembryos donated to others. Ethics Committee of the ASRM, Defining Embryo Donation: An Ethics Committee Opinion, 106 Fertility & Sterility 56 (2016). Should regulation of preembryo donations mirror gamete donation rules or are there any special concerns? See Charles P. Kindregan, Jr. & Maureen McBrien, Embryo Donation: Unresolved Legal Issues in the Transfer of Surplus Cryopreserved Embryos, 49 Vill. L. Rev. 169 (2004).

7. *Additional Commentaries.* Professor Robertson was the leading commentator on frozen embryo disputes; he served as an expert in the *Davis* trial and wrote extensively on the subject. See, e.g., John A. Robertson, Precommitment Strategies for Disposition of Frozen Embryos, 50 Emory L. J. 990 (2001). See also Jessica Berg, Owning Persons: The Application of Property Theory to Embryos and Fetuses, 40 Wake Forest L. Rev. 159 (2005); I. Glenn Cohen, The Constitution and the Rights Not to Procreate, 60 Stan. L. Rev. 1135 (2008); Janet L. Dolgin, The "Intent" of Reproduction: Reproductive Technologies and the Parent-Child Bond, 26 Conn. L. Rev. 1261

(1994); Michael T. Flannery, "Rethinking" Embryo Disposition Upon Divorce, J. of Contemp. Health L. & Pol'y 233 (2013); Dara E. Purvis, Expectant Fathers, Abortion, and Embryos, 43 J. L. Med. & Ethics 330 (2015); Ellen Waldman, The Parent Trap: Uncovering the Myth of "Coerced Parenthood" in Frozen Embryo Disputes, 53 Am. U. L. Rev. 1021 (2004) (discusses and critiques the dominance of the right to not procreate in frozen embryo disputes). See generally Annot., 87 A.L.R.5th 253 (2001).

5. "Traditional" and Gestational Surrogacy

■ **R.R. v. M.H.**
689 N.E.2d 790 (Mass. 1998)

WILKINS, C.J.

On a report by a judge in the Probate and Family Court, we are concerned with the validity of a surrogacy parenting agreement between the plaintiff (father) and the defendant (mother). Both the mother and the father are married but not to each other. A child was conceived through artificial insemination of the mother with the father's sperm, after the mother and father had executed the surrogate parenting agreement. The agreement provided that the father would have custody of the child. During the sixth month of her pregnancy and after she had received funds from the father pursuant to the surrogacy agreement, the mother changed her mind and decided that she wanted to keep the child.

The father thereupon brought this action. . . . The question of the enforceability of the surrogacy agreement is before us and, although we could defer any ruling until there is a final judgment entered, the issue is one on which we elect to comment because it is fully briefed and is of importance to more than the parties. This court has not previously dealt with the enforceability of a surrogacy agreement. . . .

The baby girl who is the subject of this action was born on August 15, 1997. . . . The defendant mother and the plaintiff father are her biological parents. The father and his wife, who live in Rhode Island, were married in June, 1989. The wife is infertile. Sometime in 1994, she and the father learned of an egg donor program but did not pursue it because the procedure was not covered by insurance and had a relatively low success rate. Because of their ages (they were both in their forties), they concluded that pursuing adoption was not feasible. In April, 1996, responding to a newspaper advertisement for surrogacy services, they consulted a Rhode Island attorney who had drafted surrogacy contracts for both surrogates and couples seeking surrogacy services. On the attorney's advice, the father and his wife consulted the New England Surrogate Parenting Advisors (NESPA), a for-profit corporation that helps infertile couples find women willing to act as surrogate mothers. They entered into a contract with NESPA in September, 1996, and paid a fee of $6,000. Meanwhile, in the spring of 1996, the mother, who was married and had two children, responded to a NESPA advertisement. She reported to NESPA that her family was complete and that she desired to allow others less fortunate than herself to have children. The mother submitted a surrogacy application to NESPA. The judge found that the mother was motivated to apply to NESPA by a desire to be pregnant, in order to earn money, and to help an infertile couple.

In October, Dr. Angela Figueroa of NESPA brought the mother together with the father and his wife. They had a seemingly informative exchange of information and views. The mother was advised to seek an attorney's advice concerning the surrogacy agreement. Shortly thereafter, the mother, the father, and his wife met again to discuss the surrogacy and other matters. The mother also met with a clinical psychologist as part of NESPA's evaluation of her suitability to act as a surrogate. The psychologist, who also evaluated the father and his wife, advised the mother to consult legal counsel, to give her husband a chance to air his concerns, to discuss arrangements for contact with the child, to consider and discuss her expectations concerning termination of the pregnancy, and to arrange a meeting between her husband and the father and his wife. The psychologist concluded that the mother was solid, thoughtful, and well grounded, that she would have no problem giving the child to the father, and that she was happy to act as a surrogate. The mother told the psychologist that she was not motivated by money, although she did plan to use the funds received for her children's education. The mother's husband told the psychologist by telephone that he supported his wife's decision.

The mother signed the surrogate parenting agreement and her signature was notarized on November 1. The father signed on November 18. The agreement stated that the parties intended that the "Surrogate shall be inseminated with the semen of Natural Father" and "that, on the birth of the child or children so conceived, Natural Father, as the Natural Father, will have the full legal parental rights of a father, and surrogate will permit Natural Father to take the child or children home from the hospital to live with he [sic] and his wife." The agreement acknowledged that the mother's parental rights would not terminate if she permitted the father to take the child home and have custody, that the mother could at any time seek to enforce her parental rights by court order, but that, if she attempted to obtain custody or visitation rights, she would forfeit her rights under the agreement and would be obligated to reimburse the father for all fees and expenses paid to her under it. . . .

The agreement provided for compensation to the mother in the amount of $10,000 "for services rendered in conceiving, carrying and giving birth to the Child." Payment of the $10,000 was to be made as follows: $500 on verification of the pregnancy; $2,500 at the end of the third month; $3,500 at the end of the sixth month; and $3,500 at the time of birth "and when delivery of child occurs." The agreement stated that no payment was made in connection with adoption of the child, the termination of parental rights, or consent to surrender the child for adoption. The father acknowledged the mother's right to determine whether to carry the pregnancy to term, but the mother agreed to refund all payments if, without the father's consent, she had an abortion that was not necessary for her physical health. The father assumed various expenses of the pregnancy, including tests, and had the right to name the child. The mother would be obliged, however, to repay all expenses and fees for services if tests showed that the father was not the biological father of the child, or if the mother refused to permit the father to take the child home from the hospital. The agreement also provided that the mother would maintain some contact with the child after the birth. The judge found that the mother entered into the agreement on her own volition after consulting legal counsel. There was no evidence of undue influence, coercion, or duress. The mother fully understood that she was contracting to give custody of the baby to the father. She sought to inseminate herself on November 30 and December 1, 1996. The attempt at conception was successful.

The lawyer for the father sent the mother a check for $500 in December, 1996, and another for $2,500 in February. In May, the father's lawyer sent the mother a check for $3,500. She told the lawyer that she had changed her mind and wanted to keep the child. She returned the check uncashed in the middle of June. The mother has made no attempt to refund the amounts that the father paid her, including $550 that he paid for pregnancy-related expenses.

Approximately two weeks after the mother changed her mind and returned the check for $3,500, and before the child was born, the father commenced this action against the mother seeking to establish his paternity, alleging breach of contract, and requesting a declaration of his rights under the surrogacy agreement. Subsequently, the wife's husband was added as a defendant. The judge appointed a guardian ad litem to represent the interests of the unborn child. Proceedings were held on . . . the mother's motion to determine whether surrogacy contracts are enforceable in Massachusetts. . . .

A significant minority of States have legislation addressing surrogacy agreements. Some simply deny enforcement of all such agreements. . . . Others expressly deny enforcement only if the surrogate is to be compensated. . . . Some States have simply exempted surrogacy agreements from provisions making it a crime to sell babies. . . . A few States have explicitly made unpaid surrogacy agreements lawful. . . . Florida, New Hampshire, and Virginia require that the intended mother be infertile. . . . New Hampshire and Virginia place restrictions on who may act as a surrogate and require advance judicial approval of the agreement. . . . Last, Arkansas raises a presumption that a child born to a surrogate mother is the child of the intended parents and not the surrogate. . . .

There are few appellate court opinions on the enforceability of traditional surrogacy agreements. . . .

The best known opinion is that of the Supreme Court of New Jersey in the *Matter of Baby M.*, 537 A.2d 1227 (N.J. 1988), where the court invalidated a compensated surrogacy contract because it conflicted with the law and public policy of the State. . . . The Baby M surrogacy agreement involved broader concessions from the mother than the agreement before us because it provided that the mother would surrender her parental rights and would allow the father's wife to adopt the child. . . . The agreement, therefore, directly conflicted with a statute prohibiting the payment of money to obtain an adoption and a statute barring enforcement of an agreement to adoption made prior to the birth of the child. . . . The court acknowledged that an award of custody to the father was in the best interests of the child, but struck down orders terminating the mother's parental rights and authorizing the adoption of the child by the husband's wife. . . . The court added that it found no "legal prohibition against surrogacy when the surrogate mother volunteers, without any payment, to act as a surrogate and is given the right to change her mind and to assert her parental rights." . . .

The case before us concerns traditional surrogacy, in which the fertile member of an infertile couple is one of the child's biological parents. Surrogate fatherhood, the insemination of the fertile wife with sperm of a donor, often an anonymous donor, is a recognized and accepted procedure. . . . If the mother's husband consents to the procedure, the resulting child is considered the legitimate child of the mother and her husband. *G. L. c. 46, §4B.* . . . Section 4B does not comment on the rights and obligations, if any, of the biological father, although inferentially he has none. In the case before us, the infertile spouse is the wife. No statute decrees the consequences of the artificial insemination of a surrogate with the sperm of a fertile husband. This situation presents different considerations from surrogate fatherhood because surrogate motherhood is never anonymous and her commitment and contribution is unavoidably much greater than that of a sperm donor.[10]

We must face the possible application of *G. L. c. 46, §4B*, to this case. Section 4B tells us that a husband who consents to the artificial insemination of his wife with the sperm of another is considered to be the father of any resulting child. In the case before us, the birth mother was married at the time of her artificial insemination. . . . It is doubtful, however, that the Legislature intended §4B to apply to the child of a married surrogate mother. . . .

Policies underlying our adoption legislation suggest that a surrogate parenting agreement should be given no effect if the mother's agreement was obtained prior to a reasonable time after the child's birth or if her agreement was induced by the payment of money. Adoption legislation is, of course, not applicable to child custody, but it does provide us with some guidance. Although the agreement makes no reference to adoption and does not concern the termination of parental rights or the adoption of the child by the father's wife, the normal expectation in the case of a surrogacy agreement seems to be that the father's wife will adopt the child with the consent of the mother (and the father). Under *G. L. c. 210, §2*, adoption requires the written consent of the father and the mother but, in these circumstances, not the mother's husband. Any such consent, written, witnessed, and notarized, is not to be executed "sooner than the fourth calendar day after the date of birth of the child to be adopted." Id. That statutory standard should be interpreted as providing that no mother may effectively agree to surrender her child for adoption earlier than the fourth day after its birth, by which time she better knows the strength of her bond with her child. Although a consent to surrender custody has less permanency than a consent to adoption, the legislative judgment that a mother should have time after a child's birth to reflect on her wishes concerning the child weighs heavily in our consideration whether to give effect to a prenatal custody agreement. No private agreement concerning adoption or custody can be conclusive in any event because a judge, passing on custody of a child, must decide what is in the best interests of the child.[11]

Adoptive parents may pay expenses of a birth parent but may make no direct payment to her. See *G. L. c. 210, §11A*. . . . Even though the agreement seeks to attribute that payment of $10,000, not to custody or adoption, but solely to the mother's services in carrying the child, the father ostensibly was promised more than those services because, as a practical matter, the mother agreed to surrender custody of the child. She could assert custody rights, according to the agreement, only if she repaid the father all amounts that she had received and also reimbursed him for all expenses he had incurred. The statutory prohibition of payment for receiving a child through adoption suggests that, as a matter of policy, a mother's agreement to surrender custody in exchange for money (beyond pregnancy-related expenses) should be given no effect in deciding the custody of the child.

10. A situation which involves considerations different from those in the case before us arises when the birth mother has had transferred to her uterus an embryo formed through in vitro fertilization of the intended parents' sperm and egg. This latter process in which the birth mother is not genetically related to the child (except coincidentally if an intended parent is a relative) has been called gestational surrogacy. . . .

11. In the case of a divorce, a judge may approve an agreement between parents concerning child custody unless the judge makes specific findings that the agreement would not be in the best interests of the child. *G. L. c. 208, §31.*

The mother's purported consent to custody in the agreement is ineffective because no such consent should be recognized unless given on or after the fourth day following the child's birth. In reaching this conclusion, we apply to consent to custody the same principle which underlies the statutory restriction on when a mother's consent to adoption may be effectively given. Moreover, the payment of money to influence the mother's custody decision makes the agreement as to custody void. Eliminating any financial reward to a surrogate mother is the only way to assure that no economic pressure will cause a woman, who may well be a member of an economically vulnerable class, to act as a surrogate. It is true that a surrogate enters into the agreement before she becomes pregnant and thus is not presented with the desperation that a poor unwed pregnant woman may confront. However, compensated surrogacy arrangements raise the concern that, under financial pressure, a woman will permit her body to be used and her child to be given away.

There is no doubt that compensation was a factor in inducing the mother to enter into the surrogacy agreement and to cede custody to the father. If the payment of $10,000 was really only compensation for the mother's services in carrying the child and giving birth and was unrelated to custody of the child, the agreement would not have provided that the mother must refund all compensation paid (and expenses paid) if she should challenge the father's right to custody. Nor would the agreement have provided that final payment be made only when the child is delivered to the father. We simply decline, on public policy grounds, to apply to a surrogacy agreement of the type involved here the general principle that an agreement between informed, mature adults should be enforced absent proof of duress, fraud, or undue influence.

We recognize that there is nothing inherently unlawful in an arrangement by which an informed woman agrees to attempt to conceive artificially and give birth to a child whose father would be the husband of an infertile wife. We suspect that many such arrangements are made and carried out without disagreement.

If no compensation is paid beyond pregnancy-related expenses and if the mother is not bound by her consent to the father's custody of the child unless she consents after a suitable period has passed following the child's birth, the objections we have identified in this opinion to the enforceability of a surrogate's consent to custody would be overcome. Other conditions might be important in deciding the enforceability of a surrogacy agreement, such as a requirement that (a) the mother's husband give his informed consent to the agreement in advance; (b) the mother be an adult and have had at least one successful pregnancy; (c) the mother, her husband, and the intended parents have been evaluated for the soundness of their judgment and for their capacity to carry out the agreement; (d) the father's wife be incapable of bearing a child without endangering her health; (e) the intended parents be suitable persons to assume custody of the child; and (f) all parties have the advice of counsel. The mother and father may not, however, make a binding best-interests-of-the-child determination by private agreement. Any custody agreement is subject to a judicial determination of custody based on the best interests of the child.

The conditions that we describe are not likely to be satisfactory to an intended father because, following the birth of the child, the mother can refuse to consent to the father's custody even though the father has incurred substantial pregnancy-related expenses. A surrogacy agreement judicially approved before conception may be a better procedure, as is permitted by statutes in Virginia and New Hampshire. A Massachusetts statute concerning surrogacy agreements, pro or con, would provide guidance to judges, lawyers, infertile couples interested in surrogate parenthood, and prospective surrogate mothers.

We do not reach but comment briefly on the mother's argument that the agreement was unconscionable. She actively sought to become a surrogate and entered into the surrogacy agreement voluntarily, advised by counsel, not under duress, and fully informed. Unconscionability is not apparent on this record.

A declaration shall be entered that the surrogacy agreement is not enforceable. Such further orders as may be appropriate, consistent with this opinion, may be entered in the Probate and Family Court.

■ CULLITON v. BETH ISRAEL DEACONESS MEDICAL CENTER
756 N.E.2d 1133 (Mass. 2001)

GREANEY, J.

We transferred this case here on our own motion to decide whether a judge in the Probate and Family Court had authority to act on the plaintiffs' complaint that sought declaratory and injunctive relief by way of a judgment ordering the defendant Beth Israel Deaconess Medical Center (hospital) "to enter MARLA CULLITON as the mother, and STEVEN CULLITON as the father [,] on the birth certificates of unborn Baby A and unborn Baby B." The children, twins, were born while the case was pending appeal. They are the genetic children of the plaintiffs, who had embryos . . . that had been created from the plaintiff Steven Culliton's sperm . . . and the plaintiff Marla Culliton's ova . . . implanted into the uterus of the defendant Melissa Carroll, who agreed to act as a gestational carrier for the plaintiffs pursuant to a gestational carrier contract with them. The judge ordered the entry of a judgment dismissing the complaint because of a "lack of clarity and certainty as to this court's authority" to grant the relief sought. We conclude that the judge had authority to decide the merits of the complaint. We also conclude that, on the facts of this case, a judgment should enter declaring that the plaintiffs are the legal parents of the children, and ordering the hospital, through its reporters, to place the plaintiffs' names on all "record[s] of birth" created pursuant to G. L. c. 46, §§1, 3, 3A, listing the plaintiffs as the mother and father, respectively, of the children.

The facts of this case are undisputed. We now summarize those facts and provide an overview of the case's procedural background. The plaintiffs and the defendant Melissa Carroll (gestational carrier), a single woman over the age of twenty-one years who had "at least one previous live birth," entered into a gestational carrier contract. Pursuant to the contract, the gestational carrier agreed to have implanted into her uterus embryos that were created from the sperm of Steven Culliton and the ova of Marla Culliton; to carry and deliver any child resulting from the embryo implantation; and, upon the birth of any child resulting from the embryo implantation, to permit the plaintiffs to have sole physical and legal custody of the child or children. For her role, the gestational carrier was to receive certain financial compensation.[6] The contract appears to have been executed because Marla "is capable of conceiving

---

6. Under the contract, the plaintiffs agreed to pay the gestational carrier for certain medical expenses, maternity clothing, travel expenses, childcare expenses, legal expenses, telephone expenses, medically necessitated lost wages, psychological counselling expenses, health insurance expenses, and living expenses. According to the contract, payment of these expenses was not conditioned "upon the termination of any parental rights or the placement of the child with [the plaintiffs]."

a child, but incapable of bearing and giving birth to a child without unreasonable risk to her health."

The gestational carrier underwent the embryo implantation and became pregnant with twins. A few months later, the plaintiffs filed a verified complaint in the Probate and Family Court seeking a declaration of paternity and maternity, as well as a prebirth order directing the hospital at which the gestational· carrier was expected to deliver to designate the plaintiffs as the father and mother of the children on their birth certificates. Together with the complaint, the plaintiffs and the gestational carrier filed a stipulation for the entry of judgment in the plaintiffs' favor. . . .

A judge in the Probate and Family Court, concluding that he did not have the authority to issue a prebirth order of parentage, ordered the entry of a judgment of dismissal. . . . The plaintiffs filed a notice of appeal, and the case was entered in the Appeals Court. That court, on motion by the plaintiffs, entered a preliminary injunction enjoining the hospital from issuing birth certificates until resolution of the appeal. The day before we transferred the case here, the twins were born. After transfer, we entered an order continuing the injunction in effect. . . .

The judge acted prudently in seeking to place this case before us as quickly as possible because, as he correctly noted, there is no direct legal "authority for issuing a pre-birth order regarding parentage under the facts of this case." Authority elsewhere is sparse and not altogether consistent [citing cases from Ohio, New Jersey, New York, and California].

The pregnancy in issue is not governed by the statutes referred to by the [trial] judge. General Laws c. 209C, for instance, establish procedures for determining paternity and maternity for children "born out of wedlock." See G. L. c. 209C, §1. . . . While the twins technically were born out of wedlock, because the gestational carrier was not married when she gave birth to them, it is undisputed that the twins were conceived by a married couple. In these circumstances the children should be presumed to be the children of marriage. . . . Conversely, problems would have arisen if the gestational carrier had been married at the time of birth, for, in those circumstances, under G. L. c. 209C, her husband would be presumed to be the father of the children to whom she gave birth. . . . Additionally, under the statute, in contested cases, one method of proving paternity involves soliciting testimony from one parent concerning the occurrence of "sexual intercourse" with the other party during the "probable period of conception." . . . As shown by the facts of this case, reproductive advances have eliminated the necessity of having sexual intercourse in order to procreate. It is apparent, after examining the paternity statute in detail, that the statute is simply an inadequate and inappropriate device to resolve parentage determinations of children born from this type of gestational surrogacy.

Nor does the adoption statute, G. L. c. 210, furnish any better guidance. While this court has previously looked to the adoption statute in deciding whether to enforce a traditional surrogacy agreement, . . . see [citing R.R. v. M.H., supra], the court did so "to assure that no economic pressure will cause a woman . . . to act as a surrogate. . . . Compensated surrogacy arrangements raise the concern that, under financial pressure, a woman will permit her body to be used and her child to be given away." . . . In such an arrangement, the surrogate is both the genetic mother of the child and the mother who carries the child through pregnancy and delivery. The child is thus, undisputedly, "her" child to be surrendered for adoption. Here, where it is undisputed that the plaintiffs were not donating an embryo or embryos to the gestational carrier, and that the twins have no genetic relation to the gestational carrier, the concerns are different. . . .

Also, in these circumstances, applying the four-day waiting period of G. L. c. 210, §2, to this gestational carrier arrangement would work unintended, and possibly detrimental, results. The duties and responsibilities of parenthood (for example, support and custody) would lie with the gestational carrier for at least four days; the gestational carrier could be free to surrender the children for adoption; and the genetic parents of the children would be forced to go through the adoption process, possibly having to wait as long as six months, see G. L. c. 210, §5A . . . , before becoming the legal parents of the children. As is evident from its provisions, the adoption statute was not intended to resolve parentage issues arising from gestational surrogacy agreements.

Contrary to the plaintiffs' contention, G. L. c. 46, §4B, does not authorize the relief sought in this case. That statute provides that "any child born to a married woman as a result of artificial insemination with the consent of her husband, shall be considered the legitimate child of the mother and such husband." G. L. c. 46, §4B. As we explained in R.R. v. M.H., supra at 510, §4B "seems to concern the status of a child born to a fertile mother whose husband, presumably infertile, consented to her artificial insemination with the sperm of another man so that the couple could have a child biologically related to the mother." The situation that §4B addresses is not present here. The statute does not apply. . . .

Here, where (a) the plaintiffs are the sole genetic sources of the twins; (b) the gestational carrier agrees with the orders sought; (c) no one, including the hospital, has contested the complaint or petition; and (d) by filing the complaint and stipulation for judgment the plaintiffs agree that they have waived any contradictory provisions in the contract (assuming those provisions could be enforced in the first place), we conclude that pursuant to the Probate and Family Court's general equity jurisdiction under G. L. c. 215, §6, the judge had authority to consider the merits of the relief sought here.[9]

This conclusion acknowledges the importance of establishing the rights and responsibilities of parents as soon as is practically possible. By enacting G. L. c. 46, which contains provisions establishing a process for the issuance of accurate birth certificates on which the "parents" of a newly born child are listed, the Legislature has also recognized and addressed, in some measure, this concern. Delays in establishing parentage may, among other consequences, interfere with a child's medical treatment in the event of medical complications arising during or shortly after birth; may hinder or deprive a child of inheriting from his legal parents should a legal parent die intestate before a postbirth action could determine parentage; may hinder or deprive a child from collecting Social Security benefits under 42 U.S.C. §402(d) (Supp. 1999); and may result in undesirable support obligations as well as custody disputes (potentially more likely in situations where the child is born with congenital malformations or anomalies, or medical disorders and diseases). . . . Our holding provides that such consequences, at least in some circumstances, can be minimized or avoided, thus

9. This conclusion takes into account a fact apparently overlooked by the plaintiffs, namely, that a hospital's reporters do not "issue" birth certificates. Rather, they furnish certain information pursuant to G. L. c. 46, §§1, 3, 3A, including the identity of the "parents" of the child born, which, in turn, is used by city and town clerks to "record" a complete "return of birth," which is commonly known as a person's birth certificate, see G. L. c. 46, §§1, 3, 3A, 4A. City or town clerks, the Commissioner of Public Health, or the State Registrar of Vital Records and Statistics may then furnish or "issue" a certified copy of the birth record to a parent. See G. L. c. 46, §§2A, 19, 19B, 19C.

furnishing a measure of stability and protection to children born through such gestational surrogacy arrangements. See E.N.O. v. L.M.M., 711 N.E.2d 886 (Mass. 1999),
cert. denied, 528 U.S. 1005 (1999) ("the court's duty as parens patriae necessitates
that its equitable powers extend to protecting the best interests of children.").

[W]e suggested [in a previous case] that a protocol for these types of cases be
established. Such a protocol becomes increasingly necessary as infertile couples,
and others, take advantage of existing and emerging assisted reproductive technologies, and as children are conceived and born through these technologies. . . .
While responding to some parentage issues arising through artificial insemination,
see G. L. c. 46, §4B, the Legislature has not enacted laws to determine parentage of
children born from other methods of reproductive technologies or assisted conception. The Legislature is the most suitable forum to deal with the questions involved
in this case, and other questions as yet unlitigated, by providing a comprehensive set
of laws that deal with the medical, legal, and ethical aspects of these practices. . . .

The judgment of dismissal is vacated. The preliminary injunction enjoining
the hospital from complying with its statutory obligations for the children is dis-
solved. A judgment is to enter declaring the plaintiffs as the legal parents of the
children and ordering the hospital, through its reporters, to place the plaintiffs'
names on its "record[s] of birth" created pursuant to G. L. c. 46, §§1, 3, 3A, listing
the plaintiffs as the mother and father, respectively, of the children.

So ordered.

Notes: Traditional and Gestational Surrogacy

1. *One Plus One Equals Three?* Do *R.R.* and *Culliton* give consistent treatment to
the legal "weight" of genetic parenthood and gestational parenthood? The modern
approach is to treat egg donation and sperm donation as equivalent legal acts with
equivalent consequences. See supra at page 812. A gamete donor is thus legally permitted to terminate his or her parental rights at the time of the donation. According to *Culliton*, a gestational surrogate may also enter into a binding agreement to
forgo whatever parental rights she might have before the birth of the child. What
prevents an egg donor who is also a gestational surrogate from entering into a binding agreement to forgo her parental rights? Why does the *R.R.* court turn instead
to the laws governing adoption for standards to be applied in traditional surrogacy
cases? Perhaps the distinction is that the parties in *Culliton* sought an agreed court
order and there was no dispute that required a court to weigh the gestational surrogate's interests. See Steven H. Snyder & Mary Patricia Byrn, The Use of Prebirth
Parentage Orders in Surrogacy Proceedings, 39 Fam. L. Q. 633 (2005). The *Culliton*
court notes the gestational carrier's agreement.

Could there be a legal or ethical basis for recognizing the gestational surrogate
as a parent? In Johnson v. Calvert, 851 P.2d 776 (Cal. 1993) (en banc), cert. denied,
510 U.S. 874 (1993), cert. dismissed by Baby Boy J. v. Johnson, 510 U.S. 938 (1993), the
California Supreme Court rejected a claim by a gestational surrogate that she should
be recognized as the mother of the resulting child and given visitation privileges. The
court found that state laws addressing the determination of maternity were ambiguous and held that the original intent of the parties should determine the outcome:

> Because two women each have presented acceptable proof of maternity, we do not
> believe this case can be decided without enquiring into the parties' intentions as

manifested in the surrogacy agreement. . . . Mark and Crispina are a couple who desired to have a child of their own genetic stock but are physically unable to do so without the help of reproductive technology. . . . The parties' aim was to bring Mark's and Crispina's child into the world, not for Mark and Crispina to donate a zygote to Anna. . . . No reason appears why Anna's later change of heart should vitiate the determination that Crispina is the child's natural mother.

We conclude that although the Act recognizes both genetic consanguinity and giving birth as means of establishing a mother and child relationship, when the two means do not coincide in one woman, she who intended to procreate the child — that is, she who intended to bring about the birth of a child that she intended to raise as her own — is the natural mother under California law. . . .

851 P.2d at 782. The court rejected Anna's claim that the surrogacy contract violated public policy, noting that gestational surrogacy is distinguishable from adoption and that public policy favored giving women the same right to enter into contracts as men.

The end result in practice is that infertile couples avoid the problems of "traditional" or "genetic" surrogacy by splitting the genetic and biological contributions: using an egg donor and a different gestational surrogate. See, e.g., Raftopol v. Ramey, 12 A.3d 783 (Conn. 2011) (gestational carrier does not have parental rights to child; domestic partner who was intended co-parent in valid gestational agreement gains status without separate adoption proceeding); J.F. v. D.B., 879 N.E.2d 740 (Ohio 2007) (gestational surrogacy contract prohibiting gestational surrogate with no genetic connection to child from asserting parental rights does not violate public policy). However, it is important to recognize that some jurisdictions have had difficulty detaching parenthood from biology or gestation. The New Jersey courts continued to struggle in the aftermath of the *Baby M* case summarized in *R.R.*, finding in a 2011 case that state law permits a declaration of maternity to a biologically or gestationally related woman but not to the intended nonbiological, nongestational mother. In re T.J.S., 16 A.3d 386 (N.J. Super. Ct. 2011) (intended mother not entitled to declaration of maternity; differential treatment of infertile husband and infertile wife under Parentage Act does not violate equal protection), aff'd, 54 A.3d 263 (N.J. 2012) (affirmed by equally divided court with per curiam and dissenting opinions). See also Kate Zernike, Court's Split Decision Provides Little Clarity on Surrogacy, N.Y. Times, Oct. 24, 2012.

Moreover, the parties to ART sometimes hope that a gestational contribution will "count" in determining parentage. Some women who are incapable of producing suitable ova may seek to bear and rear children created with donor ova. In this circumstance, the parties intend that the gestational mother serve as the legal mother, even though she has no genetic relationship with the child. The physical arrangements in these two situations are similar (woman gives birth to a child with whom she has no genetic relationship), but the parties' preliminary intentions differ. How should the courts treat disputes arising out of these arrangements? Note that the 2002 UPA contains the presumption, found in most state laws, that a woman who gives birth to a child is the child's mother. UPA §201(a)(1) (2002). The Act also includes alternate provisions applicable in states that permit gestational surrogacy. Id. §201(a)(1), (4). In addition, the UPA provides that mechanisms for challenging paternity may also be used to challenge maternity. Id. §106. Similar provisions are found in the 2017 UPA. See §201(1) (a parent child relationship is established if the individual gives birth to the child, except as provided in the UPA article governing surrogacy); Art. 6 (proceedings to adjudicate parentage). See also Soos v. Superior Court, County of Maricopa, 897 P.2d 1356 (Ariz. Ct. App. 1995) (statute that allowed biological father to prove paternity while denying genetic mother that right violates equal protection clause). Do these provisions lessen the maternal security of an intended mother who gives birth to a baby produced from a donor egg? Could the woman argue that she did not "donate" the egg? See supra at page 813 n.2. The 2017 UPA provides that genetic testing should not be used to challenge the parentage of an individual who is a parent under the UPA provisions governing assisted reproduction or surrogacy, UPA §502(b) (2017), however "donor" is still defined as an "individual who provides gametes intended for use in assisted reproduction," UPA §102(9) (2017).

In another twist, the Tennessee Supreme Court considered a case questioning the legal status of a woman who gave birth to triplets who had been conceived using IVF, donor eggs, and her male partner's sperm. In re C.K.G., 173 S.W.3d 714 (Tenn. 2005). The woman sought custody of the children when the couple separated. Her former partner objected, asserting that the woman was not the mother or a legal parent of the children because she was merely a gestational surrogate who has no genetic or legally enforceable tie to the children. The trial court held that the woman was the birth mother and legal mother; the appeals court affirmed using the intent of the parties as the legally relevant test, see Johnson v. Calvert, supra. The Tennessee Supreme Court affirmed that the woman was the legal mother on different grounds. The court rejected the intent test as straying too far from Tennessee's statutory framework and the genetics test because it would reach unintended results in cases involving egg donors. 173 S.W.3d at 724-725. The court instead adopted a "narrow" ruling limited to the specific facts and focusing on several factors: genetics, intent, gestation, and the "absence of controversy between the gestator and the genetic 'mother.'" Based on its analysis of these factors, the court decided that the woman who gave birth to the triplets was the legal mother and entitled to share custody with the genetic father. Id. at 730.

2. *Constitutional Considerations.* How does the right to procreate apply to surrogacy arrangements? How would you "unbundle" the rights to and not to procreate for the parties involved in these cases and what does that unbundling reveal about the treatment of the various parties? How would this analysis apply to claims beyond those arising from a specific dispute over parental rights? For example, does a prohibition on commercial surrogacy violate the constitutional rights to procreate of the commissioning parents? Of the surrogate?

Does the Massachusetts court in *R.R.* consider whether infertile couples have a constitutionally protected interest in the enforcement of their surrogacy arrangement? In *Baby M*, the court considered and rejected the genetic father's constitutional claims:

> Both parties argue that the Constitutions—state and federal—mandate approval of their basic claims. The source of their constitutional arguments is essentially the same: the right of privacy, the right to procreate, the right to the companionship of one's child, those rights flowing either directly from the Fourteenth Amendment or by its incorporation of the Bill of Rights, or from the Ninth Amendment, or through the penumbra surrounding all of the Bill of Rights. They are the rights of personal intimacy, of marriage, of sex, of family, of procreation. . . . The right asserted by the Sterns is the right of procreation; that asserted by Mary Beth Whitehead is the right to the companionship of her child. We find that the right of procreation does not extend as far as claimed by the Sterns. . . . The right to procreate very simply is the right to have natural children, whether through sexual intercourse or artificial insemination. It is no more than that. Mr. Stern has not been deprived of that right. Through artificial insemination of Mrs. Whitehead, Baby M is his child. The

custody, care, companionship, and nurturing that follow birth are not parts of the right to procreation; they are rights that may also be constitutionally protected, but that involve many considerations other than the right of procreation. . . .

Mrs. Whitehead, on the other hand, asserts a claim that falls within the scope of a recognized fundamental interest protected by the Constitution. As a mother, she claims the right to the companionship of her child. This is a fundamental interest, constitutionally protected. Furthermore, it was taken away from her by the action of the court below. Whether that action under these circumstances would constitute a constitutional deprivation, however, we need not and do not decide. By virtue of our decision Mrs. Whitehead's constitutional complaint—that her parental rights have been unconstitutionally terminated—is moot. . . .

In re Baby M, 537 A.2d 1227, 1253-1255 (N.J. 1988). Constitutional challenges to state surrogacy rules are relatively rare. As referenced above, note 1, equal protection claims were raised unsuccessfully in In re T.J.S. In J.R., M.R. & W.K.J. v. Utah, 261 F. Supp. 2d 1268 (D. Utah 2002), the court found that the plaintiffs had standing to challenge a portion of the then-applicable state law that prevented them from establishing that they were the legal parents of twins born as a result of a gestational surrogacy agreement. Utah's UPA now authorizes certain gestational agreements. Utah Code Ann. §78B-15-801.

3. *Traditional or "Genetic" Surrogacy Contracts.* Why does the *R.R.* court refuse to enforce the surrogacy contract? Is there a way to write an enforceable traditional surrogacy contract, in which the surrogate both contributes the egg and gestates the embryo, in Massachusetts? Are the factors the court suggests ones that a court or legislature should devise? Why does the court reject the surrogate's claim that the contract was unconscionable? What is the legal distinction between refusing to enforce a contract and declaring it unconscionable? See also A.L.S. ex rel. J.P. v. E.A.G., 2010 WL 4181449 (Minn. App. 2011) (traditional surrogate was legal and biological mother of resulting child).

What explains discomfort with surrogacy contracts? The development of private law in the nineteenth century can be viewed, under one theory, as the movement from status to contract. See H. Maine, Ancient Law (1939) (originally published in 1884). Many years before the development of doctrines tested on today's bar exams, an individual was born into a network of social relationships that established his or her legal rights and duties to others and to the state. This status-based idea of legal relationships is reflected in matters ranging in time from feudal law to the old law of master and servant to modern family law. Surrogacy contracts could be viewed as part of a continued assault on status-based law by contractarian principles. See, e.g., Janet L. Dolgin, Status and Contract in Surrogate Motherhood: An Illumination of the Surrogacy Debate, 38 Buff. L. Rev. 515 (1990).

Discomfort with traditional surrogacy arrangements is intertwined with concerns about economic exploitation. The *Baby M* court issued the classic statement regarding the need for courts to protect surrogates:

Intimated, but disputed, is the assertion that surrogacy will be used for the benefit of the rich at the expense of the poor. See, e.g., Radin, Market Inalienability, 100 Harv. L. Rev. 1849, 1930 (1987). In response it is noted that the Sterns are not rich and the Whiteheads not poor. Nevertheless, it is clear to us that it is unlikely that surrogate mothers will be as proportionately numerous among those women in the top 20 percent income bracket as among those in the bottom 20 percent. Ibid. Put differently, we doubt that infertile couples in the low-income bracket will find upper income surrogates. . . .

The point is made that Mrs. Whitehead agreed to the surrogacy arrangement, supposedly fully understanding the consequences. Putting aside the issue of how compelling her need for money may have been, and how significant her understanding of the consequences, we suggest that her consent is irrelevant. There are, in a civilized society, some things that money cannot buy. In America, we decided long ago that merely because conduct purchased by money was "voluntary" did not mean that it was good or beyond regulation and prohibition. West Coast Hotel Co. v. Parrish, 300 U.S. 379 (1937). Employers can no longer buy labor at the lowest price they can bargain for, even though that labor is "voluntary," 29 U.S.C. §206 (1982), or buy women's labor for less money than paid to men for the same job, 29 U.S.C. §206(d), or purchase the agreement of children to perform oppressive labor, 29 U.S.C. §212, or purchase the agreement of workers to subject themselves to unsafe or unhealthful working conditions, 29 U.S.C. §§651 to 678 (Occupational Safety and Health Act of 1970). There are, in short, values that society deems more important than granting to wealth whatever it can buy, be it labor, love, or life. . . .

The surrogacy contract is based on principles that are directly contrary to the objectives of our laws. It guarantees the separation of a child from its mother; it looks to adoption regardless of suitability; it totally ignores the child; it takes the child from the mother regardless of her wishes and her maternal fitness; and it does all of this, it accomplishes all of its goals, through the use of money.

Beyond that is the potential degradation of some women that may result from this arrangement. In many cases, of course, surrogacy may bring satisfaction, not only to the infertile couple, but to the surrogate mother herself. The fact, however, that many women may not perceive surrogacy negatively but rather see it as an opportunity does not diminish its potential for devastation to other women.

In sum, the harmful consequences of this surrogacy arrangement appear to us all too palpable. In New Jersey the surrogate mother's agreement to sell her child is void. Its irrevocability infects the entire contract, as does the money that purports to buy it. . . .

In re Baby M, 537 A.2d 1227, 1249-1250 (N.J. 1988). How would you describe the court's attitude toward women who wish to become surrogates? Empowering? Respectful? Paternalistic? Baby M's analysis of the evils of surrogacy can be compared with the pro-contract views of the proponents of law and economics and the views of some feminists. See, e.g., Lori Andrews, Beyond Doctrinal Boundaries: A Legal Framework for Surrogate Motherhood, 81 Virginia L. Rev. 2343 (1995); Richard Epstein, Surrogacy: The Case for Full Contractual Enforcement, 81 Va. L. Rev. 2305 (1995).

4. *Surrogacy and Intentional Parenting.* In In re Marriage of Buzzanca, a California court considered the impact of assisted reproduction involving a donated embryo and a gestational surrogate. 72 Cal. Rptr. 2d 280 (Ct. App. 1998). Luanne and John Buzzanca agreed to create a child by using a donor embryo implanted into a gestational surrogate. John filed for divorce shortly before the birth of Jaycee. John alleged that the couple did not have children; Luanne contended that they were expecting their first child from the surrogate. Id. at 282. The surrogate did not want to parent the child. The trial court found that Jaycee did not have any parents. Id. at 283. The appellate court rejected this conclusion, finding that the AI statute applied to both intended parents and that John became Jaycee's father by causing the child's conception. Id. at 284-288, 292. The intent of the parties was only relevant to a point, however, as John was barred from asserting that Luanne had prom-

ised to assume responsibility for Jaycee's care. Id. at 292. See also Doe v. Doe, 710 A.2d 1297 (Conn. 1998) (nonbiological mother given custody of child conceived as a result of a surrogacy arrangement in which her husband's sperm had been used to inseminate a third party; case subsequently superceded by legislation).

5. *State Legislative Activity and the UPA.* States have adopted a range of approaches to surrogacy. Some address surrogacy through partial or comprehensive legislation, which permits or prohibits certain practices. Other states have left the issue to the courts, which has resulted in a range of decisions permitting or disapproving various components of surrogacy arrangements. Note that a ban on surrogacy agreements is not technically a ban on surrogacy itself; the ban merely impedes the creation of enforceable agreements in which money is paid to the surrogate. While this undoubtedly has the effect of diminishing the business of surrogacy, surrogate arrangements are still possible between family members, for example, who are motivated by nonmonetary factors. In any event, the trend appears to be toward permitting gestational surrogacy arrangements, with conditions, and to disfavoring traditional or genetic surrogacy arrangements.

Although surrogacy was a controversial area for legislative reform, the Uniform Law Commission included optional surrogacy provisions in its 2002 UPA. In releasing the revised 2017 UPA, the drafters candidly noted that "there appeared to be a lack of enthusiasm for the substance of the [2002 UPA surrogacy] provisions" given that they were accepted by only 2 of the 11 states that had adopted the 2002 UPA. Over the past 15 years, a number of jurisdictions have instead adopted non-UPA surrogacy legislation. Among other problems, the 2002 UPA treated gestational and genetic surrogacy equally. The 2017 UPA follows the recent state law trends by "impo[sing] additional safeguards or requirements on genetic surrogacy agreements" and by "liberaliz[ing] the rules governing gestational surrogacy arrangements." UPA Art. 8 Comment (2017) (Surrogacy Agreements).

The 2017 UPA surrogacy provisions thus are designed to reflect the current trend in states which have authorizing surrogacy, with some modifications designed to address new considerations, such as the Supreme Court's decision in Pavan v. Smith, 137 S.Ct. 2075 (2017), see page 814. Article 8 begins with some provisions relevant to both genetic and gestational surrogacy. UPA §§801-807 (2017). These provisions establish basic definitions (§801), set eligibility criteria for surrogates and intended parents (§802), detail the process for executing a surrogacy agreement (§803), outline the core elements of the surrogacy agreement (§804), establish the impact of subsequent changes of marital status of the parties (§805), provide a process for protecting the confidentiality of the surrogacy documents (§806), and give the relevant court exclusive, continuing jurisdiction over all matters arising from the agreement during a defined time period (§807).

Section 802 can be understood as an attempt to establish eligibility criteria that will protect the parties. For example, to be eligible to serve as a surrogate, a woman must be at least 21 years of age, must previously have given birth to at least one child, must have completed a medical exam by a licensed medical doctor and a mental health consultation by a licensed mental health professional, and must have independent legal representation of her choice throughout the surrogacy arrangement. UPA §802 (2017). The requirements for intended parents are virtually identical. Id. (with the exception of the requirement of previous childbearing). How does the requirement of previous childbearing for the surrogate help to protect the parties to the agreement?

Section 804 establishes that, absent an exception provided by another provision of the UPA, the surrogate agrees to attempt to achieve pregnancy through assisted reproduction and that the "intended parent or parents, jointly and severally, immediately on birth will be the exclusive parent or parents of the child, regardless of the number of children born or gender or mental or physical condition of each child." UPA §804. This section also establishes that "the surrogate and the surrogate's spouse or former spouse . . . will have no claim to parentage of a child conceived by assisted reproduction under the agreement." Id.

The 2017 UPA then provides states with the option of enacting a framework for gestational surrogacy:

SPECIAL RULES FOR GESTATIONAL SURROGACY AGREEMENT

SECTION 808. TERMINATION OF GESTATIONAL SURROGACY AGREEMENT.

(a) A party to a gestational surrogacy agreement may terminate the agreement, at any time before an embryo transfer, by giving notice of termination in a record to all other parties. If an embryo transfer does not result in a pregnancy, a party may terminate the agreement at any time before a subsequent embryo transfer.

(b) Unless a gestational surrogacy agreement provides otherwise, on termination of the agreement under subsection (a), the parties are released from the agreement, except that each intended parent remains responsible for expenses that are reimbursable under the agreement and incurred by the gestational surrogate through the date of termination.

(c) Except in a case involving fraud, neither a gestational surrogate nor the surrogate's spouse or former spouse, if any, is liable to the intended parent or parents for a penalty or liquidated damages, for terminating a gestational surrogacy agreement under this section.

SECTION 809. PARENTAGE UNDER GESTATIONAL SURROGACY AGREEMENT.

(a) Except as otherwise provided in subsection (c) or Section 810(b) or 812, on birth of a child conceived by assisted reproduction under a gestational surrogacy agreement, each intended parent is, by operation of law, a parent of the child.

(b) Except as otherwise provided in subsection (c) or Section 812, neither a gestational surrogate nor the surrogate's spouse or former spouse, if any, is a parent of the child.

(c) If a child is alleged to be a genetic child of the woman who agreed to be a gestational surrogate, the court shall order genetic testing of the child. If the child is a genetic child of the woman who agreed to be a gestational surrogate, parentage must be determined based on [other provisions of the UPA]

(d) Except as otherwise provided in subsection (c) or Section 810(b) or 812, if, due to a clinical or laboratory error, a child conceived by assisted reproduction under a gestational surrogacy agreement is not genetically related to an intended parent or a donor who donated to the intended parent or parents, each intended parent, and not the gestational surrogate and the surrogate's spouse or former spouse, if any, is a parent of the child, subject to any other claim of parentage.

SECTION 810. GESTATIONAL SURROGACY AGREEMENT: PARENTAGE OF DECEASED INTENDED PARENT.

(a) Section 809 applies to an intended parent even if the intended parent died during the period between the transfer of a gamete or embryo and the birth of the child.

(b) Except as otherwise provided in Section 812, an intended parent is not a parent of a child conceived by assisted reproduction under a gestational surrogacy agreement if the intended parent dies before the transfer of a gamete or embryo unless: (1) the agreement provides otherwise; and (2) the transfer of a gamete or embryo occurs not later than [36] months after the death of the intended parent or birth of the child occurs not later than [45] months after the death of the intended parent.

SECTION 811. GESTATIONAL SURROGACY AGREEMENT: ORDER OF PARENTAGE.

(a) Except as otherwise provided in Sections 809(c) or 812, before, on, or after the birth of a child conceived by assisted reproduction under a gestational surrogacy agreement, a party to the agreement may commence a proceeding in the [appropriate court] for an order or judgment:

(1) declaring that each intended parent is a parent of the child and ordering that parental rights and duties vest immediately on the birth of the child exclusively in each intended parent;

(2) declaring that the gestational surrogate and the surrogate's spouse or former spouse, if any, are not the parents of the child;

(3) designating the content of the birth record in accordance with [cite applicable law of this state other than this [act]] and directing the [state agency maintaining birth records] to designate each intended parent as a parent of the child;

(4) to protect the privacy of the child and the parties, declaring that the court record is not open to inspection [except as authorized under [another section of the Act]];

(5) if necessary, that the child be surrendered to the intended parent or parents; and

(6) for other relief the court determines necessary and proper.

(b) The court may issue an order or judgment under subsection (a) before the birth of the child. The court shall stay enforcement of the order or judgment until the birth of the child.

(c) Neither this state nor the [state agency maintaining birth records] is a necessary party to a proceeding under subsection (a).

SECTION 812. EFFECT OF GESTATIONAL SURROGACY AGREEMENT.

(a) A gestational surrogacy agreement that complies with Sections 802, 803, and 804 [summarized above] is enforceable.

(b) If a child was conceived by assisted reproduction under a gestational surrogacy agreement that does not comply with Sections 802, 803, and 804, the court shall determine the rights and duties of the parties to the agreement consistent with the intent of the parties at the time of execution of the agreement. Each party to the agreement and any individual who at the time of the execution of the agreement was a spouse of a party to the agreement has standing to maintain a proceeding to adjudicate an issue related to the enforcement of the agreement.

(c) Except as expressly provided in a gestational surrogacy agreement or subsection (d) or (e), if the agreement is breached by the gestational surrogate or one or more intended parents, the non-breaching party is entitled to the remedies available at law or in equity.

(d) Specific performance is not a remedy available for breach by a gestational surrogate of a provision in the agreement that the gestational surrogate be impregnated, terminate or not terminate a pregnancy, or submit to medical procedures.

(e) Except as otherwise provided in subsection (d), if an intended parent is determined to be a parent of the child, specific performance is a remedy available for:

> (1) breach of the agreement by a gestational surrogate which prevents the intended parent from exercising immediately on birth of the child the full rights of parentage; or
>
> (2) breach by the intended parent which prevents the intended parent's acceptance, immediately on birth of the child conceived by assisted reproduction under the agreement, of the duties of parentage.

UPA §§808-812 (2017).

Does the 2017 UPA strike the correct balance in protecting the parties and facilitating gestational agreements? Are there any provisions that seem problematic? Note that §809 addresses errors in the ART process, establishing that the intended parents bear the risk of clinical or laboratory errors that result in a child who does not have the genetic heritage that the parties intended. Section 812 establishes some important standards and rights for the parties. First, §812 provides that a gestational agreement meeting the requirements for the Act will be enforceable. As importantly, where the parties have not complied with the UPA's requirements for surrogacy agreements, §812 provides that courts should use the intent of the parties as a guide for determining parental rights. This section also establishes the rights of the parties on breach, including the circumstances in which specific performance may be ordered. Should a gestational surrogate have the same right to make an abortion decision freely as other pregnant women? See Kevin Yamamoto & Shelby A. D. Moore, A Trust Analysis of a Gestational Carrier's Right to Abortion, 70 Fordham L. Rev. 93 (2001). Kristine S. Knaplund, Children of Assisted Reproduction, 45 U. Mich. J. L. Reform 899 (2012) (comparing 2002 UPA with other approaches).

The 2017 UPA's new genetic surrogacy provisions can be found at §§813-818. The regulations are considerably more stringent. Absent an exception established in the Act, a genetic surrogacy agreement must be validated by a court to be enforceable and the proceeding to validate the agreement must be initiated before the assisted reproductive activities begin. UPA §813 (2017). Gestational surrogates may withdraw consent any time before the transfer of the embryo. Genetic surrogates, in contrast, "may withdraw their consent to the agreement any time before 72 hours after the birth of a child conceived by assisted reproduction under the agreement." UPA §814 (2017). On termination, the parties are released from all obligations except that the intended parents must pay for the surrogate's expenses through the date of the termination. Non-expense compensation is not required from the intended parents and the genetic surrogate or spouse may not be held liable for termination penalties or liquidated damages. Id. The 2017 UPA also establishes rules for nonvalidated genetic surrogacy agreements, including an option for the court to validate the agreement retroactively. Where the surrogate withdraws her consent, the court is to determine parentage using the non-surrogacy/ART UPA provisions. Where the surrogate does not withdraw her consent, the court is to determine parentage based on the best interests of the child, taking the parties' intent into account. Id. The genetic surrogacy provisions also permit remedies for breach of validated agreements, including specific performance on the same terms as it is available for breaches of gestational agreements meeting the requirements of the Act. UPA §818 (2017).

6. *It Takes a Village (or, More than Two Parents).* The 2017 UPA also includes provisions relating to the number of legally recognized parents. The early court cases relating to ARTs arose when the structure of laws assumed that a child could have two parents—one mother and one father—and the courts managed the musical chairs task of assigning who would serve in these roles at the end of the ART process. As the legal system began to adopt broader conceptions of parenthood, such as with the recognition of two mothers or two fathers, questions arose about whether it might also sometimes be in the child's best interests to have more than two parents. See, D.G. and S.H. v. K.S., 133 A.3d 703 (N.J. Super. 2015) (discussing legal implications of an "agreement entered into between three friends to conceive and jointly raise a child in a tri-parenting arrangement"; court awards joint legal and joint residential custody of child to all three parties); and R. Alta Charo, And Baby Makes Three—or Four, or Five, or Six: Redefining the Family After the Reprotech Revolution, 15 Wis. Women's L. J. 231 (2000). The 2017 UPA takes up the question by providing two alternatives for states: limiting the number of parents to two or authorizing courts to "adjudicate a child to have more than two parents . . . if the court finds that failure to recognize more than two parents would be detrimental to the child." UPA §613 (2017) (alternatives A & B). Does the standard established by the UPA make sense? Why shouldn't the test be the intentions of the parties, or perhaps the best interests of the child? Would it have made any difference to the outcome of the early genetic and gestational surrogacy cases if courts had been given the option of naming more than two parents? Multiple parenting is recognized in two Canadian provinces and is under consideration in the Netherlands. The Netherlands May Let Children Have More than Two Legal Parents, The Economist, Aug. 31, 2017.

7. *Professional Guidelines and Tort Claims.* While surrogacy arrangements present the same medical risks as the gamete donation and IVF procedures discussed earlier, professional organizations recognize the process raises a broader range of ethical issues and potential conflicts of interest. Traditional, genetic surrogacy arrangements are strongly discouraged. Ethics Committee of the ASRM, Consideration of the Gestational Carrier: A Committee Opinion, 99 Fertility & Sterility 1838-1841 (2013). The ASRM recommendations for gestational surrogacy arrangements include both medical and social components. See, Ethics Committee of the ASRM, Using Family Members as Gamete Donors or Gestational Carriers, 107 Fertility & Sterility 1136 (2017). One potentially controversial standard governs the appropriateness of gestational surrogacy: "Gestational carriers may be used when a true medical condition precludes the intended parent from carrying a pregnancy or

would pose a significant risk of death or harm to the woman or fetus." Practice Committee of the ASRM, Recommendations for Practices Utilizing Gestational Carriers: A Committee Opinion, 107 Fertility & Sterility e3, e3-e4 (2017) (listing appropriate medical conditions, including "[b]iologic inability to conceive or bear a child, such as a single male or homosexual male couple"). Is this limitation justified? Could denials of service to persons falling outside the guideline be legally challenged?

There is some evidence that conflicts of interest and power imbalances affect the treatment of gestational surrogates. Gestational surrogates are more likely to receive multiple embryos, thus increasing the probabilities of multiple fetuses, with the attendant medical risks. Only 15 percent of gestational surrogates received a single embryo transfer, despite medical guidelines calling for the transfer of a single embryo. Given that a cycle of treatment involving a gestational surrogate can cost more than $60,000, some experts have suggested that the data may reflect the desire of intended parents to secure "'two for the price of one.'" Joshua Kapfhamer & Bradley Van Voorhis, Gestational Surrogacy: A Call for Safer Practice, 106 Fertility & Sterility 270 (2016) (calling on physicians to carry out their "moral, professional, and ethical obligation to ensure the safety of our patients"); and Kiran M. Perkins et al., Trends and Outcomes of Gestational Surrogacy in the United States, 106 Fertility & Sterility 435 (2016).

Could the tort system provide additional protections for participants in ART arrangements? Could the parents in *R.R.* sue the fertility clinic or psychologist for failure to screen surrogates appropriately for latent traditionally maternal instincts? What would be the damages? Could the fertility clinic be liable if a child from a surrogacy arrangement is born with a genetic defect? Could intended parents bring a claim against a gestational surrogate for smoking, drinking alcohol, or using illegal drugs? Could a gestational surrogate bring a malpractice claim based on the transfer of multiple embryos in violation of the standard of care? Note, Whole Foods for Whole Pregnancy: Regulating Surrogate Mother Behavior During Pregnancy, 23 Wm & Mary J. Women & L. 367 (2017); and Summer James et al., Avoiding Legal Pitfalls in Surrogacy Arrangements, 21 Reproductive BioMedicine 862 (2010) (reviewing legal issues for endocrinologists).

8. *Uterus Transplants.* Approximately 1/500 women are unable to carry a pregnancy, either due to the absence of a uterus, disease, or another cause. Women with uterine infertility have pursued parenthood through gestational surrogacy or adoption. After years of preliminary research, transplant attempts, and commentaries by ethicists, physicians announced the first birth of a baby who had been gestated in a woman with a transplanted uterus in 2014. What are the advantages and disadvantages of uterus transplantation? Should there be any concerns with using transplantation to address a non-life-threatening condition? Uterus transplants involve significant risks for the recipient, including surgical risks, the need to take immunosuppressive drugs, and the risk of rejection. Fetuses carried in the transplanted uterus might be exposed to additional risk. The surgery allows the recipient to have the experience (though not the full sensation) of pregnancy. Birth is accomplished via cesarean section and the donated uterus is expected to be removed after one or two births. Should these risks be considered "unnecessary" because of the available alternatives of adoption or surrogacy? Denise Grady, Uterus Transplants May Soon Help Some Infertile Women in the U.S. to Become Pregnant, N.Y. Times, Nov. 12, 2015.

The first successful transplant involved a live donor, who confronted significant medical risks along with the donor, recipient. The medical risks could be narrowed through using deceased donors, much like other organs. The first attempted transplant in the United States used a cadaveric donor, however the transplant failed due to an infection. Denise Grady, Yeast Infection Led to Removal of Transplanted Uterus, N.Y. Times, April 8, 2016; L. Johannesson & S. Järvholm, Uterus Transplantation: Current Progress and Future Prospects, 8 Int. J. Womens Health 43 (2016); and V. Lavoué et al., Which Donor for Uterus Transplants: Brain-Dead Donor or Living Donor?, 101 Transplantation 267 (2017). Some of the media commentary on this development focused on the future possible use of uterus transplantation for transgender persons or men. See Timothy F. Murphy, Assisted Gestation and Transgender Women, 29 Bioethics 389 (2015). For a discussion of the role of artificial wombs in debates about abortion and surrogacy, see Jennifer S. Hendricks, Not of Woman Born: A Scientific Fantasy, 623 Case W. Res. L. Rev. 399 (2011).

9. *Commentaries.* The surrogate motherhood controversy has generated profuse commentary in legal, medical, philosophical, and popular journals. In addition to the books and articles cited above, for summaries of the legal landscape and commentaries on **general aspects of traditional and gestational surrogacy**, (note 1), see George L. Blum, Validity of Surrogate Parenting Agreement, 19 A.L.R.7th 4 (2016); Ardis L. Campbell, Determination of Status as Legal or Natural Parents in Contested Surrogacy Births, 77 A.L.R.5th 567 (2000); Columbia Law School Sexuality & Gender Law Clinic, Surrogacy Law and Policy in the U.S. (2016) (survey of state law on surrogacy), available at: www.law.columbia.edu. There are a number of articles exploring **constitutional aspects of surrogacy** (note 2). Some recent entries include: Andrea B. Carroll, Discrimination in Baby Making: The Unconstitutional Treatment of Prospective Parents through Surrogacy, 88 Ind, L. J. 1187 (2013), along with responses by Kimberly M. Mutcherson, How Parents are Made, 88 Ind. L. J. 1207 (2013) and Radhika Rao, Hierarchies of Discrimination in Baby Making, 88 Ind. L. J. 1217 (2013). For commentaries on surrogacy drawing on **feminist and law and economics approaches** (note 3), see Sara L. Ainsworth, Bearing Children, Bearing Risks: Feminist Leadership for Progressive Regulation of Compensated Surrogacy in the United States, 89 Wash. L. Rev. 1077 (2014); Susan Frelich Appleton, Reproduction and Regret, 23 Yale J. L. & Feminism 257 (2011) (drawing together cases from abortion, surrogacy, and gamete donation); Richard A. Posner, The Ethics and Economics of Enforcing Contracts of Surrogate Motherhood, 5 J. Contemp. Health L. & Pol'y 21, 31 (1989). For more on **model legislative approaches** to surrogacy agreements (note 5), see the ABA Model Act (2008); and Christine Metteer Lorillard, Informed Choices and Uniform Decisions: Adopting the ABA's Self-Enforcing Administrative Model to Ensure Successful Surrogacy Arrangements, 16 Cardozo J. L. & Gender 237 (2010). For concerns about whether current practices adequately protect **the vulnerability of surrogates** (note 7), see Pamela Laufer-Ukeles, Mothering for Money: Regulating Commercial Intimacy, Surrogacy, Adoption, 88 Ind. L. J. 1223 (2013) along with extended responses by Richard E. Storrow, New Thinking on Commercial Surrogacy, 88 Ind. L. J. 1281 (2013) and Michele Goodwin, Reproducing Hierarchy in Commercial Intimacy, 88 Ind. L. J. 1289 (2013). For additional commentaries on **uterus transplants and artificial wombs** (note 8), see John A. Robertson, Other Women's Wombs: Uterus Transplants and Gestational Surrogacy, 3 J. L. & the Biosciences 68-86 (2016) along with commentaries; Amel Alghrani,

Uterus Transplantation: Does Procreative Liberty Encompass the Right to Gestate, 3 J. L. & the Biosciences 636 (2016); Judith Daar & Sigal Klipstein, Refocusing the Ethical Choices in Womb Transplant, 3 J. L. & the Biosciences 383 (2016); Kimberley Mutcherson, Reproductive Surrogates, Risk and the Desire for Genetic Parenthood, 3 J. L. & the Biosciences 389 (2016); and John A. Robertson, Impact of Uterus Transplant on Fetuses and Resulting Children: A Response to Daar and Klipstein, 3 J. L. & the Biosciences 710 (2016); Rebecca Roache, Infertility and Non-Traditional Families, 42 J. Med. Ethics 557 (2016); Stephen Wilkinson & Nicola Jane Williams, Should Uterus Transplants be Publicly Funded, 42 J. Med. Ethics 559 (2016); Elizabeth Yoko, Weighing the Ethics of Artificial Wombs, N.Y. Times, May 8, 2017.

Problems: Determining Parentage

The explosive growth of reproductive technologies creates an almost bewildering array of parenting possibilities. The statutes and cases in this section demonstrate that the rules governing the determination of parentage are still in flux. The most established technology—AI or IUI—is regulated by statutes that attempt to allocate parenting rights and responsibilities. Consumers of donated sperm nonetheless confront some legal uncertainties. Technologies designed to provide the female components of the reproductive process—eggs and a uterus—are less well regulated, and significant areas of legal uncertainty still remain. States appear to be moving toward treating egg donation as the equivalent of sperm donation. See 2017 UPA. Conflicts over the disposition of frozen embryos also can be difficult to resolve, with courts suggesting that they will enforce the prior agreements of progenitors but balking at the imposition of parenthood on a presently unwilling individual. Consumers and sellers of reproductive services, and their lawyers, attempt to meet the objectives of the parties within whatever legal framework is available. Intended parents typically separate gamete donation from gestational surrogacy, for example, to avoid the use of traditional, or genetic surrogates. A poor use of reproductive technology can result in substantial emotional and financial costs for the participants, as well as in professional disciplinary or malpractice liability for the health care providers and attorneys. See generally Linda S. Anderson, Adding Players to the Game: Parentage Determinations When Assisted Reproductive Technology Is Used to Create Families, 62 Ark. L. Rev. 29 (2009).

1. *Sperm Donation and AI.* Assume you are in a jurisdiction that has adopted the 2002 version of UPA's provisions governing gamete donation. Melissa and Julie wish to have and raise a child together. Their friend, David, volunteers to provide sperm that will be used to artificially inseminate Julie. How should the transaction be structured to ensure that David will not have any parental rights and obligations? How could the parties use AI and ensure that David will be considered to be the resulting child's legal father? Will Melissa have any legally recognized relationship with the child? Could such a relationship be created? Would your analysis change under the 2017 UPA?

2. *Egg Donation and Surrogacy.* Latisha and Michael Bates have been married for eight years. Pregnancy and/or the hormonal treatments necessary for egg harvesting would injure Latisha's health. The couple still wants very much to have a child, preferably one that is genetically related to Michael. They have heard about surrogacy arrangements and would like to hire a surrogate to bear their child. Assume

you are in a jurisdiction with laws like those in Massachusetts. Could the Bateses enter into a surrogacy agreement with their neighbor, Paula? What should be the terms? Will the agreement be enforceable? What type of compensation, if any, will the Bateses be able to give Paula? Who will be the parents of the resulting child? Can the parties do anything to ensure that Latisha and Michael will be considered to be the parents?

Now assume that the Bateses make a separate arrangement with an egg donor, Ala Truistic, whose egg would be fertilized with Michael's sperm and implanted in Paula's uterus for gestation. Could Ala be paid any compensation for undergoing the procedures necessary for egg donation? Could Paula be compensated for enduring the pregnancy? Who would be the mother? Consider this question first based under the Massachusetts cases, supra at pages 839-847. Then consider the 2017 UPA approach. Who would be considered to be the legal parents of any resulting child?

Suppose that Ala donates several eggs that are fertilized with Michael's sperm. The eggs are donated pursuant to a written agreement that provides that Ala is donating the eggs "for use by Michael and Latisha Bates, a married couple, for use in raising the resulting child in a loving home." Latisha files for divorce from Michael after the eggs are fertilized and the resulting embryos are frozen but before implantation into Paula. Suppose that Ala now wants to control the disposition of the frozen embryos on the theory that the donation contract has been breached. Could you make any arguments on her behalf? Suppose that Michael wants to control the disposition of the embryos on the theory that Ala's ability to exercise reproductive choices ended with her donation?

3. *Reproductive vs. Domestic Tourism.* Suppose that you are approached by a couple residing in another country. Kerry and Chris would like to obtain donor eggs and sperm and the services of a surrogate to bear a child for them. They intend to bring their child to their home country and hope to be recognized as the child's legal parents and to obtain citizenship for their child. How would you advise your clients? What concerns might you have about Kerry and Chris's plans? What precautions would you advise? See generally sources cited supra at page 805; and, e.g., Government of Canada, Who Is a Parent for Citizenship Purposes Where Assisted Human Reproduction (AHR), Including Surrogacy Arrangements, Are Involved, available at http://www.cic.gc.ca/english/resources/tools/cit/admin/id/parent-assist.asp (visited Oct. 6, 2017) ("Children born abroad through assisted human reproduction (AHR), including surrogacy arrangements, undertaken by Canadian intending parents are not eligible for Canadian citizenship by descent when no genetic lineage or gestational connection to a Canadian parent who is eligible to pass on citizenship can be established").

E. ETHICAL AND LEGAL IMPLICATIONS OF ADVANCES IN GENETICS

1. Introduction

The fifth and final section of the chapter explores the legal implications of advances in genetics and the regulation of genetic technologies. In some senses these advances have already played a significant role in the chapter's coverage of reproduction: advances in understanding heredity and genetics undercut the scientific foundation for the eugenics theories underlying the laws challenged in Buck v. Bell, supra at page 701, and Skinner v. Oklahoma, supra at page 703. Genetic testing provides the technical capacity for parents to identify the sex of a fetus and to learn whether the fetus has certain genetic anomalies; the woman carrying the fetus may decide to abort based on the results of these tests. See pages 726-727. The process greatly increases the possibility of using genetic information to shape offspring. This can be seen in Internet Web sites for sperm and egg donors, which appear to offer recipients the ability to select donors based on characteristics commonly understood to have a genetic component such as height, hair and eye color, and intelligence. IVF provides an even more direct opportunity to perform genetic testing on the preembryos and to use the results to determine which embryos will be selected for transplantation. Genetic testing can be used to screen for disabling genetic conditions as well as to select for some characteristics, see pages 727, 806.

The final section of this chapter will focus more directly on the implications of scientific discoveries in this area. Should cloning and related procedures be allowed for reproductive, research, or therapeutic purposes? Should scientists be permitted to patent life forms and genes? How should society balance the positive incentives created from intellectual property ownership rules with the need to ensure equitable access to important new developments?

2. Human Stem Cell Research

As noted supra at page 761, federal and state governments have struggled with the ethical and legal implications of research involving certain types of stem cells that are derived from human embryos. Understanding the debate requires familiarity with some basic biology. The human body contains hundreds of different types of specialized cells capable of performing different functions. Heart muscle cells, nerve cells (neurons), and liver cells all perform different functions. Certain types of stem cells are "undifferentiated" (they have not yet become specialized cells), "pluripotent" (they have the capacity to become any type of specialized cell), and "self-replicating" (they can replicate in a proper laboratory setting). Stem cells can be found in all stages of human development from embryos (up to about seven weeks of development), fetuses (from the eighth week of development to birth), children, and adults.

There are several uses for stem cells. At a basic level, researchers hope to use stem cells to understand more about the process by which stem cells are able to differentiate into one of hundreds of specialized cells in the human body. Once more is understood about this process, it is possible that researchers will be able to develop clinical applications for stem cells by, for example, using stem cells to generate differentiated cells that could be used to replace heart muscle injured in a heart attack, nerve cells for those who have suffered spinal cord injuries, insulin-producing cells for persons with diabetes. Stem cell research thus offers the tantalizing possibility of enormous tangible benefits to persons suffering from cardiovascular disease, diabetes, or spinal cord injuries, along with other conditions. Researchers hope that mastery of the process of cellular differentiation, combined with a ready supply of human stem cells, could halt or reverse the progress of these diseases. See

U.S. Department of Health and Human Services, Regenerative Medicine, at http://
stemcells.nih.gov/info/Regenerative_Medicine/. As noted above, at page 826, it
may also be possible to create gametes for use in reproduction. However, there are
significant questions about the clinical use of pluripotent stem cells, including concerns about increased cancer risks. Alan Trounson, Potential Pitfall of Pluripotent
Stem Cells, 377 N. Eng. J. Med. 490 (2017).

One specific type of stem cell research is tied to the ongoing debates about
cloning and to the destruction of embryos. The use of ordinary stem cells for treatment could give rise to an immune reaction in the recipient of the stem cells, as the
body will treat the cells as foreign matter. One way to avoid this reaction involves
using somatic cell nuclear transplantation (often referred to as SCNT in the scientific literature). This technique involves taking the genetic materials from a somatic
cell[2] from the intended recipient and transplanting this material into an oocyte (a
human egg cell) that has had its original genetic material removed. The oocyte is
then manipulated into beginning the process of cell division and the creation of
an embryo. The embryo will contain stem cells that could be extracted and used to
create specialized cells that would no longer be viewed as foreign by the recipient
and thus would not create the risk of tissue rejection and the need for the recipient to take immune-suppressing drugs. This procedure is known as "therapeutic"
cloning because, as in reproductive cloning, an embryo is created with virtually the
same genetic identity as another human being.[3] Therapeutic cloning is different
from reproductive cloning because the resulting embryo is never implanted in a
uterus with the hope of producing a human being; instead the goal is to provide
a therapeutic treatment using embryonic stem cells. Diagram 1 compares natural
reproduction, therapeutic cloning, and reproductive cloning.

Stem cell research involving human embryonic stem cells provokes debates
about fetal interests. To those who believe that personhood begins at the union of a
sperm and egg, research using embryonic stem cells involves the sacrifice of human
life for scientific progress. Furthermore, the successful development of treatments
using embryonic stem cells might require the commercialized production and
exploitation of human embryos. The use of embryonic stem cells implicates strongly
held views regarding the status of embryos and fetuses and the degree to which they
command special respect and concern. Many ethicists and others object to the creation of potential human life solely for the purpose of producing stem cells. Many
also object to the extraction of stem cells from embryos or fetuses originally created for other purposes, such as through ordinary pregnancy or the use of in vitro
fertilization, even if the potential for human life will never be realized because of a
woman's right to choose to terminate her pregnancy or because embryos created
for assisted human reproduction are no longer needed for this purpose.

2. Somatic cells are ordinary cells from the body containing a full complement of chromosomes (23 pairs) as opposed to germ-line cells (sperm and egg cells), which contain only
half of a person's chromosomes (23).

3. The cloned embryo will not be completely identical because the genetic material
found in the oocyte's mitochondria is not removed; mitochondrial DNA from the donor
oocyte therefore will be reproduced in the embryo. See, page 827.

Diagram 1: Normal Reproduction, Reproductive Cloning, and Therapeutic Cloning[4]

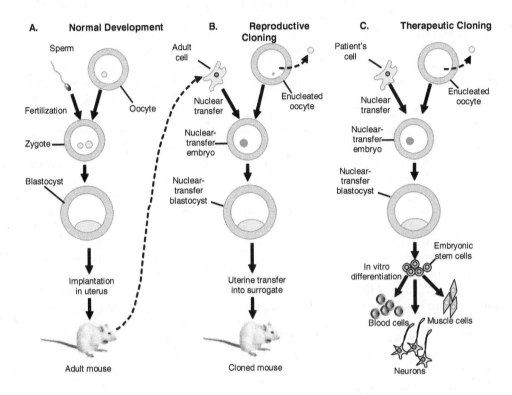

Embryonic stem cells have been easier to harvest and considered more likely to be pluripotent than adult stem cells. See generally National Institutes of Health, Stem Cell Information, available at http://stemcells.nih.gov. Embryonic stem cell research has expanded worldwide over the past decade and the first clinical trials of related therapies are now under way. See, e.g., David Cyranoski, Trials of Embryonic Stem Cells to Launch in China, 546 Nature 15 (2017); Steven D. Schwartz et al., Human Embryonic Stem Cell–Derived Retinal Pigment Epithelium in Patients with Age-Related Macular Degeneration and Stargardt's Macular Dystrophy, 385 Lancet 509 (2015) ("study provide[s] the first evidence of the medium-term to long-term safety, graft survival, and possible biological activity of pluripotent stem cell progeny in individuals with any disease.")

Researchers have developed a third approach to generating human stem cells that might be used for clinical therapies without the risk of generating an immune response. Researchers begin with cells from adults, resetting differentiated cells to create induced pluripotent stem cells that have properties similar to embryonic stem cells. Praschant Mali & Linzhao Cheng, Concise Review: Human Cell Engineering: Cellular Reprogramming and Genome Editing, 30 Stem Cells 75 (2012). It is not yet

---

4. Adapted from Konrad Hochedlinger & Rudolf Jaenisch, Nuclear Transplantation, Embryonic Stem Cells, and the Potential for Cell Therapy, 349 N. Eng. J. Med. 275 (2003).

clear whether induced pluripotent stem cells can produce the same potential benefits as embryonic stem cells. See Mo Li & Juan Carlos Izpisua Belmonte, Looking to the Future Following 10 Years of Induced Pluripotent Stem Cell Technologies, 11 Nature Protoc. 1579 (2016); Yanhong Shi et al., Induced Pluripotent Stem Cell Technology: A Decade of Progress, 16 Nature Rev. Drug Discov. 115 (2017).

The federal debate about human stem cell research has focused on funding for research involving embryonic stem cells. Federal law "prohibits NIH from funding '(1) the creation of a human embryo or embryos for research purposes; or (2) research in which a human embryo or embryos are destroyed, discarded, or knowingly subjected to risk of injury or death greater than that allowed for research on fetuses in utero under 45 C.F.R. 46.204(b) and [42 U.S.C. §289g(b)].'" Sherley v. Sebelius, 689 F.3d 776, 779 (D.C. Cir. 2012) (quoting the Dickey-Wicker Amendment inserted by Congress into appropriations bills since 2006). This language leaves open the question of whether federal funding could be used for research involving embryonic stem cells so long as the specific research project does not involve the destruction of human embryos. Id.

In 2001, President Bush authorized federal funding for research involving embryonic stem cells so long as the cell lines were already in existence at the time of the announcement and were derived from embryos originally created for use in assisted reproduction but were no longer going to be used for this purpose. Exec. Order No. 13,435, 72 Fed. Reg. 34,591 (2007) (formalizing 2001 policy announcement). Stem cell research remained a sensitive political issue through the decade, driven in part by public pleas for expansions in governmental funding from prominent individuals such as Christopher Reeve, an actor paralyzed in a riding accident; Michael J. Fox, an actor with Parkinson's disease; and former First Lady Nancy Reagan, whose husband, former President Ronald Reagan, eventually died from Alzheimer's disease.

The federal funding debate during the 2000s sparked a parallel debate in the states. The gap in federal funding sparked concerns that important stem cell research projects and leading researchers might leave the United States for other, more hospitable jurisdictions around the world. Some argued that the United States might lose access to important and potentially lucrative scientific developments. Stem cell activists began to promote state funding of stem cell research as a method of ensuring that U.S. researchers could remain at the forefront of the field. Several states provided funding and support for stem cell research — including embryonic stem cell research — through successful voter or legislative initiatives. See, e.g., the Web site for the California Institute for Regenerative Medicine, established as the result of a voter initiative, at www.cirm.ca.gov; and Mike McPhate, Waiting on the Promise of Stem Cells, N.Y. Times, May 4, 2017 (noting criticisms and challenges as Institute seeks a new round of funding).

Given limited federal involvement in human stem cell–related research during much of the 2000s, other groups generated ethical guidelines and procedures governing the derivation and use of stem cells. See National Academies, Stem Cells at the Academies (2010); and International Society for Stem Cell Research (ISSCR), Guidelines for Stem Cell Research and Clinical Translation (2016).

President Obama issued an executive order in 2009 permitting federal funding for research using stem cells from embryos where appropriate procedures and consents had been employed to develop the stem cells. Exec. Order 13,505, 74 Fed.

Reg. 10,667 (2009). See also Joel B. Finkelstein, Change in Federal Stem Cell Funding Policy Spurs Interest in Field, 101 J. Natl. Cancer Inst. 626 (2009). The approach was reflected in new federal regulations. Guidelines for Human Stem Cell Research, 74 Fed. Reg. 32,170-02 (2009). See also Sherley v. Sebelius, 689 F.3d 776, 781 (D.C. Cir. 2012) (affirming "that NIH had reasonably interpreted Dickey-Wicker's ban on funding 'research in which . . . embryos are destroyed' to allow federal funding of ESC research").

The 2009 NIH regulations focus on defining the circumstances in which federal funding will be available for stem cell research. Federal funding still cannot be used to create new lines of embryonic stem cells under the Dickey-Wicker ban. Federal funding is available only for research involving embryonic stem cells derived from IVF embryos originally created for reproductive purposes. The NIH guidelines provide paths to possible federal funding for research using embryonic stem cells created before or after the development of the federal guidelines, within or outside the United States. Ethical guidelines developed by other groups, such as the National Academies, retain their importance in the wide range of areas outside the ambit of federal funding and oversight, including the creation of the embryonic stem cells lines themselves, the use of embryonic stem cells from embryos created for research purposes (rather than for IVF), the creation of induced pluripotent human stem cells, and the use of human stem cells in various forms of non-federally funded research. President Trump reappointed Francis Collins, a supporter of stem cell research, as head of the National Institutes of Health in June 2017. As of mid-2017, the administration's stem cell research policies remained unchanged. Trump Retains Collins as NIH Director, June 6, 2017, available at: www.sciencemag.org.

Notes: Human Stem Cell Research

1. *Resources on Stem Cell Research.* Stem cell research has attracted an enormous amount of commentary from individuals and specialized, expert committees or groups. For more information about stem cell research and the implications for law and ethics see, e.g., Nefi D. Acosta & Sidney H. Golub, The New Federalism: State Policies Regarding Embryonic Stem Cell Research, 44 J. J. Med. & Ethics 419 (2016); Aileen J. Anderson & Brian J. Cummings, Achieving Informed Consent for Cellular Therapies: A Preclinical Translational Research Perspective on Regulations Versus a Dose of Reality, 44 J. L. Med & Ethics 394 (2016); Symposium, 38 J. L., Med. & Ethics 175-351 (2010); Stem Cell Symposium, 9 Yale J. Health Pol'y L. & Ethics 483-622 (2009); Russell Korobkin, Stem Cell Century: Law and Policy for a Breakthrough Technology (2009) (with contributions from Stephen R. Munzer); and the National Academies and ISSCR Web sites noted above.

2. *The Destruction of Preexisting Embryos Originally Created for Reproductive Purposes.* Many existing stem cell lines were derived from very early embryos, more scientifically known as morulae or blastocysts, originally created as a part of assisted human reproduction but no longer needed for that purpose. The NIH guidelines squarely cover using human embryonic stem cells derived in this fashion for research. The guidelines developed by the National Academies provide overlapping guidance that is more prescriptive in some areas.

Should the "intended parents" of an embryo be required to consent to the use of the embryo even if it was created solely through the use of donor gametes? The answer is "yes" under both the NIH and National Academies guidelines. Should gamete donors be required to consent to the use of the resulting embryo in research? Consent from gamete donors is not specifically required under the NIH guidelines but is required under the National Academies approach. NIH Guidelines for Human Stem Cell Research, 74 Fed. Reg. 32170-02, 32173; National Academies, Guidelines for Human Embryonic Stem Cell Research (2010), supra, at 5 & Appendix C, §3.2, 3.3 (consent requirement met by simple written agreement that embryo research is one possible use of material). See also Ethics Committee of the ASRM, Informed Consent and the Use of Gametes and Embryos for Research: A Committee Opinion, 101 Fertility & Sterility 332 (2014); Ethics Committee of the ASRM, Donating Embryos for Human Embryonic Stem Cell (hESC) Research: A Committee Opinion, 100 Fertility & Sterility 935 (2013).

3. *The Creation of Embryos for Stem Cell Research.* The NIH guidelines do not apply to the creation of embryos for research purposes, and research involving embryonic stem cells derived from embryos created for research purposes is not eligible for federal funding. The NIH guidelines attempt to ensure that individuals who have created embryos for IVF are not paid or otherwise pressured to release the embryos for research. 74 Fed. Reg. 32170-02, 32174. What rules should apply outside the context of federally funded research? See, e.g., Nefi D. Acosta & Sidney H. Golub, The New Federalism, supra; Ethics Committee of the ASRM, Donating Embryos for Human Embryonic Stem Cell (hESC) Research, supra.

Compensation for human cells, blood, and tissues is controversial and sometimes prohibited entirely. See Chapter 6.B and Flynn v. Holder, 684 F.3d 852 (9th Cir. 2012) (holding that federal ban on compensation for bone marrow donations did not apply to blood stem cells obtained through peripheral blood stem cell apheresis). But, as noted, supra, at page 812, gamete donors may be compensated. Oocyte donation is an invasive and potentially risky procedure. Is it unethical to ask women who will receive no direct medical or financial benefit to bear the risks of oocyte donation? See Dieter Egli et al., Letter, Impracticality of Egg Donor Recruitment in the Absence of Compensation, 9 Cell Stem Cell 293 (2011); Debora Spar, The Egg Trade — Making Sense of the Market for Human Oocytes, 356 New Eng. J. Med. 1289 (2007) (noting inconsistency in permitting payment to oocyte donors for reproduction but not for research). In 2009, the board, charged with administering state funds for stem cell research in New York, authorized payments to women donating oocytes for research that were comparable to the sums available to oocyte donors in assisted reproduction. Pamela Foohey, Paying Women for Their Eggs for Use in Stem Cell Research, 30 Pace L. Rev. 900 (2010). The National Academies' 2010 guidelines continued to prohibit direct payment to oocyte donors, while noting that "states and other entities may choose to set their own policies." National Academies, Guidelines for Human Embryonic Stem Cell Research (2010), supra, at 5.

4. *Regulating the Creation of Induced Pluripotent Human Stem Cells.* The NIH Human Stem Cell Guidelines note that the ordinary rules governing research on human subjects, including informed consent, privacy protection, and Institutional Review Board oversight, might apply to research involving human adult stem cells or induced pluripotent stem cells. 74 Fed. Reg. 32174, see also Chapter 3.D. The

NIH Human Stem Cell Guidelines do not focus on the specific informed consent provisions that should be used for donors of somatic cells that might be used to create human pluripotent stem cells. The National Academies' Guidelines suggest that the informed consent requirements should be the same as those used for donors in embryonic stem cell research. National Academies, Guidelines for Human Embryonic Stem Cell Research (2010), supra, at Appendix C, §3.6. For a sample consent, see Stanford University, Stanford Consent Form Template for Somatic Cell Donation for Stem Cell Research, available on the casebook Web site.

5. *Oversight vs. Regulation and the Creation of Chimeras.* Stem cell research could involve mixing human and animal cells, tissues, or genetic materials in new ways. This type of research often is described as the creation of human-animal hybrids or modern-day "chimeras," drawing on ancient Greek myths about monsters with attributes of humans and other animals. Federal regulation of stem cell research has been indirect rather than direct, using the incentive of federal funding to induce researchers toward some types of research and away from others and relying on the existing framework of human subjects research protection as a general safety net. Thus the federal regulations tie funding to certain informed consent requirements and prohibit federal funding of certain types of research, such as the introduction of human embryonic stem cells or induced pluripotent human stem cells into non-human primate blastocysts or "[r]esearch involving the breeding of animals . . . where the human stem cells might contribute" genetic material to the animal's offspring. 74 Fed. Reg. 32170-02, 32174. The National Academies' Guidelines include both procedural protections, such as the creation of institutional Embryonic Stem Cell Research Oversight Committees to review certain types of research, and outright prohibitions of certain forms of research, such as research that could introduce human neural tissue into animals or that could transmit human genes through breeding. National Academies, Guidelines for Human Embryonic Stem Cell Research (2010), supra, at Appendix C, §§1.3(b), 1.3(c), 6; see also, ISSCR, Guidelines for Stem Cell Research, supra (2.1.3.3. Prohibited Research Activities). These guidelines are voluntary. Should federal or state governments simply prohibit these types of research? See Ariz. Rev. Stat. Ann. §36-2311-2312; and Kerry Lunn Macintosh, Chimeras, Hybrids, and Cybrids: How Essentialism Distorts the Law and Stymies Scientific Research, 47 Ariz. St. L. J. 183 (2015).

There is a broad spectrum of human/non-human animal chimera research and some forms of research have substantial support. One often-discussed possibility involves addressing the persistent shortage of human donor organs with human organs developed in animals. Nicholas Wade, New Prospects for Growing Human Replacement Organs in Animals, N.Y. Times, January 26, 2017; and Sonya Levine & Laura Grabel, The Contribution of Human/Non-human Animal Chimeras to Stem Cell Research, 24 Stem Cell Res. 128 (2017). In 2016, the NIH issued requests for public comment on loosening its moratorium on funding certain forms of human/non-human research; the proposal seemed stalled as of mid-2017. See Jocelyn Kaiser, NIH Moves to Lift Moratorium on Animal-Human Chimera Research, available at: www.sciencemag.org (August 4, 2016).

6. *Stem Cell Therapies, Regulation, and Stem Cell Tourism.* Media accounts of stem cell research almost always include suggestions about the wide range of treatments that may someday be available for patients desperate for cures. The transition from research to practice clearly creates the potential for risks to health and

safety. Stem cell therapies are regulated by the U.S. Food and Drug Administration. See United States v. Regenerative Sciences, LLC, 741 F.3d 1314 (2014) (discussing applicable regulatory structure); and Barbara von Tiberstrom, Revising the Regulation of Stem Cell–Based Therapies: Critical Assessment of Potential Models, 70 Food & Drug L. J. 315 (2015). Some providers have exploited the gap between optimistic news stories and clinically–proven and approved therapies. Gina Kolata, A Cautionary Tale of 'Stem Cell Tourism,' N.Y. Times, June 22, 2016; Hermes Taylor-Weiner & Joshua Graff Zivin, Medicine's Wild West—Unlicensed Stem-Cell Clinics in the United States, 373 N. Eng. J. Med. 985 (2015). In August 2017, in a follow-up to the 21st Century Cures Act signed by President Obama in 2016, the FDA announced a new effort to speed approval of legitimate therapies while moving to reign in potentially dangerous treatments. Sheila Kaplan & Denise Grady, F.D.A. Cracks Down on 'Unscrupulous' Stem Cell Clinics, N.Y. Times, August 28, 2017. California enacted legislation requiring clinics to inform patients if treatments have not been approved by the FDA 2017 California Senate Bill No. 512, California 2017-2018 Regular Session (to be codified Cal. Bus & Prof. Code §684).

7. *Therapeutic Cloning.* Part of the controversy surrounding therapeutic cloning arises from the fact that it involves the creation of embryos that are then destroyed to extract embryonic stem cells. Should the fact that the embryos are cloned create any additional ethical concerns? Is the line between therapeutic and reproductive cloning as clear as Diagram 1 supra, would suggest? The next section will explore the cloning debate in more detail.

3. Human Reproductive Cloning

Scientists reported the first successful reproductive cloning of a mammal early in 1997. Wilmut et al., Viable Offspring Derived from Fetal and Adult Mammalian Cells, 385 Nature 810 (1997). Reproductive cloning essentially involves the creation of a sort of time-delayed nearly identical twin. An ovum's nucleus is replaced by the nucleus of a mature adult cell that contains the core genetic identity of an individual being. The ovum is induced to divide and to produce living offspring that have virtually the same genetic identity as the donor of the original genetic material ("virtually," because cloning does not now involve the transfer of genetic material found outside the nucleus in the mitochondria. See page 827.

This is not the "cloning" of late-night science fiction films—a single cell does not grow in a laboratory and give rise to an adult being with the same memories and abilities as the original being. See Nancy L. Segal, Human Cloning: Insights from Twins and Twin Research, 53 Hastings L. J. 1073 (2002). Neither Hitler nor Gandhi could be absolutely replicated. But the development of mammalian cloning nonetheless raised the significant possibility that people might now be able to pass on their genetic heritage to future generations without engaging in the shuffling and mixing of genes that occurs in sexual reproduction. This could be an important tool for persons who do not have gametes or who cannot reproduce sexually within their relationships. David Orentlicher, Beyond Cloning: Expanding Reproductive Options for Same-Sex Couples, 66 Brook. L. Rev. 651 (2000–2001).

The immediate response to the birth of Dolly, the cloned sheep, was largely negative. President Bill Clinton announced that federal funds would not be used for human reproductive cloning research. The FDA reacted swiftly, asserting jurisdiction over clinical research using cloning technology for human reproduction in 1998. Researchers were warned not to pursue human reproductive cloning without following the FDA's investigational new drug (IND) regulations.

Commentators argued that research into human reproductive cloning should be banned for a number of reasons. Would cloning stifle the normal evolutionary process, which depends on new combinations of genes created through sexual reproduction? Would cloning encourage unduly egocentric reproduction—perhaps the creation of 50 genetic copies of a wealthy real estate developer or writer of health law casebooks? Would cloning encourage reproduction for profit—50 genetic copies of LeBron James or Bill Gates? Perhaps cloning would be used to create genetically identical persons who could provide "spare parts," such as organs or tissue for their creator. See, e.g., Human Cloning Requires a Moratorium, Not a Ban, 386 Nature 1 (1997); Elizabeth Pennisi & Nigel Williams, Will Dolly Send in the Clones?, 275 Science 1415 (1997). If nothing else, negative responses to the possibility of human reproductive cloning have revealed our fears about genetic determinism and our belief that "normal" reproduction represents something different—and better—than selfish egotism.

Scientific and ethical advisory boards weighed in on reproductive cloning in the early 2000s. See, e.g., President's Council on Bioethics, Human Cloning and Human Dignity: An Ethical Inquiry (2002); National Research Council, Scientific and Medical Aspects of Human Reproductive Cloning (2002) (focusing on medical risks that make the procedure unsafe for participants and offspring). These advisory groups uniformly recommended at least a moratorium if not a permanent ban on human cloning for reproduction. The virtual uniformity of views regarding the inadvisability of human cloning reflected the fact that mammalian cloning appeared to be extraordinarily difficult to achieve and to entail significant risks of genetic and other abnormalities. This raises the possibility that the debate may become less one sided if human cloning should ever become less medically risky. When and how would researchers determine the safety of human cloning if the practice is banned? See also The Ethics Committee of the ASRM, Human Somatic Cell Nuclear Transfer and Reproductive Cloning: An Ethics Committee Opinion, 105 Fertility & Sterility e1 (2016) (human reproductive cloning currently unethical due to medical risk and availability of alternative reproduction; noting difficulty of ethical analysis if safety concerns reduced in the future).

Congress considered banning reproductive cloning in the early 2000s but the proposed legislation stalled due to a clash between lawmakers who favored permitting therapeutic cloning and those who believed that therapeutic and reproductive cloning were indistinguishable misuses of human embryos. See, e.g., George J. Annas, Cloning and the U.S. Congress, 346 New Eng. J. Med. 1599 (2002). More than a dozen states have banned human reproductive cloning. Russell A. Spivak, I. Glenn Cohen & Eli Y. Adashi, Germ Line Editing and Congressional Reaction in Context, 30 J. L. & Health 20 (2017). The U.N. General Assembly adopted a nonbinding declaration urging nations to ban reproductive and therapeutic human cloning. United Nations Declaration on Human Cloning.

Notes: Human Reproductive Cloning

1. *Cloning as Procreation?* Reproductive cloning would produce a child who, from a genetic standpoint, would be similar to an identical twin of the genetic progenitor. From one genetic perspective, the child would not be the "child" of anyone, because reproduction involves the mixing of parental genes, not the duplication of those genes. Could you even develop an argument that the U.S. Constitution's protection of procreative liberty includes a right to reproductive cloning? Should the analysis depend on whether the individual is infertile? What about the "dysfertile" e.g., gays and lesbians or single individuals who are unable to reproduce because of social rather than medical reasons? Should the Constitution treat differently someone unable to reproduce using other technologies that turns to cloning as a last resort versus someone who turns to cloning simply because they want a child that shares their complete genotype? See John A. Robertson, Why Human Reproductive Cloning Should Not in All Cases Be Prohibited, 4 N.Y.U. J. Legis. & Pub. Pol'y 35, 39 (2001) (claiming that reproductive cloning should be considered a fundamental right when the couple's gametic infertility creates the desire to employ cloning or when one partner has serious genetic disorders). Should the state be in the position of judging why individuals want to clone? How should we consider potential harm to offspring in the analysis? Does it depend on whether the problem with cloning is that it will cause children to come into existence with deficits versus having a high failure rate of non-births? What about the treatment of a cloned child under state law—to whom would the 2017 UPA assign parental rights?

2. *The Ethics of Cloning.* The President's Bioethics Advisory Council unanimously found that human reproductive cloning is unethical. President's Council Human Cloning Report ch. 5 (2002). The Council viewed human cloning as a particularly risky type of human experimentation in which it is impossible to obtain the consent of the party at the most risk, the cloned child. Unlike other groups, the Council found that "safety is not a temporary ethical concern. It is rather an enduring moral concern that might not be surmountable and should thus preclude work toward the development of cloning techniques to produce children." Id. at 14. The President's Council identified several "specific ethical issues and objections to cloning human children: (1) problems of identity and individuality; (2) concerns regarding manufacture; (3) the prospects of a new eugenics; (4) troubled family relations; and (5) effects on society [through, e.g., permitting dehumanizing practices]." Id. at 18. How would you weigh these ethical objections? How many of them do you think apply to other uses of reproductive technology?

3. *Comparing Regulatory Regimes.* Several countries have enacted comprehensive legislation designed to address assisted reproductive technologies, embryo research, and cloning. Are there any lessons in this legislation for the United States? Canada's Assisted Human Reproduction Act, http://laws.justice.gc.ca/en/A-13.4/, prohibits germ-line engineering, the creation of chimeras, human reproductive cloning, sex selection unless it is being used to treat or prevent a sex-linked disease, and creation of human embryos solely for research, as well as payment of surrogates or payment for gametes. See also Barbara von Tigerstrom, Federal Health Legislation and the Assisted Human Reproduction Act Reference, 74 Sask. L. Rev. 33 (2011) (summarizing impact of Supreme Court of Canada decision on validity of legislation). The United Kingdom has had legislation in place since 1990. The Human Fertilization

and Embryology Act creates the Human Fertilization and Embryology Authority, whose responsibilities include licensing ART clinics, gamete and embryo storage facilities, and licensing and monitoring human embryo research. Human reproductive cloning is prohibited but therapeutic cloning research is permitted. See www.hfea.gov.uk.

4. *Commentaries.* In addition to the sources noted above, see Robert A. Burt, Constitutional Constraints on the Regulation of Cloning, 9 Yale J. Health Pol'y L. & Ethics 495 (2009); Cass R. Sunstein, Is There a Constitutional Right to Clone?, 53 Hastings L. J. 987 (2002). Ronald Chester, Cloning Embryos from Adult Human Beings: The Relative Merits of Reproductive, Research and Therapeutic Uses, 39 New Eng. L. Rev. 583 (2005); Leon R. Kass & James Q. Wilson, The Ethics of Human Cloning (1998).

Problem: Human Cloning

Your client, Chris Jacobs, wants to create a child through cloning. Chris is preparing to go to an unnamed foreign country where experts believe they have perfected the process. The nucleus from some of Chris's cells will be inserted into a donor's eggs, whose nuclei have been removed. The eggs will be stimulated into developing into embryos, which will then be implanted into a gestational surrogate. The surrogate will then relinquish the child to Chris. Chris hopes to be a parent within a year. How would you counsel Chris? Do you have any ethical, professional disciplinary, or malpractice concerns? Assume that Chris brings a child back to this country. How would you go about attempting to establish that Chris is the child's parent? Examine the relevant statutes in your state. Who is the child's parent? See also I. Glenn Cohen, Medical Tourism: The View from 10,000 Feet, 40(2) Hastings Center Rep. 11 (Mar.–Apr. 2010).

4. Intellectual Property and the Ownership of Genetic Discoveries

■ DIAMOND v. CHAKRABARTY
447 U.S. 303 (1980)

Burger, C.J.

We granted certiorari to determine whether a live, human-made micro-organism is patentable subject matter under 35 U.S.C. §101.

In 1972, respondent Chakrabarty, a microbiologist, filed a patent application, assigned to the General Electric Co. The application asserted 36 claims related to Chakrabarty's invention of "a bacterium from the genus Pseudomonas containing therein at least two stable energy-generating plasmids, each of said plasmids providing a separate hydrocarbon degradative pathway." This human-made, genetically engineered bacterium is capable of breaking down multiple components of crude oil. Because of this property, which is possessed by no naturally occurring bacteria, Chakrabarty's invention is believed to have significant value for the treatment of oil spills.

Chakrabarty's patent claims were of three types: first, process claims for the method of producing the bacteria; second, claims for an inoculum comprised of a carrier material floating on water, such as straw, and the new bacteria; and third, claims to the bacteria themselves. The patent examiner allowed the claims falling into the first two categories, but rejected claims for the bacteria. His decision rested on two grounds: (1) that micro-organisms are "products of nature," and (2) that as living things they are not patentable subject matter. . . . [T]he Patent Office Board of Appeals . . . affirmed the Examiner on the second ground. Relying on the legislative history of the 1930 Plant Patent Act, in which Congress extended patent protection to certain asexually reproduced plants, the Board concluded that §101 was not intended to cover living things such as these laboratory created micro-organisms. . . .

[The case went through a circuitous appeal process finally resulting in a decision by Court of Customs and Patent Appeals reversing the patent examiner and Board of Appeals.] The Commissioner of Patents and Trademarks . . . sought certiorari, and we granted the writ. . . .

II

The Constitution grants Congress broad power to legislate to "promote the Progress of Science and useful Arts, by securing for limited Times to Authors and Inventors the exclusive Right to their respective Writings and Discoveries." Art. I, §8, cl. 8. The patent laws promote this progress by offering inventors exclusive rights for a limited period as an incentive for their inventiveness and research efforts. . . . The authority of Congress is exercised in the hope that "[t]he productive effort thereby fostered will have a positive effect on society through the introduction of new products and processes of manufacture into the economy, and the emanations by way of increased employment and better lives for our citizens." [Kewanee Oil Co. v. Bicron Corp., 416 U.S. 470, 480 (1974).]

The question before us in this case is a narrow one of statutory interpretation requiring us to construe 35 U.S.C. §101, which provides: "Whoever invents or discovers any new and useful process, machine, manufacture, or composition of matter, or any new and useful improvement thereof, may obtain a patent therefore, subject to the conditions and requirements of this title." [] Specifically, we must determine whether respondent's micro-organism constitutes a "manufacture" or "composition of matter" within the meaning of the statute.[6] . . .

III

. . . Guided by [] canons of construction, this Court has read the term "manufacture" in §101 in accordance with its dictionary definition to mean "the production of articles for use from raw or prepared materials by giving to these materials new forms, qualities, properties, or combinations, whether by hand-labor or by machinery." American Fruit Growers, Inc. v. Brogdex Co., 283 U.S. 1 (1931). . . . In choosing such expansive terms as "manufacture" and "composition of matter," modified by the comprehensive "any," Congress plainly contemplated that the patent laws would be given wide scope.

---

6. This case does not involve the other "conditions and requirements" of the patent laws, such as novelty and nonobviousness. 35 U.S.C. §101, 103.

The relevant legislative history also supports a broad construction. The Patent Act of 1793, authored by Thomas Jefferson, defined statutory subject matter as "any new and useful art, machine, manufacture, or composition of matter, or any new or useful improvement [thereof]." The Act embodied Jefferson's philosophy that "ingenuity should receive a liberal encouragement." . . . In 1952, when the patent laws were recodified, Congress replaced the word "art" with "process," but otherwise left Jefferson's language intact. The Committee Reports accompanying the 1952 Act inform us that Congress intended statutory subject matter to "include anything under the sun that is made by man."

This is not to suggest that §101 has no limits or that it embraces every discovery. The laws of nature, physical phenomena, and abstract ideas have been held not patentable. . . . Thus, a new mineral discovered in the earth or a new plant found in the wild is not patentable subject matter. Likewise, Einstein could not patent his celebrated law that $E = mc^2$; nor could Newton have patented the law of gravity. Such discoveries are "manifestations of . . . nature, free to all men and reserved exclusively to none."

Judged in this light, respondent's micro-organism plainly qualifies as patentable subject matter. His claim is not to a hitherto unknown natural phenomenon, but to a nonnaturally occurring manufacture or composition of matter—a product of human ingenuity "having a distinctive name, character [and] use." The point is underscored dramatically by comparison of the invention here with that in [Funk Brothers Seed Co. v. Kalo Inoculant Co, 333 U.S. 127, 130 (1948)]. There, the patentee had discovered that there existed in nature certain species of root-nodule bacteria which did not exert a mutually inhibitive effect on each other. He used that discovery to produce a mixed culture capable of inoculating the seeds of leguminous plants. Concluding that the patentee had discovered "only some of the handiwork of nature," the Court ruled the product nonpatentable:

> Each of the species of root-nodule bacteria contained in the package infects the same group of leguminous plants which it always infected. No species acquires a different use. The combination of species produces no new bacteria, no change in the six species of bacteria, and no enlargement of the range of their utility. Each species has the same effect it always had. The bacteria perform in their natural way. Their use in combination does not improve in any way their natural functioning. They serve the ends nature originally provided and act quite independently of any effort of the patentee.

Here, by contrast, the patentee has produced a new bacterium with markedly different characteristics from any found in nature and one having the potential for significant utility. His discovery is not nature's handiwork, but his own; accordingly it is patentable subject matter under §101.

IV

Two contrary arguments are advanced, neither of which we find persuasive. [The Court discussed arguments that congressional enactment of the] . . . 1930 Plant Patent Act, which afforded patent protection to certain asexually reproduced plants, and the 1970 Plant Variety Protection Act, which authorized protection for certain sexually reproduced plants but excluded bacteria from its protection . . .

[indicated] congressional understanding that the terms "manufacture" or "composition of matter" do not include living things; if they did, the petitioner argues, neither Act would have been necessary.... [The Court rejected these claims, noting that] Congress ... explained at length its belief that the work of the plant breeder "in aid of nature" was patentable invention....

Congress thus recognized that the relevant distinction was not between living and inanimate things, but between products of nature, whether living or not, and human-made inventions. Here, respondent's micro-organism is the result of human ingenuity and research. Hence, the passage of the Plant Patent Act affords the Government no support....

In particular, we find nothing in the exclusion of bacteria from plant variety protection to support the petitioner's position.... The legislative history gives no reason for this exclusion. As the Court of Customs and Patent Appeals suggested, it may simply reflect congressional agreement with [that court's previous holding that "bacteria were not plants for the purposes of the 1930 Act"].... Or it may reflect the fact that prior to 1970 the Patent Office had issued patents for bacteria under §101.[9]...

The petitioner's second argument is that ... genetic technology was unforeseen when Congress enacted §101. From this it is argued that resolution of the patentability of inventions such as respondent's should be left to Congress. The legislative process, the petitioner argues, is best equipped to weigh the competing economic, social, and scientific considerations involved, and to determine whether living organisms produced by genetic engineering should receive patent protection.... The subject-matter provisions of the patent law have been cast in broad terms to fulfill the constitutional and statutory goal of promoting "the Progress of Science and the useful Arts" with all that means for the social and economic benefits envisioned by Jefferson. Broad general language is not necessarily ambiguous when congressional objectives require broad terms.... Congress employed broad general language in drafting §101 precisely because such inventions are often unforeseeable.[10]

To buttress his argument, the petitioner, with the support of amicus, points to grave risks that may be generated by research endeavors such as respondent's. The briefs present a gruesome parade of horribles. Scientists, among them Nobel laureates, are quoted suggesting that genetic research may pose a serious threat to the human race, or, at the very least, that the dangers are far too substantial to permit such research to proceed apace at this time. We are told that genetic research and related technological developments may spread pollution and disease, that it may result in a loss of genetic diversity, and that its practice may tend to depreciate the

9. In 1873, the Patent Office granted Louis Pasteur a patent on "yeast, free from organic germs of disease, as an article of manufacture." And in 1967 and 1968, immediately prior to the passage of the Plant Variety Protection Act, that Office granted two patents which, as the petitioner concedes, state claims for living micro-organisms.

10. Even an abbreviated list of patented inventions underscores the point: telegraph (Morse, No. 1,647); telephone (Bell, No. 174,465); electric lamp (Edison, No. 223,898); airplane (the Wrights, No. 821,393); transistor (Bardeen & Brattain, No. 2,524,035); neutronic reactor (Fermi & Szilard, No. 2,708,656); laser (Schawlow & Townes, No. 2,929,922). See generally Revolutionary Ideas, Patents & Progress in America, United States Patent and Trademark Office (1976).

value of human life. These arguments are forcefully, even passionately, presented; they remind us that, at times, human ingenuity seems unable to control fully the forces it creates—that with Hamlet, it is sometimes better "to bear those ills we have than fly to others that we know not of."

It is argued that this Court should weigh these potential hazards in considering whether respondent's invention is patentable subject matter under §101. We disagree. The grant or denial of patents on micro-organisms is not likely to put an end to genetic research or to its attendant risks. The large amount of research that has already occurred when no researcher had sure knowledge that patent protection would be available suggests that legislative or judicial fiat as to patentability will not deter the scientific mind from probing into the unknown any more than Canute could command the tides. Whether respondent's claims are patentable may determine whether research efforts are accelerated by the hope of reward or slowed by want of incentives, but that is all.

What is more important is that we are without competence to entertain these arguments—either to brush them aside as fantasies generated by fear of the unknown, or to act on them. The choice we are urged to make is a matter of high policy for resolution within the legislative process after the kind of investigation, examination, and study that legislative bodies can provide and courts cannot. That process involves the balancing of competing values and interests, which in our democratic system is the business of elected representatives. . . .

Congress is free to amend §101 so as to exclude from patent protection organisms produced by genetic engineering. . . . Or it may choose to craft a statute specifically designed for such living things. But, until Congress takes such action, this Court must construe the language of §101 as it is. The language of that section fairly embraces respondent's invention. Accordingly, the judgment of the Court of Customs and Patent Appeals is *affirmed.*

BRENNAN, J., dissenting [joined by Justices White, Marshall, and Powell].

I agree with the Court that the question before us is a narrow one. Neither the future of scientific research, nor even, the ability of respondent Chakrabarty to reap some monopoly profits from his pioneering work, is at stake. Patents on the processes by which he has produced and employed the new living organism are not contested. The only question we need decide is whether Congress, exercising its authority under Art. I, §8, of the Constitution, intended that he be able to secure a monopoly on the living organism itself, no matter how produced or how used. Because I believe the Court has misread the applicable legislation, I dissent.

The patent laws attempt to reconcile this Nation's deep seated antipathy to monopolies with the need to encourage progress. . . . Given the complexity and legislative nature of this delicate task, we must be careful to extend patent protection no further than Congress has provided. . . . [W]e are not dealing—as the Court would have it—with the routine problem of "unanticipated inventions." . . . In [the two Plant Acts] . . . Congress has addressed the general problem of patenting animate inventions and has chosen carefully limited language granting protection to some kinds of discoveries, but specifically excluding others. . . .

Because Congress thought it had to legislate in order to make agricultural "human-made inventions" patentable and because the legislation Congress enacted is limited, it follows that Congress never meant to make items outside the scope of the legislation patentable.

Second, the 1970 Act clearly indicates that Congress has included bacteria within the focus of its legislative concern, but not within the scope of patent protection. Congress specifically excluded bacteria from the coverage of the 1970 Act. The Court's attempts to supply explanations for this explicit exclusion ring hollow. . . . It is the role of Congress, not this Court, to broaden or narrow the reach of the patent laws. This is especially true where, as here, the composition sought to be patented uniquely implicates matters of public concern.

■ MAYO COLLABORATIVE SERVICES v. PROMETHEUS LABORATORIES, INC.
566 U.S. 66 (2012)

BREYER, J.

Section 101 of the Patent Act [35 U.S.C. §101] defines patentable subject matter. It says:

> Whoever invents or discovers any new and useful process, machine, manufacture, or composition of matter, or any new and useful improvement thereof, may obtain a patent therefor, subject to the conditions and requirements of this title.

The Court has long held that this provision contains an important implicit exception. "[L]aws of nature, natural phenomena, and abstract ideas" are not patentable. Thus, the Court has written that "a new mineral discovered in the earth or a new plant found in the wild is not patentable subject matter. Likewise, Einstein could not patent his celebrated law that $E = mc^2$; nor could Newton have patented the law of gravity. Such discoveries are 'manifestations of . . . nature, free to all men and reserved exclusively to none.'" Chakrabarty, 447 U.S. 303, 309 (quoting Funk Brothers Seed Co. v. Kalo Inoculant Co., 333 U.S. 127, 130 (1948)).

"Phenomena of nature, though just discovered, mental processes, and abstract intellectual concepts are not patentable, as they are the basic tools of scientific and technological work." Gottschalk v. Benson, 409 U.S. 63, 67(1972). And monopolization of those tools through the grant of a patent might tend to impede innovation more than it would tend to promote it.

The Court has recognized, however, that too broad an interpretation of this exclusionary principle could eviscerate patent law. For all inventions at some level embody, use, reflect, rest upon, or apply laws of nature, natural phenomena, or abstract ideas. Thus, in [Diamond v. Diehr] the Court pointed out that " 'a process is not unpatentable simply because it contains a law of nature or a mathematical algorithm.'" 450 U.S. 175, 187. It added that "an application of a law of nature or mathematical formula to a known structure or process may well be deserving of patent protection." Diehr, supra, at 187. And it emphasized . . . " 'While a scientific truth, or the mathematical expression of it, is not a patentable invention, a novel and useful structure created with the aid of knowledge of scientific truth may be.'" 450 U.S. at 188 (quoting [Mackay Radio & Telegraph Co. v. Radio Corp. of America], 450 U.S. 86, 188 (1939)). See also Funk Brothers, supra, at 130 ("If there is to be invention from [a discovery of a law of nature], it must come from the application of the law of nature to a new and useful end").

Still, as the Court has also made clear, to transform an unpatentable law of nature into a patent-eligible application of such a law, one must do more than simply state the law of nature while adding the words "apply it."

The case before us lies at the intersection of these basic principles. It concerns patent claims covering processes that help doctors who use thiopurine drugs to treat patients with autoimmune diseases determine whether a given dosage level is too low or too high. The claims purport to apply natural laws describing the relationships between the concentration in the blood of certain thiopurine metabolites and the likelihood that the drug dosage will be ineffective or induce harmful side-effects. We must determine whether the claimed processes have transformed these unpatentable natural laws into patent-eligible applications of those laws. We conclude that they have not done so and that therefore the processes are not patentable.

Our conclusion rests upon an examination of the particular claims before us in light of the Court's precedents. Those cases warn us against interpreting patent statutes in ways that make patent eligibility "depend simply on the draftsman's art" without reference to the "principles underlying the prohibition against patents for [natural laws]." [Parker v. Flook, 437 U.S. 584, 593 (1978).] They warn us against upholding patents that claim processes that too broadly preempt the use of a natural law. And they insist that a process that focuses upon the use of a natural law also contain other elements or a combination of elements, sometimes referred to as an "inventive concept," sufficient to ensure that the patent in practice amounts to significantly more than a patent upon the natural law itself.

We find that the process claims at issue here do not satisfy these conditions. In particular, the steps in the claimed processes (apart from the natural laws themselves) involve well-understood, routine, conventional activity previously engaged in by researchers in the field. At the same time, upholding the patents would risk disproportionately tying up the use of the underlying natural laws, inhibiting their use in the making of further discoveries.

I

A

The patents before us concern the use of thiopurine drugs in the treatment of autoimmune diseases, such as Crohn's disease and ulcerative colitis. When a patient ingests a thiopurine compound, his body metabolizes the drug, causing metabolites to form in his bloodstream. Because the way in which people metabolize thiopurine compounds varies, the same dose of a thiopurine drug affects different people differently, and it has been difficult for doctors to determine whether for a particular patient a given dose is too high, risking harmful side effects, or too low, and so likely ineffective.

At the time the discoveries embodied in the patents were made, scientists already understood that the levels in a patient's blood of certain metabolites, including, in particular, 6-thioguanine and its nucleotides (6-TG) and 6-methyl-mercaptopurine (6-MMP), were correlated with the likelihood that a particular dosage of a thiopurine drug could cause harm or prove ineffective. But those in the field did not know the precise correlations between metabolite levels and likely harm or ineffectiveness. The patent claims at issue here set forth processes embodying researchers' findings that identified these correlations with some precision.

More specifically, the patents—U.S. Patent No. 6,355,623 ('623 patent) and U.S. Patent No. 6,680,302 ('302 patent)—embody findings that concentrations in a patient's blood of 6-TG or of 6-MMP metabolite beyond a certain level (400 and 7000 picomoles per 8 x 10^8 red blood cells, respectively) indicate that the dosage is likely too high for the patient, while concentrations in the blood of 6-TG metabolite lower than a certain level (about 230 picomoles per 8 x 10^8 red blood cells) indicate that the dosage is likely too low to be effective.

The patent claims seek to embody this research in a set of processes. Like the Federal Circuit we take as typical claim 1 of the '623 Patent, which describes one of the claimed processes as follows:

> A method of optimizing therapeutic efficacy for treatment of an immune-mediated gastrointestinal disorder, comprising:
>
> (a) administering a drug providing 6-thioguanine to a subject having said immune-mediated gastrointestinal disorder; and
>
> (b) determining the level of 6-thioguanine in said subject having said immune-mediated gastrointestinal disorder,
>
> wherein the level of 6-thioguanine less than about 230 pmol per 8 x 10^8 red blood cells indicates a need to increase the amount of said drug subsequently administered to said subject and
>
> wherein the level of 6-thioguanine greater than about 400 pmol per 8 x 10^8 red blood cells indicates a need to decrease the amount of said drug subsequently administered to said subject. '623 patent, col.20, ll.10-20, 2 App. 16.

For present purposes we may assume that the other claims in the patents do not differ significantly from claim 1.

B

Respondent, Prometheus Laboratories, Inc. (Prometheus), is the sole and exclusive licensee of the '623 and '302 patents. It sells diagnostic tests that embody the processes the patents describe. For some time petitioners, Mayo Clinic Rochester and Mayo Collaborative Services (collectively Mayo), bought and used those tests. But in 2004 Mayo announced that it intended to begin using and selling its own test—a test using somewhat higher metabolite levels to determine toxicity (450 pmol per 8 x 10^8 for 6-TG and 5700 pmol per 8 x 10^8 for 6-MMP). Prometheus then brought this action claiming patent infringement.

The District Court found that Mayo's test infringed [various aspects of the claimed patent]. . . . Nonetheless the District Court ultimately granted summary judgment in Mayo's favor. The court reasoned that the patents effectively claim natural laws or natural phenomena—namely the correlations between thiopurine metabolite levels and the toxicity and efficacy of thiopurine drug dosages—and so are not patentable.

On appeal, the Federal Circuit reversed. It pointed out that in addition to these natural correlations, the claimed processes specify the steps of (1) "administering a [thiopurine] drug" to a patient and (2) "determining the [resulting metabolite] level." These steps, it explained, involve the transformation of the human body or of blood taken from the body. Thus, the patents satisfied the Circuit's "machine or transformation test," which the court thought sufficient to "confine the patent monopoly within rather definite bounds," thereby bringing the claims into compliance with §101. 581 F.3d 1336, 1345, 1346-1347 (2009) (internal quotation marks omitted).

Mayo filed a petition for certiorari. We granted the petition, vacated the judgment, and remanded the case for reconsideration in light of Bilski, 130 S. Ct. 3218, which clarified that the "machine or transformation test" is not a definitive test of patent eligibility, but only an important and useful clue. 130 S. Ct., at 3234-3235. On remand the Federal Circuit reaffirmed its earlier conclusion. It thought that the "machine-or-transformation test," understood merely as an important and useful clue, nonetheless led to the "clear and compelling conclusion . . . that the . . . claims . . . do not encompass laws of nature or preempt natural correlations." 628 F.3d 1347, 1355 (2010). Mayo again filed a petition for certiorari, which we granted.

II

Prometheus' patents set forth laws of nature—namely, relationships between concentrations of certain metabolites in the blood and the likelihood that a dosage of a thiopurine drug will prove ineffective or cause harm. Claim 1, for example, states that if the levels of 6-TG in the blood (of a patient who has taken a dose of a thiopurine drug) exceed about 400 pmol per 8×10^8 red blood cells, then the administered dose is likely to produce toxic side effects. While it takes a human action (the administration of a thiopurine drug) to trigger a manifestation of this relation in a particular person, the relation itself exists in principle apart from any human action. The relation is a consequence of the ways in which thiopurine compounds are metabolized by the body—entirely natural processes. And so a patent that simply describes that relation sets forth a natural law.

The question before us is whether the claims do significantly more than simply describe these natural relations. To put the matter more precisely, do the patent claims add enough to their statements of the correlations to allow the processes they describe to qualify as patent-eligible processes that apply natural laws? We believe that the answer to this question is no.

A

If a law of nature is not patentable, then neither is a process reciting a law of nature, unless that process has additional features that provide practical assurance that the process is more than a drafting effort designed to monopolize the law of nature itself. A patent, for example, could not simply recite a law of nature and then add the instruction "apply the law." Einstein, we assume, could not have patented his famous law by claiming a process consisting of simply telling linear accelerator operators to refer to the law to determine how much energy an amount of mass has produced (or vice versa). Nor could Archimedes have secured a patent for his famous principle of flotation by claiming a process consisting of simply telling boat builders to refer to that principle in order to determine whether an object will float.

What else is there in the claims before us? The process that each claim recites tells doctors interested in the subject about the correlations that the researchers discovered. In doing so, it recites an "administering" step, a "determining" step, and a "wherein" step. These additional steps are not themselves natural laws but neither are they sufficient to transform the nature of the claim.

First, the "administering" step simply refers to the relevant audience, namely doctors who treat patients with certain diseases with thiopurine drugs. That audience is a pre-existing audience; doctors used thiopurine drugs to treat patients suffering from autoimmune disorders long before anyone asserted these claims. In any event, the "prohibition against patenting abstract ideas 'cannot be circumvented by attempting to limit the use of the formula to a particular technological environment.'" Bilski, supra, 130 S. Ct., at 3230 (quoting Diehr, 450 U.S., at 191-192).

Second, the "wherein" clauses simply tell a doctor about the relevant natural laws, at most adding a suggestion that he should take those laws into account when treating his patient. That is to say, these clauses tell the relevant audience about the laws while trusting them to use those laws appropriately where they are relevant to their decisionmaking (rather like Einstein telling linear accelerator operators about his basic law and then trusting them to use it where relevant).

Third, the "determining" step tells the doctor to determine the level of the relevant metabolites in the blood, through whatever process the doctor or the laboratory wishes to use. As the patents state, methods for determining metabolite levels were well known in the art. Indeed, scientists routinely measured metabolites as part of their investigations into the relationships between metabolite levels and efficacy and toxicity of thiopurine compounds. Thus, this step tells doctors to engage in well-understood, routine, conventional activity previously engaged in by scientists who work in the field. Purely "conventional or obvious" "[pre]-solution activity" is normally not sufficient to transform an unpatentable law of nature into a patent-eligible application of such a law. Flook, 437 U.S., at 590.

Fourth, to consider the three steps as an ordered combination adds nothing to the laws of nature that is not already present when the steps are considered separately. . . . Anyone who wants to make use of these laws must first administer a thiopurine drug and measure the resulting metabolite concentrations, and so the combination amounts to nothing significantly more than an instruction to doctors to apply the applicable laws when treating their patients.

The upshot is that the three steps simply tell doctors to gather data from which they may draw an inference in light of the correlations. To put the matter more succinctly, the claims inform a relevant audience about certain laws of nature; any additional steps consist of well-understood, routine, conventional activity already engaged in by the scientific community; and those steps, when viewed as a whole, add nothing significant beyond the sum of their parts taken separately. For these reasons we believe that the steps are not sufficient to transform unpatentable natural correlations into patentable applications of those regularities. . . .

3

The Court has repeatedly emphasized . . . a concern that patent law not inhibit further discovery by improperly tying up the future use of laws of nature. Thus, in *Morse* the Court set aside as unpatentable Samuel Morse's general claim for " 'the use of the motive power of the electric or galvanic current . . . however developed, for making or printing intelligible characters, letters, or signs, at any distances,'" [O'Reilly v. Morse, 15 How. 62, 86 (1854).] The Court explained:

For aught that we now know some future inventor, in the onward march of science, may discover a mode of writing or printing at a distance by means of the electric or galvanic current, without using any part of the process or combination set forth in the plaintiff's specification. His invention may be less complicated—less liable to get out of order—less expensive in construction, and in its operation. But yet if it is covered by this patent the inventor could not use it, nor the public have the benefit of it without the permission of this patentee.

These statements reflect the fact that, even though rewarding with patents those who discover new laws of nature and the like might well encourage their discovery, those laws and principles, considered generally, are "the basic tools of scientific and technological work." Benson, supra, at 67. And so there is a danger that the grant of patents that tie up their use will inhibit future innovation premised upon them, a danger that becomes acute when a patented process amounts to no more than an instruction to "apply the natural law," or otherwise forecloses more future invention than the underlying discovery could reasonably justify. See generally W. Landes & R. Posner, The Economic Structure of Intellectual Property Law 305-306 (2003) (The exclusion from patent law of basic truths reflects "both . . . the enormous potential for rent seeking that would be created if property rights could be obtained in them and . . . the enormous transaction costs that would be imposed on would-be users [of those truths]").

The laws of nature at issue here are narrow laws that may have limited applications, but the patent claims that embody them nonetheless implicate this concern. They tell a treating doctor to measure metabolite levels and to consider the resulting measurements in light of the statistical relationships they describe. In doing so, they tie up the doctor's subsequent treatment decision whether that treatment does, or does not, change in light of the inference he has drawn using the correlations. And they threaten to inhibit the development of more refined treatment recommendations (like that embodied in Mayo's test), that combine Prometheus' correlations with later discovered features of metabolites, human physiology or individual patient characteristics. The "determining" step too is set forth in highly general language covering all processes that make use of the correlations after measuring metabolites, including later discovered processes that measure metabolite levels in new ways.

We need not, and do not, now decide whether were the steps at issue here less conventional, these features of the claims would prove sufficient to invalidate them. For here, as we have said, the steps add nothing of significance to the natural laws themselves. Unlike, say, a typical patent on a new drug or a new way of using an existing drug, the patent claims do not confine their reach to particular applications of those laws. The presence here of the basic underlying concern that these patents tie up too much future use of laws of nature simply reinforces our conclusion that the processes described in the patents are not patent eligible, while eliminating any temptation to depart from case law precedent.

III

We have considered several further arguments in support of Prometheus' position. But they do not lead us to adopt a different conclusion. First, the Federal Circuit, in upholding the patent eligibility of the claims before us, relied on this

Court's determination that "[t]ransformation and reduction of an article 'to a different state or thing' is the clue to the patentability of a process claim that does not include particular machines." Benson, supra, 93 S. Ct. 253. It reasoned that the claimed processes are therefore patent eligible, since they involve transforming the human body by administering a thiopurine drug and transforming the blood by analyzing it to determine metabolite levels. 628 F.3d, at 1356-1357.

The first of these transformations, however, is irrelevant. As we have pointed out, the "administering" step simply helps to pick out the group of individuals who are likely interested in applying the law of nature. And the second step could be satisfied without transforming the blood, should science develop a totally different system for determining metabolite levels that did not involve such a transformation. Regardless, in stating that the "machine-or-transformation" test is an "important and useful clue " to patentability, we have neither said nor implied that the test trumps the "law of nature" exclusion. Bilski, supra, 130 S. Ct., at 3225-3227 (emphasis added). That being so, the test fails here.

Second, Prometheus argues that, because the particular laws of nature that its patent claims embody are narrow and specific, the patents should be upheld. Thus, it encourages us to draw distinctions among laws of nature based on whether or not they will interfere significantly with innovation in other fields now or in the future.

But the underlying functional concern here is a relative one: how much future innovation is foreclosed relative to the contribution of the inventor. A patent upon a narrow law of nature may not inhibit future research as seriously as would a patent upon Einstein's law of relativity, but the creative value of the discovery is also considerably smaller. And, as we have previously pointed out, even a narrow law of nature (such as the one before us) can inhibit future research.

In any event, our cases have not distinguished among different laws of nature according to whether or not the principles they embody are sufficiently narrow. And this is understandable. Courts and judges are not institutionally well suited to making the kinds of judgments needed to distinguish among different laws of nature. And so the cases have endorsed a bright-line prohibition against patenting laws of nature, mathematical formulas and the like, which serves as a somewhat more easily administered proxy for the underlying "building-block" concern.

Third, the Government argues that . . . other statutory provisions—those that insist that a claimed process be novel, 35 U.S.C. §102, that it not be "obvious in light of prior art," §103, and that it be "full[y], clear[ly], concise[ly], and exact[ly]" described, §112—can [address any concerns]. . . . In particular, it argues that these claims likely fail for lack of novelty under §102. . . . [The government's] approach, however, would make the "law of nature" exception to §101 patentability a dead letter. . . .

Fourth, Prometheus, supported by several amici, argues that a principle of law denying patent coverage here will interfere significantly with the ability of medical researchers to make valuable discoveries, particularly in the area of diagnostic research. That research, which includes research leading to the discovery of laws of nature, is expensive; it "ha[s] made the United States the world leader in this field"; and it requires protection. Brief for Respondent 52.

Other medical experts, however, argue strongly against a legal rule that would make the present claims patent eligible, invoking policy considerations that point in the opposite direction. The American Medical Association, the American College of Medical Genetics, the American Hospital Association, the American Society of Human Genetics, the Association of American Medical Colleges, the Association for Molecular Pathology, and other medical organizations tell us that if "claims to exclusive rights over the body's natural responses to illness and medical treatment are permitted to stand, the result will be a vast thicket of exclusive rights over the use of critical scientific data that must remain widely available if physicians are to provide sound medical care." Brief for American College of Medical Genetics et al. as Amici Curiae 7; see also App. to Brief for Association Internationale pour la Protection de la Propriete Intellectuelle et al. as Amici Curiae A6, A16 (methods of medical treatment are not patentable in most of Western Europe).

We do not find this kind of difference of opinion surprising. Patent protection is, after all, a two-edged sword. On the one hand, the promise of exclusive rights provides monetary incentives that lead to creation, invention, and discovery. On the other hand, that very exclusivity can impede the flow of information that might permit, indeed spur, invention, by, for example, raising the price of using the patented ideas once created, requiring potential users to conduct costly and time-consuming searches of existing patents and pending patent applications, and requiring the negotiation of complex licensing arrangements. At the same time, patent law's general rules must govern inventive activity in many different fields of human endeavor, with the result that the practical effects of rules that reflect a general effort to balance these considerations may differ from one field to another.

In consequence, we must hesitate before departing from established general legal rules lest a new protective rule that seems to suit the needs of one field produce unforeseen results in another. And we must recognize the role of Congress in crafting more finely tailored rules where necessary. Cf. 35 U.S.C. §§161-164 (special rules for plant patents). We need not determine here whether, from a policy perspective, increased protection for discoveries of diagnostic laws of nature is desirable. . . .

For these reasons, we conclude that the patent claims at issue here effectively claim the underlying laws of nature themselves. The claims are consequently invalid. And the Federal Circuit's judgment is reversed.

◼ HARVARD COLLEGE v. CANADA (COMMISSIONER OF PATENTS)
2002 SCC 76, 219 D.L.R. (4th) 577 (Supreme Court of Canada 2002)

BASTARACHE, J. . . .

This appeal raises the issue of the patentability of higher life forms within the context of the Patent Act, R.S.C. 1985, C. P-4. The respondent, the President and Fellows of Harvard College, seeks to patent a mouse that has been genetically altered to increase its susceptibility to cancer, which makes it useful for cancer research. The patent claims also extend to all non-human mammals which have been similarly altered. . . .

The Commissioner of Patents upheld the Patent Examiner's refusal to grant the patent. This decision was in turn upheld by the Federal Court Trial Division, but was overturned by a majority of the Federal Court of Appeal. . . . To refuse a patent, the Commissioner must be satisfied that the applicant is not "by law" entitled to the patent, wording which indicates that the Commissioner has no discretion independent of the Patent Act to consider the public interest when granting or denying a patent. . . . [Therefore], the sole question is whether Parliament intended the definition of invention, and more particularly the words "manufacture" or "composition of matter", within the context of the Patent Act,[7] to encompass higher life forms such as the oncomouse [so-called in reference to "oncology" or cancer].

II. FACTUAL BACKGROUND. . . .

On June 21, 1985, the respondent, the President and Fellows of Harvard College ("Harvard"), applied for a patent on an invention entitled "transgenic animals". The invention aims to produce animals with a susceptibility to cancer for purposes of animal carcinogenic studies. The animals can be used to test a material suspected of being a carcinogen by exposing them to the material and seeing if tumours develop. Because the animals are already susceptible to tumour development, . . . the animals will be expected to develop tumours in a shorter time period. The animals can also be used to test materials thought to confer protection against the development of cancer. . . .

The technology by which a cancer-prone mouse ("oncomouse") is produced is described in the patent application disclosure. The oncogene (the cancer-promoting gene) is obtained from the genetic code of a non-mammal source, such as a virus. A vehicle for transporting the oncogene into the mouse's chromosomes is constructed using a small piece of bacterial DNA referred to as a plasmid. The plasmid, into which the oncogene has been "spliced", is injected into fertilized mouse eggs, preferably while they are at the one-cell stage. The eggs are then implanted into a female host mouse, or "foster mother", and permitted to develop to term. . . . those [offspring] that contain the oncogene are called "founder" mice. . . .

In its patent application, the respondent seeks to protect both the process by which the oncomice are produced and the end product of the process, i.e. the founder mice and the offspring whose cells are affected by the oncogene. The process and product claims also extend to all non-human mammals. . . .

V. ANALYSIS . . .

The sole question in this appeal is whether the words "manufacture" and "composition of matter", in the context of the Patent Act [see note 7 above], are sufficiently broad to include higher life forms. If these words are not sufficiently broad to include higher life forms, it is irrelevant whether this Court believes that higher life forms such as the oncomouse ought to be patentable. . . .

Having considered the relevant factors, I conclude that Parliament did not intend to include higher life forms within the definition of invention found in the Patent Act. . . . I do not believe that a higher life form such as the oncomouse is easily understood as either a "manufacture" or a "composition of matter". For this reason, I am not satisfied that the definition of "invention" in the Patent Act is

---

7. [According to the] *Patent Act*, R.S.C. 1985, c. P-4:. . . "invention" means any new and useful art, process, machine, manufacture or composition of matter, or any new and useful improvement in any art, process, machine, manufacture or composition of matter. . . .

sufficiently broad to include higher life forms. This conclusion is supported by the fact that the patenting of higher life forms raises unique concerns which do not arise in respect of non-living inventions and which are not addressed by the scheme of the Act. Even if a higher life form could, scientifically, be regarded as a "composition of matter," . . . the patenting of higher life forms is a highly contentious and complex matter that raises serious practical, ethical and environmental concerns. [Therefore,] [a]bsent explicit legislative direction, the Court should not order the Commissioner to grant a patent on a higher life form. . . .

In *Chakrabarty*, the majority [of the U.S. Supreme Court] attributed the widest meaning possible to the phrases "composition of matter" and "manufacture" for the reason that inventions are, necessarily, unanticipated and unforeseeable. . . . I agree that the definition of invention in the Patent Act is broad. Because the Act was designed in part to promote innovation, it is only reasonable to expect the definition of invention to be broad enough to encompass unforeseen and unanticipated technology. I cannot however agree with the suggestion that the definition is unlimited in the sense that it includes "anything under the sun that is made by man". In drafting the Patent Act, Parliament chose to adopt an exhaustive definition that limits invention to any "art, process, machine, manufacture or composition of matter". Parliament did not define "invention" as "anything new and useful made by man". By choosing to define invention in this way, Parliament signalled a clear intention to include certain subject matter as patentable and to exclude other subject matter as being outside the confines of the Act. . . .

[T]he word ["manufacture"] would commonly be understood to denote a non-living mechanistic product or process. . . . In *Chakrabarty*, . . . "manufacture" was defined as "the production of articles for use from raw or prepared materials by giving to these materials new forms, qualities, properties, or combinations, whether by hand-labor or by machinery." . . . Is a mouse an "article" [or] "material" . . . ? In my view, while a mouse may be analogized to a "manufacture" when it is produced in an industrial setting, the word in its vernacular sense does not include a higher life form. . . .

As regards the meaning of the words "composition of matter", I believe that they must be defined more narrowly than was the case in *Chakrabarty*. . . . It [] is significant that the word "matter" captures but one aspect of a higher life form. As defined by the Oxford English Dictionary . . . "matter" is a "[p]hysical or corporeal substance in general, . . . contradistinguished from immaterial or incorporeal substance (spirit, soul, mind), and from qualities, actions, or conditions". . . . Higher life forms are generally regarded as possessing qualities and characteristics that transcend the particular genetic material of which they are composed. A person whose genetic make-up is modified by radiation does not cease to be him or herself. Likewise, the same mouse would exist absent the injection of the oncogene into the fertilized egg cell; it simply would not be predisposed to cancer. The fact that it has this predisposition to cancer that makes it valuable to humans does not mean that the mouse, along with other animal life forms, can be defined solely with reference to the genetic matter of which it is composed. The fact that animal life forms have numerous unique qualities that transcend the particular matter of which they are composed makes it difficult to conceptualize higher life forms as mere "composition[s] of matter". It is a phrase that seems inadequate as a description of a higher life form. . . . It simply does not follow from the objective of promoting ingenuity that all inventions must be patentable. . . .

The respondent . . . submits that there is . . . no evidentiary or legal basis for the distinction the Patent Office has made between lower life forms such as bacteria, yeast and moulds, and higher life forms such as plants and animals. . . .

[I]t is up to Parliament and not the courts to assess the validity of the distinction drawn by the Patent Office between higher life forms and lower life forms. Yet, even if this Court were to alter the status quo and find higher life forms patentable, it would be unable to avoid engaging in line-drawing. The majority of the Federal Court of Appeal, which found that the Patent Act did apply to higher life forms, was nonetheless compelled to draw a distinction between higher life forms and human beings. In doing so, it merely substituted one line, that between humans and animals, for the line preferred by the Patent Office, that between higher and lower life forms. In my opinion, the decision to move the line in this manner was ill-advised. As I stated earlier when considering the definition of invention, the patenting of all plants and animals, and not just human beings, raises several concerns that are not appropriately dealt with in the Patent Act. In addition, a judicially crafted exception from patentability for human beings does not adequately address issues such as what defines a human being and whether parts of the human body as opposed to the entire person would be patentable. . . .

Appeal allowed.

[Justice Binnie's dissenting opinion omitted. The Justices were split 5-4.]

Notes on Ownership

1. *Intellectual Property Doctrine.* As noted in *Chakrabarty,* the Patent Act establishes a broad right to patent "any new and useful [invention], . . . subject to the conditions and requirements of this title." 35 U.S.C.A. §101. Although not emphasized in *Chakrabarty,* these conditions require that the invention be "novel," "nonobvious," and "adequately enabled and described." A patent gives an inventor a monopoly over the use of the discovery for a 20-year period. The owner can profit from the discovery directly or through "licensing" the use of the discovery to third parties who pay the inventor a "royalty." The Patent Act gives patent holders the right to bring a civil action against infringers for injunctive relief and damages (usually at least what would have been the reasonable royalty payments but treble damages are possible in cases of intentional infringement). 35 U.S.C.A. §§281-287.

As emphasized by the Court in *Mayo v. Prometheus,* ownership of intellectual property creates incentives for innovation but this also can result in barriers to accessing the invention itself and to innovation in related areas. The patent owner has the right to exclude others from using the invention. If the patent holder does not make use of the patent or offer other users licenses at a reasonable fee, then the innovation may not be available to the public, defeating the overriding purpose of offering patent protection in the first place. Patent law attempts to balance these competing policy considerations by, for example, ensuring that laws of nature and abstract ideas cannot be patented. The field of intellectual property is vast, and there are numerous books, articles, and treatises. Some basic reference works can be found in note 4, below.

2. *Patenting Life Forms. Chakrabarty* was a 5-4 decision involving a closely contested question of federal statutory interpretation. Congress did not accept the

Court's implicit invitation to override its decision. See Anna Lumelsky, Diamond v. Chakrabarty: Gauging Congress's Response to Dynamic Statutory Interpretation by the Supreme Court, 39 U.S.F. L. Rev. 641 (2005). The Supreme Court of Canada's 5-4 decision in the *Harvard Mouse* case was equally controversial. As Justice Binnie noted in his dissent, "the oncomouse has been held patentable, and is now patented" in 16 jurisdictions including the United States. Two additional countries have issued patents for similar inventions. "Indeed, we were not told of any country with a patent system comparable to Canada's (or otherwise) in which a patent on the oncomouse had been applied for and been refused." 2002 SCC 76 at ¶2. The Supreme Court of Canada revisited the patentability of life forms in another 5-4 decision upholding patents for plants genetically modified to resist application of an herbicide used to control weeds. Schmeiser v. Monsanto, 2004 SCC 34 (2004). Animal patents are relatively common in the United States. See Tracie Letterman et al., Patently Cruel, 40 Brief 39 (Summer 2011) (noting 800 PTO-approved patents on live animals since approval of Harvard Mouse; summarizing current efforts to challenge animal patents).

3. *IP and the Access Debate.* Intellectual property ownership rules give patent holders monopoly power to extract significant profits from their inventions, or to block others from using, or even experimenting with, their inventions. The concept of ownership itself can be controversial. Activists in some countries and cultures have argued that intellectual property regimes have failed to protect local communities from corporations that have allegedly exploited local knowledge of traditional medicines. See, e.g., Jim Chen, There's No Such Thing as Biopiracy . . . and It's a Good Thing Too, 37 McGeorge L. Rev. 1 (2006); Daniel Robinson, Confronting Biopiracy: Challenges, Cases and International Debates (2011).

When medical technologies are involved, intellectual property rights generate considerable controversy if they threaten to retard biomedical research or block access to essential life-saving innovations. An example of this problem can be found in Chapter 6.B.2.'s discussion of Greenberg v. Miami Children's Hospital Research Institute, Inc., 264 F. Supp. 2d 1064 (S.D. Fla. 2003), at page 672, which involves a patent on the gene that causes Canavan's disease—a fatal brain disorder that is most prevalent in children of eastern and central European Jewish descent. Families affected with the disease who had provided biological samples to the researchers who discovered the gene sued (unsuccessfully) to block enforcement of patent rights because they felt the owners were obstructing access to the gene test in order to increase their profits. Patent law addresses concerns such as these in several ways.

a. *"March-In" Rights and Compulsory Licensing.* First, patents can be overridden for pressing public policy considerations. Without going into details here, various sources of law allow (1) the U.S. government to "march in" and reclaim pharmaceutical patents from private entities whose research the government funded, if the private patent holder fails to develop or market the product; (2) courts to refuse to enjoin patent infringement where the infringement serves an important public purpose; and (3) in some countries, compulsory licensing to protect public health, meaning that the government can force companies to sell essential patented medical products at reasonable prices. Exercises of these special powers are rare and controversial, however. See generally National Research Council of the Nat'l Academies, Reaping the Benefits of Genomic and Proteomic Research: Intellectual Property Rights, Innovation, and Public Health 146-147 (2006).

b. *Access to Research Materials.* There have been numerous reports of IP-fueled restrictions on access to biomedical research materials such as cell lines, cancer drugs, and gene-altered mice. The United States has at best an extremely narrow research exemption to patent rights. Madey v. Duke University, 307 F.3d 1351 (Fed. Cir. 2002) ("regardless of whether a particular institution or entity is engaged in an endeavor for commercial gain, so long as the act is in furtherance of the alleged infringer's legitimate business and is not solely for amusement, to satisfy idle curiosity, or for strictly philosophical inquiry, the act does not qualify for the very narrow and strictly limited experimental use defense"); Katherine J. Standburg, What Does the Public Get? Experimental Use and the Patent Bargain, 2004 Wis. L. Rev. 81 (2004). These concerns have resulted in various studies and recommendations, either for a more explicit research exemption in the law, or for biomedical patent holders to adopt "best practices" in their licensing and patent enforcement practices for researchers. See, e.g., Aaron D. Levine, Access to Human Embryonic Stem Cell Lines, 29 Nature Biotechnology 1079 (2011) (study finds significant delays for human embryonic stem cell researchers).

c. *Medical Process Patents.* Many countries bar patents for medical processes, such as innovations in surgical procedures or medical protocols, for public policy reasons. This is not the law in the United States. Instead, medical processes are inherently patentable, if other requirements are met (such as novelty, nonobviousness, etc.). However, medical ethics disfavor seeking patent protection, and a special statutory amendment (35 U.S.C. §287(c)) prevents patent holders from enforcing their rights against health care practitioners, making such patents generally not worth the effort. In addition, *Mayo,* supra, emphasizes that to be patentable, medical processes must do more than simply restate and apply natural laws. Commentators have noted that the reasoning in *Mayo* could be used to challenge a broad range of patents relating to medical procedures and diagnostic tests. See, e.g., Bernard Chao, Moderating *Mayo,* 107 Nw. U. L. Rev. 423 (2012). Commentators focused in particular on the implications of *Mayo* for litigation involving diagnostic tests for genes and gene mutations that are the focus of the next section of this chapter. See Jeffrey L. Fox, Industry Reels as Prometheus Falls and Myriad Faces Further Reviews, 30 Nature Biotechnology 373 (2012).

4. *Additional Commentaries.* There are a great number of important books, treatises, and commentaries on **intellectual property law** (note 1). Some key references are: Donald S. Chisum, Chisum on Patents (this 53-volume loose-leaf treatise demonstrates the breadth of the field); and Craig Allen Nord & Michael J. Madison, The Law of Intellectual Property (2017). For an international perspective, see Oliver Mills, Biotechnological Innovation, Moral Rights and Patent Law (2005). For some especially relevant publications, see Dan Burk & Mark Lemley, Policy Levers in Patent Law, 89 Va. L. Rev. 1575 (2003); Rebecca S. Eisenberg, Patents and the Progress of Science, 56 U. Chi. L. Rev. 1017 (1989); David Singh Grewal, Before Peer Production: Infrastructure Gaps and the Architecture of Openness in Synthetic Biology, 20 Stan. Tech. L. Rev. 143 (2017) (noting importance of reorienting IP to consider state support for development of infrastructure; focusing on Bio-Bricks Foundation's support of public domain strategy in synthetic biology); Sapna Kumar & Arti Rai, Synthetic Biology: The Intellectual Property Puzzle, 85 Tex. L. Rev. 1745 (2007); Arti K. Rai, Patent Validity Across the Executive Branch: Ex Ante Foundations for Policy Development, 61 Duke L. J. 1237 (2012) (exploring role of executive branch agencies, such as the NIH, in the development of patent policy,

including DNA-patenting debates); Arti Rai ed., Intellectual Property and Biotechnology (2011); Note, Recent Legislation, Patent Law, 125 Harv. L. Rev. 1290 (2012) (analyzing Leahy-Smith America Invents Act reforms, including major change from "first to invent" to "first inventor to file" priority standard and new administrative processes for patent challenges).

There are a number of important commentaries discussing different aspects of the **balance between protection of intellectual property and other important social objectives,** such as access (note 3). For more on the biopiracy debate, see Jonathan Curci, The Protection of Biodiversity and Traditional Knowledge in International Law of Intellectual Property (2010); George Frisvold & Kelly Day-Rubenstein, Bioprospecting and Biodiversity Conservation: What Happens When Discoveries Are Made?, 50 Ariz. L. Rev. 545 (2008); and Cynthia M. Ho, Access to Medicine in the Global Economy (2011). For more on the Bayh-Dole Act and "march-in" rights, (note 3(a)) see 35 U.S.C. §203; Board of Trustees of the Leland Stanford Junior University v. Roche Molecular Systems, Inc., 563 U.S. 776 (2011) (analyzing impact of Bayh-Dole Act on inventor's assignment of rights to federally funded inventions); and Daniel J. Hemel & Lisa Larrimore Ouellette, Bayh-Dole Beyond Borders, 4 J. of L. & the Biosciences 282 (2017) (discussing general critique of Bayh-Dole along with international implications). For a discussion of the judicial power to deny an injunction where infringement serves the public interest, see eBay, Inc. v. MercExchange, L.L.C., 547 U.S. 388 (2006). For more on compulsory licensing, see Richard A. Epstein, Questioning the Frequency and Wisdom of Compulsory Licensing for Pharmaceutical Patents, 78 U. Chi. L. Rev. 71 (2011); Donald Harris, TRIPS After Fifteen Years: Success or Failure, as Measured by Compulsory Licensing, 18 J. Intell. Prop. L. 367 (2011); Symposium, Patent Sovereignty and International Law, 6 UC Irvine L. Rev. 282-508 (2016). For additional material on the impact of the narrow research exemption to patents (note 3(b)), see David H. Ledbetter, Gene Patenting and Licensing: The Role of Academic Researchers and Advocacy Groups, 10 Genet. Med. 314 (2008); Nicholas Short, The Political Economy of the Research Exemption in American Patent Law, 26 Fordh. Intell. Prop. Media & Ent. L. J. 573 (2016); Principles and Guidelines for Recipients of NIH Research Grants and Contracts on Obtaining and Disseminating Biomedical Research Resources, 62 Fed. Reg. 72090 (1999); NIH, Best Practices for the Licensing of Genomic Inventions, 70 Fed. Reg. 18413 (2005); National Research Council of the Nat'l Academies, Reaping the Benefits of Genomic and Proteomic Research: Intellectual Property Rights, Innovation, and Public Health 140-144 (2006). Medical process patents (note 3(c)) are discussed in Aaron Kesselheim & Michelle Mello, Medical-Process Patents: Monopolizing the Delivery of Health Care, 355 New Eng. J. Med. 2036 (2006); Note, 13 Colum. Sci. & Tech. L. Rev. 206 (2012); Note, 91 Minn. L. Rev. 1088 (2007). See also John C. Newman & Robin Feldman, Copyright and Open Access at the Bedside, 365 New Eng. J. Med. 2447 (2011) (exploring intersection of copyright with medical practice in context of commonly used mental state examination).

5. Intellectual Property, Human Genes, and Human Stem Cells

One consequence of the Human Genome Project was the race by researchers, universities, and companies to patent human genes, diagnostic tests, and other procedures or products related to human genes. See Michael J. Malinowski & Radhika Rao, Legal Limits on Genetic Research and the Commercialization of Its Results, 54 Am. J. Comp. L. 45, 47-49 (2006) (as of 2005, "[c]ompanies and universities ha[d] obtained patents on more than 4,000 human genes, almost 20 percent of the roughly 24,000 human genes"). Human gene patents raise two different types of issues: Are these genetic discoveries patentable under the specific requirements of U.S. law? Do moral or other policy considerations justify restricting patent rights relating to genetic aspects of life forms generally or humans in particular? These are separate issues because U.S. patent law does not explicitly provide the U.S. Patent and Trademark Office (PTO) with the right to refuse patent applications based on general moral or policy grounds not otherwise found within the terms of the patent legislation. See Cynthia M. Ho, Splicing Morality and Patent Law: Issues Arising from Mixing Mice and Men, 2 Wash. U. J. L. & Pol'y 247 (2000).

As Malinowski and Rao note, determining the validity of a gene-related patent required the PTO to ensure that the patent application demonstrated an invention rather than simply the discovery of a natural phenomenon. Malinowski & Rao, supra, 54 Am. J. Comp. L. at 48-49. Relying in part on researchers' claims that they had demonstrated invention by isolating and purifying genetic DNA, the PTO initially took a relatively lenient approach to human gene patents. This led to widespread criticism that premature gene patents were preventing even more productive research efforts. Although the PTO's gene patenting policies had not been formally rejected in court, these concerns caused the PTO to toughen its standards on the secondary considerations required for patentability (such as utility, nonobviousness, and adequate description), even as it continued to view human genes as inherently patentable subject matter. U.S. Patent and Trademark Office, Utility Examination Guidelines, 66 Fed. Reg. 1092 (2001) (revised guidelines governing gene patents). For a major report on the issues, see National Research Council of the Nat'l Academies, Reaping the Benefits of Genomic and Proteomic Research: Intellectual Property Rights, Innovation, and Public Health 140-144 (2006).

The stage was set for a clash in the Supreme Court between the traditional view that gene patents were valid and the *Mayo v. Prometheus*-fueled view that at least some gene patents might be an invalid effort to patent laws of nature. The litigation involved the validity of patent claims held by Myriad Genetics on two genes (BRCA1 and BRCA2) associated with susceptibility to breast and ovarian cancer.

▪ ASSOCIATION FOR MOLECULAR PATHOLOGY et al. v. MYRIAD GENETICS, INC. et al.
564 U.S. 576 (2013)

THOMAS, J

Respondent Myriad Genetics, Inc. (Myriad), discovered the precise location and sequence of two human genes, mutations of which can substantially increase the risks of breast and ovarian cancer. Myriad obtained a number of patents based upon its discovery. This case involves claims from three of them and requires us to resolve whether a naturally occurring segment of deoxyribonucleic acid (DNA) is patent eligible under 35 U.S.C. § 101 by virtue of its isolation from the rest of the human genome. We also address the patent eligibility of synthetically created DNA known as complementary DNA (cDNA), which contains the same protein-coding information found in a segment of natural DNA but omits portions within the DNA segment that do not code for proteins. For the reasons that follow, we hold that a naturally occurring DNA segment is a product of nature and not patent eligible merely because it has been isolated, but that cDNA is patent eligible because it is not naturally occurring. We, therefore, affirm in part and reverse in part the decision of the United States Court of Appeals for the Federal Circuit.

I

Genes form the basis for hereditary traits in living organisms. The human genome consists of approximately 22,000 genes packed into 23 pairs of chromosomes. Each gene is encoded as DNA, which takes the shape of the familiar "double helix" that Doctors James Watson and Francis Crick first described in 1953. Each "cross-bar" in the DNA helix consists of two chemically joined nucleotides. . . .The nucleotide cross-bars are chemically connected to a sugar-phosphate backbone that forms the outside framework of the DNA helix. Sequences of DNA nucleotides contain the information necessary to create strings of amino acids, which in turn are used in the body to build proteins. Only some DNA nucleotides, however, code for amino acids; these nucleotides are known as "exons." Nucleotides that do not code for amino acids, in contrast, are known as "introns."

Creation of proteins from DNA involves two principal steps, known as transcription and translation. In transcription, the bonds between DNA nucleotides separate, and the DNA helix unwinds into two single strands. A single strand is used as a template to create a complementary ribonucleic acid (RNA) strand. . . .Transcription results in a single strand RNA molecule, known as pre-RNA, whose nucleotides form an inverse image of the DNA strand from which it was created. Pre–RNA still contains nucleotides corresponding to both the exons and introns in the DNA molecule. The pre-RNA is then naturally "spliced" by the physical removal of the introns. The resulting product is a strand of RNA that contains nucleotides corresponding only to the exons from the original DNA strand. The exons-only strand is known as messenger RNA (mRNA), which creates amino acids through translation. In translation, cellular structures known as ribosomes read each set of three nucleotides, known as codons, in the mRNA. Each codon either tells the ribosomes which of the 20 possible amino acids to synthesize or provides a stop signal that ends amino acid production.

DNA's informational sequences and the processes that create mRNA, amino acids, and proteins occur naturally within cells. Scientists can, however, extract DNA from cells using well known laboratory methods. These methods allow scientists to isolate specific segments of DNA—for instance, a particular gene or part of a gene—which can then be further studied, manipulated, or used. It is also possible to create DNA synthetically through processes similarly well known in the field of genetics. One such method begins with an mRNA molecule and uses the natural bonding properties of nucleotides to create a new, synthetic DNA molecule. The result is the inverse of the mRNA's inverse image of the original DNA, with one important distinction: Because the natural creation of mRNA involves splicing that removes introns, the synthetic DNA created from mRNA also contains only the exon sequences. This synthetic DNA created in the laboratory from mRNA is known as complementary DNA (cDNA).

Changes in the genetic sequence are called mutations. Mutations can be as small as the alteration of a single nucleotide — a change affecting only one letter in the genetic code. Such small-scale changes can produce an entirely different amino acid or can end protein production altogether. Large changes, involving the deletion, rearrangement, or duplication of hundreds or even millions of nucleotides, can result in the elimination, misplacement, or duplication of entire genes. Some mutations are harmless, but others can cause disease or increase the risk of disease. As a result, the study of genetics can lead to valuable medical breakthroughs.

This case involves patents filed by Myriad after it made one such medical breakthrough. Myriad discovered the precise location and sequence of what are now known as the BRCA1 and BRCA2 genes. Mutations in these genes can dramatically increase an individual's risk of developing breast and ovarian cancer. The average American woman has a 12– to 13–percent risk of developing breast cancer, but for women with certain genetic mutations, the risk can range between 50 and 80 percent for breast cancer and between 20 and 50 percent for ovarian cancer. Before Myriad's discovery of the BRCA1 and BRCA2 genes, scientists knew that heredity played a role in establishing a woman's risk of developing breast and ovarian cancer, but they did not know which genes were associated with those cancers.

Myriad identified the exact location of the BRCA1 and BRCA2 genes on chromosomes 17 and 13. Chromosome 17 has approximately 80 million nucleotides, and chromosome 13 has approximately 114 million. Within those chromosomes, the BRCA1 and BRCA2 genes are each about 80,000 nucleotides long. If just exons are counted, the BRCA1 gene is only about 5,500 nucleotides long; for the BRCA2 gene, that number is about 10,200. Knowledge of the location of the BRCA1 and BRCA2 genes allowed Myriad to determine their typical nucleotide sequence. That information, in turn, enabled Myriad to develop medical tests that are useful for detecting mutations in a patient's BRCA1 and BRCA2 genes and thereby assessing whether the patient has an increased risk of cancer.

Once it found the location and sequence of the BRCA1 and BRCA2 genes, Myriad sought and obtained a number of patents. Nine composition claims from three of those patents are at issue in this case.[2] Claims 1, 2, 5, and 6 from the '282 patent are representative. The first claim asserts a patent on "[a]n isolated DNA coding for a BRCA1 polypeptide," which has "the amino acid sequence set forth in SEQ ID NO:2." SEQ ID NO:2 sets forth a list of 1,863 amino acids that the typical BRCA1 gene encodes. Put differently, claim 1 asserts a patent claim on the DNA code that tells a cell to produce the string of BRCA1 amino acids listed in SEQ ID NO:2.

Claim 2 of the '282 patent operates similarly. It claims "[t]he isolated DNA of claim 1, wherein said DNA has the nucleotide sequence set forth in SEQ ID NO:1." Like SEQ ID NO:2, SEQ ID NO:1 sets forth a long list of data, in this instance the sequence of cDNA that codes for the BRCA1 amino acids listed in claim 1. Importantly, SEQ ID NO:1 lists only the cDNA exons in the BRCA1 gene, rather than a full

---

2. At issue are claims 1, 2, 5, 6, and 7 of U.S. Patent 5,747,282 (the '282 patent), claim 1 of U.S. Patent 5,693,473 (the '473 patent), and claims 1, 6, and 7 of U.S. Patent 5,837,492 (the '492 patent).

DNA sequence containing both exons and introns. As a result, the Federal Circuit recognized that claim 2 asserts a patent on the cDNA nucleotide sequence listed in SEQ ID NO:1, which codes for the typical BRCA1 gene.

Claim 5 of the '282 patent claims a subset of the data in claim 1. In particular, it claims "[a]n isolated DNA having at least 15 nucleotides of the DNA of claim 1." The practical effect of claim 5 is to assert a patent on any series of 15 nucleotides that exist in the typical BRCA1 gene. Because the BRCA1 gene is thousands of nucleotides long, even BRCA1 genes with substantial mutations are likely to contain at least one segment of 15 nucleotides that correspond to the typical BRCA1 gene. Similarly, claim 6 of the '282 patent claims "[a]n isolated DNA having at least 15 nucleotides of the DNA of claim 2." This claim operates similarly to claim 5, except that it references the cDNA-based claim 2. The remaining claims at issue are similar, though several list common mutations rather than typical BRCA1 and BRCA2 sequences.

Myriad's patents would, if valid, give it the exclusive right to isolate an individual's BRCA1 and BRCA2 genes (or any strand of 15 or more nucleotides within the genes) by breaking the covalent bonds that connect the DNA to the rest of the individual's genome. The patents would also give Myriad the exclusive right to synthetically create BRCA cDNA. In Myriad's view, manipulating BRCA DNA in either of these fashions triggers its "right to exclude others from making" its patented composition of matter under the Patent Act. 35 U.S.C. § 154(a)(1); see also § 271(a) ("[W]hoever without authority makes . . . any patented invention . . . infringes the patent").

But isolation is necessary to conduct genetic testing, and Myriad was not the only entity to offer BRCA testing after it discovered the genes. The University of Pennsylvania's Genetic Diagnostic Laboratory (GDL) and others provided genetic testing services to women. Petitioner Dr. Harry Ostrer, then a researcher at New York University School of Medicine, routinely sent his patients' DNA samples to GDL for testing. After learning of GDL's testing and Ostrer's activities, Myriad sent letters to them asserting that the genetic testing infringed Myriad's patents. In response, GDL agreed to stop testing and informed Ostrer that it would no longer accept patient samples. Myriad also filed patent infringement suits against other entities that performed BRCA testing, resulting in settlements in which the defendants agreed to cease all allegedly infringing activity. Myriad, thus, solidified its position as the only entity providing BRCA testing.

Some years later, petitioner Ostrer, along with medical patients, advocacy groups, and other doctors, filed this lawsuit seeking a declaration that Myriad's patents are invalid under 35 U.S.C. § 101. . . . The District Court . . . granted summary judgment to petitioners on the composition claims at issue in this case based on its conclusion that Myriad's claims, including claims related to cDNA, were invalid because they covered products of nature. The Federal Circuit reversed and this Court granted the petition for certiorari, vacated the judgment, and remanded the case in light of Mayo Collaborative Services v. Prometheus Laboratories, Inc., 566 U.S. ——, 132 S.Ct. 1289 (2012).

On remand, the Federal Circuit affirmed the District Court in part and reversed in part, with each member of the panel writing separately. . . . With respect to the merits, the court held that both isolated DNA and cDNA were patent eligible under § 101. The central dispute among the panel members was whether the act of isolating DNA—separating a specific gene or sequence of nucleotides from the rest of the chromosome—is an inventive act that entitles the individual who first isolates it to a patent. Each of the judges on the panel had a different view on that question. Although the judges expressed different views concerning the patentability of isolated DNA, all three agreed that patent claims relating to cDNA met the patent eligibility requirements of § 101. We granted certiorari.

II

Section 101 of the Patent Act provides: "Whoever invents or discovers any new and useful . . . composition of matter, or any new and useful improvement thereof, may obtain a patent therefor, subject to the conditions and requirements of this title." 35 U.S.C. § 101. We have "long held that this provision contains an important implicit exception[:] Laws of nature, natural phenomena, and abstract ideas are not patentable." Mayo, 132 S. Ct., at 1293. . . .The rule against patents on naturally occurring things is not without limits, however, for "all inventions at some level embody, use, reflect, rest upon, or apply laws of nature, natural phenomena, or abstract ideas," and "too broad an interpretation of this exclusionary principle could eviscerate patent law." 132 S. Ct., at 1293. As we have recognized before, patent protection strikes a delicate balance between creating "incentives that lead to creation, invention, and discovery" and "imped[ing] the flow of information that might permit, indeed spur, invention." 132 S. Ct., at 1305. We must apply this well-established standard to determine whether Myriad's patents claim any "new and useful . . . composition of matter," § 101, or instead claim naturally occurring phenomena.

It is undisputed that Myriad did not create or alter any of the genetic information encoded in the BRCA1 and BRCA2 genes. The location and order of the nucleotides existed in nature before Myriad found them. Nor did Myriad create or alter the genetic structure of DNA. Instead, Myriad's principal contribution was uncovering the precise location and genetic sequence of the BRCA1 and BRCA2 genes within chromosomes 17 and 13. The question is whether this renders the genes patentable.

Myriad recognizes that our decision in *Chakrabarty* is central to this inquiry. . . . The *Chakrabarty* bacterium was new "with markedly different characteristics from any found in nature," 447 U.S., at 310, due to the additional plasmids and resultant "capacity for degrading oil." Id., at 305, n. 1. In this case, by contrast, Myriad did not create anything. To be sure, it found an important and useful gene, but separating that gene from its surrounding genetic material is not an act of invention.

Groundbreaking, innovative, or even brilliant discovery does not by itself satisfy the § 101 inquiry. In Funk Brothers Seed Co. v. Kalo Inoculant Co., 333 U.S. 127 (1948), this Court considered a composition patent that claimed a mixture of naturally occurring strains of bacteria that helped leguminous plants take nitrogen from the air and fix it in the soil. . . . The Court held that the composition was not patent eligible because the patent holder did not alter the bacteria in any way. . . . His patent claim thus fell squarely within the law of nature exception. So do Myriad's. Myriad found the location of the BRCA1 and BRCA2 genes, but that discovery, by itself, does not render the BRCA genes "new . . . composition[s] of matter," § 101, that are patent eligible.

Indeed, Myriad's patent descriptions highlight the problem with its claims. . . . Many of Myriad's patent descriptions simply detail the "iterative process" of discovery by which Myriad narrowed the possible locations for the gene sequences that it sought.[6] Myriad seeks to import these extensive research efforts into the § 101 patent-eligibility inquiry. But extensive effort alone is insufficient to satisfy the demands of § 101.

Nor are Myriad's claims saved by the fact that isolating DNA from the human genome severs chemical bonds and thereby creates a nonnaturally occurring molecule. Myriad's claims are simply not expressed in terms of chemical composition, nor do they rely in any way on the chemical changes that result from the isolation of a particular section of DNA. Instead, the claims understandably focus on the genetic information encoded in the BRCA1 and BRCA2 genes. If the patents depended upon the creation of a unique molecule, then a would-be infringer could arguably avoid at least Myriad's patent claims on entire genes . . . by isolating a DNA sequence that included both the BRCA1 or BRCA2 gene and one additional nucleotide pair. Such a molecule would not be chemically identical to the molecule "invented" by Myriad. But Myriad obviously would resist that outcome because its claim is concerned primarily with the information contained in the genetic sequence, not with the specific chemical composition of a particular molecule.

Finally, Myriad argues that the PTO's past practice of awarding gene patents is entitled to deference, citing J.E.M. Ag Supply, Inc. v. Pioneer Hi–Bred Int'l, Inc., 534 U.S. 124 (2001). We disagree. [Unlike in *J.E.M.*,] Congress has not endorsed the views of the PTO in subsequent legislation. . . . Further undercutting the PTO's practice, the United States argued in the Federal Circuit and in this Court that isolated DNA was not patent eligible under § 101 and that the PTO's practice was not "a sufficient reason to hold that isolated DNA is patent-eligible." These concessions weigh against deferring to the PTO's determination.

cDNA does not present the same obstacles to patentability as naturally occurring, isolated DNA segments. As already explained, creation of a cDNA sequence from mRNA results in an exons-only molecule that is not naturally occurring. Petitioners concede that cDNA differs from natural DNA in that "the non-coding regions have been removed." They nevertheless argue that cDNA is not patent eligible because "[t]he nucleotide sequence of cDNA is dictated by nature, not by the lab technician." That may be so, but the lab technician unquestionably creates something new when cDNA is made. cDNA retains the naturally occurring exons of DNA, but it is distinct from the DNA from which it was derived. As a result, cDNA is not a "product of nature" and is patent eligible under § 101, except insofar as very short series of DNA may have no intervening introns to remove when creating

6. Myriad first identified groups of relatives with a history of breast cancer (some of whom also had developed ovarian cancer); because these individuals were related, scientists knew that it was more likely that their diseases were the result of genetic predisposition rather than other factors. Myriad compared sections of their chromosomes, looking for shared genetic abnormalities not found in the general population. It was that process which eventually enabled Myriad to determine where in the genetic sequence the BRCA1 and BRCA2 genes reside.

cDNA. In that situation, a short strand of cDNA may be indistinguishable from natural DNA.[9]

III

It is important to note what is not implicated by this decision. First, there are no method claims before this Court. Had Myriad created an innovative method of manipulating genes while searching for the BRCA1 and BRCA2 genes, it could possibly have sought a method patent. But the processes used by Myriad to isolate DNA were well understood by geneticists at the time of Myriad's patents "were well understood, widely used, and fairly uniform insofar as any scientist engaged in the search for a gene would likely have utilized a similar approach," 702 F.Supp.2d, at 202–203, and are not at issue in this case.

Similarly, this case does not involve patents on new applications of knowledge about the BRCA1 and BRCA2 genes. Judge Bryson aptly noted that, "[a]s the first party with knowledge of the [BRCA1 and BRCA2] sequences, Myriad was in an excellent position to claim applications of that knowledge. Many of its unchallenged claims are limited to such applications." 689 F.3d, at 1349.

Nor do we consider the patentability of DNA in which the order of the naturally occurring nucleotides has been altered. Scientific alteration of the genetic code presents a different inquiry, and we express no opinion about the application of § 101 to such endeavors. We merely hold that genes and the information they encode are not patent eligible under § 101 simply because they have been isolated from the surrounding genetic material.

For the foregoing reasons, the judgment of the Federal Circuit is affirmed in part and reversed in part. . . .

Justice SCALIA, concurring in part and concurring in the judgment.

I join the judgment of the Court, and all of its opinion except [the first four paragraphs of this edited opinion] and some portions of the rest of the opinion going into fine details of molecular biology. I am unable to affirm those details on my own knowledge or even my own belief. It suffices for me to affirm, having studied the opinions below and the expert briefs presented here, that the portion of DNA isolated from its natural state sought to be patented is identical to that portion of the DNA in its natural state; and that complementary DNA (cDNA) is a synthetic creation not normally present in nature.

Notes: *Myriad*, Human Gene Patents, and Stem Cell Patents

1. *The* Myriad *Decision and the Aftermath.* What is the purpose of Justice Thomas's introduction to DNA and genetics in Part I of the opinion? Intellectual property is well known for involving intricate scientific issues and the U.S. Court of Appeals for the Federal Circuit's specialized jurisdiction is justified in part by the ability to develop expertise relevant to understanding the application of patent law

---

9. We express no opinion whether cDNA satisfies the other statutory requirements of patentability. See, e.g., 35 U.S.C. §§ 102, 103, and 112.

to complex areas of human endeavor. Cf. Jason Rantanen, Empirical Analyses of Judicial Opinions: Methodology, Metrics and the Federal Circuit, 49 Conn. L. Rev. 227 (2016) (noting areas of debate and assessing the state of research on the Federal Circuit). Justice Scalia's concurrence is a particularly candid admission that Supreme Court review of patent cases can be challenging on many levels.

The Court was unanimous in holding that Myriad's discovery of the precise location and sequencing of the BRCA1 and BRCA2 genes fell within the "law of nature" exception. Identifying and isolating an "important and useful gene" from "its surrounding genetic material in not an act of invention" that would be patentable under §101 of the Patent Act. 133 S.Ct. at 2117 (majority); Id. at 2120 (Scalia, J., concurring). The Court therefore rejected the longstanding position of the U.S. Patent and Trademark Office. The patents associated with the development of cDNA were upheld as the "creation of a cDNA sequence . . . results in an exons-only molecule that is not naturally occurring," except for short strands of cDNA that are indistinguishable from natural DNA, which would not be patentable. Id. at 2119 (majority); Id. at 2120 (Scalia, J., concurring). Predictably, the Court's decision garnered praise among those who had expressed concerns about the possible negative impact of gene patents on research and innovation, see, Jeffrey M. Perkel, Gene Patents Decision: Everybody Wins, The Scientist Magazine, June 18, 2013, while eliciting expressions of concern from those concerned with incentives for investment in gene-related research, see Christopher M. Holman, In *Myriad* the Supreme Court Has, Once Again, Increased the Uncertainty of U.S. Patent Law, 32 Biotech. L. Rep. 1 (2013).

2. *Patents and Diagnostic Genetic Testing.* Some post-*Mayo, supra,* and *Myriad* commentators focused on the potential impact of these decisions on incentives for investment in diagnostic testing, including genetic testing. These concerns were reinforced by the Federal Circuit's decision to invalidate a patent on a method for non-invasive prenatal screening using fetal DNA. Sequenom v. Ariosa 788 F.3d 1371 (Fed. Cir. 2015). Some commentators noted that biotechnology companies might emphasize other legal mechanisms, such as trade secrets, to maintain control over discoveries. See Robert Cook-Deegan et al., The Next Controversy in Genetic Testing: Clinical Data as Trade Secrets?, 21 Eur. J. of Human Genetics 585 (2013). Will limits on the patentability of diagnostic tests affect the growth of precision medicine? See Rachel E. Sachs, Innovation Law and Policy: Preserving the Future of Personalized Medicine, 49 U.C. Davis L. Rev. 1881 (2016) (noting importance of multiple factors, including patent law, on incentives for innovation in diagnostic testing); see also page 181.

3. *Human Stem Cell Patents.* The controversy over human gene patents is only part of the picture. The U.S. Patent and Trademark Office has issued more than 1,000 stem cell patents. This too is controversial, not only because the patents involve human cells and sometimes the destruction of human embryos, but also because patent holders have been accused of limiting the ability of researchers to pursue potentially important research of great public benefit. The holders of patents covering two of the most useful lines of human stem cells (WARF and Geron) claimed that their patents covered all similar human stem cells, even if they were derived from other sources. The patent owners imposed significant licensing costs on researchers, including the right to receive royalties if research using the stem cells resulted in additional products with commercial value.

Again, the U.S. Patent and Trademark Office, rather than relenting on whether human stem cells are fundamentally patentable subject matter, began to question stem cell patents on more technical grounds. For example, in 2007, it revoked three such patents previously issued to the University of Wisconsin because the cells "appeared to be the same as, or obvious variations of, cells described in earlier scientific papers or in patents issued to others." Andrew Pollack, 3 Patents on Stem Cells Are Revoked in Initial Review, N.Y. Times, Apr. 3, 2007, at C2. See also John M. Golden, WARF's Stem Cell Patents and Tensions Between Public and Private Sector Approaches to Research, 38 J. L., Med. & Ethics 314 (2010). The 2011 Leahy-Smith America Invents Act (AIA) may facilitate stem cell patent challenges by reducing the standing requirements that had stymied some challenges to the WARF patents and by reducing costs. See Jacob S. Sherkow & Christopher Thomas Scott, Stem Cell Patents after the America Invents Act, 16 Cell Stem Cell 461 (2015) (noting WARF litigation and AIA creation of administrative procedures to challenge new and existing patents). Some authors have suggested that stem cells be provided sui generis treatment. See, e.g., Simon A. Rose, Semiconductor Chips, Genes, and Stem Cells: New Wine for New Bottles?, 38 Am. J. L. & Med. 113 (2012) (arguing for sui generis IP approach for "isolated genes, stem cells, and related bioproducts"). European courts have rejected patents on embryonic stem cell lines created from the destruction of embryos that had the potential to develop into human beings but permit patents for other types of stem cell lines. See, Hanna Schickl, Matthias Braun & Peter Dabrock, Ways Out of the Patenting Prohibition?, 31 Bioethics 409 (2017).

4. *Patenting Human Beings.* If human genes, cells, and tissues have been patented, should courts also allow the patenting of human beings? The America Invents Act included a provision relating to 35 U.S.C.A. §101 that mirrored previous PTO announcements and guidelines in providing that "[n]otwithstanding any other provision of law, no patent may issue on a claim directed to or encompassing a human organism." P.L. 112-29, 125 Stat. 284, 340 (2011). The U.S. PTO's guidance notes that the legislative history for the AIA makes clear that the legislation affirms rather than alters PTO policy and that it does not affect patents on "stem cells [and] animals with human genes." U.S. PTO, Manual of Patent Examining Procedure, 2105 Patentable Subject Matter—Living Subject Matter (9th ed. 2015).

5. *Additional Commentaries.* There are a number of commentaries on the **Myriad decision** (note 1). A useful collection can be found in Symposium, The Meaning of *Myriad*, 5 U.C.Irvine L. Rev. 973-1271 (2015); see also, Daniel L. Burk, Dolly and Alice, 2 J. L. and the Biosciences 606 (2015); Daniel L. Burk, The Curious Incident of the Supreme Court in Myriad Genetics, 90 Notre Dame L. Rev. 505 (2014); Christopher M. Holman, Patent Eligibility Post-Myriad: A Reinvigorated Judicial Wildcard of Uncertain Effect, 82 Geo. Wash. L. Rev., 1796 (2014); Arti K. Rai, Biomedical Patents at the Supreme Court: A Path Forward, 66 Stan. L. Rev. Online 111 (2013) (exploring *Mayo* and *Myriad* in the context of innovation policy). Additional articles on *Myriad*'s implications for **diagnostic testing** (note 2) include: Robert Cook-Deegan & Annie Niehaus, After Myriad: Genetic Testing in the Wake of Recent Supreme Court Decisions about Gene Patents, 2 Curr. Genet. Med. Rep. 223 (2014). For additional articles on **stem cell patents** (note 3) see, Yael Bregman-Eschet et al., The Ripple Effect of Intellectual Property Policy: Empirical Evidence from Stem Cell Research and Development, 19 J. Tech. L. & Pol'y 227 (2014) (reviewing differential treatment of stem cell patentability in the United States and Europe; arguing that data demonstrates European position had negative impact on

investment); Stephen Munzer, How to Integrate Administrative Law and Tort Law: The Regulation of Stem Cell Products, 64 Admin. L. Rev. 743 (2012) (suggesting revisions to FDA and tort approaches); Ned Stafford, Patents Cannot Be Given for Research Methods That Destroy Healthy Human Embryos to Obtain Stem Cells, German Court Rules, 345 BMJ e8248 (2012). For a critique of the meaning and the potential impact of the AIA provision on patenting human organisms (note 4), see Yaniv Heled, 36 Cardozo L. Rev. 241 (2014).

Problem: CRISPR, Gene Editing, and Germ-Line Modification

In 2012, researchers developed a new, efficient, relatively inexpensive and effective technique for editing genes. Anthony L. Komaroff, Gene Editing Using CRISPR: Why the Excitement?, 318 JAMA 699 (2017). CRISPR (Clustered Regularly Interspaced Short Palindromic Repeat) is RNA combined with a special nuclease, commonly Cas9, to create a kind of "molecular scissors" that can cut the two strands of DNA at a specific location so that DNA can be added or removed. The combined technology is referred to as CRISPR-Cas9. CRISPR can be used to change both the structure of genes (for example, "transform[ing] the gene for hemoglobin S (sickle cell globin) into the gene for hemoglobin") and the expression of genes (for example "shut[ting]off the production of a protein, or ramp[ing] it up"). Id. at 699. CRISPR genes were discovered as a part of research into bacterial genomes, when it was recognized that they disabled viruses by editing viral genes. Id.

CRISPR has created great excitement along with controversy and concern. One important set of questions focuses on the limits, if any, on the use of CRISPR technology. There are many concerns about CRISPR's potential uses and the adequacy of the regulatory structure in countries around the world, including the United States. As noted above, CRISPR can be "delivered" to target genes in various ways and at different stages of development. One potentially important distinction in thinking about the use of CRISPR is whether the targeted changes will focus on "somatic" gene editing or whether the changes will be capable of being passed on to future generations; that is, whether they affect the "germ-line" of the organism.

Somatic gene editing governance has three components: (1) review by the federal Recombinant DNA Advisory Committee (RAC); (2) review by institutional review boards (IRBs); and (3) "review and approval by the FDA." Jordan Paradise, U.S. Regulatory Challenges for Gene Editing, 13(1) ABA SciTech Law. 10 (2016) (describing regulatory structure). RAC and IRB review is linked to the receipt of federal funding and FDA review is required for research leading up to request for market approval. Are you concerned about any potential gaps in this regulatory scheme? Does somatic gene editing present significant risks to society that will or won't be addressed through this structure? Compare, National Academies of Sciences, Engineering & Medicine, Human Genome Editing: Science, Ethics, and Governance 34-44, 83-100 (2017) (summarizing governance and considering somatic gene editing) with Sarah Polcz & Anna Lewis, CRISPR-Cas9 and the Non-Germline Non-Controversy, 3 J. of L. & the Biosciences 413 (2016) (discussing and critiquing policy focus on germ-line editing and discussing issues raised by somatic cell gene editing). Is the distinction between somatic and germ-line engineering reasonable?

Much of the attention has been focused on whether or not CRISPR could be used to modify the germ-line, perhaps to eliminate genetic mutations associated with premature death. The discussion has strong parallels with the debate about mitochondrial replacement, which has been considered to affect the germ-line because of the pairing of the donor mitochondrial DNA with the nuclear DNA of the intended mother of the child born through the procedure. See page 827. Should the United States permit use of CRISPR to address some types of serious genetic conditions, even where the edited genes will be passed on to future generations? Compare, National Academies of Sciences, Engineering & Medicine, Human Genome Editing, supra, at 111-136 (offering recommendations and criteria for clinical trials using "heritable genome editing" in some cases) with id. at 136 (noting barrier created by federal legislation prohibiting use of funds to respond to or acknowledge submission of exemption for research "in which a human embryo is intentionally created or modified to include a heritable genetic modification"). See also, Amy Harmon, Human Gene Editing Receives Science Panel's Support, N.Y. Times, Feb. 14, 2017.

How would the Constitution treat a claim by a patient seeking to use this technology to alter embryonic DNA? Does it matter that the technology may permit germ-line alterations; that is, changes that will be inherited to future generations? Baltimore and colleagues note that even changing "a disease-causing genetic mutation to a sequence more typical among healthy people," a "straightforward scenario," raises several concerns including "the potential for unintended consequences of heritable germline modifications, because there are limits to our knowledge of human genetics, gene-environment interactions, and the pathways of disease (including the interplay between one disease and other conditions or diseases in the same patient)." Baltimore, et al., a Prudent Path Forward of Generic Engineering and Germ-line Modification, 348 Science 36, 37 (2015). Is it plausible to think that the Constitution speaks to what the state may or may not do as to such a new technology? Does it depend on one's theory of constitutional interpretation, such as Originalism or Living Constitutionalism?

CRISPR has also generated significant patent litigation. See, e.g., Andrew Pollack, Harvard and M.I.T. Scientists Win Gene-Editing Patent Fight, N.Y. Times, Feb. 15, 2017; and In re Schlich for Order to Take Discovery, 2017 WL 4155405 ("This . . . application is just one part of an ongoing patent battle between two research groups for rights to a new biotechnology breakthrough, CRISPR/Cas9"). The debate at this stage is simply about ownership, not patentability. See Deborah Ku, The Patentability of the CRISPR-Cas9 Genome Editing Tool, 16 Chi. Kent J. Intell. Prop. 408 (2017) (CRISPR would be found patentable subject matter under §101). How valuable will the CRISPR patents be? The wide range of uses for the technique makes it difficult to speculate. However, as one data point on the question of economic value, a recently approved gene therapy (created using a different technique), is being released at a cost of $475,000 per treatment. Gina Kolata, New Gene-Therapy Treatments Will Carry Whopping Price Tags, N.Y. Times, Sept. 11, 2017 (noting additional examples along with small patient base for treatments).

Problem: Patenting Chimeras

"Chimeras" in mythology were a combination of three different animals. Modern-day researchers are combining two or more different species in a variety of ways.

Hybrids can be created through genetic manipulation (inserting the gene of one species into the genes of another species) or through manipulating the combination of nuclear material from different species to create a new organism. Each cell of the new organism will have the newly inserted gene or new genetic combination. Chimeras can be created through combining the stem cells of one organism with the embryo of another; the resulting organism will have cells of different genetic heritage within it. There has been considerable attention to whether and how to limit the creation of chimeras or hybrids using human genes and/or stem cells. See Section E.2, supra. Animal-human combinations are becoming commonplace in research. One example is the development of mice with human immune systems created by the addition of human genes; another is the mixing of mouse and human stem cells to create mice with human brain cells. See, e.g., Andrew Pollack, Seeking Cures, Patients Enlist Mice Stand-Ins, N.Y. Times, Sept. 25, 2012.

Should researchers be able to patent human-animal chimeras or hybrids? The PTO rejected a patent application for a human-animal chimera in 2005, citing among other things, the Thirteenth Amendment prohibition against slavery. See U.S. Patent Application 20030079240; Mary Ann Liebert, No Patent on Embryonic Human-Animal Chimera, 24 Biotechnology L. Rep. 290 (2005); Sander Rabin, The Human Use of Humanoid Beings: Chimeras and Patent Law, 24 Nature Biotechnology 517 (2006). At what point should use of human genes or tissues result in an inability to patent? What is the definition of "human" under the Leahy-Smith Innovation Act, supra? For more on the issues, see Ryan Hagglund, Patentability of Human-Animal Chimeras, 25 Santa Clara Computer & High Tech. L. J. 51 (2008); Gregory R. Hagen & Sébastien A. Gittens, Patenting Part-Human Chimeras, Transgenics and Stem Cells for Transplantation in the United States, Canada, and Europe, 14 Rich. J. L. & Tech. 11, 16 (2008); Laura A. Keay, Morality's Move Within U.S. Patent Law: From Moral Utility to Subject Matter, 40 AIPLA Q. J. 409 (2012); Note, Presumed Sapient: A Proposed Test for the Constitutional Personhood and Patentability of Human-Animal Chimeras and Hybrids, 46 U.S.F. L. Rev. 1075 (2012).

Problem: Synthetic Biology

The cases and commentaries to date have focused on issues connected with human genes. One of the consequences of genetic research more generally is the slowly developing ability of scientists to create and use DNA segments that can be selected to create new forms of life. This research raises significant intellectual property issues. As noted by Sapna Kumar and Arti Rai, intellectual property rules have the potential to stifle development of the field. For example, "foundational patents" on basic approaches and mechanisms could block development. Or, separate, smaller "building blocks" could be held by multiple inventors in ways that create "patent thickets" or "anticommons" hindering development. Sapna Kumar & Arti Rai, Synthetic Biology: The Intellectual Property Puzzle, 85 Tex. L. Rev. 1745 (2007) (analyzing issues and potential solutions). See also, David Singh Grewal, Before Peer Production: Infrastructure Gaps and the Architecture of Openness in Synthetic Biology, 20 Stan. Tech. L. Rev. 143 (2017) (exploring public domain approaches to developing infrastructure for synthetic biology).

Beyond intellectual property rules, synthetic biology also challenges our society's general strategy of using funding carrots and voluntary guidelines to direct research toward or away from certain areas. The synthesis of new forms of life could present substantial risks and benefits. See, e.g., Carl Zimmer, Amateurs Are New Fear in Creating Mutant Virus, N.Y. Times, Mar. 5, 2012 (noting debate over publication of research reporting modification of H5N1 bird flu virus heightening transmissibility between mammals). What form of regulation seems appropriate and feasible? The National Science Advisory Board for Biosecurity (NSABB) initially recommended against publication of the H5N1 research. See Declan Butler, Post-Mortem on Mutant Flu, 484 Nature 150 (2012); Editorial, Publishing Risky Research, 485 Nature 5 (2012). Challenges to public health will provide a focus to the issues considered in Chapter 8.

Note: Concluding Thoughts

This chapter has examined the state's right to regulate individual reproductive capacity and the implications of advances in genetic technology. You are now in a position to assess whether the legal treatment of reproductive issues is united by any common constitutional theme or policy, or whether this chapter's topics are united only by their biological underpinnings. For interesting commentary that takes this perspective, see Note, Guiding Regulatory Reform in Reproduction and Genetics, 120 Harv. L. Rev. 574 (2006) (comparing and contrasting regulatory approaches to reproduction and genetics). You might also have developed some views on whether the Supreme Court has arrived at a firmer constitutional basis for judicial review of state legislation than in the *Lochner* debacle. You can appreciate the role that advances in genetics have played in reproduction along with some of the larger issues raised by the intersection of those advances with intellectual property law. You can consider the implications of advances in genetics for insurance coverage; see Chapter 9. You can look forward to being able to place the reproductive case law in context with material in other chapters. What is the nature of a person's interest in controlling reproduction? Do we have a constitutional right to control procreative capacity that is distinguishable from the right to control medical treatment? See Chapters 3, 5, and 6. How is state regulation to protect the health of pregnant women or to safeguard fetal life similar to or different from other types of state regulation? See Chapter 8.

8

█

Public Health Law

Our lives are a tenuous gift, subject to revocation by injury, illness, and death. What is the proper role of government in safeguarding people from illness or injury? Should this responsibility be exercised by federal, state, or local government? To what extent should the need to protect public health outweigh the interests of persons subjected to coercive regulation? This chapter will consider these important questions.

Section A introduces some traditional public health strategies designed to reduce the transmission of disease and to protect individuals from injury. It is important to understand the potential scope of these measures before considering their legal implications. Medical and legal approaches to solving public health threats often seem to conflict, or at least to operate with different assumptions. Even the "simple" process of identifying and assessing the severity of public health threats can raise a number of important legal and policy questions.

Section B provides a sketch of legal underpinnings for state or federal attempts to protect public health. Traditionally, states have had the primary authority and responsibility for public health under their "police power," whether exercised directly or delegated to local governmental authorities. The federal government does not have any constitutional authority to regulate to protect the public health. Instead, its power comes from the authority to regulate the relationship between the United States and foreign countries, to regulate interstate commerce, and to spend to promote the public welfare. U.S. Const. art. 1, §8. This basic constitutional division of authority has blurred over time. These constitutional rules are supplemented by some important statutory developments, particularly the widespread effect of statutes that prohibit discrimination against persons with disabilities.

International aspects of public health law are increasingly important given the need to identify and coordinate the response to global public health threats. The United States is also an active participant in developing and funding global public health initiatives targeting issues ranging from HIV to malaria.

What distinguishes "public health" law from other categories of legal regulation? It can be difficult to discern a unifying theme. Consider licensing requirements for restaurants, funding for waste treatment plants, food and drug regulations, federal support of the Centers for Disease Control and Prevention and the National Institutes of Health or for global health initiatives, rules governing quarantines and civil commitments, licensure of health care providers, and environmental regulation. It is hard to imagine a more diverse set of policies. Yet each is founded upon governmental interests in protecting health. Seen in this light, many of the topics discussed in other chapters could be considered specific examples of "public health law." State or federal attempts to control the physician-patient relationship, to control the dying process, or to regulate organ transplantation, abortion, and reproductive technologies can be justified by the need to protect the health of members of our society. The major distinction between these topics and those traditionally considered the domain of "public health law" is the identification of the "public" protected. Governmental regulations considered in Chapters 2–6 were primarily concerned with protecting the individual patient. Some of the policies discussed in Chapter 7 were additionally justified as governmental efforts to protect fetal interests. The licensing schemes applied to individual and institutional health care providers discussed in Chapter 10 are based on the need to protect vulnerable patients from exploitation. In contrast, public health policies traditionally have protected society "at large" from threats to public health. Public health focuses on the health of populations.

The range of potential public health topics is so large that only a small subset of public health policies has been selected for consideration here. In section C, we focus on traditional public health interventions. This section explores the legal authority for disease testing and reporting statutes, quarantine, commitment, and mandatory treatment. Section D focuses on restrictions on consumer choices to protect public health. The federal government's regulation of pharmaceuticals is a particularly important example of this type of regulatory structure. The medical marijuana movement provides an opportunity to consider federal-state conflicts in public health policy. The chapter concludes with an exploration of public health approaches to the "epidemic" of obesity.

The main theme that connects these different topics is the attempt to balance the state's interest in protecting the public at large with an individual's right to freedom from coercion or constraint. As you read these materials, consider whether the balance struck between public needs and individual rights is appropriate. Will the state's interest in public health always outweigh the assertion of individual interests? What role will the courts take in ensuring that the threat to health is real and that the public health measures employed are likely to reduce the risk? Consider also the wide range of threats to public health that public health entities must address. Can the same governmental agencies and statutory/regulatory framework be used to address the public health risks presented by avian influenza, bioterrorism, and obesity?

A. PUBLIC HEALTH STRATEGIES

1. *Medical and Legal Views of Public Health*

What does it mean to protect the public's health? Health professionals tend to give a four-step answer to this question. First, potential threats to public health must be understood. Scientists work to identify "injuries" to public health and to connect those harms with their causes. Suppose that your fellow law students suddenly began to experience high fevers, swelling of their extremities, lung congestion, unconsciousness, and then rapid death. Part of the medical response would be to identify the cause of this problem—perhaps exposure to a contagious disease or an environmental toxin. Similarly, suppose that scientists observed increasing rates of morbidity and mortality from lung cancer or heart disease in society. They might then attempt to identify the causes of these conditions, such as use of tobacco products or ingestion of trans fats.

The second task is to identify a mechanism for eliminating or reducing the threat. Identifying a "cure" for the malady afflicting your classmates might be a part of this task. But researchers might also try to reduce exposure to the causal agent. If the disease is spread by exposure to rodent feces, for example, public health officials would probably develop recommendations to minimize exposure to this source and to safely clean your law school's food service area. Similarly, medical authorities might develop educational or regulatory campaigns designed to discourage smoking or consumption of trans fats.

The third step is implementation. The protective mechanisms developed in step two must be implemented. Governments must be convinced to spend scarce resources and/or to create appropriate laws or regulations to address the problem. In this stage, scientists must work with other groups in society, such as political interest groups, trade associations, lobbyists, public health officials, and legislators.

The fourth step, at least ideally, involves evaluation of the policy's outcomes. Have the new rules regarding food service sanitation actually reduced the premature death rate? Do people actually have a better diet and smoke less? If not, how can these policies be improved? Empirical research into the impact of public health law is an important example of this evaluation process.

■HISTORY OF CDC
Centers for Disease Control
45 MMWR 526 (1996)

. . . When CDC's name changed in 1970, from the Communicable Disease Center to the Centers for Disease Control, CDC scientists were poised to accept new challenges. The most notable of the agency's many achievements in the following ten years was its role in global smallpox eradication, a program that finally succeeded because of the application of scientific principles of surveillance to a complex problem. In the realm of infectious diseases, CDC maintained its preeminence, identifying the Ebola virus and the sexual transmission of hepatitis B, and isolating the hepatitis C virus and the bacterium causing Legionnaires disease. The Study of the Effectiveness of Nosocomial Infection Control (SENIC) was the most expensive study the agency had ever undertaken and proved for the first time the effectiveness of recommended infection-control practices. Other studies included identification of the association of Reye's syndrome with aspirin use, the relation between liver cancer and occupational exposure to vinyl chloride, and the harmful effects of the popular liquid protein diet.

The 1980s institutionalized what is considered to be a critically important scientific activity at CDC—the collaboration of laboratorians and epidemiologists. The decade began with the national epidemic of toxic-shock syndrome, documentation of the association with a particular brand of tampons, and the subsequent withdrawal of that brand from the market. CDC collaboration with the National Center for Health Statistics (NCHS) resulted in the removal of lead from gasoline, which in turn has markedly decreased this exposure in all segments of the population. The major public health event of the 1980s was the emergence of AIDS. CDC helped lead the response to this epidemic, including characterization of the syndrome and defining risk factors for disease. . . .

The 1990s have been characterized by continuing applications of CDC's classic field-oriented epidemiology, as well as by the development of new methodologies. For example, the disciplines of health economics and decision sciences were merged to create a new area of emphasis—prevention effectiveness—as an approach for making more rational choices for public health interventions. In 1993, the investigation of hantavirus pulmonary syndrome required a melding between field epidemiology and the need for sensitivity to and involvement of American Indians and their culture. Similarly, the response to global problems with Ebola virus and plague underscore the importance of adapting these new methodologies. Other major CDC contributions to the world's health include global polio eradication efforts and efforts to prevent neural tube defects. Finally, in October 1992, Congress changed CDC's official name to the Centers for Disease Control and Prevention, to recognize CDC's leadership role in prevention. Today, CDC is both the nation's prevention agency and a global leader in public health. As the world enters the new millennium, CDC will remain the agency ready to address the challenges to its vision of healthy people in a healthy world through prevention.

■ SUMMARY OF NOTIFIABLE INFECTIOUS DISEASES AND CONDITIONS—UNITED STATES, 2015

Deborah A. Adams, et al.,
64(53) Morbidity and Mortality Weekly Rep. (Aug. 11, 2017)

BACKGROUND

. . . A notifiable infectious disease or condition is one for which regular, frequent, and timely information regarding individual cases is considered necessary for the prevention and control of the disease or condition. A brief history of the reporting of nationally notifiable infectious diseases and conditions in the United States is available at https://wwwn.cdc.gov/nndss/history.aspx. In 1961, CDC assumed responsibility for the collection of data on nationally notifiable diseases. Data are collected through NNDSS, which is neither a single surveillance system nor a method of reporting. Rather, it is a "system of systems," which is coordinated by CDC at the national level across disease-specific programs to optimize data compilation, analysis, and dissemination of notifiable disease data. Monitoring surveillance data enables public health authorities to detect sudden changes in disease or condition occurrence and distribution, identify changes in agents and host factors, and detect changes in health care practices. National-level surveillance data are compiled from case notification reports of nationally notifiable infectious diseases and conditions submitted from the state, territory, and selected local health departments to CDC.

Cases are first identified through reports of infectious diseases and conditions from the local level to the state or territory. Legislation, regulation, or other rules in those jurisdictions require health care providers, hospitals, laboratories, and others to provide information on reportable conditions to public health authorities or their agents. Case reporting at the local level protects the public's health by ensuring the proper identification and follow-up of cases. Public health workers ensure that persons who are already ill receive appropriate treatment; trace contacts who need vaccines, treatment, quarantine, or education; investigate and control outbreaks; eliminate environmental hazards; and close premises where disease transmission is believed to be ongoing.

Although infectious disease and condition reporting is mandated at the state, territory, and local levels by legislation or regulation, state and territory notification to CDC is voluntary. All U.S. state health departments, five territorial health departments, and two local health departments (New York City and District of Columbia) voluntarily notify CDC about nationally notifiable infectious diseases and conditions that are reportable in their jurisdictions . . . . Case notification of nationally notifiable infectious diseases and conditions helps public health authorities monitor the effect of these diseases and conditions, measure the disease and condition trends, assess the effectiveness of control and prevention measures, identify populations or geographic areas at high risk, allocate resources appropriately, formulate prevention strategies, and develop public health policies.

The list of nationally notifiable infectious diseases and conditions is revised periodically . . . . An infectious disease or condition might be added to the list as a new pathogen emerges, or a disease or condition might be removed as its incidence declines. Public health officials at state and territorial health departments collaborate with CDC staff in determining which infectious diseases and conditions should be considered nationally notifiable. CSTE [Council of State and Territorial Epidemiologists], with input from CDC, makes recommendations annually for additions and deletions to the list. The list of infectious diseases and conditions considered reportable in each jurisdiction varies over time and across jurisdictions. Current and historical national public health surveillance case definitions used for classifying and enumerating cases consistently at the national level across reporting jurisdictions are available at https://wwwn.cdc.gov/nndss/conditions. . . .

INTERNATIONAL HEALTH REGULATIONS

At its annual meeting in June 2007, CSTE approved a position statement that supports implementation of International Health Regulations (IHR) in the United States. CSTE approval followed the adoption of revised IHR in May 2005 by the

World Health Assembly that went into effect in the United States on July 18, 2007. This international legal instrument governs the role of the World Health Organization (WHO) and its member countries, including the United States, in identifying, responding to, and sharing information about events that might constitute a Public Health Emergency of International Concern (PHEIC). A PHEIC is an extraordinary event that constitutes a public health risk to other countries through international spread of disease and potentially requires a coordinated international response. All WHO member countries are required to notify WHO of a potential PHEIC. WHO makes the final determination about the existence of a PHEIC.

Health care providers in the United States are required to report diseases, conditions, and outbreaks determined to be reportable by local, state, or territorial law or regulation. In addition, all health care providers should work with their local, state, or territorial health agencies to identify and report events occurring in their location that might constitute a PHEIC. U.S. state and territorial departments of health report information about a potential PHEIC to the most relevant federal agency responsible for monitoring such an event. In the case of human diseases, the U.S. state or territorial departments of health notifies CDC through existing formal and informal reporting mechanisms. CDC further analyzes the event by use of the decision algorithm in Annex 2 of the IHR and notifies the U.S. Department of Health and Human Services (DHHS) Secretary's Operations Center (SOC), as appropriate. The DHHS SOC is responsible for reporting a potential PHEIC to WHO.

In the United States, DHHS has the lead role in carrying out IHR, in cooperation with multiple federal departments and agencies. When a potential PHEIC is identified, the United States has 48 hours to assess the risk for the reported event. If authorities determine that a potential PHEIC exists, the United States, as with all WHO member countries, has 24 hours to report the event to WHO.

An IHR decision algorithm (Annex 2 of the IHR) was developed to help countries determine whether an event should be reported. If any two of the following four questions are answered in the affirmative, then a potential PHEIC exists and WHO should be notified:

- Is the public health impact of the event serious?
- Is the event unusual or unexpected?
- Is there a significant risk for international spread?
- Is there a significant risk for international travel or trade restrictions?

The revised IHR reflects a conceptual shift from the use of a predefined disease list to a framework of reporting and responding to events on the basis of an assessment of public health criteria, including seriousness, unexpectedness, and international travel and trade implications. A PHEIC is an event that falls within those criteria . . . however, any one of the following four conditions always constitutes a PHEIC and do not require the use of the IHR decision instrument in Annex 2:

- severe acute respiratory syndrome (SARS),
- smallpox,
- poliomyelitis caused by wild-type poliovirus, and
- human influenza caused by a new subtype.

Examples of events that require the use of the decision instrument include, but are not limited, to cholera, pneumonic plague, yellow fever, West Nile fever, viral hemorrhagic fevers, and meningococcal disease. Other biologic, chemical, or radiologic events that fit the decision algorithm also must be reported to WHO. . . .

■ THE LAW AND THE PUBLIC'S HEALTH: A STUDY OF INFECTIOUS DISEASE LAW IN THE UNITED STATES*
Lawrence O. Gostin, Scott Burris & Zita Lazzarini
99 Colum. L. Rev. 59 (1999)

Public health is typically regarded as a scientific pursuit, and, undoubtedly, our understanding of the etiology and response to disease is heavily influenced by scientific inquiry. Less well understood is the role of law in public health. Law is an essential part of public health practice. Law defines the jurisdiction of public health officials and specifies the manner in which they may exercise their authority. The law is a tool in public health work, which is used to establish norms for healthy behavior and to help create the social conditions in which people can be healthy. The most important social debates about public health take place in legal fora—legislatures, courts, and administrative agencies—and in the law's language of rights, duties, and justice. . . .

The Institute of Medicine (IOM), in its foundational 1988 report, "The Future of Public Health" (the IOM Report), agreed that law was essential to public health, but cast serious doubt on the soundness of public health's legal basis in the United States. . . .[2]

Communicable disease control has occupied American governments from the earliest years of European settlement, and it was in response to epidemics that formal health agencies were first created. Throughout the history of the United States, each state, through the exercise of its police powers, has enacted a web of legislation to control infectious disease. These laws range from generic statutes establishing powers relating to communicable and sexually transmitted disease, to disease- specific laws relating, for example, to tuberculosis or HIV/AIDS. Although the threat of communicable diseases in America has declined throughout the last century, new diseases such as AIDS, hepatitis C, and hantavirus have emerged as major threats, and old diseases such as tuberculosis and E. coli have returned with new virulence.

Communicable disease law has deep historical roots, yet remains centrally important to legal institutions and to the public's health. Our approach to reform, however, is based on a broader notion of the determinants of health and the role of the state in promoting it, a view in which the distinction between communicable

---

* Reprinted with permission. Lawrence O. Gostin is a Professor of Law and University Professor at Georgetown University. Scott Burris is a Professor at Temple University's Beasley School of Law. Zita Lazzarini is an Associate Professor in Community Medicine and Health Care at the University of Connecticut School of Medicine.

2. Committee for the Study of the Future of Public Health, IOM, Nat'l Acad. of Sci., The Future of Public Health 1-6 (1988). . . .

and noncommunicable health threats is, in many ways, unimportant. Thus, many of our points about communicable disease law apply to public health regulation as a whole.

Our frankly utilitarian premise is that public health law ought to be as effective as possible in helping public health agencies create the conditions necessary for health. To do this, the law must reflect our best understanding of how public health agencies work to promote health, as well as the political conditions in which these agencies operate. . . .

The essential job of public health agencies is to identify what makes us healthy and what makes us sick, and then to take the steps necessary to make sure we encounter a maximum of the former and a minimum of the latter. At first glance, this would seem to be a rather uncontroversial goal, but we will show that the pursuit of public health creates fundamental social disputes virtually by definition. Public health is rooted in the biomedical and social sciences, but from the moment of asserting some collective responsibility for the population's health, through the process of defining the determinants of health and disease, to the implementation of programs, the practice of public health entails judgments that challenge deeply ingrained social attitudes and practices.

Three distinct accounts of disease and health are widely used in public health practice today. . . . The microbial model focuses on the pathogens that are the immediate causes of many illnesses. The microbial model produces interventions designed to kill the pathogen or isolate it from human beings; it also tends to produce political disputes about the proper scope and exercise of the state's power to attack the pathogen by controlling the human being who carries it. The behavioral model looks primarily at the behavior that exposes us to pathogens or that otherwise tends to produce illness and premature death. The idea that behavior is an important factor in health and disease is widely accepted, but health efforts on the behavioral model are nonetheless often controversial. When the government gives advice about how to have safer sex or how to reduce the risk of drug injection, many people see an official endorsement of what they regard as deviant behavior. When the state uses its power to discourage smoking, to require a motorcycle helmet, or even to prevent dental caries through water fluoridation, many people see unacceptable paternalism. The ecological model takes the broadest view of what makes people ill or well, seeking the causes of disease in the way society organizes itself, produces and distributes wealth, and interacts with the natural environment. Such an approach operates unavoidably as a critique of the status quo, pointing to such fundamental social causes of disease as poverty, racism, and severe income inequality. The ecological model also implicates our collective responsibility for unhealthy behavior, suggesting the importance of social factors in producing, for example, the levels of drug abuse and unsafe sex that fuel the HIV and hepatitis epidemics. Each of these models of disease and health is rooted in the sciences of medicine and epidemiology and provides complementary ways of understanding and fighting disease, but each also entails judgments about who is responsible for illness and who must change to produce health. . . .

We name five perennially significant political problems inherent in modern public health practice. The first is the problem of popular apathy about public health programs. Much of what public health agencies do is to prevent injury and disease, often by getting people at low risk to refrain from behaviors they enjoy or profit from. . . .

Second, public health agencies have a jurisdiction problem. Many societal and environmental factors that influence public health are beyond the reach of health agencies. Occupational safety, environmental protection, food safety, and the prevention of violence and accidents are normally the province of other agencies, and much of the behavior that public health tries to change—eating a diet high in fat, for example—is not subject to direct legal regulation at all.

Third, public health agencies must confront the problem of stigma and social hostility. Communicable disease control has traditionally had to deal with barriers thrown up by the social reaction to disease. In their time, diseases like cholera, yellow fever, tuberculosis, and syphilis were all attributed to sin or vice, and the shame and social risk of having such conditions often led the sick to conceal their illness and to avoid medical and public health services. The problem of stigma and social hostility has been an important factor in HIV prevention since the earliest days of the epidemic.

The fourth problem involves the legitimacy of government action in certain realms of human behavior. The problem of legitimacy arises whenever public health measures are perceived to exceed the bounds of proper government action. Whether framed in terms of paternalism, endorsement, neutrality, or simple libertarianism, the legitimacy issue turns on the belief that there are certain things government simply ought not do, no matter how laudable its objectives.

Finally, health agencies face a problem of trust. Because so much of what public health does depends upon voluntary cooperation by those at risk and the support of the population at large, health officials must appear credible in the advice they render and trustworthy in their practices. If the public perceives health officials as simply the tool of an overreaching government or suspects that they have been captured by "special interests," their ability to win compliance and support is compromised.

As if these built-in challenges were not enough, communicable disease control faces economic and structural barriers: the decline in the public health infrastructure for monitoring and controlling disease; the transformation of the health care system, including expansion of managed care and integrated delivery systems; and the emergence and resurgence of infectious disease threats. . . .

"Public health" refers both to a goal for the health of a population and to professional practices aimed at its attainment. . . . At a minimum, the goal of public health is to attain the highest level and widest distribution of physical and mental health that a society reasonably can achieve within the limits of the resources it chooses to devote to the task. . . .

Even this carefully narrowed definition places the goal of public health at the intersection of deep social fault lines. First, it posits that public health is a function of the health of populations, not individuals. Geoffrey Rose has brilliantly described the practical implications of this difference for disease prevention, including most notably the "prevention paradox." This is the apparently iron law holding that those measures that have the greatest potential for improving public health (like seatbelt use) offer little absolute benefit to any individual, while measures that heroically save individual lives (like heart transplants) make no significant contribution to the population's health. Public health, in other words, has as its chief duty the unenviable tasks of providing common goods and controlling negative externalities, both difficult at best. . . .

The ability of public health work to attract support is, however, essential to its success, for, as the definition of public health also reminds us, public health operates in a world of choices in the allocation of limited resources. The great sanitarian Herman Biggs famously remarked that "public health is purchasable," but because there will always be limits on how much we are willing to buy, public health will always turn on allocational decisions. Thus, public health, as both a goal and a practice, is as inherently political (i.e., concerned with the allocation of resources in society) as it is technological (i.e., concerned with the deployment of professional knowledge of illness).

Finally, public health's desire for optimally healthy populations builds into the definition a concern for distributive justice that must, on occasion, challenge the current distribution of wealth. A society in which the more prosperous segment of the population enjoys health conditions that are as good as any in the world, but where many are living substantially below the norm, is not a nation with good public health. . . .

Nineteenth-century sanitarians focused on providing clean water, adequate sewers, pure food, safe workplaces, and hygienic dwellings to the urban poor who were at greatest risk for the most common communicable diseases. Toward this end, boards of health were created and given increasingly broad powers to investigate and abate nuisances endangering health, and an administrative and legal infrastructure was built of food safety laws, building codes, social welfare programs, and water bureaus. But as early as the turn of this century, the escalating success of biomedical science was changing public health, moving its center away from a broad social, environmental focus to a more individualized, medical one based on germ theory. Health leaders . . . pushed for the legal authority to deploy modern "epidemiological methods" of disease control, in which pathogens were to be identified through individual testing or population screening and reporting, and then eliminated through vaccination, treatment, isolation, or quarantine. With good diagnostic tools and surveillance, disease outbreaks could be spotted early. With quick and effective treatments, patients could be rendered noninfectious with little disruption to their lives or society's business. The pathogen, not social conditions, was thought to be the problem, and through modern methods like these, the pathogen could be defeated. Health authorities sought the power to test suspected carriers, screen populations (such as marriage license applicants and newborns), trace partners, and require treatment. The social vision and reform agenda that had focused sanitary reformers on slums and sewer lines was replaced with a concern for biomedical research, vaccination, and timely medical treatment. It was in the early- to mid-twentieth century, the heyday of the microbial model of disease, that communicable disease law assumed the form in which it largely exists to this day.

Health departments are influenced by this history, even as they try to adapt to changes in social conditions and threats to health. Health departments today are generally organized to serve four "core functions": health promotion and disease prevention; assessment, data collection, and data analysis; medical services; and leadership and policy development. . . .

The main job of health agencies is to directly promote good health and prevent illness. To this end, modern public health practice deploys measures based on all three of the major models of disease causation. Health departments continue to employ traditional measures aimed at finding and controlling pathogens (e.g., testing, screening, reporting, contact tracing, vaccination, compulsory treatment, and isolation). Health departments also oversee the purity of water supplies and the hygienic conditions of food service establishments. Law provides both jurisdiction over the problem and the authority to require compliance. Law, in the form of privacy rules and due process requirements, also helps assure that measures involving the control of individuals are, and are perceived to be, rational, fair, and as harmless to the individual as possible.

Health departments also devote significant resources to changing behavior in the population. As chronic, nonmicrobial diseases such as cancer and heart disease came to dominate the mortality tables, public health focused its attention on risk-enhancing behavior such as smoking, high-fat diets, and inactivity. Significant behavioral sources of traumatic injury and death, such as teen violence and drunken driving, have also been treated as public health problems. Changing behavior has, of course, become crucial in controlling communicable diseases like HIV, as well. Risk-factor screening (for cholesterol or high blood pressure, for example), individualized counseling, and health education are standard tools of behavior change, but so is the law. Law is used to reduce unsafe behavior by both direct (e.g., helmet laws for motorcyclists and drunk driving laws) and indirect (e.g., taxes and subsidies) means, the goals of which are to make healthier behavior less costly and unhealthy behavior more expensive.

Influenced by ecological thinking about disease, public health workers have recognized the importance of addressing the social causes of unhealthy individual behavior. Individual choices depend in substantial part on the options provided by society and on the behavioral cues with which individual decisionmakers are bombarded in any social setting. They also depend upon material conditions, like the distribution of wealth and government policies. Health workers now routinely design interventions that attempt to address social factors such as stigma, discrimination, and sexism. Public health officials have become advocates of policies, such as the elimination of legal barriers to sterile hypodermic syringes and needles, that make it possible for individuals to make healthier choices. Using tools of economics and marketing, public health authorities have begun to develop programs to influence individual behavior choices by changing the prevailing social norms.

Ecological strategies address environmental problems, land use, patterns of commerce, and medical and commercial use of antimicrobials, as well as social, political, and economic conditions that influence population movement and changes in standards of living. With such broad targets, health measures aimed at ecological causes of disease quickly bring health agencies to the outer bounds of their statutory jurisdiction. . . .

Notes: An Overview of Public Health Strategies

1. *Sources of Information.* There are a broad range of measures designed to improve public health, ranging from improved sanitation to vaccination, screening programs, and education about health threats such as tobacco. There are different sources of information on all of these public health topics. The Centers for Disease Control and Prevention (CDC) is a world leader in identifying threats to public health and in developing recommendations to reduce health risks. Its pub-

lication, the aptly named Morbidity and Mortality Weekly Report (MMWR), is a major source of data on a variety of threats to public health, but particularly for data on contagious diseases. The publication is not for the fainthearted or for those with any tendencies toward hypochondria. The MMWR's pages are regularly filled with detailed case descriptions of everything from infectious diseases to the disastrous effects of ingesting commercially prepared, improperly refrigerated potato soup. The CDC maintains extensive online resources. See, e.g., CDC homepage, www.cdc.gov/; MMWR homepage, www.cdc.gov/mmwr/.

2. *Conflicts Between Medical and Legal Norms.* Where should public health policies be developed—in legislative bodies, in administrative agencies, or somewhere else? Should physicians or lawyers have primary control over the development and implementation of public health strategies? What role should the courts take in overseeing public health measures? Medical or scientific authorities and lawyers tend to have somewhat different perspectives on public health strategies. Historically, public health officials focused on the medical or scientific aspects of public health policies and paid little attention to their impact on individual liberty. The article by Professors Gostin, Burris, and Lazzarini was one of the early publications in a significant effort to study and to reform public health law that is still underway. The CDC established a public health law program, see www.cdc.gov/phlp/ and has supported a range of public health law activities, including national conferences. Professor Gostin is a leader in the reform of public health law within the United States and internationally. See Lawrence O. Gostin and Lindsay F. Wiley, Public Health Law: Power, Duty, Restraint (3d ed. 2016) [hereinafter Public Health Law].

3. *Jurisdictional Issues.* Public health threats often span jurisdictional boundaries. The federal government plays an important role in addressing threats that cross international or state boundaries, 42 U.S.C. §§264-272, but states typically manage outbreaks of disease within their borders. Federal and state public health policies and practices were tested by global health challenges in the 2010s, including significant outbreaks of Ebola in Africa and the Middle East Respiratory Syndrome (MERS) in Middle East and South Korea. The public health responses were not always clear and consistent with best practices. See pages 916-917 and 987.

The CDC issued a notice of proposed rulemaking relating to its quarantine powers in August 2016. The proposal elicited a significant number of comments: 15,800 in the 60-day public comment period. The CDC issued the Final Rule for the Control of Communicable Diseases: Interstate and Foreign, on January 19, 2017. 82 Fed. Reg. 6890-01 (2017) (amending 42 C.F.R. 70, 71). After a brief delay to permit review during the change in Presidential administrations, the Final Rule became effective on March 21, 2017. The revised Rule's objectives were to "aid public health responses to outbreaks of new or re-emerging communicable diseases and to accord due process to individuals subject to Federal public health orders." Id. at 6890. The Final Rule differed from the initial proposal in several areas, including the adoption of additional procedural safeguards, such as a "requirement for CDC to provide legal counsel for isolated or quarantined individuals qualifying as indigent who request a medical review." Id. See also, Kyle Edwards, Wendy Parmet & Scott Burris, Why the C.D.C.'s Power to Quarantine Should Worry Us, N.Y. Times, Jan. 23, 2017 (noting, among other concerns, the lack of a mechanism for speedy judicial review of federal quarantine orders).

The CDC plays an important role in collecting data from states about the incidence of disease, and the federal government is responsible for making determinations under WHO's International Health Regulations (www.who.int/topics/international_health_regulations/en/). Yet, mandatory disease reporting is established by state law, reporting to the CDC is voluntary, and there are gaps and difficulties in comparing the voluntarily reported state data. Is the constitutional balance between state and federal authority in protecting public health appropriate? Has the federal government achieved virtual authority over public health matters by tying state receipt of federal funding to compliance with federal requirements? See Rebecca Katz & Sara Rosenbaum, Challenging Custom: Rethinking National Population Surveillance Policy in a Global Public Health Age, 35 J. Health Pol. Pol'y & L. 1027 (2010) (suggesting possible expansion of federal involvement in disease surveillance); Kumanan Wilson et al., Strategies for Implementing the New International Health Regulations in Federal Countries, 86(3) Bull. World Health Organ. 215 (2008).

A different form of jurisdictional conflict arises as public health policies move beyond traditional responses to infectious diseases into addressing chronic diseases caused by behavioral choices, disparities in health related to social determinants of the health of populations, and complex threats such as climate change. Public Health Law at 531-550; CDC Health Disparities and Inequalities Report—United States, 2013, 62 MMWR 1 (2013) (Suppl. 3). As one example, public health organizations are beginning to address climate change as a new threat to public health. See CDC, Climate Change and Human Health (www.cdc.gov/climateandhealth). What are the advantages and disadvantages of addressing global warming as a public health issue? How will the public health response be affected by debates about climate change regulations in the United States? What effect does framing the issue in this way have on the federal and state governments' ability to regulate human activities that contribute to global warming? Greenhouse gas emissions are typically seen as matters for environmental regulation rather than as public health threats remedied through, e.g., nuisance actions. See, e.g., American Electric Power Co. Inc. v. Connecticut, 564 U.S. 410 (2011) (federal legislation and proposed EPA action on greenhouse gases displaces availability of nuisance claim under federal law; availability of state law nuisance claims to be determined on remand); Massachusetts et al. v. Environmental Protection Agency et al., 549 U.S. 497 (2007) (EPA has jurisdiction over greenhouse gas emissions under the Clean Air Act). The CDC and WHO focus on planning for the health care outcomes of global warming rather than on reduction or elimination of the underlying problem.

4. *The World Health Organization (WHO) and Calls to Strengthen Global Health Governance.* Although many important health threats cross national borders, the international aspects of health law have only recently become a major area of study:

> Safeguarding the population's health traditionally occurs at the national level, with a web of laws and regulations governing health services, injury and disease prevention, and health promotion. However, in a globalized world in which pathogens and lifestyle risks span borders, the need for collective action has intensified interest in international legal solutions.
>
> The law relating to global health rests primarily within the domain of public international law, which can be broadly characterized as the rules that govern the conduct and relations of countries, including their rights and obligations. Countries remain the major subjects of international law, but international organizations

and (through human rights law) individuals are also considered to be subject of international law.

There is a complex array of international norms, including those that are binding, or "hard" (e.g., treaties), and those that are nonbinding, or "soft" (e.g., codes of practice). Hard and soft legal instruments have many similarities and often take similar forms, since both forms of instruments are negotiated and adopted by countries, are administered by international organizations, and have similar compliance mechanisms, such a setting targets, monitoring progress, and reporting to governmental agencies. Soft instruments can influence domestic law and policy and are often viewed as part of the corpus of international law.

Lawrence O. Gostin & Devi Sridhar, Global Health and the Law, 370 N. Eng. J. Med. 1732, 1732 (2014) (providing broad overview of major global health law instrument and cases, as well as a discussion of future hard and soft law approaches).

The WHO and the international health law framework have been challenged by a succession of epidemics and pandemics over the past ten years. The H1N1 epidemic in 2009 provided the first opportunity to test what was then a relatively new international health law framework. H1N1 was a novel influenza virus; the impact on public health thus could have ranged from minimal to severe. The WHO attempted to use its powers under the IHR to guide the global response but the morbidity and mortality associated with the virus proved to be within normal ranges and critics charged that public health authorities overreacted to the threat. An expert review panel concluded: "The core national and local capacities called for in the IHR are not yet fully operational and are not now on a path to timely implementation worldwide. . . . The world is ill-prepared to respond to a severe influenza pandemic or to any similarly global, sustained and threatening public-health emergency." Report of the Review Committee on the Functioning of the International Health Regulations in Relation to Pandemic (H1N1) 2009, 11-12 (2011). The Review Committee noted that a number of countries failed to comply with WHO guidance regarding the lack of justification for restrictions on travel and trade. The Committee concluded: "The most important structural shortcoming of the IHR is the lack of enforceable sanctions. For example, if a country fails to explain why it has adopted more restrictive traffic and trade measures than those recommended by WHO, no legal consequences follow." Id. at 12.

The next round of challenges came with the Ebola outbreak in 2014 and the Zika epidemic in 2016. WHO was criticized for moving too slowly to address Ebola as it waited four months to declare that the outbreak was a public health emergency of international concern. Lawrence O. Gostin, Mary C. DeBartolo & Eric A. Friedman, The International Health Regulations 10 Years On, 386 Lancet 2222 (2015) (noting additional failures to declare public health emergencies for MERS and other global events). The Ebola epidemic revealed serious gaps, including a lack of health care personnel, equipment, and community trust in the health care systems of a number of affected countries. Critics also noted "[s]tate and private industry disregard for WHO temporary recommendations — particularly travel and trade restrictions and injudicious quarantines." Id. at 2225. See page 987.

The WHO declared the Zika virus a global health emergency in February 2016, even as evidence was still developing that the virus could cause microcephaly in children born to affected mothers. However, critics noted that the organization initially failed to recommend that pregnant women avoid travel to affected areas, with some suggesting the reluctance might be related to Brazil's preparations to host the Summer Olympics. Sabrina Tavernise & Donald G. McNeil, Jr., Zika Virus a Global Health Emergency, N.Y. Times, February 1, 2016. WHO did not advise people living in Zika-affected areas to delay pregnancy until late May of 2016, months after other health authorities had suggested this measure. Donald G. McNeil, Jr., Delay Pregnancy in Areas with Zika, W.H.O. Suggests, N.Y. Times, June 9, 2016 (noting as well the challenges associated with limited access to birth control or abortion in affected countries). WHO declared the Zika emergency over in November 2016 because the epidemic—while continuing to present significant seasonal risks in South America, most of North America, Asia, and elsewhere—no longer met the IHR criteria. Zika Is No Longer a Global Emergency, W.H.O. Says, N.Y. Times, Nov. 18, 2016 (noting concerns that delisting would be misunderstood by individuals at risk and governments making decisions about funding for programs). See also, Jacqueline Fox, Zika and the Failure to Act Under the Police Power, 49 Conn. L. Rev. 1211 (2017) (critiquing lack of state or federal legislative response to Zika in the United States).

As many critics have noted, the past decade of global responses to emerging health threats suggests potential issues with capacity at the WHO as well as in countries with relatively poor health infrastructure or other economic, social, or cultural barriers to protecting public health. The weakness of the global health infrastructure creates serious risks for people around the world. Given the nature of the threats to public health, should the United States work with other countries toward more powerful international institutions and standards? See Gostin, DeBartolo & Friedman, supra; and compare Lawrence O. Gostin & Eric A. Friedman, Global Health: A Pivotal Moment of Opportunity and Peril, 36 Health Affairs 20 (2017) (optimistic) with Lawrence O. Gostin, "America First": Prospects for Global Health, 95 Millbank Q. 224 (2017) (less so).

5. *Fear.* What would be your response to an apparently serious, contagious illness spreading among your classmates? Dangerous contagious diseases can create a state euphemistically called "anxiety," better known as panic or fear. Fear can motivate a wide range of responses, some helpful from a public health standpoint, but some not. Gillian K. SteelFisher, Robert J. Blendon & Narayani Lasala-Blanco, Ebola in the United States—Public Reactions and Implications, 373 N. Eng. J. Med. 789 (2015). Consider the role fear plays in the various public health strategies and responses that you will review in the remaining sections of this chapter. What should be the role of public health officials in addressing public concerns? Should courts worry more about too weak or too vigilant public health responses? See Cass R. Sunstein, Laws of Fear: Beyond the Precautionary Principle (2005); Luc Bonneux & Wim Van Damme, An Iatrogenic Pandemic of Panic, 332 BMJ 786 (2006). For more on this topic, see Albert Camus, The Plague (1947) or the portions of the Bible (especially Exodus, Deuteronomy, and Amos) dealing with plagues and public reactions to contagious diseases.

6. *Other Resources.* There are a number of excellent books and articles on public health measures from medical and legal perspectives. In addition to the **general sources** noted above (note 1), see Scott Burris et al., Making the Case for Laws That Improve Health: A Framework for Public Health Law Research, 88 Mil-

bank Q. 169 (2010); Committee on Public Health Strategies to Improve Health, Institute of Medicine, For the Public's Health: Revitalizing Law and Policy to Meet New Challenges (2011); Wendy E. Parmet, Populations, Public Health, and the Law (2009); Mark Rothstein, From SARS to Ebola: Legal and Ethical Considerations for Modern Quarantine, 12 Ind. Health L. Rev. 227 (2015); Symposium, The Intersection of Law, Science, and Policy to Protect the Public's Health, 53 Jurimetrics 254-387 (2013). For more on potential conflicts between the **norms of law and medicine** (note 2), see Jonny Anomaly, What Is an Epidemic? 42 J. L. Med. & Ethics 389 (2014) (commentary on the meaning and use of the word "epidemic"); Dan Beauchamp, The Health of the Republic: Epidemics, Medicine, and Moralism as Challenges to Democracy (1990); Allan M. Brandt, No Magic Bullet: A Social History of Venereal Disease in the United States Since 1880 (1985). There are numerous commentaries on **jurisdictional issues** and the breadth of topics potentially included within the realm of public health law (note 3). See, e.g., James G. Hodge et al., Public Health "Preemption Plus," 45 J. L. Med. & Ethics 156 (2017); Jennifer L. Pomeranz & Mark Pertschuk, State Preemption: A Significant and Quiet Threat to Public Health in the United States, 107 Am. J. Pub. Health 900 (2017). For additional resources on public health approaches to reducing health inequality, see Symposium, 2016 Public Health Law Conference — Lead, Connect, Innovate: Strategies for Achieving Health Equity, 45 J. L. Med. & Ethics 8-102 (2017). For more on public health and climate change, see Bruce Levy & Jonathan Patz, Climate Change and Public Health (2015). **International aspects** of public health law (note 4) are a growing area of interest and concern, see Lawrence O. Gostin, Global Health Law (2014); Lawrence O. Gostin & Ana S. Ayala, Global Health Security in an Era of Explosive Pandemic Potential, 9 J. Nat'l Security L. & Pol'y 53 (2016); Steven J. Hoffman, John-Arne Røttingen & Julio Frenk, Assessing Proposals for New Global Health Treaties, 105 Am. J. Pub. Health 1523 (2015); Alexandra Minna Stern & Howard Markel, International Efforts to Control Infectious Diseases, 1851 to the Present, 292 JAMA 1474 (2004); Symposium, Global Infectious Diseases: New Challenges and Solutions, 42 Am. J. L. & Med. 223-620 (2016); Symposium, Global Health and the Law, 41 J. L. Med. & Ethics 9-300 (2013).

7. *Assessing Public Health Threats.* What are the greatest threats to public health? Infectious conditions? Bioterrorism? Environmental hazards such as climate change? Dietary and lifestyle choices? How would you identify the "greatest" threat? By number of persons affected? By the severity of the harm? Now consider the appropriate role of government in responding to the risks you have identified. Should the government develop a response to one or more of these risks? What type of response seems justified: public education or using regulations to reduce risks? Where should governments apply their scarce resources and why? The next case addresses some of these issues, in the context of OSHA regulation. Although the Occupational Safety and Health Administration is not considered one of the classic public health agencies, the following case focuses on a workplace health risk peculiar to hospitals — contagious disease — that is at the core of classic public health regulation. Moreover, this case explains the fundamentals of risk assessment that are the basis for all public health measures.

2. Risk Assessment and Regulatory Competence

▌AMERICAN DENTAL ASSOCIATION v. MARTIN
984 F.2d 823 (7th Cir. 1993)

POSNER, Circuit Judge.

In 1991 the Occupational Safety and Health Administration promulgated a rule on occupational exposure to bloodborne pathogens. 29 C.F.R. §1910.1030. The rule is designed to protect health care workers from viruses, particularly those causing Hepatitis B and AIDS, that can be transmitted in the blood of patients. Promulgated after a protracted notice-and-comment rulemaking proceeding, the rule and its supporting reasons occupy 178 densely packed pages in the Federal Register. Most employers in the health care industry have accepted the rule, which in essence requires compliance with procedures for health care workers recommended by the Centers for Disease Control (since renamed the Centers for Disease Control and Prevention), the federal agency responsible for the control of contagious diseases. Many of these employers, indeed, had adopted the procedures as soon as the CDC recommended them. Three employer groups, however, challenge the rule—dentists, represented by the American Dental Association, and medical-personnel and home-health employers, both represented by the Home Health Services and Staffing Association. Medical-personnel firms supply health care workers on a temporary basis to hospitals and nursing homes, while home-health firms supply such workers to patients at home.

As of 1991, there had been only 24 confirmed cases of U.S. health care workers infected with the AIDS virus by patients since AIDS was first diagnosed in 1981. Hepatitis B is a far more common disease than AIDS, though less scary, publicized, or stigmatized. . . . Although most infected persons recover uneventfully, about 1 percent die and about 6 to 10 percent of adult (and a much higher percentage of child) victims of Hepatitis B become carriers. . . . Nonetheless, because of the greater virulence of the Hepatitis B virus (HBV) and the fact that many health care workers are not vaccinated, patient-communicated Hepatitis B kills about 200 health workers in the United States per year—roughly 100 times the number of such workers infected by patient-communicated HIV [human immunodeficiency virus]. The precautions against infection of health care workers by the two viruses is similar, except that the vaccine against HBV offers a protection that has no counterpart with regard to HIV, and contaminated laundry poses a danger of spreading HBV that also has no counterpart with regard to HIV.

OSHA's rule reflects the public-health philosophy of "universal precautions," which means precautions against the blood of every patient, not just the blood of patients known or believed likely to be carriers of HBV or HIV. The precautions are various. They include engineering controls (such as requirements for the location of sinks), work practice controls (such as standards of care in handling contaminated sharp instruments, such as needles), requirements for personal protective equipment such as gloves, masks, goggles, and gowns, requirements for housekeeping (covering such things as the cleaning of contaminated surfaces and laundry and the disposal of contaminated waste), reporting requirements, and provisions for medical care. The rule requires the employer to offer employees who are at risk of exposure to the blood of patients the Hepatitis B vaccine at the employer's own expense, though it allows the employees to decline to be vaccinated. An employee who is involved in an "exposure incident," such as being stuck with a contaminated needle, must be offered at the employer's expense a confidential blood test for HBV and HIV; that is, only the employee is entitled to the result of the test.

In deciding to impose this extensive array of restrictions on the practice of medicine, nursing, and dentistry, OSHA did not (indeed is not authorized to) compare the benefits with the costs and impose the restrictions on finding that the former exceeded the latter. Instead it asked whether the restrictions would materially reduce a significant workplace risk to human health without imperiling the existence of, or threatening massive dislocation to, the health care industry. For this is the applicable legal standard. 29 U.S.C. §655(b) (5); Industrial Union Dept., AFL-CIO v. American Petroleum Institute, 448 U.S. 607, 642-645, 655-656 (1980) (the "benzene" case) (plurality opinion); American Textile Mfrs. Institute, Inc. v. Donovan, 452 U.S. 490, 509-512, 530-536 (1981) (the "cotton dust" case). The agency focused on HBV rather than on HIV because of the minute number of health care workers who have been infected by the latter virus. It estimated that the rule would eliminate between 113 and 129 annual deaths of health care workers from Hepatitis B, and a somewhat higher figure (187 to 197) if deaths of nonworkers infected by health-care workers who (but for the rule) would be carriers are factored in as well. (In making this additional calculation, OSHA expressed an uncharacteristic, but as it seems to us commendable, concern with the indirect effects of its rule. On the other hand it did not consider the reduction in medical care that might result from the rule's effect in making the practice of medicine more costly—more on this shortly.) Most of these deaths would be avoided by the vaccine, but by no means all, because the vaccine is not a hundred percent effective and, more important, because many health care workers refuse to be vaccinated. Hence the other parts of the rule would have a positive effect even on Hepatitis B; and there is no vaccine (or cure) for AIDS.

OSHA's evaluation of the effects of the rule, relying as it does on the undoubted expertise of the Centers for Disease Control, cannot seriously be faulted, at least by judges. Hence we cannot say that the rule, viewed as a whole, flunks the test of material reduction of a significant risk to workplace health. As for the impact on the health care industry, OSHA estimated the total cost of compliance with the rule at $813 million a year, clearly not enough to break the multi-hundred-billion-dollar healthcare industry. The rule's implicit valuation of a life is high—about $4 million—but not so astronomical, certainly by regulatory standards, . . . as to call the rationality of the rule seriously into question, especially when we consider that neither Hepatitis B nor AIDS is a disease of old people. . . . Nor is death the only consequence of these diseases. AIDS causes protracted pain and disability before death, and Hepatitis B causes pain and disability and often permanent liver damage, even when the patient "recovers."

No doubt the agency's $813 million estimate is an underestimate. It ignores . . . many or most time costs. . . . But the petitioners made no effort in the rulemaking proceeding to quantify these costs or to provide any basis for supposing them to be huge.

OSHA also exaggerated the number of lives likely to be saved by the rule by ignoring lives likely to be sacrificed by it, since the increased cost of medical care, to the extent passed on to consumers, will reduce the demand for medical care, and some people may lose their lives as a result. The agency's consideration of the indirect costs of the rule is thus incomplete. How many lives the rule is likely to sacrifice, however, we do not know; and again the petitioners make no effort to come up with a number. So while $4 million doubtless underestimates the agency's implicit valuation of each life actually likely to be saved by the rule, we do not know how great the underestimate is and we cannot resolve our doubts against the agency. We add that the $4 million ignores the benefits to workers who will be spared illness — remember that 99 times as many people get Hepatitis B as die from it.

As an original matter we might have been inclined to think that the regulation of the safety of the medical and dental workplace could be left largely to the market, that doctors, dentists, and other health care workers have a stronger incentive than the government to protect themselves from health hazards at reasonable cost, that their employees are compensated in their wages for what is after all a modest risk, and that health care workers who refuse to be vaccinated against Hepatitis B are knowingly assuming the risk and should be left to bear the consequences without government interference. But the occupational safety and health law is constructed on different premises that we are not free to question, and perhaps the infectious character of HIV and HBV warrants even on narrowly economic grounds more regulation than would be necessary in the case of a noncommunicable disease. . . .

So in the main the [bloodborne pathogen] rule must be upheld. Which is not to say that it is a good rule. It may be unnecessary; it may go too far; its costs may exceed its benefits. . . . But our duty as a reviewing court of generalist judges is merely to patrol the boundary of reasonableness, and . . . OSHA's bloodborne-pathogens rule — accepted as it has been by most health care industries and based as it is on the recommendations of the nation's, perhaps the world's, leading repository of knowledge about the control of infectious diseases — does not cross it. . . .

COFFEY, Circuit Judge, concurring in part, dissenting in part.

Section 3(8) of the Occupational Safety and Health Act defines "occupational safety and health standard" as a standard which requires the adoption of practices "reasonably necessary or appropriate to provide safe or healthful employment and places of employment." 29 U.S.C. §652(8). . . .

The rule adopted can best be classified as an attempt to try to kill a fly with a sledgehammer. The rule was drafted partially in response to the public hysteria surrounding AIDS. . . . The rule was not drafted in response to an established significant risk of harm to employees. The dangers of transmitting the blood-borne pathogen hepatitis B have been well-established for years yet for reasons unexplained OSHA did not concern itself with that risk in the workplace prior to November 1987. . . . The rule unduly burdens health care employers, including but not limited to dentists, doctors and hospitals, while offering but minimal benefit to their employees, and furthermore it is estimated that it will increase health care costs some $817 million annually. Additionally, the rule duplicates the scientifically based and well-reasoned guidelines of the Centers for Disease Control and Prevention (CDC) a governmental agency medically and scientifically qualified to determine and evaluate if there is in fact a significant risk in the health care area and, if so, propose reasonable, efficient guidelines. . . .

I suggest that the United States Congress must address the question of whether there is a need to duplicate the education, investigation and prevention efforts of the CDC and state health agencies, thus increasing health care costs, and whether OSHA is the proper agency to regulate health care given their lack of experience, knowledge and expertise in comparison to the CDC and state health agencies. In the alternative, the entire rule should be remanded to OSHA. . . .

I am cognizant of the need for dental and medical regulations and safeguards to insure and prevent the spread of infection, but fail to understand why OSHA must assert authority over the health care field when it lacks the required medical knowledge, training, and experience, much less expertise. . . . There is no need for four separate entities (OSHA, CDC, state agencies, and professional organizations) to regulate the health care industry. . . . One qualified entity can most effectively and efficiently regulate the health care profession. I see no reason why the respective states are unable to continue to regulate the medical and dental profession as the states have traditionally done in the past and presently do in many other professional fields including but not limited to law, engineering and architecture. . . .

Finally, there is little doubt that lobbyists and the media in all probability have greatly impacted OSHA's rulemaking.

Notes: Risk Assessment by Legislatures, Agencies, and Courts

1. *Is Any Action Required?* Identify the risk the bloodborne pathogen rule was designed to reduce. Was this a risk in need of reduction? How would you answer that question? Posner contends, in dictum, that the whole concept of an occupational safety and health statute is unnecessary because it is in workers' own interests to practice safe work habits and because workers in unsafe workplaces may be choosing to risk injury in exchange for higher wages. Judge Coffey criticizes the bloodborne pathogen standard from a different standpoint; he argues that it provides little marginal benefit over guidelines already issued by the CDC that were already being implemented in most workplaces. In your view, is the bloodborne pathogen standard necessary and appropriate? Should the answer be influenced by the fact that the rule was precipitated by a fear of HIV even though the long-standing risk of hepatitis was much more serious? Is this a case of overreaction to irrational hysteria, or was HIV simply the impetus to take action that was long overdue? To what extent is risk assessment an essentially political determination rather than a mathematical calculation? Consumer activists and industry groups regularly lobby government to promote action (or inaction). See, e.g., Jock McCulloch & Geoffrey Tweedale, Defending the Indefensible (2008) (asbestos industry).

2. *Administrative Competence.* Assuming some action was necessary, is OSHA the correct agency to act? OSHA's bloodborne pathogen rule was a departure from OSHA's historical focus on traditional sources of risk in the workplace such as machinery and chemicals. What do you think of Judge Coffey's contention that the states or the CDC are better able to regulate the health care professions? OSHA tried but failed to regulate workplace exposure to tuberculosis in the late 1990s. See Institute of Medicine, Tuberculosis in the Workplace (2001). OSHA regulations continue to generate controversy. See generally Cass R. Sunstein, Is OSHA Unconstitutional?, 94 Va. L. Rev. 1407 (2008).

3. *Risk Assessment Literature.* The vast academic literature on risk assessment explores how and why societies and individuals choose to respond to some risks

but not others, and at what costs. For a small sampling, see Stephen Breyer, Breaking the Vicious Cycle: Toward Effective Risk Regulation (1993); Elizabeth Fisher, Risk Regulation and Administrative Constitutionalism (2010); Public Health Law at 50-64; Kip Viscusi, Fatal Tradeoffs: Public and Private Responsibilities for Risk (1992); Cass R. Sunstein, Laws of Fear: Beyond the Precautionary Principle (2005); Richard H. Thaler & Cass R. Sunstein, Nudge (2009); Matthew D. Adler, Against "Individual Risk": A Sympathetic Critique of Risk Assessment, 153 U. Pa. L. Rev. 1121 (2005); R. Keeney, Decisions About Life-Threatening Risks, 331 New Eng. J. Med. 193 (1994).

Problem: State Law, Disaster-Planning, and Bioterrorism Preparedness

The United States has been fortunate not to have experienced many large-scale public health disasters since the influenza epidemic in the early part of the 1900s. But concerns about bioterrorism spurred public health officials and researchers in the early 2000s to review the ability of state and local governments to respond to public health emergencies. Medical journals increased their coverage of illnesses and injuries associated with potential terrorist attacks after 9/11. See, e.g., Luciana Borio et al., Consensus Statement, Hemorrhagic Fever Viruses and Biological Weapons: Medical and Public Health Management, 287 JAMA 2391 (2002); Julie Louise Gerberding et al., Bioterrorism Preparedness and Response: Clinicians and Public Health Agencies as Essential Partners, 287 JAMA 898 (2002).

Attention shifted from bioterrorism to natural disasters in the aftermath of events such as the Indian Ocean tsunami (2004), Hurricane Katrina (2005), and earthquakes with serious health implications in Haiti (2010) and Japan (2011). See Symposium, 4 Harv. L. & Pol'y Rev. 263 (2010); and Symposium, 25 Health Aff. 898 (2006). Public health officials also began to devote considerable attention to planning responses to a possible new influenza pandemic. See, e.g., Leslie E. Gerwin, Planning for Pandemic: A New Model for Governing Public Health Emergencies, 37 Am. J. L. & Med. 129 (2011); Lawrence O. Gostin, Public Health Strategies for Pandemic Influenza, 295 JAMA 1700 (2006); and CDC, www.flu.gov/. According to some estimates, a new pandemic influenza could cause global mortality of 62 million people, with many of the deaths occurring in the developing world. C. J. Lopez, Estimation of Potential Global Pandemic Influenza Mortality on the Basis of Vital Registry Data from the 1918-1920 Pandemic, 368 Lancet 2211 (2006).

Professor Lawrence Gostin and other public health experts prepared the Model State Emergency Health Powers Act to facilitate discussion of the legal aspects of disaster preparedness, available on the casebook Web site (Dec. 21, 2001 version) (hereinafter MSEHPA). See also Lawrence O. Gostin et al., The Model State Emergency Health Powers Act: Planning for and Response to Bioterrorism and Naturally Occurring Infectious Diseases, 288 JAMA 622 (2002); William Martin, Legal and Public Policy Responses of States to Bioterrorism, 94 Am. J. Public Health 1093 (2004). Has your state adopted any of the MSEHPA provisions or reviewed and revised its public health emergency powers in the past 15 years?

The Model Act includes rules and procedures designed to improve detection of a public health emergency and then establishes rules and procedures that take effect only in a public health emergency. The definition of "public health emergency" is therefore critical to the Act's operation:

> A "public health emergency" is an occurrence or imminent threat of an illness or health condition that:
>> (1) is believed to be caused by any of the following:
>>> (i) bioterrorism;
>>> (ii) the appearance of a novel or previously controlled or eradicated infectious agent or biological toxin;
>>> (iii) [a natural disaster]
>>> (iv) [a chemical attack or accidental release; or]
>>> (v) [a nuclear attack or accident] . . . and
>> (2) poses a high probability of any of the following harms;
>>> (i) a large number of deaths in the affected population;
>>> (ii) a large number of serious or long-term disabilities in the affected population; or
>>> (iii) widespread exposure to an infectious or toxic agent that poses a significant risk of substantial future harm to a large number of people in the affected population.

MSEHPA §104(m) (emphasis omitted; items in brackets are optional provisions). Note that the Act attempts to give states the option of creating a single legal framework for the public health response to a wide range of crises. As you review the Act's provisions through the remainder of this chapter, consider whether you would advise a state to adopt a single framework. Should the same rules apply in a bioterrorism incident as in a natural disaster? Does that Act—created in the shadow of 9/11—give adequate and appropriate guidance for other types of health emergencies?

B. THE SOURCE AND LIMITS OF AUTHORITY TO PROTECT PUBLIC HEALTH

This section explores the fundamental source and scope of the government's authority to pursue various public health measures. The first case is an historical one that establishes the constitutional basis for constraining individual liberties. The second case looks at the limits imposed by the more contemporary concern about disability discrimination. Although each case focuses on a specific public health measure, the general principles these cases establish permeate all of the public health topics that we encounter in the remainder of the chapter.

1. Constitutional Principles

■ JACOBSON v. COMMONWEALTH OF MASSACHUSETTS
197 U.S. 11 (1905)

HARLAN, J.

This case involves the validity, under the Constitution of the United States, of certain provisions in the statutes of Massachusetts relating to vaccination.

[A Massachusetts statute permitted cities to require vaccination and revaccination of all inhabitants of a city; noncompliant citizens over the age of 21 could be charged a fine of $5.00. The city of Cambridge adopted a smallpox vaccination regulation under this statute. Jacobson refused to be vaccinated for smallpox and these proceedings were instituted against him. He was found guilty and jailed until he paid the $5.00 fine.] . . .

The authority of the state to enact this statute is to be referred to what is commonly called the police power,—a power which the state did not surrender when becoming a member of the Union under the Constitution. Although this court has refrained from any attempt to define the limits of that power, yet it has distinctly recognized the authority of a state to enact quarantine laws and "health laws of every description"; indeed, all laws that relate to matters completely within its territory and which do not by their necessary operation affect the people of other states. According to settled principles, the police power of a state must be held to embrace, at least, such reasonable regulations established directly by legislative enactment as will protect the public health and the public safety. It is equally true that the state may invest local bodies called into existence for purposes of local administration with authority in some appropriate way to safeguard the public health and the public safety. The mode or manner in which those results are to be accomplished is within the discretion of the state, subject, of course, so far as federal power is concerned, only to the condition that no rule prescribed by a state, nor any regulation adopted by a local governmental agency acting under the sanction of state legislation, shall contravene the Constitution of the United States, nor infringe any right granted or secured by that instrument. A local enactment or regulation, even if based on the acknowledged police powers of a state, must always yield in case of conflict with the exercise by the general government of any power it possesses under the Constitution, or with any right which that instrument gives or secures.

We come, then, to inquire whether any right given or secured by the Constitution is invaded by the statute as interpreted by the state court. The defendant insists that his liberty is invaded when the state subjects him to fine or imprisonment for neglecting or refusing to submit to vaccination; that a compulsory vaccination law is unreasonable, arbitrary, and oppressive, and, therefore, hostile to the inherent right of every freeman to care for his own body and health in such way as to him seems best; and that the execution of such a law against one who objects to vaccination, no matter for what reason, is nothing short of an assault upon his person. But the liberty secured by the Constitution of the United States to every person within its jurisdiction does not import an absolute right in each person to be, at all times and in all circumstances, wholly freed from restraint. There are manifold restraints to which every person is necessarily subject for the common good. . . .

Applying these principles to the present case, it is to be observed that the legislature of Massachusetts required the inhabitants of a city or town to be vaccinated only when, in the opinion of the board of health, that was necessary for the public health or the public safety. The authority to determine for all what ought to be done in such an emergency must have been lodged somewhere or in some body; and surely it was appropriate for the legislature to refer that question, in the first instance, to a board of health composed of persons residing in the locality affected, and appointed, presumably, because of their fitness to determine such questions. To invest such a body with authority over such matters was not an unusual, nor an unreasonable or arbitrary, requirement. Upon the principle of self-defense, of paramount necessity, a community has the right to protect itself against an epidemic of disease which threatens the safety of its members. It is to be observed that when the regulation in question was adopted smallpox, according to the recitals in the regulation adopted by the board of health, was prevalent to some extent in the city of Cambridge, and the disease was increasing. If such was the situation,—and nothing is asserted or appears in the record to the contrary,—if we are to attach, any value whatever to the knowledge which, it is safe to affirm, in common to all civilized peoples touching smallpox and the methods most usually employed to eradicate that disease, it cannot be adjudged that the present regulation of the board of health was not necessary in order to protect the public health and secure the public safety. Smallpox being prevalent and increasing at Cambridge, the court would usurp the functions of another branch of government if it adjudged, as matter of law, that the mode adopted under the sanction of the state, to protect the people at large was arbitrary, and not justified by the necessities of the case. We say necessities of the case, because it might be that an acknowledged power of a local community to protect itself against an epidemic threatening the safety of all might be exercised in particular circumstances and in reference to particular persons in such an arbitrary, unreasonable manner, or might go so far beyond what was reasonably required for the safety of the public, as to authorize or compel the courts to interfere for the protection of such persons. . . .

There is, of course, a sphere within which the individual may assert the supremacy of his own will, and rightfully dispute the authority of any human government,—especially of any free government existing under a written constitution, to interfere with the exercise of that will. But it is equally true that in every well-ordered society charged with the duty of conserving the safety of its members the rights of the individual in respect of his liberty may at times, under the pressure of great dangers, be subjected to such restraint, to be enforced by reasonable regulations, as the safety of the general public may demand. . . . [Citing rules governing the quarantine of persons exposed to contagious diseases and mandatory military service.] It is not, therefore, true that the power of the public to guard itself against imminent danger depends in every case involving the control of one's body upon his willingness to submit to reasonable regulations established by the constituted authorities, under the sanction of the state, for the purpose of protecting the public collectively against such danger. . . .

Looking at the propositions embodied in the defendant's rejected offers of proof, it is clear that they are more formidable by their number than by their inherent value. . . . We must assume that, when the statute in question was passed, the legislature of Massachusetts was not unaware of these opposing theories [about the safety and efficacy of vaccination], and was compelled, of necessity, to choose between them. . . . Upon what sound principles as to the relations existing between the different departments of government can the court review this action of the legislature? If there is any such power in the judiciary to review legislative action in respect of a matter affecting the general welfare, it can only be when that which the legislature has done comes within the rule that, if a statute purporting to have been enacted to protect the public health, the public morals, or the public safety, has no real or substantial relation to those objects, or is, beyond all question, a plain, palpable invasion of rights secured by the fundamental law, it is the duty of the courts to so adjudge, and thereby give effect to the Constitution. Mugler v. Kansas, 123 U.S. 623, 661.

Whatever may be thought of the expediency of this statute, it cannot be affirmed to be, beyond question, in palpable conflict with the Constitution. Nor, in view of the methods employed to stamp out the disease of smallpox, can anyone confidently assert that the means prescribed by the state to that end has no real or substantial relation to the protection of the public health and the public safety. Such an assertion would not be consistent with the experience of this and other countries whose authorities have dealt with the disease of smallpox. . . .

[T]he police power of a state, whether exercised directly by the legislature, or by a local body acting under its authority, may be exerted in such circumstances, or by regulations so arbitrary and oppressive in particular cases, as to justify the interference of the courts to prevent wrong and oppression. Extreme cases can be readily suggested. Ordinarily such cases are not safe guides in the administration of the law. It is easy, for instance, to suppose the case of an adult who is embraced by the mere words of the act, but yet to subject whom to vaccination in a particular condition of his health or body would be cruel and inhuman in the last degree. We are not to be understood as holding that the statute was intended to be applied to such a case, or, if it was so intended, that the judiciary would not be competent to interfere and protect the health and life of the individual concerned. . . . Until otherwise informed by the highest court of Massachusetts, we are not inclined to hold that the statute establishes the absolute rule that an adult must be vaccinated if it be apparent or can be shown with reasonable certainty that he is not at the time a fit subject of vaccination, or that vaccination, by reason of his then condition, would seriously impair his health, or probably cause his death. No such case is here presented. It is the cause of an adult who, for aught that appears, was himself in perfect health and a fit subject of vaccination, and yet, while remaining in the community, refused to obey the statute and the regulation adopted in execution of its provisions for the protection of the public health and the public safety, confessedly endangered by the presence of a dangerous disease.

We now decide only that the statute covers the present case, and that nothing clearly appears that would justify this court in holding it to be unconstitutional and inoperative in its application to the plaintiff in error. The judgment of the court below must be affirmed. It is so ordered. Mr. Justice BREWER and Mr. Justice PECKHAM dissent.

Notes: The State Police Power and Federalism

1. *Interpreting* Jacobson. The *Jacobson* case, while ancient in constitutional law terms, is often cited as the authoritative statement of the scope of the state's police power, Lawrence O. Gostin, *Jacobson v. Massachusetts* at 100 Years: Police Power and Civil Liberties in Tension, 95 Am. J. Public Health 576 (2005), and has guided the development of the law in areas ranging from abortion to end-of-life decisionmaking, see, e.g., Gonzales v. Carhart, 550 U.S. 124 (2007); Cruzan v. Director, Missouri Department of Health, 497 U.S. 261 (1990). Professor Gostin and Wiley argue that:

Jacobson established a floor of constitutional protection. It deemed compulsory powers constitutionally permissible only if they are exercised in conformity with five standards . . . [:]

Public Health Necessity. Public health powers are exercised under the theory that they are necessary to prevent an avoidable harm. . . . The standard of public health necessity requires, at a minimum, that the subject of the compulsory intervention actually pose a threat to the community. . . .

Reasonable Means. . . . The methods used . . . must be designed to prevent or ameliorate th[e] threat. The *Jacobson* Court adopted a means/ends test that required the demonstration of a reasonable relationship between the [public health] intervention and the achievement of a legitimate governmental objective. . . . [T]he methods adopted must have a "real and substantial relation" to protection of the public health, and cannot be "a plain, palpable invasion of rights."

Proportionality. . . . A [public health] regulation is nevertheless unconstitutional if the human burden imposed is wholly disproportionate to the expected benefit. . . .

Harm Avoidance. . . . The control measure itself . . . should not pose a health risk to its subject.

Fairness. [Although] [t]he facts in *Jacobson* did not require the Supreme Court to enunciate a standard of fairness under the Equal Protection Clause of the Fourteenth Amendment [the standard had already been established under federal law].

Public Health Law at 124-126. Do you agree with this analysis of *Jacobson*? Is the end result consistent with the current approach to judicial review under the strict scrutiny or rational basis standards? Gostin and Wiley note the possibility of a "sliding scale" for review: "As the intrusiveness and unfairness of a policy increase, so does the level of judicial scrutiny." Id. at 151. Commentators agree that public health measures will elicit even greater judicial scrutiny if they infringe on fundamental rights or operate based on suspect or quasi-suspect classifications.

Do individuals have a liberty interest in avoiding vaccination? Do individuals have a protected liberty interest in engaging in behaviors that could help spread disease? Or do individuals have a fundamental right to bodily integrity that is outweighed by the state's compelling interest in protecting public health? *Jacobson*'s discussion of these issues seems a little murky to the modern eye. The Court suggests at times that there simply is no liberty interest in conduct that puts others at risk. Yet, the Court's analysis ultimately is consistent with the more modern balancing approach: Whatever liberty interest individuals have can be outweighed where the state has a compelling interest in protecting public health, assuming the public health measure is appropriately tailored to meet that objective. Under what facts could Jacobson have avoided vaccination without penalty? For more on *Jacobson*'s relevance today, see Wendy Parmet et al., Individual Rights Versus the Public's Health — 100 Years After *Jacobson v. Massachusetts*, 352 New Eng. J. Med. 652 (2005); Michael H. Shapiro, Updating Constitutional Doctrine: An Extended Response to the Critique of Compulsory Vaccination, 12 Yale J. Health Pol'y L. & Ethics 87 (2012); and Michael Ulrich, Law and Politics, An Emerging Epidemic, 42 Am. J. L. & Med. 256 (2016). See also Phillips v. City of New York, 775 F.3d 538 (2015) (rejecting substantive due process and free exercise, and equal protection challenges to child vaccination statute); Coshow v. City of Escondido, 34 Cal. Rptr. 3d 19 (2005) (rejecting substantive due process challenge to fluoridation of drinking water).

2. *Delegation.* The police power is the power of the "state" to protect its citizens. The power is most often initially invested in the state legislature by the state constitution. The legislature therefore may pass statutes designed to protect the public. The state legislature also can delegate the power in at least two different directions. It may establish some administrative agency in the executive branch, such as a state health department, which will be given statutory authority to oversee some aspects of public health. The legislature may also delegate some portion of its authority to other political entities within the state, such as to counties, cities, or local health entities.

As an initial matter, it is important to determine whether the entity exercising the police power has the constitutional authority to do so. See Wong Wai v. Williamson, 103 F. 1 (C.C. N.D. Cal. 1900) (court notes that San Francisco Board of Supervisors, rather than the Board of Health, was the entity with authority to issue ordinances to protect public health); and page 965. Other, related questions include examining the delegation of authority from the legislature to the entity to ensure that the entity has not exceeded or improperly exercised its authority under the terms of the grant. In *Jacobson*, for example, the Court noted that the state may give some public health authority to local bodies, and that, in this case, the Massachusetts legislature had delegated to the local Board of Health the determination of when vaccinations were necessary. The delegation itself can also be challenged as "standardless" or as not providing sufficient guidance to the entity given the authority to exercise the police power.

3. *Due Process and Equal Protection.* Courts in the early 1900s were extremely deferential to a state's power to protect public health. Thus, courts would uphold a state's public health action so long as it was not "arbitrary" or "unreasonable" or "unnecessary" to protect public health. See *Jacobson*, supra. Under current constitutional law doctrines, individuals have a protected liberty interest in maintaining their own bodily integrity and in exercising at least some decisionmaking power with respect to their medical treatment. See Chapters 5-7, especially the discussions of *Cruzan* (pages 511 and 547) and *Casey* (page 728). Persons subjected to coercive state policies may also assert their First Amendment right to the free exercise of religion and their Fourth Amendment right to be free from unreasonable searches and seizures. Under the modern approach, a state may infringe a fundamental right to serve a compelling state interest only so long as the infringement is narrowly tailored to meet that interest. Consider whether and how this standard has been incorporated into modern public health decisions as you read the remaining cases in this chapter. See also Public Health Law at 115-151.

Under the equal protection clause, class-based legislation will be reviewed under one of three standards: (1) suspect classifications (those based on race, for example, or those that intrude on other fundamental rights) will be subjected to strict scrutiny; (2) quasi-suspect classifications (such as gender) will receive intermediate scrutiny; and (3) all other legislative classifications will be reviewed under the rational basis standard. There is some suggestion that the Supreme Court will apply a heightened rational basis review standard (sometimes called "rational basis with bite") to some classifications, see, e.g., Romer v. Evans, 517 U.S. 620 (1996) (Court uses "rational basis" standard to strike down state measure that specifically prejudiced persons seeking legislative bans on discrimination against homosexuals); City of Cleburne v. Cleburne Living Center, 473 U.S. 432 (1985) (invalidating application of zoning ordinance to group home for persons with mental disabilities under "rational basis" standard). But see Maxwell L. Stearns, *Obergefell, Fisher,* and the Inversion of Tiers, U. Pa. J. Const. Law. (2017) (arguing that cases reflect a five-tier approach).

4. *Statutory Construction.* Courts generally follow the rule of statutory construction that exhorts that ambiguous statutes should be construed to avoid constitutional defects. In *Jacobson,* for example, the Court grafts an exception onto the vaccination rule. What constitutional defect is remedied by this procedure?

5. *Compulsory Vaccination and Religious or Philosophical Objections.* Compulsory smallpox vaccination opened the door to broader immunization campaigns. Later programs were targeted at early vaccination of children prior to attending public school. In another classic decision, the U.S. Supreme Court held that parental religious objections to vaccination would not justify avoiding vaccination of children despite the First Amendment's protection of religious freedom. See Prince v. Massachusetts, 321 U.S. 158 at 166-167 (1944); and Workman v. Mingo County Board of Education, 2011 WL 1042330 (4th Cir. 2011) (state not required to include religious exemption in mandatory vaccination law). On religious objection to health measures generally, see Annot., 94 A.L.R.5th 613 (2001). The vaccination regimes in some states have permitted parents to refuse vaccination for their children based on religious or philosophical objections. States are considering new, more restrictive policies given problems with low immunization rates and outbreaks of preventable and risky childhood illnesses. See Erwin Chemerinsky & Michelle Goodwin, Compulsory Vaccination Laws Are Constitutional, 110 Nw. U. L. Rev. 589 (2016) (discussing California's narrow approach to immunization exemptions; arguing that states may constitutionally mandate vaccination without any exception other than medical necessity); Note, 117 Colum. L. Rev. 913 (2017).

6. *Vaccine Safety.* Childhood vaccinations continue to be controversial, despite the unified efforts of public health authorities to reassure the public about the safety and efficacy of the vaccinations. See, e.g., the CDC's Vaccine and Immunization Web site, at www.cdc.gov/vaccines/; WHO, Immunization Safety, at www.who.int/immunization_safety/en/. Use your favorite Internet search engine to find information by combining "vaccine" with "risks" or "danger." Do the "official" Web sites provide sufficient information to counteract the "scary" vaccine Web sites? Many of the comments received in response to the CDC's recent quarantine rulemaking actually related to concerns about mandatory vaccination. See, Dorit Rubinstein Reiss, Regulating in the Era of Face News: Anti-Vaccine Activists Respond to the CDC Quarantine Rule, 79 U. Pitt. L. Rev. __ (2018) (51.8 percent of sample comments indicated opposition to forced vaccination, an issue not directly raised by the regulations); Allison Kennedy et al., Confidence About Vaccines in the United States: Understanding Parents' Perceptions, 30 Health Aff. 1151 (2011); and Gregory A. Poland & Robert M. Jacobson, The Age-Old Struggle Against the Antivaccinationalists, 364 New Eng. J. Med. 97 (2011). For information on vaccine injury compensation schemes, see infra page 362.

7. *Vaccine Production and Distribution.* Vaccines must be developed, manufactured, and distributed if they are to be used to protect public health. Much of this activity occurs in the private sector as pharmaceutical companies work to discover and develop vaccines, to secure governmental approval for their use, and to establish economically beneficial manufacturing and distribution arrangements. There

are substantial concerns about whether this system is capable of meeting the public health needs of the United States and other countries. David P. Fidler & Lawrence O. Gostin, The WHO Pandemic Influenza Preparedness Framework: A Milestone in Global Governance for Health, 306 JAMA 200 (2011) (discussing new, nonbinding WHO framework for Pandemic Influenza Preparedness (PIP)).

These concerns were reinforced when vaccine production lagged in response to the H1N1 pandemic in 2009. New approaches to vaccines are being developed and implemented. See Sara Eve Crager, Improving Global Access to New Vaccines: Intellectual Property, Technology Transfer, and Regulatory Pathways, 104 Am. J. Pub. Health e85 (2014). The CDC Web site provides information on current vaccine shortages, at: https://www.cdc.gov/vaccines/hcp/clinical-resources/shortages.html. How should access to vaccines be rationed during times of shortage? Should this be seen as a medical or legal issue? Nimalan Arinaminpathy et al., Effective Use of a Limited Antiviral Stockpile for Pandemic Influenza, 6 J. Bioethical Inq. 171 (2009); and Michelle M. Mello & Troyen A. Brennan, Legal Concerns and the Influenza Vaccine Shortage, 294 JAMA 1817 (2005).

Health care providers are often given priority in vaccination schemes, at least in part because they may be at increased risk of acquiring and then passing on infection to others. Should priority access to vaccines be translated into a mandate that health care providers undergo vaccination? See Symposium, Vaccine-Preventable Diseases and Vaccinations Among Health-Care Workers, 32 Vaccine, 4813-4880 (2014). Should the existence of vaccine or treatment priorities be related to legal obligations compelling the health care providers to work during a health emergency? See Carl H. Coleman, Beyond the Call of Duty: Compelling Health Care Professionals to Work During an Influenza Pandemic, 94 Iowa L. Rev. 1 (2008); James G. Hodge, Jr. et al., Law, Medicine, and Public Health Preparedness: The Case of Ebola, 130 Pub. Health Rep. 167 (2015); and Mark A. Rothstein, Should Health Care Providers Get Treatment Priority in an Influenza Epidemic?, 38 J. L. Med. & Ethics 412 (2010).

8. *Federal Authority over Public Health.* These days we are most likely to see the federal government as a pervasive force in our lives, with its influence—for good or for bad—exerted over everything from the national defense, to the organization of our health care system, to the problem of educational standards in our local schools. Constitutionally speaking, the national government has limited powers and may exercise authority only in those areas ceded by the states to the federal government within that document. Somewhat surprisingly, given the undeniable breadth and scope of federal health and safety regulation, the federal government does not have any direct constitutional authority to protect the public health. Congress and the executive branch have not been deterred by this gap in authority. Instead, Congress has achieved many of the same objectives through the exercise of its powers to regulate the relationship between the United States and foreign countries, to regulate interstate commerce, and to spend to promote the public welfare. U.S. Const. art. 1, §8. For a sampling of federal public health initiatives, see Public Health Law at 159-161 (Table 5.2). James Hodge et al., The Pandemic and All-Hazards Preparedness Act: Improving Public Health Emergency Response, 297 JAMA 1708 (2007) (evaluating federal legislation).

9. *State vs. Federal Authority.* A state's power to regulate in order to protect the public health can also be limited by conflicts with federal authority over interstate or international matters. States often attempt to establish standards that can have a negative impact on interstate commerce. Should a state or local government be

permitted to legislate to improve roadway safety within its borders? City of Columbus v. Ours Garage & Wrecker Service, Inc., 536 U.S. 424 (2002) (preserving local tow truck rule from federal preemption despite generally broad federal preemptive authority). In general, state power in areas of federal jurisdiction, including interstate commerce, is severely restricted by federal supremacy and preemption. Compare Pliva v. Mensing, 564 U.S. 604 (2011) (state warning claim preempted by federal law governing generic drugs when impossible for manufacturer to comply with both state and federal warning requirements), with Wyeth v. Levine, 555 U.S. 555 (2009) (state failure to warn claim not preempted by FDA labeling rule for non-generic drug as possible for manufacturer to comply with both federal and state rules). See also National Meat Association v. Harris, 565 U.S. 452 (2012) (Federal Meat Inspection Act preempts application of California Penal Code provision banning sale of meat from "nonambulatory" animals to humans).

Problem: Bioterrorism and Smallpox Vaccination

Routine vaccination for smallpox ended in the early 1970s, when it appeared that the only smallpox virus on earth was safely contained in scientific laboratories in the United States and Russia. The federal government began to reconsider its vaccination policies in 2001, amidst growing concern about the threat that smallpox would be used as a weapon of bioterrorism. The initial problem was the production of new smallpox vaccine. The federal government arranged to purchase several hundred million doses of vaccine. The second issue involved the appropriate distribution strategy. The smallpox vaccine carries a significant risk of disease or death for persons with compromised immune systems (e.g., persons with HIV, or transplant recipients) as well as for people with a history of eczema or atopic dermatitis. A massive vaccination program could put millions at risk, whether or not they underwent vaccination directly, because of the live viral particles that would be shed from the vaccination sites of those who did receive the vaccine. Yet, delaying vaccination programs until after the first case of smallpox could result in thousands of preventable deaths.

What smallpox vaccine distribution policy do you favor? What ethical and/or legal constraints should govern the development and implementation of mandatory or voluntary vaccination policies? See generally CDC Smallpox, available at https://www.cdc.gov/smallpox/bioterrorism-response-planning/public-health/vaccination-strategies.html. for the most current federal plans for the distribution of smallpox vaccine in the event of a confirmed case. For a discussion of the failure of the federal government's initial smallpox vaccination campaign, see Jay Gold Rathbun, The Smallpox Vaccination Campaign of 2003: Why Did It Fail and What Are the Lessons for Bioterrorism Preparedness?, 64 La. L. Rev. 851 (2004).

2. Disability Discrimination

Despite its age, *Jacobson* still sets the basic framework for debating the constitutional legitimacy of various public health interventions. That debate has expanded in recent years, however, to incorporate a new concern, one that has a statutory origin: disability discrimination. The following case explains how concepts of disability discrimination relate to contagious diseases. As with *Jacobson*, the case's relevance extends far beyond the particular dispute since it establishes broad principles that apply throughout the public health arena.

■ SCHOOL BOARD OF NASSAU COUNTY v. ARLINE
480 U.S. 273 (1987)

BRENNAN, Justice.

Section 504 of the Rehabilitation Act of 1973, 29 U.S.C. §794 (Act), prohibits a federally funded state program from discriminating against a handicapped individual solely by reason of his or her handicap. This case presents the questions whether a person afflicted with tuberculosis, a contagious disease, may be considered a "handicapped individual" within the meaning of §504 of the Act, and, if so, whether such an individual is "otherwise qualified" to teach elementary school.

I

From 1966 until 1979, respondent Gene Arline taught elementary school in Nassau County, Florida. She was discharged in 1979 after suffering a third relapse of tuberculosis within two years. After she was denied relief in state administrative proceedings, she brought suit in federal court, alleging that the school board's decision to dismiss her because of her tuberculosis violated §504 of the Act . . . [which] reads in pertinent part:

> No otherwise qualified handicapped individual . . . shall, solely by reason of his handicap, be excluded from participation in, be denied the benefits of, or be subjected to discrimination under any program or activity receiving Federal financial assistance. . . .

29 U.S.C. §794. In 1974 Congress expanded the definition of "handicapped individual" for use in §504 to read as follows:

> [A]ny person who (i) has a physical or mental impairment which substantially limits one or more of such person's major life activities, (ii) has a record of such an impairment, or (iii) is regarded as having such an impairment.

The amended definition reflected Congress' concern with protecting the handicapped against discrimination stemming not only from simple prejudice, but also from "archaic attitudes and laws" and from "the fact that the American people are simply unfamiliar with and insensitive to the difficulties confront[ing] individuals with handicaps." S. Rep. No. 93-1297, p.50 (1974), U.S. Code Cong. & Admin. News 1974, p.6400. To combat the effects of erroneous but nevertheless prevalent perceptions about the handicapped, Congress expanded the definition of "handicapped individual" so as to preclude discrimination against "[a] person who has a record of, or is regarded as having, an impairment [but who] may at present have no actual incapacity at all." Southeastern Community College v. Davis, 442 U.S. 397, 405-406, n.6 (1979).

Petitioners concede that a contagious disease may constitute a handicapping condition to the extent that it leaves a person with "diminished physical or mental capabilities," and concede that Arline's hospitalization for tuberculosis in 1957 demonstrates that she has a record of a physical impairment. Petitioners maintain, however, that Arline's record of impairment is irrelevant in this case, since the school board dismissed Arline not because of her diminished physical capabilities, but because of the threat that her relapses of tuberculosis posed to the health of others.

We do not agree with petitioners that, in defining a handicapped individual under §504, the contagious effects of a disease can be meaningfully distinguished from the disease's physical effects on a claimant in a case such as this. Arline's contagiousness and her physical impairment each resulted from the same underlying condition, tuberculosis. It would be unfair to allow an employer to seize upon the distinction between the effects of a disease on others and the effects of a disease on a patient and use that distinction to justify discriminatory treatment.

Allowing discrimination based on the contagious effects of a physical impairment would be inconsistent with the basic purpose of §504, which is to ensure that handicapped individuals are not denied jobs or other benefits because of the prejudiced attitudes or the ignorance of others. By amending the definition of "handicapped individual" to include not only those who are actually physically impaired, but also those who are regarded as impaired and who, as a result, are substantially limited in a major life activity, Congress acknowledged that society's accumulated myths and fears about disability and disease are as handicapping as are the physical limitations that flow from actual impairment. Few aspects of a handicap give rise to the same level of public fear and misapprehension as contagiousness. Even those who suffer or have recovered from such noninfectious diseases as epilepsy or cancer have faced discrimination based on the irrational fear that they might be contagious. . . . We conclude that the fact that a person with a record of a physical impairment is also contagious does not suffice to remove that person from coverage under §504.

IV

The remaining question is whether Arline is otherwise qualified for the job of elementary schoolteacher. To answer this question in most cases, the district court will need to conduct an individualized inquiry and make appropriate findings of fact. Such an inquiry is essential if §504 is to achieve its goal of protecting handicapped individuals from deprivations based on prejudice, stereotypes, or unfounded fear, while giving appropriate weight to such legitimate concerns of grantees as avoiding exposing others to significant health and safety risks. The basic factors to be considered in conducting this inquiry are well established. In the context of the employment of a person handicapped with a contagious disease, we agree with amicus American Medical Association that this inquiry should include:

> [findings of] facts, based on reasonable medical judgments given the state of medical knowledge, about (a) the nature of the risk (how the disease is transmitted), (b) the duration of the risk (how long is the carrier infectious), (c) the severity of the risk (what is the potential harm to third parties) and (d) the probabilities the disease will be transmitted and will cause varying degrees of harm.

In making these findings, courts normally should defer to the reasonable medical judgments of public health officials. The next step in the "otherwise-qualified" inquiry is for the court to evaluate, in light of these medical findings, whether the employer could reasonably accommodate the employee. . . .

Because of the paucity of factual findings by the district court, we, like the court of appeals, are unable at this stage of the proceedings to resolve whether Arline is "otherwise qualified" for her job. . . .

We remand the case to the district court to determine whether Arline is otherwise qualified for her position. The judgment of the court of appeals is Affirmed.

[The dissenting opinion of Chief Justice Rehnquist and Justice Scalia is omitted.]

Notes: Balancing Risk Reduction with Other Values

1. *Disability Discrimination Law.* The *Arline* case was decided under the federal Rehabilitation Act of 1973, which prohibits disability-based discrimination by the federal government, federal contractors, and recipients of federal funds. 29 U.S.C. §§701-796. Congress later enacted the Americans with Disabilities Act (ADA), 42 U.S.C. §§12101-12213, to expand protection against discrimination by private employers, public entities, and public accommodations. Thus, these disability discrimination principles apply to virtually all of the different public health measures encountered in this chapter.

The two Acts have similar definitions of disability: A person is disabled under the statutes if she (1) has a physical or mental impairment that substantially limits her ability to engage in one or more major life activities; (2) has a record of such an impairment; or (3) is regarded as being impaired. 42 U.S.C. §12102(1). A person who meets one of these three tests will be protected from discrimination so long as she meets the essential qualifications and does not present a "direct threat" or a "significant risk" to the health or safety of others, with or without reasonable accommodation. See, e.g., id. at §12111(3) (defining direct threat) and §12113(b) (direct threat defense). Thus, as in *Arline*, persons with contagious diseases are protected from discrimination unless they present a significant risk to others.

How should employers and the courts assess the degree and probability of risk? In *Arline*, the Supreme Court suggested that "courts normally should defer to the reasonable medical judgments of public health officials," supra. In Bragdon v. Abbott, the Court described a more nuanced approach:

> In assessing the reasonableness of [a defendant's] actions, the views of public health authorities such as the U.S. Public Health Service, CDC, and the National Institutes of Health, are of special weight and authority. *Arline,* [480 U.S.] at 288; 28 C.F.R. pt. 36, App. B, p. 626 (1997). The views of these organizations are not conclusive, however. A health care professional who disagrees with the prevailing medical consensus may refute it by citing a credible scientific basis for deviating from the accepted norm.

524 U.S. 624, 650 (1998). See also Samuel R. Bagenstos, The Americans with Disabilities Act as Risk Regulation, 101 Colum. L. Rev. 1479 (2001).

2. *TB, HIV, and "Disability."* On remand, the district court found that Arline did not present a significant risk to the health and safety of others. Arline v. School Board of Nassau County, 692 F. Supp. 1286 (M.D. Fla. 1988). Although Arline was infected with TB, the decision was clearly potentially relevant to discrimination against persons with HIV infection or AIDS. The next question, however, was whether a person with HIV infection had a "disability" as defined in the statutes. The Supreme Court finally addressed this question in Bragdon v. Abbott, 524 U.S. 624 (1998). Sidney Abbott was infected with HIV but appeared otherwise healthy. Bragdon refused to fill Abbott's cavity in his dental office, offering to do so in a local hospital if Abbott would pay the hospital charges. Abbott brought a disability-based discrimination claim. The Court held that Abbott was a person with a disability because she had a physical impairment that substantially limited her ability to engage in the major life activity of reproduction. The "substantial limitation" was not physical inability to reproduce but the fact that HIV could be transmitted to her sexual partner or to her offspring in the process.

3. *Direct Threat.* Employers, public entities, and places of public accommodation are permitted to discriminate against a person with a disability where that person poses a significant risk to the health or safety of others. Employers have successfully relied upon the "direct threat" exclusion in a number of cases. See, e.g., Jakubowski v. Christ Hospital, 627 F.3d 195 (6th Cir. 2010) (medical resident with Asperger's Disorder); Turco v. Hoechst Celanese Corp., 101 F.3d 1090 (5th Cir. 1996) (diabetic presents direct threat in workplace with heavy machinery and dangerous chemicals). In most cases involving HIV infection, courts have rejected "direct threat" claims asserted by employers or others. See, e.g., Doe v. Deer Mountain Day Camp, 682 F. Supp. 2d 324 (S.D.N.Y. 2010) (HIV-infected applicant to basketball camp); Chalk v. United States District Court Central District of California, 840 F.2d 701 (9th Cir. 1988) (HIV-infected teacher).

Where should the burden of proof lie in "direct threat" litigation? Compare McKenzie v. Benton, 388 F.3d 1342 (10th Cir. 2004) (plaintiff has burden of proving she did not pose a direct threat), cert. denied, 544 U.S. 1048 (2005) with Branham v. Snow, 392 F.3d 896 (7th Cir. 2004) (defendant has burden of proof for the defense of direct threat). See also Leslie Francis & Anita Silvers, The Health Care Workforce: How to Understand Accommodations, 9 St. Louis U. J. Health L. & Pol'y 57 (2015).

4. *Other State and Local Laws.* Virtually every state has its own disability discrimination statutes. The great majority have already declared AIDS and HIV infection covered under these state laws. There are also more general antidiscrimination laws in most states related to public accommodations and private housing. How will other contagious diseases be treated under these statutes?

5. *Disability Discrimination and State Public Health Regulation. Jacobson* seemed to stand for the proposition that the state had broad powers to regulate to protect the public health, even when those regulations intruded on personal liberty. You might predict that courts would use a very loose standard of review when considering the constitutional validity of state public health regulation. Do the ADA and the Rehabilitation Act fundamentally change this understanding of the relative power of the state and the judiciary in public health matters? These laws prevent government from discriminating against persons with disabilities in public services and in federally funded programs. How might these principles limit the actions of public health authorities? See Crowder v. Kitagawa, 81 F.3d 1480 (9th Cir. 1996) (challenge to

state quarantine of dogs; court holds that "without reasonable modification quarantine requirement effectively prevented visually-impaired persons from enjoying the benefits of state services and activities in violation of ADA"); and Wendy F. Hensel & Leslie E. Wolf, Playing God: The Legality of Plans Denying Scarce Resources to People with Disabilities in Public Health Emergencies, 63 Fla. L. Rev. 719 (2011); Scott Burris, Rationality Review and the Politics of Public Health, 34 Vill. L. Rev. 933 (1989).

The Supreme Court's decision in Board of Trustees of the University of Alabama v. Garrett, 531 U.S. 356 (2001), cast doubt on whether and how the ADA might be applied to the states. In *Garrett*, the Court held that Congress had exceeded its Fourteenth Amendment authority in attempting to abrogate states' Eleventh Amendment immunity under Title I of the ADA. State employees were denied the ability to bring actions for money damages under the ADA in federal court. Id. Importantly, the case did not affect injunctive and declaratory relief, which remain available.

Similar concerns are raised by Title II of the ADA's prohibition against disability-based discrimination in public services. In Tennessee v. Lane, 541 U.S. 509 (2004), the Court held that Title II could be used to recover money damages in cases involving a valid exercise of congressional power to enforce the Fourteenth Amendment. See City of Boerne v. Flores, 521 U.S. 507 (1997) (setting forth test used to determine whether a congressional enactment is a valid effort to enforce the Fourteenth Amendment). Abrogation of state immunity was upheld in *Lane* because the action contested under Title II involved a fundamental right — access to the courts. In United States v. Georgia et al., the Court held that Title II of the ADA validly abrogates state sovereign immunity "for conduct that actually violates the Fourteenth Amendment." 546 U.S. 151 (2006) (emphasis omitted). See also Phiffer v. Columbia River Correctional Institute, 384 F.3d 791 (9th Cir. 2004), cert. denied, 546 U.S. 1137 (2006) (inmate suffering from osteoarthritis and osteoporosis denied accommodation for his disabilities; state not entitled to Eleventh Amendment immunity from the inmate's suit under Title II of the ADA). Case law must be monitored to determine whether and how Title II might be applied in other public health cases. The Rehabilitation Act's provisions prohibiting disability-based discrimination by recipients of federal funds might grow in importance if *Lane* signals sharp restrictions in the application of Title II of the ADA to cases involving state public services. See, e.g., Guttman v. Khalsa, 669 F.3d 1101 (10th Cir. 2012) (sovereign immunity applies to physician's claim that state revocation of his medical license violated ADA's prohibition against disability discrimination in the provision of public services or programs).

6. *Summary.* Persons seeking to challenge the validity of public health measures may look to the federal Constitution, federal statutes such as the ADA and Rehabilitation Act, state constitutions, state statutes, and state regulations. You may wish to consider each of these potential limitations on public health initiatives throughout the remainder of this chapter.

C. REGULATING MEDICAL TREATMENT TO PROTECT PUBLIC HEALTH

There are many types of governmental intervention into the treatment relationship. Much of the discussion in previous chapters might be characterized, one way or another, as governmental regulation of this important relationship. The policies examined in sections C.1-C.4 below are distinguished from those studied in earlier chapters, however, by their explicit and unique grounding in a governmental interest in protecting the community's health beyond the health of the individual. The analytical focus in these sections is the sacrifice of individual autonomy to serve the public health. Traditional public health measures often involve significant intrusions into bodily integrity, privacy, and freedom of movement. How much of a sacrifice can be exacted? In what circumstances? With what level of judicial oversight?

1. Testing and Public Health

Section A, above, discusses primary public health techniques, including the identification of threats to public health and the development of strategies to address those threats. Traditionally, public health authorities have used five strategies to respond to certain types of contagious diseases. *Testing* is used to identify persons who are infected with the disease. The individual might then be *treated*, if any treatment is available, or might be *confined* to protect others from the disease. *Reporting* allows state and federal public health officials to gather specific information about people who have been infected and also permits general epidemiological research into the rate and distribution of infection within a population of people. *Contact tracing* is used to alert people who have had contact with an infected person of the possibility of exposure to the disease. If such an individual tests positive for the relevant condition, a new round of testing, reporting, and tracing can begin.

Each of these public health strategies entails some risk to individual liberty. Mandatory testing can be physically intrusive; it also violates the concept of individual autonomy and control over one's medical care. Reporting violates the norms of confidentiality and can expose an individual to the risk of additional, more intrusive public health interventions. Contact tracing might threaten the confidentiality of the "source" individual, and can lead to additional harms. Should courts weigh the protection of public health against individual liberties in determining the validity of public health programs? These traditional public health strategies have never been employed for all contagious illnesses; instead they have been reserved for particularly serious and particularly transmissible conditions. How should public health authorities determine whether and when to employ these techniques? Mandatory reporting will be explored in section C.2. Quarantine treatment and confinement will be considered in sections C.3 and C.4. Treatment and confinement will be considered in section C.4.

■ STATE v. HANDY
44 A.3d 776 (Vt. 2012)

JOHNSON, J.

Following defendant's conviction for a sex offense, the superior court, criminal division, granted the State's motion to compel defendant to submit to testing for sexually transmitted diseases under the authority of 13 V.S.A. §3256, which does not require probable cause or a warrant for testing. On appeal, defendant argues that the statute is unconstitutional because it does not serve any special need beyond law enforcement justifying abandonment of the normal probable-cause and warrant requirements and because, even if such a special need were present, the governmental goals advanced by the statute do not outweigh his constitutionally protected privacy interests. We affirm the trial court's order compelling the testing, but we remand the matter for the court to issue an order restricting the victim's disclosure of the test results.

In November 2009, defendant was convicted of lewd or lascivious conduct as the result of his having had nonconsensual sexual intercourse with the victim in a public place on October 28, 2007. In March 2010, at the behest of the victim, the State moved for the trial court to order defendant to submit to testing for sexually transmitted diseases based on his conviction for a crime involving a sexual act that created a risk of exposing the victim to the etiologic agent for acquired immune deficiency syndrome (AIDS). Upon completion of a brief nonevidentiary hearing, the trial court issued an order concluding that it was compelled to grant the State's motion under §3256, even though it had been nearly three years since the assault occurred, and that the statute was constitutional. . . .

On appeal, defendant argues that the trial court erred by concluding that the purposes underlying §3256 represented special needs sufficient to abandon the warrant and probable-cause requirements under Article Eleven of the Vermont Constitution, and further that, even if the statute represented such special needs, those special needs did not overcome his constitutionally protected privacy rights.

Article Eleven is implicated in this case because the taking of a blood sample or cheek swab is unquestionably a search that triggers constitutional protections. Article Eleven, like the Fourth Amendment, "does not contemplate an absolute prohibition on warrantless searches or seizures, but circumstances under which warrantless searches or seizures are permitted must be jealously and carefully drawn." State v. Welch, 624 A.2d 1105, 1110 (1992). Toward that end, this Court has adopted as part of its Article Eleven jurisprudence, in the context of administrative searches, the "special needs" standard of review set forth by Justice Blackman in his dissent in O'Connor v. Ortega, 480 U.S. 709 (1987).* Similarly, other jurisdictions have applied a special-needs analysis in reviewing constitutional challenges to statutes compelling sex offenders to submit to testing, at the request of the victim, for sexually transmitted diseases. See, e.g., State v. Houey, 651 S.E.2d 314, 316-317 (2007) (applying special-needs test in rejecting constitutional challenge to federal statute allowing victims to obtain HIV testing of sexual assault perpetrators).

Under the standard adopted in [previous cases], we will abandon the probable-cause and warrant requirements only under exceptional circumstances when the State demonstrates that special needs beyond normal law enforcement make those requirements impracticable and those special needs outweigh countervailing privacy interests. It is the State's burden, then, to show both that there are special needs outside law enforcement making warrants impracticable and that those needs outweigh any countervailing privacy rights upon which the warrantless search intrudes. . . .

---

* [The special needs exception to the warrant and probable cause requirements of the Fourth Amendment is also discussed in Ferguson v. City of Charleston, 532 U.S. 67 (2001), excerpted at page 781.—EDS.]

Section 3256 addresses both the testing of the perpetrator and the testing and support of the victim of unlawful sexual conduct. . . . Upon the request of the victim "at any time after the commission of a crime involving a sexual act," the state "shall" provide to the victim various services, including "counseling regarding human immunodeficiency virus (HIV)," confidential testing "for HIV and other sexually-transmitted diseases," counseling regarding "the accuracy of the testing, and the risk of transmitting HIV and other sexually-transmitted diseases to the victim as the result of the crime involving a sexual act," and "prophylaxis treatment, crisis counseling, and support services." . . .

At issue in this appeal are the . . . subsections of the statute that concern the testing of convicted sex offenders. The victim of a sexual act "which creates a risk of transmission of the etiologic agent for AIDS" may obtain an order requiring the perpetrator "convicted" of an offense based on that act to be tested for AIDS and other sexually transmitted diseases. If the court determines that the offender has been convicted of a crime involving a sexual act with the victim, as defined in the statute, "the court shall order the test to be administered," id. §3256(c). "The results of the offender's test shall be disclosed only to the offender and the victim," and the test results and record of the court proceedings "shall be sealed," id. §3256(j).

. . . As courts in other jurisdictions have uniformly held in examining similar statutes, statutes such as these are directed at public health matters, not law enforcement, and therefore satisfy the first part of the special-needs standard. . . . Moreover, the courts have also recognized that imposing probable-cause and warrant requirements would be entirely impracticable in this context because many sexually transmitted diseases, and most particularly the AIDS virus, have no outward manifestations that would permit a probable-cause determination for obtaining a warrant. Hence, requiring probable cause and a warrant for such searches would effectively preclude the testing of sex offenders and thus negate the statute. . . .

[Next], we must balance the governmental interests forwarded by §3256 against the privacy interests invaded by the statute. We first examine the privacy interests at stake here because they are more straightforward. At the outset, we recognize that the statute's targeted class—convicted sex offenders—has greatly diminished privacy interests, particularly with respect to precluding the testing of bodily fluids forced upon their victims in criminal sexual acts. See In re Juveniles, 847 P.2d at 460 ("For sexual offenders in particular, their expectation in privacy in bodily fluids is greatly diminished because they have engaged in a class of criminal behavior which presents the potential of exposing others to the AIDS virus."). Moreover, the taking of a blood sample or a cheek swab is a relatively minimal intrusion on privacy.

On the other hand, courts have recognized "that the information obtained as the result of a positive HIV test may have a devastating impact on individuals who would prefer not to know their true status" and that "persons with AIDS are often stigmatized and subject to social disapproval." People v. Adams, 597 N.E.2d 574, 582-83 (Ill. 1992). "Mandatory testing and disclosure of HIV status thus threaten privacy interests beyond the taking of the blood sample, particularly because of the social stigma, harassment, and discrimination often suffered by individuals who have AIDS or who are HIV-positive." In re J.G., 701 A.2d 1260, 1267 (N.J. 1997).

The degree to which convicted sex offenders may be subject to this more significant invasion of privacy associated with mandatory HIV testing "is a function of how widely the results are disseminated." Gov't of Virgin Islands v. Roberts, 756 F. Supp. 898, 902 (D. V.I. 1991). "The risk of stigmatic harm therefore speaks not to whether the search should transpire in the first instance, but rather to the extent to which the private medical facts learned from the procedure should be disclosed." Id. In short, the only privacy interest of any significance in this context is the risk of public dissemination of positive test results.

We now examine the other side of the equation—the governmental interest in testing sex offenders. On its face, the statute begs several questions. How does the testing of sex offenders following conviction contribute to the state's interest in public health and, more specifically, the well-being of the victims of sex crimes? What is the nexus between testing offenders following conviction and providing relevant information to victims about their risk of contracting sexually transmitted infectious diseases? Given that testing offenders after conviction apparently would not provide any information as to when a sexually transmitted disease was contracted relative to the timing of the sex offense for which they were convicted, how does the testing further the state's public health interest?

None of these questions was addressed at the nonevidentiary hearing before the trial court. . . . [An analysis of the legislative history of the mandatory testing provision reveals that it] was a controversial proposition that had been introduced in various bills and debated and negotiated in legislative committees over several legislative sessions. . . . The medical expert testified [during the legislative process] that . . . [t]he latency period between exposure to the virus and the accumulation of sufficient antibodies to result in a positive test is normally between six weeks and six months. For a victim potentially exposed to the AIDS virus to benefit from prophylaxis treatment aimed at reducing the chances of incurring the virus, the treatment must commence within a seventy-two-hour period. Therefore, testing the offender following conviction cannot inform a decision as to whether to begin the rigorous prophylaxis treatment. Nor would such testing normally precede the six-week-to-six-month latency period during which the victim's own testing might not yet reveal the presence of the virus. Hence, neither a negative nor a positive result from the offender's testing would appear to have any value for the victim. Moreover, any positive test result from the offender would have limited value for the additional reasons that the tests do not indicate when the virus was incurred and that the chances of passing the virus on to a sexual assault victim are very small. Indeed, even those who testified in support of testing offenders acknowledged that such testing provided little or no medically useful information for victims of sexual crimes.

Faced with this testimony, the chairs of both the House and Judiciary Committees acknowledged the apparent lack of medical usefulness in testing offenders, but explained that the State of Vermont would not be eligible to receive roughly $175,000 per year in federal grants to fund testing and counseling for sexual assault victims . . . unless the statute required testing the perpetrators. This appears to be the principal driving force behind incorporating in §3256 the sections compelling the testing of sex offenders upon the request of the victim.

If retaining federal funding were the sole governmental interest supporting the challenged portion of the statute, then the constitutionality of the law would be suspect because there would be no nexus between the law's intrusion on even the diminished privacy interest here and the information obtained from that intrusion. That is not the case, however. There was additional testimony before the legislative committees in support of testing offenders unrelated to preserving federal grant money. . . . Courts have . . . recognized the psychological benefit for victims of having the perpetrator tested even if such testing, as a practical matter, provides little or no useful medical information to the victim. . . .

We concur. One hardly need document the obvious trauma and suffering endured by victims of sexual assault. . . . When that trauma is further exacerbated by a legitimate fear of contracting a life-threatening sexually transmitted disease, the desire of victims to have the perpetrator tested to allay their fears is entirely understandable and real. Therefore, although the consensus among medical experts is that testing offenders—particularly following conviction after months or even years have passed—has little or no direct medical benefit to victims, testing offenders can provide to victims some psychological benefit that outweighs the offenders' significantly diminished interest in preventing the testing of bodily fluids forced upon their unwilling victims.

Accordingly, as long as the trial court imposes restrictions that comport with the statute's obvious intent to prevent public dissemination of the perpetrator's test results, we find no constitutional infirmity to the statute. . . . To safeguard defendant's privacy interests in not having any potential positive test results disseminated publicly, we remand the matter for the court to order the victim not to disclose defendant's test results to anyone except for the victim's medical provider or counselor, who, in turn, would have an obligation to keep confidential information revealed by their patients. . . .

Notes: Testing Programs

1. *Voluntary Screening.* Voluntary screening programs present the fewest constitutional objections. A voluntary program is consistent with the norms of patient consent for medical treatment. In practice, a voluntary program can operate along a spectrum of voluntariness and consent: A patient may have an opportunity to give specific, sometimes written consent after a discussion of the test's risks and benefits. A patient can be told that testing is "routine" and will be performed unless the patient "opts out" or objects. Finally, a patient's consent to medical treatment can be deemed to cover a particular test without any specific discussion or explicit opportunity to object.

A voluntary screening program can be established through the development of professional norms of practice or through governmental intervention. When the link between maternal age and Down syndrome was recognized, for example, prenatal screening for the condition became widespread. In part because of the risk of malpractice liability, physicians began to routinely advise women of the risk of Down syndrome and to offer prenatal screening.

Governmental bodies have also required that certain screening tests be offered to selected populations. For example, newborn screening programs for genetic and other conditions are often established under state law. See Ellen Wright Clayton, State Run Newborn Screening in the Genomic Era, or How to Avoid Drowning When Drinking from a Firehose, 38 J.L. Med. & Ethics 697 (2010); Proceedings: Newborn Screening for Nontreatable Disorders, 19 Health Matrix 137-204 (2009). One particular controversial form of screening has been the collection of newborn blood spots in some states, which has led to litigation and ultimately legislative action. See Sonia M. Suter, Did You Give the Government Your Baby's DNA? Rethinking Consent in Newborn Screening, 15 Minn. J. L. Sci. & Tech. 729 (2014); Newborn Screening Saves Lives Reauthorization Act of 2014, H.R. 1281, 113th Cong. (2014) (mandating that all federally funded research on newborn dried blood spots will require informed consent in the form of parental permission with no exception, though set to sunset in 2018). Do ethnically focused testing programs create any special concerns? See Cynthia F. Hinton et al., Ethical Implications and Practical Considerations of Ethnically Targeted Screening for Genetic Disorders: The Case of Hemoglobinopathy Screening, 16 Ethnicity & Health 377 (2011). Some of these programs, while officially voluntary, can as a practical matter result in coercive testing. This is particularly so where individuals either do not understand that testing is being performed or do not understand their right to refuse the procedure. For an interesting case dealing with the liability implications of state newborn screening programs, see Creason v. State Department of Health Services, 957 P.2d 1323 (Cal. 1998).

2. *"Conditional" Screening.* Conditional screening programs occupy an uneasy middle ground between voluntary and mandatory testing programs. Conditional screening occurs where testing is required as a condition of participation in some activity or for the receipt of some benefit. Conditional screening seems most like voluntary screening where the activity or benefit is of little consequence to the individual to be tested. A rule that requires HIV screening of blood donors, for example, seems more like a voluntary testing program because no one is compelled to donate blood and the benefits of donation are largely emotional. See Cal. Health & Safety Code §§1603.3, 1644.5 (HIV screening of blood and tissue donors).

Conditional screening seems much more like mandatory screening where the activity or benefit is of great importance. Rules that require testing applicants for marriage licenses for sexually transmitted diseases or that impose HIV testing on hospital patients or in employment seem closer to mandatory testing. Certainly, a person can avoid testing, but only by refraining from participating in a valued activity. For that reason, the legal analysis of these programs is likely to be similar to that employed for traditional mandatory screening programs.

a. *Premarital Screening.* Various states in the United States and some countries have conditioned issuance of a marriage license on submission of evidence that the participants had undergone a premarital examination and testing for certain diseases. Some states have repealed their premarital testing provisions, often because they were considered to be inefficient: Not many cases of infection were identified, and transmission would often already have been accomplished via premarital sexual activity. See, e.g., N.Y. Dom. Rel. §13-a. Repealed. L. 1985, 674, §1, eff. Aug. 1, 1985. Should states consider expanding their premarital testing statutes to include mandatory HIV screening or, as science advances, genetic screening? Compare Edmund C. Tamon & Shant S. Boyajian, Learning from History: What the Public Health Response to Syphilis Teaches Us About HIV/AIDS, 26 J. Contemp. Health L. & Pol'y 253 (2010) (arguing for expansion of HIV screening akin to response to syphilis before 1945), with Michael Closen et al., Mandatory Premarital HIV Testing: Political Exploitation of the AIDS Epidemic, 69 Tul. L. Rev. 71 (1994). See also Ill. Rev. Stat. ch. 40, §204 (1987) (syphilis test requirement repealed in favor of providing brochure on sexually transmitted diseases to all seeking marriage licenses). How would you analyze the constitutionality of a statute requiring premarital testing for some sexually transmitted disease or for genetic conditions that might be inherited by offspring? The issue of mandatory premarital HIV screening has garnered recent attention in the international sphere. See, e.g., Open Society Institute, Mandatory Premarital HIV Testing: An Overview (2010); UNAIDS/WHO, Statement on HIV Testing Services (2017).

b. *Medical Testing in Private and Public Employment.* Should private entities be entitled to screen individuals for unwanted medical conditions? The ADA regulates employer use of medical examinations. The Act sets up three different rules. Employers may not impose medical exams or ask questions designed to ferret out applicants' disabilities during the pre-offer stage. Employers may ask whether an applicant will be able to perform the essential functions of a job, with or without reasonable accommodations. After extending a conditional offer of employment, the employer may require that all prospective employees undergo a medical screening exam. The exam does not need to be job related, but the employer must offer a nondiscriminatory rationale for retracting a job offer after an employment physical. Once employed, an individual may only be subjected to mandatory medical exams that are job related and consistent with business necessity. See, e.g., Deborah F. Buckman, Construction and Application of §102(d) of Americans with Disabilities Act (42 U.S.C.A. §12112(d)) Pertaining to Medical Examinations and Inquiries, 159 A.L.R. Fed. 89 (2000). Some industries face unique legal and ethical issues regarding the testing of employees. For a discussion of such issues in the National Football League, see, e.g., Jessica L. Roberts et al., Evaluating NFL Player Health and Performance: Legal and Ethical Issues, 165 Penn. L. Rev. 227 (2017).

The government-as-employer often must comply with certain constitutional rules, including those protecting individual rights as well as the ADA. See Local 1812, American Federation of Government Employees v. Department of State, 662 F. Supp. 50 (D.D.C. 1987). But see Norman-Bloodsaw v. Lawrence Berkeley Laboratory, 135 F.3d 1260 (9th Cir. 1998) (noting that employees had a protected privacy interest in intimate personal matters such as syphilis, sickle-cell trait, and pregnancy; case remanded for further fact finding regarding employee authorization and government's need for information); and Elizabeth Pendo, Race, Sex, and Genes at Work: Uncovering the Lessons of Norman-Bloodsaw, 10 Hous. J. Health L. & Pol'y 227 (2010) (providing historical background on the case along with implications for Genetic Information Nondiscrimination Act of 2008). Should the federal government require HIV screening for state department employees or military personnel? The U.S. State Department eliminated its HIV testing requirement in 2008, shortly before a scheduled trial on the issue. See Taylor v. Rice, 451 F.3d 898 (D.C. Cir. 2006); Matthew Lee, State Department Drops Ban on HIV-Positive Diplomats after Pressure from Lawsuit, Associated Press, (Feb. 16, 2008). Meanwhile, the Department of Defense reissued its regulation of mandatory HIV testing for military applicants and active duty personnel in 2013. See U.S. Department of Defense Instruction Number 6485.01 (June 7, 2013).

3. *Mandatory Screening.* Mandatory screening programs impose testing on all persons who fit within some defined group. Examples of current mandatory screening programs include: premarital testing for sexually transmitted diseases; mandatory drug testing of certain employees; mandatory HIV or other testing for those convicted of sexual offenses; and mandatory TB screening for prisoners. In each

of these cases, states have sought to enhance safety or health by identifying those who might present a risk to others. Does the rationale applied in *Handy* suggest that each of these programs will be found to be constitutional under the Fourth Amendment? Can you think of any other constitutional objections? Should HIV screening be mandated in some sports, like boxing? See Corona v. State, 100 Cal. Rptr. 3d 591 (App. 2009). HIV testing was eliminated as a mandatory component of medical screening for immigration in 2009. Julia Preston, Obama Lifts a Ban on Entry into U.S. by H.I.V.-Positive People, N.Y. Times, Oct. 30, 2009; see also Final Rule, Medical Examination of Aliens — Removal of Human Immunodeficiency Virus (HIV) Infection from Definition of Communicable Disease of Public Health Significance, 74 Fed. Reg. 56547 (Nov. 2, 2009).

a. *STD Testing for Persons Convicted of Sexual Crimes.* What public health objectives are served by testing persons convicted of sexual crimes for sexually transmitted diseases (STDs)? Will the testing program necessarily prevent future transmission of disease? Does the disclosure of the test result to the survivor of a sexual assault provide useful information? Unfortunately, as noted in *Handy*, HIV testing performed years after a sexual assault will be too late to provide useful medical information for the survivor. Were you persuaded by the *Handy* court's finding that the psychological benefits to survivors are sufficient to justify HIV testing for the perpetrators of sexual crimes? Testing convicted defendants for HIV and other STDs is very popular among legislators, in part because of the incentives created by a federal link between state HIV testing rules and eligibility for federal funds. See, e.g., N.Y. Crim. Proc. Law §390.15 (legislative history including link to federal law, since repealed, which conditioned receipt of certain federal funds on state implementation of law authorizing mandatory HIV testing of perpetrators under some circumstances).

As noted in *Handy*, mandatory testing programs generally are held to implicate the Fourth Amendment's right to be free from unreasonable searches and seizures. The Fourth Amendment requires that searches be reasonable, balancing the government's interest in the search against the individual's liberty interests. Not all searches require a warrant or individualized suspicion. Courts have developed the "special governmental needs" exception to the warrant requirement. Under this approach, applied in *Handy*, a warrantless search may be upheld where it serves some special governmental purpose important enough to outweigh an individual's reasonable expectation of privacy. As the *Handy* court noted, concerns about public health and safety easily fall within the category of "special needs." What public health objectives were supported by coercive testing of persons convicted of sexual offenses? Why does the court hold that the intrusion into individual liberty is "minimal" when balanced against the governmental need? What types of personal interests are at stake? Which is most important, the physical intrusion created by the blood test? The use of an HIV antibody test? The disclosure of the test result to others? Do you agree with the court's balancing analysis? See also Ferguson v. City of Charleston at page 781.

b. *Equal Protection.* In People v. Adams, 597 N.E.2d 574 (Ill. 1992), cited in *Handy*, the court upheld a mandatory HIV testing law applicable to persons convicted of prostitution. The court found that the testing program could be upheld under the special needs exception to the warrant requirement. In addition, the court considered and rejected the defendants' equal protection claim that the HIV testing statute is both underinclusive (because it fails to require HIV testing for certain criminal conduct that is as likely to result in the transmission of AIDS as prostitution) and overinclusive (because it includes within its scope offenses such as solicitation having no risk of AIDS transmission). The court found that the statute "does not impinge upon the exercise of a fundamental right or operate against a suspect class" and that the testing requirement "bears a rational relationship to the state interest in combating the spread of AIDS." Id. at 585-586.

c. *TB and HIV Testing in Prisons.* Contagious diseases also present complex constitutional issues within prisons. Prisoners do not lose all of their constitutional rights by virtue of their confinement. Prisoners may thus assert their right to be free from unreasonable searches, to make medical decisions, to pursue their religious beliefs, and to be free from cruel and unusual punishment. U.S. Const. amends. I, V, VIII, XIV. Prisoners may also be able to assert statutory claims, such as prohibitions against disability-based discrimination. 29 U.S.C. §794 (Rehabilitation Act provisions prohibiting disability-based discrimination by federal entities or recipients of federal funds); 42 U.S.C. §12132 (ADA prohibition of disability-based discrimination by public entities). But see pages 936-937. Prison officials are nonetheless given considerable latitude in devising prison rules that, while impinging on individual liberties, are considered reasonable in light of the prison's legitimate penological goals. See Turner v. Safley, 482 U.S. 78, 89 (1987); and Johnson v. California, 543 U.S. 499 (2005) (*Turner* applies to restriction of rights that are inconsistent with incarceration but not to policies contravening racial equality). See also Thompson v. City of Los Angeles, 885 F.2d 1439, 1447 (9th Cir. 1989) (prison officials have compelling interest in disease prevention).

Should correctional facilities be permitted to test inmates for the presence of contagious conditions? Most courts have answered affirmatively. See, e.g., Moore v. Mabus, 976 F.2d 268 (5th Cir. 1992) ("identification and segregation of HIV-positive prisoners obviously serves a legitimate penological purpose"); Hasenmeier- McCarthy v. Rose, 986 F. Supp. 464 (S.D. Ohio 1998) (forcible administration of TB test performed pursuant to legitimate penological interest in detecting and controlling communicable disease). HIV testing practices recommended by the CDC for use in correctional facilities include the provision of routine opt-out testing at entry in all facilities. Yet, a 2014 survey found that only 14 percent of U.S. state prisons provide HIV testing in accordance with the CDC's recommendations, and 37 percent require mandatory HIV testing. See Solomon et al., Survey Finds That Many Prisons and Jails Have Room to Improve HIV Testing and Coordination of Postrelease Treatment, 33 Health Affairs 434 (2014). The World Health Organization and UNAIDS have consistently opposed compulsory HIV testing, and nearly all European countries have abandoned such testing. See UNAIDS/WHO, Statement on HIV Testing Services (2017).

d. *HIV Screening for Pregnant Women and Newborns.* The risk of HIV transmission from woman to child during pregnancy is less than 30 percent without treatment. In the 1990s, proponents of mandatory or routine HIV testing for pregnant women noted that the risk of HIV transmission through pregnancy could be reduced significantly. Transmission rates drop to less than 2 percent if pregnant women are aware of their infection, take antiretroviral therapies, and use special procedures during birth and during the newborn's first days and months of life. Edward M. Connor et al., Reduction of Maternal-Infant Transmission of Human Immunodeficiency Virus Type 1 with Zidovudine Treatment, 331 New Eng. J. Med. 1173 (1994).

Given this sharp reduction in the risk of transmission, a number of states considered whether to adopt mandatory or routine maternal screening for HIV. See Comment, 45 Am. U. L. Rev. 1185 (1996); Tex. Health & Safety Code §81.090 (routine screening with "opt-out"). In the mid-2000s, public health officials recommended routine screening coupled with directive counseling. Bernard M. Branson et al., Revised Recommendations for HIV Testing of Adults, Adolescents, and Pregnant Women in Health Care Settings, 55 MMWR 1 (2006) (RR-14) (recommending directive counseling).

4. *Criminalization of HIV Transmission.* Persons who knowingly put others at risk for HIV transmission, through sexual or other activity, can be prosecuted for assault, attempted murder, or for violation of HIV-specific criminal statutes. Adeline Delavande et al., Criminal Prosecution and Human Immunodeficiency Virus-Related Risky Behavior, 53 J. L. & Econ. 741 (2010); Sun Goo Lee, Criminal Law and HIV Testing, 14 Yale J. Health Pol'y L. & Ethics 194 (2014). Prosecution is difficult unless it can be shown that the defendant knew that he or she was HIV infected. Should test results obtained from convicted defendants or prisoners be used in subsequent prosecutions to prove that the defendant must have known of his or her HIV status at the time of the risky act? See State ex rel. J. G., 701 A.2d 1260 (N.J. 1997) (answering no). HIV criminalization laws have been criticized as misguided and poor policy, particularly given the increasing availability of preventative HIV medication. Stephen Frost, HIV Criminalization Laws: A Poor Public Policy Choice in the New Era of PrEP, 6 Wake Forest J. L. & Pol'y 319 (2016); see also Rhoades v. State, 848 N.W.2d 22 (Iowa 2014) (reversing conviction for criminal transmission of HIV and ruling that Iowa's HIV criminalization statute could not be used to prosecute people living with HIV for consensual sex acts that pose no reasonable risk of transmitting HIV). In 2014, Iowa became the first state to reform its HIV criminal transmission statute, creating a new law that provides for graded offenses, which depend in part on the defendant's specific intent. See Iowa Code §706D.3(1) (2015). Efforts are also underway at the federal level to challenge state HIV criminalization laws. In March 2015, Congresswoman Barbara Lee reintroduced a new iteration of the REPEAL HIV Discrimination Act, which would require an interagency review of federal and state laws that criminalize certain actions by people living with HIV. REPEAL HIV Discrimination Act of 2015, H.R. 1586, 114th Cong. (2015).

5. *Further Reading.* For more on **mandatory STD testing of those convicted of sexual crimes** (note 3), see Michael P. Bruyere, Damage Control for Victims of Physical Assault—Testing the Innocent for AIDS, 21 Fla. St. U. L. Rev. 945 (1994); Steven Eisenstat, An Analysis of the Rationality of Mandatory Testing for the HIV Antibody: Balancing the Governmental Public Health Interests with the Individual's Privacy Interest, 52 U. Pitt. L. Rev. 327 (1991).

For more on **mandatory HIV and TB testing in correctional facilities** (note 3), see John V. Jacobi, Prison Health, Public Health: Obligations and Opportunities, 31 Am. J. L. & Med. 447 (2005); John D. Kraemer, Screening of Prisoners for HIV: Public Health, Legal, and Ethical Implications, 13 Mich. St. U. J. Med. & L. 187 (2009); James Less Pope, HIV Testing in State Correctional Systems, 22 J. L. & Health 17 (2009).

For more on **HIV and other STD testing in pregnant women** (note 3), see Zita Lazzarini & Lorilyn Rosales, Legal Issues Concerning Public Health Efforts to Reduce Perinatal HIV Transmission, 3 Yale J. Health Pol'y L. & Ethics 67 (2002); Lawrence O. Gostin, HIV Screening in Health Care Settings: Public Health and Civil Liberties in Conflict?, 296 JAMA 2023 (2006).

Problem: Routine HIV Screening for All

Should mandatory or routine HIV testing be imposed for all adults and adolescents? What would be the benefits and risks of such testing program? See Howard Libman, Screening for HIV Infection: A Healthy, "Low-Risk" 42-Year-Old Man, 306 JAMA 637 (2011); A. David Paltiel et al., Expanded Screening for HIV in the United States — An Analysis of Cost-Effectiveness, 352 New Eng. J. Med. 586 (2005); see also Samuel Bossette, Routine Screening for HIV Infection — Timely and Cost-Effective, 352 New Eng. J. Med. 620 (2005). Should the law protect the right of individuals not to know their HIV status? Cf. Christian Turner, The Burden of Knowledge, 43 Ga. L. Rev. 297 (2009).

The CDC now recommends routine HIV testing for most adolescents and adults in health care settings. The recommendations specify that patients should be told about the testing and be given an opportunity to decline. Do you agree with this approach? Bernard M. Branson et al., Revised Recommendations for HIV Testing of Adults, Adolescents, and Pregnant Women in Health Care Settings, 55 MMWR Recomm. Rep. 1 (2006) (RR-14); Matthew W. Pierce et al., Testing Public Health Ethics: Why the CDC's HIV Screening Recommendations May Violate the Least Infringement Principle, 39 J. L. Med. & Ethics 263 (2011). The CDC estimated in 2009 that 45 percent of adults between the ages of 18 and 65 had ever been tested for HIV, only a 5 percent increase over the level of testing that existed before the expansion in the CDC's guidelines in 2006. Libman, supra, at 641. What would explain the apparent resistance to the implementation of the CDC's recommendations? Would you expect that continuing stigma associated with HIV would be more or less important than legal barriers? Should insurance plans cover the costs of routine HIV screening? See Ronald Bayer & Gerald Oppenheimer, Routine HIV-Screening — What Counts as Evidence-Based Policy?, 365 New Eng. J. Med. 1265 (2011) (discussing possibility that U.S. Preventive Services Task Force ("USPSTF") might join CDC in recommending routine screening, which would result in broader insurance coverage for screening); see also Virginia Moyer, Screening for HIV: U.S. Preventive Services Task Force Recommendation Statement, 159 Ann. Intern. Med. 51 (2013) (updated USPSTF recommendation that clinicians screen adolescents and adults aged 15 to 65 years for HIV infection).

Examine your jurisdiction's rules regarding HIV testing. Could the CDC's recommendations be adopted without legislative changes? Has your state's legislation changed in response to the recommendations? See CDC, State HIV Laws, http://www.cdc.gov/hiv/policies/law/states/ (as of 2016, all but two states, Nebraska and New York, have HIV testing laws that are consistent with the CDC's recommendation); A. P. Mahajan et al., Consistency of State Statutes with the Centers for Disease Control and Prevention HIV Testing Recommendations for Health Care Settings, 150 Ann. Intern. Med. 263 (2009); Lauren E. Palmer, Solving the HIV Testing Problem: An Analysis of New York's New Legislation, 4 Alb. Gov't L. Rev. 758 (2011); Colleen Snyder, Chapter 550: Relaxing Consent Requirements for HIV Testing, 39 McGeorge L. Rev. 567 (2008). For the international debate on "opt-in" or "opt-out" testing, see Ronald Bayer & Claire Edington, HIV Testing, Human Rights, and Global AIDS Policy: Exceptionalism and Its Discontents, 34 J. Health Pol. Pol'y & L. 301 (2009). Could the CDC's recommendations be used to establish a new standard of care in medical practice with respect to HIV screening? Should physician's failure to implement HIV screening lead to liability for failure to diagnose HIV infection through proof, for example, that earlier testing would have permitted early use of antiretroviral therapies or prevented HIV transmission to others? Interestingly, although the CDC guidelines are advisory, in 2011 public health authorities implemented a new campaign to increase rates of HIV testing, called: "HIV Screening. Standard Care." See www.actagainstaids.org/; CDC, HIV Testing in Healthcare Settings. A 2016 study found that HIV testing rates remained low among high school students and young adults despite the measures taken by the CDC. Michelle Handel et al., HIV Testing Among US High School Students and Young Adults, 137 Pediatrics 1 (2016).

Problem: State Law, Disaster-Planning, and Bioterrorism Preparedness

The Model State Emergency Health Powers Act (MSEHPA) described above at pages 923-924, includes rules and procedures designed to improve detection of a public health emergency and then establishes rules and procedures that take effect only in a public health emergency. As noted above, a public health emergency is one that is caused by bioterrorism, novel infectious agents, natural disasters, or certain other enumerated events.

The Model Act includes provisions authorizing mandatory medical examinations and tests:

> Medical examination and testing. During a state of public health emergency the public health authority may perform physical examinations and/or tests as necessary for the diagnosis or treatment of individuals.
>
> (a) Medical examinations or tests may be performed by any qualified person authorized to do so by the public health authority.
>
> (b) Medical examinations or tests must not be such as are reasonably likely to lead to serious harm to the affected individual.
>
> (c) The public health authority may isolate or quarantine, pursuant to Section 604 [discussed infra at pages 984-987], any person whose refusal of medical examination or testing results in uncertainty regarding whether he or she has been exposed to or is infected with a contagious or possibly contagious disease or otherwise poses a danger to public health.

MSEHPA §602.

Evaluate the constitutionality of the Model Act's testing provisions. Should it matter how a public health emergency is declared and whether there can be judicial review of the decision? Should it matter whether public health authorities have any reason to suspect that an individual has been exposed to a contagious disease or transmissible condition? Compare the Model Act's provisions to the relevant public health statute in your own state. Do the public health authorities in your state have explicit authority to mandate medical tests or examinations? If so, do you see any similarities or differences between your state law and the Model Act? Which seems better from a legal or policy standpoint? Should the same testing rules apply in bioterrorism incidents as during natural disasters or a natural epidemic such as avian influenza? Would you recommend the adoption of the Model Act's testing provision? See Daniel S. Reich, Modernizing Local Responses to Public Health

Emergencies: Bioterrorism, Epidemics, and the Model State Emergency Health Powers Act, 19 J. Contemp. Health L. & Pol'y 379, 401-406 (2003).

2. Confidentiality, Reporting, and Contact Tracing

Testing programs, whether public or private, create opportunities for additional public health interventions. What use should be made of a test result? One possibility is that the individual tested could be counseled about the significance of the test result and given information about how to safeguard her own health or the health of others with whom she may have contact. Testing can thus be an opportunity to improve public health through targeted education. For more on testing and screening, see Public Health Law at 365-372.

Other public health interventions might proceed along a different path. State reporting statutes require specified entities to report information to state health authorities. The federal CDC collects and disseminates information about some types of health threats at the national level. See CDC's Vision for Public Health Surveillance in the 21st Century, 61 MMWR 1-40 (2012) (July 27 Supp.). Common examples of reporting statutes include those that govern gunshot wounds, suspected child abuse, and certain diseases, such as plague or HIV. See page 141. In some cases, reporting statutes are an "early warning" system that can alert public health officials to serious epidemics. More prosaically, the information could promote better health budgeting as states reallocate funds and personnel to emerging health threats. Public health officials could follow-up case reports with notices about treatment or other options. Finally, the information could be used to protect those exposed to disease. Contact tracing programs attempt to identify and notify persons who have been exposed to a person with a contagious condition.

Each of these public health strategies begins with the disclosure of an individual's health status to others. Do individuals have a right to confidentiality that protects them from disclosures about their health status? The answer may depend on the nature of the information and the public interest asserted in its disclosure.

■WHALEN v. ROE
429 U.S. 589 (1977)

STEVENS, J.

The constitutional question presented is whether the state of New York may record, in a centralized computer file, the names and addresses of all persons who have obtained, pursuant to a doctor's prescription, certain drugs for which there is both a lawful and an unlawful market.

The district court enjoined enforcement of the portions of the New York State Controlled Substances Act of 1972 which require such recording on the ground that they violate appellees' constitutionally protected rights of privacy. We noted probable jurisdiction of the appeal by the Commissioner of Health, 424 U.S. 907, and now reverse.

Many drugs have both legitimate and illegitimate uses. In response to a concern that such drugs were being diverted into unlawful channels, in 1970 the New

York legislature created a special commission to evaluate the state's drug-control laws. The commission found the existing laws deficient in several respects. There was no effective way to prevent the use of stolen or revised prescriptions, to prevent unscrupulous pharmacists from repeatedly refilling prescriptions, to prevent users from obtaining prescriptions from more than one doctor, or to prevent doctors from over-prescribing, either by authorizing an excessive amount in one prescription or by giving one patient multiple prescriptions. In drafting new legislation to correct such defects, the commission consulted with enforcement officials in California and Illinois where central reporting systems were being used effectively.

The new New York statute classified potentially harmful drugs in five schedules.[7] Drugs, such as heroin, which are highly abused and have no recognized medical use, are in Schedule I; they cannot be prescribed. Schedules II through V include drugs which have a progressively lower potential for abuse but also have a recognized medical use. Our concern is limited to Schedule II which includes the most dangerous of the legitimate drugs.[8]

With an exception for emergencies, the Act requires that all prescriptions for Schedule II drugs be prepared by the physician in triplicate on an official form. The completed form identifies the prescribing physician; the dispensing pharmacy; the drug and dosage; and the name, address, and age of the patient. One copy of the form is retained by the physician, the second by the pharmacist, and the third is forwarded to the New York State Department of Health in Albany. A prescription made on an official form may not exceed a 30-day supply, and may not be refilled.

The district court found that about 100,000 Schedule II prescription forms are delivered to a receiving room at the Department of Health in Albany each month. They are sorted, coded, and logged and then taken to another room where the data on the forms is recorded on magnetic tapes for processing by a computer. Thereafter, the forms are returned to the receiving room to be retained in a vault for a five-year period and then destroyed as required by the statute. . . .

A few days before the Act became effective, this litigation was commenced by a group of patients regularly receiving prescriptions for Schedule II drugs, by doctors who prescribe such drugs, and by two associations of physicians. After various preliminary proceedings, a three-judge district court conducted a one-day trial. Appellees offered evidence tending to prove that persons in need of treatment with Schedule II drugs will from time to time decline such treatment because of their fear that the misuse of the computerized data will cause them to be stigmatized as "drug addicts."

---

7. These five schedules conform in all material aspects with the drug schedules in the Federal Comprehensive Drug Abuse Prevention and Control Act of 1970. 21 U.S.C. §801 et seq.

8. These include opium and opium derivatives, cocaine, methadone, amphetamines, and methaqualone. Pub. Health Law §3306. These drugs have accepted uses in the amelioration of pain and in the treatment of epilepsy, narcolepsy, hyperkinesia, schizo-affective disorders, and migraine headaches.

I

The district court found that the state had been unable to demonstrate the necessity for the patient-identification requirement on the basis of its experience during the first 20 months of administration of the new statute. . . .

State legislation which has some effect on individual liberty or privacy may not be held unconstitutional simply because a court finds it unnecessary, in whole or in part. For we have frequently recognized that individual states have broad latitude in experimenting with possible solutions to problems of vital local concern.

The New York statute challenged in this case represents a considered attempt to deal with such a problem. It is manifestly the product of an orderly and rational legislative decision. It was recommended by a specially appointed commission which held extensive hearings on the proposed legislation, and drew on experience with similar programs in other states. There surely was nothing unreasonable in the assumption that the patient-identification requirement might aid in the enforcement of laws designed to minimize the misuse of dangerous drugs. For the requirement could reasonably be expected to have a deterrent effect on potential violators as well as to aid in the detection or investigation of specific instances of apparent abuse. At the very least, it would seem clear that the state's vital interest in controlling the distribution of dangerous drugs would support a decision to experiment with new techniques for control. For if an experiment fails—if in this case experience teaches that the patient-identification requirement results in the foolish expenditure of funds to acquire a mountain of useless information—the legislative process remains available to terminate the unwise experiment. It follows that the legislature's enactment of the patient-identification requirement was a reasonable exercise of New York's broad police powers. The district court's finding that the necessity for the requirement had not been proved is not, therefore, a sufficient reason for holding the statutory requirement unconstitutional.

II

Appellees contend that the statute invades a constitutionally protected "zone of privacy." The cases sometimes characterized as protecting "privacy" have in fact involved at least two different kinds of interests. One is the individual interest in avoiding disclosure of personal matters, and another is the interest in independence in making certain kinds of important decisions. Appellees argue that both of these interests are impaired by this statute. The mere existence in readily available form of the information about patients' use of Schedule II drugs creates a genuine concern that the information will become publicly known and that it will adversely affect their reputations. This concern makes some patients reluctant to use, and some doctors reluctant to prescribe, such drugs even when their use is medically indicated. It follows, they argue, that the making of decisions about matters vital to the care of their health is inevitably affected by the statute. Thus, the statute threatens to impair both their interest in the nondisclosure of private information and also their interest in making important decisions independently.

We are persuaded, however, that the New York program does not, on its face, pose a sufficiently grievous threat to either interest to establish a constitutional violation.

Public disclosure of patient information can come about in three ways. Health Department employees may violate the statute by failing, either deliberately or negligently, to maintain proper security. A patient or a doctor may be accused of a violation and the stored data may be offered in evidence in a judicial proceeding. Or, thirdly, a doctor, a pharmacist, or the patient may voluntarily reveal information on a prescription form.

The third possibility existed under the prior law and is entirely unrelated to the existence of the computerized data bank. Neither of the other two possibilities provides a proper ground for attacking the statute as invalid on its face. There is no support in the record, or in the experience of the two states that New York has emulated, for an assumption that the security provisions of the statute will be administered improperly. And the remote possibility that judicial supervision of the evidentiary use of particular items of stored information will provide inadequate protection against unwarranted disclosures is surely not a sufficient reason for invalidating the entire patient-identification program.

Even without public disclosure, it is, of course, true that private information must be disclosed to the authorized employees of the New York Department of Health. Such disclosures, however, are not significantly different from those that were required under the prior law. Nor are they meaningfully distinguishable from a host of other unpleasant invasions of privacy that are associated with many facets of health care. Unquestionably, some individuals' concern for their own privacy may lead them to avoid or to postpone needed medical attention. Nevertheless, disclosures of private medical information to doctors, to hospital personnel, to insurance companies, and to public health agencies are often an essential part of modern medical practice even when the disclosure may reflect unfavorably on the character of the patient. Requiring such disclosures to representatives of the state having responsibility for the health of the community, does not automatically amount to an impermissible invasion of privacy.

Appellees also argue, however, that even if unwarranted disclosures do not actually occur, the knowledge that the information is readily available in a computerized file creates a genuine concern that causes some persons to decline needed medication. The record supports the conclusion that some use of Schedule II drugs has been discouraged by that concern; it also is clear, however, that about 100,000 prescriptions for such drugs were being filled each month prior to the entry of the district court's injunction. Clearly, therefore, the statute did not deprive the public of access to the drugs.

Nor can it be said that any individual has been deprived of the right to decide independently, with the advice of his physician, to acquire and to use needed medication. Although the state no doubt could prohibit entirely the use of particular Schedule II drugs, it has not done so. This case is therefore unlike those in which the Court held that a total prohibition of certain conduct was an impermissible deprivation of liberty. Nor does the state require access to these drugs to be conditioned on the consent of any state official or other third party. Within dosage limits which appellees do not challenge, the decision to prescribe, or to use, is left entirely to the physician and the patient.

We hold that neither the immediate nor the threatened impact of the patient-identification requirements in the New York State Controlled Substances Act of 1972 on either the reputation or the independence of patients for whom Schedule

II drugs are medically indicated is sufficient to constitute an invasion of any right or liberty protected by the Fourteenth Amendment. . . .

Reversed.

Notes: Informational Privacy

1. *Informational vs. Decisional Privacy.* Does *Whalen* clearly establish that we have a fundamental constitutional right to maintain the privacy of our medical information? To the contrary, the Court upholds the validity of a state public health statute that required physicians to report sensitive information about individual prescription drug use. The constitutional protection of confidentiality is at best found in the margins of the decision, in the Court's suggestion that a constitutional right to privacy might have been implicated if the state's reporting mechanism had failed to protect patient information from improper disclosure. Justice Brennan concurred in the Court's opinion with the understanding that constitutional norms were implicated and that widespread dissemination of private information could only be justified by a compelling governmental objective. Justice Stewart's concurrence rested on his understanding that the opinion did not establish a constitutional right to privacy.

The technological capacity to collect and store information has increased dramatically since *Whalen.* Data that once could only be stored on mainframe computers can now be kept on laptops and moved via USB drives or email attachments. Hackers and unauthorized employees may access supposedly secure computerized information. Reed Abelson & Matthew Goldstein, Anthem Hacking Points to Security Vulnerability of Health Care Industry, N.Y. Times (Feb. 5, 2015) (detailing extent of recent health care breaches targeting medical information). Does this affect your view of whether constitutional protection for privacy is desirable and realistic? The HIPAA electronic records and confidentiality provisions discussed in Chapter 3.B create clear standards for confidentiality but offer no private right of action for breaches. But cf. Byrne v. Avery Center for Obstetrics and Gynecology, P.C., 102 A.3d 32 (Conn. 2014) (holding that HIPAA does not preempt state law tort actions alleging that a health care provider negligently disclosed a patient's medical records).

2. *Nomenclature. Whalen* suggests that the "right to privacy" encompasses both decisional and informational privacy. In recent years, the Supreme Court has retreated from the use of "privacy" as a basis for protecting individual decisionmaking from governmental intrusion. Most Justices now tend to refer to a "protected liberty interest" in making certain types of decisions free from unwarranted governmental interference. The Court has not taken the opportunity to revisit and more clearly delineate an individual's protected liberty interest in the privacy of information. The current status of the right remains, at best, unclear. See NASA v. Nelson, 131 S. Ct. 746 (2011) (assuming without deciding the existence of the right but finding no violation). See also Mark A. Rothstein, Constitutional Right to Informational Health Privacy in Critical Condition, 39 J. L. Med. & Ethics 280 (2011); and Ferguson v. City of Charleston at page 781.

3. *Confidentiality in the Courts of Appeal.* Despite *Whalen*'s unstable foundation, some courts have at least tentatively erected a constitutional confidentiality doctrine.

The debate has centered on the standard of review to be applied to state measures that intrude on individual privacy. The Tenth Circuit requires a compelling state interest for privacy intrusions. Stidham v. Peace Officer Standards & Training, 265 F.3d 1144 (10th Cir. 2001). A few federal courts of appeal have adopted an intermediate standard of review, employing a balancing test to weigh an individual's interest in privacy against the governmental objective. See Overstreet v. Lexington-Fayette Urban County Government, 305 F.3d 566 (6th Cir. 2002) (balancing test applies only when disclosure implicates fundamental rights); Denius v. Dunlap, 209 F.3d 944 (7th Cir. 2000) (noting relevance of type of information); C.N. v. Ridgewood Board of Education, 430 F.3d 159 (3d Cir. 2005) (balancing test includes consideration of seven factors); Matson v. Board of Education, 631 F.3d 57 (2d. Cir. 2011) (level of privacy related to character of medical information and associated risk to individual). Some courts of appeal apply only a rational basis standard of review. See also National Federation of Federal Employees v. Greenberg, 983 F.2d 286, 293-294 (D.C. Cir. 1993) (critique of *Whalen*'s "uncharted terrain").

Which of the following measures would likely withstand constitutional attack in which jurisdictions?

1. A statute requiring physicians to report the names and addresses of persons diagnosed with AIDS.
2. A statute requiring disclosure of a surgeon's HIV status to her patients.
3. A statute requiring persons with TB to post the information on their doors in at least 12-point type.

Commentators have argued that individual privacy is increasingly at risk because of a number of trends, including expanded governmental involvement in health care and the resurgence of dangerous contagious diseases such as HIV and TB.

4. *Statutory and Common-Law Protections.* The confidentiality of health-related information is protected by statute and common law as well. See Chapter 3.B; and Soumitra Sengupta et al., A Model for Expanded Public Health Reporting in the Context of HIPAA, 15 J. Am. Med. Inform. Assoc. 569 (2008). Yet none of these sources of protection is absolute. Each has an extensive list of express or implied exceptions. Typically, for example, physicians are permitted to disclose confidential medical information if "*required or authorized by law*," such as under HIPAA or state reporting statutes. See, e.g., 45 C.F.R. §164.512 (a), (b) (HIPAA authorization for use and disclosure without authorization or opportunity to agree or object where otherwise required by law or for certain public health activities); Tex. Occ. Code Ann. §159.004. See also FAA v. Cooper, 132 S. Ct. 1441 (2012) (exchange of information about individual's HIV status between federal agencies may have violated Privacy Act but sovereign immunity barred damage claims for emotional or mental distress).

5. *Further Reading.* For more on **informational privacy and big data** (note 1), see Amy L. Fairchild, The Democratization of Privacy: Public-Health Surveillance and Changing Conceptions of Privacy in Twentieth-Century America in History and Health Policy in the United States (Rosemary A. Stevens et al. eds., 2006); I. Glenn Cohen et al., The Legal and Ethical Concerns that Arise From Using Complex Predictive Analytics in Health Care, 33 Health Affairs 1139 (2014); Elizabeth R. Pike,

Securing Sequences: Ensuring Adequate Protections for Genetic Samples in the Age of Big Data, 37 Cardozo L. Rev. 1977 (2016). See also the discussion at 131-132.

For further reading on **the tensions between privacy, disclosure, and public health** (note 4), see Jessica Berg, All for One and One for All: Informed Consent and Public Health, 50 Hous. L. Rev. 1 (2012); Amy L. Fairchild et al., Searching Eyes: Privacy, the State, and Disease Surveillance in America (2007); Public Health Law at 316-330; Seth F. Kreimer, Sunlight, Secrets, and Scarlet Letters: The Tension Between Privacy and Disclosure in Constitutional Law, 140 U. Pa. L. Rev. 1 (1991); Neil M. Richards, Essay, The Information Privacy Law Project, 94 Geo. L. J. 1087 (2006); Daniel J. Solove, A Taxonomy of Privacy, 154 U. Pa. L. Rev. 477 (2006).

■ MIDDLEBROOKS v. STATE BOARD OF HEALTH
710 So. 2d 891 (Ala. 1998)

MADDOX, Justice.

This case presents the issue whether §22-11A-2, Ala.Code 1975, which requires physicians, dentists, and certain other persons to report cases or suspected cases of "notifiable diseases" and health conditions, such as HIV infections and AIDS cases, to the Alabama State Board of Health, is discriminatory and therefore violates the Equal Protection Clause of the Fourteenth Amendment to the Constitution of the United States.

Dr. Mark Middlebrooks, a physician practicing in Jefferson County, specializes in infectious diseases. Through his practice, Dr. Middlebrooks diagnoses and treats patients who are infected with HIV and AIDS. Under the provisions of §22-11A-2, Dr. Middlebrooks is within the class of persons required to report all cases of HIV infection and AIDS to the State Board of Health. The required reports are to include the names and addresses of persons infected.[1]

---

1. Section 22-11A-2 provides, in part:

   Each physician, dentist, nurse, medical examiner, hospital administrator, nursing home administrator, laboratory director, school principal, and day care center director shall be responsible to report cases or suspected cases of notifiable diseases and health conditions. The report shall contain such information, and be delivered in such a manner, as may be provided for from time to time by the rules of the state board of health. All medical and statistical information and reports required by this chapter shall be confidential and shall not be subject to the inspection, subpoena, or admission into evidence in any court, except proceedings brought under this chapter to compel the examination, testing, commitment or quarantine of any person or upon the written consent of the patient, or if the patient is a minor, his parent or legal guardian. Any physician or other person making any report required by this chapter or participating in any judicial proceeding resulting therefrom shall, in doing so, be immune from any civil or criminal liability, that might otherwise be incurred or imposed.

   The rules of the State Board of Health define HIV and AIDS as "notifiable diseases" and require the reporting person to give the patient's name and address and certain laboratory data. Alabama *Administrative Code*, Chapter 420-4-1 et seq.

In July 1993, Dr. Middlebrooks was contacted by officials of the Jefferson County Health Department, who requested that he comply with the reporting mandate of the statute and with the rules of the State Board of Health. . . . Dr. Middlebrooks provided certain statistical data, as the statute and regulatory rules required, but he refused to provide the names and addresses of his patients.

On September 8, 1994, the State Board of Health filed this action against Dr. Middlebrooks, seeking to compel him to disclose the names and addresses of his HIV and AIDS patients, as required by statute and rule. On March 13, 1996, the trial court entered an order compelling disclosure; Dr. Middlebrooks appealed.

Dr. Middlebrooks primarily contends that the statutory and regulatory scheme violates the Equal Protection Clause of the Fourteenth Amendment because persons or entities not listed in the statute are authorized by regulations adopted by the Federal Food and Drug Administration to sell confidential HIV-testing kits and the sellers of those kits are not required to report the names and addresses of the purchasers. Dr. Middlebrooks argues that he is subjected to discriminatory treatment because he is required to report the names and addresses of his HIV and AIDS patients while those who sell the testing kits and out-of-state testing laboratories that evaluate the test results are not required to report the names and addresses of those persons who test positive.

In order to address Dr. Middlebrooks's arguments, we believe it essential to discuss briefly the right of privacy in regard to disclosure of medical information relating to diseases such as HIV and AIDS.

The United States Supreme Court has stated:

> [D]isclosures of private medical information to doctors, to hospital personnel, to insurance companies, and to public health agencies are often an essential part of modern medical practice even when the disclosure may reflect unfavorably on the character of the patient. Requiring such disclosures to representatives of the State having responsibility for the health of the community, does not automatically amount to an impermissible invasion of privacy.

Whalen v. Roe, 429 U.S. 589, 602 (1977). In United States v. Westinghouse Electric Corp., 638 F.2d 570, 578 (3d Cir. 1980), the United States Court of Appeals for the Third Circuit established factors for a court to consider when determining "whether an invasion into an individual's records is justified." Those factors are:

> the type of record requested, the information it does or might contain, the potential for harm in any subsequent nonconsensual disclosure, the injury from disclosure to the relationship in which the record was generated, the adequacy of safeguards to prevent unauthorized disclosure, the degree of need for access, and whether there is an express statutory mandate, articulated public policy, or other recognizable public interest militating toward access. [Id.]

After weighing the *Westinghouse* factors, we hold that the prevention of the spread of HIV and AIDS is a legitimate governmental interest, and that, even in regard to HIV and AIDS, where, in some situations, the disclosure may reflect unfavorably on the character of the patient, . . . the State can require disclosure to representatives of the State having responsibility for the health of the community, and that the disclosure required by §22-11A-2 does not amount to an impermissible invasion of privacy. The statute and the regulatory rules adopted pursuant thereto have adequate safeguards to protect the medical records from unauthorized disclosure.

Now that we have determined that §22-11A-2 does not violate the right to privacy, we must decide whether Dr. Middlebrooks's constitutional right to equal protection is violated by the fact that §22-11A-2 does not apply to the stores that market and sell at-home HIV testing kits and out-of-state testing labs that analyze the results of the tests.

The purpose of the Equal Protection Clause is to prevent states from enacting legislation that treats persons "similarly situated" differently. City of Cleburne v. Cleburne Living Center, Inc., 473 U.S. 432, 439 (1985). "It does not, however, require that a statute necessarily apply equally to all persons or require that things different in fact be treated in law as though they were the same." McClendon v. Shelby County, 484 So. 2d 459, 464 (Ala. Civ. App. 1985).

We conclude that the State has made a reasonable classification in this instance. It appears to us that the out-of-state testing labs that analyze the results of the testing kits are not, as to those required to report HIV and AIDS cases under §22-11A-2, similarly situated.[3]

We conclude that the trial judge properly ordered Dr. Middlebrooks to disclose to the State Board of Health the names of his patients infected with HIV and AIDS. The judgment is, therefore, affirmed.

Notes: Reporting and Contact Tracing

1. Middlebrooks *Analysis*. What standard of review does the court apply to Dr. Middlebrooks's constitutional claims? Given the standard of review, could Dr. Middlebrooks have relied on public health experts who question whether states should require name-specific HIV reporting? Most public health officials strongly support names-based reporting. See, e.g., CDC, Guidelines for National Human Immunodeficiency Virus Case Surveillance, Including Monitoring for Human Immunodeficiency Infection and Acquired Immunodeficiency Syndrome, 48 MMWR 1 (1999) (RR-13). According to the CDC, as of mid-2016, all 50 states, the District of Columbia, and six U.S.-dependent areas use a uniform name-based HIV infection reporting system for collecting data on HIV infection. See CDC, State HIV Laws, http://www.cdc.gov/hiv/policies/law/states/. Why isn't the state reporting scheme irrational under the equal protection clause? Does it help or hurt the equal protection clause analysis if state residents can obtain anonymous HIV antibody testing at clinics in the state or if individuals are permitted to use false names when registering for testing?

---

3. We note, from the Board's brief, that Alabama, like other states, is attempting to get a waiver of the federal rule that permits the sale of testing kits within the state. In any event, it appears to us that the out-of-state testing labs do not know the identity of the persons that are being tested. The vendors of the testing kits are not similarly situated, because they merely sell the kits and have no information on whether a particular purchaser is HIV- or AIDS-positive.

2. *Reporting Requirements.* States currently require physicians to report a wide range of health conditions to public health authorities. New reporting requirements are typically added piecemeal and spread throughout the state's code of laws. See, e.g., Cal. Health & Safety Code §120250 (duty to report infectious, contagious, or communicable diseases); Cal. Penal Code §11166 (duty to report child abuse); Cal. Welf. & Inst. Code §15630 (duty to report elder or dependent adult abuse). See also pages 141-142.

3. *Contact Tracing and Partner Notification.* Contact tracing programs provide a mechanism for the notification of persons who may have been exposed to a contagious or transmissible condition. These programs have a long history, particularly for sexually transmitted diseases such as syphilis or gonorrhea and are now being applied to HIV infection. See, e.g., CDC, Recommendations for Partner Service Programs for HIV Infection, Syphilis, Gonorrhea, and Chlamydial Infection, 57 MMWR 1 (2008) (RR-9); Mary R. Reichler et al., Evaluation of Investigations Conducted to Detect and Prevent Transmission of Tuberculosis, 287 JAMA 991 (2002) (reviewing data and concluding that improvements are needed in TB contact investigation techniques); James M. Tesoriero et al., The Effect of Names-Based Reporting and Partner Notification on HIV Testing in New York State, 98 Am. J. Public Health 728 (2008) (HIV reporting not associated in decreased willingness to be tested).

Contact tracing programs typically are required to protect the confidentiality of the source individual. The programs nonetheless increase the risk that an individual's identity will be disclosed to third parties. Suppose, for example, that an individual notified about possible exposure to a sexually transmitted disease has had only one sexual partner. See Jane K. Stoever, Stories Absent from the Courtroom: Responding to Domestic Violence in the Context of HIV and AIDS, 87 N.C. L. Rev. 1157 (2009).

Consider Iowa's approach to the issues:

§141A.5. Partner Notification Program—HIV.

1. The department shall maintain a partner notification program for persons known to have tested positive for HIV infection.

2. In administering the program, the department shall provide for the following:

a. A person who tests positive for HIV infection shall receive post-test counseling, during which time the person shall be encouraged to refer for counseling and HIV testing any person with whom the person has had sexual relations or has shared drug injecting equipment.

b. The physician or other health care provider attending the person may provide to the department any relevant information provided by the person regarding any person with whom the tested person has had sexual relations or has shared drug injecting equipment.

c. (1) Devise a procedure, as a part of the partner notification program, to provide for the notification of an identifiable third party who is a sexual partner of or who shares drug injecting equipment with a person who has tested positive for HIV, by the department or a physician, when all of the following situations exist:

(a) A physician for the infected person is of the good faith opinion that the nature of the continuing contact poses an imminent danger of HIV transmission to the third party.

(b) When the physician believes in good faith that the infected person, despite strong encouragement, has not and will not warn the third party and will not participate in the voluntary partner notification program.

(2) Notwithstanding subsection 3, the department or a physician may reveal the identity of a person who has tested positive for HIV infection pursuant to this subsection only to the extent necessary to protect a third party from the direct threat of transmission. This subsection shall not be interpreted to create a duty to warn third parties of the danger of exposure to HIV through contact with a person who tests positive for HIV infection.

(3) The department shall adopt rules . . . to implement this paragraph "c". The rules shall provide a detailed procedure by which the department or a physician may directly notify an endangered third party.

3. In making contact the department shall not disclose the identity of the person who provided the names of the persons to be contacted and shall protect the confidentiality of persons contacted.

4. The department may delegate its partner notification duties under this section to local health authorities unless the local authority refuses or neglects to conduct the partner notification program in a manner deemed to be effective by the department. . . .

Iowa Code Ann. §141A.5. Does the statute reach an appropriate balance between individual liberties and public health? What can or should be done if a person refuses to name his or her contacts? See also Lawrence O. Gostin & James G. Hodge, Jr., Piercing the Veil of Secrecy in HIV/AIDS and Other Sexually Transmitted Diseases: Theories of Privacy and Disclosure in Partner Notification, 5 Duke J. Gender L. & Pol'y 9 (1998).

Eleven of twenty-four European countries reported the existence of laws or regulations that make partner notification compulsory for the health care provider, the patient, or both. These laws most often apply to HIV, syphilis, gonorrhea, chlamydia, and hepatitis B and C. Concerns about negative reaction from partners, the impact on relationships, stigma, and social repercussions were cited as barriers to partner notification. Patient referral methods requiring less interaction, for example, providing pharmacy contact slips to partners, were preferred for notifying ex-partners or casual partners. Matthew Hogben et al., Partner Services in Sexually Transmitted Disease Programs: A Review, 43 Sexually Transmitted Diseases S53 (2016).

Could email, social media, and forms of electronic communication be used to spur testing and contact notification? See David Tuller, After Hookups, E-Cards That Warn, "Get Checked," N.Y. Times, Jan., 20, 2009; Mary D. Fan, Decentralizing STD Surveillance: Toward Better Informed Sexual Consent, 12 Yale J. Health Pol'y L. & Ethics 1 (2012); Rachel Kachur et al., Reaching Patients and Their Partners Through Mobile: Text Messaging for Case Management and Partner Notification, 38 Sex. Trans. Dis. 149 (2011); and Summer McGee, Mobile Contact Tracing and Counseling for STI's: There's Not an App for That, 11 Am. J. Bioethics 3 (2011) (noting new mobile app for STD testing might increase testing while reducing use of counseling and contract tracing); but see Cornelis A. Rietmeijer et al., Evaluation of an Online Partner Notification Program, 38 Sex. Trans. Dis. 359 (2011) (finding low rates of use of Internet-based e-card notification program).

For more on contact tracing for STDs, see Matthew Hogben et al., *Partner Services in Sexually Transmitted Disease Programs: A Review*, 43 Sexually Transmitted Diseases S53 (2016); Theresa Yuricic, *An Examination of Partner Notification Laws: What Does Partner Notification Mean for HIV/AIDS in the African-American Community?*, 3 S. Regional Black L. Students Ass'n L. J. 121 (2009).

Problem: Reporting and Treatment for HIV Infection

States have gathered information for decades on persons testing positive for HIV infection. As a result, almost all states have information about positive test results along with information about the immunological status of HIV-positive individuals and their "viral load" (which, among other things, is correlated to the likelihood that the person would transmit the virus to others during, e.g., sexual activity). The emergence of therapies that seem to extend life for many people with HIV infection has created some controversy about whether and how surveillance data gathered for public health purposes could be used for clinical purposes. Should state reporting be viewed as a "one-way" process in which information is sent upward to the public health authorities or should the information collected at the state level be made available to clinicians providing care for patients? About half of all persons who know that they are infected "are not receiving regular HIV care." Amy Fairchild & Ronald Bayer, *HIV Surveillance, Public Health, and Clinical Medicine*, 365 New Eng. J. Med. 685, 686 (2011). Should confidentiality constraints governing information collected by public health authorities prevent using public health data to monitor and encourage follow-up care for HIV-infected persons? Should a state be permitted to link the public health database to clinical records so that "open[ing] a patient's electronic medical record in the state hospital system . . . triggers an automatic data query to the" public health authorities who could alert a caregiver via "an eye-catching 'point-of-care message,'" that the patient "tested positive for HIV but was not informed of the results or hasn't received a CD4 test within the past 12 months . . . [thereby] alerting the caregiver that the patient is HIV-positive and not receiving care and providing an opportunity to offer appropriate services." Id. Would the linkage have violated the privacy rights of HIV-infected patients, as those who know their status presumably should be able to decide whether or not to disclose their status to health care providers? Could the disclosure of information nonetheless be justified by the life-extending impact of appropriate HIV antiretroviral therapy? See Patricia Sweeney et al., *Shifting the Paradigm: Using HIV Surveillance Data as a Foundation for Improving HIV Care and Preventing HIV Infection*, 91 Milbank Q. 558 (2012) (arguing that although privacy concerns surrounding the uses of HIV surveillance data still exist, there are ethical concerns associated with not using HIV surveillance to maximize the benefits from HIV medical care and treatment). Could public health authorities justify the monitoring system by noting that antiretroviral therapy reduces the likelihood that an HIV-infected person will transmit the virus to others? See also Myron S. Cohen et al., *Prevention of HIV-1 Infection with Early Antiretroviral Therapy*, 365 New Eng. J. Med. 493 (2011); Stacy M. Cohen et al., *Vital Signs: HIV Prevention Through Care and Treatment—United States*, 60 MMWR 1618 (2011).

Problem: Reporting and Contact Tracing Under the MSEHPA

The MSEHPA also includes reporting and tracking provisions. The following sections are in effect whether or not a public health emergency has been declared:

ARTICLE III. MEASURES TO DETECT AND TRACK PUBLIC HEALTH EMERGENCIES

Section 301 Reporting.

(a) **Illness or health condition.** A health care provider, coroner, or medical examiner shall report all cases of persons who harbor any illness or health condition that may be potential causes of a public health emergency. Reportable illnesses and health conditions include, but are not limited to, the diseases caused by the biological agents listed in 42 C.F.R. §72, app. A (2000) and any illnesses or health conditions identified by the public health authority.

(b) **Pharmacists.** In addition to the foregoing requirements for health care providers, a pharmacist shall report any unusual or increased prescription rates, unusual types of prescriptions, or unusual trends in pharmacy visits that may be potential causes of a public health emergency. . . .

(c) **Manner of reporting.** The report shall be made electronically or in writing within [*twenty-four (24) hours*] to the public health authority. The report shall include as much of the following information as is available: the specific illness or health condition that is the subject of the report; the patient's name, date of birth, sex, race, occupation, and current home and work addresses (including city and county); the name and address of the health care provider, coroner, or medical examiner and of the reporting individual, if different; and any other information needed to locate the patient for follow-up. For cases related to animal or insect bites, the suspected locating information of the biting animal or insect, and the name and address of any known owner, shall be reported.

(d) **Animal diseases.** Every veterinarian, livestock owner, veterinary diagnostic laboratory director, or other person having the care of animals shall report animals having or suspected of having any diseases that may be potential causes of a public health emergency. . . .

(f) **Enforcement.** The public health authority may enforce the provisions of this Section in accordance with existing enforcement rules and regulations. . . .

Section 302 Tracking.
The public health authority shall ascertain the existence of cases of an illness or health condition that may be potential causes of a public health emergency; investigate all such cases for sources of infection and to ensure that they are subject to proper control measures; and define the distribution of the illness or health condition. To fulfill these duties, the public health authority shall identify exposed individuals as follows —

(a) **Identification of individuals.** Acting on information developed in accordance with Section 301 of this Act, or other reliable information, the public health authority shall identify all individuals thought to have been exposed to an illness or health condition that may be a potential cause of a public health emergency.

(b) **Interviewing of individuals.** The public health authority shall counsel and interview such individuals where needed to assist in the positive identification of exposed individuals and develop information relating to the source and spread of the illness or health condition. Such information includes the name and address (including city and county) of any person from whom the illness or health condition may have been contracted and to whom the illness or health condition may have spread.

(c) **Examination of facilities or materials.** The public health authority shall, for examination purposes, close, evacuate, or decontaminate any facility or decontaminate or destroy any material when the authority reasonably suspects that such facility or material may endanger the public health.

(d) **Enforcement.** The public health authority may enforce the provisions of this Section in accordance with existing enforcement rules and regulations. An order of the public health authority given to effectuate the purposes of this Section shall be enforceable immediately by the public safety authority. . . .

Section 303 Information sharing.

(a) Whenever the public safety authority or other state or local government agency learns of a case of a reportable illness or health condition, an unusual cluster, or a suspicious event that may be the cause of a public health emergency, it shall immediately notify the public health authority.

(b) Whenever the public health authority learns of a case of a reportable illness or health condition, an unusual cluster, or a suspicious event that it reasonably believes has the potential to be caused by bioterrorism, it shall immediately notify the public safety authority, tribal authorities, and federal health and public safety authorities.

(c) Sharing of information on reportable illnesses, health conditions, unusual clusters, or suspicious events between public health and safety authorities shall be restricted to the information necessary for the treatment, control, investigation, and prevention of a public health emergency.

MSEHPA §§301-303, available at the casebook Web site.

Evaluate the constitutionality of the Model Act's reporting and tracking provisions. Does the constitutionality of the provisions depend on the identification of a serious threat of bioterrorism or other public health emergency? Note that §303 explicitly permits public health authorities to share information with public safety officials, before the declaration of a public health emergency. Does this entanglement of public health and police functions complicate your analysis? See Ferguson v. City of Charleston, 532 U.S. 67 (2001), supra at page 781.

Would the disclosures be permissible under the federal HIPAA privacy rule? See 45 C.F.R. §164.512 (allowing disclosure for "the purpose of preventing or controlling disease") and supra at pages 139-140; Julie Bruce, Bioterrorism Meets Privacy: An Analysis of the Model State Health Powers Act and the HIPAA Privacy Rule, 12 Ann. Health L. 75 (2003); Janlori Goldman, Balancing in a Crisis? Bioterrorism, Public Health and Privacy, 38 J. Health L. 481 (2005); Andrea Wilson, Missing the Mark: The Public Health Exception to the HIPAA Privacy Rule and Its Impact on Surveillance Activity, 9 Hous. J. Health L. & Pol'y 131 (2008); Edward P. Richards, Dangerous People, Unsafe Conditions: The Constitutional Basis for Public Health Surveillance, 30 J. Legal Med. 27 (2009).

Would contact tracing be a realistic option for contagious diseases like smallpox given the large numbers of potentially exposed people and the general hysteria that might accompany the discovery of the first case? See Edward P. Richards, III, The United States Smallpox Bioterrorism Preparedness Plan: Rational Response or Potemkin Planning?, 36 Wm. Mitchell L. Rev. 5179 (2010) (expressing skepticism). What does it mean to "counsel and interview" persons under MSEHPA §302(b)? Is the reference to enforcement powers in §302(d) meant to suggest that individuals might be compelled to disclose information about possible sources and contacts?

Contact tracing made national headlines in October 2014 when Craig Spencer, a physician who had recently returned to his home in New York City after treating Ebola patients in Guinea, tested positive for the deadly virus. Spencer was placed in isolation while public health authorities attempted to retrace his steps (the night before, Spencer had ridden the subway, visited a bowling alley in Brooklyn, and taken a taxi home), and reassure an anxious public that they were not at risk of contracting the virus. See Marc Santora, Doctor in New York City is Sick with Ebola, N.Y. Times, Oct. 23, 2014.

Compare the Model Act's provisions to the relevant public health statute in your own state. Which seems better from a legal or policy standpoint? Do health care providers in your state have an obligation to report diseases related to bioterrorism? What about pharmacists? How are these measures enforced? May public health authorities and law enforcement share information? If so, do you see any similarities or differences between your state law and the Model Act? If not, would you recommend the adoption of the Model Act's provisions? See also Lawrence O. Gostin, When Terrorism Threatens Health: How Far Are Limitations on Personal and Economic Liberties Justified?, 55 Fla. L. Rev. 1105 (2003).

3. Isolation and Quarantine

"Isolation" and "quarantine" are technically different public health approaches, though the two terms are often used interchangeably to describe separating those who are or may be infected from those who are believed to be unaffected. Isolation is used to separate infected people with communicable conditions from others until the period of communicability passes. Quarantine is used to detain those who have been exposed to a disease for the incubation period of that disease so that contact with uninfected persons can be avoided (the term comes from the Italian phrase "quaranta giorni," meaning 40 days—the period of time merchant ships were sequestered after returning from infected regions).

However denominated, the concept of separation has ancient roots. In earlier centuries, the victims of disease who were believed to be dangerous to the public through some human contact (which then included most of the known afflictions of humans) were banished from the community and abandoned, beyond the campfire, the village, or the wall of the city. In urbanized areas in the Middle Ages, the practice of "quarantine" began. Voyagers were held on board ship; the local afflicted were confined to their homes. As hospitals and detention houses were developed, they were used for isolation or quarantine when other quarters were not available. With no available treatment, isolation for a temporary period until the person recovered and was no longer infectious, or until death, was the most humane alternative. In the nineteenth century and the early twentieth century, quarantine and isolation were the most common means of disease control. For a comprehensive historical analysis of the sweep of diseases and plagues from ancient times, see a wonderfully enlightening and exciting review by a leading American historian, William Hardy McNeill, Plagues and Peoples (1998), along with the excellent Norman F. Cantor, In the Wake of the Plague: The Black Death and the World It Made (2002), and Joseph B. Topinka, Yaw, Pitch, and Roll, 30 J. Legal Med. 51 (2009). The plague can now be treated effectively with antibiotics. Modern contagious diseases that spark a similar level of fear include the Ebola virus and smallpox, see page 917.

■ WONG WAI v. WILLIAMSON
103 F. 1 (C.C.N.D. Cal. 1900)

MORROW, Circuit Judge.

[A Chinese resident of San Francisco brought suit against various governmental officers, challenging the application of rules that (1) required persons of Chinese ancestry to undergo inoculation against the bubonic plague by a "serum known as 'Haffkine Prophylactic,' " and (2) prohibited uninoculated Chinese residents from traveling outside the city.] . . .

To the order to show cause [why an injunction should not be issued] . . . the defendants . . . composing the board of health of the city and county of San Francisco, have produced a copy of a resolution adopted by the board on May 18, 1900, as follows:

> Resolved, that it is the sense of this board that bubonic plague exists in the city and county of San Francisco, and that all necessary steps already taken for the prevention of its spread be continued, together with such additional measures as may be required. . . .

The defendants constituting the board of health of the city and county of San Francisco contend that they are justified in their action with respect to the matter in controversy under their authority as a board, acting pursuant to the resolution of the board of May 18, 1900. The charter of the city and county of San Francisco provides, in article 10, for a department of public health, under the management of a board of health. . . . [The charter provides, however, that the Board of Supervisors is the legislative body of the city with the power to enact ordinances.]

It thus appears that suitable provision has been made in the city charter for the necessary legislation providing rules and regulations to secure proper sanitary conditions in the city and for the protection of the public health, but we are not advised that the board of supervisors has taken any action whatever in that direction; and the resolution of the board of health furnished to the court fails to disclose the method it has adopted for that purpose, under the conditions it has declared to exist. We need not, however, dwell upon the manifest lack of legislative authority to enable the board of health to deal with this important subject. It is sufficient for the present purpose to mention the fact, as one of the features of the situation to be considered in connection with the regulations which the complainant alleges have been imposed upon him and other Chinese residents of the city by the defendants.

It appears that there are about 25,000 Chinese residents in the city of San Francisco, and, while it is well known that a large number of these people are domiciled within the area designated as the "Chinese Quarter," nevertheless there are a great many scattered over the city, engaged in various employments. No restrictions have been placed upon any of the Chinese residents in passing from one part of the city to the other; nor has any house, block, or section of the city been declared infected or unsanitary. There is, therefore, no fact established by the board of supervisors or by the board of health from which an inference might be drawn that any particular class of persons, or persons occupying a particular district, were liable to develop, or in danger of developing, the plague. The restriction is that no Chinese person shall depart from the city without being inoculated with the serum called "Haffkine Prophylactic." The city has a population of about 350,000, but the restriction does not apply to any of the inhabitants other than Chinese or Asiatics, and the inhabitants other than Chinese or Asiatics are permitted to depart from and return to the city without being subject to the inoculation imposed upon the Chinese inhabitants. This restriction, it is alleged, discriminates unreasonably against the complainant and other Chinese residents, confines them within the territorial limits of the city and county, and deprives them of their liberty, causing them great and irreparable loss and injury.

The conditions of a great city frequently present unexpected emergencies affecting the public health, comfort, and convenience. Under such circumstances, officers charged with the duties pertaining to this department of the municipal government should be clothed with sufficient authority to deal with the conditions in a prompt and effective manner. Measures of this character, having a uniform operation, and reasonably adapted to the purpose of protecting the health and preserving the welfare of the inhabitants of a city, are constantly upheld by the courts as valid acts of legislation, however inconvenient they may prove to be, and a wide discretion has also been sanctioned in their execution. But when the municipal authority has neglected to provide suitable rules and regulations upon the subject, and the officers are left to adopt such methods as they may deem proper for the occasion, their acts are open to judicial review, and may be examined in every detail to determine whether individual rights have been respected in accordance with constitutional requirements.. . . .

In the light of these well-established principles, the action of the defendants as described in the bill of complaint cannot be justified. . . . They are not based upon any established distinction in the conditions that are supposed to attend this plague, or the persons exposed to its contagion, but they are boldly directed against the Asiatic or Mongolian race as a class, without regard to the previous condition, habits, exposure to disease, or residence of the individual; and the only justification offered for this discrimination was a suggestion made by counsel for the defendants in the course of argument, that this particular race is more liable to the plague than any other. No evidence has, however, been offered to support this claim, and it is not known to be a fact. This explanation must therefore be dismissed as unsatisfactory. . .

It follows from these considerations that the defendants have failed to justify their action in the premises, and that an injunction must issue as prayed for in the bill of complaint.

■ JEW HO v. WILLIAMSON
103 F. 10 (C.C.N.D. Cal. 1900)

MORROW, Circuit Judge.

The purpose of quarantine and health laws and regulations with respect to contagious and infectious diseases is directed primarily to preventing the spread of such diseases among the inhabitants of localities. In this respect these laws and regulations come under the police power of the state, and may be enforced by quarantine and health officers, in the exercise of a large discretion, as circumstances may require. . . .

The object of all such rules and regulations is to confine the disease to the smallest possible number of people; and hence when a vessel in a harbor, a car on a railroad, or a house on land, is found occupied by persons afflicted with such a disease, the vessel, the car, or the house, as the case may be, is cut off from all communication with the inhabitants of adjoining houses or contiguous territory, that the spread of the disease may be arrested at once and confined to the least possible territory. This is a system of quarantine that is well recognized in all communities, and is provided by the laws of the various states and municipalities: That, when a contagious or infectious disease breaks out in a place, they quarantine the house or houses first; the purpose being to restrict spread to other people in the same locality. It must necessarily follow that, if a large section or a large territory is quarantined, intercommunication of the people within that territory will rather tend to spread the disease than to restrict it. If you place 10,000 persons in one territory, and confine them there, as they have been in prisons and other places, the spread of disease, of course, becomes increased, and the danger of such spread of disease is increased, sometimes in an alarming degree, because it is the constant communication of people that are so restrained or imprisoned that causes the spread of the disease. If we are to suppose that this bubonic plague has existed in San Francisco since the 6th day of March, and that there has been danger of its spreading over the city, the most dangerous thing that could have been done was to quarantine the whole city, as to the Chinese, as was substantially done in the first instance. The next most dangerous thing to do was to quarantine any considerable portion of the city, and not restrict intercommunication within the quarantined district. . . .

The court cannot but see the practical question that is presented to it as to the ineffectiveness of this method of quarantine against such a disease as this. So, upon that ground, the court must hold that this quarantine is not a reasonable regulation to accomplish the purposes sought. It is not in harmony with the declared purpose of the board of health or of the board of supervisors.

But there is still another feature of this case that has been called to the attention of the court, and that is its discriminating character; that is to say, it is said that this quarantine discriminates against the Chinese population of this city, and in favor of the people of other races. Attention is called to the fact that, while the board of supervisors has quarantined a district bounded by streets, the operation of the quarantine is such as to run along in the rear of certain houses, and that certain houses are excluded, while others are included; that, for instance, upon Stockton street, in the block numbered from 900 to 1,000, there are two places belonging to persons of another race, and these persons and places are excluded from this quarantine, although the Chinese similarly situated are included, and although the quarantine, in terms, is imposed upon all the persons within the blocks bounded by such streets. The evidence here is clear that this is made to operate against the Chinese population only, and the reason given for it is that the Chinese may communicate the disease from one to the other. That explanation, in the judgment of the court, is not sufficient. It is, in effect, a discrimination, and it is the discrimination that has been frequently called to the attention of the federal courts where matters of this character have arisen with respect to Chinese. . . .

It follows from the remarks that I have made that his quarantine cannot be continued, by reason of the fact that it is unreasonable, unjust, and oppressive, and therefore contrary to the laws limiting the police powers of the state and municipality in such matters; and, second, that it is discriminating in its character, and is contrary to the provisions of the fourteenth amendment of the constitution of the United States.

Notes: Isolation and Quarantine

1. Wong Wai *and* Jew Ho. The public health measures adopted in *Wong Wai* and *Jew Ho* combined a form of vaccination with a quarantine order restricting uninoculated Asians from leaving San Francisco. The court's decisions are relatively unique in their detailed examination and rejection of measures asserted to involve protection of the public health. What explains the result?

Consider the large number of evidentiary and legal defects cited by the court. Should it matter whether there was evidence that the bubonic plague was present within the city? (The opinion casts doubt on this factor; others have suggested that cases of plague had been reported.) Were the quarantine and inoculation orders issued by the appropriate governmental authorities? The court suggests that the orders should have been passed as ordinances by the Board of Supervisors rather than issued by the city Board of Health. What should be the effect of finding the orders to be *ultra vires?* Why were the inoculation and quarantine orders applicable only to those of Asian heritage? What standard of review would a modern court apply to an order of this type? Cf. Jed Rubenfeld, The End of Privacy, 61 Stan. L. Rev. 101, 144-148 (2008) (exploring Fourth Amendment jurisprudence including implications for quarantine and civil commitment). What types of evidence would be necessary to support a public health measure applied only to persons of a particular racial or ethnic background? Could a quarantine order prove counterproductive by causing panic or discrimination? See Mark A. Rothstein, From SARS to Ebola, 12 Ind. Health L. 227 (2015).

2. *Federal Quarantine Regulations.* The federal Public Health Service Act gives the Secretary of Health and Human Services authority over quarantines within federal jurisdiction:

§264 Regulations to Control Communicable Diseases

(a) Promulgation and enforcement by Surgeon General

The Surgeon General, with the approval of the Secretary, is authorized to make and enforce such regulations as in his judgment are necessary to prevent the introduction, transmission, or spread of communicable diseases from foreign countries into the States or possessions, or from one State or possession into any other State or possession. . . .

(b) Apprehension, detention, or conditional release of individuals

Regulations prescribed under this section shall not provide for the apprehension, detention, or conditional release of individuals except for the purpose of preventing the introduction, transmission, or spread of such communicable diseases as may be specified from time to time in Executive orders of the President upon the recommendation of the Secretary, in consultation with the Surgeon General,

(c) Application of regulations to persons entering from foreign countries

Except as provided in subsection (d) of this section, regulations prescribed under this section, insofar as they provide for the apprehension, detention, examination, or conditional release of individuals, shall be applicable only to individuals coming into a State or possession from a foreign country or a possession.

(d) Apprehension and examination of persons reasonably believed to be infected

(1) Regulations prescribed under this section may provide for the apprehension and examination of any individual reasonably believed to be infected with a communicable disease in a qualifying stage and [who is a probable source of infection who is or will be moving from state to state] . . . Such regulations may provide that if upon examination any such individual is found to be infected, he may be detained for such time and in such manner as may be reasonably necessary. . . .

42 U.S.C. §264. This authority is now delegated to the CDC, with the Surgeon General no longer involved. CDC, Final Rule for the Control of Communicable Diseases: Interstate and Foreign, 82 Fed. Reg. 6890-01 (Jan. 19, 2017) (amending 42 C.F.R. 70, 71). The current executive order includes SARS and influenza viruses capable of causing a pandemic. See CDC, Legal Authorities for Isolation and Quarantine. The threat of pandemic flu and the widely reported case of an international traveler who allegedly suffered from drug-resistant TB (explored further in note 6, infra) raised questions about the adequacy of federal rules governing quarantine. See, e.g., Symposium, The Dangerous Patient: Medical, Legal, and Public Policy Responses, 30 J. Legal Med. 1-140 (2009).

3. *State Quarantine Law.* State quarantine laws were little used and little discussed for decades. The situation changed with the advent of drug-resistant TB and the threats posed by bioterrorism and resurgent strains of influenza. Since its introduction, 38 states and the District of Columbia have enacted into law a total of 66 bills containing provisions of the MSEHPA. Mark A. Rothstein, From SARS to Ebola: Legal and Ethical Considerations for Modern Quarantine, 12 Ind. Health L. Rev. 227, 240 (2015).

4. *State Quarantines and Conflicts with Federal Law.* Where does the state's power to restrict the movement of people end? Is a state permitted to enact travel restrictions that hinder interstate commerce or immigration, two areas within the domain of federal law? Federal quarantine law specifies that: "(e) Nothing in this section . . . or the regulations . . . may be construed as superseding any provision under State law (including regulations and including provisions established by political subdivisions of States), except to the extent that such a provision conflicts with an exercise of Federal authority. . . ." 42 U.S.C. §264. Does this resolve the question?

In Compagnie Francaise de Navigation a Vapeur v. State Board of Health, Louisiana, 186 U.S. 380 (1902), the Supreme Court considered and upheld the validity of a board order barring entry of any "body or bodies of people, immigrants, soldier, or others" into cities where a quarantine had been declared. The asserted basis of this "reverse" quarantine was that the introduction of new, uninfected persons to an area would "add[] fuel to the flame." How would this case be decided today? What, if anything, has changed? Has Congress occupied the field more thoroughly than it had in the early 1900s? Has the Court changed its mind about the state's ability to enact public safety regulations that impede interstate commerce? Could a state pass a statute refusing to permit introduction of additional hazardous waste into its borders? See Chemical Waste Management v. Hunt, 504 U.S. 334, 346-347 (1992) (distinguishing permissible and impermissible state quarantine provisions that have an impact on interstate commerce, citing *Compagnie Francaise*). See also Annot., 86 A.L.R.4th 401 (1991); Eang L. Ngov, Under Containment: Preempting State Ebola Quarantine Regulations, 88 Temp. L. Rev. 1 (2015). Federal laws prohibiting disability-based discrimination might also limit the permissibility of state quarantine rules in some situations. See supra at pages 936-937.

5. *Responding to SARS.* The outbreak of Severe Acute Respiratory Syndrome (SARS) in Canada and other countries in 2003 provided a modern example of the use of quarantine and isolation. Tens of thousands of people were quarantined in places such as Toronto, Beijing, and Taiwan. See Lawrence O. Gostin & Benjamin E. Berkman, Pandemic Influenza: Ethics, Law, and the Public's Health, 59 Admin. L. 121, 171 (2007). See also Lawrence O. Gostin et al., Ethical and Legal Challenges Posed by Severe Acute Respiratory Syndrome, 290 JAMA 3229 (2003); and National Advisory Committee on SARS and Public Health, Learning from SARS: Renewal of Public Health in Canada (2003) (the Naylor Report).

6. *Federal Quarantine in Practice: The Andrew Speaker Incident.* When is it appropriate to forcibly isolate or quarantine an individual believed to be infectious in

order to prevent further spread of the disease? In May 2007, Atlanta lawyer Andrew Speaker was diagnosed with multi-drug-resistant tuberculosis (MDR-TB) and told to cancel his planned trip abroad. Instead, Speaker left for Europe, just as CDC tests diagnosed him with extensively drug-resistant TB (XDR-TB), which is significantly harder to treat. Despite continued warnings from the CDC that he should avoid traveling because he might expose others to TB, Speaker took two commercial flights and eventually landed in Montreal. He then re-entered the United States after the Border Patrol ignored a border alert. The CDC eventually tracked Speaker down, ordered him into a New York City hospital, and served him with the first federal quarantine order issued since 1963 (technically speaking, he was isolated, because he was infectious). In subsequent congressional hearings, Speaker's actions were equated with those of terrorists. See David P. Fidler, Lawrence O. Gostin & Howard Markel, Through the Quarantine Looking Glass, 35 J. L. Med. & Ethics 616 (2007); Wendy E. Parmet, Dangerous Perspectives, 30 J. Legal 83 (2009). Should Speaker have been isolated earlier? Or was the order ultimately unnecessary and a violation of his rights? How would it affect your analysis to know that Speaker's original diagnosis was correct (he never had XDR-TB only MDR-TB)? Or that his diagnosis was just luck (it was spotted during a chest X-ray for an unrelated injury, meaning that he would have otherwise traveled unaware that he had TB)? Does it matter that there were half a million cases of XDR-TB worldwide in 2004? How would the CDC's response differ if this case were to arise under its new quarantine rule?

7. *Isolation and HIV Infection.* Should persons with HIV infection be separated from the general population? Public health authorities uniformly reject the suggestion. See Karen E. Zuck, HIV and Medical Privacy: Government Infringement on Prisoners' Constitutional Rights, 9 U. Pa. J. Const. L. 1277 (2007). Segregation or isolation of persons with HIV within correctional facilities is nonetheless permitted but not required. Compare Onishea v. Hopper, 171 F.3d 1289 (11th Cir. 1999) (segregation of HIV-infected inmates does not violate Rehabilitation Act), with Glick v. Henderson, 855 F.2d 536 (8th Cir. 1988) (failure to segregate infected prisoners does not violate the Eighth Amendment's prohibition against cruel and unusual punishment). But see Henderson v. Thomas, 913 F. Supp. 2d 1267 (M.D. Ala. 2012) (categorical separation of HIV-positive inmates violates ADA and Rehabilitation Act).

8. *A New Influenza Pandemic?* How should we prepare for the possibility of a new, deadly influenza pandemic? As noted above at pages 916 and 923, a novel flu virus capable of rapid human-to-human transmission could cause millions of deaths worldwide. See also an online resource for avian and pandemic flu information managed by the Department of Health and Human Services: www.flu.gov/pandemic. Canada's experience with quarantine orders during the SARS outbreak suggests that isolation/quarantine might be important components of the public health response, although this will depend on the characteristics of the influenza virus. Neil M. Ferguson et al., Letter, Strategies for Mitigating an Influenza Epidemic, 442 Nature 448 (2006) (model shows that "case isolation or household quarantine could have a significant impact" on influenza pandemic). But see Wendy K. Mariner et al., Pandemic Preparedness: A Return to the Rule of Law, 1 Drexel L. Rev. 341 (2009) (contending that quarantine measures caused negative and counterproductive public reactions); Lawrence O. Gostin & Benjamin E. Berkman, Pandemic Influenza: Ethics, Law, and the Public's Health, 59 Admin. L. Rev. 121, 171 (2007) (noting that 30 percent of individuals quarantined later suffer from

posttraumatic stress disorder or depression). Does the current legal framework in the United States permit the use of isolation and quarantine on the scale that might be warranted from a public health standpoint? See Note, Phase Six Pandemic: A Call to Re-Evaluate Federal Quarantine Authority Before the Next Catastrophic Outbreak, 44 Ga. L. Rev. 803 (2010); Lawrence O. Gostin, Public Health Strategies for Pandemic Influenza: Ethics and the Law, 295 JAMA 1700 (2006).

4. Civil Commitment and Mandatory Treatment

Should a state be able to promote public health by requiring medical treatment? In some sense, this form of state regulation could be viewed as the most direct and effective method of health promotion. So long as the state has correctly identified an affected individual and so long as an effective treatment is available, mandatory treatment would seem to promote both the health of the individual and of those with whom the individual interacts. The apparent simplicity of this approach is matched, of course, by the serious threat to individual liberties it entails. When should the state's interest in public health outweigh the individual's rights to freedom of movement, to bodily integrity, and to make medical treatment decisions free from state coercion? Should it matter whether the illness is mental or physical?

■ADDINGTON v. TEXAS
441 U.S. 418 (1979)

BURGER, C.J.

[The appellant had a long history of temporary commitments as mentally ill (seven times between 1969 and 1975) to several Texas mental hospitals. In December 1975, appellant was arrested on charges of assault and threats against his mother. His mother filed a petition for indefinite commitment. A trial was held before a jury to determine whether the appellant was mentally ill and in need of treatment for his welfare and protection, or for the protection of others. The trial lasted six days. The appellant was found mentally ill and subject to commitment under the law based upon "clear, unequivocal and convincing evidence." The Texas Supreme Court upheld the commitment and the applicable standard of proof.]

The question in this case is what standard of proof is required by the Fourteenth Amendment to the Constitution in a civil proceeding brought under state law to commit an individual involuntarily for an indefinite period to a state mental hospital.

This Court repeatedly has recognized that civil commitment for any purpose constitutes a significant deprivation of liberty that requires due process protection. Moreover, it is indisputable that involuntary commitment to a mental hospital after a finding of probable dangerousness to self or others can engender adverse social consequences to the individual. Whether we label this phenomena "stigma" or choose to call it something else is less important than that we recognize that it can occur and that it can have a very significant impact on the individual.

The state has a legitimate interest under its *parens patriae* powers in providing care to its citizens who are unable because of emotional disorders to care for themselves; the state also has authority under its police power to protect the community from the dangerous tendencies of some who are mentally ill. Under the Texas Mental Health Code, however, the state has no interest in confining individuals involuntarily if they are not mentally ill or if they do not pose some danger to themselves or others. Since the preponderance standard creates the risk of increasing the number of individuals erroneously committed, it is at least unclear to what extent, if any, the state's interests are furthered by using a preponderance standard in such commitment proceedings.

The expanding concern of society with problems of mental disorders is reflected in the fact that in recent years many states have enacted statutes designed to protect the rights of the mentally ill. However, only one state by statute permits involuntary commitment by a mere preponderance of the evidence, Miss. Code Ann. §41-21-75 (1978 Supp.), and Texas is the only state where a court has concluded that the preponderance-of-the-evidence standard satisfies due process. We attribute this not to any lack of concern in those states, but rather to a belief that the varying standards tend to produce comparable results. As we noted earlier, however, standards of proof are important for their symbolic meaning as well as for their practical effect. . . .

Appellant urges the Court to hold that due process requires use of the criminal law's standard of proof—"beyond a reasonable doubt." . . .

There are significant reasons why different standards of proof are called for in civil commitment proceedings as opposed to criminal prosecutions. In a civil commitment state power is not exercised in a punitive sense. . . .

In addition, the "beyond a reasonable doubt" standard historically has been reserved for criminal cases. This unique standard of proof, not prescribed or defined in the Constitution, is regarded as a critical part of the "moral force of the criminal law," In re Winship, 397 U.S., at 364, and we should hesitate to apply it too broadly or casually in noncriminal cases.

The heavy standard applied in criminal cases manifests our concern that the risk of error to the individual must be minimized even at the risk that some who are guilty might go free. Patterson v. New York, 432 U.S. 197, 208 (1977). The full force of that idea does not apply to a civil commitment. It may be true that an erroneous commitment is sometimes as undesirable as an erroneous conviction, 5 J. Wigmore, Evidence §1400 (Chadbourn rev. 1974). However, even though an erroneous confinement should be avoided in the first instance, the layers of professional review and observation of the patient's condition, and the concern of family and friends generally will provide continuous opportunities for an erroneous commitment to be corrected. Moreover, it is not true that the release of a genuinely mentally ill person is no worse for the individual than the failure to convict the guilty. One who is suffering from a debilitating mental illness and in need of treatment is neither wholly at liberty nor free of stigma. See Chodoff, The Case for Involuntary Hospitalization of the Mentally Ill, 133 Am. J. Psychiatry 496, 498 (1976); Schwartz, Myers & Astrachan, Psychiatric Labeling and the Rehabilitation of the Mental Patient, 31 Arch. Gen. Psychiatry 329, 334 (1974). It cannot be said, therefore, that it is much better for a mentally ill person to "go free" than for a mentally normal person to be committed. . . .

The subtleties and nuances of psychiatric diagnosis render certainties virtually beyond reach in most situations. The reasonable-doubt standard of criminal law functions in its realm because there the standard is addressed to specific, knowable facts. Psychiatric diagnosis, in contrast, is to a large extent based on medical "impressions" drawn from subjective analysis and filtered through the experience of the diagnostician. This process often makes it very difficult for the expert physician to offer definite conclusions about any particular patient. Within the medical discipline, the traditional standard for "factfinding" is a "reasonable medical certainty." If a trained psychiatrist has difficulty with the categorical "beyond a reasonable doubt" standard, the untrained lay juror—or indeed even a trained judge—who is required to rely upon expert opinion could be forced by the criminal law standard of proof to reject commitment for many patients desperately in need of institutionalized psychiatric care. Such "freedom" for a mentally ill person would be purchased at a high price. . . .

We have concluded that the reasonable-doubt standard is inappropriate in civil commitment proceedings because, given the uncertainties of psychiatric diagnosis, it may impose a burden the state cannot meet and thereby erect an unreasonable barrier to needed medical treatment. Similarly, we conclude that use of the term *unequivocal* is not constitutionally required, although the states are free to use that standard. To meet due process demands, the standard has to inform the factfinder that the proof must be greater than the preponderance-of-the-evidence standard applicable to other categories of civil cases.

We noted earlier that the trial court employed the standard of "clear, unequivocal and convincing" evidence in appellant's commitment hearing before a jury. That instruction was constitutionally adequate. However, determination of the precise burden equal to or greater than the "clear and convincing" standard which we hold is required to meet due process guarantees is a matter of state law which we leave to the Texas Supreme Court. Accordingly, we remand the case for further proceedings not inconsistent with this opinion.

Vacated and remanded.

■ IN THE INTEREST OF J.A.D.
492 N.W.2d 82 (N.D. 1992)

VANDE WALLE, Justice.

J.A.D. appealed from an order of the county court of Stutsman County requiring that he be hospitalized and treated for mental illness for a period not to exceed 90 days. We reverse. . . .

Before a court can issue an order for an involuntary treatment, the petitioner must prove by clear and convincing evidence that the respondent is a person requiring treatment. NDCC §25-03.1-19. The determination that an individual is a "person requiring treatment" under the statutory definition is a two-step process: (1) the court must find that the individual is mentally ill, and (2) the court must find that there is a reasonable expectation that if the person is not hospitalized there exists a serious risk of harm to himself, others, or property. NDCC §25-03.1-02(10). . . . We therefore focus on the evidence that J.A.D. was mentally ill and that there was a substantial likelihood of substantial harm to J.A.D. to determine if there is clear and convincing evidence to support the findings of the trial court. . . .

The record demonstrates that J.A.D. is suffering from a mental illness. The record also fairly indicates that without treatment, J.A.D.'s mental health would be at a substantial risk of deterioration. However, as we have previously held, the need for treatment alone is not sufficient to order hospitalization. The issue is therefore whether or not this likely deterioration of J.A.D.'s mental health will predictably result in dangerousness to himself, others, or property. . . .

The record is tenuous as to whether J.A.D. poses a danger to himself, to others, or to property. Testimony at the hearing indicates that J.A.D. may be a danger to himself, though most likely not a danger to others or to property. The concern over J.A.D.'s dangerousness to himself centered around his homelessness and his ability to take care of himself, such as his resourcefulness at getting food and proper nutrition, and his propensity to seek out shelter during the winter months. . . .

Dr. Kottke's testimony that J.A.D. was in need of treatment as defined by the statutes was not clear and convincing. Dr. Kottke's conclusion, that absent commitment to the State Hospital there exists a strong risk of harm to J.A.D., was also premised on his concern that J.A.D. would not seek appropriate shelter when winter came, as it surely will, in North Dakota.

All three witnesses expressed concern that because J.A.D. was a recent arrival from the deep South he was not aware of the severe cold which the winter season may bring to North Dakota and would not seek appropriate food and shelter. These concerns were essentially premised on isolated incidents in which J.A.D. did not take advantage of shelter the caseworker had arranged, the fact that J.A.D. took shelter in abandoned buildings, that he talked about obtaining a hotplate, and the fact that he once placed food he received from the private organization in a garbage dumpster because, according to the witness, he could not remember where he obtained the food and was afraid to eat it. . . .

Not all homeless people are mentally ill and in need of treatment. Homelessness may in some instances be a product of mental illness, but it may also be the result of economic hardship or simply lifestyle choice. We cannot categorize homeless people as people in need of compulsory mental therapy simply because they do without a traditional home, kitchen, plumbing, or electricity. Homeless people may be very resourceful in obtaining food and shelter, as evidenced by J.A.D. seeking out the Salvation Army and social programs offered by the various state and private agencies in the community. J.A.D. has been receiving food and meals, and has sought shelter. Because he did not make use of the shelter which he was offered during the summer months is not necessarily indicative of a propensity to not seek shelter in the winter months. J.A.D. had the wherewithal to travel to North Dakota, and we can presume that he has the wherewithal to leave. In the winter, he may seek assistance for shelter as he has in the past, or simply leave the state for warmer locations. There is no presumption that J.A.D., as a homeless person, will neither be able to fend for himself during the winter months nor be able to take care of his needs. . . . [The court also expressed its concern with the trial court's failure to adequately consider appropriate, less restrictive alternatives to commitment.] . . .

Accordingly, we reverse the order for hospitalization and treatment.

ERICKSTAD, Chief Justice, specially concurring.

I respectfully, reluctantly concur in the result of the majority opinion, with great concern that, in our effort to find clear and convincing evidence of J.A.D.'s need for treatment, we have actually tried this case anew and found that evidence wanting. . . .

Through our very careful review of the facts and our analysis of the possible consequences of the facts, we may have deprived J.A.D. of treatment crucial to his future welfare, without providing him with a safety net of any kind, at a time, considering the season of the year, when survival as a homeless person in North Dakota could be hazardous to say the very least.

Notes: Mandatory Mental Health Treatment

1. *Trends in Mental Health Treatment.* The *Addington* case in the Supreme Court represented a high-water mark in efforts to raise the standard of proof for compulsory hospitalization of the mentally ill. In large measure, the laws on commitment of the mentally ill came full circle in some 200 years in the United States. The nineteenth-century laws were essentially modeled after criminal procedures. The person who was believed to be mentally ill was "arrested" and "charged" with being "insane" and at large and was "committed" to a mental institution, usually for life. On any escape, the patient was hunted down like a criminal and returned to the institution in chains.

In the middle years of the twentieth century, the laws concerning mental illness were largely decriminalized, and compulsory hospitalization was made considerably easier as an administrative action without judicial intervention. This was the case all over the world. The movement away from the informal system back to a much more structured, judicially sanctioned review procedure for compulsory hospitalization began in the 1970s and continued into the 1980s. Michael L. Perlin, The Hidden Prejudice: Mental Disability on Trial (2000); The Evolution of Mental Health Law (Lynda E. Frost & Richard Bonnie eds., 2001).

2. *Clear and Convincing Evidence.* Why does the Court impose this higher burden of proof for civil commitments? Should the burden apply to all aspects of the state's case, including both the diagnosis of mental illness and the requirement of dangerousness? Most jurisdictions answer both questions affirmatively. In addition to *J.A.D.*, supra, see People v. Stevens, 761 P.2d 768 (Colo. 1988); In re Richard A., 771 A.2d 572 (N.H. 2001) (reviewing standards); In the Matter of The Commitment of N.N., 679 A.2d 1174 (N.J. 1996) (discussing the constitutional constraints applicable to the commitment of minors). See also In re Jeffrey E., 281 P.3d 84 (Alaska 2012) (deferring to prediction of possible future grave disability). In most cases, the issues of commitment and treatment are intertwined. Will the same due process protections apply to "mandatory treatment," as an issue distinct from commitment? Yes. See Wetherhorn v. Alaska Psychiatric Institute, 156 P.3d 371 (Alaska 2007); Donaldson v. District Court, 847 P.2d 632 (Colo. 1993) (en banc); In re C.E., 641 N.E.2d 345 (Ill. 1994); In re W.J.C.A., 810 N.W.2d 327 (N.D. 2012). How do you reconcile this approach with the right to control one's own medical treatment described in Chapters 3 and 5?

A number of commentators have explored the law and policy governing mental health civil commitments. See generally Sara Gordon, The Danger Zone: How the Dangerousness Standard in Civil Commitment Proceedings Harms People with Serious Mental Illness, 66 Case W. Res. L. Rev. 657, 658 (2016). Should — or can — psychiatric experts be relied upon to accurately predict whether an individual poses a danger to himself or others? M. Neil Browne & Ronda R. Harrison-Spoerl,

Putting Expert Testimony in Its Epistemological Place: What Predictions of Dangerousness in Court Can Teach Us, 91 Marq. L. Rev. 1119 (2008); Barefoot v. Estelle, 463 U.S. 880 (1983) (Blackmun, J., dissenting) ("Psychiatric predictions of future dangerousness are not accurate.").

3. *Involuntary Treatment of Prisoners with Psychotropic Medications.* Do *Addington*'s due process protections apply to prisoners? In Washington v. Harper, 494 U.S. 210 (1990), the Supreme Court analyzed the constitutionality of a state policy that authorized treatment of inmates with antipsychotic drugs without a judicial hearing. The Court held that prisoners do retain a protected liberty interest in avoiding unwanted treatment. It held, however, that this due process interest was subject to the reasonableness test of Turner v. Safley, 482 U.S. 78 (1987): Policies that infringe prisoner rights will be upheld so long as they are reasonably related to legitimate penological interests. Applying this standard, the Court held that "given the requirements of the prison environment, the due process clause permits the state to treat a prison inmate who has a serious mental illness with antipsychotic drugs against his will, if the inmate is dangerous to himself or others and the treatment is in the inmate's medical interest." *Harper,* 494 U.S. at 227.

The Court also considered whether Harper had been denied his right to procedural due process. See, e.g., Morrissey v. Brewer, 408 U.S. 471, 481 (1972). The state's procedure, which included determinations through administrative hearings before the institution's own mental health care personnel (although not those involved in the direct treatment of the prisoner), was deemed to be procedurally adequate. *Harper,* 494 U.S. at 232-236. The Court rejected contentions that the decision should be made before a judge and with the assistance of counsel. Justice Blackmun, often deferential to medical authority, concurred in the majority decision, while noting that use of a formal commitment procedure would render the debate unnecessary. Id. at 236-237. Justices Stevens, Brennan, and Marshall dissented, noting that the Court had failed to recognize and protect Harper's significant liberty interests. See also Foucha v. Louisiana, 504 U.S. 71 (1992) (person acquitted by reason of insanity who subsequently was found to be without mental illness could not be committed to mental institution based on dangerousness alone).

However, the Court imposed a stricter standard to medicate the accused forcibly for the purposes of adjudging him competent to stand trial. In Sell v. United States, 539 U.S. 166 (2003), the Court deviated from the *Harper* test in finding that the government could administer antipsychotic medications to a mentally ill dentist who had been charged, but not convicted, with 62 counts of fraud and the attempted murder of an FBI agent. The Court outlined a multi-factor test, explaining that "the Constitution permits the Government involuntarily to administer antipsychotic drugs to a mentally ill defendant facing serious criminal charges in order to render that defendant competent to stand trial, but only if the treatment is medically appropriate, is substantially unlikely to have side effects that may undermine the fairness of the trial, and, taking account of less intrusive alternatives, is necessary significantly to further important governmental trial-related interests." Nonetheless, in United States v. Loughner, 672 F.3d 731 (9th Cir. 2012), the Ninth Circuit found that Loughner—who had attempted to assassinate Arizona Congresswoman Gabrielle Giffords—could be forcibly medicated under the lower *Harper* standard because he was "dangerous to himself or others." The *Harper* standard is also used to determine when it is constitutional to forcibly medicate prisoners in order to make them competent to be executed for a capital offense. See, e.g., Singleton v. Norris, 319 F.3d 1018 (8th Cir. 2003) (holding that "mandatory medication regime . . . does not become unconstitutional under *Harper* when an execution date is set" and the Eighth Amendment is not violated when a state executes a prisoner who "regained competency through appropriate medical care"). See also David M. Adams, Belief and Death: Capital Punishment and the Competence-for-Execution Requirement, 10 Crim. L. & Phil. 17 (2016) (arguing for abandonment of the competence-for-execution doctrine).

4. *Outpatient Commitment.* In-patient commitment and mandatory treatment both involve substantial invasions of individual liberty. What standards should be applied to state laws permitting "outpatient commitment," under which individuals might be required to demonstrate continued adherence to medical treatment or therapy? Could outpatient commitment be used to ensure that mentally ill patients continue to take necessary medications while in the community, thus preventing relapses and the need for inpatient commitment? In New York, "Kendra's Law" empowers courts to order participation in an "assisted outpatient treatment" (AOT) program. To do so, the court must find by clear and convincing evidence that the person suffers from a mental illness, is "unlikely to survive safely in the community without supervision," has a "history of treatment noncompliance" that has led to hospitalization or violent behavior, and is unlikely to participate voluntarily. Moreover, the possibility of non-treatment must create a serious risk of harm to the person or others and AOT must be both beneficial and the least restrictive means available. See Candice T. Player, Involuntary Outpatient Commitment: The Limits of Prevention, 26 Stan. L. & Pol'y Rev. 159 (2015); In re K. L., 806 N.E.2d 480 (N.Y. 2004) (upholding Kendra's Law). See also Mills v. Rogers, 457 U.S. 291, 299 (1982) (explaining that "the Constitution recognizes a liberty interest in avoiding the unwanted administration of antipsychotic drugs").

5. *Intellectual Disabilities.* Does commitment based on reduced intellectual abilities or developmental disabilities invoke the same constitutional concerns as commitment for mental illness? In Heller v. Doe, 509 U.S. 312 (1993), the Court considered the validity of a statutory scheme that imposed a lower burden of proof on involuntary commitments for persons who were "mentally retarded." The Court's analysis was based on a rational review standard because the litigants had failed to present their claim properly that a higher level of scrutiny should be applied. A divided Court upheld the lower commitment standard, in part because of distinctions between this form of disability and mental illness. Intellectual disabilities might be easier to diagnose, with less risk of error, for example. Similarly, Kentucky "could conclude" that persons with lower intellectual functioning were more likely to present a danger to themselves or others. In addition, treatment for this form of disability is "much less invasive" than treatment for mental illness. Justices Souter, Blackmun, and Stevens dissented, with Justice O'Connor joining in part. See Susan Lee, Heller v. Doe: Involuntary Civil Commitment and the "Objective" Language of Probability, 20 Am. J. L. & Med. 457 (1994). See also People v. Barrett, 281 P.3d 753 (Cal. 2012) (no equal protection claim where different approach to requesting jury trials for mentally ill and dangerous persons as compared with "mentally retarded" and dangerous persons); Porter v. Knickrehm, 457 F.3d 794 (8th Cir. 2006) (only minimal procedural protections required for admission of intellectually disabled

individual to state human development center when admission under voluntary authority of legal guardian); Bryan Y. Lee, The U.N. Convention on the Rights of Persons with Disabilities and Its Impact upon Involuntary Civil Commitment of Individuals with Developmental Disabilities, 44 Colum. J. L. & Soc. Probs. 393 (2011) (comparing state civil commitment standards with emerging norms from U.N. Convention).

6. For more **on the law and public policy of involuntary civil commitment**, see Lawrence O. Gostin & Lance Gable, The Human Rights of Persons with Mental Disabilities: A Global Perspective on the Application of Human Rights Principles to Mental Health, 63 Md. L. Rev. 20 (2004); Nicholas Scurich & Richard John, The Normative Threshold for Psychiatric Civil Commitment, 50 Jurimetrics 425 (2009-2010). See also Symposium, Conundrums and Controversies in Mental Health and Illness, 38 J. L. Med. & Ethics 722-806 (2010).

Problem: Civil Commitment and Drug Abuse

Should persons addicted to drugs or alcohol be subjected to civil commitment and, where available, forced treatment? Under what circumstances would such a commitment be legitimate? Is addiction a "mental illness"? In E.P. v. Alaska Psychiatric Institute, 205 P.3d 1101 (Alaska 2009), the court considered whether a person who practiced "huffing" (inhaling gas and other fumes) could be involuntarily committed.

E.P. has a history of alcohol abuse and inhaling gasoline fumes and other substances to get high ("huffing"). These actions have led to several commitments, both voluntary and involuntary to the Alaska Psychiatric Institute (API). Huffing has damaged the frontal lobe of E.P.'s brain, resulting in dementia, personality disorder, and not otherwise specified psychosis. He has poor judgment and insight, and as a result cannot grasp the severe health consequences of huffing. E.P. is addicted to huffing. . . .

Alaska law permits involuntary commitment only of those who are gravely disabled or likely to harm themselves or others as the result of mental illness. Thus, the state may involuntarily commit E.P. only if he is "mentally ill" under the statutes. Alaska Statute 47.30.915(12) defines "mental illness" as:

[A]n organic, mental, or emotional impairment that has substantive adverse effects on an individual's ability to exercise conscious control of the individual's actions or ability to perceive reality or to reason or understand; mental retardation, epilepsy, drug addiction, and alcoholism do not per se constitute mental illness, although persons suffering from these conditions may also be suffering from mental illness.

E.P.'s organic brain damage meets the first part of the statutory definition: as found by the superior courts, E.P. suffers from organic mental impairments affecting his judgment, perception of reality, and rational decision-making capabilities. The evidence supported those findings. The question is whether the statute's specific exception of "drug addiction" from the definition of "mental illness" means that E.P. is not mentally ill. We believe that it does not.

E.P.'s organic brain damage is a condition apart from, and more than, his drug addiction. While it is the result of his addiction, it has led to greatly impaired ability to exercise judgment, loss of perception of reality, and impaired ability to communicate. E.P. is not simply a drug addict, he has lost the capacity to appreciate the dangers of his addiction. . . . [B]ecause of cognitive damage, E.P. had little or no insight into the fact that huffing gas hurts him. His continued desire to huff gas stems not only from addiction, but also from his cognitive inability to understand his situation. . . .

Although Alaska law allows commitment of mentally ill people "likely to cause harm to [self] or others," it does not define that term. . . .

We conclude that E.P.'s intent to huff gas constitutes intent to cause himself bodily harm, and that it results from his mental illness. . . . We distinguish this case from one in which an addicted person with full mental capacity chooses to continue abusing harmful substances, no matter how unwise one might consider that choice. In such a case, the person's intent to harm himself by abusing substances results from drug addiction alone, which the legislature excluded from the definition of "mental illness." In this case, E.P.'s decision to harm himself by abusing substances results from his brain damage, and therefore meets the statutory standards. . . .

Id. How would you write legislation to authorize the civil commitment of sexually violent predators? What elements would the government need to prove and by what standard? How would you ensure that it would not become a mechanism for permanent detention?

Sexual predator laws have been widely enacted at the state and federal levels. In United States v. Comstock, 560 U.S. 126 (2010), the Supreme Court upheld the Adam Walsh Child Protection and Safety Act as within Congress's power under the Necessary and Proper Clause. The Act authorizes the Attorney General to petition for the civil commitment of federal prisoners who have completed their criminal sentences. To do so, the government must prove by clear and convincing evidence that the "individual (1) has previously 'engaged or attempted to engage in sexual violent conduct or child molestation,' (2) currently 'suffers from a serious mental illness, abnormality, or disorder,' and (3) 'as a result of' that . . . [condition] is 'sexually dangerous to others,' in that 'he would have serious difficulty in refraining from sexual violent conduct or child molestation if released.'" See Note, Civil Commitment, 124 Harv. L. Rev. 279 (2010).

State legislation has been subject to mixed treatment by courts. In Kansas v. Hendricks, 521 U.S. 346 (1997), the Supreme Court upheld Kansas's civil commitment statute and explicitly drew the connection between quarantining those suspected of harboring infectious diseases and incapacitating potential sexual predators. Citing *Compagnie Francaise,* Justice Thomas wrote for the majority, "A State could hardly be seen as furthering a 'punitive' purpose by involuntarily confining persons afflicted with an untreatable, highly contagious disease." However, more recently, a Minnesota federal district court found that state's civil commitment regime unconstitutional, as "a punitive system that segregates and indefinitely detains a class of potentially dangerous individuals without the safeguards of the criminal justice system" in which "no one has any realistic hope of ever getting out of this 'civil' detention." Karsjens v. Jesson, 109 F.Supp.3d 1139 (D. Minn. 2015), appeal docketed, No. 15-3485 (8th Cir. Nov. 2, 2015).

For more on state initiatives, see the National Conference of State Legislatures Web site; Kansas v. Crane, 534 U.S. 407 (2002) (states must prove individual lacks control over dangerous behavior); Lee v. Superior Court, 99 Cal. Rptr. 3d 712 (2009) (interaction of HIPAA's confidentiality provisions and court order to obtain medical records related to sexual predator law); Monica Davey, States Struggle With What to Do With Sex Offenders After Prison, N.Y. Times, Oct. 29, 2015. See also Allegra M. McLeod, Regulating Sexual Harm: Strangers, Intimates, and Social Institutional Reform, 102 Cal. L. Rev. 1553 (2014) (noting that convicted sex offenders may actually have lower recidivism rates than other types of offenders, and that less than 10 percent of the sex offenders civilly committed between 1990 and 2007 had been released); Annot., 96 A.L.R.3d 840 (2016).

Notes: Mandatory Treatment for Contagious Diseases

1. *Mandatory Treatment of Contagious Disease. Addington's* principles have been applied to cases involving involuntary treatment of persons for contagious disease. Regulations adopted in the modern era tend to include elaborate due process safeguards. The ordinance in City of New York v. Antoinette R., 165 Misc. 2d 1014, 630 N.Y.S.2d 1008 (N.Y. Sup. Ct. 1995), provides a typical example:

> The issue presented at this special proceeding is whether the respondent, a person with active tuberculosis, should be forcibly detained in a hospital setting to allow for the completion of an appropriate regime of medical treatment. . . .
>
> Due to a resurgence of tuberculosis, New York City recently revised the Health Code to permit the detention of individuals infected with TB who have demonstrated an inability to voluntarily comply with appropriate medical treatment. . . . The prerequisite for an order is that there is a substantial likelihood, based on the person's past or present behavior, that the individual cannot be relied upon to participate in or complete an appropriate prescribed course of medication or, if necessary, follow required contagion precautions for tuberculosis. Such behavior may include the refusal or failure to take medication or to complete treatment for tuberculosis, to keep appointments for the treatment of tuberculosis, or a disregard for contagion precautions.
>
> The statute provides certain due process safeguards when detention is ordered. For example, there are requirements for an appraisal of the risk posed to others and a review of less restrictive alternatives which were attempted or considered. Furthermore, there must be a court review within five days at the patient's request, and court review within 60 days and at 90-day intervals thereafter. The detainee also has the right to counsel, to have counsel provided, and to have friends or relatives notified. See Richard T. Andrias, The Criminal Justice System and the Resurgent TB Epidemic, 9 Crim. Just. 2 (Spring, 1994). . . .

165 Misc. 2d at 1014-1015.

In *Antoinette*, the city sought to apply its mandatory treatment regime to a 33-year-old woman who had repeatedly been diagnosed with TB but who had failed to complete her course of treatment after being released from the hospital. Court-ordered "directly observed therapy" (DOT) had failed when she refused to comply. The issue in the case was whether Antoinette would be forced to remain in the hospital for the estimated seven months it would take to complete treatment or whether she would be released for treatment in the home of her mother:

The mother of the respondent lives in a private home with four of her grandchildren and a newborn great-grandson, the grandchild of the respondent. The mother is willing to take the respondent into her home and provide cooperation should she be released from the hospital. Over the past two months the mother has visited her daughter on several occasions and talked with her over the phone on a daily basis. The mother has noticed a change in attitude in the respondent, that is, she is not as hostile. The mother attributes this change to the respondent's acceptance of religion. The respondent also contends that her attitude has been transformed and credits religion as her motivation. Since being detained at the hospital, she has joined various outpatient programs and attended parenting meetings. A nurses aide and the head nurse, who attend to the medical needs of the respondent, both verify that there has been an improvement in the respondent's demeanor. She is now cooperative while taking her medicines and on occasions has independently approached the nursing staff to request her medicines. Relying on her "change in attitude," the respondent opposes the order of detention and again requests the option of participating in Directly Observed Therapy to be conducted at her mother's place of residence. . . .

The petitioner's request for enforcement of the order of the Commissioner is granted. The petitioner has demonstrated through clear and convincing evidence the respondent's inability to comply with a prescribed course of medication in a less restrictive environment. The respondent has repeatedly sought medical treatment for the infectious stages of the disease and has consistently withdrawn from medical treatment once symptoms abate. She has also exhibited a pattern of behavior which is consistent with one who does not understand the full import of her condition nor the risks she poses to others, both the public and her family. On the contrary, she has repeatedly tried to hide the history of her condition from medical personnel. Although the court is sympathetic to the fact that she has recently undergone an epiphany of sorts, there is nothing in the record which would indicate that once she leaves the controlled setting of the hospital she would have the self-discipline to continue her cooperation. Moreover, her past behavior and lack of compliance with outpatient treatment when her listed residence was her mother's house, makes it all the more difficult to have confidence that her mother's good intentions will prevail over the respondent's inclinations to avoid treatments. In any event, the court will reevaluate the progress of the respondent's ability to cooperate in a less restrictive setting during its next review of the order in 90 days.

Accordingly, the respondent shall continue to be detained in a hospital setting until the petitioner or the court determines that the respondent has completed an appropriate course of medication for tuberculosis, or a change in circumstances indicates that the respondent can be relied upon to complete the prescribed course of medication without being in detention. The petitioner is further directed, pursuant to New York City Health Code §11.47 to apply to the court within 90 days for authorization to continue respondent's detention.

Id. at 1019-1020.

Assess the evidence in *Antoinette*. If you represented Antoinette, what evidence and arguments would you want to present at the next hearing? Do you think that you would be successful? See also In re Washington, 735 N.W.2d 111 (Wis. 2007) (upholding commitment of noncompliant patient with noninfectious TB found to be at "high risk of developing infectious tuberculosis"; court may take into account costs of confinement options in considering least restrictive environment; upholding commitment in jail). But see Souvannarath v. Hadden, 95 Cal. App. 4th 1115 (2002) (affirming order preventing county jail from detaining noncompliant TB patient based on California statute forbidding use of correctional facilities for quarantine or isolation). How might the five "justificatory conditions" identified by scholars as helpful to decide when public health should trump individual liberty—effectiveness, proportionality, necessity, least infringement, and public justification—apply in these cases? See James F. Childress et al., Public Health Ethics: Mapping the Terrain, 30 J. L. Med. & Ethics 170 (2002).

2. *Due Process.* Should the clear and convincing evidence standard be used for commitment and treatment orders applied to persons with contagious diseases? In which ways are the consequences and proof disputes similar to those implicated in commitment for mental illness? Most jurisdictions that have considered the issue use the clear and convincing standard and provide other due process protections. See, e.g., Greene v. Edwards, 263 S.E.2d 661 (W. Va. 1980) (clear and convincing standard applied to commitment for TB treatment). See also Public Health Law at 428-430. Can these cases be reconciled with the "right to die" jurisprudence developed in Chapter 5? Patients with contagious conditions presumably are competent. What explains the state's ability to override their treatment refusals?

3. *Americans with Disabilities Act.* Federal regulations explicitly include contagious diseases such as HIV and tuberculosis as disabilities under the ADA. 28 C.F.R. §35.104. The ADA prohibits discrimination by public entities against persons with disabilities unless those persons present a direct threat to the health or safety of others, based on an individualized assessment. 42 U.S.C. §12131; 28 C.F.R. pt. 35, App. B. The potential remains, however, to consider whether the ADA could be used to limit state control measures that "discriminate" against carriers of contagious diseases. In City of Newark v. J. S., 652 A.2d 265 (N.J. Super. Ct. Law Div. 1993), for example, the court construed the state's TB commitment statute to avoid due process and ADA claims. The court held that the city had presented clear and convincing evidence of the likelihood that J. S. presented a danger to others and approved his commitment. It rejected mandatory sputum tests and treatment, however, noting that J. S. could refuse these measures, although to do so would likely render his confinement indefinite. The court's analysis of the due process and ADA issues was heavily influenced by Professor Gostin's work. Lawrence O. Gostin, Controlling the Resurgent Tuberculosis Epidemic: A Fifty-State Survey of TB Statutes and Proposals for Reform, 269 JAMA 255 (1993). More recently, the Supreme Court held in Olmstead v. L. C., 527 U.S. 581 (1999) that "unjustified isolation . . . is properly regarded as discrimination based on disability."

4. *Directly Observed Therapy (DOT).* Directly Observed Therapy is similar to the "Outpatient Commitment" approach for persons with mental illness discussed above. DOT provides an alternative to commitment for persons with treatable, contagious conditions. In DOT, an individual is ordered to undergo treatment and is monitored to ensure that treatment is taken. A person's adherence to a drug therapy regime can be monitored by requiring the individual to appear at a health clinic daily or by daily visits from a public health worker. This strategy has some obvious advantages for both the individual and the state: The procedure is less intrusive and less expensive. It still involves a significant liberty infringement, however, and, as in *Antoinette R.*, recalcitrant persons can evade monitoring. What are your views on the use of DOT? Would you object to a program of DOT designed to ensure that you take the entire course of therapy whenever you are issued a prescription for antibiotics?

Problem: Antiretroviral Therapy and the Risk of HIV Infection

Antiretroviral therapies for HIV infection are costly, can have significant side effects, and are not a panacea. These therapies nonetheless have played an important role in extending the lives and improving the health status of persons infected with HIV. Beyond the life-extending properties of therapy for the infected individual, antiretroviral therapies also have been employed in some circumstances to reduce the risk of HIV transmission. Antiretroviral therapies designed to prevent infection by HIV have routinely been made available to health care workers and emergency response personnel who have been exposed to potentially infected blood or body fluids, to survivors of sexual assault, and to pregnant women to prevent HIV transmission to their offspring.

Recent research suggests that antiretroviral therapy can reduce the risk of HIV transmission through sexual activity or needle-sharing in two additional ways. See, e.g., Myron S. Cohen & Lindsey R. Baden, Preexposure Prophylaxis for HIV—Where Do We Go from Here?, 367 New Eng. J. Med. 459 (2012); Scott M. Hammer, Antiretroviral Treatment as Prevention, 365 New Eng. J. Med. 561 (2011). First, HIV-infected persons who are able to access and adhere to antiretroviral therapy have lower viral loads and greatly reduced rates of HIV transmission through, e.g., sexual activity. Yet, only about half of all persons who are aware of their HIV infection are receiving appropriate treatment. What factors might explain this rate of treatment, particularly given the evidence that antiretroviral therapy extends lives and reduces transmission risks? Should policymakers create additional incentives for infected persons to adhere to treatment? For example, should persons with HIV infection who engage in sexual or needle-sharing activity be shielded from potential criminal penalties for exposing others to the risk of HIV-infection if they can prove faithful use of antiretroviral therapies? Contra State v. Musser, 721 N.W.2d 734 (Iowa 2006) (upholding conviction for criminal transmission of HIV and resulting 25-year prison sentence of defendant who was receiving medical treatment for HIV).

Second, the risk of becoming infected with HIV through sexual or needle-sharing activity can be reduced if currently uninfected persons who engage in risky behaviors take antiretroviral therapies prophylactically. See Jonathan S. Jay & Lawrence O. Gostin, Ethical Challenges of Preexposure Prophylaxis for HIV, 308 J. Am. Med. Ass'n 867 (2012); Robert Steinbrook, Preexposure Prophylaxis for HIV Infection, 308 J. Am. Med. Ass'n 865 (2012). Should persons seeking to avoid HIV infection from voluntary sexual or needle-sharing activity be permitted to access antiretroviral therapies even though they are not currently infected with HIV? Should the cost of these antiretroviral therapies be reimbursable for uninfected persons under private or public health insurance programs?

When, if ever, should the right of access to these therapies be transformed into a mandate that the therapies be used? Should women who refuse antiretroviral therapy for themselves or their newborns be charged with child neglect? See N.J. Div. of Youth & Family Services v. L.V., 889 A.2d 1153 (Ch. Div. 2005) (holding mother's refusal to take medication to reduce risk of transferring virus to unborn child not act of abuse). See also In re Aaliyah W., 332 Wis.2d 318 (Wis. 2011) (detention of pregnant woman in hospital to ensure HIV treatment necessary to protect unborn child). Should HIV-infected persons who have engaged in conduct capable of transmitting the virus (e.g., through sexual activity or needle-sharing) be civilly committed or required to undergo DOT?

Problem: Public Health Emergencies, Mandatory Treatment, and Quarantine

The MSEHPA includes provisions giving state public health authorities broad powers to require treatment and to impose isolation or quarantine. These provisions undoubtedly are the most controversial in the Model Act. See, e.g., George J. Annas, Bioterrorism, Public Health, and Civil Liberties, 346 New Eng. J. Med. 1337 (2002); Lawrence O. Gostin et al., The Model State Emergency Health Powers Act: Planning for and Response to Bioterrorism and Naturally Occurring Infectious Diseases, 288 JAMA 622 (2002). See also Joseph Barbera et al., Large-Scale Quarantine Following Biological Terrorism in the United States: Scientific Examination, Logistics and Legal Limits, and Possible Consequences, 286 JAMA 2711 (2001); James G. Hodge, Jr., Public Health Emergency Legal and Ethical Preparedness, in The Oxford Handbook of U.S. Healthcare Law (I. Glenn Cohen, Allison K. Hoffman & William M. Sage eds., 2015). Review the following excerpts from the Model Act, which will only become effective when a state declares a public health emergency pursuant to the Act:

> **Section 603 Vaccination and treatment.** During a state of public health emergency the public health authority may exercise the following emergency powers over persons as necessary to address the public health emergency—
>
> (a) **Vaccination.** To vaccinate persons as protection against infectious disease and to prevent the spread of contagious or possibly contagious disease.
>
> (1) Vaccination may be performed by any qualified person authorized to do so by the public health authority.
>
> (2) A vaccine to be administered must not be such as is reasonably likely to lead to serious harm to the affected individual.
>
> (3) To prevent the spread of contagious or possibly contagious disease the public health authority may isolate or quarantine, pursuant to Section 604, persons who are unable or unwilling for reasons of health, religion, or conscience to undergo vaccination pursuant to this Section.
>
> (b) **Treatment.** To treat persons exposed to or infected with disease.
>
> (1) Treatment may be administered by any qualified person authorized to do so by the public health authority.
>
> (2) Treatment must not be such as is reasonably likely to lead to serious harm to the affected individual.
>
> (3) To prevent the spread of contagious or possibly contagious disease the public health authority may isolate or quarantine, pursuant to Section 604, persons who are unable or unwilling for reasons of health, religion, or conscience to undergo treatment pursuant to this Section.
>
> **Section 604 Isolation and quarantine.**
>
> (a) **Authorization.** During the public health emergency, the public health authority may isolate . . . or quarantine . . . an individual or groups of individuals. This includes individuals or groups who have not been vaccinated, treated, tested, or examined pursuant to Sections 602 and 603. The public health authority may also establish and maintain places of isolation and quarantine, and set

rules and make orders. Failure to obey these rules, orders, or provisions shall constitute a misdemeanor.

(b) **Conditions and principles.** The public health authority shall adhere to the following conditions and principles when isolating or quarantining individuals or groups of individuals:

(1) Isolation and quarantine must be by the least restrictive means necessary to prevent the spread of a contagious or possibly contagious disease to others and may include, but are not limited to, confinement to private homes or other private and public premises.

(2) Isolated individuals must be confined separately from quarantined individuals. . . .

(5) Isolated and quarantined individuals must be immediately released when they pose no substantial risk of transmitting a contagious or possibly contagious disease to others. . . .

(c) **Cooperation.** Persons subject to isolation or quarantine shall obey the public health authority's rules and orders; and shall not go beyond the isolation or quarantine premises. Failure to obey these provisions shall constitute a misdemeanor. . . .

Section 605 Procedures for isolation and quarantine. During a public health emergency, the isolation and quarantine of an individual or groups of individuals shall be undertaken in accordance with the following procedures.

(a) **Temporary isolation and quarantine without notice.**

(1) **Authorization.** The public health authority may temporarily isolate or quarantine an individual or groups of individuals through a written directive if delay in imposing the isolation or quarantine would significantly jeopardize the public health authority's ability to prevent or limit the transmission of a contagious or possibly contagious disease to others.

(2) **Content of directive.** The written directive shall specify the following: (i) the identity of the individual(s) or groups of individuals subject to isolation or quarantine; (ii) the premises subject to isolation or quarantine; (iii) the date and time at which isolation or quarantine commences; (iv) the suspected contagious disease if known; and (v) a copy of Article 6 and relevant definitions of this Act.

(3) **Copies.** A copy of the written directive shall be given to the individual to be isolated or quarantined or, if the order applies to a group of individuals and it is impractical to provide individual copies, it may be posted in a conspicuous place in the isolation or quarantine premises.

(4) **Petition for continued isolation or quarantine.** Within ten (10) days after issuing the written directive, the public health authority shall file a petition pursuant to Section 605(b) for a court order authorizing the continued isolation or quarantine of the isolated or quarantined individual or groups of individuals.

(b) **Isolation or quarantine with notice.**

(1) **Authorization.** The public health authority may make a written petition to the trial court for an order authorizing the isolation or quarantine of an individual or groups of individuals.

(2) **Content of petition.** A petition under subsection (b)(1) shall specify the following: (i) the identity of the individual(s) or groups of individuals subject to isolation or quarantine; (ii) the premises subject to isolation or quarantine; (iii) the date and time at which isolation or quarantine commences; (iv) the suspected contagious disease if known; (v) a statement of compliance with the conditions and principles for isolation and quarantine of Section 604(b);

and (vi) a statement of the basis upon which isolation or quarantine is justified in compliance with this Article. The petition shall be accompanied by the sworn affidavit of the public health authority attesting to the facts asserted in the petition, together with any further information that may be relevant and material to the court's consideration.

(3) **Notice.** Notice to the individuals or groups of individuals identified in the petition shall be accomplished within twenty-four (24) hours in accordance with the rules of civil procedure.

(4) **Hearing.** A hearing must be held on any petition filed pursuant to this subsection within five (5) days of filing of the petition. In extraordinary circumstances and for good cause shown the public health authority may apply to continue the hearing date on a petition filed pursuant to this Section for up to ten (10) days, which continuance the court may grant in its discretion giving due regard to the rights of the affected individuals, the protection of the public's health, the severity of the emergency and the availability of necessary witnesses and evidence.

(5) **Order.** The court shall grant the petition if, by a preponderance of the evidence, isolation or quarantine is shown to be reasonably necessary to prevent or limit the transmission of a contagious or possibly contagious disease to others. . . .

(e) **Court to appoint counsel and consolidate claims.**

(1) **Appointment.** The court shall appoint counsel at state expense to represent individuals or groups of individuals who are or who are about to be isolated or quarantined pursuant to the provisions of this Act and who are not otherwise represented by counsel. . . .

MSEHPA §§603-605, available at the casebook Web site.

Evaluate the constitutionality of the Model Act's vaccination, treatment, and quarantine provisions. Note that the "penalty" for refusing vaccination or treatment under §603 is isolation or quarantine pursuant to §604. Is the threatened loss of liberty more or less constitutionally problematic than the fine in *Jacobson*, supra at page 924? Note that the Act anticipates that licensed health care providers might not be available to care for all and merely requires states to use "qualified" persons. Section 604 describes the conditions of isolation/quarantine, while §605 focuses on the procedural prerequisites. Both sections take into account the possibility that a massive public health emergency might preclude individualized determinations and care. Public authorities are authorized to maintain "places" for quarantine, for example, and notices may be posted if individual notice is impractical. The penalty for violating the Act's quarantine/isolation provisions is a misdemeanor. Would this preclude criminal prosecution for attempted murder, for example, if a person with smallpox escaped from isolation? Should it? Section 605 permits public health authorities to impose isolation and quarantine without notice. A petition for a court order must be filed within ten days. The Act also provides a mechanism for public health authorities to secure a court order before implementing isolation/quarantine. What standard of proof is required?

Compare the Model Act's provisions to the relevant public health statute in your own state. Does your state law permit public health officials to order vaccination or treatment? Does it include provisions for isolation/quarantine, with or without a court order? If your state has comprehensive public health laws covering these issues, do you see any similarities or differences between your state law and the Model Act? Which seems better from a legal or policy standpoint? If your state does not have such laws, would you recommend the adoption of the Model Act's provisions? Do state law provisions need to be reviewed given the new federal quarantine rules? See page 914. What conflicts or opportunities to coordinate might be uncovered?

The government's ability—whether it be state, federal, or foreign—to respond effectively during a public health crisis was tested dramatically during the 2014 Ebola epidemic, introduced at the start of this chapter. The outbreak originated in West Africa, where the virus killed 55 percent of those it infected. In response, the Director-General of the World Health Organization (WHO) declared a "public health emergency of international concern," requiring nations to develop their preparedness capacities. The WHO discouraged complete travel bans in favor of exit screening to prevent potentially infected people from spreading the virus. However, African governments deployed military forces to conduct house-to-house searches, institute checkpoints, and create *cordons sanitaires*. Liberia—a country with just 51 physicians to serve its 4.3 million residents—attempted to quarantine the tens of thousands of people living in the West Point slum in Monrovia, an effort that collapsed only ten days into the 21-day plan after protests erupted. See Lawrence O. Gostin, Daniel Lucey & Alexandra Phelan, The Ebola Epidemic: A Global Health Emergency, 312 J. Am. Med. Ass'n 1095 (2014); Mark A. Rothstein, From SARS to Ebola: Legal and Ethical Considerations for Modern Quarantine, 12 Ind. Health L. Rev. 227, 240 (2015).

The United States, despite its minimal exposure to people infected with the virus, responded to the threat of outbreak in a far-from-seamless manner. With a midterm election looming, state and federal officials argued over potential policies, which included proposals to ban travelers from infected countries and quarantine all health workers returning from the region. Tensions came to a head when Kaci Hickox, a nurse who had treated Ebola patients in Sierra Leone, was ordered quarantined by New Jersey Governor Chris Christie after she showed signs of fever upon arriving at the Newark airport. She was forced to live in a tent outside a New Jersey hospital for three days before being allowed to return to her home in Maine for an in-home quarantine. Soon after, a Maine judge denied the state's request for an order forcing her to comply with the in-home quarantine. The judge found that the state had failed to prove "by clear and convincing evidence that limiting [Hickox's] movements to the degree requested" was necessary "to avoid a clear and immediate public health threat." See Jess Bidgood & Dave Philipps, Judge in Maine Eases Restrictions on Nurse, N.Y. Times, Oct. 31, 2014; Robert Gatter, Ebola, Quarantine, and Flawed CDC Policy, 23 U. Miami Bus. L. Rev. 375 (2015); James G. Hodge, Jr., Legal Myths of Ebola Preparedness and Response, 29 Notre Dame J.L. Ethics & Pub. Pol'y 355 (2015); Craig Spencer, Having and Fighting Ebola—Public Health Lessons from a Clinician Turned Patient, 372 New Eng. J. Med 1089 (2015).

Do you think the Judge acted correctly in the Hickox case? To what extent should public fear over a crisis, founded or ill-founded, be relevant to the analysis? Does the severity of symptoms associated with a particular outbreak matter for the analysis? Compare, for example, Ebola with SARS or bird flu or the Zika virus. How should the origin of the crisis—homegrown or from abroad—affect the response? Should state or federal authorities take the lead in ordering quarantines?

D. RESTRICTING CONSUMER CHOICE TO PROTECT PUBLIC HEALTH

This section of this chapter explores a newly expanding frontier in public health law: the restriction of consumer choice to protect individual and public health. This form of public health regulation has long roots, extending back into the regulation of medicinal products and devices over 100 years ago. Yet public health measures that restrict consumer choices are increasingly important as public health officials seek to attack the consequences of behavioral choices that, while borne by individuals, create significant morbidity and mortality—and increased health care expenditures—across populations. How should the law treat public health measures such as restrictions on access to unapproved drugs, rules mandating the use of motorcycle helmets, or taxes focused on foods high in sugar or fat? While proponents argue that the protection of individuals and the reduction of health care costs provide more than sufficient justification for these forms of public health regulation, opponents argue that the initiatives are the precursor to the emergence of a "nanny state" in which individuals are no longer permitted to exercise autonomy in making decisions about the acceptance of risk. When, if ever, will constitutional limits be placed on these forms of public health policies? Given the broad constitutional authority governments have to protect health and safety and to use tax to shape behavior, the policy constraints may well be political rather than constitutional in many cases. How should health law and policy experts evaluate the range of options, risks, and benefits of policies in these areas?

1. The FDA, Pharmaceutical Regulation, and the Constitution

■ ABIGAIL ALLIANCE FOR BETTER ACCESS TO DEVELOPMENTAL DRUGS v. VON ESCHENBACH
495 F.3d 695 (D.C. Cir. 2007)

GRIFFITH, Circuit Judge:

This case presents the question whether the Constitution provides terminally ill patients a right of access to experimental drugs that have passed limited safety trials but have not been proven safe and effective. The district court held there is no such right. A divided panel of this Court held there is. Because we conclude that there is no fundamental right "deeply rooted in this Nation's history and tradition" of access to experimental drugs for the terminally ill, see Washington v. Glucksberg, 521 U.S. 702, 720-21 (1997), we affirm the judgment of the district court.

I.A.

The Abigail Alliance for Better Access to Developmental Drugs (the "Alliance") is an organization of terminally ill patients and their supporters that seeks expanded access to experimental drugs for the terminally ill. The Food, Drug, and Cosmetic Act ("FDCA" or "Act"), however, generally prohibits access to new drugs unless and until they have been approved by the Food and Drug Administration ("FDA"). See 21 U.S.C. §355(a). Gaining FDA approval can be a long process. First, an experimental drug's sponsor (e.g., a drug company) must submit an application for approval. Because no drug may be approved without a finding of "substantial evidence that the drug will have the effect it purports or is represented to have," an application must contain "full reports of investigations which have been made to show whether or not such drug is safe for use and whether such drug is effective in use," id. §355(b)(1)(A). Such reports rely in large measure on clinical trials with human subjects.

But before a sponsor can even begin human testing, it must submit for the FDA's approval an investigational new drug application ("IND") containing detailed information establishing that human testing is appropriate. Once the application for human testing has been approved, several phases of clinical testing begin. The Alliance's amended complaint alleges that this testing process is an extremely lengthy one, requiring nearly seven years for the average experimental [or "investigational"] drug.

Clinical testing for safety and effectiveness requires three or sometimes four phases. See 21 C.F.R. §312.21. Phase I involves the initial introduction of a new drug into human subjects. A Phase I study usually consists of twenty to eighty subjects and is "designed to determine the metabolism and pharmacologic actions of the [new] drug in humans, the side effects associated with increasing doses, and, if possible, to gain early evidence on effectiveness." Although gathering data on effectiveness may be part of Phase I, its primary focus is to determine whether the drug is safe enough for continued human testing. See id. Phase II studies are "well controlled" and "closely monitored" clinical trials of no more than several hundred subjects, used to evaluate both the "effectiveness of the drug for a particular indication" and its "common short-term side effects and risks." Id. §312.21(b).

Phase III studies are expanded clinical trials of several hundred to several thousand subjects designed to "gather . . . additional information about effectiveness and safety that is needed to evaluate the overall benefit-risk relationship of the drug and to provide an adequate basis for physician labeling." At any time during the clinical trials, a drug sponsor is required to notify the FDA of "[a]ny adverse experience associated with the use of the drug that is both serious and unexpected," and the FDA may order a "clinical hold" halting the trials if it determines that safety concerns so warrant, id. §312.42. To guide the clinical testing process, Congress has directed the FDA to establish "[s]cientific advisory panels" to "provid[e] expert scientific advice and recommendations to the Secretary regarding a clinical investigation of a drug or the approval for marketing of a drug." . . .

Terminally ill patients need not, however, always await the results of the clinical testing process. The FDA and Congress have created several programs designed to provide early access to promising experimental drugs when warranted. For example, under the "treatment IND" program, the FDA may approve use of an investigational drug by patients not part of the clinical trials for the treatment of "serious or immediately life-threatening disease[s]" if there exists "no comparable or satisfactory alternative drug or other therapy." . . .*

B.

Concluding that the FDA's current process for early access to new drugs was inadequate to meet the needs of its terminally ill members, the Alliance submitted its own proposals to the FDA. Those proposals culminated in a "citizen petition" to the

---

* [The Court cited proposed regulations now codified as amended at 21 C.F.R. §312.300-.320.—Eds.]

FDA, arguing that there is a "different risk-benefit tradeoff facing patients who are terminally ill and who have no other treatment options." . . . Having thus been rejected by the FDA, the Alliance turned to the courts, arguing that the United States Constitution provides a right of access to experimental drugs for its members. In a complaint that mirrored much of its earlier submissions to the FDA, the Alliance argued that the FDA's lengthy clinical trials, combined with the "FDA's restrictions on pre-approval availability[,] amount to a death sentence for these [terminally ill] patients." Nor, the Alliance argues, are the FDA's exceptions to the clinical testing process sufficient to provide the terminally ill the access they need because they "are small, when they exist at all," and the ban on profits prevents many drug sponsors from participating.

"Terminally ill patients," in the Alliance's view, "are typically willing to assume risks. . . ." Before the district court, the Alliance argued that the Constitution guarantees them the right to do so. The district court rejected that argument, holding that "there is no constitutional right of access to unapproved drugs." A divided panel of this Court reversed, concluding that "where there are no alternative government-approved treatment options, a terminally ill, mentally competent adult patient's informed access to potentially life-saving investigational new drugs determined by the FDA after Phase I trials to be sufficiently safe for expanded human trials warrants protection under the Due Process Clause." Abigail Alliance for Better Access to Developmental Drugs v. von Eschenbach, 445 F.3d 470, 486 (D.C. Cir. 2006). We vacated that decision and granted rehearing en banc.

As framed by the Alliance, we now consider:

> Whether the liberty protected by the Due Process Clause embraces the right of a terminally ill patient with no remaining approved treatment options to decide, in consultation with his or her own doctor, whether to seek access to investigational medications that the [FDA] concedes are safe and promising enough for substantial human testing.

Appellants' Br. at 1.[5] That is, we must determine whether terminally ill patients have a fundamental right to experimental drugs that have passed Phase I clinical testing.

---

5. The dissent has recast the Alliance's proposed right away from the terms used in its briefs and oral argument—a right to access investigational new drugs—into a right "to try to save one's life," which has "its textual anchor in the right to life [expressed in the Fifth Amendment]." Dissent at 714-15. Regardless of how it is described, we must examine the proposed right under *Glucksberg*, which specifically cautions against the type of broad generalization the dissent now employs. See *Glucksberg*, 521 U.S. at 721 (requiring a " 'careful description' of the asserted fundamental liberty interest"). If the asserted right is so broad that it protects a person's efforts to save his life, it might subject to strict scrutiny any government action that would affect the means by which he sought to do so, no matter how remote the chance of success. The Supreme Court rejected a similar attempt to broadly define the right at issue in . . . Reno v. Flores, 507 U.S. 292, 302 (1993). The dissent suffers from the same flaw in arguing that this is about the right to save one's life, because, in the end, this case is about the right to access experimental and unproven drugs in an attempt to save one's life, which we conclude under *Glucksberg* is not deeply rooted in our Nation's history and traditions. By describing too broadly at the outset a proposed right that will cover the Alliance's more narrow claim, the dissent fails *Glucksberg*'s threshold requirement of a carefully described right. We need not pursue the arguments that follow that initial misstep.

If such a right exists, the Alliance argues that both 21 C.F.R. §312.34(b)(3) (preventing access to experimental drugs for terminally ill patients where there is insufficient evidence of effectiveness or where there is an unreasonable risk of injury) and 21 C.F.R. §312.7 (prohibiting drug manufacturers from profiting on the sale of experimental drugs) must be subjected to strict scrutiny because they interfere with a fundamental constitutional right. We do not address the broader question of whether access to medicine might ever implicate fundamental rights.

II.

The Due Process Clause of the Fifth Amendment provides that "[n]o person shall be . . . deprived of life, liberty, or property, without due process of law." U.S. CONST. amend. V. The Supreme Court has held that the protections of the Amendment "guarantee[ ] more than fair process." *Glucksberg*, 521 U.S. at 719. The Court has stated that "[t]he Clause . . . provides heightened protection against government interference with certain fundamental rights and liberty interests," (citing Planned Parenthood of Se. Pa. v. Casey, 505 U.S. 833, 851 (1992)), including "the rights to marry, to have children, to direct the education and upbringing of one's children, to marital privacy, to use contraception, to bodily integrity, and to abortion," *Glucksberg*, 521 U.S. at 720.

As such rights are not set forth in the language of the Constitution, the Supreme Court has cautioned against expanding the substantive rights protected by the Due Process Clause "because guideposts for responsible decisionmaking in this unchartered area are scarce and open-ended." Collins v. Harker Heights, 503 U.S. 115, 125 (1992). There is an additional and substantial concern that courts must also consider: "By extending constitutional protection to an asserted right or liberty interest, we, to a great extent, place the matter outside the arena of public debate and legislative action." *Glucksberg*, 521 U.S. at 720. Thus, the Supreme Court has directed courts to "exercise the utmost care whenever we are asked to break new ground in this field, lest the liberty protected by the Due Process Clause be subtly transformed into the policy preferences of the [courts' members]." Id. (and citing "history of the *Lochner* era").

In *Glucksberg*, the Supreme Court described its "established method of substantive-due-process analysis" as having "two primary features."

> First, we have regularly observed that the Due Process Clause specially protects those fundamental rights and liberties which are, objectively, deeply rooted in this Nation's history and tradition and implicit in the concept of ordered liberty, such that neither liberty nor justice would exist if they were sacrificed. Second, we have required in substantive-due-process cases a careful description of the asserted fundamental liberty interest.

We will assume arguendo that the Alliance's description of its asserted right would satisfy *Glucksberg*'s "careful description" requirement.[6] Looking to whether

---

6. We nonetheless have serious doubt about whether the Alliance's description of its proposed constitutional right could ever pass constitutional muster. The Alliance's claimed right depends on a regulatory determination that the drug is safe for testing, prompting an obvious question: How can a constitutional right be defined by an administrative regulation that is subject to change?

the Alliance has demonstrated that its right is deeply rooted in this Nation's history, tradition, and practices, the Alliance's claim for constitutional protection rests on two arguments: (1) that "common law and historical American practices have traditionally trusted individual doctors and their patients with almost complete autonomy to evaluate the efficacy of medical treatments"; and (2) that FDA policy is "inconsistent with the way that our legal tradition treats persons in all other life-threatening situations." More specifically, the Alliance argues that the concepts of self-defense, necessity, and interference with rescue are broad enough to demonstrate the existence of the fundamental right they seek—a right for "persons in mortal peril" to "try to save their own lives, even if the chosen means would otherwise be illegal or involve enormous risks."

. . . The Alliance argues that its right can be found in our history and legal traditions because "the government never interfered with the judgment of individual doctors about the medical efficacy of particular drugs until 1962," i.e., when major amendments were made to the Food, Drug, and Cosmetic Act. Appellants' Br. at 44. . . . The Alliance has little to say, however, about our Nation's history of regulating the safety of drugs. The Alliance's effort to focus on efficacy regulation ignores one simple fact: it is unlawful for the Alliance to procure experimental drugs not only because they have not been proven effective, but because they have not been proven safe. Although the Alliance contends that it only wants drugs that "are safe and promising enough for substantial human testing," i.e., drugs that have passed Phase I testing, current law bans access to an experimental drug on safety grounds until it has successfully completed all phases of testing. . . . Thus, to succeed on its claim of a fundamental right of access for the terminally ill to experimental drugs, the Alliance must show not only that there is a tradition of access to drugs that have not yet been proven effective, but also a tradition of access to drugs that have not yet been proven safe.

. . . [W]e conclude that our Nation has long expressed interest in drug regulation, calibrating its response in terms of the capabilities to determine the risks associated with both drug safety and efficacy. Drug regulation in the United States began with the Colonies and States when the Colony of Virginia's legislature passed an act in 1736 that addressed the dispensing of more drugs than was "necessary or useful" because that practice had become "dangerous and intolerable." Edward Kremers, Kremers and Urdang's History of Pharmacy 158 (4th ed. 1976). . . .

Nor were the States the only regulators of access to drugs. Although early federal regulation was not extensive, perhaps because "[n]ot until interstate commerce began its great expansion after the Civil War did the need for Federal rule-making become widely realized," Wallace F. Janssen, Outline of the History of U.S. Drug Regulation and Labeling, 36 Food Drug Cosm. L. J. 420, 425 (1981), there are early examples of federal government intervention. In 1848, the Import Drug Act, ch. 70, 9 Stat. 237 (1848), banned "imported adulterated drugs" after a congressional committee concluded that "this country had become the grand mart and receptacle of all the refuse [drug] merchandise . . . , not only from the European warehouses, but from the whole Eastern world." Wesley J. Heath, America's First Drug Regulation Regime: The Rise and Fall of the Import Drug Act of 1848, 59 Food & Drug L.J. 169, 175 (2004).

The current regime of federal drug regulation began to take shape with the Food, Drug, and Cosmetic Act of 1938, 21 U.S.C. §301 et seq. The Act required that drug manufacturers provide proof that their products were safe before they could be marketed. . . . We end our historical analysis where the Alliance would prefer it begin—with the 1962 Amendments to the FDCA. Undoubtedly, as the Alliance argues at length, Congress amended the FDCA in 1962 to explicitly require that the FDA only approve drugs deemed effective for public use. Thus, the Alliance argues that, prior to 1962, patients were free to make their own decisions whether a drug might be effective. But even assuming arguendo that efficacy regulation began in 1962, the Alliance's argument ignores our Nation's history of drug safety regulation. . . .

Nor can the Alliance override current FDA regulations simply by insisting that drugs which have completed Phase I testing are safe enough for terminally ill patients. Current law bars public access to drugs undergoing clinical testing on safety grounds. The fact that a drug has emerged from Phase I with a determination that it is safe for limited clinical testing in a controlled and closely-monitored environment after detailed scrutiny of each trial participant does not mean that a drug is safe for use beyond supervised trials.[11] FDA regulation of post-Phase I drugs is entirely consistent with our historical tradition of prohibiting the sale of unsafe drugs.

But even setting the safety issue to one side, . . . an arguably limited history of efficacy regulation prior to 1962 does not establish a fundamental right of access to unproven drugs. The amendments made to the FDCA by Congress throughout the twentieth century demonstrate that Congress and the FDA have continually responded to new risks presented by an evolving technology. Recent government efficacy regulation has reflected Congress's exercise of its well-established power to regulate in response to scientific, mathematical, and medical advances [such as the development of clinical trials during and after WW II]. . . . [C]reating constitutional rights to be free from regulation based solely upon a prior lack of regulation would undermine much of the modern administrative state, which, like drug regulation, has increased in scope as changing conditions have warranted. . . .[17]

Although it has not addressed the precise constitutional argument urged by the Alliance, we find it highly significant that the Supreme Court has rejected several similar challenges to the FDCA and related laws brought on statutory grounds. See, e.g., United States v. Rutherford, 442 U.S. 544, 552, (1979) ("we are persuaded by the legislative history and consistent administrative interpretation of the [FDCA] that no implicit exemption for drugs used by the terminally ill is necessary to attain congressional objectives"). And other courts have rejected arguments that the Constitution provides an affirmative right of access to particular medical treatments reasonably prohibited by the Government [citing, e.g., Mitchell v. Clayton, 995 F.2d

---

11. In fact, the FDA cites numerous examples in which drugs have been pulled from the market post-Phase I due to safety concerns.

17. . . . The Alliance can, of course, advocate its position vigorously before Congress and the FDA, and convince our Nation's democratic branches that the values the Alliance favors should be protected. In fact, within the last year, the political branches have responded to the concerns of the Alliance and others. The FDA recently issued a notice of proposed rulemaking [which resulted in the expansion of access to investigational new drugs for seriously ill patients outside of formal clinical trials, see 21 C.F.R. §312.300-.320].

772, 775 (7th Cir. 1993) ("most federal courts have held that a patient does not have a constitutional right to obtain a particular type of treatment or to obtain treatment from a particular provider if the government has reasonably prohibited that type of treatment or provider")]. In keeping with those decisions, we conclude that the Alliance has not provided evidence of a right to procure and use experimental drugs that is deeply rooted in our Nation's history and traditions. To the contrary, our Nation's history evidences increasing regulation of drugs as both the ability of government to address these risks has increased and the risks associated with drugs have become apparent. . .[19]

IV.

Because the Alliance's claimed right is not fundamental, the Alliance's claim of a right of access to experimental drugs is subject only to rational basis scrutiny. . . . [W]e cannot say that the government's interest does not bear a rational relation to a legitimate state interest. That conclusion is compelled by the Supreme Court's decision in United States v. Rutherford, 442 U.S. 544 (1979). In that case, terminally ill patients sought to prevent the FDA from prohibiting access to the drug laetrile, even though the drug had not been approved for public use. In rejecting a challenge by terminally ill patients claiming that the FDCA's safety requirement did not apply to them, the Supreme Court held that "[f]or the terminally ill, as for anyone else, a drug is unsafe if its potential for inflicting death or physical injury is not offset by the possibility of therapeutic benefit." See also id. at 558 (noting that history has demonstrated that numerous "resourceful entrepreneurs" might try to take advantage of an unregulated market, which "suggest[s] why Congress could reasonably have determined to protect the terminally ill, no less than other patients, from the vast range of self-styled panaceas that inventive minds can devise").

Although terminally ill patients desperately need curative treatments, as *Rutherford* holds, their deaths can certainly be hastened by the use of a potentially toxic drug with no proven therapeutic benefit. Thus, we must conclude that, prior to distribution of a drug outside of controlled studies, the Government has a rational basis for ensuring that there is a scientifically and medically acceptable level of knowledge about the risks and benefits of such a drug. We therefore hold that the FDA's policy of limiting access to investigational drugs is rationally related to the legitimate state interest of protecting patients, including the terminally ill, from potentially unsafe drugs with unknown therapeutic effects. . . .

19. As there exists no deeply rooted right, . . . we need not and do not address all of the Alliance's arguments regarding whether their proposed right is implicit in our Nation's system of ordered liberty, [but] we note a crucial difference between this case and one of the cases relied upon by the Alliance in making that argument, Cruzan v. Director, Mo. Dep't of Health, 497 U.S. 261 (1990). . . . Looking to *Cruzan*, the Alliance argues that "[i]f a patient has a fundamental right to medical self-determination that gives them the right to starve themselves to death, then surely they have a right to choose to fight for their lives even if that means taking a drug that has not yet met the FDA's full approval standards." . . . But a tradition protecting individual freedom from life-saving, but forced, medical treatment does not evidence a constitutional tradition of providing affirmative access to a potentially harmful, and even fatal, commercial good.

Our Nation's history and traditions have consistently demonstrated that the democratic branches are better suited to decide the proper balance between the uncertain risks and benefits of medical technology, and are entitled to deference in doing so. . . . Jacobson v. Massachusetts, 197 U.S. 11, 30 (1905); see also Gonzales v. Carhart, 550 U.S. 124 (2007). Consistent with that precedent, our holding today ensures that this debate among the Alliance, the FDA, the scientific and medical communities, and the public may continue through the democratic process.

ROGERS, Circuit Judge, with whom Chief Judge GINSBURG joins, dissenting:

Today, the court rejects the claim that terminally ill patients who have exhausted all government-approved treatment options have a fundamental right to access investigational new drugs. The court's opinion reflects a flawed conception of the right claimed by the Abigail Alliance for Better Access to Developmental Drugs and a stunning misunderstanding of the stakes. The court shifts the inquiry required by Washington v. Glucksberg, 521 U.S. 702 (1997), by changing the nature of the right, by conflating the right with the deprivation, and by prematurely advancing countervailing government interests. The court fails to come to grips with the Nation's history and traditions, which reflect deep respect and protection for the right to preserve life, a corollary to the right to life enshrined in the Constitution. The court confuses this liberty interest with the manner in which the Alliance alleges that the liberty has been deprived, namely by denying terminally ill patients access to investigational medications under the narrow conditions described by the Alliance. The court conflates the inquiry as to whether a fundamental right exists at all with whether the government has demonstrated a compelling interest, when strictly scrutinized, rendering its restrictive policy constitutional.

These missteps lead the court to rely upon how rights and liberties have been limited and restricted—addressing regulations to prevent fraud in the sale of misbranded and adulterated medications or safety restrictions applicable to all medicines for any palliative purpose—which says little about the historic importance of the underlying right of a person to save her own life. . . . The common law doctrines [of necessity and self defense] remain good evidence of a history and tradition of protecting life and attempts to preserve life as a deep-seated personal right. That the right may be and has been denied in the face of compelling governmental interests is no reason for conflating the two stages of the analysis and looking only to the results of past cases in order to avoid the analysis prescribed by the Supreme Court in *Glucksberg*. . . .

In the end, it is startling that the oft-limited rights to marry, to fornicate, to have children, to control the education and upbringing of children, to perform varied sexual acts in private, and to control one's own body even if it results in one's own death or the death of a fetus have all been deemed fundamental rights covered, although not always protected, by the Due Process Clause, but the right to try to save one's life is left out in the cold despite its textual anchor in the right to life. This alone is reason the court should pause about refusing to put the FDA to its proof when it denies terminal patients with no alternative therapy the only option they have left, regardless of whether that option may be a long-shot with high risks. The court is on even weaker footing when it relies upon the risks entailed in medical procedures to wrest life-and-death decisions that once were vested in patients and their physicians. The court commits a logical error of dramatic consequence by concluding that the investigational drugs are somehow not "necessary." While the potential cures may not prove sufficient to save the life of a terminally ill patient, they are surely necessary if there is to be any possibility of preserving her life. . . .

[T]he history and traditions of this Nation support the right of a terminal patient, and not the government, to make this fundamentally personal choice involving her own life. Because judicial precedents and the historical record require strict scrutiny before upsetting rights of this magnitude, the FDA must demonstrate a compelling governmental interest before its policy restricting access can survive. Accordingly, I would remand the case to the district court to make the initial determination as to whether FDA has met its burden, and I respectfully dissent.

Notes: The Scope and Constitutionality of Pharmaceutical Regulation

1. *Federal and State Regulation of Pharmaceuticals.* The federal government has enacted a complex web of food, drug, and medical device regulations under the federal authority to regulate interstate commerce. The power to regulate interstate commerce includes the power to regulate commerce to protect public health. Federal law preempts many state law claims. See, e.g., Patricia J. Zettler, Pharmaceutical Federalism, 92 Ind. L. J. 845 (2017). The regulation of drugs and medical devices is complex and detailed. See generally David G. Adams et al. eds., Food and Drug Law and Regulation (3d ed. 2015); and FDA in the Twenty-First Century (Holly Fernandez Lynch & I. Glenn Cohen eds., 2015). The Food and Drug Law Institute offers programs and resources at www.fdli.org. The discussion here will focus on the intersection between the regulation of drugs and individual access to therapy.

2. *The Drug Approval Process and Access to Experimental Therapies.* As noted in *Abigail Alliance,* new drugs must go through at least three phases of drug trials to be proven to be "safe" and "effective" in treating a particular condition. 21 U.S.C. §355; 21 C.F.R. §312.21. The fourth phase of drug trials alluded to in the opinion is the post-market surveillance trial, which is used to identify any safety or efficacy issues related to drugs across a broader population sample. See Anna B. Laakman, Collapsing the Distinction Between Experimentation and Treatment in the Regulation of New Drugs, 62 Ala. L. Rev. 305, 337-341 (2011).

Under current federal regulations, patients with serious or life-threatening illnesses may be given access to certain types of investigational new drugs under some circumstances. Regulations designed to enhance access to investigational drugs for treatment purposes, noted by the *Abigail* court, are now codified at 21 C.F.R. §312.300-320. These regulations apply to persons with life-threatening diseases or serious diseases or conditions "associated with morbidity that ha[ve] substantial impact on day-to-day functioning. . . . Whether a disease or condition is serious is . . . based on its impact on such factors as survival, day-to-day functioning, or the likelihood that the disease, if left untreated, will progress from a less severe condition to a more serious one." Id. at §312.300.

Access to investigational drugs under the regulations depends in part on a determination that there are no other treatment options, that the patient benefits outweigh the risks, and that "[p]roviding the investigational drug for the requested use will not interfere with the initiation, conduct, or completion of clinical investigations that could support marketing approval of the expanded access use or otherwise compromise the potential development of the expanded access use." 21 C.F.R. §312.305(a). Is there any constitutional problem with a regulatory regime that explicitly subordinates the needs of individual patients to the "greater good" that can result from the completion of clinical trials? See Jonathan J. Darrow et. al., Practical, Legal, and Ethical Issues in Expanded Access to Investigational Drugs, 372 N. Eng. J. Med. 279 (2015) (considering a number of issues, including impact of expanded access on clinical trials). If the *Abigail* plaintiffs had succeeded, would the need to preserve clinical trials have provided the compelling justification required to uphold the regulations in strict scrutiny review? Would this rationale apply to patients who are ineligible for clinical trials, who therefore could not be deterred from participating? See Abigail R. Moncrieff, The Freedom of Health, 159 U. Pa. L. Rev. 2209, 2243-2245 (2011). The FDA reports that 99 percent of applications for access are accepted but patients nonetheless may not be able to secure access to the drug from the manufacturer. Could patients bring claims against drug companies demanding participation in these alternative access schemes? See Cacchillo v. Insmed, 551 Fed. Appx. 592 (2d Cir. 2014) (affirming summary judgment for company).

3. *Legislative Success for "The Right to Try."* As noted in *Abigail*, the U.S. Supreme Court had not yet directly ruled on whether terminally ill patients had any constitutionally protected right to access unapproved potential therapies. The *Rutherford* decision cited in the opinion is almost solely concerned with the issue of whether the FDA's statutorily granted power to regulate the safety and effectiveness of drugs could be applied to drugs used to treat terminal conditions. On remand from the Supreme Court decision, the Tenth Circuit confronted and rejected the constitutional claim, holding that "the decision by the patient whether to have a treatment or not is a protected right, but his selection of a particular treatment, or at least a medication, is within the area of governmental interest in protecting public health." Rutherford v. United States, 616 F.2d 455, 457 (10th Cir. 1980).

The issue dramatically reemerged with the D.C. Circuit panel's initial decision in *Abigail Alliance*, 445 F.3d 470 (2006), which the decision above reversed en banc. The initial D.C. Circuit panel decision found that:

> where there are no alternative government-approved treatment options, a terminally ill, mentally competent adult patient's informed access to potentially life-saving investigational new drugs determined by the FDA after Phase I trials to be sufficiently safe for expanded human trials warrants protection under the Due Process Clause. The prerogative asserted by the FDA—to prevent a terminally ill patient from using potentially life-saving medication to which those in Phase II clinical trials have access—thus impinges upon an individual liberty deeply rooted in our Nation's history and tradition of self-preservation. . . . [W]e remand the case . . . to determine whether the FDA's policy . . . is narrowly tailored to serve a compelling governmental interest.

Id. at 486. Is restricting access to potential treatments for terminally ill patients consistent with the jurisprudence governing the termination of life-sustaining treatment? See Chapter 5. With case law on a woman's right to choose abortion? See Chapter 7.B.2. For more on the right to self-preservation, see Eugene Volokh,

Medical Self-Defense, Prohibited Experimental Therapies, and Payment for Organs, 120 Harv. L. Rev. 1813 (2007).

The fight for access moved to the legislatures. The libertarian Goldwater Institute developed "Right to Try" model legislation authorizing manufacturers to provide terminally ill patients with investigational drugs, biological products, or devices that had completed phase 1 of the clinical trial process. The model legislation requires physician certification of the patient's medical condition and the need for the unproven therapy. Patients are to provide informed consent. Manufacturers may choose whether to provide the therapy and whether to recover any costs. "Right to Try" legislation has now been adopted in 37 states. Richard Cauchi, State Laws and Legislation Related to Biologic Medications and Substitution of Biosimilars, National Conference of State Legislatures, available at: www.ncsl.org (as of September 2017). Do states have authority to legislate in this area? Rebecca Dresser, "Right to Try" Laws: The Gap between Experts and Advocates, 45(3) Hastings Center Report 9 (May–June 2015). Would the patient's informed consent preclude subsequent liability claims against the manufacturer? "Right to Try" legislation passed the U.S. Senate in August of 2017, and it was under consideration in the House as of October 2017. The federal bill includes measures designed to encourage manufacturers to participate. Robert Pear & Sheila Kaplan, Senate Passes F.D.A. Funding and 'Right to Try' Drug Bills, N.Y. Times, Aug. 3, 2017.

4. *The FDA and Drug Development Efforts.* The FDA has been criticized for unnecessary delays in the approval of important drugs. The laetrile dispute in the 1970s paved the way for vigorous protests by HIV/AIDS activists in the 1980s and 1990s. Lewis A. Grossman, AIDS Activists, FDA Regulation, and the Amendment of America's Drug Constitution, 42 Am. J. L. & Med. 687 (2016). Congress sought to speed up the development of new drugs by providing additional incentives to pharmaceutical firms. Under the Orphan Drug Act, Pub. L. No. 97-414, 96 Stat. 2049 (1983), as amended, those companies are encouraged to develop and market drugs for rare illnesses, where the relatively small number of persons affected might otherwise not constitute a sufficient market to sustain the research and development costs of providing treatment. See also 21 C.F.R. §316.1-.40. The court in *Abigail* cites the "Fast Track" program, designed to provide access to "drugs intended to treat life-threatening and severely-debilitating illnesses." Congress has since approved a number of additional programs designed to speed FDA review of various therapies. See e.g., Veronica S. Jae, Simplifying FDASIA: The "Fast Track" to Expedited Drug Approval Efficiency, 66 Admin L. Rev. 173 (2014) (discussing new "Breakthrough Therapies" program); Aaron S. Kesselheim & Jerry Avorn, New "21st Century Cures" Legislation: Speed and Ease vs. Science, 317 JAMA 581 (2017) (expressing concern about new legislation designed to reduce perceived barriers in drug approval process and to spur expedited review for regenerative therapies, such as those using human stem cells).

Any effort to speed up the approval of new drugs inevitably creates the risk that truncated studies and review will result in the release of drugs with unknown hazards and uncertain effectiveness. The ongoing debate focuses on whether the reform of the drug approval process has gone too far or not far enough in providing consumers with access to safe and effective drugs. Data from the FDA's postmarket surveillance process indicates that 32 percent of the "222 novel therapeutics approved by the FDA from 2001 through 2010 . . . were affected by a postmarket safety event."

Nicholas S. Downing et al., Postmarket Safety Events Among Novel Therapeutics Approved by the US Food and Drug Administration Between 2001 and 2010, 317 JAMA 1854 (2017). Does this help to resolve the debate, one way or another?

5. *Drug Labeling, "Off-Label Use," and the Learned Intermediary Doctrine.* Under the regulatory policy of the FDA, each prescription drug carries a package-insert label with quite elaborate information on the methods of administering the drug, conditions for which the drug is recommended, as well as warnings about contraindications for use and about known dangers and side effects. As discussed in Chapter 4, the package inserts have considerable, although not totally controlling, influence over the proper standard of accepted patient care related to the drug. Physicians may, and often do, prescribe drugs for "off-label" uses, although there has been controversy in recent years about physician discretion in this area. See, e.g., Wendy Teo, FDA and the Practice of Medicine: Looking at Off-Label Drugs, 41 Seton Hall Legis. J. 305 (2017) (discussing the FDA's deferential approach).

Should drug manufacturers be permitted to disseminate information about off-label uses to physicians? The FDA initially took the view that these communications should be severely restricted to prevent circumvention of the labeling process. Drug company off-label marketing practices generated significant litigation and very significant judgments moving into the early 2010s. For a sampling of parties and theories, see, e.g., Gardiner Harris, Pfizer Pays $2.3 Billion to Settle Marketing Case, N.Y. Times, Sept. 3, 2009; Krumplebeck v. Breg, Inc., 2012 WL 3241587 (6th Cir.) (analyzing possible liability claims related to off-label marketing in context of medical device); Thomas M. Greene, A New Weapon in Pharma Cases, Trial 40 (Nov. 2011) (RICO).

The FDA's rules restrict the freedom of drug companies to express their views. The Supreme Court historically applied low-level scrutiny to governmental regulation of commercial speech. However, in Sorrell v. IMS Health, 564 U.S. 552 (2011), the Court invalidated Vermont legislation restricting sale and disclosure of physician prescribing behavior under the First Amendment. The decision suggested that the Court might apply some form of heightened scrutiny to regulations restricting commercial speech, including the flow of information to physicians and to patients. See Symposium, Marketing Health: The Growing Role of Commercial Speech Doctrine in FDA Regulation, 37 Am. J. L. & Med. 203-421 (2011); Symposium, Commercial Speech and Public Health, 21 Health Matrix 1-230 (2011). In U.S. v. Caronia, a pharmaceutical sales consultant had been recorded speaking with physician-customers about off-label uses of a drug. He was convicted of conspiracy to introduce a misbranded drug into interstate commerce. The conviction was overturned by the Second Circuit, which held that "the FDA cannot prosecute pharmaceutical manufacturers and their representatives under the FDCA [Food, Drug, and Cosmetic Act] for speech promoting the lawful, off-label use of an FDA-approved drug." 703 F.3d 149, 168-169 (2d Cir. 2012). A New York district court subsequently held in another case that the "FDA could not prevent promotion of a drug for an unapproved use if a manufacturer's promotional statements are 'truthful.'" Jerry Avorn, Ameet Sarpatwari & Aaron S. Kesselheim, Forbidden and Permitted Statements about Medications — Loosening the Rules, 373 N. Eng. J. Med. 967 (2015) (discussing *Amarin* case, conflicting precedents and more permissive FDA policies). Could the FDA justify a restriction on truthful speech between manufacturers and physicians? Christopher Robertson & Aaron Kesselheim, Regulating Off-Label Promotion—A Critical Test, 375 N. Eng. J. Med. 2313 (2016) (arguing that *Caronia* approach should be rejected by courts and the FDA). If truthfulness is the standard, who should have the burden of proof?

6. *Direct to Consumer (DTC) Advertising.* In the prescription drug field, the courts have quite uniformly accepted the package-insert warnings to physicians as meeting the drug manufacturers' legal obligation. As discussed in Chapter 4, the physician is expected to be a "learned intermediary" between the company and the patient in protecting the patient and in providing direct information about the drug to the patient. The retail pharmacist is also a source of advice for drug consumers. These assumptions have been shaken somewhat by the expansion of direct-to-consumer (DTC) advertising by pharmaceutical companies. See Prescription-Drug Advertisements, 21 C.F.R. §202.1; and Christopher T. Robertson, New DTCA Guidance—Enough to Empower Consumers?, 373 N. Eng. J. Med. 1085 (2015). The potential for state law claims, using tort or other theories, is limited by the ability of defendants to argue that state claims are preempted by federal law. Compare Pliva v. Mensing, 565 U.S. 604 (2011) (state warning claim preempted by federal law governing generic drugs when impossible for manufacturer to comply with both state and federal warning requirements), with Wyeth v. Levine, 555 U.S. 555 (2009) (state failure to warn claim not preempted by FDA labeling rule for non-generic drug where manufacturer could comply with both). Could greater public access to drug trial data benefit consumers? Aaron S. Kesselheim & Michelle M. Mello, Confidentiality Laws and Secrecy in Medical Research: Improving Public Access to Data on Drug Safety, 26 Health Aff. 483 (2007); and Kevin Outterson, Clinical Trial Transparency—Antidote to Weaker Off-Label-Promotion Rules?, 371 N. Eng. J. Med. 1 (2014)

a. *The FDA and New Regulatory Challenges: From Tobacco to Medical Apps.* The FDA's regulatory activities frequently generate controversy. Some critics lambaste the agency for its ties to industry and alleged failure to safeguard citizens, while others lament the agency's aggressive regulatory stance and its alleged stifling of innovation. The debate can be seen in the FDA's approach to tobacco, nutritional supplements, genetic tests, and medical apps.

a) *Tobacco.* One major controversy, involving the agency's attempt to regulate tobacco, resulted in legislation in 2009 giving the FDA the power to regulate tobacco products. See Lawrence Deyton et al., Tobacco Product Regulation—A Public Health Approach, 362 New Eng. J. Med. 1753 (2010) (Family Smoking Prevention and Tobacco Control Act, 21 U.S.C. §§387-387u). There was a setback when one early initiative under the Act—an effort to require graphic warnings on cigarette packages—was found to violate the First Amendment. Eric N. Lindblom, Micah L. Berman & James F. Thrasher, FDA-Required Tobacco Product Inserts & Onserts—And the First Amendment, 72 Food & Drug L. J. 1 (2017) (discussing caselaw and making recommendations for additional action). Researchers have expressed concerns that e-cigarettes could fuel continuing and perhaps even expanding addiction to nicotine. See, Amy L. Fairchild, Ronald Bayer & James Colgove, The Renormalization of Smoking? E-Cigarettes and the Tobacco "Endgame," 370 N. Eng. J. Med. 293 (2014). The FDA moved to exert regulatory authority over all tobacco products, issuing a final rule that extended authority to e-cigarettes and other products in 2016. FDA, Deeming Tobacco Products to Be Subject to the Federal Food, Drug and Cosmetic Act, 81 Fed Reg. 28974-01 (May 10, 2016). This initiative was followed in 2017 by a new plan that would reduce the level of nicotine in cigarettes to levels that would no longer sustain addiction while encouraging development of alternative, safer products to deliver nicotine to consumers. Kenneth E. Warner & Steven A. Schroeder, FDA's Innovative Plan to Address the Enormous Toll of Smoking, 318 JAMA 1755 (2017). What are the benefits and risks of the plan to reduce nicotine in cigarettes?

b. *Dietary Supplements.* The regulation of dietary supplements has been controversial, in part because of industry claims that the supplements are more like food than they are like classic pharmaceuticals. The FDA's suggestion that it might regulate supplements as though they were drugs drew congressional action in the form of the Dietary Supplement Health and Education Act of 1994 (DSHEA). The DSHEA gives the FDA the authority to "regulate[] vitamins, minerals, herbs, amino acids, and other dietary substances. Dietary supplements are generally regulated in a manner similar to food and the FDA is authorized to prevent adulterated products from entering the market." Nutraceutical v. von Eschenbach, 459 F.3d 1033, 1035 (2006) (interpreting DSHEA; upholding FDA ban on ephedrine-alkaloid dietary supplements). A dietary supplement is adulterated if it "presents a significant or unreasonable risk of illness or injury" under suggested or ordinary use. 21 U.S.C. §342(f)(1). Nutritional supplements are also subject to adverse event reporting requirements. 21 U.S.C. §379aa-1. See generally GAO, Dietary Supplements: FDA Should Take Further Actions to Improve Oversight and Consumer Understanding (2009); Ranjani R. Starr, Too Little, Too Late: Ineffective Regulation of Dietary Supplements in the United States, 105 Amer. J. Public Health 478 (2015). As research continues to reveal the importance of the microbiome to health, should "probiotics" be regulated as food, drugs, dietary supplements, or within a different framework? See Diane E. Hoffmann et al., Probiotics: Achieving a Better Regulatory Fit, 69 Food & Drug L. J. 237 (2014).

c. *Genetic Tests.* The regulation of genetic tests is another area of controversy. The advances in genetics that made it possible to develop associations between certain genetic variants and potential health conditions raised a number of concerns for experts and policymakers. Was the information meaningful? Would efforts to market genetic testing and reporting confuse consumers about the utility of the results or would consumers be able to understand the serious limits to the information? Is it appropriate to offer consumers information about possible increased risk for serious conditions for which there is no treatment? Should the "consumers" be considered to be "patients" who required personalized counseling before and after the testing process? Should genetic tests be regulated as medical devices? Laboratory procedures and standards? Clinical practice? Ordinary consumer products? Consumer education? See GAO, Direct-to-Consumer Genetic Tests: Misleading Test Results Are Further Complicated by Deceptive Marketing and Other Questionable Practices (2010).

Genetic testing companies began marketing DTC genetic testing in the 2000s. The FDA announced in 2010 that it considered the DTC genetic tests to be medical devices and the genetic testing services to be medical interventions. Andrew Pollack, F.D.A. Faults Companies on Unapproved Genetic Tests, N.Y. Times, June 11, 2010. After failing to come to an agreement with the company, the FDA ordered 23andMe to discontinue offering its genetic analyses to consumers for a period of time. Andrew Pollack, FDA Orders Genetic Testing Firm to Stop Selling DNA Analysis Service, N.Y. Times, Nov. 25, 2013; Andrew Pollack, 23andMe Will Resume Giving Users Health Data, Oct. 21, 2015 (authorizing limited genetic testing for carrier status). The FDA authorized a broader range of genetic testing services in April 2017. Gina Kolata, F.D.A. Will Allow 23andMe to Sell Genetic Tests for Disease Risk to Consumers, N.Y. Times, Apr. 6, 2017 (authorizing testing that includes 10 disease risks for consumers). The FDA approval did not extend to "diagnostic" genetic testing: tests that are used to make clinical decisions, such as testing for BRCA. FDA, FDA Allows Marketing of First Direct-to-Consumer Tests That Provide Genetic Risk Information for Certain Conditions, April 6, 2017, available at: www.fda.gov (noting as well the specific regulatory pathways used to consider and approve the DTC genetic tests).

Take a few moments to look online for a genetic testing company. How does the company provide information about the nature of its genetic tests, the meaning of test results, the risks to individuals who may discover that they have a heightened risk for a serious, but currently untreatable, condition? Companies may use the information they collect to carry out additional research. Are consumers being given sufficient information about the commercial use of their health data? See Jennifer Abbasi, 23andMe, Big Data, and the Genetics of Depression, 317 JAMA 14 (2017); J. Scott Roberts et al., Direct-to-Consumer Genetic Testing, 20 Public Health Genomics 36 (2017) (2 percent of surveyed DTC genetic testing consumers reported regret about seeking testing; 1 percent reported harm from results).

d. *Medical "Apps."* How should the FDA respond to the plethora of health-related applications for mobile phones and the development of fitness-related wearables from watches to clothing? These developments—sometimes called "mobile health" or "mhealth"—can provide greater access to health-related information and personal data for billions of people. The FDA issued guidance to industry in 2013, indicating that it would regulate these developments as medical devices but that it would focus its regulatory attention on "apps that present greater risk to patients if they don't work as intended and on apps that cause smartphones or other mobile platforms to impact the functionality or performance of traditional medical devices." FDA, Mobile Medical Applications, available at www.fda.gov/. The regulatory structure is in flux, with multiple studies, legislative, and regulatory proposals, many of which have been focused more on loosening regulatory oversight than on "creating a regulatory framework that encourages high-value innovation while also preventing the market from being overcome with products that are ineffective or unsafe." Nathan G. Cortez, I. Glenn Cohen & Aaron S. Kesselheim, FDA Regulation of Mobile Health Technologies, 371 N. Eng. J. Med. 372, 376 (2014) (comprehensive analysis of range of mhealth products, benefits and risks, and the regulatory response). See also, Sarah Duranske, This Article Makes You Smarter! (Or, Regulating Health and Wellness Claims), 43 Amer. J. L. & Med. 7 (2017) (noting importance of Federal Trade Commission (FTC) role in addressing false claims of health products). This is a rapidly evolving area that may transform aspects of our health care system in the years ahead.

8. *Additional Commentaries.* As noted above, there are numerous treatises, loose-leaf services, journals, and commentaries focused on the **regulation of food, drugs, medical devices, biologics,** and so on (note 1). Some helpful sources include: Audrey L. Gassman, Christine P. Nguyen & Hylton V. Joffe, FDA Regulation of Prescription Drugs, 376 N. Eng. J. Med. 674 (2017); Kenneth R. Piña & Wayne L. Pines eds., A

Practical Guide to Food and Drug Law and Regulation (5th ed. 2014). For more on the **drug approval process and access to experimental therapies** (note 2), see George Annas, Cancer and the Constitution, 357 New Eng. J. Med. 4 (2007); Richard Epstein, The Erosion of Individual Autonomy in Medical Decisionmaking: Of the FDA and IRBs, 96 Geo. L. J. 559 (2008); William M. Janssen, A "Duty" to Continue Selling Medicines, 40 Am. J. L. & Med. 330 (2014); Elizabeth Weeks Leonard, Right to Experimental Treatment: FDA New Drug Approval, Constitutional Rights, and the Public's Health, 37 J. L. Med. & Ethics 269 (2009). For more on the **"right to try" and constitutional aspects** of pharmaceutical choice (note 3), see, e.g., Daniel Carpenter et al., Drug-Review Deadlines and Safety Problems, 358 New Eng. J. Med. 1354 (2008); Jennifer Couzin-Frankel & Yasmin Ogale, Once on "Fast Track," Avastin Now Derailed, 333 Science 143 (2011); Anna B. Laakman, Collapsing the Distinction Between Experimentation and Treatment in the Regulation of New Drugs, 62 Ala. L. Rev. 305, 337-341 (2011); and Special Section on "Right to Try," 51 Therapeutic Innovation and Regulatory Science 142-179 (2017). For more on the **FDA and the drug development** process (note 4), see FDA, The FDA's Drug Review Process, available at: www.fda.gov/Drugs/ResourcesForYou/Consumers/ucm143534.htm; and FDA, Fast Track, Breakthrough Therapy, Accelerated Approval, Priority Review www.fda.gov/forpatients/approvals/fast/default.htm. **Drug labeling, off-label use, and the learned intermediary doctrine** (note 5) are discussed in Chapter 4. For some additional resources about some of the risks of marketing, see Symposium, Institutional Corruption and the Pharmaceutical Industry, 41 J. L. Med. & Ethics 544-687 (2013). For more on the **Direct to Consumer** advertising (note 6), see FDA, Advertising Guidances, available at: https://www.fda.gov/Drugs/GuidanceCompliance-RegulatoryInformation/Guidances/ucm064956.htm; Jeremy A. Greene & David Herzberg, Hidden in Plain Sight: Marketing Prescription Drugs to Consumers in the Twentieth Century, 100 Am. J. Public Health 793 (2010) (tracing history of DTC advertising). There are a number of commentaries focused on the FDA's efforts relating to tobacco, dietary supplements, genetic tests, and medical applications: George J. Annas, 23andMe and the FDA, 370 N. Eng. J. Med. 985 (2014); Barbara J. Evans, The FDA and Genomic Tests—Getting Regulation Right, 372 N. Eng. J. Med. 2258 (2015); Scott Gottlieb & Mitchell Zeller, A Nicotine-Focused Framework for Public Health, 377 N. Eng. J. Med. 1111 (2017) (announcing initiative); Institute of Medicine, Dietary Supplements: A Framework for Evaluating Safety (2005); NIH, Regulation of Genetic Tests, available at: https://www.genome.gov/10002335/regulation-of-genetic-tests/ (providing overview of regulatory environment and initiatives through 2016); Lars Noah & Barbara Noah, A Drug by Any Other Name . . . ? Paradoxes in Dietary Supplement Risk Regulation, 17 Stan. L. & Pol'y Rev. 165 (2006); N. Sawicki, Compelling Images: The Constitutionality of Emotionally Persuasive Health Campaigns, 73 Md. L. Rev. 458 (2014); Kayte Spector-Bagdady, Reconceptualizing Consent for Direct-to-Consumer Health Services, 41 Amer. J. of L. & Med. 568 (2015); Symposium, 39 Amer. J. L. & Med. 199-489 (2013).

2. Federal-State Conflicts: State Regulation and Medicinal Marijuana

Possession and use of marijuana have been subject to federal and state criminal sanctions for decades. See, e.g., Controlled Substances Act (CSA), 21 U.S.C.

§§801-971. Despite this fact, patient advocacy and pro-marijuana groups successfully introduced "medicinal marijuana" laws beginning in the mid-1990s, for the most part through voter referenda. Proponents argued that the drug could be used to treat glaucoma and to reduce nausea and weight loss for persons undergoing chemotherapy. See National Academies of Sciences, Engineering, and Medicine, The Health Effects of Cannabis and Cannabinoids: The Current State of the Evidence and Recommendations for Research (2017) (reviewing evidence regarding therapeutic effects and recommending additional research). The state laws purported to shield from prosecution persons involved in prescribing, using, or possessing marijuana for specified medical purposes.

The California initiative is typical:

§11362.5. Medical use. . . .

(b)(1) The people of the State of California hereby find and declare that the purposes of the Compassionate Use Act of 1996 are as follows:

(A) To ensure that seriously ill Californians have the right to obtain and use marijuana for medical purposes where that medical use is deemed appropriate and has been recommended by a physician who has determined that the person's health would benefit from the use of marijuana in the treatment of cancer, anorexia, AIDS, chronic pain, spasticity, glaucoma, arthritis, migraine, or any other illness for which marijuana provides relief.

(B) To ensure that patients and their primary caregivers who obtain and use marijuana for medical purposes upon the recommendation of a physician are not subject to criminal prosecution or sanction.

(C) To encourage the federal and state governments to implement a plan to provide for the safe and affordable distribution of marijuana to all patients in medical need of marijuana.

(2) Nothing in this section shall be construed to supersede legislation prohibiting persons from engaging in conduct that endangers others, nor to condone the diversion of marijuana for nonmedical purposes.

(c) Notwithstanding any other provision of law, no physician in this state shall be punished, or denied any right or privilege, for having recommended marijuana to a patient for medical purposes.

(d) . . . [State criminal laws], relating to the possession of marijuana, and . . . relating to the cultivation of marijuana, shall not apply to a patient, or to a patient's primary caregiver, who possesses or cultivates marijuana for the personal medical purposes of the patient upon the written or oral recommendation or approval of a physician.

(e) For the purposes of this section, "primary caregiver" means the individual designated by the person exempted under this section who has consistently assumed responsibility for the housing, health, or safety of that person.

Cal. Health & Safety Code §11362.5. For an update on state legislation, see National Conference of State Legislatures (NCSL), State Medical Marijuana Laws, available at www.ncsl.org. As of September, 2017, 29 states "allow for comprehensive public medical marijuana and cannabis programs." Id. (along with D.C., Guam, & Puerto Rico). In addition, "18 states allow use of 'low THC, high cannabidiol (CBD)' products for medical reasons in limited situations or as a legal defense." Id. Eight states and the District of Columbia now permit access to marijuana for recreational use and nearly half the states have decriminalized possession of small amounts of marijuana. NCSL, Marijuana Overview, available at www.ncsl.org (as of Aug. 30, 2017); and Beau Kilmer, Recreational Cannabis—Minimizing the Health Risks from Legalization, 376 N. Eng. J. Med. 705 (2017).

These state marijuana initiatives are in profound conflict with federal criminal law. Controlled Substances Act (CSA), 21 U.S.C. §§801-971. In Gonzales v. Raich, 545 U.S. 1 (2005), the Supreme Court ruled that congressional authority to regulate interstate commerce included the power to prohibit the local cultivation and use of marijuana for medical purposes even in the states that permitted it. See George J. Annas, Jumping Frogs, Endangered Toads, and California's Medical Marijuana Law, 353 New Eng. J. Med. 2291 (2005); Lawrence O. Gostin, Medical Marijuana, American Federalism, and the Supreme Court, 294 JAMA 842 (2005).

After the Bush administration's aggressive campaigns against the marijuana initiatives, the Obama administration initially announced a "non-enforcement policy" under which the federal government would refrain from prosecutions against individuals complying with state medical marijuana laws. Robert A. Mikos, A Critical Appraisal of the Department of Justice's New Approach to Medical Marijuana, 22 Stan. L. & Pol'y Rev. 633 (2011). In 2013, the Department of Justice reiterated that it was deferring challenging state legalization laws. NCSL, supra. See generally, Erwin Chemerinsky et al., Cooperative Federalism and Marijuana Regulation, 62 U.C.L.A. L. Rev. 74 (2015). There have been some indications that President Trump's administration might change course, including a request that Congress end the budget rider restricting Department of Justice action against state medical marijuana programs. Avantika Chilkoti, States Keep Saying Yes to Marijuana Use. Now Comes the Federal No., N.Y. Times, Jul. 15, 2017 (noting anti-marijuana views of Attorney General Jeff Sessions).

Problem: Off-Label Marketing

In 2017, Arizona enacted a new law protecting off-label marketing:

A. Notwithstanding any other law, a pharmaceutical manufacturer or its representative may engage in truthful promotion of an off-label use of a drug, biological product or device.

B. This section does not require a health care insurer, other third-party payor or other health plan sponsor to provide coverage for the cost of any off-label use of a drug, biological product or device as a treatment.

C. Notwithstanding any other law, an official, employee or agent of this state may not enforce or apply § 32-1967 [a state law prohibiting "misbranding of a drug or device"] against or otherwise prosecute a pharmaceutical manufacturer or its representative for engaging in truthful promotion of an off-label use of a drug, biological product or device.

D. Notwithstanding any other law, the Arizona state board of pharmacy, the Arizona medical board, the Arizona board of osteopathic examiners in medicine and surgery and the department of health services may not revoke, fail to renew or take any other action against the license of a pharmaceutical manufacturer or its representative, a health care institution or a physician solely for engaging in truthful promotion of an off-label use of a drug, biological product or device.

E. For the purposes of this section: . . . .

3. "Off-label use" means the use of a United States Food and Drug Administration-approved drug, biological product or device in a manner other than the use approved by the United States Food and Drug Administration.

4. "Truthful promotion" means the sharing of information that is not misleading, not contrary to fact, and consistent with generally accepted scientific principles, between pharmaceutical manufacturers and licensed professionals who can prescribe medication within the provider's scope of practice.

Arizona R.S. §32-1997. What purposes does the law serve? Will it be effective? Should the FDA adopt a similar rule?

Problem: Antibiotics

News stories regularly cite the discovery of drug-resistant strains of bacteria. Physicians are advised to avoid inappropriate antibiotic prescribing practices. Education campaigns endeavor to reduce inappropriate prescribing by informing the public about the proper use of antibiotics. Research funding is allocated to the development of new antibiotics. The federal government attempts to foster innovation in the development of new antibiotics by implementing expedited regulatory review, more favorable drug trial pathways, and greater economic benefits for approved antibiotic drugs. Agricultural experts seek new ways to reduce antibiotic use in farming. Despite these initiatives, among many others, "[m]any commentators have emphasized the looming threat of the 'post-antibiotic era,'" Spencer Phillips Hey & Aaron S. Kesselheim, Reprioritizing Research Activity for the Post-Antibiotic Era: Ethical, Legal, and Social Considerations, 47(2) Hastings Center Rep. 16 (March–April 2017). What role can law play in establishing appropriate prescribing practices and in fostering innovation? See Online Symposium, Antibiotic Resistance, 43 J. L. Med. & Ethics 6-78 (2015) (special suppl), along with Emilie Aguirre, Contagion without Relief: Democratic Experimentalism and Regulating the Use of Antibiotics in Food-Producing Animals, 64 UCLA L. Rev. 550 (2017); Christine Ärdal, International Cooperation to Improve Access to and Sustain Effectiveness of Antimicrobials, 387 Lancet 296 (2016); and Carl Nathan & Otto Cars, Antibiotic Resistance—Problems, Progress, and Prospects, 371 N. Eng. J. Med. 1761 (2015).

Problem: Drug Importation

Drugs approved for sale in the United States are often available at lower prices in other countries. Should senior citizens and the chronically ill be able to organize drug shopping trips to Canada and Mexico and to bring drugs back into the United States? What if the bargain hunters can demonstrate that they hold a valid prescription for the drugs and that the drugs have been approved for sale in the United States? Would state legislation authorizing or facilitating the importation be invalid?

The FDA Web site includes a page devoted to consumer protection that includes links to the U.S. Customs and Border Protection restrictions on importation of prescription drugs. See https://www.fda.gov/ForConsumers/ProtectYourself/default.htm. See also United States v. Rx Depot, Inc., 438 F.3d 1052 (10th Cir.

2006) (disgorgement order related to reimportation profits upheld); and 21 U.S.C. §381(d)(1). For commentary on the reimportation issue, see generally Patricia M. Danzon et al., Commercial Importation of Prescription Drugs in the United States: Short-Run Implications, 36 J. Health Pol. Pol'y & L. 295 (2011) (concluding cost savings likely to be small and costs to foreign countries significant); Chang-fa Lo, Potential Conflict Between TRIPS and GATT Concerning Parallel Importation of Drugs and Possible Solution to Prevent Undesirable Market Segmentation, 66 Food & Drug L. J. 73 (2011); Abigail Zuger, Rx: Canadian Drugs, 349 New Eng. J. Med. 2188 (2003); Richard Frank, Prescription Drug Prices, 351 New Eng. J. Med. 1375 (2004); and Kevin Outterson, Pharmaceutical Arbitrage: Balancing Access and Innovation in International Prescription Drug Markets, 5 Yale J. Health Pol'y, L. & Ethics 193 (2005).

Problem: Opioid Epidemic

In September 2017, the CDC reported that "[o]pioid overdose deaths in the United States have been increasing since 1999, initially driven by prescription opioid misuse and more recently by heroin and other illicit opioid use." Julie K. O'Donnell, R. Matthew Gladden & Puja Seth, Trends in Deaths Involving Heroin and Synthetic Opioids Excluding Methadone — United States, 2006-2015, 66 MMWR 897 (2017) (opioid deaths quadrupled from 1999-2015). According to the Report:

> Three interconnected trends drove increases in . . . deaths involving heroin and synthetic for opioids and the United States during 2006–2015: increases in the supply and use of heroin, mixing of fentanyl into the heroin supply, and increases in deaths involving synthetic opioids without heroin. Large increases in the heroin supply coincided with increases in deaths involving heroin across all U.S. Census regions, with the largest increases in the Northeast and Midwest. In 2016, many state and local law enforcement agencies in these regions reported that heroin could be easily obtained in their communities and was the top drug threat. The increasing availability of heroin comes at a time when an estimated 2 million persons reported a substance use disorder involving misuse of prescription opioids and nearly 600,000 reported a substance use disorder involving heroin in 2015.

Id. at 900. In a response to an interim report from the President's Commission on Combatting Drug Addiction and the Opioid Crisis, President Trump announced his intention to designate the opioid epidemic a "national emergency." See Lawrence O. Gostin, James G. Hodge & Sarah A. Noe, Reframing the Opioid Epidemic as a National Emergency, 318 JAMA 1539 (2017). As Professor Gostin and his co-authors note, the designation would be consistent with "expanding conceptions of public health emergencies" and would "mobilize[ ] powers and resources that are either currently unavailable or mired in legal obstacles." Id. at 1539-1540 (noting potential benefits along with concerns about "potential for more punitive responses focused on incarnation. . . . or paternalistic interventions that deny rights.")

There are a wide range of proposals targeting opioid addiction at the federal and state levels. Consider the problem of opioid abuse in your community or state. Are there ways in which the law assists or hinders efforts to address the problem?

What legal reforms would you propose? Would you support initiatives allowing communities to open supervised injection sites? See Sarah E. Wakeman, Another Senseless Death — The Case for Supervised Injection Facilities, 376 N. Eng. J. Med. 1011 (2017). Should prescription drug monitoring programs be standardized or supplemented by a national prescription drug monitoring program? See Corey S. Davis, Jill E. Johnston & Matthew W. Pierce, Overdose Epidemic, Prescription Monitoring Programs, and Public Health: A Review of State Laws, 105 Amer. J. Public Health e9 (2015); and Joanna Shepherd, Combating the Prescription Painkiller Epidemic: A National Prescription Drug Reporting Program, 40 Amer. J. L. & Med. 85 (2014). For a different, litigation-based approach to the issues, see John Schwartz, Chicago and 2 California Counties Sue Over Marketing of Painkillers, N.Y. Times, Aug. 24, 2014; and City of Chicago v. Purdue Pharma L.P., 211 F. Supp.3d 1058 (N. D. Ill. 2016) (disposing of some claims).

3. Clashes in Values and Jurisdictional Boundaries: Public Health Regulation and the Crushing Obesity Epidemic

■PELMAN v. McDONALD'S CORPORATION
396 F.3d 508 (2d Cir. 2005)

RAKOFF, District Judge.

In this diversity action, plaintiffs Ashley Pelman and Jazlen Bradley . . . appeal from the dismissal, pursuant to Rule 12(b)(6), Fed.R.Civ.P., of Counts I-III of their amended complaint. Each of the these counts purports to allege, on behalf of a putative class of consumers, that defendant McDonald's Corporation violated . . . the New York Consumer Protection Act, during the years 1987 through 2002. Specifically, Count I alleges that the combined effect of McDonald's various promotional representations during this period was to create the false impression that its food products were nutritionally beneficial and part of a healthy lifestyle if consumed daily. Count II alleges that McDonald's failed adequately to disclose that its use of certain additives and the manner of its food processing rendered certain of its foods substantially less healthy than represented. Count III alleges that McDonald's deceptively represented that it would provide nutritional information to its New York customers when in reality such information was not readily available at a significant number of McDonald's outlets in New York visited by the plaintiffs and others. The amended complaint further alleges that as a result of these deceptive practices, plaintiffs, who ate at McDonald's three to five times a week throughout the years in question, were "led to believe[ ] that [McDonald's] foods were healthy and wholesome, not as detrimental to their health as medical and scientific studies have shown, . . . [and] of a beneficial nutritional value," and that they "would not have purchased and/or consumed the Defendant's aforementioned products, in their entire[t]y, or on such frequency but for the aforementioned alleged representations and campaigns." Finally, the amended complaint alleges that, as a result, plaintiffs have developed "obesity, diabetes, coronary heart disease, high blood pressure, elevated cholesterol intake, related cancers, and/or other detrimental and adverse health effects. . . ."

What is missing from the amended complaint, however, is any express allegation that any plaintiff specifically relied to his/her detriment on any particular representation made in any particular McDonald's advertisement or promotional material. The district court concluded that, with one exception, the absence of such a particularized allegation of reliance warranted dismissal of the . . . false advertising [claims]. As to the exception—involving McDonald's representations that its French fries and hash browns are made with 100% vegetable oil and/or are cholesterol-free—the district court found that, while the amended complaint might be read to allege implicit reliance by plaintiffs on such representations, the representations themselves were objectively nonmisleading. . . .

Plaintiffs' appellate brief . . . challenge[s] the district court's dismissal of the claims under §349 of the New York General Business Law, which makes unlawful "[d]eceptive acts or practices in the conduct of any business, trade or commerce or in the furnishing of any service in this state." Unlike a [false advertising claim], a private action brought under §349 does not require proof of actual reliance. Additionally, . . . §349 extends well beyond common-law fraud to cover a broad range of deceptive practices . . . [and] does not require proof of the same essential elements (such as reliance) as common-law fraud. . . . [T]he district court nonetheless dismissed the claims under §349 because it concluded that "[p]laintiffs have failed, however, to draw an adequate causal connection between their consumption of McDonald's food and their alleged injuries." Thus, the district court found it fatal that the complaint did not answer such questions as:

> What else did the plaintiffs eat? How much did they exercise? Is there a family history of the diseases which are alleged to have been caused by McDonald's products? Without this additional information, McDonald's does not have sufficient information to determine if its foods are the cause of plaintiffs' obesity, or if instead McDonald's foods are only a contributing factor.

This, however, is the sort of information that is appropriately the subject of discovery, rather than what is required to satisfy the limited pleading requirements of Rule 8(a), Fed.R.Civ.P. . . . So far as the §349 claims are concerned, the amended complaint more than meets the requirements of Rule 8(a). Accordingly, the district court's dismissal of those portions of Counts I-III of the amended complaint as alleged violations of §349 is VACATED, and the case is REMANDED for further proceedings consistent with this opinion. [In 2010, the district court refused to certify these claims as a class action.]

■NUTRITIONAL LABELING IN RESTAURANTS
21 U.S.C. §343

A food shall be deemed to be misbranded—[unless it meets the following requirements governing nutritional information] . . .

* * *

(H) Restaurants, retail food establishments, and vending machines
    (i) General requirements for restaurants and similar retail food establishments

Except for food described in subclause (vii), in the case of food that is a standard menu item that is offered for sale in a restaurant or similar retail food establishment that is part of a chain with 20 or more locations doing business under the same name (regardless of the type of ownership of the locations) and offering for sale substantially the same menu items, the restaurant or similar retail food establishment shall disclose the information described in subclauses (ii) and (iii).

(ii) Information required to be disclosed by restaurants and retail food establishments

Except as provided in subclause (vii), the restaurant or similar retail food establishment shall disclose in a clear and conspicuous manner—

(I)(aa) in a nutrient content disclosure statement adjacent to the name of the standard menu item, so as to be clearly associated with the standard menu item, on the menu listing the item for sale, the number of calories contained in the standard menu item, as usually prepared and offered for sale; and

(bb) a succinct statement concerning suggested daily caloric intake, as specified by the Secretary by regulation and posted prominently on the menu and designed to enable the public to understand, in the context of a total daily diet, the significance of the caloric information that is provided on the menu;

(II)(aa) in a nutrient content disclosure statement adjacent to the name of the standard menu item, so as to be clearly associated with the standard menu item, on the menu board, including a drive-through menu board, the number of calories contained in the standard menu item, as usually prepared and offered for sale; and

(bb) a succinct statement concerning suggested daily caloric intake, as specified by the Secretary by regulation and posted prominently on the menu board, designed to enable the public to understand, in the context of a total daily diet, the significance of the nutrition information that is provided on the menu board;

(III) in a written form, available on the premises of the restaurant or similar retail establishment and to the consumer upon request, the nutrition information required under clauses (C) and (D) of subparagraph (1); and

(IV) on the menu or menu board, a prominent, clear, and conspicuous statement regarding the availability of the information described in item (III). . . .

(vii) Nonapplicability to certain food

(I) In general

Subclauses (i) through (vi) do not apply to—

(aa) items that are not listed on a menu or menu board (such as condiments and other items placed on the table or counter for general use);

(bb) daily specials, temporary menu items appearing on the menu for less than 60 days per calendar year, or custom orders; or

(cc) such other food that is part of a customary market test appearing on the menu for less than 90 days, under terms and conditions established by the Secretary. . . .

Notes: Public Health Law and Obesity

1. *The Obesity "Epidemic."* News stories regularly decry the "epidemic" of obesity in the United States and other developed countries. Americans are allegedly

"addicted" to high-fat, high-calorie, processed foods that offer "empty calories" rather than balanced nutritional value. Food companies, restaurants, and TV cooking shows promote eating too many calories even as modern conveniences and sedentary pursuits such as Internet surfing have reduced our caloric needs. Advertisements for high-calorie foods and beverages, sometimes served in endless buffets, compete with media portrayals of the very thin and advertisements from companies selling amazing weight-loss solutions. Numerous studies have documented the increasing prevalence of obesity in children and adults. More than two-thirds of adult Americans are either overweight or obese. See AP, US Obesity Problem is Not Budging, New Data Shows, N.Y. Times, Oct. 13, 2017 (about 40 percent of adults and 18.5 percent of children are obese); Committee on an Evidence Framework for Obesity Prevention Decision Making, Institute of Medicine, Bridging the Evidence Gap in Obesity Prevention: A Framework to Inform Decision Making (2010).

While obesity is sometimes viewed as a health issue on its own, public health advocates typically target obesity and overweight because of associated negative health conditions. Obesity is correlated with specific diseases and conditions such as diabetes and cardiovascular disease. The GBD 2015 Obesity Collaborators, Health Effects of Overweight and Obesity in 195 Countries over 25 Years, 377 N. Eng. J. Med. 13 (2017) (noting rapid increase in the prevalence and disease burden of elevated body mass index (BMI)); Committee on Progress in Preventing Childhood Obesity, Institute of Medicine, Progress in Preventing Childhood Obesity: How Do We Measure Up? (2007). Some types of food ingredients, such as "trans fats," carry specific risks. Kelly D. Brownell & Jennifer Pomeranz, The Trans-Fat Ban—Food Regulation and Long Term Health, 370 N. Eng. J. Med. 1773 (2014) (discussing implications of FDA proposal to find trans-fats no longer "generally recognized as safe" (GRAS) for use in food); FDA, Final Determination Regarding Partially Hydrogenated Oils, 80 Fed. Reg. 34650 (2015).

The obesity debate has a strong philosophical and political overlay: Overweight individuals are sometimes portrayed as morally blameworthy by the public while efforts to prohibit or restrict unhealthy foods or to hold manufacturers or distributors of food products legally responsible are dismissed as the intrusion of the "nanny state" (or paternalism) into unfettered consumer choice. See Rogan Kersh, The Politics of Obesity, 87 Milbank Q. 295 (2009). Critics of the medicalization—and legalization—of food and weight target a range of concerns. See W.A. Bogart, Law as a Tool in "The War on Obesity": Useful Interventions, Maybe, But, First, What's the Problem?, 41 J. L. Med. & Ethics 28 (2013) (offering critical perspective that includes the risk that anti-obesity initiatives will reinforce stigma and discrimination); Michael Gard & Jan Wright eds., The Obesity Epidemic: Science, Morality and Ideology (2005).

2. *The Role of Public Health Law: Policy Options.* What should be the role of law and of public health law in particular in combating the "epidemic" of obesity? For some, the "epidemic" is at least to some extent the product of individual decision-making about food consumption and exercise. Yet consumer choice occurs within a framework of complex environmental, economic, and market forces. See, e.g., National Academies of Sciences, Engineering, and Medicine, Driving Action and Progress on Obesity Prevention and Treatment (2017) (reviewing trends and assessing initiatives). Virtually every level of government could potentially be involved in public health initiatives related to obesity and many, if not most, of the potential

initiatives have at least some legal component. Julie Ralston Aoki, Manel Kappagoda & Seth E. Mermin, Beyond the Code Book: Legal Tools for Accelerating Progress in Obesity Prevention, 41 J. L. Med. & Ethics 61 (2013) (noting that "[e]ach of the five main goals set out in" an influential Institute of Medicine report on obesity "includes recommended strategies and actions that raise questions of law and legal authority.")

Professors Gostin & Wiley have described public health strategies designed to address noncommunicable diseases, such as measures to reduce obesity, in far reaching and comprehensive terms:

> Drawing on the ecological model, advocates demand legal interventions aimed at altering the messaging environment (disclosure requirements and advertising restrictions); the retail environment (taxes, minimum prices, subsidies, and licensing restrictions); and the built environment (public spending, development, and zoning). All of these have an effect on the social environment (social norms about physical activity and consumption).

Public Health Law, at 442. Thus, governmental policies can affect access to exercise in areas ranging from the tax treatment of gym fees, to the level of physical activity required in schools, to requirements for community sidewalks and parks. The foods available for consumer choice could be directly regulated to reduce exposure to substances like trans fats or indirectly regulated through farm subsidies that reduce the costs of healthy foods or tax policies increasing the costs of unhealthy foods, mirroring the familiar taxes on tobacco and alcohol. The decisionmaking environment for consumer choice could be influenced by requiring disclosure of the nutritional value of different types of food, such as in the restaurant nutritional labeling provisions found above, which were incorporated into the ACA health reform legislation. What is the proper balance among (1) regulations designed to ensure that consumers have the information to make good food choices; (2) restrictive regulations diminishing access to certain types of foods; and (3) regulations designed to enhance opportunities for exercise? Is there any role for tort law claims as suggested by the *Pelman* litigation, above? Melissa Mortazavi, Tort as Democracy: Lessons from the Food Wars, 57 Ariz. L. Rev. 929 (2015) (arguing for symbolic impact of tort litigation).

3. *Soda Taxes.* Some measures adopted to address other behaviorally related health threats are also being considered in the fight against obesity. "Soda tax" proposals—based on the "sin taxes" applied to cigarettes and alcohol—are examples of this policy transference. Proponents of soda taxes argue that increasing the cost of these beverages will decrease consumption. The tax may also be justified as a means of generating revenue for public initiatives or to offset the health care costs associated with obesity or diabetes. Is the analogy between tobacco and sugar appropriate? Lawrence O. Gostin, 2016: The Year of the Soda Tax, 95 Milbank Q. 19 (2017) (summarizing initiatives and evidence of impact); Jennifer Falbe et al., Impact of Berkeley Excise Tax on Sugar-Sweetened Beverage Consumption, 106 Amer. J. Pub. Health 1865 (2016) (decreased consumption associated with implementation of $ 0.01/oz. tax, which may also have affected social acceptability of affected beverages). Critics of soda taxes note the relative lack of data on impact, the regressive nature of the tax (which disproportionately affects lower-income households), and

the likelihood that tax revenue will be used to support non-health-related initiatives. See, e.g., AP, County Officials Vote to Repeal Chicago-Area Soda Tax, N.Y. Times, Oct. 11, 2017 ($0.01/oz. tax repealed after two months due to litigation, threats from state about potential cuts to food stamp benefits, and complaints from store owners and consumers; $200 million impact on City budget).

4. The Impact of Nutritional Information. Public health law initiatives, like other forms of intervention designed to improve health, should be evaluated for effectiveness. What is the impact of nutritional labeling of restaurant food? Consumers might use the posted information to choose less caloric options and restaurants might have a clearer incentive to shift to lower calorie options. The preliminary evidence on the impact of restaurant labeling on consumer behavior does not support the effectiveness of this approach. T. M. Cantu-Jungles et al., A Meta-Analysis to Determine Impact of Restaurant Menu Labeling on Calories and Nutrients, 9 Nutrients (2017) (reviewing studies; menu labeling in laboratory settings reduces calorie ordered/consumed but menu labeling away-from-home did not change behavior); and Michael W. Long, Systematic Review and Meta-Analysis of the Impact of Restaurant Menu Calorie Labeling, 105 Am. J. Public Health e11 (2015) (reviewing studies; current evidence does not support a significant impact on calorie consumption). How should public health officials, policymakers, and government officials respond to these studies?

5. Regulatory Authority and Jurisdictional Conflicts. The policy options for addressing obesity raise significant jurisdictional issues. International efforts have been limited, with greater focus on providing access to food for those facing malnutrition than in addressing obesity. But see The GBD 2015 Obesity Collaborators, supra; and Joanne Stettner, International Obesity: Legal Issues, 24 Emory Int'l L. Rev. 210 (2010) (discussing WHO's global obesity strategy and initiatives related to food marketing to children).

What issues govern the level of government involved in anti-obesity policies? One important precondition to action is the existence of legislative or regulatory authority. The issue became particularly salient when New York City, under the leadership of then-Mayor Bloomberg, attempted to cap the size of containers used in the sale of sugar-sweetened beverages. The New York City Board of Health promulgated the Sugary Drinks Portion Cap Rule after vigorous public comment and debate. The measure was challenged and found to constitute lawmaking outside the regulatory authority of the Board. New York Statewide Coalition of Hispanic Chambers of Commerce v. N.Y. City Dept. of Health and Mental Hygiene, 16 N.E.3d 538 (N.Y. 2014).

Assuming that more than one level of government has the appropriate authority, what factors influence the public health law strategy? Local initiatives may be easier to "pass" and can be tailored to local values and preferences but the result can be a patchwork of regulation that may be difficult for companies to negotiate while also leaving significant portions of the public in jurisdictions with no legislation. State or national policies can be more comprehensive but may offer lower protections. State or national preemption can reduce the flexibility of localities to adopt more stringent regulations. Melissa M. Card, Local and State Governments Are Taking the Stage When It Is FDA's Curtain Call, 12 J. Food L. & Pol'y 214 (2016) (exploring impact of federal preemption); James G. Hodge, Jr. et al., Public Health "Preemption Plus," 45 J. L. Med. & Ethics 156 (2017) (noting preemption tied to supplemental policies with negative impact on localities); Jennifer L. Pomeranz & Mark Perschuk, State Preemption: A Significant and Quiet Threat to Public Health in the United States, 107 Amer. J. Pub. Health 900 (2017) (analyzing state preemption of local laws involving nutrition and other issues).

These jurisdictional issues have been particularly important for the regulation of foods and labeling requirements. The nutritional labeling provisions in the Affordable Care Act, found below, were accompanied by a strong preemption provision:

§343-1. National uniform nutrition labeling

(a) Except as provided in subsection (b) of this section, no State or political subdivision of a State may directly or indirectly establish under any authority or continue in effect as to any food in interstate commerce—...

(4) any requirement for nutrition labeling of food that is not identical to the requirement of section 343(q) of this title, except that this paragraph does not apply to food that is offered for sale in a restaurant or similar retail food establishment that is not part of a chain with 20 or more locations doing business under the same name (regardless of the type of ownership of the locations) and offering for sale substantially the same menu items unless such restaurant or similar retail food establishment complies with the voluntary provision of nutrition information requirements under section 343(q)(5)(H) (ix) of this title. . . .

(b) Upon petition of a State or a political subdivision of a State, the Secretary may exempt from subsection (a) of this section, under such conditions as may be prescribed by regulation, any State or local requirement that—

(1) would not cause any food to be in violation of any applicable requirement under Federal law,

(2) would not unduly burden interstate commerce, and

(3) is designed to address a particular need for information which need is not met by the requirements of the sections referred to in subsection (a) of this section.

Would the *Pelman* litigation survive a preemption challenge? What better explains federal adoption of the restaurant nutritional labeling rules: a desire to bring the power of federal regulation to an important problem or the need to protect the food industry from uneven and uncertain regulation and the risk of tort liability at the state and local level? Could labeling and other messaging requirements—such as those requiring that posted signs advertising sugar-sweetened beverages include health warnings—violate the First Amendment's protection of commercial speech? See American Beverage Association v. City and County of San Francisco, 871 F.3d 884 (2017) (First Amendment challenge to municipal ordinance requiring health warnings has sufficient chance of success on the merits to support issuance of a preliminary injunction).

6. *Additional Resources.* For more information on **obesity** and the **nanny state/ paternalism debate** (note 1), see CDC, Overweight and Obesity, available at www. cdc.gov and David Adam Friedman, Public Health Regulation and the Limits of Paternalism, 46 Conn. L. Rev. 1687-1770 along with Commentaries, 46 Conn. L. Rev. 1771-1936). There are a great number of commentaries and articles on **policy options** (note 2). For a sampling, see Deborah L. Rhode, Obesity and Public Policy: A Roadmap for Reform, 22 Va. J. Soc. Pol'y & L. 492 (2015); Special Issue on Physical Activity, 380 Lancet 188-196, 209-212, 219-229, 247-305 (2012); Sympo-

sium, Food and Health, 34 Health Affairs 1807-2001 (2015); Symposium, The Iron Triangle of Food Policy, 41 Amer. J. L. & Med. 223-504 (2015); Symposium, Weight of the Nation, 41 J. L. M. & Ethics 5-67 (2013); Symposium, Proceedings of the National Summit on Legal Preparedness for Obesity Prevention and Control, 37 J. L. Med. & Ethics 9-129 (2009) (special supp.). For more information and commentaries on **regulatory authority and jurisdictional conflicts** (note 5) see, FDA, Menu and Vending Machines Labeling Requirements, available at www.fda.gov/ (linking to final regulations and industry guidance); Jennifer L. Pomeranz & Sabrina Adler, Defining Commercial Speech in the Context of Food Marketing, 43 J. L. Med. & Ethics 40 (2015) (suppl); Belinda Reeve et al., State and Municipal Innovations in Obesity Policy, 105 Amer. J. Pub. Health 442 (2015); Joanna K. Sax & Neal Doran, Food Labeling and Consumer Associations with Health, Safety and Environment, 44 J. L. Med. & Ethics 630 (2016).

Problem: Helmets and the Law

Common sense suggests, and epidemiological data confirm, that motorcycle helmets can reduce dramatically the risk of injury or death associated with the use of motorcycles. Yet public debate about state helmet laws demonstrates that the reduction of deaths or injuries is not always sufficient to justify restrictions on individual liberty. What arguments can you marshal favoring or opposing the imposition of a mandatory helmet law? Are the issues similar for bicycle helmets? Should use of bicycle helmets be made mandatory? For all or just for minors? Would mandating helmet use protect public health by preventing head injuries or threaten public health by discouraging use of bicycles? Should it matter whether the law is designed to protect the safety of the rider or to reduce the costs of injuries in the health care system? Should this be a matter for state or federal lawmakers? What constitutional analysis would you apply to a law requiring cyclists of various types to wear helmets?

For excellent surveys of the issues related to motorcycles, see Alexander Busko, Zachary Hubbard & Tanya Zakrison, Motorcycle-Helmet Laws and Public Health, 376 N. Eng. J. Med. 1208 (2017); CDC, Helmet Use Among Motorcyclists Who Died in Crashes and Economic Cost Savings Associated with State Motorcycle Helmet Laws—United States, 2008-2010, 61 MMWR 425 (2012) ("Research has shown that when a state repeals its helmet law or opts for less restrictive requirements, helmet use decreases and motorcycle-related deaths, injuries, and costs increase"). One of the major criticisms of motorcycle helmet regulation is that it is "paternalistic." Cf. Marian Moser Jones & Ronald Bayer, Paternalism and Its Discontents: Motorcycle Helmet Laws, Libertarian Values, and Public Health, 97 Am. J. Public Health 208 (2007); R. George Wright, Legal Paternalism and the Eclipse of Principle, 71 U. Miami L. Rev. 194 (2016). What does "paternalism" mean in the context of law and could this be framed as a legal objection? What are the limits of a person's ability to accept risk of harm elsewhere in the law? See also Constantino v. Michigan Department of State Police, 794 F. Supp. 2d 773 (W.D. Mich. May 18, 2011) (upholding enforcement of state motorcycle helmet law); United States v. Bohn, 622 F.3d 1129 (9th Cir. 2010) (National Park Service had authority to require use of helmets).

For issues related to bicycle helmets, see Christopher S. Carpenter & Mark Stehr, Intended and Unintended Consequences of Youth Bicycle Helmet Laws, 54 J. L. & Econ. 305 (2011) (laws increase helmet use but decrease use of bicycles); Ken McLeod, Bicycle Laws in the United States—Past, Present, and Future, 42 Fordham Urb. L. J. 869 (2015); Jake Olivier & Igor Radun, Bicycle Helmet Effectiveness Is Not Overstated, 18 Traffic Inj. Prev. 755 (2017) (best available evidence indicates that helmet use is effective in reducing cycling head injury). See also State v. Portillo, 314 S.W.3d 210 (Tex. App.—El Paso 2010) (upholding city bicycle helmet ordinance against constitutional attack in state that allows motorcyclists not to wear helmets in some circumstances).

E. CONCLUSION

This chapter is a capstone in our focus on bioethical aspects of the treatment relationship. As you conclude this section, consider whether the rules developed in Chapters 5–8 consistently deal with the conflict between personal freedom and social interests. You may conclude that the chapters represent a progression of sorts, in which individuals' interests are measured against successively "weightier" social interests. In Chapter 5, the primary state interest is simply society's interest in preserving the life of the individual patient. Chapter 6 begins to look at situations where lives other than the patient's are at stake. In Chapter 7, the stakes are raised even higher on both sides of the conflict. On one side there is the notion that the individual herself owes an obligation of protection for the potential life of her fetus, and on the other side we recognize special constitutional protection for reproductive freedom. In this chapter, the state asserts the broadest interest, one that attempts to protect the health of the community as a whole. Do you think there is a matching pattern in the courts' rulings across these chapters? In other words, do individuals have consistently less freedom as the state's interests become progressively stronger?

Are the cases in this chapter united by any other common themes? Public health cases are often viewed in isolated groupings, identified by the specific public health strategy employed rather than by broader themes. Section C considered a wide range of state interventions into the treatment relationship. Does grouping these interventions together bring any clarification to your understanding of the law?

Public health challenges continue to elicit new strategies and new legal challenges to those strategies. These challenges may intensify in the future. Some scientists predict widespread outbreaks of highly lethal, antibiotic-resistant infections similar to the plagues that ravaged Europe centuries earlier. If this were to occur, would you predict greater or lesser recognition of personal liberty interests in public health matters?

This chapter also provides a useful jumping-off point for Chapter 9's discussion of health care expenditures and funding, which focuses largely on payment for individual medical care by private and public health insurance. Professor Gostin and his colleagues have observed:

> Health promotion and disease prevention have a far greater impact on health than clinical services, in part because inadequate access to biomedical intervention

is not the primary cause of premature morbidity and mortality. Evidence indicates that preventative interventions targeting behavior, the environment, and socioeconomic factors (including education, economic security, social support, and community safety) account for approximately 80% of the reduction in morbidity and mortality, whereas clinical care only accounts for 20%. This is because the burden of disease results from a combination of individual behavioral factors (e.g., smoking, diet, physical activity, and sexual behavior), the environment in which people live (e.g., environmental risk factors such as pollution, toxic chemical exposure, and contaminated food), and the social determinants of health (e.g., education, income, and housing). . . .

Despite the value of health promotion and disease prevention in improving the public's health, they have limited political and financial support. Less than 5% of health spending is devoted to health promotion and disease prevention, even though [more than half of all deaths in the United States are from "preventable conditions"].

Lawrence O. Gostin et al., Restoring Health to Health Reform: Integrating Medicine and Public Health to Advance the Population's Well-Being, 159 U. Pa. L. Rev. 1777, 1792, 1795-1796 (2011). See also David Hemenway, Why Don't We Spend Enough on Public Health?, 362 New Eng. J. Med. 1657 (2010). Gostin and his colleagues argue that integrating public health promotion for populations with medical care for individuals can reduce costs (by, e.g., lowering the rates for obesity and its related health conditions) and improve outcomes (through, e.g., reducing hospital-acquired infections). See also Glen P. Mays & Sharla A. Smith, Evidence Links Increases in Public Health Spending to Declines in Preventable Deaths, 30 Health Aff. 1585 (2011). What is the proper balance between expenditures on public health—investments in the health of populations—as opposed to expenditures on health care for individuals?

PART III

INSTITUTIONS, PROVIDERS, AND THE STATE

The organization of this book can be thought of in terms of concentric rings. We began at the center with the core treatment relationship between physician and patient. We then considered increasingly compelling external interests that might affect individual medical decisions. We continue that progression in this last part of the book by looking at the financial and institutional arrangements that surround the treatment relationship. Chapter 9 explores who pays for medical care, and under what terms. Chapter 10 explains the structure of medical facilities and how they relate to member physicians and to each other. Chapter 10 also examines the most complex layer in this set of rings: the emerging interconnections among insurers, facilities, and physicians as the marketplace for health care delivery undergoes rapid and fundamental transformation.

The themes in this part of the book do not appear as focused and tidy as in the earlier parts, for there are several fascinating threads that interweave to make a complex and colorful tapestry. The dominant theme is quite apparent, however: As our society struggles to solve the problems that confront the health care financing and delivery system, should we rely primarily on a market model that treats medicine as a consumer good, or on a social model that looks to regulatory governmental intervention to correct the perceived failures of the marketplace?

9

Health Care Financing and Reform

Our fragmented system of paying for health care makes it difficult to cover comprehensively all of the complex legal regimes created by the many different sources of insurance. Rather than dividing the world of insurance into public vs. private, and conventional vs. managed care, we have chosen to organize this chapter around the generic issues that affect all sources of insurance: who is eligible, what services are covered, how is insurance regulated, how are disputes resolved, and how are doctors and hospitals paid? Along the way, it will be necessary, however, to learn whether answers to these questions differ according to the particular source of insurance. Therefore, we begin with a description of the entire, complex financing system.

A. SOURCES OF HEALTH INSURANCE

1. The Right to Health Care

■UNCOMPENSATED HOSPITAL CARE: RIGHTS AND RESPONSIBILITIES*
Uwe Reinhardt

While honest economists long ago despaired of developing an overarching theory of distributive justice, political philosophers continue to hammer away at

---

* This reading is excerpted from the first chapter of a book by this title edited by F. Sloan, J. Blumstein & J. Perrin (1986). Reprinted with permission of Johns Hopkins University Press. The author was a well-known health economist at Princeton (and his first name is pronounced "OO-vay").

the problem. The several distinct theories of distributive justice emerging from these efforts are elegant in their internal logic, and eminently stimulating even to a skeptic. In the end, however, that literature fails as a guide towards a universally acceptable principle of justice. On the contrary, it persuades one that there cannot possibly be such a principle. For however tight the internal logic of any particular philosopher's theory of justice may be, that logic is ultimately anchored on some overarching value for which that author claims primacy on purely subjective grounds. Collectively, the political philosophers writing on the subject teach us that justice, like beauty, rests in the eye of the beholder.

Libertarian philosophers, for example, elevate individual liberty to the status of the single, overriding social value to which all other values are subordinate, and which can never justly be traded off against any subordinate value. Implicit in the libertarian's concept of "liberty" is the tenet that the individual is entitled to dispose of his or her possessions as he or she sees fit. Extreme versions of the theory—articulated, for example, in Robert Nozick's Anarchy, State, and Utopia (1974)—hold that any governmental infringement on this presumed property right is ipso facto unjust. Thus, to tax one person's wealth in order to finance another person's health care is unjust, as is a policy that compels physicians or privately owned facilities to render health care to designated individuals. In the libertarian's credo, it is the health care provider's right to determine whom to serve and whom not to serve, and also what price to exact for health services rendered. Health care providers must find this a comforting credo.

Diametrically opposed to the libertarian credo are the various theories of distributive justice espoused by egalitarian philosophers. Egalitarian philosophers elevate "equal respect for all individuals" or "equality of opportunity" to the overriding value of a just society to which all other values—among them individual liberty—are deemed subordinate. Equality of opportunity, argue these philosophers, requires as a minimum that all members of society have equal access to certain basic commodities, access to which determines an individual's range of opportunities and measure of self-respect. Health care, along with food, shelter, and education, is among these basic commodities.

The entitlements implicit in the egalitarian tenet seem rather open-ended, and as recent history in this country has shown, they certainly are. Egalitarians, however, do not glibly ignore resource constraints. They merely argue that, in the face of such constraints, need, rather than ability to pay, should be the basis for rationing. Clearly, this theory of justice implies redistribution of the sort libertarians consider coercive and hence unjust.

One's own predilections aside, it is certainly no more logically compelling to let equal opportunity triumph completely over individual liberty than it is to do the reverse. Indeed, outside the ivory tower, any prevailing sense of justice is apt to be an amalgam in which each of the pure theories is somewhat compromised. While purist philosophers may deplore such compromises, policymakers must not only countenance them but actively lead in forging the amalgam.

A remarkable and unique feature of American health policy has been its attempt to accommodate simultaneously both the egalitarian and the libertarian theories of justice in their extreme purity. No other nation in the industrialized West has been quite so bold, or quite so naive, as to attempt that feat. Ironically, no other nation finds itself, in the mid-1980s, with the unsolved problem of uncompensated indigent care at the center stage of its health policy debate. There appears to be a causal link between schizoid thinking on the ethical plane and impotence at the level of policy.

Throughout the postwar period, and possibly even earlier, our policies on the distribution of health care have been firmly rooted in the egalitarian credo: It has been a widely shared notion that health care in the United States should be distributed on the basis of medical need rather than ability to pay. Furthermore, with appeal to the overarching principle of "equal respect for all individuals," it has generally been held (at least in public debate) that the nation should aim for equality in the process of—that there should be equity in the so-called amenities accompanying the delivery of health care, including the travel and wait time during access and the degree of free choice among providers. Politicians of all ideological stripes have supported these tenets (at least none has openly questioned them), and providers have endorsed them as well.

Cynics may argue that no one seriously entertained these lofty maxims and that they were recited by politicians mainly for public consumption. Some glaring remaining inequalities in access to health care may be cited to buttress that case. But a fair reading of health legislation during the 1960s and 1970s should persuade even a skeptic that public policy in those years was motivated by a genuine desire to move the country closer to an egalitarian distribution of health care. By the end of the 1970s, few policy analysts and even fewer public officials still questioned the proposition that access to all medically necessary and technically feasible health care on equal (process) terms is one of an American citizen's basic rights.

The pursuit of an egalitarian health care system is, of course, not a uniquely American phenomenon. Most other industrialized nations have shared that goal, and some of them seem to have been rather more successful than have we in approaching it. A uniquely American phenomenon, however, has been the endeavor to extract an egalitarian distribution of health care from a delivery system still firmly grounded in libertarian principles.

To be sure, our health care delivery system does not measure up in all respects to a libertarian's dream. Some individual liberties are being compromised by government for the sake of quality control, and even the staunchest defenders of the libertarian credo, America's physicians, have from time to time enlisted the government's coercive power to protect their economic turf through occupational licensing. We share such infringements with other modern societies. But in no other modern society espousing egalitarian principles for the distribution of health care have physicians and hospitals been quite so free as they have in the United States to organize their facilities as they see fit, to practice medicine as they see fit, and to price their services as they see fit. In these realms, libertarian principles have prevailed, and every legislative attempt to compromise them for the sake of cost control or greater equity in distribution has, until very recently, been beaten back successfully, with overt appeals to the libertarian credo. "If you want an egalitarian distribution of health care," providers have said, "we endorse it heartily, and we shall do our best to bring it about—but for a fee, and we want that fee to be reasonable as we define that term."

Libertarian and egalitarian purists wrestle with one another in any democratic society. The politician's task, as noted earlier, is to fashion from this struggle a sustainable social compromise. It is on that count that American health policy has performed poorly relative to other democracies. For, in seeking to cater to both extremes among notions of distributive justice, American policymakers have bestowed upon the nation a maze of public health programs that make a Rube Goldberg contraption appear streamlined by comparison.

There has been extraordinarily generous public health insurance coverage for some services and for some individuals—replete with completely free choice of providers by patients and with virtually open-ended reimbursement formulas for providers, . . . entitlements that have, on occasion, bordered on handing providers the key to the public treasury. . . . Yet, attempts to curb that flow of public funds into private treasuries have always been decried and, until very recently, rejected as an intolerable, regulatory infringement on private liberties.

Congressional respect for this peculiar conception of "liberty" naturally carried the danger of turning any federal health program into a fiscal hemorrhage. Too timid to prevent that outcome through controls on providers, our politicians have pursued the next logical policy to contain public health budgets: They simply have left glaring gaps in health insurance coverage, particularly for the near poor and the unemployed (whose health insurance coverage typically ceases with employment). . . . [O]ne would be hard put to identify any other industrialized society today that would still visit upon an unemployed worker's family, already down on its luck in so many material and emotional ways, the added anxiety and potential real hardship of going without health insurance coverage. It happens only in America.

It has become fashionable to attribute our long-standing failures in this area to a streak of meanness in the American character. Having lived both outside and inside this nation, I do not accept that interpretation. The special genius of nations who have long settled these problems lies not in their citizens' superior character, but lies, as noted, in a political process capable of forging a more stable ethical foundation for their health care systems. In all of these nations, the providers of health care enjoy fewer liberties than do their American counterparts. But, in addition, a good many of these countries—for example, the United Kingdom, West Germany, France, Switzerland, and Holland—have been rather more tolerant of some degree of tiering in their health systems than have the champions of egalitarianism in the United States. Perhaps the time has come for Americans, too, to debate more openly—and without the customary rancor and slander—just what are the essential ingredients of a just health care system.

■ THE RIGHT TO A DECENT MINIMUM OF HEALTH CARE*
Tom L. Beauchamp & James F. Childress

The history of the right to health care has been characterized more by political rhetoric than by careful analysis. The primary question has been whether the government should be involved in health care allocation and distribution, rather than leaving these matters to the marketplace. Libertarians insist that all rights to social goods based on enforced beneficence violate the principle of respect for autonomy. Society has often allowed this libertarian-supported rule of ability to pay

---

* This excerpt is from Principles of Biomedical Ethics (4th ed. 1994).

to determine the distribution of health goods and services, but we will argue that this rule should not be allowed to serve as our only principle of distributive justice.

Two main arguments support a right to health care: (1) an argument from collective social protection and (2) an argument from fair opportunity. The first argument focuses on the similarities between health needs and other needs that have conventionally been protected by government. Threats to health are relevantly similar to threats presented by crime, fire, and polluted environments. The latter threats are conventionally resisted by collective actions and resources. . . . If government has an obligation to provide one type of essential service, then it must have an obligation to provide another. . . . However, . . . these public programs pertain to social goods, such as public health, whereas health care is largely a matter of the individual's private good. . . .

A second argument buttresses this first argument by appealing to the fair-opportunity rule. From this perspective, the justice of social institutions is gauged by their tendency to counteract lack of opportunity caused by unpredictable bad luck and misfortune over which the person has no meaningful control. Insofar as injury, disability, or disease creates profoundly significant disadvantages and reduces agents' capacity to function properly, justice is done if societal health care resources are used to counter these morally arbitrary, disadvantaging effects and to restore to persons a fair chance to use their capacities. . . .

This general guideline of fair opportunity suggests a path for giving content to the idea of a decent minimum of health care and for setting priorities in the allocation of resources. . . . The rule of fair opportunity asserts that collective moral obligations exist to provide health care at the level needed for persons to receive as fair a chance in life as possible.

Even if the arguments we have presented for a moral right to health care are rejected on grounds that justice does not support this right, a legal right or entitlement to health care can be supported on a different moral basis such as compassion and beneficence. . . . According to the "enforced beneficence argument," as Allen Buchanan terms it, beneficent citizens who do not believe that the needy have a right to health care would still establish certain health programs for the needy while coercively requiring those with the resources to sustain the programs. . . . If the goals are sufficiently fundamental and important, coercion can be morally justified to fulfil the goals independent of the existence of rights.

A directly related argument from societal beneficence focuses on the expression of social virtue and excellence in public policies, with an emphasis on creating a morally worthy society with which citizens can identify. This communitarian approach concentrates on compassion for victims of the various lotteries of life. Themes from this approach echo in the influential report of the President's Commission for the Study of Ethical Problems in Medicine and Biomedical Research on Securing Access to Health Care (1983): "The depth of a society's concern about health care can be seen as a measure of its sense of solidarity in the face of suffering and death. . . . A society's commitment to health care reflects some of its most basic attitudes about what it means to be a member of the human community."

THE SCOPE OF THE RIGHT TO HEALTH CARE

Apart from the contest between libertarian and nonlibertarian views of justice, an intractable, and ultimately the most important, problem is how to specify the entitlements and limits established by a right to health care. Two broad views have attracted wide contemporary support: a right to equal access to health care and a right to a decent minimum of health care. Both rely on egalitarian premises. The former represents a strong egalitarian perspective of equal access to all bona fide health care resources. The latter incorporates only a weak egalitarian point of view, viz., equal access to fundamental health care resources. . . . The societal obligation can be discharged at various levels, but the decent-minimum approach entails acceptance of [a] two-tiered system of health care: enforced social coverage for basic and catastrophic health needs (tier 1), together with voluntary private coverage for other health needs and desires (tier 2). . . .

Although some parties will be distressed to learn that the standard is "decent" care rather than "optimum" care, only the former can be justified in a socially funded policy. When we later . . . discuss explicit health policies such as the pioneering Oregon health plan, we will see that it is unrealistic to expect a higher level than adequate care. Rationing will also be an essential part of the process. Otherwise priorities cannot be set and maintained.

This proposal has the advantage of holding out the potential for compromise among libertarians, utilitarians, communitarians, and egalitarians, because it incorporates some moral concerns stressed by each of these theories. It guarantees basic health care for all on a premise of equal access, while allowing unequal additional purchase by individual initiative and contract. It mixes private and public forms of distribution, and it affirms collective as well as free-market methods of delivering health care. . . .

Despite these attractions, the decent-minimum proposal has proved difficult to explicate and implement. . . . Those who promote access to a decent minimum or adequate level of care usually do not specify where to set limits on expenditures for health care that confer precise entitlements. . . . [This] raises problems of whether society can fairly, consistently, and unambiguously devise a public policy that recognizes a right to care for primary needs without creating a right to exotic and expensive forms of treatment, such as liver transplants costing over $200,000 for what many deem to be marginal benefits in quality-adjusted life-years. More importantly, the model is purely programmatic until society defines what decent minimum means in operational terms. This task is, we believe, the major problem confronting health policy in the United States today.

Notes: The Right to Health Care

1. *The Right to Health Care.* Consider these additional perspectives on whether there is a moral or social right to health care, and what that right might be:

> There is a moral right to health care, but not of the sort often claimed. It is a right grounded not in purchasing power, merit, or social worth, but in human need. The right to health care finds its rationale in a social concept of the self, in a sense of common humanity, and in a knowledge of common vulnerability to disease and death. The right begins in a recognition that we all fall ill and are susceptible to disability and death. That is our nature and, whatever cultural variations there may be . . . , the root awareness we have of this is not an invention but a discovery. Second, while some illnesses are self-induced diseases generally are not the sort of things

which are distributed by merit. We are all very likely to incur needs for health care for which we are not responsible and which are, in many instances, unforeseeable. Third, health care . . . is effective. Ill health is, in sum, the sort of thing which is universally experienced, but unevenly distributed, over which we have little control or predictive powers and for which there is frequently effective help. A just society is one in which the right to health care is based on the elemental fact of human need. . . . A more complete statement of a right to health care is as follows: *A right to health care based on need means a right to equitable access based on need alone to all effective care society can reasonably afford.* [The author defines "need alone" to mean that a person's entitlement to health care depends on the person's need for care, not the person's race, wealth, status, or other social attributes. Larry R. Churchill, Rationing Health Care in America 90-94 (1987) (emphasis in original).]

[P]ermitting a noticeably lower tier of services for the poor can be based on respect for poor persons' own preferences. If poor, I will rationally and knowledgeably prefer to spend less on preserving health and saving life than if I am well off. Especially in choosing whether to cover and pay for statistically expensive, marginally beneficial procedures, lower income people will properly choose differently. To flatten out these differences through uniform health services *without* changing the basic distribution of income rides roughshod over poor people's preferences for the only lives they have to live. If wider injustice is the problem, it should be attacked by redistributing economic resources generally, not by restricting the choices of the poor when those choices are plausibly rational within their real-life context. [Paul T. Menzel, Some Ethical Costs of Rationing, 20 L. Med. & Health Care 57, 62-63 (1992).]

[T]he United States [has] never really come close to forging the chain of public policies necessary to empower consumers to purchase health care according to their respective needs and circumstances. . . . [W]here other nations have more or less arranged their health care systems so that those who want more or better care than is suitable for the median citizen must pay more for it, the United States has structured things so that lower- and middle-income premium payers bear heavy burdens so that the elite classes can continue to enjoy the style of health care to which they are accustomed. [Clark Havighurst, How the Health Care Revolution Fell Short, 65 Law & Contemp. Probs. 55, 77-78, 89 (Autumn 2002).]

2. *"Safety Net" Care for Uninsured Patients.* In the United States, health insurance is the main vehicle for providing access to affordable medical care, but insurance is not the only way. Lower-income uninsured patients have direct access to care through a number of "safety net" providers — those who, as a last resort, will take all patients regardless of their ability to pay.

Most prominently, hospitals may not refuse at least "stabilizing" treatment to emergency patients (see Chapter 2.A.1). But, beyond that, many hospitals will accept indigent uninsured patients for free or at very steep discounts. These safety net facilities include public hospitals owned by large municipalities or state medical schools, as well as (to varying degrees) nonprofit private hospitals that are tax-exempt. The United States also has a large number of "community health centers" and free clinics that provide primary care services on the safety net basis. These are supported by federal and state funds, or by charity and volunteer workers. Public hospitals and clinics are also operated by the federal government for Native Americans (the Indian Health Service), military personnel, and veterans (VA hospitals).

What are the inadequacies of such safety net systems? First, safety net providers are absent in many locations, and where they do exist, funding is usually deficient.

Several prominent suits attempting to force municipalities to better fund their public hospitals have achieved only moral victories due to procedural obstacles. See, e.g., Evelyn V. v. Kings County Hospital Center, 819 F. Supp. 183 (E.D.N.Y. 1993) (public hospital's level of service may violate state and federal statutes, but federal courts lack authority to order compliance); Tailfeather v. Board of Supervisors, 48 Cal. App. 4th 1223 (Cal. 1996) (county not obligated to adopt formal standards specifying maximum waiting times for indigents' receipt of medical care); Franklin Memorial Hospital v. Harvey, 575 F.3d 121 (1st Cir. 2009) (finding no constitutional infirmity in requiring private hospitals to provide free indigent care). But see Saint Alphonsus Regional Medical Center, Inc. v. Board of County Commissioners of Ada County, 190 P.3d 870 (Idaho 2008) (requiring county to pay some of the $187,000 medical bill incurred by an illegal immigrant). See generally Gary Jones, Regulatory Takings and Emergency Medical Treatment, 47 San Diego L. Rev. 145 (2010).

Second, most of the safety net is focused on primary care and on hospital care for acute or emergency conditions. Often lacking is any well-organized system to provide specialist outpatient services and diagnostic testing. But, where these and other deficiencies do not exist, well-coordinated, comprehensive safety net systems have been shown to provide levels of care similar to that provided by private or public insurance. See Mark A. Hall, Access to Care Provided by Better Safety Net Systems for the Uninsured, 68 Med. Care Res. Rev. 441 (2011). The Veterans Health Administration is sometimes held out as a prime example, although not without some controversy. See Adam Oliver, The Veterans Health Administration: An American Success Story?, 85 Milbank Q. 5 (2007); Phillip Longman, Best Care Anywhere: Why VA Healthcare Is Better Than Yours (2007).

3. *Further Reading*. For discussions of the **moral foundation and meaning of the right to health care**, see Norman Daniels, Just Health Care 27-29 (1985); Richard Epstein, Mortal Peril: Regulating Health Care in America (1997), which contains an extensive argument against entitlements and positive rights to health care; Timothy Jost, Disentitlement: Health Care Entitlements and the Threats That They Face (2003); Christina Ho, Are We Suffering From an Undiagnosed Health Right?, 42 Am. J. L. & Med. 743 (2016); Lindsay Wiley, From Patient Rights to Health Justice: Securing the Public's Interest in Affordable, High-Quality Health Care, 37 Cardozo Law Review 833 (2016); Sidney Watson, Metaphors, Meaning, and Health Reform, 54 St. Louis U. L. J. 1313 (2010); Einer Elhauge, Allocating Health Care Morally, 82 Cal. L. Rev. 1449 (1995); Andre Hampton, Markets, Myths, and a Man on the Moon: Aiding and Abetting America's Flight from Health Insurance, 52 Rutgers L. Rev. 987 (2000); Kevin P. Quinn, Viewing Health Care as a Common Good: Looking Beyond Political Liberalism, 73 S. Cal. L. Rev. 277 (2000); Jennifer P. Ruger, Toward a Theory of a Right to Health, 18 Yale J. L. & Human. 273 (2006); Note, Universal Access to Health Care, 108 Harv. L. Rev. 1323 (1995); Symposium, 36 J. Med. & Phil. 529 (2011); and the excerpt by Ronald Dworkin at page 1124.

For discussions of a **legal right to health care**, generally, see Mila Versteeg & Emily Zackin, American Constitutional Exceptionalism Revisited, 81 U. Chi. L. Rev. 1641 (2014) (observing that "a whopping 72% [of the world's written constitutions] include a right to health care"); Erin C. Fuse Brown. Developing a Durable Right to Health Care, 14 Minn. J. L. Sci. & Tech. 439 (2013); Abigail Moncrieff, The Freedom of Health, 159 Penn. L. Rev. 2209 (2011); Puneet K. Sandhu, A Legal Right to Health Care: What Can the United States Learn from Foreign Models of Health

Rights Jurisprudence?, 95 Cal. L. Rev. 1151 (2007) (arguing, based on experience in other countries, that a legal right to health care is justiciable); Elizabeth Weeks Leonard, State Constitutionalism and Health Care, 12 U. Pa. J. Const. L. 1327 (2010) (noting lack of enforcement of relevant state constitutional provisions); Alan Jenkins & Sabrineh Ardalan, Positive Health: The Human Right to Health Care Under the New York State Constitution, 35 Fordham Urb. L. J. 479 (2008).

For discussions of the **safety net**, see Mark Hall & Sara Rosenbaum eds., The Health Care Safety Net in a Post-Reform World (2012); Mark A. Hall, Approaching Universal Coverage with Better Safety-Net Programs for the Uninsured, 11 Yale J. Health Pol'y, L. & Ethics 9 (2011); Symposium, 31(8) Health Aff. (2012); Symposium, 26(5) Health Aff. (2007); Symposium, 25(3) Health Aff. (2006).

2. Private Health Insurance

■ THE MARKET STRUCTURE OF THE HEALTH INSURANCE INDUSTRY
D. Andrew Austin & Thomas L. Hungerford, *Congressional Research Service, 2009*

The market structure of the modern U.S. health insurance industry not only reflects the complexities and uncertainties of health care, but also its origins in the 1930s and its evolution in succeeding decades. . . . As population shifted from rural agricultural regions to industrialized urban centers, . . . [m]any workers obtained accident or sickness policies through fraternal organizations, labor unions, or private insurers. These policies were usually indemnity plans, that would pay a set cash amount in the event of a serious accident or health emergency. . . .

HOW THE "BLUES" BEGAN

The modern health insurance industry in the United States was spurred by the onset of the Great Depression. In 1929, the Baylor University Hospital in Dallas created a pre-paid hospitalization benefit plan for school teachers after a hospital executive discovered that unpaid bills accumulated by local educators were a large burden on hospital finances as well as on the teachers themselves. Unlike earlier health insurance policies, subscribers were entitled to hospital care and services rather than a cash indemnity. . . . Other hospitals in Dallas quickly followed suit with their own group hospitalization plans as a means of ensuring a steady revenue source in difficult economic times.[11] . . . Community-based plans in St. Paul, Minnesota, Washington, D.C., and Cleveland were created soon afterwards. The Blue Cross emblem, first used by the St. Paul plan, was widely adopted by other prepaid hospital benefit plans adhering to American Hospital Association (AHA) guidelines. . . .

11. Robert Cunningham III and Robert M. Cunningham Jr., *The Blues: A History of the Blue Cross and Blue Shield System* (Dekalb, IL: Northern Illinois University Press, 1997).

The health insurance market in the United States, according to many historians, was originally structured to avoid competition among providers.[15] . . . Hospital and professional groups . . . soon pushed for joint plans that required "free choice of physicians and hospital," rather than plans offered by individual hospitals. Joint plans dampened incentives for local hospitals to compete on the basis of price or generosity of plan benefits. The American Hospital Association strongly favored ' joint plans that allowed a subscriber to obtain care from any licensed local hospital and viewed single-hospital plans as a threat to the economic stability of community hospitals. . . .

Insurance coverage of physician services lagged behind the growth of Blue Cross hospital plans due to opposition from the American Medical Association (AMA) and restrictive state laws.[19] In several states, however, medical societies set up prepaid service plans to preempt proposed state or federal plans, which evolved into Blue Shield plans. . . . Blue Cross plans accelerated their growth during World War II and extended to almost all states by 1946. Wartime wage and price controls authorized in October 1942 excluded "reasonable" insurance and pension benefits. As industries struggled to expand war production, many employers used health insurance and other fringe benefits to attract new workers. In the late 1940s, the National Labor Relations Board (NLRB) successfully sued employers that refused to bargain collectively over fringe benefits, opening the way for unions to negotiate with employers over health insurance, which further helped boost enrollments in health insurance plans. . . .

[Today, most] private health insurance is offered through employers. With employer-sponsored plans, employers may simply offer health benefit plans through an insurance company for a negotiated price and bear no insurance risk. At the other extreme, the employer may self-insure and handle the plan itself, thus bearing all of the insurance risk and the administrative burden of the plan. Often, the extent of employer involvement depends on the number of employees. Research has found that 80% of large employers (500 or more employees) choose to self-insure rather than purchase coverage from a health insurer. . . .

TAX ADVANTAGES FOR EMPLOYER-PROVIDED HEALTH INSURANCE BENEFITS

. . . Health insurance is subsidized through the tax system in several ways. First, . . . [the] Internal Revenue Code of 1954 included section 106, which explicitly allowed the exclusion of employer contributions for health insurance. . . . The Joint Committee on Taxation (JCT) estimates that the federal government forgoes [over $250 billion] annually in tax revenue because of this exclusion. . . . The tax exemption for employer-provided health care made health insurance cheaper than non-exempt forms of consumption for individuals. One study found that health insurance coverage following the 1954 tax changes expanded more rapidly among employees with higher incomes, who generally had marginal tax rates, which could indicate that the tax exclusion led workers to demand more extensive or generous

15. Rosemary Stevens, *In Sickness and In Wealth: American Hospitals in the 20th Century* (New York: Basic Books, 1989), p. 156.

19. Paul Starr, *The Social Transformation of American Medicine* (New York: Basic Books, 1983), pp. 296-297.

plans. Other factors, such as rising income levels, competition for workers, and rising medical costs, also spurred growth in employer-provided health benefits. . . .

COMMERCIAL INSURERS ENTER

Before World War II, many commercial insurers doubted that hospital or medical costs were an insurable risk. Insurers traditionally considered a risk insurable only if the potential losses were definite, measurable and not subject to control by the insured. The financial risks linked to illness or injury, however, could vary depending on the judgment of medical personnel, and behavior of the insured could affect the probability of ill health in many ways. After the rapid spread of Blue Cross plans in the mid-1930s, however, several commercial insurers began to offer similar health coverage. By the 1950s, commercial health insurers had become potent competitors and began to cut into Blue Cross's market share in many parts of the country. The large-scale entry of commercial insurers into the health insurance market changed the competitive environment. . . .

[T]he commercial health insurers were not bound to set premiums using the Blue Cross community rating principle, which linked premiums to average claims costs across a geographic area rather than to the claims experience of particular groups or individuals. Therefore, commercial insurers using an "experience rating" approach were able to underbid Blue Cross for firms that employed healthier-than-average individuals, which on average were cheaper to insure.

The loss of healthier groups then raised average costs among remaining groups, which . . . compelled Blue Cross to adopt experience rating. . . . The shift toward experience rating changed the nature of competition in the health insurance market. Insurers could cut costs by shifting risks to others, by recruiting firms whose employees and their families were healthier than average, rather than finding more efficient ways of managing risks for a given pool of subscribers. . . .

By the 1980s, health researchers and policymakers had begun to view the differences between Blue Cross/Blue Shield insurers, which were organized as non-profit organizations, and for-profit commercial health insurers as having narrowed. . . . In 1994, Blue Cross/Blue Shield guidelines were amended to let affiliates reorganize as for-profit insurers, leading the way for more than a dozen Blue Cross/Blue Shield affiliates to convert to for-profit status. Other Blue Cross/Blue Shield insurers bought other insurers, merged, or restructured in other ways. At the same time, private insurers acquired HMOs and other managed care organizations. Consolidations reduced both the number of commercial and Blue Cross/Blue Shield organizations, leading to the emergence of a small number of very large insurers with strong market positions across the country. . . .

INTRODUCTION OF MEDICARE AND MEDICAID

. . . While Blue Cross/Blue Shield and commercial insurance plans covered a large portion of employees and their dependents at the end of the 1950s, many low-income and elderly people had trouble obtaining affordable health insurance or paying for health care. . . . Social Security was extended to pay providers to cover certain medical costs incurred by aged, blind, and disabled beneficiaries starting in 1950. . . . State governments, subject to certain federal requirements, retained substantial discretion over benefit levels and income limits, which were typically linked to welfare assistance programs. . . .

In 1965, the Johnson Administration worked with Ways and Means Committee Chairman Wilbur Mills to create the Medicare program, which provided health insurance for nearly all Americans over age 65. Medicare combined a compulsory hospital insurance program (Part A) with a voluntary physician services plan (Part B). While some had worried that Medicare would displace private insurers, Blue Cross organizations became fiscal intermediaries for Medicare, responsible for issuing payments to providers and other back office operations. Medicaid, created in the same 1965 act, is a means-tested program financed by federal and state funds. Each state designs and administers its own program under federal rules. Over time, Medicaid eligibility standards and federal requirements have become more complex. . . .

THE RISE OF MANAGED CARE [AND "CONSUMER-DIRECTED" CARE]

In some parts of the country, plans combining insurance with the direct provision of health care evolved into important players in local markets despite the strong opposition of the AHA and AMA. A health plan designed for southern California construction workers in the mid-1930s eventually became the Kaiser Health Plan. . . . While some of these plans prospered locally or regionally, they did not achieve national reach until the 1970s.

In 1971, President Nixon announced a program to encourage prepaid group plans that joined insurance and care functions as a way to constrain the growth of medical care costs, which had risen sharply in the years following the startup of the Medicare and Medicaid programs, and to enhance competition in the health insurance market. Advocates claimed that health maintenance organizations (HMOs), which integrate health care and health insurance functions, would have a financial motive to promote wellness and would lack incentives to overprovide care. . . .

While this ambitious goal was not reached in the 1970s, by the late 1980s policymakers and businesses began to view greater use of managed care organizations such as HMOs and similar organizations as a key strategy for controlling health care costs. In the mid-1990s, the broader use of more restrictive forms of managed care (such as stringent gatekeeper, second medical opinion, and pre-approval requirements) sparked strong consumer resistance, which forced an industry retreat from some of those strategies. Networks of providers, known as preferred provider organizations (PPOs), grew rapidly in the late 1980s and early 1990s. PPOs, often owned by hospital systems and other providers, typically contract with insurers or self-insured firms and offer discounted fee-for-service (FFS) rates. PPO enrollees who receive care outside of the network typically must obtain plan approval or pay more. Thus, PPO plans provided patients with more flexibility than staff-model HMOs, which generally did not cover care provided outside of the HMO. As various types of managed care plans such as HMOs and PPOs became widespread, more employers offered choices among competing health plans to let workers willing to pay higher premiums avoid restrictive plans. . . .

The predominant type of health insurance plan has changed dramatically over the past 25 years. Over 90% of the privately insured were covered by an indemnity or traditional "unmanaged" health insurance plan in 1980; now the share is less than 10%. Today, most people covered by private insurance are covered by some kind of managed care plan ranging from a managed indemnity plan (e.g., PPOs, where the insurers negotiate fees with providers) to a staff HMO (the insurer and the provider are the same, and patients see physicians who are on salary). . . .

In the 1990s, proponents of "consumer-directed" health care proposed measures intended to make consumers more sensitive to medical care costs. In . . . 2003 . . . Congress passed legislation to allow consumers with high-deductible health insurance plans to set up Health Savings Accounts (HSAs) that allow people to pay for out-of-pocket expenses through a tax-advantaged medical savings account. . . .

DESCRIPTION OF THE HEALTH INSURANCE MARKET

Individuals and families typically buy insurance to avoid risks by paying a known premium in order to receive benefits if an adverse event were to occur during the insurance policy's term. Most individuals are willing to pay an insurer to assume the bulk of financial risks associated with unpredictable health outcomes of uncertain severity. . . . Some insured people will become sick or injured and incur significant medical expenses. Most people, however, will remain relatively healthy, thus incurring little or no medical expenses.[54] . . . In essence, money is shifted from those who remain healthy to those who become sick or injured.

The health insurance market is tightly interrelated with other parts of the health care system. . . . Health insurers not only reimburse providers, but also typically have some control over the number and types of services covered and negotiate contracts with providers on the payments for health services. . . .

The health insurance market has many features that push it far from the economic benchmark of perfect competition. . . . How insurers design health care networks influences how consumers use health care. Consumers typically choose a primary physician who selects tests and treatments and makes referrals to medical specialists. Employers negotiate with insurers on behalf of their workers, and labor unions negotiate with employers over health benefits on behalf of their members. Health insurers, in turn, negotiate contracts with providers and handle payments for individual services. A primary physician's admitting privileges typically determine where his patient goes for non-emergency hospital care. Patients must go through a physician to obtain most medical tests and pharmaceuticals. Health care consumers typically rely on these intermediaries instead of interacting directly with other parts of the health care system. This heavy reliance on intermediaries is a key characteristic of the current health care market. . . .

Using intermediaries such as health insurers protects consumers from financial risks linked to serious medical problems, but it also insulates consumers from information about costs and prices for specific health care goods and services. When a third-party, such as a private insurer or a government, pays for the bulk of health care costs, consumers may demand more care and providers may wish to supply more care. Links among intermediaries and providers can also limit consumers' choices. For example, a person's job may limit her health insurance choices, and another person's choice of physician may limit choices among hospitals. Some fami-

---

54. A analysis of 2002 Medical Expenditure Panel Survey data found that "[h]alf of the population spends little or nothing on health care, while 5 percent of the population spends almost half of the total amount." . . . [See also National Institute for Health Care Management, The Concentration of Health Care Spending (2012).]

lies and individuals lacking these intermediaries must navigate the health insurance and health care system themselves, which may be a serious challenge. . . .

Finally, how intermediaries interact has important consequences in the health care market. For instance, employers and health insurers, which both intermediate on behalf of individuals, interact through negotiations over insurance benefits packages. Politicians can also act as intermediaries for their constituents by helping to determine reimbursement rates for public insurance programs and by changing the regulatory environment facing health insurers. . . .

MORAL HAZARD

Moral hazard, which occurs when insurance status changes behavior, is another problem in the health insurance market. Moral hazard occurs if an insured individual consumes more medical services than she would have had she been uninsured. For example, having health insurance could induce someone to seek medical care for minor conditions (e.g., a sore throat), choose a high-amenity health care setting (e.g., a more hotel-like hospital), or neglect his health (e.g., by eating fatty foods). Consequently, moral hazard leads the insurer to pay providers more for an insured person's medical services than that person would have paid out of his own pocket had he not been insured. Of course, non-monetary costs, such as the pain and inconvenience of obtaining unnecessary medical care, may help limit moral hazard among patients.

Insurers typically react to moral hazard by raising premiums to cover the costs of additional services and by limiting care, either directly (e.g., through prior approval requirements) or through cost-sharing measures such as copayments and deductibles. . . . The lack of transparency in the pricing of medical services contributes to this problem—most people do not know the cost of medical services (both what the provider normally charges and what the insurance company reimburses the provider).

THE PRINCIPAL-AGENT PROBLEM

A patient (here, a *principal*), as noted above, typically relies on a physician (an *agent*) for care and advice. The physician, or other intermediary, might face incentives to act to further their own interests, rather than those of the patient, by providing a higher quantity or lower quality of care than would be appropriate for a patient. . . . [P]ayment and incentive systems may mitigate conflicts of interests. Professional standards and professional organizations may also help mitigate those conflicts. . . .

While that arrangement may avoid some problems, it may not solve others. In fee-for-service (FFS) arrangements, physicians and other providers may face financial incentives to provide more care than would best suit the patient's interests. When insurance pays most of the costs associated with health care, providers have little financial incentive to control costs and may overprovide health care services. One study randomly selected doctors into a salary group and a fee-for-service group during a nine-month study. The results showed that doctors in the fee-for-service group scheduled more office visits than salaried doctors, and almost all of the difference was due to the fee-for-service doctors seeing well patients rather than sick patients. Defensive medicine, in which physicians or other providers order tests that may reduce the probability of medical malpractice litigation, but which provide limited therapeutic benefits to the patient, presents a similar problem. . . .

Responses to . . . moral hazard and principal-agent problems affect the structure of the health financing system. Health insurers, as noted above, use coinsurance and pre-approval requirements to limit potential moral hazard among patients. Health insurers concerned about moral hazard and principal-agent problems among providers design incentive systems to limit overprovision of care. For example, the rapid transition to managed care in the 1990s might be seen as an attempt to control costs due to moral hazard. In addition, research and development (R&D) decisions made by medical technology and pharmaceutical firms may be indirectly guided by how health insurance coverage affects choices of providers and patients. Reforms that change the health financing system without taking into account potential moral hazards that previous structures and practices were designed to mitigate could encounter unanticipated problems. . . .

■47 MILLION AND COUNTING: WHY THE HEALTH CARE MARKETPLACE IS BROKEN
Testimony of Mark A. Hall
U.S. Senate Committee on Finance Hearing (2008)

The high concentration of most medical costs in a relative few people is the single most important fact for understanding the private insurance market. It is hard to find the right words to describe this foundational statistical phenomenon in terms that are sufficiently compelling, so I will start with a graphic depiction. Arraying the population by health care spending in [2014, Figure 9.1 below] shows that

FIGURE 9.1 The Concentration of Health Care Spending

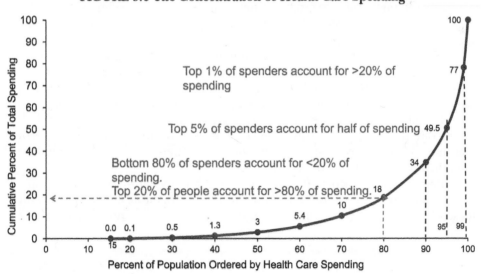

Source: NIHCM Foundation analysis from the 2009 Medical Expenditure Panel Survey.

- the top 1% [who averaged more than $100,000] accounted for [over one-fifth] of total spending
- the top 5% [who averaged more than $50,000] accounted for [almost] half of all spending
- and the top 20% . . . accounted for [over] 80% of spending.

The bottom half of the population distribution [who averaged $264 that year] incurred [3%] of total costs.

For convenience, I refer to this as "the 80/20 rule." I call it a rule because the pattern is remarkably universal. This pattern has a fractal geometry that appears wherever one looks. It holds true both for the population at large and for just about any subpopulation of any size one might choose to examine. . . . The extreme concentration of health care costs is an economic law of nature that has been observed as early as the 1930s and that will be with us for as long as anyone can foresee — regardless of how we deliver and pay for health care.

I stress the 80/20 rule because it is the most elemental fact of health insurance. It is as fundamental as gravity, and as pervasive as the weather. It is the endemic First Cause that reaches everywhere and explains just about everything of importance in the market for insurance. The high concentration of medical costs is why we need and have insurance in the first place. Pooling expenses across a population keeps them affordable for everyone, but the extreme costs at the high end also explain why insurance is so expensive, especially for those who anticipate no real need.

The extreme magnitude of differences in health risks also explains the private insurance market's most perplexing dynamics. I will describe several troubling phenomena, each of which derives from the basic fact that insurers stand to gain a great deal by avoiding or appropriately pricing people with higher risks. They also stand to lose a great deal if they do not attract a good number of lower risks. Therefore, competitive forces in health insurance markets inevitably focus on risk selection (or risk segmentation). Other points of competitive focus — such as product design, benefit coverage, sales vehicles, and care management — either have much less impact on profitability or are themselves surrogates for risk selection or segmentation. . . .

The natural dynamics of risk segmentation are so strong that risk selection occurs even without overt [screening by insurers]. Subscribers naturally sort themselves by risk to some extent, according to the covered benefits and plan features they find most attractive. Insurers and employers have learned that features such as deductibles, managed care, and particular benefits that are covered or excluded appeal differently to people with lesser versus greater health care needs. This is one reason many health policy analysts favor uniform benefits and why most employers limit their workers' choice of health plans. . . .

Risk selection practices flow directly from the very nature of how competitive markets should and must respond to highly concentrated health risks. Therefore, these effects will never be eliminated unless the market is fundamentally restructured. . . .

■ BAD MEDICINE: A GUIDE TO THE REAL COSTS AND CONSEQUENCES OF THE NEW HEALTH CARE LAW
Michael D. Tanner
Cato Institute, July 2010*

On March 21, 2010, in an extraordinary Sunday night session, the House of Representatives gave final approval to President Obama's long-sought health insurance plan in a partisan 219-212 vote. The bill had earlier passed the Senate on Christmas Eve, 2009. Not a single Republican in either chamber voted for the bill. . . . More than 2,500 pages and 500,000 words long, the Patient Protection and Affordable Care Act (PPACA) [also known as the Affordable Care Act or ACA] represents the most significant transformation of the American health care system since Medicare and Medicaid. It will fundamentally change nearly every aspect of health care from insurance to the final delivery of care.

The final legislation is, in some ways, an improvement over earlier versions. It is not the single-payer system sought by many liberals. Nor did it include the interim step of a so called "public option" that would likely have led to a single-payer system in the long run. . . . But that does not mean that this is, as the president has claimed, a "moderate" bill. It mandates that every American purchase a government-designed insurance package, while fundamentally reordering the insurance market and turning insurers into something resembling public utilities. . . .

Insurance coverage will be extended to millions more Americans as government subsidies are expanded deep into the middle class. Costs will be shifted between groups, though ultimately not reduced. And a new entitlement will be created, with the threat of higher taxes and new debt for future generations. In many ways, it has rewritten the relationship between the government and the people, moving this country closer to European-style social democracy. . . .

INDIVIDUAL AND EMPLOYER MANDATES

Perhaps the single most important piece of this legislation is its individual mandate, a legal requirement that every American obtain health insurance coverage that meets the government's definition of "minimum essential coverage." Those who don't receive such coverage through government programs, their employer, or some other group would be required to purchase individual coverage on their own. This individual mandate is unprecedented in U.S. governance. . . .

Under the new law, beginning in 2014, those who fail to obtain insurance would be subject to a tax penalty. That penalty would be quite mild at first, either $95 or one percent of annual income in 2014, whichever is greater. But it ramps up quickly after that, . . . [to] the greater of $695 or 2.5 percent of annual income. . . . Individuals will be exempt from the penalties if they . . . are unable to obtain insurance that costs less than 8 percent of their gross incomes. . . . While the law imposes penalties for failure to comply, . . . it does not contain any criminal penalties for failing to comply, and it forbids the use of liens or levies to collect the penalties.

However, the IRS . . . may withhold tax refunds to individuals who fail to comply with the mandate. . . .

The new law also contains an employer mandate, although it is watered down from the proposal that passed the House last year. . . . [B]eginning in 2014, if a company with 50 or more full-time employees (or the equivalent) does not provide health insurance to its workers, . . . the company must pay a tax penalty of $2,000 for every person they employ full time (minus 30 workers). . . . [A]s with the individual mandate, the penalty may be low enough that many businesses may find it less costly to "pay" than to "play" . . .

INSURANCE REGULATIONS

The Patient Protection and Affordable Care Act imposes a host of new federal insurance regulations that will significantly change the way the health insurance industry does business. Some of these regulatory changes are likely to be among the law's most initially popular provisions. But many are likely to have unintended consequences. Perhaps the most frequently discussed regulatory measure is the ban on insurers denying coverage because of preexisting conditions. . . . Specifically, . . . insurers would be prohibited from making any underwriting decisions based on health status, mental or physical medical conditions, claims experience, medical history, genetic information, disability, [or] other evidence of insurability. . . .

Finally, there will be limits on the ability of insurers to vary premiums on the basis of an individual's health. That is, insurers must charge the same premium for someone who is sick as for someone who is in perfect health. Insurers may consider age in setting premiums, but those premiums cannot be more than three times higher for their oldest than their youngest customers. Smokers may also be charged up to 50 percent more than nonsmokers. . . . While the ban on medical underwriting may make health insurance more available and affordable for those with preexisting conditions and reduce premiums for older and sicker individuals, it will also increase premiums for younger and healthier individuals. . . .

Perhaps the most fundamental reordering of the current insurance market is the creation of "exchanges" in each state. . . . The exchanges would function as a clearinghouse, a sort of wholesaler or middleman, matching customers with providers and products. Exchanges would also allow individuals and workers in small companies to take advantage of the economies of scale, both in terms of administration and risk pooling, which are currently enjoyed by large employers. . . . Exactly how significant the exchanges will prove to be remains to be seen. . . . However, one should be skeptical of claims that the exchange will reduce premiums. . . .

Insurance plans offered for sale within the exchanges [are] grouped into four categories based on actuarial value: bronze, the lowest cost plans, providing 60 percent of the actuarial value of a standard plan as defined by the secretary of HHS; silver, providing 70 percent of the actuarial value; gold, providing 80 percent of the actuarial value; and platinum, providing 90 percent of the actuarial value. In addition, exchanges may offer a special catastrophic plan to individuals who are under age 30 or who have incomes low enough to exempt them from the individual mandate. . . . CBO estimates that premiums for bronze plans would probably average between $4,500 and $5,000 for an individual and between $12,000 and $12,500 for family policies. The more inclusive policies would have correspondingly higher premiums. . . .

SUBSIDIES

The number one reason that people give for not purchasing insurance is that they cannot afford it. Therefore, the legislation's principal mechanism for expanding coverage (aside from the individual and employer mandates) is to pay for it, either through government-run programs such as Medicaid . . . or through subsidizing the purchase of private health insurance.

Starting in 2011, states are required to expand their Medicaid programs to cover all U.S. citizens with incomes below 133 percent of the poverty level [which is roughly $15,000 for an individual or $30,000 for a family of four]. . . . [T]he primary result of the law's Medicaid expansion would be to extend coverage to the parents in low-income families and to childless adults. In particular, single, childless men will now be eligible for Medicaid. . . .

Individuals with incomes too high to qualify for Medicaid but below 400 percent of the poverty level ($88,000 per year, for family of four) will be eligible for subsidies . . . in the form of refundable tax credits. . . . The credit is calculated on a sliding scale according to income in such a way as to limit the total proportion of income that an individual would have to pay for insurance. Thus, individuals with incomes between 133 and 200 percent of the poverty level will receive a credit covering the cost of premiums up to four percent of their income, while those earning 300-400 percent of the poverty level will receive a credit for costs in excess of 9.5 percent of their income. . . . As with many tax credits, the phase-out of these benefits creates a high marginal tax penalty as wages increase. In some cases, workers who increase their wages could actually see their after-tax income decline as the subsidies are reduced. . . .

All together, this law represents a massive increase in the welfare state, adding millions of Americans to the roll of those dependent, at least to some extent, on government largess. Yet for all the new spending, the Patient Protection and Affordable Care Act falls short of its goal of achieving universal coverage. . . . According to the Congressional Budget Office, the legislation would reduce the number of uninsured Americans by about [25] million people by 2019. . . . Supporters of the legislation point out that that would decrease the number of uninsured Americans to roughly [8] percent of non-elderly Americans, a far cry from universal coverage, but undoubtedly better than today's 15 percent. . . .

INCREASED SPENDING, INCREASED DEBT

Health-care costs are rising faster than GDP growth and now total more than $[2.5] trillion — more than Americans spend on housing, food, national defense, or automobiles. However, the Patient Protection and Affordable Care Act fails to do anything to reduce or even restrain the growth in those costs. . . . This should not come as a big surprise. The primary focus of the legislation was to expand insurance coverage. Giving more people access to more insurance, not to mention mandating that current insurance cover more services, will undoubtedly result in more spending. . . .

It is also worth noting that cost estimates for government programs have been wildly optimistic over the years, especially for health care programs. . . . There is certainly reason to believe that the costs of this law will exceed projections. For example, as discussed above, increased insurance coverage could lead to increased utilization and higher subsidy costs. At the same time, if companies choose to drop their current insurance and dump employees into subsidized coverage or Medicaid, it could substantially increase the program's costs. . . .

This is all taking place at a time when the government is facing an unprecedented budgetary crisis. The U.S. budget deficit hit $1.4 trillion in 2009, and we are expected to add as much as $9 trillion to the national debt over the next 10 years, a debt that is already in excess of $12 trillion and rising at a rate of nearly $4 billion per day. Under current projections, government spending will rise from its traditional 20-21 percent of our gross domestic product to 40 percent by 2050. That would require a doubling of the tax burden just to keep up. . . .

CONCLUSION

Health care reform was designed to accomplish three goals: (1) provide health insurance coverage for all Americans, (2) reduce insurance costs for individuals, businesses, and government, and (3) increase the quality of health care and the value received for each dollar of health care spending. . . . The legislation comes closest to success on the issue of expanding the number of Americans with insurance. . . . The law also makes some modest insurance reforms that will prohibit some of the industry's more unpopular practices. However, those changes will come at the price of increased insurance costs, especially for younger and healthier individuals, and reduced consumer choice.

At the same time, the legislation is a major failure when it comes to controlling costs. While we were once promised that health care reform would "bend the cost curve down," this law will actually *increase* U.S. health care spending. . . . Clearly the trajectory of U.S. health care spending under this law is unsustainable. Therefore, it raises the inevitable question of whether it will lead to rationing down the road.

We should be clear, however. With a few minor exceptions governing Medicare reimbursements, the law would not directly ration care or allow the government to dictate how doctors practice medicine. There is no "death board" as Sarah Palin once wrote about in her Facebook posting. Even so, . . . this law represents a fundamental shift in the debate over how to reform health care. It rejects consumer-oriented reforms in favor of a top-down, "command and control," government-imposed solution. As such, it sets the stage for potentially increased government involvement. . . . One thing is certain—the debate over health care reform is far from over. . . .

■ THE HEALTH BILL EXPLAINED AT LAST
Theodore R. Marmor & Jonathan Oberlander *
New York Review of Books, August 2010

. . . Republicans have sought to make health care reform Barack Obama's "Waterloo" . . . by scaring the public. Ominous and utterly false warnings about

---

* The authors are (or were) political science professors in the public health departments of Yale University and the University of North Carolina, respectively.

"death panels," a government "takeover" of American medicine, and "pulling the plug on grandma" followed. . . . The irony is that for all the apocalyptic rhetoric, the new health reform law is anything but radical. In fact, it closely resembles the 2006 reform in Massachusetts supported by then-governor Republican Mitt Romney. And most strikingly, it does not replace the current mix of US health insurance schemes with a single public health insurance program like Medicare. Instead, the 2010 reform legislation introduces a complex system of subsidies, mandates, regulations, and programs that build on our present patchwork arrangements. . . .

Despite such deep flaws in the US health care system, the central assumption of both the Obama administration and the Democratic leadership in Congress was that only legislation that did not seek to radically change it had a chance of success. That political calculation, in turn, was based on the view that the Clinton administration's health reform effort failed during 1993-1994 because it tried to change too much and provoked too much opposition from insurance companies and other powerful interests.

This time around, reformers hoped to reassure the large number of insured Americans who say they are satisfied with their current coverage that they had nothing to fear from change. Democrats also wanted to work with rather than fight against the health care industry. They hoped to gain support from the insurance, hospital, and pharmaceutical industries, which stood to gain financially from expanded insurance coverage and had the financial resources and political influence to undercut reforms they opposed. As a consequence, the creation of a Canadian-style health program, in which universal insurance — Medicare for all — is provided by the government, was never seriously considered. Such a reform would have caused, in the administration's view, too much disruption of prevailing arrangements and led to an inflammatory and unwinnable debate over "socialized medicine." . . .

HOW WILL THE NEW LAW WORK?

First, all Americans who earn less than 133 percent of the federal poverty level [which amounts to roughly $15,000 for an individual or $30,000 for a family of four] will become eligible for Medicaid [in states that opt to expand Medicaid]. For the first time, Medicaid will offer coverage solely on the basis of income and regardless of family circumstance — including the single adults without children who are now excluded. . . .

Most Americans under age sixty-five will continue to receive employer-sponsored coverage. As a new feature, children can stay on their parents' insurance plans until age twenty-six. New regulations banning insurers from imposing caps on both annual and lifetime payments will also benefit policyholders. Larger employers will have to offer health coverage to their workers or pay a penalty ($2,000 per worker) to the federal government. Smaller employers with fewer than fifty workers will be exempt from this requirement, and, depending on their average wage, businesses with twenty-five or fewer workers are eligible for tax credits to help them buy health insurance for their workers.

The law also expands coverage by offering subsidies to uninsured Americans to purchase insurance in newly formed health benefit exchanges. Each state is expected to set up and administer these exchanges as a regulated market for health insurance. If a state chooses not to do so, its residents can join a federally sponsored exchange. In either case, people will choose from a variety of private insurance plans within each exchange, with federal subsidies available on a sliding scale to help them pay their premiums. Those with incomes up to 400 percent of the federal poverty level (i.e., now up to about [$50,000 for singles or twice that for a family of four]) will be eligible for subsidies. In all, 29 million Americans are expected to obtain insurance through the exchanges by 2019. . . .

The insurance exchanges will be regulated extensively. Starting in 2014, insurers will not be able to deny coverage to would-be policyholders or charge them higher premiums because of their health status (though insurers can vary premiums by age). Insurers will also be prohibited from retroactively canceling coverage for sick policyholders. Most Americans will be required to obtain health insurance or pay a federal tax penalty—starting in 2014 at $95 per person or 1 percent of taxable income, whichever is greater, and then increasing to $695 or 2.5 percent of taxable income by 2016.

The CBO estimates that [about 25] million Americans will gain coverage through the expansion of Medicaid, subsidies, and insurance exchanges. This will make an enormous difference to the financial circumstances of many Americans with modest means and large medical expenses. Contrary to what conservative critics have claimed, the reform will undoubtedly mean less, not more, rationing of medical care as tens of millions of uninsured persons gain access to health insurance.

By broadening health insurance coverage, the law moves the United States closer to the principle that no one should go without access to medical care. In regulating the health insurance industry, with provisions to end discrimination on the basis of preexisting conditions, it brings about a long-overdue expansion of federal authority. In these ways and more, the Affordable Care Act is a substantial achievement.

At the same time, large gaps remain between the problems of American medicine and the remedies that Congress has adopted. Even if the Affordable Care Act were fully implemented, an estimated [30] million people would still lack insurance [by 2020]. We cannot know precisely who will be without coverage a decade from now. But analysts expect that the uninsured will be made up of three groups: undocumented immigrants who are ineligible for federal subsidies or Medicaid; Americans who still find coverage, even with subsidies, too expensive to purchase on their own but aren't poor enough to qualify for Medicaid; and healthy people who can afford to buy coverage but will instead choose the cheaper option of paying the penalty for not having insurance. In any case, the United States, alone among industrialized democracies, will likely continue to have a large uninsured population for years to come. . . .

In fact, the expansion of insurance coverage and regulation described in the law is hardly straightforward. . . . [I]nsurers whose profits are at stake can be expected to seek loopholes to evade the new regulations. According to the law, the secretary of health and human services must write the thousands of pages of regulations necessary to implement it, and these will be subject to congressional scrutiny and intense lobbying by the health care industry. . . . One consequence, then, of building on the existing system is that the new law will require coordination of a great many disparate policies if coverage goals are to be met and if the health insurance marketplace is to be transformed.

Perhaps the largest shortcoming of the reform, though, is the absence of reliable, system-wide controls on medical costs. The law takes steps to slow down the rate of increase in Medicare spending, such as cutting projected payments to hospitals. . . . Outside of Medicare, the measures to slow health care spending are far less impressive. . . . The law's strategy to contain costs additionally rests on a series of reforms aimed at improving medical care delivery and health outcomes: paying hospitals on the basis of quality; bundling payments together for inpatient and outpatient care; funding research that compares the clinical effectiveness of medical treatment options; and providing greater coverage of preventive services. It also encourages the formation of so-called accountable care organizations that create networks of primary care doctors, specialists, and hospitals to care (and receive payments) for a defined set of patients. Many of these reforms will be implemented initially in Medicare—a newly established Medicare innovations center is charged with testing payment reform—with the hope that successful policies will then spread through the private sector.

Health and Human Services Secretary Kathleen Sebelius says that "every cost-cutting idea that every health economist has brought to the table is in this bill." That is probably true—but it also shows that American health policy researchers pay scant attention to international experience. . . . The new law seems based on the hope that if a large variety of reforms are tested, at least some will succeed; but nobody knows how many will work in practice or whether they will save money at all.

We do know that other rich democracies that spend much less than the US on medical care do so largely by adopting budgetary targets for health expenditures and by tightly regulating what the governments and insurers pay hospitals, doctors, and other medical care providers. Outside of Medicare, the current reform contains no such measures.

The Obama administration, confronting enormous opposition over proposals to expand coverage, chose mostly to defer addressing the political problems of cost control. But the . . . issue cannot be avoided for long. . . . The expansion of coverage and the requirement that individuals purchase insurance, alongside rising premium costs, . . . will increase [pressure] on the federal government to moderate the growth in health care costs—especially in view of sizable budget deficits. . . . As a result, there is enormous uncertainty about how well and how long the patchwork of health reforms adopted in 2010 will hold together.

Notes: Health Care Reform—A Work in Progress

1. *"The More Things Change, . . ."* The ACA fundamentally changed how the individual health insurance market works and expanded who among those in poverty can qualify for Medicaid. However, the ACA's changes to employer-based insurance and Medicare (elderly and disabled) were modest to minor; those sources of coverage remain fundamentally the same. Also, employers have not dropped coverage nearly to the extent that many analysts predicted. Accordingly, despite all the *sturm und drang*, most people have not actually been affected very much by the ACA, at least directly. The following pie charts nicely illustrate how coverage has, and has not, changed following implementation of the ACA.

FIGURE 9.2

Insurance Coverage Prior
to Affordable Care Act (2013)

Insurance Coverage Under
the Affordable Care Act (2015)

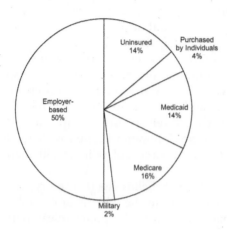

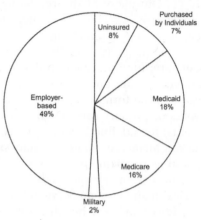

   2. *Agreeing to Disagree.* Public and political views on the ACA have been highly polarized from the beginning, both due to differences in ideology, but also due to raw partisan politics—much of which focused on President Obama. In contrast, notice the degree of commonality between the two selections presented above, which come from thoughtful policy analysts at distinctly different positions in the political spectrum. On which points do they agree? On which do they fundamentally disagree—more than simply a choice of emphasis (glass half full vs. half empty)?

   Among the full range of views, consider also those of liberal physicians who favor a "single-payer" national health insurance system:

> As much as we would like to join the celebration . . . , in good conscience we cannot. We take no comfort in seeing aspirin dispensed for the treatment of cancer. Instead of eliminating the root of the problem—the profit-driven, private health insurance industry—this costly new legislation will enrich and further entrench these firms. . . .
>
> Millions of middle-income people will be pressured to buy commercial health insurance policies costing up to 9.5 percent of their income but covering an average of only 70 percent of their medical expenses, potentially leaving them vulnerable to financial ruin if they become seriously ill. Many will find such policies too expensive to afford or, if they do buy them, too expensive to use because of the high co-pays and deductibles.
>
> Insurance firms will be handed at least $447 billion in taxpayer money to subsidize the purchase of their shoddy products. This money will enhance their financial and political power, and with it their ability to block future reform. . . .
>
> The much-vaunted insurance regulations—e.g., ending denials on the basis of pre-existing conditions—are riddled with loopholes, thanks to the central role that insurers played in crafting the legislation. Older people can be charged up to three times more than their younger counterparts. . . .

Congress and the Obama administration have saddled Americans with an expensive package of onerous individual mandates, new taxes on workers' health plans, countless sweetheart deals with the insurers and Big Pharma, and a perpetuation of the fragmented, dysfunctional, and unsustainable system that is taking such a heavy toll on our health and economy today. This bill's passage reflects political considerations, not sound health policy. . . . We pledge to continue our work for the only equitable, financially responsible and humane remedy for our health care mess: single-payer national health insurance, an expanded and improved Medicare for All.

Physicians for a National Health Program, Health Bill Leaves 23 Million Uninsured: A False Promise of Reform (Mar. 22, 2010).

3. *What Does the Public Think?* Democrats predicted that the Affordable Care Act would become popular with the American public once it took full effect. Instead, opinion has remained bitterly divided, substantially along political lines, with almost half the country viewing it unfavorably. Republican repeal-and-replace efforts, however, have apparently made the ACA more popular: by June 2017, and for the first time, more than half of the public reported favorable views on the law.

People who have gained private coverage through the ACA's exchanges are generally happy with their insurance, with 80 percent reporting that they are "very" or "somewhat" satisfied, according to surveys by the Commonwealth Fund. Many of those who have enrolled in private plans, however, are frustrated with the price of coverage, and in particular with the high deductibles that are common in exchange plans. (The average deductible in 2017 for a typical Obamacare plan was $3,572 for individuals and $7,474 for families.) Also, some people (such as younger, healthier males) are upset that they can no longer purchase more bare bones coverage (that excludes, for instance, mental health and maternity care), at rates that are adjusted for their gender and age. Thus, unless they qualify for a substantial subsidy, some people have to pay several times more for insurance than before the ACA, when they purchase individually.

Major industry interest groups (hospitals, doctors, insurers, pharmaceuticals) continue to support the ACA or at least to oppose its repeal. Their stocks have generally performed better than overall market indices since reform.

4. *What Has Health Reform Accomplished?* The ACA's most singular achievement is not universal insurance, but universal insur*ability*. Not everyone is covered, but everyone may now obtain coverage. Put another way, no one need worry about becoming uninsurable. Consider what life choices this basic guarantee enhances, from jobs to career paths to family relationships. Some analysts have detected an uptick in start-up companies, career changes, and early retirements following the ACA. Despite accusation that the ACA hurts employment, there is no evidence that it has increased job terminations or slowed job growth, nor have employers dropped health coverage in substantial numbers.

Measured against its core goal of actually expanding coverage, the ACA has been a partial success. In the glass half-full column, the National Center for Health Statistics estimates that "[i]n 2016, 28.6 million (9.0%) persons of all ages were uninsured at the time of interview—20.0 million fewer persons than in 2010." The portion of the population without insurance is lower than it has ever been in the United States.

In the half-empty column, nearly 30 million people remain uninsured. Who are they? Many are people who choose to (or feel they have to) pay the "individual mandate" tax penalty for remaining uninsured rather than purchase insurance, even when insurance is partially subsidized. In the 19 states that have chosen not to accept federal money to expand their Medicaid programs, stringent eligibility rules continue to disqualify many nonelderly adults near poverty. Even in states that have expanded, many people are unaware of their options or struggle with the enrollment process. Undocumented immigrants make up another substantial fraction of the uninsured population.

The ACA's exchanges work well in many states, especially those that chose to run their own exchanges. But the exchanges in some states (rural states in particular) have struggled to attract sufficient insurers, and insurer participation is diminishing on account of the political uncertainty over the ACA. Also, premiums in the individual market have increased sharply. Initially, these premiums were considerably lower than expected, due to intense competition among insurers for a large bolus of new enrollment. Since then, however, premiums have increased at double-digit rates in order to keep up with the level of medical costs that new enrollees are incurring. Despite these increases, average premiums on the exchanges are generally in line with, or not a great deal more than, what employers pay for similar group coverage, and premium increases have been much more moderate in states (mostly blue) that have openly embraced the ACA. Nevertheless, premiums are especially high in some parts of the country, and are expected to rise still higher as uncertainty over the ACA's fate makes healthier people more reluctant to enroll.

5. *Who Pays for All of This?* When it was enacted in 2010, the ACA was projected to cost the federal government almost $1 trillion over the first ten years. Over half of this was financed from a variety of taxes, such as taxes on medical devices and prescription drugs, increased Medicare payroll taxes for high-wage earners, and, oddly, a tax on tanning beds. Most of the remainder of the ACA's price tag was financed by reductions in Medicare payments to providers and insurers. On balance, the Congressional Budget Office projected that these tax increases and spending cuts would exceed the ACA's costs by roughly $100 billion over ten years, and would slightly reduce the federal deficit. However, the cuts to Medicare and the increase in Medicare payroll taxes used to finance the ACA make it more difficult to enact reforms needed to keep Medicare solvent for the next generation.

Partly because of the Great Recession, and partly because not all states took advantage of the Medicaid expansion, actual spending on the law's coverage provisions has been about one-third lower than anticipated. As a result, according to CBO, "repealing the ACA would increase federal budget deficits by $137 billion over the 2016–2025 period."

6. *Repeal, Replace, or Repair?* The election of Donald Trump gave Republicans unified control of the White House and Congress for the first time since the ACA's adoption. Yet Republicans were unable to muscle a repeal-and-replace bill through Congress. The political scientist Jonathan Oberlander explained where matters stood in the fall of 2017:

> The repeal-and-replace debate revealed Republicans' failure to meet another challenge: developing a decent, let alone better, alternative to Obamacare. The House-passed AHCA would have repealed the ACA's mandates, reduced insurance subsidies for low-income persons, cut taxes for wealthier persons, loosened insurance regulations, and rolled back funding for Medicaid expansion while capping

federal Medicaid spending. That combination of reforms . . . would result in tens of millions of Americans losing coverage and paying more for health insurance.

[The replacement proposals] also underscored the success of ACA policies in making insurance more accessible for persons with preexisting conditions and more affordable for lower-income Americans. . . . The fact that GOP repeal proposals would have left much of the ACA in place confirmed that reality. . . . Although Republican politicians highlighted the soaring premiums in ACA insurance exchanges in many states, in a legislative "bait and switch," their repeal plans retained the exchanges and instead targeted Medicaid, which has nothing to do with the rising premiums in the individual insurance market. . . .

Since 2010, Republicans have campaigned against a mythical Obamacare that they demonized as a disaster. The real Obamacare has serious shortcomings, but it also provides essential, popular benefits to tens of millions of Americans. . . . By comparison with the GOP's dystopian health care vision, Obamacare has never looked better. Republicans could not mobilize public support for their plan, which was the least popular major legislation of the past three decades. Instead, the Republican threats to Obamacare inspired widespread protests and a movement to protect the law. . . .

Still, Obamacare's fortunes remain uncertain. . . . [T]he president could create a self-fulfilling prophecy of ACA failure [by refusing to fund key payments to insurers as discussed below, and by declining to enforce the individual mandate]. . . . Alternatively, Democrats and Republicans could cooperate to stabilize the ACA's insurance marketplaces and adopt other reforms . . . .

Since 2010, the ACA has been an existential issue for Republicans who made its elimination a political cause. Abandoning that commitment to repeal Obamacare, and instead working with Democrats on incremental measures to improve the law, will not be easy. The demise, for now, of Senate repeal legislation will not end the Obamacare debate. But could it mark a turning point?

Jonathan Oberlander, Repeal, Replace, Repair, Retreat: Republicans' Health Care Quagmire, 377 New Engl. J. Med. 1001 (2017).

With repeal-and-replace on life support, congressional Republicans took a different approach. In the closing days of 2017, they passed a tax reform bill that (among many other things) zeroed out the individual mandate. Premiums on the exchanges are expected to surge as a result, and an estimated 13 million people could lose coverage in the coming decade. See Congressional Budget Office, Repealing the Individual Health Insurance Mandate: An Updated Estimate (Nov. 2017). The repeal is due to take effect in 2019.

7. *Further Reading.* For accounts of the law's **enactment and general descriptions of its contents**, see Washington Post, Landmark: The Inside Story of America's New Health Care Law (2010); Jonathan Gruber, Health Care Reform: What It Is, Why It's Necessary, How It Works (2011); Paul Starr, Remedy and Reaction: The Peculiar American Struggle over Health Care Reform (2011); Stuart Altman, Power, Politics and Universal Health Care (2011); John McDonough, Inside National Health Reform (2011); Lawrence Jacobs & Theda Skocpol, Health Care Reform and American Politics (2010).

For more about the Massachusetts precursor to the ACA, see Edward Zelinsky, The New Massachusetts Health Law: Preemption and Experimentation, 49 Wm. & Mary L. Rev. 229 (2008); Michael Tanner, No Miracle in Massachusetts: Why Governor Romney's Health Care Reform Won't Work (Cato Institute, 2006); Symposium, 55 U. Kan. L. Rev. 1091 (2007); Symposium, 28(4) Health Aff. w578 (July–Aug.

2009); Symposium, 36(5) Hastings Center Rep. 14 (Oct. 2006); Symposium, 354 New Eng. J. Med. 2093 (2006).

■NATIONAL FEDERATION OF INDEPENDENT BUSINESS v. SEBELIUS
567 U.S. 1 (2012)

Chief Justice ROBERTS.

Today we resolve constitutional challenges to two provisions of the Patient Protection and Affordable Care Act of 2010: the individual mandate, which requires individuals to purchase a health insurance policy providing a minimum level of coverage; and the Medicaid expansion, which gives funds to the States on the condition that they provide specified health care to all citizens whose income falls below a certain threshold. . . .

I

The individual mandate requires most Americans to maintain "minimum essential" health insurance coverage. 26 U. S. C. § 5000A. . . . Many individuals will receive the required coverage through their employer, or from a government program such as Medicaid or Medicare. But for individuals who are not exempt and do not receive health insurance through a third party, the means of satisfying the requirement is to purchase insurance from a private company.

Beginning in 2014, those who do not comply with the mandate must make a "[s]hared responsibility payment" to the Federal Government, . . . calculated as a percentage of household income, subject to a floor based on a specified dollar amount and a ceiling based on the average annual premium the individual would have to pay for qualifying private health insurance. In 2016, for example, the penalty will be 2.5 percent of an individual's household income, but no less than $695 and no more than the average yearly premium for ["bronze level"] insurance. The Act . . . bars the IRS from using several of its normal enforcement tools, such as criminal prosecutions and levies. And some individuals who are subject to the mandate are nonetheless exempt from the penalty—for example, those with income below a certain threshold and members of Indian tribes.

On the day the President signed the Act into law, Florida and 12 other States filed a complaint . . . subsequently joined by 13 more States, several individuals, and the National Federation of Independent Business. The plaintiffs alleged, among other things, that the individual mandate provisions of the Act exceeded Congress's powers under Article I of the Constitution. The District Court agreed, holding that . . . the individual mandate could not be severed from the remainder of the Act, and therefore struck down the Act in its entirety. . . . The Court of Appeals for the Eleventh Circuit . . . struck down only the individual mandate, leaving the Act's other provisions intact. . . .

III. A

The Government's first argument is that the individual mandate is a valid exercise of Congress's power under the Commerce Clause and the Necessary and

Proper Clause. According to the Government, the health care market is characterized by a significant cost-shifting problem. Everyone will eventually need health care at a time and to an extent they cannot predict, but if they do not have insurance, they often will not be able to pay for it. Because state and federal laws nonetheless require hospitals to provide a certain degree of care to individuals without regard to their ability to pay, hospitals end up receiving compensation for only a portion of the services they provide. To recoup the losses, hospitals pass on the cost to insurers through higher rates, and insurers, in turn, pass on the cost to policy holders in the form of higher premiums. Congress estimated that the cost of uncompensated care raises family health insurance premiums, on average, by over $1,000 per year.

In the Affordable Care Act, Congress addressed the problem of those who cannot obtain insurance coverage because of preexisting conditions or other health issues. It did so through the Act's "guaranteed-issue" and "community-rating" provisions. These provisions together prohibit insurance companies from denying coverage to those with such conditions or charging unhealthy individuals higher premiums than healthy individuals.

The guaranteed-issue and community-rating reforms do not, however, address the issue of healthy individuals who choose not to purchase insurance to cover potential health care needs. In fact, the reforms sharply exacerbate that problem, by providing an incentive for individuals to delay purchasing health insurance until they become sick, relying on the promise of guaranteed and affordable coverage. The reforms also threaten to impose massive new costs on insurers, who are required to accept unhealthy individuals but prohibited from charging them rates necessary to pay for their coverage. This will lead insurers to significantly increase premiums on everyone.

The individual mandate was Congress's solution to these problems. By requiring that individuals purchase health insurance, the mandate prevents cost-shifting by those who would otherwise go without it. In addition, the mandate forces into the insurance risk pool more healthy individuals, whose premiums on average will be higher than their health care expenses. This allows insurers to subsidize the costs of covering the unhealthy individuals the reforms require them to accept. The Government claims that Congress has power under the Commerce and Necessary and Proper Clauses to enact this solution.

1

. . . Given its expansive scope, it is no surprise that Congress has employed the commerce power in a wide variety of ways to address the pressing needs of the time. But Congress has never attempted to rely on that power to compel individuals not engaged in commerce to purchase an unwanted product. . . . The power to regulate commerce presupposes the existence of commercial activity to be regulated. . . . As expansive as our cases construing the scope of the commerce power have been, they all have one thing in common: They uniformly describe the power as reaching "activity." . . .

The individual mandate, however, does not regulate existing commercial activity. It instead compels individuals to become active in commerce by purchasing a product, on the ground that their failure to do so affects interstate commerce. Construing the Commerce Clause to permit Congress to regulate individuals precisely because they are doing nothing would open a new and potentially vast domain to congressional authority. Every day individuals do not do an infinite number of things. . . .

To consider [an] example in the health care market, many Americans do not eat a balanced diet, . . . [which] increases health care costs to a greater extent than the failure of the uninsured to purchase insurance. . . . Under the Government's theory, Congress could address the diet problem by ordering everyone to buy vegetables. . . . That is not the country the Framers of our Constitution envisioned. . . . Congress already enjoys vast power to regulate much of what we do. Accepting the Government's theory would give Congress the same license to regulate what we do not do, fundamentally changing the relation between the citizen and the Federal government. . . .

The individual mandate's regulation of the uninsured as a class is, in fact, particularly divorced from any link to existing commercial activity. The mandate primarily affects healthy, often young adults who are less likely to need significant health care and have other priorities for spending their money. . . . The Government, however, . . . regards it as sufficient to trigger Congress's authority that almost all those who are uninsured will, at some unknown point in the future, engage in a health care transaction. . . . The Commerce Clause is not a general license to regulate an individual from cradle to grave, simply because he will predictably engage in particular transactions. Any police power to regulate individuals as such, as opposed to their activities, remains vested in the States.

The Government argues that the individual mandate can be sustained as a sort of exception to this rule, because health insurance is a unique product. According to the Government, upholding the individual mandate would not justify mandatory purchases of items such as cars or broccoli because, as the Government puts it, "[h]ealth insurance is not purchased for its own sake like a car or broccoli; it is a means of financing health-care consumption and covering universal risks." But cars and broccoli are no more purchased for their "own sake" than health insurance. They are purchased to cover the need for transportation and food. . . . And for most of those targeted by the mandate, significant health care needs will be years, or even decades, away. The proximity and degree of connection between the mandate and the subsequent commercial activity is too lacking to justify an exception of the sort urged by the Government. . . .

2

The Government next contends that Congress has the power under the Necessary and Proper Clause to enact the individual mandate because the mandate is an "integral part of a comprehensive scheme of economic regulation"—the guaranteed-issue and community-rating insurance reforms. . . . [Interpreting the] power to "make all Laws which shall be necessary and proper for carrying into Execution" the powers enumerated in the Constitution, Art. I, § 8, cl. 18, we have been very deferential to Congress's determination that a regulation is "necessary." We have thus upheld laws that are " 'convenient, or useful' or 'conducive' to the authority's 'beneficial exercise.' " But we have also carried out our responsibility to declare unconstitutional those laws that undermine the structure of government established by the Constitution. . . .

Applying these principles, the individual mandate cannot be sustained under the Necessary and Proper Clause as an essential component of the insurance reforms. Each of our prior cases upholding laws under that Clause involved exercises of authority derivative of, and in service to, a granted power. . . . The individual mandate, by contrast, vests Congress with the extraordinary ability to create the necessary predicate to the exercise of an enumerated power, . . . reach[ing] beyond the natural limit of its authority and draw[ing] within its regulatory scope those who otherwise would be outside of it. Even if the individual mandate is "necessary" to the Act's insurance reforms, such an expansion of federal power is not a "proper" means for making those reforms effective. . . . The commerce power thus does not authorize the mandate.

[Justices Scalia, Kennedy, Thomas, and Alito concurred with, but did not join, the Commerce Clause portion (III.A) of this opinion. The other four justices dissented from this portion.]

B

That is not the end of the matter. . . . [T]he Government asks us to read the mandate not as ordering individuals to buy insurance, but rather as imposing a tax on those who do not buy that product. . . . The most straightforward reading of the mandate is that it commands individuals to purchase insurance. . . . [But] if an individual does not maintain health insurance, the only consequence is that he must make an additional payment to the IRS when he pays his taxes. . . . Under that theory, the mandate is not a legal command to buy insurance. Rather, it makes going without insurance just another thing the Government taxes, like buying gasoline or earning income. . . .

The question is not whether that is the most natural interpretation of the mandate, but only whether it is a "fairly possible" one. . . . Granting the Act the full measure of deference owed to federal statutes, it can be so read, for the reasons set forth below. . . . First, for most Americans the amount due will be far less than the price of insurance, and, by statute, it can never be more.[4] . . . While the individual mandate clearly aims to induce the purchase of health insurance, it need not be read to declare that failing to do so is unlawful. . . . Indeed, it is estimated that four million people each year will choose to pay the IRS rather than buy insurance. . . .

Neither the Act nor any other law attaches negative legal consequences to not buying health insurance, beyond requiring a payment to the IRS. . . . [Instead], the shared responsibility payment merely imposes a tax citizens may lawfully choose to pay in lieu of buying health insurance. . . .

[Justices Ginsburg, Breyer, Sotomayor, and Kagan joined this tax power portion of the opinion (III.B). The portion of the decision addressing Medicaid expansion is excerpted at page 1067.]

---

4. In 2016, for example, individuals making $35,000 a year are expected to owe the IRS about $60 for any month in which they do not have health insurance. Someone with an annual income of $100,000 a year would likely owe about $200. The price of a qualifying insurance policy is projected to be around $400 per month.

Justice GINSBURG, concurring in part and dissenting in part.

. . . Although every [person] will incur significant medical expenses during his or her lifetime, the time when care will be needed is often unpredictable. An accident, a heart attack, or a cancer diagnosis commonly occurs without warning. Inescapably, we are all at peril of needing medical care without a moment's notice. To manage the risks associated with medical care — its high cost, its unpredictability, and its inevitability — most people in the United States obtain health insurance. Many (approximately 170 million in 2009) are insured by private insurance companies. Others, including those over 65 and certain poor and disabled persons, rely on government-funded insurance programs, notably Medicare and Medicaid. Combined, private health insurers and State and Federal Governments finance almost 85% of the medical care administered to U. S. residents.

Not all U. S. residents, however, have health insurance. In 2009, approximately 50 million people were uninsured, either by choice or, more likely, because they could not afford private insurance and did not qualify for government aid. . . . Unlike markets for most products, however, the inability to pay for care does not mean that an uninsured individual will receive no care. Federal and state law, as well as professional obligations and embedded social norms, require hospitals and physicians to provide care when it is most needed, regardless of the patient's ability to pay. As a consequence, medical-care providers deliver significant amounts of care to the uninsured for which the providers receive no payment. . . .

Health-care providers do not absorb these bad debts. Instead, they raise their prices, passing along the cost of uncompensated care to those who do pay reliably: the government and private insurance companies. In response, private insurers increase their premiums, shifting the cost of the elevated bills from providers onto those who carry insurance. . . . And it is hardly just the currently sick or injured among the uninsured who prompt elevation of the price of health care and health insurance. . . . [B]ecause any uninsured person may need medical care at any moment and because health-care companies must account for that risk, every uninsured person impacts the market price of medical care and medical insurance. . . .

Aware that a national solution was required, Congress could have taken over the health-insurance market by establishing a tax-and-spend federal program like Social Security. Such a program, commonly referred to as a single-payer system (where the sole payer is the Federal Government), would have left little, if any, room for private enterprise or the States. Instead of going this route, Congress enacted the ACA, a solution that retains a robust role for private insurers and state governments. To make its chosen approach work, however, Congress had to use some new tools, including a requirement that most individuals obtain private health insurance coverage. As explained below, by employing these tools, Congress was able to achieve a practical, altogether reasonable, solution. . . .

Congress knew that encouraging individuals to purchase insurance would not suffice to solve the problem, because most of the uninsured are not uninsured by choice. Of particular concern to Congress were people who, though desperately in need of insurance, often cannot acquire it: persons who suffer from preexisting medical conditions. Before the ACA's enactment, private insurance companies took an applicant's medical history into account when setting insurance rates or deciding whether to insure an individual. Because individuals with preexisting medical conditions cost insurance companies significantly more than those without such conditions, insurers routinely refused to insure these individuals, charged them substantially higher premiums, or offered only limited coverage that did not include the preexisting illness.

To ensure that individuals with medical histories have access to affordable insurance, Congress devised a three-part solution. First, Congress imposed a "guaranteed issue" requirement, which bars insurers from denying coverage to any person on account of that person's medical condition or history. Second, Congress required insurers to use "community rating" to price their insurance policies. Community rating, in effect, bars insurance companies from charging higher premiums to those with preexisting conditions.

But these two provisions, Congress comprehended, could not work effectively unless individuals were given a powerful incentive to obtain insurance. In the 1990's, several States—including New York, New Jersey, Washington, Kentucky, Maine, New Hampshire, and Vermont—enacted guaranteed-issue and community-rating laws without requiring universal acquisition of insurance coverage. The results were disastrous. All seven states suffered from skyrocketing insurance premium costs, reductions in individuals with coverage, and reductions in insurance products and providers.

Congress comprehended that guaranteed-issue and community-rating laws alone will not work. When insurance companies are required to insure the sick at affordable prices, individuals can wait until they become ill to buy insurance. Pretty soon, those in need of immediate medical care—i.e., those who cost insurers the most—become the insurance companies' main customers. This "adverse selection" problem leaves insurers with two choices: They can either raise premiums dramatically to cover their ever-increasing costs or they can exit the market. In the seven States that tried guaranteed-issue and community-rating requirements without a minimum coverage provision, that is precisely what insurance companies did. See, e.g., Hall, An Evaluation of New York's Reform Law, 25 J. Health Pol. Pol'y & L. 71, 91-92 (2000).

Massachusetts, Congress was told, cracked the adverse selection problem. By requiring most residents to obtain insurance, the Commonwealth ensured that insurers would not be left with only the sick as customers. As a result, federal lawmakers observed, Massachusetts succeeded where other States had failed. In coupling the minimum coverage provision with guaranteed-issue and community-rating prescriptions, Congress followed Massachusetts' lead.

In sum, Congress passed the minimum coverage provision as a key component of the ACA to address an economic and social problem that has plagued the Nation for decades: the large number of U. S. residents who are unable or unwilling to obtain health insurance. Whatever one thinks of the policy decision Congress made, it was Congress' prerogative to make it. Reviewed with appropriate deference, the minimum coverage provision, allied to the guaranteed-issue and community-rating prescriptions, should survive measurement under the Commerce and Necessary and Proper Clauses. . . .

II

. . . The inevitable yet unpredictable need for medical care and the guarantee that emergency care will be provided when required are conditions nonexistent in other markets. That is so of the market for cars, and of the market for broccoli as well. Although an individual might buy a car or a crown of broccoli one day, there is no certainty she will ever do so. And if she eventually wants a car or has a craving for broccoli, she will be obliged to pay at the counter before receiving the vehicle or nourishment. She will get no free ride or food, at the expense of another consumer forced to pay an inflated price. Upholding the minimum coverage provision on the ground that all are participants or will be participants in the health-care market would therefore carry no implication that Congress may justify under the Commerce Clause a mandate to buy other products and services.

. . . The Chief Justice also calls the minimum coverage provision an illegitimate effort to make young, healthy individuals subsidize insurance premiums paid by the less hale and hardy. This complaint, too, is spurious. . . . In the fullness of time, moreover, today's young and healthy will become society's old and infirm. Viewed over a lifespan, the costs and benefits even out: The young who pay more than their fair share currently will pay less than their fair share when they become senior citizens. And even if, as undoubtedly will be the case, some individuals, over their lifespans, will pay more for health insurance than they receive in health services, they have little to complain about, for that is how insurance works. Every insured person receives protection against a catastrophic loss, even though only a subset of the covered class will ultimately need that protection. . . .

Recall that one of Congress' goals in enacting the Affordable Care Act was to eliminate the insurance industry's practice of charging higher prices or denying coverage to individuals with preexisting medical conditions. The commerce power allows Congress to ban this practice, a point no one disputes. Congress knew, however, that simply barring insurance companies from relying on an applicant's medical history would not work in practice. Without the individual mandate, Congress learned, guaranteed-issue and community-rating requirements would trigger an adverse-selection death-spiral in the health-insurance market: Insurance premiums would skyrocket, the number of uninsured would increase, and insurance companies would exit the market. When complemented by an insurance mandate, on the other hand, guaranteed issue and community rating would work as intended. . . .

Asserting that the Necessary and Proper Clause does not authorize the minimum coverage provision, The Chief Justice focuses on the word "proper," . . . declar[ing] the minimum coverage provision not "proper" because it is less "narrow in scope" than other laws this Court has upheld under the Necessary and Proper Clause. . . . The Chief Justice [fails] to explain why the [individual mandate] is more far-reaching than other implied powers this Court has found meet under the Necessary and Proper Clause. These powers include the power to enact criminal laws; the power to imprison, including civil imprisonment; and the power to create a national bank. . . . How is a judge to decide, when ruling on the constitutionality of a federal statute, whether Congress employed an "independent power," or merely a "derivative" one. Whether the power used is "substantive," or just "incidental"? The instruction The Chief Justice, in effect, provides lower courts: You will know it when you see it. . . .

Justices SCALIA, KENNEDY, THOMAS, and ALITO, dissenting.
. . . In our view, both these central provisions of the [ACA] — the Individual Mandate and Medicaid Expansion — are invalid. It follows, as some of the parties

urge, that all other provisions of the Act must fall as well. . . . The whole design of the Act is to balance the costs and benefits affecting each set of regulated parties. Thus, individuals are required to obtain health insurance. Insurance companies are required to sell them insurance regardless of patients' pre-existing conditions and to comply with a host of other regulations. And the companies must pay new taxes. States are expected to expand Medicaid eligibility and to create regulated market-places called exchanges where individuals can purchase insurance. Some persons who cannot afford insurance are provided it through the Medicaid Expansion, and others are aided in their purchase of insurance through federal subsidies available on health-insurance exchanges. The Federal Government's increased spending is offset by new taxes and cuts in other federal expenditures, including reductions in Medicare and in federal payments to hospitals. Employers with at least 50 employees must either provide employees with adequate health benefits or pay a financial exaction if an employee who qualifies for federal subsidies purchases insurance through an exchange.

In short, the Act attempts to achieve near-universal health insurance coverage by spreading its costs to individuals, insurers, governments, hospitals, and employers — while, at the same time, offsetting significant portions of those costs with new benefits to each group. . . . [The dissenters therefore conclude that a defect in any major provision should bring down the entire Act.]

— END —

Notes: Access to Private Health Insurance

1. *Who Would Have Guessed?* No one was surprised that the Supreme Court split 5-4 on the ACA's constitutionality. What was surprising, though, were the two particular bases for the ruling. In all the litigation leading up to the Supreme Court, not a single lower court (out of the dozen or so) had ruled either that the mandate is merely a tax, or that the Medicaid expansion coerces the states unless they are allowed to opt out.

Also surprising was that the four conservative dissenters declined to join Justice Roberts's opinion on the Commerce Clause issues. They dissented based on the tax issue and on severability, but elsewhere in their dissent, they expressed the same reasoning as Roberts on the Commerce Clause issues. According to several journalists, Roberts initially sided with the other conservatives, but he switched during the opinion-drafting process. Jeffrey Toobin, The Oath: The Obama White House and the Supreme Court (2012).

2. *The Way It Was.* As noted above, Congress repealed the individual mandate in late 2017 (effective 2019). Many congressional Republicans remain committed to undoing the rest of the ACA. As the debate over the future of health reform plays out, however, it is important not to lose sight of the way things were before. People not covered by group insurance could be turned down, or charged more, for the slightest reasons, including common conditions such as hay fever or ear infections. According to the Senate testimony excerpted above, "about 70 percent of people who appl[ied] for health insurance receive[d] an offer of coverage at standard rates or better. The rest [were] either declined (12%), offered higher rates (6%), or offered coverage that exclude[d] one or more particular pre-existing conditions (13%). In field studies, market testers found that conditions as common as asthma,

ear infections, and high blood pressure [created] problems obtaining coverage." Even in groups, covered people could have "pre-existing conditions" excluded for up to a year.

A dense thicket of federal and state laws tried to ameliorate the worst effects of this "medical underwriting," but only in a patchwork fashion. The federal Health Insurance Portability and Accountability Act (HIPAA) prevented group insurers (those who cover employers) from turning anyone down, but did not regulate insurance rates. That was left to the states, most of which allowed insurers to charge older or sicker people substantially more. HIPAA protected people from undergoing new waiting periods for preexisting conditions when they changed jobs, but it did not help them if they went without insurance for more than two months. Another federal law, called COBRA, allows people to stay on their employer's plan for up to three years after they leave a job, but only if they are able to pay the entire premium themselves.

3. *The Fairness of Community Rating.* Notice how the Justices differed in their characterizations of the ACA's community rating rule. Chief Justice Roberts emphasizes that the ACA requires younger, healthy people to pay more than they actually expect to incur in medical expense, on average, in order to subsidize other people. Is this a form of redistribution? If so, is it fair? Justice Ginsburg reminds us that no one knows when he or she might suffer medical misfortune, so we all face a similar set of risks from basic human frailty and brute luck. Although the magnitude of risk differs over time, Justice Ginsburg is willing to take more of a lifetime perspective.

Another principle of justice, however, might say that people who deliberately engage in risky behavior should not be allowed to force those who do not to pay their extra costs of insurance. Note that, despite community rating, the ACA allows insurers to charge smokers up to 50 percent more, and it also allows employers to pay substantial rebates to workers who participate in health-improving "wellness" programs. How much of medical costs do you speculate are caused by other voluntary behaviors? Which of these behaviors should be "punished" with higher insurance premiums or tolerated as legitimate lifestyle choices? Consider each of the following: eating meat, obesity, having children, drinking while pregnant, failing to exercise regularly, hang gliding.

Related to this debate is whether health insurance is more of a social financing mechanism for expected costs, rather than simply a private contingency fund for unexpected events. Economists observe that medical expense does not fit the classic model for insurable costs that applies to conventional insurance lines such as life, fire, and liability. These types of "casualty insurance" are designed for unpredictable, high-cost events, but most people's medical expenses are predictable to a significant extent. Nevertheless, we insure these expenses in order to make them more affordable, by spreading them more broadly across society. This is most obvious for the "social insurance" government programs of Medicare and Medicaid. But private health insurance also serves important social functions. Thus, whether to conceive of medical benefits coverage as a fundamental social good or a purely private good lies at the heart of many of the controversies explored in these notes, such as how comprehensive health insurance should be, whether insurers should be allowed to pick and choose among subscribers, and whether health insurance should be community rated.

4. *What About Employer Sponsored Coverage?* Even as the ACA transformed the individual market for health insurance, it made relatively few changes to the employer-sponsored market. The reason is simple: Employer-sponsored insurance already represents a naturally occurring form of community rating, in the sense that the premium cost is viewed as being equal for each member of the group. Even though each member contributes a different amount to the overall group cost, when the group is of sufficient size, insurers feel no need, even in unregulated markets, to assess each person's risk status in order to predict the group's overall expected medical cost (because groups' historical averages predict future expenses well enough). These and other natural economies of scale help explain why employer-based health insurance has been so successful. In a sense, the ACA's reforms are meant to help the individual and small-group market work as well as the large-group employer market already works on its own.

Tax law also strongly encourages employer-based insurance. Insurance premiums paid by employers are not taxed as income, and employees' premium contributions are paid on a pre-tax basis through payroll deduction. In contrast, individual (non-group) insurance is usually paid entirely through after-tax earnings. Is it fair that people who buy their own insurance do not receive the same tax breaks as employer-sponsored insurance? Note that the employment-based tax advantage is highly regressive, since it gives the most support to people with the greatest income. Covering people through the workplace also restricts their choices to plans that employers want to offer.

From time to time, proposals surface to decouple health insurance from employment. This could occur in several ways, to a greater or lesser degree. One idea, known as "defined contribution," is for employers to give employees a fixed budget that employees can use to shop for insurance anywhere they want, rather than the employer's paying for a benefit plan the employer selects. A second approach is to provide a tax credit (rather than deduction) to anyone who purchases health insurance, whether or not insurance comes as a job benefit.

When the ACA was adopted, many commentators predicted that employers would stop offering insurance and send their employees to the exchanges. So far, however, the ACA has had little effect on employer-based coverage. See Jean Abraham & Anne Beeson Royalty, How Has the Affordable Care Act Affected Work and Wages? (Jan. 2017). Many employees prefer employer-sponsored coverage on account of its favorable tax treatment. In addition, the exchanges in some states have struggled to attract a sufficient number of insurers, contributing to market instability. For those reasons, as well as uncertainty over the ACA's future, employers and employees have proven reluctant to disturb existing arrangements.

5. *Workplace Wellness Programs.* Although employers are generally prohibited from discriminating against their employee on the basis of health status, the ACA relaxes the community rating rules in connection with employer-sponsored "wellness programs." There are two types of wellness programs. *Participatory wellness programs* offer employees a financial incentive based on their participation alone. An employee might get a reduction in her monthly premium, for example, for filling out a detailed assessment designed to gauge her overall health. *Health-contingent wellness programs* require employees to achieve health-related targets in order to receive the financial incentive. Employees might have to go to the gym a certain number of times each month or keep their blood pressure under control. Supporters of

wellness programs have argued that a healthier workforce will reduce employer health care costs, perhaps substantially. Prior to the ACA, however, federal rules prohibiting discrimination on the basis of health status discouraged employers from adopting health-contingent wellness programs. The ACA has spurred their broader adoption by authorizing employers to offer financial incentives of up to 30 percent of the cost of the employee's premiums. Partly in response, most large employers have adopted wellness programs of one kind or another, although programs that offer extremely large incentives to promote adherence remain rare. Soeren Mattke et al., RAND Health, Workplace Wellness Programs Study (2013). Wellness is now a $6 billion industry.

Rigorous studies indicate, however, that workplace wellness programs rarely reduce spending or improve employee health. Indeed, many wellness programs actually increase expenses because employees receive unnecessary care arising as a result of their wellness screenings. Although some specialized wellness programs that target employees with chronic diseases may result in savings, such programs are not the norm. See Adrianna McIntyre et al., The Dubious Empirical and Legal Foundations of Workplace Wellness Programs, 27 Health Matrix 59 (2017).

Wellness programs have also come under fire for violating the Americans with Disabilities Act. To forestall disability discrimination, the ADA prohibits employers from asking employees about their medical histories unless their responses are "voluntary." In early 2016, the EEOC finalized a rule clarifying that a health assessment would be considered "voluntary" within the meaning of the ADA if the incentives of the wellness program stayed within the limits marked out in the ACA. 81 Fed. Reg. 31126 (2016). Critics have argued that the rule is too permissive: Because the average premium for a family plan in 2015 was $17,545, employers can offer incentives of up to $5,263 in connection with adherence to a wellness program. With potential incentives that large, it is not clear how a health assessment can be considered "voluntary." See AARP v. EEOC, 2017 WL 3614430 (D.D.C. Aug. 22, 2017) (holding that the EEOC rule is arbitrary and capricious).

In addition, wellness programs raise concerns about patient privacy. In 2013, for example, employees at Penn State were outraged when they were asked to take a health assessment that asked whether they "have recently had problems with a supervisor, a separation or a divorce, their finances or a fear of job loss; another question asks female employees whether they plan to become pregnant over the next year." Natasha Singer, On Campus, a Faculty Uprising Over Personal Data, N.Y. Times (Sept. 14, 2013).

6. *Additional Reading.* For **commentary on the Supreme Court's decision**, see The Health Care Case: The Supreme Court's Decision and Its Implications (Nathaniel Persily et al. eds. 2013); David A. Hyman, Why Did Law Professors Misunderestimate the Lawsuits Against PPACA?, 2014 U. Ill. L. Rev. 805; Josh Blackman, Unprecedented: The Constitutional Challenge to Obamacare (2013); Symposium, Health Care and the Constitution: A Forum on the Supreme Court's Affordable Care Act Decision, 81 Fordham L. Rev. 1697 (2013); Einer Elhauge, Obamacare on Trial (2012); Andrew Koppleman, The Tough Luck Constitution and the Fight over Health Care Reform (2013); Symposium, 38 J. Health Pol. Pol'y & L. 215 (2013); Martha Minow, Affordable Convergence: "Reasonable Interpretation" and the Affordable Care Act, 126 Harv. L. Rev. 117 (2012) ("Reading the two opinions . . . is a bit like traveling between two countries speaking different languages.").

On the **fairness of community rating** (note 3), see Jessica L. Roberts, "Healthism": A Critique of the Antidiscrimination Approach to Health Insurance and Health-Care Reform, 2012 U. Ill. L. Rev. 1159; Allison K. Hoffman, Three Models of Health Insurance: The Conceptual Pluralism of the Patient Protection and Affordable Care Act, 159 U. Pa. L. Rev. 1873 (2011); Deborah Stone, The Struggle for the Soul of Insurance, 18 J. Health Pol. Pol'y & L. 287 (1993); Lisa Klautzer et al., Can We Legally Pay People for Being Good?, 49 Inquiry 268 (2012).

On **insurance markets and regulation under the ACA**, see Tom Baker, Health Insurance, Risk, and Responsibility After the Patient Protection and Affordable Care Act, 159 U. Pa. L. Rev. 1577 (2011); Amy Monahan, On Subsidies and Mandates: A Regulatory Critique of the ACA, 36 J. Corp. L. 781 (2011); Allison K. Hoffman, Oil and Water: Mixing Individual Mandates, Fragmented Markets, and Health Reform, 36 Am. J. Law Med. & Ethics 7 (2010); Timothy Jost, Loopholes in the Affordable Care Act, 5 St. Louis U. J. Health L. & Pol'y 27 (2011).

On the **merits of decoupling insurance from employment** (note 4), see Edward A. Zelinsky, The Defined Contribution Paradigm, 114 Yale L. J. 451 (2004); Symposium, 38 Inquiry 175 (2001); Symposium, 25(6) Health Aff. 1474 (Dec. 2006). On the possible demerits, see David A. Hyman & Mark A. Hall, Two Cheers for Employment-Based Health Insurance, 2 Yale J. Health Pol'y L. & Ethics 23 (2002). See generally Mark V. Pauly, Health Benefits at Work (1998).

For discussions of **wellness programs** (note 5), see Symposium, 27 Health Matrix 1 (2017); Special Issue, 39 Journal of Health, Politics, Policy and Law 955 (2014); Jill R. Horwitz et al., Wellness Incentives in the Workplace: Cost Savings Through Cost Shifting to Unhealthy Workers, 32 Health Affairs 468 (2013).

An excellent textbook on **health insurance economics and regulation** generally is Michael A. Morrisey, Health Insurance (2013).

7. *Insurance Exchanges and States' Options.* Health insurance exchanges are quasi-public entities that facilitate the online sale and purchase of insurance and that determine people's eligibility for the ACA's subsidies. Under the ACA, states had the option of establishing their own insurance exchange or falling back on a federally operated exchange. The ACA's drafters anticipated that most states, even those hostile to health reform, would rather run their own exchanges than cede that authority to the federal government. But the choice of whether to establish an exchange became, in many states, a referendum on the state's support for the broader project of health reform. In the end, 34 states declined to establish exchanges. Rather unexpectedly, those choices became the subject of a second Supreme Court case over the future of the ACA.

◼ KING v. BURWELL
576 U.S. ___ (2015)

Chief Justice ROBERTS delivered the opinion of the Court [in which Justices KENNEDY, GINSBURG, BREYER, SOTOMAYOR, and KAGAN joined].

The Patient Protection and Affordable Care Act adopts a series of interlocking reforms designed to expand coverage in the individual health insurance market. First, the Act bars insurers from taking a person's health into account when deciding whether to sell health insurance or how much to charge. Second, the Act generally requires each person to maintain insurance coverage or make a payment to the Internal Revenue Service. And third, the Act gives tax credits to certain people to make insurance more affordable.

In addition to those reforms, the Act requires the creation of an "Exchange" in each State—basically, a marketplace that allows people to compare and purchase insurance plans. The Act gives each State the opportunity to establish its own Exchange, but provides that the Federal Government will establish the Exchange if the State does not.

This case is about whether the Act's interlocking reforms apply equally in each State no matter who establishes the State's Exchange. Specifically, the question presented is whether the Act's tax credits are available in States that have a Federal Exchange.

I. A.

The Patient Protection and Affordable Care Act grew out of a long history of failed health insurance reform. In the 1990s, several States began experimenting with ways to expand people's access to coverage. One common approach was to impose a pair of insurance market regulations—a "guaranteed issue" requirement, which barred insurers from denying coverage to any person because of his health, and a "community rating" requirement, which barred insurers from charging a person higher premiums for the same reason. Together, those requirements were designed to ensure that anyone who wanted to buy health insurance could do so.

The guaranteed issue and community rating requirements achieved that goal, but they had an unintended consequence: They encouraged people to wait until they got sick to buy insurance. Why buy insurance coverage when you are healthy, if you can buy the same coverage for the same price when you become ill? This consequence—known as "adverse selection"—led to a second: Insurers were forced to increase premiums to account for the fact that, more and more, it was the sick rather than the healthy who were buying insurance. And that consequence fed back into the first: As the cost of insurance rose, even more people waited until they became ill to buy it.

This led to an economic "death spiral." As premiums rose higher and higher, and the number of people buying insurance sank lower and lower, insurers began to leave the market entirely. As a result, the number of people without insurance increased dramatically. . . .

In 1996, Massachusetts adopted the guaranteed issue and community rating requirements and experienced similar results. But in 2006, Massachusetts added two more reforms: The Commonwealth required individuals to buy insurance or pay a penalty, and it gave tax credits to certain individuals to ensure that they could afford the insurance they were required to buy. The combination of these three reforms—insurance market regulations, a coverage mandate, and tax credits—reduced the uninsured rate in Massachusetts to 2.6 percent, by far the lowest in the Nation.

B.

The Affordable Care Act adopts a version of the three key reforms that made the Massachusetts system successful. First, the Act adopts the guaranteed issue and community rating requirements. . . . Second, the Act generally requires individuals to maintain health insurance coverage or make a payment to the IRS. . . . In Congress's view, that coverage requirement was "essential to creating effective health insurance markets." Congress also provided an exemption from the coverage requirement for anyone who has to spend more than eight percent of his income on health insurance. Third, the Act seeks to make insurance more affordable by giving refundable tax credits to individuals with household incomes between 100 percent and 400 percent of the federal poverty line. . . .

These three reforms are closely intertwined. As noted, Congress found that the guaranteed issue and community rating requirements would not work without the coverage requirement. And the coverage requirement would not work without the tax credits. The reason is that, without the tax credits, the cost of buying insurance would exceed eight percent of income for a large number of individuals, which would exempt them from the coverage requirement. . . .

C.

In addition to those three reforms, the Act requires the creation of an "Exchange" in each State where people can shop for insurance, usually online. An Exchange may be created in one of two ways. First, the Act provides that "[e]ach State shall . . . establish an American Health Benefit Exchange . . . for the State." Second, if a State nonetheless chooses not to establish its own Exchange, the Act provides that the Secretary of Health and Human Services "shall . . . establish and operate such Exchange within the State."

The issue in this case is whether the Act's tax credits are available in States that have a Federal Exchange rather than a State Exchange. The Act . . . provides that the amount of the tax credit depends in part on whether the taxpayer has enrolled in an insurance plan through "an Exchange established by the State under section 1311 of the Patient Protection and Affordable Care Act." The IRS addressed the availability of tax credits by promulgating a rule that made them available on both State and Federal Exchanges. . . . At this point, 16 States and the District of Columbia have established their own Exchanges; the other 34 States have elected to have HHS do so.

Petitioners are four individuals who live in Virginia, which has a Federal Exchange. They do not wish to purchase health insurance. In their view, Virginia's Exchange does not qualify as "an Exchange established by the State," so they should not receive any tax credits. That would make the cost of buying insurance more than eight percent of their income, which would exempt them from the Act's coverage requirement. . . .

II

. . . When analyzing an agency's interpretation of a statute, we often apply the two-step framework announced in Chevron U. S. A. Inc. v. Natural Resources Defense Council, Inc., 467 U. S. 837 (1984). Under that framework, we ask whether the statute is ambiguous and, if so, whether the agency's interpretation is reasonable. This approach "is premised on the theory that a statute's ambiguity constitutes an implicit delegation from Congress to the agency to fill in the statutory gaps." FDA v. Brown & Williamson Tobacco Corp., 529 U. S. 120, 159 (2000). "In extraordinary cases, however, there may be reason to hesitate before concluding that Congress has intended such an implicit delegation."

This is one of those cases. The tax credits are among the Act's key reforms, involving billions of dollars in spending each year and affecting the price of health insurance for millions of people. Whether those credits are available on Federal Exchanges is thus a question of deep "economic and political significance" that is central to this statutory scheme; had Congress wished to assign that question to an agency, it surely would have done so expressly. It is especially unlikely that Congress would have delegated this decision to the IRS, which has no expertise in crafting health insurance policy of this sort. This is not a case for the IRS.

It is instead our task to determine the correct reading of [this provision]. If the statutory language is plain, we must enforce it according to its terms. But oftentimes the "meaning—or ambiguity—of certain words or phrases may only become evident when placed in context." Brown & Williamson, 529 U. S., at 132. So when deciding whether the language is plain, we must read the words "in their context and with a view to their place in the overall statutory scheme." Our duty, after all, is "to construe statutes, not isolated provisions."

A.

We begin with the text of Section 36B. As relevant here, Section 36B allows an individual to receive tax credits only if the individual enrolls in an insurance plan through "an Exchange established by the State under [42 U. S. C. §18031]." . . . Section 18031 provides that "[e]ach State shall . . . establish an American Health Benefit Exchange . . . for the State." Although phrased as a requirement, the Act gives the States "flexibility" by allowing them to "elect" whether they want to establish an Exchange. If the State chooses not to do so, Section 18041 provides that the Secretary "shall . . . establish and operate such Exchange within the State." By using the phrase "such Exchange," Section 18041 instructs the Secretary to establish and operate the same Exchange that the State was directed to establish under Section 18031. In other words, State Exchanges and Federal Exchanges are equivalent . . . .

Second, we must determine whether a Federal Exchange is "established by the State" for purposes of Section 36B. At the outset, it might seem that a Federal Exchange cannot fulfill this requirement. . . . But when read in context, "with a view to [its] place in the overall statutory scheme," the meaning of the phrase "established by the State" is not so clear. . . . [Various technical] provisions suggest that the Act may not always use the phrase "established by the State" in its most natural sense. Thus, the meaning of that phrase may not be as clear as it appears when read out of context. . . .

The upshot of all this is that the phrase "an Exchange established by the State under [§18031]" is properly viewed as ambiguous. The phrase may be limited in its reach to State Exchanges. But it is also possible that the phrase refers to all Exchanges—both State and Federal—at least for purposes of the tax credits. . . . The Affordable Care Act contains more than a few examples of inartful drafting. . . . Several features of the Act's passage contributed to that unfortunate reality. . . . Congress passed much of the Act using a complicated budgetary procedure known as "reconciliation," which limited opportunities for debate and amendment, and bypassed the Senate's normal 60-vote filibuster requirement. As a result, the Act does not reflect the type of care and deliberation that one might expect of such significant legislation. Cf. Frankfurter, Some Reflections on the Reading of Statutes, 47 Colum. L. Rev. 527, 545 (1947) (describing a cartoon "in which a senator tells his colleagues 'I admit this new bill is too complicated to understand. We'll just have to pass it to find out what it means.' ").

Anyway, we "must do our best, bearing in mind the fundamental canon of statutory construction that the words of a statute must be read in their context and with a view to their place in the overall statutory scheme." Utility Air Regulatory Group, 573 U. S., at ___. . . .

B.

Given that the text is ambiguous, we must turn to the broader structure of the Act to determine the meaning of Section 36B. . . . Here, the statutory scheme compels us to reject petitioners' interpretation because it would destabilize the individual insurance market in any State with a Federal Exchange, and likely create the very "death spirals" that Congress designed the Act to avoid. . . . It is implausible that Congress meant the Act to operate in this manner. . . . Congress made the guaranteed issue and community rating requirements applicable in every State in the Nation. But those requirements only work when combined with the coverage requirement and the tax credits. So it stands to reason that Congress meant for those provisions to apply in every State as well. . . .

Finally, the structure of Section 36B itself suggests that tax credits are not limited to State Exchanges. Section 36B(a) initially provides that tax credits "shall be allowed" for any "applicable taxpayer." [It] then defines an "applicable taxpayer" as someone who (among other things) has a household income between 100 percent and 400 percent of the federal poverty line. Together, these two provisions appear to make anyone in the specified income range eligible to receive a tax credit. . . .

In a democracy, the power to make the law rests with those chosen by the people. Our role is more confined — "to say what the law is." Marbury v. Madison, 1 Cranch 137, 177 (1803). That is easier in some cases than in others. But in every case we must respect the role of the Legislature, and take care not to undo what it has done. A fair reading of legislation demands a fair understanding of the legislative plan.

Congress passed the Affordable Care Act to improve health insurance markets, not to destroy them. If at all possible, we must interpret the Act in a way that is consistent with the former, and avoids the latter. . . .

Justice SCALIA, with whom Justice THOMAS and Justice ALITO join, dissenting.

. . . This case requires us to decide whether someone who buys insurance on an Exchange established by the Secretary gets tax credits. You would think the answer would be obvious — so obvious there would hardly be a need for the Supreme Court to hear a case about it. . . . Words no longer have meaning if an Exchange that is not established by a State is "established by the State." It is hard to come up with a clearer way to limit tax credits to state Exchanges. . . .

The Court persists that these provisions "would make little sense" if no tax credits were available on federal Exchanges. Even if that observation were true, it would show only oddity, not ambiguity. Laws often include unusual or mismatched provisions. The Affordable Care Act spans 900 pages; it would be amazing if its provisions all lined up perfectly with each other. This Court "does not revise legislation . . . just because the text as written creates an apparent anomaly." Michigan v. Bay Mills Indian Community, 572 U. S. ___, ___ (2014). . . .

[In various places, the dissent describes the majority's analysis as "feeble," "interpretive jiggery-pokery," "outlandish[]," "indefensible," a "dismal failure," and "[p]ure applesauce."]

Even less defensible, if possible, is the Court's claim that its interpretive approach is justified because this Act "does not reflect the type of care and deliberation that one might expect of such significant legislation." . . . It is not our place to . . . make everything come out right when Congress does not do its job properly. It is up to Congress to design its laws with care, and it is up to the people to hold them to account if they fail to carry out that responsibility. Rather than rewriting the law under the pretense of interpreting it, the Court should have left it to Congress to decide what to do about the Act's limitation of tax credits to state Exchanges. If Congress values above everything else the Act's applicability across the country, it could make tax credits available in every Exchange. . . . And if Congress thinks that the present design of the Act works well enough, it could do nothing. Congress could also do something else altogether, entirely abandoning the structure of the Affordable Care Act. The Court's insistence on making a choice that should be made by Congress both aggrandizes judicial power and encourages congressional lassitude. . . .

The Act that Congress passed makes tax credits available only on an "Exchange established by the State." This Court, however, concludes that this limitation would prevent the rest of the Act from working as well as hoped. So it rewrites the law to make tax credits available everywhere. We should start calling this law SCOTUScare.

Perhaps the Patient Protection and Affordable Care Act will attain the enduring status of the Social Security Act or the Taft-Hartley Act; perhaps not. But this Court's two decisions on the Act will surely be remembered through the years. The somersaults of statutory interpretation they have performed ("penalty" means tax, . . .) will be cited by litigants endlessly, to the confusion of honest jurisprudence. And the cases will publish forever the discouraging truth that the Supreme Court of the United States favors some laws over others, and is prepared to do whatever it takes to uphold and assist its favorites.

Notes: The Exchanges

1. *Hurricane Season.* King v. Burwell was preceded by almost as much fevered anticipation as NFIB v. Sibelius. And for good reason: Had the case come out the other way, the exchanges would likely have collapsed in the 34 states that had chosen the federal default exchange. See Nicholas Bagley et al., Predicting the Fallout from King v. Burwell, 372 New Eng. J. Med. 101 (2015). Republican congressional leaders would have come under intense pressure to propose a statutory fix that President Obama would have been willing to sign into law. No one knows, though, whether such an imagined bipartisan compromise could have been achieved.

2. *Tea Leaves.* Does the Court's decision signal a desire to bring an end to judicial challenges to the ACA's fundamentals? Another flashpoint of legal controversy arose in *House of Representatives v. Price* (formerly *House v. Burwell*), where House

Republicans argued that the Obama administration was spending money to support the ACA without the required appropriation from Congress. The ACA provision in question requires insurers to give their lowest-income enrollees a discount on their out-of-pocket spending (in the forms of deductibles and copayments); in exchange, the federal government is supposed to reimburse the insurers. The Obama administration asked Congress to appropriate the needed funds, but Congress declined. To prevent the ACA's collapse, the administration then interpreted the statute to allow it to make the payments out of an existing appropriation.

The lawsuit was initially seen as a political stunt. Fights over the appropriations power are worked out between the political branches; historically, they have never been the subject of litigation. Observers on both sides of the aisle believed that the House of Representatives lacked standing to bring the case. But a federal district court disagreed, reasoning that a violation of the appropriations power would infringe on the House's constitutionally assigned powers and would thus cause it a concrete injury. House v. Burwell, 130 F.Supp.3d 53 (D.D.C. 2015). On the merits, the court also sided with the House: In its view, the ACA included no appropriation for the cost-sharing subsidies. House v. Burwell, 185 F.Supp.3d 165 (D.D.C. 2016). The court enjoined the government from making cost-sharing payments, but stayed its injunction pending appeal to the D.C. Circuit.

In October 2017, while the appeal was still pending, President Trump reversed the Obama administration's legal determination and ordered the payments to cease. Although many observers feared that the exchanges would unravel with the loss of the cost-sharing payments, the real-world consequences have been surprisingly muted. The vast majority of insurers had already raised their premiums to account for the risk that President Trump might cut off their payments, and state insurance commissioners took creative steps to shield their insurance markets from the worst effects. Higher premiums will harm those people who do not quality for premium subsidies, but the ACA protects those making less than four times the poverty level by capping their premiums at a fixed percentage of income. Although a bipartisan group of senators has proposed legislation to temporarily fund the cost-sharing payments, it is unclear as of late 2017 whether the legislation has any chance of passing.

3. *Correcting Congress's Mistakes.* The drafting anomaly in King v. Burwell was initially seen as an obvious mistake arising from the somewhat rushed manner in which its final language was hammered together. Senate committees had drafted two earlier versions, one that relied entirely on state exchanges and the other that had only a single federal exchange. Although the enacted bill merged the two ideas—states would take the lead, but with a federal fallback—drafters failed to clean up all of the exchange-related phrasing. Do you find it curious that neither the challengers nor the government openly characterized the legislative language as a mistake? Or that the Court's opinion only vaguely hints at this possibility?

Instead of claiming a drafting error, the challengers argued—implausibly and with essentially no evidentiary support—that Congress deliberately withheld subsidies from the federal fallback exchange in order to compel states to establish their own exchanges. If Congress did use subsidies in this manner, would it have amounted to unconstitutional coercion? Consider the question in light of the portion of NFIB v. Sebelius that we turn to below.

4. *The Health of the Exchanges.* The rollout of the exchanges was initially rocky. HealthCare.gov, the federally operated exchange, did not function for the first months of its operation, and a number of newly established "cooperative health

plans" failed. These growing pains notwithstanding, however, the exchanges have proven successful at enrolling people in coverage. More than 12.2 million people selected coverage for 2017 through the state and federal exchanges, and about 84 percent of them qualified for premium subsidies. See CMS, Health Insurance Marketplaces 2017 Open Enrollment Period Final Enrollment Report (Mar. 2017).

But the top-level numbers mask wide variability. In 2016, the prices for a typical silver-level exchange plan ran from a high of $719 per month in Anchorage, Alaska to a low of $186 per month in Albuquerque, New Mexico. Many rural counties have struggled to attract enough insurers to assure a competitive marketplace. Today, more than one in five exchange enrollees had a choice of only one insurer. See Cynthia Cox et al., 2017 Premium Changes and Insurer Participation in the Affordable Care Act's Health Insurance Marketplaces, Kaiser Family Foundation, Oct. 24, 2016. On the other hand, by the end of 2016, premiums and range of choice were not dramatically different for ACA individual coverage than what most employers typically pay and what most employees have to choose from.

Large premium increases for 2017, together with the withdrawal of several large insurers who were leaving the exchanges, raised questions about the long-term stability of the exchanges. Although most independent observers believed that prices in 2018 would stabilize and that the exchanges would remain viable, the election of Donald Trump has changed the calculus. The president's decision to cut off cost-sharing payments, together with concerns that the administration may not vigorously enforce the individual mandate, has sent jitters through the insurance industry.

5. *Rate Regulation.* Although the ACA imposes a host of new requirements for the individual and small-group insurance markets, it does relatively little to regulate the price of insurance. The important exception is the ACA's "medical loss ratio," which requires insurers to spend at least 80 percent of what they earn in premiums on their enrollees' medical expenses. (To an insurer, any payment for health care is a "medical loss.") If an insurer spends less than the required amount, it must remit the difference to its customers. The medical loss ratio aims to discourage insurers from denying good claims, to stop them from spending too much on sales and administration, and to prevent them from pocketing excessive profits. But the requirement is controversial. Smaller insurers, for example, may spend more on administration relative to their larger competitors, making it more difficult for them to hit the medical loss ratio.

The ACA also requires insurers to inform the federal government if they plan on increasing their premiums by more than 10 percent and to explain the reasons for the rate increase. See 76 Fed. Reg. 29964 (2011). The ACA, however, does not empower the federal government to reject unreasonable rate increases; that authority remains with the states, which vary greatly in the rigor of their rate review processes. See Department of Health and Human Services, Rate Review Annual Report (Dec. 2015).

6. *Further Reading.* For some of the voluminous commentary on King v. Burwell, see Josh Blackman, Unraveled: Obamacare, Religious Liberty, and Executive Power (2016); Abbe R. Gluck, Imperfect Statutes, Imperfect Courts: Understanding Congress's Plan in an Era of Unorthodox Lawmaking, 129 Harv. L. Rev. 62 (2015); Nicholas Bagley, Three Words and the Future of the Affordable Care Act, 40 J. Health Pol. Pol'y & L. 589 (2015); Jonathan H. Adler & Michael F. Cannon,

Taxation Without Representation: The Illegal IRS Rule to Expand Tax Credits under the PPACA 23 Health Matrix 119 (2013).

For background on House v. Price (note 2), see Nicholas Bagley, Legal Limits and the Implementation of the Affordable Care Act, 164 Penn. L. Rev. 1715, 1729-1735 (2016).

For discussion of the **medical loss ratio** (note 4), see Michael McCue et al., Impact of Medical Loss Regulation on the Financial Performance of Health Insurers, 32 Health Affairs 1546 (2013); Michael McCue & Mark A. Hall, The Federal Medical Loss Ratio Rule: Implications for Consumers in Year 3 (2013); Benjamin Day et al., The Affordable Care Act and Medical Loss Ratios: No Impact in First Three Years, 45 Int'l J. Health Servs. 127 (2015).

3. Medicaid

■ NATIONAL FEDERATION OF INDEPENDENT BUSINESS v. SEBELIUS
567 U.S. 1 (2012)

Chief Justice ROBERTS.

. . . On the day the President signed the [Patient Protection and Affordable Care] Act into law, Florida and 12 other States filed a complaint . . . subsequently joined by 13 more States . . . and the National Federation of Independent Business. The plaintiffs alleged, among other things, that . . . the Medicaid expansion, which gives funds to the States on the condition that they provide specified health care to all citizens whose income falls below a certain threshold, . . . exceeds Congress's authority under the Spending Clause . . . [because it coerces them] by threatening to withhold all of a State's Medicaid grants, unless the State accepts the new expanded funding and complies with the conditions that come with it. This, they argue, violates the basic principle that the Federal Government may not compel the States to enact or administer a federal regulatory program. . . .

Enacted in 1965, Medicaid offers federal funding to States to assist [low-income] pregnant women, children, needy families, the blind, the elderly, and the disabled in obtaining medical care. See 42 U. S. C. § 1396a(a)(10). In order to receive that funding, States must comply with federal criteria governing matters such as who receives care and what services are provided at what cost. By 1982 every State had chosen to participate in Medicaid. . . .

There is no doubt that the Act dramatically increases state obligations under Medicaid. The current Medicaid program requires States to cover only certain discrete categories of needy individuals — pregnant women, children, needy families, the blind, the elderly, and the disabled. There is no mandatory coverage for most childless adults, and the States typically do not offer any such coverage.[6] The States also enjoy considerable flexibility with respect to the coverage levels for parents of

---

6. [Actually, about half the states provide at least some coverage for low-income childless adults, but the coverage usually is more limited than Medicaid's full benefits and federal funding is provided only through special "waivers" of normal Medicaid funding rules. — EDS.]

needy families. On average States cover only those unemployed parents who make less than 37 percent of the federal poverty level, and only those employed parents who make less than 63 percent of the poverty line.[7]

The Medicaid provisions of the Affordable Care Act, in contrast, require States to expand their Medicaid programs by 2014 to cover all individuals under the age of 65 with incomes below 133 percent of the federal poverty line. . . . The Affordable Care Act provides that the Federal Government will pay 100 percent of the costs of covering these newly eligible individuals through 2016. In the following years, the federal payment level gradually decreases, to a minimum of 90 percent. In light of the expansion in coverage mandated by the Act, the Federal Government estimates that its Medicaid spending will increase by approximately $100 billion per year, nearly 40 percent above current levels. . . .

In this case, the financial "inducement" Congress has chosen is much more than "relatively mild encouragement"—it is a gun to the head. . . . [T]he Medicaid Act provides that if a State's Medicaid plan does not comply with the Act's requirements, the Secretary of Health and Human Services may declare that "further payments will not be made to the State." A State that opts out of the Affordable Care Act's expansion in health care coverage thus stands to lose not merely "a relatively small percentage" of its existing Medicaid funding, but all of it. Medicaid spending accounts for over 20 percent of the average State's total budget, with federal funds covering 50 to 83 percent of those costs. . . . The threatened loss of over 10 percent of a State's overall budget . . . is economic dragooning that leaves the States with no real option but to acquiesce in the Medicaid expansion. . . .

[T]he Government claims that the Medicaid expansion is properly viewed merely as a modification of the existing program because the States agreed that Congress could change the terms of Medicaid when they signed on in the first place. . . . Congress has in fact done so, sometimes conditioning only the new funding, other times both old and new. The Medicaid expansion, however, accomplishes a shift in kind, not merely degree.

The original program was designed to cover medical services for four particular categories of the needy: the disabled, the blind, the elderly, and needy families with dependent children. Previous amendments to Medicaid eligibility merely altered and expanded the boundaries of these [mandatory] categories. Under the Affordable Care Act, Medicaid is transformed into a program to meet the health care needs of the entire nonelderly population with income below 133 percent of the poverty level. It is no longer a program to care for the neediest among us, but rather an element of a comprehensive national plan to provide universal health insurance coverage. . . . A State could hardly anticipate that Congress's reservation of the right to "alter" or "amend" the Medicaid program included the power to transform it so dramatically. . . .

[Justices Breyer and Kagan joined this portion of the opinion (IV.A). Justices Scalia, Kennedy, Thomas, and Alito concurred with, but did not join, this portion. Thus, seven justices agreed that the Medicaid expansion is unconstitutional.]

---

7. [The federal poverty level is about $12,000 for a single person and about twice that for a family of four, with other levels similarly scaled to household size.—EDS.]

B

Nothing in our opinion precludes Congress from offering funds under the Affordable Care Act to expand the availability of health care, and requiring that States accepting such funds comply with the conditions on their use. What Congress is not free to do is to penalize States that choose not to participate in that new program by taking away their existing Medicaid funding. . . . As a practical matter, that means States may now choose to reject the expansion; that is the whole point. But that does not mean all or even any will. Some States may indeed decline to participate, either because they are unsure they will be able to afford their share of the new funding obligations, or because they are unwilling to commit the administrative resources necessary to support the expansion. Other States, however, may voluntarily sign up, finding the idea of expanding Medicaid coverage attractive, particularly given the level of federal funding the Act offers at the outset. . . .

[Justices Ginsburg, Breyer, Sotomayor, and Kagan joined this subsection B, regarding the consequence of finding the Medicaid expansion coercive. The other four justices (Scalia, Kennedy, Thomas, and Alito) dissented on the remedy, arguing instead that the consequence should be to strike down the entire Affordable Care Act. See page 1007.]

Justice GINSBURG [with whom Justice SOTOMAYOR joined], dissenting in part.

. . . Medicaid is a prototypical example of federal-state cooperation in serving the Nation's general welfare. Rather than authorizing a federal agency to administer a uniform national health-care system for the poor, Congress offered States the opportunity to tailor Medicaid grants to their particular needs, so long as they remain within bounds set by federal law. In shaping Medicaid, Congress did not endeavor to fix permanently the terms participating states must meet; instead, Congress reserved the "right to alter, amend, or repeal" any provision of the Medicaid Act. . . . And from 1965 to the present, States have regularly conformed to Congress' alterations of the Medicaid Act.

The Chief Justice's . . . conclusion rests on [the premise that] . . . the Medicaid expansion is . . . a new grant program, not an addition to the Medicaid program existing before the ACA's enactment. Congress, The Chief Justice maintains, has threatened States with the loss of funds from an old program in an effort to get them to adopt a new one. . . . The Chief Justice therefore—for the first time ever—finds an exercise of Congress' spending power unconstitutionally coercive.

Medicaid, as amended by the ACA, however, is not two spending programs; it is a single program with a constant aim—to enable poor persons to receive basic health care when they need it. . . . States have no entitlement to receive any Medicaid funds; they enjoy only the opportunity to accept funds on Congress' terms. . . . The Federal Government, therefore, is not, as The Chief Justice charges, threatening States with the loss of "existing" funds from one spending program in order to induce them to opt into another program. Congress is simply requiring States to do what States have long been required to do to receive Medicaid funding: comply with the conditions Congress prescribes for participation. . . .

Expansion has been characteristic of the Medicaid program. Akin to the ACA in 2010, the Medicaid Act as passed in 1965 augmented existing federal grant programs jointly administered with the States. Huberfeld, Federalizing Medicaid, 14 U. Pa. J. Const. L. 431, 444-445 (2011). States were not required to participate in

Medicaid. But if they did, the Federal Government paid at least half the costs. To qualify for these grants, States had to offer a minimum level of health coverage to beneficiaries of four federally funded, state-administered welfare programs: Aid to Families with Dependent Children; Old Age Assistance; Aid to the Blind; and Aid to the Permanently and Totally Disabled. At their option, States could enroll additional "medically needy" individuals; these costs, too, were partially borne by the Federal Government at the same, at least 50%, rate.

Since 1965, Congress has amended the Medicaid program on more than 50 occasions, sometimes quite sizably. Most relevant here, between 1988 and 1990, Congress required participating States to include among their beneficiaries pregnant women with family incomes up to 133% of the federal poverty level, children up to age 6 at the same income levels, and children ages 6 to 18 with family incomes up to 100% of the poverty level. These amendments added millions to the Medicaid-eligible population. . . .

Compared to past alterations, the ACA is notable for the extent to which the Federal Government will pick up the tab. Medicaid's 2010 expansion is financed largely by federal outlays. In 2014, federal funds will cover 100% of the costs for newly eligible beneficiaries; that rate will gradually decrease before settling at 90% in 2020. By comparison, federal contributions toward the care of beneficiaries eligible pre-ACA range from 50% to 83%, and averaged 57% between 2005 and 2008. . . .

Finally, any fair appraisal of Medicaid would require acknowledgment of the considerable autonomy States enjoy under the Act. . . . Subject to its basic requirements, the Medicaid Act empowers States to "select dramatically different levels of funding and coverage, alter and experiment with different financing and delivery modes, and opt to cover (or not to cover) a range of particular procedures and therapies. States have leveraged this policy discretion to generate a myriad of dramatically different Medicaid programs over the past several decades." Ruger, Of Icebergs and Glaciers, 75 Law & Contemp. Probs. 215, 233 (2012). . . .

The alternative to conditional federal spending, it bears emphasis, is not state autonomy but state marginalization. In 1965, Congress elected to nationalize health coverage for seniors through Medicare. It could similarly have established Medicaid as an exclusively federal program. Instead, Congress gave the States the opportunity to partner in the program's administration and development. . . . Congress must of course have authority to impose limitations on the States' use of the federal dollars. This Court, time and again, has respected Congress' prescription of spending conditions, and has required States to abide by them. . . . That is what makes this such a simple case, and the Court's decision so unsettling. . . .

■ MEDICAID EVOLUTION FOR THE 21ST CENTURY
John V. Jacobi
102 Ky. L.J. 357 (2014)

Medicaid was created in 1965 as a companion to Medicare. Unlike Medicare, which was intended as a contributory social insurance system for the elderly, Medicaid was intended to shore up the existing patchwork of state systems, and, funded in part by the federal government, to provide health care services to the poor. From the beginning, Medicaid recognized the historical primacy of the states as providers for the poor, but also initiated an increased regulatory role for the federal government to enforce some basic coverage principles as conditions of states' receipt of the federal funds available under the program. Like its sister program, Medicare, Medicaid did not interfere with the financial freedom of health care providers; like private health insurance coverage, it set about creating payment mechanisms that would lead providers to participate voluntarily in Medicaid as they did in private insurance programs. Medicaid, then, deviated from precursor systems: "[I]n its essential structure, Medicaid resembled not a grant program to clinics and hospitals, but instead a 'third party payment' system structured to operate like insurance, paying 'participating' health care professionals and institutions for covered services furnished to enrolled persons."

Medicaid was set up as something akin to a public insurance system, but became increasingly cabined over time by statutory and regulatory provisions that bar the states' Medicaid programs from running, as private insurance does, on a market-oriented, risk-sensitive basis. As Medicaid has developed, it has deviated more and more from the private insurance model on which it was loosely based, in three essential ways: first, those covered are mostly uninsurable in private markets; second, the services covered extend beyond those covered in commercial insurance; and third, the structure, adjusted by many amendments over the years, is much more complex than any private insurance product.

A. WHO IS COVERED?

Prior to the expansions permitted by the ACA, Medicaid enrollees have been limited to the most medically precarious: the poor and vulnerable. In short, they are exactly the people private insurers do not wish to cover. They are poor, and also "categorically eligible." That is, in addition to meeting income and assets requirements, enrollees are required to be blind, disabled, elderly, pregnant women, children, or in families with children. These groups represent predictably high-cost insureds. A child with disabilities, for example, requires about four times the health expenditures of a child without disabilities, and people over the age of sixty-five are similarly expensive to cover. In Medicaid, the elderly and people with disabilities comprise only about 25% of enrollees, but account for about 65% of the program's cost. The distribution of health care usage generally, and predictably, is very skewed toward the elderly and people with disabilities and chronic illnesses, with the most-ill 5% utilizing about half of the health care resources, and the least-ill 50% accounting for only about 3% of annual health expenditures. On the basis of their age and health history, then, Medicaid enrollees are likely to need a great deal of care and will be essentially uninsurable under the circumstances.

In addition, people in the Medicaid program raise identity issues beyond disability and age. The non-elderly enrollment in Medicaid is over 53% Black or Hispanic, although those two groups comprise only about 30% of the American population. The long history of race- and ethnicity- based health disparities in American health care strongly suggests that the overrepresentation of people of color in Medicaid will reflect poorer health outcomes—regardless of any faults of the Medicaid program itself. "For example, relative to whites, African Americans and Hispanics are less likely to receive appropriate cardiac medication . . . or to undergo coronary artery bypass surgery, even when the variations in such factors as insurance status, income, age, co-morbid conditions, and symptom expression are taken into account." In addition to the effects of race and ethnicity, socioeconomic status has a demonstrable effect on health status, independent of insurance status. Regardless of the causes of these effects, they establish that people covered by Medicaid are more medically fragile, have more complex health conditions, and are affected by determinants of poor health, independent of their access to health coverage or care.

B. What is covered?

Medicaid also differs from other health finance programs in the breadth of services covered. The program covers services included in commercial insurance, including preventive, curative, and restorative physician, pharmacy, and hospital services. In addition, however, Medicaid mandates that states cover long-term care services, home care services, transportation services to and from service providers, Federally Qualified Health Center services, and rural health clinic services. In addition, many states have added "optional" services that are not mandated, but for which the federal government will provide funding if added by a state plan. The most common of these services include dental, eyeglass, prostheses, and personal care services, as well as intermediate care facility services for individuals with intellectual disabilities.

This broad coverage fits Medicaid's programmatic mission to assist the states in fulfilling their traditional mission of serving the health needs of the poor and vulnerable. Some of the additional services included in many Medicaid programs, such as coverage of eyeglasses and dental services, simply reflect a recognition that the poor do not have the disposable income to pay for services and devices that have a relatively low expected cost. Other benefits, like intermediate care facilities for people with intellectual disabilities and home care services, reflect the need to provide services for the very conditions that give rise to the vulnerability entitling individuals to Medicaid services. The slate of covered services, then, reflects the poor, elderly, or disabled condition of Medicaid enrollees.

C. Complex structure

The structure of Medicaid is famously complex. Unlike Medicare, which is wholly federally funded and governed, Medicaid requires that the federal and state governments work in partnership—a relationship that has been notably strained recently. Its basic structure, as leading historians of Medicaid have observed, lacked coherence and clarity as a social insurance system for three reasons: first, it failed to cover all of the poor, but extended only to the categorically eligible; second, the definition and scope of medical services covered were variable from state to state; and third, the income eligibility standards varied, in some cases dramatically, from state to state. In sum, the program remained a balkanized system funded by the federal government but largely run by the states. Perhaps most critically, states retained substantial power to determine how much to pay providers for their services, and states have taken advantage of that power.

Medicaid was criticized as rather "ill-designed" and "vague" from the beginning. It paid providers on a fee-for-service basis, as did insurers. But federal payments, forming the majority of Medicaid financing, were structured as a grant-in-aid program for the states, which were largely in charge of maintaining a network of willing providers. Unlike private insurance, the Medicaid program has grown, adding components over the years ranging beyond traditional medical care to address the needs of the target population. In addition, millions of low-income elderly persons and persons with long-term disabilities qualify for both Medicaid and Medicare, and use Medicare as the primary payer for services. They rely on Medicaid, however, to pay for Medicare's coinsurance and deductibles, and for those health care services covered by Medicaid but not Medicare. One major source of Medicaid's complexity has been states' gradual movement away from the role of public insurer to the role of public payor, devolving many insurer functions to commercial HMOs.

The movement toward then-novel HMOs as fiscal and programmatic intermediaries began within five years of Medicaid's creation. California was a pioneer in the use of Medicaid HMOs. Widespread claims of fraudulent sales practices and inadequate provider networks frustrated these efforts and led federal regulators to impose relatively stringent requirements for the use of Medicaid managed care. By 1980, only about 1% of Medicaid enrollees were in HMOs. During the 1980s, however, Medicaid officials in the Reagan and George H.W. Bush administrations relaxed many of the restrictions on the use of Medicaid HMOs, although these efforts only raised the percentage of enrollees to about 12%. During the 1990s, mostly through the use of [administrative] waivers, the number of Medicaid enrollees in HMOs grew dramatically "from 9.5 percent of total Medicaid enrollment in 1991 to 40.1 percent in 1996." These waivers from usual Medicaid regulatory requirements were necessary because state managed care programs limited the range of enrollees' choice of providers and varied, by location within states, enrollees' access to services. Then, as part of the Balanced Budget Act of 1997, states obtained the authority to mandate HMO enrollment for most Medicaid beneficiaries.

In an effort to contain Medicaid costs, states have continued to move toward managed care. By 2010, most states had moved the majority of their enrollees to HMOs, and almost two-thirds of Medicaid enrollees were in managed care. For most states, the movement to HMOs for Medicaid enrollees has not resulted in the hoped-for cost savings, and the shift seems not to have improved the quality of care or access to providers. Medicaid programs have, then, largely moved from directly administering provider payments to purchasing insurance coverage for enrollees from private vendors. In other words, most states have largely privatized what had been among their most important programmatic functions: selecting, maintaining, monitoring, and compensating health care providers for many of their Medicaid enrollees. This "decentralization" of government function not only saved states the administrative and staffing costs of network formation and maintenance, but also, to some extent, relieved them of the always-delicate task of intermediating between providers and enrollees.

Notes: Medicaid

1. *Medicaid Quandaries.* The Supreme Court's decision in NFIB v. Sebelius allowed states to refuse the ACA's Medicaid expansion while retaining funding for traditional Medicaid. As of this writing, 19 states, concentrated in the South and the Great Plains, have refused the Medicaid expansion. Does it make financial sense

FIGURE 9.3 Medicaid's Role for Selected Populations

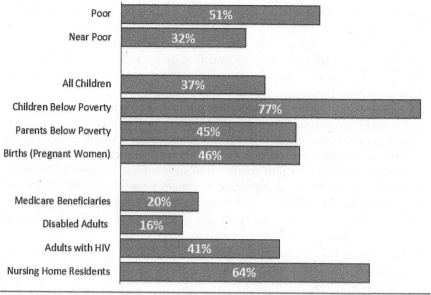

Percent with Medicaid Coverage

Population	Percent
Poor	51%
Near Poor	32%
All Children	37%
Children Below Poverty	77%
Parents Below Poverty	45%
Births (Pregnant Women)	46%
Medicare Beneficiaries	20%
Disabled Adults	16%
Adults with HIV	41%
Nursing Home Residents	64%

SOURCE: Kaiser Commission on Medicaid and the Uninsured (KCMU) and Urban Institute analysis of various federal data sources for 2013 or earlier, prior to Medicaid expansion under the ACA.

for those states to refuse the expansion considering that federal funds will pay for at least 90 percent of the costs? What other reasons might states have for refusing to expand? What effect does a refusal to expand have on physicians and hospitals? Even though Medicaid pays them substantially less than private insurance, many of them are already treating the people who would be added to Medicaid, but are doing so for almost no money, as indigent uninsured patients. See Mark Hall, States' Decisions Not to Expand Medicaid, 92 N.C. L. Rev. 1459 (2014).*

2. *Block Grants.* With Donald Trump's election, the debate over repealing and replacing the ACA has raised questions about the future of the Medicaid expansion and even about Medicaid's basic structure:

> Congressional Republicans hope to transform Medicaid from an individual entitle-ment to a block grant—a fixed sum of money that places few restrictions on the purposes that states can use it for. In some respects, block grant proposals promote federalism: they afford states more discretion about how to put Medicaid dollars

---

* See also, Jonathan Oberlander, Repeal, Replace, Repair, Retreat: Republicans' Health Care Quagmire, ___ New Engl. J. Med. ___ (2017): "Medicaid's remarkable scope (it covers more than 70 million Americans), array of sympathetic constituencies (it covers 49 percent of all children, 39 percent of births, 35 percent of persons with disabilities, and 64 percent of nursing home residents), role in financing vital medical services (including mental-health, HIV, and opioid-addiction treatments and long-term care), and importance to health system stakeholders (including hospitals, physicians, and states) means that it is not an easy mark" for funding cuts.

to work. A state, for example, could place limits on eligibility or benefits; more creatively, it could use some of its Medicaid money for lead abatement in urban cores, as Michigan has recently been allowed to do on a small scale. But the devil is in the details. A fixed block grant that increases with economy-wide inflation and is insensitive to the business cycle would not give states the fiscal flexibility necessary to cope with a recession. Over time, as well, the galloping pace of medical inflation would erode the value of the block grants, requiring states to ration access to medical care, either through cuts to benefits or to eligibility. Proposals to transform Medicaid into a block-grant program may trade on the rhetoric of states' rights, but they have the perverse effect of inhibiting state power.

Alternative approaches could mitigate the concern. Per capita grants anchored to a formula that accounted for the number of people within a state under a particular income threshold, for example, would avoid the countercyclical trap: federal outlays would then increase as more people lost their jobs and became dependent on government assistance. But because the data necessary to calculate funding levels may lag the economy by several years, a state could find itself in a financial pinch just as a recession takes hold. Nor would a per capita grant account for unanticipated cost spikes associated with the release of costly new therapies (like the new Hepatitis C drugs) or epidemics (like the Zika outbreak). Of greater concern, the size of per capita grants would have to increase with medical inflation. Yet Republicans anticipate achieving large cost reductions through Medicaid reform — suggesting that the goal is not to provide sufficient funds to cover those who are currently eligible, but instead to force states to shrink their programs through eligibility restrictions and benefit cuts.

Nicholas Bagley, Federalism and the End of Obamacare, 127 Yale L. J. F. 1 (2017). For an in-depth discussion of block grants and changing Medicaid's status as an entitlement program, see David A. Super, The Political Economy of Entitlement, 104 Colum. L. Rev. 633 (2004).

3. *Federalism on Steroids.* The intricate structure of federal and state roles in the ACA — not just under Medicaid, but also regarding the regulation of private health insurance — raises a host of federalism issues that scholars will debate for years to come. For a start, see Abbe Gluck, Intrastatutory Federalism and Statutory Interpretation: State Implementation of Federal Law in Health Reform and Beyond, 121 Yale L. J. 534, 582 (2011); I. Glenn Cohen, Conscientious Objection, Coercion, the Affordable Care Act, and U.S. States, 20 Ethical Perspectives 163 (2013); David K. Jones, Lavatories of Democracy? Health Reform and Federalism in the Trump Era, 95 Milbank Q. 470 (2017); Elizabeth McCuskey, Agency Imprimatur & Health Reform Preemption, 89 Ohio St. L. J. (2017); Nicole Huberfeld et al., Plunging into Endless Difficulties: Medicaid and Coercion in National Federation of Independent Business v. Sebelius, 93 B.U. L. Rev. 1 (2013); Elizabeth Weeks Leonard, Rhetorical Federalism: The Value of State-Based Dissent to Federal Health Reform, 39 Hofstra L. Rev. 111 (2010); Abigail Moncrieff, Cost-Benefit Federalism: Reconciling Collective Action Federalism and Libertarian Federalism in the Obamacare Litigation and Beyond, 37 Am. J. L. & Med. 288 (2012).

4. *Enforcing the Medicaid Entitlement.* For eligible beneficiaries, Medicaid creates an entitlement to medically necessary care. Paying for that care, however, puts an enormous strain on state budgets. Especially in hard times, states may try to save money by reducing their Medicaid payments to hospitals, physicians, and other providers. On average, Medicaid pays hospitals close to Medicare rates, but it pays physicians just 70 percent of what they receive from Medicare, and in some states

that figure is much lower. As payments drop, physicians or specialized facilities may refuse to see new Medicaid patients, making it difficult or impossible for those patients to secure needed care. In principle, § 30(A) of the Medicaid statute prohibits states from paying providers so little that they abandon the program. Enforcing that obligation has proven challenging, however, as the following case suggests.

■ARMSTRONG v. EXCEPTIONAL CHILD CENTER, INC.
576 U.S. ___ (2015)

Justice SCALIA delivered the opinion of the Court, except as to Part IV.

We consider whether Medicaid providers can sue to enforce § (30)(A) of the Medicaid Act, [which addresses the sufficiency of payments to health care providers].

Medicaid is a federal program that subsidizes the States' provision of medical services to "families with dependent children and of aged, blind, or disabled individuals, whose income and resources are insufficient to meet the costs of necessary medical services." § 1396-1. Like other Spending Clause legislation, Medicaid offers the States a bargain: Congress provides federal funds in exchange for the States' agreement to spend them in accordance with congressionally imposed conditions.

In order to qualify for Medicaid funding, the State of Idaho adopted, and the Federal Government approved, a Medicaid "plan," § 1396a(a), which Idaho administers through its Department of Health and Welfare. Idaho's plan includes "habilitation services"—in-home care for individuals who, "but for the provision of such services . . . would require the level of care provided in a hospital or a nursing facility or intermediate care facility for the mentally retarded the cost of which could be reimbursed under the State plan," § 1396n(c) and (c)(1). Providers of these services are reimbursed by the Department of Health and Welfare.

STATUTE

> Section 30(A) of the Medicaid Act requires Idaho's plan to:
> "provide such methods and procedures relating to the utilization of, and the payment for, care and services available under the plan . . . as may be necessary to safeguard against unnecessary utilization of such care and services and to assure that payments are consistent with efficiency, economy, and quality of care and are sufficient to enlist enough providers so that care and services are available under the plan at least to the extent that such care and services are available to the general population in the geographic area. . . .".

Respondents are providers of habilitation services to persons covered by Idaho's Medicaid plan. They sued petitioners—two officials in Idaho's Department of Health and Welfare—in the United States District Court for the District of Idaho, claiming that Idaho violates § 30(A) by reimbursing providers of habilitation services at rates lower than § 30(A) permits. [In particular, the challengers objected to basing rates on what the state's budget allowed rather than on what the state's own studies indicated that the services actually cost]. They asked the court to enjoin petitioners to increase these rates [by amounts ranging from 105 to 80 percent]. . . .

III

The power of federal courts of equity to enjoin unlawful executive action is subject to express and implied statutory limitations. "'Courts of equity can no more disregard statutory and constitutional requirements and provisions than can courts of law.'" In our view the Medicaid Act implicitly precludes private enforcement of § 30(A), and respondents cannot, by invoking our equitable powers, circumvent Congress's exclusion of private enforcement.

Two aspects of § 30(A) establish Congress's "intent to foreclose" equitable relief. First, the sole remedy Congress provided for a State's failure to comply with Medicaid's requirements—for the State's "breach" of the Spending Clause contract—is the withholding of Medicaid funds by the Secretary of Health and Human Services. As we have elsewhere explained, the "express provision of one method of enforcing a substantive rule suggests that Congress intended to preclude others." Alexander v. Sandoval, 532 U.S. 275, 290 (2001).

The provision for the Secretary's enforcement by withholding funds might not, by itself, preclude the availability of equitable relief. But it does so when combined with the judicially unadministrable nature of § 30(A)'s text. It is difficult to imagine a requirement broader and less specific than § 30(A)'s mandate that state plans provide for payments that are "consistent with efficiency, economy, and quality of care," all the while "safeguard[ing] against unnecessary utilization of . . . care and services." Explicitly conferring enforcement of this judgment-laden standard upon the Secretary alone establishes, we think, that Congress "wanted to make the agency remedy that it provided exclusive," thereby achieving "the expertise, uniformity, widespread consultation, and resulting administrative guidance that can accompany agency decisionmaking," and avoiding "the comparative risk of inconsistent interpretations and misincentives that can arise out of an occasional inappropriate application of the statute in a private action." Gonzaga Univ. v. Doe, 536 U.S. 273, 292 (2002) (Breyer, J., concurring in judgment). The sheer complexity associated with enforcing § 30(A), coupled with the express provision of an administrative remedy, § 1396c, shows that the Medicaid Act precludes private enforcement of § 30(A) in the courts.

Justice BREYER, concurring in part and concurring in the judgment.

. . . I believe that several characteristics of the federal statute before us, when taken together, make clear that Congress intended to foreclose respondents from bringing this particular action for injunctive relief.

For one thing, as the majority points out, § 30(A) of the Medicaid Act sets forth a federal mandate that is broad and nonspecific. But, more than that, § 30(A) applies its broad standards to the setting of rates. The history of ratemaking demonstrates that administrative agencies are far better suited to this task than judges. More than a century ago, Congress created the Interstate Commerce Commission, the first great federal regulatory rate-setting agency, and endowed it with authority to set "reasonable" railroad rates. It did so in part because judicial efforts to maintain reasonable rate levels had proved inadequate.

Reading § 30(A) underscores the complexity and nonjudicial nature of the rate-setting task. That provision requires State Medicaid plans to "assure that payments are consistent with efficiency, economy, and quality of care and are sufficient to enlist enough providers" to assure "care and services" equivalent to that "available to the general population in the geographic area." The methods that a state agency, such as Idaho's Department of Health and Welfare, uses to make this kind of determination may involve subsidiary determinations of, for example, the actual cost of providing quality services, including personnel and total operating expenses; changes in public expectations with respect to delivery of services; inflation; a comparison of rates paid in neighboring States for comparable services; and a comparison of any rates paid for comparable services in other public or private capacities.

At the same time, § 30(A) applies broadly, covering reimbursements provided to approximately 1.36 million doctors, serving over 69 million patients across the Nation. And States engage in time-consuming efforts to obtain public input on proposed plan amendments.

I recognize that federal courts have long become accustomed to reviewing for reasonableness or constitutionality the rate-setting determinations made by agencies. But this is not such an action. Instead, the lower courts here . . . required the State to set rates that "approximate the cost of quality care provided efficiently and economically." To find in the law a basis for courts to engage in such direct rate-setting could set a precedent for allowing other similar actions, potentially resulting in rates set by federal judges (of whom there are several hundred) outside the ordinary channel of federal judicial review of agency decisionmaking. The consequence, I fear, would be increased litigation, inconsistent results, and disorderly administration of highly complex federal programs that demand public consultation, administrative guidance and coherence for their success. I do not believe Congress intended to allow a statute-based injunctive action that poses such risks (and that has the other features I mention).

Justice SOTOMAYOR, with whom Justice KENNEDY, Justice GINSBURG, and Justice KAGAN join, dissenting.

Suits in federal court to restrain state officials from executing laws that assertedly conflict with the Constitution or with a federal statute are not novel. To the contrary, this Court has adjudicated such requests for equitable relief since the early days of the Republic. Nevertheless, today the Court holds that Congress has foreclosed private parties from invoking the equitable powers of the federal courts to require States to comply with § 30(A) of the Medicaid Act. It does so without pointing to the sort of detailed remedial scheme we have previously deemed necessary to establish congressional intent to preclude resort to equity. Instead, the Court relies on Congress' provision for agency enforcement of § 30(A) — an enforcement mechanism of the sort we have already definitively determined not to foreclose private actions — and on the mere fact that § 30(A) contains relatively broad language. As I cannot agree that these statutory provisions demonstrate the requisite congressional intent to restrict the equitable authority of the federal courts, I respectfully dissent. . . .

What is the . . . "carefully crafted and intricate remedial scheme" for enforcement of § 30(A)? The Court relies on two aspects of the Medicaid Act, but, whether considered separately or in combination, neither suffices.

First, the Court cites 42 U.S.C. § 1396c, which authorizes the Secretary of Health and Human Services (HHS) to withhold federal Medicaid payments to a State in whole or in part if the Secretary determines that the State has failed to comply with the obligations set out in § 1396a, including § 30(A). But . . . § 1396c provides no specific procedure that parties actually affected by a State's violation of its statutory obligations may invoke in lieu of [equitable remedies] — leaving them without any other avenue for seeking relief from the State. Nor will § 1396c always provide a particularly effective means for redressing a State's violations: If the State has violated § 30(A) by refusing to reimburse medical providers at a level "sufficient to enlist enough providers so that care and services are available" to Medicaid beneficiaries to the same extent as they are available to "the general population," agency action resulting in a reduced flow of federal funds to that State will often be self-defeating. See Brief for Former HHS Officials as Amici Curiae 18 (noting that HHS is often reluctant to initiate compliance actions because a "state's non-compliance creates a damned-if-you-do, damned-if-you-don't scenario where the withholding of state funds will lead to depriving the poor of essential medical assistance"). . . .

Second, perhaps attempting to reconcile its treatment of § 1396c with this longstanding precedent, the Court focuses on the particular language of § 30(A), contending that this provision, at least, is so "judicially unadministrable" that Congress must have intended to preclude its enforcement in private suits. Admittedly, the standard set out in § 30(A) is fairly broad. . . . But mere breadth of statutory language does not require the Court to give up all hope of judicial enforcement—or, more important, to infer that Congress must have done so. . . .

Of course, the broad scope of § 30(A)'s language is not irrelevant. But rather than compelling the conclusion that the provision is wholly unenforceable by private parties, its breadth counsels in favor of interpreting § 30(A) to provide substantial leeway to States, so that only in rare and extreme circumstances could a State actually be held to violate its mandate. The provision's scope may also often require a court to rely on HHS, which is "comparatively expert in the statute's subject matter." When the agency has made a determination with respect to what legal standard should apply, or the validity of a State's procedures for implementing its Medicaid plan, that determination should be accorded the appropriate deference. See, e.g., Chevron U.S.A., Inc. v. Natural Resources Defense Council, Inc., 467 U.S. 837 (1984). . . .

The Court's error today has very real consequences. Previously, a State that set reimbursement rates so low that providers were unwilling to furnish a covered service for those who need it could be compelled by those affected to respect the obligation imposed by § 30(A). Now, it must suffice that a federal agency, with many programs to oversee, has authority to address such violations through the drastic and often counterproductive measure of withholding the funds that pay for such services. Because a faithful application of our precedents would have led to a contrary result, I respectfully dissent.

Notes: Enforcing Medicaid

1. *Assuring Access After* Armstrong. The agency charged with administering Medicaid, the Centers for Medicare and Medicaid Services (CMS), believes that *Armstrong* "underscores the need for stronger non-judicial processes to ensure access, including stronger processes at both the state and federal levels for developing data on beneficiary access and reviewing the effect on beneficiary access of changes to payment methodologies." 80 Fed. Reg. 67,579 (2015). But doubts remain as to whether the Medicaid branch of CMS—a small and under-resourced agency—can effectively enforce § 30(A).

2. *The Developing Case Law.* Applying and extending *Armstrong*, the federal courts have held that those provisions of the Medicaid statute that establish broad, non-specific guidelines for state Medicaid plans cannot generally be enforced through a

private right of action. See, e.g., Davis v. Shah, 821 F.3d 231 (2d Cir. 2016). Although suits under the Administrative Procedure Act may still be brought on the ground that the federal government acted arbitrarily or capriciously in approving a state's Medicaid plan, APA review is highly deferential. See Christ the King Manor v. Burwell, 163 F.Supp.3d 123 (M.D. Pa. 2016).

Even after *Armstrong*, however, the courts have been receptive to claims that approval of a state's plan will deprive private plaintiffs of specific, unambiguous rights guaranteed under the Medicaid statute. See Planned Parenthood of Gulf Coast v. Gee, 837 F.3d 477 (5th Cir. 2016) (holding that a Medicaid provision "phrased in individual terms and in specific, judicially administrable terms" is privately enforceable); Guggenberger v. Minnesota, 198 F.Supp.3d 973 (D. Minn. 2016) ("*Armstrong* does not provide a basis for an across-the-board rejection of all private enforcement actions under the Medicaid Act's numerous varied provisions."); Planned Parenthood of Kansas v. Mosier, 2016 WL 3597457 (D. Kan. 2016); but see Does v. Gillespie, 867 F. 3d 1034 (8th Cir. 2017) (holding that an apparently specific right is not enforceable through a private cause of action).

3. *Medicaid and Immigration.* Legal immigrants are ineligible for Medicaid until they have been permanent residents for five years. Is that requirement constitutional? It certainly satisfies the rational basis standard under federal law, but at least one state court has ruled that its constitution imposes strict scrutiny of drawing such legislative lines. Finch v. Commonwealth Health Insurance Connector Authority, 459 Mass. 655 (2011). See generally Patricia Illingworth & Wendy E. Parmet, The Health of Newcomers (2017).

4. *Further Reading.* For further discussion of *Armstrong*, see Henry Paul Monaghan, A Cause of Action, Anyone?, 91 Notre Dame L. Rev. 1807 (2016); Jane Perkins, Pin the Tail on the Donkey: Beneficiary Enforcement of the Medicaid Act Over Time, 9 St. Louis U. J. Health L. & Pol'y 207 (2016); Private Rights of Action—Equitable Remedies to Enforce the Medicaid Act—Armstrong v. Exceptional Child Center, Inc., 129 Harv. L. Rev. 211 (2015).

For discussions on the occasion of **Medicaid's 50th birthday**, Sara Rosenbaum, Medicaid at 50, in The Oxford Handbook of U.S. Health Law (2017); Symposium, The Law of Medicare and Medicaid at 50, 15 Yale J. of Health Pol'y, L. & Ethics 1 (2015); Symposium, The ABCs (Accessibility, Barriers, and Challenges) of Medicaid Expansion. 9 St. Louis U. J. Health L. & Pol'y 179-296 (2016); Commonwealth Fund, Medicare at 50 Years (2015); Symposium, Medicare and Medicaid at 50, 31 JAMA 311 (2015).

4. Medicare

■REFLECTIONS ON MEDICARE AT 50: BREAKING THE CHAINS OF PATH DEPENDENCY FOR A NEW ERA
Richard L. Kaplan
23 Elder L.J. 1 (2015)

One of the enduring myths surrounding Medicare is that it is a single, integrated program created at one moment in time and largely impervious to change. That is simply not the case. For better or worse, Medicare has evolved since its original enactment in 1965 to encompass several distinct programs, usually denominated Parts A through D, that stand largely separate from one another in terms of their coverages, exclusions, and costs.

ORIGINAL PROGRAM: PART A

Medicare Part A is the original component and represents the height of the social insurance model as applied to health care for older Americans; i.e., it is structured as a mandatory program with its own dedicated source of financing. In both of these aspects, Part A is unique among Medicare's constituent components. Every person who receives income from wages, salaries, or self-employment must pay a "contribution," or tax, to fund this program, and eligibility is based on attaining a specified age—namely, 65 years—that has remain unchanged since the program's original enactment.

Medicare's tax is currently 2.9% of income from earnings, which is collected half from employees and half from employers or paid in its entirety by self-employed persons. An additional 0.9% tax is collected on earnings in excess of $200,000 per year for unmarried persons and $250,000 per year for married couples. This additional Medicare tax, it should be noted, was added only recently by the ACA. But the main point is that Medicare Part A is financed entirely from this dedicated revenue stream, with funds deposited into a "trust fund" that the federal government administers.

The scope of Medicare Part A's coverage consists of four principal components, each with its own limitations, exclusions, and cost-sharing features. Those components pertain to: (1) hospitalization, (2) nursing homes, (3) home health care, and (4) hospice care. . . .

1. HOSPITALIZATION

There is no question that most people's largest medical expenditures are likely to involve hospital stays, but Medicare Part A provides fairly comprehensive coverage for such expenditures. The program covers almost all services incurred during the first 60 days of a "spell of illness." . . . This "spell of illness" determination is important for two independent reasons. First, . . . [a]ny hospital days within a "spell of illness" after the first 60 days are subject to per-day deductibles that are adjusted annually for inflation. . . . Second, each "spell of illness" has a deductible that is also adjusted annually for inflation and [was] $1,260 in 2015. [Because of these cost-sharing obligations,] Medicare enrollees could face substantial out-of-pocket costs from repeated hospital stays. [Those large out-of-pocket costs] illustrat[e] a very important aspect of Medicare Part A—namely, that this program has no "stop loss" provision that limits how much an enrollee is obligated to pay, unlike most private health insurance plans.

For that reason, most Medicare beneficiaries obtain some type of supplemental coverage, often private policies that are usually denominated "Medigap" insurance. . . .

2. NURSING HOMES

No component of Medicare Part A is more misunderstood than its coverage of "skilled nursing facilities," more commonly called nursing homes. Medicare does indeed cover the cost of nursing homes, but under structures that reflect the state of care that such facilities provided when Medicare was first enacted, and are increasingly outdated as Americans live longer and need nursing homes for more extended periods of time. For example, Medicare covers nursing home care only if a patient is admitted to the nursing home within 30 days of that person's being discharged from a hospital. Moreover, the patient must require care in the nursing home for a condition that was treated originally in the hospital or is medically related to that condition. But today, many older people transition from their own home or apartment directly to a nursing facility without needing to go to a hospital first, especially when the underlying ailment is a neurodegenerative condition such as Alzheimer's or Parkinson's disease. . . . Clearly, Medicare's coverage of nursing homes was built on a model of post-hospitalization rehabilitative care and does not encompass the sort of long-term confinement that characterizes many older Americans' nursing home experience today.

OUT OF DATE

3. Home health care

Medicare Part A covers home health care services subject to three major caveats. First, the recipient of such care must be unable to leave his or her home without assistance from other people or devices such as canes, walkers, or wheelchairs. Second, the home health care services must be provided by a Medicare-certified home health care agency. In other words, help provided by family members, friends, neighbors, or church groups does not qualify for payment by Medicare. Third, home health care services must be provided pursuant to a written plan of care that was prepared by the patient's doctor, and that is reviewed by that doctor every 60 days.

If these requirements are met, Medicare pays for occupational, physical, and speech therapy, along with medical supplies, and "part-time and intermittent" nursing care. . . . Medicare Part A does not, however, cover many home health care services that older patients need to stay in their homes, such as around-the-clock nursing care, meal preparation, or laundry.

4. Hospice   *>6 months*

One of the less well-known coverages within Medicare Part A is hospice care for persons whose doctors have certified that they have no more than six months to live. Under this coverage, such persons can receive various home care and other benefits, including services that are generally not covered by Medicare, that attempt to mitigate a dying person's pain rather than remedy his or her underlying illness. . . .

Optional Coverage for Physicians' Charges: Part B

Medicare Part A excludes many common medical expenses, the most significant being doctors' charges. This exclusion seems unfathomable in today's world, but doctors' fees were apparently not as significant in the pre-Medicare era and were often not covered by the typical private health insurance plans that were marketed as "major medical" policies. In formulating Medicare Part A, its creators consciously tried to replicate those policies, so physicians' charges were not included in Medicare Part A.

Instead, an optional coverage called Medicare Part B was fashioned to cover such charges, as well as other less common expenses, such as ambulance service and durable medical equipment (hospital beds, wheelchairs, scooters, and so forth). Medicare Part B has no relationship to the Medicare payroll tax and is financed strictly on a current-year basis. Premiums are paid by those who have enrolled in Medicare B and are adjusted annually for inflation. In 2015, this premium is $104.90 per month, an amount that was calculated to cover approximately 25% of the program's projected costs for the coming year. The remaining 75% of the program's funding comes from general tax revenues of the federal government, which are paid by all U.S. taxpayers regardless of their age or likely enrollment in Medicare. Most of Part B's financing, in other words, comes from society as a whole, or at least that portion of society that pays income taxes. This arrangement constitutes a substantial subsidization of Medicare Part B for those who elect its coverage.

No one is required to enroll in Medicare Part B, but most eligible persons do so because of this substantial public subsidy. . . .

The Managed Care Alternative: Part C

As managed care plans were introduced into the private health insurance marketplace, this option became available to Medicare beneficiaries on a contractual basis. This approach was formalized in Medicare Part C as "Medicare + Choice" and then re-labeled "Medicare Advantage" as part of the George W. Bush Administration's initiative to boost enrollment in such plans. But regardless of the specific appellation, Medicare's managed care program essentially parallels its private sector counterpart.

For example, Medicare managed care plans promise better coordination of care and simpler paperwork when claiming benefits in exchange for restricting their enrollees to specific doctors, hospitals, home health agencies, and usually pharmacies as well. Older Americans often have established relationships with numerous physicians, so such restrictions may present a difficult dilemma. Perhaps that is why managed care plans represent only a minority of Medicare beneficiaries—approximately three in ten according to the most recent data available.

On the other hand, Medicare managed care represents a major simplification of elders' health care financing by substituting a monthly premium and modest copayments for Medicare's convoluted array of annual deductibles and unlimited coinsurance obligations. Managed care also eliminates the need for supplemental "Medigap" policies and their related claims-filing procedures. Moreover, Medicare managed care plans offer benefits that historically were not available in "traditional" Medicare, such as annual physical examinations and prescription drugs. Indeed, access to such drugs was a major reason that many older Americans enrolled in managed care plans before Medicare Part D became effective in 2006. Even today, managed care plans provide a variety of benefits that Medicare generally does not, including vision and dental care, exercise classes, and other services that are intended to keep enrollees healthy.

Adding Prescription Drugs: Part D

No single aspect of Medicare better illustrates the ossification of its programmatic development than the failure to provide generally available coverage of prescription medications until Medicare Part D took effect in 2006—four decades after Medicare was enacted! During those intervening years, pharmacological innovations included important maintenance drugs for a wide range of chronic conditions that often affect the Medicare population, such as arthritis, asthma, diabetes, heart disease, and hypertension, among others.

Moreover, when Part D was finally created, it reflected a very different orientation than Medicare Parts A and B regarding the role of government and the appeal of personal choice. Instead, Part D is a quasi-voucher approach that provides subsidies to private prescription drug plans that compete on various parameters including monthly premiums, specific drug coverage, pharmacy location, and other factors. During the annual open enrollment period, new plans become available to Medicare enrollees, though the precise number of different plans that are available to any given enrollee depends upon his or her state of residence. . . . Medicare Part D's plethora of choices has generally been popular with enrollees, despite its inherent complexity and curious financial structure. . . .

Notes: Medicare at 50

1. *Frozen in Time?* Notice the distinct resemblance between Medicare's structure, the basic contours of which were established in 1965, and the structure of the typical, provider-friendly Blue Cross/Blue Shield health plan of the 1960s. The divide between Medicare Part A and Part B resembles the historical divide between Blue Cross (hospital coverage) and Blue Shield (physician coverage), which at the time were often separate companies. Private insurance rarely covered prescription drugs in the 1960s, so neither did Medicare until 2006 (Part D). Later in the chapter, we'll also learn that, originally (until the 1980s), Medicare paid hospitals based on their actual costs and physicians based on their actual charges, similar to how the Blues treated their virtual "owners" at the time. Even to this day, Medicare contracts out most of its day-to-day administrative functions (contracting, claims payment, auditing, etc.) to private, third-party "intermediaries," which often (but not always) are actual Blues plans. The similarities between Medicare and the Blues were not an accident. The aim was to make Medicare as familiar and non-threatening as possible to the medical establishment, in order to overcome political opposition and the possible boycott of the program. Theodore R. Marmor, The Politics of Medicare (2d ed. 1999). As the story unfolds, consider how influential these historical foundations remain.

2. *The Future of Medicare.* When Medicare was first enacted, Part A was projected to cost only $9 billion a year in 1990. It actually cost $60 billion that year. Government actuaries failed to anticipate the continuing inflationary effects of Medicare's generous payment methods, the increased demand for medical services that resulted from making health insurance much more widespread, and the expanded life expectancy of the elderly. See Steven Hayward & Erik Peterson, The Medicare Monster, Reason, Jan. 1993, at 19. Yet the program remains popular.

> Medicare achieves its highest marks from the millions of elderly beneficiaries who depend on the program to pay for a substantial portion of their medical care, but surveys of public opinion also show wide-spread support for it among people under

65 [as well]. . . . [Nevertheless], given its rapid rate of growth, [Medicare] will remain at the center of government efforts to trim the massive budget deficit. [Previously,] budget-cutting exercises exacted most of their toll from providers, and they remain a prime target now. But providers are scarcely prepared to be the sole stakeholders who accept sacrifice. The only other real options are raising taxes on the general population, reducing Medicare benefits, or asking the elderly to pay more on some income-related basis. However, elected politicians of almost every stripe have shown no disposition to embrace any of these unpopular approaches, suggesting by their inaction that we can somehow have it all. That is indeed a fanciful formula for the future. . . .

John K. Iglehart, The American Health Care System: Medicare, 327 New Eng. J. Med. 1467 (1992). This analysis rings as true today as it did when it was written a quarter-century ago.

In 2016, Medicare consumed about 15 percent of the federal budget, roughly the same amount as was spent on the national defense. That figure will inevitably swell as the costs of medical care continue to increase, the population continues to age, and the baby boomers retire. Budget-conscious policymakers have considered different approaches to reducing Medicare spending, a few of which worked their way into the ACA:

> In its most controversial effort to rein in Medicare cost inflation, the ACA created a new agency known as the Independent Payment Advisory Board (IPAB). Comprising fifteen health-care experts appointed by the President who are removable only for cause, the Board has authority that is nothing short of remarkable. Starting in 2015, the Board must submit to the President and Congress annual "proposals" for cutting Medicare if spending over a five-year period increases faster than preselected targets linked to economy-wide inflation (through 2019) and economic growth (for 2020 and after). IPAB proposals are subject to few constraints: they cannot ration care, modify Medicare eligibility, or increase beneficiary cost sharing.
>
> Eight months after the Board issues a proposal, the Secretary of HHS must implement it—wholesale and without amendment—unless Congress has enacted (and the President has signed) legislation making different, but equally deep, cuts. The proposal goes into effect "[n]otwithstanding any other provision of law," meaning that Board proposals can override even preexisting congressional statutes with which they conflict. Judicial review of an IPAB proposal or its implementation is prohibited.
>
> The Board's insulation from political influence is both its principal virtue and its biggest vice. To its proponents, the Board's insulation allows it to bring policy expertise to bear on how most effectively to hold down rising Medicare costs. To its detractors, the Board is an antidemocratic abdication of congressional authority to unaccountable green-eyeshade types.

Nicholas Bagley, Bedside Bureaucrats: Why Medicare Reform Hasn't Worked, 101 Georgetown L. J. 520, 569-570 (2013). Because neither President Obama nor President Trump has appointed anyone to the IPAB, the exercise of its authorities will fall to the Secretary of HHS. Due to a recent lull in Medicare spending growth, the IPAB spending targets have not yet been exceeded. Some observers believe that could soon change, likely spurring a legal challenge to the IPAB's authority. See Coons v. Lew, 762 F.3d 891 (9th Cir. 2014) (dismissing as unripe a constitutional challenge to IPAB).

Many policymakers believe that Medicare needs a more fundamental transformation. Premium support—or, more pejoratively, the "voucherization" of Medicare—has received considerable attention, particularly from budget-conscious Republicans.

In a premium support system, the federal government would provide a payment on behalf of each Medicare beneficiary toward the purchase of a health insurance plan—either a private plan, similar a Medicare Advantage plan, or traditional Medicare. This approach is sometimes called a defined contribution or voucher approach. Under a premium support system, health plans would compete for enrollees and people on Medicare would choose among plans for their coverage—an approach that sounds similar to the current system, but is not the same. A key difference is that payments for services provided to beneficiaries in traditional Medicare would be capitated rather than the current approach that generally ties payments to the specific services that beneficiaries use.

A number of premium support proposals have been introduced in recent years; these proposals are similar in their general approach, but often differ in key policy parameters, and some are more specific than others. Premium support proposals vary in several ways, including: the role of traditional Medicare in the new system, the extent to which benefits would be defined, the rules for health insurers, and the methodology used to set payments to plans, including traditional Medicare. For example, some proposals would base the federal payment to plans on the average bid (the cost to the plan of providing all Medicare-covered services) submitted by plans in a given area while other proposals would base federal payment on the second lowest plan bid. These policy specifications have important implications for federal savings, beneficiaries' costs, the viability of private plans in markets across the country, and the sustainability of traditional Medicare.

Typically, premium support proposals would affect services covered under Medicare Parts A and B, but not Part D.

Gretchen Jacobson & Tricia Neuman, Turning Medicare into a Premium Support System: Frequently Asked Questions, Kaiser Family Foundation (July 2016). Speaker of the House Paul Ryan has expressed interest in adopting a premium support model for Medicare, but those efforts have come to naught so far.

3. *Concierge Medicine.* In general, physicians must accept Medicare's rates as full payment for the services they provide. They cannot charge their patients for the difference between their private rates and what Medicare pays—so-called "balance billing." In recent years, however, some private physicians have begun charging a substantial "retainer" fee of several thousands of dollars a year in addition to Medicare billings. In exchange, patients get "boutique" or "concierge" services, such as 24-hour direct access through cell phones or pagers and a promise that the physician will restrict his practice so as to have more time for each patient.

The legality of this arrangement is still in doubt, with physicians claiming it does not violate balance billing rules since the extra payments are for administrative or non-Medicare-covered services. What about the ethics of these boutique practices? Proponents argue that they allow physicians to regain control of their professional lives and to establish the type of personal and holistic medical practice that has long since disappeared. Critics say that concierge medicine is elitist and exploitative.

4. *Devilish Part D Details.* Enrollment in Part D prescription drug benefit plans is voluntary, i.e., Medicare-eligible individuals choose whether to pay a subsidized premium for coverage offered primarily by competing private insurers. These Part D insurers set their premiums for drug coverage at whatever they think the market will bear. This is in marked contrast to Medicare Part B, with government insurance that has the premium nationwide. For drug coverage, the government subsidizes 75 percent of the Part D premium for most Medicare beneficiaries, but pays 100 percent of the premium for low-income beneficiaries (135 percent of the federal poverty level) who are not covered by another source such as Medicaid. Payments to health plans are adjusted for health status and insurance risk, to counter adverse selection, but premiums to beneficiaries are community rated.

The private companies offering Part D submit plan designs and premium bids to the government for approval. Insurers may offer "alternate" plan designs that are "actuarially equivalent" (or better). Thus, retirees face the following dizzying array of alternatives:

- Several drug plans that provide "standard" benefit plan design
- Several other drug plans that provide "alternate" benefit plan design
- Several Medicare Advantage HMO or PPO plans that include prescription drug coverage

The standard Part D coverage has a $325 deductible and then pays for 75 percent of drug costs up to about $3,000 a year. Then, coverage ceases until total costs reach $4,700 (the "doughnut hole"), at which point 95 percent of drug costs are paid. The ACA has gradually filled the doughnut hole, which is set to disappear as of 2020. The ACA also reduces or eliminates deductibles, co-payments, and gaps in coverage for people who are below 150 percent of the federal poverty level. For the non-poor, however, drug plans are not allowed to cover the deductibles and co-payments in the standard plan.

Controversially, the legislation establishing Part D prohibits the government from regulating or negotiating drug costs. Instead, costs are whatever drug companies charge, subject to negotiation by the private drug plans. Drug plans may also adopt "formularies" that require the use of generic drugs and that refuse to cover more expensive drugs when less expensive ones are equally effective, but beneficiaries may appeal these restrictions in individual cases of medical necessity.

5. *Long-Term Care.* This chapter focuses on conventional medical insurance for hospitals and doctors and so neglects the sources of financing for long-term care insurance that covers nursing homes and home health care. The appropriate source and financing for this type of insurance will be one of the most pressing public health policy issues for decades to come. Two developments are accelerating the rate at which long-term care is increasing its portion of the nation's health care budget: the aging of the baby-boom generation and increasing life expectancy. Private insurance for nursing homes is not very extensive because of its costs. Its costs are high because most people don't consider purchasing it until they anticipate needing it. Mark Pauly, The Rational Nonpurchase of Long-Term-Care Insurance, 98 J. Pol. Econ. 153 (1990). The principal fallback is Medicaid, which requires the elderly to impoverish themselves. Various financial planning techniques are possible for sheltering assets from Medicaid "spend down" rules, but Congress is

steadily curbing these techniques. For instance, Medicaid now counts assets that the patient transferred as long as 36 months ago, that are owned jointly by the patient's spouse, or that are in a revocable trust. 42 U.S.C. §1396p. Congress also made it a criminal offense for lawyers or financial advisors to counsel clients in avoiding restrictions.

Policy analysts have explored a number of options for making private financing of nursing homes more feasible (such as "reverse mortgages" and "continuing care retirement communities") or for devising innovative hybrids between public and private financing. The coverage of home health care is somewhat more extensive under private insurance and Medicare because it is seen as an inexpensive alternative to hospital or institutional care.

The Patient Protection and Affordable Care Act was expected to make a major change in long-term care insurance, with a component known as the CLASS Act (for Community Living Assistance Services and Support). This promised to create a public insurance plan that people could contribute to through payroll deductions while they are still working, which then would pay fixed amounts for nursing homes, home care, and related services when the need arose. Before the law took effect, however, CMS actuaries proved critics to be correct, that the premiums allowed by the CLASS Act would not be sufficient to cover the promised benefits due to likely adverse selection (people more likely to contribute if they expect to need long-term care than if they don't). Therefore, Congress, with the Obama administration's support, repealed the CLASS Act in 2013 and created another study commission on long-term care.

6. *Further Reading.* For discussions of **Medicare at 50**, see Jonathan Oberlander & Theodore Marmor, Medicare at 50, in The Oxford Handbook of U.S. Health Law (2017); Medicare and Medicaid at 50: America's Entitlement Programs in the Age of Affordable Care (2015) (Alan B. Cohen et al. eds. 2015); Symposium, The Law of Medicare and Medicaid at 50, 15 Yale J. Health Pol'y L. Ethics (2015).

For **historical and political accounts of Medicare** (note 1), see Nicholas Bagley, Bedside Bureaucrats: Why Medicare Reform Hasn't Worked, 101 Georgetown L. J. 520 (2013); Henry Aaron & Jeanne Lambrew, Reforming Medicare: Options, Trade-offs, and Opportunities (2008); Timothy Stoltzfus Jost, Disentitlement: The Threats Facing Our Public Health-Care Programs and a Rights-Based Response (2003); David Hyman, Medicare Meets Mephistopheles (2006); Jonathan Oberlander, The Political Life of Medicare (2003). The most widely used source for detailed knowledge is the CCH Medicare and Medicaid Guide. See also Terry Coleman, Medicare Law (2d ed. 2006).

For discussion of **concierge medicine** (note 3), see Troyen A. Brennan, Luxury Primary Care: Market Innovation or Threat to Access?, 346 New Eng. J. Med. 1165 (2002); Jeffrey Hammond, Cash Only Doctors: Challenges and Prospects of Autonomy and Access, 80 UMKC L. Rev. 307 (2011); Note, 17 Wash. U. J. L. & Pol'y 313 (2005); Sandra J. Carnahan, Law, Medicine, and Wealth: Does Concierge Medicine Promote Health Care Choice, or Is It a Barrier to Access?, 17 Stan. L. & Pol'y Rev. 121 (2006); Frank Pasquale, The Three Faces of Retainer Care: Crafting a Tailored Regulatory Response, 7 Yale J. Health Pol'y L. & Ethics 39 (2007); Note, 66 Duke L. J. (2017).

For discussions of **Medicare Part D** (note 4), see John B. Kirkwood, Buyer Power and Healthcare Prices, 91 Wash. L. Rev. 253 (2016); Janet Cummings et al., Who Thinks That Part D Is Too Complicated?, 66 Med. Care Res. Rev. 97 (2009); Richard H. Thaler & Cass R. Sunstein, Nudge: Improving Decisions About Health,

Wealth, and Happiness, ch. 10 (2008); Jerry Avorn, Part "D" for "Defective": The Medicare Drug-Benefit Chaos, 354 New Eng. J. Med. 1339 (2006); Jonathan Oberlander, Through the Looking Glass: The Politics of the Medicare Prescription Drug, Improvement, and Modernization Act, 32 J. Health Pol. Pol'y & L. 153 (2007); John K. Iglehart, The New Medicare Prescription-Drug Benefit: A Pure Power Play, 350 New Eng. J. Med. 826 (2004); Thomas R. Oliver et al., A Political History of Medicare and Prescription Drug Coverage, 82 Milbank Q. 283 (2004); Susan Channick, The Medicare Prescription Drug, Improvement, and Modernization Act of 2003, 14 Elder L. J. 237 (2006); Symposium, 23(1) Health Aff. 1 (Jan. 2004).

For discussions of **long-term care** (note 5), see Allison K. Hoffman, Reimagining the Risk of Long-Term Care, 16 Yale J. Health Pol'y, L. & Ethics 239 (2016); Symposium, Health Care Reform, Transition, and Transformation in Long-Term Care, 8 St. Louis J. Health L & Pol'y 1 (2014); Richard Kaplan, Analyzing the Impact of the New Health Care Reform Legislation on Older Americans, 18 Elder L. J. 213 (2011); Joshua M. Wiener et al., Federal and State Initiatives to Jump Start the Market for Private Long-Term Care Insurance, 8 Elder L. J. 57 (2000); Symposium, 29 Health Aff. 6 (2010); Symposium 4 J. Health Care L. & Pol'y 159 (2001); Note, 14 Elder L. J. 485 (2006); Hal Fliegelman & Debora Fliegelman, Giving Guardians the Power to Do Medicaid Planning, 32 Wake Forest L. Rev. 341 (1997); Symposium, 31 McGeorge L. Rev. 703 (2000).

B. INSURANCE AND MANAGED CARE REGULATION

1. *The Rise of Managed Care*

■ RUSH PRUDENTIAL HMO v. MORAN
536 U.S. 355 (2002)

SOUTER, J., delivered the opinion of the Court, [which was split 5-4].

Illinois's Health Maintenance Organization Act provides . . . a right to independent medical review of certain denials of benefits.[2] The issue in this case is

2. . . . The Act defines a "Health Maintenance Organization" as "any organization formed under the laws of this or another state to provide or arrange for one or more health care plans under a system which causes any part of the risk of health care delivery to be borne by the organization or its providers." . . . In the health care industry, the term "Health Maintenance Organization" has been defined as "[a] prepaid organized delivery system where the organization *and* the primary care physicians assume some financial risk for the care provided to its enrolled members. . . . In a *pure HMO*, members must obtain care from within the system if it is to be reimbursed." Weiner & de Lissovoy, Razing a Tower of Babel: A Taxonomy for Managed Care and Health Insurance Plans, 18 J. of Health Politics, Policy and Law 75, 96 (Spring 1993) (emphasis in original). The term "Managed Care Organization" is used more broadly to refer to any number of systems combining health care delivery with financing. *Id.*, at 97. The Illinois definition of HMO does not appear to be limited to the traditional usage of that term, but instead is likely to encompass a variety of different structures (although Illinois does distinguish HMOs from pure insurers by regulating "traditional" health insurance in a different portion of its insurance laws). Except where otherwise indicated, we use the term "HMO" because that is the term used by the State and the parties.

whether the statute . . . is preempted by the Employee Retirement Income Security Act of 1974 (ERISA), 29 U.S.C. §1001 *et seq.*, [which is addressed in the next section]. We hold it is not. . . .

Debra Moran is a beneficiary under [an employee welfare benefit] plan, sponsored by her husband's employer. . . . As the [insurance policy] explains, Rush contracts with physicians "to arrange for or provide services and supplies for medical care and treatment" of covered persons. Each covered person selects a primary care physician from those under contract to Rush, while Rush will pay for medical services by an unaffiliated physician only if the services have been "authorized" both by the primary care physician and Rush's medical director.

In 1996, when Moran began to have pain and numbness in her right shoulder, Dr. Arthur LaMarre, her primary care physician, unsuccessfully administered "conservative" treatments such as physiotherapy. In October 1997, Dr. LaMarre recommended that Rush approve surgery by an unaffiliated specialist, Dr. Julia Terzis, who had developed an unconventional treatment for Moran's condition. Although Dr. LaMarre said that Moran would be "best served" by that procedure, Rush denied the request and, after Moran's internal appeals, affirmed the denial on the ground that the procedure was not "medically necessary." Rush instead proposed that Moran undergo standard surgery, performed by a physician affiliated with Rush.

In January 1998, Moran made a written demand for an independent medical review of her claim. . . . When Rush failed to provide the independent review, Moran sued in an Illinois state court to compel compliance with the state Act. Rush removed the suit to Federal District Court, arguing that the cause of action was "completely preempted" under ERISA, [a federal statute that regulates pension plans and other employee fringe benefits].

While the suit was pending, Moran had surgery by Dr. Terzis at her own expense and submitted a $94,841.27 reimbursement claim to Rush. Rush treated the claim as a renewed request for benefits and began a new inquiry to determine coverage. The three doctors consulted by Rush said the surgery had been medically unnecessary. Meanwhile, the federal court remanded the case back to state court . . . , [and] the state court enforced the state statute and ordered Rush to submit to review by an independent physician. The doctor selected was a reconstructive surgeon at Johns Hopkins Medical Center, Dr. A. Lee Dellon. Dr. Dellon decided that Dr. Terzis's treatment had been medically necessary, based on the definition of medical necessity in Rush's Certificate of Group Coverage, as well as his own medical judgment. Rush's medical director, however, refused to concede that the surgery had been medically necessary, and denied Moran's claim in January 1999. . . . The Court of Appeals for the Seventh Circuit reversed. . . . Because the decision of the Court of Appeals conflicted with the Fifth Circuit's treatment of a similar provision of Texas law in Corporate Health Ins., Inc. v. Texas Dept. of Ins., 215 F.3d 526 (2000), we granted certiorari. We now affirm.

II

To "safeguar[d] . . . the establishment, operation, and administration" of employee benefit plans, ERISA . . . contains an express preemption provision that ERISA "shall supersede any and all State laws insofar as they may now or hereafter relate to any employee benefit plan. . . ." A saving clause then reclaims a substantial

amount of ground with its provision that "nothing in this subchapter shall be construed to exempt or relieve any person from any law of any State which regulates
insurance, banking, or securities." The "unhelpful" drafting of these antiphonal
clauses occupies a substantial share of this Court's time. [See section C and Chapter
4.F.] . . .

As a law that "relates to" ERISA plans, [the Illinois statute] is saved from preemption only if it also "regulates insurance." Rush insists that the Act is not such
a law. . . . [I]n deciding whether a law "regulates insurance" under ERISA's saving
clause, we start with a "common-sense view of the matter." . . . Rush contends that
seeing an HMO as an insurer distorts the nature of an HMO, which is, after all, a
health care provider, too. This, Rush argues, should determine its characterization,
with the consequence that regulation of an HMO is not insurance regulation within
the meaning of ERISA.

The answer to Rush is, of course, that an HMO is both: it provides health
care, and it does so as an insurer. Nothing in the saving clause requires an either-or
choice between health care and insurance. . . . [I]t would ignore the whole purpose
of the HMO-style of organization to conceive of HMOs without their insurance element. . . . The HMO design goes beyond the simple truism that all contracts are,
in some sense, insurance against future fluctuations in price, R. Posner, Economic
Analysis of Law 104 (4th ed. 1992), because HMOs actually underwrite and spread
risk among their participants, a feature distinctive to insurance.

So Congress has understood from the start, when the phrase "Health Maintenance Organization" was established and defined in the HMO Act of 1973, 42
U.S.C. §300 et seq. The Act was intended to encourage the development of HMOs
as a new form of health care delivery system, and when Congress set the standards
that the new health delivery organizations would have to meet to get certain federal
benefits, the terms included requirements that the organizations bear and manage
risk. . . . This congressional understanding that it was promoting a novel form of
insurance was made explicit in the Senate Report's reference to the practices of
"health insurers to charge premium rates based upon the actual claims experience
of a particular group of subscribers," thus "raising costs and diminishing the availability of health insurance for those suffering from costly illnesses." The federal Act
responded to this insurance practice by requiring qualifying HMOs to [use community rating], and it was because of that mandate "pos[ing] substantial competitive
problems to newly emerging HMOs" that Congress authorized funding subsidies
[for qualifying HMOs]. . . .

This conception has not changed in the intervening years. Since passage of
the federal Act, States have been adopting their own HMO enabling Acts, and today,
at least 40 of them, including Illinois, regulate HMOs primarily through the States'
insurance departments, see Aspen [Wolters Kluwer], Managed Care Law Manual,
although they may be treated differently from traditional insurers, owing to their
additional role as health care providers, see, e.g., Alaska Ins. Code §21.86.010 (health
department reviews HMO before insurance commissioner grants a certificate of
authority); Ohio Rev. Code Ann. §1742.21 (health department may inspect HMO).
Finally, this view shared by Congress and the States has passed into common understanding. . . . While the original form of the HMO was a single corporation employing its own physicians, the 1980s saw a variety of other types of structures develop
even as traditional insurers altered their own plans by adopting HMO-like cost-con-

trol measures. The dominant feature is the combination of insurer and provider, and "an observer may be hard pressed to uncover the differences among products that bill themselves as HMOs, [preferred provider organizations (PPOs)], or managed care overlays to health insurance." Managed Care Law Manual, *supra*. . . . Rush cannot checkmate common sense by trying to submerge HMOs' insurance features beneath an exclusive characterization of HMOs as providers of health care. . . .

On a second tack, Rush . . . [argues] that an HMO is no longer an insurer when it arranges to limit its exposure, as when an HMO arranges for capitated contracts to compensate its affiliated physicians with a set fee for each HMO patient regardless of the treatment provided. Under such an arrangement, Rush claims, the risk is not borne by the HMO at all. . . . The problem with Rush's argument is . . . that capitation contracts do not relieve the HMO of its obligations to the beneficiary. The HMO is still bound to provide medical care to its members, and this is so regardless of the ability of physicians or [other] third-part[ies] to honor their contracts with the HMO. . . .

Nor do we see anything standing in the way of applying the . . . general state definition of HMO [to] include a contractor that provides only administrative services for a self-funded plan. Rush points out that the general definition of HMO under Illinois law includes not only organizations that "provide" health care plans, but those that "arrange for" them to be provided. . . . Rush hypothesizes a sort of medical matchmaker, bringing together [employers] and medical care providers; even if the latter bear all the risks, the matchmaker would be an HMO under the Illinois definition. . . . Even on the most generous reading of Rush's argument, however, it boils down to the bare possibility (not the likelihood) of some overbreadth in the application of [the Illinois statute] beyond orthodox HMOs. . . .

In sum, . . . HMOs have taken over much business formerly performed by traditional indemnity insurers and they are almost universally regulated as insurers under state law. . . . Thus, the Illinois HMO Act is a law "directed toward" the insurance industry, and [so is saved from ERISA preemption]. . . .

■ MEDICARE AND THE AMERICAN HEALTH CARE SYSTEM: 1996 REPORT TO CONGRESS
Prospective Payment Assessment Commission

The most common managed care models are health maintenance organizations (HMOs), preferred provider organizations (PPOs), and point-of-service (POS) plans. In a traditional HMO plan, subscribers must receive their care from a limited group of providers. PPO and POS subscribers may not be subject to the same level of plan oversight as in HMOs; Generally they may go to any provider, but their out-of-pocket payments are lower if they choose participating providers that give the insurer discounted rates.

Managed care plans use a variety of techniques to control their costs. First, they actively seek providers with lower-cost practice patterns and offer them a defined patient base in exchange for favorable payment rates. By limiting the number of providers or by creating strong financial incentives to choose certain ones, managed care plans influence which providers subscribers will use. Through this selective contracting, managed care plans can substantially affect providers' revenues. Plans' bargaining positions are strongest in areas with excess provider capacity. Providers that choose not to participate or that are not selected by the managed care plan may experience a decline in their patient volume.

In addition, managed care plans often use discounted fee-for-service rates to control their costs. They also use per case, per day, or per person payments to shift some of the financial risk of treating patients to providers. Per case or per day payments are generally made to hospitals, whereas per person payments are more often made to physicians, predominately primary care practitioners. These payment methods reward providers for delivering care efficiently, discouraging unnecessary service use.

A per person, or capitation, payment system is the most comprehensive way to shift financial risk to providers. Under capitation, providers receive a prepaid sum to furnish a defined set of services to a plan's enrollees. This creates a monetary incentive for physicians to limit patients' use of services (or encourage preventive services) because the physician receives the same payment regardless of the volume or intensity of care, or even if no care is provided at all. Many managed care plans also require primary care physicians to act as "gatekeepers" to specialty care or hospital services. Under these arrangements, the primary care physician must preauthorize any services a patient receives. While these physicians usually do not bear the full financial risk for the additional services, delegating the gatekeeping function enables managed care plans to use financial incentives to limit referrals. . . .

HOSPITALS [AND PHYSICIANS]

. . . The long-term effects of the changing environment on hospitals are still unclear. . . . Hospitals traditionally have been viewed as the hub of the health care system and often have the capital reserves necessary to finance collaborations with other providers. Those that aggressively pursue such arrangements not only can improve their chances of being the hospital of choice for inpatient services, but also can exert more influence over medical practice decisions. In areas where managed care systems exert more control, however, hospitals may be viewed as cost centers with little input into delivery decisions.

Historically, physicians determined not only which services would be provided, but where those services would be delivered. These decisions generally were made with little accountability for costs. Managed care is changing this. . . . One indication of the level of financial pressure physicians are facing is the [reduced growth] in physician income. . . . Some physicians are responding to the intensified pressures by selling their practices to hospitals or managed care organizations, and becoming employees of those entities. . . . [On the other hand,] [b]ecause physicians generate the demand for hospital services, they have leverage to assume a leadership role in arrangements with other providers. . . .

Notes: Regulation of Health Insurance and Managed Care

1. *What Is Managed Care?* In a traditional indemnity plan, a health insurer reimburses an enrollee for any qualifying medical expenses. As indemnity plans evolved,

they began remitting payment directly to physicians and hospitals, eliminating the need for enrollees to pay up front for their medical care. For patients, the chief advantage of an indemnity-style plan is the flexibility it affords them to choose their own providers. For physicians, indemnity-style plans minimize any intrusion on their medical judgments.

Prepaid medical plans—the original HMOs—operate on a different model. Instead of agreeing to pay for their enrollees' care, they promise to provide that care directly, either through an integrated delivery system controlled by the plan or through tightly affiliated hospitals and physicians. Prepaid medical plans afford patients less freedom to choose their providers and exercise more control over the practice of medicine. In exchange for that loss of flexibility, prepaid medical plans can offer cheaper coverage and may be able to improve the quality of care that their enrollees receive.

Nowadays, few insurers are pure indemnity plans or pure prepaid medical plans. Instead, virtually all insurance falls under the broad umbrella of "managed care." Discussions about managed care can get bogged down in a tangle of acronyms and arcana—closed-panel HMOs, open-panel HMOs, preferred provider organizations (PPOs), exclusive provider organizations (EPOs), and point-of-service plans (POSs) are all types of managed care plans. What really distinguishes these plans from one another, however, is the extent to which they exercise three basic management techniques: cost-containing financial incentives, narrow networks, and utilization review. See Theodore R. Marmor & Jacob S. Hacker, How Not to Think About "Managed Care," 32 U. Mich. J. L. Reform 661 (1999). We will discuss the first two of these techniques in this section, reserving consideration of utilization review until Part D.2.

Despite fierce resistance by many doctors and some patients, managed care remains the dominant form of insurance. However, enrollment has shifted rather dramatically in recent years from tightly managed HMO plans to PPO and other open network plans that give patients more options. Regardless of the form managed care takes, it raises a host of legal, ethical, and regulatory issues. For now, consider these broad inquiries: Are you concerned that insurers are interfering with medical judgment by deciding what treatments to pay for? Would you be more comfortable with a regime that let physicians and patients decide for themselves, but rewarded physicians for saving money or punished them for being excessive? Or is the answer to make patients pay much more out of pocket so that they regulate their own spending decisions?

2. *Conventional Insurance Regulation.* Historically, the states have regulated their own health insurance markets, demanding primarily that insurers maintain large capital reserves for solvency protection and to pay taxes on insurance premiums. States also regulate how insurers invest their funds, the content of insurance policies, the rates insurers charge, and whether insurers engage in fair business practices. See generally R. Jerry, Understanding Insurance Law (4th ed. 2007). States vary a great deal in how or whether they regulate insurers' premium rates.

In what ways does health insurance differ from traditional casualty insurance—say, car insurance? Health insurance does offer protection from unexpected illness or injury. But isn't it also a pooled financing mechanism for predictable medical expenses? Your car insurance doesn't help you finance the cost of automobile maintenance, purchase, and repair. Why should health insurance cover routine doctor visits, preventive care, and the like?

3. *A Brief History of Managed Care.* Precursors of managed care can be traced all the way back into the nineteenth century, mainly as industry-sponsored health clinics for employees. The most prominent early example is Kaiser-Permanente, which was started in the Pacific Northwest by industrialist Henry J. Kaiser in the 1940s to serve the many employees of his different companies. But these prepaid medical plans were fiercely resisted by the American Medical Association, which sought to protect physician independence from corporate control. The AMA went so far as to organize boycotts against prepaid medical plans: physicians were threatened with expulsion from their medical societies and from hospital medical staffs if they participated in prepaid medical plans. The AMA's zealousness attracted the attention of federal antitrust officials, and the Supreme Court eventually sustained a criminal indictment against the AMA under the antitrust laws. See AMA v. United States, 317 U.S. 519 (1943).

Although prepaid medical plans often prevailed in these and other court challenges to their legal authority, the burden of overcoming the persistent hostility of local providers delayed the rise of managed care until the 1980s. Under market pressures, this hostility has given way to resigned acceptance in some parts of the country and open embrace in others.

4. *Financial Incentives.* Although many managed care plans pay providers on a fee-for-service basis, others enter into alternative financial arrangements with providers. Prepaid medical plans like Kaiser, for example, pay a salary to their physicians. In other managed care plans, including the plan at issue in *Rush Prudential,* payments to physicians and hospitals may take the form of complex capitation and "withhold" formulae rather than simple salary:

> Here's how capitation typically works. Say an HMO has 100 enrollees, each covered by a $100 monthly premium. First, the HMO subtracts $20 from each premium to cover its administrative expenses—and pad its profits. It divides the remaining $80 equally between a physician group and a hospital. Of the doctors' $40 payment per member per month, $10 goes to the enrollee's primary care physician. The other $30 is pooled to cover specialty and inpatient care. Half of the doctors' entire capitated payment, $20, is set into a risk pool . . . to pay specialists for care as it occurs. Most groups reimburse specialists on a . . . modified fee-for-service basis, although some groups pay specialists on a capitated basis. The remaining $10 goes into a reserve to cover any unexpectedly high inpatient- or specialty-care costs. [Money left in these pools at year end is returned to the primary care physicians as a bonus, and the physicians make up any deficits.] . . .
>
> [The hospital's portion would amount to $48,000 per year (100 x $40 x 12).] In most capitated environments, the hospital could expect . . . 25 [in]-patient days per 100 enrollees. Given a cost of $1,000 per day, inpatient stays would eat up $25,000 of the hospital's risk pool. Outpatient care would account for another $12,000 of the pool, and out-of-area care $1,000 more. Thus the hospital figures on annual costs of $38,000 against a risk pool of $48,000. The hospital generally splits the resulting $10,000 bonus with the medical group as a reward to doctors for controlling utilization. Conversely, utilization could surge, saddling the hospital with annual expenses of $60,000. This deficit is also split with doctors, who pay for the loss out of the reserve pool they've established for inpatient care.

J. Johnsson, The Whys and Wherefores of Capitation, Am. Med. News, Dec. 6, 1993, at 31. Managed care plans will often mix and match these various approaches to payment. Primary care physicians might receive capitated payments, for example, even as specialists are paid on a fee-for-service basis.

From a patient's perspective, what are the advantages of salaried physicians? Or capitation? What are the risks? For a recent overview of the costs and benefits of different payment approaches, see Robert A. Berenson et al., Payment Methods: How They Work (2016).

5. *Narrow Networks.* Apart from adjusting *how* they pay for care, managed care plans can limit *who* they pay for care. To keep costs low, plans negotiate with physicians, hospitals, and other providers over how much they will pay for medical services. When they cannot reach agreement, plans may exclude providers from their coverage networks. Enrollees must then pay out of pocket if they seek treatment from an out-of-network provider. (Plans will typically include an exception for emergency services outside the coverage area.)

Because managed care plans compete with one another for customers, they have an incentive to exclude providers that demand high prices for their services. Plans use the threat of exclusion to negotiate low rates. At the same time, however, plans that exclude too many providers — or especially popular providers — may not be popular with customers. Especially in areas with a few dominant providers, plans may have little negotiating leverage. Variations in market concentration among providers and insurers explain much of the substantial geographic variation in the cost of insurance across the country. See Eric T. Roberts, Michael E. Chernew & John McWilliams, Market Share Matters: Evidence of Insurer and Provider Bargaining Over Prices, 36 Health Affairs 141 (2017).

Network restrictions are unpopular with physicians, hospitals, and patients. They restrict choice and trigger concerns that only the wealthy, who can afford to purchase gold-plated plans, will have access to the finest medical care, while everyone else will have to make do with second- and third-rate providers. These concerns have fueled particular criticism of the ACA: In response to competitive pressures, many exchange plans have very narrow networks. See Sabrina Corlette et al., Narrow Provider Networks in New Health Plans (Urban Institute, May 2014). Narrow networks, however, are also on the rise in employer-sponsored coverage. Mark Hall & Paul Fronstin, Narrow Provider Networks for Employer Plans (EBRI, Dec. 2016).

Policymakers have responded to frustrations with narrow networks in two principal ways. First, regulators in many states have adopted "network adequacy" rules requiring insurers to demonstrate that their enrollees will have reasonable access to needed services. These rules vary a great deal from state to state, and evidence suggests that compliance is spotty. Although the federal government has adopted a network adequacy rule for plans sold on the exchanges, it has left primary enforcement of the adequacy rule to state insurance regulators. See 82 Fed. Reg. 18372 (2017); Mark Hall & Paul Ginsburg, A Better Approach to Regulating Provider Network Adequacy (Brookings, 2017).

Second, some states have experimented with "any willing provider" statutes, which require managed care plans to include in their network any provider that is willing to accept the plan's standard payment and contracting terms. Interest in these statutes has grown as narrow-network plans have proliferated in the wake of the ACA. See Ashley Nobel, Health Insurers and Access to Health Care Providers: Any Willing Providers (National Conference of State Legislatures, Nov. 2014).

6. *The Managed Care Backlash.* By the late 1990s, the rise of tightly controlled HMOs had precipitated a fierce consumer backlash, stoked in part by an AMA legislative initiative known as the "Patient Protection Act." The backlash led to the adoption of a spate of laws, mainly at the state level, that attempted to limit what managed care organizations could do to constrain their costs. In addition to the independent review process described in *Rush Prudential*, examples include:

- giving subscribers more information about how HMOs work (prohibiting so-called gag clauses),
- requiring HMOs to include a PPO-type option that allows subscribers to go outside the network,
- giving physicians procedural protections when they are excluded from the network,
- requiring HMOs to pay for emergency care if a "prudent layperson" would have thought it was necessary to go to an emergency room,
- allowing patients with chronic illness to have direct access to specialists, or women to have direct access to obstetricians, without going through the gatekeeping system, and
- mandating minimum coverage provisions such as at least two days in the hospital following childbirth (prohibiting so-called drive-through deliveries).

Frank A. Sloan & Mark A. Hall, Market Failures and the Evolution of State Regulation of Managed Care, 65 Law & Contemp. Probs. 169 (Autumn 2002). The ACA has now adopted a number of these same provisions as federal law—especially for insurers that wish to qualify to sell to individuals and small groups through the new insurance exchanges.

Some commentators have seen in these enactments a broader backlash to market forces in health care:

> The essential message of all the horror stories told by patients is the anguish of abandonment. The howl of doctors, nurses, and other caregivers is moral revulsion at the callousness they are forced to enact. Backlash is a cold shudder against the market paradigm, which taken to its logical endpoint as managed care seems to be doing, respects no human bonds, shows no mercy, and has no use for kindness, loyalty, and other moral qualities of community.

Deborah Stone, Managed Care and the Second Great Transformation, 24 J. Health Pol. Pol'y & L. 1213 (1999). Prof. Stone goes on to criticize these laws for catering to the interests of people with insurance and diverting attention from the plight of those with no insurance.

A similar point is made by Prof. Havighurst, from the other end of the political spectrum. In a provocative essay, he argues that patient protection legislation is being driven by social "elites"—the portion of the public that is "most aware, affluent, influential, and politically active," supported by special interests such as physicians. Therefore, the standards set by this legislation "are designed to suit the preferences of the privileged minority and the interests of health care providers, thereby denying ordinary people the freedom to spend their limited incomes in ways that maximize their welfare." He sees this body of regulation as one of several "mechanisms through which the expensive tastes of upper middle class consumers are invisibly subsidized by persons with either lower expectations or less ability to command attention to their health problems." He concludes:

> It is especially objectionable for academic experts and self-styled "consumer advocates" claiming to represent the interests of all consumers to support the use of the judicial system and state power to deny fellow citizens alternative kinds of health care that would better meet their respective needs — not only for health care but for other things as well. To satisfy their own needs (including their need to demonstrate their symbolic aspirations for others), the political majority, other special interests, and elite movers and shakers of health policy are content to design things so that lower-income consumers have only a Hobson's choice — either pay the high cost of upper-middle-class medical care or go without any health coverage at all.

Clark Havighurst, The Backlash Against Managed Health Care: Hard Politics Make Bad Policy, 34 Ind. L. Rev. 398 (2001). However, many of these "anti-managed care" provisions are ones that HMOs themselves had adopted, under market pressures or after finding that various cost-management strategies were not effective.

7. *Points to Ponder.* What if insurers were to attempt to circumvent these laws by requiring, or encouraging, patients to receive care outside the country (and paying their travel costs for doing so)? Should states or federal exchanges ban such a requirement? See Glenn Cohen, Protecting Patients with Passports: Medical Tourism and the Patient-Protective Argument, 95 Iowa L. Rev. 1467 (2010).

The legal landscape is complicated even more by ERISA preemption. As discussed in more detail in the next section, ERISA broadly preempts any state law that relates to employee benefits, unless the state is regulating the business of insurance. *Rush Prudential* appears to hold that most types of state regulation meet the definition of insurance regulation. See, e.g., Kentucky Ass'n of Health Plans v. Miller, 538 U.S. 329 (2003) (ERISA does not preempt any-willing-provider statute). But states may not regulate employers that self-insure their workers' health care benefits.

8. *Empirical Evidence.* Deciding whether HMOs are the monsters or messiahs of medicine, and the appropriate degree of regulation or encouragement, should be influenced not only by their potential for harm but also by empirical findings on their actual performance. The following notes discuss these findings, first looking at cost containment and then at quality of care.

9. *Do HMOs Harm Quality?* "Reversing the financial incentives in the provision of health care would be dangerous to patients. . . . Incentives for economy can also be incentives for no care or inferior care. . . . The danger that HMOs will provide inferior care is particularly acute when the organization is a profit-making one, when the physician's compensation is based on a percentage of profit rather than a fixed salary, . . . when HMO enrollees have no alternative means of obtaining medical care, and when the HMO population is exclusively poor or aged." Sylvia Law, Blue Cross: What Went Wrong?, 108-109 (2d ed. 1976).

Naturally, there is another side to the story. One reason for optimism about the quality of HMO care is that there are countervailing pressures against any tendencies to over-economize. Physicians face the threat of a malpractice suit. . . . Incentives for keeping the subscriber population healthy can be built into the method of rewarding physicians. And competition among pre-paid group practice plans, or between such plans and alternative delivery systems, also limits any potential trend toward unduly low hospitalization rates. Yet the strongest force militating against excessive economizing is the strongly imbued norms of practicing good medicine under conditions of strict professional review.

Developments, The Role of Prepaid Group Practice in Relieving the Medical Care Crisis, 84 Harv. L. Rev. 887, 926 (1971). The HMO industry has developed its own, self-reported measures of quality to assist employers and subscribers in making wise insurance purchasing decisions. These "quality report cards," described at page 305, provide statistics in a comparable format about matters such as the rates of mammography and childhood immunizations, five-year survival rates after cancer, and patient satisfaction. How much confidence do you have that competitive forces will spur HMOs to improve their performance measures? Enough that you think they should be essentially self-regulated for the quality of medical outcomes, like hospitals? Would you expect these measures to be geared more to patients' interest in quality, or employers' interest in cost?

A large and elaborate study by RAND confirmed that low-income enrollees are especially vulnerable in HMOs; those who were sick at the start of the study did worse (under some but not most measures of health status) than comparable patients in fee-for-service insurance. Joseph Newhouse et al., Free for All? Lessons from the RAND Health Insurance Experiment (1993). For most people, however, numerous studies have shown that patient satisfaction and the quality of care overall are as high or higher in HMOs as elsewhere. Yet there is continuing concern over whether patients do as well in HMOs when they suffer from serious chronic illnesses that require ongoing expensive treatment, or from rare conditions that require unusually expensive drugs or special expertise that is not available in the established network.

10. *Do HMOs Save Money?* The cost containment record of HMOs has been mixed. Throughout the 1980s, HMOs engaged in "shadow pricing," namely, tracking their prices close to traditional indemnity insurance and competing instead by offering more comprehensive coverage for the same price, such as reduced patient cost-sharing (deductibles and co-payments). During the 1990s, price competition in some parts of the country (notably California and Minnesota) saw substantial (5 to 10 percent) *declines* in HMO premiums, driven mainly by drastic reductions (30 to 50 percent) in the use of hospitals. Skeptics responded, however, that HMOs achieved lower prices more through "biased" or "favorable" selection than through real efficiencies. HMOs are thought to attract relatively younger and healthier subscribers because their managed care controls are unattractive to patients with chronic illnesses and established provider relationships. Consequently, lower HMO premiums may reflect simply an artificially lower-risk pool of subscribers or "adverse selection" against traditional insurance. The actual extent of this biased selection is in dispute, though, since the lower deductibles and co-payments common in HMOs also tend to attract subscribers who expect substantial medical expenses. One study concluded that HMOs are cheaper than traditional indemnity insurance, but about

half the difference is an artifact of HMOs attracting healthier people, and the other half is due to HMOs paying lower prices to hospitals and physicians, not to HMOs delivering less care. Daniel Altman et al., Enrollee Mix, Treatment Intensity, and Cost in Competing Indemnity and HMO Plans, 22 J. Health Econ. 23 (2003).

In any event, HMOs soon lost their price advantages over other kinds of insurance, nor are they offering substantially more generous insurance. Instead, they came to look increasingly like PPOs, with similar levels of cost-sharing and more options to go outside the network or to move within the network without gatekeeping controls. Traditional unrestricted indemnity insurance has all but disappeared from the market, except under Medicare and Medicaid, and even then, managed care is making substantial inroads, as noted in sections A.3 & .4 above. One disenchanted former executive in the managed care industry has this to say about the trajectory of HMOs:

> Conventional wisdom has it that managed care has failed to live up to all but its most brutal promises. Left in the rubble are bewildered consumers, disappointed employers, enraged patients, embittered physicians, and a raft of lawsuits. . . . What once looked like a permanent reduction in health insurance premiums—thanks to a onetime round of severe price competition among managed care organizations—turned out to be an anomaly, a momentary pause in their inevitable rise. . . . In the final analysis, most "managed care" really was "managed cost" all along—but it failed to accomplish even that goal, and the U.S. health care system is worse off for the experiment.
>
> Although it is easy and occasionally fun to pick on the bad manners and various hypocrisies of managed care, it is also unfair. The nation's managed care organizations were asked to do a job that simply cannot be done. . . . As a society, we expected managed care to fix, in a few short years, the disaster in slow motion that is the U.S. health care system. We asked large, organizationally complex insurance companies to reform a century's worth of self-serving professional habits, rein in ever-expanding consumer and patient demands, and fix dysfunctional economic behaviors—all while answering to the taskmasters on Wall Street every quarter. . . . Most of us believed that these insurance companies could do well financially by doing good medically. We were wrong.

J. D. Kleinke, Oxymorons: The Myth of a U.S. Health Care System xi (2001).

11. *Further Reading.* For discussions of the **history of managed care** (note 2), see Developments, supra, 84 Harv. L. Rev. 887 (1971); R. Holley & R. Carlson, The Legal Context for the Development of Health Maintenance Organizations, 24 Stan. L. Rev. 644 (1972); Lawrence Brown, Politics and Health Care Organization: HMOs as Federal Policy (1983); John Iglehart, Physicians and the Growth of Managed Care, 331 New Eng. J. Med. 1167 (1994); Alain C. Enthoven & Laura A. Tollen, Toward a 21st Century Health System: The Contributions and Promise of Prepaid Group Practice (2004); Jan Coombs, The Rise and Fall of HMOs: An American Health Care Revolution (2005).

For discussions of the **managed care backlash** (note 6), see R. A. Dudley & H. S. Luft, Managed Care in Transition, 344 New Eng. J. Med. 1087 (2001); James C. Robinson, The End of Managed Care, 285 JAMA 2622 (2001); Mark A. Hall, The "Death" of Managed Care: A Regulatory Autopsy, 30 J. Health Pol. Pol'y & L. 427 (2005); Thomas Bodenheimer, The HMO Backlash: Righteous or Reactionary?, 335 New Eng. J. Med. 1601 (1996); Symposium, 24 J. Health Pol. Pol'y & L. 873-1257 (1999); Symposium, 16(6) Health Aff. 1 (Dec. 1997).

Both sides of **the debate over managed care patient protection laws** (note 6) are well represented in a series of articles: in favor of these laws, by Marc Rodwin, in 26 Seton Hall L. J. 1007 (1996), 32 Hous. L. Rev. 1319 (1996), and 15 Health Aff. 110 (1996); and against them, by David Hyman, in 73 S. Cal. L. Rev. 221 (2000), 78 N.C. L. Rev. 5 (1999), and 43 Vill. L. Rev. 409 (1998). See generally Russell Korobkin, The Efficiency of Managed Care "Patient Protection" Laws: Incomplete Contracts, Bounded Rationality, and Market Failure, 85 Cornell L. Rev. 1 (1999); Wendy K. Mariner, Standards of Care and Standard Form Contracts: Distinguishing Patient Rights and Consumer Rights in Managed Care, 15 J. Contemp. Health L. & Pol'y 1 (1998); William Sage, Regulating Through Information: Disclosure Laws and American Health Care, 99 Colum. L. Rev. 1701 (1999); Comment, 28 Cap. U. L. Rev. 685 (2000); Symposium, 47 St. Louis U. L.J. 21 (2003).

For discussions of **the problem of HMO underservice** (note 9), particularly in government programs, see George Anders, Health Against Wealth: HMOs and the Breakdown of Medical Trust (1996); John V. Jacobi, Canaries in the Coal Mine: The Chronically Ill in Managed Care, 9 Health Matrix 79 (1999).

For discussions of the **limited evidence that HMOs harm quality**, see Bruce E. Landon et al., Comparison of Performance of Traditional Medicare vs. Medicare Managed Care, 291 JAMA 1744 (2004); Joseph Gottfried & Frank A. Sloan, The Quality of Managed Care: Evidence from the Medical Literature, 65 Law & Contemp. Probs. 103 (Autumn 2002); Robert Miller & Harold Luft, HMO Plan Performance Update: An Analysis of the Literature, 1997-2001, 21(4) Health Aff. 1 (July 2002); James D. Reschovsky & Peter Kemper, Do HMOs Make a Difference?, 36 Inquiry 374 (2000); Symposium, 30 J. Leg. Stud. 527 (2001).

Exercise: Your Insurance

Investigate your health plan (or your family's health plan) and answer the following questions about your insurance.

- *Cost-sharing.* What is the plan's deductible? For what co-payments and co-insurance are you or your family responsible? Do the out-of-pocket payments vary for inpatient care, outpatient services, or prescription drugs?
- *Networks.* Which physicians and hospitals are in your health plan's network? Can you find an up-to-date provider directory? Are you allowed to visit out-of-network physicians? If so, under what circumstances and at what price?

2. *Consumer-Directed Health Care*

■ TRANSCRIPT OF INTERVIEW WITH JAMIE ROBINSON, Ph.D.*
Lehman Brothers Industry Expert Conference Call Series *May 17, 2002*

As we go into the new decade, the insurance industry is reevaluating whether it wants to be America's method of health care cost control. It's found that this is

* Reprinted with the permission of Prof. Robinson and the former Lehman Brothers.

a very difficult and very unappreciated job. It appears to the public that there is a tradeoff between corporate profits and individual health care, which is a very, very bad image for the industry. The insurers now want to have a completely different image, which is helping the consumer make health care choices. . . .

I think the battle is over and the providers won. The health plans don't really want to get in there and second-guess doctor decision-making. That just proved to be a turf where the providers were very strong, and had the support of the patients and the regulators. . . . There is a lot of lousy medicine being practiced out there that the insurance companies could detect, and could clean up, but they could never convince anybody that they're doing it for the right reasons rather than simply for their own profits.

They've essentially abandoned that role. Increasingly they want to see themselves as a financial services company, like a Fidelity, [which manages investment funds for retirement accounts]. . . . Fidelity offer[s] a stock fund and a bond fund and a mixed fund and employees can allocate their savings across these however they want [with the help of] some decision support tools. . . . The health plans want to do that on the health plan side. "We have our PPO product and our HMO product and our Medical Savings Account product and we're not going to try to force people to pick one or the other. We're going to give them choices. We're going to give them information about the different products, about their prices, about access and about quality. We're going to give them Internet based decision support and tools, and we're going to let them choose. After that, what happens is between the patient and their doctor and their hospital. We, the insurance company, are not going to be responsible for that." . . .

One of the reasons that the insurance industry wants to get out of managed care and go back to being like the financial services industry is that it wants to stop being continually compared to the tobacco industry. It doesn't want to be the second most hated industry in America. The industry needs to re-brand itself as a consumer friendly decision support and information industry rather than something that's trying to save money for corporations.

■ THE HEALTH CARE CRISIS AND WHAT TO DO ABOUT IT
Paul Krugman & Robin Wells
New York Review of Books, Mar. 23, 2006

. . . [H]eavy reliance on insurance disturbs some economists, who believe that doctors and patients fail to make rational decisions about spending because third parties bear the costs of medical treatment. . . . The 2004 Economic Report of the President [for instance] illustrated the alleged problem with a parable about the clothing industry:[9]

---

9. [See also the similar parable based on insuring food consumption, presented two generations earlier by Judith R. Lave & Lester B. Lave, Medical Care and Its Delivery: An Economic Appraisal, 35 Law & Contemp. Probs. 252 (Spring 1970), which is reprinted on the Web site for this casebook. — Eds.]

Suppose, for example, that an individual could purchase a clothing insurance policy with a "coinsurance" rate of 20 percent, meaning that after paying the insurance premium, the holder of the insurance policy would have to pay only 20 cents on the dollar for all clothing purchases. An individual with such a policy would be expected to spend substantially more on clothes—due to larger quantity and higher quality purchases—with the 80 percent discount than he would at the full price. . . . The clothing insurance example suggests an inherent inefficiency in the use of insurance to pay for things that have little intrinsic risk or uncertainty. . . .

But it's no use wishing that health care were sold like ordinary consumer goods, with individuals paying out of pocket for what they need. By its very nature, most health spending must be covered by insurance. The reason is simple: in any given year, most people have small medical bills, while a few people have very large bills. . . . [In any given year], health spending roughly follow[s] the "80-20 rule": 20 percent of the population account[s] for 80 percent of expenses. Half the population ha[s] virtually no medical expenses; a mere 1 percent of the population account[s] for 22 percent of expenses. . . . "Most health costs are incurred by a small proportion of the population whose expenses greatly exceed plausible limits on out-of-pocket spending." . . .

So the only way modern medical care can be made available to anyone other than the very rich is through health insurance. . . . [But] the whole system of employer-based health care is under severe strain. We can identify several reasons for that strain, but mainly it comes down to the issue of costs. Providing health insurance looked like a good way for employers to reward their employees when it was a small part of the pay package. [In 2016], however, the annual cost of coverage for a family of four is estimated by the Kaiser Family Foundation at more than [$18,000]. One way to look at it is to say that that's roughly what a worker earning minimum wage and working full time earns in a year. It's [well] more than half the annual earnings of the average Wal-Mart employee. . . . Inevitably, this creates pressure to reduce or eliminate health benefits. And companies that can't cut benefits enough to stay competitive—such as GM—find their very existence at risk. . . . [W]e may well be seeing the whole institution unraveling.

Notice that this unraveling is the byproduct of what should be a good thing: advances in medical technology, which lead doctors to spend more on their patients. This leads to higher insurance costs, which causes employers to stop providing health coverage. . . .

The "Consumer-Directed" Diversion

The view that Americans consume too much health care because insurers pay the bills leads to what is currently being called the "consumer-directed" approach to health care reform. The virtues of such an approach are the theme of John Cogan, Glenn Hubbard, and Daniel Kessler's *Healthy, Wealthy, and Wise* [2004]. The main idea is that people should pay more of their medical expenses out of pocket. And the way to reduce public reliance on insurance, reformers from the right wing believe, is to remove the tax advantages that currently favor health insurance over out-of-pocket spending. . . . Instead of raising taxes on health insurance, the [Bush] administration has decided to cut taxes on out-of-pocket spending. . . . The administration's proposals . . . focus[] on an expanded system of tax-advantaged health savings accounts. Individuals can shelter part of their income from taxes by depositing it in such accounts, then withdraw money from these accounts to pay medical bills.

What's wrong with consumer-directed health care? One immediate disadvantage is that health savings accounts, whatever their ostensible goals, are yet another tax break for the wealthy, . . . but little or nothing to lower-income Americans who face a marginal tax rate of 10 percent or less, and lack the ability to place the maximum allowed amount in their savings accounts. A deeper disadvantage is that such accounts tend to undermine employment-based health care, because they encourage adverse selection: health savings accounts are attractive to healthier individuals, who will be tempted to opt out of company plans, leaving less healthy individuals behind.

Yet another problem with consumer-directed care is that the evidence says that people don't, in fact, make wise decisions when paying for medical care out of pocket. A classic study by the Rand Corporation found that when people pay medical expenses themselves rather than relying on insurance, they do cut back on their consumption of health care — but that they cut back on valuable as well as questionable medical procedures, showing no ability to set sensible priorities.

But perhaps the biggest objection to consumer-directed health reform is that its advocates have misdiagnosed the problem. . . . Excessive consumption of routine care, or small-expense items, can't be a major source of health care inefficiency, because such items don't account for a major share of medical costs. Remember the 80-20 rule: the great bulk of medical expenses are accounted for by a small number of people requiring very expensive treatment. When you think of the problem of health care costs, you shouldn't envision visits to the family physician to talk about a sore throat; you should think about coronary bypass operations, dialysis, and chemotherapy. Nobody is proposing a consumer-directed health care plan that would force individuals to pay a large share of extreme medical expenses, such as the costs of chemotherapy, out of pocket. And that means that consumer-directed health care can't promote savings on the treatments that account for most of what we spend on health care. . . .

Notes: Patient Cost-Sharing

1. *The "Consumer-Directed" Movement.* Patients can be sensitized to the costs of treatment options in a variety of ways, loosely referred to as "consumer-directed" health care. One approach is simply to increase substantially the co-payment and deductible amounts, producing what is known as "catastrophic" insurance. "Catastrophic" refers to insurance that kicks in only after a patient has incurred a very large expense; for instance, after paying out of pocket the first $5,000 in a year.

A related idea, mentioned by Krugman and Wells, is to couple catastrophic coverage with a "savings account" that is tax-sheltered, or is subsidized by employers. Money in this account can be used only for medical expenses but is used at the patient's discretion, and unused funds can be rolled forward to future years. Originally called medical savings accounts (MSAs), they are now called health savings accounts (HSAs) or health reimbursement arrangements (HRAs). (In brief, HSA funds belong to the individual account holders whereas HRA funds belong to the employers who fund them for workers.) Under any name, the key is that contributions to these accounts are excluded from income taxation. A federal law promotes the use of health savings accounts by making them available to pay expenses covered by high-deductible "catastrophic" insurance policies — those whose deductibles range anywhere from $1,350 for individuals up to about $13,000 for a family.

Although there is no crisp definition of what counts as "catastrophic" coverage, health plans with very high deductibles have proliferated over the past decade. In 2006, just 4 percent of employees were enrolled in a plan with a deductible of at least $1,000 for an individual or $2,000 for a family. By 2016, that figure stood at 29 percent. See Kaiser Family Foundation, 2016 Employer Health Benefits Annual Survey, Fig. 8.5. These figures can be a bit misleading, however. "[O]ut-of-pocket spending has not increased as a share of total employer-sponsored insurance because the rise in deductibles has been offset by more protection [in the Affordable Care Act] against excessive out-of-pocket costs. There is more focus on the former because more people are affected by the upward pressure on deductibles, but given the extreme concentration of health spending, the latter matters just as much for the total dollars involved." Peter Orszag, U.S. Health Care Reform: Cost Containment and Improvement in Quality, 316 JAMA 493 (2016).

Most of the health plans sold on the Affordable Care Act's exchanges also impose high deductibles: the average "silver" plan in 2017, for example, had a deductible of $3,572 for an individual and $7,474 for families. Cost-sharing protections in the ACA shielded lower-income families from some of these out-of-pocket costs, but high deductibles have still emerged as a source of deep frustration with the ACA. Notwithstanding consumer dissatisfaction, the trend toward greater cost-sharing persists. A few states are even experimenting with limited cost-sharing in their Medicaid programs. See John Z. Ayanian, Michigan's Approach to Medicaid Expansion and Reform, 369 New Eng. J. Med. 1773 (2013).

2. *Every Good Idea Is Flawed.* Krugman and Wells mention several of the grounds for criticizing these initiatives. Consider also this point from a former head of CMS:

> [T]he advocates of increased [leaner insurance] seldom go the further step: inquire just why it is that there is so much health insurance around. . . . Consumers have sought the kinds of health insurance they have, not because they wish to act irrationally in the aggregate economic sense, but precisely because they don't wish to be forced to make rational trade-offs when they are confronted with medical care consumption decisions. No matter how we draw our curves or shape our abstract arguments, the elemental fact is that medical care is about living and dying, something considered by many to be of a rather different character from the purchase of tomatoes. The primary characteristic of most consumers of medical care most of the time is that they are scared. They are scared of dying, or disfigurement, or permanent disability; and these are serious matters. It is hardly fair to expect any of us to make rational decisions about matters of such import. As a society, we may be prepared to pay a substantial economic premium to insulate people from having to make such decisions.

Bruce Vladeck, The Market v. Regulation: The Case for Regulation, 59 Milbank Q. 209 (1981). Professor Robinson flags a related set of concerns:

> [The following] problems will plague a consumer-driven health care system. First, despite the widespread dissemination of information, . . . even the most

sophisticated and Internet-enabled consumer . . . will face significant obstacles in understanding the quality and even the true price of health insurance and health care services. . . . [C]onsumers vary enormously in their financial, cognitive, and cultural preparedness to navigate the complex health care system. The new paradigm fits most comfortably the educated, assertive, and prosperous and least comfortably the impoverished, meek, and poorly educated. . . . Finally, the emerging era will make transparent and render difficult the redistribution of income from rich to poor that otherwise results from the collective purchasing and administration of health insurance.

Jamie Robinson, The End of Managed Care, 285 JAMA 2622 (2001).

Which of these arguments is most convincing to you? Even if most people simply follow their physicians' advice about what care they need, is it possible that giving patients more "skin in the game" will make physicians more sensitive to costs, or will make patients more willing to abide by managed care restrictions? In other words, even if patients themselves will not "direct" care, could increased cost-sharing make medical consumers more amenable to cost-based care management? Mark A. Hall & Clark C. Havighurst, Reviving Managed Care with Health Savings Accounts, 24 Health Aff. 1490 (2005).

3. *The Evidence.* Emerging evidence suggests that the critics of consumer-directed health care may have a point. One recent study examined the effect of switching the employees of a large firm into high-deductible health plans. The switch was associated with a substantial reduction (roughly 12 percent or 13 percent) in health-care spending—but not because employees shopped for care or sought out cheaper providers. Instead, "spending reductions were due almost entirely to consumer quantity reductions across a broad range of services, including some that were likely of high value in terms of health and potential to avoid future costs." See Zarek C. Brot-Goldberg et al., What Does a Deductible Do? The Impact of Cost-Sharing on Health Care Prices, Quantities, and Spending Dynamics, Nat'l Bureau of Econ. Research (2015).

The findings echo the conclusions of the famous RAND Corporation study, which was conducted in the late 1970s and placed patients under varying degrees of financial responsibility for their care. The results reveal that cost-sharing indeed has a striking effect on utilization: A catastrophic insurance plan that required the patient to pay 95 percent of the first $1,000 successfully reduced expenditures 31 percent relative to zero out-of-pocket costs, with no discernible differences in health status for most patients. But the lowest-income participants under the cost-sharing plans scored noticeably worse on several measures of health status than did low-income participants under the free plan. Further analysis revealed that most of the cost savings came from patients' reducing their initial visits to their doctors, and that patients cut back both on necessary and unnecessary visits. Once they saw their doctors, patients who paid mostly out of pocket incurred about the same costs as those who paid nothing out of pocket. Joseph Newhouse et al., Free for All? Lessons from the RAND Health Insurance Experiment (1993). These RAND experiments suggest that people in general do not make objectively wise medical spending decisions without the advice of their doctors, but once they consult their doctors, they are inclined to follow medical advice regardless of the financial cost to them (within the $1,000 limit that was studied 30 years ago).

4. *Further Reading.* For additional and more detailed analysis of the entire **debate over consumer-directed health care**, see Timothy S. Jost, Health Care at Risk: A Critique of the Consumer-Driven Movement (2007); Carl Schneider & Mark Hall, The Patient Life: Can Consumers Direct Health Care?, 35 Am. J. L. & Med. 7 (2009); Mark A. Hall, The Legal and Historical Foundations of Patients as Medical Consumers, 96 Geo. L. J. 583 (2008); Douglass Farnsworth, Moral Hazard in Health Insurance: Are Consumer-Directed Plans the Answer?, 15 Ann. Health L. 251 (2006); Christopher Robertson, The Split Benefit: The Painless Way to Put Skin Back in the Healthcare Game, 98 Cornell L. Rev. 921 (2013). For analysis of legal issues related to consumer-directed health care, see Haavi Morreim, High-Deductible Health Plans: New Twists on Old Challenges from Tort and Contract, 59 Vand. L. Rev. 1207 (2006); Timothy S. Jost & Mark A. Hall, The Role of State Regulation in Consumer-Driven Health Care, 31 Am. J. L. & Med. 395 (2005); Mark A. Hall, Paying for What You Get, and Getting What You Pay For, 69 Law & Contemp. Probs. 159 (Autumn 2006).

For further discussions **of health savings accounts** (note 2), see Michael F. Cannon, Health Savings Accounts: Do the Critics Have a Point? (2005); Richard L. Kaplan, Who's Afraid of Personal Responsibility? Health Savings Accounts and the Future of American Health Care, 36 McGeorge L. Rev. 535 (2005); Edward J. Larson & Marc Dettmann, The Impact of HSAs on Health Care Reform: Preliminary Results After One Year, 40 Wake Forest L. Rev. 1087 (2005); Symposium, 19 St. Thomas L. Rev. 1 (2006).

C. ERISA PREEMPTION

This section introduces the broad health policy implications of the Employee Retirement Income Security Act of 1974, a federal statute better known as ERISA, whose primary aim is to regulate private pension plans and other employee fringe benefits. ERISA's main relevance for us is that it preempts certain state laws. While ERISA preemption appears quite technical and perhaps incidental to our main inquiry, it has broad importance for the structure of the health care market and the proper role of state and federal oversight. As one health law scholar has noted, "Although in its text 'hospital' appears only once and 'physician' not at all, ERISA may be the most important law [prior to the Affordable Care Act] affecting health care in the United States." William Sage, "Health Law 2000": The Legal System and the Changing Health Care Market, 15(3) Health Aff. 9 (Aug. 1996).

As you read the main case, pay careful attention to the general purpose that ERISA preemption serves and how its complex preemption provisions are crafted and interpreted. In fact, before you begin, it's a very good idea to read carefully the following statutory language that defines ERISA's scope of preemption:

> (a) Except as provided in subsection (b) of this section, the provisions of [ERISA] shall supersede any and all state laws insofar as they may now or hereafter relate to any employee benefit plan. . . .
> (b) (2)(A) Except as provided in subparagraph (B), nothing in [ERISA] shall be construed to exempt or relieve any person from any law of any state which regulates insurance, banking, or securities. (B) Neither an employee benefit plan . . .

nor any trust established under such a plan shall be deemed to be an insurance company or other insurer, bank, trust company, or investment company or to be engaged in the business of insurance or banking for purposes of any law of any State purporting to regulate insurance companies, insurance contracts, banks, trust companies, or investment companies. . . .

(c) For purposes of this section, the term *state law* includes all laws, decisions, rules, regulations, or other state action having the effect of law, of any state.

Section 514 of ERISA, 29 U.S.C. §1144.[1]

■ RETAIL INDUSTRY LEADERS ASSOCIATION v. FIELDER
475 F.3d.180 (4th Cir. 2007)

NIEMEYER, Circuit Judge

On January 12, 2006, the Maryland General Assembly enacted the Fair Share Health Care Fund Act, which requires employers with 10,000 or more Maryland employees to spend at least 8% of their total payrolls on employees' health insurance costs or pay the amount their spending falls short to the State of Maryland. Resulting from a nationwide campaign to force Wal-Mart Stores, Inc., to increase health insurance benefits for its 16,000 Maryland employees, the Act's minimum spending provision was crafted to cover just Wal-Mart. The Retail Industry Leaders Association, of which Wal-Mart is a member, brought suit against James D. Fielder, Jr., the Maryland Secretary of Labor, Licensing, and Regulation, to declare that the Act is preempted by the Employee Retirement Income Security Act of 1974 ("ERISA"), 29 U.S.C. §1144(a). . . . Because Maryland's Fair Share Health Care Fund Act effectively requires employers in Maryland covered by the Act to restructure their employee health insurance plans, it conflicts with ERISA's goal of permitting uniform nationwide administration of these plans. We conclude therefore that the Maryland Act is preempted by ERISA. . . .

[T]he Secretary contends that . . . the Act imposes a payroll tax on covered employers and offers them a credit against that tax for their healthcare spending [rather than mandating an employer's provision of health care benefits]. . . . To resolve the question whether ERISA preempts the Fair Share Act, we consider first the scope of ERISA's preemption provision, and then the nature and effect of the Fair Share Act. . . .

ERISA establishes comprehensive federal regulation of employers' provision of benefits to their employees. It does not mandate that employers provide specific

1. Even these provisions are somewhat an oversimplification because ERISA preemption actually stems from two independent statutory sources, one explicit and the other implied. These materials focus on the explicit preemption language in § 514 of the Act, which affects primarily regulatory measures. Courts have also recognized a different form of preemption, called complete preemption, emanating from § 502 (29 U.S.C. § 1132), which gives the federal courts exclusive jurisdiction over actions to enforce rights under ERISA plans. Section 502 is the basis for preempting the tort and contract actions discussed in section D.2 and Chapter 4.F. Unlike the regulatory preemption in § 514, there is no "insurance savings clause" for the judicial preemption in § 502.

employee benefits but leaves them free, for any reason at any time, to adopt, modify, or terminate welfare plans. Instead, ERISA regulates the employee benefit plans that an employer chooses to establish, setting various uniform standards, including rules concerning reporting, disclosure, and fiduciary responsibility.

The vast majority of healthcare benefits that an employer extends to its employees qualify as an "employee welfare benefit plan," which ERISA defines broadly as:

> any *plan, fund, or program* which . . . was established or is maintained for the purpose of providing for its participants or their beneficiaries, through the purchase of insurance or otherwise, . . . *medical, surgical, or hospital care or benefits, or benefits in the event of sickness, accident, disability,* death or unemployment, or vacation benefits, apprenticeship or other training programs, or day care centers, scholarship funds, or prepaid legal services. . . .

DEFINITION

29 U.S.C. §1002(1) (emphasis added). . . . Because the definition of an ERISA "plan" is so expansive, nearly any systematic provision of healthcare benefits to employees constitutes a plan.

The primary objective of ERISA was to provide a uniform regulatory regime over employee benefit plans. To accomplish this objective, §514(a) of ERISA broadly preempts "any and all State laws insofar as they may now or hereafter *relate to* any employee benefit plan" covered by ERISA. This preemption provision aims "to minimize the administrative and financial burden of complying with conflicting directives among States or between States and the Federal Government", and to reduce "the tailoring of plans and employer conduct to the peculiarities of the law of each jurisdiction." Ingersoll-Rand Co. v. McClendon, 498 U.S. 133, 142 (1990).

The language of ERISA's preemption provision-covering all laws that "relate to" an ERISA plan-is "clearly expansive." N.Y. State Conf. of Blue Cross & Blue Shield Plans v. Travelers Ins. Co., 514 U.S. 645, 655 (1995). . . . [T]he Supreme Court has held, [however,] that not all state healthcare regulations are equal for purposes of ERISA preemption. States continue to enjoy wide latitude to regulate healthcare *providers.* See, e.g., De Buono v. NYSA-ILA Med. & Clinical Servs. Fund, 520 U.S. 806 (1997) (upholding a state tax on gross receipts for patient services at hospitals, residential healthcare facilities, and diagnostic and treatment centers); Travelers (upholding a state mandate that hospitals charge certain insurers at higher rates than Blue Cross & Blue Shield). And ERISA explicitly saves state regulations of *insurance companies* from preemption. But unlike laws that regulate healthcare providers and insurance companies, state laws that mandate employee benefit structures or their administration are preempted by ERISA. . . . Thus, in *Shaw v. Delta Air Lines, Inc.,* 463 U.S. 85 (1983), the Supreme Court held that ERISA preempted a New York law requiring employers to structure their employee benefit plans to provide the same benefits for pregnancy-regulated disabilities as for other disabilities. . . . On the other hand, a state law that creates only indirect economic incentives that affect but do not bind the choices of employers or their ERISA plans is generally not preempted. . . .

At its heart, the Fair Share Act requires every employer of 10,000 or more Maryland employees to pay to the State an amount that equals the difference between what the employer spends on "health insurance costs" . . . and 8 percent of its payroll. As Wal-Mart noted by way of affidavit, it would not pay the State a sum of money that it could instead spend on its employees' healthcare. This would be the decision of any reasonable employer. . . . An employer would gain from increasing the compensation it offers employees through improved retention and performance of present employees and the ability to attract more and better new employees. In contrast, an employer would gain nothing in consideration of paying a greater sum of money to the State. . . . In effect, the only rational choice employers have under the Fair Share Act is to structure their ERISA healthcare benefit plans so as to meet the minimum spending threshold. . . .

It is a stretch to claim, as the Secretary does, that the Fair Share Act is a revenue statute of general application. When it was enacted, the General Assembly knew that it applied, and indeed intended that it apply, to one employer in Maryland: Wal-Mart. . . . [O]ther States and local governments have adopted or are considering [similar] healthcare spending mandates. . . . If permitted to stand, these laws would force Wal-Mart to tailor its healthcare benefit plans to each specific State, and even to specific cities and counties. This is precisely the regulatory balkanization that Congress sought to avoid by enacting ERISA's preemption provision. . . .

[T]he laws involved in *Travelers* . . . are inapposite because they dealt with regulations that only *indirectly* regulated ERISA plans. In *Travelers,* a New York law required hospitals to add a surcharge to the fees they demanded from most insurance companies, but the law exempted Blue Cross and Blue Shield from having to pay the surcharge. The effect of the law was to make Blue Cross and Blue Shield a cheaper and more attractive option for ERISA-covered healthcare plans to purchase. . . . In short, while the state law in *Travelers* directly regulated *hospitals'* charges to insurance companies, it only *indirectly* affected the prices ERISA plans would pay for insurance policies. . . .

Because the Act directly regulates employers' provision of healthcare benefits, it has a "connection with" covered employers' ERISA plans and accordingly is preempted by ERISA. . . .

MICHAEL, Circuit Judge, dissenting:

Maryland, like most states, is wrestling with explosive growth in the cost of Medicaid. Innovative ideas for solving the funding crisis are required, and the federal government, as the co-sponsor of Medicaid, has consistently called upon the states to function as laboratories for developing workable solutions. In response to this call and its own funding predicament, Maryland . . . require[d] very large employers, such as Wal-Mart Stores, Inc., to assume greater responsibility for employee health insurance costs that are now shunted to Medicaid. I respectfully dissent from the majority's opinion that the Maryland Act is preempted by ERISA. The Act offers a covered employer the option to pay an assessment into a state fund that will support Maryland's Medicaid program. Thus, the Act offers a means of compliance that does not impact ERISA plans, and it is not preempted.

Medicaid is a means-tested entitlement program financed by the states and federal government" that provides medical care for about 60 million Americans. . . . Medicaid was originally intended . . . to serve only as the "payer of last resort." Over time, however, Medicaid has become the payer of first resort for a large percentage of patients. In 2006 state and federal Medicaid spending totaled an estimated $320 billion. Medicaid-the fastest-growing expense for many states-dominates the state budgeting process around the country. . . .

The increase in Medicaid spending is caused in part by the decline in employer-sponsored health insurance. In Maryland's words, Medicaid "has been transformed into a corporate subsidy, with taxpayer-funded employee health care an integral component of [many] an employer's benefits program." Wal-Mart, which is subject to the Maryland Act, is cited as a company that abuses the Medicaid program. "Wal-Mart has more employees and dependents on subsidized Medicaid or similar programs than any other company nationwide." . . . In an internal company memo of fairly recent origin, Wal-Mart acknowledged that "[t]wenty-seven percent of [its employees'] children are on [Medicaid]," and an additional nineteen percent are uninsured. . . . As employers drop or fail to offer affordable family health care coverage, more and more children of low income employees are forced into Medicaid or other taxpayer-funded insurance. . . .

I respectfully dissent on the issue of ERISA preemption because . . . [a]n employer can comply with the Act either by paying assessments into the special fund or by increasing spending on employee health insurance. . . . This choice is real. The assessment does not amount to an exorbitant fee that leaves a large employer with no choice but to alter its ERISA plan offerings. . . . Th[e] choice would simply be a business judgment that Wal-Mart is free to make. Indeed, an employer close to the required statutory percentage, such as Wal-Mart, may find it easier to pay the assessment than to increase health insurance spending. . . . [Therefore,] I would hold that the Act is not preempted.

■ AMERICAN MEDICAL SECURITY, INC. v. BARTLETT
111 F.3d 358 (4th Cir. 1997)

NIEMEYER, Circuit Judge.

. . . This case presents the tension between Maryland's effort to guarantee through its regulation of insurance that employee benefit plans offer at least 28 state-mandated health benefits, and Congress' preemption, through ERISA of any state regulation that "relates to" an employee benefit plan.

ERISA is a comprehensive federal statute regulating [primarily private pension plans, but also covering other employee fringe benefit plans], including plans maintained for the purpose of providing medical or other health benefits for employees. To assure national uniformity of federal law, ERISA broadly preempts state law and assures that federal regulation will be exclusive. Section 514(a) provides that ERISA "shall supersede any and all state laws insofar as they may now or hereafter relate to any employee benefit plan" as defined by ERISA. The courts have interpreted this clause broadly to carry out Congress' purpose of displacing any state effort to regulate ERISA plans. See, e.g., FMC Corp. v. Holliday, 498 U.S. 52, 58 (1990) ("The preemption clause is conspicuous for its breadth"); Shaw v. Delta Airlines, Inc., 463 U.S. 85, 98 (1983) ("The section's preemptive scope [is] as broad as its language"). Thus, any law that "relates to" a plan is preempted by §514(a). . . .

Although ERISA's preemptive scope is broad, the "savings clause" explicitly saves from ERISA's preemption those state laws that regulate insurance. See 29 U.S.C. §1144(b)(2)(A). At the same time, however, the "deemer clause" provides that state insurance laws are not saved from preemption if they deem an employee benefit plan to be an insurance company in order to regulate it. See 29 U.S.C.

§1144(b)(2)(B); see also Pilot Life Ins. Co. v. Dedeaux, 481 U.S. 41, 45 (1987). Thus, a preempted law is saved from preemption if it regulates insurance, . . . but at bottom, state insurance regulation may not directly or indirectly regulate self-funded ERISA plans. Accordingly, although plans that provide benefits in the form of insurance may be indirectly regulated through regulation of that insurance, plans that are self-funded or self-insured may not themselves be regulated as insurance companies even if the self-funded or self-insured plan purchases stop-loss insurance to cover losses or benefits payments beyond a specified level. . . .

[Plaintiffs in this declaratory judgment action include three] Maryland employers sponsoring self-funded employee health benefit plans subject to ERISA. Each has purchased stop-loss insurance . . . to cover their plans' benefit payments above an annual $25,000-per-employee level, known as the "attachment point." . . . The employee benefit plans sponsored by these three Maryland employers contained substantially fewer benefits than the 28 mandated by Maryland for health insurance policies regulated by the Maryland Insurance Commissioner. The benefit plans sponsored by these Maryland employers did not, for example, include benefits for skilled nursing facility services, outpatient rehabilitative services, and certain organ transplants, all of which are mandated for inclusion in Maryland health insurance policies. . . .

Stop-loss insurance provides coverage to self-funded plans above a certain level of risk absorbed by the plan. It provides protection to the plan, not to the plan's participants or beneficiaries, against benefits payments over the specified level. . . . Stop-loss insurance is thus akin to "reinsurance" in that it provides reimbursement to a plan after the plan makes benefit payments.

The state of Maryland regulates health insurance, requiring that health insurance policies afford at least 28 specified benefits.[2] Apparently not wishing to be subject to state-mandated health benefits, insurance companies and their ERISA plan clients have entered into arrangements under which plans self-fund benefits and purchase stop-loss insurance to insure themselves against benefits paid beyond designated attachment points. . . . [B]y absorbing a minimal amount of initial risk and insuring the remainder through stop-loss insurance, plans are able to provide health benefits of a kind or at a level different from what state law requires of [regulated] health insurance.

Recognizing that such arrangements bypass Maryland's regulations for health insurance and intending to prevent such arrangements, the Maryland Insurance

---

2. [Included in this list are: (4) Inpatient mental health and substance abuse services . . . up to a maximum of 25 days per covered person per year in a hospital or related institution; . . . (10) Mammography services for persons ages 40 to 49 once every other calendar year, and for ages 50 and above once per calendar year; . . . (16) Chiropractic services up to 20 visits per condition per year; (17) Skilled nursing facility [and home health] services as an alternative to medically necessary inpatient hospital services up to a maximum of 100 days per year; (18) Infertility [and family planning] services . . . ; (19) Nutritional services for the treatment of cardiovascular disease, diabetes, malnutrition, cancer, cerebral vascular disease, or kidney disease up to a maximum of six visits per year per condition; (20) Autologous and nonautologous bone marrow, cornea, kidney, liver, heart, lung, heart/lung, pancreas, and pancreas/kidney transplants; . . . (25) Pregnancy and maternity services, including abortion; (26) Generic prescription drugs . . . ; (27) Controlled clinical trials. . . .]

Commissioner adopted regulations that require plans to absorb the risk of at least the first $10,000 of benefits paid to each beneficiary. . . . Justifying the regulation and explaining how low attachment points permit self-funded ERISA plans to bypass state mandates, the Insurance Commissioner stated in his order: "... The goal is obvious: As policies become available with attachment points lower than many deductibles, it became an increasingly attractive option to 'self-insure' a health plan, but to continue to shift the majority of the risk to the insurance carrier by purchasing 'stop loss' coverage." The regulations [that plaintiffs seek to declare invalid] accordingly provide that any stop-loss insurance policy with a specific attachment point below $10,000 is deemed to be a health insurance policy for purposes of Maryland's health insurance regulations and must therefore contain mandated benefits. . . .

In summary, on one side of the issue before us, the Maryland Insurance Commissioner seeks to take advantage of his right under ERISA's savings clause to regulate the business of insurance. And on the other side, the insurance companies seek to take advantage of ERISA's preemption and deemer clauses to remove self-funded plans from the reach of state insurance regulation.

III

We begin the analysis with the question of whether Maryland's regulations "relate to" ERISA employee benefit plans and thus whether they fall within ERISA's preemptive scope. A regulation relates to an employee benefit plan when it has a "connection with or reference to such a plan." *Shaw,* 463 U.S. at 96-97. The Maryland Insurance Commissioner wisely concedes that the regulations at issue do "relate to" ERISA plans. . . .

Even though Maryland's regulations relate to ERISA plans, they nevertheless may be saved from preemption if they constitute a law that "regulates insurance." . . . In determining whether a state law is one that "regulates insurance," it is not enough that it operate only on insurance companies or insurance policies. The regulation must regulate the business of insurance in the sense that the object of its regulation (1) "has the effect of transferring or spreading a policyholder's risk"; (2) "is an integral part of the policy relationship between the insurer and the insured"; and (3) "is limited to entities within the insurance industry." Metropolitan Life Insurance Company v. Massachusetts, 471 U.S. 724, 743 (1985). [That decision held that a state may, consistent with ERISA, require health insurers to include certain mandated mental health benefits in policies they sell to employers.]

In this case, the Maryland Insurance Commissioner can well argue with respect to the first *Metropolitan Life* factor that the setting of attachment points allocates risk. Higher attachment points burden plans with more risk while lower attachment points increase insurance company risk. The Commissioner might also be able to argue successfully on the second *Metropolitan Life* factor that the regulations address a practice integral to the insured-insurer relationship. . . . This factor is, however, complicated by the fact that the intended, stated, and actual effect of the regulations is to reach the relationship between ERISA plans and their participants who are not parties to the insurance contract. The third *Metropolitan Life* factor is complicated in the same way. Although the state's regulation of attachment points is limited to entities in the insurance industry, the stated purpose of the regulations is also to reach the [employer]-participant relationship, a relationship which is outside the insurance industry. . . .

We recognize that the regulations are carefully drafted to focus directly on insurance companies issuing stop-loss insurance and not on the employee benefit plans themselves. . . . The state asserts a need for this regulation because, in its absence, the loophole would allow every self-funded plan to provide coverage for fewer health benefits than state law mandates for health insurance policies. It argues that absorbing a minimal risk is simply a sham to circumvent state insurance regulation, the area carved out by ERISA in which states may act. But in seeking to address this perceived loophole, the state in fact ends up regulating self-funded employee benefit plans that are exclusively subject to ERISA. In seeking to require self-funded plans to offer coverage consistent with state insurance law, Maryland crosses the line of preemption. . . . By aiming at the [employer]-participant relationship, Maryland law violates the ERISA provision that no ERISA plan "shall be deemed to be an insurance company . . . for purposes of any law of any state purporting to regulate insurance companies [or] insurance contracts." 29 U.S.C. §1144(b)(2)(B).

The state's fear that [employers] will circumvent state regulation and offer citizens too few health benefits is understandable. But to state that fear reveals that Maryland is really concerned, not with the business of insurance and its coverage of risks, but with the benefits that ERISA plans can choose to provide their participants and beneficiaries. No matter how understandable this concern may be, only Congress may address it, not the state of Maryland through its insurance regulations. . . . If a self-funded plan insured by stop-loss insurance having an attachment point of $5,000 provided no benefit for organ transplants, the regulations would either raise plan costs by including unwanted, state-mandated insurance coverage for organ transplants or convert the self-funded plan into a fully insured plan contrary to its preference. These effects impermissibly intrude on the relationship between an ERISA plan and its participants and beneficiaries. . . .

When ERISA preempted state law relating to ERISA-covered employee benefit plans, it may have created a regulatory gap, but Maryland is without authority to fill that gap. . . .

Notes: ERISA Preemption; Mandated Benefits

1. *Does Any Law Not "Relate to" Employee Benefits?* Owing to the broad "relates to" language, the potential sweep of ERISA preemption is limited only by the bounds of one's imagination. In these materials, ERISA preemption has major impact primarily in three places (in addition to here): (1) malpractice actions against HMOs, section D.2 and Chapter 4.F; (2) contract claims for the denial of payment under health insurance; and (3) state attempts to encourage employers to offer health insurance. But, ERISA preemption is capable of cropping up almost anywhere. Consider, for instance, whether the following are potentially preempted: physicians' contract actions against managed care plans that drop them from their networks; taxation of firms that assist self-insured employers in administering their health benefits; state laws that limit health insurers' or employers' subrogation rights when employees' tort awards include medical expenses. The answer to each is "potentially, yes" (with certain qualifications). See S. Law & B. Ensminger, Negotiating Physicians' Fees: Individual Patients or Society?, 61 N.Y.U. L. Rev. 1, 80-81 (1986) ("in this judicially constructed Alice in Wonderland world, any state seeking to regulate

insurers' arrangements with physicians or providers must be prepared to litigate claims of ERISA preemption").

Broad ERISA preemption was intended to ensure uniform federal regulation of employee benefits. However, ERISA imposes substantive regulation primarily on *pension* benefits, but much less so on *welfare* benefits such as health insurance. It appears that Congress did not realize it was creating such a regulatory vacuum, but subsequent lobbying by vested interests has precluded much alteration of the status quo.

As the *Fielder* case explains, however, courts have begun to adopt a more limited interpretation of "relates to," following the Supreme Court's decision in New York State Conference of Blue Cross & Blue Shield Plans v. Travelers Insurance Co., 514 U.S. 645 (1995). *Travelers* held that ERISA does not preempt a New York statute that requires hospitals to collect surcharges from patients covered by commercial insurers, but not from patients insured by Blue Cross & Blue Shield plans. These surcharges were used to reimburse hospitals for the costs of treating patients without insurance. Blue Cross patients were not charged because Blue Cross's premiums were already more expensive than commercial insurers, due to Blue Cross's policy of accepting both healthy and sick subscribers.

The plaintiffs in *Travelers* argued that the New York statute was preempted by ERISA because it "make[s] the Blues more attractive (or less unattractive) as insurance alternatives and thus ha[s] an indirect economic effect on choices made by insurance buyers, including ERISA plans." The Supreme Court disagreed, holding that statutes that have "only an indirect economic effect on the relative costs of various health insurance packages" available to ERISA plans are not preempted by ERISA. The Court emphasized, though, that it still supports a broad reading of "relates to":

> [W]e do not hold today that ERISA preempts only direct regulation of ERISA plans, nor could we do that with fidelity to the views expressed in our prior opinions on the matter. We acknowledge that a state law might produce such acute, albeit indirect, economic effects, by intent or otherwise, as to force an ERISA plan to adopt a certain scheme of substantive coverage . . . and that such a state law might indeed be preempted under §514. But as we have shown, New York's surcharges do not fall into [that] category; they affect only indirectly the prices of insurance policies, a result no different from myriad state laws in areas traditionally subject to local regulation. . . .

In the subsequent decision mentioned in *Fielder*, the Court found no preemption even though the financial assessment was imposed directly on clinics owned and operated by self-insured employers, since the tax applied generally to all health care facilities and did not target those sponsored by employers. See DeBuono v. NYSA-ILA Medical and Clinical Services Fund, 520 U.S. 806 (1997).

2. *Gobeille.* The scope of *Travelers* remains contested. In Gobeille v. Liberty Mutual Insurance Co., 136 S.Ct. 936 (2016), the Supreme Court heard a challenge to a Vermont law requiring all insurers, public and private, to submit the prices they pay for health care to an "all payer claims database." Eighteen states have moved to establish such databases in the hope of fostering price transparency. "Depending on local policies, that transparency can serve any number of purposes. It can aid state regulators in fashioning new payment models, help researchers better understand

the effects of payment and benefits policies, and enable people with high deductibles to comparison shop." Nicholas Bagley & Christopher Koller, Transparency and the Supreme Court—Can Employers Refuse to Disclose How Much They Pay for Health Care?, 373 New Eng. J. Med. 34 (2016).

Vermont argued that the law did not "relate to" benefit plans because it did not require employers to alter their benefit plans or meaningfully intrude on their administration of those plans. By a 6 to 2 vote, the Supreme Court disagreed:

> ERISA's reporting, disclosure, and recordkeeping requirements for welfare benefit plans are extensive. ERISA plans must present participants with a plan description explaining, among other things, the plan's eligibility requirements and claims-processing procedures. Plans must notify participants when a claim is denied and state the basis for the denial. Most important for the pre-emption question presented here, welfare benefit plans governed by ERISA must file an annual report with the Secretary of Labor. The report must include a financial statement listing assets and liabilities for the previous year and, further, receipts and disbursements of funds. The information on assets and liabilities as well as receipts and disbursements must be provided to plan participants on an annual basis as well. Because welfare benefit plans are in the business of providing benefits to plan participants, a plan's reporting of data on disbursements by definition incorporates paid claims. . . .
>
> It should come as no surprise, then, that plans must keep detailed records so compliance with ERISA's reporting and disclosure requirements may be "verified, explained, or clarified, and checked for accuracy and completeness." . . .
>
> As all this makes plain, reporting, disclosure, and recordkeeping are central to, and an essential part of, the uniform system of plan administration contemplated by ERISA. The Court, in fact, has noted often that these requirements are integral aspects of ERISA. . . .
>
> The State maintains that its program has nothing to do with the financial solvency of plans or the prudent behavior of fiduciaries. This does not suffice to avoid federal pre-emption. . . . In *Travelers*, for example, the Court noted that "[b]oth the purpose and the effects of "the state law at issue "distinguish[ed] it from" laws that "function as a regulation of an ERISA plan itself." 514 U.S., at 658-659. The perceived difference here in the objectives of the Vermont law and ERISA does not shield Vermont's reporting regime from pre-emption. Vermont orders health insurers, including ERISA plans, to report detailed information about the administration of benefits in a systematic manner. This is a direct regulation of a fundamental ERISA function. Any difference in purpose does not transform this direct regulation of "a central matter of plan administration," into an innocuous and peripheral set of additional rules.

136 Sup. Ct. 944-946. The Supreme Court's decision will allow most large employers to withhold price information from the all-payer claims databases. As a result, states will likely struggle to compile a comprehensive picture of medical prices.

3. *The Insurance Savings Clause.* The extent of ERISA preemption depends on the scope of the insurance savings clause, which restores state authority. The three-point test applied in *Metropolitan Life*, which is discussed in *American Medical Security*, pinpoints only the most central core of insurance practice—risk spreading—and only when that practice relates directly to the policyholder. These two limitations exclude a broad array of important activity. In Group Life & Health Insurance Co. v. Royal Drug, 440 U.S. 205 (1979), the Court held that an insurance company's

setting the amount it is willing to pay a health care provider does not constitute the business of insurance because it fails to meet either prong of the test. Similarly, in *Union Labor Life Insurance Co. v. Pireno*, 458 U.S. 119 (1981), the Court excluded from the business of insurance the process of verifying insurance claims, because it occurs only after risk has been transferred.

Subsequent decisions, however, have taken a more relaxed approach to this issue, one that uses a "commonsense" test for what is insurance regulation, a test that does not require that all three parts of the McCarran-Ferguson test be applied in a strict or rigid fashion. For instance, *Rush Prudential HMO v. Moran*, 536 U.S. 355 (2002) (excerpted at pages 1089 and 1154), found that a state law that permits an administrative appeal of HMOs' denial of coverage does regulate insurance even though it does not necessarily affect the aspect of insurance that "spreads a policyholder's risk." In *Kentucky Ass'n of Health Plans v. Miller*, 538 U.S. 329 (2003), the Supreme Court made a "clean break" from its previous reliance on the three-part McCarran-Ferguson definition of insurance regulation. Instead, it adopted the following two-part test to capture the ordinary meaning of insurance regulation: "First, the state law must be specifically directed toward entities engaged in insurance. . . . Second . . . the state law must substantially affect the risk pooling arrangement between the insurer and insured." See also UNUM Life Insurance Co. of America v. Ward, 526 U.S. 358 (1999) (common-law rules regarding interpretation of insurance contracts regulate insurance if they are unique to insurance). Do these subsequent decisions cast doubt on *American Medical Security*'s reasoning? See Russell Korobkin, The Battle over Self-Insured Health Plans, or "One Good Loophole Deserves Another," 5 Yale J. Health Pol'y L. & Ethics 1 (2005) (arguing that this case was wrongly decided).

4. *Self-Insured Employers and the "Deemer Clause."* Owing to ERISA's "deemer clause," employers can avoid all state insurance regulation by self-funding their health care benefits rather than purchasing health insurance. This is one reason that over half of privately insured people are covered by self-funded employer plans. Self-insuring also avoids the state premium taxes that insurers pay, and it potentially reduces the overhead and profits built into insurance premiums. Self-insuring does not entirely eliminate insurers from the equation, however, because most self-insured employers hire insurance companies or other "third-party administrators" to administer claims and to use their networks of providers who have agreed to negotiated discounts. Accordingly, most people cannot tell if their employer plan is self-funded or insured. Under either arrangement, workers have the same insurance card, and they receive care from the same providers under the similar rules.

Conventionally, only large employers take a chance on self-insuring, since even one or two medical problems could bankrupt smaller employers. Although stop-loss insurance protects against that risk, its cost reduces the price advantage being sought. The smaller the employer, the more stop-loss they need to buy, so the equation usually turns negative below about 200 workers.

The ACA may have changed this calculus for small employers, however. Under its community rating rules, small firms with younger and healthier workers have to pay higher premiums in most states if they purchase regulated insurance. By self-insuring, these employers can instead purchase stop-loss coverage that is "experience-rated," meaning that it is priced based on each group's actual, expected claims. Then, if workers or family members develop a serious ongoing health problem, the employer can still jump back into the community-rated market. Imagine what this "adverse selection" would do to community premiums. What can states do to prevent this clear potential for undermining insurance market reforms? In light of *Bartlett*, could they: (1) simply prohibit the sale of stop-loss coverage to small firms, to discourage self-insuring; or (2) require that stop-loss insurance also be community rated?

5. *"Play or Pay" Laws.* The approach to avoiding ERISA preemption attempted by Maryland in its law targeting Wal-Mart is known as "play or pay," meaning that employers can avoid paying the state by "playing" fair regarding their health insurance benefits. Prior to the ACA, the play-or-pay strategy was at the heart of several states' attempts to achieve universal coverage. If ERISA bars either an employer mandate or a play-or-pay law, are states left with no other options than either an individual mandate or a government program funded by a general tax? Could they, for instance, fund universal health care through a general payroll tax that applies to all employers, but give a tax credit to employers that provide insurance?

In Golden Gate Restaurant Association v. City and County of San Francisco, 546 F.3d 639 (9th Cir. 2008), the Ninth Circuit upheld a San Francisco ordinance that required employers either to offer coverage to their employees or pay a tax penalty. The court distinguished *Fielder* on the ground that the penalty would be used to finance a public insurance program for residents whose employers did not offer health coverage. According to the court, that left employers with "a meaningful alternative": they could offer coverage directly (as a fringe benefit of employment) or indirectly (via an earmarked tax). Because an employer that chose the latter approach would have to make no changes at all to its employee benefit plan, the court concluded that ERISA did not preempt the ordinance.

How persuasive is this distinction? Eight of the 27 judges on the Ninth Circuit voted to rehear the case en banc, arguing that it opened a circuit split with *Fielder* and ran counter to the Supreme Court's case law on ERISA preemption. See Golden Gate Rest. Ass'n v. City & Cty. of San Francisco, 558 F.3d 1000 (9th Cir. 2009) (en banc). The restaurant association in *Golden Gate* asked the Supreme Court to review the case, but the ACA was adopted while the association's request was pending. Probably because the ACA obviated the need for state and local play-or-pay laws, the Supreme Court declined to hear the case. If the ACA is partly repealed (its fate remains unclear as of this writing), states and localities may attempt to extend coverage to their uninsured residents—and the legality of play-or-pay laws could again take center stage.

Notably, ERISA does not preempt more incremental state reforms, such as those that make it easier to purchase insurance or that create compensation pools for uncompensated hospital care. See generally Mary Anne Bobinski, Unhealthy Federalism: Barriers to Increasing Health Care Access for the Uninsured, 24 U.C. Davis L. Rev. 255 (1990).

6. *Mandated Insurance Benefits.* Notice in note 2 of the *American Medical Security* case the range of benefits that Maryland requires private health insurance to cover. Which of these mandated benefits are compelled by broad public policy concerns, and which are open to criticism as responses to pressure from particular interest groups? The argument against these mandates is that state legislatures too easily succumb to special interest lobbying by provider groups, thereby increasing the costs of health insurance overall and pricing more people out of the market.

The same tensions exist at the federal level. The Mental Health Parity Act requires that larger employers, including self-insured employers, who offer mental health benefits do so on par with other benefits. Larger employers are not required to offer mental health benefits, but if they do so, those benefits cannot be subject to any different limits (such as cost-sharing, number of treatments, or out-of-network restrictions) than medical benefits. Out of concern that this might prompt employers to drop mental health coverage altogether, however, the law exempts employers for whom this mandate would result in increasing insurance costs more than 1 percent.

The Affordable Care Act greatly expands the federal role in determining which benefits insurance should cover, but it also preserves an important role for the states. Insurers that cover individuals and small groups must offer a comprehensive package of "essential health benefits," including mental health and substance abuse treatment, but each state is permitted to decide what particulars that package should consist of, as long as it is generally consistent with the ACA and with what employers typically cover in that state. Larger employers and those that are self-insured are not required to offer the full set of "essential health benefits."

7. *Accidental Federalism.* Is there any sense or logic in the complicated pattern of state versus federal jurisdiction over the various aspects of health care finance and delivery covered so far in this chapter? Consider not only ERISA but also Medicaid, page 1067, and insurance regulation under the Affordable Care Act, page 1048. The ACA sets detailed requirements for how states must regulate health insurers if they do not want to turn insurance regulation over to the federal government. Moreover, while federal law leaves most aspects of physician practice to the states, it heavily regulates the privacy of medical information, Chapter 3.B, and it strongly influences hospital regulation through its conditions for Medicare participation, page 1080.

8. *Further Readings.* On **the history of ERISA's adoption** (note 1), see James A. Wooten, The Employee Retirement Income Security Act of 1974: A Political History (2004); Daniel Fox & Daniel Schaffer, Health Policy and ERISA: Interest Groups and Semiprotection, 14 J. Health Pol. Pol'y & L. 239 (1989).

For discussions of **the *Travelers* decision** (note 1), see Note, 13 Yale L. & Pol'y Rev. 339 (1995); Catherine Fisk, The Last Article About the Language of ERISA Preemption?, 33 Harv. J. Leg. 35 (1996); Karen Jordan, *Travelers Insurance*: New Support for the Argument to Restrain ERISA Preemption, 13 Yale J. on Reg. 255 (1996). Discussing whether ERISA preempts state-managed care regulation, see Donald T. Bogan, Protecting Patient Rights Despite ERISA: Will the Supreme Court Allow States to Regulate Managed Care?, 74 Tul. L. Rev. 951 (2000); Margaret Farrell, ERISA Preemption and Regulation of Managed Health Care, 23 Am. J. L. & Med. 251 (1997). For discussions of how the ACA might have shifted the ERISA terrain somewhat, see Brendan S. Maher, The Affordable Care Act, Remedy, and Litigation Reform, 63 Am. U. L. Rev. 649 (2014); Katherine T. Vukadin, Hope or Hype?: Why the Affordable Care Act's New External Review Rules for Denied ERISA Healthcare Claims Need More Reform, 60 Buff. L. Rev. 1201 (2012).

For discussions of Gobeille v. Liberty Mutual (note 2), see Erin C. Fuse Brown & Jamie King, The Double-Edged Sword of Health Care Integration: Consolidation and Cost Control, 92 Ind. L. J. 55 (2016); Elizabeth Y. McCuskey, Body of Preemption: Health Law Traditions and the Presumption Against Preemption, 89 Temp. L. Rev. 95 (2016); Edward Zelinsky, Gobeille v. Liberty Mutual: An Opportunity to Correct the Problems of ERISA Preemption, 100 Cornell L. Rev. Online 24 (2015).

For discussions about **employers using stop-loss coverage to take advantage of ERISA** (note 3), see Timothy Jost & Mark Hall, Self Insurance for Small Employers Under the Affordable Care Act: Federal and State Regulatory Options, 69 N.Y.U. Ann. Surv. Am. L. 539 (2013); K. Caster, The Future of Self-Funded Health Plans, 79 Iowa L. Rev. 413 (1994); J. Lenhart, ERISA Preemption: The Effect of Stop-Loss Insurance on Self-Insured Health Plans, 14 Va. Tax Rev. 615 (1995).

For discussions of **play-or-pay laws** (note 5), see Peter D. Jacobson, The Role of ERISA Preemption in Health Reform: Opportunities and Limits, 37 J. L. Med. & Ethics 88 (2009); Amy B. Monahan, Pay or Play Laws, ERISA Preemption, and Potential Lessons from Massachusetts, 55 Kan. L. Rev. 1203 (2007); Christen Linke Young, Note, Pay or Play Programs and ERISA Section 514: Proposals for Amending the Statutory Scheme, 10 Yale J. Health Pol'y, L. & Ethics 197 (2010)

For discussions of **mandated benefits** (note 6), see the several articles by Amy Monahan at 2007 U. Ill. L. Rev. 1361; 80 U. Colo. L. Rev. 127 (2009); and 2012 U. Ill. L. Rev. 139. See also Nicholas Bagley & Helen Levy, Essential Health Benefits and the Affordable Care Act: Law and Process, 39 J. Heath Pol., Pol'y & Law 441 (2013); Stacy Tovino, A Proposal for Comprehensive and Specific Essential Mental Health and Substance Use Disorder Benefits, 38 Am. J. L. & Med. 471 (2012).

For discussions of **federalism in health care** (note 7), see Nicholas Bagley, Federalism and the End of Obamacare, 127 Yale L. J. Forum 1 (2017); Patricia J. Zettler, Toward Coherent Federal Oversight of Medicine, 52 San Diego L. Rev. 427 (2015); Brendan S. Maher & Radha A. Pathak, Enough About the Constitution: How States Can Regulate Health Insurance Under the ACA, 31 Yale Law & Pol'y Rev. 275 (2013); Michael Doonan, American Federalism in Practice: The Formulation and Implementation of Contemporary Health Policy (2013); Lars Noah, Ambivalent Commitments to Federalism in Controlling the Practice of Medicine, 53 U. Kan. L. Rev. 149 (2004); Richard P. Nathan, Federalism and Health Policy, 24(6) Health Aff. 1458 (Nov. 2005); John D. Blum, Overcoming Managed Care Regulatory Chaos Through a Restructured Federalism, 11 Health Matrix 327 (2001).

9. *A Path Through the Maze.* Let us recapitulate the complex analysis required to answer an ERISA preemption question: (1) ERISA's preemption clause is extremely broad because so many state laws "relate to" employee benefits. (2) The insurance savings clause would reinstate most relevant state regulation, except for the fact that it sometimes is given a narrow construction. And, (3) regardless, for reasons just explained, self-insured health benefits may never be subjected to state regulation. The confusion surrounding this complicated scheme and the meaning of its various parts has deterred states from asserting more aggressive regulatory jurisdiction, even where that might be possible to do

ERISA Preemption Quiz

The following questions are supposed to have clear, settled answers for those who understand this complex law. See how you do.

Due to ERISA preemption, are any of the following true? Why or why not?

a. States may not force employers to purchase insurance.

b. States may not require self-insured employers to cover mental health services.

c. States may not regulate the rates that hospitals charge (i) insurers and HMOs, or (ii) self-insured employers.

D. HEALTH INSURANCE COVERAGE

In the previous section, we made the transition from looking at who is covered by what types of insurance, to looking at which benefits are covered. This section explores the latter topic in much greater depth. We start by examining whether it is desirable or permissible to exclude some medical conditions or treatments by assessing which medical needs are most demanding and what treatments work the best. The public policy focus here is on how insurance contracts or statutes might be rewritten, and the legal focus is on disability discrimination. Then, we go on to look at how to interpret and apply insurance contracts and statutes once they are adopted, and how to appeal coverage denials.

As you read this section, realize that, in a world of limited resources, insurance cannot pay for all beneficial medical care that anyone might need. The problem, then, is which approach to limiting insurance benefits makes the most sense, and whether discrimination law and policy allow sensible health care public policy to emerge from either market or political forces.

1. Rationing and Discrimination

■ ALEXANDER v. CHOATE
469 U.S. 287 (1985)

Justice MARSHALL delivered the opinion of the Court.

... Faced in 1980-1981 with projected state Medicaid costs of $42 million more than the state's Medicaid budget of $388 million, the directors of the Tennessee Medicaid program decided to institute a variety of cost-saving measures. Among these changes was a reduction from 20 to 14 in the number of inpatient hospital days per fiscal year that Tennessee Medicaid would pay hospitals on behalf of a Medicaid recipient. Before the new measures took effect, respondents, Tennessee Medicaid recipients, brought a class action for declaratory and injunctive relief in which they alleged, inter alia, that the proposed 14-day limitation on inpatient coverage would have a discriminatory effect on the handicapped. Statistical evidence, which petitioners do not dispute, indicated that in the 1979-1980 fiscal year, 27.4 percent of all handicapped users of hospital services who received Medicaid required more than 14 days of care, while only 7.8 percent of nonhandicapped users required more than 14 days of inpatient care.

Based on this evidence, respondents asserted that the reduction would violate §504 of the Rehabilitation Act of 1973 . . . [which] provides: "No otherwise qualified handicapped individual . . . shall, solely by reason of his handicap, be excluded from the participation in, be denied the benefits of, or be subjected to discrimination under any program or activity receiving Federal financial assistance." 29 U.S.C. §794. . . .

[The] major thrust of respondents' attack was directed at the use of any annual limitation on the number of inpatient days covered, for respondents acknowledged that, given the special needs of the handicapped for medical care, any such limitation was likely to disadvantage the handicapped disproportionately. . . . [T]he Medicaid programs of only ten states impose such restrictions.[10] Respondents therefore suggested that Tennessee follow these other states and do away with any limitation on the number of annual inpatient days covered. Instead, argued respondents, the state could limit the number of days of hospital coverage on a per-stay basis, with the number of covered days to vary depending on the recipient's illness (for example, fixing the number of days covered for an appendectomy); the period to be covered for each illness could then be set at a level that would keep Tennessee's Medicaid program as a whole within its budget. . . .

The first question the parties urge on the Court is whether proof of discriminatory animus is always required to establish a violation of §504 and its implementing regulations, or whether federal law also reaches action by a recipient of federal funding that discriminates against the handicapped by effect rather than by design. . . . Discrimination against the handicapped was perceived by Congress to be most often the product, not of invidious animus, but rather of thoughtlessness and indifference—of benign neglect. . . . For example, elimination of architectural barriers was one of the central aims of the Act, yet such barriers were clearly not erected with the aim or intent of excluding the handicapped. . . .

At the same time, the position urged by respondents—that we interpret §504 to reach all action disparately affecting the handicapped—is also troubling. Because the handicapped typically are not similarly situated to the nonhandicapped, respondents' position would in essence require each recipient of federal funds first to evaluate the effect on the handicapped of every proposed action that might touch the interests of the handicapped, and then to consider alternatives for achieving the same objectives with less severe disadvantage to the handicapped. The formalization and policing of this process could lead to a wholly unwieldy administrative and adjudicative burden. . . .

To determine which disparate impacts §504 might make actionable, . . . [we must strike] a balance between the statutory rights of the handicapped to be integrated into society and the legitimate interests of federal grantees in preserving the integrity of their programs: While a grantee need not be required to make "fundamental" or "substantial" modifications to accommodate the handicapped, it may be required to make "reasonable" ones. . . .

[A]n otherwise qualified handicapped individual must be provided with meaningful access to the benefit that the grantee offers. The benefit itself, of course, cannot be defined in a way that effectively denies otherwise qualified handicapped individuals the meaningful access to which they are entitled; to assure meaningful access, reasonable accommodations in the grantee's program or benefit may have

---

10. As of 1980 the average ceiling in those states was 37.6 days. Six states also limit the number of reimbursable days per admission, per spell of illness, or per benefit period.

to be made. In this case, the 14-day limitation will not deny respondents meaningful access to Tennessee Medicaid services or exclude them from those services.

The new limitation does not invoke criteria that have a particular exclusionary effect on the handicapped; the reduction, neutral on its face, does not distinguish between those whose coverage will be reduced and those whose coverage will not on the basis of any test, judgment, or trait that the handicapped as a class are less capable of meeting or less likely of having. Moreover, it cannot be argued that "meaningful access" to state Medicaid services will be denied by the 14-day limitation on inpatient coverage; nothing in the record suggests that the handicapped in Tennessee will be unable to benefit meaningfully from the coverage they will receive under the 14-day rule.[22] The reduction in inpatient coverage will leave both handicapped and nonhandicapped Medicaid users with identical and effective hospital services fully available for their use, with both classes of users subject to the same durational limitation. . . .

To the extent respondents further suggest that their greater need for prolonged inpatient care means that, to provide meaningful access to Medicaid services, Tennessee must single out the handicapped for more than 14 days of coverage, the suggestion is simply unsound. At base, such a suggestion must rest on the notion that the benefit provided through state Medicaid programs is the amorphous objective of "adequate health care." But Medicaid programs do not guarantee that each recipient will receive that level of health care precisely tailored to his or her particular needs. Instead, the benefit provided through Medicaid is a particular package of health care services, such as 14 days of inpatient coverage. That package of services has the general aim of assuring that individuals will receive necessary medical care, but the benefit provided remains the individual services offered—not "adequate health care."[23] . . .

Section 504 does not require the state to alter this definition of the benefit being offered simply to meet the reality that the handicapped have greater medical needs. To conclude otherwise would be to find that the Rehabilitation Act requires states to view certain illnesses, i.e., those particularly affecting the handicapped, as more important than others and more worthy of cure through government subsidization. Nothing in the legislative history of the Act supports such a conclusion. Cf. Doe v. Colautti, 592 F.2d 704 (3d Cir. 1979) (state may limit covered-private-inpatient-psychiatric care to 60 days even though state sets no limit on duration of coverage for physical illnesses). Section 504 seeks to assure evenhanded treatment and the opportunity for handicapped individuals to participate in and benefit from programs receiving federal assistance. The Act does not, however, guarantee the handicapped equal results from the provision of state Medicaid, even assuming some measure of equality of health could be constructed. . . .

---

22. The record does not contain any suggestion that the illnesses uniquely associated with the handicapped or occurring with greater frequency among them cannot be effectively treated, at least in part, with fewer than 14 days' coverage. In addition, the durational limitation does not apply to only particular handicapped conditions and takes effect regardless of the particular cause of hospitalization.

23. . . . [W]e express no opinion on whether annual limits on hospital care are in fact consistent with the Medicaid Act. . . .

We turn next to respondents' alternative contention . . . that all annual durational limitations discriminate against the handicapped because (1) the effect of such limitations falls most heavily on the handicapped and because (2) this harm could be avoided by the choice of other Medicaid plans that would meet the state's budgetary constraints without disproportionately disadvantaging the handicapped. Viewed in this light, Tennessee's current plan is said to inflict a gratuitous harm on the handicapped that denies them meaningful access to Medicaid services. . . .

On the contrary, to require that the sort of broad-based distributive decision at issue in this case always be made in the way most favorable, or least disadvantageous, to the handicapped, even when the same benefit is meaningfully and equally offered to them, would be to impose a virtually unworkable requirement on state Medicaid administrators. Before taking any across-the-board action affecting Medicaid recipients, an analysis of the effect of the proposed change on the handicapped would have to be prepared. Presumably, that analysis would have to be further broken down by class of handicap—the change at issue here, for example, might be significantly less harmful to the blind, who use inpatient services only minimally, than to other subclasses of handicapped Medicaid recipients; the state would then have to balance the harms and benefits to various groups to determine, on balance, the extent to which the action disparately impacts the handicapped. In addition, respondents offer no reason that similar treatment would not have to be accorded other groups protected by statute or regulation from disparate-impact discrimination.

It should be obvious that administrative costs of implementing such a regime would be well beyond the accommodations that are required. . . . As a result, Tennessee need not redefine its Medicaid program to eliminate durational limitations on inpatient coverage, even if in doing so the State could achieve its immediate fiscal objectives in a way less harmful to the handicapped. . . .

■ WILL CLINTON'S PLAN BE FAIR?
Ronald Dworkin
New York Review of Books, Jan. 13, 1994

Some critics deny that health-care rationing is really necessary: They argue that if the waste and greed in the American health-care system were eliminated, we could save enough money to give men and women all the medical treatment that could benefit them. But . . . the greatest contribution to the rise in medical costs in recent decades has been the availability of new, high-tech means of diagnosis, like magnetic resonance imaging and new and very expensive techniques like organ transplants and, on the horizon, monoclonal-antibody treatment for cancer. . . . Many politicians and some doctors say that much of the new technology is "unnecessary" or "wasteful." They do not mean that it provides no benefit at all. They mean that its benefit is too limited to justify its cost, and this is an argument for rationing, not an argument that rationing is unnecessary. . . . So we cannot . . . avoid the question of justice: What is "appropriate" medical care depends on what it would be unfair to withhold on the grounds that it costs too much. That question has been missing from the public debate. . . .

For millennia doctors have paid lip service, at least, to an ideal of justice in medicine which I shall call the rescue principle. It has two connected parts. The first holds that life and health are, as René Descartes put it, chief among all goods: Everything else is of lesser importance and must be sacrificed for them. The second insists that health care must be distributed on grounds of equality: that even in a society in which wealth is very unequal and equality is otherwise scorned, no one must be denied the medical care he needs just because he is too poor to afford it. These are understandable, even noble, ideals. They are grounded in a shared human understanding of the horror of pain, and, beyond that, of the indispensability of life and health to everything else we do. The rescue principle is so ancient, so intuitively attractive, and so widely supported in political rhetoric, that it might easily be thought to supply the right standard for answering questions about rationing. . . .

In past centuries, however, there was not so huge a gap between the rhetoric of the rescue principle and what it was medically possible for a community to do. But now that science has created so many vastly expensive forms of medical care, it is preposterous that a community should treat longer life as a good that it must provide at any cost—even one that would make the lives of its people barely worth living. . . .

The rescue principle does have something helpful, though negative, to say about the other question of justice, which is how health care should be distributed. It says that if rationing is necessary, it should not be done, as it now largely is in the United States, on the basis of money. But we need more positive advice: What should the basis of rationing be? The egalitarian impulse of the principle suggests that medical care should be distributed according to need. But what does that mean—how is need to be measured? Does someone "need" an operation that might save his life but is highly unlikely to do so? Is someone's need for life-saving treatment affected by the quality his life would have if the treatment were successful? Does the age of patient matter—does someone need or deserve treatment less at 70 than a younger age? Why? How should we balance the need of many people for relief from pain or incapacity against the need of fewer people for life-saving care? At one point the procedures of an Oregon commission appointed to establish medical priorities ranked tooth-capping ahead of appendectomy, because so many teeth can be capped for the price of one operation. Why was that so clearly a mistake? . . .

— END —

■ HEALTH CARE RATIONING AND DISABILITY RIGHTS
Philip G. Peters, Jr.
70 Ind. L.J. 491 (1995)

. . . Any criterion suggested for rationing health care will be controversial. The stakes are high and no popular or ethical consensus has emerged. But allocation decisions are omnipresent and their continuation is inevitable. . . . Americans have never been willing to pay for all the health care that is of any conceivable benefit, nor are they likely to do so in the future. Unfortunately, the existing mechanisms for deciding who receives what care are blunt and often irrational or unfair, reflecting the influence of wealth, employment, habit, cost, and power. . . . Common sense tells us to give priority to services that do the most good. As a result, an approach which would eliminate only the least beneficial or least cost-effective treatments has considerable potential appeal. It offers both the promise of maximizing health care outcomes from limited resources and the surface allure of scientific objectivity and nonpartisan neutrality. . . .

But rationing the least effective care has a dark side beneath its veneer of objectivity. Any health care allocation scheme which attempts to maximize health care outcomes by giving priority to the most effective treatments has the potential to disfavor disabled patients and others, such as the elderly and the frail, whose quality of life is most impaired or whose conditions are most resistant to cure. As a result, the use of effectiveness criteria to allocate health resources may be challenged as violating society's commitment to equality in general, and to protection of those with the greatest need in particular.

The resolution of this conflict between efficiency and equality has dramatic implications for health policy. . . . It arises whenever effectiveness or cost-effectiveness is used by health care providers or insurers to determine which treatments to provide or insure. Those instances range from bedside decisions by clinicians to macroallocation decisions by benefit plans about coverage of conditions such as AIDS, infertility, or mental illness. In each setting, allocations based on medical utility have the potential to disfavor some patients on the basis of their disability. . . .

I. [EFFECTIVENESS MEASURES AND THE OREGON EXPERIMENT]

Health economists have worked for decades on methodologies for calculating both the effectiveness and the cost-effectiveness of health care expenditures.[11] Originally utilized to compare the value of different treatments for the same disease, these methods were later used to compare the cost-effectiveness of treatments for different diseases. Cost-effectiveness calculations have the appeal of incorporating outcomes research, patient preferences, and expected costs into a rational and potentially sophisticated scheme for maximizing health care outcomes from the available resources. . . .

Theoretically, at least, calculating the effectiveness of a medical service is relatively straightforward. This calculation involves both an estimate of the likely outcomes and an assignment of value to those outcomes. The value assigned to an outcome is determined by the impact which the treatment is expected to have on a patient's quality of life. That value is then adjusted to reflect the probability and duration of the expected benefit. The product of this calculus is a single unit which expresses the number and quality of additional years that the treatment is likely to confer. These outcome units have been called both Quality-Adjusted Life Years ("QALYs") and Well Years. . . .

The theoretical value of these calculations cannot be overstated. They provide a common unit of measurement which permits treatments for different diseases to be compared on the basis of their expected benefit or their

---

11. American researchers initially derived the methodology from operations research in engineering and mathematics, using it in the health care setting to measure the tradeoff between survival and quality of life that is implicated by some treatment choices such as conservative care versus aggressive care. The British, most notably Alan Williams, then borrowed the concept as a way of suggesting priorities in their national health care system.

cost-effectiveness.[16] Using QALYs or their equivalents, comparisons can be made between such disparate treatments as AZT [for AIDS], autologous bone marrow transplants, infertility treatments, mammography screening, early CT scans for head pain, and heroic care for patients in persistent vegetative states. . . .

As the health economist David Hadorn has emphasized, reliable cost-effectiveness data will help health care providers minimize human suffering to the maximum extent possible with the resources society allocates to health care.[17] . . . Current insurance and clinical practices often make the same kinds of calculations regarding treatment value and cost, albeit in a more intuitive manner. . . . QALYs can help improve the process, making it more rational and, therefore, more just. . . .

QALYs may also help health decisionmakers to avoid what David Eddy has called "rationing by meat ax." By excluding the least effective treatments for conditions that ordinarily are covered by insurance, savings could be generated to fund more comprehensive coverage of treatments for conditions such as mental health that are typically excluded or restricted. Blanket restrictions on treatments for infertility or mental health, for example, could be replaced by narrower exclusions of only those treatments which are least effective.

In addition, the exclusion of whole groups of uninsured persons from programs such as Medicaid could be replaced by the exclusion of marginally effective care. Oregon, for example, replaced a Medicaid system in which a six-year-old child was eligible when a seven-year-old was not, in which pregnant women had coverage but other women did not, and in which single adults with children were covered but those without children or with a spouse were excluded. In its place, the state has instituted a system [described below] that provides protection for [all people below the poverty line] by prioritizing the treatments covered.[24] . . . This explicit attention to the difficult choices is in marked contrast to current practices, such as those of physicians who use neutral terms such as "futility" to mask intuitive judgments about the value of treatment to the patient. . . .

16. . . . John Rawls includes several helpful illustrations of comparisons based on cost-effectiveness:

> For example, a patient with severe arthritis of the hip who is unable to work and is in severe distress scores a quality of life of 0.7. . . . His expectation of life of ten years is reduced to seven quality adjusted life years. Successful hip replacement, by eliminating disability and distress, restores 3 QALYs to his total, at an average cost of pounds sterling 750 per QALY.

> Another example is a patient with renal failure undergoing renal dialysis twice a week in hospital for a year. He is unable to work and suffers moderate distress with a quality of life of 0.9. However, hemodialysis is life-saving, so every year adds 0.9 to the number of QALYs he would otherwise enjoy, at a cost of pounds sterling 14000 per QALY.

John Rawls, Castigating QALYs, 15 J. Med. Ethics 143, 144-145 (1989).

17. David C. Hadorn, Setting Health Care Priorities in Oregon: Cost-Effectiveness Meets the Rule of Rescue, 265 JAMA 2218, at 2225 (1991) (describing the original Oregon methodology and the modifications undertaken before submission to the federal government for approval). . . .

24. Compare the approach of Missouri, which spent nearly $1 million keeping Nancy Cruzan alive in a persistent vegetative state, while providing Medicaid for only 40 percent of its citizens below the poverty level. Leonard M. Fleck, Just Health Care Rationing: A Democratic Decisionmaking Approach, 140 U. Pa. L. Rev. 1597, 1611 (1992).

But measurement of medical effectiveness also presents serious methodological and ethical problems which must be surmounted before its use expands. The
methodological problems arise both from the difficulty of obtaining adequate data
about outcomes, benefits, and costs and also from predictable issues of study design.
Problems of this kind contributed to the failure of Oregon's initial attempt to prioritize medical treatments entirely on the basis of net benefit. . . .

In order to calculate a treatment's medical effectiveness, analysts must estimate its probable outcome and then place a value on that outcome. Both steps
could disfavor disabled patients. When outcomes are taken into account, patients
with preexisting disabilities, such as diabetes, cancer, or pulmonary disease, could
be disfavored because they often have more difficulty fighting unrelated illnesses
(comorbidity) than patients who are otherwise healthy.[36] For example, diabetes
reduces the probable effectiveness of some treatments for serious heart ailments.
Unchecked alcoholism, another disability, could interfere with the success of organ
transplantation. . . .

In addition, seriously disabled patients could be disfavored when values are
placed on treatment outcomes. For example, QALY use disfavors lifesaving care for
patients who are expected to be disabled after treatment, because saving the life of
a disabled person with an impaired quality of life will theoretically generate fewer
quality-adjusted life years than saving the life of a person whose quality of life after
treatment would be better. . . .

The chance that disabled patients will fare unfavorably in QALY calculations
is further accentuated by the risk that the scales used to measure quality of life will
unfairly underestimate the quality of life of disabled persons. This was precisely
the federal government's criticism of the Oregon quality of life measurements. Yet,
until the Oregon plan was submitted for federal government approval, no public attention had been called to the discriminatory potential of prioritization on
the basis of medical effectiveness. Although the Oregon plan was vilified on other
grounds (principally that only poor people would be asked to make sacrifices to
help fund an expansion of health care coverage for other poor people), virtually no
public debate on disability rights had occurred. As a result, the [first] Bush administration's rejection of the plan because of discrimination against patients with disabilities surprised most observers and caused some speculation that the administration had simply used the disability rights issue to derail a proposal which it found
objectionable for other reasons. . . .

36. See, e.g., David Orentlicher, Rationing and the Americans with Disabilities Act, 271
JAMA 308, 310 (1994) (recognizing that patients with pulmonary disease are poor candidates
for coronary bypass surgery). In another example, an HMO denied payment for a $170,000
liver transplant requested by an e-antigen positive hepatitis-B patient due to the high rate
of reinfection of e-antigen positive patients and the liver shortage. Barnett v. Kaiser Found.
Health Plan, Inc., Health Care Facility Mgmt. (CCH) ¶22,594 (N.D. Cal. 1993). The HMO's
eight-member advisory board had concluded that transplantation was not an appropriate
medical treatment for the patient's condition. The federal district court ruled that the HMO
had not abused its discretion in considering this factor, even though transplantation might be
the patient's only chance of survival. The disability rights laws were apparently not addressed.

Oregon's initial ranking of treatments . . . was based on a pure cost-effectiveness analysis, but problems with that list[44] induced the Oregon Health Services Commission to abandon that list and produce another one . . . using a more intuitive, multifactorial methodology. Nonetheless, considerations of effectiveness continued to play a crucial role . . . at three junctures. First, the Commission divided all treatments into one of seventeen different categories and then ranked these categories. A sampling of the categories illustrates the methodology: "acute fatal, treatment prevents death with full recovery" (ranked #1); "maternity care" (#2); "acute fatal, treatment prevents death without full recovery" (#3); "comfort care" (#7); "acute nonfatal, treatment causes return to previous health state" (#10); and "infertility services" (#15). These rankings gave priority to treatments which produced complete cures over those which ordinarily produce only partial recovery. In this way, the Commission retained a blunt measure of effectiveness in its ranking process. The Commission also considered cost-effectiveness as one of many factors used to create and rank these categories.

Second, the Commission used QALYs to rank treatments within the 17 categories.[51] Third and finally, the Commissioners reviewed the resulting list and adjusted some of the rankings using their "professional judgments and their interpretation of the community values." The Commissioners imposed a "reasonableness" test upon themselves, taking into account effectiveness and cost along with other factors such as public health impact, incidence of condition, and social costs. The result was a ranking of 709 treatments of which 587 were to be funded in the first year. . . .

44. . . . In David Eddy's view, Oregon's inability to estimate accurately either costs or benefits precluded reliance on its initial list. Categories of services and outcomes were defined too broadly. For example, "trouble speaking" could range from mild lisp to mutism. Duration of treatment benefits was poorly differentiated. Cost data were incomplete or inaccurate. And the list generated serious doubts whether the values assigned to treatment outcomes, especially lifesaving treatments, had been accurately measured. David M. Eddy, Oregon's Methods: Did Cost-Effectiveness Analysis Fail?, 266 JAMA 2135 (1991); David M. Eddy, Oregon's Plan: Should It Be Approved?, 266 JAMA 2439 (1991).

Counter-intuitive rankings resulted from these problems. Reportedly, "burn over large areas of the body" scored the same as an "upset stomach." Michael Astrue, then-general counsel of the Department of Health and Human Services, was startled that treatments for ectopic pregnancies and appendicitis were ranked below some dental caps and splints for temporomandibular joint disorder. . . . Unwillingness to accept the implications of cost-effectiveness analysis, especially for the prioritization of noncritical care over life-extending care, may also partially explain the adverse reaction to this list. . . .

51. Benefits were measured using Dr. Robert M. Kaplan's Quality of Well-Being ("QWB") scale. Using the results of a random telephone poll of 1,001 Oregon households in which respondents were asked to rank 23 symptoms and 6 levels of functional impairment, the Commission assigned a value to various states of health, such as requiring a wheelchair or having severe burns. The benefits associated with each treatment were then calculated by using the values for the various outcomes provided by the telephone survey and weighting those values to reflect the probability of their occurrence. Expected outcomes were ascertained by polling practitioners. Outcomes (such as death or return to former health) were estimated five years after treatment. Net benefit (QWB) scores were derived by comparing the QWB score without treatment to the QWB score with treatment. The Commission multiplied the expected QWB by the duration of the benefit (thereby obtaining a measure of quality-adjusted life years or QALYs). In most cases, duration was the patient's life expectancy.

[T]he Department of Health and Human Services ("HHS") announced that Oregon had been denied a waiver [of the usual Medicaid coverage requirements] because its plan violated the Americans with Disabilities Act ("ADA").... HHS specifically identified two instances in which disabilities had been impermissibly taken into account: (1) the ranking of alcoholic cirrhosis of the liver (#690) below other cirrhoses (#366) and (2) the ranking of extremely low birth weight babies (#708) below heavier babies (#22).

Oregon denied that it had violated the ADA, but nevertheless complied with HHS's demands. Approval was not granted until Oregon had eliminated quality of life data from its formal methodology and had abandoned the separate classification of alcoholic cirrhosis and low birth weight babies. In addition, the newly elected Clinton administration insisted that Oregon no longer disfavor infertility treatments. In March, 1993, the Oregon Commission approved a new list which was based first on mortality and then, as a tie-breaker, on cost considerations. It was then adjusted by the Commission to reflect community values, such as a preference for preventive services and a dislike for medically ineffective care....

This exchange between Oregon and the federal government has dramatic implications for health policy. Oregon's capitulation has cast a shadow over similar endeavors by other states. In its wake, considerable confusion exists about the permissible role of effectiveness in allocating health resources.... Alexander Morgan Capron, an ... advocate of rationing, was ... dire in his assessment. "As some form of rationing is an inevitable part of all health insurance," he concluded, "the ADA roadblock to rational prioritization of services by their expected benefit should be of grave concern to us all."

Was the federal government correct? Exactly what limits do the disability rights laws place on the use of effectiveness criteria? Answering these questions requires a basic understanding of the disability rights laws.

II. FEDERAL DISABILITY RIGHTS LAW

Two federal statutes protect disabled individuals from improper discrimination in health care decisionmaking: The Rehabilitation Act of 1973 and the more recent Americans with Disabilities Act of 1990 ("ADA").... Although the ADA is much more detailed than the Rehabilitation Act and the wording of the various titles of the ADA are slightly different, the basic paradigm of the two federal laws protecting disability rights can be briefly summarized. Section 504 of the Rehabilitation Act bars discrimination by any program receiving federal financial assistance or any executive agency against an "otherwise qualified" individual with a disability "by reason of her or his disability." The ADA extends this prohibition against discrimination "on the basis of" disability to state programs and private entities that do not receive federal funding.

Federal law defines disabled persons as individuals who have a "physical or mental impairment which substantially limits a major life activity," "who have a record of such an impairment," or who are "regarded as having such an impairment." The regulations list examples such as blindness, mental retardation, emotional illness, cancer, heart disease, and HIV infection....

Because functional impairment may affect a person's qualifications for some benefits, the laws governing disability rights permit consideration of a person's disability if the condition legitimately affects that person's ability to meet the essential eligibility requirements. This basic structure is quite different from civil rights legislation governing race because race is presumed to be irrelevant.

While acknowledging that disabilities are sometimes relevant, Congress also recognized that their consideration would often result in the exclusion of disabled persons who could become qualified with modest modifications of policies or practices. To prevent this, Congress required that a reasonable effort be made to accommodate the needs of disabled persons before concluding that they are ineligible. By conferring on people with disabilities this right to affirmative assistance, Congress endorsed, at least in a limited way, an egalitarian approach to distributive justice which allocates extra resources for those persons with the greatest need. . . . To summarize this basic paradigm, a disabled person is qualified to receive health benefits or services if, with reasonable accommodation, she is able to meet the "essential" or "necessary" eligibility criteria. . . .

When the issue is joined, as it was in Oregon, the statutory terms *essential* and *necessary* seem sufficiently elastic to permit courts to consider whether medical utility is a permissible basis for disfavoring disabled patients. In effect, courts would be deciding whether the objective of maximizing health outcomes is an "essential" program objective within the meaning of the equal opportunity laws. . . . HHS did exactly this in responding to the Oregon waiver request. . . .

While the legal status of rationing based on effectiveness is still uncertain, underwriting exclusions based on anticipated cost have express congressional sanction. In the ADA, Congress authorized benefits plans to engage in "the legitimate classification of risk." As a result, plans remain free to consider how various disabilities influence a person's risk of death or illness. This exclusion permits risk-bearing health plans (but not necessarily practicing physicians) to consider the anticipated cost of treating various disabilities. However, the statutory exemption for underwriting practices does not appear to sanction the use of QALYs or other measures of a given treatment's effectiveness. Unlike restrictions based on underwriting risks, eligibility restrictions based on effectiveness are not based on the risk of subscriber illness and its predicted cost. They are based, instead, on predicted outcomes. Patients whose care is relatively ineffective are not necessarily any more costly or financially risky than other patients. . . . As a result, only the cost portion of cost-effectiveness analysis has clear statutory blessing, and even then only when it is part of an underwriting process. . . .

Until the courts rule on this issue, it is possible . . . that employers will be flatly prohibited from adopting health benefits plans that discriminate on the basis of disability for nonunderwriting reasons. . . . [To overcome this objection, employers and insurers will need to establish that] the use of effectiveness criteria is vital to the goal of maximizing health outcomes from fixed resources. . . .

■ MAKING MEDICAL SPENDING DECISIONS: THE LAW, ETHICS, AND ECONOMICS OF RATIONING MECHANISMS*
Mark A. Hall

When we are ill, we desperately want our doctors to do everything within their power to heal us, regardless of the costs. Medical technology has advanced so far, however, that literal adherence to this credo for every human frailty would consume much more than our country's entire economic output,[13] and, in the process, cause economic collapse. . . . Any workable system for financing and delivering health care must face the fundamental problem of how best to allocate limited medical resources among competing beneficial uses. Someone, somewhere must decide which items of potential medical benefit are not worth the cost. . . .

It is sometimes thought that medical advances will eventually reduce medical spending by making people fundamentally healthier, but this assumption is equally flawed. Medical needs are inherently limitless because aging and illness are a permanent feature of the human condition. Much beneficial medical care results in people living to an older age where they are more frail and succumb to more chronic and expensive diseases. This does not mean we should suppress these innovations, only that the drive to conquer all forms of illness is ultimately doomed to failure. The course of history over this century demonstrates that, as medicine advances, so do both medical needs and medical spending.

For these various reasons, most policy analysts recognize that rationing in some form is desirable and inevitable. Every spending decision is necessarily a rationing decision simply because resources devoted to one person or one use are not available for someone or something else. If wants are limitless and resources are finite, it is impossible to maintain that rationing is avoidable in all its forms.

We have always rationed health care resources on a massive scale, only according to irrational and unjust principles.[14] Presently, we ration health care by denying it to those unfortunate individuals who lack insurance either because their employer does not provide it or because their level of poverty has not yet fallen to the desperate level required for Medicaid eligibility. At the same time, we heavily subsidize health insurance for the upper and middle classes through a regressive tax policy that excludes from an employee's income the value of insurance premiums contributed by employers. Moreover, for those who are fully insured, we devote vast resources to save lives and restore health once an illness or accident occurs, but we spend only microscopic amounts in comparison on basic safety, health education, and health prevention measures. . . .

The haphazard and unprincipled basis on which rationing presently occurs effectively rebuts another argument raised by critics of rationing, namely, that rationing should occur only under numerous, morally demanding conditions that presently do not exist. These critics impose unattainably Utopian prerequisites to rationing, such as developing ethically unassailable and scientifically valid ration-

13. The U.S. gross domestic product per capita is about $23,000. To see how easy it would be to spend this amount each year on maximal health care, consider that it costs about this same amount on average simply to incarcerate a prisoner (not counting the costs of building new prison space). See also Lamm, R.D., "Rationing of Health Care: Inevitable and Desirable," 140 U. Pa. L. Rev. 1511, 1512 (1992) ("[A] French study asked how much it would cost to give all the health care that is 'beneficial' to each citizen. The answer was five-and-one-half times the French gross national product.").

14. Fuchs, V.R., "The 'Rationing' of Medical Care," 311 New Eng. J. Med. 1572 (1984); Rosenblatt, R.E., "Rationing 'Normal' Health Care: The Hidden Legal Issues," 59 Texas L. Rev. 1401-1420 (1981).

ing criteria, insisting on their strict egalitarian application throughout all strata of society, and first eliminating all wasteful spending, both within medicine and elsewhere in society. These demands ignore the fact that any systematically thought-out rationing scheme, however flawed, is far superior to the thoughtless and inhumane way in which many uninsured people are now treated. A more considered form of resource allocation is the first step, not the last, toward social equity and broad-based reform. Only with some better approach to rationing will minimally acceptable access to health care become affordable for everyone.

Despite these many powerful arguments, it is still controversial to speak in terms of rationing health care. In order to avoid drawing the fire of those who oppose any use of this term, I will instead lean towards the more neutral terminology of resource allocation or spending decisions. I will not entirely refrain from the "R" word, however. Its emotional baggage can help to dramatize the pervasive necessity of making medical spending decisions. Despite their differing emotional content, both rationing and allocation can fairly be used in the generic sense that refers to either implicit or explicit denial of marginally beneficial medical treatment out of consideration for its cost. . . .

[R]egardless of the overall structure of a health care financing and delivery system, [w]hether it is regulatory or competitive, public or private, we are plagued by two basic issues: (1) Who should decide what care is not worth the costs, and (2) what criteria of benefit should be used to make this determination? The second of these problems is the one that has received more attention to date. Numerous volumes have been written on questions such as whether the short supply of transplantable organs should be distributed based simply on random draw or who has been waiting the longest, or instead based on elaborate concepts of medical need or medical benefit.[15] This literature also gives extensive thought to routine medical technologies. It explores whether medical resources generally should be rationed according to age or instead according to some more quantitative formula for effectiveness or value. Others before me have debated at length whether medical benefit should be defined by the number of lives saved, the length of life, the quality of life, or some more intermediate goal such as diagnostic certainty, and whether judgments about people's social worth can be prevented from tainting these concepts.

These are tremendously fascinating and important questions deserving of continuing inquiry, but they avoid what I see as a more fundamental question: Who should be the rationing decisionmaker? . . . [M]edical sociologist David Mechanic

---

15. Leading general discussions are found in AMA Council in Ethical and Judicial Affairs, "Ethical Considerations in the Allocation of Organs and Other Scarce Medical Resources Among Patients," 155 Archives Internal Med. 29 (1995); Blank, R.H., Rationing Medicine (1988); Churchill, L.R., Rationing Health Care in America: Perceptions and Principles of Justice (1987); Kilner, J.F., Who Lives? Who Dies?: Ethical Criteria in Patient Selection (1990); Winslow, G.R., Triage and Justice (1982). An early general discussion is contained in Note, "Scarce Medical Resources," 69 Colum. L. Rev. 620 (1969). A more recent treatment is the cogent and comprehensive analysis by Elhauge, E., "Allocating Health Care Morally," 82 Cal. L. Rev. 1449 (1994). For a thorough discussion of rationing criteria used commonly throughout society, see generally Elster, J., Local Justice: How Institutions Allocate Scarce Goods and Necessary Burdens (1992).

[f]irst articulated that health care spending decisions can be made through three fundamentally different mechanisms. Cost-sensitive treatment decisions can be made by patients, by physicians, or by third parties — primarily private and governmental insurers but also various regulatory or review organizations. Elsewhere in our economy, cost/benefit trade-offs are usually made through the purchasing decisions of individual consumers. For example, nutrition resources are allocated at both the macro and micro levels through the aggregation of countless individual decisions of how much food to buy, of what quality, and from what source. This simple market mechanism is not generally available or desirable for health care because of the unpredictability of illness and the complexities of medical judgment. . . . [W]e purchase insurance rather than pay out of pocket because we want to protect ourselves from the uncertain costs of health care and the anxiety of making spending decisions under the strain of serious illness. Moreover, even without insurance, patients make few of their medical decisions themselves because the complexity of treatment compels us to delegate extensive authority to our doctors. . . .

Insurers, either private or governmental, can make medical spending decisions through cost-sensitive rules about what treatment they will pay for. Until recently, this has seldom happened, but in 1994 Oregon became the first state to attempt explicit rule-based rationing for all of medicine. Oregon ranked over 600 condition-treatment pairings (e.g., surgery for appendicitis) according to their medical effectiveness, for purposes of allocating limited Medicaid funding. Elsewhere in this country, efforts are under way to develop a host of much more detailed and nuanced clinical practice guidelines, which could also serve as rule-based tools for third-party resource allocation. In addition to insurers' payment rules, spending decisions can be imposed by other parties who are similarly outside the doctor-patient relationship. Courts, citizen groups or other ideal democratic processes, and physician administrators who review the work of treating doctors are each able to set limits or give directions on how medical resources are spent. . . .

The third fundamental alternative for allocating medical spending authority is for physicians to incorporate cost considerations into their clinical judgment. Authorizing physicians to make cost/benefit trade-off decisions at the bedside differs from centralized, rule-based rationing because it individualizes spending decisions to the circumstances of each patient, and it operates through professional incentives rather than bureaucratic authority. Bedside rationing, however, fundamentally compromises physicians' role-based ethic, which . . . traditionally requires doctors to provide all care that offers any benefit, regardless of its cost. Physician bedside rationing is rendered even more controversial by the use of financial incentives to motivate doctors' performance. . . .

As can be seen from this summary, most of this book is taken up with what Edward Rubin [infra] terms a "microanalysis of social institutions," one that seeks to assess the relative strengths, weaknesses, and characteristics of alternative mechanisms for allocating health care resources, drawing from both political economics and social theory. . . . Accordingly, I will not be wedded to a particular analytical framework or ideological perspective. I will undertake a pragmatic analytical critique, one that seeks to clarify for each rationing mechanism its basic rationale, its inherent limits, the evidence supporting both views, the potential for harm or manipulation, and the accommodations needed to make it work.

▮RATIONING HEALTH CARE IN BRITAIN AND THE UNITED STATES
Leonard J. Nelson, III
7 J. Health & Biomed. L. 175 (2011)

Rationing is a "dirty word," "a code word for immoral, inappropriate, or greedy," and "a four letter word." And not surprisingly, rationing was at the forefront of the recent debate in the United States over health care reform. Former Governor Sarah Palin's Facebook page allegation that the Democrat's health care reform legislation included "death panels," which would ration care for the sick and elderly, was later named "lie of the year" by the fact checkers at Politifacts.com, but it did garner significant attention. . . .

Although [Sarah Palin's] claims are "sensationalistic," they draw attention to a central truth, i.e., . . . that rationing will have to be a part of any publicly subsidized program for the provision of health care to maintain fiscal sustainability. . . . Dr. [Ezekiel Emanuel, former director of bioethics at the NIH,] identified three levels of health care allocation decisions with respect to government health care decisions. First, macro-allocation decisions determine how much of the gross national product ("GNP") to spend on health care services as opposed to national defense, transportation, etc. Second, there is an intermediate level where a determination will be made as to the basic package of health care services that all citizens are entitled to receive. Third, micro-allocation decisions about which patients are eligible to receive particular services. At the intermediate level, he suggested the need for transparency in the form of "public forums to deliberate about which health services should be considered basic and should be socially guaranteed." . . .

Medicare is already engaged in stealth rationing through the Centers for Medicare and Medicaid Services' the use of National Coverage Determinations ("NCDs"), in which CMS refuses to cover expensive new technologies; CMS nevertheless denies taking cost into account in making decisions relating to coverage. . . . [I]t is unlikely that Congress will give CMS the [express] power to ration health care using a cost-effectiveness analysis. . . . As long as Medicare is a service benefit program, it will be very difficult, politically, to control costs. . . .

[D]uring the debate over health care reform, President Obama spoke of the need for a "very difficult democratic conversation" about health care at the end of life, even expressing doubt about whether his own grandmother should have been given a hip replacement when she was terminally ill. But he also acknowledged that, "It is very difficult to imagine the country making those decisions just through the normal political channels. And that's part of why you have to have some independent group that can give you guidance." . . .

The ongoing debate about the possible role of comparative effectiveness research in health care reform illustrates the political difficulty of rationing health care. . . . The 2009 federal stimulus legislation created [an agency to conduct comparative effectiveness research, which PPACA renamed] the Patient Centered Outcomes Research Institute ("PCORI"). . . . Perhaps in response to concerns about rationing, PPACA expressly precludes the Secretary of the Health and Human Services ("HHS") from relying solely on comparative effectiveness research to deny coverage or from using PCORI sponsored comparative effectiveness research "in a manner that treats extending the life of an elderly, disabled, or terminally ill individual as of lower value than extending the life of an individual who is younger, nondisabled, or not terminally ill." . . . The Secretary is also precluded from using comparative effectiveness "with the intent to discourage an individual from choosing a health care treatment based on how the individual values the tradeoff between extending the length of their life and the risk of disability." . . . [T]hese provisions have been interpreted to prohibit the PCORI "from developing or using cost-per-QALY thresholds," and these provisions have been decried as reflecting "a certain xenophobia toward the kinds of approaches used in Britain, where the National Institute of Health and Clinical Excellence ["NICE"] makes recommendations about technologies and services on the basis of cost-per-QALY thresholds." . . .

[PPACA's] continued reliance on employment-based insurance may make it more difficult to impose rationing in the Medicare program because the standard of care for all is influenced by the care provided through relatively generous employment-based plans. . . . With the exception of "grandfathered" plans, all small group and individual plans offered both within and outside of the exchanges will have to offer at least the "essential health benefits" package. This package is supposed to include the elements of a typical employer plan. [Also, the statute forbids designing "benefits in ways that discriminate against individuals because of their age, disability, or expected length of life" or that are "subject to denial . . . on the basis of the individuals' age or expected length of life or of the individuals' present or predicted disability, degree of medical dependency, or quality of life."] . . .

As noted in the Washington Post, defining the "essential health benefits" is an important and difficult task; "Draw up a package that is too bare-bones and millions of Americans could be deprived of meaningful health coverage when they need it most—undercutting a central goal of the health care law. Add in too many expensive benefits and premiums could spike to unaffordable levels." . . .

PPACA [also] establishes the Independent Payment Advisory Board ("IPAB") for the purpose of reducing the per capita rate of growth in Medicare spending. The board is to be composed of fifteen full-time members who are health care experts drawn from various fields. Beginning in 2014, IPAB is required to make annual recommendations to Congress to reduce per capita growth rates when these costs exceed a targeted per capita growth rate that the Chief Actuary of CMS sets. These recommendations will be implemented unless subsequent congressional action blocks them. Notably, a 3/5 vote in the Senate is required to change the IPAB recommendations. But there are some significant limitations on the nature of these recommendations. PPACA provides that these recommendations, "shall not include any recommendation to ration health care, . . . increase Medicare beneficiary cost-sharing[,] . . . or otherwise restrict benefits or modify eligibility criteria." Prior to 2020, the recommendation also cannot include cuts in payment rates for hospitals and suppliers, which PPACA already targets.

. . . Michael Tanner, a health policy expert at the Cato Institute, [notes] that in light of the restrictions on IPAB, it . . . "will end up as neutered as previous attempts to impose fiscal discipline on government health care programs." With all the constraints on its actions, and the possibilities for Congress to void any cuts proposed, it is unlikely IPAB will be successful in reducing costs in the Medicare program. . . .

Health policy experts customarily refer to the health care "Iron Triangle." . . . The three angles of the triangle or triad are cost, access, and quality. It has been observed that, "increasing the performance of the health care system along any one of these dimensions can compromise one or both of the other dimensions, regardless of the amount that is spent on health care." . . . The debate over the impact of PPACA on Medicare costs illustrates the constraints of the iron triangle. . . . While in theory it may be possible to increase health care access, reduce costs, and improve quality, in practice it is virtually impossible. The reduction of costs in public programs without endangering aggregate quality would have to be based on across the board rigorous application of cost-effectiveness analysis that would result in the denial of beneficial treatments to individuals. It is unlikely that Congress has the political will to impose such a regime. . . . Rationing is certainly the third rail of American politics, and the cost controls in PPACA may not be sufficient to save us from ourselves.

Notes: Health Care Rationing and Disability Discrimination

1. *Medical Effectiveness Measures.* It is important to distinguish among ordinary medical effectiveness, comparative effectiveness, cost-effectiveness, and cost-benefit analysis. Ordinary effectiveness determines simply whether a medical procedure works at all. Comparative effectiveness asks whether it works better than another method for the same condition. Cost-effectiveness analysis also asks how much it costs to achieve an increment in health improvement. And finally, cost-benefit analysis asks whether an effectiveness improvement is actually worth what it costs.

QALYs were devised so that effectiveness can be judged based on quality of life rather than simply number of lives or years of life saved. A generic unit of health improvement also allows comparisons between totally different treatments and disease conditions, such as determining whether prenatal care yields more medical benefit than liver transplants. That kind of comparative cost analysis can help to determine the best use of limited funds, but it cannot tell us what total health expenditures should be, that is, whether to do *both* prenatal care and liver transplants, or *neither* and instead spend the money on education or housing. If that decision is to be made quantitatively, it requires a cost-benefit analysis, which compares the cost of medical procedures with their benefit in terms of dollars. This is obviously much more controversial since it requires that a value be placed on human life and suffering.

None of the techniques surveyed by Philip Peters goes this far. They only ask, comparatively, whether one benefit is greater than another, not whether the expenditure is worth it at all. But, in adopting the rubric of "comparative effectiveness" rather than "cost effectiveness" in the Affordable Care Act, did Congress mean to say that costs may not be considered at all? For example, it has been estimated that the cost of administering Pap smears, which detect cervical cancer, is roughly $5,000 per additional year of life expectancy for testing every three years but $200,000–400,000 per year of life saved for annual testing. Should insurers, either public or private, be required to fund annual testing? Which would you choose as a patient paying out of pocket? See Sarah Feldman, How Often Should We Screen for Cervical Cancer?, 349 New Eng. J. Med. 1495 (2003) (recommending testing every three years after a series of negative one-year exams).

During the heat of national debate over the Affordable Care Act, political opponents raised yet another storm of controversy over a government blue ribbon panel that happened to issue a recommendation about limiting routine mammography screening to every two years for women over 50, rather than every year and starting at age 40, for women with no prior symptoms or family history of breast cancer. The panel's rationale was to reduce the medical harms from "false positive" results that lead to needless biopsies and surgeries. But, it was also influenced by studies indicating that it would cost $340,000 or more per QALY gained to screen more frequently or at younger ages. See John Schousboe et al., Personalizing Mammography by Breast Density and Other Risk Factors for Breast Cancer, 144 Ann. Intern. Med. 10 (2011).

2. *Comparative Institutional Analysis.* The approach Mark Hall takes to analyzing health care rationing is known as "comparative institutional analysis" or as "legal process theory." It is an approach that is well suited to analyzing numerous legal and public policy issues, in health care and elsewhere, and so it is employed throughout this casebook. Its focus is not so much on what is the correct answer, but on what are the best (or least worst) institutions and processes for arriving at an answer. This approach compares the strengths and weaknesses of various institutions and processes within the judicial system, the private sector, the public sector, the nonprofit sector, and professional groups, among others. For further discussion, see sources cited in note 12.

3. *The Scope of Disability Discrimination Laws.* The potential impact of disability discrimination law on many aspects of medical decisionmaking has come to light only gradually. Elsewhere, these materials explore whether the ADA prevents physicians from refusing to treat patients infected with the AIDS virus, and whether hospitals can restrict the clinical privileges of HIV-infected physicians. The main issues there are what constitutes a disability, and what is required by way of "reasonable accommodation." Here, the primary issue is what constitutes discrimination. How far might courts and agencies actually go in micromanaging medically informed decisions by covered institutions?

Most commentators believe, for example, that it would clearly violate the ADA and §504 for an employer to exclude or limit coverage for AIDS, and this is the interpretation that the EEOC has taken in a number of enforcement actions. But what about other more common, less objectionable restrictions? In *Choate* the Supreme Court cited approvingly a Second Circuit opinion holding that the limitation of mental health coverage does not violate §504. See also Modderno v. King, 82 F.3d 1059 (D.C. Cir. 1996) (disparity in coverage of mental health treatment is not disability discrimination; to rule otherwise would be "to invite challenges to virtually every exercise of the [insurer's or employer's] discretion with respect to the allocation of benefits amongst an encyclopedia of illnesses"). What is the difference between AIDS restrictions and mental health restrictions? Could it be the fact that many mental health patients are not disabled, whereas all AIDS patients are? Then what about the exclusion of experimental cancer treatment? See Henderson v. Bodine Aluminum, 70 F.3d 958 (8th Cir. 1995) (denying expensive new therapy for breast cancer is potentially discrimination where the plan covers this treatment for other cancers and there is evidence it works for breast cancer). But see Lenox v. Healthwise of Kentucky, 149 F.3d 453 (6th Cir. 1998) (no ADA violation in excluding coverage for heart transplants). See Jane Korn, Cancer and the ADA: Rethinking Disability, 74 S. Cal. L. Rev. 339 (2001).

It is also important to realize how many activities and programs the discrimination laws cover. Originally, § 504 covered federal government jobs, programs, and contractors. But § 1557 of the ACA has extended its reach to any health program or activity that receives federal financial assistance, including plans sold on the ACA's new health insurance exchanges. See 81 Fed. Reg. 31376 (May 18, 2016). The ADA's scope is somewhat different: It covers state and private entities and is divided into several titles, each of which covers different realms of activity—including employment, transportation, and public accommodations. The ADA's prohibition on disability discrimination in connection with the employment relationship extends to employer-sponsored insurance.

Health plans continue to test the limits of these antidiscrimination rules. In 2014, for example, insurers came under attack for designing health plans in a manner that discriminates against people living with HIV/AIDS. By manipulating their drug formularies, the insurers made it excessively costly and bureaucratically difficult for patients to access needed antiretroviral medication. See Douglas B. Jacobs & Benjamin D. Sommers, Using Drugs to Discriminate—Adverse Selection in the Insurance Marketplace, 372 New Eng. J. Med. 399 (2015) (finding evidence of "adverse tiering" on the exchanges). The federal government and state insurance officials have opened investigations into these practices and a number of class-action lawsuits have been filed against major insurers.

4. *Meaningful Access Without Fundamental Alteration.* Does the Supreme Court's "meaningful access to benefits" test provide a good guide for what's permissible? Meaningful access to *which* benefits? To the particular item of treatment being sought or to insurance coverage generally? See Doe v. Chandler, 83 F.3d 1150 (9th Cir. 1996) (limiting welfare for disabled recipients but not for dependent children does not discriminate against the disabled because states may craft different benefits for different programs).

Choate also speaks in terms of avoiding requirements that would fundamentally alter the nature of the product or program. This is the defense on which Philip Peters rests most of his justification for effectiveness analysis in the remainder of his article. But this issue is also largely untested in the courts. In contrast with *Choate*, see Olmstead v. L.C., 527 U.S. 581 (1999), which found a potential ADA violation where a state Medicaid plan covered long-term hospitalization for mental illness but not less restrictive community placement options, and the Court suggested that it would not be a "fundamental alteration" to require the state to expand its coverage if doing so can be "reasonably accommodated" without straining the budget for other mental health services. Compare Lovell v. Chandler, 303 F.3d 1039 (9th Cir. 2002) (finding an ADA violation where the state expanded eligibility for Medicaid up to three times the poverty level but excluded disabled participants from the increased eligibility parameters, even though the state said this was all it could afford). See Sara Rosenbaum, *Olmstead v. L.C.*: Implications for Medicaid and Other Publicly Funded Health Services, 12 Health Matrix 93 (2002).

For an argument that these distinctions fail to protect adequately against disability discrimination through disparate impact, see D. Orentlicher, Destructuring Disability: Rationing of Health Care and Unfair Discrimination Against the Sick, 31 Harv. C.R.-C.L. L. Rev. 51 (1996). According to another law professor, "the ADA is an inadequate and even inept tool for resolving whether we should tolerate cost-conscious [insurance] policies" because its concepts are so poorly suited for articulating and understanding the underlying social policy debate. Mary A. Crossley, Medical Futility and Disability Discrimination, 81 Iowa L. Rev. 179 (1995).

5. *Tossing Around the Hot Potato.* Against this backdrop of uncertainty, is there clarity in the ACA's legislative language that forbids designing "benefits in ways that discriminate against individuals because of their age, disability, or expected length of life" or that are "subject to denial . . . on the basis of the individuals' . . . present or predicted disability, degree of medical dependency, or quality of life"? As Professor Nelson notes, this appears aimed at prohibiting the government's use of QALYs to define the standard set of "essential health benefits" that private insurers must cover (in the individual and small group markets). However, another statutory provision says that "nothing . . . shall be construed to prohibit . . . [health insurers] from carrying out utilization management techniques that are commonly used as of the date of enactment of this Act." Does that mean that rationing, or cost-effectiveness analysis, is fine as long as the government does not do it?

Partly to avoid grappling with questions like these, the Obama administration adopted a rule deputizing the states to select a "benchmark plan" from among existing health plans in the state. The benefits covered under that benchmark plan would then be considered "essential" within the state. In its rulemaking, HHS explained that a national, uniform definition of essential health benefits would needlessly disrupt the market and thwart state efforts to tailor their insurance rules to local conditions. 78 Fed. Reg. 12834 (Feb. 25, 2013).

6. *Rationing Criteria and Social Values.* QALYs are objectionable on other moral grounds besides disability discrimination. As discussed most forcefully by David Hadorn and John Harris, cited by Peters, the mathematics of QALYs mean that it is equally as valuable to save ten years from one person's life as it is to save one year of life for ten people. This utilitarian logic does not fit most people's intuitions. See John Taurek, Should the Numbers Count?, 6 Phil. & Pub. Aff. 293 (1977). On the other hand, if we are to avoid use of rationing criteria that contain any controversial value judgments, we would have to adopt completely arbitrary rationing criteria such as a simple lottery, or treating whoever asks first. Most people would view these "neutral" criteria as even more irrational and objectionable. See Einer Elhauge, Allocating Health Care Morally, 82 Cal. L. Rev. 1449 (1994).

The "rescue principle" mentioned by Prof. Dworkin exists in other social arenas such as natural disasters and high-risk recreational activity, where we spend seemingly unlimited amounts responding to crisis situations when people are visibly threatened with death or disability at the same time that we neglect less expensive preventive measures that might avoid a situation in the first place. This is also known as the paradox of "statistical versus identifiable lives." If the thrust of this argument is to spend more on prevention, few would disagree, but if the thrust is to spend less on heroic measures, the argument is met with the following response:

> I will risk my life on the roads to do nothing more than secure a bag of potato chips, not to mention take the risk of eating them simply for fleeting gustatory sensations. But should I come up short in the potato chips v. life lottery, and suffer either a car or a cardiovascular accident, I do not expect society to respond by saying, "Well, tough luck, but you made an open-eyed trade-off here." No, I expect EMTs to rush

to the scene and pound on my chest and speed me to the hospital in reckless disregard of the laws set down to reduce the risk faced by other travelers in search of potato chips and other goods. This social response, I am suggesting, can be seen as a way of marking the fact that our lives are shot through with incommensurable values, and that we have to wind our way through them in a way that does its best to acknowledge their separate significance.

J. L. Nelson, Publicity and Pricelessness: Grassroots Decisionmaking and Justice in Rationing, 19 J. Med. & Phil. 333 (1994). In a similar vein, Calabresi and Bobbitt explain that rationing is more socially acceptable when the tragic choices are hidden from view, as they are when the harms are merely statistical, than when identifiable victims of rationing can clearly be seen. G. Calabresi & P. Bobbitt, Tragic Choices (1978). Does this mean that effective rationing can be done only out of public view? If so, is that a legitimate reason to promote or tolerate less explicit or "democratic" forms of rationing?

Prof. Gregg Bloche argues that health care law and policy is in a "confused, even chaotic state" because it assumes that medical resources can be allocated in a "systematically rational manner," which is not feasible or even desirable considering differing values, limitations on human rationality, and inconsistent understandings about what rationality means or requires. Instead, he urges an "inelegant" approach that "defines our aims more modestly, consistent with a picture of rationality as limited by context, discontinuous across different settings, and changeable with time." Gregg Bloche, The Invention of Health Law, 91 Cal. L. Rev. 247 (2003). Does that make things less confused? For further discussion, see sources cited in note 12.

7. *Medicaid Coverage.* Many of the decisions discussed below at page 1155 that require Medicaid to fund controversial procedures such as sex-change operations and liver transplants for former alcoholics are reasoned in terms of disability discrimination, even though they are based on the Medicaid statute. They reason that the basic standard of rationality and nonarbitrariness required by the Medicaid statute prevents covering a medically beneficial treatment for some conditions but not for others. Therefore, Medicaid must either exclude the treatment altogether or selectively exclude it under generic criteria such as medically necessary or experimental. See, e.g., Salgado v. Kirschner, 878 P.2d 659 (Ariz. 1994) (unreasonable to cover liver transplant only for children; medically relevant factors, not age alone, should determine coverage).

Imagine that you are in charge of allocating limited government health care funds. Where, if anywhere, would you want to set limits? Would you fund a liver transplant for a patient whose recovery is only 50 percent certain? For a patient with only partial liver dysfunction whose life is not at stake? For an alcoholic? Would you support lung transplants for cigarette smokers? Heart transplants for overeaters?

If the legislature appropriated an additional $5 million to use at your discretion, would you choose (1) a large expansion in low-cost prenatal care, which would help decrease the high costs of caring for premature births, or (2) a few expensive organ transplants, or (3) some of both? Which of these decisions would disability discrimination principles allow?

Oregon's adoption of the rationing list reflected an effort to answer some of these difficult questions. The effort was somewhat half-hearted, however. Many of the items eliminated from funding are fairly "small ticket," are requested only rarely, or were not covered in the first place. In other instances, physicians are able to obtain coverage by recharacterizing the patient's condition as especially serious. Accordingly, Oregon's expansion of Medicaid eligibility was financed mostly by increased taxation and legislative appropriations, not by savings from the list. Symposium, 24 J. Health Pol. Pol'y & L. 151 (1999). Does Oregon's experience suggest that saying "no" to particular treatments is impossible? Or does the program's tentativeness merely reflect the novelty of the experiment?

8. *The (Second) Oregon Experiment.* In response to budget cuts during the Great Recession, Oregon turned to a lottery method to keep costs down, enrolling in Medicaid only a fraction of those eligible to join. H. Allen et al., What the Oregon Health Study Can Tell Us About Expanding Medicaid, 29 Health Aff. 1498 (2010). As a method of allocating access to health care, is a random lottery preferable to a rationing list? If so, why?[11]

9. *Hepatitis C.* In 2014, breakthrough anti-viral drugs to treat Hepatitis C came on the market. In contrast to previous therapies, the drugs boast cure rates exceeding 90 percent and have few side effects. The drugs are so effective that prominent clinical guidelines indicate that they should be supplied to nearly everyone who has contracted Hepatitis C. But an estimated 3.2 million people are infected with the disease and the drugs are very expensive: Sovaldi, for example, was initially priced at $84,000 for a twelve-week course of treatment.

Predictably, private insurers and public programs have balked at footing the astronomical bill for these new drugs. States are under particular stress given that a disproportionate number of Hepatitis C patients are poor (and therefore enrolled in Medicaid) or imprisoned. As a result, many private insurers and most states have limited coverage for the drugs to patients whose disease has progressed far enough to lead to severe liver damage.

The coverage limitations have provoked congressional outrage and spurred litigation from patients who argue that they should not have to suffer liver damage before receiving treatment. Only recently—and, not coincidentally, as prices for the Hepatitis C drugs have begun to fall—have payers begun to relent. In 2016, an investigation by New York Attorney General yielded a settlement with seven insurers in which they agreed to cover the drugs for nearly all Hepatitis C patients. Shortly after, a federal judge in Washington State entered a preliminary injunction ordering the state's Medicaid program to pay for the drugs for any beneficiary diagnosed with Hepatitis C. See B.E. v. Teeter, 16-227 (W.D. Wash. 2016). As of this writing, a handful of states—including Massachusetts, New York, and Florida—have voluntarily dropped their Medicaid restrictions. State prison systems, however, remain under enormous strain. Peter Loftus & Gary Fields, High Cost of New Hepatitis C Drugs Strains Prison Budgets, Locks Many Out of Cure, Wall St. J., Sept. 12, 2016.

---

11. Unintentionally, Oregon's use of a lottery provided a unique opportunity to study the effects of getting Medicaid coverage. In an ongoing study, researchers are comparing those who won the lottery to those who did not, allowing them to assess Medicaid's effect on utilization, financial security, and health outcomes. Early results indicate that Medicaid leads to less financial strain and reduced levels of depression, but that it also increases use of the emergency room and may do little to reduce hypertension or cholesterol levels. See Katherine Baicker et al., The Oregon Experiment—Effects of Medicaid on Clinical Outcomes, 368 New Eng. J. Med. 1713 (2013).

10. *Race or Gender Discrimination.* Insurance restrictions can be challenged under other discrimination statutes besides disability. Suppose, for instance, that an excluded disease category has a disproportionate impact on blacks. Most commentators conclude that this alone is not illegal without some indication of racial animus or subterfuge. More compelling, however, is the argument that a treatment exclusion has a categorical effect on only one gender. In Newport News Shipbuilding v. EEOC, 462 U.S. 669 (1993), the Court held that an employer violates Title VII's prohibition of sex discrimination by providing more generous pregnancy benefits to female employees than to the wives of male employees. Similarly, would the exclusion of fertility treatment such as in vitro fertilization constitute either gender or disability discrimination? Saks v. Franklin Covey Co., 316 F.3d 337 (2d Cir. 2003) (no, because infertility is not always a disability, and plan excluded fertility treatment for both men and women).

Civil rights discrimination statutes apply to government programs as well, under Title VI. These statutes have had less effect. A series of public interest lawsuits have failed to block cities from closing public hospitals in low-income communities, with courts finding that the disparate impact on minorities does not constitute prohibited discrimination. See, e.g., Bryan v. Koch, 627 F.2d 612 (2d Cir. 1980); NAACP v. Wilmington Medical Center, 657 F.2d 1322 (3d Cir. 1981). See also Chapter 2.A.2.

11. *Impotence and Contraception.* Among the various controversies concerning what health insurance should cover, debates about contraception and sexual health have been especially lively. Following the introduction of Viagra, impotence pills for men were covered by traditional health insurance. While Viagra addresses a physical dysfunction often caused by health problems or medication side effects, it is also prescribed in more discretionary situations to enhance sexual performance. Rather than crafting sexual performance indicators or drawing age-based lines, insurers simply capped the number of Viagra pills permitted per month. (One wonders how they arrived at the cutoff.) See Alison Keith, The Economics of Viagra, 19 Health Aff. 147 (2000).

Insurers' willingness to cover Viagra highlighted the inequities of the then-common practice of not covering contraceptives for women, which are similarly important to sexual health. Although Obama administration rules under the Affordable Care Act at first mandated contraceptive coverage, the Trump administration is expected to rescind or restrict that coverage mandate. Also, the Supreme Court has recognized a right of religiously motivated employers to refuse contraceptive coverage. Burwell v. Hobby Lobby Stores, 573 U.S. __ (2014). Furthermore, many women encounter obstacles from insurance companies that restrict which types of birth control they make available. See Kaiser Family Foundation, Coverage of Contraceptive Services: A Review of Health Insurance Plans in Five States (2015).

12. *Further Readings.* For further discussions of **moral and public policy dimensions of QALYs** and other criteria for rationing, see Chapter 6.D on allocation of organ transplants; Marion Danis et al. eds., Fair Resource Allocation and Rationing at the Bedside (2015); Larry Churchill, Rationing Health Care in America (1987); Frances Kamm, Morality and Mortality (1993); John Kilner, Who Lives? Who Dies? (1990); Paul Menzel, Strong Medicine: The Ethical Rationing of Health Care (1990); Eric Rakowski, Taking and Saving Lives, 93 Colum. L. Rev. 1063 (1993); Matthew D. Adler, QALYs and Policy Evaluation: A New Perspective, 6 Yale J. Health Pol'y L. & Ethics 1 (2006); Sharona Hoffman, Unmanaged Care: Towards Moral

Fairness in Health Care Coverage, 78 Ind. L. J. 659 (2003); Norman Daniels & James E. Sabin, Setting Limits Fairly: Can We Learn to Share Medical Resources? (2000); Jennifer Prah Ruger, Health, Capability and Justice: Toward a New Paradigm of Health Ethics, Policy and Law, 15 Cornell J. L. Pub. Pol'y 403 (2006); Amy B. Monahan, Value-Based Mandated Health Benefits, 80 U. Colo. L. Rev. 127-200 (2009); Ani B. Satz, The Limits of Health Care Reform, 59 Ala. L. Rev. 1451 (2008); Symposium, 12 Value in Health S1 (2009). For a harrowing account of hospital rationing in the aftermath of Hurricane Katrina, see Sheri Fink, Five Days at Memorial: Life and Death in a Storm-Ravaged Hospital (2013).

For discussions of **comparative medical effectiveness** (note 1), see Eleanor Kinney, Comparative Effectiveness Research Under the Patient Protection and Affordable Care Act, 37 Am. J. L. & Med. 522 (2011); Richard Saver, Health Care Reform's Wild Care: The Uncertain Effectiveness of Comparative Effectiveness Research, 159 U. Pa. L. Rev. 2147 (2011); Sean Tunis, Reflections on Science, Judgment, and Value in Evidence-Based Decision Making, 26 Health Aff. w500 (2007); Note, 21 Ann. Health L. 329 (2012); Symposium, 31 Health Aff. 2225 (2012); Symposium, 29 Health Aff. 1756 (2010); Govind Persad, Priority Setting, Cost-Effectiveness, and the Affordable Care Act, 41 Am. J. L. & Med. 119 (2015).

For discussions of **Medicare's refusal to explicitly consider costs in making coverage decisions**, see Nicholas Bagley, Bedside Bureaucrats: Why Medicare Reform Hasn't Worked, 101 Geo. L. J. 519 (2013); Jacqueline Fox, The Hidden Role of Cost: Medicare Decisions, Transparency, and Public Trust, 79. U. Cin. L. Rev. 1 (2011); S. Dhruva et al., CMS's Landmark Decision on CT Colonography, 361 New Eng. J. Med. 1316 (2009); Peter Neumann, Medicare's National Coverage Decisions for Technologies, 27 Health Aff. 1620 (2008); Peter J. Neumann et al., Medicare and Cost-Effectiveness Analysis, 353 New Eng. J. Med. 1516 (2006).

For broader discussions of **the use of cost-benefit analyses in legal and regulatory settings generally**, see Matthew Adler & Eric Posner, Cost-Benefit Analysis: Legal, Economic, and Philosophical Perspectives (2001); Richard L. Revesz & Michael Livermore, How Cost-Benefit Analysis Can Better Protect the Environment and Our Health (2008); Identified versus Statistical Lives: An Interdisciplinary Perspective (I. Glenn Cohen et al. eds. 2015).

An excellent example of **institutional choice analysis** (note 2) applied to problems in health policy is Russell Korobkin, The Efficiency of Managed Care "Patient Protection" Laws: Incomplete Contracts, Bounded Rationality, and Market Failure, 85 Cornell L. Rev. 1 (1999). See also Einer Elhauge, Can Health Law Become a Coherent Field of Law? 41 Wake Forest L. Rev. 365 (2006); William M. Sage, Unfinished Business: How Litigation Relates to Health Care Regulation, 28 J. Health Pol. Pol'y & L. 387 (2003); Ezekiel Emanuel, Choice and Representation in Health Care, 56 Med. Care Res. & Rev. 1 (1999). See generally Neil Komesar, Imperfect Alternatives: Choosing Institutions in Law, Economics, and Public Policy (1995); Edward Rubin, The New Legal Process, The Synthesis of Discourse, and the Microanalysis of Institutions, 109 Harv. L. Rev. 1393 (1996).

For discussions of **ADA issues generally and in insurance coverage and medical care** (note 5), see Leslie Francis & Anita Silvers, Debilitating *Alexander v. Choate*: "Meaningful Access" to Health Care for People with Disabilities, 35 Fordham Urb. L. J. 447 (2008); Alexander Abbe, "Meaningful Access" to Health Care and the Remedies Available to Medicaid Managed Care Recipients Under the ADA and the Rehabilitation Act, 147 U. Pa. L. Rev. 1161 (1999); Mary Crossley, Becoming Visible: The ADA's Impact on Health Care for Persons with Disabilities, 52 Ala. L. Rev. 51 (2000); Mary Crossley, The Disability Kaleidoscope, 74 Notre Dame L. Rev. 521 (1999); Maxwell J. Mehlman et al., When Do Health Care Decisions Discriminate Against People with Disabilities?, 22 J. Health Pol. Pol'y & L. 1385 (1997).

For discussion of the **inevitable difficulties in balancing the ACA's competing goals in light of its various restrictions on rationing** (note 6), see Nicholas Bagley & Helen Levy, Essential Health Benefits and the Affordable Care Act: Law and Process, 39 J. Health Pol., Pol'y & L. 441 (2014); Sara Rosenbaum et al., The Essential Health Benefits Provisions of the Affordable Care Act: Implications for People with Disabilities (2011); Alan Cohen, The Debate over Health Care Rationing: Déjà Vu All Over Again?, 49 Inquiry 90 (2012); Alan Weil, The Value of Federalism in Defining Essential Health Benefits, 366 New Eng. J. Med. 366 (2012); Jesse Hill, What Is the Meaning of Health? Constitutional Implications of Defining "Medical Necessity" and "Essential Health Benefits" Under the Affordable Care Act, 38 Am. J. L. & Med. 445 (2012); Institute of Medicine, Essential Health Benefits: Balancing Coverage and Cost (2011).

For **broader discussions** of how health law addresses disability and discrimination issues more generally, see Jessica Roberts, Health Law as Disability Rights Law, 97 Minn. L. Rev. 1963 (2013); Jessica Roberts & Elizabeth Weeks Leonard, What Is (and Isn't) Healthism, 50 Ga. L. Rev. 833 (2016).

For discussions of **transplant funding** (note 7), see Lisa Deutsch, Medicaid Payment for Organ Transplants: The Extent of Mandated Coverage, 30 Colum. J. L. & Soc. Probs. 185 (1997); Clark Havighurst & Nancy King, Liver Transplantation in Massachusetts: Public Policymaking as Morality Play, 19 Ind. L. Rev. 955 (1986); Note, 79 Minn. L. Rev. 1232 (1995); Note, 89 Nw. U. L. Rev. 268 (1994).

For discussions of **the Oregon scheme and the legality of QALYs under the ADA** (note 8), see Jonathan Oberlander et al., Rationing Health Care: Rhetoric and Reality in the Oregon Health Plan, 164 Canadian Medical Ass'n J. 1583 (2001); Kevin P. Quinn, Viewing Health Care as a Common Good: Looking Beyond Political Liberalism, 73 S. Cal. L. Rev. 277 (2000); Note, 93 Colum. L. Rev. 1985 (1993); Note, 106 Harv. L. Rev. 1296 (1993).

For discussions of **the Hepatitis C drugs** (note 9), see Judith Graham, Medicaid, Private Insurers Begin to Lift Curbs on Pricey Hepatitis C Drugs, Kaiser Health News, July 5, 2016; Valerie K. Blake, An Opening for Civil Rights in Health Insurance After the Affordable Care Act, 36 B.C. J. L. & Soc. Just. 235 (2016); Hannah Brennan et al., A Prescription for Excessive Drug Pricing: Leveraging Government Patent Use for Health, 18 Yale J. L. & Tech. 275 (2016).

For discussions of **race and gender discrimination** (note 10), see Lisa Kerr, Can Money Buy Happiness? An Examination of the Coverage of Infertility Services Under HMO Contracts, 49 Case W. Res. L. Rev. 559 (1999); Carl Coleman, Conceiving Harm: Disability Discrimination in Assisted Reproductive Technologies, 50 UCLA L. Rev. 17 (2002). For a related issue, see L. Dechery, Do Employer-Provided Insurance Plans Violate Title VII When They Exclude Treatment for Breast Cancer?, 80 Minn. L. Rev. 945 (1996); Christine Nardi, When Health Insurers Deny Coverage for Breast Reconstructive Surgery: Gender Meets Disability, 1997 Wis. L. Rev. 778.

Problem: Allocation Choices in a Public Program

You are CEO of a municipal hospital, funded by the county, looking at next year's budget. This forces you to make tough allocation decisions. Due to your brilliant administrative leadership, the hospital managed to treat all patients who requested service last year, and it still has a $5 million surplus left over. After receiving recommendations from a task force, you have to choose among these three options:

(1) Return the money to the county to help them avoid an anticipated property tax increase.

(2) Buy one Very Big Fancy Machine (VBFM), which, over the course of its five-year useful life, will treat 100 patients a year, with a 1 percent better chance of saving their life compared with existing technologies. In other words, the machine is expected to save five lives at a cost of $1 million/life. On average, each person saved will live for ten more years. (Imagine a machine that helps resuscitate patients in the emergency room.)

(3) Buy 5,000 Really Simple Little Things (RSLTs), which have a 1 percent chance to extend life one year for each person who uses one. In other words, this will provide one additional year for 50 people, at a cost of $100,000 per person. (Imagine an expensive drug that does a better job of delaying but not avoiding death from cancer.)

Now, suppose you learn that patients treated with the VBFM will be left bedridden and debilitated but fully conscious, whereas RSLT patients will be left ambulatory but in pain and with diminished mental capacities. Assuming you were unfettered by the ADA, what do you do? Realizing, however, that the ADA might apply, does it potentially force you to change your mind? What factors determine what effect the ADA might have?

2. Determining What Is Medically Appropriate

Once insurance language is written, disputes do not disappear. We still must decide which treatments are actually covered by insurance in effect. The main readings view these issues from a more substantive perspective, and the notes take a more procedural look. The focus in the main readings is on private insurance; the notes include public programs as well. Regardless, the issues remain essentially the same throughout: Who should decide what is medically appropriate, and according to what criteria?

■ MOUNT SINAI HOSPITAL v. ZOREK
271 N.Y.S.2d 1012 (N.Y. Civ. Ct. 1966)

GREENFIELD, Judge.

One of the most celebrated trials of our literature was the confrontation of Portia and Shylock as they struggled with the problem of the removal of a pound of flesh. Now, once again, the removal of a pound of flesh, or more properly several pounds, has created a weighty legal problem for resolution by the court.

The hopes, despairs, and conflicts of our time, and ultimately every crisis, custom and social neurosis find reflection in the matters brought before the courts, the great mirror of our society. While not of the same magnitude as wars, depressions or the disasters of nature, the problem of obesity has persistently troubled part of mankind, but even more of womankind, ever since man first eked out more than the marginal subsistence required for bare survival, accumulated the luxury of a surplus food supply, and began to live to eat instead of eating to live.

With the plump and fleshy females portrayed by Rubens no longer in vogue, having been supplanted by the ideal of the lithe and willowy high-cheekboned model, the plight of those women whose rotundity does not conform to the ideal has been accentuated. The plaintiff cry "O! that this too too solid flesh would melt Thaw and resolve itself into a dew" is re-echoed today by the plump and portly, and has evoked a burgeoning and varied response from Elizabeth Arden, reducing pills, milk farms, steam baths and slenderizers to No-Cal and the Drinking Man's Diet.

Grace, felicity and beauty are qualities ardently sought after—but aesthetic considerations aside, excess avoirdupois also creates problems of health, vigor, longevity, hygiene and a general state of well-being that call for the arts of the medical practitioner. Obesity is definitely a medical problem. The correlation between overweight and a shortened life-span has been amply demonstrated. What a challenge to a medical Michelangelo, to liberate from beneath mountains of flesh the slender, sylphlike creature yearning to be free!

Doctor John J. Bookman was one who rose to the challenge. Among his patients was Jane Zorek, the wife of the defendant and third-party plaintiff in this action. Mrs. Zorek was 5' 2", but could not exactly be described as petite, for she had weighed well over 200 pounds. The doctor had been treating her for a number of medical problems arising from her obesity—including abscesses, cysts, and skin grafts. In 1962, when this had caused sebaceous gland trouble, he had her hospitalized. In the hospital she was put on a rigid reducing diet restricted to 800 calories a day and lost 7 1/2 pounds. The third-party defendant, Associated Hospital Service of New York, with whom Mr. Zorek had a family Blue Cross contract, on that occasion paid the expenses of Mrs. Zorek's hospital stay without a murmur of protest.

Out of the hospital, Mrs. Zorek was unable to maintain her weight loss, and was plagued by recurring boils and cysts. Hence, in May of 1963, Doctor Bookman again concluded that hospitalization was required and had her admitted to the plaintiff Mount Sinai Hospital. This time she was put on what is known as the "Duncan Regime"—a rigid starvation diet, in which the patient receives no calories at all, only fluids, vitamins and minerals. During her three weeks stay in the hospital on this stringent program, Mrs. Zorek lost 17 1/2 pounds without adverse effects.

When pressed by the hospital for payment, Mr. Zorek looked to his Blue Cross policy with Associated Hospital Service of New York for reimbursement. AHS, however, this time refused payment, contending that obesity was not within the coverage of the contract, and that Mrs. Zorek's hospital confinement was not necessary for treatment of her condition. This lawsuit then followed.

[Although] AHS argued that obesity is neither a disease nor an injury, it is clear that Blue Cross coverage is not limited only to those calamities. Since the policy spells out the "condition, disease, ailment or accidental injury" which is *excluded* from coverage, it should be plain that there *is* coverage for hospitalization resulting from any condition, disease, injury or ailment which is not excluded. While it is debatable whether or not obesity is an illness or ailment, certainly it is a "condition," and the test of coverage must be determined on other grounds.

The policy provides:

> Such Hospital Service shall be available to a Subscriber, following his admission to a hospital and during the time he is confined herein as a registered bed patient and while he is under the treatment of a physician, *when such hospital confinement is necessary for his proper treatment*. . . . However, there shall be available only such items of Hospital Service as are necessary and consistent with the diagnosis and treatment of the Condition for which such hospitalization is required. (Italics supplied.)

Under Exclusions appear the following: "A. Hospital Service Shall Not Be Provided: . . . 5. For a hospital stay or that portion of a hospital stay which is primarily for custodial, convalescent or sanitarium type care or for a rest cure."

Associated Hospital Service, the third-party defendant, argues that hospital confinement was not necessary for proper treatment of Mrs. Zorek's obese condition, and that the care rendered to her during her stay in the hospital was convalescent or sanitarium type care which the contract excludes. . . .

The words *necessary for proper treatment* call into play the exercise of judgment. "Proper" in whose eyes? The patient's, the treating physician's, the hospital's, an AHS administrator's, or a court's looking back on the events sometime afterwards? Although no cases have been brought to the court's attention directly dealing with this problem, this court concludes that the applicable standards of judgment as to the treatment prescribed must be those of the treating physician.

Only the treating physician can determine what the appropriate treatment should be for any given condition. Any other standard would involve intolerable second-guessing, with every case calling for a crotchety Doctor Gillespie to peer over the shoulders of a supposedly unseasoned Doctor Kildare. The diagnosis and treatment of a patient are matters peculiarly within the competence of the treating physician. The diagnosis may be insightful and brilliant, or it may be wide of the mark, but right or wrong, the patient under his doctor's guidance proceeds upon his theories and sustains expenses therefor. Can a hospitalization insurer rightfully decline to pay for the expenses incurred on the theory that subsequent events may have proved the diagnosis or the recommended treatment to have been wrong?

Once the treating doctor has decided on the treatment, we may of course review his judgment as to whether or not hospital confinement was necessary for the particular treatment prescribed. The doctor who orders hospital confinement for the removal of a simple splinter or the lancing of a boil has almost certainly exceeded the bounds of proper medical judgment in providing for his patient. The doctor who orders hospitalization for major surgery clearly is correct in concluding that hospital confinement is necessary for that treatment, even though he may be in egregious error in deciding that major surgery is called for. Once the treating doctor has decided on a course of treatment for which hospitalization is necessary, his judgment cannot be retrospectively challenged.

A gall-bladder or a liver condition may be treated by a radical operation or by allowing a healthy regimen and the healing passage of time to work the miracle of regeneration. Who can say with certainty which course of treatment is correct? But if the operation is decided on, can there be a denial of Blue Cross coverage because alternative courses of treatment were available?

In this case doctors might differ as to what treatment should have been given to Mrs. Zorek for obesity and related disorders. The doctor who treated her concluded the appropriate treatment for the condition would be not further home dieting, or intensive exercise, or sanitarium care, but the Duncan regime. Other doctors might disagree as to prescribing the Duncan regime, but they were not treating Mrs. Zorek. . . .

The Duncan regime is a recognized medical treatment for obesity. While there is some controversy about it, and not all doctors would choose to resort to that treatment, many reputable doctors do. Doctor Bookman chose that treatment here. He having determined, within the scope of his medical competence, that the treatment was necessary, the sole question remaining is whether hospitalization was necessary for the treatment decided on.

AHS contends that what was done for Mrs. Zorek in the hospital demonstrates that hospitalization was not necessary. Apart from restricting her intake of food and administering vitamins, the patient was permitted to continue ambulatory and was weighed daily. All these things, AHS contends, were in the nature of custodial care and could have been done at home or in any sanitarium or rest home. Looking back, Mrs. Zorek's stay was indeed uneventful. However, we must measure the necessity for hospitalization by the prospective potentialities for danger inherent in a treatment, and not by fortuitous actuality.

Dr. Bookman testified that the Duncan regime was a dangerous course of treatment, and because of the dangers involved called for careful supervision at all times. The patient's blood pressure, temperature, and body fluids had to be continuously checked to be certain that proper chemical balance was maintained, and he insisted much more than mere custodial care would be required. Indeed, severe shock and even death are known to have ensued for persons following the Duncan regime even under carefully supervised conditions, since the changes which occur may be sudden and drastic. Even the medical expert who testified for Blue Cross stated that while he personally would not recommend the Duncan regime, the reason he would not do so is because of its inherent danger. In fact, he said, it would be foolishness to place someone on a Duncan diet outside of a hospital with facilities for 24 hour supervision and a well-trained medical staff.

Fortunately, there were no adverse developments or complications for Mrs. Zorek during her hospital stay. The possibilities were ever-present however, and in any sensible society penalties are not to be imposed where common-sense precautions are taken. The court concludes that not only was hospitalization necessary once the Duncan regime was decided upon, but that it would have been medically irresponsible to have had anything less. Certainly we must presume that a busy metropolitan hospital complex like Mount Sinai was not going to make one of its much sought-after beds available for three weeks for a person who merely was seeking a "rest cure," and the kind of enforced diet she could otherwise get on a milk farm. It was medical necessity and not cosmetic vanity which dictated the hospital stay. . . .

It is the holding of this Court in construing the Blue Cross contract that when multiple courses of treatment are available, whether for the obese, the alcoholic, or the addicted, if the treating physician chooses that treatment for which hospitalization is required, and rejects those treatments which can be adequately administered in a rest home or sanitarium, then, absent a specific contractual exclusion, there is full coverage for the hospital stay. . . .

The amount of the hospital bill in this case attributed to Mrs. Zorek's treatment for obesity came to $557.90, for which sum the plaintiff, Mount Sinai Hospital, is entitled to judgment. . . .

■ BECHTOLD v. PHYSICIANS HEALTH PLAN OF NORTHERN INDIANA
19 F.3d 322 (7th Cir. 1994)

COFFEY, Circuit Judge.

BACKGROUND

. . . The parties have stipulated to the relevant facts in this case and legal issues only need be determined. Penny Jo Bechtold is a 40-year-old premenopausal adult female. She is employed by Magnavox Electronic Systems which maintains a health plan administered by the defendant Physicians Health Plan of Northern Indiana [PHP]. The plan is an "employee welfare benefit plan" as defined [by ERISA].

In October, 1991, the plaintiff was diagnosed as having breast cancer and underwent a modified radical mastectomy. The surgery disclosed heavy lymph node involvement with the breast cancer cells. After the removal of the tumor she was treated with standard chemotherapy and radiation. Her oncologist recommended that she receive heavy dose chemotherapy with an autologous bone marrow transplant (HDC/ABMT) and referred her to the Cleveland Clinic for this treatment.

HDC/ABMT is a two-step procedure. Physicians first extract ("harvest") the bone marrow cells from the patient's body and place them temporarily in frozen storage. Next, the patient undergoes a cycle of high-dose chemotherapy in hopes of killing the cancer cells. . . . [T]he patient's own ("autologous") stored marrow is [then] reinfused intravenously into the bloodstream to relieve the patient from the toxic effects of the chemotherapy. HDC/ABMT has proven effective in treating certain cancerous blood diseases such as leukemia and Hodgkin's disease but to date it has not been universally accepted treatment for solid-type tumors including breast cancer.

Before Bechtold proceeded with the treatment, PHP advised her that the HDC/ABMT treatment was not a covered service under the plan. . . . [T]he plaintiff . . . appeal[ed] the denial of benefits and received a hearing before a committee [composed of one PHP doctor, one PHP patient, and a representative of PHP management]. The committee recommended that even though the insurer had met its obligations to the plaintiff under the contract, that the insurer should change its policy and authorize payment for the procedure because the treatment was reasonable for a patient of Bechtold's age. PHP did not agree with the committee's recommendation, and refused to pay for the treatment stating that it had "lived up to its Contract obligations" under the "clear and unambiguous language in the Contract." . . .

DISCUSSION

We are aware that Mrs. Bechtold and her immediate family have undoubtedly endured a great deal of heartache, frustration, and depression during her battle with cancer.[2] there is no doubt that the policy questions posed in cases like this are of grave concern to all of us, yet we, as a court of law, are called upon to make legal determinations.[3] The issue in this case is very straightforward: Does the PHP benefit plan authorize coverage of HDC/ABMT? This is a matter of contract interpretation that does not implicate the broader policy issues involved in whether insurers should cover medical procedures that are presently of unknown medical value and extremely costly.

A claim for benefits under an ERISA-governed plan "is a matter of contract interpretation." . . . The parties have devoted considerable time arguing what the proper standard of review is in this case. In Firestone Tire & Rubber Co. v. Bruch, 489 U.S. 101 (1989), the United States Supreme Court ruled that the denial of benefits by an ERISA plan administrator must "be reviewed under the de novo standard unless the benefit plan gives the administrator or fiduciary discretionary authority to determine eligibility for benefits or to construe the plan." "[I]f a benefit plan gives discretion to an administrator or fiduciary who is operating under a conflict of interest, that conflict must be weighed as a 'facto[r] in determining whether there is an abuse of discretion.'" (quoting Restatement (Second) of Trusts §187, Comment *d* (1959)). The plaintiff argues that because PHP was operating under a conflict of interest (i.e., PHP stood to gain a greater profit if the claim was denied) we should grant less deference to PHP's determination that HDC/ABMT is experimental. We need not decide what level of deference to give to the defendant's interpretation of the contract term because under the facts in this case, even applying de novo review, the clear and unambiguous language of the policy dictates that the defendant, Physicians Health Plan of Northern Indiana, properly denied coverage for the HDC/ABMT treatment.

2. Fortunately for Mrs. Bechtold she has secondary insurance that paid for the treatment and thus this action will merely determine which of two insurers will pay for the treatment.

3. In Harris v. Mutual of Omaha Cos., 1992 WL 421489, 1992 U.S. Dist. LEXIS 21393 (S.D. Ind. Aug. 26, 1992), aff'd, 992 F.2d 706 (7th Cir. 1993), a similar case of a claimant seeking coverage for HDC/ABMT, U.S. District Judge Tinder succinctly summarized the problem facing courts in these difficult claims for medical coverage:

Despite rumors to the contrary, those who wear judicial robes are human beings, and as persons, are inspired and motivated by compassion as anyone would be. Consequently, we often must remind ourselves that in our official capacities, we have authority only to issue rulings within the narrow parameters of the law and the facts before us. The temptation to go about, doing good where we see fit, and to make things less difficult for those who come before us, regardless of the law, is strong. But the law, without which judges are nothing, abjures such unlicensed formulation of unauthorized social policy by the judiciary. Plaintiff Judy Harris well deserves, and in a perfect world would be entitled to, all known medical treatments to control the horrid disease from which she suffers. In ruling as this court must, no personal satisfaction is taken, but that the law was followed. The court will have to live with the haunting thought that Ms. Harris, and perhaps others insured by the Mutual of Omaha Companies under similar plans, may not ultimately receive the treatment they need and deserve. Perhaps the question most importantly raised about this case, and similar cases, is who should pay for the hopeful treatments that are being developed in this rapidly developing area of medical science?

DENIAL OF COVERAGE

In part, the Plan provides:

"Experimental or Unproven Procedures" means any procedures, devices, drugs or medicines or the use thereof which falls within any of the following categories: 1. Which is considered by any government agency or subdivision, including but not limited to the Food and Drug Administration, the Office of Health Technology Assessment, or Medicare Coverage Issues Manual to be: a. experimental or investigational; b. not considered reasonable and necessary; or c. any similar finding; 2. Which is not covered under Medicare reimbursement laws, regulations or interpretations; or 3. Which is not commonly and customarily recognized by the medical profession in the state of Indiana as appropriate for the condition being treated. PLAN reserves the right to change, from time to time, the procedures considered to be Experimental or Unproven. Contact PLAN to determine if a particular procedure, treatment, or device is considered to be Experimental or Unproven.

The Medicare Coverage Issues Manual (which is referenced in the PHP Plan) provides in §35-31:

C. Autologous Bone Marrow Transplantation (Effective for Services Performed on or After 04/28/89). . . . —Insufficient data exist to establish definite conclusions regarding the efficacy of autologous bone marrow transplantation for the following conditions: . . . Acute leukemia in relapse, Chronic granulocytic leukemia or Solid tumors [such as breast cancer] (other than neuroblastoma). In these cases, autologous bone marrow transplantation is not considered reasonable and necessary within the meaning of §1862(a)(1)(A) of the Act and is not covered under Medicare.

The plaintiff does not challenge the language of the Medicare Coverage Issues Manual but argues that the phrase in the Plan that PHP "reserves the right to change, from time to time, the procedures considered to be Experimental or Unproven" creates an obligation on the part of PHP to cover the contested treatment in light of recent medical research endorsing the procedure for solid tumors like breast cancer . . . rather than to hide behind outdated or inapplicable guidelines and therefore if the treatment is no longer experimental—as the plaintiff argues—she is entitled to coverage. . . .

The "right to change" the classification of procedures certainly does not obligate PHP to reclassify hourly, weekly, monthly or annually whether a treatment should be covered on the basis of competing views of medical experts (oncologists). Rather, PHP chose to link the experimental nature of a treatment to the neutral (third party) determination of the medical experts responsible for drafting the Medicare Coverage Issues Manual.[6] Clearly, PHP's intent was to avoid a case-by-case battle of the experts in which PHP would be required to reevaluate covered treatments each time a self-proclaimed "expert" publishes a new article. . . . [The contract] is . . .

6. The Medicare Coverage Issues Manual is updated when new medical data becomes available and the updates are published quarterly in the Federal Register. The provision relating to autologous bone marrow transplants for solid tumors (breast cancer) was published in the Federal Register on June 11, 1992, and was in effect at all times relevant to this proceeding (Bechtold was denied coverage in October 1992).

clear and unambiguous. Heller v. Equitable Life Assur. Soc., 833 F.2d 1253, 1257 (7th Cir. 1987) ("In the absence of a clear, unequivocal and specific contractual requirement [placing a duty on a party,] we refuse to order the same. To hold otherwise and to impose such a requirement would, in effect, enlarge the terms of the policy beyond those clearly defined in the policy agreed to by the parties.").[7] . . .

ERISA . . . does not dictate what a plan such as the PHP plan before us should cover. Hickey v. A.E. Staley Mfg., 995 F.2d 1385, at 1393 (7th Cir. 1993) ("Congress never intended ERISA to dictate the content of welfare benefit plans, much less for the federal courts to determine the content of such plans; . . . the discretion to make decisions concerning the content of the Plan rests with the Plan administrator"). Therefore, we hold that the language of the PHP Plan excludes coverage for HDC/ABMT as a treatment for breast cancer.

FULL AND FAIR REVIEW

Bechtold's second argument is that she was denied full and fair review . . . because PHP refused to accept the recommendation of its own complaints committee and instead denied the benefits based on the Plan Chief Operating Officer's disagreement with the committee's recommendation. We cannot agree with Bechtold's argument on this account because a review of the letter from PHP denying the benefits makes clear that the committee recognized that the HDC/ABMT treatment was not covered under the plan. The committee, however, recommended a change of policy by the insurer to allow coverage of the procedure because: (1) the procedure was not experimental and PHP has an express intent of providing reasonable care for patients of this type; (2) Medicare supporting claims for this type of noncovered condition, is not that of a patient of Ms. Bechtold's age; (3) supportive data suggests the proposed treatment as very appropriate. . . .

The only authority vested in the committee was to recommend whether a specific claim for benefits had been properly denied based upon the language of the policy; it was not free to cast aside the agreed upon terms of the insurance contract. . . .

CONCLUSION

As stated above, cases of this nature pose troubling social as well as ethical questions that go well beyond the legal issues. As a court of law we are empowered to decide legal issues presented by specific cases or controversies. The greater social questions must be decided by the political branches of government which can engage in legislative factfinding and benefit from public hearings and constituent expression of opinion. . . . Chesterfield Smith, the former president of the Ameri-

---

7. In Heller, . . . [w]e [noted] that [t]he insurance company seeking to [limit] coverage . . . need only incorporate a specific requirement to that effect in the policy, and we would not hesitate to enforce the same. On the other hand, insurers who fail to include this express . . . contractual requirement, and who refuse to cover an insured after entering into a binding and enforceable agreement after accepting substantial premiums, in circumstances such as those before us, cause problems not only for the insured, but for the insurance industry as well. Insurance companies, members of a service industry, . . . must conduct themselves accordingly instead of attempting to rely on the courts to correct their own deficiencies in underwriting and/or careless policy drafting.

can Bar Association once stated in a Law Day address: "Courts are being asked today to solve problems for which they are not institutionally equipped. . . . The American public perceives the courts as a jack-of-all trades available to furnish the answer to whatever may trouble them." The question of what procedures insurance companies should cover is just the type of problem to which Mr. Smith was referring.

In order to resolve the question of whether health insurance providers should cover treatments like HDC/ABMT, the prudent course of action might be to establish some sort of regional cooperative committees comprised of oncologists, internists, surgeons, experts in medical ethics, medical school administrators, economists, representatives of the insurance industry, patient advocates and politicians. Through such a collective task force perhaps some consensus might be reached concerning the definition of experimental procedures, as well as agreement on the procedures, which are so cost prohibitive that requiring insurers to cover them might result in the collapse of the healthcare industry. While such a committee would in no way be a panacea for our skyrocketing health care costs, it may help to reduce the incidence of suits in which one "expert" testifies that a procedure is experimental and another equally qualified "expert" testifies to the opposite effect. This so called battle of the experts occurs all too frequently in federal court. . . .

■ RUSH PRUDENTIAL HMO v. MORAN
536 U.S. 355 (2002)

Justice SOUTER delivered the opinion of the Court [with four justices dissenting].

Petitioner, Rush Prudential HMO, Inc., is a health maintenance organization (HMO) that contracts to provide medical services for employee welfare benefit plans covered by ERISA. Respondent Debra Moran is a beneficiary under one such plan, sponsored by her husband's employer. Rush's "Certificate of Group Coverage," issued to employees who participate in employer-sponsored plans, promises that Rush will provide them with "medically necessary" services. The terms of the certificate give Rush the "broadest possible discretion" to determine whether a medical service claimed by a beneficiary is covered under the certificate. . . .

In 1996, when Moran began to have pain and numbness in her right shoulder, Dr. Arthur LaMarre, her primary care physician, unsuccessfully administered "conservative" treatments such as physiotherapy. In October 1997, Dr. LaMarre recommended that Rush approve surgery by an unaffiliated specialist, Dr. Julia Terzis, who had developed an unconventional treatment for Moran's condition. Although Dr. LaMarre said that Moran would be "best served" by that procedure, Rush denied the request and, after Moran's internal appeals, affirmed the denial on the ground that the procedure was not "medically necessary." Rush instead proposed that Moran undergo standard surgery, performed by a physician affiliated with Rush. [Read the remainder of the facts of this case, excerpted at pages 1089-1092.]

In January 1998, Moran made a written demand for an independent medical review of her claim, as guaranteed by Illinois's HMO Act, which provides:

> Each Health Maintenance Organization shall provide a mechanism for the timely review by a physician holding the same class of license as the primary care physician, who is unaffiliated with the Health Maintenance Organization, jointly selected by the patient . . . , primary care physician and the Health Maintenance Organization

in the event of a dispute between the primary care physician and the Health Maintenance Organization regarding the medical necessity of a covered service proposed by a primary care physician. In the event that the reviewing physician determines the covered service to be medically necessary, the Health Maintenance Organization shall provide the covered service. . . .

When Rush failed to provide the independent review, Moran sued in an Illinois state court to compel compliance with the state Act. . . . [Rush claimed that ERISA preempts the state Act because the Act requires a review mechanism that is inconsistent with ERISA's process for challenging benefit denials.]

[T]his case addresses a state regulatory scheme that provides no new cause of action under state law and authorizes no new form of ultimate relief. While independent review under [the HMO Act] may well settle the fate of a benefit claim under a particular contract, the state statute does not enlarge the claim beyond the benefits available in any action brought under [ERISA]. And although the reviewer's determination would presumably replace that of the HMO as to what is "medically necessary" under this contract, the relief ultimately available would still be what ERISA authorizes in a suit for benefits. . . .

[The Act] does resemble an arbitration provision [which might be preempted] . . . to the extent that the independent reviewer considers disputes about the meaning of the HMO contract and receives "evidence" in the form of medical records, statements from physicians, and the like. But this is as far as the resemblance to arbitration goes, for the other features of review . . . give the proceeding a different character, one not at all at odds with the policy behind [ERISA preemption]. The Act does not give the independent reviewer a free-ranging power to construe contract terms, but instead, confines review to a single term: the phrase "medical necessity," used to define the services covered under the contract. This limitation, in turn, . . . [means that] the independent examiner must be a physician with credentials similar to those of the primary care physician, and is expected to exercise independent medical judgment in deciding what medical necessity requires. Accordingly, the reviewer in this case did not hold the kind of conventional evidentiary hearing common in arbitration, but simply received medical records submitted by the parties, and ultimately came to a professional judgment of his own. Once this process is set in motion, it does not resemble either contract interpretation or evidentiary litigation before a neutral arbiter, as much as it looks like a practice (having nothing to do with arbitration) of obtaining another medical opinion. The reference to an independent reviewer is similar to the submission to a second physician, which many health insurers are required by law to provide before denying coverage. . . . [O]nce [the Act] is seen as something akin to a mandate for second-opinion practice in order to ensure sound medical judgments, the preemption argument that arbitration . . . supplants judicial enforcement runs out of steam.

Notes: Insurance Coverage Disputes

1. *Medicare and Medicaid Coverage.* The coverage of public programs such as Medicare and Medicaid is defined in the same "medically necessary" and "experimental" terms as are commonly used in private insurance contracts. A related body of case law addresses whether novel or alternative treatments are covered under

these public programs, reaching similarly mixed results. In favor of coverage, one court held that Medicaid must cover a certain treatment for both early and advanced stages of AIDS, even though FDA approval of the drug was limited to the latter. The court reasoned that "it would be improper . . . to interfere with a physician's judgment of medical necessity" based on FDA drug-labeling requirements because "FDA approved indications [are] not intended to limit or interfere with the practice of medicine; . . . the package insert is only informational." Weaver v. Reagan, 886 F.2d 194, 198 (8th Cir. 1989). In another case, the court found that a sex change operation is medically necessary and nonexperimental under Medicaid. Pinneke v. Preisser, 623 F.2d 546 (8th Cir. 1980). In a third, the court ordered Medicare to cover artificial lens implants for cataract correction despite the fact they were still under research investigation, explaining that

> manufacturers and physicians working to develop [lens implants] need to be assured that they will be reimbursed for their efforts during these investigational periods. Withdrawing Medicare coverage . . . [will likely cause the lens] industry's remarkable level of invention [to] decrease dramatically. . . . [Medicare]'s stultifying regulatory strategy, with its preference for government rules over market-generated innovation, is reminiscent of the central planning apparatuses that other nations are now struggling to leave behind. . . . If this type of thinking were to prevail, the status quo would be frozen and research and development would become a thing of the past. That is not the American way.

American Society of Cataract and Refractive Surgery v. Sullivan, 772 F. Supp. 666 (D.D.C. 1991). For decisions the other way, see Goodman v. Sullivan, 891 F.2d 449 (2d Cir. 1989) (Medicare regulation denying payment for MRI scans does not impermissibly supervise or control the practice of medicine); MacKenzie Medical Supply v. Leavitt, 419 F. Supp. 2d 766 (D. Md. 2006) ("if the Secretary . . . could never deny a claim when the physician had written a prescription, [t]hat would undermine the role of the Secretary in the Medicare system").

Especially controversial have been cases involving major organ transplants (liver, heart, lung, etc.) under Medicaid. In favor of coverage, see Pereira v. Kozlowski, 996 F.2d 723 (4th Cir. 1993); Salgado v. Kirschner, 878 P.2d 659 (Ariz. 1994); Jackson v. Millstone, 801 A.2d 1034 (Md. 2002). Allowing states to limit or refuse coverage, see Dexter v. Kirschner, 984 F.2d 979 (9th Cir. 1992); Shannon v. Jack Eckerd Corp., 113 F.3d 208 (11th Cir. 1997).

2. *Appeal Procedures.* In addition to the *substance* of coverage decisions, *Moran* shows that the proper *procedures* for challenging and reviewing these decisions have been controversial under both public and private insurance. For conventional private insurance, appeal procedures at one time were fairly straightforward: If you were unhappy, you hired a lawyer and sued. Although ERISA preemption complicates which court to sue in and what the standard of review will be, these disputes were resolved essentially like any other contract dispute. But that is true only so far as *judicial* review is concerned. The decision process by the insurer at the initial stage of decision first attracted the attention of state regulators and legislators. This is especially true under managed care because then the denial of coverage does not simply affect who will pay, it often affects whether treatment will be rendered at all. Therefore, it is not sufficient for patients eventually to have their day in court. They need a prompt and fair review process on the spot.

As the *Moran* case illustrates, many states now require prompt external, independent review for all health insurers, but state law still cannot reach self-insured employers. Therefore, the Affordable Care Act implemented a uniform set of external, independent review requirements for all forms of private health insurance, including self-funded employers. These standards require that, under normal circumstances, appeals be sent to an independent physician reviewer within a week, for decision within 45 days. When that length of time would seriously jeopardize health, the review must be completed within three days. 75 Fed. Reg. 43330 (2010). Somewhat surprisingly (or perhaps not), some courts have refused to treat these independent reviews as binding on patients who decide to pursue further appeals in court. See, e.g., Alexandra H. v. Oxford Health Insurance, 833 F.3d 1299 (11th Cir. 2016).

Under Medicare and Medicaid, appeal procedures are even more complex since the analysis varies along each of the following lines, and for each of these categories there are several points of view: There are constitutional, statutory, and regulatory dimensions. Not only do each of these dimensions differ between the two programs, but within Medicare the appeal procedures differ between Part A and Part B, and within Medicaid they vary state by state. Within each program, appeal procedures also differ between fee-for-service and HMO providers. And, appeal issues differ according to what is at stake: basic eligibility or particular covered services. The issues also differ according to whether a patient is challenging a fact-based ruling in an individual case, a general substantive rule or policy decision, or a procedural rule. And, there are various levels of decision, from initial review by "fiscal intermediaries" (insurers under contract with CMS), to administrative review within CMS, to judicial review. To top it all off, a whole different set of procedures and institutions govern appeals by patients over eligibility for coverage than those that govern appeals by providers challenging how much they are paid when services are covered.

3. *Block That Metaphor.* For another court moved to literary heights by an insurance coverage dispute, see Zuckerberg v. Blue Cross & Blue Shield, 464 N.Y.S.2d 678, 683 (1983) (requiring Blue Shield to pay for a course of nutritional cancer therapy of unproven benefit that the plaintiff obtained in Mexico), rev'd on other grounds, 490 N.E.2d 839 (N.Y. 1986), where the court recited:

> A possible path was opened, had it not been taken, what then? At least, it was tried. "For of all sad words of tongue or pen, The saddest are these: 'It might have been!'" (*Maud Muller*, by John Greenleaf Whittier, stanza 53).

For a more somber view, consider the following thoughts from Judge Gladys Kessler in *Salazar v. District of Columbia*, 1996 WL 768038 (D.D.C. 1996):

> This case is about people—children and adults who are sick, poor, and vulnerable—for whom life, in the memorable words of poet Langston Hughes, "ain't been no crystal stair." It is written in the dry and bloodless language of "the law"—statistics, acronyms of agencies and bureaucratic entities, Supreme Court case names and quotes, official governmental reports, periodicity tables, etc. But let there be no forgetting the real people to whom this dry and bloodless language gives voice: anxious, working parents who are too poor to obtain medications or heart catheter procedures or lead poisoning screens for their children, AIDS patients unable to get treatment, elderly persons suffering from chronic conditions like diabetes and heart disease who

require constant monitoring and medical attention. Behind every "fact" found herein is a human face and the reality of being poor in the richest nation on earth.

And a more balanced view:

Coverage litigation has become one of the American health system's Crimeas, a designated battleground for opposing armies. On one side are arrayed individual patients with idiosyncratic needs, and the physicians and hospitals who stand ready to serve them. On the other side can be found employers, insurers and government—in each case claiming to represent the interest of beneficiaries or taxpayers as a whole by denying relief to one member or the group. This is, of course, the core challenge of managed care: creating an efficient system of population-based health management which nonetheless accounts equitably for the interests of individuals.

William Sage, Judicial Opinions Involving Health Insurance Coverage: Trompe L'Oeil or Window on the World?, 31 Ind. L. Rev. 49 (1998).

4. *The Doctor Knows Best.* Returning to the *Zorek* case from 1966, note that three weeks of hospitalization at Mount Sinai Hospital then cost $557.90. Today, this would not even buy *one day's* hospitalization. Should this fact change the outcome in *Zorek*? The *Zorek* court appears quite absolute in its statement that "only the treating physician can determine what the appropriate treatment should be for any given condition." What more prosaic phrase do we usually apply to allowing the one who is paid (or, here, a member of its medical staff) to be the sole judge of the necessity of its services? Consider the contrasting literary viewpoint found in George Bernard Shaw's preface to his play *The Doctor's Dilemma*:

That any sane nation . . . should . . . give a surgeon a pecuniary interest in cutting off your leg, is enough to make one despair of political humanity. But that is precisely what we have done. And the more appalling the mutilation, the more the mutilator is paid. Scandalized voices murmur that . . . operations are necessary. They may be. It may also be necessary to hang a man or pull down a house. But we take good care not to make the hangman and the house breaker the judges of that.

In *Black & Decker Disability Plan v. Nord*, 538 U.S. 822 (2003), the Court ruled that ERISA does not require employers to defer to the judgment of treating physicians in determining whether a worker is disabled.

5. *ERISA and Medicare.* The seminal decision holding that ERISA governs insurance contract disputes between employers and employees is Pilot Life Insurance Co. v. Dedeaux, 481 U.S. 41 (1987). Thereafter, most of these cases have shifted to the federal courts, where they are decided without a jury and without the possibility of personal injury or punitive damages. As discussed in Chapter 4.G.2, ERISA allows recovery of only the monetary value of the treatment at issue. When ERISA does not apply, state court juries have sometimes awarded punitive damages in the range of $50 million to $100 million. Most commentators believe that, although some of the punitive awards were excessive, it is unconscionable to disallow any recovery of basic compensatory damages for bodily injury when there is a clear breach of a contract for medical services.

For private insurers that offer Medicare coverage (known as Medicare Advantage), the Medicare dispute resolution process has a preemptive effect similar to that of ERISA, barring beneficiaries from pursing their grievances under state law. See Uhm v. Humana Health Plan Inc., 573 F.3d 865 (9th Cir. 2009).

6. *In Search of the "Iron Clad" Insurance Contract. Bechtold* demonstrates that the legal landscape has changed considerably since *Zorek.* This is true in several respects. First, coverage decisions under private insurance are now typically decided prior to or during the course of treatment through requests for prior authorization, rather than in the ordinary process of claims review. Second, as the result of ERISA preemption, these cases are now decided in federal court under a potentially more lenient standard of review than that governing garden-variety contract disputes. Third, insurers have rewritten contracts to make their decisions more enforceable. They declare that questions of interpretation are to be determined in the discretion of the insurer, whose decision is binding. And they more frequently exclude specific controversial treatments by name.

None of these changes has dramatically altered the favorable treatment that patients usually receive in court, however. The shift from retrospective to prospective or concurrent utilization review has introduced a different form of hardship. Now, rather than merely risking loss of money, patients risk not getting the treatment at all. As one court noted: "A mistaken conclusion about medical necessity following retrospective review will result in the wrongful withholding of payment. An erroneous decision in a prospective review process, on the other hand, in practical consequences, results in the withholding of necessary care, potentially leading to a patient's permanent disability or death." See Wickline v. State, 239 Cal. Rptr. 810, 812 (Cal. Ct. App. 1986).

Although ERISA allows a more lenient standard of review, *Bechtold* explains that ERISA requires more exacting scrutiny when insurers are under a conflict of interest. The obvious conflict of interest is that insurers usually have already collected their premium and each medical payment comes out of their bottom line. Moreover, a different part of the *Moran* opinion held that a deferential standard does not apply to reviews by independent physicians, and in *Metropolitan Life Ins. Co. v. Glenn,* 554 U.S. 105 (2008), the Court held that an insurer administering a self-funded employer plan is under a conflict of interest, even though the insurer spends the employer's money, not its own, when approving claims. Thus, even under ERISA, courts still frequently construe ambiguous terms such as *experimental* and *medically necessary* in favor of patients. See, e.g., Kunin v. Benefit Trust Life Insurance Co., 910 F.2d 534 (9th Cir. 1990) (it is arbitrary and capricious to conclude that autism is excluded as a "mental illness"); Bradley v. Empire Blue Cross & Blue Shield, 562 N.Y.S.2d 908 (N.Y. Sup. Ct. 1990) (patient likely to prevail in showing that HDC/ABMT is not experimental treatment for AIDS, even though his doctor was the only one in the country who had ever used the procedure this way and the patient had signed an informed consent form acknowledging that he was participating in an "experiment").

As for the contract technique used in *Bechtold,* other courts have ruled that incorporation by reference does not give subscribers fair notice of what is excluded, and it is particularly unconscionable to govern young policyholders with rules written for the elderly under Medicare. See, e.g., Waldrip v. Connecticut National Life Insurance Co., 573 So. 2d 1172 (5th Cir. 1991); Hyde v. Humana Insurance Co., 598 So. 2d 876 (Ala. 1992).

The contractual change that has had the most impact is assigning to the insurer the authority to make binding interpretations of ambiguous phrases. Courts have ruled that, in effect, ERISA allows the contract to nullify the usual judicial presumption against the party that drafted the contract (*contra proferentum*). To counter that move, the National Association of Insurance Commissioners proposed a model act to ban such clauses, which several states have adopted. But courts have split on whether ERISA allows this type of regulation. See Standard Insurance Co. v. Morrison, 584 F.3d 837 (9th Cir. 2009).

7. *Conflicts of Interest.* As these cases and notes suggest, various conflicts of interest permeate the arena of insurance coverage determinations. The most obvious conflict is that of the insurer who has to pay. But is an insurer under a conflict of interest if it merely administers claims and does utilization review for a self-insured employer rather than bearing the risk of medical costs itself? In this situation, the insurer is paid a per-case or per-annum administrative fee and the financial risk is borne by the employer. Does this then put the employer under a conflict of interest, or is it accurate to say that the employer has in mind the interests of the employee group as a whole? One interesting case allowed an employer and its workers to sue under ERISA for wrongly *paying out* medical benefits from a self-funded plan under the theory that this depleted the plan's assets, which otherwise would have been available to pay more legitimate claims. IT Corp. v. General American Life Insurance Co., 107 F.3d 1415 (9th Cir. 1997). What about letting committees composed of employees decide these disputes? Are they conflict-free, considering that they may trade off the interests of one patient to favor the interests of the rest of the group?

Various expressions of opinion on these issues can be found in the case law, but suffice it to say that judicial opinions are still inconsistent and evolving. One notable instance of a decision apparently affected by an insurer's conflict of interest occurred in an unreported California trial verdict that was later settled (Fox v. HealthNet). That case also involved HDC/ABMT for breast cancer. There, an HMO refused coverage and the patient later died. The case was tried under state law because her insurance came from her government job, which ERISA does not cover. Therefore, her family was free to seek punitive damages. The jury returned a whopping $89 million verdict. According to press reports, the jury was influenced by two aggravating circumstances: that the HMO's medical director received a bonus determined in part by the amount of money he saved through coverage denials, and that the HMO had recently approved this same procedure for one of its own employees.

A different type of conflict surfaced in another notable case against HealthNet. As discussed in section E.3, HMOs sometimes shift the insurance risk to treating physicians by contracting with them on a fully capitated basis. This in effect tosses the hot potato of making coverage denials to the doctor, because it is the doctor who bears most of the costs. This also minimizes the potential for coverage disputes arising in the first place, since a patient is much less likely to be presented conflicting opinions between her doctor and her insurer if the doctor simply declines to order the treatment. This new dynamic was revealed when the same lawyer who represented Mrs. Fox in the prior case began to investigate a similar case involving Mrs. DeMeurs, also with breast cancer. He found that her doctor initially recommended her for HDC/ABMT but he changed his mind after the HMO medical director called the doctor to question his initial judgment. This case was decided in arbitration, resulting in a $1 million award. In the arbitrators' opinion,

> the [HMO's] actions designed and intended to interfere with an existing doctor/patient relationship constitute extreme and outrageous behavior exceeding all bounds usually tolerated in a civilized society. It is conduct undertaken with reckless disregard of the probability of causing severe emotional distress. This conduct clearly crosses the line of appropriate communication between insurer and doctor.

Do you agree?

8. *Courts, Committees, or Congress?* Suppose we view this situation as one involving two, unavoidably competing conflicts of interest: that of the physician who is to be paid, and that of the insurer/employer who is to pay. Is there any "neutral" third party capable of resolving this conflict? Are the courts themselves neutral, given their tendency, noted by Judge Coffey, to "go about doing good where we see fit"? Is the proper, "unbiased" perspective that of the individual patient who is presently sick and has insurance, or instead that of the pool of subscribers at the point they are deciding how much insurance coverage they can afford? Which perspective are courts more likely to take? Legislatures? Employers? Panels of expert doctors? Panels like those suggested by Judge Coffey composed of various interest groups and expertise? Isn't the hearing committee that actually reviewed Ms. Bechtold's case potentially one such representative panel? See Barnett v. Kaiser Foundation Health Plan, 32 F.3d 413 (9th Cir. 1994) (advisory board composed of HMO's own doctors provides neutral, expert review). If so, why was Judge Coffey so reluctant to accept its recommendation? Which of these various processes do you have the most confidence in, considering the full range of medical conditions and expenditures that are potentially at stake?

9. *Cookbook Medicine.* Why would insurers ever have adopted such broad terms as *medically necessary* and *experimental* in the first place? One could have predicted that it would be impossible to police physicians' decisions by using their own conceptual norms. One reason contracts might contain such open-ended terms is that health insurance originated from the medical establishment itself, in the form of Blue Cross/Blue Shield. But why has this not changed now that insurers are much more aggressively competitive? Courts frequently urge insurers to make their contracts more specific if they want to reliably exclude coverage. Indeed, it is possible to make coverage terms quite specific using the detailed practice guidelines that are being produced by the health services research community in great numbers. See Clark C. Havighurst, Practice Guidelines for Medical Care: The Policy Rationale, 34 St. Louis U. L. J. 777 (1990). But how realistic is this really? The most extensive effort to date is that in Oregon, described in section D.1, which uses more than 600 treatment-condition pairings (e.g., surgery for appendicitis) to specify Medicaid coverage across the entire range of medical practice.

The difficulty with this approach is aptly captured in Aaron and Schwartz's criticism of the Oregon list as "meat-ax" rationing. All covered treatments are always covered, no matter how mild the condition or how effective the medical intervention, while excluded items are not covered at all no matter how severe the condition or how great the potential is for improvement. To achieve the desirable level of specificity would require rigorous scientific information on each of the almost 10,000 diagnostic entries in the International Classification of Diseases (10th ed.) (known as "ICD-10") and for each of the 10,000 medical interventions listed in the AMA's Common Procedural Terminology (known as "CPT" codes). Moreover, each complication and sequence of events for each of these items would have to be evaluated in all possible combinations. In other words, for two conditions, A and B, we would have to consider A alone, B alone, and AB, as well as A before B and A after B. For even a single, modestly complex disease category (say, heart disease) with only 20 conditions, this analysis would produce some 10 billion different clinical scenarios.

The practical impossibility of adequately capturing the judgmental and nuanced aspects of medical decisionmaking in a detailed, prescriptive fashion has led legal scholars to refer to this as a problem in "relational contracting." Contracts that call for the exercise of professional judgment or that define complex, ongoing service relationships present unique problems as compared with classic contractual settings that simply specify the purchase of identified products. These relational contracts require inventive and flexible contracting tools in order to accomplish their purposes. In health insurance contracts, we see a persistent desire on the part of both subscribers and insurers to use contract terms that invoke broad medical norms rather than precise clinical details. If courts insist on construing these terms against insurers, are they not forcing the parties to adopt suboptimal contracting techniques like the one used in *Bechtold* of simply cross-referencing Medicare rules designed for old people?

Perhaps there is a workable middle ground between hyperspecific contracts and the open-ended discretion conferred by "medically necessary." Consider these thoughtful comments by Prof. Sage:

> The most important thing to appreciate about "medical necessity" is that has always operated at two levels: symbolic and substantive. . . . To many physicians, the phrase "not medically necessary" means "not clinically indicated," which makes them question why a seemingly nonprofessional party such as a health plan has the right to challenge their professional opinion. To many health plans, it means "not covered even though not expressly excluded from coverage," which gives them a degree of comfort issuing denials based on established insurance practice even though such decisions outrage physicians. Consequently, decisions involving medical necessity are frequently characterized by inconsistent administration, poor communication, distrust and, if disputes arise, relatively unprincipled, results-oriented judicial resolution. . . .
>
> [M]edical necessity cannot do the heavy lifting of cost control, or of quality assurance, in health care. . . . [H]ealth plans and policymakers have paid too much attention to standardized rules for coverage decisions and too little attention to therapeutic effect. Health care is both an outcome and a process, and all parts of the process, including those involving insurers, need to be caring as well as efficient. Medical necessity determinations should indeed be scientific and equitable, but, like good medicine, should also demonstrate compassion, offer hope, promote trust, and avoid abandonment.

William M. Sage, Managed Care's Crimea: Medical Necessity, Therapeutic Benefit, and the Goals of Administrative Process in Health Insurance, 53 Duke L. J. 597, 600, 650 (2003).

10. *Can Patients Decide?* With both courts and insurers struggling with what is "medically necessary" or "experimental" in any given case, Russell Korobkin has called for putting the choice back into the patient's own hands. Under what Korobkin terms "relative value health insurance," health plans would differ in their depth of coverage. More expensive plans might cover all medically necessary care; other, cheaper plans might exclude from coverage treatments that fail to meet a cost-effectiveness threshold. Patients could select the plans that best suit them. See Russell Korobkin, Relative Value Health Insurance, 39 J. of Health Pol., Pol'y & Law 417 (2014). For a criticism of the Korobkin approach, see Nicholas Bagley et al., Correcting Signals for Innovation in Health Care, Brookings, Oct. 7, 2015.

Another proposal, endorsed by Christopher Robertson, would allow patients to decline treatments in exchange for a cash payment from their insurer:

> Instead of asking patients whether the health care consumption is better than nothing, we should ask patients if health consumption is better than whatever else they may prefer. [T]he potential reform is simple:
>
> 1. Pay a small but substantial part of the insurance benefit as cash directly to the patient-beneficiary.
>
> 2. If the patient chooses to proceed with the treatment, the patient takes the cash payment to the provider (along with any required cost-share obligation), and the insurer matches it with the balance of the insurance benefit. . . .
>
> As such, the patient would receive both a cash benefit (the payment he or she receives) and an in-kind benefit (the payment to the provider), while still perhaps remaining exposed to some portion of the cost out-of-pocket. For patients that choose to spend the money in ways other than the treatment, the insurer saves the remainder of the cost of the procedure. . . .
>
> Patients who receive a split benefit may choose to proceed with the treatment or choose to promote health in some other way, such as consuming some other treatment not covered by the insurer (e.g., acupuncture, an alternative diet regimen, a concierge doctor, or visiting nursing services), paying money to a member of the family to stay home and provide care to the dying patient, or purchasing disability insurance to help cope with the symptoms of the illness. Or patients may use the money to serve other nonmedical values, such as enhancing housing, consuming more of some luxury good, paying off other debts that are causing disutility, paying for education (for themselves or others), contributing to a charity, or whatever else may appeal to the patient.

Christopher T. Robertson, The Split Benefits: The Painless Way to Put Skin Back in the Health Care Game, 98 Cornell L. Rev. 921 (2013); see also Christopher T. Robertson, Paying for Ourselves: The Ethics, Economics, and Law of Cost-Sharing in Health Insurance (2017).

11. *Paying for Medical Research.* Another important public policy implication of these cases is, who should pay for the necessary costs of medical experimentation? Manufacturers bear most of the costs for clinical trials that test new *drugs* and *devices* subject to FDA approval. Medical *procedures*, in contrast, are not required to be tested and are not owned by anyone. If new medical and surgical techniques are tested at all, the funding usually comes from the National Institutes of Health. Remarkably, its $30 *billion* budget is sufficient only to cover the *research* expenses of clinical trials (patient recruitment, data collection and analysis, etc.), not the *clinical* costs. Conventionally, the clinical costs are paid by patients' private and public insurance. Initially, insurers used "experimental" exclusions to refuse payment only for unscientific, "alternative" medicine. Under pressure from private market forces and public program deficits, insurers also began to refuse payment for some treatments that are rendered in scientific research studies. Despite the explicitly "experimental" setting, insurers have not been uniformly successful. For instance, Medicare decided in the mid-1990s to limit what it pays for treatments during clinical research studies, but following a legal challenge, an executive order, and legislation, Medicare now pays for routine clinical costs involved in NIH-funded or FDA-focused studies, or in studies of medical devices used in life-threatening medical situations. Also, the Affordable Care Act now requires private insurers to cover treatment costs in clinical trials for cancer or "other life-threatening conditions."

12. *Further Reading.* For discussions of **medical necessity** (note 1), see Timothy P. Blanchard, "Medical Necessity" Determinations: A Continuing Healthcare Policy Problem, 37 J. Health L. 599 (2004); Muriel R. Gillick, Medicare Coverage for Technological Innovations: Time for New Criteria?, 350 New Eng. J. Med. 2199 (2004); Janet L. Dolgin, Unhealthy Determinations: Controlling "Medical Necessity," 22 Va. J. Soc. Pol'y & L. 435 (2015).

For those who are interested in **appeals procedures** (note 2), a fairly detailed overview can be found on the Web site for this book, www.health-law.org. There is also substantial scholarly commentary. The most prolific author on these topics is Professor Eleanor Kinney. *See* Eleanor Kinney, The Accidental Administrative Law of the Medicare Program, 15 Yale J. Health Pol'y L. & Ethics 111 (2015); Eleanor Kinney ed., Guide to Medicare Coverage Decision-Making and Appeals (2002); Eleanor D. Kinney, Medicare Coverage Decision-Making and Appeal Procedures, 60 Wash. & Lee L. Rev. 1461 (2003); Eleanor Kinney, Rule and Policy Making Under the Medicaid Program: A Challenge to Federalism, 51 Ohio St. L. J. 855 (1991). For general and comprehensive overviews, see also Diane Hoffmann & Virginia Rowthorn, Achieving Quality and Responding to Consumers: The Medicare Beneficiary Complaint Process, 5 Ind. Health L. Rev. 9 (2008); Maxwell Mehlman & Karen Visocan, Medicare and Medicaid: Are They Just Health Care Systems?, 29 Hous. L. Rev. 835 (1992).

For in-depth commentary and analysis, with both theoretical and philosophical analyses and numerous suggestions for improvement on the full range of these procedural issues, see Eleanor D. Kinney, Protecting American Health Care Consumers (2002); Aaron Kesselheim, What's the Appeal? Trying to Control Managed Care Medical Necessity Decisionmaking Through a System of External Appeals, 149 U. Pa. L. Rev. 873 (2001); Nan D. Hunter, Risk Governance and Deliberative Democracy in Health Care, 97 Geo. L. J. 1 (2008); Meir Katz, Towards a New Moral Paradigm in Health Care Delivery, 36 Am. J. L. & Med. 78 (2010); Won Bok Lee, Recalibrating "Experimental Treatment Exclusion": An Empirical Analysis, 83 U. Cin. L. Rev. 171 (2014).

For commentary **generally supportive of the *Bechtold* point of view** (note 4), see Mark Hall & Gerard Anderson, Health Insurers' Assessment of Medical Necessity, 140 U. Pa. L. Rev. 1637 (1992); Richard Saver, Reimbursing New Technologies: Why Are the Courts Judging Experimental Medicine?, 44 Stan. L. Rev. 1095 (1992). For **contrasting commentary, supportive of *Zorek***, see David Frankford, Food Allergy and the Health Care Financing Administration: A Story of Rage, 1 Widener L. Symp. J. 159 (1996); Sara Rosenbaum et al., Who Should Determine When Health Care Is Medically Necessary?, 340 New Eng. J. Med. 229 (1999). For **an international perspective**, see Timothy Jost, Health Care Coverage Determinations: An International Comparative Study (2004). For thorough analysis of medical, legal, and health policy issues relating to **bone marrow transplants**, see Richard A. Rettig, False Hope vs. Evidence-Based Medicine: Bone Marrow Transplantation and Breast Cancer (2005); Peter Jacobson et al., Litigating the Science of Breast Cancer Treatment, 32 J. Health Pol. Pol'y & L. 785 (2007). Considering the facts of *Zorek*, it is interesting to note that "stomach-stapling" **surgeries for obesity** constitute a growing area of dispute and litigation. See Mark A. Hall, State Regulation of Medical Necessity: The Case of Weight-Reduction Surgery, 53 Duke L. J. 653 (2004); Manny v. Central States, Southeast and Southwest Areas Pension and Health Welfare Funds, 388 F.3d 247 (7th Cir. 2004) (Posner, J.).

For discussions of **how ERISA shapes the interpretation of insurance contracts** (notes 6 and 7), see John H. Langbein, Trust Law as Regulatory Law: The *UNUM/ Provident* Scandal and Judicial Review of Benefit Denials Under ERISA, 101 Nw. U. L. Rev. 1315 (2007); Timothy Jost, "*MetLife v. Glenn*": The Court Addresses a Conflict over Conflicts in ERISA Benefit Administration, 27 Health Aff. w430 (2008); Roy Harmon & A. G. Harmon, Weighing Medical Judgments, 13 Mich. St. U. J. Med. & L. 157 (2009); Maria Hylton, Post-*Firestone* Skirmishes: "Obama Care," Discretionary Clauses and Judicial Review of ERISA Plan Administrator Decisions, 10 Wm. & Mary Pol'y Rev. 1 (2010); Mark Hall et al., Judicial Protection of Managed Care Consumers: An Empirical Study of Insurance Coverage Disputes, 26 Seton Hall L. J. 1055 (1996).

For general analysis of **which institutional actor should make coverage decisions** (note 8), see Mark A. Hall, Making Medical Spending Decisions ch.3 (1997); David Hsia, Benefits Determination Under Health Care Reform: Who Should Decide Coverage Policy?, 15 J. Leg. Med. 533 (1994).

For articles taking a **therapeutic jurisprudence or a legal process approach to analyzing coverage disputes** (note 9), see Kathy Cerminara, Dealing with Dying: How Insurers Can Help Patients Seeking Last-Chance Therapies (Even When the Answer Is "No"), 15 Health Matrix 285 (2005); Nan D. Hunter, Managed Process, Due Care: Structures of Accountability in Health Care, 6 Yale J. Health Pol'y L. & Ethics 93 (2006); Charity Scott, Therapeutic Approaches to Conflict Resolution in Health Care Settings, 21 Ga. St. U. L. Rev. 797 (2005).

For discussions of **paying for clinical medical research** (note 11), see Sandra J. Carnahan, Medicare's Coverage with Study Participation Policy: Clinical Trials or Tribulations?, 7 Yale J. Health Pol'y L. & Ethics 229 (2007); Mark Barnes & Jerald Korn, Medicare Reimbursement for Clinical Trial Services, 38 J. Health L. 609 (2005); Dina Berlyn, Routine Patient Care in Clinical Trials: Whose Cost Is It Anyway?, 16 J. L. & Health 78 (2003); Earl Steinberg et al., Insurance Coverage for Experimental Technologies, 14(4) Health Aff. 143 (Nov. 1995); Mark B. McClellan & Sean R. Tunis, Medicare Coverage of ICDs, 352 New Eng. J. Med. 222 (2005).

Notes: Peer Review Organizations and Utilization Review

1. *Medicare Peer Review.* The very first section of the Medicare statute prohibits any federal "supervision or control over the practice of medicine." 42 U.S.C. §1395. Despite this guarantee of physician autonomy, someone obviously has to scrutinize the necessity of the medical services Medicare pays for. For many years, Medicare used the mechanism of physician peer review—that is, doctors monitoring themselves—to reconcile the principle of noninterference with the need for judging medical necessity. But the peer review organizations (PROs) that Congress established to carry out that function failed to save any money and provoked intense physician blowback. See Timothy Jost, Policing Cost Containment: The Medicare Peer Review Organization Program, 14 Puget Sound L. Rev. 483 (1991).

Over time, PROs have moved away from peer review and refocused their efforts on quality improvement. In 2002, Medicare even began referring to them as Quality Improvement Organizations (QIOs). QIOs serve as government-sponsored consultants that partner with health care organizations—in particular, hospitals and nursing homes—to share data, teach best practices, and offer technical support. The QIOs bear little resemblance to the utilization-review entities that Congress once envisioned. See Nicholas Bagley, Bedside Bureaucrats: Why Medicare Reform Hasn't Worked, 101 Geo L. J. 519, 535 (2013).

2. *UR: Friend or Foe?* In the 1990s, private insurers pursued "utilization review" (UR) much more thoroughly and aggressively than they had in prior decades, leading to a backlash from physicians and patients. Consider the following:

> In the predawn hours of March 27, 1993, Esther Nesbitt was working the night shift at Kaiser's nurse hotline. She had been a nurse for 20 years, working in New York City emergency rooms early in her career. . . . On Nesbitt's desk was a *Manual of Pediatric Protocols*, including a three-page tip sheet entitled "Fever." The tip sheet was arranged much like a set of college notes, with a nine-line definition of fever at the top, an explanation of fever's causes, and only then a series of questions that parents should be asked. Down near the bottom of the first page, ninth in a list of 11 questions, was a question that many emergency-room doctors would pose right away: "Is [the] child having problems breathing?"
>
> From her perch at Kaiser's offices, Nesbitt decided after a few minutes that little James Adams wasn't in respiratory distress. . . . There would be no ambulance called, no authorization for the family to seek the closest hospital. Kaiser had given its instructions. It was up to Lamona Adams to stand in her driveway, holding her baby in the dark, and wait for her husband to come home. [The couple drove 40 miles through a severe rain storm to reach the hospital designated by Kaiser. At that point, their baby had stopped breathing. He turned out to have meningitis, a severe but easily treatable infection when caught in time. With aggressive treatment, the doctors saved his life, but they had to amputate all his hands and feet because of damage to his circulatory system.]

George Anders, Health Against Wealth: HMOs and the Breakdown of Medical Trust (1996). And, consider this physician's view:

> To call myself a vascular surgeon, I had to do well in college, then spend the next 12 years working grueling hours, depriving myself of most of the joys of young adulthood and immersing myself in other people's worst misery. . . . I now have an army of vindictive bureaucrats and largely untrained reviewers nipping at my heels, and must spend many hours a week defending myself against their overwhelmingly wrongheaded second-guessing of clinical decisions.

Stephen D. Leonard, M.D., Letter to the Editor, N.Y. Times, Apr. 28, 1992, at A16.

3. *The Legality of Prior Authorization.* Nowadays, utilization review is more often conducted on a prospective basis, prior to treatment, than as part of ordinary insurance claims review. As a result, decisions to deny coverage are likely to result in denial of treatment as well. Those denials of treatment can give rise to tort liability as well as contractual liability. The materials in Chapters 2.B.3 and 4.F consider whether physicians and hospitals are permitted to refuse treatment based on lack of insurance coverage, and whether insurers are responsible in tort when doing so leads to medical injury.

The legality of UR can also be challenged under regulatory and contract law. Because coverage denials affect treatment decisions, utilization review might be characterized as an illegal interference with medical judgment. This might occur, for instance, if the utilization reviewer making a medical necessity determination is not a licensed physician in the relevant state. The usual process is for nonmedical personnel to review coverage requests with screening criteria that flag certain requests for review by a nurse. The nurse then decides which cases to refer for physician review. Usually the request is not denied without physician review, but the physician may be in some central office out of state, and usually is not trained in the particular specialty involved, unless the insurer decides to refer the request for independent review.

Courts generally have upheld this process when challenged based on medical licensure or on general principles of interference with medical judgment. They reason that utilization reviewers do not purport to make medical treatment decisions, only payment decisions. See Morris v. District of Columbia Board of Medicine, 701 A.2d 364 (D.C. 1997) (reviewing medical appropriateness for an insurance company does not constitute the practice of medicine); Association of American Physicians and Surgeons v. Weinberger, 395 F. Supp. 125 (N.D. Ill. 1975) (three-judge court), aff'd mem., 423 U.S. 975 (1975) (medical necessity review under Medicare does not unduly interfere with physicians' judgment). But see Murphy v. Board of Medical Examiners, 949 P.2d 530 (Ariz. Ct. App. 1997) (medical licensing board has jurisdiction over insurance company doctor who allegedly exercised bad medical judgment in denying claims); State Board of Registration for Healing Arts v. Fallon, 41 S.W.3d 474 (Mo. 2001) (same). Might a utilization review requirement that denies coverage unless the patient obtains advance approval be struck down as an illegal forfeiture or penalty clause under contract law? Consider a case where it is clear the request would have been approved if submitted but the insurer denies payment simply because the patient or doctor did not follow the proper channels. Nazay v. Miller, 949 F.2d 1323, 1335 (3d Cir. 1991) (upholding insurer under ERISA, but only where the failure to obtain advance permission cost the patient a 30 percent co-payment, not complete denial of coverage).

Legal oversight of UR has resulted more through legislation than through judicial doctrine. Utilization review regulations now exist in most states. They require insurers and third-party UR firms to maintain proper licensure and expertise of personnel (including M.D.s licensed in the state), to give a prompt response to coverage requests, and sometimes to disclose the screening criteria they use.

4. *The Success of UR.* Research shows that cost-savings from UR are modest. Utilization review successfully reduces hospitalization expenses, but savings overall are muted by the administrative expense of running these programs. See Uwe Reinhardt, Spending More Through Cost Control: Our Obsessive Quest to Gut the Hospital, 15(2) Health Aff. 145 (May 1996); M. Shapiro & N. Wenger, Rethinking Utilization Review, 333 New Eng. J. Med. 1353 (1995). This anemic performance, coupled with the public and professional backlash UR engenders, has caused health insurers to cut back on the amount of UR they do.

5. *Further Readings.* For **narrative accounts** of the maddening logic and personal impact of medical necessity determinations, see Andrew Batavia, Of Wheelchairs and Managed Care, 18(6) Health Aff. 171 (Nov. 1999); Lisa Iezzoni, Boundaries, 18(6) Health Aff. 171 (Nov. 1999); Margaret Gilhooley, Broken Back: A Patient's Reflections on the Process of Medical Necessity Determinations, 40 Vill. L. Rev. 153 (1995) (a law professor's personal account of an insurer that "evicted" her from the hospital); Gerald Grumet, Health Care Rationing Through Inconvenience,

31 New Eng. J. Med. 607 (1989) (railing against the "managerial-review process in which armies of claims clerks, administrators, auditors, form processors, peer reviewers, functionaries, and technocrats of every description insinuate themselves into a complex system that authorizes, pays for and delivers medical care"). For a more neutral and academic account of how health insurance medical directors go about their work, see Thomas Bodenheimer & Lawrence Casalino, Executives with White Coats—The Work and World View of Managed-Care Medical Directors, 341 New Eng. J. Med. 1945 (1999). For the view from an actual medical director, see S. D. Boren, I Had a Tough Day Today, Hillary, 330 New Eng. J. Med. 500 (1994).

On the **legal oversight of utilization review** (note 3), see Gail Agrawal, Resuscitating Professionalism: Self-Regulation in the Medical Marketplace, 66 Mo. L. Rev. 341 (2001); Edward P. Richards, The Police Power and the Regulation of Medical Practice: A Historical Review and Guide for Medical Licensing Board Regulation of Physicians in ERISA-Qualified Managed Care Organizations, 8 Ann. Health L. 201 (1999); David L. Treuman, The Liability of Medical Directors for Utilization Review Decisions, 35 J. Health L. 105 (2002).

Problem: Choosing Health Insurance

From what you have learned so far, which of the following insurance plans do you personally prefer, assuming each one costs the same? Defend your choice (both your selection and rejections) with reasons drawn from these readings:

- Plan A: Covers the full range of medical care, subject to standard medical necessity or experimental exclusions, without any deductibles or co-payments, but you must receive all care at an HMO clinic where doctors are paid a bonus for saving money.
- Plan B: Excludes mental health services, but covers the rest of the normal range of medical care, subject to a $250 deductible and 20 percent co-payment up to a maximum of $2,000 per year. Your choice of doctor, but all expensive treatments must be submitted for prior approval by the insurer to determine medical appropriateness.
- Plan C: Covers the full range of medical care, with no major exclusions and your choice of doctor, and no prior authorization requirement, but subject to a $4,000 deductible.
- Plan D: Coverage is defined in an approach similar to the Oregon plan, but using 5,000 specific categories of inclusion and exclusion taken from the latest practice guidelines based on medical research, as selected by a national panel of politically appointed experts. No other restrictions or financial limitations.

E. PROVIDER REIMBURSEMENT

We now shift from patients to providers. Providers are affected by health insurance not only in who and what it covers, but also in how they are paid for services that are covered. The following materials reveal that various methods of provider reimbursement are important in all three arenas of legal practice: litigation, business planning, and public policy.

■ HEALTH PLAN*
Alain Enthoven
1980

Most people think of the need for medical care as an insurable event, very similar to insured hurricane or automobile collision damage. You are either sick or well. If you are sick, you go to the doctor. The doctor diagnoses your illness, applies the standard treatment, and sends the bill for his or her "usual, customary, and reasonable fee," all or most of which is paid by your insurance company. Our entire Blue Cross-Blue Shield and commercial insurance system was built on that view of the problem. Medicare and Medicaid, the public insurance systems for the elderly and poor, were built on the same model. The consequence is a financial disaster. Our society has accepted the casualty insurance model for health care financing, only to find that it contributes to excessive and excessively costly care. . . .

Many people seem to think that medical care is like mechanical engineering—that for each medical condition there is a "best treatment," a "professional standard." It is up to the doctor to know that treatment and use it. People do not fully understand the great uncertainties that pervade medical care and the variety of acceptable treatments. They think of medical care as mostly treatment for acute life-threatening conditions, as if it were accurately represented by the television dramas about the emergency room. Based on these misconceptions, we have applied to medical care a financing system that was developed for casualty (fire and collision) insurance.

The ideal case for casualty insurance is one in which the damage is caused by an act of God and the cost of repair can be determined objectively. In such a case the financial incentives inherent in insurance do not play a significant role in either the incidence of damage or the cost of repair. Insurance of houses against hurricane damage or fires caused by lightning does not bring on more storms. Collision insurance for automobiles fits the model tolerably, but much less well. Most people do not drive less carefully just because they have insurance. But those who do have insurance are likely to demand more and better repairs than those who do not—because someone else is paying the bill. Still, ordinarily, having your collision-damaged car repaired is not an open-ended task.

Medical insurance hardly fits the model at all. The element of judgment and choice in the decision to seek care and in the amount of care provided is too great. Caring for a patient can be open-ended, especially if he or she has a chronic disease. Uncertainty pervades medical diagnosis and treatment. In most cases, there is not one correct or standard treatment. There may be several accepted therapies: Most medical care is not a matter of life and death, but rather of darker or lighter shades of grey concerning the quality of life. . . .

When thinking about medical care, then, we should think in terms of a variety of legitimate treatments for each condition, with their relative merits in a particular case depending on the unique circumstances and values of the people involved. We should remember that there is pervasive uncertainty and that medicine is more an art based on judgment than a science based on calculation. Medical care deals more with the quality of life than with the quantity (length) of life. The "product" does not come in standard units. Medical care is a matter of subtle and complex judgments about more versus less, and more may often not be better. . . .

In view of this, it should not be surprising that the institutional arrangements for providing care, including the financial incentives facing the doctor, are very important. The casualty insurance model does not fit medical care at all well, because making more care free to the patient and remunerative to the doctor leads to more, and more costly, care being demanded and provided. . . .

To observe that financial incentives play an important role in the use of medical services is not to imply that they are the only, or even the most important, factor. Physicians are concerned primarily with curing their sick patients, regardless of the cost. That ethic has been instilled in them through years of arduous training. Many take a failure to cure a sick patient as a personal defeat. When we are sick, we want our doctors to be concerned with curing us and nothing else. Physicians and other health professionals are also motivated by a desire to achieve professional excellence and the esteem of their peers and the public. But their use of resources is inevitably shaped by financial incentives. Physicians who survive and prosper must ultimately do what brings in money and curtail those activities that lose money. . . .

■ REIMBURSING PHYSICIANS AND HOSPITALS*
Thomas Bodenheimer & Kevin Grumbach
272 JAMA 971 (1994)

During the course of a typical day, many physicians experience four or five distinct types of reimbursement. In this article, we describe the different ways by which physicians and hospitals are paid. Although reimbursement has many facets, from determinations of prices to processing of claims, we focus our discussion on one of its most basic elements: establishing the unit of payment. This unit-of-payment taxonomy is essential for understanding such concepts as managed care and physician-borne "risk," concepts that feature prominently in many health system reform proposals.[12]

---

* Copyright © 1994, American Medical Association.

12. [See also Robert Berenson et al., Payment Methods: How they Work (Urban Institute, June 2016).]

Units of Payment in Order of Least to Most Aggregated

Payee	Procedure	Day	Episode of Illness	Patient	Time
Physician	Fee for service	Not applicable	Surgical or obstetric fee or physician diagnosis related group	Capitation	Salary
Hospital	Fee for service	Per diem	Hospital diagnosis related group	Capitation	Global budget

Methods of payment lie along a continuum that extends from the least to the most aggregated unit. Under fee-for-service reimbursement, the unit of payment is the visit or procedure. All other reimbursement modes aggregate or bundle together several services into one unit of payment. Reimbursement by episode of illness pays physicians or hospitals one sum for all services delivered during one illness, for example, global surgical fees to physicians and DRGs for hospitals. Per diem payments to hospitals bundle all services delivered to a patient during one day. A further bundling of services is accomplished by capitation payment, in which one payment is made for each patient's treatment during a month or year. Capitation payment is generally associated with managed care. Payment based on all services delivered to all patients within a certain period includes global budget reimbursement of hospitals and salaried payment of physicians. . . .

1. Open-Ended Reimbursement

◼ ALLEN v. CLARIAN HEALTH PARTNERS, INC.
980 N.E.2d 306 (Ind. 2012)

Rucker, Justice.
. . . Abby Allen . . . sought medical treatment at Clarian North Hospital, a hospital owned by Clarian Health Partners, Inc. ("Clarian"). Before receiving treatment Allen, who is uninsured and not covered by Medicare or Medicaid, signed a form contract drafted by Clarian under which she agreed to pay all charges associated with her treatment. The contract did not specify a dollar amount for services rendered, but provided that Allen "guarantees payment of the account." Clarian provided medical treatment to Allen and then billed its "chargemaster" rates* for

---

* [A chargemaster is a comprehensive list of a hospital's prices for each of its many thousands of different services. See the casebook Web site for examples. — Eds.]

medical services and supplies in the amount of $15,641.64. [Plaintiffs' class action complaint] alleges breach of contract and seeks declaratory judgment, namely, that rates the hospital bills its uninsured patients are unreasonable and unenforceable. According to the complaint, if Allen had been insured then Clarian would have accepted $7,308.78 for the same services and supplies. The complaint alleges that Clarian charges only uninsured patients the chargemaster rates, while "[i]nsured patients and Medicare/Medicaid patients pay significantly discounted rates for the same services and supplies."

[The trial court granted the hospital's motion to dismiss, but the Court of Appeals reversed, holding] that because the contract did not contain a price term the reasonable value of services should be implied, and the issue of reasonableness requires resolution by a fact-finder. We disagree with our colleagues, and . . . we now affirm the [dismissal by] the trial court. . . .

. . . The provision of the contract at issue provides in relevant part: "In consideration of services delivered by Clarian North Medical Center and/or the physicians, the undersigned guarantees payment of the account, and agrees to pay the same upon discharge if such account is not paid by a private or governmental insurance carrier." . . .

We agree that if a contract is uncertain as to a material term such as price then Indiana courts may impute a reasonable price. . . . Restatement (Second) of Contracts § 33 (recognizing that in order to give effect to a contract, its terms must be "reasonably certain"). But "[a]n offer which appears to be indefinite may be given precision by usage of trade or by course of dealing between the parties." Id., cmt. a. A contract need not declare a specific a dollar amount for goods or services in order to be enforceable. See id. ("A telephones to his grocer, 'Send me a ten-pound bag of flour.' The grocer sends it. A has thereby promised to pay the grocer's current price therefor.").

In the context of contracts providing for health care services precision concerning price is close to impossible. As the Third Circuit has recognized, omitting a specific dollar figure is "the only practical way in which the obligations of the patient to pay can be set forth, given the fact that nobody yet knows just what condition the patient has, and what treatments will be necessary to remedy what ails him or her." DiCarlo v. St. Mary Hosp., 530 F.3d 255, 264 (3d Cir. 2008). And a leading scholarly article on the subject—while advocating for courts to "shelter" patients in the health care market—recognizes that "courts have generally tolerated low levels of specificity in medical contracts." Mark A. Hall and Carl E. Schneider, Patients as Consumers: Courts, Contracts, and the New Medical Marketplace, 106 Mich. L. Rev. 643, 646, 674 (2008).

In the context of a contract for the provision of and payment for medical services, a hospital's chargemaster rates serve as the basis for its pricing. Each hospital sets its own chargemaster rates, thus each hospital's chargemaster is unique. It is from these chargemaster prices that insurance companies negotiate with hospitals for discounts for their policyholders. . . . Many courts have addressed contracts similar to those of [plaintiffs'] and most have held that price terms in these contracts, while imprecise, are not sufficiently indefinite to justify imposition of a "reasonable" price standard. For example, the Third Circuit held that a patient's promise to pay "all charges and collection costs for services rendered" was not indefinite, and "can only refer to [the hospital's] uniform charges set forth in its Chargemaster."

Other courts have reached similar conclusions. But see Doe v. HCA Health Svcs. of Tenn., Inc., 46 S.W.3d 191, 197 (Tenn. 2001) (holding that a patient's agreement to be "financially responsible to the hospital for charges not covered by" insurance contained an indefinite price term . . .). We align ourselves with those courts that have recognized the uniqueness of the market for health care services delivered by hospitals. . . .

■ AN AMERICAN SICKNESS (2017)
Elisabeth Rosenthal

A BRIEF HISTORY OF MEDICAL CODING

Medical coding is a cryptic and constantly evolving numerical language through which the things that are done to you in a hospital or other medical office are expressed on claims and bills. (In one version called Current Procedural Terminology, or CPT, CPT 35476 means "repair venous blockage using a balloon catheter" and CPT 35475 means "repair arterial blockage," for example.)

Medical coding and coders like ours essentially don't exist in any other healthcare system. . . . A detailed itemized bill for a hip replacement in Belgium . . . is not hard to understand, even though it is in Flemish: "Twoopersoonskamer [two-bedded room] = 329 Euro / Implantaten [implant parts] = 1621, 1195 and 209 Euro." An itemized bill for the same operation at many hospitals in the United States would likely total over $100,000 and run dozens of pages, each filled with medical terminology and numerical codes you couldn't possibly comprehend. . . . .

In 1948 the World Health Organization took over stewardship . . . [of coding by creating] the International Statistical Classification of Diseases, Injuries and Causes of Death (ICD). The codes became an invaluable tool, a common language for epidemiologists and statisticians to use when tracking the world's afflictions. But in the United States, the codes gradually took on a bedrock financial function as the basis for medical billing. In 1979 the U.S. government decided to use ICD codes in adjudicating Medicare and Medicaid claims, with some modifications added specifically for that business purpose, so the U.S. version is called ICD-CM. Other insurers followed. In multiple volumes, the U.S. version not only categorized and number-coded diagnoses but also introduced codes for procedures.

The financial stakes in coding are high. If you code for "heart failure" (ICD-9-CM code 428) when you could code for "acute systolic heart failure" (code 428.21), the difference is thousands of dollars. According to a coding professional, "In order to code for the more lucrative code, you have to know how it is defined and make sure the care described in the chart meets the criterion, the definition, for that higher number." . . . Submitting a bill using the higher code without meeting those criteria could constitute fraud. The coders who work for hospitals strive to get money. The coders employed by insurers try to deny claims as overreaching. Coders who audit Medicare charts look for abuses that need to be punished.

Suddenly coding meant big bucks and a new industry thrived. For-profit colleges began offering medical coding degrees, and required internships soon followed. There are three different alphanumeric coding languages . . . and each is as different from the other as Chinese is from Russian and Russian is from French.

As a result, different degree tracks were necessary, along with professional exams, certifications, and licensure offered by competing professional organizations. . . . Highly skilled coders have contributed to higher costs for patients, because the salaries of this new layer of professionals and their years of education are reflected in our medical bills.

The international ICD system has created codes for novel diseases—Lyme disease, AIDS, and SARS —as well as for conditions like obesity, which was not considered a disease state until 2013. Until obesity was labeled a disease and had codes assigned to it, insurers in the United States could not be obligated to pay for its treatment as a medical condition. Because, in the United States, codes define not just disease states but also the procedures and treatments that the medical profession can sell, providers, insurers, and regulators lobby for and fight over each code rule and revision. Having your code as part of the lexicon matters.

In 1996, Medicare . . . made it clear that certain [procedure] codes couldn't appear on the same bill because they were inherently part of the same procedure. . . . As a rule, an anesthesiologist could not, for example, separately bill for anesthesia and checking your oxygen level during your surgery. One subsumed the other. But the government created modifier 59—a code that could be appended to other codes to allow doctors to take exceptions to that rule in rare cases. Modifier 59 could be deployed to allow for two payments in certain situations, such as when an oncology nurse needed to insert two separate IVs—one to administer chemotherapy and another because the patient appeared to be dehydrated.

And the games began.

An investigation by the HHS OIG in 2005 found massive evidence of modifier 59 abuse. Forty percent of code pairs billed with modifier 59 in 2003 weren't kosher, resulting in $59 million in overpayment. . . .

Instead of resolving the problem, [Medicare's] attempts at clarification simply created a secondary business of even more advanced coding consultants, who advised other coders as well as healthcare providers and taught courses that covered the nitty-gritty of insurers' reimbursement policies. For example, an ER doctor learned that insurers would accept a better-reimbursed code for the examination and treatment of a patient with a finger fracture (usually 99282) if a narcotic painkiller was prescribed (bump up to 99283). With that type of guidance, some surgeons stopped suturing wounds shut after their operations and instead handed off to another doctor, say, a plastic surgeon, who could therefore code and charge separately. . . .

The latest iteration of international disease codes, ICD-10, was completed in 1992 and has been used by the rest of the world for decades. Why did it take the United States until 2015 to fully deploy it? The problem was that the United States' medical billing system, and how to game it, evolved based on ICD-9. . . . Because adopting the new system in the United States would require new billing software and require every coder to go back to class, the medical industry convinced Medicare to delay adopting ICD-10 year after year. Doctors' groups warned that switching to the new system would lead to a "catastrophic" number of "unpaid Medicare claims." When it finally came into use—uneventfully—in late 2015, it created some headaches for doctors and a burst of new business for coding consultants.

Notes: Cost-Based and UCR Reimbursement

1. *Price Discrimination and Sliding Scales.* Are you surprised that Clarian Hospital bills its uninsured patients twice what it agrees to accept from patients with private insurance? This is also typical for many physicians, especially specialists. In fact, many hospitals (and some specialists) charge uninsured patients or those who are out of network three or four times what they agree to accept from insured patients, for exactly the same services. Hospitals, of course, view the insurance price as a discount, rather than the uninsured price as a mark-up, but either way, the gap between nominal charges and actual payments has widened greatly over recent years.

Based on this gap, some courts, including even the Indiana Supreme Court, have refused to measure the medical costs owed to tort victims based on hospitals' full charges, reasoning that almost no one actually pays these inflated prices. For instance, in *Stanley v. Walker,* 906 N.E.2d 852, 856-857 (Ind. 2009), the court explained:

> As more medical providers are paid under fixed payment arrangements, . . . hospital charge structures have become less correlated to hospital operations and actual payments. The Lewin Group, A Study of Hospital Charge Setting Practices i (2005). Currently, the relationship between charges and costs is "tenuous at best." In fact, *hospital executives reportedly admit that most charges have "no relation to anything, and certainly not to cost."* Hall [& Schneider], Patients as Consumers, 106 Mich. L. Rev. at 665. [Internal Footnote 3: *Indeed, amicus in this case, the Insurance Institute of Indiana, Inc., flatly says "charges billed by health care providers are effectively irrelevant to the value of the services provided. . . ."*] Thus, based on the realities of health care finance, we are unconvinced that the reasonable value of medical services is necessarily represented by either the amount actually paid or the amount stated in the original medical bill. . . .

The *Allen* court, however, held that this tort law precedent should not govern a contract action. In effect, uninsured patients are held to their agreement to pay anything that hospitals care to charge, even if the prices admittedly are unreasonable.

2. *Reasonable Costs.* When Medicare and Medicaid were first adopted in 1965, they aimed to cover hospitals' reasonable costs:

> "Reasonable cost" reimbursement, or reimbursement based on a provider's cost, means simply that the payment made to a hospital for services rendered to Medicare or Medicaid patients is calculated to reimburse the hospital for its expenses, or costs, incurred in providing such services. . . . [B]ecause the approach, as originally employed, contained a guarantee that costs incurred by a hospital would be recouped, hospitals had a clear incentive to expand services and increase costs to meet anticipated new demand, and had no incentives under the reimbursement methodology to control costs. The methodology itself was inherently inflationary in its impact on the payment obligations of the Medicare and Medicaid programs. It substantially increased the pressure to increase costs that was a function of the expanded entitlement to health care created by the programs themselves. [As a result, the annual rate of increase in both charges and costs for hospital rooms doubled in the five years following 1965, compared to the rate of increase in prior years.]

The decision to base Medicare and Medicaid reimbursement on "reasonable cost" reflected congressional concern that hospitals would be unwilling to participate voluntarily in those programs unless adequate reimbursement were assured. The approach did succeed in attracting the voluntary participation of most American hospitals. But the introduction of the Medicare and Medicaid programs stands as an example of the fiscal dangers inherent in a program that rapidly measures entitlement to services without, at the same time, taking strong measures to contain the cost impact of that expansion. . . .

Stephen M. Weiner, "Reasonable Cost" Reimbursement For Inpatient Hospital Services Under Medicare And Medicaid, 3 Am. J. L. & Med. 1 (1977).

3. *Other Litigation, and Historical Practices.* A series of class action lawsuits challenged whether this type of price discrimination is appropriate for tax-exempt "charitable" hospitals. Most courts favored the hospitals, based on a variety of somewhat technical concerns about the appropriateness of a class action and the novelty of the particular theories of liability. Beverly Cohen, The Controversy over Hospital Charges to the Uninsured—No Villains, No Heroes, 51 Vill. L. Rev. 95-148 (2006). However, the Affordable Care Act has an important new provision that requires charitable hospitals to limit charges to low-income uninsured patients eligible to no more than the lowest amounts that insurers pay.

Pharmaceutical companies have also been sued for inflating or misstating their prices. These challenges also sometimes founder on appeal, due to a variety of technical legal deficiencies in the cases. See, e.g., Astra USA v. Santa Clara County, 131 S. Ct. 1342 (2011); AstraZeneca v. Alabama, 41 So. 3d 15 (Ala. 2006). However, at least one large class action has resulted in a multi-million-dollar award. Blue Cross Blue Shield of Massachusetts v. AstraZeneca Pharmaceuticals, 582 F.3d 156 (1st Cir. 2009).

Historically, prior to widespread health insurance, physicians employed much more socially progressive forms of sliding fee scales by charging wealthy patients several times more than middle- or lower-income patients. Courts endorsed and enforced this practice, but it disappeared in the 1960s when insurers began to demand consistent pricing. See Mark A. Hall, Paying for What You Get, and Getting What You Pay For, 69 Law & Contemp. Probs. 159 (Autumn 2006); Spencer v. West, 126 So. 2d 423 (La. Ct. App. 1960); Eagle v. Snyder, 604 A.2d 253 (Pa. Super. Ct. 1992); Annot., 97 A.L.R.2d 1232 (1964).

Economists explain that physicians and hospitals would not be able to vary their charges this widely unless they possessed substantial market or monopoly power over patients without managed care insurance. What do you think is the likely source of this power? Concerns about market power have grown more acute in recent years, which have seen a sharp increase in hospital consolidation. Deploying a widely used economic metric, researchers have demonstrated that roughly half of all hospital markets are highly concentrated and another third are moderately concentrated. See David M. Cutler & Fiona Scott Morton, Hospitals, Market Share, and Consolidation, 310 JAMA 1964, 1969 (2013).

4. *Medical Debt and Bankruptcy.* Widespread practices of charging substantially more than what insurance will pay, and then aggressively pursuing collection of unpaid bills, is one reason medical debt is a leading cause of personal bankruptcies. Even patients with insurance can get stuck with huge bills because, if they seek care out of network, they are not protected by the deep discounts negotiated by insurers and therefore are obligated to pay the portion of full charges that the insurer does

not cover. Realize also that, under the common-law "necessaries doctrine," family members might be responsible for a patient's unpaid bills. E.g., Forsyth Memorial Hospital v. Chisholm, 467 S.E.2d 88 (N.C. 1996) (separation does not excuse husband's obligation to pay for wife unless hospital had actual notice at the time).

5. *Surprise Bills.* As network restrictions grow tighter, physicians and other providers have taken steps to retain their ability to charge high prices. Other portions of Elisabeth Rosenthal's book, and her reporting for the New York Times, document one apparently burgeoning practice of "drive-by doctoring," where physicians and other medical professionals assist an in-network physician or hospital in providing care. When the assisting providers are outside the patient's network, they can charge exorbitant fees for their assistance—without the patient ever realizing that she received out-of-network care. A similar problem arises when a patient goes to an in-network emergency room that is staffed exclusively by out-of-network physicians or arranges surgery with an in-network surgeon and hospital but does not realize that the anesthesiologist has refused to join the network. In specialties where patients have no real ability to pick their doctor (such as anesthesia or emergency care), physicians increasingly are refusing to give insurance plans any substantial discounts, opting instead to remain outside of most or all networks.

Some state legislatures are pushing back. In March 2014, New York passed a law limiting what out-of-network doctors can charge when they work at an in-network facility or where an in-network doctor refers a patient to their care. See N.Y. Pub. Health Law §24. California and Florida enacted similar laws in 2016. See Cal. Assembly Bill No. 72 (2016); Fla. House Bill 221 (2016). Because of ERISA preemption, however, these new state laws do not apply to self-insured employer health plans.

6. *A Rose by Any Other Name.* Rosenthal also documents another anomaly of medical billing: When treatment is at hospital-based outpatient departments, health insurance typically pays both a physician fee and a facility fee, which usually results in a substantially higher payment than if the same service were provided in an ordinary physician's office. "Dr. Ronald Anderson, a Pennsylvania rheumatologist, can inject a bursa with painkillers in his office for about $80. (Bursas are fluid-filled sacs that reduce friction around joints. When they become temporarily inflamed it is called bursitis.) But when one of his patients had the condition treated by an orthopedist at a surgicenter with ultrasound guidance, the bill was almost $5,000, most of which the insurance company paid." Elisabeth Rosenthal, An American Sickness 38 (2017). This disparity has helped to fuel the rapid growth in hospitals' employment of specialists—which not only drives up medical costs, but also exposes patients to more cost burden, since deductibles and co-payments are often substantially higher for treatment at hospital outpatient clinics than at physicians' offices.

7. *Health Insurance Fraud.* More than just inflated prices, health insurance has given rise to fraudulent or abusive billing practices that, under both public and private insurance, are estimated to cost many tens of billions of dollars each year. In the most classic form, consider the following form of Medicaid fraud:

> Nursing facilities represent convenient resident "pools" and make it lucrative for unscrupulous persons to carry out fraudulent schemes. The [Office of Inspector General (OIG)] has become aware of a number of fraudulent schemes . . . by which health care providers, including medical professionals, inappropriately bill

Medicare and Medicaid for the provision of unnecessary services and services which were not provided at all. . . . Some examples follow: One physician improperly billed $350,000 over a two-year period for comprehensive physical examinations of residents without ever seeing a single resident. A psychotherapist working in nursing facilities manipulated Medicare billing codes to charge for three hours of therapy for each resident when, in fact, he spent only a few minutes with each resident. . . . The OIG has learned about podiatrists whose entire practices consist of visits to nursing facilities. Noncovered routine care is provided, e.g., toenail clipping, but Medicare is billed for . . . toenail removals, a service that is covered but not frequently or routinely needed. . . . Investigators discovered one resident for whom bills were submitted claiming a total of 11 toenail removals.

DHHS Office of Inspector General, Special Fraud Alert: Fraud and Abuse in the Provision of Services in Nursing Facilities (1996).

In contrast with blatant manufacturing of fictitious patients or procedures, doctors or hospitals accused or convicted of fraud often believe they are doing nothing wrong because they were merely manipulating the complex bureaucratic rules of an underfunded public system in order to do what was right for their patients and receive decent reimbursement. Accordingly, various types of questionable manipulation are commonplace, even by respected doctors, who might exaggerate or fudge diagnoses in order to obtain insurance coverage for treatment they think is proper but that is not actually covered. For instance, a doctor might classify an annual check-up as an office visit for a cold, or he might classify a 15-minute visit as an "extended" office visit. Do these actions deserve felony treatment?

Regardless, fraudulent or abusive billing practices are a matter of sufficient national concern that federal law makes insurance fraud a federal crime and creates a coordinated enforcement effort that has led to a vast increase in the number of prosecutions and settlements (more than $1 billion per year by one estimate). But, this surge in federal fraud prosecution has led to an outcry of protest by physicians and hospitals over abuse of prosecutorial powers. As discussed in Chapter 10.A.2, prosecutors use the federal False Claims Act to charge that incorrect billings under Medicare, or even poor quality of care, constitute criminal fraud. Providers complain that prosecutors are seizing on technical noncompliance with immensely complex Medicare rules and paperwork requirements and relying on vague and ambiguous standards of illegality. Rather than challenge these prosecutions in court, however, providers usually agree to settle, sometimes for very large amounts in the tens or hundreds of millions of dollars, to avoid risking the legal and public consequences of being found guilty of criminal fraud.

8. *Open-Ended Reimbursement: Down but Not Out.* Medicare no longer reimburses hospitals on a reasonable cost basis. However, this is still the basis for paying some nonhospital facilities. It is also the way that Blue Cross and Medicaid historically paid hospitals and in some instances still do. Other private insurers still pay hospitals a negotiated discount from charges. Similarly, as Alain Enthoven notes, doctors traditionally were paid their "usual, customary, and reasonable" (UCR) rates—both by Medicare and Medicaid and by private insurers, although now both types of insurers pay physicians using fee schedules they determine or negotiate. Even though these open-ended forms of reimbursement have been replaced by various forms of "prospective payment," it is still important to understand traditional payment

methods, since their incentive effects are what newer payment methods are meant to counteract.

9. *Corporate Structure.* How Medicare measures allowable costs has tremendous influence not only on financial and operational management, but also on basic corporate structure. In particular, repeated waves of hospital mergers have presented regulators and courts with the issue of whether a hospital consolidation is a "bona fide" sale. If not, Medicare reimbursement can be refused either for a loss or for increased depreciation. The casebook's Web site contains further discussion of this complex issue.

10. *Further Readings.* On the **irrationality of medical prices** (note 1), Steven Brill, Bitter Pill: Why Medical Bills Are Killing Us, Time, Feb. 20, 2013; Erin C. Fuse Brown, Irrational Hospital Pricing, 14 Hous. J. Health L. & Pol'y 11 (2014); George A. Nation III, Healthcare and the Balance-Billing Problem, 61 Vill. L. Rev. 153 (2016).

For **discussions of whether exorbitant contracts should be enforced** (note 1), see Hall & Schneider, supra, 106 Mich. L. Rev. 643; Wendy Epstein, Price Transparency and Incomplete Contracts in Health Care, 67 Emory L. J. (2017); James McGrath, Overcharging the Uninsured in Hospitals: Shifting a Greater Share of Uncompensated Medical Care Costs to the Federal Government, 26 Quinnipiac L. Rev. 173 (2007); George A. Nation III, Obscene Contracts: The Doctrine of Unconscionability and Hospital Billing of the Uninsured, 94 Ky L. J. 101, 121-123 (2006). For general analysis, see Haavi Morreim, High-Deductible Health Plans: New Twists on Old Challenges from Tort and Contract, 59 Vand. L. Rev. 1207 (2006); Comment, 78 Temp. L. Rev. 493 (2005); Government Accountability Office, Health Care Price Transparency (2011); Kelly Kyanko & Susan Busch, The Out-of-Network Benefit: Problems and Policy Solutions, 49 Inquiry 352 (2012).

For discussions of **market power in the health care industry** (note 3), see Martin Gaynor et al., Making Health Care Markets Work, 317 JAMA 1313 (2017); Thomas G. McGuire, Physician Agency, *in* Anthony J. Culyer & Joseph P. Newhouse, Handbook of Health Economics 462, 482, 527 (2000); Martin Gaynor, Issues in the Industrial Organization of the Market for Physician Services, 3 J. Econ. Manag. Strat. 211 (1994); Reuben Kessel, Price Discrimination in Medicine, 1 J. L. & Econ. 20 (1958).

For more on **medical debt and bankruptcy** (note 4), see Melissa B. Jacoby et al., Rethinking the Debates over Health Care Financing: Evidence from the Bankruptcy Courts, 76 N.Y.U. L. Rev. 375 (2001); Melissa B. Jacoby & Elizabeth Warren, Beyond Hospital Misbehavior: An Alternative Account of Medical-Related Financial Distress, 100 Nw. U. L. Rev. 535 (2006); Melissa Jacoby & Mirya Holman, Managing Medical Bills on the Brink of Bankruptcy, 10 Yale J. Health Pol'y L. & Ethics 239 (2010); Symposium, 51 St. Louis U. L. J. 293 (2007); Daniel A. Austin, Medical Debt As a Cause of Consumer Bankruptcy, 67 Me. L. Rev. 1 (2015).

For discussions of **surprise medical bills** (note 5), see Mark A. Hall et al., Solving Surprise Medical Bills (Brookings, 2016); Daryl M. Berke, Drive-by-Doctoring: Contractual Issues and Regulatory Solutions to Increase Patient Protection from Surprise Medical Bills, 42 Am. J. L. & Med. 170 (2016); Erin C. Fuse Brown, Consumer Financial Protection in Health Care, 95 Wash. U. L. Rev. __ (2017).

For discussions of **the extent of medical fraud** (note 7), see Joan Krause, Following the Money in Health Care Fraud, 36 Am. J. L. & Med. 343 (2010); Michael

K. Sparrow, License to Steal: Why Fraud Plagues America's Health Care System (1999); Symposium, 51 U. Ala. L. Rev. 1 (1999); Symposium, 3 Quinnipiac Health L. J. 1 (2000); Symposium, 43 St. Louis L. Rev. 1 (1999). For more on **routine, low-level fraud**, see Victor G. Freeman et al., Lying for Patients: Physician Deception of Third-Party Payers, 159 Arch. Intern. Med. 2263 (1999); Matthew K. Wynia et al., Physician Manipulation of Reimbursement Rules for Patients: Between a Rock and a Hard Place, 283 JAMA 1858 (2000).

2. Prospective Payment

Open-ended cost-based reimbursement still exists, but both public and private insurance are rapidly moving toward various forms of prospective payment. Prospective payment systems (PPS) reverse the incentives created by retrospective reimbursement by setting a fixed rate in advance that does not vary as much according to the nature or extent of treatment given. In this regard, prospective payment mimics the incentives created by a competitive market in which, in theory, firms are "price takers," meaning that they are forced to sell at the market rate and cannot unilaterally determine their price. Therefore, providers have a profit/loss-based incentive to cut costs and attract more business. Depending on the form of payment, however, they also have an incentive to manipulate the payment system in socially unproductive ways.

There are huge differences in the degree of prospectivity and the types of manipulation created by different forms of prospective payment. These various forms are defined by the unit of payment and by the methods used to adjust the fixed rate among different patients and providers. The first form we look at is the "DRG" system under Medicare, so named because payment rates are fixed according to "diagnosis-related groups." Although the focus is on Medicare, this payment method, and other types of prospective payment, are in wide use among private insurers and other government programs. Thus, both the details and the general structure of Medicare DRGs have pervasive importance across the landscape of health care financing.

■ BEDSIDE BUREAUCRATS: WHY MEDICARE REFORM HASN'T WORKED
Nicholas Bagley
101 Geo. L. J. 519 (2013)

[T]o constrain relentless increases in Medicare expenditures, . . . Congress in 1983 adopted the "prospective payment system," still in place today, under which hospital patients are assigned at discharge, depending on their diagnosis, to differently weighted diagnosis related groups (DRGs). To determine how much to pay a hospital for a particular patient stay, the assigned DRG is multiplied by the national average cost of treating a hospital patient (subject to variations for, among other things, high- and low-wage areas).

The shift to prospective payment flipped hospitals' former financial incentives. Under the preexisting "reasonable cost" approach, a hospital earned more for long and resource-intensive stays. Under the prospective payment system, however, a hospital that spends less on a particular patient than the DRG weighted payment can retain the excess, and a hospital that spends more is in the hole. As such, it is generally in a hospital's financial interest to treat patients conservatively and discharge them quickly. Congress's hope was that prospective payment would encourage hospitals to push their physicians to adopt low-cost practice patterns.

Physicians, however, remained free to bill Medicare for their reasonable charges. And during the 1980s, physician payments began spiraling out of control. Alarmed, in 1989 Congress called for the creation of a fee schedule for physician payments. Establishing this fee schedule required estimating the relative "work" (measured with reference to time, stress, and physical and mental effort) for every medical service. Each service was then assigned a relative value unit (RVU) depending on the work that went into the service. A service that required twice as much "work" as another was assigned an RVU twice as high. To calculate what a physician was owed under the fee schedule, the RVU for the service was multiplied by a practice expense adjustment (practices in high-cost areas have a higher adjustment) and a monetary conversion factor that Congress updates each year. The end result, known as the resource-based relative value scale (RB-RVS), went into effect in 1992 and remains in effect today. . . .

More than any other change in Medicare, prospective payment has slowed the rate of cost escalation. The effect has been particularly pronounced for hospital inpatient care. Without denying its successes, however, prospective payment has not enabled Medicare to assert sufficient authority over its [physicians]. . . .

a. Cost Control. Prospective payment for inpatient hospitalizations was supposed to encourage hospitals to adjust the practice patterns of their affiliated physicians. In this respect, it has proven a qualified failure. Although hospitals have successfully encouraged early discharges, they have otherwise only modestly reshaped how physicians practice medicine. This is in large part because physicians are not usually employed by the hospitals in which they work and have a secure source of fee-for-service revenue through Medicare Part B, even for care provided in an inpatient hospital setting. As Mark McClellan observes, "[v]esting the residual rights of production [i.e., treatment] decisions in the physician, and separating physician reimbursement incentives from hospital reimbursement incentives, clearly reduces the strength of the physician–hospital agency relationship." Not only do hospitals often enjoy little leverage over physicians, but hospitals' financial incentives (decrease care intensity) are at loggerheads with those of their medical staffs' (increase care intensity). Further complicating matters, the Medicare statute prohibits hospitals from making any "payment, directly or indirectly, to a physician as an inducement to reduce or limit services provided" to Medicare beneficiaries.

Instead of pushing physicians to practice cost-conscious care, hospitals have instead cut costs in three principal ways. First, they have reduced overhead and eliminated staff, particularly nurses. Second, they have shifted patients from inpatient to outpatient settings. As other institutional providers—skilled nursing facilities, home health-care agencies, and ambulatory surgery centers—have come under prospective payment, the locus of care has lurched toward physician offices. Costs are shifted, not necessarily reduced. Third, some hospitals have inflated Medicare payments by "upcoding" patients—improperly shifting a patient's diagnosis from one DRG code to a more profitable one, [a maneuver known as "DRG creep"]. A functional bureaucracy might police this sort of manipulative behavior, but Medicare lacks a functional bureaucracy.

What's more, and contrary to expectations, prospective payment did not discourage the adoption and use of expensive new technologies of uncertain value. Under the physician fee schedule, such new technologies often involve more "work" and are thus better remunerated. Hospitals in turn compete to attract physicians who, in part for financial reasons, want to use the new technology. Because DRGs are periodically updated whenever a sufficient number of hospitals adopt a new technology, hospitals are too ready to embrace costly medical innovations without regard to their benefits. . . .

Restraining payments to physicians under the fee schedule has posed a particularly vexing challenge. . . . Part of the trouble is that the overstretched CMS bureaucracy cannot itself update the thousands of RVUs that form the backbone of the fee schedule. Out of necessity, the agency has enlisted the help of an AMA panel called the Specialty Society Relative Value Update Committee (RUC), comprising mainly physician specialists, to review codes and recommend updates. Lacking the resources and expertise necessary to push back with any force, CMS approves nine out of every ten RUC recommendations. As Uwe Reinhardt has noted, CMS has de jure authority to adjust rates, but the RUC is the de facto decision maker. The large majority of adjustments increase the RVUs for particular medical services, and most of those adjustments are for specialty services. That encourages [physicians] to provide larger volumes of these often-expensive services.

Even if it had the resources, CMS lacks the timely data it would need to update the fee schedule. As it stands, CMS must wait eighteen months or more for claims data from its carriers. . . . The payment for the service is typically pegged to the initial costs of the treatment, but those costs often decline as the treatment becomes more common. The absence of timely review means that, over time, the new procedure is overcompensated and, hence, overprovided by Medicare's physicians. In the meantime, categories of services that lack new procedures—in particular, primary care—become relatively less remunerative.

b. Quality Improvement. There is little evidence that the shift to prospective payment has pushed physicians to practice higher quality care. To the contrary, prospective payment may exacerbate some quality concerns. In the hospital setting, prospective payment rewards hospitals for providing low-quality care if such care leads to complications that generate higher DRG classifications or rapid readmissions. In addition, hospital encouragement of early discharges poses a risk that patients will be discharged "quicker and sicker," especially where too-early discharges may lead to readmissions. Hospitals have also slashed nursing staff in response to prospective payment. This too is a consequence of Medicare's architecture—the fact that physicians are paid separately from the hospitals in which they practice means that hospital administrators often find it easier to fire nurses than to shift physician practice patterns. But it's problematic. Copious research suggests that reductions in nursing staff contribute to lower quality care.

For physicians, the quality concerns are different. The fee schedule encourages physicians to overuse specialty services, some of which are harmful to patients. Consider imaging services, for example. Because of the fee-for-service incentives baked into the fee schedule, physicians who own or lease their own imaging equipment can bill for each and every scan that they order. The result has been explosive growth in the volume of inappropriate diagnostic imaging services, including CT scans. Yet CT scans involve relatively high doses of radiation and increase cancer risks. To the extent that it encourages intensive medical care of negligible value, the fee schedule is inimical to quality care.

* * *

When it comes to restraining cost growth, prospective payment remains the most successful reform in Medicare's history. But congressional inattention to the incentives and capacities of hospitals and medical societies, combined with Medicare's rickety administrative structure, has undermined its effectiveness in reshaping how physicians practice medicine. Hospitals often have little capacity to change how physicians with a separate source of revenue do their jobs. Medicare's abiding commitment to compensating for the full costs of care encourages both physicians and hospitals to adopt new and expensive technologies. . . . And a hollow central bureaucracy without access to timely data has struggled, without much success, to restrain growth in payment rates to intensive specialty services.

Notes: DRGs; Relative Value Scales; Rate Regulation

1. *The Structure and Scope of DRGs.* A DRG-type system has been implemented for hospital outpatient services and ambulatory surgical centers, and nursing homes and home health agencies are now paid according to per diem rates fixed by formula rather than through cost-based reimbursement. See generally Rick Mayes & Robert Bereneson, Medicare Prospective Payment and the Shaping of U.S. Health Care (2006).

2. *The Myth of Institutional Control.* The annual adjustment to the standardized hospital rate provides a convenient tool for continuously ratcheting down Medicare outlays: The more economizing effort hospitals exert in response to the incentives of prospective payment, the more leeway Medicare will have each year to tighten up the standardized rate. DRGs thus have the prospect of not only halting future increases in spending (relative to inflation) but also gradually eliminating the system's built-up fat. But this is true only to the extent that hospital managers actually control the costs of treatment. As Professor Bagley observes, physicians control most clinical decisions that drive hospital costs, and they are notoriously independent from institutional control.

This physician independence is not just a matter of professional and institutional culture; it is supported by various legal constraints that protect physicians from outside control. Mark A. Hall, Institutional Control of Physician Behavior: Legal Barriers to Health Care Cost Containment, 137 U. Pa. L. Rev. 431 (1988). Based on the topics covered in Chapters 10.B.1, 10.C.1, and 10.E, imagine what legal objections could be raised if a hospital were to: (1) impose mandatory treatment protocols that physicians must follow (unlicensed, corporate practice of medicine); (2) pay physicians a reward for keeping their patients' costs within DRG limits ("fraud and abuse" fee splitting); or (3) kick off the medical staff any physician who consistently loses money ("economic credentialing"). Responding to Hall's prediction, above, that courts will systematically frustrate cost containment initiatives,

Peter Jacobson argues this has not in fact occurred. Peter Jacobson, Strangers in the Night: Law and Medicine in the Managed Care Era (2002).

3. *Hospitalists.* One way that hospitals now assert more administrative control of patient care decisions is by hiring hospital-based physicians called "hospitalists" to take over primary responsibility for case management of hospitalized patients rather than having patients being seen primarily by their regular physicians. So far, hospitalist programs are voluntary, in the sense that primary care physicians can use them at their discretion; but hospitals in theory could start to insist on using their employed staff. For a general overview of ethical and public policy issues, see page 135.

4. *Adjustments to Hospital Rates.* Following the logic that hospitals should bear the brunt of only the costs they control, the Medicare DRG system has been forced to add numerous adjustments other than simply those related to patients' diagnoses. As David Frankford has explained:

> [T]he reimbursement system contains a very complicated set of mechanisms to determine this question. The most important of these adjustments is for geographic variations among hospitals in their cost of labor.... [A]ll agree that labor constitutes the most important component of a hospital's operating costs. Accordingly, the statute clearly provides for some type of "wage adjustment." To make this adjustment, [Medicare] divides the country into numerous — and hotly contested — geographic wage areas, and each area is ranked vis-a-vis a national average wage, thereby creating a "wage index" — an indexical ranking of labor costs in different locations. Each hospital is placed into a particular area, and thus its reimbursement for any case is a product of its relevant category of standardized payment amount — rural, large urban, or other urban — weighted to take into account its local labor costs....
>
> There are then "additional payment amounts" made for other factors for which hospitals are not held accountable. Teaching activities in hospitals are thought to generate increased costs indirectly, due to the treatment of more severely ill patients through use of technology and utilization patterns which differ from those prevalent in nonteaching hospitals. Accordingly, payments to teaching hospitals are increased by percentages, called the "indirect medical education adjustment," which vary with the size of the hospital and its teaching program. Somewhat related, but not completely coextensive, is an adjustment made for hospitals which treat a "disproportionate share" of indigent patients. These patients too are thought to generate higher costs because they are more severely ill at admission than the average Medicare beneficiary. Furthermore, treatment of these patients imposes higher costs because post-discharge care is often harder to arrange and because there are generally higher costs associated with operating in areas accessible to the poor.... [H]ospitals which are the sole facilities in their respective communities ... are eligible for designation as a "sole community hospital." ... [B]oth sole community hospitals and Medicare-dependent, small rural hospitals are given ... a lump sum payment that is calculated to cover their fixed costs and the costs of maintaining core staff and services.... Finally, all hospitals are paid a separate, additional amount for extraordinarily expensive cases — the so-called "outlier cases" which deviate greatly from the average case in a DRG.

David Frankford, The Complexity of Medicare's Hospital Reimbursement System: Paradoxes of Averaging, 78 Iowa L. Rev. 517, 579-584 (1993). See also Southeast Alabama Medical Center v. Sebelius, 572 F.3d 912 (D.C. Cir. 2009) (upholding factors HHS used to determine hospitals' area wage index); Anna Jacques Hospital v.

Burwell, 797 F.3d 1155 (D.C. Cir. 2015) (same). Over time, these adjustments have accounted for an increasing portion of total DRG payments. Sam Krinsky, Variation in Payment Rates under Medicare's Inpatient Prospective Payment System, 52 Health Serv. Rev. 676 (2017).

5. *The Ethics of Considering Costs.* A thorny dilemma that DRGs and other forms of prospective payment present is the ethical bind they impose on practicing physicians. Is it morally right for a doctor to be influenced by the inevitable resource constraints placed on hospitals or on society at large, if, as a result of third-party reimbursement, the doctor's patients are sheltered from these constraints? Consider the following hypothetical (but very real) problem:

> Lakeview Hospital's medical director, Jared Lapin, M.D., . . . analyzed a lengthy computer report that matched, for each physician, the revenue the hospital received with the costs incurred for treating patients in each of the DRGs in one month. While studying the 15 DRGs under Major Diagnostic Category number 14 (Pregnancy, Childbirth, and the Puerperium), [he] noticed that, . . . across all deliveries, the costs of treating Dr. Weiner's patients exceeded the revenue received from the DRG rates. But the total cost incurred in providing care to the other obstetricians' patients was considerably below revenue and hence the hospital was able to earn a "profit." . . . The reason for Dr. Weiner's comparatively poor overall "financial performance" . . . was that he performed many fewer cesarians than did his colleagues. . . . Dr. Lapin countered that "it's in all our interests to look out for the financial health of the hospital. And since it is unclear which of the two approaches benefits the patient more, I urge you to reconsider the way you handle these cases."

Was it ethical for Dr. Lapin to approach Dr. Weiner if there was no indication he was delivering poor quality care? How should financial considerations, both those related to the hospital and society at large, be weighed against physician judgment? Wasserman, The Doctor, the Patient and the DRG, 13(5) Hastings Center Rep. 23 (Oct. 1983).

6. *Discharging Patients "Quicker and Sicker."* Critics of DRGs have documented that they caused hospitals to discharge patients "quicker and sicker." But is it necessarily wrong that a patient not be allowed to remain in the hospital for the full period of recuperation? Contrast these critics with Katherine Kahn et al., The Effects of the DRG-Based Prospective Payment System on Quality of Care for Hospitalized Medicare Patients, 264 JAMA 1953 (1990) (finding no systematic effects on quality of care). CMS has attempted to prevent premature discharge by requiring that all Medicare patients be given upon admission a written statement of their rights to protest a discharge decision. Patients have a grace period of several days after written notice of discharge to remain in the hospital and appeal the decision to the local Quality Improvement Organization (formerly called Peer Review Organization).

Despite this, a surprising 20 percent of Medicare patients are readmitted to the hospital within 30 days of discharge. Often, this is not so much because of premature discharge, but because hospitals have no financial incentive to manage patients' outpatient care following discharge, such as taking their medications or returning for follow-up visits. To change this, CMS has started penalizing hospitals with excessive readmissions rates. As a result, readmissions have dropped sharply.

See Centers for Medicare and Medicaid Services, New HHS Data Shows Major Strides Made in Patient Safety, Leading to Improved Care and Savings, May 7, 2014.

7. *DRG Creep.*

In New Jersey, a study found that 26.4 percent of the patients had been misclassi-fied [to the wrong DRG]. . . . One of the most publicized examples was the softball player who had injured his finger. He had to be hospitalized for two days so that the bone in his finger could be repaired with a metal pin. The DRG category assigned to this patient was "fracture with major surgery," usually reserved for serious cases such as total hip replacement. While the patient's actual charges would have been less than $1000, the DRG classification resulted in a bill for $5,000.

P. Feldstein, Health Care Economics 296 (2d ed. 1982).

8. *Physicians' Fee Schedules.* It is critical to observe that DRGs only cover hospital costs. What difficulties would be encountered in extending DRGs to physician ser-vices? Consider the following explanation by the former head of CMS:

In view of the generally successful change in Medicare's hospital-payment system, many wonder why we cannot repeat the accomplishment with respect to Medicare payment of physicians. The answer is simple: Paying physicians is far more compli-cated. When developing a hospital-payment system for Medicare, one must handle 11 million admissions to 7,000 hospitals for 475 diagnosis-related groups. Those numbers pale in comparison to Medicare's 350 million claims from 500,000 physi-cians for 7,000 different procedure codes. Moreover, whereas hospitals can average their gains and losses under a prospective payment system across many cases, physi-cians' smaller caseloads and greater specialization make such averaging much more risky for them. These differences mean that improving the way Medicare pays physi-cians will be vastly more difficult, both analytically and administratively.

William Roper, Perspectives on Physician-Payment Reform, 319 New Eng. J. Med. 865 (1988).

9. *Public Utility Regulation.* The debate over how to slow medical spending tends to pit advocates of market-based reforms against supporters of a single-payer approach. But there is another alternative, one that treats the health care industry as a type of public utility. A public utility approach would retain the architecture of the private financing system while enabling the state to assert control over the medi-cal industry's economic excesses. The approach is not as foreign to the American health care system as it may seem at first glance:

[I]n the decades following the Second World War, the meteoric growth of the medi-cal industry prompted the enactment of federal and state laws that bore the hall-marks of public utility regulation. Collectively, these laws regulated market entry, imposed service obligations, prohibited certain forms of price discrimination and even fixed prices. In the last decades of the twentieth century, some of this econom-ic regulation gave way in the face of the resurgent belief that market forces, not state control, ought to guide the distribution of health-care services. But a durable strain of the law has always treated modern medicine as a public calling—even today.

The fit is natural. Public utility regulation aims to address the sorts of prob-lems in market ordering—supply imbalances, access restrictions, and abusive and discriminatory pricing—that have long afflicted the medical industry. Now that the

[ACA] has eased public concerns about the uninsured, the serious economic challenges facing those with insurance are likely to become more salient. Should the ACA fail to remedy a number of disturbing practices in the medical marketplace, policymakers may find public utility regulation increasingly attractive. Indeed, nascent interest in such regulation suggests that we may already be heading in that direction.

Nicholas Bagley, Medicine as a Public Calling, 114 Mich. L. Rev. 57, 59-60 (2015).

The most comprehensive form of public utility regulation would impose a global budget on hospitals and their employed physicians, as is typical for government-run hospitals. A global budget is difficult to formulate, however, when private hospitals have multiple sources of private sector income. Instead, during the 1970s, about a dozen states instituted comprehensive regulation of hospital rates, regulating what hospitals could charge private or public insurers. The purpose was both to contain costs and to more equitably spread the burden of uncompensated care borne by different hospitals. Since then, however, every one of these states except Maryland has since repealed its "all payer" hospital rate regulation, opting instead to trust in the rise of managed care to restrain medical spending. John McDonough, Tracking the Demise of State Hospital Rate Setting, 16 Health Affairs 13 (1997). The rise of dominant health care systems in many markets has rekindled interest in some quarters in a return to rate-setting.

10. *Hospital Appeals Under Medicare; Constitutionality.* There are few judicial challenges under Medicare to the basic DRG methodology because of provisions in the statute expressly precluding review of the DRG weights and severely limiting the opportunity to challenge individual hospital rates. See Skagit County Public Hospital District v. Shalala, 80 F.3d 379 (9th Cir. 1996); Palisades General Hospital Inc. v. Leavitt, 426 F.3d 400 (D.C. Cir. 2005). Query, then, whether the system has sacrificed accuracy and fairness in order to obtain deceptive legal simplicity. At the administrative level, however, administrative appeals have run so rampant that the Provider Reimbursed Review Board (PRRB) has a backlog of several years. The single matter of adjusting a hospital's rate to accurately reflect geographically determined factors (wages, rural status, etc.) became so burdensome for the PRRB that a separate review board was created for this sole purpose — the Medicare Geographic Classification Review Board. See generally David W. Thomas, Review of Medicare Reimbursement Disputes Under 42 U.S.C. §1395oo: Delineating a Unified Theory of the Provider Reimbursement Review Board's Jurisdiction and Scope of Review, 39 Duq. L. Rev. 287 (2001); Recent Development, 95 N.C.L. Rev. 1293 (2017).

Because participation in Medicare and Medicaid is voluntary, there generally are thought to be no constitutional problems with limiting reimbursement or judicial review. See, e.g., Nazareth Home of Franciscan Sisters v. Novello, 7 N.Y.3d 538 (N.Y. 2006); William Brewbaker, Health Care Price Controls and the Takings Clause, 21 Hastings Const. L.Q. 669 (1994).

11. *Further Readings.* On the **institutional control of physicians** (note 2), see Jessica Mantel, The Myth of the Independent Physician, 64 Case W. Res. 455 (2013); Theodore Ruger, Plural Constitutionalism and the Pathologies of American Health Care, 120 Yale L. J. Online 347 (2011); Robert F. Rich et al., Judicial Interpretations of Managed Care Policy 13 Elder L. J. 85 (2005).

For more on **"outlier payments" and their manipulation by hospitals** (note 4), see Elizabeth A. Weeks, Gauging the Cost of Loopholes: Health Care Pricing and Medicare Regulation in the Post-Enron Era, 40 Wake Forest L. Rev. 1215 (2005); R. Brent Rawlings & Hugh E. Aaron, The Effect of Hospital Charges on Outlier Payments Under Medicare's Inpatient Prospective Payment System: Prudent Financial Management or Illegal Conduct?, 14 Ann. Health L. 267 (2005).

For further discussion and debate on **Medicare physician payment and relative value scales** (note 8), see Miriam J. Laugesen, Fixing Medical Prices: How Physicians Are Paid (2016); Joseph P. Newhouse, Medicare Spending on Physicians: No Easy Fix in Sight, 356 New Eng. J. Med. 1883 (2007); Paul Ginsburg, Rapidly Evolving Physician-Payment Policy: More Than the SGR, 362 New Eng. J. Med. 172 (2011); Paul B. Ginsburg & Robert A. Berenson, Revising Medicare's Physician Fee Schedule—Much Activity, Little Change, 356 New Eng. J. Med. 1201 (2007); and the annual reports of MedPAC, the Medicare Payment Advisory Commission.

For recent discussions of **rate-setting and the public utility model** (note 9), see Erin C. Fuse Brown, Resurrecting Heath Care Rate Regulation, 67 Hastings L. J. 85 (2015); Robert Murray & Robert A. Berenson, Hospital Rate Setting Revisited Dumb Price Fixing or a Smart Solution to Provider Pricing Power and Delivery Reform? (2015); David M. Frankford, It's the Prices, Advanced Capitalism, and the Need for Rate Setting—Stupid, 44 J. L., Med. & Ethics (2017).

Problem: Technology Innovation

What effects are DRGs and other forms of prospective payment likely to have on technology acquisition and medical innovation? The answer depends on the type of innovation. Consider: Those that involve greater cost versus lesser costs. Those that increase admissions by finding new things to treat versus those that shorten length of stay for existing diagnoses. And, those that improve diagnostic accuracy versus those that improve treatment. Here are several concrete examples. For each, consider the technology from a perspective of when it was first introduced, that is, assuming that a specific DRG has not yet been created for it or that overall payment rates have not yet been adjusted to reflect the new technology.

1. A procedure known as "balloon angioplasty," (or P.T.C.A. for percutaneous transluminal coronary angioplasty) is an alternative to bypass surgery that involves inserting a small balloon into an artery and inflating it to clear blockage.

2. A PET (positron emission tomographer) scanner, a multi-million-dollar machine that produces images of biochemical activity inside the body, in contrast with an MRI, which depicts soft tissues, or a CAT scan, which depicts bones and hard tissue.

3. Low osmolarity contrast media, used for angiography.

4. Extracorporeal shock-wave lithotripter, a space-age machine that pulverizes kidney stones by concentrating blasts of focused shock (sound) waves, as an alternative to either surgical removal or enduring pain (sometimes excruciating) while waiting to excrete the stones naturally.

3. Capitation Payment

◼ PEGRAM v. HERDRICH
530 U.S. 211 (2000)

Justice SOUTER delivered the opinion of the Court.

The question in this case is whether treatment decisions made by a health maintenance organization, acting through its physician employees, are fiduciary acts within the meaning of the Employee Retirement Income Security Act of 1974 (ERISA). We hold that they are not.

Petitioners, Carle Clinic Association . . . , function as a health maintenance organization (HMO) organized for profit. Its owners are physicians providing pre-paid medical services to participants whose employers contract with Carle to provide such coverage. Respondent, Cynthia Herdrich, was covered by Carle through her husband's employer, State Farm Insurance Company. The events in question began when a Carle physician, petitioner Lori Pegram, examined Herdrich, who was experiencing pain in the midline area of her groin. Six days later, Dr. Pegram discovered a six by eight centimeter inflamed mass in Herdrich's abdomen. Despite the noticeable inflammation, Dr. Pegram did not order an ultrasound diagnostic procedure at a local hospital, but decided that Herdrich would have to wait eight more days for an ultrasound, to be performed at a facility staffed by Carle more than 50 miles away. Before the eight days were over, Herdrich's appendix ruptured, causing peritonitis.

Herdrich sued Pegram and Carle in state court for medical malpractice, and . . . prevailed [against] both, receiving $35,000 in compensation for her injury. . . . [She also sued in federal court under ERISA, the federal statute discussed in section C and Chapter 4.F that regulates pension plans and other fringe benefits. The ERISA suit alleged that Carle HMO's] rewarding its physician owners for limiting medical care entailed an inherent or anticipatory breach of an ERISA fiduciary duty, since these terms created an incentive to make decisions in the physicians' self-interest, rather than the exclusive interests of plan participants. . . . [This claim was dismissed by the district court but was reinstated by the Seventh Circuit.]

Whether Carle is a fiduciary when it acts through its physician owners as pleaded in the ERISA count depends on some background of fact and law about HMO organizations, medical benefit plans, fiduciary obligation, and the meaning of Herdrich's allegations. . . .

In a fee-for-service system, a physician's financial incentive is to provide more care, not less, so long as payment is forthcoming. The check on this incentive is a physician's obligation to exercise reasonable medical skill and judgment in the patient's interest. . . . The defining feature of an HMO is . . . [that it] assumes the financial risk of providing the benefits promised. . . . Like other risk-bearing organizations, HMOs take steps to control costs, [such as utilization review]. These cost-controlling measures are commonly complemented by specific financial incentives to physicians, rewarding them for decreasing utilization of health-care services, and penalizing them for what may be found to be excessive treatment. Hence, in an HMO system, a physician's financial interest lies in providing less care, not more. The check on this influence (like that on the converse, fee-for-service incentive) is the professional obligation to provide covered services with a reasonable degree of skill and judgment in the patient's interest.

The adequacy of professional obligation to counter financial self-interest has been challenged no matter what the form of medical organization. HMOs became popular because fee-for-service physicians were thought to be providing unnecessary or useless services; today, many doctors and other observers argue that HMOs often ignore the individual needs of a patient in order to improve the HMOs' bottom lines. In this case, for instance, one could argue that Pegram's decision to wait before getting an ultrasound for Herdrich, and her insistence that the ultrasound be done at a distant facility owned by Carle, reflected an interest in limiting the HMO's expenses, which blinded her to the need for immediate diagnosis and treatment.

Herdrich focuses on the Carle scheme's provision for a "year-end distribution" to the HMO's physician owners. She argues that this particular incentive device of annually paying physician owners the profit resulting from their own decisions rationing care can distinguish Carle's organization from HMOs generally, so that reviewing Carle's decisions under a fiduciary standard as pleaded in Herdrich's complaint would not open the door to like claims about other HMO structures. While the Court of Appeals agreed, we think otherwise, under the law as now written.

Although it is true that the relationship between sparing medical treatment and physician reward is not a subtle one under the Carle scheme, no HMO organization could survive without some incentive connecting physician reward with treatment rationing. The essence of an HMO is that salaries and profits are limited by the HMO's fixed membership fees. See Orentlicher, Paying Physicians More to Do Less: Financial Incentives to Limit Care, 30 U. Rich. L. Rev. 155, 174 (1996). This is not to suggest that the Carle provisions are as socially desirable as some other HMO organizational schemes; they may not be. But whatever the HMO, there must be rationing and inducement to ration.

Since inducement to ration care goes to the very point of any HMO scheme, and rationing necessarily raises some risks while reducing others (ruptured appendixes are more likely; unnecessary appendectomies are less so), any legal principle purporting to draw a line between good and bad HMOs would embody, in effect, a judgment about socially acceptable medical risk. A valid conclusion of this sort would, however, necessarily turn on facts to which courts would probably not have ready access: correlations between malpractice rates and various HMO models, similar correlations involving fee-for-service models, and so on. . . . . [S]uch complicated factfinding and such a debatable social judgment are not wisely required of courts unless for some reason resort cannot be had to the legislative process, with its preferable forum for comprehensive investigations and judgments of social value, such as optimum treatment levels and health care expenditure. We think, then, that courts are not in a position to derive a sound legal principle to differentiate an HMO like Carle from other HMOs. . . .

C

We turn now from the structure of HMOs to the requirements of ERISA. A fiduciary within the meaning of ERISA must be someone acting in the capacity of manager, administrator, or financial adviser to a "plan." . . . Rules governing collection of premiums, definition of benefits, submission of claims, and resolution of disagreements over entitlement to services are the sorts of provisions that constitute a plan. Thus, when employers contract with an HMO to provide benefits to employees subject to ERISA, the provisions of documents that set up the HMO are not, as such, an ERISA plan, but the agreement between an HMO and an employer who pays the premiums may, as here, provide elements of a plan by setting out rules under which beneficiaries will be entitled to care.

As just noted, fiduciary obligations can apply to managing, advising, and administering an ERISA plan. . . . In general terms, fiduciary responsibility under ERISA is simply stated. The statute provides that fiduciaries shall discharge their duties with respect to a plan "solely in the interest of the participants and beneficiaries." . . . These responsibilities imposed by ERISA have the familiar ring of their source in the common law of trusts: . . . "The most fundamental duty owed by the trustee to the beneficiaries of the trust is the duty of loyalty. . . . It is the duty of a trustee to administer the trust solely in the interest of the beneficiaries." 2A A. Scott & W. Fratcher, Trusts §170, 311 (4th ed. 1987).

Beyond the threshold statement of responsibility, however, the analogy between ERISA fiduciary and common law trustee becomes problematic. This is so because the trustee at common law characteristically wears only his fiduciary hat when he takes action to affect a beneficiary, whereas the trustee under ERISA may wear different hats.

Speaking of the traditional trustee, Professor Scott's treatise admonishes that the trustee "is not permitted to place himself in a position where it would be for his own benefit to violate his duty to the beneficiaries." 2A Scott, §170, at 311. Under ERISA, however, a fiduciary may have financial interests adverse to beneficiaries. Employers, for example, can be ERISA fiduciaries and still take actions to the disadvantage of employee beneficiaries, when they act as employers (e.g., firing a beneficiary for reasons unrelated to the ERISA plan), or even as plan sponsors (e.g., modifying the terms of a plan as allowed by ERISA to provide less generous benefits). . . . ERISA does require, however, that the fiduciary with two hats wear only one at a time, and wear the fiduciary hat when making fiduciary decisions. . . .

The pleadings must also be parsed very carefully to understand what acts by physician owners acting on Carle's behalf are alleged to be fiduciary in nature.[8] It will help to keep two sorts of arguably administrative acts in mind. Cf. Dukes v. U.S. Healthcare, Inc., 57 F.3d 350, 361 (3rd Cir. 1995) (discussing dual medical/administrative roles of HMOs). What we will call pure "eligibility decisions" turn on the plan's coverage of a particular condition or medical procedure for its treatment. "Treatment decisions," by contrast, are choices about how to go about diagnosing and treating a patient's condition: given a patient's constellation of symptoms, what is the appropriate medical response?

---

8. . . . The fraud claims in Herdrich's initial complaint could be read to allege breach of a fiduciary obligation to disclose physician incentives to limit care, whereas her amended complaint alleges an obligation to avoid such incentives. . . . cf. Varity Corp. v. Howe, 516 U.S. 489, 505 (1996) (holding that ERISA fiduciaries may have duties to disclose information about plan prospects that they have no duty, or even power, to change). But failure to disclose is no longer the allegation of the amended complaint. . . .

These decisions are often practically inextricable from one another. . . . This is so not merely because, under a scheme like Carle's, treatment and eligibility decisions are made by the same person, the treating physician. It is so because a great many and possibly most coverage questions are not simple yes-or-no questions, like whether appendicitis is a covered condition (when there is no dispute that a patient has appendicitis), or whether acupuncture is a covered procedure for pain relief (when the claim of pain is unchallenged). The more common coverage question is a when-and-how question. Although coverage for many conditions will be clear and various treatment options will be indisputably compensable, physicians still must decide what to do in particular cases. The issue may be, say, whether one treatment option is so superior to another under the circumstances, and needed so promptly, that a decision to proceed with it would meet the medical necessity requirement that conditions the HMO's obligation to provide or pay for that particular procedure at that time in that case. . . . In practical terms, these eligibility decisions cannot be untangled from physicians' judgments about reasonable medical treatment, and in the case before us, Dr. Pegram's decision was one of that sort. She decided (wrongly, as it turned out) that Herdrich's condition did not warrant immediate action; the consequence of that medical determination was that Carle would not cover immediate care, whereas it would have done so if Dr. Pegram had made the proper diagnosis and judgment to treat. The eligibility decision and the treatment decision were inextricably mixed, as they are in countless medical administrative decisions every day. . . .

Based on our understanding of the matters just discussed, we think Congress did not intend Carle or any other HMO to be treated as a fiduciary to the extent that it makes mixed eligibility decisions acting through its physicians. We begin with doubt that Congress would ever have thought of a mixed eligibility decision as fiduciary in nature. At common law, fiduciary duties characteristically attach to decisions about managing assets and distributing property to beneficiaries. Trustees buy, sell, and lease investment property, lend and borrow, and do other things to conserve and nurture assets. They pay out income, choose beneficiaries, and distribute remainders at termination. Thus, the common law trustee's most defining concern historically has been the payment of money in the interest of the beneficiary.

Mixed eligibility decisions by an HMO acting through its physicians have, however, only a limited resemblance to the usual business of traditional trustees. . . . [T]he physicians through whom HMOs act make just the sorts of decisions made by licensed medical practitioners millions of times every day, in every possible medical setting: HMOs, fee-for-service proprietorships, public and private hospitals, military field hospitals, and so on. The settings bear no more resemblance to trust departments than a decision to operate turns on the factors controlling the amount of a quarterly income distribution. Thus, it is at least questionable whether Congress would have had mixed eligibility decisions in mind when it provided that decisions administering a plan were fiduciary in nature. Indeed, when Congress took up the subject of fiduciary responsibility under ERISA, it concentrated on fiduciaries' financial decisions, focusing on pension plans, the difficulty many retirees faced in getting the payments they expected, and the financial mismanagement that had too often deprived employees of their benefits. Its focus was far from the subject of Herdrich's claim.

Our doubt that Congress intended the category of fiduciary administrative functions to encompass the mixed determinations at issue here hardens into conviction when we consider the consequences that would follow from Herdrich's contrary view. . . . Although Herdrich is vague about the mechanics of relief, the one point that seems clear is that she seeks the return of profit from the pockets of the Carle HMO's owners, with the money to be given to the plan for the benefit of the participants. Since the provision for profit is what makes the HMO a proprietary organization, her remedy in effect would be nothing less than elimination of the for-profit HMO. Her remedy . . . might well portend the end of nonprofit HMOs as well, since those HMOs can set doctors' salaries. A claim against a nonprofit HMO could easily allege that salaries were excessively high because they were funded by limiting care, and some nonprofits actually use incentive schemes similar to that challenged here. . . .

It is enough to recognize that the Judiciary has no warrant to precipitate the upheaval that would follow a refusal to dismiss Herdrich's ERISA claim. The fact is that for over 27 years the Congress of the United States has promoted the formation of HMO practices. . . . If Congress wishes to restrict its approval of HMO practice to certain preferred forms, it may choose to do so. But the Federal Judiciary would be acting contrary to the congressional policy of allowing HMO organizations if it were to entertain an ERISA fiduciary claim portending wholesale attacks on existing HMOs solely because of their structure, untethered to claims of concrete harm. . . .

The fiduciary is, of course, obliged to act exclusively in the interest of the beneficiary, but this translates into no rule readily applicable to HMO decisions or those of any other variety of medical practice. While the incentive of the HMO physician is to give treatment sparingly, imposing a fiduciary obligation upon him would not lead to a simple default rule, say, that whenever it is reasonably possible to disagree about treatment options, the physician should treat aggressively. After all, HMOs came into being because some groups of physicians consistently provided more aggressive treatment than others in similar circumstances, with results not perceived as justified by the marginal expense and risk associated with intervention; excessive surgery is not in the patient's best interest, whether provided by fee-for-service surgeons or HMO surgeons subject to a default rule urging them to operate. Nor would it be possible to translate fiduciary duty into a standard that would allow recovery from an HMO whenever a mixed decision influenced by the HMO's financial incentive resulted in a bad outcome for the patient. It would be so easy to allege, and to find, an economic influence when sparing care did not lead to a well patient, that any such standard in practice would allow a factfinder to convert an HMO into a guarantor of recovery. . . .

[T]he defense of any HMO would be that its physician did not act out of financial interest but for good medical reasons, the plausibility of which would require reference to standards of reasonable and customary medical practice in like circumstances. That, of course, is the traditional standard of the common law. Thus, for all practical purposes, every claim of fiduciary breach by an HMO physician making a mixed decision would boil down to a malpractice claim, and the fiduciary standard would be nothing but the malpractice standard traditionally applied in actions against physicians.

What would be the value to the plan participant of having this kind of ERISA fiduciary action? It would simply apply the law already available in state courts and federal diversity actions today, and the formulaic addition of an allegation of financial incentive would do nothing but bring the same claim into a federal court under federal-question jurisdiction. It is true that in States that do not allow malpractice actions against HMOs the fiduciary claim would offer a plaintiff a further defendant to be sued for direct liability, and in some cases the HMO might have a deeper pocket than the physician. But we have seen enough to know that ERISA was not enacted out of concern that physicians were too poor to be sued. . . .

We hold that mixed eligibility decisions by HMO physicians are not fiduciary decisions under ERISA.

■DIRECT FINANCIAL INCENTIVES IN MANAGED CARE: UNANSWERED QUESTIONS
Henry T. Greely
6 Health Matrix 53 (1996)

The diagnosis was devastating. Joyce — a health-conscious mother of a three-year-old son — had colon cancer. Twenty months and seven operations later, she was dead at age thirty-four. Her husband contends that it was greed that killed [his wife]. In a malpractice suit scheduled for trial this summer, he alleges that the financial incentives in their contracts with the HMO prompted his wife's doctors to place their interests ahead of hers. . . .

WHAT ARE DIRECT FINANCIAL INCENTIVES?

Direct financial incentives can take many forms, but the key is structuring the physician's compensation in ways that create incentives to practice economically. . . . [F]our general approaches are commonly used: salary, capitation, profit sharing, and bonus. Each can be combined with others in a variety of forms. Under a salaried system, the physician's income is set by the plan, generally annually, through a salary. . . . Under a capitated system, the physician is paid a certain amount, generally on a monthly basis, for each of the managed care plan's patients for whom she is responsible. In its purest form, if the doctor spends less than the capitated amount, she makes a profit on that patient; if she spends more, she takes a loss.

Capitation comes in a dizzying number of forms, with the variations spreading over at least two dimensions. One dimension is the range of services included in the capitation. Capitation to a primary care physician almost always will include primary care services. It may or may not include the costs of specialty or hospital services. It may include or exclude laboratory or radiological services. It could, but rarely does, include mental health services or pharmaceutical costs. If a service is excluded from the capitation agreement, its costs are not charged against the capitated physician, but are paid from some other pool of funds.

The second dimension is the degree to which the physician is at risk even for the capitated services. At the extreme, the risk could be total. A physician receiving ninety dollars per month as "global" capitation (physician services and hospital services) might be held financially responsible for the entire $150,000. . . . More commonly, however, the risk is shared. The physician might be responsible for higher costs only up to a certain point, defined either in terms of dollars per patient or patient pool (through stop-loss insurance) or in terms of a percentage of the capitated amount (through withheld funds). In the alternative, the physician, in turn, may spread the risk through capitated arrangements with other providers, such as hospitals or specialists.

A concrete example might make this more clear. Stanford University offers its employees a choice among three health maintenance organizations. . . . [In one arrangement], the University contracts with three physician groups to provide the HMO-level care. These physician groups would receive approximately ninety dollars per month to cover all physician and hospital services for a middle-aged individual. The physicians then contract with a local hospital to cover all hospital services for about forty dollars per month. The University's plan administrator withholds a percentage of the capitated payment to each physician group. This "withhold" pool is used to pay for services members receive . . . , as well as for unanticipated expenses. At the end of the year, if money remains in the "withhold" pool, it is shared between the physician group, which receives eighty percent of the pool, and the University, which keeps the balance. If no money remains in that pool, the physician group is left with only the payments it has already received, but it is not responsible for any cost overrun.

A third strategy is the bonus. The physicians may be paid during a fixed period under any system: salary, capitation, or fee-for-service. At the end of that period, physicians receive a bonus based on the plan's financial results that year and the physicians' contribution to them. The manner of determining the bonus can vary widely. [Under one] method . . . the physicians receive a negotiated share of the plan's profits. They may receive that share as owners of the plan or otherwise. . . .

In reality, all of these systems can be used and most of them can be combined. . . . For an example, return to the Stanford University [HMO plan]. The university contracts with three local physician groups and a statewide HMO to provide the HMO level of care for this plan. Each of the three physician groups is paid on a capitation basis to cover both the medical and hospital needs of the [HMO] members who come to them, but the contractual negotiations led to somewhat different outcomes. First, the amount paid to the three groups by Stanford to cover its members differs from group to group, depending on the bargains the University struck with each. . . . Then, each of the physician groups in turn contracted with a local hospital, designated by the University, to subcapitate the hospital care of their [HMO] plan members. The amount the groups have to pay the hospital varies, in part because some of the physician groups provided services in their clinics that other groups obtained through the hospital. Third, each of the groups' capitation payments are subject to a percentage withheld to cover member expenses for services obtained outside the HMO. . . .

The result is that each of the four sets of doctors participating in the HMO tier of Stanford's plan, although paid on a capitated basis, is paid differently. Because they are paid differently, the financial incentives they face in making decisions about a patient's care differ. They receive different amounts per patient. . . . Moreover, Stanford's [HMO] plan contracted not with physicians, but with physician groups. In a group practice, each physician does not "eat what he kills," a phrase from other professional organizations that is particularly jarring when used with physicians. Instead, the group as a whole decides how to pay its physician members. Therefore, even if a group has an HMO contract that provides for strict capitation, the group might, in its own compensation scheme, pay the physicians on the basis of any system: salary, profit sharing, capitation, bonus, fee-for-service, or any combination of the above. . . .

IMPLICATIONS FOR PUBLIC POLICY

What are the implications of direct financial incentives for patients and for public policy? . . . [A] capitated plan that included diagnostic tests within the capitation might lead a physician not to order an expensive magnetic resonance imaging (MRI) scan for a patient even though there was a small, but nonzero, chance the test would reveal something useful. . . . [Or] direct financial incentives [might] lead physicians to educate asthmatics better about controlling their disease, leading to fewer serious asthma attacks, better health, and fewer expensive emergency room visits and hospital admissions. . . .

To what extent are physicians adopting these [different] methods of lowering costs as a result of direct financial incentives? . . . In the absence of data, we are left with logic and anecdotes, both often misleading when looking at human affairs. . . . [A]t least three important factors will push against a physician's doing "too little." First, truly doing "too little" for a patient often will be more expensive, in the long run, than offering the proper mix of services. . . . Second, by doing too little, for whatever reason, physicians put themselves at risk for malpractice liability. . . . Third, and most important, physicians want to do the right thing for their patients. Faced with a patient who the doctor believes really needs another test, the cost of which will come out of the doctor's income, I am confident that almost all doctors, almost all of the time, will order the test. . . .

We cannot dismiss the possibility that, in some circumstances, direct financial incentives could harm patients. It seems plausible that we could identify some factors or situations that might increase the odds of such bad outcomes. At the same time, the health care world is in the midst of a complicated and rapidly changing revolution in how society buys care. At this point in that revolution, what should be done about direct financial incentives?

One set of at least partial answers has been advanced by the federal government. In the Omnibus Budget Reconciliation Act of 1986, Congress [forbade] hospitals . . . from knowingly making incentive payments to physicians to induce them to reduce or limit services [under Medicare and Medicaid,[11] but] . . . Congress repealed the prohibition [for HMOs]. In its place, Congress substituted three rules governing organizations using such incentives. 42 U.S.C. §1395mm(8). First, [Medicare and Medicaid HMOs] could not have a physician incentive plan that made specific payments to doctors to induce them to limit or reduce medically necessary services to a specific individual. Second, they had to tell [CMS] about their physician incentive plans in detail. Finally, if their plans put physicians or physician groups at "substantial risk," as defined by regulation, they had to provide stop-loss insurance to the physicians and survey their present and past members about the members' access to and satisfaction with the services they received. . . .

---

11. [The statute reads: "If a hospital . . . knowingly makes a payment, directly or indirectly, to a physician as an inducement to reduce or limit services provided with respect to [Medicare or Medicaid patients who] are under the direct care of the physician, the hospital . . . shall be subject . . . to a civil money penalty of not more than $2,000 for each such individual with respect to whom the payment is made." 42 U.S.C. §1320a-7a(b)(1).—EDS.]

[CMS] defined "substantial financial risk" as situations where a physician, or group, would have either more than twenty-five percent (for physicians or groups evaluated annually) or fifteen percent (if evaluated more frequently than annually) of its total compensation from the organization at risk, based at least in part on services the physicians did not provide directly. . . . [These] definitions for "substantial financial risk" [were chosen] solely because those seem to be near the limit of the risk amounts currently used by plans. As the current plans have no proven problems, [CMS] suggests, those percentages should be safe. This, of course, entirely avoids the questions of whether those percentages, or any percentages, are necessary. . . . There seems little reason for substantive regulation when all the regulators can say is that what they propose is consistent with what the industry already does. And, when an industry is evolving as rapidly as this one, such regulation may prove burdensome. . . . If evidence from research made it clear that some combinations of managed care incentives hurt patients, those methods could be banned or discouraged. . . .

In the long run, direct financial incentives may provide a useful solution to the problem of managing care, but only in a context where their risks are shared, and, hence, softened. . . . Thus, one way to adjust to direct financial incentives is to reconstruct medicine into a world of fairly large group practices that will be subject to those incentives. . . . I know many physicians who practice under one form of managed care with direct financial incentives: the Kaiser Permanente system. They tell me that they never feel pressure to make a treatment decision for financial reasons, but they also say that they practice differently at Kaiser than they did elsewhere and that their views of what is good medical practice have changed. . . . Physicians may use less expensive but equally effective drugs, or not keep patients in the hospitals longer than studies show is appropriate. All agree that much unnecessary, or unnecessarily expensive, care can be wrung out of the medical system.

At some point, though, when the unnecessary care has been eliminated, society still may be unwilling to pay the bill for all the appropriate care that is technically available. Under a system of care delivered by physician groups, operating under financial incentives, these rationing decisions would be made largely by the physician groups. . . . By burying the decisions in physician groups, one avoids the kinds of express allocation rules that prompt litigation—and accountability. Are physician groups the right bodies to make these rationing decisions? Compared to having them made by managed care groups? Congress? The courts? The "market"? These questions may lurk below the surface of the speculative future outlined above. . . .

Notes: Capitation, Gainsharing, and Other Physician Incentives

1. *The Ethics of Physician Incentives.* Capitation payments and other incentive plans common in HMOs raise a variety of legal and regulatory issues that are considered in other chapters (informed consent in Chapter 3.C, liability in Chapter 4, and insurance regulation in section B of this chapter). This section explores only the structure and use of capitation arrangements, and the ethical conflicts of interest they create. The following section covers additional payment innovations targeted more directly to episodes of illness, or to value-based measures of performance.

Regardless of what the law says about capitation, what about professional medical ethics? Should physicians avoid working in settings and contracting with insurers that reward them for reduced care? The following two excerpts give a flavor of this debate. The first is from a prominent physician at Boston University, Norman Levinsky, The Doctor's Master, 311 New Eng. J. Med. 1573 (1984):

> [P]hysicians are required to do everything that they believe may benefit each patient without regard to costs or other societal considerations. In caring for an individual patient, the doctor must act solely as that patient's advocate, against the apparent interests of society as a whole, if necessary. An analogy can be drawn with the role of a lawyer defending a client against a criminal charge. The attorney is obligated to use all ethical means to defend the client, regardless of the cost of prolonged legal proceedings or even of the possibility that a guilty person may be acquitted through skillful advocacy. Similarly, in the practice of medicine, physicians are obligated to do all that they can for their patients without regard to any costs to society.
>
> This [ethic] may become blurred if physicians are pressed to balance the needs of their patients with societal needs. The practitioner may make decisions for economic reasons but rationalize them as in the best interest of the individual patient. . . . It is society, not the individual practitioner, that must make the decision to limit the availability of effective but expensive types of medical care. . . . Society, through its elected officials, is entitled to decide that the resources required for [expensive treatment] are better used for other purposes. However, a physician who thinks that his or her patient may benefit from [the treatment] must make that patient aware of this opinion and assist the patient in obtaining the [treatment]. . . .

The contrasting viewpoint is from a well-known economist at MIT, Lester Thurow, Learning to Say "No," 311 New Eng. J. Med. 1569 (1984):

> [From an economic perspective], physicians must stop treatments when marginal benefits are equal to marginal costs. But where lies the point at which marginal costs equal marginal benefits? And who is to make this ethical decision? . . . One answer is that third-party payers can write rules and regulations concerning what they will and will not pay for and can prohibit their clients from buying services that are not allowed under the private or public insurance systems. . . . Such a procedure works, but it works clumsily, since no set of rules can be adjusted to the nuances of individual medical problems. It will be far better if American doctors begin to build up a social ethic and behavioral practices that help them decide when medicine is bad medicine — not simply because it has absolutely no payoff or because it hurts the patient — but also because the costs are not justified by the marginal benefits. . . .
>
> The medical profession now has professional norms concerning what constitutes bad medical practice. Those norms have to be expanded to include cases in which high costs are not justified by minor expected benefits. If such norms are developed and then legally defended against malpractice suits, it just may be possible to build up a system of doctor-imposed cost controls that will be much more flexible than any system of cost controls imposed by third-party payers could be. But if the medical profession fails to do this, sooner or later the United States will move to a system of third-party controls. Something will have to be done.

Which position do you think is more convincing?

Does it make you any more comfortable to know that physicians under financial incentives tend to adjust their practice styles across the board, for both HMO and fee-for-service patients alike? In other words, incentives do affect how physicians behave, but a physician is likely to respond impartially to all his patients rather than differentiate among them based on each patient's particular source of payment. See Rajesh Balkrishnan et al., Capitation Payment, Length of Visit, and Preventive Services, 8 Am. J. Managed Care 332 (2002); Laurence C. Baker, Managed Care Spillover Effects, 24 Annu. Rev. Public Health 435 (2003). Is this the ethical way to respond, or should patients with more generous insurance receive better service?

Commenting broadly on the attempt to regulate physician incentives, consider the following forceful commentary from another prominent health economist, James C. Robinson, Theory and Practice in the Design of Physician Payment Incentives, 79 Milbank Q. 149, 173-174 (2001):

> Physician payment mechanisms are inevitably subject to more public monitoring than compensation systems in other occupations, since we all care more about our doctor's immediate motivation than we do about our accountant's or plumber's.... The tendency to overregulate must be recognized, however. The complexity of clinical services, combined with the importance that we all ascribe to what happens between physicians and patients, is conducive to the most egregious manifestations of what legal theorists refer to as the inhospitality tradition. That which cannot be understood without effort is deemed ipso facto to be designed for fraud, monopolization, or some other antisocial purpose.... The contemporary moment in health policy is nothing short of a Dionysian rhapsody of regulation, the inhospitality tradition gone riot, the formal and final enshrinement of the doctrine that everything not mandatory is prohibited. The complexity of physician behavior, the emergence of payment methods that blend fee-for-service and capitation, the interdependence of price mechanisms with nonprice mechanisms, the salience of organization as a support for compensation systems, and the remarkable variety and continual change in all arenas suggest that public policymakers should adopt a stance of intellectual humility and a tone of cautious optimism. In physician payment, as in most other aspects of life, matters are never as good as we might hope but never as bad as we might fear.

See also Thomas P. Stossel, Regulation of Financial Conflicts of Interest in Medical Practice and Medical Research, 50 Perspect. Biol. Med. 54 (2007). Robert Kuttner observes that, "in building adequate risk-adjustment models, there are subtleties of Byzantine complexity.... Like so much else about the U.S. health system, [this] seems an astonishingly complex way to achieve some straightforward policy goals." He concludes that "the superior approach would be to cut the increasingly convoluted knot and move to a universal, unfragmented system of health insurance or a neutral form of payment for doctors, such as by salary." Robert Kuttner, The Risk-Adjustment Debate, 339 New Eng. J. Med. 1952 (1999).

2. *Risk Adjustment.* Capitation payments are rarely the same for each patient. Instead, they typically vary according to the patient's age and gender, in order to coarsely reflect how much care different types of patients usually need on average. This kind of calibration is known as "risk adjustment," and how it is done adds another major complication:

> The intent of more aggregated payment units, such as capitation, is to encourage providers to make more efficient use of resources for a set bundle of services. However, just as insurance companies and HMOs have discovered an irresistible market

logic in skimming off the healthiest subscribers, physicians . . . face a financial incentive to economize under more aggregated payment units by caring for healthier patients. Concern about this undesirable risk-skimming incentive has given rise to attempts to risk adjust reimbursement—that is, to pay at a higher rate for higher-risk patients.

Traditional fee-for-service payment has an intrinsic risk-adjustment factor. The sicker the patient, the more services provided. More services provided means greater reimbursement. In the episode-of-illness mode of payment, risk adjustment has been factored into such payment methods as the Medicare hospital DRG system. . . . Thus, DRG reimbursement is higher for a patient hospitalized for septic shock than for a patient admitted for elective cholecystectomy. . . .

Risk adjustment has been a technically greater challenge in setting capitation payments. The ideal risk-adjustment method for capitation payments would characterize each individual's health status or need for health care services to attach a higher payment rate to the higher-risk patients. For example, [an HMO] could pay a higher capitation rate for . . . HIV patients than for . . . healthy ones. Unfortunately, accurately predicting individuals' need for care is difficult. Data routinely collected during insurance enrollment, such as age, offer only a crude estimate of an individual's likelihood of using services. More accurate predictions necessitate examining an individual's medical history or current level of health, a relatively expensive proposition that often still falls short of the desired precision at estimating an individual's future health care expenses. . . . Interest in improving the "science" of risk adjustment is increasing as payers in the United States increasingly turn to capitation and other aggregated units of reimbursement.

Thomas Bodenheimer & Kevin Grumbach, Reimbursing Physicians and Hospitals, 272 JAMA 971 (1994).

Do you see the nightmare of DRGs recurring in the guise of risk adjustment? Medicare has struggled with how to implement risk adjustment for the managed care plans that its beneficiaries can purchase through Medicare Advantage. One approach pays more for patients with a history of designated chronic illnesses. The amount of extra payment is based on days of hospitalization and primary diagnoses in the prior year. Although this creates an incentive for HMOs to hospitalize their patients more in one year to increase payment in the next year, CMS claims there are sufficient checks in place to prevent this incentive from increasing costs. See Lisa Iezzoni et al., Paying More Fairly for Medicare Capitated Care, 339 New Eng. J. Med. 1933 (1998).

3. *Hospital "Gainsharing."* Carefully reread the passage in Prof. Greely's article that discusses the two federal statutes regulating physician incentives under Medicare and Medicaid. Note that the statute governing hospital-created incentives contains a flat prohibition of what has since come to be known as "gainsharing," whereas the HMO regulation is more permissive. Why should the rules about economizing incentives be much stricter for hospitals than for HMOs? The hospital statute was enacted in response to several for-profit hospitals in California that paid each doctor a percentage of the profits the hospital earned under DRGs from the doctor's Medicare patients. But, if Congress did not want money to influence decisions about hospital treatment, why did it adopt the DRG system in the first place?

If it is illegal for hospitals to split cost savings with physicians, then can hospitals not even reward physicians for identifying and eliminating wasteful practice patterns, such as not opening more surgical supplies than are needed for an operation, or using less expensive versions of particularly expensive surgical supplies? Hospital lawyers believed that such worthy purposes would avoid the statutory prohibition by focusing on more aggregate practice patterns among a group of physicians rather than on discrete treatment decisions by particular doctors. At first DHHS broadly pronounced these "gainsharing" efforts illegal, but following an outcry from hospitals and their lawyers, it subsequently declined to prosecute arrangements that contained various safeguards, limits, and oversight mechanisms to guard against abuses, similar to those under the HMO financial incentive statute. Also, regulations now clarify that the gainsharing prohibition applies only to programs that reduce medically necessary care, and the prohibition does not apply to accountable care organizations that participate in Medicare's new "shared savings" program—whose purpose, after all, is essentially the same as the gainsharing plans that DHHS initially disapproved. Still, hospitals and their lawyers often consider the rules to be too restrictive, such that gainsharing arrangements often are not worth the bother or the uncertainty of compliance. See Government Accountability Office, Implementation of Financial Incentive Programs Under Federal Fraud and Abuse Laws (2012).

4. *Disclosing Incentives.* Are you convinced by *Pegram* that it is not a proper judicial function to adjudicate financial conflicts of interest under fiduciary principles? If this claim were brought under common law, should it still be dismissed? What if the claim involves the failure to *disclose* physician incentives rather than the argument that the incentives *themselves* violate fiduciary duties? Notice in footnote 8 that even *Pegram* says that failing to disclose financial incentives might violate ERISA. See also Shea v. Esensten, 208 F.3d 712 (8th Cir. 2000) (suggesting in dictum that Minnesota would recognize an action against physicians for failing to disclose financial incentives). Prior to *Pegram*, this theory had received only mixed success in the federal courts under ERISA. See Comment, 106 Dick. L. Rev. 415 (2001). Following *Pegram*, at least one court has held that ERISA does not require disclosure of physician incentives unless the patient asks for this information, or unless the HMO knows the patient needed or wanted this information and that it would have avoided harm to the patient. Horvath v. Keystone Health Plan East, Inc., 333 F.3d 450 (3d Cir. 2003). Could this theory of liability be based simply on informed consent law? Compare Mark Hall, A Theory of Economic Informed Consent, 31 Ga. L. Rev. 31 (1997) (arguing no); with Devon C. McGraw, Financial Incentives to Limit Services: Should Physicians Be Required to Disclose These to Patients?, 83 Geo. L. J. 1821 (1995) (arguing yes).

One important decision refused to allow such a suit under state law, citing *Pegram* for support. Neade v. Portes, 739 N.E.2d 496 (Ill. 2000), discussed at page 201. However, the court held that evidence of physician incentives could be relevant in assessing medical negligence. *Neade* also observed that Illinois, like many other states, has a statute requiring disclosure of incentives but imposes this duty only on the HMO, not on the physician. See Tracy E. Miller & William M. Sage, Disclosing Physician Financial Incentives, 281 JAMA 1424-1430 (1999). Therefore, similar to *Pegram*, the *Neade* court felt that the issue should not be dealt with through common law.

Under either tort law or regulatory law, what is the optimal timing for disclosing physician incentives: when someone is deciding which health insurance to choose, when the person is picking a physician, or when the person is considering a treatment option? Federal rules implementing Medicare's shared savings program for ACOs require primary care physicians to disclose their participation in the incentive program to patients "at the point of care." 42 C.F.R. 425.312(a). How much detail should patients be given? How much is this information likely to really matter to people in making important decisions? See generally Mark A. Hall, The Theory and Practice of Disclosing HMO Physician Incentives, 65 Law & Contemp. Probs. 207 (Autumn 2002).

5. Pegram*'s Importance for Preemption.* Because *Pegram* broadly discusses the purpose and functioning of HMOs, it has importance in a number of other areas of litigation. For instance, consider what this decision has to say about the issue addressed in Chapter 4.F of whether ERISA preempts malpractice claims against HMOs, based on the Court's assumption that Pegram has tort remedies available under state law.

6. *Additional Readings.* For concerns about **global capitation and the role of financial incentives generally** (note 1), see Steffie Woolhandler & David Himmelstein, Extreme Risk: The New Corporate Proposition for Physicians, 333 New Eng. J. Med. 1706 (1995); Christopher Robertson, Effect of Financial Relationships on the Behavior of Healthcare Professionals, 40 J. L. Med. & Ethics 452 (2012).

For more on **the ethics of physicians incentives** (note 1), see Conflicts of Interest in Clinical Practice and Research (Roy Spece et al. eds., 1996); Peter A. Ubel, Pricing Life: Why It's Time for Health Care Rationing (2000); Christopher Robertson et al., Effect of Financial Relationships on the Behaviors of Health Care Professionals, 40 J. L. Med. & Ethics 452 (2012); Gail Agrawal, Resuscitating Professionalism: Self-Regulation in the Medical Marketplace, 66 Mo. L. Rev. 341 (2001); Mark A. Hall, Rationing Health Care at the Bedside, 69 N.Y.U. L. Rev. 693 (1994); William M. Sage, Physicians as Advocates, 35 Hous. L. Rev. 1529 (1999); Timothy S. Hall, Bargaining with Hippocrates: Managed Care and the Doctor-Patient Relationship, 54 S.C. L. Rev. 689 (2003); Symposium, 40 J. L. Med. & Ethics 436 (2012); and the readings and sources cited in section D.1 and Chapter 1.D.5.

For general discussion of the methods, purpose, and performance of risk adjustment (note 2), see Mark A. Hall, Risk Adjustment Under the Affordable Care Act, 20 Kan. J. L. & Pub. Pol'y 222 (2011); David Blumenthal et al., The Who, What, and Why of Risk Adjustment, 30 J. Health Pol. Pol'y & L. 453 (2005); Fred Hellinger & Herbert Wong, Selection Bias in HMOs: A Review of the Evidence, 57 Med. Care Res. Rev. 405 (2000); Symposium, Private Employers and Risk Adjustment, 38 Inquiry 242 (2001).

For discussions of **hospital gainsharing** (note 3), see Richard S. Saver, Squandering the Gain: Gainsharing and the Continuing Dilemma of Physician Financial Incentives, 98 Nw. U. L. Rev. 145 (2003); Gail Wilensky, Gain Sharing: A Good Concept Getting a Bad Name?, 26(1) Health Aff. w58 (Jan. 2007); Catherine Martin, Incentive Payment and Shared Savings Programs: The New Gainsharing, 17 BNA Health L. Rep. 1011 (2008); Anne Claiborne et al., Legal Impediments to Implementing Value-Based Purchasing in Healthcare, 35 Am. J. L. & Med. 443 (2009). For discussion of the HMO rules, see M. Hall, Physician Rationing and Agency Cost Theory, *in* Spece, supra; David Orentlicher, Paying Physicians More to Do Less: Financial Incentives to Limit Care, 30 U. Rich. L. Rev. 155, 174 (1996); Stephen R. Latham, Regulation of Managed Care Incentive Payments to Physicians, 22 Am.

J. L. & Med. 399 (1996); Douglas Blair, The "PIP" Regulations in Perspective, 29 U. Mem. L. Rev. 137 (1998).

For more on **informed consent and the disclosure of payment arrangements** (note 4), see E. Haavi Morreim, Diverse and Perverse Incentives of Managed Care: Bringing Patients into Alignment, 1 Widener L. Symp. J. 89, 123 (1996); Grant H. Morris, Dissing Disclosure: Just What the Doctor Ordered, 44 Ariz. L. Rev. 313 (2002); Susan M. Wolf, 35 Hous. L. Rev. 1631 (1999); Joan H. Krause, Reconceptualizing Informed Consent in an Era of Health Care Cost Containment, 85 Iowa L. Rev. 261 (1999). For more discussion of **"gag clauses"** (note 5), see Gordon Brand et al., The Two Faces of Gag Provisions: Patients and Physicians in a Bind, 17 Yale L. & Pol'y Rev. 249 (1998); Joan H. Krause, The Brief Life of the Gag Clause, 67 Tenn. L. Rev. 1 (1999).

For a discussion of how **fiduciary law principles** apply to these issues generally, see Peter D. Jacobson & Michael T. Cahill, Applying Fiduciary Responsibilities in the Managed Care Context, 26 Am. J. L. & Med. 155 (2000); Marc A. Rodwin, Strains in the Fiduciary Metaphor: Divided Physician Loyalties and Obligations in a Changing Health Care System, 21 Am. J. L. & Med. 241 (1995).

For general commentary on *Pegram* and the issues it raises, see Michael T. Cahill & Peter D. Jacobson, *Pegram*'s Regress: A Missed Chance for Sensible Judicial Review of Managed Care Decisions, 27 Am. J. L. & Med. 421 (2001); Peter J. Hammer, On Peritonitis, Preemption, and the Elusive Goal of Managed Care Accountability, 26 J. Health Pol. Pol'y & L. 767 (2001); Richard A. Ippolito, Freedom to Contract in Medical Care: HMOs, ERISA and Pegram v. Herdrich, 9 Sup. Ct. Econ. Rev. 1 (2001); Arnold J. Rosoff, Breach of Fiduciary Duty Lawsuits Against MCOs, 22 J. Leg. Med. 55 (2001); William Sage, UR Here: The Supreme Court's Guide for Managed Care, 19 Health Aff. 219 (2000); Jeffrey Stempel & Nadia Magdenko, Doctors, HMOs, ERISA, and the Public Interest After Pegram v. Herdrich, 36 Tort & Ins. L.J. 687 (2001); Symposium, 1 Yale J. Health Pol'y L. & Ethics (2001)

4. Value-Based Payment Innovations

■REVISITING INCENTIVE-BASED CONTRACTS
Wendy Netter Epstein
17 Yale J. Health Pol'y, L. & Ethics 1 (2017)

Incentive-based compensation has its roots in classic economic theory: rational, selfish actors who are motivated to maximize their own wealth will do their best work if they will get a financial reward for doing so. Material incentives are generally believed to be powerful motivators. The Aztecs rewarded successful warriors with land and better food. Roman warriors were rewarded in the same ways. The use of financial incentives in particular is now pervasive across very different industries, from executive compensation to professional sports and education. Common sense and economic principles both suggest that connecting pay to quality metrics will yield better results.

Incentive pay is a concept that almost everyone seems to be able to get behind. Indeed, incentive regimes are a part of the new ideological hybrid– libertarian paternalism–that encourages behavior by making it attractive without regulating it.[4] The liberal Obama Administration has firmly embraced the idea, arguing that rewarding excellence with pay improves quality. And conservatives generally support incentive pay because it is essentially a private, market-based solution. It remains to be seen if the new Trump Administration will stay the course or not, but there is reason to believe it may not.

It may be right to revisit the move to incentive pay. The history of incentive pay across industries has been mixed. Scholars and policymakers have identified a host of observed and potential mal-effects, from cherry picking easy cases or cheating on the metrics, to excessively focusing on the metrics to the detriment of overall quality of performance. . . .

The issue of how to structure reimbursement agreements is really one of how to draft contracts to maximize party performance. Economists, social scientists, and contracts scholars have contributed to an immense literature addressing the effects of contract drafting strategies on agents' cognition, compliance, and motivation to perform. This literature–theoretical, experimental, and empirical–is complicated, and at times, seemingly conflicting. Financial incentives can motivate, but can also crowd out intrinsic motivation. Contract specificity can inform goals and facilitate improved performance, while reducing the likelihood that parties will use contractual gaps to justify unethical behavior. But specificity can also cause agents to focus too narrowly and ignore hard cases, decreasing overall performance, among a host of other identified effects.

The literature suggests that the detailed, control-based contracting approach is a better fit for easily measurable, compliance-oriented tasks not requiring creativity or innovation than it is for more difficult-to-define tasks that require motivating the agent's best performance. Experience with incentive-based contracting across industries seems to bear out these predictions. . . .

The health-care industry provides a new lens through which to study this long-standing problem. . . . The general consensus in the industry is that physician financial incentives must be addressed as a part of addressing overall cost and quality concerns. . . . If the problem is that doctors' incentives are out of step with those of payers and patients, then align their incentives; pay physicians for delivering cost-effective, quality care, not for simply delivering more care.

Just as in other industries, the health-care commitment to incentive compensation evidences a commitment to a more detailed contracting approach. In a fee-for-service system, the contracts between physicians and payers are, relatively speaking, unspecific and make only limited use of control elements, such as reporting requirements and financial incentives tied to performance. . . . Importantly, it commits to payment regardless of outcome.

Incentive-based compensation, on the other hand, requires much more detailed contract drafting. The payer provides, *ex ante*, a list of metrics the physician is required to meet. The payer also defines the financial implications of meeting, exceeding, or falling short of those metrics. If fee-for-service contracts tend to be

---

4. *See* Richard Thaler & Cass Sunstein, *Libertarian Paternalism*, 93 Am. Econ. Rev. 175 (2003).

vague in task definition and tend to make limited use of control elements, incentive pay is a move to the other end of the contract-drafting spectrum: detailed task specification and extensive use of contractual control mechanisms such as reporting, monitoring, and financial incentives.

The health-care industry has been focused on how to improve this new payment model—for instance, how to determine the proper amount of the financial incentive and how to choose the correct quality metrics. This Article suggests that focus is misplaced. The key question the health-care industry should be focused on solving is not how to improve this new payment model, although that work may be useful, but rather on where and where not to use the model. The legal, economic, and behavioral literature teaches that an across-the-board approach such as the one currently being hailed in the industry will not be effective. The industry must determine, and then implement, a more nuanced approach that draws the line between tasks where incentive-pay mechanisms will be helpful and those where they will be ineffective at best or harmful at worst. Changing focus in this way is much more likely to yield successful results, even if it requires recognizing that incentive-based compensation cannot solve all of the health industry's problems. . . .

THE HEALTH INDUSTRY'S INCENTIVE-PAY SOLUTION

Linking payment with desired results has been touted by members of Congress as the panacea for health care that can save the United States $700 billion a year, while simultaneously improving quality. . . . In January 2015, the Department of Health and Human Services (HHS) publicly announced a goal of tying fifty percent of payments to alternative payment models, such as ACOs, by the end of 2018 [although the Trump administration is expected to scale back or delay that goal]. . . . The following explains how incentive-based compensation is expected to work.

In the health context specifically, the typical pay-for-performance program provides a bonus to health-care providers (or hospitals or other medical entities) if they meet or exceed agreed-upon metrics, although some are structured to penalize providers that fail to meet defined metrics. . . . Quality and performance measures differ by program, but generally fall into four categories: process, outcome, patient experience, or structure. Process metrics require providers to follow a predefined process to satisfy the metric, such as giving aspirin to heart-attack victims within a certain amount of time after the patient arrives in the emergency room. Outcome measures focus on results. Morbidity and mortality data are the classic examples. More recently, there has been a focus on defining more-specific outcome measures, such as reductions in hemoglobin A1c in diabetic patients. Patient experience measures the patients' perception of the care they receive and is usually collected by compiling the results of patient surveys. Finally, structure considers the inputs into health-care provision, from the facilities and equipment used in treatment, to the adoption of health information technology.

THE AFFORDABLE CARE ACT'S COMMITMENT TO INCENTIVE-BASED COMPENSATION

Despite the contentious political debates that surrounded and continue to surround the Affordable Care Act (ACA), there was strong bipartisan support for a key category of reform reflected in the bill: restructuring the Medicare delivery system by tying financial incentives to performance. . . . By some measures, the ACA includes forty five different provisions aimed at reforming health-care delivery to either improve the quality and/or the efficiency of health care in some way.[82] . . . The three largest initiatives are: (1) the establishment of a Shared Savings Program to benefit Accountable Care Organizations; (2) the new incentive-based compensation model for physicians (and hospitals); and (3) a pilot program to test bundled payments, among other initiatives.

A. ACCOUNTABLE CARE ORGANIZATIONS

Of all the provisions aimed at reforming the delivery model by aligning incentives, Accountable Care Organizations (ACOs) have received the most attention [and are further discussed in the next reading]. . . . An ACO is a network of care providers committed to improving quality and reducing cost through coordination of efforts. Rather than individual specialists treating one patient without collaboration (thus duplicating tests and procedures, and lacking a cohesive view of the entire patient), ACOs deliver integrated care enabled by shared medical records and other coordination. . . . By giving providers who have at least some control over cost and quality of care a bonus for cost and quality metrics improvement (and in some cases a penalty for failing to meet goals), the ACO model aligns provider incentives with governmental priorities.

Both cost savings and quality metrics play a part in determining ACO compensation. First, CMS sets a benchmark of average Medicare expenditures, taking into account a projected growth rate in expenses. CMS also sets a list of [33] quality metrics and associated benchmarks. . . . ACOs receive points on a sliding scale based on level of performance relative to the benchmarks. For instance, ACOs must report on certain preventive health measures administered to patients, such as immunizations for influenza and mammography screenings. ACOs must also report outcome measures for patients with various illnesses. For example, for patients with diabetes, ACOs must document control of Hemoglobin A1c, and for patients with hypertension, ACOs must report on patient blood pressure. . . . The quality metrics differentiate ACOs from HMOs and, in theory, prevent ACOs from saving money by rationing necessary care. . . .

B. INCENTIVE-BASED COMPENSATION FOR PHYSICIANS

The ACA also changes the method of physician [and hospital] payment through the Physician Value-Based Payment Modifier [and the Hospital (In-Patient) Value-Based Purchasing Program]. . . . The modifier adjusts fees paid to physicians [and hospitals] using data reported on quality and resource use. . . . The program started by focusing on measures of clinical processes and results of patient-satisfaction surveys, but over time has come to rely more heavily on outcome measures, such as mortality rates, rather than measures of process compliance. . . .

---

82. This does not include, for instance, the recent enactment of the Medicare Access and CHIP Reauthorization Act of 2015 and its expansion of value-based payment systems for providers.

This new adjustment was first applied in 2015 to [hospitals] group practices with one hundred or more eligible professionals, using quality reporting data from 2013. The program [was expected to] be scaled up to apply to all physicians by 2018 [but has been delayed by the Trump administration]. The program is budget neutral for the government; therefore, some [providers] will see their pay increase while others will see it decrease.

C. BUNDLED PAYMENTS

Finally, [the ACA] establishes a five-year program to test bundled payments [which has now been made ongoing since 2013]. Bundled payments mean that rather than paying per procedure or per test, reimbursement will be based on the expected costs for an entire episode of care (e.g., a single illness or course of treatment). . . . The idea is, if a predefined sum of money will be awarded for patient care and total reimbursement cannot be increased by ordering more tests or procedures, providers will think hard about whether that extra test is likely to yield valuable information before ordering it and will coordinate their efforts to avoid costly and unnecessary duplication. . . . The financial incentive in [the current] model flows directly to the hospital and not the physician, although physician behavior is intended to be targeted as well. . . .

III. INCENTIVE-BASED COMPENSATION: THE EVIDENCE SO FAR

Although incentive-based compensation is, relatively speaking, new to health care, it has long been employed in other industries, such as executive compensation, professional sports, and education. . . .The experience in these three industries . . . seems to bear out many of the predictions of the literature. While financial incentives do seem to motivate, at least according to some studies, they tend to do so best where easy-to-measure goals are closely associated with the performance the principal wishes to prompt from the agent. But . . . there are other overarching concerns. Financial incentives seem to cause focus on the metric to which compensation is tied, and in particular, promote paying attention to metrics that are easier to move, while ignoring the harder cases. Performance pay can also encourage risk-taking behavior and even cheating.

. . . [P]erformance pay works better in some contexts than others. Key attributes of successful performance pay systems appear to be: (1) easy to define and measure tasks; (2) low ability or need to cheat on the metrics; and (3) a low likelihood of crowding out already strong intrinsic motivation, either because intrinsic motivation is weak to begin with or intrinsic motivation is not particularly necessary to successful execution of the task. . . .

EARLY RESULTS OF INCENTIVE PAY IN HEALTH CARE

. . . A number of studies also assess the extent to which pay for performance can be linked to cost savings. The most salient inquiry is whether cost savings can be achieved while quality metrics are simultaneously maintained or improved. The purpose of incentive-pay models is not to achieve cost savings at the sacrifice of quality. Arguably that was the problem with HMOs. Again, results are mixed. Some are positive. . . . Others actually found that where quality improves as intended, cost increases rather than decreases. . . .

Several studies have also investigated whether incentive pay yields unintended consequences. In other words, some providers might succeed in improving quality and decreasing cost, but might do so in ways that have undesirable effects in other areas.

First, policymakers have been concerned that physician financial incentives will result in adverse selection, where physicians cherry pick the easier cases while harder cases receive less attention. . . . Second, some studies have assessed whether incentive pay tied to certain procedures or categories of care has negative spillover effects on unincentivized procedures. . . . Third, there has been concern over gaming the system or cheating on the metrics. . . . The fourth unintended consequence concerns whether the use of financial incentives affects the intrinsic motivation of providers or provider professionalism. [Studies so far are limited and inconclusive on each of these possibilities]. . . .

Relatedly, some studies have noted that the use of incentive pay has adversely affected the physician-patient relationship.[283] For instance, physicians have reported resentment toward non-compliant patients who negatively impact their compensation. In one study, physicians also reported pressure to convince patients to agree to certain treatments or to bypass the informed-consent process.

In general, it is hard to draw concrete lessons from this very preliminary and mixed data. But it at least suggests that the predictions of the incomplete contracts literature may bear out in the health industry, as they seem to do in the executive compensation, education, and professional sports examples, and that there may be additional challenges unique to the health-care context. . . . .

CONCLUSION

The health-care industry has rallied behind a far-reaching implementation of incentive pay, one that applies across delivery models, to generalist and specialty physicians, and to a wide range of procedures and diagnoses. The contracts literature suggests that this is too blunt of an approach. Task specification and control-based contracting that utilizes monitoring and financial incentives tends to work best for ensuring compliance. But it works less well for motivating consummate performance because it can signal distrust and crowd out social and professional norms that would otherwise have operated to improve performance. Task specification coupled with control mechanisms can also lead to gamesmanship and cheating on the metrics to secure increased compensation. The health-care industry should be focusing on where to implement incentive pay to capture its benefits for compliance and standardization, but minimize its negative impact on innovation and the operation of positive norms. The new Trump Administration has an opportunity to study this issue further and to claw back some of the misguided attempts to

---

283. Note that it is this concern—about the effect of incentive pay on the doctor-patient relationship—that caused Tom Price, President Trump's first Secretary of Health and Human Services, who is also a physician, to come out publicly against the use of incentive pay in health care.

implement incentive pay where it is likely to have mal-effects. These are lessons to be extrapolated to other industries, as well.

■ACCOUNTABLE CARE ORGANIZATIONS IN MEDICARE AND THE PRIVATE SECTOR: A STATUS UPDATE
Robert A. Berenson & Rachel A. Burton (2011)
WHY IS EVERYONE TALKING ABOUT ACOS?

. . . For many [health care policy analysts], the holy grail of health policy-making has been to find a model that aligns health care providers' and patients' interests. In the 1980s and '90s, some thought that health maintenance organizations (HMOs) might be such a model, but patients, encouraged by their physicians, eventually objected to HMOs' perceived intrusion into patient care decisions, causing HMOs to back off from some of their earlier approaches and to now fade from prominence.

Two decades later, the next great hope of many has become accountable care organizations (ACOs). Although known primarily as a Medicare program authorized in the Affordable Care Act (ACA), ACO-style payment arrangements have already been adopted by private insurers, even before the Centers for Medicare & Medicaid Services (CMS) issued its final regulations . . . for the Medicare Shared Savings Program, as it is called. . . . Medicare's ACO approach may influence many more health plans because it provides a model for an intermediary form of delivery: putting providers in a position somewhere between being paid solely through volume-increasing fee-for-service payments and operating within tightly managed, prospectively defined capitated budgets that place providers at full financial risk for all spending for their enrolled populations. . . . The ACO's performance on numerous quality metrics is also central to determining whether the ACO is eligible for shared savings and, if so, the amount of shared savings it receives from the sponsoring payer. . . .

In current ACO arrangements, providers generally receive bonuses if their patients' health care costs are below a projected amount based on their own historic spending, regardless of whether the level of their historic spending is high or low. The size of these bonuses depends, in part, on how much savings the ACO produces. Both the [Medicare Shared Savings Program] and private ACO contracts have been layering these bonus payments on top of traditional fee-for-service reimbursement, rather than making the leap to capitation (pre-paid fees paid per patient). . . . Several private ACO contracts [as well as Medicare] are offering providers 50 percent of the savings they generate . . . , and intend to transition their private ACO contracts to some form of capitation in coming years, as in the Pioneer ACO model being pursued by CMS' Innovation Center. . . .

[P]rivate ACO contracts are giving patients added incentives to seek care within their plan's provider network, such as by offering reduced premiums for individuals who receive care from providers taking part in such arrangements. By contrast, Medicare has so far chosen not to offer such financial incentives to Medicare beneficiaries to stay within their ACO's provider network. . . . [Medicare] beneficiaries will retain the freedom to seek care from any health care providers they choose. But if a beneficiary obtains the plurality of their primary care from a provider who belongs to an ACO, that beneficiary's total health care spending, along with care quality metrics, will be measured and used to assess whether their provider's ACO is eligible for shared savings bonus payments. ACOs will be sent lists of beneficiaries they are likely to be held accountable for under CMS' assignment algorithm on a quarterly basis. Then, at the end of the year, CMS will calculate ACOs' shared savings bonus payments based on a re-assessment of where those beneficiaries actually ended up receiving a plurality of their primary care services. CMS calls this approach "preliminary prospective assignment." . . .

WILL ACOs SAVE MONEY?

The results of the only demonstration that directly tested the ACO concept . . . suggest that ACOs will be able to improve the quality of care they deliver (at least as measured by process-oriented clinical quality measures), but will have a harder time generating savings. . . . Only two participants lowered health spending enough to receive bonuses in all five years of the demo, and three of the 10 participants received no bonus in any year of the demo. . . .

Even more disappointing, CMS' independent evaluator questioned whether demo participants generated savings by actually reducing spending or by merely raising the spending targets they had to work within by more thoroughly recording patients' diagnoses. (Under the risk-adjustment model CMS uses, spending and spending targets are adjusted based on patients' diagnoses.) . . .

The bottom line is that the [Medicare] demo does not seem to have succeeded in meaningfully reducing spending growth. However, it should not be surprising that the demo did not cause providers to dramatically alter the way they deliver care to achieve large reductions in health care spending, . . . [g]iven the initial three-year limit on CMS' commitment to the payment approach used in this demo. . . .

WILL QUALITY MEASURES PROTECT PATIENTS AGAINST HARM?

ACO proponents think that publicly available quality measures can go a long way towards protecting patients against the kind of stinting on care that patients perceived HMOs as engaging in during the 1990s. In the [Medicare Shared Savings Program], CMS will monitor ACOs through their reporting on 33 quality measures. ACOs that do not perform at the 30th percentile or percent (depending on the measure) on at least 70 percent of the measures in each of four domains would not be eligible to share in any savings they generate, and would have one year to improve performance before being terminated from the program. . . .

It is unclear whether quality measures currently are up to one of the tasks assigned them, that is, to ensure that cost savings will not be achieved by stinting on care. . . . [The measures] do not cover the full range of areas that an organization responsible for the entire continuum of care for a population of Medicare beneficiaries should address; for example, appropriate referral to specialized centers outside the ACO, when specialized expertise is needed to treat particular forms of cancer. . . .

Notes: Future Directions in Reimbursement

1. *Accountable Care Organizations.* These notes introduce ACOs as a vehicle for payment innovation. As a means to reduce costs, recent evidence suggests that

Medicare's ACO program has yielded only small savings. See J. Michael McWilliams et al., Early Performance of Accountable Care Organizations in Medicare, 374 New Eng. J. Med. 2357 (2016). That may be due in part to the weakness of the "shared savings" incentives under Medicare. As discussed more in Chapter 10, ACOs are also designed for use under private insurance, which could opt to use stronger incentives. Or, ACOs might form the nucleus for providers themselves to become insurers, or for them to contract directly with employers, thus acting as virtual insurers.

2. *Value-Based Payment Reform.* In January 2015, CMS announced an ambitious goal of tying at least 90 percent of all Medicare fee-for-service payments to quality or value metrics by the end of 2018. See Sylvia Burwell, Setting Value-Based Payment Goals—HHS Efforts to Improve U.S. Health Care, 372 New Eng. J. Med. 897 (2015). The bipartisan adoption of the Medicare Access and CHIP Reauthorization Act of 2015 (MACRA) should aid the agency's efforts to pay for value instead of quantity.

> This approach incentivizes clinicians to participate in "alternative payment models" (APMs). Examples of APMs could be accountable care organizations, bundled payment models, and medical homes. MACRA establishes specific criteria for "eligible alternative payment entities," which operate under one of these APMs. Essentially, MACRA establishes two paths for payment updates [i.e., increasing the amount that clinicians are paid each year]—a path for clinicians who participate in eligible alternative payment entities and a path for all other clinicians.
>
> Beginning in 2019 and continuing through 2024, clinicians will receive a 5 percent incentive payment if the level of revenue they receive through eligible alternative payment entities meets a certain threshold. In 2025, there will be no update and no incentive payments, and from 2026 on, clinicians meeting the revenue threshold will receive a higher update than clinicians who do not meet that threshold. Thus, how CMS defines eligible alternative payment entities and how clinicians qualify for the incentive payment are of great interest to clinicians.
>
> For clinicians who do not qualify for the APM incentive payment, a separate program exists for assessing clinicians on their performance—the Merit-based Incentive Payment System (MIPS). Performance on MIPS will determine whether clinicians will receive a bonus or a penalty on their fee-for-service (FFS) payments. Although budget neutral in aggregate, these bonuses and penalties could have a large effect on payments for individual clinicians and hence on the attractiveness of the APM and MIPS paths.

Medicare Payment Advisory Commission, June 2016 Report to Congress, at 29-30.

CMS has issued a lengthy and complex set of rules to implement MACRA, which went into effect at the beginning of 2017. See 81 Fed. Reg. 77008 (Nov. 2016). But the law is unpopular among physicians, with the MIPS program attracting particular ire:

> [P]hysicians and their staff currently spend, on average, 785.2 hours ($40,069 per physician) annually simply tracking and reporting quality measures for Medicare, Medicaid, and private health insurers. . . . In spite of the substantial time diverted from patient care and the money ($15.4 billion—roughly the amount of government spending each year on graduate medical education) that could be used for other purposes, most physicians feel that the current measures do not help them improve the care they provide. According to an October 2016 analysis of the current

misalignment of health quality measures, the Government Accountability Office concluded that: "Although hundreds of quality measures have been developed, relatively few are measures that payers, providers, and other stakeholders agree to adopt, because few are viewed as leading to meaningful improvements in quality."

Making this huge investment in measure reporting with very little return in quality improvement is wholly inconsistent with the goal of value-based health care. Furthermore, while MIPS is essentially a complex pay-for-performance system that will reward or penalize physicians based on their performance on a range of measures, analyses of pay-for-performance payments systems have shown that they have had little effect on improving the quality of care over the past decade.

John O'Shea, As MACRA Implementation Proceeds, Changes Are Needed, Health Affairs Blog (Apr. 21, 2017). Adding to the confusion is the complexity involved when a given provider or network is subject to multiple different payment methods simultaneously. Robert E. Mechanic, When New Medicare Payment Systems Collide, 374 New Eng. J. Med. 1706 (2016). Based on all of this, the influential Medicare Payment Advisory Commission (MedPAC) has recommended repeal of MIPS, to be replaced with a voluntary approach that bases performance bonuses on measurable patient outcomes. MedPAC, June 2017 Report to Congress.

If paying for performance is so hard, what other approaches could CMS take to assure that it gets good value for its money?

3. *Bundling Payment for Episodes of Care.* Currently, Medicare ACOs receive only a bonus for savings compared to benchmark standard fee-for-service payment (or possibly a penalty for costing more). But, as Prof. Epstein mentions, some policy analysts hope that ACOs will permit a move away from fee-for-service models entirely, toward paying lump sums for entire episodes of care. Doing that would also depart from having different payment methods for hospitals versus physicians, by bundling payment across all providers for a given episode of treatment, leaving to providers to negotiate how to allocate the bundled payment. Can you start to see the complexities in conducting such negotiations?

> In the early 1990s, Medicare created the Medicare Participating Heart Bypass Center Demonstration, which bundled hospital and physician payments for cardiac bypass graft surgery. The payments covered readmissions within seventy-two hours postdischarge and related physician services for a ninety-day period. Although the demonstration was considered successful, it was not renewed because of opposition from some parts of the hospital industry. . . .
>
> In its June 2008 report, MedPAC [the Medicare Payment Advisory Commission], having studied the issue for more than a year, made [these] unanimous recommendations to Congress regarding bundling [which Congress included in the 2010 health reform law]: . . . Congress should require the Secretary to create a voluntary pilot program to test the feasibility of actual bundled payment for services around hospitalization episodes for select conditions. . . . [T]he commissioners believed . . . that bundling could provide the incentive and opportunity for physicians to reduce the number of hospital visits without harming quality. Second, they intended that a bundled payment pilot would remove legal barriers that currently keep hospitals from compensating physicians for using fewer resources during a hospital stay. Third, depending upon the structure of the bundled payment, physicians would be encouraged to focus on posthospital care and the prevention of [hospital] readmissions. . . .

Whichever model proves to be the best, this type of incentive change is difficult. As noted by [MedPAC's chairman], "[we are] under no illusion that the path of policy change outlined here is easy. . . . But a continuation of the status quo is unacceptable."

Francis J. Crosson & Laura A. Tollen, Partners in Health: How Physicians and Hospitals Can Be Accountable Together (2010).

The CMS Innovation Center is charged with developing demonstration projects to test new payment approaches, including bundled payments. Initially, the Innovation Center's bundled payment initiatives were voluntary: Providers could choose whether or not to participate. The problem with voluntary demonstration projects, however, is that volunteering organizations could be—indeed, they likely are—systematically different from organizations that do not volunteer. What works for volunteers may not work for non-volunteers, making it hard to know whether the demonstration should be scaled up.

To avoid the problems of causal inference, the Innovation Center decided in late 2015 to require providers in 67 geographical areas to accept bundled payments for hip and knee replacements. See 80 Fed. Reg. 73273 (2015). And in January 2017, in the waning days of the Obama administration, the agency announced that it would also require some providers to use bundled payments for hip fractures, heart attacks, and coronary bypass surgery. 82 Fed. Reg. 180 (2017).

Resistance from hospitals and physicians to these "mandatory models" has been intense, however, and Tom Price, President Trump's first Secretary of Health and Human Services (and former physician), has been an especially vocal critic. Shortly after the change in administration, CMS announced that it would delay the newest bundled payment initiatives, perhaps indefinitely. Many in the policy community fear that the abandonment of mandatory models "would eliminate the ability to generate robust evidence on their effectiveness, dealing a severe blow to efforts to use bundled payments to improve care delivery in orthopedics and cardiac care, and to the chances for bringing bundled payments to scale nationally in the coming years." Tim Gronniger et al., How Should the Trump Administration Handle Medicare's New Bundled Payment Programs?, Health Affairs Blog, Apr. 10, 2017.

4. *Staying up to Date.* The following is a sampling of literature on these fast-paced developments, but those wanting the latest should do additional research, since payment reform, like the weather, is subject to rapid change and resists accurate forecasts.

For an overview **of initial ACO performance** (note 1), see Zirui Song & Elliott Fisher, The ACO Experiment in Infancy: Looking Back and Looking Forward, 316 JAMA 705 (2016).

For discussions of **pay for performance** (note 2), see Nita Garg, Hospital Value Based Purchasing and the Bundled Payment Initiative Under the Affordable Care Act: A Good Start, But Is it Good Enough?, 22 Ann. Health L. 171 (2013); Christopher Robertson, Susannah Rose & Aaron S. Kesselheim, Effect of Financial Relationships on the Behaviors of Health Care Professionals: A Review of the Evidence, 40 J. L. Med. & Ethics 452 (2012); Adam Candeub, Contract, Warranty and the Patient Protection and Affordable Care Act, 46 Wake Forest L. Rev. 45 (2011); David M. Cutler, Your Money or Your Life: Strong Medicine for America's Health Care

System (2004); Institute of Medicine, Rewarding Provider Performance: Aligning Incentives in Medicare (2006); David Hyman, Follow the Money: Money Matters in Health Care, Just Like Everything Else, 36 Am. J. L. & Med. 370 (2010); David A. Hyman & Charles M. Silver, The Poor State of Health Care Quality in the U.S.: Is Malpractice Liability Part of the Problem or Part of the Solution?, 90 Cornell L. Rev. 893 (2005); Bruce C. Vladeck, If Paying for Quality Is Such a Bad Idea, Why Is Everyone for It?, 60 Wash. & Lee L. Rev. 1345 (2003).

For discussions of **MACRA** (note 2), see Health Policy Brief, Medicare's New Physician Payment System (Health Affairs, April 2016); Eric C. Schneider & Cornelia J. Hall, Improve Quality, Control Spending, Maintain Access—Can the Merit-Based Incentive Payment System Deliver?, 376 New Eng. J. Med. 708 (2017); Peter Hussey et al., The Medicare Access and CHIP Reauthorization Act: Effects on Medicare Payment Policy and Spending, 36 Health Affairs 697 (2016); Jonathan Oberlander & Miriam J. Laugesen, Leap of Faith—Medicare's New Physician Payment System, 373 New Eng. J. Med. 1185 (2015).

For an especially thorough analysis of **paying for episodes of care** (note 3), see William M. Sage, Assembled Products: The Key to More Effective Competition and Antitrust Oversight in Health Care, 101 Cornell L. Rev. 609 (2016). See also Michael E. Porter & Elizabeth Olmsted Teisberg, Redefining Health Care: Creating Value-Based Competition on Results (2006); Karen Davis, Paying for Care Episodes and Care Coordination, 356 New Eng. J. Med. 1166 (2007); Francois de Brantes et al., Building a Bridge from Fragmentation to Accountability: The Prometheus Payment Model, 361 New Eng. J. Med. 1033 (2009); Francois de Brantes et al., Should Health Care Come with a Warranty?, 28(4) Health Aff. w674 (July–Aug. 2009); Symposium, 28(2) Health Aff. w205 (Jan. 2009); Symposium, 28(5) Health Aff. 1372 (Oct. 2009); Symposium, 29 Health Aff. 1284 (2010); Symposium, 30 Health Aff. 378 (2012).

F. NATIONAL HEALTH INSURANCE

■ THE HEALING OF AMERICA
T. R. Reid (2009)

. . . [F]or all the local variations, [foreign] health care systems tend to follow [four] general patterns . . . :

THE BISMARCK MODEL

This . . . is named for the Prussian chancellor Otto von Bismarck, who invented the welfare state as part of the unification of Germany in the nineteenth century. Despite its European heritage, the model would look familiar to Americans. In Bismarck countries, both health care providers and payers are private entities. The model uses private health insurance plans, usually financed jointly by employers and employees through payroll deduction. Unlike the U.S. health insurance industry, though, Bismarck-type plans are basically charities: They cover everybody, and they don't make a profit. . . . [T]ight regulation of medical services and fees gives the system much of the cost-control clout that the single-payer Beveridge Model (see below) provides.

THE BEVERIDGE MODEL

This arrangement is named after William Beveridge, a daring social reformer . . . who inspired Britain's National Health Service. In this system, . . . [t]here are no medical bills; rather, medical treatment is a public service, like the fire department or the public library. In Beveridge systems, many (sometimes all) hospitals and clinics are owned by the government [and] some doctors are government employees. . . . These systems tend to have low costs per capita, because the government, as the sole payer, controls what doctors can do and what they can charge. . . .

The Beveridge Model, with government holding almost all the cards, is probably what Americans have in mind when they talk about "socialized medicine." . . . [T]he two purest examples . . . are both found in the Western Hemisphere: Cuba and the U.S. Department of Veterans Affairs. In both of those systems, all the health care professionals work for the government in government-owned facilities, and patients receive no bills.

THE NATIONAL HEALTH INSURANCE MODEL

This system has elements of both Bismarck and Beveridge: The providers of health care are private, but the payer is a government-run insurance program that every citizen pays into. The national, or provincial, insurance plan collects monthly premiums and pays medical bills. . . . As a single payer covering everybody, the national insurance plan tends to have considerable market power to negotiate for lower prices. NHI countries also control costs by limiting the medical services they will pay for or by making patients wait to be treated. The paradigmatic NHI system is Canada's. . . .

THE OUT-OF-POCKET MODEL

. . . Most of the nations on the planet are too poor and too disorganized to provide any kind of mass medical care. The basic rule in such countries is simple, and brutal: The rich get medical care; the poor stay sick or die. . . .

These four models should be fairly easy for Americans to understand, because we have elements of all of them in our convoluted national health care apparatus. . . . And yet we're like no other country because the United States maintains so many separate systems for separate classes of people. . . .

◼ CHAOULLI v. QUEBEC
[2005] 1 S.C.R. 791, 130 C.R.R. (2d) 99, Supreme Court of Canada

DESCHAMPS, J.

Quebeckers are prohibited from taking out insurance to obtain in the private sector services that are available under Quebec's public health care plan. Is this prohibition justified by the need to preserve the integrity of the plan?

As we enter the 21st century, health care is a constant concern. The public health care system, once a source of national pride, has become the subject of frequent and sometimes bitter criticism. This appeal does not question the appropriateness of the state making health care available to all Quebeckers. On the contrary, . . . [o]nly the state can make available to all Quebeckers the social safety net consisting of universal and accessible health care.

The demand for health care is constantly increasing, and one of the tools used by governments to control this increase has been the management of waiting lists. . . . The appellants do not claim to have a solution that will eliminate waiting lists. Rather, they submit that the delays resulting from waiting lists violate their rights under the Charter of Human Rights and Freedoms ("Quebec Charter"), and the Canadian Charter of Rights and Freedoms ("Canadian Charter"). They contest the validity of the prohibition . . . on private insurance for health care services that are available in the public system. . . . In essence, the question is whether Quebeckers who are prepared to spend money to get access to health care that is, in practice, not accessible in the public sector because of waiting lists may be validly prevented from doing so by the state. For the reasons that follow, I find that the prohibition infringes the right to personal inviolability and that it is not justified by a proper regard for democratic values, public order and the general well being of the citizens of Quebec.

The validity of the prohibition is contested by the appellants, George Zeliotis and Jacques Chaoulli [pronounced "shayOOyee"]. Over the years, Mr. Zeliotis has experienced a number of health problems and has used medical services that were available in the public system, including heart surgery and a number of operations on his hip. The difficulties he encountered prompted him to speak out against waiting times in the public health care system. Mr. Chaoulli is a physician who has tried unsuccessfully to have his home delivered medical activities recognized and to obtain a licence to operate an independent private hospital. . . .

The Superior Court dismissed the motion for a declaratory judgment. . . . Piché J. was of the opinion that the purpose of the [the prohibition of private insurance contained in §11 of] the Hospital Insurance Act (s. 11 HOIA) and [§15 of] the Health Insurance Act (s. 15 HEIA) is to establish a public health system that is available to all residents of Quebec. . . . In her opinion, the enactment of these provisions was motivated by considerations of equality and human dignity. She found no conflict with the general values expressed in the Canadian Charter or in the Quebec Charter. She did find that waiting lists are long and the health care system must be improved and transformed. In her opinion, however, the expert testimony could not serve to establish with certainty that a parallel health care system would solve all the current problems of waiting times and access. . . .

In the instant case, s. 7 of the Canadian Charter and s. 1 of the Quebec Charter have numerous points in common:

CANADIAN CHARTER

7. Everyone has the right to life, liberty and security of the person and the right not to be deprived thereof except in accordance with the principles of fundamental justice.

Quebec Charter

1. Every human being has a right to life, and to personal security, inviolability and freedom. . . .

The appellant Zeliotis argues that the prohibition infringes Quebeckers' right to life. Some patients die as a result of long waits for treatment in the public system when they could have gained prompt access to care in the private sector. Were it not for s. 11 HOIA and s. 15 HEIA, they could buy private insurance and receive care in the private sector.

The Superior Court judge stated [TRANSLATION] "that there [are] serious problems in certain sectors of the health care system" (at p. 823). The evidence supports that assertion. . . . Not only is it common knowledge that health care in Quebec is subject to waiting times, but a number of witnesses acknowledged that the demand for health care is potentially unlimited and that waiting lists are a more or less implicit form of rationing. Waiting lists are therefore real and intentional. The witnesses also commented on the consequences of waiting times. Dr. Daniel Doyle, a cardiovascular surgeon, testified that when a person is diagnosed with cardiovascular disease, he or she is [TRANSLATION] "always sitting on a bomb" and can die at any moment. In such cases, it is inevitable that some patients will die if they have to wait for an operation. . . .

In the opinion of my colleagues Binnie and LeBel JJ., there is an internal mechanism that safeguards the public health system. According to them, Quebeckers may go outside the province for treatment where services are not available in Quebec. This possibility is clearly not a solution for the system's deficiencies. The evidence did not bring to light any administrative mechanism that would permit Quebeckers suffering as a result of waiting times to obtain care outside the province. The possibility of obtaining care outside Quebec is case specific and is limited to crisis situations. . . .

[Justice Deschamps concluded that the prohibition of private insurance, coupled with long waiting times, constitutes a prima facie deprivation of the rights protected by §1 of the Quebec Charter.]

Justification for the Prohibition

Section 9.1 of the Quebec Charter sets out the standard for justification. It reads as follows: "In exercising his fundamental freedoms and rights, a person shall maintain a proper regard for democratic values, public order and the general well being of the citizens of Québec." In this respect, the scope of the freedoms and rights, and limits to their exercise, may be fixed by law. . . . First, the court must determine whether the objective of the legislation is pressing and substantial. Next, it must determine whether the means chosen to attain this legislative end are reasonable and demonstrably justifiable in a free and democratic society. For this second part of the analysis, three tests must be met: (1) the existence of a rational connection between the measure and the aim of the legislation; (2) minimal impairment of the protected right by the measure; and (3) proportionality between the effect of the measure and its objective. . . .

Even if it were assumed that the prohibition on private insurance could contribute to preserving the integrity of the system, . . . prohibiting insurance contracts is by no means the only measure a state can adopt to protect the system's integrity. . . . The regimes of the provinces where a private system is authorized demonstrate that public health services are not threatened by private insurance. It can therefore be concluded that the prohibition is not necessary to guarantee the integrity of the public plan. . . .

In a number of European countries, there is no insurance paid for directly out of public funds. In Austria, services are funded through decentralized agencies that collect the necessary funds from salaries. People who want to obtain health care in the private sector in addition to the services covered by the mandatory social insurance are free to do so, but private insurance may cover no more than 80 percent of the cost billed by professionals practising in the public sector. The same type of plan exists in Germany and the Netherlands, but people who opt for private insurance are not required to pay for the public plan. Only nine percent of Germans opt for private insurance. . . . C. H. Tuohy, C. M. Flood and M. Stabile, "How Does Private Finance Affect Public Health Care Systems? Marshaling the Evidence from OECD Nations" (2004), 29 J. Health Pol. 359. . . .

The United Kingdom does not restrict access to private insurance for health care. Nor does the United Kingdom limit a physician's ability to withdraw from the public plan. However, physicians working full-time in public hospitals are limited in the amounts that they may bill in the private sector to supplement income earned in the public sector. Only 11.5 percent of Britons had taken out private insurance in 1998, and only eight percent of hospital beds in the United Kingdom are private. New Zealand has a plan similar to that of the United Kingdom with the difference that 40 percent of New Zealanders have private insurance. . . .

As can be seen from the evolution of public plans in the few [European] countries that have been examined in studies produced in the record, there are a wide range of measures that are less drastic, and also less intrusive in relation to the protected rights. . . . A measure as drastic as prohibiting private insurance contracts appears to be neither essential nor determinative. . . .

Governments have promised on numerous occasions to find a solution to the problem of waiting lists. Given the tendency to focus the debate on a sociopolitical philosophy, it seems that governments have lost sight of the urgency of taking concrete action. The courts are therefore the last line of defence for citizens. . . .

[Justice Deschamps concluded that the violation of the provincial Quebec Charter was not justified. Therefore, she declined to consider whether the prohibition also violates the national Canadian Charter. The concurring opinion, however, which follows, did address the Canadian Charter.]

McLACHLIN, the Chief Justice, and MAJOR, J. (concurring)
We concur in the conclusion of our colleague Deschamps J. that the prohibition against contracting for private health insurance violates s. 1 of the Quebec Charter of Human Rights and Freedoms. . . . [We go further and find] that the anti-insurance provision also violates s. 7 of the Canadian Charter of Rights and Freedoms ("Charter"). . . .

The [Canadian Charter] does not confer a freestanding constitutional right to health care. However, where the government puts in place a scheme to provide health care, that scheme must comply with the Charter. . . . The Canada Health Act, the Health Insurance Act, and the Hospital Insurance Act do not expressly prohibit private health services. However, they limit access to private health services by removing the ability to contract for private health care insurance to cover the same services covered by public insurance. The result is a virtual monopoly for the public health scheme. The state has effectively limited access to private health care except for the very rich, who can afford private care without need of insurance. This virtual monopoly, on the evidence, results in delays in treatment that adversely affect the citizen's security of the person. Where a law adversely affects life, liberty or security of the person, it must conform to the principles of fundamental justice. This law, in our view, fails to do so. . . .

The government defends the prohibition on medical insurance on the ground that the existing system is the only approach to adequate universal health care for all Canadians. The question in this case, however, is not whether single-tier health care is preferable to two-tier health care. . . . The mere fact that this [case] may have policy ramifications does not permit us to avoid [deciding] it. . . .

Given the ban on insurance, most Quebeckers have no choice but to accept delays in the medical system and their adverse physical and psychological consequences. Delays in the public system are widespread and have serious, sometimes grave, consequences. There was no dispute that there is a waiting list for cardiovascular surgery for life-threatening problems. . . . Inevitably, where patients have life-threatening conditions, some will die because of undue delay in awaiting surgery. The same applies to other health problems. . . . Dr. Eric Lenczner, an orthopaedic surgeon, testified that the one-year delay commonly incurred by patients requiring ligament reconstruction surgery increases the risk that their injuries will become irreparable. Dr. Lenczner also testified that 95 per cent of patients in Canada wait well over a year, and many two years, for knee replacements. . . . Even though death may not be an issue for them, these patients "are in pain," "would not go a day without discomfort" and are "limited in their ability to get around," some being confined to wheelchairs or house bound. . . .

In addition to threatening the life and the physical security of the person, waiting for critical care may have significant adverse psychological effects. . . . Studies confirm that patients with serious illnesses often experience significant anxiety and depression while on waiting lists. . . . This adverse psychological impact can have a serious and profound effect on a person's psychological integrity, and is a violation of security of the person. . . .

The principle of fundamental justice implicated in this case is that laws that affect the life, liberty or security of the person shall not be arbitrary . . . in the sense of bearing no real relation to the [government's] goal and hence being manifestly unfair. The more serious the impingement on the person's liberty and security, the more clear must be the connection. Where the individual's very life may be at stake, the reasonable person would expect a clear connection, in theory and in fact, between the measure that puts life at risk and the legislative goals. . . .

The government argues that the interference with security of the person caused by denying people the right to purchase private health insurance is necessary to providing effective health care under the public health system. It argues that if people can purchase private health insurance, they will seek treatment from private doctors and hospitals, which are not banned under the Act. According to the government's argument, this will divert resources from the public health system into private health facilities, ultimately reducing the quality of public care. . . .

This brings us to the evidence called by the appellants at trial on the experience of other developed countries with public health care systems which permit access to private health care. The experience of these countries suggests that there is no real connection in fact between prohibition of health insurance and the goal of a quality public health system. . . . [M]any western democracies that do not impose a monopoly on the delivery of health care have successfully delivered to their citizens medical services that are superior to and more affordable than the services that are presently available in Canada. . . .

In Sweden, the availability of private health care insurance appears not to have harmed the public health care system. In Germany, public health care insurance is administered by 453 Sickness Funds—private non-profit organizations structured on a regional task or occupational basis. Sickness Fund membership is compulsory for employees with gross incomes lower than approximately [$50,000], and voluntary for those with gross incomes above that level. . . . In Germany, as in Sweden, private health insurance is available to individuals at a certain income level who may voluntarily opt out of the Sickness Funds. . . . Despite the availability of alternatives, 88 per cent of the German population are covered by the public Sickness Funds. . . .

It is compelling to note that not one of the countries referred to relies exclusively on either private insurance or the public system to provide health care coverage to its citizens. Even in the United States, where the private sector is a dominant participant in the field of health care insurance, public funding accounts for 45% of total health care spending. . . .

The government undeniably has an interest in protecting the public health regime. However, given the absence of evidence that the prohibition on the purchase and sale of private health insurance protects the health care system, the rational connection between the prohibition and the objective is not made out. . . .

In sum, the prohibition on obtaining private health insurance, while it might be constitutional in circumstances where health care services are reasonable as to both quality and timeliness, is not constitutional where the public system fails to deliver reasonable services. Life, liberty and security of the person must prevail. . . .

BINNIE and LEBEL, J.J. (Dissenting)
. . . The Quebec government views the prohibition against private insurance as essential to preventing the current single-tier health system from disintegrating into a de facto two-tier system. The trial judge found, and the evidence demonstrated, that there is good reason for this fear. . . . It would be open to Quebec to adopt a U.S.-style health care system. No one suggests that there is anything in our Constitution to prevent it. But to do so would be contrary to the policy of the Quebec National Assembly, and its policy in that respect is shared by the other provinces and the federal Parliament. As stated, Quebec further takes the view that significant growth in the private health care system (which the appellants advocate) would inevitably damage the public system. Our colleagues the Chief Justice and Major J. disagree with this assessment, but governments are entitled to act on a reasonable apprehension of risk of such damage. . . . We now propose to review briefly some of the evidence supporting the findings of the trial judge. . . .

(II) THE IMPACT OF A PARALLEL PRIVATE REGIME ON GOVERNMENT SUPPORT FOR A PUBLIC SYSTEM

The experience in [European] countries shows that an increase in private funding typically leads to a decrease in government funding. At trial, Dr. Bergman explained that a service designed purely for members of society with less socio-economic power would probably lead to a decline in quality of services, a loss of political support and a decline in the quality of management. . . .

(III) Private Insurers May "Skim the Cream" and Leave the Difficult and Costly Care to the Public Sector

The evidence suggests that parallel private insurers prefer to siphon off high income patients while shying away from patient populations that constitute a higher financial risk, a phenomenon known as "cream skimming." The public system would therefore carry a disproportionate burden of patients who are considered "bad risks" by the private market by reason of age, socio-economic conditions, or geographic location. . . .

(IV) The U.S. Two-Tier System of Health Coverage

Reference has already been made to the U.S. health care system, which is the most expensive in the world, even though by some measures Americans are less healthy than Canadians. The existence of a private system has not eliminated waiting times. The availability, extent and timeliness of health care is rationed by private insurers, who may determine according to cost, not need, what is "medically necessary" health care and where and when it is to occur. Whether or not the private system in the U.S. is better managed is a matter of debate amongst policy analysts. The point here is simply that the appellants' faith in the curative power of private insurance is not borne out by the evidence put before the Court. . . .

[One additional justice concurred in each of the two secondary opinions, producing a vote of 1+3 vs. 3. Because of the difference among the majority justices over whether only the Quebec Charter was violated, or also the Canadian Charter, only the authoring Justice Deschamps signed the "majority" opinion. Therefore, this case controls only in Quebec. Another unusual aspect is that two of the Court's nine justices did not participate because they were appointed after the case had been argued.]

▪ STATEMENT INTRODUCING THE U.S. NATIONAL HEALTH INSURANCE ACT
Marcia Angell, M.D. *
Feb. 4, 2003

Americans have the most expensive health care system in the world. We spend about twice as much per person as other developed nations, and that gap is growing. That's not because we are sicker or more demanding (Canadians, for example, see their doctors more often and spend more time in the hospital). And it's not because we get better results. By the usual measures of health (life expectancy, infant

* Former Editor-in-Chief, *New England Journal of Medicine.*

mortality, immunization rates), we do worse than most other developed countries. Furthermore, we are the only developed nation that does not provide comprehensive health care to all its citizens. . . .

The underlying problem is that we treat health care like a market commodity instead of a social service. Health care is targeted not to medical need, but to the ability to pay. Markets are good for many things, but they are not a good way to distribute health care. . . . It's instructive to follow the health care dollar as it wends its way from employers toward the doctors and nurses and hospitals that actually provide medical services.

First, private insurers regularly skim off the top a substantial fraction of the premiums—anywhere from 10 to 25 percent—for their administrative costs, marketing, and profits. The remainder is then passed along a veritable gauntlet of satellite businesses that feed on the health care industry, including brokers to cut deals, disease-management and utilization review companies, drug-management companies, legal services, marketing consultants, billing agencies, information management firms, and so on and so on. Their function is often to limit services in one way or another. They, too, take a cut, including enough for their own administrative costs, marketing, and profits. I would estimate that no more than 50 cents of the health care dollar actually reaches the providers—who themselves face high overhead costs in dealing with multiple insurers. . . .

The program [that Physicians for a National Health Program] are introducing today is the very soul of simplicity and efficiency, compared with our private health care system. It is a single-payer system, that is, health care funds would be distributed by a single, public entity, so that health care could be coordinated to eliminate both gaps and overlap. In many ways, our program would be tantamount to extending Medicare to the entire population. Medicare is, after all, a government-financed single-payer system embedded within our private, market-based system. It's by far the most efficient part of our health-care system, with overhead costs of less than 3 percent, and it covers virtually everyone over the age of 65, not just some of them. Medicare is not perfect, but it is by far the most popular part of the U. S. health care system. . . .

What are the usual objections to the sort of national program we are calling for today? They are mostly based on a number of myths. Myth #1 is that we can't afford a national health care system, and if we try it, we will have to ration care. My answer is that . . . [a] single-payer system would be far more efficient, since it would eliminate excess administrative costs, profits, cost-shifting and unnecessary duplication. . . .

According to Myth #2, innovative technologies would be scarce under a single-payer system, we would have long waiting lists for operations and procedures, and in general, medical care would be threadbare and less available. This misconception is based on the fact that there are indeed waits for elective procedures in some countries with national health systems, such as the U. K. and Canada. But that's because they spend far less on health care than we do. (The U. K. spends about a third of what we do per person.) If they were to put the same amount of money as we do into their systems, there would be no waits and all their citizens would have immediate access to all the care they need. For them, the problem is not the system; it's the money. For us, it's not the money; it's the system. . . .

Myth #3 is that a single-payer system amounts to socialized medicine, which would subject doctors and other providers to onerous, bureaucratic regulations. But in fact, although a national program would be publicly funded, providers would not work for the government. That's currently the case with Medicare, which is publicly funded, but privately delivered. As for onerous regulations, nothing could be more onerous both to patients and providers than the multiple, intrusive regulations imposed on them by the private insurance industry. . . .

Myth #4 says that the government can't do anything right. Some Americans like to say that, without thinking of all the ways in which government functions very well indeed, and without considering the alternatives. I would not want to see, for example, the [National Institutes of Health], the National Park Service, or the IRS privatized. We should remember that the government is elected by the public and we are responsible for it. An investor-owned insurance company reports to its owners, not to the public.

Some people say that a single-payer system is a good idea, but politically unrealistic. That is a self-fulfilling prophecy. In my opinion, the medical profession and the public would be enthusiastic about a single-payer system if the facts were known and the myths dispelled. Yes, there would be powerful special interests opposing it and I don't underestimate them, but with courageous leadership . . . and the support of the medical profession and public, I believe there is nothing unrealistic about a National Health Insurance Program.

I want to mention one final and very important reason for enacting a national health program. We live in a country that tolerates enormous disparities in income, material possessions, and social privilege. That may be an inevitable consequence of a free market economy. But those disparities should not extend to denying some of our citizens certain essential services because of their income or social status. One of those services is health care. Others are education, clean water and air, equal justice, and protection from crime, all of which we already acknowledge are public responsibilities. We need to acknowledge the same thing for health care. Providing these essential services to all Americans, regardless of who they are, helps ensure that we remain a cohesive and optimistic country. . . .

■ THE GRASS IS NOT ALWAYS GREENER: A LOOK AT NATIONAL HEALTH CARE SYSTEMS AROUND THE WORLD
Michael Tanner *
2008

Critics of the U.S. health care system frequently point to other countries as models for reform. They point out that many countries spend far less on health care than the United States yet seem to enjoy better health outcomes. . . . In his movie *SiCKO*, Michael Moore . . . compares the U.S. system unfavorably with those of Canada, Great Britain, and France. Economist and New York Times columnist

* Director of Health and Welfare Studies, Cato Institute.

Paul Krugman also thinks the health care systems of France, Britain, and Canada are better than that of the United States. . . .

These critics contend that by adopting a similar [single-payer, national health care] system the United States could solve many of [its] problems. . . . Under such a system, health care would be financed through taxes rather than consumer payments or private insurance. Direct charges to patients would be prohibited or severely restricted. Private insurance, if allowed at all, would be limited to a few supplemental services not covered by the government plan. The government would control costs by setting an overall national health care budget and reimbursement levels.

However, a closer look at countries with national health care systems shows that those countries have serious problems of their own, including rising costs, rationing of care, lack of access to modern medical technology, and poor health outcomes. Countries whose national health systems avoid the worst of these problems are successful precisely because they incorporate market mechanisms and reject centralized government control. . . . Health care reform should be guided by the Hippocratic Oath: First, do no harm. Therefore, before going down the road to national health care, we should look more closely at foreign health care systems and examine both their advantages and their problems. . . .

TYPES OF NATIONAL HEALTH CARE SYSTEMS

National health care, or universal health care, is a broad concept and has been implemented in many different ways. There is no single model that the rest of the world follows. Each country's system is the product of its unique conditions, history, politics, and national character, and many are undergoing significant reform. . . . Some countries, such as France and Japan, impose significant cost sharing on consumers in an effort to discourage overutilization and to control costs. Other countries strictly limit the amount that consumers must pay out of pocket. Some countries permit free choice of providers, while others limit it. In some countries there is widespread purchase of alternative or supplemental private insurance, whereas in others, private insurance is prohibited or used very little. Resource allocation and prioritization vary greatly. Japan spends heavily on technology but limits reimbursement for surgery, while France has exceptionally high levels of prescription drug use. . . .

With all of that in mind, consider the following prominent national health care systems.

FRANCE

Some of the most thoughtful proponents of national health care look to France as a model of how such a program could work. . . . Ezra Klein of the *American Prospect* calls France "the closest thing to a model structure out there." The French system ranks at or near the top of most cross-country comparisons and is ranked number one by the [World Health Organization].

Although the French system is facing looming budgetary pressures, it does provide at least some level of universal coverage and manages to avoid many of the problems that afflict other national health care systems. . . . France provides a basic level of universal health insurance through a series of mandatory, largely occupation-based, health insurance funds. These funds are ostensibly private entities but are heavily regulated and supervised by the French government. Premiums (funded primarily through payroll taxes), benefits, and provider reimbursement rates are all set by the government. In these ways the funds are similar to public utilities in the United States. . . .

Payroll taxes provide the largest source of funding. Employers must pay [13.55] percent of wages for every employee. . . . In addition, there is a 5.25 general social contribution tax on income. . . . Thus, most French workers are effectively paying 18.8 percent of their income for health insurance. Finally, dedicated taxes are assessed on tobacco, alcohol, and pharmaceutical company revenues. . . .

Most services require substantial copayments, ranging from 10 to 40 percent of the cost. As a result, French consumers pay for roughly 13 percent of health care out of pocket, roughly the same percentage as U.S. consumers. Moreover, because many health care services are not covered, and because many of the best providers refuse to accept the fee schedules imposed by the insurance funds, more than 92 percent of French residents purchase complementary private insurance, [which] . . . makes up roughly 12.7 percent of all health care spending in France. . . .

Although reimbursement levels are set by the government, the amount physicians charge is not. The French system permits providers to charge more than the reimbursement schedule, and approximately one-third of French physicians do so. . . . [P]hysicians employed by hospitals, as opposed to those in private practice, do not have the same ability to charge more than the negotiated rate. The government also sets reimbursement rates for both public and private hospitals, which are generally not allowed to bill beyond the negotiated fee schedules. . . .

A 2004 poll showed that the French had the highest level of satisfaction with their health care system among all European countries. This is partly because their hybrid system has avoided many of the biggest problems of other national health care systems. Yet it also stems from French social character. For example, by a three-to-one margin, the French believe the quality of care they receive is less important than everyone having equal access to that care. This means the French experience may not be easily transferable to the United States, which has a far less egalitarian ethic. . . .

GREAT BRITAIN

Almost no one disputes that Britain's National Health Service faces severe problems, and few serious national health care advocates look to it as a model. Yet it appears in Moore's movie *SiCKO* as an example of how a national health care system should work, so it is worth examining.

The NHS is a highly centralized version of a single-payer system. The government pays directly for health care and finances the system through general tax revenues. Except for small copayments for prescription drugs, dental care, and optician services, there are no direct charges to patients. Unlike many other single-payer systems such as those in Canada and Norway, most physicians and nurses are government employees.

For years, British health policy has focused on controlling spending and in general has been quite successful, with the system spending just 7.5 percent of GDP on health care. . . . And that level of services leaves much to be desired. Waiting lists are a major problem. As many as 750,000 Britons are currently awaiting admission to NHS hospitals. These waits are not insubstantial and can impose significant risks on patients. For example, by some estimates, cancer patients can wait as long as eight months for treatment. Delays in receiving treatment are often so long that nearly 20 percent of colon cancer patients considered treatable when first diagnosed are incurable by the time treatment is finally offered. . . .

Explicit rationing also exists for some types of care, notably kidney dialysis, open heart surgery, and some other expensive procedures and technologies. Patients judged too ill or aged for the procedures to be cost-effective may be denied treatment altogether. . . .

A small but growing private health care system has emerged in the UK. About 10 percent of Britons have private health insurance. Some receive it through their employer, while others purchase it individually. In general, the insurance replicates care provided through the [national health system] and is purchased to gain access to a wider choice of providers or to avoid waiting lists. . . .

The British public is well aware of the need for reform. Nearly two-thirds of Britons (63 percent) say that the need for reform is "urgent." . . . Yet Britons are also extremely proud of their health care system and wary of any reforms that would "Americanize" it. . . .

SWITZERLAND

Of all the countries with universal health care, Switzerland has one of the most market-oriented systems. Indeed, the Swiss government actually pays for a smaller amount of total health care expenditures than the U.S. government, 24.9 percent versus 44.7 percent.

The Swiss system is based on the idea of managed competition, the same concept that underlay . . . [t]he 1993 Clinton health plan, . . . Mitt Romney's reforms in Massachusetts, and most of the proposals advocated by the current Democratic presidential candidates. Managed competition leaves the provision of health care and health insurance in private hands but creates a highly regulated artificial marketplace as a framework within which the health care industry operates. . . . Individuals have a choice of insurers within the regulated marketplace and a choice of providers. Although the government sets a standard benefits package, insurers may compete on price, cost sharing, and additional benefits. . . .

Swiss law requires all citizens to purchase a basic package of health insurance, an individual mandate. . . . Insurance is generally purchased on an individual basis. Few employers contribute to the purchase or provide insurance. . . .

Individuals can purchase expensive policies with very low deductibles and copayments, or far less expensive policies with high deductibles or extensive copayments. Thus, premiums vary according to their cost-sharing attributes and plan type. . . . Because employers do not pay for workers' health insurance, the Swiss are exposed to the full cost of their insurance purchases. As a result, many Swiss have opted for high-deductible insurance. Thus, with high deductibles and extensive copayments, the Swiss pay out of pocket for 31.5 percent of health care, twice as much as in the United States. . . .

The Swiss government offers subsidies to low-income citizens to help them purchase a policy. . . . These subsidies are designed to prevent any individual from having to pay more than 10 percent of income on insurance. . . .

Swiss insurers operate as cartels to negotiate provider reimbursements on a [regional] basis. Providers must accept the negotiated payment, and balance-billing is prohibited. If insurers and providers are unable to reach agreement on a fee schedule, canton governments are empowered to step in and impose an agreement. . . . Private hospitals negotiate reimbursement with insurance cartels and physicians in the same manner. Public hospitals are operated by cantons, which negotiate reimbursement rates with insurers and provide subsidies to the hospitals. In some cantons, individuals with only the basic insurance plan must use public hospitals; supplementary insurance is required for admission to private hospitals. . . .

The Swiss do not impose a global budget on their health care system and have therefore avoided the waiting lists common in other systems. In addition, the Swiss have a high degree of access to modern medical technology, but it has come at a cost. The Swiss spend 11.5 percent of GDP on health care, second only to the United States.

Since Swiss health care consumers are exposed to the cost consequences of their health care decisions, this trade-off between access and cost can be presumed to reflect the desires of Swiss patients. They have chosen high quality care even though it costs them more. Given that . . . Switzerland is a wealthy nation, such a decision seems entirely reasonable.

At the same time, it is notable that Swiss health care spending remains below that of the United States for nearly comparable care. Strong evidence suggests that the exposure of Swiss consumers to the cost consequences of their health care decisions has made them more conscious consumers and helped limit overall health care costs. . . .

The Swiss generally seem pleased with their system. Earlier this year, Swiss voters overwhelmingly rejected a proposal to replace the current system with a single-payer plan. . . .

CONCLUSION

. . . [It is] important to realize that no country's system would translate directly to the United States. Americans are unlikely to accept the rationing or restrictions on care and technology that many countries use to control costs. Nor are U.S. physicians likely to accept a cut in income to the levels seen in countries like France or Germany. The politics, economics, and national cultures of other countries often vary significantly from those of the United States. Their citizens are far more likely to have faith in government actions and to be suspicious of free markets. And polling suggests that citizens of many countries put social solidarity and equality ahead of quality and choice when it comes to health policy. American attitudes are quite different. . . . Even so, some important lessons can be drawn from the experiences of other countries: . . .

Those countries that have single-payer systems or systems heavily weighted toward government control are the most likely to face waiting lists, rationing, restrictions on the choice of physician, and other barriers to care. Those countries with national health care systems that work better, such as France, the Netherlands, and Switzerland, are successful to the degree that they incorporate market mechanisms such as competition, cost-consciousness, market prices, and consumer choice, and eschew centralized government control. . . .

Although no country with universal coverage is contemplating abandoning a universal system, the broad and growing trend in countries with national health care systems is to move away from centralized government control and introduce more market-oriented features. . . . Thus, even as Americans debate adopting a government-run system, countries with those systems are debating how to make their systems look more like that of the United States. . . . Therefore, if U.S. policymakers can take one lesson from national health care systems around the world, it is not to follow the road to government-run national health care, but to increase consumer incentives and control. . . .

Notes: Foreign and Single-Payer Health Care Systems

1. Chaoulli. How consistent is the *Chaoulli* decision with U.S. constitutional law? For discussion of constitutional principles applied to various aspects of health care regulation and finance, see section A of this chapter, and Chapters 2.A.1, 5.A, 7.B, and 8.C.1. In Canada, this decision generated a great deal of criticism and controversy, much of which is addressed in the excellent anthology, Colleen M. Flood et al. eds., Access to Care, Access to Justice: The Legal Debate over Private Health Insurance in Canada (2005).

Somewhat surprisingly, the Canadian Supreme Court's decision has not led to the wholesale repeal of the private insurance prohibition in Quebec, much less in other provinces. Instead, these governments have worked to shorten waiting lists and to provide targeted funding for those who are forced to seek private care outside the system for critical surgeries when waits become too long. Quebec also now allows the sale of insurance covering only select surgeries.

2. *Is Health Care Special?* Consider these thoughts on the role of government generally in health care financing and delivery:

> We must apply some modest degree of scrutiny to the proposition that health care is special: surely it is important, but so is food, clothing, shelter, education, entertainment, and all the other goods and services that are necessary to sustain life and to make the life sustained worth living. Importance, however, is not an argument for government subsidy or support, for if it were then socialism would apply to things where it matters most, and lead to the most ruinous of consequences. Instead the importance, so to speak, of importance is simple: It is important to get the right set of solutions, be it private or public, to the problem at hand. Importance does not create a presumption in favor of government, or for that matter against it. It only raises the stakes for making a correct decision in the matter at hand.

Richard A. Epstein, Why Is Health Care Special?, 40 U. Kan. L. Rev. 307 (1992).

3. *The AMA's Opposition.* Although the AMA endorsed the ACA, it has steadfastly opposed national health insurance throughout the past century. As Dr. Marcia Angell demonstrates, however, other medical groups support single-payer reforms. Why doesn't the AMA see it in its interest for the government to provide universal insurance so that everyone can pay for medical services? If you were a doctor, would you prefer the restrictions as well as the protections of a government-run system over the ravages of the unregulated managed care marketplace? Realize that the

unregulated market was much more attractive in the 1950s when organized medicine controlled health insurance through Blue Cross, when there was little antitrust scrutiny of physician collusion, and when the corporate practice of medicine doctrine more actively preserved physicians' independence from medical institutions — topics that are discussed in Chapter 10.

4. *Socialized Medicine.* Critics of government involvement in health care frequently lump all forms of involvement together as "socialized medicine." It is important, however, to distinguish whether government is merely paying for health care, or also directly delivering health care. Canada (like Medicare) does only the first, which is more accurately labeled "socialized *insurance*." As T. R. Reid notes, the U.S. analogue for true British-style socialized medicine is the Veterans Administration (VA) health care system, which covers veterans' service-related health problems. Rather than this giving the idea a bad name, many observers point to the VA as a model for efficient delivery of high-quality care:

> [The VA] runs its own hospitals and clinics, and provides some of the best-quality health care in America at far lower cost than the private sector. How does the VA do it? It turns out that there are many advantages to having a single health care organization provide individuals with what amounts to lifetime care. For example, the VA has taken the lead in introducing electronic medical records, which it can do far more easily than a private hospital chain because its patients stay with it for decades. The VA also invests heavily and systematically in preventive care, because unlike private health care providers it can expect to realize financial benefits from measures that keep its clients out of the hospital.

Paul Krugman & Robin Wells, The Health Care Crisis and What to Do About It, New York Review of Books, March 23, 2006.

Is there any reason state or federal governments couldn't do a decent job delivering care directly to people who can't afford insurance? What if government health care were as good (or bad) as student health services? Would that be "good enough for government work"?

5. *Single-payer?* During the primary campaign of 2016, Senator Bernie Sanders's proposal for a single-payer program — what he termed "Medicare for All" — generated considerable enthusiasm on the political left. Sanders's proposal called for replacing the complexities of the current system with a single, government-run program that would cover the entire range of medically necessary care for the entire population. Pointing to international experience, where state-run coverage of this sort is common, many members of the public and some influential voices in the medical community argue that single-payer would reduce administrative costs, enable government to bargain effectively for low prices, and improve coverage for the uninsured and the underinsured.

Despite this enthusiasm, most experts — even those sympathetic to single-payer — believe that it is unrealistic to hope for its adoption. The price tag for a single-payer scheme far exceeds that of the ACA and there is little appetite in Congress to support the tax increases that would be necessary to finance a vast expansion of public coverage. See John Holahan et al., Urban Institute, The Sanders Single-Payer Health Care Plan: The Effect on National Health Expenditures and Federal and Private Spending (2016). Any such proposal would also face fierce opposition from existing health insurers (which could be put out of business), the health care industry, and much of organized medicine.

6. *The Public Option.* Given the bleak political outlook for Medicare for All, some have suggested a slower, long-term effort to move toward a single-payer scheme, perhaps by incorporating a "public option" into the ACA. Glenn Hackbarth, Today's Medicare Is Built on 50 Years of Robust Compromise. Now What? Health Affairs Blog (March 8, 2016). Under the public option, the government would operate a health plan that it would then sell on the exchanges. If consumers preferred the public plan to private plans, the public option could come to dominate the market, displacing private insurance and perhaps paving the road to single-payer.

A public option appeared likely early in the congressional deliberations over the ACA, but it was dropped as part of a political compromise. Hillary Clinton resurrected the idea in her 2016 presidential run. The idea is straightforward: The government (either state or federal) would run a plan that would pay rates based on Medicare's payment schedules. The hope is that the public option would have enough bargaining leverage to entice providers to participate, even if the public option paid less than private insurers. Low payment rates would mean low premiums for the public option, and competition between the public option and private insurers would restrain prices in the private market.

Opposition to the public option is intense. Critics question whether private insurers stand a chance of competing with the government on an even footing and believe that the public option's supporters wish to use it as a Trojan horse to achieve single-payer reform. Supporters point to Medicare Advantage as proof that a public option and private insurance can coexist. They also argue that the public option may be critical in those states with limited competition among private insurers.

7. *Crowd-Out and Sliding Scales.* A major difficulty of offering a government program alongside privately purchased insurance, in order to cover people who are uninsured, is that, if the government system is halfway decent, many people who otherwise might or do purchase insurance would simply drop it in favor of the free (or greatly discounted) government program. This drop-out problem—which is also known as "crowd-out," meaning the public provision crowds out private provision—has happened at least to some extent, for instance, when states expanded Medicaid to cover children above poverty. Then, some parents with family policies through work switched to less expensive single coverage, or employers stopped offering to pay as much for family members.

Do crowd-out problems necessarily mean that a comprehensive insurance system must be either all private or all public? In theory, it is possible to construct sliding-scale eligibility and subsidy rules that reduce incentives to switch from one to the other, but doing that is substantially more complicated. This smoothing of the boundaries also confronts the basic problem encountered by any sliding scale subsidy: The more that basic needs are subsidized, the more that people stand to lose when they earn more income. Thus, income-based subsidies function like a tax, in reverse: It costs to earn more, which means there is less incentive to work. This work disincentive also exists in any kind of income tax, so it isn't necessarily crippling, but adding expensive social programs on top of income tax rates compounds the disincentive. Thus, if the scale slides too steeply, for a benefit as expensive as health insurance, people in some lower-income brackets might stand to lose almost all of any increased income, when tax effects are combined with social support. The only way to avoid this incentive at the margin is to make the social support scale up or down more gradually, but that means extending it to much greater portions of the population.

8. *Beware of What You Wish For.* Do you think national health insurance is politically feasible in the United States—at least in your lifetime? What social, economic, and political conditions might give rise to this sort of comprehensive reform? Consider these thoughts from two eminent health policy scholars:

> Any comprehensive change in the health care system is likely to result in winners and losers. Prospective losers are likely to be much more involved and effective in blocking change than prospective winners will be in promoting it. As Machiavelli, one of the shrewdest political analysts of all time, noted, "There is nothing more difficult to carry out, nor more the reformer has enemies in all those who profit by the old order, and only lukewarm defenders in all those who would profit by the new order."... What might set the stage for comprehensive reform of health care? A major war, a depression, or large-scale civil unrest might well set in motion a change in the political climate that would overpower the obstacles that prevail in normal times. A national health crisis, such as a flu pandemic, might also light the fuse of change.

Victor R. Fuchs & Ezekiel J. Emanuel, Health Care Reform: Why? What? When?, 24(6) Health Aff. 1399 (Nov. 2005).

9. *Managed Competition.* Rather than adopting a cohesive single-payer system, the United States is more likely to continue developing a "managed competition" or "voucher" approach to purchasing coverage. The health insurance exchanges created by the ACA, for instance, are a leading example of this approach, which, as Michael Tanner describes, is also used in Switzerland. As Tanner notes, the idea is widely adaptable. Republicans advocate using a managed competition voucher approach to privatizing both Medicare and Medicaid, and Medicare currently uses this approach for Part D drug coverage.

One major difficulty that exists in any managed competition framework is making sure that market forces focus on efficient delivery of quality care rather than on selecting the healthiest people and avoiding the sickest. For that to happen, competing insurers must be paid proportionately to each subscriber's actuarial risk. Otherwise, insurers will find ways to engage in covert or overt risk selection—for instance, by tailoring their marketing or plan designs and operations to attract healthier subscribers or discourage sicker ones. Unless older and sicker people are required to pay more, the only obvious way to fix this problem is to "risk adjust" the subsidized "voucher" amounts to accurately reflect each subscriber's health risk.

10. *Further Readings.* For additional readings on **foreign health care systems generally**, see Sarah Thomson et al., International Profiles of Health Care Systems (2012); David A. Rochefort & Kevin P. Donnelly, Foreign Remedies: What the Experience of Other Nations Can Tell Us About Next Steps in Reforming U.S. Health Care (2012); David Squires, The U.S. Health System in Perspective: A Comparison of Twelve Industrialized Nations (Commonwealth Fund, 2011); Daniel Callahan & Angela Wasunna, Medicine and the Market: Equity v. Choice (2006) (focusing on developing countries); Nathan Cortez, International Health Care Convergence, 26 Wis. Int'l L. J. 646 (2008); Timothy Jost, Private or Public Approaches to Insuring the Uninsured: Lessons from International Experience with Private Insurance, 76

N.Y.U. L. Rev. 419 (2001); Symposium, 30 J. Health Pol. Pol'y & L. 1 (2005); Symposium, 23(3) Health Aff. 7 (June 2004); Symposium, 28 J. Health Pol. Pol'y & L. 575 (2003). For the developments in the British NHS, see Henry J. Aaron & William B. Schwartz, Can We Say No? The Challenge of Rationing Health Care (2005); Rudolf Klein, Britain's National Health Service Revisited, 350 New Eng. J. Med. 937 (2004). On **Canada**, see Colleen Flood ed., Just Medicare (2006); Allan S. Detsky & C. David Naylor, Canada's Health Care System: Reform Delayed, 349 New Eng. J. Med. 804 (2003).

For analysis of the **implications of the *Chaoulli* case for U.S. constitutional law and public policy** (note 1), see Roy G. Spece Jr., A Fundamental Constitutional Right of the Monied to "Buy Out Of" Universal Health Care Program Restrictions Versus the Moral Claim of Everyone Else to Decent Health Care, 3 J. Health & Biomed. L. 1 (2007); Mary Anne Bobinski, The Health Insurance Debate in Canada: Lessons for the United States?, 14 Conn. Ins. L. J. 341 (2008).

For further criticism of a **government takeover of the health care finance and delivery** (note 2), see John C. Goodman et al., Lives at Risk: Single-Payer National Health Insurance Around the World (2004).

For discussions of **the AMA's resistance to government regulation** (note 2), see George Lundberg, Severed Trust: Why American Medicine Hasn't Been Fixed (2000); Robert Berenson, Do Physicians Recognize Their Own Best Interests?, 13(2) Health Aff. 185 (Apr. 1994) (critiquing as inconsistent and shortsighted the AMA's historical antipathy to government regulation).

For readings on the **socialized medicine and the Veterans Health Administration** (note 4), see Phillip Longman, The Best Care Anywhere (2d ed. 2010); Adam Oliver, The Veterans Health Administration: An American Success Story?, 85 Milbank Q. 1 (2007). For an argument to expand access to government clinics and hospitals, see Donald W. Moran, Whence and Whither Health Insurance? A Revisionist History, 24(6) Health Aff. 1415 (Dec. 2005); Mark A. Hall, Approaching Universal Coverage with Better Safety Net Programs for the Uninsured, 11 Yale J. Health Pol'y L. & Ethics (2011).

For arguments **in favor of single-payer** (note 5), see Dominic F. Caruso, David U. Himmelstein & Steffie Woolhandler, Single-Payer Health Reform: A Step Toward Reducing Structural Racism in Health Care, Harvard Public Health Review (July 2015); Adam Gaffney et al., Moving Forward from the Affordable Care Act to a Single-Payer System, 106 Am. J. Public Health 987 (2016).

For articles **questioning the political viability of single-payer** (note 5), see Jonathan Oberlander, The Virtues and Vices of Single-Payer Health Care, 374 New Eng. J. Med. 1401 (2016); Harold Pollack, Medicare for All—If It Were Politically Possible—Would Necessarily Replicate the Defects of Our Current System, 40 J. Health Politics, Policy and Law 921, 924 (August 2015).

For debate over **the public option** (note 6), see John Z. Ayanian & Richard Hirth, Going Public: Could Clinton's Health Care Proposals Work? The Conversation (2016); Jacob Hacker, There's a Simple Fix for Obamacare's Current Woes: The Public Option, Vox.com (2016); Susan Jaffe, A Public Health Insurance Plan, Health Policy Brief, Nov. 10, 2009; Victor R. Fuchs, The Proposed Government Health Insurance Company, 360 New Eng. J. Med. 2273 (2009); Michael F. Cannon,

Fannie Med? Why a "Public Option" Is Hazardous to Your Health (2009); John Holahan & Linda J. Blumberg, Is the Public Plan Option a Necessary Part of Health Reform? (2009).

For more on **crowd-out** (note 7), see Jonathan Gruber & Kosali Simon, Crowd-Out Ten Years Later: Have Recent Public Insurance Expansions Crowded Out Private Health Insurance?, 27 J. Health Econ. 201 (2008); John V. Jacobi, Medicaid Expansion, Crowd-Out, and Limits of Incremental Reform, 45 St. Louis U. L. J. 79 (2001).

The original work of the Stanford economist who first articulated the idea of **managed competition** (note 9) can be found at Alain Enthoven, Consumer Choice Health Plan: A National Health Insurance Proposal Based on Regulated Competition in the Private Sector, 298 New Eng. J. Med. 650, 709 (1978); Jackson Hole Group, Managed Competition II: A Proposal, 46 Wash. U. J. Urb. & Contemp. L. 33 (1994). See generally Paul Starr, The Logic of Health-Care Reform (1992); Walter Zelman, The Changing Health Care Marketplace (1996); Alain Enthoven, The History and Principles of Managed Competition, 12 (Supp. 1) Health Aff. 24 (Jan. 1993).

Problem: Universal Access to Health Care

Be prepared to either defend or attack each of the following propositions, using analysis and facts from the readings in this chapter.

1. A two-tier health care system—one that tolerates different standards of access and care according to wealth and social position—is morally unjustified because health care is a basic human right of fundamental importance.
2. A system of socialized medicine like that in Canada is distinctly un-American and will lead to massive rationing of services.
3. In order to have a coherent health care financing system, it is essential to sever the link between employment and insurance.
4. The best feasible way to guarantee everyone access to a decent minimum level of health care is to fund a comprehensive network of public hospitals and outpatient clinics as a safety net for those without health insurance.

Exercise: Negotiating Health Care Reform

Assume you represent the interests of one of the following groups: physicians, low-income public, upper- and middle-income public, large insurance companies and HMOs, small employers, or large employers. Now, develop your legislative lobbying position with respect to each of the following reform ideas:

1. A British-type system
2. A Canadian-type system

3. An entirely privatized system that gives each person a voucher, funded by the government, sufficient to pay for 60 to 100 percent (depending on income) of the cost of the lowest-priced insurance policy in the market, and then leaving it entirely to individual choice whether and what to buy.

Meet with representatives from the other interest groups and attempt to negotiate comprehensive health care reform.

G. ECONOMIC AND REGULATORY THEORY

As an interlude between this and the next chapter, this section addresses economic and regulatory theory in more depth, as it applies to health care public policy. In Chapter 1, we learned that American medicine is thought to be in a crisis, both because of the number of people without either public or private health insurance coverage and because of steeply escalating medical costs. This chapter has helped us to understand why this crisis arose and some of the public policy responses; the next chapter considers additional responses to the crisis in spending. These responses are sometimes focused on activating market forces and at other times on regulatory controls; often, reforms contain a mix of these objectives.

It is obvious, then, that a full understanding of these issues requires some appreciation of economic and regulatory theory. Economic theory also helps us to better understand the root of the problems that cost containment measures are designed to correct, so we can better assess how well they are likely to work. Specifically, we must be able to intelligently discuss the extent to which health care delivery should be left to market forces, whether government regulation should displace market mechanisms because of the unique attributes of medicine, or whether government should try to make the market work better. Do not expect to be able to resolve these issues. Instead, as you read these selections, focus your thoughts on the legal and public policy positions you have seen so far and ask yourself which are supported or undermined by each of the points the authors make.

For additional readings on economics versus regulation in health care, see Glenn Cohen, Holly Lynch & Christopher Robertson eds., Nudging Health: Health Law and Behavioral Economics (2016); Michael F. Cannon & Michael D. Tanner, Healthy Competition (2005); David Hyman, Improving Healthcare: A Dose of Competition (2005); Handbook of Health Economics (Anthony Culyer & Joseph P. Newhouse eds., 2000); Joseph White, Markets and Medical Care, 85 Milbank Q. (2007); Robert Field, Government as the Crucible for Free Market Health Care, 159 U. Penn. L. Rev. 1669 (2011); Ronen Avraham & K. A. D. Camara, The Tragedy of the Human Commons, 29 Cardozo L. Rev. 479 (2007); H. E. Frech, Competition and Monopoly in Medical Care (1996); Gregg Bloche, The Invention of Health Law, 91 Cal. L. Rev. 247 (2003); Symposium, Kenneth Arrow and the Changing Economics of Health Care, 26 J. Health Pol. Pol'y & L. 823 (2001); Symposium, 31 J. Health Pol. Pol'y L. 417 (2006); Symposium, 22 J. Health Pol. Pol'y & L. 382 (1997); Symposium, 13 J. Health Pol. Pol'y & L. 223-364 (1988); Symposium, 34 Vand. L. Rev. 849 (1981).

■ HEALTH PLAN*
Alain Enthoven
1980

The fundamental strategic choice for public policy on health care costs is competition or regulation. . . .

The choice between competition and regulation is a choice about the role of government. In the strategy of competition the government takes a much simpler and less intrusive role than in the regulatory approach. It seeks to set the basic framework of rules and incentives in such a way that the market (that is, the interaction of people making transactions in their own best interests) will produce the desired result. In the regulatory approach applied to health care, the government takes on a much more complex and demanding role, a role in which, in my view, it is bound to fail. In the regulatory approach government would leave today's cost-increasing incentives in place and then try to stop them from having their natural effect by direct detailed controls such as telling doctors how much they can charge for each service. In this approach direct controls are intended to substitute for rational economic incentives. In my view, the regulatory approach is like trying to make water run uphill, whereas in the competitive market approach the government is merely trying to channel the stream in its downhill course.

Procompetitive regulation is likely to be much simpler and more effective than direct controls on prices, capacity, and use of services, which act in opposition to the financial incentives. For in this case the basic incentives are pointing people in about the right direction. The regulators are attempting merely to modify the behavior of the regulated at the margin. . . .

On the other hand, under the regulatory approach, the regulators are attempting to make regulated entities behave in ways that are directly opposed to their financial interests, possibly even threatening their survival. Therefore, the incentive to attempt to bend, fight, or evade the regulations is much stronger. . . .

Regulation often raises costs to consumers. Regulators become responsible for the economic survival of the regulated. If they let a regulated entity fail, they will be blamed for denying society a needed service and for causing a loss of jobs. So they cannot force the regulated to sustain losses or even to live with less than some target rate of return on investment. So cost increases have to be "passed through" to consumers, and price controls become cost reimbursement, with all of its cost-increasing incentives.

Regulators are often "captured" by the regulated. They must get their information about the regulated industry from the regulated. The regulated firms hire high-priced lawyers and lobbyists who exert a constant pressure in their favor. The consumer interest in lower prices or better service is too diffused to allow for an effectively organized counterpressure. The formal procedures of regulation also make it very costly and time-consuming. This is especially true if there are many entities to be regulated, with many special circumstances to be considered, as is the case with physicians and hospitals. . . .

Competition, on the other hand, sets up an inexorable force for cost reduction. If company *B* can make a product of equal quality to company *A*'s, but for less cost, it can sell it for a lower price and take the business away from company *A*. If company *A* cannot match the cost reduction, it will lose profits in the short run and risk being driven out of business in the long run. Survival demands that it cut costs. It has no regulators to appeal to for protection. . . .

Competition rewards innovation and often channels it in socially desirable directions. Fortunes are made on new products and services, so innovations that lead to better services or reduced costs are encouraged. Firms that do not match their competitors' innovations often do not survive.

Market economies are the most effective in improving productivity and raising living standards. There are good reasons for this. People accept efficiency-improving changes such as closing unneeded plants or hospitals produced by impersonal market forces in the private sector. The people directly affected may not like them, but there is not much they can do about them. In the long run the whole economy benefits. But when such changes are imposed by government, those who would be harmed resist them, usually successfully, through legal and political action. . . .

In market systems producers and consumers adapt continuously and gradually to changing conditions, even in anticipation of future events. The expectation of higher gasoline prices in the future motivates people to buy cars with good mileage now. In regulatory systems the rules themselves create vested interests which make the rules very difficult to change. These factors make for great rigidity in regulated industries, in contrast to flexible adaptation in markets.

Government often responds to well-focused producer interests; competitive markets respond systematically, if imperfectly, to consumer interests. Voters base their choices on issues of decisive personal importance, on their pocketbooks if they see their livelihoods at stake. People specialize in production and diversify in consumption. To a dairy farmer, a rise in coffee prices is a minor irritant, but an increase in the price of milk (supported by government) is a "make-or-break" issue. People are therefore much more likely to pressure their representatives about the issues that affect their livelihoods than on their interests as consumers, and their companies and unions provide natural organizations for doing so. In competitive markets companies get their revenues from satisfied customers who have alternative choices. So in product and pricing decisions, business must seek to serve the desires of consumers. Thus the choice between a regulated and a competitive market system of health care services is a choice between service that responds mainly to the interests of providers or to those of consumers.

Regulation depends on coercion, on forcing people to behave in ways they consider opposed to their own best interests. The decentralized competitive market, on the other hand, leaves maximum freedom to individual providers and consumers consistent with achievement of society's purposes. As Charles Schultze put it:

Relationships in the market are a form of unanimous-consent arrangement. When dealing with each other in a buy-sell transaction, individuals can act voluntarily on the basis of mutual advantage. . . . Market-like arrangements not only minimize the need for coercion as a means of organizing society; they also reduce the need for compassion, patriotism, brotherly love, and cultural solidarity as motivating forces behind social improvement.

The development of these desirable virtues is more likely to be encouraged if we do not place too heavy a burden on people who practice them.

Moreover, the market encourages the pluralism and diversity that is valued by the American people. The regulatory approach works on the basis of uniform numerical standards. . . . [It thus tends to ignore individual differences in] a patient's needs, preferences, and lifestyle. Consider a woman who likes to ski and ride horseback and who has a partially detached retina in one eye. One ophthalmologist believes in an operation that does a minimum amount of "welding" (photocoagulation) and would minimize her loss of vision. Although that might satisfy the physician's criterion of technical excellence, it does not allow the woman to resume her athletic pursuits safely. Another ophthalmologist might propose to coagulate a complete circle around her retina. In this case the patient would lose some vision, but would have more of a guarantee that the retina will not detach again, and she could ski and ride again.

Patients suffering from severe angina pectoris (chest pain thought to be due to a lack of oxygen supply to the heart) pose another therapeutic dilemma. One doctor may recommend heart surgery; another, treatment with drugs such as nitroglycerine. For most such patients, there is no consensus among physicians today as to which is the best treatment. What is "best" in a particular case will depend on the values and needs of the patient, the skills of the doctor, and the other resources available. . . .

■ HEALTH CARE INTO THE 21ST CENTURY
Mark A. Peterson
22 J. Health Pol. Pol'y & L. 291 (1997)

What are we to make of the market transformation of health care in the United States, the core legacy of the current decade? Should we favor the dynamics of markets, standing alone, as a vehicle for reform? What are the limitations? What has motivated the restructuring of the private insurance system? What happens when the market transformation extends from private insurance to the publicly financed programs for the elderly and poor? . . . Before launching into that analysis, it is imperative to . . . [ask] what do we mean when we speak of markets in the health care setting? . . . [R]elatively few people, beyond some libertarian and right-wing politicians, believe that all matters pertaining to the delivery of medical care services should be left to the marketplace, however conceived. Some individuals may believe that health care is no different from toothpaste, but that view is shared by few analysts and citizens.

Most market advocates, such as health economists Alain Enthoven and Mark Pauly, support major interventions by the government to subsidize insurance coverage and promote improved rules of the game for an otherwise inefficient market. Analysts across the spectrum of opinion reject the simplistic dichotomies of government versus the market, or regulation versus competition. More pertinent are questions about where, when, in what form, and under what conditions both markets and government have a role.

In the health care setting, the market is more typically a reference to a set of market-like instruments or arrangements. These include privately owned or managed institutions, which can range from stockholder-owned insurance companies to nonprofit sickness funds in the German tradition. They often refer to the use of incentives embedded within institutions of whatever sort (private or public) that are designed to promote more efficient individual-level behavior. Fully capitated payments to physicians by corporate HMOs, which shift risk to the doctor and reward the utilization of fewer services, would certainly be included. But one would also have to consider the hospital payment methodology of diagnosis-related groupings (DRGs) used by a public program like Medicare. The market frequently is taken to refer to a process of decision making; for example, using competition among substitutable entities to identify and select the best choice according to some measure of utility. That competition, however, can be among private firms, nonprofit institutions, or even public agencies or employees. It can occur within an unregulated marketplace or within the bowels of the public sector. The same can be said of another market-like arrangement: contracting between relevant parties.

■ CALIFORNIA DENTAL ASS'N v. FEDERAL TRADE COMMISSION
526 U.S. 756 (1999)

SOUTER, J.

[The issue in this case is] whether a "quick look" sufficed to justify finding that certain advertising restrictions adopted by the California Dental Association violated the antitrust laws. . . . The CDA is a voluntary nonprofit association of local dental societies to which some 19,000 dentists belong, including about three-quarters of those practicing in the State. . . . [These dentists] agree to abide by a Code of Ethics (Code) including the following:

> Although any dentist may advertise, no dentist shall advertise or solicit patients in any form of communication in a manner that is false or misleading in any material respect. In order to properly serve the public, dentists should represent themselves in a manner that contributes to the esteem of the public. . . .

The CDA has issued a number of advisory opinions interpreting this section, and through separate advertising guidelines intended to help members comply with the Code and with state law the CDA has advised its dentists of disclosures they must make under state law when engaging in discount advertising. . . .

The FTC brought a complaint against the CDA, alleging that . . . the CDA had unreasonably restricted two types of advertising: price advertising, particularly discounted fees, and advertising relating to the quality of dental services. An Administrative Law Judge (ALJ) . . . found a violation of §5 of the FTC Act, [which prohibits "unfair competition and deceptive acts or practices." 15 U.S.C. §45(a)(1). We reverse and remand.] . . .

The restrictions on both discount and nondiscount advertising are, at least on their face, designed to avoid false or deceptive advertising in a market characterized by striking disparities between the information available to the professional and the patient.[9] In a market for professional services, in which advertising is relatively rare and the comparability of service packages not easily established, the difficulty for customers or potential competitors to get and verify information about the price and availability of services magnifies the dangers to competition associated with misleading advertising. What is more, the quality of professional services tends to resist either calibration or monitoring by individual patients or clients, partly because of the specialized knowledge required to evaluate the services, and partly because of the difficulty in determining whether, and the degree to which, an outcome is attributable to the quality of services (like a poor job of tooth filling) or to something else (like a very tough walnut). Patients' attachments to particular professionals, the rationality of which is difficult to assess, complicate the picture even further. The existence of such significant challenges to informed decisionmaking by the customer for professional services immediately suggests that advertising restrictions arguably protecting patients from misleading or irrelevant advertising call for more than cursory treatment as obviously comparable to classic horizontal agreements to limit output or price competition.

■ WHERE YOU STAND DEPENDS ON WHERE YOU SIT: MUSINGS ON THE REGULATION/COMPETITION DIALOGUE*
Donald R. Cohodes
7 J. Health Pol. Pol'y & L. 54 (1982)

An analysis of alternative approaches to containing medical care costs—especially an analysis oriented toward market approaches—must be firmly based on an understanding of the medical care market: why medical care is different from other products; why the nature of medical care leads to institutional factors that do not exist in other markets; why institutional arrangements that do exist and work well in other markets cause problems in the market for medical care; why governmental attempts to deal with the medical care market often have perverse or inflationary effects; and why the interaction of all these factors tends to undermine the means and the incentives for an efficient, cost-effective market for medical care.

Medical care has a number of characteristics that distinguish it from most other products in important ways:

10. "The fact that a restraint operates upon a profession as distinguished from a business is, of course, relevant in determining whether that particular restraint violates the [antitrust laws]. It would be unrealistic to view the practice of professions as interchangeable with other business activities, and automatically to apply to the professions antitrust concepts which originated in other areas. The public service aspect, and other features of the professions, may require that a particular practice, which could properly be viewed as a violation of [antitrust laws] in another context, be treated differently." Goldfarb v. Virginia State Bar, 421 U.S. 773, 788-789, n. 17, 95 S. Ct. 2004, 44 L. Ed. 2d 572 (1975).

1. *Demand for health.* Medical care services are not purchased from any desire for such services in themselves. The demand for medical care services is derived from the "demand" for good health.

2. *Medical care and health.* Medical care is only one determinant of health status, and for most people at most times it is not even a very important determinant. Environment, exercise, nutrition, and personal habits also are important factors affecting health status.

3. *Risk.* The need for medical care is unpredictable, requiring expenditures that are irregular and of uncertain magnitude.

4. *Immediacy.* The need for medical care is often immediate, allowing little time for shopping around and seeking advice or alternatives.

5. *Lack of information.* Consumers are usually ignorant of their medical care needs. They cannot possibly obtain the knowledge and training to diagnose their own medical care needs and "demand" the required services.

6. *Uncertainty.* Physicians, though highly trained and better able to diagnose needs and prescribed treatment, also are often uncertain about the appropriate services to provide.

These factors clearly hamper the operation of a normal market. . . .

Certain institutional developments and responses to the unique characteristics of medical care have further aggravated the problem. These include:

1. *Physician as agent.* Because of the consumer's uncertainty about the medical services he needs, the physician serves a dual role. Once the consumer has decided to seek care and select a physician, the physician diagnoses problems and decides on the course and place of treatment. The physician thus acts as agent for the consumer. But the physician provides more than advice; he also provides medical services. Unlike most producers, the physician may control the demand for his services. The more services he prescribes, the more fees he collects. It is this factor that makes fee-for-service pricing of physician services a concern to those who would like to see a more competitive medical care market. The problem is compounded by the uncertainty of medical science. The physician may not know exactly what the patient needs. The lack of accepted standards of medical practice, and the consequent fear of malpractice claims, leads to "[defensive] medicine"—the provision of services that may be neither warranted nor efficient. When the physician makes decisions for the consumer, there is little incentive for efficient use of resources.

2. *Third-party payment.* Due to the risk and uncertainty of incurring medical expenses, consumers purchase insurance to regularize their expenses. The predominant form of insurance purchased today is characterized by direct third-party payments of some or all medical expenses. The consequent reduction or absence of direct consumer payment for services has been found to be a significant factor affecting consumer and provider decision-making. The insulation of the consumer from direct payment for care has been shown to undermine incentives for cost-conscious consumer behavior. When a consumer pays little or nothing out-of-pocket for the services he is receiving, economic theory and empirical evidence indicate that more

service will be demanded than if out-of-pocket expenses reflect the full cost of care.

3. *Retrospective cost reimbursement.* Not only are payments made by a third party, but payments are generally based on incurred costs. This rewards physicians and hospitals with more revenues for generating more costs. In contrast to the competitive theory of economic efficiency, where producers are rewarded for lowering costs, providers of medical services are rewarded for raising costs.

Table 1. The Market for Medical Care

Assumptions Underlying a Perfectly Competitive Market	Match with Market for Medical Care	Specific Differences
Market Structure		
Large number of buyers and sellers	Mixed	Many consumers and physicians; few hospitals
Complete information (absence of uncertainty)	No	Consumer ignorance of the product risk and uncertainty of need
Firms operate independently (no one seller can influence price)	No	Price fixing (physician fee schedules); Cost reimbursement for hospitals
Free entry and exit of all producers	No	Barriers to entry (personnel licensure, hospital accreditation, certificate-of-need programs, a limited number of medical schools)
The product is homogeneous	No	Multiple, undefined products; varied quality
The consumer is the key decision-maker	No	Physicians act as agents on behalf of consumers
Market Conduct		
Firms are price-takers	No	Hospitals and physicians are price setters
Firms maximize their profits	No	In general, hospitals are nonprofit organizations which seek to maximize other objectives (growth, prestige) Similarly, physicians may have noneconomic motives, such as intellectual curiosity, esteem of peers

Together, these factors undercut virtually all normal incentives for market efficiency. Consumers trust providers to make consumption decisions; and since they often pay little or nothing *directly* for medical services, consumers have little incentive to economize. Providers are generally paid by a third party; and since they are reimbursed for their fees and incurred costs, providers have little incentive to economize. Insurers spread the costs among all subscribers, who in the end pay for this inefficiency in the *indirect* costs of their premiums. No one in this triangular flow of dollars has sufficient incentives to make economizing choices; indeed, the predominant incentives are for more and more spending.

Other institutional and attitudinal factors compound the cost-inflating incentives described above:

1. *Medical ethic.* Physicians are generally unconcerned with, and unaccountable for, the costs of services recommended and rendered. This is especially true of hospital costs. Physician training emphasizes thoroughness and the use of all available resources to help the patient, rather than the management of health care resources and the trade-off of cost and effectiveness. While difficult to change, this attitude has serious efficiency implications in a system where resources are allocated by physicians.

2. *Medical mystique.* Physicians are among the most respected members of society, and in the medical marketplace few consumers question the wisdom of physician recommendations. Moreover, the idea that "money is no object" in medical care decisions is widespread among consumers as well as physicians. Few consumers even ask about the prices of medical care. Again, these attitudes have serious implications in a system where individual consumers do not bear much of the direct costs of resource consumption.

3. *Nonprofit institutions.* In a society where health has no price, institutions are not expected to profit from illness. Large segments of the medical care industry are nonprofit, and the response to financial incentives differs from that of a profit-making industry. While profit-making firms strive to maximize earnings and thus to minimize cost per unit of output, nonprofit hospitals place more emphasis on maximizing quality of service or capital investment. The growth-with-quality imperative creates incentives for greater costs. This must be a concern in a financing system based on cost reimbursement.

These societal and institutional attitudes — that cost should not be a factor in medical decisions, that health has no price, that quality is of paramount concern — are unique to the medical care market. They create strong pressures for spending. The institutional and financing arrangements in the market offer little resistance to cost increases and little incentive for efficient resource allocation.

Some government policies also contribute to the incentives for cost-increasing behavior in the medical care sector. This happens at both the federal and state levels through direct and indirect subsidies, health care financing programs, and extensive regulation:

1. *Tax subsidies.* By exempting from taxation employer contributions to health care plans, the federal income and payroll tax structures provide an enormous ($[200 billion in 2006]) subsidy for private insurance coverage. This, in effect,

allows employees to purchase insurance with pre-tax dollars rather than after-tax dollars, an average subsidy of 30 percent of the employer's contribution. This subsidy distorts the employee's incentive for efficient health care expenditures by encouraging the purchase of more expensive, first-dollar coverage.

2. *Hidden premium costs.* The tax incentive to pay for medical insurance through employers results in substantial consumer ignorance of full premium costs. Approximately 80 percent of health insurance premiums are paid through employment-related group insurance plans. Under these group plans, on average, the employer pays two-thirds of the total premium. . . . These institutional and consumer responses to the government subsidy provide further incentives for consumers to seek more comprehensive, cost-inflating coverage than if the premium costs were paid directly.

3. *Medicare and Medicaid.* These two health care financing programs rely almost entirely on third-party, fee-for-service, and cost-reimbursement financing. They pay more on behalf of people who choose more costly systems of care, and they pay more to providers that cost more.

4. *Regulatory barriers to efficiency.* Federal and state legislatures and regulatory agencies, often with the advice of medical associations, have adopted regulations that in many respects serve as barriers to cost-reducing innovation. The use of supervised para-professionals and physician extenders for routine services, for example, has been severely restricted by regulation. Restrictive laws and practices have also inhibited the growth of alternative, more efficient health delivery systems. Even the Health Maintenance Organization Act, which was intended to spur the growth of HMOs, encumbered developing HMOs with enough restrictive "quality controls" to raise the cost of their operation and make them less competitive than they could be.

While some government policies have attempted to contain medical costs through direct economic regulation, other policies have exacerbated the inflationary pressures within the market.

A brief sketch of the medical care market cannot provide a definitive background for understanding the regulation/competition debate. However, it is essential to begin an assessment of the debate with an examination of intrinsic market characteristics. Only by distinguishing those elements that are intrinsic and cannot be changed (e.g., risk, uncertainty) from those elements that are institutional responses and may be changed (e.g., third-party cost reimbursement), and by distinguishing both from the symptoms (e.g., excess bed capacity), can the true sources of the problem be identified and effective policy alternatives be developed.

■HEALTH CARE CHOICES: PRIVATE CONTRACTS AS INSTRUMENTS OF HEALTH REFORM
Clark C. Havighurst
1995

The nature of the challenge posed by health care costs can be appreciated best by seeing the graphic demonstration in Figure 9.4.

FIGURE 9.4 Targets in the War on Health Care Costs

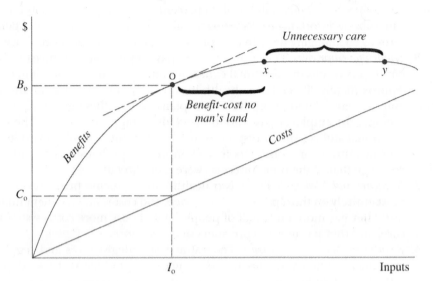

The "benefits" curve in Figure 9.4 shows heuristically the probable relation-ships between the benefits of health care (measured in dollars on the vertical axis) and the inputs needed to obtain them. It is assumed that "inputs" are all uniform and that they will be added in a sequence dictated by their ability to yield benefits. Thus, at low input levels, the benefits curve rises steeply, reflecting the true miracles of modern medical science. The curve rises more and more gradually, however, as the inputs being added yield either cures at increasingly higher cost or benefits of increasingly equivocal kinds. The curve is flat after point x, as added inputs yield no benefit, illustrating the notion of unnecessary care. (The curve actually falls after point y, showing that some medical care is positively harmful.)

The benefits curve alone cannot reveal where society or any given purchaser should stop adding inputs. Although no care should be purchased beyond point x, cost-containment efforts that stop there would not ensure an efficient level of consumption. Efficiency demands that costs be taken into account. The diagram therefore introduces a cost curve, a straight line illustrating the cumulative dollar cost of adding uniform inputs. The critical feature of this line for present purposes is its slope (rate of increase), which is reflected in the dotted parallel line having a point of tangency with the benefits curve at point o. At that point, the benefits curve is rising at exactly the same rate as the cost line. Up to that point, the inputs added yield benefits that exceed the costs incurred. Beyond point o, however, the benefits obtainable by adding additional inputs are no longer as great as the cost of those inputs. In other words, marginal costs exceed marginal benefits. Io then represents . . . the optimal (efficient) level of inputs, and Co represents the (provisionally) optimal level of spending.

The first crucial point in this demonstration is that even though adding inputs and expenditures beyond point o would improve aggregate health, that fact does not justify such additional spending; employing the same resources in other ways, dedicating them to nonhealth purpose, would increase welfare even more. This conclusion, while theoretically correct, may be hard to accept because of doubts about valuing the health benefits of individuals in dollars and trading them off against other things beneficial to other individuals. It is not proposed, however, to operationalize this calculus in making social decisions or in rationing care. Instead, the analysis here is offered simply to make the point that it is almost certainly socially wrong—in the sense that it reduces aggregate welfare—to pay for every health service that yields some benefit. This point, however, is the beginning, not the end, of the discussion.

An equally important implication of the foregoing demonstration is the obvious practical difficulty of deciding what specific services to omit and of preventing them from being rendered in particular cases. This difficulty will be encountered at whatever level the requisite actions must be taken, whether by society as a whole acting through government, by financing intermediaries, by providers of care, or by individual patients. To highlight this aspect of the problem we are setting for ourselves, the diagram labels the portion of the benefits curve between point o and point x as the benefit-cost no man's land. In this area, health care, being beneficial, will seem desirable as long as the decisionmaker—public or private, as the case may be—does not consider the true cost of providing it. The potential for conflict is clear. Precisely because anyone venturing to fight the battle for cost containment in this range is likely to draw criticism of the most intense kind, including lawsuits, the no-man's-land metaphor seems apt. Again and again in the discussion ahead, there will be occasions to ask whether the cost-containment weapons being used are capable of fighting the battle in the benefit-cost no man's land. We will discover that virtually all of the cost-containment measures in use today seek to eliminate only flat-of-the-curve care and not to take on the more dangerous challenge.

■ HEALTH CARE, MARKETS, AND DEMOCRATIC VALUES*
Rand E. Rosenblatt
34 Vand. L. Rev. 1067 (1981)

Market advocates attempt to structure the patient's relationship to health care as an economic transaction, namely, as an exchange of a commodity for money in a competitive market setting. A primary justification for increasing market competition in health care is to promote efficiency in the use and delivery of services. Some proponents argue that market competition also has value in its own right as a uniquely legitimate method of defining and promoting efficiency. It is argued that collective social decisions, however made, are inherently coercive and inevitably inefficient. Market mechanisms are said to promote only the value of individual liberty, which enables consumers to express their own preferences by their economic "votes"; otherwise, these mechanisms are considered to be value-neutral.

Despite its considerable superficial appeal, this position is misguided. The distribution of health services through competitive markets promotes at least three major and related nonneutral values. First, in a competitive market individuals are encouraged to make decisions about health care primarily from an economic perspective, as opposed to a broader, more realistic view. Second, individuals also are encouraged to perceive health care choices and health itself as an individual matter, rather than as a matter based upon a close interrelationship between individual decisions and social patterns concerning nutrition, work, environmental quality, economic opportunity, and many other factors. Last, in a competitive market, individuals in their role as citizens or government officials are encouraged to believe that the proper goal of most government policy is to encourage voluntary market transactions. As a result, issues of equality become confined to the special and limited sphere of redistributing purchasing power, the purpose of which is to permit deserving low income persons to participate in the free market. These three values may be defensible, but they certainly are not neutral, at least not in the sense of simply allowing individuals to express their own preferences. On the contrary, they are designed to exert influence over what those preferences might be, as well as to limit the kinds of social settings in which preferences can be expressed and satisfied. . . .

Health can be understood rather simply as the absence of disease and death, and health care as a "curative defense" against both. Health care, . . . however, also must be understood as a caring rather than purely a curative activity, the goal of which is to reduce pain and anxiety and increase the patient's sense of self-determination and quality of life. . . . From this perspective, a central need of health care reform is not more refined quantitative cost-benefit analyses, but rather a restructuring of the patient-provider relationship that ideally could increase the sense of self-determination and satisfaction for both. . . .

A question of great importance about the market approach to health care delivery is how it will affect people with low incomes. By their very nature, markets respond to those consumer preferences that are expressed with money, and people with the least money, therefore, tend to have their preferences given the least attention. Market advocates are aware that some number of low income people could not afford to pay for services or insurance in a competitive health care market. Consequently, they usually propose the simple solution of income transfers — typically effected through a voucher for medical care — that would be sufficient to purchase "basic or necessary" services. . . .

Despite this apparently benign intention of the market advocates, there are strong reasons to believe that poor and low income persons will suffer grievously. A society that embraces a market approach to most of its daily economic life, including the socially sensitive area of health care, is unlikely to redistribute adequate purchasing power to people in economic need. Whether it is theoretically possible for a market society to be strongly egalitarian as well need not be definitively resolved; it is sufficient to note the major reasons why the market perspective is often inconsistent with egalitarian redistribution. First, such a society, or the dominant groups within it, are likely to have a strong belief that the income distribution produced by the market is just. Moreover, they are likely to see unequal economic rewards as necessary incentives for socially desirable qualities such as hard work, risk taking, and enterpreneurial initiative. Income redistribution — even in the form of in-kind vouchers for medical care — probably will be viewed as threatening work incentives and efficient allocation of resources.

10

Regulation of Health Care Facilities and Transactions

There was a time, prior to the 1980s, when the only legal representation most hospitals and doctors required, aside from malpractice defense, was occasional tax advice. It was once common for even large hospitals to rely solely on sporadic pro bono counsel. These idyllic days are now long past. Health care law has been one of the most rapidly growing areas of legal specialization for over two decades. Despite its focus on a single industry, health care law calls on a broad array of legal talents and requires sophistication in subjects as diverse as antitrust, corporate and tax law, administrative law, and securities regulation.

This transformation in the legal climate has resulted from the strong winds of economic and organizational change that are buffeting the health care delivery system. What was once a tranquil service industry dominated by religious orders is now a dynamic sector of the economy driven by a new-found entrepreneurial fervor. "Vertical integration," "diversification," "joint venturing," and "strategic aligning" are the buzzwords that fill today's health care trade press and boardrooms. The days of solo physician practice, freestanding hospitals, and bright-line divisions among doctors, hospitals, and insurers are giving way to various forms of joint ventures, complex corporate structures, and integrated alternative delivery systems.

The driving force behind this massive restructuring is the fear that unless individual providers are affiliated with larger institutions, alliances, or ventures, their business will dwindle under intensified competition or they may be forced out of business entirely. The feeling is that the stakes are high, and the time is now, so few providers have failed to act. See generally Einer Elhauge ed., The Fragmentation of U.S. Health Care: Causes and Solutions (2010); James C. Robinson, The Corporate

Practice of Medicine (1999); Jessica Mantel, The Myth of the Independent Physician: Implications for Health Law, Policy, and Ethics, 64 Case W. Res. L. Rev. 455 (2013); Abbe R. Gluck, The New Health Care Industry: Consolidation, Integration, Competition in the Wake of the ACA, Health Aff. Blog (Feb. 24, 2016); Symposium, 36 Health Aff. 1527 (2017); Symposium, 29 Health Aff. 1284 (2010); Symposium, 25(6) J. Gen. Intern. Med. 584 (June 2010); Symposium, 67(4) Med. Care Res. Rev. (Aug. 2010); Symposium, 27 Health Aff. 1218 (2008).

Corporate Structure and Integration

It is easy enough to draw in broad outline the forces that are restructuring health care financing and delivery. It is much more difficult to classify all of the variety of forms in which these restructurings can take shape. This difficulty arises in part from the lack of a settled vocabulary of consistent usage, in part from the still developmental nature of the market, and in part from the vast complexity that is inherent in the field.

An "integrated delivery system" (IDS) is the broadest construct, including, at a minimum, a full array of hospital and physician services in both inpatient and outpatient settings. It may also include long-term-care facilities and specialized services such as mental health or physical therapy. Most important, an integrated system incorporates some form of insurance risk, either by selling insurance directly, or contracting with insurers or employers on a capitated basis.

In the simplest manifestation, this would be an ordinary staff-model HMO that owns its own hospitals, employs its own physicians, and markets its own insurance. A contrasting model is one in which physicians and hospitals remain in separately governed entities but affiliate with each other and the insurer by some commonality of ownership or contract. A holding company might tie the components together, or one of the components—usually the insurer or the hospital—might be the dominant party. A structure in which the insuring entity is the dominant party is a group- or network-model HMO. A structure in which a nonprofit hospital or its nonprofit parent is the dominant party has come to be known as the "Foundation model."[1] When hospitals and physicians stand on approximately equal footing, as in a partnership, the structure is sometimes known as a "physician-hospital organization" (PHO).

Short of full integration, affiliations between and among hospitals, doctors, and insurers can take place through a variety of contracting or partnership arrangements, in both horizontal and vertical dimensions—that is, among similar providers or between different delivery-system components. To make things even more confusing, the same term sometimes applies to substantially different arrangements. For instance, a group of physicians that contract with each other in order to

---

1. This terminology arose in California, the first state to be swept by integrated networks, so as to take advantage of a provision in the California statutes that exempts so-called foundations from a certain legal restriction that otherwise precludes the employment of physicians. Although a "foundation" is not actually any particular type of legal entity, here it is interpreted to mean a nonprofit corporation.

negotiate with insurers can be called an "independent practice association" (IPA), but this term applies to the type of HMO that contracts with a large number of physicians on a nonexclusive basis. When insurers other than HMOs do this on a fee-for-service rather than capitated basis, the structure is usually called a PPO, for preferred provider organization.

Similarly, a hospital or insurer "acquiring" a physician practice has a number of still unsettled meanings. Aside from actually employing physicians, networks can contract with them or make them equity partners (i.e., investors). One common arrangement, referred to above as a "management services organization" (MSO), is for the network to acquire the tangible assets of a physician practice—the office building, files, medical records, etc.—for a lump sum price but for the physicians themselves to remain independent contractors. They agree to treat network patients under a predetermined compensation arrangement, and the network agrees to manage their office practice (staffing, billing, etc.).

This description should not be taken as a fixed categorization, much less a "how-to" guide. The variety of organizational techniques are far too numerous, and the field of activity is far too fluid, for any such codification. Many of the structures in use are fairly conventional forms of HMOs and hospital holding companies. Others are hybrids whose names seem to change every year or two, and many of the terms just defined are used by others in different and inconsistent ways. Accountable care organizations (ACOs), for instance, were not heard or thought of before about 2008, and we still lack a fixed definition of what they are. Once defined, it may be hard to distinguish ACOs from other similar constructs that were once in vogue but have receded from prominence. What happens next is anyone's guess. The only thing that is certain about the future is that things will not stay the same.

—END—

The Scope of This Chapter

The result of this cauldron of activity, aside from a never-ending stream of new acronyms and buzz phrases, is a tremendous surge in legal work. Each of these innovative ventures must be examined against the backdrop of both traditional legal doctrine and new bodies of health care regulation. This chapter covers a range of issues that modern health care attorneys must contend with at the cutting edge of their practice field. This is necessarily a grab bag of legal issues. Because we cannot hope to convey the universe of law relevant to the multitude of organizational and operational activities of health care business, we will set aside the areas of doctrine that have more general applicability—such as contract law and securities regulation—and focus instead on the doctrinal areas of unique importance to health care. Those who desire greater detail or depth might consult one of the following multivolume treatises: Wolters Kluwer's Hospital Law Manual and Managed Care Law Manual; Carol Colborn-Loepere et al., Health Care Financial Transactions Manual; Hooper Lundy & Bookman, Treatise on Health Care Law; American Health Lawyers Association, Health Law Practice Guide.

This chapter progresses through the layers of complexity in the health care industry as follows. The chapter begins with the regulation, corporate structure, and taxation of hospitals and other facilities as discrete, freestanding institutions. It then explores how these institutions relate with physicians. Then the chapter addresses the application of antitrust law to a range of key activities and organizations. The chapter concludes with the topic of greatest complexity: the regulation of financial relationships among all components of the health care financing and delivery system. Throughout, there are two central questions: What are the motivating concerns and concepts of each discrete body of law? Are they still relevant in the rapidly changing environment in which health care institutions currently find themselves? This inquiry is not simply whether courts correctly discern the technical aspects of each separate body of law; it is whether health care law more generally suffers from a "pathology" (to quote Prof. Elhauge at page 45) of viewing each topic too parochially and dissecting problems too narrowly. The risk is that courts will fail to see the overall, interactive effects of the many strands of legal doctrine that determine how medical institutions are formed and operated and that have a major impact on our nation's health care public policy.

■ PARTNERS IN HEALTH: HOW PHYSICIANS AND HOSPITALS CAN BE ACCOUNTABLE TOGETHER
Francis J. Crosson & Laura A. Tollen (2010)*

Any approach to sustained cost reduction in health care must involve hospitals and physicians. Hospitalizations are the costliest form of care delivery, and conventional wisdom is that physician care decisions directly drive over 80 percent of total health care costs. Accordingly, there is a growing consensus that changes in payment incentives to hospitals and physicians are required, and that such changes must be more than superficial. Most such payment reforms involve either prepayment for services to be rendered, with some form of risk sharing, or episode-based payments such as case payments to physicians and hospitals together.

But there is a problem. As seen in [the figure below], advanced payment methodologies are most feasible in an environment of highly organized providers. Such payment methodologies are much less feasible in the disaggregated delivery model that exists in much of the United States today. . . .

The solution to the problem is a coordinated set of delivery system reforms that involve changes in both payment and incentives and in the structure of how hospitals and physicians are organized to provide care. The changes must address the chicken-or-the-egg dilemma that has impeded progress in delivery system integration in many parts of the country. Without payment reform, there is little motivation for disaggregated physicians to do the hard work of forming larger organizations and to work with hospital administrators. Conversely, without the existence of greater numbers of integrated organizations, payers (including Medicare) have gained little traction in developing advanced payment methodologies because so few entities are capable of receiving them and succeeding with them.

Over the past eighty years, there have been a number of carefully constructed calls for delivery system integration. In 1933, the Committee on the Costs of Medical Care recommended that the United States seek to create many more group

---

* Copyright © Jossey Bass Press. Reprinted with permission.

FIGURE 10.1 Organization and Payment Methods

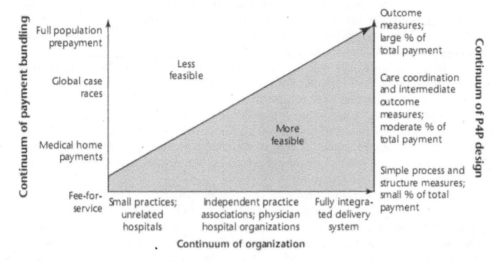

practices (modeled after the Mayo Clinic), because such practices were more efficient and less costly than solo practices. More recently, . . . in its landmark report in 2007, *A High Performance Health System for the United States,* The Commonwealth Fund Commission on a High Performance Health System called for "the U.S. [to] embark on the organization and delivery of health care services to end the fragmentation, waste, and complexity that currently exist. Physicians and other care providers should be rewarded, through financial and non-financial incentives, to band together into traditional or virtual organizations that can provide the support needed for physicians and other providers to practice 21st century medicine."

The goal then, in the context of [the figure above], is to move through both payment changes and delivery system changes over time from the "southwest" corner of the figure to somewhere closer to the "northeast" corner. There are many ideas about how to do this, discussed throughout this book. Virtually every one of these ideas for change will require increased collaboration or integration between hospitals and physicians. . . .

CLINICAL INTEGRATION

Most U.S. physicians practice medicine, at least in part, within a hospital setting but without a direct legal or financial relationship with the hospital. There are some exceptions to this model. In integrated delivery systems, such as Kaiser Permanente, . . . most physicians are employed by the group practice, which either owns or has a financial arrangement with the hospital or hospitals. Similarly, in physician hospital organizations (PHOs), the hospital and its associated physicians create a joint financial entity through which revenue is distributed. Recently, hospitals have begun to employ physicians directly in a variety of specialties. . . . In each of these settings, there is usually a sound structural, financial, and legal basis for physicians to work closely together to improve care quality and reduce unnecessary costs. . . .

In the more common setting, where the physicians and hospitals are not part of a single economic entity, the situation is quite different. In some states, the "corporate practice of medicine bar" prevents hospitals from hiring physicians. . . . In addition, a broad range of federal laws and regulations inhibits physician-hospital interrelationships, including antitrust provisions, tax-exempt organization regulations, laws intended to prevent limitation of services to Medicare beneficiaries, and "anti-kickback" and "Stark" provisions.

These regulations, as well as possible mitigation approaches, are discussed in detail [throughout this] chapter. Were there to be a significant "relaxation" of the laws and regulations that now inhibit financial arrangements between otherwise separate physicians and hospitals, it is possible that more formal integrated structures . . . might be less necessary. However, the pace of such regulatory changes is likely to be too slow to foster the type of systematic reorganization that appears to be called for now, as part of health care reform. Therefore, other, more complex proposals are under consideration. . . .

Whether . . . integration driven by a more widespread use of bundled payments, or the evolution of [Accountable Care Organizations], becomes the predominant reform dynamic in the next five or so years, there is little question that change is coming. . . . There are really only two ways to reduce [costs], either through progressive fee-for-service payment reductions to physicians and hospitals or through reorganization of care delivery and changes to payment and incentives. It is likely that only the latter choice has a simultaneous chance to improve quality. So the best hope is the most radical—to restructure and integrate. . . .

But are U.S. physicians and hospitals capable of proceeding successfully through such changes? . . . Some remember all too well the failed attempts to "integrate" in the mid-1990s to prepare for managed care prepayment, which never materialized. Many nascent organizations failed or disbanded as a consequence. Hard feelings and financial losses were the result. Currently, in many institutions, physicians and hospitals are at loggerheads over control issues or are in frank competition for patients needing complex, profitable procedures. A first step in breaking down this negative environment is to analyze what is wrong and how it could be different. . . .

Notes: Innovation Without End

1. *ACOs: Here We Go Again.* It is expected that ACOs will take multiple forms, similar to previous managed care organizations and alternative delivery structures reviewed in this and the previous chapter. Many of these existing templates are being dusted off and buffed up to respond to the new buzz. According to one astute observer, the "problem with this movie is that we've actually seen it before, and it was a colossal and expensive failure." Jeff Goldsmith, The Accountable Care Organization: Not Ready for Prime Time (Health Affairs Blog, Aug. 17, 2009). Initial reactions to Medicare's ACO rules were often negative, claiming that the potential rewards did not outweigh the business risks and administrative costs. Others, however, are more optimistic. Also, this time around, perhaps physicians will take the lead, rather than hospitals or insurers. E. J. Emanuel, Why Accountable Care Organizations Are Not 1990s Managed Care Redux, 307 JAMA 2263 (2012). But, the skeptics point out that many physician-led organizations also failed in the 1990s, and that hospitals are better able to shoulder the considerable capital costs entailed

in forming new delivery system structures. See Chapter 9.E.3 for further discussion ACA performance. Various legal issues raised by ACOs are covered throughout this chapter. For surveys, and discussion of practical issues, see note 4 below.

2. *Medical Homes vs. Retail Clinics.* Short of full-scale integration across the spectrum of care, "medical homes" provide better integration of primary care and other outpatient services, especially for people with chronic illness. Medical homes are primary care physicians or clinics that provide a fuller spectrum of services, including a comprehensive medical record and coordinated referrals to necessary specialists. From one vantage, these are kinder and gentler versions of the primary care "gatekeepers" much reviled under the first generation of managed care. It is not clear, however, whether they have potential to save money since, at least initially, medical homes require more payment than ordinary primary care, in order to support their broader range of supporting services. As with other practice innovations, the Affordable Care Act called for medical homes to be studied and encouraged, but it failed to set a firm course. At the other end of the integration spectrum, retail medical clinics are an emerging development implicating licensure, reimbursement, and corporate laws. Located in drugstores and megastores such as Walmart, they are staffed by nurse practitioners to provide simple and routine urgent care and medical screening services.

3. *Milking the System.* One reason for the huge upsurge in hospitals employing physicians is the disparity in payment rates between office-based and facility-based procedures. For exactly the same procedure, such as a colonoscopy, Medicare and private insurance typically pay considerably more when it is done at a facility, such as a hospital outpatient department, than at a physician's office. The main reason for the greater payment is that physicians practicing in office settings receive only a "professional fee," whereas at a facility the insurer also pays a facility fee. Thus, payment rates can double or triple simply by moving procedures from offices to facilities — an economic gain that strongly incentivized employment of previously independent physicians.[2] See Caroline S. Carlin, Roger Feldman & Bryan Dowd, The Impact of Provider Consolidation On Physician Prices, __ Health Econ. __ (2017).

4. *Sobering Thought of the Day.* According to one astute observer:

> [A]lmost any fix for what ails the U.S. health care system, be it a private market initiative or act of public legislation, every "solution" an entrepreneur or politician can dream up, runs headlong into the utter complexity of the system, the uncanny ability of those working in it to defend their precious turf against the solution, and the constant disconnect between what people in health care say they are going to do and what they actually end up doing. . . . The long view of our industry's history shows that health care is not changing so much as running in place, faster and faster, consuming more and more dollars as it tries to "re-engineer" itself out of its own realities.

2. Even more stimulus came from the fact that, for a while, hospitals could simply designate a physician's clinic as part of its facilities, thus escalating reimbursement without making any changes in the site of service (other than the signage). Starting in 2017, however, Medicare does not allow hospitals to claim facility fees for services performed off campus. However, the fundamental payment disparity still exists.

J. D. Kleinke, Oxymorons: The Myth of a U.S. Health Care System xii (2001) (also excerpted at page 42).

5. *Further Readings.* On **ACOs** (note 1), see Stephen Shortell et al., A Taxonomy of Accountable Care Organizations for Policy and Practice, 49(6) Health Serv. Res. 1883 (2014); Bruce Fried et al., Accountable Care Organizations: Navigating the Legal Landscape, 4 J. Health & Life Sci. L. 88 (2010); Douglas A. Hastings, Constructing Accountable Care Organizations: Some Practical Observations at the Nexus of Policy, Business, and Law, 19 BNA Health L. Rep. 883 (2010); John Hoff, How CMS's Final Regulations for Accountable Care Organizations Fall Flat (2012); Sara Kreindler et al., Interpretations of Integration in Early Accountable Care Organizations, 90 Milbank Q. 457 (2012); State Actions to Promote and Restrain Commercial Accountable Care Organizations (UC Berkeley, Oct. 2015); Symposium, 73(6) Med. Care Res. & Rev. 643 (2016); Symposium, 40(4) J. Health Pol. Pol'y L. 637 (2015); Symposium, 28 J. Contemp. Health L. & Pol'y 224 (2012); Symposium, 31 Health Aff. 2362 (2012); Symposium, 42 Seton Hall L. Rev. 1371 (2012).

On **medical homes** (note 2), see generally Anna D. Sinaiko et al., Synthesis of Research on Patient-Centered Medical Homes Brings Systematic Differences Into Relief, 36 Health Aff. 500 (2017); Symposium, 25(6) J. Gen. Intern. Med. 584 (June 2010); Symposium, 67(4) Med. Care Res. Rev. (Aug. 2010). On **retail clinics** (note 2), see William Sage, The Wal-Martization of Health Care, 28 J. Leg. Med. 503 (2007); William Sage, Out of the Box: The Future of Retail Medical Clinics, 3 Harv. L. & Pol'y Rev. 1 (online) (2009); Kaj Rozga, Retail Health Clinics: How the Next Innovation in Market-Driven Health Care Is Testing State and Federal Law, 35 Am. J. L. & Med. 205 (2009); Julie Muroff, Retail Health Care: "Taking Stock" of State Responsibilities, 30 J. Leg. Med. 151 (2009); Kristin Schleiter, Retail Medical Clinics: Increasing Access to Low Cost Medical Care Amongst a Developing Legal Environment, 19 Ann. Health L. 527 (2010); Symposium, 27(5) Health Aff. 1271 (Oct. 2008).

Problem: The History of Florence Nightingale Hospital and How It Grew*

This hypothetical serves as the basis for several of the discussion problems later in this chapter. It illustrates the profound transformations that have occurred in the health care sector over the last half century. It might be helpful in reviewing this to chart the legal measures that appear to prompt or support these organizational changes.

Florence Nightingale Hospital (FNH) is a private, nonprofit 400-bed facility employing more than 2,000 workers, with more than $100 million in annual rev-

---

* This fact scenario and many of the problems in this chapter that grow from it are based on ones originally developed by Prof. Phyllis Bernard at Oklahoma City University School of Law. The editors appreciate her permission to adapt them for use in this book.

enues. It is located on the outskirts of a metropolitan area of one million people that contains three other major tertiary care hospitals of 300 beds or more and four smaller, community hospitals of 100 to 150 beds. Currently, 38 percent of FNH's gross revenues are from Medicare, 12 percent are from Medicaid, and 40 percent from private insurance or out-of-pocket payments. The remaining 10 percent is bad debt or charity care.

Florence Nightingale Hospital was born in the 1950s as a small community hospital. It began as an effort by persons from the local church and medical communities joining forces with local business leaders to provide convenient hospital care in the growing suburbs. When the federal Hill-Burton program created a reservoir of construction loan money in the 1950s, the group of town boosters chose to apply for a construction loan to build a 100-bed facility. Its affiliation with the religious denomination has never been formalized through ownership, and the church no longer provides any significant financial support. Nevertheless, the charitable role of the hospital is taken seriously by the board of directors, which always includes one or two members of the denomination.

In the latter 1960s, increased revenues through the Medicare program enabled the hospital to obtain further construction loans, and the hospital expanded to add 100 more beds and more sophisticated inpatient services. Another wave of change swept through the health care industry in the 1980s, in response to a fundamental alteration in the way Medicare pays hospitals. Some hospitals consolidated, whereas Florence Nightingale sought to diversify operations and increase its patient base by providing a wider range of services and much larger bed capacity. Using a bond issue financed through the state, the hospital doubled in size to 400 beds. In addition, the hospital reorganized as the Florence Nightingale Healthcare Corporation in order to expand into nursing home, home health, and other related ventures.

In the 1990s the city had grown to reach Florence Nightingale Hospital's doorstep. FNH was no longer merely a suburban hospital. It became a major tertiary hospital serving the metroplex. However, revenues were beginning to dip due to the advent of managed care systems. Its average occupancy rate dropped from 85 to 70 percent.

In response, the hospital merged in 2000 with two other hospitals on the same side of town and formed the Florence Nightingale Network. The objective was to curb the loss of patients to other managed care networks by signing up a number of physicians, mainly in primary care but also in common specialties, and then marketing this network directly to employers and also to large insurance companies who would then offer the network to their customers. This effort was partially a bust, but in other ways was a great success. The idea of marketing directly to employers did not work because the network does not cover a broad enough geographic area to appeal to the largest employers, and smaller employers prefer a network that includes most of the physicians in town so they don't have to force their employees to switch doctors.

The network was a great advantage, however, in contracting with insurers. Because of employers' demands for broad networks, and regulators' requirements that managed care insurers provide adequate network capacity, insurers feel they have to include Florence Nightingale's facilities and physicians in their networks if they want to sell insurance in the region. Therefore, over the past few years, Florence Nightingale has been able to insist on double-digit increases in the payment rates from managed care plans.

Recently, however, Florence Nightingale is starting to lose some of its most profitable business to physicians on its medical staff who have opened outpatient surgery and radiology clinics. There are rumblings that some doctors might even open a competing hospital that refuses to take Medicaid or uninsured patients. And, there is talk among area physicians of starting their own ACO, in order to benefit from enhanced Medicare payments. Florence Nightingale is now considering what its next moves should be.

A. PROFESSIONAL AND FACILITY REGULATION

1. *Professional Licensure*

During the nineteenth century, snake oil salesmen and other quacks roamed the countryside preying on the gullible public with unfounded promises of miracle cures. To eliminate such practices, around the turn of the twentieth century every state began to license medical practitioners. The typical Medical Practice Act makes it a criminal offense to practice medicine without a physician's license and establishes the grounds for revocation or suspension of a license. The job of medical licensure and discipline is entrusted to a Board of Medical Examiners, which usually consists predominantly of physicians. Some alternative practitioners, such as osteopaths, chiropractors, and podiatrists, have likewise been successful in petitioning the legislature for recognition and protection through professional licensure and self-regulation. Thus, professional licensure serves a "fencing" function, one that keeps some persons from providing health care services altogether and that separates providers into different categories of professionals with at least somewhat distinct areas of permissible practice. And licensure also serves a policing function that investigates and disciplines allegedly errant providers.

■ **STATE v. MILLER**
542 N.W.2d 241 (Iowa 1995)

ANDREASEN, Justice.

Albert C. Miller appeals from his convictions for practicing medicine without a license. He urges . . . that the record contains insufficient evidence to support his convictions. We affirm the judgment of the district court.

Miller was charged by a trial information with seven counts of practicing medicine without a license. [This prosecution was brought after Mr. Miller repeatedly violated injunctions to cease treated patients as described below. Most of the offenses charged were Class D felonies.] . . .

Several persons testified at trial describing treatments they received from Miller in his home for various ailments. His usual method of treatment was to put a lock of the person's hair or a photograph of the person into a machine called a radionics device. After recording numerous readings from the device on a chart, he would treat the person by administering mild electric shocks from a "function generator," massaging the person's feet or neck, or placing large magnets next to the person. In addition, he often sold or recommended natural vitamins or nutrients to the people who visited him. Although Miller did not charge for the treatments, he consistently accepted donations of $10 for each treatment. He did not have any license to practice medicine, osteopathy, or surgery.

Dr. John Renner, M.D., Director of the Consumer Health Information Research Institute, testified as an expert witness for the state. He found the various treatments and vitamins given by Miller to his patients, while not necessarily harmful, were generally not medically useful. In his opinion the primary danger was not from the medicine itself, but from the fact it delayed appropriate, potentially beneficial, medical treatment.

On July 14, 1994, the jury returned verdicts finding Miller guilty on all seven counts. He was sentenced to a term of incarceration not to exceed five years on six counts. On the seventh count, he was sentenced to four months in the county jail. All the sentences were suspended and Miller was placed on probation for five years. . . .

We must uphold the jury's verdict unless the record lacks substantial evidence to support the charges. Substantial evidence is evidence which could convince a rational jury the defendant is guilty of the crimes charged beyond a reasonable doubt. . . .

Miller was charged with practicing medicine and osteopathic medicine in violation of Iowa Code §147.2. Two separate instructions were given to the jury defining the practice of medicine and osteopathic medicine. One instruction . . . provided the following definition:

> The practice of medicine and osteopathic medicine means holding one's self out as being able to diagnose, treat, or prescribe for any human disease, pain, injury, deformity, or physical or mental condition and who shall either offer or undertake, by any means or methods, to diagnose, treat, or prescribe for any human disease, pain, injury, deformity or physical or mental condition.

The other instruction provided that the following "persons shall be deemed to be engaged in the practice of medicine and osteopathic medicine":

1. Persons who publicly profess to be physicians or who publicly profess to assume the duties incident to the practice of medicine and osteopathic medicine.
2. Persons who prescribe, or prescribe and furnish medicine for human ailments. . . .

Miller argues that he did not publicly profess to be a physician or publicly profess to assume the duties incident to the practice of medicine and osteopathic medicine. He emphasizes that he never advertised nor described himself as a doctor; he would sometimes recommend that his customers consult a licensed physician or chiropractor; and he only met people in his home, not in an office.

We conclude there is sufficient evidence to conclude that Miller publicly professed to assume the duties incident to the practice of medicine and osteopathic medicine. We have defined the "duties incident to the practice of medicine" to include diagnosing patients' ailments and prescribing the proper treatment. Witnesses testified that they were treated by Miller for various ailments including arthritis, rash, infection, headaches, constipation, and neck, shoulder, and back pain. Although he may not have referred to himself as a doctor, he led his customers to believe that he could diagnose and treat their ailments. Even though Miller did not formally advertise his treatments, he gained a large local customer base by means of referral from one customer to another. The fact that Miller would sometimes recommend that his customers consult a licensed physician or chiropractor does not detract from the fact that he would diagnose and treat their physical conditions, at least up to a certain point.

We also conclude there was sufficient evidence that Miller routinely prescribed and furnished medicine. Miller argues that he sold or recommended only natural vitamins or nutrients. His defense, through the testimony of a witness, was that vitamins and nutrients were not medicines, but food.

We have broadly construed the statutory words "prescribe and furnish medicine" to include administering any substance or remedy in the treatment of an ailment or disease. The fact that a substance may also have value as a food "will not deprive of its character as a medicine if it be administered and employed for that purpose." State v. Bresee, 114 N.W. 45, 47 (1907).

> It is evident [the defendant] was catering to patronage of the sick who were asking relief from their ills, and, if [he] listened to their statements, assured them of [his] ability to help them out, and supplied them with [his] alleged appropriate remedies giving instructions for their application or use, this would seem to come . . . within the ordinary and usual signification attached to the words "prescribing" or "prescribing and furnishing medicines," as they are commonly used and understood. Id.

We believe Miller's actions of selling or recommending natural vitamins to his customers constitutes furnishing a substance or remedy for treating their ailments.

We conclude there is sufficient evidence to convince a rational jury beyond a reasonable doubt that Miller was guilty of practicing medicine and osteopathic medicine without a license.

[On an ironic note, the court also rejected Miller's appellate lawyers' claim that the district court had erred in permitting him to represent himself at trial. Miller had initially sought to appoint "unlicensed" counsel to represent him at trial and chose to represent himself when his request was rejected. The court held that Miller knowingly and intelligently waived his right to licensed representation.]

■ CHARACTER, COMPETENCE, AND THE PRINCIPLES OF MEDICAL DISCIPLINE

Nadia N. Sawicki
13 J. Health Care L. & Pol'y 285 (2010)

As the state agencies responsible for the licensure and discipline of physicians, medical boards serve as the gatekeepers of the medical profession. However, critics frequently question whether boards have, in fact, been living up to their potential in this regard, particularly in the context of professional discipline. Since the 1970s, state medical boards have faced criticism from a variety of sources for inappropriately screening applicants for medical licensure,[3] failing to discipline dangerous physicians, and generally being lax in their oversight duties at the expense of a vulnerable public.[7] . . .

[A] common explanation for medical boards' lax approach to professional discipline is that the boards are "captured" by professional interests or otherwise lack meaningful public oversight. Indeed, one of the most prominent criticisms of the medical profession in the 20th century has been that it is self-protective, monopolistic, and more attuned to the economic security of its members than to the welfare of the public at large. . . .

While there is likely some element of truth to the argument that medical boards discipline physicians too infrequently, this Article identifies a more substantive problem—namely, that when boards do choose to exercise their disciplinary discretion, they often focus on character-related misconduct, including criminal misconduct, that bears only a tangential relation to clinical quality and patient care. . . . In recent years, medical providers have been disciplined on grounds as varied as tax fraud, failure to facilitate review of child support obligations, soliciting sex in a public restroom, possession of marijuana for personal use, and reckless driving involving alcohol, as well as other conduct allegedly bringing the medical profession into disrepute. While these are not commendable activities by any stretch of the imagination, this Article questions whether, in light of the traditional goals of professional discipline, sanctioning physicians on these grounds (as opposed to grounds more clearly linked to clinical practice) is the most effective or efficient use of medical boards' resources. . . .

A. MEDICAL BOARD AUTHORITY: HISTORY AND PRACTICE

Among the unenumerated powers reserved to each state under the Tenth Amendment is the power to protect the health, safety, and welfare of its citizenry, commonly known as the police power. . . . As explained by the Supreme Court in *Dent v. West Virginia*, 129 U.S. 114 (1889), . . . [i]t is pursuant to their police powers that states are authorized to regulate law, medicine, and other professions, which they typically do by delegating authority to professional licensing boards.

. . . The first state medical boards were created in the late 1800s when private medical associations pushed state legislators to adopt laws regulating the practice of medicine. These efforts were driven by physicians who, fearful of incursions on their territory by "irregulars" and "quacks," were convinced that well-drafted legis-

---

3. *See* Marc T. Law & Zeynep K. Hansen, *Medical Licensing Board Characteristics and Physician Discipline: An Empirical Analysis*, 35 J. HEALTH POL. POL'Y & L. 63, 66 (2010).

7. Economists, in particular, have long made similar arguments, questioning the value of licensure and self-regulation in highly insulated and self-protective professions, like medicine. These authors and others suggest that medical quality and patient safety could be better safeguarded through market-based solutions that close the information gap between physicians and consumers. *See generally* Walter Gellhorn, *The Abuse of Occupational Licensing*, 44 U. CHI. L. REV. 6, 16-18, 22, 25 (1976) (arguing that occupational licensing impedes access to needed services and serves only to protect those who have already been licensed, rather than protect the public from incompetent professionals); Anthony Ogus, *Rethinking Self-Regulation*, 15 OXFORD J. LEGAL STUD. 97 (1995) (offering general criticism of the self-regulatory model). . . .

lation—far from being self-defeating—could serve an important role in protecting their professional interests. Though some historians suggest that professional self-protection, rather than concern for patient safety, was the driving force behind these lobbying efforts, the medical practice acts that resulted were, as a matter of law, clearly adopted pursuant to the legislative authority to protect public health and safety.

At a minimum, modern medical practice acts define the practice of medicine, establish the requirements for medical licensure, and set forth procedures for disciplinary action against licensees. . . . Modern medical boards generally include some public members but are dominated by physicians appointed by the governor.

American licensure laws are exclusive in that they grant qualified individuals the right to engage in the lawful practice of medicine and prohibit the practice of medicine by unlicensed persons. The requirements for obtaining a medical license are relatively consistent from state to state—generally, the applicant must be a graduate of an approved medical school, have completed at least one year of an approved graduate medical education program (residency or fellowship), and have passed the United States Medical Licensing Examination (USMLE). Beyond imposing educational and training requirements, many medical practice acts also require that applicants for medical licensure demonstrate good moral character. . . .

Medical boards' ongoing duties include periodic re-registration of licensees, which is typically contingent on completion of specified hours of Continuing Medical Education training. However, medical boards rarely impose additional requirements intended to ensure the quality of care, such as mandatory recertification or random practice audits, upon physicians who have already received their licenses. As a result, the most important of state medical boards' oversight responsibilities with respect to medical quality is the discipline of professional licensees.

The medical disciplinary process is generally reactive, rather than proactive. It begins when a member of the public files a complaint, or, in the case of discipline on the grounds of criminal or civil liability, when a court or law enforcement agency files a report with the medical board. The board screens, and, if appropriate, investigates the complaint; if the board finds the complaint is valid, it may exercise its discretion to pursue disciplinary action against the physician, which can range from oral or written reprimand to license revocation or suspension.

Although the substantive grounds for professional discipline vary from state to state, most state medical practice acts authorize discipline for gross incompetence, physical or mental impairment, alcohol or drug abuse, practicing without a license or aiding the unlicensed practice of medicine, as well as reciprocal discipline against those providers who have been subject to disciplinary action in other states. Moreover, most states authorize discipline under a broad category of "unprofessional conduct," which may include violations of codes of medical ethics, conduct that brings the medical profession into disrepute, or other unspecified forms of "dishonorable conduct," including criminal acts (typically felonies or crimes of "moral turpitude"). . . .

In foundational cases such as *Dent* [*v. West Virginia*] and *Schware v. Board of Bar Examiners*, 353 U.S. 232 (1957), the Supreme Court held that the criteria for licensure and discipline may not be vague, arbitrary, or unattainable, and "must have a rational connection with the applicant's fitness or capacity to practice" his profession. However, because no fundamental rights are implicated in the loss of a professional license, courts review boards' disciplinary determinations under a highly deferential standard. . . .

[T]he medical board's disciplinary authority is aimed at protecting medical consumers from the harms they may incur at the hands of incompetent or dishonest physicians. This is reflected in the sanctions that may be imposed on physicians, which range from alerting the medical board and community of a potential for harm (via a public letter of reprimand) to withdrawing the physician's right to practice (delicensure). Unlike criminal law, which is aimed at punishing wrongdoers, or civil law, which is aimed at victim compensation, professional discipline seeks to protect public welfare by incapacitating or rehabilitating dangerous physicians. . . .

A final, and related, insight . . . is [that] professional licensure and discipline standards are established to ensure a minimal level of competence, rather than to identify aspirational standards of professional conduct. . . . The appropriate view of professional licensure, then, is as a floor beyond which practitioners may not drop, rather than an ideal towards which they must strive. In other words, though we view a medical license as evidence that a physician possesses the basic tools necessary to practice medicine safely, the license does not ensure that he will actually use these tools correctly going forward. Moreover, a medical license does not distinguish the merely competent provider from the excellent provider—that distinction takes place at the marketplace level. . . .

C. Quantitative and Qualitative Concerns

Despite the fact that the theoretical underpinnings of the American medical disciplinary regime are sound, the system as it is being practically implemented boasts few supporters. . . . The most common criticism that has been traditionally levied against medical boards is that they simply do not discipline physicians often enough to have a substantial impact on patient safety and public health. . . . [E]stimates suggest that less than one-half of one percent of licensed physicians face serious discipline annually. . . .

While there may be some truth to [these] claims, . . . [t]he rate at which medical professionals face serious discipline annually is comparable to the rate of serious professional discipline in other professions, including law. It is also comparable to the rate of felony convictions among the American public. While professional boards and prosecutors certainly could be doing more to pursue those who violate professional standards or break the law, given the parallels between the rates of professional discipline and criminal conviction, the degree of invective levied at medical boards by public advocates seems disproportionate. . . .

Arguably more important in determining whether medical boards are likely to be successful in protecting the public is the qualitative issue of which physicians are being disciplined and on what substantive grounds. That is, if medical boards can pursue only 3,000 serious disciplinary actions against physicians each year, boards . . . ought to ask which is likely to have the greatest impact on patient protection, which [complaints have] the closest link to fitness to practice, and where each [case] falls on the spectrum from minimal competencies to aspirational standards. . . .

[M]edical boards rarely take disciplinary action on the basis of incompetent medical practice or poor quality of care. . . . [F]ewer than 15% of professional disciplinary actions taken between 1999 and 2008 appear to have been taken on grounds clearly related to clinical competence. . . . Although the majority of disciplinary actions are taken on unspecified grounds, the ones that are categorized tend to fall within three broad categories—drug or alcohol abuse, criminal convictions, and unspecified unprofessional conduct. . . . [B]etween 1994 and 2002, unspecified "unprofessional conduct" was the single most frequently cited ground for discipline, appearing in approximately a third of all cases. . . .

Often, when boards take serious disciplinary action on the basis of unprofessional behavior or criminal conduct, the sanctioned physicians challenge their suspensions on due process grounds, arguing that their behavior, while possibly indicative of poor personal judgment or character, is simply not relevant to their fitness to practice medicine. . . .

[D]. An Imperfect Fit with the Principles of Professional Discipline

The fact that physicians are frequently sanctioned for engaging in character-related or criminal misconduct is troubling in light of the [principle] . . . that boards ought to be primarily concerned with enforcing minimal standards of fitness to practice in an effort to protect consumers of medical services. It hardly seems obvious why . . . boards should be using their scarce resources to discipline physicians for character-related misconduct occurring outside the clinical sphere, particularly where such behavior is already subject to criminal or civil sanctions. . . . [M]ost state court decisions in disciplinary matters simply conclude that moral character broadly defined is a necessary component of fitness to practice without providing adequate support for this assertion. . . . Even *Hawker v. New York*, 170 U.S. 189 (1898), the case that speaks most directly to the issue of character-related criteria for professional licensure and discipline, offers little guidance. In *Hawker*, the Supreme Court upheld a New York state law prohibiting the practice of medicine by those who have been convicted of a felony, but provided little support for its conclusion that personal "[c]haracter is as important a qualification as knowledge" for professional practice and is therefore subject to discipline. In two brief sentences, the Court offered the following meager explanation of its conclusion: "The physician is one whose relations to life and health are of the most intimate character. It is fitting, not merely that he should possess a knowledge of diseases and their remedies, but also that he should be one who may safely be trusted to apply those remedies." . . .

Trust theorists posit that misconduct outside the clinical sphere is a legitimate subject for professional discipline if it is likely to cause public distrust of the medical profession. . . . [But] [p]atients may place faith in their physicians for any number of reasons—their religion, their affiliation with a particular hospital, their personal appearance—and it is by no means clear why a state should facilitate patient decisions that are based on non-clinical, irrelevant, or potentially discriminatory factors that have no clear link with fitness or competency to practice medicine. . . .

Much like criminal law, professional discipline serves an important signaling function for the medical community. It is the rare doctor who, in an effort to understand the boundaries of permissible professional behavior, turns first to the local law library to brush up on recent state legislation and case law. More likely, he receives periodic disciplinary updates from his state medical board, reads about cases of professional discipline in the media, and hears about the experiences of colleagues and friends. Given that some of the most public and visible cases of professional discipline deal with cases of misconduct that bear little connection to the practice of medicine, I argue that modern medical boards that discipline on character-related grounds may not be sending the most constructive signals to physicians trying to conform their behavior to the law. . . .

Notes: Professional Licensure

1. *Criminal Prosecution.* Note that the unlicensed practice of medicine is a criminal offense; persons convicted of the offense can be fined and imprisoned. Suppose that the patient of an unlicensed provider is injured in the course of receiving care. Is the provider liable in tort under a negligence per se theory? See Chapter 4.C.1. Jurisdictions may also criminalize "assisting" in the unlicensed practice of medicine. This criminal offense can have civil law implications as well. Physicians and other licensed health care professionals are subject to professional disciplinary action, such as license revocation or suspension, for assisting in the unlicensed practice of medicine. Annot., 99 A.L.R.2d 654 (1965).

2. *Physician Supply.* Most states require M.D.s to graduate from an AMA-accredited medical school (or, for foreign medical graduates, certification by the Educational Commission for Foreign Medical Graduates (ECFMG) and an internship in an AMA-approved residency program). As a result, medical licensure essentially cedes to the medical profession control of how many doctors can enter practice, since the AMA can control the size of medical school classes through the accreditation process and the ECFMG can control the certification process. Mark A. Peterson, From Trust to Political Power: Interest Groups, Public Choice, and Health Care, 26 J. Health Pol. Pol'y & L. 1145 (2001).

Allowing the medical profession to control entry into its own market creates the anticompetitive risk that the AMA will act out of economic self-interest to maintain artificial shortages. Barriers to entry into service professions tend automatically to drive up prices by creating a supply shortage. Reuben Kessel, Price Discrimination in Medicine, 1 J. L. & Econ. 20 (1959); Reuben Kessel, The A.M.A. and the Supply of Physicians, 35 Law & Contemp. Probs. 267 (Spring 1970).

Concern about physician shortages seems misplaced these days, when we are much more apt to hear about the "glut" of physicians, particularly of specialists. The ratio of physicians to citizens in the United States has been steadily increasing, rising from 146 physicians/100,000 in 1950 to 233/100,000 in 1990, to 277/100,000 in the year 2008. Some experts argue that the ideal ratio lies somewhere between 160 and 200 physicians per 100,000. More important than the total number, however, is their distribution. Policymakers are concerned that there are too few primary care physicians, who are less expensive, and too many specialists, who drive up the cost of care by providing services that could be more cheaply provided by family practitioners or other generalists. Also, the geographic distribution of physicians clearly remains problematic. Many rural areas have found it difficult to attract physicians. A similar problem can be found in some urban centers, where physicians have not been willing to establish practices that serve low-income populations. Tracy Hampton, US Medical School Enrollment Rising, but Residency Programs Too Limited, 299 JAMA 284 (2008).

3. *Defining Medical Practice.* The legislative definition of the "practice of medicine" typically is quite broad, as can be seen by examining the jury instructions in *Miller.* The breadth of the definition is important because persons who engage in the specified activities without an appropriate license are subject to criminal penalties. How far can the definition of medical practice be stretched?

The various exotic and peripheral ministrations successfully attacked under the medical licensure statutes range from the sublime to the ridiculous. Magnetism, mental suggestion, faith healing, color wave therapy, reflexology, massage, hypnotism, tattooing, and electrical hair removal all have been held to constitute the practice of medicine. See, e.g., State v. White, 560 S.E.2d 420 (S.C. 2002) (state statute restricting tattooing to licensed physicians for cosmetic or reconstructive purposes does not violate free speech and is valid exercise of police power.) Even the commonplace practice of offering nutritional advice might subject the advisor to criminal prosecution, as in *Miller.* Courts have found that some activities, such as ear piercing and cosmetic hair removal, lie outside the sometimes seemingly unlimited scope of medical practice.

The very breadth of the typical medical practice act definition suggests a trap for the unwary, who might unexpectedly confront criminal liability for engaging in seemingly innocuous activities. Do the instructions given to the jury in *Miller* provide appropriate guidance for their decision? Defendants have challenged these statutes on vagueness grounds; however, courts have been understandably reluctant to agree and have upheld the statutes by artfully using a number of different techniques of statutory construction. See People v. Rogers, 641 N.W.2d 595 (2001) (statutory definition not facially overbroad or unconstitutionally vague).

4. *Licensure vs. Credentialing.* Thinking about both the broader purposes and criticisms of licensing health care professionals, what benefits does professional licensure have over a system of accreditation or certification? Under the latter, patients would be given clear notice about who does and does not have recognized credentials, but they would be permitted to choose whether to seek care from an unaccredited or uncertified person. Health care payers, such as insurance companies, might be empowered to reject payment claims made by those lacking certification. Licensure schemes are preferred where there is a risk that consumers might not be able to exercise reasoned judgment about the qualifications of their health care providers, perhaps because of lack of knowledge, the decisionmaking deficits created by disease, or financial distress. See Timothy Stoltzfus Jost, Oversight of the Quality of Medical Care: Regulation, Management, or the Market, 37 Ariz. L. Rev. 825 (1995); Randall G. Holcombe, Eliminating Scope of Practice and Licensing Laws to Improve Health Care, 31 J. L. Med. & Ethics 236 (2003).

5. *A Right to Receive Treatment?* Do patients have any constitutionally protected interest in being able to choose to receive health care services of one type or another, from one type of provider or another? The issue was not raised in *Miller* but has been litigated elsewhere. Most courts have found that there is no fundamental right of access to treatment by unlicensed providers. See, e.g., Mitchell v. Clayton, 995 F.2d 772, 775-776 (7th Cir. 1993). The Supreme Court's ruling in the physician-assisted suicide cases, see Chapter 5.B, suggests that the Constitution does not give patients a protected interest in obtaining particular types of medical treatment. What if, however, a case could be made that the particular treatment is the only one that might work? See Chapters 2.A. and 8.C for discussion of related constitutional issues.

6. *A Right to Provide Care?* Medical practitioners have been equally unsuccessful in their attempts to claim a constitutional right to provide care. Courts uniformly have upheld state licensing regulations so long as they are rationally related to serving some legitimate state interest. In Williamson v. Lee Optical of Oklahoma, Inc., the plaintiff challenged the constitutional validity of Oklahoma's licensure provisions that made it "unlawful for any person not a licensed optometrist or ophthalmologist to fit lenses to a face or to duplicate or replace into frames lenses or other optical appliances, except upon written prescriptive authority of an Oklahoma licensed ophthalmologist or optometrist." 348 U.S. 483, 485 (1955). The district court had held a portion of the statute unconstitutional, finding in part that it unreasonably prohibited opticians from making duplicate lenses for persons whose glasses were lost or broken. The Court upheld the statute, using classic rational basis review:

> The Oklahoma law may exact a needless, wasteful requirement in many cases. But it is for the legislature, not the courts, to balance the advantages and disadvantages of the new requirement. It appears that in many cases the optician can easily supply the new frames or new lenses without reference to the old written prescription. . . . But the law need not be in every respect logically consistent with its aims to be constitutional. It is enough that there is an evil at hand for correction, and that it might be thought that the particular legislative measure was a rational way to correct it.
>
> The day is gone when this Court uses the due process clause of the Fourteenth Amendment to strike down state laws, regulatory of business and industrial conditions, because they may be unwise, improvident, or out of harmony with a particular school of thought. . . . Id. at 487-488.

The Court also rejected an equal protection claim, again stating the applicable rational basis test in classic terms:

> The problem of legislative classification is a perennial one, admitting of no doctrinaire definition. Evils in the same field may be of different dimensions and proportions, requiring different remedies. Or so the legislature may think. Or the reform may take one step at a time, addressing itself to the phase of the problem which seems most acute to the legislative mind. The legislature may select one phase of one field and apply a remedy there, neglecting the others. The prohibition of the equal protection clause goes no further than the invidious discrimination. We cannot say that that point has been reached here. . . . Id. at 489.

The rational basis approach adopted in *Lee* has been applied in nearly every case since. See, e.g., National Ass'n for the Advancement of Psychoanalysis v. California Board of Psychology, 228 F.3d 1043 (9th Cir. 2000) (upholding state's mental health licensing scheme under rational basis test); Sherman v. Cryns, 786 N.E.2d 139 (Ill. 2003) (state midwifery licensing statute is rationally related to a legitimate state interest).

States often provide an exception to the normal rules governing the practice of medicine for religious practitioners. See, e.g., Cal. Bus. & Prof. Code §2063 ("Nothing in this chapter shall be construed . . . [to] regulate, prohibit, or apply to any kind of treatment by prayer, nor interfere in any way with the practice of religion."). Is this religious exemption required by the First Amendment? Does an exemption for religious practitioners violate the First Amendment's prohibition of state estab-lishment of religion? Does the exemption for religious practitioners undercut the rationale for general licensure requirements—if the public health is at risk from "unscientific" practitioners, then shouldn't the public be protected from religious practitioners? Most academic attention focuses on the liability of parents for child neglect for the use of religious or spiritual healers. See, e.g., Jessie Hill, Whose Body, Whose Soul?, 32 Cardozo L. Rev. 1857 (2011).

7. *Alternative Healing Techniques.* Why did Miller's patients seek his assistance? Why are alternative practitioners so popular? First, of course, critics of the medi-cal system note that the appeal can be directly related to the "ills" of traditional medicine. Medical practice is expensive, impersonal, and bureaucratic. Second, alternative therapies apparently work, at least some therapies for some people. The National Institutes of Health (NIH) created the Center for Complementary and Alternative Medicine (CAM) in 1992 to fund research designed to test the efficacy of a wide range of alternative therapies. Even if the alternative therapy is scien-tifically worthless, a significant percentage of people given a placebo will experi-ence relief from their symptoms and even an improvement in their condition. See Chapter 1.B.3. Given all of this, perhaps licensure requirements keep people from seeking out potentially effective care. Does that mean alternative healers should be exempted from licensure, or should instead petition legislatures for their own licen-sure schemes? See John Lunstroth, Voluntary Self-Regulation of Complementary and Alternative Medicine Practitioners, 70 Alb. L. Rev. 209 (2006).

8. *Interprofessional Disputes.* Rules prohibiting the unlicensed practice of various professions also serve to establish boundaries between particular classes of health care providers. Persons providing health care services pursuant to statutory autho-rization are not guilty of the unlicensed practice of medicine. Thus a nurse is not engaging in the unlicensed practice of medicine when she or he makes a nursing diagnosis or provides nursing services to a patient.

Still, interprofessional turf battles are waged, particularly where nonphysician health care providers have attempted to expand their scope of practice. See, e.g., Brown v. Belinfante, 557 S.E.2d 399 (Ga. Ct. App. 2001) (oral surgeon violates den-tal practice act by performing facelift); Connecticut State Medical Society v. Con-necticut Board of Examiners of Podiatry, 546 A.2d 830 (Conn. 1988) (litigation to determine whether podiatrists can treat ankles).

9. *Physician Extenders.* Physicians often delegate functions to other types of health care practitioners, such as nurses or physician assistants. The educational training of these other health care providers can vary widely. Traditionally, nurses have performed a wide range of functions within the health care system, sometimes under the control of physicians and sometimes exercising independent, nursing judgment. Physician assistants, in contrast, have traditionally been characterized as "dependent" practitioners, who perform only tasks delegated by physicians. Many states now certify or otherwise regulate physician assistants to ensure that they are appropriately supervised.

Can physicians delegate tasks to assistants who are not independently licensed, without assisting in the unlicensed practice of medicine? Some legislatures have been extremely active in attempting to mark the bounds of appropriate delegation. Others provide physicians broad discretion to delegate tasks however they want as long as they do so consistent with proper medical standards, they supervise and retain responsibility, and the person doing the tasks does not purport to be practicing medicine. See, e.g., Tex. Occ. Code Ann. §157.001.

Nurse practitioners and physician assistants play a particularly important role in providing medical services in rural and central urban areas, where physicians are rare. Residents of these areas will often not have access to any health care unless they can be treated by "physician extenders." As a consequence, many states permit physicians to delegate more tasks, such as signing certain prescriptions, in "medically underserved" areas of the state.

Physician assistants or nurses performing delegated tasks generally do so pursuant to physician's orders, standing medical orders, standing delegation orders, or written protocols. Courts, administrative agencies, and legislatures have struggled to define when a physician's degree of supervision is inadequate. Some jurisdictions have at least partially defined the degree of required supervision by establishing periodic physician reviews (e.g., daily status reports, once a week on-site direction, etc.) and limiting the number of persons whom the physician can supervise. Should surgeons be permitted to delegate some tasks during surgery to persons not licensed to practice medicine?

10. *Telemedicine and "Mobile" Medicine.* Health care provider licensure is a matter of state law. How should this state-level system respond to the growing nationalization of health care practice, in which physicians in other states may use telemedicine or Internet technology to diagnose and recommend treatment for patients from afar? Many states have amended their licensing statutes or regulations in recent years to respond to this issue, some by tightening rules that prohibit out-of-state physicians from providing regular and ongoing direct care to patients, and others by specifying under which conditions this may be done. See note 13 below.

A related, but potentially even more revolutionary, development is "mobile medicine" in the form of small devices and apps that monitor health, facilitate self-help measures, and connect people with care advisors potentially anywhere in the world, or perhaps only through artificial intelligence. At the federal level, the FDA has indicated its intent to assert its jurisdiction over medical devices. Nathan Cortez, The Mobile Health Revolution?, 47 U.C. Davis L. Rev. 1173 (2014). At the state level, there are potential issues, not yet widely asserted, regarding whether these apps constitute diagnosis or prescription that amounts to the practice of medicine. Fazal Khan, The "Uberization" of Healthcare: The Forthcoming Legal Storm over Mobile Health Technology's Impact on the Medical Profession, 26 Health Matrix 123 (2016).

11. *Grounds for Discipline.* Despite Prof. Sawicki's criticisms, medical boards sometimes do discipline physicians who have delivered substandard, incompetent, or negligent care. When they do, boards are generally not required to prove that any patients were actually harmed. See Annot., 93 A.L.R.2d 1398 (1964); Annot., 28 A.L.R.3d 487 (1969); Annot., 22 A.L.R.4th 668 (1983).

As Prof. Sawicki notes, however, professional discipline often targets purely economic misbehavior. For instance, licensure codes often attempt to restrict the range of permissible advertising or solicitation that practitioners may use. One rationale for these restrictions is that they prevent consumer fraud and abuse. Another is that they insulate the profession from the demands of competition, which might result in price wars and lost income. States generally may not restrict truthful, nonmisleading professional advertisements without violating the First Amendment's protection of free speech. See, e.g., Virginia State Board of Pharmacy v. Virginia Citizens Consumer Council, Inc., 425 U.S. 748, 762 (1976) (striking down ban on price advertising by pharmacists); Culpepper v. Arkansas Board of Chiropractic Examiners, 36 S.W.3d 335 (Ark. 2001) (ban on direct contact by chiropractors with potential patients is unconstitutional).

What of professional disciplinary rules that forbid certain business arrangements, such as assisting in the corporate practice of medicine? See section B.3. Viewed in one light, these provisions indirectly protect patients by reducing the threat that economic motivations will override patient interests in the provider-patient relationship. Once again, however, it could readily be argued that these prohibitions serve to protect professional autonomy, regardless of the impact on patients.

12. *An Administrative Law Primer.* Complaints against medical practitioners are adjudicated initially by "hearing officers," who determine if a violation has occurred and recommend an appropriate sanction. The agency typically has an internal appeals process with the final agency determination rendered by the relevant board itself. The agency's procedures are likely to be established within its enabling legislation and within the state's Administrative Procedure Act. Alleged flaws in this process are often the main focus of any court challenges, giving rise to constitutional and statutory issues that are studied at length in Administrative Law. Some of these issues are also addressed briefly in section C.2 below, dealing with disciplinary actions by hospitals against physicians. For additional discussion, see materials on the Web site for this book, www.health-law.org, and note 13.

13. *Additional Readings.* On the *history of medical licensure*, see Lewis Grossman, The Origins of American Health Libertarianism, Yale J. Health Pol'y L. & Ethics 76 (2013).

On **scope of practice issues** (notes 8 and 9), see Barbara J. Safriet, Closing the Gap Between *Can* and *May* in Health-Care Providers' Scopes of Practice: A Primer for Policymakers, 19 Yale J. on Reg. 301 (2002); Lori B. Andrews, The Shadow Health Care System: Regulation of Alternative Health Care Providers, 32 Hous. L. Rev. 1273, 1275 (1996); Laura Hermer & William Winslade, Access to Health Care in Texas: A Patient-Centered Perspective, 35 Tex. Tech L. Rev. 33 (2004); Joy L. Delman, The Use and Misuse of Physician Extenders, 24 J. Leg. Med. 249 (2003); Symposium, 32(11) Health Aff. 1870 (2013).

On **telemedicine and mobile apps/devices** (note 10), see Roundtable on Legal Impediments to Telemedicine, 14 J. Health Care L. & Pol'y 1-117 (2011); Amar Gupta & Deth Sao, The Constitutionality of Current Legal Barriers to Telemedicine in the United States, 21 Health Matrix 385 (2011); John Blum, Internet Medicine and the Evolving Legal Status of the Physician-Patient Relationship, 24 J. Leg. Med. 413 (2003); Symposium, 33(30 Health Aff. 194 (2014); Symposium, 14 J. Health Care L. & Pol'y 1 (2011); Symposium, 46 St. Louis U. L. J. 1-110 (2002).

On **First Amendment issues** (note 11), see Jess Alderman, Words to Live By: Public Health, the First Amendment, and Government Speech, 57 Buff. L. Rev. 161 (2009); Paula Berg, Toward a First Amendment Theory of Doctor-Patient Discourse and the Right to Receive Unbiased Medical Advice, 74 B.U. L. Rev. 201, 241-243 (1994).

On **administrative and due process issues** (note 12), see Eleanor Kinney, Administrative Law of Health Care in a Nutshell (2016); J. Bruce Bennet, The Rights of Licensed Professionals to Notice and Hearing in Agency Enforcement Actions, 7 Tex. Tech Admin. L. J. 205 (2006); Annot., 10 A.L.R.5th 1 (1993); Annot., 74 A.L.R.4th 969 (1989).

Problem: Professional Licensure

Dr. Alicia Chuanski lives in an urban area in a state that has many under-populated, rural areas. She has established a thriving family practice in the city. She is interested in expanding her practice into a rural area about 90 miles from her office. She hopes to set up a satellite office, staffed with a nurse and a physician assistant. Dr. Chuanski plans to supervise the satellite office in several ways:

1. She will establish detailed protocols for the nurse and physician assistant. They both will meet with patients, take patient histories and record patient symptoms, and establish baseline heart rates, blood pressures, and temperatures. The protocols will establish diagnostic or other procedures that should be followed for patients with particular symptoms. The protocols also will establish "opt-out" points: symptoms or complaints that indicate the need to refer patients to the nearest emergency room, which is about 20 miles away. Dr. Chuanski will leave a presigned prescription pad at the satellite for the use of the nurse and physician assistant (pursuant to the protocols); prescriptions will be reviewed on a daily basis.
2. Dr. Chuanski will attempt to establish a backup relationship with a nearby physician, perhaps one who maintains an office near the hospital mentioned above.
3. Dr. Chuanski will be available for phone consultations from 12 to 1:00 P.M. and from 4:30 to 5:30 P.M. every work day. Summary reports on the day's patients will be faxed to her each evening.
4. As the price of technology decreases, Dr. Chuanski will consider establishing a video link to the satellite so that she could "see" and "examine" patients from her office in the city.
5. Dr. Chuanski will visit the satellite once every ten days or so.

Evaluate Dr. Chuanski's plans. Will the nurse and/or physician assistant be engaged in the unlicensed practice of medicine? Is Dr. Chuanski assisting in the unlicensed practice of medicine? Is Dr. Chuanski engaged in unprofessional conduct that could lead to disciplinary action? Where would you look to answer these questions? What additional information might you need to answer the questions? Can you suggest any improvements to Dr. Chuanski's plans?

2. Facility Licensure and Accreditation

■ PATIENT POWER: SOLVING AMERICA'S HEALTH CARE CRISIS
John C. Goodman & Gerald L. Musgrave
(1992)

In terms of rules, restrictions, and bureaucratic requirements, the health care sector is one of the most regulated industries in our economy. Consider Scripps Memorial Hospital, a medium-sized acute care facility in San Diego, California. As [the following] table shows, Scripps must answer to 39 governmental bodies and 7 nongovernmental bodies, and must periodically file 65 different reports, about one report for every four beds.[1] . . . Regulatory requirements intrude in a highly visible way on the activities of the medical staff and affect virtually every aspect of medical practice. Another California hospital, Sequoia Hospital in the San Francisco Bay area, has attempted to calculate how many additional employees are required as a result of government regulations. Sequoia's [administrative and nursing] staff increased by 163.6 percent [from 450 to 736] between 1966 and 1990, even though the average number of patients per day (250) did not change. . . .

Regulatory Agencies Over Scripps Memorial Hospital, 1989

Agency
Government
Occupational Safety and Health Administration
San Diego County Health Department
State Board of Equalization (hazardous waste tax return)
Internal Revenue Service
Franchise Tax Board
Secretary of State
Medicare
State Board of Equalization (sales tax return)
California Hospital Facilities Commission
State Board of Health
Environmental Protection Agency
Department of Transportation
Department of Health Services
Air Resources Board
Office of Emergency Services
Health and Welfare Agency
Air Pollution Control/Air Quality Management District
Regional Water Quality Control Board
Local Sewering Agencies
San Diego Department of Health Services

1. The hospital association in New York once claimed that its members were subject to 174 regulatory bodies, and another survey found that hospitals have to submit themselves to over 50 different inspections and reports each year, often requiring into similar matters. B. Gray, The Profit Motive and Patient Care 112 (1991). [The American Hospital Association claims that, for every hour of patient care, hospitals engage in 30 to 60 minutes of paperwork. Patients or Paperwork? The Regulatory Burden Facing America's Hospitals (2001). See also John Braithwaite & Valerie Braithwaite, The Politics of Legalism: Rules Versus Standards in Nursing-Home Regulation, 4 Soc. Leg. Stud. 307, 320 (1995) ("the people who inspect U.S. nursing homes are checking compliance with over a thousand regulations"); Christopher J. Conover, Health Care Regulation: A $169 Billion Hidden Tax (Cato Institute, 2004) (finding that health care regulation costs twice as much as its benefits are worth). See generally Robert I. Field, Health Care Regulation in America: Complexity, Confrontation and Compromise (2007).]

Agency

State Licensing Board
Board of Registered Nursing
Licensed Vocational Nursing Board
U.S. Department of Labor
Industrial Welfare Commission
Fair Employment Practice Commission
National Labor Relations Board
Immigration and Naturalization Service
Employment Development Department
Social Security Administration
Employee Retirement Income Security Requirements
State Board of Pharmacy
Drug Enforcement Agency
Food and Drug Administration
Bureau of Narcotic Enforcement
California Department of Health, Radiologic Health Branch
Nongovernment
Joint Commission on Accreditation of Hospitals
American Hospital Association
American Conference of Governmental Industrial Hygienists
California Medical Association
Radiation Safety Organization (Syncor, Inc.)
National Association of Social Workers
American College of Surgeons
San Diego and Imperial Counties Organization for Cancer Control

Note: Facility Licensing, Accreditation, and Certification

Three terms are commonly used to describe the multilevel process for inspecting and approving health care facilities by state, federal, and private agencies: licensure, accreditation, and certification. Each of these terms has a specific meaning, and each represents a different level of significance for operation within the health care community. The requirements for licensure, accreditation, and certification exert a strong regulatory force on the organization and operation of health care facilities.

Licensure is the mandatory governmental process whereby a health care facility receives the right to operate. In the United States, licensure operates on a state-by-state basis. A health care facility (as that term is defined in the statute) cannot open its doors lawfully without a license from the appropriate state agency. Licensed health care facilities include hospitals, nursing homes, ambulatory surgery centers, freestanding emergency centers, pharmacies, and, in some instances, diagnostic centers. State licensing schemes also exist for various financing systems, both for ordinary health insurance and for innovative delivery systems such as HMOs, PPOs, and utilization review systems.

Accreditation is a private voluntary approval process through which a health care organization is evaluated and can receive a designation of competence and quality. Most private accreditation for health care organizations today is done under the auspices of the Joint Commission for the Accreditation of Healthcare Organizations (called "JCAHO," "Jayco," or "Joint Commission," formerly known as the Joint Commission for the Accreditation of Hospitals). The Joint Commission is governed by the major trade associations, primarily the American Medical Association, the American Hospital Association, the American College of Surgeons, and the American College of Physicians, and its accreditation programs serve all sorts of health care organizations, although its primary participants are hospitals. Although the Joint Commission is private and purely voluntary, historically it has wielded enormous power and influence because virtually no hospital of respectable size risks the business consequences of jeopardizing its accreditation status. However, the Joint Commission's dominance of facility accreditation is starting to wane somewhat in the face of increasing competition from other accrediting bodies for nonhospital facilities.

Certification is a voluntary procedure for health care organizations to meet the qualifications for participation in government funding programs, specifically Medicare and Medicaid. Although certification is voluntary, more often than not Medicare and Medicaid certification are necessary to the economic survival of a health care organization.

The three functions of licensure, accreditation, and certification are intertwined to a considerable extent. Joint Commission accreditation, for example, frequently satisfies the requirements for both state licensing and Medicare/Medicaid certification. Where this is not the case, Medicare/Medicaid certification surveys are often performed by the same agency and personnel that conduct state licensing surveys. Not only are the three functions intertwined, but there is also a high level of congruence among the various standards and processes employed in each function. Therefore, these materials will examine all three systems interchangeably.

■ ESTATE OF SMITH v. HECKLER
747 F.2d 583 (10th Cir. 1984)

McKay, Circuit Judge.

Plaintiffs . . . brought this class action on behalf of Medicaid recipients residing in nursing homes in Colorado. They alleged that the Secretary of Health and Human Services (Secretary) has a statutory duty . . . to develop and implement a system of nursing home review and enforcement designed to ensure that Medicaid recipients residing in Medicaid certified nursing homes actually receive the optimal medical and psychosocial care that they are entitled to under the Act. The plaintiffs contended that the enforcement system developed by the Secretary is "facility oriented," not "patient oriented" and thereby fails to meet the statutory mandate. . . .

[P]laintiffs instituted the lawsuit in an effort to improve the deplorable conditions at many nursing homes. They presented evidence of the lack of adequate medical care and of the widespread knowledge that care is inadequate. Indeed, the district court concluded that care and life in some nursing homes is so bad that the homes "could be characterized as orphanages for the aged." . . . [Nevertheless] [t]he trial court denied relief. This appeal is from that judgment. . . .

An understanding of the Medicaid Act (the Act) is essential to understand plaintiffs' contentions. The purpose of the Act is to enable the federal government to assist states in providing medical assistance to "aged, blind or disabled individuals, whose income and resources are insufficient to meet the costs of necessary medical services, and . . . rehabilitation and other services to help such . . . individuals to attain or retain capabilities for independence or self care." To receive funding, a state must submit to the Secretary and have approved by the Secretary a plan for medical assistance which meets the requirements of 42 U.S.C. §1396a(a). . . . The plan must include descriptions of the standards and methods the state will use to assure that medical or remedial care services provided to the recipients "are of high quality." . . . The appropriate state agency must determine on an ongoing basis whether participating institutions meet the requirements for continued participation in the Medicaid program. . . . In conducting the review, however, the states must use federal standards, forms, methods and procedures. . . .

Among other things, the regulations provide for the frequency and general content of patients' attending physician evaluations, nursing services with policies "designed to ensure that each patient receives treatments, medications, . . . diet as prescribed . . . rehabilitative nursing care as needed, . . . is kept comfortable, clean, well-groomed, [is] protected from accident, injury, an infection, and [is] encouraged, assisted, and trained in self-care and group activities." The rehabilitative nursing care is to be directed toward each patient achieving an optimal level of self-care and independence. The regulations require a written patient care plan to be developed and maintained for each patient. . . . Finally, the regulations provide for treatment of the social and emotional needs of recipients.

The Secretary has established a procedure for determining whether state plans comply with the standards set out in the regulations. This enforcement mechanism is known as the "survey/certification" inspection system. Under this system, the states conduct reviews of nursing homes. . . . The Secretary then determines, on the basis of the survey results, whether the nursing home surveyed is eligible for certification and, thus, eligible for Medicaid funds. . . .

The plaintiffs do not challenge the substantive medical standards, or "conditions of participation," which have been adopted by the Secretary and which states must satisfy to have their plans approved. Rather, plaintiffs challenge the enforcement mechanism the Secretary has established. The plaintiffs contend that the federal forms . . . which states are required to use, evaluate only the physical facilities and theoretical capability to render quality care. They claim that . . . out of the 541 questions contained in the Secretary's form which must be answered by state survey and certification inspection teams, only 30 are "even marginally related to patient care or might require any patient observation. . . ." Plaintiffs contend that the enforcement mechanism's focus on the facility, rather than on the care actually provided in the facility, results only in "paper compliance" with the substantive standards of the Act. Thus, plaintiffs contend, the Secretary has violated her statutory duty to assure that federal Medicaid monies are paid only to facilities which meet the substantive standards of the Act—facilities which actually provide high quality medical, rehabilitative and psychosocial care to resident Medicaid recipients. . . .

Congress intended the Secretary to be responsible for assuring that federal Medicaid money is given only to those institutions that actually comply with Medicaid requirements. The Act's requirements include providing high quality medical care. . . . Being charged with this function, we must conclude that a failure to promulgate regulations that allow the Secretary to remain informed, on a continuing basis, as to whether facilities receiving federal money are meeting the requirements of the Act, is an abdication of the Secretary's duty. . . .

■ COSPITO v. HECKLER
742 F.2d 72 (3d Cir. 1984)

GARTH, Circuit Judge.

Appellants Douglas Cospito, et al., ("the Patients") are or have been patients at the Trenton Psychiatric Hospital (TPH). In 1975, TPH lost its accreditation from codefendant Joint Commission on Accreditation of [Healthcare Organizations (JCAHO or JCAH)]. As a result, codefendant Secretary of the Department of Health, Education, and Welfare (now the Department of Health and Human Services) terminated various federal benefits which were conditioned upon the beneficiaries being treated at a qualified psychiatric hospital. . . . The Patients brought this action in district court challenging the loss of their federal benefits on several constitutional grounds. . . .

Beginning in 1973, TPH was surveyed under the standards for "psychiatric facilities" recently promulgated under the auspices of JCAH. Following the 1973 survey, major deficiencies were disclosed in several areas, including patient treatment, staffing, environment, and fire safety. TPH was accredited for only one year, and was notified that these deficiencies must be corrected to maintain accreditation. In 1974, however, many of the same deficiencies were found again. A preliminary decision was made by JCAH not to accredit. At TPH's request, a resurvey was conducted in May, 1975, which again resulted in a preliminary decision not to accredit. TPH did not appeal from that decision, and the deaccreditation became final. . . .

JCAH is an Illinois not-for-profit corporation formed in 1951 for the purpose of creating and maintaining professional standards for evaluating hospital performance. The body is governed by a 22-member Board of Commissioners. Its constituent members consist of the American College of Physicians, the American College of Surgeons, the American Dental Association, the American Hospital Association, and the American Medical Association. . . .

The survey itself consists of an on-site visit conducted by a team of surveyors designated by JCAH. The surveyors evaluate the quality of the facility's environment and review its administrative records to determine whether they conform to applicable standards. . . .

JCAH accreditation, however, must be distinguished from certification by the Secretary for eligibility in federal assistance programs. While JCAH accreditation may, depending on the circumstances, be a component of certification, the two are not necessarily coextensive, and at least as a matter of terminology, we will refer to the two separately. . . .

The Patients at TPH had, before decertification by the Secretary, been the beneficiaries of three types of federally funded benefits: (1) Medicare, (2) Medicaid, and (3) Supplemental Social Security Income. . . . When TPH was decertified in 1975, all of the benefits described above were terminated, since TPH was no longer an institution eligible under Medicare and Medicaid. . . . The Patients brought suit in district court alleging that deprivation of their Medicare, Medicaid, and Social Security benefits was unconstitutional. They alleged lack of procedural due process, lack of substantive due process, lack of equal protection, and unconstitutional delegation of authority to JCAH. . . .

Our analysis of the procedural due process aspects of this case is guided by the Supreme Court's decision in O'Bannon v. Town Court Nursing Center, 447 U.S. 773 (1980), which involved facts comparable to those presented here. In *Town Court*, residents of a nursing home claimed a violation of due process when they lost federal benefits as a result of the decertification of their facility. Like the Patients here, they claimed a right to a pretermination hearing.

The Supreme Court found as a threshold matter, however, that the residents of the nursing home had not been deprived of any protectable property interest, and thus, absent this foundation, no due process right was triggered. Writing for the Court, Justice Stevens found that patients did not have a settled interest in receiving benefits at any [particular] facility, including a decertified one, and therefore there had been no deprivation of "property." . . .

[T]he only factor which even arguably distinguishes this case from *Town Court* is the fact that the Patients are unable to transfer out of TPH [because they were involuntarily committed under state mental health law]; [therefore], they are barred from receiving federal benefits at another qualified institution. Thus, they contend that there has been an actual "deprivation" of a protectable interest. Even accepting that contention, however, . . . [b]ecause any loss of benefits to the Patients was only "indirectly" caused by the Secretary's decision to decertify TPH, whatever deprivation which was suffered [by virtue of the state-law psychiatric commitment] was not the result of any [federal] governmental action. The Patients are therefore not in a position to claim any Fifth Amendment due process protection, even if they alleged a "deprivation."[17] . . .

Finally, we turn to the Patients' argument that the Medicare (and thus Medicaid) provisions improperly delegate authority to JCAH, in derogation of Congress' ultimate responsibility to establish federal policy. . . . We need not reach the question of whether delegation of such authority to a private entity breaches the constitutional barrier, since our reading of the Medicare statute, which in turn is applicable to the Medic[aid] and Social Security programs, convinces us that the Secretary retains ultimate authority over decertification decisions, through the ability to engage in a "distinct part" survey. . . .

While JCAH accreditation may, under certain circumstances, independently satisfy the statutory requirements for participation in Medicare, the Secretary is free to prescribe standards which are higher than those of the Commission, in which case JCAH accreditation would not be effective. Moreover, if the Secretary determines that, despite JCAH accreditation, a particular hospital nevertheless has serious deficiencies, he may, after appropriate notice, decertify the institution. On the other hand, if the Secretary chose to promulgate a standard lower than that of JCAH, a general hospital could presumably be certified by meeting only that lesser standard, even if it did not meet the requirements imposed by the Commission.

---

17. The district court granted summary judgment on the procedural due process claim for the reason that, in its opinion, the procedures used adequately safeguarded the Patients' interests, [a]pplying the tests of Mathews v. Eldridge, 424 U.S. 319 (1976). . . . Without disagreeing with the district court's reasoning, we note that our analysis makes it unnecessary to reach the issues addressed by the court below. . . .

The Patients argue, however, that in the case of psychiatric hospitals, the statute places JCAH accreditation in a position of ascendancy over approval by the Secretary, thus leading to the question of unconstitutional delegation to a private group. Our reading of the statute leads us to disagree. While Congress did choose to give special attention to JCAH accreditation in the context of psychiatric hospitals,[27] it still provided the "distinct part" survey as a mechanism whereby the Secretary could independently determine whether a particular institution was qualified for participation. Through consecutive or simultaneous distinct part surveys, therefore, it is possible to obtain a de novo evaluation by the Secretary on the adequacy of a hospital's facilities. . . .

Since, in effect, all actions of JCAH are subject to full review by a public official who is responsible and responsive to the political process, we find that there has been no real delegation of authority to JCAH.[29] . . .

BECKER, Circuit Judge, dissented.

Notes: Facility Regulation and Accreditation

1. *Which Facilities Are Covered?* The first question under any licensing scheme is its jurisdiction. Jurisdictional issues arise with increasing frequency as the result of innovative service delivery and ownership arrangements in the medical industry. One common issue is whether a license for a central facility such as a hospital covers satellite facilities such as urgent care centers, or whether they must be separately licensed. Another issue is whether a specialty clinic, say for abortions or for expensive diagnostic scans, can be treated as simply a physician's office, which does not require a facility license. See RIH Medical Foundation v. Nolan, 723 A.2d 1123 (R.I. 1999) (physician-owned corporation that operates physician offices is exempt from health facility licensing); Ex parte Sacred Heart Health System, 155 So. 2d 980 (Ala. 2012) (announcing five-part test to determine when a physician's office is not a regulated facility); Covenant Healthcare System, Inc. v. City of Wauwatosa, 800 N.W.2d 906 (Wis. 2011) (urgent care center is not just an expanded doctor's office, but functions more like a "hospital," for purposes of tax-exempt status). A third issue is whether an existing license covers the buyer or lessor of a health facility, and whether turning the facility's operation over to a management company requires applying for a formal transfer of the license. Often, the same questions apply generally to accreditation and certification. Usually, the only way to know the answer is to simply ask the governing authorities, since statutes and regulations frequently

---

27. The legislative history reveals that Congress intended "to support the efforts of the various professional accrediting organizations sponsored by the medical and hospital associations. . . ."

29. Our resolution of this issue renders somewhat academic the Patients' contention that it was improper for JCAH to "subdelegate" the responsibility for evaluating psychiatric hospitals to the various accreditation councils. Since we have found that no real authority was actually vested in JCAH, it follows that there could be no improper "subdelegation" of authority to divisions of the Commission. . . .

fail to flesh out these details. The consequences for wrongly interpreting licensing jurisdiction can be severe. In one case, the court refused to enforce any of the contracts entered into by an unlicensed nursing agency. U.S. Nursing Corp. v. St. Joseph Medical Center, 39 F.3d 790 (7th Cir. 1994). See also section B.3 discussing the corporate practice of medicine doctrine.

2. *Regulation Run Amok?* One possible result of excess regulation may be to spur the increasing trend, known as "medical tourism," of traveling overseas to receive medical care much more cheaply in foreign countries. See page 43 for articles reviewing the legal and public policy implications. On health care regulation generally, see Robert Field, Health Care Regulation in America: Complexity, Confrontation, and Compromise (2007); Symposium, Rethinking Regulation in an Era of Reform, 32 Hamline J. Pub. L. & Pol'y 301 (2011).

3. *Measuring Quality Through Structure or Outcomes.* The next question under any of these regulatory or quasi-regulatory schemes is their content. A detailed understanding is beyond the scope of this book. However, it is possible to convey the gist of this content in terms of Donabedian's famous distinction among structural, process, and outcome measures of quality, summarized at page 279. State licensing authorities, like the Medicaid nursing home requirements in *Estate of Smith*, do not inquire into the actual outcomes of patient treatment. Instead, facility licensure provisions typically read like a gigantic building code for the industry, specifying a host of architectural, safety, and sanitation minutiae. Similarly, the Joint Commission accreditation standards traditionally have addressed only the organizational and structural aspects of each hospital department—issues such as whether bylaws are properly drafted, whether proper committees are established, and whether administrative structures contain proper monitoring and documentation—rather than attempting any direct assessment of the actual outcomes of medical care in the hospital. This point was articulated in an Internet discussion group by someone who worked as a hospital therapist and department manager for 13 years:

> We never worried about JCAHO until the three months prior and the two days of the inspection. In the three months prior, we backdated all the documentation that we needed to get through the inspection, and in the two days they were there we spent telling them how focused we were on quality, etc. As long as the paperwork is in order, people can be dying in the halls and there could be guppies in the IV fluids; the JCAHO wouldn't notice.

For an extensive critique of the traditional structural and process measures of institutional quality and an argument for adopting outcomes measures, see Troyen Brennan & Donald Berwick, New Rules: Regulation, Markets and the Quality of American Health Care (1996), which also contains an excellent overview and historical account of licensure and accreditation. Assessing regulatory approaches in light of vastly expanded sources of information about quality and costs, see Kristin Madison, Regulating Health Care Quality in an Information Age, 40 U.C. Davis L. Rev. 1577 (2007).

More generally, "new governance" is an important intellectual movement in administrative law, which considers from an empirically informed behavioral perspective a more diverse set of tools to accomplish regulatory goals than traditional "command and control" regulation. For a review of applications to hospital, insurance, and health care regulation, see Nan D. Hunter, Risk Governance and

Deliberative Democracy in Health Care, 97 Geo. L. J. 1-60 (2008); John Blum, The Quagmire of Hospital Governance: Finding Mission in a Revised Licensure Model, 31 J. Leg. Med. 35 (2010); Symposium, 2 Regulation & Governance 1 (2008).

4. *Process and Outcomes Measures.* The *Smith* case presaged a move away from purely structural measures of quality. That decision resulted in a statutory amendment (known as OBRA '87) and an extensive set of regulations (updated in 2016) that govern in considerable detail the treatment plans, living environment, legal rights, and human dignity of nursing home patients. 42 C.F.R. §§483 et seq. These regulations are focused primarily on the process of care. In a controversial decision, the Third Circuit ruled that Medicaid's nursing home standards can form the basis for a personal injury suit against the nursing home, by the estate of a deceased patient. Grammer v. John J. Kane Regional Centers, 570 F.3d 520 (3d Cir. 2009). See generally David Bohm, Striving for Quality Care in America's Nursing Homes, 4 DePaul J. Health Care L. 317 (2001); Jennifer Brady, Long-Term Care Under Fire: A Case for Rational Enforcement, 18 J. Contemp. Health L. & Pol'y 1 (2001); Comment, 73 U. Colo. L. Rev. 1013 (2002); Symposium, 26 J. Leg. Med. 1 (2005).

Reformers have tried to move even further toward evaluating institutions based on the outcomes of treatment. For instance, CMS at one point (in 1997) proposed fundamentally revising the standards for hospital participation in Medicare and Medicaid to focus much more extensively on outcomes of care and systems for continuous quality improvement. The proposed standards would have required each patient to receive a comprehensive assessment of care needs and a coordinated plan of care within 24 hours of admission. However, the final rule (adopted in 2003) falls back on general process requirements of having "data-driven quality assessment and performance improvement" systems that "measure, analyze, and track quality indicators," and then taking unspecified "actions aimed at performance improvement" that "track performance to ensure that improvements are sustained." 42 C.F.R. §482.

The Joint Commission has also attempted to streamline accreditation standards and focus more on patient safety issues. One key feature is a self-assessment and a "sentinel event" policy that requires hospitals to take the following actions whenever there is an unexpected death or serious injury resulting from treatment: inform the patient or family, conduct a "root cause" analysis, and institute a corrective action plan. However, hospitals do not have to report these events to the Joint Commission, since doing so might compromise the hospital's ability to protect the information from discovery in lawsuits. Symposium, 35 J. Health L. 179 (2002). As a result, the Joint Commission's outcomes initiative has become simply another process measure, one that requires institutions to assess internally their bad outcomes rather than enforcing mandatory outcomes standards.

Outcomes measures of quality may find their purest expression in the accreditation of HMOs and other types of integrated delivery systems. The National Committee for Quality Assurance (NCQA) is the leading accreditation organization for these new comprehensive financing and delivery systems. From the start, it has spearheaded a focus on outcomes measures in the form of the quality report cards discussed at page 280. These report cards adopt a standard reporting format about matters such as patient satisfaction, childhood immunization rates, and other broad indicators of health status (not just medical treatment) in the covered population. The aim is to provide this information as a basis on which subscribers and employers can comparison shop based on both price and quality, thereby substituting more market-based forces for regulatory oversight.

5. *Challenging Adverse Decisions.* The third major area of concern under licensure, accreditation, and certification programs is the processes for determining compliance and challenging adverse decisions. Space limitations preclude us from covering these important aspects of public oversight and legal practice. In brief summary, substantial procedural protections are usually built into these regulatory schemes, so challenges for denial of due process usually fail. The most intense disputes arise when licensing inspectors find such glaring safety concerns that the facility is shut down immediately without a chance for correction or rebuttal. These shutdowns have been challenged as unconstitutional, but usually without success considering the patient protection concerns at stake and the ample procedural rights following a temporary shutdown.

Constitutional challenges depend on the presence of state action, which usually does not exist for private accreditation. McKeesport v. Accreditation Council for Graduate Medical Education, 24 F.3d 519 (3d Cir. 1994). Contra St. Agnes Hospital v. Riddick, 668 F. Supp. 478 (D. Md. 1987) (state action exists where private accreditation affects state licensure). Therefore, suit against accreditation organizations depends on somewhat obscure common-law theories of fairness in business dealings. There are only a few such cases, the leading ones arising in connection with physician accreditation and membership in professional societies. They reason, similar to Greisman v. Newcomb Hospital, page 1358, that when membership organizations control important economic and public interests, they must provide rational reasons and a fair process for their exclusion decisions. See Pinsker v. Pacific Coast Society of Orthodontists, 526 P.2d 253 (Cal. 1974); Falcone v. Middlesex County Medical Society, 170 A.2d 791 (N.J. 1961). See generally Robert Trefney, Judicial Intervention in Admissions Decisions of Private Professional Associations, 49 U. Chi. L. Rev. 840 (1992).

6. *The Public Role of Private Accreditation. Cospito* raises the important public policy question of whether public regulatory authorities cede too much control to private accreditation organizations that are controlled by the regulated industry. State licensure of health care facilities, like federal certification, sometimes defers to the Joint Commission, either by using its accreditation as a proxy for licensure or by incorporating many of its standards. Even if this passes constitutional muster, it still deserves critique for whether this essentially self-regulatory approach is good public policy. See generally Symposium, Private Accreditation in the Regulatory State, 57 Law & Contemp. Probs. 4 (Autumn 1994) (exploring this and a number of other important legal and public policy issues concerning accreditation). It is worth observing that, although the Joint Commission arose from the hospital industry, it has long been sufficiently independent that it sometimes receives harsh criticism from hospitals for the expense and intrusiveness of its inspections. At the same time, consumer groups lash out against the Joint Commission for its relationship with the hospital industry.

7. *Occupational Hazards and Medical Wastes.* These are not the only regulatory authorities affecting health care facilities. Because of the size, complexity, and public importance of hospitals, they are subject to numerous specialized regulatory laws and generalized laws that have special importance in the hospital setting. Two prime examples are the laws governing workers' exposure to infectious diseases and the

disposal of medical waste. For more detail, see the Web site for this book, www. health-law.org.

Research Exercise: Medicare/Medicaid Certification*

Your client is a hospital that has recently undergone a series of layoffs. A disgruntled former employee, a nurse, has complained to the state health department that the quality of patient care has suffered significantly. The hospital has had reason to be concerned about high rates of nosocomial infections (infections acquired in a hospital). There is also concern about bedsores and soiled linen. One patient's open wound was infected by maggots. The nurse's call to the state health department triggered a surprise inspection by the unit charged with overseeing certification for participation in the Medicare and Medicaid programs. It appears likely that the state Department of Health will seek summarily to terminate the hospital's status under these programs as a "participating provider" (also known as the "provider agreement"). Consult the Code of Federal Regulations or one or more of the relevant practitioner treatises (e.g., Wolters Kluwer's Medicare and Medicaid Guide or Hospital Law Manual) to determine what this means and what can be done about it.

■ UNIVERSAL HEALTH SERVICES v. UNITED STATES, ex rel. ESCOBAR AND CORREA
136 S.Ct. 1989 (2016)

Justice THOMAS.

The [federal] False Claims Act imposes significant penalties on those who defraud the Government. This case concerns a theory of False Claims Act liability commonly referred to as "implied false certification." According to this theory, when a defendant submits a claim, it impliedly certifies compliance with all conditions of payment. But if that claim fails to disclose the defendant's violation of a material statutory, regulatory, or contractual requirement, so the theory goes, the defendant has made a misrepresentation that renders the claim "false or fraudulent." This case requires us to consider this theory of liability and to clarify some of the circumstances in which the False Claims Act imposes liability.

We first hold that . . . [a] misrepresentation about compliance with a statutory, regulatory, or contractual requirement must be material to the Government's payment decision in order to be actionable under the False Claims Act. We clarify below how that rigorous materiality requirement should be enforced. . . .

I.

Enacted in 1863, the False Claims Act "was originally aimed principally at stopping the massive frauds perpetrated by large contractors during the Civil War." . . .

---

* The editors are grateful to Prof. Phyllis Bernard for permission to use this problem, which she devised.

Congress responded by imposing civil and criminal liability for 10 types of fraud on the Government, subjecting violators to double [and now triple] damages, forfeiture, and up to five years' imprisonment. . . . The Act's scienter requirement defines "knowing" and "knowingly" to mean that a person has "actual knowledge of the information," "acts in deliberate ignorance of the truth or falsity of the information," or "acts in reckless disregard of the truth or falsity of the information." And the Act defines "material" to mean "having a natural tendency to influence, or be capable of influencing, the payment or receipt of money or property." . . .

The alleged False Claims Act violations here arose within the Medicaid program . . . . [The complaint alleges that, for] five years, Yarushka Rivera, a teenage beneficiary of Massachusetts' Medicaid program, received counseling services at Arbour Counseling Services, . . . owned and operated by a subsidiary of petitioner Universal Health Services. . . . In May 2009, Yarushka had an adverse reaction to a medication that a purported doctor at Arbour prescribed after diagnosing her with bipolar disorder. Her condition worsened; she suffered a seizure that required hospitalization. In October 2009, she suffered another seizure and died. She was 17 years old.

[handwritten margin note: FACTS]

Thereafter, an Arbour counselor revealed to respondents Carmen Correa and Julio Escobar—Yarushka's mother and stepfather—that . . . of the five professionals who had treated Yarushka, only one was properly licensed. The practitioner who diagnosed Yarushka as bipolar identified herself as a psychologist with a Ph. D., but failed to mention that her degree came from an unaccredited Internet college and that Massachusetts had rejected her application to be licensed as a psychologist. Likewise, the practitioner who prescribed medicine to Yarushka, and who was held out as a psychiatrist, was in fact a nurse who lacked authority to prescribe medications absent supervision . . . . And the problem went beyond those who treated Yarushka. Some 23 Arbour employees lacked licenses to provide mental health services . . . .

[handwritten margin note: NOT LICENSED]

When submitting reimbursement claims, Arbour used payment codes corresponding to different services that its staff provided to Yarushka, such as "Individual Therapy" and "Family Therapy." Staff members also misrepresented their qualifications and licensing status to the Federal Government to obtain individual National Provider Identification numbers, which are submitted in connection with Medicaid reimbursement claims . . . .

In 2011, respondents filed a *qui tam* suit[3] in federal court alleging that Universal Health . . . submitted reimbursement claims that made representations about the specific services provided by specific types of professionals, but that failed to disclose serious violations of regulations pertaining to staff qualifications and licensing requirements for these services. . . . Universal Health thus allegedly defrauded the program, which would not have reimbursed the claims had it known that it was

---

3. [This is a suit in which a private "bounty hunting" party or "whistleblower" (referred to as the "relator") sues on behalf of the federal government to recoup falsely paid amounts. If successful, the court can award the relator up to 30 percent of the recovery. If the government chooses to intervene, it then conducts the litigation, but the relator still receives 15-25 percent of the recovery. See Section E for further discussion.]

billed for mental health services that were performed by unlicensed and unsupervised staff. The United States [initially] declined to intervene [but then briefed the case when it reached the Supreme Court].

The District Court granted Universal Health's motion to dismiss the complaint . . . [because] none of the regulations that Arbour violated was a condition of payment. The United States Court of Appeals for the First Circuit reversed in relevant part and remanded. The court observed that each time a billing party submits a claim, it "implicitly communicate[s] that it conformed to the relevant program [participation] requirements, such that it was entitled to payment." . . . In the court's view, a statutory, regulatory, or contractual requirement can be a condition of payment either by expressly identifying itself as such or by implication. The court then held that . . . the [state licensure] regulations themselves "constitute[d] dispositive evidence of materiality" because they identified [proper licensure] as an "express and absolute" condition of payment . . . .

We granted certiorari to resolve the disagreement among the Courts of Appeals over the validity and scope of the implied false certification theory of liability. The Seventh Circuit has rejected this theory, reasoning that only express (or affirmative) falsehoods can render a claim "false or fraudulent" . . . . Other courts have accepted the theory, but limit its application to cases where defendants fail to disclose violations of expressly designated conditions of payment [rather than more general "conditions of participation" in the government program]. Yet others hold that conditions of payment need not be expressly designated as such to be a basis for False Claims Act liability.

II.

We first hold that the implied false certification theory can, at least in some circumstances, provide a basis for liability. By punishing defendants who submit "false or fraudulent claims," the False Claims Act encompasses claims that make fraudulent misrepresentations, which include certain misleading omissions. When, as here, a defendant makes representations in submitting a claim but omits its violations of statutory, regulatory, or contractual requirements, those omissions can be a basis for liability if they render the defendant's representations misleading with respect to the goods or services provided. . . .

We need not resolve whether all claims for payment implicitly represent that the billing party is legally entitled to payment. The claims in this case do more than merely demand payment. They fall squarely within the rule that half-truths—representations that state the truth only so far as it goes, while omitting critical qualifying information—can be actionable misrepresentations. . . . [For example], an applicant for an adjunct position at a local college makes an actionable misrepresentation when his resume lists prior jobs and then retirement, but fails to disclose that his "retirement" was a prison stint for perpetrating a $12 million bank fraud.

So too here, by submitting claims for payment using payment codes that corresponded to specific counseling services, Universal Health represented that it had provided individual therapy, family therapy, preventive medication counseling, and other types of treatment. Moreover, Arbour staff members allegedly made further representations in submitting Medicaid reimbursement claims by using National Provider Identification numbers corresponding to specific job titles. And these representations were clearly misleading in context. Anyone informed that a social worker at a Massachusetts mental health clinic provided a teenage patient with individual counseling services would probably—but wrongly—conclude that the . . . social worker possesses the prescribed qualifications for the job. . . .

Accordingly, we hold that the implied certification theory can be a basis for liability, at least where two conditions are satisfied: first, the claim does not merely request payment, but it also makes specific representations about the goods or services provided; and second, the defendant's failure to disclose noncompliance with material statutory, regulatory, or contractual requirements makes those representations misleading half-truths.

The second question presented is whether, as Universal Health urges, a defendant should face False Claims Act liability only if it fails to disclose the violation of a contractual, statutory, or regulatory provision that the Government expressly designated a condition of payment. We conclude that the Act does not impose this limit on liability. But we also conclude that not every undisclosed violation of an express condition of payment automatically triggers liability. Whether a provision is labeled a condition of payment is relevant to but not dispositive of the materiality inquiry. . . .

A defendant can have "actual knowledge" that a condition is material without the Government expressly calling it a condition of payment. If the Government failed to specify that guns it orders must actually shoot, but the defendant knows that the Government routinely rescinds contracts if the guns do not shoot, the defendant has "actual knowledge." . . .

We now clarify how that materiality requirement should be enforced. . . . The materiality standard is demanding. The False Claims Act is not . . . a vehicle for punishing garden-variety breaches of contract or regulatory violations. A misrepresentation cannot be deemed material merely because the Government designates compliance with a particular statutory, regulatory, or contractual requirement as a condition of payment. . . . [If that were so, the] Government might respond by designating every legal requirement an express condition of payment. But billing parties are often subject to thousands of complex statutory and regulatory provisions [that are conditions of participation.] . . . . Materiality, in addition, cannot be found where noncompliance is minor or insubstantial. . . .

[P]roof of materiality can include, but is not necessarily limited to, evidence that the defendant knows that the Government consistently refuses to pay claims in the mine run of cases based on noncompliance with the particular statutory, regulatory, or contractual requirement. Conversely, . . . if the Government regularly pays a particular type of claim in full despite actual knowledge that certain requirements were violated, and has signaled no change in position, that is strong evidence that the requirements are not material.

These rules lead us to disagree with the Government's and First Circuit's view of materiality: that any statutory, regulatory, or contractual violation is material so long as the defendant knows that the Government would be entitled to refuse payment were it aware of the violation. At oral argument, the United States explained the implications of its position: If the Government contracts for health services and adds a requirement that contractors buy American-made staplers, anyone who submits a claim for those services but fails to disclose its use of foreign staplers violates the False Claims Act. To the Government, liability would attach if the defendant's use of foreign staplers would entitle the Government not to pay the claim in whole or part—irrespective of whether the Government routinely pays claims despite knowing that foreign staplers were used. Likewise, if the Government required contractors to aver their compliance with the entire U.S. Code and Code of Federal Regulations, then under this view, failing to mention noncompliance with any of those requirements would always be material. The False Claims Act does not adopt such an extraordinarily expansive view of liability. . . .

We emphasize . . . that the False Claims Act is not a means of imposing treble damages and other penalties for insignificant regulatory or contractual violations. This case centers on allegations of fraud, not medical malpractice. Respondents have alleged that Universal Health misrepresented its compliance with mental health facility requirements that are so central to the provision of mental health counseling that the Medicaid program would not have paid these claims had it known of these violations. Respondents may well have adequately pleaded a violation of [the False Claims Act]. But we leave it to the courts below to resolve this in the first instance.

Notes: Medicare Conditions of Participation; Health Care Fraud

1. *What's in a Name?* Note the distinction that previous courts had drawn between "conditions of *participation*" and "conditions of *payment*." The former refers to all regulatory requirements that providers must meet to join the program and remain in good standing. The latter refers to requirements for paying particular claims to participating providers. Other courts (and the district court in *Escobar*) had previously drawn a line between these two sets of conditions—in part because participation conditions are so numerous, technical, and potentially ambiguous. Although *Escobar* eliminates this line, it emphasizes the materiality line: conditions of either payment or participation are actionable, but only if the provider has reason to know that they actually matter to the program's reimbursement policies and practices. It remains unclear whether, on balance, the decision will end up being more restrictive or more enabling to false claims suits.

2. *Fraud on Steroids.* Expansive interpretations of what constitutes a "false" claim, and when such claims are submitted "knowingly," have led to a spate of both private and government enforcement actions. Use of *qui tam* actions by private "bounty hunting" parties have proliferated, as further discussed in Section E. Direct government enforcement actions are also numerous, resulting in several billions of dollars in recoveries each year. Most of these are not for what one would call typical "fraud," however. Instead, usually they are for legitimate services that are inappropriately billed. As further illustrated in Section E, because a single error in procedures or documentation for submitting claims can be replicated in countless numbers of claims until noticed and rectified, false claims damages can be enormous, even ruinous. Therefore, hospitals and other providers have complained bitterly that they have no choice but to agree to very large settlements, sometimes in the tens or hundreds of millions of dollars, for what they consider to be innocent behavior, honest differences of opinion, or at most only careless mistakes rather than criminal fraud.

3. *Food for Thought.* Various scholars have considered, with mixed support in the case law, whether the False Claims Act can be used to **police low quality or unnecessary care**, or even failure to obtain informed consent. See, e.g., Isaac D. Buck,

Overtreatment and Informed Consent: A Fraud-Based Solution, 43 Fla. St. U. L. Rev. 901 (2016); Isaac D. Buck, Breaking the Fever: A New Construct for Regulating Overtreatment. 48 UC Davis L. Rev. 1261 (2015); Isaac D. Buck, Caring Too Much: Misusing the False Claims Act to Target Overtreatment, 74 Ohio St. L. J. 463 (2013); Joan H. Krause, Medical Error as False Claim, 27 Am. J. L. & Med. 181 (2001).

For additional commentary and critique of **medical fraud enforcement generally**, see David Hyman, Health Care Fraud and Abuse: Market Change, Social Norms, and "The Trust Reposed in the Workmen," 30 J. Legal Stud. 531 (2002); Joan H. Krause, "Promises to Keep": Health Care Providers and the Civil False Claims Act, 23 Cardozo L. Rev. 1363 (2002); Kathleen Boozang & Simone Handler-Hutchinson, "Monitoring" Corporate Corruption: DOJ's Use of Deferred Prosecution Agreements in Health Care, 35 Am. J. L. Med. 89 (2009); Isaac D. Buck, Enforcement Overdose: Health Care Fraud Regulation in an Era of Overcriminalization and Overtreatment, 74 Md. L. Rev. 259 (2015); Anthony Kyriakakis, The Missing Victims of Health Care Fraud, 2015 Utah L. Rev. 605.

3. Certificate of Need Regulation

Certificate of need (CON) laws are another important type of facility regulation, one that operates essentially like a building permit for hospitals and other medical facilities, but with a focus on costs rather than on quality. Medical facilities must show that a need exists in the community, and that they satisfy financial feasibility and other criteria, before undertaking any of several enumerated new activities. These typically include substantial new construction, the purchase of major new equipment, the initiation of important new services, or a change in ownership. Hospitals, nursing homes, and outpatient clinics are all usually covered by this legislation, but physician offices are frequently excluded.

These laws are an outgrowth of community health planning efforts that began in the 1940s, when the country first recognized a shortage and maldistribution of hospitals. At that time, planning efforts were attached to federal grants and loans for hospital construction under the Hill-Burton Act of 1946 to make sure new hospitals were placed where they were most needed. In 1964, New York State adopted the first state CON law. It made health planning mandatory for all facilities and it was concerned with both hospital excess capacity as well as hospital shortages. The American Hospital Association quickly embraced this mandatory planning philosophy and began lobbying other states to follow suit.

CON laws became widespread after the federal government enacted the National Health Planning and Resources Development Act (NHPRDA) of 1974, 42 U.S.C. §§300k-300t-14 (repealed). NHPRDA required states to follow a model CON process in order to continue receiving certain federal funding for public health activities, and to continue participating in Medicaid. By 1980, all states had enacted some version of CON legislation. This federal initiative quickly came to an end when President Reagan signed the Omnibus Health Package of 1986 repealing NHPRDA. About a dozen states thereafter repealed their CON laws, but most states still retain this regulation and many have expended it (for instance, to cover more outpatient services). The old federal law thus remains influential on the interpretation of the state laws because it served as the model enacted by most states.

The following materials provide a glimpse of how this regulatory scheme functions in the three dozen states in which it is still active. More detailed explanation can be found on the Web site for this book, www.health-law.org. As you read the next case, consider whether the rationale for this regulation was sound when it was first enacted, and whether it remains sound today.

■ OVERLAKE HOSPITAL ASSOCIATION v. DEPARTMENT OF HEALTH

239 P.3d 1096 (Wash. 2010)

ALEXANDER, J.

Swedish Health Services (Swedish) and the Washington State Department of Health (Department) seek review of a decision of the Court of Appeals, in which that court concluded that the Department used flawed methodology in determining that there was need for an additional ambulatory surgical facility (ASF) in East King County. . . . We agree with Swedish and the Department and, consequently, reverse the Court of Appeals.

In 1979, the legislature created the certificate of need [CON] program, which authorizes the Department to control the number and types of health care services and facilities that are provided in a given planning area. The purpose behind this legislation was to ensure that such services and facilities are developed in a manner consistent with identified priorities and without unnecessary duplication. Under this statutory regime, in order for certain health care providers to establish or expand health care facilities within this state, including [ambulatory surgical facilities], they must obtain a [CON] from the Department.

In determining whether there is need for an additional ASF in a given area, the Department employs the three-step methodology . . . designed to determine: (a) the existing capacity of operating rooms in the planning area, (b) the anticipated number of surgeries in the area three years into the future, and (c) whether existing operating room capacity is sufficient to accommodate the projected number of future surgeries.

Facilities in the offices of private physicians or dentists, whether for individual or group practice, are exempt from the definition of an ASF. . . . Historically, and in the instant case, the Department excludes exempt surgical facilities in calculating step one of the methodology—existing capacity. It does, however, include surgeries performed in the exempt facilities in calculating step two-projected future need.

In November 2002, Swedish applied for a [CON] to establish a new ASF in Bellevue, Washington. Overlake Hospital Association (Overlake) and Evergreen Healthcare (Evergreen) each obtained "affected part[y]" status and submitted comments to the Department in opposition to Swedish's application. Using the methodology described above, the Department determined that there was need in East King County for an additional ASF with 5.39 outpatient operating rooms. Accordingly, it issued a [CON] to Swedish to build a five-room ASF in Bellevue.

Overlake and Evergreen requested an adjudicative proceeding before a health law judge to determine whether the Department erred. . . . In upholding the Department's decision, . . . the health law judge determined that exempt facilities should be excluded from the calculation of existing capacity, but included in the calculation of future need. . . . In holding that Swedish established need for an additional five operating room ASF in Bellevue, the health law judge took particular note of the legislature's emphasis on assuring "that all citizens have accessible health services" and indicated that "[i]f the more inclusive approach were followed, the calculation of available operating rooms would include [exempt facilities] that would not be available to many of the individuals within the health planning area." . . .

In determining whether to issue a [CON] for a new health care facility, the Department is to consider the following factors: (1) need, (2) financial feasibility, (3) structure and process of care, and (4) cost containment. Factors two, three, and four have not been at issue in this case. Rather, the focus has been on factor one — whether the Department used the proper methodology for calculating need. More specifically, the question before us is whether the Department erred in the manner in which it factored exempt facilities in its calculation of existing capacity and future need. . . . For future need, [the Department, under its rules,] must

> [p]roject number of inpatient and outpatient surgeries performed within the hospital planning area for the third year of operation. This shall be based on the current number of surgeries adjusted for forecasted growth in the population served and may be adjusted for trends in surgeries per capita. . . .
> Subtract the capacity of dedicated outpatient operating rooms from the forecasted number of outpatient surgeries. . . .
> Determine the average time per inpatient and outpatient surgery in the planning area. . . .
> Calculate the sum of inpatient and remaining outpatient . . . operating room time needed in the third year of operation.
> Net need, the ultimate question for the Department, is determined by calculating the difference, if any, between existing capacity and future need.

. . . [T]he Court of Appeals concluded that the Department acted arbitrarily and capriciously by employing the methodology it did for calculating net need, i.e., excluding exempt facilities in calculating existing capacity, while at the same time including surgeries performed at those facilities in calculating future need. . . .

We are satisfied that the public policy rationale behind the [CON] program, which convinced the health law judge that the regulation meant that exempt facilities should be excluded from existing capacity but included in future need, resolves the ambiguity. As noted above, the legislature has made clear its intent to "promote, maintain, and assure the health of all citizens in the state, provide accessible health services, health manpower, health facilities." That, in our judgment, is the overriding purpose of the [CON] program. While we agree with Overlake and Evergreen that controlling the costs of medical care and promoting prevention are also priorities, we believe that these goals are of secondary significance because, to a large extent, they would be realized by promotion and maintenance of access to health care services for all citizens. . . .

In sum, we are satisfied that the Department's interpretation of the regulation is consistent with the goal of assuring a sufficient supply of publicly available ASFs, in that the approach "does not rely on unregulated exempt [facilities] to meet any part of the public demand for the service." The Department's reasoning, we believe, was well described by a Department analyst . . . at the hearing before the health law judge as follows:

. . . The facilities that are described as exempt facilities, the use of those facilities is limited only to members of those group practices. And very frequently, we see that the use of these facilities is limited to one, sometimes two, different specialties of medicine, such as ENT [ear, nose, and throat] surgery or oral surgery or something like that. So those operating rooms are not really analogous to a generally available ambulatory surgery center, operating room, where a multitude of various services could be performed by a number of different physicians.

. . . [W]e conclude that the Department properly considered the competing policy rationales . . . and that its decision was not arbitrary or capricious. . . .

■ CERTIFICATE OF NEED IN THE POST-AFFORDABLE CARE ACT ERA

Emily Whelan Parento[4]
105 Ky. L.J. 201 (2017)

I. THE EVOLUTION OF CERTIFICATE OF NEED PROGRAMS

CON programs are a powerful force in the majority of states, serving as a gate-keeper to the supply of healthcare facilities. Under CON laws, healthcare facilities are required to obtain a permit from state health planning entities before offering new services, constructing new buildings, or purchasing new medical equipment. For example, if a hospital wishes to add additional beds to its facility, it must seek approval from the state, which will evaluate the request based on a determination of, at minimum, whether there exists sufficient public "need" for the new beds. . . . Beyond need, which is usually determined either in whole or in part by reference to a numeric formula, additional review criteria may exist, including accessibility, costs, feasibility, available economic resources, quality, and others. . . .

[A]n understanding of the underlying rationale for CON and changes in the programs over time is essential to understanding their place in the modern health-care delivery system. In most instances, the government allows market forces to determine the appropriate supply of a product, and for consumers to purchase the amount of that product that meets their needs. However, the market for healthcare services is not a normal market, and it is this recognition that led to the development of health planning authorities and ultimately to CON programs.

Following the end of World War II, "faced with the aging infrastructure of a healthcare system ill-equipped to accommodate the needs of returning soldiers and the inevitable baby boom that followed," Congress passed the Hospital Survey and Construction Act (the "Hill-Burton Act," or the "Act"), which was designed to promote public and nonprofit hospital construction and modernization . . . . As Nicholas Bagley recently observed, although the scope of the Hill-Burton Act increased

---

4. [Before joining the faculty of the University of the Pacific McGeorge School of Law, Prof. Parento was head of the Office of Health Policy in Kentucky, where she oversaw Kentucky's certificate of need program.]

rapidly throughout the 1960s, the health planning in this era "lacked regulatory bite," as planning agencies could advocate for particular facilities and services to be provided, but could not compel the private sector to build facilities or provide the needed services.[5]

. . . . [I]ncreasing health sector costs led government officials to look to additional strategies to regulate costs, including by instituting CON programs to constrain facility supply as a cost control mechanism, an approach heavily influenced by the theory of Milton Roemer that "[a] built bed is a filled bed." Under Roemer's Law, there exists a direct correlation between capacity and utilization; when combined with the availability of third-party reimbursement, oversupply of resources will create its own demand for excessive use. . . .

Congress passed the National Health Planning and Resources Development Act of 1974 ("NHPRDA"). NHPRDA provided significant funding for state health planning activities and "effectively required states to adopt certificate of need laws conforming to federal standards." By 1980, every state except Louisiana had a CON program. . . . [By] preventing more beds from being built, and later by preventing proliferation of other services deemed "unnecessary," states–and, for a time, the federal government–hoped to slow the alarming rise in healthcare expenditures. Later, and perhaps in response to criticisms that the programs were proving ineffective at achieving meaningful cost containment, additional justifications for the programs became prevalent, such as ensuring an adequate distribution of healthcare services across geographic areas and socioeconomic groups, providing states a regulatory lever to require that healthcare providers deliver sufficient and quality care for the indigent. . . .

At first glance, it is not apparent how a supply constraint mechanism can result in lower costs for a product. Conventional economic theory suggests that restricting supply of a product does not result in reduced prices–rather, assuming constant demand, prices would increase in the face of decreased supply as more people competed to purchase a product in limited supply. However, healthcare is not a normal product and the market for health services has a number of factors that render it far from efficient. Thus, the theory for the ability of CON programs to contain costs, as noted above, is that by restricting the arms race among healthcare providers to build ever newer and more expensive facilities (e.g., new hospital buildings when an older one will suffice) and to offer newer and more expensive services even when those services are not demonstrably more effective than older treatments (e.g., MRI and CT scans instead of X-rays), CON programs prevent providers from raising prices to reflect the costs of these newer facilities and treatments. This theory was reasonable at the time it was first conceived–when providers were often paid an amount equal to their cost plus a small percentage of that cost, there was no incentive for providers to keep costs low. Thus, it stood to reason that restricting the ability of providers to increase their costs via capital expenditures would result in a more reasonable rate of increase in healthcare expenditures. . . .

While laudable in intent, CON programs were largely perceived as falling short of expectations by the early 1980s, particularly as a deregulatory political climate prevailed. Costs continued to escalate, and a number of studies found that

5. Nicholas Bagley, Medicine as a Public Calling, 114 MICH. L. REV. 57, 88 (2015).

CON programs did not help contain healthcare expenditures. Moreover, as larger and more influential healthcare entities learned to navigate the often complicated and bureaucratic programs, perceptions of protectionism of incumbents further undermined support for CON. Congress, too, became skeptical of the benefits of CON and repealed NHPRDA in 1987. By 1990, eleven states repealed their programs, and by 2000, a total of fourteen states had repealed their CON laws.

Although many states repealed their programs following the repeal of the federal mandate, the trend toward full repeal has stalled. . . . While CON remains prevalent, there continues to be vigorous debate over the wisdom of these programs in states at all points along the political spectrum. In recent years, several states have reexamined the efficacy of the CON system and proposed modifications to existing CON programs. In 2009, half of the thirty-six states with CON programs had bills to repeal or reform these programs introduced in their state legislatures. . . . These efforts at CON reform have continued in the post-Affordable Care Act era. . . .

II. SKEPTICISM TOWARD CERTIFICATE OF NEED
FROM ALL QUARTERS

. . . [F]or at least the past fifteen years, the FTC and the DOJ Antitrust Division have taken an active position against the continuance of CON programs. . . . In [various] statements, the agencies opine that CON laws impede the efficient performance of healthcare markets by creating barriers to entry and expansion, to the detriment of healthcare competition and consumers. The agencies cite economic research on the effects of CON laws, as well as some of the well-known risks that CON laws entail. For example, the agencies observe that in addition to limiting entry, CON laws create opportunities for existing competitors to exploit the CON process to thwart or delay new competition; they can facilitate anticompetitive agreements among providers; and, as noted by a number of researchers who interviewed former state CON officials, the CON process itself may be susceptible to corruption. . . . .

Most recently in 2015, current FTC Commissioner Maureen K. Ohlhausen characterized certificate of need programs as a "prescription for higher costs." Ohlhausen observed that CON programs were particularly unhelpful to achieving the goals of healthcare market regulation in that they "stand out as an example of regulation that squelches the beneficial effects of competition in healthcare markets without delivering valuable public benefits in return." Noting that the cost-plus payment methodology that was in existence at the time programs began has been largely abolished in favor of negotiated rates between insurers and providers, Ohlhausen argued that as the "purported market failure that CON laws were designed to fix no longer exists," it should surprise no one that "it has proven difficult to demonstrate the benefits of a legislative scheme designed to fix an issue overtaken by subsequent events." She further explained that although the benefits of CON have been difficult to quantify, the negative results are readily apparent–CON laws operate to insulate healthcare providers from "socially beneficial" competition.

[Ohlhausen] correctly raises the question as to why CON laws are still on the books in thirty-five states even in the absence of demonstrable success at achieving their original cost containment objectives. The answer, it seems, is a combination of legislative inertia and shifting policy rationales of CON proponents to justify the continued existence of the programs. Ohlhausen observes that CON laws "insulate politically powerful incumbents from market forces, and those providers naturally are loathe to give up the special government preferences that CON laws bestow." However, she writes, incumbents cannot directly espouse to legislators that they deserve special protection at the expense of the public interest–so, instead, providers have adopted new rationales for the continued existence of CON, among them that the programs allow for improved care of the indigent.

This argument must be deconstructed to be understood, because it is not readily apparent how insulation from competition leads to better care for the poor. In essence, incumbents argue that the guarantee of restricted competition allows them to negotiate higher prices with private insurance companies, thereby conferring a larger profit margin, which allows for more resources to provide care to poorer patients without insurance. So, there is a cross-subsidization whereby providers, usually hospitals, will charge higher rates to wealthier patients and retain profitable procedures that might otherwise migrate to lower-cost venues (e.g., imaging, outpatient surgical procedures) to subsidize unprofitable areas of the business, including indigent care. The trouble, as Ohlhausen notes, is that this argument has not been proven to be correct; studies have not shown a marked difference in the provision of indigent care by hospitals in CON states as compared to those in states without the programs. . . . . Thus, she surmises that . . . arguments by CON proponents that the programs support indigent care claims "appear to be little more than an argument of convenience by politically powerful special interests attempting to protect their historical government perquisites." . . . .

Among academic scholars, it is rare to find ardent, or even lukewarm defenders of CON programs. Although the arguments for the effectiveness of CON have not been conclusively disproven, the prevailing view reflects considerable skepticism about the ability of CON programs to achieve any of their intended aims. . . . [T]here appears to widespread acknowledgement that CON programs as administered are essentially unable to be insulated from political influence. Arguing in 2010 in favor of a more evolved model of state health planning rather than turning the healthcare delivery system over to market forces, John Blum acknowledged the marked distinction between the intent and reality of CON programs:

Somewhere along the journey of C.O.N. laws, these statutes became dominated by process review and evaluation, and the core function of creating state and regional health plans dropped from the agenda of these agencies, or planning was turned over to state bureaucrats whose best efforts were foiled by political realities.[6] . . .

III. THE ABILITY OF CON PROGRAMS TO SURVIVE CONSTITUTIONAL CHALLENGE

It is not for lack of legal challenge that CON programs remain in place. Opponents have attempted a number of constitutional and other challenges to the laws, but courts have refused to overturn them.

---

6. John D. Blum, *Finding a New Regulatory Pathway for the Old Labyrinth of Health Planning*, 19 ANNALS OF HEALTH L. 213, 216 (2010).

The most obvious and common line of challenge to CON laws is under the Commerce Clause. In *Colon Health Centers of America v. Hazel*, 813 F. 3d 145 (4th Cir. 2016), out-of-state providers of medical imaging services challenged Virginia's CON law under the dormant aspect of the Commerce Clause. The Fourth Circuit rejected the challenge and affirmed the district court, which found that the law neither discriminated nor placed an undue burden on interstate commerce. The court first reiterated the well-known standard that a statute that is facially discriminatory, or discriminatory in purpose or effect, may survive strict scrutiny only if it "advances a legitimate local purpose that cannot be adequately served by reasonable nondiscriminatory alternatives." While the parties agreed the statute was not facially discriminatory, plaintiffs argued that it was discriminatory in purpose, with a primary goal to shelter existing providers (all of whom were, by definition, in state) from competition at the expense of out-of-state businesses seeking entry into the market. Rejecting this argument, the court noted that Virginia's CON law served a number of "legitimate public purposes: improving healthcare quality by discouraging the proliferation of underutilized facilities, enabling underserved and indigent populations to access necessary medical services, and encouraging cost-effective consumer spending." Accordingly, the court said it could not "discern a sinister protectionist purpose in this straightforward effort to bring medical care to all the citizens of the Commonwealth in the most efficient and professional manner."

Turning to the question of whether the law was discriminatory in effect, the court was equally unconvinced. Plaintiffs alleged that Virginia's law "systematically advantage[d] established in-state providers at the expense of new, primarily out-of-state firms," by impermissibly granting current providers "the authority to thwart the market entrance of out-of-state providers" through participation in the adversarial process as applications were evaluated (existing providers could oppose applications by new entrants at a hearing) and by allowing existing providers to file competing applications to block the approval of new entrants. The court evaluated these claims with regard to whether the plaintiffs demonstrated that Virginia's CON law, "if enforced, would negatively impact interstate commerce to a greater degree than intrastate commerce," in considering whether the CON law "erects a special barrier to market entry by non-domestic entities," but concluded that plaintiffs had not shown that they faced a special hardship compared to instate providers. The court noted repeatedly that CON programs are generally policy decisions that are properly the purview of legislators, and although the plaintiffs were frustrated by legislative policy, the court declined to take the "potentially limitless step of striking down every state regulatory program that has some alleged adverse effect on market competition." As the court observed, "[w]e live in such an interconnected economy that for any regulation some effects are almost bound to be felt out of state. To accept appellants' arguments 'would broaden the negative Commerce Clause beyond its existing scope.'"

Having rejected the plaintiffs' argument, the court determined that the law survived a rational basis review by balancing the putative local benefits against the incidental burdens on state commerce, as required by the Supreme Court in Pike v. Bruce Church, Inc., 397 U.S. 137 (1970). Virginia had put forth a number of rational reasons in support of its CON program, among them the many justifications described above–improvement in healthcare quality, indigent care, ensuring appropriate distribution of services across geographic areas, and even healthcare cost reduction. Fundamentally, the court believed that the decision over the merits of CON was a legislative one, observing that while "[t]he battle between laissez fairists and regulators is as old as the hills," these disputes are "more often over economics and politics than over law." Moreover, the court noted, "[l]egislators, not jurists, are best able to compare competing economic theories and sets of data and then weigh the result against their own political valuations of the public interests at stake."

. . . .

In short, the post-ACA healthcare market looks very different. This is true whether a state has embraced healthcare reform or resisted it. Accordingly, the historic rationale for CON programs, much of which rested on a foundation of (1) a large uninsured population requiring significant uncompensated care from providers and (2) a market in which providers were reimbursed under a FFS payment structure, must now be reexamined in view of the shifted coverage and payment landscape. Policy objectives such as cost containment via supply restrictions (on the theory that a bed built is a bed filled) and preventing overutilization of high-cost services are significantly less relevant when payment is based on the value of the service delivered rather than the quantity of services provided. Similarly, enabling cross-subsidization of profitable services to support the provision of indigent care becomes less necessary when the uninsured population is significantly reduced. . . .

The call for full-scale repeal of CON programs has largely been unsuccessful and seems likely to continue to fall on deaf ears among legislators in the states that retain CON laws. A more successful strategy for health-oriented policymakers and stakeholders is to embrace CON programs as an additional regulatory tool to drive systematic change in healthcare delivery systems, [such as preferential treatment for those who adopted interconnected electronic health records, meet objective quality metrics, or participate in value-based payment programs, as Kentucky was the first to do.] . . . .

Notes: Certificate of Need Regulation

1. *Incomplete Public Utility Regulation.* "Certificate-of-need laws establish entry controls which are similar in intent and impact to the certificate-of-public-convenience-and-necessity device widely employed in public utility and common carrier regulation." Clark Havighurst, Regulation of Health Facilities and Services by "Certificate of Need," 59 Va. L. Rev. 1143, 1153 (1973). As such, they appear to be an aggressive regulatory approach to containing health care costs. Yet it is hard to see why they might ever succeed. CON laws address primarily capital investment, not operating expenses. Thus, CON programs may slow the increase in numbers of beds, but the funds saved are simply moved to new services and equipment. Moreover, CON laws constrain only what hospitals *spend*, not what they *charge*. In the latter respect, CON programs constitute incomplete public utility regulation. Most such regulation imposes *price* controls in addition to *entry* controls. Indeed, price control would seem essential since restricting entry tends to create monopoly power. In contrast with the Fourth Circuit decision noted by Prof. Parento, one court relied on this effect of conferring state-sanctioned monopolies without controlling for monopolistic abuse to support its holding that the original North Carolina CON statute was unconstitutional. In re Certificate of Need for Ashton Park Hospital, 193

S.E.2d 729 (N.C. 1973). Other courts to consider the issue, though, have upheld the constitutionality of CON regulation.

2. *Needs vs. Wants.* When CON laws were first adopted, the CAT scanner was one of the primary examples cited of a technology much in need of centralized planning. Ironically, the capital expenditure threshold for CON review of equipment purchases has risen to the extent that CAT scanners usually require no approval. A greater irony is that the CON laws have proven inadequate for controlling even far more expensive technological devices. How has this happened? Consider the following explanation:

> Need is a medical concept, largely defined by professionals. It is subjective, rather than objective, and consequently is not a limiting, but an expansive concept. Unlike economic "demand" for goods and services, which reflects both consumers' wants and their resource limitations, medical need reflects what professionals deem desirable, rather than what patients can afford. Professionals decide what is needed according to their concept of what constitutes good care, which tends to be established according to the state of the art — what is medically possible at a given time. Virtually any medical benefit is seen as a need; medical professionals are generally guided by a more-is-better philosophy, which has been characterized as a "technological" or a "quality imperative." . . . The most obvious way to judge future need is to extrapolate from past patterns of growth for the institution or area under consideration. Historically, such projections have been the major quantitative tool of health planners. Simply applied, such methods perpetuate past patterns — including presumably inappropriate growth. . . . [T]he appropriateness of current utilization is not challenged. . . .

Randall Bovbjerg, Problems and Prospects for Health Planning: The Importance of Incentives, Standards, and Procedures in Certificate of Need, 1978 Utah L. Rev. 83. See also H. Aaron & William Schwartz, The Painful Prescription (1984) ("the prevention of all duplication would achieve only modest, one-time savings, which would not affect the subsequent rate of increases in cost."). Consider, for example, that even if CON laws can limit the number of X-ray or CAT scan machines, they do not limit the further development of different types of scanners. X-rays show bones and harder tissue in two dimensions. CAT scans do the same in three dimensions. MRIs show muscle and other soft tissue in much finer detail. PET scans reveal how organs are functioning, by identifying blood flow and metabolism. Each technology costs progressively more than the next, with PET scanners topping out at a several million dollars. Consider also proton beam therapy for cancer — which is much more precise than standard radiation therapy, but currently costs in the vicinity of $100 million per machine.

3. For review of the substantial case law challenging CON decisions, see Annot., 61 A.L.R.3d 278 (1994).

B. CORPORATE FORM

1. Nonprofit and Public Entities

Regulatory constraints on medical institutions are not always imposed from external sources. Some derive from their own internal organization. For instance, because most hospitals and some HMOs are organized as nonprofit corporations, they are subject to a special set of corporate governance and tax rules, which the next case introduces. Public hospitals are subject to similar restrictions. These ancient rules, derived from the law of charitable trusts, are becoming increasingly relevant as various health care facilities contemplate expanding their range of activities or converting to a more commercialized corporate form.

■ QUEEN OF ANGELS HOSPITAL v. YOUNGER
136 Cal. Rptr. 36 (Cal. 1977)

KAUS, Presiding Justice.

[Queen of Angels Hospital (Queen) was founded in 1927 in connection with the Catholic church. The Franciscan Sisters of the Sacred Heart, known as "the Motherhouse," is a large religious order that, for 30 years, has staffed an outpatient clinic in the hospital.] . . . In April 1971—the details will be supplied in the discussion—Queen's board of directors approved a lease to be effective May 1, 1971, between Queen as lessor and W.D.C. Services, Inc., hospital entrepreneurs, as lessee. Queen leased the hospital, excepting the outpatient clinic and a convent house, to W.D.C. for 25 years with two options for ten additional years each. The minimum annual rental guaranteed Queen was $800,000 for the first two years and one million dollars a year thereafter.

Queen intends to use a substantial portion of the lease proceeds to establish and operate additional medical clinics in East and South Central Los Angeles, which clinics will dispense free medical care, aid and advice to the poor and needy. It is not disputed that an outpatient clinic is not functionally equivalent to a hospital.

In June 1971, the Motherhouse submitted a claim for 16 million dollars for the value of the Sisters' past services to Queen's board of directors. . . . [A]n agreement was executed between Queen and the Motherhouse, effective May 1971, settling and compromising the claim for the Sisters' past services by agreeing that Queen should pay to the Motherhouse $200 per month for each Sister in the Order over the age of 70 years, . . . whether or not the particular Sister performed services at Queen of Angels Hospital. The initial annual cost of the agreement would be $309,600—in July 1971, there were 129 Sisters over the age of 70. . . .

[Queen and Motherhouse] filed a declaratory relief action against the Attorney General to determine the validity of [the] lease agreement . . . and the . . . retirement pay. . . . [The trial court ruled in favor of the plaintiffs on the issue of the lease but against the plaintiffs on the issue of the retirement pay, and so both parties appealed.]

1. THE HOSPITAL [LEASE]

The Attorney General contends that under its articles of incorporation, Queen held its assets in trust primarily for the purpose of operating a hospital, and the use of those assets exclusively for outpatient clinics would constitute an abandonment of Queen's primary charitable purpose and a diversion of charitable trust assets. . . .

The rules governing the use of the assets of a nonprofit charitable organization are well established: "(A)ll the assets of a corporation organized solely for charitable purposes must be deemed to be impressed with a charitable trust by virtue of the express declaration of the corporation's purposes. . . . It follows that . . . (a nonprofit corporation cannot) legally divert its assets to any purpose other than charitable purposes. . . ." *Pacific Home v. County of Los Angeles,* 41 Cal. 2d 844, 852, 264 P.2d 539, 543. "Since there is usually no one willing to assume the burdens of a legal action, or who could properly represent the interest of the trust or the public, the Attorney General has been empowered to oversee charities as the representative of the public." *Holt v. College of Osteopathic Physicians & Surgeons,* 61 Cal. 2d 750, 754, 40 Cal. Rptr. 244, 247, 394 P.2d 932, 935. . . .

With this apparent agreement in principle we turn to an examination of the articles of incorporation and the relevant undisputed facts. The articles of incorporation, as amended in 1941, provides in relevant part as follows:

> . . . the purposes for which said corporation is formed are:
>
> (1) To establish, . . . own, . . . maintain, . . . and operate a hospital in the City of Los Angeles, . . . to furnish, . . . hospital care, . . . and medical and surgical treatment of every kind and character, and to receive, treat and care for patients, invalids, the aged and infirm, and generally to conduct and carry on, and to do all things necessary or advisable in conducting and carrying on a hospital;
>
> (2) To perform and to foster and support acts of Christian charity particularly among the sick and ailing; to practice, foster and encourage religious beliefs and activities, particularly those of the Holy Roman Catholic Church; to house and care for unprotected and indigent sick, aged and infirm persons regardless of race, creed, sex or age;
>
> (3) To educate, . . . nurses and medical students, and to provide facilities for the same;
>
> (4) That it is a corporation which is not formed for pecuniary gain . . . and any revenue received . . . from the operation and carrying on of said hospital shall be used in improving the same . . . or shall be used in enlarging and improving said hospital and in enlarging the field and scope of its charitable, religious and educational activities;
>
> (5) To lease or purchase any real estate, . . . which may be necessary, proper or useful in carrying out the purposes or for the benefit of the hospital, or as may be deemed to be conducive to the welfare of this corporation; . . .[2]

[W]hat is most apparent in the articles of incorporation is that . . . the framework of those multiple purposes is the operation of a hospital. Clinics are not even mentioned. . . . [A]lthough Queen did operate a clinic from 1932 to the present time, that clinic was physically housed within the hospital and drew on hospital resources. . . .

Queen also represented to the public that it was a hospital. In its statement to the Franchise Tax Board, it stated that it was in the "business of running a hospital." Similar statements were made to the Internal Revenue Service and Los Angeles county tax authorities. Funds were solicited from the public for the hospital or hospital purposes. Such acts further bind Queen to its primary purpose of operating

---

2. The articles also contain a "parity clause" which provides that the corporation may generally "do all acts and things which may be necessary, proper, useful or advantageous to the full carrying out of the purposes of this corporation." . . .

a hospital. In brief, whatever else Queen of Angels Hospital Corporation may do under its articles of incorporation, it was intended to and did operate a hospital and cannot, consistent with the trust imposed upon it, abandon the operation of the hospital business in favor of clinics.

Queen's argument in response does not meet the issue. Plaintiffs point out, as we have noted, that the corporation has multiple "purposes"; that the purpose "to furnish, . . . medical and surgical treatment" is broad enough to authorize the operation of a clinic or clinics and that acts of "Christian charity" encompass all forms of medical aid, care, and advice to the poor and needy. None of the foregoing is disputed. The question is not whether Queen can use some of its assets or the proceeds from the operation of the hospital for purposes other than running a hospital; it certainly can and has. The question is whether it can cease to perform the primary purpose for which it was organized. That, we believe, it cannot do.

Moreover, the issue is not, as plaintiffs contend, whether the operation of clinics serving the poor in the areas in which they live is as worthy a use of charitable funds. . . . This corporation is bound by its articles of incorporation. Queen may maintain a hospital and retain control over its assets or it may abandon the operation of a hospital and lose those assets to the successor distributees, but it cannot do both. . . .

2. THE RETIREMENT PLAN

The trial court made the following relevant findings: . . . The property of Queen does not belong to either the Motherhouse or the Roman Catholic Church. From the inception of the hospital through 1971, services . . . provided Queen by the [M]otherhouse . . . were considered donated to Queen by both parties. Neither the Motherhouse nor the Sisters expected any further or future compensation for those services. Although the claim for compensation for past services was made in good faith and was not a dishonest claim, "there was no basis for such claim and neither the Motherhouse nor Queens had a reasonable basis for believing in the validity of the claim." The compromise of the claim—e.g., the retirement plan—"was not a proper exercise of sound business judgment or of the fiduciary duties of Queens' Board." The court concluded that . . . the retirement plan was invalid and that, if implemented, it would constitute a diversion of charitable assets.

First, although plaintiffs make much of the relationship between Queen and the Motherhouse and attempt to present this relationship in terms of Roman Catholic Canon Law, the trial court properly rejected this approach. Plaintiffs' assertion that such evidence is material reflects an attempt to bootstrap a First Amendment argument by citing . . . moral and ecclesiastic duties of Queen and the Motherhouse, and then arguing that whether the retirement plan accords with church doctrine is an internal ecclesiastic matter. Throughout, plaintiffs have sought the benefits of and conformed to the general requirements of civil law; they cannot now decline to be ruled by the principles which Queen has itself invited.

Applying neutral principles, . . . there was no reasonable basis for compromising the 16 million-dollar claim submitted by the Motherhouse for past services. Although plaintiffs attempt to analogize the pension plan to a—sometimes—enforceable promise to pay for past services, as the Attorney General points out, the compromise "bore no relationship whatsoever to a traditional retirement plan as it provided payments to all of the Sisters of the Order over the age of 70 wherever situated, regardless of whether they had ever served at Queen of Angels, or if so, how long, or when, and regardless of any other provisions being made for such Sisters through retirement plans at any of the other ten hospitals established by the Franciscan Sisters." . . .

3. [LEGAL AND BUSINESS] FEES

[The lease was negotiated by an attorney, John Brandlin, who was also a member of Queen's board of directors.] The Attorney General contends that Queen's agreement to pay [Brandlin and his business partners] 3 percent of the annual rentals for the first five years of the lease and 2 percent of the annual rentals for each year thereafter as fees for negotiating the lease is, in fact, an agreement to pay real estate brokers' fees and, since none of the recipients is licensed, the agreement is invalid. . . .

The underlying facts are as follows: During the time in which this lease was negotiated, prepared and executed, Brandlin was Queen's attorney and also a member of Queen's board of directors. The hospital was in financial difficulties and Brandlin was authorized to find out what could be done about leasing the hospital, an idea he had proposed informally. Another of Brandlin's clients was John L. Donovan, a stockbroker, through whom Brandlin met Glenn Thomason, "a kind of hospital entrepreneur" who "deals in hospitals." None of the three was licensed as a real estate broker. In late 1969, Brandlin, Donovan and Thomason had contemplated the formation of a corporation—"American Hospital Administrators"—to acquire or lease hospitals and go "public" with them, but the project never got off the ground.

In July 1970, after preliminary discussions, Brandlin was told by Sister Timothy Marie that Queen was interested in pursuing the possibility of a lease. . . . After further discussions with W.D.C. and with the Order's headquarters in Illinois, Brandlin began preparing the documents. Brandlin did all of the legal work.

The agreement presented to the Board covering the services of Thomason, Donovan and Brandlin states that the three "are entitled to reasonable compensation" for their "services." . . . Brandlin was employed on a retainer basis by Queen until about April 1971, and thereafter he billed his legal services—other than the fee in dispute—based upon an hourly rate. . . .

That Brandlin's involvement in three capacities—lawyer, trustee and frustrated entrepreneur—was legal and professional dynamite is obvious. Nevertheless, professional protocol—such as disclosure [and] disqualification as trustee when called for—appears to have been scrupulously observed. . . .

In essence, this is what happened: Brandlin rendered legal services to Queen's. These were undoubtedly of such a nature that a layman would have been required to be a licensed real estate broker. Brandlin, however, was an attorney and, as such, came within [an] exception. . . . The Attorney General claims that Queen could not obligate itself to pay Donovan and Thomason anything because they were more than mere finders [and thus were seeking a sales commission without a real estate license]. To be brief and blunt, we disagree on the facts. . . .

The judgment is reversed.

■COLUMBIA/HCA AND THE RESURGENCE OF THE FOR-PROFIT HOSPITAL BUSINESS*
Robert Kuttner**

335 New Eng. J. Med. 362 (1996)

This two-part article addresses the medical, ethical, and public-policy issues posed by the resurgence of for-profit chains and their acquisition of nonprofit community hospitals. The prime case in point is Columbia/HCA Healthcare Corporation, the largest and most aggressive of the for-profit chains, the product of three large and several smaller mergers. With 340 hospitals, 135 outpatient-surgery offices, and 200 home health care agencies in 38 states, Columbia/HCA now controls nearly half the for-profit beds, and 7 percent of all hospital beds, in the United States. The company's gross earnings exceed 20 percent of revenues, and its 1995 profits were just under $1 billion, with $20 billion in assets. . . .

Columbia's founder, Richard Scott, bought his first two hospitals in El Paso, Texas, from Healthtrust in 1988. From a base of 12 hospitals in 1991, Columbia acquired Basic American Medical (1992, 8 hospitals), Galen (1993, 71 hospitals), HCA (1994, 97 hospitals), Medical Care America (1994, 96 ambulatory surgical centers), and the rest of Healthtrust (1995, 117 hospitals) after a bidding war with NME. . . . In 1995 alone, Columbia/HCA acquired or negotiated joint ventures with 32 nonprofit hospitals. . . .

The company has targeted and achieved a formidable corporate goal of a 20 percent gross return on revenues. I was told by a Columbia/HCA executive that chief executives of company hospitals who fall short of this goal are regularly called to corporate headquarters in Nashville to explain and are ordered to redouble their efforts. Further economies at the local hospital usually follow. . . .

Columbia/HCA's most audacious recent foray [is] in Ohio. . . . In March, Blue Cross and Blue Shield of Ohio, the state's largest insurer, with annual revenues of some $2 billion, agreed to sell 85 percent ownership to Columbia for $299.5 million through a complex venture called BlueCo, legally crafted to avoid the form of a conversion, thus eliminating a payout obligation to policyholders or a charitable foundation. Because $223 million of Blue Cross and Blue Shield reserves would go to the new venture, Columbia/HCA would be buying Blue Cross and Blue Shield largely with the latter's own assets. . . . Under the proposed acquisition, Columbia/HCA will pay three top executives of Ohio Blue Cross and Blue Shield over $15 million in severance payments characterized as consulting fees and agreements not to compete, with millions more going as a consulting fee to the Blues' outside lawyer. . . .

[T]he big nonprofits are now in many ways defensively emulating Columbia/HCA and other for-profits. . . . A market culture and market idiom are becoming pervasive, even among nonprofits. Within living memory, service areas were not called markets; heads of hospitals were administrators, not chief executive officers; hospitals did not advertise for patients; and few hospital administrators spoke of

---

** The author is a respected journalist and social critic.

market share, let alone EBITDA (earnings before interest, taxes, depreciation, and amortization). All this has changed, perhaps irrevocably. . . .

[A year after this was written, Richard Scott, who subsequently became governor of Florida, was ousted by Columbia/HCA's board of directors, in part because the company's image had become so tarnished by his management style. This occurred amid a sweeping federal probe of billing practices at several of Columbia's hospitals, and was followed by criminal fraud indictments against several of Columbia's managers. The company has since dropped Columbia from its name and returned to HCA, for Hospital Corporation of America. To settle the government's fraud investigation and associated lawsuits, HCA agreed to pay a record $1.7 *billion*. See Symposium, 17(2) Health Aff. 1 (Mar.–Apr. 1998). It is still the largest hospital chain in the country.

Similar controversy subsequently erupted for another for-profit hospital chain, Tenet Healthcare, which also agreed to a very large settlement, of nearly $900 million. See Elizabeth A. Weeks, Gauging the Cost of Loopholes: Health Care Pricing and Medicare Regulation in the Post-Enron Era, 40 Wake Forest L. Rev. 1215 (2005).]

Notes: Charitable Trust Law; Public and Religious Hospitals; For-Profit Conversions

1. Queen of Angels, the hospital, was located near Hollywood and, at one time, was the birthplace for the vast majority of L.A. residents, including many movie stars. In 1985, it merged with Hollywood Presbyterian Medical Center, and was then purchased by the for-profit Tenet Health System in 1998, and sold in 2005 to Dr. Kwang Yul Cha, a Korean fertility specialist. The new management team borrowed from the hotel industry to provide concierge-type services such as valet parking and bellhop attendants. In 2007, the hospital agreed to pay a $1 million fine resulting from a federal investigation into its allegedly dumping an uninsured paraplegic patient on skid row wearing nothing more than a soiled gown and a broken colostomy bag. Richard Winton, Skid Row Dumping Suit Settled, L.A. Times, May 31, 2008.

Queen of Angels, the case, succinctly applies three distinct doctrines of nonprofit and charitable trust law: (1) *ultra vires* or charitable purpose; (2) duty of care or the business judgment rule; and (3) duty of loyalty and conflict of interest. These notes will explore each in turn.

2. *Ultra vires* ("beyond its powers") is the term sometimes used to describe the court's first holding. How would you revise the articles of incorporation to avoid this holding? Where bylaws are worded differently, courts are usually not nearly such sticklers about modifying corporate purposes, as long as the new purpose still pursues the same general charitable aims. See, e.g., Attorney General v. Hahnemann Hospital, 494 N.E.2d 1011 (Mass. 1986) (allowing hospital to devote proceeds of its sale to other health care institutions but not to "any activity that promotes the health of the general public" such as research or education). Restrictions can be even more stringent than in *Queen of Angels*, however, if the hospital has received gifts with specific strings attached. Especially troubling are gifts limited to a particular facility's location or ownership, not just to the facility type. One commentator explains:

Unrestricted gifts received by a charitable corporation must be used for a purpose for which the charitable corporation exists generally; gifts which have certain terms or conditions attached must be used in accordance with such specifications. These restrictions can be extraordinarily burdensome to the sale or lease of an entire facility, particularly since the facility might be constructed with gifts from thousands of individual donors. As an example, Professor Bloche [infra] recounts the difficulty faced by Creighton University when it sold its primary teaching hospital to American Medical International. . . . The University had to consider whether the sale of the hospital was consistent with [a] single [restricted] gift, even though it constituted only a tiny fraction of the hospital's original construction costs.

Jeffrey Heidt, Conversion of Status and Facility Closure, *in* Health Care Corporate Law: Facilities and Transactions (M. Hall & W. Brewbaker eds., 1996).

3. *Public and Religious Hospitals.* Public hospitals, those owned by government and chartered by statute, are subject to similar limitations on their powers, depending on how their corporate purposes are stated in the governing statutes. See, e.g., New York City Council v. Giuliani, 93 N.Y.2d 60 (1999) (public hospital not authorized to enter long-term sublease agreement). But see In re University Hospitals Authority, 953 S.W.2d 314 (Okla. 1997) (approving a state university hospital's long-term lease and management agreement with a for-profit company).

Queen of Angels Hospital also highlights another source of restriction for corporate transactions — religious law — which is particularly important for Catholic hospitals because of the formality of canon law. Although the court found that canon law does not *supersede* secular law, it does *supplement* secular law in practical effect. Before undertaking a major corporate transaction, a Catholic institution must receive approval from the Holy See that it satisfies the Ethical and Religious Directives for Catholic Health Facilities. This requirement stopped another effort by the Queen of Angels board to sell its hospital. The archbishop of Los Angeles refused approval, and the state attorney general ruled that the hospital's bylaws make this decision binding on the corporation. But see Kansas East Conference of the United Methodist Church v. Bethany Medical Center, 969 P.2d 859 (Kan. 1998) (Methodist church is not entitled to the proceeds from the sale of a hospital it helped to found.).

4. Cy Pres. As the court briefly notes, the *ultra vires* doctrine does not require a nonprofit board to continue running a money-losing hospital until it goes bankrupt. The board is permitted to wind up operations and transfer ownership entirely to a new corporation. In such an event, another trust law doctrine, *cy pres* ("as near as possible"), determines what alternative use to make of the proceeds from the sale. *Cy pres* precedents allow considerably more flexibility in selecting alternate charitable purposes of the same general type when the original purpose is no longer possible or practical. Should a long-term lease be treated so differently than a complete sale, especially when the lease was approved by the same religious order that founded the hospital? Should courts give nonprofit hospitals greater managerial leeway today as a result of the greatly increased competition caused by the rapid infiltration of managed care? One commentator has opined in the context of teaching hospitals that "courts should give considerable weight to the argument that intensified competitive pressures in the hospital industry are 'circumstances not . . . foreseen' by a donor and [thus a gift to a medical school would be rendered] more effective in advancing teaching and research if applied to some activity other than

hospital operations." M. Gregg Bloche, Corporate Takeover of Teaching Hospitals, 65 S. Cal. L. Rev. 1035 (1992).

Where circumstances justify invoking the *cy pres* doctrine, then the alternative uses for the proceeds are usually quite broad. As Heidt, supra, explains:

> Nonprofit hospitals that sell or lease their facilities will usually attempt to comply with these restrictions in one of three ways. First, they might use the proceeds to operate a different type of health care facility such as an outpatient clinic or long-term care facility. Second, the nonprofit can consider converting to a funding agency that supports other health care facilities or activities. For instance, the proceeds from the sale or lease of a teaching hospital might be used to fund medical research. Third, the proceeds might be used to support charitable activities at the very facility being sold or leased. Such activities include not only medical education and research, but also charity care. In structuring this latter arrangement, however, care must be taken to avoid the characterization that the nonprofit is paying a rebate to the for-profit buyer by helping the buyer to reduce its bad debt.

5. *Conversions to For-Profit.* As Kuttner explains, nonprofit health care entities, including hospitals and HMOs, are increasingly converting to for-profit status by selling out to investor-owned corporations — not so much because they are losing money but because they can make more if they have better access to capital. In one of the most notable instances, Blue Cross of California created a for-profit HMO subsidiary called WellPoint Health Networks. WellPoint was a big success, and its stock became very valuable. In 1993, California Blue Cross folded itself into Well-Point, thereby giving up its nonprofit status, but California regulators required Blue Cross to leave $3 billion of assets behind in a nonprofit foundation to support medical research and care for the poor.

In such cases, the difficult legal issue is not only what alternative uses to make of the charitable proceeds, but also whether the buyer is paying sufficient value for the business and its assets so that the past support from donors and from tax exemption is not dissipated. The bargained-for price is often not reliable because the purchasing corporation is often not at arm's length, especially when it is simply part of an internal corporate reorganization, as in the Blue Cross example. These concerns have prompted state attorneys general to assert jurisdiction over these transactions by invoking their authority under either common law or under newly enacted statutes in many states designed to regulate (or perhaps discourage) these transactions. Also, consumer advocates have sued to enforce charitable trust principles. In some cases, converting hospitals and insurers have been required to turn over to a foundation only a relatively modest sum ($50 million to $150 million), based on the net asset value of the company. In other instances, however, such as the California Blue Cross conversion, the foundation has been given full stock ownership of the new company, which avoids the need to agree to a valuation. When the foundation divests the stock, it is usually worth many times more than the company's asset value. Which measure of value is more appropriate: the historical asset value while the company was still a nonprofit, or the new equity value created by the conversion to for-profit status? See In re Manhattan Eye, Ear & Throat Hospital, 715 N.Y.S.2d 575 (Sup. Ct. 1999) (blocking a transaction similar to that in *Queen of Angels* because the sales price failed to account for the goodwill value of the hospital's name and its value as an ongoing business).

Should these conversions concern us? Perhaps the incentive that insurers and HMOs have to compromise care is much more tolerable if the nonprofit form meant that denying care to one patient is likely to help another patient who is in greater need. Because nonprofit insurers may not distribute earnings to owners, perhaps there is a greater chance their earnings will be devoted to patient care. One indication this is true is that the "medical loss ratio" (the amount of premium dollars devoted to medical care rather than to overhead) is generally higher for nonprofit HMOs than for for-profits. Also, some research studies have found that nonprofit HMOs perform notably better than for-profits on a number of measures of quality of care. Ha T. Tu & James D. Reschovsky, Assessments of Medical Care by Enrollees in For-Profit and Nonprofit Health Maintenance Organizations, 346 New Eng. J. Med. 1288 (2002). Based on these factors, Minnesota requires all HMOs to be nonprofit. See also Premera v. Kreidler, 131 P.3d 930 (Wash. App. 2006) (upholding a regulator's refusal to allow a Blue Cross plan in Washington State to convert to for-profit status).

6. *Business Judgment.* The Motherhouse pension plan was struck down as an improper "exercise of sound business judgment," which the board members are required to exercise as part of their fiduciary duty of care. Again, this appears to be an especially strict application of fiduciary rules. In contrast, the business judgment rule that applies to for-profit directors is considerably more forgiving. Other courts have rejected the stricter charitable trust scrutiny and ruled that the same leniency should be given to nonprofit as to for-profit directors, considering that they often serve for free and they increasingly are functioning in a more commercial business climate that requires broader business discretion. The leading case to this effect was decided in relation to another hospital, one whose board members were sued for investing its funds in low-interest accounts at banks affiliated with board members. Stern v. Lucy Webb Hayes National Training School for Deaconesses & Missionaries, 381 F. Supp. 1003 (D.D.C. 1974) (holding, despite the more lenient scrutiny, that fiduciary duties were violated by the conflict of interest). This liberalized business judgment rule is adopted by the Revised Model Nonprofit Corporation Act §8.30.

7. *Conflicts of Interest.* Brandlin, the Queen of Angels lawyer, ran a serious risk of violating his duty of loyalty because of the conflict of interest between his board position and his own law practice and entrepreneurship. He was saved by full disclosure and because his terms were reasonable. But for that, the transaction might have been declared void and Brandlin held liable for damages to the corporation. In Boston Children's Heart Foundation v. Nadal-Ginard, 73 F.3d 429 (1st Cir. 1996), the court upheld a $6.5 million award against a physician board member and employee who failed to disclose he was being paid to work for a competing hospital and research center at the same time.

Is it appropriate for existing board members and top management to participate in the profits realized by a conversion to for-profit status? This might occur if they take an ownership position in the new for-profit corporation, or if they are given stock as part of a severance bonus. Although the initial ownership share or severance bonus might be valued only modestly, when the for-profit decides to "go public" (sell shares in the stock market), the initial directors and managers might find themselves suddenly wealthy, as happened with Blue Cross of California and with many other recent hospital and HMO conversions like those described by Kuttner. The usual remedy for a conflict of interest is disclosure and ratification by the board, but this does not work where most or all of the board is subject to the same conflict. As a result, a state court may be asked to evaluate the fairness of the transaction to the nonprofit entity under common-law principles of fiduciary responsibility. Also, these transactions raise dangerous red flags of "private inurement" under principles of tax exemption discussed below.

8. *Further Readings.* On **religious hospitals** (note 3), see Kathleen Boozang, Deciding the Fate of Religious Hospitals in the Emerging Health Care Market, 31 Hous. L. Rev. 1429 (1995); Lisa C. Ikemoto, When a Hospital Becomes Catholic, 47 Mercer L. Rev. 1087 (1996); Lawrence Singer, Realigning Catholic Health Care: Bridging Legal and Church Control in a Consolidating Market, 72 Tulane L. Rev. 159 (1997); Comment, 17 St. Louis U. Pub. L. Rev. 157 (1999).

On **conversion to for-profit status** (note 5), see Mark A. Hall & Christopher Conover, Privatization of Blue Cross Plans: Public Benefit or Public Harm?, 27 Annu. Rev. Public Health 443 (2006); David Hyman, Hospital Conversions: Fact, Fantasy, and Regulatory Follies, 23 J. Corp. L. 741 (1998); Mark Krause, "First, Do No Harm": An Analysis of the Nonprofit Hospital Sale Acts, 45 UCLA L. Rev. 503 (1997).

On the **business judgment rule** (note 6), see Michael Peregrine & James Schwartz, The Business Judgment Rule and Other Protections for the Conduct of Not-for-Profit Directors, 33 J. Health L. 455 (2000); Mary O'Byrne, Directors' Duty of Care to Monitor Information Systems in HMOs: Some Lessons from the Oxford Health Plan, 14 J. L. & Health 45 (2000).

For discussion of the post-Enron corporate governance issues raised by **the Sarbanes-Oxley Act**, see Robert W. Friz et al., The Sarbanes-Oxley Act: Considerations for Nonprofit Health Care Organizations, 18(5) The Health Lawyer 1 (June 2006); Michael J. Myers, Juxtaposing Sarbanes-Oxley with JCAHO Governance Standards: A Shortcut to Auditable Health System Compliance?, 51 S.D. L. Rev. 465 (2006); Glenn T. Troyer et al., Governance Issues for Nonprofit Healthcare Organizations and the Implications of the Sarbanes-Oxley Act, 1 Ind. Health L. Rev. 175-211 (2004); James G. Wiehl, Roles and Responsibilities of Nonprofit Health Care Board Members in the Post-Enron Era, 25 J. Leg. Med. 411 (2004); Symposium, 3 Seattle J. Soc. Justice 205 (2004); Note, 2011 U. Ill. L. Rev. 229.

Problem: For-Profit Joint Venture

To seek shelter from the competitive storm, Florence Nightingale Hospital (FNH) is considering forming a joint venture with an existing for-profit HMO. FNH would be given 30 percent ownership of the privately held HMO, and each of its five board of trustee members would be given 1 percent ownership, in exchange for FNH contributing $10 million in capital funds, which is 35 percent of the HMO's appraised net worth. Since the HMO already owns its own nursing home, FNH will raise the capital by selling its nursing home. FNH will receive 30 percent of whatever profit distributions the HMO board chooses to make from time to time and the trustees will receive their 1 percent shares. FNH also hopes to increase its patient base for hospital admissions and to secure a better bargaining position for reimbursements from the HMO, but the HMO is making no promises about where its subscribers will be sent for hospital care, nor how it will pay FNH for hospital services to its subscribers.

Assume that FNH has articles of incorporation similar to Queen of Angels', only covering nursing home as well as hospital services, and that it has received only general, unrestricted gifts from donors. Also, assume there is no other management or personal connection between FNH and the HMO. What issues would you want to alert the hospital board to concerning whether this is a permissible venture and how the HMO can use its capital funds? Would these parties be advised to have the HMO pledge some portion of its revenues to pay for charity care services at FNH?

2. Charitable Tax Exemption

This section explores the fundamental justification for classifying various medical institutions as charitable for purposes of tax exemption. The question you should ask yourself is how nonprofit hospitals differ from their for-profit counterparts, and whether those characteristics also allow others in the health care sector to qualify for exemption. These readings then explain the detailed organizational and operational constraints that must be met in order to maintain charitable status.

■ EASTERN KENTUCKY WELFARE RIGHTS ORGANIZATION v. SIMON
506 F.2d 1278 (D.C. Cir. 1974)

JAMESON, Senior District Judge:
. . . Sections 501(a) and (c)(3) of the Internal Revenue Code of 1954 exempt from federal income tax: "(3) Corporations, and any community chest, fund, religious, or foundation, organized and operated exclusively for charitable . . . purposes, . . . no part of the net earnings of which inures to the benefit of any private shareholder or individual." . . . Other related sections of the Code provide that contributions to such tax exempt charitable organizations are deductible for purposes of computing federal income tax and estate and gift taxes.

Hospitals and other health organizations have never been expressly categorized as tax exempt organizations and have achieved that status only by qualifying as "charitable" organizations under the Code. Long established Internal Revenue Service (I.R.S.) policy held that hospitals qualified as charitable organizations under §501(c)(3) only if they provided free or below cost service to those unable to pay. This policy was articulated in Revenue Ruling 56-185, which held that a hospital could qualify for tax exempt status only if it was "operated to the extent of its financial ability for those not able to pay for the services rendered and not exclusively for those who are able and expected to pay."[2]

2. Other pertinent parts of Revenue Ruling 56-185 state: "It is normal for hospitals to charge those able to pay for services rendered in order to meet the operating expenses of the institution without denying medical care or treatment to others unable to pay. . . . It may furnish services at reduced rates which are below cost, and thereby render charity in that manner. . . . It must not, however, refuse to accept patients in need of hospital care who cannot pay for such services."

The I.R.S. modified this position in 1969 with the issuance of Revenue Ruling 69-545. The new ruling broadly defines "charitable" in terms of community benefit and holds that the promotion of health constitutes a "charitable purpose" in the "generally accepted legal sense of that term" and within the meaning of §501(c)(3) of the Code. According to the ruling, "The promotion of health . . . is one of the purposes in the general law of charity that is deemed beneficial to the community as a whole even though the class of beneficiaries eligible to receive a direct benefit from its activities does not include all members of the community, such as indigent members of the community." . . .

Based on this community benefit concept, a nonprofit hospital can qualify as a charitable organization under §501(c)(3) "by operating an emergency room open to all persons and by providing hospital care for all those persons in the community able to pay the cost thereof either directly or through third party reimbursement . . ." (e.g. private health insurance, Medicare, or Medicaid). Thus, for a hospital to qualify as a tax-exempt organization, the provision of free or below cost service to those unable to pay is no longer essential.

Alleging harm from this new ruling, the plaintiffs-appellees, a group of health and welfare organizations and indigent persons, brought this action seeking to declare Revenue Ruling 69-545 invalid and to enjoin its implementation. They submitted affidavits recounting incidents in various parts of the country involving the denial of hospital services to indigents by institutions enjoying tax exempt status as "charitable" organizations. . . .

We conclude that Revenue Ruling 69-545 is not inconsistent with 26 U.S.C. §501(c)(3) and that the modification of the prior ruling was authorized. The definition of the term *charitable* has never been static and has been broadened in recent years. . . . In promulgating Revenue Ruling 69-545, the Commissioner [relied] on an analogy to the law of charitable trusts. [T]he Commissioner cited both the Restatement (Second) of Trusts, §368 and §372,[16] and IV Scott on Trusts (3rd ed. 1967) §368 and §372 in holding that the promotion of health is a charitable purpose within the meaning of §501(c)(3).

The term *charitable* is thus capable of a definition far broader than merely the relief of the poor. The law of charitable trusts supports the broader concept. . . . While it is true that in the past Congress and the federal courts have conditioned a hospital's charitable status on the level of free or below cost care that it provided for indigents, there is no authority for the conclusion that the determination of "charitable" status was always to be so limited. Such an inflexible construction fails to recognize the changing economic, social and technological precepts and values of contemporary society.

In the field of health care, the changes have been dramatic. Hospitals in the early part of this nation's history were almshouses supported by philanthropy and serving almost exclusively the sick poor. Today, hospitals are the primary community health facility for both rich and poor. Philanthropy accounts for only a min-

---

16. The Restatement (Second) of Trusts §368 (1959) states: "Charitable purposes include: (a) the relief of poverty; (b) the advancement of education; (c) the advancement of religion; (d) the promotion of health; (e) governmental or municipal purposes; (f) other purposes the accomplishment of which is beneficial to the community."

ute percentage of the hospital's total operating costs. Those costs have soared in recent years as constant modernization of equipment and facilities is necessitated by the advances in medical science and technology. The institution of Medicare and Medicaid in the last decade combined with the rapid growth of medical and hospital insurance has greatly reduced the number of poor people requiring free or below cost hospital services. Much of that decrease has been realized since the promulgation of Revenue Ruling 56-185. Moreover, increasingly counties and other political subdivisions are providing nonemergency hospitalization and medical care for those unable to pay. Thus, it appears that the rationale upon which the limited definition of "charitable" was predicated has largely disappeared. To continue to base the "charitable" status of a hospital strictly on the relief it provides for the poor fails to account for these major changes in the area of health care....

It is important to note also that Revenue Ruling 69-545 . . . entails the operation of an emergency room open to all regardless of their ability to pay and providing hospital services to those able to pay the cost either directly or through third party reimbursement. Thus, to qualify as a tax exempt charitable organization, a hospital must still provide services to indigents.

The required provision of emergency room services is of great import to the indigent. Emergency room service is often the only means of access that the poor have to medical care. Furthermore, the fact that hospitals seeking to qualify as charities pursuant to Revenue Ruling 69-545 must accept Medicare and Medicaid patients is also significant. A large percentage of the indigent populace of the nation is now covered by either Medicare or Medicaid. In the final analysis, Revenue Ruling 69-545 may be of greater benefit to the poor than its predecessor Ruling 56-185. . . .

[On appeal, the Supreme Court dismissed this case for lack of standing under the reasoning that, even if the plaintiffs won, they may not be any better off since nonprofit hospitals would be free to relinquish their charitable status rather than agreeing to treat more indigent patients. Eastern Kentucky Welfare Rights Organization v. Simon, 426 U.S. 26 (1976).]

■ PROVENA COVENANT MEDICAL CENTER v. DEPARTMENT OF REVENUE
925 N.E.2d 1132 (Ill. 2010)

KARMEIER, J.

The central issue in this case is whether Provena Hospitals established that it was entitled to a charitable exemption under . . . the Property Tax Code . . . for various parcels of real estate it owns in Urbana, [Illinois]. The Director of Revenue determined that it had not and denied the exemption. . . . Following a hearing, the circuit court determined that Provena Hospitals was entitled to both a charitable and religious exemption. . . . [We uphold] the decision by the Department of Revenue to deny the exemption.

BACKGROUND

. . . Provena Hospitals was formed through the consolidation of four Catholic-related health-care organizations and is organized as a not-for-profit corporation under the laws of Illinois. . . . Provena Hospitals is exempt from federal income tax under section 501(c)(3) of the Internal Revenue Code. The Illinois Department of Revenue has also determined that the corporation is exempt from this state's retailers' occupation tax, service occupation tax, use tax, and service use tax. In addition, the Illinois Attorney General has concluded that the corporation "meets the qualifications of 'An Act to Regulate Solicitation and Collection of Funds for Charitable Purposes' . . . and constitutes a religious organization exempt from filing annual financial reports under those statutes."

Provena Hospitals owns and operates six hospitals, including Provena Covenant Medical Center (PCMC), a full-service hospital located in the City of Urbana . . . [serving] a 13-county area in east central Illinois. . . . Just as PCMC relies on private physicians to fill its medical staff, it utilizes numerous third-party providers to furnish other services at the hospital. . . . The company providing lab services is one of the businesses owned by Provena Enterprises, a Provena Health subsidiary. It is operated for profit. Provena Hospitals' employees do not work gratuitously. Everyone employed by the corporation, including those with religious affiliations, are paid for their services. . . .

PCMC has agreements with some private third-party payers which provide for payment at rates different from "its established rates." The payment amounts under these agreements cover the actual costs of care. The amounts PCMC receives from Medicare and Medicaid are not sufficient to cover the costs of care. . . . For 2002, PCMC calculated the difference to be $7,418,150 in the case of Medicare patients and $3,105,217 for Medicaid patients. . . .

During 2002, Provena Hospitals' "net patient service revenue" was $713,911,000. . . . Provena Hospitals' "expenses and losses" exceeded its "revenue and gains" during this period by $4,869,000. In other words, the corporation was in the red. The following year, this changed. The corporation's revenue and gains exceeded its expenses and losses by $10,548,000. . . . This surplus existed even after provision for uncollectible accounts receivable (i.e., bad debt) in the amount of $7,101,000. Virtually none of PCMC's income was derived from charitable contributions. The dollar amount of "unrestricted donations" received by PCMC for the year ending December 31, 2002, was a mere $6,938. . . . In years when PCMC realizes a net gain, the gain is "reinvested in order to sustain and further [the corporation's] charitable mission and ministry." . . .

In 2002, PCMC . . . advertised in newspapers, phone directories, event playbills, and Chamber of Commerce publications; on television and radio; and through public signage. It also advertised using "booths, tables, and/or tents at community health or nonprofit fundraising events; sponsorship of sports teams and other community events; and banner advertisements at sponsored community events." . . . None of its ads that year mentioned . . . a charity care policy in place at the hospital [which] . . . provided that the institution would "offer, to the extent that it is financially able, admission for care or treatment, and the use of the hospital facilities and services regardless of race, color, creed, sex, national origin, ancestry or ability to pay for these services." The charity policy was not self-executing. An application was required. Whether an application would be granted was determined by PCMC on a case-by-case basis using eligibility criteria based on federal poverty guidelines. A sliding scale was employed [based on income and assets]. . . .

[I]f a patient failed to obtain an advance determination of eligibility under the program, normal collection practices were followed. PCMC would look first to private insurance, if there was any, then pursue any possible sources of reimbursement from the government. Failing that, the hospital would seek payment from the patient directly. . . . Staffed by a small group of employees in Joliet, the Extended Business Office would typically make three or four phone calls and send three or four statements to patients owing outstanding balances. If a balance remained unpaid following such efforts, which typically did not extend beyond three months, Provena Hospitals would treat the account as "bad debt" and refer it to a collection agency. . . .

During 2002, the amount of aid provided by Provena Hospitals to PCMC patients under the facility's charity care program was modest. The hospital waived $1,758,940 in charges, representing an actual cost to it of only $831,724. This was equivalent to only 0.723% of PCMC's revenues for that year and was $268,276 less than the $1.1 million in tax benefits which Provena stood to receive if its claim for a property tax exemption were granted.[1] The number of patients benefitting from the charitable care program was similarly small. During 2002, only 302 of PCMC's 10,000 inpatient and 100,000 outpatient admissions were granted reductions in their bills under the charitable care program. That figure is equivalent to just 0.27% of the hospital's total annual patient census. . . .

ANALYSIS

Under Illinois law, . . . tax exemption under federal law is not dispositive of whether real property is exempt from property tax under Illinois law. . . . [The state's constitution] provides that the General Assembly may, by law, exempt from taxation property . . . "used exclusively for agricultural and horticultural societies, and for school, religious, cemetery and charitable purposes." . . . In *Methodist Old Peoples Home v. Korzen*, 233 N.E.2d 537 (Ill. 1968), we identified the distinctive characteristics of a charitable institution as follows: . . . (2) it earns no profits or dividends but rather derives its funds mainly from private and public charity and holds them in trust for the purposes expressed in the charter; (3) it dispenses charity to all who need it and apply for it; . . . and (5) it does not appear to place any obstacles in the way of those who need and would avail themselves of the charitable benefits it dispenses. . . .

There is no blanket exemption under the law for hospitals or health-care providers. Whether a particular institution qualifies as a charitable institution and is exempt from property tax is a question which must be determined on a case-by-case basis. . . . Provena Hospitals plainly fails to meet the second criterion: its funds are not derived mainly from private and public charity and held in trust for the purposes

---

1. The disparity between the amount of free or discounted care dispensed and the amount of property tax that would be saved through receipt of a charitable exemption is in no way unique to the case before us here. Excluding bad debt, "the amount of uncompensated care provided by as many as three-quarters of nonprofit hospitals is less than their tax benefits." J. Colombo, *Federal & State Tax Exemption Policy, Medical Debt & Healthcare for the Poor*, 51 St. Louis L.J. 433, 433 n.2 (2007).

expressed in the charter. They are generated, overwhelmingly, by providing medical services for a fee. . . . The only charitable donations documented in this case . . . were so small, a mere $6,938, that they barely warrant mention. Provena Hospitals likewise failed to show by clear and convincing evidence that it satisfied factors three or five. . . . When the law says that property must be "exclusively used" for charitable or beneficent purposes, it means that charitable or beneficent purposes are the primary ones for which the property is utilized. Secondary or incidental charitable benefits will not suffice, nor will it be enough that the institution professes a charitable purpose or aspires to using its property to confer charity on others. . . .

[M]ore than a century ago . . . we explained that "[t]he reason for exemptions in favor of charitable institutions is the benefit conferred upon the public by them, and a consequent relief, to some extent, of the burden upon the State to care for and advance the interests of its citizens." . . . Conditioning charitable status on whether an activity helps relieve the burdens on government is appropriate. After all, each tax dollar lost to a charitable exemption is one less dollar affected governmental bodies will have to meet their obligations directly. If a charitable institution wishes to avail itself of funds which would otherwise flow into a public treasury, it is only fitting that the institution provide some compensatory benefit in exchange. While Illinois law has never required that there be a direct, dollar-for-dollar correlation between the value of the tax exemption and the value of the goods or services provided by the charity, it is a *sine qua non* of charitable status that those seeking a charitable exemption be able to demonstrate that their activities will help alleviate some financial burden incurred by the affected taxing bodies in performing their governmental functions.

. . . To be sure, Provena Hospitals did not condition the receipt of care on a patient's financial circumstances. Treatment was offered to all who requested it, and no one was turned away by PCMC based on their inability to demonstrate how the costs of their care would be covered. The record showed, however, that during the period in question here, Provena Hospitals did not advertise the availability of charitable care at PCMC. Patients were billed as a matter of course, and unpaid bills were automatically referred to collection agencies. . . . As a practical matter, there was little to distinguish the way in which Provena Hospitals dispensed its "charity" from the way in which a for-profit institution would write off bad debt. . . .

The minimal amount of charitable care dispensed by Provena Hospitals at the PCMC complex cannot be rationalized on the grounds that the area's residents did not require additional services. For one thing, the argument that there really was no demand for additional charitable care in Champaign County is one that Provena Hospitals cannot comfortably make. . . . [A]pproximately 13.4% of Champaign County's more than 185,000 residents have incomes below the federal poverty guidelines. That amounts to nearly 25,000 people. In addition, nearly 20,000 county residents are estimated to be without any health-care coverage. There is no reason to believe that these groups of indigent and/or uninsured citizens are any healthier than the population at large. To the contrary, experience teaches that such individuals are likely to have significant unmet health-care needs. . . .

Further undermining Provena Hospitals' claims of charity is that even where it did offer discounted charges, the charity was often illusory. As described earlier in this opinion, uninsured patients were charged PCMC's "established" rates, which were more than double the actual costs of care. When patients were granted discounts at the 25% and 50% levels, the hospital was therefore still able to generate a surplus. . . . Moreover, it appears that in every case when a "charitable" discount was granted or full payment for a bill was otherwise not received, the corporation expected the short-fall to be offset by surpluses generated by the higher amounts it was able to charge other users of its facilities and services. Such "cross-subsidies" are a pricing policy any fiscally sound business enterprise might employ. We cannot fault Provena Hospitals for following this strategy. . . . We note merely that such conduct is in no way indicative of any form of charitable purpose or use of the subject property. . . .

Provena Hospitals argues that the amount of free and discounted care it provides to self-pay patients at the PCMC complex is not an accurate reflection of the scope of its charitable use of the property. In its view, its treatment of Medicare and Medicaid patients should also be taken into account because the payments it receives for treating such patients [fell $10 million short of covering] the full costs of care. . . . Accepting Medicare and Medicaid patients is optional. While it is consistent with Provena Hospitals' mission, it also serves the organization's financial interests. In exchange for agreeing to accept less than its "established" rate, the corporation receives a reliable stream of revenue and is able to generate income from hospital resources that might otherwise be underutilized. . . . Mindful of such considerations, our appellate court has held that discounted care provided to Medicare and Medicaid patients is not considered charity for purposes of assessing eligibility for a property tax exemption. . . .

Provena Hospitals asserts that assessment of its charitable endeavors should also take into account subsidies it provides for ambulance service, its support of the crisis nursery, donations made to other not-for-profit entities, volunteer initiatives it undertakes, and support it provides for graduate medical education, behavioral health services, and emergency services training. This contention is problematic for several reasons. First, while all of these activities unquestionably benefit the community, community benefit is not the test. Under Illinois law, the issue is whether the property at issue is used exclusively for a charitable purpose. . . .

With respect to the ambulance subsidy, the costs for most patients who were transported by ambulance appear to have been covered by third-party insurers. The deficit claimed by Provena may therefore result primarily from the reduced rates insurers are allowed to pay, something which clearly would not qualify as charitable in nature. . . . We further note . . . that the ambulance service provided noncharitable benefits to the institution. It complemented PCMC's emergency room, which it was required by law to provide and which was operated by a for-profit corporation, and enhanced PCMC's ability to fill its beds and cover its fixed costs.

The volunteer classes and services cited by Provena Hospitals included such items as free health screenings, wellness classes, and classes on handling grief. Again, while beneficial to the community, they were not necessarily charitable. Private for-profit companies frequently offer comparable services as a benefit for employees and customers and a means for generating publicity and goodwill for the organization. . . . In a competitive health-care environment, [offering free services] may be an effective means for increasing awareness of the hospital, encouraging others outside the immediate community to use its services.

Provena Hospitals' reliance on expenses associated with the medical residency program is also problematic. . . . [I]n addition to generating direct payments from the University, Provena Hospitals' participation in the program unquestionably adds to PCMC's prestige and enables it to supplement its medical staff with well-trained, if inexperienced, physicians. While we cannot exclude the possibility that there is some charity in this relationship, it is difficult to know in which direction such charity flows, from Provena Hospitals to the University of Illinois or vice versa. . . .

We likewise find no error in the Department of Revenue's rejection of Provena Hospitals' request for a religious exemption. . . . [M]edical care, while potentially miraculous, is not intrinsically, necessarily, or even normally religious in nature. . . .

[Two other justices joined the majority opinion, and two dissented, for a 3-2 split.]

Justice BURKE, dissenting in part.

I join that portion of the plurality opinion which holds that Provena Hospitals failed to demonstrate it was entitled to a religious exemption. . . . I do not join that portion of the plurality opinion which addresses the doctrine of charitable use. . . . By imposing a quantum of care requirement and monetary threshold, the plurality is injecting itself into matters best left to the legislature. The legislature did not set forth a monetary threshold for evaluating charitable use. We may not annex new provisions or add conditions to the language of a statute. . . . The Michigan Supreme Court in *Wexford Medical Group v. City of Cadillac*, 713 N.W.2d 734 (2006), aptly set out this principle:

> . . . To set such a threshold, significant questions would have to be grappled with. For instance, a court would have to determine how to account for the indigent who do not identify themselves as such but who nonetheless fail to pay. A court would have to determine whether facilities that provide vital health care should be treated more leniently than some other type of charity because of the nature of its work, or even if a health care provider in an undeserved area, such as petitioner, is more deserving of exemption than one serving an area of lesser need. A court would need to consider whether to premise the exemption on whether the institution had a surplus and whether providing below-cost care constitutes charity. Clearly, courts are unequipped to handle these and many other unanswered questions. Simply put, these are matters for the Legislature.

. . . Similarly, in *Medical Center Hospital of Vermont, Inc. v. City of Burlington*, 566 A.2d 1352 (1989), the Vermont Supreme Court, in rejecting the taxing authority's argument that the amount of free care dispensed must exceed revenues, concluded there was nothing in any Vermont case that required an institution to dispense *any* free care to qualify as charitable for purposes of the charitable property tax exemption. . . . The court declared: "In our opinion, pegging charitability to a stated amount of free care rendered would not be workable in determinating an organization's taxable status. Instead, uncertainty would reign. . . ." Rather, "[t]he better inquiry, it seems to us, is the one used by the trial court in this case: whether health care was made available by the plaintiff to all who needed it, regardless of their ability to pay." . . . "As plaintiff pointed out at trial, if the economy in the Burlington [VT] area were to fall off dramatically and unemployment to soar, fewer people would be covered by health care insurance through employers and, consequently, more free care would be rendered to those in need. Should the economy make a turnaround the following year, the amount of free care given might fall again should unemployment levels drop."

I find these authorities persuasive. . . .

Notes: The Basis for Health Care Tax Exemption

1. *The Benefits of Charitable Exemption.* "The voluntary [i.e., charitable nonprofit] hospital, like the government hospital, generally enjoys exemption from the federal income tax and from state and local property taxes. This has been true historically and it is true today. Any general repeal of the exemptions is most unlikely in the near future, despite the criticism of some respected authorities who see the exemptions as 'mindless subsidies' of the industry which could be carried out much more effectively in other ways. The complexities of current tax law are such, however, that even in a basically exempt industry the law impinges on many aspects of hospital operations and can be manipulated one way or another with resulting impact in hospital developments. It thus constitutes a de facto type of public regulation." A. Somers, Hospital Regulation: The Dilemma of Public Policy 38 (1969).

The requirements for maintaining tax exemption have such a strong influence because the financial stakes are so high. Hospitals own considerable real property that is subject to local property tax, and they generate a very high volume of revenues potentially subject to sales tax. Even "nonprofit" hospitals such as Provena often earn many millions of dollars a year, which would be subject to state and federal corporate income tax. Equally important, tax-exempt hospitals are eligible to use tax-exempt bond financing, which significantly lowers their capital costs. Perhaps the most obvious benefit of tax exemption — eligibility to receive tax-deductible gifts — is the least important since hospitals no longer rely substantially on donations.

2. *Unrelated Business Income.* A related concern is whether various activities of hospitals generate "unrelated business income." This is income from activities that are not connected with the hospital's exempt functions. The consequence of earning such income is not nearly so severe as finding private inurement. Usually, this merely results in an "unrelated business income tax" (UBIT) imposed only on that designated portion of income. IRC §§511-513. However, if unrelated income constitutes a "substantial portion" of the hospital's total operations, it can threaten the entire exemption. See, e.g., GCM 39684 (Sept. 28, 1984) (hospital subsidiary that provided purchasing and data processing services to nonexempt hospitals lost exemption because of "substantial, nonexempt commercial purpose").

The major decision applying the unrelated business income tax to hospital operations (which coincidentally comes from the same city as *Provena*) is Carle Foundation v. United States, 611 F.2d 1192 (7th Cir. 1980). It sets forth the general rule that income from nonhospital patients is unrelated to the institution's exempt function. Thus, for instance, a nonprofit hospital's pharmacy sales to outpatients are taxable, even if sold to patients of physicians on the medical staff with offices in the hospital's own building, because these are not hospital patients. The service exempts pharmacy and laboratory sales to nonpatients only in "unique circumstances" where the hospital is the only available source for the service to nonhospital patients. Rev. Rul. 85-110. Why is it necessary to define the hospital's exempt function so narrowly? Why not conceive of the hospital's purpose as providing health care services generally to the community at large? This seems to be another example of the IRS's antagonism toward physicians benefiting from the exemption.

3. *Charity Care vs. Community Benefit.* What do you think about the *Provena* dissent's argument that, even if hospitals no longer provide significant charity care,

it should be sufficient if they simply maintain an "open door" policy by which they accept anyone who seeks care, regardless of ability to pay? Consider the role physicians play in determining whether a patient is admitted to a hospital. Suppose a hospital does not require its physicians to accept charity cases.

The IRS further liberalized its free care policy in 1983, ruling that even free emergency services are unnecessary if an emergency room isn't needed in the community or if the hospital is a specialized one that offers limited treatment (e.g., eye hospitals or cancer hospitals). Rev. Rul. 83-187.

In a replay of the IRS's 1969 ruling, will states like Illinois change their position if national health care reform further reduces the need for charity care? In Dialysis Clinic, Inc. v. Levin, 938 N.E.2d 329 (Ohio 2010), the court held, over a dissent, that a dialysis clinic was not excused from having to show some level of charity care simply because almost all patients with kidney disease are covered by Medicare or Medicaid if they don't have private insurance.

The ACA requires tax-exempt hospitals to assess the health needs of their community, to report what community benefits they provide, and to have clear charity care policies that they publicize. It also prevents tax-exempt hospitals from charging low-income patients any more than the hospital receives from commercial insurers, and prohibits aggressive collection actions against patients who are eligible for the hospital's financial assistance policy. However, the ACA does not require hospitals to show any particular quantum of charity care or community benefit.

Prof. Jill Horwitz argues that hospitals need not provide more charity care than for-profits in order to justify tax exempt status. Instead, it suffices that they provide a broader range of services, including those that are not profitable. Jill R. Horwitz, Why We Need the Independent Sector: The Behavior, Law, and Ethics of Not-For-Profit Hospitals, 50 UCLA L. Rev. 1345 (2003). Professor Bloche argues that a charity care requirement is "deeply problematic" because it requires hospitals to fund the care for some patients by increasing charges to others. This "cost shifting" can be seen as an implicit form of "internal" taxation that is highly objectionable compared with a broad-based income tax: It is essentially a hidden tax on the sick that does a poor job of targeting resources to where they are most needed—preventive and primary care. M. Gregg Bloche, Health Policy Below the Waterline: Medical Care and the Charitable Exemption, 80 Minn. L. Rev. 299 (1995). True enough, tax exemption is not a good substitute for national health insurance, but do these imperfections justify excusing hospitals from any concrete obligation in exchange for the exemption? Other law professors argue for a looser test for exemption based on enhancing access to care in the community or promoting population health, or advancing religious missions, where this can be clearly documented. See note 8.

4. *Measuring Charity Care.* Following *Provena*, the Illinois revenue department denied exemption to several other hospitals, including Northwestern University's—causing a great stir from hospitals statewide, concerned that the new standards were too demanding or unclear. The state legislature responded in 2012 with a statute that requires hospitals to quantify that their charitable services equal or exceed what their state tax bill would have been but allows hospitals to count reimbursement shortfalls under Medicaid and from a range of essential services such as emergency rooms and burn units. A few other states have enacted similar laws requiring tax-exempt hospitals to document that the value of their charity care and other community benefits exceed either some set percentage of operations or

exceed the value of their tax exemption, but federal bills that would do the same have not advanced in Congress. However, the ACA requires tax-exempt hospitals to at least study community needs and report on how the hospital is helping to meet them.

Where states impose a charity care standard, they must next decide how to measure the amount and value of unreimbursed services. Hospitals attempt to measure this value in terms of their listed charges rather than actual costs, but these list prices are rarely charged in full to insurance companies. Sometimes, hospitals even try to count as free care these voluntary "contractual adjustments" with paying customers. See St. Margaret Seneca Place v. Board of Property Assessment, 640 A.2d 380 (Pa. 1994) (accepting this argument with respect to Medicaid payments to nursing home, but only to extent that payments were less than average costs). Do you agree with the *Provena* majority that hospitals should not be allowed to count their uncollectable accounts since this is no different than for-profit hospitals that write off their bad debts? According to one estimate, the amount of uncompensated care that nonprofit hospitals provide above and beyond what similar for-profits provide amounts to only a small fraction of the value of the charitable tax exemption. Congressional Budget Office, Nonprofit Hospitals and the Provision of Community Benefits (Dec. 2006).

5. *The Nonprofit Ethos.* Hospitals argue that the "community benefit" justification for exemption captured in the 1969 revenue ruling is warranted because nonprofit hospitals are inherently superior to their for-profit counterparts. The debate between the two hospital sectors has raged for decades, ever since large corporate chains began to acquire significant numbers of for-profit hospitals in the late 1970s. The seminal article is A. Relman, The New Medical-Industrial Complex, 303 New Eng. J. Med. 963 (1980), but the core issues go back even further, as one court explained:

> Because the "care of the sick" has traditionally been an activity regarded as charitable in American law, . . . we deem it important to scrutinize the contemporary social and economic context of such care. We are convinced that traditional assumptions bear little relationship to the economics of the medical-industrial complex of the 1980s. Nonprofit hospitals were traditionally treated as tax-exempt charitable institutions because, until late in the nineteenth century, they were true charities providing custodial care for those who were both sick and poor. The hospitals' income was derived largely or entirely from voluntary charitable donations, not government subsidies, taxes, or patient fees.[7] The function and status of hospitals began to change in the late nineteenth century; the transformation was substantially completed by the 1920s. "From charities, dependent on voluntary gifts, [hospitals]

---

7. Paul Starr, The Social Transformation of American Medicine 150 (1982). "Voluntary" hospitals, like public hospitals (which evolved from almshouses for the dependent poor), performed a "welfare" function rather than a medical or curing function: The poor were housed in large wards, largely cared for themselves, and often were not expected to recover. See id. at 145, 149, 160. Early voluntary hospitals had paternalistic, communal social structures in which patients entered at the sufferance of their benefactors, "had the moral status of children," and received more moralistic and religious help than medical treatment. Id. at 149, 158.

developed into market institutions financed increasingly out of payments from patients." The transformation was multidimensional: Hospitals were redefined from social welfare to medical treatment institutions; their charitable foundation was replaced by a business basis; and their orientation shifted to "professionals, and their patients," away from "patrons and the poor." . . .

Also of considerable significance . . . is the increasing irrelevance of the distinction between nonprofit and for-profit hospitals for purposes of discovering the element of charity in their operations. The literature indicates that two models, described below, appear to describe a large number of nonprofit hospitals as they function today. (1) The "physicians' cooperative" model describes nonprofit hospitals that operate primarily for the benefit of the participating physicians. Physicians, pursuant to this model, enjoy power and high income through their direct or indirect control over the nonprofit hospitals to which they bring their patients. The nonprofit form is believed to facilitate the control by physicians better than the for-profit form. Pauly & Redisch, The Not-For-Profit Hospital as a Physicians' Co-operative, 63 Am. Econ. Rev. 87, 88-89 (1973). This model has also been called the "exploitation hypothesis" because the physician "income maximizing" system is hidden behind the nonprofit facade of the hospital. Clark, Does the Nonprofit Form Fit the Hospital Industry?, 93 Harv. L. Rev. 1416, 1436-1437 (1980). . . . (2) The "polycorporate enterprise" model describes the increasing number of nonprofit hospital chains. Here, power is largely in the hands of administrators, not physicians. Through the creation of holding companies, nonprofit hospitals have grown into large groups of medical enterprises, containing both for-profit and nonprofit corporate entities. Nonprofit corporations can own for-profit corporations without losing their federal nonprofit tax status as long as the profits of the for-profit corporations are used to further the nonprofit purposes of the parent organization. . . . The emergence of hospital organizations with both for-profit and nonprofit components has increasingly destroyed the charitable pretentions of nonprofit organizations.

Utah County v. Intermountain Health Care, Inc., 709 P.2d 265 (Utah 1985). Documenting the court's observations, health policy researchers have produced an extensive body of empirical findings that fail to reveal any major differences in the cost or quality of care delivered by nonprofits and for-profits. See, e.g., Jill Marsteller et al., Nonprofit Conversion: Theory, Evidence, and State Policy Options, 33 Health Serv. Res. 1495 (1998); David Cutler ed., The Changing Hospital Industry (2000). Others, however, point to notable instances where profit motivation has run amok, such as Columbia/HCA, described at page 1299. The following exchange from a generation ago gives a glimpse of the still highly charged nature of this debate:

> Nonprofit hospitals . . . receive billions of dollars annually in subsidies from the rest of us taxpayers through various tax exemptions. Our research showed that nonprofit hospital chains did not provide benefits to society that justified this multibillion dollar gift. When compared with for-profits, the nonprofit hospital chains had the same prices and the same level of access for patients with no or low levels of health insurance. Moreover, they had higher costs, more employees, less efficient use of beds, and much older capital than for-profits. The net result was that the nonprofits performed less and cost much more—billions of dollars more!

Regina Herzlinger, An Author Replies, 65 Harv. Bus. Rev., Mar.–Apr. 1987, at 135, replying in support of Regina Herzlinger & William Krasker, Who Profits from Nonprofits?, 65 Harv. Bus. Rev., Jan.-Feb. 1987, at 93 (nonprofits "do more to maximize the welfare of the physicians who are their main consumers"). Uwe Reinhardt, a leading health economist, responded: "[T]his study is a truly shoddy statistical analysis. . . . The author's bias for privatization screams out from every page of the study. I'm concerned by the apparent attempt to propagate personal bias in the guise of science." N.Y. Times, Apr. 2, 1987, at 32, col. 3. A later round of this never-ending debate can be found in 25(4) Health Aff. W287 (June 2006).

Regardless of the evidence, nonprofit advocates claim that it is wrong to profit from people's medical misfortunes. Economists respond that the profit incentive is not inherently evil and may produce better service because it reacts more quickly and efficiently to consumer demands. But, absent any evidence that a systemic, material difference exists between the two hospital sectors, this debate turns to intangibles such as whether nonprofits promote a superior institutional ethos because they are devoted primarily to healing, not to generating profits. The danger of accepting this justification on faith is that even defenders of the exemption concede that "self-satisfaction and self-righteousness . . . is perhaps an occupational hazard" among nonprofit hospital administrators, who tend to "have an almost reflexive belief in the inherent superiority of voluntary health care." Id. at 4-5. Skeptics observe that hospital administrators respond more to where the money comes from than to abstract mission statements in corporate documents. At one time, nonprofits received substantial funding from donations, but now they rely almost entirely on public and private insurance, as well as borrowed capital. Because the sources of financing for both types of hospitals are nearly identical, many observers conclude that their administrative style and institutional ideology are virtually indistinguishable. Defenders of the community benefit standard respond by pointing to counterexamples such as Columbia/HCA, discussed at page 1299. They also encourage nonprofit hospitals to document their community responsiveness and social accountability by cataloguing their various public-spirited programs and activities, such as health education, free screenings, and other good works. Federal law now follows the lead of several statutes in requiring tax-exempt hospitals to conduct these community benefit assessments and file periodic reports. What do you think about the *Provena* majority's perspective that these are merely marketing devices to create good will among potential customers?

6. *What if You're Not a Hospital?* Both the federal government and the states are more demanding of *non*hospital health care enterprises. Both refuse tax exemption to physician practices. See, e.g., Covenant Healthcare System, Inc. v. City of Wauwatosa, 800 N.W.2d 906 (Wis. 2011). And clinics and nursing homes are regularly denied exemption based on a low volume of free care. Similarly, the IRS refused to give charitable status to a nonprofit pharmacy, claiming that the sale of prescriptions is too "inherently commercial" to qualify under the "promotion of health" standard. Federal Pharmacy Service v. Commissioner, 625 F.2d 804 (8th Cir. 1980). Is there any reason to distinguish between the charitable status of inpatient versus outpatient health care services, hospital versus other institutional services, or surgery versus medication?

Both states and the federal government are also distinctly hostile toward extending the charitable exemption to physician groups. Under the modern rationale for hospital exemption, is there any justification for this distinction either? The IRS's position is that physicians would personally benefit too much if their professional corporations were exempt, in violation of the private inurement and private benefit prohibitions discussed in the following readings. Reluctantly, the IRS is willing, however, to exempt medical school faculty groups and very large and prestigious physician groups such as the Mayo Clinic that run a hospital, conduct medical research, and set physician salaries through a somewhat independent governance process. See D. Bromberg, The Tax-Exempt Clinic, 8 Exempt Org. Tax Rev. 557 (1993).

7. *HMO and ACO Exemption.* Equally controversial is whether HMOs or ACOs qualify for charitable tax exemption. The materials above cite state court opinions on either side of the HMO question. Federal tax policy is somewhat confusing. For ACOs, the IRS has ruled that those participating in Medicare's "shared savings program" are eligible for exemption, but not if the ACO serves only commercial insurers, since doing only that lacks sufficient public benefit. See IRS Public Letter Ruling 201615022.

For HMOs to be tax exempt, the IRS requires them to offer open enrollment and community rating, discounted fees for low-income subscribers, and support for research and education. For a time, it was thought that these attributes were sufficient for all HMOs, based on a Tax Court decision, Sound Health Ass'n v. Commissioner, 71 T.C. 158 (1978), but a subsequent court decision drew a different line. In Geisinger Health Plan v. Commissioner, 985 F.2d 1210 (3d Cir. 1993), the court found that these factors were not sufficient for an HMO that it incorrectly classified as an IPA. (It was actually a group or network model, one that resembles a staff model except that it contracts with full-time physicians rather than employs them.) The court's major concern was that contracting for, rather than directly providing, medical services is not a charitable purpose, even though the contracting parties were part of a hospital system each of whose other components is tax exempt.[4] Does this make sense to you? It is an apparent attempt to draw some distinction between HMOs that are more like hospitals, and those that are more like ordinary insurance. Nonprofit health insurers like Blue Cross lost their exemption by virtue of a 1986 statutory enactment, §501(m). To preserve some meaningful distinction between Blue Cross and HMOs, the HMO exemption appears limited to staff model HMOs, which retain physicians full-time and own their own hospitals.

This position was affirmed by the Tenth Circuit in a case where the IRS revoked the exemption for an HMO owned by a tax-exempt hospital because, following *Geisinger*, the HMO did not operate its own medical facilities. The court ruled that "an organization cannot satisfy the community benefit requirement based solely on the fact that it offers health care services to all in the community in exchange for a fee. . . . Rather, the organization must provide some additional 'plus.'" First on the list of these "pluses" was "free or below-cost services," though the court acknowledged that "devoting surpluses to research, education and medical training" might also suffice. IHC Health Plans v. Commissioner of Internal Revenue, 325 F. 3d 1188 (10th Cir. 2003).

Commenting on this decision, Prof. Colombo says: "What the heck is going on here? . . . The only answer I have been able to come up with is that sometime after

---

4. The court also reasoned that extending free services and discounted membership to subscribers was not the same as serving the community at large, even though membership was open to the community at large.

issuing Rev. Rul. 69-545, folks at the Service realized that there were an awful lot of businesses that 'promote health' in this country by providing services or goods at a fee to anyone who can pay. . . . But instead of simply admitting that Rev. Rul. 69-545 was a well-meaning mistake and then revoking it (or limiting it to acute-care hospitals only), the Service embarked on what now is a 20-year struggle to find alternative means of limiting the scope of Rev. Rul. 69-545 while pretending that it still governs tax exemption for all health care providers. The Service's war on HMOs is one example of this struggle." John Colombo, The IHC Cases: A Catch-22 for Integral Part Doctrine, A Requiem for Rev. Rul. 69-545, 34 Exempt Org. Tax Rev. 401 (2001). See also John D. Colombo, The Failure of Community Benefit, 15 Health Matrix 29 (2005).

Are there any reasons that health policy and law might want to favor nonprofit HMOs or ACOs? Are the distinctions the IRS draws sensitive to these reasons? The loss of tax exemption is one reason given by many Blue Cross plans for converting to for-profit status in recent years. See page 1302.

To complicate matters even further (if that's possible), HMOs can still qualify for a lesser form of charitable exemption under §501(c)(4) for "social welfare" organizations. The major difference is that entities under this form of exemption are not eligible to receive tax-exempt donations or tax-exempt bond financing. However, nonprofit indemnity insurers like Blue Cross are not eligible for even this lesser status. Again, there is no easily discernible logic to this pattern. See generally Loren Rosenzweig, *Geisinger*, HMOs and Health Care Reform, 72 Taxes 20 (1994); Symposium, 9 Exempt Org. Tax Rev. 271 (1994).

8. *Further Readings.* For analysis and critique of the **federal position on hospital tax exemption**, see Mark Hall & John Colombo, The Charitable Status of Nonprofit Hospitals: Toward a Donative Theory of Tax Exemption, 66 Wash. L. Rev. 307 (1991); Jack E. Karns, Justifying the Nonprofit Hospital Tax Exemption in a Competitive Market Environment, 13 Widener L. J. 383 (2004); Comment, 20 Rev. Litig. 709 (2001); Symposium, 15 Health Matrix 5 (2005); Symposium, 25(4) Health Aff. w287 (Aug. 2006).

On **community benefits** (note 3), see John Colombo, The Role of Access in Charitable Tax Exemption, 82 Wash. U. L.Q. 343 (2004); Jessica Berg, Putting the Community Back into the "Community Benefit" Standard, 44 Ga. L. Rev. 375 (2010); Michael J. DeBoer, Religious Hospitals and the Federal Community Benefit Standard, 42 Seton Hall L. Rev. 1549 (2012); Mary Crossley, Health and Taxes: Hospitals, Community Health and the IRS, 16 Yale J. Health Pol'y L. 51 (2016); Dan Diamond, How Hospitals Got Richer off Obamacare, Politico, July 17, 2017.

On **charity care** (note 4), see Sayeh Nikpay & John Ayanian, Hospital Charity Care: Effects of New Community-Benefit Requirements, 373 New Eng. J. Med. 1687 (2015); Nancy M. Kane & William Wubbenhorst, Alternative Funding Policies for the Uninsured: Exploring the Value of Hospital Tax Exemption, 78 Milbank Q. 185 (2000); John Colombo, Federal and State Tax Exemption Policy, Medical Debt and Healthcare for the Poor, 51 St. Louis U. L. J. 433 (2007).

Regarding whether **nonprofits are superior** (note 5), see Horowitz, supra, 50 UCLA L. Rev. 1345 (2003); Daniel Fox, Policy Commercializing Nonprofits in Health: The History of a Paradox, 93 Milbank Q. 179 (2015); Kathleen Boozang & Tim Greaney, Mission, Margin and Trust in the Nonprofit Healthcare Enterprise, 5 Yale J. Health Pol'y L. & Ethics 1 (2005); Eleanor D. Kinney, For Profit Enterprise in

Health care: Can it Contribute to Health Reform?, 36 Am. J. L. & Med. 405 (2010); George Nation, Non-Profit Charitable Tax-Exempt Hospitals: Wolves in Sheep's Clothing, 42 Rutgers L. Rev. 141 (2010); David Cutler ed., The Changing Hospital Industry (2000).

On **exemption for physicians** (note 6), see John Colombo, Are Associations of Doctors Tax Exempt? Analyzing Inconsistencies in the Tax Exemption of Health Care Providers, 9 Va. Tax Rev. 469 (1990); Kenneth Levine, Obtaining 501(c)(3) Status for Professional Medical Corporations, 2 DePaul J. Health Care L. 231 (1998).

The following books cover **health care tax exemption generally** under both federal and state law: John D. Colombo et al., Charity Care for Nonprofit Hospitals (2010); T. Hyatt & B. Hopkins, The Law of Tax-Exempt Healthcare Organizations (2d ed. 2004); Douglas Mancino, Taxation of Hospitals and Health Care Organizations (2d ed. 2005). Federal tax law is further discussed in the sources cited throughout these notes. A very good general treatise is F. Hill & D. Mancino, Taxation of Exempt Organizations (2002). The best practitioner journal is the Exempt Organization Tax Review. For a broad overview of multiple issues, see David Studdert et al., Regulatory and Judicial Oversight of Nonprofit Hospitals, 356 New Eng. J. Med. 625 (2007).

■ HARDING HOSPITAL, INC. v. UNITED STATES
505 F.2d 1068 (6th Cir. 1974)

PHILLIPS, Chief Judge.

The sole issue presented in this appeal is whether Harding Hospital, Inc. (the Hospital) qualified under 501(c)(3) of the Internal Revenue Code of 1954 as an organization exempt from federal income taxes. . . .

The Hospital, a nationally recognized psychiatric institution, treats mental and nervous diseases. It utilizes a method of treatment known as milieu therapy in which a patient's total environment is controlled on an around-the-clock basis and structured toward rehabilitation.

The Hospital was originally a corporation for profit. In December 1961, its articles of incorporation were amended to adopt its present name and to qualify under Ohio law as a corporation not for profit. . . . Before amending its articles of incorporation, the Hospital had a contract with a medical partnership composed of seven doctors. This medical partnership performed all the psychiatric treatment on 90 to 95 percent of the patients admitted to the Hospital. Immediately after the Hospital's change in status in 1962, the medical partnership was incorporated as the Harding-Evans Medical Associates, Inc. (the Associates).

Starting in 1962, and for the years in question, the Hospital entered into contracts with the Associates whereby the Associates provided medical supervision in the Hospital, teaching and supervision in the residency and other training programs, and medical service to the Hospital's indigent patients without a charge or at a reduced rate. For these services, the Hospital paid the Associates an annual amount of $25,000. This amount was raised to $35,000 as of July 1, 1968. Further, the agreement provided that the Associates were to pay the Hospital $1,000 per month as rental for facilities, equipment and business office services. This rental was increased to $35,000 per year as of January 1, 1965. It subsequently was lowered to $15,000 per year as of July 1, 1968, at the same time that the amount which the Hospital paid the Associates for medical supervision was increased from $25,000 to $35,000.

Since 1963, individuals not connected with the Associates have constituted a majority of the Board of Trustees of the Hospital. During the years in question, the Board consisted of nine members, only two of whom had any connection with the Associates of the Hospital prior to the 1961 reorganization.

The Harding-Evans Foundation (the Foundation) was set up in 1959 and is an entity separate from the Hospital and the Associates. The Foundation is a tax exempt organization, the principal activity of which is to provide a residency program in the field of psychiatry for the physicians. The Foundation collects charitable funds and expends them on the residency training program at the Hospital. . . .

Section 501(a) of the Code provides that the following organizations, which are listed in §501(c)(3), are exempt from federal income taxation:

> Corporations . . . organized and operated exclusively for religious, charitable, scientific, testing for public safety, literary, or educational purposes, or for the prevention of cruelty to children or animals, no part of the net earnings of which inures to the benefit of any private shareholder or individual, no substantial part of the activities of which is carrying on propaganda, or otherwise attempting, to influence legislation, and which does not participate in, or intervene in (including the publishing or distributing of statements), any political campaign on behalf of any candidate for public office.

In the context of the present case, this section essentially imposes three requirements for exemption: (1) the corporation must be organized and operated exclusively for charitable purposes; (2) no part of its net earnings may inure to the benefit of a private individual or shareholder; and (3) it cannot engage in certain lobbying and political activities. The government stipulated that the Hospital did not offend the third requirement for exemption. . . . [W]e proceed to determine if the district court was correct in holding that the Hospital "was operated almost exclusively for the benefit of the members of the . . . Associates and was not operated exclusively for charitable purposes." . . .

Based on the five factors set forth below, we hold that the Hospital was not entitled to tax exemption under §501(c)(3) during the years in question. We do not single out any one or combination of these factors as the consideration crucial to our holding. We conclude only that all these factors, as they occurred in the aggregate in this case, require denying the appellant Hospital the tax exemption for the years in question. . . .

(1) and (2) [The court observed that the hospital received virtually no charitable donations], and did not have a specific plan or policy for the treatment of charity patients during the years in question. . . . [P]ractically all patients presented themselves as paying patients and only when their funds were exhausted did the Hospital treat them on a charitable basis.

(3) Since the doctors who were members of the Associates treated between 90 and 95 percent of the patients admitted to the Hospital, they derived substantial benefit from the existence and operation of the Hospital. This was the primary source of the doctors' professional income. Although the Hospital did not pay over

any of its net earnings to the Associates, except for the annual sum for supervision, this virtual monopoly by the Associates of the patients permitted benefits to inure to the Associates within the intendment of the statute. Sonora Community Hospital, supra, 46 T.C. at 526.

(4) Associates also benefitted from the agreement with the Hospital whereby the Associates paid $35,000 annually as rental for office space, equipment, and business office services. See the fourth requirement of Rev. Rul. 56-185. The $35,000 amount was reduced to $15,000 as of July 1, 1968. . . .

The Hospital introduced the testimony of an appraiser who indicated, in sum, that the $35,000 figure was a fair rental for the office space. That essentially meant that the Associates were not adequately compensating the Hospital for the use of the equipment and business office services (including secretarial assistance). Further, when the annual rental was reduced to $15,000, the Associates were not adequately compensating the Hospital for office space alone.

(5) The Associates also received a private benefit from the agreement whereby the Hospital paid an annual sum of either $25,000 or $35,000 to the Associates for hospital supervision. . . .

On the basis of these five factors, the judgment of the district court is affirmed.

■ HOSPITAL-PHYSICIAN JOINT VENTURES
General Counsel Memorandum [GCM] 39862 (Dec. 2, 1991)

ISSUE

Whether a hospital, tax exempt because it is described in §501(c)(3), jeopardizes its exempt status by forming a joint venture with members of its medical staff and selling to the joint venture the gross or net revenue stream derived from operation of an existing hospital department or service for a defined period of time. . . .

FACTS

[The memorandum describes several hospital/physician joint ventures that all resemble the following example:] "Z-Hospital" proposed to establish a for-profit stock corporation for certain purposes that would be jointly owned in equal shares by the hospital and physicians on its medical staff. The new corporation would in turn establish and serve as the general partner in four limited partnerships (Z-LPs). The Z-LPs were to be formed to allow medical staff physician participation in the operation of four Z-Hospital outpatient departments. The four departments, Outpatient Surgery, Outpatient Diagnostic (CT Scan, Ultrasound, etc.), Ophthalmology, and Cardiac Nuclear Medicine, represented in the aggregate about 4 percent of Z-Hospital's gross revenues.

Z-Hospital stated that it would "in effect, lease the individual departments for a limited time period to the limited partnership[s]." Apparently, the Z-LPs would pay Z-Hospital an actuarially established price (discounted to present value) for the revenue stream of each of the subject departments. In addition, the Z-LPs would pay Z-Hospital a fee for managing the facilities and reimburse the hospital for all fixed and variable costs incurred in operating the departments. [In other words, the hospital would continue to own the equipment and deliver and bill for the services, but all the money would flow through the LPs. They would pay the hospital for its existing revenue stream and reimburse the hospital for actual expenses, but they would keep any remaining revenues.] Thus, according to the hospital, physician-investors would benefit only if utilization of the facilities increased because, in effect, they shared only in profits over and above the level the hospital already received.

Z-Hospital represented that it would retain, through its interest in the for-profit corporation, an interest in each Z-LP. Fifty percent of each Z-LP would be held by the corporation and 50 percent sold to medical staff physicians [for $5,000 each]. Z-Hospital also stated that it would retain actual control of the facilities through a management agreement, and that it alone would determine the rates charged patients for services in those facilities.

The stated reason for the proposed transactions was to maintain or increase utilization of Z-Hospital's various services, both inpatient and outpatient, so that it could provide the highest level of service at the lowest price to the public. Z-Hospital told the Service that, if it carried out the transactions, its utilization rate (then 65 percent) would be maintained or increased rather than experiencing a decline. At conference, Z-Hospital's chief financial officer predicted significant adverse effects if the hospital did nothing. The hospital was located in an overbedded service area and faced competition from two nearby hospitals, one for-profit, the other non-profit. It also faced potential competition from a private physician who was planning to develop free-standing outpatient facilities to be jointly owned with other doctors. Z-Hospital argued that failure to undertake the proposed transaction would raise a probability that it would be unable to continue providing the same high level of service to the community so, it reasoned, the transaction should be viewed as furthering its charitable purposes.

Z-Hospital maintained that the ventures would help it by creating incentives for medical staff physicians to increase inpatient admissions. The ventures would also create incentives for medical staff physicians to increase referrals to ancillary departments. These factors, combined with a feared loss of outpatient department business to competitors if the ventures were not undertaken, led the hospital to believe it would be better off by proceeding than by not doing so. . . .

ANALYSIS

The joint venture arrangements described above are just one variety of an increasingly common type of competitive behavior engaged in by hospitals in response to significant changes in their operating environment. Many medical and surgical procedures once requiring inpatient care, still the exclusive province of hospitals, now are performed on an outpatient basis, where every private physician is a potential competitor. The marked shift in governmental policy from regulatory cost controls to competition has fundamentally changed the way all hospitals, for-profit and not, do business.

A driving force behind the new hospital operating environment was the federal Medicare Program's 1983 shift from cost-based reimbursement for covered inpatient hospital services to fixed, per-case, prospective payments. This change to a diagnosis-related prospective payment system (PPS) dramatically altered hospital financial incentives. . . . Hospitals realized that, in addition to attracting more patients, they needed to control utilization of ancillary hospital services, discharge

Medicare beneficiaries as quickly as is medically appropriate, and operate more efficiently. . . . Once hospital and physician economic incentives diverged, hospitals began seeking ways to stimulate loyalty among members of their medical staffs and to encourage or reward physician behaviors deemed desirable. . . . Since most medical staff physicians are not hospital employees, and typically do not provide services to or receive direct compensation from the hospitals at which they practice, managers have had to look for innovative ways to influence their behavior. . . .

Whenever a charitable organization engages in unusual financial transactions with private parties, the arrangements must be evaluated in light of applicable tax law and other legal standards. . . . We believe the transactions described above cannot withstand such scrutiny. . . . [T]hese transactions must be viewed as jeopardizing a hospital's tax exempt status for three reasons: they allow inurement of part of a charitable organization's net earnings to the benefit of private individuals; they confer more than incidental benefits on private interests; and they may well violate federal law [prohibiting referral fees. Only the first] of these reasons is discussed below. . . .

[Section 501(c)(3)] describes as charitable only an organization "no part of the net earnings of which inures to the benefit of any private shareholder or individual." . . . Violations of this prohibition are commonly referred to as private inurement, or simply, inurement.

Protecting charitable organizations against private inurement serves important purposes. A charitable organization is viewed under the common law and the Internal Revenue Code as a trust whose assets must irrevocably be dedicated to achieving charitable purposes. The inurement prohibition serves to prevent anyone in a position to do so from siphoning off any of a charity's income or assets for personal use.

The proscription against inurement generally applies to a distinct class of private interests—typically persons who, because of their particular relationship with an organization, have an opportunity to control or influence its activities. . . . While most physicians on the medical staffs of the subject hospitals presumably are not employees and do not provide any compensable services directly to the hospitals, they do have a close professional working relationship with the hospitals.[8] . . . Individually, and as a group, they largely control the flow of patients to and from the hospital and patients' utilization of hospital services while there. . . .

Even though medical staff physicians are subject to the inurement proscription, that does not mean there can be no economic dealings between them and the hospitals. The inurement proscription does not prevent the payment of reasonable compensation for goods or services. It is aimed at preventing dividend-like distributions of charitable assets or expenditures to benefit a private interest. . . . Rev. Rul. 69-383, 1969-2 C.B. 113. In that ruling, the Service approved payment to a hospital-based

---

8. When considering hospital-physician relationships, the Service should be aware that many . . . "hospital based" physicians, notably radiologists, anesthesiologists, pathologists, medical residents, and some emergency room physicians typically are employees or contractors paid by the hospital. . . . Some states have laws . . . [that] restrict hospitals' ability to employ physicians to render professional services to patients. For federal employment tax purposes, however, physicians may be classified as hospital employees notwithstanding such laws.

radiologist of a percentage of the adjusted gross revenues from the radiology department in return for management and professional services. . . . Unlike the instant cases, the hospital in Rev. Rul. 69-383 was billing (presumably on a global charge basis) and collecting for the radiologist's professional services, as well as its own facility charge. Thus, the percentage compensation at issue represented an allocation of a portion of the global charge (referred to as the "professional component") to the physician to compensate him for his services. The hospital retained the remainder (the "technical" or "facility component") as compensation for use of its facilities and equipment. This type of arrangement was typical for pathology and radiology departments prior to the 1982 enactment of changes affecting Medicare reimbursement for hospital-based physicians. See Mancino, Nonexempt Uses of Tax-Exempt Hospital Bonds, 24 J. Health & Hospital Law 73, 79-80 (1991). Due to Medicare changes, the typical arrangement today provides for even hospital-based physicians to bill separately for their professional services, while the hospital bills separately for the technical component. Thus, while never revoked, Rev. Rul. 69-383 has little relevance to most hospital-physician relationships today, including the instant cases. In these cases, only hospital revenues derived from the technical or facility component are at issue.

Even while approving the specific arrangement in Rev. Rul. 69-383, the Service cautioned that the presence of a percentage compensation arrangement will destroy the organization's exemption where it transforms the principal activity of the organization into a joint venture between it and a group of physicians or is merely a device for distributing profits to persons in control. Also, it is equally clear that, if salaries or total compensation are not reasonable, they will result in inurement. . . . There is no de minimis exception to the inurement prohibition. . . . See also Lowry Hosp. Ass'n v. Commissioner, 66 T.C. 850 (1976) (use of hospital's funds to make substantial unsecured loans to nursing home owned by hospital's founding physician inured to his benefit). . . .

The proper starting point for our analysis of the net revenue stream arrangements is to ask what the hospital gets in return for the benefit conferred on the physician-investors. Put another way, we ask whether and how engaging in the transaction furthers the hospital's exempt purposes. Here, there appears to be little accomplished that directly furthers the hospitals' charitable purposes of promoting health. No expansion of health care resources results; no new provider is created. No improvement in treatment modalities or reduction in cost is foreseeable. We have to look very carefully for any reason why a hospital would want to engage in this sort of arrangement. . . .

Whether admitted or not, we believe the hospitals engaged in these ventures largely as a means to retain and reward members of their medical staffs; to attract their admissions and referrals; and to preempt the physicians from investing in or creating a competing provider. Even putting aside any legality issues [under Medicare fraud and abuse laws], . . . the structure of these transactions is problematic. Giving (or selling) medical staff physicians a proprietary interest in the net profits of a hospital under these circumstances creates a result that is indistinguishable from paying dividends on stock. . . . We do not mean to suggest that a §501(c)(3) hospital cannot have an appropriately structured incentive compensation plan for employees in which profits are a factor in the compensation formula. . . .

Another key principle in the law of tax exempt organizations is that an entity is not organized and operated exclusively for exempt purposes unless it serves a public rather than a private interest. Thus, in order to be exempt, an organization must establish that it is not organized or operated for the benefit of private interests such as designated individuals, the creator or his family, shareholders of the organization, or persons controlled, directly or indirectly, by such private interests. However, this private benefit prohibition applies to all kinds of persons and groups, not just to those "insiders" subject to the more strict inurement proscription. . . . Any private benefit arising from a particular activity must be "incidental" in both a qualitative and quantitative sense to the overall public benefit achieved by the activity if the organization is to remain exempt. . . . Such benefits might also be characterized as indirect or unintentional. . . .

In our view, some private benefit is present in all typical hospital-physician relationships. Physicians generally use hospital facilities at no cost to themselves to provide services to private patients for which they earn a fee. The private benefit accruing to the physicians generally can be considered incidental to the overwhelming public benefit resulting from having the combined resources of the hospital and its professional staff available to serve the public. . . . In contrast, the private benefits conferred on the physician-investors by the instant revenue stream joint ventures are direct and substantial, not incidental. . . .

Similar issues and arguments were considered in GCM 37789. There, a tax exempt hospital proposed to lease to certain members of its medical staff land adjacent to the hospital upon which the physicians would construct a medical office building. The agreement called for below market rent (99 years at one dollar per year), and the hospital also proposed to lend the physicians a portion of the construction costs on fair market terms. This Office determined that a more than incidental private benefit would flow to the physicians from the below market rental and that the hospital should lose its exemption if it entered into the transaction. . . .

Thus far, our discussion has focused principally on the sales of the revenue streams involved in the instant arrangements. We also need to address the joint venture aspect. This area of the law has undergone significant change over the last decade. In Plumstead Theatre Soc'y, Inc. v. Commissioner, 74 T.C. 1324 (1980), aff'd, 675 F.2d 244 (9th Cir. 1982), the Tax Court disagreed with the Service's earlier stand [that opposed] charitable organization participation as a general partner in a limited partnership. . . . The Service no longer contends that participation as a general partner in a partnership is per se inconsistent with exemption. . . . However, close scrutiny is necessary to ensure that the obligations of the exempt organization as general partner do not conflict with its ability to pursue exclusively charitable goals. Thus, in all partnership cases, the initial focus should be on whether the joint venture organization furthers a charitable purpose. . . . This requires a finding that the benefits received by the limited partners are incidental to the public purposes served by the partnership. Hospital participation in a joint venture is inconsistent with exemption, then, if it does not further a charitable purpose or if there is inadequate protection against financial loss by the hospital or improper financial gain by the physician-investors. See [GCM 39005 (Dec. 17, 1982)]; GCM 39444 (July 18, 1985); GCM 39546 (Aug. 14, 1986). . . .

GCM 39732 considered three cases in which hospitals or affiliated exempt organizations participated as general partners in joint ventures with medical staff physicians to establish (1) a free-standing physical therapy center, (2) a free-standing ambulatory surgery center, and (3) a magnetic resonance imaging facility. . . .

[W]e concluded that participation in the partnerships (and activities) in question furthered their exempt purposes. In each case, a new health care provider or resource was made available to the community. Also, the joint venture entity itself actually became the property owner or service provider, subject to all the attendant risks, responsibilities, and potential rewards.

In the instant cases, we have moved from joint venture ownership of property and operation of an activity typically viewed as promoting the health of the community to a shell type of arrangement where the hospital continues to own and operate the facilities in question and the joint venture invests only in a profits interest. These arrangements, despite the joint venture cloak, are merely an arrangement between an exempt hospital and its medical staff physicians through which the hospital shares its net profits from designated activities with the physicians. The partnership's only true function is to purchase, receive, and distribute the net revenue stream from the activity. A hospital's participation in this type of partnership does not clearly further any exempt purpose.

In each of the cases at issue, the hospital has stated that its reasons for participating in the joint venture were to maintain or enhance utilization of its facilities. . . . In our view, there are a fixed number of individuals in a community legitimately needing hospital services at any one time. Paying doctors to steer patients to one particular hospital merely to improve its efficiency seems distant from a mission of providing needed care. We question whether the Service should ever recognize enhancing a hospital's market share vis-á-vis other providers, in and of itself, as furthering a charitable purpose. In many cases, doing so might hamper another charitable hospital's ability to promote the health of the same community. . . .

In addition, . . . the instant arrangements are distinguishable from the medical office building fact pattern in Rev. Rul. 69-464, 1969-2 C.B. 132. In that ruling, the Service recognized that leasing of office space adjacent to a hospital to members of the medical staff under the circumstances described furthers the hospital's exempt purposes by (1) increasing its efficiency, (2) encouraging fuller utilization of its facilities, and (3) improving the overall quality of its patient care. The hospital established that having members of the medical staff practicing next door would result in greater use being made of its diagnostic facilities, implying that attracting business may have been one reason for the arrangement. . . . Of course, the analysis would be completely different if, as in GCM 37789, the physicians paid below fair market rent. In the instant cases, the arrangements do not appear to result in improved patient convenience, greater accessibility of physicians, or any other direct benefit to the community. . . .

[In conclusion,] . . . participation in the subject net revenue stream purchase joint ventures is inconsistent with a hospital's continued exemption as a charitable organization. . . . Depending on the facts, revocation of the hospital's exemption might well be appropriate in such cases.

Notes: Private Inurement and Joint Ventures

1. *The Consequence of Private Inurement.* Finding private inurement can be fatal to tax exemption. Not only is the specific venture taxable, but the hospital's entire exemption can be revoked retroactive to the initiation of the venture. In the past,

the "nuclear bomb" of complete revocation was the only enforcement measure the IRS could employ. The IRS is now authorized, however, to impose "intermediate sanctions" such as a fine proportionate to the size of the venture or the degree of inurement. As a consequence, IRS enforcement of compensation, joint ventures, and conflicts of interest has greatly intensified. It now issues a virtual code of conduct that nonprofit entities must comply with or pay a series of graduated penalties. See IRC §4958; Hill & Kirschten, Federal and State Taxation of Exempt Organizations ¶2.03[3][f].

2. *Private Benefit.* Observe the differences noted in the General Counsel Memorandum (GCM) between the private inurement prohibition and the requirement that charities not operate for the private benefit of any individual. The private benefit proscription does not require monetary payment, it is not limited to "insiders," but it does have a de minimis exception. *Harding Hospital* gives one prime example of private benefit: a hospital that does not open its medical staff to all physicians in the community. The other examples—below-market office space rental, and excess compensation for administrative services—might be classified as either private inurement or private benefit.

3. *Physician Recruitment.* If it is impermissible for hospitals to secure the loyalty of their *existing* medical staff members, can they devise various incentives to attract *new* staff members? Generally, the answer to that is also no, unless the hospital is in an underserved area (such as an inner city or a remote rural setting) where it is difficult to recruit physicians. Then, if the hospital can show a need for the particular physician, the IRS has approved a list of limited recruitment incentives to assist with the transitional costs of moving and setting up a new practice. Examples include income guarantees, office support, subsidized malpractice insurance, and loan guarantees. Hermann Hospital Closing Agreement, *reprinted in* 3 BNA Health L. Rep. 1519 (1994); Rev. Rul. 97-21 (1997).

4. *Whole Hospital vs. Ancillary Joint Ventures.* The gist of the GCM appears to be that joint ventures that create new facilities may be permissible, but not those that merely reallocate revenue streams from existing operations. What if a hospital were to shift its entire operation over to a for-profit entity? At first glance, it would seem to be a foregone conclusion that this is impermissible. However, careful lawyering can do wonders in this arena. Using a vehicle known as a "whole hospital" joint venture, some for-profit hospital companies like Hospital Corporation of America (HCA, which was formerly Columbia) have been able to acquire management of nonprofit hospitals without sacrificing their tax exemption. The nonprofit entity contributes all its operating assets, including the hospital, to the joint venture, which it jointly owns, in exchange for a lump sum of money from the for-profit company. The joint venture then hires a management firm to run the hospital. In Rev. Rul. 98-15, the IRS ruled that the original nonprofit entity will retain its tax exemption if (1) it has majority control of the joint venture, (2) the agreement imposes specific operational requirements necessary to ensure that the hospital will continue meeting the community benefits test for charitable purpose, and (3) the management contract is with a firm that is unrelated to the for-profit party.

In St. David's Health Care System v. United States, 349 F.3d 232 (5th Cir. 2003), the court found that a fact issue existed over whether a nonprofit hospital had ceded operational management to HCA. The court rejected the trial court's summary judgment ruling that the particular agreement adequately protected the board's control over the hospital's charitable purpose, noting that the hospital had only a 50 percent share of the voting control over the joint venture and that the manager was paid a percentage of net revenues, which creates an incentive to maximize profits. On remand, however, the trial court found that the nonprofit hospital board did retain sufficient control because it had an "escape clause" that allowed it to back out if the management firm did not pursue charitable purposes adequately. For commentary, see Gary J. Young, Federal Tax-Exemption Requirements for Joint Ventures Between Nonprofit Hospital Providers and For-Profit Entities, 13 Ann. Health L. 327 (2004).

Although this ruling is permissive with respect to whole hospital joint ventures, the ruling raised concerns among hospital lawyers that some or all of its requirements will affect other, more traditional, joint ventures such as constructing a medical office building, or opening a satellite clinic. See Gerald Griffith, Revenue Ruling 98-15: Dimming the Future of All Nonprofit Joint Ventures?, 31 J. Health & Hosp. L. 71 (1998). For instance, in Redlands Surgical Services v. Commissioner, 113 T.C. No. 3 (July 17, 1999), aff'd per curiam, 242 F.3d 904 (9th Cir. 2001), the Tax Court applied this ruling to deny exemption to a nonprofit entity formed by an exempt hospital to purchase an outpatient surgery center. The center was purchased through a joint venture between the exempt hospital and an unrelated for-profit company that owns surgical centers across the country. The Tax Court found the absence of a charitable purpose, and an unallowable level of private benefit, because the joint venture agreement gave complete operational control to the for-profit chain, and the surgery center provided no free care to indigents and had only a minuscule amount of Medicaid business. (The lengthy full opinion in this case is well worth reading for the detail it gives about the corporate and contractual documents and entities used to form joint ventures of this sort.)

In analyzing these situations, it is important to clarify what the main issue is. Usually, the issue is *not* whether the venture *itself* is exempt, since usually it clearly is not. Rather, it is whether the nonprofit's participation in a for-profit venture jeopardizes the nonprofit's exemption. *Redlands Surgical* is an unusual case that attempts to, but fails to, obtain exemption for the joint venture. No one suggested the joint venture might threaten the hospital parent's core exemption. As long as the joint venture is ancillary to a hospital's main activity, lawyers assume that the IRS will continue to allow an exempt hospital to put a portion of its assets at risk for legitimate purposes, even if the hospital does not retain full control of the venture's operations. See generally John D. Colombo, A Framework for Analyzing Exemption and UBIT Effects of Joint Ventures, 34 Exempt Org. Tax Rev. 187 (2001).

Notes: Hospital Reorganization and Integrated Delivery Systems

1. *Holding Companies.*

For most of this century, the legal structure of the hospital was uncomplicated. Most hospitals were operated as single nonprofit organizations or, perhaps, as public corporations. As health care delivery has become more complex, however, so have the corporate structures of health care institutions. . . .

The holding company structure is usually the result of a reorganization of a single hospital corporation into a group of affiliated corporations. The resulting corporations typically include a parent holding company, a hospital subsidiary and additional subsidiaries from which other components of the reorganized health care "system" are operated—components such as outpatient facilities, or real estate holdings. . . .

Complex hospital corporate structures are a relatively recent phenomenon. Hospital reorganizations began in the 1970s and were widespread by the early 1980s. The typical restructuring involved a freestanding hospital operated through a single, usually nonprofit, corporation. The reorganization resulted in the replacement of this simple corporate structure with a "parent holding company" controlling one or more operating subsidiaries, including a hospital subsidiary. As a result of this reorganization movement, few hospitals currently operate as stand-alone corporations without the benefit of a corporate parent, a so-called sister affiliate or a subsidiary.

The earliest hospital reorganizations were motivated primarily by Medicare reimbursement incentives. Prior to the adoption of the prospective payment system (PPS) . . . [r]eorganizing the hospital along the lines of the "parent holding company" model provided a number of different reimbursement advantages. . . . As part of a corporate reorganization, departments with low Medicare usage could be placed into separate corporations, leaving the bulk of hospital overhead costs to be allocated only among the Medicare-intensive departments that remained within the primary hospital corporation. Putting the low-usage activities in legally separate entities was thought to make it more difficult for the Medicare program to succeed in challenging overhead allocations. Separate incorporation of different components of hospital operations could also be used to avoid interest income offsets, to avoid provider cost limits, or, possibly, to obtain charge-based (as opposed to cost-based) reimbursement for certain services.[4]

Because most hospitals are no longer reimbursed on a cost basis, these reasons are now largely obsolete. Nevertheless, market incentives and regulatory rules still create significant additional reasons for hospitals to consider the holding company structure advantageous. . . . For example, in some states a hospital might be required to obtain a certificate of need to build a parking garage or a medical office building, whereas a separate corporation created for these specific purposes might be able to initiate the same project without CON review. . . . [Also], nonprofit health care systems may find it advantageous to put operations that generate unrelated business income into separate taxable subsidiaries in order to avoid jeopardizing tax-exempt status.[5] . . . [Finally], [s]eparating diverse functions into distinct entities

4. See generally David Frankford, The Complexity of Medicare's Hospital Reimbursement System: Paradoxes of Averaging, 78 Iowa L. Rev. 517 (1993).

5. . . . [However,] health care delivery systems may become so obsessed with diversification that corporations are created that have nothing to do with the initial and overall mission of the system. For example, Hamot Medical Center in Erie, Pennsylvania was publicly scrutinized when an affiliate was discovered to have purchased a marina for $375,000. In a fight to maintain its tax-exempt status, the hospital argued that the affiliate was furthering the hospital's purposes "by promoting urban redevelopment." A court reviewing the tax-exempt status of the Medical Center concluded that the hospital's primary business was no longer health promotion, but funding of affiliates that competed with local businessmen. School District of City of Erie v. Hamot Medical Center, 144 Pa. Commw. Ct. 668, 602 A.2d 407 (1992). . . .

can also create more precise accountability and awareness of corporate performance. Thus, the goal of hospital reorganization is often to use separate corporations to reflect separate lines of business. . . .

Reorganization may also create competitive advantages for the health care system by providing greater flexibility for participation in the creation and operation of health care networks and other innovative transactions. . . . [T]he recent development of integrated delivery systems has made the creation of a parent corporation even more important than in the past.

Stephen Bernstein, Complex Corporate Structures, *in* Health Care Corporate Law: Facilities and Transactions (M. Hall & W. Brewbaker eds., 1996).

2. *Integrated Delivery Systems.* These reorganizations have led to a number of rulings concerning the extent to which hospital holding companies and other complex corporate structures comply with the requirements for charitable tax exemption under specialized doctrines known as the "integral part test" and the "shared service organization" rule. These rulings are summarized on the Web site for this book, www.health-law.org.

The most important application of these corporate restructuring rulings is to so-called vertically integrated networks or integrated delivery systems (IDSs), those that contain not only hospitals but also nursing homes, home health agencies, physician groups, and an HMO. The IRS's rulings at first followed a de facto rule that participating physicians may constitute no more than 20 percent of the governing board, based on obscure precedents dealing with tax-exempt bond financing. After sustained criticism, the IRS relaxed this limit to 49 percent as long as physician board members are insulated from decisions about physician compensation and other conflict of interest protections are in place. Lawyers await IRS guidance on similar issues relating to ACOs.

Is a limit on physician board membership consistent with the corporate practice of medicine doctrine? Is it consistent with realistic business planning? Hospital-based networks need to include physicians in order to offer the better management and coordination of care that health policy seeks, but hospitals find it difficult to form tight affiliations with physician groups without giving them substantial governance authority.

3. *Are Hospital-Run Systems Optimal?* Although the IRS may have relaxed somewhat its opposition to physician governance, it still appears essential that tax-exempt networks be hospital run. Otherwise, it would be difficult to invoke the generous "promotion of health" precedents that apply to hospitals and difficult to meet the free emergency service requirements. On the other hand, hospital control may not prove to be the optimal, or even a viable, organizational structure for emerging ACOs. The Friendly Hills system that received the first integrated system ruling in the 1990s abandoned its exempt status less than two years later and split up into several for-profit components owned by the physicians, and many other provider-owned networks formed in the 1990s failed or were bought out by larger insurers. A prominent health management consultant gives several, highly opinionated reasons this may have occurred:

[T]here are a lot of Walter Mitty-like fantasies of power being realized in the creation of integrated systems. Some executives believe that management is finally about to triumph over physicians. . . . My experience . . . taught me early on that physicians crave order but despise authority. . . . While many physicians fall prey to an illusion of omnicompetence and believe that their medical training endowed them with superior management judgment, most are incapable of submitting to the authority of anyone, even a fellow physician. . . . As a consequence, many lack the interpersonal skills or civility to function as part of a larger enterprise. When physicians are unhappy, they whine—deafeningly. They passively resist initiatives that they cannot overtly oppose, often doing so with dazzling flair and elegance. They will agree in public meetings and subvert privately. They wait for temporary weakness in administrative personnel and savage them. . . . In short, . . . a sizeable fraction of the current generation of private practitioners or medical school faculties are poor candidates for participating in any integrated health care enterprise. . . . One thing becomes clear.

Jeff Goldsmith, Hospital/Physician Relationships: A Constraint to Health Reform, 12(3) Health Aff. 161 (Aug. 1993). However, Goldsmith is equally dubious of hospital control:

The hospital is not the appropriate nucleus of an integrated health care system. . . . Rather, the hospital is a high-maintenance core asset whose use must be rigorously limited by managed care incentives. Outside the integrated enterprise, the hospital is merely a vulnerable vendor of a surplus commodity. Owning a lot of hospital beds in the emerging managed care world will be as advantageous as owning a lot of rubles in post-Soviet Russia.

Problem: Choosing a Corporate Form

Florence Nightingale Hospital has decided to form an HMO in which it wants to give physicians a major stake, in order to foster allegiance and encourage cost-effective treatment. You are consulted as a legal and management expert to advise the hospital on the consequences of forming the HMO as a nonprofit vs. a for-profit entity. What are the relevant considerations with respect to tax exemption, the ability to raise capital, the role of physicians, and operational constraints?

3. The Corporate Practice of Medicine

This section explores an old body of law known as the corporate practice of medicine doctrine, which now may appear archaic, but which has profound influence on the entire structure of the health care delivery system.

■ BARTRON v. CODINGTON COUNTY
2 N.W.2d 337 (S.D. 1942)

SMITH, Judge.

. . . The central question of law to be determined is whether certain exhibited bargains between Codington County and the Bartron Clinic, a corporation for profit, pursuant to which such corporation furnished medical and surgical services, and medicines to the county indigent, are illegal and unenforceable.

The "Bartron Clinic" was incorporated in February of 1929, "to conduct and operate a general medical and surgical hospital and clinic and employ duly licensed physicians, surgeons, nurses, students, and other persons to carry on the business of said corporation." Its 750 shares of capital stock were originally issued and held by duly licensed physicians and surgeons, and by nurses and other employees of the corporation. . . . Except for some minor services of an intern, all of the professional services involved herein were performed by duly licensed physicians and surgeons employed at fixed salaries by the corporation, and all charges therefor accrued to and were made by the corporation. The corporation owned all equipment used by the doctors and maintained the supply of drugs furnished patients. The corporation did not hold a license to practice medicine and surgery, nor to operate a pharmacy.

On January 3, 1933, the county and the corporation executed and delivered two contracts in writing wherein the corporation agreed to furnish hospitalization, medical and surgical services and medicine to the county for its poor persons. . . .

The court [below] found that there was not in connection with the organization of the Bartron Clinic, or at any time thereafter, any purpose or intent whatsoever on the part of Dr. Bartron or anybody else connected with said corporation to place the actual control of the practice of medicine with any person other than duly licensed physicians; that there was not at any time throughout the existence of said corporation any control, or effort to exercise control, as to the actual practice of medicine on the part of anybody other than a licensed physician and no interference, or attempted interference, by anybody other than a licensed physician, with the actual practice of medicine; that the actual purpose and intent of Dr. Bartron in promoting the organization of said corporation was to establish what amounted to a system of profit sharing, whereby the prominent and leading employees of said hospital and clinic business would have some actual interest in the success thereof.

[This case] originated as a claim before the county commissioners in aggregate amount of $3,649.63 for medicine supplied the county indigent between January 1, 1938 and September 1, 1938. . . . [T]he court found that the professional services were actually rendered by duly licensed physicians, except for a small item for intern's services, and that the medicines were prescribed by such physicians in treatment of the county poor, and that all of this was done pursuant to directions and orders of the county commissioners.

The court concluded as a matter of law . . . that it is unlawful and contrary to public policy for a corporation to practice medicine or surgery and to operate a pharmacy or sell medicine without a license as required by the statutes of South Dakota. These conclusions are challenged here by appropriate assignments of error. . . .

When conduct opposed to the public interest is made the subject of a bargain the courts ordinarily refuse to accord a party thereto a remedy predicated thereon. . . . While decision has rarely turned on the naked issue of public policy, the expressions of the courts indicate a current of opinion, to which there are but few dissentients, that such practice contravenes the public interest and is contrary to public policy.

The leading case is that of In re Cooperative Law Co., 198 N.Y. 479, 92 N.E. 15. The court said:

The practice of law is not a business open to all, but a personal right, limited to a few persons of good moral character, with special qualifications ascertained and certified after a long course of study, both general and professional, and a thorough examination by a state board appointed for the purpose. . . . The relation of attorney and client is that of master and servant in a limited and dignified sense, and it involves the highest trust and confidence. It cannot be delegated without consent, and it cannot exist between an attorney employed by a corporation to practice law for it, and a client of the corporation, for he would be subject to the directions of the corporation, and not to the directions of the client. There would be neither contract nor privity between him and the client, and he would not owe even the duty of counsel to the actual litigant. The corporation would control the litigation, the money earned would belong to the corporation, and the attorney would be responsible to the corporation only. His master would not be the client but the corporation, conducted it may be wholly by laymen, organized simply to make money and not to aid in the administration of justice which is the highest function of an attorney and counsellor at law. The corporation might not have a lawyer among its stockholders, directors, or officers. Its members might be without character, learning or standing. There would be . . . no stimulus to good conduct from the traditions of an ancient and honorable profession, and no guide except the sordid purpose to earn money for stockholders. The bar, which is an institution of the highest usefulness and standing, would be degraded if even its humblest member became subject to the orders of a money-making corporation engaged not in conducting litigation for itself, but in the business of conducting litigation for others. *The degradation of the bar is an injury to the state.* . . .

Debasement of the learned professions is in fact inimical to the public welfare. The public is the ultimate beneficiary of its professional social organisms, and of the private, as well as of the unselfish public, exercise of the skills and talents of its professional practitioners. Although the members of the legal profession in their individual capacities as officers of the courts of justice sustain a relationship to the public without parallel in the medical professions, in all other respects the services of the two professions are of equal importance to the public, and debasement of the one, in our opinion, would constitute no less a public evil than would the degradation of the other.

These professions, as they exist in our social structure, rest upon a foundation of sturdy, sterling human character which, in turn, has been and is being shaped and moulded by the impact of traditional ideals and points of view. The licensing statutes with their emphasis on character and professional conduct evidence a fixed public desire and will not only to foster, but to develop and reinforce, these basic attributes of its professional servants. . . . We are therefore persuaded that that which tends to debase the learned professions is at war with the public interest and is therefore contrary to public policy.

Does practice of the learned professions by a profit corporation functioning through duly licensed practitioners tend to debase the professions? We pause to emphasize the word *tend* because the learned trial court has found that the Bartron Clinic was innocent of any unethical intention or practice, and that its licensed officers and employees controlled its professional activities. Our present concern is with the tendency of the challenged conduct. Though the exhibited instance of that conduct has accomplished no evil, if its inherent tendency be at war with public interest, it is contrary to public policy.

Because of the rights with which the law invests a stockholder in a corporation for profit, recognition of such a means of conducting a professional business involves yielding the right of participation in control of its policies and in its earnings to lay persons. . . . The object of such a company would be to produce an earning on its fixed capital. Its trade commodity would be the professional services of its employees. Constant pressure would be exerted by the investor to promote such a volume of sales of that commodity as would produce an ever increasing return on his investment. To promote such sales it is to be presumed that the layman would apply the methods and practices in which he had been schooled in the market place. The end result seems inevitable to us, viz., undue emphasis on mere money making, and commercial exploitation of professional services. To universalize the use of this method of organizing the professions, or to permit such a use to become general, would ultimately wipe out or blight those characteristics which distinguish the business practices of the professions from those of the market place. Such an ethical, trustworthy and unselfish professionalism as the community needs and wants cannot survive in a purely commercial atmosphere. . . .

That such is the tendency of the profit corporation when used to conduct a professional practice is not a matter of mere fancy or conjecture. It is a matter of common knowledge that this form of organization has been tried in the field of dentistry and resulted in such unethical and commercial practices as induced the legislature of this and many other states to pass statutes expressly prohibiting its use.

Being convinced that the practice of the learned professions by a profit corporation tends to the commercialization and debasement of those professions, we are of the opinion that such a mode of conducting the practice is in contravention of the public interest and is against public policy. It follows that we are of the view that insofar as the bargains of the Bartron Clinic and Codington County dealt with medical and surgical services, they were illegal. [As a result, the court refused to order the county to pay for medical services it had received, but the court did allow the clinic to keep funds previously paid.]

RIGHT OF CORPORATION TO PRACTICE MEDICINE
Note, 48 Yale L.J. 346 (1938)

Efforts to obtain adequate medical care at reasonable cost have stimulated extensive experimentation with methods of medical organization. The result has been widespread development of such diversified types as private group clinics, employee health associations, county physician bureaus, health insurance plans, and medical cooperatives. Many of the sponsors of these systems have attempted to take advantage of the corporate form in order to achieve limited liability and continuity of existence. Groups of physicians have incorporated to operate their own clinic; laymen have formed corporations, hiring physicians to treat patients for profit; and aggregations of prospective patients have organized nonprofit cooperative corporations. Yet the legal existence of these corporate types has been jeopardized at one time or another by attempted application of the principle that corporations may not practice the learned professions. . . .

While numerous state statutes directly forbid the corporate practice of law, express prohibition of the corporate practice of medicine is rare. Instead, denial of the right of some corporations to practice medicine has been based upon those statutes in every state which outlaws performance of the healing art by unlicensed persons. The obvious inability of a corporate entity to meet the educational and character requirements prerequisite to a license is said to inhibit a corporation from practicing medicine. To bolster this interpretation of the statutes, courts have commonly resorted to arguments of public policy. Since the judiciary do not possess an intrinsic power to regulate the medical profession as they do the legal, the validity of this viewpoint is necessarily dependent upon the soundness of the courts' inference that state licensing statutes automatically forbid utilization of the corporate power.

Courts which profess to deny all corporations the right to have any connection with medical activities have apparently misconstrued the purpose of the state licensing statutes. These statutes are designed to preserve the public health by excluding from practice persons with inadequate ability, morality, and training. Since the diagnosis and treatment of disease are obviously purely personal functions, a corporation can perform them only through the medium of doctors. But the mere fact that a corporation employs physicians, or is operated by physicians, provides no valid basis for requiring the corporation itself to be licensed. As long as the doctors are properly licensed and their professional activities are not interfered with by unlicensed persons, the purpose of the statutes is fully effected, for no one without proper qualifications is then directly or indirectly administering to the public. This is true even though laymen may be entrusted with considerable control over administrative details. Only when lay officers or directors exercise substantial supervision over the professional activities of the physicians employed is there ground for arguing that the corporation is enabling unlicensed persons to practice medicine. Thus the real issue is not whether corporations generally are unlicensed to practice medicine, but whether in each individual case physicians are *actually* controlled in their purely professional functions by unlicensed persons in such a manner as to nullify the purpose of the licensing statutes. . . .

Even in states following [this doctrine], numerous corporations engage unchallenged in activities which have all the indicia of corporate practice of medicine as defined by the same courts. It is common knowledge that private hospitals, sanitariums, fraternal organizations, educational institutions, and industrial concerns all administer medical services to their constituents through staffs of physicians hired and paid on a full or part time basis. Similarly, salaried physicians undertake part time contract practice on behalf of various companies, particularly railroads, to treat passengers and employees. The explanation for such discrimination may be that the social utility of these types of corporate medical service has long been tacitly recognized; nevertheless, the fact remains that some corporate forms have been permitted in the face of the same state licensing statutes which are so rigorously invoked against others.

Since the legal construction of state licensing statutes is by no means inexorable, their varying application to certain corporate forms is probably attributable to the judges' evaluation of social policy arguments against corporate medical practice. Impairment of the intimate doctor-patient relationship and commercialization of the medical profession are the two general social policy objections most commonly cited by the courts. The first evil will result, it is feared, from possible restrictions upon the patient's freedom of choice of physician and from a division of the physician's loyalty between patient and corporate employer. If the old-fashioned family doctor is used as the norm, this objection might assume serious proportions. But when the challenged corporate forms are compared with the many types of corporate medical service already accepted, any distinguishing basis must be fanciful indeed. Furthermore, consistency would require that the same charge be levelled against noncorporate forms such as county, municipal, and private partnership clinics. And even if the choice of doctors should be unusually restricted within a particular corporate scheme, many patients might prefer that scheme to other types of private group medical services or to receiving inadequate or no medical treatment whatsoever. . . . Moreover, insulation of the doctor from administrative and economic cares and elimination of the patient's concern over cost may actually enhance the relationship between patient and physician.

More plausible is the second social objection to the corporate furnishing of medical service. It is feared that the profession may be commercially exploited by laymen who, not being amenable to ethical standards, are free to engage in high pressure solicitation of patients and sharp competitive advertising. But the fact that this fear may at times be well-grounded should not justify resort to the drastic measure of barring corporate medical service entirely. A more sensible solution is for the state to combine its recognized regulatory powers over corporations and professions in order to curb objectionable professional activity. And even without special regulation, the state can undoubtedly hold contract physicians to the same standard of ethics as private practitioners. Moreover, the opposition of the American Medical Association to this type of corporate medical practice assures a zealous and vigilant supervision by a body duty-bound to report to the state injurious professional activity.

. . . Some courts persist in trying to solve such cases by repeating generalizations which are meaningless in the abstract. A more realistic judicial approach would disregard the corporate form as such and inquire instead whether the actual setup is so provocative of abuses that the only solution is to deny the corporation existence altogether. However, the public interest in furthering experiments in medical care may suffer much by trusting to haphazard decisions by tribunals ill-fitted to investigate intricate specific cases. The surer method of achieving the benefits of corporate medical organization without possible attendant evils would be by enactment of legislation specifically authorizing the corporate form but carefully regulating its activities so as to insure the highest response to professional ethics by the corporation as an entity and by its physicians.

◼ BERLIN v. SARAH BUSH LINCOLN HEALTH CENTER
688 N.E.2d 106 (Ill. 1997)

NICKLES, J.

. . . The [Sara Bush Lincoln] Health Center is a nonprofit corporation duly licensed under the Hospital Licensing Act to operate a hospital. In December 1992, Dr. Berlin and the Health Center entered into a written agreement whereby the Health Center employed Dr. Berlin to practice medicine for the hospital for five years. The agreement . . . contained a restrictive covenant which prohibited Dr. Berlin from competing with the hospital by providing health services within a 50-mile radius of the Health Center for two years after the end of the employment agreement. On February 4, 1994, Dr. Berlin informed the Health Center by letter that he was resigning effective February 7, 1994 and accepting employment with the Carle Clinic . . . located approximately one mile from the Health Center. Shortly thereafter, the Health Center sought a preliminary injunction to prohibit Dr. Berlin from practicing at the Carle Clinic. . . . The circuit court, finding the entire employment agreement unenforceable, granted Dr. Berlin's motion for summary judgment. . . . [T]he circuit court determined that the Health Center, by hiring Dr. Berlin to practice medicine as its employee, violated the prohibition against corporations practicing medicine.[3] . . .

. . . The corporate practice of medicine doctrine prohibits corporations from providing professional medical services. Although a few states have codified the doctrine, the prohibition is primarily inferred from state medical licensure acts, which regulate the profession of medicine and forbid its practice by unlicensed individuals. See A. Rosoff, The Business of Medicine: Problems with the Corporate Practice Doctrine, 17 Cumb. L. Rev. 485, 490 (1987). The rationale behind the doctrine is that a corporation cannot be licensed to practice medicine because only a human being can sustain the education, training, and character-screening which are prerequisites to receiving a professional license. Since a corporation cannot receive a medical license, it follows that a corporation cannot legally practice the profession. The rationale of the doctrine concludes that the employment of physicians by corporations is illegal because the acts of the physicians are attributable to the corporate employer, which cannot obtain a medical license. See M. Hall, Institutional Control of Physician Behavior: Legal Barriers to Health Care Cost Containment, 137 U. Pa. L. Rev. 431, 509-10 (1988). The prohibition on the corporate employment of physicians is invariably supported by several public policy arguments which espouse the dangers of lay control over professional judgment, the division of the physician's loyalty between his patient and his profitmaking employer, and the commercialization of the profession. See A. Willcox, Hospitals and the Corporate Practice of Medicine, 45 Cornell L.Q. 432, 442-43 (1960).

This court first [applied] the corporate practice doctrine [to strike down a restrictive covenant] in Dr. Allison, Dentist, Inc. v. Allison, 360 Ill. 638 (1935), [whose facts were essentially the same as here, except that Dr. Allison was a dentist working for a dental office, not a physician at a hospital] . . . Soon after the *Allison* decision, this court . . . addressed the corporate practice doctrine as it pertained to [physicians working in a clinic, in a ruling essentially the same as in Bartron v. Codington County, supra] People ex rel. Kerner v. United Medical Service, Inc., 362 Ill. 442 (1936). . . . Prior to the instant action, apparently no Illinois court has . . . specifically addressed the issue of whether licensed hospitals are prohibited from employing physicians. We therefore look to other jurisdictions with reference to the application of the corporate practice of medicine doctrine to hospitals.

. . . [N]umerous jurisdictions have recognized either judicial or statutory exceptions to the corporate practice of medicine doctrine which allow hospitals

---

3. [This case challenges the legality of the employment relationship as a whole. The legality of restrictive covenants in particular has also been challenged, as discussed in the notes at page 1354. — EDS.]

to employ physicians and other health care professionals. . . . First, some states . . . determined that a hospital corporation which employs a physician is not practicing medicine, but rather is merely making medical treatment available. See, e.g., State ex rel. Sager v. Lewin, 128 Mo. App. 149, 155, 106 S.W. 581, 583 (1907); State Electro-Medical Institute v. Platner, 74 Neb. 23, 29, 103 N.W. 1079, 1081 (1905). Under the second approach, the courts of some jurisdictions determined that the corporate practice doctrine is inapplicable to nonprofit hospitals and health associations. These courts reasoned that the public policy arguments supporting the corporate practice doctrine do not apply to physicians employed by charitable institutions. See, e.g., Group Health Ass'n v. Moor, 24 F. Supp. 445, 446 (D.D.C. 1938); People ex rel. State Board of Medical Examiners v. Pacific Health Corp., 12 Cal. 2d 156, 159-61, 82 P.2d 429, 431 (1938). In the third approach, the courts of several states have determined that the corporate practice doctrine is not applicable to hospitals which employ physicians because hospitals are authorized by other laws to provide medical treatment to patients. See, e.g., Rush v. City of St. Petersburg, 205 So. 2d 11 (Fla. App. 1967); St. Francis Regional Medical Center, Inc. v. Weiss, 254 Kan. 728, 869 P.2d 606 (1994).

We find the [third] rationale . . . persuasive. . . . The Medical Practice Act contains no express prohibition on the corporate employment of physicians.[1] Rather, the corporate practice of medicine doctrine was inferred from the general policies behind the Medical Practice Act. . . . The [hospital licensing] statutes clearly authorize, and at times mandate, licensed hospital corporations to provide medical services. . . .

In addition, we find the public policy concerns which support the corporate practice doctrine inapplicable to a licensed hospital in the modern health care industry. The concern for lay control over professional judgment is alleviated in a licensed hospital, where generally a separate professional medical staff is responsible for the quality of medical services rendered in the facility.[2] Furthermore, we believe that extensive changes in the health care industry since [1936], including the emergence of corporate health maintenance organizations, have greatly altered the concern over the commercialization of health care. In addition, such concerns are relieved when a licensed hospital is the physician's employer. Hospitals have an independent duty to provide for the patient's health and welfare. See Darling v. Charleston Community Mem. Hosp., 33 Ill. 2d 326 (1965) (recognizing hospital's duty to assume responsibility for the care of its patients).

We find particularly appropriate the statement of the Kansas Supreme Court that "[i]t would be incongruous to conclude that the legislature intended a hospital to accomplish what it is licensed to do without utilizing physicians as independent contractors or employees. . . . To conclude that a hospital must do so without

TIMES CHANGING

---

1. In contrast, the Dental Practice Act, applied by this court in _Allison_, expressly prohibited a corporation from furnishing dentists and owning and operating a dental office.

2. Moreover, in the instant case, the employment agreement expressly provided that the Health Center had no control or direction over Dr. Berlin's medical judgment and practice, other than that control exercised by the professional medical staff. Dr. Berlin has never contended that the Health Center's lay management attempted to control his practice of medicine.

employing physicians is not only illogical but ignores reality." *Weiss*, 869 P.2d at 618. Accordingly, we conclude that a duly-licensed hospital possesses legislative authority to practice medicine by means of its staff of licensed physicians and is excepted from the operation of the corporate practice of medicine doctrine. Consequently, the employment agreement between the Health Center and Dr. Berlin is not unenforceable merely because the Health Center is a corporate entity. . . .

HARRISON, J. and MILLER, J., dissenting:

. . . [N]one of the statutes invoked by my colleagues supports their position. The most that can be said of those statutes is that they authorize hospitals to operate facilities for the diagnosis and care of patients and to make emergency service available regardless of ability to pay. . . . None of those endeavors, however, requires that hospitals have the power to employ physicians directly or to charge patients for the physicians' services. All may be accomplished by granting staff privileges to duly licensed private physicians, and the Hospital Licensing Act presumes that hospitals will staff their facilities in precisely that way. . . . [T]he General Assembly has expressly authorized the employment of physicians by Health Maintenance Organizations (HMOs) under the Health Maintenance Organization Act. If the General Assembly had intended to grant the same authority to hospitals, I believe that it would have been similarly straightforward and unambiguous in doing so. In addition to creating special rules for HMOs, the General Assembly has also decided to allow physicians to employ various forms of business organizations in practicing their profession. Physicians may incorporate in accordance with the Professional Service Corporation Act, they may form corporations to provide medical services under the Medical Corporation Act, they have the right to practice in a professional association organized pursuant to the Professional Association Act, and they can organize and operate limited liability companies to practice medicine under the recently amended Limited Liability Company Act. Again, however, none of these provisions pertains to hospitals, and no inference can be drawn from any of them that the General Assembly intended to alter the prohibition against the corporate practice of medicine by hospitals. . . .

Notes: Corporate Practice of Medicine and Choice of Entity

1. *The Fundamental Structure of American Medical Institutions.* This body of law may appear obscure and antiquated, but it continues to have fundamental importance for the structure of institutional and economic relationships in American medicine. Observe, for instance, that the prohibition of institutions charging for medical services explains why doctors are paid separately from hospitals and why there used to be a distinction between Blue Cross and Blue Shield and still is between Medicare Part A and Part B. This doctrine also explains why, only in North America, hospital medical staffs are independent and self-governing. Elsewhere in the world, hospital physicians are uniformly employed or compensated by the hospital.

Challenging this traditional order is hospitals' current interest in forming ACOs that better coordinate across different practice settings. This ACO movement is causing a significant increase in hospitals employing physicians who practice in the community. See R. Kocher & N. Sahni, Hospitals' Race to Employ Physicians:

The Logic Behind a Money-Losing Proposition, 364 New Eng. J. Med. 1790 (2011). Will the corporate practice of medicine doctrine permit this? For a thorough discussion of various legal and practice issues, see Leigh Walton et al., Hospitals Employing Physicians, 22(2) The Health Lawyer 1 (Dec. 2009).

2. *Legal Landmines.* Following the 1930s and 1940s, the corporate practice of medicine doctrine entered a period of relative quiescence in the courts. It still continued to thrive, though, in state attorneys general opinions during the 1950s, in response to the growing technological sophistication of medical care and hospitals' resulting relationships with radiologists, pathologists, and other hospital-based specialists. Activity at even that level slackened noticeably over the ensuing decades, leading one to consider whether the doctrine hasn't been quietly defused. However, in Professor Rosoff's apt metaphor, corporate practice prohibitions survive as "legal landmines, remnants of an old and nearly forgotten war, half-buried on a field fast being built up with new forms of health care organizations. Occasionally, usually at the instigation of those who resist the change not taking place, one is detonated, with distressing results." A. Rosoff, The Business of Medicine: Problems with the Corporate Practice Doctrine, 17 Cumb. L. Rev. 485 (1987).

Instances of modern application in addition to those discussed in *Berlin* include Conrad v. Medical Board of California, 55 Cal. Rptr. 2d 801 (Ct. App. 1996) (hospital district may not employ physicians); and Isles Wellness, Inc. v. Progressive Northern Insurance Co., 703 N.W.2d 513 (Minn. 2005) (holding after extensive debate that the doctrine is still alive and it bars the employment of chiropractors by a clinic with lay owners). However, another decision in the latter case held that violation of the doctrine does not automatically render void any contracts entered into by the clinic. 725 N.W.2d 90 (Minn. 2006).

3. *Doctrinal Foundations.* The corporate practice doctrine is founded on two distinct bases: the Medical Practice Act and common-law public policy. The courts rarely draw this distinction, however. *Bartron* is one court that did. In another portion of the opinion, the court, influenced by the Yale Note, rejected the literal terms of the Medical Practice Act as a basis for a corporate practice challenge. In doing so, it stands almost alone.

4. *Statutory Arguments.* The *Allison* decision, discussed in *Berlin,* provides an example of the typical reasoning of the statutory basis for the corporate practice prohibition: "The qualifications [to practice a profession] include personal characteristics such as honesty, guided by an upright conscience and a sense of loyalty to clients or patients. . . . These requirements are spoken of generically as that good moral character which is a prerequisite to the licensing of any professional man. No corporation can qualify. It can have neither honesty nor conscience. . . ." 196 N.E. 799, 800 (1935). Does this line of reasoning differ in form or in substance from the following?

- The actions of drivers hired by a corporation are attributed to the corporation
- An eyesight examination is required for a driver's license
- Corporations cannot take an eye exam
- Therefore, a corporation that hires drivers is guilty of driving without a license

See Sloan v. Metropolitan Health Council, 516 N.E.2d 1104, 1107 (Ind. Ct. App. 1987) (rejecting the doctrine on this basis).

5. *Public Policy Arguments.* Addressing corporate practice from a common-law public policy perspective, how far should the courts go in striking down private contractual arrangements? Many of the original and leading cases address situations of apparent quackery in the peripheral medical professions (dentistry, optometry, etc.). See Laufer, Ethical and Legal Restrictions on Contract and Corporate Practice of Medicine, 6 Law & Contemp. Probs. 521, 526 (Autumn 1939). *Bartron*, however, applies a strict rule despite the completely upright behavior of the individual doctors. Are there any countervailing harms to banning corporate practice, or should the courts lean as far as possible in the direction of a pristine practice setting? In 1979, the Federal Trade Commission (FTC) permanently enjoined the AMA from enforcing *ethical* prohibitions against corporate practice because of the anticompetitive effects of the AMA controlling the economic and organizational aspects of medical practice. American Medical Ass'n, 94 F.T.C. 980, 1015 (1979), aff'd by equally divided court, 455 U.S. 676 (1982).

How great of a concern is the threat of divided loyalty, that is, the responsibility an employed physician owes to her employer as well as to her patient? Is the loyalty any greater than that owed by one physician *partner* to another? Than that owed by a physician to other patients? Is it not possible to serve two masters so long as they do not impose inconsistent duties?

And what of the commercialization concern, that is, that introduction of a profit motive will tend to debase the profession? Clearly a profit motive exists in medical practice regardless of the organizational form of practice. Doctors are the highest paid profession in the country. What additional concerns are introduced by *incorporating* a profitable practice? Consider whether there isn't a form of hypocrisy or self-interest in keeping only nonphysicians from sharing in medicine's rich rewards.

6. *Implicit Exceptions.* The holding in *Berlin* would appear to exempt from the corporate practice prohibition all hospitals, nursing homes, and licensed outpatient clinics, but only to the extent covered by their licenses. Could a hospital operate a chain of physician offices under this rationale? In a subsequent decision, the Illinois Supreme Court refused to apply *Berlin* to a nonprofit corporation that owned physician offices as a joint venture between a hospital and a physician group because the particular corporation used did not hold a hospital license. Carter-Shields v. Alton Health Institute, 777 N.E.2d 948 (Ill. 2002). The court also refused to find an exception based on the hospital's or the corporate entity's nonprofit status, holding that "nonprofit status is unrelated to . . . safeguarding the physician's professional judgment from lay interference or protecting the public's general health and welfare."

What other exceptions to the doctrine are mentioned in *Berlin*? See, e.g., Conrad v. Medical Board of California, 55 Cal. Rptr. 2d 901 (Ct. App. 1996) (hospital district may retain physicians only as independent contractors, not as employees). Not all courts agree with these exceptions, however.

7. *PCs and LLCs.* The dissent in *Berlin* observes that exceptions to the corporate practice prohibition are sometimes explicit in licensing statutes. The most prominent example is a professional corporation (PC). Practice groups organized like the one that was invalidated in *Bartron*, that are entirely owned by member physicians, are now permitted by PC laws widely adopted during the 1960s. A PC essentially allows physicians and other licensed professionals (lawyers included) to enjoy the liability protections of corporate organization while enjoying the tax ben-

efits of practicing as a partnership. (Note, though, that tax reform legislation in the 1980s substantially restricted PC pension and retirement benefits, the major tax advantage.) See J. Philipps et al., Origins of Tax Law: The History of the Personal Service Corporation, 40 Wash. & Lee L. Rev. 433 (1983). Do these laws change the public policy recognized in *Bartron*? Cf. Sloan v. Metropolitan Health Council, 516 N.E. 2d 1104, 1107 (Ind. Ct. App. 1987) (dictum) ("We believe that the Professional Corporation Act . . . totally abolished [the] public policy [prohibiting a corporation to practice medicine], if, indeed, it ever existed.").

Professional corporation statutes typically require owners to remain liable for each other's professional negligence, as in partnerships, and they restrict ownership to professionals who have similar categories of practice licensure (M.D.s, lawyers, dentists, etc.). This gives rise to disputes over whether physicians can employ or share ownership with other licensed medical professionals. See, e.g., Columbia Physical Therapy v. Benton Franklin Orthopedic Assoc., 228 P.2d 1260 (Wash. 2010) (holding that corporate practice doctrine does not bar physician group from employing physical therapists, but only because physical therapy is a subcomponent of medical practice).

An innovation to the PC format that has gained widespread popularity is known as a professional limited liability company (PLLC). State laws authorizing limited liability companies have proliferated in response to an IRS ruling that makes it easier to avoid corporate taxation. Classically, corporations, which are taxed as entities, were distinguished from partnerships in which there is no entity-level tax, only the ordinary income tax paid by individual members. This distinction was based on certain classic attributes of corporations, such as limited liability, centralized management, and freely transferrable investment interests, which the IRS ruled could not be fully replicated by contract without incurring corporate tax. See United States v. Kintner, 216 F.2d 418 (9th Cir. 1954). It is this ruling the IRS relaxed, opening the way to a whole new species of business organizations. The modern "check-the-box" regulations allow closely held entities to choose either partnership or corporate tax treatment, regardless of their form. 26 C.F.R. §301 (1997).

This flexible taxation approach is now available to closely held business entities, regardless of the kind of entity in question. For a time, however, it was available only by virtue of special state laws that created a new breed of business entity known as "limited liability companies" (LLCs). These are hybrids of partnerships and corporations in that they limit members' liability to the extent of their investment, like corporations, but they avoid an entity-level tax, like partnerships. LLCs also offer advantages over other hybrids such as limited partnerships and subchapter S corporations. Where authorized by statute, professional LLCs mimic PCs by making this new organizational form available to licensed professionals. However, these PLLC statutes usually contain some of the same provisions on governance authority and liability exposure that are in the PC statutes.

LLCs are widely used for physician practices, as well as for law firms. However, the restrictions hamper their use for larger, multi-specialty practice groups or for vertically integrated delivery systems. Therefore, more complex arrangements have emerged, such as a limited partnership composed of LLCs. See generally Ribstein & Keatinge on Limited Liability (2d ed. 2004); Symposium, 32 Wake Forest L. Rev. 1 (1997); Symposium, 40 Wake Forest L. Rev. 751 (2005).

8. *HMO Exemptions.* The corporate practice prohibition is recognized as one of the major historical stumbling blocks in early HMO development. Developments,

The Role of Prepaid Group Practice in Relieving the Medical Care Crisis, 84 Harv. L. Rev. 887, 960-961 (1971). State HMO enabling statutes frequently provide protection from this doctrine, but it is nevertheless puzzling that the federal HMO Act initially did not include this body of state law in its preemption provision when enacted in 1973. However, 1988 amendments to the federal Act significantly broadened its preemptive provision to strike all state laws that "impose requirements that would inhibit" HMOs. 42 U.S.C. §300e-10(a)(1)(E). Does it make sense to limit this preemption to only federally qualified HMOs, to the exclusion of other innovative forms of health care financing and delivery?

9. *The Future.* The conflict between the corporate practice prohibition and the need for organizational experimentation, a dominant theme in the 1938 Yale Note, has an eerie resonance with present day circumstances. Do you agree with *Berlin* that the doctrine's public policy foundations no longer apply? Most commentators argue that the doctrine should yield to modern developments. See Nicole Huberfeld, Be Not Afraid of Change: Time to Eliminate the Corporate Practice of Medicine Doctrine, 14 Health Matrix 243 (2004); Adam Freiman, The Abandonment of the Antiquated Corporate Practice of Medicine Doctrine: Injecting a Dose of Efficiency into the Modern Health Care Environment, 47 Emory L. J. 697 (1998); M. Hall, Institutional Control of Physician Behavior: Legal Barriers to Health Care Cost Containment, 137 U. Pa. L. Rev. 431, 510 (1988); A. Rosoff, supra; Note, 7 Health Matrix 241 (1997); Note, 40 Vand. L. Rev. 445, supra. Others, however, argue that the doctrine should be revived in order to restrict the practice of medicine over the Internet—see, e.g., Brian Monnich, Bringing Order to Cybermedicine: Applying the Corporate Practice of Medicine Doctrine to Tame the Wild Wild Web, 42 B.C. L. Rev. 455 (2001)—or to protect physicians against excessive forms of managed care—see Andre Hampton, Resurrection of the Prohibition on the Corporate Practice of Medicine: Teaching Old Dogma New Tricks, 66 U. Cin. L. Rev. 489 (1998).

Problem: Hospital and Physician Contracting

Florence Nightingale Hospital (FNH) realizes that, in order to survive in the current marketplace, it must promote greater loyalty, corporate identification, and clinical integration with its physicians. It would also like to capture some of the money physicians are making from treating hospital patients. FNH could simply hire all or a portion of its medical staff, but it is concerned about the legality of doing this. Which of the following approaches would you suggest to minimize that concern, without sacrificing the business objectives?

1. Form a nonprofit subsidiary that hires as many physicians as it wants because it falls within an exception to the corporate practice prohibition. Then it can bill for all medical and hospital services, pay the physicians a salary, and keep the profits (or absorb the losses).

2. Encourage the physicians to form a for-profit entity of their own, and then contract with that entity. The billing and financial arrangements would be the same as just described (billing by hospital; contract with physicians for fixed rates that generate a profit).

3. Contract with each physician separately, but not to deliver medical services, only to manage their office practice, so that FNH would provide office space and clerical support, and would do the billing and collection for these physicians, but it would turn these revenues over to the physicians, less a 15 percent management fee.

C. MEDICAL STAFF STRUCTURE

This part of the chapter explores the structure of the relationship between physicians and health care facilities. It begins with the classic organization of the hospital medical staff, which is both central to and unique to the medical system in the United States. Later cases explore in more detail the fierce disputes that can arise over medical staff membership, and how these bodies of hospital law apply to membership in managed care networks.

■DOCTORS, PATIENTS, AND HEALTH INSURANCE: THE ORGANIZATION AND FINANCING OF MEDICAL CARE
Herman Miles Somers & Anne Ramsay Somers
1961

[Read the excerpt at page 13.]

1. Medical Staff Bylaws

Physicians' rights and status with hospitals are defined by medical staff bylaws. Virtually unique from any other kind of organization, hospitals typically have two sets of bylaws, one for the medical staff and another for the hospital administration as a whole. The next two cases explore the relationship between these two governance structures, and whether it is possible to restructure the hospital medical staff.

■ST. JOHN'S HOSPITAL MEDICAL STAFF v. ST. JOHN REGIONAL MEDICAL CENTER
245 N.W.2d 472 (S.D. 1976)

St. John's Hospital Medical Staff is an unincorporated association whose members . . . hold medical staff privileges at . . . the St. John Regional Medical Center [in] Huron, South Dakota. . . . In October 1947, as construction of the [hospital] neared completion, the Sisters of the Franciscan Order proposed certain medical staff bylaws to regulate the affairs of the physicians wanting to use the hospital. . . . The interpretation and effect of these articles formulate the main issues of this action. The "Amendment Article" provides: "These by-laws may be amended after notice given at any regular meeting of the staff. Such [amendments] . . . shall require a two-thirds majority of those present for adoption. Amendments so made shall be effective when approved by the governing body." . . .

In 1972, the [hospital] wished to make certain changes in the bylaws.[2] The attempted changes were unacceptable to the medical staff and an impasse developed, . . . [so] the board of directors of the [hospital] unilaterally adopted new medical staff bylaws which were not approved by the medical staff. The [hospital] now insists that the medical staff is bound by the bylaws so adopted. . . . The [hospital] argues that . . . the power to amend the articles must be lodged in the directors in order to avoid . . . the possibility of independent hospital liability in some future case of malpractice. After a review of the record, we find these arguments to be without merit. . . .

As a general rule, the bylaws of a corporation . . . constitute a binding contract between the corporation and its shareholders. . . . In the present case, we hold that the 1947 medical staff bylaws do constitute a contract which is, by its express terms, subject to amendment when the amendment is agreed to by both the medical staff and the [hospital]. The principles which govern the construction of contracts also govern the construction and interpretation of corporate bylaws. . . . Therefore, both the medical staff and the [hospital] are bound by them until they are amended in accordance with the procedure set out [above]. . . .

South Dakota statutes recognize the power in a corporation to delegate a voice in the adoption of new bylaws to another entity. Such is the case here. The original articles of incorporation and [hospital] bylaws authorize the medical staff to promulgate medical staff bylaws. These medical staff bylaws call for a specific amendment procedure which must be followed. The [hospital] by ignoring th[is] procedure and by not including the medical staff in the attempted bylaws amendment has breached this contractual relationship with the medical staff.

■MAHAN v. AVERA ST. LUKES

621 N.W.2d 150 (S.D. 2001)

Orthopedic Surgery Specialists (OSS) . . . commenced this action against Avera St. Lukes (ASL) alleging breach of contract. . . . ASL is part of a regional health care system sponsored by the Sisters of the Presentation of the Blessed Virgin Mary of Aberdeen, South Dakota. [It is the only facility in a 90-mile radius.] Since 1901, the Presentation Sisters have been fulfilling their mission statement "to respond to God's calling for a healing ministry . . . by providing quality health services" to the Aberdeen community. . . .

In mid-1996, ASL's neurosurgeon left Aberdeen. . . . During the process [of recruiting his replacement], ASL learned that most neurosurgeon applicants would not be interested in coming to Aberdeen if there was already an orthopedic spine surgeon practicing in the area. This was due to the small size of the community and the probable need for the neurosurgeon to supplement his or her practice by performing back and spine surgeries. . . . ASL was successful in recruiting a

2. E.g., one change would allow the Chief Executive Officer of the [hospital] to temporarily suspend the clinical privileges of a staff physician upon a determination that the action must be taken immediately in the best interests of the patient care in the [hospital]. Another change would require [hospital] approval of all officers of the medical staff.

neurosurgeon who arrived in December, 1996. Around this time, ASL learned that OSS, a group of Aberdeen orthopedic surgeons, had decided to build a day surgery center that would directly compete with ASL. During the first seven months that OSS' surgery center was open, ASL suffered a 1,000-hour loss of operating room usage.

In response, . . . [ASL's Board] closed ASL's medical staff with respect to physicians requesting privileges for [spine surgery] . . . [and] closed ASL's medical staff to applicants for orthopedic surgery privileges. . . . The effect of "closing" the staff was to preclude any new physicians from applying for privileges to use hospital facilities for the named procedures. The Board's decision did not affect those physicians that had already been granted hospital privileges, including the physician-members of OSS. . . .

In the summer of 1998, OSS recruited Dr. Mahan, a spine-fellowship trained orthopedic surgeon engaged in the practice of orthopedic surgery. . . . Mahan officially requested an application for staff privileges with ASL [but] these requests were denied due to the Board's decision. . . . Mahan and OSS commenced this action against ASL, challenging the Board's decision to close the staff. The circuit court determined that ASL had breached the Staff Bylaws by closing the staff . . . without first consulting the staff. . . . The circuit court reasoned that because [the Board had delegated power regarding medical staff issues], the Board no longer had the power to initiate actions that affected the privileges of the medical staff. . . .

It is well settled in South Dakota that "a hospital's bylaws constitute a binding contract between the hospital and the hospital staff members." St. John's, 245 N.W.2d at 474. . . . [However,] under South Dakota law, "[t]he affairs of a [nonprofit] corporation *shall* be managed by a board of directors." . . . Pursuant to its authority, the Board of ASL has delegated certain powers associated with the appointment and review of medical personnel to its medical staff. These designated powers are manifested in the Staff Bylaws. Plaintiffs now claim that the Staff Bylaws trump the decision-making ability of the Board as to all decisions relating in any way to, or incidentally affecting, medical personnel issues. We do not agree.

The circuit court failed to give sufficient weight to the fact that the Staff Bylaws are derived from the Corporate Bylaws. . . . Their legal relationship is similar to that between statutes and a constitution. They are not separate and equal sovereigns. . . . The Corporate Bylaws state that "[t]he business and the property of the Corporation shall be managed and controlled . . . by a Board of Trustees. . . ." In addition, the Corporate Bylaws provide that . . . "the Members of the Board of Trustees shall have and exercise the authority . . . to delegate to the Medical Staff the authority to *evaluate the professional competence* of staff Members and applicants for staff privileges and to hold the Medical Staff responsible for *making recommendations* to the Members of the Board of Trustees concerning initial staff appointments, reappointments and the assignment or curtailment of privileges, *all subject to the final approval of the Members of the Board of Trustees*" (emphasis added). . . .

Clearly, under these explicit powers, the Board has the authority to make business decisions without first consulting the medical staff. . . . Plaintiffs rely on the Staff Bylaws as their source of authority to assume the Board's power. Yet, even within the Staff Bylaws, there is no explicit provision granting the medical staff control over personnel issues. Instead, the circuit court found that the actions of the Board violated "the spirit of the bylaws taken as a whole." Such reliance on the "spirit of the

[Staff] bylaws" turns the corporate structure of ASL upside down. . . . ASL cannot continue to offer unprofitable, yet essential services including the maternity ward, emergency room, pediatrics and critical care units, without the offsetting financial benefit of more profitable areas such as neurosurgery. The Board . . . surely has the power to attempt to insure ASL's economic survival. . . .

[T]he circuit court determined that this was not an administrative decision by the Board. Instead it held this was a decision regarding the "granting or withholding [of] staff privileges," and that the action fell "within the provisions of the medical staff bylaws." . . . According to the circuit court, in matters of personnel, the Board has only "secondary approval authority . . . ; no actions originate with the Board itself." The circuit court further concluded that the Board is only allowed to give its "seal of approval" at the final stages of staff actions. As support for this view, the circuit court cited the Staff Bylaws . . . as follows: "Initial appointments and reappointments to the Medical staff shall be made by the Governing Body. The Governing Body shall act on appointments, reappointment, or revocation of appointment only after there has been recommendation from the Medical Staff as provided in these Bylaws." The circuit court also cited a provision in the Credentialing Manual to support its claim that the Board has essentially only rubber stamp authority. That provision states that "[t]he Board shall either accept or reject the recommendation of the Credentials and Executive Committee. . . ." Finally, the circuit court found that the procedure for hearings and appellate review [by the Board] was further evidence that the Board was not allowed to originate any actions relating to the medical staff, it was only allowed to hear appeals.

These provisions have been misconstrued by the circuit court. . . . The purpose of this limited delegation of authority was to obtain input from the staff on areas of its expertise. Decisions relating to the competence, training, qualifications and ethics of a particular physician are matters for which the medical staff is uniquely qualified, while the Board admittedly has limited expertise in those areas. Under the Corporate Bylaws, it is *only* in those confined areas of expertise that the staff has any authority at all. . . . [T]he medical staff gives recommendations to the Board on issues relating to appointment and privileges. However, this case is not about appointments or the assignment or curtailment of privileges. It is about an administrative decision to close ASL's staff for certain procedures; therefore, the medical staff has no part in the decision and the Staff Bylaws do not apply. . . . The procedure for hearings and review only applies if a decision by the Board "will adversely affect [the practitioner's] appointment to or status as a member of the Medical Staff or his exercise of clinical privileges. . . ." The disputed action by the Board did not affect any physician's appointment or status as a member of the staff. . . .

Within its broad powers of management, some of the business decisions made by the Board will undoubtedly impinge upon matters that relate to or affect the medical staff of the hospital. This fact is unavoidable. However, merely because a decision of the Board affects the staff does not give the staff authority to overrule a valid business decision made by the Board. Allowing the staff this amount of administrative authority would effectively cripple the governing Board of ASL. . . .

In its decision, the circuit court attempted to distinguish between this present situation and the situation wherein a hospital enters into an exclusive contract. We find this attempt to be unpersuasive. An exclusive contract arises when the hospital contracts with an outside physician or group of physicians, whereby the hospital agrees that the physician or group of physicians shall be the only personnel allowed to use certain facilities in the hospital, such as radiology units or emergency room units. Such exclusive contracts are common practice for most hospitals today, and have been almost universally found valid and enforceable, even if not explicitly provided for in corporate bylaws. In the past, ASL has closed several areas of its facility to physicians not part of an exclusive contract. Such areas include anesthesiology, radiology, emergency room care, pathology, EKG interpretation, pulmonary function interpretation and cardiac cathe[te]rization. Plaintiffs do not allege that the prior exclusive contracts entered into by ASL are invalid. . . . Yet there is no logical reason why ASL could close certain areas of its facility to all but a few physicians (via an exclusive contract), yet not be allowed to close its facilities to any new orthopedic surgeons performing certain, named procedures. . . .

The circuit court also concluded that ASL must accept an application from any doctor wishing to have privileges at ASL . . . if the staff is satisfied [that the doctor is qualified] . . . Such a construction of the Staff Bylaws reaches a result that is contrary to the Corporate Bylaws and common sense. Are we to force ASL to grant privileges to every qualified physician that may stand at its doorstep and announce that he or she will henceforth be using the hospital's facilities, simply because the staff said they could? . . . The result reached by the circuit court . . . is impractical in a corporate business environment. Imagine the confusion and lack of clear lines of management authority that would ensue at the hospital if the Board had only the minimal amount of control over its medical staff that the circuit court would give it. . . .

Hospitals have legally defined responsibilities and duties. . . . [T]he negligent act of a doctor can impute liability to a hospital under a theory of *respondeat superior* . . . [Also], separate liability for negligence attaches to a hospital when it has breached its own standards, or those available in the same or similar community or hospitals generally, such as allowing a known incompetent doctor to remain on staff. . . . It would be completely illogical to first impose a duty of reasonable care upon a hospital, and then later strip the hospital of the ability and power to implement the policies and programs required to fulfill that duty. . . . Therefore, the circuit court's judgment is reversed.

Notes: Hospital and Medical Staff Bylaws; Exclusive Contracts; Economic Credentialing

1. *The "Two-Headed Monster."* Notice how the medical staff credentialing process was caricatured in *Mahan*. The court ridiculed the idea that the hospital has to "grant privileges to every qualified physician that may stand at its doorstep and announce that he or she will henceforth be using the hospital's facilities, simply because the staff said they could? . . . [This] is impractical in a corporate business environment. Imagine the confusion and lack of clear lines of management authority that would ensue at the hospital if the Board had only th[is] minimal amount of control over its medical staff. . . ." "Allowing the staff this amount of administrative authority would effectively cripple the governing Board." Yet many hospital administrators would say that this is precisely how hospitals have traditionally functioned, because hospitals are essentially required to maintain "open" medical staffs, and hospital boards are expected to, and do, simply "rubber stamp" medical staff recommendations. In the view of one experienced lawyer:

The internal organization of hospitals has remained essentially uniform and un-changed for the past seventy years.[1] Today, as in the past, the hospital is composed of three independent lines of authority: the medical staff, the management, and the board of directors.[2] . . . The self-governing medical staff is a feature of hospitals found only in the United States and Canada.[3] . . . The thesis of this article is that the self-governing medical staff model is an anachronistic mode of hospital organiza-tion that generally impedes the delivery of high-quality, cost-effective care. As other commentators have suggested, the law has imposed an organizational structure on hospitals that conflicts with the current regulatory agenda of promoting such care.[4] . . . Consequently, federal and state laws should be amended or repealed to allow hospitals to organize themselves according to their own managerial vision of hospi-tal organization.

Thaddeus J. Nodzenski, A Critical Analysis of the Self-Governing Medical Staff, 43 Okla. L. Rev. 591, 592 (1990). The unique structure of American hospitals has been described as "attractive as a two-headed monster" and as "stable as a three-legged stool." See H. L. Smith, Two Lines of Authority Are One Too Many, 84 Modern Hosp., March 1955, at 59.

2. *Is the Paradigm Shifting?* Many commentators have noticed a possible para-digm shift in progress. They see in decisions like *Mahan* the potential demise of the independent medical staff, to be replaced by an ordinary employment con-tract model that gives the hospital much greater control over medical as well as managerial policy. See Nodzenski, supra; Lawrence Casalino et al., Hospital-Physi-cian Relations: Two Tracks and the Decline of the Voluntary Medical Staff Model, 27(5) Health Aff. 1305 (Oct. 2008). This development is also mirrored in financing structures like HMOs and other integrated delivery systems that combine hospital and physician services under a single capitation payment. Others observe that the increased sense of urgency to improve the quality of care has led to renewed calls for hospital management to assert more authority over the medical staff. John D. Blum, Feng Shui and the Restructuring of the Hospital Corporation: A Call for Change in the Face of the Medical Error Epidemic, 14 Health Matrix 5 (2004); Symposium, 12 Ann. Health L. 179 (2003).

Observe, though, that Nodzenski, who applauds increased authority of medi-cal institutions, works for the hospital industry. Are his views sound nevertheless? The subordination of physicians is vehemently opposed by organized medicine, for reasons articulated in the discussion of the corporate practice of medicine doc-trine in section B.3. Consider what weapons physicians have in their legal arsenal to oppose fundamental structuring of the hospital medical staff. Realize that this orga-nizational structure emerged as the result of accreditation standards set by the Joint

---

1. Harris, Regulation and Internal Control in Hospitals, 55 Bull. N.Y. Acad. Med. 88, 90-92 (Jan. 1979).

2. See Hall, Institutional Control of Physician Behavior: Legal Barriers to Health Care Cost Containment, 137 Pa. L. Rev. 431, 505-506 (1988).

3. The Report of the Joint Task Force on Hospital-Medical Staff Relationships of the AMA and the AHA 10 (1985).

4. See generally Clark Havighurst, Doctors and Hospitals: An Antitrust Perspective on Traditional Relationships, 1984 Duke L.J. 1071, 1087-1092; Hall, supra n.2, at 528-532.

Commission (JCAHA), which require separate medical staff bylaws that are under the control of member physicians. In 2010, after years of sometimes acrimonious deliberation, the Joint Commission revised its medical staff standards to reinforce the elements of self-governance. 23(2) The Health Lawyer 10 (Dec. 2010). This self-governing structure is also embedded in law to the extent that many hospital licensing statutes incorporate the Joint Commission standards by reference. Other legal sources explored throughout this chapter support this structure less visibly. Consider, for instance, the impact of the charitable tax exemption, or the corporate practice of medicine doctrine, on how doctors relate to hospitals. Note also that this dual line of authority is mirrored in the structure of insurance, which pays hospitals separately from physicians, and which results in Blue Cross vs. Blue Shield, and Medicare Part A vs. Part B.

3. *Hospitalists.* Assuming that the traditional medical staff structure remains intact at least on paper, how far can a hospital feasibly go in circumventing this structure? Could a hospital use exclusive contracts for the entire array of medical services? It is not possible to consider this question fully until other bodies of law are explored, such as tax exemption and referral fee prohibitions that are discussed in sections B.2 and E, and even then the answer is far from clear. The issue may be joined, however, by the growing use of physicians known as "hospitalists" — hospital-based primary care physicians who replace patients' regular physicians in managing care when the patients are hospitalized, as is the practice in European hospitals. Hospitals view this hospitalist system as an effective way to impose greater manage-rial discipline on patient care decisions, in order to improve scheduling, reduce costs, and increase quality. Primary care physicians like the convenience of being able to concentrate their attention on their office-based practice, especially under HMO payment structures that do not reward them, or may even penalize them, for hospital care. However, many physicians view this as an invasion of their established patient relationships, and specialists see this as a threat to their source of referrals and income. So far, hospitalist programs are voluntary, in the sense that primary care physicians can use them at their discretion, but hospitals in theory could start to insist on using their employed staff.

4. *Bylaws Are Binding.* Are *St. John's* and *Mahan* in conflict? If not, how are they reconciled? If so, which has the better argument? Can you possibly justify *Mahan*'s statement that "this case is not about appointments or the assignment or curtail-ment of [clinical] privileges. It is about an administrative decision. . . . The disputed action by the Board did not affect any physician's appointment or status as a mem-ber of the staff"? What if this action were taken right after the orthopedic physician group had just hired a new physician who was in the process of applying for staff privileges? Is *Mahan* limited to a circumstance of dire economic or medical neces-sity? Does it turn on the wording of the particular bylaws used by that hospital?

Many other courts have agreed with *St. John's* that medical staff bylaws con-stitute a contract and cannot be amended or ignored unilaterally by the hospital board. For instance, this was the holding in a suit involving a different Avera hospi-tal, Medical Staff of Avera Marshall Regional Medical Center v. Avera Marshall, 857 N.W.2d 695 (Minn. 2014). Yet, most courts also agree with *Mahan* that hospitals are free to enter unilaterally into exclusive contracts or stop admitting new members to a portion or all of the medical staff. E.g., Garibaldi v. Applebaum, 742 N.E.2d 279 (Ill. 2000) (awarding an exclusive contract is an administrative decision and so does not require a medical staff hearing for excluded physicians because the decision is not necessarily based on physician competence); Radiation Therapy Oncology, P.C. v. Providence Hospital, 906 So. 2d 904 (Ala. 2005) (hospital board may close cancer radiation staff as a "valid business decision," related in part to quality of care); City of Cookeville v. Humphrey, 126 S.W.3d 897 (Tenn. 2004) (bylaws require only "consultation" and not approval by medical staff prior to hospital adopting exclusive contract that closed the radiology staff). But see Kessel v. Monongalia County General Hospital Co., 600 S.E.2d 321 (W. Va. 2004) (exclusive contract by a public hospital for anesthesia services infringes on the physicians' right to practice and patients' rights to choose their own physicians (even anesthesiologists!)).

Courts reconcile these two lines of authority in two ways: (1) They distinguish, as *Mahan* did, between administrative decisions reserved to the hospital board versus medical decisions made by the medical staff. When the reasons for action are economic, they fall in the board's realm to act unilaterally. How well does this square with *St John's*? (2) Courts also distinguish between the possession of clinical privileges and the right to exercise those privileges, reasoning that medical staff bylaws protect only the former, not the latter. This distinction arises in exclusive contract cases, where the hospital picks a certain set of physicians to staff a portion of the hospital, such as the emergency room or the room where anesthesia is administered. The result is that not only new doctors but also existing doctors lose the ability to practice in those areas of the hospital. Courts uphold this nonetheless by reasoning that, technically, the non-contracting doctors still retain their status as members of the medical staff and are entitled to practice in other areas of the hospital. One court said that "such reasoning simply defies logic. Hospital privileges are not, in reality, some amorphous grant [of status]. . . . They are instead quite specific descriptions of very particular acts a doctor is permitted to do in that facility. Precluding a doctor from performing those acts is, as Plaintiffs here assert, very much a denial or termination of hospital privileges." Aluko v. Charlotte-Mecklenburg Hospital Authority, 959 F. Supp. 729 (W.D.N.C. 1997). However, this court also "recognize[d] the very real needs that hospitals . . . have to respond in a rapidly changing health care market with its unique blend of savage competition and heavy-handed governmental regulation." The court reconciled these competing considerations by reasoning that it is not the form of restriction that matters (denial of staff privileges vs. limiting use of the facilities); rather, it is the reason given for the restriction: quality of care vs. an economic reason. Where the physicians' "professional reputations are intact, . . . there is no foreclosure of opportunity to practice their profession nor bar to seeking privileges in other institutions." Is this reasoning convincing? In today's marketplace, might not a reputation for being a high-cost or inefficient physician potentially be just as damaging as having a reputation for poor quality? For a thorough analysis of these and other cases, see Bryan A. Liang, An Overview and Analysis of Challenges to Medical Staff Exclusive Contracts, 18 J. Leg. Med. 1 (1997). See generally Annot., 74 A.L.R.3d 1268 (1974).

5. *Economic Credentialing.* The focus in these cases on hospitals' motivation for closing departments or using exclusive contracts points to a broader issue of immense importance to health care law and public policy—whether hospitals can explicitly consider economic factors in choosing physicians, in addition to, or instead of, quality-of-care factors. In the trade, this is known as "economic credentialing." The decisions discussed in the next section express the traditional attitude

that only quality factors are relevant, but they arose before cost concerns became so paramount. Now that public policy embodies cost concerns as well, can they be included in the balance of considerations? Indeed, it appears from some cases that financially motivated exclusions are *easier* to justify than those motivated by quality concerns, because only the latter must be pursued through the medical staff hearing process and justified under the bylaws. If one is concerned about patient care, shouldn't this distinction cut in exactly the opposite direction?

This issue remains largely unsettled, however. In those jurisdictions that require economically based exclusions to be pursued through the bylaws process, two obstacles remain: (1) the need to amend traditional quality-based medical staff bylaws to make sure economic concerns are allowable criteria for reviewing physicians; (2) the legal uncertainty over whether economic concerns can *trump* quality concerns. Physicians who are excluded from contracts and medical staff membership because their treatment patterns are too expensive will likely complain that the hospital is sacrificing high quality for low costs. Hospitals have been able to avoid this charge by arguing that cost savings do not in fact compromise quality (e.g., swapping one good high-cost doctor for another good low-cost doctor), or by arguing that lower-cost treatment produces higher quality (e.g., reducing the risks of unnecessary surgery or medication). See, e.g., Knapp v. Palos Community Hospital, 465 N.E.2d 554 (Ill. App. Ct. 1984) (physician whose costs were 31 percent higher than others also had serious quality problems from overutilization of tests and medication).

Another form of economic credentialing is known as "conflict credentialing," in which hospitals refuse privileges to physicians who establish specialty facilities that compete with the hospital's services, under the theory that there is an economic conflict of interest between the two parties. In an important ruling, the Arkansas Supreme Court held that it violates public policy and constitutes an unfair trade practice for a general hospital to exclude from its staff any physician with an ownership interest in a competing specialty hospital. Baptist Health v. Murphy, 373 S.W.3d 269 (Ark. 2010).

6. *Further Readings.* For discussion of the nature, status, and powers of the **hospital medical staff** (note 1), see William Brewbaker, Antitrust Conspiracy Doctrine and the Hospital Enterprise, 74 B.U. L. Rev. 67 (1994); James F. Blumstein, Of Doctors and Hospitals: Setting the Analytical Framework for Managing and Regulating the Relationship, 4 Ind. Health L. Rev. 209 (2007); Lawton Burns et al., History of Physician-Hospital Collaboration, *in* Crosson & Tollen, page 1250. Discussing the increasing **tensions between hospitals and their medical staffs**, see John D. Blum, Beyond the Bylaws: Hospital-Physician Relationships, Economics, and Conflicting Agendas, 53 Buff. L. Rev. 459 (2005); Robert Berenson et al., Hospital-Physician Relations: Cooperation, Competition, or Separation?, 26(1) Health Aff. w31 (Jan. 2006); Symposium, 26(1) Health Aff. w31 (Dec. 2006).

For discussions of **hospitalists** (note 3), including ethical and public policy issues, see Hoangmai Pham, Hospitalists and Care Transitions, 27(5) Health Aff. 1315 (Oct. 2008); J. Coffman & T. G. Rundall, The Impact of Hospitalists on the Cost and Quality of Inpatient Care in the United States: A Research Synthesis, 62 Med. Care Res. Rev. 379 (2005); R. M. Wachter & L. Goldman, The Hospitalist Movement 5 Years Later, 287 JAMA 487 (2002); David Meltzer, Hospitalists and the Doctor-Patient Relationship, J. Leg. Stud. 589 (2001).

On **economic credentialing** (note 5), see Beverly Cohen, An Examination of the Right of Hospitals to Engage in Economic Credentialing, 77 Temp. L. Rev. 705 (2004); Elizabeth A. Weeks, The New Economic Credentialing: Protecting Hospitals from Competition by Medical Staff Members, 36 J. Health L. 247 (2003); Comment, 88 Marq. L. Rev. 413 (2004); Blum, supra, 53 Buff. L. Rev. 459 (2005).

Notes: Physician Employment; Labor Law

1. *Covenants Not to Compete.* As illustrated by Berlin v. Sarah Bush Lincoln Health Center, page 1338, physician contracts, both with hospitals and with medical clinics and groups, also usually contain restrictive covenants that prevent them from practicing with competitors in the vicinity for a defined period of time. Physicians have been somewhat more successful in attacking these contract provisions. Covenants not to compete, in this and other employment contexts, are viewed with suspicion by the courts because they tend to contravene public policies in favor of free trade and the right to work. Nevertheless, these covenants are upheld if they are reasonable as to duration, geographic scope, and the range of activities covered, and if they are not otherwise contrary to the public interest.

The issue of greatest relevance in the medical context is whether it violates public policy to restrain the practice of a physician whose specialized services are much needed in the community. For example, in Dick v. Geist, 693 P.2d 1133 (Idaho Ct. App. 1985), the court refused to enforce a restrictive covenant that would have excluded the two doctors who rendered 90 percent of the neonatal care in the community. One court refused to enforce a restriction against a general practitioner who left an HMO and took 167 of his patients with him, even though there was no local shortage of physicians. The court was particularly disturbed by a penalty clause that assessed $700 for each patient the doctor took with him. The court reasoned that this "financial wedge . . . needlessly hindered the continuation of existing and successful doctor/patient relationships . . . vital to the provision of health care." Humana v. Jacobson, 614 So. 2d 520 (Fla. Dist. Ct. App. 1992). See also Murfreesboro Medical Clinic, P.A. v. David Udom, 166 S.W.3d 674 (Tenn. 2005) ("The right of a person to choose the physician that he or she believes is best able to provide treatment is so fundamental that we can not allow it to be denied because of an employer's restrictive covenant."). However, another line of cases has reasoned that hospitals have an interest in the protection of their own patient relationships, or that the public interest is equally well served if a doctor is allowed to treat different patients in another part of the state. Concord Orthopaedics v. Forbes, 702 A.2d 1273 (N.H. 1997); Sisters of Charity Health System v. Farrago, 21 A.3d 110 (Maine 2011).

2. *Labor Laws.* In addition to the *private* law rights of *individual* doctors, the law is also concerned with the *public* law rights of *groups* of health care employees. By convention, the former set of issues is labeled "employment law" and the latter "labor law." Other employment law issues relating to "at will" employment, wrongful discharge, and various employment discrimination laws are explored at pages 1365 and 1375. The remainder of these notes survey labor law.

The National Labor Relations Act (NLRA), 29 U.S.C. §§151 et seq., establishes a comprehensive regulatory scheme, administered by the National Labor Relations Board (NLRB), to protect employees' rights to form a union, to require their employer to bargain with the union in good faith and honor collective bargaining agreements, and to strike if they are dissatisfied with the terms or conditions of their employment. Employed physicians' efforts to unionize must clear a critical hurdle. The Supreme Court has interpreted the NLRA as excluding from its protections "managerial employees," those who assist management in setting and implementing policy. NLRB v. Bell Aerospace, 416 U.S. 267 (1974). In NLRB v. Yeshiva University, 444 U.S. 672 (1980), the Court determined in a 5-4 vote that this exclusion applies to professional employees—in that case, university professors—who serve on important committees and heavily influence hiring decisions. In Delphic dictum, however, the Court cautioned that not all employed professionals are ipso facto managers: "[E]mployees whose decisionmaking is limited to the routine discharge of professional duties in projects to which they have been assigned cannot be excluded from coverage. . . . Only if an employee's activities fall outside the scope of the duties routinely performed by similarly situated professionals will he be found aligned with management." 444 U.S. at 690.

The meaning of this distinction for employed doctors remains a matter of considerable dispute. In FHP and Union of American Physicians and Dentists, 274 N.L.R.B. 1141 (1985), the NLRB determined that all 70 doctors employed by an HMO were "managerial" and therefore not able to unionize because they served on numerous peer review and patient care committees that formulate and effectuate clinical policy. Even though these are the same committees typically found in a hospital, a prior decision ruled that the employed physicians at a teaching hospital (ironically, at Yeshiva University's medical school) were not managerial because clinical policy there was merely advisory, and department chairs exercised most of the managerial power. Montefiore Hospital, 261 NLRB 569 (1982). The NLRB subsequently applied the *Montefiore* precedent to HMOs, finding physicians are not managerial. E.g., New York University Medical Center, 324 NLRB 887 (1997).

3. *Physician Unions.* Although the disturbing specter of a physician strike is virtually unheard of, labor union activity in the health care sector has increased considerably. Most of this activity involves nonphysicians such as nurses and technicians, but even among physicians there has been interest in unionizing as a way to counteract loss of clinical and economic autonomy. In 1999, the AMA's House of Delegates took the unprecedented step of calling for the AMA to form a national bargaining unit under federal law to represent employed physicians and residents. The politically conservative leadership of the AMA has long opposed the formation of a union, but the AMA membership insisted on this move to give physicians a stronger voice against HMOs and hospitals, and to preempt efforts by other labor organizations that are eager to take the lead in forming physician unions. It is important to realize, though, that the NLRA covers only employees. This limitation would seem to exclude independent physicians on hospital or HMO medical staffs from the NLRA's protections. 329 NLRB No. 55 (1999). Despite this limitation, physician unionizing is still of pressing importance due to the great increase in physician employment, especially by hospitals or health systems.

One advantage physicians seek by unionizing is protection from the antitrust laws, by virtue of the antitrust exemption for labor activities. 15 U.S.C. §17. (Otherwise, every employee strike over wages would constitute per se price fixing.) Subsequent sections of these materials describe the antitrust difficulties physicians face when they organize into groups to negotiate with insurance companies, HMOs and

PPOs over reimbursement rates. See section D.2. As a result, some doctors have attempted to label their negotiating groups "unions." The flaw in this tactic is that doctors traditionally have not been employees of insurance plans; they are, at best, independent contractors. Therefore, their collective actions could result in huge damages or even criminal sentences. See AMA v. United States, 317 U.S. 519 (1943) (rejecting labor exemption claim made by physicians who boycotted an HMO). To avoid this, physicians have sought legislative authority to engage in collective bargaining with HMOs (but not strikes or boycotts), in order to offset HMO market power. The physicians' first victory was in Texas in 1999; but so far, similar legislative proposals have not been adopted at the national level. Although state law cannot give physician unions the same status they have under federal labor law, it might (or might not) achieve the same objective of conferring an exemption from antitrust laws using the "state-action immunity" doctrine mentioned on page 1410.

4. *Nurse Managers.* The "managerial employee" exclusion from the NLRA's protections has surprisingly proven troublesome for nurses as well. Nurse employees in hospitals and nursing homes historically had no problem qualifying unless they held explicitly supervisory positions. In 1994, the Supreme Court ruled, however, that nurses employed in a nursing home exercised sufficient de facto supervision over nurses' aides to meet the managerial exclusion because they controlled work assignments. Health Care & Retirement Corp. of America v. NLRB, 511 U.S. 571 (1994). The NLRB, however, has resisted following this precedent, for instance, by finding that hospital "charge nurses" do not have managerial status. In NLRB v. Kentucky River Community Care, 532 U.S. 706 (2001), the Court reversed the NLRB again, holding that it read the Act too narrowly in ruling that supervising nurses at a mental health facility are not managers. Yet, the NLRB once again resisted, ruling that only full-time charge nurses qualify as managers, and not those who have these responsibilities only part time. Oakwood Healthcare Inc., 348 NLRB No. 37 (2006).

5. *Disruption of Patient Care; Definition of Bargaining Units.* Until 1974, nonprofit hospitals, which constitute the bulk of the industry, were not covered by the NLRA. In that year, however, Congress amended the Act with provisions directed specifically to the health care industry. 29 U.S.C. §§152, 158, 169, 183. In doing so, Congress expressed a concern that union activity not disrupt patient care. Specifically, both the Senate and the House stated that "due consideration should be given by the Board to preventing proliferation of bargaining units in the health care industry" because too many unions within a single institution would pose an excessive risk of crippling, repetitive strikes. 1974 U.S. Code Cong. & Admin. News 3950. This "nonproliferation" directive has been a constant thorn in the side of the NLRB's numerous attempts to determine the appropriate scope of hospital bargaining units for nurses and other nonphysician employees. See, e.g., NLRB v. HMO International, 678 F.2d 806 (9th Cir. 1982) (improper to exclude vocational nurses from RN's union) (noting the "nearly perfect record of reversals of the NLRB by the court of appeals in review of health care bargaining units").

In response to a series of court reversals, the NLRB, which is notorious for deciding all policy issues in adjudication, took the extraordinary step of initiating a rulemaking proceeding to define the proper approach to health care unit determinations. Its final regulations allow up to eight, but only eight, separate bargaining units in any hospital, regardless of local circumstances: RNs, physicians, other professionals, technicians, clerical, maintenance, security guards, and others. 29 C.F.R.

§103.30. These rules generated intense opposition from health care management, which perceives that carving units into this many divisions greatly increases the ease of unionizing. The rule was upheld by the Supreme Court, however. American Hospital Ass'n v. NLRB, 499 U.S. 606 (1991). In nonhospital health care facilities, the proper size of bargaining units remains unsettled. See, e.g., Specialty Healthcare and Rehabilitation Center, 357 NLRB 83 (2011) (allowing nursing assistants at a nursing home to organize separately from other service workers).

6. *Further Readings.* For general discussions of labor law issues in the health care industry, see Grace Budrys, When Doctors Join Unions (1997); William Brewbaker, Physician Unions and the Future of Competition in the Health Care Sector, 33 U.C. Davis L. Rev. 545 (2000); Note, 9 J. Health & Biomed. L. 117 (2013); Comment, 36 Hous. L. Rev. 951 (1999); Comment, 19 Cardozo L. Rev. 1125 (1997); Note, 34 Colum. J.L. & Soc. Probs. 1-48 (2000); Note, 42 Ariz. L. Rev. 803-833 (2000); Note, 52 Vand. L. Rev. 1051 (1999).

Problem: Economic Credentialing

You are the lawyer for Florence Nightingale Community Hospital. The administrator approaches you about how best to amend the bylaws so that the hospital can get rid of doctors who are costing the hospital too much money under Medicare and HMO insurance. The administrator is concerned about which removal actions can be defended in court and which bylaw amendments are politically feasible with physicians. Advise the administrator on each of these options:

- Amend the Hospital Bylaws to give the hospital board authority to remove doctors from the medical staff for any reason, regardless of the medical staff's own recommendations, as long as the medical staff is first consulted.
- Amend the Medical Staff Bylaws to declare that an additional criterion for medical staff membership is to practice an efficient style of medicine that avoids wasting medical resources or providing unnecessary care.
- Amend the Medical Staff Bylaws to declare that any physician who consistently loses money for the hospital will be removed from the medical staff.
- Forget about amending any bylaws. Instead, go after physicians who are economic losers based on their general medical competence and their unwillingness to be cooperative.
- Keep but supplant the entire medical staff structure by limiting who can practice in each department through one-year renewable contracts with the 200 best doctors out of the present 300.

2. Medical Staff Disputes

Access to a hospital is essential for most physicians to carry on a practice. Hospitals, on the other hand, are coming under increasing legal and economic pressure to monitor who joins the medical staff. From the intersection of these two competing interests springs a powerful flow of litigation, in the health care field, second only to malpractice. These materials explore which legal theories are available to physicians wanting to challenge their exclusion, and how much scrutiny courts impose on these decisions. We begin with common-law doctrine, first as applied to hospitals and then to HMOs. Following that is antitrust law. As you read the first two cases, try to identify what species of common law is being used to review staffing decisions by private hospitals, and attempt to articulate what hospitals have to show to justify their decisions.

■ GREISMAN v. NEWCOMB HOSPITAL
192 A.2d 817 (N.J. 1963)

JACOBS, Judge.

In 1958, the plaintiff graduated from the Philadelphia College of Osteopathy with the degree of doctor of osteopathy. [See nn.3 and 4 in Weiss v. York Hospital at page 1384 for a definition of osteopathy.] He served an internship, took the full medical boards in New York, and was given an unqualified license to practice medicine and surgery in that state. Thereafter, he was admitted to practice in Michigan, Florida and New Jersey. His New Jersey admission by the State Board of Medical Examiners constituted an unrestricted license to practice medicine and surgery within the borders of our State. See Falcone v. Middlesex Co. Medical Soc., 34 N.J. 582, 170 A.2d 791 (1961). In July 1959, he began the general practice of medicine in the City of Vineland and, in November 1959, he opened an office in Newfield which is in the Vineland metropolitan area. Until January 1962 he also engaged in the practice of medicine from his home in Vineland. He is the only licensed physician in Newfield, is the plant physician for a Newfield company engaged in heavy industrial work and for an additional company engaged in the making of glassware, and is the school physician for Newfield's public school as well as for a Catholic school in the same community. He states that he is the only osteopathic physician fully licensed to practice general medicine and surgery in the metropolitan Vineland area which is said to have a population approximating 100,000; the defendants state that there is another osteopathic physician practicing in Vineland but the suggested variance is of no real significance here.

In 1961, the plaintiff sought to file an application for admission to the courtesy staff of the Newcomb Hospital which is located in Vineland about a mile from his home. The hospital was incorporated in 1921, is operated as a general hospital, and is the only hospital in the Vineland metropolitan area. Its certificate of incorporation sets forth the purposes for which it was formed including . . . the care of sick and injured persons residing in the vicinity of Vineland. . . . The hospital is a nonprofit corporation and its governing body is a Board of Trustees consisting of not less than 15 members. It solicits and receives funds annually in the form of charitable contributions and has received funds from the Ford Foundation. Several years ago, it constructed a new building, the cost being borne almost entirely by public subscription. It receives funds from the City of Vineland for the treatment of indigent patients from within the city, and funds from the County of Cumberland for the treatment of indigent patients from other areas in the county. It receives tax exemptions available to nonprofit corporations operated for charitable and like purposes. It is eligible for federal funds under the Hill-Burton Act.

Despite suitable requests, the Newcomb Hospital refused to permit the plaintiff to file any application for admission to its courtesy staff. In taking that course it did not question his personal or professional qualifications nor did it purport to exercise a discretion in the process of administrative screening and selection. It rested entirely on a provision in the hospital bylaws which sets forth that an applicant for membership on the courtesy staff must be a graduate of a medical school approved by the American Medical Association and must be a member of the County Medical Society. The American Medical Association has long rejected schools of osteopathy, though the original supporting reasons have been largely dissipated. See Report of the Committee for the Study of Relations Between Osteopathy and Medicine, 158 JAMA 736 (1955). Admittedly, the plaintiff is not a graduate of a medical school approved by the American Medical Association and, because of his schooling, his application to the County Medical Society was never acted upon. The school he graduated from is an accredited school of osteopathy, has been approved as in good standing by the New Jersey State Board of Medical Examiners, and has long given the full traditional medical course as well as osteopathic teaching. . . .

The Law Division found that the Newcomb Hospital did not confine itself to any specialized branch of medicine and had assumed the position and status of the only general hospital open to the public within the convenient accessibility of the inhabitants of the metropolitan area of Vineland, including Newfield; that the plaintiff had suffered economic and other harm because he was not permitted to admit his patients to the hospital or to serve them professionally once they were admitted, or to use the emergency room services of the hospital; that his patients suffered restriction in their choice of physicians or hospital facilities because of the plaintiff's inability to attend them professionally at the hospital, and that this was not minimized by the fact that the plaintiff was permitted to visit them at the hospital without, however, any opportunity to read their charts or prescribe for them. . . .

The defendants contend that the Newcomb Hospital is a private rather than a public hospital, that it may in its discretion exclude physicians from its medical staff, and that no legal ground exists for judicial interference with its refusal to consider the plaintiff's application for membership. . . . Broad judicial expressions may, of course, be found to the effect that hospitals such as Newcomb are private in nature and that their staff admission policies are entirely discretionary. They are private in the sense that they are nongovernmental but they are hardly private in other senses. Newcomb is a nonprofit organization dedicated by its certificate of incorporation to the vital public use of serving the sick and injured, its funds are in good measure received from public sources and through public solicitation, and its tax benefits are received because of its nonprofit and nonprivate aspects. It constitutes a virtual monopoly in the area in which it functions and it is in no position to claim immunity from public supervision and control because of its allegedly private nature. Indeed, in the development of the law, activities much less public than the hospital activities of Newcomb, have commonly been subjected to judicial (as well as legislative) supervision and control to the extent necessary to satisfy the felt needs of the times. See Munn v. Illinois, 94 U.S. 113 (1877); German Alliance Ins. Co. v. Lewis, 233 U.S. 389 (1914); Nebbia v. New York, 291 U.S. 502 (1934).

During the course of history, judges have often applied the common law so as to regulate private businesses and professions for the common good; perhaps the most notable illustration is the duty of serving all comers on reasonable terms which was imposed by the common law on innkeepers, carriers, farriers and the like. See Falcone v. Middlesex Co. Medical Soc., supra, 34 N.J., at p. 594; Messenger et al. v. Pennsylvania R.R. Co., 36 N.J.L. 407 (Sup. Ct. 1873). In the *Messenger* case Chief Justice Beasley, speaking for the former Supreme Court, noted that a railroad, though a private corporation, is engaged in a "public employment," that it "owes a duty to the community" and that under considerations of public policy it must be held under obligation to serve without discrimination. On appeal, Justice Bedle, speaking for the Court of Errors and Appeals, expressed the view that although railroad corporations are private, they hold their property "as a quasi-public trust," and that as trustees they must conduct their operations in such manner so as to insure to every member of the community the equal enjoyment of the means of transportation.

Implemented by specific legislation, the supervision of private businesses and professions for the public good has gone far beyond the early common law fields. In Munn v. Illinois, supra, a state's imposition of maximum charges for the storage of grain in warehouses was sustained in an opinion which stressed that the private property was devoted "to a public use" and was therefore subject to public regulation; in German Alliance Insurance Co. v. Lewis, supra, a state's fixing of fire insurance rates was upheld on the ground that the business of insurance was "so far affected with a public interest" as to justify its regulation; and in Nebbia v. New York, supra, a state's extensive regulation of its milk industry was upheld in an opinion by Justice Roberts which frankly recognized that there is no closed class or category of businesses affected with a public interest, that the phrase means no more than that an industry, for adequate reason, is subject to control for the public good, and that "upon proper occasion and by appropriate measures the state may regulate a business in any of its aspects." . . .

It is evident that . . . similar policy considerations apply with equal strength and call for a declaration that . . . Dr. Greisman is entitled to have his application evaluated on its own individual merits without regard to the bylaw requirement rejected by the Law Division. His personal and professional qualifications are not in dispute here; he lives in Vineland, has an office in Newfield in the Vineland metropolitan area, has an unrestricted license to practice medicine and surgery, and is engaged in the general practice of medicine. All he seeks, at this juncture, is simply permission to file his application for membership on the courtesy staff of the Newcomb Hospital and have it considered to the end that, if he is passed on favorably in accordance with the hospital's valid bylaws, he and his patients, as such, will have hospital facilities when needed.

The Newcomb Hospital is the only hospital in the Vineland metropolitan area and it is publicly dedicated, primarily to the care of the sick and injured of Vineland and its vicinity and, thereafter to the care of such other persons as may be accommodated. Doctors need hospital facilities and a physician practicing in the metropolitan Vineland area will understandably seek them at the Newcomb Hospital. Furthermore, every patient of his will want the Newcomb Hospital facilities to be readily available. It hardly suffices to say that the patient could enter the hospital under the care of a member of the existing staff, for his personal physician would have no opportunity of participating in his treatment; nor does it suffice to say that there are other hospitals outside the metropolitan Vineland area, for they may be too distant or unsuitable to his needs and desires. All this indicates very pointedly that, while the managing officials may have discretionary powers in the selection of the medical staff, those powers are deeply imbedded in public aspects, and are rightly viewed . . . as fiduciary powers to be exercised reasonably and for the public good.

It must be borne in mind that we are not asked to pass on a discretionary exercise of judgment but only on the validity of the bylaw requirement. Therefore, we need not concern ourselves with any of the larger issues relating to discretionary limits or the general lengths to which a hospital may go in conditioning staff admissions on the approval of outside bodies. Viewed realistically, our proper concern here is whether the hospital had the right to exclude consideration of the plaintiff, solely because he was a doctor of osteopathy and had not been admitted, because of his osteopathic schooling, to his County Medical Society. . . . In this day there should be no hesitancy in rejecting as arbitrary, the stand that a doctor of osteopathy, though fully licensed by state authority and reputably engaged in the general practice of medicine and as the local school and plant physician, is nonetheless automatically, and without individual evaluation, to be considered unfit for staff membership at the only available hospital in the rather populous metropolitan area where he resides and practices. The public interest and considerations of fairness and justness point unerringly away from the hospital's position and we agree fully with the Law Division's judgment rejecting it.

Hospital officials are properly vested with large measures of managing discretion and to the extent that they exert their efforts toward the elevation of hospital standards and higher medical care, they will receive broad judicial support. But they must never lose sight of the fact that the hospitals are operated not for private ends but for the benefit of the public, and that their existence is for the purpose of faithfully furnishing facilities to the members of the medical profession in aid of their service to the public. They must recognize that their powers, particularly those relating to the selection of staff members, are powers in trust which are always to be dealt with as such. While reasonable and constructive exercises of judgment should be honored, courts would indeed be remiss if they declined to intervene where, as here, the powers were invoked at the threshold to preclude an application for staff membership, not because of any lack of individual merit, but for a reason unrelated to sound hospital standards and not in furtherance of the common good.

Affirmed.

■ NANAVATI v. BURDETTE TOMLIN MEMORIAL HOSPITAL
526 A.2d 697 (N.J. 1987)

POLLOCK, J.

This appeal arises out of the revocation of the staff privileges of Suketu H. Nanavati (Dr. Nanavati) as a cardiologist at Burdette Tomlin Memorial Hospital (the hospital). . . .

The background of this case is a dispute between Dr. Nanavati and Dr. Robert Sorensen, who at the time was the chief of cardiology, chairman of the Department of Medicine, and a member of the Board of Governors at the hospital. The dispute originated over the allocation of the reading of electrocardiograms (ECGs or EKGs), which, at $5 per reading, produced an annual income of approximately $75,000. Burdette Tomlin is the only hospital in Cape May County, and when he was granted staff privileges, Dr. Nanavati was the only board-certified cardiologist in the county. Before the arrival of Dr. Nanavati in 1979, Dr. Sorensen, an internist, enjoyed a virtual monopoly on reading ECGs. Dr. Nanavati was allowed to read ECGs one day each week, but when he requested an additional day, Dr. Sorensen rejected his request. The rejection stimulated Dr. Nanavati into criticizing Dr. Sorensen, who retaliated. As the discord between the two doctors escalated, Dr. Nanavati allegedly committed a series of violations of the hospital's bylaws. On August 2, 1982, the medical staff executive committee "voted unanimously to act toward the revocation of Dr. Nanavati's medical staff privileges." That action marked the beginning of lengthy proceedings before the hospital authorities and before federal and state courts in this state.

Pursuant to the hospital bylaws, the chairman of the medical staff executive committee requested the hospital executive committee to take corrective action. The executive committee forwarded the request to the chief of the Department of Medicine, who appointed an ad hoc committee to investigate the matter. The charges against Dr. Nanavati were captioned as "Acts of Disruptive Behavior" and "Failure to Cooperate with Hospital Personnel Regarding the Use of Facilities Especially During the Summer Months and the Emergent Admissions Procedures."

Underlying these charges is the contention that Dr. Nanavati caused disruption in violation of a bylaw provision requiring a staff doctor to

> be of a temperament and disposition that will enable him to work in harmony with his colleagues on the Medical Staff; with the professional, technical, and other personnel in the hospital, and with the administration, accepting criticism without resentment and offering it in a spirit and manner that is constructive and devoid of offense and malice. . . .

The further allegation is that Dr. Nanavati violated a bylaw provision that a staff member "must enjoy the reputation of being an ethical and conscientious practitioner and must strictly abide by the Code of Ethics. . . ." At no time has the hospital questioned Dr. Nanavati's technical competence.

On August 23, 1982, the ad hoc committee "found against Dr. Nanavati on all charges and specifications" and recommended as the only appropriate punishment "his discharge from the Medical Staff of Burdette Tomlin Memorial Hospital, together with the permanent deprivation of Burdette Memorial Hospital privileges." The executive committee of the medical staff affirmed that finding, and Dr. Nanavati appealed to an ad hoc committee of the medical staff, which unanimously found against him and recommended that he be dismissed from the staff of the hospital. In November, the hospital administrator advised Dr. Nanavati of the revocation of his staff privileges.

Dr. Nanavati immediately filed an action in the Chancery Division, which found that the proceedings had not been conducted in accordance with the hospital's bylaws, enjoined the revocation of Dr. Nanavati's privileges, and remanded the matter for further proceedings to be conducted in accordance with the hospital's bylaws. The Board of Governors thereupon appointed a hearing committee, which recommended on April 15, 1983, "that the action of the medical staff in dismissing Dr. Nanavati be affirmed." Two weeks later, on April 29, the board affirmed the hearing committee's recommendation. . . .

[On appeal] the Chancery Division independently reviewed the record by a preponderance-of-the-evidence standard. The court determined that Dr. Nanavati's staff privileges should not be revoked on the ground of disharmony, absent a showing of actual interference with patient care, and concluded that the record did not support any such showing. Consequently, the court issued a permanent injunction against revocation of his privileges.

Although the Appellate Division affirmed the trial court's finding that the hospital proceedings were invalid, it disagreed with other portions of the trial court's opinion and held that the trial court, in reviewing the revocation of hospital staff privileges, should not have made independent findings of fact, but should have determined whether the hospital's decision was supported by sufficient credible evidence. In addition, the Appellate Division ruled that mere disharmony, although an insufficient ground by itself, is a relevant consideration in revocation proceedings. . . .

We granted Dr. Nanavati's petition for certification to determine the appropriate standard of review of the decision by a hospital to terminate a physician's staff privileges and to determine further whether actual interference with patient care is required in order to terminate those privileges. . . .

Twenty-five years ago we rejected the notion that decisions of private hospitals concerning staff privileges were beyond judicial review. Greisman v. Newcomb Hosp., 192 A.2d 817. By analogy to private businesses affected by the public interest, we ruled that courts should intervene when a hospital denied staff membership "for a reason unrelated to sound hospital standards and in furtherance of the common good." In reaching that conclusion, we also declared that "reasonable and constructive exercises of judgment should be honored. . . ." Thus, courts should sustain a hospital's standard for granting staff privileges if that standard is rationally related to the delivery of health care. A decision is so related if it advances the interests of the public, particularly patients; the hospital; or those who are essential to the hospital's operations, such as doctors and nurses.

Although not quite so deferential when reviewing individual decisions denying staff privileges, courts still apply a relaxed standard of review to those decisions. The test for judicial review of such a decision is whether it is supported by "sufficient reliable evidence, even though of a hearsay nature, to justify the result."

We have previously explained the difference between the two tests by analogy to judicial review of administrative actions. Setting a standard for admission to staff privileges is roughly analogous to the kind of policy decision reflected in administrative rulemaking. Carrying forward the analogy, a hospital's use of that standard to decide a particular case is like quasi-judicial agency action. . . .

Underlying the more relaxed standard is our growing awareness that courts should allow hospitals, as long as they proceed fairly, to run their own business. That sense is tempered by the recognition that doctors need staff privileges to serve their patients, and that the public interest requires that hospitals treat doctors fairly in making decisions about those privileges. . . .

In prior cases, we have considered the denial of privileges to new applicants. . . . Although we have not previously decided a case involving the *revocation* of privileges, . . . [n]onetheless, the standard of judicial review should remain the same. . . .

[I]f a hospital is to care for its patients, the staff, particularly doctors and nurses, must work together. As important as cooperation is to other corporations, it is even more critical in a modern hospital, where no single doctor cares for all the needs of any one patient. Hospital doctors depend on their colleagues, nurses, technicians, and other employees for total patient care. . . . Consequently, a hospital may adopt a bylaw providing that the inability of a doctor to work with nurses and other doctors is a ground for denying or terminating staff privileges. . . .

Doctors, like other people, have quirks, and some doctors are more disagreeable than others. The mere fact that a doctor is irascible, however, does not constitute good cause for termination of his or her hospital privileges. McElhinney v. William Booth Memorial Hosp., 544 S.W.2d 216, 218 (Ky. 1977). Nor should allegations of "disharmony" ever be used as a ruse to deny or terminate staff privileges because of a doctor's race, religion, color, or gender. Likewise, a doctor should not be cut off from staff membership merely because he or she has criticized hospital practices and other doctors. . . . A hospital need not wait for a disruptive doctor to harm a patient before terminating his or her privileges. Nonetheless, more should be required than general complaints of a physician's inability to cooperate with others. To constitute disruptive behavior meriting termination of staff privileges, hospital authorities should present concrete evidence of specific instances of misbehavior, such as unjustified altercations with other doctors or nurses, violations of hospital routines or rules, breaches of professional standards, or the commission of some other act that will adversely affect health care delivery. . . .

The judgment of the Appellate Division is affirmed as modified, and the cause is remanded to the hospital.

Notes: Judicial Review of Medical Staff Disputes

1. *Overiew.* Why might a hospital want to exclude a doctor? More doctors, after all, mean more patients. If it is in a hospital's economic interest to exclude only bad doctors, why should we bother to scrutinize the hospital's decision at all?

In addressing these questions, the principal focus of these notes will be the common-law fairness theory announced in *Greisman.* The notes explore first whether any judicial review is available, and then the scope of review. As *Nanavati* indicates, it is helpful to divide the scope of judicial review into two components—procedural and substantive—and, further, to divide substantive review into (a) the rationale for the general membership criteria contained in the bylaws and (b) the evidence supporting the application of the bylaws to an individual physician. The primary focus of these notes is on the next-to-last issue: the substantive validity of general criteria.

2. *Other Legal Causes of Action.* There are many other causes of action potentially available to excluded physicians besides common-law fairness. Pursued below in section D.1 are challenges under the federal antitrust laws. State antitrust statutes and common-law unfair competition theories are another hook for the same hat. Under tort law, excluded physicians can allege defamation, e.g., Purgess v. Sharrock, 33 F.3d 134 (2d Cir. 1994) ($5.1 million damages), civil conspiracy, Nashville Memorial Hospital v. Brinkley, 534 S.W.2d 318 (Tenn. 1976), or tortious interference with contract, supra. The prior section also discusses the use of contract law to require hospitals to adhere to their bylaws when reviewing the credentials of existing medical staff members. Several states create statutory causes of action. See, e.g., N.Y. Pub. Health Law §2901-c(1) (McKinney); Egan v. St. Anthony's Medical

Center, 244 S.W.3d 169 (Mo. 2008) (implied statutory action). Doctors excluded from public hospitals can bring constitutional claims. Caine v. Hardy, 905 F.2d 858 (5th Cir. 1990). Finally, claims can be brought under the civil rights statutes that protect against discrimination based on suspect classifications such as race or disability, even though physicians, technically speaking, are not employees of the hospital. See, e.g., Doe v. St. Joseph's Hospital, 788 F.2d 411 (7th Cir. 1986) (Title VII action applies); Ambrosino v. Metropolitan Life Insurance Co., 899 F. Supp. 438 (N.D. Cal. 1995) (state law version of the ADA governs a physician excluded due to past drug dependency). But see Alexander v. Rush Medical Center, 101 F.3d 487 (7th Cir. 1996) (no Title VII action exists where physician is independent contractor); Jimenez v. WellStar Health System, 596 F.3d 1304 (11th Cir. 2010) (no civil rights violation in a state where bylaws do not constitute a contract). For further discussion, see the Web site for this book, www.health-law.org.

Observe that each of these alternative legal theories is limited by elements of the cause of action that do not restrain the common-law fairness theory. But, even under that theory, if bylaws constitute a contract, can they be used to require physicians to waive any right to sue over credentialing decisions? See Estate of Blume v. Marian Health Center, 516 F.3d 705 (8th Cir. 2008) (such a provision does not violate public policy, in the absence of any claim that civil rights were violated).

3. *Constitutional Issues.* Care must be taken to distinguish the *common-law* fairness theory articulated in *Greisman* from *constitutional* due process and equal protection. While the content of the doctrines may (or may not) be the same, their origins are distinctly different. Only public hospitals, that is, those *owned* by state or municipal authorities, are subject to the Constitution; it is well settled that the extensive involvement of private hospitals with public funding and regulation is not sufficient to constitute state action. Blum v. Yaretsky, 457 U.S. 991 (1982); Philips v. Pitt County Memorial Hospital, 572 F.3d 176 (4th Cir. 2009).

A constitutional theory that has not succeeded, even at public hospitals, is the *substantive* due process argument that "all licensed physicians have a constitutional right to practice their profession. It is not incumbent on the state to maintain a hospital for the private practice of medicine." Hayman v. City of Galveston, 273 U.S. 414, 417 (1926).

4. *Judicial Review, Pro and Con.* The *Greisman* public-facility theory has not won uniform acceptance. Consider the validity of the following objection to the quasi-public facility theory:

> It is far from clear today why hospitals are under any greater obligation than typical employers to account to the courts for the fairness with which they screen applicants for professional positions or why health care professionals deserve any special legal help in surmounting marketplace barriers to their pursuit of a livelihood. The due process requirements that common-law courts have required private hospitals to observe in allocating staff privileges are in fact anomalous and find weak support in the common-law ground in which they are rooted.

Clark Havighurst, Doctors and Hospitals: An Antitrust Perspective on Traditional Relationships, 1984 Duke L. J. 1071, 1099-1100.

The following are a sampling of cases pro and con: *Pro judicial review*—Silver v. Castle Memorial Hospital, 497 P.2d 564 (Haw. 1972); Barrows v. Northwestern

Memorial Hospital, 525 N.E.2d 50 (Ill. 1988); Mahmoodian v. United Hospital Center, 404 S.E.2d 750 (W. Va. 1991). *Contra judicial review*—Pepple v. Parkview Memorial Hospital, 536 N.E.2d 274 (Ind. 1989); Lakeside Community Hospital v. Levenson, 710 P.2d 727, 728 (Nev. 1985); Medical Center Hospitals v. Terzis, 367 S.E.2d 728 (Va. 1988). Canada, which is virtually the only other country with a medical staff structure similar to ours, follows the New Jersey approach. The leading case is Abouna v. Foothills Provincial General Hospital, [1978] 2 W.W.R. 130. See generally Craig W. Dallon, Understanding Judicial Review of Hospitals' Physician Credentialing and Peer Review Decisions, 73 Temp. L. Rev. 597 (2000); K. Van Tassel, Does the Hospital Peer Review Hearing Process Negatively Impact Healthcare Quality, Cost and Access?, 40 Pepperdine L. Rev. 911 (2013); Nicholas Bagley, Medicine as a Public Calling, 114 Mich. L. Rev. 57, 88 (2015).

5. *Monopoly Status.* In examining how faithful this body of law is to the common carrier/innkeeper precedent on which it is based, consider whether excluded physicians should be able to demand judicial review of the fairness of a private hospital's decision even if they (and their patients) have the choice of several other hospitals in town, or should the public-facility theory apply only where hospitals exercise monopoly power in their local markets? *Barrows*, supra, 525 N.E.2d 50 (Ill. 1988) (the former); Kelly v. St. Vincent Hospital, 692 P.2d 1350 (N.M. Ct. App. 1984) (the latter). Given that the great majority of all municipalities in the United States with an acute care hospital have only one or two, usually with similar medical staff membership, is it appropriate to overlook this technicality in those locations where there is effective competition?

6. *Physician Access vs. Patient Access.* Note that the common-law public service duties of common carriers were owed to their *customers*, not to their employees. As *Greisman* recognizes, then, excluded doctors have cause to complain only by virtue of their control over patient admissions to hospitals. Consequently, should the public-facility doctrine apply to doctors such as anesthesiologists and consulting specialists who do not admit patients? No one appears to have considered this issue.

7. *Extensions of the Quasi-Public Theory.* It is fascinating to speculate what other applications might exist for a doctrine as novel as this. One case has extended the quasi-public facility theory to physician (as opposed to hospital) services, holding that a patient refused service by the only practice group in town after lodging a complaint against one of the doctors in the group may maintain an action alleging an arbitrary refusal to serve. Leach v. Drummond Medical Group, 192 Cal. Rptr. 650 (Ct. App. 1983). Consider, also, whether private hospitals owe common-law fairness duties to their *employed* physicians. Ezekial v. Winkley, 572 P.2d 32 (Cal. 1977) (yes for existing employees but not for applicants).

And what about possible hospital duties extending directly to *patients*? Chapter 2.A.1 explains that the quasi-public characterization has been used by a few courts to prevent hospitals from refusing patients for arbitrary or invidious reasons. But can a hospital set limits on which services or accommodations it offers? For instance, could this doctrine be used by a woman in labor to demand that her husband be allowed to attend the birth? Hulit v. St. Vincent's Hospital, 520 P.2d 99 (Mont. 1974) (holding no, but only after finding that the hospital rule was "reasonable" and "fair"). Finally, if ancient common-law precedents are to be given full force in this context, note that common carriers were subject to heightened liability for accidents and to judicial scrutiny for the reasonableness of their rates!

8. *Valid and Invalid Criteria.* Among the numerous possible criteria for medical staff membership, those that are usually upheld include possessing a license to practice medicine, having board certification, or having satisfactory references. Criteria that are usually struck down include being a member in the local medical society and having a recommendation from one or more current members of the medical staff. See American Health Lawyers Ass'n, Peer Review Guidebook (5th ed. 2016); Annot., 37 A.L.R.3d 645 (1971).

9. *Deference to Medical Judgment.* Is *Nanavati* consistent with the following frequently quoted standard of review?

> No court should substitute its evaluation of such matters for that of the Hospital Board. . . . Human lives are at stake, and the governing board must be given discretion in its selection so that it can have confidence in the competence and moral commitment to its staff. The evaluation of professional proficiency of doctors is best left to the specialized expertise of their peers, subject only to limited judicial surveillance. . . . In short, so long as staff selections are administered with fairness, geared by a rationale compatible with hospital responsibility, and unencumbered with irrelevant considerations, a court should not interfere.

Sosa v. Board of Managers, 437 F.2d 173 (5th Cir. 1971). See also Branch v. Hempstead County Memorial Hospital, 539 F. Supp. 908 (W.D. Ark. 1982) ("this court does not intend . . . to become a super hospital governing board"); Sadler v. Dimensions Healthcare Corp., 836 A.2d 655 (Md. 2003) (applying a corporate law "business judgment" rule).

10. *The Hard Cases.* In *Greisman*, the hospital did not attempt to defend its exclusion of osteopaths on the basis of a quality-of-care rationale. If it had, what justification would suffice? Is it necessary to establish *poor* quality of care, or only a relative *difference* in the quality of care? Which of the following exclusionary policies do you think are valid?

- A hospital limits staff membership to licensed physicians (M.D.s or D.O.s), which necessarily excludes other licensed health professionals such as clinical psychologists, podiatrists, nurse midwives, and chiropractors. Shaw v. Hospital Authority, 614 F.2d 946 (5th Cir. 1985) (constitutionally permissible to exclude podiatrists).

- A tertiary care hospital limits staff membership to specialists who are board eligible or board certified, which necessarily excludes general practitioners, including many osteopaths. Silverstein v. Gwinnett Hospital Authority, 861 F.2d 1560 (11th Cir. 1988) (valid); Armstrong v. Board of Directors, 553 S.W.2d 77 (Tenn. 1977) (invalid).

- A Christian Science hospital excludes physicians who do not practice according to its religious beliefs. Cf. Watkins v. Mercy Medical Center, 520 F.2d 894 (9th Cir. 1975) (Catholic hospital may refuse to have abortions performed on premises, but may not exclude abortionists from staff).

- A hospital excludes osteopaths because they are trained under a different medical philosophy. Hayman v. City of Galveston, 273 U.S. 414, 417 (1926) (sufficient to pass constitutional muster); Stern v. Tarrant County Hospital District, 778 F.2d 1052 (5th Cir. 1985) (en banc) (same); Petrocco v. Dover General Hospital, 642 A.2d 1016 (N.J. Super. 1994) (permissible under *Greisman* for hospital to exclude chiropractors where it gave the issue careful thought and rational justification).

It may assist you in answering these questions to employ an equal protection type of analysis by asking what level of scrutiny do physician exclusion decisions warrant—minimum "rational basis," strict "compelling interest," or intermediate "substantial basis" scrutiny? Do you see any indication that courts heighten their level of scrutiny in response to suspicions about the genuineness of the asserted reasons for physician exclusion? Professor Havighurst, above, argues that medical staff decisions should be presumed valid when they appear to be made independently by the hospital motivated by its own business concerns, but should be scrutinized when it appears that physicians controlled or influenced the decision for competitive or personal reasons. Does this appear consistent with what the courts are doing?

11. *Disruptive Physicians.* Courts no longer seem to deliberate as closely as the *Nanavati* case did before upholding hospital decisions to discipline disruptive physicians. It now appears that a documented series of unprofessional behavior will suffice, regardless of whether patient care is actually threatened. See, e.g., Sternberg v. Nanticoke Memorial Hospital, 15 A.3d 1225 (Del. 2011); Guier v. Teton County Hospital District, 248 P.3d 623 (Wyo. 2011). This low-tolerance position is supported by the Joint Commission, which in 2009 adopted a standard that requires hospitals to police disruptive behavior.

12. *Economic Credentialing.* The debate in physician exclusion cases usually turns on whether the decision was motivated by the public interest in quality of care or by the existing doctors' interest in limiting competition. But what about the *hospital's* interest? Is it ever allowed to exclude a physician to advance its private economic interest, so long as that interest does not conflict with the public interest? In one limited context, courts have allowed explicitly self-interested hospital motives. They have held that a hospital has a "right to take reasonable measures to protect itself" against exposure to joint and several liability with a doctor by requiring all medical staff members to carry a certain level of insurance. Holmes v. Hoemako Hospital, 573 P.2d 477 (Ariz. 1977). See Annot., 7 A.L.R.4th 1238 (1977).

With the mounting pressure for improved efficiency in medical treatment, it is widely predicted that this question will take on much broader significance. Hospitals are contemplating using economic criteria in the credentialing process to screen out wasteful doctors. The notes at page 1353 explore whether a body of law premised on excluding physicians for poor quality will accommodate physician exclusion for *excessive* quality. Assuming this is generally permissible, what evidence will be necessary in the particular case that a physician's treatment patterns are excessively costly: that the doctor's patients are more expensive than average, the most expensive of all, much more expensive than anyone else's? Will courts entertain objections by the doctor that his patients are especially difficult cases and therefore costly because (a) he is such a terrific doctor he gets all the hard cases; (b) he's been in practice longer and so naturally his patients are older and therefore sicker on average; (c) random luck of the draw? See Sokol v. Akron General Medical Center, 173 F.3d 1026 (6th Cir. 1999) (split decision on whether objections like these undermine statistics showing that a surgeon's patients died more frequently than those of other surgeons).

13. *Procedural Protections.* Much of the case law on medical staff disputes concerns only whether the excluded doctor received procedural due process. See, e.g.,

Kiester v. Humana Hospital Alaska, 843 P.2d 1219 (Alaska 1992); Silver v. Castle Memorial Hospital, 497 P.2d 564 (Haw. 1972); American Health Lawyers Ass'n, Peer Review Guidebook (1995). Physician credentialing usually proceeds through several stages: investigation by a departmental or hospitalwide credentialing committee; vote by the medical staff as a whole and/or its executive committee; consideration of the medical staff recommendation by the hospital board; and an evidentiary review hearing if the board's decision is negative. Courts require that an excluded physician, whether an applicant or an existing staff member, be given notice of the charges, an opportunity to present evidence, and the right to confront and cross-examine opposing witnesses. The decisionmakers in this quasi-adjudicatory hearing may not be exposed to ex parte communication and must not have prejudged the merits. Much of this law is codified in the Health Care Quality Improvement Act of 1986, discussed at page 1409, which imposes fair procedure requirements as a condition for conferring an immunity on those who participate in the hospital peer review process. The major respects in which this act differs from the case law are (1) it allows the challenged physician representation by counsel, and (2) it disqualifies from the hearing panel anyone who is in "direct economic competition" with the physician. 42 U.S.C. §11112(b). Observe, though, that this Act's procedural steps are not mandatory or exclusive; they only create a safe harbor that establishes one manner in which a hospital can qualify for immunity. Cf. Owens v. New Britain General Hospital, 643 A.2d 233 (Conn. 1994) (only substantial, not strict, compliance with bylaw procedures is required). Nevertheless, the procedures specified in the Act have quickly become the industry standard in practice.

What problems do these requirements present for a small rural hospital? See Applebaum v. Board of Directors, 163 Cal. Rptr. 831 (Ct. App. 1980) (procedures unfair where five physicians served on both the initial review committee and the hearing committee); A. Southwick, The Law of Hospital and Health Care Administration 618 (2d ed. 1988) ("In hospitals having a relatively small medical staff the risk of bias and partiality increases. A hearing panel composed of persons from outside the hospital may then be necessary.").

3. Membership in Managed Care Networks

HMOs have also been drawn into disputes arising from physician selection decisions. When they exclude physicians from their networks, the stakes from the physicians' point of view can be just as high, but the reasons may differ, as may the available legal theories for judicial review. Think carefully about whether HMO physicians should have the same legal theory of action as hospital physicians, and, if not, which exclusion decisions and reasons are valid or invalid as a result.

■ POTVIN v. METROPOLITAN LIFE INSURANCE CO.
997 P.2d 1153 (Cal. 2000)

KENNARD, Judge.

After removal from defendant insurance company's "preferred provider" lists, plaintiff physician brought this action. Citing the common law right to fair procedure, which forbids arbitrary expulsions from private organizations under certain circumstances, plaintiff alleged he should have been given reasonable notice and an opportunity to be heard before his removal.

We first applied the common law doctrine of fair procedure in the late 19th century. . . . Some 50 years later, relying on the general principles underlying this doctrine, we held that a union could not arbitrarily deny full membership privileges to African-American workers. Thereafter, in the 1960's and 1970's, we extended the doctrine in a trio of decisions . . . involv[ing] the exclusion of a dentist from professional organizations [and] a hospital's expulsion of a surgical resident. The general principles this court enunciated in the[se] decisions apply in this case as well.

On September 10, 1990, Metropolitan Life Insurance (MetLife) entered into an agreement with Dr. Louis E. Potvin, an obstetrician and gynecologist, to include him as one of 16,000 participants on two of its preferred provider lists. Potvin had practiced medicine for more than 35 years; he was a past president of the Orange County Medical Association; and he held full staff privileges at Mission Regional Hospital, where he had served as Chairman of the Obstetrics and Gynecology Department for nine years. . . . The agreement . . . provided for termination by either party "at any time, with or without cause, by giving thirty (30) days prior written notice to the other party."

On July 22, 1992, MetLife notified Potvin in writing that effective August 31, 1992, it was terminating his preferred provider status . . . without cause. MetLife then stated that even though it did not have to give a reason, Potvin's "delistment from the provider network was related to the fact that [he] did not meet [MetLife's] current selection and retention standard for malpractice history." At the time, MetLife would not include or retain on its preferred provider lists any physician who had more than two malpractice lawsuits, or who had paid an aggregate sum of $50,000 in judgment or settlement of such actions. Potvin's patients had sued him for malpractice on four separate occasions, all predating his 1990 agreement with MetLife. In three of these actions, the plaintiffs had abandoned their claims, while the fourth case had settled for $713,000.

After MetLife failed to respond to Potvin's request for a hearing, Potvin filed this lawsuit. . . . Potvin alleged that MetLife's termination of his preferred provider status devastated his practice, reducing it to "a small fraction" of his former patients. He asserted that he was required to reveal his termination to other insurers and managed care entities, which then removed him from their preferred provider lists, and that he suffered rejection by "physician groups . . . dependent upon credentialling by MetLife" and by current MetLife preferred provider physicians, who ceased referring patients to him. The trial court granted MetLife's motion for summary judgment. . . .

II

The purpose of the common law right to fair procedure is to protect, in certain situations, against arbitrary decisions by private organizations. As this court has held, this means that, when the right to fair procedure applies, the decisionmaking "must be both substantively rational and procedurally fair." . . . In James v. Marinship Corp. 25 Cal.2d 721, 155 P.2d 329 (1944), . . . we upheld an injunction restraining the labor union and the employer, a Marin County shipbuilder, from "discharging or causing the discharge of . . . Negro employees because they are not members of a labor union with which their employer has a closed shop agreement, but which will not grant Negroes full membership privileges." . . . We explained: "It was well established at common law that innkeepers and common carriers were under a duty to furnish accommodations to all persons, in absence of some reasonable ground. . . . Where, as here, a labor union has attained a monopoly of the labor supply through closed shop agreements, such a union, like a public service business, may not unreasonably discriminate against Negro workers for the sole reason [of their race]." . . . Thereafter, . . . we went on to say: "one may not be expelled from membership in a private association without charges, notice and hearing. This common law protection against arbitrary expulsion, judicially declared, is of broader application and has been extended not only to labor unions [citations] and professional and trade organizations [citations], but to mutual benefit societies [citations] and other fraternal and social groups [citations]. The underlying theme of these decisions, variously stated, is that membership in an association, with its associated privileges, once attained, is a valuable interest which cannot be arbitrarily withdrawn. Thus, they comport with the broader principle that one on whom an important benefit or privilege has already been conferred may enjoy legal protections not available to an initial applicant for the same benefit." Exekial v. Winkley, 752 P.2d 32 (Cal. 1977). . . .

Plaintiff here points out that when an insurance company with fiduciary obligations to its insureds maintains a list of preferred provider physicians to render medical services to the insureds, a significant public interest is affected. One practical effect of the health care revolution, which has made quality care more widely available and affordable through health maintenance organizations and other managed care entities, is that patients are less free to choose their own doctors for they must obtain medical services from providers approved by their health plan. . . .

Our conclusion that the relationship between insurers and their preferred provider physicians significantly affects the public interest does not necessarily mean that every insurer wishing to remove a doctor from one of its preferred provider lists must comply with the common law right to fair procedure. The obligation to do so arises only when the insurer possesses power so substantial that the removal significantly impairs the ability of an ordinary, competent physician to practice medicine or a medical specialty in a particular geographic area, thereby affecting an important, substantial economic interest. . . . Here, plaintiff's amici curiae, the American Medical Association and the California Medical Association, . . . predict that in the near future no more than a handful of health care entities will dominate the managed care industry. If participation in managed care arrangements is a practical necessity for physicians generally and if only a handful of health care entities have a virtual monopoly on managed care, removing individual physicians from preferred provider networks controlled by these entities could significantly impair those physicians' practice of medicine.

Here, Potvin alleged that among the adverse effects of removal from MetLife's preferred provider lists were rejection by "physician groups which were dependent upon credentialing by MetLife" and devastation of his practice, which was reduced to "a small fraction" of his former patients. Proof of these allegations might establish that, in terminating a physician's preferred provider status, MetLife wields power so substantial as to significantly impair an ordinary, competent physician's ability to practice medicine or a medical specialty in a particular geographic area, thereby affecting an important, substantial economic interest. . . . We therefore agree with Potvin that the "without cause" termination clause is unenforceable to the extent it purports to limit an otherwise existing right to fair procedure under the common law.

BROWN, J., dissenting.

With its decision today, the majority, in effect, declares that it is the public policy of this state that physicians are entitled to a minimum income. . . . What is the majority's authority for declaring this public policy, for singling out physicians for such special treatment? . . . Historically, the common law duty to serve arose in response to the fact that in the 15th century those engaged in certain public callings, for example, innkeepers and carriers, exercised virtual monopolies. "When the weary traveller reaches the wayside inn in the gathering dusk, if the host turn him away what shall he do? Go on to the next inn? It is miles away, and the roads are infested with robbers. The traveller would be at the mercy of the innkeeper, who might practice upon him any extortion, for the guest would submit to anything almost, rather than be put out into the night." (Wyman, The Law of the Public Callings as a Solution to the Trust Problem (1904) 17 Harv. L.Rev. 156, 159.) . . . Under the standard announced by the majority today, an insurer need not exercise monopoly power before the burdens of the common law right of fair procedure are imposed on it. Rather, . . . it is sufficient if the insurer has any significant share of a regional market. . . .

History has confirmed this court's judgment that the racial discrimination practiced by the union in *Marinship* was "an act against which the law has definitely set its face." However, it trivializes *Marinship* to suggest that anything like the same degree of public policy consensus has developed with regard to the question at bar. According to Dr. Potvin, the average physician who practices his specialty, obstetrics/gynecology, has been sued for malpractice 2.3 times. Metropolitan Life Insurance Company (MetLife) wishes to restrict its preferred provider lists to physicians with a slightly better than average malpractice history, to those who have not been sued more than twice. Potvin, by contrast, has been sued 4 times—nearly twice the average. Now the majority's public policy antennae may be more sensitive than mine, but I suspect the jury is still out on the question of whether an insurer should be able to control its costs by restricting its preferred provider lists to physicians with slightly better than average malpractice histories. That, surely, is a business judgment, and if the insurer makes the wrong judgment by depriving itself of doctors that patients insist upon, then the market will punish the insurer and force it to retreat from the impracticable standard. . . .

[T]his court has made doctors a protected class. Until the economy turned around recently, one could hardly open a newspaper without reading of yet another company that had laid off thousands of its employees. However, no one suggested that textile workers or bank employees, for example, had a right to a hearing before losing their jobs. The layoffs certainly affected "important, substantial economic interest[s]" of theirs. Indeed, they may well have exhausted their savings and lost their homes. And yet textile workers and bank employees must fend for themselves, while doctors are treated by the majority as if they are entitled to a minimum income. . . .

The majority insists that, "[o]ur decision here does not apply to employer-employee contractual relations. Rather, it applies only to an insurer's decision to remove individual physicians from its preferred providers lists." However, employers will not be comforted, for why wouldn't the majority's opinion apply to employer-employee contractual relations? . . . For that matter, why wouldn't the majority's opinion apply to the admission to, as well as the removal of physicians from, an insurer's preferred provider lists? . . .

The out-of-state case upon which the majority relies [Harper v. Healthsource New Hampshire, 674 A.2d 962 (N.H. 1996)] . . . provides little support for the majority's refusal to enforce the "without cause" termination clause of Potvin's contract with MetLife. . . . [U]nder the *Harper* rule, a physician terminated pursuant to a "without cause" provision is entitled to review only if "the physician believes that the decision to terminate was, in truth, made in bad faith or based upon some factor that would render the decision contrary to public policy." Indeed, under the *Harper* rule, the "without cause" termination provision of MetLife's contract with Dr. Potvin should be enforced because there is no showing that MetLife's decision was "made in bad faith or based upon some other factor that would render the decision contrary to public policy." Certainly it is not contrary to public policy for a business enterprise to seek to minimize its costs. Any successful business must do so, and in this era of spiraling health care costs, health care providers have a special societal responsibility to do so. . . . Therefore, to be competitive, a medical insurer would be wise to restrict its preferred provider lists to physicians with better than average malpractice histories, and, by his own admission, Dr. Potvin's malpractice history was considerably worse than average.

In conclusion, the judgment of the trial court granting MetLife's motion for summary judgment should have been affirmed.

[The decision was 4-3.]

Notes: Managed Care Contracting; Employment at Will; Interference with Doctor/Patient Relationship

1. *Medical Staff Disputes Deja Vu?* Managed care contracts between physicians and HMOs or PPOs usually contain some of the same due process hearing protections as do medical staff bylaws. This is also increasingly being required by state insurance regulations and by industry accreditation standards adopted by the National Committee for Quality Assurance. Managed care physician networks, therefore, have taken on many of the same structural attributes of hospital medical staffs. John Blum, The Evolution of Physician Credentialing into Managed Care Selective Contracting, 22 Am. J. L. & Med. 173 (1996). There are two key differences, however. First, insurers retain the option in managed care contracts to use either for-cause or no-cause termination, and only the former invokes due process protections. Second, these due process protections apply, for the most part, only to physicians once they join the network. HMOs and PPOs are still free to reject physician applicants at the outset without judicial review of their reasons or process. Observe, though, tort law and state insurance regulation require managed care networks to review physicians' credentials before enrolling them. See Chapters 4.F.2 and 9.B. If this initial credentialing is commonplace, can due process requirements be far behind?

Despite physicians' concerns over no-cause terminations, physicians themselves often insist on putting these provisions in their managed care contracts. Can you imagine why? Suppose you were a doctor about to be terminated for good cause. What would you prefer? Realize that HMOs with formal peer review processes who seek immunity under the Health Care Quality Improvement Act must report to the National Practitioner Data Bank any adverse actions "based on competence or professional conduct." Lawyers also insist on no-cause provisions in part to comply with the referral fee laws that, for complex reasons, make it difficult to enter into short-term renewable contracts with doctors (the fear being that contract renewal will be used as an inducement to refer more business). An indefinite contract with no-cause termination therefore may be the only feasible way to maintain flexibility for both parties.

2. *"Deselection."* The unfortunate term that has emerged for terminating physicians from managed care networks is "deselection." Did the California Supreme Court disagree with the *substantive* reason for deselecting Dr. Potvin, or only the lack of procedural protections? As the dissent notes, other courts have allowed physicians to object only when they allege that the reason for termination violates public policy, as would be the case with an allegation of racial discrimination. More common are allegations that insurers retaliate against physicians for challenging insurers' limitations on coverage:

> Several California doctors have told the [California Medical Association (CMA)] that when they protested denials of treatment or UR policy with IPAs, PPOs, large group practices or integrated delivery systems, the organizations retaliated by exercising their right to terminate the physician without cause. One doctor reported denial of a necessary MRI scan. Repeated appeals by the doctor eventually overturned the UR decision, but the physician was terminated from the plan two weeks later. Another physician reported challenging a managed care plan's program that required his ill patients to travel long distances for second opinions. After listening to his criticisms, the plan terminated the doctor's contract. . . .
>
> HMO interests paint a different scenario. They say physicians challenge UR denials as a defensive medicine tactic, motivated by self-interest, to the detriment of cost-containment strategies and quality assurance initiatives. . . . But physician advocates still see the issue as part of an ominous trend that could be replayed across the country. . . . CMA pressed for state legislation that . . . provides legal recourse for doctors who can prove that they were fired from a managed care organization because they challenged a denial of necessary treatment or otherwise advocated on behalf of their patients. . . . "The legislators agreed with us that it was imperative to preserve the physician's role as the patient's advocate," said CMA General Counsel.

Brian McCormick, What Price Patient Advocacy?, Am. Med. News, Mar. 28, 1994. The California statute, Cal. Bus. & Prof. Code §2056, has been adopted in a number of other states. Under the common-law fairness theory, is it permissible to terminate a physician for being excessively costly, or for simply not being among the lowest-cost providers?

> Anecdotal evidence of physician deselection has received considerable publicity over the past year or two. . . . Reports range from one insurer's decision to drop more than 100 physicians from its network to another . . . [that] dropped 600 specialists from its HMO network, including most of its African American physi-

cians. . . . One plan's approach, which has received substantial publicity, may typify what others are doing. The Blue Cross Blue Shield plan based in Washington, D.C., uses a profiling system called Pro/File that compares resource consumption by each practice with that of other doctors in the same specialty and the same region. Pro/File considers a broad array of utilization measures (e.g., numbers of laboratory tests and office visits and what they call long-range utilization), but not patient outcomes. An adjustment for case mix is implemented by comparing groups of patients with similar diseases, ages, and treatments. Critics claim that small sample size is a significant problem and that Pro/File judges only resource consumption and not quality of care. . . .

Physician Payment Review Commission, Annual Report to Congress 226 (1995). Minority physicians have been especially hard hit by deselection in some instances, it appears, because HMOs perceived that their patients are less profitable or because HMOs didn't wish to market themselves in certain locations. See Note, The Impact of Managed Care on Doctors Who Serve Poor and Minority Patients, 108 Harv. L. Rev. 1625 (1995).

3. *Other States, Other Cases, and Other Theories.* Cases like *Potvin* are still few and far between. When they do arise, courts more commonly adopt the legal theory mentioned in the dissent, which allows physicians to challenge no-cause terminations only if they can show the true reason violates public policy. This is an extension of the "whistleblower" suits that arise under employment law, where courts have recognized a public policy exception to the "employment at will" doctrine.

Under either theory of action, should courts exert as much scrutiny as they do over hospital staffing decisions? Does the level of scrutiny depend on the theory of review? Is *Potvin* saying that HMOs are "quasi-public" facilities, relying on the same factors invoked in *Greisman*? If not, what level of scrutiny is justified by the public policy limitation proposed by the dissent? One way to think about this is to consider, under each of these theories, who bears the burden of proof to show exactly what? For instance, under the dissent's public policy theory, should HMOs be allowed to exclude osteopaths from their networks? Does the dissent's theory require the HMO to provide any due process procedures?

Is the dissent correct that the majority's theory might also apply to physicians who are refused initial admission into managed care networks? Under the majority's approach, are there any substantive grounds that would not require due process procedures? In another California case, the court held that it was illegal to summarily remove a physician from a network even though he had been disciplined by the state licensing board for prior substance abuse, improperly prescribing Demerol, and treating patients under the influence of drugs. The court reasoned that the insurer failed to show that the physician was presently impaired or a threat to patients. Ambrosino v. Metropolitan Life Insurance Co., 899 F. Supp. 438 (N.D. Cal. 1995).

For analysis of the full range of issues, see Linda C. Fentiman, Patient Advocacy and Termination from Managed Care Organizations, 82 Neb. L. Rev. 508 (2003); Mark A. Kadzielski, Provider Deselection and Decapitation in a Changing Healthcare Environment, 41 St. Louis U. L. J. 891 (1997); Brian A. Liang, Deselection under Harper v. Healthsource: A Blow for Maintaining Patient-Physician Relationships in the Era of Managed Care?, 72 Notre Dame L. Rev. 799 (1997); William M. Sage, Physicians as Advocates, 35 Hous. L. Rev. 1529 (1999); Bethany J. Spielman, Managed Care Regulation and the Physician-Advocate, 47 Drake L. Rev. 713 (1999); Note, 49 Rutgers L. Rev. 1397 (1997); Note, 48 Wm. & Mary L. Rev. 677 (2006).

4. *Interference with the Doctor/Patient Relationship.* In this body of law, to what extent should courts be concerned with patients' interests in addition to physicians'? If a patient's physician is excluded from the patient's HMO, what option does the patient have? Does the HMO have a "monopoly" over the patient's business? In one case, the court ruled that patients do not have a right to challenge the termination of their physician, because they can be treated by other physicians in the network. Maltz v. Aetna Health Plans of New York, 114 F.3d 9 (2d Cir. 1997). However, in Harper v. Healthsource New Hampshire, 674 A.2d 962 (N.H. 1996), the court noted that "the termination of [Dr. Harper's] relationship with [the HMO] affects more than just his own interest. Several relationships in our society stand on a different footing from the rest. The most visible are those between wife and husband, lawyer and client, pastor and penitent, and physician and patient. In these relationships, society values truthfulness in communication above other competing interests, such as evidence in the search for truth in legal actions. Evidentiary privileges protect communication within these relationships from being revealed in litigation because society has determined that the relationship 'ought to be sedulously fostered.'"

This viewpoint suggests another possible theory of action. Tort law recognizes an action for tortious interference with advantageous relationships. Doctors whose clinical privileges are limited by a hospital often argue that the hospital interfered with their economic relationships with patients. Viewed as a business tort, this often fails because hospitals are pursing their own appropriate business interests and therefore lack the requisite bad motive. If the restriction of privileges is seen as interfering with something more sacred, however, these claims may have a greater chance of success. In Baptist Health v. Murphy, 210 Ark. 358 (2010), the court found tortious interference where a general hospital excluded physicians who owned competing specialty hospitals, reasoning that this policy "affronts the sense of justice, decency, and reasonableness [and] impinges on fundamentally important public policies without adequate countervailing justification . . . because [it] would disrupt the patient-physician relationship, discouraged specialty hospitals, [and] suppressed competition. . . . Baptist wanted to force patients to choose between it and the [excluding] physician[s], . . . [whose] interest was in patient-physician relationships and the continuity of care. [This interest] outweighed Baptist's interest in protecting its economic viability because no evidence supported Baptist's purported need for the Policy." See generally Annot., 87 A.L.R.4th 845 (1991).

5. *Immunity Laws.* There has been little litigation yet over whether the federal Health Care Quality Improvement Act discussed below creates an immunity from damages for formal peer review decisions by HMOs. It appears that immunity does not apply to no-cause contract terminations or to decisions based on economic grounds, but does apply to formal peer review actions based on quality concerns. Cf. Alexander v. Memphis IPA, 870 S.W.2d 278 (Tenn. 1993) (state immunity statute applies to peer review by IPA). Also, there is an unresolved possibility that these suits are preempted by ERISA, the federal law discussed in Chapter 9.C that overrides certain state laws affecting employer-provided health insurance. Compare Zuniga v. Blue Cross and Blue Shield of Michigan, 52 F.3d 1395 (6th Cir. 1995) (ERISA preempts breach of contract and due process claims by physician removed from a PPO) with Napoletano v. CIGNA Healthcare of Connecticut, 680 A.2d 127 (Conn. 1996) (ERISA does not preempt a similar action).

6. *Wrongful Discharge.* The public policy limitation on at-will employment and for-cause termination applies to nonphysicians as well. For some reason, these

wrongful discharge cases seem to crop up with some regularity in the hospital industry, in the form of "whistleblower" cases, where an employee is fired in retaliation for reporting, for example, workplace safety problems to the proper authorities. See, e.g., Margiotta v. Christian Hospital, 315 S.W.3d 342 (Mo. 2010) (terminated after reporting hospital safety violations); Van v. Portneuf Medical Center, 212 P.3d 982 (Idaho 2009) (terminated after reporting unsafe helicopter). Also, observe that public hospitals are subject to constitutional as well as contractual restrictions in their employment decisions. Waters v. Churchill, 511 U.S. 661 (1994).

7. *Conscientious Objection.* Consider whether public policy should limit the ability to discipline medical employees for exercising conscientious objection to assisting in particular medical procedures, such as abortions or termination of life support. Most states have "conscience clause" statutes that expressly prohibit discharge for refusal to perform abortions, and federal law enforces a similar prohibition against providers and institutions that receive certain forms of federal health care funding. See pages 110 and 527.

8. *Negotiating Managed Care Contracts.* Most physicians belong to several (sometimes many dozens) of overlapping managed care networks. Once these networks are formed, insurers then market them to employers and to other insurers, thereby binding physicians to payment and coverage terms that may vary from one purchaser to the next. In deciding whether to sign these contracts, physicians must grapple with many crucial issues in addition to no-cause termination clauses. Other issues include their basic service obligation and payment rights, whether they can limit the number of patients they accept, whether they must indemnify the HMO for liability arising from patient care, and how disputes are resolved. The following exercise provides an opportunity to sample some of these issues.

Exercise: Negotiating a Managed Care Contract*

Florence Nightingale Hospital (FNH) is described at page 1254. One of its competitors established a successful IPA-model HMO two years ago. Fearing loss of patients, FNH is forming the Florence Nightingale Managed Care Network (the Network). The objective is to sign up a number of physicians, mainly in primary care but also in common specialties, and then to market this network to these two sources: (1) large employers who provide health insurance to their workers on a self-insured basis and (2) large regional or national insurance companies (such as Blue Cross) who then offer the Network to their customers.

The Network is approaching each physician group individually and asking them to sign up nonexclusively, leaving them free to sign up with other networks or HMOs. The contract excerpts below contain some common sticking points in these negotiations. Read each pairing of contract options and determine what is at stake. Then, assume the position of lawyer/negotiator for either (a) the Network or (b) a physician group who wants to sign up but is concerned about the details. Meet with a representative from the other side and see if you can hammer out a deal, either adopting one version or the other, or making any changes you want.

---

* This exercise is adapted from one developed by Jan Yarborough, a North Carolina lawyer.

COMPENSATION

A. In exchange for providing Covered Services,* Physician shall receive usual, customary, and reasonable rates that similarly situated physicians charge for like services, less a discount of 15 percent; provided, however, that Physician agrees that the Network shall receive his or her "most favored" discount, such that, if Physician gives a greater discount to another network, insurer, employer, or health plan, Physician shall extend the same discount to the Florence Nightingale Network.

B. In exchange for providing Covered Services,* Physician shall receive the same compensation the Network pays other similarly situated physicians for like services, which will be according to a proprietary fee schedule maintained by the Network and which the Network shall be free to modify from time to time as it deems fit, so long as it applies the fee schedule consistently to all physicians in the Network who are similarly situated.

AVAILABILITY OF PHYSICIAN'S SERVICES

A. Physician agrees to provide or arrange all Covered Services* sought by Members in return for the compensation stated above. Physician shall provide such services on a twenty-four per day, seven day per week basis. During the term of this Agreement, Physician must have and maintain full and unrestricted medical staff privileges at a hospital which is under contract with Network.

B. Physician shall provide Covered Services* sought by Members in the same manner provided to persons who are not Members in return for the compensation stated above. During the term of this Agreement, Physician must have and maintain medical staff privileges at a hospital in the geographic area covered by the Network.

INDEMNIFICATION

A. Physician agrees to indemnify and hold harmless the Network against any negligent act or claim made with respect to items or services provided by Physician under this Agreement. The Network agrees to indemnify and hold harmless Physician against any negligent act or claim made with respect to items or services provided under this Agreement to the extent that the Network is solely responsible for the negligent act or claim.

B. [No indemnification clause at all. Each party is left to bear its own liability.]

TERM AND TERMINATION

A. This Agreement may not be terminated as to any Physician prior to its expiration unless said Physician loses his or her license to practice medicine. Provided, however, the Physician shall have the option to terminate this Agreement in the event of the failure of the MCO to make payments when due.

B. This Agreement may be terminated by either party at any time without cause by written notice given at least one-hundred-twenty (120) days in advance of

---

* "Covered Services" is defined as "those health care services which the Network may be obligated to provide any employer or individual under a health insurance or health benefits plan sold by or on behalf of the network."

the effective date of termination without the need for prior consent of, or notice to any Member, Participating Provider, or other third party.

D. ANTITRUST LAW

Note: Introduction to Antitrust Law

Until the 1980s, the health care industry was remarkably complacent about the antitrust laws. Physicians openly threatened boycotts to enforce their interests; hospitals had few qualms about dividing markets with each other; and the AMA ruled supreme over the economics and organization of medical practice. No one thought to challenge this conduct because it was considered that the learned professions did not engage in the type of trade that is subject to antitrust scrutiny, that health care is an inherently local enterprise not subject to federal jurisdiction, and that lofty considerations of ethical practice and quality of care removed health care decisionmaking from base concerns of economic efficiency.

However, Supreme Court decisions systematically upset each of these assumptions. In Goldfarb v. Virginia State Bar, 421 U.S. 773, 787 (1975), the Court held that there was no antitrust exemption for professionals: "The nature of an occupation, standing alone, does not provide sanctuary from the Sherman Act." In Hospital Building Company v. Trustees of Rex Hospital, 425 U.S. 738 (1976), the Court held that hospital activities can meet the interstate commerce prerequisite to antitrust jurisdiction. And in American Medical Ass'n v. FTC, 455 U.S. 676 (1982), the Supreme Court upheld without opinion an FTC injunction against the AMA using its code of professional ethics to ban physician advertising and certain physician contractual arrangements.

The result of suddenly exposing an entire industry that was once exempt from antitrust law has been an explosion of litigation and counseling. Health care antitrust cases pop up all over the health care landscape faster than dandelions after a spring rain. Law firms have created new health care practice groups and old antitrust litigators have found an area of revival in an otherwise sluggish specialty. Antitrust liability can be a frightening prospect to physicians, hospitals, and insurers. Violations can be privately enforced in civil damage actions brought by injured plaintiffs, defendants face the possibility of treble damages, and losing defendants must pay the plaintiff's attorney fees. To top it off, professional liability insurance rarely covers antitrust exposure. Enforcement authority is also lodged in the FTC, which is empowered to bring civil injunction actions, and in the Department of Justice (DOJ), which, in addition, may prosecute criminal violations (although this almost never happens in health care cases). Both agencies also issue advisory rulings and general interpretative guidelines.

Health care antitrust cases have emerged with such force and prominence that antitrust analysis can no longer be reserved to the litigation specialist. Health care lawyers must have a working understanding of this area of the law in order to advise their clients effectively on how to plan their activities in advance to minimize antitrust exposure. Yet it is not possible in the course of this survey text to cover the entirety of a field as complex as health care antitrust.[5] Materials in this chapter and elsewhere explore some basic principles governing the more prominent areas of litigation. This section examines group boycott law in the context of the exclusion of practitioners from hospital medical staffs and managed care networks. The next section contains a discussion of the price-fixing ramifications of structuring various collaborations and joint ventures, and the following section explores antitrust merger doctrine as applied to hospitals and physicians. The following is a summary of antitrust law as it relates primarily to the first category of disputes, but it also explains principles that apply generally to all types of antitrust theories.

Physicians frequently challenge medical staff membership and network formation decisions under federal antitrust laws, contending that exclusion from the hospital or from a managed care network constitutes a concerted refusal to deal, which is pejoratively known as a group boycott. The primary basis for these suits is §1 of the Sherman Act, 15 U.S.C. §1:

> Every contract, combination . . . or conspiracy in restraint of trade or commerce among the several states, or with foreign nations, is declared to be illegal.

The three elements of a §1 action, evident from the face of the statute, are (1) concerted, as opposed to unilateral, action; (2) an unreasonable restraint of trade; and (3) interstate commerce. A general overview of these three elements may be helpful to the uninitiated reader prior to tackling the principal cases.

1. *Conspiracy.* No Sherman Act §1 violation exists if the challenged activity is unilateral in nature, that is, if it is the action of a single entity. The theory underlying §1 is that competitive harm exists only where two or more economic actors collude to subvert the forces of competition. When a single hospital or HMO excludes a physician, concerted action is not readily apparent, even though many individual doctors and administrators within the hospital or HMO participate in the exclusion decision. The Supreme Court has clearly held that "[t]he officers of a single firm are not separate economic actors pursuing separate economic interests, so agreements among them do not suddenly bring together economic power that was previously pursing divergent goals. Coordination within a firm is as likely to result from an effort to compete as from an effort to stifle competition." Copperweld Corp. v. Independence Tube Corp., 467 U.S. 752, 769 (1984). This reasoning is referred to as the "intra-enterprise conspiracy rule": No conspiracy ordinarily can exist within a single business enterprise.

---

5. For more comprehensive overviews, see Carl Ameringer, The Health Care Revolution: From Monopoly to Market Power (2008); Clark Havighurst & Barak Richman, The Provider Monopoly Problem in Health Care, 89 Or. L. Rev. 847 (2011); Thomas L. Greaney, Competition Policy and Organizational Fragmentation in Health Care, 71 U. Pitt. L. Rev. 217 (2009); Deborah Haas-Wilson, Managed Care and Monopoly Power: The Antitrust Challenge (2003); Spencer Weber Waller, How Much of Health Care Antitrust Is Really Antitrust? 48 Loy. U. Chi. L. Rev. 643 (2017); Martin Gaynor, Farzad Mostashari & Paul B. Ginsburg, Making Health Care Markets Work: Competition Policy for Health Care (Brookings, Apr. 2017); National Academy of Social Insurance, Addressing Pricing Power in Health Care Markets (Apr. 2015); Thomas L. Greaney, Chicago's Procrustean Bed: Applying Antitrust Law in Health Care, 71 Antitrust L.J. 857 (2004); William M. Sage & Peter J. Hammer, A Copernican View of Health Care Antitrust, 65 Law & Contemp. Probs. 241 (Autumn 2002); Symposium, 7 Hous. J. Health L. & Pol'y 183 (2007); Symposium, 31 J. Health Pol. Pol'y L. 417 (2006).

There are exceptions to this intra-enterprise conspiracy rule, however. A combination or conspiracy may exist within a single enterprise if one or more of its members have different, outside economic interests that are separate from the firm's. In such a situation, it is no longer the case that the various corporate actors are pursuing a single economic purpose, and, therefore, the potential for harmful collusion exists even within a single firm. For instance, the Supreme Court held in American Needle Inc. v. National Football League, 130 S. Ct. 2201 (2010) that although the NFL is a single enterprise for many purposes, it is a collection of competing teams when it comes to licensing logos and therefore an exclusive license for marketing all teams' apparel is subject to §1 scrutiny.

In the health care context, suppose a malpractice insurance company owned and operated by obstetricians were to deny coverage to a doctor because he worked with midwives. There would be no conspiracy if the company simply thought the doctor posed an excessive insurance risk, but a conspiracy would exist if the corporate actors were motivated by an outside interest unrelated to the concerns of insurance, namely to suppress competition from midwives.[6] Likewise, the threshold issue in hospital or HMO exclusion cases is whether the economic interest that medical staff members have in competition with excluded practitioners (and with each other) results in the concerted behavior required to invoke Sherman Act §1. If not, a claim must be stated under Sherman Act §2 concerning monopolization. Its elements are more restrictive and are covered only briefly in these materials.

2. *Unreasonable Restraint of Trade.* If concerted action is present, then the core substantive question becomes whether the challenged conduct results in an unreasonable restraint of trade. This is a complex and difficult inquiry, one that is not capable of completely accurate summation. Nevertheless, some preliminary analysis is useful before encountering the case law. First, observe that the language of the Sherman Act provides no useful guidance; it prohibits "*every* contract . . . in restraint of trade," which, taken literally, is an impossibility since *every* contract in fact restrains trade at least to some small extent by precluding the contracting parties from dealing with someone else for the subject matter of the contract. To make sense of the statute, courts have found it necessary to add a judicial gloss so that it prohibits only *unreasonable* restraints of trade. This generates what is known as the "rule of reason" test of illegality: A restraint is illegal only if its anticompetitive harms outweigh its procompetitive benefits. Such a finding often requires a complex, lengthy, and expensive inquiry. To avoid engaging in this burdensome undertaking in every case, the courts have crafted what is known as the "per se rule" of illegality: Certain restraints are automatically illegal if it is clear from their general nature that they are anticompetitive in the vast majority of situations. The primary example of per se illegality is horizontal price fixing, that is, price fixing among competitors.

In general, the *horizontal/vertical distinction* is crucial to characterizing and analyzing particular arrangements subject to antitrust challenge. A vertical arrangement is aligned up and down the chain of distribution for the good or service in question. A horizontal arrangement is one that exists among competitors at one level of this chain. For manufactured goods, the vertical chain is usually manufacturer-wholesaler-retailer. For medical services, the vertical alignment, generally speaking,

---

6. These facts are suggested by Nurse Midwifery Associates v. Hibbett, 918 F.2d 605 (6th Cir. 1990), which found allegations similar to these to be sufficient to go to trial.

is insurer-hospital-doctor. Practices or restraints that are only in a vertical alignment are, for the most part, much less of a concern for antitrust law because they are usually imposed by a single actor and they do not obviously restrain competition in the various affected horizontal levels. For instance, a manufacturer who restricts its dealers to certain cities or states so they don't compete with each other over its products imposes a vertical market division that enhances its ability to compete with other manufacturers. Therefore, it is judged under the rule of reason, whereas the same arrangement agreed to among the dealers themselves and imposed on the manufacturer would be a per se illegal horizontal market division.

In the context of medical staff disputes, plaintiffs attempt to invoke the rule of per se illegality for medical staff or network exclusion decisions by characterizing these decisions as both a horizontal and a vertical *group boycott* among the hospital and members of the medical staff, all of whom agree not to deal with the plaintiff. Unfortunately for litigants and for students of health care antitrust, there is considerable confusion about the precise application and boundaries of the per se rule against group boycotts. Despite several Supreme Court precedents declaring boycotts per se illegal, "exactly what types of activity fall within the forbidden category is . . . far from certain." Northwest Wholesale Stationers Inc. v. Pacific Stationery and Printing Co., 472 U.S. 284, 294 (1985). In this case, the Court explained that "the mere allegation of a concerted refusal to deal does not suffice because not all concerted refusals to deal are predominantly anticompetitive." Therefore, "a plaintiff seeking application of the per se rule must present a threshold case that the challenged activity falls into a category likely to have predominantly anticompetitive effects." Id. at 297. This intermediate stance between per se illegality and rule of reason balancing is sometimes known as the "quick look" approach, in that it requires the court to make an initial assessment of a practice's likely competitive impact before deciding which way to characterize it.[7] How this general directive

---

7. In a major 5-4 decision, California Dental Ass'n v. FTC, 526 U.S. 756 (1999), excerpted at page 1238, the Supreme Court created considerable confusion about the appropriate standard of review in health care antitrust cases and in Sherman Act §1 cases generally. The FTC and the Ninth Circuit had ruled that it was illegal for the California Dental Association to ban most forms of price and quality information in advertising by dentists. (For instance, dentists could not claim in general terms that they offer discounted prices or are especially good with children.) This ban was struck down using both the per se rule and a "quick look" version of the rule of reason, finding no plausible pro-competitive justifications asserted for conduct that otherwise appeared to be a restraint of trade. The Supreme Court reversed and remanded for further consideration, holding that neither the per se rule, the full-blown rule of reason, nor the particular version of the "quick look" standard of review used in this case were appropriate in this particular case. Instead, the Court wanted to see a "less quick look" than had been given, explaining that each case requires "an enquiry meet for the case, looking to a restraint's circumstances, details, and logic." The Court appears to be saying that the standard of review and the burden of proof in §1 cases do not fall into discrete categories but must be viewed as a continuum in which the standard and burden are adjusted to the particulars of each case, at least for categories of cases that have not yet received clear Supreme Court pronouncements. Needless to say, this makes it even more difficult to predict how particular arrangements and activities will be evaluated by the courts or the antitrust enforcement agencies in the future. See Marina Lao, The Rule of Reason and Horizontal Restraints Involving Professionals, 68 Antitrust L. J. 499 (2000).

might apply to medical staff disputes is the second principal issue explored in the following section.

When restraints are judged under the rule of reason, two key issues emerge in medical cases. The first is what role *quality of patient care* plays in proper antitrust analysis. There are several possibilities explored below. Enhanced quality of care could be a relevant competitive benefit to be weighed in the balance of competitive effects pro and con. Quality of care could also be viewed as a noneconomic benefit that outweighs the competitive harms from the restraint. Or, medical markets might be thought to be so infused with noneconomic quality concerns that they deserve a sweeping exemption or extraordinarily lenient scrutiny under antitrust laws. You will see from the readings below that considerable confusion still reigns over these central questions.

A related point of confusion is whether the competitive impact of a restraint is to be judged more by the parties' *subjective motivation and purpose*, or instead by the likely *effects* of their actions. Black-letter law states that actual probable effects, not intent, should control the analysis, such that a good intent will not save a bad act nor will a bad intent impugn a harmless act. Nevertheless, courts still frequently place great weight on subjective intent, either in predicting the restraint's likely effects or in deciding how to characterize the nature of the restraint (e.g., as vertical vs. horizontal, or as price fixing vs. refusal to deal). Often, motive comes strongly into play in distinguishing "ancillary" from "naked" restraints. An ancillary restraint is one that occurs as a side effect of pursuing a primarily procompetitive purpose, whereas a naked restraint occurs where the core purpose of the activity is anticompetitive. For instance, a hospital or HMO that excludes chiropractors from the medical staff might be viewed as engaging in either a naked or an ancillary restraint depending on how one conceives of its primary purpose: making it more difficult for alternative providers to compete with M.D.s, or protecting its own reputation by not associating with nonphysicians. Naked restraints are obviously much harder to defend.

Yet another generic analytical issue that is critical in health care antitrust is *market power.* A given arrangement creates greater or lesser anticompetitive concerns according to the power that the parties have to raise prices, restrict output, or lower quality. If they lack this power, competitive forces will discipline any adverse consequences because the offenders will lose business to other firms—either those presently in the market or those that might enter in order to exploit the competitive opportunity created by the restraint. Therefore, market power—measured in terms of market share and barriers to market entry—is critical to assessing the likely effects of a restraint of trade. Courts increasingly are ruling that, under the rule of reason, defendants need not offer any justification for their behavior whatsoever unless the plaintiff makes a threshold showing of market power.

The easiest way to gauge market power is to measure the actor's market share. Market power tends to increase the smaller or more compact the market is. Therefore, a given restraint is worse when the market within which it occurs is smaller because it has a larger proportionate impact. *Defining the relevant market* is therefore critical to deciding many antitrust cases. Markets are defined in two dimensions: the relevant product (or service) and the relevant geography. Medical markets tend to be small and highly concentrated because service delivery is inherently local and because hospitals are large dominant institutions. Thus, it is easy to imagine a market for hospital services with only a single hospital. Simply put, this is a monopoly and so, by definition, anything the hospital does has serious competitive consequences because it enjoys extreme market power. Therefore, defendants in many health care antitrust cases struggle to characterize the market in terms that enlarge its *geographic or product scope*. They also attempt to show that, despite large market share, their market power is diminished by unique attributes of medical markets.

3. *Interstate Commerce.* Because antitrust litigation is usually long, complex, expensive, high stakes, and of an uncertain outcome, defendants are eager to find defects in the plaintiff's case that avoid trial or even discovery. The elements of the action just summarized rarely result in dismissing a claim at the pleadings stage. Therefore, a more forceful defense is to claim absence of federal jurisdiction. In order for federal antitrust jurisdiction to attach, a restraint must have a substantial effect on interstate commerce. Initially, this requirement too was controversial in this body of law because health care delivery, like other types of personal service, appears inherently local in nature, in contrast with the manufacture and distribution of products. The Supreme Court resolved, however, that a competitive impact on even small local medical markets has interstate effects because reimbursement, equipment, and supplies frequently cross state lines, even if patients do not. Summit Health v. Pinhas, 500 U.S. 322 (1991). Also, even if federal jurisdiction were lacking, most states have antitrust statutes similar to the federal laws, and some state attorneys general are notably active in enforcing these laws.

Still, courts often have a strong instinct that a single doctor should not be able to make a federal case out of a staffing decision at a single hospital or HMO. This instinct can express itself in some of the standard defenses outlined above or in other, somewhat more obscure, defenses summarized in the notes following these cases.

1. Medical Staff Boycotts

■ WEISS v. YORK HOSPITAL
745 F.2d 786 (3d Cir. 1984)

BECKER, Circuit Judge.

This antitrust case arises from the refusal to grant hospital staff privileges to a physician. The plaintiff, Malcolm Weiss, is an osteopath[2] who was denied staff privileges at York (Pennsylvania) Hospital. Dr. Weiss brought this suit, both individually and as representative of the class of all osteopathic physicians in the York Medical

---

2. Dorland's Illustrated Medical Dictionary defines Osteopathy as

> a system of therapy . . . based on the theory that the body is capable of making its own remedies against disease. . . . It utilizes generally accepted physical, medicinal and surgical methods of diagnosis while placing chief emphasis on the importance of normal body mechanics and manipulative methods of detecting and correcting faulty structure.

Osteopathic physicians signify their degree as D.O. [See Joel Howell, The Paradox of Osteopathy, 341 New Eng. J. Med. 1465 (1999). —EDS.]

Service Area (York MSA), against York Hospital (York), the York Medical and Dental Staff, and ten individual physicians who served on the York Medical Staff Executive Committee and the York Judicial Review Committee. York is controlled by, and, at the time Dr. Weiss applied for staff privileges, was exclusively staffed by doctors who graduated from allopathic medical schools.[3]

The gravamen of Weiss' lawsuit is that, although allopaths (hereinafter referred to as medical doctors or M.D.s) and osteopaths (D.O.s) are equally trained and qualified to practice medicine,[4] his application for staff privileges at York hospital was turned down solely because of his status as an osteopath. . . . In Weiss' submission, this scheme to exclude D.O.s from York Hospital was motivated by a desire to restrict the ability of D.O.s to compete with M.D.s, thereby increasing the profits of the M.D.s. [The jury found that the medical staff, but not the hospital, violated §1 of the Sherman Act.] . . .

II. The Facts

A. Hospital Services in the York MSA

There are two providers of in-patient hospital services in the York MSA: York, which is run by M.D.s, and Memorial Hospital (Memorial), which is run by D.O.s. York is by far the larger of the two, with approximately 450 beds and 2,500 employees. Memorial has 160 beds. The testimony at trial established that York had a market share of 80 percent of the patient-days of hospitalization in the York MSA.

---

3. Allopathy is defined as a system of remedial treatment in which it is sought to cure a disease by producing, through medicines, a condition incompatible with the disease. See Funk & Wagnalls New Standard Dictionary of the English Language (1942). Allopathy constitutes the common or "regular" system of medical practice. Allopathic doctors, signify their degree as M.D.

4. At trial Dr. Merle S. Bacastow, an M.D. and the Vice-President of Medical Affairs at York, testified that at least since the mid-1960s there has been no difference in terms of medical training and ability to provide medical care between graduates of osteopathic medical schools and graduates of allopathic medical schools. This observation is born out by the fact that osteopaths and allopaths are equally qualified for state licensure to practice medicine and surgery within the Commonwealth of Pennsylvania. . . . See also Blackstone, The A.M.A. and The Osteopaths: A Study of the Power of Organized Medicine, 22 Antitrust Bulletin 405, 408-414 (1977). Professor Blackstone concludes that in general D.O.s receive somewhat shorter, less expensive, and less specialized training than today's highly specialized M.D.s. He states that this difference may justify limitations on the privileges of osteopaths that are similar to limitations imposed upon general practice M.D.s and family practitioners, but that it would not seem to justify the total exclusion of osteopaths. See id. at 411; Kissam, Webber, Bigers, and Holzgraefe, Antitrust and Hospital Privileges: Testing the Conventional Wisdom, 70 Calif. L. Rev. 595, 641 n.218 (1982) [hereinafter cited as Antitrust and Hospital Privileges]; Dolan & Ralston, Hospital Admitting Privileges and the Sherman Act, 18 Houston L. Rev. 707, 728 (1981) ("Osteopaths undergo training regimens quite similar to that of M.D. practitioners, except that greater emphasis is placed on family practice and on some manipulative practices. Regardless of the situation 30 years ago, it is highly unlikely that any significant qualitative difference between the two groups exists today."). [See also Enders, Federal Antitrust Issues Involved in the Denial of Medical Staff Privileges, 17 Loy. U. Chi. L. J. 331 (1986).—Eds.]

In addition to York's overall market dominance, testimony at trial established that certain complex, highly technical "tertiary care" services and facilities are, for a number of reasons, only available at York. Included among the services offered only at York are therapeutic radiology, open heart surgery, cardiac catheterization, renal dialysis, neo-natal intensive care, short-term acute psychiatric care, monitored stroke treatment, audiology, burn care, cardiopulmonary laboratory, cardiopulmonary rehabilitation, electroencephalography, genetic counseling, prosthetic service, speech therapy, computerized axial tomography (CAT scan), and infusion aspirator. . . .

[I]n early 1976, Weiss and another osteopath named Dr. Michael Zittle, both of whom were engaged in family practice in the York MSA, applied for staff privileges at York. Dr. Weiss informed representatives of the York medical staff that if York excluded him because of his osteopathic training he would institute legal action.

The York medical staff considered the applications and Weiss' threat of legal action, and in November of 1976 amended its bylaws to permit admission of osteopaths at York. Dr. Weiss contends that the amendment of the bylaws was purely cosmetic, and that since 1976 the York medical staff has engaged in a deliberate covert policy of discrimination against osteopaths. . . .

D. DOCTOR WEISS' APPLICATION FOR STAFF PRIVILEGES

In 1976 Doctors Weiss and Zittle applied for staff privileges in York's Family Practice Department. In accordance with the procedures outlined above, the Family Practice Department Credentials Committee and the chairman of the Family Practice Department considered the applications. On January 17, 1977, the department recommended that they be accepted. The Medical Staff Credentials Committee then reviewed the applications and also recommended acceptance. The Medical Staff Executive Committee, however, did not approve either application. Instead, it took the unusual step of deciding to conduct a further investigation. The Committee made extensive oral and written inquiries concerning the professional competence and moral character of both Weiss and Zittle. No such survey had ever before been conducted by the hospital before. Ultimately the investigation turned up some questions about Dr. Weiss' personality. The investigation also raised some glimmer of a question about Dr. Weiss' medical competence, but the sole "evidence" that was adduced was hearsay, often second or third level hearsay. Nevertheless, the Medical Staff Executive Committee, apparently based on this "new evidence," decided not to recommend Weiss for staff privileges.

On June 30, 1977, the hospital Board of Directors considered the recommendations of the various committees which had considered Weiss' and Zittle's applications. The board voted to approve Zittle's application and deny Weiss' application. . . . The Credentials Committee's written report is revealing in both its assessment of the "evidence" against Weiss, and in its frank recognition of the "controversy" at York over the admission of D.O.s to staff privileges:

> The Committee invited Dr. Weiss to discuss the reactivation of his application and to direct certain questions to him. He was told of the developments in the past and precisely how his application has been handled and of the problems

that had arisen. He was specifically told that almost everybody with whom we spoke acknowledged him to be an intelligent, competent, conscientious physician whose care of his patients in the Hospital was quite competent. He was told that the Chairman of his Department suggested that he probably was the best general practitioner. However, almost everyone to whom we spoke acknowledged that he has had personality problems in the past which have caused him to have difficult interpersonal relations with other members of the staff. He was told that because of this personality problem, his application was rejected. It was further explained to him that because of the controversy that accompanied the application of osteopaths to the York Hospital, it was felt that acceptance of his application would jeopardize that endeavor. We explained to Dr. Weiss that his admission to the staff would be met in some instances with outright hostility and in others with indifference and it was a matter of real concern to the Committee how he would react to this sort of reception. . . .

IV. The Sherman Act Claims

We now turn to the substantive-law questions presented by this appeal. . . .

A. Section 1 of the Sherman Act

In order to establish a violation of §1 of the Sherman Act, 15 U.S.C. §1 (1982), a plaintiff must establish three elements: (1) a contract, combination, or conspiracy; (2) restraint of trade; and (3) an effect on interstate commerce. Each of these three elements has been the subject of extensive analysis by the courts, and we now turn to a discussion of that case law and its application to the facts of this case, taking the elements up in turn.

1. Proof of an Agreement: Is There a Sufficient Number of Conspirators?

In order to establish a violation of §1, a plaintiff must prove that two or more distinct entities agreed to take action against the plaintiff. Before the district court, Weiss contended that the hospital and its medical staff were legally distinct entities and therefore capable of conspiring in violation of §1. He also asserted that the doctors who joined together to form the medical staff were separate economic entities who competed against each other so that, as a matter of law, the medical staff was a "combination" of doctors within the meaning of §1. Finally, Weiss argued that even if the individual doctors who made up York's medical staff were deemed by the court to be the equivalent of "officers or employees" of the hospital and therefore ordinarily not capable of conspiring with the hospital, nevertheless the doctors were acting for their own benefit in discriminating against osteopaths, and therefore fell within an exception to the ordinary rule that "officers or employees of the same firm do not provide the plurality of actors imperative for a §1 conspiracy." Copperweld Corp. v. Independence Tube Corp., 467 U.S. 752 (1984).

The district court concluded, and instructed the jury, that the medical staff was an "unincorporated division" of the hospital, and as such the two were legally a "single entity" incapable of conspiring. . . . However, . . . the district court held the defendant medical staff liable to the plaintiff class under §1. On the question who conspired with the medical staff, the court stated only:

The York Hospital Medical and Dental Staff conspired with another person or entity to deny or impede reasonable, fair, equal, and full access to staff privileges at York Hospital by osteopathic physicians other than Plaintiff Weiss.

We agree with the plaintiffs that, as a matter of law, the medical staff is a combination of individual doctors and therefore that any action taken by the medical staff satisfies the "contract, combination, or conspiracy" requirement of §1. . . .

Antitrust policy requires the courts to seek the economic substance of an arrangement, not merely its form. The "substance" of an arrangement often depends on the economic incentive of the parties. The York medical staff is a group of doctors, all of whom practice medicine in their individual capacities, and each of whom is an independent economic entity in competition with other doctors in the York medical community. Each staff member, therefore, has an economic interest separate from and in many cases in competition with the interests of other medical staff members. Under these circumstances, the medical staff cannot be considered a single economic entity for purposes of antitrust analysis. . . . In substance, the medical staff is a group of individual doctors in competition with each other and with other physicians in the York MSA, who have organized to regulate the provision of medical care at York hospital. Where such associations exist, their actions are subject to scrutiny under §1 of the Sherman Act in order to insure that their members do not abuse otherwise legitimate organizations to secure an unfair advantage over their competitors. . . .

Finally, we deal with the plaintiff's assertion that the district court erred in charging the jury that the hospital could not conspire with its medical staff. The district court found that the medical staff was an unincorporated division of the hospital, and as such the court determined that the two could not conspire. Although we do not necessarily agree with the district court's characterization of the medical staff as an unincorporated division of the hospital, we agree with its basic conclusion that, with respect to the issues in this case, the hospital could not, as a matter of law, conspire with the medical staff. The medical staff was empowered to make staff privilege decisions on behalf of the hospital. As such, with regard to these decisions, the medical staff operated as an officer of a corporation would in relation to the corporation. Although the members of the medical staff had independent economic interests in competition with each other, the staff as an entity had no interest in competition with the hospital. Accordingly, we conclude that the district court correctly charged the jury that there could not be a conspiracy between the hospital and the medical staff.

2. Proof of Restraint of Trade

a. Introduction

Read literally, §1 prohibits every agreement "in restraint of trade." In United States v. Joint Traffic Ass'n, 171 U.S. 505, 19 S. Ct. 25, 43 L. Ed. 259 (1898), the Supreme Court recognized that Congress could not have intended a literal interpretation of the word *every,* and since Standard Oil Co. of New Jersey v. United States, 221 U.S. 1, 31 S. Ct. 502, 55 L. Ed. 619 (1911), courts have analyzed most restraints under the so-called rule of reason. As its name suggests, the rule of reason requires the factfinder to decide whether, under all the circumstances of the case, the restrictive practice imposes an unreasonable restraint on competition.[52]

The courts have also, however, applied a rule of per se illegality to certain types of business practices. The development of per se rules has resulted from a recognition that the case-by-case approach inherent in the rule of reason has significant costs, and that certain types of business practices almost always have anticompetitive effects without offsetting pro-competitive effects. In applying the per se rules, a court eschews the ordinary evaluation of the effect of the challenged practice, and concentrates instead on the question whether the practice falls within one of the categories of practices condemned by the per se rule. In this case, the plaintiffs argued that the actions of the defendants were the equivalent of a boycott, or as it is sometimes called, a concerted refusal to deal, and thus illegal per se. We now turn to that inquiry.

b. Is Defendants' Exclusionary Conduct the Equivalent of a Concerted Refusal to Deal ("Boycott")?

The jury found that the defendants had engaged in a policy of discrimination against Dr. Weiss and the other D.O.s in the York MSA by applying unfair, unequal, and unreasonable procedures in reviewing their applications. In addition, the district court concluded that this unfair, unreasonable, and unequal treatment "could reasonably be anticipated [by the defendants] to cause osteopathic physicians to refrain from applying for staff privileges at the York Hospital." The question before us is whether these actions should properly be characterized as a "group boycott" or "concerted refusal to deal," in which case they are illegal per se under §1. If the defendants' actions cannot be so characterized, the rule of reason analysis would apply and the outcome of the case could be different. We conclude that the defendants' actions, as found in the district court, are the equivalent of a concerted refusal to deal.

The classic example of a concerted refusal to deal is the situation in which businesses at one level of production or distribution, e.g., retailers, use the threat of a boycott to induce businesses at another level, e.g., manufacturers, not to deal with competitors of the retailers. As Professor Sullivan has observed, "The boycotting group members, in effect, say to their suppliers or to their customers, 'If you don't stop dealing with non-group members, we will stop dealing with you.' If continued trade with group members is more important to a supplier or customer than is trading with non-group members, this threat will be effective." L. Sullivan, Handbook of the Law of Antitrust §83, at 230 (1977).

---

52. Justice Brandeis provided the classic statement of the rule of reason in Board of Trade of City of Chicago v. United States, 246 U.S. 231, 238, 38 S. Ct. 242, 244, 62 L. Ed. 683 (1918):

> The true test of legality is whether the restraint imposed is such as merely regulates and perhaps thereby promotes competition or whether it is such as may suppress or even destroy competition. To determine that question the court must ordinarily consider the facts peculiar to the business to which the restraint was imposed; its condition before and after the restraint and its effect; the nature of the restraint and its effect, actual or probable. The history of the restraint, the evil believed to exist, the reason for adopting the particular remedy, the purpose or end sought to be attained, are all relevant facts.

In this case York is a provider of hospital services; for the purpose of our analysis, the equivalent of the manufacturer in the example of a classical boycott. Similarly, the M.D.s are the equivalent of the retailers in the example, in the sense that physicians require access to a hospital in order to effectively treat patients. The difficulty with this analogy, at first blush, is that there is no evidence that the M.D.s have used coercion for the purpose of inducing York to exclude their competitors, the D.O.s. . . . In this case, however, because of the M.D.s' control over York's admission decisions, no coercion is necessary. . . .

[At this point, the court's opinion becomes somewhat confused. The following explanation may help to clarify the issues: The paradigm boycott case involves a "secondary boycott" (i.e., a boycott aimed at one party in order to exclude or discipline a third party) because competitors usually lack any ready means to boycott the target firm directly. A classic secondary boycott would have occurred here if the medical staff had threatened to leave the hospital if Dr. Weiss were admitted. An ordinary medical staff exclusion case differs from this paradigm only because doctors don't need to use this indirect threat if they possess the ability to keep out the unwanted practitioner themselves, that is, to engage in primary rather than a secondary boycott. — Eds.]

We recognize that the facts of this case do not precisely fit into the mold of the classical refusal to deal. The refusal to deal is less than total insofar as York admitted Dr. Zittle and a number of other osteopaths. Arguably then, what is at issue is not a boycott but mere discrimination, which sounds less like a per se antitrust violation. However, given the evidence of the different standards applied to osteopaths and M.D.s and the second-class citizenship afforded D.O.s upon admission to staff privileges at York, and in view of the adverse impact of these factors upon D.O. applications for York staff privileges, we are satisfied that the restrictive policy is, in purpose and effect, sufficiently close to the traditional boycott, that the characterization is appropriate.

The Medical Staff is, however, entitled to exclude individual doctors, including osteopaths, on the basis of their lack of professional competence or unprofessional conduct. If York's policy toward D.O.'s could be viewed as a form of industry self-regulation of this type, the rule of reason, rather than a per se rule, would be applicable. See generally L. Sullivan, Handbook of the Law of Antitrust §§86-88 (1977). We recognize, therefore, that in many cases involving exclusion from staff privilege, courts will, more or less openly, have to utilize a rule of reason balancing approach. This case is different, however, because York has not contended that osteopaths as a group are less qualified than M.D.s. See supra n.4. In the absence of such a contention, or another legitimate explanation for the discrimination, we conclude that a per se rule should be applied, since the effect of the practice is identical to that of the traditional boycott, and plainly anticompetitive.

Congruent with the foregoing discussion, the Supreme Court has adopted an exception to application of the per se rule of illegality where the case involves a learned profession and where the restriction is justified on "public service or ethical norm" grounds. Thus, unlike most cases where characterization of some activity as a classical boycott ends the inquiry, here, because the medical profession is involved, the rule of reason analysis may still control, as a "built-in" exception. We now turn to a discussion of this potential "escape hatch" to see if it can extricate the defendants from the "cut" of the per se rule.

c. The "Learned Profession" Exception

In Goldfarb v. Virginia State Bar, 421 U.S. 773, 788 n.17, (1975), in which the Supreme Court made clear that the medical profession is not exempt from the antitrust laws, the Court stated that the "public service aspect, and other features of the professions, may require that a particular practice, which could properly be viewed as a violation of the Sherman Act in another context, be treated differently." In Arizona v. Maricopa County Medical Society, 457 U.S. 332, 348-349 (1982), the Court partially explained this exception by stating that conduct which is normally subject to per se condemnation under §1 will instead be subject to rule of reason analysis where the challenged conduct is "premised on public service or ethical norms." In *Maricopa*, because the defendants did not attempt to justify their price fixing arrangements on either of these grounds, but instead attempted to argue that the maximum price levels were pro-competitive, the Court held that the per se rule controlled and consequently found that the defendants' conduct violated §1.

In this case, the defendants have offered no "public service or ethical norm" rationale for their discriminatory treatment of D.O.s. Indeed, their defense at trial was that they did not discriminate against D.O.s. Since the jury believed otherwise, we conclude that the per se rule governs this case. . . .[61]

---

61. Several circuit court opinions have held the rule of reason analysis, not the per se rule of illegality, controls in boycott cases involving the learned professions. We believe these cases are readily distinguishable from the instant case. In Wilk v. American Medical Ass'n, 719 F.2d 207 (7th Cir. 1983), a case involving the refusal of M.D.s to deal with chiropractors, the Seventh Circuit stated: "[B]oycotts are illegal per se only if used to enforce agreements that are themselves illegal per se—for example price fixing agreements." Id. at 221 (quoting Marrese v. American Academy of Orthopaedic Surgeons, 706 F.2d 1488, 1495 (7th Cir. 1983)). Since the court could find no per se illegal purpose for the A.M.A.'s medical ethics principle 3, which in essence provided that M.D.'s should not associate with chiropractors, it concluded that the rule of reason analysis governed in that case. We believe that the Seventh Circuit was correct in utilizing a rule of reasons analysis in the *Wilk* case because the defendants were plainly asserting a "public service or ethical norm" justification for their concerted refusal to deal with chiropractors. In Virginia Academy of Clinical Psychologists v. Blue Shield of Va., 624 F.2d 476, 484-485 (4th Cir. 1980), the Fourth Circuit stated: "Because of the special considerations involved in the delivery of health services, we are not prepared to apply a per se rule of illegality to medical plans which refuse or condition payments to competing or potentially competing providers." . . . [A] "medical necessity" justification was apparently raised by the defendants, and in our view that would have been sufficient to bring the defendants within the purview of Maricopa's exception for conduct based on "public service or ethical norms." Finally, in Kreuzer v. American Academy of Periodontology, 735 F.2d 1479 (D.C. Cir. 1984), the D.C. Circuit Court held that the rule of reason analysis governed a §1 challenge to a rule promulgated by the American Academy of Periodontology (AAP) that limited membership in the AAP to licensed dentists who practice periodontics exclusively, and who do not practice other forms of dentistry. The court labeled the effect of the AAP's rule a "group boycott" but concluded that "[w]hen a conspiracy of this sort is alleged in the context of one of the learned professions, the nature and extent of its anticompetitive effect are often too uncertain to be amendable to per se treatment." . . . [See also Betkerur v. Aultman Hospital Ass'n, 78 F.3d 1079 (6th Cir. 1996) (no per se horizontal boycott existed where independent obstetricians agreed to designate one neonatologist for most of their referrals; the relationship between the two kinds of doctors was vertical, not horizontal, and no economic motives were apparent). —EDS.]

V. CONCLUSION

In summary, we reach the following conclusions. First, we find that the district court's decision that the medical staff violated Sherman Act §1 as to the plaintiff class is supported by sufficient evidence, and we therefore will affirm the district court on this point. . . . [W]e also agree that the issuance of an injunction by the district court in this case was proper.

ALLEGB1578

■ HASSAN v. INDEPENDENT PRACTICE ASSOCIATES
698 F. Supp. 679 (E.D. Mich. 1988)

NEWBLATT, District Judge.

Before the court are defendants' Motion for Summary Judgment. . . . Plaintiffs Shawky Hassan and Fikria Hassan are allergists who practice through the Allergy & Asthma Center, P.C., a professional corporation wholly owned by the Drs. Hassan. Defendant Independent Practice Associates, P.C., (IPA) is an organization of physicians and osteopaths who provide medical care to subscribers of Genesee Health Care, Inc., doing business as Health Plus of Michigan (Health Plus), a state licensed, federally qualified health maintenance organization (HMO). . . . Plaintiffs allege . . . that IPA's participation in plaintiffs' separation from IPA and the group's subsequent refusal to readmit the doctors, constitute an illegal group boycott. . . .

IPA is the corporation through which the group of doctors that treat patients who subscribe to Health Plus practice. It is owned by the physicians who comprise the group. Health Plus, the HMO insurance contractor here, was formed by the Genesee County Medical Society in 1979. Its Board of Directors is made up of subscribers, the public and physicians. Health Plus is funded by subscribers who pay a fixed premium per month. With this money, Health Plus pays service providers, such as IPA, on a computed basis and also a fixed amount per member per month. IPA members are paid primarily on a fee-for-services basis, which the IPA determines according to a set maximum fee schedule. . . .

Defendants concede that IPA exists only to serve Health Plus patients. . . . Health Plus has experienced substantial growth since 1979 and its patient market share is 20 percent of the population in the area of Genesee-Lapeer-Shiawassee counties. . . . There is no evidence that IPA physicians cannot also belong to other such organizations.

Defendants contend that they face a competitive market. For example, they contend that the largest portion of Health Plus's membership is represented by General Motors (GM) employees. In order to obtain the GM business, defendants must compete on an annual basis by obtaining both GM and UAW approval as an authorized insurer and then, further, convince the employees to choose the Health Plus program. Thus, GM, the union, and the workers must be satisfied as to both price charged and benefits offered. . . . This has resulted in actions [to cut costs such as] denying physicians' applications for membership and terminations or resignations of physicians. . . .

Plaintiffs joined IPA in 1979, and until October of 1981, they were the only allergy specialists to provide such service to Health Plus subscribers. In 1980, a review of billing records revealed a high incidence of lab tests performed by plaintiffs and prompted the IPA's Care, Quality and Cost Committee to request justification for those tests from plaintiff Shawky Hassan. Moreover, the Committee began setting guidelines for allergy testing which prohibited routine testing. Further, in October of 1981, an IPA survey of allergy testing procedures indicated that plaintiffs performed far more tests than two other specialists, and a review of patient charts failed to satisfy the IPA that the Hassans' level of testing was justified. . . .

Health Plus sent out a notice that subscribers could no longer see the Drs. Hassan. . . . In August of 1983, the Hassans applied to IPA on behalf of their newly established Urgent Care Family Clinic to provide emergency care to IPA members. . . . On January 6, 1984, all of plaintiffs' applications were denied without explanation. The Hassan Clinic lost money and, in 1985, it was closed. . . .

1. WAS THERE A CONSPIRACY?

. . . [E]ach physician in IPA has a practice or other profession independent of IPA or Health Plus. The inferences from the undisputed facts lead the court to the conclusion that there is at least a question of fact as to whether there was a conspiracy to exclude plaintiffs from IPA. First, Health Plus was created by physicians, the Genesee County Medical Society, who are members of IPA. Moreover, although IPA members may not dominate the Health Plus Board of Directors, one third of its members belong to IPA. . . . [T]here is at least an inference which must be viewed in a light most favorable to plaintiffs, that IPA members have effective control. . . .

2. IS THERE A PER SE VIOLATION?

Defendants next argue that Northwest Wholesale Stationers, Inc. v. Pacific Stationery Printing, Co., 472 U.S. 284 (1985) precludes treatment of this case under the per se illegal group boycott rule. . . . In *Northwest Wholesale Stationers*, . . . a cooperative buying agency expelled a member without procedural means for challenging the expulsion.[40] . . . The Court [refused to apply the per se categorization, explaining: "A plaintiff seeking application of the per se rule must present a threshold case that the challenged activity falls into a category likely to have predominantly anticompetitive effects. The mere allegation of a concerted refusal to deal does not suffice because not all concerted refusals to deal are predominantly anticompetitive."] . . . Thus, the court in *Northwest Wholesalers* required that, [before invoking the per se rule], those plaintiffs . . . make a threshold showing (1) whether that practice is [not] justified by plausible arguments that it is intended to enhance overall efficiency and make markets more competitive; and (2) a showing that defendant possesses — (a) market power, and (b) exclusive access to an element essential to effective competition. . . .

---

40. Northwest was a purchasing cooperative of approximately 100 office supply retailers which acted as a primary wholesaler for the retailers. In 1978, members of Northwest voted to expel Pacific, offering no explanation at the time nor giving Pacific notice, a hearing, or any other opportunity to challenge the decision. Pacific contended that the expulsion was a group boycott and a per se violation of §1.

The court agrees with defendants that the acts of expulsion and the refusal to readmit plaintiffs are justified by enhancing efficiency and making the market more competitive. First, despite plaintiffs' counsel's contentions at the hearing, the record shows that plaintiffs do not dispute the fact that IPA adopted its allergy testing policy to prevent excessive use of costly tests and that plaintiffs disagreed with this policy. It is also undisputed that cost containment objectives are procompetitive. . . .

Although plaintiffs contend that defendants' decisions or policies as to allergy testing were incorrect, that is irrelevant. The issue is not whether the decisions were correct but "whether there are plausible arguments that they were intended to enhance overall efficiency and make markets more competitive." Northwest, 472 U.S. 284 at 294. . . . Finally, plaintiffs contend that the decision to deny membership to plaintiffs was made by primary care physicians who were interested in providing allergy care themselves. Not only is there no evidence of this, but allegations that defendants' motives were manifestly anticompetitive are more properly considered under a rule of reason analysis. . . .

[As for market power,] 20 percent market share is not sufficient market power in light of the competition from other providers in the relevant market. However, market share does not always indicate whether a firm really has market power. There-fore, other factors must also be examined and these support defendants' position.

First, there are no significant barriers to entry into this market—that is, the market for health care finance.[47] In Ball Memorial Hosp., Inc. v. Mutual Hosp. Ins., 784 F.2d 1325, 1335 (6th Cir. 1986), the Seventh Circuit stated that:

> The insurance industry is not like the steel industry, in which a firm must take years to build a costly plant before having anything to sell. The "productive asset" of the insurance business is money, which may be supplied on a moment's notice, plus the ability to spread risk, which many firms possess and which has no geographic boundary. In this case, defendants' expert has stated in his affidavit that any health care insurer in Michigan may serve patients in this market. Plaintiffs have not iden-tified any barriers to entry and, in fact, Greater Flint HMO and PPO, Trust, have recently entered the market.

. . . Plaintiffs, however, argue that defendants have market power through the percentage of physicians (75 percent) in this market who are members of IPA. . . . The authority they cite does not apply because it is concerned with a different prob-lem—that of deterring the establishment of new HMOs. Those concerns would only come into play if IPA was able to affiliate with physicians on an exclusive basis. There is simply nothing in the record to indicate that IPA physicians are not free to affiliate with other providers.[50] . . . Accordingly, plaintiffs are not entitled to a find-ing of per se illegality.

47. Although plaintiffs contend that the relevant market is the "prepaid market share," which includes only HMOs, the relevant market "consists of the . . . services with which de-fendants' product competes." In this case, Health Plus must compete with the other sources of health care financing. . . .

50. If there was exclusive affiliation, there would be a barrier to entry. [It can be seen from this discussion that antitrust law favors physicians contracting with networks on a non-mutually exclusive basis or under contracts of very short duration. However, another body of law regulating "referral fees" is hostile to these types of contracts. See page 1427 for further discussion of exclusive dealing in managed care networks. —Eds.]

3. RULE OF REASON

Defendants next contend that there is no unreasonable restraint of trade as no significant anticompetitive effect has resulted from the plaintiffs' expulsion or resignation, and subsequent rejection for readmittance, from IPA. The test under the rule of reason is whether competition in the overall market has been harmed, the antitrust laws not having been intended to protect merely individual competitors. . . .

In this case, the undisputed facts indicate that there has been no anticompetitive impact on the overall market. First, as indicated above, IPA does not have significant market power. . . . Even assuming that defendants did have the requisite market power, there is no evidence that the exclusion of plaintiffs had an impact on overall competition . . . because the substitution of one company for another "does not limit competition in any substantial sense." . . .

The plaintiffs' expulsion or departure from IPA was followed (or shortly preceded) by the admittance of two new allergists. . . . Moreover, there is no indication that plaintiffs left the market, so the end result is that the public has just as many allergists from which to choose. Even if the plaintiffs were to leave the tri-county market, there is no reason to believe that they would not be easily replaced so that the market would be served by enough allergists. . . . Finally, competition is not harmed because there are a sufficient number of allergists and primary care physicians who can provide allergy services in the tri-county area. . . .

Next, plaintiffs claim that defendants' motives in excluding plaintiffs from IPA were anticompetitive.[56] Plaintiffs present no evidence of an anticompetitive motive other than that several doctors, primary care physicians who were involved in the decision stood to benefit from plaintiffs' exclusion. Not only does this ignore the fact that several allergists were admitted shortly before and after plaintiffs' expulsion, but it also ignores the rule of reason's requirement of injury to overall competition, not just to individual competitors. Thus, plaintiffs have failed to satisfy the requirements under the rule of reason. . . .

Having disposed of all plaintiffs' claims, judgment in this case shall hereby be entered for defendants.

Notes: Medical Staff Boycotts; Exclusion from Managed Care Networks

1. *Medical Staff Conspiracies. Weiss* ruled that all physicians participating in a medical staff credentialing decision constitute a "walking conspiracy" as a matter of law. Granted that some physicians on the York Hospital medical staff have an independent interest in competition with Dr. Weiss, is this true of neurosurgeons, pathologists, or specialists who are not engaged in a general practice? Even for those doctors who potentially are in direct competition—in Dr. Weiss' case, say, general and family practitioners—should the court find a conspiracy as a matter of law? Individual doctors might in fact ignore their competitive interests in making a

---

56. Plaintiffs rely on FTC v. Indiana Federation of Dentists, 476 U.S. 447 (1986), for the proposition that "where clear anticompetitive motives are present and no clear competitive benefits exist, an extended market analysis is not required."

staffing decision. Following *Weiss*, several courts have held that no conspiracy exists unless special facts are shown. In one, the court held that pediatricians who voted to exclude nurse midwives were acting merely as agents of a single hospital because nurse midwives compete only with obstetricians, not pediatricians. As for the obstetricians, conspiracy would not be presumed; the midwives must show at least the possibility that they acted for other than legitimate reasons. Nurse Midwifery Ass'n v. Hibbett, 918 F.2d 605 (6th Cir. 1990).

In contrast with its holding as a matter of law that a conspiracy existed *within* the medical staff, *Weiss* held that the medical staff *as an entity* cannot, as a matter of law, conspire with the hospital because it is part of the hospital. But if members of the medical staff conspire with each other by virtue of their independent stake in the decision, why not with the hospital as well? Compare Bolt v. Halifax Hospital Medical Center, 891 F.2d 810 (11th Cir. 1990) ("we hold that a hospital and the members of its medical staff are all legally capable of conspiring with one another" because "a hospital and the members of its medical staff are legally separate entities").

Which of these approaches best captures the realities of the hospital/medical staff relationship, the typical reasons for peer review, and who controls the decisionmaking? For a detailed analysis of these issues, see William Brewbaker, Antitrust Conspiracy Doctrine and the Hospital Enterprise, 74 B.U. L. Rev. 67 (1994) ("given the typical economic and managerial independence of physicians from hospitals, . . . [concerted action exists unless] it can be demonstrated that the medical staff acted in a purely advisory role").

2. *Monopolies.* Where concerted action is not found and Sherman Act §1 is not implicated, an antitrust claim might still be stated under various §2 theories covering unilateral refusals to deal. Usually, unilateral refusals are beyond reproach, even if the hospital or HMO enjoys a monopoly, because the antitrust laws do not proscribe monopolies per se, nor do they proscribe the lawful exercise of monopoly power rightfully obtained. Antitrust law prohibits only obtaining monopoly power in certain unfair ways, or abusing that power in certain ways. Depending on the circumstances, a monopolist's unilateral refusal to deal might be considered abusive. However, understanding the qualifications embedded in the previous two sentences is largely beyond the scope of these materials. The one §2 theory of particular note for hospital exclusions is the "essential facilities doctrine." This is based on a smattering of cases holding that, where access to a particular facility is essential for others to compete, the facility must be offered to all competitors on fair and reasonable terms. This doctrine applies, however, only where the hospital in question enjoys a monopoly position in the market.

3. *Different Levels of Scrutiny.* In order for the *Weiss* court to impose a rule of per se illegality, it first characterized the medical staff's decision as a class-based exclusion of all osteopaths not premised on any quality-of-care justification. How strong is the evidence for this characterization? Consider that the medical staff did amend its bylaws to allow in osteopaths and it in fact extended privileges to Dr. Zittle, a D.O. who applied at the same time as Dr. Weiss. Consider also the stated justification relating to Dr. Weiss' personality.

Where the exclusion is not class-based but is directed unambiguously to the professional competence of a single practitioner, plaintiffs have rarely succeeded. *Weiss* is unique in applying a per se rule because the jury found that the hospital's justification for an individual exclusion was a pretext, and the hospital did not offer any justification for a class-based exclusion of all osteopaths (which it believed it had not engaged in but the jury found it had). When exclusions *are* premised on quality of care, the *Weiss* court concedes that the rule of reason applies. Although rule of reason cases are usually long and complex, in hospital disputes courts usually find ways to dismiss the case quickly, on the pleadings or on motion for summary judgment, without going to trial. As one court explained:

> The cases involving staffing at a single hospital are legion. Hundreds, perhaps thousands of pages in West publications are devoted to the issues those circumstances present. Those cases invariably analyze those circumstances under the rule of reason — there is nothing obviously anticompetitive about a hospital choosing one staffing pattern over another or in restricting the staffing to some rather than many, or all. A hospital has an unquestioned right to exercise some control over the identity and number to whom it accords staff privileges. Malpractice concerns, quality of care, market perceptions, cost, and administrative considerations may all impact those decisions. Those hundreds or thousands of pages almost always come to the same conclusion: the staffing decision at a single hospital was not a violation of §1 of the Sherman Act. [Citations to 28 cases omitted.]
>
> The reasons advanced for that conclusion are varied. Insufficient nexus to interstate commerce, lack of standing, lack of antitrust injury, failure to show a detrimental effect on competition, the inability of a hospital to conspire with its staff, and insufficient market power in the relevant market are among the reasons relied upon for denying section 1 relief. Sometimes the conclusion follows a motion to dismiss; more often the decision is one of summary judgment, but often it appears that the record relied upon is the absence of facts indicating special circumstances raising antitrust concerns. . . .
>
> Before we enlist this court in the micromanagement of the staffing arrangements at [this hospital] under the aegis of the antitrust laws, we need better reasons than the plaintiffs have given us. . . . "If the law were otherwise, many a physician's workplace grievance with a hospital would be elevated to the status of an antitrust action. To keep the antitrust laws from becoming so trivialized, the reasonableness of a restraint is evaluated based on its impact on competition as a whole within the relevant market." Oksanen v. Page Memorial Hospital, 945 F.2d 696, 708 (4th Cir. 1991).

BCB Anesthesia Care v. Passavant Memorial Area Hospital Ass'n, 36 F.3d 664 (7th Cir. 1994) (dismissing at the pleadings stage a complaint by three nurse anesthetists that the hospital conspired with a physician anesthetist to terminate their contract for anesthesiology services). This is consistent with a general trend in antitrust decisions toward making it easier for defendants to obtain summary judgment where the plaintiff's basic theory "simply makes no economic sense." Matsushita Electrical Industrial Co. v. Zenith Radio Corp., 475 U.S. 574 (1986).

A few courts since *Weiss* have found, however, that intensive review of hospitals' staffing decisions is justified under antitrust law. For example, one court reversed the grant of summary judgment to a hospital that excluded a doctor on quality grounds after he set up a competing clinic explaining:

> [Dr.] Miller contends that his hospital staff privileges were revoked and his applications for reinstatement denied because defendants wished to stifle his competition. He contends that . . . he was treated more severely than other physicians whose

competence was in question but who presented no economic threat to the defendants. Defendants' argument that they revoked Miller's staff privileges because of his professional incompetence and unprofessional conduct is a defense they may present before the jury which, if convinced, will absolve them of any antitrust liability. It is inappropriate and unprecedented, however, to . . . defer to the manner in which defendants themselves, who are parties in interest, weighed the evidence and drew inferences.

Miller v. Indiana Hospital, 843 F.2d 139 (3d Cir. 1987). It appears from the remainder of the opinion that the court envisioned a de novo jury decision on the hospital's actual motives, not on the doctor's actual competence. Where the motives are more clearly appropriate, then courts are almost always deferential to the hospitals' assessment of competence. This pattern in the case law contrasts with frequent statements by the courts that legality is tested more by anticompetitive effects than by anticompetitive motives. On remand, the district court in *Miller* granted summary judgment to the hospital based on a lack of market impact, even though this was the only hospital in the county.

4. *Standing and Injury to Competition.* Courts at first expressed their hostility to hearing these antitrust disputes by finding no federal jurisdiction due to the lack of any impact on interstate commerce, but as summarized in the introduction, this route was closed off by the Supreme Court in 1991. Subsequently, courts have sometimes ruled based on lack of standing, holding that if there were any injury to competition, it would be suffered by patients or by hospitals, not by the excluded doctor. See Todorov v. DCH Healthcare Authority, 921 F.2d 1438 (10th Cir. 1991) (the reduced competition that theoretically might result from a hospital's exclusive contract for CT scans would injure only consumers, not the excluded neurologist; his only injury is the inability to share in the allegedly illegal profits); Balaklaw v. Lovell, 14 F.3d 793 (2d Cir. 1994) (physician who lost exclusive contract has no standing to complain that he was replaced; remedy sought would not increase consumer choice); cf. Brunswick Corp. v. Pueblo Bowl-O-Mat, 429 U.S. 477 (1977) (competitor lacks standing to challenge merger of bowling alleys). More commonly, however, courts simply rule as in *Hassan* that no injury to competition exists and therefore no violation occurs if the doctors who remain possess no significant market power. A single competitor's loss of patients to another doctor or hospital does not harm the patients, nor does it necessarily threaten to raise prices or worsen quality. In a phrase, antitrust law, in contrast with tort law, is concerned with harm to competition, not harm to competitors.

The instinct that single-physician staffing decisions should not create a federal antitrust case is also captured in the Health Care Quality Improvement Act, discussed at page 1409, which immunizes peer review of individual physicians based on quality concerns. This qualified immunity extends, however, only to damages actions, not to injunctive relief, and it does not cover exclusions (1) of nonphysicians, (2) of groups of physicians, or (3) based on economic or administrative concerns.

5. *Using Outside Reviewers.* For hospitals concerned that the antitrust exposure for aggressive peer review is still too intense, Professors Blumstein and Sloan offer an inviting solution: "hospitals concerned about antitrust exposure could avoid liability by . . . using outside professional consultants for quality assurance. . . . [The]

lack of [outside reviewers'] competitive status with staff physicians would remove such peer-review activities from coverage under §1 of the Sherman Act. No capacity to conspire would exist." James Blumstein & Frank Sloan, Antitrust and Hospital Peer Review, 51 Law & Contemp. Probs. 7, 39-53 (Spring 1988). See also Mathews v. Lancaster General Hospital, 87 F.3d 624 (3d Cir. 1996) (no conspiracy as a matter of law despite possible economic motivation where hospital board acted independently and obtained outside review by independent consultant). Why do you suppose outside review is not more common, considering that it appears to create a nearly iron-clad defense against §1 antitrust claims? See Brewbaker, supra ("JCAHO standards may fairly be read to prohibit a governing body's unilateral decision to retain an external peer reviewer.").

6. *Further Readings.* For additional academic commentary on these lines of cases, proposing various degrees of scrutiny, standards of legality, and burdens of proof, see n.4 in *Weiss*; Blumstein & Sloan supra (advocating that, for certain "cartel-behavior" decisions, courts should take "a precautionary prophylactic approach . . . requiring defendants to establish an overriding procompetitive justification . . . [that] is not just theoretical but factually demonstrable."); Clark Havighurst, Doctors and Hospitals: An Antitrust Perspective on Traditional Relationships, 1984 Duke L. J. 1071, 1133-1134, 1157 ("To ensure that hospitals have reasonable freedom of action, . . . summary judgment or a directed verdict would be appropriate if documentary evidence and affidavits showed that the hospital's action reflected its [own] corporate concerns. . . . Under this test, a court would not concern itself . . . with whether the ostensible motives for the actions taken were the real motives or whether the adverse effect of the hospital action on competition among practitioners was outweighed by its actual contribution to fulfilling the hospital's objectives."). For an empirical analysis of this body of case law, see Peter J. Hammer & William M. Sage, Antitrust, Health Care Quality, and the Courts, 102 Colum. L. Rev. 545 (2002). See generally 89 A.L.R. Fed. 419 (1988).

7. *Exclusion from Managed Care Networks.* The paradigm boycott case consists of a hospital excluding practitioners for ostensibly quality-of-care reasons, but *Hassan* illustrates that this body of law also applies to exclusion by insurers and managed care networks, and exclusions based on economic grounds. Antitrust law is more familiar with these conventional commercial contexts and so, although these developments are somewhat novel in the industry, the legal analysis is in some ways easier. For a decision similar to *Hassan*, see Capital Imaging Associates v. Mohawk Valley Medical Associates, 996 F.2d 537 (2d Cir. 1993) (holding that member physicians of an IPA are capable of conspiring among themselves in deciding to award an exclusive radiology contract, but dismissing antitrust claim because of the IPA's small market share and consequent absence of any likely impact on prices or quality).

Levine v. Central Florida Medical Affiliates, 72 F.3d 1538 (11th Cir. 1996), presents perhaps the most startling set of facts. There, a general internist was able to earn $724,000 a year despite his exclusion from one of the area's largest PPOs. He complained that, had the exclusion not occurred, he would have been able to "score a [financial] touchdown." The court obviously found that the PPO lacked market power. The case is interesting for the way it treats a leading Supreme Court decision of importance for defining markets. Eastman Kodak v. Image Technical Services, 504 U.S. 451 (1992), held that a separate market could exist for the parts required to repair a Kodak brand photocopy machine depending on whether Kodak parts are interchangeable with parts for other brands. If not interchangeable, once the Kodak machine is purchased the buyers are locked into that brand's repair parts. Similarly, Dr. Levine argued that the PPO has extreme power in a small market because subscribers to a managed care network are locked into an "aftermarket" of network providers. The court observed, however, that subscribers in a PPO can go outside the network, only at extra costs that providers such as Levine were free to make up through discounts, and that subscribers were generally able to change health insurance once a year. See generally James Ponsoldt & Lance McMillian, The Judicial Legitimization of Horizontal Price-Fixing Among Partially Integrated Health Care Providers: An Antitrust/Health Care Case Study, 50 Ala. L. Rev. 465 (1999). For additional discussion of market definition for managed care entities, see section D.3.

8. *Illegal "Tie-Ins."* The Supreme Court has, so far, spoken directly on physician exclusion issues in only one case, Jefferson Parish Hospital District v. Hyde, 466 U.S. 2 (1984), but it was decided on a more obscure antitrust theory relating to "tie-ins." In that case, a physician challenged an exclusive contract for anesthesiology services that kept him from practicing in the hospital. He argued that requiring surgery patients to use the services of only designated anesthesiologists constituted a per se illegal tie-in: Surgery patients were forced to use only designated anesthesiologists even if they might want someone else. Surprisingly, the Court seemed to agree that surgery and anesthesia are indeed separate services, but it rejected the tie-in claim nevertheless because the hospital lacked the requisite market power to force the packaged sale on the patient.

9. *Reimbursement Limits.* A related line of cases are those concerning health insurers' limitations on reimbursement for certain medical services. Chiropractors, for instance, would be severely affected if Blue Cross/Blue Shield refused to pay for their services. However, if Blue Cross/Blue Shield merely determines on its own the terms under which it is willing to do business and separately reaches an agreement with individual providers, there is no horizontal conspiracy—or is there? Law professor Sylvia Law, in her influential study Blue Cross: What Went Wrong? (2d ed. 1976), explains that providers historically have dominated the Blues and used them to enforce their economic interests. See Virginia Academy of Clinical Psychologists v. Blue Shield, 624 F.2d 476 (4th Cir. 1980) (§1 violation established by Blue Shield's refusal to reimburse psychiatrists directly); Hahn v. Oregon Physicians' Service, 868 F.2d 1022 (9th Cir. 1988) (physician-controlled HMO that excluded podiatrists can be challenged as group boycott). Where insurers are not controlled by physicians, however, most courts conclude that they are free to unilaterally pay or not pay for whatever medical services and in whatever amounts they want. E.g., American Chiropractic Ass'n v. Trigon Healthcare, Inc., 367 F.3d 212 (4th Cir. 2004) (no conspiracy in limiting payments to chiropractors).

Nevertheless, in a bold move the Affordable Care Act (§2706) prohibits any health plan from "discriminating" against any category of licensed health care provider. Thus, regardless of antitrust law, insurers no longer may flatly refuse to pay alternative providers. However, the statute does not require that health plans include alternative practitioners in their contracted networks (which means the law has meaning only for health plans that cover out-of-network care). Also, the government has interpreted this anti-discrimination requirement narrowly to allow health plans to pay alternative practitioners less, and to set "medical management" limits on the "frequency, method, treatment or setting" for their services. CMS, Affordable Care Act Implementation FAQs (Sept. 15, 2013).

■ **CALIFORNIA DENTAL ASS'N v. FEDERAL TRADE COMMISSION**
526 U.S. 756 (1999)

[Read the excerpt at page 1238, and the footnote on page 1382.]

■ **THE ROLE OF QUALITY OF HEALTH CARE CONSIDERATIONS IN ANTITRUST ANALYSIS**
Thomas E. Kauper
51 Law & Contemp. Probs. 273 (Spring 1988)

For decades, health care services markets have functioned, for better or worse, without the constraints imposed on markets by competitive market pressures. . . . Self-regulation has been the norm. Actors in these markets long assumed that the antitrust laws were of little or no relevance to their conduct. As a result, health care services markets have been characterized by a variety of structures and actions which in most other industries would raise serious antitrust questions. The introduction of antitrust policy into these markets has therefore resulted in direct challenges to a broad range of conduct within a short period of time. . . . In virtually every instance, the concern over quality of care is likely to be raised in justification for the conduct under antitrust attack.

A doctor is denied hospital staff privileges. Hospitals deny access to midwives or chiropractors, or enter into exclusive contracts with providers for the performance of specialized services. Groups of local hospitals, acting on their own or through regional planning groups, determine which hospitals will have emergency or burn treatment facilities. Doctors agree on, or communicate about, the amounts they will accept in reimbursement from insurers, or collaborate to resist other efforts by insurers to reduce costs. A hospital is denied accreditation by an accrediting group which relies in part on judgments by other hospitals. A physician is denied specialist certification by an organization made up of such specialists. A hospital (or group of hospitals) opposes the issuance of a certificate of need to a potential competitor. . . . Running through this broad range of cases is a single issue which is the central focus of this study. When, if ever, should an antitrust court weigh the impact of conduct on quality of care? . . .

II. QUALITY OF CARE: A FRAMEWORK FOR ANALYSIS

A quality-of-care "defense" can mean a number of quite different things. First, the [defendants] may seek recognition of a limited professional services exemption from the antitrust laws. Adverse competitive effects then would have no antitrust consequences. Second, the [defendants] may contend that even if the [action] in question has adverse price and output effects, those effects are offset in some way by the social and economic benefits of avoiding deaths and physical harm to [patients].

Such a justification proceeds on the premise that quality of care is a national goal to be achieved even at the cost of competition. . . . Third, the [defendants] may assert that . . . quality of care is a relevant competitive factor or that there are no adverse price and output effects because of the preservation of a high quality of care. . . . [This] is a quite different argument from either the first or second; it is consistent with the view that antitrust analysis is confined to an examination of price and output effects. Fourth, the [defendant] may contend that its [action] is saved by a good purpose. In cases where violation may depend on the presence of an anticompetitive intent, a good purpose may negate the presence of the bad. . . .

The quality-of-care "defense" is thus not a single contention, but a series of distinctly different arguments. . . . But courts confronted with quality-of-care claims have too often failed to understand these differences. The result has been analytical confusion, much of which can be attributed to the Supreme Court. . . .

This confusion began with the Supreme Court's decision in Goldfarb v. Virginia State Bar Association, 421 U.S. 773 (1975), which found that the use of recommended fee schedules by the Fairfax County (Virginia) Bar Association violated §1 of the Sherman Act. The Court rejected the contention that the "learned professions" were not engaged in "trade or commerce" and were not therefore covered by the Sherman Act, noting that "the public service aspect of professional practice [is not] controlling in determining whether §1 includes professions." While *Goldfarb* dealt specifically with lawyers, it opened the door for the application of the antitrust laws to a wide variety of restraints involving health care markets. But in a now well-known footnote [17], inserted perhaps out of an abundance of caution, the Court sowed the seeds for the confusion about the relevance of quality-of-care concerns. [F]ootnote [17] states:

> The fact that a restraint operates upon a profession as distinguished from a business is, of course, relevant in determining whether that particular restraint violates the Sherman Act. It would be unrealistic to view the practice of professions as interchangeable with other business activities, and automatically apply to the professions antitrust concepts which originated in other areas. The public service aspect, and other features of the professions, may require that a particular practice, which could properly be viewed as a violation of the Sherman Act in another context, be treated differently. . . .

So the antitrust laws apply to the professions, but not quite. . . . *Goldfarb* was followed by the decision in National Society of Professional Engineers v. United States, 435 U.S. 679 (1978). The canons of ethics of the Society prohibited competitive bidding. This, according to the government, was tantamount to price-fixing. In defense, the Society asserted that the prohibition was necessary because competitive bidding would result in "inferior work with consequent risk to public safety and health," a contention contrary to the repeated earlier assertions by the Court, noted above, that it is competition which assures quality. The Court's conclusion in *Professional Engineers* that the Society's ban on competitive bidding could not be justified on quality-of-service grounds is hardly surprising. . . . *Professional Engineers* makes clear that antitrust rules are directed solely to the *competitive* effects of the restraint. . . . But the Court went on:

> We adhere to the view expressed in *Goldfarb* that, by their nature, professional services may differ significantly from other business services, and, accordingly, the nature

of the competition in such services may vary. Ethical norms may serve to regulate and promote this competition, and thus fall within the Rule of Reason.

While verbally adhering to the *Goldfarb* footnote, this reservation is more precise. Rather than public service, the touchstone is the nature of the competition. If professional services differ from others, the differences are in the markets themselves. Evaluation of competitive effects must take such differences into account. . . .

The Supreme Court's trilogy of health care antitrust cases following *Goldfarb*—Arizona v. Maricopa County Medical Society, 457 U.S. 332 (1981). Jefferson Parish Hospital District No. 2 v. Hyde, 466 U.S. 2 (1984), and FTC v. Indiana Federation of Dentists, 476 U.S. 447 (1986)—leaves little doubt about the general applicability of the antitrust laws to health care activities and considerable doubt about how they are to be applied. . . .

The final case in the trilogy is *Indiana Federation of Dentists*, where protection of the quality of dental care was the primary justification offered by defendants. At issue was a collective refusal by Indiana dentists, through the Indiana Federation, to supply X-rays along with claim forms to a number of dental care insurers. In order to contain dental care cost, insurers operated under policies limiting payments to the cost of the "least expensive yet adequate treatment," and often insisted that patient X-rays be submitted as part of the claims review process. . . . [T]he Federation attempted to justify its action on quality-of-care grounds, asserting that because X-rays alone do not furnish an adequate basis for evaluating dental problems, insurers who rely solely on X-rays would decline to pay for treatment which was in the best interest of the patient. . . . The Court declined to apply a per se rule, noting, inter alia, that "we have been slow to condemn rules adopted by professional associations as reasonable per se," but found that the [FTC's] findings of anticompetitive effects were sufficient. . . . The decision gives little comfort to those urging that antitrust analysis in health care markets should take into account a variety of non-economic factors.

Can the quality-of-care strands taken from *Goldfarb* through *Indiana Federation of Dentists* be woven into a coherent whole? The questions are being narrowed, and the nature of inquiry is now more sharply focused. A clear pattern is emerging. First, and most obvious, the Supreme Court has never found professional activity having adverse price and output effects justified by concerns over the quality of service provided. Second, justifications based on the view that competition will necessarily result in quality deterioration are unacceptable. . . . The Court's repeated assertions that professional conduct, and conduct in health care markets in particular, should be evaluated under standards that differ significantly from those more generally applied has created confusion. . . . These imprecise references to public service and ethical norms have allowed lower courts to treat quality-of-care issues in a variety of inconsistent ways, and in a manner reflecting biases more than consistent principles of antitrust analysis. . . .

Despite the confusion caused by the *Goldfarb* footnote and its progeny, the Court in its health care cases is generally moving in a direction in which quality of care is simply a factor in the analysis of adverse competitive effects. . . . Market structures and forces may be different in health care markets, and these differences may be relevant in evaluating the price and output effects of particular conduct, but the antitrust principles applied remain the same. . . .

Firms compete not only on price, but also on quality of product or service. Both are integral factors in the consumer's decision to buy. . . . The most obvious example is a hospital's denial of staff privileges to a physician who is simply incompetent, or has a public reputation of incompetence. The hospital will contend that the effect of its action is to prevent debasement of the quality of care its patients receive. It is not, however, acting out of some purely altruistic, public service concern. The presence of such a physician on the staff will damage the hospital's reputation, and thus its ability to compete. It may also injure the reputation of other members of the staff through association, although this effect is less obvious. If these effects are strong enough, the hospital may lose patients not only through consumer choice but because other physicians, fearful for their own reputations, leave the staff, taking their patients with them. . . .

A court called upon to decide such a case need not consider these effects unless the denial of staff privileges is likely to have adverse price and output effects in the market served by the denied physician. In most cases, such effects are likely only when . . . the number of competing physicians with such privileges is small. Under these circumstances, the denial of entry may protect a cartel among those already established. Few denials of staff privileges to individual physicians (or other providers) are likely to have such adverse price and output effects.[131] But where they do, the reputational effects of granting privileges become relevant and should be treated in the same manner as [cost] efficiencies. The likelihood of these effects must be evaluated on the record. The problems of defining quality should not be an obstacle here. The focus is more on reputation than quality as such. It is not necessary to define quality in some absolute sense. . . .

Courts and commentators on occasion have suggested that with some types of conduct, a predicate to antitrust liability is a determination that the conduct was accompanied by a purpose to injure competition. . . . [But] [p]urpose is relevant only as a guide to a judgment about effects, both adverse and beneficial. Where those who know a market act for the avowed purpose of restraining it, their intention is some evidence that adverse effects will occur. Similarly, an unambiguous intention to promote efficiency is probative in determining whether conduct does so. . . . The role of purpose is evidentiary. Standing alone, it can neither justify nor condemn. . . .

Purpose is often relied upon in evaluating agreements among competitors to which rules involving boycotts might be applied. The reason apparently lies in those rules themselves. Traditionally, boycotts have been described as per se violations, illegal without consideration of effects. Until very recently the definition of boycott, for the purpose of this rule has been far too broad. . . . Virtually any professional association rule which is enforced through a denial of benefits, such as staff privileges or accreditation, can be described as a boycott. Emphasis on purpose in health care cases of this type has added flexibility and mitigated the harshness of the per se rule. With the Supreme Court's reformulations of boycott doctrine in Northwest Wholesale Stationers, Inc. v. Pacific Stationery & Printing Co., 472 U.S. 284 (1985),

---

131. Adverse effects are more likely where an entire class of competitors or potential competitors (e.g., podiatrists, nurse-midwives) are denied hospital access. . . .

and FTC v. Indiana Federation of Dentists, there is less need for such reliance on the parties' purposes. These decisions move in the direction of effects analysis.[156] . . .

III. TRANSLATING THEORY INTO REALITY: A CASE STUDY

This section examines two decisions, Wilk v. American Medical Association[200] and Koefoot v. American College of Surgeons, 652 F. Supp. 882 (N.D. Ill. 1987), in which the boundaries of a quality-of-care, or patient care, defense, if any, are explored in depth. In both cases, the defendants placed primary reliance on the legitimacy of their efforts to guard the public in general, and their own patients in particular, against what, in their perception, was a significant threat to the quality of care provided. No other decisions discuss the issue as carefully or exhaustively. . . .

A. WILK

In *Wilk*, plaintiff chiropractors asserted that the American Medical Association and its members conspired among themselves and with other groups including the American Hospital Association, American College of Surgeons, American College of Physicians, American College of Radiology, American Academy of Orthopedic Surgeons, and the Joint Committee on Accreditation of Hospitals (JCAH) to conduct a nationwide boycott of chiropractic providers. While the facts are complex, the central feature of the alleged boycott was a 1966 AMA resolution stating: "It is the position of the medical profession that chiropractic is an unscientific cult whose practitioners lack the necessary training and background to diagnose and treat human disease." . . . The effect of the actions of the AMA and its co-conspirators was to discourage cooperation between chiropractors and physicians in the form of referrals, consultations, and the sharing of clinical and research results, and to deny chiropractors hospital facilities, including X-ray and laboratory facilities. . . .

Throughout the litigation, the defendants insisted that they had acted to protect the public health and safety from what they believed to be a form of quackery, a type of treatment without foundation in science. . . .

The court of appeals found the [trial court's] per se instructions erroneous. . . . Relying on *Goldfarb*'s reservations, the court noted that an ethical standard dealing with the role of scientific method presented sufficiently novel questions to avoid per se analysis. . . .

Had the appellate court stopped at this point, its analysis would have been fully consistent with conventional antitrust doctrine, . . . [b]ut the court then con-

---

156. In *Northwest Wholesale Stationers*, the Court held that the per se rule did not apply to expulsion from a purchasing cooperative made up of plaintiff's competitors absent a showing that the cooperative "possesses market power or unique access to a business element necessary for effective competition." 472 U.S. at 298. Without such a showing, a court could not: find that the expulsion was per se illegal. The Court also noted that in prior cases in which it had applied a per se rule, the practices were not justified "by plausible arguments that were intended to enhance overall efficiency." . . . The boycott analysis in *Indiana Federation of Dentists* is similar, although qualified by the observation that "we have been slow to condemn rules of professional associations as unreasonable per se."

200. 719 F.2d 207 (1983). Following reversal by the court of appeals, the case was retried in a bench trial. Wilk v. American Medical Ass'n, 671 F. Supp. 1465 (N.D. Ill. 1987).

cluded that in accord with *Goldfarb*'s reservation it was free "to modify the rule of reason test in a case involving a certain kind of question of ethics for the medical profession." . . . In the court's words, "a value independent of the values attributed to unrestrained competition must enter the equation." If the defendants' dominant motive was a concern over scientific method in the care of patients, their conduct was reasonable even if competition was restricted. [The court constructed a four-part affirmative defense that tested the sincerity and objectivity of this motive and whether the defendants chose the least restrictive means of achieving their purpose. The trial court found in a bench trial that the least restrictive means test was not met because the defendants could have achieved their purpose through education. The court ordered sweeping injunctive relief requiring the trade associations to tell their members they are free to make individual decisions about whether to associate with chiropractors.] . . .

B. KOEFOOT[223]

Over half of all board certified surgeons in the country are members of the American College of Surgeons (ACS). . . . Board certification or status as an ACS fellow is required to hold staff privileges in hospitals accredited by JCAH. . . . The "itinerant surgery" rule of the ACS prohibits:

> [t]he performance of surgical operations (except on patients whose chances of recovery would be prejudiced by removal to another hospital) under circumstances in which the responsibility for diagnosis or care of the patient is delegated to another who is not fully qualified to undertake it.

The effect of the rule is that ACS surgeons may delegate responsibility for postoperative care only to other surgeons.

Dr. Koefoot is a general surgeon who performs surgery in three hospitals in Grand Island, Nebraska, and in several community hospitals some 20 minutes away. He gives postoperative care to his patients in Grand Island, but delegates responsibility for such care to nonsurgeon general practitioners in the community hospitals. After his expulsion from ACS for violating the itinerant surgery rule, he filed an antitrust suit against ACS, attacking the rule as a form of market allocation used by ACS members to block entry, as a boycott of non-surgeons, and as a tie-in between surgery and post-operative care. . . . ACS has defended the rule as a legitimate ethical canon adopted to enhance the quality of care provided surgical patients. . . .

[T]he trial court held that the itinerant surgery violation was not a per se violation and set an agenda for the trial under the rule of reason. A "facially legitimate ethical canon," defined as a rule of professional practice that establishes standards of care "without reference to the economic interests of professionals," is not per se illegal. . . .

The trial court then dealt with the relevance of evidence offered by ACS to establish (1) that their motive was to safeguard the quality of patient care, and (2) that the practice of itinerant surgery was in fact harmful. As to the first, the court found *Wilk*'s patient care motive doctrine inapplicable. . . . [T]he later Supreme

---

223. Koefoot v. American College of Surgeons, 610 F. Supp. 1298, 1301 (N.D. Ill. 1985).

Court decisions in *Jefferson Parish* and *Indiana Federation of Dentists* . . . suggest that . . . [m]otive evidence is relevant and admissible, but only for the limited purpose of evaluating effect. Evidence that itinerant surgery was in fact harmful is relevant only to establish ACS's intent. . . . Because harm evidence is of limited relevance, and is a type of evidence that is likely to be prejudicial, the court concluded that its quality and quantity must be severely limited. . . .

Uncomfortable with the *Wilk* patient-care-motive justification, the court confined it to cases involving allegations of pure quackery. It is apparent that the court was determined not to make judgments about the medical consequences of itinerant surgery and feared that evidence about harm would distract the jury from its assignment to focus solely on competitive efforts. [After trial, the jury found that the rule had no anticompetitive effect.] . . .

C. [ANALYSIS]

. . . [The *Wilk* court was correct that] the AMA nonaffiliation rule and related actions cannot be . . . characterized as procompetitive . . . protection of reputation for quality. Physicians do have a legitimate competitive interest in reputation. And particular physicians could well decide that their competitive stance would be damaged by affiliation with chiropractors. But an *agreement* not to affiliate could be so justified only if a physician's ability to compete is impaired if *other* physicians affiliate with chiropractors. If such affiliation is harmful to reputation, however, affiliation by others would appear to enhance the competitive posture of those who reject it. . . .

[The *Wilk* court was wrong, however, to construct a special patient care affirmative defense.] Invariably, denial of access to these alternative providers is explained as a measure to protect the public from inferior care, [but this is] an explanation which in this broad sense is not cognizable in an antitrust case. . . . There is no single quality-of-care defense in health care antitrust cases. To the extent such a defense might be predicated on a balancing of social gains against adverse price and output effects, it is inconsistent with the focus on competitive effects which is central in antitrust analysis. Nor can such a defense be based on a dominant laudable purpose. Intent is relevant only as a predictor of effect. Where effect is established, intent is no longer of consequence.

Conduct that promotes efficiency, ameliorates the effects of market failures or imperfections, or increases quality rivalry among providers is, to this extent, procompetitive and may improve quality of care by enhancing the competitive process. Any further accommodation of quality-of-care concerns is a direct challenge to the central role of the market in the determination of quality, and therefore to the relevance of antitrust itself. It is for legislatures, not courts, to grant antitrust exemptions or otherwise displace the application of the antitrust laws.

Notes: Quality of Care as a Defense; Allied Health Professionals; Professional Society Rules

1. On balance, does antitrust law or the common law fairness doctrine do a better job of subjecting hospitals and HMOs to the proper level of scrutiny for their staffing decisions? Does your answer differ with respect to matters of procedure and matters of substance?

2. *Other Readings.* For additional discussions of the role that quality of care plays in health care antitrust analysis, see Peter J. Hammer & William M. Sage, Antitrust, Health Care Quality, and the Courts, 102 Colum. L. Rev. 545 (2002); William M. Sage & Peter J. Hammer, A Copernican View of Health Care Antitrust, 65 Law & Contemp. Probs. 241 (Autumn 2002).

3. If only competitive effects are relevant to antitrust analysis, why is a Catholic hospital allowed to exclude abortionists? (Possibly because of overriding First Amendment concerns. Or, because such a policy does not advance the economic interests of member physicians, it does not constitute a conspiracy.)

Should Congress's 1986 enactment of an *explicit* qualified immunity in the Health Care Quality Improvement Act, discussed below, resolve any further debate about whether the courts should find an *implied* patient care affirmative defense?

4. *Recognition for Allied Health Professionals.* Both the *Weiss* case above and the *Wilk* case discussed by Prof. Kauper manifest the traditional medical establishment's longstanding hostility to competing schools of practitioners that are founded on less scientific theories of medicine. Chiropractors and osteopaths are only two among the several allied health professions that are engaged in active struggles to achieve professional recognition and hospital access. Similar challenges have been mounted by podiatrists, clinical psychologists, nurse anesthetists, and midwives, usually without success. See, e.g., Minnesota Ass'n of Nurse Anesthetists, 208 F.3d 2000 (8th Cir. 2000) (rejecting a boycott challenge to several hospitals' decisions to contract only with physician groups for anesthesia services).

An important indirect effect of this antitrust pressure has been to force a revision of the JCAHO accreditation standards. Prior to 1984, JCAHO standards were read as prohibiting hospitals from extending staff privileges to practitioners other than doctors and dentists. However, in that year, the JCAHO adopted an amendment that allowed hospitals to "include other licensed individuals permitted by law and by the hospital to provide patient care services independently." For a survey of these developments, see C. Dodd, Exclusion of Nonphysician Health Care Providers from Integrated Delivery Systems, 64 U. Cin. L. Rev. 983 (1996).

In some states, allied health professionals have won their contest in the legislature by obtaining statutory enactments that require hospitals to grant them equal consideration in extending clinical privileges. Representative is D.C. Code Ann. §44-507, which requires individual, nondiscriminatory consideration of the credentials of podiatrists, psychologists, nurse anesthetists, nurse midwives, and nurse practitioners. See also Ohio Rev. Code Ann §3701.351(B).

5. *Codes of Professional Ethics. California Dental Ass'n* and the *Koefoot* and *Indiana Federation of Dentists* cases discussed by Prof. Kauper are examples of the several challenges to various ethical restrictions in medical professional codes. The most prominent of these is American Medical Ass'n v. FTC, 94 FTC 980, 1015 (1979), enforced 638 F.2d 443 (2d Cir. 1980), aff'd mem. by an equally divided Court, 455 U.S. 676 (1982), which invalidated ethical prohibitions against advertising and certain physician contractual arrangements. For additional commentary, see the articles cited in note 2 above, and Clark Havighurst & Nancy King, Private Credentialing of Health Care Personnel: An Antitrust Perspective, 9 Am. J. L. & Med. 131, 263 (1983).

Problem: Medical Staff Boycotts of Allied Health Professionals

Centerville Psychiatric (CP) is a for-profit psychiatric hospital in a large town with two other free-standing psychiatric hospitals and with four general hospitals that have smaller psychiatric units. CP attempts to distinguish itself from its competitors by claiming to offer better doctors and more state-of-the-art structured treatment programs that combine intensive counseling and drug therapy for acute episodes of serious mental illness (so-called nervous breakdowns). This treatment approach contrasts with that in general hospitals, which is unstructured, much shorter in duration, and often administered by nonspecialists, and contrasts with other specialized psychiatric hospitals that offer long-term custodial treatment for more chronic conditions.

Consistent with its long-standing bylaws, CP's medical staff presently consists of only board-certified psychiatrists, which are specially trained M.D.s. Alfred Zock, Ph.D. is a psychologist of good reputation with an active counseling and therapy practice in Centerville. He has decided to break the mold by applying for medical staff privileges at CP. The major practical difference between psychiatrists and psychologists is that only the former can prescribe drugs; psychologists are limited by state licensing laws to "couch therapy." In the past, psychologists have been allowed to see CP patients who were under their care before coming to CP, but only if a staff psychiatrist approved and supervised the psychologist. Dr. Zock would like to admit his own patients directly and treat them at CP without supervision or prior approval. He has admitting privileges at one of the general hospitals in town, but he finds their facilities unsatisfactory.

The existing psychiatrists oppose Dr. Zock's admission because they like things the way they are, for both clinical and financial reasons. The hospital administration is also not in favor, partly because it does not want to antagonize its medical staff in a competitive hospital market where they can take their patients elsewhere, and partly because reimbursement rates under managed care insurance are usually higher for drug therapy than for counseling. On the other hand, it is clear many patients would prefer their own psychologist to be their primary physician.

As lawyer for CP, advise it on the safest way to exclude Dr. Zock. Consider whether to use primarily quality or economic criteria, whether to act under the existing bylaws, or to change them and then consider Dr. Zock individually. Consider what procedures to follow in making these decisions.

Note: Peer Review Immunity

After reading about all these lawsuits arising from medical staff disputes, both under the common-law fairness doctrine and under antitrust law, it may surprise you to learn that a federal statute confers broad immunity on participants in hospital and HMO credentialing or peer review processes. Known as the Health Care Quality Improvement Act, 42 U.S.C. §§11101-11152, the statute's purpose is to promote more aggressive policing of the quality of care. It does so by immunizing from monetary damages any participant in a qualified peer review proceeding. This immunity applies both to state law and to federal theories of liability, including antitrust, but not to a violation of the civil rights statutes. Similar immunity statutes exist in many states, and state statutes also usually protect information generated by peer review activities from being released to the public or in litigation. See page 348.

These immunity and confidentiality statutes have had some impact, but they have not eliminated this body of litigation because these statutes are subject to a number of important limitations. We will illustrate by focusing on the federal statute. First, it does not bar suit for injunctive relief. Second, to qualify for immunity, the proceedings must be conducted in a fashion that is procedurally and substantively fair. Thus, at least some review of the merits of the decision and the fairness of the process is still required in order to invoke the protection of the statute, although at an earlier stage of the litigation and subject to certain presumptions and burdens of proof that favor the defendants. Third, immunity is available only for actions against individual physicians based on quality-of-care concerns. In other words, immunity is not available for actions against nonphysicians, against classes of physicians, or based on economic considerations. It should be clear by now that the immunity statute would have precluded little, if any, of the litigation reviewed in the preceding sections.

A fuller exploration of these issues, and an illustrative case, can be found on the Web site for this book, www.health-law.org. The Web site also explains another, more specialized immunity known as "state action immunity" that applies only to antitrust cases. For additional discussion of the Health Care Quality Improvement Act immunity and similar state statutes, see Charity Scott, Medical Peer Review, Antitrust, and the Effect of Statutory Reform, 50 Md. L. Rev. 316 (1991) ("the Act appears to immunize only conduct that would not be actionable under the antitrust laws in the first place. . . . Remarkably, of the few . . . [antitrust] cases that courts have said were proper for jury resolution, only a handful could even in theory have qualified for immunity.").

2. Price-Fixing Law

■ ARIZONA v. MARICOPA COUNTY MEDICAL SOCIETY
457 U.S. 332 (1982)

Justice STEVENS delivered the opinion of the Court.

The question presented is whether §1 of the Sherman Act, 26 Stat. 209, as amended, 15 U.S.C. §1, has been violated by agreements among competing physicians setting, by majority vote, the maximum fees that they may claim in full payment for health services provided to policyholders of specified insurance plans. The United States Court of Appeals for the Ninth Circuit held that the question could not be answered without evaluating the actual purpose and effect of the agreements at a full trial. Because the undisputed facts disclose a violation of the statute, we granted certiorari and now reverse.

I

In October 1978, the state of Arizona filed a civil complaint against two county medical societies and two "foundations for medical care" that the medical societies had organized. The complaint alleged that the defendants were engaged in illegal price-fixing conspiracies. . . .

The Maricopa Foundation for Medical Care is a nonprofit Arizona corporation composed of licensed doctors of medicine, osteopathy, and podiatry engaged in private practice. Approximately 1,750 doctors, representing about 70 percent of the practitioners in Maricopa County, are members. The Maricopa Foundation was organized in 1969 for the purpose of promoting fee-for-service medicine and to provide the community with a competitive alternative to existing health insurance plans. The foundation performs three primary activities. It establishes the schedule of maximum fees that participating doctors agree to accept as payment in full for services performed for patients insured under plans approved by the foundation. It reviews the medical necessity and appropriateness of treatment provided by its members to such insured persons. It is authorized to draw checks on insurance company accounts to pay doctors for services performed for covered patients. In performing these functions, the foundation is considered an "insurance administrator" by the Director of the Arizona Department of Insurance. Its participating doctors, however, have no financial interest in the operation of the foundation.

The Pima Foundation for Medical Care, which includes about 400 member doctors, performs similar functions. For the purposes of this litigation, the parties seem to regard the activities of the two foundations as essentially the same. No challenge is made to their peer review or claim administration functions. Nor do the foundations allege that these two activities make it necessary for them to engage in the practice of establishing maximum-fee schedules. . . .

The fee schedules limit the amount that the member doctors may recover for services performed for patients insured under plans approved by the foundations. To obtain this approval the insurers—including self-insured employers as well as insurance companies—agree to pay the doctors' charges up to the scheduled amounts, and in exchange the doctors agree to accept those amounts as payment in full for their services. The doctors are free to charge higher fees to uninsured patients, and they also may charge any patient less than the scheduled maxima. A patient who is insured by a foundation-endorsed plan is guaranteed complete coverage for the full amount of his medical bills only if he is treated by a foundation member. He is free to go to a nonmember physician and is still covered for charges that do not exceed the maximum-fee schedule, but he must pay any excess that the nonmember physician may charge.

The impact of the foundation fee schedules on medical fees and on insurance premiums is a matter of dispute. The state of Arizona contends that the periodic upward revisions of the maximum-fee schedules have the effect of stabilizing and enhancing the level of actual charges by physicians, and that the increasing level of their fees in turn increases insurance premiums. The foundations, on the other hand, argue that the schedules impose a meaningful limit on physicians' charges, and that the advance agreement by the doctors to accept the maxima enables the insurance carriers to limit and to calculate more efficiently the risks they underwrite and therefore serves as an effective cost-containment mechanism that has saved patients and insurers millions of dollars. Although the Attorneys General of 40 different states, as well as the Solicitor General of the United States and certain organizations representing consumers of medical services, have filed amicus curiae briefs supporting the state of Arizona's position on the merits, we must assume that the respondents' view of the genuine issues of fact is correct.

This assumption presents, but does not answer, the question whether the Sherman Act prohibits the competing doctors from adopting, revising, and agreeing to use a maximum-fee schedule in implementation of the insurance plans.

III

The respondents recognize that our decisions establish that price-fixing agreements are unlawful on their face. But they argue that the per se rule does not govern this case because the agreements at issue are horizontal and fix maximum prices, are among members of a profession, are in an industry with which the judiciary has little antitrust experience, and are alleged to have procompetitive justifications. Before we examine each of these arguments, we pause to consider the history and the meaning of the per se rule against price-fixing agreements.

Section 1 of the Sherman Act of 1890 literally prohibits *every* agreement "in restraint of trade." In United States v. Joint Traffic Assn., 171 U.S. 505 (1898), we recognized that Congress could not have intended a literal interpretation of the word *every*; since Standard Oil Co. of New Jersey v. United States, 221 U.S. 1 (1911), we have analyzed most restraints under the so-called rule of reason. As its name suggests, the rule of reason requires the factfinder to decide whether under all the circumstances of the case the restrictive practice imposes an unreasonable restraint on competition.

The elaborate inquiry into the reasonableness of a challenged business practice entails significant costs. Litigation of the effect or purpose of a practice often is extensive and complex. Judges often lack the expert understanding of industrial market structures and behavior to determine with any confidence a practice's effect on competition. And the result of the process in any given case may provide little certainty or guidance about the legality of a practice in another context.

The costs of judging business practices under the rule of reason, however, have been reduced by the recognition of per se rules. Once experience with a particular kind of restraint enables the Court to predict with confidence that the rule of reason will condemn it, it has applied a conclusive presumption that the restraint is unreasonable. As in every rule of general application, the match between the presumed and the actual is imperfect. For the sake of business certainty and litigation efficiency, we have tolerated the invalidation of some agreements that a fullblown inquiry might have proved to be reasonable. . . .

[P]rice-fixing agreements are unlawful per se under the Sherman Act and . . . "no showing of so-called competitive abuses or evils which those agreements were designed to eliminate or alleviate may be interposed as a defense." United States v. Socony-Vacuum Oil Co., 310 U.S. 150, 218 (1940). In that case, a glut in the spot market for gasoline had prompted the major oil refiners to engage in a concerted effort to purchase and store surplus gasoline in order to maintain stable prices. Absent the agreement, the companies argued, competition was cutthroat and self-defeating. The argument did not carry the day:

> Any combination which tampers with price structures is engaged in an unlawful activity. . . . The Act places all such schemes beyond the pale and protects that vital

part of our economy against any degree of interference. . . . Nor has the Act created or authorized the creation of any special exception in favor of the oil industry. Whatever may be its peculiar problems and characteristics, the Sherman Act, so far as price-fixing agreements are concerned, establishes one uniform rule applicable to all industries alike. . . . Under the Sherman Act a combination formed for the purpose and with the effect of raising, depressing, fixing, pegging, or stabilizing the price of a commodity in interstate or foreign commerce is illegal per se.

Over the objection that maximum-price-fixing agreements were not the "economic equivalent" of minimum-price-fixing agreements, [we held in] Albrecht v. Herald Co., 390 U.S. 145 (1968):

Maximum and minimum price fixing may have different consequences in many situations. But schemes to fix maximum prices, by substituting the perhaps erroneous judgment of a seller for the forces of the competitive market, may severely intrude upon the ability of buyers to compete and survive in that market. Competition, even in a single product, is not cast in a single mold. Maximum prices may be fixed too low for the dealer to furnish services essential to the value which goods have for the consumer or to furnish services and conveniences which consumers desire and for which they are willing to pay. Maximum price fixing may channel distribution through a few large or specifically advantaged dealers who otherwise would be subject to significant nonprice competition. Moreover, if the actual price charged under a maximum price scheme is nearly always the fixed maximum price, which is increasingly likely as the maximum price approaches the actual cost of the dealer, the scheme tends to acquire all the attributes of an arrangement fixing minimum prices.

We have not wavered in our enforcement of the per se rule against price fixing. Indeed, in our most recent price-fixing case we summarily reversed the decision of another Ninth Circuit panel that a horizontal agreement among competitors to fix credit terms does not necessarily contravene the antitrust laws. Catalano, Inc. v. Target Sales, Inc., 446 U.S. 643 (1980). . . . The per se rule "is grounded on faith in price competition as a market force [and not] on a policy of low selling prices at the price of eliminating competition." Rahl, Price Competition and the Price Fixing Rule—Preface and Perspective, 57 Nw. U. L. Rev. 137, 142 (1962). In this case the rule is violated by a price restraint that tends to provide the same economic rewards to all practitioners regardless of their skill, their experience, their training, or their willingness to employ innovative and difficult procedures in individual cases. Such a restraint also may discourage entry into the market and may deter experimentation and new developments by individual entrepreneurs. It may be a masquerade for an agreement to fix uniform prices, or it may in the future take on that character.

Nor does the fact that doctors—rather than nonprofessionals—are the parties to the price-fixing agreements support the respondents' position. In Goldfarb v. Virginia State Bar, 421 U.S. 773, 788, n.17 (1975), we stated that the "public service aspect, and other features of the professions, may require that a particular practice, which could properly be viewed as a violation of the Sherman Act in another context, be treated differently." See National Society of Professional Engineers v. United States, 435 U.S. 679, 696 (1978). The price-fixing agreements in this case, however, are not premised on public service or ethical norms. The respondents do not argue, as did the defendants in *Goldfarb* and *Professional Engineers*, that the quality of the professional service that their members provide is enhanced by the price restraint. The respondents' claim for relief from the per se rule is simply that the doctors' agreement not to charge certain insureds more than a fixed price facilitates the successful marketing of an attractive insurance plan. But the claim that the price restraint will make it easier for customers to pay does not distinguish the medical profession from any other provider of goods or services. . . .

The respondents' principal argument is that the per se rule is inapplicable because their agreements are alleged to have procompetitive justifications. The argument indicates a misunderstanding of the per se concept. The anticompetitive potential inherent in all price-fixing agreements justifies their facial invalidation even if procompetitive justifications are offered for some. Those claims of enhanced competition are so unlikely to prove significant in any particular case that we adhere to the rule of law that is justified in its general application. Even when the respondents are given every benefit of the doubt, the limited record in this case is not inconsistent with the presumption that the respondents' agreements will not significantly enhance competition. . . .

It is true that a binding assurance of complete insurance coverage — as well as most of the respondents' potential for lower insurance premiums — can be obtained only if the insurer and the doctor agree in advance on the maximum fee that the doctor will accept as full payment for a particular service. Even if a fee schedule is therefore desirable, it is not necessary that the doctors do the price fixing.[26] The record indicates that the Arizona Comprehensive Medical/Dental Program for Foster Children is administered by the Maricopa Foundation pursuant to a contract under which the maximum-fee schedule is prescribed by a state agency rather than by the doctors. This program and the Blue Shield plan challenged in Group Life & Health Insurance Co. v. Royal Drug Co., 440 U.S. 205 (1979), indicate that insurers are capable not only of fixing maximum reimbursable prices but also of obtaining binding agreements with providers guaranteeing the insured full reimbursement of a participating provider's fee. In light of these examples, it is not surprising that nothing in the record even arguably supports the conclusion that this type of insurance program could not function if the fee schedules were set in a different way.

The most that can be said for having doctors fix the maximum prices is that doctors may be able to do it more efficiently than insurers. The validity of that assumption is far from obvious, but in any event there is no reason to believe that any savings that might accrue from this arrangement would be sufficiently great to affect the competitiveness of these kinds of insurance plans. It is entirely possible that the potential or actual power of the foundations to dictate the terms of such insurance plans may more than offset the theoretical efficiencies upon which the respondents' defense ultimately rests. . . .

---

26. . . . [T]his case [does not] present the question whether an insurer may, consistent with the Sherman Act, fix the fee schedule and enter into bilateral contracts with individual doctors. . . . In an amicus curiae brief, the United States expressed its opinion that such an arrangement would be legal unless the plaintiffs could establish that a conspiracy among providers was at work. . . .

IV

Having declined the respondents' invitation to cut back on the per se rule against price fixing, we are left with the respondents' argument that their fee schedules involve price fixing in only a literal sense. For this argument, the respondents rely upon Broadcast Music, Inc. v. Columbia Broadcasting System, Inc., 441 U.S. 1 (1979).

In *Broadcast Music,* we were confronted with an antitrust challenge to the marketing of the right to use copyrighted compositions derived from the entire membership of the American Society of Composers, Authors and Publishers (ASCAP). The so-called blanket license was entirely different from the product that any one composer was able to sell by himself. Although there was little competition among individual composers for their separate compositions, the blanket-license arrangement did not place any restraint on the right of any individual copyright owner to sell his own compositions separately to any buyer at any price. But a "necessary consequence" of the creation of the blanket license was that its price had to be established. We held that the delegation by the composers to ASCAP of the power to fix the price for the blanket license was not a species of the price-fixing agreements categorically forbidden by the Sherman Act. The record disclosed price fixing only in a "literal sense."

This case is fundamentally different. Each of the foundations is composed of individual practitioners who compete with one another for patients. Neither the foundations nor the doctors sell insurance, and they derive no profits from the sale of health insurance policies. The members of the foundations sell medical services. Their combination in the form of the foundation does not permit them to sell any different product. Their combination has merely permitted them to sell their services to certain customers at fixed prices and arguably to affect the prevailing market price of medical care.

The foundations are not analogous to partnerships or other joint arrangements in which persons who would otherwise be competitors pool their capital and share the risks of loss as well as the opportunities for profit. In such joint ventures, the partnership is regarded as a single firm competing with other sellers in the market. The agreement under attack is an agreement among hundreds of competing doctors concerning the price at which each will offer his own services to a substantial number of consumers. It is true that some are surgeons, some anesthesiologists, and some psychiatrists, but the doctors do not sell a package of three kinds of services. If a clinic offered complete medical coverage for a flat fee, the cooperating doctors would have the type of partnership arrangement in which a price-fixing agreement among the doctors would be perfectly proper. But the fee agreements disclosed by the record in this case are among independent competing entrepreneurs. They fit squarely into the horizontal price-fixing mold.

The judgment of the court of appeals is reversed.

Justices BLACKMUN and O'CONNOR took no part in this case [due to conflicts of interest].

Justice POWELL, with whom THE CHIEF JUSTICE and Justice REHNQUIST join, dissenting.

The medical care plan condemned by the Court today is a comparatively new method of providing insured medical services at predetermined maximum costs. It involves no coercion. Medical insurance companies, physicians, and patients alike are free to participate or not as they choose. On its face, the plan seems to be in the public interest. . . .

It is settled law that once an arrangement has been labeled as "price fixing" it is to be condemned per se. But it is equally well settled that this characterization is not to be applied as a talisman to every arrangement that involves a literal fixing of prices. Many lawful contracts, mergers, and partnerships fix prices. But our cases require a more discerning approach. . . . In Broadcast Music, Inc. v. Columbia Broadcasting System, Inc., supra, there was minimum price fixing in the most "literal sense." We nevertheless agreed, unanimously, that an arrangement by which copyright clearinghouses sold performance rights to their entire libraries on a blanket rather than individual basis did not warrant condemnation on a per se basis. Individual licensing would have allowed competition between copyright owners. But we reasoned that licensing on a blanket basis yielded substantial efficiencies that otherwise could not be realized. Indeed, the blanket license was itself "to some extent, a different product."

In sum, the fact that a foundation-sponsored health insurance plan literally involves the setting of ceiling prices among competing physicians does not, of itself, justify condemning the plan as per se illegal. Only if it is clear from the record that the agreement among physicians is "so plainly anticompetitive that no elaborate study of [its effects] is needed to establish [its] illegality" may a court properly make a per se judgment. National Society of Professional Engineers v. United States, supra, at 692. . . .

In a complex economy, complex economic arrangements are commonplace. It is unwise for the Court, in a case as novel and important as this one, to make a final judgment in the absence of a complete record and where mandatory inferences create critical issues of fact.

Notes: Price-Fixing Antitrust Liability; Managed Care Networks; Joint Ventures

1. *Foundation Plans.* Medical society "foundation plans," such as those considered in *Maricopa County*, arose in the 1970s as a way for the medical profession to resist the introduction of alternative financing and delivery systems such as HMOs. These arrangements illustrate the AMA's continuing "strategy of preemption and cooptation [through] professionally sponsored reforms." Clark Havighurst, Professional Restraints on Innovation in Health Care Financing, 1978 Duke L. J. 303. It is therefore not surprising that the Court found these plans to have anticompetitive potential, especially where they include most of the doctors in town. This ruling is borne out by subsequent developments in Phoenix, where the number of PPOs and HMOs increased from 1 to 18 within three years of the *Maricopa County* decision.

2. *Managed Care Provider Networks. Maricopa County*'s importance for health care markets extends far beyond the particular "foundation plans" the Court ruled on. Observe that these largely defunct foundations plans were structurally identical to

present-day PPOs, which are now the dominant form of health insurance. PPOs give subscribers a discount if they seek care from doctors and hospitals within the preferred network, rather than allowing the completely free choice of providers, or forcing patients to use *only* contracted providers. Providers agree to accept discounted payments in exchange for the prospect of a higher volume of business, and they agree to abide by certain utilization review protocols. More recently, we have also seen the formation of ACOs (accountable care organizations), in which providers affiliate not only to provide more competitive pricing, but also to coordinate care and contract for more value-based payment methods than traditional fee-for-service. Does *Maricopa County* remain convincing in the present-day climate where ACOs, PPOs, and other types of provider networks are seen as *pro*competitive innovations? Note that, due to recusals, the majority opinion has the support of only four justices.

One potential way to distinguish the *Maricopa County* arrangement from current market arrangements is whether the impetus for the formation of a provider network comes from purchasers rather than from providers. In a purchaser-based network, an employer or insurance company approaches doctors and hospitals individually and negotiates with each separately. But sometimes, providers take the initiative by jointly agreeing to offer their services as a package to employers or insurers. In the past, they have done so mainly on a discounted fee-for-service basis, through what are known as Independent Practice Associations (IPAs). These provider-initiated networks raise the distinct aura of per se illegal price fixing, yet it may be necessary for groups of providers to cooperate in order for potentially procompetitive activity to flourish, especially if providers are to be organized in a manner (such as ACOs) that permits different forms of payment such as capitation or outcomes-based payment incentives.

Thus, the primary legal concern for managed care provider networks is whether this can be done in a way that avoids price-fixing antitrust liability.

3. *Antitrust Enforcement Guidelines.* Both the DOJ and the FTC have enforcement authority over the antitrust laws. These agencies, in exercising their prosecutorial discretion, have taken a substantially more encouraging position against provider networks. In a joint set of "Statements of Antitrust Enforcement Policy in Health Care," called the "DOJ/FTC Antitrust Guidelines," the two agencies establish the following safety zones for physician (not hospital) networks:

> By developing and implementing mechanisms that encourage physicians to collaborate in practicing efficiently as part of the network, many physician network joint ventures promise significant procompetitive benefits for consumers of health care services. . . . To qualify for [an] antitrust safety zone, the physicians participating in a physician network joint venture must share substantial financial risk. . . . Risk sharing provides incentive for the physicians to cooperate in controlling costs and improving quality by managing the provision of services by network physicians. The following are examples of situations in which participants in a physician network joint venture can share substantial financial risk:
>
> > (1) agreement by the venture to provide services to a health plan at a "capitated" rate; or . . .
> > (2) use by the venture of significant financial incentives for its physician participants, as a group, to achieve specified cost-containment goals . . . [such as]

withholding from all physician participants a substantial amount of the compensation due to them, with distribution of that amount to the physician participants based on group performance in meeting the cost-containment goals. . . .

Physician network joint ventures that fall outside the antitrust safety zone . . . do not necessarily raise substantial antitrust concerns. . . . [They] will be analyzed under the rule of reason, and will not be viewed as per se illegal, if the physicians' integration through the network is likely to produce significant efficiencies that benefit consumers, and any price agreements are reasonably necessary to realize those efficiencies. . . .

Physician network joint ventures that do not involve the sharing of substantial financial risk may also involve sufficient [clinical] integration to demonstrate that the venture is likely to produce sufficient efficiencies. Such [clinical] integration can be evidenced by the network implementing an active and ongoing program to evaluate and modify practice patterns . . . and to create a high degree of interdependence and cooperation among the physicians to control costs and ensure quality. . . .

In contrast to integrated physician network joint ventures, such as these, . . . there have been arrangements among physicians that have taken the form of networks, but which in purpose or effect were little more than efforts by their participants to prevent or impede competitive forces from operating in the market. . . . Determining that an arrangement is merely a vehicle to fix prices or engage in naked anticompetitive conduct is a factual inquiry that must be done on a case-by-case basis to determine the arrangement's true nature and likely competitive effects. . . . In assessing the competitive environment, the Agencies would consider such market factors as the number, types, and size of managed care plans operating in the area [and] the extent of physician participation in those plans. If in the relevant market there are many other networks or many physicians who would be available to form competing networks or to contract directly with health plans, it is unlikely that the joint venture would raise significant competitive concerns. . . . The Agencies will consider a broad range of possible cost savings, including improved cost controls, case management and quality assurance, economies of scale, and reduced administrative or transaction costs. . . .

Some networks that are not substantially integrated use a variety of "messenger model" arrangements to facilitate contracting between providers and payers and avoid price-fixing agreements among competing network providers. Arrangements that are designed simply to minimize the costs associated with the contracting process, and that do not result in collective determination by the competing network providers on prices or price-related terms, are not per se illegal price fixing. . . . For example, network providers may use an agent or third party to convey to purchasers information obtained individually from the providers about the prices or price-related terms that the providers are willing to accept. In some cases, the agent may convey to the providers all contract offers made by purchasers, and each provider then makes an independent, unilateral decision to accept or reject the contract offers. In others, the agent may have received from individual providers some authority to accept contract offers on their behalf. . . . The Agencies will examine whether the agent facilitates collective decision-making by network providers, rather than independent, unilateral, decisions.[65] . . .

_____

65. Use of an intermediary or "independent" third party to convey collectively determined price offers to purchasers or to negotiate agreements with purchasers, or giving to individual providers an opportunity to "opt" into, or out of, such agreements does not negate the existence of an agreement.

Are the DOJ/FTC Antitrust Guidelines consistent with *Maricopa County*? See generally Scott Danzis, Revising the Revised Guidelines: Incentives, Clinically Integrated Physician Networks, and the Antitrust Laws, 87 Va. L. Rev. 531 (2001).

Observe that these safe harbors do not apply to "multi-provider" networks; that is, those that contain hospitals. Why might the antitrust risks be greater or different when hospitals are present?

4. *Joint Venture Techniques.* The *Maricopa County* decision and the enforcement guidelines suggest three possible avenues for organizing a provider network to avoid a per se price-fixing charge:

a. *Financial or clinical integration.* No horizontal price fixing exists if doctors integrate into a single economic entity that bears substantial financial risk. This can occur through true corporate integration in which doctors invest capital and form a joint business enterprise. Or, it can occur through contractual joint venture arrangements. In the latter case, the focus is on the degree of financial risk sharing or clinical integration. The DOJ/FTC Guidelines give examples, but provide no quantification. A portion of Hassan v. Independent Practice Associates omitted from the excerpt at page 1392 held that a "risk withhold" payment system that placed 12 to 25 percent of the physicians' payments at risk succeeded in classifying an IPA physician network as a "legitimate joint venture" under *Maricopa County*, thus escaping per se condemnation. This escape hatch raises a number of additional questions.

First, is it necessary for all doctors to share substantial risk for all of their services, or only for some or most? Payment schemes for specialists often differ substantially from those for primary care physicians. In two simultaneous consent orders (St. Joseph's and Danbury), the DOJ indicated that it is sufficient if the controlling physicians bear substantial risk; physicians who are paid by the network only as subcontractors may be reimbursed on a fee-for-service basis. 60 Fed. Reg. 51,809, 52,015 (1995).

Second, are there other ways to establish integration besides financial risk sharing? After vehement argument from the AMA and others, the DOJ and FTC revised their initial guidelines to allow a showing of *clinical* integration to suffice, as quoted above. Observe how clinical integration is defined. Illustrations include utilization review, quality assurance, practice guidelines, and physician credentialing. Are these enough to demonstrate that physicians in different offices are practicing as a coordinated clinical enterprise, or are they merely "window dressing" as found in *Maricopa County*? In the first ruling to find clinical integration, the FTC ruled in February 2002 (letter regarding MedSouth, Inc.) that it would not constitute a per se violation for more than half the doctors in one part of Denver to jointly negotiate with insurers, as long as they did so on a nonexclusive basis (i.e., each doctor could opt out and negotiate independently). The FTC found clinical integration to exist because the doctors proposed to share medical information, develop practice guidelines, monitor performance, and reduce utilization. The FTC also "concluded that the joint contracting appears to be sufficiently related to, and reasonably necessary for, the achievement of the potential benefits [of clinical integration] to be regarded as ancillary to the operation of the venture." Does that sound plausible to you? Especially noteworthy is the FTC's 2009 approval of the TriState Health Partners joint venture between the only hospital in Hagerstown, Maryland and most of the area's 300 physicians, finding enough indicia of increased clinical interaction among participating providers. For commentary, see Taylor Burke & Sara Rosenbaum, Accountable Care Organizations: Implications for Antitrust Policy (Robert Wood Johnson Foundation, 2010), *reprinted in* 19 BNA Health L. Rep. 358 (2010); Thomas B. Leary, The Antitrust Implications of "Clinical Integration:" An Analysis of FTC Staff's Advisory Opinion to MedSouth, 47 St. Louis U. L. Rev. 223 (2003); Comment, 14 Ann. Health L. 125 (2005).

The third problem is that full-scale integration may not be the most attractive option for physicians, either from a business or from a legal antitrust perspective. From a business perspective, when provider groups assume substantial financial risk for medical treatment, they may as a result fall within the jurisdiction of state health insurance regulations that require them to maintain large capital reserves to protect consumers against their insolvency. See Chapter 9.B. From a legal perspective, consider what new antitrust problems would exist if 70 percent of the doctors in Phoenix had formed a joint venture. See the discussion of merger law that follows. On the other hand, what antitrust issues would exist if PPO physicians selectively limited membership to a smaller number of competitors? See the discussion of boycott law in section D.1; Reazin v. Blue Cross & Blue Shield of Kansas, 899 F.2d 951 (10th Cir. 1990) ($7.8 million verdict sustained in favor of hospital excluded by a PPO).

b. *Creation of a new product.* A second way to avoid per se price fixing, based on the reasoning of the *Broadcast Music* (*BMI*) case discussed in *Maricopa County*, is for physicians to attempt to form a new product. In *BMI*, the Court used the new product characterization to justify its holding that a "blanket license" for a library of music compositions did not constitute price fixing even though numerous music composers collectively agreed to market their compositions through a joint agency rather than dealing individually with each radio station and nightclub singer. See also NCAA v. Board of Regents, 468 U.S. 85 (1984) ("horizontal restraints on competition are essential if [an organized college football league] is to be available at all"). Why did the Court reject the Foundation plans' argument that the bulk sale of physician services to insurance companies and large employers, coupled with claims processing, quality assurance, and utilization review, constitutes a new health care product? What did the Court indicate would suffice to meet the new product test?

The DOJ/FTC Antitrust Guidelines do not speak in terms of a "new product," but instead analyze the *BMI* issue in terms of procompetitive efficiencies. The guidelines leave open the possibility that a network lacking financial integration may still be able to avoid per se condemnation if, after what some commentators call a "quick look" review, it appears not to be a "naked" restraint but instead is a "legitimate" joint venture. In such a case, the agencies will then weigh the procompetitive benefits against the anticompetitive harms. The agencies remain skeptical, however, that a network will actually survive this scrutiny if it in fact lacks financial and clinical integration. Therefore, it still appears necessary to show that a network does something more than merely facilitate marketing of physician services.

c. *The "messenger" model.* The easiest way to avoid per se condemnation is to show that no horizontal price agreement exists at all. This is so if physicians individually respond to unilateral price offers from potential buyers. See n.26 in the opinion. The "messenger model" is an attempt to capitalize on this notion by using the physician network as merely a means to communicate and coordinate individual offers, counteroffers, and acceptances. The difficulty is that such coordinated price negotiations could easily be viewed as constituting an implicit horizontal agreement among the doctors, especially where most of them end up agreeing to the same prices. Consider, for instance, whether doctors could legally agree in advance to be bound by the best price a joint negotiator is capable of obtaining from each purchaser? The DOJ and FTC have taken a strict stance against versions of the messenger model that resemble this "black box" variation. In various rulings, they have looked with disfavor on price negotiations initiated by quotes from the providers rather than bids from the purchasers, and they have ruled against an arrangement where physicians are bound in advance to negotiators' best prices unless they opt out. North Texas Specialty Physicians v. FTC, 528 F.3d 346 (5th Cir. 2008). This still leaves intact the possibility of an "opt-in" messenger arrangement, and at least one court has ruled that even an "opt-out" arrangement is legal where a nonphysician risk-bearing entity (e.g., an HMO) takes the initiative in formulating the fee schedule. Levine v. Central Florida Medical Affiliates, 72 F.3d 1538 (11th Cir. 1996).

5. *Safe Harbors for ACOs.* The FTC's rulings on "clinical integration" lay the groundwork for the government's emerging position on the new ACOs that are expected to take shape, to participate in Medicare's new "shared savings" program outlined on page 1209. Some commentators fear that when independent hospitals and doctors form ACOs, this will lead to greater market power, thereby driving up health care costs and insurance premiums. See, e.g., T. Greaney, The Affordable Care Act and Competition Policy: Antidote or Placebo? 89 Or. L. Rev. 811 (2011). Others complain that antitrust law is a major barrier to providers forming more effective coordination and integration of care.

Attempting to walk this fence, the DOJ and FTC issued a special set of antitrust guidelines for ACOs, building on their more general guidelines above. 76 Fed. Reg. 67026 (2011). In brief:

1. Qualifying ACOs are automatically regarded as clinically integrated, and thus subject to only rule of reason scrutiny;
2. A safe harbor applies to ACOs whose providers constitute less than 30 percent of the local market in each category or service, or, in rural areas, no more than one hospital or one physician per specialty;[8]
3. ACOs that fall outside the safe harbor are warned to avoid certain activities that raise competitive concerns, or to seek specific agency approval for such arrangements, but agency review is not mandatory. These activities of concern include interfering with insurers' cost-savings efforts, or requiring participating providers to deal with the ACO exclusively.

See Deborah Feinstein et al., ACOs and Antitrust Enforcement: Promoting Competition and Innovation, 40 J. Health Pol. Pol'y & L. 873 (2015); T. Greaney, Regulators as Market-Makers: ACOs and Competition Policy, 46 Ariz. L. J. 1 (2014).

6. *Virtual Merger: Beware.* Antitrust enforcers have also turned their attention to the price-fixing implications of what are known as "virtual mergers" or "joint

---

8. In addition, to receive safe harbor protection: ACOs may not contract exclusively with just one insurer; and participation by hospitals and rural physicians must be nonexclusive, meaning they are free to join other ACOs. Also, the guidelines provide detailed instructions for computing market boundaries and shares.

operating agreements." In these arrangements, two or more entities attempt to accomplish the substance of a merger without actual common corporate ownership, through detailed agreements that provide for joint or coordinated operations and management. Sometimes, this is done to avoid various corporate law restrictions that prevent complete merger, for instance, between religious and non-religious hospitals, but sometimes this is done because the boards of the different entities simply can't agree on a full merger but still want to attempt joint operations. In such cases, the parties run the risk of per se illegal price fixing if the contractual arrangements do not create sufficient financial or corporate integration. For instance, in Medical Center at Elizabeth Place v. Atrium Health System, 817 F.3d 934 (6th Cir. 2016), the court surprised health lawyers by ruling (in a 2-1 decision) that a carefully constructed joint operating agreement did not create a single entity for antitrust purposes, thus exposing the participating hospitals to potentially per se liability in their managed care contracting. The court emphasized that, despite consolidating many of their operations, the participating hospitals did not give up their separate "corporate consciousness" but remained competitive rivals in important respects, analogizing to the NFL, which, the Supreme Court held is engaged in concerted action when it coordinates licensing for the teams' logo'ed sportswear. American Needle v. National Football League, 560 U.S. 183 (2010).

■ OCEAN STATE PHYSICIANS HEALTH PLAN, INC. v. BLUE CROSS & BLUE SHIELD OF RHODE ISLAND
883 F.2d 1101 (1st Cir. 1989)

LEVIN H. CAMPBELL, Chief Judge.

. . . Defendant Blue Cross, a nonprofit corporation established in 1939, has long been the largest health insurer in Rhode Island. It purchases health services from physicians, hospitals, and other health care providers on behalf of its subscribers. . . . Plaintiff Ocean State is a for-profit health maintenance organization (HMO) that began operations in 1984. Like Blue Cross, Ocean State contracts with physicians to provide medical care to its subscribers, and then pays its contracted physicians on a fee-for-service basis. . . . Eighty percent of the shares of the Ocean State corporation are owned by its participating physicians. A physician may participate in more than one health insurance program. . . .

Apparently because Ocean State provided more coverage and charged lower premiums, many subscribers switched from Blue Cross to Ocean State. By the spring of 1986, Blue Cross had lost approximately 30,000 of its 543,015 enrollees, while Ocean State's enrollment had exceeded all expectations, growing to 70,000. . . . [T]o meet the challenge presented by Ocean State, Blue Cross instituted a three-pronged attack:

First, Blue Cross launched its own HMO "look-alike," dubbed HealthMate, which it marketed to employers who were offering the Ocean State plan to their employees. Like Ocean State, HealthMate provided 15 percent more coverage than the standard Blue Cross plan, including such added benefits as office visits, prescription drugs, and "good health" benefits. . . .

Second, Blue Cross instituted an "adverse selection" policy of pricing. "Adverse selection" refers to the tendency for younger and healthier people to opt for HMOs such as Ocean State when they are made available, leaving older and sicker people (on the average) in the standard Blue Cross pool. Because of such adverse selection, Blue Cross expected the health care costs for standard Blue Cross to be higher in those employer groups that offered an HMO option than in those employer groups that did not. . . . Blue Cross instituted a pricing plan that took account of this projected difference in health expenses. Under this policy, employers were offered three different rates for traditional Blue Cross coverage. The rate was lowest for an employer who offered only traditional Blue Cross, intermediate for an employer who also offered a competing HMO (usually Ocean State) and HealthMate, and highest for an employer who also offered a competing HMO but declined to offer HealthMate.

Third, Blue Cross initiated a policy, which it called "Prudent Buyer," of not paying a physician more for any service or procedure than that physician was accepting from any other health care cost provider (such as Ocean State). Blue Cross established this policy after it became apparent that Ocean State's contracting physicians were accepting about 20 percent less for their services from Ocean State than they were receiving from Blue Cross. . . . After the implementation of Prudent Buyer, about 350 of Ocean State's 1,200 physicians resigned, in many cases apparently in order to avoid a reduction in their Blue Cross fees. . . .

Ocean State alleged that Blue Cross's conduct violated, inter alia, §2 of the Sherman Act, which makes it unlawful to "monopolize . . . any part of the trade or commerce among the several States." Ocean State charged that Blue Cross launched HealthMate not because it was a viable long-term product, but in order to put Ocean State out of business. Through the adverse selection policy, Ocean State claimed, Blue Cross was able to raise its rates for standard Blue Cross for employer groups offering HealthMate—which, in turn, influenced employers not to make HealthMate available. Finally, Ocean State claimed that Blue Cross instituted the Prudent Buyer policy not in order to save money, but rather to induce physicians to resign from Ocean State. . . .

After a lengthy trial, the jury found Blue Cross "guilty" on the §2 claim, but it awarded no damages on this claim. . . . [T]he district court granted Blue Cross's motion for judgment notwithstanding the verdict. . . .

B. The Effect of the McCarran-Ferguson Act

The McCarran-Ferguson Act ("the Act"), 15 U.S.C. §§1012(b), 1013(b), exempts from the antitrust laws all conduct that is (1) part of the "business of insurance"; (2) "regulated by state law"; and (3) not in the form of "boycott, coercion, or intimidation." Blue Cross argued to the district court that both the introduction of HealthMate and the use of the adverse selection rate factors—but not the Prudent Buyer policy—were exempted from antitrust scrutiny by the Act. . . .

The Supreme Court has identified "three criteria relevant in determining whether a particular practice is part of the 'business of insurance' exempted from the antitrust laws": first, whether a particular practice has the effect of transferring or spreading a policyholder's risk; second, whether the practice is an integral part of the policy relationship between the insurer and the insured; and third, whether the practice is limited to entities within the insurance industry. Union Labor Life Insurance Co. v. Pireno, 458 U.S. 119 (1982). See also Group Life & Health Insurance Co. v. Royal Drug Co., 440 U.S. 205 (1979). . . .

Both HealthMate and the adverse selection policy qualify as the "business of insurance" under these criteria. HealthMate is an insurance policy which operates by spreading policyholders' risk; adverse selection is a pricing policy that inherently involves risk-spreading. Both HealthMate and adverse selection directly involve the relationship between the insurer (Blue Cross) and the insured (its policyholders). Such policies are, more or less by definition, limited to entities in the "insurance industry" as broadly construed. Accord Health Care Equalization Committee v. Iowa Medical Society, 851 F.2d 1020, 1029 (8th Cir. 1988).

Ocean State . . . bases [its] argument [against immunity] on a misreading of *Royal Drug*. In that case, the Supreme Court characterized Blue Shield's contacts with its health care providers as "merely arrangements for the purchase of goods and services by Blue Shield." But the Court took care to distinguish Blue Shield's provider contracts from its subscriber contracts. . . . This distinction was emphasized in Justice Brennan's dissenting opinion: "Neither the Court . . . nor the parties challenge the fact that the . . . policy offered by Blue Shield to its policyholders—as distinguished from the contract between Blue Shield and the [providers]—is the 'business of insurance.' " . . . [Based on this distinction], we conclude that the challenged actions of Blue Cross with respect to HealthMate and adverse selection are exempt from antitrust scrutiny under the McCarran-Ferguson Act.

C. THE PRUDENT BUYER POLICY

The Prudent Buyer policy involves Blue Cross's relationships not with its subscribers but with its provider physicians. Blue Cross makes no claim that this policy is protected by the McCarran-Ferguson exemption. We agree with the district court, however, that the Prudent Buyer policy . . . as a matter of law, [is] not violative of §2 of the Sherman Act.

Section 2 of the Sherman Act makes it unlawful to "monopolize . . . any part of the trade or commerce among the several states." 15 U.S.C. §2. The offense of monopolization has two elements: (1) the possession of monopoly power in the relevant market and (2) the willful acquisition or maintenance of that power as distinguished from growth or development as a consequence of a superior product, business acumen, or historic accident. United States v. Grinnell Corp., 384 U.S. 563 (1966). On this appeal, Blue Cross does not dispute its monopoly power in the market for health care insurance in Rhode Island. Ocean State, for its part, concedes that Blue Cross acquired its historical advantages legitimately. The issue in dispute is whether Blue Cross maintained its monopoly position through improper means.

Section 2 does not prohibit vigorous competition on the part of a monopoly. To the contrary, the primary purpose of the antitrust laws is to encourage competition. What §2 does prohibit is "exclusionary" conduct by a monopoly, often defined as "behavior that not only (1) tends to impair the opportunities of rivals, but also (2) either does not further competition on the merits or does so in an unnecessarily restrictive way." 3 P. Areeda & D. Turner, Antitrust Law ¶626b at 78. . . .

In the case at hand, the record amply supports Blue Cross's view that Prudent Buyer was a bona fide policy to ensure that Blue Cross would not pay more than any competitor paid for the same services. . . . Blue Cross estimated that it saved $1,900,000 through this policy. We agree with the district court that such a policy of insisting on a supplier's lowest price—assuming that the price is not "predatory" or below the supplier's incremental cost—tends to further competition on the merits and, as a matter of law, is not exclusionary. It is hard to disagree with the district court's view: "As a naked proposition, it would seem silly to argue that a policy to pay the same amount for the same service is anticompetitive, even on the part of one who has market power. This, it would seem, is what competition should be all about."

This conclusion is also compelled by this court's holding in Kartell v. Blue Shield of Massachusetts, 749 F.2d 922 (1st Cir. 1984), that a health insurer's unilateral decisions about the prices it will pay providers do not violate the Sherman Act—unless the prices are "predatory" or below incremental cost—even if the insurer is assumed to have monopoly power in the relevant market. Kartell concerned Blue Shield of Massachusetts's ban on balance billing, a price policy according to which Blue Shield paid participating physicians only if they agreed not to make any additional charges to the subscriber. We held that, for antitrust purposes, a health insurer like Blue Shield must be viewed "as itself the purchaser of the doctors' purchases." As such, the insurer—like any buyer of goods or services—is lawfully entitled to bargain with its providers for the best price it can get. "[E]ven if the buyer has monopoly power, an antitrust court . . . will not interfere with a buyer's (nonpredatory) determination of price." . . .

Ocean State argues that Kartell is a "vertical" case (involving the effects of Blue Shield's policy on its provider physicians), while the present case is "horizontal" (involving the effects of Blue Cross's policy on its competitor, Ocean State). But the distinction is of no consequence. In both cases the challenged activity is the price that the buyer offers to the seller. . . . Even a monopoly can engage in a competitive course of conduct, so long as it does so for valid business reasons (such as the desire to get the lowest possible price), rather than in order to smother competition. . . .

[E]ven if we assume for argument's sake that Blue Cross selectively applied Prudent Buyer [only to Ocean State physicians], its conduct remains legitimate. It was primarily Ocean State physicians who were selling their services at a lower price to another provider (Ocean State) than to Blue Cross. Indeed, it was Ocean State's lower pricing policy—in particular, its 1986 decision not to return its participating physicians' withholds for 1985—that gave rise to Prudent Buyer. Therefore, it seems only logical—and not illegitimate—for Blue Cross to have focused its efforts in applying Prudent Buyer on Ocean State physicians. . . .

Finally, Ocean State points to evidence in the record that Blue Cross officials hoped that Prudent Buyer—together with HealthMate and adverse selection—would have the effect of destroying or weakening Ocean State. For example, there was testimony that Blue Cross's president had expressed—in none-too-polite terms—a desire to emasculate Ocean State. Another Blue Cross executive wrote in a handwritten note that "not one guy in the state isn't going to know the implication of signing with Ocean State." . . . The jury may reasonably have concluded, on the basis of this and other evidence, that Blue Cross's leadership desired to put Ocean State out of business. But the desire to crush a competitor, standing alone, is insufficient to make out a violation of the antitrust laws. . . . As long as Blue Cross's course of conduct was itself legitimate, the fact that some of its executives hoped to see Ocean State disappear is irrelevant. Under these circumstances Blue Cross is no more guilty of an antitrust violation than a boxer who delivers a perfectly legal punch—hoping that it will kill his opponent—is guilty of attempted murder. . . .

Notes: Vertical Restraints by Insurers

1. *Horizontal Conspiracy vs. Vertical Pricing.* The *Kartell* decision discussed in *Ocean State* was written by Justice Breyer when he sat on the First Circuit. Prior to that, he was an antitrust professor at Harvard. Justice Breyer offered the following important distinction elsewhere in his opinion:

> There is no suggestion that Blue Shield's fee schedule reflects, for example, an effort by, say, one group of doctors to stop other doctors from competing with them. Cf. Virginia Academy of Clinical Psychologists v. Blue Shield of Virginia, 624 F.2d 476 (4th Cir. 1980) (Blue Shield found to be a combination, not of policyholders, but of physicians [with respect to decision not to cover services of psychologists]).... *Maricopa* [therefore] is simply not on point.... [It] involved a horizontal agreement among competing doctors about what to charge.

Considering the origins of Blue Cross/Blue Shield, however, a few older decisions have agreed with *Virginia Academy* by finding that Blue Cross in particular constitutes a "walking horizontal conspiracy" among its controlling doctors. Glen Eden Hospital v. Blue Cross & Blue Shield of Michigan, 740 F.2d 423 (6th Cir. 1984) (possible conspiracy). Also, it is always possible to find that, in a particular case, an insurer and providers have conspired even apart from the insurer's internal structure. E.g., West Penn Allegheny Health System, v. UPMC, 627 F.3d 85 (3d Cir. 2010) (reinstating claim that Blue Cross and the area's dominant hospital conspired against smaller hospital); Reazin v. Blue Cross & Blue Shield of Kansas, 899 F.2d 951 (10th Cir. 1990) ($7.8 million verdict sustained in favor of hospital excluded by a PPO). And, apart from antitrust law, the new ACA prohibits any health plan (including self-insured employers) from "discriminating" against any category of licensed health care provider. What exactly this regulatory law means for insurers' many pricing decisions remains to be seen, but, in today's health care market structure, most courts agree with *Kartell* that insurers' vertical pricing decisions are beyond *antitrust* reproach. E.g., SmileCare Dental Group v. Delta Dental Plan, 88 F.3d 780 (9th Cir. 1996) (insurer can prevent dentists from waiving co-payments).

The focus of these notes is on areas of special importance to health care where insurers' cost-containment initiatives might pose antitrust violations in a *vertical* dimension. Challenges might arise either under a §1 rule of reason analysis, or under the §2 monopolization theory outlined in *Ocean State*, depending on whether the action is wholly unilateral or involves a vertical agreement. Other types of vertical restraints and §2 theories relevant to health care markets—more to hospitals than to insurers—are discussed in the notes at pages 1396 and 1400 in terms of "unilateral refusals to deal," the "essential facilities" doctrine, and illegal "tie-ins." For general commentary see Peter J. Hammer & William M. Sage, Monopsony as an Agency and Regulatory Problem in Health Care, 71 Antitrust L.J. 949 (2004).

2. *Most Favored Nation Clauses.* The "prudent buyer" policy at issue in *Ocean State* is more commonly known as a "most favored nation clause." Many antitrust experts consider this aspect of the decision to be wrong, or at least overstated. See Arnold Celnicker, A Competitive Analysis of Most Favored Nations Clauses in Contracts Between Health Care Providers and Insurers, 69 N.C. L. Rev. 863 (1991). To understand why, consider the following scenario: A dominant insurer with market

power attempts to ward off a new insurer by insisting that the dominant's participating physicians and hospitals contract exclusively with it, that is, they lose all of their existing business if they take any of the new business. This would clearly constitute a potential antitrust violation if there were no legitimate business reason for demanding exclusivity (such as that exclusive arrangements foster better-quality service or lower prices). See Aspen Skiing Co. v. Aspen Highlands Skiing Corp., 472 U.S. 585 (1985) (sustaining jury finding that monopolist illegally excluded competitor by refusing to give the competitor's customers the same all-inclusive lift ticket discount package it gave its own customers). The main difference between this extreme scenario and *Ocean State* is that the most favored nation provision made it very expensive, but not impossible, to do business with the new insurer: Physicians who accepted the insurer's terms in effect had to discount all their business by 20 percent.

Most favored nation provisions obviously make it more difficult for a new insurer to stimulate downward pressure on prices for physicians' services and, ultimately, for its own insurance product. Thus, these vertical restraints potentially have horizontal effects. Accordingly, the DOJ and FTC take a dim view of these agreements. See Beth Ann Wright, How MFN Clauses Used in the Health Care Industry Unreasonably Restrain Trade Under the Sherman Act, 18 J. L. & Health 29 (2003); Cascade Health Solutions v. PeaceHealth, 515 F.3d 883 (9th Cir. 2007) (ordering new trial because of jury instructions in a $16.2 million antitrust verdict against a hospital's use of a most favored nation's provision with a health care facility plan). Is it possible to justify *Ocean State* nevertheless based on its unique facts, in which, with respect to HMO insurance in particular, Blue Cross was doing badly in the market and its only response was to meet Ocean State's price where they competed head to head? Doesn't this justification turn on an assessment of Blue Cross' motive and purpose, and are these not quintessential factual issues for the jury to resolve?

3. *Exclusive Contracts.* For reasons explained in the preceding note, the DOJ and FTC also take a dim view of exclusivity agreements in managed care agreements and joint ventures, preferring that providers remain free to participate nonexclusively in several networks or arrangements. This can be seen in their health care antitrust enforcement guidelines. Under the general guideline:

> The Agencies will not challenge, absent extraordinary circumstances, an *exclusive* physician network joint venture comprising *20 percent or less* of the physicians in each physician specialty with active hospital staff privileges who practice in the relevant geographic market. . . . The Agencies will not challenge, absent extraordinary circumstances, a *nonexclusive* physician network joint venture comprising *30 percent or less* of the physicians in each physician specialty with active hospital staff privileges who practice in the relevant geographic market. In relevant markets with less than four [or five] physicians in a particular specialty, a . . . physician network joint venture otherwise qualifying for the antitrust safety zone may include one physician from that specialty [on a nonexclusive basis]. . . . The Agencies will determine whether a physician network joint venture is exclusive or nonexclusive by its physician participants' activities and not simply by the terms of the contractual relationship . . . [using] the following indicia of nonexclusivity, among others: . . . (2) that physicians in the network actually . . . contract with other networks or managed care plans. . . .

Statements of Antitrust Enforcement Policy in Health Care, 5 BNA Health L. Rep. 1295 (emphasis added). This viewpoint is echoed in the more recent guidelines for ACOs. See page 1421. See also *Hassan*, excerpted at page 1392. Others argue, however, that exclusive arrangements can be procompetitive when used to form tighter clinical and financial bonds among providers that make different networks more distinctive. According to several leading scholars, preserving freedom to choose too often has been used by providers to resist market power from insurers, by keeping them from engaging in competitive bidding. Charles Weller, "Free Choice" as a Restraint of Trade in American Health Care Delivery and Insurance, 69 Iowa L. Rev. 1351 (1984).

4. *Monopolization.* When vertical restraints are challenged under §2, it is necessary to establish the existence (or at least the "dangerous probability") of monopoly power. (Sometimes, the technical term *monopsony* is used to describe a *buyer* as opposed to *seller* monopoly.) Blue Cross has a very large market share in many states, especially in the Northeast. See, e.g., *Reazin*, supra (60 percent market share sufficient to support finding of monopolization); *Kartell*, supra (75 percent market share presumed to be a monopoly for sake of argument). Other courts, however, have found no monopoly power despite large market share because competing insurers elsewhere in the state or the nation face few inherent barriers to entering the same market or expanding their existing market share. The leading discussion is Ball Memorial Hospital v. Mutual Hospital Insurance Co., 784 F.2d 1325 (7th Cir. 1986) (no market power despite 50 to 80 percent market share). Is this a realistic assessment given the start-up capital costs of (1) complying with state insurance regulations concerning solvency and (2) assembling a managed care network of providers? The issue of market share and market power in managed care settings is considered further in the following section.

3. Antitrust Merger Law

■ **FTC v. TENET HEALTH CARE CORP.**
   186 F.3d 1045 (8th Cir. 1999)

BEAM, Circuit Judge.

Tenet Healthcare and Poplar Bluff Physicians Group, Inc., doing business as Doctors' Regional Medical Center (collectively, Tenet) appeal the district court's order enjoining the merger of two hospitals in Poplar Bluff, Missouri. . . . The district court found a substantial likelihood that the merger would substantially lessen competition between acute care hospitals in Poplar Bluff, Missouri, in violation of section 7 of the Clayton Act, 15 U.S.C. §15. We reverse.

Poplar Bluff is a city of 17,000 people in southeastern Missouri. It is located in Butler County, which has a population of 40,000. It is the largest city in several counties and has numerous major employers and manufacturing operations. Sikeston, Missouri, and Cape Girardeau, Missouri, both towns with populations of over 40,000 are forty and sixty miles away from Poplar Bluff. The population in the area surrounding Poplar Bluff is concentrated in Scott and Stoddard Counties, which lie between Poplar Bluff and Cape Girardeau. Poplar Bluff is within a few hours' drive of several large metropolitan centers including St. Louis, Missouri, Memphis, Tennessee, and Jonesboro, Arkansas.

Tenet Healthcare Corporation presently owns Lucy Lee Hospital in Poplar Bluff. Lucy Lee is a general acute care hospital that provides primary and secondary care services.[1] Lucy Lee has 201 licensed beds, 185 of which are staffed. It operates ten outpatient clinics in the surrounding counties. Its average daily census was 75 in 1994, 76 in 1995 and 104 in 1996. Doctors' Regional Medical Center in Poplar Bluff is presently owned by a group of physicians. It is also a general acute care hospital providing primary and secondary care services. It has 230 licensed beds, of which 187 are staffed. Its average census in 1994 was 106, in 1995 was 99, in 1996 was 95 and in 1997 was 77. It also operates several rural health clinics in the area. Though profitable, both hospitals are underutilized and have had problems attracting specialists to the area.

Tenet recently entered into an agreement to purchase Doctors' Regional for over forty million dollars. Tenet plans to operate Doctors' Regional as a long-term care facility and to consolidate inpatient services at Lucy Lee. It plans to employ more specialists at the merged facility and to offer higher quality care in a comprehensive, integrated delivery system that would include some tertiary care.[2] Pursuant to the Hart-Scott-Rodino Act, 15 U.S.C. §18a, the hospitals filed a premerger certification with the FTC. Shortly thereafter, the FTC filed a complaint alleging that the hospitals' merger would lessen competition for primary and secondary inpatient hospitalization services in the area. . . .

The evidence adduced at the hearing shows that Lucy Lee and Doctors' Regional are the only two hospitals in Poplar Bluff, other than a Veteran's Hospital. . . . There are several [larger, regional] hospitals in the surrounding area [that] offer the same or a greater range of services. . . . In addition, there are smaller rural hospitals located in nearby towns, . . . [which] have fewer than fifty beds and provide only primary care.

Lucy Lee's and Doctors' Regional's patient bases are composed primarily of patients who are covered by Medicare and Medicaid and thus remain largely insensitive to price differentials. Most of the remaining patient admissions at Lucy Lee and Doctors' Regional are covered by health insurance, under a plan administered by a managed care organization.[5] These organizations include health maintenance

---

1. Primary care involves relatively simple medical or surgical procedures. Secondary care is somewhat more complex, including procedures such as hernia repair or patient services related to a heart attack.

2. A comprehensive, integrated healthcare delivery system is one that provides service along the spectrum of healthcare: inpatient clinics, home health, hospitalization, inpatient and outpatient surgery, and short- and long-term convalescent or rehabilitation care. Tertiary care is sophisticated, complex, or high-tech care that includes, for example, open heart surgery, oncology surgery, neurosurgery, high-risk obstetrics, neonatal intensive care, and trauma services. Quaternary care is even more sophisticated and includes organ transplants.

5. Another form of healthcare coverage is traditional indemnity insurance. Traditional indemnity insurers cover a percentage of an insured's healthcare costs, with the remainder covered by the insured. Indemnity insurance is not implicated in this case, because it has become virtually nonexistent in the Poplar Bluff area. Historically, indemnity insurers have not attempted to gain discounts from providers.

organizations (HMOs)[6] and preferred provider organizations (PPOs).[7] Hospitals are willing to discount their stated rates to managed care payers in order to entice the managed care entity to send its enrollees to that hospital. Managed care organizations have had a presence in Poplar Bluff for approximately fifteen years. Most employers in the Poplar Bluff area either subscribe to or administer a PPO. Both Lucy Lee and Doctors' Regional have entered into discount agreements with numerous managed care entities and employers.

The hospitals in Cape Girardeau, on the other hand, refused to negotiate with managed care plans until recently, when, at the insistence of area employers, Southeast Missouri Hospital entered into a discount arrangement with HealthLink, a managed care organization. Healthcare prices in Cape Girardeau have historically been significantly higher than prices in Poplar Bluff. However, there is also a perception of higher quality service at Cape Girardeau hospitals. Since the entry of managed care in the Cape Girardeau market, there has been some reduction in prices. . . . Cape Girardeau hospitals now [advertise] in Poplar Bluff.

Market participants, specifically, employers, health plans and network providers testified that they had negotiated substantial discounts and favorable per diem rates with either or both Lucy Lee and Doctors' Regional as a result of "playing the two hospitals off each other." These managed care organizations and employers testified that if the merged entity were to raise its prices by ten percent, the health plans would have no choice but to simply pay the increased price. They testified that they perceive it is essential for the plans to include a Poplar Bluff hospital in their benefit packages because their enrollees would not travel to other towns for primary and secondary inpatient treatment. They stated that their employees and subscribers find it convenient to use a Poplar Bluff hospital; are loyal to their physicians in Poplar Bluff and would not be amenable to a health benefit plan that did not include a Poplar Bluff hospital.

The evidence shows that patient choice of hospitals is determined by many variables, including patient/physician loyalty, perceptions of quality, geographic proximity and, most importantly or determinatively, access to hospitals through an insurance plan. Managed care organizations have been able to influence or change patient behavior with financial incentives in other healthcare markets. This practice is known as "steering." Representatives of Poplar Bluff managed care entities testified, however, that they did not believe such efforts would be successful in the Poplar Bluff market, . . . in spite of the fact that such tactics had been successful in other markets. . . .

Lucy Lee and Doctors' Regional obtain ninety percent of their patients from zip codes within a fifty-mile radius of Poplar Bluff. In eleven of the top twelve zip

6. An HMO generally charges a set fee which covers all of an enrollee's healthcare needs, including hospitalizations. HMO enrollees are required to obtain care only from those physicians and hospitals who provide a discounted rate to the HMO. HMOs often have their own clinics and enrollees are obligated to go to those clinics for care. In addition, HMOs often consult with hospitals to ensure that costs of hospitalization remain as low as possible.

7. In a PPO, the PPO negotiates discounted rates with certain physicians or hospitals and then provides financial incentives, such as low deductibles or low co-payments, to its enrollees to use those providers.

codes, however, significant patient admissions—ranging from 22% to 70%—were to hospitals other than those in Poplar Bluff. There is no dispute that Poplar Bluff residents travel to St. Louis, Memphis, and Jonesboro for tertiary care. . . . [T]he FTC presented the testimony . . . based on an analysis of DRG data[9] that patients seeking care outside Poplar Bluff were seeking a more sophisticated level of service than that available in Poplar Bluff. . . . The evidence also shows, however, that significant numbers of patients in the Poplar Bluff service area travel to other towns for primary and secondary treatment that is also available in Poplar Bluff.

The evidence shows that the healthcare industry is rapidly changing. The emergence and growth of managed care—a system in which a third-party monitors healthcare resources and expenditures—has had a large impact on healthcare. This monitoring has caused a corresponding decline in the number and length of inpatient admissions. Many procedures that formerly required a hospital stay are now performed on an outpatient basis. Another trend has been growth of outreach efforts such as rural clinics to extend the service area of a hospital. Patient loyalty to a certain doctor has diminished as patients' out-of-pocket expenditures have increased. . . .

DISCUSSION

The determination of a relevant market is a necessary predicate to the finding of an antitrust violation. . . . A relevant market consists of two components: a product market and a geographic market. *See* Department of Justice, Federal Trade Commission, Antitrust Division, 1992 Horizontal Merger Guidelines, 57 Fed.Reg. 41552. The parties agree that the relevant product market at issue in this case is the delivery of primary and secondary inpatient hospital care services. They disagree, however, on the relevant geographic market.

A geographic market is the area in which consumers can practically turn for alternative sources of the product and in which the antitrust defendants face competition. . . . A properly defined geographic market includes potential suppliers who can readily offer consumers a suitable alternative to the defendant's services. Determination of the relevant geographic market is highly fact sensitive. . . . A monopolization claim often succeeds or fails strictly on the definition of the product or geographic market. . . .

The FTC proposes a relevant geographic market that essentially matches its service area: a fifty-mile radius from downtown Poplar Bluff. It is from this service area that the two hospitals obtain ninety percent of their patients. A service area, however, is not necessarily a merging firm's geographic market for purposes of antitrust analysis. The FTC's proposed geographic market includes four other hospitals:

---

9. A DRG is a numerical code that serves to classify patients into one of 503 clinically cohesive groups that demonstrate similar consumption of hospital resources and length of stay patterns. These classifications are used by the federal government in administering Medicare and Medicaid programs and by insurers to evaluate reimbursement, utilization of resources, treatment protocols, related conditions, and demographic distribution. Examples of DRGs would be "extracranial vascular procedures," "chronic obstructive pulmonary disease," and "specific cerebral vascular disorders."

a Tenet-owned regional hospital in Kennett, Missouri, and three rural hospitals. The FTC contends that its evidence shows that the merged entity will have a post-merger market share of eighty-four percent of this geographic market.[10] Tenet, on the other hand, proposes a relevant geographic market that encompasses a sixty-five mile radius from downtown Poplar Bluff in addition to Barnes Hospital in St. Louis. The proposed area includes [20] hospitals. . . .

Because we conclude that the FTC produced insufficient evidence of a well-defined relevant geographic market, we find that it did not show that the merged entity will possess such market power. . . . The evidence in this case falls short of establishing a relevant geographic market that excludes the Sikeston or Cape Girardeau areas. The evidence shows that hospitals in either or both of these towns, as well as rural hospitals throughout the area, are practical alternatives for many Poplar Bluff consumers. In adopting the FTC's position, the district court improperly discounted the fact that over twenty-two percent of people in the most important zip codes already use hospitals outside the FTC's proposed market for treatment that is offered at Poplar Bluff hospitals. . . . If patients use hospitals outside the service area, those hospitals can act as a check on the exercise of market power by the hospitals within the service area. The FTC's contention that the merged hospitals would have eighty-four percent of the market for inpatient primary and secondary services within a contrived market area that stops just short of including a regional hospital (Missouri Delta in Sikeston) that is closer to many patients than the Poplar Bluff hospitals, strikes us as absurd. The proximity of many patients to hospitals in other towns, coupled with the compelling and essentially unrefuted evidence that the switch to another provider by a small percentage of patients would constrain a price increase, shows that the FTC's proposed market is too narrow. . . .

The district court rejected the Cape Girardeau hospitals as practicable alternatives because they were more costly. In so doing, it underestimated the impact of nonprice competitive factors, such as quality. The evidence shows that one reason for the significant amount of migration from the Poplar Bluff hospitals to either Sikeston, Cape Girardeau, or St. Louis is the actual or perceived difference in quality of care. . . . As the district court noted, healthcare decisions are based on factors other than price. It is for that reason that, although they are less expensive, HMOs are not always an employer's or individual's choice in healthcare services. See Blue Cross and Blue Shield United of Wisconsin v. Marshfield Clinic, 65 F.3d 1406, 1412, 1410 (7th Cir. 1995) (Posner, J.) (noting "[g]enerally you must pay more for higher quality" and "the HMO's incentive is to keep you healthy if it can but if you get very sick, and are unlikely to recover to a healthy state involving few medical expenses, to let you die as quickly and cheaply as possible.") . . .

We further find that although Tenet's efficiencies defense may have been properly rejected by the district court, the district court should nonetheless have considered evidence of enhanced efficiency in the context of the competitive effects of the merger. The evidence shows that a hospital that is larger and more efficient than Lucy Lee or Doctors' Regional will provide better medical care than either

---

10. An inference of monopoly power can be drawn from an 84% market share. . . . Market shares of less than 60% are generally not sufficient to create an inference of monopoly power.

of those hospitals could separately. The merged entity will be able to attract more highly qualified physicians and specialists and to offer integrated delivery and some tertiary care. . . . [Therefore,] the merged entity may well enhance competition in the greater Southeast Missouri area. . . .

The district court also relied on the seemingly outdated assumption of doctor-patient loyalty that is not supported by the record. The evidence shows, and the district court acknowledged, that the issue of access to a provider through an insurance plan is determinative of patient choice. Essentially, the evidence shows that patients will choose whatever doctors or hospitals are covered by their health plan. Undeniably, although many patients might prefer to be loyal to their doctors, it is, unfortunately, a luxury they can no longer afford. . . . As much as many patients long for the days of old-fashioned and local, if expensive and inefficient, health-care, recent trends in healthcare management have made the old healthcare model obsolete.

The reality of the situation in our changing healthcare environment may be that Poplar Bluff cannot support two high-quality hospitals. Third-party payers have reaped the benefit of a price war in a small corner of the market for healthcare services in Southeastern Missouri, at the arguable cost of quality to their subscribers. . . . We are mindful that competition is the driving force behind our free enterprise system and that, unless barriers have been erected to constrain the normal operation of the market, a court ought to exercise extreme caution because judicial intervention in a competitive situation can itself upset the balance of market forces, bringing about the very ills the antitrust laws were meant to prevent. This appears to have even more force in an industry, such as healthcare, experiencing significant and profound changes.

■ SAINT ALPHONSUS MEDICAL CENTER v. ST. LUKE'S HEALTH SYSTEM
778 F.3d 775 (9th Cir. 2015)

HURWITZ, Circuit Judge:

This case arises out of the 2012 merger of two health care providers in Nampa, Idaho; [Saltzer Medical Group and St. Luke's Health System]. . . . Although the district court believed that the merger was intended to improve patient outcomes and might well do so, the judge nonetheless found that the merger violated § 7 [of the Clayton Act] and ordered divestiture.

As the district court recognized, the job before us is not to determine the optimal future shape of the country's health care system, but instead to determine whether this particular merger violates the Clayton Act. In light of the careful factual findings by the able district judge, we affirm the judgment below.

I. BACKGROUND

Nampa, the second-largest city in Idaho, is some twenty miles west of Boise and has a population of approximately 85,000. Before the merger at issue, St. Luke's Health Systems, an Idaho-based, not-for-profit health care system, operated an emergency clinic in the city. Saltzer Medical Group, the largest independent multi-specialty physician group in Idaho, had thirty-four physicians practicing at its offices in Nampa. The only hospital in Nampa was operated by Saint Alphonsus Health System . . . . The largest adult primary care physician ("PCP") provider in the Nampa market was Saltzer, which had sixteen PCPs. St. Luke's had eight PCPs and Saint Alphonsus nine. Several other PCPs had solo or small practices.

Saltzer had long had the goal of moving toward integrated patient care and risk-based reimbursement. After unsuccessfully attempting several informal affiliations, . . . Saltzer sought a formal partnership with a large health care system. In 2012, St. Luke's acquired Saltzer's assets and entered into a five-year professional service agreement ("PSA") with the Saltzer physicians. Saltzer received a $9 million payment for goodwill. The initial PSA contained hortatory language about the parties' desire to move away from fee-for-service reimbursement, but included no provisions for implementing that goal. . . .

C. PROCEDURAL HISTORY

. . . [St. Alphonsus sued in 2012, alleging] anticompetitive effects in the relevant markets for "primary care physician services," "general acute-care inpatient services," "general pediatric physician services," and "outpatient surgery services." . . . In March 2013, the FTC and the State of Idaho filed a complaint in the district court seeking to enjoin the merger pursuant to the Federal Trade Commission Act, the Clayton Act, and Idaho law.[1] This complaint alleged anticompetitive effects only in the adult PCP market. The district court consolidated this case with the one filed by [St. Alphonsus], and after a nineteen-day bench trial, found the merger prohibited . . . because of its anticompetitive effects on the Nampa adult PCP market.

The district court expressly noted the troubled state of the U.S. health care system, found that St. Luke's and Saltzer genuinely intended to move toward a better health care system, and expressed its belief that the merger would "improve patient outcomes" if left intact. Nonetheless, the court found that the "huge market share" of the post-merger entity "creates a substantial risk of anticompetitive price increases" in the Nampa adult PCP market. Rejecting an argument by St. Luke's that anticipated post-merger efficiencies excused the potential anticompetitive price effects, the district court ordered divestiture. This appeal followed. . . .

III. THE CLAYTON ACT § 7 ANALYSIS

The great Yankee catcher Yogi Berra is reputed (likely apocryphally) to have said that it's "tough to make predictions, especially about the future." Yet that is precisely what this case requires. Because § 7 of the Clayton Act bars mergers whose effect "may be substantially to lessen competition, or to tend to create a monopoly," judicial analysis necessarily focuses on "probabilities, not certainties." This "requires not merely an appraisal of the immediate impact of the merger upon competition, but a prediction of its impact upon competitive conditions in the future . . .

---

1. The Idaho Competition Act is "construed in harmony" with federal antitrust law, Idaho Code §§ 48–102(3), –106, and the district court held that the antitrust analysis is the same for each. The parties do not contend otherwise.

B. THE RELEVANT MARKET

.. .. Although the parties agree that the relevant product market in this case is adult PCPs, St. Luke's vigorously disputes the district court's determination that Nampa is the relevant geographic market. We find no clear error in that factual finding. . . . A common method to determine the relevant geographic market, and the one used by the district court, is to find whether a hypothetical monopolist could impose a "small but significant nontransitory increase in price" ("SSNIP") in the proposed market [without driving away much business]. . . .

Market definition thus perforce focuses on the anticipated behavior of buyers and sellers. In the health care industry, insurance companies effectively act both as buyers and sellers. Noting that "the vast majority of health care consumers are not direct purchasers of health care—the consumers purchase health insurance and the insurance companies negotiate directly with the providers," the district court correctly focused on the "likely response of insurers to a hypothetical demand by all the PCPs in a particular market for a [SSNIP]."[2]

The district court found that a hypothetical Nampa PCP monopolist could profitably impose a SSNIP on insurers. Citing testimony that Nampa residents "strongly prefer access to local PCPs," the court found that "commercial health plans need to include Nampa PCPs in their networks to offer a competitive product." "Given this dynamic—that health plans must offer Nampa Adult PCP services to Nampa residents to effectively compete—Nampa PCPs could band together and successfully demand a [SSNIP] (or reimbursement increase) from health plans."

St. Luke's argues that the district court erred by considering only the current behavior of Nampa consumers, not their likely response to a SSNIP. St. Luke's is of course correct that geographic market definition involves prospective analysis—it predicts consumer response to a hypothetical price increase. But that is precisely what the district court did. The court not only examined present Nampa consumer behavior, but also concluded that it would not change in the event of a SSNIP.

This determination was supported by the record. Evidence was presented that insurers generally need local PCPs to market a health care plan, and that this is true in particular in the Nampa market. For example, Blue Cross of Idaho has PCPs in every zip code in which it has customers, and the executive director of the Idaho Physicians Network testified that it could not market a health care network in Nampa that did not include Nampa PCPs. Evidence also indicated that consumers would not change their behavior in the event of a SSNIP. Experts testified that because health care consumers only pay a small percentage of health care costs out of pocket, the impact of a SSNIP likely would not register. Similarly, there was testimony that consumers choose physicians on factors other than price. The court was unconvinced by evidence that insurers could defend against a SSNIP by steering consumers to non-Nampa PCPs. . . .

---

2. This "two-stage model" of health care competition is "the accepted model." John J. Miles, 1 Health Care & Antitrust L. § 1:5 (2014). In the first stage, providers compete for inclusion in insurance plans. See Gregory Vistnes, Hospitals, Mergers, and Two–Stage Competition, 67 Antitrust L.J. 671 (2000). In the second stage, providers seek to attract patients enrolled in the plans. Because patients are "largely insensitive" to price, the second stage "takes place primarily over non-price dimensions." Thus, antitrust analysis focuses on the first stage.

C. THE PLAINTIFFS' CASE

Once the relevant geographic market is determined, a prima facie case is established if the plaintiff proves that the merger will probably lead to anticompetitive effects in that market. The district court held that the plaintiffs established a prima facie case because of the post-merger entity's: (1) market share; (2) ability to negotiate higher PCP reimbursement rates with insurers; and (3) ability to "charge more [ancillary] services at the higher hospital billing rates." The court also found that "entry into the market has been very difficult and would not be timely to counteract the anticompetitive effects of the Acquisition." St. Luke's does not challenge the barriers-to-entry finding; we review the others in turn for clear error. . . .

The district court calculated the post-merger Herfindahl-Hirschman Index (HHI0 [a measure of market concentration] in the Nampa PCP market as 6,219, and the increase as 1,607. St. Luke's does not challenge these findings. As the district court correctly noted, these HHI numbers "are well above the thresholds for a presumptively anticompetitive merger (more than double and seven times their respective thresholds, respectively)." The district court also found that St. Luke's would likely use its post-merger power to negotiate higher reimbursement rates from insurers for PCP services. . . .

Because St. Luke's and Saltzer had been each other's closest substitutes in Nampa, the district court found the acquisition limited the ability of insurers to negotiate with the merged entity. Pre-acquisition internal correspondence indicated that the merged companies would use this increased bargaining power to raise prices. . . .

3. Ancillary Services

The district court's finding that St. Luke's would raise prices in the hospital-based ancillary services market[3] is more problematic. The court found that St. Luke's would "exercise its enhanced bargaining leverage from the acquisition to charge more services at the higher hospital-based billing rates." Because insurers and providers typically negotiate for all services as part of the same contract, the district court found that St. Luke's increased leverage with respect to PCP services would allow it to demand higher fees for ancillary services.

The problem with this conclusion is that the district court made no findings about St. Luke's' market power in the ancillary services market. Absent such a finding, it is difficult to conclude that the merged entity could easily demand anticompetitive prices for such services. Perhaps the court was suggesting that St. Luke's would engage in tying, "a device used by a seller with market power in one product market to extend its market power to a distinct product market." Although various

---

3. Ancillary services, such as x-rays and diagnostic testing, are sometimes performed by doctors in conjunction with PCP examinations. Before the merger, Saltzer provided many ancillary services at its physicians' offices. Insurance companies and Medicare often offer higher reimbursements for ancillary services performed at a hospital-based outpatient facility.

antitrust statutes address tying, Clayton Act § 7 does not expressly prohibit the practice. . . .

D. [THE POST–MERGER EFFICIENCIES DEFENSE]

Because the plaintiffs established a prima facie case, the burden shifted to St. Luke's to "cast doubt on the accuracy of the Government's evidence as predictive of future anticompetitive effects." The rebuttal evidence focused on the alleged pro-competitive effects of the merger, particularly the contention that the merger would allow St. Luke's to move toward integrated care and risk-based reimbursement.[4]

The Supreme Court has never expressly approved an efficiencies defense to a § 7 claim [and has several times ruled or reasoned in ways that appear inconsistent with this defense]. . . .Notwithstanding the Supreme Court's statements, four of our sister circuits (the Sixth, D.C., Eighth, and Eleventh) have suggested that proof of post-merger efficiencies could rebut a Clayton Act § 7 prima facie case. The FTC has also cautiously recognized the defense, noting that although competition ordinarily spurs firms to achieve efficiencies internally, "a primary benefit of mergers to the economy is their potential to generate significant efficiencies and thus enhance the merged firm's ability and incentive to compete, which may result in lower prices, improved quality, enhanced service, or new products." Merger Guidelines § 10. However, none of the reported appellate decisions have actually held that a § 7 defendant has rebutted a prima facie case with an efficiencies defense; thus, even in those circuits that recognize it, the parameters of the defense remain imprecise. . . .

We remain skeptical about the efficiencies defense in general and about its scope in particular. It is difficult enough in § 7 cases to predict whether a merger will have future anticompetitive effects without also adding to the judicial balance a prediction of future efficiencies. . . . Nonetheless, we assume, as did the district court, that because § 7 of the Clayton Act only prohibits those mergers whose effect "may be substantially to lessen competition," a defendant can rebut a prima facie case with evidence that the proposed merger will create a more efficient combined entity and thus increase competition. For example, if two small firms were unable to match the prices of a larger competitor, but could do so after a merger because of decreased production costs, a court recognizing the efficiencies defense might reasonably conclude that the transaction likely would not lessen competition. . . . The [Clayton] Act focuses on "competition," so any defense must demonstrate that the prima facie case "portray[s] inaccurately the merger's probable effects on

---

4. The district court found that a core reason for high health care costs is the prevalent fee-for-service reimbursement model, based on the apparently uncontested opinions of expert witnesses. Experts have recommended moving toward integrated care and risk-based reimbursement. "In an integrated delivery system, [PCPs] and specialty physicians work as a team, with PCPs managing patient care and specialty physicians consulting and providing care as needed." Risk-based reimbursement (also known as capitation) means that "providers receive reimbursement from insurers in the form of a set amount for each patient rather than a payment for each service rendered. The set amount is based on the average expected health care utilization for the patients given such factors as their age and medical history." "Capitation motivates providers to consider the costs of treatment as they will share in the savings if they can keep actual costs below the set amount they receive."

competition." In other words, a successful efficiencies defense requires proof that a merger is not, despite the existence of a prima facie case, anticompetitive. . . .

St. Luke's argues that the merger would benefit patients by creating a team of employed physicians with access to Epic, the electronic medical records system used by St. Luke's. The district court found that, even if true, these predicted efficiencies were insufficient to carry St. Luke's' burden of rebutting the prima facie case. We agree.

It is not enough to show that the merger would allow St. Luke's to better serve patients. The Clayton Act focuses on competition, and the claimed efficiencies therefore must show that the prediction of anticompetitive effects from the prima facie case is inaccurate. Although the district court believed that the merger would eventually "improve the delivery of health care" in the Nampa market, the judge did not find that the merger would increase competition or decrease prices. Quite to the contrary, the court, even while noting the likely beneficial effect of the merger on patient care, held that reimbursement rates for PCP services likely would increase. Nor did the court find that the merger would likely lead to integrated health care or a new reimbursement system; the judge merely noted the desire of St. Luke's to move in that direction.

. . . [Moreover], [t]he court found "no empirical evidence to support the theory that St. Luke's needs a core group of employed primary care physicians beyond the number it had before the Acquisition to successfully make the transition to integrated care," and that "a committed team can be assembled without employing physicians." The court also found that the shared electronic record was not a merger-specific benefit because data analytics tools are available to independent physicians. . . .

But even if we assume that the claimed efficiencies were merger-specific, the defense would nonetheless fail. At most, the district court concluded that St. Luke's might provide better service to patients after the merger. That is a laudable goal, but the Clayton Act does not excuse mergers that lessen competition or create monopolies simply because the merged entity can improve its operations. . . ..

St. Luke's nonetheless argues that the district court erred in ordering divestiture because (1) divestiture will not actually restore competition; (2) divestiture eliminates the transaction's procompetitive benefits; and (3) a proposed conduct remedy was preferable. We find no abuse of discretion in the district court's choice of remedy. . . .

Notes: Hospital, Physician, and Insurer Mergers

1. *You Can't Win Them All. Tenet* is emblematic of the remarkable string of losses in hospital merger cases the federal government suffered prior to this decade. Prof. Greaney gives this explanation:

Segments of the judiciary are openly hostile toward applying traditional competition concepts to the health care sector . . . [and so] have dealt a number of important setbacks to government agencies and private plaintiffs litigating antitrust matters. A close examination of these cases reveals an admixture of factors ranging from plain judicial error, to subtle changes in legal doctrine, to a shifting jurisprudence that is increasingly deferential to professionalism in health market interactions. An undercurrent has been that a backlash against managed care has contributed to decisions that shield providers from the antitrust laws.

The unfavorable reception to antitrust cases in court appears to have had a corresponding chilling effect upon federal enforcement efforts. . . . Cases involving serious misconduct have resulted in mild civil sanctions rather than criminal prosecutions, and the overall level of investigatory and advisory activity appears to have declined. . . .

The most pronounced change in the law has been in merger enforcement. . . . Since 1995 federal and state enforcers have lost all seven cases litigated in federal court. . . . [T]he government's failures in court have undoubtedly encouraged consolidation across the health care industry. Because they may supply precedent on issues such as market definition, the hospital merger decisions are likely to have a profound impact in other areas of antitrust concern such as physician consolidation, network formation, and restraints of trade. Experienced attorneys giving advice to physicians and hospitals see a judicial imprimatur for consolidation. As one practitioner put it, the cases "make almost any merger worth trying."

Thomas L. Greaney, Whither Antitrust? The Uncertain Future of Competition Law in Health Care, 21(2) Health Aff. 185 (Mar. 2002).

St. Luke's reflects the government's more recent track record. For another decision applying a similar analysis, see FTC v. Penn State Hershey, Medical Center, 838 F.3d 327 (3d Cir. 2016) (enjoining the merger of the two largest hospitals in the Harrisburg, Pennsylvania area).

2. *Undoing Mistakes.* The FTC, not wanting to let the courts have the last word, has adopted a policy of challenging mergers several years after they are consummated if evidence shows that actual effects have been adverse for competition. In the first such case, the FTC ordered partial divestiture in a merger that was approved four years earlier of the only two hospitals in Evanston, Illinois (which borders Chicago), based on evidence that the merger allowed the hospital to increase its payment rates under managed care contracts. However, the FTC declined to order a corporate breakup. Instead, it ruled only that the two facilities must conduct certain of their operations separately, such as negotiating for managed care contracts. In re Evanston Northwestern Healthcare Corporation, No. 9315 (FTC, Aug. 2, 2007). More generally, note 10 cites the increasing evidence that both horizontal and vertical mergers among providers tend to drive prices up, and that claimed efficiencies are rarely achieved.

3. *Joint Ventures and Other Transactions.* Merger analysis and related monopolization charges are not restricted to outright acquisitions. They are also relevant to a variety of contractual networks and joint venture arrangements. Consider, for instance, a sole community hospital's forming of a joint venture with its medical staff to enter into managed care contracts with insurers and employers, or a joint venture between the only two hospitals in town to purchase and share the town's only MRI scanner. One issue, discussed in the previous section, is whether or not a joint venture has sufficient integration to avoid scrutiny under Sherman Act §1; if not, the joint venture might constitute a "walking conspiracy," incurring *per se* liability. But, if the venture is viewed as a single enterprise, the participants still need to consider whether its creation violates merger law.

For this second purpose, the DOJ/FTC Antitrust Enforcement Guidelines, quoted at page 1417, create safe harbors of either 20 or 30 percent market share for physician networks depending on whether the physician affiliations are exclusive or nonexclusive. The product market is defined in terms of the number of physicians practicing in the specialty. The guidelines also observe that joint ventures between competitors to purchase expensive high-tech equipment have never been challenged by the agencies and are not likely to be if efficiency justifications can be given for cost-sharing. However, in one notable decision, the Eleventh Circuit held that a dominant hospital monopolized the market for "durable medical equipment" (wheelchairs, oxygen equipment, and other items used in patients' homes) by entering into a joint venture with one equipment supplier and then having the hospitals' nurses steer its patients to that supplier when they left the hospital. Key Enterprises v. Venice Hospital, 919 F.2d 1550 (11th Cir. 1990).

4. *Geographic Markets.* In contrast with *Tenet's* treatment of the geographic market definition, Judge Posner had the following to say about a proposed merger of two of the three hospitals in Rockford, Illinois:

> It is always possible to take pot shots at a market definition (we have just taken one), and the defendants do so with vigor and panache. Their own proposal, however, is ridiculous—a ten-county area in which it is assumed (without any evidence and contrary to common sense) that Rockford residents, or third-party payors, will be searching out small, obscure hospitals in remote rural areas if the prices charged by the hospitals in Rockford rise above competitive levels. . . . For highly exotic or highly elective hospital treatment, patients will sometimes travel long distances, of course. But for the most part hospital services are local. People want to be hospitalized near their families and homes, in hospitals in which their own—local—doctors have hospital privileges.

United States v. Rockford Memorial Corp., 898 F.2d 1278 (7th Cir. 1990). See also William G. Kopit, Price Competition in Hospital Markets: The Significance of Managed Care, 35 J. Health L. 291, 319 (2002) ("The assertions [in *Tenet*] in support of the defendant's market definition are completely without factual support").

5. *Product Market Definition.* The second aspect of market determination is defining the relevant product. Note that the *St. Luke's* court distinguished between the market for primary care and the market for "ancillary" services. Similarly, the DOJ/FTC Guidelines treat each practice specialty as a distinct market, and the ACO Guidelines instruct how specialties are to be defined.

For hospitals, although *Tenet* did not contest the issue, how was the product market defined in that case and how might it have differed? Compare *Rockford Memorial,* supra:

> If you need a kidney transplant, or a mastectomy, or if you have a stroke or a heart attack or a gunshot wound, you will go (or be taken) to an acute-care hospital for inpatient treatment. The fact that for other services you have a choice between inpatient care at such a hospital and outpatient care elsewhere places no check on the prices of the services we have listed. . . . If you need your hip replaced, you can't decide to have chemotherapy instead because it's available on an outpatient basis at a lower price. . . . Hospitals can and do distinguish between the patient who wants a coronary bypass and the patient who wants a wart removed from his foot; these services are not in the same product market merely because they have a common provider.

6. *Insurance Markets.* Consider how the market definition issues might differ when antitrust cases involve insurers rather than providers. Because insurers can sell

nationally, it is possible to argue for a national market, but the need to meet regulatory requirements in each state tends to restrict insurance markets to no greater than a state and the surrounding region. Should insurance markets be even smaller, however, due to the fact that, to be competitive, insurers need to contract with local providers?

Regarding product markets, should "Medicare Advantage" insurance be considered a separate market from commercial insurance? And, for commercial insurance, are there separate markets for employers versus individuals, or for employers that do and do not self-insure (and thus contract for administrative services and network access). According to some courts, market share is defined not only by *existing* competitors but also by *potential* competitors. See, e.g., Little Rock Cardiology Clinic v. Baptist Health, 591 F.3d 591 (8th Cir. 2009) (refusing to limit market definition to patients covered only by private insurance, reasoning that patients can also opt to pay for cardiology services out of pocket); City of New York v. Group Health Inc., 649 F.3d 151 (2d Cir. 2011) (refusing to limit market to the insurers currently offered to New York City employees).

Some insight into government policy on these questions is provided by the Justice Department's decisions in 2016 to block two separate mergers among four of the five largest insurers in the country: Aetna with Humana, and Cigna with Anthem (the largest Blue Cross conglomerate). The DOJ distinguished among all of the different product markets just noted, and considered geographic markets to be as small as a single county for some products (although national for very large employers, and metropolitan areas for most commercial insurance). It remains to be seen whether these positions will be upheld in court or altered by the Trump administration.

7. *Antitrust Two-Step.* As both of these cases indicate, it is necessary to analyze hospital and physician mergers in the context of not only their own markets, but also the insurance markets that determine how they are paid. The *St. Luke's* decision refers to this as the "two-stage model." Notice, for instance, the *Tenet* court's description of hospitals in neighboring Cape Girardeau for refusing to contract with managed care plans, at least for a time. This happens regularly around the country, even in metropolitan areas. Hospitals or physician groups that control a significant share of the market have learned that when push comes to shove, insurers will often back down and give in to demands for higher rates. Insurers often feel they can't afford to have major gaps in their networks because larger employers look for insurers that cover most doctors and hospitals in the area.

Coupled with providers' market power is a regulatory requirement in most states that managed care plans maintain adequate hospital and physician networks (both primary care and specialists) in each county where they do business. At an extreme, having a major gap in the network may mean giving up a license to sell the product in certain counties. More commonly, however, regulators allow managed care plans to continue doing business but require them to pay non-network providers their full, non-discounted rates if the local network does not have adequate capacity for the number of people enrolled locally. Therefore, regulators constrain the ability of HMOs to send people long distances for care.

Based on these considerations, some economists believe that market concentration among insurers has the pro-competitive benefit of forcing dominant hospitals and provider groups to be more willing to negotiate. Other economists, however, disagree, as did the DOJ in its 2016 decision (just noted) to block mergers among some large national insurers—in part because larger insurers that obtain price concessions do not necessarily pass those savings on to consumers. See Leemore S. Dafny, Evaluating the Impact of Health Insurance Industry Consolidation (Commonwealth Fund, Nov. 2015); Richard Scheffler & Daniel Arnold, Insurer Market Power Lowers Prices in Numerous Concentrated Provider Markets, 36 Health Aff. 1539 (2017); Kate Ho & Robin S. Lee, Insurer Competition in Health Care Markets, 85 Econometrica 379 (2017).

8. *Natural Monopolies.* Observe that market share statistics are not the sole consideration. A hospital merger even in a highly concentrated market is unlikely to lessen competition and, indeed, might help competition if one or both of the hospitals would not survive financially without the merger, or if a merged hospital would offer better service at lower cost. These arguments are known as the "failing firm" defense and the "efficiencies" defense. Although *Tenet* did not find that these arguments were sustained as affirmative defenses, the court did note that "the reality of the situation . . . may be that Poplar Bluff cannot support two high-quality hospitals." This suggests the presence of "natural monopoly" conditions. In line with this thinking, the DOJ/FTC Antitrust Enforcement Guidelines establish a safe harbor for mergers between two hospitals, no matter how small the market, where one has fewer than 100 beds and 40 patients a day.

9. *Are Nonprofits Different?* For a time, it was disputed whether the FTC has jurisdiction over nonprofit entities, due to the wording of the FTC's governing statute. Although the Supreme Court rejected this argument as an absolute defense in *California Dental Ass'n*, above, the substance of the argument sometimes surfaces when nonprofit hospitals argue they are not likely to abuse market power since they are not driven by a profit motive. On this score, one district relied heavily on the difference in nonprofit governance in approving the merger of the two dominant hospitals in a medium-sized town (Grand Rapids). The court observed that having community and business leaders on the nonprofit hospital board dampens the incentive to raise prices, and it pointed to research that markets dominated by nonprofit hospitals have lower prices. The court concluded:

> In the real world, hospitals are in the business of saving lives, and managed care organizations are in the business of saving dollars. Managed care organizations' interest in maintaining a competitive edge cannot be allowed to trump either hospitals' conscientious endeavors to continue to provide comprehensive, high quality health care . . . or the consumer public's right to receive the same. Permitting defendant hospitals to achieve the efficiencies of scale that would clearly result from the proposed merger would enable the . . . combined entity to continue the quest for establishment of world-class health facilities in West Michigan, a course the Court finds clearly and unequivocally would ultimately be in the best interests of the consumer public as a whole.

FTC v. Butterworth Health Corp., 946 F. Supp. 1285 (W.D. Mich. 1996), aff'd, 121 F.3d 708 (6th Cir. 1997). However, in the *Rockford* case discussed above, the court reasoned to the contrary:

> [T]he defendants contend that they have no incentive to act anti-competitively because . . . monopoly profits garnered by a not-for-profit company cannot be distributed to anyone, let alone corporate decisionmakers. Instead, any excess of rev-

enues over expense must be farmed back into the firm's operation. . . . The court rejects the defendants' narrow view as to the motivation behind anti-competitive action. . . . The not-for-profit decisionmaker may desire more money for a new piece of equipment or to hire a new specialist or for a better office, salary or title, or just to keep the firm afloat in particularly lean or dangerous times. . . . Simply put, decisionmakers need not be solely interested in the attainment of profit to act anti-competitively."

717 F. Supp. 1284.

10. *Further Readings.* On the government's **track record in court** (note 1), see Barak D. Richman, Antitrust and Nonprofit Hospital Mergers: A Return to Basics, 156 U. Pa. L. Rev. 121 (2007); Thomas L. Greaney, Thirty Years of Solicitude: Antitrust Law and Physician Cartels, 7 Hous. J. Health L. & Pol'y (2007); Jennifer R. Conners, A Critical Misdiagnosis: How Courts Underestimate the Anticompetitive Implications of Hospital Mergers, 91 Cal. L. Rev. 543 (2003); Casenote, 130 Harv. L. Rev. 1736 (2017).

For analysis of the **legal issues in the *St. Luke's* case**, see T. Greaney & D. Ross, Navigating Through the Fog of Vertical Merger Law, 91 Wash. L. Rev. 191 (2016); Roger Blair et al., Hospital Mergers and Economic Efficiency, 91 Wash. L. Rev. 1 (2016).

Addressing how **states could take a more prominent enforcement or oversight role**, see Erin Fuse Brown & Jaime King, The Double-Edged Sword of Health Care Integration: Consolidation and Cost Control, 92 Ind. L. J. 55 (2016).

On the **empirical effects of hospital and physician mergers** (note 2), see Erin Fuse Brown, Jaime King & David Cutler, Hospitals, Market Share, and Consolidation, 310 JAMA 1964 (2013); Jeff Goldsmith et al., Integrated Delivery Networks: In Search of Benefits and Market Effects (NASI, Feb. 2015); David Dranove & Andrew Sfekas, The Revolution in Health Care Antitrust: New Methods and Provocative Implications, 87 Milbank Q. 607 (2009); Kristin Madison, Hospital Mergers in an Era of Quality Improvement, 7 Hous. J. Health L. & Pol'y 265 (2007); Note, 90 B.U. L. Rev. 431 (2010); Symposium, 36 Health Aff. 1527 (2017).

On antitrust analysis for **nonprofit hospitals** (note 8), see Barak D. Richman, The Corrosive Combination of Nonprofit Monopolies and U.S.-Style Health Insurance: Implications for Antitrust and Merger Policy, 69 Law & Contemp. Probs. 139 (Autumn 2006); Clark Havighurst & Barak Richman, The Provider Monopoly Problem in Health Care, 89 Or. L. Rev. 847 (2011).

Problem: Rural Hospital Merger*

Rural County has a population of 15,000, a small primary care hospital, and ten physicians, including seven general and family practitioners, an obstetrician, a pediatrician, and a general surgeon. All the physicians are solo practitioners. The nearest urban area is about 60 miles away in Big City, which has a population of 300,000, and three major hospitals to which patients from Rural County are referred

---

* This problem is excerpted directly from the DOJ/FTC antitrust guidelines.

or transferred for higher levels of hospital care. However, Big City is too far away for most residents of Rural County to use for services available in Rural County.

Insurance Company, which operates throughout the state, is attempting to offer "managed care" programs in all areas of the state, and has asked the local physicians in Rural County to form an IPA to provide services under the program to covered persons living in the county. No other managed care plan has attempted to enter the county previously.

Initially, two of the general practitioners and two of the specialists express interest in forming a network, but Insurance Company says that it intends to market its plan to the larger local employers, who need broader geographic and specialty coverage for their employees. Consequently, Insurance Company needs more of the local general practitioners and the one remaining specialist in the IPA in order to provide adequate geographic, specialty, and backup coverage to subscribers in Rural County. Eventually, four of the seven general practitioners and the one remaining specialist join the IPA and agree to provide services to Insurance Company's subscribers under contracts providing for capitation. While the physicians' participation in the IPA is structured to be nonexclusive, no other managed care plan has yet entered the local market or approached any of the physicians about joining a different provider panel. In discussing the formation of the IPA with the Insurance Company, a number of the physicians have made clear their intention to continue to practice outside the IPA and have indicated they would be interested in contracting individually with other managed care plans when those plans expand into Rural County. Insurance Company requests your legal advice about whether this network formation is likely to be challenged by the federal government.

E. REFERRAL FEE LAWS

Many of the transactions and relationships surveyed in this chapter are affected by an entirely different set of laws that happen to be motivated by the same concerns about excess commercialization and distorting incentives: the collection of federal and state laws that prohibit or regulate referral fees. By referral fees, we mean explicit or implicit incentives to generate or refer medical business. These referral fee laws are unfortunately but unavoidably complex, and they have effects that permeate the medical enterprise. They are taken very seriously by lawyers, doctors, and institutions because their violation can result in denial of payment, inability to enforce contracts, or even criminal penalties. As you become acquainted with this highly specialized body of law, try first to focus on the gist of what it prohibits and why, and then begin to consider its less obvious applications and implications.

■ UNITED STATES v. GREBER
760 F.2d 68 (3d Cir. 1985)

Weis, Circuit Judge.

In this appeal, defendant argues that payments made to a physician for professional services in connection with tests performed by a laboratory cannot be the basis of Medicare fraud. We do not agree and hold that if one purpose of the payment was to induce future referrals, the Medicare statute has been violated. . . .

Defendant is an osteopathic physician who is board certified in cardiology. In addition to hospital staff and teaching positions, he was the president of Cardio-Med, Inc., an organization which he formed. The company provides physicians with diagnostic services, one of which uses a Holter-monitor. This device, worn for approximately 24 hours, records the patient's cardiac activity on a tape. A computer operated by a cardiac technician scans the tape, and the data is later correlated with an activity diary the patient maintains while wearing the monitor.

Cardio-Med billed Medicare for the monitor service and, when payment was received, forwarded a portion to the referring physician. The government charged that the referral fee was 40 percent of the Medicare payment, not to exceed $65 per patient.

Based on Cardio-Med's billing practices, counts 18-23 of the indictment charged defendant with having tendered remuneration or kickbacks to the referring physicians in violation of [the Medicare fraud statute]. . . . The proof as to the Medicare fraud counts was that defendant had paid a Dr. Avallone and other physicians "interpretation fees" for the doctors' initial consultation services, as well as for explaining the test results to the patients. There was evidence that physicians received "interpretation fees" even though defendant had actually evaluated the monitoring data. Moreover, the fixed percentage paid to the referring physician was more than Medicare allowed for such services.

The government also introduced testimony defendant had given in an earlier civil proceeding. In that case, he had testified that ". . . if the doctor didn't get his consulting fee, he wouldn't be using our service. So the doctor got a consulting fee." . . .

I. Medicare Fraud

The Medicare fraud statute was amended [in] 1977. Congress, concerned with the growing problem of fraud and abuse in the system, wished to strengthen the penalties to enhance the deterrent effect of the statute. To achieve this purpose, the crime was upgraded from a misdemeanor to a felony. . . . A particular concern was the practice of giving "kickbacks" to encourage the referral of work. Testimony before the congressional committee was that "physicians often determine which laboratories would do the test work for their medicaid patients by the amount of the kickbacks and rebates offered by the laboratory. . . . Kickbacks take a number of forms including cash, long-term credit arrangements, gifts, supplies and equipment, and the furnishing of business machines."

To remedy the deficiencies in the statute and achieve more certainty, the present version of 42 U.S.C. §[1320a-7b(b), Social Security Act §1128B(b)(2)] was enacted. It provides:

> [W]hoever knowingly and willfully offers or pays any remuneration (including any kickback, bribe or rebate) directly or indirectly, overtly or covertly in cash or in kind to induce such person— . . . to purchase, lease, order, or arrange for or recommend purchasing . . . or ordering any . . . service or item for which payment may be made . . . under [Medicare or Medicaid] shall be guilty of a felony.

The district judge instructed the jury that the government was required to prove that Cardio-Med paid to Dr. Avallone some part of the amount received from Medicare; that defendant caused Cardio-Med to make the payment; and did so knowingly and willfully as well as with the intent to induce Dr. Avallone to use Cardio-Med's services for patients covered by Medicare. The judge further charged that even if the physician interpreting the test did so as a consultant to Cardio-Med, that fact was immaterial if a purpose of the fee was to induce the ordering of services from Cardio-Med.

Defendant contends that the charge was erroneous. He insists that absent a showing that the only purpose behind the fee was to improperly induce future services, compensating a physician for services actually rendered could not be a violation of the statute. The government argues that Congress intended to combat financial incentives to physicians for ordering particular services patients did not require.

The language and purpose of the statute support the government's view. Even if the physician performs some service for the money received, the potential for unnecessary drain on the Medicare system remains. The statute is aimed at the inducement factor.

The text refers to "any remuneration." That includes not only sums for which no actual service was performed but also those amounts for which some professional time was expended. "Remunerates" is defined as "to pay an equivalent for service." Webster Third New International Dictionary (1966). By including such items as kickbacks and bribes, the statute expands "remuneration" to cover situations where no service is performed. That a particular payment was a remuneration (which implies that a service was rendered) rather than a kickback, does not foreclose the possibility that a violation nevertheless could exist. . . .

We conclude that the more expansive reading is consistent with the impetus for the 1977 amendments and therefore hold that the district court correctly instructed the jury. If the payments were intended to induce the physician to use Cardio-Med's services, the statute was violated, even if the payments were also intended to compensate for professional services.

■ LIMITATION ON CERTAIN PHYSICIAN REFERRALS
*42 U.S.C. §1395nn**

(a) Prohibition of certain referrals.

(1) In general. Except as provided in subsection (b) of this section, if a physician (or an immediate family member of such physician) has a financial relationship with an entity specified in paragraph (2), then the physician may not make a referral to the entity for the furnishing of designated health services [under Medicare or Medicaid and the entity may not seek payment for such services]. . . .

(2) Financial relationship specified. A financial relationship of a physician (or an immediate family member of such physician) with an entity specified in this paragraph is—

---

* This statute is known as the Stark Law, after its sponsor, Rep. Pete Stark. It was enacted in 1993.

(A) except as provided in subsections (c) and (d) of this section, an ownership or investment interest in the entity [through equity or debt], or

(B) except as provided in subsection (e) of this section, a compensation arrangement between the physician (or an immediate family member of such physician) and the entity. . . .

(b) General exceptions to both ownership and compensation arrangement prohibitions. Subsection (a)(1) of this section shall not apply in the following cases:

(1) Physicians' services. In the case of physicians' services provided personally by (or under the personal supervision of) another physician in the same group practice as the referring physician.

(2) In-office ancillary services. In the case of services . . . that are [billed by and] furnished personally by the referring physician, personally by a physician who is a member of the same group practice as the referring physician, or personally by individuals who are directly supervised by the physician or by another physician in the group practice. . . .

(c) General exception related only to ownership or investment prohibition for ownership in publicly traded securities and mutual funds. Ownership of the following shall not be considered to be an ownership or investment interest described in subsection (a)(2)(A) of this section: Ownership of investment securities which may be purchased on terms generally available to the public and which are [publicly traded on the stock exchanges] or [are] in a corporation that [has] . . . stockholder equity exceeding $75,000,000. . . .

(d) Additional exceptions related only to ownership or investment prohibition. The following, if not otherwise excepted under subsection (b) of this section, shall not be considered to be an ownership or investment interest described in subsection (a)(2)(A) of this section: . . .

(2) Rural provider. . . . [I]f substantially all of the designated health services furnished by such entity are furnished to individuals residing in [a] rural area.

(3) Hospital ownership. In the case of designated health services provided by a hospital if the referring physician is authorized to perform services at the hospital, and the ownership or investment interest is in the hospital itself (and not merely in a subdivision of the hospital). [The ACA placed a moratorium on this "whole-hospital" exception — denying it to any new hospitals or hospital expansions starting in 2012, but grandfathering existing arrangements. — Eds.]

(e) Exceptions relating to other compensation arrangements. The following shall not be considered to be a compensation arrangement described in subsection (a)(2)(B) of this section:

(1) Rental of office space; rental of equipment. Payments made by a lessee to a lessor for the use of premises [or equipment] if —

(i) the lease is set out in writing, signed by the parties, and specifies the premises covered by the lease,

(ii) the space [or equipment] rented or leased does not exceed that which is reasonable and necessary for the legitimate business purposes of the lease or rental and is used exclusively by the lessee when being used by the lessee, . . .

(iii) the lease provides for a term of rental or lease for at least one year,

(iv) the rental charges over the term of the lease are set in advance, are consistent with fair market value, and are not determined in a manner that takes into account the volume or value of any referrals or other business generated between the parties,

(v) the lease would be commercially reasonable even if no referrals were made between the parties, and

(vi) the lease meets such other requirements as the Secretary may impose by regulation as needed to protect against program or patient abuse.

(2) Bona fide employment relationships. Any amount paid by an employer to a physician (or an immediate family member of such physician) who has a bona fide employment relationship with the employer for the provision of services if—

(A) the employment is for identifiable services,

(B) the amount of the remuneration under the employment is consistent with the fair market value of the services and is not determined in a manner that takes into account (directly or indirectly) the volume or value of any referrals by the referring physician, [and]

(C) the remuneration is provided pursuant to an agreement which would be commercially reasonable even if no referrals were made to the employer. . . .

(3) Personal service arrangements. [This subsection covers independent contractors, and requires terms that reflect fair market and are unrelated to the volume of services, similar to the two exceptions above for leases and employment. The contract must cover at least 1 year, and must provide for fixed compensation set in advance.] . . .

(5) Physician recruitment. In the case of remuneration which is provided by a hospital to a physician to induce the physician to relocate to the geographic area served by the hospital in order to be a member of the medical staff of the hospital, if the physician is not required to refer patients to the hospital, and the amount of the remuneration under the arrangement is not determined in a manner that takes into account (directly or indirectly) the volume or value of any referrals by the referring physician. . . .

(g) Sanctions. [Medicare and Medicaid services delivered in arrangements that violate this section will not be paid for. Also, a knowing violation can result in the imposition of civil monetary penalties or exclusion from the Medicare and Medicaid programs.]

(h) Definitions and special rules. For purposes of this section: . . .

(1) The term "compensation arrangement" means any arrangement involving any remuneration between a physician . . . and an entity. . . . The term "remuneration" includes any remuneration, directly or indirectly, overtly or covertly, in cash or in kind. . . .

(3) The term "fair market value" means the value in arms length transactions . . . and, in the case of a lease of space, not adjusted to reflect the additional value the prospective lessee or lessor would attribute to the proximity or convenience to the lessor where the lessor is a potential source of patient referrals to the lessee. . . .

(5) . . . [T]he request by a physician for the item or service, . . . [or] the establishment of a plan of care by a physician which includes the provision of the designated health service, . . . constitutes a "referral" by the "referring physician." [The definition then clarifies that no referral occurs when certain specialists such as radiologists or pathologists order their own services or services rendered under their supervision.]

(6) Designated health services. The term "designated health services" means any of the following items or services: clinical laboratory services, physical therapy services, occupational therapy services, radiology services, . . . durable medical equipment and supplies, . . . home health services, . . . outpatient prescription drugs, and inpatient and outpatient hospital services. [Note that this list does not include basic physician services but only specified "ancillary" services

that physicians might provide or arrange for. The inclusion of hospital services covers only the facility's services (nursing care, testing, use of operating room, etc.) and not physicians' personal professional time.]

■U.S. ex rel. DRAKEFORD v. TUOMEY HEALTHCARE SYSTEM
792 F.3d 364, 382. (4th Cir. 2015)

Diaz, Circuit Judge:

In a *qui tam* action in which the government intervened, a jury determined that Tuomey Healthcare . . . knowingly submitted 21,730 false claims to Medicare for reimbursement. The district court then entered final judgment for the government and awarded damages and civil penalties totaling $237,454,195. . . . [W]e affirm the district court's judgment.

I. A.

Tuomey [pronounced "TOO-mee"] is a nonprofit hospital located in Sumter, South Carolina, a small, largely rural community that is a federally-designated, medically-underserved area. At the time of the events leading up to this lawsuit, most of the physicians that practiced at Tuomey were not directly employed by the hospital, but instead were members of independent specialty practices.

Beginning around 2000, doctors who previously performed outpatient surgery at Tuomey began doing so in their own offices or at off-site surgery centers. The loss of this revenue stream was a source of grave concern for Tuomey because it collected substantial facility fees from patients who underwent surgery at the hospital's outpatient center. ... To stem this loss, Tuomey sought to negotiate part-time employment contracts with a number of local physicians.

In drafting the contracts, Tuomey was well aware of the constraints imposed by the Stark Law. While we discuss the provisions of that law in greater detail below, in broad terms, [it] prohibits physicians from making referrals to entities where "[t]he referring physician . . . receives aggregate compensation . . . that varies with, or takes into account, the volume or value of referrals or other business generated by the referring physician for the entity furnishing" the designated health services. 42 C.F.R. § 411.354. Pursuant to the Stark Law, [a] hospital may not submit for payment a Medicare claim for services rendered pursuant to a prohibited referral.

Beginning in 2003, Tuomey sought the advice of its longtime counsel, Nexsen Pruet, [which conferred with a physician compensation expert, a former Inspector General for the US Department of Health and Human Services, and another prominent healthcare law firm. Under the contracts Nexsen Pruet drafted, each physician's base salary] . . . was adjusted from year to year based on the amount the physician collected from all services rendered the previous year. The bulk of the physicians' compensation was earned in the form of a productivity bonus, which paid the physicians 80 percent of the amount of their collections for that year. The physicians were also eligible for an incentive bonus of up to seven percent of their earned productivity bonus. In addition, Tuomey [paid for medical malpractice insurance, employment taxes, and billing and collections costs].

The contracts had ten-year terms, during which physicians could maintain their private practices, but were required to perform outpatient surgical procedures exclusively at the hospital. Physicians could not own any interest in a facility located in Sumter that provided ambulatory surgery services . . . .

Tuomey ultimately entered into part-time employment contracts with nineteen physicians. Tuomey, however, was unable to reach an agreement with Dr. Michael Drakeford, an orthopedic surgeon. Drakeford believed that the proposed contracts violated the Stark Law because the physicians were being paid in excess of their collections . . . and thus the government would view it as an unlawful payment for the doctor's facility-fee-generating referrals.

To address Drakeford's concerns, Tuomey suggested a joint venture as an alternative business arrangement, whereby "doctors would become investors . . . in . . . a management company that would provide day-to-day management of the outpatient surgery center," and both Tuomey and its co-investors would "receive payments based on that management [structure]." Drakeford, however, declined that option.

Unable to break the stalemate in their negotiations, in May 2005, Tuomey and Drakeford sought the advice of Kevin McAnaney, an attorney . . . [who had formerly served in the Office of Counsel to the DHHS Inspector General]. In that position, McAnaney wrote a "substantial portion" of the regulations implementing the Stark Law. McAnaney advised the parties that the proposed employment contracts raised significant "red flags" under the Stark Law. . . . McAnaney also warned Tuomey that the contracts presented "an easy case to prosecute" for the government.

Drakeford ultimately declined to enter into a contract with Tuomey. He later sued the hospital under the *qui tam* provisions[5] of the [federal False Claims Act (FCA)], alleging that because the part-time employment contracts violated the Stark Law, Tuomey had knowingly submitted false claims for payment to Medicare. As was its right, the government intervened in the action . . . .

[An initial trial found that the hospital had violated the Stark Law, but not the False Claims Act, presumably because its violation of Stark was not "knowing or reckless," but the Fourth Circuit reversed and remanded for a new trial, based in part on the initial judge excluding testimony about Kevin McAnaney's view of the contracts' legality. In the second trial, the] jury found that Tuomey violated both the Stark Law and the FCA. It further found that Tuomey had submitted 21,730 false claims to Medicare with a total value of $39,313,065. The district court trebled the actual damages and assessed an additional civil penalty, both actions required by the FCA. From the resulting judgment of $237,454,195, Tuomey appeals.

II. B.

. . . The Stark Law is intended to prevent overutilization of services by physicians who [stand] to profit from referring patients to facilities or entities in which they [have] a financial interest. The statute prohibits a physician from making a referral to an entity, such as a hospital, with which he or she has a financial relation-

---

5. [This "whistleblower" law, 31 U.S.C. §3729, allows private parties to sue on behalf of the government to recoup money paid under any claim that was knowingly false or fraudulent. Successful qui tam "relators" (as they are called) can earn a bounty of 15-30 percent of the recovered amounts.]

ship, for the furnishing of designated health services. If the physician makes such a referral, the hospital may not submit a bill for reimbursement to Medicare. Similarly, the government may not make any payment for a designated health service provided in violation of the Stark Law. . . .

Inpatient and outpatient hospital services are considered designated health services under the law. A referral includes "the request by a physician for the item or service." A referral does not include "any designated health service personally performed or provided by the referring physician." However, there is a referral when the hospital bills a "facility fee" (also known as a "facility component" or "technical component") "in connection with the personally performed service."

A financial relationship constitutes a prohibited "indirect compensation arrangement," if . . . "[t]he referring physician . . . receives aggregate compensation . . . that varies with, or takes into account, the volume or value of referrals or other business generated by the referring physician for the entity furnishing" the designated health services . . . . The statute, however, does not bar indirect compensation arrangements where: (1) the referring physician is compensated at fair market value for "services and items actually provided"; (2) the compensation arrangement is "not determined in any manner that takes into account the volume or value of referrals"; [and] (3) the compensation arrangement is "commercially reasonable" . . . .

. . . A reasonable jury could find that Tuomey violated the Stark Law when it paid aggregate compensation to physicians that varied with or took into account the volume or value of actual or anticipated referrals to Tuomey. . . . There are two different components of the physicians' compensation that we believe so varied. First, each year, the physicians were paid a base salary that was adjusted upward or downward depending on their collections from the prior year. In addition, the physicians received the bulk of their compensation in the form of a productivity bonus, pegged at eighty percent of the amount of their collections. . . . In sum, the more procedures the physicians performed at the hospital, the more facility fees Tuomey collected, and the more compensation the physicians received in the form of increased base salaries and productivity bonuses. . . .

Tuomey next argues that . . . it did not knowingly violate the FCA. Specifically, Tuomey claims that because it reasonably relied on the advice of counsel, no reasonable jury could find that Tuomey possessed the requisite intent to violate the FCA. Because the record here is replete with evidence indicating that Tuomey shopped for legal opinions approving of the employment contracts, while ignoring negative assessments, we disagree. . . .

McAnaney's testimony, summarized above, is alone sufficient to sweep aside Tuomey's claim of error. . . . According to McAnaney, compensation arrangements under which the contracting physicians are paid in excess of their collections were "basically a red flag to the government." He noted that similar cases had previously been prosecuted, although all of them were ultimately settled. McAnaney also pointed out that the ten-year term of the contracts, combined with the thirty-mile, two-year noncompete provision, would reinforce the government's view that Tuomey was "paying [the physicians] above fair market value for referrals." . . .

Nonetheless, a defendant may avoid liability under the FCA if it can show that it acted in good faith on the advice of counsel. . . . Tuomey contends that it provided full and accurate information regarding the proposed employment contracts to [their law firm] Hewson, who in turn advised Tuomey that the contracts did not run afoul of the Stark Law. But as the government aptly notes, "[i]n determining whether Tuomey reasonably relied on the advice of its counsel, the jury was entitled to consider all the advice given to it by any source."

. . . Tuomey defends its dismissal of McAnaney's warnings by claiming that his opinion was tainted by undue influence exerted by Drakeford and his counsel. But there was evidence before the jury suggesting that Tuomey also tried to procure a favorable opinion from McAnaney. . . . Thus, a reasonable jury could conclude that Tuomey ignored McAnaney because it simply did not like what he had to say. . . .

IV.

Finally, Tuomey makes several challenges to the $237,454,195 judgment entered against it. . . . A defendant found liable under the FCA must pay the government "a civil penalty of" not less than $5,500 and not more than $11,000 "plus 3 times the amount of damages which the Government sustains because of that person." In this case, the jury found that Tuomey had submitted 21,730 false claims, for which it awarded actual damages of $39,313,065, which the district court trebled. The district court then added a civil penalty of $119,515,000 to that sum, which it calculated by multiplying the number of false claims by the $5,500 statutory minimum penalty. . . .

According to Tuomey, the civil penalty assessed was improperly inflated because the jury was permitted to take into account both inpatient and outpatient procedures performed by the contracting physicians. . . . Tuomey is incorrect.

It is true that the contracts solely addressed compensation for outpatient procedures. . . . [However, if] a physician has a financial relationship with a hospital, then the Stark Law prohibits the physician from making any referral to that hospital for the furnishing of designated health services. . . . Inpatient hospital services are designated health services. And a referral includes "the request or establishment of a plan of care by a physician which includes the provision of the designated health service." Plainly, then, inpatient services constitute a prohibited referral for the furnishing of designated health services, and the district court properly instructed the jury to factor them into the damages calculation.

Tuomey also asserts that the jury's damage award is flawed because the government . . . did not identify the "referring physician," and thus failed to prove that the alleged false claims came about through a prohibited referral. . . . . [However,] several courts have accepted that the "'attending/operating' physician identified in [Medicare claims form] qualifies as a referring physician," . . . [and that] the fact that one of the physicians with whom the hospital has a financial relationship is identified as an "operating" or "attending" physician is sufficient evidence that the physician was also the "referring physician" absent evidence to the contrary. . . .

Tuomey next argues that the district court erroneously assessed the penalty based on [each of] the 21,730 [claims] forms Tuomey submitted to Medicare for reimbursement. . . . Instead, Tuomey asserts that the number of false claims should be limited to four [based on the number of times the hospital submitted annual reconciliations for aggregate Medicare payments]. Tuomey provides no Stark Law case to support its argument. Rather, each time Tuomey submitted to Medicare a [claims] form asking for reimbursement for a prohibited referral, it was knowingly asking the government to pay an amount that, by law, it could not pay. Consequently, we find the district court did not err in finding that each [claims] form constituted a separate claim.

Tuomey also . . . argues that the true measure [of actual damages] is not the sum total of all claims the government paid (as the court instructed the jury), but rather the difference (if any) between the true value of the services provided by Tuomey and what the government actually paid. According to Tuomey, since "there was no evidence that the Government did not get what it paid for[,] . . . there were no actual damages under the FCA." Here again, Tuomey's view of the law is incorrect.

The Stark Law prohibits the government from paying any amount of money for claims submitted in violation of the law. . . . The Stark Law expresses Congress's judgment that all services provided in violation of that law are medically unnecessary. By reimbursing Tuomey for services that it was legally prohibited from paying, the government has suffered injury equivalent to the full amount of the payments. . . .

C.

Finally, Tuomey argues that the district court's award of $237,454,195, consisting of damages and a civil penalty, is unconstitutional under the Excessive Fines Clause of the Eighth Amendment and the Due Process Clause of the Fifth Amendment. While the award is substantial, we cannot say that it is unconstitutional. ...

[T]he Supreme Court has directed courts to evaluate the degree of reprehensibility of the defendant's conduct by considering whether [among other factors not present here] "... the conduct involved repeated actions or was an isolated incident; and the harm was the result of intentional malice, trickery, or deceit, [rather than] mere accident." Clearly, Tuomey's conduct "involved repeated actions" as it submitted 21,730 false claims. Thus, while the penalty is certainly severe, it is meant to reflect the sheer breadth of the fraud Tuomey perpetrated upon the federal government. . . .

Next, we consider the disparity between actual harm and the punitive damages award. . . . Here, we can properly regard the entire civil penalty, $119,515,000, as punitive. On the other hand, the actual damages of $39,313,065 are entirely compensatory. As discussed above, the additional sum of $78,626,130 resulting from the trebling of actual damages is a hybrid of compensatory and punitive damages. . . . Assuming further that Drakeford receives the minimum amount allotted by the statute–that is fifteen percent of the total recovery–the relator would be entitled to $11,793,920 of the trebled award, leaving $66,832,210 to be allocated to punitive damages. By this calculation, the portion of damages that is compensatory is $51,106,985 and the $186,347,210 balance is punitive. . . .

[The Supreme Court] has suggested that "an award of more than four times the amount of compensatory damages might be close to the line of constitutional impropriety." Here, the ratio of punitive damages to compensatory damages is approximately 3.6-to-1 . . . . We therefore conclude that the damages award is constitutional under the Fifth and Eighth Amendments.

Finally, we do not discount the concerns raised by our concurring colleague regarding the result in this case. But having no found no cause to upset the jury's verdict in this case and no constitutional error, it is for Congress to consider whether changes to the Stark Law's reach are in order.

WYNN, Circuit Judge, concurring:

. . . I agree with the majority that the jury's determination that Tuomey violated both the Stark Law and the False Claims Act must stand. Our standard of review at this juncture is a highly deferential one. . . . Nevertheless, I am troubled by the picture this case paints: An impenetrably complex set of laws and regulations that will result in a likely death sentence for a community hospital in an already medically underserved area. . . .

"The Stark Law is a strict liability statute so it is immaterial whether one intended to violate the law; an inadvertent violation can trigger liability." Paula Tironi, The "Stark" Reality: Is the Federal Physician Self-Referral Law Bad for the Health Care Industry?, 19 Annals Health L. 235, 237-38 (2010). Individuals and entities that violate the Stark Law can be subject to severe monetary penalties and exclusion from federal health care programs. These "steep civil sanctions and program exclusions may be ruinous. Health care providers are open to extensive liability, their financial security resting uneasily upon a combination of their attorneys' wits [and] prosecutorial discretion." Jo-Ellyn Sakowitz Klein, The Stark Laws: Conquering Physician Conflicts of Interest?, 87 Geo. L. J. 499, 503-04 (1998).

Despite attempts to establish "bright line" rules so that physicians and healthcare entities could "ensure compliance and minimize . . . costs," 66 Fed. Reg. 860 (2001), the Stark Law has proved challenging to understand and comply with. Indeed, "[t]he Stark law is infamous among health care lawyers and their clients for being complicated, confusing, and counterintuitive; for producing results that defy common sense, and sometimes elevating form over substance. . . . Charles B. Oppenheim, The Stark Law: Comprehensive Analysis (AHLA 5th ed. 2014). . . .

Against this problematic backdrop, the availability of an advice of counsel defense should perhaps be especially robust in Stark Law cases prosecuted under the False Claims Act. . . . In the context of the Stark Law, it is easy to see how even diligent counsel could wind up giving clients incorrect advice. Between the law's being amended to have a broader scope but then narrowed with various exceptions, along with the promulgation and amendment of copious associated rules and regulations, "the Stark Law bec[ame] a classic example of a moving target. For lawyers, who must depend on the predictability of the law when they give counsel to their clients, such unpredictability [i]s an unusually heavy burden." Steven D. Wales, The Stark Law: Boon or Boondoggle? An Analysis of the Prohibition on Physician Self-Referrals, 27 Law & Psychol. Rev. 1, 21.

In this case, there can be no doubt that Tuomey sought and followed the advice of its long-time counsel, Nexsen Pruet. . . . Nevertheless, as the majority opinion notes, "a reasonable jury could have concluded that Tuomey was . . . no longer acting in good faith reliance on the advice of its counsel when it refused to give full consideration to McAnaney's negative assessment of the" contracts. . . .

This case is troubling. It seems as if, even for well-intentioned health care providers, the Stark Law has become a booby trap rigged with strict liability and potentially ruinous exposure—especially when coupled with the False Claims Act. Yet . . . the jury did not act irrationally when it determined that Tuomey violated both the Stark Law and the False Claims Act. Accordingly, I must concur in the outcome reached by the majority.

[Note: To avoid bankruptcy, Tuomey hospital was subsequently purchased by a larger hospital chain, and the sales proceeds were used to settle with the government for $72.4 million. The government also assessed a $1 million fine against the hospital's former CEO.]

■ A PUBLIC POLICY DISCUSSION: TAKING THE MEASURE OF THE STARK LAW
American Health Lawyers Association Public Interest Committee (2009)*

The Stark Law starts with an extremely broad prohibition. All physician referrals to an entity are prohibited unless the physician's financial relationships with that entity fit within one or more exceptions. Given the equally broad definition of financial relationships, the Stark Law has virtually ubiquitous application in the healthcare delivery system. The practical implications of the Law are greatly magnified by the fact that where the entity has a non-excepted financial relationship with a physician, the entity is prohibited from billing for any designated health services referred to it by that physician. In addition, the Stark Law is a strict liability statute in that the referral prohibition and the prohibition on billing are not dependent on the parties' intent. . . .

The strict liability provisions of the Stark Law combined with its breadth have yielded both positive and negative results. . . . [The Law] is credited with eliminating physician ownership of freestanding diagnostic centers and blamed for encouraging physicians to provide an ever growing range of services through their group practices. The Law has made it more difficult for physicians to have an ownership interest in a provider of designated health services but prompted an expansion of leasing and management services arrangements. . . .

The proscriptive structure of the Stark Law requires the creation of an exception for each and every permissible financial relationship. Given the dynamics of the healthcare industry, the Law is destined to impede changes that involve relationships that do not fit within existing exceptions. This, in turn, creates pressure for an ever-increasing number of exceptions, enhancing the complexity of the law and undermining the industry's ability to understand and comply with its provisions. The mechanical application of the Stark Law can also result in overpayment liabilities that are highly disproportionate to the conduct giving rise to the offense.

On the other hand, the Stark Law's broad prohibition and lack of an intent element make it easier for CMS and government enforcement agencies to use. . . . The sharp rise in the number of Stark-based False Claims Act cases is a testament to the utility of the statute. . . .

* Reprinted with permission, Copyright © American Health Lawyers. In its role as a public resource on health law, the AHLA from time to time convenes panels of experts representing diverse viewpoints to explore issues of significance to the health law and health policy communities. The views expressed in this paper are a summary of the positions expressed by such experts and should not be construed as an endorsement of any position by the AHLA or its members.

The Dangers of Disproportionality. The risk that a Stark violation might result in a level of exposure that could effectively bankrupt a hospital is a scenario that haunts administrators. For example:

> [A]ssume that in 2001, a hospital enters into a medical director agreement with its most productive cardiac surgeon. The terms of the agreement are commercially reasonable and the compensation is set at fair market value. In 2002, the medical director agreement expires but the hospital mistakenly assumes that the agreement automatically renewed and continues to pay the surgeon. The surgeon also thinks the written agreement is still in place and continues to provide the services and submits weekly timesheets documenting the hours devoted to his medical director duties. In 2009, the hospital discovers that the medical director agreement expired in 2002. Under the Stark Law, the hospital has had a non-excepted financial relationship with the cardiac surgeon for the past seven years and all reimbursement that the hospital received during that period for services provided to Medicare [or Medicaid] patients pursuant to referrals from that cardiac surgeon are subject to recoupment by the government.

The repayment liability in this instance could be millions of dollars. If the hospital made the same type of faulty assumption with respect to five agreements, the potential exposure grows accordingly. If this Stark violation is used as the basis for a False Claims Act case, civil penalties and treble damages could also be recovered.[6] In short, the hospital's total exposure flowing from an expired medical director agreement could well be ruinous. . . .

While the potential exposure for a Stark violation is enormous, historically the likelihood of enforcement has been low. CMS has not been actively seeking recoupment based on violations of the Stark Law. Enforcement of Stark through the False Claims Act is random and often not the sole or even primary focus of the government's case. The risk of a hospital facing disproportional penalties for an innocent Stark violation, however, is exacerbated to the extent that prosecutorial discretion has been effectively abdicated to whistleblowers under the *qui tam* provisions of the FCA. Given all these factors, the industry has viewed Stark enforcement as akin to lightning striking—unpredictable but deadly. . . . [M]ost hospitals, even when faced with a claim with little merit, will settle rather than roll the dice in a government enforcement action. . . .

[*Dealing with Technical Violations.*] As noted above, there is general consensus that the Stark Law is exceedingly complex and highly technical. . . . Some participants noted that the complexity of the Stark Law arises in part from its history of "reactive" rulemaking. According to this perspective, the cycle has been that (1) the agency promulgates an exception or a rule, (2) following implementation, someone identifies a potentially abusive practice in the industry; and (3) the agency reacts, not by taking a different tact, but by either amending the existing rule or creating "an exception to the exception" to address the perceived concern. Although this

---

6. [In part, this is because the Fraud Enforcement and Recovery Act of 2009 defines "false claim" to include the knowing retention of overpayments that were thought to be proper at the time the claim was made, but which are later discovered to be improper. —EDS.]

cycle may seem logical, it has resulted in a maze of regulatory definitions, special rules, and exceptions. . . .

Several participants in the Convener Session noted that when confronted with evidence of a Stark violation, providers' [options are to]: . . .

- Do nothing.
- Fix the problem and don't look back.
- Fix the problem and return the entire "overpayment."
- Identify a government agency, make a disclosure and attempt to negotiate a compromise.

All options pose substantial risks. . . . Disclosure to [CMS,] the Department of Justice or local US Attorney's Office could be viewed as an admission of wrongdoing and neither [CMS,] the DOJ nor the US Attorneys are known for their willingness to compromise claims for less than the face amount of the repayment obligation. . . .

Given the backdrop of potentially ruinous liability under the FCA, . . . the industry has been casting about for a practical means of addressing Stark violations once they are identified. . . . [S]everal participants suggested that CMS establish a Stark self-disclosure protocol to give the industry a practical means of addressing Stark violations once they are identified.

Notes: Referral Fees

1. *Sources of Law.* There are four sources of referral fee prohibitions, two federal and two state.[9] The most threatening are the two federal statutes discussed in the principal readings (the Stark law, and the Medicare/Medicaid fraud and abuse statute, which is also called the "anti-kickback statute"). Many states also criminalize referral fees or prohibit physician referral arrangements. In California, for instance, "the . . . receipt or acceptance, by any [physician] of any rebate, refund, commission . . . or other consideration, whether in the form of money or otherwise, as compensation or inducement for referring patients . . . to any person . . . is unlawful . . . and is punishable [as a felony]." Cal. Bus. & Prof. Code §650. Finally, state medical practice acts frequently enumerate fee splitting as one of the grounds for revocation or suspension of a physician's license to practice. A typical statute allows disciplinary action by the board of medical examiners for "division of fees . . . received for professional services with any person for bringing or referring a patient." See generally Note, 43 Brandeis L. J. 465 (2005).

Litigation under the state laws is becoming more common, as a basis for challenging the legality of various business arrangements, some of which are very common. See, e.g.:

- Medical school's 10 percent "dean's tax" on its clinical departments' revenue constitutes illegal "fee splitting" with respect to part-adjunct, part-time faculty.

---

9. In addition, in contrast with prohibitions of referral incentives is the related prohibition of "gainsharing" incentives to reduce Medicare or Medicaid services, which is quoted and discussed in Chapter 9.E.3.

Odrich v. Trustees of Columbia University, 764 N.Y.S.2d 448 (N.Y. App. Div. 2003).

- Courts differ on whether ordinary office management contracts are illegal in which physicians pay a percentage of revenues or profits for running their business operations. Compare, e.g., Necula v. Glass, 647 N.Y.S.2d 501 (1996) (illegal) *with* Epic Medical Management v. Paquette, 244 Cal.App.4th 504 (2015) (legal).
- Physicians who resell prescription drugs at a markup do not violate the state's anti-kickback statute. Wright v. Jeckle, 144 P.3d 301 (2006).

Also, consider whether "Groupons" for doctors might be illegal fee-splitting. Michael Bolongna, Online Coupons from Doctors: Fee-Splitting?, 20 BNA Health L. Rep. 1513 (2011) (discussing legality of Groupons for doctors).

Representative Stark introduced his law after increased attention to the abuses that result when physicians own or invest in the medical facilities where they practice or to which physicians refer business. This ownership interest in the facility means they profit not only from their own service fees but also from the earnings of the facility. This extra incentive to in essence refer business to themselves causes increased utilization of the facilities. Several studies have shown, for instance, that physicians who own or invest in clinical laboratories or expensive diagnostic equipment such as MRI scanners order from 40 to 100 percent more tests of this nature than do other doctors with similar patients.

Although the aim of the Stark self-referral statute is essentially the same as the anti-kickback statute, its structure is fundamentally different. First, it is primarily civil, not criminal; the main effect is to disallow payment for medical services in arrangements that violate the statute. Second, it does not have the same large gray areas of legal uncertainty; under Stark, you are either on base or you are out, whereas anti-kickback liability depends on a more subjective intent to induce referrals.

2. *Seeking Safety Under the Anti-Kickback Statute.* Greber v. United States rules that any intent to induce referrals poisons the arrangement, even if payments are in exchange for physicians' services. However, close attention to the facts suggest that the decision may not be this ominous. Do you see any indications that the "interpretation services" were a bogus front to disguise what was in reality a true kickback scheme? Nevertheless, several other Circuits have adopted the same broad interpretation of the federal statute, dashing the hopes of those who initially read that decision as limited. United States v. Borrasi, 639 F.3d 774 (7th Cir. 2011). Only the First Circuit has made a conviction at least marginally more difficult by requiring a showing that there be a "primary" rather than merely an "incidental" purpose to induce referrals.

Under the broader interpretation of the anti-kickback statute, wouldn't it potentially be a felony punishable by five years' imprisonment for a rural hospital to recruit a badly needed specialist to the community, for a doctor to discount his services by waiving insurance deductibles and coinsurance, or for a health care institution to pay its doctors a bonus as a reward for efficient practice? As startling as this may seem, a case can be made that each of these activities falls within the literal terms of the statute and entails at least some intent to induce referrals. Enticing a physician to join the medical staff necessarily involves implicit or explicit incentives to refer the physician's patients to that hospital. Price discounts can be characterized as payments to refer one's patients to one's self for treatment. And efficiency bonuses can induce doctors to admit patients to a particular hospital or encourage them to direct patients to a particular insurance plan. Beverly Cohen, An Examination of the Right of Hospitals to Engage in Economic Credentialing, 77 Temp. L. Rev. 705 (2004).

To reduce legal uncertainty, the Department of Health and Human Services (DHHS) has issued a series of "safe harbor" regulations specifying payment practices that are deemed legal under the anti-kickback statute despite their potential referral incentive. 42 C.F.R. §1001.952. These safe harbors track fairly closely the particular financial relationships that the Stark Law allows as exceptions to its general prohibition. Among the more important ones are those covering physician recruitment, space rental, management contracts, price discounts, certain joint ventures, and physician investments in certain health care entities. In addition, private parties may seek a ruling from DHHS about whether it will challenge particular transactions under the anti-kickback statute (but not under Stark).

The difficulty with these safe harbors and Stark exceptions is that they identify only a limited list of uncontroversial and conventional transactions, and thus they provide little guidance for novel, unanticipated business arrangements that fall outside their scope. Many of the private rulings have also been extremely cautious. For instance, in one ruling (subsequently reversed by regulation), DHHS stated that hospitals may not restock ambulance supplies for free since this might act as an inducement to bring patients to one emergency room rather than another, and in another ruling, it said that an ambulance company may not give nursing homes a discount on some of their patients for fear this might induce nursing homes to refer other, non-discounted patients to the ambulance company. Also, the DHHS ruled that it is potentially illegal for a hospice to offer free services to terminally ill patients who do not have insurance coverage. Some rulings have been more permissive. One approved a joint venture arrangement in which physicians own or invest in an outpatient surgery clinic. Nevertheless, this ruling was limited to surgery because the facility fee is only a small fraction of the procedure fee that surgeons earn regardless of their investment in the facility; therefore, having a stake in the facility fee creates very little added incentive to perform more surgeries.

3. *What's a Lawyer to Do?* Safe harbor regulations and private rulings on particular transactions help to reduce uncertainty over what is and is not a "kickback," but to a great extent, the health care industry must simply rely on the government's good sense to exercise discretion in choosing to challenge only truly abusive arrangements. Is it comforting that federal prosecutors simply overlook the fact that so many accepted and socially beneficial relationships in the health care industry potentially violate a felony statute? Professor Blumstein provides a colorful metaphor for this legal state of affairs:

> [T]he modern American healthcare industry is akin to a speakeasy—conduct that
> is illegal is rampant and countenanced by law enforcement officials because the law
> is so out of sync with the conventional norms and realities of the marketplace. . . .
> This poses a formidable civil liberties concern as prosecutors exercise enormous
> prosecutorial discretion, which is subject to abuse.

The Fraud and Abuse Statute in an Evolving Healthcare Marketplace: Life in the Health Care Speakeasy, 22 Am. J. L. & Med. 205 (1996).

Also, consider the dilemma that lawyers face in giving advice under these ambiguous laws. In Kansas the U.S. Attorney prosecuted two lawyers who drafted agreements under which a hospital paid physicians to manage nursing home patients, an arrangement that was found to be a criminal violation of the anti-kickback statute. United States v. Lahue, 261 F.3d 993 (9th Cir. 2001). The prosecutor presented evidence that some of the physicians overbilled Medicare and solicited kickbacks for recruiting patients. However, in dismissing the case against the lawyers, the trial judge ruled (March 9, 1999) that they tried in good faith to structure an arrangement that they thought complied with the law, and they should not be faulted for technical failures or other people's hidden motivations, considering the complexity, ambiguity, and evolving nature of this law. See Stuart M. Gerson & Jennifer E. Gladieux, Advice of Counsel: Eroding Confidentiality in Federal Health Care Law, 51 Ala. L. Rev. 163 (1999).

In the *Tuomey* case, however, which was decided on the more strictly worded Stark Law, former members of the hospital's board of trustees sued their lawyers for malpractice in giving the flawed advice that led to the disastrous legal outcome.

4. *Whistleblowing and Fessing Up.* In *Tuomey*, note the motivation of the physician who initially brought the situation to light. This illustrates that every disappointed business partner, disgruntled employee, patient, or lawyer is a potential bounty hunter under the referral fee statutes. Also, note the handsome "bounty" reward that went to Dr. Drakeford. Plaintiffs' lawyers who pursue such cases naturally would receive a substantial share of such awards.

Congress finally heard the cries for help from the health care industry and its lawyers. The ACA required that CMS adopt a "self-disclosure protocol" that allows CMS to reduce refunds when providers voluntarily reveal previously unknown technical Stark violations. According to one analysis, the approach CMS took "is so punitive and difficult to navigate that very few health-care providers have made disclosures, despite specific legal requirements to do so." Jean Veilleux, Catching Flies with Vinegar: A Critique of the Centers for Medicare and Medicaid Self-Disclosure Program, 22 Health Matrix 169 (2012).

5. *Separating the Wheat from the Chaff.* Is it possible in a health care system as complex as ours to intelligently regulate which potentially distorting incentives are allowable and which are not? See David Frankford, Creating and Dividing the Fruits of Collective Economic Activity: Referrals Among Health Care Providers, 89 Colum. L. Rev. 1861, 1937 (1989) ("Laws like [this] are absolutely incapable of logically defining, much less policing against, inflated prices. [T]hey fail even to create a language for comprehensible debate. They simply obfuscate the issues."). Is any kind of physician payment incentive completely beyond reproach? Even straight salary has the perverse effect of inducing physicians to spend less time with patients or to make excessive referrals to other doctors. Consider the following from the prestigious Institute of Medicine's influential report For-Profit Enterprise in Health Care 153 (B. Gray ed., 1986):

> All compensation systems—from fee-for-service to capitation or salary—present some undesirable incentives for providing too many services, or too few. No system will work without some degree of integrity, decency, and ethical commitment on the

part of professionals. Inevitably, we must presume some underlying professionalism that will constrain the operation of unadulterated self-interest.

Realizing this, could it be dangerous to single out individual incentives from the overall mix of counteracting incentives and regulate each one (or only some of them) in isolation? Even unadulterated referral fees might be beneficial if they are used to counteract the incentive that general practitioners have to not refer patients to specialists when needed. Mark Pauly, The Ethics and Economics of Kickbacks and Fee Splitting, 10 Bell J. Econ. 344 (1974) ("it is possible for fee splitting to offer incentives which actually improve patient welfare"). Dr. Arnold S. Relman, former editor of the New England Journal of Medicine, would respond:

> The situation is different when physicians seek income beyond fee for service and make business arrangements with other providers of services to their patients. Such arrangements introduce a new and unnecessary conflict, which strains the physician's fiduciary commitment to the patient. Unlike the conflicts of interest in the fee-for-service system, these new arrangements are usually not fully disclosed to the patient, and therefore are more difficult to control.

Dealing with Conflicts of Interest, 313 New Eng. J. Med. 749, 750 (1985). Do the rule of necessity and the absence of disclosure justify felony imprisonment?

Regardless, these laws are not written to prohibit only unnecessary and undisclosed incentives. Another way, then, to draw sensible distinctions is to determine whether a transaction implicates these laws' core purposes. Mark A. Hall, Making Sense of Referral Fee Statutes, 13 J. Health Pol. Pol'y & L. 623 (1988). Referral fee statutes are intended to prevent three abuses: ordering unnecessary services, increasing charges for needed services, and influencing with financial considerations the decision of where best to refer a patient. To illustrate with the most common target of referral fee criticism, a clinical laboratory kickback to doctors who order tests might induce doctors to order unnecessary tests, increase a lab's billings for tests that are necessary, or persuade doctors to send tests to an inferior lab.

One might reason, then, that a less blatant practice does not violate referral fee statutes if the practice does not conflict with any of the three mentioned purposes, even though the practice might fall within the literal language of these sweeping prohibitions. For example, one might think that the waiver of insurance deductibles and co-payments should not be prosecuted because this practice does not result in any increased costs to the government; indeed, it reduces costs for beneficiaries.

This purpose-based analysis provides only limited guidance, however. Any incentive that has a referral aspect in a literal sense will always conflict with at least one of the stated purposes—namely, the potential to influence *where* a patient is referred. Moreover, incentives usually have some impact on whether a service should be ordered at all. For instance, on the question of waiving co-payments and deductibles, DHHS issued a safe harbor regulation that allows such price discounts by hospitals and HMOs, but not by doctors. It reasoned that deductibles and co-payments are meant to deter ordering unnecessary care, and only hospital care is sufficiently urgent that reducing patient cost-sharing is not likely to increase program costs.

An alternative definitional model is to determine whether or not referral fees are earned through arm's-length non-referral services paid at fair market value. A classic situation is the rental of hospital space and equipment to in-house pharmacies and radiologists in exchange for a percentage of their gross receipts. Since hospital pharmacies and radiologists obtain their patients from the hospital, these rental payments have the clear potential to induce referrals. Courts and regulators analyzing this situation have distinguished between earned and unearned referral fees: Fees incidentally related to a referral are valid if they do not exceed the fair market value of legitimate non-referral services bargained for at arm's length. Hall, Making Sense of Referral Fee Statutes, supra. This conceptual guide is prominent in a wide variety of anti-kickback safe harbor regulations and Stark Law exceptions.

The utility of the fair market guide is weakened, however, by the fact that referral-neutral reference points to judge market value are often lacking in the medical marketplace, since the market value of a service or relationship often stems precisely from the business it generates. Consider, for instance, a hospital that seeks to recruit badly needed new physicians. Although this may be good for the community, it is also good for the hospital's business. Any "market value" for new physicians surely must reflect, in part, the increased admissions that hospitals expect.

Therefore, safe harbor rules and exceptions often stress a more subjective assessment of whether the fees in question are intended to generate referrals. But, because purity of intent is difficult to prove, the safest route, also reflected in the rules, is often to structure payments so that their amount does not depend on the number and value of referrals made. But, sometimes, this simply is not possible. For instance, when hospitals or HMOs consider purchasing physician office practices, in order to employ the physicians, the true market value of the practice obviously depends in part on components such as good will, customer lists, patient records, and employee contracts that relate directly to how much existing patients are likely to continue seeing the physician. This calls into question the legality of any amount paid in excess of simply the hard assets of the office practice.

6. *Impact on Organizational Form.* Professor Frankford, above, argues that the referral fee prohibition distorts health care institutional arrangements by concentrating more power within medical institutions. This is because "referrals" do not occur within institutions, only between them, and the safe harbors are more protective of larger than smaller institutions. In short, there is less legal exposure if health care institutions grow to absorb more physicians and sources of payment. 89 Colum. L. Rev. 1861. In this regard, referral fee laws might be seen as an unnatural stimulus for fully integrated rather than more loosely formed delivery systems.

Professor Blumstein, above, observes that these laws also threaten various contractual arrangements that are transitional states between no integration and full integration. Casting into doubt the financial relationships that exist in partially or "virtually" integrated models (such as hospital/physician joint ventures and physician office management contracts) makes the movement toward full integration more difficult.

Observe, also, that the referral law's bias toward complete integration is at odds with the corporate practice of medicine doctrine, which prohibits physician employment, and it is in tension with tax exemption law that imposes greater scrutiny when doctors are "insiders." Also, the safe harbors protect physician ownership in for-profit entities, but have no equivalent protection for physicians who are insiders in nonprofits, which discourages adoption of the nonprofit form.

Critics have also observed that referral fee prohibitions make little sense in the context of bundled or capitated payment systems because these laws were meant to address the abuses of fee-for-service reimbursement, and incentives within managed care systems are likely to reduce costs in the long run by encouraging more efficient practice patterns. Recognizing this, a 1999 safe harbor protects providers who practice under capitation and other "at risk" incentives that discourage overutilization. Similarly, a 2011 ruling protects provider payments within ACOs that participate in the Medicare shared savings program. And, a 2015 law protects the sharing of payments among providers under Medicare's new approach that bundles payment based on certain episodes of illness (see Chapter 9.E.4).

7. *Further Readings.* For description and analysis of the **safe harbors and the exceptions** to the self-referral statute, as well as the effect these statutes have on contemporary business arrangements, see Rebecca Olavarria, MACRA and Stark: Strange Bedfellows at the Heart of Health Care Reform, 62 Wayne L. Rev. 131 (2017); Nancy L. Zisk, Investing in Health Care, 36 Seattle U. L. Rev. 189 (2012); Alice G. Gosfield, Medicare and Medicaid Fraud and Abuse (2015); Patrick Sutton, The Stark Law in Retrospect, 20 Ann. Health L. 15 (2011); Jean M. Mitchell, The Prevalence of Physician Self-Referral Arrangements After Stark II, 26(3) Health Aff. W415 (Apr. 2007); James Belanger & Scott Bennett, The Continued Expansion of the False Claims Act, 4 J. Health & Life Sci. L. 26 (2010); Robert Lower & Robert Stone, Off with Their Heads! Summary Execution for Technical Stark Violations—And a Proposal to Commute the Sentence, 3 Health & Life Sci. L. 112 (2010); Leigh Walton et al., Hospital Syndications: Opportunities and Options, or Poised for Extinction?, 21(4) The Health Lawyer 1 (Apr. 2009); Paul DeMuro, Eye of the Storm: The Government's Focus on Hospital-Physician Arrangements, 21(5) The Health Lawyer 30 (June 2009).

For a sampling of the burgeoning literature on *qui tam* **health care actions**, see Dayna Matthew, *Qui Tam* Litigation Under the False Claims Act, 69 Wash. & Lee L. Rev. 365 (2012); Beverly Cohen, KABOOM! The Explosion of *Qui Tam* False Claims Under the Health Reform Law, 116 Penn. St. L. Rev. 77 (2011); A. Kesselheim & D. Studdert, Whistleblower-Initiated Enforcement Actions Against Health Care Fraud and Abuse in the U.S., 149 Ann. Intern. Med. 342 (2008). See section A.2 for additional discussion of the **False Claims Act**.

8. *A Look Back.* Look back over this chapter as well as Chapter 9 to observe the many ways in which federal and state regulation of health care fail to achieve a coordinated and purposeful public policy. One searching for imperfections might justifiably assert that health care corporate and regulatory law suffers from each of the following pathologies:

- ERISA unthinkingly creates a regulatory vacuum that is only erratically filled by state or federal insurance regulation.
- State corporate practice of medicine law is anachronistic and unpredictable.
- Insurance regulation fails to achieve a level playing field between traditional and innovative forms of health care delivery, and confuses consumer protection with provider protection.

- Tax exemption law discourages the formation of nonprofit HMOs and is too lenient on hospitals.
- Fraud and abuse law deters legitimate ventures and fails to see that incentives in a fee-for-service era are fundamentally different than those in an era of bundled payment and pay-for-performance.
- The details of each of these particular bodies of law point in inconsistent directions on fundamental questions such as how tightly integrated financing and delivery systems should be and the proper role of physicians in their ownership and management.

In your view, are these hypothetical criticisms valid?

Problem: Medicare/Medicaid Fraud and Abuse

You are outside counsel to the Florence Nightingale Healthcare Corporation, which among its other operations owns a durable medical equipment (DME) subsidiary, which sells equipment for home use such as crutches, wheel chairs, and oxygen concentrators. You learn that the subsidiary has had certain business practices about which you have some question under the Medicare and Medicaid Anti-Fraud and Abuse provisions:

- Salesmen regularly offer home health agency employees a "premium" whenever their clients order DME from the subsidiary.
- The subsidiary offers "rebates" to patients who use its equipment.
- The subsidiary pays hospital and home health agency personnel for assisting its patients in learning how to use its products.
- Some arterial blood gas test results may have been "massaged a bit" by the DME in order to facilitate Medicare payment for oxygen concentrators.

What advice would you give?

Problem: Reverse Referral Fees

You are outside counsel to the Florence Nightingale Healthcare Corporation (FNHC), which is concerned that expenses in some of its ancillary departments are causing it to lose money under Medicare and HMO insurance. It would like to start charging its hospital-based physicians for some of the costs of running their departments. Its current relationship with these physicians is one in which they have exclusive contracts to work in these departments, but no money changes hands between them. The hospital handles all billing, staffing, and overhead, but it bills separately for facility charges vs. professional fees, and the physicians keep all the professional fees the hospital collects on their behalf. This is the standard practice in the industry. FNHC has the following suggestions for changing this arrangement:

- Have the radiology group pay for services, supplies, personnel, utilities, maintenance, and billing services furnished by the hospital. In a nonhospital, office-based setting, this package would normally cost about $100,000 to $150,000 per year. The hospital will charge the radiology group only $25,000 at first, but increase the charges to $100,000 over four years. Payments are due only if the hospitals' gross revenue derived from radiology services exceeds $1,000,000 in the previous year.
- The hospital's clinical laboratory, under the direction of the pathology group, would pay the hospital a 20 percent fee for "specimen collection and handling services" when a physician on the FNHC medical staff orders a test from the clinical lab.

What advice would you give?

Comprehensive Review Problem: Forming an Integrated Delivery System

Review the introductory discussion at page 1248 and the description of Florence Nightingale Hospital at page 1254. Now, consider the following methods the hospital might pursue for closer affiliation with physicians, in order to begin to form an integrated delivery system or an accountable care organization. Suppose this affiliation was undertaken either to market a comprehensive managed care insurance plan and participate in the Medicare shared savings program, or, less ambitiously, to establish an outpatient clinic. How would each of three possible integration/affiliation models fare under each of several business and legal factors that have been reviewed in this chapter? Fill in the following chart by indicating whether each business or legal factor would view each arrangement favorably (+), negatively (–), or in neutral/mixed way (/).

	Physician Autonomy	Clinical and Financial Integration	Corporate Practice of Medicine	Antitrust	Referral Fee Law	Tax Exempt
Corporate Ownership The hospital's corporate parent buys out physician practices and employs the physicians.						
Physician-Hospital Organization (PHO) Hospital and several physician groups form joint-venture partnership, contribute equal capital, and split the proceeds.						
Management Services Organization (MSO) Hospital contracts with independent physicians to provide office management services and to act as negotiating agent with insurers/ employers.						

Glossary of Organizational Terms and Acronyms

In previous generations, it was necessary to learn a specialized vocabulary to study law and medicine. This is still true, but in the past that vocabulary was purely medical. Today, it includes many obscure organizational terms as well. This is a selected glossary of organizational terms and acronyms, adapted from the Prospective Payment Assessment Commission, 1996 Report to Congress.

ACA	Affordable Care Act of 2010
ACO	Accountable Care Organization
AFDC	Aid to Families with Dependent Children
AHA	American Hospital Association
AHRQ	Agency for Health Care Research and Quality
AMA	American Medical Association
CDHC	Consumer-Directed (or Driven) Health Care
CMS	Center for Medicare and Medicaid Services
COBRA	Consolidated Omnibus Budget Reconciliation Act of 1985
CON	Certificate of Need
DHHS	*See* HHS
DRG	Diagnosis-Related Group
ERISA	Employee Retirement Income Security Act of 1974
ESRD	End-Stage Renal Disease
FDA	Food and Drug Administration
HCFA	Health Care Financing Administration, now CMS
HHS	Health and Human Services, Department of
HIPAA	Health Insurance Portability and Accountability Act

HIV	Human Immunodeficiency Virus
HMO	Health Maintenance Organization
HRA or HSA	Healthcare Reimbursement or Health Savings Account (*see also* MSA)
IDS	Integrated Delivery System
IPA	Independent Practice Association
JCAHO	Joint Commission on Accreditation of Healthcare Organizations
MSA	Medical Savings Account
MSO	Management Services Organization
NCQA	National Committee for Quality Assurance
OBRA	Omnibus Budget Reconciliation Act
PHO	Physician-Hospital Organization
POS	Point of Service
PPACA	Patient Protection and Affordable Care Act
PPO	Preferred Provider Organization
PPS	Prospective Payment System
RBRVS	Resource-Based Relative Value Scale
SNF	Skilled Nursing Facility
SSI	Supplemental Security Income
TEFRA	Tax Equity and Fiscal Responsibility Act of 1982
UR/UM	Utilization Review, or Utilization Management

Accountable Care Organization (ACO)—An organization or network of physicians and/or hospitals that is able to receive payment from public or private insurers on a bundled basis that holds the provider group collectively responsible for the cost and quality of patients' care.

Adverse Selection—A term of art in insurance economics that describes the tendency of people who expect to have greater need for insurance to have more interest in purchasing insurance.

Community Rating—A method of determining an insurance premium structure that reflects expected utilization by the population as a whole, rather than by specific groups.

Consumer-Driven Health Care (CDHC)—An alternative to managed care, which seeks to activate patients to be cost-conscious consumers at the point of treatment, by requiring them to pay more out of pocket, and by providing better information about treatment options and costs.

Cost Shifting—Increasing revenues from some payers to offset uncompensated care losses and lower net payments from other payers.

Diagnosis-Related Groups (DRGs)—A system for determining case mix, used for payment under Medicare's PPS and by some other payers. The DRG system classifies patients into groups based on the principal diagnosis, type of surgical procedure, presence or absence of significant comorbidities or complications, and other relevant criteria. DRGs are intended to categorize patients into groups that are clinically meaningful and homogeneous with respect to resource use. Medicare's PPS currently uses 490 mutually exclusive DRGs, each of which is assigned a relative weight that compares its cost lines to the average for all DRGs.

Fee-for-Service—A method of reimbursing health care providers in which payment is made for each unit of service rendered.

Fiscal Intermediary—An insurer or other private company that the government contracts with to administer Medicare or Medicaid payments to providers.

Gainsharing—An awkward term referring to hospital arrangements that reward physicians for their participation in initiatives or programs that save costs or improve quality.

Health Maintenance Organization (HMO)—A managed care plan that integrates financing and delivery of a comprehensive set of health care services to an enrolled population. HMOs may contract with, directly employ, or own participating health care providers. Enrollees are usually required to choose from among these providers and in return have limited co-payments. Providers may be paid through capitation, salary, per diem, or prenegotiated fee-for-service rates.

Health Savings Account (HSA)—A tax-sheltered account, similar to an IRA, and also known as a Healthcare Reimbursement Account (HRA) or Medical Savings Account (MSA), that is used to pay for medical expenses. It is coupled with high-deductible or "catastrophic" insurance, such that the HSA can pay for most ordinary expenses and insurance is used only for very expensive treatment.

Integrated Delivery System (IDS)—Any number of different arrangements among doctors, hospitals, other medical facilities, and insurers in which a full range of medical services is offered to employers, subscribers, or insurers. Includes conventional arrangements such as HMOs, as well as more innovative arrangements known as PHOs, PSNs, or MSOs, which are discussed in Chapter 10.

Managed Care—Any system of health service payment or delivery arrangements in which the health plan or provider attempts to control or coordinate health service use to contain health expenditures, improve quality, or both. Arrangements often involve a defined delivery system of providers having some form of contractual relationship with the plan.

Moral Hazard—A term from insurance economics describing the fact that insurance makes people less concerned about the costs of their behavior than for costs that are covered by insurance.

Peer Review Organization (PRO)—An organization that contracts with HCFA to investigate the quality of health care furnished to Medicare beneficiaries and to educate beneficiaries and providers. PROs also conduct limited review of medical records and claims to evaluate the appropriateness of care provided.

Physician-Hospital Organization (PHO)—A joint venture or affiliation among one or more hospitals and physicians or physician groups. The venture might encompass the full range of medical services, or only one or a few services.

Point-of-Service (POS)—A health plan allowing the enrollee to choose to receive a service from a participating or a nonparticipating provider, with different benefit levels associated with one or the other types of providers.

Preferred Provider Organization (PPO)—A health plan with a network of providers whose services are available to enrollees at lower cost than the services of non-network providers. PPO enrollees may self-refer to any network provider at any time.

Prospective Payment—A method of paying health care providers in which rates are established in advance. Providers are paid these rates regardless of the costs they actually incur.

Prospective Payment System (PPS) — Medicare's acute care hospital payment method for inpatient care. Prospective per case payment rates are set at a level intended to cover operating costs for treating a typical inpatient in a given diagnosis-related group. Payments for each hospital are adjusted for differences in area wages, teaching activity, care to the poor, and other factors.

Relative Value Scale — An index that assigns weights to each medical service; the weights represent the relative amount to be paid for each service. The relative value scale used in the development of the Medicare Physician Fee Schedule consists of three cost components, physician work, practice expense, and malpractice expense.

Risk Adjustment — A method to assess the relative severity or likelihood of medical conditions for different groups of patients, in order to adjust comparative measures of quality or cost. Risk adjustment is used, for instance, to increase or reduce payments to health plans to compensate for health care expenditures that are expected to be higher or lower than average. Risk adjustment is also used to determine whether differences in medical outcomes are due to patients' underlying conditions or instead to how providers treat them.

Uncompensated Care — Care rendered by hospitals or other providers without payment from the patient or a government-sponsored or private insurance program. It includes both charity care, which is provided without the expectation of payment, and bad debts, for which the provider has made an unsuccessful effort to collect payment due from the patient.

Utilization Review (UR) — A review of services delivered by a health care provider to evaluate the appropriateness, necessity, and quality of the prescribed services. The review can be performed on a prospective, concurrent, or retrospective basis.

Table of Cases

Primary cases are indicated by italics.

Index